WHO WAS WHO

A CUMULATED INDEX

1897–1980

WHO'S WHO

*An annual biographical dictionary
first published in 1849*

WHO WAS WHO

VOL. I   1897–1915
VOL. II   1916–1928
VOL. III   1929–1940
VOL. IV   1941–1950
VOL. V   1951–1960
VOL. VI   1961–1970
VOL. VII   1971–1980

Published by
ADAM & CHARLES BLACK

WHO WAS WHO

A
CUMULATED
INDEX
1897–1980

ADAM AND CHARLES BLACK
LONDON

FIRST PUBLISHED 1981
BY A. AND C. BLACK (PUBLISHERS) LIMITED
35 BEDFORD ROW LONDON WC1

COPYRIGHT © 1981 A. & C. BLACK (PUBLISHERS) LTD

ISBN 0–7136–2177–X

PRINTED IN GREAT BRITAIN BY
LATIMER TREND & COMPANY LTD, PLYMOUTH

PREFACE

THIS INDEX has been prepared to give easy access to the seven volumes of *Who Was Who* for those who may come upon a name, in newspapers, journals, diaries or memoirs, which was obviously so familiar to the writer that he saw no need to explain it; for those who know that an entry should appear in one of the seven volumes, but do not know which volume—because the date of death is not to hand; for researchers in social and political history. The entries thus brought into one list are far from uniform; they range from very brief to expansive, from very personal to official in tone; but they are alike in that they were compiled, for the most part, by their subjects, published in their lifetimes, and sent for correction each year. They give at worst a clue, at best a full answer, to the enquirer seeking to turn a name into a person.

In the eighty-four years of publication recorded there have been many changes, not so much of editorial policy as in the sort of person whose name and career attracted general public interest. *Who's Who* has reflected this interest faithfully; an invitation to have an entry has always signified the compilers' response thereto, rather than the capricious accolade sometimes supposed.

In the earlier days of *Who's Who* consistency seems, not surprisingly, to have been thought relatively unimportant. The result is a wide variety of forms of heading to entries, which required adaptation to fit into a single list. A form has been chosen for the Index which leaves no doubt as to which entry is referred to, but which is not necessarily exactly as printed in the book. Individuals preferred to appear under styles such as The MacDermot, or, in the case of titles, with forms or numberings not now regarded as correct. They spelt their names (for example) M'Taggart, Mactaggart or McTaggart. Where it is conceivable that a name might be hard to find a cross-reference is given, as it is to the part of a double surname under which an entry appears from the other part. There are also cross-references from pseudonyms, maiden names, married names, and other forms appearing in entries.

For hereditary peerages the Index gives the title only; where for any reason one holder of the title is missing from the sequence this is indicated. For life peerages, courtesy titles, and the titles of Lords of Session it gives the forenames and family name also; life peers have a cross-reference under their former names if these differ from their eventual title, and Lords of Session also have a cross-reference to their judicial titles from their family names and forenames. Baronets appear in alphabetical order among other entries; if there are two or more baronetcies of the same surname they are distinguished by the date of creation, and any missing from the sequences are noted.

In the case of names preceded by prefixes such as von or de, which may appear under the prefix or under the main part of the name in *Who Was Who*, the Index gives them as they appear in the book with no cross-reference to the other possible form.

It has always been necessary to include some entries in Addenda to the volumes of *Who Was Who*, because the compilers did not learn of the deaths in question until the main part of the volumes had been completed; such entries might later be transferred to another volume, and in these cases both appearances of the entry are indexed. Where entries appear in the Addenda they are distinguished by (A) after the volume number. There were, however, occasions, particularly in the earlier years, when an entry was removed from *Who's Who* and included in *Who Was Who* by mistake; when the mistake was discovered the entry was returned to *Who's Who* but remained. also, wrongly, in *Who Was Who*. In these cases the earlier, incorrect, appearance of the name has not been indexed. In the course of preparation of the Index a number of entries have been found without a date of death appended. Where possible the dates have been discovered and included; they will be added to the volumes of *Who Was Who* as new editions are published. Because the dates were not known some entries will be found in the wrong volumes of *Who Was Who*.

It is normal for entries once included in *Who's Who* to remain until death, but there has been one major exception to this. In 1943 the paper shortage was so acute that, even though the book was treated generously by the authorities, it became necessary to reduce the number of entries sharply. Very few of those entries then deleted were ever returned to *Who's Who*, and they do not appear in *Who Was Who*.

A

A. K. H. B.; *see* Boyd, Very Rev. A. K. H.

Aalto, Alvar; *see* Aalto, H. A. H.

Aalto, (Hugo) Alvar (Henrik), 1898–1976, vol. VII

Aaltonen, Wäinö Valdemar, 1894–1966, vol. VI

Abadie, Major Eustace Henry Egremont, 1877–1914, vol. I

Abadie, Captain George Howard Fanshawe, *died* 1904, vol. I

Abadie, Maj.-Gen. Henry Richard, 1841–1915, vol. I

Abady, Jacques, 1872–1964, vol. VI

Abayomi, Sir Kofo Adekunle, 1896–1979, vol. VII

Abbas, Kuli Khan (Nawab), 1864–1938, vol. III

Abbay, Col Bryan Norman, 1881–1947, vol. IV

Abbay, Rev. Richard, 1844–1924, vol. II

Abbe, Cleveland, 1838–1916, vol. II

Abbey, Edwin Austin, 1852–1911, vol. I

Abbey, Lt-Col Walter Bulmer Tate, 1872–1949, vol. IV

Abbey, William Henry, 1864–1943, vol. IV

Abbiss, Sir George, 1884–1966, vol. VI

Abbot, Charles Greeley, 1872–1973, vol. VII

Abbot, Lt-Col Frederick William, 1862–1942, vol. IV

Abbott, Albert, 1872–1950, vol. IV

Abbott, Albert Holden, 1871–1934, vol. III

Abbott, Alexander Crever, 1860–1935, vol. III

Abbott, Arthur, 1879–1955, vol. V

Abbott, Hon. Sir Charles (Arthur Hillas) Lempriere, 1889–1960, vol. V

Abbott, Charles Lydiard Aubrey, 1886–1975, vol. VII

Abbott, Charles Theodore, *died* 1956, vol. V

Abbott, Claude Colleer, 1889–1971, vol. VII

Abbott, Edwin, 1878–1947, vol. IV

Abbott, Rev. Edwin Abbott, 1838–1926, vol. II

Abbott, Evelyn Robins, 1873–1950, vol. IV

Abbott, Francis Charles, 1867–1938, vol. III

Abbott, Frank Frost, 1860–1924, vol. II

Abbott, Brig.-Gen. Henry Alexius, 1849–1924, vol. II

Abbott, Rt Rev. Henry Pryor Almon, 1881–1945, vol. IV

Abbott, Col Rev. Preb. Herbert Alldridge, 1881–1962, vol. VI

Abbott, Col Herbert Edward Stacy, 1855–1939, vol. III

Abbott, John Sutherland, 1900–1979, vol. VII

Abbott, Hon. Sir Joseph Palmer, 1842–1901, vol. I

Abbott, Brig.-Gen. Leonard Henry, 1875–1949, vol. IV

Abbott, Rev. Lyman, 1835–1922, vol. II

Abbott, Percival William Henry, 1869–1954, vol. V

Abbott, Lt-Col Percy Phipps, 1869–1940, vol. III

Abbott, Brig. Reginald Stuart, 1882–1964, vol. VI

Abbott, Rt Rev. Robert Crowther, 1869–1927, vol. II

Abbott, Thomas Charles, *died* 1927, vol. II

Abbott, Rev. Thomas Kingsmill, *died* 1912, vol. I

Abbott, Rev. Thomas Kingsmill, 1829–1913, vol. I

Abbott, William, 1891–1963, vol. VI

Abdool Raoof, Khan Bahadur Sir Muhammad, *died* 1947, vol. IV

Abdoolcader, Sir Husein Hasanally, 1890–1974, vol. VII

Abdul, Sir Husain Sahib, Khan Bahadur Mirza, vol. III

Abdul Maliki, Alhaji, 1914–1969, vol. VI

Abdul Qaiyum, Nawab Sir Sahibzada, 1866–1937, vol. III

Abdul Razak bin Hussein, Hon. Tun Haji, 1922–1976, vol. VI

Abdulrahman Khan, Ameer of Afghanistan, *died* 1901, vol. I

Abdussamad Khan, Sahibzada Sir, 1874–1943, vol. IV

Abdy, Sir Anthony Charles Sykes, 3rd Bt, 1848–1921, did not have an entry in Who's Who.

Abdy, Brig.-Gen. Anthony John, 1856–1924, vol. II

Abdy, Sir Henry Beadon, 4th Bt, 1853–1921, vol. II

Abdy, Richard Combe, *died* 1938, vol. III

Abdy, Sir Robert Henry Edward, 5th Bt, 1896–1976, vol. VII

Abdy, Sir William Neville, 2nd Bt, 1844–1910, vol. I

à Beckett, Ada Mary; *see* à Beckett, Mrs T. A.

àBeckett, Sir Albert, 1840–1904, vol. I

A'Beckett, Arthur William, 1844–1909, vol. I

A'Beckett, Hon. Sir Thomas, 1837–1919, vol. II

à Beckett, Mrs Thomas Archibald, (Ada Mary à Beckett), 1872–1948, vol. IV

Abel, Arthur Lawrence, 1895–1978, vol. VII

Abel, Sir Frederick Augustus, 1st Bt, 1826–1902, vol. I

1

Abel, Henry George, 1875–1945, vol. IV
Abel Smith, Sir Alexander, 1904–1980, vol. VII
Abel Smith, Desmond, 1892–1974, vol. VII
Abel-Smith, Geoffrey Samuel, *died* 1926, vol. II
Abel-Smith, Brig.-Gen. Lionel, 1870–1946, vol. IV
Abel Smith, Reginald Henry Macaulay, 1890–1964, vol. VI
Abell, George Foster, 1875–1946, vol. IV
Abell, Lt-Col Robert Lloyd, 1889–1957, vol. V
Abell, Thomas Bertrand, 1880–1956, vol. V
Abell, Sir Westcott Stile, 1877–1961, vol. VI
Abend, Hallett, 1884–1955, vol. V
Abensur, Isaac Aaron, 1861–1937, vol. III
Abeokuta, The Alake of, (Ademola II), Sir Ladapo Ademola, 1873–1962, vol. VI
Aberconway, 1st Baron, 1850–1934, vol. III
Aberconway, 2nd Baron, 1879–1953, vol. V
Abercorn, 2nd Duke of, 1838–1913, vol. I
Abercorn, 3rd Duke of, 1869–1953, vol. V
Abercorn, 4th Duke of, 1904–1979, vol. VII
Abercorn, Dowager Duchess of; (Rosalind Cecilia Caroline), 1869–1958, vol. V
Abercrombie, Captain Alexander Ralph, 1896–1918, vol. II
Abercrombie, Col Charles Murray, 1874–1933, vol. III
Abercrombie, George Francis, 1896–1978, vol. VII
Abercrombie, Sir John Robertson, 1888–1960, vol. V
Abercrombie, Lascelles, 1881–1938, vol. III
Abercrombie, Sir (Leslie) Patrick, 1879–1957, vol. V
Abercrombie, Michael, 1912–1979, vol. VII
Abercrombie, Sir Patrick; *see* Abercrombie, Sir L. P.
Abercrombie, Peter Henderson, 1867–1950, vol. IV
Abercromby, 4th Baron, 1838–1917, vol. II
Abercromby, 5th Baron, 1841–1924, vol. II
Abercromby, Bt-Col Sir George William, 8th Bt, 1886–1964, vol. VI
Abercromby, Sir Robert Alexander, 9th Bt, 1895–1972, vol. VII
Aberdare, 2nd Baron, 1851–1929, vol. III
Aberdare, 3rd Baron, 1885–1957, vol. V
Aberdeen and Temair, 1st Marquess of, 1847–1934, vol. III
Aberdeen and Temair, 2nd Marquis of, 1879–1965, vol. VI
Aberdeen and Temair, 3rd Marquis of, 1883–1972, vol. VII
Aberdeen and Temair, 4th Marquess of, 1908–1974, vol. VII
Aberdeen and Temair, Marchioness of; (Ishbel Maria), 1857–1939, vol. III
Abergavenny, 1st Marquess of, 1826–1915, vol. I (A)
Abergavenny, 2nd Marquess of, 1853–1927, vol. II
Abergavenny, 3rd Marquess of, 1854–1938, vol. III
Abergavenny, 4th Marquess of, 1883–1954, vol. V
Aberhart, Hon. William, 1878–1943, vol. IV
Abernethy, James Smart, 1907–1976, vol. VII
Abertay, 1st Baron, *died* 1940, vol. III
Abinash Chandra Sen, Rai Bahadur, 1870–1922, vol. II
Abingdon, 7th Earl of, 1836–1928, vol. II

Abinger, 4th Baron, 1871–1903, vol. I
Abinger, 5th Baron, 1872–1917, vol. II
Abinger, 6th Baron, 1876–1927, vol. II
Abinger, 7th Baron, 1878–1943, vol. IV
Ablett, Thomas Robert, *died* 1945, vol. IV
Abney, Sir William de Wiveleslie, 1843–1921, vol. II
Abrahall, Bennet H.; *see* Hoskyns-Abrahall.
Abrahall, Sir Theo Chandos H.; *see* Hoskyns-Abrahall
Abraham, Ashley Perry, 1876–1951, vol. V
Abraham, Rt Rev. C. T., 1857–1945, vol. IV
Abraham, Rt Rev. Charles John, 1814–1903, vol. I
Abraham, Edgar Gaston Furtado, 1880–1955, vol. V
Abraham, George Dixon, 1872–1965, vol. VI
Abraham, James Johnston, 1876–1963, vol. VI
Abraham, Sir John Bradley, 1881–1945, vol. IV
Abraham, John Conrad, 1889–1939, vol. III
Abraham, Rt Rev. Philip Selwyn, 1897–1955, vol. V
Abraham, Phineas Simon, *died* 1921, vol. II
Abraham, William, 1840–1915, vol. I
Abraham, Rt Hon. William, 1842–1922, vol. II
Abraham, Maj.-Gen. Sir William Ernest Victor, 1897–1980, vol. VII
Abrahams, Sir Adolphe, 1883–1967, vol. VI
Abrahams, Major Sir Arthur Cecil, 1878–1944, vol. IV
Abrahams, Bertram, 1870–1908, vol. I
Abrahams, Gerald, 1907–1980, vol. VII
Abrahams, Harold Maurice, 1899–1978, vol. VII
Abrahams, Israel, 1858–1925, vol. II
Abrahams, Sir Lionel, 1869–1919, vol. II
Abrahams, Louis Barnett, 1839–1918, vol. II
Abrahams, Rt Hon. Sir Sidney Solomon, 1885–1957, vol. V
Abrahamson, Sir Martin Arnold, 1870–1962, vol. VI
Abram, Sir George Stewart, 1866–1928, vol. II
Abram, John Hill, *died* 1933, vol. III
Abramson, Major Albert, 1876–1944, vol. IV
Abruzzi, Duke of; Prince Luigi Amedeo Giuseppé Maria Ferdinando Francesco, 1873–1933, vol. III
Abubakr, Seiyid Sir, bin Sheik al Kaf, *died* 1965, vol. VI
Achard, Marcel, 1899–1974, vol. VII
Acharya, Sir Vijaya Ragahava, 1875–1953, vol. V
Acheampong, Ignatius Kutu, 1931–1979, vol. VII
Acheson, Capt. Albert Edward, 1862–1945, vol. IV
Acheson, Andrew Basil, 1895–1959, vol. V
Acheson, Anne Crawford, *died* 1962, vol. VI
Acheson, Dean, 1893–1971, vol. VII
Acheson, Maj.-Gen. Hon. Edward Archibald Brabazon, 1844–1921, vol. II
Acheson, Edward Goodrich, 1856–1931, vol. III
Acheson, Sir James Glasgow, 1889–1973, vol. VII
Acheson, Hon. Patrick George Edward Cavendish-, 1883–1957, vol. V
Achurch, Janet, (Janet Achurch Sharp), *died* 1916, vol. II
Ackerley, Rev. Frederick George, 1871–1954, vol. V

2

Ackermann, Gerald, 1876–1960, vol. V (A), vol. VI
Ackers, Benjamin St John, 1839–1915, vol. I
Ackland, Robert Craig, died 1923, vol. II
Ackland, William Alfred, 1875–1940, vol. III (A), vol. IV
Ackland, Major William Robert, 1863–1949, vol. IV
Acklom, Captain Cecil Ryther, 1872–1937, vol. III
Acklom, Maj. Spencer, died 1918, vol. II
Ackner, Brian Gerard Conrad, 1918–1966, vol. VI
Ackner, Conrad A., died 1976, vol. VII
Ackroyd, Sir Cuthbert Lowell, 1st Bt, 1892–1973, vol. VII
Ackroyd, Sir Edward James, 1838–1904, vol. I
Ackroyd, Thomas Raven, 1861–1946, vol. IV
Acland, Col Alfred Dyke, 1858–1937, vol. III
Acland, Arthur Geoffrey Dyke, 1909–1964, vol. VI
Acland, Rt Hon. Sir Arthur Herbert Dyke, 13th Bt (cr 1644), 1847–1926, vol. II
Acland, Lt-Gen. Arthur Nugent F.; see Floyer-Acland.
Acland, Sir (Charles) Thomas Dyke, 12th Bt (cr 1644), 1842–1919, vol. II
Acland, Engr-Rear-Adm. Edward Leopold Dyke, 1878–1968, vol. VI
Acland, F. A., 1861–1950, vol. IV (A), vol. V
Acland, Rt Hon. Sir Francis Dyke, 14th Bt (cr 1644), 1874–1939, vol. III
Acland, Captain Frank E. Dyke, 1857–1943, vol. IV
Acland, Henry Dyke, 1867–1942, vol. IV
Acland, Sir Henry Wentworth Dyke, 1st Bt (cr 1890), 1815–1900, vol. I
Acland, Captain Sir Hubert Guy Dyke, 4th Bt (cr 1890), 1890–1978, vol. VII
Acland, Col Sir Hugh Thomas Dyke, 1874–1956, vol. V
Acland, Sir Reginald Brodie Dyke, 1856–1924, vol. II
Acland, Rt Rev. Richard Dyke, 1881–1954, vol. V
Acland, Theodore Dyke, 1851–1931, vol. III
Acland, Rev. Theodore William Gull, 1890–1960, vol. V
Acland, Sir Thomas; see Acland, Sir C. T. D.
Acland, Rt Hon. Sir Thomas Dyke, 11th Bt (cr 1644), 1809–1898, vol. I
Acland, Adm. Sir William Alison Dyke, 2nd Bt (cr 1890), 1847–1924, vol. II
Acland, Sir William Henry Dyke, 3rd Bt (cr 1890), 1888–1970, vol. VI
Acland-Troyte, Lt-Col Sir Gilbert John, 1876–1964, vol. VI
Acomb, Henry Waldo, 1891–1962, vol. VI
A'Court-Repington, Lt-Col Charles; see Repington.
A'Court-Repington, Charles Henry Wyndham, 1819–1903, vol. I
Acton, 1st Baron, 1834–1902, vol. I
Acton, 2nd Baron, 1870–1924, vol. II
Acton, Hon. Sir Edward, 1865–1945, vol. IV
Acton, Dame (Ellen) Marian, died 1971, vol. VII
Acton, Fitzmaurice, 1874–1921, vol. II
Acton, Frederick, 1845–1935, vol. III
Acton, Harry Burrows, 1908–1974, vol. VII
Acton, Lt-Col Hugh William, 1883–1935, vol. III
Acton, John Adams, died 1910, vol. I

Acton, Dame Marian; see Acton, Dame E. M.
Acton, Murray A.; see Adams-Acton
Acton, Maj.-Gen. Thomas Heward, 1917–1977, vol. VII
Acton, Lt-Col William Maxwell, 1878–1939, vol. III
Acworth, Captain Bernard, 1885–1963, vol. VI
Acworth, Harry Arbuthnot, 1849–1933, vol. III
Acworth, Col Louis Raymond, 1872–1934, vol. III
Acworth, Sir William Mitchell, 1850–1925, vol. II
Adair, Cecil; see Everett-Green, Evelyn.
Adair, Adm. Charles Henry, 1851–1920, vol. II
Adair, Sir Charles William, 1822–1897, vol. I
Adair, Mrs Cornelia, died 1922, vol. II
Adair, Edward Robert, 1888–1967, vol. VI
Adair, Sir Frederick Edward Shafto, 4th Bt, 1860–1915, vol. I
Adair, Gilbert Smithson, 1896–1979, vol. VII
Adair, Sir Hugh Edward, 3rd Bt, 1815–1902, vol. I
Adair, Brig.-Gen. Hugh Robert, 1863–1946, vol. IV
Adair, Sir (Robert) Shafto, 5th Bt, 1862–1949, vol. IV
Adair, Sir Shafto; see Adair, Sir R. S.
Adair, Rear-Adm. Thomas Benjamin Stratton, died 1928, vol. II
Adair, Gen. Sir William Thompson, 1850–1931, vol. III
Adam, Hon. Lord; James Adam, 1824–1914, vol. I
Adam, Sir Charles Elphinstone, 1st Bt (cr 1882), 1859–1922, vol. II
Adam, Charles Fox Frederick, 1852–1913, vol. I
Adam, Captain Charles Keith, 1891–1971, vol. VII
Adam, Rev. David Stow, 1859–1925, vol. II
Adam, Edwin, 1862–1931, vol. III
Adam, Eric Graham Forbes, 1888–1925, vol. II
Adam, Sir Frank Forbes, 1st Bt (cr 1917), 1846–1926, vol. II
Adam, Maj.-Gen. Frederick Archibald, 1860–1924, vol. II
Adam, Frederick Edward Fox, 1887–1969, vol. VII
Adam, Major Frederick Loch, 1864–1907, vol. I
Adam, Mrs George, (H. Pearl Adam), 1882–1957, vol. V
Adam, George Jefferys, 1883–1930, vol. III
Adam, H. Pearl; see Adam, Mrs George.
Adam, Captain Herbert Algernon, 1872–1920, vol. II
Adam, J. Millen, 1853–1941, vol. IV
Adam, James, 1860–1907, vol. I
Adam, Sir James, 1870–1949, vol. IV
Adam, John Hunter, 1882–1958, vol. V
Adam, Mme Juliette, 1836–1936, vol. III
Adam, Karl, 1876–1966, vol. VI
Adam, Kenneth, 1908–1978, vol. VII
Adam, Neil Kensington, died 1973, vol. VII
Adam, Patrick William, 1854–1929, vol. III
Adam, Major William Augustus, 1865–1940, vol. III
Adami, John George, 1862–1926, vol. II
Adami, Sir Leonard Christian, 1874–1952, vol. V
Adamic, Louis, 1899–1951, vol. IV
Adams, 1st Baron, 1890–1960, vol. V
Adams, Alexander Annan, 1884–1955, vol. V

Adams, Hon. Alexander Samuel, 1861–1937, vol. III

Adams, Rev. Arthur, 1852–1926, vol. II

Adams, Arthur Henry, 1872–1936, vol. III

Adams, Sir Arthur Robert, 1861–1937, vol. III

Adams, Beale, died 1939, vol. III

Adams, Bernard, died 1965, vol. VI

Adams, Brooks, 1848–1927, vol. II

Adams, Captain Bryan Fullerton, 1887–1971, vol. VII

Adams, Charles Edward, 1870–1945, vol. IV

Adams, Charles Francis, 1835–1915, vol. I

Adams, Charles Kingsley, 1899–1971, vol. VII

Adams, Dartrey; see Adams, H. D. C.

Adams, David, 1871–1943, vol. IV

Adams, David Morgan, 1875–1942, vol. IV

Adams, Miss E. Proby, died 1945, vol. IV

Adams, Ephraim Douglass, 1865–1930, vol. III

Adams, Sir Ernest Charles, 1886–1974, vol. VII

Adams, Col Francis, 1874–1945, vol. IV

Adams, Sir Francis Boyd, 1888–1974, vol. VII

Adams, Rev. Francis John, 1858–1929, vol. III

Adams, Frank Dawson, 1859–1942, vol. IV

Adams, Frederick James, 1885–1957, vol. V

Adams, George Burton, 1851–1925, vol. II

Adams, George Francis, 1870–1921, vol. II

Adams, Col Gofton Gee, 1861–1936, vol. III

Adams, Sir Grantley Herbert, 1898–1971, vol. VII

Adams, Major Sir Hamilton John G.; see Goold-Adams.

Adams, (Harold) Richard, 1912–1978, vol. VII

Adams, Harry William, 1868–1947, vol. IV

Adams, Henry, 1846–1935, vol. III

Adams, Henry Carter, 1851–1921, vol. II

Adams, Henry Charles, 1873–1952, vol. V

Adams, Col Sir Henry Edward Fane G.; see Goold-Adams.

Adams, Captain Henry George Homer, 1879–1960, vol. V

Adams, Ven. Henry Joseph, 1870–1946, vol. IV

Adams, Comdr Henry William Allen, 1884–1962, vol. VI

Adams, Herbert, 1858–1945, vol. IV

Adams, Herbert, 1874–1958, vol. V

Adams, Herbert Louis, 1910–1972, vol. VII

Adams, (Howard) Dartrey (Charles), 1897–1958, vol. V

Adams, James Alexander, died 1930, vol. III

Adams, James Elwin Cokayne, 1876–1961, vol. VI

Adams, James Truslow, 1878–1949, vol. IV

Adams, Rev. James Williams, died 1903, vol. I

Adams, Comdr Sir Jameson Boyd, 1880–1962, vol. VI

Adams, Sir John, 1857–1934, vol. III

Adams, John, 1872–1950, vol. IV

Adams, Sir John Coode-, 1859–1934, vol. III

Adams, Ven. John Michael G.; see Goold-Adams.

Adams, John Roland, 1894–1961, vol. VI

Adams, Captain Joseph Ebenezer, 1878–1926, vol. II

Adams, Joseph Robert George, 1859–1919, vol. II

Adams, Katharine; see Webb, Katharine.

Adams, Louis, 1853–1931, vol. III

Adams, Marcus Algernon, 1875–1959, vol. V

Adams, Col Noel Percy, 1882–1954, vol. V

Adams, Paul, 1903–1972, vol. VII

Adams, Philip Edward Homer, 1879–1948, vol. IV

Adams, Rev. Reginald Arthur, 1864–1939, vol. III

Adams, Rev. Reginald Samuel, died 1928, vol. II

Adams, Richard; see Adams, H. R.

Adams, Richard, 1846–1908, vol. I

Adams, Maj.-Gen. Sir Robert Bellew, 1856–1928, vol. II

Adams, Rev. Canon Samuel Trerice, died 1936, vol. III

Adams, Samuel Vyvyan Trerice, 1900–1951, vol. V

Adams, Sidney Herbert; see Sidney, Herbert.

Adams, Stanley John, 1893–1965, vol. VI

Adams, Stephen; see Maybrick, Michael.

Adams, Sydney, 1905–1980, vol. VII

Adams, Sir Theodore Samuel, 1885–1961, vol. VI

Adams, Thomas, died 1929, vol. III

Adams, Thomas, 1871–1940, vol. III

Adams, Sir Walter, 1906–1975, vol. VII

Adams, Most Rev. Walter Robert, 1877–1957, vol. V

Adams, Walter Sydney, 1876–1956, vol. V

Adams, Wilfrid George, 1885–1936, vol. III

Adams, William B.; see Bridges-Adams.

Adams, William Dacres, 1864–1951, vol. V

Adams, William Davenport, 1851–1904, vol. I

Adams, William George Stewart, 1874–1966, vol. VI

Adams, William Grylls, 1836–1915, vol. I

Adams, William Henry, 1844–1928, vol. II (A), vol. III

Adams, Rev. Canon William John Telia Phythian P.; see Phythian-Adams.

Adams, Rear-Adm. William Leslie Graham, 1901–1963, vol. VI

Adams, William Thomas, 1884–1949, vol. IV

Adams-Acton, Murray, 1886–1971, vol. VII

Adams-Beck, John Melliar, 1909–1979, vol. VII

Adams-Connor, Captain Harry George, 1859–1939, vol. III

Adamson, Lt-Col Charles Henry Ellison, 1846–1930, vol. III

Adamson, Sir Harvey, 1854–1941, vol. IV

Adamson, Col Henry Mackenzie, 1861–1939, vol. III

Adamson, Horatio George, 1865–1955, vol. V

Adamson, Mrs Jennie Laurel, died 1962, vol. VI

Adamson, John, 1865–1918, vol. II

Adamson, John, 1886–1969, vol. VI

Adamson, Sir John Ernest, 1867–1950, vol. IV

Adamson, John Evans, 1884–1961, vol. VI

Adamson, Col John George, 1855–1932, vol. III

Adamson, John William, 1857–1947, vol. IV

Adamson, Joy-Friederike Victoria, 1910–1980, vol. VII

Adamson, Sir Kenneth Thomas, 1904–1976, vol. VII

Adamson, Lawrence Arthur, 1860–1932, vol. III

Adamson, Robert, died 1902, vol. I

Adamson, Lt-Col and Hon. Col Robert Hay, 1869–1936, vol. III

Adamson, Robert Stephen, 1885–1965, vol. VI

Adamson, William, 1830–1910, vol. I

Adamson, Sir William, 1832–1917, vol. II
Adamson, Rt Hon. William, 1863–1936, vol. III
Adamson, William Murdoch, 1881–1945, vol. IV
Adcock, (Arthur) St John, 1864–1930, vol. III
Adcock, Sir Frank Ezra, 1886–1968, vol. VI
Adcock, Sir Hugh, 1847–1920, vol. II
Adcock, St John; see Adcock, A. St J.
Addams, Jane, 1860–1935, vol. III
Addams Williams, Christopher, 1877–1944, vol. IV
Adderley, Sir Augustus John, 1835–1905, vol. I
Adderley, Hubert John Broughton-, 1860–1931, vol. III
Adderley, Hon. and Rev. James Granville, 1861–1942, vol. IV
Adderley, Hon. Reginald Edmund, 1857–1934, vol. III
Addington, 2nd Baron, 1842–1915, vol. I
Addington, 3rd Baron, 1883–1966, vol. VI
Addington, 4th Baron, 1884–1971, vol. VII
Addinsell, Richard Stewart, 1904–1977, vol. VII
Addis, Sir Charles Stewart, 1861–1945, vol. IV
Addis, Sir William, 1901–1978, vol. VII
Addis, Rev. William E., 1844–1917, vol. II
Addison, 1st Viscount, 1869–1951, vol. V
Addison, 2nd Viscount, 1904–1976, vol. VII
Addison, Adm. Sir (Albert) Percy, 1875–1952, vol. V
Addison, D'Arcy Wentworth, 1872–1955, vol. V
Addison, Maj.-Gen. George Henry, 1876–1964, vol. VI
Addison, Sir James, 1879–1949, vol. IV
Addison, John Edmund Wentworth, 1838–1907, vol. I
Addison, Sir Joseph, 1879–1953, vol. V
Addison, Brig. Leonard Joseph Lancelot, 1902–1975, vol. VII
Addison, Margaret E. T., 1868–1940, vol. III (A), vol. IV
Addison, Oswald Lacy, 1874–1942, vol. IV
Addison, Adm. Sir Percy; see Addison, Adm. Sir A. P.
Addison, Hon. William, 1890–1966, vol. VI
Addison, William Innes, 1857–1912, vol. I
Addison, Rev. William Robert Fountaine, died 1962, vol. VI
Addison-Smith, Chilton Lind, 1875–1955, vol. V
Addison-Smith, George Lind, 1870–1934, vol. III
Addy, Sidney Oldall, 1848–1933, vol. III
Adeane, Charles Robert Whorwood, 1863–1943, vol. IV
Adeane, Col Sir Robert Philip Wyndham, 1905–1979, vol. VII
Adeler, Max, (Charles Heber Clark), 1841–1915, vol. I
Adenauer, Konrad, 1876–1967, vol. VI
Adeney, Bernard, died 1966, vol. VI
Adeney, Walter Frederick, 1849–1920, vol. II
Aderemi I; see Ife.
Adermann, Rt Hon. Sir Charles Frederick, 1896–1979, vol. VII
Adey, William James, 1874–1956, vol. V
Adie, Edward Percival, 1890–1977, vol. VII
Adie, William John, 1886–1935, vol. III
Adie-Shepherd, Harold Richard Bowman, 1904–1979, vol. VII

Adjaye, Sir Edward; see Asafu-Adjaye.
Adkin, Harry Kenrick K.; see Knight-Adkin.
Adkin, Rev. Walter Kenrick K.; see Knight-Adkin.
Adkins, Sir Ryland; see Adkins, Sir W. R. D.
Adkins, Sir (William) Ryland Dent, 1862–1925, vol. II
Adlam, George Henry Joseph, 1876–1946, vol. IV
Adlam, Lt-Col Tom Edwin, 1893–1975, vol. VII
Adler, Alfred, 1870–1937, vol. III
Adler, Cyrus, 1863–1940, vol. III
Adler, Elkan Nathan, 1861–1946, vol. IV
Adler, Felix, 1851–1933, vol. III
Adler, Very Rev. Hermann, 1839–1911, vol. I
Adler, Rev. Michael, 1868–1944, vol. IV
Adler, Miss N., died 1950, vol. IV
Adler, Saul, 1895–1966, vol. VI
Adlercron, Brig.-Gen. Rodolph Ladeveze, 1873–1966, vol. VI
Adoo, Julius S.; see Sarkodee-Adoo.
Adrian, 1st Baron, 1889–1977, vol. VII
Adrian, Alfred Douglas, 1845–1922, vol. II
Adrian, Frederick Obadiah, 1836–1909, vol. I
Adrian, Lady; (Hester Agnes), 1899–1966, vol. VI
Adrian, Max, 1903–1973, vol. VII
Adshead, Prof. Stanley Davenport, 1868–1946, vol. IV
Ady, Julia, (Mrs Henry Ady), died 1924, vol. II
Adye, Frederick James, 1874–1945, vol. IV
Adye, Gen. Sir John, 1819–1900, vol. I
Adye, Maj.-Gen. Sir John, 1857–1930, vol. III
Adye, Col Walter, 1858–1915, vol. I
Æ; see Russell, G. W.
Aehrenthal, Count Alois, 1854–1912, vol. I
Aelen, Most Rev. John, 1853–1929, vol. III
Aeron-Thomas, Gwilym Ewart, 1885–1958, vol. V
Affleck, Sir Frederick Danby James, 8th Bt, 1856–1939, vol. III
Affleck, Sir James Ormiston, died 1922, vol. II
Affleck, John Barr, 1878–1941, vol. IV
Affleck, Sir Robert, 7th Bt, 1852–1919, vol. II
Afghanistan, Ameer of; see Abdulrahman Khan.
Aflalo, Frederick George, 1870–1918, vol. II
Afsur-Ul-Mulk, Afsur-ud-Dowla, Afsur Jung, Mirza Mahomed Ali Beg, Khan Bahadur, Nawab, Maj.-Gen., died 1930, vol. III
Aga Khan (III), HH Rt Hon. Aga Sultan Sir Mahomed Shah, 1877–1957, vol. V
Agar, Sir Arthur Kirwan, 1877–1942, vol. IV
Agar, Captain Augustus Willington Shelton, 1890–1968, vol. VI
Agar, Charles Phipp, 1886–1963, vol. VI
Agar, Col Edward, 1859–1930, vol. III
Agar, Sir Francis, 1859–1934, vol. III
Agar, Hon. Francis William Arthur, 1873–1936, vol. III
Agar, Herbert Sebastian, 1897–1980, vol. VII
Agar, Lt-Col John Arnold Shelton, died 1951, vol. V
Agar, Wilfred Eade, 1882–1951, vol. V
Agar-Robartes, Hon. Thomas Charles Reginald, 1880–1915, vol. I (A)
Agarwala, Sir Clifford Manmohan, 1890–1964, vol. VI
Agassiz, Alexander, 1835–1910, vol. I

Agate, James Evershed, 1877–1947, vol. IV
Aggey, Most Rev. John Kwao Amuzu, 1908–1972, vol. VII
Aglen, Ven. Anthony Stocker, 1836–1908, vol. I
Aglen, Sir Francis Arthur, 1869–1932, vol. III
Aglionby, Col Arthur, 1832–1911, vol. I
Aglionby, Rev. Canon Francis Keyes, 1848–1937, vol. III
Aglionby, Rt Rev. John Orfeur, 1884–1963, vol. VI
Agnew, Alan Graeme, 1887–1962, vol. VI
Agnew, Sir Andrew, 1882–1955, vol. V
Agnew, Sir Andrew Noel, 9th Bt (cr 1629), 1850–1928, vol. II
Agnew, (Sir) Fulque Melville Gerald Noel, 10th Bt (cr 1629), 1900–1975, vol. VII
Agnew, Sir George William, 2nd Bt (cr 1895), 1852–1941, vol. IV
Agnew, Comdr Hugh Ladas, 1894–1975, vol. VII
Agnew, Hon. Sir James Wilson, 1815–1901, vol. I
Agnew, Hon. John Hume, 1863–1908, vol. I
Agnew, Sir John Stuart, 3rd Bt (cr 1895), 1879–1957, vol. V
Agnew, Sir Norris Montgomerie, 1895–1973, vol. VII
Agnew, Sir Patrick Dalreagle, 1868–1925, vol. II
Agnew, Philip Leslie, 1863–1938, vol. III
Agnew, Col Quentin Graham Kinnaird, 1861–1937, vol. III
Agnew, Sir Stair, 1831–1916, vol. II
Agnew, Sir William, 1st Bt (cr 1895), 1825–1910, vol. I
Agnew, Sir William Fischer, 1847–1903, vol. I
Agnew, Vice-Adm. Sir William Gladstone, 1898–1960, vol. V
Agnew, William Lockett, 1858–1918, vol. II
Agnon, Shmuel Yosef Halevi, 1888–1970, vol. VI
Agostini, L. E., 1858–1918, vol. II
Agron, Gershon, 1893–1959, vol. V
Agronsky, Gershon; see Agron, G.
Aguet, Gustave Charles, died 1927, vol. II
Ahearne, Christopher Dominic, 1886–1964, vol. VI
Ahern, Maj.-Gen. Donal Maurice, 1911–1966, vol. VI
Ahern, Maj.-Gen. Timothy Michael Richard, 1908–1980, vol. VII
Aherne, Rev. David, 1871–1941, vol. IV
Ahlefeldt-Laurvig, Count Preben Ferdinand, 1872–1946, vol. IV
Ahlmann, Hans Wilhelmson, 1889–1974, vol. VII
Ahmad, Hon. Ahsanuddin, 1859–1918, vol. II
Ahmad, Maulvi Sir Nizam-ud-Din-Niwab Nizamat Jung Bahadur, 1871–1955, vol. V
Ahmad, Maulvi Sir Rafiuddin, 1865–1954, vol. V
Ahmad, Sir Zia-Uddin, 1879–1947, vol. IV
Ahmad Khan, Sardar Sahibzada Sir Sultan, 1864–1936, vol. III
Ahmed, Fakhruddin Ali, 1905–1977, vol. VII
Ahmed, Kabeerud-Din, 1888–1939, vol. III (A), vol. IV
Ahmed, Sir Syed Sultan, 1880–1963, vol. VI
Aicard, Jean, 1848–1921, vol. II
Aickin, Very Rev. George Ellis, died 1937, vol. III
Aickin, Thomas Reginald, 1886–1948, vol. IV (A)
Aide, Charles Hamilton, 1826–1907, vol. I

Aiken, Conrad Potter, 1889–1973, vol. VII
Aiken, John Elliott, 1909–1977, vol. VII
Aiken, John Macdonald, died 1961, vol. VI
Aikenhead, Brig. David Francis, 1895–1955, vol. V
Aikins, Hon. Sir James Albert Manning, 1851–1929, vol. III
Aikman, Sir Alexander, 1886–1968, vol. VI
Aikman, David Wann, 1863–1931, vol. III
Aikman, George, 1830–1905, vol. I
Aikman, Robert Gordon, 1905–1962, vol. VI
Aikman, Sir Robert Smith, died 1917, vol. II
Aikman, Col Thomas S. G. H. Robertson-, 1860–1948, vol. IV
Ailesbury, 5th Marquess of, 1842–1911, vol. I
Ailesbury, 6th Marquess of, 1873–1961, vol. VI
Ailesbury, 7th Marquess of, 1904–1974, vol. VII
Ailsa, 3rd Marquess of, 1847–1938, vol. III
Ailsa, 4th Marquess of, 1872–1943, vol. IV
Ailsa, 5th Marquess of, 1875–1956, vol. V
Ailsa, 6th Marquess of, 1882–1957, vol. V
Ailwyn, 1st Baron, 1855–1924, vol. II
Ailwyn, 2nd Baron, 1886–1936, vol. III
Ailwyn, 3rd Baron, 1887–1976, vol. VII
Ainger, Rev. Alfred, 1837–1904, vol. I
Ainger, Arthur Campbell, 1841–1919, vol. II
Ainley, Henry Hinchcliffe, 1879–1945, vol. IV
Ainley-Walker, Ernest William, 1871–1955, vol. V
Ainscough, Sir Thomas Martland, 1886–1976, vol. VII
Ainsley, John William, 1899–1976, vol. VII
Ainslie, Ainslie Douglas, 1838–1929, vol. III
Ainslie, Ven. Alexander Colvin, died 1903, vol. I
Ainslie, Lt-Col Charles Marshall, 1878–1940, vol. III
Ainslie, Charlotte, 1863–1960, vol. V
Ainslie, Grant Duff Douglas, 1865–1948, vol. IV
Ainslie, Lt-Col Henry Sandys, 1869–1948, vol. IV
Ainslie, James Percival, 1899–1973, vol. VII
Ainslie, Rev. Richard Montague, 1858–1924, vol. II
Ainsworth, Alfred Richard, 1879–1959, vol. V
Ainsworth, Bt Col Charles, 1874–1956, vol. V
Ainsworth, David, 1842–1906, vol. I
Ainsworth, Harry, 1888–1965, vol. VI
Ainsworth, John, 1864–1946, vol. IV
Ainsworth, Sir John Stirling, 1st Bt, 1844–1923, vol. II
Ainsworth, Maj.-Gen. Sir Ralph Bignell, 1875–1952, vol. V
Ainsworth, Mrs Robert; see Brunskill, Muriel.
Ainsworth, Sir Thomas, 2nd Bt, 1886–1971, vol. VII
Ainsworth, Lt-Col William John, 1873–1945, vol. IV
Ainsworth-Davis, James Richard, 1861–1934, vol. III
Ainsworth-Davis, John Creyghton, 1895–1976, vol. VII
Ainsworth Dickson, Thomas, 1881–1935, vol. III
Aird, Ian, 1905–1962, vol. VI
Aird, Sir John, 1st Bt, 1833–1911, vol. I
Aird, Sir John, 2nd Bt, 1861–1934, vol. III
Aird, Sir John, 1855–1938, vol. III
Aird, Col Sir John Renton, 3rd Bt, 1898–1973, vol. VII

Airedale, 1st Baron, 1835–1911, vol. I
Airedale, 2nd Baron, 1863–1944, vol. IV
Airedale, 3rd Baron, 1882–1958, vol. V
Airey, Sir Edwin, 1878–1955, vol. V
Airey, Paymr Rear-Adm. Frederick W. I., 1861–1922, vol. II
Airey, Harold M.; see Morris-Airey.
Airey, Col Henry Parke, 1844–1911, vol. I
Airey, Sir James Talbot, 1812–1898, vol. I
Airey, John Robinson, died 1937, vol. III
Airey, Col Robert Berkeley, 1874–1933, vol. III
Airlie, 8th Earl of, 1856–1900, vol. I
Airlie, 12th (de facto 9th) Earl of, 1893–1968, vol. VI
Airlie, Countess of; (Mabell), 1866–1956, vol. V
Airy, Anna, 1882–1964, vol. VI
Airy, Rev. Basil Reginald, 1845–1924, vol. II
Airy, Osmund, 1845–1928, vol. II
Airy, Wilfrid, died 1925, vol. II
Aitchison, Rt Hon. Lord; Craigie Mason Aitchison, 1882–1941, vol. IV
Aitchison, Gen. Charles Terrington, 1825–1919, vol. II
Aitchison, Craigie Mason; see Aitchison, Rt Hon. Lord.
Aitchison, Sir David, 1892–1975, vol. VII
Aitchison, George, 1825–1910, vol. I
Aitchison, George, 1877–1954, vol. V
Aitchison, James, 1899–1968, vol. VI
Aitchison, James Edward Tierney, 1835–1898, vol. I
Aitchison, Patrick Edward, 1881–1945, vol. IV
Aitchison, Sir Stephen, 1st Bt, 1863–1942, vol. IV
Aitchison, Sir Stephen Charles de Lancey, 3rd Bt, 1923–1958, vol. V
Aitchison, Sir Walter de Lancey, 2nd Bt, 1892–1953, vol. V
Aitken, Alexander Craig, 1895–1967, vol. VI
Aitken, Cecil Edward, 1888–1959, vol. V
Aitken, Charles, 1869–1936, vol. III
Aitken, Edward Hamilton, 1851–1909, vol. I
Aitken, George Atherton, 1860–1917, vol. II
Aitken, George Benjamin Johnston, died 1942, vol. IV
Aitken, George Lewis, 1864–1940, vol. III
Aitken, Henry, 1851–1931, vol. III
Aitken, Hon. J. G. W., died 1921, vol. II
Aitken, Sir James, 1880–1948, vol. IV
Aitken, James Hume, 1890–1955, vol. V
Aitken, John, died 1919, vol. II
Aitken, John E., died 1957, vol. V
Aitken, John Hobson, 1851–1923, vol. II
Aitken, Col John James, 1878–1946, vol. IV
Aitken, Major Nigel Woodford, 1882–1863, vol. VI
Aitken, Sir Robert, 1863–1924, vol. II
Aitken, Rev. Canon Robert Aubrey, 1870–1941, vol. IV
Aitken, Robert Grant, 1864–1951, vol. V
Aitken, Stephen Rowan, 1883–1943, vol. IV
Aitken, Col William, 1846–1917, vol. II
Aitken, Rev. William Hay Macdowall Hunter, 1841–1927, vol. II
Aitken, Sir William Traven, 1905–1964, vol. VI
Aiton, Sir Arthur; see Aiton, Sir J. A.

Aiton, Sir (John) Arthur, 1864–1950, vol. IV
Aiyangar, Sir Venbakam B.; see Bashyam Aiyangar.
Aiyar, Sir C. P. R.; see Ramaswami Aiyar.
Aiyar, N. Chandrasekhara, 1888–1957, vol. V
Aiyar, Sir Theagaraja; see Sadasiva Aiyar.
Aiyer, Sir Pazhamarneri Sundaram Sivaswamy, 1864–1946, vol. IV
Ajasa, Sir Kitoyi, 1866–1937, vol. III
Akbar, Hon. M. T., 1880–1944, vol. IV (A)
Aked, Charles Frederic, 1864–1941, vol. IV
Akeley, Carl Ethan, 1864–1926, vol. II
Akenhead, David, 1894–1978, vol. VII
Akenhead, Rev. Edmund, died 1931, vol. III
Akerman, John Camille, died 1950, vol. IV
Akerman, Hon. Sir John William, 1825–1905, vol. I
Akerman, Air Vice-Marshal Walter Joseph Martin, 1901–1964, vol. VI
Akerman, Maj.-Gen. William Philip Jopp, 1888–1971, vol. VII
Akers, Sir Wallace Alan, 1888–1954, vol. V
Akhurst, Captain Algernon Frederic, 1893–1972, vol. VII
Akrill-Jones, Rev. Canon David, 1868–1945, vol. IV
Alabaster, Sir Chaloner, 1838–1898, vol. I
Alabaster, Sir Chaloner Grenville, died 1958, vol. V
Alagappa Chettiar, Sir Ramanatha, 1909–1957, vol. V
Alanbrooke, 1st Viscount, 1883–1963, vol. VI
Alanbrooke, 2nd Viscount, 1920–1972, vol. VII
Alba, 17th Duque de, 1878–1953, vol. V
Alban, Sir Frederick John, 1882–1965, vol. VI
Alban Davies, Jenkin, 1901–1968, vol. VI
Albanesi, Mme, (Effie Henderson), 1859–1936, vol. III
Albani, Dame Emma, 1852–1930, vol. III
Albee, Ernest, 1865–1927, vol. II
Albemarle, 8th Earl of, 1858–1942, vol. IV
Albemarle, 9th Earl of, 1882–1979, vol. VII
Albert-Buisson, François, 1881–1961, vol. VI
Albertini, Luigi, 1871–1941, vol. IV
Alberts, Col Johannes Joachim, 1872–1947, vol. IV
Albery, Sir Bronson James, 1881–1971, vol. VII
Albery, Sir Irving James, 1879–1967, vol. VI
Albery, Michael James, 1910–1975, vol. VII
Albright, George Stacey, 1855–1945, vol. IV
Albright, William Foxwell, 1891–1971, vol. VII
Albu, Sir George, 1st Bt, 1857–1935, vol. III
Albu, Major Sir George Werner, 2nd Bt, 1905–1963, vol. VI
Albu, Leopold, died 1938, vol. III
Alcazar, Sir Henry Albert, 1860–1930, vol. III
Alchin, Gordon, died 1947, vol. IV
Alcock, Lt-Col Alfred William, 1859–1933, vol. III
Alcock, Charles William, 1842–1907, vol. I
Alcock, Henry, 1886–1948, vol. VI
Alcock, Rev. Preb. John Mark, died 1955, vol. V
Alcock, Captain Sir John William, 1892–1919, vol. II
Alcock, Nathaniel Henry, 1871–1913, vol. I
Alcock, Reginald, 1868–1944, vol. IV

Alcock, Sir Rutherford, 1809–1897, vol. I
Alcock, Sir Walter Galpin, 1861–1947, vol. IV
Alcorn, George Oscar, 1850–1930, vol. III
Aldam, Col William St Andrew W.; see Warde-Aldam.
Aldanov, Mark, 1889–1957, vol. V
Alden, Henry Mills, 1836–1919, vol. II
Alden, John H., 1900–1976, vol. VII
Alden, Sir Percy, 1865–1944, vol. IV
Aldenham, 1st Baron, 1819–1907, vol. I
Aldenham, 2nd Baron, 1846–1936, vol. III
Aldenham, 3rd Baron, 1879–1939, vol. III
Aldenham, 4th Baron, and Hunsdon of Hunsdon, 2nd Baron, 1888–1969, vol. VI
Alder, Kurt, 1902–1958, vol. V
Alder, Wilfred, died 1962, vol. VI
Alderdice, Hon. Frederick Charles, 1872–1936, vol. III
Alderman, Edwin Anderson, 1861–1931, vol. III
Alderman, Harry Graham, 1895–1962, vol. VI
Alderman, Major Robert Edward, 1887–1934, vol. III
Alderman, Col Walter William, 1874–1935, vol. III
Aldersey, Captain Ralph, 1890–1971, vol. VII
Alderson, Rt Rev. Cecil William, 1900–1968, vol. VI
Alderson, Sir Charles Henry, 1831–1913, vol. I
Alderson, Sir Edward Hall, 1864–1951, vol. V
Alderson, Lt-Gen. Sir Edwin Alfred Hervey, 1859–1927, vol. II
Alderson, Rev. Frederick Cecil, 1836–1907, vol. I
Alderson, Sir George Beeton, 1844–1926, vol. II
Alderson, Sir Harold George, 1891–1978, vol. VII
Alderson, Vice-Adm. William John Standly, died 1946, vol. IV
Alderton, George Edwin Lisle, 1888–1969, vol. VI (AII)
Aldham, Rev. Canon Vernon Harcourt, 1843–1929, vol. III
Aldin, Cecil Charles Windsor, 1870–1935, vol. III
Aldington, Charles, died 1922, vol. II
Aldington, Hubert Edward, 1883–1967, vol. VI
Aldington, Richard, 1892–1962, vol. VI
Aldred-Brown, George Ronald Pym, 1896–1946, vol. IV
Aldren Turner, John William; see Turner.
Aldrich, Gertrude; see Lawrence, G.
Aldrich, Adm. Pelham, 1844–1930, vol. III
Aldrich, Thomas Bailey, 1836–1906, vol. I
Aldrich, Winthrop Williams, 1885–1974, vol. VII
Aldrich-Blake, Dame Louisa Brandreth, 1865–1925, vol. II
Aldridge, Lt-Col Arthur Russell, 1864–1947, vol. IV
Aldridge, Sir Frederick, 1891–1966, vol. VI
Aldridge, Major John Barttelot, 1871–1909, vol. I
Aldridge, Very Rev. John Mullings, died 1920, vol. II
Aldridge, Leonard, 1892–1952, vol. V
Aldworth, Lt-Col W., died 1900, vol. I
Alekhine, Alexander; see Alekhine, A. A.
Alekhine, (Aljechin) Alexander, 1892–1946, vol. IV
Alers Hankey, Richard Lyons, 1906–1969, vol. VI
Alexander of Hillsborough, 1st Earl, 1885–1965, vol. VI

Alexander of Hillsborough, Countess; (Esther Ellen), died 1969, vol. VI
Alexander of Tunis, 1st Earl, 1891–1969, vol. VI
Alexander, Mrs; see Hector, Annie Alexander.
Alexander, Alexander, 1849–1928, vol. II
Alexander, Rev. Archibald, 1874–1942, vol. IV
Alexander, Rev. Archibald Browning Drysdale, 1855–1931, vol. III
Alexander, Arthur Harvey, 1843–1905, vol. I
Alexander, Col Aubrey de Vere, 1849–1923, vol. II
Alexander, Boyd, 1873–1910, vol. I
Alexander, Lt-Col Boyd Francis, 1834–1917, vol. II
Alexander, Charles; see Alexander, R. C.
Alexander, Brig.-Gen. Charles Henry, 1856–1946, vol. IV
Alexander, Charles McCallon, 1867–1920, vol. II
Alexander, Rear-Adm. Charles Otway, 1888–1970, vol. VI
Alexander, Maj.-Gen. Sir Claud, 1st Bt (cr 1886), 1831–1899, vol. I
Alexander, Sir Claud, 2nd Bt (cr 1886), 1867–1945, vol. IV
Alexander, Conel Hugh O'Donel, 1909–1974, vol. VII
Alexander, Conel W. O'D. L., 1879–1920, vol. II
Alexander, Cyril Wilson, 1879–1947, vol. IV
Alexander, David, died 1944, vol. IV
Alexander, David, 1906–1972, vol. VII
Alexander, David Lindo, 1842–1922, vol. II
Alexander, Sir Douglas, 1st Bt (cr 1921), 1864–1949, vol. IV
Alexander, Major Dudley Henry, 1863–1931, vol. III
Alexander, Edward Bruce, 1872–1955, vol. V
Alexander, Maj.-Gen. Edward Currie, 1875–1964, vol. VI
Alexander, Edwin, 1870–1926, vol. II
Alexander, Eleanor Jane, died 1939, vol. III
Alexander, Ernest Edward, 1872–1946, vol. IV
Alexander, Maj.-Gen. Ernest Wright, 1870–1934, vol. III
Alexander, Lt-Col Francis David, 1878–1956, vol. V
Alexander, Sir Frank Samuel, 1st Bt (cr 1945), 1881–1959, vol. V
Alexander, Frederick Matthias, 1869–1955, vol. V
Alexander, Frederick William, 1859–1937, vol. III
Alexander, Sir George, 1858–1918, vol. II
Alexander, George Edward, 1865–1931, vol. III
Alexander, Gilchrist Gibb, 1871–1958, vol. V
Alexander, Harold Vincent, 1886–1950, vol. IV
Alexander, Col Harvey, 1859–1936, vol. III
Alexander, Lt-Col Heber Maitland, 1881–1942, vol. IV
Alexander, Henry, 1841–1914, vol. I
Alexander, Sir Henry, 1875–1940, vol. III
Alexander, Henry Clay, 1902–1969, vol. VI
Alexander, Maj.-Gen. Henry Lethbridge, 1878–1944, vol. IV
Alexander, Maj.-Gen. Henry Templer, 1911–1977, vol. VII
Alexander, Herbert, 1874–1946, vol. IV
Alexander, Lt-Col Hon. Herbrand Charles, 1888–1965, vol. VI

Alexander, James Browning, 1888–1962, vol. VI
Alexander, Rt Hon. Sir James Ulick F. C.; see Alexander, Rt Hon. Sir Ulick.
Alexander, Very Rev. John, 1833–1908, vol. I
Alexander, Hon. John, 1876–1941, vol. IV
Alexander, Col John Donald, 1867–1922, vol. II
Alexander, John W., 1856–1915, vol. I (A)
Alexander, Joseph Gundry, 1848–1918, vol. II
Alexander, Sir Lionel Cecil William, 6th Bt (cr 1809), 1885–1956, vol. V
Alexander, Lt-Col Maurice, 1889–1945, vol. IV
Alexander, Peter, died 1969, vol. IV
Alexander, Reginald Gervase, 1859–1916, vol. II
Alexander, (Richard) Charles, 1884–1968, vol. VI
Alexander, Robert, died 1923, vol. II
Alexander, Lt-Col Robert Donald Thain, 1878–1969, vol. VI
Alexander, Robert Edward, 1874–1946, vol. IV
Alexander, Maj.-Gen. Ronald Okeden, 1888–1949, vol. IV
Alexander, Samuel, 1859–1938, vol. III
Alexander, Rev. Sidney Arthur, 1866–1948, vol. IV
Alexander, Sir Sidney Robert, 1863–1929, vol. III
Alexander, Stanley Walker, 1895–1980, vol. VII
Alexander, Thomas, died 1933, vol. III
Alexander, Thomas Hood Wilson, 1878–1941, vol. IV
Alexander, Rt Hon. Sir Ulick, 1889–1973, vol. VII
Alexander, Walter, 1895–1964, vol. VI
Alexander, Most Rev. William, 1824–1911, vol. I
Alexander, William, died 1921, vol. II
Alexander, Brig.-Gen. Sir William, 1874–1954, vol. V
Alexander, William Cleverly, 1840–1916, vol. II
Alexander, Rev. William Menzies, died 1929, vol. III
Alexander, Lt-Col William Nathaniel Stuart, 1874–1956, vol. V
Alexander, Col Hon. William Sigismund Patrick, 1895–1972, vol. VII
Alexander-Sinclair, Adm. Sir Edwyn Sinclair, 1865–1945, vol. IV
Alexandrowicz, Charles Henry, 1902–1975, vol. VII
Alfieri, Ernest, 1864–1913, vol. I
Alfieri, Maj.-Gen. Frederick John, 1892–1961, vol. VI
Alford, Charles Richard, 1816–1898, vol. I
Alford, Rev. Preb. Charles Symes Leslie, 1885–1963, vol. VI
Alford, Sir Edward Fleet, 1850–1905, vol. I
Alford, (Edward) John (Gregory), 1890–1960, vol. V (A)
Alford, Lt-Col Henry, died 1955, vol. V
Alford, Rev. Henry Powell, died 1921, vol. II
Alford, John; see Alford, E. J. G.
Alford, Rev. Josiah George, 1847–1924, vol. II
Alford, Sir Robert Edmund, 1904–1979, vol. VII
Algeo, Sir Arthur, 1903–1967, vol. VI
Alger, John Goldworth, 1836–1907, vol. I
Algie, Sir Ronald Macmillan, 1888–1978, vol. VII
Ali, Abdullah Yusuf, 1872–1953, vol. V
Ali, Khan Bahadur Nawab Sir Chaudri Fazal, died 1942, vol. IV
Ali, (Chaudri) Mohamad, 1905–1980,vol. VII

Ali, Mir Aula, died 1898, vol. I
Ali, Mohamad; see Ali, C. M.
Ali, Mohammed, 1909–1963, vol. VI
Ali, Rt Hon. (Syed) A.; see Ameer-Ali.
Ali, Syed Waris A.; see Ameer Ali.
Ali, Sir Torick A.; see Ameer Ali.
Ali Chowdhuri, Hon. Nawab Bahadur Syed Nawab, 1863–1929, vol. III
Ali-Rajpur, Raja of, 1881–1948, vol. IV (A), vol. V
Alington, 1st Baron, 1825–1904, vol. I
Alington, 2nd Baron, 1859–1919, vol. II
Alington, 3rd Baron, 1896–1940, vol. III
Alington, Adrian Richard, 1895–1958, vol. V
Alington, Vice-Adm. Argentine Hugh, 1876–1945, vol. IV
Alington, Adm. Arthur Hildebrand, 1839–1925, vol. II
Alington, Very Rev. Cyril Argentine, 1872–1955, vol. V
Alington, Hon. Mrs Cyril, (Hester Margaret), 1874–1958, vol. V
Alington, Hon. Hester Margaret; see Alington, Hon. Mrs Cyril.
Alison, Sir Archibald, 2nd Bt, 1826–1907, vol. I
Alison, Sir Archibald, 3rd Bt, 1862–1921, vol. II
Alison, Comdr Sir Archibald, 4th Bt, 1888–1967, vol. VI
Alison, David, died 1955, vol. V
Alison, Sir Frederick Black, 5th Bt, 1893–1970, vol. VI
Alison, John, 1861–1952, vol. V
Allan of Kilmahew, Baron (Life Peer); Robert Alexander Allan, 1914–1979, vol. VII
Allan, Albert, 1893–1948, vol. IV
Allan, Archibald Russell Watson, 1878–1959, vol. V
Allan, Arthur Percy, 1868–1927, vol. II
Allan, Charles Edward, 1861–1929, vol. III
Allan, Donald James, 1907–1978, vol. VII
Allan, Douglas Alexander, 1896–1967, vol. VI
Allan, F. L., 1893–1964, vol. VI
Allan, Francis John, 1858–1932, vol. III
Allan, George William, 1860–1940, vol. III
Allan, Sir Harold Egbert, 1894–1953, vol. V
Allan, Sir Henry Marshman H.; see Havelock-Allan.
Allan, Sir Henry Ralph Moreton H.; see Havelock-Allan.
Allan, Captain Henry Samuel, 1892–1979, vol. VII
Allan, Sir Henry Spencer Moreton H.; see Havelock-Allan.
Allan, Hugh A., 1857–1938, vol. III
Allan, Col Sir Hugh Montagu, 1860–1951, vol. V
Allan, Rev. J. B., 1873–1932, vol. III
Allan, Hon. John, 1866–1936, vol. III
Allan, John, died 1955, vol. V
Allan, John, 1927–1979, vol. VII
Allan, John Steele, 1889–1979, vol. VII (AII
Allan, Maud, died 1956, vol. V
Allan, Philip Bertram Murray, 1884–1973, vol. VII
Allan, Sir Robert George, 1879–1972, vol. VII
Allan, Robert W., died 1942, vol. IV
Allan, Maj.-Gen. William, 1832–1918, vol. II
Allan, Sir William, 1837–1903, vol. I

Allan, Lt-Col William David, 1879–1961, vol. VI

Allanby, Ven. Christopher Gibson, *died* 1917, vol. II

Allanson, Col Cecil John Lyons, 1877–1943, vol. IV

Allanson, Harry Llewelyn Lyons, 1876–1955, vol. V

Allard, Sir George Mason, 1866–1953, vol. V

Allard, Hon. Jules, 1859–1945, vol. IV

Allardyce, Elsie Elizabeth, (Lady Allardyce), *died* 1962, vol. VI

Allardyce, Brig. John Grahame Buchanan, 1878–1949, vol. IV

Allardyce, Robert Moir, 1882–1951, vol. V

Allardyce, Sir William Lamond, 1861–1930, vol. III

Allason, Maj.-Gen. Sir Richard B.; *see* Bannatine-Allason.

Allason, Brig.-Gen. Walter, 1875–1960, vol. V

Allberry, Albert Spenser, 1880–1949, vol. IV

Allbon, Charles F., 1856–1926, vol. II (A), vol. III

Allbutt, Rt Hon. Sir Clifford; *see* Allbutt, Rt Hon. Sir T. C.

Allbutt, Rt Hon. Sir (Thomas) Clifford, 1836–1925, vol. II

Allchin, Sir Geoffrey Cuthbert, 1895–1968, vol. VI

Allchin, Thomas, 1848–1936, vol. III

Allchin, Sir William Henry, 1846–1911, vol. I

Allcock, Rev. Arthur Edmund, 1851–1924, vol. II

Allcott, Walter Herbert, 1880–1951, vol. V

Allcroft, Herbert John, 1865–1911, vol. I

Allden, John Eric, 1886–1949, vol. IV

Allderidge, Charles Donald, 1889–1958, vol. V

Alldis, Rev. Canon John, 1849–1930, vol. III

Alldridge, Thomas Joshua, 1847–1916, vol. II

Allen of Hurtwood, 1st Baron, 1889–1939, vol. III

Allen of Hurtwood, Lady; (Marjory), 1897–1976, vol. VII

Allen, A. Stuart, 1890–1957, vol. V

Allen, Sir (Albert) George, 1888–1956, vol. V

Allen, Brig.-Gen. Alfred James Whitacre, 1857–1939, vol. III

Allen, Arthur Acland, 1868–1939, vol. III

Allen, Maj.-Gen. Arthur Samuel, 1894–1959, vol. V

Allen, Rev. Barten Wilcockson, *died* 1940, vol. III

Allen, Basil Copleston, 1870–1935, vol. III

Allen, Benjamin, 1845–1929, vol. III

Allen, Rear-Adm. Sir Bertram Cowles, 1875–1957, vol. V

Allen, Sir Carleton Kemp, 1887–1966, vol. VI

Allen, Lt-Col Carleton Woodford, 1878–1938, vol. III

Allen, Col Sir Charles, 1852–1920, vol. II

Allen, Air Vice-Marshal Charles Edward Hamilton, 1899–1975, vol. VII

Allen, Charles Francis Egerton, 1847–1927, vol. II

Allen, Major Rt Hon. Charles Peter, 1861–1930, vol. III

Allen, Charles Peter Selwyn, 1917–1977, vol. VII

Allen, Charles Turner, 1877–1958, vol. V

Allen, Clarence Edgar, 1871–1951, vol. V

Allen, Derek Fortrose, 1910–1975, vol. VII

Allen, Edgar Johnson, 1866–1942, vol. IV

Allen, Edgar Malpas, 1883–1967, vol. VI

Allen, Lt-Col Edward, 1859–1933, vol. III

Allen, Edward H.; *see* Heron-Allen.

Allen, Col Edward Watts, 1883–1965, vol. VI

Allen, Edwin Hopkins, 1878–1967, vol. VI

Allen, Ernest Joshua, 1871–1955, vol. V

Allen, Sir Ernest King, 1864–1937, vol. III

Allen, F. M.; *see* Downey, Edmund.

Allen, Sir Francis Raymond, 2nd Bt, 1910–1939, vol. III

Allen, Frank, 1874–1965, vol. VI

Allen, Sir Frederick Charles, 1st Bt, 1864–1934, vol. III

Allen, Frederick Lewis, 1890–1954, vol. V

Allen, Frederick Martin Brice, 1898–1972, vol. VII

Allen, Sir George; *see* Allen, Sir A. G.

Allen, Engr Rear-Adm. George Bennett, 1888–1948, vol. IV

Allen, George Berney, 1862–1917, vol. II

Allen, Rev. George Kendall, 1883–1975, vol. VII

Allen, George Thomas, 1852–1940, vol. III

Allen, Sir George Vance, 1894–1970, vol. VI

Allen, Rt Rev. Gerald Burton, 1885–1956, vol. V

Allen, Grant, 1848–1899, vol. I

Allen, Rear-Adm. Hamilton Colclough, 1883–1964, vol. VI

Allen, Harold Major, 1911–1977, vol. VII

Allen, Harold Tuckwell, 1879–1950, vol. IV

Allen, Sir Harry Brookes, 1854–1926, vol. II

Allen, Harry Epworth, 1894–1958, vol. V

Allen, Henry George, *died* 1908, vol. I

Allen, Brig. Henry Isherwood, 1887–1979, vol. VII

Allen, Henry Seymour, 1847–1928, vol. II

Allen, Maj.-Gen. Henry Tureman, 1859–1930, vol. III

Allen, Herbert Stanley, 1873–1954, vol. V

Allen, Herbert Warner, 1881–1968, vol. VI

Allen, Rev. Canon Herbert William, *died* 1944, vol. IV

Allen, Hervey, 1889–1949, vol. IV

Allen, Lt-Col Hugh Morris, 1867–1932, vol. III

Allen, Sir Hugh Percy, 1869–1946, vol. IV

Allen, Inglis, 1879–1943, vol. IV

Allen, Very Rev. James, 1802–1897, vol. I

Allen, Col Hon. Sir James, 1855–1942, vol. IV

Allen, James Lane, 1849–1925, vol. II

Allen, Vice-Adm. John Derwent, 1875–1958, vol. V

Allen, John Edsall, 1861–1944, vol. IV

Allen, John Ernest, 1872–1962, vol. VI

Allen, John Romilly, 1847–1907, vol. I

Allen, Sir John Sandeman, 1865–1935, vol. III

Allen, Col John Sandeman, 1892–1949, vol. IV

Allen, Col John Woolley, 1865–1942, vol. IV

Allen, Leslie Holdsworth, 1879–1964, vol. VI

Allen, Comdt Mary Sophia, 1878–1964, vol. VI

Allen, Col Newton Seymour, 1857–1934, vol. III

Allen, Norman Percy, 1903–1972, vol. VII

Allen, Sir Oswald Coleman, 1887–1959, vol. V

Allen, Percy Stafford, 1869–1933, vol. III

Allen, Maj.-Gen. Ralph Edward, 1846–1910, vol. I

Allen, Raymond Cecil, 1872–1937, vol. III

Allen, Raymond Seaforth Stirling, 1905–1974, vol. VII

Allen, Rev. Richard Watson, 1833–1914, vol. I
Allen, Richard William, 1876–1921, vol. II
Allen, Sir Richard William, 1867–1955, vol. V
Allen, Captain Robert Calder, 1812–1903, vol. I
Allen, Lt-Col Robert Candlish, 1881–1942, vol. IV
Allen, Col Robert Franklin, 1860–1916, vol. II
Allen, Sir Roger, 1909–1972, vol. VII
Allen, Sir Ronald Wilberforce, 1889–1936, vol. III
Allen, Col Sir Stephen Shepherd, 1882–1964, vol. VI
Allen, Sydney Scholefield, 1898–1974, vol. VII
Allen, Rev. Thomas, 1837–1912, vol. I
Allen, Very Rev. Thomas, 1873–1927, vol. II
Allen, Sir Thomas, 1864–1943, vol. IV
Allen, Thomas Carleton, 1852–1927, vol. II
Allen, Thomas Palmer, 1899–1979, vol. VII
Allen, Sir Walter Macarthur, 1870–1943, vol. IV
Allen, Wilfred Baugh, 1849–1922, vol. II
Allen, William, 1892–1941, vol. IV
Allen, William, 1870–1945, vol. IV
Allen, Major William Barnsley, 1892–1933, vol. III
Allen, William Edward David, 1901–1973, vol. VII
Allen, William Gilbert, 1892–1970, vol. VI
Allen, Sir William Guilford, 1898–1977, vol. VI
Allen, William Henry, 1844–1926, vol. II
Allen, Lt-Col Sir William James, 1866–1947, vol. IV
Allen, Major William Lynn, 1871–1914, vol. I
Allen, William Philip, 1888–1958, vol. V
Allen, William Shepherd, 1831–1915, vol. I
Allen, Rev. Willoughby Charles, 1867–1953, vol. V
Allen-Williams, Brig.-Gen. Sir Arthur John, 1869–1949, vol. IV
Allenby, 1st Viscount, 1861–1936, vol. III
Allenby, Captain Frederick Claude Hynman, 1864–1934, vol. III
Allenby, Adm. Reginald Arthur, 1861–1936, vol. III
Allendale, 1st Baron, 1829–1907, vol. I
Allendale, 1st Viscount, 1860–1923, vol. II
Allendale, 2nd Viscount, 1890–1956, vol. V
Allerton, 1st Baron, 1840–1917, vol. II
Allerton, 2nd Baron, 1867–1925, vol. II
Allerton, Air Cdre Ord Denny, died 1977, vol. VII
Alletson, Major G. C., died 1928, vol. II
Alleyne, Maj.-Gen. Sir James, died 1899, vol. I
Alleyne, Sir John Gay Newton, 3rd Bt, 1820–1912, vol. I
Allfrey, Lt-Gen. Sir Charles Walter, 1895–1964, vol. VI
Allfrey, Major Edward Mortimer, 1886–1957, vol. V
Allfrey, Captain Maurice Charles, 1916–1942, vol. IV
Allgeyer, Rt Rev. Emile Auguste, 1856–1924, vol. II
Allgood, Maj.-Gen. George, 1827–1907, vol. I
Allgood, Brig.-Gen. William Henry Loraine, 1868–1957, vol. V
Allhusen, (Augustus) Henry (Eden), 1867–1925, vol. II
Allhusen, Beatrice May, died 1918, vol. II
Allhusen, Lt-Col. Frederick Henry, 1872–1957, vol. V

Allhusen, Henry; see Allhusen, A. H. E.
Allhusen, William Hutt, 1845–1923, vol. II
Allies, Mary H. A., 1852–1927, vol. II
Allin, Norman, 1884–1973, vol. VII
Allin, Samuel John Henry Wallis, 1871–1933, vol. III
Allingham, Helen, (Mrs William Allingham), 1848–1926, vol. II
Allingham, Herbert William, died 1904, vol. I
Allingham, Margery Louise, 1904–1966, vol. VI
Allingham, Mrs William; see Allingham, H.
Allinson, Adrian Paul, 1890–1959, vol. V
Allison, Sir Charles William, 1886–1972, vol. VII
Allison, Rev. David, died 1940, vol. III
Allison, James, 1865–1951, vol. V
Allison, James Anthony, 1915–1976, vol. VII
Allison, Sir John; see Allison, Sir W. J.
Allison, Captain John Hamilton, 1902–1968, vol. VI
Allison, John William, died 1934, vol. III
Allison, Philip Rowland, 1907–1974, vol. VII
Allison, Sir Richard John, 1869–1958, vol. V
Allison, Richard Sydney, 1899–1978, vol. VII
Allison, Sir Robert Andrew, 1838–1926, vol. II
Allison, William, 1851–1925, vol. II
Allison, Sir (William) John, 1903–1966, vol. VI
Alliston, Sir Frederick Prat, 1832–1912, vol. I
Allitsen, Frances, died 1912, vol. I
Allitt, Sir (John) William, 1896–1972, vol. VII
Allitt, Sir William; see Allitt, Sir J. W.
Allix, Charles Peter, 1842–1920, vol. II
Allman, George James, 1812–1898, vol. I
Allman, George Johnston, 1824–1904, vol. I
Allman, Robert, 1854–1917, vol. II, vol. III
Allmand, Arthur John, 1885–1951, vol. V
Allnutt, Col Edward Bruce, 1885–1972, vol. VII
Allnutt, Rev. George Herbert, 1843–1919, vol. II
Allom, Sir Charles Carrick, 1865–1947, vol. IV
Allott, Eric Newmarch, 1899–1980, vol. VII
Allport, Alfred, 1867–1949, vol. IV
Allsebrook, George Clarence, 1877–1957, vol. V
Allsop, Hon. Sir James Joseph Whittlesea, 1887–1963, vol. VI
Allsop, Kenneth, 1920–1973, vol. VII
Allsop, Lt-Col William Gillian, 1874–1951, vol. V
Allsopp, Hon. Alfred Percy, 1861–1929, vol. III
Allsopp, Hon. Frederic Ernest, 1857–1928, vol. II
Allsopp, Hon. George Higginson, 1846–1907, vol. I
Allsopp, Captain Hon. Herbert Tongue, 1855–1920, vol. II
Allsopp, Samuel Ranulph, 1899–1975, vol. VII
Allsup, Major Edward Saunders, 1879–1928, vol. II
Allt, Wilfrid Greenhouse, 1889–1969, vol. VI
Allum, Frederick Warner, 1869–1963, vol. VI
Allum, Horace Benjamin, 1884–1966, vol. VI
Allum, Sir John Andrew Charles, 1889–1972, vol. VII
Allward, Walter Seymour, 1876–1955, vol. V
Allwood, James, died 1933, vol. III
Allwork, Rev. Robert Long, 1863–1919, vol. II
Allworthy, Rev. Thomas Bateson, 1879–1964, vol. VI
Alma-Tadema, Miss Anna, died 1943, vol. IV

11

Alma-Tadema, Laura Theresa, (Lady Alma-Tadema), *died* 1909, vol. I

Alma-Tadema, Miss Laurence, *died* 1940, vol. III

Alma-Tadema, Sir Lawrence, 1836–1912, vol. I

Almedingen, E. M., 1898–1971, vol. VII

Almond, Hely Hutchinson, 1832–1903, vol. I

Almond, Sir James, 1891–1964, vol. VI

Almond, Hon. Col Ven. John Macpherson, 1872–1939, vol. III (A), vol. IV

Almond, W. Douglas, *died* 1916, vol. II

Alness, 1st Baron, 1868–1955, vol. V

Alpass, Joesph Herbert, 1873–1969, vol. VI

Alpe, Frank Theodore, *died* 1952, vol. V

Alsop, James Willcox, 1846–1921, vol. II

Alsop, Ralph, *died* 1950, vol. IV

Alstead, Robert, 1873–1946, vol. IV

Alston, Alexander Rowland, 1863–1945, vol. IV

Alston, Rt Rev. Arthur Fawssett, 1872–1954, vol. V

Alston, Rt Hon. Sir Beilby Francis, 1868–1929, vol. III

Alston, Sir Charles Ross, 1862–1937, vol. III

Alston, Sir Francis Beilby, 1820–1905, vol. I

Alston, Brig.-Gen. Francis George, 1878–1961, vol. VI

Alston, Hilda, (Lady Alston), *died* 1945, vol. IV

Alston, Captain Hubert George, 1866–1939, vol. III

Alston, Leonard, 1875–1953, vol. V

Alston, Brig. Llewilyn Arthur Augustus, 1890–1968, vol. VI

Alston, Rowland Crewe, 1852–1933, vol. III

Alston Roberts West, Gen. Sir Michael Montgomerie; *see* West.

Alt, Col William John, 1840–1908, vol. I

Altham, Captain Edward, 1882–1950, vol. IV

Altham, Lt-Gen. Sir Edward Altham, 1856–1943, vol. IV

Altham, Harry Surtees, 1888–1965, vol. VI

Althaus, Frederick Rudolph, 1895–1975, vol. VII

Althaus, Friedrich, 1829–1897, vol. I

Altman, Sir Albert Joseph, 1839–1912, vol. I

Alton, Ernest Henry, *died* 1952, vol. V

Alton, Sir Francis Cooke, 1856–1926, vol. II

Altrincham, 1st Baron, 1879–1955, vol. V

Alun Roberts, Robert, 1894–1969, vol. VI

Aluwihare, Sir Richard, 1895–1976, vol. VII

Alvarez, Justin Charles William, 1859–1934, vol. III

Alvarez de Rocafuarte, Marguerite; *see* D'Alvarez, Madame.

Alverstone, 1st Viscount, 1842–1915, vol. I (A)

Alves, Duncan Elliott, 1870–1940, vol. III

Alves, Lt-Col Henry Malcolm Jerome, 1883–1940, vol. III

Alvingham, 1st Baron, 1889–1955, vol. V

Alvord, Clarence Walworth, 1868–1928, vol. II

Alwar, HH Raj Rishi Shri Sewai Sir Jey Singhji Veerendra Shiromani Dev, Bharat Dharam Prabhakar, Maharaj of, 1882–1937, vol. III

Aly Khan, Shah, 1911–1960, vol. V

Amand de Mendieta, Rev. Emmanuel Alexandre, 1907–1976, vol. VII

Amar Singh, Gen. Raja Sir, 1864–1909, vol. I

Amarjit Singh, Lt-Col Maharajkumar, 1893–1944, vol. IV

Ambedkar, Bhimrao Ramji, 1893–1956, vol. V

Ambler, Air Vice-Marshal Geoffrey Hill, 1904–1978, vol. VII

Ambrose, Robert, 1855–1940, vol. III

Ambrose, Brig. Robert Denis, 1896–1974, vol. VII

Ambrose, William, 1832–1908, vol. I

Amcotts, Lt-Comdr John C.; *see* Cracroft-Amcotts.

Amcotts, Lt-Col Sir Weston C.; *see* Cracroft-Amcotts.

Ameer-Ali, Rt Hon. (Syed), 1849–1928, vol. II

Ameer Ali, (Syed) Waris, 1886–1975, vol. VII

Ameer Ali, Sir Torick, 1891–1975, vol. VII

Amery, Rt Hon. Leopold Stennett, 1873–1955, vol. V

Amery, William Bankes, 1883–1951, vol. V

Ames, Sir Cecil Geraint, 1897–1977, vol. VII

Ames, Frederick, 1836–1918, vol. II

Ames, Sir Herbert Brown, 1863–1954, vol. V

Ames, Jennifer; *see* Greig, Maysie.

Ames, John Richard Woodland, 1872–1947, vol. IV

Ames, Lt-Col Oswald Henry, 1862–1927, vol. II

Ames, Percy W., 1853–1919, vol. II

Amherst, 3rd Earl, 1836–1910, vol. I

Amherst, 4th Earl, 1856–1927, vol. II

Amherst of Hackney, 1st Baron, 1835–1909, vol. I

Amherst of Hackney, Baroness (2nd in line), 1857–1919, vol. II

Amherst of Hackney, 3rd Baron, 1912–1980, vol. VII

Amherst, Rev. Hon. Percy Arthur, 1839–1910, vol. I

Amherst, Hon. Sybil Margaret, *died* 1926, vol. II

Ami, Henry M., 1858–1931, vol. III

Amies, Sir Arthur Barton Pilgrim, 1902–1976, vol. VII

Amigo, Most Rev. Peter E., 1864–1949, vol. IV

Amin, All Hajj Mohammud; *see* Keane, John Fryer Thomas.

Ammon, 1st Baron, *died* 1960, vol. V

Amod, Thakor of, Sardar Nawab Sir Naharsinhji Ishwarsinhji, *died* 1945, vol. IV

Amor, Arthur Joseph, 1897–1966, vol. VI

Amory, Sir Ian Murray Heathcoat Heathcoat-, 2nd Bt, 1865–1931, vol. III

Amory, Major Sir John Heathcoat-, 3rd Bt, 1894–1972, vol. VII

Amory, Sir John Heathcoat H.; *see* Heathcoat-Amory.

Amos, Major Herbert Gilbert Maclachlan, 1866–1924, vol. II

Amos, Sir Maurice Sheldon, 1872–1940, vol. III

Amphlett, Major Charles Grove, 1862–1921, vol. II

Amphlett, Richard Holmden, 1847–1925, vo l.II

Ampthill, 2nd Baron, 1869–1935, vol. III

Ampthill, 3rd Baron, 1896–1973, vol. VII

Ampthill, Lady; (Margaret), 1874–1957, vol. V

Amshewitz, J. H., 1882–1942, vol. IV

Amulree, 1st Baron, 1860–1942, vol. IV

Amundsen, Captain Roald, 1872–1928, vol. II

Amwell, 1st Baron, 1876–1966, vol. VI

Amyand, Arthur; *see* Haggard, Major E. A.

Amyot, Lt-Col Hon. George Elie, 1856–1940, vol. III

Amyot, Lt-Col John Andrew, 1867–1940, vol. III

Ancaster, 1st Earl of, 1830–1910, vol. I

Ancaster, 2nd Earl of, 1867–1951, vol. V

Anda, Géza, 1921–1976, vol. VII

Anderson, Hon. Lord; Andrew Macbeth Anderson, 1862–1936, vol. III

Anderson, Dame Adelaide Mary, 1868–1936, vol. III

Anderson, Sir Alan Garrett, 1877–1952, vol. V

Anderson, Alan Orr, 1879–1958, vol. V

Anderson, Alexander, 1850–1904, vol. I

Anderson, Alexander, 1845–1909, vol. I

Anderson, Alexander, 1858–1936, vol. III

Anderson, Alexander, 1888–1954, vol. V

Anderson, Maj.-Gen. Alexander Dingwall, 1843–1916, vol. II

Anderson, Sir Alexander Greig, *died* 1961, vol. VI

Anderson, Sir Alexander James, 1879–1965, vol. VI

Anderson, Alexander Knox, 1892–1955, vol. V

Anderson, Alexander Richard, *died* 1933, vol. III

Anderson, Maj.-Gen. Alexander Vass, 1895–1963, vol. VI

Anderson, Maj.-Gen. Alfred, 1842–1909, vol. I

Anderson, Andrew Macbeth; *see* Anderson, Hon. Lord.

Anderson, Andrew Newton, 1880–1950, vol. IV

Anderson, Archibald Stirling Kennedy, 1887–1972, vol. VII

Anderson, Arthur Emilius David, 1886–1967, vol. VI

Anderson, Arthur Ingham, 1916–1976, vol. VII

Anderson, Sir Arthur Robert, 1860–1924, vol. II

Anderson, Maj.-Gen. Arthur William Leslie, 1842–1929, vol. III

Anderson, Sir Athol Lancelot, 1875–1955, vol. V

Anderson, Sir Austin Innes, 1897–1973, vol. VII

Anderson, Brig.-Gen. Austin Thomas, *died* 1949, vol. IV

Anderson, Lt-Col Barton Edward, 1881–1927, vol. II

Anderson, C. Goldsborough, 1865–1936, vol. III

Anderson, Charles, 1876–1944, vol. IV

Anderson, Major Charles, 1886–1954, vol. V

Anderson, Lt-Gen. Sir Charles Alexander, 1857–1940, vol. III

Anderson, Charles Buxton, 1879–1953, vol. V

Anderson, Charles Martin, 1918–1961, vol. VI

Anderson, Rt Rev. Charles Palmerston, 1865–1930, vol. III

Anderson, Clinton Presba, 1895–1975, vol. VII

Anderson, Sir Colin Skelton, 1904–1980, vol. VII

Anderson, Daniel Elie, *died* 1928, vol. II

Anderson, Gen. David, 1821–1909, vol. I

Anderson, Sir David, 1880–1953, vol. V

Anderson, David; *see* Hon. Lord St Vigeans.

Anderson, David Dick, 1889–1980, vol. VII

Anderson, David Martin, 1880–1955, vol. V

Anderson, Adm. Sir (David) Murray, 1874–1936, vol. III

Anderson, Lt-Gen. Sir Desmond Francis, 1885–1967, vol. VI

Anderson, Sir Donald Forsyth, 1906–1973, vol. VII

Anderson, Sir Donald George, 1917–1975, vol. VII

Anderson, Sir Duncan Law, 1901–1980, vol. VII

Anderson, Edith Muriel, (Lady Anderson), *died* 1958, vol. V

Anderson, Col Edmund Bullar, 1857–1935, vol. III

Anderson, Sir Edward Arthur, 1908–1979, vol. VII

Anderson, Rev. Edward Erskine, 1872–1950, vol. IV

Anderson, Lt-Col Edward Philip, 1883–1934, vol. III

Anderson, Elizabeth Garrett, 1836–1917, vol. II

Anderson, Emily, 1891–1962, vol. VI

Anderson, Col Eric Litchfield Brooke, 1889–1959, vol. V

Anderson, Eric Oswald, 1870–1935, vol. III

Anderson, Rt Rev. Ernest Augustus, 1859–1945, vol. IV

Anderson, Major Ernest Chester, 1863–1913, vol. I

Anderson, Lt-Col Francis, 1888–1925, vol. II

Anderson, Sir Francis, 1858–1941, vol. IV

Anderson, Brig.-Gen. Sir Francis James, *died* 1920, vol. II

Anderson, Francis Sheed, 1897–1966, vol. VI

Anderson, Frank, 1889–1959, vol. V

Anderson, Sir Frederick, 1884–1961, vol. VI

Anderson, Rev. Frederick Ingall, *died* 1961, vol. VI

Anderson, Lt-Col Frederick Jasper, 1886–1957, vol. V

Anderson, Sir George, 1845–1923, vol. II

Anderson, Sir George, 1876–1943, vol. IV

Anderson, Dr George Cranston, 1879–1944, vol. IV

Anderson, Major George Denis, 1885–1971, vol. VII

Anderson, George Henry Garstin, 1896–1959, vol. V

Anderson, Hon. George James, 1860–1935, vol. III

Anderson, George Knox, 1854–1941, vol. IV

Anderson, Sir Gilmour M.; *see* Menzies Anderson.

Anderson, Lt-Col Guy Willoughby, 1885–1949, vol. IV

Anderson, Gen. Harry Cortlandt, 1826–1921, vol. II

Anderson, Lt-Gen. Sir Hastings; *see* Anderson, Lt-Gen. Sir W. H.

Anderson, Henry Aiken, 1851–1936, vol. III

Anderson, Major Henry Graeme, 1882–1925, vol. II

Anderson, Lt-Col Henry Stewart, 1872–1961, vol. VI

Anderson, Gen. Sir Horace Searle, 1833–1907, vol. I

Anderson, Hugh Alfred, 1867–1933, vol. III

Anderson, Sir Hugh Kerr, 1865–1928, vol. II

Anderson, Ian, 1891–1970, vol. VI

Anderson, J. Wemyss, 1868–1930, vol. III

Anderson, James, 1881–1915, vol. I

Anderson, James, 1857–1932, vol. III

Anderson, Col James, 1872–1955, vol. V

Anderson, James B., 1886–1938, vol. III

Anderson, Col James Dalgliesh, 1877–1947, vol. IV

Anderson, James Drummond, 1852–1920, vol. II

Anderson, Sir James Drummond, 1886–1968, vol. VI

Anderson, James Maitland, 1852–1927, vol. II

Anderson, James S., 1891–1976, vol. VII
Anderson, Hon. James Thomas Milton, 1878–1946, vol. IV
Anderson, James Wallace, *born* 1848, vol. II
Anderson, John, 1833–1900, vol. I
Anderson, John, 1840–1910, vol. I
Anderson, Sir John, 1858–1918, vol. II
Anderson, Sir John, 1852–1924, vol. II
Anderson, John, 1886–1935, vol. III
Anderson, Lt-Col John, 1852–1936, vol. III
Anderson, John, 1855–1938, vol. III
Anderson, Sir John, 1st Bt (*cr* 1920), 1878–1963, vol. VI
Anderson, Sir John, 1908–1965, vol. VI
Anderson, Most Rev. John George, 1866–1943, vol. IV
Anderson, John George Clark, 1870–1952, vol. V
Anderson, John Gerard, 1836–1912, vol. I
Anderson, John Hubback, 1883–1950, vol. IV
Anderson, Rt Rev. John Ogle, 1912–1969, vol. VI
Anderson, John William Stewart, 1874–1920, vol. II
Anderson, Joseph, 1832–1916, vol. II
Anderson, Major Joseph Ringland, 1894–1961, vol. VI
Anderson, Rev. K. C., vol. II
Anderson, Gen. Sir Kenneth Arthur Noel, 1891–1959, vol. V
Anderson, Sir Kenneth Skelton, 1st Bt (*cr* 1919), 1866–1942, vol. IV
Anderson, Dame Kitty, 1903–1979, vol. VII
Anderson, Maj.-Gen. Louis Edward, 1861–1941, vol. IV
Anderson, Louisa Garrett, 1873–1943, vol. IV
Anderson, Mark Louden, 1895–1961, vol. VI
Anderson, Martin Cynicus, 1854–1932, vol. III
Anderson, Mary Reid; *see* Macarthur, M. R.
Anderson, Sir Maurice Abbot, 1861–1938, vol. III
Anderson, Maxwell, 1888–1959, vol. V
Anderson, Captain Sir Maxwell Hendry Maxwell-, 1879–1951, vol. V
Anderson, Melville Best, 1851–1933, vol. III
Anderson, Adm. Sir Murray; *see* Anderson, Adm. Sir D. M.
Anderson, Maj.-Gen. Nelson Graham, 1875–1945, vol. IV
Anderson, Lt-Col Sir Neville, 1881–1963, vol. VI
Anderson, Ven. Nicol Keith, 1882–1953, vol. V
Anderson, Air Vice-Marshal Norman Russel, *died* 1948, vol. IV
Anderson, Col Patrick Campbell, 1894–1965, vol. VI
Anderson, Peter Corsar, 1871–1955, vol. V
Anderson, Peter John, *died* 1926, vol. II
Anderson, Richard John, 1848–1914, vol. I
Anderson, Lt-Gen. Sir Richard Neville, 1907–1979, vol. VII
Anderson, Sir Robert, 1841–1918, vol. II
Anderson, Sir Robert, 1st Bt (*cr* 1911), 1837–1921, vol. II
Anderson, Sir Robert Albert, 1866–1942, vol. IV
Anderson, Major Robert Grenville G.; *see* Gayer-Anderson.
Anderson, Brig. Robert Heath, 1882–1940, vol. III
Anderson, Brig.-Gen. Sir Robert Murray

McCheyne, 1867–1940, vol. III (A), vol. IV
Anderson, Rt Hon. Sir Robert Newton, 1871–1948, vol. IV
Anderson, Sir Robert Rowand, 1834–1921, vol. II
Anderson, Roger Charles, 1883–1976, vol. VII
Anderson, Col Rowland James Percy, 1873–1950, vol. IV
Anderson, Major Roy Dunlop, 1878–1932, vol. III
Anderson, Rudolph Martin, 1876–1961, vol. VI
Anderson, Rupert Darnley, 1859–1944, vol. IV
Anderson, Samuel Boyd, 1878–1934, vol. III
Anderson, Sherwood, *died* 1941, vol. IV
Anderson, Stanley, 1884–1966, vol. VI
Anderson, Brig.-Gen. Stuart Milligan, 1879–1954, vol. V
Anderson, Tempest, 1846–1913, vol. I
Anderson, Theodore Farnworth, 1901–1979, vol. VII
Anderson, Thomas, 1844–1926, vol. II
Anderson, Thomas Alexander Harvie, *died* 1953, vol. V
Anderson, Thomas David, 1853–1932, vol. III
Anderson, Col Thomas Gayer G.; *see* Gayer-Anderson.
Anderson, Sir Thomas M'Call, 1836–1908, vol. I
Anderson, Thomas Scott, 1853–1919, vol. II
Anderson, Brig. Thomas Stephen James, 1909–1969, vol. VI
Anderson, Maj.-Gen. Thomas Victor, 1881–1972, vol. VII
Anderson, Lt-Gen. Sir (Warren) Hastings, 1872–1930, vol. III
Anderson, Maj.-Gen. Warren Melville, 1894–1973, vol. VII
Anderson, Sir William, 1835–1898, vol. I
Anderson, William, 1842–1900, vol. I
Anderson, William, 1831–1913, vol. I
Anderson, Col William, 1886–1944, vol. IV
Anderson, William, 1889–1955, vol. V
Anderson, William Alexander, 1890–1971, vol. VII
Anderson, Maj.-Gen. William Beaumont, 1877–1959, vol. V
Anderson, William Blair, 1877–1959, vol. V
Anderson, William C., *died* 1919, vol. II
Anderson, Col William Campbell, 1868–1926, vol. II
Anderson, Brig.-Gen. William Christian, 1867–1942, vol. IV
Anderson, William Galloway Macdonald, 1905–1978, vol. VII
Anderson, William Geddes, 1858–1932, vol. III
Anderson, Brig. William Henniker, 1880–1958, vol. V
Anderson, Sir William Hewson, 1897–1968, vol. VI
Anderson, Sir William John, 1846–1908, vol. I
Anderson, Rt Rev. William Louis, 1892–1972, vol. VII
Anderson, Lt-Col William Maurice, 1873–1946, vol. IV
Anderson, Lt-Col William Menzies, 1883–1940, vol. III
Anderson, Col William Patrick, 1851–1927, vol. II
Anderson, Col William Robert le Geyt, 1850–1908, vol. I

Anderson, William Thomas, 1872–1948, vol. IV
Anderson, Very Rev. W(illiam) White, 1888–1956, vol. V
Anderson-Morshead, Lt-Col Rupert Henry, *died* 1918, vol. II
Andersson, Lt-Col Sir C. Llewellyn, 1861–1948, vol. IV
Anderton, Sir Francis Robert Ince, 1859–1950, vol. IV
Anderton, Francis Swithin, 1868–1909, vol. I
Andoe, Vice-Adm. Sir Hilary Gustavus, 1841–1905, vol. I
Andrade, Edward Neville da Costa, 1887–1971, vol. VII
Andreades, Andrew, 1876–1935, vol. III
Andreae, Herman Anton, 1876–1965, vol. VI
Andrew, Engr-Captain George Edward, 1869–1945, vol. IV
Andrew, Alistair Hugh, 1908–1947, vol. IV
Andrew, George, 1873–1956, vol. V
Andrew, Engr-Capt. George Edward, 1869–1945, vol. IV
Andrew, Ian Graham, 1893–1962, vol. VI
Andrew, Sir John, 1896–1968, vol. VI
Andrew, John Harold, 1887–1961, vol. VI
Andrew, Brig. Leslie Wilton, 1897–1969, vol. VI
Andrew, Col Richard Hynman, 1885–1964, vol. VI
Andrew, Samuel Ogden, 1868–1952, vol. V
Andrew, Walter Jonathan, *died* 1934, vol. III
Andrew, William Monro, 1895–1973, vol. VII
Andrew, Rev. Canon William Shaw, 1884–1963, vol. VI
Andrewes, Major Francis Edward, 1878–1920, vol. II
Andrewes, Sir Frederick William, 1859–1932, vol. III
Andrewes, Rev. Canon Gerrard Thomas, 1855–1941, vol. IV
Andrewes, Rev. John Brereton, *died* 1920, vol. II
Andrewes, Adm. Sir William Gerrard, 1899–1974, vol. VII
Andrews, Albert Andrew, 1896–1976, vol. VII
Andrews, Lt-Col Cecil Rollo Payton, 1870–1951, vol. V
Andrews, Rev. Charles Freer, 1871–1940, vol. III
Andrews, Charles M'Lean, 1863–1943, vol. IV
Andrews, Charles William, 1866–1924, vol. II
Andrews, Cyril Frank Wilton, 1892–1978, vol. VII
Andrews, Edward Gordon, *died* 1915, vol. II
Andrews, Sir Edwin Arthur C.; *see* Chapman-Andrews.
Andrews, Hon. Elisha Benjamin, 1844–1917, vol. II
Andrews, Ernest Clayton, 1870–1948, vol. IV
Andrews, Sir Ernest Herbert, 1873–1961, vol. VI
Andrews, Captain Francis Arthur Lavington, 1869–1944, vol. IV
Andrews, Rev. George Whitefield, 1833–1931, vol. III
Andrews, Henry Russell, 1871–1942, vol. IV
Andrews, Rev. Herbert T., 1864–1928, vol. II
Andrews, Hugh, *died* 1926, vol. II
Andrews, Rt Hon. Sir James, 1st Bt, 1877–1951, vol. V
Andrews, James Frank, 1848–1922, vol. II

Andrews, James Peter, 1902–1968, vol. VI
Andrews, John Alban, *died* 1964, vol. VI
Andrews, John Launcelot, 1893–1968, vol. VI
Andrews, Rt Hon. John Miller, 1871–1956, vol. V
Andrews, Joseph Ormond, 1873–1909, vol. I
Andrews, Lewis Yelland, 1896–1937, vol. III
Andrews, Sir Linton; *see* Andrews, Sir W. L.
Andrews, Norman Roy F.; *see* Fox-Andrews.
Andrews, Surgeon Captain Octavius William, 1865–1936, vol. III
Andrews, Rear-Adm. Robert Walter Benjamin, 1876–1965, vol. VI
Andrews, Roland Stuart, 1897–1961, vol. VI
Andrews, Roy Chapman, 1884–1960, vol. V
Andrews, Thomas, 1847–1907, vol. I
Andrews, Rt Hon. Thomas, 1843–1916, vol. II
Andrews, Rt Rev. Walter, 1852–1932, vol. III
Andrews, Wilfrid, 1892–1975, vol. VII
Andrews, William, 1848–1908, vol. I
Andrews, Rt Hon. William Drennan, 1832–1924, vol. II
Andrews, William Horner, 1887–1953, vol. V
Andrews, Sir (William) Linton, 1886–1972, vol. VII
Andrews-Speed, James, 1876–1939, vol. III
Andric, Ivo, 1892–1975, vol. VII
Andrus, Brig.-Gen. Thomas Alchin, 1872–1959, vol. V
Anethan, Baroness Albert d', *died* 1935, vol. III
Aney, Madhao Shrihari, 1880–1968, vol. VI
Angas, Sir (John) Keith, 1900–1977, vol. VII
Angas, Sir Keith; *see* Angas, Sir J. K.
Angas, Major Lawrence Lee Bazley, 1893–1973, vol. VII
Angel, John, 1881–1960, vol. V
Angell, Col Frederick John, 1861–1922, vol. II
Angell, James Burrill, 1829–1916, vol. II
Angell, James Rowland, 1869–1949, vol. IV
Angell, Sir Norman, 1874–1967, vol. VI
Angellier, Auguste Jean, 1848–1911, vol. I
Angers, Hon. Sir Auguste Réal, 1837–1919, vol. II
Angers, Hon. Eugène-Réal, 1883–1956, vol. V
Angier, Sir Theodore Vivian Samuel, 1843–1935, vol. III
Anglesey, 4th Marquess of, 1835–1898, vol. I
Anglesey, 5th Marquess of, 1875–1905, vol. I
Anglesey, 6th Marquess of, 1885–1947, vol. IV
Angless, Violet B.; *see* Brunton-Angless.
Anglin, Arthur H., 1850–1934, vol. III
Anglin, Arthur Whyte, 1867–1955, vol. V
Anglin, Rt Hon. Francis Alexander, 1865–1933, vol. III
Angliss, Hon. Sir William Charles, 1865–1957, vol. V
Angst, Sir Henry, 1847–1922, vol. II
Angus, Alfred Henry, 1873–1957, vol. V
Angus, Henry Brunton, 1867–1927, vol. II
Angus, J. Mortimer, 1850–1945, vol. IV
Angus, Richard Bladworth, 1831–1922, vol. II
Angus, Rev. Samuel, 1881–1943, vol. IV
Angus, Sir William, *died* 1912, vol. I
Angus, Col William Mathwin, 1851–1934, vol. III
Angwin, Col Sir (Arthur) Stanley, 1883–1959, vol. V

15

Angwin, Hugh Thomas Moffitt, 1888–1949, vol. IV
Angwin, Col Sir Stanley; see Angwin, Col Sir A. S.
Angwin, Hon. William Charles, 1863–1944, vol. IV
Anley, Brig.-Gen. Barnett Dyer Lempriere Gray, 1873–1954, vol. V
Anley, Brig.-Gen. Frederick Gore, 1864–1936, vol. III
Anley, Col Henry Augustus, 1864–1942, vol. IV
Anley, Major Philip Francis Ross, 1874–1956, vol. V
Ann, Sir Edwin Thomas, 1852–1913, vol. I
Annaly, 3rd Baron, 1857–1922, vol. II
Annaly, 4th Baron, 1885–1970, vol. VI
Annan, William, 1872–1952, vol. V
Annand, James, 1843–1906, vol. I
Annandale, Charles, 1843–1915, vol. I
Annandale, Nelson; see Annandale, T. N.
Annandale, Thomas, 1838–1907, vol. I
Annandale, (Thomas) Nelson, died 1924, vol. II
Anne, Ernest Lambert Swinburne, 1852–1939, vol. III
Anne, George Charlton, 1886–1960, vol. V
Annesley, 5th Earl, 1831–1908, vol. I
Annesley, 6th Earl, 1884–1914, vol. I
Annesley, 7th Earl, 1861–1934, vol. III
Annesley, 8th Earl, 1894–1957, vol. V
Annesley, 9th Earl, 1900–1979, vol. VII
Annesley, Captain Hon. Arthur, 1880–1914, vol. I
Annesley, Lt-Gen. Sir Arthur Lyttelton L.; see Lyttelton-Annesley.
Annesley, Col Arthur Stephen Robert, 1869–1939, vol. III
Annesley, Lt-Col James Howard Adolphus, 1868–1919, vol. II
Annesley, Captain John Campbell, 1895–1964, vol. VI
Annesley, Lt-Col William Henry, 1876–1934, vol. III
Annesley, Major William Richard Norton, 1863–1914, vol. I
Annett, Engr-Captain George Lewis, 1887–1980, vol. VII
Annett, Henry Edward, 1871–1945, vol. IV (A), vol. V
Anningson, Bushell, died 1916, vol. II
Annois, Leonard Lloyd, 1906–1966, vol. VI
Anns, Bryan Herbert, 1929–1975, vol. VII
Anrep, Gleb V., 1891–1955, vol. V
Anscomb, Major Allen-Mellers, born 1849, vol. II
Ansell, Rev. Preb. George Frederick James, 1886–1951, vol. V
Ansell, James Lawrence Bunting, died 1978, vol. VII
Ansell, John, 1874–1948, vol. IV
Ansell, William Henry, 1872–1959, vol. V
Ansell, William James David, 1858–1920, vol. II
Ansermet, Ernest, 1883–1969, vol. VI
Anslow, 1st Baron, 1850–1933, vol. III
Anson, Viscount; Thomas William Arnold Anson, 1913–1958, vol. V
Anson, Rt Rev. and Hon. Adelbert John Robert, 1840–1909, vol. I
Anson, Captain Hon. Alfred, 1876–1944, vol. IV

Anson, Rear-Adm. Algernon Horatio, 1854–1913, vol. I
Anson, Maj.-Gen. Sir Archibald Edward Harbord, 1826–1925, vol. II
Anson, Adm. Charles Eustace, 1859–1940, vol. III
Anson, Hon. Claud, 1864–1947, vol. IV
Anson, Sir Denis George William, 4th Bt, 1888–1914, did not have an entry in Who's Who.
Anson, Sir Edward Reynell, 6th Bt, 1902–1951, vol. V
Anson, Hon. Frederic William, 1862–1917, vol. II
Anson, Lt-Col Hon. Sir George Augustus, 1857–1947, vol. IV
Anson, George H., died 1957, vol. V
Anson, Ven. George Henry Greville, died 1898, vol. I
Anson, Sir (George) Wilfrid, 1893–1974, vol. VII
Anson, Rev. Harold, 1867–1954, vol. V
Anson, Sir John Henry Algernon, 5th Bt, 1897–1918, vol. II
Anson, Sir Wilfrid; see Anson, Sir G. W.
Anson, Rt Hon. Sir William Reynell, 3rd Bt, 1843–1914, vol. I
Ansorge, Sir Eric Cecil, 1887–1977, vol. VII
Ansorge, William John, 1850–1913, vol. I
Anstead, Rudolph David, 1876–1962, vol. VI
Anstey, Most Rev. Arthur Henry, died 1955, vol. V
Anstey, Brig. Edgar Carnegie, 1882–1958, vol. V
Anstey, F.; see Guthrie, T. A.
Anstey, Hon. Frank, 1865–1940, vol. III
Anstey, Gilbert Tomkins, 1889–1974, vol. VII
Anstey, Percy, 1876–1920, vol. II
Anstey, Vera, 1889–1976, vol. VII
Anstey, Engr-Rear-Adm. William John, 1860–1936, vol. III
Anstice, Hon. Col Sir Arthur, 1846–1929, vol. III
Anstice, Vice-Adm. Sir Edmund Walter, 1899–1979, vol. VII
Anstice, Lt-Col Sir Robert Henry, 1843–1922, vol. II
Anstie, James, 1836–1924, vol. II
Anstruther, Brig. Alexander Meister, 1902–1969, vol. VI
Anstruther, Arthur Wellesley, 1864–1938, vol. III
Anstruther, Col Charles Frederick St Clair, 1855–1925, vol. II
Anstruther, Hon. Dame Eva Isabella Henrietta, 1869–1935, vol. III
Anstruther, George Elliot, 1870–1940, vol. III
Anstruther, Henry Torrens, 1860–1926, vol. II
Anstruther, Col Philip Noel, 1891–1960, vol. V
Anstruther, Sir Ralph William, 6th Bt (cr 1694), 1858–1934, vol. III
Anstruther, Adm. Robert Hamilton, 1862–1938, vol. III
Anstruther, Lt-Col Robert Hamilton Lloyd-, 1841–1914, vol. I
Anstruther, Sir Windham Charles James Carmichael, 8th Bt (cr 1700 and 1798), 1824–1898, vol. I
Anstruther, Sir Windham Eric Francis Carmichael-, 11th Bt (cr 1700 and 1798), 1900–1980, vol. VII

Anstruther, Sir Windham Frederick Carmichael-, 10th Bt (cr 1700 and 1798), 1902–1928, vol. II

Anstruther, Sir Windham Robert Carmichael, 9th Bt (cr 1700 and 1798), 1877–1903, vol. I

Anstruther-Gough-Calthorpe, Sir FitzRoy Hamilton, 1st Bt, 1872–1957, vol. V

Anstruther-Gray, Lt-Col William, 1859–1938, vol. III

Anstruther-Thomson, John, 1818–1904, vol. I

Antelme, Hon. Sir Celicourt, 1818–1899, vol. I

Anthonisz, James Oliver, 1860–1921, vol. II

Anthonisz, Peter Daniel, 1822–1903, vol. I

Anthony, Henry Montesquieu, 1873–1949, vol. IV

Anthony, Herbert Douglas, 1892–1968, vol. VI

Anthony, Irvin, 1890–1971, vol. VII

Anthony, Sir John, died 1935, vol. III

Anthony, Philip Arnold, 1873–1949, vol. IV

Anthony, Maj.-Gen. Richard William, 1874–1940, vol. III

Anthony, Maj.-Gen. William Samuel, 1874–1943, vol. IV

Antill, Maj.-Gen. John Macquarie, 1866–1937, vol. III

Antony, Jonquil, 1912–1980, vol. VII

Antrim, 11th Earl of, 1851–1918, vol. II

Antrim, 12th Earl of, 1878–1932, vol. III

Antrim, 13th Earl of, 1911–1977, vol. VII

Antrobus, Sir Cosmo Gordon, 5th Bt, 1859–1939, vol. III

Antrobus, Dame Edith Marion, died 1944, vol. IV

Antrobus, Sir Edmund, 3rd Bt, 1818–1899, vol. I

Antrobus, Sir Edmund, 4th Bt, 1848–1915, vol. I

Antrobus, Edward Gream, 1860–1940, vol. III

Antrobus, John Coutts, 1829–1916, vol. II

Antrobus, Captain Sir Philip Humphrey, 6th Bt, 1876–1968, vol. VI

Antrobus, Sir Reginald Laurence, 1853–1942, vol. IV

Antrobus, Lt-Col Ronald Henry, 1891–1980, vol. VII

Anwyl, Sir Edward, 1866–1914, vol. I

Anwyl, Rev. John Bodvan, 1875–1949, vol. IV (A), vol. V

Anwyl-Davies, Thomas, died 1971, vol. VII

Anwyl-Passingham, Col Augustus Mervyn Owen, 1880–1955, vol. V

Anzon Caccamisi, Baronne; See Marchesi, Blanche

Aoki, Viscount, 1844–1914, vol. I

Apcar, Sir Apcar Alexander, 1851–1913, vol. I

Ap Ellis, Gp Captain Augustine, 1886–1969, vol. VI

Aplin, Harold D'Auvergne, 1879–1958, vol. V

Aplin, Major John George Orlebar, died 1915, vol. I

Aplin, Col Philip John Hanham, 1858–1927, vol. II

Aplin, Col Stephen Lushington, 1863–1940, vol. III

Appelbe, Brig.-Gen. Edward Benjamin, 1855–1935, vol. III

Apperley, (George Owen) Wynne, 1884–1960, vol. V

Apperley, Newton Wynne, 1846–1925, vol. II

Apperley, Wynne; see Apperley, G. O. W.

Apperly, Sir Alfred, 1839–1913, vol. I

Apperly, Herbert, died 1932, vol. III

Apperson, George Latimer, 1857–1937, vol. III

Appleby, Sir Alfred, 1866–1952, vol. V

Appleby, Lt-Col Charles Bernard, 1905–1975, vol. VII

Appleby, Lt-Col John Pringle, 1891–1966, vol. VI

Appleby, Sir Robert Rowland, 1887–1966, vol. VI

Applegarth, Robert, 1834–1924, vol. II

Appleton, Arthur Beeny, died 1950, vol. IV

Appleton, Sir Edward Victor, 1892–1965, vol. VI

Appleton, George Webb, 1845–1909, vol. I

Appleton, Brig. Gilbert Leonard, 1894–1970, vol. VI

Appleton, Rev. Richard, 1849–1909, vol. I

Appleton, William, 1846–1906, vol. I

Appleton, Sir William, 1889–1958, vol. V

Appleton, William Archibald, 1859–1940, vol. III

Appleton, William Thomas, 1859–1930, vol. III

Appleyard, Maj.-Gen. Frederick Ernest, 1829–1911, vol. I

Appleyard, Col Kenelm Charles, 1894–1967, vol. VI

Appleyard, Rollo, 1867–1943, vol. IV

Applin, Captain Arthur, died 1949, vol. IV

Applin, Lt-Col Reginald Vincent Kempenfelt, 1869–1957, vol. V

Apponyi, Count Albert, 1846–1933, vol. III

Apps, Rear-Adm. Edgar Stephen, 1893–1958, vol. V

Apps, Engr-Captain William Richard, 1862–1947, vol. IV

ap Rhys Pryce, Gen. Sir Henry Edward, 1874–1950, vol. IV

Apsey, Sir John, 1859–1930, vol. III

Apsley, Lord; Allen Algernon Bathurst, 1895–1942, vol. IV

Apsley, Lady; (Violet Emily Mildred), died 1966, vol. VI

Apthorp, Major Shirley East, 1882–1937, vol. III

Arabi, Sayed Ahmed Pasha, 1841–1911, vol. I

Arbab Dost Muhammad Khan, Khan Bahadur Sir, died 1931, vol. III

Arber, Agnes, (Mrs E. A. Newell Arber), 1879–1960, vol. V

Arber, Mrs E. A. Newell; see Arber, Agnes.

Arber, Edward, 1836–1912, vol. I

Arber, Edward Alexander Newell, 1870–1918, vol. II

Arberry, Arthur John, 1905–1969, vol. VI

Arbuckle, Hon. Sir William, 1839–1915, vol. I

Arbuckle, Sir William Forbes, 1902–1966, vol. VI

Arbuthnot, Brig. Alexander George, 1873–1961, vol. VI

Arbuthnot, Sir Alexander John, 1822–1907, vol. I

Arbuthnot, Sir Charles George, 1824–1899, vol. I

Arbuthnot, Charles George, 1846–1928, vol. II

Arbuthnot, Vice-Adm. Charles Ramsay, 1850–1913, vol. I

Arbuthnot, Clifford William Ernest, died 1974, vol. VII

Arbuthnot, Brig.-Gen. Sir Dalrymple, 5th Bt, 1867–1941, vol. IV

Arbuthnot, Captain Ernest Kennaway, 1876–1945, vol. IV

Arbuthnot, Adm. Sir Geoffrey Schomberg, 1885–1957, vol. V

Arbuthnot, Ven. George, 1846–1922, vol. II
Arbuthnot, Sir George Gough, 1847–1929, vol. III
Arbuthnot, Gerald Archibald, 1872–1916, vol. II
Arbuthnot, Maj.-Gen. Henry Thomas, 1834–1919, vol. II
Arbuthnot, James Woodgate, 1848–1927, vol. II
Arbuthnot, Major John Bernard, 1875–1950, vol. IV
Arbuthnot, Major Sir Robert Dalrymple, 6th Bt, 1919–1944, vol. IV
Arbuthnot, Robert Edward Vaughan, 1871–1922, vol. II
Arbuthnot, Rear-Adm. Sir Robert Keith, 4th Bt, 1864–1916, vol. II
Arbuthnot, Robert Wemyss Muir, 1889–1962, vol. VI
Arbuthnot-Leslie of Warthill, William, 1878–1956, vol. V
Arbuthnott, 11th Viscount of, 1845–1914, vol. I
Arbuthnott, 12th Viscount of, 1849–1917, vol. II
Arbuthnott, 13th Viscount of, 1847–1920, vol. II
Arbuthnott, 14th Viscount of, 1882–1960, vol. V
Arbuthnott, 15th Viscount of, 1897–1966, vol. VI
Arbuthnott, Hon. David, 1820–1901, vol. I
Arbuthnott, John Campbell, 1858–1923, vol. II
Arbuthnott, Robert, 1900–1980, vol. VII
Arcedeckne-Butler, Maj.-Gen. St John Desmond, 1896–1959, vol. V
Arch, Joseph, 1826–1919, vol. II
Archambeault, Hon. Sir Horace, 1857–1918, vol. II
Archambeault, Rt Rev. Joseph Alfred, 1859–1913, vol. I
Archbold, William Arthur Jobson, 1865–1947, vol. IV
Archdale, Brig. Arthur Somerville, 1882–1948, vol. IV
Archdale, Rt Hon. Edward, 1850–1916, vol. II
Archdale, Rt Hon. Sir Edward Mervyn, 1st Bt, 1853–1943, vol. IV
Archdale, Rev. Canon Eyre William Preston, 1871–1955, vol. V
Archdale, Helen Alexander, 1876–1949, vol. IV
Archdale, Brig.-Gen. Hugh James, 1854–1921, vol. II
Archdale, Vice-Adm. Sir Nicholas Edward, 2nd Bt, 1881–1955, vol. V
Archdale, Major Theodore Montgomery, 1873–1918, vol. II
Archdale, Rev. Thomas Hewan, died 1924, vol. II
Archdall, Rev. Canon Henry Kingsley, 1886–1976, vol. VII
Archdall, Rt Rev. Mervyn, 1833–1913, vol. I
Archer, Allan; see Archer, H. A. F. B.
Archer, Lt-Col Charles, 1861–1941, vol. IV
Archer, Adm. Sir Ernest Russell, 1891–1958, vol. V
Archer, Francis Kentdray, 1882–1962, vol. VI
Archer, Sir Geoffrey Francis, 1882–1964, vol. VI
Archer, George, 1896–1960, vol. V
Archer, Sir Gilbert, 1882–1948, vol. IV
Archer, Major Henry, 1883–1917, vol. II
Archer, (Henry) Allan (Fairfax Best), 1887–1950, vol. IV
Archer, Captain Hugh Edward Murray, 1879–1930, vol. III
Archer, James, 1822–1904, vol. I

Archer, Col James Henry L.; see Lawrence-Archer.
Archer, Sir John, 1860–1949, vol. IV
Archer, John Beville, 1893–1948, vol. IV
Archer, John Mark, 1908–1965, vol. VI
Archer, Wing Comdr John Oliver, 1887–1968, vol. VI
Archer, Norman Ernest, 1892–1970, vol. VI
Archer, Richard Lawrence, 1874–1953, vol. V
Archer, Col Samuel Arthur, 1871–1943, vol. IV
Archer, Thomas, 1823–1905, vol. I
Archer, Walter E., 1855–1917, vol. II
Archer, William, 1856–1924, vol. II
Archer, William George, 1907–1979, vol. VII
Archer, William John, 1861–1934, vol. III
Archer-Hind, Richard Dacre, 1849–1910, vol. I
Archer Houblon, Mrs Doreen, 1899–1977, vol. VII
Archer-Houblon, Col George Bramston; see Houblon.
Archer-Jackson, Lt-Col Basil, 1884–1965, vol. VI
Archer-Shee, Lt-Col Sir Martin, 1873–1935, vol. III
Archey, Sir Gilbert Edward, 1890–1974, vol. VII
Archibald, 1st Baron, 1898–1975, vol. VII
Archibald, Col (temp. Brig.) Gordon King, died 1942, vol. IV
Archibald, James, 1863–1946, vol. IV
Archibald, Very Rev. John, died 1916, vol. II
Archibald, John Gordon, 1885–1970, vol. VI
Archibald, Hon. John Sprott, 1843–1932, vol. III
Archibald, Myles, 1898–1961, vol. VI
Archibald, Raymond Clare, 1875–1957, vol. V
Archibald, Sir Robert George, 1880–1953, vol. V
Archibald, Sir William Frederick Alphonse, 1846–1922, vol. II
Arcot, Prince of, 1882–1952, vol. V
Ardagh, Lt-Col George Hutchings, 1863–1930, vol. III
Ardagh, Maj.-Gen. Sir John Charles, 1840–1907, vol. I
Arden, Lt-Col John Henry Morris, 1875–1918, vol. II
Arden-Clarke, Sir Charles Noble, 1898–1962, vol. VI
Arden-Close, Col Sir Charles Frederick, 1865–1952, vol. V
Arden Wood, William Henry Heton, 1858–1932, vol. III
Ardilaun, 1st Baron, 1840–1915, vol. I
Ardill, Rev. John Roche, died 1947, vol. IV (A)
Arditi, Luigi, 1822–1903, vol. I
Ardizzone, Edward Jeffrey Irving, 1900–1979, vol. VII
Ardron, John, 1843–1919, vol. II
Ardwall, Hon. Lord; Andrew Jameson, 1845–1911, vol. I
Arenberg, Auguste Louis Alberic, Prince D', 1837–1924, vol. II
Arendzen, Rev. John, 1873–1954, vol. V
Arensky, Antony Stepanovich, 1861–1906, vol. I (A)
Argenti, Philip Pandely, died 1974, vol. VII
Argles, Rev. Canon George Marsham, 1841–1920, vol. II
Argyle, Lt-Col Edward Percy, 1875–1935, vol. III

Argyle, Hon. Sir Stanley Seymour, 1867–1940, vol. III

Argyll, 8th Duke of, 1823–1900, vol. I

Argyll, 9th Duke of, 1845–1914, vol. I

Argyll, 10th Duke of, 1872–1949, vol. IV

Argyll, 11th Duke of, 1903–1973, vol. VII

Aria, Mrs, 1866–1931, vol. III

Ariff, Sir Kamil Mohamed, 1893–1960, vol. V

Aris, Lt-Col Charles John, 1874–1931, vol. III

Aris, Ernest Alfred, 1882–1963, vol. VI

Aris, Major Herbert, 1868–1952, vol. V

Arisugawa, Prince Takehito, 1862–1913, vol. I

Arkell, Rev. Anthony John, 1898–1980, vol. VII

Arkell, Reginald, died 1959, vol. V

Arkell, William Joscelyn, 1904–1958, vol. V

Arkle, Harry, 1893–1973, vol. VII

Arkwright, Rev. Ernest Henry, 1868–1950, vol. IV

Arkwright, Esme Francis Wigsell, 1882–1934, vol. III

Arkwright, Francis, 1846–1915, vol. I

Arkwright, Frederic Charles, 1853–1923, vol. II

Arkwright, John Hungerford, 1833–1905, vol. I

Arkwright, John Peter, 1864–1931, vol. III

Arkwright, Sir John Stanhope, 1872–1954, vol. V

Arkwright, Sir Joseph Arthur, 1864–1944, vol. IV

Arkwright, Richard, 1835–1918, vol. II

Arkwright, Maj.-Gen. Robert Harry Bertram, 1903–1971, vol. VII

Arkwright, William, 1857–1925, vol. II

Arlen, Michael, 1895–1956, vol. V

Arlen, Stephen Walter, 1913–1972, vol. VII

Arliss, George, 1868–1946, vol. IV

Arliss, Vice-Adm. Stephen Harry Tolson, 1895–1954, vol. V

Armaghdale, 1st Baron, 1850–1924, vol. II

Armand, Louis, 1905–1971, vol. VII

Armbruster, Charles Hubert, 1874–1957, vol. V

Armes, Col Reginald John, 1876–1948, vol. IV

Armfelt, Roger Noel, 1897–1955, vol. V

Armfield, Constance, (Mrs Maxwell Armfield); see Smedley, Constance.

Armfield, Maxwell Ashby, died 1972, vol. VII

Armitage, Captain Albert Borlase, 1864–1943, vol. IV

Armitage, Bernard William, 1890–1976, vol. VII

Armitage, Sir Cecil; see Armitage, Sir S. C.

Armitage, Captain Sir Cecil Hamilton, 1869–1933, vol. III

Armitage, Cecil Henry, 1877–1955, vol. V

Armitage, Gen. Sir (Charles) Clement, 1881–1973, vol. VII

Armitage, Major Charles Leathley, 1871–1951, vol. V

Armitage, Gen. Sir Clement; see Armitage, Gen. Sir Charles C.

Armitage, Rev. Cyril Moxon, 1900–1966, vol. VI

Armitage, Brig.-Gen. Edward Hume, 1859–1949, vol. IV

Armitage, Elkanah, 1844–1929, vol. III

Armitage, Ella Sophia, 1841–1931, vol. III

Armitage, Francis Paul, 1875–1953, vol. V

Armitage, Frank, 1872–1955, vol. V

Armitage, Rev. George, 1856–1948, vol. IV

Armitage, Hugh Traill, 1881–1963, vol. VI

Armitage, John, 1910–1980, vol. VII

Armitage, Robert, 1866–1944, vol. IV

Armitage, Rev. Robert, 1857–1954, vol. V

Armitage, Sir (Stephen) Cecil, 1889–1962, vol. VI

Armitage, Valentine Leathley, 1888–1964, vol. VI

Armitage, Ven. William James, 1860–1929, vol. III

Armitage-Smith, George, died 1923, vol. II

Armitage-Smith, Sir Sydney Armitage, 1876–1932, vol. III

Armitstead, 1st Baron, 1824–1915, vol. I (A)

Armitstead, Ven. John Hornby, 1868–1941, vol. IV

Armitstead, Rev. John Richard, 1829–1918, vol. II

Armour, Donald John, died 1933, vol. III

Armour, Eric Norman, 1877–1934, vol. III

Armour, George Denholm, 1864–1949, vol. IV

Armour, Rev. James Brown, 1842–1928, vol. II

Armour, Hon. John Douglas, 1830–1903, vol. I (A)

Armour, Jonathan Ogden, 1863–1927, vol. II

Armour, Margaret; see MacDougall, Margaret.

Armour, Rev. Samuel Crawford, 1839–1929, vol. III

Armour, Rt Rev. Thomas Makinson, 1890–1963, vol. VI

Armour, William, 1903–1979, vol. VII

Armour-Hannay, Samuel Beveridge, 1856–1919, vol. II

Arms, John Taylor, 1887–1953, vol. V

Armstead, Henry Hugh, 1828–1905, vol. I

Armstrong, 1st Baron cr 1887, 1810–1900, vol. I (up to the 5th edition of vol. I this entry is headed in error by the first three lines of the following entry: Armstrong, Sir Alexander)

Armstrong, 1st Baron cr 1903, 1863–1941, vol. IV

Armstrong, 2nd Baron cr 1903, 1892–1972, vol. VII

Armstrong of Sanderstead, Baron (Life Peer); William Armstrong, 1915–1980, vol. VII

Armstrong, Sir Alexander, 1818–1899, vol. I

Armstrong, Sir Alfred Norman, 1899–1966, vol. VI

Armstrong, Sir Andrew Harvey, 3rd Bt, 1866–1922, vol. II

Armstrong, Anthony (A. A.); see Willis, A. A.

Armstrong, Arthur Henry, 1893–1972, vol. VII

Armstrong, Arthur Leopold, 1888–1973, vol. VII

Armstrong, Col Bertie Harold Olivier, 1873–1950, vol. IV

Armstrong, Sir Charles Herbert, 1862–1949, vol. IV

Armstrong, Brig.-Gen. Charles Johnstone, 1872–1934, vol. III

Armstrong, David; see Clewes, Winston.

Armstrong, Edmond Arrenton, 1899–1966, vol. VI

Armstrong, Edmund Clarence Richard, 1879–1923, vol. II

Armstrong, Rev. Sir Edmund Frederick, 2nd Bt, 1836–1899, vol. I

Armstrong, Edmund La Touche, 1864–1946, vol. IV

Armstrong, Edward, 1846–1928, vol. II

Armstrong, Lt-Col Edward, 1869–1951, vol. V

Armstrong, Maj.-Gen. Edward Francis Hunter, 1834–1917, vol. II

Armstrong, Edward Frankland, 1878–1945, vol. IV

Armstrong, Hon. Ernest Howard, vol. III

Armstrong, F. A. W. T., 1849–1920, vol. II
Armstrong, Francis Edwin, 1879–1921, vol. II
Armstrong, Sir Francis Philip, 3rd Bt, 1871–1944, vol. IV
Armstrong, Major Francis Savage Nesbitt S.; see Savage-Armstrong.
Armstrong, Frederick Ernest, 1884–1962, vol. VI
Armstrong, Captain Sir George Carlyon Hughes, 1st Bt, 1836–1907, vol. I
Armstrong, George Eli, 1854–1933, vol. III
Armstrong, Sir George Elliot, 2nd Bt, 1866–1940, vol. III
Armstrong, George Francis S.; see Savage-Armstrong.
Armstrong, George Frederick, 1842–1900, vol. I
Armstrong, George Gilbert, 1870–1945, vol. IV
Armstrong, George James, 1901–1972, vol. VII
Armstrong, Col Gerald Denne, 1865–1931, vol. III
Armstrong, Sir Gloster; see Armstrong, Sir H. G.
Armstrong, Sir Godfrey, 1882–1964, vol. VI
Armstrong, Hamilton Fish, 1893–1973, vol. VII
Armstrong, Captain Harold Courtenay, 1892–1943, vol. IV
Armstrong, Sir (Harry) Gloster, 1861–1938, vol. III
Armstrong, Rt Hon. Henry Bruce, 1844–1943, vol. IV
Armstrong, Henry Edward, 1848–1937, vol. III
Armstrong, Rev. James, died 1928, vol. II
Armstrong, James Shelley Phipps, 1899–1971, vol. VII
Armstrong, John, 1893–1973, vol. VII
Armstrong, Surg.-Dentist John Alexander, 1862–1928, vol. II
Armstrong, Brig. John Cardew, 1887–1953, vol. V
Armstrong, Col John Cecil, 1870–1961, vol. VI
Armstrong, Sir John Dunamace H.; see Heaton-Armstrong.
Armstrong, John Elliot, 1875–1962, vol. VI
Armstrong, Vice-Adm. John Garnet, 1870–1949, vol. IV
Armstrong, Hon. John Ignatius, 1908–1977, vol. VII
Armstrong, John Warneford Scobell, 1877–1960, vol. V
Armstrong, Katharine Fairlie, 1892–1969, vol. VI
Armstrong, Louis Daniel, 1900–1971, vol. VII
Armstrong, Martin Donisthorpe, 1882–1974, vol. VII
Armstrong, Dame Nellie; see Melba, Dame Nellie.
Armstrong, Sir Nesbitt William, 4th Bt, 1875–1953, vol. V
Armstrong, Col Oliver Carleton, 1859–1932, vol. III
Armstrong, Sir Richard Harold, 1874–1950, vol. IV
Armstrong, Gen. St George Bewes, 1871–1956, vol. V
Armstrong, Samuel, 1878–1959, vol. V
Armstrong, Rev. Simon Carter, 1856–1942, vol. IV
Armstrong, Thomas, 1832–1911, vol. I
Armstrong, Thomas, 1899–1978, vol. VII
Armstrong, Thomas Graves Lowry Herbert, 1856–1940, vol. III
Armstrong, Rt Rev. Thomas Henry, 1857–1930, vol. III

Armstrong, Thomas Mandeville Emerson, 1869–1922, vol. II
Armstrong, Wallace Edwin, 1896–1980, vol. VII
Armstrong, Sir Walter, 1850–1918, vol. II
Armstrong, Rev. Walter H., 1873–1949, vol. IV
Armstrong, William, 1882–1952, vol. V
Armstrong, William Charles H.; see Heaton-Armstrong.
Armstrong, Hon. William Drayton, 1861–1936, vol. III
Armstrong, William George, 1859–1941, vol. IV
Armstrong, Sir William Herbert Fletcher, 1892–1950, vol. IV
Armstrong Cowan, Sir Christopher; see Cowan, Sir C. G. A.
Armstrong-Jones, Sir Robert; see Jones.
Armstrong-Jones, Ronald Owen Lloyd, 1899–1966, vol. VI
Armytage, Rev. Canon Duncan, 1889–1954, vol. V
Armytage, Sir George, 5th Bt, 1819–1899, vol. I
Armytage, Brig.-Gen. Sir George Ayscough, 7th Bt, 1872–1953, vol. V
Armytage, Sir George John, 6th Bt, 1842–1918, vol. II
Armytage, Percy, 1853–1934, vol. III
Armytage, Lt-Col Vivian Bartley G.; see Green-Armytage.
Arnason, Frú Barbara; see Moray Williams, B.
Arnaud, Emile, 1864–1921, vol. II
Arnaud, Yvonne, 1895–1958, vol. V
Arnavon, Jacques, 1877–1949, vol. IV
Arnell, Charles Christopher, 1881–1948, vol. IV
Arnett, Edward John, died 1940, vol. III
Arnheim, Edward Henry Silberstein Von, died 1925, vol. II
Arnison, William Christopher, 1837–1899, vol. I
Arno, Peter, 1906–1968, vol. VI
Arnold, 1st Baron, 1878–1945, vol. IV
Arnold, Sir Alfred, 1835–1908, vol. I
Arnold, Col Alfred James, 1866–1933, vol. III
Arnold, Maj.-Gen. Allan Cholmondeley, 1893–1962, vol. VI
Arnold, Sir Arthur, 1833–1902, vol. I
Arnold, Arthur, 1891–1961, vol. VI
Arnold, Bening Mourant, 1884–1955, vol. V
Arnold, Edmund George, 1865–1939, vol. III
Arnold, Edward Augustus, 1857–1942, vol. IV
Arnold, Edward Carleton, died 1949, vol. IV
Arnold, Edward Vernon, 1857–1926, vol. II
Arnold, Sir Edwin, 1832–1904, vol. I
Arnold, Edwin Lester, died 1935, vol. III
Arnold, Sir Frederick Blackmore, 1906–1968, vol. VI
Arnold, George Frederick, died 1917, vol. II
Arnold, Henry Fraser James Coape-, 1846–1923, vol. II
Arnold, Gen. of the Army Henry H., 1886–1950, vol. IV
Arnold, Rev. Henry James Lawes, 1854–1928, vol. II
Arnold, Lt-Col Herbert Tollemache, 1867–1943, vol. IV
Arnold, Ivor Deiniol Osborn, 1895–1952, vol. V
Arnold, Major John Effingham, 1882–1939, vol. III

Arnold, John Oliver, 1858–1930, vol. III
Arnold, Ralph Crispian Marshall, 1906–1970, vol. VI
Arnold, Reginald Edward, 1853–1938, vol. III
Arnold, Ronald Nathan, 1908–1963, vol. VI
Arnold, Col Stanley, 1844–1906, vol. I
Arnold, Thomas, 1823–1900, vol. I
Arnold, Thomas George, 1866–1944, vol. IV
Arnold, Thomas James, 1879–1945, vol. IV
Arnold, Sir Thomas Walker, 1864–1930, vol. III
Arnold, Thurman Wesley, 1891–1969, vol. VI
Arnold, Tom, (Thomas Charles Arnold), *died* 1969, vol. VI
Arnold, Sir William Henry, 1903–1973, vol. VII
Arnold, William R., 1872–1929, vol. III
Arnold-Forster, Rear-Adm. Forster Delafield, 1876–1958, vol. V
Arnold-Forster, Major Francis Anson, 1890–1966, vol. VI
Arnold-Forster, Comdr Hugh Christopher, 1890–1965, vol. VI
Arnold-Forster, Rt Hon. Hugh Oakeley, 1855–1909, vol. I
Arnoldi, Frank, *born* 1848, vol. III
Arnoldi, Col Frank Fauquier, 1889–1953, vol. V
Arnott, Rev. Henry, *died* 1931, vol. III
Arnott, Sir John, 1st Bt, 1817–1898, vol. I
Arnott, John, 1871–1942, vol. IV
Arnott, Sir John Alexander, 2nd Bt, 1853–1940, vol. III
Arnott, Col John Maclean, 1869–1945, vol. IV
Arnott, Sir Lauriston John, 3rd Bt, 1890–1958, vol. V
Arnott, Leonard, 1887–1943, vol. IV
Arnott, Sir Robert John, 4th Bt, 1896–1966, vol. VI
Arnott, Maj.-Gen. Stanley, 1888–1972, vol. VII
Arnott, Brig.-Gen. William, 1860–1929, vol. III
Arnould, Francis Graham, 1875–1941, vol. IV
Aron, Robert, 1905–1975, vol. VII
Aronson, Victor Rees, 1880–1951, vol. V
Arp, Jean Hans, 1887–1966, vol. VI
Arran, 5th Earl of, 1839–1901, vol. I
Arran, 6th Earl of, 1868–1958, vol. V
Arran, 7th Earl of, 1903–1958, vol. V
Arrhenius, Svante August, 1859–1927, vol. II
Arrol, Sir William, 1839–1913, vol. I
Arrow, Gilbert John, 1873–1948, vol. IV
Arrowsmith, Hugh, 1888–1972, vol. VII
Arrowsmith, Rev. Preb. Walter Gordon, 1888–1964, vol. VI
Arrowsmith-Brown, Lt-Col James Arnold, 1882–1937, vol. III
Arsenault, Hon. Aubin Edmond, 1870–1969, vol. VI
Artemus Jones, Sir Thomas; *see* Jones.
Arthur, Sir Allan, 1857–1923, vol. II
Arthur, Col Sir Charles Gordon, 1884–1953, vol. V
Arthur, Major Christopher Geoffrey, 1882–1943, vol. IV
Arthur, Sir George Compton Archibald, 3rd Bt, 1860–1946, vol. IV
Arthur, Sir George Malcolm, 4th Bt, 1908–1949, vol. IV
Arthur, Col John Maurice, 1877–1954, vol. V

Arthur, Captain Leonard Robert Sunskersett, *died* 1903, vol. I
Arthur, Col Lionel Francis, 1876–1952, vol. V
Arthur, Sir (Oswald) Raynor, 1905–1973, vol. VII
Arthur, Sir Raynor; *see* Arthur, Sir O. R.
Arthur, Hon. Richard, 1865–1932, vol. III
Artsibashev, Michel Petrovitch, 1878–1927, vol. II
Arunachalam, Sir Ponnambalam, 1853–1924, vol. II
Arundale, George Sydney, 1878–1945, vol. IV
Arundel and Surrey, Earl of; Philip Joseph Mary Fitzalan-Howard, 1879–1902, vol. I
Arundel, Sir Arundel Tagg, 1843–1929, vol. III
Arundell of Wardour, 12th Baron, 1831–1906, vol. I
Arundell of Wardour, 13th Baron, 1834–1907, vol. I
Arundell of Wardour, 14th Baron, 1859–1921, vol. II
Arundell of Wardour, 15th Baron, 1861–1939, vol. III
Arundell of Wardour, 16th Baron, 1907–1944, vol. IV
Arur Singh, Sir Sardar Bahadur Sardar, 1863–1926, vol. II
Arwyn, Baron (Life Peer); Arwyn Randall Arwyn, 1897–1978, vol. VII
Asafu-Adjaye, Sir Edward Okyere, 1903–1976, vol. VII
Asbury, William, 1889–1961, vol. VI
Asch, Sholem, 1880–1957, vol. V
Asche, Oscar, 1872–1936, vol. III
Ascoli, Frank David, 1883–1958, vol. V
Ascroft, Peter Byers, 1906–1965, vol. VI
Ascroft, Robert, 1847–1899, vol. I
Ascroft, Sir William, 1832–1916, vol. II
Ascroft, Sir William Fawell, 1876–1954, vol. V
Ash, Audrey B., *died* 1958, vol. V
Ash, Edwin Lancelot Hopewell-, 1881–1964, vol. VI
Ash, Rt Rev. Fortescue Leo, 1882–1956, vol. V
Ash, Graham Baron, 1889–1980, vol. VII
Ash, Major William Claudius Casson, 1870–1916, vol. II
Ashbee, C. R., 1863–1942, vol. IV
Ashbolt, Sir Alfred Henry, 1870–1930, vol. III
Ashbourne, 1st Baron, 1837–1913, vol. I
Ashbourne, 2nd Baron, 1868–1942, vol. IV
Ashbridge, Sir Noel, 1889–1975, vol. VII
Ashbrook, 7th Viscount, 1830–1906, vol. I
Ashbrook, 8th Viscount, 1836–1919, vol. II
Ashbrook, 9th Viscount, 1870–1936, vol. III
Ashburner, Maj.-Gen. George Elliot, 1820–1907, vol. I
Ashburner, Lt-Col Lionel Forbes, 1874–1923, vol. II
Ashburner, Lionel Robert, 1827–1907, vol. I
Ashburner, Walter, 1864–1936, vol. III
Ashburnham, 5th Earl of, 1840–1913, vol. I
Ashburnham, 6th Earl of, 1855–1924, vol. II
Ashburnham, Sir Anchitel, 8th Bt, 1828–1899, vol. I
Ashburnham, Sir Anchitel Piers, 9th Bt; *see* Ashburnham-Clement.
Ashburnham, Sir Cromer, 1831–1917, vol. II
Ashburnham, Sir Fleetwood, 11th Bt, 1869–1953, vol. V

Ashburnham, Hon. John, 1845–1912, vol. I
Ashburnham, Sir Reginald, 10th Bt, 1865–1944, vol. IV
Ashburnham-Clement, Sir Anchitel Piers, 9th Bt, 1861–1935, vol. III
Ashburton, 5th Baron, 1866–1938, vol. III
Ashburton, Lady; (Louisa), *died* 1903, vol. I
Ashby, Arthur Wilfred, 1886–1953, vol. V
Ashby, Col George Ashby, 1856–1937, vol. III
Ashby, Hugh Tuke, 1880–1952, vol. V
Ashby, Sir James William Murray, 1822–1911, vol. I
Ashby, Very Rev. Paul Ogilvie, 1867–1937, vol. III
Ashby, Robert Claude, 1876–1963, vol. VI
Ashby, Thomas, 1874–1931, vol. III
Ashby-Sterry, Joseph, *died* 1917, vol. II
Ashcombe, 1st Baron, 1828–1917, vol. II
Ashcombe, 2nd Baron, 1867–1947, vol. IV
Ashcombe, 3rd Baron, 1899–1962, vol. VI
Ashcroft, Alec Hutchinson, 1887–1963, vol. VI
Ashcroft, D(udley) Walker, 1904–1963, vol. VI
Ashcroft, Thomas, 1890–1961, vol. VI
Ashdown, Baron (Life Peer); Arnold Silverstone, 1911–1977, vol. VII
Ashdown, Arthur Durham, 1872–1953, vol. V
Ashdown, Sir Curtis George, 1876–1933, vol. III
Ashdown, Sir George Henry, 1857–1924, vol. II
Ashdown, Rt Rev. Hugh Edward, 1904–1977, vol. VII
Ashe, Rear-Adm. Edward Percy, 1852–1914, vol. I
Asher, Alexander, 1835–1905, vol. I
Asher, Amy, (Mrs Peter Asher); *see* Shuard, A.
Asher, Sir Augustus Gordon Grant, 1861–1930, vol. III
Asher, Florence May, 1888–1977, vol. VII
Asher, Samuel Garcia, 1868–1938, vol. III
Ashfield, 1st Baron, 1874–1948, vol. IV
Ashfield, Percy John, 1870–1946, vol. IV
Ashford, Bailey K., *died* 1934, vol. III
Ashford, Sir Cyril Ernest, 1867–1951, vol. V
Ashford, Hon. William George, 1874–1925, vol. II
Ashkanasy, Maurice, 1901–1971, vol. VII
Ashley; *see* Harinden, A. E.
Ashley, Lord; Anthony Ashley-Cooper, 1900–1947, vol. IV
Ashley, Rt Hon. (Anthony) Evelyn Melbourne, 1836–1907, vol. I
Ashley, Hon. Cecil, 1849–1932, vol. III
Ashley, Rt Hon. Evelyn Melbourne; *see* Ashley, Rt Hon. A. E. M.
Ashley, Francis Noel, 1884–1976, vol. VII
Ashley, Lt-Col Frank, 1870–1923, vol. II
Ashley, Frederick Morewood, 1846–1933, vol. III
Ashley, Henry V., 1872–1945, vol. IV
Ashley, Sir Percy Walter Llewellyn, 1876–1945, vol. IV
Ashley, Walter, 1893–1937, vol. III
Ashley, Sir William James, 1860–1927, vol. II
Ashley-Brown, Ven. William, 1887–1970, vol. VI
Ashley-Scarlett, Lt-Col Henry, 1886–1976, vol. VII
Ashlin, George C., 1837–1922, vol. II
Ashmall, Rev. Francis James, 1856–1948, vol. IV
Ashman, Sir Frederick Herbert, 2nd Bt, 1875–1916, vol. II
Ashman, Sir Herbert, 1st Bt, 1854–1914, vol. I

Ashmead-Bartlett, Ellis, 1881–1931, vol. III
Ashmead-Bartlett, Sir Ellis; *see* Bartlett.
Ashmore, Hon. Lord; John Wilson, 1857–1932, vol. III
Ashmore, Sir Alexander Murray, 1855–1906, vol. I
Ashmore, Maj.-Gen. Edward Bailey, 1872–1953, vol. V
Ashmore, Major Edwin James Caldwell, 1893–1959, vol. V
Ashmore, Vice-Adm. Leslie Haliburton, 1893–1974, vol. VII
Ashmore, William Caldwell, 1866–1931, vol. III
Ashton, 1st Baron, 1842–1930, vol. III
Ashton, Baroness; (Florence Maude), 1856–1944, vol. IV
Ashton of Hyde, 1st Baron, 1855–1933, vol. III
Ashton, Algernon Bennet Langton, 1859–1937, vol. III
Ashton, Arthur Jacob, 1855–1925, vol. II
Ashton, Lt-Col Edward Malcolm, 1895–1978, vol. VII
Ashton, Lt-Gen. Ernest Charles, 1873–1957, vol. V
Ashton, Harry, 1882–1952, vol. V
Ashton, Helen, (Mrs Arthur Jordan), 1891–1958, vol. V
Ashton, Captain Henry Gordon Gooch, 1870–1951, vol. V
Ashton, Sir Hubert, 1898–1979, vol. VII
Ashton, Hon. James, 1864–1939, vol. III
Ashton, Engr Rear-Adm. James, 1883–1951, vol. V
Ashton, Rt Rev. John William, 1866–1964, vol. VI
Ashton, Julian Rossi, 1851–1942, vol. IV
Ashton, Margaret, 1856–1937, vol. III
Ashton, Sir Ralph Percy, 1860–1921, vol. II
Ashton, Teddy; *see* Clarke, Charles Allen.
Ashton, Rt Hon. Thomas, 1844–1927, vol. II
Ashton, Thomas Southcliffe, 1889–1968, vol. VI
Ashton, Sir William, 1881–1963, vol. VI
Ashton-Gwatkin, Frank Trelawny Arthur, 1889–1976, vol. VII
Ashton-Gwatkin, Rev. Walter Henry Trelawny; *see* Gwatkin.
Ashtown, 3rd Baron, 1868–1946, vol. IV
Ashtown, 4th Baron, 1897–1966, vol. VI
Ashtown, 5th Baron, 1901–1979, vol. VII
Ashwanden, Col Sydney William Louis, 1878–1947, vol. IV
Ashwell, Lena, *died* 1957, vol. V
Ashwin, Sir Bernard Carl, 1896–1975, vol. VII
Ashworth, Ernest Horatio, 1870–1934, vol. III
Ashworth, Harold Kenneth, 1903–1978, vol. VII
Ashworth, James Hartley, 1874–1936, vol. III
Ashworth, Sir John Percy, 1906–1975, vol. VII
Ashworth, Philip Arthur, 1853–1921, vol. II
Ashworth, Air Comdt Dame Veronica Margaret, 1910–1977, vol. VII
Aske, Sir Robert William, 1st Bt, 1872–1954, vol. V
Askew, Claude Arthur Cary, *died* 1917, vol. II
Askew, William George, 1890–1968, vol. VI
Askew-Robertson, Watson, 1834–1907, vol. I
Askew Robertson, William Haggerston, 1868–1942, vol. IV
Askuran, Sir Shantidas, 1882–1950, vol. IV (A), vol. V

Askwith, 1st Baron, 1861–1942, vol. IV
Askwith, Lady; (Ellen), *died* 1962, vol. VI
Askwith, Arthur Vivian, 1893–1971, vol. VII
Askwith, Rev. Edward Harrison, 1864–1946, vol. IV
Askwith, Col Henry Francis, 1865–1938, vol. III
Askwith, Rt Rev. Wilfred Marcus, 1890–1962, vol. VI
Askwith, Ven. William Henry, 1843–1911, vol. I
Aslett, Alfred, 1847–1928, vol. II
Aslin, Charles Herbert, 1893–1959, vol. V
Asman, Rev. Harry Newbitt, 1877–1950, vol. IV
Aspden, Hartley, 1858–1940, vol. III
Aspell, Sir John, 1854–1938, vol. III
Aspinall, Sir Algernon Edward, 1871–1952, vol. V
Aspinall, Arthur, 1901–1972, vol. VII
Aspinall, Butler, 1861–1935, vol. III
Aspinall, Sir John Audley Frederick, 1851–1937, vol. III
Aspinall, John Bridge, 1877–1932, vol. III
Aspinall, Major John Ralph, 1878–1947, vol. IV
Aspinall, Ven. Noël Lake, 1861–1934, vol. III
Aspinall, Lt-Col Robert Lowndes, 1869–1916, vol. II
Aspinall, Lt-Col Robert Stivala, 1895–1954, vol. V
Aspinall-Oglander, Brig.-Gen. Cecil Faber, 1878–1959, vol. V
Asquith of Bishopstone, Baron (Life Peer); Cyril Asquith, 1890–1954, vol. V
Asquith of Yarnbury, Baroness (Life Peeress); Helen Violet Bonham Carter, 1887–1969, vol. VI
Asquith, Hon. Anthony, 1902–1968, vol. VI
Asquith, Hon. Arthur Melland, 1883–1939, vol. III
Asquith, Lady Cynthia, *died* 1960, vol. V
Asquith, Cyril Edward, 1902–1967, vol. VI
Asquith, Hon. Herbert, 1881–1947, vol. IV
Asquith, Raymond, 1878–1916, vol. II
Asser, Gen. Sir John; *see* Asser, Gen. Sir J. J.
Asser, Gen. Sir (Joseph) John, 1867–1949, vol. IV
Asser, Brig.-Gen. Verney, 1873–1944, vol. IV
Assheton, Ralph, 1830–1907, vol. I
Assheton, Sir Ralph Cockayne, 1st Bt, 1860–1955, vol. V
Assheton, Richard, 1863–1915, vol. I (A)
Assheton-Smith, Sir Charles Garden, 1st Bt, 1851–1914, vol. I
Assheton-Smith, George W. Duff, *died* 1904, vol. I
Astbury, Arthur Ralph, 1880–1973, vol. VII
Astbury, Lt-Comdr Frederick Wolfe, 1872–1954, vol. V
Astbury, Rev. George, *died* 1926, vol. II
Astbury, Rev. Canon (Harold) Stanley, 1889–1962, vol. VI
Astbury, Herbert Arthur, 1870–1968, vol. VI
Astbury, Rt Hon. Sir John Meir, 1860–1939, vol. III
Astbury, Rev. Canon Stanley; *see* Astbury, Rev. Canon H. S.
Astbury, William Thomas, 1898–1961, vol. VI
Astell, Maj.-Gen. Charles Edward, *died* 1901, vol. I
Astell, Richard John Vereker, 1890–1969, vol. VI
Astell, Captain Somerset Charles Godfrey Fairfax, 1866–1917, vol. II
Asterley Jones, Philip; *see* Jones.

Astley, Bertram Frankland Frankland-Russell-, 1857–1904, vol. I
Astley, Major Delaval Graham L'Estrange, 1868–1951, vol. V
Astley, Henry Jacob Delaval Frankland-Russell-, 1888–1912, vol. I
Astley, Hubert Delaval, 1860–1925, vol. II
Astley, Rev. Hugh John Dukinfield, 1856–1930, vol. III
Astley, Kathleen Mary; *see* Astley, Mrs Reginald.
Astley, Mrs Reginald, (Kathleen Mary Astley), *died* 1973, vol. VII
Astley, Reginald Basil, 1862–1942, vol. IV
Astley-Corbett, Sir Francis Edmund George, 4th Bt, 1859–1939, vol. III
Astley-Corbett, Sir (Francis) Henry (Rivers), 5th Bt, 1915–1943, vol. IV
Astley-Corbett, Sir Henry; *see* Astley-Corbett, Sir F. H. R.
Astley-Rushton, Vice-Adm. Edward Astley; *see* Rushton.
Aston, Alfred Withall, 1852–1929, vol. III
Aston, Rev. Canon Basil, 1880–1957, vol. V
Aston, Bernard Cracroft, 1871–1951, vol. IV
Aston, Francis William, 1877–1945, vol. IV
Aston, Maj.-Gen. Sir George Grey, 1861–1938, vol. III
Aston, Theodore, *died* 1910, vol. I
Aston, William George, 1841–1911, vol. I
Astor, 1st Viscount, 1848–1919, vol. II
Astor, 2nd Viscount, 1879–1952, vol. V
Astor, 3rd Viscount, 1907–1966, vol. VI
Astor, Viscountess; (Nancy), *died* 1964, vol. VI
Astor of Hever, 1st Baron, 1886–1971, vol. VII
Astor, John Jacob, 1864–1912, vol. I
Astor, Hon. Michael Langhorne, 1916–1980, vol. VII
Asturias, Miguel Angel, 1899–1974, vol. VII
Atatürk, Kamâl, 1881–1938, vol. III
Atcherley, Air Vice-Marshal David Francis William, 1904–1952, vol. V
Atcherley, Col Sir Llewellyn William, 1871–1954, vol. V
Atcherley, Air Marshal Sir Richard Llewellyn Roger, 1904–1970, vol. VI
Atchison, Major Charles Ernest, 1875–1917, vol. II
Atchley, Chewton, 1850–1922, vol. II
Atchley, Shirley Clifford, 1871–1936, vol. III
Athawes, Edward James, *died* 1902, vol. I
Athelstan-Johnson, Wilfrid, 1876–1939, vol. III
Athenagoras, Archbishop, (Archbishop of Thyateira), *died* 1962, vol. VI
Athenagoras, Spyrou, 1886–1972, vol. VII
Athenagoras, Theodoritos, 1912–1979, vol. VII
Atherley, Major Evelyn George Hammond, 1852–1935, vol. III
Atherley-Jones, Llewellyn Archer, 1851–1929, vol. III
Atherton, Gertrude Franklin, *died* 1948, vol. IV
Atherton, Ray, 1885–1960, vol. V
Atherton, Col Thomas James, 1856–1920, vol. II
Athill, Charles Harold, *died* 1922, vol. II
Athill, Lt-Col Francis Remi Imbert, 1880–1958, vol. V

Athlone, 1st Earl of, 1874–1957, vol. V
Athlumney, 6th Baron, 1865–1929, vol. III
Atholl, 7th Duke of, 1840–1917, vol. II
Atholl, 8th Duke of, 1871–1942, vol. IV
Atholl, 9th Duke of, 1879–1957, vol. V
Atholl, Duchess of; (Katharine Marjory), *died* 1960, vol. V
Atholstan, 1st Baron, 1848–1938, vol. III
Atkey, Sir Albert (Reuben), 1867–1947, vol. IV
Atkey, Oliver Francis Haynes, *died* 1960, vol. V
Atkin, Baron (Life Peer); James Richard Atkin, 1867–1944, vol. IV
Atkin, Charles, *died* 1934, vol. III
Atkin, Peter Wilson, 1859–1931, vol. III
Atkins, Maj.-Gen. Sir Alban Randell Crofton, 1870–1926, vol. II
Atkins, Alexander Robert; *see* Atkins, R.
Atkins, Charles Norman, 1885–1960, vol. V
Atkins, Col Ernest Clive, 1870–1953, vol. V
Atkins, Frederick Anthony, 1864–1929, vol. III
Atkins, Henry Gibson, 1871–1942, vol. IV
Atkins, Ian Robert, 1912–1979, vol. VII
Atkins, Sir Ivor Algernon, 1869–1953, vol. V
Atkins, Col Sir John, 1875–1963, vol. VI
Atkins, John Black, 1871–1954, vol. V
Atkins, John William Hey, 1874–1951, vol. V
Atkins, Malcolm Ramsay, 1881–1960, vol. V
Atkins, Robert, 1886–1972, vol. VII
Atkins, Thomas Frederick B.; *see* Burnaby-Atkins.
Atkins, William Ringrose Gelston, 1884–1959, vol. V
Atkinson, Baron (Life Peer); John Atkinson, 1844–1932, vol. III
Atkinson, Major Sir Arthur Joseph, *died* 1959, vol. V
Atkinson, Brig.-Gen. Ben, 1872–1942, vol. IV
Atkinson, Cecil Hewitt, 1894–1954, vol. V
Atkinson, Hon. Cecil Thomas, 1876–1919, vol. II
Atkinson, Ven. Charles Frederic, 1855–1942, vol. IV
Atkinson, Charles Milner, 1854–1920, vol. II
Atkinson, Hon. Sir Cyril, 1874–1967, vol. VI
Atkinson, Donald, 1886–1963, vol. VI
Atkinson, Rev. Edward, *died* 1915, vol. I
Atkinson, Ven. Edward Dupré, 1855–1937, vol. III
Atkinson, Sir Edward Hale Tindal, 1878–1957, vol. V
Atkinson, Surgeon-Captain Edward Leicester, 1882–1929, vol. III
Atkinson, Sir Edward Tindal, 1847–1930, vol. III
Atkinson, Major Edward William, 1873–1920, vol. II
Atkinson, Lt-Gen. Sir Edwin Henry de Vere, 1867–1947, vol. IV
Atkinson, Rt Hon. Sir Fenton, 1906–1980, vol. VII
Atkinson, Brig.-Gen. Francis Garnett, 1857–1941, vol. IV
Atkinson, Frank Buddle, 1866–1953, vol. V
Atkinson, Frank Stuart, 1899–1971, vol. VII
Atkinson, George, *died* 1941, vol. IV
Atkinson, Major George Prestage, 1885–1929, vol. III
Atkinson, Henry John Farmer-, 1828–1913, vol. I
Atkinson, Rev. Canon Henry Sadgrove, *died* 1927, vol. II

Atkinson, Henry Tindal, *died* 1918, vol. II
Atkinson, Rev. J. Augustus, *died* 1911, vol. I
Atkinson, Lt-Col John, *died* 1945, vol. IV
Atkinson, John Mitford, 1856–1917, vol. II
Atkinson, Sir John Nathaniel, 1857–1931, vol. III
Atkinson, Maj.-Gen. John Richard Breeks, 1844–1926, vol. II
Atkinson, Meredith, 1883–1929, vol. III
Atkinson, Robert, 1883–1952, vol. V
Atkinson, Thomas Dinham, 1864–1948, vol. IV
Atkinson, Thomas John Day, 1882–1949, vol. IV
Atkinson, Vivian Buchanan, 1886–1960, vol. V
Atkinson, Sir William Nicholas, 1850–1930, vol. III
Atkinson-Willes, Adm. Sir George Lambart, 1847–1921, vol. II
Atlay, James Beresford, 1860–1912, vol. I
Atlay, Rev. Marcus Ethelbert, *died* 1934, vol. III
Atlay, Sir Wilfrid, 1866–1929, vol. III
Atta, Nana Sir Ofori, 1881–1943, vol. IV
Attenborough, Charles Leete, 1853–1937, vol. III
Attenborough, Frederick L., 1887–1973, vol. VII
Attenborough, Walter Annis, 1850–1932, vol. III
Atterbury, Sir Frederick, 1853–1919, vol. II
Attewell, Humphrey Cooper, 1894–1972, vol. VII
Attfield, John, 1835–1911, vol. I
Atthill, Major Anthony William Maunsell, 1861–1926, vol. II
Atthill, Lombe, 1827–1910, vol. I
Attlee, 1st Earl, 1883–1967, vol. VI
Attlee, Wilfrid Henry Waller, 1876–1962, vol. VI
Attwater, Harry Lawrence, 1885–1961, vol. VI
Attwell, Mabel Lucie, (Mrs Harold Earnshaw), 1879–1964, vol. V
Attwood, Harold Augustus F.; *see* Freeman-Attwood.
Attygalle, Sir Nicholas, 1894–1970, vol. VI (AII)
Atukorala, Nandasara Wijetilaka, 1915–1969, vol. VI
Atwater, Albert William, 1856–1929, vol. III
Atwood, Clare, 1866–1962, vol. VI
Aubin, Charles Walter Duret, 1894–1972, vol. VII
Auboyneau, Adm. Philippe Marie Joseph Raymond, 1899–1961, vol. VI
Aubrey, Brig. Herbert Arthur Reginald, 1883–1954, vol. V
Aubrey, Rev. Melbourn Evans, 1885–1957, vol. V
Aubrey, Sir Stanley James, 1883–1962, vol. VI
Aubrey, William Hickman Smith, 1858–1916, vol. II
Aubrey-Fletcher, Rt Hon. Sir Henry; *see* Fletcher.
Aubrey-Fletcher, Major Sir Henry Lancelot, 6th Bt, 1887–1969, vol. VI
Aubrey-Fletcher, Sir Lancelot, 5th Bt, 1846–1937, vol. III
Auchinleck, William Douglas, 1848–1932, vol. III
Auckland, 5th Baron, 1859–1917, vol. II
Auckland, 6th Baron, 1895–1941, vol. IV
Auckland, 7th Baron, 1891–1955, vol. V
Auckland, 8th Baron, 1892–1957, vol. V
Auden, George Augustus, 1872–1957, vol. V
Auden, Henry William, 1867–1940, vol. III
Auden, Rev. Thomas, 1836–1920, vol. II
Auden, Wystan Hugh, 1907–1973, vol. VII
Audette, Hon. Louis Arthur, 1856–1942, vol. IV

Audiffret-Pasquier, Duc d', (Edmé Armand Gaston), 1823–1905, vol. I
Audland, Brig. Edward Gordon, 1896–1976, vol. VII
Audley, Baroness (22nd in line), 1858–1942, vol. IV
Audley, 23rd Baron, 1913–1963, vol. VI
Audley, Baroness (24th in line), 1911–1973, vol. VII
Audsley, Matthew Thomas, 1891–1975, vol. VII
Auer, Leopold, 1845–1930, vol. III
Aufrecht, Theodor, 1821–1907, vol. I
Augagneur, Victor, 1855–1931, vol. III
Aulard, Alphonse, 1849–1928, vol. II
Auld, Maj.-Gen. Robert, 1848–1911, vol. I
Auld, Lt- Col Samue lJames Manson, 1884–1963, vol. VI
Ault, Norman, 1880–1950, vol. IV
Aumonier, Stacy, 1887–1928, vol. II
Aung, Maung Myat Tun, died 1920, vol. II
Auriol, Vincent, 1884–1966, vol. VI
Aurobindo, Sri, 1872–1950, vol. IV
Austen, Gen. Sir Alfred Reade G.; see Godwin-Austen.
Austen, Col Arthur Robert, 1860–1939, vol. III
Austen, Major Ernest Edward, 1867–1938, vol. III
Austen, Rev. George, 1839–1933, vol. III
Austen, Harold Cholmley Mansfield, 1878–1975, vol. VII
Austen, Harold William Colmer, 1868–1943, vol. IV
Austen, Henry Haversham G.; see Godwin-Austen.
Austen, Sir William Chandler R.; see Roberts-Austen.
Austen, Winifred M. L., died 1964, vol. VI
Austen-Cartmell, James; see Cartmell.
Austen-Leigh, Charles Edward, 1833–1916, vol. II
Austen-Leigh, Richard Arthur, 1872–1961, vol. VI
Austin, 1st Baron, 1866–1941, vol. IV
Austin, Alfred, 1835–1913, vol. I
Austin, Maj.-Gen. Arthur Bramston, 1893–1967, vol. VI
Austin, Hon. Austin Albert, 1855–1925, vol. II
Austin, Vice-Adm. Sir Francis Murray, 1881–1953, vol. V
Austin, Frederic, 1872–1952, vol. V
Austin, Frederick Britten, 1885–1941, vol. IV
Austin, George Wesley, 1891–1975, vol. VII
Austin, Sir Harold Bruce Gardiner, 1877–1943, vol. IV
Austin, Sir Herbert, 1867–1929, vol. III
Austin, Brig.-Gen. Herbert Henry, 1868–1937, vol. III
Austin, James Valentine, 1850–1914, vol. I
Austin, Sir John, 1st Bt, 1824–1906, vol. I
Austin, Brig.-Gen. John Gardiner, died 1956, vol. V
Austin, John Langshaw, 1911–1960, vol. V
Austin, Sir John Worroker, died 1980, vol. VII (AII)
Austin, Mary Hunter, died 1934, vol. III
Austin, Michael, 1855–1916, vol. II
Austin, Reginald McPherson, 1887–1950, vol. IV
Austin, Robert Sargent, 1895–1973, vol. VII
Austin, Roland, 1874–1954, vol. V
Austin, Roland Gregory, 1901–1974, vol. VII

Austin, Sir Thomas, 1887–1976, vol. VII
Austin, Warren Robinson, 1877–1962, vol. VI
Austin, Sir William Michael Byron, 2nd Bt, 1871–1940, vol. III
Austral, Florence, 1894–1968, vol. VI
Auten, Captain Harold, died 1964, vol. VI
Auty, Robert, 1914–1978, vol. VII
Ava, Earl of; Archibald James Leofric Temple Blackwood, 1863–1900, vol. I
Avebury, 1st Baron, 1834–1913, vol. I and I (A)
Avebury, 2nd Baron, 1858–1929, vol. III
Avebury, 3rd Baron, 1915–1971, vol. VII
Aveling, Arthur Francis, 1893–1954, vol. V
Aveling, Charles, 1873–1959, vol. V
Aveling, Claude, 1869–1943, vol. IV
Aveling, Francis Arthur Powell, 1875–1941, vol. IV
Avenol, Joseph Louis Anne, 1879–1952, vol. V
Averill, Most Rev. Alfred Walter, 1865–1957, vol. V
Avery, Charles Harold, 1867–1943, vol. IV
Avery, Brig. Henry Esau, 1885–1961, vol. VI
Avery, Major Leonard, died 1953, vol. V
Avery, Thomas, 1862–1940, vol. III
Avery, Sir William Beilby, 1st Bt, died 1908, vol. I
Avery, Sir William Eric Thomas, 2nd Bt, 1890–1918, vol. II
Aves, Ernest, 1857–1917, vol. II
Avezathe, Gerald Henry, 1889–1966, vol. VI
Avis, John, 1851–1936, vol. III
Avon, 1st Earl of, 1897–1977, vol. VII
Avonmore, 6th Viscount, 1866–1910, vol. I
Avory, Rt Hon. Sir Horace Edmund, 1851–1935, vol. III
Awbery, Stanley Stephen, 1888–1969, vol. VI
Awdry, Rev. Charles Hill, died 1910, vol. I
Awdry, Sir Richard Davis, 1843–1916, vol. II
Awdry, Rt Rev. William, 1842–1910, vol. I
Axford, Surg.-Rear-Adm. Walter Godfrey, 1861–1942, vol. IV
Axon, Sir Albert Edwin, 1898–1974, vol. VII
Axon, William Edward Armytage, 1846–1913, vol. I
Ayala, Ramon Pérez de, 1880–1962, vol. VI
Aydelotte, Frank, 1880–1956, vol. V
Ayers, Charles William, 1880–1965, vol. VI
Ayers, Hon. Sir Henry, 1821–1897, vol. I
Ayers, Engineer Captain Robert Bell, 1863–1940, vol. III
Ayerst, Rev. George Haughton, 1863–1931, vol. III
Ayerst, Rev. William, 1830–1904, vol. I
Aykroyd, Sir Alfred Hammond, 2nd Bt (cr 1920), 1894–1965, vol. VI
Aykroyd, Sir Frederic Alfred, 1st Bt (cr 1929), 1873–1949, vol. IV
Aykroyd, Wallace Ruddell, 1899–1979, vol. VII
Aykroyd, Sir William Henry, 1st Bt (cr 1920), 1865–1947, vol. IV
Aylen, Rt Rev. Charles Arthur William, 1882–1972, vol. VII
Aylen, Helena Constance; see Romanne-James.
Ayles, Rev. Herbert Henry Baker, 1861–1940, vol. III

Ayles, Walter Henry, 1879–1953, vol. V
Aylesford, 8th Earl of, 1851–1924, vol. II
Aylesford, 9th Earl of, 1908–1940, vol. III (A), vol. IV
Aylesford, 10th Earl of, 1886–1958, vol. V
Aylesworth, Hon. Sir Allen Bristol, 1854–1952, vol. V
Ayliff, Henry Kiell, died 1949, vol. IV
Ayling, Sir William Bock, 1867–1946, vol. IV
Aylmer, 7th Baron, 1814–1901, vol. I
Aylmer, 8th Baron, 1842–1923, vol. II
Aylmer, 9th Baron, 1880–1970, vol. VI (AII)
Aylmer, 10th Baron, 1883–1974, vol. VII
Aylmer, 11th Baron, 1886–1977, vol. VII
Aylmer, Sir Arthur Percy Fitzgerald, 12th Bt (cr 1622), 1858–1928, vol. II
Aylmer, Col Edmund Kendal Grimston, 1859–1931, vol. III
Aylmer, Sir Felix, 1889–1979, vol. VII
Aylmer, Lt-Gen. Sir Fenton John, 13th Bt (cr 1622), 1862–1935, vol. III
Aylmer, Sir Gerald (Arthur) Evans-Freke, 14th Bt (cr 1622), 1869–1939, vol. III
Aylmer, Gerald Percy Vivian, 1856–1936, vol. III
Aylmer, Rear-Adm. Henry Evans-Freke, 1878–1933, vol. III
Aylmer-Jones, Sir Felix E.; see Aylmer, Sir Felix.
Aylward, Florence, 1862–1950, vol. IV
Aylward, Francis, 1911–1978, vol. VII
Aylwen, Sir George, 1st Bt, died 1967, vol. VI
Aynsley, Charles Murray, 1821–1901, vol. I
Aynsley, Sir Charles Murray M.; see Murray-Aynsley.
Ayre, Sir Amos Lowrey, 1885–1952, vol. V
Ayre, Captain Leslie Charles Edward, 1886–1979, vol. VII
Ayre, Sir Wilfrid, 1890–1971, vol. VII
Ayres, Sir Reginald John, 1900–1966, vol. VI
Ayres, Ruby Mildred, 1883–1955, vol. V
Ayrton, Hertha, died 1923, vol. II
Ayrton, Maxwell; see Ayrton, O. M.
Ayrton, Michael, 1921–1975, vol. VII
Ayrton, (Ormrod) Maxwell, died 1960, vol. V
Ayrton, William Edward, 1847–1908, vol. I
Ayscough, Florence, died 1942, vol. IV
Ayscough, John; see Bickerstaffe-Drew, Rt Rev. Mgr Count F. B. D.
Ayscough, Rev. Thomas Ayscough, 1830–1920, vol. II
Ayson, Hugh Fraser, 1884–1948, vol. IV
Aytoun, Col Andrew, 1860–1945, vol. IV
Ayub Khan, Field-Marshal Mohammad; see Khan, Field-Marshal M. A.
Azariah, Rt Rev. Vedanayakam Samuel, 1874–1945, vol. IV
Azcarate y Florez, Pablo de, 1890–1971, vol. VII
Azizuddin Ahmad, Kazi Sir, 1861–1940, vol. III
Azizul Huque, Khan Bahadur Sir M., 1892–1947, vol. IV
Azopardi, James Frendo, 1866–1938, vol. III
Azopardi, Sir Vincent Frendo, 1865–1919, vol. II

B

Ba, Sir Maung, died 1937, vol. III
Baba, Hon. Sir Khem Singh Beda, 1830–1905, vol. I
Babb, S. Nicholson, 1874–1957, vol. V
Babbage, Maj.-Gen. Henry Prevost, 1824–1918, vol. II
Babbitt, Irving, 1865–1933, vol. III
Baber, Edward Cresswell, died 1910, vol. I
Baber, Lt-Col John Barton, 1892–1967, vol. VI
Baber Shum Shere Jung Bahadur Rana, General, 1888–1960, vol. V
Babington, Rt Hon. Sir Anthony Brutus, 1877–1972, vol. VII
Babington, Col David Melville, 1863–1929, vol. III
Babington, Captain Gervase, 1890–1948, vol. IV
Babington, Lt-Gen. Sir James Melville, 1854–1936, vol. III
Babington, Air Marshal Sir John Tremayne; see Tremayne, Air Marshal Sir J. T.
Babington, Air Marshal Sir Philip, 1894–1965, vol. VI
Babington, Very Rev. Richard, 1869–1952, vol. V
Babington, Col Stafford Charles, 1866–1951, vol. V
Babonau, Col Alexander Frederick, 1882–1949, vol. IV
Babtie, Lt-Gen. Sir William, 1859–1920, vol. II
Baby-Casgrain, Hon. Col Hon. Joseph Philippe; see Casgrain.
Bacchus, Captain Roy, 1883–1951, vol. V
Bach, Guido R., died 1905, vol. I
Bacharach, Alfred Louis, 1891–1966, vol. VI
Bachauer, Gina, (Mrs Alec Sherman), 1913–1976, vol. VII
Bache, Miss Constance, died 1903, vol. I
Bacheller, Irving, 1859–1950, vol. IV (A), vol. V
Bacher, William, 1850–1913, vol. I
Back, Ven. Hugh Cairns Alexander, 1863–1928, vol. II
Back, Ivor, died 1951, vol. V
Backhaus, Wilhelm, 1884–1969, vol. VI
Backhouse, Sir Edmund Trelawny, 2nd Bt, 1873–1944, vol. IV
Backhouse, Col Edward Henry Walford, 1895–1973, vol. VII
Backhouse, Major Sir John Edmund, 3rd Bt, 1909–1944, vol. IV
Backhouse, Sir Jonathan Edmund, 1st Bt, 1849–1918, vol. II
Backhouse, Lt-Col Julius Batt, 1854–1911, vol. I
Backhouse, Lt-Col Miles Roland Charles, 1878–1962, vol. VI
Backhouse, Adm. Oliver, 1876–1943, vol. IV
Backhouse, Adm. of the Fleet Sir Roger Roland Charles, 1878–1939, vol. III
Backhouse, Thomas Mercer, 1903–1955, vol. V
Bacon, Benjamin Wisner, 1860–1932, vol. III
Bacon, Sir Edward Denny, 1860–1938, vol. III
Bacon, Edwin Munroe, 1844–1916, vol. II
Bacon, Frederic, 1880–1943, vol. IV
Bacon, Frederick Joseph, 1853–1929, vol. III
Bacon, Gertrude, (Mrs T. J. Foggitt), 1874–1949, vol. IV

Bacon, Sir Hickman Beckett, 11th Bt, 1855–1945, vol. IV
Bacon, Janet Ruth, 1891–1965, vol. VI
Bacon, John Henry Frederick, 1865–1914, vol. I
Bacon, John Mackenzie, 1846–1904, vol. I
Bacon, Sir Nicholas Henry, 12th Bt, 1857–1947, vol. IV
Bacon, Adm. Sir Reginald Hugh Spencer, 1863–1947, vol. IV
Bacon, Sir Roger Sewell, 1895–1962, vol. VI
Bacon, Comdr Sidney Kendrick, 1871–1950, vol. IV
Bacot, Arthur William, 1866–1922, vol. II
Badcock, Gen. Sir Alexander Robert, 1844–1907, vol. I
Badcock, Brig.-Gen. Francis Frederick, 1867–1926, vol. II
Badcock, Brig. Gerald Eliot, 1883–1966, vol. VI
Badcock, Isaac, 1842–1906, vol. I
Badcock, Jasper Capper, 1840–1924, vol. II
Badcock, Paymaster Captain Kenneth Edgar, 1886–1947, vol. IV
Baddeley, Angela; see Clinton-Baddeley, M. A.
Baddeley, Col Charles Edward, 1861–1923, vol. II
Baddeley, Sir Frank Morrish, 1874–1966, vol. VI
Baddeley, Sir John Beresford, 3rd Bt, 1899–1979, vol. VII
Baddeley, John Halkett, 1920–1972, vol. VII
Baddeley, Sir John James, 1st Bt, 1842–1926, vol. II
Baddeley, Hon. John Marcus, 1881–1953, vol. V
Baddeley, Sir (John) William, 2nd Bt, 1869–1951, vol. V
Baddeley, Sir Vincent Wilberforce, 1874–1961, vol. VI
Baddeley, Sir William; see Baddeley, Sir J. W.
Badè, William Frederic, 1871–1936, vol. III
Badeley, 1st Baron, 1874–1951, vol. V
Badeley, Rt Rev. Walter Hubert, 1894–1960, vol. V
Baden-Powell, 1st Baron, 1857–1941, vol. IV
Baden-Powell, 2nd Baron, 1913–1962, vol. VI
Baden-Powell, Agnes, 1858–1945, vol. IV
Baden-Powell, Major Baden Fletcher Smyth, 1860–1937, vol. III
Baden-Powell, Baden Henry, 1841–1901, vol. I
Baden-Powell, Frank Smyth, 1850–1933, vol. III
Baden-Powell, Sir George Smyth, 1847–1898, vol. I
Baden-Powell, Lady; (Olave), 1889–1977, vol. VII
Baden-Powell, Warington, died 1921, vol. II
Badenoch, Sir (Alexander) Cameron, 1889–1973, vol. VII
Badenoch, Sir Cameron; see Badenoch, Sir A. C.
Badenoch, Rev. George Roy, 1830–1912, vol. I
Bader, Hubert Eugène, 1902–1936, vol. III
Badger, Rev. Canon George Edwin, 1868–1948, vol. IV
Badgerow, Sir George W., 1872–1937, vol. III
Badham, Edward Leslie, died 1944, vol. IV
Badham, Rev. Leslie Stephen Ronald, 1908–1975, vol. VII
Badham-Thornhill, Col George, 1876–1958, vol. V
Badley, John Haden, 1865–1967, vol. VI
Badock, Sir Stanley Hugh, 1867–1945, vol. IV
Badock, Sir Walter, 1854–1931, vol. III
Baekeland, Leo Hendrik, 1863–1944, vol. IV

Baerlein, Edgar M., 1879–1971, vol. VII
Baerlein, Henry, 1875–1960, vol. V, vol. VI
Bagchi, Satischandra, 1882–1939, vol. III (A), vol. IV
Bagenal, Hope; see Bagenal, P. H. E.
Bagenal, (Philip) Hope (Edward), 1888–1979, vol. VII
Baggaley, Ernest James, 1900–1978, vol. VII
Baggallay, Claude, 1853–1906, vol. I
Baggallay, Ernest, 1850–1931, vol. III
Baggallay, Rev. Frederick, 1855–1928, vol. II
Baggallay, Lt-Col Richard Romer Claude, 1884–1975, vol. VII
Bagge, Sir Alfred Thomas, 3rd Bt, 1843–1916, vol. II
Bagge, Sir Alfred William Francis, 4th Bt, 1875–1939, vol. III
Bagge, Sir (John) Picton, 5th Bt, 1877–1967, vol. VI
Bagge, Sir Picton; see Bagge, Sir J. P.
Bagge, Major Sir Richard Ludwig, 1872–1933, vol. III
Bagge, Stephen Salisbury, 1859–1950, vol. IV
Baggott, Ven. Louis John, 1891–1965, vol. VI
Baghot de la Bere, Stephen, 1877–1927, vol. II
Bagley, Edward Albert Ashton, 1876–1961, vol. VI
Bagnall, Hon. Sir Arthur; see Bagnall, Hon. Sir W. A.
Bagnall, Sir John, 1888–1954, vol. V
Bagnall, Hon. Sir (William) Arthur, 1917–1976, vol. VII
Bagnall-Wild, Ralph Bagnall, 1845–1925, vol. II
Bagnall-Wild, Brig.-Gen. Ralph Kirkby, 1873–1953, vol. V
Bagnold, Col Arthur Henry, 1854–1943, vol. IV
Bagot, 4th Baron, 1857–1932, vol. III
Bagot, 5th Baron, 1866–1946, vol. IV
Bagot, 6th Baron, 1877–1961, vol. VI
Bagot, 7th Baron, 1894–1973, vol. VII
Bagot, 8th Baron, 1897–1979, vol. VII
Bagot, Sir Alan Desmond, 1st Bt, 1896–1920, vol. II
Bagot, Col Charles Hervey, 1847–1911, vol. I
Bagot, Sir Charles Samuel, 1828–1906, vol. I
Bagot, (Sir) Josceline FitzRoy (1st Bt, but died before the passing under the Great Seal of the Patent of Baronetage), 1854–1913, vol. I
Bagot, Richard, 1860–1921, vol. II
Bagot, Theodosia, (Lady Bagot), 1865–1940, vol. III
Bagot, Major Hon. Walter Lewis, 1864–1927, vol. II
Bagot-Chester, Col Heneage Charles, 1836–1912, vol. I
Bagrit, Sir Leon, 1902–1979, vol. VII
Bagshawe, Arthur Clement, 1874–1937, vol. III
Bagshawe, Sir Arthur William Garrard, 1871–1950, vol. IV
Bagshawe, Most Rev. Edward Gilpin, 1829–1915, vol. I
Bagshawe, Edward Leonard, 1876–1955, vol. V
Bagshawe, Francis John Edward, 1877–1953, vol. V
Bagshawe, Col Frederick William, 1868–1945, vol. IV

Bagshawe, Lt-Col Herbert Vale, 1874–1962, vol. VI
Bagshawe, Thomas Wyatt, 1901–1976, vol. VII
Bagshawe, William Henry Gunning, 1825–1901, vol. I
Bagster, Robert, 1847–1924, vol. II
Baguley, Sir John Minty, 1880–1964, vol. VI
Bagwell, John, 1874–1946, vol. IV
Bagwell, Lt-Col John, 1884–1949, vol. IV
Bagwell, Richard, 1840–1918, vol. II
Bahadur Shamsher Jang Bahadur Rana, Commanding-General, 1892–1977, vol. VII
Bahauddin Khan, Resaldar Major, 1833–1901, vol. I
Bahawalpur, Ameer of, 1904–1966, vol. VI
Bahawalpur, Nawab of, 1883–1907, vol. I
Bahr, Sir Philip M.; see Manson-Bahr.
Bahrain, Ruler of; HH Shaikh Sir Hamed bin Isa Al Khalifah, died 1942, vol. IV
Bahrain, Ruler of, HH Shaikh Sulman bin Hamad Al Khalifah, died 1961, vol. V
Baig, Mirza Sir Abbas Ali, died 1932, vol. III
Baigent, Rt Rev. Mgr William Joseph, 1857–1930, vol. III
Baikie, Alfred, 1861–1947, vol. IV
Baikie, Brig.-Gen. Sir Hugh Archie Dundas Simpson-, 1871–1924, vol. II
Baikie, Rev. James, 1866–1931, vol. III
Baildon, Henry Bellyse, died 1907, vol. I
Bailey, Sir Abe, 1st Bt, 1864–1940, vol. III
Bailey, Col Alfred John, 1867–1940, vol. III
Bailey, Arnold Savage, 1881–1935, vol. III
Bailey, Arthur, 1903–1979, vol. VII
Bailey, Arthur Charles John, 1886–1951, vol. V
Bailey, Captain Arthur Harold, 1873–1925, vol. II
Bailey, Charles Thomas Peach, 1882–1968, vol. VI
Bailey, Cyril, 1871–1957, vol. V
Bailey, Sir Edward Battersby, 1881–1965, vol. VI
Bailey, Ernest Edmond, 1907–1956, vol. V
Bailey, Lt-Col Francis William, 1871–1932, vol. III
Bailey, Lt-Col Frederick George Glyn, 1880–1951, vol. V
Bailey, Frederick Manson, 1827–1915, vol. I
Bailey, Lt-Col Frederick Marshman, 1882–1967, vol. VI
Bailey, George Buchanan, 1898–1969, vol. VI
Bailey, Air Cdre George Cyril, 1890–1972, vol. VII
Bailey, Sir George Edwin, 1879–1965, vol. VI
Bailey, Sir George Leader, 1882–1953, vol. V
Bailey, George Leo, 1901–1979, vol. VII
Bailey, Gertrude Mary, 1870–1941, vol. IV
Bailey, Hamilton, 1894–1961, vol. VI
Bailey, Rev. Henry, 1815–1906, vol. I
Bailey, Henry Christopher, 1878–1961, vol. VI
Bailey, Hon. Herbert Crawshay, died 1936, vol. III
Bailey, Horace Thomas, 1852–1945, vol. IV
Bailey, Miss (Irene) Temple, died 1953, vol. V
Bailey, Sir James, 1840–1910, vol. I
Bailey, John, 1889–1957, vol. V
Bailey, Sir John, 1898–1969, vol. VI
Bailey, John Cann, 1864–1931, vol. III
Bailey, John E., 1897–1958, vol. V
Bailey, John Frederick, 1866–1938, vol. III
Bailey, Rev. J(ohn) H(enry) Shackleton, 1875–1956, vol. V

Bailey, Sir John Milner, 2nd Bt, 1900–1946, vol. IV
Bailey, John Walter, 1845–1930, vol. III
Bailey, Kenneth, 1909–1963, vol. VI
Bailey, Kenneth Claude, 1896–1951, vol. V
Bailey, Sir Kenneth Hamilton, 1898–1972, vol. VII
Bailey, Liberty Hyde, 1858–1954, vol. V
Bailey, Lionel Danyers, 1879–1967, vol. VI
Bailey, Philip James, 1816–1902, vol. I
Bailey, Sir Reginald Greenwood, 1894–1953, vol. V
Bailey, Richard William, 1885–1957, vol. V
Bailey, Sir Rowland, 1852–1930, vol. III
Bailey, Sidney Alfred, 1886–1972, vol. VII
Bailey, Adm. Sir Sidney Robert, 1882–1942, vol. IV
Bailey, Stanley John, 1901–1980, vol. VII
Bailey, Miss Temple; see Bailey, I. T.
Bailey, Victor Albert, 1895–1964, vol. VI
Bailey, Hon. Brig.-Gen. Vivian Telford, 1868–1938, vol. III
Bailey, Walter M.; see Milne-Bailey.
Bailey, Wilfrid Norman, 1893–1961, vol. VI
Bailey, Rt Hon. William Frederick, 1857–1917, vol. II
Bailey, Sir William Henry, 1838–1913, vol. I
Bailey, William Henry, born 1855, vol. II
Bailey, Sir William Thomas, 1873–1949, vol. IV
Bailey, Lt-Col E. Wyndham-Grevis, died 1920, vol. II
Bailhache, Sir Clement Meacher, 1856–1924, vol. II
Bailie, Thomas, 1885–1957, vol. V
Bailie, Maj.-Gen. Thomas Maubourg, 1844–1918, vol. II
Baillet-Latour, Comte de; Henry, 1876–1942, vol. IV
Baillie, Sir Adrian William Maxwell, 6th Bt, 1898–1947, vol. IV
Baillie, Rev. Albert Victor, 1864–1955, vol. V
Baillie, Col Augustus Charles, 1861–1939, vol. III
Baillie, Rev. Donald Macpherson, 1887–1954, vol. V
Baillie, Sir Duncan Colvin, 1856–1919, vol. II
Baillie, Col Duncan Gus, 1872–1968, vol. VI
Baillie, Hon. Evan; see Baillie, Hon. G. E. M.
Baillie, Sir Frank, 1875–1921, vol. II
Baillie, Lt-Col Frederick David M.; see Murray Baillie.
Baillie, Sir Gawaine George Stuart, 5th Bt, 1893–1914, vol. I
Baillie, Hon. (George) Evan (Michael), 1894–1941, vol. IV
Baillie, George Henry, 1901–1970, vol. VI (AII)
Baillie, Col Hugh Frederick, 1879–1941, vol. IV
Baillie, Sir James Black, 1872–1940, vol. III
Baillie, Gen. James Cadogan Parkison, 1835–1928, vol. II
Baillie, James Evan Bruce, 1859–1931, vol. III
Baillie, Very Rev. John, 1886–1960, vol. V
Baillie, John Gilroy, 1896–1960, vol. V
Baillie, Lady Maud L. E., 1896–1975, vol. VII
Baillie, Sir Robert Alexander, 4th Bt, 1859–1907, vol. I
Baillie, Ronald Hugh, 1863–1948, vol. IV
Baillie-Gage, Thomas Robert; see Gage.

28

Baillie-Grohman, Vice-Adm. Harold Tom, 1888–1978, vol. VII

Baillie-Grohman, William A., 1851–1921, vol. II (A)

Baillie-Hamilton, Hon. Charles William, 1900–1939, vol. III

Baillie-Hamilton, Sir William Alexander, 1844–1920, vol. II

Baillie Reynolds, Paul Kenneth; *see* Reynolds.

Baillie-Saunders, Margaret, 1873–1949, vol. IV

Baillieu, 1st Baron, 1889–1967, vol. VI

Baillieu, 2nd Baron, 1915–1973, vol. VII

Baillon, Maj.-Gen. Joseph Aloysius, 1895–1951, vol. V

Baily, Francis Evans, *died* 1962, vol. VI

Baily, Francis Gibson, 1868–1945, vol. IV

Baily, J. T. Herbert, 1865–1914, vol. I

Baily, Rev. Johnson, 1835–1915, vol. I (A)

Baily, Leslie, 1906–1976, vol. VII

Baily, Robert Edward Hartwell, 1885–1973, vol. VII

Bain, Sir (Albert) Ernest, 1875–1939, vol. III

Bain, Alexander, 1818–1903, vol. I

Bain, David, 1855–1933, vol. III

Bain, Donald Charles, 1913–1964, vol. VI

Bain, Sir Ernest; *see* Bain, Sir A. E.

Bain, Francis William, 1863–1940, vol. III

Bain, Sir Frederick, 1889–1950, vol. IV

Bain, Sir James, 1817–1898, vol. I

Bain, James Robert, 1851–1913, vol. I

Bain, Robert Nisbet, 1854–1909, vol. I

Bain, William Alexander, 1905–1971, vol. VII

Bain-Marais, Colin, 1893–1942, vol. VI

Bainbridge, Col Sir Edmond, 1841–1911, vol. I

Bainbridge, Maj.-Gen. Sir (Edmund) Guy (Tulloch), 1867–1943, vol. IV

Bainbridge, Emerson, 1845–1911, vol. I

Bainbridge, Francis Arthur, 1874–1921, vol. II

Bainbridge, Maj.-Gen. Frederick Thomas, 1834–1915, vol. I (A)

Bainbridge, Maj.-Gen. Sir Guy; *see* Bainbridge, Maj.-Gen. Sir E. G. T.

Bainbridge, Herbert William, 1862–1940, vol. III

Bainbridge, Rev. Howard Gurney D.; *see* Daniell-Bainbridge.

Bainbridge, Rear-Adm. John Hugh, 1845–1901, vol. I

Bainbridge, Col Norman Bruce, 1869–1935, vol. III

Bainbridge, Brig.-Gen. Percy Agnew, 1864–1934, vol. III

Bainbridge, Brig.-Gen. William Frank, 1873–1953, vol. V

Bainbrigge, Rev. Philip Thomas, *died* 1919, vol. II

Baines, Ven. Albert, *died* 1951, vol. V

Baines, Sir Frank, 1877–1933, vol. III

Baines, Frederick Ebenezer, 1832–1911, vol. I

Baines, Rt Rev. Frederick Samuel, *died* 1939, vol. III

Baines, Rt Rev. Henry Wolfe, 1905–1972, vol. VII

Baines, Hubert, 1874–1953, vol. V

Baines, Lt-Col J. C., 1876–1928, vol. II

Baines, Sir Jervoise Athelstane, 1847–1925, vol. II

Baines, Matthew Talbot, 1863–1925, vol. II

Baines, William, 1899–1922, vol. II

Baines, William Henry, 1879–1958, vol. V

Bainton, Edgar Leslie, 1880–1956, vol. V

Baird, Sir Alexander, 1st Bt (*cr* 1897), 1849–1920, vol. II

Baird, Brig.-Gen. Alexander Walter Frederic, 1876–1931, vol. III

Baird, Rev. Andrew Cumming, 1883–1940, vol. III

Baird, Col Andrew Wilson, 1842–1908, vol. I

Baird, Sir David, 3rd Bt (*cr* 1809), 1832–1913, vol. I

Baird, Sir David, 4th Bt (*cr* 1809), 1865–1941, vol. IV

Baird, Gen. Sir Douglas; *see* Baird, Gen. Sir H. B. D.

Baird, Douglas H., *died* 1940, vol. III

Baird, Edith Elina Helen, *died* 1924, vol. II

Baird, Brig.-Gen. Edward William David, 1864–1956, vol. V

Baird, Rear-Adm. Sir George Henry, 1871–1924, vol. II

Baird, Hon. George Thomas, 1847–1917, vol. II

Baird, Gen. Sir (Harry Beauchamp) Douglas, 1877–1963, vol. VI

Baird, James Craig, 1906–1973, vol. VII

Baird, Sir James Hozier Gardiner, 9th Bt (*cr* 1695), 1883–1966, vol. VI

Baird, John, 1906–1965, vol. VI

Baird, John George Alexander, 1854–1917, vol. II

Baird, Sir John Kennedy Erskine, 1832–1908, vol. I

Baird, John L., 1888–1946, vol. IV

Baird, Percy Johnstone, 1877–1956, vol. V

Baird, Sir Robert Hugh Hanley, 1855–1934, vol. III

Baird, William, 1848–1918, vol. II

Baird, Major Sir William, 1874–1956, vol. V

Baird, William Arthur, 1879–1933, vol. III

Baird, William George, 1889–1975, vol. VII

Baird, William James, 1893–1961, vol. VI

Baird, Sir William James Gardiner, 8th Bt (*cr* 1695), 1854–1921, vol. II

Baird, Sir William MacDonald, 1881–1946, vol. IV

Baird-Smith, David, *died* 1951, vol. V

Bairnsfather, Captain Bruce, 1888–1959, vol. V

Bainsfather, Captain George Edward Beckwith, 1855–1945, vol. IV

Bairstow, Arthur William, 1855–1943, vol. IV

Bairstow, Sir Edward C., 1874–1946, vol. IV

Bairstow, Sir Leonard, 1880–1963, vol. VI

Bajpai, Sir Girja Shankar, 1891–1954, vol. V

Bajpai, Sir Seetla Prasad, Rai Bahadur, 1865–1947, vol. IV

Baker, Rev. Albert Edward, 1884–1962, vol. VI

Baker, Alfred, *died* 1942, vol. IV

Baker, Sir Alfred, 1870–1943, vol. IV

Baker, Alfred Thomas, 1873–1936, vol. III

Baker, Mrs Alice, *died* 1935, vol. III

Baker, Alma; *see* Baker, C. A.

Baker, Andrew Clement, 1842–1913, vol. I

Baker, Arthur, 1861–1939, vol. III

Baker, Major Arthur Brander, 1868–1918, vol. II

Baker, Arthur Harold, 1890–1962, vol. VI

Baker, Brig.-Gen. Arthur Slade, 1863–1943, vol. IV

Baker, Sir Augustine FitzGerald, 1851–1922, vol. II

Baker, Sir Benjamin, 1840–1907, vol. I

Baker, Lt-Col (Bernard) Granville, 1870–1957, vol. V
Baker, Bevan Braithwaite B.; see Bevan-Baker.
Baker, Air Marshal Sir Brian Edmund, 1896–1979, vol. VII
Baker, Bryant, 1881–1970, vol. VI
Baker, Vice-Adm. Casper Joseph, 1852–1918, vol. II
Baker, Col Cecil Norris, 1869–1934, vol. III
Baker, Charles, 1851–1934, vol. III
Baker, (Charles) Alma, 1857–1941, vol. IV
Baker, Charles Ernest S.; see Smalley-Baker.
Baker, Charles Gaffney, 1907–1969, vol. VI
Baker, Charles Henry Collins, 1880–1959, vol. V
Baker, Charles Maurice, 1872–1952, vol. V
Baker, Lt-Col Sir Dodington George Richard S.; see Sherston-Baker.
Baker, Rt Rev. Donald, 1882–1968, vol. VI
Baker, Doris Manning, died 1971, vol. VII
Baker, Edmund Wilfrid, 1869–1953, vol. V
Baker, Edward Charles Stuart, 1864–1944, vol. IV
Baker, Lt-Col Edward Mervyn, 1875–1925, vol. II
Baker, Rev. Edward Morgan, 1874–1940, vol. III
Baker, Sir Edward Norman, 1857–1913, vol. I
Baker, Major Edwin Godfrey Phipps, 1885–1963, vol. VI
Baker, Rev. Eric Wilfred, 1899–1973, vol. VII
Baker, Ernest A., 1869–1941, vol. IV
Baker, Flora May, 1882–1949, vol. IV
Baker, Francis Douglas, 1884–1958, vol. V
Baker, Frederick Grenfell, died 1930, vol. III
Baker, Sir Frederick Spencer Arnold, 1885–1963, vol. VI
Baker, Field-Marshal Sir Geoffrey Harding, 1912–1980, vol. VII
Baker, Col George, 1840–1910, vol. I
Baker, George Arthur, 1885–1976, vol. VII
Baker, Hon. George Barnard, 1834–1910, vol. I
Baker, Air Vice-Marshal George Brindley Aufrere, 1894–1968, vol. VI
Baker, George Edwin, 1876–1960, vol. V
Baker, George Fisher, 1840–1931, vol. III
Baker, George Philip, 1879–1951, vol. V
Baker, Sir George Sherston, 4th Bt (cr 1796), 1846–1923, vol. II
Baker, Lt-Col Granville; see Baker, Lt-Col B. G.
Baker, Granville Edwin Lloyd L.; see Lloyd-Baker.
Baker, Rt Hon. Harold Trevor, 1877–1960, vol. V
Baker, Henry, 1893–1975, vol. VII
Baker, Henry Frederick, died 1956, vol. V
Baker, Hon. Sir Henry Seymour, 1890–1968, vol. VI
Baker, Henry William Clinton-; see Clinton-Baker.
Baker, H(enry) Wright, 1893–1969, vol. VI
Baker, Sir Herbert, 1862–1946, vol. IV
Baker, Herbert Arthur, 1875–1946, vol. IV
Baker, Herbert Brereton, 1862–1935, vol. III
Baker, J. Percy, 1859–1930, vol. III
Baker, Sir Jack Croft, 1894–1962, vol. VI
Baker, James, 1847–1920, vol. II
Baker, Adm. Sir Lewis C.; see Clinton-Baker.
Baker, James H., 1848–1925, vol. II
Baker, Lt-Gen. James Mitchell, 1878–1956, vol. V
Baker, Maj.-Gen. Jasper, 1877–1964, vol. VI

Baker, Joanna Constance, (Mrs Noel Baker); see Scott-Moncrieff, J. C.
Baker, Sir John, 1828–1909, vol. I
Baker, Sir John, 1861–1939, vol. III
Baker, John, 1867–1939, vol. III
Baker, John Alfred, 1882–1957, vol. V
Baker, John Gilbert, 1834–1920, vol. II
Baker, Ven. John Percy, 1871–1947, vol. IV
Baker, Air Chief Marshal Sir John Wakeling, 1897–1978, vol. VII
Baker, Joseph Allen, 1852–1918, vol. II
Baker, Julian Levett, 1873–1958, vol. V
Baker, Lawrence James, 1827–1921, vol. II
Baker, Adm. Sir Lewis C; see Clinton-Baker.
Baker, Newton Diehl, 1871–1937, vol. III
Baker, Olive Katherine Lloyd L.; see Lloyd-Baker.
Baker, Oliver, 1856–1939, vol. III
Baker, Percy M., 1872–1935, vol. III
Baker, Lt-Col Sir Randolf Littlehales, 4th Bt (cr 1802), 1879–1959, vol. V
Baker, Ray Stannard, 1870–1946, vol. IV
Baker, Reginald George Gillam, 1887–1971, vol. VII
Baker, Reginald Tustin, 1900–1966, vol. VI
Baker, Hon. Sir Richard Chaffey, 1842–1911, vol. I
Baker, Richard Thomas, 1854–1941, vol. IV
Baker, Major Robert Joseph, 1857–1931, vol. III
Baker, Rev. Stanley, 1868–1950, vol. VI
Baker, Sir Stanley, 1928–1976, vol. VII
Baker, Stephen Leonard, 1888–1978, vol. VII
Baker, Rev. Sir Talbot Hastings Bendall, 3rd Bt (cr 1802), 1820–1900, vol. I
Baker, Sir Thomas, died 1926, vol. II
Baker, Col Thomas MacDonald, 1894–1976, vol. VII
Baker, Lt-Gen. Thomas Norris, 1833–1915, vol. I
Baker, Walter John, 1876–1930, vol. III
Baker, Walter Reginald, 1852–1929, vol. III
Baker, Will C., vol. III
Baker, Rev. William, 1841–1910, vol. I
Baker, William, 1849–1920, vol. II
Baker, Ven. William Arthur, 1870–1950, vol. IV
Baker, Sir William Frederick, 1844–1929, vol. III
Baker, Ven. William George, died 1923, vol. II
Baker, Adm. William Henry Baker, 1862–1932, vol. III
Baker, Lt-Gen. Sir William Henry Goldney, 1888–1964, vol. VI
Baker, Rev. William James Furneaux Vashon, 1851–1932, vol. III
Baker, Sir William Thomas Webb, 1873–1948, vol. IV
Baker, Rev. William Wing Carew, 1860–1930, vol. III
Baker-Carr, Brig.-Gen. Christopher D'Arcy Bloomfield Saltern, 1878–1949, vol. IV
Baker-Carr, Major Robert George Teesdale, 1867–1931, vol. III
Baker-Wilbraham, Sir George Barrington; see Wilbraham.
Baker Wilbraham, Sir Randle John; see Wilbraham.
Bakewell, James Herbert, died 1931, vol. III

Bakker, Cornelis Jan, 1904–1960, vol. V
Bakst, Leon, 1868–1924, vol. II
Balasinor, Nawab of, 1894–1945, vol. IV
Balbo, Maresciallo dell'Aria Italo, 1896–1940, vol. III
Balch, Emily Greene, 1867–1961, vol. VI
Balchin, Brig. Nigel Marlin, 1908–1970, vol. VI
Balcon, Sir Michael, 1896–1977, vol. VII
Bald, Major A. Campbell, died 1905, vol. I
Bald, Lt-Col John Arthur, 1876–1960, vol. V
Bald, Robert Cecil, 1901–1965, vol. VI
Balderston, John Lloyd, 1889–1954, vol. V
Baldock, Maj.-Gen. Thomas Stanford, 1854–1937, vol. III
Baldock, William, 1850–1933, vol. III
Baldrey, Lt-Col Frank Shelson Headon, 1869–1935, vol. III
Baldry, Alfred Lys, 1858–1939, vol. III
Baldry, Walter Burton Burton-; see Burton-Baldry.
Baldwin of Bewdley, 1st Earl, 1867–1947, vol. IV
Baldwin of Bewdley, 2nd Earl, 1899–1958, vol. V
Baldwin of Bewdley, 3rd Earl, 1904–1976, vol. VII
Baldwin, Sir Archer Ernest, 1883–1966, vol. VI
Baldwin, Rev. Edward Curtis, 1844–1941, vol. IV
Baldwin, Ernest H. F., 1909–1969, vol. VI
Baldwin, Engr-Rear-Adm. George William, 1871–1955, vol. V
Baldwin, Brig.-Gen. Guy Melfort, 1865–1945, vol. IV
Baldwin, Sir Harry, 1862–1931, vol. III
Baldwin, James Mark, 1861–1934, vol. III
Baldwin, Air Marshal Sir John Eustace Arthur, 1892–1975, vol. VII
Baldwin, Lt-Col Sir John Grey, 1867–1939, vol. III
Baldwin, John Herbert Lacy, 1863–1945, vol. IV
Baldwin, Joseph Mason, 1878–1945, vol. IV
Baldwin, Nelson Mills, 1923–1980, vol. VII
Baldwin, Hon. Simeon Eben, 1840–1927, vol. II
Baldwin-Webb, Col James, died 1940, vol. III
Bale, Edwin, 1838–1923, vol. II
Bale, Hon. Sir Henry, 1854–1910, vol. I
Balewa, Alhaji Rt Hon. Sir Abubakar T.; see Tafawa Balewa.
Balfour, 1st Earl of, 1848–1930, vol. III
Balfour, 2nd Earl of, 1853–1945, vol. IV
Balfour, 3rd Earl of, 1902–1968, vol. VI
Balfour of Burleigh, 6th Lord, 1849–1921, vol. II
Balfour of Burleigh, 11th (de facto 7th) Lord, 1883–1967, vol. VI
Balfour, Alfred, 1885–1963, vol. VI
Balfour, Brig.-Gen. Sir Alfred Granville, 1858–1936, vol. III
Balfour, Alice Blanche, died 1936, vol. III
Balfour, Sir Andrew, 1873–1931, vol. III
Balfour, Ven. Andrew Jackson, 1845–1923, vol. II
Balfour, Col Arthur Macintosh, 1862–1936, vol. III
Balfour, Charles Barrington, 1862–1921, vol. II
Balfour, Major Charles James, 1889–1939, vol. III
Balfour, Captain Christopher Egerton, 1872–1907, vol. I
Balfour, Edward, 1849–1927, vol. II
Balfour, Brig. Edward William Sturgis, 1884–1955, vol. V

Balfour, Col Eustace James Anthony, died 1911, vol. I
Balfour, Lady Frances, 1858–1931, vol. III
Balfour, Lt-Col Francis Cecil Campbell, 1884–1965, vol. VI
Balfour, Rt Rev. Francis Richard Townley, 1846–1924, vol. II
Balfour, Lt-Col Frederick Robert Stephen, 1873–1945, vol. IV
Balfour, George, 1872–1941, vol. IV
Balfour, Sir Graham, 1858–1929, vol. III
Balfour, Henry, 1863–1939, vol. III
Balfour, Sir Isaac Bayley, 1853–1922, vol. II
Balfour, Hon. James, 1830–1913, vol. I
Balfour, Hon. James Moncreiff, 1878–1960, vol. V
Balfour, James William, 1827–1907, vol. I
Balfour, Col John Edmond Heugh, 1863–1952, vol. V
Balfour, Lt-Col Kenneth Robert, 1863–1936, vol. III
Balfour, Margaret Ida, died 1945, vol. IV
Balfour, Lt-Col Oswald Herbert Campbell, died 1953, vol. V
Balfour, Patrick; see Kinross, 3rd Baron.
Balfour, Lt-Gen. Sir Philip Maxwell, 1898–1977, vol. VII
Balfour, Sir Robert, 1st Bt, 1844–1929, vol. III
Balfour, Rev. Robert Gordon, 1826–1905, vol. I
Balfour, Col William Edward Ligonier, 1855–1934, vol. III
Balfour-Browne, John Hutton; see Browne.
Balfour-Browne, Vincent R., died 1963, vol. VI
Balfour-Browne, William Alex Francis, 1874–1967, vol. VI
Balfour-Melville, Leslie Melville, 1854–1937, vol. III
Baliol Scott, Edward, 1873–1963, vol. VI
Baliol Scott, Napier, 1903–1956, vol. V
Ball, Sir Albert, 1862–1946, vol. IV
Ball, Sir Arthur; see Ball, Sir C. A. K.
Ball, Air Vice-Marshal Sir Benjamin, 1912–1977, vol. VII
Ball, Sir (Charles) Arthur (Kinahan), 2nd Bt, 1877–1945, vol. IV
Ball, Sir Charles Bent, 1st Bt, 1851–1916, vol. II
Ball, Charles Francis, 1869–1933, vol. III
Ball, Major Charles James Prior, 1893–1973, vol. VII
Ball, Rev. Charles Richard, died 1918, vol. II
Ball, E. Bruce, 1873–1944, vol. IV
Ball, Sir Edmund Lancaster, 1883–1971, vol. VII
Ball, Ernest, died 1927, vol. II
Ball, Eustace Alfred R.; see Reynolds-Ball.
Ball, Major George Joseph, 1880–1952, vol. V
Ball, Sir (George) Joseph, 1885–1961, vol. VI
Ball, Harry Standish, 1888–1941, vol. IV
Ball, James Barry, died 1926, vol. II
Ball, Sir James Benjamin, 1867–1920, vol. II
Ball, James Dyer, 1847–1919, vol. II
Ball, John, 1861–1940, vol. III
Ball, John, 1872–1941, vol. IV
Ball, Rt Hon. John Thomas, 1815–1898, vol. I
Ball, Sir Joseph; see Ball, Sir G. J.
Ball, Sir Nigel Gresley, 3rd Bt, 1892–1978, vol. VII

Ball, Sir Robert Stawell, 1840–1913, vol. I
Ball, Thomas, 1846–1922, vol. II
Ball, Very Rev. Thomas Isaac, *died* 1916, vol. II
Ball, Walter William Rouse, 1850–1925, vol. II
Ball, Wilfrid, 1853–1917, vol. II
Ball, Willet, 1873–1962, vol. VI
Ball, William Antony, 1904–1973, vol. VII
Ball, Sir William Girling, *died* 1945, vol. IV
Ball, Sir William Valentine, 1874–1960, vol. V
Ballance, Sir Charles Alfred, 1856–1936, vol. III
Ballance, Rear-Adm. Frank Arthur, 1902–1978, vol. VII
Ballance, Sir Hamilton Ashley, 1867–1936, vol. III
Ballantine-Dykes, Col Frescheville Hubert; *see* Dykes.
Ballantrae, Baron (Life Peer); Bernard Edward Fergusson, 1911–1980, vol. VII
Ballantyne, Archibald Morton, 1908–1977, vol. VII
Ballantyne, Arthur James, 1876–1954, vol. V
Ballantyne, Sir Henry, 1855–1941, vol. IV
Ballantyne, Horatio, 1871–1956, vol. V
Ballantyne, John Andrew, 1912–1960, vol. V
Ballantyne, John William, 1861–1923, vol. II
Ballard, Albert, 1888–1969, vol. VI
Ballard, Lt-Col Basil W.; *see* Woods Ballard.
Ballard, Bristow Guy, 1902–1975, vol. VII
Ballard, Brig.-Gen. Colin Robert, 1868–1941, vol. IV
Ballard, Edward, 1820–1897, vol. I
Ballard, Rev. Frank, *died* 1931, vol. III
Ballard, Rev. Frank Hewett, *died* 1959, vol. V
Ballard, Adm. George Alexander, 1862–1948, vol. IV
Ballard, Henry, 1840–1919, vol. II
Ballard, Brig. James Archibald William, 1905–1978, vol. VII
Ballard, Philip Boswood, 1865–1950, vol. IV
Ballentine, Maj.-Gen. John Steventon, 1897–1965, vol. VI
Ballin, Ada S., *died* 1906, vol. I
Ballingall, Lt-Col Henry Miller, 1878–1936, vol. III
Ballinger, Sir John, 1860–1933, vol. III
Ballou, Henry Arthur, 1872–1937, vol. III
Balls, William Lawrence, 1882–1960, vol. V
Bally, Maj.-Gen. John Ford, 1845–1912, vol. I
Balme, Archibald Hamilton, *died* 1942, vol. IV
Balme, Harold, *died* 1953, vol. V
Balmforth, Rev. Canon Henry, 1890–1977, vol. VII
Balrampur, Maharaja Bahadur of, 1879–1921, vol. II
Balsdon, John Percy Vyvian Dacre, 1901–1977, vol. VII
Balston, Thomas, 1883–1967, vol. VI
Baly, Edward Charles Cyril, 1871–1948, vol. IV
Balzani, Count Ugo, 1847–1916, vol. II
Bam, Lt-Col Pieter Canzius van Blommestein; *see* Stewart-Bam of Ards.
Bamber, Col Charles James, 1855–1941, vol. IV
Bamber, John, 1915–1976, vol. VII
Bamber, Captain Wyndham Lerrier, *died* 1924, vol. II
Bambridge, Sir George, 1883–1961, vol. VI
Bambridge, Henry James, 1881–1956, vol. V
Bambridge, Rev. Joseph John, *died* 1923, vol. II

Bambridge, Thomas, vol. III
Bamfield, Lt-Gen. Albert Henry, 1830–1908, vol. I
Bamfield, Maj.-Gen. Harold John Kinahan, *died* 1959, vol. V
Bamford, Major Edward, 1887–1928, vol. II
Bamford, Sir Eric St John, 1891–1957, vol. V
Bamford, Lt-Col Harry William Morrey, 1882–1968, vol. VI
Bamford, Percival Clifford, 1886–1960, vol. V
Bamford, Rt Rev. Thomas Ambrose, 1861–1945, vol. IV
Bamford-Slack, Sir John, 1857–1909, vol. I
Bampton, Rev. Joseph M., 1854–1933, vol. III
Banarji, Hon. Sir Pramada Charan, *died* 1930, vol. III
Banatvala, Col Sir Hormasjee Eduljee, 1859–1932, vol. III
Banbury of Southam, 1st Baron, 1850–1936, vol. III
Banbury, Brig.-Gen. Walter Edward, 1863–1927, vol. II
Bancroft, Claude Keith, 1885–1919, vol. II
Bancroft, Edgar Addison, 1857–1925, vol. II
Bancroft, Elias, *died* 1924, vol. II
Bancroft, George Pleydell, 1868–1956, vol. V
Bancroft, Hubert Howe, 1832–1918, vol. II
Bancroft, Marie Effie, (Lady Bancroft), 1839–1921, vol. II
Bancroft, Sir Oswald Lawrance, 1888–1964, vol. VI
Bancroft, Sir Squire Bancroft, 1841–1926, vol. II
Bandaranaike, Sir Solomon Dias, 1862–1946, vol. IV
Bandaranaike, Solomon West Ridgeway Dias, 1899–1959, vol. V
Bandon, 4th Earl of, 1850–1924, vol. II
Bandon, 5th Earl of, 1904–1979, vol. VII
Bandon, Countess of; (Georgina), 1853–1942, vol. IV
Banerjea, A. C., 1894–1979, vol. VII
Banerjea, Pramathanath, 1881–1960, vol. V (A)
Banerjea, Sir Surendranath, 1848–1925, vol. II
Banerjee, Sir Gooroo Dass, 1844–1919, vol. II
Banerjee, Sarat Chandra, 1870–1932, vol. III
Banerji, Sir Albion Rajkumar, 1871–1950, vol. IV
Banerji, Amiya Charan, 1891–1968, vol. VI (AII)
Banes, George Edward, 1828–1907, vol. I
Banfield, John William, *died* 1945, vol. IV
Banfield, Col Rees John Francis, 1850–1926, vol. II
Banford, Leslie Jackson, *died* 1961, vol. VI
Bangor, 5th Viscount, 1828–1911, vol. I
Bangor, 6th Viscount, 1868–1950, vol. IV
Bangs, John Kendrick, 1862–1922, vol. II
Banister, Col Fitzgerald Muirson, 1853–1928, vol. II
Banister, George Henry, *died* 1934, vol. III
Banister, John Bright, 1880–1938, vol. III
Banister, Rt Rev. William, 1855–1928, vol. II
Bankart, Sir Alfred Seymour, 1870–1933, vol. III
Bankart, Surg. Rear-Adm. Sir Arthur Reginald, 1868–1943, vol. IV
Bankart, Arthur Sydney Blundell, 1879–1951, vol. V
Bankart, Vice-Adm. Sir (George) Harold, 1893–1964, vol. VI

32

Bankart, Vice-Adm. Sir Harold; *see* Bankart, Vice-Adm. Sir G. H.
Bankes, Rev. Eldon Surtees, 1829–1915, vol. I
Bankes, Rt Hon. Sir John Eldon, 1854–1946, vol. IV
Bankes, Ralph George Scott, 1900–1948, vol. IV
Bankes, Ralph Vincent, *died* 1921, vol. II
Bankes, Robert Wynne, 1887–1975, vol. VII
Bankes, Walter Ralph, 1853–1904, vol. I
Bankes-Williams, Ivor Maredydd, 1896–1974, vol. VII
Banks, Col Hon. Charles Arthur, 1885–1961, vol. VI
Banks, Col Cyril, 1901–1969, vol. VI
Banks, Sir Donald, 1891–1975, vol. VII
Banks, Edward Bernard, 1901–1968, vol. VI
Banks, Elizabeth, *died* 1938, vol. III
Banks, Mrs George Linnaeus, 1821–1897, vol. I
Banks, Lt-Col Henry John Archibald, 1869–1939, vol. III
Banks, Sir John, *died* 1908, vol. I
Banks, Sir John Garnett, 1889–1974, vol. VII
Banks, Rev. John Shaw, 1835–1917, vol. II
Banks, Leslie James, 1890–1952, vol. V
Banks, Sir Reginald Mitchell, 1880–1940, vol. III
Banks, Rev. Samuel John Sherbrooke, 1861–1941, vol. IV
Banks, Sir Thomas Macdonald; *see* Banks, Sir Donald.
Banks, Sir William Mitchell, 1842–1904, vol. I
Banks-Davis, Henry John, 1867–1936, vol. III
Bannatine-Allason, Maj.-Gen. Sir Richard, 1855–1940, vol. III
Bannatyne, Rev. Colin A., 1849–1920, vol. II
Bannatyne, Maj.-Gen. Neil Charles, 1880–1970, vol. VI
Bannatyne, Sir Robert Reid, 1875–1956, vol. V
Banner, Major Sir Harmood H.-; *see* Harmood-Banner.
Banner, Hubert Stewart, 1891–1964, vol. VI
Banner, Sir John Sutherland H.; *see* Harmood-Banner.
Bannerman of Kildonan, Baron (Life Peer); John MacDonald Bannerman, 1901–1969, vol. VI
Bannerman, Sir Alexander, 11th Bt, 1871–1934, vol. III
Bannerman, Lt-Col Sir Arthur D'Arcy Gordon, 12th Bt, 1866–1955, vol. V
Bannerman, Charles Edward Woolhouse, 1884–1943, vol. IV
Bannerman, David Armitage, 1886–1979, vol. VII
Bannerman, Sir George, 10th Bt, 1827–1901, vol. I
Bannerman, Rt Hon. Sir Henry C.; *see* Campbell-Bannerman.
Bannerman, Gen. William, 1828–1914, vol. I
Bannerman, Maj.-Gen. William Burney, 1858–1924, vol. II
Banning, Lt-Col Stephen Thomas, 1859–1935, vol. III
Bannister, Rev. Arthur Thomas, 1862–1936, vol. III
Bannister, Charles Olden, 1876–1955, vol. V
Bannister, Frank Kenneth, 1909–1975, vol. VII

Bannister, Frederick Allan, 1901–1970, vol. VI
Bannister, Rev. Henry Marriott, 1854–1919, vol. II
Banon, Brig.-Gen. Frederick Lionel, 1862–1950, vol. IV
Bansda, ex-Maharaja Saheb of, 1888–1951, vol. V
Banswara, Maharawal of, 1888–1944, vol. IV (A), vol. V
Banta, Arthur Mangun, 1877–1946, vol. IV (A), vol. V
Banting, Sir Frederick Grant, 1891–1941, vol. IV
Banting, Air Vice-Marshal George Gaywood, 1898–1973, vol. VII
Bantock, George Granville, *died* 1913, vol. I
Bantock, Sir Granville, 1868–1946, vol. IV
Banton, George, 1856–1932, vol. III
Barbé, Louis A., 1845–1926, vol. II
Barbenson, Nicholas Peter Le Cocq, 1838–1928, vol. II
Barber, Arthur Vavasour, *died* 1957, vol. V
Barber, Rev. Benjamin Aquila, 1876–1946, vol. IV
Barber, Charles Alfred, 1860–1933, vol. III
Barber, Lt-Col Charles Harrison, 1877–1965, vol. VI
Barber, Lt-Gen. Sir Colin Muir, 1897–1964, vol. VI
Barber, Donald, 1905–1957, vol. V
Barber, Ven. Edward, 1841–1914, vol. I
Barber, Sir (Edward) Fairless, 1873–1958, vol. V
Barber, Elizabeth; *see* Barber, M. E.
Barber, Eric Arthur, 1888–1965, vol. VI
Barber, Sir Fairless; *see* Barber, Sir E. F.
Barber, Maj.-Gen. Frederick Charles, *died* 1908, vol. I
Barber, Maj.-Gen. George Walter, 1868–1951, vol. V
Barber, Sir George William, 1858–1945, vol. IV
Barber, Harold Wordsworth, 1886–1955, vol. V
Barber, Sir Henry; *see* Barber, Sir W. H.
Barber, Sir Herbert William, 1887–1978, vol. VII
Barber, Horace Newton, 1914–1971, vol. VII
Barber, Captain James William, *died* 1962, vol. VI
Barber, Leslie Claud Seton, 1894–1968, vol. VI
Barber, Mary, 1911–1965, vol. VI
Barber, (Mary) Elizabeth, 1911–1979, vol. VII
Barber, Ohio C., 1841–1920, vol. II
Barber, Percival Ellison, *died* 1959, vol. V
Barber, Sir Philip; *see* Barber, Sir T. P.
Barber, Philip Stanley, 1895–1973, vol. VII
Barber, Rev. Thomas Gerrard, *died* 1952, vol. V
Barber, Sir (Thomas) Philip, 1st Bt (*cr* 1960), 1876–1961, vol. VI
Barber, William Charles, *died* 1921, vol. II
Barber, William David, *died* 1952, vol. V
Barber, W(illiam) Edmund, *died* 1958, vol. V
Barber, Sir (William) Henry, 1st Bt (*cr* 1924), 1860–1927, vol. II
Barber, Rev. William Theodore Aquila, 1858–1945, vol. IV
Barber-Starkey, William Joseph Starkey, 1847–1924, vol. II
Barberton, Ivan Graham Mitford-, 1896–1976, vol. VII
Barbier, Paul, *died* 1921, vol. II
Barbier, Paul, 1873–1947, vol. IV

Barbieri, Bishop Guido Bastiani Pascucci, 1836–1910, vol. I
Barbirolli, Sir John Giovanni Battista, 1899–1970, vol. VI
Barbour, A. H. Freeland, 1856–1927, vol. II
Barbour, Sir David Miller, 1841–1928, vol. II
Barbour, George, 1841–1919, vol. II
Barbour, George Brown, 1890–1977, vol. VII (AII)
Barbour, George Freeland, 1882–1946, vol. IV
Barbour, Harold Adrian Milne, 1874–1938, vol. III
Barbour, Rt Hon. Sir John Milne, 1st Bt, 1868–1951, vol. V
Barbour, Major Robert, 1876–1928, vol. II
Barbusse, Henri, 1873–1935, vol. III
Barchard, Col Charles Henry, died 1902, vol. I
Barclay, Alfred Ernest, 1876–1949, vol. IV
Barclay, Sir Cecil; see Barclay, Sir R. C. de B.
Barclay, Rt Hon. Sir Colville Adrian de Rune, 1869–1929, vol. III
Barclay, Brig. Cyril Nelson, 1896–1979, vol. VII
Barclay, Edward Exton, 1860–1948, vol. IV
Barclay, Florence L., 1862–1920, vol. II
Barclay, Sir George Head, 1862–1921, vol. II
Barclay, Sir Harry John, 1861–1933, vol. III
Barclay, Col Henry Albert, 1858–1947, vol. IV
Barclay, Hugh Gurney, 1851–1936, vol. III
Barclay, Rev. Humphrey Gordon, died 1955, vol. V
Barclay, Rev. James, 1844–1920, vol. II
Barclay, John, 1845–1936, vol. III
Barclay, John Stephen, 1908–1968, vol. VI
Barclay, Major Maurice Edward, 1886–1962, vol. VI
Barclay, Sir Noton; see Barclay, Sir R. N.
Barclay, Col Reginald, 1861–1945, vol. IV
Barclay, Robert, 1837–1913, vol. I
Barclay, Robert Buchanan, 1843–1919, vol. II
Barclay, Sir (Robert) Cecil de Belzim, 13th Bt, 1862–1930, vol. III
Barclay, Robert Francis, 1867–1948, vol. IV
Barclay, Robert Leatham, 1869–1939, vol. III
Barclay, Sir (Robert) Noton, 1872–1957, vol. V
Barclay, Robert Wyvill, 1880–1951, vol. V
Barclay, Sir Thomas, 1839–1921, vol. II
Barclay, Rev. Thomas, 1849–1935, vol. III
Barclay, Sir Thomas, 1853–1941, vol. IV
Barclay, William, 1907–1978, vol. VII
Barclay, William Singer, 1871–1947, vol. IV
Barclay-Harvey, Sir (Charles) Malcolm, 1890–1969, vol. VI
Barclay-Harvey, Sir Malcolm; see Barclay-Harvey, Sir C. M.
Barclay-Smith, Edward, died 1945, vol. IV
Barclay-Smith, (Ida) Phyllis, died 1980, vol. VII
Barclay-Smith, Phyllis; see Barclay-Smith, I. P.
Barcroft, John Coleraine Hanbury, 1908–1958, vol. V
Barcroft, Sir Joseph, 1872–1947, vol. IV
Barcŷnska, Countess Hélène Armiger Barclay, died 1930, vol. III
Bardill, Ralph William, 1876–1935, vol. III
Bardoux, Jacques, 1874–1959, vol. V
Bardsley, Rt Rev. Cyril Charles Bowman, 1870–1940, vol. III
Bardsley, Rev. Ernest John, 1868–1948, vol. IV

Bardsley, Rt Rev. John Wareing, 1835–1904, vol. I
Bardsley, Rev. Joseph Udell Norman, 1868–1928, vol. II
Bardsley, Robert Vickers, 1890–1952, vol. V
Bardswell, Charles William, 1832–1902, vol. I
Bardswell, Hugh Rosser, 1874–1962, vol. VI
Bardswell, Noel Dean, 1871–1938, vol. III
Bardwell, Thomas Newman Frederick, 1850–1931, vol. III
Bardwell, Captain William Scot, 1892–1968, vol. VI
Bare, Lt-Col Alfred Raymund, 1886–1967, vol. VI
Bare, Captain Arnold Edwin, 1880–1917, vol. II
Barea, Arturo, 1897–1957, vol. V
Barefoot, Lt-Col George Henry, 1864–1924, vol. II
Barff, Rev. Albert, died 1913, vol. I
Barff, Henry Ebenezer, 1857–1925, vol. II
Barff, Rev. Henry Tootai, 1834–1917, vol. II
Barff, Stafford Edward Douglas, 1909–1976, vol. VII
Barfoot, Most Rev. Walter Foster, 1893–1978, vol. VII
Barford, Edward, 1898–1980, vol. VII
Barge, Lt-Col Kenneth, 1883–1971, vol. VII
Barger, George, 1878–1939, vol. III
Bargone, Frédéric Charles; see Farrère, Claude.
Barham, Col Arthur Saxby, 1869–1952, vol. V
Barham, Ven. Charles Mitchell, died 1935, vol. III
Barham, Rt Rev. E(dward) Lawrence, 1901–1973, vol. VII
Barham, Sir George, 1836–1913, vol. I
Barham, George Titus, 1860–1937, vol. III
Baria, Raja of, 1886–1949, vol. IV
Barillon, Rt Rev. Emile, 1860–1935, vol. III
Baring, Brig.-Gen. Hon. Everard, 1865–1932, vol. III
Baring, Hon. Francis Henry, 1850–1915, vol. I
Baring, Sir Godfrey, 1st Bt, 1871–1957, vol. V
Baring, Godfrey Nigel Everard, 1870–1934, vol. III
Baring, Major Hon. Guy Victor, 1873–1916, vol. II
Baring, Harold Herman John, 1869–1927, vol. II
Baring, Hon. Hugo, 1876–1949, vol. IV
Baring, Wing Comdr Hon. Maurice, 1874–1945, vol. IV
Baring, Walter, 1844–1915, vol. I
Baring, Hon. Windham, 1880–1922, vol. II
Baring-Gould, Sabine, 1834–1924, vol. II
Bark, Sir Peter, 1869–1937, vol. III
Barker, Aldred Farrer, 1868–1964, vol. VI
Barker, Sir Alport; see Barker, Sir T. W. A.
Barker, Anthony Raine, 1880–1963, vol. VI
Barker, Arthur Edward James, died 1916, vol. II
Barker, Augustine, 1887–1937, vol. III
Barker, Bertie Thomas Percival, 1877–1961, vol. VI
Barker, Cecil; see Barker, H. C. J.
Barker, Sir (Charles Frederic) James, 1914–1980, vol. VII
Barker, Col Charles William Panton, 1857–1926, vol. II
Barker, Air Vice-Marshal Clifford Cockcroft, 1909–1977, vol. VII
Barker, Captain Sir David W., 1858–1941, vol. IV
Barker, Douglas William Ashley, 1905–1978, vol. VII
Barker, Edward Harrison, 1851–1919, vol. II

Barker, Sir Ernest, 1874–1960, vol. V
Barker, Col Ernest Francis William, 1877–1961, vol. VI
Barker, Sir Francis Henry, 1865–1922, vol. II
Barker, Col Sir Francis William James, 1841–1924, vol. II
Barker, Lt-Col Frederic Allan, 1882–1959, vol. V
Barker, Hon. Sir Frederic Eustace, 1838–1916, vol. II
Barker, Lt-Col Frederick George, 1866–1951, vol. V
Barker, Maj.-Gen. Sir George, 1849–1930, vol. III
Barker, George, 1858–1936, vol. III (A), vol. IV
Barker, Gen. Sir George Digby, 1833–1914, vol. I
Barker, Rev. Canon Gilbert David, 1882–1958, vol. V
Barker, Harley Granville G.; see Granville-Barker.
Barker, (Harold) Cecil James, 1893–1974, vol. VII
Barker, Helen G.; see Granville-Barker.
Barker, Sir Henry Edward, 1872–1942, vol. IV
Barker, Henry James, 1852–1934, vol. III (A), vol. IV
Barker, Sir Herbert Atkinson, 1869–1950, vol. IV
Barker, J. Ellis, 1870–1948, vol. IV
Barker, Sir James; see Barker, Sir C. F. J.
Barker, Sir John, 1st Bt, 1840–1914, vol. I
Barker, John, died 1970, vol. VI
Barker, John Edward, 1832–1912, vol. I
Barker, Lt-Col John Stafford, 1879–1959, vol. V
Barker, Maj.-Gen. John Stewart Scott, 1853–1918, vol. II
Barker, Very Rev. Joseph, 1834–1924, vol. II
Barker, Lancelot Elliot, 1908–1972, vol. VII
Barker, Lewellys F., 1867–1943, vol. IV
Barker, Dame Lilian Charlotte, 1874–1955, vol. V
Barker, Louis William, 1879–1954, vol. V
Barker, Lt-Gen. Michael George Henry, 1884–1960, vol. V
Barker, Rev. Peter, died 1937, vol. III
Barker, Lt-Col Randle Barnett-, 1870–1918, vol. II
Barker, Sir Rayner Childe, 1858–1945, vol. IV
Barker, Maj.-Gen. Richard Ernest, 1888–1962, vol. VI
Barker, Sir Robert Beacroft, 1890–1960, vol. V, vol. VI
Barker, Lt-Col Robert Hewitt, 1887–1961, vol. VI
Barker, Captain Roland Auriol, 1892–1954, vol. V
Barker, Ronald Ernest, 1920–1976, vol. VII
Barker, Sir Ross; see Barker, Sir W. R.
Barker, Rev. Rowland Vectis, 1846–1926, vol. II
Barker, Dame Sara Elizabeth, 1904–1973, vol. VII
Barker, Sydney George, 1887–1942, vol. IV
Barker, Thomas Vipond, 1881–1931, vol. III
Barker, Sir (Thomas William) Alport, died 1956, vol. V
Barker, Tom Battersby, died 1968, vol. VI
Barker, Sir (Wilberforce) Ross, 1874–1957, vol. V
Barker, Very Rev. William, 1838–1917, vol. II
Barker, Lt-Col William Arthur John, 1879–1924, vol. II
Barker, Lt-Col William George, 1894–1930, vol. III
Barker, William Henry, 1882–1929, vol. III
Barker, Wright, died 1941, vol. IV

Barker-Benfield, Brig. Karl Vere, 1892–1969, vol. VI
Barker-Mill, William Claude Frederick V.; see Vaudrey-Barker-Mill.
Barkla, Charles Glover, 1877–1944, vol. IV
Barkley, Alben William, 1877–1956, vol. V
Barkley, Col Macdonald, 1871–1956, vol. V
Barkley, William Henry, 1869–1942, vol. IV
Barkly, Sir Henry, 1815–1898, vol. I
Barkway, Rt Rev. James Lumsden, 1878–1968, vol. VI
Barlee, Sir Kenneth William, died 1956, vol. V
Barley, Frederick, died 1915, vol. I
Barley, Lt-Col Leslie John, 1890–1979, vol. VII
Barling, Sir Gilbert; see Barling, Sir H. G.
Barling, Sir (Harry) Gilbert, 1st Bt, 1855–1940, vol. III
Barling, Joseph, born 1839, vol. III
Barling, Lt-Col Seymour Gilbert, died 1960, vol. V
Barlow, Sir Alan; see Barlow, Sir J. A. N.
Barlow, Rt Hon. Sir Anderson M.; see Montague-Barlow.
Barlow, Adm. Charles James, 1848–1921, vol. II
Barlow, Rt Rev. Christopher George, 1858–1915, vol. I (A)
Barlow, Disney Charles, 1880–1965, vol. VI
Barlow, Francis John, 1869–1940, vol. III
Barlow, Sir Frank Herbert, 1918–1979, vol. VII
Barlow, George Thomas, 1865–1919, vol. II
Barlow, Rev. Henry Theodore Edward, 1863–1906, vol. I
Barlow, Sir Hilaro William Wellesley, 5th Bt (cr 1803), 1861–1941, vol. IV
Barlow, Horace M., 1884–1954, vol. V
Barlow, James, 1921–1973, vol. VII
Barlow, Sir (James) Alan (Noel), 2nd Bt (cr 1900), 1881–1968, vol. VI
Barlow, Rev. James William, 1826–1913, vol. I
Barlow, Jane, died 1917, vol. II
Barlow, Col John, died 1924, vol. II
Barlow, John, 1853–1943, vol. IV (A)
Barlow, Sir John Emmott, 1st Bt (cr 1907), 1857–1932, vol. III
Barlow, Percy, 1867–1931, vol. III
Barlow, Ralph Mitford Marriott, 1904–1977, vol. VII
Barlow, Sir Richard Hugh, 6th Bt (cr 1803), 1904–1946, vol. IV
Barlow, Sir Richard Wellesley, 4th Bt (cr 1803), 1836–1904, vol. I
Barlow, Sir Robert, 1891–1976, vol. VII
Barlow, Sir Thomas, 1st Bt (cr 1900), 1845–1945, vol. IV
Barlow, Sir Thomas D., 1883–1964, vol. VI
Barlow, Walter Sydney L.; see Lazarus-Barlow.
Barlow, William, 1834–1915, vol. I
Barlow, William, 1845–1934, vol. III
Barlow, William H., 1812–1902, vol. I
Barltrop, Ernest William, 1893–1957, vol. V
Barman, Christian August, 1898–1980, vol. VII
Barnaby, Sir Nathaniel, 1829–1915, vol. I
Barnard, 9th Baron, 1854–1918, vol. II
Barnard, 10th Baron, 1888–1964, vol. VI
Barnard, Andrew Bigoe, 1862–1928, vol. II

Barnard, Beverley Gayer, 1916–1973, vol. VII
Barnard, Sir Charles Loudon, 1823–1902, vol. I
Barnard, Rev. Charles William, *died* 1928, vol. II
Barnard, Brig.-Gen. Cyril Darcy Vivien C.; *see* Cary-Barnard.
Barnard, Sir Edmund Broughton, 1856–1930, vol. III
Barnard, Eric, 1891–1980, vol. VII
Barnard, Francis Pierrepont, 1854–1931, vol. III
Barnard, Hon. Sir Frank Stillman, 1856–1936, vol. III
Barnard, Vice-Adm. Sir Geoffrey, 1902–1974, vol. VII
Barnard, George Grey, 1863–1938, vol. III
Barnard, George Henry, 1868–1948, vol. IV
Barnard, Sir Herbert, 1831–1920, vol. II
Barnard, Brig.-Gen. J. H., 1846–1901, vol. I
Barnard, Joseph Edwin, *died* 1949, vol. IV
Barnard, Joseph Terence Owen, 1872–1936, vol. III
Barnard, Leonard William, 1870–1951, vol. V
Barnard, Rev. Percy Mordaunt, 1868–1941, vol. IV
Barnard, Hon. William Edward, 1886–1958, vol. V
Barnard, William George, 1892–1956, vol. V
Barnard, Maj.-Gen. William Osborne, 1838–1920, vol. II
Barnard, William Tyndall, *died* 1923, vol. II
Barnardiston, Col Nathaniel, 1832–1916, vol. II
Barnardiston, Maj.-Gen. Nathaniel Walter, 1858–1919, vol. II
Barnardiston, Lt-Col Samuel John Barrington, 1875–1924, vol. II
Barnardo, Fleming; *see* Barnardo, F. A. F.
Barnardo, (Frederick Adolphus) Fleming, 1874–1962, vol. VI
Barnardo, Thomas John, 1845–1905, vol. I
Barnato, Henry Isaac, *died* 1908, vol. I
Barnato, Woolf, 1895–1948, vol. IV
Barnby, 1st Baron, 1841–1929, vol. III
Barne, Rt Rev. George Dunsford, 1879–1954, vol. V
Barne, Major Miles, 1874–1917, vol. II
Barne, Brig. William Bradley Gosset, 1880–1951, vol. V
Barneby, William Theodore, 1873–1946, vol. IV
Barnell, Herbert Rex, 1907–1973, vol. VII
Barnes, Alexander, 1855–1924, vol. II
Barnes, Rt Hon. Alfred, 1887–1974, vol. VII
Barnes, Alfred Edward, 1881–1956, vol. V
Barnes, Alfred Schwartz, 1868–1949, vol. IV
Barnes, Anthony Charles, 1891–1974, vol. VII
Barnes, Gen. Ardley Henry Falwasser, 1837–1910, vol. I
Barnes, Rev. Canon Arthur Hubert, *died* 1952, vol. V
Barnes, Arthur Kentish, 1872–1954, vol. V
Barnes, Rt Rev. Mgr Arthur Stapylton, 1861–1936, vol. III
Barnes, Barry K., (Nelson Barry Mackintosh Barnes), 1906–1965, vol. VI
Barnes, Bernard, 1890–1950, vol. IV
Barnes, Bertie Frank, 1888–1965, vol. VI
Barnes, Captain Charles Roper Gorell, 1896–1918, vol. II
Barnes, Edwin Clay, 1864–1941, vol. IV

Barnes, Air Cdre Eric Delano, 1900–1957, vol. V
Barnes, Rt Rev. Ernest William, 1874–1953, vol. V
Barnes, Fancourt, *died* 1908, vol. I
Barnes, Frank, *died* 1960, vol. V
Barnes, Col Frank Purcell, 1880–1956, vol. V
Barnes, Sir Frederic Gorell, 1856–1939, vol. III
Barnes, Frederick Dallas, 1843–1899, vol. I
Barnes, Rt Hon. George Nicoll, 1859–1940, vol. III
Barnes, Sir George Reginald, 1904–1960, vol. V
Barnes, Sir George Stapylton, 1858–1946, vol. IV
Barnes, Harold Charles Edward, 1871–1940, vol. III
Barnes, Major Harry, 1870–1935, vol. III
Barnes, Harry Cheetham, 1898–1961, vol. VI (AII)
Barnes, Harry Elmer, 1889–1968, vol. VI
Barnes, Henry, 1842–1921, vol. II
Barnes, Howard Turner, 1873–1950, vol. IV (A)
Barnes, Sir Hugh Shakespear, 1853–1940, vol. III
Barnes, Major Humphry Aston, 1900–1940, vol. III
Barnes, Col James, 1866–1936, vol. III
Barnes, Sir James Horace, 1891–1969, vol. VI
Barnes, Sir (James) Sidney, 1881–1952, vol. V
Barnes, John Frederick Evelyn, 1851–1925, vol. II
Barnes, John Morrison, 1913–1975, vol. VII
Barnes, Sir Kenneth Ralph, 1878–1957, vol. V
Barnes, Nelson Barry Mackintosh; *see* Barnes, Barry K.
Barnes, Col Osmond, 1834–1930, vol. III
Barnes, Rev. Peter, 1856–1921, vol. II
Barnes, Maj.-Gen. Sir Reginald Walter Ralph, 1871–1946, vol. IV
Barnes, Richard Cumberland, 1912–1970, vol. VI (AII)
Barnes, Sir Sidney; *see* Barnes, Sir J. S.
Barnes, Stanley, 1875–1955, vol. V
Barnes, Sir Thomas James, 1888–1964, vol. VI
Barnes, Hon. Walter Henry, 1858–1933, vol. III
Barnes, Walter Mayhew, 1871–1950, vol. IV
Barnes, Air Vice-Marshal William Edward, 1897–1958, vol. V
Barnes, Rev. William Emery, 1859–1939, vol. III
Barnes-Lawrence, Rev. Arthur Evelyn, 1851–1931, vol. III
Barnes-Lawrence, Herbert Cecil, 1852–1921, vol. II
Barnett, Lt-Col Alfred George, 1883–1955, vol. V
Barnett, Alfred John, 1857–1943, vol. IV
Barnett, Rev. Arthur Thomas, 1858–1941, vol. IV
Barnett, Sir Ben Lewis, 1894–1979, vol. VII
Barnett, Cecil Guy, 1881–1959, vol. V
Barnett, Charles Edward, 1848–1937, vol. III
Barnett, Cyril Harry, 1919–1970, vol. VI
Barnett, Rev. Ernest Judd, 1859–1955, vol. V
Barnett, Sir Geoffrey Morris, 1902–1970, vol. VI
Barnett, George Alfred, *died* 1903, vol. I
Barnett, Col George Henry, 1880–1942, vol. IV
Barnett, Sir George Percy, 1894–1965, vol. VI
Barnett, Harry Villiers, 1858–1928, vol. II
Barnett, Dame Henrietta Octavia, 1851–1936, vol. III
Barnett, Lt-Col Henry N.; *see* Norman Barnett.
Barnett, Rev. Herbert, 1851–1937, vol. III
Barnett, John Francis, 1837–1916, vol. II
Barnett, Lionel David, 1871–1960, vol. V

Barnett, Sir Louis Edward, 1865–1946, vol. IV
Barnett, Rev. Maurice, 1917–1980, vol. VII
Barnett, Percy Arthur, 1858–1941, vol. IV
Barnett, Major Sir Richard Whieldon, 1863–1930, vol. III
Barnett, Rev. Samuel Augustus, 1844–1913, vol. I
Barnett, Rev. T. Ratcliffe, 1868–1946, vol. IV
Barnett-Barker, Lt-Col Randle; see Barker.
Barnett-Clarke, Very Rev. Charles William, died 1916, vol. II
Barnewall, Sir John Robert, 11th Bt, 1850–1936, vol. III
Barnewall, Sir Reginald Aylmer John de Barneval, 10th Bt, 1838–1909, vol. I
Barnewall, Sir Reginald J., 12th Bt, 1888–1961, vol. VI
Barnewall, Hon. Reginald Nicholas Francis, 1897–1918, vol. II
Barnham, Henry Dudley, 1854–1936, vol. III
Barnhill, Alexander Perley, 1863–1935, vol. III
Barnicoat, John Wallis, 1814–1905, vol. I
Barnie, Marian, (Mrs Donald Barnie); see Veitch, Marian.
Barnish, Captain Geoffrey Howard, 1887–1941, vol. IV
Barns, Rev. John Wintour Baldwin, 1912–1974, vol. VII
Barns, Thomas Alexander, 1881–1930, vol. III
Barnsley, Brig.-Gen. Sir John, 1858–1926, vol. II
Barnsley, Maj.-Gen. Robert Eric, 1886–1968, vol. VI
Barnston, Sir Harry, 1st Bt, 1870–1929, vol. III
Baroda, HH Maharaja Gaekwar Sir Sayaji Rao III, 1863–1939, vol. III
Baroda, Maharaja of, 1908–1968, vol. VI
Baroja Nessi, Pio, (Don Pio Baroja), 1872–1956, vol. V
Baron, Sir Barclay Josiah, died 1919, vol. II
Baron, Bernhard, 1850–1929, vol. III
Baron, Sir Bernhard; see Baron, Sir L. B.
Baron, Cyril Faudel Joseph, 1903–1978, vol. VII
Baron, Sir Edward S., 1892–1962, vol. VI
Baron, Sir (Louis) Bernhard, 1st Bt, 1876–1934, vol. III
Baron-Suckling, Rev. Charles William, 1862–1944, vol. IV
Barotseland, Litunga of, 1888–1968, vol. VI
Barr, Alexander Wallace, 1886–1949, vol. IV
Barr, Amelia Edith, 1831–1919, vol. II
Barr, Archibald, 1855–1931, vol. III
Barr, Lt-Col Sir David William Keith, 1846–1916, vol. II
Barr, Sir George William, 1881–1956, vol. V
Barr, Comdr James, 1855–1937, vol. III
Barr, Sir James, 1849–1938, vol. III
Barr, Rev. James, 1862–1949, vol. IV
Barr, Sir James, 1884–1952, vol. V
Barr, James Angus Evan Abbot, 1862–1923, vol. II
Barr, James Gordon, 1908–1963, vol. VI
Barr, John, 1859–1940, vol. III
Barr, Mark, 1871–1950, vol. IV
Barr, Robert, died 1912, vol. I
Barr, Thomas, 1846–1916, vol. II
Barr, Venie, died 1947, vol. IV

Barr Smith, Sir Tom Elder, 1904–1968, vol. VI
Barraclough, Frank, 1901–1974, vol. VII
Barraclough, Sir Henry; see Barraclough, Sir S. H. E.
Barraclough, Sir (Samuel) Henry (Egerton), 1874–1958, vol. V
Barran, Sir John, 1st Bt, 1821–1905, vol. I
Barran, Sir John Leighton, 3rd Bt, 1904–1974, vol. VII
Barran, Sir John Nicholson, 2nd Bt, 1872–1952, vol. V
Barran, Sir Rowland Hirst, 1858–1949, v9l. IV
Barrand, Arthur Rhys, 1861–1941, vol. IV
Barratt, Sir Albert, 1860–1941, vol. IV
Barratt, Air Chief Marshal Sir Arthur Sheridan, 1891–1966, vol. VI
Barratt, Sir Charles, 1910–1971, vol. VII
Barratt, Captain Sir Francis Henry Godolphin L., 2nd Bt; see Layland-Barratt.
Barratt, Sir Francis Layland-, 1st Bt, 1860–1933, vol. III
Barratt, Col Herbert James, 1858–1952, vol. V
Barratt, John Arthur, 1857–1944, vol. IV
Barratt, John Oglethorpe Wakelin, 1862–1956, vol. V
Barratt, Reginald, 1861–1917, vol. II
Barratt, Major Stanley George Reeves E.; see Elton-Barratt.
Barratt, Sir Sydney, 1898–1975, vol. VII
Barratt, Rev. Thomas H., 1870–1951, vol. V
Barratt, Maj.-Gen. William Cross, 1862–1940, vol. III
Barratt, William Donald, 1883–1955, vol. V
Barraud, Francis, died 1924, vol. II
Barrell, Francis Richard, 1860–1915, vol. I (A)
Barres, Maurice, 1862–1923, vol. II
Barret, Rt Rev. John Patrick, 1878–1946, vol. IV
Barrett, Major Alexander Gould, 1866–1954, vol. V
Barrett, Field Marshal Sir Arthur Arnold, 1857–1926, vol. II
Barrett, Ashley William, died 1939, vol. III
Barrett, Lt-Col Cyril Charles Johnson, 1884–1933, vol. III
Barrett, Col Dacre Lennard, 1858–1941, vol. IV
Barrett, Rev. Daniel William, died 1925, vol. II
Barrett, Edith Helen, died 1939, vol. III
Barrett, Brig.-Gen. Edward Alfred M.; see Moulton-Barrett.
Barrett, Edward Ivo Medhurst, 1879–1950, vol. IV
Barrett, Florence Elizabeth, (Lady Barrett), died 1945, vol. IV
Barrett, Francis E. H. Joyce, died 1925, vol. II
Barrett, Frank, 1848–1926, vol. II
Barrett, Frank Ashley, died 1954, vol. V
Barrett, Rev. George Slatyer, 1839–1916, vol. II
Barrett, Col Henry Walter, 1857–1949, vol. IV
Barrett, Herbert Roper, 1873–1943, vol. IV
Barrett, Rev. Hugh S.; see Scott-Barrett.
Barrett, Lt-Col Sir James William, 1862–1945, vol. IV
Barrett, Col John Cridlan, 1897–1977, vol. VII
Barrett, Group Captain John Francis Tufnell, 1898–1941, vol. IV
Barrett, Norman Rupert, 1903–1979, vol. VII

Barrett, Robert John, 1861–1942, vol. IV
Barrett, Thomas J., 1841–1914, vol. I
Barrett, William, 1863–1931, vol. III
Barrett, Very Rev. William Edward Colvile, 1880–1956, vol. V
Barrett, Sir William Fletcher, 1844–1925, vol. II
Barrett, Sir William Scott, 1843–1921, vol. II
Barrett, Wilson, 1846–1904, vol. I
Barrett-Lennard, Sir Fiennes, *died* 1963, vol. VI
Barrett-Lennard, Lt-Col John, 1863–1935, vol. III
Barrett-Lennard, Sir Richard Fiennes; *see* Lennard.
Barrett-Lennard, Sir Thomas, 2nd Bt; *see* Lennard.
Barrett-Lennard, Sir Thomas, 3rd Bt; *see* Lennard.
Barrett-Lennard, Sir Thomas Richard F.; *see* Lennard.
Barrie, Alexander Baillie, 1906–1957, vol. V
Barrie, Sir Charles, 1840–1921, vol. II
Barrie, Rt Hon. Hugh T., 1860–1922, vol. II
Barrie, James, 1862–1932, vol. III
Barrie, Sir James Matthew, 1st Bt, 1860–1937, vol. III
Barringer, Paul Brandon, 1857–1941, vol. IV
Barrington, 8th Viscount, 1825–1901, vol. I
Barrington, 9th Viscount, 1848–1933, vol. III
Barrington, 10th Viscount, 1873–1960, vol. V
Barrington, Hon. Bernard; *see* Barrington, Hon. W. B. L.
Barrington, Hon. Sir (Bernard) Eric (Edward), 1847–1918, vol. II
Barrington, Sir Charles Bacon, 6th Bt, 1902–1980, vol. VII (AII)
Barrington, Sir Charles Burton, 5th Bt, 1848–1943, vol. IV
Barrington, Charles George, 1827–1911, vol. I
Barrington, Claud, 1893–1960, vol. V
Barrington, E.; *see* Beck, L. A.
Barrington, Emilie Isabel, *died* 1933, vol. III
Barrington, Hon. Sir Eric; *see* Barrington, Hon. Sir B. E. E.
Barrington, John Harcourt, 1907–1973, vol. VII
Barrington, Hon. Rupert Edward Selborne, 1877–1975, vol. VII
Barrington, Sir Vincent Hunter Barrington K.; *see* Kennett-Barrington.
Barrington, Hon. (Walter) Bernard (Louis), 1876–1959, vol. V
Barrington, Hon. Sir William Augustus Curzon, 1842–1922, vol. II
Barrington-Fleet, George Rutland, 1853–1922, vol. II
Barrington-Kennett, Lt-Col Brackley Herbert Barrington, 1846–1919, vol. II
Barrington-Ward, Frederick Temple, 1880–1938, vol. III
Barrington-Ward, John Grosvenor, 1894–1946, vol. IV
Barrington-Ward, Sir Lancelot Edward, 1884–1953, vol. V
Barrington-Ward, Rev. Mark James, *died* 1924, vol. II
Barrington-Ward, Sir Michael; *see* Barrington-Ward, Sir V. M.
Barrington-Ward, Robert M'Gowan, 1891–1948, vol. IV

Barrington-Ward, Sir (Victor) Michael, 1887–1972, vol. VII
Barrios, Benjamin, 1878–1929, vol. III
Barron, Claud Alexander, 1871–1948, vol. IV
Barron, Donovan Allaway, 1907–1980, vol. VII
Barron, Elwyn Alfred, *died* 1929, vol. III
Barron, Evan Macleod, 1879–1965, vol. VI
Barron, Maj.-Gen. Frederick Wilmot, 1880–1963, vol. VI
Barron, Gladys Caroline, *died* 1967, vol. VI
Barron, Maj.-Gen. Sir Harry, 1847–1921, vol. II
Barron, Sir Henry Page-Turner, 2nd Bt, 1824–1900, vol. I
Barron, James, 1847–1919, vol. II
Barron, Brig.-Gen. Netterville Guy, 1867–1945, vol. IV
Barron, Oswald, 1868–1939, vol. III
Barron, Wilfrid Philip S.; *see* Shepherd-Barron.
Barron, Col Willie Netterville, 1872–1930, vol. III
Barrow, Albert Boyce, *died* 1939, vol. III
Barrow, Sir Alfred, 1850–1928, vol. II
Barrow, Adm. Arthur, 1853–1914, vol. I
Barrow, Col Arthur Frederick, 1850–1903, vol. I
Barrow, Rear-Adm. Benjamin Wingate, 1878–1966, vol. VI
Barrow, Gen. Sir Edmund George, 1852–1934, vol. III
Barrow, Sir Francis Laurence John, 4th Bt, 1862–1950, vol. IV
Barrow, Gen. Sir George de Symons, 1864–1959, vol. V
Barrow, Maj.-Gen. Harold Percy Waller, 1876–1957, vol. V
Barrow, John, 1808–1898, vol. I
Barrow, Sir John Croker, 3rd Bt, 1833–1900, vol. I
Barrow, Hon. Sir Malcolm Palliser, 1900–1973, vol. VII
Barrow, Oscar Theodore, 1854–1937, vol. III
Barrow, Sir Reuben Vincent, 1838–1918, vol. II
Barrow, Sir Samuel, 1859–1935, vol. III
Barrow, Walter, 1867–1954, vol. V
Barrow, Sir Wilfrid John Wilson Croker, 5th Bt, 1897–1960, vol. V
Barrowclough, Rt Hon. Sir Harold Eric, 1894–1972, vol. VII
Barrows, William Leonard, 1905–1976, vol. VII
Barrs, Alfred George, 1853–1934, vol. III
Barry, Rt Rev. Alfred, 1826–1910, vol. I
Barry, Brig. Arthur Gordon, 1885–1942, vol. IV
Barry, Lt-Col Arthur John, 1859–1944, vol. IV
Barry, Lt-Col Cecil Charles Stewart, 1867–1933, vol. III
Barry, Charles, 1887–1963, vol. VI
Barry, Charles David, *died* 1928, vol. II
Barry, Rt Hon. Charles Robert, 1825–1897, vol. I
Barry, Adm. Sir Claud Barrington, 1891–1951, vol. V
Barry, Sir (Claude) Francis, 3rd Bt, 1883–1970, vol. VI
Barry, David Thomas, 1870–1955, vol. V
Barry, E. L. M.; *see* Milner-Barry.
Barry, Edward, 1852–1927, vol. II (A), vol. III
Barry, Lt-Col Edward, 1896–1952, vol. V

Barry, Sir Edward Arthur, 2nd Bt, 1858–1949, vol. IV

Barry, Sir Francis; see Barry, Sir C. F.

Barry, Sir Francis Tress, 1st Bt, 1825–1907, vol. I

Barry, Rt Rev. (Frank) Russell, 1890–1976, vol. VII

Barry, Sir Gerald Reid, 1898–1968, vol. VI

Barry, Geraldine Mary, 1897–1978, vol. VII

Barry, Rear-Adm. Sir Henry Deacon, 1849–1908, vol. I

Barry, Rt Rev. Hugh Van Lynden O.; see Otter-Barry.

Barry, Iris, 1895–1969, vol. VI

Barry, Hon. Lt-Col James, died 1920, vol. II

Barry, Major James D., died 1941, vol. IV

Barry, Hon. Jeremiah Hayes, 1858–1946, vol. IV

Barry, Rt Rev. John, 1875–1938, vol. III

Barry, John Arthur, 1850–1911, vol. I

Barry, Sir John Edmond, 1828–1919, vol. II

Barry, Hon. Sir John Vincent William, 1903–1969, vol. VI

Barry, Sir John Wolfe Wolfe-, 1836–1918, vol. II

Barry, Sir Patrick Redmond, 1898–1972, vol. VII

Barry, Ralph Brereton, 1856–1920, vol. II

Barry, Redmond, 1866–1913, vol. I

Barry, Richard Fitzwilliam, 1861–1916, vol. II (A), vol. III

Barry, Sir Rupert Rodney Francis Tress, 4th Bt, 1910-1977, vol. VII

Barry, Rt Rev. Russell; see Barry, Rt Rev. F. R.

Barry, Col Stanley Leonard, 1873–1943, vol. IV

Barry, Col Thomas David Collis, died 1943, vol. IV

Barry, Rt Rev. Thomas Francis, 1841–1920, vol. II

Barry, Most Rev. William, 1872–1929, vol. III

Barry, Rt Rev. Mgr William Francis, 1849–1930, vol. III

Barry, William James, 1864–1952, vol. V

Barry, William Whitmore O.; see Otter-Barry.

Barry-Doyle, Rt Rev. Mgr Richard; see Doyle.

Barrymore, 1st Baron, 1843–1925, vol. II

Barrymore, Ethel, 1879–1959, vol. V

Barrymore, John, 1882–1942, vol. IV

Barrymore, Lionel, 1878–1954, vol. V

Barson, Derek Emmanuel, 1922–1980, vol. VII

Barstow, Maj.-Gen. Arthur Edward, 1888–1942, vol. IV

Barstow, Sir George Lewis, 1874–1966, vol. VI

Barstow, Maj.-Gen. Henry, 1876–1952, vol. V

Barstow, Major John Nelson, 1890–1936, vol. III

Barstow, Mrs Montague; see Baroness Orczy.

Barstow, Percy Gott, 1883–1969, vol. VI

Barter, Lt-Gen. Sir Charles St Leger, 1857–1931, vol. III

Barter, Captain Frederick, died 1953, vol. V

Barter, Geoffrey Herbert, 1901–1952, vol. V

Barter, Rev. Herbert Francis Treseder, 1869–1949, vol. IV

Barter, Sir Percy, 1886–1975, vol. VII

Barter, Sir Richard, 1837–1916, vol. II

Barth, Lt-Col Sir Jacob William, 1871–1941, vol. IV

Barth, Karl, 1886–1968, vol. VI

Bartholome, Albert, 1848–1928, vol. II

Bartholomew, Maj.-Gen. Arthur Wollaston, 1878–1945, vol. IV

Bartholomew, Sir Clarence Edward, 1879–1946, vol. IV

Bartholomew, Col Hugh John, 1871–1938, vol. III

Bartholomew, James Rankin, 1887–1951, vol. V (A)

Bartholomew, John, 1870–1937, vol. III

Bartholomew, John, 1890–1962, vol. VI

Bartholomew, John George, 1860–1920, vol. II

Bartholomew, Gen. Sir William Henry, 1877–1962, vol. VI

Barthorpe, Major Sir Frederick James, died 1942, vol. IV

Bartle, Anita, died 1962, vol. VI

Bartleet, Rev. Edwin Berry, 1872–1946, vol. IV

Bartleet, Rev. Samuel Edwin, 1835–1924, vol. II

Bartleman, Maj.-Gen. Woodburn Francis, 1840–1924, vol. II

Bartlet, James Vernon, 1863–1940, vol. III

Bartlet, Rev. T. J., 1833–1915, vol. I

Bartlett, Lt-Col Alfred James Napier, 1884–1956, vol. V

Bartlett, Ven. Arthur Robert, 1851–1923, vol. II

Bartlett, Cdre Charles Alfred, 1868–1945, vol. IV

Bartlett, Sir Charles John, 1889–1955, vol. V

Bartlett, Rev. Charles Oldfeld, 1858–1937, vol. III

Bartlett, Rt Rev. David Daniel, 1900–1977, vol. VII

Bartlett, Rev. Canon Donald Mackenzie Maynard, 1873–1969, vol. VI

Bartlett, Ellis A.; see Ashmead-Bartlett.

Bartlett, Sir Ellis Ashmead-, 1849–1902, vol. I

Bartlett, Sir Frederic Charles, 1886–1969, vol. VI

Bartlett, George Bertram, 1880–1944, vol. IV

Bartlett, Sir Herbert Henry, 1st Bt, 1842–1921, vol. II

Bartlett, Sir Herbert Henry, 1st Bt, 1842–1921, vol. II

Bartlett, Humphrey Edward Gibson, 1880–1951, vol. V

Bartlett, Joseph Leslie, 1889–1968, vol. VI

Bartlett, Paul Wayland, 1865–1925, vol. II

Bartlett, W. H., 1858–1932, vol. III

Bartlett-Burdett-Coutts, Rt Hon. William Lehman Ashmead; see Burdett-Coutts.

Bartley, Lt-Col Bryan Cole, died 1968, vol. VI

Bartley, Sir Charles, 1882–1968, vol. VI

Bartley, Sir George Christopher Trout, 1842–1910, vol. I

Bartley, Sir John, 1886–1954, vol. V

Bartley, Patrick, 1909–1956, vol. V

Bartley, William, 1885–1961, vol. VI

Bartley-Denniss, Lt-Col Cyril Edmund Bartley, 1882–1955, vol. V

Bartley-Denniss, Sir Edmund Robert Bartley, 1854–1931, vol. III

Bartók, Béla, 1881–1945, vol. IV

Bartolo, Hon. Sir Augustus, 1883–1937, vol. III

Bartolomé, Adm. Sir Charles Martin de, 1871–1941, vol. IV

Barton, Most Rev. Arthur William, 1881–1962, vol. VI

Barton, Arthur Willoughby, 1899–1976, vol. VII

Barton, Lt-Col Baptist Johnston, 1876–1944, vol. IV

Barton, Major Basil Kelsey, 1879–1958, vol. V
Barton, Cecil James Juxon Talbot, 1891–1980, vol. VII
Barton, Cecil Molyneux, 1883–1962, vol. VI
Barton, Major Charles Gerard, 1860–1919, vol. II
Barton, Lt-Col Charles Walter, 1876–1950, vol. IV
Barton, Clarence, 1892–1957, vol. V
Barton, Rt Hon. Sir (Dunbar) Plunket, 1st Bt, 1853–1937, vol. III
Barton, Rt Hon. Sir Edmund, 1849–1920, vol. I (A), vol II (A),
Barton, Edwin Alfred, 1863–1953, vol. V
Barton, Edwin Henry, 1858–1925, vol. II
Barton, Adm. Ernest Gillbe, 1861–1938, vol. III
Barton, Captain Francis Rickman, 1865–1947, vol. IV
Barton, Frederick Sherbrooke, 1895–1969, vol. VI
Barton, Maj.-Gen. Sir Geoffry, 1844–1922, vol. II
Barton, Rev. George Aaron, 1859–1942, vol. IV
Barton, George Alexander Heaton, 1865–1924, vol. II
Barton, George Samuel Horace, 1883–1962, vol. VI
Barton, Guy Trayton, 1908–1977, vol. VII
Barton, Sir Harold Montague, 1882–1962, vol. VI
Barton, Ven. Harry Douglas, 1898–1968, vol. VI
Barton, Lt-Col Sir Henry Baldwin, 1869–1952, vol. V
Barton, Sir John George, 1850–1937, vol. III
Barton, Rt Rev. Mgr John Mackintosh Tilney, 1898–1977, vol. VII
Barton, John Saxon, 1875–1961, vol. VI
Barton, Joseph Edwin, 1875–1959, vol. V
Barton, Lt-Col Leslie Eric, 1889–1952, vol. V
Barton, Col Maurice Charles, 1852–1939, vol. III
Barton, Rt Hon. Sir Plunket; see Barton, Rt Hon. Sir D. P.
Barton, Richard, 1850–1927, vol. II
Barton, Lt-Col Richard Lionel, 1875–1942, vol. IV
Barton, Robert Childers, 1881–1975, vol. VII
Barton, Rose, died 1929, vol. III
Barton, Samuel Saxon, died 1957, vol. V
Barton, Sir Sidney, 1876–1946, vol. IV
Barton, Rev. Walter John, died 1955, vol. V
Barton, Wilfred Alexander, 1880–1953, vol. V
Barton, Sir William, 1862–1957, vol. V
Barton, William Henry, 1869–1928, vol. II
Barton, Lt-Col William Hugh, 1874–1945, vol. IV
Barton, Sir William Pell, 1871–1956, vol. V
Bartram, Rev. Henry, 1849–1934, vol. III
Bartram, Sir Robert Appleby, 1835–1925, vol. II
Barttelot, Adm. Sir Brian Herbert Fairbairn, 1867–1942, vol. IV
Barttelot, Major Sir Walter Balfour, 3rd Bt, 1880–1918, vol. II
Barttelot, Lt-Col Sir Walter de Stopham, 4th Bt, 1904–1944, vol. IV
Barttelot, Sir Walter George, 2nd Bt, 1855–1900, vol. I
Barty, James Webster, 1841–1915, vol. I
Baruch, Bernard Mannes, 1870–1965, vol. VI
Barwell, Rev. Arthur Henry Sanxay, 1834–1913, vol. I
Barwell, Claud Foster, 1912–1971, vol. VII
Barwell, Harold Shuttleworth, 1875–1959, vol. V

Barwell, Hon. Sir Henry Newman, 1877–1959, vol. V
Barwick, George Frederick, 1853–1931, vol. III
Barwick, Sir John Storey, 1st Bt, 1840–1915, vol. I
Barwick, Sir John Storey, 2nd Bt, 1876–1953, vol. V
Barwick, Sir Richard Llewellyn, 3rd Bt, 1916–1979, vol. VII
Barzellotti, Giacomo, 1844–1917, vol. II
Basden, Rev. George Thomas, 1873–1944, vol. IV
Basedow, Herbert, 1881–1933, vol. III
Bashford, Ernest Francis, 1873–1923, vol. II
Bashford, Sir Henry Howarth, 1880–1961, vol. VI
Bashford, James W., 1849–1919, vol. II
Bashford, John Laidlay, died 1908, vol. I
Bashford, Major Lindsay, 1881–1921, vol. II
Bashyam Aiyangar, Sir Venbakam, died 1908, vol. I
Basing, 2nd Baron, 1860–1919, vol. II
Basing, 3rd Baron, 1890–1969, vol. VI
Baskcomb-Harrison, Captain Henry Neville; see Harrison.
Baskerville, Beatrice; see Guichard, B. C.
Baskerville, Rev. C. G., 1830–1921, vol. II
Baskerville, Lt-Col Charles Herbert Lethbridge, 1860–1946, vol. IV
Baskerville, Geoffrey, 1870–1944, vol. IV
Baskerville, Rev. Canon George Knyfton, 1867–1941, vol. IV
Baskerville, Ralph Hopton, 1883–1918, vol. II
Baskett, Charles H., 1872–1953, vol. V
Baskett, Sir Ronald Gilbert, 1901–1972, vol. VII
Bason, Fred, (Frederick Thomas Bason), 1907–1973, vol. VII
Bass, Hamar Alfred, 1842–1898, vol. I
Bass, John Stuart, 1905–1954, vol. V
Bass, Col Philip de Salis, 1862–1936, vol. III
Bass, Sir William Arthur Hamar, 2nd Bt, 1879–1952, vol. V
Bassano, 3rd Duc de, 1844–1906, vol. I
Basser, Sir Adolph, 1887–1964, vol. VI
Basset, Alfred Barnard, 1854–1930, vol. III
Basset, Arthur Francis, 1873–1950, vol. IV
Basset, Maj.-Gen. Richard Augustin Marriott, 1891–1954, vol. V
Basset, Ronald Lambart, 1898–1972, vol. VII
Bassett, Arthur Tilney, 1869–1964, vol. VI
Bassett, George Arthur, 1884–1971, vol. VII
Bassett, Henry, 1881–1965, vol. VI
Bassett, Herbert Harry, 1874–1939, vol. III (A), vol. IV
Bassett, John Harold, died 1974, vol. VII
Bassett, John Spencer, 1867–1928, vol. II
Bassett, Ralph Henry, 1896–1962, vol. VI
Bassett, Sir Walter Eric, 1892–1978, vol. VII
Bassett-Smith, Surg.-Rear-Adm. Sir Percy W., 1861–1927, vol. II
Bastable, Charles F., 1855–1945, vol. IV
Bastard, Bt Col Reginald, 1880–1960, vol. V
Bastard, Rev. William Pollexfen, 1832–1915, vol. I
Bastian, Henry Charlton, 1837–1915, vol. I (A)
Bastin, Maj.-Gen. George Edward Restalic, 1902–1960, vol. V
Bastyan, Lt-Gen. Sir Edric Montague, 1903–1980, vol. VII

40

Bastyan, Maj.-Gen. Kenneth Cecil Orville, 1906–1975, vol. VII
Basu, Bhupendra Nath, 1859–1924, vol. II
Basu, Hon. Bijay Kumar, 1885–1937, vol. III
Batchelor, Rev. Alfred Williams, 1864–1961, vol. VI
Batchelor, Denzil Stanley, 1906–1969, vol. VI
Batchelor, Hon. Egerton Lee, 1865–1911, vol. I
Batchelor, Ferdinand Campion, died 1916, vol. II
Batchelor, Francis Malcolm, 1865–1937, vol. III
Batchelor, Col Gordon Guthrie Malcolm, 1908–1976, vol. VII
Batchelor, Sir Stanley Lockhart, 1868–1938, vol. III
Batchelor, Lt-Col Vivian Allan, 1882–1960, vol. V
Bate, Col Albert Louis Frederick, 1862–1924, vol. II
Bate, Maj.-Gen. (Alfred) Christopher, 1927–1980, vol. VII
Bate, Maj.-Gen. Christopher; see Bate, Maj.-Gen. A. C.
Bate, Captain Claude Lindsay, died 1957, vol. V
Bate, Edward Raoul, 1859–1948, vol. IV
Bate, Francis, died 1950, vol. IV
Bate, Sir Henry Newel, 1828–1917, vol. II
Bate, Very Rev. Herbert Newell, 1871–1941, vol. IV
Bate, John Pawley, 1857–1921, vol. II
Bate, Percy, 1868–1913, vol. I
Bate, Col Thomas Elwood Lindsay, 1852–1937, vol. III
Bate, Brig.-Gen. Thomas Reginald Fraser, 1881–1964, vol. VI
Bateman, 2nd Baron, 1826–1901, vol. I
Bateman, 3rd Baron, 1856–1931, vol. III
Bateman, Sir Alfred Edmund, 1844–1929, vol. III
Bateman, Alys, died 1924, vol. II
Bateman, Rev. Arthur Fitzroy D.; see Dobbie-Bateman.
Bateman, Arthur Leonard, 1879–1957, vol. V
Bateman, Brig.-Gen. Bernard Montague, 1865–1937, vol. III
Bateman, Maj.-Gen. Donald Roland Edwin Rowan, 1901–1969, vol. VI
Bateman, Edward Louis, 1834–1909, vol. I
Bateman, Francis John Harvey, died 1920, vol. II
Bateman, Sir Frederic, 1824–1904, vol. I
Bateman, George Cecil, 1882–1963, vol. VI
Bateman, Lt-Col Harold Henry, 1888–1974, vol. VII
Bateman, Harry, 1882–1946, vol. IV
Bateman, Henry Mayo, 1887–1970, vol. VI
Bateman, James, died 1959, vol. V
Bateman, John, 1839–1910, vol. I
Bateman, Rev. William Fairbairn La Trobe-, 1845–1926, vol. II
Bateman, Rev. William Henry Fraser, 1855–1923, vol. II
Bateman-Champain, Brig.-Gen. Hugh Frederick, 1869–1933, vol. III
Bateman-Champain, Rt Rev. John Norman, 1880–1950, vol. IV
Bateman-Hanbury, Rev. Hon. Arthur Allen, 1829–1919, vol. II

Bateman-Hanbury, Captain Hon. Charles Stanhope Melville, 1877–1931, vol. III
Bateman-Hanbury, Major Edward Reginald, 1859–1907, vol. I
Bater, Rev. Alfred Brenchly, died 1933, vol. III
Bates, Sir Alfred, 1897–1979, vol. VII
Bates, Arlo, 1850–1918, vol. II
Bates, Arthur Henry, died 1947, vol. IV
Bates, Lt-Col Austin Graves, 1891–1961, vol. VI
Bates, Major Cecil Robert, 1882–1935, vol. III
Bates, Brig.-Gen. Sir (Charles) Loftus, 1863–1951, vol. V
Bates, Rt Hon. Sir Dawson; see Bates, Rt Hon. Sir R. D.
Bates, Sir Edward Bertram, 3rd Bt (cr 1880), 1877–1903, vol. I
Bates, Sir Edward Percy, 2nd Bt (cr 1880), 1845–1899, vol. I
Bates, Air Vice-Marshal Eric Cecil, 1906–1975, vol. VII
Bates, Brig.-Gen. Francis Stewart Montague, 1876–1954, vol. V
Bates, Frederic Alan, 1884–1957, vol. V
Bates, Harry, 1851–1899, vol. I
Bates, Henry Montague, 1849–1928, vol. II
Bates, Henry Thomas Roy, 1902–1958, vol. V
Bates, Herbert Ernest, 1905–1974, vol. VII
Bates, Leslie Fleetwood, 1897–1978, vol. VII
Bates, Air Vice-Marshal Sir Leslie John Vernon, 1896–1966, vol. VI
Bates, Brig.-Gen. Sir Loftus; see Bates, Brig.-Gen. Sir C. L.
Bates, Ven. Mansel Harry, 1912–1980, vol. VII
Bates, Oric, 1883–1918, vol. II
Bates, Sir Percy Elly, 4th Bt (cr 1880), 1879–1946, vol. IV
Bates, Rt Hon. Sir (Richard) Dawson, 1st Bt (cr 1937), 1876–1949, vol. IV
Bates, Rev. Canon T., 1842–1911, vol. I
Bates, Thorpe, 1883–1958, vol. V
Bateson, Sir Alexander Dingwall, 1866–1935, vol. III
Bateson, Lt-Col David Mayhew, 1906–1975, vol. VII
Bateson, Sir Dingwall Latham, 1898–1967, vol. VI
Bateson, Frederick Wilse, 1901–1978, vol. VII
Bateson, Col John Holgate, 1880–1956, vol. V
Bateson, Rev. Joseph Harger, 1865–1935, vol. III
Bateson, Mary, 1865–1906, vol. I
Bateson, Rear-Adm. Stuart Latham, 1898–1980, vol. VII
Bateson, William, 1861–1926, vol. II
Batey, Joseph, 1867–1949, vol. IV
Batey, Rowland William John S.; see Scott-Batey.
Bath, 5th Marquess of, 1862–1946, vol. IV
Bath, Engr-Rear-Adm. George Clark, 1862–1925, vol. II
Bath, Hon. Thomas Henry, 1875–1956, vol. V
Bather, Francis Arthur, 1863–1934, vol. III
Bather, Ven. Henry Francis, 1832–1905, vol. I
Bather, Rear-Adm. Rowland Henry, 1873–1961, vol. VI
Batho, Sir Charles Albert, 1st Bt, 1872–1938, vol. III

Batho, Cyril, 1885–1951, vol. V
Bathurst, 7th Earl, 1864–1943, vol. IV
Bathurst, Lt-Col Hon. (Allen) Benjamin, 1872–1947, vol. IV
Bathurst, Lt-Col Hon. Benjamin; see Bathurst, Lt-Col Hon. A. B.
Bathurst, Charles, 1836–1907, vol. I
Bathurst, Ven. Frederick, died 1910, vol. I
Bathurst, Major Sir Frederick Edward William Hervey-, 5th Bt, 1870–1956, vol. V
Bathurst, Sir Frederick Thomas Arthur Hervey, 4th Bt, 1833–1900, vol. I
Bathurst, Hon. William Ralph Seymour, 1903–1970, vol. VI
Batiffol, Pierre Henry, 1861–1929, vol. III
Batley, Mabel Terry; see Lewis, M. T.
Batson, Col Herbert, 1853–1941, vol. IV
Batson, Reginald George, 1885–1974, vol. VII
Batt, Rear-Adm. Charles Ernest, 1874–1958, vol. V
Batt, Francis Raleigh, 1890–1961, vol. VI
Batt, Lt-Col Reginald Cossley, 1872–1952, vol. V
Batt, Lt-Col William Elliott, 1882–1971, vol. VII
Batt, William Loren, 1885–1965, vol. VI
Battcock, Col Grenville Arthur, 1882–1964, vol. VI
Batten, Adm. Alexander William Chisholm, 1851–1925, vol. II
Batten, Frederick Eustace, 1865–1918, vol. II
Batten, (Harry) Mortimer, 1888–1958, vol. V
Batten, Col Herbert Cary George, 1849–1926, vol. II
Batten, Col Herbert Copeland Cary, 1884–1963, vol. VI
Batten, Herbert Ernest, 1877–1950, vol. IV
Batten, Sir John Kaye, 1865–1938, vol. III
Batten, Col John Mount, 1843–1916, vol. II
Batten, John Winterbotham, 1831–1901, vol. I
Batten, Lauriston Leonard, 1863–1934, vol. III
Batten, Mortimer; see Batten, H. M.
Batten, Maj.-Gen. Richard Hutchison, 1908–1972, vol. VII
Batterbee, Sir Harry Fagg, 1880–1976, vol. VII
Battersby, Edmund James, 1911–1978, vol. VII
Battersby, Rev. Preb. Gerald William, 1911–1961, vol. VI
Battersby, Henry Francis Prevost, died 1949, vol. IV
Battersby, Maj.-Gen. John Prevost, 1826–1917, vol. II
Battersby, Maj.-Gen. Thomas Preston, died 1941, vol. IV
Battersby, Thomas Stephenson Francis, 1855–1933, vol. III
Battersea, 1st Baron, 1843–1907, vol. I
Battersea, Lady; (Constance), 1843–1931, vol. III
Battershill, Sir William Denis, 1896–1959, vol. V
Battey, Mrs E. J.; see White, E. E. McI.
Batthyany-Strattmann, HSH Edmund, 1826–1914, vol. I
Battine, Lt-Col Reginald St Clair, 1869–1942, vol. IV
Battiscombe, Rear-Adm. Albert H. W., 1831–1918, vol. II
Battistini, Mattia, 1858–1928, vol. II

Battle, George Frederick Newsum, 1897–1966, vol. VI
Battle, William Henry, died 1936, vol. III
Battley, John Rose, 1880–1952, vol. V
Batty, Archibald Douglas George Staunton, 1877–1961, vol. VI
Batty, Rt Rev. Basil Staunton, died 1952, vol. V
Batty, Rt Rev. Francis de Witt, 1879–1961, vol. VI
Batty, Herbert, 1849–1923, vol. II
Batty, James Henly, 1868–1946, vol. IV
Batty, Tom, 1906–1980, vol. VII
Batty-Smith, Henry, died 1927, vol. II
Battye, Maj.-Gen. Arthur, 1839–1909, vol. I
Battye, Aubyn Bernard Rochfort T.; see Trevor-Battye.
Battye, Col Basil Condon, 1882–1932, vol. III
Battye, Lt-Col Clinton Wynyard, 1874–1917, vol. II
Battye, Maj.-Gen. Henry Doveton, 1833–1915, vol. I
Battye, Brig. Ivan Urmston, 1875–1953, vol. V
Battye, James Sykes, 1871–1954, vol. V
Battye, Lt-Col Montague M'Pherson, 1836–1929, vol. III
Battye, Major Richmond Keith Molesworth, 1905–1958, vol. V
Battye, Lt-Col Walter Rothney, 1874–1943, vol. IV
Baty, Charles Witcomb, 1900–1979, vol. VII
Baty, Thomas, 1869–1954, vol. V
Bauchop, Lt-Col Arthur, 1871–1915, vol. I
Baud, Rt Rev. Joseph A., 1890–1980, vol. VII (AII)
Baudains, Captain George La Croix, 1892–1942, vol. IV
Baudains, Captain Philip, 1836–1909, vol. I
Baudouin, Charles, 1893–1963, vol. VI
Baudrillart, Cardinal Henri Marie Alfred, 1859–1942, vol. IV
Bauer, Louis Hopewell, 1888–1964, vol. VI (AII)
Baugh, Charles Herbert, 1881–1953, vol. V
Baugh, Captain George Johnstone, 1862–1924, vol. II
Baughan, Edward Algernon, 1865–1938, vol. III
Baughan, William Frederick, 1834–1908, vol. I
Baulkwill, Sir Pridham; see Baulkwill, Sir R. P.
Baulkwill, Sir (Reginald) Pridham, 1895–1974, vol. VII
Baulkwill, Rev. William Robert Kellaway, 1860–1915, vol. I
Baum, Vicki, 1896–1960, vol. V
Baumann, Arthur Anthony, 1856–1936, vol. III
Baume, Eric; see Baume, F. E.
Baume, Frederick Ehrenfried, (Eric Baume), 1900–1967, vol. VI
Baumer, Lewis C. E., 1870–1963, vol. VI
Baverstock, Rev. Alban Henry, 1871–1950, vol. IV
Bavin, John Thomas, died 1937, vol. III
Bavin, Hon. Sir Thomas Rainsford, 1874–1941, vol. IV
Bawden, Sir Frederick Charles, 1908–1972, vol. VII
Bax, Sir Arnold Edward Trevor, 1883–1953, vol. V
Bax, Clifford, 1886–1962, vol. VI
Bax, Ernest Belfort, 1854–1926, vol. II

Bax, Adm. Robert Nesham, *died* 1969, vol. VI
Bax-Ironside, Sir Henry George Outram, 1859–1929, vol. III
Baxendale, Col Joseph Francis Noel, 1877–1957, vol. V
Baxendale, Joseph William, 1848–1915, vol. I
Baxter, Sir (Arthur) Beverley, 1891–1964, vol. VI
Baxter, Cdre Sir Arthur James, 1890–1951, vol. V
Baxter, Sir Beverley; *see* Baxter, Sir A. B.
Baxter, Charles William, 1895–1969, vol. VI
Baxter, Frederick William, 1897–1980, vol. VII
Baxter, George Herbert, 1894–1962, vol. VI
Baxter, Sir George Washington, 1st Bt, 1853–1926, vol. II
Baxter, Herbert James, 1900–1974, vol. VII
Baxter, James, 1886–1964, vol. VI
Baxter, James Houston, 1894–1973, vol. VII
Baxter, James Sinclair, *died* 1933, vol. III
Baxter, John Babington Macaulay, 1868–1946, vol. IV
Baxter, Rev. Michael Paget, 1834–1910, vol. I
Baxter, Sir Thomas, 1878–1951, vol. V
Baxter, Thomas Tennant, 1894–1947, vol. IV
Baxter, William, 1911–1979, vol. VII
Baxter, Sir William James, 1845–1918, vol. II
Baxter, Wynne Edwin, 1844–1920, vol. II
Bayard, Brig.-Gen. Reginald, 1860–1925, vol. II
Bayer, Sir Horace, 1878–1965, vol. VI
Bayes, Gilbert, 1872–1952, vol. V
Bayes, Walter, 1869–1956, vol. V
Bayfield, Rev. Matthew Albert, 1852–1922, vol. II
Bayford, 1st Baron, 1867–1940, vol. III
Bayford, Major Edmund Heseltine, 1873–1942, vol. IV
Bayford, Robert Augustus, 1838–1922, vol. II
Bayford, Robert Frederic, 1871–1951, vol. V
Baykov, Alexander M., 1899–1963, vol. VI
Baylay, Brig.-Gen. Sir Atwell Charles, 1879–1957, vol. V
Baylay, Brig.-Gen. Frederick, 1865–1956, vol. V
Bayles, Herbert Laurence, 1886–1940, vol. III
Bayley, Col Arthur George, 1878–1949, vol. IV
Bayley, Charles Butterworth, 1876–1926, vol. II
Bayley, Charles Clive, 1864–1923, vol. II
Bayley, Sir Charles Stuart, 1854–1935, vol. III
Bayley, Lt-Col Edward Charles, 1867–1924, vol. II
Bayley, Brig.-Gen. Gerald Edward, 1874–1955, vol. V
Bayley, Sir H. Dennis R.; *see* Readett-Bayley.
Bayley, Lt-Col Hadrian, *died* 1931, vol. III
Bayley, Sir John, 1852–1952, vol. V
Bayley, Maj.-Gen. Kennett, 1903–1967, vol. VI
Bayley, Col Lionel Seton, 1875–1940, vol. III
Bayley, Sir Lyttelton Holyoake, 1827–1910, vol. I
Bayley, Sir Steuart Colvin, 1836–1925, vol. II
Bayley, Lt-Col Steuart Farquharson, 1863–1938, vol. III
Bayley, Thomas, 1846–1906, vol. I
Bayley, Vernon Thomas, 1908–1966, vol. VI
Bayley, Victor, 1880–1972, vol. VII
Bayliffe, Col Alfred Danvers, 1873–1942, vol. IV
Baylis, Rev. Frederick, *died* 1935, vol. III
Baylis, Harry Arnold, 1889–1972, vol. VII
Baylis, Lilian Mary, 1874–1937, vol. III

Baylis, T. Henry, 1817–1908, vol. I
Bayliss, Edwin, 1894–1971, vol. VII
Bayliss, William, 1886–1963, vol. VI
Bayliss, Sir William Maddock, 1860–1924, vol. II
Bayliss, Sir Wyke, 1835–1906, vol. I
Bayly, Lt-Col Abingdon Robert, 1871–1952, vol. V
Bayly, Ada Ellen, 1857–1903, vol. I
Bayly, Maj.-Gen. Sir Alfred William Lambart, 1856–1928, vol. II
Bayly, Edward, 1865–1934, vol. III
Bayly, Major Edward Archibald Theodore, 1877–1959, vol. V
Bayly, Francis Albert, *died* 1911, vol. I
Bayly, Hugh Wansey, 1873–1946, vol. IV
Bayly, Gen. John, 1821–1905, vol. I
Bayly, Adm. Sir Lewis, 1857–1938, vol. III
Bayly, Col Richard Kerr, 1838–1903, vol. I
Bayly, William Reynolds, 1867–1937, vol. III
Bayne, Charles Gerwien, 1860–1947, vol. IV
Bayne, Charles S., 1876–1952, vol. V
Bayne, Charles Walter, 1872–1937, vol. III
Bayne, Ven. Percy Matheson, 1865–1942, vol. IV
Bayne, Rt Rev. Stephen Fielding, Jr, 1908–1974, vol. VII
Bayne, Thomas Wilson, 1845–1931, vol. III
Bayne, William, *died* 1922, vol. II
Bayne-Jardine, Brig. Christian West, 1888–1959, vol. V
Baynes, Rt Rev. Arthur Hamilton, 1854–1942, vol. IV
Baynes, Sir Christopher William, 4th Bt, 1847–1936, vol. III
Baynes, Dorothy Julia C.; *see* Colston-Baynes.
Baynes, Edward Stuart Augustus, 1889–1972, vol. VII
Baynes, Edward William, 1880–1962, vol. VI
Baynes, Frederic William Wilberforce, 1889–1967, vol. VI
Baynes, Frederick, 1848–1917, vol. II
Baynes, Lt-Gen. George Edward, 1823–1906, vol. I
Baynes, Helton Godwin, 1882–1943, vol. IV
Baynes, Hon. Joseph, 1842–1925, vol. II
Baynes, Keith Stuart, 1887–1977, vol. VII
Baynes, Norman Hepburn, 1877–1961, vol. VI
Baynes, Robert Edward, 1849–1921, vol. II
Baynes, Sir Rory Malcolm Stuart, 6th Bt, 1886–1979, vol. VII
Baynes, Sir William Edward Colston, 5th Bt, 1876–1971, vol. VII
Baynes, Sir William John Walter, 3rd Bt, 1820–1897, vol. I
Baynham, Brig. Cuthbert Theodore, 1889–1966, vol. VI
Baynham, Captain Sir Walter de Mouchet, 1876–1936, vol. III
Bazarrabusa, Byabasakuzi Timothy, 1912–1966, vol. VI
Bazeley, Rev. William, 1843–1925, vol. II
Bazett, Henry Cuthbert, 1885–1950, vol. IV
Bazin, René François Nicolas Marie, *died* 1932, vol. III
Bazley, Sir Thomas Sebastian, 2nd Bt, 1829–1919, vol. II

Bazley-White, John, 1847–1927, vol. II
Bea, H.E. Cardinal Agostino, 1881–1968, vol. VI
Beach, Charles Fisk, 1854–1934, vol. III
Beach, Col Gerald, 1881–1955, vol. V
Beach, Rex, 1877–1949, vol. IV
Beach, Col Thomas Boswall, 1866–1941, vol. IV
Beach, Lady Victoria Alexandrina H.; see Hicks-Beach.
Beach, William Frederick H.; see Hicks Beach.
Beach, Maj.-Gen. William Henry, 1871–1952, vol. V
Beach, Major William Whitehead H.; see Hicks Beach.
Beach, William Wither Bramston H.; see Hicks-Beach.
Beachcomber; see Morton, J. C. A. B. M.
Beachcroft, Sir Charles Porten, 1871–1927, vol. II
Beachcroft, Maurice; see Beachcroft, P. M.
Beachcroft, Sir Melvill; see Beachcroft, Sir R. M.
Beachcroft, (Philip) Maurice, 1879–1969, vol. VI
Beachcroft, Sir (Richard) Melvill, 1846–1926, vol. II
Beadle, Sir Gerald Clayton, 1899–1976, vol. VII
Beadle, Rt Hon. Sir Hugh; see Beadle, Rt Hon. Sir T. H. W.
Beadle, James Prinsep Barnes, 1863–1947, vol. IV
Beadle, Rt Hon. Sir (Thomas) Hugh (William), 1905–1980, vol. VII
Beadnell, Surg. Rear-Adm. Charles Marsh, 1872–1947, vol. IV
Beadnell, Hugh John Llewellyn, 1874–1944, vol. IV
Beadon, Lt-Col Henry Cecil, 1869–1959, vol. V
Beadon, Bt Col Lancelot Richmond, 1875–1922, vol. II
Beadon, Col Roger Hammet, 1887–1945, vol. IV
Beaglehole, John Cawte, 1901–1971, vol. VII
Beak, Maj.-Gen. Daniel Marcus William, 1891–1967, vol. VI
Beak, George Bailey, 1872–1934, vol. III
Beal, Vice-Adm. Alister Francis, 1875–1962, vol. VI
Beal, Charles, 1841–1921, vol. II
Beal, Col Henry, 1843–1905, vol. I
Beal, Col Robert, died 1907, vol. I
Beal, Rev. T. Gilbert, 1865–1948, vol. IV
Beale, Charles Gabriel, died 1912, vol. I
Beale, Dame Doris Winifred, 1889–1971, vol. VII
Beale, Dorothea, 1831–1906, vol. I
Beale, George Galloway, 1868–1936, vol. III
Beale, Lt-Col Henry Yelverton, 1860–1930, vol. III
Beale, Sir John Field, 1874–1935, vol. III
Beale, Lionel Smith, 1828–1906, vol. I
Beale, Sir Louis, 1879–1971, vol. VII
Beale, Peyton Todd Bowman, 1864–1957, vol. V
Beale, Sir Samuel Richard, 1881–1964, vol. VI
Beale, Sir William Phipson, 1st Bt, 1839–1922, vol. II
Beale-Browne, Brig.-Gen. Desmond John Edward, 1870–1953, vol. V
Beales, Arthur Charles Frederick, 1905–1974, vol. VII
Beales, Reginald Edwin, 1909–1980, vol. VII
Beall, Lt-Col Edward Metcalfe, 1877–1950, vol. IV
Beall, Captain George, 1840–1918, vol. II

Beals, Carlyle Smith, 1899–1979, vol. VII
Beaman, Bt Lt-Col Ardern Arthur Hulme, 1886–1950, vol. IV
Beaman, Ardern George Hulme, 1857–1929, vol. III
Beaman, Sir Frank Clement Offley, 1858–1928, vol. II
Beaman, Lt-Col Winfrid Kelsey, died 1929, vol. III
Beament, Brig. Arthur Warwick, 1898–1966, vol. VI
Beamish, Wing-Comdr Francis Victor, 1903–1942, vol. IV
Beamish, Air Marshal Sir George Robert, 1905–1967, vol. VI
Beamish, Rear-Adm. Henry Hamilton, 1829–1901, vol. I
Beamish, Rear-Adm. Tufton Percy Hamilton, 1874–1951, vol. V
Bean, Rev. Alexander Henry Stillingfleet, 1849–1929, vol. III
Bean, Charles Edwin Woodrow, 1879–1968, vol. VI
Bean, Sir Edgar Layton, 1893–1977, vol. VII
Bean, Sir George, 1855–1924, vol. II
Bean, Hon. Sir George Joseph, 1915–1973, vol. VII
Bean, John Harper, 1885–1963, vol. VI
Bean, William Jackson, 1863–1947, vol. IV
Beane, Sir Francis Adams, 1872–1959, vol. V
Beanland, Maj.-Gen. Douglas, 1893–1963, vol. VI
Beanlands, Rev. Arthur John, 1857–1917, vol. II
Bearblock, Engr Rear-Adm. Charles William John, 1865–1929, vol. III
Bearcroft, Col Edward Hugh, 1852–1932, vol. III
Bearcroft, Adm. John Edward, 1851–1931, vol. III
Beard, Charles A., 1874–1948, vol. IV
Beard, Charles Thomas, 1858–1918, vol. II
Beard, Maj.-Gen. Edmund Charles, 1894–1974, vol. VII
Beard, Lt-Col George John Allen, died 1922, vol. II
Beard, James Robert, 1885–1962, vol. VI
Beard, John, 1871–1950, vol. IV
Beard, John Stanley Coombe, 1890–1970, vol. VI
Beard, Sir Lewis, 1858–1933, vol. III
Beard, Sidney Hartnoll, 1862–1938, vol. III
Beard, Wilfred Blackwell, 1892–1967, vol. VI
Beardmore, Rt Rev. Harold, 1898–1968, vol. VI
Beards, Samuel Arthur, died 1975, vol. VII
Beardsell, Sir William Arthur, 1865–1940, vol. III
Beardsley, Aubrey, 1874–1898, vol. I
Beardsworth, Air Vice-Marshal George Braithwaite, 1904–1959, vol. V
Beare, Daniel Robert O'S.; see O'Sullivan-Beare.
Beare, Ernest Edwin, 1877–1956, vol. V
Beare, John Isaac, died 1918, vol. II
Beare, Josias Crocker, 1881–1962, vol. VI
Beare, Sir Thomas Hudson, 1859–1940, vol. III
Beare, William, 1900–1963, vol. VI
Bearn, Edward Gordon, 1887–1945, vol. IV
Bearne, Catherine Mary, died 1923, vol. II
Bearne, Lt-Col Lewis Collinwood, 1878–1940, vol. III
Bearsted, 1st Viscount, 1853–1927, vol. II
Bearsted, 2nd Viscount, 1882–1948, vol. IV
Beasley, Cyril George, 1901–1956, vol. V
Beasley, Sir (Horace) Owen (Compton), 1877–1960, vol. V

Beasley, Rt Hon. John Albert, 1895–1949, vol. IV
Beasley, Sir Owen; *see* Beasley, Sir H. O. C.
Beath, John Henry, 1835–1904, vol. I
Beaton, Lt-Col Angus John, 1858–1945, vol. IV
Beaton, Sir Cecil Walter Hardy, 1904–1980, vol. VII
Beatson, Col Charles Henry, 1851–1938, vol. III
Beatson, Maj.-Gen. Finlay Cochrane, 1855–1933, vol. III
Beatson, Sir George Thomas, 1848–1933, vol. III
Beatson, Maj.-Gen. Sir Stuart Brownlow, 1854–1914, vol. I
Beatson-Bell, Col John, 1866–1929, vol. III
Beattie, Lt-Col Alexander Elder, 1888–1951, vol. V
Beattie, Rt Hon. Sir Andrew, *died* 1923, vol. II
Beattie, Sir Carruthers; *see* Beattie, Sir J. C.
Beattie, Charles Innes, 1875–1952, vol. V
Beattie, Francis, 1885–1945, vol. IV
Beattie, Sir James, 1861–1933, vol. III
Beattie, James Martin, 1868–1955, vol. V
Beattie, John, *died* 1960, vol. V
Beattie, John, 1899–1976, vol. VII
Beattie, Sir (John) Carruthers, 1866–1946, vol. IV
Beattie, Captain Kenneth Adair, 1883–1940, vol. III
Beattie, Rt Rev. Philip Rodger, 1912–1960, vol. V
Beattie, Robert, 1873–1940, vol. III
Beattie, Captain Stephen Halden, 1908–1975, vol. VII
Beattie, Hon. Col Rev. William, 1873–1943, vol. IV
Beattie-Brown, William, 1831–1909, vol. I
Beatty, 1st Earl, 1871–1936, vol. III
Beatty, 2nd Earl, 1905–1972, vol. VII
Beatty, Sir (Alfred) Chester, 1875–1968, vol. VI
Beatty, Major Charles Harold Longfield, 1870–1917, vol. II
Beatty, Sir Chester; *see* Beatty, Sir A. C.
Beatty, Sir Edward Wentworth, 1877–1943, vol. IV
Beatty, Maj.-Gen. Sir Guy Archibald Hastings, 1870–1954, vol. V
Beatty, Haslitt Michael, *died* 1916, vol. II
Beatty, James, 1870–1947, vol. IV
Beatty, Sir Kenneth James, *died* 1966, vol. VI
Beatty, Brig.-Gen. Lionel Nicholson, 1867–1929, vol. III
Beatty, Pakenham Thomas, 1855–1930, vol. III
Beatty, Rose Mabel, 1879–1932, vol. III
Beatty, Wallace, 1853–1923, vol. III
Beatty, Wing-Comdr William Dawson, 1884–1941, vol. IV
Beaty-Pownall, Adm. Charles Pipon, 1872–1938, vol. III
Beaubien, Hon. Charles Philippe, 1870–1949, vol. IV
Beaubien, De Gaspé, 1881–1969, vol. VI (AII)
Beaubien, Justine Lacoste, (Mme L. de G. Beaubien), 1877–1967, vol. VI
Beauchamp, 7th Earl, 1872–1938, vol. III
Beauchamp, 8th Earl, 1903–1979, vol. VII
Beauchamp, Sir Brograve Campbell, 2nd Bt (*cr* 1911), 1897–1976, vol. VII
Beauchamp, Sir Edward, 1st Bt (*cr* 1911), 1849–1925, vol. II
Beauchamp, Col Sir Frank, 1st Bt (*cr* 1918), 1866–1950, vol. IV

Beauchamp, Sir Harold, 1858–1938, vol. III
Beauchamp, Rt Rev. Mgr Henry, 1884–1948, vol. IV
Beauchamp, Henry King, 1866–1907, vol. I
Beauchamp, Col Sir Horace George Proctor-, 6th Bt (*cr* 1744), 1856–1915, vol. I (A)
Beauchamp, Rev. Sir Ivor Cuthbert Proctor-, 8th Bt (*cr* 1744), 1900–1971, vol. VII
Beauchamp, Rev. Sir Montagu Harry Proctor-, 7th Bt (*cr* 1744), 1860–1939, vol. III
Beauchamp, Sir Reginald William Proctor-, 5th Bt (*cr* 1744), 1853–1912, vol. I
Beauchamp, Sir Sydney, 1861–1921, vol. II
Beauchesne, Arthur, 1876–1959, vol. V
Beauclerk, Lord William de Vere, 1883–1954, vol. V
Beauclerk, William Nelthorpe, 1849–1908, vol. I
Beaufort, 8th Duke of, 1824–1899, vol. I
Beaufort, 9th Duke of, 1847–1924, vol. II
Beaufort, Sir Leicester Paul, 1853–1926, vol. II
Beaufoy, Henry Mark, 1887–1958, vol. V
Beaufoy, Mark Hanbury, 1854–1922, vol. II
Beaufoy, Samuel Leslie George, 1899–1961, vol. VI
Beauman, Brig.-Gen. Archibald Bentley, 1888–1977, vol. VII
Beaumarchais, Jacques Delarüe Caron de, 1913–1979, vol. VII
Beaumont, Baroness (11th in line), 1894–1971, vol. VII
Beaumont, Cyril William, 1891–1976, vol. VII
Beaumont, Rev. Francis Morton, 1838–1915, vol. I
Beaumont, Air Cdre Frank, 1896–1968, vol. VI
Beaumont, Sir George Arthur Hamilton, 11th Bt, 1881–1933, vol. III
Beaumont, George Ernest, 1888–1974, vol. VII
Beaumont, Sir George Howland William, 10th Bt, 1851–1914, vol. I
Beaumont, Henry Frederick, 1833–1913, vol. I
Beaumont, Sir Henry Hamond Dawson, 1867–1949, vol. IV
Beaumont, Hon. Hubert, 1864–1922, vol. II
Beaumont, Captain Hubert, *died* 1948, vol. IV
Beaumont, Hugh, 1908–1973, vol. VII
Beaumont, James Buchan, 1925–1973, vol. VII
Beaumont, Rt Hon. Sir John William Fisher, 1877–1974, vol. VII
Beaumont, Kenneth Macdonald, 1884–1965, vol. VI
Beaumont, Adm. Sir Lewis Anthony, 1847–1922, vol. II
Beaumont, Michael Wentworth, 1903–1958, vol. V
Beaumont, Hon. Ralph Edward Blackett, 1901–1977, vol. VII
Beaumont, Roberts, *born* 1862, vol. II
Beaumont, Somerset Archibald, 1836–1921, vol. II
Beaumont, W(illiam) Comyns, 1879–1955, vol. V
Beaumont, Sir William Henry, 1851–1930, vol. III
Beaumont, William Worby, 1848–1929, vol. III
Beaumont-Nesbitt, Maj.-Gen. Frederick George, 1893–1971, vol. VII
Beaumont-Thomas, Col Lionel, 1893–1942, vol. IV
Beaurepaire, Sir Frank, 1891–1956, vol. V
Beavan, Arthur Henry, 1844–1907, vol. I
Beavan, Margaret, *died* 1931, vol. III

Beaven, Rt Rev. Frederic Hicks, 1855–1941, vol. IV
Beaver, Sir Hugh Eyre Campbell, 1890–1967, vol. VI
Beaver, James Addams, 1837–1914, vol. I
Beaverbrook, 1st Baron, 1879–1964, vol. VI
Beavis, Arthur Beagley, 1867–1934, vol. III
Beavis, Maj.-Gen. Leslie Ellis, 1895–1975, vol. VII
Beazeley, Lt-Col George Adam, 1870–1961, vol. VI
Beazley, Sir (Charles) Raymond, 1868–1955, vol. V
Beazley, Col Sir Geoffrey; see Beazley, Col Sir J. G. B.
Beazley, Sir Hugh Loveday, 1880–1964, vol. VI
Beazley, Col Sir (James) Geoffrey (Brydon), 1884–1962, vol. VI
Beazley, Sir John Davidson, 1885–1970, vol. VI
Beazley, John Godfrey, 1885–1948, vol. IV
Beazley, Patrick Langford, 1859–1923, vol. II
Beazley, Sir Raymond; see Beazley, Sir C. R.
Beazley, Lt-Col Walter Edwin, 1886–1969, vol. VI
Bebb, Rev. Llewellyn John Montfort, 1862–1915, vol. I (A)
Bebbington, Bernard Nicolas, 1910–1980, vol. VII
Bebbington, Rev. John Henry, died 1936, vol. III
Bebel, Ferdinand August, 1840–1913, vol. I
Beberrua, 3rd Count of, born 1839, vol. III
Bech, Joseph, 1887–1975, vol. VII
Becher, Maj.-Gen. Andrew Cracroft, 1858–1929, vol. III
Becher, Dame Ethel Hope, died 1948, vol. IV
Becher, Sir Eustace William Windham Wrixon-, 4th Bt, 1859–1934, vol. III
Becher, Lt-Col Henry Wrixon-, 1866–1951, vol. V
Becher, Sir John Wrixon-, 3rd Bt, 1828–1914, vol. I
Becher, Rear-Adm. Otto Humphrey, 1908–1977, vol. VII
Becher, Gen. Septimus Harding, 1817–1908, vol. I
Béchervaise, Albert Eric, 1884–1969, vol. VI
Beck, Col Hon. Sir Adam, 1857–1925, vol. II
Beck, Sir (Arthur) Cecil (Tyrrell), 1878–1932, vol. III
Beck, Arthur Clement, 1865–1949, vol. IV
Beck, Sir Cecil; see Beck, Sir A. C. T.
Beck, Lt-Col Charles Harrop, 1861–1910, vol. I.
Beck, Conrad, died 1944, vol. IV
Beck, Diana Jean Kinloch, 1902–1956, vol. V
Beck, Edward Anthony, 1848–1916, vol. II
Beck, Maj.-Gen. Edward Archibald, 1880–1974, vol. VII
Beck, Rev. Edward Josselyn, 1832–1924, vol. II
Beck, Egerton, 1858–1941, vol. IV
Beck, Rev. Frederick John, died 1922, vol. II
Beck, Most Rev. George Andrew, 1904–1978, vol. VII
Beck, Harvey Mortimer, 1868–1948, vol. IV
Beck, Hon. James Montgomery, 1861–1936, vol. III
Beck, Hon. Sir Johannes Henricus Meiring, 1855–1919, vol. II
Beck, John Melliar A.; see Adams-Beck.
Beck, Mrs L. Adams, died 1931, vol. III
Beck, Hon. Nicholas Du Bois Dominic, 1857–1928, vol. II
Beck, Captain Oliver Lawrence, died 1947, vol. IV
Beck, Sir Raymond, 1861–1953, vol. V

Beck, Very Rev. William Ernest, 1884–1957, vol. V
Beck, William Hopkins, 1892–1957, vol. V
Becke, George Louis, 1848–1913, vol. I
Becke, Major Sir Jack, 1878–1962, vol. VI
Becke, Brig.-Gen. John Harold Whitworth, 1879–1949, vol. IV
Becker, Sir Ellerton; see Becker, Sir J. E.
Becker, Sir Frederick Edward Robert, 1871–1936, vol. III
Becker, Harry Thomas Alfred, 1892–1980, vol. VII
Becker, Sir (Jack) Ellerton, 1904–1979, vol. VII
Becker, Neal Dow, 1883–1955, vol. V
Becker, Sir Walter Frederick, 1855–1927, vol. II
Beckett, Arthur, died 1943, vol. IV
Beckett, Brig.-Gen. Charles Edward, 1849–1925, vol. II
Beckett, Maj.-Gen. Clifford Thomason, 1891–1972, vol. VII
Beckett, Sir Eric; see Beckett, Sir W. E.
Beckett, Sir Eric Frederick, 1895–1971, vol. VII
Beckett, Geoffrey Bernard, 1903–1965, vol. VI
Beckett, Hon. Sir Gervase; see Beckett, Hon. Sir W. G.
Beckett, Harold, 1891–1952, vol. V
Beckett, James, 1891–1970, vol. VI
Beckett, Lt-Col John Douglas Mortimer, 1881–1918, vol. II
Beckett, John Warburton, 1894–1964, vol. VI (AII)
Beckett, Ronald Brymer, 1891–1970, vol. VI
Beckett, Hon. Rupert Evelyn, 1870–1955, vol. V
Beckett, Col Stephen, 1840–1921, vol. II
Beckett, Captain Walter Napier Thomason, 1893–1941, vol. IV
Beckett, Walter Ralph Durie, 1864–1917, vol. II
Beckett, Sir (William) Eric, 1896–1966, vol. VI
Beckett, Hon. Sir (William) Gervase, 1st Bt, 1866–1937, vol. III
Beckett, Brig.-Gen. William Thomas Clifford, 1862–1956, vol. V
Beckles, Rt Rev. Edward Hyndman, died 1902, vol. I
Beckles, Gordon, 1901–1954, vol. V
Beckwith, Brig.-Gen. Arthur Thackeray, 1875–1942, vol. IV
Beckwith, Edward George Ambrose, died 1935, vol. III
Beckwith, Air Vice-Marshal William Flint, 1913–1971, vol. VII
Beckwith-Smith, Maj.-Gen. Merton, 1890–1942, vol. IV
Bective, Countess of; (Alice), died 1928, vol. II
Bedale, Rev. Frederick, died 1924, vol. II
Bedale, Rear-Adm. Sir John Leigh, 1891–1964, vol. VI
Bedale, Rev. Stephen Frederick Burstal, 1888–1961, vol. VI
Beddall, Maj.-Gen. Walter Samuel, 1894–1973, vol. VII
Beddard, Arthur Philip, died 1939, vol. III
Beddard, Frank Evers, 1858–1926, vol. II
Beddington, Brig. Sir Edward Henry Lionel, 1884–1966, vol. VI
Beddington, Frances Ethel, (Mrs Claude Beddington), died 1963, vol. VI

Beddington, Gerald Ernest, 1867–1958, vol. V
Beddington, Jack, 1893–1959, vol. V
Beddington, Reginald, 1877–1962, vol. VI
Beddington, Maj.-Gen. William Richard, 1893–1975, vol. VII
Beddington-Behrens, Sir Edward, 1897–1968, vol. VI
Beddoe, John, 1826–1911, vol. I
Beddome, Col Richard Henry, died 1910, vol. I
Beddow, Lt-Col Arnold Bellamy, 1883–1965, vol. VI
Beddy, James Patrick, 1900–1976, vol. VII
Beddy, Brig. Percy Langdon, died 1945, vol. IV
Bedell, Frederick, 1868–1958, vol. V (A)
Bedells, Charles Herbert, 1862–1943, vol. IV
Bedford, 11th Duke of, 1858–1940, vol. III
Bedford, 12th Duke of, 1888–1953, vol. V
Bedford, Duchess of; (Mary du Caurroy), 1865–1937, vol. III
Bedford, Vice-Adm. Arthur Edward Frederick, 1881–1949, vol. IV
Bedford, Lt-Col Sir Charles Henry, 1866–1931, vol. III
Bedford, Davis Evan, 1898–1978, vol. VII
Bedford, Adm. Sir Frederick George Denham, 1838–1913, vol. I
Bedford, Henry Hall, 1847–1930, vol. III
Bedford, Herbert, 1867–1945, vol. IV
Bedford, Mrs Herbert; see Lehmann, Liza.
Bedford, James Douglas Hardy, 1884–1960, vol. V
Bedford, John, 1903–1980, vol. VII
Bedford, Richard Perry, 1883–1967, vol. VI
Bedford, Maj.-Gen. Sir Walter George Augustus, 1858–1922, vol. II
Bedford, Rev. William Campbell Riland, 1852–1922, vol. II
Bedford, Rev. William Kirkpatrick Riland, 1826–1905, vol. I
Bedi, Raja Sir Baba Gurbukhsh Singh, died 1945, vol. IV
Bedier, Joseph, 1864–1938, vol. III
Bedingfeld, Sir Henry Edward P.; see Paston-Bedingfeld.
Bedingfeld, Sir Henry George P.; see Paston-Bedingfeld.
Bedson, Peter Phillips, 1853–1943, vol. IV
Bedson, Sir Samuel Phillips, 1886–1969, vol. VI
Bedwell, Cyril Edward Alfred, died 1950, vol. IV
Bedwell, Rev. Francis, died 1925, vol. II
Bedwell, Horace, 1868–1954, vol. V
Beebe, William, 1877–1962, vol. VI
Beeby, Sir George Stephenson, 1869–1942, vol. IV
Beech, Francis William, 1885–1969, vol. VI
Beech, Lt-Col John Robert, 1860–1915, vol. I (A)
Beecham, Sir Joseph, 1st Bt, 1848–1916, vol. II
Beecham, Sir Thomas, 2nd Bt, 1879–1961, vol. VI
Beecher, Rev. Patrick A., 1870–1940, vol. III
Beecher, Willis Judson, 1838–1912, vol. I
Beechey, Rev. St Vincent, 1841–1905, vol. I
Beeching, Maj.-Gen. Frank, 1839–1916, vol. II
Beeching, Very Rev. Henry Charles, 1859–1919, vol. II
Beechman, Captain Alec; see Beechman, Captain N. A.

Beechman, Captain Nevil Alexander, (Captain Alec Beechman), died 1965, vol. VI
Beeding, Francis; see Saunders, H. A. St G.
Beeman, Christina May, died 1935, vol. III
Beeman, Engr Rear-Adm. Sir Robert, died 1963, vol. VI
Beeman, Brig. William Gilbert, 1884–1953, vol. V
Beer, Sir Frederick Tidbury T.; see Tidbury-Beer.
Beer, Harry, 1896–1970, vol. VI
Beer, Ven. Henry, 1844–1937, vol. III
Beer, Col James Henry Elias, 1848–1925, vol. II
Beer Bikram Singh, Rajkumar, died 1923, vol. II
Beerbohm, Sir Max, 1872–1956, vol. V
Beere, Mrs Bernard, (Fanny Mary), 1856–1915, vol. I
Beernaert, Auguste Marie François, 1829–1912, vol. I
Beery, Wallace, died 1949, vol. IV
Beesly, Edward Spenser, 1831–1915, vol. I
Beesly, Lewis Rowland, 1912–1978, vol. VII
Beeson, Cyril Frederick Cherrington, 1889–1975, vol. VII
Beeston, Col Joseph Livesley, 1859–1921, vol. II
Beet, Rev. Joseph Agar, 1840–1924, vol. II
Beetham, Sir Edward Betham, 1905–1979, vol. VII
Beeton, Alan, 1880–1942, vol. IV
Beeton, Sir Mayson, died 1947, vol. IV
Beeton, William Hugh, 1903–1976, vol. VII
Beets, Nicolas, 1814–1903, vol. I
Beevor, Charles Edward, 1854–1908, vol. I
Beevor, Sir Hugh Reeve, 5th Bt, 1858–1939, vol. III
Beevor, Rt Rev. Humphry, 1903–1965, vol. VI
Beevor, Comdr Sir Thomas Lubbock, 6th Bt, 1897–1943, vol. IV
Beevor, Lt-Col Walter Calverley, 1858–1927, vol. II
Begas, Reinhold, 1831–1911, vol. I
Begbie, Maj.-Gen. Elphinstone Waters, 1842–1915, vol. I (A)
Begbie, Col Francis Warburton, died 1922, vol. II
Begbie, Major George Edward, 1868–1907, vol. I
Begbie, Harold, 1871–1929, vol. III
Begbie, Rt Rev. Herbert Gordon Smirnoff, 1905–1973, vol. VII
Begbie, Ven. Herbert Smirnoff, 1871–1951, vol. V
Begbie, Sir James, 1859–1934, vol. III
Begg, Col Charles Mackie, died 1919, vol. II
Begg, Ferdinand Faithfull, 1847–1926, vol. II
Begg, Jean, 1887–1971, vol. VII
Begg, John Henderson, 1844–1911, vol. I
Begg, Col Robert B.; see Burns-Begg.
Begg, Rev William H.; see Henderson-Begg.
Beggs, Engr-Captain James, died 1949, vol. IV
Beggs, Hon. Theodore, 1859–1940, vol. III
Begin, His Eminence Cardinal Louis Nazaire, 1840–1925, vol. II
Behan, Brendan, 1923–1964, vol. VI
Behan, Sir Harold Garfield, 1901–1979, vol. VII (AII)
Behan, Sir John Clifford Valentine, 1881–1957, vol. V
Beharrell, Sir Edward; see Beharrell, Sir G. E.
Beharrell, Sir George; see Beharrell, Sir J. G.
Beharrell, Sir (George) Edward, 1899–1972, vol. VII

47

Beharrell, Sir (John) George, 1873–1959, vol. V
Behr, Fritz Bernhard, 1842–1927, vol. II
Behram, Sir Jehangir Bomonji B.; see Bomon-Behram.
Behrend, George L., 1868–1950, vol. IV
Behrens, Sir Charles, 1848–1925, vol. II
Behrens, Major Clive, 1871–1935, vol. III
Behrens, Edgar Charles, 1885–1975, vol. VII
Behrens, Sir Edward B.; see Beddington-Behrens.
Behrens, Gustav, 1846–1936, vol. III
Behrens, Sir Leonard Frederick, 1890–1978, vol. VII
Behrens, Walter, 1856–1922, vol. II
Behrman, S. N., 1893–1973, vol. VII
Beibitz, Rev. Joseph Hugh, 1868–1936, vol. III
Beilby, Sir George Thomas, 1850–1924, vol. II
Beinart, Ben Zion, 1914–1979, vol. VII
Beique, Hon. Frederic Liguori, 1845–1933, vol. III
Beirne, Hon. Thomas Charles, 1860–1949, vol. IV
Beit, Alfred, 1853–1906, vol. I
Beit, Sir Otto John, 1st Bt, 1865–1930, vol. III
Beith, Maj.-Gen. John Hay, 1876–1952, vol. V
Beith, Hon. Robert, 1843–1922, vol. II
Béjot, Eugène, died 1931, vol. III
Békésy, Dr Georg von, 1899–1972, vol. VII
Beland, Hon. Henri, 1869–1935, vol. III
Belasco, David, 1859–1931, vol. III
Belch, Alexander, died 1967, vol. VI
Belcher, Rev. Arthur Hayes, 1876–1947, vol. IV
Belcher, Sir Charles Frederic, 1876–1970, vol. VI
Belcher, Captain Douglas Walter, 1889–1953, vol. V
Belcher, Major Ernest Albert, 1871–1949, vol. IV
Belcher, George Frederick Arthur, 1875–1947, vol. IV
Belcher, Lt-Col Harold Thomas, 1875–1917, vol. II
Belcher, John, 1841–1913, vol. I
Belcher, John William, 1905–1964, vol. VI
Belcher, Major Robert, 1849–1919, vol. II
Belcher, Rev. Thomas Waugh, 1831–1910, vol. I
Belcher, Rt Rev. Wilfrid Bernard, died 1963, vol. VI
Belcourt, Hon Napoleon Antoine, 1860–1932, vol. III
Belden, Rev. Albert David, 1883–1964, vol. VI
Belfield, Sir Henry Conway, 1855–1923, vol. II
Belfield, Lt-Gen. Sir Herbert Eversley, 1857–1934, vol. III
Belfield, Lt-Col Sydney, 1862–1946, vol. IV
Belfield, Major William Seymour, died 1924, vol. II (A), vol. III
Belfrage, Sydney Henning, 1871–1950, vol. IV
Belgion, (Harold) Montgomery, 1892–1973, vol. VII
Belgion, Montgomery; see Belgion, H. M.
Belgrave, Sir Charles Dalrymple, 1894–1969, vol. VI
Belhaven and Stenton, 10th Lord, 1840–1920, vol. II
Belhaven and Stenton, 11th Lord, 1871–1950, vol. IV
Belhaven and Stenton, 12th Lord, 1903–1961, vol. VI
Belhaven, Master of; Hon. Ralph Gerard Alexander Hamilton, 1883–1918, vol. II

Belilios, Emanuel Raphael, 1837–1905, vol. I
Belisario, John Colquhoun, 1900–1976, vol. VII
Béliveau, Most Rev. Arthur, 1870–1955, vol. V
Beljame, Alexandre, died 1906, vol. I
Belk, John Thomas, 1837–1901, vol. I
Belk, Lt-Col William, 1869–1952, vol. V
Bell, Adam Carr, 1847–1912, vol. I
Bell, Captain Adolphus Edmund, 1850–1927, vol. II
Bell, Adrian Hanbury, 1901–1980, vol. VII
Bell, Alexander Foulis, 1876–1940, vol. III
Bell, Alexander Graham, 1847–1922, vol. II
Bell, Andrew Beatson, 1831–1913, vol. I
Bell, Andrew James, 1856–1932, vol. III
Bell, Lt-Comdr Archibald Colquhoun, died 1958, vol. V
Bell, Archibald Græme, 1868–1948, vol. IV
Bell, Rev. Archibald William, 1870–1938, vol. III
Bell, Sir Arthur Capel Herbert, 1904–1977, vol. VII
Bell, Arthur Doyne Courtenay, 1900–1970, vol. VI
Bell, Arthur George, died 1916, vol. II
Bell, Maj.-Gen. Arthur Henry, 1871–1956, vol. V
Bell, Col Arthur Hugh, 1878–1968, vol. VI
Bell, Maj.-Gen. Sir Arthur Lynden L.; see Lynden-Bell.
Bell, Arthur William, 1868–1935, vol. III
Bell, Aubrey FitzGerald, 1881–1950, vol. IV
Bell, Rev. Benjamin, 1845–1930, vol. III
Bell, Sir (Bernard) Humphrey, died 1959, vol. V
Bell, Bertram Charles, 1893–1941, vol. IV
Bell, Sir Charles Alfred, 1870–1945, vol. IV
Bell, Rev. Canon Charles Carlyle, 1868–1954, vol. V
Bell, Rev. Charles Dent, 1818–1898, vol. I
Bell, Charles Francis, 1871–1966, vol. VI
Bell, Charles Frederick Moberly, 1847–1911, vol. I
Bell, Captain Charles Leigh de Hauteville, 1903–1972, vol. VII
Bell, Sir Charles William M.; see Morrison-Bell.
Bell, Claude Waylen, 1891–1964, vol. VI
Bell, Sir Claude William Hedley M.; see Morrison-Bell.
Bell, Clive, 1881–1964, vol. VI
Bell, Sir Clive M.; see Morrison-Bell.
Bell, Cyril Francis, 1883–1957, vol. V
Bell, Sir Douglas James, 1904–1974, vol. VII
Bell, Sir Eastman, 2nd Bt (cr 1909), 1884–1955, vol. V
Bell, Edward, 1844–1926, vol. II
Bell, Col Edward, 1866–1937, vol. III
Bell, Edward Allen, 1884–1959, vol. V
Bell, Col Edward Horace Lynden L.; see Lynden-Bell.
Bell, Sir (Edward) Peter (Stubbs), 1902–1957, vol. V
Bell, Edward Price, 1869–1943, vol. IV
Bell, Enid Moberly, 1881–1967, vol. VI
Bell, Eric Temple, 1883–1960, vol. V
Bell, Ernest, 1851–1933, vol. III
Bell, Sir Ernest Albert Seymour, died 1955, vol. V
Bell, Lt-Col Ernest FitzRoy M.; see Morrison-Bell.
Bell, Lt-Col Eustace Widdrington M.; see Morrison-Bell.
Bell, Eva Mary, died 1959, vol. V

Bell, Hon. Sir Francis Dillon, *died* 1898, vol. I
Bell, Sir Francis Gordon, 1887–1970, vol. VI
Bell, Rt Hon. Sir Francis Henry Dillon, 1851–1936, vol. III
Bell, Francis Jeffrey, *died* 1924, vol. II
Bell, Frank, 1878–1961, vol. VI
Bell, Sir Frederick Archibald, 1891–1972, vol. VII
Bell, Col Frederick Charles, 1883–1971, vol. VII
Bell, Captain Frederick Secker, 1897–1973, vol. VII
Bell, Lt-Col Frederick William, *died* 1954, vol. V
Bell, Hon. George Alexander, 1856–1927, vol. II
Bell, Rev. George Charles, *died* 1913, vol. I
Bell, Rev. Canon George Fancourt, 1874–1952, vol. V
Bell, Col George James Hamilton, 1861–1930, vol. III
Bell, Col Hon. Sir George John, 1872–1944, vol. IV
Bell, Rt Rev. George Kennedy Allen, 1883–1958, vol. V
Bell, Rev. Preb. George Milner, 1872–1947, vol. IV
Bell, Gertrude Margaret Lowthian 1868–1926, vol. II
Bell, Grace Effingham Laughton, (Mrs Harry Graham Bell), *died* 1975, vol. VII
Bell, Major Graham Airdrie, 1874–1929, vol. III
Bell, Harold Arthur, 1918–1978, vol. VII
Bell, Sir (Harold) Idris, 1879–1967, vol. VI
Bell, Lt-Col Sir Harold W.; *see* Wilberforce-Bell.
Bell, Harry Charles Purvis, 1851–1937, vol. III
Bell, Mrs Harry Graham; *see* Bell, G. E. L.
Bell, Rev. Henry, 1838–1919, vol. II
Bell, Sir Henry, 1st Bt (*cr* 1909), 1848–1931, vol. III
Bell, Henry, *died* 1935, vol. III
Bell, Henry McGrady, 1880–1958, vol. V
Bell, Lt-Col Henry Stanley, 1874–1949, vol. IV
Bell, (Henry Thomas) Mackenzie, 1856–1930, vol. III
Bell, Henry Thurburn Montague, 1873–1949, vol. IV
Bell, Herbert Clifford Francis, 1881–1966, vol. VI
Bell, Herbert Wright, 1857–1936, vol. III
Bell, Sir Hesketh, 1864–1952, vol. V
Bell, Sir Hugh, 2nd Bt (*cr* 1885), 1844–1931, vol. III
Bell, Sir Hugh Francis, 4th Bt (*cr* 1885), 1923–1970, vol. VI
Bell, Sir Humphrey; *see* Bell, Sir B. H.
Bell, Sir Idris; *see* Bell, Sir H. I.
Bell, Isaac, 1879–1964, vol. VI
Bell, James, 1825–1908, vol. I
Bell, Rev. James, *died* 1918, vol. II
Bell, Sir James, 1st Bt (*cr* 1895), 1850–1929, vol. III
Bell, Sir James, 1866–1937, vol. III
Bell, Sir James, 1878–1948, vol. IV
Bell, James, 1872–1955, vol. V
Bell, James Alan, 1894–1968, vol. VI
Bell, Maj.-Gen. Sir James Alexander, 1856–1926, vol. II
Bell, Rev. James Allen, *died* 1934, vol. III
Bell, James Mackintosh, 1877–1934, vol. III
Bell, James Young, 1877–1966, vol. VI
Bell, Sir John, 2nd Bt (*cr* 1895), 1876–1943, vol. IV
Bell, John, 1890–1958, vol. V
Bell, Col John B.; *see* Beatson-Bell.

Bell, Sir John Charles, 1st Bt (*cr* 1908), 1844–1924, vol. II
Bell, Sir John Ferguson, 1856–1937, vol. III
Bell, John Joy, 1871–1934, vol. III
Bell, John Keble, 1875–1928, vol. II
Bell, Ven. John White, *died* 1928, vol. II (A), vol. III
Bell, Lt-Col John William, 1844–1928, vol. II
Bell, Sir John William Anderson, 1873–1938, vol. III
Bell, Joseph, 1837–1911, vol. I
Bell, Hon. Joshua Thomas, 1863–1911, vol. I
Bell, Julia, 1879–1979, vol. VII
Bell, Rev. Kenneth Norman, 1884–1951, vol. V
Bell, Laird, 1883–1965, vol. VI
Bell, Lilian, *died* 1929, vol. III
Bell, Louis, 1864–1923, vol. II
Bell, Sir Lowthian, 1st Bt (*cr* 1885), 1816–1904, vol. I
Bell, Mackenzie; *see* Bell, H. T. M.
Bell, Col Mark Sever, 1843–1906, vol. I
Bell, Mrs Mary Taylor Watson, *died* 1943, vol. IV
Bell, Lt-Col Matthew Gerald Edward, 1871–1926, vol. II
Bell, Col Sir Maurice Hugh Lowthian, 3rd Bt (*cr* 1885), 1871–1944, vol. IV
Bell, Nancy R. E., *died* 1933, vol. III
Bell, Rev. Sir Nicholas Dodd Beatson, 1867–1936, vol. III
Bell, Norris Garrett, 1860–1937, vol. III
Bell, Oliver, 1898–1952, vol. V
Bell, Sir Peter; *see* Bell, Sir E. P. S.
Bell, Maj.-Gen. Peter Harvey, 1886–1963, vol. VI
Bell, Richard, 1859–1930, vol. III
Bell, Robert, 1841–1917, vol. II
Bell, Robert, 1845–1926, vol. II
Bell, Robert, 1863–1937, vol. III
Bell, Robert Anning, 1863–1933, vol. III
Bell, Sir Robert Duncan, 1878–1953, vol. V
Bell, Robert Stanley Warren, 1871–1921, vol. II
Bell, Sir Stanley, 1899–1972, vol. VII
Bell, Very Rev. Thomas, 1820–1917, vol. II
Bell, Sir Thomas, 1865–1952, vol. V
Bell, Sir Thomas Hugh; *see* Bell, Sir Hugh.
Bell, Thomas Reid Davys, *died* 1948, vol. IV
Bell, Hon. Valentine Græme, 1839–1908, vol. I
Bell, Walter George, *died* 1942, vol. IV
Bell, Col William, 1829–1913, vol. I
Bell, Rev. William, *died* 1918, vol. II
Bell, William, 1860–1946, vol. IV
Bell, William Abraham, 1841–1920, vol. II
Bell, William B.; *see* Blair-Bell.
Bell, Lt-Col William Cory Heward, 1875–1961, vol. VI
Bell, Rev. Canon William Godfrey, 1880–1953, vol. V
Bell, Sir William James, *died* 1913, vol. I
Bell-Irving, Lt-Col Andrew, 1855–1929, vol. III
Bell-Irving, James Jardine, 1859–1936, vol. III
Bell-Irving, John, 1846–1925, vol. II
Bell-Smith, Frederic Marlett, 1846–1923, vol. II
Bell-Smyth, Brig.-Gen. John Ambard, 1868–1922, vol. II
Bellairs, Comdr Carlyon, 1871–1955, vol. V

Bellairs, Hamon D'Albini, *died* 1932, vol. III
Bellairs, Rear-Adm. Roger Mowbray, 1884–1959, vol. V
Bellairs, Lt-Gen. Sir William, 1828–1913, vol. I
Bellamy, Albert, *died* 1931, vol. III
Bellamy, Charles Vincent, 1867–1938, vol. III
Bellamy, Dennis, 1894–1964, vol. VI
Bellamy, Edward, 1850–1898, vol. I
Bellamy, Rev. James, 1819–1909, vol. I
Bellamy, Sir Joseph Arthur, 1845–1918, vol. II
Bellamy, Lt-Col Robert, 1871–1927, vol. II
Bellamy, Brig. Robert Hugh, 1910–1972, vol. VII
Bellars, Rear-Adm. Edward Gerald Hyslop, 1894–1955, vol. V
Bellasis, Edward, 1852–1922, vol. II
Bellasis, Captain Richard O.; *see* Oliver-Bellasis.
Bellenger, Captain Rt Hon. Frederick John, 1894–1968, vol. VI
Bellerby, Rev. Alfred Courthope Benson, 1888–1979, vol. VII
Bellerby, Major John Rotherford, 1896–1977, vol. VII
Belleroche, Albert de, 1864–1944, vol. IV
Bellessort, André, 1861–1942, vol. IV
Bellew, 3rd Baron, 1855–1911, vol. I
Bellew, 4th Baron, 1857–1935, vol. III
Bellew, 5th Baron, 1889–1975, vol. VII
Bellew, Lt-Col Sir Charles Christopher G.; *see* Grattan-Bellew.
Bellew, Captain Edward Donald, 1882–1961, vol. VI
Bellew, Sir Henry Christopher G.; *see* Grattan-Bellew.
Bellew, Hon. Richard Eustace, 1858–1933, vol. III
Belley, Hon. L. G., 1863–1930, vol. III
Bellhouse, Sir Gerald, 1867–1946, vol. IV
Bellingham, Brig.-Gen. Sir Edward Henry Charles Patrick, 5th Bt, 1879–1956, vol. V
Bellingham, Sir Henry, 4th Bt, 1846–1921, vol. II
Bellingham, Sir Roger Carroll Patrick Stephen, 6th Bt, 1911–1973, vol. VII
Bellman, Sir Harold, 1886–1963, vol. VI
Bello, Alhaji Sir Ahmadu, 1909–1966, vol. VI
Belloc, Hilaire; *see* Belloc, J. H. P.
Belloc, (Joseph) Hilaire (Pierre), 1870–1953, vol. V
Belloc, Marie Adelaide, (Mrs Belloc Lowndes), 1868–1947, vol. IV
Bellot, Hugh Hale, 1890–1969, vol. VI
Bellot, Hugh Hale Leigh, 1860–1928, vol. II
Bellville, Captain George Ernest, 1879–1967, vol. VI
Belmont, August, 1853–1924, vol. II
Belmont, Perry, 1851–1947, vol. IV
Belmore, 4th Earl of, 1835–1913, vol. I
Belmore, 5th Earl of, 1870–1948, vol. IV
Belmore, 6th Earl of, 1873–1949, vol. IV
Belmore, 7th Earl of, 1913–1960, vol. V
Beloe, Vice-Adm. Sir (Isaac) William (Trant), 1909–1966, vol. VI
Beloe, Rev. Robert Douglas, 1868–1931, vol. III
Beloe, Vice-Adm. Sir William; *see* Beloe, Vice-Adm. Sir I. W. T.
Belper, 2nd Baron, 1840–1914, vol. I
Belper, 3rd Baron, 1883–1956, vol. V

Belsey, Sir Francis Flint, 1837–1914, vol. I
Belshaw, Edward, *died* 1916, vol. II
Belstead, 1st Baron, 1882–1958, vol. V
Belt, Comdr Francis Walter, 1862–1938, vol. III
Belton, Rev. Francis George, *died* 1962, vol. VI
Belton, Leslie James, 1897–1949, vol. IV
Bemelmans, Ludwig, 1898–1962, vol. VI
Bemont, Charles, 1848–1939, vol. III (A), vol. IV
Bemrose, Sir Henry Howe, 1827–1911, vol. I
Ben-Gurion, David, 1886–1973, vol. VII
Benares, Maharajah Bahadur of, 1855–1931, vol. III
Benares, Maharaja of, 1874–1939, vol. III
Benas, Bertram Benjamin Baron, *died* 1968, vol. VI
Benavente, Jacinto, 1866–1954, vol. V
Benbow, Sir Henry, 1838–1916, vol. II
Bence-Jones, Col Philip Reginald, 1897–1972, vol. VII
Bence-Lambert, Col Guy Lenox, 1856–1930, vol. III
Benckendorff, Count de, Alexandre, 1849–1917, vol. II
Bencraft, Sir Henry William Russell, 1858–1943, vol. IV
Benda, Wladyslaw Theodor, 1873–1948, vol. IV, vol. V
Bendall, Cecil, 1856–1906, vol. I
Bendall, Ernest Alfred, 1846–1924, vol. II
Bendall, Col Frederic William Duffield, 1882–1953, vol. V
Bender, Rev. A. P., 1863–1937, vol. III
Bender, William E. G., 1885–1961, vol. VI
Bendern, Count; Arnold Maurice, 1879–1968, vol. VI
Bendit, Gladys; *see* Presland, John.
Benecke, Paul V. M., 1868–1944, vol. IV
Benedict, Ruth Fulton, 1887–1948, vol. IV
Benedite, Leonce, *died* 1925, vol. II
Beneš, Dr Eduard, 1884–1948, vol. IV
Benét, Stephen Vincent, 1898–1943, vol. IV
Benét, William Rose, 1886–1950, vol. IV
Benett, Lt-Col Henry Cleeve, 1877–1941, vol. IV
Benfield, Brig. Karl Vere B.; *see* Barker-Benfield.
Benger, Berenger, 1868–1935, vol. III
Bengough, Guy Dunstan, 1876–1945, vol. IV
Bengough, Maj.-Gen. Sir Harcourt Mortimer, 1837–1922, vol. II
Benham, Frederic Charles Courtenay, *died* 1962, vol. VI
Benham, Sir Gurney; *see* Benham, Sir W. G.
Benham, Rev. William, 1831–1910, vol. I
Benham, Sir William Blaxland, 1860–1950, vol. IV
Benham, Sir (William) Gurney, 1859–1944, vol. IV
Benians, Ernest Alfred, 1880–1952, vol. V
Benin, Oba of; Akenzua II; Godfrey Okoro, 1899–1978, vol. VII
Benjamin, Arthur, 1893–1960, vol. V
Benjamin, Sir Benjamin, 1834–1905, vol. I
Benjamin, Lewis S., 1874–1932, vol. III
Benjamin, Louis Edmund, 1865–1935, vol. III
Benjamin-Constant, Jean Joseph, 1845–1902, vol. I
Benka-Coker, Sir Salako Ambrosius, 1900–1965, vol. VI
Benn, Alfred William, 1843–1916, vol. II

Benn, Engr Rear-Adm. Edward Piercy St John, 1872–1947, vol. IV

Benn, Sir Ernest John Pickstone, 2nd Bt (cr 1914), 1875–1954, vol. V

Benn, Ion Bridges Hamilton, 1887–1956, vol. V

Benn, Captain Sir Ion Hamilton, 1st Bt (cr 1920), 1863–1961, vol. VI

Benn, Sir John Williams, 1st Bt (cr 1914), 1850–1922, vol. II

Benn, Lt-Col Robert Arthur Edward, 1867–1940, vol. III

Bennet, Sir Edward, 1880–1958, vol. V

Bennet, Edward Armstrong, died 1977, vol. VII

Bennet, Maj.-Gen. John, 1893–1976, vol. VII

Bennet-Clark, Thomas Archibald, 1903–1975, vol. VII

Bennett, 1st Viscount, 1870–1947, vol. IV

Bennett of Edgbaston, 1st Baron, 1880–1957, vol. V

Bennett, Sir Albert Edward, 1900–1972, vol. VII

Bennett, Sir Albert James, 1st Bt, 1872–1945, vol. IV

Bennett, Alexander John Munro, 1868–1943, vol. IV

Bennett, Lt-Col Alfred Charles, died 1915, vol. I

Bennett, Alfred Gordon, 1901–1962, vol. VI

Bennett, Col Alfred Joshua, 1865–1946, vol. IV

Bennett, Alfred Rosling, 1850–1928, vol. II

Bennett, Alfred William, 1833–1902, vol. I

Bennett, Andrew Percy, 1866–1943, vol. IV

Bennett, Arnold; see Bennett, E. A.

Bennett, Arthur, 1862–1931, vol. III

Bennett, Cecil Harry Andrew, 1898–1967, vol. VI

Bennett, Engr-Rear-Adm. Cecil Reginald Percival, 1896–1976, vol. VII

Bennett, Sir Charles Alan, 1877–1943, vol. IV

Bennett, Lt-Col Charles Hugh, 1867–1932, vol. III

Bennett, Lt-Col Sir C(harles) Wilfrid, 2nd Bt, 1898–1952, vol. V

Bennett, Sir Courtenay Walter, 1855–1937, vol. III

Bennett, Cyril, 1928–1976, vol. VII

Bennett, Edward H., 1837–1907, vol. I

Bennett, (Enoch) Arnold, 1867–1931, vol. III

Bennett, Sir Ernest Nathaniel, died 1947, vol. IV

Bennett, Captain (Eugene) Paul, 1892–1970, vol. VI

Bennett, Sir Francis Sowerby, 1863–1950, vol. VI

Bennett, Very Rev. Frank Selwyn Macaulay, 1866–1947, vol. IV

Bennett, Rt Rev. Frederick Augustus, 1872–1950, vol. IV

Bennett, Rev. Frederick George, died 1937, vol. III

Bennett, Frederick Henry C.; see Curtis-Bennett.

Bennett, Geoffrey Thomas, died 1943, vol. IV

Bennett, Rev. George, 1855–1930, vol. III

Bennett, Rt Rev. George Henry, 1875–1946, vol. IV

Bennett, George John, 1863–1930, vol. III

Bennett, George Lovett, 1846–1916, vol. II

Bennett, George Macdonald, 1892–1959, vol. V

Bennett, George Wheatley, 1845–1921, vol. II

Bennett, Lt-Gen. Gordon; see Bennett, Lt-Gen. H. G.

Bennett, Henry Currie L.; see Leigh-Bennett.

Bennett, Sir Henry Curtis, 1846–1913, vol. I

Bennett, Lt-Gen. (Henry) Gordon, 1887–1962, vol. VI

Bennett, Sir Henry Honywood C.; see Curtis-Bennett.

Bennett, Rev. Henry Leigh, 1833–1912, vol. I

Bennett, Henry Stanley, 1889–1972, vol. VII

Bennett, James Allan Jamieson, 1903–1973, vol. VII

Bennett, James Gordon, 1841–1918, vol. II

Bennett, Engr Rear-Adm. James Martin Cameron, died 1922, vol. II

Bennett, Sir John, 1814–1897, vol. I

Bennett, Sir John, 1876–1948, vol. IV

Bennett, John, 1909–1975, vol. VII

Bennett, Sir John (Cecil) Sterndale, 1895–1969, vol. VI

Bennett, John Colburn, 1897–1969, vol. VI

Bennett, Hon. Sir John R., 1866–1941, vol. IV

Bennett, John Reginald William, 1888–1971, vol. VII

Bennett, John Still, 1911–1970, vol. VI

Bennett, Sir John Thorne Masey, 1894–1949, vol. IV

Bennett, John Wheeler W.; see Wheeler-Bennett.

Bennett, Sir John Wheeler W.; see Wheeler-Bennett.

Bennett, Kenneth Geoffrey, 1911–1974, vol. VII

Bennett, Sir Noel C.; see Curtis-Bennett.

Bennett, Sir Norman Godfrey, 1870–1947, vol. IV

Bennett, Captain Paul; see Bennett, Captain E. P.

Bennett, Percy Raymond L.; see Leigh-Bennett.

Bennett, Sir Reginald, died 1944, vol. IV

Bennett, Reginald Robert, 1879–1966, vol. VI

Bennett, Rex George, 1885–1972, vol. VII

Bennett, Robert Augustus, 1855–1929, vol. III

Bennett, Maj.-Gen. Roland Anthony, 1899–1974, vol. VII

Bennett, Rev. Canon Ronald Du Pré G.; see Grange-Bennett.

Bennett, Seymour John, 1848–1930, vol. III

Bennett, T. C. S.; see Sterndale-Bennett.

Bennett, T. Izod, 1887–1946, vol. IV

Bennett, Thomas Henry, died 1900, vol. I

Bennett, Sir Thomas Jewell, 1852–1925, vol. II

Bennett, Sir Thomas Penberthy, 1887–1980, vol. VII

Bennett, Comdr Thomas William, 1872–1939, vol. III

Bennett, Thomas William Westropp, 1867–1962, vol. VI

Bennett, Hon. Walter, 1864–1934, vol. III

Bennett, Lt-Col Sir Wilfrid; see Bennett, Lt-Col Sir C. W.

Bennett, Col William, 1835–1912, vol. I

Bennett, William, 1854–1935, vol. III

Bennett, William, 1873–1937, vol. III

Bennett, William Exall Tempest, 1858–1937, vol. III

Bennett, William H., 1859–1925, vol. II

Bennett, William Hart, 1861–1918, vol. II

Bennett, Sir William Henry, 1852–1931, vol. III

Bennett, Sir William James, 1896–1971, vol. VII

Bennett-Edwards, Mrs; see Edwards, Mrs B.

Bennett-Goldney, Francis, 1865–1918, vol. II

Benney, Ernest Alfred Sallis, 1894–1966, vol. VI

Benning, Captain Charles Stuart, 1884–1924, vol. II

Bennion, Claud, 1886–1976, vol. VII
Benoit, Pierre, 1886–1962, vol. VI
Benoy, Brig. James Francis, 1896–1972, vol. VII
Benoy, Maj.-Gen. John Meredith, 1896–1977, vol. VII
Benskin, Gladys, (Mrs Joseph Benskin), died 1978, vol. VII
Benskin, Col Joseph, 1883–1953, vol. V
Bensley, Benjamin Arthur, 1875–1934, vol. III
Bensley, Col Clement Henry, 1870–1940, vol. III
Bensley, Edward von Blomberg, 1863–1939, vol. III
Bensly, Rev. William James, 1874–1943, vol. IV
Benson, Arthur Christopher, 1862–1925, vol. II
Benson, Arthur Henry, 1852–1912, vol. I
Benson, Air Cdre Constantine Evelyn, died 1960, vol. V
Benson, Rear-Adm. Cyril Herbert Gordon, 1884–1974, vol. VII
Benson, Edward Frederic, 1867–1940, vol. III
Benson, Hon. (Eleanor) Theodora Roby, 1906–1968, vol. VI
Benson, Sir Frank, 1878–1952, vol. V
Benson, Sir Frank Robert, 1858–1939, vol. III
Benson, Frank Weston, 1862–1951, vol. V
Benson, Maj.-Gen. Sir Frederick William, 1849–1916, vol. II
Benson, Sir George, 1889–1973, vol. VII
Benson, Guy Holford, 1888–1975, vol. VII
Benson, Hon. Lt-Col Henry Wightman, 1855–1935, vol. III
Benson, Sir J. Hawtrey, 1843–1931, vol. III
Benson, James Bourne, 1848–1930, vol. III
Benson, Rev. John Peter, died 1944, vol. IV
Benson, Margaret J., died 1936, vol. III
Benson, Rev. Niale Shane Trevor, 1911–1980, vol. VII
Benson, Percy George Reginald, 1872–1961, vol. VI
Benson, Surg.-Gen. Percy Hugh, 1852–1933, vol. III
Benson, Philip de Gylpyn, 1883–1931, vol. III
Benson, Preston, 1896–1975, vol. VII
Benson, Col Ralph Hawtrey Rohde, 1880–1943, vol. IV
Benson, Sir Ralph Sillery, 1851–1920, vol. II
Benson, Lt-Col Sir Rex Lindsay, 1889–1968, vol. IV
Benson, Rev. Richard Meux, 1824–1915, vol. I
Benson, Brig.-Gen. Riou Philip, 1863–1939, vol. III
Benson, Brig. Robert, 1881–1952, vol. V
Benson, Vice-Adm. Robert Edmund Ross, died 1927, vol. II
Benson, Robert Henry, 1850–1929, vol. III
Benson, Very Rev. Mgr Robert Hugh, 1871–1914, vol. I
Benson, Col Starling Meux, 1846–1933, vol. III
Benson, Stella, 1892–1933, vol. III
Benson, Stephen Riou, died 1961, vol. VI
Benson, Hon. Theodora; see Benson, Hon. E. T. R.
Benson, Ven. Thomas M., died 1921, vol. II
Benson, Col Wallace, died 1951, vol. V
Benson, William Arthur Smith, 1854–1924, vol. II
Benson, William Denman, 1848–1919, vol. II
Benson, Col William George Sackville, 1861–1954, vol. V

Benson, William John, died 1941, vol. IV
Benson, William Noël, 1885–1957, vol. V
Benstead, Sir John, 1897–1979, vol. VII
Bensusan, Samuel Levy, 1872–1958, vol. V
Bent, Col Arthur Milton, 1870–1940, vol. III
Bent, Col Charles Edward, 1880–1955, vol. V
Bent, Rear-Adm. Eric Ritchie, 1888–1949, vol. IV
Bent, James Theodore, 1852–1897, vol. I
Bent, Mabel Virginia Anna, (Mrs Theodore Bent), died 1929, vol. III
Bent, Mrs Theodore; see Bent, M. V. A.
Bent, Hon. Sir Thomas, 1838–1909, vol. I
Bentall, Gerald Chalmers, 1903–1971, vol. VII
Benthall, Sir Edward Charles, 1893–1961, vol. VI
Benthall, Major John Lawrence, 1868–1947, vol. IV
Benthall, Michael Pickersgill, 1919–1974, vol. VII
Bentham, Ethel, died 1931, vol. III
Bentham, George Jackson, 1863–1929, vol. III
Bentham, Percy George, 1883–1936, vol. III
Bentinck, Baron Adolph Willem Carel, 1905–1970, vol. VI
Bentinck, Arthur Harold Walter, died 1964, vol. VI
Bentinck, Lt-Col Lord Charles C.; see Cavendish-Bentinck.
Bentinck, Rev. Charles D., 1866–1940, vol. III
Bentinck, Rev. Sir Charles Henry, 1879–1955, vol. V
Bentinck, Frederick Cavendish-, 1856–1948, vol. IV
Bentinck, Lord Henry Cavendish, 1863–1931, vol. III
Bentinck, Lady Norah, died 1939, vol. III
Bentinck, Adm. Sir Rudolph Walter, 1869–1947, vol. IV
Bentinck, Baron Walter Guy, 1864–1957, vol. V
Bentinck, Lord William Augustus Cavendish-, 1865–1903, vol. I
Bentinck, Count William Charles Philip Otho, 1848–1912, vol. I
Bentley, Alfred, died 1923, vol. II
Bentley, Arthur Owen, 1898–1943, vol. IV
Bentley, Bertram Henry, 1873–1946, vol. IV
Bentley, Charles Albert, 1873–1949, vol. IV
Bentley, Rt Rev. David Williams Bentley, died 1970, vol. VI
Bentley, Edmund Clerihew, 1875–1956, vol. V
Bentley, Col Francis I., 1868–1938, vol. III
Bentley, Frederic Herbert, 1905–1980, vol. VII
Bentley, Nicolas Clerihew, 1907–1978, vol. VII
Bentley, Phyllis Eleanor, 1894–1977, vol. VII
Bentley, Richard, 1854–1936, vol. III
Bentley, Walter Owen, 1888–1971, vol. VII
Bentley-Buckle, Lt-Col Arthur William; see Buckle.
Bentliff, Hubert David, 1891–1953, vol. V
Bentliff, Walter David, 1859–1940, vol. III
Benton, Sir John, 1850–1927, vol. II
Benton, William, 1900–1973, vol. VII
Bentwich, Helen Caroline, (Mrs Norman Bentwich), 1892–1972, vol. VII
Bentwich, Herbert, 1856–1932, vol. III
Bentwich, Norman, 1883–1971, vol. VII
Benuarrat, 7th Baron of, 1870–1935, vol. III
Benyon, Sir Henry Arthur, 1st Bt, 1884–1959, vol. V
Benyon, James Herbert, 1849–1935, vol. III

Benyon, Vice-Adm. Richard, 1892–1968, vol. VI
Benziger, August, 1867–1955, vol. V
Benzinger, Immanuel G. A., *born* 1865, vol. III
Beoku-Betts, Sir Ernest Samuel, 1895–1957, vol. V
Berar, State of; Gen. HH the Prince of, 1907–1970, vol. VI (AII)
Berard, Victor, 1864–1931, vol. III
Bercovici, Konrad, *died* 1961, vol. VI
Berendsen, Sir Carl August, *died* 1973, vol. VII
Berens, Alexander Augustus, 1842–1926, vol. II
Berenson, Bernhard, 1865–1959, vol. V
Beresford, 1st Baron, 1846–1919, vol. II
Beresford, Ven. Alfred Richard Angland, *died* 1936, vol. III
Beresford, Cecil Hugh W., *died* 1912, vol. I
Beresford, Col Charles Edward de la Poer, 1850–1921, vol. II
Beresford, Rev. Charles John, 1868–1936, vol. III
Beresford, Denis R. P.; *see* Pack-Beresford.
Beresford, George de la Poer, 1831–1906, vol. I
Beresford, Maj.-Gen. Sir George de la Poer, *died* 1964, vol. VI
Beresford, Jack, 1899–1977, vol. VII
Beresford, Rev. John, 1839–1918, vol. II
Beresford, John Baldwyn, 1888–1940, vol. III
Beresford, Maj.-Gen. John Beresford, *born* 1828, vol. II
Beresford, John Davys, 1873–1947, vol. IV
Beresford, John George M.; *see* Massy-Beresford.
Beresford, John Stuart, 1845–1926, vol. II
Beresford, Lord Marcus de la Poer, 1848–1922, vol. II
Beresford, Marcus Henry de la Poer, 1857–1934, vol. III
Beresford, Lt-Gen. Mostyn de la Poer, 1835–1911, vol. I
Beresford, Hon. Seton Robert de la Poer Horsley, 1868–1928, vol. II
Beresford, Tristram de la Poer, 1887–1962, vol. VI
Beresford, Lady William, *died* 1909, vol. I
Beresford, Lord William Leslie de la Poer, 1847–1900, vol. I
Beresford-Peirse, Major Sir Henry Bernard de la Poer, 4th Bt, 1875–1949, vol. IV
Beresford-Peirse, Sir Henry Campbell de la Poer, 5th Bt, 1905–1972, vol. VII
Beresford-Peirse, Sir Henry Monson de la Poer, 3rd Bt, 1850–1926, vol. II
Beresford-Peirse, Lt-Gen. Sir Noel Monson de la Poer, 1887–1953, vol. V
Beresford-Peirse, Rev. Richard Windham de la Poer, 1876–1952, vol. V
Beresford-Peirse, Rev. Canon Windham de la Poer, 1858–1940, vol. III
Berg, Alban, 1885–1935, vol. III
Berger, Francesco, 1834–1933, vol. III
Berget, Baron Alphonse, 1860–1933, vol. III
Bergh, Rt Rev. Frederick Thomas, 1840–1924, vol. II
Bergholt, Ernest George Binckes, 1856–1925, vol. II
Bergin, Osborn Joseph, *died* 1950, vol. IV
Bergin, William, 1864–1942, vol. IV

Bergius, Friedrich Karl Rudolph, 1884–1949, vol. IV
Bergne, Sir John Henry Gibbs, 1842–1908, vol. I
Bergson, Henri Louis, 1859–1941, vol. IV
Beringer, Oscar, 1844–1922, vol. II
Beringer, Mrs Oscar, 1856–1936, vol. III
Berkeley, 8th Earl, 1865–1942, vol. IV
Berkeley, Baroness (15th in line), 1840–1899, vol. I
Berkeley, Baroness (16th in line), 1875–1964, vol. VI
Berkeley, Rt Rev. Alfred Pakenham, 1862–1938, vol. III
Berkeley, Lt-Col Arthur Mowbray, 1870–1937, vol. III
Berkeley, Lt-Col Christopher Robert, 1877–1959, vol. V
Berkeley, Sir Comyns, 1865–1946, vol. IV
Berkeley, Sir Ernest James Lennox, 1857–1932, vol. III
Berkeley, Essex Digby, 1843–1936, vol. III
Berkeley, Maj.-Gen. Frederick George, 1841–1906, vol. I
Berkeley, Sir George, 1819–1905, vol. I
Berkeley, Sir Henry Spencer, 1851–1918, vol. II
Berkeley, Maj.-Gen. James Cavan, 1839–1926, vol. II
Berkeley, Sir Maurice Julian, *died* 1931, vol. III
Berkeley, Captain Reginald Cheyne, 1890–1935, vol. III
Berkeley, Robert Valentine, 1853–1940, vol. III
Berkeley, Stanley, *died* 1909, vol. I
Berkin, John Phillip, 1905–1979, vol. VII
Berle, Adolf Augustus, 1895–1971, vol. VII
Berliner, Emile, 1851–1929, vol. III
Berlyn, Alfred, *died* 1936, vol. III
Berlyn, Mrs Alfred, *died* 1943, vol. IV
Berlyn, Bernard Henry Alfred Forbes, 1886–1936, vol. III
Bermingham, Engr-Rear-Adm. Cecil Henry Alec, 1870–1938, vol. III
Bernacchi, Louis Charles, 1876–1942, vol. IV
Bernadotte, Count Folke, 1895–1948, vol. IV
Bernal, Frederic, 1828–1924, vol. II
Bernal, Lt-Col Greville Hugh Woodlee, *died* 1922 vol. II
Bernal, John Desmond, 1901–1971, vol. VII
Bernal, Ralph, 1867–1938, vol. III
Bernard, Albert Victor, 1885–1955, vol. V
Bernard, Andrew Milroy F.; *see* Fleming-Bernard.
Bernard, Anthony, 1891–1963, vol. VI
Bernard, Hon. Charles Brodrick Amyas, 1904–1977, vol. VII
Bernard, Sir Charles Edward, 1837–1901, vol. I
Bernard, Sir Dallas Gerald Mercer, 1st Bt, 1888–1975, vol. VII
Bernard, Lt-Gen. Sir Denis Kirwan, 1882–1956, vol. V
Bernard, Col Sir Edgar Edwin, 1866–1931, vol. III
Bernard, Rev. Edward Russell, 1842–1921, vol. II
Bernard, Rt Rev. Eustace Anthony M.; *see* Morrogh Bernard.
Bernard, Francis Georgius, 1908–1978, vol. VII
Bernard, Lt-Col Francis Tyringham H.; *see* Higgins Bernard.

Bernard, Jean-Jacques, 1888–1972, vol. VII
Bernard, Most Rev. and Rt Hon. John Henry, 1860–1927, vol. II
Bernard, Col Joseph Francis, 1871–1953, vol. V
Bernard, Oliver Percy, 1881–1939, vol. III
Bernard, Percy Brodrick, 1844–1912, vol. I
Bernard, Lt-Col Ronald Percy Hamilton, 1875–1921, vol. II
Bernard, Col Ronald Playfair St Vincent, 1888–1943, vol. IV
Bernard, Rev. Thomas Dehany, 1815–1904, vol. I
Bernard, Adm. Vivian Henry Gerald, 1868–1934, vol. III
Bernard, Lt-Col William Kingsmill, 1872–1933, vol. III
Bernays, Charles Arrowsmith, 1862–1940, vol. III
Bernays, Comdr Leopold Arthur, died 1917, vol. II
Bernays, Lewis Adolphus, 1831–1908, vol. I
Bernays, Lewis Edward, 1886–1972, vol. VII
Bernays, Robert Hamilton, 1902–1945, vol. IV
Berners, Baroness (7th in line), 1835–1917, vol. II
Berners, 8th Baron, 1855–1918, vol. II
Berners, 14th (de facto 9th) Baron, 1883–1950, vol. IV
Berners, John Anstruther, died 1934, vol. III
Berners, Brig.-Gen. Ralph Abercrombie, 1871–1949, vol. IV
Berney, Sir Henry, 1862–1953, vol. V
Berney, Sir Henry Hanson, 9th Bt, 1843–1907, vol. I
Berney, Captain Sir Thomas Reedham, 10th Bt, 1893–1975, vol. VII
Berney-Ficklin, Maj.-Gen. Horatio Pettus Mackintosh, 1892–1961, vol. VI
Bernhardt, Sarah, 1845–1923, vol. II
Bernier, Captain Joseph Elzear, 1852–1934, vol. III
Bernier, Hon. Michel Esdras, 1841–1921, vol. II
Bernier, Hon. Thomas Alfred, 1844–1909, vol. I
Bernstein, Henri, 1876–1953, vol. V
Bernstorff, Count John, 1862–1939, vol. III
Berrangé, Major Christian Anthony Lawson, 1864–1922, vol. II
Berridge, Harold, 1872–1949, vol. IV
Berridge, Sir Thomas Henry Devereux, 1857–1924, vol. II
Berrie, John Archibald Alexander, 1887–1962, vol. VI
Berrow, William Lewis, 1862–1928, vol. II
Berry, Lt-Col Alfred Eugene, 1869–1932, vol. III
Berry, Arthur, 1862–1929, vol. III
Berry, Rev. Charles Albert, 1852–1899, vol. I
Berry, Rev. Edward Arthur, 1871–1949, vol. IV
Berry, (Frances) May Dickinson, 1857–1934, vol. III
Berry, Sir George Andreas, 1853–1940, vol. III
Berry, Hon. Sir Graham, 1822–1904, vol. I
Berry, Henry, 1883–1956, vol. V
Berry, Henry Fitz-Patrick, born 1847, vol. II
Berry, Sir (Henry) Vaughan, 1891–1979, vol. VII
Berry, Very Rev. Hugh Frederick, died 1961, vol. VI (AII)
Berry, Prof. Jack, 1918–1980, vol. VII (AII)
Berry, Sir James, 1860–1946, vol. IV
Berry, John Stanley, 1915–1975, vol. VII

Berry, John William Edward, 1901–1971, vol. VII
Berry, Martha McChesney, 1866–1942, vol. IV
Berry, May Dickinson; see Berry, F. M. D.
Berry, Richard James Arthur, 1867–1962, vol. VI
Berry, Robert, 1825–1903, vol. I
Berry, Rev. Sidney Malcolm, 1881–1961, vol. VI
Berry, Rt Rev. Thomas Sterling, 1854–1931, vol. III
Berry, Trevor T.; see Thornton-Berry.
Berry, Sir Vaughan; see Berry, Sir H. V.
Berry, Sir Walter Wheeler, 1857–1933, vol. III
Berry, Sir William John, 1865–1937, vol. III
Berry, Hon. Sir William Bisset-, 1839–1922, vol. II
Berry, William Grinton, 1873–1926, vol. II
Berryman, Sir Frederick Henry, 1869–1952, vol. V
Berryman, John, 1914–1972, vol. VII
Berryman, Montague Levander, 1899–1974, vol. VII
Berteau, Francis Cyrus, 1856–1945, vol. IV
Berteaux, Henry Maurice, 1852–1911, vol. I
Bertenshaw, Eric Strickland, 1888–1957, vol. V
Berthon, Rear-Adm. Charles Pierre, 1893–1965, vol. VI
Berthon, Rev. Edward Lyon, 1813–1899, vol. I
Berthon, Henry Edward, 1862–1948, vol. IV
Berthoud, Edward Henry, 1876–1955, vol. V
Berthoulat, Georges, 1859–1930, vol. III
Bertie of Thame, 1st Viscount, 1844–1919, vol. II
Bertie of Thame, 2nd Viscount, 1878–1954, vol. V
Bertie, Rev. Hon. Alberic Edward, 1846–1928, vol. II
Bertie, Major Hon. Arthur Michael, 1886–1957, vol. V
Bertie, Lt-Col Hon. George Aubrey Vere, 1850–1926, vol. II
Bertie, Col Hon. Reginald Henry, 1856–1950, vol. IV
Bertillon, Alphonse, 1853–1914, vol. I
Bertouch, Baroness de, Beatrice, died 1931, vol. III
Bertram, Brig.-Gen. Sir Alexander, 1853–1926, vol. II
Bertram, Anthony, 1897–1978, vol. VII
Bertram, Sir Anton, 1869–1937, vol. III
Bertram, Edith, (Lady Bertram), died 1959, vol. V
Bertram, Francis George Lawder, 1875–1938, vol. III
Bertram, Sir George Clement, 1841–1915, vol. I (A)
Bertram, Julius, 1866–1944, vol. IV
Bertram, Louis John, 1859–1940, vol. III
Bertram, Neville Rennie, 1909–1974, vol. VII
Bertram, Lt-Col William Robert, 1888–1970, vol. VI
Bertrand, Cavalier Léon, 1897–1980, vol. VII
Bertrand, Louis Marie Emile, 1866–1941, vol. IV
Beruete y Moret, Aureliano de, 1878–1922, vol. II (A), vol. III
Berwick, 7th Baron, 1847–1897, vol. I
Berwick, 8th Baron, 1877–1947, vol. IV
Berwick, 9th Baron, 1897–1953, vol. V
Berwick, T., 1826–1915, vol. I
Berwick, William Edward Hodgson, 1888–1944, vol. IV
Besant, Annie, 1847–1933, vol. III
Besant, Arthur Digby, 1869–1960, vol. V

Besant, Sir Walter, 1836–1901, vol. I
Besant, William Henry, 1828–1917, vol. II
Besicovitch, Abram Samoilovitch, 1891–1970, vol. VI
Besier, Rudolf, 1878–1942, vol. IV
Besley, Edward Thomas Edmonds, 1826–1901, vol. I
Besley, Rev. Walter Philip, 1870–1934, vol. III
Besly, Ernest Francis Withers, 1891–1965, vol. VI
Besly, Maurice, 1888–1945, vol. IV
Besnard, Paul Albert, 1849–1934, vol. III
Bessborough, 7th Earl of, 1821–1906, vol. I
Bessborough, 8th Earl of, 1851–1920, vol. II
Bessborough, 9th Earl of, 1880–1956, vol. V
Bessell-Browne, Brig.-Gen. Alfred Joseph; see Browne.
Bessemer, Sir Henry, 1813–1898, vol. I
Best, Charles Herbert, 1899–1978, vol. VII
Best, Edna, 1900–1974, vol. VII
Best, Elsdon, 1856–1931, vol. III
Best, George Percival, 1872–1953, vol. V
Best, Captain Humphrey Willie, 1884–1959, vol. V
Best, Hon. James William, 1882–1960, vol. V
Best, Rev. John Dugdale, 1856–1933, vol. III
Best, Sir John Victor Hall, died 1972, vol. VII
Best, Ven. Joseph, 1880–1965, vol. VI
Best, Hon. Margaret, 1872–1941, vol. IV
Best, Adm. Hon. Sir Matthew Robert, 1878–1940, vol. III
Best, Rt Hon. Richard, died 1939, vol. III
Best, Richard Irvine, 1872–1959, vol. V
Best, Hon. Robert Rainy, 1834–1903, vol. I
Best, Hon. Sir Robert Wallace, 1856–1946, vol. IV
Best, Sir Thomas Alexander Vans, 1870–1941, vol. IV
Beste, Captain Sir Henry Aloysius Bruno D.; see Digby-Beste.
Besterman, Theodore Deodatus Nathaniel, 1904–1976, vol. VII
Betham, Lt-Col Sir Geoffrey Lawrence, 1889–1963, vol. VI
Betham, Brig.-Gen. Robert Mitchell, 1864–1939, vol. III
Betham-Edwards, Matilda; see Edwards.
Bethel, Albert, born 1874, vol. III
Bethell, 1st Baron, 1861–1945, vol. IV
Bethell, 2nd Baron, 1902–1965, vol. VI
Bethell, 3rd Baron, 1928–1967, vol. VI
Bethell, Captain Adrian, 1890–1941, vol. IV
Bethell, Hon. (Albert) Victor, 1864–1927, vol. II
Bethell, Adm. Hon. Sir Alexander Edward, 1855–1932, vol. III
Bethell, Col Alfred Bryan, 1875–1956, vol. V
Bethell, Col Edward Hugh, 1854–1940, vol. III
Bethell, George Richard, 1849–1919, vol. II
Bethell, Brig.-Gen. Henry Arthur, 1861–1939, vol. III
Bethell, Maj.-Gen. Sir (Hugh) Keppel, 1882–1947, vol. IV
Bethell, Maj.-Gen. Sir Keppel; see Bethell, Maj.-Gen. Sir H. K.
Bethell, Hon. Richard, 1883–1929, vol. III
Bethell, Sir Thomas Robert, died 1957, vol. V
Bethell, Hon. Victor; see Bethell, Hon. A. V.

Bethell, William, 1847–1926, vol. II
Bethune, Rev. Charles James Stewart, 1838–1932, vol. III
Bethune, Lt-Gen. Sir Edward Cecil, 1855–1930, vol. III
Bethune, Francis John, 1860–1954, vol. V
Bethune, Lt-Col Henry Alexander, 1866–1946, vol. IV
Bethune, Henry Leonard, 1858–1939, vol. III
Bethune, Rev. John Walter, 1882–1960, vol. V
Bethune, Strachan, 1821–1910, vol. I
Bethune-Baker, Rev. James Franklin, 1861–1951, vol. V
Betjemann, Gilbert H., 1840–1921, vol. II
Bett, Rev. Henry, 1876–1953, vol. V
Bett, Surg. Rear-Adm. William, 1863–1946, vol. IV
Bettany, Frederick George, 1868–1942, vol. IV
Betteridge, Don; see Newman, Bernard.
Bettington, Gp Captain (Arthur) Vere, 1881–1950, vol. IV
Bettington, Gp Captain Vere; see Bettington, Gp Captain A. V.
Bettmann, Siegfried, 1863–1951, vol. V
Betts, Mrs E. M.; see Hayes, Gertrude.
Betts, Edward William, 1881–1980, vol. VII
Betts, Captain Ernest Edward Alexander, 1877–1951, vol. V
Betts, Sir Ernest Samuel B.; see Beoku-Betts.
Betts, Frederick Pimlott, 1853–1930, vol. III
Betts, James Anthony, 1897–1980, vol. VII
Betts, Reginald Robert, 1903–1961, vol. VI
Betts, William Andrew, 1866–1945, vol. IV
Betty, Vice-Adm. Arthur K.; see Kemmis Betty.
Betty, Lt-Col Paget K.; see Kemmis Betty.
Betuel, Herbert William Norman, 1908–1980, vol. VII
Beuttler, Brig. V. O., 1886–1948, vol. IV
Bevan, Sir Alfred H., died 1900, vol. I
Bevan, Rt Hon. Aneurin, 1897–1960, vol. V
Bevan, Anthony Ashley, 1859–1933, vol. III
Bevan, Cosmo, 1863–1935, vol. III
Bevan, Sir David Martyn E.; see Evans Bevan.
Bevan, Rt Rev. Edward Latham, 1861–1934, vol. III
Bevan, Edwyn Robert, 1870–1943, vol. IV
Bevan, Francis Augustus, 1840–1919, vol. II
Bevan, Frederick Charles, born 1856, vol. III
Bevan, Captain George Parker, 1878–1920, vol. II
Bevan, Ven. Henry Edward James, 1854–1935, vol. III
Bevan, Ven. Hugh Henry Molesworth, 1884–1970, vol. VI
Bevan, John Henry, 1894–1978, vol. VII
Bevan, John Sage, 1900–1978, vol. VII
Bevan, Lawrence Emlyn Douglas, 1903–1972, vol. VII
Bevan, Major Rev. Llewelyn David, 1842–1918, vol. II
Bevan, Hon. Dame Maud Elizabeth, 1856–1944, vol. IV
Bevan, Rear-Adm. Sir Richard Hugh Loraine, 1885–1976, vol. VII
Bevan, Robert Alexander Polhill, 1901–1974, vol. VII

Bevan, Stuart James, *died* 1935, vol. III
Bevan, Wilfred, 1866–1940, vol. III
Bevan, Ven. William Latham, 1821–1908, vol. I
Bevan-Baker, Bevan Braithwaite, 1890–1963, vol. VI
Bevan-Lewis, William, 1847–1929, vol. III
Bevenot, Clovis, *died* 1925, vol. II
Beveridge, 1st Baron, 1879–1963, vol. VI
Beveridge, Lady; (Janet), 1876–1959, vol. V
Beveridge, Alexander William Morton, *died* 1959, vol. V
Beveridge, Maj.-Gen. Arthur Joseph, 1893–1959, vol. V
Beveridge, Erskine, 1851–1920, vol. II
Beveridge, Rev. John, 1857–1943, vol. IV
Beveridge, Maj.-Gen. Sir Wilfred William Ogilvy, 1864–1962, vol. VI
Beverley, Rt Rev. Alton Ray, 1884–1956, vol. V
Beverley, Frank, *died* 1972, vol. VII
Bevers, Edmund Cecil, 1876–1961, vol. VI
Beves, Donald Howard, 1896–1961, vol. VI
Beves, Brig.-Gen. Percival Scott, 1868–1924, vol. II
Beville, Lt-Col Charles Hamilton, 1865–1934, vol. III
Beville, Lt-Col Francis Granville, 1867–1923, vol. II
Beville, Gen. Sir George Francis, 1837–1913, vol. I
Bevin, Rt Hon. Ernest, 1881–1951, vol. V
Bevin, Dame Florence Anne, *died* 1968, vol. VI
Bevir, Sir Anthony, 1895–1977, vol. VII
Bevir, Vice-Adm. Oliver, 1891–1967, vol. VI
Bewerunge, Rev. Henry, *born* 1862, vol. II
Bewes, Lt-Col Arthur Edward, 1871–1922, vol. II
Bewes, Wyndham Austis, 1857–1942, vol. IV
Bewick, Ralph Martin, 1861–1934, vol. III
Bewick-Copley, Brig.-Gen. Sir Robert Calverley Alington Bewicke, 1855–1923, vol. II
Bewley, Col Alfred William, 1866–1939, vol. III
Bewley, Sir Edmund Thomas, 1837–1908, vol. I
Bewley, Henry, 1860–1945, vol. IV
Bewley, Thomas Kenneth, 1890–1943, vol. IV
Bewley, William Fleming, 1891–1976, vol. VII
Bewoor, Sir Gurunath Venkatesh, *died* 1950, vol. IV
Bews, John William, 1884–1938, vol. III
Bewsher, Brig. Frederick William, 1886–1950, vol. IV
Bewsher, Paul, 1894–1966, vol. VI
Bewsher, Lt-Col William Dent, 1868–1942, vol. IV
Bex, Charles James, *died* 1940, vol. III
Beyen, Johan Willem, 1897–1976, vol. VII
Beyers, Brig.-Gen. Hon. Christian Frederick, 1869–1914, vol. I
Beyers, Hon. Fredrik William, 1867–1938, vol. III
Beyfus, Gilbert Hugh, 1885–1960, vol. V
Beynon, Albert Gwyn, 1908–1978, vol. VII
Beynon, Major Godfrey Evan Schaw P.; *see* Protheroe-Beynon.
Beynon, Brig.-Gen. Henry Lawrence Norman, 1868–1950, vol. IV
Beynon, Sir John Wyndham, 1st Bt, *died* 1944, vol. IV
Beynon, Maj.-Gen. Sir William George Lawrence, 1866–1955, vol. V

Bezzant, Rev. Canon James Stanley, 1897–1967, vol. VI
Bhabha, H. J., 1852–1941, vol. IV
Bhabha, Homi Jehangir, 1909–1966, vol. VI
Bhagat, Lt-Gen. Premindra Singh, 1918–1975, vol. VII
Bhalja, Govardhan Shankerlal, 1895–1948, vol. IV (A), vol. V
Bhandari, Rai Bahadur Sir Gopal Das, 1860–1927, vol. II
Bhandarkar, Devadatta Ramkrishna, 1875–1950, vol. IV (A), vol. V
Bhandarkar, Sir Ramkrishna Gopal, 1837–1925, vol. II
Bhanot, Harnam Dass, 1897–1948, vol. IV
Bharatpur, Maharaja of, 1899–1929, vol. III
Bhatawadekar, Sir Bhalchandra Krishna, *born* 1852, vol. III
Bhatnagar, Sir Shanti Swarupa, 1895–1955, vol. V
Bhatt, Ramchandra Madhavram, 1874–1936, vol. III
Bhavnagar, HH Maharaja of, 1875–1919, vol. II
Bhopal, HH Nawab Shah Jahan Begum, 1838–1901, vol. I
Bhopal, HH Nawab Sultan Jehan Begum, 1858–1930, vol. III
Bhopal, Ruler of, 1894–1960, vol. V
Bhore, Sir Joseph William, 1878–1960, vol. V
Bhownagree, Sir Mancherjee Merwanjee, 1851–1933, vol. III
Bhutan, Maharajah of, 1861–1926, vol. II
Bhutto, Zulfikar Ali, 1928–1979, vol. VII
Biagi, Guido, 1855–1925, vol. II
Biancardi, Lt Col Nicola G.; *see* Grech-Biancardi.
Bibby, Arthur Wilson, 1846–1935, vol. III
Bibby, Major Brian; *see* Bibby, Major F. B. F.
Bibby, Frank, 1857–1923, vol. II
Bibby, Major (Frank) Brian (Frederic), 1893–1929, vol. III
Bibby, John Hartley, 1864–1938, vol. III
Bibby, Joseph, 1851–1940, vol. III
Bibesco, Prince Antoine, 1878–1951, vol. V
Bice, Hon. Sir John George, 1853–1923, vol. II
Bicester, 1st Baron, 1867–1956, vol. V
Bicester, 2nd Baron, 1898–1968, vol. VI
Bickerdyke, John, (Charles Henry Cook), 1858–1933, vol. III
Bickerstaffe, Sir John, 1848–1930, vol. III
Bickerstaffe-Drew, Rt Rev. Mgr Count Francis Browning Drew, 1858–1928, vol. II
Bickersteth, Rt Rev. Edward, 1850–1897, vol. I
Bickersteth, Rt Rev. Edward Henry, 1825–1906, vol. I
Bickersteth, Rev. Canon Edward Monier, 1882–1976, vol. VII
Bickersteth, Geoffrey Langdale, 1884–1974, vol. VII
Bickersteth, John Burgon, 1888–1979, vol. VII
Bickersteth, John Joseph, 1850–1932, vol. III
Bickersteth, John Richard, 1897–1967, vol. VI
Bickersteth, Rev. Kenneth Julian Faithfull, 1885–1962, vol. VI
Bickersteth, Rev. Montagu Cyril, 1858–1936, vol. III

Bickersteth, Robert Alexander, 1862–1924, vol. II
Bickersteth, Rev. Samuel, 1857–1937, vol. III
Bickerton, Alexander William, 1842–1929, vol. III
Bickerton, John Myles, 1894–1977, vol. VII
Bickerton, Reginald Ernest, 1870–1949, vol. IV
Bicket, Sir Alexander, 1853–1931, vol. III
Bicket, Brig.-Gen. William Neilson, 1883–1978, vol. VII
Bickford, Adm. Andrew Kennedy, 1844–1927, vol. II
Bickford, Major Arthur Louis, 1870–1916, vol. II
Bickford, Brig.-Gen. Edward, 1861–1949, vol. IV
Bickford, Rt Rev. Mgr Francis P., 1889–1968, vol. VI
Bickford, Captain William George Hastings, died 1932, vol. III
Bickford, Rev. William Pennington, 1874–1941, vol. IV
Bickford, Col William Wilfrid, 1871–1951, vol. V
Bickley, Francis Lawrance, 1885–1976, vol. VII
Bickley, William Gee, 1893–1969, vol. VI
Bicknell, Rev. Edward John, died 1934, vol. III
Bicknell, Lt-Col Henry Percy Frank, 1879–1940, vol. III
Bidder, George Parker, 1863–1953, vol. V
Bidder, Maurice McClean, 1879–1934, vol. III
Biddle, A. J. Drexel, 1874–1948, vol. IV
Biddle, Maj.-Gen. Anthony J. Drexel, 1896–1961, vol. VI
Biddle, Francis, 1886–1968, vol. VI
Biddle, Major Fred Leslie, 1885–1917, vol. II
Biddle, Maj.-Gen. John, 1859–1936, vol. III
Biddle, Sir Reginald Poulton, 1888–1970, vol. VI
Biddlecombe, Rev. Stuart Holman, 1879–1944, vol. IV
Biddulph, 1st Baron, 1834–1923, vol. II
Biddulph, 2nd Baron, 1869–1949, vol. IV
Biddulph, 3rd Baron, 1898–1972, vol. VII
Biddulph, Assheton, 1850–1916, vol. II
Biddulph, Sir Francis Henry, 9th Bt, 1882–1980, vol. VII
Biddulph, Brig.-Gen. Harry, 1872–1952, vol. V
Biddulph, Lt-Col Hope, 1866–1940, vol. III
Biddulph, Gen. Sir Michael Anthony Shrapnel, 1823–1904, vol. I
Biddulph, Gen. Sir Robert, 1835–1918, vol. II
Biddulph, Sir Theophilus George, 8th Bt, 1874–1948, vol. IV
Biddulph, Thomas Henry Stillingfleet, 1846–1919, vol. II
Bidie, Surg.-Gen. George, 1830–1913, vol. I
Bidlake, Rev. Walter, 1865–1938, vol. III
Bidwell, Rt Rev. Edward John, 1866–1941, vol. IV
Bidwell, Hayward John, 1849–1931, vol. III
Bidwell, Leonard Arthur, 1865–1912, vol. I
Bidwell, Rt Rev. Mgr Manuel John, died 1930, vol. III
Bidwell, Rear-Adm. Roger Edward Shelford, 1899–1968, vol. VI
Bidwell, Shelford, 1848–1909, vol. I
Biermans, Rt Rev. John Henry Mary, 1871–1941, vol. IV
Biernacki, Roderick Korneli, died 1943, vol. IV
Biffen, Sir Rowland, 1874–1949, vol. IV

Bigelow, John, 1817–1911, vol. I
Bigelow, Melville Madison, 1846–1921, vol. II
Bigelow, Poultney, 1855–1954, vol. V
Bigg, Rev. Charles, 1840–1908, vol. I
Bigg, Henry Robert Heather, 1853–1911, vol. I
Biggam, Maj.-Gen. Sir Alexander Gordon, 1888–1963, vol. VI
Biggar, Maj.-Gen. James Lyons, 1856–1922, vol. II
Biggar, Oliver Mowat, 1876–1948, vol. IV
Biggart, Sir John Henry, 1905–1979, vol. VII
Biggart, Sir Thomas, died 1949, vol. IV
Bigge, Sir Amherst S.; see Selby-Bigge, Sir L. A.
Bigge, Sir John Amherst S.; see Selby-Bigge.
Bigge, Col Thomas Arthur Hastings, 1866–1955, vol. V
Bigge, Maj.-Gen. Thomas Scovell, 1837–1914, vol. I
Bigge, Sir William Egelric, died 1916, vol. II
Bigger, Sir Edward Coey, 1861–1942, vol. IV
Bigger, Joseph Warwick, 1891–1951, vol. V
Biggs, Sir (Albert) Ashley, died 1938, vol. III
Biggs, Sir Arthur Worthington, 1846–1928, vol. II
Biggs, Sir Ashley; see Biggs, Sir A. A.
Biggs, Christopher Thomas Ewart E.; see Ewart-Biggs.
Biggs, George Nixon, 1881–1922, vol. II
Biggs, Col Henry Vero, 1860–1925, vol. II
Biggs, Hermann M., 1859–1923, vol. II
Biggs, Vice-Adm. Sir Hilary Worthington, 1905–1976, vol. VII
Biggs, Rt Rev. Huyshe Wolcott Y.; see Yeatman-Biggs.
Biggs, Leonard Vivian, 1873–1944, vol. IV
Bigham, Hon. Sir (Frank) Trevor R., 1876–1954, vol. V
Bigham, Hon. Sir Trevor; see Bigham, Hon. Sir F. T. R.
Bigland, Alfred, 1855–1936, vol. III
Bigland, Eileen Anne Carstairs, (Mrs E. W. Bigland), 1898–1970, vol. VI
Bigland, Rt Rev. Mgr John, 1871–1945, vol. IV
Bigland, Percy, died 1926, vol. II
Bignold, Sir Arthur, 1839–1915, vol. I
Bignold, Sir (Charles) Robert, 1892–1970, vol. VI
Bignold, Sir Robert; see Bignold, Sir C. R.
Bigsby, Sydney Herbert, 1885–1946, vol. IV
Bigsworth, Air Cdre Arthur Wellesley, 1885–1961, vol. VI
Bigwood, Sir Cecil, 1863–1947, vol. IV
Bigwood, James, died 1919, vol. II
Bijawar State, HH Bharat Dharm-indu Maharajah Sawai Sir Sawant Singh Bahadur, 1877–1940, vol. III (A), vol. IV
Bikaner, Maharajah of; General HH Maharaja-dhiraj Sri Ganga Singbji Bahadur, 1880–1943, vol. IV
Bikaner, Maharajah of; Lt-Gen. HH Maharaja-dhiraj Raj Rajeshwar Narendra Shiromani (Sri Sadul Singhji Bahadur), 1902–1950, vol. IV
Bilaspur (Kehlur) State, Chief HH Raja Bije Chand, 1873–1931, vol. III
Bilbrough, Rt Rev. Harold Ernest, 1867–1950, vol. IV
Biles, Sir John Harvard, 1854–1933, vol. III

57

Bilgrami, Syed Akeel, Nawab Sir Akeel Jung Bahadur, 1874–1945, vol. IV
Bilgrami, Sayyid Ali, Shamsul Ulama, 1853–1911, vol. I
Bilgrami, Syed Hossain, 1842–1926, vol. II
Bilgrami, Sayyid Sir Mehdi Husain, Nawab Mahdi Yar Jang Bahadur, *died* 1948, vol. IV
Biliotti, Sir Alfred, 1833–1915, vol. II
Bilkey, Paul Ernest, 1878–1962, vol. VI
Bill, Charles, 1843–1915, vol. I (A)
Bill, Rt Rev. Sydney Alfred, 1884–1964, vol. VI
Bille, Frank Ernest, 1832–1918, vol. II
Billen, Rev. Albert Victor, *died* 1961, vol. VI
Billett, Rev. Canon Frederick, *died* 1941, vol. IV
Billimoria, Sir Shapoorjee, 1877–1958, vol. V
Billing, Rt Rev. Claudius, *died* 1898, vol. I
Billing, N. Pemberton, 1880–1948, vol. IV
Billingham, Col John Alfred Lawrence, 1868–1955, vol. V
Billinghurst, Alfred John, 1880–1963, vol. VI
Billings, Rear-Adm. Frederick Stewart, 1900–1980, vol. VII
Billington, Mary Frances, *died* 1925, vol. II
Billington, William, *died* 1932, vol. III
Billington, Lt-Col Lawson, 1882–1954, vol. V
Billmeir, Jack Albert, 1900–1963, vol. VI
Billson, Alfred, 1839–1907, vol. I
Billson, Hon. Alfred Arthur, 1858–1930, vol. III
Billson, Herbert George, 1871–1938, vol. III
Bilsborrow, Most Rev. James Romanus, 1862–1931, vol. III
Bilsborrow, Rt Rev. John, 1837–1903, vol. I
Bilsland, 1st Baron, 1892–1970, vol. VI
Bilsland, Sir William, 1st Bt, 1847–1921, vol. II
Bilton, Lt-Col Lewis Leonard, *died* 1954, vol. V
Binder, Sir Bernhard Heymann, 1876–1966, vol. VI
Bindley, Rev. Thomas Herbert, 1861–1931, vol. III
Bindloss, Harold, 1866–1945, vol. IV
Bindoff, Stanley Thomas, 1908–1980, vol. VII
Bing, Geoffrey Henry Cecil, 1909–1977, vol. VII
Bing, Gertrud, 1892–1964, vol. VI
Bingen, Sir Eric Albert, 1898–1972, vol. VII
Bingham, Col Sir Albert Edward, 2nd Bt, 1868–1945, vol. IV
Bingham, Hon. Albert Yelverton, 1840–1907, vol. I
Bingham, Captain Alexander Gordon, 1873–1933, vol. III
Bingham, Rear-Adm. Hon. Barry; *see* Bingham, Rear-Adm. Hon. E. B. S.
Bingham, Maj.-Gen. Hon. Sir Cecil Edward, 1861–1934, vol. III
Bingham, Col Charles Henry Marion, 1873–1957, vol. V
Bingham, Lt-Col Hon. Denis; *see* Bingham, Lt-Col Hon. J. D. Y.
Bingham, Rear-Adm. Hon. (Edward) Barry (Stewart), 1881–1939, vol. III
Bingham, Maj.-Gen. Hon. Sir Francis Richard, 1863–1935, vol. III
Bingham, Lt-Col Hon. (John) Denis (Yelverton), *died* 1940, vol. III
Bingham, Sir John Edward, 1st Bt, 1839–1915, vol. I
Bingham, Lionel John, 1878–1919, vol. II

Bingham, Brig.-Gen. Oswald Buckley Bingham Smith-, 1868–1949, vol. IV
Bingham, Lt-Col Ralph Charles, 1885–1977, vol. VII
Bingham, Rear-Adm. Hon. Richard, 1847–1924, vol. II
Bingham, Robert Worth, 1871–1937, vol. III
Bingham, Lt-Col Samuel, *died* 1941, vol. IV
Bingley, 1st Baron, 1870–1947, vol. IV
Bingley, Adm. Sir Alexander Noel Campbell, 1905–1972, vol. VII
Bingley, Lt-Gen. Sir Alfred Horsford, 1865–1944, vol. IV
Bingley, Henry Campbell Alchorne, *died* 1939, vol. III
Bingley, Col Robert Albert Glanville, 1902–1976, vol. VII
Binnall, Rev. Canon Peter Blannin Gibbons. 1907–1980, vol. VII
Binney, Anthony Lockhart, 1890–1973, vol. VII
Binney, Lt-Col Edward Victor, 1885–1942, vol. IV
Binney, Sir Frederick George; *see* Binney, Sir G.
Binney, Sir George, 1900–1972, vol. VII
Binney, Adm. Sir Hugh; *see* Binney, Adm. Sir T. H.
Binney, James, 1868–1935, vol. III
Binney, Captain Ralph Douglas, 1888–1944, vol. IV
Binney, Adm. Sir (Thomas) Hugh, 1883–1953, vol. V
Binney, Rev. William Hibbert, 1857–1916, vol. II
Binnie, Sir Alexander Richardson, 1839–1917, vol. II
Binnie, Rev. Alfred Jonathan, *died* 1926, vol. II
Binnie, James, 1842–1930, vol. III
Binnie, Thomas Inglis, 1874–1954, vol. V
Binnie, William James Eames, 1867–1949, vol. IV
Binning, Col Lord; George Baillie-Hamilton, 1856–1917, vol. II
Binning, Sir Arthur William, 1861–1931, vol. III
Binning, Lt-Col Joseph, 1845–1913, vol. I
Binns, Arthur, 1861–1952, vol. V
Binns, Sir Arthur Lennon, 1891–1971, vol. VII
Binns, Asa, 1873–1946, vol. IV
Binns, Sir Bernard Ottwell, 1898–1953, vol. V
Binns, Sir Frank, 1898–1954, vol. V
Binns, Joseph, 1900–1975, vol. VI
Binns, Kenneth, 1882–1969, vol. VI
Binns, Rev. Leonard Elliott Elliott-, 1885–1963, vol. VI
Binns, Percy, *died* 1920, vol. II
Binny, Graham, *died* 1929, vol. III
Binny, Major Steuart Scott, 1871–1916, vol. II
Binstead, Arthur Morris, 1861–1914, vol .I
Binstead, Herbert Ernest, 1869–1937, vol. III
Binstead, Mary, *died* 1928, vol. II
Binyon, Basil, 1885–1977, vol. VII
Binyon, Laurence, 1869–1943, vol. IV
Bion, Frederick Fleetwood, 1870–1949, vol. IV
Birch, Sir Alan; *see* Birch, Sir J. A.
Birch, Albert Edward Henry, 1868–1954, vol. V
Birch, Sir Arthur, 1837–1914, vol. I
Birch, Claude Churchill, 1846–1940, vol. III
Birch, David; *see* Birch, W. H. D.

Birch, De Burgh, 1852–1937, vol. III
Birch, Col Edward Massy, 1875–1964, vol. VI
Birch, Sir Ernest Woodford, 1857–1929, vol. III
Birch, Francis Lyall, 1889–1956, vol. V
Birch, George Henry, 1842–1904, vol. I
Birch, Henry William, 1854–1927, vol. II
Birch, Gen. Sir (James Frederick) Noel, 1865–1939, vol. III
Birch, Major James Richard Kemmis, 1859–1907, vol. I
Birch, Sir (John) Alan, 1909–1961, vol. VI
Birch, Rev. John George, born 1839, vol. II
Birch, John Henry Stopford, died 1949, vol. IV
Birch, Gen. Sir Noel; see Birch, Gen. Sir J. F. N.
Birch, Lt-Col Percy Yates, 1884–1939, vol. III
Birch, S. J. Lamorna, 1869–1955, vol. V
Birch, Walter de Gray, 1842–1924, vol. II
Birch, (William Henry) David, 1894–1968, vol. VI
Birch, Wyndham Lindsay, 1879–1950, vol. IV
Birch-Reynardson, Col Charles; see Reynardson.
Birch-Reynardson, Lt-Col Henry T.; see Reynardson.
Birchall, Sir John Dearman, 1875–1941, vol. IV
Birchall, Sir Raymond; see Birchall, Sir W. R.
Birchall, Sir (Walter) Raymond, 1888–1968, vol. VI
Bircham, Sir Bernard Edward H.; see Halsey-Bircham.
Bircham, Sir Bertram Okeden, 1877–1961, vol. VI
Bircham, Major Humphry Francis William, 1875–1916, vol. II
Birchenough, Charles, 1882–1973, vol. VII
Birchenough, Very Rev. Godwin, 1880–1953, vol. V
Birchenough, Sir Henry, 1st Bt, 1853–1937, vol. III
Birchenough, Mabel, (Lady Birchenough), died 1936, vol. III
Bird, Sir Alfred Frederick, 1849–1922, vol. II
Bird, Archibald John, 1872–1939, vol. III
Bird, Col Arthur James Glover, 1883–1962, vol. VI
Bird, Hon. Bolton Stafford, 1840–1924, vol. II
Bird, Sir Charles Hayward, 1862–1944, vol. IV
Bird, Christopher John, 1855–1922, vol. II
Bird, Cuthbert Hilton G.; see Golding-Bird.
Bird, Sir C(yril) Handley, 1896–1969, vol. VI
Bird, Rt Rev. Cyril Henry G.; see Golding-Bird.
Bird, (Cyril) Kenneth, 1887–1965, vol. VI
Bird, Sir Donald Geoffrey, 3rd Bt, 1906–1963, vol. VI
Bird, Elliott Beverley S.; see Steeds-Bird.
Bird, Eric Leslie, 1894–1965, vol. VI
Bird, Sir Ernest Edward, 1877–1945, vol. IV
Bird, Ernest Roy, 1883–1933, vol. III
Bird, Sir F. Hugh W. S.; see Stonehewer Bird.
Bird, Col Frederic Dougan, 1858–1929, vol. III
Bird, Captain Frederic Godfrey, 1868–1919, vol. II
Bird, Gen. Sir George Corrie, 1838–1907, vol. I
Bird, Harington; see Bird, J. A. H.
Bird, Sir Harry, 1862–1944, vol. IV
Bird, Sir Henry Busby, 1856–1929, vol. III
Bird, Henry Edward, 1830–1908, vol. I
Bird, Sir James, 1863–1925, vol. II
Bird, Squadron Comdr Sir James, 1883–1946, vol. IV
Bird, Rev. James Grant, died 1920, vol. II

Bird, James William Fairbridge, 1858–1938, vol. III
Bird, (John Alexander) Harington, died 1936, vol. III
Bird, Rev. John Turnbull, 1862–1930, vol. III
Bird, Lt-Col John Wilfred, 1872–1938, vol. III
Bird, Kenneth; see Bird, C. K.
Bird, Captain Oliver, 1880–1963, vol. VI
Bird, Lt-Col Robert, 1866–1918, vol. II
Bird, Sir Robert Bland, 2nd Bt, 1876–1960, vol. V
Bird, Rev. Samuel William Elderfield, died 1926, vol. II
Bird, Col Spencer Godfrey, 1854–1926, vol. II
Bird, Col Stanley, 1864–1938, vol. III
Bird, Col Stanley G., 1837–1905, vol. I
Bird, Terence Frederick, 1906–1979, vol. VII
Bird, Tom, died 1932, vol. III
Bird, Maj.-Gen. Sir Wilkinson Dent, 1869–1943, vol. IV
Bird, Sir William Barrott Montfort, 1855–1950, vol. IV
Bird, William Seymour, 1846–1919, vol. II
Birdwood, 1st Baron, 1865–1951, vol. V
Birdwood, 2nd Baron, 1899–1962, vol. VI
Birdwood, Lt-Col George Christopher McDowall, 1863–1944, vol. IV
Birdwood, Sir George Christopher Molesworth, 1832–1917, vol. II
Birdwood, Herbert Mills, 1837–1907, vol. I
Birkbeck, Sir Edward, 1st Bt, 1838–1907, vol. I
Birkbeck, Geoffrey, 1875–1954, vol. V
Birkbeck, Harold Edward, 1902–1977, vol. VII
Birkbeck, Henry, 1853–1930, vol. III
Birkbeck, Major Henry Anthony, 1885–1956, vol. V
Birkbeck, Col Oliver, 1893–1952, vol. V
Birkbeck, Maj.-Gen. Theodore Henry, 1911–1976, vol. VII
Birkbeck, Maj.-Gen. Sir William Henry, 1863–1929, vol. III
Birkbeck, William John, 1859–1916, vol. II
Birkenhead, 1st Earl of, 1872–1930, vol. III
Birkenhead, 2nd Earl of, 1907–1975, vol. VII
Birkenruth, Adolphus, 1861–1940, vol. III
Birkett, 1st Baron, 1883–1962, vol. VI
Birkett, Brig.-Gen. Herbert Stanley, 1864–1942, vol. IV
Birkett, Brig. Richard Maule, 1882–1942, vol. IV
Birkett, Sir Thomas William, 1871–1957, vol. V
Birkin, Sir Alexander Russell, 4th Bt, 1861–1942, vol. IV
Birkin, Lt-Col Charles Wilfrid, 1865–1932, vol. III
Birkin, Sir Henry Ralph Stanley, 3rd Bt, 1896–1933, vol. III
Birkin, Lt-Col Richard Leslie, 1863–1936, vol. III
Birkin, Sir Stanley; see Birkin, Sir T. S.
Birkin, Sir Thomas Isaac, 1st Bt, 1831–1922, vol. II
Birkin, Sir (Thomas) Stanley, 2nd Bt, 1857–1931, vol. III
Birkinshaw, Air Cdre George William, 1896–1977, vol. VII
Birkmyre, Sir Archibald, 1st Bt, 1875–1935, vol. III
Birks, Falconer Moffat, 1885–1960, vol. V
Birley, Lt-Col Bevil Langton, 1884–1943, vol. IV

Birley, Sir Frank, 1883–1940, vol. III
Birley, James Leatham, 1884–1934, vol. III
Birley, Leonard, 1875–1951, vol. V
Birley, Norman Pellew, 1891–1980, vol. VII
Birley, Captain Sir Oswald Hornby Joseph, 1880–1952, vol. V
Birley, Mrs Percy Langton, 1875–1956, vol. V
Birley, Col Richard Kennedy, 1845–1914, vol. I
Birley, Rt Rev. Thomas Howard, *died* 1949, vol. IV
Birmingham, George A.; *see* Hannay, Rev. James O.
Birnage, Arthur, 1874–1953, vol. V
Birnam, Hon. Lord; (Thomas) David King Murray, 1884–1955, vol. V
Birnie, Col Eugene St John, 1900–1976, vol. VII
Birnie, Captain Harry Charles, 1882–1943, vol. IV
Biron, Sir Chartres, 1863–1940, vol. III
Birrell, Rt Hon. Augustine, 1850–1933, vol. III
Birrell, Col Edwin Thomas Fairweather, 1874–1944, vol. IV
Birrell, Hon. Frederick William, *died* 1939, vol. III
Birrell, John, 1836–1902, vol. I
Birrell-Gray, Major William; *see* Gray, Major W. B.
Birt, Francis Bradley B.; *see* Bradley-Birt.
Birt, Guy Capper, 1884–1972, vol. VII
Birt, Rev. Canon Roderick Harold Capper, 1882–1975, vol. VII
Birt, Sir William, 1834–1911, vol. I
Birtchnell, Sir Cyril Augustine, 1887–1967, vol. VI
Birtwistle, Brig.-Gen. Arthur, 1877–1937, vol. III
Birtwistle, George, 1877–1929, vol. III
Birtwistle, Ivor Treharne, 1892–1976, vol. VII
Bisat, William S., 1886–1973, vol. VII
Bischoff, Thomas Hume, 1886–1951, vol. V
Bischoffesheim, Henry Louis, 1829–1908, vol. I
Biscoe, Rev. Cecil Earle T.; *see* Tyndale-Biscoe.
Biscoe, Lt-Col Sir Hugh Vincent, 1881–1932, vol. III
Biscoe, Brig.-Gen. Julian Dallas Tyndale T.; *see* Tyndale-Biscoe.
Biscoe, Walter Treweeke, 1892–1969, vol. VI
Biscoe, Lt-Gen. William Walters, 1841–1920, vol. II
Bisdee, Lt-Col John Hutton, 1869–1930, vol. III
Bisgood, Joseph John, 1861–1927, vol. II
Bishop, Arthur Henry Burdick, *died* 1969, vol. VI
Bishop, Lt-Comdr Francis Charles, 1905–1965, vol. VI
Bishop, Sir (Frank) Patrick, 1900–1972, vol. VII
Bishop, Frederic Sillery, *died* 1913, vol. I
Bishop, Captain Frederick Edward, 1872–1931, vol. III
Bishop, George Walter, 1886–1965, vol. VI
Bishop, Henry, *died* 1939, vol. III
Bishop, Mrs Isabella Luey, 1832–1904, vol. I
Bishop, John, 1828–1913, vol. I
Bishop, Joseph Bucklin, 1847–1928, vol. II
Bishop, Julius, 1855–1932, vol. III
Bishop, Laurence Arthur, 1895–1954, vol. V
Bishop, Matilda Ellen, 1844–1913, vol. I
Bishop, Sir Patrick; *see* Bishop, Sir F. P.
Bishop, Peter Maxwell Farrow, 1904–1979, vol. VII
Bishop, Hon. Robert Kirby, 1853–1930, vol. III

Bishop, Theodore Bendysh Watson, 1886–1967, vol. VI
Bishop, W. Follen, 1856–1936, vol. III
Bishop, Walter Frederick, 1879–1955, vol. V
Bishop, Air Marshal William Avery, 1894–1956, vol. V
Bishop, Sir William Poole, 1894–1977, vol. VII
Bismarck, Prince Herbert von, 1849–1904, vol. I
Bispham, David, 1857–1921, vol. II
Bispham, James Webb, *died* 1956, vol. V
Bisschop, Willem Roosegaarde, 1866–1944, vol. IV
Bisseker, Rev. Harry, 1878–1965, vol. VI
Bisset, Vice-Adm. Arthur William La Touche, 1892–1956, vol. V
Bisset, Captain Sir James Gordon Partridge, 1883–1967, vol. VI
Bisset, Sir Murray, 1876–1931, vol. III
Bisset, Col Sir William Sinclair Smith, 1843–1916, vol. II
Bisset-Berry, Hon. Sir William; *see* Berry.
Bisset-Smith, George Tulloch, 1863–1922, vol. II
Bissett, Maj.-Gen. Frederic William Lyon, 1888–1961, vol. VI
Bisson, Laurence Adolphus, 1897–1965, vol. VI
Biswambhar Ray, Rai Bahadur (Vidyabenode), 1855–1930, vol. III
Biswas, Rt Rev. Nirod Kumar, 1905–1948, vol. IV
Bithell, Jethro, 1878–1962, vol. VI
Bizet, George; *see* Bisset-Smith, George Tulloch.
Bjoerling, Jussi, 1911–1960, vol. V
Björnson, Björnstjerne, 1832–1910, vol. I
Blache, Jules Adolphe Lucien, 1893–1970, vol. VI
Blachford, Lady; (Georgina Mary), *died* 1900, vol. I
Black, Sir Alec, 1st Bt (*cr* 1918), 1872–1942, vol. IV
Black, Alexander William, 1859–1906, vol. I
Black, Andrew, 1850–1916, vol. II
Black, Sir Archibald Campbell, *died* 1962, vol. VI
Black, Rt Hon. Arthur, 1888–1968, vol. VI
Black, Arthur John, 1855–1936, vol. III
Black, Sir Arthur William, 1863–1947, vol. IV
Black, Charles Crofton, 1880–1937, vol. III
Black, Lt-Col Claud Hamilton Griffith, *died* 1946, vol. IV
Black, Colin Mackenzie, 1877–1943, vol. IV
Black, Davidson, 1884–1934, vol. III
Black, Donald Harrison, 1899–1978, vol. VII
Black, Ebenezer Charlton, 1861–1927, vol. II
Black, Francis, *died* 1939, vol. III
Black, Sir Frederick William, 1863–1930, vol. III
Black, Hon. George, 1873–1965, vol. VI
Black, Major George Cumine Strahan, 1882–1951, vol. V
Black, George Norman, 1907–1955, vol. V
Black, Rev. Canon Gibson James Hunter Monahan, 1867–1950, vol. IV
Black, Henry, 1875–1960, vol. V, vol. VI
Black, Rev. Hugh, 1868–1953, vol. V
Black, Hugo LaFayette, 1886–1971, vol. VII
Black, Rt Rev. James, 1894–1968, vol. VI
Black, Very Rev. James Macdougall, 1879–1949, vol. IV
Black, James Watt, 1840–1918, vol. II
Black, John Bennett, 1883–1964, vol. VI

Black, Col John Campbell Lamont, 1869–1950, vol. IV
Black, Sir John Paul, 1895–1965, vol. VI
Black, John Stewart, 1865–1930, vol. III
Black, John Sutherland, 1846–1923, vol. II
Black, John Wycliffe, 1862–1951, vol. V
Black, Kenneth, 1879–1959, vol. V
Black, Ladbroke Lionel Day, 1877–1940, vol. III
Black, Sir Misha, 1910–1977, vol. VII
Black, Robert Alastair Lucien, 1921–1967, vol. VI
Black, Sir Robert Andrew Stransham, 2nd Bt, 1902–1979, vol. VII
Black, Sir Robert James, 1st Bt (*cr* 1922), 1860–1925, vol. II
Black, Sir Samuel, 1830–1910, vol. I
Black, Sydney, 1908–1968, vol. VI
Black, Thomas Porteous, 1878–1915, vol. I
Black, Maj.-Gen. Walter Clarence, 1867–1930, vol. III
Black, William, 1841–1898, vol. I
Black, Hon. William Anderson, 1847–1934, vol. III
Black, Maj.-Gen. William Campbell, 1846–1931, vol. III
Black, William Charles, 1890–1959, vol. V (A)
Black, William George, 1857–1932, vol. III
Black, William John, 1872–1941, vol. IV
Black, Maj.-Gen. Sir Wilsone, 1837–1909, vol. I
Blackadder, William, 1877–1940, vol. III
Blackader, Alexander Dougall, 1847–1932, vol. III
Blackader, Maj.-Gen. Charles Guinand, 1869–1921, vol. II
Blackbourne, Rev. Jacob, 1862–1936, vol. III
Blackburn, Hon. Lord; Robert Francis Leslie Blackburn, 1864–1944, vol. IV
Blackburn, Sir Arthur Dickinson, 1887–1970, vol. VI
Blackburn, Brig. Arthur Seaforth, 1892–1960, vol. V
Blackburn, Lt-Col Sir Charles Bickerton, 1874–1972, vol. VII
Blackburn, Lt-Col Charles Cautley, 1867–1938, vol. III
Blackburn, Henry, 1830–1897, vol. I
Blackburn, Col John Edward, 1851–1927, vol. II
Blackburn, Maurice McCrae, 1880–1944, vol. IV
Blackburn, Robert Francis Leslie; *see* Blackburn, Hon. Lord.
Blackburn, Sir Thomas, *died* 1974, vol. VII
Blackburn, Vernon, *died* 1907, vol. I
Blackburn, William Ernest, 1873–1951, vol. V
Blackburne, Lt-Col Charles Harold, 1876–1918, vol. II
Blackburne, Rev. Foster Grey, *died* 1909, vol. I
Blackburne, Gertrude Mary Ireland, 1861–1951, vol. V
Blackburne, Very Rev. Harry William, 1878–1963, vol. VI
Blackburne, Joseph Henry, 1841–1924, vol. II
Blackburne, Sir Kenneth William, 1907–1980, vol. VII
Blackburne, Very Rev. Lionel Edward, 1874–1951, vol. V
Blackburne, Col Robert Ireland, 1850–1930, vol. III

Blackden, Col Leonard Shadwell, 1863–1937, vol. III
Blacker, Carlos Paton, 1895–1975, vol. VII
Blacker, Edward Carew, 1863–1932, vol. III
Blacker, Col Frederick St John, 1881–1942, vol. IV
Blacker, Sir George, 1865–1948, vol. IV
Blacker, Maj.-Gen. George Patrick Demaine, 1906–1974, vol. VII
Blacker, Harold Alfred Cecil, 1889–1944, vol. IV
Blacker, L(atham) V(alentine) Stewart, *died* 1964, vol. VI
Blacker, Lt-Col Stewart William Ward, 1865–1935, vol. III
Blacket, Wilfred, 1859–1937, vol. III
Blackett, Baron (Life Peer); Patrick Maynard Stuart Blackett, 1897–1974, vol. VII
Blackett, Sir Basil Phillott, 1882–1935, vol. III
Blackett, Sir Charles Douglas, 9th Bt, 1904–1968, vol. VI
Blackett, Sir Edward William, 7th Bt, 1831–1909, vol. I
Blackett, Adm. Henry, 1867–1952, vol. V
Blackett, Sir Hugh Douglas, 8th Bt, 1873–1960, vol. V
Blackett, Rev. Selwyn, 1854–1935, vol. III
Blackett, Col William Cuthbert, 1859–1935, vol. III
Blackett Ord, Ven. Charles Edward, 1858–1931, vol. III
Blackford, 1st Baron, 1862–1947, vol. IV
Blackford, 2nd Baron, 1887–1972, vol. VII
Blackford, 3rd Baron, 1923–1977, vol. VII
Blackham, Maj.-Gen. Robert James, *died* 1951, vol. V
Blackie, Rt Rev. Ernest Morell, 1867–1943, vol. IV
Blackie, Walter Wilfrid, 1860–1953, vol. V
Blacking, Randoll; *see* Blacking, W. H. R.
Blacking, (William Henry) Randoll, 1889–1958, vol. V
Blackledge, Geoffrey Glynn, 1894–1964, vol. VI
Blackledge, Rev. Canon George Robert, 1868–1935, vol. III
Blackley, Rev. William Lewery, 1830–1902, vol. I
Blacklock, Maj.-Gen. Cyril Aubrey, 1870–1936, vol. III
Blacklock, Donald Breadalbane, 1879–1955, vol. V
Blacklock, John William Stewart, *died* 1973, vol. VII
Blackman, Aylward Manley, 1883–1956, vol. V
Blackman, Frederick Frost, 1866–1947, vol. IV
Blackman, Geoffrey Emett, 1903–1980, vol. VII
Blackman, Vernon Herbert, 1872–1967, vol. VI
Blackman, Winifred Susan, *died* 1950, vol. IV
Blackmore, Sir Charles Henry, 1880–1967, vol. VI
Blackmore, Col Lindsay William Saul, 1896–1973, vol. VII
Blackmore, Richard D., 1825–1900, vol. I (A)
Blackmur, Richard Palmer, 1904–1965, vol. VI
Blackshaw, J. F., 1875–1943, vol. IV
Blackshaw, Maurice Bantock, 1903–1975, vol. VII
Blackshaw, Rev. William, 1866–1953, vol. V
Blackton, James Stuart, 1875–1941, vol. IV
Blackwell, Sir (Cecil) Patrick, 1881–1944, vol. IV
Blackwell, Elizabeth, 1821–1910, vol. I
Blackwell, Sir Ernley Robertson Hay, 1868–1941, vol. IV

Blackwell, Francis Samuel, 1869–1951, vol. V
Blackwell, Major Francis Victor, *died* 1928, vol. II
Blackwell, John Humphrey, 1895–1979, vol. VII
Blackwell, Sir Patrick; *see* Blackwell, Sir C. P.
Blackwell, Richard, 1918–1980, vol. VII
Blackwell, Thomas Francis, 1838–1907, vol. I
Blackwell, Thomas Geoffrey, 1884–1943, vol. IV
Blackwell, Maj.-Gen. William Richard, 1877–1946, vol. IV
Blackwood, Lt-Col Albemarle Price, 1881–1921, vol. II
Blackwood, Algernon Henry, 1869–1951, vol. V
Blackwood, Lord Basil; *see* Blackwood, Lord I.B.G.T.
Blackwood, Rt Rev. Donald Burns, 1884–1967, vol. VI (AII)
Blackwood, Sir Francis, 4th Bt, 1838–1924, vol. II
Blackwood, Sir Francis Elliot Temple, 6th Bt, 1901–1979, vol. VII
Blackwood, Captain Frederick Herbert, 1885–1926, vol. II
Blackwood, George William, 1876–1942, vol. IV
Blackwood, Sir Henry Palmer Temple, 5th Bt, 1896–1948, vol. IV
Blackwood, Lord (Ian) Basil (Gawaine Temple), 1870–1917, vol. II
Blackwood, James H., 1878–1951, vol. V
Blackwood, Captain Maurice Baldwin Raymond, 1882–1941, vol. IV
Blackwood, William, 1836–1912, vol. I
Blackwood, William, 1878–1958, vol. V
Blackwood-Price, Rev. Canon Edward Hyde, 1875–1940, vol. III
Blades, Hon. Lord; Daniel Patterson Blades, 1888–1959, vol. V
Blades, Daniel Patterson; *see* Blades, Hon. Lord.
Blades, Major Walter William, 1863–1943, vol. IV
Bladin, Air Vice-Marshal Francis Masson, 1898–1978, vol. VII
Bladon, Air Cdre Graham Clarke, 1899–1967, vol. VI
Blagden, Charles Otto, 1864–1949, vol. IV
Blagden, Rt Rev. Claude Martin, 1874–1952, vol. V
Blagden, Rev. Henry, 1832–1922, vol. II
Blagden, John Basil, 1901–1964, vol. VI
Blagrove, Col Henry John, 1854–1925, vol. II
Blaikie, Leonard, 1873–1951, vol. V
Blaikie, Walter Biggar, 1847–1928, vol. II
Blaikie, Rev. William Garden, 1820–1899, vol. I
Blaikley, John Barnard, 1906–1975, vol. VII
Blaiklock, George, 1856–1943, vol. IV
Blain, Hon. Sir Eric Herbert, 1904–1969, vol. VI
Blain, Sir Herbert Edwin, 1870–1942, vol. IV
Blain, William, *died* 1908, vol. I
Blain, Sir William Arbuthnot, 1833–1911, vol. I
Blaine, Sir Charles Frederick, *died* 1915, vol. I
Blaine, Brig. Charles Herbert, 1883–1958, vol. V
Blaine, Sir Robert Stickney, *died* 1897, vol. I
Blair; *see* Blair-Fish, W. W.
Blair, Alexander, 1864–1944, vol. IV
Blair, Lt-Col Alexander Stevenson, 1865–1936, vol. III
Blair, Hon. Andrew George, 1844–1907, vol. I

Blair, Andrew James Fraser, (Hamish Blair), 1872–1935, vol. III
Blair, Hon. Sir Archibald William, 1875–1952, vol. V
Blair, Brig.-Gen. Arthur, 1869–1947, vol. IV
Blair, Gen. Charles Renny, 1837–1912, vol. I
Blair, Charles Samuel, 1859–1939, vol. III
Blair, David, 1932–1976, vol. VII
Blair, Rt Rev. Sir David H.; *see* Hunter-Blair.
Blair, Duncan MacCallum, 1896–1944, vol. IV
Blair, Captain Sir Edward H.; *see* Hunter-Blair.
Blair, Dame Emily Mathieson, *died* 1963, vol. VI
Blair, Eric Arthur; *see* Orwell, George.
Blair, Brig.-Gen. Everard Macleod, 1866–1939, vol. III
Blair, Col Frederick Gordon, 1852–1943, vol. IV
Blair, Hamish; *see* Blair, A. J. F.
Blair, Gen. James, 1828–1905, vol. I
Blair, Col James Molesworth, 1880–1925, vol. II
Blair, James Richard, 1890–1958, vol. V
Blair, Hon. Sir James William, 1871–1944, vol. IV
Blair, Kenneth Gloyne, 1882–1952, vol. V
Blair, Rt Rev. Laurence Frederick Devaynes, *died* 1925, vol. II
Blair, Oliver Robin, 1925–1975, vol. VII
Blair, Patrick James, 1865–1932, vol. III
Blair, Col Sir Patrick James, 1891–1972, vol. VII
Blair, Sir Reginald, 1st Bt, 1881–1962, vol. VI
Blair, Sir Robert, 1859–1935, vol. III
Blair, Robert Kerr, 1876–1942, vol. IV
Blair, Maj.-Gen. Walter Charles H.; *see* Hunter-Blair.
Blair, Very Rev. William, 1830–1916, vol. II
Blair-Bell, William, 1871–1936, vol. III
Blair-Fish, Wallace Wilfrid, 1889–1968, vol. VI
Blais, Rt Rev. Andrew Albert, 1842–1919, vol. II
Blake, Captain Sir Acton; *see* Blake, Captain Sir H. A.
Blake, Sir Arthur Ernest, 1869–1935, vol. III
Blake, Arthur John J.; *see* Jex-Blake.
Blake, Col Arthur Maurice, *born* 1852, vol. II
Blake, Lt-Col Arthur O'Brien ffrench, 1879–1973, vol. VII
Blake, Comdr Sir Cuthbert Patrick, 6th Bt (*cr* 1772), 1885–1975, vol. VII
Blake, Hon. Edward, 1833–1912, vol. I
Blake, Sir Edward; *see* Blake, Sir F. E. C.
Blake, Edwin Holmes, 1873–1956, vol. V
Blake, Sir Ernest Edward, 1845–1920, vol. II
Blake, Sir Francis Douglas, 1st Bt (*cr* 1907), 1856–1940, vol. III
Blake, Sir (Francis) Edward (Colquhoun), 2nd Bt (*cr* 1907), 1893–1950, vol. IV
Blake, Francis Gilman, 1887–1952, vol. V
Blake, Vice-Adm. Sir Geoffrey, 1882–1968, vol. VI
Blake, George, 1893–1961, vol. VI
Blake, Lt-Col Sir (George) Reginald, 1882–1949, vol. IV
Blake, Maj.-Gen. Gilbert Alan, 1887–1971, vol. VII
Blake, Henrietta J.; *see* Jex-Blake.
Blake, Sir Henry Arthur, 1840–1918, vol. II
Blake, Gen. Henry William, 1815–1908, vol. I
Blake, Henry Wollaston, 1815–1899, vol. I

Blake, Captain Sir (Herbert) Acton, 1857–1926, vol. II
Blake, Herbert Frederick, 1866–1946, vol. IV
Blake, Jack Percy, *died* 1950, vol. IV
Blake, Rev. James Edward Huxley, 1863–1933, vol. III
Blake, Rev. James Martindale, 1863–1934, vol. III
Blake, Rev. John Frederick, 1839–1906, vol. I
Blake, Sir John Lucian, 1898–1954, vol. V
Blake, Katharine J.; *see* Jex-Blake.
Blake, Louisa Brandreth A.; *see* Aldrich-Blake.
Blake, Col Maurice Charles Joseph, 1837–1917, vol. II
Blake, Major Napoleon Joseph Rodolph, 1853–1926, vol. II
Blake, Nicholas; *see* Day-Lewis, Cecil.
Blake, Sir Patrick James Graham, 5th Bt (*cr* 1772), 1861–1930, vol. III
Blake, Lt-Col Sir Reginald; *see* Blake, Lt-Col Sir G. R.
Blake, Sophia J.; *see* Jex-Blake.
Blake, Lt-Col Terence Joseph Edward, 1886–1921, vol. II
Blake, Sir Thomas Patrick Ulick John Harvey, 15th Bt (*cr* 1622), 1870–1925, vol. II
Blake, Very Rev. Thomas William J.; *see* Jex-Blake.
Blake, Sir Ulick Temple, 16th Bt (*cr* 1622), 1904–1963, vol. VI
Blake, Vernon, 1875–1930, vol. III
Blake, Brig.-Gen. William Alan, 1878–1959, vol. V
Blake-Daly, John Archer; *see* Daly.
Blake-Humfrey, Rev. John, 1847–1930, vol. III
Blake-Reed, Sir John Seymour, 1882–1966, vol. VI
Blakelock, Denys Martin, 1901–1970, vol. VI
Blakely, Hon. Arthur, 1886–1972, vol. VII
Blakeman, Joan, (Mrs L. T. Blakeman); *see* Woodward, Joan.
Blakeman, John, 1881–1942, vol. IV
Blakeman, Leslie Thompson, 1904–1975, vol. VII
Blakemore, Frederick, 1906–1955, vol. V
Blakeney, Edward Henry, *died* 1955, vol. V
Blakeney, Col Herbert Norwood, 1871–1946, vol. IV
Blakeney, Rev. Richard, 1857–1946, vol. IV
Blakeney, Rev. Robert Bibby, 1865–1948, vol. IV
Blakeney, Brig.-Gen. Robert Byron Drury, 1872–1952, vol. V
Blakeney, Col William Edward Albemarle, *died* 1942, vol. IV
Blaker, Cedric, 1889–1965, vol. VI
Blaker, Harry Rowsell, 1872–1953, vol. V
Blaker, Sir John George, 1st Bt, 1854–1926, vol. II
Blaker, Sir Reginald, 2nd Bt, 1900–1975, vol. VII
Blaker, Richard, 1893–1940, vol. III
Blaker, Richard Henry, 1866–1940, vol. III
Blaker, Col William Frederick, 1877–1933, vol. III
Blakesley, Major Henry J., *died* 1931, vol. III
Blakesley, Thomas H., 1847–1929, vol. III
Blakeway, Ven. Charles Edward, 1868–1922, vol. II
Blakeway, Lt-Col Sir Denys Brooke, 1870–1933, vol. III

Blakeway, Brig.-Gen. John Prestwich, 1867–1936, vol. III
Blakey, James, 1851–1929, vol. III
Blakiston, Sir Arthur Frederick, 7th Bt, 1892–1974, vol. VII
Blakiston, Sir (Arthur) Norman (Hunter), 8th Bt, 1899–1977, vol. VII
Blakiston, Sir Charles Edward, 6th Bt, 1862–1941, vol. IV
Blakiston, Cuthbert Harold, 1879–1949, vol. IV
Blakiston, Rev. Cyril Ralph Noel, 1880–1941, vol. IV
Blakiston, Rev. Herbert Edward Douglas, 1862–1942, vol. IV
Blakiston, Sir Horace Nevile, 5th Bt, 1861–1936, vol. III
Blakiston, John Francis, 1882–1965, vol. IV
Blakiston, Sir Norman; *see* Blakiston, Sir A. N. H.
Blakiston, Wilfrid Robert Louis, 1876–1955, vol. V
Blakiston-Houston, Major Charles, 1868–1935, vol. III
Blakiston-Houston, John, 1829–1920, vol. II
Blakiston-Houston, Maj.-Gen. John, 1881–1959, vol. V
Blamey, Col Edwin Herbert, 1877–1936, vol. III
Blamey, Field Marshal Sir Thomas Albert, 1884–1951, vol. V
Blampied, Edmund, 1886–1966, vol. VI
Blanc, Edmond, 1861–1920, vol. II
Blanc, Sir Henry Jules, 1831–1911, vol. I
Blanc, Hippolyte Jean, 1844–1917, vol. II
Blanche, Rt Rev. Gustave, 1848–1916, vol. II
Blanche, Jaques Emile, 1862–1942, vol. IV
Blanco, Alfredo Ernesto, 1877–1945, vol. IV
Blanco White, George Rivers; *see* White.
Bland, Charles Heber, 1886–1966, vol. VI
Bland, E.; *see* Nesbit, E.
Bland, E. Beatrice, 1868–1951, vol. V
Bland, Brig.-Gen. Edward Humphry, 1866–1945, vol. IV
Bland, Edward Maltby, 1878–1946, vol. IV
Bland, Rev. Edward Michael, 1851–1936, vol. III
Bland, Francis Armand, 1882–1967, vol. VI
Bland, Francis Lawrence, 1873–1941, vol. IV
Bland, Sir (George) Nevile Maltby, 1886–1972, vol. VII
Bland, Lt-Col John Edward Michael, 1899–1976, vol. VII
Bland, John Otway Percy, 1863–1945, vol. IV
Bland, Sir Nevile; *see* Bland, Sir G. N. M.
Bland, Robert Norman, 1859–1948, vol. IV
Bland, Sir Thomas Maltby, 1906–1968, vol. VI
Bland, William Archdale, 1862–1934, vol. III
Bland, Col William St Colum, 1868–1950, vol. IV
Bland-Sutton, Sir John, 1st Bt, 1855–1936, vol. III
Blandford, Marchioness of; (Albertha Frances Anne), 1847–1932, vol. III
Blandford, George Fielding, 1829–1911, vol. I
Blandford, Laurence James, 1876–1944, vol. IV
Blandford, Hon. Sydney Dara, 1868–1929, vol. III
Blandy, Beatrice Charlotte, *died* 1950, vol. IV
Blandy, Sir Edmond Nicolas, *died* 1942, vol. IV
Blandy, Air Cdre Lyster Fettiplace, 1874–1964, vol. VI

Blandy, Richard Denis, 1891–1964, vol. VI
Blane, Brig.-Gen. Charles Forbes, 1859–1930, vol. III
Blane, Comdr Sir Charles Rodney, 4th Bt, 1879–1916, vol. II
Blane, Gilbert Gordon, 1851–1928, vol. II
Blane, Lt-Gen. Sir Seymour John, 3rd Bt, 1833–1911, vol. I
Blane, Thomas Andrew, 1881–1940, vol. III
Blane, William, 1864–1936, vol. III
Blanesborough, Baron (Life Peer); Robert Younger, 1861–1946, vol. IV
Blaney, Thomas, 1823–1903, vol. I
Blanford, William Thomas, 1832–1905, vol. I
Blank, Abraham Lewis, 1891–1967, vol. VI
Blankenberg, Sir Reginald Andrew, 1876–1960, vol. V (A)
Blantyre, 12th Baron, 1818–1900, vol. I
Blaserna, Pietro, *died* 1918, vol. II
Blatch, Sir William Bernard, 1887–1965, vol. VI
Blatchford, Robert, 1851–1943, vol. IV
Blatherwick, Col Sir Thomas, 1887–1950, vol. IV
Blathwayt, Raymond, 1855–1935, vol. III
Blathwayt, Robert Wynter, 1850–1936, vol. III
Blaxland, Maj.-Gen. Alan Bruce, 1892–1963, vol. VI
Blaxland, Rev. George Cuthbert, 1852–1930, vol. III
Blaxland, Vice-Adm. John Edric, 1847–1935, vol. III
Blaxter, Kenneth William, 1895–1964, vol. VI
Blaydes, Frederick Henry Marvell, 1818–1908, vol. I
Blaylock, Col Harry Woodburn, 1878–1928, vol. II
Bleackley, Horace William, 1868–1931, vol. III
Bleackley, Engr Rear-Adm. Hubert, 1886–1950, vol. IV
Blease, W. Lyon, 1884–1963, vol. VI
Bleck, Edward Charles, 1861–1919, vol. II
Bledisloe, 1st Viscount, 1867–1958, vol. V
Bledisloe, 2nd Viscount, 1899–1979, vol. VII
Blee, David, 1899–1979, vol. VII
Blegen, Carl William, 1887–1971, vol. VII
Blencowe, Rev. Alfred James, *died* 1928, vol. II
Blenkin, Very Rev. George Wilfrid, 1861–1924, vol. II
Blenkinsop, Maj.-Gen. Sir Alfred Percy, 1865–1936, vol. III
Blenkinsop, Arthur, 1911–1979, vol. VII
Blenkinsop, Edward Robert Kaye, 1871–1954, vol. V
Blenkinsop, Maj.-Gen. Sir Layton John, 1862–1942, vol. IV
Blennerhassett, Sir Arthur Charles Francis Bernard, 5th Bt, 1871–1915, vol. I
Blennerhassett, Col Blennerhassett Montgomerie, 1849–1926, vol. II
Blennerhassett, Sir Marmaduke Charles Henry Joseph, 6th Bt, 1902–1940, vol. III
Blennerhassett, Rt Hon. Sir Rowland, 4th Bt, 1839–1909, vol. I
Blennerhassett, Rowland Ponsonby, 1850–1913, vol. I

Blennerhassett, William Lewis Rowland Paul Sebastian, 1882–1958, vol. V
Bleriot, Louis, 1872–1936, vol. III
Blewett, Francis Richard, *born* 1869, vol. II
Blewitt, Maj.-Gen. William Edward, 1854–1939, vol. III
Bligh, Sir Edward Clare, 1887–1976, vol. VII
Bligh, John Murray, *died* 1968, vol. VI
Bligh, Sir Timothy James, 1918–1969, vol. VI
Blight, Francis James, 1858–1935, vol. III
Blind, Karl, 1826–1907, vol. I
Blind, Rudolf, 1850–1916, vol. II
Blindell, Sir James, 1884–1937, vol. III
Bliss, 4th Baron, 1869–1926, vol. II
Bliss, Sir Arthur, 1891–1975, vol. VII
Bliss, Major Charles, 1871–1914, vol. I
Bliss, Cuthbert Vivian, 1878–1963, vol. VI
Bliss, Col Ernest William, 1869–1934, vol. III
Bliss, Sir Henry William, 1840–1919, vol. II
Bliss, Rev. Howard S., 1860–1920, vol. II
Bliss, Rev. John Worthington, 1832–1917, vol. II
Bliss, Joseph, 1853–1939, vol. III
Bliss, Brig. Philip Wheeler, 1887–1966, vol. VI
Bliss, Gen. Tasker Howard, 1853–1930, vol. III
Bliss, Col Thomas Gordon, 1869–1949, vol. IV
Bliss, Rev. W. H., 1834–1919, vol. II
Bliven, Bruce, 1889–1977, vol. VII
Blixen Finecke, Karen; *see* Dinesen, Isak.
Bloch, Ernest, 1880–1959, vol. V
Bloch, Jean de, *died* 1902, vol. I
Bloch, Sir Maurice, *died* 1964, vol. VI
Bloch, Olaf F., *died* 1944, vol. IV
Block, Sir Adam Samuel James, 1856–1941, vol. IV
Block, Brig. Allen Prichard, 1899–1973, vol. VII
Block, Comdr Leslie Kenneth Allen, 1906–1980, vol. VII
Blockey, Air Vice-Marshal Paul Sandland, 1905–1963, vol. VI
Blodget, Cornelia Otis, (Mrs A. S. Blodget); *see* Skinner, C. O.
Blofeld, Rev. Stuart, 1872–1950, vol. IV
Blofeld, Thomas Calthorpe, 1836–1908, vol. I
Blois, Captain Sir Gervase Ralph Edmund, 10th Bt, 1901–1968, vol. VI
Blois, Sir Ralph Barrett Macnaghten, 9th Bt, 1866–1950, vol. IV
Blois-Johnson, Lt-Col Thomas Gordon; *see* Johnson.
Blom, Eric Walter, 1888–1959, vol. V
Blomefield, Edward Hugh, 1952–1938, vol. III
Blomefield, Sir Thomas Wilmot Peregrine, 4th Bt, 1848–1928, vol. II
Blomfield, Arthur Conran, 1863–1935, vol. III
Blomfield, Sir Arthur William, 1829–1899, vol. I
Blomfield, Maj.-Gen. Charles James, 1855–1928, vol. II
Blomfield, Charles James, *died* 1932, vol. III
Blomfield, Douglas John, 1885–1979, vol. VII
Blomfield, Joseph, 1870–1948, vol. IV
Blomfield, Sir Reginald, 1856–1942, vol. IV
Blomfield, Wing Comdr Richard Graham, 1890–1940, vol. III
Blomfield, Rear-Adm. Sir Richard Massie, 1835–1921, vol. II

Blomfield, Maj.-Gen. Valentine, 1898–1980, vol. VII
Blomfield, Rev. William Ernest, 1862–1934, vol. III
Blommers, Johannes Bernardus, 1845–1914, vol. I
Blond, Neville, 1896–1970, vol. VI
Blondin, Lt-Col Hon. Pierre Edouard, 1874–1943, vol. IV
Blood, Alexander, died 1933, vol. III
Blood, Gen. Sir Bindon, 1842–1940, vol. III
Blood, Sir Hilary Rudolph Robert, 1893–1967, vol. VI
Blood, Lancelot Ivan Neptune Lloyd-, 1896–1951, vol. V
Blood, Brig. William Edmund Robarts, 1897–1976, vol. VII
Blood, Brig. William Holcroft, 1887–1976, vol. VII
Blood-Smyth, Rev. William A., 1853–1940, vol. IV
Bloomfield, Lady; (Georgiana), 1822–1905, vol. I
Bloomfield, Maurice, 1855–1928, vol. II (A), vol. III
Blore, Rev. George John, 1835–1916, vol. II
Blore, Lt-Col Herbert Richard, 1871–1955, vol. V
Blosse, Sir David Edward L.; see Lynch-Blosse.
Blosse, Sir Henry L.; see Lynch-Blosse.
Blosse, Sir Robert Cyril Lynch-, 13th Bt, 1887–1951, vol. V
Blosse, Sir Robert Geoffrey Lynch-, 14th Bt, 1915–1963, vol. VI
Blosse, Sir Robert Lynch, 12th Bt, 1861–1942, vol. IV
Blouët, Paul; see O'Rell, Max.
Bloundelle-Burton, John Edward, died 1917, vol. II
Blount, Austin Ernest, 1870–1954, vol. V
Blount, Air Vice-Marshal Charles Hubert Boulby, 1893–1940, vol. III
Blount, Col Edward Augustine, died 1936, vol. III
Blount, Sir Edward Charles, 1809–1905, vol. I
Blount, Edward Francis Riddell-, 1865–1943, vol. IV
Blount, Sir Edward Robert, 11th Bt, 1884–1978, vol. VII
Blount, Vice-Adm. George Ronald, 1877–1964, vol. VI
Blount, Lt-Gen. Harold, 1881–1967, vol. VI
Blount, Sir Walter Aston, 10th Bt, 1876–1958, vol. V
Blount, Sir Walter de Sodington, 9th Bt, 1833–1915, vol. I (A)
Blow, Detmar, 1867–1939, vol. III
Blow, Horatio John Hooper, 1855–1933, vol. III
Blow, Very Rev. Norman John, 1915–1950, vol. IV (A), vol. V
Blow, Sydney, died 1961, vol. VI
Blowers, Arthur R., 1868–1954, vol. V
Blowitz, Henri Georges Stephane Adolphe Opper de, 1832–1903, vol. I
Bloxam, John Astley, died 1926, vol. II
Blucher von Wahlstatt, Prince; see Wahlstatt.
Blum, Léon, 1872–1950, vol. IV
Blumberg, Gen. Sir Herbert Edward, 1869–1934, vol. III
Blumenfeld, Ralph David, 1864–1948, vol. IV
Blumenthal, George, 1858–1941, vol. IV
Blumenthal, Jacques, 1829–1908, vol. I
Blumhardt, J. F., died 1922, vol. II

Blundell, Lt-Col Bryan Seymour Moss-, 1878–1932, vol. III
Blundell, Charles Joseph W.; see Weld-Blundell.
Blundell, Rev. Canon E. K., 1886–1961, vol. VI
Blundell, Edward, 1842–1932, vol. III
Blundell, Mrs Francis, died 1930, vol. III
Blundell, Francis Nicholas, 1880–1936, vol. III
Blundell, Col Frederick Blundell Moss, 1873–1964, vol. VI
Blundell, Henry B. H.; see Blundell-Hollinshead-Blundell.
Blundell, Henry Seymour Moss-, 1871–1947, vol. IV
Blundell, Col John Eyles, 1843–1931, vol. III
Blundell, Lionel Alleyne, 1910–1975, vol. VII
Blundell, Maj.-Gen. Richard H. B.; see Blundell-Hollinshead-Blundell.
Blundell, Sir Robert Henderson, 1901–1967, vol. IV
Blundell-Hollinshead-Blundell, Henry, 1831–1906, vol. I
Blundell-Hollinshead-Blundell, Maj.-Gen. Richard, 1835–1912, vol. I
Blunden, Edmund Charles, 1896–1974, vol. VII
Blunden, Sir John, 5th Bt, 1880–1923, vol. II
Blunden, Sir William, 4th Bt, 1840–1923, vol. II
Blundstone, Ferdinand V., 1882–1951, vol. V
Blunt, Rev. Alexander Colvin, died 1920, vol. II
Blunt, Rt Rev. Alfred Walter Frank, 1879–1957, vol. V
Blunt, Lt-Col Allan St John, 1880–1931, vol. III
Blunt, Arthur Powlett, 1883–1946, vol. IV
Blunt, Col Charles Jasper, died 1933, vol. III
Blunt, Col Conrad Edward Grant, 1868–1948, vol. IV
Blunt, Davenport Fabian Cartwright, died 1965, vol. VI
Blunt, Denzil Layton, 1891–1968, vol. VI
Blunt, Sir Edward Arthur Henry, 1877–1941, vol. IV
Blunt, Col Ernest, 1851–1932, vol. III
Blunt, Brig. Gerald Charles Gordon, 1883–1967, vol. VI
Blunt, Sir John Elijah, 1832–1916, vol. II
Blunt, Captain Sir John Harvey, 8th Bt, 1839–1922, vol. II
Blunt, Sir John Harvey, 9th Bt, 1872–1938, vol. III
Blunt, Sir John Lionel Reginald, 10th Bt, 1908–1969, vol. VI
Blunt, John Silvester, 1874–1943, vol. IV
Blunt, Reginald, 1857–1944, vol. IV
Blunt, Sir Richard David Harvey, 11th Bt, 1912–1975, vol. VII
Blunt, Rt Rev. Richard Lefevre, 1833–1910, vol. I
Blunt, Wilfrid Scawen, 1840–1922, vol. II
Blunt, Sir William, 7th Bt, 1826–1902, vol. I
Blunt, Rear-Adm. William Frederick, 1870–1928, vol. II
Blyth, 1st Baron, 1841–1925, vol. II
Blyth, 2nd Baron, 1868–1943, vol. IV
Blyth, 3rd Baron, 1905–1977, vol. VII
Blyth, Alexander Wynter, died 1921, vol. II
Blyth, Alfred Carleton, 1865–1936, vol. III
Blyth, Benjamin Hall, 1849–1917, vol. II

Blyth, Lt-Col Charles Frederick Tolmé, 1868–1950, vol. IV

Blyth, Rt Rev. George Francis Popham, *died* 1914, vol. I

Blyth, Lt-Col James, 1869–1925, vol. II

Blyth, James, 1864–1933, vol. III

Blyth, James Pattison C.; *see* Currie-Blyth.

Blyth, Ormond Alfred, 1879–1947, vol. IV

Blyth, Robert Henderson, 1919–1970, vol. VI

Blyth, Rev. Thomas Allen, 1844–1913, vol. I

Blythe, Ernest, 1889–1975, vol. VII

Blythe, Wilfred Lawson, 1896–1975, vol. VII

Blythswood, 1st Baron, 1837–1908, vol. I

Blythswood, 2nd Baron, 1839–1916, vol. II

Blythswood, 3rd Baron, 1845–1918, vol. II

Blythswood, 4th Baron, 1870–1929, vol. III

Blythswood, 5th Baron, 1877–1937, vol. III

Blythswood, 6th Baron, 1881–1940, vol. III

Blythswood, 7th Baron, 1919–1940, vol. III

Blyton, Enid Mary, *died* 1968, vol. VI

Boag, Sir George Townsend, 1884–1969, vol. VI

Board, Air Cdre Andrew George, 1878–1973, vol. VII

Board, Sir (Archibald) Vyvyan, 1884–1973, vol. VII

Board, Ernest, 1877–1934, vol. III

Board, Peter, 1858–1945, vol. IV

Board, Sir Vyvyan; *see* Board, Sir A. V.

Board, Sir William John, 1869–1946, vol. IV

Boardman, Adm. Frederick Ross, 1843–1927, vol. II

Boardman, Paymaster Captain John Cogswell, *died* 1942, vol. IV

Boas, Franz, 1858–1942, vol. IV

Boas, Frederick S., 1862–1957, vol. V

Boas, Guy, 1896–1966, vol. VI

Boase, Lt-Gen. Allan Joseph, 1894–1964, vol. VI

Boase, Col. George Orlebar, 1881–1966, vol. VI

Boase, Thomas Sherrer Ross, 1898–1974, vol. VII

Boase, William Norman, 1870–1938, vol. III

Bocquet, Guy Sutton, 1882–1961, vol. VI

Bocquet, Roscoe, 1839–1920, vol. II

Boddam, Maj.-Gen. Welby Wraughton, 1832–1906, vol. I

Boddam-Whetham, Rear-Adm. Edye Kington, 1887–1944, vol. IV

Boddam-Whetham, Major Sydney A., 1885–1925, vol. II

Boddie, Rear-Adm. Ronald Charles, 1886–1967, vol. VI

Boddington, Rev. Edward Henry, *died* 1920, vol. II

Boddis, Alfred Charles, 1895–1958, vol. V

Bode, Major Louis William, 1860–1936, vol. III

Boden, Rev. Charles John, 1853–1937, vol. III

Bodenham-Lubienski, Count Louis, 1852–1909, vol. I

Bodenstein, Helgard Dewald Johannes, 1881–1943, vol. IV

Bodet, Jaime T.; *see* Torres Bodet.

Bodington, Rev. Charles, 1836–1918, vol. II

Bodington, Ven. Eric James, 1862–1929, vol. III

Bodington, Sir Nathan, 1848–1911, vol. I

Bodinnar, Sir John Francis, *died* 1958, vol. V

Bodkin, Sir Archibald Henry, 1862–1957, vol. V

Bodkin, Gilbert Edwin, 1886–1955, vol. V

Bodkin, Matthias M'Donnell, 1850–1933, vol. III

Bodkin, Thomas Patrick, 1887–1961, vol. VI

Bodkin, Fr William, 1867–1930, vol. III

Bodkin, Hon. Sir William Alexander, 1883–1964, vol. VI

Bodle, Brig.-Gen. William, 1855–1924, vol. II

Bodley, George Frederick, 1827–1907, vol. I

Bodley, John Edward Courtenay, 1853–1925, vol. II

Body, Rev. George, 1840–1911, vol. I

Body, Maj.-Gen. Kenneth Marten, 1883–1973, vol. VII

Boegner, Marc, 1881–1970, vol. VI

Boevey, Sir Francis Hyde Crawley-, 6th Bt, 1868–1928, vol. II

Boevey, Sir Lance (Launcelot Valentine Hyde) C.; 7th Bt; *see* Crawley-Boevey.

Boevey, Sir Thomas Hyde Crawley, 5th Bt, 1837–1912, vol. I

Boffa, Sir Paul, 1890–1962, vol. VI

Bogart, Humphrey de Forest, 1899–1957, vol. V

Boger, Lt-Col Dudley Coryndon, *died* 1935, vol. III

Boger, Major R. W., 1868–1910, vol. I

Bogert, Clarence Atkinson, 1864–1949, vol. IV

Bogert, Ven. James John, 1835–1920, vol. II

Boggis-Rolfe, Douglass Horace, 1874–1966, vol. VI

Bogle, Very Rev. Andrew Nisbet, *died* 1957, vol. V

Bogle, Lt-Col John Savile, 1872–1940, vol. III

Bogle, Lockhart, *died* 1900, vol. I

Bogle-Smith, Col Steuart, 1859–1921, vol. II

Bohane, (Albert) Edward, 1873–1940, vol. III

Bohane, Edward; *see* Bohane, A. E.

Bohlen, Charles Eustis, 1904–1974, vol. VII

Bohr, Niels Henrik David, 1885–1962, vol. VI

Boileau, Sir Edmond Charles, 7th Bt, 1903–1980, vol. VII

Boileau, Col Etienne Ronald Partridge, 1870–1947, vol. IV

Boileau, Sir Francis George Manningham, 2nd Bt, 1830–1900, vol. I

Boileau, Sir Francis James, 5th Bt, 1871–1945, vol. IV

Boileau, Col Francis William, 1835–1915, vol. I (A)

Boileau, Col Frank Ridley Farrer, 1867–1914, vol. I

Boileau, Sir Gilbert George Benson, 6th Bt, 1898–1978, vol. VII

Boileau, Brig.-Gen. Guy Hamilton, 1870–1962, vol. VI

Boileau, Hugh Evan Ridley, 1906–1952, vol. V

Boileau, Sir Maurice Colborne, 3rd Bt, 1865–1937, vol. III

Boileau, Sir Raymond Frederic, 4th Bt, 1868–1942, vol. IV

Boillot, Félix, 1880–1961, vol. VI

Bois, Col John, 1881–1941, vol. IV

Bois, Sir Stanley, 1864–1938, vol. III

Boisragon, Col Guy Hudleston, 1864–1931, vol. III

Boissier, Arthur Paul, 1882–1953, vol. V

Boissier, Rev. George John, 1857–1929, vol. III

Boissier, Léopold, 1893–1968, vol. VI

Boissier, Marie Louis Gaston, 1823–1908, vol. I

Boito, Arrigo, 1842–1918, vol. II

Bojer, Johan, 1872–1959, vol. VI

Bok, Edward William, 1863–1930, vol. III

Bolam, Rev. Cecil Edward, 1875–1960, vol. V

Bolam, Sir Robert, *died* 1939, vol. III
Boland, Sir (Edward) Rowan, 1898–1972, vol. VII
Boland, Harry, *died* 1922, vol. II
Boland, John Pius, 1870–1958, vol. V
Boland, Sir Rowan; *see* Boland, Sir E. R.
Bolden, John Leonard, 1841–1929, vol. III
Boldero, Sir Harold Esmond Arnison, 1889–1960, vol. VI
Boldrewood, Rolf, (Thomas Alexander Browne), 1826–1915, vol. I
Bole, Hon. W. Norman, 1846–1923, vol. II
Boles, Lt-Col Dennis Coleridge, 1885–1958, vol. V
Boles, Lt-Col Sir Dennis Fortescue, 1st Bt, 1861–1935, vol. III
Boles, Sir Gerald Fortescue, 2nd Bt, 1900–1945, vol. IV
Boles, Rev. Richard Henry, 1855–1929, vol. III
Bolingbroke, 5th Viscount, **and St John,** 6th Viscount, 1820–1900, vol. I (the entry is incorrect)
Bolingbroke, 6th Viscount, **and St John,** 7th Viscount, 1896–1974, vol. VII
Bolingbroke, Leonard George, 1859–1927, vol. II
Bolitho, Lt-Col Sir Edward Hoblyn Warren, *died* 1969, vol. VI
Bolitho, Hector; *see* Bolitho, Henry H.
Bolitho, (Henry) Hector, 1897–1974, vol. VII
Bolitho, Captain Richard John Bruce, 1889–1965, vol. VI
Bolitho, Thomas Bedford, 1835–1915, vol. I
Bolitho, Thomas Robins, 1840–1925, vol. II
Bolitho, Lt-Col William Edward Thomas, 1862–1919, vol. II
Bolland, Robert William, 1915–1974, vol. VII
Bollard, Hon. R. F., *died* 1927, vol. II
Bolling, Cunliffe Lawrance, 1898–1938, vol. III
Bols, Major Louis Jean, 1867–1909, vol. I
Bols, Lt-Gen. Sir Louis Jean, 1867–1930, vol. III
Bolst, Captain Clifford Charles Alan Lawrence E.; *see* Erskine-Bolst.
Bolster, Francis, *died* 1941, vol. IV
Bolster, Rev. Robert Crofts, *died* 1918, vol. II
Bolster, Captain Thomas Charles Carpenter, *died* 1955, vol. V
Bolt, Rev. G. H., 1863–1947, vol. IV
Bolt, George Thomas, 1900–1971, vol. VII
Bolter, Albert Ernest, 1856–1933, vol. III
Bolton, 4th Baron, 1845–1922, vol. II
Bolton, 5th Baron, 1869–1944, vol. IV
Bolton, 6th Baron, 1900–1963, vol. VI
Bolton, Arthur Thomas, 1864–1945, vol. IV
Bolton, Charles, *died* 1947, vol. IV
Bolton, Brig. Charles Arthur, 1882–1964, vol. VI
Bolton, Rev. Charles Nelson, 1844–1918, vol. II
Bolton, Charles Walter, 1850–1919, vol. II
Bolton, Lt-Col Edward Frederick, 1879–1977, vol. VII
Bolton, Edward Richards, 1878–1939, vol. III
Bolton, Sir Edwin, 1st Bt, 1858–1931, vol. III
Bolton, Elizabeth, 1878–1961, vol. VI
Bolton, Sir Frederic, 1851–1920, vol. II
Bolton, Gambier, *died* 1928, vol. II
Bolton, Guy, 1884–1979, vol. VII
Bolton, Herbert, *died* 1936, vol. III

Bolton, Sir (Horatio) Norman, 1875–1965, vol. VI
Bolton, Sir John Brown, 1902–1980, vol. VII (AII)
Bolton, Joseph Cheney, 1819–1901, vol. I
Bolton, Joseph Shaw, 1867–1946, vol. IV
Bolton, Louis Hamilton, 1884–1953, vol. V
Bolton, Sir Norman; *see* Bolton, Sir H. N.
Bolton, Thomas Dolling, 1841–1906, vol. I
Bolton, Thomas Henry, 1841–1916, vol. II
Bolton, Brig.-Gen. William Kinsey, 1861–1941, vol. IV
Bomanji, Sir Dhunjibhoy, *died* 1937, vol. III
Bomford, Surg.-Gen. Sir Gerald, 1851–1915, vol. I
Bomford, Sir Hugh, 1882–1939, vol. III
Bomon-Behram, Sir Jehangir Bomonji, 1868–1949, vol. IV
Bompas, Cecil Henry, 1868–1956, vol. V
Bompas, Henry Mason, 1836–1909, vol. I
Bompas, Rt Rev. William Carpenter, 1834–1906, vol. I
Bonaparte, Hon. Charles Joseph, 1851–1921, vol. II
Bonaparte, HIH Prince Roland, 1858–1924, vol. II
Bonaparte-Wyse, Andrew Nicholas, 1870–1940, vol. III
Bonar, Henry Alfred Constant, 1861–1935, vol. III
Bonar, James, 1852–1941, vol. IV
Bonavia, Hon. Edgar, 1868–1927, vol. II
Boncour, Joseph P.; *see* Paul-Boncour.
Bond, Carrie Jacobs-, 1862–1946, vol. IV
Bond, Brig.-Gen. Charles Earbery, 1877–1953, vol. V
Bond, Charles John, *died* 1939, vol. III
Bond, Rev. Charles Watson, 1839–1922, vol. II
Bond, Lt-Col Chetwynd Rokeby Alfred, 1863–1944, vol. IV
Bond, Engr Captain Edmund Edward, 1865–1943, vol. IV
Bond, Edward, 1844–1920, vol. II
Bond, Sir Edward Augustus, 1815–1898, vol. I
Bond, Francis, *died* 1918, vol. II
Bond, Maj.-Gen. Sir Francis George, 1856–1930, vol. III
Bond, Frederick Bligh, 1864–1945, vol. IV
Bond, Henry, 1853–1938, vol. III
Bond, Henry Coulson, 1864–1937, vol. III
Bond, Sir Hubert, 1870–1945, vol. IV
Bond, Col James Henry Robinson, 1871–1943, vol. IV
Bond, Ven. John, 1841–1912, vol. I
Bond, Maj.-Gen. John Arthur Mallock, 1891–1959, vol. V
Bond, John Wentworth Garneys, 1865–1948, vol. IV
Bond, Joshua Walter MacGeough, 1831–1905, vol. I
Bond, Lt-Gen. Sir Lionel Vivian, 1884–1961, vol. VI
Bond, Sir Ralph Stuart, 1871–1968, vol. VI
Bond, Lt-Col Reginald Copleston, 1866–1936, vol. I, vol. III
Bond, Surg. Vice-Adm. Sir Reginald St George Smallridge, 1872–1955, vol. V
Bond, Maj.-Gen. Richard Lawrence, 1890–1979, vol. VII
Bond, Richard Warwick, 1857–1943, vol. IV

Bond, Rt Hon. Sir Robert, 1857–1927, vol. II
Bond, Rev. Robert, *died* 1952, vol. V
Bond, Stanley Shaw, 1877–1943, vol. IV
Bond, Sir Walter Adrian M.; *see* Macgeough Bond.
Bond, Walter Fitzgerald; *see* Fitzgerald, Walter.
Bond, Most Rev. William Bennett, 1815–1906, vol. I
Bond, Maj.-Gen. William Dunn, 1836–1919, vol. II
Bond, William Langley, 1873–1947, vol. IV
Bond, William Linskill, 1892–1950, vol. IV
Bond, William Ralph Garneys, 1880–1952, vol. V
Bondfield, Rt Hon. Margaret Grace, 1873–1953, vol. V
Bone, Sir David William, 1874–1959, vol. V
Bone, Rev. Frederic James, 1844–1917, vol. II
Bone, Gertrude Helena, (Lady Bone), *died* 1962, vol. VI
Bone, Engr-Rear-Adm. Howard, 1869–1955, vol. V
Bone, James, 1872–1962, vol. VI
Bone, John Wardle, 1869–1949, vol. IV
Bone, Sir Muirhead, 1876–1953, vol. V
Bone, Phyllis Mary, 1894–1972, vol. VII
Bone, Group Captain Reginald John, 1888–1972, vol. VII
Bone, Stephen, 1904–1958, vol. V
Bone, William Arthur, 1871–1938, vol. III
Bonet Maury, Amy-Gaston, 1842–1919, vol. II
Bonfield, John Martin, 1915–1976, vol. VII
Bonham, Lt-Col Charles Barnard, 1871–1943, vol. IV
Bonham, Major Sir Eric Henry, 3rd Bt, 1875–1937, vol. III
Bonham, Sir George Francis, 2nd Bt, 1847–1927, vol. II
Bonham, Col John, 1834–1928, vol. II
Bonham, Major Walter Floyd, *died* 1905, vol. I
Bonham-Carter, Alfred, *died* 1910, vol. I
Bonham-Carter, Arthur Thomas, 1869–1916, vol. II
Bonham-Carter, Gen. Sir Charles, 1876–1955, vol. V
Bonham Carter, Rear-Adm. Sir Christopher Douglas, 1907–1975, vol. VII
Bonham-Carter, Air Cdre David William Frederick, 1901–1974, vol. VII
Bonham-Carter, Sir Edgar, 1870–1956, vol. V
Bonham Carter, Helen Violet; *see* Baroness Asquith of Yarnbury.
Bonham-Carter, Ian Malcolm, 1882–1953, vol. V
Bonham Carter, Sir Maurice, 1880–1960, vol. V
Bonham-Carter, Adm. Sir Stuart Sumner, 1889–1972, vol. VII
Bonheur, Rosa, (Marie Rosalie Bonheur), 1822–1899, vol. I
Bonhote, Rev. Edward Frederic, 1888–1972, vol. VI
Boni, Giacomo, 1859–1925, vol. II
Boniwell, Martin Charles, 1883–1967, vol. VI
Bonn, Leo, 1850–1929, vol. III
Bonn, Sir Max J., 1877–1943, vol. IV
Bonnar, John Calderwood, 1888–1956, vol. V
Bonnat, Leon, *died* 1922, vol. II
Bonner, Rev. Carey, 1859–1938, vol. III
Bonner, Charles George, 1884–1951, vol. V
Bonner, Sir George Albert, 1862–1952, vol. V

Bonner, Hypatia Bradlaugh, 1858–1935, vol. III
Bonner, Captain Singleton, 1879–1917, vol. II
Bonner-Smith, David; *see* Smith.
Bonnet, Georges, 1889–1973, vol. VII
Bonnetard, Sir France; *see* Bonnetard, Sir N. P. F.
Bonnetard, Sir (Nicholas Patrick) France, 1907–1969, vol. VI
Bonney, Rev. Edwin, 1873–1946, vol. IV
Bonney, Rev. Thomas George, 1833–1923, vol. II
Bonney, Victor, *died* 1953, vol. V
Bonsal, Stephen, 1865–1951, vol. V
Bonsall, Arthur Charles, 1859–1924, vol. II (A), vol. III
Bonsall, Major Hugh Edward, *died* 1928, vol. II
Bonser, Rev. Henry, 1884–1966, vol. VI
Bonser, Rt Hon. Sir John Winfield, 1847–1914, vol. I
Bonser, Wilfrid, 1887–1971, vol. VII
Bonsey, Henry Dawes, *died* 1919, vol. II
Bonsey, Rev. William, 1845–1909, vol. I
Bonsor, Sir Bryan Cosmo, 3rd Bt, 1916–1977, vol. VII
Bonsor, Sir Cosmo; *see* Bonsor, Sir H. C. O.
Bonsor, Sir (Henry) Cosmo (Orme), 1st Bt, 1848–1929, vol. III
Bonsor, Major Sir Reginald, 2nd Bt, 1879–1959, vol. V
Bonus, Maj.-Gen. Joseph, 1836–1926, vol. II
Bonus, Col William John, 1862–1943, vol. IV
Bonvalot, Pierre Gabriel, 1853–1933, vol. III
Bonwick, Alfred James, 1883–1949, vol. IV
Bonython, Hon. Sir (John) Langdon, 1848–1939, vol. III
Bonython, Sir (John) Lavington, 1875–1960, vol. V
Bonython, Sir Lavington; *see* Bonython, Sir J. L.
Booker, Lt-Col George Edward Nussey, *died* 1938, vol. III
Booker, Sir William Lane, 1824–1905, vol. I
Bookey, Col John Trench Brownrigg, 1847–1921, vol. II
Boome, Brig.-Gen. Edward Herbert, 1865–1945, vol. IV
Boon, Sir Geoffrey Pearl, 1888–1970, vol. VI
Boon, Quartermaster George, 1846–1927, vol. II
Boon, John, 1859–1928, vol. II
Boord, Sir Arthur; *see* Boord, Sir W. A.
Boord, Sir Richard William, 3rd Bt, 1907–1975, vol. VII
Boord, Sir (Thomas) William, 1st Bt, 1838–1912, vol. I
Boord, Sir William; *see* Boord, Sir T. W.
Boord, Sir (William) Arthur, 2nd Bt, 1862–1928, vol. II
Boos, Sir Werner James, 1911–1974, vol. VII
Boose, Major James Rufus, 1859–1936, vol. III
Boosey, Leslie Arthur, 1887–1979, vol. VII
Boot, Rev. Alfred, 1854–1937, vol. III
Boot, Sir Horace, 1873–1943, vol. IV
Boot, William Henry James, *died* 1918, vol. II
Booth, Alfred, 1893–1965, vol. VI
Booth, Sir Alfred Allen, 1st Bt (*cr* 1916), 1872–1948, vol. IV
Booth, Sir Arthur; *see* Booth, Sir G. A. W.
Booth, Mrs Bramwell, (Florence Eleanor), 1861–1957, vol. V

Booth, Rt Hon. Charles, 1840–1916, vol. II
Booth, Charles, 1868–1938, vol. III
Booth, Sir Charles H., 1853–1939, vol. III
Booth, Hon. Charles Lutley S.; see Sclater-Booth.
Booth, Sir Charles Sylvester, 1897–1970, vol. VI
Booth, Edgar Harold, 1893–1963, vol. VI
Booth, Dame Edith; see Evans, Dame Edith.
Booth, Eva G.; see Gore-Booth.
Booth, Evangeline Cory, died 1950, vol. IV
Booth, Florence Eleanor; see Booth, Mrs Bramwell.
Booth, Rear-Adm. Sir Francis Fitzgerald H.; see Haworth-Booth.
Booth, Frederick Handel, 1867–1947, vol. IV
Booth, Sir (G.) Arthur W., 1879–1972, vol. VII
Booth, George Macaulay, 1877–1971, vol. VII
Booth, Sir Henry William Gore-, 5th Bt (cr 1760), 1843–1900, vol. I
Booth, James William, died 1953, vol. V
Booth, John Bennion, 1880–1961, vol. VI
Booth, John Reginald Trevor, 1883–1963, vol. VI
Booth, Most Rev. Joseph John, 1886–1965, vol. VI
Booth, Sir Josslyn (Augustus Richard) Gore-, 6th Bt (cr 1760), 1869–1944, vol. IV
Booth, Very Rev. Lancelot Parker, died 1925, vol. II
Booth, Leonard William, 1856–1923, vol. II
Booth, Mary Booth, 1885–1969, vol. VI
Booth, Major Sir Paul, 1884–1963, vol. VI
Booth, Sir Philip, 2nd Bt (cr 1916), 1907–1960, vol. V
Booth, S. Lawson, died 1928, vol. II
Booth, W. Bramwell, 1856–1929, vol. III
Booth, W. S., 1896–1972, vol. VII
Booth, Col Hon. Walter Dashwood S.; see Sclater-Booth.
Booth, Walter Reynolds, 1891–1963, vol. VI
Booth, Rev. William, 1829–1912, vol. I
Booth-Gravely, Sir Walter, 1882–1971, vol. VII
Booth Tucker, Frederick St George de Lautour, 1853–1929, vol. III
Boothby, Sir Brooke, 11th Bt, 1856–1913, vol. I
Boothby, Sir Charles Francis, 12th Bt, 1858–1926, vol. II
Boothby, Captain Evelyn Leonard Beridge, 1876–1937, vol. III
Boothby, Captain Frederick Lewis Maitland, 1881–1940, vol. III
Boothby, Guy Newell, 1867–1905, vol. I
Boothby, Rev. Sir Herbert Cecil, 13th Bt, 1863–1935, vol. III
Boothby, Comdr Hubert Basil, 1863–1941, vol. IV
Boothby, Josiah, 1837–1916, vol. II
Boothby, Sir Robert Tuite, 1871–1941, vol. IV
Boothby, Sir Seymour William Brooke, 14th Bt, 1866–1951, vol. V
Boothby, Cdre William Osbert, 1866–1913, vol. I
Boothman, Air Chief Marshal Sir John Nelson, 1901–1957, vol. V
Booty, Arthur Ernest, 1875–1932, vol. III
Booty, Vice-Adm. Edward Leonard, 1871–1949, vol. IV
Boppe, Lucien, 1834–1909, vol. I (A)
Bor, Gen. James Henry, 1857–1914, vol. I
Bor, Max; see Adrian, Max.

Bor, Norman Loftus, 1893–1972, vol. VII
Borah, William Edgar, 1865–1940, vol. III
Boraston, Sir John, 1851–1920, vol. II
Boraston, Lt-Col John Herbert, 1885–1969, vol. VI
Borchgrevink, Carsten E., 1864–1934, vol. III
Bordeaux, Henry, 1870–1963, vol. VI
Borden, Rev. Byron Crane, 1850–1929, vol. III
Borden, Hon. Sir Frederick William, 1847–1917, vol. II
Borden, Mary, (Lady Spears), died 1968, vol. VI
Borden, Rt Hon. Sir Robert Laird, 1854–1937, vol. III
Bordes, Charles, 1865–1909, vol. I, vol. I (A)
Bordet, Jules, 1870–1961, vol. VI
Bordonaro, Antonio Chiaramonte, 1877–1932, vol. III
Boreel, Sir Alfred, 12th Bt, 1883–1964, vol. VI
Boreel, Sir Francis William Robert, 11th Bt, 1882–1941, vol. VI
Boreel, Sir Jacob Willem Gustaaf, 10th Bt, 1852–1937, vol. III
Boreham, Ven. Frederick, 1888–1966, vol. VI
Borenius, Tancred, 1885–1948, vol. IV
Borg, Sir George, 1887–1954, vol. V
Borg, Raphael, 1840–1903, vol. I
Borg Olivier, George, 1911–1980, vol. VII
Borgeaud, Charles, 1861–1940, vol. III
Boring, Edwin Garrigues, 1886–1968, vol. VI
Borland, John Ernest, died 1937, vol. III
Borland, Captain John MacInnes, 1869–1946, vol. IV
Borland, Kenneth Alexander, died 1948, vol. IV
Borland, Rev. William, 1867–1945, vol. IV
Born, Max, 1882–1970, vol. VI
Borradaile, Col George William, 1838–1927, vol. II
Borradaile, Brig.-Gen. Harry Benn, 1860–1948, vol. IV
Borradaile, Lancelot Alexander, 1872–1945, vol. IV
Borradaile, Rev. Robert Hudson, died 1914, vol. I
Borrajo, Edward Marto, 1853–1909, vol. I
Borrett, Adm. George Holmes, died 1952, vol. V
Borrett, Maj.-Gen. Herbert Charles, 1841–1919, vol. II
Borrett, Lt-Gen. Sir Oswald Cuthbert, 1878–1950, vol. IV
Borrowes, Sir Erasmus Dixon, 9th Bt, 1831–1898, vol. I
Borrowes, Sir Eustace Dixon, 11th Bt, 1866–1939, vol. III
Borrowes, Lt-Col Sir Kildare Dixon, 10th Bt, 1852–1924, vol. II
Borschette, Albert, 1920–1976, vol. VII
Borthwick, 17th Baron, 1867–1910, vol. I
Borthwick, Albert William, died 1937, vol. III
Borthwick, Lt-Col Alexander, 1839–1914, vol. I
Borthwick, Captain Alfred Edward, 1871–1955, vol. V
Borthwick, Algernon Malcolm, 1907–1975, vol. VII
Borthwick, Brig.-Gen. Francis Henry, 1883–1977, vol. VII
Borthwick, Henry, 1868–1937, vol. III
Borthwick, Sir Thomas, 1st Bt, 1835–1912, vol. I
Borthwick, Sir Thomas Banks, 2nd Bt; see Whitburgh.

Borthwick, William Henry, 1832–1928, vol. II
Borton, Air Vice-Marshal Amyas Eden, 1886–1969, vol. VI
Borton, Lt-Col Arthur Drummond, 1883–1933, vol. III
Borton, Col Charles Edward, 1857–1924, vol. II
Borton, Neville Travers, 1870–1938, vol. III
Borwick, 1st Baron, 1845–1936, vol. III
Borwick, 2nd Baron, 1880–1941, vol. IV
Borwick, 3rd Baron, 1886–1961, vol. VI
Borwick, Lt-Col George Oldroyd, 1879–1964, vol. VI
Borwick, Leonard, 1868–1925, vol. II
Borwick, Lt-Col Malcolm, 1882–1957, vol. V
Bosanquet, Sir Albert; see Bosanquet, Sir F. A.
Bosanquet, Bernard, 1848–1923, vol. II
Bosanquet, Bernard James Tindal, 1877–1936, vol. III
Bosanquet, Adm. Sir Day Hort, 1843–1923, vol. II
Bosanquet, Sir (Frederick) Albert, 1837–1923, vol. II
Bosanquet, Major George Richard Bosanquet S.; see Smith-Bosanquet.
Bosanquet, Adm. George Stanley, 1835–1914, vol. I
Bosanquet, Helen, 1860–1925, vol. II
Bosanquet, Captain Henry Theodore Augustus, 1870–1959, vol. V
Bosanquet, Sir Oswald Vivian, 1866–1933, vol. III
Bosanquet, Robert Carr, 1871–1935, vol. III
Bosanquet, Robert Holford Macdowall, died 1912, vol. I
Bosanquet, Sir Ronald Courthope; see Bosanquet, Sir S. R. C.
Bosanquet, Sir (Samuel) Ronald Courthope, 1868–1952, vol. V
Bosanquet, Theodora, 1880–1961, vol. VI
Bosanquet, Vivian Henry Courthope, 1872–1943, vol. IV
Bosanquet, William Cecil, died 1941, vol. IV
Boscawen, Rt Hon. Sir Arthur Sackville Trevor G.; see Griffith-Boscawen.
Boscawen, Major Hon. George Edward, 1888–1918, vol. II
Boscawen, Hon. Hugh le Despencer, 1844–1908, vol. I
Boscawen, Hon. John Richard De Clare, 1860–1915, vol. I (A)
Bosch, Carl, 1874–1940, vol. III
Bose, Sir Bipin Krishna, 1851–1933, vol. III
Bose, Rai Bahadur C.; see Chunilal Bose.
Bose, Sir Jagadis Chunder, 1858–1937, vol. III
Bose, Sir Kailas Chandra, Rai Bahadur, died 1927, vol. II
Bose, Satyendranath, 1894–1974, vol. VII
Bossom, Baron (Life Peer); Alfred Charles Bossom, 1881–1965, vol. VI
Bostock, Rev. Charles, 1869–1943, vol. IV
Bostock, Geoffrey, 1880–1961, vol. VI
Bostock, Henry, died 1923, vol. II
Bostock, Henry John, 1870–1956, vol. V
Bostock, Hon. Hewitt, 1864–1930, vol. III
Bostock, John, 1916–1977, vol. VII
Bostock, Col John Southey, 1875–1930, vol. III
Bostock, Samuel, died 1938, vol. III

Bostock, Air Vice-Marshal William Dowling, 1892–1968, vol. VI
Boston, 6th Baron, 1860–1941, vol. IV
Boston, 7th Baron, 1889–1958, vol. V
Boston, 8th Baron, 1897–1972, vol. VII
Boston, 9th Baron, 1897–1978, vol. VII
Boston, Sir Henry (Josiah) Lightfoot, 1898–1969, vol. VI
Boswall, Sir George Lauderdale H.; see Houstoun-Boswall.
Boswall, Sir George Reginald H.; see Houstoun-Boswall.
Boswall, Major Sir Gordon H.; see Houstoun-Boswall.
Boswall, Sir (Thomas) Randolph H.; see Houstoun-Boswall.
Boswall, Sir William Evelyn H.; see Houstoun-Boswall.
Boswell, Alexander Bruce, 1884–1962, vol. VI
Boswell, Arthur Radcliffe, born 1838, vol. II
Boswell, Maj.-Gen. John James, 1835–1908, vol. I
Boswell, Captain Lennox Albert Knox, 1898–1975, vol. VII
Boswell, Percy George Hamnall, 1886–1960, vol. V
Bosworth, George Herbert, 1896–1979, vol. VII
Bosworth, Col William John, 1858–1923, vol. II
Bosworth-Smith, Nevil Digby, 1886–1964, vol. VI
Bosworth Smith, Reginald Montagu, 1872–1944, vol. IV
Boteler, Sir Edgar Collins Boehm, 2nd Bt, 1869–1928, vol. II
Botha, Colin Graham, 1883–1973, vol. VII
Botha, Rt Hon. Louis, 1863–1919, vol. II
Botham, Arthur William, 1874–1963, vol. VI
Bothamley, Rev. Hilton, died 1919, vol. II
Bothamley, Rev. Canon Westley, 1861–1933, vol. III
Bothe, Walther, 1891–1957, vol. V
Bott, Alan John, died 1952, vol. V
Bott, Lt-Col Robert Henry, 1882–1938, vol. III
Botteley, James, born 1839, vol. III
Botterell, Percy Dumville, 1880–1952, vol. V
Bottome, Phyllis, (Mrs A. E. Forbes Dennis), 1884–1963, vol. VI
Bottomley, Albert Ernest, 1873–1950, vol. IV
Bottomley, Sir Cecil; see Bottomley, Sir W. C.
Bottomley, Edwin, died 1929, vol. III
Bottomley, Gordon, 1874–1948, vol. IV
Bottomley, Col Herbert, 1866–1926, vol. II (A), vol. III
Bottomley, James H., 1857–1934, vol. III
Bottomley, James Thomson, 1845–1926, vol. II
Bottomley, John Mellor, 1888–1960, vol. V (A)
Bottomley, Air Chief Marshal Sir Norman Howard, 1891–1970, vol. VI
Bottomley, William Beecroft, 1863–1922, vol. II
Bottomley, Sir (William) Cecil, 1878–1954, vol. V
Boucaut, Hon. Sir James Penn, 1831–1916, vol. II
Bouch, Thomas, 1882–1963, vol. VI
Bouchard, Hon. T. Damien, died 1962, vol. VI
Bouche-Leclercq, Auguste, 1842–1923, vol. II
Boucher, Lt-Col Benjamin Hamilton, 1864–1928, vol. II
Boucher, Rev. Charles Estcourt, 1856–1940, vol. III

Boucher, Maj.-Gen. Sir Charles Hamilton, 1898–1951, vol. V
Boucher, Rear-Adm. Maitland Walter Sabine, 1888–1963, vol. VI
Boucher, Maj.-Gen. Valentine, 1904–1961, vol. VI
Boucherett, Emilia Jessie, 1825–1905, vol. I
Bouchier, Air Vice-Marshal Sir Cecil Arthur, 1895–1979, vol. VII
Boucicault, Dion, 1859–1929, vol. III
Boughey, Rev. Anchitel Harry Fletcher, 1849–1936, vol. III
Boughey, Charles Lovell Fletcher, 1887–1934, vol. III
Boughey, Sir Francis, 8th Bt, 1848–1927, vol. II
Boughey, Rev. Sir George, 5th Bt, 1837–1910, vol. I
Boughey, Col George Fletcher Ottley, 1844–1918, vol. II
Boughey, Sir George Menteth, 9th Bt, 1879–1959, vol. V
Boughey, Maj.-Gen. John, 1845–1932, vol. III
Boughey, Sir Richard James, 10th Bt, 1925–1978, vol. VII
Boughey, Rev. Sir Robert, 7th Bt, 1843–1921, vol. II
Boughey, Sir Thomas Fletcher, 4th Bt, 1836–1906, vol. I
Boughey, Sir William Fletcher, 6th Bt, 1840–1912, vol. I
Boughton, Rev. Canon Charles Henry Knowler, 1883–1943, vol. IV
Boughton, Sir Charles Henry Rouse-, 11th Bt, 1825–1906, vol. I
Boughton, Sir Edward Hotham Rouse-, 13th Bt, 1893–1963, vol. VI
Boughton, George Henry, 1833–1905, vol. I
Boughton, Rutland, 1878–1960, vol. V
Boughton, Sir William St Andrew Rouse-, 12th Bt, 1853–1937, vol. III
Boughton-Knight, Charles Andrew R.; see Rouse-Boughton-Knight.
Bougle, C., died 1940, vol. III
Bouguereau, Adolphe William, 1825–1905, vol. I
Boulanger, Nadia Juliette, 1887–1979, vol. VII
Bould, John, 1855–1938, vol. III
Boulden, Rev. Alfred William, 1849–1920, vol. II
Boulenger, Charles L., 1885–1940, vol. III
Boulenger, Edward George, 1888–1946, vol. IV
Boulenger, George Albert, died 1937, vol. III
Boulger, Demetrius Charles, 1853–1928, vol. II
Boulger, Dorothy Henrietta, 1847–1923, vol. II
Boulger, George Simonds, 1853–1922, vol. II
Boulnois, Charles, 1832–1912, vol. I
Boulnois, Edmund, 1838–1911, vol. I
Boulter, Rev. Canon John Sidney, 1890–1969, vol. VI
Boulter, Robert, 1885–1973, vol. VII
Boulter, Stanley Carr, 1852–1917, vol. II
Boulter, Rev. Walter Easton, 1874–1936, vol. III
Boulton, A. C. Forster, 1862–1949, vol. IV
Boulton, Lt-Col Aubrey Holmes, 1882–1932, vol. III
Boulton, Major Charles Percy, 1867–1916, vol. II
Boulton, Sir (Denis Duncan) Harold (Owen), 3rd Bt (cr 1905), 1892–1968, vol. VI

Boulton, Maj.-Gen. Harold, 1872–1955, vol. V
Boulton, Sir Harold; see Boulton, Sir D. D. H. O.
Boulton, Sir Harold Edwin, 2nd Bt (cr 1905), 1859–1935, vol. III
Boulton, Percy, 1840–1909, vol. I
Boulton, Sir Samuel Bagster, 1st Bt (cr 1905), 1830–1918, vol. II
Boulton, Sidney, 1855–1932, vol. III
Boulton, William Savage, 1867–1954, vol. V
Boulton, Sir William Whytehead, 1st Bt (cr 1944), 1873–1949, vol. IV
Boumphrey, Geoffrey Maxwell, 1894–1969, vol. VI
Bouquet, Rev. Alan Coates, 1884–1976, vol. VII
Bourcard, Gustave Amaury René, 1846–1925, vol. II (A), vol. III
Bourcart, Charles Daniel, 1860–1940, vol. III
Bourchier, Arthur, 1864–1927, vol. II
Bourchier, Rev. Basil Graham, 1881–1934, vol. III
Bourchier, Lt-Gen. Eustace Fane, 1822–1902, vol. I
Bourchier, Sir George, 1821–1898, vol. I
Bouchier, James David, 1850–1920, vol. II
Bourchier, Col Hon. Murray William James, 1881–1937, vol. III
Bourchier, Violet, (Mrs Arthur Bourchier); see Vanbrugh, Violet.
Bourchier, Very Rev. William Chadwick, died 1924, vol. II
Bourdelle, Antoine; see Bourdelle, E. A.
Bourdelle, (Emile) Antoine, 1861–1929, vol. III
Bourdillon, Sir Bernard Henry, 1883–1948, vol. IV
Bourdillon, Francis Bernard, 1883–1970, vol. VI
Bourdillon, Francis William, 1852–1921, vol. III
Bourdillon, Sir James Austin, 1848–1913, vol. I
Bourdillon, Lancelot Gerard, 1888–1950, vol. IV
Bourdillon, Robert Benedict, 1889–1971, vol. VII
Bourgeois, Emile, 1857–1934, vol. III
Bourgeois, Jeanne; see Mistinguett.
Bourgeois, Léon Victor Auguste, 1851–1925, vol. II
Bourget, Paul, 1852–1935, vol. III
Bourinot, Sir John George, 1837–1903, vol. I
Bourke, Hon. Algernon Henry, 1854–1922, vol. II
Bourke, Ven. Cecil Frederick Joseph, died 1910, vol. I
Bourke, Edmund, 1857–1939, vol. III
Bourke, Maj.-Gen. Sir George Deane, 1852–1936, vol. III
Bourke, Rev. Hon. George Wingfield, 1829–1903, vol. I
Bourke, Major Sir Harry L.; see Legge-Bourke.
Bourke, Lt-Col Henry Beresford, 1855–1921, vol. II
Bourke, John Francis, 1889–1967, vol. VI
Bourke, Lt-Col John Joseph, 1865–1933, vol. III
Bourke, Matthew J., died 1936, vol. III
Bourke, Hon. Maurice Archibald, 1853–1900, vol. I
Bourke, Lt-Comdr Roland, 1885–1958, vol. V
Bourke, Hon. Terence Theobald, 1865–1923, vol. II
Bourke, Gp Captain Ulick John Deane, 1884–1948, vol. IV
Bourke-White, Margaret, 1906–1971, vol. VII
Bourne, Gen. Sir Alan George Barwys, 1882–1967, vol. VI
Bourne, Aleck William, 1886–1974, vol, VII
Bourne, Sir Alfred Gibbs, 1859–1940, vol. III
Bourne, Rev. Charles William, 1846–1927, vol. II

Bourne, Edward John, 1922–1974, vol. VII
Bourne, His Eminence Cardinal Francis, 1861–1935, vol. III
Bourne, Sir Frederick Chalmers, 1891–1977, vol. VII
Bourne, Sir Frederick Samuel Augustus, 1854–1940, vol. III
Bourne, Geoffrey, 1893–1970, vol. VI
Bourne, George; see Sturt, G.
Bourne, Rev. George Hugh, died 1925, vol. II
Bourne, Gilbert Charles, 1861–1933, vol. III
Bourne, Sir (Henry) Roland (Murray), 1874–1931, vol. III
Bourne, Hugh Clarence, died 1909, vol. I
Bourne, Kenneth Morison, 1893–1968, vol. VI
Bourne, Captain Rt Hon. Robert Croft, 1888–1938, vol. III
Bourne, Sir Roland; see Bourne, Sir H. R. M.
Bourne, Thomas Johnstone, 1864–1947, vol. IV
Bourne, Rev. William St Hill, 1846–1929, vol. III
Bourns, Newcome Whitelaw, died 1927, vol. II
Bousfield, Edward George Paul, 1880–1957, vol. V
Bousfield, Guy William John, 1893–1974, vol. VII
Bousfield, Rt Rev. Henry Brougham, 1832–1902, vol. I
Bousfield, Lt-Col Henry Richings, 1863–1930, vol. III
Bousfield, Col Hugh Delabere, 1872–1951, vol. V
Bousfield, Sir William, 1842–1910, vol. I
Bousfield, William Robert, 1854–1943, vol. IV
Boussac, Marcel, 1889–1980, vol. VII
Boustead, Rev. Canon Harry Wilson, 1858–1942, vol. IV
Boustead, Col Sir Hugh; see Boustead, Col Sir J. E. H.
Boustead, Col Sir (John Edmund) Hugh, 1895–1980, vol. VII
Boutens, Dr Peter Cornelis, 1870–1943, vol. IV
Boutflour, Robert, 1890–1961, vol. VI
Boutflower, Rt Rev. Cecil Henry, 1863–1942, vol. IV
Boutflower, Rev. Douglas Samuel, died 1940, vol. III
Boutroux, Emile, 1845–1921, vol. II
Bouveret, Pascal Adolph Jean D.; see Dagnan-Bouveret.
Bouverie, Rev. Hon. Bertrand P.; see Pleydell-Bouverie.
Bouverie, Hon. Duncombe P.; see Pleydell-Bouverie.
Bouverie, Col Hon. Stuart P.; see Pleydell-Bouverie.
Bouverie-Pusey, Philip Francis, died 1933, vol. III
Bovell, Sir (Conrad Swire) Kerr, 1913–1973, vol. VII
Bovell, Sir Henry Alleyne, 1854–1938, vol. III
Bovell, Vice-Adm. Henry Cecil, 1893–1963, vol. VI
Bovell, John Redman, 1855–1928, vol. II (A), vol. III
Bovell, Sir Kerr; see Bovell, Sir C. S. K.
Bovell-Jones, Thomas Boughton, 1906–1967, vol. VI
Bovenschen, Sir Frederick Carl, died 1977, vol. VII
Bovey, Henry Taylor, died 1912, vol. I

Bovill, Major Anthony Charles Stevens, 1888–1943, vol. IV
Bovill, Charles Harry, 1878–1918, vol. II
Bovill, Edward William, 1892–1966, vol. VI
Boville, Thomas Cooper, 1860–1948, vol. IV
Bowater, Sir Dudley; see Bowater, Sir T. D. B.
Bowater, Sir Eric Vansittart, 1895–1962, vol. VI
Bowater, Major Sir Frank H., 1st Bt (cr 1939), 1866–1947, vol. IV
Bowater, Sir Frederick William, 1867–1924, vol. II
Bowater, Sir Rainald Vansittart, 2nd Bt (cr 1914), 1888–1945, vol. IV
Bowater, Sir T. Vansittart, 1st Bt (cr 1914), 1862–1938, vol. III
Bowater, Sir (Thomas) Dudley Blennerhassett, 3rd Bt (cr 1914), 1889–1972, vol. VII
Bowater, Sir William Henry, 1855–1932, vol. III
Bowcher, Frank, died 1938, vol. III
Bowden, Sir Frank, 1st Bt, 1848–1921, vol. II
Bowden, Captain Frank Lake, 1863–1906, vol. I
Bowden, Frank Philip, 1903–1968, vol. VI
Bowden, Major George Robert Harland, died 1927, vol. II
Bowden, Rev. Canon Guy Arthur George, 1909–1974, vol. VII
Bowden, Sir Harold, 2nd Bt, 1880–1960, vol. V
Bowden, Col James Hubert Thomas C.; see Cornish-Bowden.
Bowden, Lt-Col John, died 1948, vol. IV
Bowden, Norman Henry Martin, 1879–1968, vol. VI
Bowden, Vivian Gordon, 1884–1942, vol. IV
Bowden, Walter, 1859–1919, vol. II
Bowden, William Douglas, 1875–1944, vol. IV
Bowden-Smith, Adm. Sir Nathaniel, 1838–1921, vol. II
Bowden Smith, Vice-Adm. William, 1874–1962, vol. VI
Bowdler, Audley; see Bowdler, W. A.
Bowdler, Lt-Col Basil Wilfred Bowdler, 1873–1960, vol. V
Bowdler, Col Cyril William Bowdler, 1839–1918, vol. II
Bowdler, (William) Audley, 1884–1969, vol. VI
Bowdon, John Erdeswick B.; see Butler-Bowdon.
Bowell, Hon. Sir Mackenzie, 1823–1917, vol. II
Bowen, Sir Albert, 1st Bt, 1858–1924, vol. II
Bowen, Lt-Col Alfred John Hamilton, 1885–1917, vol. II
Bowen, Arthur Charles M.; see Mainwaring-Bowen.
Bowen, Col Arthur Winniett Nunn, died 1964, vol. VI
Bowen, Catherine Drinker, died 1973, vol. VII
Bowen, Hon. Sir Charles Christopher, 1830–1917, vol. II
Bowen, Major Charles Otway Cole, 1867–1910, vol. I
Bowen, Rev. David, died 1928, vol. II (A), vol. III
Bowen, David, 1885–1950, vol. IV
Bowen, Edmund John, 1898–1980, vol. VII
Bowen, Major Sir Edward Crowther, 2nd Bt, 1885–1937, vol. III
Bowen, Edward Ernest, 1836–1901, vol. I

Bowen, Elizabeth Dorothea Cole, 1899–1973, vol. VII
Bowen, Sir George Bevan, 1858–1940, vol. III
Bowen, Rt Hon. Sir George Ferguson, 1821–1899, vol. I
Bowen, Col Herbert Walter, 1870–1944, vol. IV
Bowen, Col Hildred Edward W.; see Webb-Bowen.
Bowen, Horace G., died 1902, vol. I
Bowen, Ira Sprague, 1898–1973, vol. VII
Bowen, Ivor, died 1934, vol. III
Bowen, James Bevan, 1828–1905, vol. I
Bowen, Air Cdre James Bevan, 1883–1969, vol. VI
Bowen, Sir John Cuthbert Grenside, 1860–1932, vol. III
Bowen, Sir John Edward Mortimer, 3rd Bt, 1918–1939, vol. III
Bowen, Sir John Poland, died 1955, vol. V
Bowen, Sir (John) William, 1876–1965, vol. VI
Bowen, Marjorie; see Long, M. G.
Bowen, Norman Levi, 1887–1956, vol. V
Bowen, Owen, 1873–1967, vol. VI
Bowen, Air Vice-Marshal Sir Tom Ince W.; see Webb-Bowen.
Bowen, Trevor Alfred, died 1964, vol. VI
Bowen, Sir William; see Bowen, Sir J. W.
Bowen, Lt-Col William Allan, 1879–1937, vol. III
Bowen, Hon. and Rev. William Edward, 1862–1938, vol. III
Bowen, William Henry, died 1963, vol. VI
Bowen, William Herbert, 1843–1937, vol. III
Bowen, Maj.-Gen. William Oswald, 1898–1961, vol. VI
Bowen, York, 1884–1961, vol. VI
Bowen-Buscarlet, Air Vice-Marshal Sir Willett Amalric Bowen, 1898–1967, vol. VI
Bowen-Davies, Alan, 1907–1974, vol. VII
Bowen-Jones, Sir John Bowen; see Jones.
Bowen-Rowlands, Ernest Brown, 1866–1951, vol. V
Bower, Sir Alfred Louis, 1st Bt, died 1948, vol. IV
Bower, Sir Edmund Ernest N.; see Nott-Bower.
Bower, Frederick Orpen, 1855–1948, vol. IV
Bower, Lt-Col George Haddon, 1871–1950, vol. IV (A)
Bower, George Spencer, 1854–1928, vol. II
Bower, Sir Graham John, 1848–1933, vol. III
Bower, Maj.-Gen. Sir Hamilton, 1858–1940, vol. III
Bower, Comdr John Graham, 1886–1940, vol. III
Bower, Sir John Reginald Hornby N.; see Nott-Bower.
Bower, Sir Percival, 1880–1948, vol. IV
Bower, Rev. Richard, 1845–1911, vol. I
Bower, Major Sir Robert Lister, 1860–1929, vol. III
Bower, Comdr Robert Tatton, 1894–1975, vol. VII
Bower, Sir (William) Guy N.; see Nott-Bower.
Bower, Captain Sir William N.; see Nott-Bower.
Bowerbank, Sir Fred Thompson, 1880–1960, vol. V
Bowering, John, 1894–1973, vol. VII
Bowerley, Amelia M., died 1916, vol. II
Bowerley, Walter, 1876–1952, vol. V
Bowerman, Rt Hon. Charles William, 1851–1947, vol. IV
Bowers, Sir Edward Hardman, 1854–1914, vol. I

Bowers, Frederick Gatus, 1882–1937, vol. III
Bowers, Rt Rev. John Phillips Allcot, 1854–1926, vol. II
Bowers, Ven. Percy Harris, 1856–1922, vol. II
Bowers, Col Percy Lloyd, 1879–1943, vol. IV
Bowes, Frederick, 1867–1958, vol. V
Bowes, Col Hugh, died 1952, vol. V
Bowes, Robert Kenneth, 1904–1958, vol. V
Bowes, Brig.-Gen. William Hely, 1858–1932, vol. III
Bowes-Lyon, Hon. Sir David, 1902–1961, vol. VI
Bowes-Lyon, Hon. Francis, 1856–1948, vol. IV
Bowes-Lyon, Maj.-Gen. Sir (Francis) James (Cecil), 1917–1977, vol. VII
Bowes-Lyon, Captain Geoffrey Francis, 1886–1951, vol. V
Bowes-Lyon, Maj.-Gen. Sir James; see Bowes-Lyon, Maj.-Gen. Sir F. J. C.
Bowes-Lyon, Hon. John, 1886–1930, vol. III
Bowes-Lyon, Hon. Michael Claude Hamilton, 1893–1953, vol. V
Bowes Lyon, Captain Ronald George, 1893–1960, vol. V
Bowhill, Air Chief Marshal Sir Frederick William, 1880–1960, vol. V
Bowie, James Alexander, 1888–1949, vol. IV
Bowie, John, died 1941, vol. IV
Bowie, Robert Forbes, 1860–1940, vol. III
Bowie, Sir William Tait, 1876–1949, vol. IV
Bowker, Sir Leslie Cecil Blackmore, died 1965, vol. VI
Bowker, Lt-Col William James, 1869–1931, vol. III
Bowlby, Sir Anthony Alfred, 1st Bt, 1855–1929, vol. III
Bowlby, Arthur Salvin, 1872–1932, vol. III
Bowlby, Captain Cuthbert Francis Bond, 1895–1969, vol. VI
Bowlby, Rev. Henry Thomas, 1864–1940, vol. III
Bowle, Horace Edgar, 1886–1978, vol. VII
Bowle-Evans, Maj.-Gen. Charles Harford, 1867–1942, vol. IV
Bowler, Air Vice-Marshal Thomas Geoffrey, 1895–1974, vol. VII
Bowles, Baron (Life Peer); Francis George Bowles, 1902–1970, vol. VI
Bowles, Maj.-Gen. Frederick Augustus, 1851–1931, vol. III
Bowles, Brig.-Gen. Frederick Gilbert, died 1947, vol. IV
Bowles, George Frederic Stewart, 1877–1955, vol. V
Bowles, Hon. Brig.-Gen. Henry, 1854–1932, vol. III
Bowles, Sir Henry Ferryman, 1st Bt, 1858–1943, vol. IV
Bowles, Thomas Gibson, 1844–1922, vol. II
Bowley, Sir Arthur Lyon, 1869–1957, vol. V
Bowling, Paymaster-in-Chief Thomas Henry Lovelace, 1839–1922, vol. II
Bowling, Air Vice-Marshal Victor Swanton, 1908–1971, vol. VII
Bowly, Rev. Charles Henry, 1845–1913, vol. I
Bowly, Col William Arthur Travell, 1880–1957, vol. V

Bowman, Alexander, *died* 1941, vol. IV
Bowman, Archibald Allan, 1883–1936, vol. III
Bowman, Herbert Lister, 1874–1942, vol. IV
Bowman, Humphrey Ernest, 1879–1965, vol. VI
Bowman, Isaiah, 1878–1950, vol. IV
Bowman, Sir James, 1st Bt, 1898–1978, vol. VII
Bowman, Laurence George, 1866–1950, vol. IV
Bowman, Rev. Sir Paget Mervyn, 3rd Bt, 1873–1955, vol. V
Bowman, Robert Ritchie, 1883–1970, vol. VI (AII)
Bowman, Thomas, *died* 1945, vol. IV
Bowman, Sir William Paget, 2nd Bt, 1845–1917, vol. II
Bowman-Manifold, Maj.-Gen. Sir (Michael) Graham Egerton; *see* Manifold.
Bown, Rev. George Herbert, 1871–1918, vol. II
Bowra, Cecil Arthur Verner, 1869–1947, vol. IV
Bowra, Sir (Cecil) Maurice, 1898–1971, vol. VII
Bowra, Sir Maurice; *see* Bowra, Sir C. M.
Bowran, Rev. John George, 1869–1946, vol. IV
Bowring, Sir Charles Calvert, 1872–1945, vol. IV
Bowring, Sir Clement, 1844–1907, vol. I
Bowring, Edgar Alfred, 1826–1911, vol. I
Bowring, Rev. Edgar Francis, 1854–1931, vol. III
Bowring, Hon. Sir Edgar Rennie, 1858–1943, vol. IV
Bowring, Sir Frederick Charles, 1857–1936, vol. III
Bowring, Col Frederick Thomas Nelson Spratt, 1847–1934, vol. III
Bowring, Adm. Humphrey Wykeham, 1874–1952, vol. V
Bowring, Lewin Bentham, 1824–1910, vol. I
Bowring, Theodore Louis, 1901–1967, vol. VI
Bowring, Sir Thomas Benjamin, 1847–1915, vol. I (A)
Bowring, Walter Andrew, 1875–1950, vol. IV
Bowring, Walter Armiger, 1874–1931, vol. III
Bowring, Sir William Benjamin, 1st Bt, 1837–1916, vol. II
Bowron, Sir Edward, 1857–1923, vol. II
Bowser, Ernest William, 1887–1969, vol. VI (AII)
Bowser, Hon. Sir John, 1856–1936, vol. III
Bowser, Rev. Sidney W., 1853–1928, vol. II
Bowser, William John, 1867–1933, vol. III
Bowstead, Rev. Canon Christopher J. K., 1844–1924, vol. II
Bowstead, John, 1897–1969, vol. VI
Bowyear, Vice-Adm. George le Geyt, *died* 1903, vol. I
Bowyear, Henry William Thomas, 1852–1936, vol. III
Bowyer, Sir Eric Blacklock, 1902–1964, vol. VI
Bowyer, Sir George Henry, 9th and 5th Bt, 1870–1950, vol. IV
Bowyer, John Francis, 1893–1974, vol. VII
Bowyer-Smijth, Sir William; *see* Smijth.
Bowyer-Smyth, Sir Alfred John; *see* Smyth.
Bowyer-Smyth, Captain Sir Philip Weyland; *see* Smyth.
Box, Charles Richard, *died* 1951, vol. V
Box, Rev. George Herbert, 1869–1933, vol. III
Boxall, Sir Alleyne Alfred, 1st Bt, 1855–1927, vol. II
Boxall, Col Sir Alleyne Percival, 2nd Bt, 1882–1945, vol. IV

Boxall, Col Sir Charles Gervaise, 1852–1914, vol. I
Boxall, William Percival Gratwicke, 1848–1931, vol. III
Boxer, Maj.-Gen. Edward M., *died* 1898, vol. I
Boxer, Rear-Adm. Henry Percy, 1885–1961, vol. VI
Boxer, Captain Herbert Martyn, 1882–1962, vol. VI
Boxshall, Col Henry Edwin, 1863–1936, vol. III
Boxwell, Lt-Col Ambrose, 1876–1959, vol. V
Boyagian, Henry Samuel Rogers, 1875–1947, vol. IV
Boyce, Arthur Cyril, 1867–1942, vol. IV
Boyce, Austin Alexander Rodney, 1870–1948, vol. IV (A)
Boyce, Col Charles Edward, 1882–1963, vol. VI
Boyce, Ven. Francis Bertie, 1884–1931, vol. III
Boyce, Francis Stewart, 1872–1940, vol. III
Boyce, Air Cdre George Harold, 1894–1975, vol. VII
Boyce, Sir (Harold) Leslie, 1st Bt, 1895–1955, vol. V
Boyce, Brig.-Gen. Harry Augustus, 1870–1954, vol. V
Boyce, Sir Leslie; *see* Boyce, Sir H. L.
Boyce, Sir Richard Leslie, 2nd Bt, 1929–1968, vol. VI
Boyce, Robert Henry, 1834–1909, vol. I
Boyce, Sir Rubert, 1863–1911, vol. I
Boyce, Sarah, 1863–1939, vol. III
Boyce, Rev. Walter, 1853–1936, vol. III
Boyce, Maj.-Gen. Sir William George Bertram, 1868–1937, vol. III
Boycott, Arthur Edwin, 1877–1938, vol. III
Boycott, Rev. Desmond M.; *see* Morse-Boycott.
Boycott, Lt-Col T. A. W.; *see* Wight-Boycott.
Boyd, Alexander Michael, 1905–1973, vol. VII
Boyd, Alexander Stuart, 1854–1930, vol. III
Boyd, Sir Alexander William K.; *see* Keown-Boyd.
Boyd, Alfred Ernest, *died* 1949, vol. IV
Boyd, Very Rev. Andrew Kennedy Hutchison, 1825–1899, vol. I
Boyd, Sir Archibald John, 1888–1959, vol. V
Boyd, Ven. Charles, 1842–1914, vol. I
Boyd, Col Charles Augustus R.; *see* Rochfort-Boyd.
Boyd, Charles Walter, 1869–1919, vol. II
Boyd, David Runciman, 1872–1955, vol. V
Boyd, Adm. Sir Denis William, 1891–1965, vol. VI
Boyd, Sir Donald James, 1877–1953, vol. V
Boyd, Douglas Thornley, 1896–1964, vol. VI
Boyd, Edmund Blaikie, 1894–1946, vol. IV
Boyd, Edward Charles Percy, 1871–1949, vol. IV
Boyd, Ernest, 1887–1946, vol. IV
Boyd, Francis Darby, 1866–1922, vol. II
Boyd, Rev. Francis Leith, 1856–1927, vol. II
Boyd, Frank M., 1863–1950, vol. IV
Boyd, Maj.-Gen. Sir Gerald Farrell, 1877–1930, vol. III
Boyd, Rev. Halbert Johnstone, 1872–1957, vol. V
Boyd, Sir Harry Robert, 1876–1940, vol. III
Boyd, Henry, 1831–1922, vol. II
Boyd, Henry, *died* 1942, vol. IV
Boyd, Lt-Col Henry Alexander, 1877–1943, vol. IV

Boyd, Lt-Col Henry Charles R.; see Rochfort-Boyd.
Boyd, Rev. Herbert Buchanan, died 1941, vol. IV
Boyd, Maj.-Gen. Ian Herbert Fitzgerald, 1907–1978, vol. VII
Boyd, James, 1888–1944, vol. IV
Boyd, James, 1888–1963, vol. VI
Boyd, James, died 1970, vol. VI
Boyd, James Dixon, 1907–1968, vol. VI
Boyd, Sir John, died 1967, vol. VI
Boyd, Hon. Sir John Alexander, 1837–1916, vol. II
Boyd, Col John Alexander, 1857–1931, vol. III
Boyd, Sir John Smith, 1886–1963, vol. VI
Boyd, Maj.-Gen. Julius Middleton, 1837–1919, vol. II
Boyd, Lachlan Macpherson, 1904–1980, vol. VII
Boyd, Martin à Beckett, 1893–1972, vol. VII
Boyd, Mary Stuart, died 1937, vol. III
Boyd, Maurice James, 1911–1979, vol. VII
Boyd, Col Mossom Archibald, 1860–1943, vol. IV
Boyd, Air Vice-Marshal Owen Tudor, 1889–1944, vol. IV
Boyd, Robert, 1890–1959, vol. V
Boyd, Rt Rev. Robert McNeil, 1890–1958, vol. V
Boyd, Ven. Robert Wallace, died 1921, vol. II
Boyd, Sidney Arthur, 1880–1966, vol. VI
Boyd, Ven. Sydney Adolphus, 1857–1947, vol. IV
Boyd, Col Thomas Crawford, 1886–1967, vol. VI
Boyd, Thomas Herbert, 1890–1941, vol. IV
Boyd, Thomas J. L. Stirling, 1886–1973, vol. VII
Boyd, Sir Thomas Jamieson, 1818–1902, vol. I
Boyd, Rt Hon. Sir Walter, 1st Bt, 1833–1918, vol. II
Boyd, Sir Walter Herbert, 2nd Bt, 1867–1948, vol. IV
Boyd, William, 1876–1961, vol. VI (AII)
Boyd, William, 1874–1962, vol. VI
Boyd, Rev. William Grenville, 1867–1941, vol. IV
Boyd Carpenter, Major Sir Archibald Boyd, 1873–1937, vol. III
Boyd-Carpenter, Henry John, 1865–1923, vol. II
Boyd-Carpenter, Captain John Peers, 1871–1936, vol. III
Boyd Carpenter, Rt Rev. William, 1841–1918, vol. II
Boyd-Moss, Brig.-Gen. Lionel Boyd, 1875–1940, vol. III
Boyd Orr, 1st Baron, 1880–1971, vol. VII
Boyd-Rochfort, Captain George Arthur, 1880–1940, vol. III
Boyd-Wilson, Edwin John, 1886–1973, vol. VII
Boyden, Rev. A. H., died 1940, vol. III (A), vol. IV
Boyer, Hon. Arthur, 1851–1922, vol. II
Boyer, Rear-Adm. (S) George Christopher Aubin, 1862–1949, vol. IV
Boyer, Sir Richard James Fildes, 1891–1961, vol. VI
Boyes, Charles Edward, 1866–1920, vol. II
Boyes, Sir George Thomas Henry, died 1910, vol. I
Boyes, Rear-Adm. Hector, 1881–1960, vol. V
Boyes, Maj.-Gen. John Edward, 1843–1915, vol. I
Boyes, John Henry, 1886–1958, vol. V
Boyle, Sir Alexander George, 1872–1943, vol. IV
Boyle, Adm. Hon. Sir Algernon Douglas Edward Harry, 1871–1949, vol. IV

Boyle, Air Cdre Archibald Robert, 1887–1949, vol. IV
Boyle, (Arthur) Brian, 1913–1965, vol. VI
Boyle, Brian; see Boyle, A. B.
Boyle, Sir Cavendish, 1849–1916, vol. II
Boyle, Col Cecil Alexander, 1888–1941, vol. IV
Boyle, Sir Courtenay, 1845–1901, vol. I
Boyle, Daniel, 1859–1925, vol. II
Boyle, Sir Edward, 1st Bt, 1849–1909, vol. I
Boyle, Sir Edward, 2nd Bt, 1878–1945, vol. IV
Boyle, Rear-Adm. Edward Courtney, 1883–1967, vol. VI
Boyle, Comdr Edward Louis Dalrymple, 1864–1923, vol. II
Boyle, Very Rev. George David, 1828–1901, vol. I
Boyle, Harry, 1863–1937, vol. III
Boyle, Captain Harry Lumsden, died 1955, vol. V
Boyle, Henry Edmund Gaskin, 1875–1941, vol. IV
Boyle, Captain James, 1850–1931, vol. III
Boyle, James, 1863–1936, vol. III
Boyle, John Andrew, 1916–1978, vol. VII
Boyle, Air Cdre Hon. John David, 1884–1974, vol. VII
Boyle, John R., 1870–1936, vol. III
Boyle, Col Lionel Richard Cavendish, 1851–1920, vol. II
Boyle, Richard Vicars, 1822–1908, vol. I
Boyle, Maj.-Gen. Robert, 1823–1899, vol. I
Boyle, Robert Colquhoun, 1877–1934, vol. III
Boyle, Vice-Adm. Hon. Robert Francis, 1863–1922, vol. II
Boyle, Robert William, 1883–1955, vol. V
Boyle, Brig.-Gen. Roger Courtenay, 1863–1944, vol. IV
Boyle, Vincent, 1891–1956, vol. V
Boyle, Hon. Walter John Harry, 1869–1939, vol. III
Boyle, Lt-Col Hon. William George, 1830–1908, vol. I
Boyle, William Lewis, 1859–1918, vol. II
Boyle, Rev. William Skinner, 1844–1915, vol. I
Boyne, 8th Viscount, 1830–1907, vol. I
Boyne, 9th Viscount, 1864–1942, vol. IV
Boyne, Robert John, died 1938, vol. III
Boynton, Sir Griffith Henry, 12th Bt, 1849–1937, vol. III
Boynton, Sir Griffith Wilfrid Norman, 13th Bt, 1889–1966, vol. VI
Boynton, Sir Henry Somerville, 11th Bt, 1844–1899, vol. I
Boynton, Captain Thomas Lamplugh W.; see Wickham-Boynton.
Boys, Sir Charles Vernon, 1855–1944, vol. IV
Boys, Sir Francis Theodore, 1870–1952, vol. V
Boys, Geoffrey Vernon, 1893–1945, vol. IV
Boys, Guy Ponsonby, 1871–1950, vol. IV
Boys, Henry Ward, 1874–1955, vol. V
Boys, Rt Rev. John, 1900–1972, vol. VII
Boys, Brig.-Gen. Reginald Harvey Henderson, 1867–1945, vol. III
Boys-Smith, Winifred L., died 1939, vol. III
Boyson, Sir John Alexander, 1846–1926, vol. II
Boyton, Sir James, 1855–1926, vol. II
Bozman, Geoffrey Stephen, 1896–1973, vol. VII

Brabant, Maj.-Gen. Sir Edward Yewd, 1839–1914, vol. I
Brabant, Rev. Frank Herbert, 1892–1972, vol. VII
Brabazon of Tara, 1st Baron, 1884–1964, vol. VI
Brabazon of Tara, 2nd Baron, 1910–1974, vol. VII
Brabazon, Maj.-Gen. Sir John Palmer, 1843–1922, vol. II
Brabin, Sir Daniel James, 1913–1975, vol. VII
Brabner, Rupert Arnold, 1911–1945, vol. IV
Brabourne, 2nd Baron, 1857–1909, vol. I
Brabourne, 3rd Baron, 1885–1915, vol. I
Brabourne, 4th Baron, 1863–1933, vol. III
Brabourne, 5th Baron, 1895–1939, vol. III
Brabourne, 6th Baron, 1922–1943, vol. IV
Brabrook, Sir Edward William, 1839–1930, vol. III
Brace, Col Henry Fergusson, 1888–1948, vol. IV
Brace, Sir Ivor Llewellyn, 1898–1952, vol. V
Brace, Rt Hon. William, 1865–1947, vol. IV
Bracegirdle, Rear-Adm. Sir Leighton Seymour, 1881–1970, vol. VI (AII)
Bracewell, Rev. Canon William, 1872–1954, vol. V
Bracewell-Smith, Sir George, (Sir Guy); see Smith.
Bracewell-Smith, Sir Guy; see Smith.
Bracken, 1st Viscount, 1901–1958, vol. V
Bracken, Clio Hinton, died 1925, vol. II
Bracken, Sir Geoffrey Thomas Hirst, 1879–1951, vol. V
Brackenbury, Arthur Jocelyn, 1876–1935, vol. III
Brackenbury, Rev. Basil V. F., 1889–1965, vol. VI
Brackenbury, Sir Cecil Fabian, 1881–1958, vol. V
Brackenbury, Rt Hon. Gen. Sir Henry, 1837–1914, vol. I
Brackenbury, Sir Henry Britten, 1866–1942, vol. IV
Brackenbury, Col Henry Langton, 1868–1920, vol. II
Brackenbury, Hereward Irenius, died 1938, vol. III
Brackenbury, Adm. John William, 1842–1918, vol. II
Brackenbury, Laura, 1868–1937, vol. III
Brackenbury, Col Maule Campbell, 1844–1915, vol. I
Brackenridge, Sir Alexander, 1893–1964, vol. VI
Brackett, Oliver, 1875–1941, vol. IV
Brackley, Air Cdre Herbert George, 1894–1948, vol. IV
Bradbeer, Sir Albert Frederick, 1890–1963, vol. VI
Bradbury, 1st Baron, 1872–1950, vol. IV
Bradbury, John Buckley, 1841–1930, vol. III
Bradbury, Surg. Rear-Adm. William, 1884–1966, vol. VI
Bradby, Godfrey Fox, 1863–1947, vol. IV
Braddell, Darcy; see Braddell, T. A. D.
Braddell, Octavius Henry, 1843–1921, vol. II
Braddell, Sir Roland St John, 1880–1966, vol. VI
Braddell, (Thomas Arthur) Darcy, 1884–1970, vol. VI
Braddell, Sir Thomas de Multon Lee, 1856–1927, vol. II
Braddock, Mrs Elizabeth Margaret, 1899–1970, vol. VI
Braddock, Geoffrey Frank, 1881–1966, vol. VI
Braddock, Thomas, 1887–1976, vol. VII
Braddon, Rt Hon. Sir Edward Nicholas Coventry, 1829–1904, vol. I

Braddon, Hon. Sir Henry Yule, 1863–1955, vol. V
Braddon, Mary Elizabeth, (Mrs John Maxwell), 1837–1915, vol. I
Brade, Sir Reginald Herbert, 1864–1933, vol. III
Bradfield, Lt-Gen. Sir Ernest W. C., 1880–1963, vol. VI
Bradfield, Rt Rev. Harold William, 1898–1960, vol. V
Bradfield, John Job Crew, 1867–1943, vol. IV
Bradfield, William Walter, 1879–1925, vol. II
Bradford, 3rd Earl of, 1819–1898, vol. I
Bradford, 4th Earl of, 1845–1915, vol. I
Bradford, 5th Earl of, 1873–1957, vol. V
Bradford, Rev. E. E., 1860–1944, vol. IV
Bradford, Adm. Sir Edward Eden, 1858–1935, vol. III
Bradford, Major Sir Edward Montagu Andrew, 3rd Bt (cr 1902), 1910–1952, vol. V
Bradford, Col Sir Edward Ridley Colborne, 1st Bt (cr 1902), 1836–1911, vol. I
Bradford, Lt-Col Sir Evelyn Ridley, 2nd Bt (cr 1902), 1869–1914, vol. I
Bradford, Sir James, 1841–1930, vol. III
Bradford, Sir John Ridley Evelyn, 4th Bt (cr 1902), 1941–1954, vol. V
Bradford, Sir John Rose, 1st Bt (cr 1931), 1863–1935, vol. III
Bradford, Ven. Richard Bleaden, 1913–1980, vol. VII
Bradford, Lt-Col Roland Boys, 1892–1917, vol. II
Bradford, Samuel Clement, 1878–1948, vol. IV
Bradford, Sir Thomas Andrews, 1886–1966, vol. VI
Bradford, William Vincent, 1883–1974, vol. VII
Bradford, Lt-Gen. Wilmot Henry, 1815–1914, vol. I
Bradley, Miss; see Field, Michael.
Bradley, Albert James, 1899–1972, vol. VII
Bradley, Andrew Cecil, 1851–1935, vol. III
Bradley, Arthur Granville, 1850–1943, vol. IV
Bradley, Col Sir (Augustus) Montague, 1865–1953, vol. V
Bradley, Brig.-Gen. Charles Edward, 1852–1931, vol. III
Bradley, Rev. Charles Lister, 1880–1957, vol. V
Bradley, Col Edward de Winton Herbert, 1889–1964, vol. VI
Bradley, Francis Ernest, died 1933, vol. III
Bradley, Francis Herbert, 1846–1924, vol. II
Bradley, Rear-Adm. Frederic Cyril, 1888–1957, vol. V
Bradley, Lt-Col Frederick Gardner, 1860–1935, vol. III
Bradley, Gladys Lilian, died 1978, vol. VII
Bradley, Henry, 1845–1923, vol. II
Bradley, Herbert, 1856–1923, vol. II
Bradley, Herbert Dennis, 1878–1934, vol. III
Bradley, Sir Kenneth Granville, 1904–1977, vol. VII
Bradley, Leslie Ripley, 1892–1968, vol. VI
Bradley, Col Sir Montague; see Bradley, Col Sir A. M.
Bradley, Orlando Charnock, 1871–1937, vol. III
Bradley, Peter Colley S.; see Sylvester-Bradley.
Bradley, Reginald Livingstone, 1894–1977, vol. VII

Bradley, Lt-Col Robert Anstruther, *died* 1965, vol. VI

Bradley, Thomas John, 1857–1936, vol. III

Bradley, Thomas Losco, 1869–1930, vol. III

Bradley, William, 1903–1972, vol. VII

Bradley-Birt, Francis Bradley, 1874–1963, vol. VI

Bradly, Henry George, 1876–1938, vol. III

Bradnack, Brian Oswald, 1898–1973, vol. VII

Bradney, George Preston, 1877–1959, vol. V

Bradney, Col Sir Joseph Alfred, 1859–1933, vol. III

Bradshaw, Surg.-Maj.-Gen. Sir A. Frederick, 1834–1923, vol. II

Bradshaw, Mrs Albert S., *died* 1938, vol. III

Bradshaw, Brig.-Gen. Charles Richard, 1873–1940, vol. III

Bradshaw, Constance H., *died* 1961, vol. VI

Bradshaw, Eric, 1909–1961, vol. VI

Bradshaw, Evelyn, 1862–1952, vol. V

Bradshaw, George Fagan, 1887–1960, vol. V

Bradshaw, Brig. George Rowley, 1898–1976, vol. VII

Bradshaw, Harold Chalton, 1893–1943, vol. IV

Bradshaw, Maj.-Gen. Laurence Julius Elliott, 1857–1929, vol. III

Bradshaw, Octavius, 1845–1928, vol. II

Bradshaw, Thomas R., 1857–1927, vol. II

Bradshaw, William, 1844–1927, vol. II

Bradshaw, Sir William, *died* 1955, vol. V

Bradshaw, William Graham, 1861–1941, vol. IV

Bradshaw, Maj.-Gen. William Pat Arthur, 1897–1966, vol. VI

Bradshaw-Isherwood, John Henry; *see* Isherwood.

Bradstock, Major George, *died* 1966, vol. VI

Bradstreet, Sir Edmond Simon, 6th Bt, 1820–1905, vol. I

Bradstreet, Sir Edward Simon Victor, 7th Bt, 1856–1924, vol. II

Bradwell, Baron (Life Peer); Thomas Edward Neil Driberg, 1905–1976, vol. VII

Brady, Sir Andrew N.; *see* Newton-Brady.

Brady, Sir Francis William, 2nd Bt, 1824–1909, vol. I

Brady, George Stewardson, 1832–1921, vol. II

Brady, Major Gerald Charles Jervis, *died* 1941, vol. IV

Brady, Rev. Canon Henry Westby, 1884–1934, vol. III

Brady, Patrick Joseph, 1868–1943, vol. IV

Brady, Sir Robert Maziere, 3rd Bt, 1854–1909, vol. I

Brady, Sir Thomas Francis, 1824–1904, vol. I

Brady, Thomas John Bellingham, 1841–1910, vol. I

Brady, Major Sir William Longfield, 4th Bt, 1864–1927, vol. II

Brækstad, H. L., 1845–1915, vol. I

Bragg, Sir Lawrence; *see* Bragg, Sir W. L.

Bragg, Sir William Henry, 1862–1942, vol. IV

Bragg, Sir (William) Lawrence, 1890–1971, vol. VII

Bragge, Rev. Charles Albert, *died* 1923, vol. II

Braham, Dudley Disraeli, 1875–1951, vol. V

Braham, Harry Vincent, 1886–1938, vol. III

Braidwood, Harold Lithgow, 1872–1949, vol. IV

Brailey, William A., *died* 1915, vol. I

Brailsford, Henry Noel, 1873–1958, vol. V

Brain, 1st Baron, 1895–1966, vol. VI

Brain, Dennis, 1921–1957, vol. V

Brain, Sir Francis William Thomas, 1855–1921, vol. II

Brain, Sir Hugh Gerner, 1890–1976, vol. VII

Brain, Lawrence L.; *see* Lewton-Brain.

Brain, Reginald T., 1894–1971, vol. VII

Braine, Brig. Herbert Edmund Reginald Rubens, 1876–1942, vol. IV

Braintree, 1st Baron, 1884–1961, vol. VI

Brais, F. Philippe, 1894–1972, vol. VII

Braithwaite, Major Sir Albert Newby, 1893–1959, vol. V

Braithwaite, Charles, *died* 1941, vol. IV

Braithwaite, Air Vice-Marshal Francis Joseph St George, 1907–1956, vol. V

Braithwaite, Col Francis Powell, 1875–1952, vol. V

Braithwaite, Major John, 1871–1940, vol. III

Braithwaite, Sir John Bevan, 1884–1973, vol. VII

Braithwaite, Sir Joseph Gurney, 1st Bt, 1895–1958, vol. V

Braithwaite, Vice-Adm. Lawrence Walter, 1878–1961, vol. VI

Braithwaite, Dame Lilian, 1873–1948, vol. IV

Braithwaite, Rev. Philip Richard Pipon, 1849–1933, vol. III

Braithwaite, Robert, 1824–1917, vol. II

Braithwaite, Gen. Sir Walter Pipon, 1865–1945, vol. IV

Braithwaite, Warwick, 1896–1971, vol. VII

Braithwaite, William Charles, 1862–1922, vol. II

Braithwaite, Brig.-Gen. William Garnett, 1870–1937, vol. III

Braithwaite, William John, 1875–1938, vol. III

Brake, Sir Francis, 1889–1960, vol. V

Brake, Brig.-Gen. Herbert Edward John, 1866–1936, vol. III

Brakenridge, Col Francis John, 1871–1955, vol. V

Brakspear, Sir Harold, 1870–1934, vol. III

Braley, Rev. Evelyn Foley, 1884–1963, vol. VI

Bramah, David, 1875–1947, vol. IV

Bramah, Ernest, *died* 1942, vol. IV

Brambell, Francis William Rogers, 1901–1970, vol. VI

Bramble, Paymaster Rear-Adm. James, 1850–1930, vol. III

Brame, John Samuel Strafford, 1871–1952, vol. V

Brameld, Rev. William Arthur, *died* 1922, vol. II

Bramley, Frank, 1857–1915, vol. I

Bramley, Fred, 1874–1925, vol. II

Bramley, Rev. Henry Ramsden, 1833–1917, vol. II

Bramley-Moore, Rev. William, 1831–1918, vol. II

Brampton, 1st Baron, 1817–1907, vol. I

Bramsdon, Sir Thomas Arthur, 1857–1935, vol. III

Bramston, Sir John, 1832–1921, vol. II

Bramston, Rev. John Trant, *died* 1931, vol. III

Bramwell, Sir Byrom, 1847–1931, vol. III

Bramwell, Edward George, 1865–1944, vol. IV

Bramwell, Edwin, 1873–1952, vol. VI

Bramwell, Sir Frederick Joseph, 1st Bt, 1818–1903, vol. I

Bramwell, John Crighton, 1889–1976, vol. VII

Bramwell, John Milne, 1852–1925, vol. II

Bramwell Davis, Maj.-Gen. Ronald Albert, 1905–1974, vol. VII

Branch, Sir (Charles Ernest) St John, *died* 1939, vol. III

Branch, James, 1845–1918, vol. II

Branch, Sir St John; *see* Branch, Sir C. E. St J.

Branch, Ven. Samuel Edmund, 1861–1932, vol. III

Brancker, Air Vice-Marshal Sir Sefton; *see* Brancker, Air Vice-Marshal Sir W. S.

Brancker, Air Vice-Marshal Sir (William) Sefton, 1877–1930, vol. III

Brand, 1st Baron, 1878–1963, vol. VI

Brand, Hon. Arthur George, 1853–1917, vol. II

Brand, Hon. Charles, 1855–1912, vol. I

Brand, Maj.-Gen. Charles Henry, 1873–1961, vol. VI

Brand, (Charles) Neville, 1895–1951, vol. V

Brand, Air Vice-Marshal Sir (Christopher Joseph) Quintin, 1893–1968, vol. VI

Brand, Sir David, 1837–1908, vol. I

Brand, Hon. Sir David, 1912–1979, vol. VII

Brand, Col David Ernest, 1884–1948, vol. IV

Brand, Ferdinand, 1846–1922, vol. II

Brand, Sir Harry F., 1873–1951, vol. V

Brand, Adm. Hon. Sir Hubert George, 1870–1955, vol. V

Brand, James, 1843–1907, vol. I

Brand, Engr-Captain James John Cantley, 1880–1952, vol. V

Brand, Lt-Col John Charles, 1885–1929, vol. III

Brand, Neville; *see* Brand, C. N.

Brand, Air Vice-Marshal Sir Quintin; *see* Brand, Air Vice-Marshal Sir C. J. Q.

Brand, Hon. Roger, 1880–1945, vol. IV

Brand, Rear-Adm. Hon. Thomas Seymour, 1847–1916, vol. II

Brandeis, Louis Dembitz, 1856–1941, vol. IV

Brander, George Maconachie, 1906–1977, vol. VII

Brander, Col Herbert Ralph, 1861–1933, vol. III

Brander, Maj.-Gen. Maxwell Spieker, 1884–1972, vol. VII

Brander, William Browne, 1880–1951, vol. V

Brandes, George, 1842–1927, vol. II

Brandin, Louis M., 1874–1940, vol. III

Brandis, Sir Dietrich, 1824–1907, vol. I

Brandon, Very Rev. Lowther E., *died* 1933, vol. III

Brandon, Col Oscar Gilbert, 1876–1968, vol. VI

Brandon, Rev. Samuel George Frederick, 1907–1971, vol. VII

Brandon, Captain Vivian R., 1882–1944, vol. IV

Brandram, Rosina, *died* 1907, vol. I

Branfill Harrison, Col Cholmeley Edward Carl; *see* Harrison.

Branfoot, Surg.-Gen. Sir Arthur Mudge, 1848–1914, vol. I

Brangwyn, Sir Frank, 1867–1956, vol. V

Branly, Edouard, 1844–1940, vol. III

Branner, John Casper, 1850–1922, vol. II

Brannigan, Owen, 1908–1973, vol. VII

Branson, Rt Hon. Sir George Arthur Harwin, 1871–1951, vol. V

Branson, William Philip Sutcliffe, 1874–1950, vol. IV

Brant, Richard William, 1852–1934, vol. III

Branthwaite, Robert Welsh, 1859–1929, vol. III

Braque, Georges, 1882–1963, vol. VI

Brash, James Couper, 1886–1958, vol. V

Brash, William Bardsley, 1877–1952, vol. V

Brasher, William Kenneth, 1897–1972, vol. VII

Braslau, Sophie, *died* 1935, vol. III

Brass, Sir Leslie Stuart, 1891–1958, vol. V

Brassey, 1st Earl, 1836–1918, vol. II

Brassey, 2nd Earl, 1863–1919, vol. II

Brassey of Apethorpe, 1st Baron, 1870–1958, vol. V

Brassey of Apethorpe, 2nd Baron, 1905–1967, vol. VI

Brassey, Albert, 1844–1918, vol. II

Brassey, Lt-Col Edgar Hugh, 1878–1946, vol. IV

Brassey, Captain Harold Ernest, 1877–1916, vol. II

Brassey, Captain Robert Bingham, 1875–1946, vol. IV

Brassington, William Salt, 1859–1939, vol. III

Bratton, Rt Rev. Theodore Du Bose, 1862–1944, vol. IV

Braude, Ernest Alexander Rudolph, 1922–1956, vol. V

Braun, Adolphe Armand, 1869–1938, vol. III

Braund, Sir Henry Benedict Linthwaite, 1893–1969, vol. VI

Braunholtz, Eugen Gustav Wilhelm, 1859–1941, vol. IV

Braunholtz, Gustav Ernst Karl, 1887–1967, vol. VI

Braunholtz, Hermann Justus, 1888–1963, vol. VI

Bray, Maj.-Gen. Sir Claude Arthur, 1858–1934, vol. III

Bray, Sir Denys de Saumarez, 1875–1951, vol. V

Bray, Sir Edward, 1849–1926, vol. II

Bray, Sir Edward Hugh, 1874–1950, vol. IV

Bray, Francis Edmond, 1882–1950, vol. IV

Bray, Frederick, 1895–1977, vol. VII

Bray, Col George Arthur Theodore, 1864–1933, vol. III

Bray, Col Hubert Alaric, 1867–1935, vol. III

Bray, Captain Sir Jocelyn, 1880–1964, vol. VI

Bray, Rt Rev. Patrick Albert, 1883–1953, vol. V

Bray, Sir Reginald More, 1842–1923, vol. II

Bray, Brig.-Gen. Robert Napier, 1872–1921, vol. II

Braybrooke, 5th Baron, 1823–1902, vol. I

Braybrooke, 6th Baron, 1827–1904, vol. I

Braybrooke, 7th Baron, 1855–1941, vol. IV

Braybrooke, 8th Baron, 1918–1943, vol. IV

Brayden, William Henry, 1865–1933, vol. III

Braye, 5th Baron, 1849–1928, vol. II

Braye, 6th Baron, 1874–1952, vol. V

Braye, Philip George, 1894–1956, vol. V

Brayley, Baron (Life Peer); (John) Desmond Brayley, 1917–1977, vol. VII

Brayn, Sir Richard, 1850–1912, vol. I

Brayne, Albert Frederic Lucas, 1884–1970, vol. VI

Brayne, Charles Valentine, 1877–1964, vol. VI

Brayne, Frank Lugard, 1882–1952, vol. V

Brayshay, Sir Maurice William, 1883–1959, vol. V

Brazel, Claude Hamilton, 1894–1959, vol. V

Brazier-Creagh, Col George Washington, 1858–1942, vol. IV

Brazil, Angela, 1868–1947, vol. IV

Brazza, Pierre Paul François Camille de, Count de Savorgnan, 1852–1905, vol. I

Breadalbane, 1st Marquis of, 1851–1922, vol. II
Breadalbane, 8th Earl of, 1885–1923, vol. II
Breadalbane and Holland, 9th Earl of, 1889–1959, vol. V
Breading, Lt-Col George Remington, 1877–1942, vol. IV
Breadner, Air Chief Marshal Lloyd Samuel, 1894–1952, vol. V
Breadner, Robert Walker, 1865–1935, vol. III
Breakey, Air Vice-Marshal John Denis, died 1965, vol. VI
Breaks, Rear-Adm. James, 1895–1968, vol. VI
Breakspeare, W. A., died 1914, vol. I
Brealey, William Ramsden, 1889–1949, vol. IV
Breasted, James Henry, 1865–1935, vol. III
Brebner, Sir Alexander, 1883–1979, vol. VII
Brebner, Arthur, 1870–1922, vol. II
Brebner, John Bartlet, 1895–1957, vol. V
Brebner, Percy James, 1864–1922, vol. II
Brechin, Sir Herbert Archbold, 1903–1979, vol. VII
Brecon, 1st Baron, 1905–1976, vol. VII
Bredius, Abraham, 1855–1946, vol. IV
Bredon, Sir Robert Edward, 1846–1918, vol. II
Bree, Rt Rev. Herbert, 1828–1899, vol. I
Bree, Ven. William, 1822–1917, vol. II
Breech, Ernest Robert, 1897–1978, vol. VII
Breeks, Brig.-Gen. Richard William, 1863–1920, vol. II
Breen, Air Marshal John Joseph, 1896–1964, vol. VI
Breen, Timothy Florence, 1885–1966, vol. VI
Breene, Very Rev. Richard Simmons, 1886–1974, vol. VII
Breese, Air-Cdre Charles Dempster, 1889–1941, vol. IV
Breese, Major Charles Edward, 1867–1932, vol. III
Breithaupt, Hon. Louis Orville, 1890–1960, vol. V
Brema, Marie, died 1925, vol. II
Bremer, Walther Erich Emanuel Friedrich, 1887–1926, vol. II
Bremner, Alexander, 1890–1944, vol. IV
Bremner, Brig.-Gen. Arthur Grant, 1867–1950, vol. IV (A)
Bremner, Lt-Col Claude E. U., 1891–1965, vol. VI
Bremner, Captain Donald, 1864–1935, vol. III
Bremond, L'Abbé Henri, 1865–1933, vol. III
Brenan, Byron, 1847–1927, vol. II
Brenan, James, 1837–1907, vol. I
Brenan, Sir John Fitzgerald, 1883–1953, vol. V
Brenan, Terence Vincent, 1887–1974, vol. VII
Brenchley, Winifred Elsie, 1883–1953, vol. V
Brend, William A., 1873–1944, vol. IV
Brennan, Charles John, 1876–1972, vol. VII
Brennan, Hon. Frank, died 1950, vol. IV
Brennan, Joseph, 1887–1976, vol. VII
Brennan, Louis, 1852–1932, vol. III
Brennan, Very Rev. Nicholas J., 1854–1928, vol. II
Brennan, Maj.-Gen. William Brian Francis, 1907–1977, vol. VII
Brent, Rt Rev. Charles Henry, 1862–1929, vol. III
Brentano, Heinrich von, 1904–1964, vol. VI
Brentford, 1st Viscount, 1865–1932, vol. III
Brentford, 2nd Viscount, 1896–1958, vol. V
Brereton, Alfred, 1849–1926, vol. II

Brereton, Austin, 1862–1922, vol. II
Brereton, Cloudesley, 1863–1937, vol. III
Brereton, Brig.-Gen. Edward Fitzgerald, died 1937, vol. III
Brereton, Very Rev. Eric Hugh, 1889–1962, vol. VI
Brereton, Bt Lt-Col Frederick Sadleir, 1872–1957, vol. V
Brereton, John Le Gay, 1871–1933, vol. III
Brereton, Maud Adeline Cloudesley-, died 1946, vol. IV
Brereton, Reginald Hugh, 1861–1944, vol. IV
Brereton, William Westropp, 1845–1924, vol. II
Bressey, Sir Charles Herbert, 1874–1951, vol. V
Breteuil, Marquis de; Henri Charles Joseph, 1848–1916, vol. II
Bretherton, Frederick S.; see Stapleton-Bretherton.
Bretherton, Major George Howard, 1860–1904, vol. I
Breton, Jules, 1827–1906, vol. I
Breton, Virginie Demont, 1859–1935, vol. III
Bretscher, Egon, 1901–1973, vol. VII
Brett, Arthur Cyril Adair, 1882–1936, vol. III
Brett, Sir Cecil Michael Wilford, 1852–1938, vol. III
Brett, Major Charles Arthur Hugh, 1865–1914, vol. I
Brett, Sir Charles Henry, 1839–1926, vol. II
Brett, Cyril Templeton, 1885–1960, vol. V
Brett, Francis William, 1885–1936, vol. III
Brett, Lt-Gen. George H., 1886–1963, vol. VI
Brett, George Platt, 1858–1936, vol. III
Brett, George Sidney, 1879–1944, vol. IV
Brett, Sir Henry, 1843–1927, vol. II
Brett, Henry James, 1878–1963, vol. VI
Brett, Very Rev. Henry Robert, 1868–1932, vol. III
Brett, James; see Brett, L. J.
Brett, John, 1831–1902, vol. I
Brett, Lt-Col John Aloysius, 1879–1955, vol. V
Brett, (Louis) James, 1910–1975, vol. VII
Brett, Lt-Col Hon. Maurice Vyner Baliol, 1882–1934, vol. III
Brett, Hon. Robert George, 1851–1929, vol. III
Brett, Brig. Rupert John, 1890–1963, vol. VI
Brett, Sir Wilford, 1824–1901, vol. I
Brett, William Bailie, 1889–1947, vol. IV
Brett Young, Francis; see Young, F. B.
Brettell, Frederick Gilbert, 1884–1965, vol. VI
Bretton, Very Rev. William Frederick, 1909–1971, vol. VII
Breuil, Abbé Henri Édouard Prosper, 1877–1961, vol. VI
Breul, Karl Herman, 1860–1932, vol. III
Breun, J. E., 1862–1921, vol. II
Brevitt, Sir Horatio, 1847–1933, vol. III
Brew, Robert John, 1838–1911, vol. I (A)
Brewer, Sir (Alfred) Herbert, 1865–1928, vol. II
Brewer, David J., died 1910, vol. I
Brewer, Rev. E. Cobham, 1810–1897, vol. I
Brewer, Rev. Edward, died 1922, vol. II
Brewer, Sir Henry Campbell, 1885–1963, vol. VI
Brewer, Sir Herbert; see Brewer, Sir A. H.
Brewer, Rt Rev. Leigh Richmond, 1839–1916, vol. II
Brewerton, Elmore, 1867–1962, vol. VI

Brewill, Lt-Col Arthur William, 1861–1923, vol. II
Brewin, Arthur Winbolt, 1867–1946, vol. IV
Brewin, Elizabeth Maud, (Mrs P. K. Brewin); see Pepperell, E. M.
Brewis, Captain Charles Richard Wynn, 1874–1953, vol. V
Brewis, Rev. John Salusbury, died 1972, vol. VII
Brewis, Nathaniel Thomas, died 1924, vol. II
Brewitt, Rev. James C., 1843–1905, vol. I
Brews, Alan; see Brews, R. A.
Brews, (Richard) Alan, 1902–1965, vol. VI
Brewster, Adolph Brewster, 1854–1937, vol. III
Brewster, Rt Rev. Benjamin, 1860–1941, vol. IV
Brewster, Rt Rev. Chauncey Bunce, 1848–1941, vol. IV
Brewster, Edward John, died 1931, vol. III
Brewster, Willoughby Staples, 1860–1932, vol. III
Brewtnall, Edward Frederick, 1846–1902, vol. I
Breymann, Dr Hermann Wilhelm, died 1910, vol. I
Brian, Percy Wragg, 1910–1979, vol. VII
Briand, Aristide, 1862–1932, vol. III
Briant, Bruce Edgar Dutton, 1895–1959, vol. V
Briant, Frank, 1865–1934, vol. III
Brice, Arthur John Hallam Montefiore, died 1927, vol. II
Brice, Rev. Edward Henry, died 1952, vol. V
Brice, Seward, 1846–1914, vol. I
Brickdale, Sir Charles F.; see Fortescue-Brickdale.
Brickdale, Eleanor F.; see Fortescue-Brickdale.
Brickdale, John Matthew F.; see Fortescue-Brickdale.
Brickell, Daniel Francis Horseman, 1893–1967, vol. VI
Brickman, Brig. Ivan Pringle, 1891–1980, vol. VII
Brickwell, Alfred James, 1870–1937, vol. III
Brickwood, Sir John, 1st Bt, 1852–1932, vol. III
Brickwood, Sir Rupert Redvers, 2nd Bt, 1900–1974, vol. VII
Bridge, Ann, (Lady O'Malley), 1891–1974, vol. VII
Bridge, Adm. Sir (Arthur) Robin (Moore), 1894–1971, vol. VII
Bridge, Brig. Charles Edward Dunscomb, 1886–1961, vol. VI
Bridge, Brig.-Gen. Sir Charles Henry, 1852–1926, vol. II
Bridge, Adm. Sir Cyprian Arthur George, 1839–1924, vol. II
Bridge, Frank, 1879–1941, vol. IV
Bridge, Sir Frederick, 1844–1924, vol. II
Bridge, George Wilfred, 1894–1971, vol. VII
Bridge, Sir John, 1824–1900, vol. I
Bridge, John Crosthwaite, 1877–1947, vol. IV
Bridge, Joseph Cox, 1853–1929, vol. III
Bridge, Joseph James Rabnett, 1875–1959, vol. V
Bridge, Peter Gonzalez, 1885–1942, vol. IV
Bridge, Adm. Sir Robin; see Bridge, Adm. Sir A. R. M.
Bridge, Roy Arthur Odell, 1911–1978, vol. VII
Bridge, Maj.-Gen. Thomas Field Dunscomb, 1847–1934, vol. III
Bridge, Thomas William, 1848–1909, vol. I
Bridgeford, Lt-Gen. Sir William, 1894–1971, vol. VII
Bridgeman, 1st Viscount, 1864–1935, vol. III

Bridgeman, Viscountess; (Caroline Beatrix), died 1961, vol. VI
Bridgeman, Brig.-Gen. Hon. Francis Charles, 1846–1917, vol. II
Bridgeman, Adm. Sir Francis Charles Bridgeman-, 1848–1929, vol. III
Bridgeman, Hon. Geoffrey John Orlando, 1898–1974, vol. VII
Bridgeman, Col Hon. Henry George Orlando, 1882–1972, vol. VII
Bridgeman, Hon. Sir Maurice Richard, 1904–1980, vol. VII
Bridgeman, Reginald Francis Orlando, 1884–1968, vol. VI
Bridgeman-Bridgeman, Adm. Sir Francis Charles; see Bridgeman.
Bridger, Rev. John, died 1911, vol. I
Bridges, 1st Baron, 1892–1969, vol. VI
Bridges, Col Arthur Holroyd, 1871–1953, vol. V
Bridges, Daisy Caroline, 1894–1972, vol. VII
Bridges, Sir Ernest Arthur, 1880–1953, vol. V
Bridges, Col Francis Doveton, 1871–1954, vol. V
Bridges, Col George, died 1962, vol. VI
Bridges, Rev. Sir George Talbot, 1818–1899, vol. I
Bridges, Lt-Gen. Sir (George) Tom (Molesworth), 1871–1939, vol. III
Bridges, Rear-Adm. Henry Dalrymple, 1881–1955, vol. V
Bridges, Col James Whiteside, 1863–1930, vol. III
Bridges, John Henry, 1832–1906, vol. I
Bridges, John Henry, 1852–1925, vol. II
Bridges, Lt-Col Lionel Forbes, 1871–1937, vol. III
Bridges, Robert, 1844–1930, vol. III
Bridges, Robert, 1858–1941, vol. IV
Bridges, Roy, 1885–1952, vol. V
Bridges, Lt-Gen. Sir Tom; see Bridges, Lt-Gen. Sir G. T. M.
Bridges, Rear-Adm. Walter Bogue, 1843–1917, vol. II
Bridges, Brig.-Gen. William Throsby, 1861–1915, vol. I
Bridges-Adams, William, 1889–1965, vol. VI
Bridgewater, Francis Matthew, 1851–1915, vol. I
Bridgford, Col Sir Robert, 1836–1905, vol. I
Bridgford, Brig.-Gen. Robert James, 1869–1954, vol. V
Bridgland, Albert Stanford, died 1944, vol. IV
Bridgland, Sir Aynsley Vernon, 1893–1966, vol. VI
Bridgman, Leonard Logoz, 1895–1980, vol. VII
Bridgman, Percy W., 1882–1961, vol. VI
Bridie, James, (O. H. Mavor), 1888–1951, vol. V
Bridport, 1st Viscount, 1814–1904, vol. I
Bridport, 2nd Viscount, 1839–1924, vol. II
Bridport, 3rd Viscount, 1911–1969, vol. VI
Briercliffe, Sir Rupert, 1889–1975, vol. VII
Brierley, Col Sir Charles Isherwood, 1879–1940, vol. III
Brierley, Edgar, 1858–1927, vol. II
Brierley, Col Geoffrey Teale, died 1961, vol. VI
Brierley, J., 1843–1914, vol. I
Brierley, Rev. Canon John, 1886–1964, vol. VI
Brierley, William Broadhurst, 1889–1963, vol. VI
Brierly, James Leslie, 1881–1955, vol. V
Brieux, Eugene, 1858–1932, vol. III

Briffa, Col Alfred, 1868–1952, vol. V
Briffault, Robert Stephen, 1876–1948, vol. IV
Brigden, James Bristock, 1887–1950, vol. IV (A)
Brigg, Sir John, 1834–1911, vol. I
Briggs, Albert William, 1900–1971, vol. VII
Briggs, Sir (Alfred) George (Ernest), 1900–1976, vol. VII
Briggs, Arthur Beecham, 1883–1937, vol. III
Briggs, Prof. Charles Augustus, 1841–1913, vol. I
Briggs, Lt-Gen. Sir Charles James, 1865–1941, vol. IV
Briggs, Adm. Sir Charles John, 1858–1951, vol. V
Briggs, D. H. Currer, 1893–1974, vol. VII
Briggs, Lt-Col Ernest, 1881–1947, vol. IV
Briggs, Ernest Edward, 1866–1913, vol. I
Briggs, Sir George; see Briggs, Sir A. G. E.
Briggs, Rev. Canon George Wallace, 1875–1959, vol. V
Briggs, Harold; see Briggs, W. J. H.
Briggs, Captain Harold Douglas, 1877–1944, vol. IV
Briggs, Lt-Gen. Sir Harold Rawdon, 1894–1952, vol. V
Briggs, Hon. Sir Henry, born 1844, vol. II
Briggs, Henry, 1883–1935, vol. III
Briggs, Henry, died 1944, vol. IV
Briggs, James, 1855–1933, vol. III
Briggs, Sir John Henry, 1808–1897, vol. I
Briggs, Martin Shaw, 1882–1977, vol. VII
Briggs, Col Norman, 1891–1960, vol. V
Briggs, Percy, 1903–1980, vol. VII
Briggs, Rev. Rawdon, 1853–1936, vol. III
Briggs, Brig. Rawdon, 1892–1960, vol. V
Briggs, Thomas, 1847–1934, vol. III
Briggs, (W. J.) Harold, 1870–1945, vol. IV
Briggs, Waldo Raven, 1883–1956, vol. V
Briggs, William, 1861–1932, vol. III
Briggs, Col William Hilton, 1871–1951, vol. V
Brighouse, Harold, 1882–1958, vol. V
Brighouse, Sir Samuel, died 1940, vol. III
Bright, Alfred Ernest, 1869–1938, vol. III
Bright, Allan Heywood, 1862–1941, vol. IV
Bright, Sir Charles, 1863–1937, vol. III
Bright, Charles Edward, 1829–1915, vol. I
Bright, Mrs Golding; see Egerton, George.
Bright, Ven. Hugh, 1867–1935, vol. III
Bright, Rt Rev. Humphrey Penderell, 1903–1964, vol. VI
Bright, Rt Hon. Jacob, 1821–1899, vol. I
Bright, James Franck, 1832–1920, vol. II
Bright, John Albert, 1848–1924, vol. II
Bright, Sir Joseph, 1849–1918, vol. II
Bright, Mary Chavelita; see Egerton, George.
Bright, Brig.-Gen. Reginald Arthur, 1870–1942, vol. IV
Bright, Major Richard George Tyndall, 1872–1944, vol. IV
Bright, Rev. William, 1824–1901, vol. I
Bright, William Robert, 1857–1908, vol. I
Brighten, Lt-Col Edgar William, 1880–1966, vol. VI
Brightman, Rev. Frank Edward, 1856–1932, vol. III

Brightmore, A. W., 1864–1927, vol. II
Brigstocke, Charles Reginald, 1876–1951, vol. V
Brigstocke, Geoffrey Reginald William, 1917–1974, vol. VII
Brigstocke, George Edward, died 1971, vol. VII
Brill, Abraham Arden, 1874–1948, vol. IV
Brillant, Jules-André, 1888–1973, vol. VII
Brimacombe, Richard William, 1867–1930, vol. III
Brimble, Lionel John Farnham, 1904–1965, vol. VI
Brims, Charles William, 1877–1944, vol. IV
Brinckman, Major Sir Theodore Ernest Warren, 4th Bt, 1898–1954, vol. V
Brinckman, Col Sir Theodore Francis, 3rd Bt, 1862–1937, vol. III
Brinckman, Sir Theodore Henry, 2nd Bt, 1830–1905, vol. I
Brind, Adm. Sir (Eric James) Patrick, 1892–1963, vol. VI
Brind, Gen. Sir John Edward Spencer, 1878–1954, vol. V
Brind, Adm. Sir Patrick; see Brind, Adm. Sir E. J. P.
Brindle, Harry, died 1976, vol. VII
Brindle, Rt Rev. Robert, 1837–1916, vol. II
Brindley, Harold Hulme, 1865–1944, vol. IV
Brine, Edgar, 1856–1932, vol. III
Brink, Lt-Gen. George Edwin, 1889–1971, vol. VII
Brinkley, Captain Frank, 1841–1912, vol. I
Brinkley, Captain John Turner, 1855–1928, vol. II
Brinson, Derek Neilson, 1921–1974, vol. VII
Brinson, J. Paul, died 1927, vol. II
Brinton, Lt-Col John Chaytor, 1867–1956, vol. V
Brinton, Selwyn, died 1940, vol. III
Brisbane, Arthur, 1864–1936, vol. III
Brisbane, Sir (Hugh) Lancelot, 1893–1966, vol. VI
Brisbane, Sir Lancelot; see Brisbane, Sir H. L.
Brisco, Sir Aubrey Hylton, 6th Bt, 1873–1957, vol. V
Brisco, Sir Hylton Musgrave Campbell, 7th Bt, 1886–1968, vol. VI
Brisco, Sir Hylton Ralph, 5th Bt, 1871–1922, vol. II
Brisco, Sir Musgrave Horton, 4th Bt, 1833–1909, vol. I
Briscoe, Sir Alfred Leigh, 2nd Bt, 1870–1921, vol. II
Briscoe, Arthur John Trevor, 1873–1943, vol. IV
Briscoe, Sir Charlton; see Briscoe, Sir J. C.
Briscoe, Major Edward William, 1857–1928, vol. II
Briscoe, Henry Vincent Aird, 1888–1961, vol. VI
Briscoe, Hugh Kynaston, 1879–1956, vol. V
Briscoe, Sir (John) Charlton, 3rd Bt, 1874–1960, vol. V
Briscoe, Sir John James, 1st Bt, 1836–1919, vol. II
Briscoe, John Potter, 1848–1926, vol. II
Briscoe, Percy Charles, died 1951, vol. V
Briscoe, Captain Richard George, 1893–1957, vol. V
Briscoe, William Richard Brunskill, 1855–1930, vol. III
Brise, Archibald Weyland R.; see Ruggles-Brise.
Brise, Col Sir Edward Archibald R.; see Ruggles-Brise.
Brise, Sir Evelyn John R.; see Ruggles-Brise.
Brise, Maj.-Gen. Sir Harold Goodeve R.; see Ruggles-Brise.

Brise, Col Sir Samuel Ruggles, 1825–1899, vol. I
Brisson, Adolphe, *died* 1925, vol. II
Brisson, Henri, 1835–1912, vol. I
Brisson, Rosalind, (Mrs F. Brisson); *see* Russell, R.
Bristol, 3rd Marquis of, 1834–1907, vol. I
Bristol, 4th Marquis of, 1863–1951, vol. V
Bristol, 5th Marquess of, 1870–1960, vol. V
Bristol, Hon. Edmund, 1861–1927, vol. II
Bristol, Major Everett, 1888–1976, vol. VII
Bristow, Sir Charles Holditch, 1887–1967, vol. VI
Bristow, Ernest, 1873–1968, vol. VI
Bristow, Frederick George, *died* 1945, vol. IV
Bristow, Very Rev. John, *died* 1909, vol. I
Bristow, Rev. Richard Rhodes, *died* 1914, vol. I
Bristow, Sir Robert Charles, 1880–1966, vol. VI
Bristow, Walter Rowley, 1882–1947, vol. IV
Bristowe, Ethel Susan Graham, 1866–1952, vol. V
Bristowe, Samuel Botelen, *died* 1897, vol. I
Bristowe, William Syer, 1901–1979, vol. VII
Brittain, Alida Luisa, (Lady Brittain), *died* 1943, vol. IV
Brittain, Rev. Canon Arthur Henry Barrett, 1854–1911, vol. I
Brittain, Frederick, *died* 1969, vol. VI
Brittain, Sir Harry E., 1873–1974, vol. VII
Brittain, Sir Herbert, 1894–1961, vol. VI
Brittain, John, 1849–1913, vol. I
Brittain, Vera, 1896–1970, vol. VI
Brittain, Rear-Adm. Wilfred Geoffrey, 1903–1979, vol. VII
Brittain, William Henry, 1835–1922, vol. II
Brittain, William James, 1905–1977, vol. VII
Brittan, Maj.-Gen. Charles Gisborne, 1860–1939, vol. III
Britten, Baron (Life Peer); (Edward) Benjamin Britten, 1913–1976, vol. VII
Britten, Benjamin; *see* Baron Britten.
Britten, Comdr Sir Edgar Theophilus, 1874–1936, vol. III
Britten, Forester Richard John, 1928–1977, vol. VII
Britten, James, 1846–1924, vol. II
Britten, Rear-Adm. Richard Frederick, 1843–1910, vol. I
Brittlebank, Lt-Col Joseph William Forster, 1876–1944, vol. IV
Britton, Major Arthur Henry Daniel, 1875–1934, vol. III
Britton, Hon. Byron Moffat, 1833–1921, vol. II
Britton, Brig. Edwin John James, 1880–1955, vol. V
Britton, George Bryant, 1863–1929, vol. III
Britton, Hubert Thomas Stanley, 1892–1960, vol. V
Britton, Rev. Canon John, 1881–1948, vol. IV
Britton, Major Philip William Poole C.; *see* Carlyon-Britton.
Brittorous, Brig. Francis Gerard Russell, 1896–1974, vol. VII
Broad, Lt-Gen. Sir Charles Noel Frank, 1882–1976, vol. VII
Broad, Charlie Dunbar, 1887–1971, vol. VII
Broad, Francis Alfred, 1874–1956, vol. V
Broad, George Alexander, 1844–1915, vol. I (A)
Broad, Philip, 1903–1966, vol. VI
Broad, William Henry, 1875–1948, vol. IV

Broadbent, A., *died* 1919, vol. II (A), vol. III
Broadbent, Albert, 1867–1912, vol. I
Broadbent, Benjamin, 1850–1925, vol. II
Broadbent, Maj.-Gen. Sir Edward Nicholson, 1875–1944, vol. IV
Broadbent, Captain Harvey William, 1864–1942, vol. IV
Broadbent, Henry, 1852–1935, vol. III
Broadbent, Col John, 1872–1938, vol. III
Broadbent, Sir John, 2nd Bt, 1865–1946, vol. IV
Broadbent, Col John Edward, 1845–1931, vol. III
Broadbent, Joseph Edward, 1883–1948, vol. IV
Broadbent, Walter, *died* 1951, vol. V
Broadbent, Sir William Henry, 1st Bt, 1835–1907, vol. I
Broadbridge, 1st Baron, 1869–1952, vol. V
Broadbridge, 2nd Baron, 1895–1972, vol. VII
Broadbridge, Stanley Robertson, 1928–1978, vol. VII
Broadfoot, Col Archibald, 1843–1926, vol. II
Broadfoot, Hon. Sir Walter James, 1881–1965, vol. VI
Broadfoot, Major William, 1841–1922, vol. II
Broadhead, Rt Rev. Mgr Joseph, 1860–1929, vol. III
Broadhurst, Sir Edward Tootal, 1st Bt, 1858–1922, vol. II
Broadhurst, George H., 1866–1952, vol. V
Broadhurst, Henry, 1840–1911, vol. I
Broadhurst, Mary Adelaide, *died* 1928, vol. II
Broadley, Alexander Meyrick, 1847–1916, vol. II
Broadley, Henry Broadley Harrison-, 1853–1914, vol. I
Broadmead, Sir Philip Mainwaring, 1893–1977, vol. VII
Broadrick, Edward George, 1864–1929, vol. III
Broadus, Edmund Kemper, 1876–1936, vol. III
Broadway, Sir Alan Brice, 1873–1948, vol. IV
Broadway, Leonard Marsham, 1903–1974, vol. VII
Broadwood, Brig.-Gen. Arthur, 1849–1928, vol. II
Broadwood, Bertha Marion, 1846–1935, vol. III
Broadwood, Captain Evelyn Henry Tschudi, 1889–1975, vol. VII
Broadwood, Lt-Gen. Robert George, 1862–1917, vol. II
Broatch, Surg. Rear-Adm. George Thomas, 1862–1945, vol. IV
Brock, Baron (Life Peer); Russell Claude Brock, 1903–1980, vol. VII
Brock, Alan Francis C.; *see* Clutton-Brock.
Brock, Lt-Col Alec Walter Saumarez, 1878–1949, vol. IV
Brock, Arthur C.; *see* Clutton-Brock.
Brock, Charles Edmund, 1870–1938, vol. III
Brock, Captain Donald Carey, 1891–1970, vol. VI
Brock, Dame Dorothy; *see* Brock, Dame M. D.
Brock, Adm. Sir Frederic Edward Errington, 1854–1929, vol. III
Brock, Brig.-Gen. Henry Jenkins, 1870–1933, vol. III
Brock, Air Cdre Henry Le Marchant, 1889–1964, vol. IV
Brock, Henry Matthew, 1875–1960, vol. V
Brock, Sir Laurence George, 1879–1949, vol. IV

Brock, Dame (Madeline) Dorothy, 1886–1969, vol. VI

Brock, Adm. of the Fleet Sir Osmond de Beauvoir, 1869–1947, vol. IV

Brock, Reginald Walter, 1874–1935, vol. III

Brock, Sir Thomas, 1847–1922, vol. II

Brockbank, A. E., 1862–1958, vol. V

Brockbank, Russell Partridge, 1913–1979, vol. VII

Brocket, 1st Baron, 1866–1934, vol. III

Brocket, 2nd Baron, 1904–1967, vol. VI

Brockholes, John William F.; see Fitzherbert-Brockholes.

Brockholes, William Joseph F.; see Fitzherbert-Brockholes.

Brockhurst, Gerald Leslie, died 1978, vol. VII

Brockie, Thomas, 1906–1976, vol. VII

Brockington, Rev. Alfred Allen, 1872–1938, vol. III

Brockington, Leonard Walter, 1888–1966, vol. VI

Brockington, Sir William Allport, 1871–1959, vol. V

Brocklebank, Sir Aubrey, 3rd Bt, 1873–1929, vol. III

Brocklebank, Sir (Clement) Edmund (Royds), 1882–1949, vol. IV

Brocklebank, Sir Edmund; see Brocklebank, Sir C. E. R.

Brocklebank, Captain Henry Cyril Royds, 1874–1957, vol. V

Brocklebank, Major John Jasper, 1875–1942, vol. IV

Brocklebank, Sir John Montague, 5th Bt, 1915–1974, vol. VII

Brocklebank, Mary Petrena; see Brocklebank, Mrs Thomas.

Brocklebank, Sir Thomas, 1st Bt, 1814–1906, vol. I

Brocklebank, Sir Thomas, 2nd Bt, 1848–1911, vol. I

Brocklebank, Thomas, 1841–1919, vol. II

Brocklebank, Mrs Thomas, (Mary Petrena Brocklebank), 1849–1937, vol. III

Brocklebank, Sir Thomas Aubrey Lawies, 4th Bt, 1899–1953, vol. V

Brocklehurst, Charles Douglas Fergusson P.; see Phillips Brocklehurst.

Brocklehurst, Rev. Canon George, 1868–1946, vol. IV

Brocklehurst, Captain Henry Dent, 1855–1932, vol. III

Brocklehurst, Major John Henry Dent-, 1882–1949, vol. IV

Brocklehurst, Sir Philip Lancaster, 1st Bt, 1827–1904, vol. I

Brocklehurst, Sir Philip Lee, 2nd Bt, 1887–1975, vol. VII

Brocklehurst, Robert Walter Douglas Phillips, 1861–1948, vol. IV

Brocklehurst, William Brocklehurst, 1851–1929, vol. III

Brockman, Brig.-Gen. David Henry D.; see Drake-Brockman.

Brockman, Sir Digby Livingstone D.; see Drake-Brockman.

Brockman, Maj.-Gen. Edmund Alfred D.; see Drake-Brockman.

Brockman, Sir Edward Lewis, 1865–1943, vol. IV

Brockman, Edward Phillimore, died 1977, vol. VII

Brockman, Engr Rear-Adm. Henry Stafford, 1884–1958, vol. V

Brockman, Sir Henry Vernon D.; see Drake-Brockman.

Brockman, Lt-Col Ralph Evelyn D.; see Drake-Brockman.

Brockman, Ralph St Leger, 1889–1975, vol. VII

Brockwell, Esca Powys Butler, died 1934, vol. III

Brockwell, Rev. Canon John Cornthwaite, 1843–1927, vol. II

Brockwell, Maurice Walter, 1869–1958, vol. V

Broderick, Sir John Joyce, 1882–1933, vol. III

Broderick, Brig. Ralph Alexander, 1888–1971, vol. VII

Brodetsky, Selig, 1888–1954, vol. V

Brodeur, Hon. Louis Philippe, 1862–1924, vol. II

Brodeur, Rear-Adm. Victor Gabriel, 1892–1976, vol. VII

Brodhurst, Henry William Frederick Cottingham, 1856–1943, vol. IV

Brodhurst, James George Joseph P.; see Penderel-Brodhurst.

Brodie, Captain Sir Benjamin Collins, 4th Bt, 1888–1971, vol. VII

Brodie, Sir Benjamin Vincent Sellon, 3rd Bt, 1862–1938, vol. III

Brodie, Captain Ewen James, 1878–1914, vol. I

Brodie, George Bernard, 1839–1919, vol. II

Brodie, Harry Cunningham, 1875–1956, vol. V

Brodie of Brodie, Ian, 1868–1943, vol. IV

Brodie, Rabbi Sir Israel, 1895–1979, vol. VII

Brodie, John A., 1858–1934, vol. III

Brodie, Rt Rev. Matthew Joseph, 1864–1943, vol. IV

Brodie, Neil, 1900–1968, vol. VI

Brodie, Thomas Gregor, 1866–1916, vol. II

Brodie, Thomas Vernor Alexander, 1907–1975, vol. VII

Brodie, Bt Major Walter Lorrain, 1884–1918, vol. II

Brodrick, Rev. Hon. Alan, 1840–1909, vol. I

Brodrick, Alan Houghton, died 1973, vol. VII

Brodrick, Hon. Arthur Grenville, 1868–1934, vol. III

Brodrick, Hon. George Charles, 1831–1903, vol. I

Brodrick, Sir Thomas, 1856–1925, vol. II

Brodrick, William John Henry, 1874–1964, vol. VI

Brodrick, Brig. William Le Couteur, 1888–1973, vol. VII

Brodsky, Adolph, 1851–1929, vol. III

Brogan, Colm, 1902–1977, vol. VII

Brogan, Sir Denis William, 1900–1974, vol. VII

Broglie, Duc de, Maurice, 1875–1960, vol. V

Broke-Smith, Brig. Philip William Lilian, 1882–1963, vol. VI

Bromage, Lt-Col John Aldhelm Raikes, 1891–1955, vol. V

Bromby, Rt Rev. Charles Henry, 1814–1907, vol. I

Bromet, Mary (Mrs Alfred Bromet); see Pownall, Mary.

Bromfield, Rev. George Henry Worth, 1842–1920, vol. II

Bromfield, Major Harry Hickman, 1869–1916, vol. II

Bromfield, Louis, 1896–1956, vol. V

Bromfield, William, 1868–1950, vol. IV

Bromhead, Lt-Col Alfred Claude, 1876–1963, vol. VI

Bromhead, Col Sir Benjamin Parnell, 4th Bt, 1838–1935, vol. III

Bromhead, Col Charles James, 1840–1922, vol. II

Bromilow, Maj.-Gen. (David) George, 1884–1959, vol. V

Bromilow, Maj.-Gen. George; *see* Bromilow, Maj.-Gen. D. G.

Bromilow, Brig.-Gen. Walter, 1863–1939, vol. III

Bromilow, Rev. William E., 1857–1929, vol. III

Bromley, Rear-Adm. Sir Arthur, 8th Bt, 1876–1961, vol. VI

Bromley, Rear-Adm. Arthur Charles Burgoyne, *died* 1909, vol. I

Bromley, Sir Henry, 5th Bt, 1849–1905, vol. I

Bromley, Sir John, 1849–1915, vol. I

Bromley, John, 1876–1945, vol. IV

Bromley, Lancelot, 1885–1949, vol. IV

Bromley, Sir Maurice, 7th Bt; *see* Bromley-Wilson.

Bromley, Sir Robert, 6th Bt, 1874–1906, vol. I

Bromley, Sir Rupert Howe, 9th Bt, 1910–1966, vol. VI

Bromley-Davenport, Dame Lilian Emily Isabel Jane, *died* 1972, vol. VII

Bromley-Davenport, Mrs Muriel Coomber, 1879–1956, vol. V

Bromley-Davenport, Brig.-Gen. Sir William, 1862–1949, vol. IV

Bromley-Derry, Henry, 1885–1954, vol. V

Bromley-Martin, Granville Edward, *died* 1941, vol. IV

Bromley-Wilson, Sir Maurice, 7th Bt, 1875–1957, vol. V

Brommage, Joseph Charles, 1897–1972, vol. VII

Bromwich, Engr Rear-Adm. George Herbert, 1871–1965, vol. VI

Bromwich, T. J. I'anson, *died* 1929, vol. III

Bronk, Detlev Wulf, 1897–1975, vol. VII

Bronowski, Jacob, 1908–1974, vol. VII

Bronson, Howard Logan, 1878–1968, vol. VI

Broodbank, Sir Joseph Guinness, 1857–1944, vol. IV

Brook, Rev. Canon Alfred Eyre-, *died* 1949, vol. IV

Brook, Barnaby; *see* Brooks, W. C.

Brook, Charles, 1866–1930, vol. III

Brook, Clive, 1887–1974, vol. VII

Brook, Rev. David, 1854–1933, vol. III

Brook, Donald Charles, 1894–1976, vol. VII

Brook, Sir Dryden, 1884–1971, vol. VII

Brook, Maj.-Gen. Edmund Smith, 1845–1910, vol. I

Brook, Edward Jonas, 1865–1924, vol. II

Brook, Captain Edward William, 1895–1963, vol. VI

Brook, Lt-Col Sir Frank, 1883–1960, vol. V

Brook, Herbert Arthur, 1855–1925, vol. II

Brook, Cdre James Kenneth, 1889–1976, vol. VII

Brook, John Herbert, 1912–1963, vol. VI

Brook, Bt Col Reginald James, 1885–1965, vol. VI

Brook, Rt Rev. Richard, 1880–1969, vol. VI

Brook, Rev. Victor John Knight, 1887–1974, vol. VII

Brook, Air Vice-Marshal William Arthur Darville, 1901–1953, vol. V

Brook-Jackson, Rev. Canon Edwin, 1877–1936, vol. III

Brooke of Oakley, 1st Baron, 1869–1944, vol. IV

Brooke, Rev. Alan England, 1863–1939, vol. III

Brooke, Sir (Arthur) Douglas, 4th Bt (*cr* 1822), 1865–1907, vol. I

Brooke, Captain Basil Richard, 1882–1929, vol. III

Brooke, Sir Basil Stanlake, 5th Bt (*cr* 1822); *see* Brookeborough, 1st Viscount.

Brooke, Rear-Adm. Sir Basil Vernon, 1876–1945, vol. IV

Brooke, (Bernard) Jocelyn, 1908–1966, vol. VI

Brooke, Lt-Gen. Sir Bertram Norman Sergison-, 1880–1967, vol. VI

Brooke, Sir Charles Johnson; *see* Sarawak, Rajah of.

Brooke, Col Charles Louis, 1868–1938, vol. III

Brooke, Sir Charles Vyner, 1874–1963, vol. VI

Brooke, Brig.-Gen. Christopher Robert Ingham, 1869–1948, vol. IV

Brooke, Sir Douglas; *see* Brooke, Sir A. D.

Brooke, Sir Edward Geoffrey de C.; *see* de Capell Brooke.

Brooke, Lt-Col Edward William Saurin, 1873–1954, vol. V

Brooke, Emma Frances, *died* 1926, vol. II

Brooke, Sir Francis Hugh, 2nd Bt (*cr* 1903), 1882–1954, vol. V

Brooke, Rt Rev. Francis Key, 1852–1918, vol. II

Brooke, Rt Hon. Frank, 1851–1920, vol. II

Brooke, Maj.-Gen. Geoffrey Francis Heremon, 1884–1966, vol. VI

Brooke, George Cyril, 1884–1934, vol. III

Brooke, Lt-Col George Frank, *born* 1878, vol. II

Brooke, Sir George Frederick, 1st Bt (*cr* 1903), 1849–1926, vol. III

Brooke, Gilbert Edward, 1873–1936, vol. III

Brooke, Col Harry Morris Mitchelson, 1868–1934, vol. III

Brooke, Captain Sir Harry Vesey, 1845–1921, vol. II

Brooke, Brig.-Gen. Hugh Fenwick, 1871–1948, vol. IV

Brooke, Rev. James Mark Saurin, 1842–1918, vol. II

Brooke, Jocelyn; *see* Brooke, B. J.

Brooke, Sir John Arthur, 1st Bt (*cr* 1919), 1844–1920, vol. II

Brooke, John Henry, *died* 1902, vol. I

Brooke, John Kendall, 1856–1939, vol. III

Brooke, Sir John Reeve, 1880–1937, vol. III

Brooke, Ven. Joshua Ingham, 1836–1906, vol. I

Brooke, Gp-Captain Kennedy Gerard, 1882–1959, vol. V

Brooke, Leonard Leslie, 1862–1940, vol. III

Brooke, Brig.-Gen. Lionel Godolphin, 1849–1931, vol. III

Brooke, Margaret, (Lady Brooke); *see* Sarawak, Ranee of.

Brooke, Nevile John, 1891–1968, vol. VI
Brooke, Ven. Richard, *died* 1926, vol. II
Brooke, Col Richard Edward Frederic H.; *see* Howard-Brooke.
Brooke, Sir Richard Marcus, 8th Bt (*cr* 1662), 1850–1920, vol. II
Brooke, Major Sir Robert Weston, 2nd Bt (*cr* 1919), 1885–1942, vol. IV
Brooke, Col Ronald George, 1866–1930, vol. III
Brooke, Rev. Stopford Augustus, 1832–1916, vol. II
Brooke, Stopford W. W., 1859–1938, vol. III
Brooke, Sir Thomas, 1st Bt (*cr* 1899), 1830–1908, vol. I
Brooke, Major Victor Reginald, 1873–1914, vol. I
Brooke, Brig. Walter Headfort, 1887–1975, vol. VII
Brooke, Sir William Robert, 1842–1924, vol. II
Brooke, Willie, 1896–1939, vol. III
Brooke, Zachary Nugent, 1883–1946, vol. IV
Brooke-Hitching, Sir Thomas Henry, 1858–1926, vol. II
Brooke-Hunt, Violet, *died* 1910, vol. I
Brooke-Pechell, Sir Alexander; *see* Brooke-Pechell, Sir A. A.
Brooke-Pechell, Sir (Augustus) Alexander, 7th Bt, 1857–1937, vol. III
Brooke-Pechell, Sir George Samuel; *see* Pechell.
Brooke-Pechell, Sir Samuel George; *see* Pechell.
Brooke-Popham, Air Chief Marshal Sir Robert; *see* Popham.
Brookeborough, 1st Viscount, 1888–1973, vol. VII
Brooker, Brig.-Gen. Edward Part, 1866–1946, vol. IV
Brookes, Hon. and Rev. Edgar Harry, 1897–1979, vol. VII
Brookes, Captain Sir Ernest Geoffrey, 1889–1969, vol. VI
Brookes, Ernest Roy, 1904–1972, vol. VII
Brookes, Mabel Balcombe, (Lady Brookes), *died* 1975, vol. VII
Brookes, Sir Norman Everard, 1877–1968, vol. VI
Brookes, Warwick, *died* 1935, vol. III
Brookfield, Col Arthur Montagu, 1853–1940, vol. III
Brookfield, Charles Hallam Elton, 1857–1913, vol. I
Brookfield, G. Piers, 1894–1975, vol. VII
Brooking, Allan John, 1934–1980, vol. VII
Brooking, Maj.-Gen. Sir Harry Triscott, 1864–1944, vol. IV
Brooking, Adm. Patrick W. B., 1896–1964, vol. VI
Brookman, Sir George, 1853–1927, vol. II
Brooks, Sir (Arthur) David, 1864–1930, vol. III
Brooks, Captain Arthur William, 1887–1941, vol. IV
Brooks, Collin; *see* Brooks, W. C.
Brooks, Gen. Sir Dallas; *see* Brooks, Gen. Sir R. A. D.
Brooks, Sir David; *see* Brooks, Sir A. D.
Brooks, Eric St John; *see* Brooks, W. E. St J.
Brooks, Ernest Walter, 1863–1955, vol. V
Brooks, Hon. Mrs Florence, *died* 1934, vol. III
Brooks, Francis, 1861–1936, vol. III
Brooks, Ven. Frederick Richard, *died* 1912, vol. I
Brooks, Frederick Tom, 1882–1952, vol. V

Brooks, Rt Rev. Gerald Henry, 1905–1974, vol. VII
Brooks, Herbert, 1842–1918, vol. II
Brooks, I. M., *died* 1971, vol. VII
Brooks, James, 1825–1901, vol. I
Brooks, Sir James Henry, 1863–1941, vol. IV
Brooks, John Birtwhistle Tyrrell, 1889–1962, vol. VI
Brooks, Hon. Marshall Jones, 1855–1944, vol. IV
Brooks, Ralph Terence St J.; *see* St John-Brooks.
Brooks, Gen. Sir (Reginald Alexander) Dallas, *died* 1966, vol. VI
Brooks, Ronald Clifton, 1899–1980, vol. VII
Brooks, Sydney, 1872–1937, vol. III
Brooks, Thomas Judson, 1880–1958, vol. V
Brooks, Lt-Col T(homas) Marshall, 1893–1967, vol. VI
Brooks, Van Wyck, 1886–1963, vol. VI
Brooks, Hon. William, 1858–1937, vol. III
Brooks, (William) Collin, 1893–1959, vol. V
Brooks, Sir William Cunliffe, 1st Bt, 1819–1900, vol. I
Brooks, (William) Eric St John, 1883–1955, vol. V
Brooksbank, Sir Edward Clitherow, 1st Bt, 1858–1943, vol. IV
Broom, Cyril George Mitchell, 1889–1968, vol. VI
Broom, Sir James Thomson, 1866–1931, vol. III
Broom, Robert, 1866–1951, vol. V
Brooman-White, Major Charles James, 1883–1954, vol. V
Brooman-White, Richard Charles, 1912–1964, vol. VI
Broome, Viscount; Henry Franklin Chevallier Kitchener, 1878–1928, vol. II
Broome, Francis Napier, 1891–1980, vol. VII (AII)
Broome, Harold Holkar, 1875–1958, vol. V
Broome, Mary Ann, (Lady Broome), *died* 1911, vol. I
Broome, Maj.-Gen. Ralph Champneys, 1860–1915, vol. I
Broome, Hon. William, 1852–1930, vol. III
Broomfield, Sir Robert Stonehouse, *died* 1957, vol. V
Brophy, John, 1899–1965, vol. VI
Bros, James Reader White, 1841–1923, vol. II
Brosio, Manlio, 1897–1980, vol. VII
Broster, Dorothy Kathleen, *died* 1950, vol. IV
Broster, Lennox Ross, *died* 1965, vol. VI
Brotchie, James Rayner, 1909–1956, vol. V
Brotherhood, Stanley, 1876–1938, vol. III
Brotherton, 1st Baron, 1856–1930, vol. III
Brotherton, Charles Frederick Ratcliffe, 1882–1949, vol. IV
Brotherton, Harry George, 1890–1980, vol. VII (AII)
Brotherton, John, 1867–1941, vol. IV
Brough, Maj.-Gen. Alan, 1876–1956, vol. V
Brough, Bennett Hooper, 1860–1908, vol. I
Brough, Bertram C., *died* 1938, vol. III
Brough, Charles Allan La Touche, *died* 1925, vol. II
Brough, Major John, *died* 1917, vol. II
Brough, Joseph, 1852–1925, vol. II
Brough, Lionel, 1836–1909, vol. I
Brough, Mary Bessie, 1863–1937, vol. III

Brough, Robert, 1872–1905, vol. I
Broughall, Rt Rev. Lewis Wilmot Bovell, 1876–1958, vol. V
Brougham and Vaux, 3rd Baron, 1836–1927, vol. II
Brougham and Vaux, 4th Baron, 1909–1967, vol. VI
Brougham, Harold de Vaux, 1858–1930, vol. III
Brougham, Very Rev. Henry, 1827–1913, vol. I
Brougham, Captain Hon. Henry, 1883–1927, vol. II
Brougham, James Rigg, 1826–1919, vol. II
Broughshane, 1st Baron, died 1953, vol. V
Broughton, Sir Alfred Davies Devonsher, 1902–1979, vol. VII
Broughton, Major Sir Delves; see Broughton, Major Sir H. J. D.
Broughton, Sir Delves Louis, 10th Bt, 1857–1914, vol. I
Broughton, Sir Henry Delves, 9th Bt, 1808–1899, vol. I
Broughton, Rev. Henry Ellis, died 1924, vol. II
Broughton, Major Sir (Henry John) Delves, 11th Bt, 1888–1942, vol. IV
Broughton, Leonard Gaston, 1864–1936, vol. III
Broughton, Miss Rhoda, 1840–1920, vol. II
Broughton, Urban Hanlon, 1857–1929, vol. III
Broughton-Adderley, Hubert John; see Adderley.
Broughton-Head, Leslie Charles, died 1961, vol. VI
Broun, Sir (James) Lionel, 11th Bt, 1875–1962, vol. VI
Broun, John Alexander, 1856–1935, vol. III
Broun, Sir Lionel; see Broun, Sir J. L.
Broun, Sir William, 10th Bt, 1848–1918, vol. II
Broun Lindsay, Major Sir (George) Humphrey (Maurice), 1888–1964, vol. VI
Broun Lindsay, Major Sir Humphrey; see Broun Lindsay, Major Sir G. H. M.
Brounger, Captain Kenneth, 1881–1942, vol. IV
Brounger, Richard Ernest, 1849–1922, vol. II
Brousson, Louis Maurice, died 1920, vol. II
Brouwer, Luitzen Egbertus Jan, 1881–1966, vol. VI
Browder, Earl Russell, 1891–1973, vol. VII
Browell, Col William Basil, 1870–1935, vol. III
Browett, Sir Leonard, 1884–1959, vol. V
Brown, A. Curtis, 1866–1945, vol. IV
Brown, Rev. A. Douglas, 1874–1940, vol. III
Brown, Adrian John, 1852–1919, vol. II
Brown, Alan Brock, 1911–1980, vol. VII
Brown, Alan Grahame, 1913–1972, vol. VII
Brown, Brig. Alan Ward, 1909–1971, vol. VII
Brown, Albert Joseph, 1861–1938, vol. III
Brown, Hon. Alexander, 1851–1926, vol. II
Brown, Alexander Crum, 1838–1922, vol. II
Brown, Col Alexander Denis B.; see Burnett-Brown.
Brown, Sir Alexander Hargreaves, 1st Bt, 1844–1922, vol. II
Brown, Alexander Kellock, 1849–1922, vol. II
Brown, Alfred Barratt, 1887–1947, vol. IV
Brown, Alfred Reginald R.; see Radcliffe-Brown.
Brown, Sir Alfred W., 1883–1955, vol. V
Brown, Sir Algernon; see Brown, Sir T. A.
Brown, Allan, 1884–1969, vol. VI
Brown, Anthony Geoffrey Hopwood G.; see Gardner-Brown.
Brown, Rev. Archibald Geikie, 1844–1922, vol. II

Brown, Armitage Noel B.; see Bryan-Brown.
Brown, Sir Arnesby; see Brown, Sir J. A. A.
Brown, Arthur, 1884–1939, vol. III
Brown, Arthur, 1921–1979, vol. VII
Brown, Rev. Arthur Ernest, 1882–1952, vol. V
Brown, Wing Comdr Arthur James, 1884–1949, vol. IV
Brown, Lt-Col Arthur Miles W.; see Weber-Brown.
Brown, Sir Arthur W.; see Whitten-Brown.
Brown, Ashley Geikie, died 1957, vol. V
Brown, Major Cecil, born 1867, vol. II
Brown, Cecil Jermyn, 1886–1945, vol. IV
Brown, Air Vice-Marshal Cecil Leonard Morley, 1895–1955, vol. V
Brown, Cedric C.; see Clifton Brown.
Brown, Charles, 1849–1929, vol. III
Brown, Charles, 1884–1940, vol. III
Brown, Rev. Charles, 1855–1947, vol. IV
Brown, Sir Charles Gage, 1826–1908, vol. I
Brown, Charles Herbert, 1868–1942, vol. IV
Brown, Lt-Col Charles John, died 1939, vol. III
Brown, Col Charles Turner, 1875–1939, vol. III (A), vol. IV
Brown, Christopher Wilson, 1891–1949, vol. IV
Brown, Col Claude R.; see Russell-Brown.
Brown, Captain Claude Wreford W.; see Wreford-Brown.
Brown, Air Vice-Marshal Colin Peter, 1898–1965, vol. VI
Brown, David, died 1935, vol. III
Brown, David Hownam, 1879–1961, vol. VI
Brown, Eden Tatton, 1877–1961, vol. VI
Brown, Dame Edith Mary, died 1956, vol. V
Brown, Sir Edward, 1851–1939, vol. III
Brown, Edward Clifton C.; see Clifton-Brown.
Brown, Edward Percy, 1911–1972, vol. VII
Brown, Edward Thomas, 1879–1943, vol. IV
Brown, Eric, died 1939, vol. III
Brown, Maj.-Gen. Eric Gilmour, 1900–1967, vol. VI
Brown, Ernest, 1878–1949, vol. IV
Brown, Rt Hon. Ernest, 1881–1962, vol. VI
Brown, Lt-Col Ernest C.; see Craig-Brown.
Brown, Rev. Ernest Faulkner, 1854–1933, vol. III
Brown, Ernest William, 1866–1938, vol. III
Brown, (Everard) Kenneth, 1879–1958, vol. V
Brown, F. Gregory, 1887–1941, vol. IV
Brown, Rev. Francis, 1849–1916, vol. II
Brown, Vice-Adm. Francis Clifton, 1874–1963, vol. VI
Brown, Francis David Wynyard, 1915–1967, vol. VI
Brown, Francis Y.; see Yeats-Brown.
Brown, Sir Frank, 1857–1931, vol. III
Brown, Sir Frank Herbert, 1868–1959, vol. V
Brown, Frank James, 1865–1958, vol. V
Brown, Frank Leslie, 1896–1977, vol. VII
Brown, Frank Percival, 1877–1958, vol. V
Brown, Frederick, 1851–1941, vol. IV
Brown, Adm. Frederick Dundas G.; see Gilpin-Brown.
Brown, Col Frederick John, 1857–1941, vol. IV
Brown, George, born 1844, vol. II
Brown, George, 1847–1934, vol. III

Brown, George, 1872–1946, vol. IV
Brown, George Clifford, 1879–1944, vol. IV
Brown, George Edward, 1872–1934, vol. III
Brown, Rt Rev. George Francis G.; see Graham Brown.
Brown, Rear-Adm. George Herbert Hempson, 1893–1977, vol. VII
Brown, Rev. George James C.; see Cowley-Brown.
Brown, Sir (George) Lindor, 1903–1971, vol. VII
Brown, George Mackenzie, 1869–1946, vol. IV
Brown, Col Sir George McLaren, 1865–1939, vol. III
Brown, George Ronald Pym A.; see Aldred-Brown.
Brown, Sir George Thomas, 1827–1906, vol. I
Brown, Hon. George William, 1860–1919, vol. II
Brown, Gerard Baldwin, 1849–1932, vol. III
Brown, H. Harris, 1864–1948, vol. IV
Brown, Major Harold, died 1918, vol. II
Brown, Harold, 1895–1969, vol. VI
Brown, Harold Arrowsmith, died 1968, vol. VI
Brown, Engr Vice-Adm. Sir Harold Arthur, 1878–1968, vol. VI
Brown, Harold George, 1876–1949, vol. IV
Brown, Harold John, died 1975, vol. VII
Brown, Sir Harry Percy, 1878–1967, vol. VI
Brown, Haydn, died 1936, vol. III
Brown, Helen Gilman, 1869–1942, vol. IV
Brown, Henry Billings, 1836–1913, vol. I
Brown, Major Henry Coddington, 1876–1958, vol. V
Brown, Sir Henry Isaac Close, 1874–1962, vol. VI
Brown, Sir Herbert, 1869–1946, vol. IV
Brown, Herbert Charles, 1874–1940, vol. III (A), vol. IV
Brown, Horace T., 1848–1925, vol. II
Brown, Horatio Robert Forbes, 1854–1926, vol. II
Brown, Brig.-Gen. Howard Clifton, 1868–1946, vol. IV
Brown, Hubert Sydney, 1898–1949, vol. IV
Brown, Ivor John Carnegie, 1891–1974, vol. VII
Brown, J. H.; see Hullah-Brown.
Brown, Rt Hon. James, 1862–1939, vol. III
Brown, James, died 1941, vol. IV
Brown, Lt-Col James Arnold A.; see Arrowsmith-Brown.
Brown, James Arthur Kinnear, 1902–1971, vol. VII
Brown, Sir James Birch, 1888–1936, vol. VI
Brown, Lt-Col James C.; see Cross Brown.
Brown, James Campbell, died 1910, vol. I
Brown, James Clifton, 1841–1917, vol. II
Brown, Hon. James Drysdale, died 1922, vol. II
Brown, James Duff, 1862–1914, vol. I
Brown, Major James Pearson, 1868–1942, vol. IV
Brown, Sir James Raitt, 1892–1979, vol. VII
Brown, Brig. James Sutherland, 1881–1951, vol. V
Brown, Rev. (James) Wilson (Davy), 1839–1922, vol. II
Brown, Jethro; see Brown, W. J.
Brown, John, 1844–1905, vol. I
Brown, Very Rev. John, 1850–1919, vol. II
Brown, John, 1830–1922, vol. II
Brown, Sir John, died 1928, vol. II
Brown, Lt-Gen. Sir John, 1880–1958, vol. V

Brown, John, 1890–1977, vol. VII
Brown, John A. H.; see Harvie-Brown.
Brown, Sir (John Alfred) Arnesby, 1866–1955, vol. V
Brown, Paymaster-Commander John Edwin Ambrose, 1879–1931, vol. III
Brown, John Frank, 1856–1941, vol. IV
Brown, Captain Sir John Hargreaves P.; see Pigott-Brown.
Brown, John James Graham, died 1925, vol. II
Brown, John Macdonald, died 1935, vol. III
Brown, Sir John McLeavy, 1842–1926, vol. II
Brown, John Macmillan, 1846–1935, vol. III
Brown, John Mason, 1900–1969, vol. VI
Brown, Very Rev. John Pierce, 1843–1925, vol. II
Brown, Sir John Rankine, died 1946, vol. IV
Brown, John T. T., died 1933, vol. III
Brown, Rev. John Thomas, 1860–1929, vol. III
Brown, John Wesley, 1873–1944, vol. IV
Brown, Rev. Johnston Carnegie, 1862–1930, vol. III
Brown, Joseph, 1809–1902, vol. I
Brown, Sir Joseph, died 1919, vol. II
Brown, Joseph Pearce, 1850–1936, vol. III
Brown, Kenneth; see Brown, E. K.
Brown, Sir Kenneth Alfred Leader, 1906–1978, vol. VII
Brown, Laurence Morton, 1854–1910, vol. I
Brown, Leonard Graham, 1888–1950, vol. IV
Brown, Air Vice-Marshal Sir Leslie Oswald, 1893–1978, vol. VII
Brown, Lilian Kate Rowland-, 1863–1959, vol. V
Brown, Lilian Mabel Alice, (Lady Richmond Brown), died 1946, vol. IV
Brown, Sir Lindor; see Brown, Sir G. L.
Brown, Mary M. Annesley, 1856–1932, vol. III
Brown, Maud Frances F.; see Forrester-Brown.
Brown, Sir Melville Richmond, 3rd Bt, 1866–1944, vol. IV
Brown, Meredith Jemima, died 1908, vol. I
Brown, Michael George Harold, 1907–1969, vol. VI
Brown, Montagu Y.; see Yeats-Brown.
Brown, Nicol Paton, 1853–1934, vol. III
Brown, Rev. Nigel Mackenzie M.; see Morgan-Brown.
Brown, Lt-Col Sir Norman Seddon S.; see Seddon-Brown.
Brown, Lt-Col Oscar, 1864–1932, vol. III
Brown, Pamela Mary, 1917–1975, vol. VII
Brown, Sir Percival, 1901–1962, vol. VI
Brown, Percy, 1872–1955, vol. V
Brown, Captain Percy George, 1874–1954, vol. V
Brown, Brig.-Gen. Percy Wilson, 1876–1954, vol. V
Brown, Sir Peter Boswell, 1866–1948, vol. IV
Brown, Peter Hume, 1850–1918, vol. II
Brown, Raymond Gordon, 1912–1962, vol. VI
Brown, Reginald, died 1936, vol. III
Brown, Richard, 1844–1910, vol. I
Brown, Richard King, 1864–1942, vol. IV
Brown, Sir Robert Charles, 1836–1925, vol. II
Brown, Robert Cunyngham, 1867–1945, vol. IV
Brown, Major Sir Robert Hanbury, 1849–1926, vol. II
Brown, Robert J.; see Jardine-Brown.

Brown, Robert Neal R.; *see* Rudmose-Brown.
Brown, Robert Sidney, 1889–1959, vol. V
Brown, Lt-Col Robert Tilbury, 1873–1928, vol. II
Brown, Robson Christie, 1898–1971, vol. VII
Brown, Ronald David S.; *see* Stewart-Brown.
Brown, Ronald S.; *see* Stewart-Brown.
Brown, Samuel Edward, 1868–1929, vol. III
Brown, Sir Samuel Harold, 1903–1965, vol. VI
Brown, Samuel Lombard, *died* 1939, vol. III
Brown, Sidney George, 1873–1948, vol. IV
Brown, Spencer C.; *see* Curtis Brown.
Brown, Sir Stuart Kelson, 1885–1952, vol. V
Brown, Rear-Adm. Sydney, 1899–1970, vol. VI
Brown, Rev. Sydney Lawrence, 1880–1947, vol. IV
Brown, T. Austen, *died* 1924, vol. II
Brown, Sir (Thomas) Algernon, 1900–1960, vol. V
Brown, Thomas Brown R.; *see* Rudmose-Brown.
Brown, Thomas C.; *see* Craig-Brown.
Brown, Thomas Edwin Burton, 1833–1911, vol. I
Brown, Thomas G.; *see* Graham Brown.
Brown, Thomas James; *see* Brown, Tom.
Brown, Rt Hon. Thomas Watters, 1879–1944, vol. IV
Brown, Tom, (Thomas James Brown), 1886–1970, vol. VI
Brown, Hon. Villiers, 1843–1915, vol. I (A)
Brown, Vincent, *died* 1933, vol. III
Brown, Walter, 1886–1957, vol. V
Brown, Lt-Col Walter Henry, 1867–1928, vol. II
Brown, Walter Hugh, *died* 1950, vol. IV
Brown, Sir Walter L.; *see* Langdon-Brown.
Brown, Walter Russell, 1879–1966, vol. VI
Brown, William, 1850–1929, vol. III
Brown, William, 1856–1945, vol. IV
Brown, William, 1881–1952, vol. V
Brown, William, 1888–1975, vol. VII
Brown, Ven. William A.; *see* Ashley-Brown.
Brown, William Adams, 1865–1943, vol. IV
Brown, William B.; *see* Beattie-Brown.
Brown, Brig.-Gen. William Baker, 1864–1947, vol. IV
Brown, Sir William Barrowclough, 1893–1947, vol. IV
Brown, Rt Rev. William F., 1862–1951, vol. V
Brown, Very Rev. William Henry, *died* 1924, vol. II
Brown, William Henry, 1845–1918, vol. II
Brown, Rt Rev. Mgr William Henry, 1852–1934, vol. III
Brown, William Herbert, *died* 1927, vol. II
Brown, Col Sir William James, 1832–1918, vol. II
Brown, Very Rev. William James, 1889–1970, vol. VI
Brown, (William) Jethro, 1868–1930, vol. III
Brown, William John, *died* 1960, vol. V
Brown, William John, 1911–1977, vol. VII
Brown, William Lowe L.; *see* Lowe-Brown.
Brown, William Marshall, 1868–1936, vol. III
Brown, Rt Rev. William Montgomery, 1855–1937, vol. III
Brown, Sir William Nicholson, 1865–1939, vol. III
Brown, Sir William R.; *see* Robson Brown.
Brown, Sir William Richmond, 2nd Bt, 1840–1906, vol. I
Brown, Sir William Roger, 1831–1902, vol. I

Brown, Sir William Scott, 1890–1968, vol. VI
Brown, Sir William Slater, 1845–1917, vol. II
Brown, Rev. William Tom, 1865–1939, vol. III
Brown, Rev. Wilson; *see* Brown, Rev. J. W. D.
Browne, Col Abraham Walker, 1854–1939, vol. III
Browne, Hon. Sir Albert, 1860–1923, vol. II
Browne, Captain Alexander Crawford, *died* 1942, vol. IV
Browne, Alfred John J.; *see* Jukes-Browne.
Browne, Brig.-Gen. Alfred Joseph Bessell-, 1877–1947, vol. IV
Browne, Lt-Col Alfred Percy, 1868–1930, vol. III
Browne, Maj.-Gen. Andrew Smythe Montague, 1836–1916, vol. II
Browne, Lt-Gen. Sir Arthur George Frederic, 1851–1935, vol. III
Browne, Rt Rev. Arthur Heber, 1864–1951, vol. V
Browne, Rt Rev. Arthur Henry Howe, *died* 1961, vol. VI
Browne, Arthur Scott, 1866–1946, vol. IV
Browne, Rev. Barrington Gore, *died* 1914, vol. I
Browne, Sir Benjamin Chapman, 1839–1917, vol. II
Browne, Maj.-Gen. Beverley Wood, *died* 1948, vol. IV
Browne, Rev. Bevil; *see* Browne, Rev. W. B.
Browne, Sir Buckston; *see* Browne, Sir G. B.
Browne, Charles Edward, *born* 1861, vol. III
Browne, Sir Charles Ernest Christopher, 1871–1953, vol. V
Browne, Charles Macaulay, 1846–1911, vol. I
Browne, Col Charles Michael, 1878–1929, vol. III
Browne, Lt-Col Cuthbert Garrard, 1883–1951, vol. V
Browne, Daniel F., *died* 1913, vol. I
Browne, Denis, 1903–1965, vol. VI
Browne, Sir Denis John Wolko, 1892–1967, vol. VI
Browne, Brig.-Gen. Desmond John Edward B.; *see* Beale-Browne.
Browne, Edith A., *died* 1963, vol. VI
Browne, Sir Edmond, 1857–1928, vol. II
Browne, Maj.-Gen. Edward George, 1863–1952, vol. V
Browne, Edward Granville, 1862–1926, vol. II
Browne, Edward Raban C.; *see* Cave-Browne.
Browne, E(lliott) Martin, 1900–1980, vol. VII
Browne, Col Sir Eric G.; *see* Gore-Browne.
Browne, Francis James, *died* 1963, vol. VI
Browne, Sir Francis G.; *see* Gore-Browne.
Browne, Major Frederick Macdonnell, 1873–1915, vol. I (A)
Browne, George, *died* 1919, vol. II
Browne, Sir (George) Buckston, 1850–1945, vol. IV
Browne, Maj.-Gen. George Fitzherbert, 1851–1935, vol. III
Browne, Rt Rev. George Forrest, 1833–1930, vol. III
Browne, Col George Herbert Stewart, 1866–1944, vol. IV
Browne, Rev. George Rickards, 1854–1921, vol. II
Browne, George Sinclair, 1880–1946, vol. IV
Browne, George Stephenson, *died* 1970, vol. VI
Browne, Sir George Washington, 1853–1939, vol. III
Browne, Comdr Godfrey G.; *see* Gore-Browne.

Browne, Gordon Frederick, 1858–1932, vol. III
Browne, Sir Granville St John O.; see Orde Browne.
Browne, Hamilton Edward, 1860–1933, vol. III
Browne, Harold Carlyon Gore, 1844–1919, vol. II
Browne, Col Harold William Alexander Francis C; see Crichton-Browne.
Browne, Henry Doughty, died 1907, vol. I
Browne, Henry George G.; see Gore-Browne.
Browne, Rev. Henry J., 1853–1941, vol. IV
Browne, Gen. Henry Ralph, 1828–1917, vol. II
Browne, Henry William Langley, 1848–1928, vol. II
Browne, Maj.-Gen. Herbert Jose Pierson, 1872–1953, vol. V
Browne, Gen. Horace Albert, 1832–1914, vol. I
Browne, Maj.-Gen. James, 1840–1917, vol. II
Browne, Brig. James Clendinning, 1878–1953, vol. V
Browne, Sir James C.; see Crichton-Browne.
Browne, Gen. Sir James Frankfort Manners, 1823–1911, vol. I
Browne, John Campbell McClure, 1912–1978, vol. VII
Browne, John Edward Stevenson, 1910–1976, vol. VII
Browne, Brig.-Gen. John Gilbert, 1878–1968, vol. VI
Browne, John Hutton Balfour-, 1845–1921, vol. II
Browne, Sir John Walton, 1845–1923, vol. II
Browne, Major John William, 1857–1938, vol. III
Browne, Julius Basil, 1892–1947, vol. IV
Browne, Kathleen A., died 1943, vol. IV
Browne, Leonard Foster, 1887–1960, vol. V
Browne, Maurice, 1881–1955, vol. V
Browne, Col Maurice, 1884–1961, vol. VI
Browne, Most Rev. Michael, died 1980, vol. VII
Browne, His Eminence Cardinal Michael David 1887–1971, vol. VII
Browne, Nassau Blair, died 1940, vol. III (A), vol. IV
Browne, Philip Austin, 1898–1961, vol. VI
Browne, Sir Philip Henry, 1877–1950, vol. IV
Browne, Maj.-Gen. Reginald Spencer, 1856–1943, vol. IV
Browne, Richard Charles, 1911–1980, vol. VII
Browne, Rt Rev. Robert, 1844–1935, vol. III
Browne, Col Samuel Haslett, 1850–1933, vol. III
Browne, Gen. Sir Samuel James, 1824–1901, vol. I
Browne, Col Sherwood Dighton, 1862–1947, vol. IV
Browne, Dame Sidney Jane, 1850–1941, vol. IV
Browne, Lt-Col Sir Stewart G.; see Gore-Browne.
Browne, Maj.-Gen. Swinton John, 1837–1914, vol. I
Browne, Thomas Alexander; see Boldrewood, R.
Browne, Air Marshal Sir Thomas Arthur W.; see Warne-Browne.
Browne, Thomas George, 1888–1963, vol. VI
Browne, Ven. Thomas Robert, 1889–1978, vol. VII
Browne, Tom, 1872–1910, vol. I
Browne, Vincent R. B.; see Balfour-Browne.
Browne, Major Walter Hamilton, 1875–1933, vol. III
Browne, Ven. Walter Marshall, 1885–1959, vol. V

Browne, Rt Rev. Wilfred G.; see Gore-Browne.
Browne, William, died 1924, vol. II
Browne, William Alex Francis B.; see Balfour-Browne.
Browne, Rev. (William) Bevil, 1845–1928, vol. II
Browne, Maj.-Gen. William C.; see Cave-Browne.
Browne, Lt-Col William Percy, 1893–1972, vol. VII
Browne, Surg.-Gen. William Richard, 1850–1924, vol. II
Browne, Wynyard Barry, 1911–1964, vol. VI
Browne-Cave, Sir Clement Charles C.; see Cave-Browne-Cave.
Browne-Cave, Rev. Sir Genille C.; see Cave-Browne-Cave.
Browne-Cave, Air Vice-Marshal Henry Meyrick C.; see Cave-Browne-Cave.
Browne-Cave, Sir Mylles C.; see Cave.
Browne-Cave, Captain Sir Reginald Ambrose C.; see Cave-Browne-Cave.
Browne-Cave, Sir Rowland Henry C.; see Cave-Browne-Cave.
Browne-Cave, Sir Thomas C.; see Cave-Browne-Cave.
Browne-Cave, Wing Comdr Thomas Reginald C.; see Cave-Browne-Cave.
Browne Clayton, Hon. Brig.-Gen. Robert Clayton, 1870–1939, vol. III
Browne-Mason, Col Hubert Oliver Browne, 1872–1930, vol. III
Browne-Synge-Hutchinson, Col Edward Douglas, 1861–1940, vol. III
Browne-Wilkinson, Rev. Arthur Rupert, 1889–1961, vol. VI
Brownell, Franklin; see Brownell, P. F.
Brownell, (Peleg) Franklin, 1857–1946, vol. IV
Brownell, Reginald Samuel, 1893–1961, vol. VI
Brownell, William Crary, 1851–1928, vol. II
Brownfield, Vice-Adm. Leslie Newton, 1901–1968, vol. VI
Brownfield, Surg. Rear-Adm. Owen Deane, 1891–1955, vol. V
Browning, Mrs Adeline Elizabeth, 1869–1950, vol. IV
Browning, Amy Katherine, died 1978, vol. VII
Browning, Andrew, 1889–1972, vol. VII
Browning, Carl Hamilton, 1881–1972, vol. VII
Browning, Rev. Charles William, 1855–1930, vol. III
Browning, Colin Arrott Robertson, 1833–1908, vol. I
Browning, Lt-Gen. Sir Frederick Arthur Montague, 1896–1965, vol. VI
Browning, Lt-Col Frederick Henry, died 1929, vol. III
Browning, Col George Dansey-, 1870–1941, vol. IV
Browning, Lt-Col Herbert Arrott, 1861–1951, vol. V
Browning, Sir Jeffrey, 1862–1933, vol. III
Browning, Maj.-Gen. Langley, 1891–1974, vol. VII
Browning, Col Montague Charles, 1837–1905, vol. I
Browning, Adm. Sir Montague Edward, 1863–1947, vol. IV
Browning, Oscar, 1837–1923, vol. II

Browning, Robert, 1902–1974, vol. VII
Browning, Sidney, *died* 1928, vol. II
Browning, Lt-Col Winthrop Benjamin, 1855–1934, vol. III
Brownjohn, Gen. Sir Nevil Charles Dowell, 1897–1973, vol. VII
Brownlee, John Donald Mackenzie, *died* 1969, vol. VI
Brownlee, John Edward, 1884–1961, vol. VI
Brownlees, Sir Anthony Culling, 1817–1897, vol. I
Brownlie, James Thomas, 1865–1938, vol. III
Brownlow, 3rd Earl, 1844–1921, vol. II
Brownlow, 5th Baron, 1867–1927, vol. II
Brownlow, 6th Baron, 1899–1978, vol. VII
Brownlow, Lt-Col Celadon Charles, 1843–1925, vol. II
Brownlow, Field-Marshal Sir Charles Henry, 1831–1916, vol. II
Brownlow, Col Charles William, 1862–1924, vol. II
Brownlow, Brig.-Gen. d'Arcy Charles, 1869–1938, vol. III
Brownlow, Lt-Gen. Henry Alexander, 1831–1914, vol. I
Brownlow, Rt Rev. William Robert, 1830–1901, vol. I
Brownlow, Maj.-Gen. William Vesey, 1841–1926, vol. II
Brownrigg, Rt Rev. Abraham, 1836–1928, vol. II
Brownrigg, Charles Edward, 1865–1942, vol. IV
Brownrigg, Vice-Adm. Sir Douglas Egremont Robert, 4th Bt, 1867–1939, vol. III
Brownrigg, Henry John Brodrick, 1828–1904, vol. I
Brownrigg, Adm. Sir (Henry John) Studholme, 1882–1943, vol. IV
Brownrigg, Sir Henry Moore, 3rd Bt, 1819–1900, vol. I
Brownrigg, Very Rev. John Studholme, 1841–1930, vol. III
Brownrigg, Col Metcalfe Studholme, 1845–1924, vol. II
Brownrigg, Adm. Sir Studholme; *see* Brownrigg, Adm. Sir H. J. S.
Brownrigg, Captain Thomas Marcus, 1902–1967, vol. VI
Brownrigg, Lt-Gen. Sir W. Douglas S., 1886–1946, vol. IV
Bruce of Melbourne, 1st Viscount, 1883–1967, vol. VI
Bruce, Vice-Adm. Alan Cameron, 1873–1947, vol. IV
Bruce, Alexander, 1854–1911, vol. I
Bruce, Alexander, 1836–1920, vol. II
Bruce, Rev. Alexander Balmain, 1831–1899, vol. I
Bruce, Sir Alexander Carmichael, 1850–1926, vol. II
Bruce, Hon. Alice Moore, 1867–1951, vol. V
Bruce, Col Andrew Macrae, 1842–1920, vol. II
Bruce, Sir Charles, 1836–1920, vol. II
Bruce, Lt-Col Charles Edward, 1876–1950, vol. IV
Bruce, Brig.-Gen. Hon. Charles Granville, 1866–1939, vol. III
Bruce, Charles Mathewes, 1875–1939, vol. III
Bruce, Very Rev. Charles Saul, *died* 1913, vol. I

Bruce, Brig.-Gen. Clarence Dalrymple, 1862–1934, vol. III
Bruce, Rev. David, *died* 1911, vol. I
Bruce, Maj.-Gen. Sir David, 1855–1931, vol. III
Bruce, Col Hon. David, 1888–1964, vol. VI
Bruce, David Kirkpatrick Este, 1898–1977, vol. VII
Bruce, Rev. Douglas William, 1885–1953, vol. V
Bruce, Col Edward, *died* 1911, vol. I
Bruce, Eric Henry Stuart, 1855–1935, vol. III
Bruce, Rev. Francis Rosslyn Courtenay, 1871–1956, vol. V
Bruce, Rt Hon. Sir Gainsford, 1834–1912, vol. I
Bruce, George Gordon, 1891–1976, vol. VII
Bruce, Col Sir Gerald Trevor, 1872–1953, vol. V
Bruce, Rt Hon. Sir H. Hervey, 3rd Bt (*cr* 1804), 1820–1907, vol. I
Bruce, Adm. Sir Henry Harvey, 1862–1948, vol. IV
Bruce, Henry James, 1880–1951, vol. V
Bruce, Lt-Gen. Sir Henry Le Geyt, 1824–1899, vol. I
Bruce, Hon. Henry Lyndhurst, 1881–1915, vol. I
Bruce, Herbert, 1877–1935, vol. III
Bruce, Col Hon. Herbert Alexander, *died* 1963, vol. VI
Bruce, Captain Sir Hervey John William, 6th Bt (*cr* 1804), 1919–1971, vol. VII
Bruce, Sir Hervey Juckes Lloyd, 4th Bt (*cr* 1804), 1843–1919, vol. II
Bruce, Sir Hervey Ronald, 5th Bt (*cr* 1804), 1872–1924, vol. II
Bruce, Howard, 1879–1961, vol. VI
Bruce, Adm. Sir James Andrew Thomas, 1846–1921, vol. II
Bruce, John, 1837–1907, vol. I
Bruce, Sir John, 1905–1975, vol. VII
Bruce, Maj.-Gen. John Geoffrey, 1896–1972, vol. VII
Bruce, Hon. John Hamilton, 1889–1964, vol. VI
Bruce, John Mitchell, 1846–1929, vol. III
Bruce, Joseph Percy, 1861–1934, vol. III
Bruce, Marcus James Henry, 1890–1956, vol. V
Bruce, Sir Michael William Selby, 11th Bt (*cr* 1629), 1894–1957, vol. V
Bruce, Hon. Randolph; *see* Bruce, Hon. Robert R.
Bruce, Richard Isaac, 1840–1924, vol. II
Bruce, Col Robert, 1825–1899, vol. I
Bruce, Rev. Robert, 1829–1908, vol. I
Bruce, Rev. Robert, *died* 1915, vol. I
Bruce, Sir Robert, 1855–1931, vol. III
Bruce, Robert, *died* 1949, vol. IV
Bruce, Sir Robert, 1871–1955, vol. V
Bruce, Major Hon. Robert, 1882–1959, vol. V
Bruce, Robert Elton Spencer, 1936–1971, vol. VII
Bruce, Hon. (Robert) Randolph, 1863–1942, vol. IV
Bruce, Rev. Rosslyn; *see* Bruce, Rev. F. R. C.
Bruce, Tamara, (Mrs H. J. Bruce); *see* Karsavina, T.
Bruce, Brig.-Gen. Thomas, *died* 1966, vol. VI
Bruce, Thomas Dundas Hope, 1885–1940, vol. III
Bruce, Hon. Victoria Alexandrina Katherine, 1898–1951, vol. V
Bruce, Sir Wallace, 1878–1944, vol. IV

Bruce, Captain Wilfrid Montagu, 1874–1953, vol. V

Bruce, Ven. William Conybeare, *died* 1919, vol. II

Bruce, Sir William Cuningham, 9th Bt (*cr* 1629), 1825–1906, vol. I

Bruce, William Ironside, *died* 1921, vol. II

Bruce, William Napier, 1858–1936, vol. III

Bruce, William Speirs, 1867–1921, vol. II

Bruce, Rev. William Straton, 1846–1933, vol. III

Bruce, Sir William Waller, 10th Bt (*cr* 1629), 1856–1912, vol. I

Bruce-Gardner, Sir Charles, 1st Bt, 1887–1960, vol. V

Bruce-Joy, Albert, *died* 1924, vol. II

Bruce Lockhart, Sir Robert Hamilton, 1887–1970, vol. VI

Bruce Mitford, Terence; *see* Mitford.

Bruce-Porter, Sir (Harry Edwin) Bruce, 1869–1948, vol. IV

Bruce-Williams, Maj.-Gen. Sir Hugh Bruce; *see* Williams.

Bruche, Maj.-Gen. Sir Julius Henry, 1873–1961, vol. VI

Bruchesi, Most Rev. Paul, 1855–1939, vol. III

Brudenell, George Lionel Thomas, 1880–1962, vol. VI

Bru-de-Wold, Col Hilmar Theodore, 1842–1913, vol. I

Bruen, Adm. Edward Francis, 1866–1952, vol. V

Bruen, Rt Hon. Henry, 1828–1912, vol. I

Bruford, Robert, 1868–1939, vol. III

Brugha, Cathal; *see* Burgess, Charles.

Bruhl, L. Burleigh, 1861–1942, vol. IV

Brühl, Paul, *born* 1855, vol. III

Brummer, Rev. Nicolaas Johannes, 1866–1947, vol. IV

Brumwell, George Murray, 1872–1963, vol. VI

Brumwell, Rev. Percy Middleton, 1881–1963, vol. VI

Brun, Constantin, 1860–1945, vol. IV

Brunault, Rt Rev. Joseph Simon-Hermann, 1857–1937, vol. III

Brundage, Avery, 1887–1975, vol. VII

Brundle, Frank Walter, 1890–1963, vol. VI

Brundrett, Sir Frederick, 1894–1974, vol. VII

Brundrit, Reginald Grange, 1883–1960, vol. V

Brune, Charles Glynn P.; *see* Prideaux-Brune.

Brune, Col Charles Robert P.; *see* Prideaux-Brune.

Brune, Sir Humphrey Ingelram P.; *see* Prideaux-Brune.

Bruneau, Hon. Arthur Aimé, 1864–1940, vol. III (A), vol. IV

Bruneau, Louis Charles Bonaventure Alfred, 1857–1934, vol. III

Brunel, Adrian Hope, 1892–1958, vol. V

Brunetiere, Ferdinand, 1849–1906, vol. I

Brunger, Captain Robert, 1893–1918, vol. II

Brüning, Heinrich, 1885–1970, vol. VI

Brunker, Brig.-Gen. Capel Molyneux, 1858–1936, vol. III

Brunker, Edward George, 1871–1951, vol. V

Brunker, Maj.-Gen. Sir James Milford Sutherland, 1854–1942, vol. IV

Brunner, Emil, 1889–1966, vol. VI

Brunner, Ernst August, *died* 1920, vol. II

Brunner, Rt Rev. George, 1889–1969, vol. VI

Brunner, Sir John Fowler, 2nd Bt, 1865–1929, vol. III

Brunner, Rt Hon. Sir John Tomlinson, 1st Bt, 1842–1919, vol. II

Brunner, Roscoe, 1871–1926, vol. II

Brunot, Ferdinand, *died* 1938, vol. III

Brunskill, Maj.-Gen. Gerald, 1897–1964, vol. VI

Brunskill, Gerald FitzGibbon, 1866–1918, vol. II

Brunskill, Hubert Fawcett, 1873–1951, vol. V

Brunskill, Lt-Col John Handfield, 1875–1940, vol. III

Brunskill, Muriel, 1899–1980, vol. VII

Brunskill, Ven. Thomas Redmond, 1870–1936, vol. III

Brunt, Sir David, 1886–1965, vol. VI

Bruntnell, Albert, 1866–1929, vol. III

Brunton, Frederick William, 1879–1953, vol. V

Brunton, Sir (James) Stopford (Lauder), 2nd Bt, 1884–1943, vol. IV

Brunton, John Stirling, 1903–1977, vol. VII

Brunton, Sir Lauder; *see* Brunton, Sir T. L.

Brunton, Sir Stopford; *see* Brunton, Sir J. S. L.

Brunton, Sir (Thomas) Lauder, 1st Bt, 1844–1916, vol. II

Brunton, Sir William, 1867–1938, vol. III

Brunton-Angless, Violet, 1878–1951, vol. V

Brunwin-Hales, Rev. Canon G. T., 1859–1932, vol. III

Brunyate, Sir James Bennett, 1871–1951, vol. V

Brunyate, Sir William Edwin, 1867–1943, vol. IV

Bruton, Charles Lamb, 1890–1969, vol. VI

Bruton, Rear-Adm. Charles William, 1875–1952, vol. V

Bruton, Sir James, 1848–1933, vol. III

Brutton, Charles Phipps, 1899–1964, vol. VI

Bruxner, Lt-Col Sir Michael Frederick, 1882–1970, vol. VI (AII)

Bruyne, Pieter Louis de, 1845–1917, vol. II

Bryan, Charles Walter Gordon, 1883–1954, vol. V

Bryan, George Hartley, 1864–1928, vol. II

Bryan, Col Sir Herbert, 1865–1950, vol. IV

Bryan, Rev. J. Ingram, 1868–1953, vol. V

Bryan, Walter Burr-, *died* 1940, vol. III

Bryan, Col William Booth, *died* 1914, vol. I

Bryan, William Jennings, 1860–1925, vol. II

Bryan-Brown, Armitage Noel, 1900–1968, vol. VI

Bryans, Rev. John Lonsdale, 1853–1945, vol. IV

Bryant, Charles David Jones, 1883–1937, vol. III

Bryant, Charles William, *died* 1935, vol. III

Bryant, Sir Francis Morgan, 1859–1938, vol. III

Bryant, Frederick, 1878–1942, vol. IV

Bryant, Frederick Beadon, 1858–1922, vol. II

Bryant, Col Frederick Carkeet, 1879–1956, vol. V

Bryant, Lt-Col George Herbert, 1883–1952, vol. V

Bryant, Captain Henry Grenville, 1872–1915, vol. I

Bryant, J. H., 1867–1906, vol. I

Bryant, Marguerite, (Mrs Munn), 1870–1962, vol. VI

Bryant, Sophie, 1850–1922, vol. II

Bryant, Thomas, 1828–1914, vol. I

Bryce, 1st Viscount, 1838–1922, vol. II

Bryce, Viscountess; (Elizabeth Marion), *died* 1939, vol. III
Bryce, Alexander Joshua Caleb, 1868–1940, vol. III
Bryce, Lt-Col Edward Daniel, 1879–1936, vol. III
Bryce, Rev. George, 1844–1931, vol. III
Bryce, James McKie, *died* 1946, vol. IV
Bryce, John Annan, *died* 1923, vol. II
Bryce, Thomas Hastie, 1862–1946, vol. IV
Bryce, William Kirk, 1867–1954, vol. V
Bryceson, Sir Arthur Benjamin, 1861–1943, vol. IV
Bryden, Henry Anderson, 1854–1937, vol. III
Bryden, Robert, 1865–1939, vol. III
Brydon, James Herbert, 1881–1960, vol. V
Brymer, Ven. Frederick Augustus, *died* 1917, vol. II
Brymer, William Ernest, 1840–1909, vol. I
Brymner, William, *born* 1855, vol. III
Bryson, Charles; *see* Barry, Charles.
Bryson, George Murray, 1904–1970, vol. VI
Buber, Martin, 1878–1965, vol. VI
Buccleuch, 6th Duke of, **and Queensberry**, 8th Duke of, 1831–1914, vol. I
Buccleuch, 7th Duke of, **and Queensberry**, 9th Duke of, 1864–1935, vol. III
Buccleuch, 8th Duke of, **and Queensberry**, 10th Duke of, 1894–1973, vol. VII
Buchan, 13th Earl of, 1815–1899, vol. I
Buchan, 14th Earl of, 1850–1934, vol. III
Buchan, 15th Earl of, 1878–1960, vol. V
Buchan, Hon. Alastair Francis, 1918–1976, vol. VII
Buchan, Alexander, 1829–1907, vol. I
Buchan, Anna, *died* 1948, vol. IV
Buchan, Lt-Col Charles Forbes, 1869–1954, vol. V
Buchan, Brig. David Adye, 1890–1950, vol. IV
Buchan, Captain James Ivory, 1885–1958, vol. V
Buchan, Brig.-Gen. Lawrence, 1847–1909, vol. I
Buchan-Hepburn, Sir Archibald, 4th Bt, 1852–1929, vol. III
Buchan-Hepburn, Sir John Karslake Thomas, 5th Bt, 1894–1961, vol. VI
Buchanan, Sir Alexander Wellesley George Thomas L.; *see* Leith-Buchanan.
Buchanan, Captain Angus, 1886–1954, vol. V
Buchanan, Lt-Col Arthur Louis Hamilton, 1866–1925, vol. II
Buchanan, Arthur William Patrick, 1870–1939, vol. III
Buchanan, Sir David Carrick Robert C.; *see* Carrick-Buchanan.
Buchanan, David William Ramsay C.; *see* Carrick-Buchanan.
Buchanan, Hon. Sir (Ebenezer) John, 1844–1930, vol. III
Buchanan, Brig. Edgar James Bernard, 1892–1979, vol. VII
Buchanan, Sir Eric Alexander, 3rd Bt, 1848–1928, vol. II
Buchanan, George, 1827–1906, vol. I
Buchanan, Rt Hon. George, 1890–1955, vol. V
Buchanan, Sir George Cunningham, 1865–1940, vol. III
Buchanan, Sir George Hector L.; *see* Leith-Buchanan.

Buchanan, Sir George Hector Macdonald L.; *see* Leith-Buchanan.
Buchanan, Sir George Seaton, 1869–1936, vol. III
Buchanan, Rt Hon. Sir George William, 1854–1924, vol. II
Buchanan, Lt-Gen. Henry James, 1830–1903, vol. I
Buchanan, Rear-Adm. Herbert James, 1902–1965, vol. VI
Buchanan, J. Courtney, 1877–1949, vol. IV
Buchanan, Jack, *died* 1957, vol. V
Buchanan, Sir James, 2nd Bt, 1840–1901, vol. I
Buchanan, Rev. John, *died* 1945, vol. IV
Buchanan, Hon. Sir John; *see* Buchanan, Hon. Sir E. J.
Buchanan, Sir John Cecil Rankin, 1896–1976, vol. VII
Buchanan, John Lee, 1831–1922, vol. II
Buchanan, John Nevile, 1887–1969, vol. VI
Buchanan, Sir John Scoular, 1883–1966, vol. VI
Buchanan, John Young, 1844–1925, vol. II
Buchanan, Joseph Andrew William, *died* 1929, vol. III
Buchanan, Maj.-Gen. Sir Kenneth Gray, 1880–1973, vol. VII
Buchanan, Brig.-Gen. Kenneth James, 1863–1933, vol. III
Buchanan, Leslie, 1868–1943, vol. IV
Buchanan, Lewis Mansergh, 1836–1908, vol. I
Buchanan, Rev. Louis George, 1871–1952, vol. V
Buchanan, Milton Alexander, 1878–1952, vol. V
Buchanan, Robert, 1841–1901, vol. I
Buchanan, Robert J. M., *died* 1925, vol. II
Buchanan, Rev. Robert M., 1871–1945, vol. IV
Buchanan, Robert Ogilvie, 1894–1980, vol. VII
Buchanan, Ven. Thomas Boughton, 1833–1924, vol. II
Buchanan, Rt Hon. Thomas Ryburn, 1846–1911, vol. I
Buchanan, Hon. Sir Walter Clarke, 1838–1924, vol. II
Buchanan, Sir Walter James, 1861–1924, vol. II
Buchanan, Hon. William A., 1876–1954, vol. V
Buchanan-Dunlop, Col Henry Donald, 1878–1950, vol. IV
Buchanan-Jardine, Captain Sir John William; *see* Jardine.
Buchanan-Riddell, Sir John Walter; *see* Riddell.
Buchanan-Riddell, Sir Walter Robert; *see* Riddell.
Buchanan-Smith, Sir Walter, 1879–1944, vol. IV
Buchanan-Wollaston, Vice-Adm. Herbert Arthur; *see* Wollaston.
Bucher, Gen. Sir Francis Robert Roy; *see* Bucher, Gen. Sir R.
Bucher, Frederick Newell, *died* 1964, vol. VI
Bucher, Gen. Sir Roy, 1895–1980, vol. VII
Buchheim, Charles Adolphus, 1828–1900, vol. I
Büchler, Adolph, 1867–1939, vol. III
Buchman, Frank N. D., 1878–1961, vol. VI
Buck, Sir Edward Charles, 1838–1916, vol. II
Buck, Edward Clarke, 1873–1950, vol. IV (A)
Buck, Sir Edward John, *died* 1948, vol. IV
Buck, George Stucley; *see* Stucley, Sir G. S.
Buck, Pearl S., 1892–1973, vol. VII
Buck, Sir Percy Carter, 1871–1947, vol. IV

Buck, Sir Peter Henry, *died* 1951, vol. V
Buckell, Sir Robert, 1841–1925, vol. II
Buckeridge, Surg. Rear-Adm. Guy Leslie, 1877–1944, vol. IV
Buckham, Bernard, 1882–1963, vol. VI
Buckham, Sir George Thomas, 1863–1928, vol. II
Buckhurst, John William, 1853–1943, vol. IV
Buckingham and Chandos, Duchess of; (Alice Anne), *died* 1931, vol. III
Buckingham, Rev. Frederick Finney, *died* 1934, vol. III
Buckingham, Sir Henry Cecil, 1867–1931, vol. III
Buckingham, Col Sir James, 1843–1912, vol. I
Buckinghamshire, 7th Earl of, 1860–1930, vol. III
Buckinghamshire, 8th Earl of, 1906–1963, vol. VI
Buckland, 1st Baron, 1877–1928, vol. II
Buckland, Captain Arthur Edgar, 1890–1969, vol. VI
Buckland, Charles Edward, 1847–1941, vol. IV
Buckland, Geoffrey Ronald Aubert, 1889–1968, vol. VI
Buckland, Brig. Gerald Charles Balfour, 1884–1967, vol. VI
Buckland, Sir Henry, 1870–1957, vol. V
Buckland, Sir Philip Lindsay, 1874–1952, vol. V
Buckland, Maj.-Gen. Sir Reginald Ulick Henry, 1864–1933, vol. III
Buckland, Sir Thomas, 1848–1947, vol. IV
Buckland, William Warwick, 1859–1946, vol. IV
Buckle, Comdr Archibald Walter, *died* 1927, vol. II
Buckle, Lt-Col Arthur William Bentley-, 1860–1923, vol. II
Buckle, Maj.-Gen. Charles Randolph, 1835–1920, vol. II
Buckle, Maj.-Gen. Christopher Reginald, 1862–1952, vol. V
Buckle, Adm. Claude Edward, 1839–1930, vol. III
Buckle, Col Cuthbert, *died* 1971, vol. VII
Buckle, George Earle, 1854–1935, vol. III
Buckle, John, *died* 1925, vol. II
Buckle, Rev. Martin Brereton, 1853–1915, vol. I
Buckle, Major Matthew Perceval, 1869–1914, vol. I
Buckler, Georgina Grenfell, (Mrs William Buckler), *died* 1953, vol. V
Buckler, William Hepburn, 1867–1952, vol. V
Buckleton, Sir Henry, 1864–1934, vol. III
Buckley, Abel, 1835–1908, vol. I
Buckley, Lt-Col Albert, 1877–1965, vol. VI
Buckley, Col Arthur Dashwood Bulkeley, 1860–1915, vol. I
Buckley, Brig.-Gen. Basil Thorold, 1874–1954, vol. V
Buckley, Charles William, 1874–1955, vol. V
Buckley, Sir Edmund, 1st Bt, 1834–1910, vol. I
Buckley, Sir Edmund, 2nd Bt, 1861–1919, vol. II
Buckley, Edward Duncombe Henry, 1860–1931, vol. III
Buckley, Ven. Eric Rede, 1868–1948, vol. IV
Buckley, Rev. Felix J., 1834–1911, vol. I
Buckley, Rear-Adm. Frederic Arthur, 1887–1952, vol. V
Buckley, Lt-Col George Alexander Maclean, 1866–1937, vol. III

Buckley, Howard; *see* Buckley, W. H.
Buckley, Maj.-Gen. Sir Hugh Clive, 1880–1962, vol. VI
Buckley, Rev. James Monroe, 1836–1920, vol. II
Buckley, Ven. James Rice, 1849–1924, vol. II
Buckley, John J., 1863–1939, vol. III
Buckley, John Joseph Cronin, 1904–1972, vol. VII
Buckley, Rev. Jonathan Charles, *died* 1927, vol. II
Buckley, Llewellyn Eddison, 1866–1944, vol. IV
Buckley, Lt-Col Percy Neville, 1867–1953, vol. V
Buckley, Robert Burton, 1847–1927, vol. II
Buckley, Ven. Thomas Richard, 1859–1936, vol. III
Buckley, Wilfred, 1873–1933, vol. III
Buckley, William, 1859–1937, vol. III
Buckley, (William) Howard, 1909–1974, vol. VII
Buckley, Brig. William Percy, 1887–1968, vol. VI
Buckman, Edwin, 1841–1930, vol. III
Buckman, Rosina, *died* 1948, vol. IV
Buckmaster, 1st Viscount, 1861–1934, vol. III
Buckmaster, 2nd Viscount, 1890–1974, vol. VII
Buckmaster, Charles A., 1854–1949, vol. IV
Buckmaster, Engr Rear-Adm. Frederick Henry, 1883–1947, vol. IV
Buckmaster, George Alfred, 1859–1937, vol. III
Buckmaster, Martin A., 1862–1960, vol. V
Bucknall, Lt-Gen. Gerard Corfield, 1894–1980, vol. VII
Bucknill, Rt Hon. Sir Alfred Townsend, 1880–1963, vol. VI
Bucknill, Sir John Alexander Strachey, 1873–1926, vol. II
Bucknill, Sir John Charles, 1817–1897, vol. I
Bucknill, Rt Hon. Sir Thomas Townsend, 1845–1915, vol. I (A), vol. II
Buckrose, J. E., *died* 1931, vol. III
Buckston, George Moreton, 1881–1942, vol. IV
Buckston, Rev. Henry, 1834–1916, vol. II
Buckton, Baron (Life Peer); Samuel Storey, 1896–1978, vol. VII
Buckton, Ernest James, 1883–1973, vol. VII
Buckton, Ven. Thomas Frederick, 1858–1933, vol. III
Buckworth-Herne-Soame, Sir Charles; *see* Soame.
Buckworth-Herne-Soame, Sir Charles Burnett; *see* Soame.
Budd, Alfred, *died* 1927, vol. II
Budd, Sir Cecil Lindsay, 1865–1945, vol. IV
Budd, Hon. Sir Harry Vincent, 1900–1979, vol. VII
Budd, Herbert Ashwin, 1881–1950, vol. IV
Budd, John Wreford, 1838–1922, vol. II
Budden, Rev. Charles William, 1878–1952, vol. V
Budden, Lt-Col F. H., 1887–1953, vol. V
Budden, Henry Ebenezer, 1871–1944, vol. IV
Budden, Lionel, 1891–1966, vol. VI
Budden, Lionel Bailey, 1887–1956, vol. V
Buddo, Hon. David, 1856–1937, vol. III
Budge, Sir Ernest A. Wallis, 1857–1934, vol. III
Budge, Sir Henry Sinclair Campbell, 1874–1946, vol. IV
Budge, Rev. Ronald Henderson Gunn, 1909–1976, vol. VII
Budgen, Rear-Adm. Douglas Adams, *died* 1947, vol. IV
Budgett, Hubert Maitland, 1882–1951, vol. V

Budworth, Maj.-Gen. Charles Edward Dutton, *died* 1921, vol. II
Budworth, Rev. Richard Dutton, 1867–1937, vol. III
Buell, Lt-Col William Senkler, 1868–1941, vol. IV
Buer, Mabel Craven, 1881–1942, vol. IV
Buesst, Captain Aylmer, 1883–1970, vol. VI
Buganda, Kabaka (King) of, 1896–1939, vol. III
Buganda, HH The Kabaka of, 1924–1969, vol. VI
Buhl, Frants Peter William, 1850–1932, vol. III
Buick, Thomas Lindsay, *died* 1938, vol. III
Buisson, Ferdinand, 1841–1932, vol. III
Buisson, François A.; *see* Albert-Buisson.
Buist, Maj.-Gen. David Simson, 1829–1908, vol. I
Buist, Col Herbert John Martin, 1868–1956, vol. V
Buist, H(ugo) Massac, 1878–1966, vol. VI
Buist, Robert Cochrane, 1860–1939, vol. III
Bulfin, Gen. Sir Edward Stanislaus, 1862–1939, vol. III
Bulganin, Marshal Nikolai Alexandrovich, 1895–1975, vol. VII
Bulkeley, Lt-Col C. Rivers, 1840–1934, vol. III
Bulkeley, Lt-Col Henry Charles, 1860–1938, vol. III
Bulkeley, John Pierson, *died* 1958, vol. V
Bulkeley, Sir Richard Henry Williams-, 12th Bt, 1862–1942, vol. IV
Bulkeley, Captain Thomas Henry Rivers, 1876–1914, vol. I
Bulkeley-Evans, William, 1870–1952, vol. V
Bulkeley-Owen, Rev. Thomas M. Bulkeley, *died* 1910, vol. I
Bull, A. J., 1875–1950, vol. IV
Bull, Archibald William Major, 1888–1970, vol. VI
Bull, Bartle, 1902–1950, vol. IV
Bull, George, 1864–1929, vol. III
Bull, George Lucien, 1876–1972, vol. VII
Bull, Henry Cecil Herbert, 1892–1964, vol. VI
Bull, Rev. Paul Bertie, 1864–1942, vol. IV
Bull, René, *died* 1942, vol. IV
Bull, Sir Stephen John, 2nd Bt, 1904–1942, vol. IV
Bull, Rt Hon. Sir William, 1st Bt, 1863–1931, vol. III
Bull, William Charles, 1858–1933, vol. III
Bull, William Perkins, 1870–1948, vol. IV
Bullard, Sir Edward Crisp, 1907–1980, vol. VII
Bullard, Sir Harry, 1841–1903, vol. I
Bullard, John Eric, 1903–1961, vol. VI
Bullard, Rev. John Vincent, 1869–1941, vol. IV
Bullard, Sir Reader William, 1885–1976, vol. VII
Bullard, Lt-Gen. Robert Lee, 1861–1947, vol. IV
Bulleid, C. H., 1883–1956, vol. V
Bulleid, G. Lawrence, 1858–1933, vol. III
Bulleid, Oliver Vaughan Snell, 1882–1970, vol. VI
Bullen, Arthur Henry, 1857–1920, vol. II
Bullen, Frank Thomas, 1857–1915, vol. I
Bullen, Rt Rev. Herbert Guy, 1896–1937, vol. III
Bullen, Keith Edward, 1906–1976, vol. VII
Bullen, Percy Sutherland, 1867–1958, vol. V
Bullen-Smith, Col George Moultrie, 1870–1934, vol. III
Buller, Sir Alexander, 1834–1903, vol. I
Buller, Arthur Henry Reginald, 1874–1944, vol. IV
Buller, Arthur Tremayne, 1850–1917, vol. II

Buller, Dame (Audrey Charlotte) Georgiana, 1883–1953, vol. V
Buller, Charles William Dunbar-, 1847–1924, vol. II
Buller, Rear-Adm. Francis Alexander Waddilove, 1879–1943, vol. IV
Buller, Dame Georgiana; *see* Buller, Dame A. C. G
Buller, Adm. Sir Henry Tritton, 1873–1960, vol. V
Buller, Brig.-Gen. Hon. Sir Henry Y.; *see* Yarde-Buller.
Buller, Major Herbert Cecil, 1882–1916, vol. II
Buller, Lt-Col John Dashwood, 1878–1961, vol. VI
Buller, Lt-Col Sir Mervyn Edward M.; *see* Manningham-Buller.
Buller, Sir Morton Edward Manningham-, 2nd Bt, 1825–1910, vol. I
Buller, Ralph Buller H.; *see* Hughes-Buller.
Buller, Gen. Rt Hon. Sir Redvers Henry, 1839–1908, vol. I
Buller, Sir Walter Lawry, 1838–1906, vol. I
Buller, Lt-Col Walter Thomas More, 1886–1938, vol. III
Buller, Hon. Walter Y.; *see* Yarde-Buller.
Bullerwell, William, 1916–1977, vol. VII
Bullett, Gerald William, 1893–1958, vol. V
Bullin, Major Sir Reginald, 1879–1969, vol. VI
Bullinger, Ethelbert William, 1837–1913, vol. I
Bullitt, William Christian, 1891–1967, vol. VI
Bulloch, John Malcolm, 1867–1938, vol. III
Bulloch, William, 1868–1941, vol. IV
Bullock, Rev. Charles, 1829–1911, vol. I
Bullock, Charles, *died* 1952, vol. V
Bullock, Sir Christopher Llewellyn, 1891–1972, vol. VII
Bullock, Lt-Col Edward George T.; *see* Troyte-Bullock.
Bullock, Sir Ernest, 1890–1979, vol. VII
Bullock, Ernest Henry, 1911–1957, vol. V
Bullock, Fred, 1878–1946, vol. IV
Bullock, Frederick Shore, 1847–1914, vol. I
Bullock, Lt-Gen. Sir George Mackworth, 1851–1926, vol. II
Bullock, Guy Henry, 1887–1956, vol. V
Bullock, Captain Sir (Harold) Malcolm, 1st Bt, 1890–1966, vol. VI
Bullock, Brig. Humphry, 1899–1959, vol. V
Bullock, Captain Sir Malcolm; *see* Bullock, Captain Sir H. M.
Bullock, Ralph, 1868–1946, vol. IV
Bullock, Rev. Richard, 1839–1918, vol. II
Bullock, Samuel, 1844–1922, vol. II
Bullock, Shan F., 1865–1935, vol. III
Bullock, Thomas Lowndes, 1845–1915, vol. I
Bullock, Walter Ll., 1890–1944, vol. IV
Bullock, Ven. William, 1885–1944, vol. IV
Bullock, Willoughby, 1882–1950, vol. IV
Bullock-Marsham, Brig. Francis William; *see* Marsham.
Bullock-Marsham, Robert H.; *see* Marsham.
Bullock-Webster, Rev. George Russell, 1858–1934, vol. III
Bullough, Sir George, 1st Bt, 1870–1939, vol. III
Bullough, Major Ian, *died* 1936, vol. III
Bulman, Henry Herbert, 1871–1928, vol. II

Bulman, Oliver Meredith Boone, 1902–1974, vol. VII
Bulman, Paul Ward Spencer, 1896–1963, vol. VI
Bulmer, Edward Frederick, 1865–1941, vol. IV
Bulmer, James Alfred, *died* 1914, vol. I
Bulmer, Sir James William, 1881–1936, vol. III
Bulstrode, Herbert Timbrell, *died* 1911, vol. I
Bulteel, Major Sir John Crocker, 1890–1956, vol. V
Bulwer, Gen. Sir Edward Earle Gascoyne, 1829–1910, vol. I
Bulwer, Sir Henry Ernest Gascoyne, 1836–1914, vol. I
Bulwer, James Redfoord, 1820–1899, vol. I
Bulwer, William Dering Earle, 1856–1915, vol. I (A)
Bulwer, Brig.-Gen. William Earle Gascoyne Lytton, 1829–1910, vol. I
Bulyea, George Hedley Vicars, 1859–1928, vol. II
Bun Behari Kapur, Raja Bahadur, 1853–1924, vol. II
Bunbury, Cecil Edward Francis, 1864–1932, vol. III
Bunbury, Sir Charles Henry Napier, 11th Bt (*cr* 1681), 1886–1963, vol. VI
Bunbury, Evelyn James, 1888–1965, vol. VI
Bunbury, Sir Henry Charles John, 10th Bt (*cr* 1681), 1855–1930, vol. III
Bunbury, Sir Henry Noel, 1876–1968, vol. VI
Bunbury, Maj.-Gen. Sir Herbert Napier, 1851–1922, vol. II
Bunbury, Rev. Sir John Richardson, 3rd Bt (*cr* 1787), 1813–1909, vol. I
Bunbury, Sir Mervyn William Richardson-, 4th Bt (*cr* 1787), 1874–1952, vol. V
Bunbury, Brig. Noël Louis St Pierre, 1890–1971, vol. VII
Bunbury, Rt Rev. Thomas, *died* 1907, vol. I
Bunbury, Brig.-Gen. Vesey Thomas, 1859–1934, vol. III
Bunbury, Maj.-Gen. William Edwin, 1858–1925, vol. II
Bunce, John Thackray, 1828–1899, vol. I
Bunch, John L., *died* 1941, vol. IV
Bunche, Ralph J., 1904–1971, vol. VII
Bund, John William W.; *see* Willis-Bund.
Bundey, Hon. Sir Henry; *see* Bundey, Hon. Sir W. H.
Bundey, Hon. Sir (William) Henry, 1838–1909, vol. I
Bundi, HH Maharao Raja, 1869–1927, vol. II
Bundi, HH Maharao Raja of, 1893–1945, vol. IV
Bundy, Edgar, *died* 1922, vol. II
Bune, John, *died* 1925, vol. II
Bunin, Ivan, 1870–1953, vol. V
Bunker, Lt-Col Sidney Waterfield, 1889–1968, vol. VI
Bunning, Arthur John Farrant, 1895–1968, vol. VI
Bunning, Herbert, 1863–1937, vol. III
Bunny, Rupert Charles Wolston, 1864–1947, vol. IV
Bunoz, Rt Rev. Emile Marie, 1864–1945, vol. IV
Bunt, Rev. Frederick Darrell, 1902–1977, vol. VII
Buntine, James Robertson, 1841–1920, vol. II
Bunting, D. G.; *see* George, Daniel.
Bunting, Sir Percy, 1836–1911, vol. I

Burbank, Luther, 1849–1926, vol. II
Burbidge, Rev. Frederick William, 1840–1915, vol. I
Burbidge, Frederick William Thomas, 1847–1905, vol. I
Burbidge, Hon. George W., *died* 1908, vol. I
Burbidge, Sir John Richard Woodman, 4th Bt, 1930–1974, vol. VII
Burbidge, Sir Richard, 1st Bt, 1847–1917, vol. II
Burbidge, Sir Richard Grant Woodman, 3rd Bt, 1897–1966, vol. VI
Burbidge, Sir (Richard) Woodman, 2nd Bt, 1872–1945, vol. IV
Burbidge, Sir Woodman; *see* Burbidge, Sir R. W.
Burbury, Samuel Hawksley, 1831–1911, vol. I
Burch, Maj.-Gen. Frederick Whitmore, 1893–1977, vol. VII
Burch, George James, 1852–1914, vol. I
Burch, Lt-Col William Edward Scarth, *died* 1940, vol. III
Burchardt, Frank A., 1902–1958, vol. V
Burchnall, Joseph Langley, 1892–1975, vol. VII
Burckhardt, Charles James, 1891–1974, vol. VII
Burd, Rev. Frederick, 1826–1915, vol. I
Burd, Rev. Prebendary John, 1828–1918, vol. II
Burd, Rt Rev. Walter, 1888–1939, vol. III
Burden, 1st Baron, 1885–1970, vol. VI
Burden, Frederick Parker, 1874–1971, vol. VII
Burden, Col Henry, 1867–1953, vol. V
Burder, Brig.-Gen. Ernest Sumner, 1866–1946, vol. IV
Burdett, Sir Charles Coventry, 9th Bt, 1902–1940, vol. III
Burdett, Sir Francis, 8th Bt, 1869–1951, vol. V
Burdett, Sir Henry, 1847–1920, vol. II
Burdett, Sir Henry Aylmer, 10th Bt, 1881–1943, vol. IV
Burdett, Osbert, 1885–1936, vol. III
Burdett, Scott Langshaw, 1897–1961, vol. VI
Burdett-Coutts, Baroness (1st in line), 1814–1906, vol. I
Burdett-Coutts, Rt Hon. William Lehman Ashmead Bartlett-, 1851–1921, vol. II
Burditt, George Frederick, 1862–1933, vol. III
Burdon, Sir Ernest, 1881–1957, vol. V
Burdon, Major Sir John Alder, 1866–1933, vol. III
Burdon, Rt Rev. John Shaw, 1826–1907, vol. I
Burdon, Rowland, 1857–1944, vol. IV
Burdon-Sanderson, Sir John Scott, 1st Bt, 1828–1905, vol. I (A)
Burdwan, Maharajadhiraja Bahadur of, 1881–1941, vol. IV
Bureau, Jacques, 1860–1933, vol. III
Buret, Captain Theobald John Claud P.; *see* Purcell-Buret.
Burford, George Henry, 1856–1937, vol. III
Burge, Sir Charles Henry, 1846–1921, vol. II
Burge, Rt Rev. Hubert Murray, 1862–1925, vol. II
Burge, Milward Rodon Kennedy, 1894–1968, vol. VI
Burger, Schalk William, *died* 1918, vol. II
Burges, Lt-Col Dan, 1873–1946, vol. IV
Burges, Ven. Ernest Travers, 1851–1921, vol. II
Burges, Col Ynyr Henry, 1834–1908, vol. I

Burgess, Arthur Henry, 1874–1948, vol. IV
Burgess, Arthur James Wetherall, 1879–1957, vol. V
Burgess, Charles, (Cathal Brugha), *died* 1922, vol. II
Burgess, Lt-Col Charles Roscoe, 1874–1966, vol. VI (AII)
Burgess, Clarkson Leo, 1902–1975, vol. VII
Burgess, Duncan, 1850–1917, vol. II
Burgess, Rev. Francis, 1879–1948, vol. IV
Burgess, (Frank) Gelett, 1866–1951, vol. V
Burgess, Rt Rev. Frederick, 1853–1925, vol. II
Burgess, Frederick George, *died* 1951, vol. V
Burgess, Frederick William, 1855–1945, vol. IV
Burgess, Gelett; *see* Burgess, F. G.
Burgess, Geoffrey, 1906–1972, vol. VII
Burgess, Rt Hon. Henry Givens, 1859–1937, vol. III
Burgess, Herbert Edward, 1863–1948, vol. IV
Burgess, James, 1832–1916, vol. II
Burgess, James John Haldane, 1862–1927, vol. II
Burgess, John Bagnold, 1830–1897, vol. I
Burgess, Norman Francis Clifford, 1902–1940, vol. III
Burgess, Robert Nelson, 1867–1945, vol. IV
Burgess, Russell Brian, 1931–1979, vol. VII
Burgess, Sir Thomas Arthur Collier, 1906–1977, vol. VII
Burgess, Thomas J. W., 1849–1926, vol. II
Burgess, Hon. William Henry, 1847–1917, vol. II
Burgess, William Leslie, 1886–1954, vol. V
Burgess, Maj.-Gen. Sir William Livingstone Hatchwell S.; *see* Sinclair-Burgess.
Burgett, Rt Rev. Arthur Edward, 1869–1942, vol. IV
Burgh, 5th Baron, 1866–1926, vol. II
Burgh, 8th (otherwise 6th) Baron, 1906–1959, vol. V
Burghard, Frédéric François, 1864–1947, vol. IV
Burghclere, 1st Baron, 1846–1921, vol. II
Burghclere, Lady; (Winifred Henrietta Christina), 1864–1933, vol. III
Burgin, Rt Hon. Edward Leslie, 1887–1945, vol. IV
Burgin, George B., 1856–1944, vol. IV
Burgis, Sir Edwin Cooper, 1878–1966, vol. VI
Burgis, Lawrence Franklin, 1892–1972, vol. VII
Burgmann, Rt Rev. Ernest Henry, 1885–1967, vol. VI
Burgoyne, Lt-Col Sir Alan Hughes, 1880–1929, vol. III
Burgoyne, Major Gerald Achilles, 1874–1936, vol. III
Burgoyne, Sir John, 1875–1969, vol. VI
Burgoyne, Col Sir John Montagu, 10th Bt, 1832–1921, vol. II
Burhop, Eric Henry Stoneley, 1911–1980, vol. VII
Burke, Rt Rev. Mgr Alfred Edward, 1862–1927, vol. II
Burke, Col Bernard Bruce, 1876–1938, vol. III
Burke, Major Charles James, 1882–1917, vol. II
Burke, Edmund Haviland, *died* 1914, vol. I
Burke, Edmund Tytler, 1888–1941, vol. IV
Burke, Captain Sir Gerald Howe, 7th Bt (*cr* 1797), 1893–1954, vol. V
Burke, Lt-Col Gerald Tyler, 1882–1952, vol. V

Burke, Harold Arthur, 1852–1942, vol. IV
Burke, Sir Henry Farnham, 1859–1930, vol. III
Burke, Sir Henry George, 5th Bt (*cr* 1797), 1859–1910, vol. I
Burke, Henry Lardner, 1850–1927, vol. II
Burke, Col Herbert Francis Lardner, 1883–1950, vol. IV
Burke, Captain James Henry Thomas, 1853–1902, vol. I
Burke, Sir John, *died* 1922, vol. II
Burke, John Benjamin Butler, 1871–1946, vol. IV
Burke, Kathleen, 1887–1958, vol. V
Burke, Rt Rev. Maurice Francis, 1845–1923, vol. II
Burke, Lt-Col Sir Richard John Charles, 1878–1960, vol. V
Burke, Sir Roland; *see* Burke, Sir U. R.
Burke, Sir Theobald Hubert, 13th Bt (*cr* 1628), 1833–1909, vol. I
Burke, Thomas, 1886–1945, vol. IV
Burke, Sir Thomas Mallachy, 6th Bt (*cr* 1797), 1864–1913 (this entry was not transferred to Who was Who).
Burke, Thomas Michael, 1870–1949, vol. IV
Burke, Sir (Ulick) Roland, 1872–1958, vol. V
Burke, Wilfrid Andrew, *died* 1968, vol. VI
Burkett, Sir William Robert, 1840–1908, vol. I
Burkhardt, Col Valentine Rodolphe, 1884–1967, vol. VI
Burkhart, Harvey J., 1864–1946, vol. IV
Burkill, Isaac Henry, 1870–1965, vol. VI
Burkitt, Col Bernard Maynard H.; *see* Humble-Burkitt.
Burkitt, Francis Crawford, 1864–1935, vol. III
Burkitt, Francis Holy, 1880–1952, vol. V
Burkitt, Miles Crawford, 1890–1971, vol. VII
Burkitt, Ven. Robert Scott Bradshaw, 1857–1940, vol. III (A), vol. IV
Burkitt, Robert William, 1908–1976, vol. VII
Burland, Col Jeffrey Hale, 1861–1914, vol. I
Burland, John Burland H.; *see* Harris-Burland.
Burland, Col William Watt, 1877–1935, vol. III
Burleigh, Bennet, *died* 1914, vol. I
Burleigh, Captain Cecil Wills, 1870–1940, vol. III
Burleson, Rt Rev. Hugh Latimer, 1865–1933, vol. III
Burlingame, Edward Livermore, 1848–1922, vol. II
Burls, Sir Edwin Grant, 1844–1926, vol. II
Burlton, Lt-Col Philip Sykes Murphy, 1865–1950, vol. IV
Burman, Sir John Bedford, 1867–1941, vol. IV
Burmester, Adm. Sir Rudolf Miles, 1875–1956, vol. V
Burn, Col Alexander Henderson, 1885–1949, vol. IV
Burn, Very Rev. Andrew Ewbank, 1864–1927, vol. II
Burn, Lt-Col Charles Pelham Maitland, 1880–1925, vol. II
Burn, Sir Clive; *see* Burn, Sir R. C. W.
Burn, Dugald Stuart, 1877–1951, vol. V
Burn, Sir George, 1847–1932, vol. III
Burn, Col Harold Septimus, *died* 1970, vol. VI
Burn, Sir Harry Harrison, 1888–1961, vol. VI
Burn, Brig.-Gen. Henry Pelham, 1882–1958, vol. V

Burn, Rev. John Henry, 1858–1937, vol. III
Burn, Sir Joseph, 1871–1950, vol. IV
Burn, Sir Richard, 1871–1947, vol. IV
Burn, Rev. Robert, 1829–1904, vol. I
Burn, Sir (Roland) Clive (Wallace), 1882–1955, vol. V
Burn, Sir Sidney, 1881–1963, vol. VI
Burn, William Laurence, 1904–1966, vol. VI
Burn-Murdoch, Hector, 1881–1958, vol. V
Burn-Murdoch, Rev. Canon James McGibbon, 1828–1904, vol. I
Burn-Murdoch, Maj.-Gen. Sir John Francis, 1859–1931, vol. III
Burn-Murdoch, W. G., 1862–1939, vol. III
Burnaby, Major Algernon Edwyn, 1868–1938, vol. III
Burnaby, Davy; see Burnaby, G. D.
Burnaby, Lt-Col Eustace Beaumont, 1842–1916, vol. II
Burnaby, (George) Davy, 1881–1949, vol. IV
Burnaby, Lt-Col Hugo Beaumont, 1874–1916, vol. II
Burnaby, Rev. John, 1891–1978, vol. VII
Burnaby-Atkins, Thomas Frederick, 1836–1918, vol. II
Burnage, Col Granville John, 1858–1945, vol. IV
Burnand, Sir Francis Cowley, 1836–1917, vol. II
Burnand, Sir Frank; see Burnand, Sir R. F.
Burnand, Sir (Richard) Frank, 1887–1969, vol. VI
Burnand, Victor Wyatt, 1868–1940, vol. III
Burnard, Major Charles Francis, 1876–1931, vol. III
Burne, Lt-Col Alfred Higgins, 1886–1959, vol. V
Burne, Gen. Henry Knightley, died 1901, vol. I
Burne, Sir Lewis Charles, 1898–1978, vol. VII
Burne, Lt-Col Lindsay Eliott Lumley, 1877–1944, vol. IV
Burne, Col Newdigate Halford Marriot, 1872–1950, vol. IV (A), vol. V
Burne, Maj.-Gen. Sir Owen Tudor, 1837–1909, vol. I
Burne, Brig.-Gen. Rainald Owen, 1871–1923, vol. II
Burne, Richard Higgins, 1868–1953, vol. V
Burne, Ven. Richard Vernon Higgins, 1882–1970, vol. VI
Burne-Jones, Sir Edward Coley, 1st Bt, 1833–1898, vol. I
Burne-Jones, Sir Philip, 2nd Bt, 1861–1926, vol. II
Burnell, Lt-Col Charles Desborough, 1876–1969, vol. VI
Burnell-Nugent, Brig.-Gen. Frank, 1880–1942, vol. IV
Burnet, Rev. Amos, 1857–1926, vol. II
Burnet, John, 1863–1928, vol. II
Burnet, Sir John James, 1857–1938, vol. III
Burnet, John Rudolph Wardlaw, 1886–1941, vol. IV
Burnet, Sir Robert William, 1851–1931, vol. III
Burnett of Leys, Major Sir Alexander Edwin, 14th Bt (cr 1626), 1881–1959, vol. V
Burnett, Col Allan Harrington, 1884–1966, vol. VI
Burnett, Cecil Ross, 1872–1933, vol. III

Burnett, Gen. Sir Charles John, 1843–1915, vol. I (A)
Burnett, Brig.-Gen. Charles Kenyon, 1868–1950, vol. IV
Burnett, Air Chief Marshal Sir Charles Stuart, 1882–1945, vol. IV
Burnett, Sir David, 1st Bt (cr 1913), 1851–1930, vol. III
Burnett, Sir Digby Vere, died 1958, vol. V
Burnett, Maj.-Gen. Edward John Sidney, 1921–1978, vol. VII
Burnett, Sir (Edward) Napier, 1872–1923, vol. II
Burnett, Mrs Frances Hodgson, 1849–1924, vol. II
Burnett, George Murray, 1921–1980, vol. VII
Burnett, Dame Ivy C.; see Compton-Burnett.
Burnett of Leys, Maj.-Gen. Sir James Lauderdale Gilbert, 13th Bt (cr 1626), 1880–1953, vol. V
Burnett, Major John Chaplyn, 1863–1943, vol. IV
Burnett, Brig. John Curteis, 1882–1968, vol. VI
Burnett, John George, 1876–1962, vol. VI
Burnett, Col Sir Leslie Trew, 2nd Bt (cr 1913), 1884–1955, vol. V
Burnett, Dame Maud, 1863–1950, vol. IV
Burnett, Sir Napier; see Burnett, Sir E. N.
Burnett, Adm. Sir Robert Lindsay, 1887–1959, vol. V
Burnett, Lt-Col Robert Richardson, 1897–1975, vol. VII
Burnett of Leys, Sir Thomas, 12th Bt (cr 1626), 1840–1926, vol. II
Burnett, William Freshfield, 1865–1935, vol. III
Burnett, William George Esterbrooke, 1886–1978, vol. VII
Burnett-Brown, Col Alexander Denis, 1894–1966, vol. VI
Burnett-Hitchcock, Lt-Gen. Sir Basil Ferguson; see Hitchcock.
Burnett-Stuart, George Eustace, 1876–1938, vol. III
Burnett-Stuart, Gen. Sir John Theodosius, 1875–1958, vol. V
Burney, Lt-Col Arthur Edward Cave, 1883–1931, vol. III
Burney, Admiral of the Fleet Sir Cecil, 1st Bt, 1858–1929, vol. III
Burney, Ven. Charles, died 1907, vol. I
Burney, Charles, 1840–1912, vol. I
Burney, Comdr Sir (Charles) Dennistoun, 2nd Bt, 1888–1968, vol. VI
Burney, Rev. Charles Fox, 1868–1925, vol. II
Burney, Comdr Sir Dennistoun; see Burney, Comdr Sir C. D.
Burney, Brig.-Gen. Herbert Henry, 1858–1932, vol. III
Burney, Brig.-Gen. Percy de Sausmarez, 1863–1934, vol. III
Burney, Sydney Bernard, died 1951, vol. V
Burnham, 1st Baron, 1833–1916, vol. II
Burnham, 1st Viscount (and 2nd Baron), 1862–1933, vol. III
Burnham, 3rd Baron, 1864–1943, vol. IV
Burnham, 4th Baron, 1890–1963, vol. VI
Burnham, Lady; (Marie Enid), died 1979, vol. VII
Burnham, Cecil, 1887–1965, vol. VI
Burnham, John Charles, 1866–1943, vol. IV

Burnie, James, 1882–1975, vol. VII

Burniston, Surg. Rear-Adm. Hugh Somerville, 1870–1962, vol. VI

Burnley, James, *died* 1919, vol. II

Burns, Sir Alan Cuthbert, 1887–1980, vol. VII

Burns, Cecil Delisle, 1879–1942, vol. IV

Burns, Cecil Laurence, 1863–1929, vol. III

Burns, David, 1884–1969, vol. VI

Burns, George, 1903–1970, vol. VI

Burns, Henry Stuart Mackenzie, 1900–1971, vol. VII

Burns, Col Hon. Sir James, 1846–1923, vol. II

Burns, James, 1859–1929, vol. III

Burns, Rev. James, 1865–1948, vol. IV

Burns, Rt Hon. John, 1858–1943, vol. IV

Burns, John George, 1880–1950, vol. IV

Burns, Brig. Lionel Bryan Douglas, 1895–1966, vol. VI

Burns, Very Rev. Michael John, 1863–1949, vol. IV

Burns, Philip Leonard, 1896–1968, vol. VI

Burns, Robert, 1869–1941, vol. IV

Burns, Robert, 1859–1951, vol. V

Burns, Robert, 1912–1971, vol. VII

Burns, Rev. Thomas, 1853–1938, vol. III

Burns, William, 1884–1970, vol. VI

Burns, William Alexander, 1921–1972, vol. VII

Burns-Begg, Col Robert, 1872–1918, vol. II

Burns-Lindow, Lt-Col Isaac William, 1868–1946, vol. IV

Burnside, Rev. Frederick, *died* 1904, vol. I

Burnside, Helen Marion, 1844–1923, vol. II

Burnside, Robert Bruce, 1862–1929, vol. III

Burnside, Rev. Walter Fletcher, 1874–1949, vol. IV

Burnside, William, 1852–1927, vol. II

Burnside, William Snow, *died* 1920, vol. II

Burnyeat, William John Dalzell, 1874–1916, vol. II

Burpee, Lawrence Johnston, 1873–1946, vol. IV

Burr, Alfred, 1855–1952, vol. V

Burr, Rear-Adm. John Leslie, 1847–1917, vol. II

Burr, Malcolm, 1878–1954, vol. V

Burr-Bryan, Walter; *see* Bryan, W. B.

Burra, Edward, 1905–1976, vol. VII

Burrage, Alfred McLelland, 1889–1956, vol. V

Burrard, Major Sir Gerald, 8th Bt, 1888–1965, vol. VI

Burrard, Col Harry George, 1871–1963, vol. VI

Burrard, Sir Harry Paul, 6th Bt, 1846–1933, vol. III

Burrard, Col Sir Sidney Gerald, 7th Bt, 1860–1943, vol. IV

Burrard, Col William Dutton, 1861–1938, vol. III

Burrell, Sir Charles Raymond, 6th Bt, 1848–1899, vol. I

Burrell, Harry James, 1873–1945, vol. IV

Burrell, John Percy, 1910–1972, vol. VII

Burrell, Lancelot S. T., 1883–1938, vol. III

Burrell, Hon. Martin, 1858–1938, vol. III

Burrell, Sir Merrik Raymond, 7th Bt, 1877–1957, vol. V

Burrell, Percy Saville, 1871–1958, vol. V

Burrell, Robert Eric, 1890–1968, vol. VI

Burrell, Sir William, 1861–1958, vol. VI

Burridge, Frederick Vango, 1869–1945, vol. IV

Burridge, Captain Robert Archibald Morison, *died* 1957, vol. V

Burrington, Arthur, *died* 1924, vol. II

Burrough, Adm. Sir Harold Martin, 1888–1977, vol. VII

Burroughes, Dorothy Mary Burroughes-, *died* 1963, vol. VI

Burroughs, Edgar Rice, 1875–1950, vol. IV

Burroughs, Rt Rev. Edward Arthur, 1882–1934, vol. III

Burroughs, Lt-Gen. Frederick William Traill, 1831–1905, vol. I

Burroughs, John, 1837–1921, vol. II

Burroughs, Ronald Arthur, 1917–1980, vol. VII

Burroughs, Rev. William Edward, 1845–1931, vol. III

Burroughs-Fowler, Walter, *died* 1930, vol. III

Burrow, Edward John, 1869–1935, vol. III

Burrow, Joseph le Fleming, 1888–1967, vol. VI

Burrowes, Lt-Col Algernon St Leger, 1847–1925, vol. II

Burrowes, Rt Rev. Arnold Brian, 1896–1963, vol. VI

Burrowes, Brig.-Gen. Arnold Robinson, 1867–1949, vol. IV

Burrowes, Herbert Alleyne Nathanael, 1870–1933, vol. III

Burrowes, Thomas Cosby, 1856–1925, vol. II (A), vol. III

Burrowes, Thomas Fraser, *died* 1947, vol. IV

Burrowes, William Henry Aglionby, *died* 1922, vol. II

Burrows, Albert, 1919–1972, vol. VII

Burrows, Alfred John, *died* 1957, vol. V

Burrows, Christine Mary Elizabeth, 1872–1959, vol. V

Burrows, Col Edmund Augustine, 1855–1927, vol. II

Burrows, Sir Ernest Pennington, 3rd Bt, 1851–1917, vol. II

Burrows, Rev. Francis Henry, 1857–1928, vol. II

Burrows, Sir Frederick Abernethy, 2nd Bt, 1845–1904, vol. I

Burrows, Sir Frederick John, 1887–1973, vol. VII

Burrows, Gen. George Reynolds Scott, 1827–1917, vol. II

Burrows, George Thomas, 1876–1949, vol. IV

Burrows, Harold, 1875–1955, vol. V

Burrows, Comdr Henry Montagu, 1899–1979, vol. VII

Burrows, Brig. Hollis Martin, 1884–1952, vol. V

Burrows, Rt Rev. Leonard Hedley, 1857–1940, vol. III

Burrows, Lionel Burton, 1883–1970, vol. VI

Burrows, Rev. Millar, 1889–1980, vol. VII

Burrows, Captain Montagu, 1819–1905, vol. I

Burrows, Lt-Gen. Montagu Brocas, 1894–1967, vol. VI

Burrows, Sir Robert Abraham, 1884–1964, vol. VI

Burrows, Sir Roland, 1882–1952, vol. V

Burrows, Ronald Montagu, 1867–1920, vol. II

Burrows, Sir Stephen Montagu, 1856–1935, vol. III

Burrows, Theodore Arthur, 1857–1929, vol. III

Burrows, Rt Rev. Winfrid Oldfield, 1858–1929, vol. III

Burry, Bessie P.; *see* Pullen-Burry.

Burstall, Frederick William, 1865–1934, vol. III
Burstall, Lt-Gen. Sir Henry Edward, 1870–1945, vol. IV
Burstall, Sara Annie, 1859–1939, vol. III
Burston, Maj.-Gen. Sir Samuel Roy, 1888–1960, vol. V
Burt, Brig.-Gen. Alfred, 1875–1949, vol. IV
Burt, Alfred LeRoy, 1888–1971, vol. VII
Burt, Sir Bryce Chudleigh, 1881–1943, vol. IV
Burt, Sir Charles, 1832–1913, vol. I
Burt, Charles Kingsley J.; see Johnstone-Burt.
Burt, Sir Cyril Lodowic, 1883–1971, vol. VII
Burt, Sir George Mowlem, 1884–1964, vol. VI
Burt, Rear-Adm. Gerald George Percy, 1888–1965, vol. VI
Burt, Henry, 1844–1940, vol. III
Burt, Rev. Henry Chadwick, 1871–1959, vol. V (A)
Burt, Sir Henry Parsall, 1857–1936, vol. III
Burt, Hugh Armitage, 1911–1976, vol. VII
Burt, Col John Marshall, 1860–1931, vol. III
Burt, Sir John Mowlem, 1845–1918, vol. II
Burt, Joseph Barnes, died 1953, vol. V
Burt, Octavius, 1849–1940, vol. III
Burt, Hon. Septimus, 1847–1919, vol. II
Burt, Rt Hon. Thomas, 1837–1922, vol. II
Burtchaell, Lt-Gen. Sir Charles Henry, 1866–1932, vol. III
Burtchaell, George Dames, 1853–1921, vol. II
Burton, 1st Baron, 1837–1909, vol. I
Burton, Baroness (2nd in line), 1873–1962, vol. VI
Burton, Alan Chadburn, 1904–1979, vol. VII
Burton, Rev. Arthur Daniel, 1852–1933, vol. III
Burton, Arthur Davis, 1887–1962, vol. VI
Burton, Maj.-Gen. Benjamin, 1855–1921, vol. II (A), vol. III
Burton, Sir Bunnell Henry, 1858–1943, vol. IV
Burton, Sir Charles William Cuffe, 5th Bt, 1823–1902, vol. I
Burton, Claud Peter Primrose, 1916–1957, vol. V
Burton, Brig. Colin, 1883–1945, vol. IV
Burton, Donald, 1892–1966, vol. VI
Burton, Brig.-Gen. Edmund Boteler, 1861–1942, vol. IV
Burton, Rev. Canon Edwin Hubert, 1870–1925, vol. II
Burton, Eli Franklin, 1879–1948, vol. IV
Burton, Rev. Ernest De Witt, 1856–1925, vol. II
Burton, Gen. Sir Fowler, 1822–1904, vol. I
Burton, Sir Francis Charles Edward D.; see Denys-Burton.
Burton, Frank Ernest, 1865–1948, vol. IV
Burton, Sir Frederick William, 1816–1900, vol. I
Burton, Captain Sir Geoffrey Duke, 1893–1954, vol. V
Burton, Sir Geoffrey Pownall, 1884–1972, vol. VII
Burton, Rt Rev. George Ambrose, 1852–1931, vol. III
Burton, Major Sir Gerald Arthur Fowler, 1869–1930, vol. III
Burton, Captain Gerard William, 1879–1915, vol. I (A)
Burton, Harold, 1901–1966, vol. VI
Burton, Harold Hitz, 1888–1964, vol. VI
Burton, Rt Hon. Henry, 1866–1935, vol. III

Burton, Henry, 1907–1952, vol. V
Burton, Rev. Henry Darwin, 1858–1943, vol. IV
Burton, Col Henry Walter, 1876–1947, vol. IV
Burton, Rev. Canon Humphrey Phillipps Walcot, 1888–1957, vol. V
Burton, John Adam Gib, 1888–1962, vol. VI
Burton, John Edward B.; see Bloundelle-Burton.
Burton, John Frederick, 1870–1937, vol. III
Burton, Rev. John James, 1849–1927, vol. II
Burton, Rev. John Richard, 1847–1939, vol. III
Burton, Rt Rev. Lewis William, 1852–1940, vol. III (A), vol. IV
Burton, Sir Montague, 1885–1952, vol. V
Burton, Sir Pomeroy, 1869–1947, vol. IV
Burton, Brig.-Gen. Reginald George, 1864–1951, vol. V
Burton, Brig-Gen. St George Edward William, died 1943, vol. IV
Burton, Rt Rev. Spence, 1881–1966, vol. VI
Burton, William, died 1954, vol. V
Burton, Sir William James Miller, 1862–1946, vol. IV
Burton, Sir William Parker, 1864–1942, vol. IV
Burton-Baldry, Walter Burton, 1888–1940, vol. III
Burton-Chadwick, Sir Robert, 1st Bt, 1869–1951, vol. V
Burton-Fanning, Frederick William, 1863–1937, vol. III
Burtt Davy, Joseph, 1870–1940, vol. III
Burwash, Lachlin Taylor, 1874–1940, vol. III
Burwash, Rev. N., 1839–1918, vol. II
Bury, Viscount; Derek William Charles Keppel, 1911–1968, vol. VI
Bury, Lt-Col Charles Kenneth Howard, 1883–1963, vol. VI
Bury, Francis George, died 1926, vol. II
Bury, Sir George, 1866–1958, vol. V
Bury, George Wyman, 1874–1920, vol. II
Bury, Rt Rev. Herbert, died 1933, vol. III
Bury, John Bagnell, 1861–1927, vol. II
Bury, Judson Sykes, died 1944, vol. IV
Bury, Lindsay Edward, 1882–1952, vol. V
Bury, Oliver R. H., died 1946, vol. IV
Bury, Ralph Frederic, 1876–1954, vol. V
Bury, Rev. William, 1839–1920, vol. II
Buscarlet, Air Vice-Marshal Sir Willett Amalric Bowen B.; see Bowen-Buscarlet.
Busch, Adolf, 1891–1952, vol. V
Busch, Fritz, 1890–1951, vol. V
Bush, Frank Whittaker, 1825–1903, vol. I
Bush, Harry, 1883–1957, vol. V
Bush, Col Harry Stebbing, 1871–1942, vol. IV
Bush, Irving T., 1869–1948, vol. IV
Bush, Col (James) Paul, 1857–1930, vol. III
Bush, Rear-Adm. James Tobin, 1874–1949, vol. IV
Bush, Brig.-Gen. John Ernest, 1858–1943, vol. IV
Bush, Col Paul; see Bush, Col J. P.
Bush, Adm. Sir Paul Warner, 1855–1930, vol. III
Bush, Raymond G. W., 1885–1972, vol. VII
Bush, Reginald Edgar James, 1869–1956, vol. V
Bush, Robert Edwin, 1855–1939, vol. III
Bush, Rev. Thomas Cromwell, died 1919, vol. II
Bush, Vannevar, 1890–1974, vol. VII
Bushby, Sir Edmund Fleming, 1879–1943, vol. IV

Bushby, Geoffrey Henry, 1899–1935, vol. III
Bushby, Henry Jeffreys, 1820–1903, vol. I
Bushby, Thomas, *died* 1916, vol. II
Bushby, Walter Edwin, 1889–1963, vol. VI
Bushe, Sir Grattan; *see* Bushe, Sir H. G.
Bushe, Sir (Henry) Grattan, 1886–1961, vol. VI
Bushe, Robert Gervase, 1851–1927, vol. II
Bushe, Seymour Coghill Hort, 1853–1922, vol. II
Bushe, Brig.-Gen. Thomas Francis, 1858–1951, vol. V
Bushe-Fox, Joscelyn Plunket, 1880–1954, vol. V
Bushe-Fox, Loftus Henry Kendal, 1863–1916, vol. II
Bushell, Stephen Wootton, 1844–1908, vol. I
Bushell, W. F., 1885–1974, vol. VII
Bushell, Rev. William Done, 1838–1917, vol. II
Bushman, Maj.-Gen. Sir Henry Augustus, 1841–1930, vol. III
Bushnell, Frank George, 1868–1941, vol. IV
Bushnell, Geoffrey Hext Sutherland, 1903–1978, vol. VII
Bushnell, George Herbert, 1896–1973, vol. VII
Busia, Kofi Abrefa, 1913–1978, vol. VII
Busk, Air Cdre Clifford Westly, 1898–1970, vol. VI
Busk, Sir Edward Henry, 1844–1926, vol. II
Busk, Henrietta, 1845–1936, vol. III
Busk, Mrs Mary, 1854–1935, vol. III
Busoni, Ferruccio Benvenuto, 1866–1924, vol. II
Bussau, Hon. Sir (Albert) Louis, 1884–1947, vol. IV
Bussau, Hon. Sir Louis; *see* Bussau, Hon. Sir A. L.
Bussé, John, 1903–1956, vol. V
Bussell, Rev. Frederick William, 1862–1944, vol. IV
Bussell, Ven. William John, *died* 1936, vol. III
Bussey, Ernest William, 1891–1958, vol. V
Bussey, Harry Youngman, 1858–1951, vol. V
Bussy, (George Francis) Philip, 1871–1933, vol. III
Bussy, Philip; *see* Bussy, G. F. P.
Bustamante, Rt Hon. and Exc. Sir Alexander; *see* Bustamante, Rt Hon. and Exc. Sir W. A.
Bustamante, Rt Hon. and Exc. Sir (William) Alexander, 1884–1977, vol. VII
Busteed, Bde-Surgeon Henry Elmsley, 1833–1912, vol. I
Buston, Brig.-Gen. Philip Thomas, 1853–1938, vol. III
Buswell, Col Ferberd Richard, *died* 1937, vol. III
Buswell, Ven. Henry Dison, 1839–1940, vol. III
Buszard, Marston Clarke, 1837–1921, vol. II
Butchart, Bt Lt-Col Henry Jackson, 1882–1971, vol. VII
Butcher, Arthur Douglas Deane, 1884–1944, vol. IV
Butcher, Very Rev. Charles Henry, 1833–1907, vol. I
Butcher, Maj.-Gen. Sir George James, 1860–1939, vol. III
Butcher, Sir Herbert Walter, 1st Bt, 1901–1966, vol. VI
Butcher, Paymaster Captain Reginald, 1880–1935, vol. III
Butcher, Rt Rev. Reginald Albert Claver, 1905–1975, vol. VII
Butcher, Samuel Henry, 1850–1910, vol. I
Butcher, William Deane, 1846–1919, vol. II

Bute, 3rd Marquess of, 1847–1900, vol. I
Bute, 4th Marquess of, 1881–1947, vol. IV
Bute, 5th Marquess of, 1907–1956, vol. V
Butler, Rev. Alexander Douglas, *died* 1926, vol. II
Butler, Alfred J., 1850–1936, vol. III
Butler, Alfred Trego, 1880–1946, vol. IV
Butler, Col Arnold Charles Paul, 1890–1973, vol. VII
Butler, Arthur Gardiner, 1844–1925, vol. II
Butler, Col Arthur Graham, 1872–1949, vol. IV
Butler, Rev. Arthur Gray, 1831–1909, vol. I
Butler, (Arthur) Hugh (Montagu), 1873–1943, vol. IV
Butler, Arthur John, 1844–1910, vol. I
Butler, Arthur Stanley, 1854–1923, vol. II
Butler, Arthur Stanley George, 1888–1965, vol. VI
Butler, Lt-Col Arthur Townley, 1867–1948, vol. IV
Butler, Lt-Col Charles Henry, 1881–1941, vol. IV
Butler, Sir (Charles) Owen, 1896–1968, vol. VI
Butler, Rt Rev. Cuthbert; *see* Butler, Rt Rev. E. C.
Butler, Sir Cyril Kendall, 1864–1936, vol. III
Butler, Rev. Dugald, 1862–1926, vol. II
Butler, Rt Rev. (Edward) Cuthbert, 1858–1934, vol. III
Butler, Sir Edwin John, 1874–1943, vol. IV
Butler, Eliza Marian, 1885–1959, vol. V
Butler, Elizabeth, (Lady Butler), 1846–1933, vol. III
Butler, Maj.-Gen. Ernest Reuben Charles, 1864–1959, vol. V
Butler, Captain Hon. Francis Almeric, 1872–1925, vol. II
Butler, Frank Hedges, 1855–1928, vol. II
Butler, Sir Frederick George Augustus, 1873–1961, vol. VI
Butler, Sir Geoffrey, 1887–1929, vol. III
Butler, Sir George Beresford, 1857–1924, vol. II
Butler, George Grey, 1852–1935, vol. III
Butler, Sir Gerald Snowden, 1885–1969, vol. VI
Butler, Sir Harcourt; *see* Butler, Sir S. H.
Butler, Sir Harold Beresford, 1883–1951, vol. V
Butler, Harold Edgeworth, 1878–1951, vol. V
Butler, Harold Edwin, 1893–1973, vol. VII
Butler, Maj.-Gen. Henry, *died* 1907, vol. I
Butler, Rev. Henry Montagu, 1833–1918, vol. II
Butler, Herbert William, 1897–1971, vol. VII
Butler, Rev. Hercules Scott, 1850–1928, vol. II
Butler, Hon. (Horace) Somerset Edmond, 1903–1962, vol. VI
Butler, Hugh; *see* Butler, A. H. M.
Butler, Hugh Montagu, 1890–1972, vol. VII
Butler, Hugh Myddleton, 1857–1943, vol. IV
Butler, Lt-Col Humphrey, 1894–1953, vol. V
Butler, James Bayley, *died* 1964, vol. VI
Butler, Sir James Ramsay Montagu, 1889–1975, vol. VII
Butler, Rev. Lord (James) Theobald Bagot John, 1852–1929, vol. III
Butler, John Alfred Valentine, 1899–1977, vol. VII
Butler, Captain John Fitzhardinge Paul, 1888–1916, vol. II
Butler, Josephine, 1828–1906, vol. I
Butler, Kathleen Teresa Blake, 1883–1950, vol. IV
Butler, Brig.-Gen. Hon. Lesley James Probyn, 1876–1955, vol. V

Butler, Maria, 1868–1901, vol. I
Butler, Matthew Joseph, 1856–1933, vol. III
Butler, Gen. Sir Mervyn Andrew Haldane, 1913–1976, vol. VII
Butler, Mildred, *died* 1941, vol. IV
Butler, Hon. Sir Milo Broughton, 1906–1979, vol. VII
Butler, Sir Montagu Sherard Dawes, 1873–1952, vol. V
Butler, Sir Nevile Montagu, 1893–1973, vol. VII
Butler, Nicholas Murray, 1862–1947, vol. IV
Butler, Sir Owen; *see* Butler, Sir C. O.
Butler, Lt-Col Patrick Richard, 1880–1967, vol. VI
Butler, Sir Paul Dalrymple, 1886–1955, vol. V
Butler, Pierce Essex O'B.; *see* O'Brien-Butler.
Butler, Sir Reginald; *see* Butler, Sir R. R. F.
Butler, Comdr Sir (Reginald) Thomas, 2nd Bt (*cr* 1922), 1901–1959, vol. V
Butler, Hon. Sir Richard, 1850–1925, vol. II
Butler, Col Richard Barry, *died* 1957, vol. V
Butler, Lt-Col Richard F.; *see* Fowler-Butler.
Butler, Lt-Gen. Sir Richard Harte Keatinge, 1870–1935, vol. III
Butler, Richard Jago, 1848–1931, vol. III
Butler, Hon. Sir Richard Layton, 1885–1966, vol. VI
Butler, Sir Richard Pierce, 11th Bt (*cr* 1628), 1872–1955, vol. V
Butler, Richard William, 1844–1928, vol. II
Butler, Maj.-Gen. Robert Henry F.; *see* Fowler-Butler.
Butler, Sir (Robert) Reginald Frederick, 1st Bt (*cr* 1922), 1866–1933, vol. III
Butler, Major Hon. Robert Thomas Rowley Probyn, 1882–1938, vol. III
Butler, Rudolph Maximilian, 1872–1943, vol. IV
Butler, Maj.-Gen. St John Desmond A.; *see* Arcedeckne-Butler.
Butler, Samuel, 1835–1902, vol. I
Butler, Slade, *died* 1923, vol. II
Butler, Hon. Somerset; *see* Butler, Hon. H. S. E.
Butler, Sir (Spencer) Harcourt, 1869–1938, vol. III
Butler, Spencer Perceval, 1828–1915, vol. I
Butler, Maj.-Gen. Stephen Seymour, 1880–1964, vol. VI
Butler, Col Sydney George, 1874–1940, vol. III
Butler, Rev. Lord Theobald; *see* Butler, Rev. Lord J. T. B. J.
Butler, Maj.-Gen. Hon. Theobald Patrick Probyn, 1884–1970, vol. VI
Butler, Theobald Richard Fitzwalter, 1894–1976, vol. VII
Butler, Thomas, *died* 1937, vol. III
Butler, Comdr Sir Thomas; *see* Butler, Comdr Sir R. T.
Butler, Major Thomas Adair, 1836–1901, vol. I
Butler, Captain Sir Thomas Dacres, 1845–1937, vol. III
Butler, Thomas Harrison, 1871–1945, vol. IV
Butler, Sir Thomas Pierce, 10th Bt (*cr* 1628), 1836–1909, vol. I
Butler, Rear-Adm. Vernon Saumarez, 1885–1954, vol. V
Butler, Victor Spencer, 1900–1969, vol. VI

Butler, William F. T., *died* 1930, vol. III
Butler, Rt Hon. Sir William Francis, 1838–1910, vol. I
Butler, Brig.-Gen. William John Chesshyre, 1864–1946, vol. IV
Butler, Sir William Waters, 1st Bt (*cr* 1926), 1866–1939, vol. III
Butler-Bowdon, John Erdeswick, 1850–1929, vol. III
Butler Brockwell, Esca Powys; *see* Brockwell, E. P. B.
Butler-Henderson, Hon. Eric Brand, 1884–1953, vol. V
Butler-Smythe, Albert Charles, 1852–1936, vol. III
Butlin, Sir Henry Guy Trentham, 2nd Bt, 1893–1916, vol. II
Butlin, Sir Henry Trentham, 1st Bt, 1845–1912, vol. I
Butlin, Sir William, 1851–1923, vol. II
Butlin, Sir William Edmund, 1899–1980, vol. VII
Butt, Sir Alfred, 1st Bt, 1878–1962, vol. VI
Butt, Charles Sinclair, 1900–1973, vol. VII
Butt, Dame Clara, 1873–1936, vol. III
Butt, John Everett, 1906–1965, vol. VI
Butt, Most Rev. Joseph, 1869–1944, vol. IV
Buttenshaw, Hon. Ernest Albert, 1876–1950, vol. IV, vol. V
Butter, Archibald Edward, 1874–1928, vol. II
Butterfield, Fred, *died* 1935, vol. III
Butterfield, Sir Frederick William Louis d'Hilliers Roosevelt Theodore, *died* 1943, vol. IV
Butterfield, Sir Harry Durham, 1898–1976, vol. VII
Butterfield, Sir Herbert, 1900–1979, vol. VII
Butterfield, Robert William Fitzmaurice, 1889–1967, vol. VI
Butterfield, William, 1814–1900, vol. I
Butters, Sir John Henry, 1885–1969, vol. VI
Butterworth, Alan, 1864–1937, vol. III
Butterworth, Sir Alexander Kaye, 1854–1946, vol. IV
Butterworth, Arthur Reginald, 1850–1924, vol. II
Butterworth, Comdr Henry, 1866–1926, vol. II
Butterworth, Reginald, 1879–1951, vol. V
Butterworth, Col Reginald Francis Amherst, 1876–1960, vol. V
Butterworth, Hon. W. Walton, 1903–1975, vol. VII
Butti, Rt Rev. Mgr Peter L., *died* 1932, vol. III
Button, Frederick Stephen, 1873–1948, vol. IV
Button, Howard, 1875–1965, vol. VI
Button, Sir Howard Stransom, 1873–1943, vol. IV
Butts, S., *died* 1906, vol. I
Buxton, 1st Earl, 1853–1934, vol. III
Buxton, Countess; (Mildred), *died* 1955, vol. V
Buxton, Alfred Fowell, 1854–1952, vol. V
Buxton, Alfred St Clair, 1854–1920, vol. II
Buxton, Major Anthony, 1881–1970, vol. VI
Buxton, Comdr Bernard, 1882–1923, vol. II
Buxton, Charles Roden, 1875–1942, vol. IV
Buxton, Denis Alfred Jex, 1895–1964, vol. VI
Buxton, Dudley Wilmot, *died* 1931, vol. III
Buxton, Edward Gurney, 1865–1929, vol. III
Buxton, Edward North, 1840–1924, vol. II
Buxton, Francis William, 1847–1911, vol. I
Buxton, Geoffrey Powell, 1852–1929, vol. III
Buxton, Gladys, 1891–1971, vol. VII

Buxton, Rt Rev. Harold Jocelyn, 1880–1976, vol. VII
Buxton, Henry Fowell, 1876–1949, vol. IV
Buxton, James Basil, *died* 1954, vol. V
Buxton, John Henry, 1849–1934, vol. III
Buxton, Col John Lawrence, 1877–1951, vol. V
Buxton, Leonard Halford Dudley, 1889–1939, vol. III
Buxton, Lionel Gurney, 1876–1962, vol. VI
Buxton, Patrick Alfred, 1892–1955, vol. V
Buxton, Richard; *see* Shanks, Edward.
Buxton, Captain Richard Gurney, 1887–1972, vol. VII
Buxton, Robert Vere, 1883–1953, vol. V
Buxton, Captain Roden Henry Victor, 1890–1970, vol. VI
Buxton, Sir Thomas Fowell, 3rd Bt, 1837–1915, vol. I (A)
Buxton, Sir Thomas Fowell, 5th Bt, 1889–1945, vol. IV
Buxton, Sir (Thomas Fowell) Victor, 4th Bt, 1865–1919, vol. II
Buxton, Sir Victor; *see* Buxton, Sir T. F. V.
Buxton, William Leonard, 1894–1964, vol. VI
Buzacott, Charles Hardie, 1835–1918, vol. II
Buzacott, William James, 1866–1937, vol. III
Buzzard, Rear-Adm. Sir Anthony Wass, 2nd Bt, 1902–1972, vol. VII
Buzzard, Lt-Col Charles Norman, 1873–1961, vol. VI
Buzzard, Sir (Edward) Farquhar, 1st Bt, 1871–1945, vol. IV
Buzzard, Brig.-Gen. Frank Anstie, 1875–1950, vol. IV
Buzzard, Thomas, 1831–1919, vol. II
Byam, Maj.-Gen. William, 1841–1906, vol. I
Byam, William, 1882–1963, vol. VI
Byass, Bt Col Sir Geoffrey Robert Sidney, 2nd Bt, 1895–1976, vol. VII
Byass, Col Harry Nicholl, 1863–1956, vol. V
Byass, Sir Sidney Hutchinson, 1st Bt, 1862–1929, vol. III
Byatt, Edwin, 1888–1948, vol. IV
Byatt, Sir Horace Archer, 1875–1933, vol. III
Byers, Sir John William, *died* 1920, vol. II
Byers, Joseph Austen, 1895–1977, vol. VII
Byers, Mrs Margaret, *died* 1912, vol. I
Byford, Sir John, 1860–1931, vol. III
Byles, William Hounsom, 1872–1928, vol. II
Byles, Sir William Pollard, 1839–1917, vol. II
Byng, 1st Viscount, 1862–1935, vol. III
Byng, Lt-Col Hon. Antony Schomberg, 1876–1934, vol. III
Byng, Col Hon. Charles Cavendish George, 1849–1918, vol. II
Byng, Hon. Ivo Francis, 1874–1949, vol. IV
Byng, L. C.; *see* Cranmer-Byng.
Byng, Major Hon. Lionel Francis George, 1858–1915, vol. I
Byng, Lady Mary Elizabeth Agnes; *see* Mauny-Talvande, Countess of.
Byng, Hon. Sydney, 1844–1920, vol. II
Bynner, Witter, 1881–1968, vol. VI
Byrd, Rear-Adm. Richard E., 1888–1957, vol. V

Byrde, Ven. Louis, *died* 1917, vol. II
Byrne, Alfred, 1882–1956, vol. V
Byrne, Brian Oswald D.; *see* Byrne, Donn.
Byrne, Donn, 1889–1928, vol. II
Byrne, Sir Edmund Widdrington, 1844–1904, vol. I
Byrne, Most Rev. Edward J., 1872–1940, vol. III
Byrne, Rt Rev. Mgr Frederick, *born* 1834, vol. II
Byrne, Col Frederick Joseph, 1873–1929, vol. III
Byrne, Col Henry, 1840–1915, vol. I (A)
Byrne, Rt Rev. Herbert Kevin, 1884–1978, vol. VII
Byrne, Rt Rev. James, 1870–1938, vol. III
Byrne, James Patrick, 1854–1935, vol. III
Byrne, Lt-Col John Dillon, 1875–1925, vol. II
Byrne, Brig.-Gen. Sir Joseph Aloysius, 1874–1942, vol. IV
Byrne, Hon. Sir Laurence Austin, 1896–1965, vol. VI
Byrne, Louis Campbell, *died* 1923, vol. II
Byrne, Patrick Sarsfield, 1913–1980, vol. VII
Byrne, Rev. Peter, *born* 1840, vol. II
Byrne, Air Cdre Reginald, 1888–1965, vol. VI
Byrne, Richard, *died* 1942, vol. IV
Byrne, Rt Hon. Sir William Patrick, 1859–1935, vol. III
Byrnes, James Francis, 1879–1972, vol. VII
Byrnes, Hon. Sir Percy Thomas, 1893–1973, vol. VII
Byrnes, Hon. Thomas Joseph, 1860–1898, vol. I
Byrom, Charles Reginald, 1878–1952, vol. V
Byrom, Thomas Emmett, 1871–1956, vol. V
Byron, 9th Baron, 1855–1917, vol. II
Byron, 10th Baron, 1861–1949, vol. IV
Byron, Captain Augustus William, 1856–1939, vol. III
Byron, Paymaster Rear-Adm. Charles Edgar, *died* 1940, vol. III
Byron, Edmund, 1843–1921, vol. II
Byron, Brig.-Gen. John, 1872–1944, vol. IV
Byron, Brig.-Gen. Hon. John Joseph, *died* 1935, vol. III
Byron, Col Richard, 1870–1939, vol. III
Byron, Robert, 1905–1941, vol. IV
Byrt, Albert Henry, 1881–1966, vol. VI
Bythesea, Rear-Adm. John, 1827–1906, vol. I
Bywater, Hector Charles, 1884–1940, vol. III
Bywater, Ingram, 1840–1914, vol. I
Bywater, Thomas Lloyd, 1905–1979, vol. VII
Bywaters, Hubert William, 1881–1966, vol. VI

C

Cabell, James Branch, 1879–1958, vol. V
Cable, 1st Baron, 1859–1927, vol. II
Cable, Boyd, *died* 1943, vol. IV
Cable, Eric Grant, 1887–1970, vol. VI
Cable, George Washington, 1844–1925, vol. II
Caborne, Captain Warren Frederick, 1849–1924, vol. II
Cabot, Sir Daniel Alfred Edmond, *died* 1974, vol. VII
Cabot, Lt-Col Hugh, 1872–1945, vol. IV
Cabrol, Rt Rev. Fernand, 1855–1937, vol. III

Caccamisi, Baronne Anzon; *see* Marchesi, Blanche.
Caccia, Anthony, 1869–1962, vol. VI
Caclamanos, Demetrius, 1872–1949, vol. IV
Cacoyannis, Hon. Sir Panayotis Loizou, 1893–1980, vol. VII
Cadbury, Barrow, 1862–1958, vol. V
Cadbury, Edward, 1873–1948, vol. IV
Cadbury, Sir Egbert, 1893–1967, vol. VI
Cadbury, Dame Elizabeth Mary, (Mrs George Cadbury), 1858–1951, vol. V
Cadbury, George, 1839–1922, vol. II
Cadbury, Henry Joel, 1883–1974, vol. VII
Cadbury, Henry Tylor, 1882–1952, vol. V
Caddell, Col Henry Mortimer, 1875–1944, vol. IV
Caddy, Adrian, 1879–1966, vol. VI
Caddy, Col Hector Osman, 1882–1935, vol. III
Cade, Sir Stanford, 1895–1973, vol. VII
Cadell, Alan, 1841–1921, vol. II
Cadell, Lt-Gen. Charles Alexander Elliott, 1888–1951, vol. V
Cadell, Francis Campbell Boileau, 1883–1937, vol. III
Cadell, Lt-Col Harry Ernest, 1867–1939, vol. III
Cadell, Henry Moubray, 1860–1934, vol. III
Cadell of Grange, Col Henry Moubray, 1892–1967, vol. VI
Cadell, Sir Patrick Robert, 1871–1961, vol. VI
Cadell, Sir Robert, 1825–1897, vol. I
Cadell, Col Thomas, 1835–1919, vol. II
Cadenhead, James, 1858–1927, vol. II
Cadge, William, *died* 1903, vol. I
Cadic, Edouard, 1858–1914, vol. I
Cadman, 1st Baron, 1877–1941, vol. IV
Cadman, 2nd Baron, 1909–1966, vol. VI
Cadman, Hon. Sir Alfred Jerome, *died* 1905, vol. I
Cadman, James, 1878–1947, vol. IV
Cadman, John Heaton, 1839–1906, vol. I
Cadman, Rev. Samuel Parkes, 1864–1936, vol. III
Cadman, Rev. William Healey, 1891–1965, vol. VI
Cadogan, 5th Earl, 1840–1915, vol. I
Cadogan, 6th Earl, 1869–1933, vol. III
Cadogan, Rt Hon. Sir Alexander George Montagu, 1884–1968, vol. VI
Cadogan, Hon. Sir Edward Cecil George, 1880–1962, vol. VI
Cadogan, Hon. Frederick William, 1821–1904, vol. I
Cadogan, Hon. William George Sydney, 1879–1914, vol. I
Cadoux, Cecil John, 1883–1947, vol. IV
Cafe, T. Watt, 1856–1925, vol. II
Cafe, Gen. William Martin, 1826–1906, vol. I
Caffery, Jefferson, 1886–1974, vol. VII
Caffieri, H., *died* 1932, vol. III
Caffyn, Kathleen Mannington, *died* 1926, vol. II
Caffyn, Sir Sydney Morris, 1901–1976, vol. VII
Cahan, Hon. Charles Hazlitt, 1861–1944, vol. IV
Cahan, J(ohn) Flint, 1912–1961, vol. VI
Cahill, Rt Rev. John Baptist, 1841–1910, vol. I
Cahill, Sir (Joseph) Robert, 1879–1953, vol. V
Cahill, Sir Robert; *see* Cahill, Sir J. R.
Cahill, Most Rev. Thomas Vincent, 1913–1978, vol. VII

Cahill, Lt-Col William Geoffrey, 1854–1931, vol. III
Cahn, Sir Julien, 1st Bt, *died* 1944, vol. IV
Cahusac, Col William Fremantle, 1857–1930, vol. III
Caie, John Morrison, 1878–1949, vol. IV
Caillard, Alfred, 1841–1900, vol. I
Caillard, Sir Vincent Henry Penalver, 1856–1930, vol. III
Caillaux, Joseph, *died* 1944, vol. IV
Cain, Sir Ernest, 2nd Bt, 1891–1969, vol. VI
Cain, Georges, *died* 1919, vol. II
Cain, John Cannell, 1871–1921, vol. II
Cain, Sir Jonathan Robert, 1869–1938, vol. III
Cain, Major Robert Henry, 1909–1974, vol. VII
Cain, Sir William, 1st Bt, 1864–1924, vol. II
Caine, Sir Derwent Hall, 1st Bt, 1891–1971, vol. VII
Caine, Gordon Ralph H.; *see* Hall Caine.
Caine, Sir Hall, 1853–1931, vol. III
Caine, William, 1873–1925, vol. II
Caine, William Ralph Hall, 1865–1939, vol. III
Caine, William Sproston, 1842–1903, vol. I
Caines, Clement Guy, 1882–1952, vol. V
Caird, Sir Andrew, 1870–1956, vol. V
Caird, David, 1863–1934, vol. III
Caird, Edward, 1835–1908, vol. I
Caird, Francis M., *died* 1926, vol. II
Caird, Sir James, 1st Bt (*cr* 1928), 1864–1954, vol. V
Caird, Sir James Key, 1st Bt (*cr* 1913), 1837–1916, vol. II
Caird, Very Rev. John, 1820–1898, vol. I
Caird, Mrs Mona, *died* 1932, vol. III
Cairncross, Maj.-Gen. John, 1835–1914, vol. I
Cairnes, Captain William Elliot, 1862–1902, vol. I
Cairnes, William Plunket, 1857–1925, vol. II
Cairney, John, 1898–1966, vol. VI
Cairns, 3rd Earl, 1863–1905, vol. I
Cairns, 4th Earl, 1865–1946, vol. IV
Cairns, Very Rev. David Smith, 1862–1946, vol. IV
Cairns, Sir Hugh William Bell, 1896–1952, vol. V
Cairns, James, 1885–1939, vol. III
Cairns, John, 1859–1923, vol. II
Cairns, John Arthur Robert, *died* 1933, vol. III
Cairns, T., *died* 1908, vol. I
Cairns, William Murray, 1866–1949, vol. IV
Caithness, 17th Earl of, 1857–1914, vol. I
Caithness, 18th Earl of, 1862–1947, vol. IV
Caithness, 19th Earl of, 1906–1965, vol. VI
Cakobau, Ratu Sir Etuate Tui-Vanuavou Tugi, 1908–1973, vol. VII
Caldecot, Ivone K.; *see* Kirkpatrick-Caldecot.
Caldecote, 1st Viscount, 1876–1947, vol. IV
Caldecott, Rev. Alfred, 1850–1936, vol. III
Caldecott, Sir Andrew, 1884–1951, vol. V
Caldecott, Lt-Col Ernest Lawrence, 1874–1927, vol. II
Caldecott, Maj.-Gen. Francis James, 1842–1926, vol. II
Calder, Alexander, 1898–1976, vol. VII
Calder, George, 1894–1968, vol. VI
Calder, George Alexander, 1859–1945, vol. IV
Calder, James, 1869–1940, vol. III
Calder, Col (Hon.) James, 1898–1968, vol. VI
Calder, Hon. James Alexander, 1868–1956, vol. V

Calder, Sir James Charles, 1869–1962, vol. VI
Calder, James William, 1914–1975, vol. VII
Calder, Sir John Alexander, 1889–1974, vol. VII
Calder, Air Vice-Marshal Malcolm Frederick, 1907–1978, vol. VII (AII)
Calder, Robert, 1838–1912, vol. I
Calder, Ven. William, 1848–1923, vol. II
Calder, Sir William Moir, 1881–1960, vol. V
Calder-Marshall, Sir Robert, 1877–1955, vol. V
Calderon, George, 1868–1915, vol. I (A)
Calderon, Philip H., died 1898, vol. I
Calderon, W. Frank, 1865–1943, vol. IV
Calderwood, Henry, 1830–1897, vol. I
Calderwood, W. L., 1865–1950, vol. IV
Caldwell, Alexander Francis Somerville, 1873–1940, vol. III
Caldwell, Francis, 1860–1934, vol. III
Caldwell, Maj.-Gen. Frederick Crofton H.; see Heath-Caldwell.
Caldwell, Rt Hon. James, 1839–1925, vol. II
Caldwell, John, 1903–1974, vol. VII
Caldwell, Peter Christopher, 1927–1979, vol. VII
Caldwell, Robert Nixon, 1888–1967, vol. VI
Caldwell, Col Robert Townley, 1843–1914, vol. I
Caldwell, Thomas Fisher, 1866–1940, vol. III
Caldwell, William, 1863–1942, vol. IV
Caledon, 4th Earl of, 1846–1898, vol. I
Caledon, 5th Earl of, 1885–1968, vol. VI
Caledon, 6th Earl of, 1920–1980, vol. VII
Calhoun, Eleanor; see Lazarovich-Hrebelianovich.
Calkin, Lance, 1859–1936, vol. III
Call, Frank Oliver, 1878–1956, vol. V
Callaghan, Sir Alfred John, 1865–1940, vol. III
Callaghan, Maj.-Gen. Cecil Arthur, 1890–1967, vol. VI
Callaghan, Admiral of the Fleet Sir George Astley, 1852–1920, vol. II
Callahan, James Morton, 1864–1956, vol. V
Callan, John Bartholomew, 1882–1951, vol. V
Callander, Lt-Gen. Sir Colin Bishop, 1897–1979, vol. VII
Callander, George Frederick William, 1848–1916, vol. II
Callander, Sir James, 1877–1952, vol. V
Callander, John Graham, 1873–1938, vol. III
Callander, Thomas, 1877–1959, vol. V
Callander, Major William Henry Burn, 1890–1967, vol. VI
Callas, Maria, 1923–1977, vol. VII
Callaway, Charles, 1838–1915, vol. I (A)
Callaway, Air Vice-Marshal William Bertram, 1889–1974, vol. VII
Callcott, F. T., died 1923, vol. II
Callender, Hugh Longbourne, 1863–1930, vol. III
Callender, Lt-Col David Aubrey, 1868–1953, vol. V
Callender, Eustace Maud, 1864–1952, vol. V
Callender, Sir Geoffrey Arthur Romaine, 1875–1946, vol. IV
Callender, Sir Thomas Octavius, 1855–1938, vol. III
Calley, Hon. Maj.-Gen. Thomas Charles Pleydell, 1856–1932, vol. III
Callow, Charles Thomas Cheslyn, 1852–1933, vol. III

Callow, Graham, 1894–1960, vol. V
Callow, William, 1812–1908, vol. I
Callwell, Maj.-Gen. Sir Charles Edward, 1859–1928, vol. II
Calman, William Thomas, 1871–1952, vol. V
Calmette, Leon Charles Albert, 1863–1933, vol. III
Calnan, Denis, died 1939, vol. III
Calry, 6th Count de, 1854–1950, vol. IV (A), vol. V
Calthorpe, 6th Baron, 1829–1910, vol. I
Calthorpe, 7th Baron, 1831–1912, vol. I
Calthorpe, 8th Baron, 1862–1940, vol. III
Calthorpe, 9th Baron, 1924–1945, vol. IV
Calthorpe, Sir FitzRoy Hamilton A. G.; see Anstruther-Gough-Calthorpe.
Calthorpe, Hon. Frederick Somerset Gough-, 1892–1935, vol. III
Calthorpe, Admiral of the Fleet Hon. Sir Somerset Arthur Gough-, 1864–1937, vol. III
Calthrop, Sir Calthrop Guy Spencer, 1st Bt, 1870–1919, vol. II
Calthrop, Col Christopher William C.; see Carr-Calthrop.
Calthrop, Dion Clayton, 1878–1937, vol. III
Calve, Emma, 1866–1942, vol. IV
Calver, Sir Robert Henry Sherwood, died 1963, vol. VI
Calverley, 1st Baron, 1877–1955, vol. V
Calverley, 2nd Baron, 1914–1971, vol. VII
Calverley, Joseph Ernest Goodfellow, 1872–1953, vol. V
Calvert, Albert Frederick, 1872–1946, vol. IV
Calvert, Albert Spencer, 1897–1953, vol. V
Calvert, Archibald Motteux, 1827–1906, vol. I
Calvert, Mrs Charles, 1836–1921, vol. III
Calvert, Edwin George Bleakley, died 1976, vol. VII
Calvert, Rt Rev. George Reginald, 1900–1976, vol. VII
Calvert, Hubert, 1875–1961, vol. VI
Calvert, James, died 1932, vol. III
Calvert, Lt-Col John Telfer, died 1944, vol. IV
Calvert, Sir Joseph, 1853–1931, vol. III
Calvert, Rear-Adm. Thomas Frederick Parker, 1883–1938, vol. III
Calvert, William Archibald, 1868–1943, vol. IV
Calvert, William Robinson, 1882–1949, vol. IV
Calvert-Jones, Maj.-Gen. Percy George, 1894–1977, vol. VII
Calwell, Rt Hon. Arthur Augustus, 1896–1973, vol. VII
Cam, Helen Maud, 1885–1968, vol. VI
Camacho, Sir Maurice Vivian, 1885–1941, vol. IV
Cambage, Richard Hind, 1859–1928, vol. II
Camber-Williams, Rev. Robert, 1860–1924, vol. II
Cambon, Paul, 1843–1924, vol. II
Cambon, Roger, 1881–1970, vol. VI
Cambridge, 2nd Duke of, 1819–1904, vol. I
Cambridge, 1st Marquess of, 1868–1927, vol. II
Cambridge, Ada, 1844–1926, vol. II
Cambridge, Sir Arthur Wallace P.; see Pickard-Cambridge.
Cambridge, Elizabeth; see Hodges, Barbara K.
Cambridge, Rev. Octavius P.; see Pickard-Cambridge.

Cambridge, William Adair P.; see Pickard-Cambridge.
Camden, 4th Marquess of, 1872–1943, vol. IV
Cameron, Rev. A. D., died 1946, vol. IV
Cameron, Alexander Gordon, 1886–1944, vol. IV
Cameron, Alexander T., 1882–1947, vol. IV
Cameron, Rev. Allan Thomas, 1870–1932, vol. III
Cameron, Archibald, 1902–1964, vol. VI
Cameron, Gen. Sir Archibald Rice, 1870–1944, vol. IV
Cameron, Rev. Archibald Stuart, died 1936, vol. III
Cameron, Col Aylmer, 1833–1909, vol. I
Cameron, Basil; see Cameron, G. B.
Cameron, Major Cecil Aylmer, 1883–1924, vol. II
Cameron, Sir Charles, 1st Bt, 1841–1924, vol. II
Cameron, Charles, 1886–1968, vol. VI
Cameron, Sir Charles Alexander, 1830–1921, vol. II
Cameron, Rev. Charles Leslie L.; see Lovett-Cameron.
Cameron, Charlotte, died 1946, vol. IV
Cameron, Sir Cornelius, 1896–1975, vol. VII
Cameron, Col Hon. Cyril St Clair, 1857–1941, vol. IV
Cameron, Vice-Adm. Cyril St Clair, 1879–1973, vol. VII
Cameron, Sir David Young, 1865–1945, vol. IV
Cameron of Lochiel, Donald, 1835–1905, vol. II
Cameron, Donald Andreas, 1856–1936, vol. III
Cameron, Sir Donald Charles, 1872–1948, vol. IV
Cameron, Lt-Col Sir Donald Charles, 1879–1960, vol. V (A), vol. VI
Cameron, Sir Donald Charles, 1877–1962, vol. VI
Cameron, Lt-Col Donald Hay, 1867–1932, vol. III
Cameron, Hon. Donald Norman, died 1931, vol. III
Cameron, Maj.-Gen. Donald Roderick, 1834–1921, vol. II
Cameron of Lochiel, Col Sir Donald Walter, 1876–1951, vol. V
Cameron, Hon. Sir Douglas Colin, 1854–1921, vol. II
Cameron, Sir Edward John, 1858–1947, vol. IV
Cameron, Edward Robert, 1857–1931, vol. III
Cameron, Elizabeth Dorothea Cole, (Mrs Alan Charles Cameron); see Bowen, E. D. C.
Cameron, Emily; see Cameron, Mrs Lovett.
Cameron, Lt-Col Ewan Cornwallis, 1865–1932, vol. III
Cameron, Sir Ewen, 1841–1908, vol. I
Cameron of Lundavra, Col Ewen Allan, 1877–1958, vol. V
Cameron, Hon. Sir Ewen Paul, 1892–1964, vol. VI
Cameron, Finlay James, 1880–1954, vol. V
Cameron, (George) Basil, 1884–1975, vol. VII
Cameron, Lt-Col George Cecil Minett Sorell-, 1871–1947, vol. IV
Cameron, Ven. George Henry, 1861–1940, vol. III
Cameron, Hector Charles, 1878–1958, vol. V
Cameron, Sir Hector Clare, 1843–1928, vol. II
Cameron, Hugh, 1835–1918, vol. II
Cameron, Col Hugh Alan, 1871–1929, vol. III
Cameron, Irving Heward, 1855–1933, vol. III
Cameron, Isabella Douglas, died 1945, vol. IV
Cameron, Col James Black, 1882–1946, vol. IV

Cameron, Sir James Davidson Stuart, 1900–1969, vol. VI
Cameron, James Nield, 1884–1960, vol. V
Cameron, James Spottiswoode, died 1918, vol. II
Cameron, John, 1873–1960, vol. V
Cameron, Sir John, 2nd Bt, 1903–1968, vol. VI
Cameron, John Donald, 1858–1923, vol. II
Cameron, Adm. John Ewen, 1874–1939, vol. III
Cameron, John Forbes, 1873–1952, vol. V
Cameron, John Gordon Patrick, 1885–1970, vol. VI
Cameron, Rev. John Kennedy, 1860–1944, vol. IV
Cameron, Col John Philip, 1879–1950, vol. IV
Cameron, John Robson, 1845–1907, vol. I
Cameron, Col Kenneth, 1863–1939, vol. III (A), vol. IV
Cameron, Mrs Lovett, (Emily), died 1921, vol. II
Cameron, Captain Ludovick Charles Richard Duncombe-Jewell, 1866–1947, vol. IV
Cameron, Malcolm Graeme, 1857–1925, vol. II
Cameron, Matthew Brown, 1867–1952, vol. V
Cameron, Major Sir Maurice Alexander, 1855–1936, vol. III
Cameron, Murdoch, died 1930, vol. III
Cameron, Maj.-Gen. Neville John Gordon, 1873–1955, vol. V
Cameron, Brig. Orford Somerville, 1878–1958, vol. V
Cameron, Robert, 1825–1913, vol. I
Cameron, Maj.-Gen. Roderic Duncan, 1893–1975, vol. VII
Cameron, Sir Roderick William, 1825–1900, vol. I
Cameron, Sir Roy, 1899–1966, vol. VI
Cameron, Samuel J., 1878–1959, vol. V
Cameron, Thomas Wright Moir, 1894–1980, vol. VII (AII)
Cameron, William, died 1954, vol. V
Cameron, Gen. Sir William Gordon, 1827–1913, vol. I
Cameron, William Lochiel Sapte Lovett, 1854–1938, vol. III
Cameron, Rt Rev. William Mouat, 1854–1915, vol. I (A)
Cameron-Head, Francis Somerville Cameron, 1896–1957, vol. V
Cameron-Head, James, 1851–1922, vol. II
Cameron-Ramsay-Fairfax-Lucy, Major Sir Brian Fulke; see Fairfax-Lucy.
Cameron-Ramsay-Fairfax-Lucy, Sir Henry William; see Fairfax-Lucy.
Cameron-Swan, Captain Donald, 1863–1951, vol. V
Camidge, Rt Rev. Charles Edward, 1838–1911, vol. I
Camilleri, Emanuel, 1887–1968, vol. VI (AII)
Camilleri, Rt Rev. Giovanni M., born 1843, vol. II
Camm, Dom Bede, 1864–1942, vol. IV
Camm, Sir Sydney, 1893–1966, vol. VI
Cammaerts, Emile, died 1953, vol. V
Cammell, Major Gerald Arthur, 1889–1933, vol. III
Cammidge, Percy John, 1872–1956, vol. V (A)
Camoys, 4th Baron, 1856–1897, vol. I
Camoys, 5th Baron, 1884–1968, vol. VI
Camoys, 6th Baron, 1913–1976, vol. VII
Camp, Harold Robert, 1893–1968, vol. VI

Camp, Instr Captain J., 1877–1962, vol. VI
Camp, Samuel James, 1876–1936, vol. III
Campagnac, E. T., died 1952, vol. V
Campbell, Captain Alexander, 1839–1914, vol. I
Campbell, Sir Alexander, 6th Bt (cr 1667), 1841–1914, vol. I
Campbell, Lt-Col Alexander, 1881–1941, vol. IV
Campbell, Alexander, died 1961, vol. VI
Campbell, Sir Alexander, 1892–1963, vol. VI
Campbell, Brig. Alexander Donald Powys, 1894–1974, vol. VII
Campbell, Maj.-Gen. Sir (Alexander) Douglas, 1899–1980, vol. VII
Campbell, Lt-Col Alexander George, 1889–1936, vol. III
Campbell, Maj.-Gen. Alexander H. E., 1835–1929, vol. III
Campbell, Alexander McCulloch, 1879–1955, vol. V
Campbell, Sir Alexander Thomas Cockburn-, 5th Bt (cr 1821), 1872–1935, vol. III
Campbell, Adm. Alexander Victor, 1874–1957, vol. V
Campbell, Lt-Col Sir Alexander William Dennistoun, 4th Bt (cr 1831), 1848–1931, vol. III
Campbell, Maj.-Gen. Alfred Edward, 1901–1973, vol. VII
Campbell, Alistair, 1907–1974, vol. VII
Campbell, Very Rev. Andrew James, 1875–1950, vol. IV
Campbell, Hon. Angus Dudley, 1895–1967, vol. VI
Campbell, Lord Archibald, 1846–1913, vol. I
Campbell, Lady Archibald; (Janey Sevilla), died 1923, vol. II
Campbell, Hon. Archibald, 1846–1913, vol. I
Campbell, Archibald, 1877–1963, vol. VI
Campbell, Sir Archibald Augustus Ava, 4th Bt (cr 1831), 1879–1916, vol. II
Campbell, Sir Archibald Ava, 3rd Bt (cr 1831), 1844–1913, vol. I
Campbell, Archibald Duncan, 1919–1975, vol. VII
Campbell, Rt Rev. Archibald Ean, 1856–1921, vol. II
Campbell, Maj.-Gen. Archibald Edwards, 1834–1921, vol. II
Campbell, Sir Archibald Henry, 1870–1948, vol. IV
Campbell, Major Archibald James Hamilton Douglas, 1884–1936, vol. III
Campbell, Rt Rev. Archibald Rollo G.; see Graham-Campbell.
Campbell, Sir Archibald Spencer Lindsey, 5th Bt (cr 1808), 1852–1941, vol. IV
Campbell, Archibald Y., 1885–1958, vol. V
Campbell, Sir Archibald Young Gipps, 1872–1957, vol. V
Campbell, Arnold Everitt, 1906–1980, vol. VII (AII)
Campbell, Lt-Col Aylmer MacIver, 1837–1915, vol. I
Campbell, Beatrice Stella; see Campbell, Mrs Patrick.
Campbell, Brig. Sir Bruce Atta, 1888–1954, vol. V
Campbell, C. S., died 1923, vol. II
Campbell, Lt-Col Hon. Sir Cecil James Henry, 1891–1952, vol. V
Campbell, Vice-Adm. Sir Charles, 1847–1911, vol. I

Campbell, Charles Arthur, 1897–1974, vol. VII
Campbell, Charles Douglas, 1905–1975, vol. VII
Campbell, Sir (Charles) Duncan Macnair, 2nd Bt (cr 1939), 1906–1954, vol. V
Campbell, Lt-Col Charles Ferguson, died 1925, vol. II
Campbell, Charles Graham, 1880–1971, vol. VII
Campbell, Lt-Col Charles Lionel Kirwan, 1873–1918, vol. II
Campbell, Sir Charles Ralph, 11th Bt (cr 1628), 1850–1919, vol. II
Campbell, Sir Charles Ralph, 12th Bt (cr 1628), 1881–1948, vol. IV
Campbell, Hon. Sir Charles Rudolph, 1885–1969, vol. VI
Campbell, Charles Stewart, 1875–1942, vol. IV
Campbell, Charles William, 1861–1927, vol. II
Campbell, Captain Claude Henry, 1878–1916, vol. II
Campbell, Lady Colin, died 1911, vol. I
Campbell, Rev. Colin, 1848–1931, vol. III
Campbell, Colin, 1851–1933, vol. III
Campbell, Sir Colin, 1891–1979, vol. VII
Campbell, Colin Algernon, 1874–1957, vol. V
Campbell, Ven. Colin Arthur Fitzgerald, 1863–1916, vol. II
Campbell, Col Colin Charles, 1842–1929, vol. III
Campbell, Colin George, 1852–1911, vol. I
Campbell, Colin George Pelham, 1872–1955, vol. V
Campbell, Sir David, 1889–1978, vol. VII
Campbell, Rt Hon. Sir David Callender, 1891–1963, vol. VI
Campbell, Gen. Sir David Graham Muschet, 1869–1936, vol. III
Campbell, Col David Wilkinson, 1832–1903, vol. I
Campbell, Most Rev. Donald Alphonsus, 1894–1963, vol. VI
Campbell, Ven. Donald F., 1886–1933, vol. III
Campbell, Donald Malcolm, 1921–1967, vol. VI
Campbell, Dorothy, (Mrs Alan Campbell); see Parker, D.
Campbell, Maj.-Gen. Sir Douglas; see Campbell, Maj.-Gen. Sir A. D.
Campbell, Douglas Colin, 1891–1957, vol. V
Campbell, Douglas Graham, 1867–1918, vol. II
Campbell, Douglas Mason, 1905–1978, vol. VII
Campbell, Lt-Col Duncan, 1880–1954, vol. V
Campbell, Sir Duncan Alexander Dundas, 3rd Bt (cr 1831), 1856–1926, vol. II
Campbell, Major Duncan Elidor, died 1930, vol. III
Campbell, Captain Duncan Lorn, 1881–1923, vol. II
Campbell, Sir Duncan John Alfred, 5th Bt (cr 1831), 1854–1932, vol. III
Campbell, Captain Duncan Lorn, 1881–1923, vol. II
Campbell, Sir Duncan Macnair; see Campbell, Sir C. D. M.
Campbell, Col Edmund George, 1893–1972, vol. VII
Campbell, Rev. Edward Fitzhardinge, 1880–1957, vol. V
Campbell, Sir Edward Taswell, 1st Bt (cr 1939), 1879–1945, vol. IV
Campbell, Captain Sir Eric Francis Dennistoun, 6th Bt (cr 1831), 1892–1963, vol. VI

Campbell, Major Hon. Eric Octavius, 1885–1918, vol. II

Campbell, Esther Helen, (Mrs Mungo Campbell); see McCracken, E. H.

Campbell, Evan Roy, 1908–1980, vol. VII

Campbell, Ewen, 1897–1975, vol. VII

Campbell, Sir Francis Alexander, 1852–1911, vol. I

Campbell, Sir Francis J., 1832–1914, vol. I

Campbell, Col Frederick, 1843–1926, vol. II

Campbell, Gen. Sir Frederick, 1860–1943, vol. IV

Campbell, Maj.-Gen. Frederick Lorn, 1850–1931, vol. III

Campbell, George Archibald, 1875–1964, vol. VI

Campbell, Engr Captain George Douglas, 1884–1972, vol. VII

Campbell, Col George Frederick Colin, 1858–1937, vol. III

Campbell, Lord George Granville, 1850–1915, vol. I

Campbell, Sir George Ilay, 6th Bt (cr 1808), 1894–1967, vol. VI

Campbell, George James, 1842–1931, vol. III

Campbell, Brig.-Gen. George Polding, 1864–1928, vol. II

Campbell, Sir George Riddoch, 1887–1965, vol. VI

Campbell, Col George Tupper Campbell C.; see Carter-Campbell.

Campbell, Vice-Adm. George William McOran, 1877–1948, vol. IV

Campbell, Sir George William Robert, 1835–1905, vol. I

Campbell, Sir Gerald, 1879–1964, vol. VI

Campbell, Gerald FitzGerald, 1862–1933, vol. III

Campbell, Gertrude Elizabeth; see Campbell, Lady Colin.

Campbell, Vice-Adm. Gordon, 1886–1953, vol. V

Campbell, Sir Gordon Huntly, 1864–1953, vol. V

Campbell, Grace Margaret; see Wilson, G. M.

Campbell, Gen. Gunning Morehead, died 1920, vol. II

Campbell, Major Sir Guy Colin, 4th Bt (cr 1815), 1885–1960, vol. V

Campbell, Lt-Col Sir Guy Theophilus, 3rd Bt (cr 1815), 1854–1931, vol. III

Campbell, H. Donald, 1879–1969, vol. VI

Campbell, Sir Harold Alfred Maurice, 1892–1959, vol. V

Campbell, Harold Ernest, 1902–1980, vol. VII

Campbell, Captain Sir Harold George, 1888–1969, vol. VI

Campbell, Harry, died 1938, vol. III

Campbell, Lt-Col Harry La Trobe, born 1881, vol. II

Campbell, Brig. Hector, 1877–1972, vol. VII

Campbell, Sir Henry, 1856–1924, vol. II

Campbell, Henry Alexander, 1851–1907, vol. I

Campbell, Rt Rev. and Rt Hon. Henry Colville M.; see Montgomery Campbell.

Campbell, Adm. Sir Henry Hervey, 1865–1933, vol. III

Campbell, Rear-Adm. Henry John Fletcher, 1837–1914, vol. I

Campbell, Henry Johnstone, 1859–1935, vol. III

Campbell, Lt-Col Hon. Henry Walter, 1835–1910, vol. I

Campbell, Ven. Herbert Ernest, died 1930, vol. III

Campbell, Brig.-Gen. Herbert M.; see Montgomery-Campbell.

Campbell, Col Hon. Ian Malcolm, 1883–1962, vol. VI

Campbell of Airds, Bt Col Ian Maxwell, 1870–1954, vol. V

Campbell, Vice-Adm. Sir Ian Murray Robertson, 1898–1980, vol. VII

Campbell, Sir Ian Vincent Hamilton, 7th Bt (cr 1831), 1895–1978, vol. VII

Campbell, Ignatius Roy Dunnachie, 1901–1957, vol. V

Campbell, Captain Hon. Ivan, 1859–1917, vol. II

Campbell, Sir James, 5th Bt (cr 1667), 1818–1903, vol. I

Campbell, Sir James, 1842–1925, vol. II

Campbell, James, 1895–1957, vol. V

Campbell, Rt Hon. James Alexander, 1825–1908, vol. I

Campbell, Maj.-Gen. James Alexander, 1886–1964, vol. VI

Campbell, James Argyll, 1884–1944, vol. IV

Campbell, Sir James Clark, 1882–1964, vol. VI

Campbell, Rear-Adm. James Douglas, 1882–1954, vol. V

Campbell, James Duncan, 1833–1907, vol. I

Campbell, James Hugh, 1889–1934, vol. III

Campbell, James Lang, 1858–1936, vol. III

Campbell, Sir James Macnabb, 1846–1903, vol. I

Campbell, Very Rev. James Montgomery, 1859–1937, vol. III

Campbell, Dame Janet Mary, died 1954, vol. V

Campbell, Surg.-Maj. John, 1817–1904, vol. I

Campbell, Lt-Col John, 1872–1928, vol. II

Campbell, Sir John, 1862–1929, vol. III

Campbell, Maj.-Gen. John, 1871–1941, vol. IV

Campbell, Sir John, 1874–1944, vol. IV

Campbell, Mrs John; see Campbell, May Eudora.

Campbell, Sir John Alexander Coldstream, 7th Bt (cr 1667), 1877–1960, vol. V

Campbell, Captain Hon. John Beresford, 1866–1915, vol. I (A)

Campbell, Lt-Col Sir John Bruce Stuart, 2nd Bt (cr 1913), 1877–1943, vol. IV

Campbell, John Dermot, 1898–1945, vol. IV

Campbell, John Edward, 1862–1924, vol. II

Campbell, Lt-Col John Edward Robert, 1855–1936, vol. III

Campbell, John Gordon Drummond, 1864–1935, vol. III

Campbell, Brig.-Gen. John Hasluck, died 1921, vol. II

Campbell, Lt-Col John Hay, 1871–1946, vol. IV

Campbell, Sir John Home-Purves Hume-, 1879–1960, vol. V

Campbell, Sir John Logan, 1817–1912, vol. I

Campbell, Rev. John McLeod, died 1961, vol. VI

Campbell, John Macmaster, 1859–1939, vol. III

Campbell, (John) Maurice (Hardman), 1891–1973, vol. VII

Campbell, J(ohn) Menzies, 1887–1974, vol. VII

Campbell, John Ross, 1894–1969, vol. VI

Campbell, Sir John Stratheden, 1863–1928, vol. II
Campbell, Brig.-Gen. John Vaughan, 1876–1944, vol. IV
Campbell, Maj.-Gen. Sir John William, 1st Bt (cr 1913) (styled 8th, of Ardnamurchan), 1836–1915, vol. I
Campbell, Rev. Joseph William Robert, 1853–1935, vol. III
Campbell, Kenneth, died 1943, vol. IV
Campbell of Strachur, Lt-Col Kenneth John, 1878–1965, vol. VI
Campbell, Lt-Col Kenneth Rankin, 1863–1931, vol. III
Campbell, Lawson; see Campbell, W. L.
Campbell, Brig.-Gen. Leslie Warner Yule, 1867–1946, vol. IV
Campbell, Captain Leveson Granville Byron Alexander, 1881–1951, vol. V
Campbell, Rev. Lewis, 1830–1908, vol. I
Campbell, Lloyd, died 1950, vol. IV
Campbell, Maj.-Gen. Lorn Robert Henry Dick, 1846–1913, vol. I
Campbell, Sir Louis Hamilton, 14th Bt (cr 1628), 1885–1970, vol. VI
Campbell, Sir Malcolm, 1848–1935, vol. III
Campbell, Major Sir Malcolm, 1885–1948, vol. IV
Campbell, Col Rev. Malcolm Sydenham Clarke, 1863–1949, vol. IV
Campbell, Hon. Sir Marshall, 1849–1918, vol. II
Campbell, Maurice; see Campbell, J. M. H.
Campbell, May Eudora, (Mrs John Campbell), died 1975, vol. VII
Campbell, Lt-Col Montagu Douglas, 1852–1916, vol. II
Campbell, Sir Nigel Leslie, died 1948, vol. IV
Campbell, Sir Norman Dugald Ferrier, 13th Bt (cr 1628), 1883–1968, vol. VI
Campbell, Sir Norman Montgomery Abercromby, 10th Bt (cr 1628, of Auchinbreck), 1846–1901, vol. I
Campbell, Norman Robert, 1880–1949, vol. IV
Campbell, Lt-Col Norman St Clair, 1877–1949, vol. IV
Campbell, Mrs Patrick, 1865–1940, vol. III
Campbell, Patrick; see Glenavy, 3rd Baron.
Campbell, Percy Gerald Cadogan, 1878–1960, vol. VI (AI)
Campbell, Peter, 1856–1951, vol. V
Campbell, Lt-Col Hon. Ralph Alexander, 1877–1945, vol. IV
Campbell, Rev. Reginald John, 1867–1956, vol. V
Campbell, (Renton) Stuart, 1908–1966, vol. VI
Campbell, Richard Hamilton, died 1923, vol. II
Campbell, Richard Mitchelson, 1897–1974, vol. VII
Campbell, Very Rev. Richard Stewart Dobbs, died 1913, vol. I
Campbell, Richard Vary, 1840–1901, vol. I
Campbell, Maj.-Gen. Robert Dallas, 1832–1916, vol. II
Campbell, Robert Garrett, 1858–1931, vol. III
Campbell, Brig. Robert Morris, 1883–1949, vol. IV
Campbell, Col Sir Robert Neil, 1854–1928, vol. II
Campbell, Robert Peel William, 1853–1929, vol. III
Campbell, Robert Richmond, 1901–1972, vol. VII

Campbell, Lt-Col Robert Wemyss, died 1939, vol. III
Campbell, Maj.-Gen. Robin Hasluck, 1894–1964, vol. VI
Campbell, Sir Rollo Frederick G.; see Graham-Campbell.
Campbell, Col Ronald Bruce, 1878–1963, vol. VI
Campbell, Rt Hon. Sir Ronald Hugh, 1883–1953, vol. V
Campbell, Major Roy Neil Boyd, 1884–1950, vol. IV
Campbell, Samuel George, 1861–1926, vol. II
Campbell, Sidney George, 1875–1956, vol. V
Campbell, Sidney Scholfield, 1909–1974, vol. VII
Campbell, Lt-Col Spurgeon, 1870–1935, vol. III
Campbell, Rev. Canon Stephen, died 1918, vol. II
Campbell, Stuart; see Campbell, R. S.
Campbell, Sybil, 1889–1977, vol. VII
Campbell, Hon. Thane A., 1895–1978, vol. VII
Campbell, Thomas Joseph, died 1946, vol. IV
Campbell, Ven. Thomas Robert Curwen, 1843–1911, vol. I
Campbell, Lt-Gen. Sir Walter, 1864–1936, vol. III
Campbell, Captain Sir Walter Douglas Somerset, 1853–1919, vol. II
Campbell, Lt-Col Sir Walter Fendall, 1894–1973, vol. VII
Campbell, Walter Stanley, 1887–1957, vol. V
Campbell, Gen. Sir William, 1847–1918, vol. II
Campbell, Rev. William, 1841–1921, vol. II
Campbell, William, 1889–1953, vol. V
Campbell, William, 1895–1976, vol. VII
Campbell, William; see Skerrington, Hon. Lord.
Campbell, Sir William Andrewes Ava, 5th Bt (cr 1831), 1880–1949, vol. IV
Campbell, Major William Charles, died 1958, vol. V
Campbell, William Gordon, 1891–1974, vol. VII
Campbell, Maj.-Gen. William Henry McNeile V.; see Verschoyle-Campbell.
Campbell, Col William Kentigern Hamilton, 1865–1917, vol. II
Campbell, Major William Lachlan, died 1937, vol. III
Campbell, (William) Lawson, 1890–1970, vol. VI
Campbell, Brig.-Gen. William MacLaren, 1864–1924, vol. II
Campbell, William Middleton, 1849–1919, vol. II
Campbell, Brig.-Gen. William Nevile, 1863–1933, vol. III
Campbell, Lt-Gen. Sir William Pitcairn, 1856–1933, vol. III
Campbell, Major William Robinson, 1879–1915, vol. I
Campbell-Bannerman, Rt Hon. Sir Henry, 1836–1908, vol. I
Campbell-Colquhoun, William Erskine, 1866–1922, vol. II
Campbell-Johnston, Malcolm, 1871–1931, vol. III
Campbell-Orde, Sir John William Powlett; see Orde.
Campbell-Orde, Major Sir Simon Arthur; see Orde.
Campbell Swinton, Brig. Alan Henry; see Swinton.

Campbell-Walter, Rear-Adm. Keith McNeil, 1904–1976, vol. VII

Camperdown, 3rd Earl of, 1841–1918, vol. II

Camperdown, 4th Earl of, 1845–1933, vol. III

Campinchi, César, 1882–1941, vol. IV

Campion, 1st Baron, 1882–1958, vol. V

Campion, Bernard, *died* 1952, vol. V

Campion, Cecil; *see* Campion, J. C.

Campion, Col Douglas John Montriou, 1883–1963, vol. VI

Campion, George, 1846–1926, vol. II

Campion, George Goring, 1862–1946, vol. IV

Campion, Rev. Canon Herbert Roper, 1868–1941, vol. IV

Campion, Rear-Adm. Hubert, 1825–1900, vol. I

Campion, (John) Cecil, 1907–1971, vol. VII

Campion, Sidney Ronald, 1891–1978, vol. VII

Campion, Col William Henry, 1836–1923, vol. II

Campion, William Magan, *died* 1898, vol. I

Campion, Col Sir William Robert, 1870–1951, vol. V

Campling, Rev. Canon William Charles, 1888–1973, vol. VII

Campney, Hon. Ralph Osborne, 1894–1967, vol. VI

Camps, Francis Edward, 1905–1972, vol. VII

Camrose, 1st Viscount, 1879–1954, vol. V

Camsell, Charles, 1876–1958, vol. V

Camus, Albert, 1913–1960, vol. V

Cana, Frank Richardson, 1865–1935, vol. III

Canaway, Arthur Pitcairn, 1857–1949, vol. IV

Canby, Henry Seidel, 1878–1961, vol. VI

Cancellor, Henry Lannoy, 1862–1929, vol. III

Candler, Edmund, 1874–1926, vol. II

Candlish, Joseph John, 1855–1913, vol. I

Candy, Rear-Adm. Algernon Henry Chester, 1877–1959, vol. V

Candy, Sir Edward Townshend, 1845–1913, vol. I

Candy, George, 1841–1899, vol. I

Candy, Major Henry Augustus, 1842–1911, vol. I

Candy, Hugh Charles Herbert, *died* 1935, vol. III

Candy, Maj.-Gen. Ronald Herbert, *died* 1972, vol. VII

Cane, Arthur Beresford, 1864–1939, vol. III

Cane, Sir Cyril Hubert, 1891–1959, vol. V

Cane, Lucy Mary, (Mrs Arthur Beresford Cane), *died* 1926, vol. II

Cane, Robert Alexander Gordon, 1893–1975, vol. VII

Canfield, Dorothy, (Dorothea Frances Canfield Fisher), 1879–1958, vol. V

Canfield, James Hulme, 1847–1909, vol. I

Canham, Ven. Thomas Henry, *died* 1947, vol. IV

Cann, Hon. John Henry, 1860–1940, vol. III

Cann, Percy Walter, 1884–1973, vol. VII

Cann, Sir William Moore, 1856–1947, vol. IV

Cannan, Charles, 1858–1919, vol. II

Cannan, Edwin, 1861–1935, vol. III

Cannan, Gilbert, 1884–1955, vol. V

Cannan, Maj.-Gen. James Harold, 1882–1976, vol. VII

Cannan, Joanna, (Mrs H. J. Pullein-Thompson), 1898–1961, vol. VI

Cannell, John, vol. III

Canney, Maurice Arthur, 1872–1942, vol. IV

Canning, Col Albert, 1861–1960, vol. V

Canning, Hon. Albert Stratford George, 1832–1916, vol. II

Canning, Rev. Clifford Brooke, 1882–1957, vol. V

Canning, Hon. Conway Stratford George, 1854–1926, vol. II

Canning, Sir Ernest R., 1876–1966, vol. VI

Canning, Frederick, 1882–1968, vol. VI

Canning, Hugh, *died* 1927, vol. II

Canning, Sir Samuel, 1823–1908, vol. I

Cannon, Annie Jump, 1863–1941, vol. IV

Cannon, George Harry Franklyn, 1885–1966, vol. VI

Cannon, Henry White, 1850–1934, vol. III

Cannon, Herbert Graham, 1897–1963, vol. VI

Cannon, James, 1864–1944, vol. IV

Cannon, Hon. Lawrence Arthur Dumoulin, 1877–1939, vol. III

Cannon, Lawrence John, 1852–1921, vol. II

Cannon, Sir Leslie, 1920–1970, vol. VI

Cannon, Hon. Lucien, 1887–1950, vol. IV

Cannon, Walter Bradford, 1871–1945, vol. IV

Cannot, Brig.-Gen. Fernand Gustave Eugene, 1873–1941, vol. IV

Canny, Sir Gerald Bain, 1881–1954, vol. V

Canny, Col James Clare Macnamara, 1877–1942, vol. IV

Cantan, Major Henry Thomas, 1868–1916, vol. II

Cantelli, Guido, 1920–1956, vol. V

Canter, Bernard Hall, 1906–1969, vol. VI

Canterbury, 4th Viscount, 1839–1914, vol. I

Canterbury, 5th Viscount, 1879–1918, vol. II

Canterbury, 6th Viscount, 1872–1941, vol. IV

Canterbury, Archbishop of; Most Rev. Frederick Temple, 1821–1902, vol. I (A)

Cantlie, Adm. Sir Colin, 1888–1967, vol. VI

Cantlie, Sir James, 1851–1926, vol. II

Cantlie, Sir Keith, 1886–1977, vol. VII

Cantlie, Lt-Gen. Sir Neil, 1892–1975, vol. VII

Canton, William, 1845–1926, vol. II

Cantor, Eddie, 1892–1964, vol. VI

Cantrell, Robert, 1849–1936, vol. III

Cantwell, Most Rev. John Joseph, 1874–1947, vol. IV

Canuck, Janey; *see* Murphy, Emily F.

Canziani, Estella Louisa Michaela, 1887–1964, vol. VI

Capablanca, José R., 1888–1942, vol. IV

Cape, Captain Charles Scarvell, *born* 1866, vol. III

Cape, Col Edmund Graves Meredith, 1878–1962, vol. VI

Cape, (Herbert) Jonathan, 1879–1960, vol. V

Cape, Jonathan; *see* Cape, H. J.

Cape, Thomas, 1868–1947, vol. IV

Capek, Karel, 1890–1938, vol. III

Capel, Air Vice-Marshal Arthur John, 1894–1979, vol. VII

Capel, Hon. Reginald Algernon, 1830–1906, vol. I

Capel, Mgr Thomas John, 1836–1911, vol. I

Capel Cure, Col Herbert; *see* Cure.

Capell, Col Algernon Essex, 1869–1952, vol. V

Capell, Richard, 1885–1954, vol. V

Capellini, Giovanni, *born* 1833, vol. II

Capener, Norman Leslie, 1898–1975, vol. VII

Capes, Bernard, *died* 1918, vol. II

Capes, Rev. William Wolfe, 1834–1914, vol. I
Capewell, Arthur, 1902–1957, vol. V
Capey, Reco, 1895–1961, vol. VI
Capon, Norman Brandon, 1892–1975, vol. VII
Capon, Maj.-Gen. Philip John Lauriston, 1902–1964, vol. VI
Caporn, Arthur Cecil, 1884–1953, vol. V
Cappel, Sir Albert James Leppoc, 1836–1924, vol. II
Cappel, Edward Louis, 1856–1936, vol. III
Cappell, Daniel Fowler, 1900–1976, vol. VII
Capper, Alfred Octavius, died 1921, vol. II
Capper, Major Charles Francis, 1902–1964, vol. VI
Capper, David Sing, died 1926, vol. II
Capper, Sir Derrick; see Capper, Sir W. D.
Capper, John Brainerd, 1855–1936, vol. III
Capper, Maj.-Gen. Sir John Edward, 1861–1955, vol. V
Capper, Stewart Henbest, 1859–1925, vol. II
Capper, Maj.-Gen. Sir Thompson, 1863–1915, vol. I (A)
Capper, Col William, 1856–1934, vol. III
Capper, Sir (William) Derrick, 1912–1977, vol. VII
Cappon, James, 1854–1939, vol. III
Capps, Frederick Cecil Wray, 1898–1970, vol. VI
Capron, Athol John, 1859–1937, vol. III
Capron, Frederick Hugh, 1857–1955, vol. V
Caproni, Gianni, 1886–1957, vol. V
Capus, Alfred; see Capus, V. M. A.
Capus, (Vincent Marie) Alfred, 1858–1922, vol. II
Carbery, 9th Baron, 1868–1898, vol. I
Carbery, 10th Baron, 1892–1970, vol. VI (AII)
Carbery, Col Andrew Robert Dillon, 1868–1948, vol. IV
Carbone, Sir Guiseppe, 1839–1913, vol. I
Carbonell, Rev. Canon Francis Rohde, 1849–1919, vol. II
Carbutt, Lt-Col Clive Lancaster, 1876–1948, vol. IV
Carcano, Miguel Angel, 1889–1978, vol. VII
Cardale, Vice-Adm. C. S., 1841–1904, vol. I
Cardell, John, 1857–1937, vol. III (A)
Cardell, J(ohn) D(ouglas) Magor, 1896–1966, vol. VI
Cardell-Oliver, Hon. Dame (Annie) Florence (Gillies), died 1965, vol. VI
Cardell-Oliver, Hon. Dame Florence; see Cardell-Oliver, Hon. Dame A. F. G.
Carden, Major D'Arcy Vandeleur, 1892–1936, vol. III
Carden, Major Sir Frederick Henry Walter, 3rd Bt (cr 1887), 1873–1966, vol. VI
Carden, Sir Frederick Walter, 2nd Bt (cr 1887), 1833–1909, vol. II
Carden, Major Henry Charles, 1855–1915, vol. I (A)
Carden, Sir Herbert, died 1941, vol. IV
Carden, Col John, 1870–1915, vol. I (A), vol. I
Carden, Rev. John, 1882–1934, vol. III
Carden, Sir John Craven, 5th Bt (cr 1787), 1854–1931, vol. III
Carden, Captain Sir John Valentine, 6th Bt (cr 1787), 1892–1935, vol. III
Carden, Sir Lionel Edward Gresley, 1851–1915, vol. I (A)
Carden, Col Louis Peile, 1860–1942, vol. IV
Carden, Adm. Sir Sackville Hamilton, 1857–1930, vol. III
Carden Roe, Brig. William, 1894–1977, vol. VII
Cardew, Sir Alexander Gordon, 1861–1937, vol. III
Cardew, Claud Ambrose, 1870–1959, vol. V
Cardew, Evelyn Roberta, (Lady Cardew), died 1953, vol. V
Cardew, Col Sir Frederic, 1839–1921, vol. II
Cardew, Rev. Prebendary Frederic Anstruther, 1866–1942, vol. IV
Cardew, Lt-Col George Ambrose, died 1941, vol. IV
Cardew, Col George Hereward, 1861–1949, vol. IV
Cardigan and Lancastre, Countess of; (Adeline Louise Maria), died 1915, vol. I
Cardin, James Joseph, 1839–1917, vol. II
Cardinall, Sir Allan Wolsey, 1887–1956, vol. V
Cardon, Philip Vincent, 1889–1965, vol. VI
Cardot, Rt Rev. Alexander, 1857–1925, vol. II
Cardozo, Benjamin N., 1870–1938, vol. III
Cardozo, Henry O'Connell, 1839–1905, vol. I
Carducci, Giosue, 1835–1907, vol. I
Cardus, Sir Neville, 1889–1975, vol. VII
Cardwell, George, 1882–1962, vol. VI
Cardwell, Rev. John Henry, 1842–1921, vol. II
Care, Henry Clifford, 1892–1979, vol. VII
Carew, 3rd Baron, 1860–1923, vol. II
Carew, 4th Baron, 1863–1926, vol. II
Carew, 5th Baron, 1860–1927, vol. II
Carew, Charles Robert Sydenham, 1853–1939, vol. III
Carew, Major George Albert Lade, 1862–1937, vol. III
Carew, Sir Henry Palk, 9th Bt, 1870–1934, vol. III
Carew, Mrs James; see Terry, Dame Ellen.
Carew, James Laurence, died 1903, vol. I
Carew, Lt-Gen. Sir Reginald Pole, 1849–1924, vol. II
Carew, Sir Thomas Palk, 10th Bt, 1890–1976, vol. VII
Carew-Gibson, Harry Frederick, 1869–1953, vol. V
Carew Hunt, Rear-Adm. Geoffrey Harry, 1917–1979, vol. VII
Carew Hunt, Captain Roland Cecil, 1880–1959, vol. V
Carew-Hunt, Lt-Col Thomas Edward, 1874–1950, vol. IV
Carey, Rev. Albert Darell T.; see Tupper-Carey.
Carey, Brig.-Gen. Arthur Basil, 1872–1961, vol. VI
Carey, Sir Bernard Sausmarez, 1864–1919, vol. II
Carey, Maj.-Gen. Carteret Walter, 1853–1932, vol. III
Carey, Cecil William Victor, 1887–1976, vol. VII
Carey, Charles William, 1862–1943, vol. IV
Carey, Clive; see Carey, F. C. S.
Carey, Maj.-Gen. Constantine Phipps, 1835–1906, vol. I
Carey, (Francis) Clive (Savill), 1883–1968, vol. VI
Carey, Frank Stanton, 1860–1928, vol. II
Carey, Maj.-Gen. George Glas Sandeman, 1867–1948, vol. IV
Carey, Gordon Vero, 1886–1969, vol. VI
Carey, Brig.-Gen. Harold Eustace, 1874–1944, vol. IV
Carey, Col Herbert Clement, 1865–1948, vol. IV

Carey, Herbert Simon, 1856–1947, vol. IV
Carey, Rt Rev. Kenneth Moir, 1908–1979, vol. VII
Carey, Maj.-Gen. Laurence Francis de Vic, 1904–1972, vol. VII
Carey, Brig.-Gen. Octavius William, 1865–1938, vol. III
Carey, Rosa Nouchette, 1840–1909, vol. I
Carey, Sir Thomas Godfrey, 1832–1906, vol. I
Carey, Sir Victor Gosselin, 1871–1957, vol. V
Carey, Captain Walter, died 1932, vol. III
Carey, Rt Rev. Walter Julius, 1875–1955, vol. V
Carey, Brig. Walter Louis John, 1872–1953, vol. V
Carey, Lt-Col Wilfrid Leathes de Mussenden, 1881–1937, vol. III
Carey, Col William, 1833–1905, vol. I
Carey, Sir Willoughby Langer, 1875–1933, vol. III
Carey Taylor, Alan; see Taylor.
Cargill, Featherston, 1870–1959, vol. V
Cargill, Air Comdt Dame Helen Wilson, 1896–1969, vol. VI
Cargill, Sir John Traill, 1st Bt, 1867–1954, vol. V
Cargill, Lionel Vernon, died 1955, vol. V
Cargill Thompson, William David James, 1930–1978, vol. VII
Carill-Worsley, Philip Ernest T.; see Tindal-Carill-Worsley.
Carington, Herbert Hanbury Smith-, 1851–1917, vol. II
Carington, Neville Woodford S.; see Smith-Carington.
Carington, Lt-Col Rt Hon. Sir William Henry Peregrine, 1845–1914, vol. I
Carisbrooke, 1st Marquess of, 1886–1960, vol. V
Carkeek, Sir Arthur, 1861–1933, vol. III
Carlaw, John, died 1934, vol. III
Carlebach, Col Sir Philip, 1873–1949, vol. IV
Carles, William Richard, 1848–1929, vol. III
Carless, Albert, died 1936, vol. III
Carleton, Hon. Brig.-Gen. Frank Robert Crofton, 1856–1924, vol. II
Carleton, Brig.-Gen. Frederick Montgomerie, 1867–1922, vol. II
Carleton, Ven. George Dundas, 1877–1961, vol. VI
Carleton, Major Guy Audouin, 1859–1941, vol. IV
Carleton, Gen. Henry Alexander, 1814–1900, vol. I
Carleton, Rev. James George, 1848–1918, vol. II
Carleton, John Dudley, 1908–1974, vol. VII
Carleton, Brig.-Gen. Lancelot Richard, 1861–1937, vol. III
Carleton, Brig.-Gen. Montgomery Launcelot, 1861–1942, vol. IV
Carleton, Maj.-Gen. Richard Langford L.; see Leir-Carleton.
Carlier, Edmond William Wace, 1861–1940, vol. III
Carlile, Sir Edward, 1845–1917, vol. II
Carlile, Sir (Edward) Hildred, 1st Bt (cr 1917), 1852–1942, vol. IV
Carlile, Sir Hildred; see Carlile, Sir E. H.
Carlile, Rev. John Charles, died 1941, vol. IV
Carlile, Sir Walter; see Carlile, Sir W. W.
Carlile, Sir (William) Walter, 1st Bt (cr 1928), 1862–1950, vol. IV
Carlile, Rev. Wilson, 1847–1942, vol. IV
Carlill, Harold Flamank, 1875–1959, vol. V

Carlill, Hildred, died 1942, vol. IV
Carlin, Gaston, died 1922, vol. II
Carline, George, 1855–1920, vol. II
Carline, Sydney W., 1888–1929, vol. III
Carling, Sir Ernest Rock, 1877–1960, vol. V
Carling, Rt Hon. Sir John, 1828–1911, vol. I
Carlingford, 1st Baron, 1823–1898, vol. I
Carlisle, 9th Earl of, 1843–1911, vol. I
Carlisle, 10th Earl of, 1867–1912 (this entry was not transferred to Who was Who).
Carlisle, 11th Earl of, 1895–1963, vol. VI
Carlisle, Rt Hon. Alexander Montgomery, 1854–1926, vol. II
Carlisle, Rt Rev. Arthur, 1881–1943, vol. IV
Carlisle, Lt-Col Denton; see Carlisle, Lt-Col J. C. D.
Carlisle, Engr Rear-Adm. Frank Scott, 1882–1941, vol. IV
Carlisle, Lt-Col (John Charles) Denton, 1888–1972, vol. VII
Carlisle, R. H., 1865–1941, vol. IV
Carlos, Don; Duke of Madrid, 1848–1909, vol. I
Carlow, Viscount; George Lionel Seymour, 1907–1944, vol. IV
Carlow, Charles Augustus, died 1954, vol. V
Carlton, Sir Arthur, died 1931, vol. III
Carlton, C. Hope, 1889–1951, vol. V
Carlyle, Rev. Alexander James, 1861–1943, vol. IV
Carlyle, Edward Irving, 1871–1952, vol. V
Carlyle, Sir Robert Warrand, 1859–1934, vol. III
Carlyon, Sir Alexander Keith, 1848–1936, vol. III
Carlyon-Britton, Major Philip William Poole, 1863–1938, vol. III
Carman, Bliss, 1861–1929, vol. III
Carmichael, 1st Baron, 1859–1926, vol. II
Carmichael, Alexander, died 1912, vol. I
Carmichael, Captain Hon. Ambrose Campbell, 1872–1953, vol. V
Carmichael, Claude Dundas James, 1862–1915, vol. I
Carmichael, Sir Duncan, 1866–1923, vol. II
Carmichael, Sir Eardley Charles William G. C.; see Gibson-Craig-Carmichael.
Carmichael, Edward Arnold, 1896–1978, vol. VII
Carmichael, Rev. Frederic Falkiner, 1831–1919, vol. II
Carmichael, Sir George, 1866–1936, vol. III
Carmichael, George Chapman, 1924–1970, vol. VI
Carmichael, Captain Sir Henry Thomas G. C.; see Gibson-Craig-Carmichael.
Carmichael, James, 1846–1927, vol. II
Carmichael, Sir James, 1858–1934, vol. III
Carmichael, James, 1894–1966, vol. VI
Carmichael, James, died 1972, vol. VII
Carmichael, Lt-Col Sir James Forrest Halkett, 1868–1934, vol. III
Carmichael, Sir James Morse, 3rd Bt, 1844–1902, vol. I
Carmichael, John Murray G.; see Gibson-Carmichael.
Carmichael, Leonard, 1898–1973, vol. VII
Carmichael, Mary, died 1935, vol. III
Carmichael, Mary Gertrude, (Lady Carmichael), died 1941, vol. IV

Carmichael, Montgomery, 1857–1936, vol. III
Carmichael, Norman Scott, 1883–1951, vol. V
Carmichael, Sir William G. C.; see Gibson-Craig-Carmichael, Sir A. H. W.
Carmichael Anstruther, Sir Windham Charles James; see Anstruther.
Carmichael-Anstruther, Sir Windham Eric Francis; see Anstruther.
Carmichael-Anstruther, Sir Windham Frederick; see Anstruther.
Carmichael Anstruther, Sir Windham Robert; see Anstruther.
Carmichael-Ferrall, John, 1855–1923, vol. II
Carmody, Very Rev. William P., died 1938, vol. III
Carmont, Hon. Lord; John Francis Carmont, 1880–1965, vol. VI
Carmont, John Francis; see Carmont, Hon. Lord.
Carnac, Charles James R.; see Rivett-Carnac.
Carnac, Sir Claud James R.; see Rivett-Carnac.
Carnac, Rev. Sir George R.; see Rivett-Carnac.
Carnac, Sir Henry George Crabbe R.; see Rivett-Carnac.
Carnac, Vice-Adm. James William R.; see Rivett-Carnac.
Carnac, Col John Henry R.; see Rivett-Carnac.
Carnac, Col Percy Temple R.; see Rivett-Carnac.
Carnac, Sir William Percival R.; see Rivett-Carnac.
Carnarvon, 5th Earl of, 1866–1923, vol. II
Carncross, Hon. Sir Walter Charles Frederick, 1855–1940, vol. III
Carnduff, Sir Herbert William Cameron, 1862–1915, vol. I
Carnegie, Andrew, 1835–1919, vol. II
Carnegie, Hon. Charles, 1883–1906, vol. I
Carnegie, Col David, 1868–1949, vol. IV
Carnegie, Air Vice-Marshal David Vaughan, 1897–1964, vol. VI
Carnegie, Hon. David Wynford, 1871–1900, vol. I
Carnegie, Lt-Col Hon. Douglas George, 1870–1937, vol. III
Carnegie, Sir Francis, 1874–1946, vol. IV
Carnegie, Lady Helena Mariota, 1865–1943, vol. IV
Carnegie, Rt Hon. Sir Lancelot Douglas, 1861–1933, vol. III
Carnegie, Louise, (Mrs Andrew Carnegie), 1857–1946, vol. IV
Carnegie, Rev. William Hartley, 1860–1936, vol. III
Carnegy, Gen. Alexander, 1829–1900, vol. I
Carnegy, Col Charles Gilbert, 1864–1928, vol. II
Carnegy of Lour, Lt-Col Elliott; see Carnegy of Lour, Lt-Col U. E. C.
Carnegy, Rev. Canon Patrick Charles Alexander, 1893–1969, vol. VI
Carnegy, Maj.-Gen. Sir Philip Mainwaring, 1858–1927, vol. II
Carnegy of Lour, Lt-Col (Ughtred) Elliott (Carnegy), 1886–1973, vol. VII
Carnock, 1st Baron, 1849–1928, vol. II
Carnock, 2nd Baron, 1883–1952, vol. V
Carnwath, 12th Earl of, 1847–1910, vol. I
Carnwath, 15th (de facto 13th) Earl of, 1883–1931, vol. III
Carnwath, 16th (de facto 14th) Earl of, 1851–1941, vol. IV

Carnwath, Thomas, 1878–1954, vol. V
Caroe, William Douglas, 1857–1938, vol. III
Carolus-Duran, Emile Auguste, 1838–1917, vol. II
Caron, Hon. Joseph Edouard, 1866–1930, vol. III
Caron, Hon. Sir Joseph Philippe Rene Adolphe, 1842–1908, vol. I
Carozzi, Joseph L., 1866–1933, vol. III
Carpendale, Vice-Adm. Sir Charles Douglas, 1874–1968, vol. VI
Carpendale, Major Frederic Maxwell-, 1887–1958, vol. V
Carpenter, Captain Alfred, 1847–1925, vol. II
Carpenter, Vice-Adm. Alfred Francis Blakeney, 1881–1955, vol. V
Carpenter, Major Sir Archibald Boyd B.; see Boyd Carpenter.
Carpenter, Charles Claude, 1858–1938, vol. III
Carpenter, Brig.-Gen. Charles Murray, 1870–1942, vol. IV
Carpenter, David, 1866–1935, vol. III
Carpenter, Edward, 1844–1929, vol. III
Carpenter, Sir Eric Ashton, 1896–1973, vol. VII
Carpenter, Geoffrey Douglas Hale, 1882–1953, vol. V
Carpenter, George, 1859–1910, vol. I
Carpenter, Lt-Gen. George, 1877–1952, vol. V
Carpenter, Rev. George Herbert, 1865–1939, vol. III
Carpenter, George Lyndon, 1872–1948, vol. IV
Carpenter, Sir H. C. Harold, 1875–1940, vol. III
Carpenter, Ven. Harry William, 1854–1936, vol. III
Carpenter, Henry John B.; see Boyd-Carpenter.
Carpenter, Ven. Horace John, 1887–1965, vol. VI
Carpenter, Rev. J. Estlin, 1844–1927, vol. II
Carpenter, Rev. James Nelson, died 1949, vol. IV (A), vol. V
Carpenter, Maj.-Gen. John Owen, 1894–1967, vol. VI
Carpenter, Captain John Peers B.; see Boyd-Carpenter.
Carpenter, Percy Frederick, 1901–1964, vol. VI
Carpenter, Percy Henry, 1879–1962, vol. VI
Carpenter, Rhys, 1889–1980, vol. VII
Carpenter, Rev. Spencer Cecil, 1877–1959, vol. V
Carpenter, Adm. Hon. Walter Cecil, 1834–1904, vol. I
Carpenter, Sir Walter Randolph, 1877–1954, vol. V
Carpenter, Rt Rev. William B.; see Boyd Carpenter.
Carpenter-Garnier, John, 1839–1926, vol. II
Carpenter-Garnier, Rt Rev. Mark Rodolph, 1881–1969, vol. VI
Carpentier, Général d'Armée Marcel Maurice, 1895–1977, vol. VII
Carpmael, Kenneth S., 1885–1975, vol. VII
Carpmael, Raymond, 1875–1950, vol. IV
Carr, Alwyn C. E., died 1940, vol. III
Carr, Sir Arthur Strettell C.; see Comyns Carr.
Carr, Sir Cecil Thomas, 1878–1966, vol. VI
Carr, Rt Rev. Charles Lisle, 1871–1942, vol. IV
Carr, Air Marshal Sir (Charles) Roderick, 1891–1971, vol. VII
Carr, Charles Telford, 1905–1976, vol. VII
Carr, Brig.-Gen. Christopher D'Arcy Bloomfield Saltern B.; see Baker-Carr.

Carr, David, 1847–1920, vol. II
Carr, Rev. Edmund, 1826–1916, vol. II
Carr, Edward Arthur, 1903–1966, vol. VI
Carr, Col Edward Elliott, 1854–1926, vol. II
Carr, Sir Emsley, 1867–1941, vol. IV
Carr, Francis Howard, 1874–1969, vol. VI
Carr, Frank Arnold, 1873–1942, vol. IV
Carr, Rev. Frederick Robert, 1869–1952, vol. V
Carr, George Shadwell Quartano, 1866–1905, vol. I
Carr, Gilbert Harry, 1884–1954, vol. V
Carr, Harry Lascelles, 1907–1943, vol. IV
Carr, Lt-Col Henry Arbuthnot, 1872–1951, vol. V
Carr, Adm. Henry John, 1839–1914, vol. I
Carr, Henry Lascelles, 1841–1902, vol. I
Carr, Henry Marvell, 1894–1970, vol. VI
Carr, Herbert Wildon, 1857–1931, vol. III
Carr, Maj.-Gen. Howard, 1863–1944, vol. IV
Carr, Howard, 1880–1960, vol. V
Carr, Sir Hubert Winch, 1877–1955, vol. V
Carr, J. W. Comyns, 1849–1916, vol. II
Carr, Rev. James Haslewood, 1831–1915, vol. I
Carr, Hon. John, 1819–1913, vol. I
Carr, John Dickson, died 1977, vol. VII
Carr, John Walter, 1862–1942, vol. IV
Carr, John Wesley, 1862–1939, vol. III
Carr, Lt-Gen. Laurence, 1886–1954, vol. V
Carr, Norman Alexander, 1899–1970, vol. VI
Carr, Rev. Owen Charles, died 1929, vol. III
Carr, Major Robert George Teesdale B.; see Baker-Carr.
Carr, Air Marshal Sir Roderick; see Carr, Air Marshal Sir C. R.
Carr, Rupert Ellis, 1910–1974, vol. VII
Carr, Theodore; see Carr, W. T.
Carr, Most Rev. Thomas Joseph, 1839–1917, vol. II
Carr, Rev. Walter Raleigh, 1843–1907, vol. I
Carr, Sir William, 1872–1949, vol. IV
Carr, Sir William Emsley, 1912–1977, vol. VII
Carr, Rev. William Henry, 1857–1932, vol. III
Carr, Surg. Rear-Adm. William James, 1883–1966, vol. VI
Carr, Col William Moncrieff, 1886–1956, vol. V
Carr, Sir William St John, 1848–1928, vol. II
Carr, (William) Theodore, 1866–1931, vol. III
Carr-Calthrop, Col Christopher William, 1844–1934, vol. III
Carr-Gomm, Francis Culling, 1834–1919, vol. II
Carr-Gomm, Hubert William Culling, 1877–1939, vol. III
Carr-Hall, Col Ralph Ellis; see Hall.
Carr-Saunders, Sir Alexander Morris, 1886–1966, vol. VI
Carr-White, Maj.-Gen. Percy, 1865–1934, vol. III
Carrara, Arthur Charles, died 1949, vol. IV
Carre, Major Ralph G. Riddell, 1868–1941, vol. IV
Carrel, Alexis, 1873–1944, vol. IV
Carrick, 5th Earl of, 1835–1901, vol. I
Carrick, 6th Earl of, 1851–1909, vol. I
Carrick, 7th Earl of, 1873–1931, vol. III
Carrick, 8th Earl of, 1903–1957, vol. V
Carrick, Alexander, died 1966, vol. VI
Carrick-Buchanan, Sir David Carrick Robert, 1825–1904, vol. I

Carrick-Buchanan, David William Ramsay, 1834–1925, vol. II
Carrier, Philippe Leslie Caro, 1893–1975, vol. VII
Carrigan, William, died 1951, vol. V
Carrington, 4th Baron, 1852–1929, vol. III
Carrington, 5th Baron, 1891–1938, vol. III
Carrington, Brig. Charles Ronald Brownlow, 1880–1948, vol. IV
Carrington, Very Rev. Charles Walter, 1859–1941, vol. IV
Carrington, Maj.-Gen. Sir Frederick, 1844–1913, vol. I
Carrington, Lt-Gen. Sir Harold; see Carrington, Lt-Gen. Sir R. H.
Carrington, Very Rev. Henry, 1814–1906, vol. I
Carrington, Vice-Adm. John Walsh, 1879–1964, vol. VI
Carrington, Sir John Worrell, 1847–1913, vol. I
Carrington, Most Rev. Philip, 1892–1975, vol. VII
Carrington, Richard, 1921–1971, vol. VII
Carrington, Lt-Gen. Sir (Robert) Harold, 1882–1964, vol. VI
Carrington, Roger Clifford, 1905–1971, vol. VII
Carrington, Sir William Speight, 1904–1975, vol. VII
Carritt, Edgar Frederick, 1876–1964, vol. VI
Carroll, Sir Alfred Thomas, (Sir Turi Carroll), 1890–1975, vol. VII
Carroll, Rt Rev. Francis P., 1890–1967, vol. VI
Carroll, Francis Patrick, 1887–1955, vol. V
Carroll, Col Frederick Fitzgerald, died 1932, vol. III
Carroll, Hon. Henry George, 1865–1939, vol. III
Carroll, Sir James, died 1905, vol. I
Carroll, Hon. Sir James, 1857–1926, vol. II
Carroll, Sir John Anthony, 1899–1974, vol. VII
Carroll, Most Rev. John J., 1865–1949, vol. IV
Carroll, Brig.-Gen. John William Vincent, 1869–1927, vol. II
Carroll, Lewis, (Rev. Charles L. Dodgson), 1832–1898, vol. I
Carroll, Paul Vincent, 1900–1968, vol. VI
Carroll, Sydney Wentworth, 1877–1958, vol. V
Carroll, Sir Turi; see Carroll, Sir Alfred Thomas.
Carroll, Rev. William Alexander, 1863–1935, vol. III
Carron, Baron (Life Peer); William John Carron, 1902–1969, vol. VI
Carrow, Comdr John Hinton, 1890–1973, vol. VII
Carruthers, Adam, 1857–1937, vol. III
Carruthers, Agnes Lucy Mary, 1872–1961, vol. VI
Carruthers, (Alexander) Douglas (Mitchell), died 1962, vol. VI
Carruthers, Engr-Rear-Adm. David John, 1867–1940, vol. III
Carruthers, Douglas; see Carruthers, A. D. M.
Carruthers, Lt-Col Francis John, 1868–1945, vol. IV
Carruthers, Lt-Col James, 1876–1936, vol. III
Carruthers, Rev. James E., 1848–1932, vol. III
Carruthers, John Bennett, 1869–1910, vol. I
Carruthers, Hon. Sir Joseph Hector M'Neil, 1857–1932, vol. III
Carruthers, Brig.-Gen. Robert Alexander, 1862–1945, vol. IV

Carruthers, Violet Rosa; see Markham, V. R.
Carruthers, William, 1830–1922, vol. II
Carruthers, Sir William, 1858–1936, vol. III
Carslaw, Horatio Scott, 1870–1954, vol. V
Carson, Baron (Life Peer); Rt Hon. Sir Edward Henry Carson, 1854–1935, vol. III
Carson, Col Charles John Lloyd, 1866–1953, vol. V
Carson, Sir Charles William Charteris, 1874–1945, vol. IV
Carson, Brig. Sir Frederick, 1886–1960, vol. V
Carson, Herbert William, 1870–1930, vol. III
Carson, Howard Adams, 1842–1931, vol. III
Carson, Maj.-Gen. Sir John Wallace, 1864–1922, vol. II
Carson, Rev. Joseph, died 1898, vol. I
Carson, Lionel, 1873–1937, vol. III
Carson, Murray, 1865–1917, vol. II
Carson, Sir Norman John, 1877–1964, vol. VI
Carson, Rachel Louise, 1907–1964, vol. VI
Carson, Thomas Henry, 1843–1917, vol. II
Carson, Captain Hon. Walter Seymour, 1890–1946, vol. IV
Carswell, Catherine Roxburgh, 1879–1946, vol. IV
Carswell, Donald, 1882–1940, vol. III
Cart de Lafontaine, Lt-Col Henry Philip L., 1884–1963, vol. VI
Cartan, Elie Joseph, 1869–1951, vol. V
Carte, D'Oyly, 1844–1901, vol. I
Carte, Rupert D'Oyly; see D'Oyly Carte.
Carte, Col Thomas Elliott, 1861–1945, vol. IV
Carter, Albert Charles Robinson, 1864–1957, vol. V
Carter, Albert Thomas, 1861–1946, vol. IV
Carter, Alexander Scott, 1879–1969, vol. VI (AII)
Carter, Alfred B.; see Bonham-Carter.
Carter, Alfred Henry, 1849–1918, vol. II
Carter, Col Alfred Henry, 1856–1934, vol. III
Carter, Ven. Anthony Basil, 1881–1942, vol. IV
Carter, Sir Archibald; see Carter, Sir R. H. A.
Carter, Arthur Herbert, 1890–1979, vol. VII
Carter, Hon. Arthur John, 1847–1917, vol. II
Carter, Arthur Thomas B.; see Bonham-Carter.
Carter, Major Aubrey John, 1872–1914, vol. I
Carter, Maj.-Gen. Beresford Cecil Molyneux, 1872–1923, vol. II
Carter, Captain (S) Bernard, 1885–1954, vol. V
Carter, Gen. Sir Charles B.; see Bonham-Carter.
Carter, Brig.-Gen. Charles Herbert Philip, 1864–1943, vol. IV
Carter, Rev. Charles Sydney, 1876–1963, vol. VI
Carter, Sir Christopher Douglas B.; see Bonham Carter.
Carter, Rev. Cyril Robert, 1863–1930, vol. III
Carter, Air Cdre David William Frederick B.; see Bonham Carter.
Carter, Desmond, died 1939, vol. III
Carter, Col Duncan Campbell, 1856–1942, vol. IV
Carter, Sir Edgar B.; see Bonham-Carter.
Carter, Edward Henry, 1876–1953, vol. V
Carter, Col Ernest Augustus Frederick, 1858–1934, vol. III
Carter, Maj.-Gen. Sir Evan Eyare, 1866–1933, vol. III

Carter, Brig.-Gen. Francis Charles, 1858–1931, vol. III
Carter, Rev. Francis Edward, 1851–1935, vol. III
Carter, Francis Edward, 1886–1977, vol. VII
Carter, Frank W., 1870–1933, vol. III
Carter, Sir Frank Willington, 1865–1945, vol. IV
Carter, Franklin, 1837–1919, vol. II
Carter, Frederick, died 1967, vol. VI
Carter, Sir Frederick Bowker Terrington, 1819–1900, vol. I
Carter, Frederick William, 1870–1952, vol. V
Carter, Sir George John, 1860–1922, vol. II
Carter, George Stuart, 1893–1969, vol. VI
Carter, Sir Gerald Francis, 1881–1959, vol. V
Carter, Sir Gilbert Thomas G.; see Gilbert-Carter.
Carter, Lt-Col Godfrey Lambert, 1868–1932, vol. III
Carter, Lt-Col Sir Gordon, 1853–1941, vol. IV
Carter, Col Harry Molyneux, 1850–1914, vol. I
Carter, Rev. Henry, 1874–1951, vol. V
Carter, Rev. Henry Child, 1875–1954, vol. V
Carter, Captain Herbert Augustine, 1874–1916, vol. II
Carter, Herbert James, 1858–1940, vol. III (A), vol. IV
Carter, Hester Marion, 1867–1944, vol. IV
Carter, Howard, 1873–1939, vol. III
Carter, Hugh Hoyles, died 1919, vol. II
Carter, Humphrey G.; see Gilbert-Carter.
Carter, Huntly, died 1942, vol. IV
Carter, Ian Malcolm B.; see Bonham-Carter.
Carter, Rev. John, 1861–1944, vol. IV
Carter, John Corrie, 1839–1927, vol. II
Carter, Lt-Col John Fillis Carré, 1882–1944, vol. IV
Carter, John Hilton, died 1926, vol. II
Carter, John Ridgely, 1865–1944, vol. IV
Carter, Maj.-Gen. Sir John Thomas, 1855–1939, vol. III
Carter, John Waynflete, 1905–1975, vol. VII
Carter, Sir Maurice B.; see Bonham-Carter.
Carter, Sir Morris; see Carter, Sir W. M.
Carter, Norman St Clair, 1875–1963, vol. VI
Carter, Octavius Cyril, 1893–1964, vol. VI
Carter, Reginald, 1868–1936, vol. III
Carter, Rei Alfred Deakin, 1856–1938, vol. III
Carter, Sir (Richard Henry) Archibald, 1887–1958, vol. V
Carter, Robert Brudenell, 1828–1918, vol. II
Carter, Lt-Col Robert Markham, 1875–1961, vol. VI
Carter, Adm. Sir Stuart Sumner B.; see Bonham-Carter.
Carter, Hon. Thomas Fortescue, 1855–1945, vol. IV
Carter, Vivian, 1878–1956, vol. V
Carter, W. Horsfall, 1900–1976, vol. VII
Carter, Walter, 1883–1964, vol. VI
Carter, Walter, 1873–1975, vol. VII
Carter, Wilfred George, died 1969, vol. VI
Carter, William, 1836–1913, vol. I
Carter, Sir William, 1848–1932, vol. III
Carter, William, died 1932, vol. III
Carter, William, 1867–1940, vol. III
Carter, William Edward, 1885–1965, vol. VI
Carter, Col William Graydon, 1857–1938, vol. III

Carter, William Henry, 1868–1944, vol. IV
Carter, Most Rev. William Marlborough, 1850–1941, vol. IV
Carter, Sir (William) Morris, 1873–1960, vol. V
Carter-Campbell, Col George Tupper Campbell, 1869–1921, vol. II
Carter-Cotton, Francis, 1847–1919, vol. II
Carteret, Captain Charles Edward M. de; see Malet de Carteret.
Carteret, Lt-Col E. C. M. de; see Malet de Carteret.
Carteret, Reginald M. de; see Malet de Carteret.
Carthew, Lt-Col Thomas Walter Colby, 1880–1955, vol. V
Carthew-Yorstoun, Brig.-Gen. Archibald Morden, 1855–1929, vol. III
Cartier De Marchienne, Baron de, 1871–1946, vol. IV
Cartland, J. Ronald H., 1907–1940, vol. III
Cartland, Major John Howard, 1849–1940, vol. III
Cartledge, Jack Pickering, 1900–1966, vol. VI
Cartmel, Lt-Col Alfred Edward, 1893–1974, vol. VII
Cartmel-Robinson, Sir Harold Francis, 1889–1957, vol. V
Cartmell, Sir Harry, died 1923, vol. II
Cartmell, James Austen-, 1862–1921, vol. II
Carton, Richard Claude, 1856–1928, vol. II
Carton, Richard Paul, 1836–1907, vol. I
Carton, Ronald Lewis, 1888–1960, vol. V
Carton de Wiart, Lt-Gen. Sir Adrian, 1880–1963, vol. VI
Carton de Wiart, Count Edmund, 1876–1959, vol. VI (A1)
Carton de Wiart, Comte Henry, 1869–1951, vol. V
Carton de Wiart, Léon Constant Ghislain, 1854–1915, vol. I
Carton de Wiart, Rt Rev. Mgr Maurice E., 1872–1935, vol. III
Cartwright, Albert, 1868–1956, vol. V
Cartwright, (Aubrey) Ralph Thomas, 1880–1936, vol. III
Cartwright, Beatrice, died 1947, vol. IV
Cartwright, Charles Frederic, 1846–1929, vol. III
Cartwright, Sir Charles Henry, 1865–1959, vol. V
Cartwright, Col Charles Marling, 1862–1946, vol. IV
Cartwright, Sir Chauncy, 1853–1933, vol. III
Cartwright, Rt Hon. Sir Fairfax Leighton, 1857–1928, vol. II
Cartwright, Lt-Col Francis Lennox, 1874–1957, vol. V
Cartwright, Brig.-Gen. Garnier Norton, 1868–1924, vol. II
Cartwright, Brig.-Gen. George Strachan, 1866–1959, vol. V
Cartwright, Col Henry Antrobus, 1887–1957, vol. V
Cartwright, Lt-Col Henry Aubrey, 1858–1945, vol. IV
Cartwright, Sir Henry Edmund, 1821–1899, vol. I
Cartwright, J. R., died 1919, vol. II
Cartwright, Rev. Canon James Lawrence, 1889–1978, vol. VII
Cartwright, Lt-Col John Rogers, 1882–1942, vol. IV
Cartwright, Julia; see Ady, J.

Cartwright, Ralph Thomas; see Cartwright, A. R. T.
Cartwright, Rt Hon. Sir Richard John, 1835–1912, vol. I
Cartwright, Lt-Col Robert, 1860–1942, vol. IV
Cartwright, Thomas Robert Brook Leslie-Melville, 1830–1921, vol. II
Cartwright, Sir William Bramwell, 1876–1958, vol. V
Cartwright, William Cornwallis, 1826–1915, vol. I (A)
Cartwright-Taylor, Gen. Sir Malcolm Cartwright, 1911–1969, vol. VI
Caruana, Col Alfred Joseph, 1865–1953, vol. V
Caruana, Most Rev. Maurus, 1867–1943, vol. IV
Carus, Dr Paul, 1852–1919, vol. II
Carus-Wilson, Mrs C. Ashley, (Mary Louisa Georgina), died 1935, vol. III
Carus-Wilson, Charles Ashley, 1860–1942, vol. IV
Carus-Wilson, Eleanora Mary, 1897–1977, vol. VII
Caruso, Enrico, 1873–1921, vol. II
Carvell, John Eric Maclean, 1894–1978, vol. VII
Carver, Rev. Alfred James, 1826–1909, vol. I
Carver, David Dove, 1903–1974, vol. VII
Carver, Captain Edmund Clifton, 1873–1942, vol. IV
Carver, Rev. George Albert, 1862–1930, vol. III
Carver, Sir Stanley Roy, 1897–1967, vol. VI
Carver, Sydney Ralph Pitts, died 1940, vol. III
Carver, Thomas Gilbert, 1848–1906, vol. I
Carver, Col William Henton, 1868–1961, vol. VI
Carvill, Patrick George Hamilton, 1839–1924, vol. II
Carwardine, Thomas, died 1947, vol. IV
Cary, (Arthur) Joyce (Lunel), 1888–1957, vol. V
Cary, Sir (Arthur Lucius) Michael, 1917–1976, vol. VII
Cary, Joyce; see Cary, A. J. L.
Cary, Max, 1881–1958, vol. V
Cary, Sir Michael; see Cary, Sir A. L. M.
Cary, Hon. Philip Plantagenet, 1895–1968, vol. VI
Cary, Sir Robert Archibald, 1st Bt, 1898–1979, vol. VII
Cary, Maj.-Gen. Rupert Tristram Oliver, 1896–1980, vol. VII
Cary-Barnard, Brig.-Gen. Cyril Darcy Vivien, 1876–1933, vol. III
Cary-Elwes, Rt Rev. Dudley Charles, 1868–1932, vol. III
Cary-Elwes, Valentine Dudley Henry; see Elwes.
Caryll, Ivan, died 1921, vol. II
Carysfort, 5th Earl of, 1836–1909, vol. I
Casadesus, Robert, 1899–1972, vol. VII
Casalis, Jeanne de, 1898–1966, vol. VI
Casals, Pablo, 1876–1973, vol. VII
Casartelli, Rt Rev. Louis Charles, 1852–1925, vol. II
Casault, Hon. Sir Louis Napoleon, 1822–1908, vol. I
Case, Col Horace Akroyd, 1879–1968, vol. VI
Case, Robert Hope, 1857–1944, vol. VII
Case, Thomas, 1844–1925, vol. II
Casella, Alfredo, 1883–1947, vol. IV
Casement, Maj.-Gen. Francis, 1881–1967, vol. VI
Casement, Adm. John Moore, 1877–1952, vol. V

Casey, Baron (Life Peer); Richard Gardiner Casey, 1890–1976, vol. VII
Casey, Captain Denis Arthur, 1889–1968, vol. VI
Casey, Hon. James Joseph, 1831–1913, vol. I
Casey, Rt Rev. Patrick, 1873–1940, vol. III
Casey, Thomas Worrall, 1869–1949, vol. IV
Casey, Most Rev. Timothy, 1862–1931, vol. III
Casey, William Francis, 1884–1957, vol. V
Casgrain, Alexandre Chase-, 1879–1941, vol. IV
Casgrain, Hon. Col Hon. Joseph Philippe Baby-, born 1856, vol. III
Casgrain, Rev. Philippe Henri Duperron, 1864–1942, vol. IV
Casgrain, Rt Hon. Thomas Chase, 1852–1916, vol. II
Cash, J. Theodore, 1854–1936, vol. III
Cash, Col Sir Reginald John, 1892–1959, vol. V
Cash, Sir Thomas James, 1888–1978, vol. VII
Cash, Sir William, 1891–1964, vol. VI
Cash, Rt Rev. William Wilson, 1880–1955, vol. V
Cash-Reed, Bellamy Alexander, 1888–1965, vol. VI
Cashin, Hon. Sir Michael Patrick, 1864–1926, vol. II
Cashman, Rt Rev. David John, 1912–1971, vol. VII
Cashmore, Herbert Maurice, 1882–1972, vol. VII
Casimir-Perier, Jean Paul Pierre, 1847–1907, vol. I
Caslon, Vice-Adm. Clifford, 1896–1973, vol. VII
Caspersz, Charles P., 1855–1951, vol. V
Cass, Major Charles Herbert Davis, 1858–1929, vol. III
Cass, Brig. Edward Earnshaw Eden, 1898–1968, vol. VI
Cass, Rev. Gilbert Henning, 1873–1931, vol. III
Cass, Sir John, 1832–1898, vol. I
Cass, Col Walter Edmund Hutchinson, 1876–1931, vol. III
Cassal, Col Charles Edward, 1858–1921, vol. II
Cassar De Sain, 9th Marquess, 1880–1927, vol. II
Cassar De Sain, 10th Marquess, 1907–1958, vol. V
Cassatt, Alexander Johnston, 1839–1906, vol. I
Cassel, Rt Hon. Sir Ernest, 1852–1921, vol. II
Cassel, Rt Hon. Sir Felix, 1st Bt, 1869–1953, vol. V
Cassel, Sir Francis Edward, 2nd Bt, 1912–1969, vol. VI
Cassel, Gustav, 1866–1945, vol. IV
Cassells, Alexander, 1883–1967, vol. VI
Cassells, Hugh Hutchison, 1886–1950, vol. IV
Cassells, Thomas, 1902–1944, vol. IV
Cassels, Brig. George Hamilton,1882–1944, vol. IV
Cassels, Brig.-Gen. Gilbert Robert, 1870–1951, vol. V
Cassels, Sir James Dale, 1877–1972, vol. VII
Cassels, Gen. Sir Robert Archibald, 1876–1959, vol. V
Cassels, Hon. Sir Walter, 1845–1923, vol. II
Cassels, Walter Richard, 1826–1907, vol. I
Cassels, Walter Seton, 1873–1932, vol. III
Cassels, Rt Rev. William Wharton, 1858–1925, vol. II
Casserly, Col Gordon, died 1947, vol. IV
Cassia, Francis Joseph Nicholas Paul S.; see Sant-Cassia.
Cassidy, David Mackay, 1846–1936, vol. III
Cassidy, Sir Jack Evelyn, 1894–1975, vol. VII

Cassidy, John, 1860–1939, vol. III
Cassidy, Sir Maurice Alan, 1880–1949, vol. IV
Cassie, William Riach, 1861–1908, vol. I
Cassin, René, 1887–1976, vol. VII
Casson, Elizabeth, 1881–1954, vol. V
Casson, Herbert Alexander, 1867–1952, vol. V
Casson, Brig.-Gen. Hugh Gilbert, 1866–1951, vol. V
Casson, Rev. Canon John, 1869–1955, vol. V
Casson, Sir Lewis, 1875–1969, vol. VI
Casson, Stanley, 1889–1944, vol. IV
Casson, Dame Sybil; see Thorndike, Dame Sybil.
Casswell, Joshua David, died 1963, vol. VI
Castaing, Jacques C. de; see Chastenet de Castaing.
Castéja, Marie Emmanuel Alvar de Biaudos-Scarisbrick, the Marquis de, 1849–1911, vol. I
Castellani, Marchese Count Aldo, 1877–1971, vol. VII
Castenskiold, H. Grevenkop, 1862–1921, vol. II
Castillejo, José, 1877–1945, vol. IV
Castle, Baron (Life Peer); Edward Cyril Castle, 1907–1979, vol. VII
Castle, Agnes, died 1922, vol. II
Castle, Edgar Bradshaw, 1897–1973, vol. VII
Castle, Egerton, 1858–1920, vol. II
Castle, Marcellus Purnell, 1849–1917, vol. II
Castle, Lt-Col Reginald Wingfield, 1874–1952, vol. V
Castle, Walter Frances Raphael, 1892–1926, vol. II
Castle, William, 1833–1911, vol. I
Castle Stewart (styled Castlestewart), 5th Earl, 1837–1914, vol. I
Castle Stewart (styled Castlestewart), 6th Earl, 1841–1921, vol. II
Castle Stewart, 7th Earl, 1889–1961, vol. VI
Castlemaine, 5th Baron, 1863–1937, vol. III
Castlemaine, 6th Baron, 1864–1954, vol. V
Castlemaine, 7th Baron, 1904–1973, vol. VII
Castleman-Smith, Col Edward Castleman, died 1943, vol. IV
Castletown, 2nd Baron, 1849–1937, vol. III
Catarinich, John, 1882–1974, vol. VII
Catchpool, Egerton St John Pettifor, 1890–1971, vol. VII
Cater, Sir (Alexander) Norman (Ley), 1880–1957, vol. V
Cater, Sir John James, 1885–1962, vol. VI
Cater, Sir Norman; see Cater, Sir A. N. L.
Cates, Arthur, 1829–1901, vol. I
Cathcart, 3rd Earl, 1828–1905, vol. I
Cathcart, 4th Earl, 1856–1911, vol. I
Cathcart, 5th Earl, 1862–1927, vol. II
Cathcart, Col Hon. Augustus Murray, 1830–1914, vol. I
Cathcart, Charles Walker, 1853–1932, vol. III
Cathcart, Edward Provan, 1877–1954, vol. V
Cathcart, George Clark, died 1951, vol. V
Cathcart, Sir Reginald Archibald Edward, 6th Bt, 1838–1916, vol. II
Cathcart, Robert, died 1907, vol. I
Cathcart, William Taylor, 1859–1940, vol. III
Cathels, Rt Rev. David, 1853–1925, vol. II
Cather, Willa Sibert, 1876–1947, vol. IV
Cathery, Edmund, 1852–1929, vol. III

Catlin, Sir George Edward Gordon, 1896–1979, vol. VII
Catling, Thomas, 1838–1920, vol. II
Catlow, Sir John William, died 1947, vol. IV
Catnach, Agnes, 1891–1979, vol. VII
Caton, Richard, died 1926, vol. II
Caton-Jones, Col Frederick William, 1860–1944, vol. IV
Cator, Maj.-Gen. Albemarle Bertie Edward, 1877–1932, vol. III
Cator, Sir Geoffrey Edmund, 1884–1973, vol. VII
Cator, Lt-Col Henry John, 1897–1965, vol. VI
Cator, John, 1862–1944, vol. IV
Cator, Lt-Col Philip James, 1901–1944, vol. IV
Cator, Sir Ralph Bertie Peter, 1861–1945, vol. IV
Cator, Rev. William Lumley Bartie, died 1918, vol. II
Catroux, Gén. Georges, 1877–1969, vol. VI
Cattanach, William, 1863–1932, vol. III
Catterall, Arthur, 1884–1943, vol. IV
Catterall, Sir Robert, 1880–1962, vol. VI
Catterns, Basil Gage, 1886–1969, vol. VI
Catterson-Smith, John Keats, 1882–1945, vol. IV
Cattley, M. H., died 1958, vol. V
Catto, 1st Baron, 1879–1959, vol. V
Catton, Bruce, 1899–1978, vol. VII
Catty, Col Thomas Claude, 1879–1967, vol. VI
Caulcutt, Sir John, 1876–1943, vol. IV
Caulfeild, Major Algernon Montgomerie, 1858–1915, vol. I (A)
Caulfeild, Algernon Thomas St George, 1869–1933, vol. III
Caulfeild, Brig.-Gen. Charles Trevor, 1863–1947, vol. IV
Caulfeild, Francis St George, 1852–1933, vol. III
Caulfeild, Vice-Adm. Francis Wade, 1872–1947, vol. IV
Caulfeild, Brig.-Gen. Francis William John, 1859–1938, vol. III
Caulfeild, Col Gordon Napier, 1862–1922, vol. II
Caulfeild, Brig.-Gen. James Edward Wilmot Smyth, 1850–1925, vol. II
Caulfeild, Captain James Montgomerie, 1855–1946, vol. IV
Caulfield, Sidney Burgoyne Kitchener, died 1964, vol. VI
Caullery, Maurice, 1868–1958, vol. V
Caulton, Rt Rev. Sidney Gething, 1895–1976, vol. VII
Caumont, Rt Rev. Mgr Fortunatus Henry, 1871–1930, vol. III
Caunt, Ven. Frederic, died 1933, vol. III
Caunter, Brig.-Gen. James Eales, 1859–1937, vol. III
Causer, William Sidney, died 1958, vol. V
Causton, Rev. Francis Jervoise, died 1932, vol. III
Cautley, 1st Baron, 1863–1946, vol. IV
Cautley, Edmund, died 1944, vol. IV
Cauty, Sir Arthur Belcher, 1870–1954, vol. V
Cavalieri, Lina, 1874–1944, vol. IV
Cavan, 9th Earl of, 1839–1900, vol. I
Cavan, 10th Earl of, 1865–1946, vol. IV
Cavan, 11th Earl of, 1878–1950, vol. IV
Cavanagh, Captain John Duncan Macaulay, 1881–1957, vol. V

Cavaye, Maj.-Gen. William Frederick, died 1926, vol. II
Cave, 1st Viscount, 1856–1928, vol. II
Cave, Countess; (Anne), died 1938, vol. III
Cave, Rev. Alfred, 1847–1900, vol. I
Cave, Arthur Wilson, died 1930, vol. III
Cave, Sir Basil Shillito, 1865–1931, vol. III
Cave, Sir Charles Daniel, 1st Bt (cr 1896), 1832–1922, vol. II
Cave, Sir Charles Henry, 2nd Bt (cr 1896), 1861–1932, vol. III
Cave, Charles John Philip, 1871–1950, vol. IV
Cave, Edmund, 1859–1946, vol. IV
Cave, Sir Edward Charles, 3rd Bt (cr 1896), 1893–1946, vol. IV
Cave, Edward Watkins, died 1948, vol. IV
Cave, Captain George Ellis, 1867–1938, vol. III
Cave, Air Vice-Marshal Henry Meyrick C.-B.; see Cave-Browne-Cave.
Cave, Adm. John Halliday, 1827–1913, vol. I
Cave, Hon. Sir Lewis William, 1832–1897, vol. I
Cave, Sir Mylles Cave-Browne-, 11th Bt (cr1641), 1822–1907, vol. I
Cave, Rev. Sydney, 1883–1953, vol. V
Cave, Sir Thomas C.-B.; see Cave-Browne-Cave.
Cave, Wing Comdr Thomas Reginald C.-B.; see Cave-Browne-Cave.
Cave, Sir Thomas Sturmy, 1846–1936, vol. III
Cave, Walter F., died 1939, vol. III
Cave-Browne, Edward Raban, 1835–1907, vol. I
Cave-Browne, Maj.-Gen. William, 1884–1967, vol. VI
Cave-Browne-Cave, Sir Clement Charles, 15th Bt (cr 1641), 1896–1945, vol. IV
Cave-Browne-Cave, Rev. Sir Genille, 12th Bt (cr 1641), 1869–1929, vol. III
Cave-Browne-Cave, Air Vice-Marshal Henry Meyrick, 1887–1965, vol. VI
Cave-Browne-Cave, Sir Mylles; see Cave.
Cave-Browne-Cave, Captain Sir Reginald Ambrose, 13th Bt (cr 1641), 1860–1930, vol. III
Cave-Browne-Cave, Sir Rowland Henry, 14th Bt (cr 1641), 1865–1943, vol. IV
Cave-Browne-Cave, Sir Thomas, 1835–1924, vol. II
Cave-Browne-Cave, Wing Comdr Thomas Reginald, 1885–1969, vol. VI
Caven, Rev. Principal, 1830–1904, vol. I
Caven, Robert Martin, 1870–1934, vol. III
Cavenagh, Prof. Francis Alexander, 1884–1946, vol. IV
Cavendish; see Jones, Henry.
Cavendish, Brig.-Gen. Alfred Edward John, 1859–1943, vol. IV
Cavendish, Lord Charles A. F., 1905–1944, vol. IV
Cavendish, Major Frederick George, 1891–1936, vol. III
Cavendish, Brig.-Gen. Frederick William Lawrence Sheppard Hart, 1878–1931, vol. III
Cavendish, Captain Lord John Spencer, 1875–1914, vol. I
Cavendish, Col Ralph Henry Voltelin, 1887–1968, vol. VI
Cavendish, Richard Charles Alexander, 1885–1941, vol. IV

Cavendish, Rt Hon. Lord Richard Frederick, 1871–1946, vol. IV
Cavendish, Brig.-Gen. Hon. William Edwin, 1862–1931, vol. III
Cavendish-Acheson, Hon. Patrick George Edward; see Acheson.
Cavendish-Bentinck, Lt-Col Lord Charles, 1868–1956, vol. V
Cavendish-Bentinck, Frederick; see Bentinck.
Cavendish-Bentinck, Lord William Augustus; see Bentinck.
Cavill, William Victor, died 1959, vol. V
Caw, Sir James Lewis, 1864–1950, vol. IV
Cawadias, Alexander Pocnagioti, died 1971, vol. VII
Cawdor, 2nd Earl, 1817–1898, vol. I
Cawdor, 3rd Earl, 1847–1911, vol. I
Cawdor, 4th Earl, 1870–1914, vol. I
Cawdor, 5th Earl, 1900–1970, vol. VI
Cawley, 1st Baron, 1850–1937, vol. III
Cawley, 2nd Baron, 1877–1954, vol. V
Cawley, Rev. Frederick, 1884–1978, vol. VII
Cawley, George, 1848–1927, vol. II
Cawley, Harold Thomas, 1878–1915, vol. I (A)
Cawley, Hon. Oswald, 1882–1918, vol. II
Cawood, Herbert Harry, 1890–1957, vol. V
Cawood, Sir Walter, 1907–1967, vol. VI
Cawston, Sir John Westerman, 1859–1927, vol. II
Cawthorn, Maj.-Gen. Sir Walter Joseph, 1896–1970, vol. VI (AII)
Cawthorne, Sir Terence Edward, 1902–1970, vol. VI
Cawthra-Elliot, Maj.-Gen. Harry Macintire, 1867–1949, vol. IV
Cay, Armistead, 1872–1957, vol. V
Cayley, Hon. Maj.-Gen. Douglas Edward, 1870–1951, vol. V
Cayley, Adm. George Cuthbert, 1866–1944, vol. IV
Cayley, Sir George Everard Arthur, 9th Bt, 1861–1917, vol. II
Cayley, Captain Harry Francis, 1873–1954, vol. V
Cayley, Dep. Surg.-Gen. Henry, 1834–1904, vol. I
Cayley, Sir Kenelm Henry Ernest, 10th Bt, 1896–1967, vol. VI
Cayley, Sir Richard, 1833–1908, vol. I
Cayley, Maj.-Gen. Sir Walter de Sausmarez, 1863–1952, vol. V
Cayley, William, 1836–1916, vol. II
Cayley-Robinson, Frederic; see Robinson.
Cayzer, Sir August Bernard Tellefsen, 1st Bt (cr 1921), 1876–1943, vol. IV
Cayzer, Sir Charles, 1st Bt (cr 1904), 1843–1916, vol. II
Cayzer, Sir Charles William, 2nd Bt (cr 1904), 1869–1917, vol. II
Cayzer, Sir Charles William, 3rd Bt (cr 1904), 1896–1940, vol. III
Cayzer, Major Harold Stanley, 1882–1948, vol. IV
Cayzer, Major John Sanders, 1871–1908, vol. I
Cayzer, Sir Nigel John, 4th Bt (cr 1904), 1920–1943, vol. IV
Cazalet, Edward Alexander, died 1923, vol. II
Cazalet, Peter Victor Ferdinand, 1907–1973, vol. VII
Cazalet, Lt-Col Victor Alexander, 1896–1943, vol. IV

Cazalet, William Marshall, 1865–1932, vol. III
Cazamian, Louis, 1877–1965, vol. VI
Cazenove, Brig. Arnold de Lerisson, died 1969, vol. VI
Cazenove, Philip Henry de Lerisson, 1901–1978, vol. VII
Ceadel, Eric Bertrand, 1921–1979, vol. VII
Cecil of Chelwood, 1st Viscount, 1864–1958, vol. V
Cecil, Algernon, 1879–1953, vol. V
Cecil, Lord Arthur, 1851–1913, vol. I
Cecil, Ean Francis, 1880–1942, vol. IV
Cecil, Col Lord Edward Herbert, 1867–1918, vol. II
Cecil, Lord Eustace Brownlow Henry, 1834–1921, vol. II
Cecil, Henry; see Leon, H. C.
Cecil, Lord John Pakenham Joicey-, 1867–1942, vol. IV
Cecil, Rev. Philip Henry, 1918–1977, vol. VII
Cecil, Victor Alexander G.; see Gascoyne-Cecil.
Cecil, Lord William, 1854–1943, vol. IV
Cecil, Hon. William Amherst, 1886–1914, vol. I
Cecil, Rt Rev. Lord William Gascoyne-, 1863–1936, vol. III
Cecil-Williams, Sir John Lias Cecil, 1892–1964, vol. VI
Cederström, Baron Rolf, died 1947, vol. IV
Cederström, Baroness Rolf; see Patti, Mme Adelina.
Céitinn, Seán; see Keating, John.
Cellier, Jacobus Stephanus, born 1878, vol. III
Cemlyn-Jones, Sir E. Wynne, 1888–1966, vol. VI
Cenez, Rt Rev. Jules Joseph, 1865–1944, vol. IV
Centlivres, Hon. Albert van de Sandt, 1887–1966, vol. VI
Ceram, C. W.; see Marek, K. W.
Cerf, Bennett, 1898–1971, vol. VII
Cerny, Jaroslav, 1898–1970, vol. VI
Cerretti, His Eminence Cardinal Bonaventura, 1872–1933, vol. III
Cerutty, Charles John, 1870–1941, vol. IV
Cervera, Adm. Pascual Cervera y Topete, 1839–1909, vol. I
Chadburn, George Haworthe, 1870–1950, vol. IV
Chadburn, Maud Mary, died 1957, vol. V
Chads, Adm. Sir Henry, 1819–1906, vol. I
Chads, Maj.-Gen. William John, 1830–1915, vol. I (A)
Chadwell, Rt Rev. Arthur Ernest, 1892–1967, vol. VI
Chadwick, Brig. Cecil Arthur Harrop, 1901–1970, vol. VI
Chadwick, Rev. Charles Egerton, 1880–1958, vol. V
Chadwick, Sir David Thomas, 1876–1954, vol. V
Chadwick, Edward Marion, 1840–1921, vol. II
Chadwick, Rt Rev. George Alexander, 1840–1923, vol. II
Chadwick, Hector Munro, 1870–1947, vol. IV
Chadwick, Sir James, 1891–1974, vol. VII
Chadwick, John Courtenay Chasman, 1846–1932, vol. III
Chadwick, Nora Kershaw, 1891–1972, vol. VII
Chadwick, Osbert, 1844–1913, vol. I
Chadwick, Rev. Canon Robert, died 1927, vol. II
Chadwick, Sir Robert B.; see Burton-Chadwick.

Chadwick, Roy, 1893–1947, vol. IV
Chadwick, Rev. Samuel, 1860–1932, vol. III
Chadwick, Sir Thomas, 1888–1969, vol. VI
Chadwick, Rev. William Edward, died 1934, vol. III
Chadwyck-Healey, Sir Charles Edward Heley, 1st Bt, 1845–1919, vol. II
Chadwyck-Healey, Sir Edward Randal, 3rd Bt, 1898–1979, vol. VII
Chadwyck-Healey, Sir Gerald Edward, 2nd Bt, 1873–1955, vol. V
Chadwyck-Healey, Oliver Nowell, 1886–1960, vol. V
Chaffey, Hon. Frank A., 1888–1940, vol. III
Chaffey, Col Ralph Anderson, 1856–1925, vol. II
Chain, Sir Ernst Boris, 1906–1979, vol. VII
Chaine, Lt-Col William, 1838–1916, vol. II
Chaliapin, Fedor Ivanovitch, 1873–1938, vol. III
Chalkley, Alfred Philip, 1886–1959, vol. V
Chalkley, Sir (Harry) Owen, 1882–1958, vol. V
Chalkley, Sir Owen; see Chalkley, Sir H. O.
Challacombe, Rev. William Allen, died 1951, vol. V
Challe, Général d'Armée Aérienne Maurice, 1905–1979, vol. VII
Challen, Charles, 1894–1960, vol. V
Challenor, Brig.-Gen. Edward Lacy, 1873–1935, vol. III
Challinor, William Francis, 1882–1967, vol. VI
Challis, John Humphrey Thornton, 1896–1958, vol. V
Chalmer, Col Francis George, 1884–1951, vol. V
Chalmer, Col Reginald, 1844–1911, vol. I
Chalmers, 1st Baron, 1858–1938, vol. III
Chalmers, Albert John, 1870–1920, vol. II
Chalmers, Sir Alfred John George, 1845–1937, vol. III
Chalmers, Archibald Kerr, 1856–1942, vol. IV
Chalmers, Archibald MacDonald, 1883–1977, vol. VII
Chalmers, Arthur Morison, 1862–1949, vol. IV
Chalmers, Sir Charles, 1861–1924, vol. II
Chalmers, Sir David Patrick, died 1899, vol. I
Chalmers, Lt-Col Frederick Roydon, 1881–1943, vol. IV
Chalmers, Sir Mackenzie Dalzell, 1847–1927, vol. II
Chalmers, P. MacGregor, 1859–1922, vol. II
Chalmers, Patrick Reginald, died 1942, vol. IV
Chalmers, Rev. Reginald, 1893–1974, vol. VII
Chalmers, Thomas Andrew, died 1944, vol. IV
Chalmers, Rear-Adm. William Scott, 1888–1971, vol. VII
Chamba, Raja of, 1869–1919, vol. II
Chamberlain, Arthur, died 1913, vol. I
Chamberlain, Rt Hon. (Arthur) Neville, 1869–1940, vol. III
Chamberlain, Rt Hon. Sir Austen; see Chamberlain, Rt Hon. Sir J. A.
Chamberlain, Basil Hall, 1850–1935, vol. III
Chamberlain, Gen. Sir Crawford Trotter, 1821–1902, vol. I
Chamberlain, Digby, 1896–1962, vol. VI
Chamberlain, Fernley John, 1879–1958, vol. V
Chamberlain, Francis Walter, 1892–1970, vol. VI
Chamberlain, Rt Rev. (Frank) Noel, 1900–1975, vol. VII

Chamberlain, Sir Henry Hamilton Erroll, 4th Bt, 1857–1936, vol. III
Chamberlain, Henry Richardson, 1859–1911, vol. I
Chamberlain, Sir Henry Wilmot, 5th Bt, 1899–1980, vol. VII (AII)
Chamberlain, Houston Stewart, 1855–1927, vol. II
Chamberlain, Ivy Muriel, (Lady Chamberlain), died 1941, vol. IV
Chamberlain, Rt Hon. Joseph, 1836–1914, vol. I
Chamberlain, Rt Hon. Sir (Joseph) Austen, 1863–1937, vol. III
Chamberlain, Rt Hon. Neville; see Chamberlain, Rt Hon. A. N.
Chamberlain, Field-Marshal Sir Nevile Bowles, 1820–1902, vol. I
Chamberlain, Col Sir Neville Francis Fitzgerald, 1856–1944, vol. IV
Chamberlain, Rt Rev. Noel; see Chamberlain, Rt Rev. F. N.
Chamberlain, Ven. Thomas, born 1854, vol. II
Chamberlain, Sir William, 1877–1944, vol. IV
Chamberlayne, Air Cdre Paul Richard Tankerville James Michael Isidore Camille, 1898–1972, vol. VII
Chamberlayne, Tankerville, 1843–1924, vol. II
Chamberlayne, Gen. William John, 1821–1910, vol. I
Chamberlin, Arthur George, died 1925, vol. II
Chamberlin, Edson J., died 1924, vol. II
Chamberlin, Frederick, 1870–1943, vol. IV
Chamberlin, Sir George, 1846–1928, vol. II
Chamberlin, Sir Michael, 1891–1972, vol. VII
Chamberlin, Peter Hugh Girard, 1919–1978, vol. VII
Chambers, Rev. Arthur, died 1918, vol. II
Chambers, Adm. Bertram Mordaunt, 1866–1945, vol. IV
Chambers, Maj.-Gen. Brooke Rynd, 1834–1915, vol. I
Chambers, Charles Edward Stuart, 1859–1936, vol. III
Chambers, Charles Haddon, 1860–1921, vol. II
Chambers, Sir Cornelius, 1862–1941, vol. IV
Chambers, Sir Edmund Kerchever, 1866–1954, vol. V
Chambers, Rev. Frederick Charles, 1860–1933, vol. III
Chambers, Rt Rev. George Alexander, died 1963, vol. VI
Chambers, George Frederick, 1841–1915, vol. I
Chambers, Sir George Henry, 1816–1903, vol. I
Chambers, George Lawson, 1852–1934, vol. III
Chambers, Helen, died 1935, vol. III
Chambers, James, died 1917, vol. II
Chambers, John Ferguson, 1894–1941, vol. IV
Chambers, Major John Reginald, 1882–1953, vol. V
Chambers, Jonathan David, 1898–1970, vol. VI
Chambers, Surg. Vice-Adm. Sir Joseph, 1864–1935, vol. III
Chambers, Lt-Col Joseph Charles, 1857–1940, vol. III (A), vol. IV
Chambers, Julius, 1850–1920, vol. II
Chambers, Lloyd Eld, 1863–1930, vol. III
Chambers, Sir Newman Pitts-, died 1922, vol. II

Chambers, Raymond Wilson, 1874–1942, vol. IV
Chambers, Rev. Robert Halley, 1853–1934, vol. III
Chambers, Maj.-Gen. Robert Macdonald, 1833–1924, vol. II
Chambers, Robert Sharp Borgnis H.; see Hammond-Chambers.
Chambers, Robert William, 1865–1933, vol. III
Chambers, Sir Theodore Gervase, 1871–1957, vol. V
Chamier, Sir Edward Maynard Des Champs, 1866–1945, vol. IV
Chamier, Maj.-Gen. Francis Edward Archibald, 1833–1923, vol. II
Chamier, Brig.-Gen. George Daniel, 1860–1920, vol. II
Chamier, Air Cdre Sir John Adrian, 1883–1974, vol. VII
Chamier, Lt-Col Richard Outram, 1888–1980, vol. VII
Chamier, Lt-Gen. Stephen, 1834–1910, vol. I
Chaminade, Cécile, died 1944, vol. IV
Chamney, Lt-Col Henry, 1861–1947, vol. IV
Champain, Brig.-Gen. Hugh Frederick B.; see Bateman-Champain.
Champain, Rt Rev. John Norman B.; see Bateman-Champain.
Champion, Arthur Mortimer, 1885–1950, vol. IV
Champion, Frank Clive, 1907–1976, vol. VII
Champion, Sir Harry George, 1891–1979, vol. VII
Champion, Henry Hyde, 1859–1928, vol. II
Champion, Captain John Pelham, 1883–1955, vol. V
Champion, Pierre, 1880–1942, vol. IV
Champion de Crespigny, Captain Claude, 1873–1910, vol. I
Champion de Crespigny, Sir Claude, 4th Bt, 1847–1935, vol. III
Champion de Crespigny, Brig.-Gen. Sir Claude Raul, 5th Bt, 1878–1941, vol. IV
Champion-de Crespigny Col Sir (Constantine) Trent, 1882–1952, vol. V
Champion de Crespigny, Comdr Sir Frederick Philip, 7th Bt, 1884–1947, vol. IV
Champion de Crespigny, Lt-Col George Harrison, 1863–1945, vol. IV
Champion de Crespigny, Sir Henry, 6th Bt, 1882–1946, vol. IV
Champion de Crespigny, Air Vice-Marshal Hugh Vivian, 1897–1969, vol. VI
Champion de Crespigny, Rose, (Mrs Philip Champion de Crespigny), died 1935, vol. III
Champion-de Crespigny, Col Sir Trent; see Champion-de Crespigny, Col Sir C. T.
Champion de Crespigny, Sir Vivian Tyrell, 8th Bt, 1907–1952, vol. V
Champness, Captain Charles Henry, 1889–1963, vol. VI
Champness, Henry Robert, 1852–1923, vol. II
Champness, Major Sir William Henry, 1873–1956, vol. V
Champneys, Basil, 1842–1935, vol. III
Champneys, Sir Francis Henry, 1848–1930, vol. III
Champneys, Rev. Francis Weldon, died 1929, vol. III

Champneys, Captain Sir Weldon D.; see Dalrymple-Champneys.
Champtaloup, Sydney Taylor, 1880–1921, vol. II
Chance, Sir Arthur, 1859–1928, vol. II
Chance, Frederick Selby, 1886–1946, vol. IV
Chance, Sir Frederick William, 1852–1932, vol. III
Chance, George Ferguson, 1854–1933, vol. III
Chance, James Frederick, 1856–1938, vol. III
Chance, Sir James Timmins, 1st Bt, 1814–1902, vol. I
Chance, Kenneth Macomb, 1879–1966, vol. VI
Chance, Kenneth Miles, 1893–1980, vol. VII
Chance, Miles; see Chance, K. M.
Chance, Brig.-Gen. Oswald Kesteven, 1880–1935, vol. III
Chance, Percival Vincent, 1888–1970, vol. VI
Chance, Sir Robert Christopher, 1883–1960, vol. V,
Chance, Thomas Williams, 1872–1954, vol. V
Chance, Walter Lucas, 1880–1963, vol. VI
Chance, Sir William, 2nd Bt, 1853–1935, vol. III
Chancellor, Alexander Richard, 1869–1959, vol. V
Chancellor, Edwin Beresford, 1868–1937, vol. III
Chancellor, Henry George, 1863–1945, vol. IV
Chancellor, Lt-Col Sir John Robert, 1870–1952, vol. V
Chand, Masheerud-dowal Rai Bahadur N.; see Nanak Chand.
Chandavarkar, Sir Narayen Ganesh, 1855–1923, vol. II
Chandavarkar, Sir Vithal Narayan, 1887–1959, vol. V
Chandler, Alfred, 1853–1923, vol. II
Chandler, Rt Rev. Arthur, 1860–1939, vol. III
Chandler, Frederick George, died 1942, vol. IV
Chandler, Hon. Sir Gilbert Lawrence, 1903–1974, vol. VII
Chandler, Sir John Beals, 1887–1962, vol. VI
Chandler, Sir John DeLisle, 1889–1967, vol. VI
Chandler, Louise; see Moulton, Mrs.
Chandler, Pretor Whitty, 1858–1941, vol. IV
Chandler, Raymond Thornton, 1888–1959, vol. V
Chandler, Sir William Kellman, 1857–1940, vol. III
Chandos, 1st Viscount, 1893–1972, vol. VII
Chandos, 2nd Viscount, 1920–1980, vol. VII
Chandos-Pole, Brig.-Gen. Harry Anthony, died 1934, vol. III
Chandy, Ven. Jacob, born 1852, vol. III
Chaney, Henry James, 1842–1906, vol. I
Chaney, Maj.-Gen. James E., 1885–1967, vol. VI
Channell, Rt Hon. Sir Arthur Moseley, 1838–1928, vol. II
Channer, Col Bernard, 1846–1916, vol. II
Channer, Frederick Francis Ralph, 1875–1950, vol. IV
Channer, Gen. George Nicholas, 1843–1905, vol. I
Channer, Maj.-Gen. George Osborne De Renzy, 1890–1969, vol. VI
Channing of Wellingborough, 1st Baron, 1841–1926, vol. II
Channing, Edward, 1856–1931, vol. III
Channon, Harold John, 1897–1979, vol. VII
Channon, Sir Henry, 1897–1958, vol. V
Chant, Clarence Augustus, 1865–1956, vol. V

Chant, Mrs Laura Ormiston, 1848–1923, vol. II
Chanter, Hon. John Moore, 1845–1931, vol. III
Chapais, Hon. Sir Thomas, 1858–1946, vol. IV
Chapel, Sir William, 1870–1950, vol. IV (A)
Chapin, Harold, 1886–1915, vol. I (A)
Chapin, Captain Sidney H., 1875–1918, vol. II
Chapleau, Hon. Sir Joseph Adolphe, 1840–1898, vol. I
Chapleau, Samuel Edmour St Onge, 1839–1921, vol. II
Chaplin, 1st Viscount, 1840–1923, vol. II (A)
Chaplin, 2nd Viscount, 1877–1949, vol. IV
Chaplin, Alan Geoffrey Tunstal, 1908–1967, vol. VI
Chaplin, Arnold; see Chaplin, T. H. A.
Chaplin, Sir Charles Spencer, 1889–1977, vol. VII
Chaplin, Sir Drummond Percy; see Chaplin, Sir F. D. P.
Chaplin, Sir (Francis) Drummond Percy, 1866–1933, vol. III
Chaplin, Frederick Leslie, 1905–1977, vol. VII
Chaplin, Sir George Frederick, 1900–1975, vol. VII
Chaplin, Brig.-Gen. James Graham, 1873–1956, vol. V
Chaplin, Col John Worthy, 1840–1920, vol. II
Chaplin, (T. H.) Arnold, 1864–1944, vol. IV
Chaplin, Rev. W. Knight, 1863–1951, vol. V
Chaplin, William Robert, 1888–1974, vol. VII
Chapman, Abel, 1851–1929, vol. III
Chapman, Captain Alexander Colin, 1897–1970, vol. VI
Chapman, Alfred Chaston, 1869–1932, vol. III
Chapman, Allan, 1897–1966, vol. VI
Chapman, Brig.-Gen. Archibald John, 1862–1950, vol. IV
Chapman, Sir Arthur, 1851–1918, vol. II
Chapman, Sir Arthur Wakefield, 1849–1926, vol. II
Chapman, Hon. Sir Austin, 1864–1926, vol. II
Chapman, Sir Benjamin Rupert, 6th Bt, 1865–1914 (this entry was not transferred to Who was Who).
Chapman, Rev. C., 1828–1922, vol. II
Chapman, Cecil Maurice, 1852–1938, vol. III
Chapman, Charles Williams, 1843–1941, vol. IV
Chapman, Rear-Adm. Cuthbert Godfrey, 1862–1931, vol. III
Chapman, David Leonard, 1869–1958, vol. V
Chapman, Col David Phelips, 1855–1939, vol. III
Chapman, Dorothy, 1878–1967, vol. VI
Chapman, Edmund Pelly, 1867–1923, vol. II
Chapman, Edward, died 1906, vol. I
Chapman, Gen. Sir Edward Francis, 1840–1926, vol. II
Chapman, Edward Henry, 1874–1933, vol. III
Chapman, Rev. Edward William, 1841–1919, vol. II
Chapman, Captain Ernest John Collis, 1876–1958, vol. V
Chapman, Fitzroy Tozer, 1880–1976, vol. VII
Chapman, Frank M., 1864–1945, vol. IV
Chapman, Ven. Frank Robert, died 1924, vol. II
Chapman, Col Frederic Hamilton, 1863–1925, vol. II
Chapman, Frederick, 1864–1943, vol. IV
Chapman, Sir Frederick Revans, 1849–1936, vol. III
Chapman, Lt-Col Frederick S.; see Spencer Chapman.

Chapman, Guy Patterson, 1889–1972, vol. VII
Chapman, Maj.-Gen. Hamilton, 1835–1926, vol. II
Chapman, Henry, died 1908, vol. I
Chapman, Sir Henry, died 1947, vol. IV
Chapman, Henry George, 1879–1934, vol. III
Chapman, Rt Rev. Henry Palmer, 1865–1933, vol. III
Chapman, Col Herbert Alexander, 1858–1939, vol. III
Chapman, Mrs Hester Wolferstan, (Mrs R. L. Griffin), 1899–1976, vol. VII
Chapman, Air Vice-Marshal Hubert Huntlea, 1910–1972, vol. VII
Chapman, Rev. Hugh Boswell, died 1933, vol. III
Chapman, Rev. James, 1849–1913, vol. I
Chapman, James Ernest, died 1941, vol. IV
Chapman, Rt Rev. John; see Chapman, Rt Rev. H. P.
Chapman, Maj.-Gen. John Austin, 1896–1963, vol. VI
Chapman, Brig.-Gen. Lawrence Joseph, 1867–1930, vol. III
Chapman, Lewis, 1890–1963, vol. VI
Chapman, Martin, 1846–1924, vol. II
Chapman, Sir Montagu Richard, 5th Bt (cr 1782), 1853–1907, vol. I
Chapman, Mrs Murray, (Olive Chapman), died 1977, vol. VII
Chapman, Olive; see Chapman, Mrs Murray.
Chapman, Oscar Littleton, 1896–1978, vol. VII
Chapman, Rev. Percy Hugh, 1866–1953, vol. V
Chapman, Col Philip Francis, 1870–1956, vol. V
Chapman, Col Sir Robert, 1st Bt (cr 1958), 1880–1963, vol. VI
Chapman, Robert Barclay, 1829–1909, vol. I
Chapman, Robert Hall, 1890–1953, vol. V
Chapman, Sir Robert William, 1866–1942, vol. IV
Chapman, Robert William, 1881–1960, vol. V
Chapman, Air Chief Marshal Sir Ronald I.; see Ivelaw-Chapman.
Chapman, Sir Samuel, died 1947, vol. IV
Chapman, Sydney, 1888–1970, vol. VI
Chapman, Sir Sydney John, 1871–1951, vol. V
Chapman, Rt Rev. Thomas Alfred, 1867–1949, vol. IV
Chapman, Thomas Algernon, 1842–1921, vol. II
Chapman, Sir Thomas Robert Tighe, 7th Bt (cr 1782), 1846–1919, vol. II
Chapman, William Arthur, 1849–1917, vol. II
Chapman, Major William P.; see Percy-Chapman.
Chapman-Andrews, Sir Edwin Arthur, 1903–1980, vol. VII
Chapman-Huston, Major Desmond Wellesley William Desmond Mountjoy, died 1952, vol. V
Chappel, Rev. William Haighton, 1860–1922, vol. II
Chappell, Sir Ernest, 1864–1943, vol. IV
Chappell, Robert Kingsley, 1884–1937, vol. III
Chappell, T. Stanley, died 1933, vol. III
Chapple, Charles Roberts, 1874–1965, vol. VI
Chapple, Frederic, 1845–1924, vol. II
Chapple, Harold, 1881–1945, vol. IV
Chapple, Paymaster Rear-Adm. Sir John Henry George, 1859–1925, vol. II
Chapple, William Allan, 1864–1936, vol. III

Chapuis, Mgr Marie Auguste, 1869–1930, vol. III
Charbonneau, Most Rev. Joseph, *died* 1959, vol. V
Charbonneau, Napoleon, 1853–1916, vol. II
Charcot, Dr Jean Baptiste Etienne Auguste, 1867–1936, vol. III
Chari, P. N., vol. III
Charkhari, HH Maharaja Dhiraj Sipah-Darul-Mulk Sir Malkhan Sinh Ju Dev Bahadur, 1872–1908, vol. I
Charkhari State, HH Maharaja-Dhiraja Sipahdar-ul-Mulk Arimardan Singh Ju Deo Bahadur, 1903–1941, vol. IV
Charlemont, 7th Viscount, 1830–1913, vol. I
Charlemont, 8th Viscount, 1880–1949, vol. IV
Charlemont, 9th Viscount, 1887–1964, vol. VI
Charlemont, 10th Viscount, 1881–1967, vol. VI
Charlemont, 11th Viscount, 1884–1971, vol. VII
Charlemont, 12th Viscount, 1887–1979, vol. VII
Charles, Captain Sir Allen Aitchison Havelock, 2nd Bt, 1887–1936, vol. III
Charles, Rt Hon. Sir Arthur, 1839–1921, vol. II
Charles, Sir Arthur Eber Sydney, 1910–1965, vol. VI
Charles, Enid, 1894–1972, vol. VII
Charles, Brig. Eric Montagu Seton, 1878–1964, vol. VI
Charles, Sir Ernest Bruce, 1871–1950, vol. IV
Charles, Rev. George B., 1862–1936, vol. III
Charles, Rev. James Hamilton, 1854–1939, vol. III
Charles, Lt-Gen. Sir (James) Ronald (Edmondston), 1875–1955, vol. V
Charles, Cdre Sir James Thomas Walter, 1865–1928, vol. II
Charles, Sir John Alexander, *died* 1971, vol. VII
Charles, John James, 1845–1912, vol. I (A)
Charles, John Roger, 1872–1962, vol. VI
Charles, Sir Noel Hughes Havelock, 3rd Bt, 1891–1975, vol. VII
Charles, Maj.-Gen. Sir Richard Havelock, 1st Bt, 1858–1934, vol. III
Charles, Ven. Robert Henry, 1855–1931, vol. III
Charles, Robert Henry, 1882–1951, vol. V
Charles, Robert Lonsdale, 1916–1977, vol. VII
Charles, Lt-Gen. Sir Ronald; *see* Charles, Lt-Gen. Sir J. R. E.
Charles, Captain Ulick de Burgh, 1884–1947, vol. IV
Charles-Roux, François, 1879–1961, vol. VI
Charlesworth, Albany Hawke, 1854–1914, vol. I
Charlesworth, Col Henry, 1851–1926, vol. II
Charlesworth, John, 1893–1957, vol. V
Charlesworth, John Kaye, 1889–1972, vol. VII
Charlesworth, Lilian E., *died* 1970, vol. VI
Charlesworth, Rev. Martin Percival, 1895–1950, vol. IV
Charleton, Henry Charles, 1870–1959, vol. V
Charley, Col Harold Richard, 1875–1956, vol. V
Charley, Sir Philip Belmont, 1893–1976, vol. VII
Charley, Sir William Thomas, 1833–1904, vol. I
Charlot, André Eugene Maurice, 1882–1956, vol. V
Charlton, Archibald Campbell, 1877–1952, vol. V
Charlton, Brig.-Gen. Claud Edward Charles Graham, *died* 1961, vol. VI
Charlton, Adm. Sir Edward Francis Benedict, 1865–1937, vol. III

Charlton, George, 1899–1979, vol. VII
Charlton, Henry Buckley, 1890–1961, vol. VI
Charlton, Hon. John, 1829–1910, vol. I
Charlton, John, *died* 1917, vol. II
Charlton, Air Cdre Lionel Evelyn Oswald, 1879–1958, vol. V
Charlton, Matthew, 1866–1948, vol. IV
Charlton, Captain William Henry, 1876–1950, vol. IV
Charlton-Meyrick, Col Sir Thomas, 1st Bt, 1837–1921, vol. II
Charmes, Francis, 1848–1916, vol. II
Charnock, George Frederick, 1860–1929, vol. III
Charnwood, 1st Baron, 1864–1945, vol. IV
Charnwood, 2nd Baron, 1901–1955, vol. V
Charoux, Siegfried Joseph, 1896–1967, vol. VI
Charpentier, Gustave, 1860–1956, vol. V
Charques, Mrs Dorothy, (Mrs S. A. G. Emms), 1899–1976, vol. VII
Charrington, Captain Eric, 1872–1927, vol. II
Charrington, Lt-Col Francis, 1858–1921, vol. II
Charrington, Frederick Nicholas, 1850–1936, vol. III
Charrington, John, 1856–1939, vol. III
Charrington, Sir John, 1886–1977, vol. VII
Charrington, John Arthur Pepys, 1905–1979, vol. VII
Charrington, Spencer, 1818–1904, vol. I
Charrington, Lt-Col Sydney Herbert, 1878–1954, vol. V
Charry, Sir Vembakkam C. D.; *see* Desika-Charry.
Chart, Edwin, 1848–1926, vol. II
Charteris, Very Rev. Archibald Hamilton, 1835–1908, vol. I
Charteris, Archibald Hamilton, 1874–1940, vol. III
Charteris, Hon. Sir Evan, 1864–1940, vol. III
Charteris, Francis James, 1875–1964, vol. VI
Charteris, Hon. Guy Lawrence, 1886–1967, vol. VI
Charteris, Hugo Francis Guy, 1922–1970, vol. VI
Charteris, Brig.-Gen. John, 1877–1946, vol. IV
Charteris, Col Nigel Keppel, 1878–1967, vol. VI
Charters, Col Alexander Burnet, 1876–1948, vol. IV
Chase, Beatrice; *see* Parr, Olive Katharine.
Chase, Rev. Drummond Percy, 1820–1902, vol. I
Chase, Rt Rev. Frederic Henry, 1853–1925, vol. II
Chase, Rt Rev. George Armitage, 1886–1971, vol. VII
Chase, Lewis, 1873–1937, vol. III (A), vol. IV
Chase, Marian, 1844–1905, vol. I
Chase, Mary Ellen, 1887–1973, vol. VII
Chase, William Henry, 1880–1965, vol. VI
Chase, Col William St Lucian, 1856–1908, vol. I
Chase-Casgrain, Alexandre; *see* Casgrain.
Chastel De Boinville, Rev. Basil William, *died* 1943, vol. IV
Chastenet de Castaing, Jacques, 1893–1978, vol. VII
Chasteney, Howard Everson, 1888–1947, vol. IV
Chatelain, Henri Louis, 1877–1915, vol. I
Chater, Maj.-Gen. Arthur Reginald, 1896–1979, vol. VII
Chater, Sir Catchick Paul, 1846–1926, vol. II
Chater, Daniel, 1870–1959, vol. V
Chater, Col Vernor, 1842–1928, vol. II
Chatfeild-Clarke, Sir Edgar, 1863–1925, vol. II

Chatfield, 1st Baron, 1873–1967, vol. VI
Chatfield, Adm. Alfred John, 1831–1910, vol. I
Chatfield, George Ernle, 1875–1930, vol. III
Chatfield-Taylor, Hobart Chatfield, 1865–1945, vol. IV
Chatham, William, 1859–1940, vol. III
Chattaway, Edward, 1873–1956, vol. V
Chattaway, Frederick Daniel, died 1944, vol. IV
Chatterjee, Sir Atul Chandra, 1874–1955, vol. V
Chatterjee, Gopal Chunder, 1873–1953, vol. V
Chatterji, Sir Nalini Ranjan, died 1942, vol. IV
Chatterji, Sir Protul Chandra, 1848–1917, vol. II
Chatterton, Sir Alfred, 1866–1958, vol. V
Chatterton, Edward Keble, 1878–1944, vol. IV
Chatterton, Rt Rev. Eyre, 1863–1950, vol. IV
Chatterton, Col Frank Beauchamp Macaulay, 1873–1934, vol. III
Chatterton, Col Frank William, 1839–1924, vol. II
Chatterton, Frederick, died 1934, vol. III
Chattisham, 1st Baron, 1886–1945, vol. IV
Chattock, Arthur Prince, 1860–1934, vol. III
Chau Tsun-Nin, Sir, 1893–1971, vol. VII
Chaubal, Sir Mahadev Bhaskar, 1857–1933, vol. III
Chaudhuri, Asutosh, 1860–1924, vol. II
Chaumeix, André, 1874–1955, vol. V
Chauncy, Col Charles Henry Kemble, died 1945, vol. IV
Chauvel, Gen. Sir Henry George, 1865–1945, vol. IV
Chauvel, Jean Michel Henri, 1897–1979, vol. VII
Chauvel, Ven. John Henry Allan, 1895–1946, vol. IV
Chavasse, Rt Rev. Christopher Maude, 1884–1962, vol. VI
Chavasse, Rt Rev. Francis James, 1846–1928, vol. II
Chavasse, Sir Thomas Frederick, 1854–1913, vol. I
Chave, Captain Sir Benjamin, 1870–1954, vol. V
Chave, Elmer Hargreaves, 1891–1957, vol. V
Chawner, William, 1848–1911, vol. I
Chaworth-Musters, Col John Nevile, 1890–1970, vol. VI
Chaytor, Alfred Henry, 1869–1931, vol. III
Chaytor, Lt-Col Clervaux Alexander, died 1941, vol. IV
Chaytor, Col D'Arcy, 1873–1960, vol. V
Chaytor, Sir Edmund Hugh, 6th Bt, 1876–1935, vol. III
Chaytor, Maj.-Gen. Sir Edward Walter Clervaux, 1868–1939, vol. III
Chaytor, Rev. Henry John, 1871–1954, vol. V
Chaytor, Lt-Col John Clervaux, 1888–1964, vol. VI
Chaytor, Sir Walter Clervaux, 5th Bt, 1874–1913, vol. I
Chaytor, Sir William Henry Clervaux, 7th Bt, 1914–1976, vol. VII
Chaytor, Sir William Henry Edward, 4th Bt, 1867–1908, vol. I
Cheadle, Walter Butler, 1835–1910, vol. I
Cheape, Brig.-Gen. (George) Ronald (Hamilton), 1881–1957, vol. V
Cheape, Lt-Col Hugh Annesley Gray-, 1878–1918, vol. II
Cheape, James, 1853–1943, vol. IV
Cheape, Brig.-Gen. Ronald; see Cheape, Brig.-Gen. G. R. H.
Cheatle, Arthur Henry, 1866–1929, vol. III

Cheatle, Sir (George) Lenthal, 1865–1951, vol. V
Cheatle, Sir Lenthal; see Cheatle, Sir G. L.
Checkley, Frank S., died 1918, vol. II
Cheeseman, A. K. A.; see Wymark, Patrick Carl.
Cheeseman, Harold Ambrose Robinson, 1889–1961, vol. VI
Cheeseman, Lt-Col William Joseph Robert, 1894–1938, vol. III
Cheesewright, William Frederick, died 1934, vol. III
Cheesman, Rev. Alfred Hunter, 1864–1941, vol. IV
Cheesman, Evelyn; see Cheesman, L. E.
Cheesman, (Lucy) Evelyn, 1881–1969, vol. VI
Cheesman, Col Robert Ernest, 1878–1962, vol. VI
Cheetham, Rev. Canon Frederic Philip, 1890–1970, vol. VI
Cheetham, Maj.-Gen. Geoffrey, 1891–1962, vol. VI
Cheetham, Rt Rev. Henry, 1827–1899, vol. I
Cheetham, Rt Hon. John Frederick, 1835–1916, vol. II
Cheetham, Sir Milne, 1869–1938, vol. III
Cheetham, Ven. Samuel, 1827–1908, vol. I
Cheiro; see Hamon, Count Louis.
Cheke, Sir Marcus John, 1906–1960, vol. V
Chelmick, William George Hamar, 1882–1969, vol. VI
Chelmsford, 1st Viscount, 1868–1933, vol. III
Chelmsford, 2nd Viscount, 1903–1970, vol. VI
Chelmsford, Viscountess; (Frances Charlotte), 1869–1957, vol. V
Chelmsford, 2nd Baron, 1827–1905, vol. I
Chelsea, Viscount; Edward George Humphry John Cadogan, 1903–1910, vol. I
Chelsea, Viscount; Henry Arthur Cadogan, 1868–1908, vol. I
Chenevix-Trench, Anthony, 1919–1979, vol. VII
Chenevix-Trench, Col Arthur Henry, 1884–1968, vol. VI
Chenevix-Trench, Charles Godfrey, 1877–1964, vol. VI
Chenevix-Trench, Lt-Col George Frederick, 1859–1937, vol. III
Chenevix-Trench, Col Lawrence, 1883–1958, vol. V
Chenevix-Trench, Brig. Ralph, 1885–1974, vol. VII
Chenevix-Trench, Lt-Col Sir Richard Henry, 1876–1954, vol. V
Cheney, E. John, 1862–1921, vol. II
Cheng, F. T.; see Cheng, Tien-Hsi.
Cheng, Tien-Hsi, (F. T. Cheng), 1884–1970, vol. VI
Chéret, Jules, 1836–1932, vol. III
Chermside, Lt-Gen. Sir Herbert Charles, 1850–1929, vol. III
Cherrington, Rt Rev. Cecil Arthur, died 1950, vol. IV
Cherry, Sir Benjamin Lennard, 1869–1932, vol. III
Cherry, Colin; see Cherry, E. C.
Cherry, (Edward) Colin, 1914–1979, vol. VII
Cherry, Sir John Arnold, 1879–1950, vol. IV
Cherry, Rt Hon. Richard Robert, 1859–1923, vol. II
Cherry, Sir Thomas MacFarland, 1898–1966, vol. VI
Cherry-Garrard, Maj.-Gen. Apsley, 1832–1907, vol. I
Cherry-Garrard, Apsley George Benet, 1886–1959, vol. V

Cherwell, 1st Viscount, *died* 1957, vol. V

Chesebrough, Robert Augustus, 1837–1933, vol. III

Chesham, 3rd Baron, 1850–1907, vol. I

Chesham, 4th Baron, 1894–1952, vol. V

Cheshire, Frederic John, 1860–1939, vol. III

Cheshire, Geoffrey Chevalier, 1886–1978, vol. VII

Cheshire, Rt Rev. Joseph Blount, 1850–1932, vol. III

Cheshire, Comdt Dame Mary Kathleen, 1902–1972, vol. VII

Cheshire, Air Chief Marshal Sir Walter Graemes, 1907–1978, vol. VII

Chesney, Col Alexander George, 1858–1939, vol. III

Chesney, Lt-Col Clement Hope Rawdon, 1883–1962, vol. VI

Chesney, Col Harold Frank, 1859–1920, vol. II

Chesney, Kathleen, 1899–1976, vol. VII

Chesser, Elizabeth Sloan, *died* 1940, vol. III

Chesser, Eustace, 1902–1973, vol. VII

Chesshire, Rev. Reginald Stanley Pargeter, 1869–1940, vol. III

Chesson, Nora; *see* Hopper, N.

Chester, Cecil Harry, 1900–1964, vol. VI

Chester, Sir George, 1886–1949, vol. IV

Chester, Col Heneage Charles B.; *see* Bagot-Chester.

Chester-Master, Rev. Harold, 1889–1948, vol. IV

Chester-Master, Lt-Col Richard, 1870–1917, vol. II

Chester-Master, Thomas William Chester, 1841–1914, vol. I

Chester-Master, Col William Alfred, 1903–1963, vol. VI

Chesterfield, 10th Earl of, 1854–1933, vol. III

Chesterfield, 11th Earl of, 1855–1935, vol. III

Chesterfield, 12th Earl of, 1889–1952, vol. V

Chesterton, Ada Elizabeth, (Mrs Cecil Chesterton), *died* 1962, vol. VI

Chesterton, Cecil Edward, 1879–1918, vol. II

Chesterton, Gilbert Keith, 1874–1936, vol. III

Cheston, Charles Sidney, *died* 1960, vol. V

Cheston, Evelyn, *died* 1929, vol. III

Chetham-Strode, Edward David, 1871–1958, vol. V

Chetham-Strode, Warren, 1896–1974, vol. VII

Chettiar, Rajah Sir Annamalai Chettiar of Chettinad, 1881–1948, vol. IV

Chettiar, Sir M. C. T. M.; *see* Muthiah Chettiar.

Chettiar, Sir Ramanatha A.; *see* Alagappa Chettiar.

Chettle, Major Henry Francis, 1882–1958, vol. V

Chettur, Govinda Krishna, 1898–1936, vol. III (A), vol. V

Chetty, Amatyasiromani Sir Bernard T. T.; *see* Thumboo Chetty.

Chetty, Sir Krishnarajapur Palligondé P.; *see* Puttanna Chetty.

Chetty, Sir Shanmukham, 1892–1953, vol. V

Chetwode, 1st Baron, 1869–1950, vol. IV

Chetwode, Adm. Sir George Knightley, 1877–1957, vol. V

Chetwynd, 7th Viscount, 1823–1911, vol. I

Chetwynd, 8th Viscount, 1863–1936, vol. III

Chetwynd, 9th Viscount, 1904–1965, vol. VI

Chetwynd, Sir (Arthur Henry) Talbot, 7th Bt, 1887–1972, vol. VII

Chetwynd, Sir George, 4th Bt, 1849–1917, vol. II

Chetwynd, Sir (George) Guy, 5th Bt, 1874–1935, vol. III

Chetwynd, Sir Guy; *see* Chetwynd, Sir George G.

Chetwynd, Henry Goulburn Willoughby, 1858–1909, vol. I

Chetwynd, Hon. Richard Walter, 1859–1908, vol. I

Chetwynd, Sir Talbot; *see* Chetwynd, Sir A. H. T.

Chetwynd, Sir Victor James Guy, 6th Bt, 1902–1938, vol. III

Chetwynd-Stapylton, Col Bryan Henry, *died* 1958, vol. V

Chetwynd-Stapylton, Granville Brian, 1887–1964, vol. VI

Chetwynd-Stapylton, Lt-Gen. Granville George, 1823–1915, vol. I

Chetwynd-Stapylton, Rev. William, 1825–1919, vol. II

Chevalier, Albert, 1861–1923, vol. II

Chevalier, Maurice, 1888–1972, vol. VII

Chevallier, Captain Barrington Henry, 1851–1930, vol. III

Chevassût, Rev. Frederick George, *died* 1932, vol. III

Chevassût, Rev. Canon Frederick George, 1889–1974, vol. VII

Chevis, Sir William, 1864–1939, vol. III

Chevrillon, André, 1864–1957, vol. V

Chew, Frederic Robert Gansel, 1907–1970, vol. VI

Cheylesmore, 2nd Baron, 1843–1902, vol. I

Cheylesmore, 3rd Baron, 1848–1925, vol. II

Cheylesmore, 4th Baron, 1893–1974, vol. VII

Cheyne, Brig. Douglas Gordon, 1889–1966, vol. VI

Cheyne, James, 1894–1973, vol. VII

Cheyne, Sir John, 1841–1907, vol. I

Cheyne, Col Sir Joseph Lister, 2nd Bt, 1888–1957, vol. V

Cheyne, Rev. Thomas Kelly, 1841–1915, vol. I

Cheyne, Sir Watson; *see* Cheyne, Sir William W.

Cheyne, Sir (William) Watson, 1st Bt, 1852–1932, vol. III

Cheyney, Peter, (Major Reginald Evelyn Peter Southouse-Cheyney), 1896–1951, vol. V

Cheyney, Major Reginald Evelyn Peter Southouse-; *see* Cheyney, Peter.

Chhajju Ram Chowdhry, Sir, *born* 1865, vol. V

Chhatarpur, Sir Maharaja of, 1866–1932, vol. III

Chhotu Ram, Rao Bahadur Chaudhri Sir, *died* 1945, vol. IV

Chhota Udepur, Maharawal Shri Natwarsinhji Fatehsinhji, Raja of, 1906–1946, vol. IV

Chiang, Yee, 1903–1977, vol. VII

Chiang Kai-Shek, Generalissimo, 1887–1975, vol. VII

Chiasson, Rt Rev. Patrice Alexandre, 1867–1942, vol. IV

Chiazzari, Comdr Nicholas William, 1868–1929, vol. III

Chichele-Plowden, Sir Trevor John Chichele, 1846–1905, vol. I

Chichester, 4th Earl of, 1838–1902, vol. I

Chichester, 5th Earl of, 1844–1905, vol. I

Chichester, 6th Earl of, 1871–1926, vol. II

Chichester, 7th Earl of, 1905–1926, vol. II

Chichester, 8th Earl of, 1912–1944, vol. IV
Chichester, Lt-Col Alan, died 1947, vol. IV
Chichester, Maj.-Gen. Sir Arlington Augustus, 1863–1948, vol. IV
Chichester, Sir Arthur, 8th Bt, 1822–1898, vol. I
Chichester, Lt-Col Arthur O'Neill Cubitt, 1889–1972, vol. VII
Chichester, Most Rev. Aston, 1879–1962, vol. VI
Chichester, Rear-Adm. Sir Edward, 9th Bt, 1849–1906, vol. I
Chichester, Rev. Edward Arthur, 1849–1925, vol. II
Chichester, Sir Edward George, 10th Bt, 1888–1940, vol. III
Chichester, Sir Francis, 1901–1972, vol. VII
Chichester, Hon. Sir Gerald Henry Crofton, 1886–1939, vol. III
Chichester, Lord Henry Fitzwarine, 1834–1928, vol. II
Chichester, Col R. P. D. S., died 1921, vol. II
Chichester, Maj.-Gen. Robert Bruce, 1825–1902, vol. I
Chichester-Clark, Captain James Lenox, 1884–1933, vol. III
Chichester-Constable, Brig. Raleigh Charles Joseph, 1890–1963, vol. VI
Chichester-Constable, Walter George Raleigh, 1863–1942, vol. IV
Chichester Smith, Charles Henry, 1897–1966, vol. VI
Chick, Sir (Alfred) Louis, 1904–1972, vol. VII
Chick, Dame Harriette, 1875–1977, vol. VII
Chick, Herbert George, 1882–1951, vol. V
Chick, Sir Louis; see Chick, Sir A. L.
Chiene, George Lyall, 1873–1951, vol. V
Chiene, John, 1843–1923, vol. II
Chiesman, Sir Walter Eric, 1900–1973, vol. VII
Chifley, Rt Hon. Joseph Benedict, 1885–1951, vol. V
Chignell, Rev. Hugh Scott, died 1950, vol. IV
Chilcott, Rear-Adm. Ronald Evered, 1876–1935, vol. III
Chilcott, Lt-Comdr Sir Warden Stanley, 1871–1942, vol. IV
Chilcott, William Winsland, 1848–1915, vol. I
Child, Arthur, 1852–1902, vol. I
Child, Sir Coles, 1st Bt (cr 1919), 1862–1929, vol. III
Child, Major Sir (Coles) John, 2nd Bt (cr 1919), 1906–1971, vol. VII
Child, Harold Hannyngton, 1869–1945, vol. IV
Child, Lieut Herbert Alexander, died 1914, vol. I
Child, Brig.-Gen. Sir Hill; see Child, Brig.-Gen. Sir S. H.
Child, Major Sir John; see Child, Major Sir C. J.
Child, Rev. Robert Leonard, 1891–1971, vol. VII
Child, Brig.-Gen. Sir (Smith) Hill, 2nd Bt (cr 1868), 1880–1958, vol. V
Childe, Rev. Christopher Venn, died 1937, vol. III
Childe, Col Ralph Bromfield Willington F.; see Fisher-Childe.
Childe, V. Gordon, 1892–1957, vol. V
Childe, Wilfred Rowland Mary, 1890–1952, vol. V
Childe-Pemberton, William Shakespear, 1859–1924, vol. II

Childers, Charles Edward Eardley, 1851–1931, vol. III
Childers, Col Edmund Spencer Eardley, 1854–1919, vol. II
Childers, Lt-Comdr Erskine, 1870–1922, vol. II
Childers, Erskine Hamilton, 1905–1974, vol. VII
Childers, Lt-Col Hugh Francis Eardley, 1886–1941, vol. IV
Childs, Maj.-Gen. Sir (Borlase Elward) Wyndham, 1876–1946, vol. IV
Childs, William Macbride, 1869–1939, vol. III
Childs, Maj.-Gen. Sir Wyndham; see Childs, Maj.-Gen. Sir B. E. W.
Childs-Clarke, Col Charles, 1861–1934, vol. III
Childs-Clarke, Rev. Septimus John, 1876–1964, vol. VI
Chilston, 1st Viscount, 1851–1926, vol. II
Chilston, 2nd Viscount, 1876–1947, vol. IV
Chilton, Rev. Arthur, 1864–1947, vol. IV
Chilton, Charles, 1860–1929, vol. III
Chilton, Donovan, 1909–1978, vol. VII
Chilton, Vice-Adm. Francis George Gillilan, 1879–1964, vol. VI
Chilton, Sir Henry Getty, 1877–1954, vol. V
Chilton, Lt-Gen. Sir Maurice Somerville, 1898–1956, vol. V
Chilvers, Rev. H. Tydeman, 1872–1963, vol. VI
Chimay, Lt-Col Prince Alphonse de, 1899–1973, vol. VII
China, William Edward, 1895–1979, vol. VII
Chinda, Count Sutemi, 1856–1929, vol. III
Chinn, Wilfred Henry, 1901–1970, vol. VI
Chinnery, E. W. Pearson, 1887–1972, vol. VII
Chinnery-Haldane, James Brodrick, 1868–1941, vol. IV
Chinnery-Haldane, Rt Rev. James Robert Alexander, 1842–1906, vol. I
Chinoy, Hon. Fazulbhoy Meherally, died 1915, vol. I
Chinoy, Sir Rahimtoola Meherally, 1882–1957, vol. V
Chinoy, Sir Sultan Meherally, 1885–1968, vol. VI
Chintamani, Sir Chirravoori Yajneswara, 1880–1941, vol. IV
Chipman, Warwick Fielding, 1880–1967, vol. VI
Chippindall, Lt-Gen. Edward, 1827–1902, vol. I
Chippindall, Sir Giles Tatlock, 1893–1969, vol. VI
Chirgwin, Rev. Arthur Mitchell, 1885–1966, vol. VI
Chirico, Giorgio de, 1888–1978, vol. VII
Chirnside, Captain John Percy, 1865–1944, vol. IV
Chirol, Sir Valentine, 1852–1929, vol. III
Chisholm, Rt Rev. Aeneas, 1836–1918, vol. II
Chisholm, Sir (Albert) Roderick, 1897–1967, vol. VI
Chisholm, Ven. Alexander, 1887–1975, vol. VII
Chisholm, Alexander Hugh, 1890–1977, vol. VII
Chisholm, Dame Alice, 1856–1954, vol. V
Chisholm, Brock; see Chisholm, G. B.
Chisholm, Catherine, 1878–1952, vol. V
Chisholm, Hon. Christopher P., 1854–1934, vol. III
Chisholm, (George) Brock, 1896–1971, vol. VII
Chisholm, George Goudie, 1850–1930, vol. III
Chisholm, Hugh, 1866–1924, vol. II
Chisholm, Col Hugh Alexander, 1883–1940, vol. III (A), vol. IV

Chisholm, John, 1857–1929, vol. III
Chisholm, Most Rev. John Wallace, 1922–1975, vol. VII
Chisholm, Hon. Sir Joseph Andrew, 1863–1950, vol. IV
Chisholm, Dr Murdoch, died 1929, vol. III
Chisholm, Sir Roderick; see Chisholm, Sir A. R.
Chisholm, Roderick William, 1925–1979, vol. VII
Chisholm, Ronald George, 1910–1972, vol. VII
Chisholm, Sir Samuel, 1st Bt, 1836–1923, vol. II
Chisholm, William Wilson, 1854–1935, vol. III
Chitham, Sir Charles Carter, 1886–1972, vol. VII
Chitnavis, Sir Gangadhar Madhav, 1863–1929, vol. III
Chitnavis, Sir Shankar Madhavi, 1863–1931, vol. III
Chitral, Major HH Muhammad Sir Nasir-ul-Mulk, Mehtar of, 1898–1943, vol. IV
Chittenden, Frederick James, 1873–1950, vol. IV
Chittenden, Russell Henry, 1856–1943, vol. IV
Chitty, Anthony Merlott, 1907–1976, vol. VII
Chitty, Sir Arthur, 1864–1948, vol. IV
Chitty, Arthur Whatley, 1824–1905, vol. I
Chitty, Sir Charles William, 1859–1932, vol. III
Chitty, Sir Henry Willes; see Chitty, Sir T. H. W.
Chitty, Sir Joseph Henry Pollock, 1861–1942, vol. IV
Chitty, Rt Hon. Sir Joseph William, 1828–1899, vol. I
Chitty, Sir (Thomas) Henry Willes, 2nd Bt, 1891–1955, vol. V
Chitty, Sir Thomas Willes, 1st Bt, 1855–1930, vol. III
Chitty, Rev. Walter Henry, 1867–1940, vol. III
Chitty, Col Walter Willis, 1866–1933, vol. III
Chivers, Edgar Warren, 1906–1979, vol. VII
Chivers, Stephen Oswald, 1899–1975, vol. VII
Chlapowska, Helena M.; see Modjeska-Chlapowska.
Choate, Joseph Hodges, 1832–1917, vol. II
Chodat, Robert, 1865–1934, vol. III
Choksy, Khan Bahadur Sir Nasarvanji Hormasji, 1861–1939, vol. III
Cholmeley, Sir Hugh Arthur Henry, 3rd Bt (cr 1806), 1839–1904, vol. I
Cholmeley, Major Sir Hugh John Francis Sibthorp, 5th Bt (cr 1806), 1906–1964, vol. VI
Cholmeley, Sir Montague Aubrey Rowley, 4th Bt (cr 1806), 1876–1914, vol. I
Cholmeley, Norman Goodford, 1863–1947, vol. IV
Cholmeley, Robert Francis, 1862–1947, vol. IV
Cholmondeley, 4th Marquess of, 1858–1923, vol. II
Cholmondeley, 5th Marquess of, 1883–1968, vol. VI
Cholmondeley, Lord George Hugo, 1887–1958, vol. V
Cholmondeley, Rev. Hon. Henry Pitt, 1820–1905, vol. I
Cholmondeley, Brig.-Gen. Hugh Cecil, 1852–1941, vol. IV
Cholmondeley, Mary, died 1925, vol. II
Cholmondeley-Pennell, Henry; see Pennell.
Chomley, Arthur Wolfe, 1837–1914, vol. I
Chomley, Charles Henry, 1868–1942, vol. IV
Chope, Brig. Arthur John Herbert, 1884–1942, vol. IV

Chopping, Col Arthur, 1871–1951, vol. V
Chopra, Iqbal Chand, 1896–1976, vol. VII
Choquette, Rt Rev. Mgr Charles Philippe, died 1947, vol. IV
Choquette, Hon. Philippe Auguste, born 1854, vol. III
Chorley, 1st Baron, 1895–1978, vol. VII
Chorlton, Alan Ernest Leofric, 1874–1946, vol. IV
Chorlton, Rev. Samuel, died 1911, vol. I
Chotzner, Alfred James, 1873–1958, vol. V
Chou En-Lai, 1898–1976, vol. VII
Chouinard, Honore Julien Jean Baptiste, 1850–1928, vol. II
Chow, Sir Shou-Son, 1861–1959, vol. V
Chowdhury, Maharaja Sir Manmatha Nath Ray, died 1939, vol. III
Chown, Maj.-Gen. Ernest Edward, 1864–1922, vol. II
Chown, John, died 1922, vol. II
Choyce, Charles Coley, 1875–1937, vol. III
Chree, Charles, 1860–1928, vol. II
Chree, Sir William, 1858–1936, vol. III
Chrimes, Sir Bertram; see Chrimes, Sir W. B.
Chrimes, Sir (William) Bertram, 1883–1972, vol. VII
Christ, George Elgie, 1904–1972, vol. VII
Christelow, Allan, 1911–1975, vol. VII
Christensen, Elsa, (Mrs Adolph Christensen); see Stralia, E.
Christian, Adm. Arthur Henry, died 1926, vol. II
Christian, Bertram, died 1953, vol. V
Christian, Rear-Adm. Charles Arbuthnot, 1862–1937, vol. III
Christian, Edmund Brown Viney, 1864–1938, vol. III
Christian, Brig.-Gen. Gerard, 1867–1930, vol. III
Christian, Adm. Henry, 1828–1916, vol. II
Christian, Henry A., 1876–1951, vol. V
Christian, Brig.-Gen. Sydney Ernest, 1867–1931, vol. III
Christian, Lt-Col William Francis, 1879–1954, vol. V
Christiansen, Arthur, 1904–1963, vol. VI
Christie, Dame Agatha Mary Clarissa, 1891–1976, vol. VII
Christie, Alexander Wishart, 1871–1955, vol. V
Christie, Col Archibald, 1889–1962, vol. VI
Christie, Augustus Langham, 1857–1930, vol. III
Christie, Maj.-Gen. Campbell Manning, 1893–1963, vol. VI
Christie, Daniel Hall, 1881–1965, vol. VI
Christie, Dugald, 1855–1936, vol. III
Christie, Harold Alfred Hunter, 1884–1960, vol. V
Christie, Hon. Sir Harold George, 1896–1973, vol. VII
Christie, Herbert Bertram, 1863–1916, vol. II
Christie, Brig.-Gen. Herbert Willie Andrew, 1868–1946, vol. IV
Christie, James, died 1960, vol. V (A)
Christie, James Archibald, 1873–1958, vol. V
Christie, James Roberton, 1866–1932, vol. III
Christie, John, 1882–1962, vol. VI
Christie, John Denham, died 1950, vol. IV
Christie, John Traill, 1899–1980, vol. VII
Christie, Joseph MacNaughtan, 1871–1936, vol. III

Christie, Gp-Captain Malcolm Grahame, 1881–1971, vol. VII
Christie, Richard Copley, 1830–1901, vol. I
Christie, Sir William Henry Mahoney, 1845–1922, vol. II
Christie, William Langham, 1830–1913, vol. I
Christie, Very Rev. William Leslie, 1858–1931, vol. III
Christie, William Lorenzo, 1858–1962, vol. VI
Christie-Miller, Col Sir Geoffry, 1881–1969, vol. VI
Christie-Miller, Samuel Vandeleur, 1911–1968, vol. VI
Christie-Miller, Sydney Richardson, 1874–1931, vol. III
Christison, Sir Alexander, 2nd Bt, 1828–1918, vol. II
Christison, Sir Robert Alexander, 3rd Bt, 1870–1945, vol. IV
Christmas, E. W., died 1918, vol. II
Christoffelsz, Arthur Eric, born 1890, vol. VII
Christoffelsz, William Sperling, 1846–1937, vol. III
Christopher, Rev. Alfred Millard William, 1820–1913, vol. I
Christopher, Col Charles de Lona, 1885–1942, vol. IV
Christopher, Eleanor Caroline, 1873–1959, vol. V
Christopher, Sir George Perrin, 1890–1977, vol. VII
Christopher, Maj.-Gen. Leonard William, 1848–1927, vol. II
Christophers, Bt Col Sir Richard; see Christophers, Bt Col Sir S. R.
Christophers, Bt Col Sir (Samuel) Rickard, 1873–1978, vol. VII
Christopherson, Douglas, 1869–1944, vol. IV
Christopherson, John Brian, 1868–1955, vol. V
Christopherson, Very Rev. Noel Charles, died 1968, vol. VI
Christopherson, Stanley, died 1949, vol. IV
Christy, Cuthbert, 1863–1932, vol. III
Christy, Stephen Henry, 1879–1914, vol. I
Chrystal, George, 1851–1911, vol. I
Chrystal, Sir George William, 1880–1944, vol. IV
Chrystall, Brig. John Inglis, 1887–1960, vol. V
Chubb, Sir Cecil Herbert Edward, 1st Bt, 1876–1934, vol. III
Chubb, Hon. Charles Edward, 1845–1930, vol. III
Chubb, Gilbert Charles, died 1966, vol. VI
Chubb, Harry Emory, 1880–1960, vol. V
Chubb, Sir John Corbin, 2nd Bt, 1904–1957, vol. IV
Chubb, Sir Lawrence Wensley, 1873–1948, vol. IV
Chudoba, František, 1878–1941, vol. IV
Chula-Chakrabongse of Thailand, HRH Prince, 1908–1963, vol. VI
Chulaparambil, Rt Rev. Alexander, 1877–1951, vol. V
Chunilal Bose, Rai Bahadur, 1861–1930, vol. III
Church, Rev. Alfred John, 1829–1912, vol. I
Church, Major Archibald George, 1886–1954, vol. V
Church, Arthur Frederick, 1868–1939, vol. III
Church, Arthur Harry, died 1937, vol. III
Church, Sir Arthur Herbert, 1834–1915, vol. I
Church, Col Arthur John Bromley, 1869–1954, vol. V
Church, Rev. Charles Marcus, died 1915, vol. I

Church, Eric Edmund Raitt, 1907–1972, vol. VII
Church, Brig. Sir Geoffrey Selby, 2nd Bt, 1887–1979, vol. VII
Church, Col George Earl, 1835–1910, vol. I
Church, Col George Ross Marryat, 1868–1940, vol. III
Church, Rev. Leslie Frederic, 1886–1961, vol. VI
Church, Richard Thomas, 1893–1972, vol. VII
Church, Robert William, 1882–1923, vol. II
Church, Samuel Harden, 1858–1943, vol. IV
Church, Maj.-Gen. Thomas Ross, 1831–1926, vol. II
Church, Vice-Adm. William Drummond, died 1937, vol. III
Church, Sir William Selby, 1st Bt, 1837–1928, vol. II
Churcher, Col Sir Arthur, 1871–1951, vol. V
Churchill, 1st Viscount, 1864–1934, vol. III
Churchill, 2nd Viscount, 1890–1973, vol. VII
Churchill, Surg.-Gen. Alexander Ferrier, 1839–1928, vol. II
Churchill, Col Arthur Gillespie, 1860–1940, vol. III
Churchill, Clementine Ogilvy S.; see Baroness Spencer-Churchill.
Churchill, Captain Edward George Spencer-, 1876–1964, vol. VI
Churchill, Lord Edward Spencer-, 1853–1911, vol. I
Churchill, George Percy, 1877–1973, vol. VII
Churchill, Harry Lionel, 1860–1924, vol. II
Churchill, Lord Ivor Charles Spencer, 1898–1956, vol. V
Churchill, Jennie Spencer; see Churchill, Lady Randolph Spencer.
Churchill, Brig. John Atherton, 1887–1965, vol. VI
Churchill, John Strange Spencer, 1880–1947, vol. IV
Churchill, Peter Morland, 1909–1972, vol. VII
Churchill, Hon. Randolph Frederick Edward Spencer, 1911–1968, vol. VI
Churchill, Lady Randolph Spencer, died 1921, vol. II
Churchill, Rev. Robert Reginald, 1890–1970, vol. VI
Churchill, Lt-Col Seton, died 1933, vol. III
Churchill, Sidney John Alexander, 1862–1921, vol. II
Churchill, Stella, died 1954, vol. V
Churchill, William, 1859–1920, vol. II (A), vol. III
Churchill, William Foster Norton, 1898–1963, vol. VI
Churchill, Winston, 1871–1947, vol. IV
Churchill, Rt Hon. Sir Winston Leonard Spencer, 1874–1965, vol. VI
Churchman, Air Cdre Allan Robert, 1896–1970, vol. VI
Churchman, Sir William Alfred, 1st Bt, died 1947, vol. IV
Churchward, Captain Alaric Watts, 1845–1929, vol. III
Churchward, George Jackson, died 1933, vol. III
Churchward, Rev. Marcus Wellesley, 1860–1940, vol. III
Churchward, Col Paul Rycaut Stanbury, 1858–1935, vol. III
Churchward, Percy Albert, 1862–1924, vol. II

Churchward, William Brown, 1844–1920, vol. II
Churston, 2nd Baron, 1846–1910, vol. I
Churston, 3rd Baron, 1873–1930, vol. III
Churton, Rt Rev. Edward Townson, 1841–1912, vol. I
Churton, Rt Rev. Henry Norris, 1843–1904, vol. I
Churton, Ven. Theodore Townson, 1853–1915, vol. I
Churton, Lt-Col William Arthur Vere, 1876–1949, vol. IV
Chute, Ven. Anthony William, 1884–1958, vol. V
Chute, Sir Charles Lennard, 1st Bt, 1879–1956, vol. V
Chute, Ven. John Chaloner, 1881–1961, vol. VI
Chuter-Ede, Baron (Life-Peer); James Chuter Chuter-Ede, 1882–1965, vol. VI
Ciano, Conte Cortellazzo, Galeazzo, 1903–1944, vol. IV
Cilcennin, 1st Viscount, 1903–1960, vol. V
Cilea, Francesco, 1866–1950, vol. IV
Cippico, Count Antonio, 1877–1935, vol. III
Clague, Sir John, 1882–1958, vol. V
Clampett, Ven. Albert Wyndham, 1860–1953, vol. V
Clancarty, 5th Earl of, 1868–1929, vol. III
Clancarty, 6th Earl of, 1891–1971, vol. VII
Clancarty, 7th Earl of, 1902–1975, vol. VII
Clancey, John Charles, 1854–1932, vol. III
Clancy, Rt Rev. John, 1856–1912, vol. I
Clancy, John Joseph, 1847–1928, vol. II
Clancy, Sir John Sydney James, 1895–1970, vol. VI (AII)
Clanmorris, 5th Baron, 1852–1916, vol. II
Clanmorris, 6th Baron, 1879–1960, vol. V
Clanricarde, 2nd Marquis of, 1832–1916, vol. II
Clanwilliam, 4th Earl of, 1832–1907, vol. I
Clanwilliam, 5th Earl of, 1873–1953, vol. V
Clapham, Sir Alfred William, 1883–1950, vol. IV
Clapham, Edward William, *died* 1943, vol. IV
Clapham, Sir John Harold, 1873–1946, vol. IV
Clapin, Adolphus Philip, 1828–1914, vol. I
Clapp, Sir Harold Winthrop, 1875–1952, vol. V
Clappen, Air Cdre Donald William, 1895–1978, vol. VII
Clapperton, Alan Ernest, *died* 1931, vol. III
Clapperton, T. J., 1879–1962, vol. VI
Clarabut, Maj.-Gen. Reginald Blaxland, 1893–1977, vol. VII
Clare, Captain Chapman James, 1853–1940, vol. III
Clare, Sir Harcourt E., 1854–1922, vol. II
Clare, Henry Lewis, 1858–1920, vol. II
Clare, Mary, (Mrs L. Mawhood), 1892–1970, vol. VI
Clare, Octavius Leigh, 1841–1912, vol. I
Clare, Lt-Col Oliver Cecil, 1881–1933, vol. III
Clarendon, 5th Earl of, 1846–1915, vol. I
Clarendon, 6th Earl of, 1877–1955, vol. V
Clarendon, Very Rev. Thomas William, 1855–1934, vol. III
Claretie, Jules Arsène Arnaud, 1840–1913, vol. I
Clarina, 4th Baron, 1830–1897, vol. I
Clarina, 5th Baron, 1837–1922, vol. II
Clarina, 6th Baron, 1880–1952, vol. V
Clark, Adrian, 1889–1944, vol. IV

Clark, Albert Curtis, 1859–1937, vol. III
Clark, Alec Fulton Charles, 1898–1979, vol. VII
Clark, Alfred, 1873–1950, vol. IV
Clark, Alfred Alexander G.; *see* Gordon Clark.
Clark, Alfred Joseph, 1885–1941, vol. IV
Clark, Sir Allen George, 1898–1962, vol. VI
Clark, Andrew, *died* 1913, vol. I
Clark, Sir Andrew Edmund James, 3rd Bt (*cr* 1883), 1898–1979, vol. VII
Clark, Andrew Rutherfurd Clark, 1828–1899, vol. I
Clark, Sir Arthur; *see* Clark, Sir W. A. W.
Clark, Arthur Campbell S.; *see* Stuart-Clark.
Clark, Arthur L., 1873–1956, vol. V
Clark, Sir Beresford; *see* Clark, Sir J. B.
Clark, Rt Rev. Bernard T., *died* 1916, vol. II
Clark, Vice-Adm. Sir Bouverie Francis, 1842–1922, vol. II
Clark, Brig. Cecil Horace, 1880–1958, vol. V
Clark, Charles Alexander, 1860–1939, vol. III
Clark, Rear-Adm. Charles Carr, 1902–1965, vol. VI
Clark, Lt-Col Charles Watson, *died* 1944, vol. IV
Clark, Christopher, 1875–1942, vol. IV
Clark, Cosmo; *see* Clark, J. C.
Clark, Lt-Col Craufurd Alexander G.; *see* Gordon-Clark.
Clark, Col D'Arcy Melville, *died* 1964, vol. VI
Clark, Donald George, 1868–1935, vol. III
Clark, Edmund Graham, 1889–1954, vol. V
Clark, Edwin Charles, 1835–1917, vol. II
Clark, Lt-Col Edwin Kitson, 1866–1943, vol. IV
Clark, Sir Ernest, 1864–1951, vol. V
Clark, Francis, 1864–1940, vol. III
Clark, Rev. Francis E., *died* 1927, vol. II
Clark, Rev. Francis Storer, 1836–1909, vol. I
Clark, Rt Rev. (Frederick) Patrick, 1908–1954, vol. V
Clark, Gavin Brown, 1846–1930, vol. III
Clark, George Albert, 1894–1963, vol. VI
Clark, George Ernest, *died* 1919, vol. II
Clark, Sir George Ernest, 2nd Bt (*cr* 1917), 1882–1950, vol. IV
Clark, Sir George Norman, 1890–1979, vol. VII
Clark, Brig. George Philip, 1901–1977, vol. VII
Clark, George Sidney Roberts K.; *see* Kitson Clark.
Clark, Sir George Smith, 1st Bt (*cr* 1917), 1861–1935, vol. III
Clark, Gowan Cresswell Strange, 1856–1929, vol. III
Clark, Harold Frederick, *died* 1957, vol. V
Clark, Henry, 1829–1900, vol. I
Clark, Henry Herbert G.; *see* Gordon Clark.
Clark, Sir Henry Laurence U.; *see* Urling Clark.
Clark, Rev. Henry W., 1869–1949, vol. IV
Clark, Captain Henry William Alfred, *died* 1935, vol. III
Clark, James, 1859–1915, vol. I
Clark, James, *died* 1935, vol. III
Clark, James, *died* 1943, vol. IV
Clark, James, (Jim Clark), 1936–1968, vol. VI
Clark, James John, 1870–1936, vol. III
Clark, Captain James Lenox C.; *see* Chichester-Clark.

Clark, James Oscar Max, 1877–1958, vol. V
Clark, Col Sir James Richardson Andrew, 2nd Bt (cr 1883), 1852–1948, vol. IV
Clark, James Robert, 1844–1919, vol. II
Clark, James T.; see Towers-Clark.
Clark, James Walker, 1858–1936, vol. III
Clark, James William, 1851–1921, vol. II
Clark, John, died 1931, vol. III
Clark, John, 1903–1977, vol. VII
Clark, Brig.-Gen. John Arthur, died 1976, vol. VII
Clark, Sir (John) Beresford, 1902–1968, vol. VI
Clark, John Brown, 1861–1947, vol. IV
Clark, (John) Cosmo, 1897–1967, vol. VI
Clark, Sir John Forbes, 2nd Bt (cr 1837), 1821–1910, vol. I
Clark, Lt-Gen. John George Walters, 1892–1948, vol. IV
Clark, Sir John Maurice, 2nd Bt (cr 1886), 1859–1924, vol. II
Clark, John Maurice, 1884–1963, vol. VI
Clark, John Murray, 1860–1929, vol. III
Clark, Sir John S.; see Stewart-Clark.
Clark, John William, 1851–1929, vol. III
Clark, John Willis, 1833–1910, vol. I
Clark, Joseph, 1834–1926, vol. II
Clark, Col Joseph Arthur Myles Ariel, 1872–1935, vol. III
Clark, Kenneth MacKenzie, 1868–1932, vol. III
Clark, Latimer, 1822–1898, vol. I
Clark, Sir Marcus; see Clark, Sir R. M.
Clark, Mrs Margaret; see Storm, Lesley.
Clark, Rt Rev. Patrick; see Clark, Rt Rev. F. P.
Clark, Col Percy William, 1888–1943, vol. IV
Clark, Philip Lindsey, 1889–1977, vol. VII
Clark, Sir (Reginald) Marcus, 1883–1953, vol. V
Clark, Col Robert, 1859–1940, vol. III (A), vol. IV
Clark, Sir Stewart S.; see Stewart-Clark.
Clark, Rev. Canon Stuart Harrington, 1869–1947, vol. IV
Clark, Sir Thomas, 1st Bt (cr 1886), 1823–1900, vol. I
Clark, Sir Thomas, 3rd Bt (cr 1886), 1886–1977, vol. VII
Clark, Thomas Archibald B.; see Bennet-Clark.
Clark, Thomas Campbell, (Tom C. Clark), 1899–1977, vol. VII
Clark, Sir Wilfrid Edward Le Gros, 1895–1971, vol. VII
Clark, William Andrews, 1839–1925, vol. II
Clark, Sir (William) Arthur (Weir), 1908–1967, vol. VI
Clark, William Clifford, 1889–1952, vol. V
Clark, Brig. William Ellis, 1877–1969, vol. VI
Clark, Hon. William George, 1865–1948, vol. IV
Clark, Rev. William Gilchrist; see Clark-Maxwell.
Clark, Sir William Henry, 1876–1952, vol. V
Clark, Sir William Mortimer, 1836–1917, vol. III
Clark, Sir William Ovens, 1849–1937, vol. III
Clark, Rt Rev. William Reid, died 1925, vol. II
Clark, Rev. William Robinson, died 1912, vol. I
Clark-Hall, Air Marshal Sir Robert Hamilton, 1883–1964, vol. VI
Clark-Kennedy, John William James; see Kennedy.
Clark-Kennedy of Knockgray, Lt-Col William Hew; see Kennedy of Knockgray.

Clark-Maxwell, Rev. William Gilchrist, 1865–1935, vol. III
Clarke, Lt-Col Albert Edward Stanley, 1879–1926, vol. II
Clarke, Col Alexander Ross, 1828–1914, vol. I
Clarke, Alfred Henry, 1860–1942, vol. IV
Clarke, Hon. Sir Andrew, 1824–1902, vol. I
Clarke, Andrew B., died 1940, vol. III
Clarke, Vice-Adm. Arthur Calvert, 1848–1926, vol. II
Clarke, Rev. Arthur Frederic, 1848–1932, vol. III
Clarke, Col Arthur Lionel Crisp, 1874–1935, vol. III
Clarke, Captain Sir Arthur Wellesley, 1857–1932, vol. III
Clarke, Astley Vavasour, 1870–1945, vol. IV
Clarke, Austin, 1896–1974, vol. VII
Clarke, Sir Basil, 1879–1947, vol. IV
Clarke, Rev. Basil Fulford Lowther, 1908–1978, vol. VII
Clarke, Brig. Bowcher Campbell Senhouse, 1882–1969, vol. VI
Clarke, Sir Campbell, 1835–1902, vol. I
Clarke, Maj.-Gen. Sir Campbell; see Clarke, Maj.-Gen. Sir E. M. C.
Clarke, Sir Caspar Purdon, 1846–1911, vol. I
Clarke, Rev. Sir Charles, 2nd Bt (cr 1831), 1812–1899, vol. I
Clarke, Charles Agacy, 1872–1939, vol. III
Clarke, Charles Allen, 1863–1935, vol. III
Clarke, Charles Baron, 1832–1906, vol. I
Clarke, Col Charles C.; see Childs-Clarke.
Clarke, Charles Cyril, 1882–1968, vol. VI
Clarke, Charles Goddard, 1849–1908, vol. I
Clarke, Bt-Col (Charles Henry Geoffrey) Mansfield, 1873–1919, vol. II
Clarke, Charles Kirk, died 1924, vol. II
Clarke, Gen. Sir Charles Mansfield, 3rd Bt (cr 1831), 1839–1932, vol. III
Clarke, Sir Charles Noble A.; see Arden-Clark.
Clarke, Rear-Adm. Sir (Charles) Philip, 1898–1966, vol. VI
Clarke, Ven. Charles Philip Stewart, 1871–1947, vol. IV
Clarke, Hon. Sir Charles Pitcher, 1857–1926, vol. II
Clarke, Very Rev. Charles William B.; see Barnett-Clarke.
Clarke, Comdr Courtney; see Clarke, Comdr H. C. C.
Clarke, Dennis Robert, 1902–1967, vol. VI
Clarke, Sir Douglas, 1901–1969, vol. VI
Clarke, Brig. Dudley Wrangel, 1899–1974, vol. VII
Clarke, Sir Edgar C.; see Chatfeild-Clarke.
Clarke, Edith, 1844–1926, vol. II
Clarke, Edward Ashley Walrond, 1860–1913, vol. I
Clarke, Edward de Courcy, 1880–1958, vol. V
Clarke, Captain Edward Denman, 1898–1966, vol. VI
Clarke, Rt Hon. Sir Edward George, 1841–1931, vol. III
Clarke, Lt-Col Sir Edward Henry St Lawrence, 4th Bt (cr 1804), 1857–1926, vol. II
Clarke, Edward Henry Scamander, 1856–1947, vol. IV

Clarke, Major Edward John Arundell, 1868–1932, vol. III
Clarke, Edward Lionel Alexander, 1837–1917, vol. II
Clarke, Maj.-Gen. Sir (Edward Montagu) Campbell, 1885–1971, vol. VII
Clarke, Sir Ernest, 1856–1923, vol. II
Clarke, Ernest, died 1932, vol. III
Clarke, (Ernest) Meredyth H.; see Hyde-Clarke.
Clarke, Sir Ernest Michael, 1868–1956, vol. V
Clarke, Hon. Sir Fielding, 1851–1928, vol. II
Clarke, Hon. Sir Francis Grenville, 1879–1955, vol. V
Clarke, Frank Edward, 1886–1938, vol. III
Clarke, Frank Wigglesworth, 1847–1931, vol. III
Clarke, Sir Fred, 1880–1952, vol. V
Clarke, Brig. Frederick Arthur Stanley, 1892–1972, vol. VII
Clarke, Ven. Frederick James, 1858–1937, vol. III
Clarke, Hon. Sir Frederick James, 1859–1944, vol. IV
Clarke, Frederick Seymour, 1855–1932, vol. III
Clarke, Sir Frederick William Alfred, 1857–1927, vol. II
Clarke, Sir Geoffrey, died 1950, vol. IV
Clarke, George, 1878–1944, vol. IV
Clarke, Gen. George Calvert, 1814–1900, vol. I
Clarke, George Johnson, died 1917, vol. III
Clarke, Brig.-Gen. Goland Vanhalt, 1875–1944, vol. IV
Clarke, Very Rev. Harold George Michael, 1898–1978, vol. VII
Clarke, Henry, 1854–1936, vol. III
Clarke, Brig.-Gen. Henry Calvert Stanley, 1872–1943, vol. IV
Clarke, Comdr H(enry) C(ecil) Courtney, 1890–1968, vol. VI
Clarke, Adm. Henry James Langford, 1866–1944, vol. IV
Clarke, Most Rev. Henry Lowther, 1850–1926, vol. II
Clarke, Herbert, 1863–1925, vol. II
Clarke, Ven. Herbert Lovell, 1881–1962, vol. VI
Clarke, Sir Horace William, 1883–1963, vol. VI
Clarke, Sir Humphrey Orme, 5th Bt (cr 1831), 1906–1973, vol. VII
Clarke, Isabel Constance, died 1951, vol. V
Clarke, Col J. de W. L.; see Lardner-Clarke.
Clarke, J. Jackson, died 1940, vol. III (A), vol. IV
Clarke, James Greville, 1854–1901, vol. I
Clarke, Rev. John, died 1923, vol. II
Clarke, John, died 1939, vol. III
Clarke, John Courtenay, 1880–1939, vol. III
Clarke, Rev. John Erskine, 1827–1920, vol. II
Clarke, John Henry, 1852–1931, vol. III
Clarke, John Joseph, 1879–1969, vol. VI
Clarke, Brig.-Gen. John Louis Justice, 1870–1944, vol. IV
Clarke, John Mason, 1857–1925, vol. II
Clarke, John Smith, 1885–1959, vol. V
Clarke, Col John Thomas, 1870–1947, vol. IV (A)
Clarke, Joseph Percival, 1862–1930, vol. III
Clarke, Col Lancelot Fox, 1858–1925, vol. II

Clarke, Captain Lionel Altham G.; see Graham-Clarke.
Clarke, Hon. Lionel H., 1859–1922, vol. II
Clarke, Loftus Otway, 1871–1954, vol. V
Clarke, Louis Colville Gray, 1881–1960, vol. V, vol. VI
Clarke, Bt-Col Mansfield; see Clarke, Bt-Col C. H. G. M.
Clarke, Lt-Col Sir Marshal, 1841–1909, vol. I
Clarke, Adm. Sir Marshal Llewelyn, 1887–1959, vol. V
Clarke, Mary Gavin, 1881–1976, vol. VII
Clarke, Mrs Mary Victoria Cowden, 1809–1898, vol. I
Clarke, Lt-Col Matthew John, 1895–1954, vol. V
Clarke, Maude Violet, 1892–1935, vol. III
Clarke, Meredyth H.; see Hyde-Clarke, E. M.
Clarke, Rear-Adm. Noel Edward Harwood, 1904–1980, vol. VII
Clarke, Rt Rev. Norman Harry, 1892–1974, vol. VII
Clarke, Sir Orme Bigland, 4th Bt (cr 1831), 1880–1949, vol. IV
Clarke, Sir Percival, 1872–1936, vol. III
Clarke, Rear-Adm. Sir Philip; see Clarke, Rear-Adm. Sir C. P.
Clarke, Sir Philip Haughton, 11th Bt (cr 1617), 1819–1898, vol. I
Clarke, Col Sir Ralph Stephenson, 1892–1970, vol. VI
Clarke, Sir Reginald, 1876–1956, vol. V
Clarke, Col Reginald Graham, 1879–1959, vol. V
Clarke, Sir Richard William Barnes, 1910–1975, vol. VII
Clarke, Robert Coningsby, 1879–1934, vol. III
Clarke, Col Robert Ffoulke Noel, died 1904, vol. I
Clarke, Lt-Col Robert Joyce, 1874–1949, vol. IV
Clarke, Sir Rupert Turner Havelock, 2nd Bt (cr 1882), 1865–1926, vol. II
Clarke, Sir Selwyn S.; see Selwyn-Clarke.
Clarke, Rev. Septimus John C.; see Childs-Clarke.
Clarke, Rev. Sidney Lampard, 1871–1945, vol. IV
Clarke, Somers, 1841–1926, vol. II
Clarke, Lt-Gen. Somerset Molyneux W.; see Wiseman-Clarke.
Clarke, Maj.-Gen. Sir Stanley de Astel Calvert, 1837–1911, vol. I
Clarke, Stephenson Robert, 1862–1948, vol. IV
Clarke, Rev. Sydney Herbert, 1894–1974, vol. VII
Clarke, Ven. Thomas, 1907–1965, vol. VI
Clarke, Col Thomas Cecil Arthur, 1898–1979, vol. VII
Clarke, Col Thomas Henry Matthews, 1869–1941, vol. IV
Clarke, Tom, 1884–1957, vol. V
Clarke, Lt-Gen. Sir Travers Edwards, 1871–1962, vol. VI
Clarke, William, 1842–1918, vol. II
Clarke, William Bruce, died 1914, vol. I
Clarke, William Eagle, 1853–1938, vol. III
Clarke, Sir William Henry, died 1930, vol. III
Clarke, Sir William Henry, 1847–1930, vol. III
Clarke, Sir William John, 1st Bt (cr 1882), 1831–1897, vol. I
Clarke, William John, 1857–1951, vol. V

Clarke, Rev. William Kemp Lowther, 1879–1968, vol. VI

Clarke, Hon. William Lionel Russell, 1876–1954, vol. V

Clarke, Brig. William Stanhope, 1899–1973, vol. VII

Clarke, Maj.-Gen. Willoughby Charles Stanley, 1833–1909, vol. I

Clarke Hall, Edna (Lady Clarke Hall), 1879–1979, vol. VII

Clarke-Jervoise, Sir Arthur Henry; see Jervoise.

Clarke-Jervoise, Sir Dudley Alan Lestock; see Jervoise.

Clarke Taylor, Air Vice-Marshal James; see Taylor.

Clarke-Thornhill, Thomas Bryan, 1857–1934, vol. III

Clarke-Travers, Sir Guy Francis Travers; see Travers.

Clarkson, Anthony; see Clarkson, G. W. A.

Clarkson, Lt-Col Bertie St John, 1868–1954, vol. V

Clarkson, (George Wensley) Anthony, 1912–1977, vol. VII

Clarkson, Rt Rev. George William, 1897–1977, vol. VII

Clarkson, Mabel, died 1950, vol. IV

Clarkson, Patrick Wensley, 1911–1969, vol. VI

Clarkson, Rev. Peter, 1871–1936, vol. III

Clarkson, Randolph Norman Macgregor, 1889–1967, vol. VI

Clarkson, Engr-Vice-Adm. Sir William, 1859–1934, vol. III

Clarry, Sir Reginald, 1882–1945, vol. IV

Claudel, Paul, 1868–1955, vol. V

Claughton, Sir Gilbert Henry, 1st Bt, 1856–1921, vol. II

Claughton, Sir Harold, 1882–1969, vol. VI

Claus, Emile, 1849–1924, vol. II

Clause, William Lionel, 1887–1946, vol. IV

Clausen, Sir George, 1852–1944, vol. IV

Clausen, Raymond John, died 1966, vol. VI

Clauson, 1st Baron, 1870–1946, vol. IV

Clauson, Sir Gerard Leslie Makins, 1891–1974, vol. VII

Clauson, Major Sir John Eugene, 1866–1918, vol. II

Clavering, Sir Albert, 1887–1972, vol. VII

Clavering, Col Charles Warren N.; see Napier-Clavering.

Clavering, Maj.-Gen. Noel Warren N.; see Napier-Clavering.

Claxton, Hon. Brooke, 1898–1960, vol. V

Claxton, Thomas Folkes, 1874–1952, vol. V

Clay, Sir Arthur Temple Felix, 4th Bt, 1842–1928, vol. II

Clay, Brig.-Gen. Bertie Gordon, 1874–1937, vol. III

Clay, Charles Felix, 1861–1947, vol. IV

Clay, Sir Charles Travis, 1885–1978, vol. VII

Clay, Lt-Col Ernest Charles, 1872–1955, vol. V

Clay, Sir Felix, 5th Bt, 1871–1941, vol. IV

Clay, Sir Geoffrey Fletcher, 1895–1969, vol. VI

Clay, Col Henry, 1872–1945, vol. IV

Clay, Sir Henry, 1883–1954, vol. V

Clay, Lt-Col Rt Hon. Herbert Henry S.; see Spender-Clay.

Clay, Col John, died 1962, vol. VI

Clay, Rev. John Harden, died 1923, vol. II

Clay, Sir Joseph Miles, 1881–1949, vol. IV

Clay, Gen. Lucius DuBignon, 1897–1978, vol. VII

Clay, Reginald S., died 1954, vol. V

Clay, William Henry, 1841–1921, vol. II

Clay, Rev. William Leslie, 1863–1928, vol. II

Clayden, Arthur William, 1855–1944, vol. IV

Clayden, Peter William, 1827–1902, vol. I

Claydon, Rev. Canon Ernest Henry Beales, 1863–1930, vol. III

Claye, Sir Andrew Moynihan, 1896–1977, vol. VII

Claye, Rev. Canon Arthur Needham, 1863–1956, vol. V

Clayhills, George, 1877–1914, vol. I

Clayson, Rev. Canon Jesse Alec Maynard, 1905–1971, vol. VII

Clayton, Rev. Albert, died 1907, vol. I

Clayton, Arthur Ross, 1876–1963, vol. VI

Clayton, Sir Christopher; see Clayton, Sir G. C.

Clayton, Colin, 1895–1975, vol. VII

Clayton, Edward, 1856–1938, vol. III

Clayton, Edward Chapman, 1837–1935, vol. III

Clayton, Major Edward Francis, 1864–1922, vol. II

Clayton, Major Sir Edward Gilbert, 1841–1917, vol. II

Clayton, Maj.-Gen. Edward Hadrill, 1899–1962, vol. VI

Clayton, Col Edward Robert, 1877–1957, vol. V

Clayton, Edwin, 1887–1973, vol. VII

Clayton, Col Sir Fitz-Roy Augustus Talbot, 1834–1913, vol. I

Clayton, Col Forrester, 1878–1942, vol. IV

Clayton, Sir Francis Hare, 1869–1956, vol. V

Clayton, Frederick, 1872–1932, vol. III

Clayton, Lt-Gen. Sir Frederick Thomas, 1855–1933, vol. III

Clayton, Most Rev. Geoffrey Hare, 1884–1957, vol. V

Clayton, Sir (George) Christopher, 1869–1945, vol. IV

Clayton, Brig.-Gen. Sir Gilbert Falkingham, 1875–1929, vol. III

Clayton, Harold, 1874–1963, vol. VI

Clayton, Sir Harold Dudley, 10th Bt (cr 1732), 1877–1951, vol. V

Clayton, Col Hon. Sir Hector Joseph Richard, 1885–1975, vol. VII

Clayton, Rev. Horace Evelyn, 1853–1916, vol. II

Clayton, Sir Hugh Byard, 1877–1947, vol. IV

Clayton, Brig. Sir Iltyd Nicholl, 1886–1955, vol. V

Clayton, Rev. John Francis, 1883–1947, vol. IV

Clayton, Rear-Adm. John Wittewronge, 1888–1952, vol. V

Clayton, Joseph, 1868–1943, vol. IV

Clayton, Rt Rev. Lewis, 1838–1917, vol. II

Clayton, Lt-Col Muirhead Collins, 1892–1957, vol. V

Clayton, Col Patrick Andrew, 1896–1962, vol. VI

Clayton, Rev. Philip Thomas Byard, 1885–1972, vol. VII

Clayton, Reginald John Byard, 1875–1962, vol. VI

Clayton, Hon. Brig.-Gen. Robert Clayton B.; see Browne Clayton.

Clayton, Lt-Col William Kitson, *died* 1937, vol. III
Clayton, William Lockhart, 1880–1966, vol. VI
Clayton, Sir William Robert, 6th Bt (*cr* 1732), 1842–1914, vol. I
Clayton-East, Sir George Frederick Lancelot, 8th Bt and 4th Bt; *see* East.
Clayton East, Sir Gilbert Augustus Clayton, 7th Bt and 3rd Bt; *see* East.
Clayton East Clayton, Sir Robert Alan, 9th Bt (*cr* 1732), and 5th Bt (*cr* 1838), 1908–1932, vol. III
Clayton-Greene, W. H., *died* 1926, vol. II
Cleary, Rt Rev. Henry William, 1859–1929, vol. III
Cleary, Ven. Robert, *died* 1919, vol. II
Cleary, Hon. Sir Timothy Patrick, 1900–1962, vol. VI
Cleary, Sir William Castle, 1886–1971, vol. VII
Cleather, Edward Gordon, 1872–1967, vol. VI
Cleaton, John Davies, *died* 1901, vol. I
Cleave, John, 1837–1928, vol. II
Cleave, John Kyrie Frederick, 1861–1947, vol. IV
Cleaver, Sir Frederick, 1875–1936, vol. III
Cleaver, Col Frederick Holden, 1875–1944, vol. IV
Cleaver, Reginald; *see* Cleaver, T. R.
Cleaver, (Thomas) Reginald, *died* 1954, vol. V
Clee, Sir Charles Beaupré Bell, 1893–1980, vol. VII
Cleeve, Brig. Francis Charles Frederick, 1896–1975, vol. VII
Cleeve, Lt-Col Herbert, 1870–1948, vol. IV
Cleeve, Lucas, (Mrs Howard Kingscote), *died* 1908, vol. I
Cleeve, Col Stewart Dalrymple, 1856–1939, vol. III
Cleeve, Sir Thomas Henry, 1844–1908, vol. I
Cleeve, Maj.-Gen. William Frederick, 1853–1922, vol. II
Clegg, Sir (Alfred) Rowland, 1872–1957, vol. V
Clegg, Sir James Travis T.; *see* Travis-Clegg.
Clegg, Rev. James Whitehead, *died* 1930, vol. III
Clegg, Sir John Charles, 1850–1937, vol. III
Clegg, Rear-Adm. John Harry Kay, 1884–1962, vol. VI
Clegg, Sir Robert Bailey, 1865–1929, vol. III
Clegg, Sir Rowland; *see* Clegg, Sir A. R.
Clegg, Sir William Edwin, 1852–1932, vol. III
Clegg, William Henry, *died* 1945, vol. IV
Cleghorn, Isabel, *died* 1922, vol. II
Cleghorn, Surg.-Gen. James, 1841–1920, vol. II
Cleland, Sir Charles, 1867–1941, vol. IV
Cleland, Brig. Sir Donald Mackinnon, 1901–1975, vol. VII
Cleland, Edward Erskine, 1869–1943, vol. IV (A)
Cleland, James William, 1874–1914, vol. I
Cleland, John, 1835–1924, vol. II
Cleland, Sir John Burton, 1878–1971, vol. VII
Clemenceau, Georges, 1841–1929, vol. III
Clemens, Benjamin, *died* 1957, vol. V
Clemens, Samuel Langhorne; *see* Twain, Mark.
Clemens, Sir William James, 1873–1941, vol. IV
Clement, Sir Anchitel Piers A.; *see* Ashburnham-Clement.
Clement, Ernest Wilson, 1860–1941, vol. IV
Clement, Sir Thomas, *died* 1956, vol. V
Clementi, Sir Cecil, 1875–1947, vol. IV
Clements, Arthur; *see* Baker, Andrew Clement.
Clements, Arthur Frederick, 1877–1968, vol. VI

Clements, Bernard; *see* Clements, W. D. B.
Clements, Rev. Jacob, 1820–1898, vol. I
Clements, Kay, (Dorothy Katharine), (Lady Clements); *see* Hammond, Kay.
Clements, Maj.-Gen. Ralph Arthur Penrhyn, 1855–1909, vol. I
Clements, Col Robert William, *died* 1941, vol. IV
Clements, (William Dudley) Bernard, 1880–1942, vol. IV
Clemesha, Lt-Col William Wesley, 1871–1958, vol. V
Cleminson, Frederick John, 1878–1943, vol. IV
Cleminson, Henry Millican, 1885–1970, vol. VI
Clemmey, Sir William Henry, 1846–1933, vol. III
Clemow, Frank Gerard, *died* 1939, vol. III
Clemson, Brig.-Gen. William Fletcher, 1866–1946, vol. IV
Clerici, Charles John Emil, *died* 1938, vol. III
Clerk, Sir Dugald, 1854–1932, vol. III
Clerk, Sir George Douglas, 8th Bt, 1852–1911, vol. I
Clerk, Sir George James Robert, 9th Bt, 1876–1943, vol. IV
Clerk, Rt Hon. Sir George Russell, 1874–1951, vol. V
Clerk, Gen. Sir Godfrey, 1835–1908, vol. I
Clerk, Maj.-Gen. Henry, 1821–1913, vol. I
Clerk, Hugh Edward, 1859–1942, vol. IV
Clerk, Col John, *died* 1919, vol. II
Clerk-Rattray, Lt-Gen. Sir James, 1832–1910, vol. I
Clerke, Agnes Mary, 1842–1907, vol. I
Clerke, Major Augustus Basil Holt, 1871–1949, vol. IV
Clerke, Ellen Mary, 1840–1906, vol. I
Clerke, Sir William Francis, 11th Bt, 1856–1930, vol. III
Clermont-Ganneau, Charles Simon, *born* 1846, vol. II
Clery, Arthur Edward, *died* 1932, vol. III
Clery, Maj.-Gen. Carleton Buckley Laming, 1869–1937, vol. III
Clery, Lt-Gen. Sir Francis, 1838–1926, vol. II
Clery, Surg.-Gen. James Albert, 1846–1920, vol. II
Cleugh, Eric Arthur, 1894–1964, vol. VI
Cleveland, Duchess of; (Catherine Lucy Wilhelmina), 1819–1901, vol. I
Cleveland, Sir Charles Raitt, 1866–1929, vol. III
Cleveland, Grover, 1837–1908, vol. I
Cleveland, Adm. Henry Forster, 1834–1924, vol. II
Cleveland, Col Henry Francis, 1863–1938, vol. III
Cleveland, Sydney Dyson, 1898–1975, vol. VII
Cleveland-Stevens, William, 1881–1957, vol. V
Cleverly, Charles F. M., *died* 1921, vol. II
Cleverly, Sir Osmund Somers, 1891–1966, vol. VI
Clewer, Maj.-Gen. Donald, 1892–1945, vol. IV
Clewes, Winston, 1906–1957, vol. V
Cleworth, Ralph, 1896–1975, vol. VII
Cleworth, Rev. Thomas Ebenezer, 1854–1909, vol. I
Clibborn, Col John, 1847–1938, vol. III
Clifden, 5th Viscount, 1829–1899, vol. I
Clifden, 6th Viscount, 1844–1930, vol. III
Clifden, 7th Viscount, 1883–1966, vol. VI

Clifden, 8th Viscount, 1887–1974, vol. VII

Cliff, Eric Francis, 1884–1969, vol. VI

Cliffe, Anthony Loftus, 1861–1922, vol. II

Cliffe, Michael, 1904–1964, vol. VI

Clifford of Chudleigh, 9th Baron, 1851–1916, vol. II

Clifford of Chudleigh, 10th Baron, 1858–1943, vol. IV

Clifford of Chudleigh, 11th Baron, 1887–1962, vol. VI

Clifford of Chudleigh, 12th Baron, 1889–1964, vol. VI

Clifford, Rt Rev. Alfred, 1849–1931, vol. III

Clifford, Captain Hon. Sir Bede Edmund Hugh, 1890–1969, vol. VI

Clifford, Sir Charles, died 1936, vol. III

Clifford, Sir Charles Lewis, 3rd Bt, 1885–1938, vol. III

Clifford, Edward C., died 1910, vol. I

Clifford, Elizabeth Lydia Rosabelle, (Lady Clifford), (Mrs Henry de la Pasture), died 1945, vol. IV

Clifford, Vice-Adm. Sir Eric George Anderson, 1900–1964, vol. VI

Clifford, Col Esmond Humphrey Miller, 1895–1970, vol. VI

Clifford, Ethel, died 1959, vol. V

Clifford, Frederick, 1828–1904, vol. I

Clifford, Sir George Hugh Charles, 2nd Bt, 1847–1930, vol. III

Clifford, Henry Charles, 1861–1947, vol. IV

Clifford, Brig.-Gen. Henry Frederick Hugh, 1867–1916, vol. II

Clifford, Sir Hugh, 1866–1941, vol. IV

Clifford, James Lowry, 1901–1978, vol. VII

Clifford, Rev. John, 1836–1923, vol. II

Clifford, Julian, 1877–1921, vol. II

Clifford, Rev. Sir Lewis Arthur Joseph, 5th Bt, 1896–1970, vol. VI

Clifford, Maj.-Gen. Richard Melville, 1841–1915, vol. I (A)

Clifford, Lt-Gen. Robert Cecil Richard, 1839–1930, vol. III

Clifford, Rev. Robert Rowntree, 1867–1943, vol. IV

Clifford, Sir Walter Lovelace, 4th Bt, 1852–1944, vol. IV

Clifford, Brig.-Gen. Walter Rees, 1866–1947, vol. IV

Clifford, Major Wigram, 1876–1917, vol. II

Clifford, Mrs William Kingdom, (Lucy Clifford), died 1929, vol. III

Clift, Hon. James Augustus, 1857–1923, vol. II

Clift, Col Sir Sidney William, 1885–1951, vol. V

Clifton, Baroness (17th in line), 1900–1937, vol. III

Clifton, Augustus Wykeham, 1829–1915, vol. I

Clifton, John Talbot, 1868–1928, vol. II

Clifton, Leon James Thomas, 1912–1978, vol. VII

Clifton, Lt-Col Percy Robert, 1872–1944, vol. IV

Clifton, Robert Bellamy, 1836–1921, vol. II

Clifton, Robert Cecil, 1854–1931, vol. III

Clifton, Violet Mary, (Mrs Talbot Clifton), 1883–1961, vol. VI

Clifton Brown, Cedric, 1887–1968, vol. VI

Clifton-Brown, Edward Clifton, 1870–1944, vol. IV

Climie, Robert, 1868–1929, vol. III

Climo, Lt-Gen. Sir Skipton Hill, 1868–1937, vol. III

Clinch, George, 1860–1921, vol. II

Clinton, 20th Baron, 1834–1904, vol. I

Clinton, 21st Baron, 1863–1957, vol. V

Clinton, David Osbert F.; see Fynes-Clinton.

Clinton, Lord Edward William Pelham-, 1836–1907, vol. I

Clinton, Rev. Henry Joy F.; see Fynes-Clinton.

Clinton, Michael Denys Arthur, 1918–1976, vol. VII

Clinton, Osbert Henry F.; see Fynes-Clinton.

Clinton, Ven. Thomas William, died 1926, vol. II

Clinton-Baddeley, Madeline Angela, (Angela Baddeley), 1904–1976, vol. VII

Clinton-Baker, Henry William, 1865–1935, vol. III

Clinton-Baker, Adm. Sir Lewis, 1866–1939, vol. III

Clipperton, Sir Charles Bell Child, 1864–1927, vol. II

Clissitt, William Cyrus, 1898–1977, vol. VII

Clissold, Major Harry, died 1917, vol. II

Clitherow, Lt-Col John Bourchier S.; see Stracey-Clitherow.

Clitherow, Richard, 1902–1947, vol. IV

Clive, Viscount; Mervyn Horatio Herbert, 1904–1943, vol. IV

Clive, Viscount; Percy Robert Herbert, 1892–1916, vol. II

Clive, Gen. Edward Henry, 1837–1916, vol. II

Clive, Lt-Col Hon. George Herbert Windsor W.; see Windsor-Clive.

Clive, Lt-Gen. Sir (George) Sidney, 1874–1959, vol. V

Clive, Lt-Col George W.; see Windsor-Clive.

Clive, Col Harry, 1880–1963, vol. VI

Clive, Captain Percy Archer, 1873–1918, vol. II

Clive, Rt Hon. Sir Robert Henry, 1877–1948, vol. IV

Clive, Lt-Gen. Sir Sidney; see Clive, Lt-Gen. Sir G. S.

Cloake, Philip Cyril, 1890–1969, vol. VI

Clodd, Edward, 1840–1930, vol. III

Clode, Sir Walter Baker, 1856–1937, vol. III

Cloete, (Edward Fairly) Stuart (Graham), 1897–1976, vol. VII

Cloete, Col Evelyn, 1863–1943, vol. IV

Cloete, Hendrik, 1851–1920, vol. II

Cloete, Lt-Gen. Josias Gordon, 1840–1907, vol. I

Cloete, Stuart; see Cloete, E. F. S. G.

Cloete, William Broderick, 1851–1915, vol. I

Clogg, Rev. Bertram; see Clogg, Rev. F. B.

Clogg, Rev. (Frank) Bertram, 1884–1955, vol. V

Clogg, Herbert Sherwell, died 1932, vol. III

Clogstoun, Herbert Cunningham, 1857–1936, vol. III

Clonbrock, 4th Baron, 1834–1917, vol. II

Clonbrock, 5th Baron, 1869–1926, vol. II

Cloncurry, 4th Baron, 1840–1928, vol. II

Cloncurry, 5th Baron, 1847–1929, vol. III

Clonmell, 6th Earl of, 1847–1898, vol. I

Clonmell, 7th Earl of, 1877–1928, vol. II

Clonmell, 8th Earl of, 1853–1935, vol. III

Cloran, Hon. Henry Joseph, 1855–1928, vol. II

Clore, Sir Charles, 1904–1979, vol. VII

Close, Col Sir Charles Frederick A.; see Arden-Close.

Close, Etta, *died* 1945, vol. IV
Close, Adm. Francis Arden, 1829–1918, vol. II
Close, Brig.-Gen. Geoffrey Dominic, 1866–1942, vol. IV
Close, Harold Arden, 1863–1932, vol. III
Close, Col Lewis Henry, 1869–1924, vol. II
Close, Major Maxwell Archibald, 1853–1935, vol. III
Close, Ralph William, 1867–1945, vol. IV
Close, S. P., vol. II
Clothier, Henry Williamson, 1878–1958, vol. V
Clothier, Wilfrid, 1887–1967, vol. VI
Cloudesley-Brereton, Maud Adeline; *see* Brereton.
Clough, Lt-Col Alfred Herrick Butler, 1856–1935, vol. III
Clough, Arthur Harold, 1897–1967, vol. VI
Clough, Blanche Athena, 1861–1960, vol. V
Clough, (Ernest Marshall) Owen, 1873–1964, vol. VI
Clough, Frederic Horton, 1878–1957, vol. V
Clough, Howard James Butler, 1890–1967, vol. VI
Clough, Sir John, 1836–1922, vol. II
Clough, Owen; *see* Clough, E. M. O.
Clough, Sir Robert, 1873–1965, vol. VI
Clough, Tom, 1867–1943, vol. IV
Clough, Walter Owen, 1846–1922, vol. II
Clough, William, 1862–1937, vol. III
Clouston, David, 1872–1948, vol. IV
Clouston, Sir Edward Seaborne, 1st Bt, 1849–1912, vol. I
Clouston, J. Storer, 1870–1944, vol. IV
Clouston, Sir Thomas Smith, 1840–1915, vol. I
Cloutier, Rt Rev. Francis Xavier, 1848–1933, vol. III
Cloutman, Sir Brett Mackay, 1891–1971, vol. VII
Clover, Maj.-Gen. Frederick Sherwood, 1894–1962, vol. VI
Clow, Sir Andrew Gourlay, 1890–1957, vol. V
Clow, Paymaster Rear-Adm. George James, *died* 1932, vol. III
Clow, Lt-Col William, 1863–1934, vol. III
Clow, William McCallum, 1853–1930, vol. III
Clowes, Lt-Gen. Cyril Albert, 1892–1968, vol. VI
Clowes, Frank, 1848–1923, vol. II
Clowes, Geoffrey Swinford Laird, 1883–1937, vol. III
Clowes, Col George Charles Knight, 1882–1941, vol. IV
Clowes, Sir Harold, 1903–1968, vol. VI
Clowes, Maj.-Gen. Norman, 1893–1980, vol. VII
Clowes, Lt-Col Peter Legh, 1853–1925, vol. II
Clowes, Samuel, 1864–1928, vol. II
Clowes, William Archibald, 1866–1937, vol. III
Clowes, Sir William Laird, 1856–1905, vol. I
Clubb, Hon. William Reid, 1884–1962, vol. VI
Clubbe, Sir Charles Percy Barlee, *died* 1932, vol. III
Clucas, Sir Frederick; *see* Clucas, Sir G. F.
Clucas, Sir (George) Frederick, 1870–1937, vol. III
Cluer, Albert Rowland, 1852–1942, vol. IV
Clune, Most Rev. Patrick Joseph, 1864–1935, vol. III
Clunes, Alec Sheriff de Moro, 1912–1970, vol. VI
Clunie, James, 1889–1974, vol. VII
Clunies-Ross, Sir Ian, 1899–1959, vol. V

Cluny Macpherson; *see* Macpherson, A. C.
Cluny Macpherson; *see* Macpherson, Brig. A. D.
Cluny Macpherson, *see* Macpherson, Brig.-Gen. E. H. D.
Cluse, William Sampson, 1875–1955, vol. V
Clute, Hon. Roger Conger, 1848–1921, vol. II
Clutsam, George H., 1866–1951, vol. V
Clutterbuck, Sir Alexander; *see* Clutterbuck, Sir P. A.
Clutterbuck, Sir (Peter) Alexander, 1897–1975, vol. VII
Clutterbuck, Sir Peter Henry, 1868–1951, vol. V
Clutton, Sir George Lisle, 1909–1970, vol. VI
Clutton, Henry Hugh, 1850–1909, vol. I
Clutton-Brock, Alan Francis, *died* 1976, vol. VII
Clutton-Brock, Arthur, 1868–1924, vol. II
Clwyd, 1st Baron, 1863–1955, vol. V
Clyde, Rt Hon. Lord; Rt Hon. James Avon Clyde, 1863–1944, vol. IV
Clyde, Rt Hon. Lord; Rt Hon. James Latham McDiarmid Clyde, 1898–1975, vol. VII
Clyde, Col Sir David, 1894–1966, vol. VI
Clyde, Rt Hon. James Avon; *see* Clyde, Rt Hon. Lord.
Clyde, Rt Hon. James Latham McDiarmid; *see* Clyde, Rt Hon. Lord.
Clyde, William McCallum, 1901–1972, vol. VII
Clydesmuir, 1st Baron, 1894–1954, vol. V
Clyne, Hon. Sir Thomas Stuart, 1887–1967, vol. VI
Clynes, Rt Hon. John Robert, 1869–1949, vol. IV
Coad, Maj.-Gen. Aubrey; *see* Coad, Maj.-Gen. B. A.
Coad, Maj.-Gen. Basil Aubrey, 1906–1980, vol. VII
Coad, Rev. Canon William Samuel, 1882–1965, vol. VI
Coade, Thorold Francis, 1896–1963, vol. VI
Coaker, Hon. Sir William Ford, 1871–1938, vol. III
Coakes, Ven. E. Lloyd, 1853–1930, vol. III
Coape-Arnold, Henry Fraser James; *see* Arnold.
Coape-Smith, Maj.-Gen. Henry, 1829–1921, vol. II
Coast, James Percy Chatterton, 1880–1962, vol. VI
Coatalen, Louis Hervé, 1879–1962, vol. VI
Coate, Rev. Harry, *died* 1939, vol. III
Coaten, Arthur Wells, 1879–1939, vol. III (A), vol. IV
Coates, Abraham George, 1861–1928, vol. II
Coates, Albert, 1882–1953, vol. V
Coates, Sir Albert Ernest, 1895–1977, vol. VII
Coates, Captain Sir Clive Milnes-, 2nd Bt (*cr* 1911), 1879–1971, vol. VII
Coates, David Wilson, 1886–1968, vol. VI
Coates, Dora; *see* Meeson, D.
Coates, Major Sir Edward Feetham, 1st Bt (*cr* 1911), 1853–1921, vol. II
Coates, Eric, 1886–1957, vol. V
Coates, Sir Eric Thomas, 1897–1968, vol. VI
Coates, Florence Earle, *died* 1927, vol. II
Coates, George James, 1869–1930, vol. III
Coates, Henry, 1880–1963, vol. VI
Coates, Sir James Hugh Buchanan, 1851–1935, vol. III
Coates, John, 1865–1941, vol. IV
Coates, Rev. John Rider, 1879–1956, vol. V

Coates, Joseph Edward, 1883–1973, vol. VII
Coates, Rt Hon. Joseph Gordon, 1878–1943, vol. IV
Coates, Sir Leonard James, 1883–1944, vol. IV
Coates, Rev. Percy, died 1925, vol. II
Coates, Brig.-Gen. Reginald Carlyon, 1869–1958, vol. V
Coates, Maj.-Gen. Thomas Seymour, 1879–1954, vol. V
Coates, Wells Wintemute, 1895–1958, vol. V
Coates, Col Sir William, 1860–1962, vol. VI
Coates, Sir William Frederick, 1st Bt (cr 1921), 1866–1932, vol. III
Coates, Sir William Henry, 1882–1963, vol. VI
Coath, Howell Lang L.; see Lang-Coath.
Coatman, John, 1889–1963, vol. VI
Coats, Major Andrew, 1862–1930, vol. III
Coats, George, 1876–1915, vol. I (A)
Coats, Col George Henry Brook, 1852–1919, vol. II
Coats, Sir James, 1st Bt (cr 1905), 1834–1913, vol. I
Coats, Sir James Stuart, 3rd Bt (cr 1905), 1894–1966, vol. VI
Coats, Rev. Jervis, 1844–1921, vol. II
Coats, Joseph, 1846–1899, vol. I
Coats, Robert Hamilton, 1874–1960, vol. V
Coats, Rev. Robert Hay, 1873–1956, vol. V
Coats, Air Cdre Rowland, 1904–1974, vol. VII
Coats, Sir Stuart Auchincloss, 2nd Bt (cr 1905), 1868–1959, vol. V
Coats, Sir Thomas Coats Glen Glen-, 2nd Bt (cr 1894), 1878–1954, vol. V
Coats, Sir Thomas Glen G., 1st Bt; see Glen-Coats.
Coats, Rev. Walter William, 1856–1941, vol. IV
Coats, William Hodge, 1866–1928, vol. II
Coatsworth, Emerson, 1854–1943, vol. IV
Cobb, Lt-Col Charles, 1884–1947, vol. IV
Cobb, Sir Cyril Stephen, 1861–1938, vol. III
Cobb, Captain Edward Charles, 1891–1957, vol. V
Cobb, Maj.-Gen. Edwyn Harland Wolstenholme, 1902–1955, vol. V
Cobb, Frederick Arthur, 1901–1950, vol. IV
Cobb, Geoffry Edward Wheatly, 1858–1931, vol. III
Cobb, Gerard Francis, 1838–1904, vol. I
Cobb, Col Henry Frederick, 1881–1939, vol. III
Cobb, Henry Venn, 1864–1949, vol. IV
Cobb, Ivo Geikie-, 1887–1953, vol. V
Cobb, Sir John Francis Scott, 1922–1977, vol. VII
Cobb, John Leslie, 1923–1977, vol. VII
Cobb, John Rhodes, 1899–1952, vol. V
Cobb, John William, 1873–1950, vol. IV
Cobb, Rear-Adm. Robert Harborne, 1900–1978, vol. VII
Cobb, Thomas, 1854–1932, vol. III
Cobb, Rev. William Frederick G.; see Geikie-Cobb.
Cobban, Alfred, 1901–1968, vol. VI
Cobban, James MacLaren, 1849–1903, vol. I
Cobbe, Gen. Sir Alexander Stanhope, 1870–1931, vol. III
Cobbe, Frances Power, 1822–1904, vol. I
Cobbe, Col Henry Hercules, 1869–1939, vol. III
Cobbe, Hon. John George, died 1944, vol. IV

Cobbett, Louis, 1862–1947, vol. IV
Cobbett, Pitt, died 1919, vol. II
Cobbett, Sir Walter Palmer, 1871–1955, vol. V
Cobbett, Walter Willson, 1847–1937, vol. III
Cobbett, Sir William, 1846–1926, vol. II
Cobbold, Lt-Col Ernest Cazenove, 1866–1932, vol. III
Cobbold, Lady Evelyn, died 1963, vol. VI
Cobbold, Felix Thornley, 1841–1909, vol. I
Cobbold, Herbert St George, died 1944, vol. IV
Cobbold, John Dupuis, 1861–1929, vol. III
Cobbold, Lt-Col John Murray, 1897–1944, vol. IV
Cobden, Lt-Col George Gough, 1878–1949, vol. IV
Cobden-Ramsay, Louis Eveleigh Bawtree, 1873–1962, vol. VI
Cobham, 8th Viscount, 1842–1922, vol. II
Cobham, 9th Viscount, 1881–1949, vol. IV
Cobham, 10th Viscount, 1909–1977, vol. VII
Cobham, 15th Baron, 1880–1933, vol. III
Cobham, 16th Baron, 1885–1951, vol. V
Cobham, Sir Alan John, 1894–1973, vol. VII
Cobham, Claude Delaval, 1842–1915, vol. I
Cobham, Brig.-Gen. Horace Walter, died 1958, vol. V
Cobham, Ven. John Lawrence, 1873–1960, vol. V, vol. VI
Cobley, Walter Henry, 1850–1938, vol. III
Coborn, Charles, (Colin Whitton McCallum), 1852–1945, vol. IV
Coburn, Sir (Marmaduke) Robert, 1885–1966, vol. VI
Coburn, Sir Robert; see Coburn, Sir M. R.
Cochin, Rajah of, died 1932, vol. III
Cochin, Maharaja of, 1861–1941, vol. IV
Cochin, Maharaja of, died 1943, vol. IV
Cochin, Henry Denys Benoit Marie, 1854–1922, vol. II
Cochran, Alexander, died 1961, vol. VI
Cochran, Sir Charles Blake, 1872–1951, vol. V
Cochran, Vice-Adm. Charles Home, 1850–1930, vol. III
Cochran-Patrick, Major Charles Kennedy; see Patrick.
Cochran-Patrick, Sir Neil James Kennedy, 1866–1958, vol. V
Cochrane of Cults, 1st Baron, 1857–1951, vol. V
Cochrane of Cults, 2nd Baron, 1883–1968, vol. VI
Cochrane, Alfred, 1865–1948, vol. IV
Cochrane, Dame Anne Annette Minnie, died 1943, vol. IV
Cochrane, Rear-Adm. Archibald, 1874–1952, vol. V
Cochrane, Captain Hon. Sir Archibald Douglas, 1885–1958, vol. V
Cochrane, Hon. Sir Arthur Auckland Leopold Pedro, 1824–1905, vol. I
Cochrane, Sir Arthur William Steuart, 1872–1954, vol. V
Cochrane, Vice-Adm. Basil Edward, 1841–1922, vol. II
Cochrane, Sir Cecil Algernon, 1869–1960, vol. V
Cochrane, Mrs Catherine, 1849–1934, vol. III
Cochrane, Charles Walter Hamilton, 1876–1932, vol. III

Cochrane, Sir Desmond Oriel Alastair George Weston, 3rd Bt (cr 1903), 1918–1979, vol. VII

Cochrane, Rev. Canon Edmund Lewis, 1876–1955, vol. V

Cochrane, Rear-Adm. Sir Edward Owen, 1881–1972, vol. VII

Cochrane, Captain Sir Ernest Cecil, 2nd Bt (cr 1903), 1873–1952, vol. V

Cochrane, Captain Hon. Ernest Grey Lambton, 1834–1911, vol. I

Cochrane, Hon. Francis, 1852–1919, vol. II

Cochrane, Helen Lavinia, died 1946, vol. IV

Cochrane, Sir Henry, 1st Bt (cr 1903), died 1904, vol. I

Cochrane, Brig.-Gen. James Kilvington, 1873–1948, vol. IV

Cochrane, Maj.-Gen. James Rupert, 1904–1978, vol. VII

Cochrane, Col John Ernest Charles James, 1870–1938, vol. III

Cochrane, Julia Dorothy, (Hon. Lady Cochrane), died 1971, vol. VII

Cochrane, Lt-Col R. C., 1871–1925, vol. III

Cochrane, Air Chief Marshal Hon. Sir Ralph Alexander, 1895–1977, vol. VII

Cochrane, Sir Stanley Herbert, 1st Bt (cr 1915), 1877–1949, vol. IV

Cochrane, Col Thomas Henry, 1867–1950, vol. IV

Cochrane, Col William Francis Dundonald, 1847–1928, vol. II

Cock, Rev. Albert A., 1883–1953, vol. V

Cock, F. William, 1858–1943, vol. IV

Cock, Gerald, 1887–1973, vol. VII

Cock, Henry, died 1922, vol. II

Cock, Julia, died 1914, vol. I

Cockayne, Edward Alfred, 1880–1956, vol. V

Cockayne, Leonard, 1855–1934, vol. III

Cockbill, Ven. Charles Shipley, 1888–1965, vol. VI

Cockburn, Archibald William, 1887–1969, vol. VI

Cockburn, Col Charles Douglas L.; see Learoyd-Cockburn.

Cockburn, Sir Edward Cludde, 8th Bt, 1834–1903, vol. I

Cockburn, Major Ernest Radcliffe, 1875–1955, vol. V

Cockburn, Col George, 1856–1925, vol. II

Cockburn, Sir George Jack, 1848–1927, vol. II

Cockburn, Major H. Z. C., died 1913, vol. I

Cockburn, Henry, 1859–1927, vol. II

Cockburn, Gen. Henry Alexander, 1831–1922, vol. II

Cockburn, Very Rev. James Hutchison, 1882–1973, vol. VII

Cockburn, Sir James Stanhope, 10th Bt, 1867–1947, vol. IV

Cockburn, Hon. Sir John Alexander, 1850–1929, vol. III

Cockburn, Lt-Col Sir John Brydges, 11th Bt, 1870–1949, vol. IV

Cockburn, Nathaniel Clayton, 1866–1924, vol. II

Cockburn, Sir Robert, 9th Bt, 1861–1938, vol. III

Cockburn, Captain William, 1893–1970, vol. VI

Cockburn, Sir William Robert Marshall, 1891–1957, vol. V

Cockburn-Campbell, Sir Alexander Thomas; see Campbell.

Cockcraft, Lt-Col Louis William la Trobe, 1880–1963, vol. VI

Cockcroft, Sir John Douglas, 1897–1967, vol. VI

Cocke, Sir Hugh, died 1958, vol. V

Cockell, Seton F.; see Forbes-Cockell.

Cocker, William Hollis, 1896–1962, vol. VI

Cockeram, William Henry, 1857–1946, vol. IV

Cockerell, Douglas Bennett, 1870–1945, vol. IV

Cockerell, Horace Abel, 1832–1908, vol. I

Cockerell, Sir Sydney Carlyle, 1867–1962, vol. VI

Cockerill, Brig.-Gen. Sir George Kynaston, 1867–1957, vol. V

Cockerline, Sir Walter Herbert, 1856–1941, vol. IV

Cockey, Air Cdre Leonard Herbert, 1893–1978, vol. VII

Cockin, Rt Rev. Frederic Arthur, 1888–1969, vol. VI

Cockin, Ven. John Irwin Browne, 1850–1924, vol. II

Cocking, William Trusting, 1862–1912, vol. I

Cockram, George, 1861–1950, vol. IV

Cockran, William Bourke, 1854–1923, vol. II

Cocks, Hon. Sir Arthur Alfred Clement, 1862–1943, vol. IV

Cocks, Charles Sebastian Somers, 1870–1951, vol. V

Cocks, Frederick Seymour, 1882–1953, vol. V

Cocks, George Arthur, died 1933, vol. III

Cocks, Rev. Henry Lawrence S.; see Somers-Cocks.

Cocks, John Sebastian S.; see Somers Cocks.

Cocks, Philip Alphonso Somers, 1862–1940, vol. III

Cockshutt, Col Hon. Henry, 1868–1944, vol. IV

Cocoto, Spiridon George, 1843–1916, vol. II

Cocteau, Jean, 1889–1963, vol. VI

Codd, Rt Rev. William, 1864–1938, vol. III

Coddington, Fitzherbert John Osbourne, 1881–1956, vol. V

Coddington, Col Herbert Adolphe, 1864–1939, vol. III

Coddington, Sir William, 1st Bt, 1830–1918, vol. II

Code, Rev. Canon George Brereton, 1886–1946, vol. IV

Code Holland, Robert Henry; see Holland.

Coderre, Louis, 1865–1935, vol. III

Codling, Sir William Richard, 1879–1947, vol. IV

Codner, Maurice Frederick, 1888–1958, vol. V

Codrington, Lt-Gen. Sir Alfred Edward, 1854–1945, vol. IV

Codrington, Sir Christopher William Gerald Henry, 2nd Bt (cr 1876), 1894–1979, vol. VII

Codrington, Engr-Comdr Claude Alexander, 1877–1955, vol. V

Codrington, Col Sir Geoffrey Ronald, 1888–1973, vol. VII

Codrington, Sir Gerald William Henry, 1st Bt (cr 1876), 1850–1929, vol. III

Codrington, Brig.-Gen. Hubert Walter, 1864–1940, vol. III

Codrington, Robert Edward, 1869–1908, vol. I

Codrington, Rev. Robert Henry, 1830–1922, vol. II
Codrington, Sir William, 5th Bt (*cr* 1721), 1829–1904 (this entry was not transferred to Who was Who).
Codrington, William Melville, 1892–1963, vol. VI
Codrington, Sir William Richard, 7th Bt (*cr* 1721), 1904–1961, vol. VI
Codrington, Lt-Col Sir William Robert, 6th Bt (*cr* 1721), 1867–1932, vol. III
Cody, Rev. Henry John, 1868–1951, vol. V
Coe, Captain; *see* Mitchell, Edward Card.
Coen, Sir Terence Bernard C.; *see* Creagh Coen.
Coffey, Christopher, 1902–1976, vol. VII
Coffey, Denis Joseph, *died* 1945, vol. IV
Coffey, George, 1857–1916, vol. II
Coffey, Rt Rev. John, *died* 1904, vol. I
Coffey, Rev. Peter, 1876–1943, vol. IV
Coffey, Hon. Thomas, 1843–1914, vol. I
Coffey, Thomas Malo, 1894–1968, vol. VI
Coffin, Col Campbell, 1867–1952, vol. V
Coffin, Charles Hayden, 1862–1935, vol. III
Coffin, Maj-Gen. Clifford, 1870–1959, vol. V
Coffin, Rev. Henry Sloane, 1877–1954, vol. V
Coffin, Major John Edward P.; *see* Pine-Coffin.
Coffin, Gen. Roger P.; *see* Pine-Coffin.
Coffin, Walter Harris, 1853–1916, vol. II
Cofman-Nicoresti, Carol Adolph, 1881–1938, vol. III (A), vol. IV
Cogan, Rev. Horace Barbut, *died* 1933, vol. III
Coghill, Col Charles Edward, 1861–1948, vol. IV
Coghill, Douglas Harry, 1855–1928, vol. II
Coghill, Sir Egerton Bushe, 5th Bt, 1853–1921, vol. II
Coghill, Rev. Canon Ernest Arthur, 1859–1941, vol. IV
Coghill, Sir John Joscelyn, 4th Bt, 1826–1905, vol. I
Coghill, Col Kendal, 1832–1919, vol. II
Coghill, Nevill Henry Kendal Aylmer, 1899–1980, vol. VII
Coghlan, Col Charles, 1852–1921, vol. II
Coghlan, Hon. Sir Charles Patrick John, 1863–1927, vol. II
Coghlan, Rt Rev. Mgr John, 1887–1963, vol. VI
Coghlan, Hon. Sir Timothy Augustine, 1857–1926, vol. II
Cogswell, Mark James, *died* 1934, vol. III
Cogswell, Rev. Canon William, 1845–1917, vol. II
Cohalan, Most Rev. Daniel, 1858–1952, vol. V
Cohalan, Most Rev. Daniel, 1884–1965, vol. VI
Cohan, George Michael, 1878–1942, vol. IV
Cohen, Baron (Life Peer); Lionel Leonard Cohen, 1888–1973, vol. VII
Cohen of Birkenhead, 1st Baron, 1900–1977, vol. VII
Cohen of Brighton, Baron (Life Peer); Lewis Coleman Cohen, 1897–1966, vol. VI
Cohen, Sir Andrew Benjamin, 1909–1968, vol. VI
Cohen, Rt Hon. Arthur, 1830–1914, vol. I
Cohen, Arthur S.; *see* Sefton-Cohen.
Cohen, Augustus, *died* 1903, vol. I
Cohen, Sir Benjamin Arthur, 1862–1942, vol. IV
Cohen, Sir Benjamin Louis, 1st Bt, *died* 1909, vol. I
Cohen, Major Sir Brunel; *see* Cohen, Major Sir J. B. B.

Cohen, Lt-Col Charles Waley, 1879–1963, vol. VI
Cohen, Clifford Theodore, 1906–1972, vol. VII
Cohen, Sir Edgar Abraham, 1908–1973, vol. VII
Cohen, Rabbi Francis Lyon, 1862–1934, vol. III
Cohen, Hannah F., *died* 1946, vol. IV
Cohen, Brig. Hon. Harold Edward, 1881–1946, vol. IV
Cohen, Harriet, *died* 1967, vol. VI
Cohen, Harry F.; *see* Freeman-Cohen.
Cohen, Hon. Henry Emanuel, 1840–1912, vol. I
Cohen, Hon. Henry Isaac, 1872–1942, vol. IV
Cohen, Sir Herbert Benjamin, 2nd Bt, 1874–1968, vol. IV
Cohen, Isaac Michael, 1884–1951, vol. V
Cohen, Israel, 1879–1961, vol. VI
Cohen, Major Sir (Jack Benn) Brunel, 1886–1965, vol. VI
Cohen, Col Jacob Waley, 1874–1948, vol. IV
Cohen, Sir John Edward, 1898–1979, vol. VII
Cohen, Joseph L., *died* 1940, vol. III
Cohen, Julius Berend, 1859–1935, vol. III
Cohen, Sir Karl Cyril, *died* 1973, vol. VII
Cohen, Sir Leonard Lionel, 1858–1938, vol. III
Cohen, Sir Lewis, 1849–1933, vol. III
Cohen, Marcel, 1884–1974, vol. VII
Cohen, Mary Gwendolen, (Mrs Arthur M. Cohen), 1893–1962, vol. VI
Cohen, Mrs Nathaniel Louis, *died* 1917, vol. II
Cohen, Reuben, 1880–1958, vol. V
Cohen, Sir Robert Waley, 1877–1952, vol. V
Cohen, Sir Samuel Sydney, 1869–1948, vol. IV
Cohn, Jefferson Davis, 1881–1951, vol. V
Coit, Stanton, 1857–1944, vol. III
Cokayne, George Edward, 1825–1911, vol. I
Coke, Adm. Sir Charles Henry, 1854–1945, vol. IV
Coke, Captain Desmond, 1879–1931, vol. III
Coke, Brig.-Gen. Edward Beresford, 1850–1924, vol. II
Coke, Brig.-Gen. Edward Sacheverell D'Ewes, 1872–1941, vol. IV
Coke, Hon. Henry John, 1827–1916, vol. II
Coke, Col Jacynth d'Ewes FitzErcald, 1879–1963, vol. VI
Coke, Sir John, 1807–1897, vol. I
Coke, Captain John Gilbert de Odingsells, 1874–1937, vol. III
Coke, Major Hon. Sir John Spencer, 1880–1957, vol. V
Coke, Maj.-Gen. John Talbot, 1841–1912, vol. I
Coke, Captain Hon. Reginald, 1883–1969, vol. VI
Coke, Major Hon. Richard, 1876–1964, vol. VI
Coke, Comdr Hon. Roger, 1886–1960, vol. V
Coke, Mrs Talbot, 1843–1922, vol. II
Coke, Lt-Col Wenman Clarence Walpole, 1828–1907, vol. I
Coke Wallis, Leonard George, 1900–1974, vol. VII
Coker, Col Edmund Rogers, 1844–1914, vol. I
Coker, Ernest George, 1869–1946, vol. IV
Coker, Sir Salako Ambrosius B.; *see* Benka-Coker.
Colahan, Nicholas Whistler, *died* 1930, vol. III
Colam, Sir Harold Nugent, 1882–1956, vol. V
Colam, Robert Frederick, *died* 1942, vol. IV
Colban, Erik, 1876–1956, vol. V
Colbeck, Edmund Henry, 1865–1942, vol. IV

Colbert, John Patrick, 1898–1975, vol. VII

Colborne, Col Hon. Francis Lionel Lydstone, 1855–1924, vol. II

Colborne, Surg. Rear-Adm. William John, 1865–1945, vol. IV

Colborne, Surg. Rear-Adm. William John, died 1971, vol. VII

Colby, Col Cecil John Herbert S.; see Spence-Colby.

Colby, Charles W., 1867–1955, vol. V

Colby, Sir Geoffrey Francis Taylor, 1901–1958, vol. V

Colchester, 3rd Baron, 1842–1919, vol. II

Colchester-Wemyss, Sir Francis, 1872–1954, vol. V

Colchester Wemyss, Maynard Willoughby, 1846–1930, vol. III

Colclough, Rear-Adm. (S) Beauchamp Urquhart, 1867–1949, vol. IV

Coldrick, William, 1896–1975, vol. VII

Coldridge, Ward, 1864–1926, vol. II

Coldstream, Sir John, 1877–1954, vol. V

Coldstream, John Phillips, 1842–1909, vol. I

Coldstream, Col William Menzies, 1869–1943, vol. IV

Coldwell, Hon. George Robson, 1858–1924, vol. II

Coldwell-Smith, Lt-Col Frederick Lawrence, 1895–1967, vol. VI (AII)

Cole, Viscount; Michael Galbraith Lowry Cole, 1921–1956, vol. V

Cole, Baron (Life Peer); George James Cole, 1906–1979, vol. VII

Cole, Air Vice-Marshal Adrian Trevor, 1895–1966, vol. VI

Cole, Alan Summerly, 1846–1934, vol. III

Cole, Alfred Clayton, 1854–1920, vol. II

Cole, Vice-Adm. Sir Antony Bartholomew, 1909–1967, vol. VI

Cole, Brig.-Gen. Arthur Willoughby George Lowry, 1860–1915, vol. I

Cole, Major Aubrey du Plat Thorold, 1877–1939, vol. III

Cole, Madame Belle, died 1904, vol. I

Cole, Charles Woolsey, 1906–1978, vol. VII

Cole, Col Sir Edward Hearle, 1863–1949, vol. IV

Cole, Edward Nicholas, 1909–1977, vol. VII

Cole, Rev. Edward Pattinson, died 1926, vol. II

Cole, Eric Kirkham, 1901–1966, vol. VI

Cole, Francis Joseph, 1872–1959, vol. V

Cole, George, died 1913, vol. I

Cole, George Douglas Howard, 1889–1959, vol. V

Cole, Lt-Gen. Sir George Sinclair, 1911–1973, vol. VII

Cole, Maj.-Gen. George Wynne, 1836–1908, vol. I

Cole, Grenville Arthur James, 1859–1924, vol. II

Cole, Harold William, 1884–1959, vol. V

Cole, Lt-Col Henry W.; see Wells-Cole.

Cole, Lt-Col Sir Henry Walter George, died 1932, vol. III

Cole, Maj.-Gen. Sir Herbert Covington, died 1959, vol. V

Cole, John, 1903–1975, vol. VII

Cole, Rev. John Francis, died 1921, vol. II

Cole, Dame Margaret Isabel, 1893–1980, vol. VII

Cole, Sir Noel, 1892–1975, vol. VII

Cole, Norman John, 1909–1979, vol. VII

Cole, Percival Pasley, died 1948, vol. IV

Cole, Percy Frederick, 1882–1968, vol. VI

Cole, Reginald John Vicat; see Cole, John.

Cole, Rex Vicat, 1870–1940, vol. III

Cole, Gp Captain Robert Arthur Alexander, 1901–1949, vol. IV

Cole, Rev. Robert Eden George, died 1921, vol. II

Cole, Robert Henry, 1866–1926, vol. II

Cole, Ven. Robert Henry, died 1934, vol. III

Cole, Robert Langton, 1858–1928, vol. II

Cole, Sophie, 1862–1947, vol. IV

Cole, Lt-Col Stanley James, 1884–1949, vol. IV

Cole, Rev. Theodore Edward Fortescue, died 1944, vol. IV

Cole, Thomas Loftus, died 1961, vol. VI

Cole, Walton Adamson, 1912–1963, vol. VI

Cole, Rev. William John, died 1933, vol. III

Cole-Deacon, Gerald John, 1890–1968, vol. VI

Cole-Hamilton, Lt-Col Claud George; see Hamilton.

Cole-Hamilton, Air Vice-Marshal John Beresford, 1894–1945, vol. IV

Colebatch, Hon. Sir Hal Pateshall, 1872–1953, vol. V

Colebrook, Edward Hilder, 1898–1977, vol. VII

Colebrook, Leonard, 1883–1967, vol. VI

Colebrooke, 1st Baron, 1861–1939, vol. III

Colefax, Sir Arthur, died 1936, vol. III

Colegate, Sir Arthur, died 1956, vol. V

Coleman, Arthur Philemon, 1852–1939, vol. III

Coleman, Lt-Gen. Sir Charles; see Coleman, Lt-Gen. Sir C. F. C.

Coleman, Charles James, died 1908, vol. I

Coleman, Lt-Gen. Sir (Cyril Frederick) Charles, died 1974, vol. VII

Coleman, D'Alton Corry, 1879–1956, vol. V

Coleman, Ephraim Herbert, 1890–1961, vol. VI

Coleman, Frank, 1876–1962, vol. VI

Coleman, Lt-Col George Burdett, died 1923, vol. II

Coleman, Herbert Cecil, 1893–1956, vol. V

Coleman, Rev. James, 1831–1913, vol. I

Coleman, Rt Rev. John Aloysius, 1887–1947, vol. IV, vol. V

Coleman, Leslie Charles, died 1954, vol. V

Coleman, Rt Rev. Michael Edward, 1902–1969, vol. VI

Coleman, Rev. Canon Noel Dolben, 1891–1948, vol. IV

Colenbrander, Col Johann William, 1859–1918, vol. II

Coleraine, 1st Baron, 1901–1980, vol. VII

Coleridge, 2nd Baron, 1851–1927, vol. II

Coleridge, 3rd Baron, 1877–1955, vol. V

Coleridge, Christabel Rose, 1843–1921, vol. II

Coleridge, Ernest Hartley, 1846–1920, vol. II

Coleridge, Hon. Gilbert James Duke, 1859–1953, vol. V

Coleridge, Lt-Col Hugh Fortescue, 1859–1928, vol. II

Coleridge, Gen. Sir John Francis Stanhope Duke, 1878–1951, vol. V

Coleridge, Miss Mary Elizabeth, 1861–1907, vol. I

Coleridge, Hon. Stephen, 1854–1936, vol. III

Coleridge, Wilfrid Duke, 1889–1956, vol. V
Coleridge-Taylor, Samuel, 1875–1912, vol. I
Coles, Col Arthur Horsman, 1856–1931, vol. III
Coles, Charles, 1853–1926, vol. II
Coles, Charles, 1878–1947, vol. IV
Coles, Edward Horsman, 1865–1948, vol. IV
Coles, Sir George James, 1885–1977, vol. VII
Coles, Gordon Robert, 1913–1975, vol. VII
Coles, Hon. Sir Jenkin, 1842–1911, vol. I
Coles, John, *died* 1919, vol. II
Coles, Col Morton Calverley, 1863–1943, vol. IV
Coles, Sir Richard James, 1862–1935, vol. III
Coles, Sherard Osborn C.; *see* Cowper-Coles.
Coles, Rev. Vincent Stuckey Stratton, 1845–1929, vol. III
Coles, Air Marshal Sir William Edward, 1913–1979, vol. VII
Coles, Major William Hewett, 1882–1955, vol. V
Colette, 1873–1954, vol. V
Coley, Frederic Collins, *died* 1928, vol. II
Colfox, Lt-Col Sir Philip; *see* Colfox, Lt-Col Sir W. P.
Colfox, Lt-Col Sir (William) Philip, 1st Bt, 1888–1966, vol. VI
Colgan, Most Rev. Joseph, 1824–1911, vol. I
Colgrain, 1st Baron, 1866–1954, vol. V
Colgrain, 2nd Baron, 1891–1973, vol. VII
Colijn, Hendrikus, 1869–1944, vol. IV
Colivet, Michael Patrick, 1884–1955, vol. V
Coll, Sir Anthony Michael, 1861–1931, vol. III
Collard, Maj.-Gen. Albert Sydney, 1876–1938, vol. III (A), vol. IV
Collard, Col Alexander Arthur Lysons, 1871–1947, vol. IV
Collard, Major Alfred Stephen, 1865–1941, vol. IV
Collard, Allan Ovenden, 1861–1928, vol. II
Collard, Vice-Adm. Bernard St G., 1876–1962, vol. VI
Collard, Lt-Col Charles Edwin, *died* 1942, vol. IV
Collard, Sir George, 1840–1921, vol. II
Collard, Gp Captain Richard Charles Marler, 1911–1962, vol. VI
Collcutt, Thomas Edward, 1840–1924, vol. II
Colledge, Lionel, 1883–1948, vol. IV
Collen, Lt-Col Edwin Henry Ethelbert, 1875–1943, vol. IV
Collen, Lt-Gen. Sir Edwin Henry Hayter, 1843–1911, vol. I
Coller, Frank Herbert, 1866–1938, vol. III
Colles, Comdr Sir Dudley, 1889–1976, vol. VII
Colles, Henry Cope, 1879–1943, vol. IV
Colles, Ramsay, 1862–1919, vol. II
Colles, William Morris, *died* 1926, vol. II
Collet, Clara E., 1860–1948, vol. IV
Collet, Sir Mark Edlmann, 2nd Bt, 1864–1944, vol. IV
Collet, Sir Mark Wilks, 1st Bt, 1816–1905, vol. I
Collet, Sir Wilfred, 1856–1929, vol. III
Colleton, Sir Robert Augustus William, 9th Bt, 1854–1938, vol. III
Collett, Charles Benjamin, 1871–1952, vol. V
Collett, Sir Charles Henry, 1st Bt, 1864–1938, vol. III
Collett, Sir Henry, 1836–1901, vol. I

Collett, Sir Henry Seymour, 2nd Bt, 1893–1971, vol. VII
Collett, Col Hon. Herbert Brayley, 1877–1947, vol. IV
Collett, Col John Henry, 1876–1942, vol. IV
Collett, Rt Rev. Dom Martin, 1879–1948, vol. IV
Collette, Charles, 1842–1924, vol. II
Colley, David Isherwood, 1916–1975, vol. VII
Colley, Richard, 1893–1964, vol. VI
Colley, Robert D.; *see* Davies-Colley.
Collie, J. Norman, 1859–1942, vol. IV
Collie, Sir John, 1860–1935, vol. III
Collie, Ruth, *died* 1936, vol. III
Collier, Maj.-Gen. Angus Lyell, 1893–1971, vol. VII
Collier, Charles Saint John, 1880–1944, vol. IV
Collier, Constance, 1880–1955, vol. V
Collier, Dorothy Josephine, 1894–1972, vol. VII
Collier, Lt-Col Ernest Victor, 1878–1964, vol. VI
Collier, Frank Simon, 1900–1964, vol. VI
Collier, Frederick William, 1851–1925, vol. II
Collier, Sir George Herman, 1856–1941, vol. IV
Collier, Horace Stansfield, *died* 1930, vol. III
Collier, James, 1846–1925, vol. II (A), vol. III
Collier, James, 1870–1935, vol. III
Collier, Hon. John, 1850–1934, vol. III
Collier, John Francis, 1829–1913, vol. I
Collier, Joseph, *died* 1967, vol. VI
Collier, Air Cdre Kenneth Dowsett Gould, 1892–1971, vol. VII
Collier, Sir Laurence, 1890–1976, vol. VII
Collier, Hon. Margaret Isabella; *see* Galletti di Cadilhac, Countess.
Collier, Marie Elizabeth, 1927–1971, vol. VII
Collier, Mayo, 1857–1931, vol. III
Collier, Most Rev. Patrick, 1880–1964, vol. VI
Collier, Peter Fenelon, 1849–1909, vol. I
Collier, Hon. Philip, 1874–1948, vol. IV
Collier, Rev. Samuel Francis, 1855–1921, vol. II
Collier, Rev. Thomas Grey, 1844–1933, vol. III
Collier, William, 1856–1935, vol. III
Collier, William Douglas, 1894–1953, vol. V
Collin, Annie Rosalie, 1852–1957, vol. V
Collindridge, Frank, *died* 1951, vol. V
Colling, Rev. James, *died* 1929, vol. III
Collinge, Walter E., *died* 1947, vol. IV
Collingridge, George Rooke, 1867–1944, vol. IV
Collingridge, William, 1854–1927, vol. II
Collings, Albert Henry, *died* 1947, vol. IV
Collings, Col Alfred Henry, 1847–1933, vol. III
Collings, Col Godfrey Disney, 1855–1941, vol. IV
Collings, Rt Hon. Jesse, 1831–1920, vol. II
Collingwood, Arthur, 1879–1952, vol. V
Collingwood, Bertram James, *died* 1934, vol. III
Collingwood, Sir Charles Arthur, 1887–1964, vol. VI
Collingwood, Brig.-Gen. Clennell William, 1873–1960, vol. V
Collingwood, Cuthbert, 1826–1908, vol. I
Collingwood, Rt Rev. Mgr Canon Cuthbert, 1908–1980, vol. VII
Collingwood, Col Cuthbert George, 1848–1933, vol. III
Collingwood, Sir Edward Foyle, 1900–1970, vol. VI

Collingwood, George Trevor, 1863–1922, vol. II
Collingwood, Robin George, 1889–1943, vol. IV
Collingwood, Sir William, 1855–1928, vol. II
Collingwood, William Gershom, 1854–1932, vol. III
Collins, Baron (Life Peer); Richard Henn Collins, 1842–1911, vol. I
Collins, Alfred Tenison, 1852–1945, vol. IV
Collins, Sir Archibald John, 1890–1955, vol. V
Collins, Lt-Col Arthur, 1845–1911, vol. I
Collins, Arthur, 1880–1952, vol. V
Collins, Arthur Ernest, 1871–1926, vol. II
Collins, Brig. Arthur Francis St Clair, 1892–1980, vol. VII
Collins, Arthur Jefferies, 1893–1976, vol. VII
Collins, Sir Arthur John Hammond, 1834–1915, vol. I
Collins, Arthur Pelham, 1863–1932, vol. III
Collins, Bernard Abdy, 1880–1951, vol. V
Collins, Charles, died 1921, vol. II
Collins, Maj.-Gen. Charles Edward E.; see Edward-Collins.
Collins, Cyril George, 1880–1947, vol. IV
Collins, Dale, 1897–1956, vol. V
Collins, Sir D(aniel) George, 1869–1959, vol. V
Collins, Maj.-Gen. Dennis Joseph, died 1939, vol. III
Collins, Douglas, 1912–1972, vol. VII
Collins, Douglas Henry, 1907–1964, vol. VI
Collins, Maj.-Gen. Sir Dudley Stuart, 1881–1959, vol. V
Collins, Edward Treacher, 1862–1932, vol. III
Collins, Adm. Sir Frederick (Basset) E.; see Edward-Collins.
Collins, Sir George; see Collins, Sir D. G.
Collins, George Edward, 1880–1968, vol. VI
Collins, Adm. Sir (George) Frederick (Basset) E.; see Edward-Collins.
Collins, Hon. George Thomas, 1839–1926, vol. II
Collins, Brig. Gerald E.; see Edward-Collins.
Collins, Sir Godfrey Ferdinando Stratford, 1888–1952, vol. V
Collins, Rt Hon. Sir Godfrey P., 1875–1936, vol. III
Collins, Herbert Frederick, 1890–1967, vol. VI
Collins, Herbert Jeffery, 1907–1968, vol. VI
Collins, Horatio John, 1894–1963, vol. VI
Collins, Sir James Patrick, 1891–1964, vol. VI
Collins, James Richard, 1869–1934, vol. III
Collins, John Churton, 1848–1908, vol. I
Collins, John Henry, 1880–1952, vol. V
Collins, Rt Rev. John J., 1857–1934, vol. III
Collins, John Philip, died 1954, vol. V
Collins, John Rupert, died 1965, vol. VI
Collins, Maj.-Gen. John Stratford, 1851–1908, vol. I
Collins, Joseph Thomas, 1863–1938, vol. III
Collins, Brig. Lionel Peter, 1878–1957, vol. V
Collins, Mabel; see Cook, Mrs M.
Collins, Mark, vol. III
Collins, Michael, 1890–1922, vol. II
Collins, Patrick, 1859–1943, vol. IV
Collins, Rev. Percy Herbert, died 1941, vol. IV
Collins, Rear-Adm. Ralph, 1877–1957, vol. V

Collins, Rev. Reginald Francis, 1851–1933, vol. III
Collins, Rt Rev. Richard, 1857–1924, vol. II
Collins, Lt-Col Hon. Richard Henn, 1873–1952, vol. V
Collins, Sir Robert Hawthorn, 1841–1908, vol. I
Collins, Maj.-Gen. Robert John, 1880–1950, vol. IV
Collins, Col Robert Joseph, 1848–1924, vol. II
Collins, Sir Robert Muirhead, 1852–1927, vol. II
Collins, Seymour John, 1906–1970, vol. VI
Collins, Sir Stephen, 1847–1925, vol. II
Collins, Hon. Sir Stephen Ogle H.; see Henn-Collins.
Collins, Sir Thomas, 1860–1944, vol. IV
Collins, Most Rev. Thomas Gibson George, 1873–1927, vol. II
Collins, Victor John; see Baron Stonham.
Collins, Rt Rev. W. E., 1867–1911, vol. I
Collins, Lt-Col William Alexander, 1873–1945, vol. IV
Collins, Sir William Alexander Roy, 1900–1976, vol. VII
Collins, Col Hon. William Edward, 1853–1934, vol. III
Collins, Sir William Henry, died 1947, vol. IV
Collins, Sir William Job, 1859–1946, vol. IV
Collins, Col Comdt Hon. William Richard, 1876–1944, vol. IV
Collins, William Wiehe, 1862–1951, vol. V
Collinson, Alfred Howe, 1866–1927, vol. II
Collinson, Col Harold, 1876–1945, vol. IV
Collinson, Lt-Col John, 1859–1901, vol. I
Collinson, Joseph, 1871–1952, vol. V
Collinson, Thomas Henry, 1858–1928, vol. II
Collinson, William Edward, 1889–1969, vol. VI
Collip, James Bertram, 1892–1965, vol. VI
Collis, Edgar Leigh, 1870–1957, vol. V
Collis, Maj.-Gen. Francis William, 1839–1905, vol. I
Collis, Maj.-Gen. Sir James Norman C.; see Cooke-Collis.
Collis, Maurice, 1889–1973, vol. VII
Collis, Very Rev. Maurice Henry Fitzgerald, 1859–1947, vol. IV
Collis, Lt-Col Robert Henry, 1874–1930, vol. III
Collis, Col William C.; see Cooke-Collis.
Collis, William Robert FitzGerald, 1900–1975, vol. VII
Collishaw, Air Vice-Marshal Raymond, 1893–1976, vol. VII
Collison, Bt Col Charles Sydney, 1871–1935, vol. III
Collison, Levi, 1875–1965, vol. VI (AII)
Collison, Ven. William Henry, 1847–1922, vol. II
Collisson, Rev. William Alexander Houston, 1865–1920, vol. II
Collister, Sir Harold James, 1885–1950, vol. IV
Colls, John Howard, died 1910, vol. I
Collyer, Ven. Daniel, 1848–1924, vol. II
Collyer, Maj.-Gen. John Johnston, 1870–1941, vol. IV
Collyer, Robert, 1823–1912, vol. I
Collyer, William Robert, 1842–1928, vol. II
Collymore, Sir Allan; see Collymore, Sir E. A.

140

Collymore, Sir (Ernest) Allan, 1893–1962, vol. VI
Colman, Cecil, 1878–1954, vol. V
Colman, Lt-Col Frederick Gordon Dalziel, *died* 1969, vol. VI
Colman, Sir (George) Stanley, *died* 1966, vol. VI
Colman, Grace Mary, 1892–1971, vol. VII
Colman, Sir Jeremiah, 1st Bt (*cr* 1907), 1859–1942, vol. IV
Colman, Sir Jeremiah, 2nd Bt (*cr* 1907), 1886–1961, vol. VI
Colman, Sir Nigel Claudian Dalziel, 1st Bt (*cr* 1952), *died* 1966, vol. VI
Colman, Col Percy Edward, 1875–1951, vol. V
Colman, Ronald, 1891–1958, vol. V
Colman, Russell James, 1861–1946, vol. IV
Colman, Sir Stanley; *see* Colman, Sir G. S.
Colmer, Joseph Grose, 1856–1937, vol. III
Colmore, G.; *see* Weaver, Mrs Baillie.
Colmore, Wing-Comdr Reginald Blayney Bulteel, 1888–1930, vol. III
Colmore, Thomas Milnes, 1845–1916, vol. II
Colnaghi, Sir Dominic Ellis, 1834–1908, vol. I
Colomb, Brig.-Gen. George Henry Cooper, 1862–1934, vol. III
Colomb, Vice-Adm. Philip Howard, 1831–1899 vol. I
Colomb, Adm. Philip Howard, 1867–1958, vol. V
Colomb, Rupert Palmer, 1869–1955, vol. V
Colombos, C(onstantine) John, *died* 1968, vol. VI
Colonne, Edouard, 1838–1910, vol. I
Colquhoun, Col Sir Alan John, 6th Bt *cr* 1786 (styled 13th Bt, *cr* 1625), 1838–1910, vol. I
Colquhoun, Archibald Ross, 1848–1914, vol. I
Colquhoun, Brian; *see* Colquhoun, C. B. H.
Colquhoun, (Cecil) Brian (Hugh), 1902–1977, vol. VII
Colquhoun, Ethel M., (Mrs Tawse Jollie), *died* 1950, vol. IV (A), vol. V
Colquhoun, Sir Iain, 7th Bt (*cr* 1786), 1887–1948, vol. IV
Colquhoun, Sir James, 5th Bt *cr* 1786 (styled 12th Bt, *cr* 1625), 1844–1907, vol. I
Colquhoun, Major Julian Campbell, 1870–1937, vol. III
Colquhoun, Col Malcolm Alexander, 1870–1950 vol. IV
Colquhoun, Robert, 1914–1962, vol. VI
Colquhoun, Ven. William, *died* 1920, vol. II
Colquhoun, William Erskine C.; *see* Campbell-Colquhoun.
Colquhoun, Comdr William Jarvie, 1859–1908, vol. I
Colson, Charles, 1839–1915, vol. I
Colson, Charles Henry, 1864–1939, vol. III
Colson, Francis Henry, 1857–1943, vol. IV
Colson, Rev. Francis Tovey, 1858–1929, vol. III
Colson, Surg. Vice-Adm. Sir Henry St Clair, 1887–1968, vol. VI
Colson, Lionel Hewitt, 1887–1943, vol. IV
Colson, Percy, 1873–1952, vol. V
Colson, Phyllis Constance, 1904–1972, vol. VII
Colston, Sir Charles Blampied, 1891–1969, vol. VI
Colston-Baynes, Dorothy Julia, *died* 1973, vol. VII
Colt, Rev. Sir Edward Harry Dutton, 8th Bt, 1850–1931, vol. III

Colt, George Frederick Russell, 1837–1909, vol. I
Colt, Sir Henry Archer, 9th Bt, 1882–1951, vol. V
Coltart, Captain Cyril George Bucknill, 1889–1964, vol. VI
Colthurst, Sir George Oliver, 7th Bt, 1882–1951, vol. V
Colthurst, Sir George St John, 6th Bt, 1850–1925, vol. II
Colthurst, Captain Sir Richard St John Jefferyes, 8th Bt, 1887–1955, vol. V
Colthurst-Vesey, Captain Charles Nicholas, 1860–1915, vol. I (A)
Coltman-Rogers, Muriel Augusta Gillian, *died* 1952, vol. V
Colton, Hon. Sir John, 1823–1902, vol. I
Colton, William Robert, 1867–1921, vol. II
Colum, Padraic, 1881–1972, vol. VII
Colvile, Ernest Frederick, 1879–1967, vol. VI
Colvile, Lt-Gen. Sir Fiennes Middleton, 1832–1917, vol. II
Colvile, Brig.-Gen. George Northcote, 1867–1940, vol. III
Colvile, Lancelot Edward, 1876–1947, vol. IV
Colvile, Comdr Mansel Brabazon Fiennes, 1887–1942, vol. IV
Colvill, Lt-Col David Chaigneau, 1898–1979, vol. VII
Colvill, Robert Frederick Stewart, 1860–1936, vol. III
Colville of Culross, 1st Viscount, 1818–1903, vol. I
Colville of Culross, 2nd Viscount, 1854–1928, vol. II
Colville of Culross, 3rd Viscount, 1888–1945, vol. IV
Colville, Brig.-Gen. Arthur Edward William, 1857–1942, vol. IV
Colville, Lady Cynthia; *see* Colville, Lady H. C.
Colville, Hon. George Charles, 1867–1943, vol. IV
Colville, Lady (Helen) Cynthia, 1884–1968, vol. VI
Colville, Maj.-Gen. Sir Henry Edward, 1852–1907, vol. I
Colville, Rev. James, *died* 1953, vol. V
Colville, John, 1852–1901, vol. I
Colville, Lt-Col John Ross, 1878–1935, vol. III
Colville, Norman Robert, 1893–1974, vol. VII
Colville, Comdr Sir Richard, 1907–1975, vol. VII
Colville, Adm. Hon. Sir Stanley Cecil James, 1861–1939, vol. III
Colville, Col Hon. Sir William James, 1827–1903, vol. I
Colvin, Arthur Edmund, 1884–1966, vol. VI (AII)
Colvin, Sir Auckland, 1838–1908, vol. I
Colvin, Sir C. Preston, 1879–1950, vol. IV
Colvin, Col Cecil Hodgson, 1858–1938, vol. III
Colvin, Sir Elliot Graham, 1861–1940, vol. III
Colvin, Lt-Col Elliot James Dowell, 1885–1950, vol. IV
Colvin, Lt-Col Forrester Farnell, 1860–1936, vol. III
Colvin, Sir George Lethbridge, 1878–1962, vol. VI
Colvin, Major Hugh, 1887–1962, vol. VI
Colvin, Ian Duncan, 1877–1938, vol. III
Colvin, Col J. M. C., 1870–1945, vol. IV
Colvin, Sir Preston; *see* Colvin, Sir C. P.

Colvin, Adm. Sir Ragnar Musgrave, 1882–1954, vol. V

Colvin, Brig.-Gen. Sir Richard Beale, 1856–1936, vol. III

Colvin, Sir Sidney, 1845–1927, vol. II

Colvin, Thomas, 1863–1940, vol. III (A), vol. IV

Colvin, Sir Walter Mytton, 1847–1908, vol. I

Colvin, Very Rev. William Evans, died 1949, vol. IV

Colvin-Smith, Surg.-Gen. Sir Colvin, 1829–1913, vol. I

Colwell, Gen. George Harrie Thorn, 1841–1913, vol. I

Colwell, Hector Alfred, 1875–1946, vol. IV

Colwell, Rev. James, 1860–1930, vol. III

Colwyn, 1st Baron, 1859–1946, vol. IV

Colwyn, 2nd Baron, 1914–1966, vol. VI

Colyer, Air Marshal Douglas, 1893–1978, vol. VII

Colyer, Sir Frank, 1866–1954, vol. V

Colyer-Fergusson, Sir Thomas Colyer, 3rd Bt, 1865–1951, vol. V

Combe, Maj.-Gen. Boyce Albert, 1841–1920, vol. II

Combe, Charles, 1836–1920, vol. II

Combe, Charles Harvey, 1863–1935, vol. III

Combe, Captain Christian, 1858–1940, vol. III

Combe, George Alexander, 1877–1933, vol. III

Combe, Air Vice-Marshal Gerard, 1902–1979, vol. VII

Combe, Harvey Trewythen Brabazon, 1852–1923, vol. II

Combe, Lt-Col Herbert, 1878–1931, vol. III

Combe, Maj.-Gen. John Frederick Boyce, 1895–1967, vol. VI

Combe, Brig.-Gen. Lionel, 1861–1950, vol. IV

Combe, Sir Ralph Molyneux, 1872–1946, vol. IV

Combe, Richard Henry, 1829–1900, vol. I

Combe, Simon Harvey, 1903–1965, vol. VI

Comben, Robert Stone, 1868–1957, vol. V

Comber, Henry Gordon, 1869–1935, vol. III

Comber, Norman Mederson, 1888–1953, vol. V

Combermere, 4th Viscount, 1887–1969, vol. VI

Combes, Emile, 1839–1921, vol. II

Combridge, Annie, 1862–1949, vol. IV

Comerford, Lt-Col Augustine Ambrose, 1886–1944, vol. IV

Comfort, Mrs Bessie; see Marchant, Bessie.

Comins, Ven. Richard Blundell, died 1919, vol. II

Commerell, Sir John Edmund, 1829–1901, vol. I

Commings, Maj.-Gen. Percy Ryan Conway, 1880–1958, vol. V

Commins, Andrew, 1829–1916, vol. II

Common, Sir Andrew; see Common, Sir L. A.

Common, Andrew Ainslie, 1841–1903, vol. I

Common, Frank Breadon, 1891–1969, vol. VI

Common, Sir (Lawrence) Andrew, 1889–1953, vol. V

Commons, John Rogers, 1862–1945, vol. IV

Commy, Rt Rev. John, 1843–1911, vol. I

Comparetti, Domenico, 1835–1927, vol. II

Comper, Sir (John) Ninian, 1864–1960, vol. V, vol. VI

Comper, Sir Ninian; see Comper, Sir J. N.

Compston, Rev. Herbert Fuller Bright, 1866–1931, vol. III

Compston, John Albert, died 1930, vol. III

Compton, Rt Rev. Lord Alwyne, 1825–1906, vol. I

Compton, Lord Alwyne Frederick, 1855–1911, vol. I

Compton, Arthur Holly, 1892–1962, vol. VI

Compton, Brig.-Gen. Charles William, 1869–1933, vol. III

Compton, Col Lord Douglas James Cecil, 1865–1944, vol. IV

Compton, Edward Robert Francis, 1891–1977, vol. VII

Compton, Fay, 1894–1978, vol. VII

Compton, Henry Francis, 1872–1943, vol. IV

Compton, Herbert Eastwick, 1853–1906, vol. I

Compton, Joseph, 1881–1937, vol. III

Compton, Joseph, 1891–1964, vol. VI

Compton, Karl Taylor, 1887–1954, vol. V

Compton, Maurice, 1908–1974, vol. VII

Compton, Captain Walter Burge, died 1932, vol. III

Compton, Rev. William Cookworthy, 1854–1936, vol. III

Compton-Burnett, Dame Ivy, 1892–1969, vol. VI

Compton Mackenzie, Faith; see Mackenzie, Lady.

Compton-Rickett, Arthur, 1869–1937, vol. III

Compton-Rickett, Rt Hon. Sir Joseph, 1847–1919, vol. II

Compton-Thornhill, Sir Anthony John; see Thornhill.

Comrie, John Dixon, 1875–1939, vol. III

Comrie, Leslie John, 1893–1950, vol. IV

Comyn, Lt-Col Edward Walter, 1868–1949, vol. IV

Comyn, Henry Ernest Fitzwilliam, 1854–1941, vol. IV

Comyn, Col Lewis James, 1878–1961, vol. VI

Comyn, Michael, 1877–1952, vol. V

Comyn-Platt, Sir Thomas; see Platt.

Comyns, Henry Joseph, 1868–1943, vol. IV

Comyns, Louis, died 1962, vol. VI

Comyns Carr, Sir Arthur Strettell, 1882–1965, vol. VI

Conacher, Hamilton, 1881–1939, vol. III

Conacher, Mungo, 1901–1977, vol. VII

Conan Doyle, Adrian Malcolm, 1910–1970, vol. VI

Conant, James Bryant, 1893–1978, vol. VII

Conant, Sir Roger John Edward, 1st Bt, 1899–1973, vol. VII

Concanon, Col Henry, 1861–1926, vol. II

Conde, Harold Graydon, died 1959, vol. V

Conder, Charles, 1868–1909, vol. I

Conder, Claude Reignier, 1848–1910, vol. I

Conder, Rev. Canon Edward Baines, 1872–1936, vol. III

Condon, Edward Uhler, 1902–1974, vol. VII

Conerney, Very Rev. John Pirrie, died 1940, vol. III (A), vol. IV

Conesford, 1st Baron, 1892–1974, vol. VII

Coneybeer, Hon. Frederick William, 1859–1950, vol. IV

Congdon, Col Arthur Edward Osmond, died 1924, vol. II

Conger, Edwin H., 1843–1907, vol. I

Congleton, 4th Baron, 1839–1906, vol. I

Congleton, 5th Baron, 1890–1914, vol. I

Congleton, 6th Baron, 1892–1932, vol. III
Congleton, 7th Baron, 1925–1967, vol. VI
Congreve, Cecil Ralph Townshend, 1876–1952, vol. V
Congreve, Comdr Sir Geoffrey, 1st Bt, died 1941, vol. IV
Congreve, John, 1872–1957, vol. V
Congreve, Gen. Sir Walter Norris, 1862–1927, vol. II
Coningham, Air Marshal Sir Arthur, 1895–1948, vol. IV
Coningham, Maj.-Gen. Frank Evelyn, 1870–1934, vol. III
Coningham, Captain Herbert John, 1867–1936, vol. III
Coningsby, Eric Alfred, 1909–1955, vol. V
Conklin, Edwin Grant, 1863–1952, vol. V
Conlay, William Lance, 1869–1927, vol. II
Connal, Benjamin Michael, 1861–1944, vol. IV
Connal, Col Kenneth Hugh Munro, 1870–1949, vol. IV
Connally, Thomas Terry; see Connally, Tom.
Connally, Tom, (Thomas Terry Connally), 1877–1963, vol. VI
Connard, Philip, 1875–1958, vol. V
Connaught, Prince Arthur of, 1883–1938, vol. III
Connaught, HRH Princess Arthur of; see Fife, Duchess of.
Connaught and Strathearn, 2nd Duke of, 1914–1943, vol. IV
Connel, John Arthur, 1903–1961, vol. VI
Connell, Rev. Alexander, 1866–1920, vol. II
Connell, Sir Charles, 1900–1972, vol. VII
Connell, Major Hugh John, 1884–1934, vol. III
Connell, Sir Isaac, 1858–1935, vol. III
Connell, James MacLuckie, 1867–1947, vol. IV
Connell, Jim, died 1929, vol. III
Connell, John, (John Henry Robertson), 1909–1965, vol. VI
Connell, Rev. Robert, 1852–1936, vol. III
Connell, Sir Robert Lowden, 1867–1936, vol. III
Connell, Walter Thomas, 1873–1964, vol. VI
Connellan, Joseph, died 1967, vol. VI (AII)
Connelly, Sir Francis Raymond, 1895–1949, vol. IV
Connelly, Marc, 1890–1980, vol. VII
Connely, Willard, 1888–1967, vol. VI
Connemara, 1st Baron, 1827–1901, vol. I
Conner, Henry Daniel, 1859–1925, vol. II
Conner, Lewis Atterbury, 1867–1950, vol. IV (A), vol. V
Connibere, Sir Charles Wellington, died 1941, vol. IV
Connolly, Col Benjamin Bloomfield, 1845–1924, vol. II
Connolly, Cyril Vernon, 1903–1974, vol. VII
Connolly, Air Cdre Hugh Patrick, 1915–1968, vol. VI
Connolly, Hon. Sir James Daniel, 1869–1962, vol. VI
Connolly, Martin, 1874–1945, vol. IV
Connolly, Richard Joseph, 1873–1948, vol. IV
Connolly, Thomas James D.; see Doull-Connolly.
Connolly, William Patrick Joseph, died 1935, vol. III

Connor, Dame (Annie) Jean, 1899–1968, vol. VI
Connor, Comdr Edward Richard, died 1903, vol. I
Connor, Francis Richard, 1870–1956, vol. V
Connor, Maj.-Gen. Sir Frank Powell, died 1954, vol. V
Connor, Captain Harry George A.; see Adams-Connor.
Connor, Dame Jean; see Connor, Dame A. J.
Connor, Col John Colpoys, 1867–1936, vol. III
Connor, Rev. Muirhead Mitchell, died 1930, vol. III
Connor, Ralph, (Rev. Charles W. Gordon), 1860–1937, vol. III
Connor, Sir William Neil, 1909–1967, vol. VI
Conolly, Major Edward Michael, 1874–1956, vol. V
Conolly, Brig. John James Pollock, 1896–1950, vol. IV
Conor, William, 1881–1968, vol. VI
Conrad, Joseph, 1857–1924, vol. II
Conran-Smith, Sir Eric Conran, 1890–1960, vol. V
Conroy, Charles O'Neill, 1871–1946, vol. IV
Conroy, Sir Diarmaid William, 1913–1978, vol. VII
Conroy, J. G., died 1915, vol. I
Conroy, Sir John, 3rd Bt, 1845–1900, vol. I
Conry, Major James Lionel Joyce, 1873–1914, vol. I
Conry, Brig. John de Lisle, 1882–1971, vol. VII
Consett, Rear-Adm. Montagu William Warcop Peter, 1871–1945, vol. IV
Considine, Sir Heffernan James Fritz, 1846–1912, vol. I
Constable, Hon. Lord; Andrew Henderson Briggs Constable, 1865–1928, vol. II
Constable, Andrew Henderson Briggs; see Constable, Hon. Lord.
Constable, Frank Challice, 1846–1937, vol. III
Constable, Sir Henry Marmaduke S.; see Strickland-Constable.
Constable, Brig. Raleigh Charles Joseph C.; see Chichester-Constable.
Constable, Walter George Raleigh C.; see Chichester-Constable.
Constable, William George, 1887–1976, vol. VII
Constable-Maxwell-Scott, Mary Monica; see Scott, Hon. Mrs Maxwell.
Constanduros, Mabel, died 1957, vol. V
Constant, Hayne, 1904–1968, vol. VI
Constant, Jean Joseph B.; see Benjamin-Constant.
Constantine, Baron (Life Peer); Learie Nicholas Constantine, 1901–1971, vol. VII
Constantine, Maj.-Gen. Charles Francis, died 1953, vol. V
Constantine, Sir George Baxandall, 1902–1969, vol. VI
Constantinides, Most Rev. Michael, 1892–1958, vol. V
Contandin, Fernand Joseph Désiré; see Fernandel.
Conti, Italia, died 1946, vol. IV
Converse, Frederick Shepherd, 1871–1940, vol. III (A), vol. IV
Conway of Allington, 1st Baron, 1856–1937, vol. III
Conway, Brig. Albert Edward, 1891–1974, vol. VII
Conway, Arthur William, 1875–1950, vol. IV (A)
Conway, Conway Joseph, died 1953, vol. V

Conway, Edward Joseph, 1894–1968, vol. VI
Conway, Essie Ruth, *died* 1934, vol. III
Conway, James, 1915–1974, vol. VII
Conway, Lt-Col John Marcus Hobson, *died* 1940, vol. III
Conway, Marmaduke Percy, 1885–1961, vol. VI
Conway, Moncure Daniel, 1832–1907, vol. I
Conway, Robert Russ, 1863–1950, vol. IV
Conway, Prof. Robert Seymour, 1864–1933, vol. III
Conway, His Eminence Cardinal William, 1913–1977, vol. VII
Conway-Gordon, Col Esme Cosmo William, 1875–1962, vol. VI
Conway-Gordon, Col Gwynnedd, 1868–1936, vol. III
Conway-Gordon, Lt-Gen. Lewis, 1863–1933, vol. III
Conwy, Rear-Adm. Rafe Grenville Rowley-, 1875–1951, vol. V
Conybeare, Alfred Edward, 1875–1952, vol. V
Conybeare, Charles Augustus Vansittart, 1853–1919, vol. II
Conybeare, Charles Frederick Pringle, 1860–1927, vol. II
Conybeare, Rear-Adm. Crawford James Markland, 1854–1937, vol. III
Conybeare, Frederick Cornwallis, 1856–1924, vol. II
Conybeare, Sir John Josias, 1888–1967, vol. VI
Conybeare, John William Edward, 1843–1931, vol. III
Conybeare, Very Rev. William James, 1871–1955, vol. V
Conyers, Dorothea, 1873–1949, vol. IV
Conyers, Evelyn Augusta, *died* 1944, vol. IV
Conyers, Sir James Reginald, 1879–1948, vol. IV
Conyngham, 4th Marquess, 1857–1897, vol. I
Conyngham, 5th Marquess, 1883–1906, vol. I
Conyngham, 6th Marquess, 1890–1974, vol. VII
Conyngham, Col Sir Gerald Ponsonby L.; *see* Lenox-Conyngham.
Conyngham, Sir William Fitzwilliam L.; *see* Lenox-Conyngham.
Cooch, Col Charles, 1829–1917, vol. II
Cooch Behar, Maharaja Bhup Bahadur of, 1886–1922, vol. II
Coode, Sir Bernard Henry, 1887–1962, vol. VI
Coode, Rear-Adm. Charles Penrose Rushton, 1870–1939, vol. III
Coode, Captain Percival, *died* 1902, vol. I
Coode-Adams, Sir John; *see* Adams.
Cook, Air Vice-Marshal Albert Frederick, 1901–1980, vol. VI
Cook, Sir Albert Ruskin, 1870–1951, vol. V
Cook, Albert Stanburrough, 1853–1927, vol. II
Cook, Arthur Bernard, 1868–1952, vol. V
Cook, Arthur James, 1885–1931, vol. III
Cook, Arthur Kemball, 1851–1928, vol. II
Cook, Rev. Canon Arthur Malcolm, 1883–1964, vol. VI
Cook, Arthur Willsteed, *died* 1930, vol. III
Cook, Sir Basil (Alfred) Kemball-, 1876–1949, vol. IV

Cook, Sir Charles Archer, 1849–1934, vol. III
Cook, Col Charles Chesney, 1866–1937, vol. III
Cook, Charles Henry; *see* Bickerdyke, John.
Cook, Edgar T., 1880–1953, vol. V
Cook, Sir Edmund Ralph, *died* 1942, vol. IV
Cook, Sir Edward Mitchener, 1881–1955, vol. V
Cook, Sir Edward Tyas, 1857–1919, vol. II
Cook, Ven. Edwin Arthur, 1888–1972, vol. VII
Cook, Lt-Col Edwin Berkeley, 1869–1914, vol. I
Cook, Elsie, (Mrs E. Thornton Cook), *died* 1960, vol. V
Cook, Ernest Benjamin, 1879–1952, vol. V
Cook, Sir Ernest Henry, 1855–1945, vol. IV
Cook, Sir Francis, 1st Bt, 1817–1901, vol. I
Cook, Sir Francis Ferdinand Maurice, 4th Bt, 1907–1978, vol. VII
Cook, Frank, 1888–1972, vol. VII
Cook, Frank Allan Grafton, 1902–1973, vol. VII
Cook, Sir Frederick Charles, 1875–1947, vol. IV
Cook, Sir Frederick Lucas, 2nd Bt, 1844–1920, vol. II
Cook, Lt-Col George Trevor-Roper, 1877–1918, vol. II
Cook, Gilbert, 1885–1951, vol. V
Cook, Sir Henry, 1848–1928, vol. II
Cook, Henry Caldwell, 1886–1939, vol. III
Cook, Ven. Henry Lucas, *died* 1928, vol. II
Cook, Brig.-Gen. Henry Rex, 1863–1950, vol. IV
Cook, Sir Herbert Frederick, 3rd Bt, 1868–1939, vol. III
Cook, Herbert George Graham, 1864–1939, vol. III
Cook, Maj.-Gen. James, 1844–1928, vol. II
Cook, James Allan, 1858–1930, vol. III
Cook, Hon. James H.; *see* Hume-Cook.
Cook, Sir James Wilfred, 1900–1975, vol. VII
Cook, John Gilbert, 1911–1979, vol. VII
Cook, John Irvine, 1892–1952, vol. V
Cook, Rt Hon. Sir Joseph, 1860–1947, vol. IV
Cook, Mrs Mabel, (Mabel Collins), 1851–1927, vol. II
Cook, Percival Robert, 1867–1939, vol. III
Cook, Stanley Arthur, 1873–1949, vol. IV
Cook, Stanley Smith, 1875–1952, vol. V
Cook, Hon. Sir Tasker Keech, 1867–1937, vol. III
Cook, Sir Theodore Andrea, 1867–1928, vol. II
Cook, Thomas Fotheringham, 1908–1952, vol. V
Cook, Thomas Reginald Hague, 1866–1925, vol. II
Cook, Lt-Col Thomas Russell Albert Mason, 1902–1970, vol. VI
Cook, Rt Rev. Thomas William, 1866–1928, vol. II
Cook, Sir William, 1834–1908, vol. I
Cooke, Col Alfred Fothergill, 1871–1946, vol. IV
Cooke, Rev. Alfred Hands, *died* 1937, vol. III
Cooke, Amos John, 1885–1961, vol. VI
Cooke, Lt-Gen. Anthony Charles, 1826–1905, vol. I
Cooke, Lt-Col Aubrey St John, 1872–1935, vol. III
Cooke, Brig.-Gen. Bertram Hewett Hunter, 1874–1946, vol. IV
Cooke, Brian K.; *see* Kennedy-Cooke.
Cooke, Sir Charles Arthur John, 11th Bt, 1905–1978, vol. VII
Cooke, Rev. Canon Charles Edward, 1860–1939, vol. III

Cooke, Charles John Bowen, 1859–1920, vol. II

Cooke, Charles Wallwyn Radcliffe-, *died* 1911, vol. I

Cooke, Christopher Herbert, 1899–1979, vol. VII

Cooke, Sir Clement K.; *see* Kinloch-Cooke.

Cooke, Conrad William, 1843–1926, vol. II

Cooke, Air Marshal Sir Cyril Bertram, 1895–1972, vol. VII

Cooke, Deryck Victor, 1919–1976, vol. VII

Cooke, Sir Douglas; *see* Cooke, Sir J. D.

Cooke, Sir (Edward) Marriott, 1852–1931, vol. III

Cooke, Rev. George Albert, 1865–1939, vol. III

Cooke, Henry Arthur, 1862–1946, vol. IV

Cooke, Sir Henry Frank, 1900–1973, vol. VII

Cooke, Sir Henry P.; *see* Paget-Cooke.

Cooke, Lt-Gen. Sir Herbert Fothergill, 1871–1936, vol. III

Cooke, Isaac, 1846–1922, vol. II

Cooke, Sir (James) Douglas, *died* 1949, vol. IV

Cooke, Rear-Adm. John Ernest, 1899–1980, vol. VII

Cooke, John Fitzpatrick, *died* 1930, vol. III

Cooke, Rear-Adm. John Gervaise Beresford, 1911–1976, vol. VII

Cooke, John Hunt, 1828–1908, vol. I

Cooke, John Sholto Fitzpatrick, 1906–1975, vol. VII

Cooke, Sir Leonard, 1901–1976, vol. VII

Cooke, Rev. Leslie Edward, 1908–1967, vol. VI

Cooke, Lewis Henry, *died* 1929, vol. III

Cooke, Sir Marriott; *see* Cooke, Sir E. M.

Cooke, Michael Joseph, 1881–1960, vol. V

Cooke, Mordecai Cubitt, 1825–1913, vol. I

Cooke, Oliver Dayrell Paget P.; *see* Paget-Cooke.

Cooke, Col Philip Ralph D.; *see* Davies-Cooke.

Cooke, Philip Tatton Davies-, 1863–1946, vol. IV

Cooke, Rev. Canon Robert Herbert Michael, 1864–1939, vol. III

Cooke, Robert Victor, 1902–1978, vol. VII

Cooke, Roger Gresham, 1907–1970, vol. VI

Cooke, Maj.-Gen. Ronald Basil Bowen Bancroft, 1899–1971, vol. VII

Cooke, Rupert C.; *see* Croft-Cooke.

Cooke, Hon. Sir Samuel Burgess Ridgway, 1912–1978, vol. VII

Cooke, Maj.-Gen. Sidney Arthur, 1903–1977, vol. VII

Cooke, Sir Stenson, 1874–1942, vol. IV

Cooke, Temple, 1851–1925, vol. II

Cooke, Theodore, 1836–1910, vol. I

Cooke, William Charles Cyril, 1881–1966, vol. VI

Cooke, William Cubitt, 1866–1951, vol. V

Cooke, William Ernest, 1863–1947, vol. IV

Cooke, William Henry, 1843–1921, vol. II

Cooke, Sir William Henry Charles Wemyss, 10th Bt, 1872–1964, vol. VI

Cooke-Collis, Maj.-Gen. Sir James; *see* Cooke-Collis, Maj.-Gen. Sir W. J. N.

Cooke-Collis, Col William, 1847–1933, vol. III

Cooke-Collis, Maj.-Gen. Sir (William) James Norman, 1876–1941, vol. IV

Cooke-Hurle, Col Edward Forbes; *see* Hurle.

Cooke-Hurle, John A.; *see* Hurle.

Cooke-Taylor, Richard Whately, 1842–1918, vol. II

Cooke-Yarborough, George Eustace, 1876–1938, vol. III

Cooke-Yarborough, Rev. John James; *see* Yarborough.

Cookman, Anthony Victor, 1894–1962, vol. VI

Cookson, Sir Charles Alfred, 1829–1906, vol. I

Cookson, Charles Lisle Stirling, 1855–1919, vol. II

Cookson, Christopher, *died* 1948, vol. IV

Cookson, Captain Claude Edward, 1879–1963, vol. VI

Cookson, Clive, 1879–1971, vol. VII

Cookson, Maj.-Gen. George Arthur, 1860–1929, vol. III

Cookson, Henry Anstey, 1886–1949, vol. IV

Cookson, John Blencowe, 1843–1910, vol. I

Cookson, Lt-Col John Cookson F.; *see* Fife-Cookson.

Cookson, Col Philip Blencowe, 1871–1928, vol. II

Cookson, Sydney Spencer S.; *see* Sawrey-Cookson.

Coolidge, Archibald Cary, 1866–1928, vol. II

Coolidge, Calvin, 1872–1933, vol. III

Coolidge, William Augustus Brevoort, 1850–1926, vol. II

Coolidge, William David, 1873–1975, vol. VII

Cools-Lartigue, Alexander Raphael, 1899–1973, vol. VII

Coomaraswamy, Ananda K., 1877–1947, vol. IV

Coomaraswamy, Sir Velupillai, 1892–1972, vol. VII

Coombe, Sir Thomas Melrose, 1877–1959, vol. V

Coomber, John Edward, 1901–1963, vol. VI

Coombes, Very Rev. George Frederick, 1856–1922, vol. II

Coombs, Carey Franklin, 1879–1932, vol. III

Coombs, Captain Thomas Edward, 1884–1953, vol. V

Coombs, William Harry, 1893–1969, vol. VI

Coombs, William Heron, 1851–1931, vol. III

Coombs, Rev. Canon William Joseph Mundy, 1871–1966, vol. VI

Coop, Hubert, 1872–1953, vol. V

Coop, Rev. James Ogden, 1869–1928, vol. II

Coope, Edward Jesser, 1849–1918, vol. II

Cooper of Culross, 1st Baron, 1892–1955, vol. V

Cooper, Sir Alfred, 1838–1908, vol. I

Cooper, Sir Alfred, 1846–1916, vol. II

Cooper, Alfred B., 1863–1936, vol. III

Cooper, Rt Rev. Alfred Cecil, *died* 1964, vol. VI

Cooper, Alfred Heaton, *died* 1929, vol. III

Cooper, Rev. Alfred William Francis, *died* 1920, vol. II

Cooper, Alice J., *died* 1917, vol. II

Cooper, Captain Archibald Frederick, 1885–1975, vol. VII

Cooper, Archibald Samuel, 1871–1942, vol. IV

Cooper, Rev. Arthur Nevile, 1850–1943, vol. IV

Cooper, Sir Astley Paston P.; *see* Paston-Cooper.

Cooper, Austin Edwin, 1869–1954, vol. V

Cooper, Bryan Ricco, 1884–1930, vol. III

Cooper, Very Rev. Cecil Henry Hamilton, 1871–1942, vol. IV

Cooper, Charles Alfred, 1829–1916, vol. II

Cooper, Maj.-Gen. Charles Duncan, 1849–1929, vol. III

Cooper, Col Charles James, *died* 1931, vol. III

Cooper, Sir Charles Naunton Paston P., 4th Bt (cr 1821); see Paston-Cooper.
Cooper, Sir Clive F.; see Forster-Cooper.
Cooper, Major Colin, 1892–1938, vol. III
Cooper, Sir Daniel, 1st Bt (cr 1863), 1821–1902, vol. I
Cooper, Sir Daniel, 2nd Bt (cr 1863), 1848–1909, vol. I
Cooper, Sir Daniel; see Cooper, Sir W. G. D.
Cooper, David, 1855–1940, vol. III
Cooper, Sir Dhanjishah Bomanjee, died 1947, vol. IV
Cooper, Sir Edward Ernest, 1st Bt (cr 1920), 1848–1922, vol. II
Cooper, Edward Henry, 1827–1902, vol. I
Cooper, Edward Herbert, 1867–1910, vol. I
Cooper, Maj.-Gen. Edward Joshua, 1858–1945, vol. IV
Cooper, Sir Edwin, 1874–1942, vol. IV
Cooper, Sir Ernest Herbert, 1877–1962, vol. VI
Cooper, Francis Alfred, 1860–1933, vol. III
Cooper, Sir Francis D'Arcy, 1st Bt (cr 1941), 1882–1941, vol. IV
Cooper, Hon. Frank Arthur, 1872–1949, vol. IV
Cooper, Col Frank Sandiford, 1873–1936, vol. III
Cooper, Frank Shewell, 1864–1949, vol. IV
Cooper, Frank Towers, 1863–1915, vol. I
Cooper, Rev. Frederic Wilson, 1860–1941, vol. IV
Cooper, Gary Frank James, 1901–1961, vol. VI
Cooper, Sir George Alexander, 1st Bt (cr 1905, of Hursley), 1856–1940, vol. III
Cooper, Captain Sir George James Robertson, 2nd Bt (cr 1905, of Hursley), 1890–1961, vol. VI
Cooper, George Joseph, died 1909, vol. I
Cooper, Gerald Melbourne, 1892–1947, vol. IV
Cooper, Giles Stannus, 1918–1966, vol. VI
Cooper, Dame Gladys, 1888–1971, vol. VII
Cooper, Sir Guy; see Cooper, Sir H. G.
Cooper, Harold H.; see Hinton-Cooper.
Cooper, Sir (Harold) Stanford, 1889–1976, vol. VII
Cooper, Col Harry, 1847–1928, vol. II
Cooper, Sir Henry, 1873–1962, vol. VI
Cooper, Henry, 1877–1947, vol. IV
Cooper, Rt Rev. Henry Edward, 1845–1916, vol. II
Cooper, Sir (Henry) Guy, 1890–1975, vol. VII
Cooper, Sir Henry Lovick, 5th Bt (cr 1821), 1875–1959, vol. V
Cooper, Henry St John, 1869–1926, vol. II
Cooper, Very Rev. James, 1846–1922, vol. II
Cooper, James, 1882–1949, vol. IV
Cooper, Sir James Alexander, died 1936, vol. III
Cooper, Rev. James Hughes, died 1909, vol. I
Cooper, James Lees, 1907–1980, vol. VII
Cooper, Rev. Canon James Sidmouth, 1869–1961, vol. VI
Cooper, John Paul, died 1933, vol. III
Cooper, Lance Harries, 1890–1972, vol. VII
Cooper, Col Lyall Newcomen, died 1929, vol. III
Cooper, Malcolm Edward, 1907–1977, vol. VII
Cooper, Margaret, died 1922, vol. III
Cooper, Sir Patrick Ashley, 1887–1961, vol. VI
Cooper, Percival Martin, 1887–1951, vol. V
Cooper, Hon. Sir Pope Alexander, 1848–1923, vol. II

Cooper, Sir Richard Ashmole, 2nd Bt (cr 1905, of Shenstone Court), 1874–1946, vol. IV
Cooper, Brig.-Gen. Richard Joshua, 1860–1938, vol. III
Cooper, Sir Richard Powell, 1st Bt (cr 1905, of Shenstone Court), 1847–1913, vol. 1
Cooper, Sir Robert Elliott-, 1845–1942, vol. IV
Cooper, Robert Higham, 1878–1944, vol. IV
Cooper, Robert William, 1877–1970, vol. VI
Cooper, Sir Stanford; see Cooper, Sir H. S.
Cooper, Rev. Canon Sydney, 1862–1942, vol. IV
Cooper, Hon. Sir Theo, 1850–1925, vol. II
Cooper, Rev. Thomas John, 1837–1911, vol. I
Cooper, Thomas Sidney, 1803–1902, vol. I
Cooper, Rev. Vincent King, 1849–1922, vol. II
Cooper, Hon. Sir Walter Jackson, 1892–1973, vol. VII
Cooper, Wilbraham Villiers, 1876–1955, vol. V
Cooper, Sir William Charles, 3rd Bt (cr 1863), 1851–1925, vol. II
Cooper, William Edward Deck, 1877–1962, vol. VI
Cooper, Lt-Col Sir William Earnshaw, 1843–1924, vol. II
Cooper, Sir (William George) Daniel, 4th Bt (cr 1863), 1877–1954, vol. V
Cooper, Sir William Herbert, 3rd Bt (cr 1905, of Shenstone Court), 1901–1970, vol. VI
Cooper, William Ranson, 1868–1926, vol. II
Cooper, Lt-Col William Weldon H.; see Herring-Cooper.
Cooper-Key, Major Sir Aston, 1861–1930, vol. III
Cooper-Key, Captain Edmund Moore Cooper, 1862–1933, vol. III
Coopland, George William, 1875–1975, vol. VII
Cooray, Edmund Joseph, 1907–1979, vol. VII
Coote, Rev. Sir Algernon, 11th Bt, 1817–1899, vol. I
Coote, Sir Algernon Charles Plumptre, 12th Bt, 1847–1920, vol. II
Coote, Captain Sir Colin Reith, 1893–1979, vol. VII
Coote, Sir Eyre, 1857–1925, vol. II
Coote, Rt Rev. Mgr Canon George, 1881–1961, vol. VI
Coote, Howard, 1865–1943, vol. IV
Coote, Rear-Adm. Sir John Ralph, 14th Bt, 1905–1978, vol. VII
Coote, Sir Ralph Algernon, 13th Bt, 1874–1941, vol. IV
Coote, William, 1863–1924, vol. II
Coote, William Alexander, 1842–1919, vol. II
Cope, 1st Baron, 1870–1946, vol. IV
Cope, Sir Alfred, died 1954, vol. V
Cope, Sir Anthony, 13th Bt (cr 1611), 1842–1932, vol. III
Cope, Sir Anthony Mohun Leckonby, 15th Bt (cr 1611), 1927–1966, vol. VI
Cope, Sir Arthur Stockdale, 1857–1940, vol. III
Cope, Charles Elvey, died 1943, vol. IV
Cope, Captain Sir Denzil, 14th Bt (cr 1611), 1873–1940, vol. III
Cope, John Hautenville, died 1942, vol. IV
Cope, Sir Mordaunt Leckonby, 16th Bt (cr 1611), 1878–1972, vol. VII

Cope, Sir Ralph, 1862–1949, vol. IV
Cope, Sir Thomas, 1st Bt (cr 1918), 1840–1924, vol. II
Cope, Brig.-Gen. Sir Thomas George, 2nd Bt (cr 1918), 1884–1966, vol. VI
Cope, Sir (Vincent) Zachary, 1881–1974, vol. VII
Cope, Sir Zachary; see Cope, Sir V. Z.
Copeau, Jacques, 1879–1949, vol. IV
Copeland, Edwin Bingham, 1873–1964, vol. VI
Copeland, Hon. Henry, 1839–1904, vol. I
Copeland, Ida, (Mrs Ronald Copeland), died 1964, vol. VI
Copeland, Ralph, 1837–1905, vol. I
Copeland, (Richard) Ronald (John), died 1958, vol. V
Copeland, Ronald; see Copeland, Richard R. J.
Copeland, Theodore Benfey, 1878–1952, vol. V
Copeman, Col Charles Edward Fraser, died 1949, vol. IV
Copeman, Constance Gertrude, 1864–1953, vol. VI
Copeman, Lt-Col Hugh Charles, 1862–1955, vol. V
Copeman, Vice-Adm. Sir Nicholas Alfred, 1906–1969, vol. VI
Copeman, Sydney A. Monckton, 1862–1947, vol. IV
Copeman, William Sydney Charles, 1900–1970, vol. VI
Copinger, Walter Arthur, 1847–1910, vol. I
Copland, Col Alexander, 1833–1908, vol. I
Copland, Sir Douglas Berry, 1894–1971, vol. VII
Copland, Harold W.; see Wallace-Copland.
Copland, Sir William Robertson, 1838–1907, vol. I
Copland, William Wallace, 1853–1922, vol. II
Copland-Griffiths, Brig. Felix Alexander Vincent, 1894–1967, vol. VI
Copland Simmons, Rev. Frederic Pearson; see Simmons.
Copland-Sparkes, Rear-Adm. Robert, 1851–1924, vol. II
Coplans, Major Myer, died 1961, vol. VI
Copleston, Rt Rev. Ernest Arthur, died 1933, vol. III
Copleston, Frederick Selwyn, 1850–1935, vol. III
Copleston, Most Rev. Reginald Stephen, 1845–1925, vol. II
Copleston, Waters Edward, died 1949, vol. IV
Coplestone, Frederick, 1850–1932, vol. III
Copley, Ethel Leontine; see Gabain, E. L.
Copley, John, 1875–1950, vol. IV
Copley, Mrs John; see Gabain, Ethel Leontine.
Copley, Very Rev. John Robert, died 1923, vol. II
Copley, Brig.-Gen. Sir Robert Calverley Alington Bewicke B.; see Bewicke-Copley.
Copley, Samuel William, 1859–1937, vol. III
Copnall, Bainbridge; see Copnall, E. B.
Copnall, (Edward) Bainbridge, 1903–1973, vol. VII
Coppard, Alfred Edgar, 1878–1957, vol. V
Coppee, François Edouard Joachim, 1842–1908, vol. I
Coppel, Elias Godfrey, 1896–1978, vol. VII
Coppel, Rt Rev. Francis Stephen, 1867–1933, vol. III
Coppin, Hon. George, 1820–1906, vol. I
Copping, Arthur E., 1865–1941, vol. IV

Copping, Harold, died 1932, vol. III
Coppinger, Rear-Adm. Robert Henry, 1877–1967, vol. VI
Coppinger, Maj.-Gen. Walter Valentine, 1875–1957, vol. V
Coppleson, Sir Victor Marcus, 1893–1965, vol. VI
Copplestone, Bennet; see Kitchin, F. H.
Coppock, Sir Richard, 1885–1971, vol. VII
Copson, Edward Thomas, 1901–1980, vol. VII
Copus, George Frederick, 1868–1949, vol. IV
Coquelin, Benoit Constant, (Coquelin aîné), 1841–1909, vol. I
Coquelin, Ernest Alexandre Honoré, (Coquelin cadet), 1848–1909, vol. I
Corah, Sir John Harold, 1884–1978, vol. VII
Corbally, Elias, 1868–1933, vol. III
Corban, Maj.-Gen. William Watts, 1829–1916, vol. II
Corbet, Maj.-Gen. Arthur Domville, 1847–1918, vol. II
Corbet, Eustace Kynaston, 1854–1920, vol. II
Corbet, Hon. Frederick Hugh Mackenzie, 1862–1916, vol. II
Corbet, Sir Gerald Vincent, 6th Bt, 1868–1955, vol. V
Corbet, Hon. Mrs (Katherine), 1861–1950, vol. IV
Corbet, Reginald, 1857–1945, vol. IV
Corbet, Sir Roland James, 5th Bt, 1892–1915, vol. I
Corbet, Sir Walter Orlando, 4th Bt, 1856–1910, vol. I
Corbet, William Joseph, 1824–1909, vol. I
Corbett, Adm. Charles Frederick, 1867–1955, vol. V
Corbett, Charles Henry Joseph, 1853–1935, vol. III
Corbett, Edward, 1843–1918, vol. II
Corbett, (Edward) James, (Jim Corbett), 1875–1955, vol. V
Corbett, Sir Francis Edmund George A.; see Astley-Corbett.
Corbett, Sir (Francis) Henry (Rivers) A.; see Astley-Corbett.
Corbett, Rev. Frederick St John, 1862–1919, vol. II
Corbett, Sir Geoffrey Latham, 1881–1937, vol. III
Corbett, Captain Godfrey Edwin, 1871–1929, vol. III
Corbett, Harvey Wiley, 1873–1954, vol. V
Corbett, J. Soden, 1871–1935, vol. III
Corbett, James; see Corbett, E. J.
Corbett, Rt Rev. James Francis, 1840–1912, vol. I
Corbett, Jim; see Corbett, E. J.
Corbett, John, 1817–1901, vol. I
Corbett, Rev. John Reginald, 1844–1920, vol. II
Corbett, Sir Julian Stafford, 1854–1922, vol. II
Corbett, Col Robert de la Cour, 1844–1904, vol. I
Corbett, Captain Roland, 1881–1938, vol. III
Corbett, Thomas Lorimer, 1854–1910, vol. I
Corbett, Captain Sir Vincent Edwin Henry, 1861–1936, vol. III
Corbett, William John, died 1941, vol. IV
Corbett-Smith, Arthur, 1879–1945, vol. IV
Corbett-Winder, Major William John, 1875–1950, vol. IV
Corbin, (André) Charles, 1881–1970, vol. VI
Corbin, Charles; see Corbin, A. C.

Corbin, John, 1870–1959, vol. V
Corbishley, Rev. Thomas, 1903–1976, vol. VII
Corby, Henry, died 1917, vol. II
Corbyn, Ernest Nugent, 1881–1961, vol. VI
Corcoran, Sir John A., 1862–1932, vol. III
Corcoran, Rev. Timothy, 1872–1943, vol. IV
Cordeaux, Captain Edward Cawdron, 1894–1963, vol. VI
Cordeaux, Col Edward Kyme, 1866–1946, vol. IV
Cordeaux, Major Sir Harry Edward Spiller, 1870–1943, vol. IV
Cordellis, Mrs M.; see Groom, Gladys Laurence.
Corder, Lt-Col Arthur Annerley, died 1923, vol. II
Corder, Frederick, 1852–1932, vol. III
Corder, Paul Walford, 1879–1942, vol. IV
Corder, Philip, 1891–1961, vol. VI
Cordes, Thomas, 1826–1901, vol. I
Cordier, Andrew Wellington, 1901–1975, vol. VII
Cordiner, George Ritchie Mather, died 1957, vol. V
Cordiner, Thomas Smith, 1902–1965, vol. VI
Cordingley, Charles, 1862–1914, vol. I
Cordingley, Air Vice-Marshal Sir John Walter, 1890–1977, vol. VII
Cordingley, Reginald Annandale, 1896–1962, vol. VI
Cordingly, Rt Rev. Eric William Bradley, 1911–1976, vol. VII
Cordon, Cecil Gilbert William, died 1952, vol. V
Core, Thomas Hamilton, 1836–1910, vol. I
Corea, Sir Claude; see Corea, Sir G. C. S.
Corea, Sir (George) Claude (Stanley), 1894–1962, vol. VI
Corelli, Marie, 1855–1924, vol. II
Corfe, Rt Rev. Charles John, 1843–1921, vol. II
Corfiato, Hector Othon, died 1963, vol. VI
Corfield, Rt Rev. Bernard Conyngham, 1890–1965, vol. VI
Corfield, Rev. Claud Evelyn Lacey, died 1926, vol. II
Corfield, Sir Conrad Laurence, 1893–1980, vol. VII
Corfield, Col Frederick Alleyne, 1884–1939, vol. III
Corfield, Gerald Frederick Conyngham, 1886–1961, vol. VI
Corfield, William Henry, 1843–1903, vol. I
Cori, Gerty T., 1896–1957, vol. V
Cork and Orrery, 9th Earl of, 1829–1904, vol. I
Cork and Orrery, 10th Earl of, 1861–1925, vol. II
Cork and Orrery, 11th Earl of, 1864–1934, vol. III
Cork and Orrery, 12th Earl of, 1873–1967, vol. VI
Cork, Philip Clark, 1854–1936, vol. III (A), vol. IV
Corke, Sir John Henry, died 1927, vol. II
Corker, Maj.-Gen. Thomas Martin, 1856–1937, vol. III
Corkery, Daniel, 1878–1964, vol. VI
Corkey, Very Rev. Rt Hon. Robert, 1881–1966, vol. VI
Corkhill, Percy Fullerton, died 1959, vol. V
Corkill, Norman Lace, 1898–1966, vol. VI
Corkill, Thomas Frederick, 1893–1965, vol. VI
Corkran, Alice, died 1916, vol. II
Corkran, Maj.-Gen. Sir Charles Edward, 1872–1939, vol. III
Corkran, Sir Victor Seymour, 1873–1934, vol. III

Corless, Richard, 1884–1967, vol. VI
Corlett, John, 1841–1915, vol. I
Corlette, Major Hubert Christian, 1869–1956, vol. V
Corlette, Brig. James Montagu Christian, 1880–1969, vol. VI (AII)
Cormack, Benjamin George, 1866–1936, vol. III
Cormack, James Maxwell Ross, 1909–1975, vol. VII
Cormack, John Dewar, 1870–1935, vol. III
Cornaby, Rev. William Arthur, 1860–1921, vol. II
Cornelius, Percival, 1874–1960, vol. V
Cornell, Katharine, 1898–1974, vol. VII
Corner, Edred Moss, 1873–1950, vol. IV
Corner, George, 1869–1947, vol. IV
Corner, Engr Rear-Adm. John Thomas, 1849–1912, vol. I
Cornewall, Sir Geoffrey, 6th Bt, 1869–1951, vol. V
Cornewall, Rev. Sir George Henry, 5th Bt, 1833–1908, vol. I
Cornewall, Sir William Francis, 7th Bt, 1871–1962, vol. VI
Corney, Bolton Glanvill, 1851–1924, vol. II
Corney, Leonard George, 1886–1955, vol. V
Cornford, Frances Crofts, 1886–1960, vol. V
Cornford, Francis Macdonald, 1874–1943, vol. IV
Cornford, Leslie Cope, died 1927, vol. II
Cornil, Georges, 1863–1944, vol. IV
Cornish, Rt Rev. Charles Edward, 1842–1936, vol. III
Cornish, Charles John, 1859–1906, vol. I
Cornish, Rev. Ebenezer Darrel, 1849–1922, vol. II
Cornish, Francis Warre, 1839–1916, vol. II
Cornish, George Augustus, 1874–1960, vol. V
Cornish, Rt Rev. George Kestell K.; see Kestell-Cornish.
Cornish, Henry Dauncey, 1877–1948, vol. IV
Cornish, Herbert, 1862–1945, vol. IV
Cornish, Hubert Warre, 1872–1934, vol. III
Cornish, Rt Rev. John Rundle, 1837–1918, vol. II
Cornish, Josiah Easton, 1841–1912, vol. I
Cornish, Rt Rev. Robert Kestell K.; see Kestell-Cornish.
Cornish, Vaughan, 1862–1948, vol. IV
Cornish-Bowden, Col James Hubert Thomas, 1870–1938, vol. III
Cornwall, Ven. Alan Whitmore, 1858–1932, vol. III
Cornwall, Rt Hon. Sir Edwin, 1st Bt, 1863–1953, vol. V
Cornwall, Ernest, 1875–1966, vol. VI
Cornwall, Lt-Col John Wolfran, 1870–1947, vol. IV
Cornwall, Sir Reginald Edwin, 2nd Bt, 1887–1962, vol. VI
Cornwall, Maj.-Gen. Richard Frank, 1902–1967, vol. VI
Cornwall-Jones, Brig. Arthur Thomas, 1900–1980, vol. VII
Cornwallis, 1st Baron, 1864–1935, vol. III
Cornwallis, Sir Kinahan, 1883–1959, vol. V
Cornwallis-West, Major George F. M., 1874–1951, vol. V
Cornwallis-West, William Cornwallis; see West.
Cornwell, Ven. Leonard Cyril, 1893–1971, vol. VII
Corrance, Frederick Snowden, died 1906, vol. I

Corrie, Major Alfred Wynne, 1856–1919, vol. II

Corrie, Sir Owen Cecil Kirkpatrick, 1882–1965, vol. VI

Corrie, Maj.-Gen. William Taylor, 1838–1931, vol. III

Corrigan, Most Rev. Michael Augustine, 1839–1902, vol. I

Corrigan, Rev. Terence Edward, 1915–1975, vol. VII

Corry, Adm. Hon. Armar L.; see Lowry-Corry.

Corry, Lt-Col Sir Henry Charles L.; see Lowry-Corry.

Corry, Col Hon. Henry William L.; see Lowry-Corry.

Corry, Major John Beaumont, 1874–1914, vol. I

Corry, Brig.-Gen. Noel Armar L.; see Lowry-Corry.

Corry, Sir William, 2nd Bt, 1859–1926, vol. II

Corsan, Brig. Reginald Arthur, 1893–1942, vol. IV

Corser, Captain Charles Huskisson, 1886–1962, vol. VI

Corser, Haden, 1845–1906, vol. I

Corson, Rear-Adm. Eric Reid, 1887–1972, vol. VII

Corstorphine, George Steuart, 1868–1919, vol. II

Cortelyou, George Bruce, 1862–1940, vol. III

Cortie, Rev. Father Aloysius Laurence, 1859–1925, vol. II

Cortis-Stanford, Gp Captain C. E., 1874–1933, vol. III

Cortissoz, Royal, 1869–1948, vol. IV

Cortlandt, Lyn, 1926–1979, vol. VII

Cortot, Alfred, 1877–1962, vol. VI

Corwin, Edward Samuel, 1878–1963, vol. VI

Cory, Ven. Alexander, 1890–1973, vol. VII

Cory, Ven Charles Page, 1859–1942, vol. IV

Cory, Sir Clifford John, 1st Bt (cr 1907), 1859–1941, vol. IV

Cory, Elizabeth Cansh, (Lady Cory), died 1956, vol. V

Cory, Lt-Col Evan James Trevor, 1863–1957, vol. V

Cory, Sir George Edward, 1862–1935, vol. III

Cory, Lt-Gen. Sir George Norton, 1874–1968, vol. VI

Cory, Sir Herbert; see Cory, Sir J. H.

Cory, Sir Herbert George Donald, 2nd Bt (cr 1919), 1879–1935, vol. III

Cory, Sir (James) Herbert, 1st Bt (cr 1919), 1857–1933, vol. III

Cory, John, 1828–1910, vol. I

Cory, John Herbert, 1889–1939, vol. III

Cory, Percy Albert, 1870–1936, vol. III

Cory, Richard, 1830–1914, vol. I

Cory, Surg. Rear-Adm. Robert Francis Preston, 1885–1961, vol. VI

Cory, Mrs Theodore; see Graham, W.

Cory, Sir Vyvyan Donald, 3rd Bt (cr 1919), 1906–1941, vol. IV

Cory, William Wallace, 1865–1943, vol. IV

Cory, Winfred; see Graham, W.

Cory-Wright, Sir Arthur Cory, 2nd Bt, 1869–1951, vol. V

Cory-Wright, Sir Cory Francis, 1st Bt, 1839–1909, vol. I

Cory-Wright, Sir Geoffrey, 3rd Bt, 1892–1969, vol. VI

Coryndon, Sir Robert Thorne, 1870–1925, vol. II

Coryton, Frederick, 1850–1924, vol. II

Coryton, William, 1847–1919, vol. II

Cosby, Dudley Sydney Ashworth, 1862–1923, vol. II

Cosby, Col Robert Ashworth Godolphin, 1837–1920, vol. II

Cosgrave, Rev. Francis Herbert, 1880–1971, vol. VII

Cosgrave, Col L. Moore, 1890–1971, vol. VII

Cosgrave, MacDowel, died 1925, vol. II

Cosgrave, Mary Josephine, died 1941, vol. IV

Cosgrave, Sir William Alexander, 1879–1952, vol. V

Cosgrave, Rev. William Frederick, 1857–1936, vol. III

Cosgrave, William Thomas, 1880–1965, vol. VI

Cosgrove, Dame Gertrude Ann, 1882–1962, vol. VI

Cosgrove, Hon. Sir Robert, 1884–1969, vol. VI

Cossar, George Carter, 1880–1942, vol. IV

Cossimbazar, Maharaja Srischandra Nandy, 1897–1952, vol. V

Costain, Rev. Alfred James, 1881–1963, vol. VI

Costain, Sir Richard Rylandes, 1902–1966, vol. VI

Costain, Thomas Bertram, 1885–1965, vol. VI

Costaki, Anthopoulos Pasha, 1838–1902, vol. I

Coste, John Henry, 1871–1949, vol. IV

Costeker, Captain John Henry Dives, 1879–1915, vol. I

Costello, Desmond Patrick, 1912–1964, vol. VI

Costello, Brig.-Gen. Edmund W., 1873–1949, vol. IV

Costello, John Aloysius, 1891–1976, vol. VII

Costello, Sir Leonard Wilfred James, 1881–1972, vol. VII

Coster, Howard, (Howard Sydney Musgrave Coster), died 1959, vol. V

Costigan, Captain Charles Telford, died 1917, vol. II

Costigan, Hon. John, 1835–1916, vol. II

Costigan, Rev. John, 1916–1978, vol. VII

Costin, Maj.-Gen. Eric Boyd, 1889–1971, vol. VII

Costin, William Conrad, 1893–1970, vol. VI

Costley-White, Cyril Grove, 1913–1979, vol. VII

Costley-White, Very Rev. Harold, 1878–1966, vol. VI

Cot, Pierre Donatien Alphonse, 1911–1977, vol. VII

Cotes, Lt-Col Charles James, 1847–1913, vol. I

Cotes, Everard, 1862–1944, vol. IV

Cotes, Mrs Everard, (Sara Jeanette Cotes), died 1922, vol. II

Cotes, Sir Merton Russell, 1835–1921, vol. II

Cotes-Preedy, Digby, 1875–1942, vol. IV

Cotman, Frederic George, 1850–1920, vol. II

Cotsworth, Moses B., 1859–1943, vol. IV

Cottam, Rev. Maj.-Gen. Algernon Edward, 1893–1964, vol. VI

Cottell, Col Reginald James Cope, 1858–1924, vol. II

Cottenham, 4th Earl of, 1874–1919, vol. II

Cottenham, 5th Earl of, 1901–1922 (this entry was not transferred to Who was Who).

Cottenham, 6th Earl of, 1903–1943, vol. IV
Cottenham, 7th Earl of, 1907–1968, vol. VI
Cotter, Col Edward, 1892–1961, vol. VI
Cotter, Maj.-Gen. Francis Gibson, 1857–1928, vol. II
Cotter, Lt-Col Harry John, 1871–1921, vol. II
Cotter, Sir James Laurence, 5th Bt, 1887–1924, vol. II
Cotter, Most Rev. William Timothy, 1866–1940, vol. III
Cotterell, Cecil Bernard, 1875–1957, vol. V
Cotterell, Gilbert Thorp, 1891–1963, vol. VI
Cotterell, Sir Henry Geers, 3rd Bt, 1834–1900, vol. I
Cotterell, Sir John Richard Geers, 4th Bt, 1866–1937, vol. III
Cotterell, Mabel, died 1968, vol. VI
Cotterell, Lt-Col Sir Richard Charles Geers, 5th Bt, 1907–1978, vol. VII
Cotterill, James Henry, 1836–1922, vol. II
Cotterill, Sir (Joseph) Montagu, 1851–1933, vol. III
Cotterill, Sir Montagu; see Cotterill, Sir J. M.
Cottesloe, 2nd Baron, 1830–1918, vol. II
Cottesloe, 3rd Baron, 1862–1956, vol. V
Cottet, Charles, died 1925, vol. II
Cottier, Sir Charles Edward, 1869–1928, vol. II
Cottingham, Lt-Col Edward Roden, 1866–1930, vol. III
Cottingham, Dame Margaret; see Teyte, Dame Maggie.
Cottington-Taylor, Dorothy Daisy, died 1944, vol. IV
Cottle, Adela, 1861–1940, vol. III
Cotton, Lt-Col Arthur Egerton, 1876–1922, vol. II
Cotton, Brig.-Gen. Arthur Stedman, 1873–1952, vol. V
Cotton, Sir Arthur Thomas, 1803–1899, vol. I
Cotton, Baron Francis C.; see Carter-Cotton.
Cotton, Charles, 1856–1939, vol. III
Cotton, Sir Charles Andrew, 1885–1970, vol. VI (AII)
Cotton, Charles William Egerton, died 1931, vol. III
Cotton, Sir Evan; see Cotton, Sir H. E. A.
Cotton, Maj.-Gen. Frederic Conyers, 1807–1901, vol. I
Cotton, Sir George, 1842–1905, vol. I
Cotton, Sir George Frederick, 1877–1943, vol. IV
Cotton, Sir (Harry) Evan Auguste, 1868–1939, vol. III
Cotton, Rev. Henry Aldrich, 1835–1927, vol. II
Cotton, Sir Henry John Stedman, 1845–1915, vol. I (A)
Cotton, Jack, 1903–1964, vol. VI
Cotton, Rev. (James) Stapleton, 1849–1932, vol. III
Cotton, James Sutherland, 1847–1918, vol. II
Cotton, Sir James Temple, 1879–1965, vol. VI
Cotton, Leo Arthur, 1883–1963, vol. VI
Cotton, Montagu Arthur Finch, 1885–1915, vol. I
Cotton, Percy Horace Gordon P.; see Powell-Cotton.
Cotton, Adm. Richard Greville Arthur Wellington S.; see Stapleton-Cotton.

Cotton, Col Hon. Richard Southwell George S.; see Stapleton-Cotton.
Cotton, Lt-Col Ronald Egerton, 1876–1932, vol. III
Cotton, Rev. Stapleton; see Cotton, Rev. J. S.
Cotton, Captain Stapleton, 1831–1908, vol. I
Cotton, Thomas Forrest, died 1965, vol. VI
Cotton, Lt-Col Vere Egerton, 1888–1970, vol. VI
Cotton, William Francis, 1847–1917, vol. II
Cotton, Sir William James Richmond, 1822–1902, vol. I
Cotton-Jodrell, Col Sir Edward Thomas Davenant, 1847–1917, vol. II
Cottrell, Brig. Arthur Foulkes Baglietto, 1891–1962, vol. VI
Cottrell, Sir Edward Baglietto, 1896–1976, vol. VII
Cottrell, Leonard, 1913–1974, vol. VII
Cottrell, Lt-Col Reginald Foulkes, 1885–1924, vol. II
Cottrell, Tom Leadbetter, 1923–1973, vol. VII
Cottrell, William Henry, 1863–1926, vol. II
Cottrell-Dormer, Charles Walter, 1860–1945, vol. IV
Cottrell-Hill, Maj.-Gen. Robert Charles, 1903–1965, vol. VI
Cotts, Sir Campbell Mitchell; see Cotts, Sir W. C. M.
Cotts, Sir (William) Campbell Mitchell-, 2nd Bt, 1902–1964, vol. VI
Cotts, Sir William Dingwall Mitchell, 1st Bt, 1871–1932, vol. III
Coty, René, 1882–1962, vol. VI
Coubertin, Pierre de Fredi, Baron de, 1863–1937, vol. III
Coubrough, Anthony Cathcart, 1877–1963, vol. VI
Couch, Sir Arthur Thomas Q.; see Quiller-Couch.
Couch, Rt Hon. Sir Richard, 1817–1905, vol. I
Couch, William Charles Milford, 1894–1975, vol. VII
Couchman, Sir Francis Dundas, 1864–1948, vol. IV
Couchman, Col George Henry Holbeche, 1859–1936, vol. III
Couchman, Brig. Sir Harold John, 1882–1956, vol. V
Couchman, Malcolm Edward, 1869–1938, vol. III
Couchman, Rev. Reginald Henry, 1874–1948, vol. IV
Coudenhove-Kalergi, Richard N., 1894–1972, vol. VII
Coudert, Most Rev. Antony, 1861–1929, vol. III
Coudurier de Chassaigne, Joseph, 1878–1961, vol. VI
Coué, Emile, died 1926, vol. II
Coughlan, Cornelius, 1828–1915, vol. II
Coulcher, Mary Caroline, 1852–1925, vol. II
Couldrey, Robert Charles, 1890–1974, vol. VII
Couling, Samuel, 1859–1922, vol. II
Coull, Hon. William, 1857–1918, vol. II
Coulson, Charles Alfred, 1910–1974, vol. VII
Coulson, Lt-Col Frank Morris, 1880–1953, vol. V
Coulson, Frederick Raymond, 1864–1922, vol. II
Coulson, Lt-Col John, 1873–1929, vol. III
Coulson, William Lisle B., 1840–1911, vol. I
Coultas, Frederick George, 1888–1961, vol. VI

Coultas, William Whitham, 1890–1973, vol. VII
Coulter, Very Rev. Isaac, 1851–1934, vol. III
Coulter, Ven. J. W., 1867–1956, vol. V
Coulter, Robert Millar, 1857–1927, vol. II
Coulthard, Rev. Canon Hugh Robert, 1860–1939, vol. III
Coulton, George Gordon, 1858–1947, vol. IV
Couper, Sir George Ebenezer Wilson, 2nd Bt, 1824–1908, vol. I
Couper, Major Sir George Robert Cecil, 5th Bt, 1898–1975, vol. VII
Couper, Sir Guy, 4th Bt, 1889–1973, vol. VII
Couper, James Brown, died 1946, vol. IV
Couper, John, died 1918, vol. II
Couper, Sir John C., 1867–1937, vol. III
Couper, John Duncan Campbell, 1876–1962, vol. VI
Couper, Leslie, 1871–1929, vol. III
Couper, Sir Ramsay George Henry, 3rd Bt, 1855–1949, vol. IV
Couper, Sir Thomas, 1878–1954, vol. V
Couper, Maj.-Gen. Sir Victor Arthur, 1859–1938, vol. III
Couperus, Louis, 1863–1923, vol. II
Coupland, Sir Reginald, 1884–1952, vol. V
Coupland, Sidney, 1849–1930, vol. III
Coupland, William Chatterton, 1838–1915, vol. I
Courage, Brig.-Gen. Anthony, 1875–1944, vol. IV
Courage, James Francis, 1903–1963, vol. VI
Courage, Lt-Col John Hubert, 1891–1967, vol. VI
Courage, John Michell, 1868–1931, vol. III
Courage, Comdr Rafe Edward, 1902–1960, vol. V
Courchesne, Most Rev. Georges, 1880–1950, vol. IV (A), vol. V
Courlander, Alphonse, 1881–1914, vol. I
Cournos, John, 1881–1966, vol. VI
Courroux, George Augustus, 1852–1923, vol. II
Court, Emily, died 1957, vol. V
Court, Sir Josiah, 1841–1938, vol. III
Court, William Henry Bassano, 1904–1971, vol. VII
Courtauld, Augustine, 1904–1959, vol. V
Courtauld, Major John Sewell, 1880–1942, vol. IV
Courtauld, Samuel, 1876–1947, vol. IV
Courtauld, Samuel Augustine, 1865–1953, vol. V
Courtauld, Sir Stephen Lewis, 1883–1967, vol. VI
Courtauld, Sir William Julien, 1st Bt, 1870–1940, vol. III
Courtauld Thomson, 1st Baron, 1865–1954, vol. V
Courtenay, Lord; Henry Reginald Courtenay, 1836–1898, vol. I
Courtenay, Col Arthur Henry, 1852–1927, vol. II
Courtenay, Brig.-Gen. Edward Reginald, 1853–1919, vol. II
Courtenay, Henry, died 1921, vol. II
Courtenay, Sir Irving; see Courtenay, Sir J. I.
Courtenay, Sir (John) Irving, 1837–1912, vol. I
Courtenay, Rt Rev. Reginald, 1813–1906, vol. I
Courthope, 1st Baron, 1877–1955, vol. V
Courthope, William John, 1842–1917, vol. II
Courthope-Munroe, Sir Harry, 1860–1951, vol. V
Courtice, Col James George, died 1939, vol. III
Courtis, Sir John Wesley, 1859–1939, vol. III
Courtneidge, Dame Cicely, 1893–1980, vol. VII
Courtney of Penwith, 1st Baron, 1832–1918, vol. II

Courtney, Air Chief Marshal Sir Christopher Lloyd, 1890–1976, vol. VII
Courtney, Col Edward Arthur Waldegrave, 1868–1926, vol. II
Courtney, Maj.-Gen. Edward Henry, 1836–1913, vol. I
Courtney, Rt Rev. Frederick, 1837–1918, vol. II
Courtney, Lt-Col Frederick Harold, 1875–1937, vol. III
Courtney, Gp Captain Ivon Terence, 1885–1978, vol. VII
Courtney, Janet Elizabeth, 1865–1954, vol. V
Courtney, John Mortimer, 1838–1920, vol. II
Courtney, Dame Kathleen D'Olier, 1878–1974, vol. VII
Courtney, Col Richard Edmond, 1870–1919, vol. II
Courtney, Victor Desmond, 1894–1970, vol. VI (AII)
Courtney, William Leonard, 1850–1928, vol. II
Courtney, William Prideaux, 1845–1913, vol. I
Courtown, 5th Earl of, 1823–1914, vol. I
Courtown, 6th Earl of, 1853–1933, vol. III
Courtown, 7th Earl of, 1877–1957, vol. V
Courtown, 8th Earl of, 1908–1975, vol. VII
Coury, Captain Gabriel George, 1896–1956, vol. V
Cousens, Col Robert Baxter, 1880–1943, vol. IV
Cousins, Arthur George, 1882–1949, vol. IV
Cousins, Clarence W., died 1954, vol. V
Cousins, Donald, 1900–1964, vol. VI
Cousins, Edmund Richard John Ratcliffe, 1888–1955, vol. V
Cousins, Sir Harry, 1852–1935, vol. III
Cousins, Herbert H., 1869–1949, vol. IV
Cousins, John Ratcliffe, 1863–1928, vol. II
Cousins, William Henry, 1833–1917, vol. II
Coussey, Sir James Henley, died 1958, vol. V
Coussirat, Rev. Daniel, 1841–1907, vol. I
Coussmaker, Col Lannoy John, 1883–1937, vol. III
Coutanche, Baron (Life Peer); Alexander Moncrieff Coutanche, 1892–1973, vol. VII
Coutts, Charles Ronald Vawdrey, 1876–1938, vol. III
Coutts, Francis James Henderson, 1865–1949, vol. IV
Coutts, James, 1852–1913, vol. I
Coutts, Rt Hon. William Lehman Ashmead Bartlett-B.; see Burdett-Coutts.
Coutts, William Strachan, 1873–1963, vol. VI
Coutts Donald, William, 1906–1974, vol. VII
Covell, Maj.-Gen. Sir Gordon, 1887–1975, vol. VII
Coverdale, Ralph, 1918–1975, vol. VII
Couvreur, Mme Jessie, died 1897, vol. I
Couzens, Sir George Edwin, 1851–1925, vol. II
Couzens, Sir Henry Herbert, died 1944, vol. IV
Cove, Captain George Edward, 1889–1967, vol. VI
Cove, William George, 1888–1963, vol. VI
Coventry, 9th Earl of, 1838–1930, vol. III
Coventry, 10th Earl of, 1900–1940, vol. III
Coventry, Bernard, 1859–1929, vol. III
Coventry, Col Hon. Charles John, 1867–1929, vol. III
Coventry, Henry Arthur, 1852–1925, vol. II
Coventry, Henry Robert Beauclerk, 1871–1953, vol. V

Coventry, Hon. Henry Thomas, 1868–1934, vol. III
Coventry, Rev. Henry William, *died* 1920, vol. II
Coventry, Millis, 1838–1930, vol. III
Coventry, R. M. G., *died* 1914, vol. I
Coventry, Hon. Sir Reginald, 1869–1940, vol. III
Covernton, Alfred Laurence, 1872–1961, vol. VI
Covernton, James Gargrave, 1868–1957, vol. V
Covington, Stenton, 1856–1935, vol. III
Covington, Walter George, *died* 1939, vol. III
Covington, Rev. William, *died* 1908, vol. I
Cowan, Sir Christopher (George) Armstrong, 1889–1979, vol. VII
Cowan, Sir Darcy Rivers Warren, 1885–1958, vol. V
Cowan, Rev. David Galloway, *died* 1921, vol. II
Cowan, Dugald M'Coig, 1865–1933, vol. III
Cowan, Rev. Henry, 1844–1932, vol. III
Cowan, Sir Henry, 1862–1932, vol. III
Cowan, Sir (Henry) Kenneth, 1900–1971, vol. VII
Cowan, Col Henry Vivian, 1854–1918, vol. II
Cowan, James, 1870–1943, vol. IV
Cowan, Col James Henry, 1856–1943, vol. IV
Cowan, James Macfarlane, 1912–1967, vol. VI
Cowan, Captain James William Alston, 1868–1899, vol. I
Cowan, Sir John, 1st Bt (*cr* 1894), 1814–1900, vol. I
Cowan, John, 1849–1926, vol. II
Cowan, Hon. John, 1847–1927, vol. II
Cowan, Sir John, 1844–1929, vol. III
Cowan, John, 1869–1935, vol. III
Cowan, John, 1870–1947, vol. IV
Cowan, Hon. Sir John, 1866–1953, vol. V
Cowan, Sir Kenneth; *see* Cowan, Sir H. K.
Cowan, Lt-Col Percy John, *died* 1954, vol. V
Cowan, Samuel, 1835–1914, vol. I
Cowan, Thomas William, 1840–1926, vol. II
Cowan, Adm. Sir Walter Henry, 1st Bt (*cr* 1921), 1871–1956, vol. V
Cowan, William Christie, 1878–1950, vol. IV (A)
Cowan-Douglas, Hugh, 1895–1960, vol. V
Cowans, Gen. Sir John Steven, 1862–1921, vol. II
Coward, Sir Cecil Allen, 1845–1938, vol. III
Coward, Sir Henry, 1849–1944, vol. IV
Coward, Sir (John Charles) Lewis, 1852–1930, vol. III
Coward, Sir Noel, 1899–1973, vol. VII
Coward, Thomas Alfred, 1867–1933, vol. III
Cowderoy, Most Rev. Mgr Cyril Conrad, 1905–1976, vol. VII
Cowdray, 1st Viscount, 1856–1927, vol. II
Cowdray, 2nd Viscount, 1882–1933, vol. III
Cowdroy, Joan Alice, *died* 1946, vol. IV
Cowell, Maj.-Gen. Sir Ernest Marshall, 1886–1971, vol. VII
Cowell, Frank Richard, 1897–1978, vol. VII
Cowell, George, 1836–1927, vol. II
Cowell, Very Rev. George Young, 1838–1930, vol. III
Cowell, Hubert Russell, *died* 1967, vol. VI
Cowell, Rev. Maurice Byles, *died* 1919, vol. II
Cowell, Philip Herbert, *died* 1949, vol. IV
Cowell, Sibert Forrest, 1863–1949, vol. IV
Cowell, Stuart Jasper, 1891–1971, vol. VII

Cowell-Stepney, Sir Emile Algernon Arthur Keppel, 2nd Bt, 1834–1909, vol. I
Cowen, Sir Frederic Hyman, 1852–1935, vol. III
Cowen, John Edward, 1873–1938, vol. III
Cowen, Joseph, 1831–1899, vol. I
Cowen, Richard John, 1871–1928, vol. II
Cowgill, John Vincent, 1888–1959, vol. V
Cowgill, Rt Rev. Joseph Robert, 1860–1936, vol. III
Cowham, Hilda, *died* 1964, vol. VI
Cowie, Brig.-Gen. Alexander Hugh, 1860–1933, vol. III
Cowie, Very Rev. Benjamin Morgan, *died* 1900, vol. I
Cowie, Maj.-Gen. Charles Henry, 1861–1941, vol. IV
Cowie, Col Henry Edward Colvin, 1872–1963, vol. VI
Cowie, Major Hugh Norman Ramsay, 1872–1915, vol. I
Cowie, Rev. James Ratchford de Wolfe, 1855–1935, vol. III
Cowie, Rt Rev. William Garden, 1831–1902, vol. I
Cowie, William Patrick, *died* 1924, vol. II
Cowland, Rear-Adm. Geoffrey; *see* Cowland, Rear-Adm. W. G.
Cowland, Bt Lt-Col Walter Storey, 1888–1942, vol. IV
Cowland, Rear-Adm. (William) Geoffrey, 1895–1966, vol. VI
Cowley, 3rd Earl, 1866–1919, vol. II
Cowley, 4th Earl, 1890–1962, vol. VI
Cowley, 5th Earl, 1921–1968, vol. VI
Cowley, 6th Earl, 1946–1975, vol. VII
Cowley, Hon. Sir Alfred Sandlings Cowley, 1848–1926, vol. II
Cowley, Sir Arthur Ernest, 1861–1931, vol. III
Cowley, Air Vice-Marshal Arthur Thomas Noel, 1888–1960, vol. V
Cowley, Herbert, 1885–1967, vol. VI
Cowley, John Duncan, 1897–1944, vol. IV
Cowley, Sir Percy; *see* Cowley, Sir W. P.
Cowley, Sir (William) Percy, 1886–1958, vol. V
Cowley-Brown, Rev. George James, 1832–1924, vol. II
Cowlin, Sir Francis Nicholas, 1868–1945, vol. IV
Cowling, Donald George, 1904–1975, vol. VII
Cowling, George H., 1881–1946, vol. IV
Cowper, 7th Earl, 1834–1905, vol. I
Cowper, Cecil, 1856–1916, vol. II
Cowper, Frank, 1849–1930, vol. III
Cowper, Frank Cadogan, 1877–1958, vol. V
Cowper, Henry Swainson, 1865–1941, vol. IV
Cowper, Maj.-Gen. Maitland, 1859–1932, vol. III
Cowper, Lt-Col Malcolm Gordon, 1877–1931, vol. III
Cowper, Sydney, 1854–1922, vol. II
Cowper-Coles, Sherard Osborn, *died* 1936, vol. III
Cowtan, Air Vice-Marshal Frank Cuninghame, 1888–1950, vol. IV
Cox, A. W., 1857–1919, vol. II
Cox, Adelaide, 1860–1945, vol. IV
Cox, Col Alexander Temple, 1836–1907, vol. I
Cox, Alfred, 1866–1954, vol. V

152

Cox, Alfred Innes, 1894–1970, vol. VI
Cox, Rev. Alfred Peachey, 1862–1930, vol. III
Cox, Arthur Frederick, 1849–1925, vol. II
Cox, Arthur Henry, 1888–1971, vol. VII
Cox, Arthur Hubert, 1884–1961, vol. VI
Cox, Arthur Sambell, 1876–1951, vol. V
Cox, Captain Bernard Thomas, 1884–1935, vol. III
Cox, Rt Rev. Charles, 1848–1936, vol. III
Cox, Maj.-Gen. Charles Frederick, 1863–1947, vol. IV
Cox, Lt-Col Sir (Charles) Henry (Fortnom), 1880–1953, vol. V
Cox, Charles Leslie, 1880–1963, vol. VI
Cox, Sir Charles Thomas, 1858–1933, vol. III
Cox, Maj.-Gen. Charles Vyvyan, 1819–1903, vol. I
Cox, Cuthbert Eustace Connop, 1885–1958, vol. V
Cox, Cuthbert Machell, 1881–1962, vol. VI
Cox, E. Albert, 1876–1955, vol. V
Cox, Col Edgar William, 1882–1918, vol. II
Cox, Edmund Charles, 1856–1935, vol. III
Cox, Bt-Col Sir (Edward) Geoffrey Hippisley, 1884–1954, vol. V
Cox, Lt-Col Edward Henry, 1863–1925, vol. II
Cox, Hon. Sir (Edward) Owen, 1866–1932, vol. III
Cox, Lt-Col Edwin Charles, 1868–1958, vol. V
Cox, Euan Hillhouse Methven, 1893–1977, vol. VII
Cox, Major Eustace R.; see Richardson-Cox.
Cox, Francis Albert, 1862–1920, vol. II
Cox, Bt-Col Sir Geoffrey Hippisley; see Cox, Bt Col Sir E. G. H.
Cox, Maj.-Gen. George, 1838–1909, vol. I
Cox, Hon. George Albertus, 1840–1914, vol. I
Cox, Rt. Rev. George Bede, 1854–1938, vol. III
Cox, George Henry, 1848–1935, vol. III
Cox, George Lissant, 1879–1967, vol. VI
Cox, Rev. Sir George William, 14th Bt (cr 1706), 1827–1902, vol. I
Cox, Gen. Sir H. Vaughan, 1860–1923, vol. II
Cox, Major Harding, died 1944, vol. IV
Cox, Harold, 1859–1936, vol. III
Cox, Lt-Col Sir Henry; see Cox, Lt-Col Sir C. H. F.
Cox, Rev. Heraclitus Matthew, 1861–1938, vol. III
Cox, Sir Herbert Charles Fahie, 1893–1973, vol. VII
Cox, Hugh Bertram, 1861–1930, vol. III
Cox, Irwin Edward Bainbridge, 1838–1922, vol. II
Cox, Sir Ivor Richard, 1891–1964, vol. VI
Cox, Rev. James Taylor, 1865–1948, vol. IV
Cox, John Charles, 1843–1919, vol. II
Cox, John Hugh, 1870–1922, vol. II
Cox, John S.; see Snead-Cox.
Cox, Sir John William, 1821–1901, vol. I
Cox, Leslie Reginald, 1897–1965, vol. VI
Cox, Sir Lionel; see Cox, Sir W. H. L.
Cox, Rev. Lionel Edgar, 1868–1945, vol. IV
Cox, Maj.-Gen. Lionel Howard, 1893–1949, vol. IV
Cox, Louisa Belle, (Lady Cox), died 1956, vol. V
Cox, Dame Marjorie Sophie, 1893–1979, vol. VII
Cox, Brig. Sir Matthew Henry, 1892–1966, vol. VI
Cox, Maj.-Gen. Maurice L.; see Lea-Cox.
Cox, Rt Hon. Michael Francis, 1852–1926, vol. II
Cox, Sir Montagu Hounsel, 1873–1936, vol. III
Cox, Hon. Sir Owen; see Cox, Hon. Sir E. O.

Cox, Palmer, 1840–1924, vol. II
Cox, Percy Stuart, 1868–1929, vol. III
Cox, Maj.-Gen. Sir Percy Zachariah, 1864–1937, vol. III
Cox, Sir Reginald Henry, 1st Bt (cr 1921), died 1922, vol. II
Cox, Sir Reginald Kennedy K.; see Kennedy-Cox.
Cox, Robert, 1845–1899, vol. I
Cox, S. Herbert, died 1920, vol. II
Cox, Lt-Col St John Augustus, 1869–1936, vol. III
Cox, Stephen, 1870–1943, vol. IV
Cox, Thomas, 1865–1947, vol. IV
Cox, Sir Thomas S.; see Skewes-Cox.
Cox, William Edward, 1880–1960, vol. V
Cox, Sir (William Henry) Lionel, 1864–1921, vol. II
Cox, Ven. William Lang Paige, 1855–1934, vol. III
Cox, Lt-Col Sir William Thomas, 1881–1939, vol. III
Cox-Davies, Rachael Annie, 1863–1944, vol. IV
Cox-Edwards, Rev. John Cox, died 1926, vol. II
Cox-Taylor, Col Herbert James; see Taylor.
Coxe, Henry Reynell Holled, 1863–1938, vol. III
Coxe, Rev. Seymour Richard, 1842–1922, vol. II
Coxen, Maj.-Gen. Walter Adams, 1870–1949, vol. IV
Coxen, Sir William George, 1st Bt, 1867–1946, vol. IV
Coxhead, Brig.-Gen. James Alfred, 1851–1929, vol. III
Coxhead, Lt-Col Thomas Langhorne, 1864–1939, vol. III
Coxwell, Charles Blake, 1889–1967, vol. VI
Coyajee, Sir Jahangir Cooverjee, 1875–1943, vol. IV (A), vol. V
Coyle, James Vincent, 1864–1948, vol. IV
Coyle, William Thomas, died 1951, vol. V
Cozens-Hardy, 1st Baron, 1838–1920, vol. II
Cozens-Hardy, 2nd Baron, 1868–1924, vol. II
Cozens-Hardy, 3rd Baron, 1873–1956, vol. V
Cozens-Hardy, 4th Baron, 1907–1975, vol. VII
Cozens-Hardy, Archibald, 1869–1957, vol. IV
Cozens-Hardy, Edgar Wrigly, 1872–1945, vol. IV
Cozzens, James Gould, 1903–1978, vol. VII
Crabb, Edward, 1853–1914, vol. I
Crabbe, Sir Cecil Brooksby, 1898–1971, vol. VII
Crabbe, Brig.-Gen. Eyre Macdonnell Stewart, 1852–1905, vol. I
Crabbe, Herbert Ernest, 1867–1940, vol. III
Crabbe, Col Sir John Gordon, 1892–1961, vol. VI
Crabbe, Vice-Adm. Lewis Gonne Eyre, 1882–1951, vol. V
Crabbe, Rt Rev. Reginald Percy, 1883–1964, vol. VI
Crabtree, Harold, 1884–1956, vol. V
Crace, Adm. Sir John Gregory, 1887–1968, vol. VI
Crackanthorpe, Dayrell Montague, died 1950, vol. IV
Crackanthorpe, Montague Hughes, 1832–1913, vol. I
Cracknall, Walter Borthwick, 1850–1902, vol. I
Cracroft-Amcotts, Lt-Comdr John, died 1956, vol. V
Cracroft-Amcotts, Lt-Col Sir Weston, 1888–1975, vol. VII

153

Craddock, Col Alexander Bainbridge, 1893–1962, vol. VI

Craddock, Sir Beresford; see Craddock, Sir G. B.

Craddock, Charles Egbert; see Murfree, Mary Noailles.

Craddock, George, 1897–1974, vol. VII

Craddock, Sir (George) Beresford, 1898–1976, vol. VII

Craddock, Sir Reginald Henry, 1864–1937, vol. III

Craddock, Lt-Gen. Sir Richard Walter, 1910–1977, vol. VII

Craddock, Sir Walter Merry, 1883–1972, vol. VII

Cradock, Rear-Adm. Sir Christopher G. F. M., 1862–1914, vol. I

Cradock, Lt-Col Montagu, 1859–1929, vol. III

Cradock, Major Sheldon William Keith, 1858–1922, vol. II

Cradock-Hartopp, Sir Charles Edward; see Hartopp.

Cradock-Hartopp, Sir Charles (William Everard); see Hartopp.

Cradock-Hartopp, Sir Frederick; see Hartopp.

Cradock-Hartopp, Sir George Francis Fleetwood; see Hartopp.

Cradock-Watson, Henry, 1864–1951, vol. V

Crafer, Rev. Thomas Wilfrid, 1870–1949, vol. IV

Craft, Percy Robert, died 1934, vol. III

Crafts, Wilbur Fisk, 1850–1922, vol. II

Cragg, Ven. Herbert Wallace, 1910–1980, vol. VII

Cragg, Major William Gilliat, 1883–1956, vol. V

Craggs, Sir John George, 1856–1928, vol. II

Craib, William Grant, 1882–1933, vol. III

Craies, William Feilden, 1854–1911, vol. I

Craig, Alexander, died 1935, vol. III

Craig, Major Sir Algernon Tudor T.; see Tudor-Craig.

Craig, Sir Archibald, died 1927, vol. II

Craig, Sir Archibald Charles G.; see Gibson-Craig.

Craig, Maj.-Gen. Archibald Maxwell, 1895–1953, vol. V

Craig, Sir Arthur John Edward, 1886–1972, vol. VII

Craig, Barry; see Craig, F. B.

Craig, Captain Rt Hon. Charles Curtis, 1869–1960, vol. V

Craig, Edward Gordon, 1872–1966, vol. VI

Craig, Edward Hubert Cunningham, 1874–1946, vol. IV

Craig, Edwin Stewart, 1865–1939, vol. III

Craig, Elizabeth Josephine, 1883–1980, vol. VII

Craig, Sir Ernest, 1st Bt, 1859–1933, vol. III

Craig, Sir (Ernest) Gordon, 1891–1966, vol. VI

Craig, Frank, 1874–1918, vol. II

Craig, Frank Barrington, (Barry Craig), 1902–1951, vol. V

Craig, George, 1873–1947, vol. IV

Craig, Sir Gilfrid Gordon, 1871–1953, vol. V

Craig, Sir Gordon; see Craig, Sir E. G.

Craig, Very Rev. Graham, died 1904, vol. I

Craig, Herbert James, 1869–1934, vol. III

Craig, J. Humbert, died 1944, vol. IV

Craig, James, 1851–1931, vol. III

Craig, Lt-Col James, 1864–1931, vol. III

Craig, Sir James, 1861–1933, vol. III

Craig, James A., died 1958, vol. V

Craig, James Alfred, 1858–1942, vol. IV

Craig, James Douglas, 1882–1950, vol. IV

Craig, Sir James Henry G.; see Gibson-Craig.

Craig, James Ireland, 1868–1952, vol. V

Craig, Sir John, 1874–1957, vol. V

Craig, John, 1898–1977, vol. VII

Craig, John Douglas, 1887–1968, vol. VI

Craig, Col John Francis, 1856–1927, vol. II

Craig, Sir John Herbert McCutcheon, 1885–1977, vol. VII

Craig, John Manson, 1896–1970, vol. VI

Craig, Sir (John) Walker, 1847–1926, vol. II

Craig, Sir Marshall Millar, 1880–1957, vol. V

Craig, Sir Maurice, 1866–1935, vol. III

Craig, Col Noel Newman Lombard, died 1968, vol. VI

Craig, Lt-Comdr Norman Carlyle, 1868–1919, vol. II

Craig, Rev. Oswald, 1867–1935, vol. III

Craig, R. Hunter, 1839–1913, vol. I

Craig, Col Robert Annesley, 1869–1932, vol. III

Craig, S. E., died 1904, vol. I

Craig, Thomas Joseph Alexander, 1881–1970, vol. VI

Craig, Sir Walker; see Craig, Sir J. W.

Craig, Dep. Surg.-Gen. William Maxwell, 1859–1914, vol. I

Craig, William Stuart McRae, 1903–1975, vol. VII

Craig-Brown, Lt-Col Ernest, 1871–1966, vol. VI

Craig-Brown, Thomas, 1844–1922, vol. II

Craigavon, 1st Viscount, 1871–1940, vol. III

Craigavon, 2nd Viscount, 1906–1974, vol. VII

Craigavon, Viscountess; (Cecil Mary Nowell Dering), died 1960, vol. V

Craighead, Edwin Boone, 1861–1920, vol. II (A), vol. III

Craigie, Rev. Charles Edward, died 1922, vol. II

Craigie, James, 1899–1978, vol. VII

Craigie, John, 1857–1919, vol. II

Craigie, Major Patrick George, 1843–1930, vol. III

Craigie, Pearl Mary Teresa; see Hobbes, John Oliver.

Craigie, Rt Hon. Sir Robert Leslie, 1883–1959, vol. V

Craigie, Adm. Robert William, 1849–1911, vol. I

Craigie, Sir William A., 1867–1957, vol. V

Craigmyle, 1st Baron, 1850–1937, vol. III

Craigmyle, 2nd Baron, 1883–1944, vol. IV

Craik, Sir George Lillie, 2nd Bt, 1874–1929, vol. III

Craik, Rt Hon. Sir Henry, 1st Bt, 1846–1927, vol. II

Craik, Sir Henry Duffield, 3rd Bt, 1876–1955, vol. V

Craik, Lt-Col James, 1871–1942, vol. IV

Craik, Robert, 1829–1906, vol. I

Cram, Ralph Adams, 1863–1942, vol. IV

Cramb, Alexander Charles, 1874–1956, vol. V

Cramb, J. A., 1862–1913, vol. I

Cramer, William, 1878–1945, vol. IV

Cramer-Roberts, Major Marmaduke Torin; see Roberts.

Cramp, Charles Henry, 1828–1913, vol. I

Cramp, Concemore Thomas, 1876–1933, vol. III
Cramp, Karl Reginald, 1878–1956, vol. V
Cramp, William, 1876–1939, vol. III
Cramp, Sir William Dawkins, 1840–1927, vol. II
Crampton, Vice-Adm. Denis Burke, 1873–1936, vol. III
Crampton, Brig.-Gen. Fiennes Henry, 1862–1938, vol. III
Crampton, Harold Percy, 1878–1969, vol. VI
Crampton, Col Philip John Ribton, 1860–1932, vol. III
Cran, Marion, 1875–1942, vol. IV
Cranage, Very Rev. David Herbert Somerset, 1866–1957, vol. V
Cranbrook, 1st Earl of, 1814–1906, vol. I
Cranbrook, 2nd Earl of, 1839–1911, vol. I
Cranbrook, 3rd Earl of, 1870–1915, vol. I (A)
Cranbrook, 4th Earl of, 1900–1978, vol. VII
Crane, Sir Alfred Victor, 1892–1955, vol. V
Crane, Lt-Col Charles Paston, died 1939, vol. III
Crane, Sir Edmund Frank, 1886–1957, vol. V
Crane, Robert Newton, 1848–1927, vol. II
Crane, Walter, 1845–1915, vol. I
Crane, Sir William, 1874–1959, vol. V
Cranfield, Arthur Leslie, 1892–1957, vol. V
Cranko, John, 1927–1973, vol. VII
Crankshaw, Lt-Col Sir Eric Norman Spencer, 1885–1966, vol. VI
Cranmer-Byng, L., 1872–1945, vol. IV
Cranston, Robert, died 1906, vol. I
Cranston, Brig.-Gen. Sir Robert, 1843–1923, vol. II
Cranston, William Patrick, 1913–1967, vol. VI
Cranstoun, Lady; (Elizabeth), died 1899, vol. I
Cranstoun, Charles Joseph Edmondstoune-, 1877–1950, vol. IV
Cranstoun, James, died 1931, vol. III
Cranswick, Rt Rev. Geoffrey Franceys, 1894–1978, vol. VII
Cranswick, Rt Rev. George Harvard, 1882–1954, vol. V
Cranworth, 1st Baron, died 1902, vol. I
Cranworth, 2nd Baron, 1877–1964, vol. VI
Craske, A(rthur) H(ugh) Glenn, 1904–1967, vol. VI
Craske, Rt Rev. Frederick William Thomas, 1901–1971, vol. VII
Craske, Glenn; see Craske, A. H. G.
Craske, Lt-Col John, 1869–1936, vol. III
Craster, Sir Edmund; see Craster, Sir H. H. E.
Cra'ster, Lt-Col Edmund Henry Bertram, 1869–1942, vol. IV
Craster, Col George, 1878–1958, vol. V
Craster, Maj.-Gen. George Ayton, 1830–1912, vol. I
Craster, Sir (Herbert Henry) Edmund, 1879–1959, vol. V
Craster, Sir John Montagu, 1901–1975, vol. VII
Cra'ster, Col Shafto Longfield, 1862–1943, vol. IV
Craster, Thomas William, 1860–1938, vol. III
Crathorne, 1st Baron, 1897–1977, vol. VII
Craufurd, Rev. Alexander Henry, 1843–1917, vol. II
Craufurd, Sir Alexander John Fortescue, 7th Bt, 1876–1966, vol. VI

Craufurd, Sir Charles William Frederick, 4th Bt, 1847–1939, vol. III
Craufurd, Mrs Eleanor Louisa Houison, died 1950, vol. IV
Craufurd, Brig.-Gen. Sir (George) Standish (Gage), 5th Bt, 1872–1957, vol. V
Craufurd, Sir James Gregan, 8th Bt, 1886–1970, vol. VI
Craufurd, Brig.-Gen. John Archibald Houison, 1862–1933, vol. III
Craufurd, Sir Quentin Charles Alexander, 6th Bt, 1875–1957, vol. V
Craufurd, Col Robert Quentin, 1880–1943, vol. IV
Craufurd, Brig.-Gen. Sir Standish; see Craufurd, Brig.-Gen. Sir G. S. G.
Craufurd-Stuart, Lt-Col Charles Kennedy; see Stuart.
Cravath, Paul Drennan, 1861–1940, vol. III
Craven, 4th Earl of, 1868–1921, vol. II
Craven, 5th Earl of, 1897–1932, vol. III
Craven, 6th Earl of, 1917–1965, vol. VI
Craven, Brig.-Gen. Arthur Julius, 1867–1933, vol. III
Craven, Arthur Scott, (Captain Arthur Keedwell Harvey James), 1875–1917, vol. II
Craven, Avery O., 1886–1980, vol. VII
Craven, Comdr Sir Charles Worthington, 1st Bt, 1884–1944, vol. IV
Craven, Sir Derek Worthington Clunes, 2nd Bt, 1910–1946, vol. IV
Craven, Rt Rev. George L., 1884–1967, vol. VI
Craven, Ven. James Brown, 1850–1924, vol. II
Craven, Hon. Osbert William, 1848–1923, vol. II
Craven, Sir Robert Martin, 1824–1903, vol. I
Craven, Major Hon. Rupert Cecil, 1870–1959, vol. V
Craven, Lt-Col Waldemar Sigismund Dacre, 1880–1928, vol. II
Craven, William George, 1835–1906, vol. I
Craven-Ellis, William, died 1959, vol. V
Craw, Sir Henry Hewat, 1882–1964, vol. VI
Crawford, 26th Earl of, and Balcarres, 9th Earl of, 1847–1913, vol. I
Crawford, 27th Earl of, and Balcarres, 10th Earl of, 1871–1940, vol. III
Crawford, 28th Earl of, and Balcarres, 11th Earl of, 1900–1975, vol. VII
Crawford, Brig. Alastair Wardrop Euing, 1896–1978, vol. VII
Crawford, Alexander W., 1866–1933, vol. III
Crawford, Andrew, 1871–1936, vol. III
Crawford, Archibald, 1882–1960, vol. V
Crawford, Arthur Muir, 1882–1962, vol. VI
Crawford, Arthur Travers, 1835–1911, vol. I
Crawford, Captain Charles Wispington Glover, died 1934, vol. III
Crawford, Colin Grant, 1890–1959, vol. V
Crawford, Donald, 1837–1919, vol. II
Crawford, Very Rev. Edward Patrick, 1846–1912, vol. I
Crawford, Col Edward William, 1879–1961, vol. VI
Crawford, Mrs Emily, died 1915, vol. I (A)
Crawford, Sir Ferguson; see Crawford, Sir W. F.

Crawford, Sir Francis Collum, 1862–1934, vol. III
Crawford, Francis Marion, 1854–1909, vol. I
Crawford, Sir Frederick, 1906–1978, vol. VII
Crawford, Lt-Col Frederick Hugh, 1861–1952, vol. V
Crawford, Col George Rainier, 1862–1915, vol. I
Crawford, Lt-Col Gilbert Stewart, 1868–1953, vol. V
Crawford, Henry Leighton, 1855–1931, vol. III
Crawford, Sir Homewood, 1850–1936, vol. III
Crawford, James Archibald, 1905–1953, vol. V
Crawford, Joan, died 1977, vol. VII
Crawford, Very Rev. John, died 1924, vol. II
Crawford, John Balfour, 1887–1962, vol. VI
Crawford, John Dawson, 1861–1946, vol. IV
Crawford, Lt-Col John Halket, 1868–1936, vol. III
Crawford, Maj.-Gen. John Scott, 1889–1978, vol. VII
Crawford, Gen. Sir Kenneth Noel, 1895–1961, vol. VI
Crawford, Lawrence, 1867–1951, vol. V
Crawford, Captain Lawrence Hugh, died 1918, vol. II
Crawford, Osbert Guy Stanhope, 1886–1957, vol. V
Crawford, Col Raymund, 1858–1927, vol. II
Crawford, Sir Richard Frederick, 1863–1919, vol. II
Crawford, Col Richmond Irvine, 1839–1910, vol. I
Crawford, Robert, died 1946, vol. IV
Crawford, Col Robert Duncan, died 1936, vol. III
Crawford, Col Rt Hon. Robert Gordon S.; see Sharman-Crawford.
Crawford, Susan Fletcher, died 1919, vol. II
Crawford, Rev. Thomas, 1860–1937, vol. III
Crawford, Thomas Clark, 1886–1955, vol. V
Crawford, Col Vincent James, 1877–1932, vol. III
Crawford, Sir (Walter) Ferguson, 1894–1978, vol. VII
Crawford, Sir William, 1840–1922, vol. II
Crawford, Lt-Col William Loftus, 1868–1951, vol. V
Crawford, William Neil Kennedy Mellon, 1910–1978, vol. VII
Crawford, Sir William S., 1878–1950, vol. IV
Crawfurd, Major Horace Evelyn, 1882–1958, vol. V
Crawfurd, Rt Rev. Lionel Payne, 1864–1934, vol. III
Crawfurd, Oswald, 1834–1909, vol. I
Crawfurd, Sir Raymond Henry Payne, 1865–1938, vol. III
Crawfurd-Price, Walter Harrington, 1881–1967, vol. VI
Crawfurd-Stirling-Stuart, William, 1854–1938, vol. III
Crawhall, Joseph, died 1913, vol. I
Crawhall, Rev. Thomas Emerson, 1866–1934, vol. III
Crawley, Alfred Ernest, 1869–1924, vol. II
Crawley, Rev. Canon Arthur Stafford, 1876–1948, vol. IV
Crawley, Cecil, 1862–1931, vol. III
Crawley, Francis, 1853–1914, vol. I
Crawley, Frank C., 1871–1935, vol. III

Crawley, Major Sir Philip Arthur Sambrooke, 1869–1933, vol. III
Crawley, Col Richard Parry, 1876–1933, vol. III
Crawley, William John Chetwode, 1844–1916, vol. II
Crawley-Boevey, Sir Francis Hyde; see Boevey.
Crawley-Boevey, Sir Lance, (Launcelot Valentine Hyde), 7th Bt, 1900–1968, vol. VI
Crawshaw, 1st Baron, 1825–1908, vol. I
Crawshaw, 2nd Baron, 1853–1929, vol. III
Crawshaw, 3rd Baron, 1884–1946, vol. IV
Crawshaw, Lionel Townsend, died 1949, vol. IV
Crawshay, Lt-Col Codrington Howard Rees, 1882–1937, vol. III
Crawshay, Captain Geoffrey Cartland Hugh, 1892–1954, vol. V
Crawshay-Williams, Lt-Col Eliot, 1879–1962, vol. VI
Craxton, Harold, 1885–1971, vol. VII
Cray, Rev. Canon Frank Maynard, 1898–1967, vol. VI
Creagh, Maj.-Gen. Arthur Gethin, 1855–1941, vol. IV
Creagh, Col Arthur Henry Dopping, 1866–1941, vol. IV
Creagh, Charles Vandeleur, 1842–1917, vol. II
Creagh, Col George Washington B.; see Brazier-Creagh.
Creagh, Rear-Adm. James Vandeleur, 1883–1956, vol. V
Creagh, Maj.-Gen. Sir Michael O'Moore, 1892–1970, vol. VI
Creagh, Gen. Sir O'Moore, 1848–1923, vol. II
Creagh, Lt-Col Peter H., 1882–1933, vol. III
Creagh Coen, Sir Terence Bernard, 1903–1970, vol. VI
Creagh-Osborne, Captain F.; see Osborne.
Creak, Captain Ettrick William, 1835–1920, vol. II
Crealock, Major John Mansfield, died 1959, vol. V
Creamer, Amos Albert, 1917–1978, vol. VII
Crean, Sir Bernard Arthur, 1881–1956, vol. V
Crean, Eugene, 1856–1939, vol. III
Crean, Major Thomas Joseph, 1873–1923, vol. II
Crease, Hon. Sir Henry Pering Pellew, 1823–1905, vol. I
Crease, Maj.-Gen. Sir John Frederick, died 1907, vol. I
Crease, Captain Thomas Evans, 1875–1942, vol. IV
Creasey, Gordon Leonard, 1873–1943, vol. IV
Creasey, John, 1908–1973, vol. VII
Creasy, Adm. of the Fleet Sir George Elvey, 1895–1972, vol. VII
Creasy, Harold Thomas, 1873–1950, vol. IV
Creasy, Leonard, 1854–1922, vol. II
Cree, Maj.-Gen. Gerald, 1862–1932, vol. III
Cree, Kate; see Rorke, K.
Creed, Clarence James, 1894–1955, vol. V
Creed, Edward ffolliott, 1893–1947, vol. IV
Creed, Rev. John Martin, 1889–1940, vol. III
Creed, Hon. John Mildred, 1842–1930, vol. III
Creed, Richard Stephen, 1898–1964, vol. VI
Creed, Sir Thomas Percival, 1897–1969, vol. VI
Creedy, Sir Herbert James, 1878–1973, vol. VII
Creelman, James, 1859–1915, vol. I

Creelman, Col John Jennings, 1882–1949, vol. IV
Crees, James Harold Edward, 1882–1941, vol. IV
Cregan, Rev. James, 1857–1935, vol. III
Creighton, Charles, 1847–1927, vol. II
Creighton, Rev. Cuthbert, 1876–1963, vol. VI
Creighton, Donald Grant, 1902–1979, vol. VII
Creighton, James George Aylwin, 1850–1930, vol. III
Creighton, Rear-Adm. Sir Kenelm Everard Lane, 1883–1963, vol. VI
Creighton, Mrs Louise, 1850–1936, vol. III
Creighton, Rt Rev. Mandell, 1843–1901, vol. I
Cremer, Herbert William, 1893–1970, vol. VI
Cremer, Robert Wyndham K.; see Ketton-Cremer.
Cremer, Sir William Randal, 1838–1908, vol. I
Cremieu-Javal, Paul, 1857–1927, vol. II
Crerar, Gen. Henry Duncan Graham, 1888–1965, vol. VI
Crerar, Sir James, 1877–1960, vol. V
Crerar, Hon. Thomas Alexander, 1876–1975, vol. VII
Cresswell, Rev. Cyril Leonard, 1890–1974, vol. VII
Cresswell, Col George Francis Addison, 1852–1926, vol. II
Cresswell, Herbert Osborn, 1860–1919, vol. II
Cresswell, Col Pearson Robert, 1834–1905, vol. I
Cresswell, Stuart Cornwallis, died 1959, vol. V
Cressy-Marcks, Violet Olivia, (Mrs Francis Fisher), died 1970, vol. VI
Creston, Dormer; see Colston-Baynes, D. J.
Creswell, Sir Archibald; see Creswell, Sir K. A. C.
Creswell, Col Edmund Fraser, 1876–1941, vol. IV
Creswell, Lt-Col Hon. Frederic Hugh Page, 1866–1948, vol. IV
Creswell, Rear-Adm. George Hector, 1889–1967, vol. VI
Creswell, Harry Bulkeley, 1869–1960, vol. V
Creswell, John Edwards, 1864–1928, vol. II
Creswell, Sir (Keppel) Archibald (Cameron), 1879–1974, vol. VII
Creswell, Margaret Susan, died 1936, vol. III
Creswell, Vice-Adm. Sir William Rooke, 1852–1933, vol. III
Creswell, William Thomas, 1872–1946, vol. IV
Creswick, Col Sir Nathaniel, 1831–1917, vol. II
Creswick, Paul, 1866–1947, vol. II
Cretney, Sir Godfrey; see Cretney, Sir W. G.
Cretney, Sir (William) Godfrey, 1912–1971, vol. VII
Crew, Albert, died 1942, vol. IV
Crew, Francis Albert Eley, 1886–1973, vol. VII
Crewdson, Bernard Francis, 1887–1966, vol. VI
Crewdson, Rev. George, 1840–1920, vol. II
Crewdson, Bt-Col William Dillworth, 1897–1972, vol. VII
Crewdson, Wilson, 1856–1918, vol. II
Crewe, 1st Marquess of, 1858–1945, vol. IV
Crewe, Marchioness of; (Margaret Etrenne Hannah), died 1967, vol. VI
Crewe, Bertie Gibson, 1884–1971, vol. VII
Crewe, Brig.-Gen. Hon. Sir Charles Preston, 1858–1936, vol. III
Crewe, Major James Hugh Hamilton D.; see Dodds Crewe.

Crewe, Sir Vauncey Harpur, 10th Bt, 1846–1924, vol. II
Crewe-Read, Col Randulph Offley, died 1932, vol. III
Creyke, Ralph, 1849–1908, vol. I
Cribbett, Sir George; see Cribbett, Sir W. C. G.
Cribbett, Sir (Wilfrid Charles) George, 1897–1964, vol. VI
Crichton, Hon. Arthur Owen, 1876–1970, vol. VI
Crichton, Lt-Col Hon. Charles Frederick, 1841–1918, vol. II
Crichton, Lady Emma, died 1936, vol. III
Crichton, Col Hon. Sir George Arthur Charles, 1874–1952, vol. V
Crichton, Lt-Col Gerald Charles Lawrence, 1900–1969, vol. VI
Crichton, Brig. Henry Coventry Maitland-Makgill-, 1880–1953, vol. V
Crichton, Col Hon. Sir Henry George Louis, 1844–1922, vol. II
Crichton, Air Cdre Henry Lumsden, 1890–1952, vol. V
Crichton, Captain Hon. James Archibald, 1877–1956, vol. V
Crichton, Engr Captain Peter Thomson, 1863–1935, vol. III
Crichton, Lt-Col Richmond Trevor, 1865–1934, vol. III
Crichton, Sir Robert, 1881–1950, vol. IV
Crichton-Browne, Col Harold William Alexander Francis, 1866–1937, vol. III
Crichton-Browne, Sir James, 1840–1938, vol. III
Crichton-Maitland, Maj.-Gen. David M.; see Makgill-Crichton-Maitland.
Crichton-Miller, Hugh, 1877–1959, vol. V
Crichton-Stuart, Lord Colum Edmund, 1886–1957, vol. V
Crichton-Stuart, Lord Ninian Edward, 1883–1915, vol. I (A)
Crick, Rt Rev. Douglas Henry, died 1973, vol. VII
Crick, Rt Rev. Philip Charles Thurlow, 1882–1937, vol. III
Crick, Very Rev. Thomas, 1885–1970, vol. VI
Crick, Hon. William P., died 1908, vol. I
Cridland, Frank, 1873–1954, vol. V
Crilly, Daniel, 1857–1923, vol. II
Crimmin, Col John, 1859–1945, vol. IV
Cripps, Col Arthur William, 1862–1945, vol. IV
Cripps, Sir Cyril Thomas, 1892–1979, vol. VII
Cripps, Sir Edward Stewart, 1885–1955, vol. V
Cripps, Major Sir Frederick William Beresford, 1873–1959, vol. V
Cripps, Henry William, died 1899, vol. I
Cripps, Dame Isobel, 1891–1979, vol. VII
Cripps, Major Hon. Leonard Harrison, died 1959, vol. V
Cripps, Hon. Lionel, 1863–1950, vol. IV
Cripps, Rt Hon. Sir (Richard) Stafford, 1889–1952, vol. V
Cripps, Rt Hon. Sir Stafford; see Cripps, Rt Hon. Sir R. S.
Cripps, W. Harrison, died 1923, vol. II
Cripps, William Parry, 1903–1972, vol. VII
Crisp, Col Rev. Alan Percy, 1889–1972, vol. VII

Crisp, Sir Frank, 1st Bt, 1843–1919, vol. II
Crisp, Sir Frank Morris, 2nd Bt, 1872–1938, vol. III
Crisp, Frederick Arthur, 1851–1922, vol. II
Crisp, Sir Harold, 1874–1942, vol. IV
Crisp, Sir John Wilson, 3rd Bt, 1873–1950, vol. IV
Crispe, Thomas Edward, died 1911, vol. I
Crispi, Francesco, 1819–1901, vol. I
Crispin, Edward Smyth, 1874–1958, vol. V
Crispin, Geoffrey Hollis, 1905–1976, vol. VII
Critchell, James Troubridge, 1850–1917, vol. II
Critchett, Sir George Anderson, 1st Bt, died 1925, vol. II
Critchett, Sir (George) Montague, 2nd Bt, 1884–1941, vol. IV
Critchett, Sir Montague; see Critchett, Sir G. M.
Critchley, Alexander, 1893–1974, vol. VII
Critchley, Brig.-Gen. Alfred Cecil, 1890–1963, vol. VI
Critchley-Waring, Captain Arthur Cunliffe Bernard, 1886–1930, vol. III
Crittall, Francis Henry, died 1935, vol. III
Croal, John P., 1852–1932, vol. III
Croce, Benedetto, 1866–1952, vol. V
Crockatt, James Laird, 1876–1936, vol. III
Crockatt, Brig. Norman Richard, 1894–1956, vol. V
Crocker, George, 1846–1923, vol. II
Crocker, Brig.-Gen. George Delamain, died 1938, vol. III
Crocker, Henry Radcliffe, 1845–1909, vol. I
Crocker, Lt-Col Herbert Edmund, 1877–1962, vol. VI
Crocker, Gen. Sir John Tredinnick, 1896–1963, vol. VI
Crocker, Brig.-Gen. Sydney Francis, 1864–1952, vol. V
Crocker, Sir William Charles, 1886–1973, vol. VII
Crocker, Rear-Adm. (S) William Ernest, died 1951, vol. V
Crocket, Henry Edgar, died 1926, vol. II
Crocket, James, 1878–1944, vol. IV
Crocket, Oswald Smith, 1868–1945, vol. IV
Crockett, Sir James Henry Clifden, 1848–1931, vol. III
Crockett, Samuel Rutherford, 1860–1914, vol. I
Crockett, Rev. William Shillinglaw, 1866–1945, vol. IV
Crocombe, Leonard Cecil, 1890–1968, vol. VI
Croft, 1st Baron, 1881–1947, vol. IV
Croft, Sir Alfred Woodley, 1841–1925, vol. II
Croft, Sir Arthur, 1886–1961, vol. VI
Croft, Sir Frederick Leigh, 3rd Bt (cr 1818), 1860–1930, vol. III
Croft, Henry Herbert Stephen, 1842–1923, vol. II
Croft, Sir Herbert Archer, 10th Bt (cr 1671), 1868–1915, vol. I
Croft, Sir Herbert George Denman, 9th Bt (cr 1671), 1838–1902, vol. I
Croft, Sir Hugh Matthew Fiennes, 12th Bt (cr 1671), 1874–1954, vol. V
Croft, Sir James Herbert, 11th Bt (cr 1671), 1907–1941, vol. IV

Croft, Sir John Frederick, 2nd Bt (cr 1818), 1828–1904, vol. I
Croft, Sir John William Graham, 4th Bt (cr 1818), 1910–1979, vol. VII
Croft, Major Owen George Scudamore, 1880–1956, vol. V
Croft, Richard Benyon, 1843–1912, vol. I
Croft, Sir William Dawson, 1892–1964, vol. VI
Croft, Brig.-Gen. William Denman, 1879–1968, vol. VI
Croft-Cooke, Rupert, 1903–1979, vol. VII
Croft-Murray, Edward, 1907–1980, vol. VII
Crofton, 3rd Baron, 1834–1911, vol. I
Crofton, 4th Baron, 1866–1942, vol. IV
Crofton, 5th Baron, 1926–1974, vol. VII
Crofton, Brig.-Gen. Cyril Randell, 1867–1941, vol. IV
Crofton, Vice-Adm. Edward George L.; see Lowther-Crofton.
Crofton, Major Sir Henry; see Crofton, Major Sir M. R. H.
Crofton, Sir Hugh Denis, 5th Bt (cr 1801), 1878–1902, vol. I
Crofton, Lt-Gen. James, 1826–1908, vol. I
Crofton, Sir Malby, 3rd Bt (cr 1838), 1857–1926, vol. II
Crofton, Major Sir (Malby Richard) Henry, 4th Bt (cr 1838), 1881–1962, vol. VI
Crofton, Col Morgan, 1850–1916, vol. II
Crofton, Sir Morgan George, 4th Bt (cr 1801), 1850–1900, vol. I
Crofton, Sir Morgan George, 6th Bt (cr 1801), 1879–1958, vol. V
Crofton, Morgan William, 1826–1915, vol. I
Crofton, Sir Richard Marsh, 1891–1955, vol. V
Crofton, Brig. Roger, 1888–1972, vol. VII
Crofton, Rt Hon. Sir Walter Frederic, 1815–1897, vol. I
Crofts, Surg.-Gen. Aylmer Martin, 1854–1915, vol. I
Crofts, Ernest, 1847–1911, vol. I
Crofts, Freeman Wills, 1879–1957, vol. V
Crofts, John Ernest Victor, 1887–1972, vol. VII
Crofts, Lt-Col Leonard Markham, 1867–1942, vol. IV
Crofts, Major Richard, 1859–1916, vol. II
Crofts, Thomas Robert Norman, 1874–1949, vol. IV
Crofts, Rev. William John H.; see Humble-Crofts.
Croiset, Alfred, 1845–1923, vol. II
Croisset, Francis de, 1885–1937, vol. III
Croke, Air Cdre Lewis George Le Blount, 1894–1971, vol. VII
Croke, Most Rev. Thomas W., 1824–1902, vol. I
Croker, Mrs B. M., died 1920, vol. II
Croker, Engr Rear-Adm. Edward James O'Brien, 1881–1960, vol. V
Croker, Maj.-Gen. Sir Henry Leycester, 1864–1938, vol. III
Croker, Richard, 1841–1922, vol. II
Croker, Captain Thomas Joseph, 1876–1956, vol. V
Crole, Charles Stewart, died 1916, vol. II
Crole, Gerard Lake, 1855–1927, vol. II

Croll, David Gifford, 1885–1948, vol. IV
Croly, Very Rev. Daniel George Hayes, *died* 1916, vol. II
Cromartie, Countess of (3rd in line), 1878–1962, vol. VI
Cromb, David Lyall, 1875–1961, vol. VI
Crombie, Alan Douglas, 1894–1958, vol. V
Crombie, Bde-Surg. Lt-Col Alexander, 1845–1906, vol. I
Crombie, Col David Campbell, 1877–1952, vol. V
Crombie, George Edmond, 1908–1972, vol. VII
Crombie, Sir James Ian Cormack, 1902–1969, vol. VI
Crombie, Rear-Adm. John Harvey Forbes, 1900–1972, vol. VII
Crombie, John William, 1858–1908, vol. I
Cromer, 1st Earl of, 1841–1917, vol. II
Cromer, 2nd Earl of, 1877–1953, vol. V
Cromie, Captain Charles Francis, 1858–1907, vol. I
Cromie, Comdr Francis Newton Allen, 1882–1918, vol. II
Cromie, Robert, 1856–1907, vol. I
Cromie, Rev. William Patrick, *died* 1927, vol. II
Crommelin, Andrew Claude de la Cherois, 1865–1939, vol. III
Crommelin, May de la Cherois, *died* 1930, vol. III
Crompton, James Shaw, 1853–1916, vol. II
Crompton, John Gilbert Frederic, 1869–1919, vol. II
Crompton, Richmal; *see* Lamburn, R. C.
Crompton, Robert, 1869–1958, vol. V
Crompton, Col Rookes Evelyn Bell, 1845–1940, vol. III
Crompton-Roberts, Lt-Col Henry Roger; *see* Roberts.
Cromwell, 5th Baron, 1893–1966, vol. VI
Crone, Anne, 1915–1972, vol. VII
Crone, Col Desmond Roe, 1900–1974, vol. VII
Crone, John Smyth, 1858–1945, vol. IV
Cronin, Rt Rev. Mgr Francis, 1879–1939, vol. III
Cronin, Henry Francis, 1894–1977, vol. VII
Cronin, Rt Rev. Mgr Michael, 1871–1943, vol. IV
Cronje, Gen. Piet A., 1835–1911, vol. I
Cronshaw, Cecil John Turrell, 1889–1961, vol. VI
Cronshaw, Rev. Christopher, *died* 1921, vol. II
Cronshaw, Rev. George Bernard, *died* 1928, vol. II
Cronshaw, Rev. Herbert Priestley, 1863–1930, vol. III
Cronwright, Samuel Cron, 1863–1936, vol. III (A), vol. IV
Cronwright Schreiner, Mrs S. C.; *see* Schreiner, Olive.
Cronyn, Captain St John, 1901–1973, vol. VII
Crook, Charles W., 1862–1926, vol. II
Crook, Thomas Mewburn, 1869–1949, vol. IV
Crook, William Montgomery, 1860–1945, vol. IV
Crooke, Lt-Col Charles Douglas Parry, 1870–1948, vol. IV
Crooke, Adm. Sir (Henry) Ralph, 1875–1952, vol. V
Crooke, Sir (John) Smedley, *died* 1951, vol. V
Crooke, Adm. Sir Ralph; *see* Crooke, Adm. Sir H. R.

Crooke, Sir Smedley; *see* Crooke, Sir J. S.
Crooke, William, 1848–1923, vol. II
Crooke-Lawless, Surg. Lt-Col Sir Warren Roland; *see* Lawless.
Crookenden, Col Arthur, 1877–1962, vol. VI
Crookenden, Harry Mitten, 1862–1947, vol. IV
Crookes, Sir William, 1832–1919, vol. II
Crookham, Rev. William Thomas Rupert, *died* 1945, vol. IV
Crooks, Sir James, 1858–1940, vol. III
Crooks, James, 1901–1980, vol. VII
Crooks, Captain Robert Crawford, 1894–1951, vol. V
Crooks, Rt Hon. William, 1852–1921, vol. II
Crookshank, 1st Viscount, 1893–1961, vol. VI
Crookshank, Col Chichester de Windt, *died* 1958, vol. V
Crookshank, Francis Graham, 1873–1933, vol. III
Crookshank, Harry Maule, 1849–1914, vol. I
Crookshank, Henry, 1893–1972, vol. VII
Crookshank, Maj.-Gen. Sir Sydney D'Aguilar, 1870–1941, vol. IV
Croom, Sir Halliday; *see* Croom, Sir J. H.
Croom, Sir (J.) Halliday, 1847–1923, vol. II
Croom-Johnson, Hon. Sir Reginald Powell, *died* 1957, vol. V
Croome, Honor Renée Minturn, 1908–1960, vol. V
Croome, William Iveson, 1891–1967, vol. VI
Cropper, Anthony Charles, 1912–1967, vol. VI
Cropper, Charles James, 1852–1924, vol. II
Cropper, Rev. James, *died* 1938, vol. III
Cropper, James Winstanley, 1879–1956, vol. V
Crosbie, Lt-Gen. Adolphus Brett, *died* 1916, vol. II
Crosbie, George, 1864–1934, vol. III
Crosbie, Henry, 1852–1928, vol. II
Crosbie, Brig.-Gen. James Dayrolles, 1865–1947, vol. IV
Crosbie, Hon. Sir John Chalker, 1876–1932, vol. III
Crosbie, Robert Edward Harold, 1886–1950, vol. IV
Crosbie, Sir William Edward Douglas, 8th Bt, 1855–1936, vol. III
Crosby, Bing; *see* Crosby, H. L.
Crosby, Very Rev. Ernest Henry L.; *see* Lewis-Crosby.
Crosby, Fanny, 1820–1915, vol. I
Crosby, Harry Lillis, (Bing Crosby), 1904–1977, vol. VII
Crosby, Sir Josiah, 1880–1958, vol. V
Crosby, Sir Thomas Boor, 1830–1916, vol. II
Crosby, William, 1832–1910, vol. I
Crosfield, Sir Arthur Henry, 1st Bt, 1865–1938, vol. III
Crosfield, Bertram Fothergill, 1882–1951, vol. V
Crosfield, Domini, (Lady Crosfield), *died* 1963, vol. VI
Crosfield, Lt-Col George Rowlandson, 1877–1962, vol. VI
Crosland, Rt Hon. Anthony; *see* Crosland, Rt Hon. C. A. R.
Crosland, Rt Hon. (Charles) Anthony (Raven), 1918–1977, vol. VII
Crosland, Brig. Harold Powell, 1893–1973, vol. VII
Crosland, Sir Joseph, 1826–1904, vol. I

Crosland, Joseph Beardsell, 1874–1935, vol. III
Crosland, T. W. H., 1868–1924, vol. II
Crosland, Brig. Walter Hugh, 1894–1960, vol. V
Cross, 1st Viscount, 1823–1914, vol. I
Cross, 2nd Viscount, 1882–1932, vol. III
Cross, Ada, (Mrs George Frederick Cross); see
  Cambridge, A.
Cross, Sir Alexander, 1st Bt (cr 1912), 1847–1914,
  vol. I
Cross, Sir Alexander, 3rd Bt (cr 1912), 1880–1963,
  vol. VI
Cross, Alexander George, 1858–1919, vol. II
Cross, Sir (Alfred) Rupert (Neale), 1912–1980,
  vol. VII
Cross, Alfred William Stephens, 1860–1932, vol. III
Cross, Arthur Lyon, 1873–1940, vol. III (A), vol. IV
Cross, Rev. Hon. Charles Francis, 1860–1937,
  vol. III
Cross, Charles Frederick, 1855–1935, vol. III
Cross, Adm. Charles Henry, died 1915, vol. I
Cross, Charles Wilson, died 1928, vol. II
Cross, Francis John Kynaston, 1865–1950, vol. IV
Cross, Francis Richardson, died 1931, vol. III
Cross, Rev. Frank Leslie, 1900–1968, vol. V
Cross, Herbert S.; see Shepherd-Cross.
Cross, Col James Albert, 1876–1952, vol. V
Cross, Hon. John Edward, 1858–1921, vol. II
Cross, Kenneth Mervyn Baskerville, 1890–1968,
  vol. VI
Cross, Rev. Leslie Basil, 1895–1974, vol. VII
Cross, Mark; see Pechey, Archibald T.
Cross, Richard Basil, 1881–1952, vol. V
Cross, Rev. Robert Nicol, 1883–1970, vol. VI
Cross, Rt Hon. Sir Ronald Hibbert, 1st Bt (cr
  1941), 1896–1968, vol. VI
Cross, Sir Rupert; see Cross, Sir A. R. N.
Cross, Rev. Thomas George, died 1932, vol. III
Cross, Sir William Coats, 2nd Bt (cr 1912), 1877–
  1947, vol. IV
Cross Brown, Lt-Col James, 1884–1969, vol. VI
Crosse, Ven. Arthur B., 1830–1909, vol. I
Crosse, Rev. Arthur John William, 1857–1948,
  vol. IV
Crosse, Lt-Col Charles Robert, 1851–1921, vol. II
Crosse, Ven. Edmond Francis, 1858–1941, vol. IV
Crosse, Rev. Canon Ernest Courtenay, 1887–1955,
  vol. V
Crosse, Rev. Frank Parker, 1897–1979, vol. VII
Crosse, Herbert D. H., 1863–1908, vol. I
Crossfield, Robert Sands, 1904–1978, vol. VII
Crossing, William, 1847–1928, vol. II
Crossley, Madame Ada, died 1929, vol. III
Crossley, Anthony Crommelin, 1903–1939, vol. III
Crossley, Arthur William, 1869–1927, vol. II
Crossley, Edward; see Crossley, J. E.
Crossley, Lt-Col Henry Joseph, 1874–1936, vol. III
Crossley, (Joseph) Edward, 1908–1969, vol. VI
Crossley, Sir Julian Stanley, 1899–1971, vol. VII
Crossley, Sir Kenneth Irwin, 2nd Bt, 1877–1957,
  vol. V
Crossley, Rt Rev. Owen Thomas Lloyd, 1860–
  1926, vol. II
Crossley, Thomas Hastings Henry, 1846–1926,
  vol. II

Crossley, Sir William John, 1st Bt, 1844–1911,
  vol. I
Crossley-Holland, Frank William, 1878–1956,
  vol. V
Crossman, Hon. Sir (Charles) Stafford, 1870–1941,
  vol. IV
Crossman, Maj.-Gen. Francis Lindisfarne Morley,
  1888–1947, vol. IV
Crossman, Col George Lytton, 1877–1947, vol. IV
Crossman, Percy, 1872–1929, vol. III
Crossman, Rt Hon. Richard Howard Stafford,
  1907–1974, vol. VII
Crossman, Hon. Sir Stafford; see Crossman, Hon.
  Sir C. S.
Crossman, Sir William, 1830–1901, vol. I
Crossman, Sir William Smith, 1854–1929, vol. III
Crosswell, Noel Alfred, 1909–1964, vol. VI
Crosthwait, Col Herbert Leland, 1867–1940,
  vol. III
Crosthwaite, Arthur Tinley, 1880–1951, vol. V
Crosthwaite, Sir Bertram Maitland, 1880–1974,
  vol. VII
Crosthwaite, Cecil, 1909–1978, vol. VII
Crosthwaite, Lt-Col Charles Gilbert, 1878–1940,
  vol. III
Crosthwaite, Sir Charles Haukes Todd, 1835–1915,
  vol. I
Crosthwaite, Lt-Col Henry Robert, 1876–1956,
  vol. V
Crosthwaite, Sir Hugh Stuart, 1879–1952, vol. V
Crosthwaite, Robert, 1868–1953, vol. V
Crosthwaite, Rt Rev. Robert Jarratt, 1837–1925,
  vol. II
Crosthwaite, Sir Robert Joseph, 1841–1917, vol. II
Crosthwaite, W. M., died 1956, vol. V
Crosthwaite, Sir William Henry, 1880–1968, vol. VI
Crosthwaite-Eyre, Sir Oliver Eyre, 1913–1978,
  vol. VII
Crotch, William Walter, 1874–1947, vol. IV
Crothers, Thomas Wilson, 1850–1921, vol. II
Crotty, Rt Rev. Horace, 1886–1952, vol. V
Crouch, Lt-Col Ernest George, 1875–1935, vol. III
Crouch, Henry Arthur, 1870–1955, vol. V
Crouch, Col Hon. Richard Armstrong, 1869–1949,
  vol. IV, vol. V
Crouch, Robert Fisher, 1904–1957, vol. V
Croudace, Rev. William Darnell, 1848–1942, vol. IV
Crousaz, Engr Rear-Adm. Augustus George, 1884–
  1977, vol. VII
Crouse, Russel, 1893–1966, vol. VI
Crow, Sir Alwyn Douglas, 1894–1965, vol. VI
Crow, Douglas Arthur, 1889–1945, vol. IV
Crow, Francis Edward, 1863–1939, vol. III
Crowden, Rev. Charles, 1836–1936, vol. III
Crowden, Guy Pascoe, 1894–1966, vol. VI
Crowder, Sir John Ellenborough, 1890–1961,
  vol. VI
Crowdy, Edith Frances, died 1947, vol. IV
Crowdy, James Fuidge, 1876–1934, vol. III
Crowdy, Mary, died 1961, vol. VI
Crowdy, Dame Rachel Eleanor, (Dame Rachel
  Thornhill), died 1964, vol. VI
Crowe, Sir Edward Thomas Frederick, 1877–1960,
  vol. V

Crowe, Eric Eyre, 1905–1952, vol. V
Crowe, Eyre, 1824–1910, vol. I
Crowe, Sir Eyre, 1864–1925, vol. II
Crowe, F. J. W., 1864–1931, vol. III
Crowe, Captain Fritz H. E., *died* 1904, vol. I
Crowe, Brig.-Gen. John Henry Verinder, 1862–1948, vol. IV
Crowe, Col Mordaunt Abingdon Carlisle, 1867–1939, vol. III
Crowe, Percy Robert, 1904–1979, vol. VII
Crowe, Philip Kingsland, 1908–1976, vol. VII
Crowe, Maj.-Gen. Thomas Carlisle, 1830–1917, vol. II
Crowe, William Henry, 1844–1925, vol. II
Crowest, Frederick J., 1860–1927, vol. II
Crowfoot, Rev. John Henchman, 1841–1926, vol. II
Crowfoot, John Winter, 1873–1959, vol. V
Crowley, James, *died* 1946, vol. IV
Crowley, John, *died* 1934, vol. III
Crowley, Ralph Henry, 1869–1953, vol. V
Crowley, Rt Rev. Timothy, 1880–1946, vol. IV
Crowley, Dep. Insp.-Gen. Timothy Joseph, *died* 1912, vol. I
Crowly, Joseph Patrick, 1859–1917, vol. II
Crown, Jennifer Brigit, (Mrs Leon Crown); *see* Vyvyan, J. B.
Crowther, Baron (Life Peer); Geoffrey Crowther, 1907–1972, vol. VII
Crowther, Charles, 1876–1964, vol. VI
Crowther, Edward, 1897–1979, vol. VII
Crowther, Henry, 1848–1937, vol. III
Crowther, James Arnold, 1883–1950, vol. IV
Crowther-Smith, Vivian Francis, 1875–1961, vol. VI
Croxton, Arthur, *died* 1956, vol. V
Croysdale, Sir James, 1886–1971, vol. VII
Croysdill, Clifford William, 1874–1935, vol. III
Crozier, Maj.-Gen. Baptist Barton, 1878–1957, vol. V
Crozier, Douglas James Smyth, 1908–1976, vol. VII
Crozier, Rev. Edward Travers, *died* 1940, vol. III
Crozier, Brig.-Gen. Frank Percy, 1879–1937, vol. III
Crozier, George, *died* 1914, vol. I
Crozier, Most Rev. John Baptist, 1853–1920, vol. II
Crozier, John Beattie, 1849–1921, vol. II
Crozier, Rt Rev. John Winthrop, 1879–1966, vol. VI
Crozier, Major Sir Thomas Henry, *died* 1948, vol. IV
Crozier, William Percival, 1879–1944, vol. IV
Cru, Robert L., 1884–1944, vol. IV
Cruddas, Bt Col Bernard, 1882–1959, vol. V
Cruddas, Col Hamilton Maxwell, 1874–1955, vol. V
Cruddas, Lt-Col Hugh Wilson, 1868–1916, vol. II
Cruddas, Maj.-Gen. Ralph Cyril, 1900–1979, vol. VII
Cruddas, William Donaldson, 1831–1912, vol. I
Cruickshank, Alexander Walmsley, 1851–1925, vol. II
Cruickshank, Rev. Alfred Hamilton, 1862–1927, vol. II

Cruickshank, Ernest William Henderson, 1888–1964, vol. VI
Cruickshank, Dame Joanna Margaret, *died* 1958, vol. V
Cruickshank, John, 1884–1966, vol. VI
Cruickshank, John Cecil, 1899–1956, vol. V
Cruickshank, Col Martin Melvin, 1888–1964, vol. VI
Cruickshank, Robert, 1899–1974, vol. VII
Cruickshank, Sir William Dickson, 1845–1929, vol. III
Cruickshank, Robert James, 1898–1956, vol. V
Cruise, Sir Francis Richard, 1834–1912, vol. I
Cruise, Sir Richard Robert, *died* 1946, vol. IV
Crum, Rev. John Macleod Campbell, 1872–1958, vol. V
Crum, Maj.-Gen. Vernon Forbes E.; *see* Erskine Crum.
Crum, Sir Walter Erskine, 1874–1923, vol. II
Crum, Walter Ewing, 1865–1944, vol. IV
Crumly, Patrick, vol. II
Crump, Basil Woodward, 1866–1945, vol. IV
Crump, Charles George, 1862–1935, vol. III
Crump, Edwin Samuel, 1882–1961, vol. VI
Crump, Frederick Octavius, 1840–1900, vol. I
Crump, Sir Henry Ashbrooke, 1863–1941, vol. IV
Crump, Rev. John Herbert, 1849–1924, vol. II
Crump, Leslie Maurice, 1875–1929, vol. III
Crump, Sir Louis Charles, 1869–1960, vol. V
Crump, Norman Easedale, 1896–1964, vol. VI
Crump, Sir William John, 1850–1923, vol. II
Crundall, Sir William Henry, 1847–1934, vol. III
Cruse, Rt Rev. John Howard, 1908–1979, vol. VII
Crutchley, Arthur Felton, 1883–1966, vol. VI
Crutchley, Maj.-Gen. Sir Charles, 1856–1920, vol. II
Crutchley, Ernest Tristram, 1878–1940, vol. III
Crutchley, Percy Edward, 1855–1940, vol. III
Crutchley, William Caius, 1848–1923, vol. II
Crute, Robert, 1907–1967, vol. VI (AII)
Cruttwell, Charles Robert Mowbray Fraser, 1887–1941, vol. IV
Cruttwell, Rev. Charles Thomas, 1847–1911, vol. I
Crymble, Percival Templeton, 1880–1970, vol. VI
Cubbon, William, 1865–1955, vol. V
Cubitt, Sir Bertram Blakiston, 1862–1942, vol. IV
Cubitt, Hon. (Charles) Guy, 1903–1979, vol. VII
Cubitt, Edward George, 1860–1933, vol. III
Cubitt, Hon. Guy; *see* Cubitt, Hon. C. G.
Cubitt, Thomas, 1870–1947, vol. IV
Cubitt, Gen. Sir Thomas Astley, 1871–1939, vol. III
Cubitt, Col William George, 1835–1903, vol. I
Cuckney, Air Vice-Marshal Ernest John, 1896–1965, vol. VI
Cudlip, Mrs Pender; *see* Thomas, Annie.
Cudlipp, Percy, 1905–1962, vol. VI
Cudmore, Sir Arthur Murray, 1870–1951, vol. V
Cudmore, Hon. Sir Collier Robert, 1885–1971, vol. VII
Cuff, Maj.-Gen. Brian, 1889–1970, vol. VI
Cuffe, Sir Charles Frederick Denny Wheeler-, 2nd Bt, 1832–1915, vol. I

Cuffe, Surg.-Gen. Sir Charles M'Donough, 1842–1915, vol. I (A)

Cuffe, Sir George Eustace, 1892–1962, vol. VI

Cuffe, Col James Aloysius Francis, 1876–1957, vol. V

Cuffe, Sir Otway Fortescue Luke Wheeler-, 3rd Bt, 1866–1934, vol. III

Cuffe, Hon. Otway Frederick Seymour, 1853–1912, vol. I

Cuke, Sir Hampden Archibald, 1892–1968, vol. VI

Culbertson, Ely, 1891–1955, vol. V

Cull, Vice-Adm. Sir Malcolm Giffard Stebbing, 1891–1962, vol. VI

Cullen, Hon. Lord; William James Cullen, 1859–1941, vol. IV

Cullen of Ashbourne, 1st Baron, 1864–1932, vol. III

Cullen, Mrs Alice, (Mrs William Reynolds), died 1969, vol. VI

Cullen, Rt Rev. Archibald Howard, 1887–1968, vol. VI

Cullen, Brian; see Cullen, J. B.

Cullen, Brig.-Gen. Ernest Henry Scott, 1869–1951, vol. V

Cullen, (James) Brian, 1905–1972, vol. VII

Cullen, Rev. John, 1836–1914, vol. I

Cullen, Kenneth Douglas, 1889–1956, vol. V

Cullen, Rt Rev. Matthew, 1864–1936, vol. III

Cullen, Comdr Percy, 1861–1918, vol. II

Cullen, William, 1867–1948, vol. IV

Cullen, William James; see Cullen, Hon. Lord.

Cullen, Hon. Sir William Portus, 1855–1935, vol. III

Culley, Rev. Arnold Duncan, 1867–1947, vol. IV

Culley, Gp Captain Stuart Douglas, 1895–1975, vol. VII

Cullinan, Edward Revill, 1901–1965, vol. VI

Cullinan, Sir Frederick Fitzjames, 1845–1913, vol. I

Cullinan, Sir Thomas Major, 1862–1936, vol. III

Cullinan, Paymaster-Rear-Adm. William Frederick, 1876–1937, vol. III

Culling, James William Henry, 1870–1949, vol. IV

Culling, Maj.-Gen. John Chislett, 1858–1938, vol. III

Cullingworth, Charles James, 1841–1908, vol. I

Cullis, Charles Edgar, 1899–1964, vol. VI

Cullis, Charles Gilbert, 1871–1941, vol. IV

Cullis, Winifred Clara, 1875–1956, vol. V

Cullum, George Gery Milner-Gibson, 1857–1921, vol. II

Cullum, Ridgwell, 1867–1943, vol. IV

Culme-Seymour, Sir Michael; see Seymour.

Culme-Seymour, Vice-Adm. Sir Michael; see Seymour.

Culpin, Ewart Gladstone, 1877–1946, vol. IV

Culpin, Millais, 1874–1952, vol. V

Culshaw, John Royds, 1924–1980, vol. VII

Culverwell, Cyril Tom, 1895–1963, vol. VI

Culverwell, Edward Parnall, 1855–1931, vol. III

Cumber, William John, 1878–1974, vol. VII

Cumberbatch, Elkin Percy, 1880–1939, vol. III

Cumberbatch, Henry Alfred, 1858–1918, vol. II

Cumberbatch, Sir Hugh Douglas, 1897–1951, vol. V

Cumberbatch, Isaac William, 1888–1971, vol. VII

Cumberland, Maj.-Gen. Charles Edward, 1830–1920, vol. II

Cumberland, Major Charles Sperling, 1847–1922, vol. II

Cumberland, Gerald, 1879–1926, vol. II

Cumberlege, Geoffrey Fenwick Jocelyn, 1891–1979, vol. VII

Cumbrae-Stewart, Francis William Sutton, 1865–1938, vol. III

Cumine, Alexander, died 1909, vol. I

Cuming, Sir Arthur Herbert, died 1941, vol. IV

Cuming, Edward William Dirom, 1862–1941, vol. IV

Cuming, Col Helier Brohier, 1867–1950, vol. IV (A)

Cuming, Adm. Robert Stevenson Dalton, 1852–1940, vol. III

Cumings, John Nathaniel, 1905–1974, vol. VII

Cumming, Alexander Neilson, died 1913, vol. I

Cumming, Major Sir Alexander Penrose G.; see Gordon-Cumming.

Cumming, Brig. Arthur Edward, 1896–1971, vol. VII

Cumming, Col Charles Chevin, 1875–1947, vol. IV

Cumming, Miss Constance Frederica G.; see Gordon-Cumming.

Cumming, Sir Duncan Cameron, 1903–1979, vol. VII

Cumming, Rev. James, died 1946, vol. IV

Cumming, Sir John Ghest, 1868–1958, vol. V

Cumming, Sir Kenneth William, 7th Bt, 1837–1915, vol. I

Cumming, Captain Sir Mansfield, 1859–1923, vol. II

Cumming, Col William Gordon, 1842–1908, vol. I

Cumming, Sir William Gordon G.; see Gordon-Cumming.

Cummings, Arthur John, died 1957, vol. V

Cummings, David Charles, 1861–1942, vol. IV

Cummings, Edward Estlin, 1894–1962, vol. VI

Cummings, William Hayman, 1831–1915, vol. I

Cummins, Ashley; see Cummins, W. E. A.

Cummins, Geraldine Dorothy, 1890–1969, vol. VI

Cummins, Maj.-Gen. Harry Ashley Vane, 1870–1953, vol. V

Cummins, Major Henry Alfred, 1864–1938, vol. III

Cummins, Henry Ashley Travers, 1847–1926, vol. II

Cummins, Herbert Ashley Cunard, 1871–1943, vol. IV

Cummins, Maj.-Gen. James Turner, 1843–1912, vol. I

Cummins, Rt Rev. John Ildefonsus, 1850–1938, vol. III

Cummins, Col Stevenson Lyle, 1873–1949, vol. IV

Cummins, Walter Herbert, 1881–1953, vol. V

Cummins, (William Edward) Ashley, died 1923, vol. II

Cumont, Franz Valery Marie, 1868–1947, vol. IV

Cumpston, John Howard Lidgett, 1880–1954, vol. V

Cunard, Sir Bache, 3rd Bt, 1851–1925, vol. II

Cunard, Sir Edward, 5th Bt, 1891–1962, vol. VI

Cunard, Ernest Haliburton, 1862–1926, vol. II

Cunard, Sir Gordon, 4th Bt, 1857–1933, vol. III
Cunard, Sir Henry Palmes, 6th Bt, 1909–1973, vol. VII
Cundall, Charles, 1890–1971, vol. VII
Cundall, Frank, 1858–1937, vol. III
Cundall, Herbert Minton, 1848–1940, vol. III
Cundall, Joseph Leslie, 1906–1964, vol. VI
Cundell, Edric, 1893–1961, vol. VI
Cundiff, Sir William, 1861–1935, vol. III
Cuneo, Cyrus Cincinatto, died 1916, vol. II
Cuningham, Maj.-Gen. Charles Alexander, 1842–1925, vol. II
Cuningham, Granville Carlyle, 1847–1927, vol. II
Cuningham, Surg.-Gen. James Macnabb, 1829–1905, vol. I
Cuningham, Sir William John, 1848–1929, vol. III
Cuninghame, Sir Alfred Edward F., 12th Bt (cr 1630); see Fairlie-Cuninghame.
Cuninghame, Sir Charles Arthur F., 11th Bt (cr 1630); see Fairlie-Cuninghame.
Cuninghame, Lt-Col Edward William Montgomery, 1878–1935, vol. III
Cuninghame, Sir Hussey Burgh Fairlie-, 14th Bt (cr 1630), 1890–1939, vol. III
Cuninghame, J. C., 1851–1917, vol. II
Cuninghame, Col John Anstruther Smith, 1852–1921, vol. II
Cuninghame, Sir Thomas Andrew Alexander Montgomery-, 10th Bt (cr 1722), 1877–1945, vol. IV
Cuninghame, Sir (W.) Andrew Malcolm Martin Oliphant Montgomery-, 11th Bt (cr 1672), 1929–1959, vol. V
Cuninghame, Sir William Edward Fairlie-, 13th Bt (cr 1630), 1856–1929, vol. III
Cuninghame, Sir William James Montgomery-, 9th Bt (cr 1672), 1834–1897, vol. I
Cuninghame, Lt-Col William Wallace Smith, 1889–1959, vol. V
Cunliffe, 1st Baron, 1855–1919, vol. II
Cunliffe, 2nd Baron, 1899–1963, vol. VI
Cunliffe, Sir Cyril Henley, 8th Bt, 1901–1969, vol. VI
Cunliffe, Sir Ellis; see Cunliffe, Sir R. E.
Cunliffe, Sir Foster Hugh Egerton, 6th Bt, 1875–1916, vol. II
Cunliffe, Brig.-Gen. Frederick Hugh Gordon, 1861–1955, vol. V
Cunliffe, Hon. Geoffrey, 1903–1978, vol. VII
Cunliffe, Sir Herbert; see Cunliffe, Sir J. H.
Cunliffe, Sir John Robert Ellis, 1886–1967, vol. VI
Cunliffe, John William, 1865–1946, vol. IV
Cunliffe, Sir (Joseph) Herbert, 1867–1963, vol. VI
Cunliffe, Sir Robert Alfred, 5th Bt, 1839–1905, vol. I
Cunliffe, Sir (Robert) Ellis, 1858–1927, vol. II
Cunliffe, Sir Robert Neville Henry, 7th Bt, 1884–1949, vol. IV
Cunliffe, Thomas, 1895–1966, vol. VI
Cunliffe-Owen, Brig.-Gen. Charles, 1863–1932, vol. III
Cunliffe-Owen, Lt-Col F., died 1946, vol. IV
Cunliffe-Owen, Sir Hugo, 1st Bt, 1870–1947, vol. IV

Cunning, Joseph, 1872–1948, vol. IV
Cunningham of Hyndhope, 1st Viscount, 1883–1963, vol. VI
Cunningham, Sir (Alexander) Frederick (Douglas), 1852–1935, vol. III
Cunningham, Alfred, 1870–1918, vol. II
Cunningham, Alfred G., 1870–1951, vol. V
Cunningham, Lt-Col Aylmer Basil, 1879–1940, vol. III (A), vol. IV
Cunningham, Rev. Bertram Keir, 1871–1944, vol. IV
Cunningham, Brysson, 1868–1950, vol. IV
Cunningham, Sir Charles Banks, 1884–1967, vol. VI
Cunningham, Daniel John, 1850–1909, vol. I
Cunningham, Col David Douglas, 1843–1914, vol. I
Cunningham, E. Margaret, 1872–1940, vol. III
Cunningham, Ebenezer, 1881–1977, vol. VII
Cunningham, Edward Charles, 1872–1929, vol. III
Cunningham, Sir Edward Sheldon, 1859–1957, vol. V
Cunningham, Sir Frederick; see Cunningham, Sir A. F. D.
Cunningham, Sir George, 1888–1964, vol. VI
Cunningham, George Charles, 1883–1950, vol. IV
Cunningham, Brig.-Gen. George Glencairn, 1862–1943, vol. IV
Cunningham, Sir George M.; see Miller-Cunningham.
Cunningham, Gordon Herriot, 1892–1962, vol. VI
Cunningham, Sir Graham, 1892–1978, vol. VII
Cunningham, Sir Henry Stewart, 1832–1920, vol. II
Cunningham, Rt Rev. Jack, 1926–1978, vol. VII
Cunningham, Rt Rev. James, 1910–1974, vol. VII
Cunningham, Lt-Col John, died 1968, vol. VI
Cunningham, Engr-Rear-Adm. John Edward Greig, 1878–1954, vol. V
Cunningham, Rt Rev. John F., 1842–1919, vol. II (A), vol. III
Cunningham, John Francis, died 1932, vol. III
Cunningham, Adm. of the Fleet Sir John Henry Dacres, 1885–1962, vol. VI
Cunningham, John Jeffrey, 1907–1959, vol. V
Cunningham, Rev. Canon John Manstead, 1879–1947, vol. IV
Cunningham, John Richard, 1876–1942, vol. IV
Cunningham, Lt-Col John Sydney, 1876–1943, vol. IV
Cunningham, Joseph Thomas, 1859–1935, vol. III
Cunningham, Sir Knox; see Cunningham, Sir S. K.
Cunningham, Lallie S. C., died 1937, vol. III
Cunningham, Marta, died 1937, vol. III
Cunningham, Mary Elizabeth, died 1939, vol. III
Cunningham, Patrick, died 1960, vol. V
Cunningham, Rt Hon. Samuel, 1862–1946, vol. IV
Cunningham, Sir (Samuel) Knox, 1st Bt, 1909–1976, vol. VII
Cunningham, Wilfred Bertram, 1882–1960, vol. V
Cunningham, Ven. William, 1849–1919, vol. II
Cunningham, William Allison, died 1939, vol. III
Cunningham, Maj.-Gen. Sir William Henry, 1883–1959, vol. V
Cunningham, William Ross, 1890–1953, vol. V
Cunningham Craig, Edward Hubert; see Craig.

163

Cunningham-Reid, Captain Alec Stratford, *died* 1977, vol. VII

Cunninghame, Sir James Fraser, 1870–1952, vol. V

Cunninghame Graham, Comdr Charles Elphinstone Fleeming, 1854–1917, vol. II

Cunninghame Graham, Robert Bontine, 1852–1936, vol. III

Cunnington, Cecil Willett, 1878–1961, vol. VI

Cunnington, Maud Edith, 1869–1951, vol. V

Cunnison, Sir Alexander, 1879–1959, vol. V

Cunnison, David Keith, 1881–1972, vol. VII

Cunygham, Major Sir Colin Keith Dick-, 11th Bt, 1908–1941, vol. IV

Cunyngham, Maj.-Gen. James Keith D.; *see* Dick-Cunyngham.

Cunyngham of Lamburghtoun, Sir Robert Keith Alexander Dick-, 9th Bt, 1836–1897, vol. I

Cunyngham, Lt-Col William Henry Dick-, *died* 1900, vol. I

Cunyngham, Sir William Stewart-Dick-, 10th Bt, 1871–1922, vol. II

Cunynghame, Sir David; *see* Cunynghame, Sir H. D. St L. B. S.

Cunynghame, Sir Francis George Thurlow, 9th Bt, 1835–1900, vol. I

Cunynghame, Sir (Henry) David St Leger Brooke Selwyn, 11th Bt, 1905–1978, vol. VII

Cunynghame, Sir Henry Hardinge, 1848–1935, vol. III

Cunynghame, Sir Percy, 10th Bt, 1867–1941, vol. IV

Curci, Amelita G.; *see* Galli-Curci.

Cure, Sir Edward Capel, 1866–1923, vol. II

Cure, Col Herbert Capel, 1859–1909, vol. I

Curgenven, Sir Arthur Joseph, 1876–1965, vol. VI

Curie, Jean F. J.; *see* Joliot-Curie.

Curie, Madame Marie, 1867–1934, vol. III

Curie, Pierre, 1859–1906, vol. I

Curle, Alexander Ormiston, 1866–1955, vol. V

Curle, James, 1862–1944, vol. IV

Curle, Richard Henry Parnell, 1883–1968, vol. VI

Curlewis, Ethel; *see* Turner, E.

Curlewis, Rt Hon. John Stephen, 1863–1940, vol. III

Curling, Brig.-Gen. Bryan James, 1877–1955, vol. V

Curling, Rev. Joseph James, 1844–1906, vol. I

Curling, Rev. Canon Thomas Higham, 1872–1944, vol. IV

Curnick, Captain Alfred James, 1865–1936, vol. III

Curnock, Rev. Nehemiah, 1840–1915, vol. I (A)

Curnow, John, 1846–1902, vol. I

Curphey, Col Sir Aldington George, 1880–1958, vol. V

Curran, Charles, 1903–1972, vol. VII

Curran, Sir Charles John, 1921–1980, vol. VII

Curran, John Adye, 1837–1919, vol. II

Curran, Pete, 1860–1910, vol. I

Curran, Thomas, *died* 1913, vol. I

Curran, Thomas Bartholomew, 1870–1929, vol. III

Curre, Augusta, (Lady Curre), *died* 1956, vol. V

Curre, John Mathew, 1859–1919, vol. II

Curre, Sir William Edward Carne, 1855–1930, vol. III

Currer Briggs, D. H.; *see* Briggs.

Currey, Adm. Bernard, *died* 1936, vol. III

Currey, Rear-Adm. Harry Philip, 1902–1979, vol. VII

Currey, Henry Latham, 1863–1945, vol. IV

Currey, Brig. Henry Percivall, 1886–1969, vol. VI

Currey, Rear-Adm. Hugh Schomberg, 1876–1955, vol. V

Currie, 1st Baron, 1834–1906, vol. I

Currie, Agnes Jean, 1899–1968, vol. VI

Currie, Major Hon. Sir Alan; *see* Currie, Major Hon. Sir H. A.

Currie, Brig.-Gen. Arthur Cecil, *died* 1942, vol. IV

Currie, Gen. Sir Arthur William, 1875–1933, vol. III

Currie, Captain Bertram Francis George, 1899–1959, vol. V

Currie, David, 1870–1933, vol. III

Currie, Sir Donald, 1825–1909, vol. I

Currie, Brig. Douglas Hendrie, 1892–1966, vol. VI

Currie, Sir Edmund Hay, 1834–1913, vol. I

Currie, Very Rev. Edward Reid, 1844–1921, vol. II

Currie, Maj.-Gen. Fendall, 1841–1920, vol. II

Currie, Rev. Sir Frederick Larkins, 2nd Bt, 1823–1900, vol. I

Currie, Sir Frederick Reeve, 3rd Bt, 1851–1930, vol. III

Currie, George Boyle Hanna, 1905–1978, vol. VII

Currie, Lt-Col George Selkirk, 1889–1975, vol. VII

Currie, George Welsh, 1870–1950, vol. IV

Currie, Harry Augustus Frederick, 1866–1912, vol. I

Currie, Major Hon. Sir (Henry) Alan, 1868–1942, vol. IV

Currie, Rev. Hugh Penton, 1854–1903, vol. I

Currie, Lt-Col Ivor Bertram Fendall, 1872–1924, vol. II

Currie, Sir James, 1868–1937, vol. III

Currie, Sir James Thomson, 1868–1943, vol. IV

Currie, John Ronald, *died* 1949, vol. IV

Currie, Laurence, 1867–1934, vol. III

Currie, Mark Mainwaring Lee, 1882–1951, vol. V

Currie, Mary Montgomerie, (Lady Currie), 1843–1905, vol. I

Currie, Patrick, 1883–1949, vol. IV

Currie, Col Ryves Alexander Mark, 1875–1920, vol. II

Currie, Col Thomas, 1851–1931, vol. III

Currie, Sir Walter Louis Rackham, 4th Bt, 1856–1941, vol. IV

Currie, Sir Walter Mordaunt Cyril, 5th Bt, 1894–1978, vol. VII

Currie, Sir William Crawford, 1884–1961, vol. VI

Currie, Major William Leopold, 1856–1929, vol. III

Currie-Blyth, James Pattison, 1824–1908, vol. I

Currin, Richard William, 1872–1942, vol. IV

Curry, Aaron Charlton, 1887–1957, vol. V

Curry, Comdr Hugh Fortescue, 1890–1932, vol. III

Curry, Brig.-Gen. Montagu Crichton, *died* 1931, vol. III

Cursetjee, Maj.-Gen. Sir Heerajee Jehangir Manockjee, 1885–1964, vol. VI

Cursiter, Stanley, 1887–1976, vol. VII

Cursley, Norman Sharpe, 1898–1972, vol. VII

Cussen, Hon. Sir Leo Finn Bernard, 1859–1933, vol. III

Cust, Aleen Isabel, *died* 1937, vol. III

Cust, Col Sir Archer; *see* Cust, Col Sir L. G. A.

Cust, Very Rev. Arthur Perceval Purey-, 1828–1916, vol. II

Cust, Sir Charles Leopold, 3rd Bt, 1864–1931, vol. III

Cust, Mrs Henry, (Emmeline Mary Elizabeth), (Nina), *died* 1955, vol. V

Cust, Henry John Cockayne, 1861–1917, vol. II

Cust, Adm. Sir Herbert Edward Purey-, 1857–1938, vol. III

Cust, Col Sir (Lionel George) Archer, 1896–1962, vol. VI

Cust, Sir Lionel Henry, 1859–1929, vol. III

Cust, Nina; *see* Cust, Mrs Henry.

Cust, Sir Reginald John, 1828–1912, vol. I

Cust, Brig. Richard Brownlow P.; *see* Purey-Cust.

Cust, Robert Henry Hobart, 1861–1940, vol. III

Cust, Robert Needham, 1821–1909, vol. I

Cust, Rev. Canon William Arthur Purey-, 1855–1938, vol. III

Custance, Col Frederic Hambleton, 1844–1925, vol. II

Custance, Adm. Sir Reginald Neville, 1847–1935, vol. III

Custance, Rear-Adm. Wilfred Neville, 1884–1939, vol. III

Custard, Reginald G.; *see* Goss-Custard.

Custard, Walter Henry Goss, 1871–1964, vol. VI

Cutbill, Col Reginald Heaton Locke, 1878–1956, vol. V

Cutforth, Sir Arthur Edwin, 1881–1958, vol. V

Cutforth, Maj.-Gen. Sir Lancelot Eric, 1899–1980, vol. VII

Cuthbert, Very Rev. Father, 1866–1939, vol. III

Cuthbert, David, 1866–1953, vol. V

Cuthbert, Maj.-Gen. Gerald James, 1861–1931, vol. III

Cuthbert, Harold David, 1909–1959, vol. V

Cuthbert, Hon. Sir Henry, 1829–1907, vol. I

Cuthbert, Captain James Harold, 1876–1915, vol. I (A)

Cuthbert, Lt-Col Thomas Wilkinson, *died* 1936, vol. III

Cuthbert, William Nicolson, *died* 1960, vol. V

Cuthbertson, Clive, 1863–1943, vol. IV

Cuthbertson, David, 1856–1935, vol. III

Cuthbertson, Brig.-Gen. Edward Boustead, 1880–1942, vol. IV

Cuthbertson, Henry, 1859–1903, vol. I

Cuthbertson, Sir John Neilson, 1829–1905, vol. I

Cutlack, Col William Philip, 1881–1965, vol. VI

Cutler, Edward, 1831–1916, vol. II

Cutler, Elliott Carr, 1888–1947, vol. IV

Cutler, John, 1839–1924, vol. II

Cuttle, William Linsdell, 1896–1958, vol. V

Cuyler, Sir Charles, 4th Bt, 1867–1919, vol. II

Cuyler, Sir George Hallifax, 5th Bt, 1876–1947, vol. IV

Cuyler, Rev. Theodore Ledyard, *died* 1909, vol. I

Cynan; *see* Evans-Jones, Rev. Sir Albert.

Czaplicka, Marie Antoinette, *died* 1921, vol. II

D

Dabbs, George Henry Roque, 1846–1913, vol. I

D'Abernon, 1st Viscount, 1857–1941, vol. IV

Dabholkar, Sir Vasantrao Anandrao, 1881–1933, vol. III

Dabney, Hon. Charles William, 1855–1945, vol. IV

d'Abo, Gerard Louis, 1884–1962, vol. VI

d'Abreu, Alphonso Liguori, 1906–1976, vol. VII

Dacca, Nawab Bahadur, Sir Khwaya Salimulla, *died* 1915, vol. I

D'Ache, Caran, (Emmanuel Poire), *died* 1909, vol. I

D'Costa, Sir Alfred Horace, 1873–1967, vol. VI

Da Costa, Brig.-Gen. Evan Campbell, 1871–1949, vol. IV

Da Costa, John, 1867–1931, vol. III

Dacre, Air Cdre George Bentley, 1891–1962, vol. VI

Dadabhoy, Sir Maneckji Byramji, 1865–1953, vol. V

Dadd, Frank, 1851–1929, vol. III

D'Aeth, Rear-Adm. Arthur Cloudesley Shovel H.; *see* Hughes D'Aeth.

D'Aeth, John, 1853–1922, vol. II

Da Fano, Corrado Donato, 1879–1927, vol. II

Da Fano, Dorothea, (Mrs C. D. Da Fano); *see* Landau, D.

Dafoe, Allan Roy, 1883–1943, vol. IV

Dafoe, John Wesley, 1866–1944, vol. IV

Daga, Sir Dewan Bahadur Kasturchand, 1855–1917, vol. II

Daga, Raja Rai Bahadur Sir Seth Bisesardass, 1877–1941, vol. IV (A), vol. V

Daggar, George, *died* 1950, vol. IV

Daggett, William Ingledew, 1900–1980, vol. VII

Daglish, Eric Fitch, 1892–1966, vol. VI

Daglish, Hon. Henry, 1866–1920, vol. II

Dagnan-Bouveret, Pascal Adolph Jean, 1852–1929, vol. III

D'Aguilar, Sir Charles Lawrence, 1821–1912, vol. I

Dahl, Knut, 1871–1953, vol. V

Dain, Charles Kenneth, 1879–1950, vol. IV (A)

Dain, George Rutherford, 1884–1954, vol. V

Dain, Sir Guy; *see* Dain, Sir H. G.

Dain, Sir (Harry) Guy, 1870–1966, vol. VI

Dain, Sir John Rutherford, 1883–1957, vol. V

Daines, Percy, *died* 1957, vol. V

Daintree, Captain John Dodson, 1864–1952, vol. V

Dakers, A. W., 1868–1947, vol. IV

Dakers, Jane, (Mrs Andrew Dakers); *see* Lane, J.

Dakin, Henry Drysdale, 1880–1952, vol. V

Dakin, William John, 1883–1950, vol. IV

Dakin, William Radford, 1860–1935, vol. III

Dakyns, George Doherty, 1856–1939, vol. III (A), vol. IV

Dakyns, Winifred, 1875–1960, vol. V

Daladier, Edouard, 1884–1970, vol. VI

Dalal, Sir Ardeshir Rustomji, 1884–1949, vol. IV

Dalal, Sirdar Sir Bamanjee Ardeshir, 1854–1932, vol. III

Dalal, Sir Barjor Jamshedji, 1871–1936, vol. III

Dalal, Sir Dadiba Merwanjee, 1870–1941, vol. IV

Dalal, Sir Ratanji Dinshaw, 1868–1957, vol. V

d'Albe, Edmund Edward F.; see Fournier d'Albe.

D'Albert, Eugen, 1864–1932, vol. III

D'Albiac, Air Marshal Sir John Henry, 1894–1963, vol. VI

Dalbiac, Philip Hugh, 1855–1927, vol. II

d'Albuquerque, Nino Pedroso, 1894–1969, vol. VI

Dalby, Rev. Francis Higgs, 1853–1933, vol. III

Dalby, Maj.-Gen. Thomas Gerald, 1880–1963, vol. VI

Dalby, W. Ernest, died 1936, vol. III

Dalby, Sir William Bartlett, 1840–1918, vol. II

Dalcroze, Emile J.; see Jaques-Dalcroze.

Daldy, Ven. Alfred Edward, 1865–1935, vol. III

Daldy, Frederick Francis, 1857–1928, vol. II

Dale, Adm. Alfred Taylor, 1840–1925, vol. II

Dale, Sir Alfred William Winterslow, 1855–1921, vol. II

Dale, Rt Rev. Basil Montague, 1903–1976, vol. VII

Dale, Benjamin James, 1885–1943, vol. IV

Dale, Charles Ernest, 1867–1956, vol. V

Dale, Major Claude Henry, 1882–1946, vol. IV

Dale, Darley; see Steele, F. M.

Dale, Sir Edgar Thorniley, 1886–1966, vol. VI

Dale, Francis Richard, 1883–1976, vol. VII

Dale, Frank Harry, 1871–1918, vol. II

Dale, Brig.-Gen. George Arthur, 1866–1940, vol. III

Dale, Harold Edward, 1875–1954, vol. V

Dale, Rev. Harold Montague, 1873–1951, vol. V

Dale, Henry Angley L.; see Lewis-Dale.

Dale, Sir Henry Hallett, 1875–1968, vol. VI

Dale, Henry Sheppard, 1852–1921, vol. II

Dale, James A., 1874–1951, vol. V

Dale, Sir James Backhouse, 2nd Bt, 1855–1932, vol. III

Dale, John Ainsworth, 1887–1938, vol. III

Dale, John Gilbert, 1869–1926, vol. II

Dale, Louise Mary, (Lady Mulleneux-Grayson), died 1954, vol. V

Dale, Ven. Canon Percy John, 1876–1957, vol. V

Dale, Rev. Thomas F., died 1923, vol. II

Dale, Rev. William, 1841–1924, vol. II

Dalen, Nils Gustaf, 1869–1937, vol. III

Daley, Sir Allen; see Daley, Sir W. A.

Daley, Sir Denis Leo, 1888–1965, vol. VI

Daley, Sir (William) Allen, 1887–1969, vol. VI

Dalgety, Arthur William Hugh, 1899–1972, vol. VII

Dalgety, Col Edmund Henry, 1847–1914, vol. I

Dalgety, Major Frederick John, 1866–1926, vol. II

Dalgleish, Wing Comdr James William O.; see Ogilvy-Dalgleish.

Dalgleish, Oakley Hedley, 1910–1963, vol. VI

Dalgleish, Walter Scott, 1834–1897, vol. I

Dalgleish, Sir William Ogilvy, 1st Bt, 1832–1913, vol. I

Dalgliesh, Richard, 1844–1922, vol. II

Dalgliesh, Theodore Irving, died 1941, vol. IV

Dalglish, Rear-Adm. Robin Campsie, 1880–1934, vol. III

Dalhoff, Most Rev. T., died 1906, vol. I

Dalhousie, 14th Earl of, 1878–1928, vol. II

Dalhousie, 15th Earl of, 1904–1950, vol. IV

Dalison, Maj.-Gen. John Bernard, 1898–1964, vol. VI

Dalison, Rev. Canon Roger William H., 1860–1939, vol. III

Dallapiccola, Luigi, 1904–1975, vol. VII

Dallas, Lt-Col Alexander Egerton, 1869–1949, vol. IV

Dallas, Surg.-Gen. Alexander Morison, 1830–1912, vol. I

Dallas, Maj.-Gen. Alister Grant, 1866–1931, vol. III

Dallas, Lt-Col Charles Mowbray, 1861–1936, vol. III

Dallas, Hon. Francis Henry, 1865–1920, vol. II

Dallas, George, 1878–1961, vol. VI

Dallas, Sir George Edward, 3rd Bt, 1842–1918, vol. II

Dallin, Cyrus Edwin, 1861–1944, vol. IV

Dallinger, Rev. William Henry, 1842–1909, vol. I

Dally, John Frederick Halls, died 1944, vol. IV

Dalmahoy, Maj.-Gen. Patrick Carfrae, 1840–1926, vol. II

Dalmahoy, Patrick Carfrae, 1872–1928, vol. II

Dalmahoy, Patrick James Edward, 1896–1963, vol. VI

Dalmeny, Lord; Archibald Ronald Primrose, 1910–1931, vol. III

Dalrymple, Rt Hon. Sir Charles, 1st Bt (cr 1887), 1839–1916, vol. II

Dalrymple, Sir (Charles) Mark, 3rd Bt (cr 1887), 1915–1971, vol. VII

Dalrymple, Sir David Charles Herbert, 2nd Bt (cr 1887), 1879–1932, vol. III

Dalrymple, Hon. David Hay, 1840–1912, vol. II

Dalrymple, Sir Edward Arthur E.; see Elphinstone-Dalrymple.

Dalrymple, Col Sir Francis Napier E.; see Elphinstone-Dalrymple.

Dalrymple, Sir Hew (Clifford) Hamilton-, 9th Bt (cr 1697), 1888–1959, vol. V

Dalrymple, Hon. Sir Hew Hamilton, 1857–1945, vol. IV

Dalrymple, James, 1859–1934, vol. III

Dalrymple, Joseph, 1869–1949, vol. IV

Dalrymple, Sir Mark; see Dalrymple, Sir C. M.

Dalrymple, Sir Robert Graeme E.; see Elphinstone-Dalrymple.

Dalrymple, Sir Walter Hamilton-, 8th Bt (cr 1697), 1854–1920, vol. II

Dalrymple, Col Sir William, 1864–1941, vol. IV

Dalrymple, Maj.-Gen. William Liston, 1845–1938, vol. III

Dalrymple-Champneys, Captain Sir Weldon, 2nd Bt, 1892–1980, vol. VII

Dalrymple-Hamilton, Adm. Sir Frederick Hew George, 1890–1974, vol. VII

Dalrymple-Hamilton, Col Hon. North de Coigny, 1853–1906, vol. I

Dalrymple-Hamilton, Col Sir North Victor Cecil, 1883–1953, vol. V

Dalrymple Hay, Sir Charles John, 5th Bt, 1865–1952, vol. V

Dalrymple-Hay, Sir Harley Hugh, 1861–1940, vol. III

Dalrymple-Horn-Elphinstone, Sir Græme Hepburn; see Elphinstone.

Dalrymple-White, Lt-Col Sir Godfrey Dalrymple, 1st Bt, 1866–1954, vol. V

Dalton, Baron (Life Peer); Edward Hugh John Neale Dalton, 1887–1962, vol. VI

Dalton, Rev. Prebendary Arthur Edison, 1853–1938, vol. III

Dalton, Charles, 1850–1913, vol. I

Dalton, Hon. Charles, 1850–1933, vol. III

Dalton, Captain Charles G.; *see* Grant-Dalton.

Dalton, Sir Cornelius Neale, 1842–1920, vol. II

Dalton, Lt-Col Duncan G.; *see* Grant-Dalton.

D'Alton, Rt Rev. Edward A., 1860–1941, vol. IV

Dalton, Emilie Hilda; *see* Dalton, Mrs John E.

Dalton, Surg.-Rear-Adm. Frederick James Abercrombie, 1868–1940, vol. III

Dalton, Frederick Thomas, 1855–1927, vol. II

Dalton, Sir Henry, 1891–1966, vol. VI

Dalton, Rev. Herbert Andrew, 1852–1928, vol. II

Dalton, Adm. Hubert G.; *see* Grant-Dalton.

Dalton, Maj.-Gen. James Cecil, 1848–1931, vol. III

D'Alton, His Eminence Cardinal John, *died* 1963, vol. VI

Dalton, Sir John Cornelius, *died* 1959, vol. V

Dalton, Mrs John E., (Emilie Hilda Dalton), 1886–1950, vol. IV

Dalton, Rev. John Neale, 1839–1931, vol. III

Dalton, John Patrick, 1886–1965, vol. VI

Dalton, Comdr (E) Lionel Sydney, 1902–1941, vol. IV

Dalton, Sir Llewelyn Chisholm, 1879–1945, vol. IV

Dalton, Norman, *died* 1923, vol. II

Dalton, Ormonde Maddock, 1866–1945, vol. IV

Dalton, Sir Robert William, 1882–1961, vol. VI

Dalton, Seymour Berkeley P.; *see* Portman-Dalton.

Dalton, Thomas Wilson Fox, 1886–1977, vol. VII

Dalton, William Bower, 1868–1965, vol. VI

Dalton-Morris, Air Marshal Sir Leslie, 1906–1976, vol. VII

D'Alvarez, Marguerite, 1886–1953, vol. V

D'Alviella, Count Goblet, 1846–1925, vol. II

Dalwood, Hubert, 1924–1976, vol. VII

Dalwood, Lt-Col John H.; *see* Hall-Dalwood.

Daly, Maj.-Gen. Arthur Crawford, 1871–1936, vol. III

Daly, Ashley Skeffington, 1882–1977, vol. VII

Daly, Augustin, 1838–1899, vol. I

Daly, Lt-Col Sir Clive Kirkpatrick, 1888–1966, vol. VI

Daly, Major Denis St George, 1862–1942, vol. IV

Daly, Lt-Col Francis Augustus Bonner, 1855–1946, vol. IV

Daly, Francis Charles, 1868–1945, vol. IV

Daly, Very Rev. Henry Edward, *died* 1949, vol. IV

Daly, Ven. Henry Varian, 1838–1925, vol. II

Daly, Lt-Col Sir Hugh, 1860–1939, vol. III

Daly, Ivan de Burgh, 1893–1974, vol. VII

Daly, John Archer Blake-, 1835–1917, vol. II (A), vol. III

Daly, Col Louis Dominic, 1885–1967, vol. VI

Daly, Lt-Col Ludger Jules Olivier G.; *see* Gingras-Daly.

Daly, Hon. Sir Malachy Bowes, 1836–1920, vol. II

Daly, Sir Oscar Bedford, 1880–1953, vol. V

Daly, Col Patrick Joseph, 1872–1931, vol. III

Daly, Col Thomas, *died* 1917, vol. II

Daly, Thomas Denis, 1890–1956, vol. V

Daly Lewis, Edward; *see* Lewis.

Dalyell of the Binns, Lt-Col Gordon, 1887–1953, vol. V

Dalyell, Major Sir James Bruce Wilkie-, 9th Bt, 1867–1935, vol. III

Dalyell, Lt-Gen. John Thomas, 1827–1919, vol. II

Dalyell, Ralph, 1834–1915, vol. I

Dalzell, Lord; Robert Hippisley Dalzell, 1877–1904, vol. I

Dalzell, Lt-Col John Norton, 1897–1957, vol. V

Dalzell, Reginald Alexander, 1865–1928, vol. II

Dalziel of Kirkcaldy, 1st Baron, 1868–1935, vol. III

Dalziel of Wooler, 1st Baron, 1854–1928, vol. II

Dalziel, Edward, 1817–1905, vol. I

Dalziel, George, 1815–1902, vol. I

Dalziel, Gilbert, 1853–1930, vol. III

Dalziel, Sir Kennedy, 1861–1924, vol. II

Dalziel, Walter Watson, 1900–1967, vol. VI

Dam, (Carl Peter) Henrik, 1895–1976, vol. VII

Dam, Henrik; *see* Dam, C. P. H.

D'Amade, Albert, 1856–1941, vol. IV

Damant, Lt-Col Frederick Hugh, 1864–1926, vol. II

Damant, Captain Guybon Chesney Castell, *died* 1963, vol. VI

d'Ambrumenil, Sir Philip, 1886–1974, vol. VII

Damiano, Most Rev. Celestine Joseph, *died* 1967, vol. VI

D'Amico Inguanez, Baroness Mary Frances Carmen Maria Teresa Sceberras Trigona, 1865–1947, vol. IV

Damle, Keshav Govind, 1868–1930, vol. III

Dampier, Adm. Cecil Frederick, 1868–1950, vol. IV

Dampier, Henry Lucius, 1828–1913, vol. I

Dampier, Sir William Cecil Dampier, 1867–1952, vol. V

Damrosch, Walter, 1862–1950, vol. IV

Dana, Charles L., 1852–1935, vol. III

Dana, John Cotton, 1856–1929, vol. III

Dana, Paul, 1852–1930, vol. III

Dana, Robert Washington, 1868–1956, vol. V

Danby, Vice-Adm. Sir Clinton Francis Samuel, 1882–1945, vol. IV

Danby, Frank, 1864–1916, vol. II

Danby, Rev. Herbert, 1889–1953, vol. V

Dance, Sir George, *died* 1932, vol. III

Dance, James, 1907–1971, vol. VII

Dancer, Sir Thomas Johnston, 7th Bt, 1852–1933, vol. III

Danckwerts, Rt Hon. Sir Harold Otto, 1888–1978, vol. VII

Danckwerts, Rear-Adm. Victor Hilary, *died* 1944, vol. IV

Danckwerts, William Otto Adolph Julius, 1853–1914, vol. I

Dandie, James Naughton, 1894–1976, vol. VII

Dando, Kenneth Walter, 1921–1980, vol. VII

Dandridge, Cecil Gerald Graham, 1890–1960, vol. V

Dandurand, Rt Hon. Raoul, 1861–1942, vol. IV

Dandy, Rev. Henry Edward, *died* 1930, vol. III

Dandy, James Edgar, 1903–1976, vol. VII
Dane, Clemence Winifred Ashton, *died* 1965, vol. VI
Dane, Lt-Col James Auchinleck, 1883–1927, vol. II
Dane, Sir Louis William, 1856–1946, vol. IV
Dane, Richard Martin, 1852–1903, vol. I
Dane, Sir Richard Morris, 1854–1940, vol. III
Dane, William Surrey, 1892–1978, vol. VII
Danesfort, 1st Baron, 1853–1935, vol. III
Dangar, Rev. James George, 1841–1917, vol. II
Danger, Frank Charles, 1873–1943, vol. IV
Dangerfield, Roland Edmund, 1897–1964, vol. VI
Dangin, François T.; *see* Thureau-Dangin.
Dangin, Paul Marie Pierre T.; *see* Thureau-Dangin.
Danglow, Rabbi Jacob, 1880–1962, vol. VI
Daniel, Sir Augustus Moore, 1866–1950, vol. IV
Daniel, Rev. Charles Henry Olive, 1836–1919, vol. II
Daniel, Lt-Col Charles James, 1861–1949, vol. IV
Daniel, Lt-Col Edward Yorke, 1865–1941, vol. IV
Daniel, Rev. Canon Evan, 1837–1904, vol. I
Daniel, Henry Cave, 1896–1980, vol. VII
Daniel, Brig. James Alfred, 1893–1959, vol. V
Daniel, Sir John, 1870–1938, vol. III
Daniel, (John) Stuart, 1912–1977, vol. VII
Daniel, Hon. John Waterhouse, 1845–1933, vol. III
Daniel, Stuart; *see* Daniel, J. S.
Daniel, Thomas Ernest, 1898–1968, vol. VI
Daniel, Rev. Wilson Eustace, 1841–1924, vol. II
Daniel-Rops, Henry, 1901–1965, vol. VI
Daniell, Major Edward Henry Edwin, 1868–1914, vol. I
Daniell, Very Rev. Edward M., 1864–1952, vol. V
Daniell, Emily Hilda, (Mrs J. A. H. Daniell); *see* Young, E. H.
Daniell, Major Francis Edward Lloyd, 1874–1916, vol. II
Daniell, Brig.-Gen. Frederick Francis Williamson, 1866–1937, vol. III
Daniell, Rev. George William, 1853–1931, vol. III
Daniell, John, 1878–1963, vol. VI
Daniell, Maj.-Gen. Sir John Frederic, 1859–1943, vol. IV
Daniell, Percy John, 1889–1946, vol. IV
Daniell, Lt-Col William Augustus Bampfylde, 1875–1956, vol. V
Daniell-Bainbridge, Rev. Howard Gurney, *died* 1950, vol. IV
Daniels, Charles Wilberforce, *died* 1927, vol. II
Daniels, George William, 1878–1937, vol. III
Daniels, Harold Griffith, 1874–1952, vol. V
Daniels, Lt-Col Harry, 1884–1953, vol. V
Daniels, Sir Percy, 1875–1951, vol. V
Daniels, Sidney Reginald, 1873–1937, vol. III
Danielsen, Col Frederick Gustavus, 1874–1951, vol. V
Danks, Sir Aaron Turner, 1861–1928, vol. II
Danks, Ven. William, 1845–1916, vol. II
Dann, Alfred Clarence, 1893–1953, vol. V
Dann, Brig.-Gen. William Rowland Harris, 1876–1957, vol. V
Dannreuther, Edward, 1844–1905, vol. I
Dannreuther, Rear-Adm. Hubert Edward, 1880–1977, vol. VII

Dannreuther, Sir Sigmund, 1873–1965, vol. VI
D'Annunzio, Gabriele, 1864–1938, vol. III
Dansey, Lt-Col Sir Claude Edward Marjoribanks, 1876–1947, vol. IV
Dansey, Col Francis Henry, 1878–1953, vol. V
Dansey-Browning, Col George; *see* Browning.
Danson, Rt Rev. Ernest Denny Logie, 1880–1946, vol. IV
Danson, Sir Francis Chatillon, 1855–1926, vol. II
Danter, Harold Walter Phillips, 1886–1976, vol. VII
Danvers, Frederick Charles, 1833–1906, vol. I
Danvers, Sir Juland, 1826–1902, vol. I
d'Aranyi, Jelly, *died* 1966, vol. VI
Darbhanga, Maharajadhiraja of, 1907–1962, vol. VI
Darbishire, Charles William, 1875–1925, vol. II
Darbishire, Helen, 1881–1961, vol. VI
Darbishire, Otto Vernon, 1870–1934, vol. III
Darboux, Jean Gaston, 1842–1917, vol. II
Darby, Very Rev. John Lionel, 1831–1919, vol. II
Darby, William Evans, 1844–1922, vol. II
Darbyshire, Most Rev. John Russell, 1880–1948, vol. IV
Darbyshire, Ruth Eveline, *died* 1946, vol. IV
Darbyshire, Taylor, 1875–1943, vol. IV
D'Arcy, Most Rev. Charles Frederick, 1859–1938, vol. III
D'Arcy, Dame Constance Elizabeth, *died* 1950, vol. IV
D'Arcy, Rev. George James Audomar, 1861–1941, vol. IV
D'Arcy, Lt-Gen. John Conyers, 1894–1966, vol. VI
D'Arcy, Very Rev. Martin Cyril, 1888–1976, vol. VII
D'Arcy, William Knox, 1849–1917, vol. II
Darcy de Knayth, Baroness (16th in line), 1865–1929, vol. III
Darcy de Knayth, 17th Baron; *see* Clive, Viscount, (vol. IV)
D'Arcy-Irvine, Rt Rev. Gerard Addington, 1862–1932, vol. III
D'Arcy-Irvine, Adm. Sir St George Caufield; *see* Irvine.
Dare, Adm. Sir Charles Holcombe, 1854–1924, vol. II
Dare, Edith Graham, 1883–1969, vol. VI
Dare, Robert Westley H.; *see* Hall-Dare.
Darell, Lt-Col Harry Francis, 1872–1934, vol. III
Darell, Sir Lionel Edward, 5th Bt, 1845–1919, vol. II
Darell, Sir Lionel Edward Hamilton Marmaduke, 6th Bt, 1876–1954, vol. V
Darell, Sir Oswald; *see* Darell, Sir W. O.
Darell, Brig.-Gen. William Harry Verelst, 1878–1954, vol. V
Darell, Sir (William) Oswald, 7th Bt, 1910–1959, vol. V
Daresbury, 1st Baron, 1867–1938, vol. III
Darewski, Herman, *died* 1947, vol. IV
Dargan, William J., *died* 1944, vol. IV
Dark, Sidney, 1874–1947, vol. IV
Darke, Harold Edwin, 1888–1976, vol. VII
Darke, Rear-Adm. Reginald Burnard, 1885–1962, vol. VI

169

Darlan, Amiral de la Flotte Jean François, 1881–1942, vol. IV
Darley, Sir Bernard D'Olier, 1880–1953, vol. V
Darley, Cecil West, 1842–1928, vol. II
Darley, Air Cdre Charles Curtis, 1890–1962, vol. VI
Darley, Rt Hon. Sir Frederick Matthew, 1830–1910, vol. I
Darley, Major Henry Read, 1865–1931, vol. III
Darley, J. F., died 1932, vol. III
Darley, Lt-Col James Russell, 1868–1951, vol. V
Darling, 1st Baron, 1849–1936, vol. III
Darling, Rev. Charles Brian Auchinleck, 1905–1978, vol. VII
Darling, Col Charles Henry, 1852–1931, vol. III
Darling, Charles Robert, 1870–1942, vol. IV
Darling, Maj.-Gen. Douglas Lyall, 1914–1978, vol. VII
Darling, Rev. Canon Edward M.; see Moore Darling.
Darling, Frank, 1850–1923, vol. II
Darling, Sir Frank F.; see Fraser Darling.
Darling, Frederick, 1884–1953, vol. V
Darling, George Kenneth, 1879–1964, vol. VI
Darling, Ven. James George Reginald, 1868–1938, vol. III
Darling, Major Hon. John Clive, 1887–1933, vol. III
Darling, Major John Collier S.; see Stormonth-Darling.
Darling, John Ford, 1864–1938, vol. III
Darling, Major John May, 1878–1942, vol. IV
Darling, Hon. Joseph, 1870–1946, vol. IV
Darling, Sir Malcolm Lyall, 1880–1969, vol. VI
Darling, Moir Tod Stormonth; see Hon. Lord Stormonth-Darling.
Darling, Sir William Young, 1885–1962, vol. VI
Darlington, Edwin, 1839–1928, vol. II
Darlington, Col Sir Henry Clayton, 1877–1959, vol. V
Darlington, Rt Rev. James Henry, 1856–1930, vol. III
Darlington, Rev. John, 1868–1947, vol. IV
Darlington, Rev. Joseph, 1850–1939, vol. III
Darlington, Reginald Ralph, 1903–1977, vol. VII
Darlington, William Aubrey, 1890–1979, vol. VII
Darlow, Rev. Thomas Herbert, 1858–1927, vol. II
Darnley, 7th Earl of, 1851–1900, vol. I
Darnley, 8th Earl of, 1859–1927, vol. II
Darnley, 9th Earl of, 1886–1955, vol. V
Darnley, 10th Earl of, 1915–1980, vol. VII
Darracott, Sir William, 1860–1947, vol. IV
Darrah, Henry Zouch, 1854–1909, vol. I
Darrell, Hon. Richard Darrell, 1827–1904, vol. I
Darroch, Alexander, 1862–1924, vol. II
Darrow, Clarence, 1857–1938, vol. III
Dart, Rt Rev. John, 1837–1910, vol. I
Dart, Rev. John Lovering Campbell, 1882–1961, vol. VI
Dart, Thurston, 1921–1971, vol. VII
Dartmouth, 6th Earl of, 1851–1936, vol. III
Dartmouth, 7th Earl of, 1881–1958, vol. V
Dartmouth, 8th Earl of, 1888–1962, vol. VI
Dartnell, Maj.-Gen. Sir John George, 1838–1913, vol. I

Dartrey, 1st Earl of, 1817–1897, vol. I
Dartrey, 2nd Earl of, 1842–1920, vol. II
Dartrey, 3rd Earl of, 1855–1933, vol. III
Darvall, Air Marshal Sir Lawrence, 1898–1968, vol. VI
Darvil-Smith, Major Percy George, 1880–1962, vol. VI
Darvill, Harold Edgar, 1908–1972, vol. VII
Darwall, Lt-Gen. Robert Henry, 1879–1956, vol. V
Darwen, 1st Baron, 1885–1950, vol. IV
Darwin, Bernard, 1876–1961, vol. VI
Darwin, Sir Charles Galton, 1887–1962, vol. VI
Darwin, Squadron Leader Charles John Wharton, 1894–1941, vol. IV
Darwin, Col Charles Waring, 1855–1928, vol. II
Darwin, Sir Francis, 1848–1925, vol. II
Darwin, Sir George Howard, 1845–1912, vol. I
Darwin, Sir Horace, 1851–1928, vol. II
Darwin, John Henry, 1884–1962, vol. VI
Darwin, Major Leonard, 1850–1943, vol. IV
Darwin, Robert Vere; see Darwin, Sir Robin.
Darwin, Sir Robin, 1910–1974, vol. VII
Darwin, Ruth, died 1972, vol. VII
Darwood, Sir John William, 1873–1951, vol. V
Daryngton, 1st Baron, 1867–1949, vol. IV
Das, Sir Kedarnath; see Kedarnath Das.
Das, Hon. M. S., 1848–1934, vol. III
Das, Hon. Satish Ranjan, 1872–1928, vol. II
Das, Sudhi Ranjan, 1894–1977, vol. VII
Dasent, Arthur Irwin, died 1939, vol. III
Dasent, Sir John Roche, 1847–1914, vol. I
Dasgupta, Surendra Nath, 1887–1952, vol. V
Dash, Sir Arthur Jules, 1887–1974, vol. VII
Dashwood, Arthur George Frederick, 1860–1922, vol. II
Dashwood, Charles James, 1843–1919, vol. II
Dashwood, Col Edmund William, 1858–1946, vol. IV
Dashwood, Elizabeth Monica, 1890–1943, vol. IV
Dashwood, Sir George John Egerton, 6th Bt (cr 1684), 1851–1933, vol. III
Dashwood, Sir Henry George Massy, 8th Bt (cr 1684), 1908–1972, vol. VII
Dashwood, Sir Henry Thomas Alexander, 1878–1959, vol. V
Dashwood, Sir John Lindsay, 10th Bt (cr 1707), 1896–1966, vol. VI
Dashwood, Maj.-Gen. Richard Lewes, died 1905, vol. I
Dashwood, Major Sir Robert Henry Seymour, 7th Bt (cr 1684), 1876–1947, vol. IV
Dashwood, Sir Robert John, 9th Bt (cr 1707), 1859–1908 (this entry was not transferred to Who was Who).
Datar Singh, Sardar Bahadur Sir, died 1973, vol. VII
Datia, HH Maharajah Sir Govind Singh Bahadur, died 1951, vol. V
Datia, HH Maharajah Sir Lockindar Bhawani Singh Bahadur, 1846–1907, vol. I
Datta, Surendra Kumar, 1878–1942, vol. IV
Daubeney, Brig.-Gen. Edward Kaye, 1858–1932, vol. III
Daubeney, Gen. Sir Henry Charles Barnston, 1810–1903, vol. I

Daubeny, Sir Peter Lauderdale, 1921–1975, vol. VII
Daubeny, Col Reginald Ernest, 1877–1935, vol. III
Dauber, J. H., died 1915, vol. I
Daubney, Robert, 1891–1977, vol. VII
Daudet, Alphonse, 1840–1897, vol. I
Daudet, Léon, 1867–1942, vol. IV
Dauglish, Captain Edward Heath, 1882–1950, vol. IV
Dauglish, Rt Rev. John, 1879–1952, vol. V
Daukes, Lt-Col Sir Clendon Turberville, 1879–1947, vol. IV
Daukes, Rt Rev. Francis Whitfield, 1877–1954, vol. V
Daukes, Frederick Clendon, 1848–1915, vol. I
Daukes, Sidney Herbert, 1879–1947, vol. IV
Daunt, Very Rev. Ernest George, 1909–1966, vol. VI
Daunt, Lt-Col Richard Algernon Craigie, 1872–1928, vol. II
Daunt, Maj.-Gen. William, 1831–1899, vol. I
Daunt, Ven. William, 1841–1919, vol. II
Dauntesey, Lt-Col William Bathurst, 1864–1937, vol. III
Davar, Sir Dinsha Dhurjibhai, 1856–1916, vol. II
Daven-Thomas, Rev. Canon Dennis; see Thomas.
Davenport, Charles Benedict, 1866–1944, vol. IV
Davenport, Major Cyril James H., 1848–1941, vol. IV
Davenport, Frederic Richard, 1872–1952, vol. V
Davenport, Hon. Sir George Arthur, 1893–1970, vol. VI
Davenport, Harold, 1907–1969, vol. VI
Davenport, Sir Henry Edward, 1866–1941, vol. IV
Davenport, Major John Lewes, 1910–1964, vol. VI
Davenport, Dame Lilian Emily Isabel Jane B.; see Bromley-Davenport.
Davenport, Muriel Coomber B.; see Bromley-Davenport.
Davenport, Robert Cecil, 1893–1961, vol. VI
Davenport, Vice-Adm. Robert Clutterbuck, 1882–1965, vol. VI
Davenport, Sir Samuel, 1818–1906, vol. I
Davenport, Brig.-Gen. Sir William B.; see Bromley-Davenport.
Daventry, 1st Viscountess, 1869–1962, vol. VI
Daverin, John, 1851–1922, vol. II
Davey, Baron (Life Peer); Horace Davey, 1833–1907, vol. I
Davey, Maj.-Gen. Basil Charles, 1897–1959, vol. V
Davey, Comdr Charles Henry, 1879–1940, vol. III
Davey, George, 1911–1959, vol. V
Davey, Henry, 1843–1928, vol. II
Davey, Herbert, 1871–1931, vol. III
Davey, Lt-Col Hon. Horace Scott, 1865–1935, vol. III
Davey, Lt-Col James Edgar, 1873–1969, vol. VI
Davey, Rev. J(ames) Ernest, 1890–1960, vol. V, vol. VI
Davey, Rev. James Penry, 1878–1939, vol. III
Davey, Rev. Thomas Arthur Edwards, died 1944, vol. IV
Davey, Thomas Herbert, 1899–1978, vol. VII
Davey, Very Rev. William Harrison, 1825–1917, vol. II

Davey, William Kendall, 1887–1968, vol. VI
David, Rt Rev. Albert Augustus, 1867–1950, vol. IV
David, Alexander Jones, 1851–1929, vol. III
David, Ven. Arthur Evan, 1861–1913, vol. I
David, Lt-Col Sir Edgeworth; see David, Lt-Col Sir T. W. E.
David, Sir Edgeworth Beresford, 1908–1965, vol. VI
David, Herman Francis, 1905–1974, vol. VII
David, Hon. Laurent Olivier, 1840–1926, vol. II
David, Sir Percival Victor, 2nd Bt, 1892–1964, vol. VI
David, Rev. Richard, died 1947, vol. IV (A)
David, Sir Sassoon, 1st Bt, 1849–1926, vol. II
David, Lt-Col Sir (Tannatt William) Edgeworth, 1858–1934, vol. III
David, Bt-Col Thomas Jenkins, 1881–1926, vol. II
David, W. T., died 1948, vol. IV
David-Weill, David, 1871–1952, vol. V
Davidge, Cecil William, 1863–1936, vol. III
Davidge, William Robert, died 1961, vol. VI
Davids, Caroline A. F. Rhys, died 1942, vol. IV
Davids, Thomas William Rhys, 1843–1922, vol. II
Davidson, 1st Viscount, 1889–1970, vol. VI
Davidson, 1st Baron, 1848–1930, vol. III
Davidson, Rev. Alan Munro, 1894–1959, vol. V
Davidson, Albert, 1869–1932, vol. III
Davidson, Maj.-Gen. Alexander Elliott, 1880–1962, vol. VI
Davidson, Air Vice-Marshal Sir Alexander Paul, 1894–1971, vol. VII
Davidson, Vice-Adm. Alexander Percy, 1868–1930, vol. III
Davidson, Sir Alfred Charles, 1882–1952, vol. V
Davidson, Allan Douglas, 1873–1932, vol. III
Davidson, Sir Andrew, 1892–1962, vol. VI
Davidson, Rev. Andrew Bruce, 1840–1902, vol. I
Davidson, Andrew Hope, 1895–1967, vol. VI
Davidson, Very Rev. (Andrew) Nevile, 1899–1976, vol. VII
Davidson, Col Sir Arthur, 1856–1922, vol. II
Davidson, Sir Charles, 1878–1927, vol. II
Davidson, Charles Findlay, 1911–1967, vol. VI
Davidson, Lt-Col Charles George Francis, 1884–1956, vol. V
Davidson, Col Charles John Lloyd, 1858–1941, vol. IV
Davidson, Sir Charles Peers, 1841–1929, vol. III
Davidson, Charles Rundle, 1875–1970, vol. VI
Davidson, Brig.-Gen. Charles Steer, 1866–1942, vol. IV
Davidson, Sir Colin George Watt, 1878–1954, vol. V
Davidson, Sir Colin John, 1878–1930, vol. III
Davidson, Lt-Col Colin Keppel, 1895–1943, vol. IV
Davidson, Col Sir David, 1811–1900, vol. I
Davidson, Brig. Douglas Stewart, 1892–1958, vol. V
Davidson, Duncan, 1865–1917, vol. II
Davidson, Brig. Edmund, 1875–1945, vol. IV
Davidson, Sir Edward; see Davidson, Sir W. E.
Davidson, Lt-Col Edward Humphrey, 1886–1962, vol. VI

Davidson, Rt Rev. Edwin John, 1899–1958, vol. V
Davidson, Ethel Sarah, 1877–1939, vol. III
Davidson, Maj.-Gen. Francis Henry Norman, 1892–1973, vol. VII
Davidson, Frederick Lewis Maitland, *died* 1936, vol. III
Davidson, George, *died* 1928, vol. II
Davidson, Major George Harry, 1866–1927, vol. II
Davidson, Ven. Gilbert Farquhar, 1871–1930, vol. III
Davidson, Col James, 1853–1932, vol. III
Davidson, Ven. James, *died* 1933, vol. III
Davidson, Lt-Col James, 1865–1933, vol. III
Davidson, James, 1885–1945, vol. IV
Davidson, James, 1875–1959, vol. V
Davidson, Sir James Inglis, 1852–1934, vol. III
Davidson, James Leigh S.; *see* Strachan-Davidson.
Davidson, Sir James Mackenzie, 1856–1919, vol. II
Davidson, (James) Norman, 1911–1972, vol. VII
Davidson, James Walker, 1872–1939, vol. III
Davidson, James Wightman, 1915–1973, vol. VII
Davidson, Jo, 1883–1952, vol. V
Davidson, John, 1869–1905, vol. I
Davidson, John, 1857–1909, vol. I
Davidson, Col John, 1845–1917, vol. II
Davidson, John, 1878–1957, vol. V
Davidson, John, 1882–1960, vol. V
Davidson, Maj.-Gen. Sir John Humphrey, 1876–1954, vol. V
Davidson, John Wallace Ord, 1888–1973, vol. VII
Davidson, Col Sir Jonathan Roberts, 1874–1961, vol. VI
Davidson, Major Leslie Evan Outram, 1882–1925, vol. II
Davidson, Sir Leybourne Francis Watson, 1859–1934, vol. III
Davidson, Lindsay Gordon, 1893–1965, vol. VI
Davidson, Sir Lionel, 1868–1944, vol. IV
Davidson, Dame Margaret A., 1871–1964, vol. VI
Davidson, Mark George, 1859–1933, vol. III
Davidson, Maurice, 1883–1967, vol. VI
Davidson, Very Rev. Nevile; *see* Davidson, Very Rev. A. N.
Davidson, Sir Nigel George, 1873–1961, vol. VI
Davidson, Norman; *see* Davidson, J. N.
Davidson, Lt-Col Peers, 1870–1920, vol. II
Davidson, Lt-Col Percival, 1874–1930, vol. III
Davidson, Randall George, 1874–1963, vol. VI
Davidson, Rev. Richard, 1876–1944, vol. IV
Davidson, Robert, 1831–1913, vol. I
Davidson, Robert, 1888–1952, vol. V
Davidson, Sir Samuel C., *died* 1921, vol. II
Davidson, Maj.-Gen. Sisley Richard, 1869–1952, vol. V
Davidson, Col Stuart, 1859–1941, vol. IV
Davidson, Thomas, 1856–1923, vol. II
Davidson, Sir Walter Edward, 1859–1923, vol. II
Davidson, Sir (William) Edward, 1853–1923, vol. II
Davidson, Col William Leslie, 1850–1915, vol. I
Davidson, William Leslie, 1848–1929, vol. III
Davidson, William Tennent Gairdner, 1889–1949, vol. IV
Davidson-Houston, Major Charles Elrington Duncan, 1873–1915, vol. I (A)

Davidson-Houston, Lt-Col Wilfred Bennett, 1870–1960, vol. V
Davidson-Smith, Maj.-Gen. E.; *see* Smith.
Davie, Major Arthur Francis Ferguson-, 1867–1916, vol. II
Davie, Rt Rev. Charles James F.; *see* Ferguson-Davie.
Davie, Sir Henry Augustus Ferguson-, 1865–1946, vol. IV
Davie, Sir John Davie Ferguson-, 2nd Bt, 1830–1907, vol. I
Davie, Thomas Benjamin, 1895–1955, vol. V
Davie, Sir William Augustus Ferguson-, 3rd Bt, 1833–1915, vol. I
Davie, Major Sir William John F., 4th Bt; *see* Ferguson-Davie.
Davies, 1st Baron, 1880–1944, vol. IV
Davies, 2nd Baron, 1915–1944, vol. IV
Davies, Aaron, 1830–1915, vol. I (A)
Davies, Alan B.; *see* Bowen-Davies.
Davies, Sir Alan Meredyth H.; *see* Hudson-Davies.
Davies, Albert Edward, 1900–1953, vol. V
Davies, Albert Emil, 1875–1950, vol. IV
Davies, Alfred, 1848–1907, vol. I
Davies, Sir Alfred Thomas, 1881–1941, vol. IV
Davies, Sir Alfred Thomas, 1861–1949, vol. IV
Davies, Alice Hollingdrake, 1878–1968, vol. VI
Davies, Rt Hon. Sir Arthian; *see* Davies, Rt Hon. Sir W. A.
Davies, Arthur Cecil, 1889–1947, vol. IV
Davies, Arthur Charles F.; *see* Fox-Davies.
Davies, (Arthur Edward) Miles, 1903–1977, vol. VII
Davies, Adm. Sir Arthur John, *died* 1954, vol. V
Davies, Rev. Arthur Llywelyn, *died* 1957, vol. V
Davies, Lt-Gen. Arthur Matcham, 1832–1908, vol. I
Davies, Arthur Templer, 1858–1929, vol. III
Davies, Arthur Vernon, *died* 1942, vol. IV
Davies, Very Rev. Arthur Whitcliffe, *died* 1966, vol. VI
Davies, Arthur William, 1878–1969, vol. VI
Davies, Ashton, 1874–1958, vol. V
Davies, Ben, 1858–1943, vol. IV
Davies, Rev. Canon Benjamin, 1880–1941, vol. IV
Davies, Bernard Noël L.; *see* Langdon-Davies.
Davies, Brian H.; *see* Humphreys-Davies.
Davies, Cecil Bertrand, 1876–1960, vol. VI
Davies, Sir Charles; *see* Davies, Sir R. C.
Davies, Rev. Charles Douglas Percy, *died* 1931, vol. III
Davies, Hon. Charles Ellis, 1848–1921, vol. II
Davies, Brig.-Gen. Charles Henry, 1867–1954, vol. V
Davies, Charles Llewelyn, 1860–1927, vol. II
Davies, Brig. Charles Stafford P.; *see* Price-Davies.
Davies, Lt-Col Charles Stewart, 1880–1946, vol. IV
Davies, Clara Novello, 1861–1943, vol. IV
Davies, Rt Hon. Clement, 1884–1962, vol. VI
Davies, Sir Colin R.; *see* Rees-Davies.
Davies, Cuthbert Collin, 1896–1974, vol. VII
Davies, Rt Rev. Daniel, 1863–1928, vol. II
Davies, Daniel James, 1880–1946, vol. IV

Davies, Sir Daniel Thomas, 1899–1966, vol. VI
Davies, Ven. David, 1858–1930, vol. III
Davies, David, 1862–1932, vol. III
Davies, Sir David, 1870–1958, vol. V
Davies, Sir David, 1889–1964, vol. VI
Davies, David, 1877–1966, vol. VI
Davies, David Alban, 1873–1951, vol. V
Davies, Rt Rev. David E.; see Edwardes-Davies.
Davies, David F.; see Ffrangcon-Davies.
Davies, Rt Rev. David Henry S.; see Saunders-Davies.
Davies, Ven. David John, 1879–1935, vol. III
Davies, David Lewis, died 1937, vol. III
Davies, David Percy, 1891–1946, vol. IV
Davies, David Samuel, died 1933, vol. III
Davies, Sir David Sanders, 1852–1934, vol. III
Davies, David Vaughan, 1911–1969, vol. VI
Davies, Derek George G.; see Gill-Davies.
Davies, Edward, died 1920, vol. II
Davies, Col Edward Campbell, died 1919, vol. II
Davies, Edward Gwynfryn, 1904–1980, vol. VII (AII)
Davies, Edward Harold, 1867–1947, vol. IV
Davies, Sir (Edward) John, 1898–1969, vol. VI
Davies, Ellis William, 1871–1939, vol. III
Davies, Eric John W.; see Warlow-Davies.
Davies, Ernest, 1873–1946, vol. IV
Davies, Ernest Herbert, died 1934, vol. III
Davies, Ernest James, 1875–1935, vol. III
Davies, Ernest S.; see Salter Davies.
Davies, Rev. Ernest William, 1901–1978, vol. VII
Davies, Rev. Evan Thomas, died 1927, vol. II
Davies, Evan Thomas, 1878–1969, vol. VI
Davies, Evan Tom, 1904–1973, vol. VII
Davies, Fanny, 1861–1934, vol. III
Davies, Francis, 1897–1965, vol. VI
Davies, Gen. Sir Francis John, 1864–1948, vol. IV
Davies, Rev. (Francis Maurice) Russell, 1871–1956, vol. V
Davies, Rev. Francis Parry W.; see Watkin-Davies.
Davies, Rev. Frederick Charles, died 1929, vol. III
Davies, Frederick William Samuel, died 1919, vol. II
Davies, Sir George Edmund, 1857–1932, vol. III
Davies, Major Sir George Frederick, 1875–1950, vol. IV
Davies, Maj.-Gen. George Freshfield, 1872–1936, vol. III
Davies, George Maitland Lloyd, 1880–1949, vol. IV
Davies, Ven. George Middlecott, 1858–1937, vol. III
Davies, Rev. Gerald Stanley, 1845–1927, vol. II
Davies, Rev. Gilbert Austin, 1868–1948, vol. IV
Davies, Gwendoline Elizabeth, died 1951, vol. V
Davies, Harold Whitridge, died 1946, vol. IV
Davies, Haydn, 1905–1976, vol. VII
Davies, Hector Leighton, 1894–1980, vol. VII
Davies, Lt-Col Henry, 1867–1923, vol. II
Davies, Sir Henry, 1856–1936, vol. III
Davies, Lt-Gen. Henry Fanshawe, 1837–1914, vol. I
Davies, Henry J.; see Jones-Davies.
Davies, Maj.-Gen. Henry Lowrie, 1898–1975, vol. VII
Davies, Henry Meirion, 1875–1950, vol. IV (A), vol. V

Davies, Maj.-Gen. Henry Rodolph, 1865–1950, vol. IV
Davies, Sir (Henry) Walford, 1869–1941, vol. IV
Davies, Col Sir Horatio David, 1842–1912, vol. I
Davies, Sir Howell; see Davies, Sir H. W.
Davies, Hubert Henry, died 1917, vol. II
Davies, Hugh Morriston, 1879–1965, vol. VI
Davies, James Henry W.; see Wootton-Davies.
Davies, Jenkin A.; see Alban Davies.
Davies, Sir John; see Davies, Sir E. J.
Davies, John Bowen, 1876–1943, vol. IV
Davies, Sir John Cecil, 1864–1927, vol. II
Davies, John Cledwyn, died 1952, vol. V
Davies, John David Griffith, 1899–1953, vol. V
Davies, John Edward Henry, died 1939, vol. III
Davies, Rt Hon. John Emerson Harding, 1916–1979, vol. VII
Davies, Hon. Sir John George, 1846–1913, vol. I
Davies, John Humphreys, died 1926, vol. II
Davies, Rev. John J., 1863–1938, vol. III
Davies, John L.; see Langdon-Davies.
Davies, Rev. John Llewelyn, 1826–1916, vol. II
Davies, John Llewelyn, 1888–1959, vol. V
Davies, Hon. Sir John Mark, died 1919, vol. II
Davies, J(ohn) Prysor, 1900–1959, vol. V
Davies, John Robert, 1856–1934, vol. III
Davies, Sir John Thomas, 1881–1938, vol. III
Davies, Very Rev. John Thomas, 1881–1966, vol. VI
Davies, Rev. John Timothy, died 1931, vol. III
Davies, Rev. (John) Trevor, 1907–1974, vol. VII
Davies, Sir Joseph, 1866–1954, vol. V
Davies, Joseph Edward, 1876–1958, vol. V
Davies, Very Rev. Joseph Gwyn, 1890–1952, vol. V
Davies, Joshua David, 1889–1966, vol. VI
Davies, Sir Leonard Twiston, 1894–1953, vol. V
Davies, Lewis, 1886–1971, vol. VII
Davies, Maj.-Gen. Llewelyn Alberic Emilius P.; see Price-Davies.
Davies, Rt Hon. Sir Louis Henry, 1845–1924, vol. II
Davies, Margaret, (Lady Davies); see Kennedy, Margaret.
Davies, Sir Martin, 1908–1975, vol. VII
Davies, Mrs Mary, 1855–1930, vol. III
Davies, Hon. Sir Matthew Henry, 1850–1912, vol. I
Davies, Miles; see Davies, A. E. M.
Davies, N. P.; see Prescott-Davies.
Davies, Owen Picton, 1872–1940, vol. III
Davies, Bt-Col Owen Stanley, died 1926, vol. II
Davies, Col Percy George, died 1947, vol. IV
Davies, Rev. Philip Latimer, 1864–1928, vol. II
Davies, Rev. R. W. F. S.; see Singers-Davies.
Davies, Rachael Annie C.; see Cox-Davies.
Davies, Randall Robert Henry, 1866–1946, vol. IV
Davies, Reginald, 1887–1971, vol. VII
Davies, Sir (Reginald) Charles, 1886–1958, vol. V
Davies, Rhisiart Morgan, 1903–1958, vol. V
Davies, Rhys, 1903–1978, vol. VII
Davies, Rhys John, 1877–1954, vol. V
Davies, Sir Richard, 1853–1939, vol. III
Davies, Vice-Adm. Richard Bell, died 1966, vol. VI
Davies, Richard Humphrey, 1872–1970, vol. VI

Davies, Col Richard Hutton, *died* 1918, vol. II
Davies, Robert Gwyneddon, 1870–1928, vol. II
Davies, Sir Robert Henry, 1824–1902, vol. I
Davies, Sir Robert John, 1900–1967, vol. VI
Davies, Robert Malcolm Deryck, 1918–1967, vol. VI
Davies, Rev. Robert Owen, 1857–1929, vol. III
Davies, Rev. Russell; *see* Davies, Rev. F. M. R.
Davies, Ven. Samuel Morris, 1879–1963, vol. VI
Davies, Sarah Emily, 1830–1921, vol. II
Davies, Rev. Sidney Edmund, *died* 1918, vol. II
Davies, Rt Rev. Stephen Harris, 1883–1961, vol. VI
Davies, Stephen Owen, 1886–1972, vol. VII
Davies, Sydney John, 1891–1967, vol. VI
Davies, T. Witton, 1851–1923, vol. II
Davies, Sir Thomas, 1858–1939, vol. III
Davies, Thomas A.; *see* Anwyl-Davies.
Davies, Col Thomas Arthur Harkness, 1857–1942, vol. IV
Davies, Thomas H.; *see* Hart-Davies.
Davies, Thomas Walton, 1907–1948, vol. IV
Davies, Timothy, 1857–1951, vol. V
Davies, Rev. Trevor; *see* Davies, Rev. J. T.
Davies, Tudor, *died* 1958, vol. V
Davies, Sir Walford; *see* Davies, Sir H. W.
Davies, Walter, 1865–1939, vol. III
Davies, Hon. Brig.-Gen. Walter Percy Lionel, 1871–1952, vol. V
Davies, Col Warburton Edward, 1879–1956, vol. V
Davies, Rev. Canon Watkin, 1869–1943, vol. IV
Davies, Sir William, 1863–1935, vol. III
Davies, William, 1899–1968, vol. VI
Davies, Rt Hon. Sir (William) Arthian, 1901–1979, vol. VII
Davies, William Frank de Rolante, *died* 1942, vol. IV
Davies, Sir William George, 1828–1898, vol. I
Davies, William Henry, 1871–1940, vol. III
Davies, Sir (William) Howell, 1851–1932, vol. III
Davies, William John, 1848–1934, vol. IV
Davies, William John, 1891–1975, vol. VI
Davies, William John Abbott, 1890–1967, vol. VI
Davies, Sir William Llewelyn, 1887–1952, vol. V
Davies, Sir William Rees-, 1863–1939, vol. III
Davies, William Robert, 1870–1949, vol. IV
Davies, William Thomas Frederick, 1860–1947, vol. IV
Davies, William Tudor, *died* 1978, vol. VII
Davies, William Watkin, 1895–1973, vol. VII
Davies, Wyndham Matabele, 1893–1972, vol. VII
Davies-Colley, Robert, *died* 1955, vol. V
Davies-Cooke, Col Philip Ralph, 1896–1974, vol. VII
Davies-Cooke, Philip Tatton; *see* Cooke.
Davies-Evans, Herbert, *died* 1928, vol. II
Davies-Gilbert, Mrs Grace Catherine Rose, *died* 1951, vol. V
d'Avigdor-Goldsmid, Major Sir Henry Joseph, 2nd Bt, 1909–1976, vol. VII
d'Avigdor-Goldsmid, Sir Osmond Elim, 1st Bt, 1877–1940, vol. III
Davin, Nicholas Flood, 1843–1901, vol. I
Daviot, Gordon, *died* 1952, vol. V

Davis, Alexander, 1861–1945, vol. IV
Davis, Sir Alfred George Fletcher H.; *see* Hall-Davis.
Davis, Anthony Tilton, 1931–1978, vol. VII
Davis, Archibald William, 1900–1979, vol. VII
Davis, Arthur Henry, 1886–1931, vol. III
Davis, Arthur J., 1878–1951, vol. V
Davis, Sir Charles, 1st Bt, 1878–1950, vol. IV
Davis, Ven. Charles Henderson, *died* 1915, vol. I
Davis, Sir Charles Henry, 1847–1938, vol. III
Davis, Charles Henry H.; *see* Hart-Davis.
Davis, Col Charles Herbert, 1872–1922, vol. II
Davis, Sir Charles Thomas, 1873–1938, vol. III
Davis, David, 1877–1930, vol. III
Davis, Sir David, 1859–1938, vol. III
Davis, Ven. David Grimaldi, *died* 1936, vol. III
Davis, Dwight Filley, 1879–1945, vol. IV
Davis, Sir Edmund, *died* 1939, vol. III
Davis, Edward David Darelan, 1880–1976, vol. VII
Davis, Air Vice-Marshal Edward Derek, 1895–1955, vol. V
Davis, Adm. Edward Henry Meggs, 1846–1929, vol. III
Davis, Eliza Jeffries, 1875–1943, vol. IV
Davis, Elmer Holmes, 1890–1958, vol. V
Davis, Sir Ernest, 1872–1962, vol. VI
Davis, Very Rev. Evans, 1848–1918, vol. II
Davis, Col Evans Greenwood, 1885–1951, vol. V
Davis, F. W., *died* 1919, vol. II
Davis, Francis John, 1900–1980, vol. VII
Davis, Francis Robert Edward, 1887–1960, vol. V
Davis, Hon. Frank Roy, 1888–1948, vol. IV
Davis, Sir George Francis, 1883–1947, vol. IV
Davis, Col George M'Bride, 1846–1909, vol. I
Davis, Sir Gilbert, 2nd Bt, 1901–1973, vol. VII
Davis, Sir Godfrey, 1890–1968, vol. VI
Davis, Lt-Col Gronow John, 1869–1919, vol. II
Davis, H. Haldin; *see* Haldin-Davis.
Davis, Lt-Col Harold James Norman, 1882–1960, vol. V
Davis, Henry John B.; *see* Banks-Davis.
Davis, Henry William Banks, 1833–1914, vol. I
Davis, Henry William Carless, 1874–1928, vol. II
Davis, Sir Herbert, 1891–1972, vol. VII
Davis, Herbert John, 1893–1967, vol. VI
Davis, Captain Herbert Ludlow, 1887–1951, vol. V
Davis, James; *see* Hall, Owen.
Davis, James Corbett, 1870–1957, vol. V
Davis, James Richard A.; *see* Ainsworth-Davis.
Davis, Col John, 1834–1902, vol. I
Davis, John Creyghton A.; *see* Ainsworth-Davis.
Davis, John King, 1884–1967, vol. VI
Davis, John Merle, 1875–1960, vol. V
Davis, John Samuel Champion, 1859–1926, vol. II
Davis, John William, 1873–1955, vol. V
Davis, Leslie John, 1899–1980, vol. VII
Davis, Lucien, 1860–1941, vol. IV
Davis, Dame Margaret; *see* Rutherford, Dame M.
Davis, Sir Mortimer Barnett, 1866–1928, vol. II
Davis, Lt-Col Nathaniel N.; *see* Newnham-Davis.
Davis, Rt Rev. Nathaniel William Newnham, 1903–1966, vol. VI
Davis, Nicholas Darnell, 1846–1915, vol. I (A)
Davis, Hon. Norman H., *died* 1944, vol. IV

Davis, R. Bramwell, 1849–1923, vol. II
Davis, Ralph, 1915–1978, vol. VII
Davis, Richard Harding, 1864–1916, vol. II
Davis, Sir Robert Henry, 1870–1965, vol. VI
Davis, Maj.-Gen. Ronald Albert B.; see Bramwell Davis.
Davis, Rushworth Kennard, 1883–1969, vol. VI
Davis, Sir Spencer; see Davis, Sir S. S.
Davis, Sir (Steuart) Spencer, 1875–1950, vol. IV
Davis, Hon. Thomas C., 1889–1960, vol. V
Davis, Thomas Frederick, 1891–1974, vol. VII
Davis, Rev. Canon Thomas Henry, 1867–1947, vol. IV
Davis, Val, 1854–1930, vol. III
Davis, Vernon Mansfield, 1855–1931, vol. III
Davis, Major William Hathaway, 1881–1928, vol. II (A), vol. III
Davis, William Morris, 1850–1934, vol. III
Davis-Goff, Sir Ernest William; see Goff.
Davis-Goff, Sir Herbert William; see Goff.
Davis-Goff, Sir William Goff; see Goff.
Davison, Archibald Thompson, 1883–1961, vol. VI
Davison, Charles, 1858–1940, vol. III
Davison, Charles Stewart, 1855–1942, vol. IV (A), vol. V
Davison, Major Douglas Stewart, 1888–1929, vol. III
Davison, Frederick Charles, 1851–1935, vol. III
Davison, Rev. Gilderoy, 1892–1954, vol. V
Davison, Mrs J. W.; see Goddard, Arabella.
Davison, John Armstrong, 1906–1966, vol. VI
Davison, John Clarke, 1875–1946, vol. IV
Davison, John Emanuel, 1870–1927, vol. II
Davison, Rt Hon. Sir Joseph, 1868–1948, vol. IV
Davison, Maj.-Gen. Kenneth Stewart, 1856–1934, vol. III
Davison, Rev. Leslie, 1906–1972, vol. VII
Davison, Ralph, 1914–1977, vol. VII
Davison, Sir Ronald Conway, 1884–1958, vol. V
Davison, T. Raffles, 1853–1937, vol. III
Davison, Rev. Canon William Holmes, 1884–1955, vol. V
Davison, William Theophilus, 1846–1935, vol. III
Davisson, Clinton J., 1881–1958, vol. V
Davitt, Michael, 1846–1906, vol. I
Davray, Henry D., 1873–1944, vol. IV
Davson, Sir Charles Simon, 1857–1933, vol. III
Davson, Sir Edward, 1st Bt, died 1937, vol. III
Davson, Lt-Col Harry Miller, 1872–1961, vol. VI
Davson, Sir Henry Katz, 1830–1909, vol. I
Davson, Lt-Col Sir Ivan Buchanan, 1884–1947, vol. IV
Davy, Col Cecil William, 1868–1957, vol. V
Davy, Francis Herbert Mountjoy Nelson H.; see Humphrey-Davy.
Davy, Georges Ambroise, 1883–1976, vol. VII
Davy, Sir Henry, 1855–1922, vol. II
Davy, Sir James Stewart, 1848–1915, vol. I (A)
Davy, Joseph B.; see Burtt Davy.
Davy, Lila, 1873–1949, vol. IV
Davy, Maurice John Bernard, 1892–1950, vol. IV
Davy, Lt-Col Philip Claude Tresilian, 1877–1951, vol. V
Davy, Richard, 1838–1920, vol. II

Davy, Sir William, 1863–1939, vol. III
Davys, Rev. Owen William, died 1914, vol. I
Daw, Sir John Edward, 1866–1959, vol. V
Daw, Sydney Ernest Henry, 1897–1963, vol. VI
Daw, Sir William Herbert, 1859–1941, vol. IV
Dawbarn, Charles, 1871–1925, vol. II
Dawbarn, Graham Richards, 1893–1976, vol. VII
Dawber, Sir Guy, 1861–1938, vol. III
Dawe, Sir Arthur James, 1891–1950, vol. IV
Dawe, Carlton, died 1935, vol. III
Dawes, Sir (Albert) Cecil, 1890–1959, vol. V
Dawes, Sir Cecil; see Dawes, Sir A. C.
Dawes, Brig.-Gen. Charles Gates, 1865–1951, vol. V
Dawes, Edgar Rowland, 1902–1973, vol. VII
Dawes, Sir Edwyn Sandys, 1838–1903, vol. I
Dawes, Lt-Col George William Patrick, 1880–1960, vol. V
Dawes, Brig. Hugh Frank, 1884–1965, vol. VI
Dawes, James Arthur, 1866–1921, vol. II
Dawes, Rt Rev. Nathaniel, 1843–1910, vol. I
Dawes, William Charles, 1865–1920, vol. II
Dawkins, Lady Bertha Mabel, 1866–1943, vol. IV
Dawkins, Charles John Massey, 1905–1975, vol. VII
Dawkins, Maj.-Gen. Sir Charles Tyrwhitt, 1858–1919, vol. II
Dawkins, Charles William, 1870–1948, vol. IV
Dawkins, Sir Clinton Edward, 1859–1905, vol. I
Dawkins, Brig.-Gen. Henry Stopford, 1856–1933, vol. III
Dawkins, Sir Horace Christian, 1867–1944, vol. IV
Dawkins, Col John Wyndham George, 1861–1913, vol. I
Dawkins, Richard MacGillivray, 1871–1955, vol. V
Dawkins, Sir William Boyd, 1837–1929, vol. III
Dawnay, Col Alan Geoffrey Charles, 1888–1938, vol. III
Dawnay, Sir Archibald Davis, died 1919, vol. II
Dawnay, Lt-Col Cuthbert Henry, 1891–1964, vol. VI
Dawnay, Maj.-Gen. Sir David, 1903–1971, vol. VII
Dawnay, Hon. Eustace Henry, 1850–1928, vol. II (A), vol. III
Dawnay, Maj.-Gen. Guy Payan, 1878–1952, vol. V
Dawnay, Major Hon. Hugh, 1875–1914, vol. I
Dawnay, Lt-Col Hon. Lewis Payn, 1846–1910, vol. I
Dawnay, Hon. William Frederick, 1851–1904, vol. I
Dawood, Khan Sahib Sir Adamjee Hajee, died 1948, vol. IV
Dawson of Penn, 1st Viscount, 1864–1945, vol. IV
Dawson, A. J., 1872–1951, vol. V
Dawson, Very Rev. Abraham Dawson, 1826–1905, vol. I
Dawson, Aimée Evelyn, (Lady Dawson), died 1946, vol. IV
Dawson, Albert, 1866–1930, vol. III
Dawson, Col Algernon Cecil, 1849–1934, vol. III
Dawson, Alistair Benedict, 1922–1978, vol. VII
Dawson, Sir Arthur James, 1859–1943, vol. IV
Dawson, Maj.-Gen. Arthur Peel, 1888–1958, vol. V
Dawson, Sir (Arthur) Trevor, 1st Bt (cr 1920), 1866–1931, vol. III

Dawson, Sir Benjamin, 1st Bt (*cr* 1929), 1878–1966, vol. VI
Dawson, Sir Bernard; *see* Dawson, Sir J. B.
Dawson, Christopher, 1889–1970, vol. VI
Dawson, Coningsby, 1883–1959, vol. V
Dawson, Brig.-Gen. Sir Douglas Frederick Rawdon, 1854–1933, vol. III
Dawson, Hon. Edward Stanley, 1843–1919, vol. II
Dawson, Rev. Edwin Collas, *died* 1925, vol. II
Dawson, Gen. Francis, 1827–1911, vol. I
Dawson, Captain Francis Evelyn M.; *see* Massy-Dawson.
Dawson, Frank Harold, 1896–1972, vol. VII
Dawson, Lt-Col Frederick Stewart, *died* 1920, vol. II
Dawson, Geoffrey, 1874–1944, vol. IV
Dawson, George Mercer, 1849–1901, vol. I
Dawson, George W., 1868–1959, vol. V
Dawson, Air Vice-Marshal Grahame George, *died* 1944, vol. IV
Dawson, Col Harry Leonard, 1854–1920, vol. II
Dawson, Harry Medforth, 1875–1939, vol. III
Dawson, Lt-Col Henry King, 1871–1941, vol. IV
Dawson, Comdr Sir Hugh Trevor, 2nd Bt (*cr* 1920), 1893–1976, vol. VII
Dawson, Hugh W., *died* 1939, vol. III
Dawson, Sir J. William, 1820–1899, vol. I
Dawson, James Alexander, 1880–1956, vol. V
Dawson, Rev. James Edward le Strange, 1853–1930, vol. III
Dawson, John Miles, 1871–1948, vol. IV
Dawson, Sir (Joseph) Bernard, 1883–1965, vol. VI
Dawson, (Sir) Lawrence Saville, 2nd Bt (*cr* 1929), 1908–1974, vol. VII
Dawson, Lucy, *died* 1958, vol. V
Dawson, M. Damer, 1875–1920, vol. II
Dawson, Nelson, *died* 1941, vol. IV
Dawson, Rear-Adm. Sir Oswald Henry, 1882–1950, vol. IV
Dawson, Peter, 1882–1961, vol. VI
Dawson, Sir Philip, *died* 1938, vol. III
Dawson, Richard Cecil, 1865–1955, vol. V
Dawson, Brig.-Gen. Robert, 1861–1930, vol. III
Dawson, Robert Arthur, *died* 1948, vol. IV
Dawson, Maj.-Gen. Robert Boyd, 1916–1977, vol. VII
Dawson, Robert MacGregor, 1895–1958, vol. V
Dawson, Col Rupert George, 1887–1975, vol. VII
Dawson, Sidney Stanley, *died* 1926, vol. II
Dawson, Lt-Col Thomas Henry, 1878–1956, vol. V
Dawson, Sir Trevor; *see* Dawson, Sir A. T.
Dawson, Sir Vernon, 1881–1958, vol. V
Dawson, Maj.-Gen. Vesey John, 1853–1930, vol. III
Dawson, Warren Royal, 1888–1968, vol. VI
Dawson, Warrington, 1878–1962, vol. VI
Dawson, Comdr William, 1831–1911, vol. I
Dawson, William Harbutt, 1860–1948, vol. IV
Dawson, Rev. William James, 1854–1928, vol. II
Dawson, William Richard, 1864–1950, vol. IV
Dawson, Major William Robert Aufrère, 1891–1918, vol. II
Dawson, Rev. Canon William Rodgers, 1871–1936, vol. III
Dawson, William Siegfried, 1891–1975, vol. VII

Dawson Scott, Catharine Amy, *died* 1934, vol. III
Dawson-Scott, Gen. Robert Nicholl, 1836–1922, vol. II
Dawson-Walker, Rev. Dawson, 1868–1934, vol. III
Day, Sir (Albert) Cecil, 1885–1963, vol. VI
Day, Sir Albert James Taylor, 1892–1972, vol. VII
Day, Rev. Alfred E. Bloxsome, 1873–1951, vol. V
Day, Vice-Adm. Sir Archibald, 1899–1970, vol. VI
Day, Bernard, *died* 1952, vol. V
Day, Sir Cecil; *see* Day, Sir A. C.
Day, Charles, 1868–1949, vol. IV
Day, Rev. Charles V. P., 1864–1922, vol. II
Day, Clive, 1871–1951, vol. V
Day, Edith, 1896–1971, vol. VII
Day, Edmund Ezra, 1883–1951, vol. V
Day, Rev. Edward Rouviere, 1867–1948, vol. IV
Day, Edward Victor Grace, 1896–1968, vol. VI
Day, Rev. Ernest Hermitage, 1866–1946, vol. IV
Day, Frank Parker, 1881–1950, vol. IV (A)
Day, Harold Benjamin, 1880–1959, vol. V
Day, Col Harry, 1880–1939, vol. III
Day, Rev. Henry, 1865–1951, vol. V
Day, Rt Rev. Mgr James, 1869–1946, vol. IV
Day, James Nathaniel Da' Russell, 1849–1933, vol. III
Day, James Roscoe, *died* 1923, vol. II
Day, John Adam, 1901–1966, vol. VI
Day, Rt Hon. Sir John Charles, 1826–1908, vol. I
Day, Rev. John Duncan, 1882–1954, vol. V
Day, Most Rev. John Godfrey Fitzmaurice, 1874–1938, vol. III
Day, Lewis Foreman, 1845–1910, vol. I
Day, Rev. Louis Ernest, 1866–1935, vol. III
Day, Rt Rev. Maurice, 1843–1923, vol. II
Day, Rt Rev. Maurice FitzGerald, 1816–1904, vol. I
Day, Col Maurice Fitzmaurice, *died* 1952, vol. V
Day, Very Rev. Maurice William, 1858–1916, vol. II
Day, Lt-Col Noel Arthur Lacy, 1882–1932, vol. III
Day, Samuel Henry, 1854–1944, vol. IV
Day, Captain Selwyn Mitchell, 1873–1938, vol. III
Day, Theodora, *died* 1976, vol. VII
Day, W. Cave, 1862–1924, vol. II
Day-Lewis, Cecil, 1904–1972, vol. VII
Daynes, John Norman, 1884–1966, vol. VI
Dayrell, Elphinstone, 1869–1917, vol. II
Deacon, Rev. A. W. N., 1847–1915, vol. I
Deacon, George Frederick, 1843–1909, vol. I
Deacon, Gerald John C.; *see* Cole-Deacon.
Deacon, Sir Henry Wade, 1852–1932, vol. III
Deacon, John Francis William, 1859–1941, vol. IV
Deacon, Stuart, 1868–1947, vol. IV
Deacon, Walter, *died* 1955, vol. V
Deacon, Col William Thomas, 1850–1916, vol. II (A), vol. II
Deadman, H. E., 1843–1925, vol. II
Deakin, Hon. Alfred, 1856–1919, vol. II
Deakin, Rt Hon. Arthur, 1890–1955, vol. V
Deakin, Ralph, 1888–1952, vol. V
Dealtry, Lawrence Percival, 1896–1963, vol. VI
Dealy, Jane M.; *see* Lewis, Jane.
Dealy, Brig.-Gen. John Anderson, 1865–1935, vol. III

De Amicis, Edmondo, 1846–1908, vol. I
Dean, Arthur, 1903–1968, vol. VI
Dean, Hon. Sir Arthur, 1893–1970, vol. VI
Dean, Arthur Edis, 1883–1961, vol. VI
Dean, Arthur Wellesley, 1857–1929, vol. III
Dean, Sir Arthur William Henry, 1892–1976, vol. VII
Dean, Bashford, 1867–1928, vol. II
Dean, Basil, *died* 1978, vol. VII
Dean, Comdr Brian, 1895–1976, vol. VII
Dean, Engr Rear-Adm. Francis Edward, 1881–1965, vol. VI
Dean, Frederic William Charles, 1867–1942, vol. IV
Dean, Frederick William, 1884–1959, vol. V
Dean, George, 1863–1914, vol. I
Dean, Brig.-Gen. George Henry, 1859–1953, vol. V
Dean, Gertrude Mary, 1878–1962, vol. VI
Dean, Gordon Evans, 1905–1958, vol. V
Dean, Henry Edwin, 1881–1973, vol. VII
Dean, Henry Percy, *died* 1931, vol. III
Dean, Henry Roy, 1879–1961, vol. VI
Dean, Herbert Samuel, 1870–1942, vol. IV
Dean, Sir Maurice Joseph, 1906–1978, vol. VII
Dean, Lt-Comdr Percy Thompson, 1877–1939, vol. III
Dean, William Reginald, 1896–1973, vol. VII
Dean-Leslie, John, 1860–1946, vol. IV
Deane, Rev. Anthony Charles, 1870–1946, vol. IV
Deane, Rev. Canon Arthur Mackreth, 1837–1926, vol. II
Deane, Augustus Henry, 1851–1928, vol. II
Deane, Maj.-Gen. Sir Dennis, 1874–1953, vol. V
Deane, Major Donald Victor, 1902–1978, vol. VII
Deane, Edgar Ernest, 1860–1933, vol. III
Deane, Rt Rev. Frederic Llewellyn, 1868–1952, vol. V
Deane, Sir George Campbell, 1873–1948, vol. IV (A), vol. V
Deane, Col George Williams, 1850–1931, vol. III
Deane, Lt-Col Sir Harold Arthur, 1854–1908, vol. I
Deane, Sir Henry Bargrave, 1846–1919, vol. II
Deane, Hermann Frederick Williams, 1858–1921, vol. II
Deane, Major James, 1863–1942, vol. IV
Deane, Rt Hon. Sir James Parker, 1812–1902, vol. I
Deane, Nora Bryan, 1902–1973, vol. VII
Deane, Percy Edgar, 1890–1946, vol. IV
Deane, Captain Richard Burton, 1848–1930, vol. III
Deane, Col Richard Woodforde, 1859–1940, vol. III
Deane, Lt-Col Robert, 1879–1969, vol. VI
Deane, Col Thomas, 1841–1907, vol. I
Deane, Sir Thomas Manly, 1851–1933, vol. III
Deane, Sir Thomas Newenham, 1830–1899, vol. I
Deane, Walter Meredith, 1840–1906, vol. I
Deane, William, 1894–1972, vol. VII
Deanesly, Margaret, 1885–1977, vol. VII
Deans, Harris, 1886–1961, vol. VI
Deans, Richard Storry, *died* 1938, vol. III
Deans, Engr-Rear-Adm. William Jordan, *died* 1947, vol. IV

Dearbergh, Geoffrey Frederick, 1924–1979, vol. VII
Dearden, Harold, 1883–1962, vol. VI
Deare, Maj.-Gen. Benjamin Hobbs, 1867–1940, vol. III
Dearing, George Edmund, 1911–1968, vol. VI
Dearlove, Rev. William John, 1869–1935, vol. III
Dearmer, Mabel, 1872–1915, vol. I
Dearmer, Rev. Percy, 1867–1936, vol. III
Deas, J. A. Charlton, 1874–1951, vol. V
Dease, Edmund Gerald, 1829–1904, vol. I
Dease, Major Edmund J., 1861–1945, vol. IV
Dease, Col Sir Gerald Richard, 1831–1903, vol. I
Deasy, Major Henry Hugh Peter, 1866–1947, vol. IV
De'Ath, Lt-Col Ian Dudley, 1918–1960, vol. V
De Azcarate, Pablo; *see* Azcarate.
De Bathe, Sir Christopher Albert, 6th Bt, 1905–1941, vol. IV
De Bathe, Gen. Sir Henry Perceval, 4th Bt, 1823–1907, vol. I
De Bathe, Sir Hugo Gerald, 5th Bt, 1871–1940, vol. III
De Bathe, Patrick Wynne, 1876–1930, vol. III
de Bazus, Baroness; *see* Leslie, Mrs Frank.
de Beer, Sir Gavin Rylands, 1899–1972, vol. VII
de Belabre, Louis Fradin, Baron, 1862–1945, vol. IV
Debenham, Sir Ernest Ridley, 1st Bt, 1865–1952, vol. V
Debenham, Frank, 1883–1965, vol. VI
Debenham, Sir Piers Kenrick, 2nd Bt, 1904–1964, vol. VI
De Bernochi, Francesco, 1887–1962, vol. VI
de Berry, Brig.-Gen. Philip Patrick Evelyn, 1872–1938, vol. III
De Bildt, Baron, 1850–1931, vol. III
de Blank, Most Rev. Joost, 1908–1968, vol. VI
de Blaquiere, 6th Baron, 1856–1920, vol. II
de Blogue, Rev. Oswald William Charles, 1874–1959, vol. V
de Boer, Henry Speldewinde, 1889–1957, vol. V
De Boinville, Rev. Basil William C.; *see* Chastel De Boinville.
Debono, Massimiliano, 1852–1932, vol. III
De Boucherville, Hon. Sir Charles Eugene Boucher, 1822–1915, vol. I
de Brath, Lt-Gen. Sir Ernest, 1858–1933, vol. III
de Brett, Hon. Brig.-Gen. Harry Simonds, 1870–1965, vol. VI
De Brigard, Camilo, 1906–1972, vol. VII
de Bruyne, Pieter Louis; *see* Bruyne.
De Bucy, 11th Marquess, *died* 1929, vol. III
de Bunsen, Rt Hon. Sir Maurice William Ernest, 1st Bt, 1852–1932, vol. III
de Burgh, Captain Charles, 1886–1973, vol. VII
de Burgh, Gen. Sir Eric, 1881–1973, vol. VII
de Burgh, Lt-Col Thomas John, 1851–1931, vol. III
de Burgh, Col Ulick George Campbell, 1855–1922, vol. II
de Burgh, William George, 1866–1943, vol. IV
Debus, Heinrich, 1824–1915, vol. I (A)
Debussy, Claude Achille, 1862–1918, vol. II
De Butts, Brig. Frederick Cromie, 1888–1977, vol. VII

Debye, Peter Joseph William, 1884–1966, vol. VI
de Candole, Rt Rev. Henry Handley Vully, 1895–1971, vol. VII
de Candole, Very Rev. Henry Lawe Corry Vully, 1868–1933, vol. III
de Candolle, Maj.-Gen. Raymond, died 1935, vol. III
de Capell Brooke, Sir Edward Geoffrey, 6th Bt, 1880–1968, vol. VI
Decarie, Hon. Jeremie L., 1870–1927, vol. II
de Carteret, Rt Rev. George Frederick Cecil, 1886–1932, vol. III
de Carteret, Samuel Laurence, 1885–1956, vol. V
De Celles, Alfred Duclos, 1844–1925, vol. II
de Chair, Adm. Sir Dudley Rawson Stratford, 1864–1958, vol. V
de Chair, Rev. Frederick Blackett, 1888–1932, vol. III
Dechamps, Jules, 1888–1968, vol. VI
de Chazal, Hon. Pierre Edmond, 1837–1914, vol. I (A)
Dechene, Hon. F. G. M., died 1902, vol. I
Decie, Brig.-Gen. Cyril Prescott-, 1865–1953, vol. V
Decies, 4th Baron, 1865–1910, vol. I
Decies, 5th Baron, 1866–1944, vol. IV
de Clifford, 25th Baron, 1884–1909, vol. I
de Colyar, Henry Anselm, died 1925, vol. II
de Comarmond, Sir Joseph Henri Maxime, 1899–1957, vol. V
Decoppet, Camille, 1862–1925, vol. II
de Cordova, Rudolph, died 1941, vol. IV
de Courcy-Perry, Sir Gerald Raoul, 1836–1903, vol. I
De Courville, Albert Pierre, (Albert Peter Hugh), 1887–1960, vol. V
de Crespigny, Captain Claude C.; see Champion de Crespigny.
de Crespigny, Sir Claude C.; see Champion de Crespigny.
de Crespigny, Brig.-Gen. Sir Claude Raul C.; see Champion de Crespigny.
de Crespigny, Col Sir (Constantine) Trent C.; see Champion-de Crespigny.
de Crespigny, Comdr Sir Frederick Philip C.; see Champion de Crespigny.
de Crespigny, Lt-Col George Harrison C.; see Champion de Crespigny.
de Crespigny, Sir Henry C.; see Champion de Crespigny.
de Crespigny, Air Vice-Marshal Hugh Vivian C.; see Champion de Crespigny.
de Crespigny, Rose C.; see Champion de Crespigny.
de Crespigny, Col Sir Trent C.; see Champion-de Crespigny.
de Crespigny, Sir Vivian Tyrell C.; see Champion de Crespigny.
De Curel, Viscomte François, 1854–1928, vol. II
Deed, Rev. Canon John George, 1842–1923, vol. II
Deedes, Rev. Arthur Gordon, 1861–1916, vol. II
Deedes, Ven. Brook, 1847–1922, vol. II
Deedes, Rev. Cecil, 1843–1920, vol. II
Deedes, Gen. Sir Charles Parker, 1879–1969, vol. VI

Deedes, John Gordon, 1892–1962, vol. VI
Deedes, Percy Gordon, 1899–1973, vol. VII
Deedes, Lt-Gen. Sir Ralph Bouverie, 1890–1954, vol. V
Deedes, Maj.-Gen. William Henry, 1839–1915, vol. I (A)
Deedes, Brig.-Gen. Sir Wyndham Henry, 1883–1956, vol. V
Deeley, Sir Anthony Meyrick M.; see Mallaby-Deeley.
Deeley, Sir Guy Meyrick Mallaby M.; see Mallaby-Deeley.
Deeley, Sir Harry Mallaby M.; see Mallaby-Deeley.
Deeping, (George) Warwick, died 1950, vol. IV
Deeping, Warwick; see Deeping, G. W.
Deer, George, 1890–1974, vol. VII
Deerhurst, Viscount; George William Reginald Victor Coventry, 1900–1927, vol. II
Deering, William Henry, 1848–1925, vol. II
Deeves, Thomas William, 1893–1977, vol. VII
de Falbe, Brig. Gen. Vigant William, 1867–1940, vol. III
De Falla, Manuel, 1876–1946, vol. IV
de Ferranti, Sebastian Ziani, 1864–1930, vol. III
de Ferranti, Sir Vincent Ziani, 1893–1980, vol. VII
De Ferrieres, 3rd Baron, 1823–1908, vol. I
De Filippi, Cav. Filippo, 1869–1938, vol. III
de Fonblanque, Maj.-Gen. Philip, 1885–1940, vol. III
De Fonseka, Sir (Deepal) Susanta, 1900–1963, vol. VI
De Fonseka, Sir Susanta; see De Fonseka, Sir D. S.
De Foville, Alfred, 1842–1913, vol. I
de Frece, Lady; see Tilley, Vesta.
de Frece, Sir Walter, 1870–1935, vol. III
De Freitas, Sir Anthony, 1869–1940, vol. III
De Freycinet, C. L., died 1923, vol. II
De Freyne, 4th Baron, 1855–1913, vol. I
De Freyne, 5th Baron, 1879–1915, vol. I
De Freyne, 6th Baron, 1884–1935, vol. III
Degacher, Maj.-Gen. Henry James, died 1902, vol. I
de Gale, Hugh Otway, 1891–1966, vol. VI
De Garston, Edward Mervyn, 1869–1939, vol. III
Degas, Hilaire Germain Edgard, 1834–1917, vol. II
De Gasperi, Alcide, 1881–1954, vol. V
de Gaulle, Gén. Charles André Joseph Marie, 1890–1970, vol. VI
De Geer, Baron Gerard, 1858–1943, vol. IV
De Gerlache De Gomery, Baron, 1866–1934, vol. III
de Gex, Col Francis J., 1861–1917, vol. II
De Giberne, Agnes; see Giberne, Agnes.
De Glanville, Sir Oscar James Lardner, died 1942, vol. IV (A), vol. V
De Glehn, Wilfrid Gabriel, 1870–1951, vol. V
De Greef, Arthur, 1862–1940, vol. III (A), vol. IV
de Grey, Nigel, 1886–1951, vol. V
de Grunwald, Anatole, 1910–1967, vol. VI
De Gruyther, Leslie, died 1937, vol. III
de Guingand, Maj.-Gen. Sir Francis W., 1900–1979, vol. VII
d'Egville, Major Alan Hervey, 1891–1951, vol. V

d'Egville, Sir Howard, *died* 1965, vol. VI

de Gylpyn, Very Rev. Edwin, 1821–1906, vol. I

de Haan, Edward Peter Nayler, 1919–1977, vol. VII

de Haas, Wander Johannes, 1878–1960, vol. V

Dehan, Richard; *see* Graves, Clotilde I. M.

de Havilland, Captain Sir Geoffrey, 1882–1965, vol. VI

de Havilland, Col Thomas Lyttleton, 1872–1939, vol. III

Dehlavi, Sir Ali Mahomed Khan, 1871–1952, vol. V

Dehlavi, Samiulla Khan, 1913–1976, vol. VII

Dehn, Adolf Arthur, 1895–1968, vol. VI

Dehn, Paul Edward, 1912–1976, vol. VII

de Hochepied, 10th Baron, 1900–1945, vol. IV

de Hochepied Larpent, Maj.-Gen. Lionel Henry Planta, 1834–1907, vol. I

de Hoghton, Sir Anthony; *see* de Hoghton, Sir H. P. A. M.

de Hoghton, Sir Cuthbert, 12th Bt, 1880–1958, vol. V

de Hoghton, Sir (Henry Philip) Anthony (Mary), 13th Bt, 1919–1978, vol. VII

de Hoghton, Sir James, 11th Bt, 1851–1938, vol. III

de Horsey, Adm. Sir Algernon Frederick Rous, 1827–1922, vol. II

de Horsey, Adm. Spencer, 1863–1937, vol. III

De Horsey, Lt-Gen. William Henry Beaumont, 1826–1915, vol. I

Deichmann, Baron Adolph Wilhelm, 1831–1907, vol. I

Deighton, Frederick, 1854–1924, vol. II

de Jersey, Rear-Adm. Gilbert Carey, 1905–1974, vol. VII

de Jersey, Rt Rev. Norman Stewart, 1866–1934, vol. III

De Jersey, Col William Grant, 1853–1935, vol. III

de Joux, Lt-Col John Sedley Newton, 1876–1949, vol. IV

De Kalb, Courtenay, 1861–1931, vol. III

de Kantzow, Comdr Arthur Henry, *died* 1928, vol. I

de Kerillis, Henri, 1889–1958, vol. V

De Keyser, Sir Polydore, 1832–1897, vol. I

Dekobra, Maurice, 1885–1973, vol. VII

de la Bedoyere, Count Michael, 1900–1973, vol. VII

De la Bere, Henry D., 1861–1937, vol. III

De La Bere, Brig. Sir Ivan, 1893–1970, vol. VI

de la Bere, Captain Richard Norman, 1869–1922, vol. II

De la Bère, Sir Rupert, 1st Bt, 1893–1978, vol. VII

de la Bere, Stephen B.; *see* Baghot de la Bere.

de Labilliere, Rt Rev. Paul Fulcrand Delacour, 1879–1946, vol. IV

Delacombe, Lt-Col Addis, 1865–1941, vol. IV

Delacourt-Smith, Baron (Life Peer); Charles George Percy Smith, 1917–1972, vol. VII

Delafaye, Sir Louis Victor, 1842–1920, vol. II

de la Ferte, Air Chief Marshal Sir Philip Bennet J.; *see* Joubert de la Ferte.

Delafield, E. M.; *see* Dashwood, Elizabeth M.

Delafield, Max Everard, 1886–1974, vol. VII

de Lafontaine, Lt-Col Henry Philip L. C.; *see* Cart de Lafontaine.

Delaforce, Brig.-Gen. Edwin Francis, 1870–1954, vol. V

de La Fosse, Sir Claude Fraser, 1868–1950, vol. IV

de La Fosse, Maj.-Gen. Henry George, *died* 1905, vol. I

Delage, Hon. Cyrille Fraser, 1869–1957, vol. V

Delage, Yves, 1854–1920, vol. II

De la Gorce, Pierre, 1846–1934, vol. III

Delahaye, Col James Viner, 1890–1948, vol. IV

de la Hey, Rev. Richard Willis, 1872–1942, vol. IV

Delalle, Rt Rev. Henry, 1869–1949, vol. IV

Delamain, Lt-Gen. Sir Walter Sinclair, 1862–1932, vol. III

De La Mare, Walter, 1873–1956, vol. V

Delamere, 3rd Baron, 1870–1931, vol. III

Delamere, 4th Baron, 1900–1979, vol. VII

De La Mothe, Sir Joseph Terence, 1876–1953, vol. V

Delamothe, Hon. Sir Peter Roylance, 1906–1973, vol. VII

De Lancey Forth, Lt-Col Nowell Barnard, 1879–1933, vol. III

Deland, Margaret, 1857–1945, vol. IV

Delaney, Colin John, 1897–1969, vol. VI (AII)

De Laney, Brig.-Gen. Matthew A., 1874–1936, vol. III

de Lange, Daniel, 1841–1918, vol. II

Delano, William Adams, 1874–1960, vol. V

Delano-Osborne, Maj.-Gen. Osborne Herbert, 1879–1958, vol. V

Delany, Mgr Patrick, 1853–1926, vol. II

Delany, Rev. William, 1835–1924, vol. II

Delany, William P., 1855–1916, vol. II

Delap, Rev. Alexander, *died* 1906, vol. I

Delap, Col George Goslett, 1873–1945, vol. IV

de la Pasture, Elizabeth Lydia Rosabelle, (Mrs Henry de la Pasture); *see* Clifford, E. L. R.

de la Poer, Edmond, 1841–1915, vol. I

de la Poer, John William Rivallon de Poher, 1882–1939, vol. III

De la Pryme, Ven. Alexander George, 1870–1935, vol. III

de Lara, Adelina, (Lottie Adelina de Lara Shipwright), 1872–1961, vol. VI

De Lara, Isidore, 1858–1935, vol. III

de la Ramée, Marie Louise; *see* Ouida.

Delarey, Gen. Hon. Jacobus Hendrik, 1848–1914, vol. I

Delargey, His Eminence Cardinal Reginald John, 1914–1979, vol. VII

de Largie, Hon. Hugh, 1859–1947, vol. IV

Delargy, Captain Hugh James, 1908–1976, vol. VII

de la Roche, Mazo, 1885–1961, vol. VI

de la Rue, Sir Ernest, 1852–1929, vol. III

de la Rue, Sir Evelyn Andros, 2nd Bt, 1879–1950, vol. IV

de la Rue, Stuart Andros, 1883–1927, vol. II

de la Rue, Sir Thomas Andros, 1st Bt, 1849–1911, vol. I

de la Rue, Warren William, 1847–1921, vol. II

de Laszlo, Patrick David, 1909–1980, vol. VII

de Laszowski-Gerard, Emily; *see* Gerard.

de Lattre de Tassigny, Général d'Armée Jean Joseph Marie Gabriel, 1889–1952, vol. V de Lavis-Trafford, Marcus Antonius Johnston, 1880–1960, vol. V

De la Voye, Brig.-Gen. Alexander Edwin, 1871–1940, vol. III

Delavoye, Col Alexander Marin, 1845–1917, vol. II

De La Warr, 8th Earl, 1869–1915, vol. I (A)

De La Warr, 9th Earl, 1900–1976, vol. VII

Delbridge, Rt Rev. Graham Richard, 1917–1980, vol. VII

Delcasse, Théophile, 1852–1923, vol. II

Delderfield, Ronald Frederick, 1912–1972, vol. VII

Deledda, Grazia, 1875–1936, vol. III

De Lemos, Charles Herman, 1855–1928, vol. II (A), vol. III

Delepine, Sheridan, 1855–1921, vol. II

Delevingne, Sir Malcolm, 1868–1950, vol. IV

De L'Hôpital, René le Brun (Count), 1877–1929, vol. III

De L'Isle and Dudley, 2nd Baron, 1828–1898, vol. I

De L'Isle and Dudley, 3rd Baron, 1853–1922, vol. II

De L'Isle and Dudley, 4th Baron, 1854–1945, vol. IV

De L'Isle and Dudley, 5th Baron, 1859–1945, vol. IV

de Lisle, Gen. Sir Beauvoir, 1864–1955, vol. V

de Lisle, Edwin Joseph Lisle March Phillipps, 1852–1920, vol. II

de Lisle, Everard March Phillipps, died 1947, vol. IV

De Lisle, Brig.-Gen. George de Saumarez, 1862–1954, vol. V

De Lisle, Leopold Victor, 1826–1910, vol. I

de Lisser, Herbert George, 1878–1944, vol. IV

Delius, Frederick, 1862–1934, vol. III

Dell, Draycot Montagu, 1888–1940, vol. III

Dell, Ethel M., 1881–1939, vol. III

Della Taflia, Marchioness, died 1953, vol. V

Della Torre Alta, Il Marchese Albert Félix Schmitt, 1873–1954, vol. V

Deller, Alfred, 1912–1979, vol. VII

Deller, Sir Edwin, 1883–1936, vol. III

Deller, Captain Harold Arthur, 1897–1976, vol. VII

Delme-Radcliffe, Brig.-Gen. Sir Charles, 1864–1937, vol. III

Delme-Radcliffe, Sir Ralph Hubert John, 1877–1963, vol. VI

Delmege, Alfred Gideon, 1846–1923, vol. II

Delmer, (Denis) Sefton, 1904–1979, vol. VII

Delmer, Sefton; see Delmer, D. S.

de Longueuil, 8th Baron, 1856–1931, vol. III

de Longueuil, 9th Baron, 1861–1938, vol. III

De Lotbinière, Maj.-Gen. Alain Chartier Joly; see Joly De Lotbinière.

de Lotbinière, Brig.-Gen. Henri Gustave J.; see Joly de Lotbinière.

de Lotbinière, Hon. Sir Henry Gustave J.; see Joly de Lotbinière.

de Lotbiniere-Harwood, Charles Auguste; see Harwood.

de Loynes, John Barraclough, 1909–1969, vol. VI

Delpech, Reginald George Marius, 1881–1935, vol. III

Delprat, Guillaume Daniel, 1856–1937, vol. III

del Re, Cavaliere Arundel, 1892–1974, vol. VII

del Riego, Teresa, 1876–1968, vol. VI

del Tufo, Sir (Moroboë) Vincent, 1901–1961, vol. VI

Delury, Justin Sarsfield, 1884–1968, vol. VI

Delves, Robert Harvey Addington, 1873–1952, vol. V

Delysia, Alice, 1889–1979, vol. VII

de Marees-Van Swinderen, Jonkheer Rene; see Van Swinderen.

de Margerie, Emmanuel, 1862–1953, vol. V

de Margerie, Pierre, 1861–1942, vol. IV

de Mauley, 3rd Baron, 1843–1918, vol. II

de Mauley, 4th Baron, 1846–1945, vol. IV

de Mauley, 5th Baron, 1878–1962, vol. VI

De Mel, Sir Henry Lawson, 1877–1936, vol. III

De Mel, Most Rev. (Hiyanirindu) Lakdasa Jacob, 1902–1976, vol. VII

De Mel, Most Rev. Lakdasa Jacob; see De Mel, Most Rev. H. L. J.

de Mendieta, Rev. Emmanuel Alexandre A.; see Amand de Mendieta.

de Meric, Rear-Adm. Martin John Coucher, 1887–1943, vol. IV

Demers, Marie Joseph, 1871–1940, vol. III (A), vol. IV

Demetriadi, Sir Stephen, 1880–1952, vol. V

deMille, Cecil Blount, 1881–1959, vol. V

de Miranda, Comtesse; see Nilsson, Mme Christine.

De Mole, Lancelot Eldin, 1880–1950, vol. IV

de Moleyns, Thomas, 1807–1900, vol. I

de Moleyns, Maj.-Gen. Townsend Aremberg, 1838–1926, vol. II

de Montalt, 1st Earl, 1817–1905, vol. I

de Monte, Frank Thomas, 1879–1950, vol. IV

de Montherlant, Henry; see Montherlant.

de Montmorency, Sir Angus; see de Montmorency, Sir H. A.

de Montmorency, Hon. Francis Raymond, 1835–1910, vol. I

de Montmorency, Sir Geoffrey Fitzhervey, 1876–1955, vol. V

de Montmorency, Sir (Hervey) Angus, 16th Bt, 1888–1959, vol. V

de Montmorency, Major Hervey Guy Francis Edward, 1868–1942, vol. IV

de Montmorency, James Edward Geoffrey, 1866–1934, vol. III

De Montmorency, Captain John Pratt, 1873–1960, vol. V

de Montmorency, Sir Miles Fletcher, 17th Bt, 1893–1963, vol. VI

de Montmorency, Hon. Raymond Hervey, 1867–1900, vol. I

de Montmorency, Sir Reginald D'Alton Lodge, 18th Bt, 1899–1979, vol. VII

de Montmorency, Reymond Hervey, 1871–1938, vol. III

de Montmorency, Ven. Waller, 1841–1924, vol. II

De Morgan, William Frend, 1839–1917, vol. II

de Morley, 21st Baron, 1844–1918, vol. II

Dempsey, Sir Alexander, 1852–1920, vol. II

Dempsey, Gen. Sir Miles Christopher, 1896–1969, vol. VI

Dempster, Francis Erskine, 1858–1941, vol. IV

Dempster, Col Reginald Hawkins H.; *see* Hall-Dempster.

Denbigh, 9th Earl of, and Desmond, 8th Earl of, 1859–1939, vol. III

Denbigh, 10th Earl of, and Desmond, 9th Earl of, 1912–1966, vol. VI

Denby, Elizabeth Marian, *died* 1965, vol. VI

Denby, Sir Ellis, 1856–1939, vol. III

Dence, Ernest Martin, 1873–1937, vol. III

Dench, William George, 1888–1963, vol. VI

Dendy, Arthur, 1865–1925, vol. II

Dendy, Edward Evershed, 1861–1929, vol. III

Dendy, Mary, 1855–1933, vol. III

Dendy, Brig. Murray Heathfield, 1885–1951, vol. V

Dene, Col Arthur Pollard, *died* 1945, vol. IV

Deneke, Margaret Clara Adèle, 1882–1969, vol. VI

de Neuflize, Baron Jean, 1850–1928, vol. II

Deneys, Comdr James Godfrey Wood, 1897–1962, vol. VI

Denham, 1st Baron, 1886–1948, vol. IV

Denham, Algernon, *died* 1961, vol. VI

Denham, Hon. Digby Frank, 1859–1944, vol. IV

Denham, Sir Edward Brandis, 1876–1938, vol. III

Denham, Godfrey Charles, 1883–1956, vol. V

Denham, Harold Arthur, 1878–1921, vol. II

Denham, Henry George, 1880–1943, vol. IV

Denham, Humphrey John, 1893–1970, vol. VI

Denham, Sir James, *died* 1927, vol. II

Denham, William Smith, 1878–1964, vol. VI

Denham-White, Lt-Col Arthur; *see* White.

Denholm, John, 1853–1937, vol. III

Deniker, Joseph, 1852–1918, vol. II

Dening, Sir Esler; *see* Dening, Sir M. E.

Dening, Lt-Gen. Sir Lewis, 1848–1911, vol. I

Dening, Sir (Maberly) Esler, 1897–1977, vol. VII

Dening, Maj.-Gen. Roland, 1888–1978, vol. VII

Denis de Vitré, Col Percy Theodosius, 1870–1940, vol. III

Denison, Rear-Adm. Hon. Albert Denison Somerville, 1835–1903, vol. I

Denison, Captain Edward C., 1888–1960, vol. V

Denison, Col George Taylor, 1839–1925, vol. II

Denison, Hon. Harold Albert, 1856–1948, vol. IV

Denison, Captain Hon. Henry, 1849–1936, vol. III

Denison, Brig.-Gen. Henry, 1847–1938, vol. III

Denison, Rev. Henry Phipps, 1848–1940, vol. III

Denison, Sir Hugh Robert, 1865–1940, vol. III

Denison, Adm. John, 1853–1939, vol. III

Denison, Robert Beckett, 1879–1951, vol. V

Denison, Maj.-Gen. Septimus Julius Augustus, 1859–1937, vol. III

Denison, William Evelyn, 1843–1916, vol. II

Denison-Pender, Sir John Denison; *see* Pender.

de Niverville, Air Vice-Marshal Joseph Lionel Elphege Albert, 1897–1968, vol. VI (AII)

Denman, 3rd Baron, 1874–1954, vol. V

Denman, 4th Baron, 1905–1971, vol. VII

Denman, Lady; (Gertrude Mary), 1884–1954, vol. V

Denman, Sir Arthur, 1857–1931, vol. III

Denman, George Lewis, 1854–1929, vol. III

Denman, John Leopold, 1882–1975, vol. VII

Denman, Hon. Sir Richard Douglas, 1st Bt, 1876–1957, vol. V

Denne, Major William Henry, 1876–1917, vol. II

Dennehy, Sir Harold George, 1890–1956, vol. V

Dennehy, Maj.-Gen. Sir Thomas, 1829–1915, vol. I

Dennehy, William Francis, *died* 1918, vol. II (A), vol. III

Dennett, Richard Edward, 1857–1921, vol. II

Denney, Rev. James, 1856–1917, vol. II

Denning, Sir Howard, 1885–1943, vol. IV

Denning, Vice-Adm. Sir Norman Egbert, 1904–1979, vol. VII

Denning, William Frederick, 1848–1931, vol. III

Dennis, Mrs A. E. Forbes; *see* Bottome, Phyllis.

Dennis, Sir Alfred Hull, 1858–1947, vol. IV

Dennis, Geoffrey Pomeroy, 1892–1963, vol. VI

Dennis, Sir (Herbert) Raymond, 1878–1939, vol. III

Dennis, Rev. Canon Herbert Wesley, *died* 1938, vol. III

Dennis, Rev. James Shepard, 1842–1914, vol. I

Dennis, Surg.-Rear-Adm. John Jeffreys, 1858–1958, vol. V

Dennis, Col John Stoughton, 1856–1938, vol. III

Dennis, John William, 1865–1949, vol. IV

Dennis, Maj.-Gen. Meade Edward, 1893–1965, vol. VI

Dennis, Col Meade James Crosbie, 1865–1945, vol. IV

Dennis, Sir Raymond; *see* Dennis, Sir H. R.

Dennis, Ven. Thomas John, 1869–1917, vol. II

Dennis, Trevor, 1882–1950, vol. IV

Dennis, William, 1856–1920, vol. II

Dennison, Major Charles George, *born* 1844, vol. III

Dennison, Major Gilbert, 1883–1957, vol. V

Dennison, Robert, 1879–1951, vol. V

Dennison, Adm. Robert Lee, 1901–1980, vol. VII

Dennison, Thomas Andrews, 1906–1972, vol. VII

Denniss, Charles Sherwood, 1860–1917, vol. II

Denniss, Lt-Col Cyril Edmund Bartley B.; *see* Bartley-Denniss.

Denniss, Sir Edmund Robert Bartley B.; *see* Bartley-Denniss.

Denniss, George Hamson, 1854–1940, vol. III (A), vol. IV

Denniston, Alexander Guthrie, 1881–1961, vol. VI

Denniston, John Dewar, 1887–1949, vol. IV

Denniston, Hon. Sir John Edward, 1845–1919, vol. II

Denniston, Sir Robert, 1890–1946, vol. IV

Dennistoun, Lt-Col Ian Onslow, 1879–1938, vol. III

Dennistoun, Lt-Col James George, 1871–1939, vol. III

Dennistoun, Hon. Robert Maxwell, 1864–1952, vol. V

Denny, Sir Archibald, 1st Bt (*cr* 1913), 1860–1936, vol. III

Denny, Barbara Mary, (Mrs Edward Denny), 1880–1965, vol. VI

Denny, Captain Sir Cecil Edward, 6th Bt (*cr* 1782), 1850–1928, vol. II

Denny, Major Ernest Wriothesley, 1872–1949, vol. IV

Denny, Frederick Anthony, 1860–1941, vol. IV
Denny, Col Henry Cuthbert, 1858–1934, vol. III
Denny, Rev. Sir Henry Lyttelton Lyster, 7th Bt (cr 1782), 1878–1953, vol. V
Denny, Henry Samuel, died 1938, vol. III
Denny, Comdr Herbert Maynard, 1876–1957, vol. V
Denny, Surg. Rear-Adm. Herbert Reginald Harry, 1876–1943, vol. IV
Denny, James Runciman, 1908–1978, vol. VII
Denny, John M'Ausland, 1858–1922, vol. II
Denny, Sir Maurice Edward, 2nd Bt (cr 1913), 1886–1955, vol. V
Denny, Adm. Sir Michael Maynard, 1896–1972, vol. VII
Denny, Sir Robert Arthur, 5th Bt (cr 1782), 1838–1921, vol. II
Denny, Rev. William Henry, died 1907, vol. I
Denny, Hon. William Joseph, died 1946, vol. IV
Dennys, Col George William Patrick, 1857–1924, vol. II
Dennys, Lt-Col Sir Hector Travers, 1864–1922, vol. II
Dennys, Gen. Julius Bentall, 1822–1907, vol. I
Densham, Sir Harry Percival, 1866–1933, vol. III
Densmore, Emmet, 1837–1912, vol. I
Dent, Alan Holmes, 1905–1978, vol. VII
Dent, Sir Alfred, 1844–1927, vol. II
Dent, Brig.-Gen. Bertie Coore, 1872–1960, vol. V
Dent, Charles Enrique, 1911–1976, vol. VII
Dent, Clinton Thomas, 1850–1912, vol. I
Dent, Adm. Douglas Lionel, 1869–1959, vol. V
Dent, Edward Joseph, 1876–1957, vol. V
Dent, Sir Francis Henry, 1866–1955, vol. V
Dent, Frederick James, 1905–1973, vol. VII
Dent, George Irving, 1918–1976, vol. VII
Dent, Lt-Col H. F., 1839–1916, vol. II
Dent, Rear-Adm. John, 1899–1973, vol. VII
Dent, John James, 1856–1936, vol. III
Dent, Lt-Col John Ralph Congreve, 1884–1969, vol. VI
Dent, Major John William, 1857–1943, vol. IV
Dent, Rev. Joseph Jonathan Dent, 1829–1907, vol. I
Dent, Major Joseph Leslie, 1889–1917, vol. II
Dent, Joseph Mallaby, 1849–1926, vol. II
Dent, Maj.-Gen. Wilkinson, 1883–1934, vol. III
Dent-Brocklehurst, Major John Henry; see Brocklehurst.
Denton, Sir George Chardin, 1851–1928, vol. II
Denton, Mrs H. S., died 1953, vol. V
Denton, William, 1844–1915, vol. I
Denton-Thompson, Merrick Arnold Bardsley, 1888–1969, vol. VI
Denville, Alfred, 1876–1955, vol. V
Denyer, Charles Leonard, 1887–1969, vol. VI
Denyer, Stanley Edward, 1869–1931, vol. III
Denys, Sir (Charles) Peter, 4th Bt (cr 1813), 1899–1960, vol. V
Denys, Sir Peter; see Denys, Sir C. P.
Denys-Burton, Sir Francis Charles Edward, 3rd Bt (cr 1813), 1849–1922, vol. II
Denza, Luigi, 1846–1922, vol. II
de Paravicini, Percy J., 1862–1921, vol. II

de Pass, Sir Eliot Arthur, 1851–1937, vol. III
de Pauley, Rt Rev. William Cecil, 1893–1968, vol. VI
De Pencier, Most Rev. Adam Urias, 1866–1949 vol. IV
Depew, Chauncey Mitchell, 1834–1928, vol. II
d'Epinay, Charles Adrien Prosper; see Epinay.
de Pourtalès, Count Guy, 1881–1941, vol. IV
De Pree, Maj.-Gen. Hugo Douglas, 1870–1943, vol. IV
de Putron, Air Cdre Owen Washington, 1893–1980, vol. VII
Deramore, 3rd Baron, 1865–1936, vol. III
Deramore, 4th Baron, 1870–1943, vol. IV
Deramore, 5th Baron, 1903–1964, vol. VI
De Ramsey, 2nd Baron, 1848–1925, vol. II
Derby, 16th Earl of, 1841–1908, vol. I
Derby, 17th Earl of, 1865–1948, vol. IV
Derbyshire, Sir Harold, 1886–1972, vol. VII
Derbyshire, Job Nightingale, 1866–1954, vol. V
De Renzy, Sir Annesley Charles Castriot, 1829–1914, vol. I
De Renzy-Martin, Lt-Col Edward Cuthbert, 1883–1974, vol. VII
Derham, Maj.-Gen. Frank Plumley, 1885–1957, vol. V
Derham, Brig.-Gen. Frank Seymour, 1858–1941, vol. IV
Derham, Hon. Frederick Thomas, 1844–1922, vol. II
de Rhé-Philipe, Maj.-Gen. Arthur Terence, 1905–1971, vol. VII
Dering, Sir Anthony Myles Cholmeley, 11th Bt, 1901–1958, vol. V
Dering, Comdr Claud Lacy Yea, 1885–1943, vol. IV
Dering, Sir Henry Edward, 10th Bt, 1866–1931, vol. III
Dering, Sir Henry Nevill, 9th Bt, 1839–1906, vol. I
Dering, Sir Herbert Guy, 1867–1933, vol. III
Dering, Lt-Col Sir Rupert Anthony Yea, 12th Bt, 1915–1975, vol. VII
d'Erlanger, Baron Emile Beaumont, 1866–1939, vol. III
d'Erlanger, Baron Frederic A., 1868–1943, vol. IV
d'Erlanger, Sir Gerard John Regis Leo, 1906–1962, vol. VI
d'Erlanger, Leo Frederic Alfred, 1898–1978, vol. VII
de Robeck, 4th Baron, 1823–1904, vol. I
de Robeck, 5th Baron, 1859–1929, vol. III
de Robeck, 6th Baron, 1895–1965, vol. VI
de Robeck, Adm. of the Fleet Sir John Michael, 1st Bt, 1862–1928, vol. II
de Ros, 24th Baron, 1827–1907, vol. I
de Ros, Baroness (25th in line), 1854–1939, vol. III
de Ros, Baroness (26th in line), 1879–1956, vol. V
de Rothschild, Anthony Gustav; see Rothschild.
de Rougemont, Brig.-Gen. Cecil Henry, 1865–1951, vol. V
de Rougemont, Charles Irving, 1864–1939, vol. III
Deroulède, Paul, 1846–1914, vol. I
Derrick, Col George Alexander, 1860–1945, vol. IV

Derrick, Thomas, *died* 1954, vol. V
Derrig, Thomas; *see* O'Deirg, Tomás.
Derriman, Captain G. L., *died* 1915, vol. I
Derry, Cyril, 1895–1964, vol. VI
Derry, Henry B.; *see* Bromley-Derry.
Derry, Henry Forster H.; *see* Handley-Derry.
Derry, John, 1854–1937, vol. III
Derry, Ven. Percy A., 1859–1928, vol. II
de Rutzen, Baron; John Frederick Foley, 1909–1944, vol. IV
de Rutzen, Sir Albert, 1831–1913, vol. I
Derviche-Jones, Lt-Col Arthur Daniel, 1873–1940, vol. III
Derville, Major Max T.; *see* Teichman-Derville.
Derwent, 1st Baron, 1829–1916, vol. II
Derwent, 2nd Baron, 1851–1929, vol. III
Derwent, 3rd Baron, 1899–1949, vol. IV
Derwent, William Raymond, 1883–1960, vol. V
de Sabata, Victor, 1892–1967, vol. VI
de Sales La Terrière, Col Fenwick Bulmer, 1856–1925, vol. II
De Salis, Sir Cecil Fane, 1857–1948, vol. IV
De Salis, Rt Rev. Charles Fane, 1860–1942, vol. IV
De Salis, Lt-Col Edward Augustus Alfred, 1874–1943, vol. IV
De Salis, Rev. Henry Jerome, 1828–1915, vol. I
de Salis, Lt-Col John Eugene, 8th Count De Salis, 1891–1949, vol. IV
de Salis, John Francis Charles, Count de Salis, 1864–1939, vol. III
De Salis, Rodolph Fane, 1854–1931, vol. III
De Salis, Adm. Sir William Fane, 1858–1939, vol. III
de Saram, John Henricus, 1844–1920, vol. II
Desart, 4th Earl of, 1845–1898, vol. I
Desart, 5th Earl of, 1848–1934, vol. III
Desart, Ellen Odette, 1857–1933, vol. III
de Satgé, Lt-Col Sir Henry Valentine Bache, 1874–1964, vol. VI
De Saumarez, 4th Baron, 1843–1937, vol. III
De Saumarez, 5th Baron, 1889–1969, vol. VI
de Sausmarez, Annie Elizabeth, (Lady de Sausmarez), *died* 1947, vol. IV
De Sausmarez, Brig.-Gen. Cecil, 1870–1966, vol. VI
de Sausmarez, Sir Havilland Walter de; *see* Sausmarez.
de Sausmarez, (Lionel) Maurice, 1915–1969, vol. VI
de Sausmarez, Maurice; *see* de Sausmarez, L. M.
Desbarats, George Joseph, 1861–1944, vol. IV
Desborough, 1st Baron, 1855–1945, vol. IV
Desborough, Arthur Peregrine Henry, 1868–1949, vol. IV
Desborough, Maj.-Gen. John, 1824–1918, vol. II
Desborough, Vincent Robin d'Arba, 1914–1978, vol. VII
Descamps, Baron, *died* 1933, vol. III
Desch, Cecil Henry, 1874–1958, vol. V
Deschanel, Paul Eugène Louis, 1856–1922, vol. II
de Segonzac, A. D.; *see* Dunoyer de Segonzac,
de Selincourt, Anne Douglas, (Mrs Basil de Selincourt); *see* Sedgwick, A. D.
de Selincourt, Aubrey, 1894–1962, vol. VI
de Selincourt, Martin, 1864–1950, vol. IV
des Forges, Sir Charles Lee, 1879–1972, vol. VII

des Graz, Charles Geoffrey Maurice, 1893–1953, vol. V
Des Graz, Sir Charles Louis, 1860–1940, vol. III
Deshon, Col Charles John, 1840–1929, vol. III
Deshon, Edward, 1836–1924, vol. II
Deshon, Lt-Gen. Frederick George Thomas, 1818–1913, vol. I
Deshon, H. F., 1858–1924, vol. II
Deshumbert, Marius, 1856–1943, vol. IV
De Sica, Vittorio, 1901–1974, vol. VII
Desika-Charry, Sir Vembakkam C., *born* 1861, vol. II
Desikachari, Diwan Bahadur Sir Tirumalai, 1868–1940, vol. III (A), vol. IV
de Silva, Sir Albert Ernest, 1887–1957, vol. VI (AI)
de Silva, Sir Arthur Marcellus, 1879–1957, vol. V
de Silva, Rt Hon. Lucien Macull Dominic, 1893–1962, vol. VI
Desjardins, Hon. Alphonse, 1841–1912, vol. II
Deslandes, Sir Charles Frederick, 1884–1957, vol. V
Deslandes, Baronne M., vol. III
de Smidt, Lt-Col Errol Mervyn, 1877–1931, vol. III
de Smidt, Henry, 1845–1919, vol. II
de Smith, Stanley Alexander, 1922–1974, vol. VII
Desmond, Astra, (Lady Neame), 1893–1973, vol. VII
Desmond, John, *died* 1938, vol. III
Desmond, Shaw, 1877–1960, vol. V, vol. VI
de Soissons, Louis, 1890–1962, vol. VI
de Sola, Rev. Meldola, 1853–1918, vol. II
De Soveral, Marquess (Sir), *died* 1922, vol. II
de Soyres, Rev. John, 1849–1905, vol. I
de Soysa, Rt Rev. Charles Harold Wilfred, *died* 1971, vol. VII
de Soysa, Sir (Lambert) Wilfred (Alexander), 1884–1968, vol. VI
de Soysa, Sir Wilfred; *see* de Soysa, Sir L. W. A.
de Soyza, Gunasena, 1902–1961, vol. VI
Despard, Captain Herbert John, 1860–1937, vol. III
Despencer-Robertson, Lt-Col James Archibald St George Fitzwarenne, 1893–1942, vol. IV
d'Esperey, Franchet, 1856–1942, vol. IV
Dessaulles, Hon. George Casimir, 1827–1930, vol. III
de Stein, Sir Edward, 1887–1965, vol. VI
de Stacpoole, 4th Duke, 1860–1929, vol. III
de Stacpoole, 5th Duke, 1886–1965, vol. VI
d'Esterre, Elsa, *died* 1935, vol. III
Destinn, Emmy, 1878–1930, vol. III
D'Estournelles de Constant, Baron, 1852–1924, vol. II
Des Vœux, Sir Charles Champagné, 6th Bt, 1827–1914, vol. I
Des Vœux, Lt-Gen. Sir Charles Hamilton, 1853–1911, vol. I
Des Vœux, Sir Edward Alfred, 8th Bt, 1864–1941, vol. IV
Des Vœux, Sir Frederick, 7th Bt, 1857–1937, vol. III
Des Vœux, Sir George William, 1834–1909, vol. I
Des Vœux, Lt-Col Henry Bertram, 1868–1930, vol. III
Des Vœux, Lt-Col Henry J., 1876–1940, vol. III

Des Vœux, Lt-Col Herbert, 1864–1945, vol. IV
Des Vœux, Lt-Col Sir Richard de Bacquencourt; see Des Vœux, Lt-Col Sir W. R. de B.
Des Vœux, Sir William; see Des Vœux, Sir G. W.
Des Vœux, Lt-Col Sir (William) Richard de Bacquencourt, 9th Bt, 1911–1944, vol. IV
De Tabley, Lady; (Elizabeth), died 1915, vol. I
Detaille, Edouard, died 1912, vol. I
de Teissier, Baron Henry de Teissier, 1862–1931, vol. III
Deterding, Sir Henri Wilhelm August, 1866–1939, vol. III
de Thieusies, Vicomte Alain O.; see Obert de Thieusies.
Dethridge, George James, 1864–1938, vol. III
Dethridge, Hon. George Leo, 1903–1978, vol. VII
Detmold, Edward J., 1883–1957, vol. V
Detmold, Maurice, 1883–1908, vol. I
de Torrenté, Henry, 1893–1962, vol. VI
De Trafford, Lieut Augustus Francis, died 1904, vol. I
De Trafford, (Charles) Edmund, 1864–1951, vol. V
De Trafford, Edmund; see De Trafford, C. E.
de Trafford, Captain Sir Humphrey Edmund, 4th Bt, 1891–1971, vol. VII
de Trafford, Sir Humphrey Francis, 3rd Bt, 1862–1929, vol. III
de Trafford, Sigismund Cathcart, 1853–1936, vol. III
Dettmann, Herbert Stanley, 1875–1940, vol. III
Deuchar, William, 1849–1923, vol. II
Deutsch, John James, 1911–1976, vol. VII
Deutsch, Otto Erich, 1883–1967, vol. VI
Deutscher, Isaac, 1907–1967, vol. VI
Devadhar, Gopal Krishna, 1871–1935, vol. III
Devadoss, Sir David Muthiah, 1868–1955, vol. V
De Valera, Eamon, 1882–1975, vol. VII
Devals, Rt Rev. Adrian, 1882–1945, vol. IV
Devas, Anthony, 1911–1958, vol. V
Devas, Charles Stanton, 1848–1906, vol. I
Devas, Rev. Francis Charles, 1877–1951, vol. V
Devaux, J. Louis, 1884–1943, vol. IV
de Vaux, Father Roland, 1903–1971, vol. VII
de Veber, Hon. Leverett George, 1849–1925, vol. II
Devenish, Rev. Robert Cecil Silvester, 1888–1973, vol. VII
Devenish, Very Rev. Robert Jones Sylvester, died 1916, vol. II
Devenish-Meares, Maj.-Gen. William Lewis, 1832–1907, vol. I
Dever, Hon. James, 1825–1904, vol. I
de Vere, Aubrey Thomas, 1814–1902, vol. I
de Vere, Robert Stephen Vere, 1872–1936, vol. III
de Vere, Sir Stephen Edward, 4th Bt, 1812–1904, vol. I
Deverell, Field Marshal Sir Cyril John, 1874–1947, vol. IV
Devereux, Rev. Edward Robert Price, died 1941, vol. IV
Devereux, Sir Joseph, 1816–1903, vol. I
Devereux, Wallace Charles, 1893–1952, vol. V
Devers, Gen. Jacob Loucks, 1887–1979, vol. VII
de Versan, Raoul Couturier, 1848–1936, vol. III

De Vesci, 5th Viscount, 1881–1958, vol. V
de Veulle, Henry Marett, 1847–1930, vol. III
de Villiers, 1st Baron, 1842–1914, vol. I
de Villiers, 2nd Baron, 1871–1934, vol. III
de Villiers, Hon. Sir Etienne; see de Villiers, Hon. Sir J. E. R.
de Villiers, Sir (H.) Nicolas, 1902–1958, vol. V
de Villiers, Maj.-Gen. Isaac Pierre, 1891–1967, vol. VI
de Villiers, Jacob, 1868–1932, vol. III
de Villiers, Hon. Sir (Jean) Etienne (Reenen), 1875–1947, vol. IV
de Villiers, Sir John Abraham Jacob, 1863–1931, vol. III
Devine, Alexander, 1865–1930, vol. III
Devine, George Alexander Cassady, 1910–1966, vol. VI
Devine, Henry, 1879–1940, vol. III
Devine, Sir Hugh Berchmans, died 1959, vol. V
Devine, Major James Arthur, 1869–1939, vol. III
Devine, Rev. Minos, 1871–1937, vol. III
De Vinne, Theodore Low, 1828–1914, vol. I
Devitt, Sir Philip Henry, 1st Bt (cr 1931), 1876–1947, vol. IV
Devitt, Sir Thomas Lane, 1st Bt (cr 1916), 1839–1923, vol. II
Devlin, Hon. Charles Ramsay, 1858–1914, vol. I
Devlin, Emmanuel, 1872–1921, vol. II
Devlin, Joseph, 1872–1934, vol. III
de Voil, Very Rev. Walter Harry, 1893–1964, vol. VI
Devon, 14th Earl of, 1870–1927, vol. II
Devon, 15th Earl of, 1872–1935, vol. III
Devon, 16th Earl of, 1875–1935, vol. III
Devon, James, 1866–1939, vol. III
Devonport, 1st Viscount, 1856–1934, vol. III
Devonport, 2nd Viscount, 1890–1973, vol. VII
Devons, Ely, 1913–1967, vol. VI
Devonshire, 9th Duke of, 1868–1938, vol. III
Devonshire, 10th Duke of, 1895–1950, vol. IV
Devonshire, Sir James Lyne, 1863–1946, vol. IV
DeVoto, Bernard Augustine, 1897–1955, vol. V
de Vries, Hugo, 1848–1935, vol. III
Dew, Col Sir Armine Brereton, 1867–1941, vol. IV
Dew, Armine Roderick, 1906–1945, vol. IV
Dew, Sir Harold Robert, 1891–1962, vol. VI
De Waal, Hon. Daniel, 1873–1938, vol. III
De Waal, Brig. Pieter, 1899–1977, vol. VII
Dewar, 1st Baron, 1864–1930, vol. III
Dewar, Hon. Lord; Arthur Dewar, died 1917, vol. II
Dewar, Rev. Alexander, 1864–1943, vol. IV
Dewar, Arthur; see Dewar, Hon. Lord.
Dewar, Douglas, 1875–1957, vol. V
Dewar, George A. B., 1862–1934, vol. III
Dewar, Sir James, 1842–1923, vol. II
Dewar, John, 1883–1964, vol. VI
Dewar, John Arthur, 1891–1954, vol. V
Dewar, Vice-Adm. Kenneth Gilbert Balmain, 1879–1964, vol. VI
Dewar, Rev. Canon Lindsay, 1891–1976, vol. VII
Dewar, Michael Bruce Urquhart, 1886–1950, vol. IV
Dewar, Robert, 1882–1956, vol. V

Dewar, Vice-Adm. Robert Gordon Douglas, *died* 1948, vol. IV

Dewar, Thomas Finlayson, 1866–1929, vol. III

Dewar, William McLachlan, 1905–1979, vol. VII

Dewas State, Maharaja Tukoji Rao Puar, 1888–1937, vol. III

de Watteville, Lt-Col Herman Gaston, 1875–1963, vol. VI

de Watteville, John Edward, 1892–1976, vol. VII

Dewdney, Rt Rev. Alfred Daniel Alexander, 1863–1945, vol. IV

Dewdney, Ven. Arthur John Bible, *died* 1946, vol. IV

de Wend-Fenton, West Fenton, 1881–1920, vol. II

de Wesselow, Owen Lambert Vaughan, 1883–1959, vol. V

De Wet, Gen. Hon. Christian Rudolf, 1854–1922, vol. II

De Wet, Sir Jacobus Albertus, 1840–1911, vol. I

De Wet, Sir Jacobus Petrus, 1838–1900, vol. I

De Wet, Rt Hon. Nicolas Jacobus, 1873–1960, vol. V

de Wet, Captain Thomas Oloff, 1869–1940, vol. III

Dewey, (Alexander) Gordon, 1890–1953, vol. V

Dewey, Cyril Marston, 1907–1973, vol. VII

Dewey, Rt Rev. Mgr Edward, 1884–1965, vol. VI

Dewey, George, 1837–1917, vol. II

Dewey, Gordon; *see* Dewey, A. G.

Dewey, John, 1859–1952, vol. V

Dewey, Kenneth Thomas, 1902–1961, vol. VI

Dewey, Rev. Sir Stanley Daws, 2nd Bt, 1867–1948, vol. IV

Dewey, Sir Thomas Charles, 1st Bt, 1840–1926, vol. II

Dewey, Thomas Edmund, 1902–1971, vol. VII

Dewhurst, Captain Gerard Powys, 1872–1956, vol. V

Dewhurst, Lt-Comdr Harry, 1866–1931, vol. III

Dewhurst, Wynford, *died* 1941, vol. IV

Dewick, Rev. E. C., 1884–1958, vol. V

De Windt, Harry, 1856–1933, vol. III

Dewing, Maj.-Gen. Maurice Nelson, 1896–1976, vol. VII

de Winton, Brig.-Gen. Charles, 1860–1943, vol. IV

de Winton, Charles Henry, 1856–1936, vol. III

de Winton, Sir Francis Walter, 1835–1901, vol. I

de Winton, Ven. Frederic Henry, 1852–1932, vol. III

de Winton, Walter Bernard, 1850–1944, vol. IV

de Winton, Wilfred Seymour, 1856–1929, vol. III

DeWitt, Norman Wentworth, 1876–1958, vol. V

Dewolfe, Rev. Henry Todd, 1867–1947, vol. IV

Dewrance, Sir John, 1858–1937, vol. III

Dewsnup, Ernest Ritson, 1874–1950, vol. IV

Dexter, Walter, 1877–1944, vol. IV

Dexter, Walter, 1876–1958, vol. V

Dey, George Goodair, 1876–1955, vol. V

Dey, Helen, 1888–1968, vol. VI

Deym, Count; Franz de Paula, 1838–1903, vol. I

D'Eyncourt, Edmund Charles T.; *see* Tennyson-D'Eyncourt.

D'Eyncourt, Adm. Edwin Clayton Tennyson, *died* 1903, vol. I

D'Eyncourt, Sir Eustace Henry William T.; *see* Tennyson-D'Eyncourt.

d'Eyncourt, Sir Gervais T.; *see* Tennyson d'Eyncourt, Sir E. G.

de Young, Michel Harry, 1849–1925, vol. II

de Zouche, Dorothy Eva, 1886–1969, vol. VI

De Zoysa, Sir Cyril, 1897–1978, vol. VII

Dhar, Lt-Col HH Maharaja Sir Udaji Rao Puar Major, Bahadur, 1886–1926, vol. II

Dharampur, Maharana of, 1863–1921, vol. II

D'Harcourt, Robert, 1881–1965, vol. VI (AII)

d'Hardelot, Guy; *see* Rhodes, Mrs Helen.

d'Hautpoul, Marquis, 1859–1934, vol. III

D'Herelle, Felix H., 1873–1949, vol. IV

Dhingra, Sir Behari Lal, 1873–1936, vol. III

Dholpur, Maharaj Rana of, 1893–1954, vol. V

Dholpur, Captain HH, 1883–1911, vol. I

Dhondup, Rai Bahadur Norbhu, *died* 1943, vol. IV

Dhrangadhra, Maharaja Raj Saheb of, 1889–1942, vol. IV

Diack, Sir Alexander Henderson, 1862–1929, vol. III

Diaghileff, Serge de, 1872–1929, vol. III

Diamond, Arthur Sigismund, 1897–1978, vol. VII

Diamond, Charles, 1858–1934, vol. III

Diamond, George le Boutillier, 1893–1964, vol. VI

Diamond, Sir William Henry, 1865–1941, vol. IV

Diaz, Maresciallo d'Italia Armando, 1861–1928, vol. II

Diaz, Sir Porfirio, 1830–1915, vol. I

Dibben, Major Cecil Reginald, 1885–1965, vol. VI

Dibblee, George Binney, 1868–1952, vol. V

Dibbs, Hon. Sir George Richard, 1834–1904, vol. I

Dibbs, Sir Thomas Allwright, 1832–1923, vol. II

Dibden, Edgar, 1888–1971, vol. VII

Dibdin, Aubrey, 1892–1958, vol. V

Dibdin, Charles, 1849–1910, vol. I

Dibdin, Edward Rimbault, 1853–1941, vol. IV

Dibdin, Sir Lewis Tonna, 1852–1938, vol. III

Dibdin, Sir Robert William, 1848–1933, vol. III

Dibdin, William Joseph, 1850–1925, vol. II

Dible, James Henry, *died* 1971, vol. VII

Dible, James Kenneth Victor, 1890–1976, vol. VII

Dible, William Cuthbert, 1886–1971, vol. VII

Dibley, Rear-Adm. Albert Kingsley, 1890–1958, vol. V

Dicconson, Hon. Robert Joseph Gerard-, 1857–1918, vol. II

Dicey, Albert Venn, 1835–1922, vol. II

Dicey, Edward, 1832–1911, vol. I

Dick, Bt Col Alan Macdonald, 1884–1970, vol. VI

Dick, Brig.-Gen. Archibald Campbell Douglas, 1847–1927, vol. II

Dick, Col Sir Arthur Robert, 1860–1943, vol. IV

Dick, Charles George Cotsford, 1846–1911, vol. I

Dick, Lt-Col Dighton Hay Abercromby, 1869–1941, vol. IV

Dick, George Paris, 1866–1941, vol. IV

Dick, Gladys; *see* Ripley, G.

Dick, Henry Charles, 1872–1946, vol. IV

Dick, Col James Adam, 1866–1942, vol. IV

Dick, Sir James Nicholas, 1832–1920, vol. II

Dick, John, 1902–1970, vol. VI

Dick, John Lawson, 1870–1944, vol. IV

Dick, Captain Quintin, 1847–1923, vol. II
Dick, Brig.-Gen. Robert Nicholas, 1879–1967, vol. VI
Dick, Sir W(illiam) R.; see Reid Dick.
Dick-Cunyngham, Major Sir Colin Keith; see Cunyngham.
Dick-Cunyngham, Maj.-Gen. James Keith, 1877–1935, vol. III
Dick-Cunyngham of Lamburghtoun, Sir Robert Keith Alexander; see Cunyngham.
Dick-Cunyngham, Lt-Col William Henry; see Cunyngham.
Dick-Lauder, Sir George William Dalrymple; see Lauder.
Dick-Lauder, Lt-Col Sir John North Dalrymple; see Lauder.
Dick-Lauder, Sir Thomas North; see Lauder.
Dick-Read, Grantly; see Read.
Dicken, Adm. Charles Gauntlett, 1854–1937, vol. III
Dicken, Charles Shortt, 1841–1902, vol. I
Dicken, Charles Vernon, 1881–1955, vol. V
Dicken, Rear-Adm. Edward Bernard Cornish, 1888–1964, vol. VI
Dicken, Col William Popham, 1834–1912, vol. I
Dickens, Craven Hildesley, died 1900, vol. I
Dickens, Adm. Sir Gerald Charles, 1879–1962, vol. VI
Dickens, Sir Henry Fielding, 1849–1933, vol. III
Dickens, Mary Angela, died 1948, vol. IV
Dickens, Air Cdre Thomas Charles, 1906–1972, vol. VII
Dickenson, Lt-Col Edward Stanley Newton, died 1910, vol. I
Dickenson, Rev. Lenthall Greville T.; see Trotman-Dickenson.
Dickeson, Sir Richard, 1823–1900, vol. I
Dickey, Rev. Charles A., died 1910, vol. I
Dickey, Edward Montgomery O'Rorke, 1894–1977, vol. VII
Dickey, Robert H. F., 1856–1915, vol. I
Dickie, Archibald Campbell, 1868–1941, vol. IV
Dickie, Captain David, 1880–1930, vol. III
Dickie, Rev. James F., 1845–1933, vol. III
Dickie, Very Rev. John, 1875–1942, vol. IV
Dickie, Maj.-Gen. John Elford, 1856–1939, vol. III
Dickie, William, 1856–1919, vol. II
Dickin, Maria Elisabeth, 1870–1951, vol. V
Dickins, Bruce, 1889–1978, vol. VII
Dickins, Brig. Frederick, 1879–1975, vol. VII
Dickins, Frederick Victor, 1838–1915, vol. I
Dickins, Rev. Henry Compton, 1838–1920, vol. II
Dickins, Col Spencer William Scrase-, 1862–1919, vol. II
Dickins, Rev. Thomas Bourne, 1832–1919, vol. II
Dickins, Col Vernon William Frank, 1867–1942, vol. IV
Dickins, Ven. William Arthur, died 1921, vol. II
Dickins, Maj.-Gen. William Drummond S.; see Scrase-Dickins.
Dickinson, 1st Baron, 1859–1943, vol. IV
Dickinson, Sir Alwin Robinson, 1873–1944, vol. IV
Dickinson, Anne Hepple, 1877–1959, vol. V

Dickinson, Arthur Harold, 1892–1978, vol. VII
Dickinson, Sir Arthur Lowes, 1859–1935, vol. III
Dickinson, Ven. Charles Henry, 1871–1930, vol. III
Dickinson, Croft; see Dickinson, W. C.
Dickinson, Maj.-Gen. Douglas Povah, 1886–1949, vol. IV
Dickinson, Frederic William, 1856–1922, vol. II
Dickinson, Gladys, 1895–1964, vol. VI
Dickinson, Goldsworthy Lowes, 1862–1932, vol. III
Dickinson, Henry Douglas, 1899–1969, vol. VI
Dickinson, Very Rev. Hercules Henry, 1827–1905, vol. I
Dickinson, James, died 1933, vol. III
Dickinson, Sir John, 1848–1933, vol. III
Dickinson, John Alfred Ernst, 1859–1933, vol. III
Dickinson, Major Neville Hope Campbell, 1862–1935, vol. III
Dickinson, Hon. Richard Sebastian Willoughby, 1897–1935, vol. III
Dickinson, Robert Edmund, 1862–1947, vol. IV
Dickinson, Thomas Vincent, 1858–1941, vol. IV
Dickinson, Lt-Col William, 1831–1917, vol. II
Dickinson, W(illiam) Croft, 1897–1963, vol. VI
Dickinson, William Howship, 1832–1913, vol. I
Dickinson, Col William Vicris, 1856–1917, vol. II
Dicks, Captain Henry Leage, 1870–1942, vol. IV
Dicksee, Sir Francis Bernard, (Frank), 1853–1928, vol. II
Dicksee, Frank; see Dicksee, Sir F. B.
Dicksee, Herbert, 1862–1942, vol. IV
Dicksee, Lawrence Robert, 1864–1932, vol. III
Dickson, Rt Hon. Lord; Scott Dickson, 1850–1922, vol. II
Dickson, Bonner William Arthur, 1887–1976, vol. VII
Dickson, Charles Gordon, 1884–1963, vol. VI
Dickson, Gen. Sir Collingwood, 1817–1904, vol. I
Dickson, Rev. Canon Daniel Eccles Lucas, died 1924, vol. II
Dickson, Air Vice-Marshal Edward Dalziel, 1895–1979, vol. VII
Dickson, Maj.-Gen. Edward Thompson, 1850–1938, vol. III
Dickson, Frank, 1862–1936, vol. III
Dickson, Lt-Col George Arthur Hamilton, died 1918, vol. II
Dickson, Lt-Col Harold Richard Patrick, 1881–1959, vol. V
Dickson, Rev. Henry Granville, 1844–1929, vol. III
Dickson, Henry Newton, 1866–1922, vol. II
Dickson, James, 1859–1941, vol. IV
Dickson, James Douglas Hamilton, 1849–1931, vol. III
Dickson, James Hill, 1863–1938, vol. III
Dickson, Hon. Sir James Robert, 1832–1901, vol. I
Dickson, Maj.-Gen. John Baillie Ballantyne, 1842–1925, vol. II
Dickson, John Harold, 1898–1967, vol. VI
Dickson, Col John Herbert, 1867–1938, vol. III
Dickson, John Robert, 1884–1937, vol. III
Dickson, Lt-Col Maurice Rhynd, 1882–1940, vol. III
Dickson, Norman Bonnington, 1868–1944, vol. IV

Dickson, Rear-Adm. Robert Kirk, 1898–1952, vol. V

Dickson, Scott; see Dickson, Rt Hon. Lord.

Dickson, Spencer Stuart, 1873–1951, vol. V

Dickson, Thomas A.; see Ainsworth Dickson.

Dickson, Rt Hon. Thomas Alexander, 1833–1909, vol. I

Dickson, Rev. Thomas Knox Whitaker, died 1931, vol. III

Dickson, Thomas S., 1885–1935, vol. III

Dickson, Brig.-Gen. William Edmund Ritchie, 1871–1957, vol. V

Dickson, Rev. William Edward, 1823–1910, vol. I

Dickson, William Elliot Carnegie, 1878–1954, vol. V

Dickson, William Everard, died 1945, vol. IV

Dickson, William Kirk, 1860–1949, vol. IV

Dickson, Rev. William Purdie, 1823–1901, vol. I

Dickson, Lt-Gen. William Thomas, 1830–1909, vol. I

Dickson Wright, Arthur; see Wright.

Diddams, Harry John Charles, 1864–1929, vol. III

Didon, Very Rev. Fr Henri, 1840–1900, vol. I

Didsbury, Brian, 1926–1970, vol. VI

Dieckhoff, Hans Heinrich, 1884–1952, vol. V

Diederichs, Hon. Nicolaas, 1903–1978, vol. VII

Diefenbaker, Rt Hon. John George, 1895–1979, vol. VII

Diehl, Alice Mangold, died 1912, vol. I

Diels, Otto, 1876–1954, vol. V

Diesel, Rudolf, died 1913, vol. I

Digan, Lt-Col Augustine J., 1878–1926, vol. II

Digby, 10th Baron, 1846–1920, vol. II

Digby, 11th Baron, 1894–1964, vol. VI

Digby, Comdr Edward Aylmer, 1883–1935, vol. III

Digby, Col Hon. Everard Charles, 1852–1914, vol. I

Digby, Col Frederick James Bosworth Digby Wingfield, 1885–1952, vol. V

Digby, Hon. Gerald Fitzmaurice, 1858–1942, vol. IV

Digby, John Kenelm Digby Wingfield, 1859–1904, vol. I

Digby, Sir Kenelm Edward, 1836–1916, vol. II

Digby, Kenelm George, 1890–1944, vol. IV

Digby, Kenelm Hutchinson, 1884–1954, vol. V

Digby, Hon. Robert Henry, 1903–1959, vol. V

Digby, Samuel, died 1925, vol. II

Digby, Rev. Stephen Harold Wingfield, 1872–1942, vol. IV

Digby, William, 1849–1904, vol. I

Digby-Beste, Captain Sir Henry Aloysius Bruno, 1883–1964, vol. VI

Diggines, Sir William Ewart, 1881–1952, vol. V

Diggle, F. Holt, 1886–1942, vol. IV

Diggle, Rt Rev. John William, 1847–1920, vol. II

Diggle, Joseph Robert, 1849–1917, vol. II

Diggle, Captain Neston William, 1880–1963, vol. VI

Diggle, Rev. Reginald Fraser, 1889–1975, vol. VII

Diggle, Wadham Neston, 1848–1934, vol. III

Dignan, Most Rev. John, died 1953, vol. V

Dilhorne, 1st Viscount, 1905–1980, vol. VII

Dilke, Beaumont Albany F.; see Fetherston-Dilke.

Dilke, Rt Hon. Sir Charles Wentworth, 2nd Bt, 1843–1911, vol. I

Dilke, Sir Charles Wentworth, 3rd Bt, 1874–1918, vol. II

Dilke, Emilia Francis, (Lady Dilke), 1840–1904, vol. I

Dilke, Sir Fisher Wentworth, 4th Bt, 1877–1944, vol. IV

Dill, Field-Marshal Sir John Greer, 1881–1944, vol. IV

Dill, Very Rev. S. Marcus, 1843–1924, vol. II

Dill, Sir Samuel, 1844–1924, vol. II

Dill-Russell, Patrick Wimberley, 1910–1977, vol. VII

Dilley, Sir Arthur George, 1854–1938, vol. III

Dilling, Walter James, 1886–1950, vol. IV

Dillingham, Cyril Claud, 1886–1943, vol. IV

Dillon, 17th Viscount, 1844–1932, vol. III

Dillon, 18th Viscount, 1875–1934, vol. III

Dillon, 19th Viscount, 1881–1946, vol. IV

Dillon, 20th Viscount, 1911–1979, vol. VII

Dillon, Hon. Conrad, 1845–1901, vol. I

Dillon, Captain Constantine Theobold Francis, 1873–1920, vol. II

Dillon, Emile Joseph, 1854–1933, vol. III

Dillon, Frank, 1823–1909, vol. I

Dillon, Frederick, 1887–1965, vol. VI

Dillon, Lt-Col George Frederick Horace, 1859–1906, vol. I

Dillon, Hon. Harry Lee Stanton; L., see Lee-Dillon.

Dillon, Major Henry Mountford, 1881–1918, vol. II

Dillon, John, 1851–1927, vol. II

Dillon, Sir John Fox, 7th Bt, 1843–1925, vol. II

Dillon, Malcolm, 1859–1945, vol. IV

Dillon, Gen. Sir Martin Andrew, 1826–1913, vol. I

Dillon, Comdr Stafford Harry, 1887–1935, vol. III

Dillon, Thomas, 1884–1971, vol. VII

Dillwyn-Llewelyn, Sir John Talbot; see Llewelyn.

Dillwyn-Venables-Llewelyn, Sir Charles Leyshon; see Venables-Llewelyn.

Dillwyn-Venables-Llewelyn, Brig. Sir Michael; see Venables-Llewelyn, Brig. Sir C. M. D.

Dilnot, Frank, 1875–1946, vol. IV

Dilworth, W. J., 1863–1922, vol. II

Dilworth-Harrison, Ven. Talbot, 1886–1975, vol. VII

Di Maria, Most Rev. Pietro, 1865–1937, vol. III

Dimbleby, Richard, 1913–1965, vol. VI

Dimmer, Lt-Col John Henry Stephen, 1884–1918, vol. II

Dimmitt, Hon. James Albert, 1888–1957, vol. V

Dimnet, Very Rev. Abbé Ernest, 1866–1954, vol. V

Dimoline, Hon. Brig. Harry Kenneth, 1903–1972, vol. VII

Dimoline, Maj.-Gen. William Alfred, 1897–1965, vol. VI

Dimond, Maj.-Gen. William Elliot Randal, 1893–1960, vol. V

Dimont, Rev. Canon Charles Tunnacliff, 1872–1953, vol. V

Dimsdale, 6th Baron of the Russian Empire, 1828–1898, vol. I

Dimsdale, 7th Baron of the Russian Empire, 1856–1928, vol. II

Dimsdale, Mrs Helen Easdale, 1907–1977, vol. VII

Dimsdale, Sir John Holdsworth, 2nd Bt, 1874–1923, vol. II

Dimsdale, Sir John Holdsworth, 3rd Bt, 1901–1978, vol. VII

Dimsdale, Rt Hon. Sir Joseph Cockfield, 1st Bt, 1849–1912, vol. I

Dimsey, Surg. Rear-Adm. Edgar Ralph, 1861–1930, vol. III

Dinajpur, Bahadur of, 1860–1919, vol. II

D'Indy, (Paul Marie Théodore) Vincent, 1851–1931, vol. III

D'Indy, Vincent; see D'Indy, P. M. T. V.

Dines, Henry George, 1891–1964, vol. VI

Dines, William Henry, 1855–1927, vol. II

Dinesen, Isak, (Karen Blixen Finecke), 1885–1962, vol. VI

Dinesen, Thomas, 1892–1979, vol. VII

Dingle, Aylward Edward, died 1947, vol. IV

Dingle, Herbert, 1890–1978, vol. VII

Dingle, Percival Alfred, 1881–1963, vol. VI

Dingle, Sir Philip Burrington, 1906–1978, vol. VII

Dingley, Allen Roy, 1892–1978, vol. VII

Dingli, Sir Adriano, 1817–1900, vol. I

Dingwall-Fordyce, Alexander, 1875–1940, vol. III

Dinneen, Rev. Patrick Stephen, died 1934, vol. III

Dinshaw, Sir Hormusjee Cowasjee, 1857–1939, vol. III

Dinwiddie, Melville, 1892–1975, vol. VII

Dinwoody, Very Rev. Leofric Matthews H.; see Hay-Dinwoody.

Diogenes; see Brown, W. J.

Dionne, Narcisse-Eutrope, 1848–1917, vol. II

Dior, Christian Ernest, 1905–1957, vol. V

Diósy, Arthur, 1856–1923, vol. II

Dippie, Herbert, 1885–1945, vol. IV

Dircks, Rudolf, died 1936, vol. III

Dirksen, Herbert von, 1882–1955, vol. V

Disbrowe-Wise, Lt-Col Henry Edward Disbrowe; see Wise.

Disher, Maurice Willson, 1893–1969, vol. VI

Disney, Lt-Col Henry Anthony Patrick, 1893–1974, vol. VII

Disney, Henry William, 1858–1925, vol. II

Disney, Hon. Sir James, 1896–1952, vol. V

Disney, Walter E., 1901–1966, vol. VI

Disraeli, Coningsby Ralph, 1867–1936, vol. III

Distant, William Lucas, 1845–1922, vol. II

Disturnal, William Josiah, died 1923, vol. II

Ditchfield, Rt Rev. John Edwin W.; see Watts-Ditchfield

Ditchfield, R.ev. Peter Hampson, 1854–1930, vol. III

Ditmars, Raymond Lee, 1876–1942, vol. IV

Ditmas, Lt-Col Francis Ivan Leslie, 1876–1969, vol. VI

Ditzen, Rudolf, 1893–1947, vol. IV

Dive, Lt-Col Gilbert Henry, 1882–1939, vol. III

Diver, Captain Cyril Roper Pollock, 1892–1969, vol. VI

Diver, (Kathrrine Helen) Maud, died 1945, vol. IV

Diver, Maud; see Diver, K. H. M.

Divers, Edward, 1837–1912, vol. I

Divers, Brig. Sydney Thomas, 1896–1979, vol. VII

Dix, Comdr Charles Cabry, 1881–1951, vol. V

Dix, Dorothy Knight; see Waddy, D. K.

Dix, G. E. A., see Dix, Rev. Dom Gregory.

Dix, Rev. G. H., died 1932, vol. III

Dix, Rev. Dom Gregory, (G. E. A. Dix), 1901–1952, vol. V

Dixey, Arthur Carlyne Niven, 1889–1954, vol. V

Dixey, Charles Neville Douglas, 1881–1947, vol. IV

Dixey, Frederick Augustus, 1855–1935, vol. III

Dixey, Sir Harry Edward, 1853–1927, vol. II

Dixey, Marmaduke; see Howard, Geoffrey.

Dixie, Sir (Alexander Archibald Douglas) Wolstan, 13th Bt, 1910–1975, vol. VII

Dixie, Sir Alexander Beaumont Churchill, 11th Bt, 1851–1924, vol. II

Dixie, Sir Douglas; see Dixie, Sir G. D.

Dixie, Lady Florence, 1857–1905, vol. I

Dixie, Sir (George) Douglas, 12th Bt, 1876–1948, vol. IV

Dixie, Sir Wolstan; see Dixie, Sir A. A. D. W.

Dixon, Alfred Cardew, 1865–1936, vol. III

Dixon, Sir Alfred Herbert, 1st Bt (cr 1918), died 1920, vol. II

Dixon, Amzi Clarence, 1854–1925, vol. II

Dixon, Andrew Francis, died 1936, vol. III

Dixon, Arthur Frederic William, 1892–1948, vol. IV

Dixon, Arthur Lee, 1867–1955, vol. V

Dixon, Sir Arthur Lewis, 1881–1969, vol. VI

Dixon, Augustus Edward, 1860–1946, vol. IV

Dixon, Maj.-Gen. Bernard Edward Cooke, 1896–1973, vol. VII

Dixon, Campbell; see Dixon, G. C.

Dixon, Cecil Edith Mary, 1891–1979, vol. VII

Dixon, Charles, 1858–1926, vol. II

Dixon, Charles, 1872–1934, vol. III

Dixon, Charles Harvey, 1862–1923, vol. II

Dixon, Sir Charles William, 1888–1976, vol. VII

Dixon, Rt Hon. Sir Daniel, 1st Bt (cr 1903), 1844–1907, vol. I

Dixon, Maj.-Gen. Edward George, 1837–1918, vol. II

Dixon, Ella Nora Hepworth, died 1932, vol. III

Dixon, Sir Francis Netherwood, 1879–1968, vol. VI

Dixon, Lt-Col Frederick Alfred, 1880–1925, vol. II

Dixon, George, 1820–1898, vol. I

Dixon, Col Sir George, 1st Bt (cr 1919), 1842–1924, vol. II

Dixon, (George) Campbell, 1895–1960, vol. V

Dixon, Gertrude Caroline, 1886–1966, vol. VI

Dixon, Col Graham Patrick, 1873–1947, vol. IV

Dixon, Harold Baily, 1852–1930, vol. III

Dixon, Harry, 1861–1941, vol. IV

Dixon, Brig.-Gen. Sir Henry Grey, 1850–1933, vol. III

Dixon, Henry Horatio, 1869–1953, vol. V

Dixon, Henry Sydenham, 1848–1931, vol. III

Dixon, Ven. Henry Thomas, 1874–1939, vol. III

Dixon, Rt Rev. Horace Henry, 1869–1964, vol. VI

Dixon, Hubert John, 1895–1971, vol. VII

Dixon, Sir John, 2nd Bt (cr 1919), 1886–1976, vol. VII

Dixon, John Edwin F.; *see* Fowler-Dixon.
Dixon, Most Rev. John Harkness, 1888–1972, vol. VII
Dixon, John Reginald, 1886–1972, vol. VII
Dixon, Captain Kennet, *died* 1927, vol. II
Dixon, Kevin, 1902–1959, vol. V
Dixon, Maj.-Gen. Matthew Charles, 1821–1905, vol. I
Dixon, Lt-Col Oscar, 1883–1966, vol. VI
Dixon, Rt Hon. Sir Owen, 1886–1972, vol. VII
Dixon, Sir Pierson John, 1904–1965, vol. VI
Dixon, Sir Raylton, 1838–1901, vol. I
Dixon, Engr-Vice-Adm. Sir Robert Bland, 1867–1939, vol. III
Dixon, Sir Samuel G.; *see* Gurney-Dixon.
Dixon, Stephen Mitchell, *died* 1940, vol. III
Dixon, Rev. Thomas Harold, *died* 1963, vol. VI
Dixon, Rt Hon. Sir Thomas James, 2nd Bt (*cr* 1903), 1868–1950, vol. IV
Dixon, Walter Ernest, 1870–1931, vol. III
Dixon, Lt-Col William, 1868–1958, vol. V
Dixon, William Gray, 1854–1928, vol. II
Dixon, William Macneile, 1866–1946, vol. IV
Dixon, Sir William Vibart, 1850–1930, vol. III
Dixon-Hartland, Sir Frederick Dixon, 1st Bt, 1832–1909, vol. I
Dixon-Spain, John Edward, *died* 1955, vol. V
Dixon-Wright, Rev. Henry Dixon, 1870–1916, vol. II
Dixson, Sir Hugh, 1841–1926, vol. II
Dixson, Sir William, 1870–1952, vol. V
Dixwell-Oxenden, Sir Percy Dixwell Nowell; *see* Oxenden.
Doak, Sir James, 1904–1975, vol. VII
Doane, Rt Rev. W. Crosswell, 1832–1913, vol. I
Dobb, Harry, 1867–1928, vol. II
Dobb, Maurice Herbert, 1900–1976, vol. VII
Dobbie, Edward David, 1857–1915, vol. I
Dobbie, Sir James Johnston, 1852–1924, vol. II
Dobbie, Sir Joseph, 1862–1943, vol. IV
Dobbie, William, 1878–1950, vol. IV
Dobbie, Lt-Gen. Sir William George Sheddon, 1879–1964, vol. VI
Dobbie, William Herbert, 1851–1941, vol. IV
Dobbie, Brig.-Gen. William Hugh, 1859–1922, vol. II
Dobbie-Bateman, Rev. Arthur Fitzroy, 1897–1974, vol. VII
Dobbin, Sir Alfred Graham, 1853–1942, vol. IV
Dobbin, Gertrude; *see* Page, G.
Dobbin, Brig.-Gen. Herbert Thomas, 1878–1946, vol. IV
Dobbin, Lt-Col Leonard George William, 1871–1936, vol. III
Dobbin, Lt-Col William James Knowles, 1856–1926, vol. II
Dobbs, Cecil Moore, 1882–1969, vol. VI
Dobbs, Col Charles Fairlie, 1872–1936, vol. III
Dobbs, Sir Henry Robert Conway, 1871–1934, vol. III
Dobbs, Lt-Col Richard Conway, 1878–1957, vol. V
Dobbs, Richard Heyworth, 1905–1980, vol. VII
Dobell, Lt-Gen. Sir Charles Macpherson, 1869–1954, vol. V

Dobell, Clifford, 1886–1949, vol. IV
Dobell, Air Cdre Frederic Osborne Storey, 1912–1965, vol. VI
Dobell, Rev. Joseph, 1844–1908, vol. I
Dobell, Hon. Richard Reid, 1837–1902, vol. I
Dobell, Sir William, 1899–1970, vol. VI
Dobie, Very Rev. George Nelson, *died* 1933, vol. III
Dobie, Marryat Ross, 1888–1973, vol. VII
Dobie, William Jardine, 1892–1956, vol. V
Dobinson, Charles Henry, 1903–1980, vol. VII
Doble, Rev. Gilbert Hunter, 1880–1945, vol. IV
Dobree, Alfred, 1864–1937, vol. III
Dobrée, Lt-Col Bonamy, 1891–1974, vol. VII
Dobree, Claude Hatherley, *died* 1960, vol. V, vol. VI
Dobree, George, 1873–1907, vol. I
Dobree, Rev. Osmond, 1832–1929, vol. III
Dobson, Alban Tabor Austin, 1885–1962, vol. VI
Dobson, Hon. Alfred, 1848–1908, vol. I
Dobson, Sir Arthur Dudley, 1841–1934, vol. III
Dobson, Sir Benjamin Alfred, 1847–1898, vol. I
Dobson, Bernard Henry, 1881–1945, vol. IV
Dobson, Rear-Adm. Claude Congreve, 1885–1940, vol. III
Dobson, Cowan, *died* 1980, vol. VII
Dobson, Lt-Col Francis George, 1879–1941, vol. IV
Dobson, Frank, 1888–1963, vol. VI
Dobson, George, *died* 1938, vol. III
Dobson, Gordon Miller Bourne, 1889–1976, vol. VII
Dobson, Henry Austin, 1840–1921, vol. II
Dobson, Henry John, 1858–1928, vol. II
Dobson, John Frederic, 1875–1947, vol. IV
Dobson, Lt-Col Joseph Henry, 1878–1954, vol. V
Dobson, Mildred Eaton, *died* 1952, vol. V
Dobson, Raymond Francis Harvey, 1925–1980, vol. VII
Dobson, Richard Rhimes, 1877–1960, vol. V
Dobson, Sir Roy Hardy, 1891–1968, vol. VI
Dobson, Sydney George, 1883–1969, vol. VI
Dobson, Thomas William, 1853–1935, vol. III
Dobson, William Charles Thomas, 1817–1898, vol. I
Dobson, Sir William Lambert, 1833–1898, vol. I
Dobson, Col Sir William Warrington, 1861–1941, vol. IV
Docker, Sir Bernard Dudley Frank, 1896–1978, vol. VII
Docker, Frank Dudley, 1862–1944, vol. IV
Docker, Ludford Charles, 1860–1940, vol. III
Docker, Rev. Wilfrid Brougham, 1882–1956, vol. V
Dockrell, Benjamin Morgan, 1860–1920, vol. II
Dockrell, Sir Maurice Edward, 1850–1929, vol. III
Dockrill, Col Walter R., 1877–1942, vol. IV
Dod, Brig.-Gen. Owen Cadogan W.; *see* Wolley-Dod.
Dodd, Brig. Arthur Harvey Russell, 1883–1955, vol. V
Dodd, Catherine I., *died* 1932, vol. III
Dodd, Charles Edward Shuter, 1891–1974, vol. VII
Dodd, Rev. Charles Harold, 1884–1973, vol. VII
Dodd, Cyril, *died* 1913, vol. I
Dodd, Sir Edward James, 1909–1966, vol. VI

Dodd, Sir Edwin, *died* 1933, vol. III
Dodd, Francis, 1874–1949, vol. IV
Dodd, Frederick Henry, 1890–1950, vol. IV
Dodd, Major George, 1872–1914, vol. I
Dodd, Henry Work, *died* 1921, vol. II
Dodd, Col John Richard, 1858–1930, vol. III
Dodd, Sir John Samuel, 1904–1973, vol. VII
Dodd, Norris Edward, 1879–1968, vol. VI
Dodd, Sir Robert John Sherwood, 1878–1950, vol. IV
Dodd, Stanley, *died* 1946, vol. IV
Dodd, Col Wilfrid T., *died* 1942, vol. IV
Dodd, Rt Hon. William Huston, 1844–1930, vol. III
Dodds, Sir Charles; *see* Dodds, Sir E. C.
Dodds, Sir (Edward) Charles, 1st Bt, 1899–1973, vol. VII
Dodds, Eric Robertson, 1893–1979, vol. VII
Dodds, George Elliott, 1889–1977, vol. VII
Dodds, Harold Willis, 1889–1980, vol. VII (AII)
Dodds, Jackson, 1881–1961, vol. VI
Dodds, Sir James Leishman, 1891–1972, vol. VII
Dodds, Sir James Miller, 1861–1935, vol. III
Dodds, Hon. Sir John Stokell, 1848–1914, vol. I
Dodds, Rev. Canon Matthew Archbold, 1864–1928, vol. II
Dodds, Norman Noel, 1903–1965, vol. VI
Dodds, Stephen Roxby, 1881–1943, vol. IV
Dodds, Maj.-Gen. Thomas Henry, 1873–1943, vol. IV
Dodds, Brig.-Gen. William Okell Holden, 1867–1934, vol. III
Dodds Crewe, Major James Hugh Hamilton, 1880–1956, vol. V
Dodge, Bayard, 1888–1972, vol. VII
Dodge, Grenville Mellen, 1831–1916, vol. II
Dodge, John Bigelow, 1894–1960, vol. V
Dodgson, Campbell, 1867–1948, vol. IV
Dodgson, Rev. Charles L.; *see* Carroll, Lewis.
Dodgson, Brig.-Gen. Colquhoun Scott, 1867–1947, vol. IV
Dodgson, Sir David Scott, 1821–1898, vol. I
Dodgson, Major Heathfield Butler, 1863–1937, vol. III
Dodgson, John Arthur, 1890–1969, vol. VI
Dodington, Brig.-Gen. Wilfred Marriott-, 1871–1931, vol. III
Dods, Alexander Waddell, *died* 1952, vol. V
Dods, Lt-Col Joseph Espie, 1874–1930, vol. III
Dods, Marcus, 1834–1909, vol. I
Dods, Marcus, *died* 1935, vol. III
Dods-Withers, Isobelle, 1876–1939, vol. III
Dodson, Sir Gerald, 1884–1966, vol. VI
Dodson, John Michael, 1919–1977, vol. VII
Dodson, Rev. Canon Thomas Hatheway, 1862–1931, vol. III
Dodsworth, Sir Claude Matthew S., 7th Bt; *see* Smith-Dodsworth.
Dodsworth, Sir (Leonard) Lumley (Savage), 1890–1968, vol. VI
Dodsworth, Sir Lumley; *see* Dodsworth, Sir Leonard L. S.
Dodsworth, Sir Matthew Blayney Smith, 6th Bt, 1856–1931, vol. III

Dodwell, David William, 1898–1980, vol. VII
Dodwell, Henry Herbert, 1879–1946, vol. IV
Doel, James, 1804–1902, vol. I
Doggart, Arthur Robert, 1866–1932, vol. III
Doherty, Rt Hon. Charles Joseph, 1855–1931, vol. III
Doherty, F. C., *died* 1959, vol. V
Doherty, William David, 1893–1966, vol. VI
Doherty-Holwell, Captain Raymond Vernon; *see* Holwell.
Dohnányi, Ernest, 1877–1960, vol. V
Doidge, Sir Frederick Widdowson, 1884–1954, vol. V
Doig, Henry Stuart, 1874–1931, vol. III
Doig, Peter, 1882–1952, vol. V
d'Oisly, (Emile) Maurice, 1882–1949, vol. IV
d'Oisly, Maurice; *see* d'Oisly, E. M.
Doke, Clement Martyn, 1893–1980, vol. VII
Dolamore, William Henry, *died* 1938, vol. III
Doland, Lt-Col George Frederick, 1872–1946, vol. IV
Dolbey, Robert Valentine, 1878–1937, vol. III
Dolby, Major Sir George Alexander, 1854–1939, vol. III
Dolgorouki, Prince Alexis, 1846–1915, vol. I
Dolgorouki, Princess Alexis, (Frances), *died* 1919, vol. II
Doll, William Alfred Millner, 1885–1977, vol. VII
Dollan, Sir Patrick Joseph, *died* 1963, vol. VI
Dollfuss, Engelbert, 1892–1934, vol. III
Dollman, John Charles, 1851–1934, vol. III
Dolman, Eric Charles, 1903–1969, vol. VI
Dolman, Frederick, *born* 1867, vol. II
Dolmetsch, Arnold, 1858–1940, vol. III
Dolphin, Albert Edward, 1895–1972, vol. VII
Dolphin, Lt-Comdr Edgar H., *died* 1930, vol. III
Dolphin, Rear-Adm. George Verner Motley, 1902–1979, vol. VII
Dolphin, John Robert Vernon, 1905–1973, vol. VII
Dolton, David, *died* 1932, vol. III
Domagk, Gerhard, 1895–1964, vol. VI
Domenichetti, Richard, *died* 1901, vol. I
Dominguez, Florencio L., *died* 1910, vol. I
Dominguez, Don Vicente J., *died* 1916, vol. II
Dominy, Reginald Hugh, *died* 1953, vol. V
Domvile, Adm. Sir Barry Edward, 1878–1971, vol. VII
Domvile, Sir Compton Edward, 1842–1924, vol. II
Domvile, Sir Compton Meade, 4th Bt, 1857–1935, vol. III
Domvile, Sir Hugo Compton Domvile P.; *see* Poë Domvile.
Domville, Rear-Adm. Sir Cecil; *see* Domville, Rear-Adm. Sir W. C. H.
Domville, Captain Sir Cecil Lionel, 6th Bt, 1892–1930, vol. III
Domville, Lt-Col Hon. James, 1842–1921, vol. II
Domville, Sir James Henry, 5th Bt, 1889–1919, vol. II
Domville, Rear-Adm. Sir (William) Cecil H., 4th Bt, 1849–1904, vol. I
Domville-Fife, Charles William, 1887–1960, vol. V (A)
Don, Rev. Alan Campbell, 1885–1966, vol. VI

Don, Charles Davidson, 1874–1959, vol. V
Don, Air Vice-Marshal Francis Percival, 1886–1964, vol. VI
Don, Sir William, 1861–1926, vol. II
Don, Surg.-Gen. William Gerard, 1836–1920, vol. II
Don-Wauchope, Sir John Douglas; *see* Wauchope.
Donachy, Frank, 1899–1970, vol. VI
Donald, Alexander Douglas, *died* 1948, vol. IV
Donald, Archibald, 1860–1937, vol. III
Donald, Charles, 1896–1955, vol. V
Donald, Maj.-Gen. Colin George, 1854–1939, vol. III
Donald, Douglas, 1865–1953, vol. V
Donald, Douglas Alexander, *died* 1975, vol. VII
Donald, Air Marshal Sir Grahame, 1891–1976, vol. VII
Donald, Sir James, 1873–1957, vol. V
Donald, Sir James Bell, 1879–1971, vol. VII
Donald, Sir John Stewart, 1861–1948, vol. IV
Donald, Mary Jane; *see* Longstaff, M. J.
Donald, Maxwell Bruce, 1897–1978, vol. VII
Donald, Sir Robert, 1861–1933, vol. III
Donald, William C.; *see* Coutts Donald.
Donaldson, Rev. Canon Alexander Edward, 1878–1960, vol. V
Donaldson, Rev. Augustus Blair, 1841–1903, vol. I
Donaldson, Comdr Charles Edward McArthur, 1903–1964, vol. VI
Donaldson, Eion Pelly, 1896–1963, vol. VI
Donaldson, Rev. Frederic Lewis, 1860–1953, vol. V
Donaldson, Sir George, 1845–1925, vol. II
Donaldson, Sir Hay Frederick, 1856–1916, vol. II
Donaldson, Sir James, 1831–1915, vol. I
Donaldson, John Coote, 1895–1980, vol. VII
Donaldson, Adm. Leonard Andrew Boyd, 1875–1956, vol. V
Donaldson, Malcolm, 1884–1973, vol. VII
Donaldson, Mary Ethel Muir, 1876–1958, vol. V
Donaldson, Norman Patrick, 1878–1955, vol. V
Donaldson, Robert, *died* 1933, vol. III
Donaldson, Rt Rev. St Clair George, 1863–1935, vol. III
Donaldson, William, 1838–1924, vol. II
Donaldson-Hudson, Lt-Col Ralph Charles, 1874–1941, vol. IV
Donat, (Frederick) Robert, 1905–1958, vol. V
Donat, Robert; *see* Donat, F. R.
Doncaster, Leonard, 1877–1920, vol. II
Doncaster, Sir Robert, 1872–1955, vol. V
Done, Brig.-Gen. Herbert Richard, 1876–1950, vol. IV
Done, William Edward Pears, 1883–1976, vol. VII
Donegall, 5th Marquess of, 1822–1904 (this entry was not transferred to Who was Who).
Donegall, 6th Marquis of, 1903–1975, vol. VII
Donegan, Lt-Col James Francis, 1863–1934, vol. III
Donelan, Captain Anthony J., 1846–1924, vol. II
Donelan, James, *died* 1922, vol. II
Doneraile, 6th Viscount, 1866–1941, vol. IV
Doneraile, 7th Viscount, 1869–1956, vol. V
Doneraile, 8th Viscount, 1878–1957, vol. V
Dönges, Theophilus Ebenhaézer, 1898–1968, vol. VI

Donington, 3rd Baron, 1859–1927, vol. II
Donkin, Sir Bryan; *see* Donkin, Sir H. B.
Donkin, Bryan, 1835–1902, vol. I
Donkin, Sir (Horatio) Bryan, 1845–1927, vol. II
Donkin, Richard Sims, 1836–1919, vol. II
Donkin, Sydney Bryan, 1871–1952, vol. V
Donn-Byrne, Brian Oswald; *see* Byrne, Donn.
Donnan, Frederick George, 1870–1956, vol. V
Donnan, James, 1837–1915, vol. I
Donnay, Maurice, 1859–1945, vol. IV
Donne, Col Benjamin Donisthorpe Alsop, 1856–1907, vol. I
Donne, Col Henry Richard Beadon, 1860–1949, vol. IV
Donne, Thomas Edward, 1859–1945, vol. IV
Donne, Ven. William, 1845–1914, vol. I
Donnelly, Alex. E., *died* 1958, vol. V
Donnelly, Sir Arthur Telford, 1890–1954, vol. V
Donnelly, Desmond Louis, 1920–1974, vol. VII
Donnelly, Harry Hill, 1909–1969, vol. VI
Donnelly, Sir John Fretcheville Dykes, 1834–1902, vol. I
Donnelly, Rt Rev. Nicholas, 1837–1920, vol. II
Donnelly, Patrick, *died* 1947, vol. IV
Donner, Anna Maria, (Lady Donner), *died* 1935, vol. III
Donner, Sir Edward, 1st Bt, 1840–1934, vol. III
Donner, Ossian, 1866–1957, vol. V
Donnet, Sir James John Louis, 1816–1905, vol. I
Donnithorne, Rev. Vyvyan Henry, 1886–1968, vol. VI
Donoghue, Stephen, (Steve), 1884–1945, vol. IV
Donohoe, Martin Henry, 1869–1927, vol. II
Donohue, Col William Edward, 1861–1945, vol. IV
Donoughmore, 5th Earl of, 1848–1900, vol. I
Donoughmore, 6th Earl of, 1875–1948, vol. IV
Donovan, Baron (Life Peer); Terence Norbert Donovan, 1898–1971, vol. VII
Donovan, Dame Florence May; *see* Hancock, Dame F. M.
Donovan, Francis Desmond, 1894–1948, vol. IV
Donovan, John, 1891–1971, vol. VII
Donovan, John Thomas, 1878–1922, vol. II
Donovan, John Thomas, 1885–1973, vol. VII
Donovan, Robert, 1862–1934, vol. III
Donovan, Maj.-Gen. Sir William, 1850–1934, vol. III
Donovan, Maj.-Gen. William J., 1883–1959, vol. V
Dontenwill, Most Rev. Augustin, 1857–1931, vol. III
Doodson, Arthur Thomas, 1890–1968, vol. VI
Doogan, P. C., *died* 1906, vol. I
Doolette, Sir George Philip, 1840–1924, vol. II
Doolin, William, 1887–1962, vol. VI
Dooner, Lt-Col William Dundas, 1876–1927, vol. II
Dooner, Col William Toke, *died* 1926, vol. II
Doorly, Sir Charles William, 1875–1942, vol. IV
Doorly, Most Rev. Edward, 1870–1950, vol. IV
Doorly, Rev. Canon Wiltshire Stokely, *died* 1932, vol. III
Dopping-Hepenstal, Major Lambert John, 1859–1928, vol. II
Dopping-Hepenstal, Col Maxwell Edward, 1872–1965, vol. VI

Doran, Alban Henry Griffiths, 1849–1927, vol. II
Doran, Maj.-Gen. Beauchamp John Colclough, 1860–1943, vol. IV
Doran, Edward, 1892–1945, vol. IV
Doran, Edward Anthony, *died* 1922, vol. II
Doran, Sir Henry Francis, 1856–1928, vol. II
Doran, Gen. Sir John, 1824–1903, vol. I
Doran, Brig. John Crampton Morton, 1880–1957, vol. V
Doran, Brig.-Gen. Walter Robert Butler, 1861–1945, vol. IV
Dorchester, 4th Baron, 1822–1897, vol. I
Dorchester, Baroness (5th in line), 1846–1925, vol. II
Dorchester, 6th Baron, 1876–1963, vol. VI
Dore, Gp Captain Alan Sydney Whitehorn, 1882–1953, vol. V
Dore, Ernest, *died* 1950, vol. IV
Doré, Victor, 1880–1954, vol. V
Dorey, Edgar Aleck, 1886–1976, vol. VII
Dorey, Stanley Fabes, 1891–1972, vol. VII
Dorez, Léon Louis Marie, 1864–1922, vol. II (A), vol. III
Dorington, Hubert, 1878–1935, vol. III
Dorington, Rt Hon. Sir John Edward, 1st Bt, 1832–1911, vol. I
Doris, William, 1860–1926, vol. II
Dorland, Arthur Garratt, 1887–1980, vol. VII
Dorling, Captain Henry Taprell, 1883–1968, vol. VI
Dorling, Vice-Adm. James Wilfred Sussex, 1889–1966, vol. VI
Dorling, Col Lionel, 1860–1925, vol. II
Dorman, Sir Arthur John, 1st Bt, 1848–1931, vol. III
Dorman, Sir Bedford Lockwood, 2nd Bt, *died* 1956, vol. V
Dorman, Brig. Edward Mungo, 1885–1967, vol. VI
Dorman, Surg.-Gen. John Cotter, 1852–1944, vol. IV
Dorman-Smith, Col Rt Hon. Sir Reginald Hugh, 1899–1977, vol. VII
Dormer, 12th Baron, 1830–1900, vol. I
Dormer, 13th Baron, 1862–1920, vol. II
Dormer, 14th Baron, 1864–1922, vol. II
Dormer, 15th Baron, 1903–1975, vol. VII
Dormer, Sir Cecil Francis Joseph, 1883–1979, vol. VII
Dormer, Charles Walter C.; *see* Cottrell-Dormer.
D'Ormesson, Count Wladimir Olivier Marie François de Paule Le Fèvre, 1888–1973, vol. VII
Dornhorst, Frederick, 1849–1927, vol. II
Dorrell, Bt Lt-Col George Thomas, *died* 1971, vol. VII
Dorrien, Gen. Sir Horace Lockwood S.; *see* Smith-Dorrien.
Dorrien, Lady (Olive Crofton) S.; *see* Smith-Dorrien.
Dorrien, Rev. Walter Montgomery S.; *see* Smith-Dorrien.
Dorrien-Smith, Major Edward Pendarves, 1879–1937, vol. III
Dorrien-Smith, Thomas Algernon, 1846–1918, vol. II
Dorrity, Rev. David, *died* 1926, vol. II
Dorté, Philip Hoghton, 1904–1970, vol. VI

Dorward, Alan James, 1889–1956, vol. V
Dorward, Maj.-Gen. Sir Arthur Robert Ford, 1848–1934, vol. III
Dos Passos, John, 1896–1970, vol. VI
Dott, Norman McOmish, 1897–1973, vol. VII
Dottin, Henri Georges, 1863–1928, vol. II (A), vol. III
Dottridge, Edwin Thomas, 1876–1947, vol. IV
Doubleday, Rt Rev. Arthur, 1865–1951, vol. V
Doubleday, Frederic Nicklin, 1885–1971, vol. VII
Doubleday, Sir Leslie, 1887–1975, vol. VII
Doudney, Sarah, 1843–1926, vol. II
Dougal, Daniel, 1884–1948, vol. IV
Dougall, Lily, 1858–1923, vol. II
Dougan, James Lockhart, 1874–1941, vol. IV
Dougan, Thomas Wilson, *died* 1907, vol. I
Dougherty, HE Cardinal Denis J., *died* 1951, vol. V
Dougherty, Rt Hon. Sir James Brown, 1844–1934, vol. III
Doughty, Sir Arthur, *died* 1936, vol. III
Doughty, Sir Charles, 1878–1956, vol. V
Doughty, Charles John Addison, 1902–1973, vol. VII
Doughty, Charles Montagu, 1843–1926, vol. II
Doughty, Sir George, 1854–1914, vol. I
Doughty, Rear-Adm. Henry Montagu, 1870–1921, vol. II
Doughty-Tichborne, Sir Anthony Joseph Henry Doughty; *see* Tichborne.
Doughty-Tichborne, Sir Henry Alfred Joseph; *see* Tichborne.
Doughty-Tichborne, Sir Joseph Henry Bernard; *see* Tichborne.
Doughty-Wylie, Major Charles Hotham Montagu; *see* Wylie.
Douglas of Barloch, 1st Baron, 1889–1980, vol. VII
Douglas of Kirtleside, 1st Baron, 1893–1969, vol. VI
Douglas, Hon. Sir Adyl, 1815–1906, vol. I
Douglas, Lord Alfred Bruce, 1870–1945, vol. IV
Douglas, Andrew, *died* 1935, vol. III
Douglas, Very Rev. Canon Lord Archibald, 1850–1938, vol. III
Douglas, Archibald Campbell, 1872–1943, vol. IV
Douglas, Adm. Sir Archibald Lucius, 1842–1913, vol. I
Douglas, Col Archibald Philip, 1867–1953, vol. V
Douglas, Lt-Col Archibald Vivian Campbell, 1902–1977, vol. VII
Douglas, Arthur, 1850–1920, vol. II
Douglas, Rt Rev. Hon. Arthur Gascoigne, 1827–1905, vol. I
Douglas, Arthur Henry Johnstone-, 1846–1923, vol. II
Douglas, Sir Arthur Percy, 5th Bt (*cr* 1777), 1845–1913, vol. I
Douglas, Campbell Mellis, *died* 1909, vol. I
Douglas, Carstairs Cumming, 1866–1940, vol. III
Douglas, Cecil George, 1854–1919, vol. II
Douglas, Lt-Col Charles Edward, 1855–1943, vol. IV
Douglas, Charles Mackinnon, 1865–1924, vol. II
Douglas, Gen. Sir Charles Whittingham Horsley, 1850–1914, vol. I

Douglas, Claude, 1852–1945, vol. IV
Douglas, Claude Gordon, 1882–1963, vol. VI
Douglas, Clifford Hugh, 1879–1952, vol. V
Douglas, David, 1823–1916, vol. II
Douglas, Brig.-Gen. Douglas Campbell, 1864–1927, vol. II
Douglas, Rt Rev. Edward, 1901–1967, vol. VI
Douglas, Hon. Edward Archibald, 1877–1947, vol. IV
Douglas, Rev. Evelyn Keith, 1859–1920, vol. II
Douglas, Francis John, 1858–1934, vol. III
Douglas, Sir George Brisbane, 5th Bt (cr 1786), 1856–1935, vol. III
Douglas, Rev. George Cunninghame Monteath, 1826–1904, vol. I
Douglas, Adm. Hon. George Henry, 1821–1905, vol. I
Douglas, Very Rev. George James Cosmo, died 1973, vol. IV
Douglas, (George) Keith, 1903–1949, vol. IV
Douglas, Lt-Col George Stuart, 1879–1947, vol. IV
Douglas, Rt Rev. Gerald Wybergh, 1875–1934, vol. III
Douglas, Rev. Hon. Henry, 1822–1907, vol. I
Douglas, Maj.-Gen. Henry Edward Manning, 1875–1939, vol. III
Douglas, Vice-Adm. Sir (Henry) Percy, 1876–1939, vol. III
Douglas, Horace James, 1866–1962, vol. VI
Douglas, Hugh C.; see Cowan-Douglas.
Douglas, Irvine; see Douglas, R. I.
Douglas, James, 1826–1904, vol. I
Douglas, James, 1837–1910, vol. I
Douglas, James, 1837–1918, vol. II
Douglas, James, 1867–1940, vol. III
Douglas, Maj.-Gen. James Archibald, 1862–1932, vol. III
Douglas, James Archibald, 1884–1978, vol. VII
Douglas, Sir James Boyd, 1893–1964, vol. VI
Douglas, James G., 1887–1954, vol. V
Douglas, Sir James Louis Fitzroy Scott, 6th Bt (cr 1786), 1930–1969, vol. VI
Douglas, Hon. James Moffat, 1839–1921, vol. II
Douglas, James Sholto Cameron, 1879–1931, vol. III
Douglas, Major Sir James Stewart, 6th Bt (cr 1777), 1859–1940, vol. III
Douglas, Major James Wightman, 1873–1937, vol. III
Douglas, Hon. John, 1828–1904, vol. I
Douglas, Rev. Canon John Albert, died 1956, vol. V
Douglas, Maj.-Gen. John Primrose, 1908–1975, vol. VII
Douglas, Katharine Greenhill, 1908–1979, vol. VII
Douglas, Keith; see Douglas, G. K.
Douglas, Sir Kenneth, 4th Bt (cr 1831), 1868–1954, vol. V
Douglas, Lewis Williams, 1894–1974, vol. VII
Douglas, Lloyd C., 1877–1951, vol. V
Douglas, Lt-Col Montagu William, 1863–1957, vol. V
Douglas, Norman, 1868–1952, vol. V
Douglas, Col Norman, 1887–1968, vol. VI

Douglas, O.; see Buchan, Anna.
Douglas, Vice-Adm. Sir Percy; see Douglas, Vice-Adm. Sir H. P.
Douglas, Reginald Stair, 1877–1933, vol. III
Douglas, Lt-Col Robert Jeffray, 1869–1916, vol. II
Douglas, Sir Robert Kennaway, 1838–1913, vol. I
Douglas, Captain Robert Langton, 1864–1951, vol. V
Douglas, Rev. Robert Noel, 1868–1957, vol. V
Douglas, Major Robert Vaughan, 1881–1922, vol. II
Douglas, Col Roderick, 1898–1965, vol. VI
Douglas, (Ronald) Irvine, 1899–1973, vol. VII
Douglas, Adm. Sholto, 1833–1913, vol. I
Douglas, Captain Sholto Grant, 1867–1956, vol. V
Douglas, Major Sholto William, 1870–1959, vol. V
Douglas, Captain Stewart Ranken, 1871–1936, vol. III
Douglas, Maj.-Gen. Sir William, 1858–1920, vol. II
Douglas, Brig.-Gen. William Charles, 1862–1938, vol. III
Douglas, William Douglas Robinson-, 1851–1921, vol. II
Douglas, William Orville, 1898–1980, vol. VII
Douglas, Comdr William Ramsay Binny, died 1919, vol. II
Douglas, Sir William Scott, 1890–1953, vol. V
Douglas-Hamilton, Rev. Hamilton Anne, 1853–1929, vol. III
Douglas-Hamilton, Lord Malcolm Avendale, 1909–1964, vol. VI
Douglas-Hamilton, Percy Seymour, 1875–1940, vol. III
Douglas-Henry, Major James, 1881–1943, vol. IV
Douglas-Jones, Sir Crawford Douglas, 1874–1956, vol. V
Douglas-Pennant, Hon. Alan George Sholto, 1890–1915, vol. I
Douglas-Pennant, Hon. Charles, 1877–1914, vol. I
Douglas-Pennant, Adm. Hon. Sir Cyril Eustace, 1894–1961, vol. VI
Douglas-Pennant, Captain Hon. George Henry, 1876–1915, vol. I
Douglas-Pennant, Hon. Violet Blanche, died 1945, vol. IV
Douglas-Scott, Lord Charles Thomas Montagu; see Scott.
Douglas-Scott-Montagu, Hon. Robert Henry, 1867–1916, vol. II
Douglass of Cleveland, Baron (Life Peer); Harry Douglass, 1902–1978, vol. VII
Douglass, Sir James Nicholas, 1826–1898, vol. I
Douglass, Walter John, 1863–1945, vol. IV
Douglass, William Tregarthen, died 1913, vol. I
Douie, Charles Oswald Gaskell, 1896–1953, vol. V
Douie, Col Francis McCrone, 1886–1935, vol. III
Douie, Sir James McCrone, 1854–1935, vol. III
Doull, Rt Rev. Alexander John, 1870–1937, vol. III
Doull, John, 1878–1969, vol. VI (AII)
Doull-Connolly, Thomas James, 1878–1949, vol. IV (A)
Doulton, Sir Henry, 1820–1897, vol. I
Doulton, Henry Lewis, 1853–1930, vol. III
Doumer, Paul, 1857–1932, vol. III

Doumergue, Emile, 1844–1937, vol. III
Doumergue, Gaston, 1863–1937, vol. III
Doumic, Rene, *died* 1937, vol. III
Douthwaite, Arthur Henry, 1896–1974, vol. VII
Douthwaite, James Lungley, 1877–1960, vol. V
Douty, Edward Henry, 1861–1911, vol. I
Dove, Dame Frances, 1847–1942, vol. IV
Dove-Edwin, George Frederick, 1896–1973, vol. VII
Dove-Wilson, Sir John Carnegie; *see* Wilson.
Dover, Rev. Thomas Birkett, 1846–1926, vol. II
Dovercourt, 1st Baron, 1878–1961, vol. VI
Doverdale, 1st Baron, 1836–1925, vol. II
Doverdale, 2nd Baron, 1872–1935, vol. III
Doverdale, 3rd Baron, 1904–1949, vol. IV
Doveton, Frederick Bazett, 1841–1911, vol. I
Dow, Alexander Warren, 1873–1948, vol. IV
Dow, David Rutherford, 1887–1979, vol. VII
Dow, Sir Hugh, 1886–1978, vol. VII
Dow, Samuel, 1908–1976, vol. VII
Dow, Thomas Millie, *died* 1919, vol. II
Dowbiggin, Sir Herbert Layard, 1880–1966, vol. VI
Dowdall, Hon. Mary Frances Harriet, 1876–1939, vol. III
Dowdall, Harold Chaloner, 1868–1955, vol. V
Dowdall, Sir Laurence Charles Edward Downing, 1851–1936, vol. III
Dowden, Major Charles Henry, 1880–1937, vol. III
Dowden, Edward, 1843–1913, vol. I
Dowden, Rt Rev. John, 1840–1910, vol. I
Dowden, John Wheeler, 1866–1936, vol. III
Dowding, 1st Baron, 1882–1970, vol. VI
Dowding, Vice-Adm. Sir Arthur Ninian, 1886–1966, vol. VI
Dowding, Cdre John Charles Keith, 1891–1965, vol. VI
Dowding, Gen. Townley Ward, 1847–1927, vol. II
Dowell, Brig.-Gen. Arthur John William, 1861–1943, vol. IV
Dowell, Col George Cecil, 1862–1949, vol. IV
Dowell, Bt Lt-Col George William, 1860–1940, vol. III
Dowell, Sir William Montagu, 1825–1912, vol. I
Dower, Col Alan Vincent Gandar, 1898–1980, vol. VII
Dowker, Gen. Howard Codrington, 1829–1912, vol. I
Dowler, Lt-Gen. Sir Arthur Arnhold Bullick, 1895–1963, vol. VI
Dowley, Francis Michael, 1885–1948, vol. IV
Dowling, Geoffrey Barrow, 1891–1976, vol. VII
Dowling, Most Rev. John Pius, 1860–1940, vol. III
Dowling, Vice-Adm. Sir Roy Russell, 1901–1969, vol. VI
Dowling, Rev. Theodore Edward, 1837–1921, vol. II
Dowling, Rt Rev. Thomas Joseph, 1840–1924, vol. II
Down, Lt-Comdr Sir Charles Edward, 1857–1927, vol. II
Down, Lt-Gen. Sir Ernest Edward, 1902–1980, vol. VII
Down, Air Cdre Harold Hunter, 1895–1974, vol. VII

Down, Captain Richard Thornton, 1882–1944, vol. IV
Downe, 8th Viscount, 1844–1924, vol. II
Downe, 9th Viscount, 1872–1931, vol. III
Downe, 10th Viscount, 1903–1965, vol. VI
Downer, Ven. George William, *died* 1912, vol. I
Downer, Sir Harold George, 1871–1935, vol. III
Downer, Hon. Sir John William, 1844–1915, vol. I
Downer, William James, 1851–1939, vol. III
Downes, Sir Arthur Henry, 1851–1938, vol. III
Downes, Commissary-Gen. Arthur William, *died* 1905, vol. I
Downes, Very Rev. Edmund Audley, 1877–1950, vol. IV
Downes, Sir Joseph, 1848–1925, vol. II
Downes, Maj.-Gen. Major Francis, 1834–1923 vol. II
Downes, Rev. Robert Percival, 1842–1924, vol. II
Downes, Maj.-Gen. Rupert Major, 1885–1945, vol. IV
Downes, Col William Knox, 1855–1911, vol. I
Downes-Shaw, Sir (Archibald) Havergal, 1884–1961, vol. VI
Downes-Shaw, Sir Havergal; *see* Downes-Shaw, Sir A. H.
Downey, Edmund, *died* 1937, vol. III
Downey, Most Rev. Richard, 1881–1953, vol. V
Downham, 1st Baron, 1853–1920, vol. II
Downham, Rev. Isaac, *died* 1923, vol. II
Downie, Major Fairbairn, 1880–1949, vol. IV
Downie, Sir Harold Frederick, 1889–1966, vol. VI
Downie, Captain John, *died* 1921, vol. II
Downie, John P., *died* 1945, vol. IV
Downie, Hon. John Wallace, 1876–1940, vol. III
Downie, Walker, *died* 1921, vol. II
Downing, Arthur Matthew Weld, 1850–1917, vol. II
Downing, Col Cameron Macartney Harwood, 1845–1926, vol. II
Downing, Rev. Edward Andrew, *died* 1931, vol. III
Downing, George Henry, 1878–1940, vol. III (A), vol. IV
Downing, Henry Philip Burke, 1865–1947, vol. IV
Downing, Richard Ivan, 1915–1975, vol. VII
Downing, Sir Stanford Edwin, 1870–1933, vol. III
Downing, Rev. Thomas William, 1864–1932, vol. III
Downs, Edgar, *died* 1963, vol. VI
Downs, James, 1856–1941, vol. IV
Downshire, 6th Marquess of, 1871–1918, vol. II
Dowse, Rt Rev. Charles Benjamin, *died* 1934, vol. III
Dowse, Maj.-Gen. John Cecil Alexander, 1891–1964, vol. VI
Dowse, Rev. John Clarence, *died* 1930, vol. III
Dowse, Very Rev. William, 1856–1939, vol. III
Dowsett, Col Ernest Blair, *died* 1951, vol. V
Dowson, Sir Ernest MacLeod, 1876–1950, vol. IV
Dowson, Sir Hubert Arthur, 1866–1946, vol. IV
Dowson, Joseph Emerson, 1844–1940, vol. III
Dowson, Sir Oscar Follett, 1879–1961, vol. VI
Dowty, Sir George Herbert, 1901–1975, vol. VII
Doxat, Major Alexis Charles, 1867–1942, vol. IV
Doxford, Sir William Theodore, 1841–1916, vol. II

Doxiadis, Constantinos Apostolos, 1913–1975, vol. VII
Doyen, E., 1859–1916, vol. II
Doyle, Adrian Malcolm C.; *see* Conan Doyle.
Doyle, Sir Arthur Conan, 1859–1930, vol. III
Doyle, Col Sir Arthur Havelock James, 4th Bt, 1858–1948, vol. IV
Doyle, Charles Francis, 1866–1928, vol. II
Doyle, Edward, 1892–1965, vol. VI
Doyle, Lt-Col Eric Edward, 1886–1937, vol. III
Doyle, Sir Everard Hastings, 3rd Bt, 1852–1933, vol. III
Doyle, Hon. Henry Martin, *died* 1929, vol. III
Doyle, Major Ignatius Purcell, 1863–1923, vol. II
Doyle, John Andrew, 1844–1907, vol. I
Doyle, Lt-Col John Francis Innes Hay, 1873–1919, vol. II
Doyle, Joseph, 1891–1974, vol. VII
Doyle, Lynn, (Leslie Alexander Montgomery), 1873–1961, vol. VI
Doyle, Sir Nicholas G.; *see* Grattan-Doyle.
Doyle, Rt Rev. Mgr Richard Barry-, 1878–1933, vol. III
Doyle, Very Rev. Thomas, 1853–1926, vol. II
Doyle-Jones, F. W., *died* 1938, vol. III
D'Oyly, Sir Charles Hastings, 12th Bt, 1898–1962, vol. VI
D'Oyly, Sir Charles Walters, 9th Bt, 1822–1900, vol. I
D'Oyly, Sir Hadley; *see* D'Oyly, Sir H. H.
D'Oyly, Sir (Hastings) Hadley, 11th Bt, 1864–1948, vol. IV
D'Oyly, Sir Warren Hastings, 10th Bt, 1838–1921, vol. II
D'Oyly Carte, Rupert, 1876–1948, vol. IV
D'Oyly-Hughes, Captain Guy, 1891–1940, vol. III
Doyne, Charles Mervyn, 1839–1924, vol. II
Doyne, Dermot Henry, 1871–1942, vol. IV
Doyne, Philip Geoffry, 1886–1959, vol. V
Doyne, Robert Walter, 1857–1916, vol. II
Drachmann, Holger, 1846–1908, vol. I
Drage, Sir Benjamin, *died* 1952, vol. V
Drage, Geoffrey, 1860–1955, vol. V
Drage, Lt-Col William Henry, 1855–1915, vol. I (A)
Drago, Luis Maria, 1859–1921, vol. II
Drake, Brig.-Gen. Bernard Francis, 1862–1954, vol. V
Drake, Bernard Harpur, 1876–1941, vol. IV
Drake, Donald Henry Charles, 1887–1974, vol. VII
Drake, Sir Eugen John Henry Vanderstegen M.; *see* Millington-Drake.
Drake, Rev. F. W., *died* 1930, vol. III
Drake, Sir Francis George Augustus Fuller-Eliott-, 2nd Bt, 1837–1916, vol. II
Drake, Lt-Col Francis Richard, 1862–1935, vol. III
Drake, Sir Garrard Tyrwhitt-; *see* Drake, Sir H. G. T.
Drake, Harold William, 1889–1973, vol. VII
Drake, Col Henry Dowrish, 1859–1931, vol. III
Drake, Sir (Hugh) Garrard Tyrwhitt-, 1881–1964, vol. VI
Drake, Hon. James George, 1850–1941, vol. IV
Drake, John Alexander, 1878–1952, vol. V

Drake, John Collard Bernard, 1884–1975, vol. VII
Drake, Maurice, 1875–1923, vol. II
Drake, Hon. Montague W. Tyrwhitt-, *died* 1908, vol. I
Drake, Lt-Col Reginald John, *died* 1948, vol. IV
Drake, Robert James, *died* 1916, vol. II
Drake, Samuel Bingham, *died* 1935, vol. III
Drake, Captain Thomas Oakley, 1863–1928, vol. II
Drake, Col William Hacche, 1873–1956, vol. V
Drake, William James, 1872–1919, vol. II
Drake, William Wyckham Tyrwhitt, 1851–1919, vol. II
Drake-Brockman, Brig.-Gen. David Henry, 1868–1960, vol. V
Drake-Brockman, Sir Digby Livingstone, 1877–1959, vol. V
Drake-Brockman, Maj.-Gen. Edmund Alfred, 1884–1949, vol. IV
Drake-Brockman, Sir Henry Vernon, 1865–1933, vol. III
Drake-Brockman, Lt-Col Ralph Evelyn, 1875–1952, vol. V
Drakoules, Platon Soterios, 1858–1942, vol. IV
Draper, Bernard Montagu, 1875–1950, vol. IV
Draper, Charles, 1869–1952, vol. V
Draper, Brig.-Gen. Denis Colbarn, 1873–1951, vol. V
Draper, Herbert James, *died* 1920, vol. II
Draper, Ruth, 1884–1956, vol. V
Draper, Hon. Thomas Percy, 1864–1946, vol. IV
Draper, William Franklin, 1842–1910, vol. I
Draper, William H., Jr, 1894–1974, vol. VII
Draper, Rev. William Henry, 1855–1933, vol. III
Drawbell, James Wedgwood, 1899–1979, vol. VII
Drawbridge, Rev. Cyprian Leycester, 1868–1937, vol. III
Drax, Adm. Hon. Sir Reginald Aylmer Ranfurly P. E. E.; *see* Plunkett-Ernle-Erle-Drax.
Drayson, Rear-Adm. Edwin Howard, 1889–1977, vol. VII
Drayson, Brig. Fitz-Alan George, 1888–1964, vol. VI
Drayton, Edward Rawle, 1859–1927, vol. II
Drayton, Miss Gertrude Drayton Grimké, 1880–1941, vol. IV
Drayton, Harley; *see* Drayton, Harold Charles.
Drayton, Harold Charles, (Harley Drayton), *died* 1966, vol. VI
Drayton, Sir Henry Lumley, 1869–1950, vol. IV
Drayton, Sir Robert Harry, 1892–1963, vol. VI
Dreaper, Surg. Rear-Adm. George Albert, 1863–1927, vol. II
Dreaper, William Porter, 1868–1938, vol. III
Dredge, James, 1840–1906, vol. I
Dreiser, Theodore, 1871–1945, vol. IV
Drennan, Basil St George, 1903–1976, vol. VII
Drennan, (C.) Max, 1870–1935, vol. III
Drennan, Max; *see* Drennan, C. M.
Dreschfeld, Julius, 1846–1907, vol. I
Dresdel, Sonia, *died* 1976, vol. VII
Dressel, Dettmar, 1878–1961, vol. VI
Dressel, Otto, 1880–1941, vol. IV
Dresser, Henry Eeles, 1838–1915, vol. I (A)
Dresser, Horatio Willis, 1866–1954, vol. V

Drever, James, 1873–1950, vol. IV (A)

Drew, Brig.-Gen. Arthur Blanshard Hawley, 1865–1947, vol. IV

Drew, Air Cdre Bertie Clephane Hawley, 1880–1969, vol. VI

Drew, Clifford Luxmoore, *died* 1919, vol. II

Drew, Douglas, 1867–1931, vol. III

Drew, Maj.-Gen. Francis Barry, *died* 1905, vol. I

Drew, Rt Rev. Mgr Count Francis Browning Drew B.; *see* Bickerstaffe-Drew.

Drew, Brig. Francis Greville, 1892–1962, vol. VI

Drew, Lt-Col Hon. George Alexander, 1894–1973, vol. VII

Drew, Lt-Col George Barry, 1868–1930, vol. III

Drew, Rev. Harry, *died* 1910, vol. I

Drew, Gen. Henry Rawlins, 1822–1906, vol. I

Drew, Lt-Col Horace Robert Hawley, 1871–1936, vol. III

Drew, Maj.-Gen. Sir James Syme, 1883–1955, vol. V

Drew, Hon. John Michael, 1865–1947, vol. IV

Drew, Mary, 1847–1927, vol. II

Drew, Sir Thomas, 1838–1910, vol. I

Drew, Vice-Adm. Thomas Bernard, *died* 1960, vol. V

Drew, William Wilson, *died* 1923, vol. II

Drew-Wilkinson, Clennell Frank Massy, 1877–1956, vol. V

Drewe, Basil, 1894–1974, vol. VII

Drewe, Sir Cedric, 1896–1971, vol. VII

Drewe, Rev. Ernest, *died* 1935, vol. III

Drewitt, Frederic George Dawtrey, 1848–1942, vol. IV

Drewry, Arthur, 1891–1961, vol. VI

Drewry, Lt George Leslie, 1894–1918, vol. II

Dreyer, Adm. Sir Frederic Charles, 1878–1956, vol. V

Dreyer, Georges, 1873–1934, vol. III

Dreyer, John Louis Emil, 1852–1926, vol. II

Dreyer, Maj.-Gen. John Tuthill, 1876–1959, vol. V

Dreyfus, Henry, 1882–1944, vol. IV

Driberg, Thomas Edward Neil; *see* Baron Bradwell.

Driesch, Hans, 1867–1941, vol. IV

Dring, Sir William Arthur, 1859–1912, vol. I

Drinkwater, George, 1852–1930, vol. III

Drinkwater, George Carr, 1880–1941, vol. IV

Drinkwater, John, 1882–1937, vol. III

Drinkwater, Sir William Leece, 1812–1909, vol. I

Driscoll, Lt-Col Daniel Patrick, 1862–1934, vol. III

Driscoll, Very Rev. James, 1870–1927, vol. II

Driver, Sir Godfrey Rolles, 1892–1975, vol. VII

Driver, John Edmund, 1900–1965, vol. VI

Driver, Rev. Samuel Rolles, 1846–1914, vol. I

Droch; *see* Bridges, Robert.

Drogheda, 9th Earl of, 1846–1908, vol. I

Drogheda, 10th Earl of, 1884–1957, vol. V

Dromgoole, Charles, *died* 1927, vol. II

Dron, Robert Wilson, 1869–1932, vol. III

Droop, John Percival, 1882–1963, vol. VI

Drought, Rev. Charles Edward, 1847–1917, vol. II

Drought, Charles W.; *see* Worster-Drought.

Drower, Sir Edwin Mortimer, 1880–1951, vol. V

Drower, Ethel May Stefana, (Lady Drower), 1879–1972, vol. VII

Drower, John Edmund, 1853–1945, vol. IV

Drown, Thomas Messinger, 1842–1904, vol. I

Druce, George Claridge, 1850–1932, vol. III

Drucker, Adolphus, 1868–1903, vol. I

Drucquer, Sir Leonard, 1902–1975, vol. VII

Drucquer, Maurice Nathaniel, 1876–1970, vol. VI

Drughorn, Sir John Frederick, 1st Bt, 1862–1943, vol. IV

Druitt, Rt Rev. Cecil Henry, 1874–1921, vol. II

Druitt, Sir Harvey; *see* Druitt, Sir W. A. H.

Druitt, Sir (William Arthur) Harvey, 1910–1973, vol. VII

Drum, Col Lorne, 1871–1933, vol. III

Drummond, Allan Harvey, 1845–1913, vol. I

Drummond, Andrew Cecil, 1865–1913, vol. I

Drummond, Arthur, 1871–1951, vol. V

Drummond, Rev. Arthur Hislop, 1843–1925, vol. II

Drummond, Arthur William Henry H.; *see* Hay-Drummond.

Drummond, Col Hon. Charles Rowley H.; *see* Hay-Drummond.

Drummond, Cyril Augustus, 1873–1945, vol. IV

Drummond, Sir David, 1852–1932, vol. III

Drummond, Lady Edith, 1854–1937, vol. III

Drummond, Adm. Edmund Charles, 1841–1911, vol. I

Drummond, Vice-Adm. Hon. Edmund Rupert, 1884–1965, vol. VI

Drummond, Sir Francis Dudley Williams, 1863–1935, vol. III

Drummond, Maj.-Gen. Sir Francis Henry Rutherford, 1857–1919, vol. II

Drummond, Lt-Comdr Geoffrey Heneage, 1886–1941, vol. IV

Drummond, Hon. Sir George Alexander, 1829–1910, vol. I

Drummond, George Henry, 1883–1963, vol. VI

Drummond, Captain George Robinson Bridge, 1845–1917, vol. II

Drummond, Hon. Mrs Geraldine Margaret, *died* 1956, vol. V

Drummond, Hamilton, *died* 1935, vol. III

Drummond, Henry, 1851–1897, vol. I

Drummond, Lt-Col Henry E. S. H.; *see* Stirling Home Drummond.

Drummond, Lt-Col Henry Edward Stirling-Home-, 1846–1911, vol. I

Drummond, Brig.-Gen. Sir Hugh Henry John, 1st Bt, 1859–1924, vol. II

Drummond, Isabella Martha, *died* 1949, vol. IV

Drummond, Sir Jack Cecil, 1891–1952, vol. V

Drummond, Rev. James, 1835–1918, vol. II

Drummond, James, 1869–1940, vol. III

Drummond, Sir James Hamlyn Williams-, 4th Bt, 1857–1913 (this entry was not transferred to Who was Who).

Drummond, Sir James Hamlyn Williams Williams-, 5th Bt, 1891–1970, vol. VI

Drummond, James Montagu Frank, 1881–1965, vol. VI

Drummond, Maj.-Gen. Laurence George, 1861–1946, vol. IV

Drummond, Lister Maurice, 1856–1916, vol. II
Drummond, Malcolm, 1856–1924, vol. II
Drummond, Captain Maldwin, 1872–1929, vol. III
Drummond, Col Hon. Sir Maurice Charles Andrew, 1877–1957, vol. V
Drummond, Michael, 1850–1921, vol. II (A), vol. III
Drummond, Air Marshal Sir Peter Roy Maxwell, 1894–1945, vol. IV
Drummond, Rev. Robert J., 1858–1951, vol. V
Drummond, Rev. Robert Skiell, 1828–1911, vol. I
Drummond, Sir Victor Arthur Wellington, 1833–1907, vol. I
Drummond, Sir Walter James, 1891–1965, vol. VI
Drummond, Col William, 1880–1960, vol. V
Drummond, Rev. William Hamilton, 1863–1945, vol. IV
Drummond, William Henry, 1854–1907, vol. I
Drummond, Sir William Hugh Dudley Williams-, 6th Bt, 1901–1976, vol. VII
Drummond-Hay, Francis Edward; see Hay.
Drummond-Hay, Sir Francis Ringler; see Hay.
Drummond-Willoughby, Brig.-Gen. Hon. Charles Strathavon Heathcote; see Willoughby.
Drury, Sir Alan Nigel, 1889–1980, vol. VII
Drury, Alfred, 1856–1944, vol. IV
Drury, Amy Gertrude (Lady Drury), died 1953, vol. V
Drury, Adm. Sir Charles Carter, 1846–1914, vol. I
Drury, Maj.-Gen. Charles William, 1856–1913, vol. I
Drury, George Thorn-, 1860–1931, vol. III
Drury, Henry Cooke, 1860–1944, vol. IV
Drury, Henry George, 1839–1941, vol. IV
Drury, Rev. John Frederick William, 1858–1923, vol. II
Drury, Lt-Col Richard Frederick, 1866–1956, vol. V
Drury, Rev. Thomas William Ernest, died 1960, vol. V
Drury, Rt Rev. Thomas Wortley, 1847–1926, vol. II
Drury, William D., 1857–1928, vol. III
Drury, Lt-Col William Price, 1861–1949, vol. IV
Drury-Lowe, Sir Drury Curzon, 1830–1908, vol. I
Drury-Lowe, Vice-Adm. Sidney Robert, 1871–1945, vol. IV
Druso; see Lumley, Lyulph.
Dryburgh, Edward Gelderd, 1909–1965, vol. VI
Dryden, Sir Alfred Erasmus, 5th and 8th Bt, 1821–1912, vol. I
Dryden, Sir Arthur, 6th and 9th Bt, 1852–1938, vol. III
Dryden, Sir Henry Edward Leigh, 4th and 7th Bt, 1818–1899, vol. I
Dryden, Hon. John, 1840–1909, vol. I
Dryden, Sir Noel Percy Hugh, 7th and 10th Bt, 1910–1970, vol. VI
Dryerre, Henry, 1881–1959, vol. V
Dryfoos, Orvil E., 1912–1963, vol. VI
Dryhurst, Frederic John, died 1931, vol. III
Dryland, Alfred, 1865–1946, vol. IV
Drysdale, Rev. A. H., 1837–1924, vol. II
Drysdale, Arthur, 1857–1922, vol. II

Drysdale, Charles Vickery, 1874–1961, vol. VI
Drysdale, Learmont, 1866–1909, vol. I
Drysdale, Sir Matthew Watt, 1892–1962, vol. VI
Drysdale, Sir William, 1819–1900, vol. I
Drysdale, Lt-Col William, 1876–1916, vol. II
D'Silva, John Leonard, 1910–1973, vol. VII
D'Souza, Most Rev. Albert V., 1904–1977, vol. VII
D'Souza, Frank, 1883–1960, vol. V
Dube, Bhugwandin, 1876–1938, vol. III
Dubilier, William, 1888–1969, vol. VI
Dubois, Paul, 1829–1905, vol. I
Dubois, Théodore, died 1924, vol. II
Du Bois, William Edward Burghardt, 1868–1963, vol. VI
Du Boisrouvray, Rt Rev. Bernard, 1877–1970, vol. VI (AII)
Dubose, William Porcher, 1836–1918, vol. II
Dubost, Antonin, 1844–1921, vol. II
Du Boulay, George Cornibert, 1883–1951, vol. V
Du Boulay, Ven. Henry Houssemayne, 1840–1925, vol. II
Du Boulay, Sir James Houssemayne, 1868–1945, vol. IV
Dubs, Homer H., 1892–1969, vol. VI
Dubuc, Arthur Edouard, 1880–1944, vol. IV
Dubuc, Sir Joseph, 1840–1914, vol. I (A)
Du Buisson, Very Rev. John Clement, 1871–1938, vol. III
Du Cane, Sir Edmund Frederick, 1830–1903, vol. I
Du Cane, Col Hubert John, 1859–1916, vol. II
Ducane, Gen. Sir John Philip, 1865–1947, vol. IV
Ducat, Col Charles Merewether, 1860–1934, vol. III
Ducat, Ven. William Methven Gordon, died 1922, vol. II
Du Chaillu, Paul Belloni, 1835–1903, vol. I
Duchemin, Rt Rev. Mgr Charles L. H., 1886–1965, vol. VI
Duchemin, Henry Pope, died 1950, vol. IV
Duchesne, Jacques; see Saint-Denis, M. J.
Duchesne, Mgr Louis Marie Olivier, 1843–1922, vol. II
Ducie, 3rd Earl of, 1827–1921, vol. II
Ducie, 4th Earl of, 1834–1924, vol. II
Ducie, 5th Earl of, 1875–1952, vol. V
Duck, Vet. Col Sir Francis, 1845–1934, vol. III
Duckett, Sir George Floyd, 3rd Bt, 1811–1902, vol. I
Duckett, Lt-Col John Steuart, 1876–1952, vol. V
Duckham, Sir Arthur McDougall, 1879–1932, vol. III
Duckworth, Sir Dyce, 1st Bt, 1840–1928, vol. II
Duckworth, Sir Edward Dyce, 2nd Bt, 1875–1945, vol. IV
Duckworth, Francis R. G., 1881–1964, vol. VI
Duckworth, Frederick Victor, 1901–1974, vol. VII
Duckworth, Sir George Herbert, 1868–1934, vol. III
Duckworth, Sir James, 1840–1915, vol. I
Duckworth, James, 1869–1937, vol. III
Duckworth, John, 1863–1946, vol. IV
Duckworth, Rev. Robinson, 1834–1911, vol. I
Duckworth, Rev. William Arthur, 1829–1917, vol. II

Duckworth, William Rostron, 1879–1952, vol. V
Duckworth, Wynfrid Laurence Henry, 1870–1956, vol. V
Duckworth-King, Col Sir Dudley Gordon Alan, 5th Bt, 1851–1909, vol. I
Duckworth-King, Sir George Henry James, 6th Bt, 1891–1952, vol. V
Duckworth-King, Sir John Richard, 7th Bt, 1899–1972, vol. VII
Duclos, Arnold Willard, 1874–1947, vol. IV
Duclos, Hon. Joseph Adolphe, 1873–1933, vol. III
Du Cros, Alfred, 1868–1946, vol. IV
Du Cros, Sir Arthur Philip, 1st Bt, 1871–1955, vol. V
Du Cros, Sir (Harvey) Philip, 2nd Bt, 1898–1975, vol. VII
Du Cros, Sir Philip; see Du Cros, Sir H. P.
du Cros, William Harvey, 1846–1918, vol. II
Duddell, W., 1872–1917, vol. II
Dudden, Rev. Frederick Homes, 1874–1955, vol. V
Dudding, Rear-Adm. Horatio Nelson, 1849–1917, vol. II
Dudding, Surg. Rear-Adm. John Scarbrough, 1877–1951, vol. V
Dudeney, Mrs Henry, died 1945, vol. IV
Dudeney, Henry Ernest, 1857–1930, vol. III
Dudgeon, Major Cecil Randolph, 1885–1970, vol. VI
Dudgeon, Sir Charles John, 1855–1928, vol. II
Dudgeon, Maj.-Gen. Frederick Annesley, 1866–1943, vol. IV
Dudgeon, Gerald Cecil, 1867–1930, vol. III
Dudgeon, Leonard Stanley, 1876–1938, vol. III
Dudgeon, Lt-Col Robert Francis, 1851–1932, vol. III
Dudgeon, Brig.-Gen. Robert Maxwell, 1881–1962, vol. VI
Dudley, 2nd Earl of, 1867–1932, vol. III
Dudley, 3rd Earl of, 1894–1969, vol. VI
Dudley, 12th Baron, 1872–1936, vol. III
Dudley, 13th Baron, 1910–1972, vol. VII
Dudley, Sir Alan Alves, 1907–1971, vol. VII
Dudley, Donald Reynolds, 1910–1972, vol. VII
Dudley, Col George de Someri, 1874–1941, vol. IV
Dudley, Harold Ward, 1887–1935, vol. III
Dudley, Rev. Owen Francis, 1882–1952, vol. V
Dudley, Roland, 1879–1964, vol. VI
Dudley, Surg. Vice-Adm. Sir Sheldon Francis, 1884–1956, vol. V
Dudley, Sir Willem Edward, died 1938, vol. III
Dudok, Willem Marinus, 1884–1974, vol. VII
Duerden, J. E., died 1937, vol. III
Duesbury, Rt Rev. Charles Leonard T.; see Thornton-Duesbury.
Duff, Major Adrian G.; see Grant-Duff.
Duff, Maj.-Gen. Alan Colquhoun, 1896–1973, vol. VII
Duff, Adm. Sir Alexander Ludovic, 1862–1933, vol. III
Duff, Archibald, 1845–1934, vol. III
Duff, Bt Lt-Col Arthur Abercromby S.; see Scott-Duff.
Duff, Adm. Sir Arthur Allan Morison, 1874–1952, vol. V

Duff, Sir Arthur Cuninghame G.; see Grant-Duff.
Duff, Gen. Sir Beauchamp, 1855–1918, vol. II
Duff, Lt-Col Benjamin Michael, 1840–1926, vol. II
Duff, Col Charles de Vertus, 1870–1950, vol. IV
Duff, Col Charles Edward, 1858–1936, vol. III
Duff, Sir (Charles) Michael (Robert Vivian), 3rd Bt, 1907–1980, vol. VII
Duff, Sir (Charles) Patrick, 1889–1972, vol. VII
Duff, Charles St Lawrence, 1894–1966, vol. VI
Duff, David, 1883–1959, vol. V
Duff, Edith Florence G.; see Grant-Duff.
Duff, Edward Gordon, 1863–1924, vol. II
Duff, Sir Evelyn G.; see Grant-Duff.
Duff, Francis Bluett, 1875–1947, vol. IV
Duff, Garden Alexander, 1853–1933, vol. III
Duff, Lt-Col Sir Garden Beauchamp, 1st Bt, 1879–1952, vol. V
Duff, Col George Mowat, 1862–1935, vol. III
Duff, Sir Hector Livingston, 1872–1954, vol. V
Duff, James Augustine, 1872–1943, vol. IV
Duff, Sir James Fitzjames, 1898–1970, vol. VI
Duff, Hon. James Stoddart, 1856–1916, vol. II
Duff, John, 1850–1921, vol. II
Duff, John Robert Keitley, 1862–1938, vol. III
Duff, John Wharton Wharton-, 1845–1935, vol. III
Duff, John Wight, 1866–1944, vol. IV
Duff, Rt Hon. Sir Lyman Poore, 1865–1955, vol. V
Duff, Sir Michael; see Duff, Sir C. M. R. V.
Duff, Rt Hon. Sir Mountstuart Elphinstone Grant, 1829–1906, vol. I
Duff, Sir Patrick; see Duff, Sir C. P.
Duff, Stanley Lewis, 1881–1943, vol. IV
Duff, Thomas Duff Gordon, 1848–1923, vol. II
Duff-Dunbar, Lt-Comdr Kenneth James; see Dunbar.
Duff Gordon, Sir Cosmo Edmund, 5th Bt; see Gordon.
Duff-Gordon, Sir Douglas Frederick, 7th Bt, 1892–1964, vol. VI
Duff-Gordon, Sir Henry William, 6th Bt, 1866–1953, vol. V
Duff-Sutherland-Dunbar, Sir George, 6th Bt; see Dunbar.
Duff-Sutherland-Dunbar, Sir George Cospatrick, 7th Bt, 1906–1963, vol. VI
Dufferin and Ava, 1st Marquess of, 1826–1902, vol. I
Dufferin and Ava, 2nd Marquess of, 1866–1918, vol. II
Dufferin and Ava, 3rd Marquess of, 1875–1930, vol. III
Dufferin and Ava, 4th Marquess of, 1909–1945, vol. IV
Dufferin and Ava, Marchioness of; (Hariot), died 1936, vol. III
Duffes, Arthur Paterson, 1880–1968, vol. VI
Duffey, Sir George Frederick, 1843–1903, vol. I
Duffield, Anne, died 1976, vol. VII
Duffield, Mary Elizabeth, 1819–1914, vol. I
Duffield, William Bartleet, died 1918, vol. II
Duffus, Brig.-Gen. Edward John, 1866–1937, vol. III
Duffy, Hon. Sir Charles Gavan, 1816–1903, vol. I

Duffy, Charles Gavan, 1855–1932, vol. III
Duffy, Hon. Sir Charles Leonard G.; *see* Gavan-Duffy.
Duffy, Rt Hon. Sir Frank Gavan, 1852–1936, vol. III
Duffy, George Gavan, 1882–1951, vol. V
Duffy, Hon. H. Thomas, *died* 1903, vol. I
Duffy, Thomas G.; *see* Gavan-Duffy.
Dufy, Raoul, 1877–1953, vol. V
Dugan of Victoria, 1st Baron, 1877–1951, vol. V
Dugas, Calixter Aimé, 1845–1918, vol. II
Dugas, François Octave, 1857–1918, vol. II (A), vol. III
Dugdale, Amy Katherine; *see* Browning, A. K.
Dugdale, Col Arthur, 1869–1941, vol. IV
Dugdale, Blanche Elizabeth Campbell; *see* Dugdale, Mrs Edgar Trevelyan Stratford.
Dugdale, Mrs Edgar Trevelyan Stratford, (Blanche Elizabeth Campbell Dugdale), *died* 1948, vol. IV
Dugdale, Col Frank, 1857–1925, vol. II
Dugdale, Frederick Brooks, *died* 1902, vol. I
Dugdale, James Broughton, 1855–1927, vol. II
Dugdale, Rt Hon. John, 1905–1963, vol. VI
Dugdale, John Stratford, 1835–1920, vol. II
Dugdale, Rev. Sydney, *died* 1942, vol. IV
Dugdale, Thomas Cantrell, 1880–1952, vol. V
Dugdale, Sir William Francis Stratford, 1st Bt, 1872–1965, vol. VI
Dugdale, Major William Marshall, 1881–1952, vol. V
Duggan, Alfred Leo, 1903–1964, vol. VI
Duggan, Edmund John, *died* 1936, vol. III
Duggan, Rear-Adm. Eyre Sturdy, 1891–1956, vol. V
Duggan, George Chester, *died* 1969, vol. VI
Duggan, Major Harold Joseph, 1896–1942, vol. IV
Duggan, Hubert John, 1904–1943, vol. IV
Duggan, Col Sir Jamshedji, 1884–1957, vol. V
Dugmore, Arthur Radclyffe, 1870–1955, vol. V
Dugmore, Rev. Ernest Edward, 1843–1925, vol. II
Dugmore, Lt-Col William Francis Brougham Radclyffe, 1868–1917, vol. II
Duguid, Charles, 1864–1923, vol. II
Duguid, Maj.-Gen. David Robertson, 1888–1973, vol. VII
Duguid, John Bright, 1895–1980, vol. VII
Duguid-McCombie, Col William McCombie, 1874–1970, vol. VI
Duhamel, Georges, 1884–1966, vol. VI
Duhig, Sir James, 1871–1965, vol. VI
Duhm, Bernhard Laward, 1847–1928, vol. II
Duigan, Maj.-Gen. Sir John Evelyn, 1882–1950, vol. IV
Dukas, Paul, 1865–1935, vol. III
Duke, Lt-Col Augustus Cecil Hare, *died* 1943, vol. IV
Duke, Brig. Cecil Leonard Basil, 1896–1963, vol. VI
Duke, Sir Charles Beresford, 1905–1978, vol. VII
Duke, Hon. Edgar Mortimer, 1895–1965, vol. VI
Duke, Rev. Edward St Arnaud, 1854–1939, vol. III
Duke, Sir (Frederick) William, 1863–1924, vol. II
Duke, Herbert Lyndhurst, 1883–1966, vol. VI
Duke, Sir James, 2nd Bt, 1865–1935, vol. III

Duke, James Buchanan, 1857–1925, vol. II
Duke, Brig. Jesse Pevensey, 1890–1980, vol. VII
Duke, Sir Norman; *see* Duke, Sir R. N.
Duke, Reginald Franklyn Hare, 1887–1929, vol. III
Duke, Sir (Robert) Norman, 1893–1969, vol. VI
Duke, Sir William; *see* Duke, Sir F. W.
Duke, Most Rev. William Mark, 1879–1971, vol. VII
Duke, Winifred, *died* 1962, vol. VI
Duke-Elder, Sir Stewart, 1898–1978, vol. VII
Dukes, Ashley, 1885–1959, vol. V
Dukes, Cuthbert Esquire, 1890–1977, vol. VII
Dukes, Sir Paul, 1889–1967, vol. VI
Dukeston, 1st Baron, 1881–1948, vol. IV
Dulac, Edmund, 1882–1953, vol. V
Dulanty, John Whelan, *died* 1955, vol. V
Duleep Singh, Prince Frederick, 1868–1926, vol. II
Duleep Singh, Prince Victor Albert Jay, 1866–1918, vol. II
Dulles, Allen Welsh, 1893–1969, vol. VI
Dulles, John Foster, 1888–1959, vol. V
Dulverton, 1st Baron, 1880–1956, vol. V
Dumarchey, Pierre; *see* MacOrlan, Pierre.
Dumaresq, Rear-Adm. John Saumarez, 1873–1922, vol. II
Dumas, Hugh Charles Sowerby, 1865–1940, vol. III
Dumas, Sir Lloyd, 1891–1973, vol. VII
Dumas, Adm. Philip Wylie, 1868–1948, vol. IV
Dumas, Sir Russell John, 1887–1975, vol. VII
du Maurier, Sir Gerald, 1873–1934, vol. III
du Maurier, Lt-Col Guy Louis Busson, 1865–1915, vol. I
Dumayne, Sir Frederick George, 1852–1930, vol. III
Dumbell, Sir Alured, 1835–1900, vol. I
Dumbell, Lt-Col Charles Harold, 1878–1935, vol. III
Dumbleton, Gen. Charles, 1824–1916, vol. II
Duminy, Jacobus Petrus, 1897–1980, vol. VII
Dummett, Robert Bryan, 1912–1977, vol. VII
Dummett, Sir Robert Ernest, 1872–1941, vol. IV
Du Moulin, Rt Rev. John Philip, 1834–1911, vol. I
Dumpleton, Cyril Walter, 1897–1966, vol. VI
Dumraon, Zamindar of, *died* 1933, vol. III
Dun, Robert Hay, 1870–1947, vol. IV
Dun, William Gibb, *died* 1927, vol. II
Dunalley, 4th Baron, 1851–1927, vol. II
Dunalley, 5th Baron, 1877–1948, vol. IV
Dunbabin, Robert Leslie, 1869–1949, vol. IV
Dunbabin, Thomas, 1883–1973, vol. VII
Dunbabin, Thomas James, 1911–1955, vol. V
Dunbar of Mochrum, Sir Adrian Ivor, 12th Bt (*cr* 1694), 1893–1977, vol. VII
Dunbar, Sir Alexander, 1888–1955, vol. V
Dunbar, Sir Alexander James, 4th Bt (*cr* 1814), 1870–1900, vol. I
Dunbar, Alexander Robert, 1904–1980, vol. VII
Dunbar, Sir Archibald, 6th Bt (*cr* 1700), 1803–1898, vol. I
Dunbar, Sir (Archibald) Edward, 9th Bt (*cr* 1700), 1889–1969, vol. VI
Dunbar, Sir Archibald Hamilton, 7th Bt (*cr* 1700), 1828–1910, vol. I
Dunbar, Sir Basil Douglas H.; *see* Hope-Dunbar.

Dunbar, Paymaster Rear-Adm. Charles Augustus Royer Flood, 1849–1939, vol. III

Dunbar, Sir Charles Dunbar H.; *see* Hope-Dunbar.

Dunbar, (Rev.) Sir Charles Gordon-Cumming, 8th Bt (*cr* 1700), 1844–1916, vol. II

Dunbar, Maj.-Gen. Claude Ian Hurley, 1909–1971, vol. VII

Dunbar, Sir Drummond Miles, 7th Bt (*cr* 1697), 1845–1903, vol. I

Dunbar, Sir Edward; *see* Dunbar, Sir A. E.

Dunbar, Evelyn Mary, *died* 1960, vol. V

Dunbar, Sir Frederick George, 5th Bt (*cr* 1814), 1875–1937, vol. III

Dunbar, Sir George Alexander Drummond, 8th Bt (*cr* 1697), 1879–1949, vol. IV

Dunbar, Sir George Cospatrick D. S., 7th Bt; *see* Duff-Sutherland-Dunbar.

Dunbar, Sir George Duff-Sutherland-, 6th Bt, 1878–1962, vol. VI

Dunbar, Sir James George Hawker Rowland, 10th Bt (*cr* 1694), 1862–1953, vol. V

Dunbar, Sir John Greig, 1906–1978, vol. VII

Dunbar, Major John Telfer, *died* 1957, vol. V

Dunbar, Lt-Comdr Kenneth James Duff-, 1886–1916, vol. II

Dunbar, Sir Loraine Geddes, 1865–1943, vol. IV

Dunbar, Sir Richard Fredrick Roberts, 1900–1965, vol. VI

Dunbar, Sir Richard Sutherland, 11th Bt (*cr* 1694), 1873–1953, vol. V

Dunbar, Robert, 1895–1970, vol. VI

Dunbar, Robert Haig, *died* 1919, vol. II

Dunbar, Sir Uthred James Hay, 8th Bt (*cr* 1694), 1843–1904, vol. I

Dunbar, Sir William Cospatrick, 9th Bt (*cr* 1694), 1844–1931, vol. III

Dunbar-Buller, Charles William; *see* Buller.

Dunbar Kilburn, Bertram Edward, 1872–1948, vol. IV

Dunbar-Nasmith, Adm. Sir Martin Eric; *see* Nasmith.

Dunboyne, 24th Baron, 1839–1899, vol. I

Dunboyne, 25th Baron, 1844–1913, vol. I

Dunboyne, 26th Baron, 1874–1945, vol. IV

Duncalfe, Sir Roger, 1884–1961, vol. VI

Duncan, Col Sir Alan Gomme Gomme-, 1893–1963, vol. VI

Duncan, Alexander, *died* 1943, vol. IV

Duncan, Alexander Mitchell, 1888–1965, vol. VI

Duncan, Alexander Robert, 1844–1927, vol. II

Duncan, Alfred Charles, 1886–1979, vol. VII

Duncan, Andrew, *died* 1912, vol. I

Duncan, Rt Hon. Sir Andrew Rae, 1884–1952, vol. V

Duncan, Charles, 1865–1933, vol. III

Duncan, Sir (Charles Edgar) Oliver, 3rd Bt (*cr* 1905), 1892–1964, vol. VI

Duncan, Claude Woodruff, *died* 1945, vol. IV

Duncan, Colin; *see* Duncan, P. C.

Duncan, Sir David, *died* 1923, vol. II

Duncan, David, 1839–1923, vol. II

Duncan, Surg. Rear-Adm. David, 1900–1974, vol. VII

Duncan, Edmondstoune, 1866–1920, vol. II

Duncan, Ellen, vol. III

Duncan, Maj.-Gen. Francis John, *died* 1960, vol. V

Duncan, Sir Frederick William, 2nd Bt (*cr* 1905), 1859–1929, vol. III

Duncan, Captain George, 1863–1937, vol. III

Duncan, Rev. George, *died* 1932, vol. III

Duncan, George, *died* 1949, vol. IV

Duncan, George B., 1869–1941, vol. IV

Duncan, Very Rev. George Simpson, 1884–1965, vol. VI

Duncan, Sir Harold Handasyde, 1885–1962, vol. VI

Duncan, Sir Hastings; *see* Duncan, Sir J. H.

Duncan, Maj.-Gen. Henry Clare, 1876–1961, vol. VI

Duncan, Sir James, *died* 1926, vol. II

Duncan, Sir James Alexander Lawson, 1st Bt (*cr* 1957), 1899–1974, vol. VII

Duncan, James Archibald, 1858–1911, vol. I

Duncan, Lt-Col James Fergus, *died* 1941, vol. IV

Duncan, Sir (James) Hastings, 1855–1928, vol. II

Duncan, James Lindsay, 1905–1954, vol. V

Duncan, Jane, 1910–1976, vol. VII

Duncan, Sir John, 1846–1914, vol. I

Duncan, John, *died* 1945, vol. IV

Duncan, Maj.-Gen. Sir John, 1872–1948, vol. IV

Duncan, Comdr John Alexander, 1878–1943, vol. IV

Duncan, John Douglas Grace, 1899–1969, vol. VI

Duncan, John Hudson E.; *see* Elder-Duncan.

Duncan, Hon. Sir John James, 1845–1913, vol. I

Duncan, John Murray, *died* 1922, vol. II

Duncan, Sir John Norman Valette; *see* Duncan, Sir Val.

Duncan, John Shiels, 1886–1949, vol. IV

Duncan, Rev. Joseph, 1843–1915, vol. I (A)

Duncan, Joseph Forbes, 1879–1964, vol. VI

Duncan, Leland Lewis, 1862–1923, vol. II

Duncan, Col Macbeth Moir, 1866–1942, vol. IV

Duncan, Norman, 1871–1916, vol. II

Duncan, Sir Oliver; *see* Duncan, Sir C. E. O.

Duncan, Rt Hon. Sir Patrick, 1870–1943, vol. IV

Duncan, (Peter) Colin, 1895–1979, vol. VII

Duncan, Lt-Col Ronald Cardew, 1886–1963, vol. VI

Duncan, Sir Surr William, 1st Bt (*cr* 1905), 1834–1908, vol. I

Duncan, Sir Thomas Andrew, 1873–1960, vol. V

Duncan, Hon. Thomas Young, 1836–1914, vol. II

Duncan, Sir Val, (John Norman Valette), 1913–1975, vol. VII

Duncan, Hon. Sir Walter Gordon, 1885–1963, vol. VI

Duncan, Brig. William Edmonstone, 1890–1969, vol. VI

Duncan, William Jolly, 1894–1960, vol. V

Duncan-Hughes, Captain John Grant; *see* Hughes.

Duncan-Jones, Very Rev. Arthur Stuart, 1879–1955, vol. V

Duncan-Jones, Austin Ernest, 1908–1967, vol. VI

Duncanson, Sir John McLean, 1897–1963, vol. VI

Duncombe, Alfred Charles, 1843–1925, vol. II

Duncombe, Col (Charles) William (Ernest), 1862–1945, vol. IV

Duncombe, Maj.-Gen. Charles Wilmer, 1838–1911, vol. I

Duncombe, Sir Everard (Philip Digby) Pauncefort-, 3rd Bt (*cr* 1859), 1885–1971, vol. VII

Duncombe, Col Sir George Augustus, 1st Bt (*cr* 1919), 1848–1933, vol. III

Duncombe, Hon. Hubert Ernest Valentine, 1862–1918, vol. II

Duncombe, Walter Henry Octavius, 1846–1917, vol. II

Duncombe, Col William; *see* Duncombe, Col C. W. E.

Duncombe, Rev. William Duncombe Van der Horst, *died* 1925, vol. II

Dundas, Hon. Lord; David Dundas, 1854–1922, vol. II

Dundas of Dundas, Adam Duncan, 1903–1951, vol. V

Dundas, Sir Ambrose Dundas Flux, 1899–1973, vol. VII

Dundas of Dundas, Adm. Sir Charles, 1859–1924, vol. II

Dundas, Hon. Sir Charles Cecil Farquharson, 1884–1956, vol. V

Dundas, Sir Charles Henry, 4th Bt (*cr* 1821), 1851–1908, vol. I

Dundas, Rev. Charles Leslie, 1847–1932, vol. III

Dundas, David; *see* Dundas, Hon. Lord.

Dundas, Lt-Col Frederick Charles, 1868–1941, vol. IV

Dundas, Lord George Heneage Lawrence, 1882–1968, vol. VI

Dundas, George Smythe, 1842–1909, vol. I

Dundas, Sir George Whyte Melville, 5th Bt (*cr* 1821), 1856–1934, vol. III

Dundas, Sir Henry Herbert Philip, 3rd Bt (*cr* 1898), 1866–1930, vol. III

Dundas, Sir Henry Matthew, 5th Bt (*cr* 1898), 1937–1963, vol. VI

Dundas, Lt-Col James Colin, 1883–1966, vol. VI

Dundas, Sir James Durham, 6th Bt (*cr* 1898), 1905–1967, vol. VI

Dundas, Vice-Adm. John George Lawrence, 1893–1952, vol. V

Dundas, Hon. Kenneth Robert, 1882–1915, vol. I

Dundas, Major Laurance Charles, 1857–1908, vol. I

Dundas, Captain Lawrence Leopold, *died* 1939, vol. III

Dundas, Col Sir Lorenzo George, 1837–1917, vol. II

Dundas, Brig. Patrick Henry, 1871–1936, vol. III

Dundas, Sir Philip, 4th Bt (*cr* 1898), 1899–1952, vol. V

Dundas, Sir Robert, 1st Bt (*cr* 1898) 1823–1909, vol. I

Dundas, Lt-Col Sir Robert, 2nd Bt (*cr* 1898), 1857–1910, vol. I

Dundas, Robert Hamilton, 1884–1960, vol. V

Dundas, Rev. Robert J., 1832–1904, vol. I

Dundas, Robert Thomas, *died* 1948, vol. IV

Dundas, Sir Sidney James, 3rd Bt (*cr* 1821), 1849–1904, vol. I

Dundas, Sir Thomas Calderwood, 7th Bt (*cr* 1898), 1906–1970, vol. VI

Dundas, William Charles Michael, 1873–1933, vol. III

Dundas, William John, 1849–1921, vol. II

Dundas-Grant, Sir James; *see* Grant.

Dundee, Col William John Daniell, 1862–1940, vol. III

Dundon, John, *died* 1952, vol. V

Dundonald, 12th Earl of, 1852–1935, vol. III

Dundonald, 13th Earl of, 1886–1958, vol. V

Dunedin, 1st Viscount, 1849–1942, vol. IV

Dunedin, Viscountess; (Jean Elmslie), *died* 1944, vol. IV

Dunfee, Col Vickers, 1861–1927, vol. II

Dunfield, Sir Brian Edward Spencer, 1888–1968, vol. VI

Dunham, E. K., 1860–1923, vol. II

Dunhill, Alfred, 1872–1959, vol. V

Dunhill, Thomas Frederick, 1877–1946, vol. IV

Dunhill, Sir Thomas Peel, 1876–1957, vol. V

Dunk, Susan S.; *see* Spain-Dunk.

Dunkerley, Ven. William Herbert Cecil, *died* 1922, vol. II

Dunkerly, John Samuel, 1881–1931, vol. III

Dunkin, Edwin, 1821–1898, vol. I

Dunkin, Major George William, 1886–1942, vol. IV

Dunkley, Rev. Charles, 1847–1936, vol. III

Dunkley, Sir Herbert Francis, 1886–1963, vol. VI (AII)

Dunleath, 2nd Baron, 1854–1931, vol. III

Dunleath, 3rd Baron, 1886–1956, vol. V

Dunlop, Alexander Johnstone, 1848–1921, vol. II

Dunlop, Mrs Annie Isabella, 1897–1973, vol. VII

Dunlop, Charles Robertson, 1876–1932, vol. III

Dunlop, Major Colin Napier Buchanan, 1877–1915, vol. I (A)

Dunlop, Rt Rev. David Colin, 1897–1968, vol. VI

Dunlop, Maj.-Gen. Dermott, 1898–1980, vol. VII

Dunlop, Sir Derrick Melville, 1902–1980, vol. VII

Dunlop, Ernest McMurchie, 1893–1969, vol. VI

Dunlop, Rev. Francis Wallace, 1875–1932, vol. III

Dunlop, Col Frank Passy, 1877–1940, vol. III

Dunlop, Col Henry Donald B.; *see* Buchanan-Dunlop.

Dunlop, Hugh Alexander, 1903–1954, vol. V

Dunlop, James Crauford, *died* 1944, vol. IV

Dunlop, James Marcus Muntz, *died* 1938, vol. III

Dunlop, James Matthew, 1867–1949, vol. IV

Dunlop, Col James William, 1854–1923, vol. II

Dunlop, Hon. John, 1837–1916, vol. II

Dunlop, Sir John Kinninmont, 1892–1974, vol. VII

Dunlop, Louis Vandalle, 1878–1954, vol. V

Dunlop, Ven. Maxwell Tulloch, 1898–1964, vol. VI

Dunlop, Sir Nathaniel, 1830–1919, vol. II

Dunlop, Robert, *died* 1935, vol. III

Dunlop, Sir Robert William Layard, 1869–1962, vol. VI

Dunlop, Ronald Offory, 1894–1973, vol. VII

Dunlop, Col Samuel, 1838–1917, vol. II

Dunlop, Engr Rear-Adm. Samuel Harrison, 1884–1950, vol. IV

Dunlop, Sir Thomas, 1st Bt, 1855–1938, vol. III

Dunlop, Sir Thomas, 2nd Bt, 1881–1963, vol. VI

Dunlop, Bt Col Sir Thomas Charles, 1878–1960, vol. V

Dunlop, Sir Thomas Dacre, 1883–1963, vol. VI
Dunlop, Col William Bruce, 1877–1933, vol. III
Dunlop, Major William Hugh, 1857–1924, vol. II
Dunlop, William Louis Martial, 1882–1948, vol. IV
Dunlop, William Wallace, 1846–1930, vol. III
Dunmore, 7th Earl of, 1841–1907, vol. I
Dunmore, 8th Earl of, 1871–1962, vol. VI
Dunmore, 9th Earl of, 1939–1980, vol. VII
Dunn, Albert Edward, 1864–1937, vol. III
Dunn, Rt Rev. Andrew Hunter, 1839–1914, vol. I
Dunn, Captain Arthur Edward, 1876–1927, vol. II
Dunn, Charles William, 1877–1966, vol. VI
Dunn, Lt-Col Cuthbert Lindsay, 1875–1956, vol. V
Dunn, Edward, 1880–1945, vol. IV
Dunn, Most Rev. Edward Arthur, 1870–1955, vol. V
Dunn, Col Henry Nason, 1864–1952, vol. V
Dunn, Hugh Percy, 1854–1931, vol. III
Dunn, James B., 1861–1930, vol. III
Dunn, Sir James Hamet, 1st Bt (*cr* 1921), 1875–1956, vol. V
Dunn, James Nicol, 1856–1919, vol. II
Dunn, James Stormont, 1879–1965, vol. VI
Dunn, John Freeman, 1874–1954, vol. V
Dunn, Sir John Henry, 2nd Bt (*cr* 1917), 1890–1971, vol. VII
Dunn, John Messenger, 1838–1904, vol. I
Dunn, John Shaw, 1883–1944, vol. IV
Dunn, John Thomas, 1858–1939, vol. III
Dunn, Louis Albert, 1858–1918, vol. II
Dunn, Naughton, 1884–1939, vol. III
Dunn, Patrick Smith, 1848–1932, vol. III
Dunn, Peter Douglas Hay, 1892–1965, vol. VI
Dunn, Sir Philip Gordon, 2nd Bt (*cr* 1921), 1905–1976, vol. VII
Dunn, Piers Duncan Williams, 1896–1957, vol. V
Dunn, Stanley Gerald, 1879–1964, vol. VI
Dunn, Rt Rev. Thomas, 1870–1931, vol. III
Dunn, Rev. Thomas Shelton, 1875–1949, vol. IV
Dunn, Thomas Smith, 1836–1916, vol. II
Dunn, Sir William, 1st Bt (*cr*1895), 1833–1912, vol. I
Dunn, William, 1876–1949, vol. IV
Dunn, Sir William Henry, 1st Bt (*cr* 1917), 1856–1926, vol. II
Dunn, William Norman, 1873–1961, vol. VI
Dunne, Arthur Mountjoy, 1859–1947, vol. IV
Dunne, Lt-Col Edward Marten, 1864–1944, vol. IV
Dunne, Finley Peter, 1867–1936, vol. III
Dunne, Major Francis Plunkett Neville, 1872–1931, vol. III
Dunne, Rt Rev. Mgr James J., 1859–1934, vol. III
Dunne, Lt-Col James Stuart, 1877–1955, vol. V
Dunne, Sir John, 1825–1906, vol. I
Dunne, Rt Rev. John, 1846–1917, vol. II
Dunne, Gen. Sir John Hart, 1835–1924, vol. II
Dunne, Captain John J., 1837–1910, vol. I
Dunne, Rt Rev. John Mary, 1843–1919, vol. II
Dunne, John William, *died* 1949, vol. IV
Dunne, Sir Laurence Rivers, 1893–1970, vol. VI
Dunne, Philip Russell Rendel, 1904–1965, vol. VI
Dunne, Col William, 1855–1932, vol. III
Dunnell, Sir Francis; *see* Dunnell, Sir R. F.
Dunnell, Sir (Robert) Francis, 1st Bt, 1868–1960, vol. V

Dunnett, George Sinclair, 1906–1964, vol. VI
Dunnett, Sir James Macdonald, 1877–1953, vol. V
Dunnicliff, Rev. Canon Edward Frederick Holwell, 1901–1963, vol. VI
Dunnicliff, Horace Barratt, *died* 1958, vol. V
Dunnico, Rev. Sir Herbert, 1876–1953, vol. V
Dunnill, W. F., *died* 1936, vol. III
Dunning, Albert Elijah, 1844–1923, vol. II
Dunning, Hon. Charles Avery, 1885–1958, vol. V
Dunning, Sir Edwin Harris, 1858–1923, vol. II
Dunning, J. Thomson, 1851–1931, vol. III
Dunning, James, 1873–1931, vol. III
Dunning, John Ray, 1907–1975, vol. VII
Dunning, Sir Leonard, 1st Bt, 1860–1941, vol. IV
Dunning, Rev. Thomas George, 1885–1975, vol. VII
Dunning, William Archibald, *died* 1922, vol. II
Dunning, Sir William Leonard, 2nd Bt, 1903–1961, vol. VI
Dunnington-Jefferson, Lt-Col Sir John Alexander, 1st Bt, 1884–1979, vol. VII
Dunoyer de Segonzac, André, 1884–1974, vol. VII
Dunphie, Sir Alfred Edwin, *died* 1938, vol. III
Dunraven and Mount-Earl, 4th Earl of, 1841–1926, vol. II
Dunraven and Mount-Earl, 5th Earl of, 1857–1952, vol. V
Dunraven and Mount-Earl, 6th Earl of, 1887–1965, vol. VI
Dunrossil, 1st Viscount, 1893–1961, vol. VI
Duns, John, 1820–1909, vol. I
Dunsandle and Clan-Conal, 4th Baron, 1849–1911, vol. I
Dunsany, 17th Baron, 1853–1899, vol. I
Dunsany, 18th Baron, 1878–1957, vol. V
Dunsford, Brig.-Gen. Francis Pearson Shaw, 1866–1931, vol. III
Dunsheath, Percy, 1886–1979, vol. VII
Dunsmuir, Hon. James, 1851–1921, vol. II
Dunstaffnage, The Captain of, 1888–1958, vol. V
Dunstan, Hon. Sir Albert Arthur, *died* 1950, vol. IV
Dunstan, Albert Ernest, 1878–1964, vol. VI
Dunstan, Edgar Grieve, 1890–1963, vol. VI
Dunstan, Ven. Ephraim, vol. II
Dunstan, Malcolm James Rowley, 1863–1938, vol. III
Dunstan, Victor Joseph, 1899–1970, vol. VI
Dunstan, William, 1895–1957, vol. V
Dunstan, Sir Wyndham Rowland, 1861–1949, vol. IV
Dunsterville, Col Arthur Bruce, 1859–1943, vol. IV
Dunsterville, Brig. Knightley Fletcher, 1883–1958, vol. V
Dunsterville, Col Knightley Stalker, 1857–1935, vol. III
Dunsterville, Maj.-Gen. Lionel Charles, 1865–1946, vol. IV
Dunsterville, Lt-Gen. Lionel D'Arcy, 1830–1912, vol. I
Dunton, Walter Theodore W.; *see* Watts-Dunton.
Duntze, Sir George Alexander, 4th Bt, 1839–1922, vol. II
Duntze, Sir George Puxley, 5th Bt, 1873–1947, vol. IV
Dunville, Lt-Col John, 1866–1929, vol. III

Dunville, Robert Grimshaw, 1838–1910, vol. I
Dunwoodie, Lallah Bessie, died 1950, vol. IV
Dunwoody, Robert Browne, 1879–1966, vol. VI
Duparc, Marie Eugene Henri, 1848–1933, vol. III
du Parcq, Baron (Life Peer); Herbert du Parcq, 1880–1949, vol. IV
Duperier, Maj.-Gen. Henry William, 1851–1940, vol. III
Du-Plat-Taylor, Francis Maurice Gustavus, 1878–1954, vol. V
du Plat-Taylor, Lt-Col St John Louis Hyde; see Taylor.
du Pont, Lammot, 1880–1952, vol. V
Du Port, Lt-Col Osmond Charteris, 1875–1929, vol. III
Dupplin, Viscount; Edmund Alfred Rollo George Hay, 1879–1903, vol. I
Duppuy, Rt Rev. Charles Ridley, died 1944, vol. IV
Dupré, August, 1835–1907, vol. I
Dupré, Hon. Maurice, 1888–1941, vol. IV
Du Pre, William Baring, 1875–1946, vol. IV
Dupree, Sir Vernon, 3rd Bt, 1884–1971, vol. VII
Dupree, Sir Victor, 4th Bt, 1887–1976, vol. VII
Dupree, Col Sir William, 2nd Bt, 1882–1953, vol. V
Dupree, Col Sir William Thomas, 1st Bt, 1856–1933, vol. III
Dupuis, Charles George, 1886–1940, vol. III
Dupuis, Raymond, 1907–1970, vol. VI (AII)
Dupuis, Rev. Theodore Crane, 1830–1914, vol. I
Dupuy, Charles Alexander, 1851–1923, vol. II
Dupuy, Jean, died 1919, vol. II
Dupuy, Paul, died 1927, vol. II
Dupuy, Pierre, 1896–1969, vol. VI
Duran, Emile Auguste C.; see Carolus-Duran.
Durand, Brig. Sir Alan Algernon Marion, 3rd Bt, 1893–1971, vol. VII
Durand, Col Algernon George Arnold, 1854–1923, vol. II
Durand, Sir Edward Law, 1st Bt, 1845–1920, vol. II
Durand, Major Sir Edward Percy Marion, 2nd Bt, 1884–1955, vol. V
Durand, Rt Hon. Sir (Henry) Mortimer, 1850–1924, vol. II
Durand, Rt Hon. Sir Mortimer; see Durand, Rt Hon. Sir H. M.
Duranleau, Alfred, 1871–1951, vol. V
Durant, Rt Rev. Henry Bickersteth, died 1932, vol. III
Duranty, Walter, died 1957, vol. V
Durbhunga, Maharajadhiraj of, 1860–1929, vol. III
Durbin, Evan Frank Mottram, 1906–1948, vol. IV
Durden, James, died 1964, vol. VI
Duret, Rt Rev. Augustin, 1846–1920, vol. II
Durga Gati, Banerji, died 1903, vol. I
Durham, 3rd Earl of, 1855–1928, vol. II
Durham, 4th Earl of, 1855–1929, vol. III
Durham, 5th Earl of, 1884–1970, vol. VI
Durham, Frances Hermia, 1873–1948, vol. IV
Durham, Lt-Col Frank Rogers, died 1947, vol. IV
Durham, Herbert Edward, 1866–1945, vol. IV
Durham, Mary Edith, 1863–1944, vol. IV
Durham, Rev. Thomas Charles, 1825–1904, vol. I
Durham, Rev. William Edward, 1857–1921, vol. II
Durley, Richard John, 1868–1948, vol. IV

Durnford, Lt-Gen. Cyril Maton Periam, 1891–1965, vol. VI
Durnford, Hugh George Edmund, 1886–1965, vol. VI
Durnford, Adm. Sir John, 1849–1914, vol. I
Durnford, Vice-Adm. John Walter, 1891–1967, vol. VI
Durnford, Richard, 1843–1934, vol. III
Durnford, Robert Chichester, 1895–1918, vol. II
Durnford, Sir Walter, 1847–1926, vol. II
Durning-Lawrence, Sir Edwin, 1st Bt, 1837–1914, vol. I
Durrant, Sir Arthur Isaac, 1864–1939, vol. III
Durrant, Frederick Chester W.; see Wells-Durrant.
Durrant, Maj.-Gen. James Murdoch Archer, 1885–1963, vol. VI
Durrant, Sir William Henry Estridge, 6th Bt, 1872–1953, vol. V
Durrant, Sir William Robert Estridge, 5th Bt, 1840–1912, vol. I
Durrant, William Scott, 1860–1932, vol. III
Durell, Col Arthur James Vavasor, 1871–1945, vol. IV
Durell, Henry E. Le Vavasseur dit, died 1921, vol. II
Durell, Rev. John Carlyon Vavasour, 1870–1946, vol. IV
Durst, Alan Lydiat, 1883–1970, vol. VI
Durst, Rev. William, 1838–1922, vol. II
Durston, Air Marshal Sir Albert, 1894–1959, vol. V
Durston, Sir Albert John, 1846–1917, vol. II
Durward, Archibald, 1902–1964, vol. VI
Durward, James, 1892–1971, vol. VII
Dury, Theodore Seton, 1854–1932, vol. III
Duse, Signora Eleonora, 1861–1924, vol. II
Duthie, George Ian, 1915–1967, vol. VI
Duthie, Sir John, 1858–1922, vol. II
Duthie, Sir William Smith, 1892–1980, vol. VII
du Toit, Alexander Logie, died 1948, vol. IV
du Toit, F. J., 1897–1961, vol. VI
du Toit, Very Rev. Lionel Meiring Spafford, 1903–1979, vol. VII
du Toit, P. J., 1888–1967, vol. VI
Dutoit, Rev. S. J., 1849–1911, vol. I
Dutt, Palme; see Dutt, R. P.
Dutt, (Rajani) Palme, 1896–1974, vol. VII
Dutt, Romesh Chunder, 1848–1909, vol. I
Dutt, William Alfred, 1870–1939, vol. III
Dutton, Alan Hart, 1913–1974, vol. VII
Dutton, Vice-Adm. Hon. Arthur Brandreth Scott, 1876–1932, vol. III
Dutton, Col Hon. Charles, 1842–1909, vol. I
Dutton, Eric Aldhelm Torlogh, 1895–1973, vol. VII
Dutton, Sir Ernest R.; see Rowe-Dutton.
Dutton, Sir Frederick, 1855–1930, vol. III
Dutton, Lt-Col Hugh Reginald, 1875–1950, vol. IV
Duval, Herbert Philip, died 1929, vol. III
Duveen, 1st Baron, 1869–1939, vol. III
Duveen, Claude Henry, 1903–1976, vol. VII
Duveen, Edward Joseph, died 1944, vol. IV
Duveen, Sir Geoffrey, 1883–1975, vol. VII
Duveen, Sir Joseph Joel, 1843–1908, vol. I
Du Vernet, Most Rev. Frederick Herbert, 1860–1924, vol. II

du Vigneaud, Vincent, 1901–1978, vol. VII
Dvorak, Pan Antonin, 1841–1904, vol. I
Dwelly, Very Rev. Frederick William, 1881–1957, vol. V
Dwight, Rev. Timothy, 1828–1916, vol. II
Dwyer, Edward, *died* 1916, vol. II
Dwyer, Lt-Col Ernest, 1880–1957, vol. V
Dwyer, Sir F. Conway, 1860–1935, vol. III
Dwyer, Sir John Patrick, 1880–1966, vol. VI
Dwyer, Rt Rev. Joseph Wilfred, 1869–1939, vol. III
Dwyer, Rt Rev. Patrick Vincent, 1858–1931, vol. III
Dwyer, Hon. Sir Walter, 1875–1950, vol. IV, vol. V
Dwyer-Hampton, Lt-Col Bertie Cunynghame, 1872–1967, vol. VI
Dyall, Clarence George, 1858–1941, vol. IV
Dyall, Franklin, 1870–1950, vol. IV
Dyas, Col James Ridgeway, 1862–1933, vol. III
Dyce, Col George Hugh Coles, 1846–1921, vol. II
Dyde, Samuel Walters, 1862–1947, vol. IV
Dye, Sidney, 1900–1958, vol. V
Dye, William David, 1887–1932, vol. III
Dyer, Sir Alfred, 1865–1947, vol. IV
Dyer, Ven. Alfred Saunders, 1853–1906, vol. I
Dyer, Arthur Reginald, 1877–1951, vol. V
Dyer, Bernard, 1856–1948, vol. IV
Dyer, Charles Edward, *died* 1937, vol. III
Dyer, Edward Jerome, *died* 1943, vol. IV
Dyer, Col George Nowers, *died* 1955, vol. V
Dyer, Maj.-Gen. Godfrey Maxwell, 1898–1979, vol. VII
Dyer, Henry, 1848–1918, vol. II
Dyer, Hugh Marshall, 1860–1938, vol. III
Dyer, James Ferguson, 1880–1940, vol. III
Dyer, Sir John Lodovick Swinnerton, 13th Bt, 1914–1940, vol. III
Dyer, Captain Sir John Swinnerton, 12th Bt, 1891–1917, vol. II
Dyer, Ven. Joseph Perry, 1855–1926, vol. II
Dyer, Sir Leonard Schroeder Swinnerton, 15th Bt, 1898–1975, vol. VII
Dyer, Sir Leonard Whitworth Swinnerton, 14th Bt, 1875–1947, vol. IV
Dyer, Brig.-Gen. Reginald Edward Harry, 1864–1927, vol. II
Dyer, Robert Morton, 1878–1936, vol. III
Dyer, Sidney Reginald, *died* 1934, vol. III
Dyer, Major Stewart Barton Bythesea, 1875–1917, vol. II
Dyer, Sir Thomas Swinnerton, 11th Bt, 1859–1907, vol. I
Dyer, Sir William Turner T.; *see* Thiselton-Dyer.
Dyett, Sir Gilbert Joseph Cullen, 1891–1964, vol. VI
Dyke, Sir Arthur James, 1872–1933, vol. III
Dyke, Rev. Edwin Francis, 1842–1919, vol. II
Dyke, Lt-Col John Samuel, 1859–1927, vol. II
Dyke, Sir Oliver Hamilton Augustus Hart, 8th Bt, 1885–1969, vol. VI
Dyke, Sidney Campbell, 1886–1975, vol. VII
Dyke, Rt Hon. Sir William Hart, 7th Bt, 1837–1931, vol. III
Dykes, David Oswald, 1876–1942, vol. IV
Dykes, Frederick James, 1880–1957, vol. V
Dykes, Col Frescheville Hubert Ballantine-, 1881–1949, vol. IV

Dykes, Rev. James Oswald, 1835–1912, vol. I
Dykes, Brig. Vivian, 1898–1943, vol. IV
Dykes, William Rickatson, 1877–1926, vol. II
Dykstra, John, 1898–1972, vol. VII
Dyment, Clifford Henry, 1914–1971, vol. VII
Dymoke, Frank Scaman, 1862–1946, vol. IV
Dymott, Rev. Sidney Edward, *died* 1924, vol. II
Dynes, Brig. Ernest, 1903–1968, vol. VI
Dynevor, 6th Baron, 1836–1911, vol. I
Dynevor, 7th Baron, 1873–1956, vol. V
Dynevor, 8th Baron, 1899–1962, vol. VI
Dynham, Edward, 1843–1914, vol. I
Dysart, 9th Earl of, 1859–1935, vol. III
Dysart, Countess of (10th in line), 1889–1975, vol. VII
Dyson, Sir (Charles) Frederick, 1854–1934, vol. III
Dyson, Sir Cyril Douglas, 1895–1976, vol. VII
Dyson, Edward Trevor, 1886–1969, vol. VI
Dyson, Sir Frank Watson, 1868–1939, vol. III
Dyson, Sir Frederick; *see* Dyson, Sir C. F.
Dyson, Sir George, 1883–1964, vol. VI
Dyson, Lt-Col Harry Hugo Bernard, 1869–1939, vol. III
Dyson, Herbert Kempton, 1880–1944, vol. IV
Dyson, William, 1849–1928, vol. II
Dyson, William, 1871–1947, vol. IV
Dyson, William Henry, 1883–1938, vol. III

E

Eacott, Rev. Canon Henry James Theodore, 1882–1943, vol. IV
Eade, Charles Stanley, 1903–1964, vol. VI
Eade, Sir Peter, 1825–1915, vol. I
Eades, Sir Thomas, 1888–1971, vol. VII
Eadie, Dennis, 1875–1928, vol. II
Eadie, William Ewing, 1896–1976, vol. VII
Eady, Sir (Crawfurd) Wilfrid Griffin, 1890–1962, vol. VI
Eady, George Hathaway, *died* 1941, vol. IV
Eady, Sir Wilfrid; *see* Eady, Sir C. W. G.
Eagar, Waldo McGillycuddy, 1884–1966, vol. VI
Eager, Sir Clifden Henry Andrews, 1882–1969, vol. VI
Eagles, Rev. Charles Frederick, 1851–1931, vol. III
Eagles, Gen. Henry Cecil, 1855–1927, vol. II
Eaglesome, Sir John, 1868–1950, vol. IV
Eagleston, Arthur John, 1870–1944, vol. IV
Eakin, Rev. Thomas, 1871–1958, vol. V
Eales, Herbert, 1857–1927, vol. II
Eales, John Frederick, 1881–1936, vol. III
Eales, Shirley, 1883–1963, vol. VI
Eames, Alfred Edward, *died* 1924, vol. II
Eames, James Bromley, 1872–1916, vol. II
Eames, Sir William, 1821–1910, vol. I
Eames, Maj.-Gen. William L'Estrange, 1863–1956, vol. V
Eardley, Joan Kathleen Harding, 1921–1963, vol. VI
Eardley-Russell, Lt-Col Edmund Stuart Eardley Wilmot, 1869–1918, vol. II
Eardley-Wilmot, Col Arthur, 1856–1940, vol. III

Eardley-Wilmot, Captain Cecil F., 1855–1916, vol. II
Eardley-Wilmot, Rev. Ernest Augustus, 1848–1932, vol. III
Eardley-Wilmot, Hugh Eden, 1850–1926, vol. II
Eardley-Wilmot, Sir John, 4th Bt, 1882–1970, vol. VI
Eardley-Wilmot, May, 1883–1970, vol. VI
Eardley-Wilmot, Maj.-Gen. Revell, 1842–1922, vol. II
Eardley-Wilmot, Sir Sainthill, 1852–1929, vol. III
Eardley-Wilmot, Rear-Adm. Sir Sydney Marow, 1847–1929, vol. III
Earengey, William George, died 1961, vol. VI
Earl, Sir Austin, 1888–1958, vol. V
Earl, Frederick, 1857–1945, vol. IV
Earle, Rt Rev. Alfred, 1827–1918, vol. II
Earle, Lt-Col Sir Algernon; see Earle, Lt-Col Sir T. A.
Earle, Sir Archdale, 1861–1934, vol. III
Earle, Arthur, 1838–1919, vol. II
Earle, Mrs C. W., (Maria Theresa Villiers), 1836–1925, vol. II
Earle, Charles Westwood, 1871–1950, vol. IV
Earle, Edward Mead, 1894–1954, vol. V
Earle, Brig. Eric Greville, 1893–1965, vol. VI
Earle, Sir George Foster, 1890–1965, vol. VI
Earle, Gerald Frederick, 1864–1944, vol. IV
Earle, Sir Hardman Alexander Mort, 5th Bt, 1902–1979, vol. VII
Earle, Lt-Col Sir Henry, 3rd Bt (cr 1869), 1854–1939, vol. III
Earle, Herbert Gastineau, 1882–1946, vol. IV
Earle, Rev. John, 1824–1903, vol. I
Earle, Hon. John, 1865–1932, vol. III
Earle, Gen. John March, 1825–1914, vol. I
Earle, Sir Lionel, 1866–1948, vol. IV
Earle, Col Maxwell, 1871–1953, vol. V
Earle, Rev. Canon Richard Cobden, 1867–1942, vol. IV
Earle, Col Robert Gilmour, 1874–1957, vol. V
Earle, Sir Thomas, 2nd Bt (cr 1869), 1820–1900, vol. I
Earle, Lt-Col Sir (Thomas) Algernon, 4th Bt (cr 1869), 1860–1945, vol. IV
Earle, Rev. Sir William, 11th Bt (cr 1629), died 1910, vol. I
Early, Stephen T., 1889–1951, vol. V
Earnshaw, Albert, 1865–1920, vol. II
Earnshaw, Mabel Lucie, (Mrs Harold Earnshaw); see Attwell, M. L.
Earp, Charles Anthony, 1871–1933, vol. III
Earp, Frank Russell, 1871–1955, vol. V
Earp, Hon. George Frederick, died 1933, vol. III
Earp, Thomas Wade, 1892–1958, vol. V
Eason, Sir Herbert Lightfoot, 1874–1949, vol. IV
Eason, John, 1874–1964, vol. VI
Eassie, Brig.-Gen. Fitzpatrick, 1864–1943, vol. IV
Eassie, Maj.-Gen. William James Fitzpatrick, 1899–1974, vol. VII
East, Sir Alfred, 1849–1913, vol. I
East, Gen. Sir Cecil James, 1837–1908, vol. I
East, Col Charles Conran, 1866–1942, vol. IV
East, Charles Frederick Terence, 1894–1967, vol. VI

East, Sir George Frederick Lancelot Clayton-, 8th Bt (cr 1732), and 4th Bt (cr 1838), 1872–1926, vol. II
East, Sir Gilbert Augustus Clayton, 7th Bt (cr 1732), and 3rd Bt (cr 1838), 1846–1925, vol. II
East, Hubert Frazer, 1893–1959, vol. V
East, Col Lionel William Pellew, 1866–1918, vol. II
East, Sir Norwood; see East, Sir W. N.
East, Sir (William) Norwood, 1872–1953, vol. V
Easten, Sir Stephen, died 1936, vol. III
Easter, Rev. Canon Arthur John Talbot, 1893–1969, vol. VI
Easterbrook, James, 1851–1923, vol. II
Easterbrook, John Thomas, died 1934, vol. III
Easterfield, Sir Thomas Hill, 1866–1949, vol. IV
Eastes, Arthur Ernest, 1877–1948, vol. IV
Eastham, Leonard Ernest Sydney, 1893–1977, vol. VII
Eastham, Sir Tom, died 1967, vol. VI
Eastlake, Charles Locke, died 1906, vol. I
Eastman, George, 1854–1932, vol. III
Eastman, Gen. William Inglefield, 1856–1941, vol. IV
Easton, Brig.-Gen. Frederick Arthur, 1871–1949, vol. IV
Easton, Col George, 1868–1946, vol. IV
Easton, Hugh, died 1965, vol. VI
Easton, John Murray, 1889–1975, vol. VII
Easton, Lt-Col Philip George, 1878–1960, vol. V
Eastwood, Benjamin, 1863–1943, vol. IV
Eastwood, Charles, 1868–1940, vol. III
Eastwood, Frank Sandford, 1895–1971, vol. VII
Eastwood, Harold, 1880–1941, vol. IV
Eastwood, Harold Edmund, 1889–1960, vol. V
Eastwood, Col Hugh de Crespigny, 1863–1934, vol. III
Eastwood, Col John Charles Basil, 1862–1934, vol. III
Eastwood, John Francis, 1887–1952, vol. V
Eastwood, Reginald Allen, 1893–1964, vol. VI
Eastwood, Lt-Gen. Sir T. Ralph, 1890–1959, vol. V
Eaton, Rev. Arthur Wentworth Hamilton, 1849–1937, vol. III
Eaton, Cecil; see Eaton, W. C.
Eaton, Cyrus Stephen, 1883–1979, vol. VII
Eaton, Sir Fred A., 1838–1913, vol. I
Eaton, Hon. Herbert Edward, 1895–1962, vol. VI
Eaton, Sir John Craig, 1876–1922, vol. II
Eaton, Col Sir Richard William, 1876–1942, vol. IV
Eaton, (Walter) Cecil, 1875–1958, vol. V
Eayrs, Rev. George, 1864–1926, vol. II
Ebbels, Brig. Wilfred Austin, 1898–1976, vol. VII
Ebbisham, 1st Baron, 1868–1953, vol. V
Ebblewhite, Ernest Arthur, 1867–1947, vol. IV
Ebbs, William Alexander, 1890–1960, vol. V
Ebbutt, Norman, 1894–1968, vol. VI
Ebden, Mrs Agnes, died 1930, vol. III
Eberle, George Strachan John Fuller, 1881–1968, vol. VI
Ebers, Georg Maurice, 1837–1898, vol. I
Ebert, Carl Anton Charles, 1887–1980, vol. VII
Eberts, Hon. David MacEwen, 1850–1924, vol. II
Eberts, Edmond Melchior, 1873–1945, vol. IV
Eborall, Sir Arthur; see Eborall, Sir E. A.

Eborall, Sir (Ernest) Arthur, 1878–1967, vol. VI
Ebrahim, Sir Currimbhoy; *see* Ebrahim, Sir H. C.
Ebrahim, Sir Currimbhoy, 1st Bt, 1840–1924, vol. II
Ebrahim, Sir Fazulbhoy Currimbhoy, 1873–1970, vol. VI (AII)
Ebrahim, Sir (Huseinali) Currimbhoy, 3rd Bt, 1903–1952, vol. V
Ebrahim, Sir Mahomedbhoy Currimbhoy, 2nd Bt, 1867–1928, vol. II
Ebrington, Viscount; Hugh Peter Fortescue, 1920–1942, vol. IV
Ebsworth, Brig. Wilfrid Algernon, 1897–1978, vol. VII
Ebury, 2nd Baron, 1834–1918, vol. II
Ebury, 3rd Baron, 1868–1921, vol. II
Ebury, 4th Baron, 1883–1932, vol. III
Ebury, 5th Baron, 1914–1957, vol. V
Eccles, Lt-Col Cuthbert John, 1870–1922, vol. II
Eccles, James Ronald, 1874–1956, vol. V
Eccles, Adm. Sir John Arthur Symons, 1898–1966, vol. VI
Eccles, Rev. Canon John Charles, *born* 1845, vol. II
Eccles, Sir Josiah, 1897–1967, vol. VI
Eccles, Launcelot William Gregory, 1890–1955, vol. V
Eccles, Miss O'C.; *see* O'Conor-Eccles, Miss.
Eccles, Maj.-Gen. Ronald Whalley, 1912–1975, vol. VII
Eccles, William Henry, 1875–1966, vol. VI
Eccles, William McAdam, *died* 1946, vol. IV
Echegaray, José, 1833–1916, vol. II
Echlin, Sir Henry Frederick, 8th Bt, 1846–1923, vol. II
Echlin, Sir John Frederick, 9th Bt, 1890–1932, vol. III
Echlin, Sir Thomas, 7th Bt, 1844–1906, vol. I
Eck, Rev. Herbert Vincent Shortgrave, *died* 1934, vol. III
Eckener, Hugo, 1868–1954, vol. V
Eckersley, Eva Mary, 1871–1944, vol. IV
Eckersley, Peter Pendleton, 1892–1963, vol. VI
Eckersley, Peter Thorp, 1904–1940, vol. III
Eckersley, Roger Huxley, 1885–1955, vol. V
Eckersley, Thomas Lydwell, 1886–1959, vol. V
Eckhoff, Nils Lovold Bjarne Victor, 1902–1969, vol. VI
Eckman, Samuel, Jr, *died* 1976, vol. VII
Eckstein, Captain Sir Bernard, 2nd Bt, 1894–1948, vol. IV
Eckstein, Sir Frederick, 1st Bt, 1857–1930, vol. III
Ecroyd, William Farrer, 1827–1915, vol. I (A)
Eddington, Sir Arthur Stanley, 1882–1944, vol. IV
Eddis, Sir Basil Eden Garth, *died* 1971, vol. VII
Eddis, Brig. Bruce Lindsay, 1883–1966, vol. VI
Eddison, Eric Rucker, 1882–1945, vol. IV
Eddison, John Edwin, 1842–1929, vol. III
Eddowes, Alfred, *died* 1946, vol. IV
Eddowes, Rev. Canon Edmund Edward, 1871–1963, vol. VI
Eddowes, Rev. John, 1826–1905, vol. I
Eddy, Sir (Edward) George, 1878–1967, vol. VI
Eddy, Sir George; *see* Eddy, Sir E. G.
Eddy, Sir (John) Montague, 1881–1949, vol. IV

Eddy, John Percy, 1881–1975, vol. VII
Eddy, Mary Baker Glover, *died* 1910, vol. I
Eddy, Sir Montague; *see* Eddy, Sir J. M.
Ede, Comdr Lionel James Spencer, 1903–1956, vol. V
Ede, Very Rev. William Moore, *died* 1935, vol. III
Edelman, Maurice, 1911–1975, vol. VII
Edelsten, Col John Arthur, 1863–1931, vol. III
Edelsten, Adm. Sir John Hereward, 1891–1966, vol. VI
Edelston, Sir Thomas Dugald, 1878–1955, vol. V
Eden, Brig.-Gen. Archibald James Fergusson, 1872–1956, vol. V
Eden, Charles William Guy, 1874–1947, vol. IV
Eden, Denis, 1878–1949, vol. IV
Eden, Rev. Frederick Nugent, 1857–1926, vol. II
Eden, Hon. George, 1861–1924, vol. II
Eden, Rt Rev. George Rodney, 1853–1940, vol. III
Eden, Guy E. Morton, *died* 1954, vol. V
Eden, Helen Parry, 1885–1960, vol. V
Eden, Rev. Robert Allan, 1839–1912, vol. I
Eden, Robert H. H., *died* 1932, vol. III
Eden, Col Schomberg Henley, 1873–1934, vol. III
Eden, Thomas Watts, 1863–1946, vol. IV
Eden, Sir Timothy Calvert, 8th Bt, 1893–1963, vol. VI
Eden, Sir William, 7th and 5th Bt, 1849–1915, vol. I
Eden, Brig.-Gen. William Rushbrooke, 1873–1920, vol. II
Edenborough, Eric John Horatio, 1893–1965, vol. VI
Eder, Montagu David, *died* 1936, vol. III
Edgar, Clifford Blackburn, 1857–1931, vol. III
Edgar, Sir Edward Mackay, 1st Bt, 1876–1934, vol. III
Edgar, Frederick Percy, 1884–1972, vol. VII
Edgar, George, 1877–1918, vol. II
Edgar, Gilbert Harold Samuel, 1898–1978, vol. VII
Edgar, Lt-Gen. Hector Geoffrey, 1903–1978, vol. VII
Edgar, Hon. Sir James David, 1841–1899, vol. I
Edgar, John, *died* 1922, vol. II
Edgar, Sir John Ware, 1839–1902, vol. I
Edgar, Pelham, 1871–1948, vol. IV
Edgar, William C., 1856–1932, vol. III
Edgar, Surg. Rear-Adm. William Harold, 1885–1959, vol. V
Edgcumbe, Aubrey Pearce; *see* Edgcumbe, J. A. P.
Edgcumbe, Sir (Edward) Robert Pearce, 1851–1929, vol. III
Edgcumbe, (John) Aubrey Pearce, 1886–1974, vol. VII
Edgcumbe, Maj.-Gen. Oliver Pearce, 1892–1956, vol. V
Edgcumbe, Richard, 1843–1937, vol. III
Edgcumbe, Sir Robert Pearce; *see* Edgcumbe, Sir E. R. P.
Edge, Frederick, 1863–1937, vol. III
Edge, James Broughton, *died* 1926, vol. II
Edge, Rt Hon. Sir John, 1841–1926, vol. II
Edge, Maj.-Gen. John Dallas, 1848–1937, vol. III
Edge, John Henry, 1841–1916, vol. II
Edge, Sir Knowles, 1853–1931, vol. III

Edge, Samuel Rathbone, 1848–1936, vol. III
Edge, Selwyn Francis, 1868–1940, vol. III
Edge, Captain Sir William, 1st Bt, 1880–1948, vol. IV
Edge-Partington, Rev. Canon Ellis Foster, 1885–1957, vol. V
Edgedale, Samuel Richards, 1897–1966, vol. VI
Edgell, Beatrice, 1871–1948, vol. IV
Edgell, George Harold, 1887–1954, vol. V
Edgell, Vice-Adm. Sir John Augustine, 1880–1962, vol. VI
Edgerley, Catherine Mabel, died 1946, vol. IV
Edgerley, Sir Steyning William, 1857–1935, vol. III
Edgeworth, Francis H., 1864–1943, vol. IV
Edgeworth, Francis Ysidro, 1845–1926, vol. II
Edgeworth, Lt-Col Kenneth Essex, 1880–1972, vol. VII
Edgeworth-Johnstone, Lt-Col Sir Walter, died 1936, vol. III
Edghill, Rev. John Cox, died 1917, vol. II
Edginton, May, died 1957, vol. V
Edgley, Sir Norman George Armstrong, 1888–1960, vol. V
Edie, Arthur George, 1872–1937, vol. III
Edie, Rev. William, 1865–1936, vol. III
Edington, Alexander Robert, 1895–1964, vol. VI
Edington, George Henry, 1870–1943, vol. IV
Edington, James William, died 1939, vol. III
Edington, William Gerald, 1895–1968, vol. VI
Edis, Sir Robert William, 1839–1927, vol. II
Edison, Thomas Alva, 1847–1931, vol. III
Edkins, John Sydney, 1863–1940, vol. III
Edlin, Sir Peter Henry, 1819–1903, vol. I
Edlmann, Major Ernest Elliot, 1868–1915, vol. I
Edlmann, Col Francis Joseph Frederick, 1885–1950, vol. IV
Edman, Irwin, 1896–1954, vol. V
Edman, Pehr Victor, 1916–1977, vol. VII
Edmeades, Major Henry, 1875–1952, vol. V
Edmeades, Lt-Col James Frederick, 1843–1917, vol. II
Edmeades, Lt-Col William Allaire, 1880–1942, vol. IV
Edmond, Colin Alexander, 1888–1956, vol. V
Edmond, James, 1859–1933, vol. III
Edmond, John Philip, 1850–1906, vol. I
Edmondes, Ven. Frederic William, 1840–1918, vol. II
Edmonds, Cecil John, 1889–1979, vol. VII
Edmonds, Air Vice-Marshal Charles Humphrey Kingsman, 1891–1954, vol. V
Edmonds, Edward Alfred Jubal, 1907–1974, vol. VII
Edmonds, Edward Reginald, 1901–1979, vol. VII
Edmonds, Garnham, 1866–1946, vol. IV
Edmonds, Brig.-Gen. Sir James Edward, 1861–1956, vol. V
Edmonds, Rev. Walter John, 1834–1914, vol. I
Edmonds, William Stanley, 1882–1969, vol. VI
Edmondson, George D'Arcy, 1904–1976, vol. VII
Edmondstoune-Cranstoun, Charles Joseph; see Cranstoun.
Edmonstone, Sir Archibald, 5th Bt, 1867–1954, vol. V

Edmonstone, Sir (Archibald) Charles, 6th Bt, 1898–1954, vol. V
Edmonstone, Sir Charles; see Edmonstone, Sir A. C.
Edmunds, Arthur, 1874–1945, vol. IV
Edmunds, Rev. Horace Vaughan, 1886–1958, vol. V
Edmunds, Humfrey Henry, 1890–1962, vol. VI
Edmunds, Lewis Humfrey, 1860–1941, vol. IV
Edmunds, Nellie M. Hepburn, died 1953, vol. V
Edmunds, Sir Percy James, 1890–1959, vol. V
Edmunds, Walter, died 1930, vol. III
Edmundson, Rev. George, 1848–1930, vol. III
Edridge, Col Frederick Lockwood, 1831–1913, vol. I
Edridge, Sir Frederick Thomas, 1843–1921, vol. II
Edridge-Green, Frederick William, died 1953, vol. V
Edsall, Rt Rev. Samuel Cook, 1860–1917, vol. II
Edser, Edwin, died 1932, vol. III
Edvina, Madame Marie Louise, died 1948, vol. IV
Edward, A. S., 1852–1915, vol. I
Edward-Collins, Maj.-Gen. Charles Edward, 1881–1967, vol. VI
Edward-Collins, Adm. Sir Frederick; see Edward-Collins, Adm. Sir G. F. B.
Edward-Collins, Adm. Sir (George) Frederick (Basset), 1883–1958, vol. V
Edwards-Collins, Brig. Gerald, 1885–1968, vol. VI
Edwardes, Lt-Col Alexander Coburn, 1873–1948, vol. IV
Edwardes, Arthur Henry Francis, 1885–1951, vol. V
Edwardes, Lt-Col Hon. Cuthbert Ellison, 1838–1911, vol. I
Edwardes, George, 1852–1915, vol. I (A)
Edwardes, Sir Henry Hope, 10th Bt, 1829–1900, vol. I
Edwardes, Gen. Sir Stanley de Burgh, 1840–1918, vol. II
Edwardes, Col Stanley Malcolm, 1863–1937, vol. III
Edwardes, Stephen Meredyth, 1873–1927, vol. II
Edwardes, Tickner, 1865–1944, vol. IV
Edwardes-Davies, Rt Rev. David, 1897–1950, vol. IV
Edwardes-Ker, Lt-Col Douglas Rous, 1886–1979, vol. VII
Edwards, Agustin, 1878–1941, vol. IV
Edwards, Alfred, 1888–1958, vol. V
Edwards, Most Rev. Alfred George, 1848–1937, vol. III
Edwards, Maj.-Gen. Sir Alfred Hamilton Mackenzie, 1862–1944, vol. IV
Edwards, Rev. Canon Allen, 1844–1917, vol. II
Edwards, (Allen) Clement, 1869–1938, vol. III
Edwards, Arthur James Howie, 1884–1944, vol. IV
Edwards, Arthur John Charles, 1883–1963, vol. VI
Edwards, (Arthur) Trystan, 1884–1973, vol. VII
Edwards, Arthur Tudor, died 1946, vol. IV
Edwards, Lt-Col Sir Bartle Mordaunt Marsham, 1891–1977, vol. VII
Edwards, Hon. Sir Bassett; see Edwards, Hon. Sir W. B.

Edwards, Mrs Bennett-, 1844–1936, vol. III
Edwards, Ven. Bickerton Cross, 1874–1949, vol. IV
Edwards, Brig. Brian Bingay, 1895–1947, vol. IV
Edwards, Rt Hon. Sir Charles, 1867–1954, vol. V
Edwards, Charles Alfred, 1882–1960, vol. V
Edwards, Charles Lewis, 1865–1928, vol. II
Edwards, Lt-Comdr Charles Peter, 1885–1960, vol. V
Edwards, Brig.-Gen. Christopher Vaughan, 1875–1955, vol. V
Edwards, Clement; see Edwards, A. C.
Edwards, Corwin D., 1901–1979, vol. VII
Edwards, Lt-Col Cosmo Grant Niven, 1896–1964, vol. VI
Edwards, D., 1858–1916, vol. II
Edwards, Sir David, 1892–1966, vol. VI
Edwards, Rev. Father Douglas Allen, 1893–1953, vol. V
Edwards, Ebby, 1884–1961, vol. VI
Edwards, Rev. Canon Edgar Thomas, 1880–1935, vol. III
Edwards, Edward, 1865–1933, vol. III
Edwards, Edward John Rogers, 1891–1965, vol. VI
Edwards, Rev. Ellis, 1844–1915, vol. I
Edwards, Enoch, 1852–1912, vol. I
Edwards, Evangeline Dora, 1888–1957, vol. V
Edwards, Brig.-Gen. Fitz-James Maine, 1861–1929, vol. III
Edwards, Lt-Col Rt Hon. Sir Fleetwood Isham, 1842–1910, vol. I
Edwards, Sir Francis, 1st Bt (cr 1907), 1852–1927, vol. II
Edwards, Lt-Gen. Frederick Charles, 1870–1947, vol. IV
Edwards, Frederick Laurence, 1903–1962, vol. VI
Edwards, Frederick Swinford, 1853–1939, vol. III
Edwards, Frederick Wallace, 1888–1940, vol. III
Edwards, G. Spencer, died 1916, vol. II
Edwards, Geoffrey Richard, 1891–1961, vol. VI
Edwards, Sir George, 1850–1933, vol. III
Edwards, George, 1854–1946, vol. IV
Edwards, Sir (George) Tristram, 1882–1960, vol. V
Edwards, Sir George William, 1818–1902, vol. I
Edwards, Gordon, 1899–1976, vol. VII
Edwards, Sir Goronwy; see Edwards, Sir J. G.
Edwards, Brig.-Gen. Graham Thomas George, 1864–1943, vol. IV
Edwards, Col Guy Janion, 1881–1962, vol. VI
Edwards, Gwilym Arthur, 1881–1963, vol. VI
Edwards, (H. C.) Ralph, 1894–1977, vol. VII
Edwards, Lt-Comdr Harington Douty, died 1916, vol. II
Edwards, Air Marshal Harold, 1892–1952, vol. V
Edwards, Lt-Col Harold Walter, 1887–1973, vol. VII
Edwards, Sir Henry, 1820–1897, vol. I
Edwards, Sir Henry Charles Serrell Priestley, 4th Bt (cr 1866), 1893–1963, vol. VI
Edwards, Sir Henry Coster Lea, 2nd Bt (cr 1866), 1840–1896, vol. I
Edwards, Henry John, 1869–1923, vol. II
Edwards, Col Herbert Ivor Powell, 1884–1946, vol. IV
Edwards, Captain Hugh, died 1916, vol. II

Edwards, Sir Ifan ab Owen, 1895–1970, vol. VI
Edwards, Very Rev. Irven David, 1907–1973, vol. VII
Edwards, Lt-Col Ivo Arthyr Exley, 1881–1947, vol. IV (A)
Edwards, Lt-Gen. Sir James Bevan, 1834–1922, vol. II
Edwards, Rt Hon. John; see Edwards, Rt Hon. L. J.
Edwards, John, died 1954, vol. V
Edwards, John, 1882–1960, vol. V
Edwards, Sir John Bryn, 1st Bt (cr 1921), 1889–1922, vol. II
Edwards, Brig.-Gen. John Burnard, 1857–1937, vol. III
Edwards, Rev. John Cox C.; see Cox-Edwards.
Edwards, Vice-Adm. John Douglas, 1871–1952, vol. V
Edwards, John Francis H.; see Hall-Edwards.
Edwards, Sir (John) Goronwy, 1891–1976, vol. VII
Edwards, Sir John Henry Priestley Churchill, 3rd Bt (cr 1866), 1889–1942, vol. IV
Edwards, John Hugh, died 1945, vol. IV
Edwards, John Passmore, 1823–1911, vol. I
Edwards, Rev. John Rosindale W.; see Wynne-Edwards.
Edwards, Joseph, 1854–1931, vol. III
Edwards, Joshua Price, 1898–1966, vol. VI
Edwards, Laura Selina, (Lady Edwards), died 1919, vol. II
Edwards, Sir Lawrence, 1896–1968, vol. VI
Edwards, Rt Hon. (Lewis) John, 1904–1959, vol. V
Edwards, Lionel D. R., 1878–1966, vol. VI
Edwards, Engr Rear-Adm. Macleod Gamul Arthur, 1884–1957, vol. V
Edwards, Rev. Maldwyn Lloyd, 1903–1974, vol. VII
Edwards, Matilda Betham-, died 1919, vol. II
Edwards, Rev. Maurice Henry, 1886–1961, vol. VI
Edwards, Rt Hon. Ness, 1897–1968, vol. VI
Edwards, Osman, 1864–1936, vol. III
Edwards, Sir Owen Morgan, 1858–1920, vol. II
Edwards, Ralph; see Edwards, H. C. R.
Edwards, Adm. Sir Ralph Alan Bevan, 1901–1963, vol. VI
Edwards, Brig.-Gen. Richard Fielding, 1866–1942, vol. IV
Edwards, Robert Hamilton, born 1872, vol. III
Edwards, Sir Robert Meredydd W.; see Wynne-Edwards.
Edwards, Captain Roderick Latimer Mackenzie, 1900–1975, vol. VII
Edwards, Lt-Col Roderick Mackenzie, died 1940, vol. III
Edwards, Sir Ronald Stanley, 1910–1976, vol. VII
Edwards, Rev. Canon Rowland Alexander, 1890–1973, vol. VII
Edwards, Rev. Thomas, vol. II
Edwards, Rev. Thomas Charles, 1837–1900, vol. I
Edwards, Sir Tristram; see Edwards, Sir G. T.
Edwards, Trystan; see Edwards, A. T.
Edwards, Walter James, 1900–1964, vol. VI
Edwards, Lt-Col Walter Manoel, 1885–1971, vol. VII

Edwards, Wilbraham Tollemache Arthur, 1836–1929, vol. III
Edwards, Wilfred Norman, 1890–1956, vol. V
Edwards, William, 1851–1940, vol. III
Edwards, William, 1874–1969, vol. VI
Edwards, Lt-Col William Bickerton, 1870–1933, vol. III
Edwards, Hon. William Cameron, 1844–1921, vol. II
Edwards, Col William Egerton, 1875–1921, vol. II
Edwards, Brig.-Gen. Willam Frederick Savery, 1872–1941, vol. IV
Edwards, Rev. Canon William George, 1858–1942, vol. IV
Edwards, Rev. William Gilbert, 1846–1936, vol. III
Edwards, Major William Mordaunt Marsh, 1855–1912, vol. I
Edwards, William Powell, 1854–1935, vol. III
Edwards, Hon. Maj.-Gen. Sir William Rice, 1862–1923, vol. II
Edwards, William Stuart, 1880–1944, vol. IV
Edwards, Hon. Sir (Worley) Bassett, 1850–1927, vol. II
Edwards-Heathcote, Justinian Heathcote; *see* Heathcote.
Edwards-Moss, Sir John Edwards, 2nd Bt, 1850–1935, vol. III
Edwards-Moss, Sir Thomas, 3rd Bt, 1874–1960, vol. V
Edwin, George Frederick D.; *see* Dove-Edwin.
Edye, Sir Benjamin Thomas, 1884–1962, vol. VI
Eeles, Francis Carolus, 1876–1954, vol. V
Eestermans, Fabian Anthony, 1858–1931, vol. III
Effingham, 3rd Earl of, 1837–1898, vol. I
Effingham, 4th Earl of, 1866–1927, vol. II
Effingham, 5th Earl of, 1873–1946, vol. IV
Egan, Sir Henry Kelly, 1848–1925, vol. II
Egan, Hon. Maurice Francis, 1852–1924, vol. II
Egan, Col Michael Henry, 1865–1940, vol. III
Egan, Rt Rev. T. Erkenwald, 1856–1939, vol. III
Egan, Major William, 1881–1929, vol. III
Egan, William Henry, 1869–1943, vol. IV
Egbert, Hon. William, 1857–1936, vol. III
Egerton, 1st Earl, 1832–1909, vol. I
Egerton of Tatton, 3rd Baron, 1845–1920 (this entry was not transferred to Who was Who).
Egerton of Tatton, 4th Baron, 1874–1958, vol. V
Egerton, Sir Alfred Charles Glyn, 1886–1959, vol. V
Egerton, Col Sir Alfred Mordaunt, 1843–1908, vol. I
Egerton, Lady Alice, 1923–1977, vol. VII
Egerton, Lt-Col Arthur Frederick, 1866–1942, vol. IV
Egerton, Sir Brian, 1857–1940, vol. III
Egerton, Rev. Sir Brooke de Malpas Grey-, 13th Bt, 1845–1945, vol. IV
Egerton, Charles Augustus, *died* 1912, vol. I
Egerton, Field-Marshal Sir Charles Comyn, 1848–1921, vol. II
Egerton, Charles William, 1862–1939, vol. III
Egerton, Rt Hon. Sir Edwin Henry, 1841–1916, vol. II
Egerton, Rear-Adm. Frederick Wilbraham, 1838–1909, vol. I

Egerton, George, (Mrs Golding Bright), (Mary Chavelita), 1859–1945, vol. IV
Egerton, Adm. Sir George le Clerc, 1852–1940, vol. III
Egerton, Major George M. L., 1837–1898, vol. I
Egerton, Maj.-Gen. Granville George Algernon, 1859–1951, vol. V
Egerton, Vice-Adm. (Henry) Jack, 1892–1972, vol. VII
Egerton, Hugh Edward, 1855–1927, vol. II
Egerton, Comdr Hugh Sydney, 1890–1969, vol. VI
Egerton, Vice-Adm. Jack; *see* Egerton, Vice-Adm. H. J.
Egerton, Lady Mabelle, 1865–1927, vol. II
Egerton, Sir Philip Henry Brian Grey-, 12th Bt, 1864–1937, vol. III
Egerton, Sir Philip Reginald le Belward G.; *see* Grey Egerton.
Egerton, Lt-Gen. Sir Raleigh Gilbert, 1860–1931, vol. III
Egerton, Sir Reginald Arthur, 1850–1930, vol. III
Egerton, Sir Robert Eyles, 1857–1912, vol. I
Egerton, Hon. Thomas Henry Frederick, 1876–1953, vol. V
Egerton, Sir Walter, 1858–1947, vol. IV
Egerton, Rear-Adm. Wilfrid Allan, 1881–1931, vol. III
Egerton, William Francis, 1868–1949, vol. IV
Egerton, Rev. William Henry, 1811–1910, vol. I
Egerton, Vice-Adm. Wion De Malpas, 1879–1943, vol. IV
Egerton-Warburton, Geoffrey, 1888–1961, vol. VI
Egerton-Warburton, John, 1883–1915, vol. I
Egerton-Warburton, Piers, 1839–1914, vol. I
Eggar, Sir Arthur, 1877–1958, vol. V
Eggar, Sir Henry Cooper, 1851–1941, vol. IV
Eggar, James, 1880–1962, vol. VI
Eggeling, H. Julius, 1842–1918, vol. II
Eggers, Henry Howard, 1903–1980, vol. VII
Egginton, Wycliffe, 1875–1951, vol. V
Eggleston, Edward, 1837–1902, vol. I
Eggleston, Sir Frederic William, 1875–1954, vol. V
Eglington, Rev. Canon Arthur, 1871–1925, vol. II
Eglington, William, 1858–1933, vol. III
Eglinton and Winton, 15th Earl of, 1848–1919, vol. II
Eglinton and Winton, 16th Earl of, 1880–1945, vol. IV
Eglinton and Winton, 17th Earl of, 1914–1966, vol. VI
Egmont, 7th Earl of, 1845–1897, vol. I
Egmont, 8th Earl of, 1856–1910, vol. I
Egmont, 9th Earl of, 1858–1929, vol. III
Egmont, 10th Earl of, 1873–1932, vol. III
Egmont, Countess of; (Lucy), *died* 1932, vol. III
Egremont, 1st Baron, and Leconfield, 6th Baron, 1920–1972, vol. VII
Eha; *see* Aitken, E. H.
Ehrenburg, Ilya, 1891–1967, vol. VI
Ehrenberg, Victor Leopold, 1891–1976, vol. VII
Ehrhardt, Albert, 1862–1929, vol. III
Ehrlich, Georg, 1897–1966, vol. VI
Ehrlich, Paul, 1854–1915, vol. I
Eichholz, Alfred, 1869–1933, vol. III

Eiffel, Alexandre Gustave, 1832–1923, vol. II
Einaudi, Luigi, 1874–1961, vol. VI
Einstein, Albert, 1879–1955, vol. V
Einstein, Alfred, 1880–1952, vol. V
Einthoven, Willem, 1860–1927, vol. II
Einzig, Paul, 1897–1973, vol. VII
Eisdell, Hubert Mortimer, 1882–1948, vol. IV
Eisenberg, Maurice, 1902–1972, vol. VII
Eisenhower, Gen. Dwight David, 1890–1969, vol. VI
Eisenschitz, Robert Karl, 1898–1968, vol. VI
Eking, Maj.-Gen. Harold Cecil William, 1903–1978, vol. VII
Ekins, Emily Helen, 1879–1964, vol. VI
Ekwall, Bror Oscar Eilert, 1877–1964, vol. VI
Eland, John Shenton, 1872–1933, vol. III
Elcho, Lord; Iain David Charteris, 1945–1954, vol. V
Elcock, William Dennis, 1910–1960, vol. V
Elder, Sir James Alexander MacKenzie, 1869–1946, vol. IV
Elder, John Munro, 1860–1922, vol. II
Elder, John Rawson, 1880–1962, vol. VI
Elder, William, 1864–1931, vol. III
Elder, William Alexander, 1881–1946, vol. IV (A)
Elder, Rear-Adm. William Leslie, 1874–1961, vol. VI
Elder, Sir (William) Stewart D.; see Duke-Elder.
Elder-Duncan, John Hudson, 1877–1938, vol. III
Elderton, Ethel Mary, 1878–1954, vol. V
Elderton, Captain Ferdinand Halford, 1865–1942, vol. IV
Elderton, Sir Thomas Howard, 1886–1970, vol. VI
Elderton, Sir William Palin, 1877–1962, vol. VI
Eldon, 3rd Earl of, 1845–1926, vol. II
Eldon, 4th Earl of, 1899–1976, vol. VII
Eldred, Paymaster-Captain Edward Henry, 1864–1929, vol. III
Eldridge, Captain George Bernard, died 1944, vol. IV
Eley, Col Edward Henry, 1874–1949, vol. IV
Eley, Sir Frederick, 1st Bt, 1866–1951, vol. V
Eley, Rt Rev. Stanley Albert Hallam, 1899–1970, vol. VI
Elford, William Joseph, 1900–1952, vol. V
Elgar, Sir Edward, 1st Bt, 1857–1934, vol. III
Elgar, Francis, 1845–1909, vol. I
Elgee, Captain Cyril Hammond, 1871–1917, vol. II
Elgee, Frank, 1880–1944, vol. IV
Elger, Major Edward Gwyn, 1864–1929, vol. III
Elgin, 9th Earl of, and Kincardine, 13th Earl of, 1849–1917, vol. II
Elgin, 10th Earl of, and Kincardine, 14th Earl of, 1881–1968, vol. VI
Elgood, Sir Frank Minshull, 1865–1948, vol. IV
Elgood, George S., 1851–1943, vol. IV
Elgood, Lt-Col Percival George, 1863–1941, vol. IV
Elhorst, Hendrik Jan, born 1861, vol. II
Elias, David Henry, 1882–1953, vol. V
Eliash, Mordecai, 1892–1950, vol. IV
Elibank, 1st Viscount, 1840–1927, vol. II
Elibank, 2nd Viscount, 1877–1951, vol. V
Elibank, 3rd Viscount, 1879–1962, vol. VI
Elibank, 13th Lord, 1902–1973, vol. VII

Eliot, Lord; Edward Henry John Cornwallis Elliot, 1885–1909, vol. I
Eliot, Hon. Arthur Ernest Henry, 1874–1936, vol. III
Eliot, Rt Hon. Sir Charles Norton Edgcumbe, 1862–1931, vol. III
Eliot, Charles William, 1834–1926, vol. II
Eliot, Edward Carlyon, died 1940, vol. III
Eliot, Ven. Edward Francis Whately, 1864–1943, vol. IV
Eliot, Sir John, 1839–1908, vol. I
Eliot, Laurence Stirling, 1845–1922, vol. II
Eliot, Lt-Col Nevill, 1880–1957, vol. V
Eliot, Very Rev. Philip Frank, 1835–1917, vol. II
Eliot, Rt Rev. Philip Herbert, 1862–1946, vol. IV
Eliot, Vice-Adm. Ralph, 1881–1958, vol. V
Eliot, Hon. Reginald Huyshe H.; see Huyshe-Eliot.
Eliot, Rev. Samuel Atkins, 1862–1950, vol. IV (A), vol. V
Eliot, Thomas Stearns, 1888–1965, vol. VI
Eliot, Rev. W., 1832–1910, vol. I
Eliot, Sir Whately, 1841–1927, vol. II
Eliott of Stobs, Sir Arthur Boswell, 9th Bt, 1856–1926, vol. II
Eliott, Lt-Col Francis Augustus Heathfield, 1867–1937, vol. III
Eliott, Lt-Col Francis Hardinge, 1862–1928, vol. II
Eliott of Stobs, Sir Gilbert Alexander Boswell, 10th Bt, 1885–1958, vol. V
Eliott of Stobs, Sir William Francis Augustus, 8th Bt, 1827–1910, vol. I
Eliott Lockhart, Sir Allan Robert, 1905–1977, vol. VII
Eliott-Lockhart, Lt-Col Percy Clare, 1867–1915, vol. I
Elkan, Benno, 1877–1960, vol. V
Elkan, Lt-Col Clarence John, 1877–1940, vol. III
Elkan, John, 1849–1927, vol. II
El'Kanemi, Alhaji Sir Umar Ibn Muhammed El'Amin, 1873–1967, vol. VI
Elkington, Frederick Pellatt, 1874–1940, vol. III (A), vol. IV
Elkington, John St Clair, died 1963, vol. VI
Elkington, John Simeon, born 1841, vol. II
Elkington, Reginald Lawrence, 1898–1975, vol. VII
Elkington, Col Robert James Goodall, 1867–1939, vol. III
Elkins, Sir Anthony Joseph, 1904–1978, vol. VII
Elkins, Stephen Benton, 1841–1911, vol. I
Elkins, Maj.-Gen. William Henry Pferinger, 1883–1964, vol. VI
Elkins, William Lukens, 1832–1903, vol. I
Elland, Percy, 1908–1960, vol. V
Ellenberger, Lt-Col Jules, 1871–1973, vol. VII
Ellenborough, 4th Baron, 1856–1902, vol. I
Ellenborough, 5th Baron, 1841–1915, vol. I (A)
Ellenborough, 6th Baron, 1849–1931, vol. III
Ellenborough, 7th Baron, 1889–1945, vol. IV
Ellerman, Sir John Reeves, 1st Bt, 1862–1933, vol. III
Ellerman, Sir John Reeves, 2nd Bt, 1909–1973, vol. VII
Ellershaw, Brig.-Gen. Arthur, 1869–1929, vol. III
Ellershaw, Rev. Henry, 1863–1932, vol. III

Ellerton, Air Cdre Alban Spenser, 1894–1978, vol. VII

Ellerton, Rev. Arthur John Bicknell, 1865–1928, vol. II

Ellerton, Sir Cecil; see Ellerton, Sir F. C.

Ellerton, Sir (Frederick) Cecil, 1892–1962, vol. VI

Ellerton, Adm. Walter Maurice, 1870–1948, vol. IV

Ellery, Lt-Col Robert Lewis John, 1827–1908, vol. I

Elles, Lt-Gen. Sir Edmond Roche, 1848–1934, vol. III

Elles, Gen. Sir Hugh Jamieson, 1880–1945, vol. IV

Ellesmere, 3rd Earl of, 1847–1914, vol. I

Ellesmere, 4th Earl of, 1872–1944, vol. II

Ellice, Major Edward Charles, 1858–1934, vol. III

Ellicott, Arthur Becher, 1849–1931, vol. III

Ellicott, Langford Pannell, 1903–1972, vol. VII

Ellicott, Rosalind, died 1924, vol. II

Ellinger, Barnard, died 1947, vol. IV

Ellingford, Herbert Frederick, 1876–1966, vol. VI

Ellington, Duke; see Ellington, Hon. E. K.

Ellington, Hon. Edward Kennedy, (Duke), 1899–1974, vol. VII

Ellington, Marshal of the Royal Air Force Sir Edward Leonard, 1877–1967, vol. VI

Elliot, Maj.-Gen. Sir Alexander James Hardy, 1825–1909, vol. I

Elliot, Alison, 1891–1939, vol. III

Elliot, Hon. Arthur Ralph Douglas, 1846–1923, vol. II

Elliot, Sir Charles, 4th Bt, 1873–1911, vol. I

Elliot, Sir Duncan; see Elliot, Sir J. D.

Elliot, Major Sir Edmund Halbert, 1854–1926, vol. II

Elliot, Lt-Gen. Sir Edward Locke, 1850–1938, vol. III

Elliot, Sir Francis Edmund Hugh, 1851–1940, vol. III

Elliot, Frederick Augustus Hugh, 1847–1910, vol. I

Elliot, Frederick Barnard, 1877–1950, vol. IV

Elliot, Rev. Frederick Roberts, 1840–1918, vol. II

Elliot, Sir George, 1812–1901, vol. I

Elliot, Sir George, 3rd Bt, 1867–1904, vol. I

Elliot, Sir George, 1868–1956, vol. V

Elliot, Rev. Canon George Edward, 1851–1916, vol. II

Elliot, Maj.-Gen. Gilbert Minto, 1897–1969, vol. VI

Elliot, Brig.-Gen. Gilbert Sutherland McDowell, 1863–1937, vol. III

Elliot, Maj.-Gen. Harry Macintire C.; see Cawthra-Elliot.

Elliot, Rt Hon. Sir Henry George, 1817–1907, vol. I

Elliot, Sir Henry George, 1826–1912, vol. I

Elliot, Lt-Col Henry Hawes, 1891–1972, vol. VII

Elliot, Maj.-Gen. Henry Riversdale, 1836–1921, vol. II

Elliot, Hubert William Arthur, 1891–1967, vol. VI

Elliot, Hugh, 1881–1930, vol. III

Elliot, Hon. Hugh Frederick Hislop, 1848–1932, vol. III

Elliot, Sir (James) Duncan, 1862–1956, vol. V

Elliot, James Robert McDowell, 1896–1980, vol. VII

Elliot, Margaret, died 1901, vol. I

Elliot, Captain Mark F.; see Fogg Elliot.

Elliot, Maj.-Gen. Minto, 1833–1909, vol. I

Elliot, Robert H., 1837–1914, vol. I

Elliot, Lt-Col Robert Henry, died 1936, vol. III

Elliot, Rt Hon. Walter Elliot, 1888–1958, vol. V

Elliot, Walter Travers S.; see Scott-Elliot.

Elliot, Col William, 1861–1936, vol. III

Elliot, Air Chief Marshal Sir William, 1896–1971, vol. VII

Elliot, Col William Henry Wilson, 1864–1934, vol. III

Elliot, Lt-Col William Scott, 1873–1943, vol. IV

Elliott, Adshead, 1869–1922, vol. II

Elliott, Albert George, 1889–1975, vol. VII

Elliott, Lt-Col Alfred Charles, 1870–1952, vol. V

Elliott, Rt Rev. Alfred George, 1828–1915, vol. I

Elliott, Algernon, 1848–1934, vol. III

Elliott, Anthony; see Elliott, T. A. K.

Elliott, Rt Rev. Anthony Blacker, 1887–1970, vol. VI (AII)

Elliott, Archibald Campbell, 1861–1913, vol. I

Elliott, Sir Bignell George, 1857–1933, vol. III

Elliott, Sir Charles Alfred, 1835–1911, vol. I

Elliott, Sir Charles Bletterman, 1841–1911, vol. I

Elliott, Col Charles Hazell, 1882–1956, vol. V

Elliott, Charles Hugh Babington, 1852–1943, vol. IV

Elliott, Rev. Canon Charles Lister Boileau, 1864–1940, vol. III

Elliott, Christopher, 1849–1933, vol. III

Elliott, Clarence, 1881–1969, vol. VI

Elliott, Sir Claude Aurelius, 1888–1973, vol. VII

Elliott, (Colin) Fraser, 1888–1969, vol. VI

Elliott, David Lee L.; see Lee-Elliott.

Elliott, Edward Cassleton, 1881–1967, vol. VI

Elliott, Maj.-Gen. Edward Draper, 1838–1918, vol. II

Elliott, Edwin Bailey, 1851–1937, vol. III

Elliott, Ven. Francis William Thomas, died 1930, vol. III

Elliott, Frank Herbert, 1878–1966, vol. VI

Elliott, Frank Louis Dumbell, 1874–1939, vol. III

Elliott, Fraser; see Elliott, C. F.

Elliott, George, 1860–1916, vol. II

Elliott, Sir George Samuel, died 1925, vol. II

Elliott, Col Gilbert Charles Edward, 1872–1934, vol. III

Elliott, Maj.-Gen. Harold Edward, 1878–1931, vol. III

Elliott, Sir Ivo D'Oyly, 2nd Bt, 1882–1961, vol. VI

Elliott, Sir James Sands, 1880–1959, vol. V

Elliott, Mrs John; see Elliott, M. H.

Elliott, Col John, 1824–1911, vol. I

Elliott, Hon. John Campbell, 1872–1941, vol. IV

Elliott, Rev. John Robert Underwood, 1843–1936, vol. III

Elliott, John Wilson, 1886–1957, vol. V

Elliott, Maud Howe, (Mrs John Elliott), 1854–1948, vol. IV

Elliott, Vice-Adm. Sir Maurice Herbert, 1897–1972, vol. VII

Elliott, Robert Charles Dunlop, 1886–1950, vol. IV
Elliott, Rt Rev. Robert Cyril Hamilton, 1890–1977, vol. VII
Elliott, Rowley, 1877–1944, vol. IV
Elliott, Rev. Canon Spencer Hayward, 1883–1967, vol. VI
Elliott, (Thomas) Anthony (Keith), 1921–1976, vol. VII
Elliott, Sir Thomas Henry, 1st Bt, 1854–1926, vol. II
Elliott, Thomas Renton, 1877–1961, vol. VI
Elliott, Rev. Canon Wallace Harold, died 1957, vol. V
Elliott, Col William, 1879–1947, vol. IV
Elliott, William John, 1890–1940, vol. III
Elliott, Rev. William Thompson, 1880–1940, vol. III
Elliott-Binns, Rev. Leonard Elliott; see Binns.
Elliott-Cooper, Sir Robert; see Cooper.
Ellis, Sir Alan Edward, 1890–1960, vol. V
Ellis, Sir Albert Fuller, 1869–1951, vol. V
Ellis, Col Alfred Charles Samuel Burdon, 1876–1955, vol. V
Ellis, Anthony Louis, died 1944, vol. IV
Ellis, Arthur, 1856–1918, vol. II
Ellis, Maj.-Gen. Sir Arthur Edward Augustus, 1837–1907, vol. I
Ellis, Arthur Isaac, 1883–1963, vol. VI
Ellis, Arthur Thomas, 1892–1964, vol. VI
Ellis, Sir Arthur William Mickle, died 1966, vol. VI
Ellis, Lt-Comdr Bernard Henry, 1885–1918, vol. II
Ellis, Sir (Bertram) Clough W.; see Williams-Ellis.
Ellis, Col Charles Conyngham, 1852–1921, vol. II
Ellis, Sir Charles Drummond, 1895–1980, vol. VII
Ellis, Sir Charles Edward, 1852–1937, vol. III
Ellis, Lt-Col Sir Charles Henry Brabazon H.; see Heaton-Ellis.
Ellis, Charles Howard, 1895–1975, vol. VII
Ellis, Col Clarence Isidore, 1871–1961, vol. VI
Ellis, Rear-Adm. (E.) Clement, died 1953, vol. V
Ellis, Colin Dare Bernard, 1895–1969, vol. VI
Ellis, Lt-Col Conyngham Richard Cecil, 1863–1938, vol. III
Ellis, David, 1874–1937, vol. III
Ellis, Rt Rev. Edward, 1899–1979, vol. VII
Ellis, Vice-Adm. Sir Edward Henry Fitzhardinge H.; see Heaton-Ellis.
Ellis, Engr Rear-Adm. Ernest Frank, 1855–1944, vol. IV
Ellis, Ernest Tetley, 1893–1953, vol. V
Ellis, Sir Evelyn Campbell, 1865–1920, vol. II
Ellis, Francis Newman, 1855–1934, vol. III
Ellis, Francis Robert, 1849–1915, vol. I (A)
Ellis, Captain Frederick, 1826–1906, vol. I
Ellis, Sir Geoffrey; see Ellis, Sir R. G.
Ellis, Gerald Edward Harold, 1878–1967, vol. VI
Ellis, Rev. Canon Henry, 1909–1972, vol. VII
Ellis, Henry Arthur Augustus, died 1934, vol. III
Ellis, Henry Havelock, 1859–1939, vol. III
Ellis, Lt-Col Henry L.; see Leslie-Ellis.
Ellis, Col Herbert Charles, 1874–1952, vol. V
Ellis, Sir Herbert Mackay, 1851–1912, vol. I
Ellis, Sir Howard; see Ellis, Sir S. H.
Ellis, Rt Hon. John Edward, 1841–1910, vol. I

Ellis, J(ohn) Hugh, 1909–1959, vol. V
Ellis, Sir (John) Whittaker, 1st Bt (cr 1882), 1829–1912, vol. I
Ellis, Sir Joseph Baxter, died 1918, vol. II
Ellis, Hon. Sir Kevin, 1908–1975, vol. VII
Ellis, Major Lionel Frederic, 1885–1970, vol. VI
Ellis, Lyle Fullam, 1887–1951, vol. V
Ellis, Malcolm Henry, 1890–1969, vol. VI (AII)
Ellis, Mary Baxter, 1892–1968, vol. VI
Ellis, Maj.-Gen. Philip George Saxon G.; see Gregson-Ellis.
Ellis, Brig. Richard Stanley, 1884–1962, vol. VI
Ellis, Richard White Bernard, 1902–1966, vol. VI
Ellis, Sir (Robert) Geoffrey, 1st Bt (cr 1932), 1874–1956, vol. V
Ellis, Robert Powley, 1845–1918, vol. II
Ellis, Robinson, 1834–1913, vol. I
Ellis, Rt Rev. Rowland, 1841–1911, vol. I
Ellis, Sir (Samuel) Howard, 1889–1949, vol. IV
Ellis, Lt-Col Sherman Gordon Venn, 1880–1937, vol. III
Ellis, Stewart Marsh, died 1933, vol. III
Ellis, T. Mullett, 1850–1919, vol. II
Ellis, Thomas Edward, 1859–1899, vol. I
Ellis, Thomas Iorwerth, 1899–1970, vol. VI
Ellis, Sir Thomas Ratcliffe R.; see Ratcliffe-Ellis.
Ellis, Tristram, 1844–1922, vol. II
Ellis, Valentine Herbert, died 1953, vol. V
Ellis, Very Rev. Vorley Spencer, 1882–1977, vol. VII
Ellis, Walter Devonshire, 1871–1957, vol. V
Ellis, Sir Whittaker; see Ellis, Sir J. W.
Ellis, William, 1828–1916, vol. II
Ellis, William, 1868–1947, vol. IV
Ellis, William Barker, died 1934, vol. III
Ellis, William C.; see Craven-Ellis.
Ellis, Rev. Hon. William Charles, 1835–1923, vol. II
Ellis, Lt-Col W(illiam) Francis, 1878–1953, vol. V
Ellis, Sir William Henry, 1860–1945, vol. IV
Ellis, William Hodgson, 1845–1921, vol. II
Ellis, Col William Montague, 1862–1952, vol. V
Ellis-Fermor, Una Mary, 1894–1958, vol. V
Ellis-Griffith, Sir Elis Arundell; see Griffith, Sir E. A. E.
Ellis-Griffith, Rt Hon. Sir Ellis Jones; see Griffith.
Ellis-Rees, Sir Hugh, 1900–1974, vol. VII
Ellison, Rear-Adm. Alfred Astley, 1874–1932, vol. III
Ellison, Ven. Charles Ottley, 1898–1978, vol. VII
Ellison, Lt-Gen. Sir Gerald Francis, 1861–1947, vol. IV
Ellison, Grace Mary, died 1935, vol. III
Ellison, Rev. John Henry Joshua, 1855–1944, vol. IV
Ellison, Captain Richard Todd, died 1932, vol. III
Ellison, William, 1911–1978, vol. VII
Ellison, William Augustine, 1855–1917, vol. II
Ellison, Rev. Canon William Frederick Archdall, 1864–1936, vol. III
Ellison-Macartney, John William; see Macartney.
Ellison-Macartney, Rt Hon. Sir William Grey; see Macartney.
Ellissen, Lt-Col Sir Herbert, 1876–1952, vol. V

Elliston, Col George Sampson, 1844–1921, vol. II
Elliston, Sir George Sampson, 1875–1954, vol. V
Elliston, Guy, 1872–1918, vol. II
Elliston, Julian Clement Peter, 1911–1970, vol. VI
Elliston, William Alfred, 1840–1908, vol. I
Elliston, William Rowley, 1869–1954, vol. V
Ellson, George, 1875–1949, vol. IV
Ellsworth, Lincoln, 1880–1951, vol. V
Ellwood, Bt Col Arthur Addison, 1886–1943, vol. IV
Ellwood, George Montague, 1875–1955, vol. V
Elman, Mischa, 1891–1967, vol. VI
Elmhirst, Dorothy Whitney, 1887–1968, vol. VI
Elmhirst, Captain Edward Pennell, 1845–1916, vol. II
Elmhirst, Leonard Knight, died 1974, vol. VII
Elmitt, Lt-Col T. F., 1871–1938, vol. III
Elmsley, Maj.-Gen. James Harold, 1878–1954, vol. V
Elmslie, Christiana Deanes, 1869–1961, vol. VI
Elmslie, Brig.-Gen. Frederick Baumgardt, 1855–1936, vol. III
Elmslie, Noel, 1876–1956, vol. V
Elmslie, Reginald Cheyne, 1878–1940, vol. III
Elmslie, Rev. William Alexander Leslie, 1885–1965, vol. VI
Elnor, Rev. William George, died 1956, vol. V
Elphick, Ronald, 1918–1977, vol. VII
Elphinstone, 16th Lord, 1869–1955, vol. V
Elphinstone, 17th Lord, 1914–1975, vol. VII
Elphinstone of Glack, Sir Alexander Logie, 10th Bt (cr 1701), 1880–1970, vol. VI
Elphinstone, Archibald Howard L., 1865–1936, vol. III
Elphinstone, Sir Arthur Percy Archibald, 11th Bt (cr 1628), born 1863 (this entry was not transferred to Who was Who).
Elphinstone, Sir (George) Keith (Buller), 1865–1941, vol. IV
Elphinstone, Sir Græme Hepburn Dalrymple-Horn-, 4th Bt (cr 1828), 1841–1900, vol. I
Elphinstone, Sir Howard Graham, 4th Bt (cr 1816), 1898–1975, vol. VII
Elphinstone, Sir Howard Warburton, 3rd Bt (cr 1816), 1830–1917, vol. II
Elphinstone, Sir Keith; see Elphinstone, Sir G. K. B.
Elphinstone, Rev. Kenneth John Tristram, 1911–1980, vol. VII
Elphinstone, Kenneth Vaughan, 1878–1963, vol. VI
Elphinstone, Sir Lancelot Henry, 1879–1965, vol. VI
Elphinstone, Rev. Maurice Curteis, 1874–1969, vol. VI
Elphinstone, Hon. Mountstuart William, 1871–1957, vol. V
Elphinstone, Sir Nicholas, 10th Bt (cr 1628), 1825–1907, vol. I
Elphinstone-Dalrymple, Sir Edward Arthur, 6th Bt, 1877–1913, vol. I
Elphinstone-Dalrymple, Col Sir Francis Napier, 7th Bt, 1882–1956, vol. V
Elphinstone-Dalrymple, Sir Robert Graeme, 5th Bt, 1844–1908, vol. I

Elrington, Rev. Charles Andrew, 1856–1936, vol. III
Elrington, Gen. Frederick Robert, 1819–1904, vol. I
Elsden, John Pascoe, 1887–1950, vol. IV
Else, Joseph, 1874–1955, vol. V
Elsee, Rev. Charles, died 1960, vol. V
Elsee, Rev. Henry John, died 1936, vol. III
Elsey, Rt Rev. William Edward, 1880–1966, vol. VI
Elsley, Rev. William James, 1870–1942, vol. IV
Elsmie, Maj.-Gen. Alexander Montagu Spears, 1869–1958, vol. V
Elsmie, George Robert, 1838–1909, vol. I
Elsner, Col Otto William Alexander, 1871–1953, vol. V
Elstob, Rev. John George, died 1926, vol. II
Elstob, Lt-Col Wilfrith, died 1918, vol. II
Eltisley, 1st Baron, 1879–1942, vol. IV
Elton, 1st Baron, 1892–1973, vol. VII
Elton, Sir Ambrose, 9th Bt, 1869–1951, vol. V
Elton, Sir Arthur Hallam Rice, 10th Bt, 1906–1973, vol. VII
Elton, Charles Isaac, 1839–1900, vol. I
Elton, Sir Edmund Harry, 8th Bt, 1846–1920, vol. II
Elton, Col Frederick Coulthurst, 1836–1920, vol. II
Elton, Maj.-Gen. Henry Strachan, 1841–1934, vol. III
Elton, Oliver, 1861–1945, vol. IV
Elton, Lt-Col William M.; see Marwood-Elton.
Elton-Barratt, Major Stanley George Reeves, 1900–1973, vol. VII
Eltringham, Harry, 1873–1941, vol. IV
Elveden, Viscount; Arthur Onslow Edward Guinness, 1912–1945, vol. IV
Elverston, Sir Harold, 1866–1941, vol. IV
Elvey, Lewis Edgar, 1908–1974, vol. VII
Elvey, Maurice, 1887–1967, vol. VI
Elvin, Sir Arthur J., 1899–1957, vol. V
Elvin, Herbert Henry, 1874–1949, vol. IV
Elvin, Ven. John Elijah, 1900–1964, vol. VI
Elwes, Simon, 1902–1975, vol. VII
Elwell, Col Francis Edwin, 1858–1922, vol. II (A), vol. III
Elwell, Frederick William, 1870–1958, vol. V
Elwes, Arthur Henry Stuart, 1858–1908, vol. I
Elwes, Rt Rev. Dudley Charles Cary-; see Cary-Elwes.
Elwes, Ven. Edward Leighton, 1848–1930, vol. III
Elwes, Lt-Col Frederick Fenn, 1875–1962, vol. VI
Elwes, Gervase Henry, 1866–1921, vol. II
Elwes, Henry John, 1846–1922, vol. II
Elwes, Sir Richard Everard Augustine, 1901–1968, vol. VI
Elwes, Valentine Dudley Henry Cary-, 1832–1909, vol. I
Elwes, Ven. William Weston, died 1901, vol. I
Elwin, Rt Rev. Edmund Henry, 1871–1909, vol. I
Elwin, Verrier, 1902–1964, vol. VI
Elwood, Hon. Edward Lindsey, born 1868, vol. II
Ely, 5th Marquess of, 1851–1925, vol. II
Ely, 6th Marquess of, 1854–1935, vol. III
Ely, 7th Marquess of, 1903–1969, vol. VI
Ely, Paul, 1897–1975, vol. VII

Emanuel, Frank Lewis, 1865–1948, vol. IV
Emanuel, Joseph George, 1871–1958, vol. V
Emanuel, Samuel Henry, died 1925, vol. II
Emanuel, Walter, 1869–1915, vol. I
Emard, Most Rev. Mgr Joseph Medard, 1853–1927, vol. II
Emberton, John James, 1893–1976, vol. VII
Emberton, Lt-Col Sir (John) Wesley, 1896–1967, vol. VI
Emberton, Joseph, 1889–1956, vol. V
Emberton, Lt-Col Sir Wesley; see Emberton, Lt-Col Sir J. W.
Embleton, Dennis, 1881–1944, vol. IV
Embling, Air Vice-Marshal John Robert André, 1913–1959, vol. V
Embry, Air Chief Marshal Sir Basil Edward, 1902–1977, vol. VII
Embury, Brig.-Gen. Hon. John Fletcher Leopold, 1875–1943, vol. IV
Embury, Lt-Col P. Robinson, 1865–1952, vol. V
Emden, Alfred, 1849–1911, vol. I
Emden, Alfred Brotherston, 1888–1979, vol. VII
Emden, Walter, 1847–1913, vol. I
Emdin, Engr Rear-Adm. Archie Russell, 1865–1950, vol. IV
Emerson, Hon. Charles H., 1864–1919, vol. II
Emerson, Hon. Sir Edward; see Emerson, Hon. Sir L. E.
Emerson, Ven. Edward Robert, 1838–1926, vol. II
Emerson, Edward Waldo, 1844–1930, vol. III
Emerson, Hon. George Henry, 1853–1916, vol. II
Emerson, Maj.-Gen. Henry Horace Andrews, 1881–1957, vol. V
Emerson, Sir Herbert William, 1881–1962, vol. VI
Emerson, Hon. Sir (Lewis) Edward, 1890–1949, vol. IV
Emerson, Very Rev. Norman David, 1900–1966, vol. VI
Emerson, Major Norman Zeal, 1872–1928, vol. II
Emerson, Sir Ralf Billing, 1897–1965, vol. VI
Emerson, Robert Jackson, died 1944, vol. IV
Emerson, Thomas, 1870–1956, vol. V
Emerson, Sir William, 1843–1924, vol. II
Emery, Douglas, 1915–1974, vol. VII
Emery, George Edwin, 1859–1937, vol. III
Emery, Henry Crosby, 1872–1924, vol. II
Emery, Walter Bryan, 1903–1971, vol. VII
Emery, Walter d'Este, died 1923, vol. II
Emery, Ven. William, 1825–1910, vol. I
Emery, Brig.-Gen. William Basil, 1871–1945, vol. IV
Emery, Winifred, (Isabel Winifred Maud Emery Maude), died 1924, vol. II
Emett, Frederick William, 1865–1935, vol. III
Emley, Herbert Barnes, 1891–1948, vol. IV
Emly, 2nd Baron, 1858–1932, vol. III
Emlyn-Jones, Hugh, 1902–1970, vol. VI
Emlyn-Jones, John Emlyn, 1889–1952, vol. V
Emlyn Williams, Arthur; see Williams.
Emmerson, Hon. Henry Robert, 1853–1914, vol. I
Emmet of Amberley, Baroness (Life Peer); Evelyn Violet Elizabeth Emmet, 1899–1980, vol. VII
Emmet, Rev. Cyril William, 1875–1923, vol. II
Emmony, Harry Oliver, 1897–1956, vol. V

Emmott, 1st Baron, 1858–1926, vol. II
Emmott, Charles Ernest George Campbell, 1898–1953, vol. V
Emmott, George Henry, 1855–1916, vol. II
Emms, Mrs Dorothy, (Mrs S. A. G. Emms); see Charques, Mrs D.
Emrys-Evans, John; see Evans.
Emrys-Evans, Paul Vychan, 1894–1967, vol. VI
Emrys-Roberts, Edward, 1878–1924, vol. II
Emslie, John William, 1901–1973, vol. VII
Emslie, Rosalie, 1891–1977, vol. VII
Emtage, William Thomas Allder, 1862–1942, vol. IV
Encombe, Viscount; John Scott, 1870–1900, vol. I
Endicott, Very Rev. James, 1865–1954, vol. V
Endicott, William, 1865–1941, vol. IV
Enever, Sir Francis Alfred, 1893–1966, vol. VI
Enfield, Sir Ralph Roscoe, 1885–1973, vol. VII
Engelbach, Alfred H. H., 1850–1928, vol. II
Engelbach, Archibald Frank, 1881–1961, vol. VI
Engelbach, Mrs Florence, died 1951, vol. V
Engelbach, Lewis William, 1837–1908, vol. I
Engelbach, Reginald, 1888–1946, vol. IV
Engelhard, Charles William, 1917–1971, vol. VII
Engelmann, Franklin, 1908–1972, vol. VII
England, Col Abraham, 1867–1949, vol. IV
England, Rev. Arthur Creyke, 1872–1946, vol. IV
England, Maj.-Gen. Edward Lutwyche, 1839–1910, vol. I
England, Edwin Bourdieu, 1847–1936, vol. III
England, Edwin Thirlwall, died 1945, vol. IV
England, E(ric) C. Gordon, 1891–1976, vol. VII
England, Henry Barren, 1855–1942, vol. IV
England, Rear-Adm. Hugh Turnour, 1884–1978, vol. VII
England, Lt-Col Norman Ayrton, 1886–1939, vol. III
England, Peter Tiarks Ede, 1925–1978, vol. VII
England, Philip Remington, 1879–1959, vol. V
England, Sir Russell, died 1970, vol. VI
Engledow, Charles John, 1860–1933, vol. III (A), vol. IV
Engleheart, Lt-Col Evelyn Linzee, 1862–1943, vol. IV
Engleheart, Sir John Gardner Dillman, 1823–1923, vol. II
English, Alexander Emanuel, 1871–1962, vol. VI
English, Sir Crisp, died 1949, vol. IV
English, Douglas, 1870–1939, vol. III
English, Lt-Col Ernest Robert Maling, 1874–1941, vol. IV
English, Col Frederick Paul, 1859–1946, vol. IV
English, Sir John; see English, Sir W. J.
English, Joseph Sandys, 1890–1971, vol. VII
English, Comdr Reginald Wastell, 1894–1980, vol. VII
English, Lt-Col William John, 1882–1941, vol. IV
English, Sir (William) John, 1903–1973, vol. VII
Ennes Ulrich, Ruy, 1883–1966, vol. VI
Ennever, William Joseph, 1869–1947, vol. IV
Ennis, George Francis Macdaniel, 1868–1933, vol. III
Ennis, John Matthew, vol. II
Ennis, Lawrence, 1871–1938, vol. III

Ennisdale, 1st Baron, 1878–1963, vol. VI
Enniskillen, 4th Earl of, 1845–1924, vol. II
Enniskillen, 5th Earl of, 1876–1963, vol. VI
Ennor, Sir Arnold Hughes, (Sir Hugh Ennor), 1912–1977, vol. VII
Ennor, Sir Hugh; see Ennor, Sir A. H.
Enock, Charles Reginald, 1868–1970, vol. VI
Enraght, Rev. Canon Hawtrey James, 1871–1938, vol. III
Enright, Adm. Sir Philip King, 1894–1960, vol. V
Enslin, Brig.-Gen. Barend Gotfried Leopold, 1879–1955, vol. V
Ensor, Arthur Hinton, 1891–1977, vol. VII
Ensor, Maj.-Gen. Howard, 1874–1942, vol. IV
Ensor, Sir Robert Charles Kirkwood, 1877–1958, vol. V
Enthoven, Mrs (Augusta) Gabrielle (Eden), 1868–1950, vol. IV
Enthoven, Mrs Gabrielle; see Enthoven, Mrs A. G. E.
Enthoven, Reginald Edward, 1869–1952, vol. V
Entrican, Lt-Col James, 1864–1935, vol. III
Entwisle, John Bertie Norreys, 1856–1945, vol. IV
Entwistle, Major Sir Cyril Fullard, 1887–1974, vol. VII
Entwistle, William James, died 1952, vol. V
Ephraim, Lee, died 1953, vol. V
Epinay, Charles Adrien Prosper d', 1836–1914, vol. I
Epps, Sir George Selby Washington, 1885–1951, vol. V
Eppstein, Rev. William Charles, 1864–1928, vol. II
Epstein, Sir Jacob, 1880–1959, vol. V
Epstein, Mortimer, died 1946, vol. IV
Erasmus, Hon. François Christiaan, 1896–1967, vol. VI
Erdelyi, Arthur, 1908–1977, vol. VII
Erhard, Ludwig, 1897–1977, vol. VII
Eriks, Sierd Sint, died 1966, vol. VI
Erith, Rev. Canon Lionel Edward Patrick, 1885–1939, vol. III
Erith, Raymond Charles, 1904–1973, vol. VII
Erlanger, Joseph, 1874–1965, vol. VI
Erle, Twynihoe William, 1828–1908, vol. I
Erne, 4th Earl of, 1839–1914, vol. I
Erne, 5th Earl of, 1907–1940, vol. III
Ernest, Maurice, 1872–1955, vol. V
Ernle, 1st Baron, 1851–1937, vol. III
Ernst, Harold Clarence, died 1922, vol. II
Ernst, Max, 1891–1976, vol. VII
Ernst, Morris Leopold, 1888–1976, vol. VII
Ernst, Noel Edward, 1891–1965, vol. VI
Ernst, Oswald Herbert, 1842–1926, vol. II
Ernst, William Gordon, 1897–1939, vol. III
Errington, Sir Eric, 1st Bt (cr 1963), 1900–1973, vol. VII
Errington, Lt-Col Francis Henry Launcelot, 1857–1942, vol. IV
Errington, Sir George, 1st Bt (cr 1885), 1839–1920, vol. II
Errington, Col Roger, 1887–1960, vol. V
Errock, Michael Warden, 1921–1970, vol. VI
Erroll, 20th Earl of, 1852–1927, vol. II
Erroll, 21st Earl of, 1876–1928, vol. II

Erroll, 22nd Earl of, 1901–1941, vol. IV
Erroll, Countess of (23rd in line), 1926–1978, vol. VII
Erskine, 5th Baron, 1841–1913, vol. I
Erskine, 6th Baron, 1865–1957, vol. V
Erskine of Rerrick, 1st Baron, 1893–1980, vol. VII
Erskine, Lord; John Francis Ashley Erskine, 1895–1953, vol. V
Erskine, Col Sir Arthur Edward, 1881–1963, vol. VI
Erskine, David, died 1922, vol. II
Erskine, Sir Derek Quicke, 1905–1977, vol. VII
Erskine, Major Esmé Nourse, 1885–1962, vol. VI
Erskine, Sir ffolliott Williams, 3rd Bt, 1850–1912, vol. I
Erskine, Hon. Francis Walter, 1899–1972, vol. VII
Erskine, Maj.-Gen. George Elphinstone, 1841–1912, vol. I
Erskine, George Oswald Harry Erskine Biber, 1857–1931, vol. III
Erskine, Gen. Sir George Watkin Eben James, 1899–1965, vol. VI
Erskine, Col Henry Adeane, 1857–1953, vol. V
Erskine, Sir Henry David, 1838–1921, vol. II
Erskine, Maj.-Gen. (Hon.) Ian David, 1898–1973, vol. VII
Erskine, James; see Rosslyn, 5th Earl of.
Erskine, Adm. of the Fleet Sir James Elphinstone, 1838–1911, vol. I
Erskine, Brig.-Gen. James Francis, 1862–1936, vol. III
Erskine, Sir James Malcolm Monteith, 1863–1944, vol. IV
Erskine, John, 1879–1951, vol. V
Erskine, Lt-Col Keith David, 1863–1914, vol. I
Erskine, Keith David, 1907–1974, vol. VII
Erskine, Robert, 1874–1933, vol. III
Erskine, Hon. Ruaraidh, 1869–1960, vol. V
Erskine, Adm. Seymour Elphinstone, 1863–1945, vol. IV
Erskine, Mrs Steuart, died 1948, vol. IV
Erskine, Sir Thomas, 2nd Bt, 1824–1902, vol. I
Erskine, Col Thomas Harry, 1860–1924, vol. II
Erskine, Sir Thomas Wilfred Hargreaves John, 4th Bt, 1880–1944, vol. IV
Erskine, Walter Hugh, 1870–1948, vol. IV
Erskine, Rt Hon. Sir William Augustus Forbes, 1871–1952, vol. V
Erskine-Bolst, Captain Clifford Charles Alan Lawrence, 1878–1946, vol. IV
Erskine Crum, Maj.-Gen. Vernon Forbes, 1918–1971, vol. VII
Erskine-Hill, Sir Alexander Galloway, 1st Bt, 1894–1947, vol. IV
Erskine-Murray, Lt-Col Arthur, 1877–1948, vol. IV
Erskine-Wyse, Marjorie Anne, (Mrs Michael Erskine-Wyse), 1914–1976, vol. VII
Ertz, Edward, 1862–1954, vol. V
Ervine, St John Greer, 1888–1971, vol. VII
Escombe, Captain Harold, died 1933, vol. III
Escombe, Rt Hon. Harry, 1838–1899, vol. I
Escombe, Captain William Malcolm Lingard, 1891–1973, vol. VII

Escott, Sir (Ernest) Bichkam S.; see Sweet-Escott.
Escott, Thomas Hay Sweet, died 1924, vol. II
Escreet, Ven. Charles Ernest, 1852–1919, vol. II
Escritt, Leonard Bushby, 1902–1973, vol. VII
Esdaile, Arundell James Kennedy, 1880–1956, vol. V
Esdaile, Katharine Ada, 1881–1950, vol. IV
Esher, 1st Viscount, 1815–1899, vol. I
Esher, 2nd Viscount, 1852–1930, vol. III
Esher, 3rd Viscount, 1881–1963, vol. VI
Esler, Erminda Rentoul, decd, vol. II
Esmarch, Johannes Friedrich August von, 1823–1908, vol. I
Esmond, Eva; see Moore, E.
Esmond, Henry V., died 1922, vol. II
Esmonde, John, 1862–1915, vol. I
Esmonde, Captain Sir John Lymbrick, 14th Bt, 1893–1958, vol. V
Esmonde, Lt-Col Sir Laurence Grattan, 13th Bt, 1863–1943, vol. IV
Esmonde, Sir Osmond Thomas Grattan, 12th Bt, 1896–1936, vol. III
Esmonde, Sir Thomas Henry Grattan, 11th Bt, 1862–1935, vol. III
Espin, Rev. John, 1836–1905, vol. I
Espin, Rev. Thomas Espinell, died 1912, vol. I
Espin, Rev. Thomas Henry Espinell Compton, 1858–1934, vol. III
Espinas, Alfred, 1844–1922, vol. II
'Espinasse, Paul Gilbert, 1900–1975, vol. VII
Espitalier-Noel, Andre; see Noel.
Esplen, Sir John, 1st Bt, 1863–1930, vol. III
Espley, Arthur James, died 1971, vol. VII
Esposito, Michele, 1855–1929, vol. III
Essame, Maj.-Gen. Hubert, 1896–1976, vol. VII
Essell, Col Frederick Knight, 1864–1951, vol. V
Essendon, 1st Baron, 1870–1944, vol. IV
Essendon, 2nd Baron, 1903–1978, vol. VII
Essenhigh, Reginald Clare, 1890–1955, vol. V
Essery, William Joseph, 1860–1955, vol. V
Essex, 7th Earl of, 1857–1916, vol. II
Essex, 8th Earl of, 1884–1966, vol. VI
Essex, Air Vice-Marshal Bertram Edward, 1897–1959, vol. V
Essex, Sir (Richard) Walter, 1857–1941, vol. IV
Essex, Sir Walter; see Essex, Sir R. W.
Esslemont, George Birnie, 1860–1917, vol. II
Esson, Col James Jacob, 1869–1940, vol. III
Esson, William, 1838–1916, vol. II
Estall, Thomas, 1848–1920, vol. II
Estaunie, Édouard, 1862–1942, vol. IV
Estcourt, 1st Baron, 1839–1915, vol. I
Estcourt, Rev. Edmund Walter S.; see Sotheron-Estcourt.
Estcourt, Captain Thomas Edmund S.; see Sotheron-Estcourt.
Estell, Hon. John, 1861–1928, vol. II
Estey, James Wilfred, 1889–1956, vol. V
Etchells, Ernest Fiander, 1876–1927, vol. II
Etchells, Frederick, died 1973, vol. VII
Etches, Major Charles Edward, 1872–1944, vol. IV
Eteson, Surg.-Gen. Alfred, died 1910, vol. I
Eteson, Col Harold Carleton Wetherall, 1863–1947, vol. IV

Ethe, C. Hermann, 1844–1917, vol. II
Etheridge, Col Cecil de Courcy, 1860–1940, vol. III
Etheridge, Rt Rev. Edward Harold, 1872–1954, vol. V
Etheridge, Robert, died 1903, vol. I
Etherington, Col Frederick, 1878–1955, vol. V
Etherington-Smith, John Henry, 1841–1923, vol. II
Etherton, Sir George Hammond, 1876–1949, vol. IV
Etherton, Col P. T., 1879–1963, vol. VI
Ettles, William James M'Culloch, 1869–1918, vol. II
Etzel, Franz, 1902–1970, vol. VI (AII)
Euan-Smith, Col Sir Charles Bean; see Smith.
Eucken, Rudolf, 1846–1926, vol. II
Eugenie, Empress, 1826–1920, vol. II
Eugster, Lt-Col Oscar Lewis, 1880–1930, vol. III
Eumorfopoulos, George, 1863–1939, vol. III
Eurich, Frederick William, 1867–1945, vol. IV
Eustace, Maj.-Gen. Alexander Henry, 1863–1939, vol. III
Eustace, Major Charles Legge Eustace R.; see Robertson-Eustace.
Eustace, Edward Arthur Rawlins, 1899–1972, vol. VII
Eustace, Maj.-Gen. Sir Francis John William, 1849–1925, vol. II
Eustace, Lt-Col Henry Montague, 1863–1926, vol. II
Eustace, Adm. John Bridges, 1861–1947, vol. IV
Eustace, John Curtis Wernher, 1906–1972, vol. VII
Eustace, Mrs Marjory Edith R.; see Robertson-Eustace.
Eustace, Robert William Barrington R.; see Robertson-Eustace.
Eustace-Jameson, Lt-Col John; see Jameson.
Eustice, John, 1864–1943, vol. IV
Euston, Earl of; Henry James Fitzroy, 1848–1912, vol. I
Evan-Jones, Cecil Artimus, 1912–1978, vol. VII
Evan-Jones, Rev. Canon Richard, 1849–1925, vol. II
Evan-Thomas, Adm. Sir Hugh, 1862–1928, vol. II
Evan-Thomas, Llewelyn, 1859–1947, vol. IV
Evans, 1st Baron, 1903–1963, vol. VI
Evans, Alan Frederick Reginald, 1891–1960, vol. V
Evans, Ven. Albert Owen, 1864–1937, vol. III
Evans, Vice-Adm. Sir Alfred Englefield, 1884–1944, vol. IV
Evans, Sir Alfred Henry, 1847–1938, vol. III
Evans, Annie Lloyd-, died 1938, vol. III
Evans, Arthur; see Evans, H. A.
Evans, Sir Arthur, 1851–1941, vol. IV
Evans, Col Sir Arthur, 1898–1958, vol. V
Evans, Rev. Canon Arthur Fitz-Gerald, 1854–1933, vol. III
Evans, Arthur Henry, died 1950, vol. IV
Evans, Rev. Arthur Norman, 1900–1975, vol. VII
Evans, Rev. Arthur Robertson, died 1923, vol. II
Evans, Rev. Arthur Wade W.; see Wade-Evans.
Evans, Bernard Walter, 1843–1922, vol. II
Evans, Captain Bertram Sutton, died 1919, vol. II
Evans, Brig. Brian P.; see Pennefather-Evans.
Evans, Caradoc, died 1945, vol. IV

Evans, Cecil Herbert, 1898–1957, vol. V
Evans, Sir Charles Arthur Lovatt, died 1968, vol. VI
Evans, Charles Barnard, died 1920, vol. II
Evans, Charles Glyn, 1883–1961, vol. VI
Evans, Maj.-Gen. Charles Harford B.; see Bowle-Evans.
Evans, Col Charles Robert, 1873–1956, vol. V
Evans, Charles Seddon, 1883–1944, vol. IV
Evans, Charles Tunstall, 1903–1980, vol. VII
Evans, Col Charles William Henry, 1851–1909, vol. I
Evans, Brig.-Gen. Cuthbert, 1871–1934, vol. III
Evans, Rt Rev. Daniel Ivor, 1900–1962, vol. VI
Evans, Rev. Daniel Silvan, 1818–1903, vol. I
Evans, Sir David, 1849–1907, vol. I
Evans, Ven. David, died 1910, vol. I
Evans, David, 1874–1948, vol. IV
Evans, David Charles Exton, 1878–1938, vol. III
Evans, Sir (David) Emrys, 1891–1966, vol. VI
Evans, David Morgan, 1892–1977, vol. VII
Evans, David Owen, 1876–1945, vol. IV
Evans, Sir (David) Rowland, died 1953, vol. V
Evans, Maj.-Gen. David Sydney Carlyon, 1893–1955, vol. V
Evans, Sir David William, 1866–1926, vol. II
Evans, Air Chief Marshal Sir Donald Randell, 1912–1975, vol. VII
Evans, Rev. E. Gwyn, 1898–1958, vol. V
Evans, Sir E. Vincent, died 1934, vol. III
Evans, Dame Edith, (Dame Edith Mary Booth), died 1976, vol. VII
Evans, Sir Edward, 1846–1917, vol. II
Evans, Maj.-Gen. Sir Edward, 1872–1949, vol. IV
Evans, Edward, 1883–1960, vol. V
Evans, Edward Francis Herbert, 1873–1958, vol. V
Evans, Col Edward Stokes, 1855–1926, vol. II
Evans, Edward Victor, 1882–1964, vol. VI
Evans, Sir Edwin, died 1928, vol. II
Evans, Edwin, 1874–1945, vol. IV
Evans, Einion, 1896–1969, vol. VI
Evans, Ellen, 1891–1953, vol. V
Evans, Emily, died 1958, vol. V
Evans, Emlyn Hugh Garner, 1911–1963, vol. VI
Evans, Sir Emrys; see Evans, Sir D. E.
Evans, Ven. Eric Herbert, 1902–1977, vol. VII
Evans, Ernest, 1885–1965, vol. VI
Evans, Sir Evan Gwynne G.; see Gwynne-Evans.
Evans, Evan Jenkin, 1882–1944, vol. IV
Evans, Evan Laming, 1871–1945, vol. IV
Evans, Evan William, 1860–1925, vol. II
Evans, Sir Evelyn Ward, 3rd Bt (cr 1902), 1883–1970, vol. VI
Evans, Major Fisher Henry Freke, 1868–1961, vol. VI
Evans, Sir Francis Henry, 1st Bt (cr 1902), 1840–1907, vol. I
Evans, Frank Dudley, 1883–1941, vol. IV
Evans, Frankis Tilney, 1900–1974, vol. VII
Evans, Captain Frederic James, 1867–1945, vol. IV
Evans, Rev. Canon Frederic James, died 1946, vol. IV
Evans, Rev. Frederic Rawlins, 1842–1927, vol. II
Evans, Sir Frederick, 1849–1939, vol. III

Evans, Frederick Buisson, 1874–1952, vol. V
Evans, Sir Geoffrey, 1883–1963, vol. VI
Evans, Geoffrey A., 1886–1951, vol. V
Evans, Rear-Adm. George Hammond, 1917–1980, vol. VII
Evans, Col George Henry, 1863–1948, vol. IV
Evans, Rev. George Simon T.; see Tudor-Evans.
Evans, Rev. George William, 1867–1938, vol. III
Evans, Lt-Col Granville P.; see Pennefather-Evans.
Evans, Griffith, 1835–1935, vol. III
Evans, Griffith Conrad, 1887–1973, vol. VII
Evans, Sir Griffith Humphrey Pugh, 1840–1902, vol. I
Evans, Griffith Ivor, 1889–1966, vol. VI
Evans, Sir Guildhaume M.; see Myrddin-Evans.
Evans, Harold Muir, 1866–1947, vol. IV
Evans, Lt-Col Harrie Smalley, 1887–1971, vol. VII
Evans, Rev. Henry, died 1924, vol. II
Evans, (Henry) Arthur, 1903–1965, vol. VI
Evans, Henry Farrington, 1845–1931, vol. III
Evans, Rt Rev. Henry St John Tomlinson, 1905–1956, vol. V
Evans, Major Herbert, 1868–1931, vol. III
Evans, Herbert D.; see Davies-Evans.
Evans, Herbert Edgar, 1884–1970, vol. VI (AII)
Evans, Herbert McLean, 1882–1971, vol. VII
Evans, Herbert Walter Lloyd, 1877–1956, vol. V
Evans, Gen. Sir Horace Moule, 1841–1923, vol. II
Evans, Brig.-Gen. Horatio James, 1850–1932, vol. III
Evans, Howard, 1839–1915, vol. I
Evans, Ifor Leslie, 1897–1952, vol. V
Evans, Illtyd Buller P.; see Pole-Evans.
Evans, Rev. J. T., 1878–1950, vol. IV
Evans, Major James John Pugh, 1885–1974, vol. VII
Evans, Dame Joan, died 1977, vol. VII
Evans, Sir John, 1823–1908, vol. I
Evans, Lt-Col John, died 1930, vol. III
Evans, Col John, 1868–1942, vol. IV
Evans, John, 1875–1961, vol. VI
Evans, John Cayo, 1879–1958, vol. V
Evans, Rev. John David, died 1912, vol. I
Evans, John Emrys-, 1853–1931, vol. III
Evans, John Gwenogvryn, 1852–1930, vol. III
Evans, Sir John Harold, 1904–1973, vol. VII
Evans, John Howell, 1870–1962, vol. VI
Evans, John Jameson, 1871–1941, vol. III
Evans, John Owain, 1875–1943, vol. IV
Evans, Rev. John Thomas, 1869–1940, vol. III
Evans, John William, died 1930, vol. III
Evans, Hon. Sir John William, 1855–1943, vol. IV
Evans, Rev. John Young, 1865–1941, vol. IV
Evans, Rev. Joseph David Samuel P.; see Parry-Evans.
Evans, Rt Rev. Kenneth Charles, 1903–1970, vol. VI
Evans, Rt. Hon. Sir Laming W.; see Worthington-Evans.
Evans, L(eonard) G(lyde) Lavington, 1888–1976, vol. VII
Evans, Rev. Leonard Hugh, 1863–1939, vol. III
Evans, Maj.-Gen. Leopold Exxel, 1837–1916, vol. II

Evans, Lewis, 1853–1930, vol. III
Evans, Rev. Lewis Herbert, 1870–1942, vol. IV
Evans, Lewis Noel Vincent, 1886–1967, vol. VI
Evans, Brig.-Gen. Lewis Pugh, 1881–1962, vol. VI
Evans, Sir Lincoln, 1889–1970, vol. VI
Evans, Mgr Canon Lionel Ella, 1882–1942, vol. IV
Evans, Lt-Col Llewelyn, *died* 1963, vol. VI
Evans, Maurice Smethurst, 1854–1920, vol. II (A), vol. III
Evans, Meredith Gwynne, 1904–1952, vol. V
Evans, Merlyn Oliver, 1910–1973, vol. VII
Evans, Rev. Sir Murland de Grasse, 2nd Bt (*cr* 1902), *died* 1946, vol. IV
Evans, Nevil Norton, 1865–1948, vol. IV
Evans, Ven. Owen, *died* 1914, vol. I
Evans, Patrick Fleming, 1851–1902, vol. I
Evans, Paul Vychan E.; *see* Emrys-Evans.
Evans, Col Percy, 1868–1945, vol. IV
Evans, Percy William, 1882–1951, vol. V
Evans, Peter MacIntyre, 1859–1944, vol. IV
Evans, Dame Regina Margaret, *died* 1969, vol. VI
Evans, (Richard) Stanley, 1883–1949, vol. IV
Evans, Richard Thomas, 1890–1946, vol. IV
Evans, Richardson, 1846–1928, vol. II
Evans, Sir Robert Charles, 1878–1961, vol. VI
Evans, Maj.-Gen. Roger, 1886–1968, vol. VI
Evans, Sir Rowland; *see* Evans, Sir D. R.
Evans, Samuel T. G., 1829–1904, vol. I
Evans, Rt Hon. Sir Samuel Thomas, 1859–1918, vol. II
Evans, Sir Shirley W.; *see* Worthington-Evans, Sir W. S. W.
Evans, Stanley; *see* Evans, R. S.
Evans, Rev. Canon Stanley George, 1912–1965, vol. VI
Evans, Stanley Norman, 1898–1970, vol. VI
Evans, T. Hopkin, 1879–1940, vol. III
Evans, Thomas, *died* 1943, vol. IV
Evans, Col Thomas Dixon Byron, 1860–1908, vol. I
Evans, Very Rev. Thomas Frye Lewis, 1845–1920, vol. II
Evans, Major Sir Thomas John Carey, 1884–1947, vol. IV
Evans, Rev. Thomas Jones, 1856–1921, vol. II
Evans, Maj.-Gen. Thomas Julian Penrhys, 1854–1921, vol. II
Evans, Timothy, 1875–1945, vol. IV
Evans, Trefor Ellis, 1913–1974, vol. VII
Evans, Ulick Richardson, 1889–1980, vol. VII
Evans, Brig.-Gen. Usher Williamson, 1864–1946, vol. IV
Evans, Sir Walter, 1855–1935, vol. III
Evans, Sir Walter Harry, 1st Bt (*cr* 1920), 1872–1954, vol. IV
Evans, Walter Jenkin, 1856–1927, vol. II
Evans, Walter John, 1864–1939, vol. III
Evans, Brig.-Gen. Wilfrid Keith, 1878–1934, vol. III
Evans, William, 1847–1918, vol. II
Evans, William, 1841–1919, vol. II
Evans, William, *died* 1936, vol. III
Evans, Brig.-Gen. William, 1871–1944, vol. IV
Evans, William B.; *see* Bulkeley-Evans.

Evans, Sir William G.; *see* Gwynne-Evans.
Evans, William H., 1873–1934, vol. III
Evans, Brig. William Harry, 1876–1956, vol. V
Evans, William James, 1861–1944, vol. IV
Evans, William Percival, 1864–1959, vol. V
Evans, Sir (William) Shirley (Worthington) W.; *see* Worthington-Evans.
Evans, Willmott Henderson, *died* 1938, vol. III
Evans Bevan, Sir David Martyn, 1st Bt, 1902–1973, vol. VII
Evans-Freke, Hon. Ralfe, 1897–1969, vol. VI
Evans-Gordon, Col Kenmure Alick Garth, 1885–1960, vol. V
Evans-Gwynne, Brig. Alfred Howel, 1882–1949, vol. IV
Evans-Jones, Rev. Sir Albert, 1895–1970, vol. VI
Evans-Lombe, Vice-Adm. Sir Edward Malcolm, 1901–1974, vol. VII
Evans-Pritchard, Sir Edward Evan, 1902–1973, vol. VII
Evanson, Maj.-Gen. Arthur Charles Tarver, 1895–1957, vol. V
Evatt, Maj.-Gen. Sir George Joseph Hamilton, 1843–1921, vol. II
Evatt, Rt Hon. Herbert Vere, 1894–1965, vol. VI
Evatt, Brig.-Gen. John Thorold, 1861–1949, vol. IV
Eve, Arthur Stewart, 1862–1948, vol. IV
Eve, Frank Cecil, *died* 1952, vol. V
Eve, Sir Frederic Samuel, *died* 1916, vol. II
Eve, George W., *died* 1914, vol. I
Eve, Rt Hon. Sir Harry Trelawney, 1856–1940, vol. III
Eve, Sir Herbert Trustram, 1865–1936, vol. III
Evelegh, Maj.-Gen. Vyvyan, 1898–1958, vol. V
Evelyn, John Harcourt Chichester, 1876–1922, vol. II
Evelyn, William John, 1822–1908, vol. I
Even, Col George Eusebe, 1855–1924, vol. II
Evennett, Henry Outram, 1901–1964, vol. VI
Everard, Captain Andrew Robert Guy, *died* 1925, vol. II (A), vol. III
Everard, Bernard, 1879–1963, vol. VI
Everard, Edward Everard Earle W.; *see* Welby-Everard.
Everard, Sir Lindsay; *see* Everard, Sir W. L.
Everard, Col Sir Nugent Talbot, 1st Bt, 1849–1929, vol. III
Everard, Major Sir Richard William, 2nd Bt, 1874–1929, vol. III
Everard, Sir (William) Lindsay, *died* 1949, vol. IV
Everett, Adm. Sir Allan Frederic, 1868–1938, vol. III
Everett, Rev. Bernard Charles Spencer, 1874–1943, vol. IV
Everett, Dorothy, 1894–1953, vol. V
Everett, Col Edward, 1837–1920, vol. II
Everett, Harry Poore, 1862–1955, vol. V
Everett, Maj.-Gen. Sir Henry Joseph, 1866–1951, vol. V
Everett, Joseph David, 1831–1904, vol. I
Everett, Sir Percy Winn, 1870–1952, vol. V
Everett, Richard Marven Hale, 1909–1978, vol. VII
Everett, Robert Lacey, 1833–1916, vol. II

Everett, Col Sir William, 1844–1908, vol. I
Everett-Green, Evelyn, 1856–1932, vol. III
Everidge, John, *died* 1955, vol. V
Everingham, Ven. William, 1856–1919, vol. II
Everitt, Sir Clement, 1873–1934, vol. III
Everitt, Major Sydney George, 1860–1932, vol. III
Evers, H(enry) Harvey, 1893–1979, vol. VII
Evershed, 1st Baron, 1899–1966, vol. VI
Evershed, Arthur, 1836–1919, vol. II
Evershed, John, 1864–1956, vol. V
Evershed, Sydney, 1825–1903, vol. I
Evershed, Sir Sydney Herbert, 1861–1937, vol. III
Evershed, Rear-Adm. Walter, 1907–1969, vol. VI
Eversley, 1st Baron, 1831–1928, vol. II
Eversley, William Pinder, 1850–1918, vol. II
Every, Rt Rev. Edward Francis, 1862–1941, vol. IV
Every, Sir Edward Oswald, 11th Bt, 1886–1959, vol. V
Eves, Sir Charles, 1864–1936, vol. III
Eves, Charles Washington, 1838–1899, vol. I
Eves, Sir Hubert Heath, 1883–1961, vol. VI
Eves, Reginald Grenville, 1876–1941, vol. IV
Evetts, Sir George, 1882–1958, vol. V
Evill, Lt-Col Charles Ariel, 1874–1954, vol. V
Evill, Air Chief Marshal Sir Douglas Claude Strathern, 1892–1971, vol. VII
Evington, Rt Rev. Henry, 1848–1912, vol. I
Evoe; *see* Knox, E. G. V.
Ewan, Col Thomas George, 1856–1937, vol. III
Ewart, Alfred James, 1872–1937, vol. III
Ewart, Adm. Arthur Wartensleben, 1862–1922, vol. II
Ewart, Lt-Gen. Charles Brisbane, 1827–1903, vol. I
Ewart, David, 1841–1921, vol. II
Ewart, David Shanks, 1901–1965, vol. VI
Ewart, Lt-Col Ernest Andrew; *see* Cable, Boyd.
Ewart, Captain Frank Rowland, 1874–1906, vol. I
Ewart, George Arthur, 1886–1942, vol. IV
Ewart, Maj.-Gen. Sir Henry Peter, 1st Bt, 1838–1928, vol. II
Ewart, James Cossar, 1851–1933, vol. III
Ewart, Gen. Sir John Alexander, 1821–1904, vol. I
Ewart, Sir John Murray, 1884–1939, vol. III
Ewart, John S., 1849–1933, vol. III
Ewart, Lt-Gen. Sir John Spencer, 1861–1930, vol. III
Ewart, Sir Joseph, 1831–1906, vol. I
Ewart, Sir Lavens Mathewson Algernon, 4th Bt, 1885–1939, did not have an entry in Who's Who.
Ewart, Richard, 1904–1953, vol. III
Ewart, Maj.-Gen. Sir Richard Henry, 1864–1928, vol. II
Ewart, Sir Talbot, 5th Bt, 1878–1959, vol. V
Ewart, William, 1848–1929, vol. III
Ewart, William Herbert Lee, 1881–1953, vol. V
Ewart, Sir William Quartus, 2nd Bt, 1844–1919, vol. II
Ewart-Biggs, Christopher Thomas Ewart, 1921–1976, vol. VII
Ewbank, Sir Robert Benson, 1883–1967, vol. VI
Ewart, Sir Robert Heard, 3rd Bt, 1879–1939, vol. III
Ewbank, Brig.-Gen. William, 1865–1930, vol. III
Ewen, Sir David Alexander, 1884–1957, vol. V

Ewen, Hon. Guy Seymour, 1871–1936, vol. III
Ewer, Col George Guy, 1883–1965, vol. VI
Ewert, Alfred, 1891–1969, vol. VI
Ewing, Sir Alexander William Gordon, 1896–1980, vol. VII
Ewing, Sir Alfred; *see* Ewing, Sir J. A.
Ewing, Alfred Cyril, 1899–1973, vol. VII
Ewing, Sir Archibald Ernest O.; *see* Orr-Ewing.
Ewing, Charles Lindsay O.; *see* Orr-Ewing.
Ewing, Sir Ian Leslie O.; *see* Orr Ewing.
Ewing, Rev. J. C. R., 1854–1925, vol. II
Ewing, James, 1884–1975, vol. VII
Ewing, Major James Alexander O.; *see* Orr-Ewing.
Ewing, Sir (James) Alfred, 1855–1935, vol. III
Ewing, Rev. John William, 1864–1951, vol. V
Ewing, Brig.-Gen. Sir Norman Archibald O.; *see* Orr Ewing.
Ewing, Hon. Norman Kirkwood, 1870–1928, vol. II
Ewing, Peter Dewar, *died* 1932, vol. III
Ewing, Rev. Robert, 1847–1908, vol. I
Ewing, Robert, 1871–1957, vol. VI
Ewing, Hon. Sir Thomas Thomson, *died* 1920, vol. II
Ewing, Rev. William, 1857–1932, vol. III
Ewing, Sir William O.; *see* Orr-Ewing.
Ewins, Arthur James, 1882–1957, vol. V
Exeter, 4th Marquess of, 1849–1898, vol. I
Exeter, 5th Marquess of, 1876–1956, vol. V
Exham, Lt-Col Harold, 1884–1950, vol. IV
Exham, Maj.-Gen. Kenneth Godfrey, 1903–1974, vol. VII
Exham, Col Richard, 1848–1915, vol. I
Exham, Col Simeon Hardy, 1850–1926, vol. II
Exley, J. R. Granville, 1878–1967, vol. VI
Exmouth, 4th Viscount, 1861–1899, vol. I
Exmouth, 5th Viscount, 1890–1922, vol. II
Exmouth, 6th Viscount, 1828–1923, vol. II
Exmouth, 7th Viscount, 1863–1945, vol. IV
Exmouth, 8th Viscount, 1868–1951, vol. V
Exmouth, 9th Viscount, 1908–1970, vol. VI
Exon, Charles, 1862–1962, vol. VI
Eyles, Sir Alfred, 1856–1945, vol. IV
Eyles, Sir George Lancelot, 1849–1919, vol. II
Eyles, Leonora; *see* Eyles, M. L.
Eyles, (Margaret) Leonora, 1889–1960, vol. V
Eyre, Rev. Alfred Collet, 1851–1929, vol. III
Eyre, Most Rev. Charles, 1817–1902, vol. I
Eyre, Ven. Christopher Benson, 1849–1928, vol. II
Eyre, Col Edmund Henry, 1838–1919, vol. II
Eyre, Edward John, 1815–1901, vol. I
Eyre, Rev. Edward Vincent, 1851–1925, vol. II
Eyre, Col Henry, 1834–1904, vol. I
Eyre, Col Henry Robert, 1842–1904, vol. I
Eyre, John, *died* 1927, vol. II
Eyre, Ven. John Rashdall, *died* 1912, vol. I
Eyre, John William Henry, 1869–1944, vol. IV
Eyre, Sir Oliver Eyre C.; *see* Crosthwaite-Eyre.
Eyre-Brook, Rev. Canon Alfred; *see* Brook.
Eyre-Matcham, Col William Eyre, 1865–1938, vol. III
Eyre-Todd, George, 1862–1937, vol. III
Eyres, Adm. Cresswell John, 1862–1949, vol. IV
Eyres, Sir Harry Charles Augustus, 1856–1944, vol. IV

Eyres, Harry Maurice, 1898–1962, vol. VI
Eyston, Charles Turbervile, 1868–1938, vol. III
Eyston, Captain George Edward Thomas, 1897–1979, vol. VII
Eyston, John Joseph, 1867–1916, vol. II
Eyston, Thomas More, 1902–1940, vol. III
Eyton, Alan John F. W.; *see* Fairbairn-Wynne-Eyton.
Eyton, Lt-Col Charles Reginald M.; *see* Morris-Eyton.
Eyton, Frank, 1894–1962, vol. VI
Ezard, Bernard John Bycroft, 1900–1976, vol. VII
Ezechiel, Sir Percy Hubert, 1875–1950, vol. IV
Ezra, Sir Alwyn, 1900–1974, vol. VII
Ezra, Sir David, 1871–1947, vol. IV

F

Faber, 1st Baron, 1847–1920, vol. II
Faber, Sir Geoffrey Cust, 1889–1961, vol. VI
Faber, George Henry, 1839–1910, vol. I
Faber, Knud, 1862–1956, vol. V
Faber, Oscar, 1886–1956, vol. V
Faber, Lt-Col Walter Vavasour, 1857–1928, vol. II
Fabre, Hon. Hector, 1834–1910, vol. I
Fabre, Jean Henri, 1823–1915, vol. I (A)
Fachiri, Adila Adrienne Adalbertina Marina, *died* 1962, vol. VI
Fadden, Rt Hon. Sir Arthur William, 1895–1973, vol. VII
Faed, John, 1819–1902, vol. I
Faed, Thomas, 1826–1900, vol. I
Fagan, Lt-Col Bernard Joseph, 1874–1939, vol. III
Fagan, Betty Maud Christian, *died* 1932, vol. III
Fagan, Brian Walter, 1893–1971, vol. VII
Fagan, Charles Edward, 1855–1921, vol. II
Fagan, Lt-Col Christopher George Forbes, 1856–1943, vol. IV
Fagan, Maj.-Gen. Sir Edward Arthur, 1871–1955, vol. V
Fagan, Hon. Henry Allan, 1889–1963, vol. VI
Fagan, James Bernard, 1873–1933, vol. III
Fagan, Maj.-Gen. James Lawtie, 1843–1919, vol. II
Fagan, Sir John, 1843–1930, vol. III
Fagan, Hon. Mark, 1873–1947, vol. IV
Fagan, Sir Patrick James, 1865–1942, vol. IV
Fagan, William Bateman, *died* 1948, vol. IV
Fage, Arthur, 1890–1977, vol. VII
Fagge, Charles Herbert, 1873–1939, vol. III
Fagge, Sir John Charles, 9th Bt, 1866–1930, vol. III
Fagge, Sir John Harry Lee, 10th Bt, 1868–1940, vol. III
Fagge, Sir John William Charles, 8th Bt, 1830–1909, vol. I
Faguet, Emile, 1847–1916, vol. II
Fahey, Edward Henry, *died* 1907, vol. I
Fahey, Rt Rev. Mgr Jerome, 1843–1920, vol. II
Fahie, Sen. Comdr Pauline Mary de Peauly, *died* 1947, vol. IV
Fahy, Francis Patrick, 1880–1953, vol. V
Faichnie, Col Douglas Charles, *died* 1938, vol. III
Fair, Hon. Sir Arthur, *died* 1970, vol. VI (AII)

Fair, Lt-Col Frederick Kendall, 1868–1953, vol. V
Fair, Lt-Col James George, 1864–1946, vol. IV
Fairbairn, Sir Andrew, 1828–1901, vol. I
Fairbairn, Andrew Martin, 1838–1912, vol. I
Fairbairn, Sir Arthur Henderson, 3rd Bt, 1852–1915, vol. I
Fairbairn, Vice-Adm. Bernard William Murray, 1880–1960, vol. V
Fairbairn, Sir George, 1855–1943, vol. IV
Fairbairn, James, *died* 1950, vol. IV
Fairbairn, Hon. James Valentine, 1897–1940, vol. III
Fairbairn, John Shields, 1868–1944, vol. IV
Fairbairn, Richard Robert, 1867–1941, vol. IV
Fairbairn, Stephen, (Steve), 1862–1938, vol. III
Fairbairn, Thomas Charles, 1874–1978, vol. VII
Fairbairn, Sir Thomas Gordon, 4th Bt, 1854–1931, vol. III
Fairbairn, Sir William Albert, 5th Bt, 1902–1972, vol. VII
Fairbairn, William Ronald Dodds, 1889–1964, vol. VI
Fairbairn-Wynne-Eyton, Alan John, *died* 1960, vol. V
Fairbank, Sir (Harold Arthur) Thomas, 1876–1961, vol. VI
Fairbank, Sir Thomas; *see* Fairbank, Sir H. A. T.
Fairbank, Sir William, 1850–1929, vol. III
Fairbanks, Charles Warren, 1852–1918, vol. II
Fairbanks, Douglas, *died* 1939, vol. III
Fairbrother, Ven. Rupert, *died* 1947, vol. IV
Fairbrother, William Henry, 1859–1927, vol. II
Fairbrother, Col William Tomes, 1856–1924, vol. II
Fairburn, Charles Edward, 1887–1945, vol. IV
Fairburn, Harold, 1884–1973, vol. VII
Fairchild, Rev. John, *died* 1942, vol. IV
Fairclough, Col Brereton, 1870–1945, vol. IV
Fairclough, Henry Rushton, 1862–1938, vol. III
Faire, Sir Arthur William, 1854–1933, vol. III
Faire, Sir Samuel, 1849–1931, vol. III
Fairey, Sir (Charles) Richard, 1887–1956, vol. V
Fairey, Sir Richard; *see* Fairey, Sir C. R.
Fairfax, 11th Lord, 1830–1900, vol. I
Fairfax of Cameron, 12th Lord, 1870–1939, vol. III
Fairfax of Cameron, 13th Lord, 1923–1964, vol. VI
Fairfax, Col Bryan Charles, 1873–1950, vol. IV
Fairfax, Hon. Charles Edmund, 1876–1939, vol. III (A), vol. IV
Fairfax, Guy Thomas, 1870–1934, vol. III
Fairfax, James Griffyth, 1886–1976, vol. VII
Fairfax, Sir James Oswald, 1863–1928, vol. II
Fairfax, Sir James Reading, 1834–1919, vol. II
Fairfax, Comdr William George Astell R.; *see* Ramsay-Fairfax.
Fairfax, Sir William George Herbert Taylor Ramsay-, 2nd Bt, 1831–1902, vol. I
Fairfax-Lucy, Major Sir Brian Fulke Cameron-Ramsay-, 5th Bt, 1898–1974, vol. VII
Fairfax-Lucy, Captain Sir (Henry) Montgomerie (Ramsay), 4th Bt, 1896–1965, vol. VI
Fairfax-Lucy, Sir Henry William Cameron-Ramsay-, 3rd Bt, 1870–1944, vol. IV
Fairfax-Lucy, Captain Sir Montgomerie; *see* Fairfax-Lucy, Captain Sir H. M. R.

Fairfield, 1st Baron, 1863–1945, vol. IV
Fairfield, (Josephine) Letitia Denny, 1885–1978, vol. VII
Fairfield, Letitia; see Fairfield, J. L. D.
Fairfield, Sir Ronald McLeod, 1911–1978, vol. VII
Fairgrieve, James, 1870–1953, vol. V
Fairhaven, 1st Baron, 1896–1966, vol. VI
Fairhaven, 2nd Baron, 1900–1973, vol. VII
Fairholme, Edward George, died 1956, vol. V
Fairholme, George Frederick, 1858–1940, vol. III
Fairholme, Brig.-Gen. William Ernest, 1860–1920, vol. II
Fairhurst, Frank, 1892–1953, vol. V
Fairhurst, James Ashton, 1867–1944, vol. IV
Fairless, Benjamin F., 1890–1962, vol. VI
Fairless, Margaret, died 1968, vol. VI
Fairley, Sir Andrew Walker, died 1965, vol. VI
Fairley, Sir Neil Hamilton, 1891–1966, vol. VI
Fairlie, James Ogilvy Reginald, 1848–1916, vol. II
Fairlie, Margaret, died 1963, vol. VI
Fairlie, Reginald Francis Joseph, 1883–1952, vol. V
Fairlie-Cuninghame, Sir Alfred Edward, 12th Bt, 1852–1901, vol. I
Fairlie-Cuninghame, Sir Charles Arthur, 11th Bt, 1846–1897, vol. I
Fairlie-Cuninghame, Sir Hussey Burgh; see Cuninghame.
Fairlie-Cuninghame, Sir William Edward; see Cuninghame.
Fairtlough, Major Edward Charles D'Heillemer, 1869–1925, vol. II
Fairtlough, Maj.-Gen. Eric Victor Howard, 1887–1944, vol. IV
Fairtlough, Col Frederick Howard, 1860–1915, vol. I (A)
Fairway, Sidney; see Daukes, S. H.
Fairweather, Sir Charles Edward Stuart, 1889–1963, vol. VI
Fairweather, Lt-Col James McIntyre, 1876–1917, vol. II
Fairweather, Sir Wallace, 1853–1939, vol. III
Faisal, King; see Saudi Arabia, HM the King of.
Faisandier, Rt Rev. Augustin, 1853–1935, vol. III
Faithfull, Lilian Mary, 1865–1952, vol. V
Faiyaz Ali Khan, Nawab, Sir Mumtazud-Dowlah, 1851–1922, vol. II
Falb, Rudolph, 1838–1903, vol. I
Falcon, Michael, 1888–1976, vol. VII
Falcon, Thomas Adolphus, 1872–1944, vol. IV
Falconbridge, Hon. Sir Glenholme, 1846–1920, vol. II
Falconbridge, John Delatre, 1875–1968, vol. VI
Falconer, Lt-Col Alexander Robertson, 1874–1955, vol. V
Falconer, Arthur Wellesley, died 1954, vol. V
Falconer, J. B., died 1924, vol. II
Falconer, James, 1856–1931, vol. III
Falconer, John Downie, 1876–1947, vol. IV
Falconer, Sir John Ireland, 1879–1954, vol. V
Falconer, Lanoe; see Hawker, M. E.
Falconer, Murray Alexander, 1910–1977, vol. VII
Falconer, Sir Robert Alexander, 1867–1943, vol. IV
Falconer Jameson, Mrs; see Buckrose, J. E.

Falconio, HE Cardinal Diomed, 1842–1917, vol. II
Falk, Bernard, 1882–1960, vol. V
Falk, Oswald Toynbee, 1879–1972, vol. VII
Falke, Otto von, 1862–1943, vol. IV
Falkiner, Rt Hon. Sir Frederick Richard, 1831–1908, vol. I (A)
Falkiner, Sir Leslie Edmond Percy Riggs, 7th Bt, 1866–1917, vol. II
Falkland, 12th Viscount, 1845–1922, vol. II
Falkland, 13th Viscount, 1880–1961, vol. VI
Falkner, Brig. Eric Felton, 1880–1956, vol. V
Falkner, John Meade, 1858–1932, vol. III
Falkner, Rev. Thomas Felton, 1847–1924, vol. II
Fall, Captain Ernest Matson, 1883–1955, vol. V
Falla, Norris Stephen, 1883–1945, vol. IV
Falla, Sir Robert Alexander, 1901–1979, vol. VII
Fallada, Hans; see Ditzen, Rudolf.
Fallas, Carl, 1885–1962, vol. VI
Falle, Lt-Col Philip Vernon Le Geyt, 1885–1936, vol. III
Falle, Very Rev. Samuel, 1854–1937, vol. III
Fallieres, Armand, 1841–1931, vol. III
Fallis, Lt-Col Rev. George Oliver, 1885–1952, vol. V
Fallon, Rt Rev. Michael Francis, 1867–1931, vol. III
Falloon, C. H., 1875–1959, vol. V
Fallows, Rt Rev. Gordon; see Fallows, Rt Rev. W. G.
Fallows, Rt Rev. (William) Gordon, 1913–1979, vol. VII
Falls, Major Sir Charles Fausset, 1860–1936, vol. III
Falls, Captain Cyril Bentham, 1888–1971, vol. VII
Falls, Lt-Col Horace Edward, 1874–1937, vol. III
Falmouth, 7th Viscount, 1847–1918, vol. II
Falmouth, 8th Viscount, 1887–1962, vol. VI
Falwasser, Arthur Thomas, 1873–1959, vol. V
Fancourt, Col St John Fancourt Michell, 1847–1917, vol. II
Fancourt, Ven. Thomas, 1840–1919, vol. II
Fane, Lady Augusta, died 1950, vol. IV
Fane, Col Cecil, 1875–1960, vol. V
Fane, Cecil Francis William, 1856–1914, vol. I
Fane, Adm. Sir Charles George, 1837–1909, vol. I
Fane, Sir Edmund Douglas Veitch, 1837–1900, vol. I
Fane, Frederick William, 1857–1933, vol. III
Fane, Lenox; see Clifton, Baroness.
Fane, Major Hon. Mountjoy John Charles Wedderburn, 1900–1963, vol. VI
Fane, Captain Octavius Edward, 1886–1918, vol. II
Fane, Rt Hon. Sir Spencer Cecil Brabazon P.; see Ponsonby-Fane.
Fane, Sydney Algernon, 1867–1929, vol. III
Fane, Maj.-Gen. Sir Vere Bonamy, 1863–1924, vol. II
Fane, Violet; see Currie, Mary Montgomerie, Lady.
Fane De Salis, Sir Cecil; see De Salis.
Fane De Salis, Rt Rev. Charles; see De Salis.
Fane De Salis, Rodolph; see De Salis.
Fane De Salis, Adm. Sir William; see De Salis.
Faning, Joseph Eaton, 1850–1927, vol. II

Fanner, John Lewis, 1921–1975, vol. VII
Fanning, Frederick William B.; see Burton-Fanning.
Fanning, Sir Roland Francis Nichol, 1829–1919, vol. II
Fanshawe, Sir Arthur Dalrymple, 1847–1936, vol. III
Fanshawe, Sir Arthur Upton, 1848–1931, vol. III
Fanshawe, Vice-Adm. Basil Hew, 1868–1929, vol. III
Fanshawe, Lt-Gen. Sir Edward Arthur, 1859–1952, vol. V
Fanshawe, Sir Edward Gennys, 1814–1906, vol. I
Fanshawe, Maj.-Gen. Sir Evelyn Dalrymple, 1895–1979, vol. VII
Fanshawe, Rev. Gerald Charles, 1870–1924, vol. II
Fanshawe, Captain Guy Dalrymple, died 1962, vol. VI
Fanshawe, Herbert Charles, 1852–1923, vol. II
Fanshawe, Lt-Gen. Sir Hew Dalrymple, 1860–1957, vol. V
Fanshawe, Brig. Lionel Arthur, 1874–1962, vol. VI
Fanshawe, Col Reginald Winnington, 1871–1932, vol. III
Fanshawe, Maj.-Gen. Sir Robert, 1863–1946, vol. IV
Fantham, Annie; see Porter, A.
Fantham, Harold Benjamin, died 1937, vol. III
Faraday, Wilfred Barnard, 1874–1953, vol. V
Fardell, Sir George; see Fardell, Sir T. G.
Fardell, Sir (Thomas) George, 1833–1917, vol. II
Farewell, Captain Michael Warren, 1868–1953, vol. V
Farey-Jones, Frederick William, 1904–1974, vol. VII
Farfan, Brig. Arthur Joseph Thomas, 1882–1953, vol. V
Fargher, John Adrian, 1901–1977, vol. VII
Fargus, Brig.-Gen. Harold, 1873–1962, vol. VI
Fargus, Lt-Col Nigel Harry Skinner, 1881–1962, vol. VI
Faridoonji Jamshedji, Nawab Sir Faridoon Jung, 1849–1928, vol. II
Farie, Rear-Adm. James Uchtred, died 1957, vol. V
Faringdon, 1st Baron, 1850–1934, vol. III
Faringdon, 2nd Baron, 1902–1977, vol. VII
Faris, Desmond William George, 1901–1957, vol. V
Farjeon, B. L., died 1903, vol. I
Farjeon, Eleanor, 1881–1965, vol. VI
Farjeon, Herbert, 1887–1945, vol. IV
Farjeon, Joseph Jefferson, 1883–1955, vol. V
Farleigh, John, 1900–1965, vol. VI
Farley, Albert Henry, 1887–1954, vol. V
Farley, Brig. Edward Lionel, 1889–1968, vol. VI
Farley, Sir Edwin Wood Thorp, 1864–1939, vol. III
Farley, HE Cardinal John, 1842–1918, vol. II
Farlow, Sir Sydney Nettleton K.; see King-Farlow.
Farman, Air Vice-Marshal Edward Crisp, 1897–1966, vol. VI
Farman, Henry, 1874–1958, vol. V
Farmar, Maj.-Gen. George Jasper, 1872–1958, vol. V
Farmar, Col Harold Mynors, 1878–1961, vol. VI

Farmer, Charles Edward, 1847–1935, vol. III
Farmer, Emily, died 1905, vol. I
Farmer, Ernest Harold, died 1952, vol. V
Farmer, Sir Francis Mark, died 1922, vol. II
Farmer, Col George Devey, 1866–1928, vol. II
Farmer, Henry George, 1882–1965, vol. VI
Farmer, John, 1835–1901, vol. I
Farmer, Sir John Bretland, 1865–1944, vol. IV
Farmer, John Cotton, 1886–1952, vol. V
Farmer, Norman William, 1901–1971, vol. VII
Farmer, Sir William, 1831–1908, vol. I
Farmer-Atkinson, Henry John; see Atkinson.
Farmiloe, Ven. William Thomas, 1863–1946, vol. IV
Farnall, Edmund Waterton, 1855–1918, vol. II
Farnall, Harry de la Rosa Burrard, 1852–1929, vol. III
Farnan, R. P., died 1962, vol. VI
Farnborough, Louisa Johanna, (Lady Farnborough), died 1901, vol. I
Farncomb, Rear-Adm. Harold Bruce, 1899–1971, vol. VII
Farndale, Joseph, 1865–1954, vol. V
Farndale, Rev. William Edward, 1881–1966, vol. VI
Farnell, Lewis Richard, 1856–1934, vol. III
Farnham, 10th Baron, 1849–1900, vol. I
Farnham, 11th Baron, 1879–1957, vol. V
Farnol, Jeffery; see Farnol, John J.
Farnol, (John) Jeffery, 1878–1952, vol. V
Farnsworth, William Charles, 1892–1964, vol. VI
Farquhar, 1st Earl, 1844–1923, vol. II
Farquhar, Alfred, 1852–1928, vol. II
Farquhar, Sir Arthur, 1815–1908, vol. I
Farquhar, Adm. Sir Arthur Murray, 1855–1937, vol. III
Farquhar, Major Francis Douglas, 1874–1915, vol. I
Farquhar, George Neil, 1896–1948, vol. IV
Farquhar, Very Rev. George Taylor Shillito, died 1927, vol. II
Farquhar, Gilbert, 1850–1920, vol. II
Farquhar, Sir Harold Lister, 1894–1953, vol. V
Farquhar, Sir Henry Thomas, 4th Bt, 1838–1916, vol. II
Farquhar, John Nicol, 1861–1929, vol. III
Farquhar, Joseph, 1854–1929, vol. III
Farquhar, Adm. Richard Bowles, 1859–1948, vol. IV
Farquhar, Sir Robert Townsend-, 6th Bt, 1841–1924, vol. II
Farquhar, Sir Walter Randolph Fitzroy, 5th Bt, 1878–1918, vol. II
Farquhar, Sir Walter Rockcliffe, 3rd Bt, 1810–1900, vol. I
Farquharson, Alexander Charles, 1864–1951, vol. V
Farquharson, Alexander Haldane, 1867–1936, vol. III
Farquharson, Bt Lt-Col Arthur Spenser Loat, died 1942, vol. IV
Farquharson, Sir Arthur Wildman, died 1947, vol. IV
Farquharson, Lt-Col David Lorraine Wilson-, 1862–1938, vol. III
Farquharson, Eric Leslie, 1905–1970, vol. VI

Farquharson, Lt-Gen. Henry Douglas, 1868–1947, vol. IV
Farquharson, James Miller, 1825–1906, vol. I
Farquharson, Col Sir John, 1839–1905, vol. I
Farquharson, John Malcolm, 1864–1936, vol. III
Farquharson, Joseph, 1846–1935, vol. III
Farquharson, Mrs Ogilvie-, died 1912, vol. I
Farquharson, Rt Hon. Robert, 1836–1918, vol. II
Farr, Clinton Coleridge, 1866–1943, vol. IV
Farr, Captain John, 1882–1951, vol. V.
Farr, William Edward, 1872–1923, vol. II
Farran, Sir Charles Frederick, 1840–1898, vol. I
Farran, Major George Lambert, died 1925, vol. II
Farrand, Livingston, 1867–1939, vol. III
Farrant, Sir Geoffrey Upcott, 1881–1964, vol. VI
Farrant, Henry Gatchell, 1864–1946, vol. IV
Farrant, Reginald Douglas, 1877–1952, vol. V
Farrant, Sir Richard, 1835–1906, vol. I
Farrar, Rev. Adam Story, died 1905, vol. I
Farrar, Rev. Charles Frederick, died 1931, vol. III
Farrar, Hon. Ernest Henry, 1879–1952, vol. V
Farrar, Very Rev. Frederic William, 1831–1903, vol. I
Farrar, Sir George Herbert, 1st Bt, 1859–1915, vol. I
Farrar, Geraldine, 1882–1967, vol. VI
Farrar, Captain John Percy, 1857–1929, vol. III
Farrar, Rev. Piercy Austin, 1873–1947, vol. IV
Farrar, Rt Rev. Walter, 1865–1916, vol. II
Farrell, Hon. Edward Matthew, 1854–1931, vol. III
Farrell, Frank James, 1877–1937, vol. III
Farrell, James A., 1863–1943, vol. IV
Farrell, James Gordon, 1935–1979, vol. VII
Farrell, James Patrick, 1865–1921, vol. II
Farrell, James T., 1904–1979, vol. VII
Farrell, Jerome; see Farrell, W. J.
Farrell, Joseph Jessop, 1866–1949, vol. IV
Farrell, Michael James, 1926–1975, vol. VII
Farrell, Robert Hamilton, 1895–1959, vol. V
Farrell, Sir Thomas, died 1900, vol. I
Farrell, (Wilfrid) Jerome, 1882–1960, vol. V
Farren, Most Rev. Neil, 1893–1980, vol. VII (AII)
Farren, Sir Richard Thomas, 1817–1909, vol. I
Farren, William, 1853–1937, vol. III
Farren, Sir William Scott, 1892–1970, vol. VI
Farrer, 1st Baron, 1819–1899, vol. I
Farrer, 2nd Baron, 1859–1940, vol. III
Farrer, 3rd Baron, 1893–1948, vol. IV
Farrer, 4th Baron, 1904–1954, vol. V
Farrer, 5th Baron, 1910–1964, vol. VI
Farrer, Augustine John Daniel, 1872–1954, vol. V
Farrer, Rev. Austin Marsden, 1904–1968, vol. VI
Farrer, Bryan, 1858–1944, vol. IV
Farrer, Claude St Aubyn, died 1940, vol. III
Farrer, Edmund Hugh, 1876–1955, vol. V
Farrer, Hon. Dame Frances Margaret, 1895–1977, vol. VII
Farrer, Harold Marson, 1882–1943, vol. IV
Farrer, Rev. Canon Henry Richard William, 1859–1933, vol. III
Farrer, Hon. Noel Maitland, 1867–1929, vol. III
Farrer, Philip Tonstall, 1877–1966, vol. VI
Farrer, Reginald, 1880–1920, vol. II
Farrer, Roland John, 1873–1956, vol. V

Farrer, Ven. Walter, 1862–1934, vol. III
Farrer, Sir William James, died 1911, vol. I
Farrère, Claude, (Frédéric Charles Bargone), 1876–1957, vol. V
Farrington, Vice-Adm. Alexander, 1869–1933, vol. III
Farrington, Benjamin, 1891–1974, vol. VII
Farrington, Sir Henry Anthony, 6th Bt, 1871–1944, vol. IV
Farrington, Col Malcolm Charles, 1835–1925, vol. II
Farrington, Sir William Hicks, 5th Bt, 1838–1901, vol. I
Farris, Hon. John Wallace de Beque, 1878–1970, vol. VI
Farrow, G. Martin, 1896–1969, vol. VI (AII)
Farrow, Leslie William, 1888–1978, vol. VII
Farson, Negley, 1890–1960, vol. V
Farthing, Rt Rev. John Cragg, 1861–1947, vol. IV
Farthing, Walter John, 1889–1954, vol. V
Farwell, Sir Christopher John Wickens, 1877–1943, vol. IV
Farwell, Rt Hon. Sir George, 1845–1915, vol. I (A)
Fasken, Maj.-Gen. Charles Grant Mansell, 1855–1928, vol. II
Fasken, Brig.-Gen. William Henry, 1863–1943, vol. IV
Fass, Sir Ernest; see Fass, Sir H. E.
Fass, Sir (Herbert) Ernest, died 1969, vol. VI
Fasson, Brig.-Gen. Disney John Menzies, 1864–1931, vol. III
Fateh Ali Khan, Hon. Sir Hajee, Nawab Kizilbash, 1862–1923, vol. II
Fathers, Henry, 1860–1937, vol. III
Faucit, Helen, (Lady Martin), 1820–1898, vol. I
Fauconberg and Conyers, Baroness (13th in line), (Countess of Yarborough), 1863–1926, vol. II
Faudel-Phillips, Sir Benjamin Samuel, 2nd Bt, 1871–1927, vol. II
Faudel-Phillips, Sir George Faudel, 1st Bt, 1840–1922, vol. II
Faudel-Phillips, Sir Lionel Lawson Faudel, 3rd Bt, 1877–1941, vol. IV
Faught, Surg.-Maj.-Gen. John George, 1832–1910, vol. I
Faulds, Archibald Galbraith, 1860–1940, vol. III
Faulkner, Sir Alfred Edward, 1882–1963, vol. VI
Faulkner, Rt Hon. (Arthur) Brian (Deane), 1921–1977, vol. VII
Faulkner, Rt Hon. Brian; see Faulkner, Rt Hon. A. B. D.
Faulkner, Major George Aubrey, died 1930, vol. III
Faulkner, Hon. George Everett, 1855–1931, vol. III
Faulkner, Harry, 1892–1971, vol. VII
Faulkner, Rear-Adm. Hugh Webb, 1900–1969, vol. VI
Faulkner, Hon. James Albert, 1877–1944, vol. IV
Faulkner, John, 1871–1958, vol. V
Faulkner, Odin T., 1890–1958, vol. V
Faulkner, Vincent Clements, 1888–1975, vol. VII
Faulkner, William, 1897–1962, vol. VI
Faull, Joseph Horace, 1870–1961, vol. VI
Faunce, Brig. Bonham, 1872–1961, vol. VI
Faunce, William Herbert Perry, 1859–1930, vol. III

Faunthorpe, Lt-Col John Champion, 1872–1929, vol. III
Faunthorpe, Rev. John Pincher, 1839–1924, vol. II
Fauré, Gabriel, 1845–1924, vol. II
Faure, Hon. Sir Pieter Hendrik, 1848–1914, vol. I
Fausset, Rev. Andrew Robert, 1821–1910, vol. I
Fausset, Hugh I'Anson, 1895–1965, vol. VI
Fausset, Rev. William Yorke, died 1914, vol. I
Faussett, Captain Sir Bryan Godfrey G.; see Godfrey-Faussett.
Faussett, Brig. Bryan Trevor G.; see Godfrey-Faussett.
Faussett, Brig.-Gen. Edmund Godfrey G.; see Godfrey-Faussett.
Faussett, Lt-Col Owen Godfrey G.; see Godfrey Faussett.
Fauteux, Rt Hon. Gérald; see Fauteux, Rt Hon. J. H. G.
Fauteux, Rt Hon. (Joseph Honoré) Gérald, 1900–1980, vol. VII (AII)
Faux, Col Edward, 1857–1937, vol. III
Favell, Richard, died 1918, vol. II
Faviell, Captain Douglas, 1884–1947, vol. IV
Faviell, Lt-Col William Frederick Oliver, 1882–1950, vol. IV
Faville, Air Vice-Marshal Roy, 1908–1980, vol. VII
Fawcett, Charles Bungay, 1883–1952, vol. V
Fawcett, Sir Charles Gordon Hill, 1869–1952, vol. V
Fawcett, Douglas; see Fawcett, E. D.
Fawcett, Edgar, 1847–1904, vol. I
Fawcett, Edmund Alderson Sandford, 1868–1938, vol. III
Fawcett, Edward, 1867–1942, vol. IV
Fawcett, (Edward) Douglas, 1866–1960, vol. V
Fawcett, Edward Pinder, 1874–1954, vol. V
Fawcett, Sir Henry; see Fawcett, Sir J. H.
Fawcett, Henry Heath, 1863–1925, vol. II
Fawcett, John, 1866–1944, vol. IV
Fawcett, Sir (John) Henry, 1831–1898, vol. I
Fawcett, Sir Luke, 1881–1960, vol. V
Fawcett, Dame Millicent, 1847–1929, vol. III
Fawcett, Lt-Col P. H., 1867–1925, vol. II (A), vol. III
Fawcett, Philippa Garrett, died 1948, vol. IV
Fawcett, William, died 1941, vol. IV
Fawcett, Sir William Claude, 1868–1935, vol. III
Fawcett, Maj.-Gen. William James, 1848–1943, vol. IV
Fawcett, William Milner, 1832–1908, vol. I
Fawcus, Lt-Col Arthur, 1886–1936, vol. III
Fawcus, George Ernest, 1885–1958, vol. V
Fawcus, Lt-Gen. Sir Harold Ben, 1876–1947, vol. IV
Fawcus, Louis Reginald, 1887–1971, vol. VII
Fawdry, Reginald Charles, 1873–1965, vol. VI
Fawdry, Air Cdre Thomas, 1891–1968, vol. VI
Fawke, Sir Ernest John, died 1928, vol. II
Fawkes, Archibald Walter, 1855–1941, vol. IV
Fawkes, Frederick Hawksworth, 1870–1936, vol. III
Fawkes, Rear-Adm. George Barney Hamley, 1903–1967, vol. VI
Fawkes, Rowland Beattie, 1894–1965, vol. VI

Fawkes, Rupert Edward Francis, 1879–1967, vol. VI
Fawkes, Adm. Sir Wilmot Hawksworth, 1846–1926, vol. II
Fawsitt, Charles Edward, 1878–1960, vol. V (A)
Fay, Charles Ernest, 1846–1931, vol. III
Fay, Charles Ryle, 1884–1961, vol. VI
Fay, Rt Rev. Cyril Damian, 1903–1975, vol. VII
Fay, Sir Sam, 1856–1953, vol. V
Fay, Sidney Bradshaw, 1876–1967, vol. VI
Fayle, Lindley Robert Edmundson, 1903–1972, vol. VII
Fayolle, Emile, 1852–1928, vol. II
Fayrer, Sir Joseph, 1st Bt, 1824–1907, vol. I
Fayrer, Sir Joseph, 2nd Bt, 1859–1937, vol. III
Fayrer, Sir Joseph Herbert Spens, 3rd Bt, 1899–1976, vol. VII
Fazan, Sidney Herbert, 1888–1979, vol. VII
Fea, Allan, 1860–1956, vol. V
Fearfield, Joseph, 1883–1941, vol. IV
Fearnley, Thomas, 1880–1961, vol. VI
Fearnley-Whittingstall, Francis Herbert, 1894–1945, vol. IV
Fearnley-Whittingstall, William Arthur, 1903–1959, vol. V
Fearnsides, Edwin Greaves, 1883–1919, vol. II
Fearnsides, William George, 1879–1968, vol. VI
Fearon, Daniel Robert, 1835–1919, vol. II
Fearon, John Francis, 1867–1940, vol. III
Fearon, Percy Hutton, (Poy), 1874–1948, vol. IV
Fearon, Rev. William Andrewes, 1841–1924, vol. II
Fearon, William Robert, 1892–1959, vol. V
Feather, Baron (Life Peer); Victor Grayson Hardie Feather, 1908–1976, vol. VII
Feather, Norman, 1904–1978, vol. VII
Featherstone, Eric Kellett, 1896–1965, vol. VI
Featherstone, Henry Walter, 1894–1967, vol. VI
Feavearyear, Sir Albert Edgar, 1896–1953, vol. V
Fechteler, Adm. William Morrow, 1896–1967, vol. VI
Fedden, Sir (Alfred Hubert) Roy, 1885–1973, vol. VII
Fedden, (Henry) Robin Romilly, 1908–1977, vol. VII
Fedden, Katharine Waldo Douglas, died 1939, vol. III
Fedden, Robin Romilly; see Fedden, H. R. R.
Fedden, Romilly, died 1939, vol. III
Fedden, Sir Roy; see Fedden, Sir A. H. R.
Fedden, Walter Fedde, died 1952, vol. V
Feetham, Brig.-Gen. Edward, 1863–1918, vol. II
Feetham, Rt Rev. John Oliver, 1873–1947, vol. IV
Feetham, Hon. Richard, 1874–1965, vol. VI
Fegen, Rear-Adm. Frederick Fogarty, 1855–1911, vol. I
Fegen, Col Magrath Fogarty, 1858–1935, vol. III
Fehr, Frank Emil, 1874–1948, vol. IV
Fehr, Henry Charles, died 1940, vol. III
Fehrenbacher, Rt Rev. Bruno, 1895–1965, vol. VI
Feilden, Cecil William Montague, 1863–1902, vol. I
Feilden, Major Granville Cholmondeley, 1863–1939, vol. III

Feilden, Major Guy; *see* Feilden, Major P. H. G.
Feilden, Maj.-Gen. Sir Henry Broome, 1834–1926, vol. II
Feilden, Col Henry Wemyss, 1838–1921, vol. II
Feilden, Major (Percy Henry) Guy, 1870–1944, vol. IV
Feilden, Lt-Col Randle Montague, 1871–1965, vol. VI
Feilden, Theodore John Valentine, 1863–1955, vol. V
Feilden, Col Wemyss Gawne Cunningham, 1870–1943, vol. IV
Feilden, Sir William Henry, 4th Bt, 1866–1946, vol. IV
Feilden, Rev. William Leyland, *died* 1907, vol. I
Feilden, Sir William Leyland, 3rd Bt, 1835–1912, vol. I
Feilden, Sir William Morton Buller, 5th Bt, 1893–1976, vol. VII
Feilding, Viscount; Lt-Col Rudolph Edmund Aloysius Feilding, 1885–1937, vol. III
Feilding, Maj.-Gen. Sir Geoffrey Percy Thynne, 1866–1932, vol. III
Feilding, Hon. Sir Percy Robert Basil, 1827–1904, vol. I
Feilding, Lt-Col Rowland Charles, *died* 1945, vol. IV
Feiling, Anthony, 1885–1975, vol. VII
Feiling, Sir Keith Grahame, 1884–1977, vol. VII
Feisal, King, *died* 1933, vol. III
Felberman, Louis, 1861–1927, vol. II
Feldman, Rev. Dayan Asher, 1873–1950, vol. IV
Feldman, William Moses, *died* 1939, vol. III
Felgate, Air Vice-Marshal Frank Westerman, 1901–1974, vol. VII
Felix, Arthur, 1887–1956, vol. V
Felkin, Mrs A. L.; *see* Fowler, Hon. Ellen Thorneycroft.
Felkin, Alfred Laurence, 1856–1942, vol. IV
Fell, Sir Arthur, 1850–1934, vol. III
Fell, Aubrey Llewellyn Coventry, 1869–1948, vol. IV
Fell, Sir Bryan Hugh, 1869–1955, vol. V
Fell, Eleanor, *died* 1946, vol. IV
Fell, Sir Godfrey Butler Hunter, 1872–1955, vol. V
Fell, Herbert Granville, 1872–1951, vol. V
Fell, John Robert Massey, 1890–1969, vol. VI
Fell, Lt-Gen. Sir Matthew Henry Gregson, 1872–1959, vol. V
Fell, Vice-Adm. Sir Michael Frampton, 1918–1976, vol. VII
Fell, Brig.-Gen. Robert Black, 1859–1934, vol. III
Fell, Sheila Mary, 1931–1979, vol. VII
Fell, Thomas Edward, 1873–1926, vol. II
Fell-Smith, Charlotte, *died* 1937, vol. III
Felling, Sir Christian Ludolph Neethling, 1880–1928, vol. II
Fellowes, Hon. Coulson Churchill, 1883–1915, vol. I (A)
Fellowes, Daisy, (Hon. Mrs Reginald Fellowes), *died* 1962, vol. VI
Fellowes, Rev. Edmund Horace, 1870–1951, vol. V
Fellowes, Sir Edward Abdy, 1895–1970, vol. VI
Fellowes, Vice-Adm. Sir John, 1843–1912, vol. I

Fellowes, Air Cdre Peregrine Forbes Morant, 1883–1955, vol. V
Fellowes, Rear-Adm. Sir Thomas Hounsom Butler, 1827–1923, vol. II
Fellows, Brig.-Gen. Bertram Charles, 1877–1956, vol. V
Fellows, Col Bruce; *see* Fellows, Col R. B.
Fellows, Col (Robert) Bruce, 1830–1922, vol. II
Fells, John Manger, 1858–1925, vol. II
Fels, Willi, 1858–1946, vol. IV (A)
Feltham, John Alric Percy, 1862–1929, vol. III
Feltin, HE Cardinal Maurice, 1883–1975, vol. VII
Felton, Sir John Robinson, 1880–1962, vol. VI
Felton, Mrs Monica, 1906–1970, vol. VI
Felton, Samuel Morse, 1853–1930, vol. III
Fenby, Charles, 1905–1974, vol. VII
Fenby, Thomas Davis, 1875–1956, vol. V
Fendall, Brig.-Gen. Charles Pears, 1860–1933, vol. III
Fendall, Percy Paul Wentworth, 1879–1910, vol. I
Fendick, Rev. George Harold, 1883–1962, vol. VI
Fenn, Col Ernest Harrold, 1850–1916, vol. II
Fenn, Frederick, 1868–1924, vol. II
Fenn, George Manville, 1831–1909, vol. I
Fenn, Harold Robert Backwell, 1894–1974, vol. VII
Fenn, John Cyril Douglas, 1879–1927, vol. II
Fenn, William Wallace, 1862–1932, vol. III
Fennelly, Sir Daniel; *see* Fennelly, Sir R. D.
Fennelly, Sir (Reginald) Daniel, 1890–1969, vol. VI
Fennelly, Most Rev. Thomas, 1845–1927, vol. II
Fenner, Tan Sri Sir Claude Harry, 1916–1978, vol. VII
Fenning, Captain Edward George, 1878–1932, vol. III
Fenton, Brig.-Gen. Alexander Bulstrode, 1856–1942, vol. IV
Fenton, Charles; *see* Fenton, T. C.
Fenton, Ferrar, *born* 1832, vol. II
Fenton, Henry John Horstman, 1854–1929, vol. III
Fenton, James, 1884–1962, vol. VI
Fenton, Hon. James Edward, 1864–1950, vol. IV
Fenton, James Stevenson, 1891–1975, vol. VII
Fenton, Sir John Charles, 1880–1951, vol. V
Fenton, Sir Michael William, 1862–1941, vol. IV
Fenton, Sir Myles, 1830–1918, vol. II
Fenton, Rt Rev. Patrick, 1837–1918, vol. II
Fenton, Richard, 1899–1959, vol. V
Fenton, Roy Pentelow, 1918–1979, vol. VII
Fenton, (Thomas) Charles, *died* 1927, vol. II
Fenton, West Fenton de W.; *see* de Wend-Fenton.
Fenton, Col Sir William Charles, 1891–1976, vol. VII
Fenton, William Hugh, 1854–1928, vol. II
Fenton, William James, 1868–1957, vol. V
Fenwick, Bedford, 1855–1939, vol. III
Fenwick, Mrs Bedford; *see* Fenwick, Ethel Gordon.
Fenwick, Rt Rev. Charles, 1850–1918, vol. II
Fenwick, Maj.-Gen. Charles Philip, 1891–1954, vol. V
Fenwick, Christian Bedford, 1888–1969, vol. VI
Fenwick, E. Hurry, 1856–1944, vol. IV
Fenwick, Edward Nicholas Fenwick-, 1847–1908, vol. I

Fenwick, Major Ernest Guy, 1867–1937, vol. III
Fenwick, Ethel Gordon, (Mrs Bedford Fenwick), 1857–1947, vol. IV
Fenwick, Sir George, 1847–1929, vol. III
Fenwick, Hon. Sir (George) Townsend, 1846–1927, vol. II
Fenwick, Lt-Col Gerard, 1868–1935, vol. III
Fenwick, Col Henry Thomas, 1863–1939, vol. III
Fenwick, Col Percival Clennell, 1870–1958, vol. V
Fenwick, Thomas FitzRoy Phillipps, 1856–1938, vol. III
Fenwick, Hon. Sir Townsend; see Fenwick, Hon. Sir G. T.
Fenwick-Fenwick, Edward Nicholas; see Fenwick.
Fenwick-Palmer, Lt-Col Roderick George, 1892–1968, vol. VI
Fenwicke, William Soltau, died 1944, vol. IV
Ferard, Arthur George, 1858–1943, vol. IV
Ferard, Henry Cecil, 1864–1936, vol. III
Ferard, John Edward, 1869–1944, vol. IV
Ferard, Reginald Herbert, 1866–1934, vol. III
Ferber, Edna, died 1968, vol. VI
Ferens, Rt Hon. Thomas Robinson, 1847–1930, vol. III
Ferens, Rev. Canon William, 1859–1935, vol. III
Fergus, Andrew Freeland, 1858–1932, vol. III
Fergus, John F., 1865–1943, vol. IV
Fergus, Hon. Thomas, 1851–1914, vol. I (A)
Ferguson, Alexander Stewart, 1883–1958, vol. V
Ferguson, Brig.-Gen. Algernon Francis Holford, 1867–1943, vol. IV
Ferguson, Allan, 1880–1951, vol. V
Ferguson, Lt-Col Sir Arthur George, 1862–1935, vol. III
Ferguson, Maj.-Gen. Augustus Klingner, 1898–1965, vol. VI
Ferguson, Charles Edward Hamilton, died 1958, vol. V
Ferguson, Hon. Sir David Gilbert, 1861–1941, vol. IV
Ferguson, Sir David Gordon, 1895–1969, vol. VI
Ferguson, Hon. Donald, 1839–1909, vol. I
Ferguson, Sir Edward Alexander James J.; see Johnson-Ferguson.
Ferguson, Sir Edward Brown, 1892–1967, vol. VI
Ferguson, Erne Cecil, 1911–1968, vol. VI
Ferguson, Fergus James, 1878–1948, vol. IV
Ferguson, Frederic Sutherland, 1878–1967, vol. VI
Ferguson, Col George Andrew, 1872–1933, vol. III
Ferguson, Lt-Col George Arthur, 1835–1924, vol. II
Ferguson, Hon. (George) Howard, 1870–1946, vol. IV
Ferguson, Sir Gordon; see Ferguson, Sir D. G.
Ferguson, Harry George, 1884–1960, vol. V
Ferguson, Sir (Henry) Lindo, 1858–1948, vol. IV
Ferguson, Herbert, 1874–1953, vol. V
Ferguson, Hon. Howard; see Ferguson, Hon. G. H.
Ferguson, Sir (Jabez) Edward J.; see Johnson-Ferguson.
Ferguson of Kinmundy, James, 1857–1917, vol. II
Ferguson, James, 1879–1949, vol. IV
Ferguson, James Haig, 1862–1934, vol. III

Ferguson, Very Rev. John, died 1902, vol. I
Ferguson, John, 1842–1913, vol. I
Ferguson, John, 1854–1916, vol. II
Ferguson, Sir John, 1870–1932, vol. III
Ferguson, John, 1854–1939, vol. III
Ferguson, Hon. Sir John Alexander, 1882–1969, vol. VI
Ferguson, John Calvin, 1866–1945, vol. IV
Ferguson, Col John David, 1866–1961, vol. VI
Ferguson, Major Sir John Frederick, 1891–1975, vol. VII
Ferguson, John Macrae, 1849–1919, vol. II
Ferguson, Joshua, 1870–1951, vol. V
Ferguson, Sir Lindo; see Ferguson, Sir H. L.
Ferguson, Col Nicholas Charles, 1862–1930, vol. III
Ferguson, Rachel, 1893–1957, vol. V
Ferguson, Richard Saul, 1837–1900, vol. I
Ferguson, Samuel Fergus, 1897–1971, vol. VII
Ferguson, Engr Rear-Adm. Samuel Pringle, 1871–1938, vol. III
Ferguson, Thomas, 1900–1977, vol. VII
Ferguson, William Alexander, 1902–1973, vol. VII
Ferguson, William Bates, 1853–1937, vol. III
Ferguson, Rev. Canon William Harold, 1874–1950, vol. IV
Ferguson, William Nassau, 1869–1928, vol. II (A), vol. III
Ferguson-Davie, Major Arthur Francis; see Davie.
Ferguson-Davie, Rt Rev. Charles James, 1872–1963, vol. VI
Ferguson-Davie, Sir Henry Augustus; see Davie.
Ferguson-Davie, Sir John Davie; see Davie.
Ferguson-Davie, Sir William Augustus; see Davie.
Ferguson-Davie, Major Sir William John, 4th Bt, 1863–1947, vol. IV
Ferguson Jones, Hugh; see Jones.
Fergusson, Col Arthur Charles, 1871–1958, vol. V
Fergusson, Bernard Edward; see Baron Ballantrae.
Fergusson, Gen. Sir Charles, 7th Bt (cr 1703), 1865–1951, vol. V
Fergusson, Sir Donald; see Fergusson, Sir J. D. B.
Fergusson, Sir Ewen MacGregor Field, 1897–1974, vol. VII
Fergusson, Lt-Col Herbert Chaworth, 1865–1939, vol. III
Fergusson, Rt Hon. Sir James, 6th Bt (cr 1703), 1832–1907, vol. I
Fergusson of Kilkerran, Sir James, 8th Bt (cr 1703), 1904–1973, vol. VII
Fergusson, Adm. Sir James Andrew, 1871–1942, vol. IV
Fergusson, Surg. Rear-Adm. James Herbert, 1874–1948, vol. IV
Fergusson, Sir James Ranken, 2nd Bt (cr 1866), 1835–1924, vol. II
Fergusson, John, 1835–1912, vol. I
Fergusson, Sir (John) Donald (Balfour), 1891–1963, vol. VI
Fergusson, John Douglas, 1909–1979, vol. VII
Fergusson, Rev. John Moore, 1863–1944, vol. IV
Fergusson, Sir Louis Forbes, 1878–1962, vol. VI
Fergusson, Sir Thomas Colyer C., 3rd Bt (cr 1866); see Colyer-Fergusson.

Fergusson, Lt-Col Vivian Moffatt, *died* 1926, vol. II
Fergusson, Col William James Smyth, 1864–1934, vol. III
Fermi, Enrico, 1901–1954, vol. V
Fermor, Sir Lewis Leigh, 1880–1954, vol. V
Fermor, Una Mary E.; *see* Ellis-Fermor.
Fermor-Hesketh, Sir Thomas George; *see* Hesketh.
Fermoy, 2nd Baron, 1850–1920, vol. II
Fermoy, 3rd Baron, 1852–1920, vol. II
Fermoy, 4th Baron, 1885–1955, vol. V
Fernald, Chester Bailey, 1869–1938, vol. III
Fernandel, (Fernand Joseph Désiré Contandin), 1903–1971, vol. VII
Fernando, Sir Ernest Peter Arnold, 1904–1956, vol. V
Fernando, Sir Hilarion Marcus, 1864–1935, vol. III
Fernando, Hugh Norman Gregory, 1910–1976, vol. VII
Fernow, Bernhard Eduard, *born* 1851, vol. II
Fernyhough, Col Hugh Clifford, 1872–1947, vol. IV
Ferraby, H. C., 1884–1942, vol. IV
Ferrall, John C.; *see* Carmichael-Ferrall.
Ferrand, Major James Brian Patrick, 1895–1934, vol. III
Ferranti, Sir Vincent Ziani de; *see* de Ferranti.
Ferrar, Lt-Col Henry Minchin, 1863–1949, vol. IV
Ferrar, Lt-Col Michael Lloyd, 1876–1971, vol. VII
Ferrari, Ermanno W.; *see* Wolf-Ferrari.
Ferraro, Rev. Preb. Francis William, 1888–1963, vol. VI
Ferraro, Vincenzo Consolato Antonino, 1907–1974, vol. VII
Ferrero, Gen. Annibale, 1839–1902, vol. I
Ferrero, Baron Augusto, vol. II
Ferrero, Guglielmo, 1871–1942, vol. IV
Ferrers, 10th Earl, 1847–1912, vol. I
Ferrers, 11th Earl, 1864–1937, vol. III
Ferrers, 12th Earl, 1894–1954, vol. V
Ferrers, Rev. Norman Macleod, 1829–1903, vol. I
Ferri, Enrico, 1856–1929, vol. III
Ferrier, Sir David, 1843–1928, vol. II
Ferrier, Sir Grant; *see* Ferrier, Sir H. G.
Ferrier, Sir (Harold) Grant, 1905–1976, vol. VII
Ferrier, Maj.-Gen. James Archibald, 1854–1934, vol. III
Ferrier, Kathleen, 1912–1953, vol. V
Ferrier, Thomas Archibald, 1877–1968, vol. VI
Ferris, Hon. Rt Rev. Mgr Francis, 1860–1931, vol. III
Ferris, Rev. Thomas Boys Barraclough, 1845–1931, vol. III
Ferris, Rev. William Bridger, *died* 1931, vol. III
Ferryman, Lt-Col Augustus Ferryman M.; *see* Mockler-Ferryman.
Ferryman, Col Eric Edward M.; *see* Mockler-Ferryman.
Fessenden, Clementina, *died* 1918, vol. II
Festetics de Tolna, Prince, 1850–1933, vol. III
Festing, Major Arthur Hoskyns-, 1870–1915, vol. I
Festing, Maj.-Gen. Edward Robert, 1839–1912, vol. I
Festing, Brig.-Gen. Francis Leycester, 1877–1948, vol. IV

Festing, Field Marshal Sir Francis Wogan, 1902–1976, vol. VII
Festing, Gabrielle, *died* 1924, vol. II
Festing, Major Harold England, 1886–1923, vol. II
Festing, Rt Rev. John Wogan, 1837–1902, vol. I
Fethers, Hon. Col Wilfrid Kent, 1885–1976, vol. VII
Fetherston, Rev. Sir George Ralph, 6th Bt, 1852–1923, vol. II
Fetherston-Dilke, Beaumont Albany, 1875–1968, vol. VI
Fetherston-Godley, Brig. Sir Francis William Crewe, 1893–1976, vol. VII
Fetherstonhaugh, Lt-Col Edward Phillips, 1879–1959, vol. V
Fetherstonhaugh, Frederick Barnard, 1864–1945, vol. IV
Fetherstonhaugh, Godfrey, 1858–1928, vol. II
Fetherstonhaugh, Captain Herbert Howard, *died* 1937, vol. III
Fetherstonhaugh, Adm. Hon. Sir Herbert M.; *see* Meade-Fetherstonhaugh.
Fetherstonhaugh, Hon. Keith Turnour-, 1848–1930, vol. III
Fetherstonhaugh, Lt-Col Timothy, 1869–1945, vol. IV
Fetherstonhaugh, Lt-Col Sir Timothy, 1899–1969, vol. VI
Fetherstonhaugh, Brig. William Albany, 1876–1947, vol. IV
Fetherstonhaugh-Whitney, Henry Ernest William, 1847–1921, vol. II
Fetterolf, Adam H., 1841–1912, vol. I
Feuchtwanger, Lion, 1884–1958, vol. V
Feversham, 1st Earl of, 1829–1915, vol. I
Feversham, 2nd Earl of, 1879–1916, vol. II
Feversham, 3rd Earl of, 1906–1963, vol. VI
Few, Bt Col Robert Jebb, 1876–1965, vol. VI
Fewtrell, Maj.-Gen. Albert Cecil, 1885–1950, vol. IV
ffarington, Henry Nowell, 1868–1947, vol. IV
ffennell, Raymond William, 1871–1944, vol. IV
Ffinch, Benjamin Traill, 1840–1910, vol. I
Ffinch, Captain Matthew Benjamin Dipnall, *died* 1951, vol. V
Ffinch, Rev. Matthew Mortimer, 1838–1920, vol. II
ffolkes, Captain Sir (Edward John) Patrick (Boschetti), 6th Bt, 1899–1960, vol. V
Ffolkes, Sir Everard; *see* Ffolkes, Sir W. E. B.
Ffolkes, Rev. Sir Francis Arthur Stanley, 5th Bt, 1863–1938, vol. III
ffolkes, Captain Sir Patrick; *see* ffolkes, Captain Sir E. J. P. B.
Ffolkes, Sir (William) Everard Browne, 4th Bt, 1861–1930, vol. III
Ffolkes, Sir William Hovell Browne, 3rd Bt, 1847–1912, vol. I
Fforde, Sir Cecil Robert, *died* 1951, vol. V
ffoulkes, Charles John, 1868–1947, vol. IV
ffoulkes, Captain Edmund Andrew, 1867–1949, vol. IV
Ffoulkes, William Wynne, *died* 1903, vol. I
Ffrangcon-Davies, David, 1850–1918, vol. II

ffrench, 6th Baron, 1868–1955, vol. V
ffrench, Rev. James Frederick Metge, *died* 1914, vol. I
ffrench, Hon. John Martin Valentine, 1872–1946, vol. IV
Ffrench, Peter, 1844–1929, vol. III
Ffrench-Blake, Lt-Col Arthur O'Brien; *see* Blake.
Ffrench-Mullen, Lt-Col John Lawrence William, 1868–1951, vol. V
Fiaschi, Col Thomas Henry, 1853–1927, vol. II
Ficklin, Maj.-Gen. Horatio Pettus Mackintosh B.; *see* Berney-Ficklin.
Fiddament, Air Vice-Marshal Arthur Leonard, 1896–1976, vol. VII
Fiddes, Edward, 1864–1942, vol. IV
Fiddes, Sir George Vandeleur, 1858–1936, vol. III
Fiddes, Sir James Raffan, 1883–1961, vol. VI
Fidler, Henry, *died* 1912, vol. I
Fiedler, Hermann George, 1862–1945, vol. IV
Field, 1st Baron, 1813–1907, vol. I
Field, Allan Bertram, 1875–1962, vol. VI
Field, Adm. Sir (Arthur) Mostyn, 1855–1950, vol. IV
Field, Bradda, *died* 1957, vol. V
Field, Lt-Col Sir Donald Moyle, 1881–1956, vol. V
Field, Adm. Edward, 1828–1912, vol. I
Field, Edward, 1898–1978, vol. VII
Field, Sir Ernest Wensley Lapthorn, 1889–1974, vol. VII
Field, Frank Meade, 1863–1943, vol. IV
Field, Adm. of the Fleet Sir Frederick Laurence, 1871–1945, vol. IV
Field, Frederick William, 1884–1960, vol. V
Field, George David, 1887–1975, vol. VII
Field, Guy Cromwell, 1887–1955, vol. V
Field, Henry St John, 1883–1949, vol. IV
Field, Gen. Sir John, 1821–1899, vol. I
Field, Major Kenneth Douglas, *born* 1880, vol. II
Field, Brig. Leonard Frank, 1898–1978, vol. VII
Field, Marshall, 1893–1956, vol. V
Field, Mary, (Mrs Agnes Mary Hankin), 1896–1968, vol. VI
Field, Michael, *died* 1914, vol. I
Field, Adm. Sir Mostyn; *see* Field, Adm. Sir A. M.
Field, Gp Captain Roger Martin, 1890–1974, vol. VII
Field, Roland Alfred Reginald, *died* 1969, vol. VI
Field, Sid, (Sidney Arthur Field), 1904–1950, vol. IV
Field, Rev. Thomas, 1855–1936, vol. III
Field, Walter, *died* 1902, vol. I
Field, William, 1848–1935, vol. III
Field, Hon. Winston Joseph, 1904–1969, vol. VI
Fielden, Lt-Col Edward Anthony, 1886–1972, vol. VII
Fielden, Edward Brocklehurst, *died* 1942, vol. IV
Fielden, Air Vice-Marshal Sir Edward Hedley, 1903–1976, vol. VII
Fielden, Captain Harold, 1868–1937, vol. III
Fielden, Lionel, 1896–1974, vol. VII
Fielden, Thomas, 1854–1897, vol. I
Fielden, Thomas Perceval, *died* 1974, vol. VII
Fielden, Victor George Leopold, 1867–1946, vol. IV

Fieldhouse, William John, 1858–1928, vol. II
Fielding, Sir Charles William, 1863–1941, vol. IV
Fielding, Marjorie, 1892–1956, vol. V
Fielding, Col Thomas Evelyn, 1873–1937, vol. III
Fielding, Rt Hon. William Stevens, 1848–1929, vol. III
Fielding-Hall, Harold, 1859–1917, vol. II
Fielding-Ould, Robert, 1872–1951, vol. V
Fields, Dame Gracie, 1898–1979, vol. VII
Fields, John Charles, 1863–1932, vol. III
Fienburgh, Wilfred, 1919–1958, vol. V
Fiennes, Hon. Sir Eustace Edward, 1st Bt, 1864–1943, vol. IV
Fiennes, Gerard Yorke Twisleton-Wykeham, 1864–1926, vol. II
Fiennes, Lt-Col Sir Ranulph Twisleton-Wykeham-, 2nd Bt, 1902–1943, vol. IV
Fife, Duchess of (2nd in line), 1891–1959, vol. V
Fife, Col Sir Aubone, 1846–1920, vol. II
Fife, Charles William D.; *see* Domville-Fife.
Fife, Herbert Legard, *died* 1941, vol. IV
Fife, Lt-Col Ronald D'Arcy, 1868–1946, vol. IV
Fife-Cookson, Lt-Col John Cookson, 1844–1911, vol. I
Fifoot, Cecil Herbert Stuart, 1899–1975, vol. VII
Figg, Sir Clifford, 1890–1947, vol. IV
Figg, Captain Donald Whitly, *died* 1917, vol. II
Figgins, James Hugh Blair, 1893–1956, vol. V
Figgis, Rev. J. B., *died* 1916, vol. II
Figgis, Rev. John Neville, 1866–1919, vol. II
Fihelly, Hon. John Arthur, 1883–1945, vol. IV
Fildes, Sir Henry, 1870–1948, vol. IV
Fildes, Sir Luke, 1843–1927, vol. II
Fildes, Sir Paul, 1882–1971, vol. VII
Filene, Edward A., *died* 1937, vol. III
Filgate, John Victor Opynschae M.; *see* Macartney-Filgate.
Filgate, Captain Richard Alexander Baillie, 1877–1967, vol. VI
Filgate, Lt-Col Townley Richard, 1854–1931, vol. III
Filgate, William de Salis, 1834–1916, vol. II
Filliter, Douglas Freeland Shute, 1884–1968, vol. VI
Filliter, Freeland, 1814–1902, vol. I
Filmer, Sir Robert Marcus, 10th Bt, 1878–1916, vol. II
Filomena; *see* Miller, Florence Fenwick.
Filon, Louis Napoleon George, 1875–1937, vol. III
Filose, Lt-Col Clement, 1853–1938, vol. III
Filose, Lt-Col Sir Michael, 1836–1925, vol. II
Finberg, Alexander Joseph, 1866–1939, vol. III
Finberg, Herbert Patrick Reginald, 1900–1974, vol. VII
Finburgh, Samuel, 1867–1935, vol. III
Fincastle, Viscount; Edward David Murray, 1908–1940, vol. III
Finch, Charles Hugh, 1866–1954, vol. V
Finch, Sir Ernest Frederick, 1884–1960, vol. V, vol. VI
Finch, Surg. Rear-Adm. Ernest James, 1868–1934, vol. III
Finch, Rt Hon. George Henry, 1835–1907, vol. I
Finch, George Ingle, 1888–1970, vol. VI

Finch, Lt-Col Hamilton Walter Edward, 1868–1935, vol. III

Finch, Major John Philip Gordon, 1898–1965, vol. VI

Finch, Peter, (Peter Ingle-Finch), 1916–1977, vol. VII

Finch, Wilfred Henry Montgomery, 1883–1939, vol. III

Finch, Col Sir William Heneage W.; see Wynne Finch.

Finch, Rev. William Robert W.; see Wykes-Finch.

Finch Hatton, Brig.-Gen. Edward Heneage, 1868–1940, vol. III

Finch-Hatton, Hon. Harold, 1856–1904, vol. I

Finck, Henry T., 1854–1926, vol. II

Finck, Herman, 1872–1939, vol. III

Findlater, Alexander, died 1931, vol. III

Findlater, Jane Helen, died 1946, vol. IV

Findlater, Mary, 1865–1963, vol. VI

Findlater, Sir William Huffington, 1824–1906, vol. I

Findlay, Adam Fyfe, 1869–1962, vol. VI

Findlay, Alexander, 1874–1921, vol. II

Findlay, Alexander, 1874–1966, vol. VI

Findlay, Alexander John, 1886–1976, vol. VII

Findlay, Sir Charles Stewart, 1874–1951, vol. V

Findlay, Sir Edmund; see Findlay, Sir J. E. R.

Findlay, Col George de Cardonnel Elmsall, 1889–1967, vol. VI

Findlay, Rev. George Gillanders, 1849–1919, vol. II

Findlay, George Hugo, 1888–1966, vol. VI

Findlay, George William Marshall, 1893–1952, vol. V

Findlay, Col Harold, 1875–1939, vol. III

Findlay, Harriet, (Lady Findlay), died 1954, vol. V

Findlay, James Thomas, 1875–1927, vol. III

Findlay, Surg.-Maj. John, 1851–1920, vol. II

Findlay, Col John, 1869–1946, vol. IV

Findlay, Sir (John) Edmund (Ritchie), 2nd Bt, 1902–1962, vol. VI

Findlay, Hon. Sir John George, 1862–1929, vol. III

Findlay, John Ritchie, 1824–1898, vol. I

Findlay, Sir John Ritchie, 1st Bt, 1866–1930, vol. III

Findlay, Joseph John, 1860–1940, vol. III

Findlay, Leonard, 1878–1947, vol. IV

Findlay, Sir Mansfeldt de Cardonnel, 1861–1932, vol. III

Findlay, Brig.-Gen. Neil Douglas, 1859–1914, vol. I

Findlay, Lt-Col Sir Roland Lewis, 3rd Bt, 1903–1979, vol. VII

Findlay, William, 1880–1953, vol. V

Findlay, Lt-Col William Henri de la Tour d'Auvergne, 1864–1941, vol. IV

Findlay-Hamilton, George Douglas, 1861–1941, vol. IV

Findon, Benjamin William, 1859–1943, vol. IV

Finegan, Most Rev. Patrick, 1858–1937, vol. III

Finer, Herman, 1898–1969, vol. VI

Finer, Sir Morris, 1917–1974, vol. VII

Fingall, 11th Earl of, 1859–1929, vol. III

Fink, Hon. Theodore, 1855–1942, vol. IV

Finlaison, Alexander John, 1840–1900, vol. I

Finlaison, Maj.-Gen. John Bruce, 1870–1950, vol. IV

Finlay, 1st Viscount, 1842–1929, vol. III

Finlay, 2nd Viscount, 1875–1945, vol. IV

Finlay, Bernard, 1913–1980, vol. VII (AII)

Finlay, Sir (Campbell) Kirkman, 1875–1937, vol. III

Finlay, David White, died 1923, vol. II

Finlay, Sir George Panton, 1886–1970, vol. VI (AII)

Finlay, Ian Archibald, 1878–1925, vol. II

Finlay, James Fairbairn, died 1930, vol. III

Finlay, Major John, 1833–1912, vol. I

Finlay, Very Rev. John, 1842–1921, vol. II

Finlay, Sir Kirkman; see Finlay, Sir C. K.

Finlay, Rev. Peter, 1851–1929, vol. III

Finlay, Rev. Thomas A., 1848–1940, vol. III

Finlay, Thomas Victor William, 1899–1980, vol. VII

Finlay-Freundlich, Erwin, 1885–1964, vol. VI

Finlayson, George Daniel, 1882–1955, vol. V

Finlayson, Surg. Captain Henry William, 1864–1944, vol. IV

Finlayson, Horace Courtenay Forbes, 1885–1969, vol. VI

Finlayson, John Rankine, died 1935, vol. III

Finlayson, Lt-Col Robert Alexander, 1857–1940, vol. III

Finlayson, General Sir Robert G.; see Gordon-Finlayson.

Finlayson, Lt-Col Walter Taylor, 1877–1928, vol. II

Finletter, Hon. Thomas Knight, 1893–1980, vol. VII

Finley, David Edward, 1890–1977, vol. VII

Finley, Frederick Gault, 1861–1940, vol. III

Finley, John Huston, 1863–1940, vol. III

Finlow, Robert Steel, 1877–1953, vol. V

Finn, Alexander, 1847–1919, vol. II

Finn, Frank, 1868–1932, vol. III

Finn, Brig.-Gen. Harry, 1852–1924, vol. II

Finnegan, Thomas, 1901–1964, vol. VI

Finnemore, Sir Donald Leslie, 1889–1974, vol. VII

Finnemore, Joseph, 1860–1939, vol. III

Finnemore, Robert Isaac, 1842–1906, vol. I

Finney, Samuel, 1857–1935, vol. III

Finney, Sir Stephen, 1852–1924, vol. II

Finney, Victor Harold, died 1970, vol. VI

Finnigan, Surg. Rear-Adm. Charles Joseph, 1901–1967, vol. VI

Finnis, Adm. Frank, 1851–1918, vol. II

Finnis, Col Frank Alexander, 1880–1941, vol. IV

Finnis, Col Henry, 1853–1929, vol. III

Finnis, Gen. Sir Henry, 1890–1945, vol. IV

Finnis, Rev. Herbert Robert, 1854–1936, vol. III

Finnis, Sidney Alexander, 1908–1969, vol. VI

Finny, Maj.-Gen. Charles Morgan, 1886–1955, vol. V

Finny, John Magee, 1841–1922, vol. II

Finot, Jean, 1856–1922, vol. II

Finsen, Niels Ryberg, died 1904, vol. I

Finucane, John, 1843–1902, vol. I

Finucane, Rt Hon. Michael, died 1911, vol. I

Finzi, Gerald, 1901–1956, vol. V

Finzi, Neville Samuel, 1881–1968, vol. VI

Firbank, Arthur Annesley Ronald, 1886–1926, vol. II

Firbank, Sir Joseph Thomas, 1850–1910, vol. I

Firebrace, Comdr Sir Aylmer Newton George, 1886–1972, vol. VII

Firman, Lt-Col Robert Bertram, 1859–1936, vol. III

Firminger, Ven. Walter K., 1870–1940, vol. III

Firth, Sir Algernon Freeman, 2nd Bt, 1856–1936, vol. III

Firth, Arthur Charles Douglas, died 1948, vol. IV

Firth, Sir Charles Harding, 1857–1936, vol. III

Firth, Col Sir Charles Henry, 1836–1910, vol. I

Firth, Rev. Edward Harding, 1863–1936, vol. III

Firth, Sir Harriss, 1876–1950, vol. IV

Firth, James Brierley, 1888–1966, vol. VI

Firth, John B., 1868–1943, vol. IV

Firth, Rev. Canon John D'Ewes Evelyn, 1900–1957, vol. V

Firth, Joseph, died 1931, vol. III

Firth, Col Sir Robert Hammill, 1858–1931, vol. III

Firth, Sir Thomas Freeman, 1st Bt, 1825–1909, vol. I

Firth, Sir William John, 1881–1957, vol. V

Fischer, Rt Hon. Abraham, 1850–1913, vol. I

Fischer, Edwin, 1886–1960, vol. V

Fischer, Elsa; see Stralia, E.

Fischer, Ernst Kuno Berthold, 1824–1907, vol. I

Fischer, Hans, 1881–1945, vol. III

Fischer, Harry Robert, 1903–1977, vol. VII

Fischer, John, 1910–1978, vol. VII

Fischer, Louis, 1896–1970, vol. VI

Fischer, Percy Ulrich, 1878–1957, vol. V

Fischer, Thomas Halhed, 1830–1914, vol. I

Fiset, Maj.-Gen. Hon. Sir Eugene Marie Joseph, 1874–1951, vol. V

Fiset, Jean Baptiste Romuald, 1843–1917, vol. II, vol. III

Fish, Anne Harriet, (Mrs Walter Sefton), died 1964, vol. VI

Fish, Elizabeth, died 1944, vol. IV

Fish, Sir (Eric) Wilfred, 1894–1974, vol. VII

Fish, Ven. Lancelot John, 1861–1924, vol. II

Fish, Stuyvesant, 1851–1923, vol. II

Fish, Wallace Wilfrid B.; see Blair-Fish.

Fish, Walter George, 1874–1947, vol. IV

Fish, Sir Wilfred; see Fish, Sir E. W.

Fishenden, Margaret White, died 1977, vol. VII

Fishenden, Richard Bertie, 1880–1956, vol. V

Fisher, 1st Baron, 1841–1920, vol. III

Fisher, 2nd Baron, 1868–1955, vol. V

Fisher of Camden, Baron (Life Peer); Samuel Fisher, 1905–1979, vol. VII

Fisher of Lambeth, Baron (Life Peer); Most Rev. and Rt Hon. Geoffrey Francis Fisher, 1887–1972, vol. VII

Fisher, A. Hugh, 1867–1945, vol. IV

Fisher, Mrs A. O.; see Peterson, Margaret.

Fisher, Alfred George Timbrell, died 1967, vol. VI

Fisher, Allan George Barnard, 1895–1976, vol. VII

Fisher, Rt Hon. Andrew, 1862–1928, vol. II

Fisher, Mrs Arabella B., 1840–1929, vol. III

Fisher, Arthur Bedford K.; see Knapp-Fisher.

Fisher, Brig. Arthur Francis, 1899–1972, vol. VII

Fisher, Ben, died 1939, vol. III

Fisher, Rev. Canon Bernard Horatio Parry, 1875–1953, vol. V

Fisher, Lt-Gen. Sir Bertie Drew, 1878–1972, vol. VII

Fisher, Rev. Cecil Edward, 1838–1925, vol. II

Fisher, Col Cecil James, 1890–1961, vol. VI

Fisher, Brig. Charles Alexander, 1872–1934, vol. III

Fisher, Charles Browning, died 1929, vol. III

Fisher, Hon. Charles Douglas, 1921–1978, vol. VII

Fisher, Maj.-Gen. Donald Rutherford Dacre, 1890–1962, vol. VI

Fisher, Dorothea Frances Canfield; see Canfield, Dorothy.

Fisher, Adm. Sir Douglas Blake, 1890–1963, vol. VI

Fisher, Sir Edward Francis K.; see Knapp-Fisher.

Fisher, Lt-Gen. Edward Henry, 1822–1910, vol. I

Fisher, Edwin, 1883–1947, vol. IV

Fisher, Francis Marion Bates, 1877–1960, vol. V

Fisher, Col Francis Torriano, 1863–1938, vol. III

Fisher, Frank Lindsay, died 1947, vol. IV

Fisher, Frederic Henry, 1849–1926, vol. II

Fisher, Rev. Frederic Horatio, 1837–1915, vol. I

Fisher, Adm. Sir Frederic William, 1851–1943, vol. IV

Fisher, Vice-Adm. Frederick Charles, 1877–1958, vol. V

Fisher, Frederick Victor, 1870–1954, vol. V

Fisher, Rt Rev. George Carnac, 1844–1921, vol. II

Fisher, George Park, 1827–1909, vol. I

Fisher, Brig. Sir Gerald Thomas, 1887–1965, vol. VI

Fisher, Sir Godfrey Arthur, 1885–1969, vol. VI

Fisher, Captain Harold, 1877–1914, vol. I

Fisher, Rt Hon. Herbert Albert Laurens, 1865–1940, vol. III

Fisher, Irving, 1867–1947, vol. IV

Fisher, James Maxwell McConnell, 1912–1970, vol. VI

Fisher, Inspector-Gen. James W., died 1919, vol. II

Fisher, Rev. John, 1862–1930, vol. III

Fisher, Brig.-Gen. John, 1862–1942, vol. IV

Fisher, John Campbell, 1880–1943, vol. IV

Fisher, John Cartwright Braddon, 1911–1968, vol. VI

Fisher, Maj.-Gen. John Frederick Lane, 1832–1917, vol. II

Fisher, John Henry, 1856–1937, vol. III

Fisher, John Herbert, 1867–1933, vol. III

Fisher, John Lenox, 1899–1976, vol. VII

Fisher, Brig. John Malcolm, 1890–1943, vol. IV

Fisher, Rev. John Martyn, 1873–1939, vol. III

Fisher, Joseph R., 1855–1939, vol. III

Fisher, Lt-Col Julian Lawrence, 1877–1953, vol. V

Fisher, Kenneth, 1882–1945, vol. III

Fisher, Rt Rev. Leonard Noel, 1881–1963, vol. VI

Fisher, Mark, died 1923, vol. II

Fisher, Matthew George, 1888–1965, vol. VI

Fisher, Sir (Norman Fenwick) Warren, 1879–1948, vol. IV

Fisher, Norman George, 1910–1972, vol. VII

Fisher, Rev. Philip John, 1883–1961, vol. VI

Fisher, Rev. Robert, 1848–1933, vol. III
Fisher, Rev. Robert, 1855–1938, vol. III
Fisher, Rev. Robert Howie, 1861–1934, vol. III
Fisher, Sir Ronald Aylmer, 1890–1962, vol. VI
Fisher, S. Melton, 1860–1939, vol. III
Fisher, Sophie Florence Lothrop; see Wavertree, Lady.
Fisher, Sir Stanley, 1867–1949, vol. IV
Fisher, Col Stanley Howe, 1891–1967, vol. VI
Fisher, Hon. Sydney Arthur, 1850–1921, vol. II
Fisher, Sydney Humbert, 1887–1980, vol. VII
Fisher, Theodore, 1863–1949, vol. IV
Fisher, Comdr Sir Thomas, 1883–1925, vol. II
Fisher, Rt Rev. Thomas Cathrew, 1871–1929, vol. III
Fisher, Vardis, 1895–1968, vol. VI (AII)
Fisher, Violet Olivia; see Cressy-Marcks, V. O.
Fisher, W. R., 1846–1910, vol. I
Fisher, Rev. Walter Henry, died 1931, vol. III
Fisher, Sir Walter Newton, 1844–1932, vol. III
Fisher, Sir Warren; see Fisher, Sir N. F. W.
Fisher, Adm. William Blake, 1853–1926, vol. II
Fisher, William James, died 1924, vol. II
Fisher, Adm. Sir William Wordsworth, 1875–1937, vol. III
Fisher, Sir Woolf, 1912–1975, vol. VII
Fisher-Childe, Col Ralph Bromfield Willington, 1854–1936, vol. III
Fisher Prout, Margaret, died 1963, vol. VI
Fisher-Rowe, Edward Rowe, 1832–1909, vol. I
Fisher-Rowe, Col Herbert Mayow, 1870–1938, vol. III
Fisher-Smith, Sir George Henry, 1846–1931, vol. III
Fishwick, Lt-Col Henry, 1835–1914, vol. I
Fisk, Sir Ernest Thomas, 1886–1965, vol. VI
Fiske, Baron (Life Peer); William Geoffrey Fiske, 1905–1975, vol. VII
Fiske, Rear-Adm. Bradley Allen, 1854–1942, vol. IV
Fiske, Rt Rev. Charles, 1868–1942, vol. IV
Fiske, John, 1842–1901, vol. I
Fisken, Archibald Clyde Wanliss, 1897–1970, vol. VI (AII)
Fison, Alfred Henry, 1857–1923, vol. II
Fison, Captain Sir (Francis) Geoffrey, 2nd Bt, 1873–1948, vol. IV
Fison, Sir Frederick William, 1st Bt, 1847–1927, vol. II
Fison, Captain Sir Geoffrey; see Fison, Captain Sir F. G.
Fison, Sir Guy; see Fison, Sir W. G.
Fison, Rt Rev. Joseph Edward, 1906–1972, vol. VII
Fison, Sir (William) Guy, 3rd Bt, 1890–1964, vol. VI
Fitch, Sir Cecil Edwin, 1870–1940, vol. III
Fitch, Charles Francis, 1860–1947, vol. IV
Fitch, Clyde, 1865–1909, vol. I
Fitch, Ven. Edward Arnold, died 1965, vol. VI
Fitch, Sir Joshua Girling, 1824–1903, vol. I
Fitchett, Very Rev. Alfred Robertson, died 1929, vol. III
Fitchett, Frederick, 1851–1930, vol. III
Fitchett, Rt Rev. William Alfred Robertson, 1872–1952, vol. V

Fitchett, Rev. William Henry, died 1928, vol. II
Fithian, Sir Edward William, 1845–1936, vol. III
Fitt, Mary; see Freeman, Kathleen.
Fitton, Col Sir Charles Vernon, 1894–1967, vol. VI
Fitton, Col Guy William, 1862–1939, vol. III
Fitton, Hedley, 1857–1929, vol. III
Fitton, Col Hugh Gregory, 1863–1916, vol. II
Fitton, James, 1864–1952, vol. V
FitzAlan of Derwent, 1st Viscount, 1855–1947, vol. IV
FitzAlan of Derwent, 2nd Viscount, 1883–1962, vol. VI
FitzClarence, Lt-Col Charles, 1865–1914, vol. I
FitzClarence, Hon. Harold Edward, 1870–1926, vol. II
Fitze, Sir Kenneth Samuel, 1887–1960, vol. V
FitzGeorge, Rear-Adm. Sir Adolphus Augustus Frederick, 1846–1922, vol. II
Fitzgeorge, Col Sir Augustus Charles Frederick, 1847–1933, vol. III
Fitzgerald, Sir (Adolf) Alexander, 1890–1969, vol. VI (AII)
Fitzgerald, Sir Alexander; see Fitzgerald, Sir A. A.
FitzGerald, Sir Arthur Henry Brinsley, 4th Bt (cr 1880), 1885–1967, vol. VI
Fitzgerald, Lt-Col Brinsley, 1859–1931, vol. III
Fitzgerald, Adm. Charles Cooper Penrose, 1841–1921, vol. II
FitzGerald, Charles Edward, 1843–1916, vol. II
FitzGerald, Col Sir Charles John Oswald, 1840–1912, vol. I
FitzGerald, Hon. David, 1847–1920, vol. II
Fitzgerald, Denis P., 1871–1947, vol. IV
FitzGerald, Captain Lord Desmond, 1888–1916, vol. II
Fitzgerald, Desmond, died 1947, vol. IV
Fitzgerald, Desmond Fitzjohn Lloyd, 1862–1936, vol. III
Fitz-Gerald, Desmond Windham Otho, 1901–1949, vol. IV
Fitzgerald, Edward, 1874–1969, vol. VI (AII)
Fitzgerald, Major Edward Arthur, 1871–1931, vol. III
Fitz-Gerald, Hon. Evelyn Charles Joseph, died 1946, vol. IV
Fitzgerald, Maj.-Gen. Fitzgerald Gabbett, died 1954, vol. V
Fitzgerald, Francis John, 1864–1939, vol. III
FitzGerald, Lt-Col Lord Frederick, 1857–1924, vol. II
Fitzgerald, Garrett Ernest, 1894–1970, vol. VI
FitzGerald, Col George Alfred, 1868–1959, vol. V
Fitzgerald, Sir George Cumming, 5th Bt (cr 1822), 1823–1908, vol. I
Fitzgerald, George Francis, 1851–1901, vol. I
FitzGerald, Hon. George Parker, 1843–1917, vol. II
Fitzgerald, Sir Gerald; see Fitzgerald, Sir W. G. S. V.
Fitzgerald, Hon. Gerald, 1849–1925, vol. II
FitzGerald, Gerald A. R., 1844–1925, vol. II
Fitzgerald, Lt-Col Gerald James, 1869–1944, vol. IV
FitzGerald, Maj.-Gen. Gerald Michael, 1889–1957, vol. V

Fitzgerald, Sir Gerald Seymour Vesey; *see* Fitzgerald, Sir W. G. S. V.

FitzGerald, Brig.-Gen. Herbert Swayne, 1856–1924, vol. II

Fitzgerald, J., *died* 1909, vol. I

Fitzgerald, James Foster-Vesey-, 1846–1907, vol. I

Fitzgerald, Sir John, 1857–1930, vol. III

FitzGerald, Hon. John Donohoe, 1848–1918, vol. II

FitzGerald, John Foster V.; *see* Vesey-FitzGerald.

Fitzgerald, John Gerald, 1882–1940, vol. III (A), vol. IV

Fitzgerald, Sir John Joseph, 2nd Bt, 1876–1957, vol. V (A)

Fitzgerald, Sir John Peter Gerald Maurice, 3rd Bt (*cr* 1880), 1884–1957, vol. V

Fitzgerald, Rear-Adm. John Uniacke Penrose, 1888–1940, vol. III

FitzGerald, John Vesey V.; *see* Vesey-FitzGerald.

Fitzgerald, Marion; *see* Fitzgerald, Mrs Robert.

FitzGerald, Lord Maurice, 1852–1901, vol. I

FitzGerald, Sir Maurice, 2nd Bt (*cr* 1880), 1844–1916, vol. II

FitzGerald, Maurice F., *died* 1927, vol. II

Fitzgerald, Rev. Canon Maurice Henry, 1877–1963, vol. VI

Fitzgerald, Maurice Pembroke, *died* 1952, vol. V

Fitzgerald, Michael, 1851–1918, vol. II

Fitzgerald, Lt-Col Oswald Arthur Gerald, *died* 1916, vol. II

Fitz-Gerald, Sir Patrick Herbert, 1899–1978, vol. VII

Fitzgerald, Brig.-Gen. Percy Desmond, 1875–1933, vol. III

FitzGerald, Percy Seymour Vesey, *died* 1924, vol. II

Fitzgerald, Sir Raymond; *see* Fitzgerald, Sir W. R.

FitzGerald, Richard Charles, 1905–1959, vol. V

Fitzgerald, Rt Rev. Richard Joseph, 1881–1956, vol. V

Fitzgerald, Mrs Robert, (Marion), 1860–1928, vol. II

Fitzgerald, Sir Robert Uniacke-Penrose-, 1st Bt (*cr* 1896), 1839–1919, vol. II

FitzGerald, Hon. Rowan Robert, *born* 1847, vol. II

Fitzgerald, Seymour Gonne V.; *see* Vesey-Fitzgerald.

Fitz-Gerald, Shafto Justin Adair, 1859–1925, vol. II

Fitzgerald, Thomas, 1879–1959, vol. V

Fitzgerald, Sir Thomas Naghten, 1838–1908, vol. I

FitzGerald, Lord Walter, 1858–1923, vol. II

Fitzgerald, Walter, 1898–1949, vol. IV

Fitzgerald, Walter, (Walter Fitzgerald Bond), 1896–1976, vol. VII

Fitzgerald, Sir (William) Gerald Seymour Vesey, 1841–1910, vol. II

Fitzgerald, Most Rev. William Michael, 1906–1971, vol. VII

Fitzgerald, Sir (William) Raymond, 1890–1964, vol. VI

Fitzgerald, William Walter Augustine, *died* 1936, vol. III

Fitzgerald-Kenney, James C., 1878–1956, vol. V

Fitzgibbon, Edmond Gerald, 1825–1905, vol. I

FitzGibbon, Brig. Francis, 1883–1964, vol. VI

Fitzgibbon, Rt Hon. Gerald, 1837–1909, vol. I

Fitzgibbon, Gerald, *died* 1942, vol. IV

FitzGibbon, Gibbon, 1877–1952, vol. V

Fitzgibbon, Henry, 1824–1909, vol. I

Fitzgibbon, Henry Macaulay, 1855–1942, vol. IV

FitzGibbon, John, 1849–1919, vol. II

Fitz-Hardinge, 2nd Baron, 1826–1896, vol. I

Fitzhardinge, 3rd Baron, 1830–1916, vol. II

Fitzherbert, Basil Thomas, 1836–1919, vol. II

Fitzherbert, Maj.-Gen. Edward Herbert, 1885–1979, vol. VII

FitzHerbert, Ven. Henry Edward, 1882–1958, vol. V

Fitzherbert, Adm. Sir Herbert, 1885–1958, vol. V

Fitzherbert, Sir Hugo Meynell, 6th Bt, 1872–1934, vol. III

Fitz Herbert, Lt-Col Norman, 1858–1943, vol. IV

Fitzherbert, Rev. Sir Richard, 5th Bt, 1846–1906, vol. I

Fitzherbert, Sir William, 7th Bt, 1874–1963, vol. VI

Fitzherbert-Brockholes, John William, 1889–1963, vol. VI

Fitzherbert-Brockholes, William Joseph, 1851–1924, vol. II

Fitzhugh, Maj.-Gen. Alfred, 1837–1929, vol. III

Fitzhugh, Captain Terrick Charles, 1876–1939, vol. III

Fitzmaurice, 1st Baron, 1846–1935, vol. III

Fitzmaurice, Gerald Henry, 1865–1939, vol. III

Fitzmaurice, Rev. Sir Henry, 1886–1952, vol. V

Fitzmaurice, Sir Maurice, 1861–1924, vol. II

Fitz Maurice, Vice-Adm. Sir Maurice Swynfen, 1870–1927, vol. II

Fitzmaurice, Nicholas, 1887–1960, vol. V

Fitzmaurice, Vice-Adm. Sir Raymond, 1878–1943, vol. IV

Fitzmaurice, Brig.-Gen. Robert, 1866–1952, vol. V

Fitzpatrick, Rt Rev. Mgr Bartholomew, 1847–1925, vol. II

Fitzpatrick, Rt Hon. Sir Charles, 1851–1942, vol. IV

Fitzpatrick, Sir Dennis, 1837–1920, vol. II

Fitzpatrick, Brig.-Gen. Sir (Ernest) Richard, 1878–1949, vol. IV

Fitzpatrick, Lt-Col Geoffrey Henry Julian, 1873–1939, vol. III

Fitz Patrick, Herbert Lindsay, 1868–1949, vol. IV

Fitz-Patrick, Horace James, 1894–1967, vol. VI

Fitzpatrick, Sir James Alexander Ossory, 1879–1937, vol. III

Fitzpatrick, Sir (James) Percy, 1862–1931, vol. III

Fitzpatrick, Brig. Noel Trew, 1888–1938, vol. III

Fitzpatrick, Sir Percy; *see* Fitzpatrick, Sir J. P.

Fitzpatrick, Brig.-Gen. Sir Richard; *see* Fitzpatrick, Brig.-Gen. Sir E. R.

Fitzpatrick, Rev. Thomas Cecil, 1861–1931, vol. III

Fitzpatrick, Thomas William, *died* 1965, vol. VI

Fitzpatrick, William Francis Joseph, 1854–1940, vol. III

Fitzroy, Sir Almeric William, 1851–1935, vol. III

Fitzroy, Rev. Lord Charles Edward, 1857–1911, vol. I

FitzRoy, Sir Charles Edward, 1876–1954, vol. V

Fitzroy, Captain Rt Hon. Edward Algernon, 1869–1943, vol. IV

FitzRoy, Lord Frederick John, 1823–1919, vol. II

Fitzsimmons, William J., 1845–1913, vol. I

Fitzsimons, Frederick William, 1875–1951, vol. V

Fitzsimons, Robert Allen, 1892–1978, vol. VII

Fitzwalter, 20th Baron, 1860–1932, vol. III

Fitzwilliam, 6th Earl, 1815–1902, vol. I

Fitzwilliam, 7th Earl, 1872–1943, vol. IV

Fitzwilliam, 8th Earl, 1910–1948, vol. IV

Fitzwilliam, 9th Earl, 1883–1952, vol. V

Fitzwilliam, 10th Earl, 1904–1979, vol. VII

Fitzwilliam, Captain Hon. Sir Charles Wentworth-; see Fitzwilliam, Captain Hon. Sir W. C. W.

Fitzwilliam, George Charles Wentworth-, died 1935, vol. III

Fitzwilliam, Captain Hon. Sir (William) Charles Wentworth-, 1848–1925, vol. II

Fitzwilliam, Hon. William Henry Wentworth-, 1840–1920, vol. II

Fitzwilliams, Duncan Campbell Lloyd, 1878–1954, vol. V

Fitzwilliams, Col Edward Crawford Lloyd, 1872–1936, vol. III

Fitzwygram, Sir Frederick Loftus Francis, 5th Bt, 1884–1920, vol. II

Fitzwygram, Sir Frederick Wellington John, 4th Bt, 1823–1904, vol. I

Flack, Harvey, 1912–1966, vol. VI

Flack, Martin, 1882–1931, vol. III

Fladgate, Maj.-Gen. Courtenay William, 1890–1958, vol. V

Fladgate, Sir Francis; see Fladgate, Sir W. F.

Fladgate, Sir (William) Francis, 1853–1937, vol. III

Flagstad, Kirsten, 1895–1962, vol. VI

Flaherty, Robert Joseph, 1884–1951, vol. V

Flammarion, Camille, 1842–1925, vol. II

Flanagan, Lt-Col Edward Martyn Woulfe, 1870–1954, vol. V

Flanagan, Rev. J., 1851–1918, vol. II

Flanagan, William Henry, 1871–1944, vol. IV

Flanders, Allan David, 1910–1973, vol. VII

Flanders, Michael, 1922–1975, vol. VII

Flandin, Pierre Etienne, 1889–1958, vol. V

Flannery, Sir Harold Fortescue, 2nd Bt, 1883–1959, vol. V

Flannery, Sir James F.; see Fortescue-Flannery.

Flather, James Henry, 1853–1928, vol. II

Flatt, Leslie Neeve, 1889–1957, vol. V

Flavelle, Sir Ellsworth; see Flavelle, Sir J. E.

Flavelle, Sir (Joseph) Ellsworth, 2nd Bt, 1892–1977, vol. VII

Flavelle, Sir Joseph Wesley, 1st Bt, 1858–1939, vol. III

Flavin, Michael Joseph, 1861–1944, vol. IV

Flaxman, Brig. Sir Hubert James Marlowe, 1893–1976, vol. VII

Fleck, 1st Baron, 1889–1968, vol. VI

Flecker, H. L. O., 1896–1958, vol. V

Flecker, Rev. William Herman, 1859–1941, vol. IV

Fleet, Rear-Adm. Ernest James, 1850–1935, vol. III

Fleet, George Rutland B.; see Barrington-Fleet.

Fleet, Vice-Adm. Henry Louis, 1850–1923, vol. II

Fleet, John Faithfull, 1847–1917, vol. II

Fleetwood-Hesketh, Charles Hesketh; see Hesketh.

Fleetwood-Walker, Bernard, 1893–1965, vol. VI

Fleischmann, Louis, 1868–1954, vol. V

Fleming, Hon. Lord; David Pinkerton Fleming, 1877–1944, vol. IV

Fleming, Sir Alexander, 1881–1955, vol. V

Fleming, Sir Ambrose; see Fleming, Sir J. A.

Fleming, Sir Andrew Fleming Hudleston le, 8th Bt, 1855–1925, vol. II

Fleming, Rev. Archibald, 1863–1941, vol. IV

Fleming, Rt Rev. Archibald Lang, 1883–1953, vol. V

Fleming, Col Archibald Nicol, 1870–1948, vol. IV

Fleming, Sir Arthur Percy Morris, 1881–1960, vol. V

Fleming, Major Charles Christie, 1864–1917, vol. II

Fleming, Charles James, 1839–1904, vol. I

Fleming, Rev. David, died 1920, vol. II

Fleming, David Hay, 1849–1931, vol. III

Fleming, David Pinkerton; see Fleming, Hon. Lord.

Fleming, Dorothy Leigh; see Sayers, D. L.

Fleming, Edward G.; see Gibson Fleming,

Fleming, Edward Lascelles, died 1950, vol. IV

Fleming, Edward Vandermere, 1869–1947, vol. IV

Fleming, Sir Francis, 1842–1922, vol. II

Fleming, Col Frank, 1876–1964, vol. VI

Fleming, Frederick, vol. II

Fleming, Geoffrey Balmanno, 1882–1952, vol. V

Fleming, George; see Fletcher, Constance.

Fleming, George, 1833–1901, vol. I

Fleming, Maj.-Gen. George, 1879–1957, vol. V

Fleming, Rev. Herbert James, 1873–1926, vol. II

Fleming, Horace, 1872–1941, vol. IV

Fleming, Very Rev. Horace Townsend, died 1909, vol. I

Fleming, Ian Lancaster, 1908–1964, vol. VI

Fleming, Rev. James, died 1908, vol. I

Fleming, James, 1841–1922, vol. II

Fleming, James Alexander, 1855–1926, vol. II

Fleming, Rev. James George Grant, 1895–1978, vol. VII

Fleming, Sir John, 1847–1925, vol. II

Fleming, Sir (John) Ambrose, 1849–1945, vol. IV

Fleming, Rev. John Dick, died 1938, vol. III

Fleming, Col John Gibson, 1880–1936, vol. III

Fleming, Lt-Col John Kenneth Sprot, 1874–1944, vol. IV

Fleming, John Marcus, 1911–1976, vol. VII

Fleming, Rev. John Robert, 1858–1937, vol. III

Fleming, Maxwell, 1871–1935, vol. III

Fleming, Patrick D., died 1928, vol. II

Fleming, Peter; see Fleming, R. P.

Fleming, Major Philip, 1889–1971, vol. VII

Fleming, Richard Evelyn, 1911–1977, vol. VII

Fleming, Robert, 1845–1933, vol. III

Fleming, Robert Alexander, 1862–1947, vol. IV

Fleming, (Robert) Peter, 1907–1971, vol. VII

Fleming, Lt-Col Samuel, 1865–1925, vol. II

Fleming, Sir Sandford, 1827–1915, vol. I

Fleming, Sir Thomas Henry, 1863–1933, vol. III

Fleming, Valentine, 1882–1917, vol. II

Fleming, Wilfrid Louis Remi, 1869–1944, vol. IV

Fleming, William Arnot, 1879–1970, vol. VI

Fleming-Bernard, Andrew Milroy, 1871–1953, vol. V

Fleming-Sandes, Alfred James Terence, 1894–1961, vol. VI

Flemming, Hon. James Kidd, 1868–1927, vol. II

Flemming, Percy, *died* 1941, vol. IV

Flemwell, George Jackson, 1865–1928, vol. II

Flenley, Ralph, 1886–1969, vol. VI

Flers, Marquis de, (Robert de Flers), 1872–1927, vol. II

Fletcher, Air Cdre Albert, *died* 1956, vol. V

Fletcher, Alfred Ewen, 1841–1915, vol. I (A)

Fletcher, Sir Angus Somerville, 1883–1960, vol. V

Fletcher, Sir (Arthur George) Murchison, 1878–1954, vol. V

Fletcher, Banister, 1833–1899, vol. I

Fletcher, Sir Banister Flight, *died* 1953, vol. V

Fletcher, Benton; *see* Fletcher, G. H. B.

Fletcher, Sir Carteret Ernest, 1868–1934, vol. III

Fletcher, Charles Brunsdon, 1859–1946, vol. IV

Fletcher, Charles John, 1843–1914, vol. I

Fletcher, Charles Robert Leslie, 1857–1934, vol. III

Fletcher, Clarence George Eugene, 1875–1929, vol. III

Fletcher, Constance, 1858–1938, vol. III

Fletcher, Rev. Canon Denis, 1881–1942, vol. IV

Fletcher, Hon. Edward Ernest, vol. II

Fletcher, Surg. Rear-Adm. Edward Ernest, 1886–1968, vol. VI

Fletcher, Sir (Edward) Lionel, 1876–1968, vol. VI

Fletcher, Lt-Col Edward Walter, 1899–1958, vol. V

Fletcher, Sir Ernest Edward, 1869–1940, vol. III

Fletcher, Ernest Tertius Decimus, 1891–1961, vol. VI

Fletcher, Sir Frank, 1870–1954, vol. V

Fletcher, Frank, 1867–1956, vol. V

Fletcher, Frank Morley, 1866–1949, vol. IV

Fletcher, Frank Thomas Herbert, 1898–1977, vol. VII

Fletcher, George Hamilton, 1860–1930, vol. III

Fletcher, (George Henry) Benton, *died* 1944, vol. IV

Fletcher, Hanslip, 1874–1955, vol. V

Fletcher, Harold Roy, 1907–1978, vol. VII

Fletcher, Lt-Col Sir Henry Arthur, 1843–1925, vol. II

Fletcher, Rt Hon. Sir Henry Aubrey-, 4th Bt, 1835–1910, vol. I

Fletcher, Major Sir Henry Lancelot A.; *see* Aubrey-Fletcher.

Fletcher, Henry Prather, 1873–1959, vol. V

Fletcher, Herbert Morley, *died* 1950, vol. IV

Fletcher, Herbert Phillips, 1872–1917, vol. II

Fletcher, J. K.; *see* Kebty-Fletcher.

Fletcher, J. S., 1863–1935, vol. III

Fletcher, Sir James, 1886–1974, vol. VII

Fletcher, James Douglas, 1857–1927, vol. II

Fletcher, Rev. James Michael John, 1852–1940, vol. III

Fletcher, Lt-Col John, 1815–1902, vol. I

Fletcher, John, 1827–1903, vol. I

Fletcher, Rev. John Charles Ballett, *died* 1926, vol. II

Fletcher, John Gould, 1886–1950, vol. IV (A), vol. V

Fletcher, Sir John Samuel, 1st Bt, 1841–1924, vol. II

Fletcher, Sir Lancelot A.; *see* Aubrey-Fletcher.

Fletcher, Sir Lazarus, 1854–1921, vol. II

Fletcher, Leonard Ralph, 1917–1974, vol. VII

Fletcher, Sir Lionel; *see* Fletcher, Sir E. L.

Fletcher, Michael Scott, 1868–1947, vol. IV

Fletcher, Sir Murchison; *see* Fletcher, Sir A. G. M.

Fletcher, Rev. Philip, 1848–1928, vol. II

Fletcher, Rev. Reginald James, 1865–1932, vol. III

Fletcher, Rev. Robert, *died* 1921, vol. II

Fletcher, Ven. Robert Crompton, 1850–1917, vol. II

Fletcher, Sir Walter, 1892–1956, vol. V

Fletcher, Sir Walter Morley, 1873–1933, vol. III

Fletcher, Surg.-Maj. William, 1863–1933, vol. III

Fletcher, Major William Alfred Littledale, 1869–1919, vol. II

Fletcher, William Charles, 1865–1959, vol. V

Fletcher, Rev. Canon William Dudley Saul, 1863–1948, vol. IV

Fletcher, Ven. William Henry, *died* 1926, vol. II

Fletcher, William Younger, 1830–1913, vol. I

Fletcher-Twemlow, George Fletcher; *see* Twemlow.

Fletcher-Watson, P., 1842–1907, vol. I

Flett, Sir John Smith, 1869–1947, vol. IV

Fleure, Herbert John, 1877–1969, vol. VI

Fleuriau, Aimé Joseph de, 1870–1938, vol. III

Flew, John Douglas Score, 1902–1972, vol. VII

Flew, Rev. Robert Newton, 1886–1962, vol. VI

Flewett, Rt Rev. William Edward, 1861–1938, vol. III

Flexner, Abraham, 1866–1959, vol. V

Flexner, Simon, 1863–1946, vol. IV

Flick, Brig.-Gen. Charles Leonard, 1869–1948, vol. IV

Flight, Claude, 1881–1955, vol. V

Flinn, D. Edgar, 1850–1926, vol. II

Flinn, Major William Henry, 1895–1973, vol. VII

Flint, Abraham John, 1903–1971, vol. VII

Flint, Alexander, 1877–1932, vol. III

Flint, Austin, 1836–1915, vol. I (A)

Flint, Charles Ranlett, 1850–1934, vol. III

Flint, Ethelbert Rest, 1880–1956, vol. V

Flint, Henry Thomas, 1890–1971, vol. VII

Flint, Joseph, 1855–1925, vol. II

Flint, Rev. Robert, 1838–1910, vol. I

Flint, Robert Purves, 1883–1947, vol. IV

Flint, Ven. Stamford R. R.; *see* Raffles-Flint.

Flint, Thomas Barnard, 1847–1919, vol. II

Flint, Sir William Russell, 1880–1969, vol. VI

Flintoff, Lt-Col Thomas, 1851–1907, vol. I

Flitcroft, Sir Thomas Evans, 1861–1938, vol. III

Floersheim, Cecil L. F., 1871–1936, vol. III

Flood, Maj.-Gen. Arthur S.; *see* Solly-Flood.

Flood, Maj.-Gen. Sir Frederick Richard S.; *see* Solly-Flood.

Flood, John Ernest William, 1886–1940, vol. III

Flood, Brig.-Gen. Richard Elles S.; *see* Solly-Flood.

Flood, Chevalier William Henry Grattan, 1859–1928, vol. II

Florence, Lt-Col Henry Louis, 1843–1916, vol. II

Florence, Mary S.; *see* Sargant-Florence.

Florey, Baron (Life Peer); Howard Walter Florey, 1898–1968, vol. VI
Floud, Bernard Francis Castle, 1915–1967, vol. VI
Floud, Sir Francis Lewis Castle, 1875–1965, vol. VI
Floud, Peter Castle, 1911–1960, vol. V
Flower, Sir Archibald Dennis, died 1950, vol. IV
Flower, Benjamin Orange, 1858–1918, vol. II
Flower, Sir Cyril Thomas, 1879–1961, vol. VI
Flower, Sir Ernest Francis Swan, 1865–1926, vol. II
Flower, Lt-Col Sir Fordham, 1904–1966, vol. VI
Flower, Major Horace John, 1883–1919, vol. II
Flower, Sir Newman; see Flower, Sir W. N.
Flower, Robin Ernest William, 1881–1946, vol. IV
Flower, Major Victor Augustine, 1875–1917, vol. II
Flower, Rev. Walker, died 1910, vol. I
Flower, Sir (Walter) Newman, 1879–1964, vol. VI
Flower, Sir William Henry, 1831–1899, vol. I
Flowerdew, Herbert, 1866–1917, vol. II
Flowerdew, Richard Edward, 1886–1971, vol. VII
Flowerdew, Spencer Pelham, 1881–1959, vol. V
Flowers, Hon. Frederick, 1864–1928, vol. II
Floyd, Alfred Ernest, 1877–1974, vol. VII
Floyd, Charles Murray, 1905–1971, vol. VII
Floyd, Brig. Sir Henry Robert Kincaid, 5th Bt, 1899–1968, vol. VI
Floyd, Captain Sir Henry Robert Peel, 4th Bt, 1855–1915, vol. I
Floyd, Major Sir John, 3rd Bt, 1823–1909, vol. I
Floyd, Sir John Duckett, 6th Bt, 1903–1975, vol. VII
Floyer-Acland, Lt-Gen. Arthur Nugent, 1885–1980, vol. VII
Fludyer, Sir Arthur John, 5th Bt, 1844–1922, vol. II
Fludyer, Col Henry, 1847–1920, vol. II
Flugel, John Carl, 1884–1955, vol. V
Flux, Sir Alfred William, 1867–1942, vol. IV
Flynn, Alfred Axen Leonard, died 1943, vol. IV
Flynn, Sir Charles Joseph, 1884–1938, vol. III
Flynn, Hon. Edmund James, 1847–1927, vol. II
Flynn, Sir J. Albert; see Flynn, Sir J(oshua) Albert.
Flynn, James Christopher, 1852–1922, vol. II
Flynn, Sir J(oshua) Albert, 1863–1933, vol. III
Flynn, Theodore Thomson, died 1968, vol. VI
Flynn, Rt Rev. Thomas Edward, 1880–1961, vol. VI
Foad, Roland Walter, 1908–1978, vol. VII
Foakes-Jackson, Rev. Frederick John, 1855–1941, vol. IV
Foch, Field-Marshal Ferdinand, 1851–1929, vol. III
Fogarty, Air Chief Marshal Sir Francis, 1899–1973, vol. VII
Fogarty, Most Rev. Michael, 1859–1955, vol. V
Fogarty, Rt Rev. Nelson Wellesley, 1871–1933, vol. III
Fogarty, Sir Reginald Francis Graham, 1892–1967, vol. VI
Fogazzaro, Antonio, 1842–1911, vol. I
Fogerty, Elsie, died 1945, vol. IV
Fogg, Charles William Eric, 1903–1939, vol. III
Fogg, Ven. Peter Parry, 1832–1920, vol. II
Fogg Elliot, Captain Mark, 1898–1950, vol. IV
Foggie, David, 1878–1948, vol. IV

Foggin, Lancelot Middleton, 1876–1968, vol. VI
Foggitt, Mrs T. J.; see Bacon, Gertrude.
Fogh, Torkel W.; see Weis-Fogh.
Fokker, A. H. G., 1890–1939, vol. III
Foletta, George Gotardo, 1892–1973, vol. VII
Foley, 5th Baron, 1850–1905, vol. I
Foley, 6th Baron, 1852–1918, vol. II
Foley, 7th Baron, 1898–1927, vol. II
Foley, Blanchard, 1869–1950, vol. IV
Foley, Most Rev. Daniel, 1865–1941, vol. IV
Foley, Sir (Ernest) Julian, 1881–1966, vol. VI
Foley, Major Francis Edward, 1884–1958, vol. V
Foley, Rear-Adm. Francis John, 1855–1911, vol. I
Foley, Col Frank Wigram, 1865–1949, vol. IV
Foley, Guy Francis, 1896–1970, vol. VI
Foley, Rt Rev. Mgr John, died 1937, vol. III
Foley, Sir Julian; see Foley, Sir E. J.
Foley, Rt Rev. Patrick, 1858–1926, vol. II
Foley, Paul Henry, 1857–1928, vol. II
Foley, Hon. Sir St George Gerald, 1814–1897, vol. I
Foley-Phillipps, Sir Richard Foley, 4th Bt, 1920–1962, vol. VI
Folger, Henry C., 1857–1930, vol. III
Folger, Col Karl Creighton, died 1941, vol. IV
Foligno, Cesare, 1878–1963, vol. VI
Foljambe, Rt Hon. Francis John Savile, 1830–1917, vol. II
Foljambe, George Savile, 1856–1920, vol. II
Folkard, Charles James, 1878–1963, vol. VI
Folkard, Henry Coleman, died 1914, vol. I
Folker, Horace S.; see Shepherd-Folker.
Foll, Hon. Hattil Spencer, 1890–1977, vol. VII
Follett, Cathleen; see Mann, C.
Follett, Sir Charles John, 1838–1921, vol. II
Follett, Lt-Col Gilbert Burrell Spencer, 1878–1918, vol. II
Follett, Lt-Col Henry Spencer, 1866–1940, vol. III
Follett, Lt-Col Robert Spencer, 1882–1941, vol. IV
Follett, Col Robert William Webb, 1844–1921, vol. II
Folley, Sydney John, 1906–1970, vol. VI
Follick, Mont, 1887–1958, vol. V
Follows, Lt-Col John Henry, 1869–1938, vol. III
Fooks, Sir Raymond Hatherell, 1888–1978, vol. VII
Foord, Francis Layton, 1874–1942, vol. IV
Foord, Rev. James, died 1932, vol. III
Foord-Kelcey, Air Vice-Marshal Alick, 1913–1973, vol. VII
Foot, Arthur Edward, 1901–1968, vol. VI
Foot, Adm. Cunningham Robert de Clare, 1864–1940, vol. III
Foot, Rt Hon. Sir Dingle Mackintosh, 1905–1978, vol. VII
Foot, Rt Hon. Isaac, 1880–1960, vol. V
Foot, Brig.-Gen. Richard Mildmay, 1865–1933, vol. III
Foot, Robert William, 1889–1973, vol. VII
Foot, Stephen Henry, 1887–1966, vol. VI
Foot, Maj.-Gen. William, 1889–1971, vol. VII
Foote, Col F. O. Barrington, 1850–1911, vol. I
Foote, John Alderson, 1848–1922, vol. II
Foote, Adm. Sir Randolph Frank Olive, 1853–1931, vol. III

Footner, Col Foster Lake, 1881–1953, vol. V

Foott, Col Cecil Henry, 1876–1942, vol. IV

Foottet, Frederick Francis, *died* 1935, vol. III

Forain, Jean Louis, 1852–1931, vol. III

Forber, Sir Edward Rodolph, 1878–1960, vol. V

Forber, Janet Elizabeth, (Lady Forber), 1877–1967, vol. VI

Forbes, 19th Lord, 1829–1914, vol. I

Forbes, 20th (styled 21st) Lord, 1841–1916, vol. II

Forbes, 21st (styled 22nd) Lord, 1882–1953, vol. V

Forbes, Alexander, 1860–1942, vol. IV

Forbes, Archibald, 1838–1900, vol. I

Forbes, Archibald Jones, 1873–1901, vol. I

Forbes, Arthur, 1843–1919, vol. II

Forbes, Maj.-Gen. Arthur, 1869–1930, vol. III

Forbes, Arthur C., 1866–1950, vol. IV

Forbes, Arthur Harold, 1885–1967, vol. VI

Forbes, Hon. Brig.-Gen. Sir Arthur William, 1858–1935, vol. III

Forbes, Athol; *see* Phillips, Rev. Forbes Alexander.

Forbes, Lt-Col Atholl Murray Hay, 1870–1942, vol. IV

Forbes, Lt-Col Hon. Bertram Aloysius, 1882–1960, vol. V

Forbes of Pitsligo, Sir Charles Hay Hepburn, 10th Bt (*cr* 1626), 1871–1927, vol. II

Forbes, Admiral of the Fleet Sir Charles Morton, 1880–1960, vol. V

Forbes, Sir Charles Stewart, 5th Bt (*cr* 1823), 1867–1927, vol. II

Forbes of Callendar, Charles William, 1871–1948, vol. IV

Forbes, Sir Courtenay; *see* Forbes, Sir V. C. W.

Forbes, Daniel, *born* 1853, vol. II

Forbes, Bt Col Hon. Donald Alexander, 1880–1938, vol. III

Forbes, Sir Douglas Stuart, 1890–1973, vol. VII

Forbes, Rev. Edward Archibald, 1869–1929, vol. III

Forbes, Elizabeth Adela, 1859–1912, vol. I

Forbes, Esther, *died* 1967, vol. VI

Forbes, Lt-Col Frederick William Dempster, 1883–1957, vol. V

Forbes, George, 1849–1936, vol. III

Forbes, Sir George Arthur D. Ogilvie-, 1891–1954, vol. V

Forbes, Sir George Stuart, 1849–1940, vol. III

Forbes, Lt-Gen. George Wentworth, 1820–1907, vol. I

Forbes, Rt Hon. George William, 1869–1947, vol. IV

Forbes, Gordon Stewart Drummond, 1868–1915, vol. I

Forbes, Most Rev. Mgr Guillaume, 1865–1940, vol. III

Forbes, Harry, 1866–1937, vol. III

Forbes, Lady Helen Emily, 1874–1926, vol. II

Forbes, Henry Ogg, 1851–1932, vol. III

Forbes of Pitsligo, Sir Hugh Stuart-, 11th Bt (*cr* 1626), 1896–1937, vol. III

Forbes, Col Ian Rose-Innes Joseph, 1875–1957, vol. V

Forbes, James, *died* 1919, vol. II

Forbes, James Graham, 1873–1941, vol. IV

Forbes, James Wright, 1866–1947, vol. IV

Forbes, (Joan) Rosita, (Mrs Arthur T. McGrath), *died* 1967, vol. VI

Forbes, John, 1838–1904, vol. I

Forbes, Gen. Sir John, 1817–1906, vol. I

Forbes, John Colin, 1846–1925, vol. II

Forbes, Lt-Col John Foster, 1835–1914, vol. I

Forbes, Col John Greenlaw, 1837–1910, vol. I

Forbes, Lt-Comdr John Hay, 1906–1940, vol. III (A), vol. IV

Forbes, John Houblon, 1852–1935, vol. III

Forbes, Rev. John T., 1857–1936, vol. III

Forbes, Air Chief Comdt Dame Katherine Jane Trefusis; *see* Watson-Watt, Air Chief Comdt Dame K. J. T.

Forbes, Mansfield Duval, 1889–1936, vol. III

Forbes, Nevill, 1883–1929, vol. III

Forbes, Captain Hon. Reginald George Benedict, 1877–1908, vol. I

Forbes, Robert Jaffrey, 1878–1958, vol. V

Forbes, Col Ronald Foster, 1881–1936, vol. III

Forbes, Rosita; *see* Forbes, J. R.

Forbes, Stanhope Alexander, 1857–1947, vol. IV

Forbes, Sir (Victor) Courtenay (Walter), 1889–1958, vol. V

Forbes, Hon. Mrs Walter R. D., (Eveline Louisa Michell), *died* 1924, vol. II

Forbes, William, 1833–1914, vol. I

Forbes, Sir William, 1856–1936, vol. III

Forbes of Pitsligo, Sir William Stuart, 9th Bt (*cr* 1626), 1835–1906 (this entry was not transferred to Who was Who).

Forbes, Brig.-Gen. Willoughby Edward Gordon, 1851–1926, vol. II

Forbes-Cockell, Seton, 1927–1971, vol. VII

Forbes-Leith of Fyvie, Col Sir Charles Rosdew, 1st Bt, 1859–1930, vol. III

Forbes-Leith of Fyvie, Sir Ian; *see* Forbes-Leith of Fyvie, Sir R. I. A.

Forbes-Leith of Fyvie, Sir (Robert) Ian (Algernon), 2nd Bt, 1902–1973, vol. VII

Forbes-Robertson, Col James, 1884–1955, vol. V

Forbes-Robertson, Jean, 1905–1962, vol. VI

Forbes-Robertson, John, 1822–1903, vol. I

Forbes-Robertson, Sir Johnston, 1853–1937, vol. III

Forbes-Sempill, Major Hon. Douglas, 1865–1908, vol. I

Forbes-Trefusis, Major Hon. John Frederick Hepburn-Stuart-; *see* Trefusis.

Ford, Ven. A. Lockett, 1853–1945, vol. IV

Ford, Col Arthur, 1834–1913, vol. I

Ford, Arthur Clow, *died* 1952, vol. V

Ford, Maj.-Gen. Barnett, *died* 1907, vol. I

Ford, Col Sir Bertram, 1869–1955, vol. V

Ford, Charles, 1844–1927, vol. II

Ford, Lt-Col Charles Hopewell, 1864–1950, vol. IV

Ford, Cdre Charles Musgrave, 1887–1974, vol. VII

Ford, Rt Hon. Sir Clare; *see* Ford, Rt Hon. Sir F. C.

Ford, Vice-Adm. Sir Denys Chester, 1890–1967, vol. VI

Ford, Edward Onslow, 1852–1901, vol. I

Ford, Ernest A. C., 1858–1919, vol. II

Ford, Rev. Ernest Robert, 1863–1942, vol. IV

Ford, Ford Madox, 1873–1939, vol. III
Ford, Sir (Francis Charles) Rupert, 5th Bt, 1877–1948, vol. IV
Ford, Rt Hon. Sir (Francis) Clare, 1830–1899, vol. I
Ford, Hon. Frank, 1873–1965, vol. VI
Ford, Ven. Frank Edward, 1902–1976, vol. VII
Ford, Col Frederick Samuel Lampson, 1869–1944, vol. IV
Ford, Rev. Gabriel Estwick, vol. II
Ford, Brig. Geoffrey Noel, 1883–1964, vol. VI
Ford, Ven. George Adam, died 1930, vol. III
Ford, Rev. George Paget, 1883–1950, vol. IV
Ford, Henry, 1863–1947, vol. IV
Ford, Henry Justice, 1860–1941, vol. IV
Ford, Hugh Alexander, 1885–1966, vol. VI
Ford, Isaac N., 1848–1912, vol. I
Ford, Sir James, 1863–1943, vol. IV
Ford, Jeremiah Denis Matthias, 1873–1958, vol. V
Ford, John, died 1917, vol. II
Ford, John, (Sean O'Feeney), 1895–1973, vol. VII
Ford, Maj.-Gen. John Randle Minshull-, 1881–1948, vol. IV
Ford, Very Rev. Lionel George Bridges Justice, 1865–1932, vol. III
Ford, Sir Patrick Johnstone, 1st Bt, 1880–1945, vol. IV
Ford, Paul Leicester, 1865–1902, vol. I
Ford, Maj.-Gen. Sir Reginald, 1868–1951, vol. V
Ford, Gen. Sir Richard Vernon Tredinnick, 1878–1949, vol. IV
Ford, Surg.-Gen. Sir Richard William, 1857–1925, vol. II
Ford, Sir Rupert; see Ford, Sir F. C. R.
Ford, Sir Theodore Thomas, 1829–1920, vol. II
Ford, Brig. Vincent Tennyson Randle, 1885–1957, vol. V
Ford, W. J., 1853–1904, vol. I
Ford, Walter Armitage Justice, 1861–1938, vol. III
Ford, Adm. Sir Wilbraham Tennyson Randle, 1880–1964, vol. VI
Ford, William, 1821–1905, vol. I
Ford, Worthington Chauncey, 1858–1941, vol. IV
Ford-Hutchinson, Lt-Col George Higginson, 1863–1933, vol. III
Forde, Lt-Col Bernard, 1865–1939, vol. III
Forde, Daryll, 1902–1973, vol. VII
Forde, Sir Henry J., 1863–1929, vol. III
Forde, Rev. Hugh, died 1929, vol. III
Forde, Col Lionel, 1860–1926, vol. II
Forde, Rt Hon. William Brownlow, 1823–1902, vol. I
Forder, Rev. Frank George, 1883–1930, vol. III
Fordham, Edward Snow, 1858–1919, vol. II
Fordham, Sir George; see Fordham, Sir H. G.
Fordham, Sir (Herbert) George, 1854–1929, vol. III
Fordham, Montague Edward, 1864–1948, vol. IV
Fordham, Lt-Col Reginald Sydney Walter, 1897–1976, vol. VII
Fordham, Brig. William Marshall, 1875–1959, vol. V
Fordyce, Alexander D.; see Dingwall-Fordyce.
Fordyce, Christian James, 1901–1974, vol. VII
Foreman, Sir Henry, 1852–1924, vol. II
Foreman, James Kenneth, 1928–1980, vol. VII

Forest Smith, John, died 1973, vol. VII
Forester, 5th Baron, 1842–1917, vol. II
Forester, 6th Baron, 1867–1932, vol. III
Forester, 7th Baron, 1899–1977, vol. VII
Forester, Cecil Scott, 1899–1966, vol. VI
Forester, Hon. Charles Cecil Orlando Weld-, 1869–1937, vol. III
Forester, Major Hon. Edric Alfred Cecil Weld-, 1880–1963, vol. VI
Forester, Francis William, 1860–1942, vol. IV
Forester, Lt-Comdr Wolstan Beaumont Charles W.; see Weld-Forester.
Forestier, Amédée, died 1930, vol. III
Forestier-Walker, Sir (Charles) Leolin, 1st Bt, 1866–1934, vol. III
Forestier-Walker, Lt-Col Claude Edward; see Walker.
Forestier-Walker, Gen. Sir Frederick William Edward Forestier; see Walker.
Forestier-Walker, Sir George Ferdinand; see Walker.
Forestier-Walker, Major Sir George Ferdinand; see Walker.
Forestier-Walker, Maj.-Gen. Sir George Townshend; see Walker.
Forestier-Walker, Sir Leolin; see Forestier-Walker, Sir C. L.
Forestier-Walker, Bt-Col Roland Stuart; see Walker.
Forgan, Very Rev. James Rae, 1876–1966, vol. VI
Forgan, Robert, 1891–1976, vol. VII
Forget, Sir Guy Joseph, 1902–1972, vol. VII
Forget, Sir (Joseph David) Rodolphe, 1861–1919, vol. II
Forget, Sir Rodolphe; see Forget, Sir J. D. R.
Forman, Rev. Adam, 1876–1977, vol. VII
Forman, Brig.-Gen. Arthur Baron, 1873–1951, vol. V
Forman, Lt-Col Douglas Evans, 1872–1949, vol. IV
Forman, E. Baxter, died 1925, vol. II
Forman, Harry Buxton, 1842–1917, vol. II
Forman, Brig. James Francis Robert, 1899–1969, vol. VI
Forman, John Calder, 1884–1975, vol. VII
Forman, Justus Miles, 1875–1915, vol. I
Forman, Rev. Thomas Pears Gordon, 1885–1965, vol. VI
Formby, George, 1904–1961, vol. VI
Formilli, Cesare T. G., died 1942, vol. IV
Formosa, Mgr Canon John, 1869–1941, vol. IV
Forneret, Ven. George Augustus, died 1927, vol. II (A), vol. III
Forrer, Ludwig, 1845–1921, vol. II
Forres, 1st Baron, 1860–1931, vol. III
Forres, 2nd Baron, 1888–1954, vol. V
Forres, 3rd Baron, 1922–1978, vol. VII
Forrest, 1st Baron, 1847–1918, vol. II
Forrest, Andrew Bryson, 1884–1951, vol. V
Forrest, Archibald Stevenson, 1869–1963, vol. VI
Forrest, Sir Charles, 5th Bt, 1857–1928, vol. II
Forrest, Major Charles Evelyn, 1876–1915, vol. I (A)
Forrest, Rev. David William, died 1918, vol. II
Forrest, George, 1922–1968, vol. VI

Forrest, Col George Atherley William, 1846–1904, vol. I
Forrest, George Topham, *died* 1945, vol. IV
Forrest, Sir George William, 1846–1926, vol. II
Forrest, Gilbert Alexander, 1912–1977, vol. VII
Forrest, Sir James, 4th Bt, 1853–1899, vol. I
Forrest, Lt-Col James, 1859–1939, vol. III
Forrest, Col John Vincent, 1873–1953, vol. V
Forrest, Sir John William, 1867–1951, vol. V
Forrest, Richard Haddow, 1908–1977, vol. VII
Forrest, Robert Edward Treston, *died* 1914, vol. I
Forrest, Very Rev. Robert William, *died* 1908, vol. I
Forrest, Sir Walter, 1869–1939, vol. III
Forrest, Lt-Col William, 1868–1921, vol. II
Forrest, Rev. William, 1867–1936, vol. III
Forrest, Gen. William Charles, 1819–1902, vol. I
Forrest, Sir William Croft, *died* 1928, vol. II
Forrestal, James, 1892–1949, vol. IV
Forrester, Charles, 1895–1980, vol. VII
Forrester, Rev. Canon John Charles, 1874–1933, vol. III
Forrester, Joseph, 1871–1967, vol. VI
Forrester, Peter, 1864–1941, vol. IV
Forrester-Brown, Maud Frances, *died* 1970, vol. VI
Forrow, Air Cdre Henry Edward, *died* 1959, vol. V
Forsdyke, Sir (Edgar) John, 1883–1979, vol. VII
Forsdyke, Sir John; *see* Forsdyke, Sir E. J.
Forsey, Charles Benjamin, 1819–1908, vol. I
Forsey, George Frank, 1889–1974, vol. VII
Forsey, Sir John, 1856–1915 vol. I
Forshaw, John Henry, 1895–1973, vol. VII
Forshaw, Thomas, 1888–1976, vol. VII
Forson, A. J., 1872–1950, vol. IV (A)
Forssmann, Werner Theodor Otto, 1904–1979, vol. VII
Forster, 1st Baron, 1866–1936, vol. III
Forster, Lady; (Rachel Cecily), *died* 1962, vol. VI
Forster of Harraby, 1st Baron, 1888–1972, vol. VII
Forster, Lt-Gen. Alfred Leonard, *died* 1963, vol. VI
Forster, Arnold John, 1885–1968, vol. VI
Forster, Very Rev. Arthur Newburgh H.; *see* Haire-Forster.
Forster, Lt-Gen. Bowes Lennox, 1837–1919, vol. II
Forster, Sir Charles, 2nd Bt (*cr* 1874), 1841–1914, vol. I
Forster, Brig. David, 1878–1959, vol. V
Forster, Edward Morgan, 1879–1970, vol. VI
Forster, Edward Seymour, 1879–1950, vol. IV
Forster, Rear-Adm. Forster Delafield A.; *see* Arnold-Forster.
Forster, Major Francis Anson A.; *see* Arnold-Forster.
Forster, Sir (Francis) Villiers, 3rd Bt (*cr* 1874), 1850–1930, vol. III
Forster, Lt-Col George Norman Bowes, 1872–1918, vol. II
Forster, Rear-Adm. Herbert Acheson, *died* 1975, vol. VII
Forster, Comdr Hugh Christopher A.; *see* Arnold-Forster.
Forster, Rt Hon. Hugh Oakeley A.; *see* Arnold-Forster.

Forster, Maj.-Gen. John Burton, 1855–1938, vol. III
Forster, John Wycliffe Lowes, *died* 1938, vol. III
Forster, Lancelot, 1882–1968, vol. VI
Forster, Sir Martin Onslow, 1872–1945, vol. IV
Forster, Lady Mary Louise Elizabeth; *see* Hamilton and Brandon, Duchess of.
Förster, Max Theodor Wilhelm, 1869–1954, vol. V
Forster, Sir Ralph Collingwood, 1st Bt (*cr* 1912), 1850–1930, vol. III
Forster, Ralph George Elliott, 1865–1931, vol. III
Forster, Sir Robert, 4th Bt (*cr* 1794), 1827–1904, vol. I
Forster, Robert Henry, 1867–1923, vol. II
Forster, Sir Sadler; *see* Forster, Sir S. A. S.
Forster, Sir (Samuel Alexander) Sadler, 1900–1973, vol. VII
Forster, Sir Samuel John, 1873–1940, vol. III
Forster, Sir Thomas Edwards, 1859–1939, vol. III
Forster, Sir Villiers; *see* Forster, Sir F. V.
Forster, Maj.-Gen. William Charles Hughan, 1874–1939, vol. III
Forster, Rev. William Thomlinson, *died* 1929, vol. III
Forster-Cooper, Sir Clive, 1880–1947, vol. IV
Forsyth, Andrew Russell, 1858–1942, vol. IV
Forsyth, Ven. David, 1845–1933, vol. III
Forsyth, David, 1877–1941, vol. IV
Forsyth, Lt-Col Fredrick Richard Gerrard, 1882–1962, vol. VI
Forsyth, Gordon M., 1879–1952, vol. V
Forsyth, Ian McMillan, 1892–1969, vol. VI
Forsyth, James Alexander, 1921–1968, vol. VI
Forsyth, Lt-Col James Archibald Charteris, *died* 1922, vol. II
Forsyth, John Andrew Cairns, 1876–1935, vol. III
Forsyth, Maj.-Gen. John Keatly, 1867–1928, vol. II
Forsyth, Neil, 1866–1915, vol. I
Forsyth, Rev. Peter Taylor, 1848–1921, vol. II
Forsyth, Robert Sutherland, 1880–1942, vol. IV
Forsyth, Thomas Miller, 1871–1958, vol. V
Forsyth, William, 1812–1899, vol. I
Forsyth, Major William Henry, 1882–1929, vol. III
Fort, George Seymour, 1858–1951, vol. V
Fort, Sir Hugh, *died* 1919, vol. II
Fort, Richard, 1856–1918, vol. II
Fort, Richard, 1907–1959, vol. V
Forte, Major Herbert Augustus Nourse, 1868–1938, vol. III
Fortescue, 3rd Earl, 1818–1905, vol. I
Fortescue, 4th Earl, 1854–1932, vol. III
Fortescue, 5th Earl, 1888–1958, vol. V
Fortescue, 6th Earl, 1893–1977, vol. VII
Fortescue, Rev. Adrian, 1874–1923, vol. II
Fortescue, Col Archer I.; *see* Irvine-Fortescue.
Fortescue, Cecil Lewis, 1881–1949, vol. IV
Fortescue, Brig.-Gen. Hon. Charles Granville, 1861–1951, vol. V
Fortescue, Hon. Dudley Francis, 1820–1909, vol. I
Fortescue, Brig.-Gen. Francis Alexander, 1858–1942, vol. IV
Fortescue, George Knottesford, 1847–1912, vol. I
Fortescue, John Bevill, 1850–1938, vol. III

Fortescue, Hon. Sir John William, 1859–1933, vol. III
Fortescue, Laurence Knottesford-, 1845–1924, vol. II
Fortescue, Captain Hon. Sir Seymour John, 1856–1942, vol. IV
Fortescue, Rev. Vincent, 1849–1932, vol. III
Fortescue, Hon. Lady; (Winifred), 1888–1951, vol. V
Fortescue-Brickdale, Sir Charles, 1857–1944, vol. IV
Fortescue-Brickdale, Eleanor, died 1945, vol. IV
Fortescue-Brickdale, John Matthew, died 1921, vol. II
Fortescue-Flannery, Sir James, 1st Bt, 1851–1943, vol. IV
Forteviot, 1st Baron, 1856–1929, vol. III
Forteviot, 2nd Baron, 1885–1947, vol. IV
Forth, Francis Charles, died 1919, vol. II
Forth, Lt-Col Nowell Barnard De Lancey; see De Lancey Forth.
Fortin, Ven. Octave, 1842–1927, vol. II
Fortington, Harold Augustus, 1890–1944, vol. IV
Fortnum, Charles Drury Edward, 1820–1899, vol. I
Fortune, Allan Stewart, 1895–1975, vol. VII
Fortune, Maj.-Gen. Sir Victor Morven, 1883–1949, vol. IV
Forward, Ernest Alfred, 1877–1959, vol. V
Forwood, Rt Hon. Sir Arthur Bower, 1st Bt, 1836–1898, vol. I
Forwood, Sir Dudley Baines, 2nd Bt, 1875–1961, vol. VI
Forwood, Sir William Bower, 1840–1928, vol. II
Fosbery, Hon. Edmund Walcott, 1834–1919, vol. II
Fosbery, Lt-Col George Vincent, died 1907, vol. I
Fosbery, Major Widenham Francis Widenham, 1869–1935, vol. III
Fosbrooke, Ven. Henry Leonard, died 1950, vol. IV
Fosdick, Rev. Harry Emerson, 1878–1969, vol. VI
Fosdick, Raymond Blaine, 1883–1969, vol. VI
Foskett, Rt Rev. Reginald, 1909–1973, vol. VII
Foss, Brig. Charles Calveley, 1885–1953, vol. V
Foss, Hubert James, 1899–1953, vol. V
Foss, Rt Rev. Hugh James, 1848–1932, vol. III
Foster, Sir (Albert) Ridgeby, 1907–1973, vol. VII
Foster, Alfred Edye Manning, died 1939, vol. III
Foster, Col Alfred James, 1864–1959, vol. V
Foster, Captain Alwyn, 1874–1953, vol. V
Foster, Rev. Arthur Austin, 1869–1942, vol. IV
Foster, Lt-Col Arthur Wellesley, 1855–1929, vol. III
Foster, Sir Augustus Vere, 4th Bt (cr 1831), 1873–1947, vol. IV
Foster, Sir Berkeley; see Foster, Sir H. W. B.
Foster, Birket, 1825–1899, vol. I
Foster, Rev. Canon Charles, 1907–1972, vol. VII
Foster, Rev. Charles Wilmer, 1866–1935, vol. III
Foster, Sir Clement Le Neve, 1841–1904, vol. I
Foster, Captain Sir Edward, 1881–1958, vol. V
Foster, Edward William Perceval, 1850–1932, vol. III
Foster, Ernest, died 1919, vol. II

Foster, Very Rev. Ernest, 1867–1925, vol. II
Foster, E(rnest) Marshall, 1907–1970, vol. VI
Foster, F(ermian) Le Neve, 1888–1972, vol. VII
Foster, Francis; see Foster, Major R. F.
Foster, Sir Frank Savin, 1879–1964, vol. VI
Foster, Geoffrey Norman, 1884–1971, vol. VII
Foster, George Carey, 1835–1919, vol. II
Foster, Rt Hon. Sir George Eulas, 1847–1931, vol. III
Foster, Hon. George G., 1860–1931, vol. III
Foster, George Ralph Cunliffe, 1869–1936, vol. III
Foster, Gilbert, 1855–1906, vol. I
Foster, Maj.-Gen. Gilbert Lafayette, 1874–1940, vol. III
Foster, Gordon Bentley, 1885–1963, vol. VI
Foster, Sir Gregory; see Foster, Sir T. G.
Foster, Lt-Col Harold William Alexander, died 1960, vol. V
Foster, Rt Hon. Sir Harry Braustyn Hylton H.; see Hylton-Foster.
Foster, Sir Harry Seymour, 1855–1938, vol. III
Foster, Maj.-Gen. Henry Nedham, 1878–1951, vol. V
Foster, Sir (Henry William) Berkeley, 4th Bt (cr 1838), 1892–1960, vol. V
Foster, Herbert Anderton, 1853–1930, vol. III
Foster, Rev. Herbert Charles, died 1926, vol. II
Foster, Rev. Canon Herbert Henry, 1864–1927, vol. II
Foster, Sir Hugh Matheson, 1886–1955, vol. V
Foster, Ivor, 1870–1959, vol. V
Foster, Rev. James, died 1926, vol. II
Foster, John, 1832–1910, vol. I
Foster, Rev. John, 1898–1973, vol. VII
Foster, John Frederick, 1903–1975, vol. VII
Foster, Maj.-Gen. John Hulbert, 1925–1980, vol. VII
Foster, (John) Kenneth, died 1930, vol. III
Foster, John Stuart, 1890–1964, vol. VI
Foster, John Watson, 1836–1917, vol. II
Foster, Joseph, 1844–1905, vol. I
Foster, Joshua James, died 1923, vol. II
Foster, Kenneth; see Foster, J. K.
Foster, Leslie Thomas, 1905–1979, vol. VII
Foster, Sir Michael, 1836–1907, vol. I
Foster, Michael George, 1864–1934, vol. III
Foster, Major Montagu Amos, 1861–1940, vol. III
Foster, Sir Montagu Richard William, died 1935, vol. III
Foster, Muriel, died 1937, vol. III
Foster, Sir Norris Tildasley, 1855–1925, vol. II
Foster, Major Percy John, 1873–1969, vol. VI
Foster, Philip Stanley, 1885–1965, vol. VI
Foster, Philip Staveley, 1865–1933, vol. III
Foster, Major Reginald Francis, 1896–1975, vol. VII
Foster, Gen. Sir Richard Foster Carter, 1879–1965, vol. V
Foster, Hon. Richard Witty, 1856–1932, vol. III
Foster, Sir Ridgeby; see Foster, Sir A. R.
Foster, Robert Frederick, 1853–1945, vol. IV
Foster, Robert John, 1850–1925, vol. II
Foster, Air Chief Marshal Sir Robert Mordaunt, 1898–1973, vol. VII

Foster, Robert Spence, 1891–1947, vol. IV
Foster, Sidney, 1885–1958, vol. V
Foster, Brig. Thomas Francis Vere, 1885–1967, vol. VI
Foster, Sir (Thomas) Gregory, 1st Bt (*cr* 1930), *died* 1931, vol. III
Foster, Thomas Henry, 1888–1970, vol. VI
Foster, Sir Thomas Saxby Gregory, 2nd Bt (*cr* 1930), 1899–1957, vol. V
Foster, Sir Tom Scott, 1845–1918, vol. II
Foster, Brig.-Gen. Turville Douglas, 1865–1915, vol. I
Foster, Vere, 1819–1900, vol. I
Foster, Major Wilfrid Lionel, 1874–1958, vol. V
Foster, Sir William, 2nd Bt (*cr* 1838), 1825–1911, vol. I
Foster, William, 1887–1947, vol. IV
Foster, Sir William, 1863–1951, vol. V
Foster, Sir William Edward, 1846–1921, vol. II
Foster, Air Vice-Marshal William Foster Mac-Neece, 1889–1978, vol. VII
Foster, Col William Henry, 1848–1908, vol. I
Foster, William Henry, 1846–1924, vol. II
Foster, Bt-Col William James, 1881–1927, vol. II
Foster, Maj.-Gen. William Wasbrough, *died* 1954, vol. V
Foster, Sir William Yorke, 3rd Bt (*cr* 1838), 1860–1948, vol. IV
Foster Pegg, Rev. Canon Henry, 1857–1940, vol. III
Foster-Skeffington, Hon. Oriel John Clotworthy Whyte-Melville; *see* Skeffington.
Foster-Vesey-Fitzgerald, James; *see* Fitzgerald.
Fothergill, (Charles) Philip, 1906–1959, vol. V
Fothergill, John Rowland, 1876–1957, vol. V
Fothergill, Philip; *see* Fothergill, C. P.
Fothergill, William Edward, 1865–1926, vol. II
Fotheringham, Rev. David Ross, 1872–1939, vol. III
Fotheringham, John Knight, 1874–1936, vol. III
Fotheringham, John Taylor, 1860–1940, vol. III (A), vol. IV
Fothringham, Walter Thomas James S. S.; *see* Scrymsoure-Steuart-Fothringham.
Fottrell, Sir George, 1849–1925, vol. II
Fouché, Jacobus Johannes, 1898–1980, vol. VII
Fouché, Leo, 1880–1949, vol. IV
Fouhy, David Emmet, 1891–1967, vol. VI
Foulds, John H., *died* 1939, vol. III
Foulds, Linton Harry, 1897–1952, vol. V
Foulerton, Alexander Grant Russell, 1863–1931, vol. III
Foulger, Robert Edward, 1899–1969, vol. VI
Foulis, Sir Archibald Charles Liston, 12th Bt, 1903–1961, vol. VI
Foulis, Sir Charles James Liston, 11th Bt, 1873–1936, vol. III
Foulis, Douglas Ainslie, 1885–1969, vol. VI
Foulis, Sir William Liston-, 10th Bt, 1869–1918, vol. II
Foulkes, Gen. Charles, 1903–1969, vol. VI
Foulkes, Maj.-Gen. Charles Howard, 1875–1969, vol. VI
Foulkes, Hedworth; *see* Foulkes, P. H.

Foulkes, P. Hedworth, 1871–1965, vol. VI
Foulsham, Sir Charles Sidney, 1892–1955, vol. V
Fountain, Sir Henry, 1870–1957, vol. V
Fountaine, Vice-Adm. Charles Andrew, 1879–1946, vol. IV
Fournier d'Albe, Edmund Edward, 1868–1933, vol. III
Foweraker, A. Moulton, 1873–1942, vol. IV
Fowke, Frank Rede, 1847–1927, vol. II (A), vol. III
Fowke, Sir Frederick Ferrers Conant, 3rd Bt, 1879–1948, vol. IV
Fowke, Sir Frederick Thomas, 2nd Bt, 1816–1897, vol. I
Fowke, Lt-Gen. Sir George Henry, 1864–1936, vol. III
Fowke, Villiers Loftus Philip, 1887–1940, vol. III
Fowkes, Maj.-Gen. Charles Christopher, 1894–1966, vol. VI
Fowlds, Hon. Sir George, 1860–1934, vol. III
Fowle, Brig. Francis Ernlé, 1893–1969, vol. VI
Fowle, Col Frederick Trenchard Thomas, 1853–1914, vol. I
Fowle, Col Sir (Henry) Walter Hamilton, 1871–1954, vol. V
Fowle, Col John, 1862–1923, vol. II
Fowle, Brig. John Le Clerc, 1893–1978, vol. VII
Fowle, Col Thomas Ernlé, 1862–1932, vol. III
Fowle, Sir Trenchard Craven William, 1884–1940, vol. III
Fowle, Col Sir Walter Hamilton; *see* Fowle, Col Sir H. W. H.
Fowler, Alfred, 1868–1940, vol. III
Fowler, Maj.-Gen. Charles Astley, 1865–1940, vol. III
Fowler, Lt Charles Wilson, 1859–1907, vol. I
Fowler, Adm. Cole Cortlandt, *died* 1936, vol. III
Fowler, Lt-Col Edward Gardiner, 1879–1953, vol. V
Fowler, Hon. Ellen Thorneycroft, *died* 1929, vol. III
Fowler, Maj.-Gen. Francis John, 1864–1939, vol. III
Fowler, George Herbert, 1861–1940, vol. III
Fowler, Sir George Jefford, 1858–1937, vol. III
Fowler, George Merrick, 1852–1935, vol. III
Fowler, Harold North, 1859–1955, vol. V
Fowler, Sir Henry, 1870–1938, vol. III
Fowler, Henry Watson, 1858–1933, vol. III
Fowler, Sir James Kingston, 1852–1934, vol. III
Fowler, James Stewart, 1870–1925, vol. II
Fowler, Sir John, 1st Bt (*cr* 1890), 1817–1898, vol. I
Fowler, Sir John Arthur, 2nd Bt (*cr* 1890), 1854–1899, did not have an entry in Who's Who.
Fowler, Sir John Edward, 3rd Bt (*cr* 1890), 1885–1915, vol. I
Fowler, Lt-Gen. Sir John Sharman, 1864–1939, vol. III
Fowler, Rev. Joseph Thomas, 1833–1924, vol. II
Fowler, Matthew, 1845–1898, vol. I
Fowler, Rev. Sir Montague, 4th Bt (*cr* 1890), 1858–1933, vol. III
Fowler, Sir Ralph Howard, 1889–1944, vol. IV
Fowler, Rees John, 1894–1974, vol. VII

Fowler, Robert, *died* 1926, vol. II
Fowler, Robert MacLaren, 1906–1980, vol. VII
Fowler, Sir Thomas, 2nd Bt (*cr* 1885), 1868–1902, vol. I
Fowler, Rev. Thomas, *died* 1904, vol. I
Fowler, Walter B.; *see* Burroughs-Fowler.
Fowler, William, 1828–1905, vol. I
Fowler, William Hope, 1876–1933, vol. III
Fowler, William Warde, 1847–1921, vol. II
Fowler, Rev. William Weekes, 1849–1923, vol. II
Fowler-Butler, Lt-Col Richard, 1865–1931, vol. III
Fowler-Butler, Maj.-Gen. Robert Henry, 1838–1919, vol. II
Fowler-Dixon, John Edwin, 1850–1943, vol. IV
Fowweather, Frank Scott, 1892–1980, vol. VII
Fox, Rev. Canon Adam, 1883–1977, vol. VII
Fox, Lt-Col Arthur Claude, 1868–1917, vol. II
Fox, Arthur Wilson, 1861–1909, vol. I
Fox, Ven. (Benjamin) George (Burton), 1913–1978, vol. VII
Fox, Bernard Joshua, 1885–1977, vol. VII
Fox, Major Brabazon Hubert Maine, 1868–1940, vol. III
Fox, Rear-Adm. Cecil Henry, 1873–1963, vol. VI
Fox, Captain Charles, 1890–1977, vol. VII
Fox, Sir (Charles) Douglas, 1840–1921, vol. II
Fox, Sir Charles Edmund, 1854–1918, vol. II
Fox, Lt-Col Charles J., 1857–1930, vol. III
Fox, Major Charles Vincent, 1877–1928, vol. II
Fox, Sir Cyril Fred, 1882–1967, vol. VI
Fox, Sir Cyril Sankey, 1886–1951, vol. V
Fox, Sir Douglas; *see* Fox, Sir C. D.
Fox, Douglas Gerard Arthur, 1893–1978, vol. VII
Fox, Hon. Mrs Eleanor Birch W.; *see* Wilson-Fox.
Fox, Dame Evelyn Emily Marion, 1874–1955, vol. V
Fox, Sir Francis, 1844–1927, vol. II
Fox, Sir Frank, 1874–1960, vol. V
Fox, Ven. George; *see* Fox, Ven. B. G. B.
Fox, Rev. George, *died* 1911, vol. I
Fox, Sir Gifford Wheaton Grey, 2nd Bt, 1903–1959, vol. V
Fox, Sir Gilbert Wheaton, 1st Bt, 1863–1925, vol. II
Fox, H. B. Earle, *died* 1920, vol. II
Fox, Harold Munro, 1889–1967, vol. VI
Fox, Sir Harry Halton, 1872–1936, vol. III
Fox, Henry Benedict, 1875–1944, vol. IV
Fox, Rev. Henry Elliott, 1841–1926, vol. II
Fox, Henry Wilson-, 1863–1921, vol. II
Fox, Sir John, 1882–1970, vol. VI
Fox, Sir John Charles, 1855–1943, vol. IV
Fox, Major John Charles Ker, 1851–1929, vol. III
Fox, John Howard, 1864–1951, vol. V
Fox, Sir John Jacob, 1874–1944, vol. IV
Fox, John Junior, 1863–1919, vol. II
Fox, Major Sir John St Vigor, 1879–1968, vol. VI
Fox, John Scott, 1852–1918, vol. II
Fox, John Shirley S.; *see* Shirley-Fox.
Fox, Joscelyn Plunket B.; *see* Bushe-Fox.
Fox, Sir Lionel Wray, 1895–1961, vol. VI
Fox, Loftus Henry Kendal B.; *see* Bushe-Fox.
Fox, Col Sir Malcolm, 1843–1918, vol. II
Fox, R. Fortescue, *died* 1940, vol. III

Fox, Richard Hodding, 1876–1966, vol. VI
Fox, Robert Barclay, 1873–1934, vol. III
Fox, Sir Robert Eyes, 1861–1924, vol. II
Fox, Brig.-Gen. Robert Fanshawe, 1862–1939, vol. III
Fox, Sir Sidney Joseph, *died* 1962, vol. VI
Fox, Terence Robert Corelli, 1912–1962, vol. VI
Fox, Thomas Colcott, 1849–1916, vol. II
Fox, Rt Rev. Thomas Martin, 1893–1967, vol. VI (AII)
Fox, Surg.-Gen. Thomas William, 1830–1908, vol. I
Fox, Uffa, 1898–1972, vol. VII
Fox, Wilfrid S., *died* 1962, vol. VI
Fox, William Sherwood, 1878–1967, vol. VI
Fox-Andrews, Norman Roy, 1894–1971, vol. VII
Fox-Davies, Arthur Charles, 1871–1928, vol. II
Fox-Pitt, Douglas, *died* 1922, vol. II
Fox-Pitt-Rivers, Augustus Henry Lane, 1820–1900, vol. I
Fox-Strangways, Maurice Walter, 1862–1938, vol. III
Fox-Symons, Sir Robert, 1870–1932, vol. III
Fox-Williams, Jack, 1893–1970, vol. VI
Foxcroft, Captain Charles Talbot, *died* 1929, vol. III
Foxcroft, Frederick Walter, 1858–1916, vol. II
Foxcroft, Miss H. C., *died* 1950, vol. IV
Foxell, Rev. William James, 1857–1933, vol. III
Foxlee, Richard William, 1885–1961, vol. VI
Foxley, Barbara, *died* 1958, vol. V
Foxton, Col Hon. Justin Fox Greenlaw, 1849–1916, vol. I, vol. II
Foxwell, Arthur, 1853–1909, vol. I
Foxwell, Herbert Somerton, 1849–1936, vol. III
Foy, Ernest Rudolph, *died* 1951, vol. V
Foy, Hon. James Joseph, 1847–1916, vol. II
Foy, Sir Thomas Arthur Wyness, 1895–1971, vol. VII
Foylan, Rt Rev. Michael, 1907–1976, vol. VII
Foyle, Gilbert Samuel, 1886–1971, vol. VII
Foyle, William Alfred, 1885–1963, vol. VI
Fraenkel, Eduard, 1888–1970, vol. VI
Frames, Col Percival R.; *see* Ross-Frames.
Frampton, Algernon de Kewer, 1904–1974, vol. VII
Frampton, E. Reginald, *died* 1923, vol. II
Frampton, Sir George James, 1860–1928, vol. II
Frampton, Henry James, 1897–1980, vol. VII
Frampton, Rev. Samuel, 1862–1943, vol. IV
Frampton, Walter, 1871–1939, vol. III
France, Anatole; *see* France, J. A. T.
France, Captain George Frederick Hayhurst H.; *see* Hayhurst-France.
France, Gerald Ashburner, 1870–1935, vol. III
France, (Jacques) Anatole (Thibault), 1844–1924, vol. II
France, Rev. Canon Walter Frederick, 1887–1963, vol. VI
France-Hayhurst, William Hosken; *see* Hayhurst.
Francia, Col John Lewis, 1864–1934, vol. III
Francillon, Robert Edward, 1841–1919, vol. II
Francis, Arthur Gordon, 1880–1958, vol. V
Francis, Augustus Lawrence, 1848–1925, vol. II
Francis, Sir Brooke; *see* Francis, Sir C. G. B.

Francis, Lt-Col Charles John Henry Watson, 1879–1959, vol. V
Francis, Charles King, 1851–1925, vol. II
Francis, Sir (Cyril Gerard) Brooke, 1883–1971, vol. VII
Francis, Francis, died 1941, vol. IV
Francis, Grant Richardson, 1868–1940, vol. III (A), vol. IV
Francis, Very Rev. Henry, died 1924, vol. II
Francis, Herbert William Sidney, 1880–1968, vol. VI
Francis, James Schreiber, 1843–1915, vol. I
Francis, Sir John, 1864–1937, vol. III
Francis, Major John, 1879–1960, vol. V
Francis, Lt-Col John Clement Wolstan, 1888–1978, vol. VII
Francis, John Collins, 1838–1916, vol. II
Francis, John Gordon Loveband, 1907–1976, vol. VII
Francis, Rt Rev. Joseph Marshall, 1862–1939, vol. III
Francis, Hon. Sir Josiah, 1890–1964, vol. VI
Francis, M. E.; see Blundell, Mrs F.
Francis, Major Norton, 1871–1939, vol. III
Francis, Richard Henry, 1897–1961, vol. VI
Francis, Brig.-Gen. Sidney Goodall, 1874–1955, vol. V
Francis-Williams, Baron (Life Peer); Edward Francis Williams, 1903–1970, vol. VI
Francis-Williams, William St John, 1871–1930, vol. III
Franck, Harry Alverson, 1881–1962, vol. VI
Franck, James, 1882–1964, vol. VI
Franck, Sir Louis, 1868–1937, vol. III
Francke, Paul Mortimer, 1866–1929, vol. III
Franckenstein, Sir George, 1878–1953, vol. V
Francklin, John Liell, 1844–1915, vol. I (A)
Francklin, Captain Philip, died 1914, vol. I
Franco Bahamonde, General Don Francisco, 1892–1975, vol. VII
François-Poncet, André, 1887–1978, vol. VII
Franey, John Sharman, 1864–1947, vol. IV
Frangulis, A. F., 1888–1975, vol. VII
Frank, Bruno, 1887–1945, vol. IV
Frank, Glenn, 1887–1940, vol. III
Frank, Sir Howard, 1st Bt, 1871–1932, vol. III
Frank, Sir Howard Frederick, 2nd Bt, 1923–1944, vol. IV
Frank, Leonhard, 1882–1961, vol. VI
Frank, Sir Peirson; see Frank, Sir T. P.
Frank, Tenney, 1876–1939, vol. III
Frank, Sir (Thomas) Peirson, 1881–1951, vol. V
Frankau, Sir Claude Howard Stanley, 1883–1967, vol. VI
Frankau, Captain Gilbert, 1884–1952, vol. V
Frankau, Mrs Julia; see Danby, Frank.
Frankau, Pamela, 1908–1967, vol. VI
Frankel, Benjamin, 1906–1973, vol. VII
Frankfort de Montmorency, 3rd Viscount, 1835–1902, vol. I
Frankfort de Montmorency, 4th Viscount, 1868–1917, vol. II
Frankfort, Henri, 1897–1954, vol. V
Frankfurter, Felix, 1882–1965, vol. VI

Frankland, Cecil J., 1884–1942, vol. IV
Frankland, Sir Edward, 1825–1899, vol. I
Frankland, Edward Percy, 1884–1958, vol. V
Frankland, Sir Frederick William Francis George, 10th Bt, 1868–1937, vol. III
Frankland, Grace C., (Mrs Percy Frankland), 1858–1946, vol. IV
Frankland, Percy Faraday, 1858–1946, vol. IV
Frankland, Major Hon. Sir Thomas William Assheton, 11th Bt, 1902–1944, vol. IV
Frankland-Payne-Gallwey, Sir John; see Gallwey.
Frankland-Russell-Astley, Bertram Frankland; see Astley.
Frankland-Russell-Astley, Henry Jacob Delaval; see Astley.
Franklen, Sir Thomas Mansel, 1840–1928, vol. II
Franklin, Arthur Ellis, 1857–1938, vol. III
Franklin, Surg.-Gen. Sir Benjamin, 1844–1917, vol. II
Franklin, David, 1908–1973, vol. VII
Franklin, Ernest Louis, 1859–1950, vol. IV
Franklin, Fabian, died 1939, vol. III
Franklin, Sir George, 1853–1916, vol. II
Franklin, George Cooper, 1846–1919, vol. II
Franklin, Bt-Col George Denne, 1877–1946, vol. IV
Franklin, Brig.-Gen. Harold Scott Erskine, 1878–1948, vol. IV
Franklin, Hon. Mrs Henrietta, 1866–1964, vol. VI
Franklin, Hon. James Thomas, 1854–1940, vol. III
Franklin, John Lewis, 1904–1972, vol. VII
Franklin, Kenneth James, 1897–1966, vol. VI
Franklin, Sir Leonard, 1862–1944, vol. IV
Franklin, Philip, died 1951, vol. V
Franklin, Sir Reginald Hector, 1893–1957, vol. V
Franklin, Richard Penrose, 1884–1942, vol. IV
Franklin, Col Will Hodgson, 1871–1941, vol. IV
Frankling, Herbert George, 1876–1962, vol. VI
Franklyn, Brig. Geoffrey Ernest Warren, 1889–1967, vol. VI
Franklyn, Gen. Sir Harold Edmund, 1885–1963, vol. VI
Franklyn, Lt-Gen. Sir William Edmund, 1856–1914, vol. I
Franks, Sir Augustus Wollaston, 1826–1897, vol. I
Franks, Lt-Col George Despard, died 1918, vol. II
Franks, Maj.-Gen. Sir George McKenzie, 1868–1958, vol. V
Franks, Sir John Hamilton, 1848–1915, vol. I
Franks, Sir Kendal, 1851–1920, vol. II
Franks, Col Kendal Fergusson, 1886–1944, vol. IV
Franks, Captain Norman, 1843–1923, vol. II
Franks, Rev. Robert Sleightholme, 1871–1964, vol. VI
Franks, Maj.-Gen. William Astell, 1838–1929, vol. III
Franks, William Temple, 1863–1926, vol. II
Franqueville, Amable Charles Franquet, Comte de, 1840–1919, vol. II
Fransella, Albert, died 1935, vol. III
Franzos, Carl Emile, 1848–1904, vol. I
Fraser of Allander, 1st Baron, 1903–1966, vol. VI
Fraser of Lonsdale, Baron (Life Peer); William Jocelyn Ian Fraser, 1897–1974, vol. VII

Fraser, Agnes Frances MacNab, 1859–1944, vol. IV

Fraser, Major Hon. Alastair Thomas Joseph, 1877–1949, vol. IV

Fraser, Alexander Brodie, 1871–1936, vol. III

Fraser, Alexander Campbell, 1819–1914, vol. I

Fraser, Maj.-Gen. Alexander Donald, 1884–1960, vol. V

Fraser, Rev. Alexander Garden, 1873–1962, vol. VI

Fraser, Sir Andrew Henderson Leith, 1848–1919, vol. II

Fraser, Mrs Angela Zelia, (Alice Spinner), died 1925, vol. II

Fraser, Sir Angus, 1909–1963, vol. VI

Fraser, Major Arthur Ion, 1879–1917, vol. II

Fraser, Sir (Arthur) Ronald, 1888–1974, vol. VII

Fraser, Lt-Col Cecil, 1885–1951, vol. V

Fraser, Sir Charles Frederick, 1850–1925, vol. II

Fraser, Charles Ian, 1903–1963, vol. VI

Fraser, Sir Colin, 1875–1944, vol. IV

Fraser, Colin Neil, 1905–1979, vol. VII

Fraser, Hon. Sir David MacDowall, 1825–1906, vol. I

Fraser, Lt-Col Sir Denholm de Montalt Stuart, 1889–1956, vol. V

Fraser, Very Rev. Donald, 1870–1933, vol. III

Fraser, Sir Drummond Drummond, 1867–1929, vol. III

Fraser, Rev. Duncan, 1814–1912, vol. I

Fraser, Duncan, 1880–1966, vol. VI

Fraser, Very Rev. Duncan, 1903–1977, vol. VII

Fraser, Surg.-Maj.-Gen. Duncan Alexander Campbell, 1831–1912, vol. I

Fraser, Sir Edward Cleather, 1853–1927, vol. II

Fraser, Sir Edward Henry, 1851–1921, vol. II

Fraser, Eric Malcolm, 1896–1960, vol. V, vol. VI

Fraser, Sir Everard Duncan Home, 1859–1922, vol. II

Fraser, Francis Charles, 1903–1978, vol. VII

Fraser, Sir Francis Richard, 1885–1964, vol. VI

Fraser, Frederick William, 1870–1936, vol. III

Fraser, Galloway, died 1925, vol. II

Fraser, Rear-Adm. Hon. George, 1887–1970, vol. VI

Fraser, Col George Ireland, 1876–1929, vol. III

Fraser, George M., 1862–1938, vol. III

Fraser, Gilbert, born 1848, vol. II

Fraser, Sir Gordon, 1873–1934, vol. III

Fraser, Captain Gordon Colquhoun, 1866–1952, vol. V

Fraser, Hanson Werry, 1850–1929, vol. III

Fraser, Col Henry Francis, 1872–1949, vol. IV

Fraser, Henry Lumsden Forbes, 1877–1951, vol. V

Fraser, Henry Ralph, 1896–1963, vol. VI

Fraser, Col Herbert Cecil, died 1943, vol. IV

Fraser, Col Howard Alan Denholm, 1867–1948, vol. IV

Fraser, Hon. Sir Hugh, died 1927, vol. II

Fraser, Mrs Hugh, died 1922, vol. II (A), vol. III

Fraser, Air Vice-Marshal Hugh Henry Macleod, 1895–1962, vol. VI

Fraser, Sir Hugh Stein, 1863–1944, vol. IV

Fraser, Ian George Inglis, 1923–1980, vol. VII

Fraser, Captain Ian Mackenzie, 1854–1922, vol. II

Fraser, Rev. James, 1842–1913, vol. I

Fraser, James, 1861–1936, vol. III

Fraser, Rev. James, 1883–1966, vol. VI

Fraser, James Alexander L.; see Lovat-Fraser.

Fraser, James Duncan, 1915–1965, vol. VI

Fraser, Lt-Col James Johnson, 1876–1939, vol. III

Fraser, Lt-Col James Wilson, 1862–1943, vol. IV

Fraser, John, 1820–1911, vol. I

Fraser, John, born 1852, vol. II

Fraser, John, died 1925, vol. II

Fraser, John, 1882–1945, vol. IV

Fraser, Sir John, 1st Bt (cr 1943), 1885–1947, vol. IV

Fraser, Lt-Col John Edward, 1877–1934, vol. III

Fraser, Sir John Foster, 1868–1936, vol. III

Fraser, Sir John George, 1840–1927, vol. II (A)

Fraser, Sir John George, 1864–1941, vol. IV

Fraser, John Henry Pearson, 1874–1949, vol. IV

Fraser, Sir John Hugh Ronald, 1878–1943, vol. IV

Fraser, Sir (John) Malcolm, 1st Bt (cr 1921), 1878–1949, vol. IV

Fraser, Rear-Adm. John Stewart Gordon, 1883–1973, vol. VII

Fraser, Kate, 1877–1957, vol. V

Fraser, Major Sir Keith Alexander, 5th Bt (cr 1806), 1867–1935, vol. III

Fraser, Sir Keith Charles Adolphus, 6th Bt (cr 1806), 1911–1979, vol. VII

Fraser, Kenneth, 1874–1941, vol. IV

Fraser, Sir Kenneth Barron, 1897–1969, vol. VI

Fraser, Leon, 1889–1945, vol. IV

Fraser, Lindley Macnaghten, 1904–1963, vol. VI

Fraser, Lovat, 1871–1926, vol. II

Fraser, Brig.-Gen. Lyons David, 1868–1926, vol. II

Fraser, Sir Malcolm; see Fraser, Sir J. M.

Fraser, Hon. Sir Malcolm, died 1900, vol. I

Fraser, Malcolm, 1873–1949, vol. IV

Fraser, Marjory Kennedy, died 1930, vol. III

Fraser, Mary, died 1940, vol. III

Fraser, Sir Matthew Pollock, died 1937, vol. III

Fraser, Captain Norman, 1879–1914, vol. I

Fraser, Rt Hon. Peter, 1884–1950, vol. IV

Fraser, Rt Rev. Robert, 1858–1914, vol. I

Fraser, Ronald; see Fraser, Sir A. R.

Fraser, Hon. Sir Simon, 1832–1919, vol. II

Fraser, Sir Stuart Mitford, 1864–1963, vol. VI

Fraser, Maj.-Gen. Sir Theodore, 1865–1953, vol. V

Fraser, Maj.-Gen. Sir Thomas, 1840–1922, vol. II

Fraser, Col Thomas, 1872–1951, vol. V

Fraser, Sir Thomas Richard, 1841–1920, vol. II

Fraser, Sir William, 1816–1898, vol. I

Fraser, Rev. William, 1851–1919, vol. II

Fraser, Hon. Sir William, 1840–1923, vol. II

Fraser, Brig. Hon. William, 1890–1964, vol. VI

Fraser, William Alexander, died 1933, vol. III

Fraser, Maj.-Gen. William Archibald Kenneth, 1886–1969, vol. VI

Fraser, Sir William Augustus, 4th Bt (cr 1806), 1826–1898, vol. I

Fraser, William Donald, 1890–1941, vol. IV

Fraser, William Henry, 1853–1916, vol. II

Fraser, William Henry, died 1966, vol. VI

Fraser, W(illiam) Lionel, died 1965, vol. VI

Fraser, William Stuart, 1876–1954, vol. V

Fraser Darling, Sir Frank, 1903–1979, vol. VII
Fraser-Harris, David Fraser, 1867–1937, vol. III
Fraser-Simson, Harold, 1878–1944, vol. IV
Fraser-Tytler, Edward Grant, 1856–1918, vol. II
Fraser-Tytler, Sir James Macleod Bannatyne, 1821–1914, vol. I
Fraser-Tytler, Bt Col Neil, 1889–1937, vol. III
Fraser-Tytler, Lt-Col Sir William Kerr, 1886–1963, vol. VI
Frayling, Frederick George, *born* 1846, vol. II
Frazer, Alastair Campbell, 1909–1969, vol. VI
Frazer, Hon. Charles Edward, 1880–1913, vol. I
Frazer, Hon. Sir Francis Vernon, 1880–1948, vol. IV
Frazer, Col George Stanley, 1865–1950, vol. IV (A), vol. V
Frazer, Sir James George, 1854–1941, vol. IV
Frazer, John Ernest Sullivan, 1870–1946, vol. IV
Frazer, Robert, 1878–1947, vol. IV
Frazer, Robert Alexander, 1891–1959, vol. V
Frazer, Robert Watson, 1854–1921, vol. II
Frazer, Sir Thomas, 1884–1969, vol. VI
Frazer, William Miller, 1864–1961, vol. VI
Frazer, William Mowll, 1888–1958, vol. V
Freake, Sir Charles Arland Maitland, 4th Bt, 1904–1951, vol. V
Freake, Sir Frederick Charles Maitland, 3rd Bt, 1876–1950, vol. IV
Freake, Sir Thomas George, 2nd Bt, 1848–1920, vol. II
Fream, William, *died* 1906, vol. I
Fréchette, Achille, 1847–1927, vol. II
Frechette, Louis, 1839–1908, vol. I
Frecheville, William, 1854–1940, vol. III
Frederic, Harold, 1856–1898, vol. I
Frederick, Lt-Col Sir Charles Arthur Andrew, 1861–1913, vol. I
Frederick, Sir Charles Edward, 7th Bt, 1843–1913 (this entry was not transferred to Who was Who).
Frederick, Sir Charles Edward St John, 8th Bt, 1876–1938, vol. III
Frederick, Lt-Col Sir Edward Boscawen, 9th Bt, 1880–1956, vol. V
Frederick, Captain George Charles, 1855–1951, vol. V
Freedman, Barnett, 1901–1958, vol. V
Freedman, Maurice, 1920–1975, vol. VII
Freeland, Maj.-Gen. Sir Henry Francis Edward, 1870–1946, vol. IV
Freeland, Lt-Gen. Sir Ian Henry, 1912–1979, vol. VII
Freeland, Col John Cavendish, 1877–1944, vol. IV
Freeling, Sir Charles Edward Luard, 9th Bt, 1858–1941, vol. IV
Freeling, Sir Clayton Pennington, 8th Bt, 1857–1927, vol. II
Freeling, Sir Harry, 6th Bt, 1852–1914, vol. I
Freeling, Rev. Sir James Robert, 7th Bt, 1825–1916, vol. II
Freeman, Anthony Mallows; *see* Freeman, P. A. M.
Freeman, Edward Bothamley, 1838–1921, vol. II
Freeman, Col Ernest Carrick, 1860–1932, vol. III

Freeman, Comdr Frederick Arthur Peere W.; *see* Williams-Freeman.
Freeman, George Mallows, 1850–1934, vol. III
Freeman, George Robert, 1875–1972, vol. VII
Freeman, George Sydney, 1879–1938, vol. III
Freeman, Harry, 1888–1959, vol. V
Freeman, Rev. Herbert Bentley, 1855–1950, vol. IV
Freeman, James E., 1871–1929, vol. III
Freeman, Rt Rev. James Edward, 1866–1943, vol. IV
Freeman, John, 1880–1929, vol. III
Freeman, John, 1877–1962, vol. VI
Freeman, John Joseph, 1851–1937, vol. III
Freeman, Kathleen, 1897–1959, vol. V
Freeman, Patrick, 1919–1978, vol. VII
Freeman, Percy Tom, 1891–1956, vol. V
Freeman, Peter, 1888–1956, vol. V
Freeman, (Philip) Anthony Mallows, 1892–1971, vol. VII
Freeman, Sir Philip Horace, 1878–1933, vol. III
Freeman, Sir Ralph, 1880–1950, vol. IV
Freeman, Richard Austin, 1862–1943, vol. IV
Freeman, Sterry Baines, 1875–1953, vol. V
Freeman, Air Chief Marshal Sir Wilfrid Rhodes, 1st Bt, 1888–1953, vol. V
Freeman, William Marshall, 1868–1953, vol. V
Freeman-Attwood, Harold Augustus, 1897–1963, vol. VI
Freeman-Cohen, Harry, *died* 1904, vol. I
Freeman-Mitford, Hon. Clement Bertram Ogilvy, 1876–1915, vol. I
Freeman-Mitford, Major Hon. Thomas David F.; *see* Mitford.
Freer, A. M. G.; *see* Goodrich-Freer.
Freer, Charles L., 1854–1919, vol. II
Freer, Ven. T. Henry, 1833–1904, vol. I
Freer Smith, Sir Hamilton Pym, 1845–1929, vol. III
Freese-Pennefather, Harold Wilfrid Armine, 1907–1967, vol. VI
Freeston, Sir Brian; *see* Freeston, Sir L. B.
Freeston, Charles Lincoln, 1865–1942, vol. IV
Freeston, Sir (Leslie) Brian, 1892–1958, vol. V
Freestun, Col William Humphrey May, 1878–1964, vol. VI
Freeth, Sir Evelyn, 1846–1911, vol. I
Freeth, Francis Arthur, 1884–1970, vol. VI
Freeth, Maj.-Gen. George Henry Basil, 1872–1949, vol. IV
Freeth, Rt Rev. Robert Evelyn, 1886–1979, vol. VII
Freke, Cecil George, 1887–1974, vol. VII
Freke, Hon. Ralfe E.; *see* Evans-Freke.
Fremantle, Gen. Sir Arthur James Lyon, 1835–1901, vol. I
Fremantle, Charles Albert, 1878–1952, vol. V
Fremantle, Hon. Sir Charles William, 1834–1914, vol. I
Fremantle, Adm. Hon. Sir Edmund Robert, 1836–1929, vol. III
Fremantle, Francis David Eardley, 1906–1968, vol. VI
Fremantle, Sir Francis Edward, 1872–1943, vol. IV
Fremantle, Henry Eardley Stephen, 1874–1931, vol. III
Fremantle, John Morton, 1876–1936, vol. III

Fremantle, Sir Selwyn Howe, 1869–1942, vol. IV

Fremantle, Adm. Sir Sydney Robert, 1867–1958, vol. V

Fremantle, Very Rev. Hon. William Henry, 1831–1916, vol. II

Frémiet, Emmanuel, 1824–1910, vol. I (A)

French, Alice Octave Thanet, 1850–1934, vol. III

French, Gen. Arthur, 1840–1928, vol. II

French, Major Arthur Cecil, 1896–1974, vol. VII

French, Col Arthur Harwood, 1876–1939, vol. III

French, Hon. Charles, 1851–1925, vol. II

French, Brig. Charles Newenham, 1875–1959, vol. V

French, Daniel Chester, 1850–1931, vol. III

French, Daniel O'Connell, 1843–1902, vol. I

French, Lt-Col Hon. (Edward) Gerald, 1883–1970, vol. VI

French, Edward Henry, 1850–1935, vol. III

French, Sir Edward Lee, 1857–1916, vol. II

French, Francis Coope, 1868–1940, vol. III

French, Rev. Francis Laurence, 1868–1936, vol. III

French, Captain Sir Frederick Edward, 1882–1947, vol. IV

French, Frederick George, 1889–1963, vol. VI

French, Maj.-Gen. Sir George Arthur, 1841–1921, vol. II

French, Col George Arthur, 1865–1950, vol. IV

French, Lt-Col Hon. Gerald; see French, Lt-Col Hon. E. G.

French, Sir Henry Leon, 1883–1966, vol. VI

French, Herbert Stanley, 1875–1951, vol. V

French, Captain Sir Houston, 1853–1932, vol. III

French, Sir James Weir, 1876–1953, vol. V

French, Maj.-Gen. John, 1906–1978, vol. VII

French, John Gay, died 1951, vol. V

French, Brig. John Linnaeus, 1896–1953, vol. V

French, Sir John Russell, 1847–1921, vol. II

French, Lewis, 1873–1945, vol. IV

French, Percy, 1854–1920, vol. II

French, Rev. Reginald, 1883–1961, vol. VI

French, Reginald Thomas George, 1881–1965, vol. VI

French, Sir Somerset Richard, 1848–1929, vol. III

French, Adm. Sir Wilfred Frankland, 1880–1958, vol. V

French, William Innes, 1910–1971, vol. VII

Frend, Charles Herbert, 1909–1977, vol. VII

Frend, Col George, 1857–1923, vol. II

Frere, Sir Bartle Compton Arthur, 1854–1933, vol. III

Frere, Sir Bartle Henry Temple, 1862–1953, vol. V

Frere, Rev. Hugh Corrie, 1857–1938, vol. III

Frere, Brig. Jasper Gray, 1894–1974, vol. VII

Frere, John Tudor, 1843–1918, vol. II

Frere, Noel Gray, 1885–1955, vol. V

Frere, Rt Rev. Walter Howard, 1863–1938, vol. III

Frere, William Edward, 1840–1900, vol. I

Freshfield, Douglas William, 1845–1934, vol. III

Freshwater, Douglas Hope, died 1945, vol. IV

Fresnay, Pierre, (Pierre Laudenbach), 1897–1975, vol. VII

Fressanges, Air Marshal Sir Francis J., 1902–1975, vol. VII

Freud, Sigmund, 1856–1939, vol. III

Freund, Sir Otto K.; see Kahn-Freund.

Freundlich, Erwin F.; see Finlay-Freundlich.

Freundlich, Herbert Max Finlay, 1880–1941, vol. IV

Frew, Rev. Dr, 1813–1910, vol. I

Frew, Air Vice-Marshal Sir Matthew Brown, 1895–1974, vol. VII

Frew, Engr Rear-Adm. Sir Sidney Oswell, died 1972, vol. VII

Frewen, Col Edward, 1850–1919, vol. II

Frewen, Adm. Sir John Byng, 1911–1975, vol. VII

Frewen, Moreton, 1853–1924, vol. II

Frewen-Laton, Col Stephen, 1857–1933, vol. III

Frewer, Rev. George Ernest, 1852–1935, vol. III

Frewer, Rt Rev. John, 1883–1974, vol. VII

Freyberg, 1st Baron, 1889–1963, vol. VI

Freyberg, Lady; (Barbara), died 1973, vol. VII

Freyberg, Captain Geoffrey Herbert, 1881–1966, vol. VI

Freyer, Sir Peter J., died 1921, vol. II

Freyer, Lt-Col Samuel Forster, 1858–1947, vol. IV

Frick, Henry Clay, 1849–1919, vol. II

Fricker, Edward T., died 1917, vol. II

Friederichs, Hulda, died 1927, vol. II

Friedlander, Max J., 1867–1958, vol. V

Friedlander, Michael, died 1910, vol. I

Friedman, Ignaz, 1882–1948, vol. IV

Friend, Maj.-Gen. Arthur Leslie Irvine, 1886–1961, vol. VI

Friend, John Albert Newton, 1881–1966, vol. VI

Friend, Maj.-Gen. Rt Hon. Sir Lovick Bransby, 1856–1944, vol. IV

Frigon, Augustin, 1888–1952, vol. V

Friml, Rudolf, 1879–1972, vol. VII

Fripp, Sir Alfred Downing, 1865–1930, vol. III

Fripp, Alfred Ernest, 1866–1938, vol. III

Fripp, Charles E., 1854–1906, vol. I

Frisby, Major Cyril Hubert, 1885–1961, vol. VI

Frisby, Lt-Col Lionel Claud, 1889–1936, vol. III

Frisch, Otto Robert, 1904–1979, vol. VII

Frisch, Ragnar Anton Kittil, 1895–1973, vol. VII

Friswell, Sir Charles Hain, 1871–1926, vol. II

Frith, Col Cyril Halsted, 1877–1946, vol. IV

Frith, Brig.-Gen. Gilbert Robertson, 1873–1958, vol. V

Frith, Col Herbert Cokayne, 1861–1942, vol. IV

Frith, W. S., died 1924, vol. II

Frith, Walter, died 1941, vol. IV

Frith, William Powell, 1819–1909, vol. I

Fritsch, Felix Eugen, 1879–1954, vol. V

Frizell, Rev. Charles William, died 1920, vol. II

Frizell, Brig.-Gen. Charles William, 1888–1951, vol. V

Frizelle, Sir Joseph, 1841–1921, vol. II

Frodsham, Rt Rev. George Horsfall, 1863–1937, vol. III

Frohawk, Frederick William, 1861–1946, vol. IV

Frohman, Charles, 1860–1915, vol. I

Frood, Hester, 1882–1971, vol. VII

Froom, Sir Arthur Henry, 1873–1964, vol. VI

Frossard, Rev. Canon Edward Louis, 1887–1968, vol. VI

Frost, Edward Granville Gordon, 1886–1971, vol. VII

Frost, Edward Purkis, 1842–1922, vol. II
Frost, Brig.-Gen. Frank Dutton, *died* 1968, vol. VI
Frost, Hon. Sir John, 1828–1918, vol. II
Frost, Lt-Col John Meadows, 1885–1923, vol. II
Frost, Sir John Meadows, 1856–1935, vol. III
Frost, Mark Edwin Pescott, 1859–1953, vol. V
Frost, Captain Meadows, 1875–1954, vol. V
Frost, Percival, 1817–1898, vol. I
Frost, Robert, 1874–1963, vol. VI
Frost, Sir Thomas Gibbons, 1820–1904, vol. I
Frostick, James Arthur, 1857–1931, vol. III
Froude, Ashley Anthony, 1863–1949, vol. IV
Froude, Robert Edmund, 1846–1924, vol. II
Frowde, Henry, 1841–1927, vol. II
Frowen, Brig. John Harold, 1898–1980, vol. VII
Frumkin, Gad, 1887–1960, vol. VI
Fry, (Anna) Ruth, 1878–1962, vol. VI
Fry, Col Arthur Brownfield, 1873–1954, vol. V
Fry, Augustine Sargood, 1890–1962, vol. VI
Fry, Cecil Roderick, 1890–1952, vol. V
Fry, Charles Burgess, 1872–1956, vol. V
Fry, Rev. Canon Charles Edward Middleton, 1882–1950, vol. IV
Fry, Maj.-Gen. Charles Irwin, 1858–1931, vol. III
Fry, Rt Hon. Sir Edward, 1827–1918, vol. II
Fry, Francis Gibson, 1864–1914, vol. I
Fry, Francis James, 1835–1918, vol. II
Fry, Sir Frederick Morris, 1851–1943, vol. IV
Fry, Sir Geoffrey Storrs, 1st Bt (*cr* 1929), 1888–1960, vol. V
Fry, George Samuel, 1853–1938, vol. III
Fry, Sir Henry James Wakely, 1849–1920, vol. II
Fry, Henry Kenneth, 1886–1959, vol. VI (AI)
Fry, Sir John Pease, 2nd Bt (*cr* 1894), 1864–1957, vol. V
Fry, Major Sir Leslie Alfred Charles, 1908–1976, vol. VII
Fry, Rt Hon. Lewis, 1832–1921, vol. II
Fry, Lewis G., 1860–1933, vol. III
Fry, Margery; *see* Fry, S. M.
Fry, Matthew Wyatt Joseph, *died* 1943, vol. IV
Fry, Oliver Armstrong, 1855–1931, vol. III
Fry, Sir Penrose; *see* Fry, Sir T. P.
Fry, Peter George, 1875–1925, vol. II
Fry, Roger E., 1866–1934, vol. III
Fry, Ruth; *see* Fry, A. R.
Fry, (Sara) Margery, 1874–1958, vol. V
Fry, Sir Theodore, 1st Bt (*cr* 1894), 1836–1912, vol. I
Fry, Sir (Theodore) Penrose, 3rd Bt (*cr* 1894), 1892–1971, vol. VII
Fry, Theodore Wilfrid, 1868–1947, vol. IV
Fry, Thomas, 1889–1958, vol. V
Fry, Very Rev. Thomas Charles, 1846–1930, vol. III
Fry, Maj.-Gen. Sir William, 1858–1934, vol. III
Fry, Sir William, 1853–1939, vol. III
Fry, Sir William Kelsey, 1889–1963, vol. VI
Fry, Windsor, *died* 1947, vol. IV
Fryar, Samuel, 1863–1938, vol. III
Frye, Frederick Robert, 1851–1942, vol. IV
Frye, Jack, 1914–1975, vol. VII
Fryer, Sir Charles Edward, 1850–1920, vol. II
Fryer, Edward Harpur, 1879–1948, vol. IV

Fryer, Sir Frederic William Richards, 1845–1922, vol. II
Fryer, Herbert, 1877–1957, vol. V
Fryer, Lt-Gen. Sir John, 1838–1917, vol. II
Fryer, Sir John Claud Fortescue, 1886–1948, vol. IV
Fryer, Walter John, 1871–1933, vol. III
Fuad, Mustafa Ziai, Bey, 1888–1968, vol. VI
Fuchs, Carl, 1865–1951, vol. V
Fuchs, Emile, 1866–1929, vol. III
Fudge, Edward George, 1888–1961, vol. VI
Fukushima, Gen. Baron, 1853–1919, vol. II
Fulford, Dame Catherine, *died* 1960, vol. V
Fulford, Francis, 1861–1926, vol. II
Fulford, Rev. Frederick John, 1860–1927, vol. II
Fulford, Henry English, 1859–1929, vol. III
Fullagar, Sir Wilfred Kelsham, 1892–1961, vol. VI
Fullard, George, 1923–1973, vol. VI
Fullbrook-Leggatt, Maj.-Gen. Charles St Quentin Outen; *see* Leggatt.
Fuller, Lt-Col Albert George Hubert, *died* 1969, vol. VI
Fuller, Maj.-Gen. Algernon Clement, 1885–1970, vol. VI
Fuller, Rev. Arthur Rose, 1874–1959, vol. V
Fuller, Sir Bampfylde; *see* Fuller, Sir J. B.
Fuller, Sir Benjamin John, 1875–1952, vol. V
Fuller, Maj.-Gen. Cuthbert Graham, 1874–1960, vol. V
Fuller, Adm. Sir Cyril Thomas Moulden, 1874–1942, vol. IV
Fuller, Sir Francis Charles, 1866–1944, vol. IV
Fuller, Brig.-Gen. Francis George, 1869–1961, vol. VI
Fuller, Francis Matthew, 1899–1963, vol. VI
Fuller, George Pargiter, 1833–1927, vol. II
Fuller, Hon. Sir George Warburton, 1861–1940, vol. III
Fuller, Henry Roxburgh, *died* 1929, vol. III
Fuller, Air Cdre Herbert Francis, 1893–1967, vol. VI
Fuller, James Franklin, 1835–1924, vol. II
Fuller, Gen. John Augustus, 1828–1902, vol. I
Fuller, Maj.-Gen. John Frederick Charles, 1878–1966, vol. VI
Fuller, Rt Rev. John Latimer, 1870–1950, vol. IV
Fuller, Sir John Michael Fleetwood, 1st Bt, 1864–1915, vol. I
Fuller, Sir (Joseph) Bampfylde, 1854–1935, vol. III
Fuller, Leonard J., 1891–1973, vol. VII
Fuller, Melville Weston, 1833–1910, vol. I
Fuller, Brig.-Gen. Richard Woodfield, 1861–1938, vol. III
Fuller, Sir Thomas Ekins, 1831–1910, vol. I
Fuller, Walter Everard, 1879–1942, vol. IV
Fuller, William Fleetwood, 1865–1947, vol. IV
Fuller-Eliott-Drake, Sir Francis George Augustus; *see* Drake.
Fuller-Maitland, J. A., 1856–1936, vol. III
Fuller-Maitland, William, 1844–1932, vol. III
Fullerton, Andrew, *died* 1934, vol. III
Fullerton, Adm. Sir Eric John Arthur, *died* 1962, vol. VI
Fullerton, Harold Williams, 1905–1970, vol. VI

Fullerton, Hugh, 1851–1922, vol. II
Fullerton, Brig. John Parke, 1894–1977, vol. VII
Fullerton, Adm. Sir John Reginald Thomas, 1840–1918, vol. II
Fullerton, John Skipwith Herbert, 1865–1940, vol. III
Fullerton, Rev. William Young, 1857–1932, vol. III
Fulleylove, John, 1847–1908, vol. I
Fullwood, John, died 1931, vol. III
Fülop-Miller, René, 1891–1963, vol. VI
Fulton, Alexander Strathern, 1888–1976, vol. VII
Fulton, Sir Edmund McGilldowny Hope, 1848–1913, vol. I
Fulton, Eustace Cecil, 1880–1954, vol. V
Fulton, Sir Forrest, 1846–1925, vol. II
Fulton, Forrest, 1913–1971, vol. VII
Fulton, Frederick John, 1862–1936, vol. III
Fulton, Lt-Col Harry Townsend, 1869–1918, vol. II
Fulton, Lt-Col J. D. B., 1876–1915, vol. I (A)
Fulton, John Farquhar, 1899–1960, vol. V
Fulton,Robert Burwell, 1849–1918, vol. II
Fulton, Sir Robert Fulton, 1844–1927, vol. II
Fulton, Thomas Alexander Wemyss, 1855–1929, vol. III
Fulton, Rev. William, 1876–1952, vol. V
Funch, Christian Holger, 1865–1915, vol. I (A)
Funk, Isaac Kaufman, 1839–1912, vol. I
Funsten, Rt Rev. James Bowen, died 1918, vol. II
Funston, Brig.-Gen. Frederick, 1865–1917, vol. II
Furber, Lt-Col Cecil Tidswell, 1883–1943, vol. IV
Furber, Douglas, 1885–1961, vol. VI
Furber, Edward Price, 1864–1940, vol. III
Furkert, Frederick William, 1876–1949, vol. IV
Furley, Sir John, 1836–1919, vol. II
Furley, John Talfourd, 1878–1956, vol. V
Furlong, Hon. L. O'Brien, 1856–1908, vol. II
Furlong, Robert O'Brien, 1842–1917, vol. II
Furneaux, Rev. Henry, 1829–1900, vol. I
Furneaux, Rev. William Mordaunt, 1848–1928, vol. II
Furness, 1st Baron, 1852–1912, vol. I
Furness, 1st Viscount, 1883–1940, vol. III
Furness, Sir Christopher, 2nd Bt, 1900–1974, vol. VII
Furness, George James, 1868–1936, vol. III
Furness, George James Barnard, 1900–1962, vol. VI
Furness, Horace Howard, 1833–1912, vol. I
Furness, Reginald Albert, died 1951, vol. V
Furness, Sir Robert Allason, 1883–1954, vol. V
Furness, Sir Robert Howard, 1880–1959, vol. V
Furness, Stephen Noel, 1902–1974, vol. VII
Furness, Sir Stephen Wilson, 1st Bt, 1872–1914, vol. I
Furness-Smith, Sir Cecil, 1890–1971, vol. VII
Furney, Brig. John Leared, 1872–1936, vol. III
Furniss, Harry, 1854–1925, vol. II
Furniss, John Mawdsley, 1877–1956, vol. V
Furnivall, Baroness (19th in line), 1900–1968, vol. VI
Furnivall, Lt-Col Charles Hilton, 1873–1946, vol. IV
Furnivall, Frederick James, 1825–1910, vol. I
Furnivall, Percy, 1868–1938, vol. III

Furse, Ven. Charles Wellington, 1821–1900, vol. I
Furse, Charles Wellington, 1868–1904, vol. I
Furse, Rear-Adm. (John) Paul (Wellington), 1904–1978, vol. VII
Furse, Dame Katharine, 1875–1952, vol. V
Furse, Rt Rev. Michael Bolton, 1870–1955, vol. V
Furse, Rear-Adm. Paul; see Furse, Rear-Adm. J. P. W.
Furse, Major Sir Ralph Dolignon, 1887–1973, vol. VII
Furse, Roger Kemble, 1903–1972, vol. VII
Furse, Lt-Gen. Sir William T., 1865–1953, vol. V
Furst, Herbert Ernest Augustus, 1874–1945, vol. IV
Furtwängler, Wilhelm, 1886–1954, vol. V
Fussell, Edward Coldham, 1901–1978, vol. VII
Fust, Herbert J.; see Jenner-Fust.
Fyers, Major Hubert Alcock Nepean, 1862–1951, vol. V
Fyfe, Sir Cleveland, 1888–1959, vol. V
Fyfe, David Theodore, 1875–1945, vol. IV
Fyfe, H. Hamilton, 1869–1951, vol. V
Fyfe, Thomas Alexander, 1852–1928, vol. II
Fyfe, Sir William Hamilton, 1878–1965, vol. VI
Fyffe, Rev. David, 1866–1929, vol. III
Fyffe, Lt-Gen. Sir Richard Alan, 1912–1972, vol. VII
Fyffe, Rt Rev. Rollestone Sterritt, 1868–1964, vol. VI
Fyleman, Rose, died 1957, vol. V
Fyler, Maj.-Gen. Arthur Roderic, 1911–1980, vol. VII
Fyler, Adm. Herbert Arthur Stevenson, 1864–1934, vol. III
Fynes-Clinton, David Osbert, 1909–1978, vol. VII
Fynes-Clinton, Rev. Henry Joy, 1875–1959, vol. V
Fynes-Clinton, Osbert Henry, died 1941, vol. IV
Fynn, Hon. Sir Percival Donald Leslie, 1872–1940, vol. III
Fynne, Robert John, died 1953, vol. V
Fysh, Sir Hudson; see Fysh, Sir W. H.
Fysh, Hon. Sir Philip Oakley, 1835–1919, vol. II
Fysh, Sir (Wilmot) Hudson, 1895–1974, vol. VII
Fyson, Rt Rev. Philip Kemball, 1846–1928, vol. II
Fyvie, Isabella; see Mayo, Mrs John H.

G

Gabain, Ethel Leontine, (Mrs John Copley), died 1950, vol. IV
Gabbatt, John Percy, 1880–1956, vol. V
Gabin, Jean, (Alexis Jean Montgorge), 1904–1976, vol. VII
Gabor, Dennis, 1900–1979, vol. VII
Gable, Clark, died 1960, vol. V
Gabriel, Lt-Col Cecil Hamilton, 1879–1947, vol. IV
Gabriel, Col Sir (Edmund) Vivian, 1875–1950, vol. IV
Gabriel, Col Sir Vivian; see Gabriel, Col Sir E. V.
Gabriel, William Bashall, died 1975, vol. VII
Gadd, Cyril John, 1893–1969, vol. VI
Gaddum, Arthur Graham, 1874–1948, vol. IV
Gaddum, Sir John Henry, 1900–1965, vol. VI

Gaddum, Captain Walter Frederick, 1888–1956, vol. V

Gadie, Lt-Col Sir Anthony, *died* 1948, vol. IV

Gadow, Hans Friedrich, 1855–1928, vol. II

Gadsby, Henry, 1842–1907, vol. I

Gadsby, John, 1884–1970, vol. VI

Gadsby, W. H., *died* 1924, vol. II

Gadsden, Cecil Holroyd, 1887–1957, vol. V

Gadsden, Edward Holroyd, 1859–1920, vol. II

Gadsdon, Sir Laurence Percival, 1897–1967, vol. VI (AII)

Gaffney, Thomas Burke, 1839–1927, vol. II

Gagarin, Col Yuri Alexeyevich, 1934–1968, vol. VI

Gage, Col Aella Molyneux Berkeley, 1863–1937, vol. III

Gage, Andrew Thomas, 1871–1945, vol. IV

Gage, Hon. Lyman Judson, 1836–1927, vol. II

Gage, Brig.-Gen. Moreton Foley, 1873–1953, vol. V

Gage, Thomas Robert Baillie-, 1842–1914, vol. I

Gage, Sir William James, 1849–1921, vol. II

Gaggero, Sir George, 1897–1978, vol. VII

Gagnon, Rt Rev. Mgr Cyrille, *died* 1945, vol. IV

Gahan, Charles Joseph, 1862–1939, vol. III

Gahan, Frank, 1890–1971, vol. VII

Gaiger, Sydney Herbert, 1884–1934, vol. III

Gailey, James Hamilton, 1869–1938, vol. III

Gailor, Rt Rev. Thomas Frank, 1856–1935, vol. III

Gaimes, John Austin, 1886–1921, vol. II

Gainer, Sir Donald St Clair, 1891–1966, vol. VI

Gainer, Rev. Canon Harry, 1858–1920, vol. II

Gainford, 1st Baron, 1860–1943, vol. IV

Gainford, 2nd Baron, 1889–1971, vol. VII

Gainsborough, 3rd Earl of, 1850–1926, vol. II

Gainsborough, 4th Earl of, 1884–1927, vol. II

Gainsborough, Hugh, 1893–1980, vol. VII

Gair, Col Sinclair, 1856–1939, vol. III

Gair, Walter Burgh, 1854–1951, vol. V

Gairdner, Arthur Charles Dalrymple, 1872–1950, vol. IV

Gairdner, Eric Dalrymple, 1878–1933, vol. III

Gairdner, James, 1828–1912, vol. I

Gairdner, Rev. Canon W. H. Temple, 1873–1928, vol. II

Gairdner, Sir William Tennant, 1824–1907, vol. I

Gairns, James Mather, 1880–1935, vol. III

Gaisford, Hugh William, 1874–1954, vol. V

Gaisford, Lt-Col Sir Philip, 1891–1973, vol. VII

Gaisford, Brig.-Gen. Richard Boileau, 1854–1924, vol. II

Gaisford-St Lawrence, Julian Charles, 1862–1932, vol. III

Gait, Sir Edward Albert, 1863–1950, vol. IV

Gaither, H. Rowan, Jr, 1909–1961, vol. VI

Gaitskell, Maj.-Gen. Frederick, 1806–1901, vol. I

Gaitskell, Rt Hon. Hugh Todd Naylor, 1906–1963, vol. VI

Gajjumal, Rai Sahib Lala, *born* 1857, vol. II

Galabin, Alfred Lewis, 1843–1913, vol. I

Galbraith, Angus, 1846–1915, vol. I (A)

Galbraith, Very Rev. George, 1829–1911, vol. I

Galbraith, James Francis Wallace, 1872–1945, vol. IV

Galbraith, Lt-Col James Ponsonby, 1881–1950, vol. IV

Galbraith, Samuel, 1853–1936, vol. III

Galbraith, Vivian Hunter, 1889–1976, vol. VII

Galbraith, Walter, 1839–1906, vol. I

Galbraith, Maj.-Gen. Sir William, 1837–1906, vol. I

Galbraith, Col William Campbell, 1870–1946, vol. IV

Galdos, Benito Perez, 1845–1920, vol. II

Gale, Anthony Eugene Myddelton, 1901–1959, vol. V

Gale, Arthur James Victor, 1895–1978, vol. VII

Gale, Rev. Canon Courtenay James Randolph, 1857–1937, vol. III

Gale, Brig. Henry John Gordon, 1883–1944, vol. IV

Gale, Brig.-Gen. Henry Richmond, 1866–1930, vol. III

Gale, Lt-Gen. Sir Humfrey Myddelton, 1890–1971, vol. VII

Gale, Rev. Isaac Sadler, *died* 1915, vol. I (A)

Gale, James, 1833–1907, vol. I

Gale, Kenneth Frederick, 1914–1969, vol. VI

Gale, Sir Laurence George, 1905–1969, vol. VI

Gale, Norman, *died* 1942, vol. IV

Gale, Lt-Col Robert, 1887–1937, vol. III

Gale, Walter Frederick, 1865–1945, vol. IV

Gale, Zona, 1874–1939, vol. III

Galea, Robert V., 1882–1962, vol. VI (AII)

Galer, Sir Bertram; *see* Galer, Sir F. B.

Galer, Sir (Frederic) Bertram, 1873–1968, vol. VI

Galer, John Maxcey, 1839–1919, vol. II

Gales, Sir Robert Richard, 1864–1948, vol. IV

Gales, Wilfred Appleby, 1860–1937, vol. III

Galipeault, Hon. Antonin, 1879–1971, vol. VII

Gall, William James, 1867–1938, vol. III

Gallacher, William, 1876–1951, vol. V

Gallacher, William, 1881–1965, vol. VI

Gallagher, Lt-Col Albert Ernest, 1872–1940, vol. III

Gallagher, Sir James Michael, 1860–1926, vol. II

Gallagher, Rt Rev. John, 1846–1923, vol. II

Gallagher, John Andrew, 1919–1980, vol. VII

Gallagher, Sir William, 1851–1933, vol. III

Gallaher, Major Alexander, *died* 1938, vol. III

Gallaher, Thomas, 1840–1927, vol. II

Gallannaugh, Bertram William Leonard, 1900–1957, vol. V

Gallarati Scotti, Tommaso, 1878–1966, vol. VI

Gallardo, Angel, 1867–1934, vol. III

Galleghan, Brig. Sir Frederick Gallagher, 1897–1971, vol. VII

Galletti di Cadilhac, Countess, (Hon. Margaret Isabella Collier), 1846–1928, vol. II

Galli-Curci, Amelita, 1882–1963, vol. VI

Gallichan, Walter M., *died* 1946, vol. IV

Gallico, Paul William, 1897–1976, vol. VII

Gallie, Maj.-Gen. James Stuart, 1870–1943, vol. IV

Gallieni, Joseph, 1849–1916, vol. II

Gallienne, Wilfred Hansford, 1897–1956, vol. V

Gallier, William Henry, 1855–1946, vol. IV

Galliffet, Marquis de; Gaston Alexandre Auguste, 1830–1909, vol. I

Galliher, Hon. William Alfred, 1860–1934, vol. III

Gallon, Tom, 1866–1914, vol. I

Gallon, William Anthony, 1898–1962, vol. VI
Gallop, Constantine, *died* 1967, vol. VI
Gallop, Rev. Edward Jordan, 1850–1928, vol. II
Gallop, Rodney Alexander, 1901–1948, vol. IV
Galloway, 10th Earl of, 1835–1901, vol. I
Galloway, 11th Earl of, 1836–1920, vol. II
Galloway, 12th Earl of, 1892–1978, vol. VII
Galloway, Countess of; (Mary Arabella Arthur Cecil), *died* 1903, vol. I
Galloway, Alexander, 1901–1965, vol. VI
Galloway, Lt-Gen. Sir Alexander, 1895–1977, vol. VII
Galloway, Adm. Arthur Archibald Campbell, 1855–1918, vol. II
Galloway, Sir David, 1858–1943, vol. IV
Galloway, Col Frank Lennox, 1869–1949, vol. IV
Galloway, George, *died* 1933, vol. III
Galloway, Sir James, *died* 1922, vol. II
Galloway, Maj.-Gen. John Mawby Clossey, 1840–1916, vol. II
Galloway, Maj.-Gen. Rudolf William, 1891–1976, vol. VII
Galloway, Sir William, *died* 1927, vol. II
Galloway, William Johnson, 1866–1931, vol. III
Gallwey, Col Edmond Joseph, 1850–1927, vol. II
Gallwey, Sir John Frankland-Payne-, 4th Bt, 1889–1955, vol. V
Gallwey, Hon. Sir Michael Henry, 1826–1912, vol. I
Gallwey, Sir Ralph William Frankland Payne-, 3rd Bt, 1843–1916, vol. II
Gallwey, Sir Reginald Frankland Payne-, 5th Bt, 1889–1964, vol. II
Gallwey, Maj.-Gen. Sir Thomas Joseph, 1852–1933, vol. III
Gallwey, Sir Thomas Lionel, 1821–1906, vol. I
Gallwey, Captain William Thomas Frankland Payne-, 1881–1914, vol. I (A), vol. II
Galpin, Rev. Arthur John, 1861–1926, vol. II
Galpin, Rev. Francis William, 1858–1945, vol. IV
Galsworthy, Sir Edwin Henry, 1831–1920, vol. II
Galsworthy, John, 1867–1933, vol. III
Galt, Alexander, 1854–1938, vol. III
Galt, Alexander Casimir, 1853–1936, vol. III
Galt, Sir Thomas, 1815–1901, vol. I
Galton, Rt Rev. Compton Theodore, 1855–1931, vol. III
Galton, Sir Douglas, 1822–1899, vol. I
Galton, Sir Francis, 1822–1911, vol. I
Galton, Frank Wallis, 1867–1952, vol. V
Galtrey, Albert Sidney, *died* 1935, vol. III
Galway, 7th Viscount, 1844–1931, vol. III
Galway, 8th Viscount, 1882–1943, vol. IV
Galway, 9th Viscount, 1929–1971, vol. VII
Galway, 10th Viscount, 1894–1977, vol. VII
Galway, 11th Viscount, 1900–1980, vol. VII
Galway, Lt-Col Sir Henry Lionel, 1859–1949, vol. IV
Gamage, Albert Walter, 1855–1930, vol. III
Gamage, Sir Leslie, 1887–1972, vol. VII
Gambier, Kenyon; *see* Lathrop, L. A.
Gambier-Parry, Major Ernest, 1853–1936, vol. III
Gambier-Parry, Maj.-Gen. Michael Denman, 1891–1976, vol. VII

Gambier-Parry, Brig. Sir Richard, 1894–1965, vol. VI
Gambier-Parry, Thomas Robert, 1883–1935, vol. III
Gamble, Rev. Arthur Mellor, 1899–1975, vol. VII
Gamble, Sir David, 1st Bt, 1823–1907, vol. I
Gamble, Sir David, 3rd Bt, 1876–1943, vol. IV
Gamble, Adm. Sir Douglas Austin, 1856–1934, vol. III
Gamble, Adm. Edward Harpur, 1849–1925, vol. II
Gamble, Frederick William, 1869–1926, vol. II
Gamble, Brig. Geoffrey Massey, 1896–1970, vol. VI
Gamble, Very Rev. Henry Reginald, *died* 1931, vol. III
Gamble, James Sykes, 1847–1925, vol. II
Gamble, Rev. John, 1859–1929, vol. III
Gamble, Sir Josias Christopher, 2nd Bt, 1848–1908, vol. I
Gamble, Sir Reginald Arthur, 1862–1930, vol. III
Gamble, Brig.-Gen. Richard Narrien, 1860–1937, vol. III
Gamble, Robert Edward, 1922–1975, vol. VII
Gamble, Victor Felix, 1886–1952, vol. V
Gamblin, Sir George Henry, 1870–1930, vol. III
Game, Henry Clement, *died* 1966, vol. VI
Game, Air Vice-Marshal Sir Philip Woolcott, 1876–1961, vol. VI
Gamelin, Général Maurice, 1872–1958, vol. V
Games, Ven. Joshua H.; *see* Hughes-Games.
Gamgee, Arthur, 1841–1909, vol. I
Gamlen, John Charles Blagdon, 1885–1952, vol. V
Gamley, Henry Snell, 1865–1928, vol. II
Gamlin, Lionel James, 1903–1967, vol. VI
Gammans, Sir David; *see* Gammans, Sir L. D.
Gammans, Sir (Leonard) David, 1st Bt, 1895–1957, vol. V
Gammell, Lt-Gen. Sir James Andrew Harcourt, 1892–1975, vol. VII
Gammell, Sir Sydney James, 1867–1946, vol. IV
Gammie, John, 1896–1968, vol. VI
Gammon, John Charles, 1887–1973, vol. VII
Gamon, Hugh Reece Percival, 1880–1953, vol. V
Gamow, George, 1904–1968, vol. VI
Gandhi, Mohandas Karamchand, 1869–1948, vol. IV
Gandhi, Nagardas P., 1886–1960, vol. VI (AI)
Gandier, Rev. Alfred, 1861–1932, vol. III
Gandolfi, Duke, 1846–1906, vol. I
Gandolfi, Duke, 1899–1937, vol. III
Gandy, Eric Worsley, 1879–1958, vol. V
Gandy, Henry Garnett, 1860–1939, vol. III
Gane, Sir Irving Blanchard, 1892–1972, vol. VII
Ganesh Datta Shastri, *born* 1861, vol. III
Ganga Ram, Rai Bahadur Sir Lala, 1851–1927, vol. II
Gange, Edwin Stanley, 1871–1944, vol. IV
Gangulee, Nagendra Nath, 1889–1954, vol. V
Ganguly, Most Rev. Theotonius A., 1920–1977, vol. VII
Ganley, Mrs Caroline Selina, 1879–1966, vol. VI
Gann, Thomas William Francis, *died* 1938, vol. III
Ganneau, Charles Simon C.; *see* Clermont-Ganneau.

Gannon, Brig. Jack Rose Compton, 1882–1980, vol. VII
Gannon, Hon. James Conley, 1860–1924, vol. II
Gannon, Rev. Patrick Joseph, 1879–1953, vol. V
Gant, Hon. Tetley, 1856–1928, vol. II
Ganz, Wilhelm, 1833–1914, vol. I
Garbe, Louis Richard, died 1957, vol. V
Garbett, Sir Colin Campbell, 1881–1972, vol. VII
Garbett, Most Rev. and Rt. Hon. Cyril Forster, 1875–1955, vol. V
Garbett, Lt-Col Hubert Champion, 1873–1939, vol. III
Garbett, Captain Leonard Gillilan, 1879–1974, vol. VII
Garcia, Manuel, 1805–1906, vol. I
Garcke, Emile, 1856–1930, vol. III
Garcke, Sidney, 1885–1948, vol. IV
Garçon, Maurice, 1889–1967, vol. VI
Gard, William Henry, 1854–1936, vol. III
Garde, Engr Captain Robert Boles, 1863–1921, vol. II
Garden, Mary, 1874–1967, vol. VI
Gardiner, Sir Alan Henderson, 1879–1963, vol. VI
Gardiner, Alfred G., 1865–1946, vol. IV
Gardiner, Col Bernard Calwoodley, 1879–1932, vol. III
Gardiner, Sir Chittampalam Abraham, 1899–1960, vol. V
Gardiner, Edward Rawson, 1859–1929, vol. III
Gardiner, Rev. Frederic Evelyn, died 1928, vol. II
Gardiner, Sir Frederick Crombie, 1855–1937, vol. III
Gardiner, Hon. Frederick George, 1874–1935, vol. III
Gardiner, Frederick William, 1849–1918, vol. II
Gardiner, Gp Captain George Cecil, 1892–1940, vol. III
Gardiner, Col Henry Lawrence, 1860–1946, vol. IV
Gardiner, Gen. Sir (Henry) Lynedoch, 1820–1897, vol. I
Gardiner, Henry Rolf, 1902–1971, vol. VII
Gardiner, James, 1860–1924, vol. II
Gardiner, Rt Hon. James Garfield, 1883–1962, vol. VI
Gardiner, John, 1852–1932, vol. III
Gardiner, John Stanley, 1872–1946, vol. IV
Gardiner, Linda, died 1941, vol. IV
Gardiner, Gen. Sir Lynedoch; see Gardiner, Gen. Sir H. L.
Gardiner, Brig. Richard, 1874–1957, vol. V
Gardiner, Sir Robert Septimus, 1856–1939, vol. III
Gardiner, Robert Strachan, 1874–1950, vol. IV
Gardiner, Samuel Rawson, 1829–1902, vol. I
Gardiner, Sir Thomas Robert, 1883–1964, vol. VI
Gardiner, Rev. Thory Gage, 1857–1941, vol. IV
Gardiner, Walter, 1859–1941, vol. IV
Gardiner, Rev. Canon William, 1848–1925, vol. II
Gardiner, William Dundas, 1830–1900, vol. I
Gardner, Hon. Mrs Alan, (Nora Beatrice), died 1944, vol. IV
Gardner, Col Alan Coulstoun, 1846–1907, vol. I
Gardner, Alice, 1854–1927, vol. II
Gardner, Arthur Duncan, 1884–1978, vol. VII
Gardner, Benjamin, 1896–1956, vol. V

Gardner, Benjamin Walter, 1865–1948, vol. IV
Gardner, Sir Charles B.; see Bruce-Gardner.
Gardner, Lt-Col Charles James Hookham, 1875–1962, vol. VI
Gardner, Christopher Thomas, 1842–1914, vol. I
Gardner, Edmund, 1874–1960, vol. V
Gardner, Edmund Garratt, 1869–1935, vol. III
Gardner, Eric Stanley, 1889–1970, vol. VI
Gardner, Sir Ernest, 1846–1925, vol. II
Gardner, Ernest Arthur, 1862–1939, vol. III
Gardner, Major Fitzroy, 1856–1936, vol. III
Gardner, Francis William, 1891–1976, vol. VII
Gardner, Frank Matthias, 1908–1980, vol. VII (AII)
Gardner, Ven. George Lawrence Harter, died 1925, vol. II
Gardner, Sir George William Hoggan, 1903–1975, vol. VII
Gardner, Henry Willoughby, 1861–1948, vol. IV
Gardner, J. Starkie, 1844–1930, vol. III
Gardner, James Clark Molesworth, 1894–1970, vol. VI
Gardner, James Patrick, 1883–1937, vol. III
Gardner, Rt Hon. Sir James Tynte Agg, 1846–1928, vol. II
Gardner, John Addyman, 1867–1946, vol. IV
Gardner, John Dunn, 1811–1903, vol. I
Gardner, Hon. Mrs Nora Beatrice; see Gardner, Hon. Mrs Alan.
Gardner, Percy, 1846–1937, vol. III
Gardner, Sir Robert, 1838–1920, vol. II
Gardner, Robert Cotton Bruce, 1889–1964, vol. VI
Gardner, Walter Myers, 1861–1939, vol. III
Gardner, William, 1845–1926, vol. II
Gardner, William Henry, 1895–1977, vol. VII
Gardner-Brown, Anthony Geoffrey Hopwood, 1913–1978, vol. VII
Gardyne, Lt-Col Charles G.; see Greenhill-Gardyne.
Garfit, William, 1840–1920, vol. II
Garforth, Rear-Adm. Edmund St John, 1836–1920, vol. II
Garforth, Captain Francis Edmund Musgrave, 1874–1953, vol. V
Garforth, Sir William Edward, 1845–1921, vol. II
Garforth, William Henry, 1856–1931, vol. III
Garioch, Lord, (Master of Mar); David Charles of Mar, 1944–1967, vol. VI
Garland, Sir Archibald, 1867–1937, vol. III
Garland, Charles Alexander Spencer, 1861–1914, vol. I
Garland, Charles Samuel, 1887–1960, vol. V
Garland, Charles Tuller, died 1921, vol. II
Garland, Rev. David John, 1864–1939, vol. III
Garland, Col Ernest Alfred Crowder, 1857–1938, vol. III
Garland, Hamlin, 1860–1940, vol. III
Garland, Hon. John, 1863–1921, vol. II
Garland, Lester V. L.; see Lester-Garland.
Garland, Patrick Joseph, 1867–1929, vol. III
Garmonsway, George Norman, 1898–1967, vol. VI
Garmoyle, Viscount; Hugh Wilfrid John Cairns, 1907–1942, vol. IV
Garnar, Sir James Wilson, 1871–1957, vol. V
Garneau, Sir George; see Garneau, Sir J. G.

Garneau, Sir (John) George, 1864–1944, vol. IV
Garneau, Hon. Némèse, 1847–1937, vol. III
Garner, Col Cathcart, 1861–1928, vol. II
Garner, Frederic Horace, 1893–1964, vol. VI
Garner, Sir Harry Mason, 1891–1977, vol. VII
Garner, John Nance, 1868–1967, vol. VI
Garner, Robert Livingston, 1894–1975, vol. VII
Garner, Walter Wesley, 1864–1938, vol. III
Garner, William, 1870–1953, vol. V
Garner, William Edward, 1889–1960, vol. V
Garnett, Bernard John, 1913–1977, vol. VII
Garnett, Edward, 1868–1937, vol. III
Garnett, Frank Walls, died 1922, vol. II
Garnett, Sir George, 1871–1955, vol. V
Garnett, Rear-Adm. Herbert Neville, 1875–1960, vol. V
Garnett, (James Clerk) Maxwell, 1880–1958, vol. V
Garnett, Lucy M. J., died 1934, vol. III
Garnett, Martha, 1869–1946, vol. IV
Garnett, Maxwell; see Garnett, J. C. M.
Garnett, Col Reginald, 1844–1910, vol. I
Garnett, Richard, 1835–1906, vol. I
Garnett, Robert Singleton, died 1932, vol. III
Garnett, Walter James, 1889–1958, vol. V
Garnett, William, 1850–1932, vol. III
Garnett, Lt-Col William Brooksbank, 1875–1946, vol. IV
Garnett, William James, 1878–1965, vol. VI
Garnier, Col Alan Parry, 1886–1963, vol. VI
Garnier, Rev. Edward Southwell, 1850–1938, vol. III
Garnier, John C.; see Carpenter-Garnier.
Garnier, Rt Rev. Mark Rodolph C.; see Carpenter-Garnier.
Garnier, Lt-Col Walter Keppel, 1882–1969, vol. VI
Garnsey, Sir Gilbert Francis, 1883–1932, vol. III
Garnsworthy, Baron (Life Peer); Charles James Garnsworthy, 1906–1974, vol. VII
Garofalo, Baron Raffaele, 1851–1934, vol. III
Garran, Hon. Andrew, 1825–1901, vol. I
Garran, Sir Robert Randolph, 1867–1957, vol. V
Garrard, Maj.-Gen. Apsley C.; see Cherry-Garrard.
Garrard, Apsley George Benet C.; see Cherry-Garrard.
Garrard, Hon. Jacob, 1846–1931, vol. III
Garratt, Brig.-Gen. Sir Francis Sudlow, 1859–1928, vol. II
Garratt, Geoffrey Theodore, 1888–1942, vol. IV
Garratt, Lt-Col John Arthur Thomas, 1842–1919, vol. II
Garratt, Rev. Samuel, 1817–1906, vol. I
Garraway, Sir Edward Charles Frederick, 1865–1932, vol. III
Garrett, Lt-Gen. Sir (Alwyn) Ragnar, 1900–1977, vol. VII
Garrett, Col Arthur Newson Bruff, 1868–1942, vol. IV
Garrett, Sir (Arthur) Wilfrid, 1880–1967, vol. VI
Garrett, Rev. Charles, 1823–1900, vol. I
Garrett, Sir Douglas Thornbury, 1883–1949, vol. IV
Garrett, Col Edmund, 1840–1914, vol. I
Garrett, Edmund William, 1850–1936, vol. III

Garrett, F. Edmund, 1865–1907, vol. I
Garrett, Lt-Col Sir Frank, 1869–1952, vol. V
Garrett, Rev. George Henry St Patrick, 1855–1937, vol. III
Garrett, George Mursell, 1834–1897, vol. I
Garrett, Herbert Leonard Offley, 1881–1941, vol. IV
Garrett, Sir Hugh; see Garrett, Sir J. H.
Garrett, John Walter Percy, 1902–1966, vol. VI
Garrett, Sir (Joseph) Hugh, 1880–1978, vol. VII
Garrett, Captain Peter Bruff, 1866–1950, vol. IV
Garrett, Philip Leslie, 1888–1978, vol. VII
Garrett, R. W., 1853–1925, vol. II
Garrett, Lt-Gen. Sir Ragnar; see Garrett, Lt-Gen. Sir A. R.
Garrett, Sir Ronald Thornbury, 1888–1972, vol. VII
Garrett, Samuel, 1850–1923, vol. II
Garrett, Sir Wilfrid; see Garrett, Sir A. W.
Garrett, William, 1890–1967, vol. VI
Garrett, Sir William Herbert, 1900–1977, vol. VII
Garrick, Hon. Sir James Francis, 1836–1907, vol. I
Garrick, Rev. James Percy, died 1919, vol. II
Garrison, Lindley Miller, 1864–1932, vol. III
Garrod, Sir Alfred Baring, 1819–1907, vol. I
Garrod, Air Chief Marshal Sir (Alfred) Guy (Roland), 1891–1965, vol. VI
Garrod, Sir Archibald Edward, 1857–1936, vol. III
Garrod, Dorothy Annie Elizabeth, 1892–1968, vol. VI
Garrod, Geoffrey, 1886–1974, vol. VII
Garrod, Rev. Canon George Watts, 1857–1936, vol. III
Garrod, Air Chief Marshal Sir Guy; see Garrod, Air Chief Marshal Sir A. G. R.
Garrod, Heathcote William, 1878–1960, vol. V
Garrod, Lawrence Paul, 1895–1979, vol. VII
Garrod, William Henry Edward, 1892–1967, vol. VI
Garrow, Alexander, 1923–1966, vol. VI
Garrow, Hon. James Thompson, 1843–1916, vol. II
Garrow, Col Robert G., 1876–1932, vol. III
Garsia, Lt-Col Herbert George Anderson, 1871–1965, vol. VI
Garsia, Lt-Col Michael Clare, 1838–1903, vol. I
Garsia, Lt-Col Willoughby Clive, 1881–1961, vol. VI
Garside, Captain Frederick Rodney, 1897–1940, vol. III
Garside, Oswald, 1869–1942, vol. IV
Garson, Alexander Denis, 1904–1968, vol. VI
Garstang, Cecil, 1904–1979, vol. VII
Garstang, John, 1876–1956, vol. V
Garstang, Walter, 1868–1949, vol. IV
Garsten, John Henry, 1838–1903, vol. I
Garstin, Brig.-Gen. Alfred Allan, 1850–1937, vol. III
Garstin, Charles Fortescue, 1880–1969, vol. VI
Garstin, Crosbie Alfred Norman, 1887–1930, vol. III
Garstin, John Ribton, 1836–1917, vol. II (A), vol. III
Garstin, Lt-Col William Arthur MacDonell, 1882–1975, vol. VII

Garstin, Sir William Edmund, 1849–1925, vol. II
Garth, Rt Hon. Sir Richard, 1820–1903, vol. I
Garth, Thomas Colleton, 1822–1907, vol. I
Garth, Sir William, 1854–1923, vol. II
Garthwaite, Brig. Clive Charlton, 1909–1979, vol. VII
Garthwaite, Sir William, 1st Bt, 1874–1956, vol. V
Gartlan, Maj.-Gen. Gerald Ion, 1889–1975, vol. VII
Garton, Lt-Col James Archibald, 1891–1969, vol. VI
Garton, John William, 1895–1971, vol. VII
Garton, Sir Richard Charles, 1857–1934, vol. III
Gartside-Tipping, Col Robert Francis, 1852–1926, vol. II
Garvagh, 3rd Baron, 1852–1915, vol. I
Garvagh, 4th Baron, 1878–1956, vol. V
Garvan, Sir John Joseph, 1873–1927, vol. II
Garvice, Charles, died 1920, vol. II
Garvice, Major Chudleigh, 1875–1921, vol. II
Garvie, Rev. Alfred Ernest, 1861–1945, vol. IV
Garvin, James Louis, died 1947, vol. IV
Garvin, Thomas, 1843–1922, vol. II
Garvin, Sir Thomas Forrest, 1881–1940, vol. III
Garwood, Edmund Johnston, 1864–1949, vol. IV
Garwood, Lt-Col Henry Percy, 1882–1956, vol. V
Garwood, Engr-Rear-Adm. Hugh Sydney, 1872–1948, vol. IV
Garwood, Lt-Col John Reginald, 1873–1948, vol. IV
Gary, Elbert Henry, died 1927, vol. II
Gary, Romain, 1914–1980, vol. VII
Gascoigne, Sir Alvary Douglas Frederick, 1893–1970, vol. VI
Gascoigne, Lt-Col Cecil Claud Hugh Orby, 1877–1929, vol. III
Gascoigne, Brig.-Gen. Sir (Ernest) Frederick (Orby), 1873–1944, vol. IV
Gascoigne, Col Frederic Richard Thomas Trench, 1851–1937, vol. III
Gascoigne, Brig.-Gen. Sir Frederick; see Gascoigne, Brig.-Gen. Sir E. F. O.
Gascoigne, Hubert Claude Victor, died 1959, vol. V
Gascoigne, John Henry, 1856–1928, vol. II
Gascoigne, Laura Gwendolen, died 1949, vol. IV
Gascoigne, Maj.-Gen. Sir William Julius Gascoigne, 1844–1926, vol. II
Gascoyne-Cecil, Victor Alexander, 1891–1977, vol. VII
Gascoyne-Cecil, Rt Rev. Lord William; see Cecil.
Gaselee, Gen. Sir Alfred, 1844–1918, vol. II
Gaselee, Sir Stephen, 1882–1943, vol. IV
Gask, George Ernest, 1875–1951, vol. V
Gask, Rear-Adm. (S) Walter, 1870–1949, vol. IV
Gaskain, John Stuart Hinton, 1910–1971, vol. VII
Gaskell, Ven. Albert Fisher, 1874–1950, vol. IV
Gaskell, Surg. Vice-Adm. Sir Arthur, 1871–1952, vol. V
Gaskell, Rt Hon. Charles George Milnes, 1842–1919, vol. II
Gaskell, Lady Constance M.; see Milnes Gaskell.
Gaskell, Evelyn Milnes, 1877–1931, vol. III
Gaskell, George Percival, 1868–1934, vol. III
Gaskell, Helen Mary, died 1940, vol. III

Gaskell, Henry Melville, 1879–1954, vol. V
Gaskell, Maj.-Gen. Herbert Stuart, 1882–1957, vol. V
Gaskell, Sir Holbrook, 1878–1951, vol. V
Gaskell, Col Joseph, 1849–1930, vol. III
Gaskell, Col Joseph Gerald, 1885–1959, vol. V
Gaskell, Walter Holbrook, 1847–1914, vol. I
Gaskell, William, 1874–1954, vol. V
Gaskin, Arthur J., 1862–1928, vol. II
Gasking, Mrs Ella Hudson, died 1966, vol. VI
Gaskoin, Charles Jacinth Bellairs, died 1955, vol. V
Gasquet, His Eminence Cardinal Francis Aidan, 1846–1929, vol. III
Gass, John Bradshaw, 1855–1939, vol. III
Gass, Sir Neville Archibald, 1893–1965, vol. VI
Gasser, Herbert Spencer, 1888–1963, vol. VI
Gasson, Sir Lionel Bell, 1889–1977, vol. VII
Gaster, Moses, 1856–1939, vol. III
Gastrell, Lt-Col Everard Huddleston, 1898–1960, vol. V
Gastrell, Sir William Houghton-, 1852–1935, vol. III
Gastrell, William Shaw Harriss, 1862–1948, vol. IV
Gatacre, Maj.-Gen. Sir John, 1841–1932, vol. III
Gatacre, Maj.-Gen. Sir William Forbes, 1843–1906, vol. I
Gatehouse, Maj.-Gen. Alexander Hugh, 1895–1964, vol. VI
Gatenby, James Brontë, 1892–1960, vol. V
Gater, Sir George Henry, 1886–1963, vol. VI
Gates, Caleb Frank, 1857–1946, vol. IV
Gates, Edward, died 1965, vol. VI
Gates, Sir Frank Campbell, 1862–1947, vol. IV
Gates, Horace Frederick Alfred, 1903–1962, vol. VI
Gates, Lewis Edwards, 1860–1924, vol. II
Gates, Percy, died 1940, vol. III
Gates, R(eginald) Ruggles, 1882–1962, vol. VI
Gates, Sidney Barrington, 1893–1973, vol. VII
Gates, Sylvester Govett, 1901–1972, vol. VII
Gates, Walter George, died 1936, vol. III
Gatey, Joseph, 1855–1912, vol. I
Gathorne-Hardy, Hon. Alfred Erskine, 1845–1918, vol. II
Gathorne-Hardy, Col Hon. Charles Gathorne, 1841–1919, vol. II
Gathorne-Hardy, Gen. Hon. Sir Francis; see Gathorne- Hardy, Gen. Hon. Sir J. F.
Gathorne-Hardy, Geoffrey Malcolm, 1878–1972, vol. VII
Gathorne-Hardy, Lady Isobel, 1875–1963, vol. VI
Gathorne-Hardy, Gen. Hon. Sir (John) Francis, 1874–1949, vol. IV
Gathorne-Hardy, Hon. Robert, 1902–1973, vol. VII
Gati, Banerji D.; see Durga Gati.
Gatley, Clement Carpenter, 1881–1936, vol. III
Gatley, John, 1845–1934, vol. III
Gatliff, Gen. Albert Farrar, 1857–1927, vol. II
Gatling, Richard Jordan, 1818–1903, vol. I
Gatt, Hon. Camillo, vol. II
Gatt, Hon. Lorenzo, 1857–1938, vol. III
Gatti, Sir John M., 1872–1929, vol. III
Gattie, Alfred Warwick, 1856–1925, vol. II
Gattie, Vernon Rodney Montagu, 1885–1966, vol. VI

Gatty, Rev. Alfred, 1813–1903, vol. I
Gatty, Sir Alfred Scott S.; see Scott-Gatty.
Gatty, Nicholas Comyn, 1874–1946, vol. IV
Gatty, Sir Stephen Herbert, 1849–1922, vol. II
Gaudet, Col Frederick Mondelet, 1867–1947, vol. IV
Gaudin, Engr-Rear-Adm. Edouard, died 1945, vol. IV
Gaughran, Rt Rev. Laurence, 1842–1928, vol. II
Gaughren, Rt Rev. Matthew, 1843–1914, vol. I (A)
Gaul, Walter Miller, 1867–1938, vol. III
Gaul, Rt Rev. William Thomas, died 1928, vol. II
Gauld, David, died 1936, vol. III
Gault, Brig. A(ndrew) Hamilton, 1882–1958, vol. V
Gault, James, 1850–1927, vol. II
Gault, Brig. Sir James Frederick, 1902–1977, vol. VII
Gaumont, Léon Ernest, 1864–1946, vol. IV
Gaunt, Lt-Col Cecil Robert, 1863–1938, vol. III
Gaunt, Sir Edwin, 1818–1903, vol. I
Gaunt, Adm. Sir Ernest Frederick Augustus, 1865–1940, vol. III
Gaunt, Adm. Sir Guy Reginald Archer, 1870–1953, vol. V
Gaunt, Mary, died 1942, vol. IV
Gaunt, Percy Reginald, 1875–1926, vol. II
Gaunt, Walter Henry, 1874–1951, vol. V
Gaunt, William, 1900–1980, vol. VII
Gauntlett, Major Eric Gerald, 1885–1972, vol. VII
Gauntlett, Sir Frederic; see Gauntlett, Sir M. F.
Gauntlett, Sir (Mager) Frederic, 1873–1964, vol. VI
Gaussen, Maj.-Gen. Charles de Lisle, 1896–1971, vol. VII
Gaussen, Brig.-Gen. James Robert, 1871–1959, vol. V
Gaussen, Perceval David Campbell, 1862–1928, vol. II
Gauthier, Most Rev. Charles Hugh, 1843–1922, vol. II
Gauthier, Rt Rev. George, 1871–1940, vol. III
Gauthier-Villars, Henry, 1859–1931, vol. III
Gautier, C. Lucien, 1850–1924, vol. II
Gautier, Judith, died 1917, vol. II
Gauvain, (Catherine Joan) Suzette, (Mrs R. O. Murray), died 1980, vol. VII
Gauvain, Sir Henry, 1878–1945, vol. IV
Gauvain, Suzette; see Gauvain, C. J. S.
Gauvain, W., died 1910, vol. I
Gavan-Duffy, Hon. Sir Charles Leonard, 1882–1961, vol. VI
Gavan-Duffy, Thomas, 1867–1932, vol. III
Gavey, Sir John, 1842–1923, vol. II
Gavin, Ethel, died 1918, vol. II
Gavin, Michael, 1843–1919, vol. II
Gavin, Sir William, 1886–1968, vol. VI
Gavin, William Aloysius, died 1948, vol. IV
Gavito, Vicente S.; see Sanchez-Gavito.
Gawan Taylor, Henry, 1855–1928, vol. II
Gawne, Ewan Moore, 1889–1978, vol. VII
Gawsworth, John, 1912–1970, vol. VI
Gawthorpe, Brig. John Bernard, 1891–1979, vol. VII
Gay, Maj.-Gen. Sir Arthur William, 1863–1944, vol. IV

Gay, Edwin Francis, 1867–1946, vol. IV
Gay, Maisie, 1883–1945, vol. IV
Gayda, Virginio, 1885–1944, vol. IV
Gaye, Sir Arthur Stretton, 1881–1960, vol. V
Gaye, Rev. Herbert Charles, died 1931, vol. III
Gayer, Arthur David, 1903–1951, vol. V
Gayer-Anderson, Major Robert Grenville, 1881–1945, vol. IV
Gayer-Anderson, Col Thomas Gayer, 1881–1960, vol. V
Gayford, Air Cdre Oswald Robert, 1893–1945, vol. IV
Gayley, Charles Mills, 1858–1932, vol. III
Gaze, Alfred Harold, 1885–1954, vol. V
Geach, William Foster, 1859–1940, vol. III (A), vol. IV
Geake, Charles, 1867–1919, vol. II
Geard, John Reginald, 1861–1934, vol. III
Geary, Major Benjamin Handley, 1891–1976, vol. VII
Geary, Lt-Col Hon. George Reginald, 1874–1954, vol. V
Geary, Lt-Gen. Sir Henry Le Guay, 1837–1918, vol. II
Geary, Sir William Nevill Montgomerie, 5th Bt, 1859–1944, vol. IV
Gebbie, Sir Frederick St John, 1871–1939, vol. III
Geddes, 1st Baron, 1879–1954, vol. V
Geddes, 2nd Baron, 1907–1975, vol. VII
Geddes, Rt Hon. Sir Eric Campbell, 1875–1937, vol. III
Geddes, Ewan, died 1935, vol. III
Geddes, Lt-Col George Hessing, 1864–1933, vol. III
Geddes, Irvine Campbell, 1882–1962, vol. VI
Geddes, Brig.Gen. John Gordon, 1863–1919, vol. II
Geddes, Norman Bel, 1893–1958, vol. V
Geddes, Sir Patrick, 1854–1932, vol. III
Geddes, Col Robert James, 1858–1928, vol. II
Geddes, Rt Rev. William Archibald, 1894–1947, vol. IV
Geddes, Sir William Duguid, 1828–1900, vol. I
Geddie, John, 1848–1937, vol. III
Geddie, John Liddell, 1881–1969, vol. VI
Geddis, Sir William Duncan, 1896–1971, vol. VII
Geden, Alfred Shenington, 1857–1936, vol. III
Gedge, Rev. Edward Lionel, 1861–1932, vol. III
Gedge, Rev. Hugh Somerville, 1844–1923, vol. II
Gedge, Montagu Lathom, 1899–1958, vol. V
Gedge, Sydney, 1829–1923, vol. II
Gedye, George Eric Rowe, 1890–1970, vol. VI
Gedye, Nicholas George, 1874–1947, vol. IV
Gee, Col Ernest Edward, 1888–1959, vol. V
Gee, Lt-Col Frederick William, 1863–1930, vol. III
Gee, Harry Percy, 1874–1962, vol. VI
Gee, Very Rev. Henry, died 1938, vol. III
Gee, Hubert George, 1909–1959, vol. V
Gee, Rev. Richard, 1817–1902, vol. I
Gee, Captain Robert, 1876–1960, vol. V
Gee, Samuel Jones, died 1911, vol. I
Gee, William Winson Haldane, 1857–1928, vol. II
Geen, Burnard, 1882–1966, vol. VI
Geen, Harry, died 1939, vol. III

Geer, Ven. George Thomas, 1844–1918, vol. II
Geffen, John Lionel Henry, 1925–1975, vol. VII
Geijer, Eric Neville, *died* 1941, vol. IV
Geikie, Sir Archibald, 1835–1924, vol. II
Geikie, Rev. Cunningham, 1824–1906, vol. I
Geikie, James, 1839–1915, vol. I
Geikie-Cobb, Ivo; *see* Cobb.
Geikie-Cobb, Rev. William Frederick, 1857–1941, vol. IV
Geil, William Edgar, *died* 1925, vol. II
Geldart, Rev. Ernest, 1848–1929, vol. III
Geldart, Rev. James William, 1837–1914, vol. I
Geldart, William Martin, 1870–1922, vol. II
Gelder, Sir Alfred; *see* Gelder, Sir W. A.
Gelder, Sir (William) Alfred, 1855–1941, vol. IV
Gell, Hon. Mrs Edith Mary, 1860–1944, vol. IV
Gell, Rt Rev. Frederick, *died* 1902, vol. I
Gell, Herbert George, 1856–1931, vol. III
Gell, Sir James, 1823–1905, vol. I
Gell, Philip Lyttelton, 1852–1926, vol. II
Gell, Rev. Canon William, 1859–1939, vol. III
Gell, William Charles Coleman, 1888–1969, vol. VI
Gell, William John, 1893–1961, vol. VI
Gellert, Leon, 1892–1977, vol. VII
Gellibrand, Maj.-Gen. Sir John, 1872–1945, vol. IV
Gelsthorpe, Rt Rev. (Alfred) Morris, 1892–1968, vol. VI
Gelsthorpe, Rt Rev. Morris; *see* Gelsthorpe, Rt Rev. A. M.
Gem, Rev. Hubert Arnold, *died* 1936, vol. III
Gemmell, Sir Arthur Alexander, 1892–1960, vol. V
Gemmell, George Harrison, 1860–1941, vol. IV
Gemmell, Samson, *died* 1913, vol. I
Gemmell, Lt-Col William Alexander Stewart, 1874–1932, vol. III
Gemmill, James Fairlie, *died* 1926, vol. II
Gemmill, Lt-Col William, 1878–1918, vol. II
Genée-Isitt, Dame Adeline, 1878–1970, vol. VI
Genese, Robert William, 1848–1928, vol. II
Genevoix, Maurice Charles Louis, 1890–1980, vol. VII
Genn, Leo John, 1905–1978, vol. VII
Genn, Captain Otto Hermann H.; *see* Hawke-Genn.
Gennadius, Joannes, 1844–1932, vol. III
Gennings, John Frederick, 1885–1955, vol. V
Genochio, Henry, 1862–1933, vol. III
Gent, Sir Edward; *see* Gent, Sir G. E. J.
Gent, Sir (Gerard) Edward (James), 1895–1948, vol. IV
Gent, John, 1844–1927, vol. II
Gentele, (Claes-) Göran Herman Arvid, 1920–1972, vol. VII
Gentele, Göran; *see* Gentele, C.-G. H. A.
Gentili, Most Rev. Charles, 1842–1917, vol. I, vol. II
Gentle, Francis Steward, 1894–1962, vol. VI
Gentle, Sir Frederick William, 1892–1966, vol. VI
Gentle, Sir William Benjamin, 1864–1948, vol. IV
Gentles, Thomas A., 1867–1943, vol. IV
Gentner, Wolfgang, 1906–1980, vol. VII (AII)
Gentry, Jack Sydney Bates, 1899–1978, vol. VII
Geoffrion, Aimé, 1872–1946, vol. IV

Geoffrion, Victor, 1851–1923, vol. II
Geoghegan, Col Francis Edward, 1869–1945, vol. IV
Geoghegan, Hon. James, *died* 1951, vol. V
Geoghegan, Joseph, 1888–1948, vol. IV
Geoghegan, Col Norman Meredith, 1876–1962, vol. VI
Geoghegan, Brig.-Gen. Stannus, 1866–1929, vol. III
George, Sir Anthony Hastings, 1886–1944, vol. IV
George, Ven. Christopher Owen, 1891–1977, vol. VII
George, Daniel, 1890–1967, vol. VI
George, Edward Claudius Scotney, 1865–1936, vol. III
George, Sir Edward James, *died* 1950, vol. IV
George, Sir Ernest, 1839–1922, vol. II
George, Frank Bernard, 1899–1974, vol. VII
George, Rev. Canon George Frank, 1873–1942, vol. IV
George, Hereford B., 1838–1910, vol. I
George, Hugh Shaw, 1892–1967, vol. VI
George, Sir John Clarke, 1901–1972, vol. VII
George, Mary Dorothy, *died* 1971, vol. VII
George, Lady Megan L.; *see* Lloyd George.
George, Air Vice-Marshal Sir Robert Allingham, 1896–1967, vol. VI
George, Rt Rev. Mgr Thomas, 1872–1943, vol. IV
George, Thomas Neville, 1904–1980, vol. VII
George, W. L., 1882–1926, vol. II
George, Senator Walter Franklin, 1878–1957, vol. V
George, Hon. William James, 1853–1931, vol. III
George, William R., 1866–1936, vol. III
Georges, Sir (James) Olva, 1890–1976, vol. VII
Georges, Sir Olva; *see* Georges, Sir J. O.
Gepp, Maj.-Gen. Sir Cyril; *see* Gepp, Maj.-Gen. Sir E. C.
Gepp, Maj.-Gen. Sir (Ernest) Cyril, 1879–1964, vol. VI
Gepp, Sir Herbert William, 1877–1954, vol. V
Gepp, Rev. Nicolas Parker, *died* 1921, vol. II
Geraghty, Sir William, 1917–1977, vol. VII
Gerahty, Sir Charles Cyril, 1888–1978, vol. VII
Gerald, William John, 1850–1923, vol. II
Gerard, 2nd Baron, 1851–1902, vol. I
Gerard, 3rd Baron, 1883–1953, vol. V
Gerard, Amelia Louise, 1878–1970, vol. VI
Gerard, Bt Col Charles Robert Tolver Michael, 1894–1971, vol. VII
Gerard, Dorothea; *see* Longard de Longgarde, D.
Gerard, Emily de Laszowski-, 1849–1905, vol. I
Gerard, Hon. James Watson, 1867–1951, vol. V
Gerard, Father John, 1840–1912, vol. I
Gerard, Gen. Sir Montagu Gilbert, 1843–1905, vol. I
Gerard-Dicconson, Hon. Robert Joseph; *see* Dicconson.
Gerardy, Jean, 1877–1929, vol. III
Géraud, Charles Joseph André, 1882–1974, vol. VII
Gerbrandy, Pieter S., 1885–1961, vol. VI
Gere, Charles March, 1869–1957, vol. V
Gerhard, Roberto Juan René, 1896–1970, vol. VI
Gerhardie, William Alexander, 1895–1977, vol. VII

Gerhardt, Elena, 1883–1961, vol. VI
Gericke van Herwijnen, Baron, *died* 1930, vol. III
Germaine, Robert Arthur, *died* 1905, vol. I
German, Sir Edward, 1862–1936, vol. III
German, Major Sir James, 1879–1958, vol. V
German, William Manley, 1851–1933, vol. III
Germanos, Strenopoulos, 1872–1951, vol. V
Gerome, Jean Leon, 1824–1904, vol. I
Gerothwohl, Maurice Alfred, 1877–1941, vol. IV
Gerrans, Henry Tresawna, 1858–1921, vol. II
Gerrard, Sir (Albert) Denis, 1903–1965, vol. VI
Gerrard, Charles Robert, *died* 1964, vol. VI
Gerrard, Sir Denis; *see* Gerrard, Sir A. D.
Gerrard, Air Cdre Eugene Louis, 1881–1963, vol. VI
Gerrard, Major Frederick Wernham, 1887–1974, vol. VII
Gerrard, Maj.-Gen. John Joseph, 1867–1938, vol. III
Gerry, Hon. Elbridge Thomas, 1837–1927, vol. II
Gershwin, George, 1898–1937, vol. III
Gertler, Mark, 1892–1939, vol. III
Gerty, Paymaster Captain Francis Hamilton, 1876–1955, vol. V
Gervais, Hon. Honoré Hippolyte Achille, 1864–1915, vol. I (A), vol. III
Gervers, Brig. Francis Richard Soutter, 1873–1971, vol. VII
Gervis, Henry, 1837–1924, vol. II
Gervis, Henry, 1863–1941, vol. IV
Gervis-Meyrick, Sir George Augustus Eliott Tapps; *see* Meyrick.
Gery, Henry Theodore W.; *see* Wade-Gery.
Gesell, Arnold, 1880–1961, vol. VI
Gethin, Sir Richard Charles Percy, 7th Bt, 1847–1921, vol. II
Gethin, Col Sir Richard Walter St Lawrence, 8th Bt, 1878–1946, vol. IV
Gettins, Lt-Col Joseph Holmes, 1873–1954, vol. V
Getty, J(ean) Paul, 1892–1976, vol. VII
Geyer, Albertus Lourens, 1894–1969, vol. VI
Geyl, Pieter, 1887–1966, vol. VI
Ghislain, Léon; *see* Carton de Wiart, L. C. G.
Ghormley, Vice-Adm. Robert Lee, 1883–1958, vol. V
Ghosal, Mrs Srimati Svarna Kumari Devi, 1857–1932, vol. III
Ghose, Sir Bipin Behary, 1868–1934, vol. III
Ghose, Sir Charu Chunder, 1874–1934, vol. III
Ghose, Sir Chunder Madhub, 1838–1918, vol. II
Ghose, Hemendra Prasad, 1876–1962, vol. VI
Ghose, Sir Rashbehary, 1845–1921, vol. II
Ghose, Sir Sarat Kumar, 1879–1963, vol. VI
Ghosh, Sir Jnan Chandra, 1894–1959, vol. V
Ghulam Mohammed, 1895–1956, vol. V
Ghuznavi, Hon. Alhadj Nawab Bahadur Sir Abdelkerim Abu Ahmed Kahan of Dilduar, 1872–1939, vol. III
Giacometti, Alberto, 1901–1966, vol. VI
Giannini, Amadeo Peter, 1870–1949, vol. IV
Gib, Gen. Sir William Anthony, 1827–1915, vol. I
Gibb, Sir Alexander, 1872–1958, vol. V
Gibb, Alistair Monteith, 1901–1955, vol. V
Gibb, Andrew Dewar, *died* 1974, vol. VII

Gibb, Sir Claude Dixon, 1898–1959, vol. V
Gibb, Maj.-Gen. Sir Evan, 1877–1947, vol. IV
Gibb, Sir George Stegmann, 1850–1925, vol. II
Gibb, Sir Hamilton Alexander Rosskeen, 1895–1971, vol. VII
Gibb, James, 1844–1910, vol. I
Gibb, Rev. James, 1857–1935, vol. III
Gibb, James A. T., 1842–1922, vol. II
Gibb, James Rattray, 1884–1946, vol. IV
Gibb, Rev. John, 1835–1915, vol. I
Gibb, Col John Hassard Stewart, 1859–1933, vol. III
Gibb, Malcolm Couper, 1861–1938, vol. III
Gibb, Maurice Sylvester, 1878–1950, vol. IV
Gibb, Robert, 1845–1932, vol. III
Gibb, Robertson Fyffe, 1868–1944, vol. IV
Gibb, Lt-Col Ronald Charles, 1873–1946, vol. IV
Gibb, Thomas George, 1915–1980, vol. VII
Gibbard, George, 1886–1960, vol. V
Gibbard, Maj.-Gen. Thomas Wykes, 1865–1957, vol. V
Gibberd, George Frederick, *died* 1976, vol. VII
Gibbes, Cuthbert Chapman, 1850–1927, vol. II
Gibbes, Sir Edward Osborne-, 3rd Bt, 1850–1931, vol. III
Gibbes, Sir Philip Arthur Osborne-, 4th Bt, 1884–1940, vol. III
Gibbes, Reginald Prescott, 1867–1933, vol. III
Gibbings, Robert John, 1889–1958, vol. V
Gibbins, Frederick William, 1861–1937, vol. III
Gibbins, Rev. Henry de Beltgens, 1865–1907, vol. I
Gibbins, Joseph, 1888–1965, vol. VI
Gibbins, Theodore, 1876–1952, vol. V
Gibbon, Col Charles Monk, 1877–1937, vol. III
Gibbon, Sir Douglas Stuart, 1882–1960, vol. V
Gibbon, Sir Gwilym; *see* Gibbon, Sir I. G.
Gibbon, Sir (Ioan) Gwilym, 1874–1948, vol. IV
Gibbon, Brig.-Gen. James Aubrey, 1864–1947, vol. IV
Gibbon, Rev. James Morgan, *died* 1932, vol. III
Gibbon, Brig. John Houghton, 1878–1960, vol. V
Gibbon, Perceval, 1879–1926, vol. II
Gibbon, Thomas Mitchell, *died* 1921, vol. II
Gibbon, Sir William Duff, 1837–1919, vol. II
Gibbon, Lt-Col William Duff, 1880–1955, vol. V
Gibbons, Major Sir Alexander Doran, 7th Bt, 1873–1956, vol. V
Gibbons, Sir Charles, 6th Bt, 1828–1909, vol. I
Gibbons, Major Edward Stephen, 1883–1918, vol. II
Gibbons, Cdre George, *died* 1959, vol. V
Gibbons, Sir George Christie, 1848–1918, vol. II
Gibbons, His Eminence Cardinal James, 1834–1921, vol. II
Gibbons, James Francis, 1890–1957, vol. V
Gibbons, James Samuel, 1850–1914, vol. I
Gibbons, John Lloyd, 1837–1919, vol. II
Gibbons, Sir Thomas Clarke Pilling, 1868–1934, vol. III
Gibbons, Lt-Col Sir Walter, 1871–1933, vol. III
Gibbons, Sir William, 1841–1930, vol. III
Gibbons, Col William Ernest, 1898–1976, vol. VII
Gibbons, Sir William Kenrick, 1876–1957, vol. V
Gibbs, Dame Anstice Rosa, 1905–1978, vol. VII

Gibbs, Antony, 1842–1907, vol. I
Gibbs, Major Arthur Hamilton, *died* 1964, vol. VI
Gibbs, Cecil Armstrong, 1889–1960, vol. V
Gibbs, Charles, *died* 1943, vol. IV
Gibbs, Sir Charles Henry, 1854–1924, vol. II
Gibbs, Edward Mitchel, 1847–1935, vol. III
Gibbs, Hon. Sir Geoffrey Cokayne, 1901–1975, vol. VII
Gibbs, George Howard, 1889–1969, vol. VI
Gibbs, Captain George Louis Downall, 1882–1956, vol. V
Gibbs, Hon. Henry L., 1861–1907, vol. I
Gibbs, Col James Alec Charles, 1867–1930, vol. III
Gibbs, John Herbert, 1872–1962, vol. VI
Gibbs, Ven. Hon. Kenneth Francis, 1856–1935, vol. III
Gibbs, Brig. Lancelot Merivale, 1889–1966, vol. VI
Gibbs, Very Rev. Michael McCausland, 1900–1962, vol. VI
Gibbs, Hon. Michael Patrick, 1870–1943, vol. IV
Gibbs, Sir Philip, 1877–1962, vol. VI
Gibbs, Rev. Thomas Crook, *died* 1914, vol. I
Gibbs, Hon. Vicary, 1853–1932, vol. III
Gibbs, Walter George, 1872–1929, vol. III
Gibbs, Lt-Col William, 1877–1963, vol. VI
Gibbs, William Edward, 1889–1934, vol. III
Gibbs-Smith, Very Rev. Oswin Harvard, 1901–1969, vol. VI
Giberne, Agnes, 1845–1939, vol. III
Giblin, Major Lyndhurst Falkiner, 1872–1951, vol. V
Giblin, Col Wilfrid Wanostrocht, 1872–1951, vol. V
Gibney, James, 1847–1908, vol. I (A), vol. III
Gibney, Rt Rev. Matthew, 1838–1925, vol. II
Gibson, Hon. Lord; Robert Gibson, 1886–1965, vol. VI
Gibson, Sir Ackroyd Herbert, 3rd Bt (*cr* 1926), 1893–1975, vol. VII
Gibson, Rt Rev. Alan George Sumner, 1856–1922, vol. II
Gibson, Alexander Boyce, 1900–1972, vol. VII
Gibson, Alexander George, 1875–1950, vol. IV
Gibson, Alexander James, 1876–1960, vol. VI (AI)
Gibson, Andrew, 1864–1933, vol. III
Gibson, Arnold Hartley, 1878–1959, vol. V
Gibson, Arnold Mackenzie, *died* 1956, vol. V
Gibson, Sir Basil; *see* Gibson, Sir E. B.
Gibson, Charles Dana, 1867–1944, vol. IV
Gibson, Sir Charles Granville, 1880–1948, vol. IV
Gibson, Charles R., 1870–1931, vol. III
Gibson, Charles Stanley, 1884–1950, vol. IV
Gibson, Charles William, 1889–1977, vol. VII
Gibson, Sir Christopher Herbert, 2nd Bt (*cr* 1931), 1897–1962, vol. VI
Gibson, Clement William Osmund, 1878–1963, vol. VI
Gibson, Rear-Adm. Cuthbert Walter Sumner, 1890–1971, vol. VII
Gibson, Rt Rev. Edgar Charles Sumner, 1848–1924, vol. II
Gibson, Sir Edmund Currey, 1886–1974, vol. VII
Gibson, Hon. Edward Graves Mayne, 1873–1928, vol. II

Gibson, Elizabeth, 1869–1931, vol. III
Gibson, Sir (Ernest) Basil, 1877–1962, vol. VI
Gibson, Hon. Sir Frank Ernest, 1879–1965, vol. VI
Gibson, George, 1885–1953, vol. V
Gibson, George Alexander, 1854–1913, vol. I
Gibson, George Alexander, 1858–1930, vol. III
Gibson, George Herbert Rae, 1881–1932, vol. III
Gibson, Wing Comdr Guy Penrose, 1918–1944, vol. IV
Gibson, Harold, 1884–1961, vol. VI
Gibson, Harold Charles Lehrs, 1897–1960, vol. V
Gibson, Harry Frederick C.; *see* Carew-Gibson.
Gibson, Harvey Dow, 1882–1950, vol. IV
Gibson, Sir Henry James, 1860–1950, vol. IV
Gibson, Sir Herbert, 1st Bt (*cr* 1926), 1851–1932, vol. III
Gibson, Sir Herbert, 1st Bt (*cr* 1931), 1863–1934, vol. III
Gibson, Herbert Mellor, 1896–1954, vol. V
Gibson, Hope, 1859–1928, vol. II
Gibson, Sir (Horace) Stephen, 1897–1963, vol. VI
Gibson, Rear-Adm. Isham Worsley, 1882–1950, vol. IV
Gibson, James, 1864–1943, vol. IV
Gibson, Rt Rev. James Byers, 1881–1952, vol. V
Gibson, Sir James Puckering, 1st Bt (*cr* 1909), 1849–1912, vol. I
Gibson, John Ashley, 1885–1948, vol. IV
Gibson, Rev. John Campbell, *died* 1919, vol. II
Gibson, John Constant, 1861–1939, vol. III
Gibson, Rt Hon. John George, 1846–1923, vol. II
Gibson, Rev. John George, 1859–1927, vol. II
Gibson, John Gibson, 1889–1970, vol. VI
Gibson, Rev. John Monro, 1838–1921, vol. II
Gibson, Maj.-Gen. Sir John Mortson, 1842–1929, vol. III
Gibson, Rev. John Paul S. R., *died* 1964, vol. VI
Gibson, Sir John Watson, 1885–1947, vol. IV
Gibson, Sir Kenneth Lloyd, 2nd Bt (*cr* 1926), 1888–1967, vol. VI
Gibson, Sir Leslie Bertram, 1896–1952, vol. V
Gibson, Major Lewis, 1880–1935, vol. III
Gibson, Margaret Dunlop, *died* 1920, vol. II
Gibson, Very Rev. Matthew Sayer, *died* 1971, vol. VII
Gibson, Michael Joseph, 1876–1953, vol. V
Gibson, Myra Macindoe, 1886–1966, vol. VI
Gibson, Rt Rev. Percival William, 1893–1970, vol. VI
Gibson, Maj.-Gen. Ralph Burgess, 1894–1962, vol. VI
Gibson, Raymond Evelyn, 1878–1969, vol. VI
Gibson, Rev. Richard Hudson, *died* 1904, vol. I
Gibson, Robert; *see* Gibson, Hon. Lord.
Gibson, Sir Robert, 1864–1934, vol. III
Gibson, Rt Rev. Robert Atkinson, 1846–1919, vol. II
Gibson, Robert Clarence, 1892–1959, vol. V
Gibson, Robert John H.; *see* Harvey-Gibson.
Gibson, Sir Stephen; *see* Gibson, Sir H. S.
Gibson, Strickland, 1877–1958, vol. V
Gibson, Rt Rev. Theodore Sumner, 1885–1953, vol. V
Gibson, Thomas, 1875–1925, vol. II

Gibson, Very Rev. Thomas B., 1847–1927, vol. II
Gibson, Walcot, 1864–1941, vol. IV
Gibson, Sir Walter Matthew, 1856–1940, vol. III
Gibson, Wilfrid, 1878–1962, vol. VI
Gibson, Hon. William, 1849–1914, vol. I
Gibson, Lt-Col William, 1887–1969, vol. VI
Gibson, William John, 1865–1944, vol. IV
Gibson, William Pettigrew, 1902–1960, vol. V
Gibson, William Ralph Boyce, 1869–1935, vol. III
Gibson, William Sumner, 1876–1946, vol. IV
Gibson, William Victor Halliday, 1884–1954, vol. V
Gibson, Sir William Waymouth, 1873–1971, vol. VII
Gibson-Carmichael, John Murray, 1860–1923, vol. II
Gibson-Craig, Sir Archibald Charles, 4th Bt, 1883–1914, vol. I
Gibson-Craig, Sir James Henry, 3rd Bt, 1841–1908, vol. I
Gibson-Craig-Carmichael, Sir (Archibald Henry) William, 14th Bt (and 7th Bt), 1917–1969, vol. VI
Gibson-Craig-Carmichael, Sir Eardley Charles William, 13th Bt (and 6th Bt), 1887–1939, vol. III
Gibson-Craig-Carmichael, Captain Sir Henry Thomas, 5th Bt (and 12th Bt), 1885–1926, vol. II
Gibson-Craig-Carmichael, Sir William; see Gibson-Craig-Carmichael, Sir A. H. W.
Gibson Fleming, Edward, 1885–1962, vol. VI
Gibsone, Maj.-Gen. William Waring Primrose, 1872–1957, vol. V
Gick, Sir William John, 1877–1948, vol. IV
Giddens, George, 1855–1920, vol. II
Giddings, Franklin Henry, 1855–1931, vol. III
Giddings, William John Peter, 1861–1938, vol. III (A), vol. IV
Giddy, Harry Douglas, 1887–1959, vol. V
Gide, André Paul Guillaume, 1869–1951, vol. V
Gide, Prof. Charles, 1847–1932, vol. III
Gideon, Col James Henry, 1862–1958, vol. V
Gidhour, Maharaja Bahadur Chandra Mauleshvar Prasad Singh, 1890–1937, vol. III
Gidhour, Maharajah Sir Ravneswar Prasad Singh, Bahadur of, 1860–1923, vol. II
Gidney, Sir Claude Henry, 1887–1968, vol. VI
Gidney, Lt-Col Sir Henry Albert John, 1873–1942, vol. IV
Gie, S. F. N., 1884–1945, vol. IV
Gielgud, Lt-Col Lewis Evelyn, 1894–1953, vol. V
Gieseking, Walter Wilhelm, 1895–1956, vol. V
Giffard, Very Rev. Agnew Walter Giles, 1869–1947, vol. IV
Giffard, Adm. George Augustus, 1849–1925, vol. III
Giffard, George Campbell, 1853–1932, vol. III
Giffard, Gen. Sir George James, 1886–1964, vol. VI
Giffard, Maj.-Gen. Sir Gerald Godfray, 1867–1926, vol. II
Giffard, Hardinge Frank, died 1908, vol. I
Giffard, Sir Henry Alexander, 1838–1927, vol. II
Giffard, Walter Thomas Courtenay, 1839–1926, vol. II
Giffard, Col William Carter, 1859–1921, vol. II
Giffen, Edmund, 1902–1963, vol. VI

Giffen, Sir Robert, 1837–1910, vol. I
Gifford, 3rd Baron, 1849–1911, vol. I
Gifford, 4th Baron, 1857–1937, vol. III
Gifford, 5th Baron, 1899–1961, vol. VI
Gifford, Charles Edwin, 1843–1922, vol. II
Gifford, Ven. Edwin Hamilton, 1820–1905, vol. I
Gifford, Hon. Maurice Raymond, 1859–1910, vol. I
Gifford, Walter Sherman, 1885–1966, vol. VI
Gift, Theo.; see Boulger, D. H.
Gigli, Beniamino, 1890–1957, vol. V
Gilbert, Albert, died 1927, vol. II
Gilbert, Sir Alfred, 1854–1934, vol. III
Gilbert, Brig.-Gen. Arthur Robert, 1863–1937, vol. III
Gilbert, Sir Bernard William, 1891–1957, vol. V
Gilbert, Carew Davies, died 1913, vol. I
Gilbert, Cass, 1859–1934, vol. III
Gilbert, Charles E. L., died 1937, vol. III
Gilbert, Rev. Charles Robert, 1851–1919, vol. II
Gilbert, Charles W.; see Web-Gilbert.
Gilbert, Edmund William, 1900–1973, vol. VII
Gilbert, Mrs Grace Catherine Rose D.; see Davies-Gilbert.
Gilbert, Sir Henry; see Gilbert, Sir J. H.
Gilbert, Sir Ian Anderson J.; see Johnson-Gilbert.
Gilbert, James Daniel, 1864–1941, vol. IV
Gilbert, Jean, died 1942, vol. IV
Gilbert, Sir John, 1817–1897, vol. I
Gilbert, Sir John Thomas, 1829–1898, vol. I
Gilbert, Sir John William, 1871–1934, vol. III
Gilbert, Sir (Joseph) Henry, 1817–1901, vol. I
Gilbert, Sir (Joseph) Trounsell, 1888–1975, vol. VII
Gilbert, Keith Reginald, 1914–1973, vol. VII
Gilbert, Brig. Leonard, 1889–1966, vol. VI
Gilbert, Lt-Col Leonard Erskine, 1874–1946, vol. IV
Gilbert, Rosa, (Lady Gilbert), (Rosa Mulholland), died 1921, vol. II
Gilbert, Hon. S. Parker, 1892–1938, vol. III
Gilbert, Adm. Thomas Drummond, 1870–1962, vol. VI
Gilbert, Rev. Thomas Morrell, died 1928, vol. II
Gilbert, Sir Trounsell; see Gilbert, Sir J. T.
Gilbert, Walter, 1871–1946, vol. IV
Gilbert, William Gladstone, 1877–1964, vol. VI
Gilbert, Sir William Schwenck, 1836–1911, vol. I
Gilbert-Carter, Sir Gilbert Thomas, 1848–1927, vol. II
Gilbert-Carter, Humphrey, 1884–1969, vol. VI
Gilbertson, Rev. Canon Arthur Deane, 1883–1964, vol. VI
Gilbertson, Rev. Lewis, 1857–1928, vol. II
Gilbey, Lt-Col Alfred, 1859–1927, vol. II
Gilbey, Sir (Henry) Walter, 2nd Bt, 1859–1945, vol. IV
Gilbey, Tresham, 1862–1947, vol. IV
Gilbey, Sir Walter, 1st Bt, 1831–1914, vol. I
Gilbey, Sir Walter; see Gilbey, Sir H. W.
Gilchrist, Alexander Fitzmaurice, 1878–1956, vol. V
Gilchrist, Archibald, 1877–1932, vol. III
Gilchrist, Archibald Daniel, 1877–1964, vol. VI
Gilchrist, Douglas Alston, died 1927, vol. II

Gilchrist, Sir James Albert, 1884–1965, vol. VI
Gilchrist, John Dow Fisher, 1866–1926, vol. II
Gilchrist, Percy Carlyle, 1851–1935, vol. III
Gilchrist, Philip Thomson, 1865–1956, vol. V
Gilchrist, Captain Robert Allister, 1921–1973, vol. VII
Gilchrist, Robert Murray, 1868–1917, vol. II
Gilchrist, Robert Niven, 1888–1972, vol. VII
Gilchrist, Lt-Col Walter Fellowes Cowan, 1879–1943, vol. IV
Gilchrist, William James, 1879–1955, vol. V
Gilchrist-Clark, Rev. William; see Clark-Maxwell, Rev. W. G.
Gildea, Col Sir James, 1838–1920, vol. II
Gildea, Rev. William, 1833–1925, vol. II
Gilder, Jeannette Leonard, 1849–1916, vol. II
Gilder, Joseph B., 1858–1936, vol. III (A), vol. IV
Gilder, Richard Watson, 1844–1909, vol. I
Gildersleeve, Basil Lanneau, 1831–1924, vol. II
Gildersleeve, Virginia Crocheron, 1877–1965, vol. VI
Gilding, Henry Percy, 1895–1973, vol. VII
Giles, Rev. Alan Stanley, 1902–1975, vol. VII
Giles, Sub-Lt Alfred Edward Boscawen, died 1917, vol. II
Giles, Arthur Edward, 1864–1935, vol. III
Giles, Bertram, 1874–1928, vol. II
Giles, Carl P.; see Prausnitz Giles.
Giles, Sir Charles Tyrrell, 1850–1940, vol. III
Giles, Edward, 1849–1938, vol. III
Giles, Maj.-Gen. Edward Douglas, 1879–1966, vol. VI
Giles, Col Frank Lucas Netlam, 1879–1930, vol. III
Giles, G. C. T., died 1976, vol. VII
Giles, George Henry, 1904–1965, vol. VI
Giles, Major Godfrey Douglas, 1857–1941, vol. IV
Giles, Herbert Allen, 1845–1935, vol. III
Giles, John Laurent, 1901–1969, vol. VI
Giles, Lancelot, 1878–1934, vol. III
Giles, Lionel, 1875–1958, vol. V
Giles, Margaret M.; see Jenkin, Mrs Bernard.
Giles, Lt-Col Sir Oswald Bissill, 1888–1970, vol. VI
Giles, Peter, 1860–1935, vol. III
Giles, Peter Broome, 1850–1928, vol. II
Giles, Robert, 1846–1928, vol. II
Giles, Sir Robert Sidney, 1865–1944, vol. IV
Gilford, Hastings, 1861–1941, vol. IV
Gilhooly, James Peter, 1847–1916, vol. II
Gilkes, Antony Newcombe, 1900–1977, vol. VII
Gilkes, Rev. Arthur Herman, died 1922, vol. II
Gilkes, Christopher Herman, 1898–1953, vol. V
Gilks, John Langton, 1880–1971, vol. VII
Gill, Alfred Henry, 1856–1914, vol. I
Gill, Allen, died 1933, vol. III
Gill, Andrew John Mitchell-, 1847–1921, vol. II
Gill, Sir Archibald Joseph, 1889–1976, vol. VII
Gill, Arthur Edmund, 1864–1932, vol. III
Gill, Sir Charles Frederick, 1851–1923 vol. II
Gill, Rt Rev. Charles Hope, 1861–1946, vol. IV
Gill, Colin Unwin, 1892–1940, vol. III
Gill, Conrad, 1883–1968, vol. VI
Gill, Sir David, 1843–1914, vol. I
Gill, Col Douglas Howard, 1877–1949, vol. IV
Gill, Eric, 1882–1940, vol. III

Gill, Rev. Ernest Compton, 1854–1912, vol. I
Gill, Ernest Walter Brudenell, 1883–1959, vol. V
Gill, Sir Frank, 1866–1950, vol. IV
Gill, Frederick Gordon, 1881–1940, vol. III
Gill, Col Gordon Harry, 1882–1962, vol. VI
Gill, Sir Harry; see Gill, Sir T. H.
Gill, Hubert Alexander, 1881–1954, vol. V
Gill, Ven. Hugh Stowell, 1830–1912, vol. I
Gill, Major James Herbert Wainwright, 1876–1951, vol. V
Gill, James Lester Willis, 1871–1939, vol. III
Gill, L. Upcott, 1846–1919, vol. II
Gill, MacDonald, 1884–1947, vol. IV
Gill, Air Cdre Napier John, 1890–1948, vol. IV
Gill, Robert Carey Chapple, 1875–1960, vol. VI (AI)
Gill, Major Robert Harwar, 1877–1938, vol. III
Gill, Cdre Sir Roy, 1887–1967, vol. VI
Gill, Stanley, 1926–1975, vol. VII
Gill, Thomas, 1849–1923, vol. II
Gill, Sir (Thomas) Harry, 1885–1955, vol. V
Gill, Thomas Patrick, 1858–1931, vol. III
Gill, Col William Smith, 1865–1957, vol. V
Gill-Davies, Derek George, 1913–1974, vol. VII
Gillam, Brig.-Gen. Reynold Alexander, 1872–1942, vol. IV
Gillam, Major William Albert, 1870–1938, vol. III
Gillan, Lt-Col Sir George V. B., 1890–1974, vol. VII
Gillan, Sir Robert Woodburn, 1867–1943, vol. IV
Gillanders, Jeannie Kathleen, 1896–1971, vol. VII
Gillanders, Hon. John Gordon, 1895–1946, vol. IV
Gillatt, Lt-Col John Maxwell, died 1937, vol. III
Gillen, Francis James, 1856–1912, vol. I
Gillen, Stanley James, 1911–1978, vol. VII
Gillespie, A. Lockhart, 1865–1904, vol. I
Gillespie, Charles Melville, 1866–1955, vol. V
Gillespie, Brig.-Gen. Ernest Carden Freeth, 1871–1942, vol. IV
Gillespie, Brig. Dame Helen Shiels, 1898–1974, vol. VII
Gillespie, Very Rev. Henry J., 1851–1936, vol. III
Gillespie, Ven. Henry Richard Butler, 1880–1943, vol. IV
Gillespie, Sir John, 1822–1901, vol. I
Gillespie, Very Rev. John, 1836–1912, vol. I
Gillespie, Peter, 1873–1929, vol. III
Gillespie, Sir Robert, died 1901, vol. I
Gillespie, Robert Alexander, 1848–1917, vol. II
Gillespie, Robert Dick, 1897–1945, vol. IV
Gillespie, Sir Robert Winton, died 1945, vol. IV
Gillespie, Col Rollo St John, 1872–1952, vol. V
Gillespie, Thomas Haining, 1876–1967, vol. VI
Gillespie, Maj.-Gen. William John, 1840–1931, vol. III
Gillespy, Rev. Francis Roebuck, 1880–1962, vol. VI
Gillett, Col Sir Alan; see Gillett, Col Sir W. A.
Gillett, Rev. Canon Charles Scott, 1880–1957, vol. V
Gillett, Charles William, 1901–1968, vol. VI
Gillett, Sir Edward Bailey, 1888–1978, vol. VII
Gillett, Lt-Col Edward Scott, 1877–1952, vol. V
Gillett, Eric Walkey, 1893–1978, vol. VII
Gillett, Frederick Huntington, 1851–1935, vol. III

Gillett, Sir George Masterman, 1870–1939, vol. III
Gillett, Rev. Gresham F., 1867–1940, vol. III
Gillett, Sir Harold; see Gillett, Sir S. H.
Gillett, Sir Michael Cavenagh, 1907–1971, vol. VII
Gillett, Adm. Owen Francis, 1863–1938, vol. III
Gillett, Sir Stuart, 1903–1971, vol. VII
Gillett, Sir (Sydney) Harold, 1st Bt, 1890–1976, vol. VII
Gillett, Major William, 1839–1925, vol. II
Gillett, Col Sir (William) Alan, 1879–1959, vol. V
Gillette, William, 1857–1937, vol. III
Gilliam, Laurence Duval, 1907–1964, vol. VI
Gilliat, Algernon Earle, 1884–1970, vol. VI
Gilliat, Rev. E., 1841–1915, vol. I (A)
Gilliat, John Saunders, 1829–1912, vol. I
Gilliat-Smith, Bernard Joseph, 1883–1973, vol. VII
Gilliat-Smith, Guy Basil, 1885–1933, vol. III
Gilliatt, Sir William, 1884–1956, vol. V
Gillibrand, Brig. Albert, 1884–1942, vol. IV
Gillick, Ernest George, died 1951, vol. V
Gillick, Mary, died 1965, vol. VI
Gillie, Rev. Robert Calder, 1865–1941, vol. IV
Gillies, Alexander, 1907–1977, vol. VII
Gillies, Arthur Hunter Denholm, 1890–1953, vol. V
Gillies, Brig. Frederick George, 1881–1955, vol. V
Gillies, Sir Harold Delf, 1882–1960, vol. V
Gillies, Hugh, 1903–1978, vol. VII
Gillies, Captain James, 1873–1938, vol. III
Gillies, Rev. James Robertson, 1855–1938, vol. III
Gillies, John, 1895–1976, vol. VII
Gillies, Marshall Macdonald, 1901–1976, vol. VII
Gillies, Sir William George, 1898–1973, vol. VII
Gillies, William King, 1875–1952, vol. V
Gillies, Hon. William Neal, 1868–1928, vol. II
Gilligan, Albert, 1874–1939, vol. III
Gilligan, Arthur Edward Robert, 1894–1976, vol. VII
Gilligan, Frank William, 1893–1960, vol. V
Gillilan, Major Edward Gibson, 1880–1947, vol. IV
Gillingham, Rev. Canon Frank Hay, 1875–1953, vol. V
Gillis, Hon. Duncan, 1834–1903, vol. I
Gillis, William, 1859–1929, vol. III
Gillitt, Lt-Col William, 1879–1962, vol. VI
Gillman, Clement, 1882–1946, vol. IV
Gillman, Herbert Francis Webb, died 1918, vol. II
Gillman, Russell Davis, died 1910, vol. I
Gillman, Gen. Sir Webb, 1870–1933, vol. III
Gillmor, Rev. Fitzwilliam, 1867–1934, vol. III
Gillmore, Ven. Charles Albert, died 1939, vol. III
Gillon, Stair Agnew, 1877–1954, vol. V
Gillot, E. Louis, born 1867, vol. II
Gillott, Hon. Sir Samuel, 1838–1913, vol. I
Gillson, Brig.-Gen. Godfrey, 1867–1937, vol. III
Gillson, Lt-Col Robert Moore Thacker, 1878–1939, vol. III
Gilman, Sir Charles Rackham, 1833–1911, vol. I
Gilman, Charlotte Perkins, 1860–1935, vol. III
Gilman, Daniel Coit, 1831–1909, vol. I
Gilman, Edward Wilmot Francis, 1876–1955, vol. V
Gilman, Harold John Wilde, 1878–1919, vol. II

Gilman, Horace James, 1907–1976, vol. VII
Gilmartin, Most Rev. Thomas P., 1861–1939, vol. III
Gilmer, Dame Elizabeth May, 1880–1960, vol. V
Gilmore, Hon. George Crosby, 1859–1937, vol. III
Gilmore, Dame Mary, 1865–1962, vol. VI
Gilmour, David, died 1946, vol. IV
Gilmour, James Pinkerton, 1860–1941, vol. IV
Gilmour, Sir John, 1st Bt (cr 1897), 1845–1920, vol. II
Gilmour, Lt-Col Rt Hon. Sir John, 2nd Bt (cr 1897), 1876–1940, vol. III
Gilmour, Major John, 1884–1943, vol. IV
Gilmour, Sir John Little, 2nd Bt (cr 1926), 1899–1977, vol. VII
Gilmour, Brig.-Gen. Sir Robert Gordon, 1st Bt (cr 1926), 1857–1939, vol. III
Gilmour, Lady Susan, 1870–1962, vol. VI
Gilmour, Thomas Lennox, 1859–1936, vol. III
Gilmour, William Ewing, 1854–1924, vol. II
Gilmour, William Henry, 1869–1942, vol. IV
Gilpin, Archibald, 1906–1959, vol. V
Gilpin, Sir Edmund Henry; see Gilpin, Sir Harry.
Gilpin, Brig.-Gen. Frederic Charles Almon, 1860–1950, vol. IV
Gilpin, Sir Harry, (Edmund Henry), 1876–1950, vol. IV
Gilpin, Peter Valentine, 1858–1928, vol. II
Gilpin-Brown, Adm. Frederick Dundas, 1866–1934, vol. III
Gilray, Colin Macdonald, 1885–1974, vol. VII
Gilray, Thomas, 1851–1920, vol. II
Gilroy, Rev. James, 1859–1931, vol. III
Gilroy, His Eminence Cardinal Sir Norman Thomas, 1896–1977, vol. VII
Gilruth, John Anderson, 1871–1937, vol. III
Gilson, Lt-Col Charles Hugh, 1870–1930, vol. III
Gilson, Major Charles J. L., 1878–1943, vol. IV
Gilson, Etienne Henry, 1884–1978, vol. VII
Gilson, Julius Parnell, 1868–1929, vol. III
Gilson, Paul, 1865–1942, vol. IV
Gilson, Robert Cary, 1863–1939, vol. III
Gilstrap, Lt-Col John MacR.; see MacRae-Gilstrap.
Gilzean, Andrew, 1877–1957, vol. V
Gilzean-Reid, Sir Hugh; see Reid.
Gimblett, Charles Leonard, 1890–1957, vol. V
Gimlette, Lt-Col George Hart Desmond, 1855–1930, vol. III
Gimlette, Surg. Rear-Adm. Sir Thomas Desmond, 1857–1943, vol. IV
Gimson, Christopher, 1886–1975, vol. VII
Gimson, Sir Franklin Charles, 1890–1975, vol. VII
Gimson, Col Thomas William, 1904–1979, vol. VII
Gingell, Overy Francis, 1916–1966, vol. VI
Gingras-Daly, Lt-Col Ludger Jules Olivier, 1876–1919, vol. II
Ginnell, Laurence, 1854–1923, vol. II
Ginner, Charles, 1878–1952, vol. V
Ginnett, Louis, died 1946, vol. IV
Ginsberg, Morris, 1889–1970, vol. VI
Ginsburg, Benedict William, 1859–1933, vol. III
Ginsburg, Christian David, 1831–1914, vol. I
Ginwala, Sir Padamji Pestonji, 1875–1962, vol. VI

Giolitti, Giovanni, 1842–1928, vol. II
Giordano, Umberto, 1867–1948, vol. IV
Giovanetti, Constantine William, 1868–1940, vol. III
Gipps, Sir Reginald Ramsay, 1831–1908, vol. I
Gipson, Lawrence Henry, 1880–1971, vol. VII
Girard, Robert George, 1859–1921, vol. II
Giraud, Surg.-Maj.-Gen. Charles Herve, died 1918, vol. II
Giraud, Gen. Henri Honoré, 1879–1949, vol. IV
Girault, Charles Louis, 1851–1932, vol. III
Girdlestone, Cuthbert Morton, 1895–1975, vol. VII
Girdlestone, Gathorne Robert, died 1950, vol. IV
Girdlestone, Rev. Robert Baker, 1836–1923, vol. II
Girdwood, Brig.-Gen. Austin Claude, 1875–1951, vol. V
Girdwood, Maj.-Gen. Sir Eric Stanley, 1876–1963, vol. VI
Girdwood, Gilbert P., 1832–1917, vol. II
Giri, Varahagiri Venkata, 1894–1980, vol. VII
Giri de Teremala di Fogliano, Count Piero Mariano, 1885–1962, vol. VI
Girling, James Lawrence, 1901–1969, vol. VI
Girling, John Henry, died 1948, vol. IV
Girling, William Henry, 1872–1958, vol. V
Girouard, Hon. Désiré, 1836–1911, vol. I
Girouard, Col Sir (Edouard) Percy Cranwill, 1867–1932, vol. III
Girouard, Hon. Jean, 1856–1940, vol. III (A), vol. IV
Girouard, Col Sir Percy; see Girouard, Col. Sir E. P. C.
Girtin, Thomas, 1874–1960, vol. V
Gisborne, Henry Paterson, 1888–1953, vol. V
Gisborne, Lt-Col Lionel Guy, 1866–1928, vol. II
Gisborough, 1st Baron, 1856–1938, vol. III
Gisborough, 2nd Baron, 1889–1951, vol. V
Gishford, Anthony Joseph, 1908–1975, vol. VII
Gissing, Algernon, 1860–1937, vol. III
Gissing, George, 1857–1903, vol. I
Gittins, Henry, 1858–1937, vol. III
Gittins, Robert John, 1895–1934, vol. III
Giuffrida-Ruggeri, Vincenzo, born 1872, vol. II
Given, Ernest Cranstoun, 1870–1961, vol. VI
Given, Brig. Thomas Frederick, 1894–1952, vol. V
Givens, Hon. Thomas, 1864–1928, vol. II
Gjellerup, Karl, died 1919, vol. II
Gladding, Donald, 1888–1971, vol. VII
Gladstone, 1st Viscount, 1854–1930, vol. III
Gladstone of Hawarden, 1st Baron, 1852–1935, vol. III
Gladstone of Hawarden, Lady; (Maud Ernestine), died 1941, vol. IV
Gladstone, Sir Albert Charles, 5th Bt, 1886–1967, vol. VI
Gladstone, Charles Andrew, (6th Bt, but did not use the title), 1888–1968, vol. VI
Gladstone, Adm. Sir Gerald Vaughan, 1901–1978, vol. VII
Gladstone, Helen, 1849–1925, vol. II
Gladstone, Sir Hugh Steuart, 1877–1949, vol. IV
Gladstone, Sir John Evelyn, 4th Bt, 1855–1945, vol. IV
Gladstone, John Hall, 1827–1902, vol. I

Gladstone, Sir John Robert, 3rd Bt, 1852–1926, vol. II
Gladstone, Reginald John, 1865–1947, vol. IV
Gladstone, Robert, 1833–1919, vol. II
Gladstone, Samuel Steuart, 1837–1909, vol. I
Gladstone, Rev. Stephen Edward, 1844–1920, vol. II
Gladstone, Rt Hon. William Ewart, 1809–1898, vol. I
Gladstone, William Glynne Charles, 1885–1915, vol. I
Glaisher, James Whitbread Lee, 1848–1928, vol. II
Glaister, John, 1856–1932, vol. III
Glaister, John, 1892–1971, vol. VII
Glaister, Rev. William, died 1919, vol. II
Glancey, Rt Rev. Mgr Michael Francis, 1854–1925, vol. II
Glancy, Sir Bertrand James, 1882–1953, vol. V
Glancy, Sir Reginald Isidore Robert, 1874–1939, vol. III
Glanely, 1st Baron, 1868–1942, vol. IV
Glanfield, Sir Robert, 1862–1924, vol. II
Glantawe, 1st Baron, 1835–1915, vol. I
Glanusk, 1st Baron, 1858–1906 (this entry was not transferred to Who was Who).
Glanusk, 2nd Baron, 1864–1928, vol. II
Glanusk, 3rd Baron, 1891–1948, vol. IV
Glanville, Mrs Edythe Mary, 1876–1959, vol. V
Glanville, Brig.-Gen. Francis, 1862–1938, vol. III
Glanville, Harold James, 1854–1930, vol. III
Glanville, Harold James Abbott, 1884–1966, vol. VI
Glanville, James Edward, 1891–1958, vol. V
Glanville, Stephen Ranulph Kingdon, 1900–1956, vol. V
Glanville, Sir William Henry, 1900–1976, vol. VII
Glascock, Lancelot Colin Bradford, 1875–1931, vol. III
Glascott, John Richard Donovan, 1877–1938, vol. III
Glaser, Dorothy, (Mrs O. C. Glaser); see Wrinch, D.
Glasfurd, Col Alexander Inglis Robertson, 1870–1942, vol. IV
Glasgow, 7th Earl of, 1833–1915, vol. I (A)
Glasgow, 8th Earl of, 1874–1963, vol. VI
Glasgow, Brig.-Gen. Alfred Edgar, 1870–1950, vol. IV
Glasgow, Edwin, 1874–1955, vol. V
Glasgow, Ellen, 1874–1945, vol. IV
Glasgow, George, 1891–1958, vol. V
Glasgow, Raymond Charles R.; see Robertson-Glasgow.
Glasgow, Maj.-Gen. Hon. Sir (Thomas) William, 1876–1955, vol. V
Glasgow, Maj.-Gen. Hon. Sir William; see Glasgow, Maj.-Gen. Hon. Sir T. W.
Glasgow, Brig.-Gen. William James Theodore, 1862–1944, vol. IV
Glasier, Major Frank Bedford, 1872–1940, vol. III
Glaspell, Susan, 1882–1948, vol. IV
Glass, David Victor, 1911–1978, vol. VII
Glass, Frederick James, 1881–1930, vol. III
Glass, George William, 1877–1967, vol. VI
Glass, James George Henry, 1843–1911, vol. I
Glass, William Mervyn, 1885–1965, vol. VI

Glasse, Alfred Onslow, 1889–1977, vol. VII
Glasse, John, 1848–1918, vol. II
Glassey, Alec Ewart, 1887–1970, vol. VI
Glassington, Charles William, 1857–1922, vol. II
Glauert, Hermann, 1892–1934, vol. III
Glazebrook, Hugh de T., 1855–1937, vol. III
Glazebrook, Rev. Michael George, 1853–1926, vol. II
Glazebrook, Philip Kirkland, 1880–1918, vol. II
Glazebrook, Sir Richard Tetley, 1854–1935, vol. III
Glazebrook, William Rimington, 1864–1954, vol. V
Glazier, Edward Victor Denis, 1912–1972, vol. VII
Glazounow, Alexander Constantinovich, 1865–1936, vol. III
Gleadowe, George Edward Yorke, 1856–1903, vol. I
Gleadowe, Reginald Morier Yorke, 1888–1944, vol. IV
Gleadowe-Newcomen, Col Arthur Hills, 1853–1928, vol. II
Gledhill, Gilbert, 1889–1946, vol. IV
Gleed, Sir John Wilson, 1865–1946, vol. IV
Gleeson, Most Rev. Edmund, 1869–1956, vol. V
Glegg, Sir Alexander, 1848–1933, vol. III
Glegg, Alexander Lindsay, 1882–1975, vol. VII
Glegg, Edward Maxwell, 1849–1927, vol. II
Gleichen, Maj.-Gen. Lord (Albert) Edward Wilfred, 1863–1937, vol. III
Gleichen, Maj.-Gen. Lord Edward; see Gleichen, Maj.-Gen. Lord A. E. W.
Gleichen, Lady Feodora, died 1922, vol. II
Gleichen, Lady Helena, died 1947, vol. IV
Glen, Alexander, 1850–1913, vol. I
Glen, Sir Alexander, 1893–1972, vol. VII
Glen, John Mackenzie, 1885–1976, vol. VII
Glen, Randolph Alexander, died 1934, vol. III
Glen-Coats, Sir Thomas Coats Glen, 2nd Bt; see Coats.
Glen-Coats, Sir Thomas Glen, 1st Bt, 1846–1922, vol. II
Glenarthur, 1st Baron, 1852–1928, vol. II
Glenarthur, 2nd Baron, 1883–1942, vol. IV
Glenarthur, 3rd Baron, 1909–1976, vol. VII
Glenavy, 1st Baron, 1851–1931, vol. III
Glenavy, 2nd Baron, 1885–1963, vol. VI
Glenavy, 3rd Baron, 1913–1980, vol. VII
Glenconner, 1st Baron, 1859–1920, vol. II
Glenday, Roy Goncalves, 1889–1957, vol. V
Glenday, Sir Vincent Goncalves, 1891–1970, vol. VI
Glendenning, Raymond Carl, 1907–1974, vol. VII
Glendinning, Henry, 1863–1938, vol. III
Glendinning, John Clements, 1866–1949, vol. IV
Glendinning, Rt Hon. Robert Graham, 1844–1928, vol. II
Glendyne, 1st Baron, 1849–1930, vol. III
Glendyne, 2nd Baron, 1878–1967, vol. VI
Glenesk, 1st Baron, 1830–1908, vol. I
Glenn, Very Rev. Henry Patterson, 1858–1923, vol. II
Glenn, Robert George, 1844–1900, vol. I
Glenn, Air Vice-Marshal Robert William Lowry, 1901–1970, vol. VI
Glennie, Brig. Edward Aubrey, 1889–1980, vol. VII
Glennie, Rev. Herbert John, 1860–1926, vol. II

Glennie, Adm. Sir Irvine Gordon, 1892–1980, vol. VII
Glennie, Vice-Adm. Robert Woodyear, 1868–1930, vol. III
Glenny, Alexander Thomas, 1882–1965, vol. VI
Glenny, William James, 1873–1963, vol. VI
Glenravel, 1st Baron, 1858–1937, vol. III
Glentanar, 1st Baron, 1849–1918, vol. II
Glentanar, 2nd Baron, 1894–1971, vol. VII
Glentoran, 1st Baron, 1880–1950, vol. IV
Glentworth, Viscount; Edmond William Claude Gerard de Vere, 1894–1918, vol. II
Glin, 28th Knight of; see Fitz-Gerald, Desmond Windham Otho.
Glindoni, Henry Gillard, died 1913, vol. I
Gloag, Lt-Gen. Archibald Robertson, 1831–1914, vol. I
Gloag, Paton J., 1823–1906, vol. I
Gloag, William Ellis; see Kincairney, Hon. Lord.
Gloag, William Murray, 1865–1934, vol. III
Glossop, Clifford William Hudson, 1901–1975, vol. VII
Glossop, Rev. George Henry Pownall, 1858–1925, vol. II
Glossop, Vice-Adm. John Collings-Taswell, 1871–1934, vol. III
Gloster, Brig.-Gen. Gerald Meade, 1864–1928, vol. II
Glover, Sir (Edward) Otho, 1876–1956, vol. V
Glover, Elizabeth Rosetta, (Lady Glover), died 1927, vol. II
Glover, Sir Ernest William, 1st Bt, 1864–1934, vol. III
Glover, George Wright, 1884–1918, vol. II
Glover, Maj.-Gen. Sir Guy de Courcy, 1887–1967, vol. VI
Glover, Halcott, died 1949, vol. IV
Glover, Sir Harold Matthew, 1885–1961, vol. VI
Glover, Henry Percy, died 1938, vol. III
Glover, James Alison, 1876–1963, vol. VI
Glover, James Grey, died 1908, vol. I
Glover, James Mackey, 1861–1931, vol. III
Glover, Sir John, 1829–1920, vol. II
Glover, Maj.-Gen. Malcolm, 1897–1970, vol. VI
Glover, Sir Otho; see Glover, Sir E. O.
Glover, Richard, 1837–1919, vol. II
Glover, Ronald Everett, died 1975, vol. VII
Glover, Terrot Reaveley, 1869–1943, vol. IV
Glover, Thomas, 1862–1942, vol. IV
Glover, Col William Reid, 1882–1959, vol. V
Glubb, Maj.-Gen. Sir Frederic Manley, 1857–1938, vol. III
Gluckman, Max, 1911–1975, vol. VII
Gluckmann, Grigory, 1898–1973, vol. VII
Gluckstein, Isidore Montague, 1890–1975, vol. VII
Gluckstein, Sir Louis Halle, 1897–1979, vol. VII
Gluckstein, Montague, 1854–1922, vol. II
Gluckstein, Major Montague, 1886–1958, vol. V
Gluckstein, Sir Samuel, 1880–1958, vol. V
Glunicke, Maj.-Gen. R. C. A., 1886–1963, vol. VI
Glyn, 1st Baron, 1885–1960, vol. V
Glyn, Hon. Alice Coralie, died 1928, vol. II
Glyn, Sir Arthur Robert, 7th Bt (cr 1759), 1870–1942, vol. IV

Glyn, Mrs Clayton, (Elinor), *died* 1943, vol. IV
Glyn, Rt Rev. Hon. Edward Carr, 1843–1928, vol. II
Glyn, Elinor; *see* Glyn, Mrs Clayton.
Glyn, Sir Francis Maurice Grosvenor, 1901–1969, vol. VI
Glyn, Rev. Frederick Ware, *died* 1918, vol. II
Glyn, Col Geoffrey Carr, 1864–1933, vol. III
Glyn, Hon. George Edward Dudley Carr, 1896–1930, vol. III
Glyn, Sir Gervas Powell, 6th Bt (*cr* 1759), 1862–1921, vol. II
Glyn, Lt-Gen. Sir John Plumptre Carr, 1837–1912, vol. I
Glyn, Sir Julius Richard, 1824–1905, vol. I
Glyn, Lewis Edmund, 1849–1919, vol. II
Glyn, Maurice George Carr, 1872–1920, vol. II
Glyn, Hon. Pascoe Charles, 1833–1904, vol. I
Glyn, Sir Richard Fitzgerald, 4th Bt (*cr* 1800) and 8th Bt (*cr* 1759), 1875–1960, vol. V
Glyn, Sir Richard George, 3rd Bt (*cr* 1800), 1831–1918, vol. II
Glyn, Col Sir Richard Hamilton, 5th Bt and 9th Bt, 1907–1980, vol. VII
Glyn, Lt-Gen. Richard Thomas, *died* 1900, vol. I
Glyn, Hon. Sidney Carr, 1835–1916, vol. II
Glyn Hughes, Hugh Llewelyn; *see* Hughes.
Glyn-Jones, Sir Hildreth, 1895–1980, vol. VII
Glyn-Jones, Sir William Samuel, 1869–1927, vol. II
Glynn, Air Cdre Arthur Samuel, 1885–1967, vol. VI
Glynn, Ernest E., *died* 1929, vol. III
Glynn, Sir Joseph Aloysius, 1869–1951, vol. V
Glynn, Hon. Patrick M'Mahon, 1855–1931, vol. III
Glynn, Lt-Col Thomas George Powell, 1863–1949, vol. IV
Glynn, Thomas Robinson, *died* 1931, vol. III
Glynton, Col Gerard Maxwell, *died* 1942, vol. IV
Gnien Is-Sultan, Paul Nicholas Apap-Pace-Bologna, 5th Marquis of, 1880–1955, vol. V
Goad, Harold Elsdale, 1878–1956, vol. V
Goad, Col Howard, 1857–1923, vol. II
Goadby, Sir Kenneth Weldon, 1873–1958, vol. V
Gobeil, Antoine, *born* 1854, vol. II
Goble, Leslie Herbert, 1901–1969, vol. VI
Goble, Air Vice-Marshal Stanley James, 1891–1948, vol. IV
Goble, Warwick, *died* 1943, vol. IV
Godber, 1st Baron, 1888–1976, vol. VII
Godber of Willington, Baron (Life Peer); Joseph Bradshaw Godber, 1914–1980, vol. VII
Godbout, Hon. Joseph, 1851–1923, vol. III
Godbout, Hon. Joseph Adélard, 1892–1956, vol. V
Godby, Col Charles, 1863–1956, vol. V
Goddard, Baron (Life Peer); Rayner Goddard, 1877–1971, vol. VII
Goddard, Alexander, 1867–1956, vol. V
Goddard, Arabella, (Mrs Davison), 1836–1922, vol. II
Goddard, Arthur, 1853–1920, vol. II
Goddard, Rt Hon. Sir Daniel Ford, 1850–1922, vol. II
Goddard, Ernest Hope, 1879–1939, vol. III
Goddard, Lt-Col Gerald Hamilton, 1873–1948, vol. IV

Goddard, Brig.-Gen. Henry Arthur, 1871–1955, vol. V
Goddard, Sir Holland; *see* Goddard, Sir J. H.
Goddard, Sir (Joseph) Holland, *died* 1958, vol. V
Goddard, Thomas Herbert, 1885–1967, vol. VI
Godding, Insp.-Gen. Charles Cane, *died* 1939, vol. III
Gödel, Kurt, 1906–1978, vol. VII
Godfray, Col Sir James, 1816–1897, vol. I
Godfray, Brig.-Gen. John William, 1850–1921, vol. II
Godfrey, Brig. Arthur Harry Langham, 1896–1942, vol. IV
Godfrey, Captain Charles, *died* 1903, vol. I
Godfrey, Charles, 1873–1924, vol. II
Godfrey, Sir Dan, 1868–1939, vol. III
Godfrey, Ernest Henry, 1862–1952, vol. V
Godfrey, Sir George Cochrane, 1871–1945, vol. IV
Godfrey, Vice-Adm. Harry Rowlandson, 1875–1947, vol. IV
Godfrey, Sir John Albert, 1889–1973, vol. VII
Godfrey, Sir John Ernest, 6th Bt, 1864–1935, vol. III
Godfrey, Sir John Fermor, 4th Bt, 1828–1900, vol. I
Godfrey, Adm. John Henry, 1888–1971, vol. VII
Godfrey, Hon. John M., 1871–1943, vol. IV
Godfrey, John Thomas, 1857–1911, vol. I
Godfrey, Sir Joseph Edward, 1858–1938, vol. III
Godfrey, Air Cdre Kenneth Walter, 1907–1979, vol. VII
Godfrey, Percy, 1859–1945, vol. IV
Godfrey, Robert Samuel, 1876–1953, vol. V
Godfrey, Lt-Col Stuart Hill, 1861–1941, vol. IV
Godfrey, Sir Walter, 1907–1976, vol. VII
Godfrey, Walter Hindes, 1881–1961, vol. VI
Godfrey, His Eminence Cardinal William, 1889–1963, vol. VI
Godfrey, Sir William Cecil, 5th Bt, 1857–1926, vol. II
Godfrey, Sir William Maurice, 7th Bt, 1909–1971, vol. VII
Godfrey, General Sir William Wellington, 1880–1952, vol. V
Godfrey-Faussett, Captain Sir Bryan Godfrey, 1863–1945, vol. IV
Godfrey-Faussett, Brig. Bryan Trevor, 1896–1970, vol. VI
Godfrey-Faussett, Brig.-Gen. Edmund Godfrey, 1868–1942, vol. IV
Godfrey Faussett, Lt-Col Owen Godfrey, 1866–1915, vol. I
Godkin, Edward Lawrence, *died* 1902, vol. I
Godlee, Sir Rickman John, 1st Bt, 1849–1925, vol. II
Godley, Gen. Sir Alexander John, 1867–1957, vol. V
Godley, Alfred Denis, 1856–1925, vol. II
Godley, Hon. Eveline Charlotte, *died* 1951, vol. V
Godley, Brig.-Gen. Francis Clements, 1858–1941, vol. IV
Godley, Brig. Sir Francis William Crewe F.; *see* Fetherston-Godley.
Godley, Lt-Col Godfrey Archibald, 1871–1935, vol. III

Godley, Major Harry Crewe, 1861–1907, vol. I
Godley, John Cornwallis, 1861–1946, vol. IV
Godman, Dame Alice Mary, died 1944, vol. IV
Godman, Col Arthur Fitzpatrick, 1842–1930, vol. III
Godman, Air Cdre Arthur Lowthian, 1877–1956, vol. V
Godman, Col Charles Bulkeley, 1849–1941, vol. IV
Godman, Frederick Du Cane, 1834–1919, vol. II
Godman, Col John, 1886–1978, vol. VII
Godman, Major Laurence, 1880–1917, vol. II
Godman, Maj.-Gen. Richard Temple, 1832–1912, vol. I
Godman, Col Sherard Haughton, 1865–1938, vol. III
Godowsky, Leopold, 1870–1938, vol. III
Godsall, Walter Douglas, 1901–1964, vol. VI
Godsell, Sir William, 1838–1924, vol. II
Godson, Sir Augustus Frederick, 1835–1906, vol. I
Godson, Clement, 1845–1913, vol. I
Godwin, Sir Arthur, 1852–1921, vol. II
Godwin, Lt-Gen. Sir Charles Alexander Campbell, 1873–1951, vol. V
Godwin-Austen, Gen. Sir Alfred Reade, 1889–1963, vol. VI
Godwin-Austen, Henry Haversham, 1834–1923, vol. II
Goe, Rt Rev. Field Flowers, 1832–1910, vol. I
Goehr, Walter, 1903–1960, vol. V
Goenka, Rai Bahadur Sir Badridas, 1883–1973, vol. VII
Goenka, Rai Bahadur Sir Hariram, 1862–1935, vol. III
Goeppert Mayer, Maria; see Mayer.
Goethals, George Washington, 1858–1928, vol. II
Goetze, Sigismund Christian Hubert, 1866–1939, vol. III
Goff, Col Algernon Hamilton Stannus, 1863–1936, vol. III
Goff, Major Cecil Willie Trevor Thomas, 1860–1907, vol. I
Goff, Sir Ernest William Davis-, 3rd Bt, 1904–1980, vol. VII
Goff, Sir Herbert William Davis-, 2nd Bt, 1870–1923, vol. II
Goff, Sir Park, 1st Bt, 1871–1939, vol. III
Goff, Captain Reginald Stannus, 1882–1965, vol. VI
Goff, Rt Hon. Sir Reginald William, 1907–1980, vol. VII
Goff, Col Robert Charles, died 1922, vol. II
Goff, Thomas Clarence Edward, 1867–1949, vol. IV
Goff, Sir William Goff Davis-, 1st Bt, 1838–1918, vol. II
Goffe, Sir Herbert, 1870–1939, vol. III
Gogarty, Col Henry Edward, 1868–1955, vol. V
Gogarty, Oliver St John, 1878–1957, vol. V
Goitein, Hugh, 1896–1976, vol. VII
Gokhale, Hon. Gopal Krishna, 1866–1915, vol. I
Gold, Major Sir Archibald Gilbey, 1870–1935, vol. III
Gold, Sir Charles, 1837–1924, vol. II
Gold, Ernest, 1881–1976, vol. VII
Gold, Sir Harcourt Gilbey, 1876–1952, vol. V

Gold, Henry, 1835–1900, vol. I
Gold, James Herbert, 1885–1974, vol. VII
Golden, Lt-Col Harold Arthur, 1896–1976, vol. VII
Goldfinch, Sir Arthur Horne, 1866–1945, vol. IV
Goldfinch, Sir Philip Henry Macarthur, 1884–1943, vol. IV
Goldfrap, Brig. Harold Wyn, 1884–1940, vol. III
Goldhawk, Rev. Ira G., died 1967, vol. VI
Goldie, Archibald Hayman Robertson, 1888–1964, vol. VI
Goldie, Barré Algernon Highmore, 1870–1949, vol. IV
Goldie, Rt Rev. Frederick, 1914–1980, vol. VII
Goldie, Rt Hon. Sir George Dashwood Taubman, 1846–1925, vol. II
Goldie, Major Kenneth Oswald, 1882–1938, vol. III
Goldie, Captain Mark Leigh, 1875–1915, vol. I
Goldie, Sir Noel Barré, 1882–1964, vol. VI
Goldie, Robert George, 1893–1971, vol. VII
Goldie-Taubman, Sir John Senhouse, 1838–1898, vol. I
Golding, Frank Yeates, 1867–1938, vol. III
Golding, Rev. Harry, 1889–1969, vol. VI
Golding, Captain John, 1871–1943, vol. IV
Golding, Louis, 1895–1958, vol. V
Golding, Captain Thomas, 1860–1937, vol. III
Golding-Bird, Cuthbert Hilton, 1848–1939, vol. III
Golding-Bird, Rt Rev. Cyril Henry, 1876–1955, vol. V
Goldman, Charles Sydney, 1868–1958, vol. V
Goldmann, Edwin E., 1862–1913, vol. I
Goldmark, Karl, 1832–1915, vol. I
Goldney, Maj.-Gen. Claude Le Bas, 1887–1978, vol. VII
Goldney, Francis B.; see Bennett-Goldney.
Goldney, Sir Frederick Hastings, 3rd Bt, 1845–1940, vol. III
Goldney, Sir Gabriel, 1st Bt, 1813–1900, vol. I
Goldney, Col George Francis Bennett, 1879–1953, vol. V
Goldney, Sir Henry Hastings, 4th Bt, 1886–1974, vol. VII
Goldney, Hon. Sir John Tankerville, 1846–1920, vol. II
Goldney, Sir Prior, 2nd Bt, 1843–1925, vol. II
Goldney, Col Thomas Holbrow, 1847–1915, vol. I
Goldring, Douglas, 1887–1960, vol. V
Goldsbrough, George Ridsdale, 1881–1963, vol. VI
Goldsbrough, Giles Forward, died 1933, vol. III
Goldschmidt, Otto, 1829–1907, vol. I
Goldschmidt, Lt-Col Sidney George, 1869–1949, vol. IV
Goldsmid, Col Albert Edward Williamson, 1846–1904, vol. I
Goldsmid, Sir Frederic John, 1818–1908, vol. I
Goldsmid, Major Sir Henry Joseph d'A.; see d'Avigdor-Goldsmid.
Goldsmid, Sir Osmond Elim d'A.; see d'Avigdor-Goldsmid.
Goldsmid, Sidney Hoffnung, 1863–1930, vol. III
Goldsmid-Montefiore, Claude Joseph; see Montefiore.
Goldsmid-Stern-Salomons, Sir David Lionel; see Salomons.

Goldsmith, Sir Allen John Bridson, 1909–1976, vol. VII
Goldsmith, Edward, 1868–1951, vol. V
Goldsmith, Francis, 1874–1940, vol. III
Goldsmith, Frank, 1878–1967, vol. VI
Goldsmith, Rt Rev. Frederick, 1853–1932, vol. III
Goldsmith, Col George Mills, 1876–1937, vol. III
Goldsmith, Col Harry Dundas, 1878–1955, vol. V
Goldsmith, Herbert Symonds, 1873–1945, vol. IV
Goldsmith, John Mills, 1845–1912, vol. I
Goldsmith, Rev. Malcolm George, 1849–1940, vol. III
Goldsmith, Vice-Adm. Sir Malcolm Lennon, 1880–1955, vol. V
Goldsmith, Col Perry Gladstone, 1874–1951, vol. V
Goldsmith, Rev. Sidney Willmer, 1869–1939, vol. III
Goldsmith, Captain Sir William Burgess, 1837–1912, vol. I
Goldsmith, William Noel, 1893–1975, vol. VII
Goldstein, Baron W. van, 1831–1901, vol. I
Goldstone, Sir Frank Walter, 1870–1955, vol. V
Goldsworthy, Captain Ivan Ernest Goodman, 1894–1970, vol. VI
Goldsworthy, Walter Tuckfield, 1837–1911, vol. I
Goldwyn, Samuel, 1882–1974, vol. VII
Goligher, Hugh Garvin, 1873–1958, vol. V
Goligher, William Alexander, 1870–1941, vol. IV
Golightly, Col Robert Edmund, 1856–1935, vol. III
Golla, Frederick Lucian, 1878–1968, vol. VI
Gollan, Sir Alexander, died 1902, vol. I
Gollan, Eliza Margaret; see Rita.
Gollan, Sir Henry Cowper, 1868–1949, vol. IV
Gollan, Herbert Roy, 1892–1968, vol. VI
Gollan, Spencer Herbert, 1860–1934, vol III
Gollancz, Rev. Sir Hermann, 1852–1930, vol. III
Gollancz, Sir Israel, 1863–1930, vol. III
Gollancz, Sir Victor, 1893–1967, vol. VI
Gollin, Alfred, 1861–1946, vol. IV
Golsworthy, Arnold, 1865–1939, vol. III
Gomez, Alice, died 1922, vol. II
Gomm, Francis Culling C.; see Carr-Gomm.
Gomm, Hubert William Culling C.; see Carr-Gomm.
Gomme, Arnold Wycombe, 1886–1959, vol. V
Gomme, Sir (George) Laurence, 1853–1916, vol. II
Gomme, Sir Laurence; see Gomme, Sir G. L.
Gomme-Duncan, Col Sir Alan Gomme; see Duncan.
Gompers, Samuel, 1850–1924, vol. II
Gompertz, Frank Priestly V.; see Vincent-Gompertz.
Gompertz, Sir Henry Hessey Johnston, 1867–1930, vol. III
Gompertz, Brig. Martin Louis Alan, 1886–1951, vol. V
Gonard, Samuel Alexandre, 1896–1975, vol. VII
Gondal, HH Maharaja of, 1865–1944, vol. IV
Gonner, Sir Edward Carter Kersey, 1862–1922, vol. II
Gonner, Rev. Eric Peter, died 1930, vol. III
Gonthier, George, 1869–1943, vol. IV
Gonzalez-Llubera, Ignacio Miguel, 1893–1962, vol. VI

Gooch, Sir Alfred Sherlock, 9th Bt (cr 1746), 1851–1899, vol. I
Gooch, Brian Sherlock, 1904–1968, vol. VI
Gooch, Charles Edmund, 1870–1937, vol. III
Gooch, Sir Daniel Fulthorpe, 3rd Bt (cr 1866), 1869–1926, vol. II
Gooch, Edwin George, 1889–1964, vol. VI
Gooch, George Gordon, 1893–1967, vol. VI (AII)
Gooch, George Peabody, 1873–1968, vol. VI
Gooch, Sir Henry Cubitt, 1871–1959, vol. V
Gooch, Sir Henry Daniel, 2nd Bt (cr 1866), 1841–1897, vol. I
Gooch, Henry Martyn, 1874–1957, vol. V
Gooch, Brig. Richard Frank Sherlock, 1906–1973, vol. VII
Gooch, Col Sir Robert Eric Sherlock, 11th Bt (cr 1746), 1903–1978, vol. VII
Gooch, Sir Thomas Vere Sherlock, 10th Bt (cr 1746), 1881–1946, vol. IV
Good, Alan Paul, 1906–1953, vol. V
Good, Christopher Frank, died 1949, vol. IV
Good, James Winder, 1877–1930, vol. III
Good, Percy, died 1950, vol. IV
Goodacre, Hugh George, 1865–1952, vol. V
Goodall, Alexander, 1876–1941, vol. IV
Goodall, Edward A., 1819–1908, vol. I
Goodall, Edward Basil Herbert, 1885–1936, vol. III
Goodall, Lt-Col Edwin, 1863–1944, vol. IV
Goodall, Frederick, 1822–1904, vol. I
Goodall, Rev. John William, died 1932, vol. III
Goodall, Joseph Strickland, 1874–1934, vol. III
Goodall, Rev. Canon Robert William, 1862–1938, vol. III
Goodall, Sir Stanley Vernon, 1883–1965, vol. VI
Gooday, John Francis Sykes, died 1915, vol. I
Goodbody, Col Cecil Maurice, 1874–1936, vol. III
Goodbody, Francis Woodcock, 1870–1938, vol. III
Goodchild, George, 1888–1969, vol. VI
Goodchild, George Frederick, 1871–1956, vol. V
Goodchild, Norman Walter, 1901–1970, vol. VI
Goodchild, Sir William Alfred Cecil, 1885–1940, vol. III
Goodden, Abington, 1901–1978, vol. VII
Goodden, Rev. Edward Wyndham, 1847–1924, vol. II
Goodden, Col John Bernhard Harbin, 1876–1951, vol. V
Goode, Sir Charles Henry, 1827–1922, vol. II
Goode, Sir Richard Allmond Jeffrey, 1873–1953, vol. V
Goode, Samuel Walter, 1878–1935, vol. III
Goode, Sir William Athelstane Meredith, died 1944, vol. IV
Gooden, Rev. Malcolm Cecil Whitridge, 1894–1969, vol. VI
Gooden, Stephen, 1892–1955, vol. V
Goodenough, Ethel Mary, died 1946, vol. IV
Goodenough, Sir Francis William, 1872–1940, vol. III
Goodenough, Frederick Cranfurd, 1866–1934, vol. III
Goodenough, Rear-Adm. Michael Grant, 1904–1955, vol. V

Goodenough, Adm. Sir William Edmund, 1867–1945, vol. IV

Goodenough, Lt-Gen. Sir William Howley, 1833–1898, vol. I

Goodenough, Sir William Macnamara, 1st Bt, 1899–1951, vol. V

Gooderham, Col Sir Albert, 1861–1935, vol. III

Gooderham, Very Rev. Hector Bransby, 1901–1977, vol. VII

Goodeve, Mrs Arthur, (Florence Everilda), *died* 1916, vol. II

Goodeve, Hon. Arthur Samuel, 1860–1920, vol. II

Goodeve, Sir Charles Frederick, 1904–1980, vol. VII

Goodeve, Florence Everilda; *see* Goodeve, Mrs Arthur.

Goodey, Tom, 1885–1953, vol. V

Goodfellow, Lt-Gen. Charles Augustus, 1836–1915, vol. I

Goodfellow, Keith Frank, 1926–1977, vol. VII

Goodfellow, Col Napier George Barras, 1878–1963, vol. VI

Goodfellow, Thomas Ashton, *died* 1937, vol. III

Goodfellow, Gen. W. W., 1833–1901, vol. I

Goodfellow, Sir William, 1880–1974, vol. VII

Goodhart, Arthur Lehman, 1891–1978, vol. VII

Goodhart, Sir Ernest Frederic, 2nd Bt, 1880–1961, vol. VI

Goodhart, Comdr Francis Herbert Heveningham, 1884–1917, vol. II

Goodhart, Gordon Wilkinson, 1882–1948, vol. IV

Goodhart, Sir James Frederic, 1st Bt, 1845–1916, vol. II

Goodhart, Sir John Gordon, 3rd Bt, 1916–1979, vol. VII

Goodhart, Leander McC.; *see* McCormick-Goodhart.

Goodhart-Rendel, Harry Stuart, 1887–1959, vol. V

Goodier, Most Rev. Alban, 1869–1939, vol. III

Goodier, Rev. Joseph Hulme, *died* 1920, vol. II

Goodland, Col Herbert Tom, 1874–1956, vol. V

Goodlet, Brian Laidlaw, 1903–1961, vol. VI

Goodliffe, Francis Foster, *died* 1925, vol. II

Goodman, Col Albert William, 1880–1937, vol. III

Goodman, Rev. Arthur Worthington, 1871–1951, vol. V

Goodman, Bruce Wilfred, 1906–1974, vol. VII

Goodman, Cyril, *died* 1938, vol. III

Goodman, George, 1821–1908, vol. I

Goodman, Hon. Sir Gerald Aubrey, 1862–1921, vol. II

Goodman, Brig.-Gen. Sir Godfrey Davenport, 1868–1957, vol. V

Goodman, Lt-Col Harry Russell, 1875–1936, vol. III

Goodman, John, 1862–1935, vol. III

Goodman, Maude, *died* 1938, vol. III

Goodman, Neville Marriott, 1898–1980, vol. VII

Goodman, Paul, 1875–1949, vol. IV

Goodman, Reginald Ernest, 1886–1968, vol. VI

Goodman, Robert Gwelo, *died* 1939, vol. III

Goodman, Sydney Charles Nichols, 1868–1936, vol. III

Goodman, Sir Victor Martin Reeves, 1899–1967, vol. VI

Goodman, Vyvian Edwin, 1889–1961, vol. VI

Goodman, Maj.-Gen. Walter Rutherfoord, 1899–1976, vol. VII

Goodman, Sir William George Toop, 1872–1961, vol. VI

Goodman, Hon. Sir William Meigh, 1847–1928, vol. II

Goodrich, A., 1840–1919, vol. II

Goodrich, Carter, 1897–1971, vol. VII

Goodrich, Edwin Stephen, 1868–1946, vol. IV

Goodrich, Henry E., 1887–1961, vol. VI

Goodrich, Adm. Sir James Edward Clifford, 1851–1925, vol. II

Goodrich, Dame Matilda, *died* 1972, vol. VII

Goodrich-Freer, A. M., *died* 1931, vol. III

Goodridge, Major Edwin, 1903–1969, vol. VI

Goodridge, Rear-Adm. Walter Somerville, 1849–1929, vol. III

Goodsall, David Henry, *died* 1906, vol. I

Goodship, Harold Edwin, 1877–1951, vol. V

Goodson, Sir Alfred Lassam, 1st Bt, 1867–1940, vol. III

Goodson, Arthur, 1913–1975, vol. VII

Goodson, Katharine, *died* 1958, vol. V

Goodwin, Albert, *died* 1932, vol. III

Goodwin, Aubrey, 1889–1964, vol. VI

Goodwin, Col Frank, 1857–1943, vol. IV

Goodwin, Engr-Rear-Adm. Frank Rheuben, 1875–1966, vol. VI

Goodwin, Major George Alfred, 1857–1945, vol. IV

Goodwin, Engr Vice-Adm. Sir George Goodwin, 1862–1945, vol. IV

Goodwin, Harvey, 1850–1917, vol. II

Goodwin, Lt-Gen. Sir John; *see* Goodwin, Lt-Gen. Sir T. H. J. C.

Goodwin, Nathaniel Carl, 1857–1919, vol. II

Goodwin, Shirley, 1880–1927, vol. II

Goodwin, Sir Stuart Coldwell, 1886–1969, vol. VI

Goodwin, Lt-Col Thomas Frederick, 1904–1965, vol. VI

Goodwin, Lt-Gen. Sir (Thomas Herbert) John (Chapman), 1871–1960, vol. V

Goodwin, William, 1873–1953, vol. V

Goodwin, William Lawton, 1856–1941, vol. IV

Goodwin, Lt-Col William Richard, 1882–1930, vol. III

Goodwin, Col William Richard Power, 1875–1958, vol. V

Goodwin, Sir William V. S. Gradwell, 1865–1942, vol. IV

Goodwin-Tomkinson, Joseph; *see* Tomkinson.

Goodwyn, Rev. Canon Frederick Wildman, 1850–1931, vol. III

Goodwyn, Major Henry Edward, 1855–1929, vol. III

Goodwyn, Lt-Col Norton James, 1861–1906, vol. I

Goodyear, Robert Arthur Hanson, 1877–1948, vol. IV

Goodyear, William Henry, 1846–1923, vol. II

Goold, Sir George Ignatius, 6th Bt, 1903–1967, vol. VI

Goold, Sir (George) Patrick, 5th Bt, 1878–1954 (this entry was not transferred to Who was Who).
Goold, Sir James Stephen, 4th Bt, 1848–1926, vol. II
Goold-Adams, Major Sir Hamilton John, 1858–1920, vol. II
Goold-Adams, Col Sir Henry Edward Fane, 1860–1935, vol. III
Goold-Adams, Ven. John Michael, 1850–1922, vol. II
Goolden, Rear-Adm. Francis Hugh Walter, 1885–1950, vol. IV
Goonetilleke, Sir Oliver Ernest, 1892–1978, vol. VII
Goosman, Hon. Sir Stanley; see Goosman, Hon. Sir W. S.
Goosman, Hon. Sir (William) Stanley, 1890–1969, vol. VI
Goossens, Sir Eugene, 1893–1962, vol. VI
Gopathi Narayanaswami Chetty, Diwan Bahadur Sir, 1881–1945, vol. IV
Gordon, Lt-Col Adrian Charles, 1889–1917, vol. II
Gordon, Alban Goodwin, 1890–1947, vol. IV
Gordon, Alec Knyvett, 1870–1951, vol. V
Gordon, Hon. Sir Alexander, 1858–1942, vol. IV
Gordon, Alexander, 1886–1965, vol. VI
Gordon, Lt-Gen. Sir Alexander Hamilton, 1859–1939, vol. III
Gordon, Alexander Morison, 1846–1913, vol. I
Gordon, Rev. Alexander Reid, 1872–1930, vol. III
Gordon, Lt-Col Rt Hon. Sir Alexander Robert Gisborne, 1882–1967, vol. VI
Gordon, Brig.-Gen. Alister Fraser, 1872–1917, vol. II
Gordon, Major Archibald Alexander, 1867–1949, vol. IV
Gordon, Sir (Archibald) Douglas, 1888–1966, vol. VI
Gordon, Sir Archibald McDonald, 1892–1974, vol. VII
Gordon, Rev. Hon. Arthur, died 1919, vol. II
Gordon of Ellon, Arthur John Lewis, 1847–1918, vol. II
Gordon, Brig. Barbara Masson, 1913–1980, vol. VII
Gordon, Lt-Gen. Sir Benjamin Lumsden, 1833–1916, vol. II
Gordon, Surg.-Gen. Sir Charles Alexander, 1821–1899, vol. I
Gordon, Sir Charles Blair, 1867–1939, vol. III
Gordon, Sir Charles Edward, 7th Bt (cr 1706), 1835–1910, vol. I
Gordon, Rev. Charles W.; see Connor, Ralph.
Gordon, Christie Wilson, 1911–1979, vol. VII
Gordon, Christopher Martin P.; see Pirie-Gordon.
Gordon, Major Colin Lindsay, died 1940, vol. III
Gordon, Cora Josephine, died 1950, vol. IV
Gordon, Sir Cosmo (Edmund) Duff, 5th Bt (cr 1813), 1862–1931, vol. III
Gordon, Crawford, 1914–1967, vol. VI
Gordon, Very Rev. Daniel Miner, 1845–1925, vol. II
Gordon, Hon. Sir David John, 1865–1946, vol. IV
Gordon, Donald, 1901–1969, vol. VI
Gordon, Donald James, 1915–1977, vol. VII
Gordon, Sir Douglas; see Gordon, Sir A. D.

Gordon, Douglas; see Gordon, G. C. D.
Gordon, Sir Douglas Frederick D.; see Duff-Gordon.
Gordon, Hon. and Rev. Douglas H.; see Hamilton-Gordon.
Gordon, Douglas John, 1900–1959, vol. V
Gordon, Major Duncan Forbes, born 1849, vol. II
Gordon, Lt-Col Edward Hyde Hamilton-, died 1955, vol. V
Gordon, Eric V., 1896–1938, vol. III
Gordon, Col Esme Cosmo William C.; see Conway-Gordon.
Gordon, Lt-Col Evelyn Boscawen, 1877–1963, vol. VI
Gordon, Sir Eyre, 1884–1972, vol. VII
Gordon, Francis Frederick, 1866–1922, vol. II
Gordon, Lt-Col Francis Lewis, 1878–1920, vol. II
Gordon, Maj.-Gen. Hon. Sir Frederick, 1861–1927, vol. II
Gordon, Sir Garnet Hamilton, 1904–1975, vol. VII
Gordon, George Angier, 1853–1929, vol. III
Gordon, Col George Grant, 1836–1912, vol. I
Gordon, Col George Grant, 1863–1926, vol. II
Gordon, Col George Hamilton, 1875–1961, vol. VI
Gordon, George Stuart, 1881–1942, vol. IV
Gordon, George V. H. M., died 1914, vol. I
Gordon, Lord Granville Armyne, 1856–1907, vol. I
Gordon, (Granville Cecil) Douglas, 1883–1930, vol. III
Gordon, Col Gwynnedd C.; see Conway-Gordon.
Gordon, Hampden Charles, died 1960, vol. V
Gordon, Harry Panmure, 1837–1902, vol. I
Gordon, Henry Erskine, 1849–1929, vol. III
Gordon, Captain Sir Henry Robert, 1886–1969, vol. VI
Gordon, Henry W.; see Wolrige-Gordon.
Gordon, Sir Henry William D., 6th Bt; see Duff-Gordon.
Gordon, Brig.-Gen. Herbert, 1869–1951, vol. V
Gordon, Herbert Ford, 1882–1963, vol. VI
Gordon, Sir Home Seton, 11th Bt (cr 1631), 1845–1906, vol. I
Gordon, Sir Home Seton Charles Montagu, 12th Bt (cr 1631), 1871–1956, vol. V
Gordon, James Charles Maitland-, 1850–1915, vol. I (A)
Gordon, Rt Rev. James Geoffrey, 1881–1938, vol. III
Gordon, James Scott, 1867–1946, vol. IV
Gordon, Jan, 1882–1944, vol. IV
Gordon, Rt Hon. John, 1849–1922, vol. II
Gordon, Lt-Col John, 1870–1938, vol. III
Gordon, Col John Charles Frederick, 1849–1923, vol. II
Gordon, Lt-Col John de la Hay, 1887–1959, vol. V
Gordon, Hon. John Edward, 1850–1915, vol. I
Gordon, Brig. John Evison, 1901–1977, vol. VII
Gordon, Rt Hon. John Fawcett, 1879–1965, vol. VI
Gordon, Col John Gordon W.; see Wolridge-Gordon.
Gordon, Hon. Sir John Hannah, 1850–1923, vol. II
Gordon, Gen. Sir John James Hood, 1832–1908, vol. I

Gordon, Brig. John Keily, 1883–1976, vol. VII
Gordon, Brig.-Gen. John Lewis Randolph, 1867–1953, vol. V
Gordon, John Rutherford, 1890–1974, vol. VII
Gordon, John William, 1853–1936, vol. III
Gordon, Maj.-Gen. Joseph Maria, 1856–1929, vol. III
Gordon, Col Kenmure Alick Garth E.; see Evans-Gordon.
Gordon, Kenneth, 1897–1955, vol. V
Gordon, Brig.-Gen. Laurence George Frank, 1864–1943, vol. IV
Gordon, Captain Lewis, 1883–1915, vol. I (A)
Gordon, Lewis, died 1935, vol. III
Gordon, Lt-Gen. Lewis C.; see Conway-Gordon.
Gordon, Sir Lionel Eldred Pottinger S. (3rd Bt); see Smith-Gordon.
Gordon, Sir Lionel Eldred Pottinger S. (4th Bt); see Smith-Gordon.
Gordon, Sir Lionel Eldred S.; see Smith-Gordon.
Gordon, Maj.-Gen. Lochinvar Alexander Charles, 1864–1927, vol. II
Gordon, Col Louis Augustus, 1857–1935, vol. III
Gordon, Dame Maria M. O.; see Ogilvie Gordon.
Gordon, Mervyn Henry, 1872–1953, vol. V
Gordon, Captain Oliver Loudon, 1896–1973, vol. VII
Gordon, Percival Hector, 1884–1975, vol. VII
Gordon, Col Philip Cecil Harcourt, 1864–1920, vol. II
Gordon, Lt-Col Ramsay Frederick Clayton, 1864–1943, vol. IV
Gordon, Reginald Hugh Lyall, 1863–1924, vol. II
Gordon, Richard J., 1881–1966, vol. VI
Gordon, Air Cdre Robert, 1882–1954, vol. V
Gordon, Robert Abercromby, died 1954, vol. V
Gordon, Sir Robert Charles, 8th Bt (cr 1706), 1862–1939, vol. III
Gordon, Sir Robert Glendonwyn, 9th Bt (cr 1625), 1824–1908, vol. I
Gordon, Captain Robert W.; see Wolrige Gordon.
Gordon, Captain Roderick Cosmo, 1902–1975, vol. VII
Gordon, Roland Graham, 1880–1958, vol. V
Gordon, Ronald Grey, 1889–1950, vol. IV
Gordon, Rupert Montgomery, 1893–1961, vol. VI
Gordon, Seton, 1886–1977, vol. VII
Gordon, Col Stannus Verner, 1846–1933, vol. III
Gordon, Thomas Eagleson, died 1929, vol. III
Gordon, Gen. Sir Thomas Edward, 1832–1914, vol. I
Gordon, Sir Thomas Stewart, 1882–1949, vol. IV
Gordon, Victor, 1884–1928, vol. II
Gordon, Vivian; see Bowden, V. G.
Gordon, Walter Maxwell, died 1951, vol. V
Gordon, Webster Boyle, 1859–1943, vol. IV
Gordon, Hon. Wesley Ashton, 1884–1943, vol. IV
Gordon, Sir William, 6th Bt (cr 1706), 1830–1906, vol. I
Gordon, Maj.-Gen. William, 1831–1909, vol. I
Gordon, Gen. William, 1824–1917, vol. II
Gordon, William, 1863–1929, vol. III
Gordon, Col William Alexander, 1869–1936, vol. III

Gordon, Col William Eagleson, 1866–1941, vol. IV
Gordon, Major Sir William Eden Evans, 1857–1913, vol. I
Gordon, Adm. William Everard Alphonso, 1817–1906, vol. I
Gordon, Col William Fanshawe Loudon, 1872–1931, vol. III
Gordon, William Smith, 1902–1967, vol. VI
Gordon, William Thomas, 1884–1950, vol. IV
Gordon Clark, Alfred Alexander, 1900–1958, vol. V
Gordon-Clark, Lt-Col Craufurd Alexander, 1864–1950, vol. IV
Gordon Clark, Henry Herbert, 1861–1951, vol. V
Gordon-Cumming, Major Sir Alexander Penrose, 5th Bt, 1893–1939, vol. III
Gordon-Cumming, Miss Constance Frederica, 1837–1924, vol. II
Gordon-Cumming, Sir William Gordon, 4th Bt, 1848–1930, vol. III
Gordon-Finlayson, Gen. Sir Robert, 1881–1956, vol. V
Gordon-Hall, Col Frederick William George, 1861–1942, vol. IV
Gordon-Hall, Lt-Col Gordon Charles William, 1875–1940, vol. III
Gordon-Ives, Col Gordon Maynard, 1837–1907, vol. I
Gordon-Lennox, Col Lord Algernon Charles, 1847–1921, vol. II
Gordon Lennox, Lady Algernon, (Blanche), died 1945, vol. IV
Gordon-Lennox, Lord Bernard Charles, died 1914, vol. I
Gordon-Lennox, Cosmo Charles, 1869–1921, vol. II
Gordon-Lennox, Lord Esme Charles, 1875–1949, vol. IV
Gordon-Lennox, Rt Hon. Lord Walter Charles, 1865–1922, vol. II
Gordon-Luhrs, Lt-Col Henry; see Luhrs.
Gordon-Smith, Sir Allan Gordon, 1881–1951, vol. V
Gordon-Smith, Frederic, 1886–1967, vol. VI
Gordon-Smith, Richard, 1858–1918, vol. II
Gordon-Stables, William, 1840–1910, vol. I
Gordon-Taylor, Sir Gordon, died 1960, vol. V
Gordon-Walker, Baron (Life Peer); Patrick Chrestien Gordon Walker, 1907–1980, vol. VII
Gordon-Watson, Maj.-Gen. Sir Charles Gordon, 1874–1949, vol. IV
Gore, A. Wentworth, 1868–1928, vol. II
Gore, Surg.-Gen. Albert H., 1839–1901, vol. I
Gore, Rev. Arthur, 1829–1913, vol. I
Gore, Col Arthur Franis Gore P. K.; see Percy-Knox-Gore.
Gore, Rt Rev. Charles, 1853–1932, vol. III
Gore, Col Charles Clitherow, 1839–1926, vol. II
Gore, Charles Henry, 1862–1945, vol. IV
Gore, Lt-Gen. Edward Arthur, 1839–1912, vol. I
Gore, Sir Francis Charles, 1846–1940, vol. III
Gore, Lt-Col Francis William George, 1855–1938, vol. III
Gore, Lt-Col Frederic Lawrence, 1884–1952, vol. V
Gore, George, 1826–1908, vol. I

Gore, Lt-Col J. C., 1852–1926, vol. II
Gore, John Ellard, 1845–1910, vol. I
Gore, John Kearns, 1924–1980, vol. VII
Gore, Sir Ralph; see Gore, Sir St G. R.
Gore, Lt-Col Sir Ralph St George Brian, 11th Bt, 1908–1973, vol. VII
Gore, Sir Ralph St George Claude, 10th Bt, 1877–1961, vol. VI
Gore, Col Robert Clements, 1867–1918, vol. II
Gore, Sir (St George) Ralph, 12th Bt, 1914–1973, vol. VII
Gore, Col Sir St John Corbet, 1859–1949, vol. IV
Gore, Hon. Seymour Fitzroy O.; see Ormsby-Gore.
Gore-Booth, Eva, died 1926, vol. II
Gore-Booth, Sir Henry William; see Booth.
Gore-Booth, Sir Josslyn Augustus Richard; see Booth.
Gore-Browne, Col Sir Eric, 1885–1964, vol. VI
Gore-Browne, Sir Francis, 1860–1922, vol. II
Gore-Browne, Comdr Godfrey, 1863–1900, vol. I
Gore-Browne, Henry George, 1830–1912, vol. I
Gore-Browne, Lt-Col Sir Stewart, 1883–1967, vol. VI
Gore-Browne, Rt Rev. Wilfred, died 1928, vol. II
Gore-Langton, Hon. Chandos Graham T.; see Temple-Gore-Langton.
Gore-Langton, Major Gerald Wentworth, died 1937, vol. III
Gore-Langton, Hon. Henry Powell, 1854–1913, vol. I
Gorell, 1st Baron, 1848–1913, vol. I
Gorell, 2nd Baron, 1882–1917, vol. II
Gorell, 3rd Baron, 1884–1963, vol. VI
Gorer, Peter Alfred, 1907–1961, vol. VI
Gorgas, William Crawford, 1854–1920, vol. II
Gorges, Sir (Edmond) Howard (Lacam), 1872–1924, vol. II
Gorges, Brig.-Gen. Edmund Howard, 1868–1949, vol. IV
Gorges, Sir Howard; see Gorges, Sir E. H. L.
Gorham, Maurice Anthony Coneys, 1902–1975, vol. VII
Goring, Sir Charles Craven, 10th Bt, 1841–1897, vol. I
Goring, Captain Sir Forster Gurney, 12th Bt, 1876–1956, vol. V
Goring, Sir Harry Yelverton, 11th Bt, 1841–1911, vol. I
Göring, Field-Marshal Hermann, 1893–1946, vol. IV
Goring-Jones, Lt-Col Michael Durwas; see Jones.
Gorky, Maxim, (Alexei Maximovitch Pieshkov), 1868–1936, vol. III
Gorle, Major Harry Vaughan, 1868–1937, vol. III
Gorman, Albert, 1883–1959, vol. V
Gorman, Arthur Pue, 1839–1906, vol. I
Gorman, Sir Eugene, 1891–1973, vol. VII
Gorman, Sir William, died 1964, vol. VI
Gorman, Ven. William Charles, 1826–1916, vol. II
Gormanston, 14th Viscount, 1837–1907, vol. I
Gormanston, 15th Viscount, 1879–1925, vol. II
Gormanston, 16th Viscount, 1914–1940, vol. III (A), vol. IV

Gorringe, Lt-Gen. Sir George F., 1868–1945, vol. IV
Gorringe, Rev. Reginald Ernest Pennington, 1871–1959, vol. V
Gorst, Sir Eldon, 1861–1911, vol. I (A)
Gorst, Elliot Marcet, 1885–1973, vol. VII
Gorst, Rev. Ernest Freeland, 1871–1942, vol. IV
Gorst, Mrs Harold, (Nina Cecilia Francesca), 1869–1926, vol. II
Gorst, Harold E., 1868–1950, vol. IV
Gorst, Rt Hon. Sir John Eldon, 1835–1916, vol. I, vol. II
Gorst, Nina Cecilia Francesca; see Gorst, Mrs Harold.
Gort, 4th Viscount, 1819–1900, vol. I
Gort, 5th Viscount, 1849–1902, vol. I
Gort, 6th Viscount, 1886–1946, vol. IV
Gort, 7th Viscount, 1888–1975, vol. VII
Gorton, Rt Rev. Neville Vincent, 1888–1955, vol. V
Gorton, Brig.-Gen. Reginald St George, 1866–1944, vol. IV
Gorvin, John Henry, 1886–1960, vol. V
Gos, Charles, 1885–1949, vol. IV
Goschen, 1st Viscount, 1831–1907, vol. I
Goschen, 2nd Viscount, 1866–1952, vol. V
Goschen, 3rd Viscount, 1906–1977, vol. VII
Goschen, Maj.-Gen. Arthur Alec, 1880–1975, vol. VII
Goschen, Charles Hermann, 1839–1915, vol. I
Goschen, Sir Edward Henry, 2nd Bt, 1876–1933, vol. III
Goschen, Hon. George Joachim, 1893–1916, vol. II
Goschen, Sir Harry, (William Henry Neville), 1865–1945, vol. IV
Goschen, Kenneth, 1882–1939, vol. III
Goschen, Rt Hon. Sir William Edward, 1st Bt, 1847–1924, vol. II
Goschen, Hon. Sir William Henry, 1870–1943, vol. IV
Goschen, Sir William Henry Neville; see Goschen, Sir Harry.
Gosford, 4th Earl of, 1841–1922, vol. II
Gosford, 5th Earl of, 1877–1954, vol. V
Gosford, 6th Earl of, 1911–1966, vol. VI
Gosling, Sir Audley Charles, 1836–1913, vol. I
Gosling, Cecil, 1870–1944, vol. IV
Gosling, Col Charles, 1868–1917, vol. II
Gosling, Frederick; see Hamlyn, F.
Gosling, Col George, 1842–1915, vol. I (A)
Gosling, Major George Edward, 1889–1938, vol. III
Gosling, Harry, 1861–1930, vol. III
Gosling, Herbert, 1841–1929, vol. III
Gosling, John Thomas, 1868–1933, vol. III
Gosling, Reginald George, 1899–1958, vol. V
Gosling, Richard Henry, 1853–1930, vol. III
Gosling, Major William Richard, 1891–1968, vol. VI
Goss, Alan; see Goss, W. A. B.
Goss, John, 1894–1953, vol. V
Goss, (William) Alan (Belcher), 1908–1963, vol. VI
Goss-Custard, Reginald, 1877–1956, vol. V
Gossage, Alfred Milne, died 1948, vol. IV
Gossage, Air Marshal Sir Leslie, 1891–1949, vol. IV

Gosse, Alfred Hope, 1882–1956, vol. V
Gosse, Sir Edmund, 1849–1928, vol. II
Gosse, Sir James Hay, 1876–1952, vol. V
Gosse, Laura Sylvia, 1881–1968, vol. VI
Gosse, Philip, 1879–1959, vol. V
Gosselin, Rt Rev. Mgr Amédée, 1863–1941, vol. IV
Gosselin, L. L. T.; see Lenotre, G.
Gosselin, Sir Martin le Marchant Hadsley, 1847–1905, vol. I
Gosselin, Major Sir Nicholas, 1839–1917, vol. II
Gosselin-Grimshawe, Hellier Robert Hadsley, 1849–1924, vol. II
Gosset, Lt-Col Allen Butler, 1868–1948, vol. IV
Gosset, Ven. Charles Hilgrove, died 1923, vol. II
Gosset, Francis Russell, 1849–1930, vol. III
Gosset, Col Francis William, 1876–1931, vol. III
Gosset, Maj.-Gen. Sir Matthew William Edward, 1839–1909, vol. I
Gossip, Alex, 1862–1952, vol. V
Gossip, Rev. Arthur John, 1873–1954, vol. V
Gossling, Archibald George, 1878–1950, vol. IV
Gostling, Col Ernest Victor, 1872–1922, vol. II
Gotch, Francis, 1853–1913, vol. I
Gotch, John Alfred, 1852–1942, vol. IV
Gotch, Thomas Cooper, 1854–1931, vol. III
Gothard, Sir Clifford Frederic, 1893–1979, vol. VII
Gotley, George Rainald H.; see Henniker-Gotley.
Gott, Sir Benjamin S., died 1933, vol. III
Gott, Sir Charles Henry, 1866–1965, vol. VI
Gott, Rt Rev. John, 1830–1906, vol. I
Gott, Lt-Gen. William Henry Ewart, 1897–1942, vol. IV
Gotto, Basil, 1866–1954, vol. V
Gotto, Brig. Christopher Hugh, 1888–1959, vol. V
Götz, Sir Frank Léon Aroha, 1892–1970, vol. VI (AII)
Goudeket, Mme Maurice; see Colette.
Goudge, Rev. Henry Leighton, 1866–1939, vol. III
Goudge, James Alfred, 1862–1955, vol. V
Goudie, Hon. Sir George Louis, 1866–1949, vol. IV
Goudie, William John, 1868–1945, vol. IV
Goudy, Henry, 1848–1921, vol. II
Gouge, Sir Arthur, 1890–1962, vol. VI
Gough, 3rd Viscount, 1849–1919, vol. II
Gough, 4th Viscount, 1892–1951, vol. V
Gough, Col Alan Percy George, 1863–1930, vol. III
Gough, Rev. Preb. Alfred William, 1862–1931, vol. III
Gough, Sir (Arthur) Ernest, 1878–1974, vol. VII
Gough, Col (Charles) Frederick (Howard), 1901–1977, vol. VII
Gough, Sir Charles John Stanley, 1832–1912, vol. I
Gough, Rev. Edwin Spencer, 1845–1927, vol. II
Gough, Sir Ernest; see Gough, Sir A. E.
Gough, Frederic Harrison, born 1863, vol. II
Gough, Col Frederick; see Gough, Col. C. F. H.
Gough, Adm. Frederick William, 1824–1908, vol. I
Gough, Harold Robert, 1889–1975, vol. VII
Gough, Lt-Col Henry Worsley Worsley-, 1874–1957, vol. V
Gough, Herbert John, 1890–1965, vol. VI
Gough, Gen. Sir Hubert de la Poer, 1870–1963, vol. VI

Gough, Lt-Col Hugh Augustus Keppel, 1871–1950, vol. IV
Gough, Gen. Sir Hugh Henry, 1833–1909, vol. I
Gough, Maj.-Gen. Hugh Sutlej, 1848–1920, vol. II
Gough, Jethro, 1903–1979, vol. VII (AII)
Gough, Brig.-Gen. John Edmond, 1871–1915, vol. I
Gough, William, 1876–1947, vol. IV
Gough-Calthorpe, Hon. Frederick Somerset; see Calthorpe.
Gough-Calthorpe, Admiral of the Fleet Hon. Sir Somerset Arthur; see Calthorpe.
Gouin, Hon. Sir Lomer, 1861–1929, vol. III
Goulburn, Brig.-Gen. Cuthbert Edward, 1860–1944, vol. IV
Goulburn, Maj.-Gen. Edward Henry, 1903–1980, vol. VII
Goulburn, Very Rev. Edward Meyrick, 1818–1897, vol. I
Gould, Hon. Sir Albert John, 1847–1936, vol. III
Gould, Alec Carruthers, 1870–1948, vol. IV
Gould, Sir Alfred Pearce, 1852–1922, vol. II
Gould, Barbara Ayrton, died 1950, vol. IV
Gould, Sir Basil John, 1883–1956, vol. V
Gould, Charles, died 1909, vol. I
Gould, Edward, 1837–1922, vol. II
Gould, Edward Blencowe, 1847–1916, vol. II
Gould, Edwin, 1866–1933, vol. III
Gould, Eric Lush Pearce, 1886–1940, vol. III
Gould, Sir Francis Carruthers, 1844–1925, vol. II
Gould, Frederick, 1879–1971, vol. VII
Gould, Frederick James, 1855–1938, vol. III
Gould, George Jay, 1864–1923, vol. II
Gould, Rev. George Pearce, 1848–1921, vol. II
Gould, Gerald, 1885–1936, vol. III
Gould, Ven. Henry George, 1851–1914, vol. I
Gould, Herbert Ross, 1887–1954, vol. V
Gould, Howard Gould, 1871–1959, vol. V
Gould, James Childs, 1882–1944, vol. IV
Gould, James Nutcombe, died 1899, vol. I
Gould, Nathaniel, 1857–1919, vol. II
Gould, Col Philip, 1870–1942, vol. IV
Gould, Rev. Reginald Freestone, 1860–1939, vol. III
Gould, Sir Robert Macdonald, died 1971, vol. VII
Gould, Lt-Comdr Rupert Thomas, 1890–1948, vol. IV
Gould, Sabine B.; see Baring-Gould.
Goulden, Charles Bernard, 1879–1953, vol. V
Goulden, Mark, died 1980, vol. VII
Goulden, Richard Reginald, died 1932, vol. III
Goulder, George Frederick, 1863–1942, vol. IV
Goulding, Henry Raynor, 1859–1934, vol. III
Goulding, Captain Sir Lingard; see Goulding, Captain Sir W. L. A.
Goulding, Rt Hon. Sir William Joshua, 1st Bt, 1856–1925, vol. II
Goulding, Captain Sir (William) Lingard Amphlett, 2nd Bt, 1883–1935, vol. III
Gouldsmith, Edmund, 1852–1932, vol. III
Gouldsmith, Rev. Herbert, died 1940, vol. III
Goument, Charles Ernest Vear, 1857–1941, vol. IV
Gour, Sir Hari Singh, 1866–1949, vol. IV
Gouraud, Gen. Henri, 1867–1946, vol. IV

Gourielli, Princess; see Rubinstein, Helena.
Gourlay, Charles, died 1926, vol. II
Gourlay, Brig. Kenneth Ian, 1891–1970, vol. VI
Gourlay, William Robert, 1874–1938, vol. III
Gourley, Sir Edward Temperley, 1828–1902, vol. I
Govan, Raymond Eustace Grant, 1891–1940, vol. III
Gover, Brig. Charles Rhodes, 1881–1942, vol. IV
Gover, John Mahan, died 1947, vol. IV
Govett, Ven. D. S., 1827–1912, vol. I
Govett, Ven. Henry, 1819–1903, vol. I
Govett, John Romaine, 1897–1956, vol. V
Govindan Nair, Diwan Bahadur Chettur, 1881–1945, vol. IV (A), vol. V
Gow, Alexander, 1869–1955, vol. V
Gow, Alexander Edward, 1884–1952, vol. V
Gow, Andrew Carrick, 1848–1920, vol. II
Gow, Andrew Sydenham Farrar, 1886–1978, vol. VII
Gow, Charles, 1846–1929, vol. III
Gow, Rev. Henry, 1861–1938, vol. III
Gow, Rev. James, 1854–1923, vol. II
Gow, Leonard, 1859–1936, vol. III
Gow, Lt-Col Peter Fleming, 1885–1949, vol. IV
Gow, William, 1853–1919, vol. II
Gow, William John, 1863–1933, vol. III
Gowan, Miss E. M., died 1934, vol. III
Gowan, Sir Hyde Clarendon, 1878–1938, vol. III
Gowan, Hon. Sir James Robert, 1815–1909, vol. I
Gowans, Surg. Rear-Adm. Francis Jollie, 1880–1952, vol. V
Gowans, Hon. Lt-Col James, 1872–1936, vol. III (A), vol. IV
Gowen, Rev. Herbert H., died 1960, vol. VI (AI)
Gower, Major Lord Alistair St Clair Sutherland L.; see Levson Gower.
Gower, Arthur Francis Gresham L.; see Leveson Gower.
Gower, Col Charles Cameron L.; see Levson-Gower.
Gower, Frederick Neville Sutherland L.; see Leveson-Gower.
Gower, Sir George Granville L.; see Leveson Gower.
Gower, Granville Charles Gresham L.; see Leveson Gower.
Gower, Sir Henry Dudley Gresham L.; see Leveson Gower.
Gower, Ivon Llewellyn Owen, 1874–1955, vol. V
Gower, Sir Patrick; see Gower, Sir R. P. M.
Gower, Col Philip L.; see Leveson Gower.
Gower, Sir (Robert) Patrick (Malcolm), 1887–1964, vol. VI
Gower, Sir Robert Vaughan, 1880–1953, vol. V
Gower, Rt Hon. Lord Ronald Sutherland-, 1845–1916, vol. II
Gowers, Sir Ernest Arthur, 1880–1966, vol. VI
Gowers, Sir William Frederick, 1875–1954, vol. V
Gowers, Sir William Richard, 1845–1915, vol. I
Gowing, Ven. Ellis Norman, 1883–1960, vol. V
Gowing, Lionel Francis, 1859–1925, vol. II
Gowing, Richard, 1831–1899, vol. I
Gowland, William, 1842–1922, vol. II
Gowlland, Lt-Col Edward Lake, 1876–1942, vol. IV

Gowrie, 1st Earl of, 1872–1955, vol. V
Graaff, Sir David Pieter de Villiers, 1st Bt, 1859–1931, vol. III
Graaff, Sir Jacobus Arnoldus Combrinck, died 1927, vol. II
Grabham, George Walter, 1882–1955, vol. V
Grabham, Michael Comport, 1840–1935, vol. III
Grace, Sir Gilbert; see Grace, Sir O. G.
Grace, Rev. Canon Harold Myers, 1888–1967, vol. VI
Grace, Harvey, 1874–1944, vol. IV
Grace, Adm. Henry Edgar, 1876–1937, vol. III
Grace, James E., 1850–1908, vol. I
Grace, John, 1886–1972, vol. VII
Grace, Leo Bernard Aloysius, 1903–1969, vol. VI
Grace, Hon. Morgan Stanislaus, died 1903, vol. I
Grace, Sir (Oliver) Gilbert, 1896–1968, vol. VI
Grace, Sir Percy Raymond, 4th Bt, 1831–1903, vol. I
Grace, Sir Raymond Eustace, 6th Bt, 1903–1977, vol. VII
Grace, Col Sheffield Hamilton-, 1834–1915, vol. I
Grace, Ven. Thomas Samuel, 1850–1918, vol. II
Grace, Sir Valentine Raymond, 5th Bt, 1877–1945, vol. IV
Grace, Rear-Adm. Walter Keir Campbell, 1890–1964, vol. VI
Grace, Wilfrid Arnold, 1895–1964, vol. VI
Grace, William Gilbert, 1848–1915, vol. I (A)
Gracey, Gen. Sir Douglas David, 1894–1964, vol. VI
Gracey, Captain George Frederick Handel, 1878–1958, vol. V
Gracey, Hugh Kirkwood, 1868–1929, vol. III
Gracey, Col Thomas, 1843–1921, vol. II
Gracias, HE Cardinal Valerian, 1900–1978, vol. VII
Gracie, Alan James, 1904–1973, vol. VII
Gracie, Sir Alexander, 1860–1930, vol. III
Gracie, Captain Henry Stewart, 1901–1979, vol. VII
Gradwell, Leo Joseph Anthony, 1899–1969, vol. VI
Gradwell, Robert Bernard George Ashhurst, 1858–1935, vol. III
Graeme, Sir Egerton Hood Murray H.; see Hamond-Graeme.
Graeme, Sir Graham Eden William H.; see Hamond-Graeme.
Græme, Patrick Neale Sutherland, 1877–1958, vol. V
Græme-Sutherland, Alexander Malcolm, 1845–1908, vol. I
Graff, Stephen John, 1842–1940, vol. III
Grafftey-Smith, Sir Anthony Paul, 1903–1960, vol. V
Grafton, 7th Duke of, 1821–1918, vol. II
Grafton, 8th Duke of, 1850–1930, vol. III
Grafton, 9th Duke of, 1914–1936, vol. III
Grafton, 10th Duke of, 1892–1970, vol. VI
Graham, Captain Alan Crosland, 1896–1964, vol. VI
Graham, Captain Lord Alastair Mungo, 1886–1976, vol. VII
Graham, Alexander, 1861–1941, vol. IV
Graham, Allan James, died 1941, vol. IV
Graham, Angus, 1892–1979, vol. VII

Graham, Anthony George M.; see Maxtone-Graham.

Graham, Sir Aubrey Gregor, 1867–1947, vol. IV

Graham, Sir Cecil William Noble, 1872–1945, vol. IV

Graham, Comdr Charles Elphinstone Fleeming C.; see Cunninghame Graham.

Graham, Rt Rev. Charles Morice, 1834–1912, vol. I

Graham, Lt-Col Charles Percy, 1881–1961, vol. VI

Graham, Flt-Lt Charles Walter, 1893–1916, vol. II

Graham, Sir Clarence Johnston, 1st Bt (cr 1964), 1900–1966, vol. VI

Graham, Sir Claverhouse Frederick Charles, died 1924, vol. II

Graham, Constantine, 1882–1934, vol. III

Graham, Rear-Adm. Cosmo Moray, died 1946, vol. IV

Graham, Sir Crosland; see Graham, Sir J. C.

Graham, Brig.-Gen. Cuthbert Aubrey Lionel, 1882–1957, vol. V

Graham, Lt-Col David James, 1871–1929, vol. III

Graham, Donald, 1844–1901, vol. I

Graham, Maj.-Gen. Douglas Alexander Henry, 1893–1971, vol. VII

Graham, Brig. Lord (Douglas) Malise, 1883–1974, vol. VII

Graham, Douglas William, 1866–1936, vol. III

Graham, Duncan MacGregor, 1867–1942, vol. IV

Graham, E. J., died 1918, vol. II

Graham, Maj.-Gen. Sir Edward Ritchie Coryton, 1858–1951, vol. V

Graham, Ennis; see Molesworth, Mary Louisa.

Graham, Rt Rev. Eric, 1888–1964, vol. VI

Graham, Sir Fergus; see Graham, Sir Frederick F.

Graham, Captain Francis, 1894–1918, vol. II

Graham, Sir Frederick, 1848–1923, vol. II

Graham, Sir (Frederick) Fergus, 5th Bt (cr 1783), 1893–1978, vol. VII

Graham, George, born 1838, vol. II

Graham, George, 1881–1949, vol. IV

Graham, George, 1882–1971, vol. VII

Graham, Very Rev. George Frederick, 1877–1962, vol. VI

Graham, Sir George Goldie, 1892–1974, vol. VII

Graham, Rt Hon. George Perry, 1859–1943, vol. IV

Graham, Rev. George R., 1850–1927, vol. II

Graham, Sir Gerald, 1831–1899, vol. I

Graham, Gilbert Maxwell Adair, 1883–1960, vol. V

Graham, (Godfrey) Michael, 1898–1972, vol. VII

Graham, Major Sir Guy; see Graham, Major Sir R. G.

Graham, H. E.; see Hamilton, Col. E. G.

Graham, Hamilton Maurice H.; see Howgrave-Graham.

Graham, Lt-Gen. Hamilton Maximillian Christian Williams, 1866–1934, vol. III

Graham, Harold, 1889–1963, vol. VI

Graham, Captain Harry J. C., 1874–1936, vol. III

Graham, Harry Robert, 1850–1933, vol. III

Graham, Captain Harry S. C., 1874–1936, vol. III

Graham, Lady Helen Violet, 1879–1945, vol. IV

Graham, Major Henry Archibald Roger, 1892–1970, vol. VI

Graham, Rev. Henry Burrans, 1909–1963, vol. VI

Graham, Henry Grey, 1843–1906, vol. I

Graham, Rt Rev. Henry Grey, 1874–1959, vol. V

Graham, Sir Henry John Lowndes, 1842–1930, vol. III

Graham, Col Herman Witsius-Gore, 1859–1932, vol. III

Graham, Lt-Col Howard Boyd, 1891–1965, vol. VI (AII)

Graham, Hugh, died 1975, vol. VII

Graham, Sir James, 1856–1913, vol. I

Graham, Gen. Sir James; see Graham, Gen. Sir S. J.

Graham, James, 1870–1961, vol. VI

Graham, Maj.-Gen. Sir James Drummond, 1875–1958, vol. V

Graham, James Edward, died 1929, vol. III

Graham, James M.; see Maxtone Graham.

Graham, John, 1844–1918, vol. II

Graham, John, 1879–1958, vol. V

Graham, Rev. John; see Graham, Rev. Jonathan J. D.

Graham, Very Rev. John Anderson, 1861–1942, vol. IV

Graham, John Cameron, died 1929, vol. III

Graham, Sir John Frederick Noble, 2nd Bt (cr 1906), 1864–1936, vol. III

Graham, John Fuller, 1872–1946, vol. IV

Graham, Sir John Gibson, 1896–1964, vol. VI

Graham, Maj.-Gen. John Gordon, 1833–1911, vol. I

Graham, Sir John Hatt Noble, 1st Bt (cr 1906), 1837–1926, vol. II

Graham, Captain John Irvine, 1862–1947, vol. IV

Graham, Sir John James, 1847–1928, vol. II

Graham, Ven. John Malcolm Alexander, died 1931, vol. III

Graham, Sir (John) Reginald (Noble), 3rd Bt (cr 1906), 1892–1980, vol. VII

Graham, John William, 1859–1932, vol. III

Graham, Rev. (Jonathan) John Drummond, died 1965, vol. VI

Graham, Joseph, 1828–1902, vol. I

Graham, Sir (Joseph) Crosland, 1866–1946, vol. IV

Graham, Col Lancelot, 1864–1932, vol. III

Graham, Sir Lancelot, 1880–1958, vol. V

Graham, Brig. Lancelot Cecil Torbock, 1890–1962, vol. VI

Graham, Col Malcolm David, 1865–1941, vol. IV

Graham, Brig. Lord Malise; see Graham, Brig. Lord D. M.

Graham, Col Malise, 1884–1929, vol. III

Graham, Michael; see Graham, G. M.

Graham, Michael, 1847–1925, vol. II

Graham, Maj.-Gen. Sir Miles William Arthur Peel, 1895–1976, vol. VII

Graham, Sir Montrose Stuart, 11th Bt (cr 1629), 1875–1939, vol. III

Graham, Sir Montrose Stuart, 12th Bt (cr 1629), 1904–1975, vol. VII

Graham, Norval Bantock, 1870–1944, vol. IV

Graham, P. Anderson, died 1925, vol. II

Graham, Peter, *died* 1921, vol. II
Graham, Sir Reginald; *see* Graham, Sir J. R. N.
Graham, Major Sir (Reginald) Guy, 9th Bt (*cr* 1662), 1878–1940, vol. III
Graham, Sir Reginald Henry, 8th Bt (*cr* 1662), 1835–1920, vol. II
Graham, Richard Brockbank, 1893–1957, vol. V
Graham, Sir Richard James, 4th Bt (*cr* 1783), 1859–1932, vol. III
Graham, Sir Robert, 1846–1929, vol. III
Graham, Sir Robert, 1876–1947, vol. IV
Graham, Robert Arthur, 1870–1940, vol. III
Graham, Col Robert Blackall, 1874–1944, vol. IV
Graham, Robert Bontine C.; *see* Cunninghame Graham.
Graham, Robert Henry, 1870–1956, vol. V
Graham, Robert James Douglas, *died* 1950, vol. IV (A)
Graham, Sir Robert James Stuart, 10th Bt (*cr* 1629), 1845–1917, vol. II
Graham, Col Robert M.; *see* Mould-Graham.
Graham, Air Vice-Marshal Ronald, 1896–1967, vol. VI
Graham, Rt Hon. Sir Ronald William, 1870–1949, vol. IV
Graham, Rose, 1875–1963, vol. VI
Graham, Gen. Sir (S.) James, 1837–1917, vol. II
Graham, Stanley Galbraith, 1895–1975, vol. VII
Graham, Stephen, 1884–1975, vol. VI
Graham, Sydney, 1879–1966, vol. VI
Graham, Maj.-Gen. Sir Thomas, 1842–1925, vol. II
Graham, Hon. Sir Thomas Lynedoch, 1860–1940, vol. III
Graham, Thomas Ottiwell, 1883–1966, vol. VI
Graham, Tom, *died* 1906, vol. I
Graham, Sir Wallace, 1848–1917, vol. II
Graham, Walter Armstrong, 1868–1949, vol. IV
Graham, Adm. Walter Hodgson Bevan, 1849–1931, vol. III
Graham, Sir William, 1825–1907, vol. I
Graham, William, *died* 1911, vol. I
Graham, Sir William, 1861–1932, vol. III
Graham, Rt Hon. William, 1887–1932, vol. III
Graham, William, 1862–1943, vol. IV
Graham, William, 1896–1955, vol. V
Graham, Col William James, 1890–1971, vol. VII
Graham, William Murray, 1884–1956, vol. V
Graham, William Perceval Gore, 1861–1918, vol. II
Graham, Winifred, (Mrs Theodore Cory), *died* 1950, vol. IV
Graham Brown, Rt Rev. George Francis, 1891–1942, vol. IV
Graham Brown, Thomas, *died* 1965, vol. VI
Graham-Campbell, Rt Rev. Archibald Rollo, 1903–1978, vol. VII
Graham-Campbell, Sir Rollo Frederick, 1868–1946, vol. IV
Graham-Clarke, Captain Lionel Altham, 1867–1914, vol. I
Graham-Harrison, Sir William Montagu, 1871–1949, vol. IV
Graham-Hodgson, Sir Harold Kingston; *see* Hodgson.
Graham-Little, Sir Ernest Gordon; *see* Little.

Graham-Montgomery, Sir Basil Templer; *see* Montgomery.
Graham-Montgomery, Rev. Sir Charles Percy; *see* Montgomery.
Graham-Moon, Sir Wilfred; *see* Moon.
Graham-Smith, George Stuart, *died* 1950, vol. IV
Graham-Stewart, Alexander, 1879–1944, vol. IV
Graham-Vivian, Preston; *see* Graham-Vivian, R. P.
Graham-Vivian, (Richard) Preston, 1896–1979, vol. VII
Grahame, Rt Hon. Sir George Dixon, 1873–1940, vol. III
Grahame, Lt-Col John Crum, 1870–1952, vol. V
Grahame, Kenneth, 1859–1932, vol. III
Grahame, Thomas George, 1861–1922, vol. II
Grahame-Thomson, Leslie; *see* MacDougall, L. G.
Grahame-White, Claude, 1879–1959, vol. V
Grain, Sir Peter, 1864–1947, vol. IV
Grainger, F.; *see* Hill, Headon.
Grainger, Percy Aldridge, 1882–1961, vol. VI
Grainger, Surg.-Gen. Thomas, 1862–1931, vol. III
Grainger-Stewart, Brig. Thomas, 1896–1979, vol. VII
Gramigna, Rt Rev. Fr Petronius, 1844–1917, vol. II
Granard, 8th Earl of, 1874–1948, vol. IV
Grand, Maj.-Gen. Laurence Douglas, 1898–1975, vol. VII
Grand, Sarah, *died* 1943, vol. IV
Grand' Combe, Félix de; *see* Boillot, Félix.
Grande, Julian, 1874–1946, vol. IV
Grane, Rev. William Leighton, 1855–1952, vol. V
Granet, Col Edward John, 1858–1918, vol. II
Granet, Sir Guy; *see* Granet, Sir W. G.
Granet, Sir (William) Guy, 1867–1943, vol. IV
Grange-Bennett, Rev. Canon Ronald du Pré, 1901–1972, vol. VII
Granger, Frank Stephen, 1864–1936, vol. III
Granger, Sir (Hugh) Rupert, 1890–1959, vol. V
Granger, Sir Rupert; *see* Granger, Sir H. R.
Granger, Col Thomas Arthur, *died* 1942, vol. IV
Granger, Sir Thomas Colpitts, 1852–1927, vol. II
Grannum, Sir Edward Allan, 1869–1956, vol. V
Grannum, Edward Thomas, 1843–1922, vol. II
Grannum, Reginald Clifton, 1872–1946, vol. IV
Gransden, Sir Robert, 1893–1972, vol. VII
Grant, Rt Hon. Lord; William Grant, 1909–1972, vol. VII
Grant, Sir (Albert) William, 1891–1965, vol. VI
Grant, Sir Alexander, 1st Bt (*cr* 1924), 1864–1937, vol. III
Grant, Alexander, 1866–1941, vol. IV
Grant, Captain Alexander, 1872–1961, vol. VI
Grant, Col Alexander Brown, 1840–1921, vol. II
Grant, Adm. Alfred Ernest Albert, 1861–1933, vol. III
Grant, Sir (Alfred) Hamilton, 12th Bt (*cr* 1688), 1872–1937, vol. III
Grant, Sir Allan John, 1875–1955, vol. V
Grant, Air Marshal Sir Andrew, 1890–1967, vol. VI
Grant, Col Sir Arthur, 10th Bt (*cr* 1705), 1879–1931, vol. III
Grant, Sir Arthur Henry, 9th Bt (*cr* 1705), 1849–1917, vol. II

Grant, Arthur James, 1862–1948, vol. IV
Grant, Major Sir Arthur Lindsay, 11th Bt (*cr* 1705), 1911–1944, vol. IV
Grant, Engr Rear-Adm. Arthur Robert, 1870–1952, vol. V
Grant, Rev. (Arthur) Rowland (Harry), 1882–1961, vol. VI
Grant, Rev. Cecil, 1870–1946, vol. IV
Grant, Sir Charles, *died* 1903, vol. I
Grant, Charles Frederick, 1878–1966, vol. VI
Grant, Charles Graham, *died* 1935, vol. III
Grant, Col Charles James William, *died* 1932, vol. III
Grant, Gen. Sir Charles John Cecil, 1877–1950, vol. IV
Grant, Corrie, 1850–1924, vol. II
Grant, Rev. Cyril Fletcher, *died* 1916, vol. II
Grant, Douglas; *see* Grant, W. D. B.
Grant, Lt-Gen. Douglas Gordon Seafield St John, 1829–1907, vol. I
Grant, Comdr Duncan, 1882–1955, vol. V
Grant, Sir Duncan Alexander, 13th Bt (*cr* 1688), 1928–1961, vol. VI
Grant, Duncan James Corrowr, 1885–1978, vol. VII
Grant, Adm. Sir (Edmund) Percy (Fenwick George), 1867–1952, vol. V
Grant, Lt-Col Edward James, 1854–1928, vol. II
Grant, Sir Francis Cullen, 12th Bt (*cr* 1705), 1914–1966, vol. VI
Grant, Francis Henry Symons, 1883–1963, vol. VI
Grant, Sir Francis James, 1863–1953, vol. V
Grant, Frederick, 1890–1954, vol. V
Grant, Captain George Bertram M.; *see* Macpherson-Grant.
Grant, Sir George M.; *see* Macpherson-Grant.
Grant, Very Rev. George Monro, 1835–1902, vol. I
Grant, Gordon, 1907–1979, vol. VII
Grant, Sir Hamilton; *see* Grant, Sir A. H.
Grant, Lt-Gen. Harold George, 1884–1950, vol. IV
Grant, Adm. Sir Heathcoat Salusbury, 1864–1938, vol. III
Grant, Henry Eugene Walter, 1855–1934, vol. III
Grant, Gen. Sir Henry Fane, 1848–1919, vol. II
Grant, Adm. Henry William, 1870–1949, vol. IV
Grant, Col Hugh Gough, 1845–1922, vol. II
Grant, Maj.-Gen. Ian Cameron, 1891–1955, vol. V
Grant, Ian Dingwall, 1891–1962, vol. VI
Grant, Sir James Alexander, 1831–1920, vol. II
Grant, Sir James Augustus, 1st Bt (*cr* 1926), 1867–1932, vol. III
Grant, Sir James Dundas-, 1854–1944, vol. IV
Grant, James William Hamilton, 1876–1934, vol. III
Grant, Col John Duncan, 1877–1967, vol. VI
Grant, John Leslie, 1890–1975, vol. VII
Grant, Sir John M.; *see* Macpherson-Grant.
Grant, John Peter, 1860–1927, vol. II
Grant, John Peter, 1885–1963, vol. VI
Grant, John Sharp, 1909–1974, vol. VII
Grant, Rt Rev. Kenneth, 1900–1959, vol. V
Grant, Sir Kerr, 1878–1967, vol. VI
Grant, Leonard Bishopp, 1882–1974, vol. VII

Grant, Adm. Sir Lowther; *see* Grant, Adm. Sir W. L.
Grant, Sir Ludovic James, 11th Bt (*cr* 1688), 1862–1936, vol. III
Grant, Hon. MacCallum, *died* 1928, vol. II
Grant, Col Maurice Harold, *died* 1962, vol. VI
Grant, Neil Forbes, 1882–1970, vol. VI
Grant, Rear-Adm. Noel, 1868–1920, vol. II
Grant, Adm. Sir Percy; *see* Grant, Adm. Sir E. P. F. G.
Grant, Peter Forbes, 1921–1974, vol. VII
Grant, Maj.-Gen. Sir Philip Gordon, 1869–1943, vol. IV
Grant, Lt-Gen. Sir Robert, 1837–1904, vol. I
Grant, Robert, 1842–1910, vol. I
Grant, Robert, 1852–1940, vol. III (A), vol. IV
Grant, Major Robert Francis Sidney, 1877–1927, vol. II
Grant, Sir Robert McVitie, 2nd Bt (*cr* 1924), 1894–1947, vol. IV
Grant, Sir Robert William L.; *see* Lyall Grant.
Grant, Brig.-Gen. Ronald Chas., 1864–1951, vol. V
Grant, Rev. Rowland; *see* Grant, Rev. A. R. H.
Grant, Col Samuel Charles Norton, 1854–1939, vol. III
Grant, Lt-Gen. Seafield Falkland Murray Treasure, 1834–1910, vol. I
Grant, Lady Sybil, *died* 1955, vol. V
Grant, William; *see* Grant, Rt Hon. Lord.
Grant, Sir William; *see* Grant, Sir A. W.
Grant, William, 1863–1919, vol. II
Grant, Brig.-Gen. William, 1870–1939, vol. III
Grant, William, 1863–1946, vol. IV
Grant, Rt Hon. William, *died* 1949, vol. IV
Grant, (William) Douglas (Beattie), 1921–1969, vol. VI
Grant, William Lawson, 1872–1935, vol. III
Grant, Adm. Sir (William) Lowther, 1864–1929, vol. III
Grant, William Robert O.; *see* Ogilvie-Grant.
Grant-Dalton, Captain Charles, 1884–1952, vol. V
Grant-Dalton, Lt-Col Duncan, 1881–1969, vol. VI
Grant-Dalton, Adm. Hubert, 1862–1934, vol. III
Grant-Duff, Major Adrian, 1869–1914, vol. I
Grant-Duff, Sir Arthur Cuninghame, 1861–1948, vol. IV
Grant-Duff, Edith Florence, (Lady Grant-Duff), *died* 1937, vol. III
Grant-Duff, Sir Evelyn, 1863–1926, vol. II
Grant Lawson, Col Sir Peter; *see* Lawson.
Grant-Sturgis, Sir Mark Beresford Russell, 1884–1949, vol. IV
Grant-Suttie, Sir George; *see* Suttie.
Grant-Suttie, Col Hubert Francis; *see* Suttie.
Grant Watson, Herbert Adolphus, 1881–1971, vol. VII
Grant-Wilson, Sir Wemyss, 1870–1953, vol. V
Grantchester, 1st Baron, 1893–1976, vol. VII
Grantham, Sir Alexander William George Herder, 1899–1978, vol. VII
Grantham, Vincent Alpe, 1889–1968, vol. VI
Grantham, Sir William, 1835–1911, vol. I
Grantham, William Wilson, 1866–1942, vol. IV
Grantley, 5th Baron, 1855–1943, vol. IV

Grantley, 6th Baron, 1892–1954, vol. V
Granville, 3rd Earl, 1872–1939, vol. III
Granville, 4th Earl, 1880–1953, vol. V
Granville, Countess; (Rose Constance), 1890–1967, vol. VI
Granville, Alexander, 1874–1929, vol. III
Granville, Col Bernard, *died* 1933, vol. III
Granville, Captain Dennis, 1863–1929, vol. III
Granville, Rev. Roger, 1848–1911, vol. I
Granville-Barker, Harley Granville, 1877–1946, vol. IV
Granville-Barker, Helen, *died* 1950, vol. IV
Granville-Sharp, Gilbert; *see* Sharp.
Granville-Smith, Stuart Hayne, 1901–1977, vol. VII
Gras, Norman Scott Brien, 1884–1956, vol. V
Grasett, Lt-Gen. Sir (Arthur) Edward, 1888–1971, vol. VII
Grasett, Lt-Gen. Sir Edward; *see* Grasett, Lt-Gen. Sir A. E.
Grasett, Col Henry James, 1847–1930, vol. III
Gratiaen, Edward Frederick Noel, 1904–1973, vol. VII
Grattan, Col Henry William, 1872–1952, vol. V
Grattan, John Henry Grafton, 1878–1951, vol. V
Grattan, Col O'Donnel Colley, 1855–1929, vol. III
Grattan-Bellew, Lt-Col Sir Charles Christopher, 4th Bt, 1887–1948, vol. IV
Grattan-Bellew, Sir Henry Christopher, 3rd Bt, 1860–1942, vol. IV
Grattan-Doyle, Sir Nicholas, 1862–1941, vol. IV
Grattidge, Captain Harry, 1890–1979, vol. VII
Gratton, Norman Murray Gladstone, 1886–1965, vol. VI
Gratwicke, George Frederick, 1850–1912, vol. I
Grau, Maurice, 1849–1907, vol. I
Grauer, Albert Edward, 1906–1961, vol. VI
Graul, Isidore, 1894–1962, vol. VI
Graumann, Sir Harry, 1868–1938, vol. III
Gravely, Sir Walter B.; *see* Booth-Gravely.
Graves, 4th Baron, 1847–1904, vol. I
Graves, 5th Baron, 1847–1914, vol. I
Graves, 6th Baron, 1871–1937, vol. III
Graves, 7th Baron, 1877–1963, vol. VI
Graves, Alfred Perceval, 1846–1931, vol. III
Graves, Arnold F., 1847–1930, vol. III
Graves, Col Benjamin Chamney, 1845–1905, vol. I
Graves, Captain Sir Cecil George, 1892–1957, vol. V
Graves, Rt Rev. Charles, 1812–1899, vol. I
Graves, Rev. Charles Edward, 1839–1920, vol. II
Graves, Charles L., 1856–1944, vol. IV
Graves, Charles Patrick Ranke, 1899–1971, vol. VII
Graves, Clotilde Inez Mary, 1863–1932, vol. III
Graves, Rt Rev. Frederick Rogers, 1858–1940, vol. III (A), vol. IV
Graves, George, 1876–1949, vol. IV
Graves, Sir Hubert Ashton, 1894–1972, vol. VII
Graves, John George, 1865–1945, vol. IV
Graves, Marjorie, *died* 1961, vol. VI
Graves, Rev. Michael, 1855–1931, vol. III
Graves, Philip Perceval, 1876–1953, vol. V
Graves, Richard Massie, 1880–1960, vol. V
Graves, Robert Ernest, 1866–1922, vol. II
Graves, Sir Robert Windham, 1858–1934, vol. III

Graves, Rev. Walter Eccleston, *died* 1922, vol. II
Graves-Sawle, Sir Charles John; *see* Sawle.
Gravina, Conte Manfredi, 1883–1932, vol. III
Gray, Lady, (19th in line), 1841–1918, vol. II
Gray, 20th Lord, 1864–1919, vol. II
Gray, Lady (21st in line, shown as 22nd), 1866–1946, vol. IV
Gray, Master of; Hon. Lindsay Stuart Campbell-Gray, 1894–1945, vol. IV
Gray, Alan, 1855–1935, vol. III
Gray, Sir Albert, 1850–1928, vol. II
Gray, Albert Alexander, 1868–1936, vol. III
Gray, Sir Alexander, *died* 1933, vol. III
Gray, Sir Alexander, 1882–1968, vol. VI
Gray, Air Vice-Marshal Alexander, 1896–1980, vol. VII
Gray, Sir Alexander George, 1884–1968, vol. VI
Gray, Andrew, 1847–1925, vol. II
Gray, Sir Archibald Montague Henry, 1880–1967, vol. VI
Gray, Arthur, 1852–1940, vol. III
Gray, Col Arthur Claypon Horner, 1878–1963, vol. VI
Gray, A(rthur) Herbert, 1868–1956, vol. V
Gray, Arthur Wellesley, 1876–1944, vol. IV
Gray, Lt-Col Clive Osric Vere, 1882–1945, vol. IV
Gray, David, 1906–1976, vol. VII
Gray, Donald, 1893–1943, vol. IV
Gray, Douglas S., 1890–1959, vol. V
Gray, Rev. Edward Dundas McQueen, 1854–1932, vol. III
Gray, Edward Francis, 1871–1960, vol. V
Gray, Rev. Edward Ker, 1842–1903, vol. I
Gray, Sir Ernest, 1857–1932, vol. III
Gray, Ethel, *died* 1962, vol. VI
Gray, Frances Ralph, *died* 1935, vol. III
Gray, Frank, 1880–1935, vol. III
Gray, Brig.-Gen. Frederick William Barton, 1867–1931, vol. III
Gray, George Buchanan, 1865–1922, vol. II
Gray, Lt-Col George Douglas, *died* 1946, vol. IV
Gray, George Kruger, 1880–1943, vol. IV
Gray, Sir George Mervyn, 1910–1973, vol. VII
Gray, Hon. George Wilkie, 1844–1924, vol. II
Gray, Harold St George, 1872–1963, vol. VI
Gray, Sir Harold William Stannus, 1867–1951, vol. V
Gray, Rt Rev. Henry Allen, *died* 1939, vol. III
Gray, Sir Henry McIlree Williamson, 1870–1938, vol. III
Gray, Rev. Herbert Branston, 1851–1929, vol. III
Gray, Rev. Horace, 1874–1938, vol. III
Gray, Howard Alexander, 1870–1942, vol. IV
Gray, James, 1877–1968, vol. VI
Gray, Sir James, 1891–1975, vol. VII
Gray, James Andrew, 1890–1966, vol. VI
Gray, James Cooke, 1847–1902, vol. I
Gray, James Gordon, *died* 1934, vol. III
Gray, James Hugo, 1909–1941, vol. IV
Gray, James Hunter, 1867–1925, vol. II
Gray, James Neville, *died* 1959, vol. V
Gray, Lt-Col John Anselm Samuel, 1874–1950, vol. IV
Gray, Sir John Milner, 1889–1970, vol. VI

Gray, Joseph Alexander, 1884–1966, vol. VI
Gray, Rev. Joseph Henry, 1856–1932, vol. III
Gray, Leonard Thomas Miller, 1893–1969, vol. VI
Gray, Louis Harold, 1905–1965, vol. VI
Gray, Maxwell, (M. G. Tuttiett), died 1923, vol. II
Gray, Milner, 1871–1943, vol. IV
Gray, Norah Neilson-, died 1931, vol. III
Gray, Sir Reginald, 1851–1935, vol. III
Gray, Robert Whytlaw W.; see Whytlaw-Gray.
Gray, Ronald, 1868–1951, vol. V
Gray, Sir Samuel Brownlow, 1823–1910, vol. I
Gray, Theodore Grant, 1884–1964, vol. VI
Gray, Thomas, 1869–1932, vol. III
Gray, Vernon Foxwell, 1882–1978, vol. VII
Gray, Lt-Col Sir Vivian Beaconsfield, 1885–1948, vol. IV
Gray, Sir Walter, 1848–1918, vol. II
Gray, Sir William, 1823–1898, vol. I
Gray, Sir William, 2nd Bt, 1895–1978, vol. VII
Gray, Lt-Col William A.; see Anstruther-Gray.
Gray, Major William Bain, 1886–1949, vol. IV
Gray, Major William Birrell-, 1872–1940, vol. III
Gray, Rt Rev. William Crane, 1835–1919, vol. II
Gray, Sir William Cresswell, 1st Bt, 1867–1924, vol. II
Gray, Maj.-Gen. William du Gard, 1856–1932, vol. III
Gray, William Forbes, 1874–1950, vol. IV
Gray, Very Rev. William Henry, 1825–1908, vol. I
Gray, Ven. William James, 1874–1960, vol. V
Gray, Col William Lewis, 1864–1924, vol. II
Gray-Cheape, Lt-Col Hugh Annesley; see Cheape.
Gray Horton, Lt-Col W(illiam); see Horton.
Gray-Smith, James Maclaren, 1832–1900, vol. I
Grayburn, Sir Vandeleur Molyneux, 1881–1943 vol. IV
Graydon, Newenham Arthur Eustace, died 1914, vol. I
Grayfoot, Col Blenman Buhot, died 1916, vol. II
Grayson, Sir Denys Henry Harrington, 2nd Bt, 1892–1955, vol. V
Grayson, Lt-Col Sir Henry Mulleneux, 1st Bt, 1865–1951, vol. V
Grazebrook, Brig. George Charles, 1873–1930, vol. III
Grazebrook, Henry Broome Durley, 1884–1969, vol. VI
Grazebrook, Brig. Tom Neville, 1904–1967, vol. VI
Grazebrook, William, died 1955, vol. V
Greany, Surg.-Gen. John Philip, 1851–1919, vol. II
Greany, Captain John Wingate, 1892–1916, vol. II
Greathed, Rear-Adm. Bernard Wilberforce, 1891–1961, vol. VI
Greatorex, Adm. Clement, 1869–1937, vol. III
Greaves, Rt Rev. Arthur Ivan, 1873–1959, vol. V
Greaves, Sir Ewart; see Greaves, Sir W. E.
Greaves, Gen. Sir George Richards, 1831–1922, vol. II
Greaves, Sir John Bewley, 1890–1977, vol. VII
Greaves, Sir John Brownson, 1900–1965, vol. VI
Greaves, John Ernest, 1847–1945, vol. IV
Greaves, Robert William, 1909–1979, vol. VII
Greaves, Sir (William) Ewart, 1869–1956, vol. V
Greaves, Sir William Herbert, 1857–1936, vol. III

Greaves, William Michael Herbert, 1897–1955, vol. V
Greaves-Lord, Sir Walter, 1878–1942, vol. IV
Grech-Biancardi, Lt-Col Nicola, died 1913, vol. I
Greely, Maj.-Gen. Adolphus Washington, 1844–1935, vol. III
Green, Sir Alan Michael, 1885–1958, vol. V
Green, Albert, 1874–1941, vol. IV
Green, Hon. Albert Ernest, 1869–1940, vol. III
Green, Alice Sophia Amelia, died 1929, vol. III
Green, Anna Katharine; see Rohlfs, Mrs Charles.
Green, Major Arthur Dowson, 1874–1914, vol. I
Green, Brig.-Gen. Arthur Frank Umfreville, 1878–1964, vol. VI
Green, Arthur George, 1864–1941, vol. IV
Green, Rt Rev. Arthur Vincent, 1857–1944, vol. IV
Green, Col Bernard Charles, 1866–1925, vol. II
Green, Cecil Alfred, 1908–1980, vol. VII
Green, Rt Rev. Charles Alfred Howell, 1864–1944, vol. IV
Green, Charles Edward, 1866–1920, vol. II
Green, Rev. Charles Edward Maddison, died 1911, vol. I
Green, Charles L.; see Leedham-Green.
Green, David, died 1918, vol. II
Green, Engr Rear-Adm. Sir (Donald) Percy, 1866–1950, vol. IV
Green, Brig.-Gen. Edgar Walter Butler, 1869–1938, vol. III
Green, Rev. Edmund Tyrrell-, 1864–1937, vol. III
Green, Sir Edward, 1st Bt (cr 1886), 1831–1923, vol. II
Green, Col Sir Edward Arthur Lycett, 3rd Bt (cr 1886), 1886–1941, vol. IV
Green, Sir (Edward) Lycett, 2nd Bt (cr 1886), 1860–1940, vol. III
Green, Ernest, 1885–1977, vol. VII
Green, Col Ernest Edward, 1878–1956, vol. V
Green, Miss Evelyn E.; see Everett-Green.
Green, Everard, 1844–1926, vol. II
Green, Sir Francis Haydn, 2nd Bt (cr 1901), 1871–1956, vol. VII
Green, Francis Henry Knethell, 1900–1977, vol. VII
Green, Sir Frank, 1st Bt (cr 1901), 1835–1902, vol. I
Green, Sir Frederick, 1845–1927, vol. II
Green, Frederick Charles, 1891–1964, vol. VI
Green, Sir Frederick Daniel, 1869–1932, vol. III
Green, Frederick Ernest, 1867–1922, vol. II
Green, Frederick Lawrence, 1902–1953, vol. V
Green, Rev. Frederick Wastie, 1884–1953, vol. V
Green, Frederick William E.; see Edridge-Green.
Green, Geoffrey, 1918–1978, vol. VII
Green, Sir George, 1843–1916, vol. II
Green, George Alfred Lawrence, died 1949, vol. IV
Green, Sir George Arthur Haydn, 4th Bt (cr 1901), 1884–1959, vol. V
Green, George Comerford, died 1940, vol. III
Green, George Conrad, 1897–1976, vol. VII
Green, George Henry, 1881–1956, vol. V
Green, George Norman, 1906–1968, vol. VI
Green, Lt-Col Harold Philip, 1877–1944, vol. IV
Green, Harry Norman, 1903–1967, vol. VI

Green, Henry, 1905–1973, vol. VII
Green, Brig.-Gen. Henry Clifford Rodes, 1872–1935, vol. III
Green, Mrs Hetty Howland Robinson, 1835–1916, vol. II
Green, Rev. James, 1868–1948, vol. IV
Green, Rev. James Paul Weston, *born* 1876, vol. III
Green, John Alfred, 1867–1922, vol. II
Green, Adm. Sir John Frederick Ernest, 1866–1948, vol. IV
Green, Sir John Little, 1862–1953, vol. V
Green, Joseph Frederick, 1855–1932, vol. III
Green, Joseph Reynolds, *died* 1914, vol. I
Green, Kathleen (Mary) Haydn, *died* 1944, vol. IV
Green, Hon. Sir Kenneth; *see* Green, Hon. Sir R. K.
Green, Leonard, 1890–1963, vol. VI
Green, Captain Leonard Henry, 1885–1966, vol. VI
Green, Rev. Sir Leonard Henry Haydn, 3rd Bt (*cr* 1901), 1879–1958, vol. V
Green, Sir Lycett; *see* Green, Sir E. L.
Green, Col Malcolm Scrimshire, 1824–1906, vol. I
Green, Max Sullivan, 1864–1922, vol. II
Green, Brig. Michael Arthur, 1891–1971, vol. VII
Green, Engr Rear-Adm. Sir Percy; *see* Green, Engr Rear-Adm. Sir D. P.
Green, Rev. Canon Peter, 1871–1961, vol. VI
Green, P(hilip) M(arion) Kirby, 1905–1969, vol. VI
Green, Hon. Sir (Richard) Kenneth, 1907–1961, vol. VI
Green, Hon. Robert Francis, 1861–1946, vol. IV
Green, Roland, 1895–1972, vol. VII
Green, Ronald Bramble, 1895–1973, vol. VII
Green, Ronald Frank, 1905–1971, vol. VII
Green, Rev. Samuel Walter, 1853–1926, vol. II
Green, Maj.-Gen. Sebert Francis St David's, 1868–1930, vol. III
Green, Thomas Ernest, 1872–1937, vol. III
Green, Thomas Farrimond, 1899–1966, vol. VI
Green, Vincent, *died* 1958, vol. V
Green, Rev. W. C., 1832–1914, vol. I
Green, Walford Davis, 1869–1941, vol. IV
Green, Walter Henry, 1878–1958, vol. V
Green, Brig.-Gen. Wilfrith Gerald Key, 1872–1937, vol. III
Green, Sir William, 1836–1897, vol. I
Green, Maj.-Gen. William, 1882–1947, vol. IV
Green, William, 1873–1952, vol. V
Green, William Allan McInnes, 1896–1972, vol. VII
Green, William Curtis, 1875–1960, vol. V
Green, Maj.-Gen. Sir William Henry Rodes, 1823–1912, vol. I
Green, William Kirby, 1876–1945, vol. IV
Green, Rev. William Spotswood, 1847–1919, vol. II
Green, Lt-Gen. Sir (William) Wyndham, 1887–1979, vol. VII
Green, Lt-Gen. Sir Wyndham; *see* Green, Lt-Gen. Sir W. W.
Green-Armytage, Lt-Col Vivian Bartley, 1882–1961, vol. VI
Green-Price, Sir John, 4th Bt, 1908–1964, vol. VI
Green-Price, Sir Richard Dansey, 2nd Bt, 1838–1909, vol. I

Green-Price, Major Sir Robert Henry, 3rd Bt, 1872–1962, vol. VI
Green-Wilkinson, Most Rev. Francis Oliver, 1913–1970, vol. VI
Green-Wilkinson, Lt-Gen. Frederick, *died* 1913, vol. I
Green-Wilkinson, Brig.-Gen. Lewis Frederic, 1865–1950, vol. IV
Greenacre, Sir Benjamin Wesley, 1832–1911, vol. I
Greenacre, Brig. Walter Douglas Campbell, 1900–1978, vol. VII
Greenall, Cyril Edward, *died* 1939, vol. III
Greenall, Thomas, 1857–1937, vol. III
Greenaway, Sir Percy Walter, 1st Bt, 1874–1956, vol. V
Greenaway, Sir Thomas Moore, 1902–1980, vol. VII (AII)
Greenbank, Percy, 1878–1968, vol. VI
Greenberg, Leopold, 1885–1964, vol. VI
Greenberg, Leopold J., *died* 1931, vol. III
Greene, 1st Baron, 1883–1952, vol. V
Greene, Benjamin Buck, 1808–1902, vol. I
Greene, Charles Henry, 1865–1942, vol. IV
Greene, Rt Hon. Sir Conyngham, 1854–1934, vol. III
Greene, Sir (E.) Walter, 1st Bt, 1842–1920, vol. II
Greene, Sir Edward Allan, 3rd Bt, 1882–1966, vol. VI
Greene, Col Hon. Edward Mackenzie, 1857–1944, vol. IV
Greene, Eric Gordon, 1904–1966, vol. VI
Greene, Gen. Francis Vinton, *died* 1921, vol. II
Greene, Geoffrey Philip, 1868–1930, vol. III
Greene, George Arthur, 1853–1921, vol. V
Greene, George Ball, 1872–1945, vol. IV
Greene, Rev. Godfrey George, 1860–1929, vol. III
Greene, Sir Graham; *see* Greene, Sir W. G.
Greene, H. Barrett, 1861–1927, vol. II
Greene, Harry Plunket, 1865–1936, vol. III
Greene, Henry David, 1843–1915, vol. I (A)
Greene, Jerome Davis, 1874–1959, vol. V
Greene, Brig.-Gen. John, 1878–1956, vol. V
Greene, John Arch, *died* 1934, vol. III
Greene, John Arthur, 1879–1945, vol. IV
Greene, Maurice Cherry, 1881–1959, vol. V
Greene, Sir Raymond; *see* Greene, Sir W. R.
Greene, W. H. C.; *see* Clayton-Greene.
Greene, Sir Walter; *see* Greene, Sir E. W.
Greene, Hon. Sir Walter M.; *see* Massy-Greene.
Greene, Sir (Walter) Raymond, 2nd Bt, 1869–1947, vol. IV
Greene, Very Rev. William Conyngham, *died* 1910, vol. I
Greene, Sir (William) Graham, 1857–1950, vol. IV
Greene, William Pomeroy Crawford, 1884–1959, vol. V
Greene Kelly, Sir Henry, 1865–1934, vol. III
Greener, Lt-Col Herbert, 1862–1943, vol. IV
Greenfield, Sir Cornelius Ewen MacLean, 1906–1980, vol. VII
Greenfield, Brig. Hector Robert Hume, 1893–1975, vol. VII
Greenfield, Sir Henry Challen, 1885–1967, vol. VI
Greenfield, Herbert, 1869–1949, vol. IV (A), vol. V

Greenfield, Brig.-Gen. Richard Menteith, 1856–1916, vol. II
Greenfield, Stanley Samuel, 1873–1956, vol. V
Greenfield, William Smith, 1846–1919, vol. II
Greenhalgh, Mrs Stobart; see Stobart, Mrs St Clair.
Greenham, Alfred Howard, 1895–1966, vol. VI
Greenham, Robert Duckworth, 1906–1976, vol. VII
Greenhill, 1st Baron, 1887–1967, vol. VI
Greenhill, Sir George, 1847–1927, vol. II
Greenhill-Gardyne, Lt-Col Charles, 1831–1923, vol. II
Greenhough, Col Frederick Harry, 1871–1953, vol. V
Greenhow, William Thomas, 1831–1921, vol. II
Greenidge, Charles Wilton Wood, 1889–1972, vol. VII
Greenish, Henry George, 1855–1933, vol. III
Greenland, Rev. William Kingscote, 1868–1957, vol. V
Greenleaves, Herbert Leslie, 1897–1975, vol. VII
Greenlees, James Robertson Campbell, 1878–1951, vol. V
Greenley, William Alfred, 1884–1949, vol. IV
Greenly, Edward, 1861–1951, vol. V
Greenly, Edward Howorth, 1837–1926, vol. II
Greenly, Lt-Col Sir John Henry Maitland, 1885–1950, vol. IV
Greenly, Maj.-Gen. Walter Howorth, 1875–1955, vol. V
Greenshields, James Naismith, 1853–1937, vol. III
Greenshields, R. A. E., died 1942, vol. IV
Greenslade, David Rex Willman, 1916–1977, vol. VII
Greenslade, Rev. Stanley Lawrence, 1905–1977, vol. VII
Greenstreet, Reginald Hawkins, 1858–1930, vol. III
Greenstreet, William John, 1861–1930, vol. III
Greenup, Rev. Albert William, 1866–1952, vol. V
Greenway, 1st Baron, 1857–1934, vol. III
Greenway, 2nd Baron, 1888–1963, vol. VI
Greenway, 3rd Baron, 1917–1975, vol. VII
Greenway, Maj.-Gen. Charles William, 1900–1968, vol. VI
Greenway, John Dee, 1896–1967, vol. VI
Greenwell, Allan, 1860–1944, vol. IV
Greenwell, Sir Bernard Eyre, 2nd Bt, 1874–1939, vol. III
Greenwell, Sir Francis, 1852–1931, vol. III
Greenwell, Captain Sir Peter McClintock, 3rd Bt, 1914–1978, vol. VII
Greenwell, Col Thomas George, 1894–1967, vol. VI
Greenwell, Sir Walpole Lloyd, 1st Bt, 1847–1919, vol. II
Greenwell, Rev. William, 1820–1918, vol. II
Greenwell, Col William Basil, 1881–1964, vol. VI
Greenwood, 1st Viscount, 1870–1948, vol. IV
Greenwood, Viscountess; (Marjery), 1886–1968, vol. VI
Greenwood, Rt Hon. Arthur, 1880–1954, vol. V
Greenwood, Col Charles Francis Hill, 1871–1944, vol. IV
Greenwood, Frederick, died 1909, vol. I
Greenwood, Sir G. George, 1850–1928, vol. II
Greenwood, George David, 1881–1953, vol. V

Greenwood, Brig. Harold Gustave Francis, 1894–1978, vol. VII
Greenwood, Col Harry, 1881–1948, vol. IV
Greenwood, Henry Harold, 1873–1962, vol. VI
Greenwood, Hubert John, 1867–1932, vol. III
Greenwood, Sir James Mantle, 1902–1969, vol. VI
Greenwood, John Eric, 1891–1975, vol. VII
Greenwood, John Frederic, 1885–1954, vol. V
Greenwood, John French, 1904–1968, vol. VI
Greenwood, Major, 1880–1949, vol. IV
Greenwood, Ranolf Nelson, 1889–1977, vol. VII
Greenwood, Robert Morrell, died 1947, vol. IV
Greenwood, Rev. Sydney, died 1926, vol. II
Greenwood, Thomas, 1851–1908, vol. I
Greenwood, Rt Rev. Tom, 1903–1974, vol. VII
Greenwood, Walter, 1903–1974, vol. VII
Greenwood, William, 1875–1925, vol. II
Greenwood, William Frederick, 1861–1933, vol. III
Greer, Rt Rev. David Hummell, 1844–1919, vol. II
Greer, Sir (Edmund) Wyly, 1862–1957, vol. V
Greer, Sir Francis Nugent, 1869–1925, vol. II
Greer, Brig.-Gen. Frederick Augustus, 1871–1958, vol. V
Greer, Rev. George Samuel, died 1921, vol. II
Greer, Sir Harry, 1876–1947, vol. IV
Greer, Sir Henry, 1855–1934, vol. III
Greer, Joseph, 1854–1922, vol. II
Greer, Richard Townsend, 1854–1942, vol. IV
Greer, Thomas Macgregor, 1853–1928, vol. II
Greer, Rt Rev. William Derrick Lindsay, 1902–1972, vol. VII
Greer, Sir Wyly; see Greer, Sir E. W.
Greeson, Surgeon Vice-Adm. Sir (Clarence) Edward, 1888–1979, vol. VII
Greeson, Surg. Vice-Adm. Sir Edward; see Greeson, Surg. Vice-Adm. Sir C. E.
Greet, Sir Philip Ben, 1857–1936, vol. III
Greeves, R(eginald) Affleck, 1878–1966, vol. VI
Greffulhe, Comtesse, died 1952, vol. V
Greg, Lt-Col Alexander, 1867–1952, vol. V
Greg, Col Ernest William, 1862–1934, vol. III
Greg, John Ronald, 1866–1950, vol. IV
Greg, Lionel Hyde, 1879–1945, vol. IV
Greg, Sir Robert Hyde, 1876–1953, vol. V
Greg, Sir Walter Wilson, 1875–1959, vol. V
Gregg, Miss; see Grier, Sydney C.
Gregg, Sir Cornelius Joseph, died 1959, vol. V
Gregg, Edward Andrew, 1881–1969, vol. VI
Gregg, Sir Henry, 1859–1928, vol. II
Gregg, Humphrey P.; see Procter-Gregg.
Gregg, Very Rev. James Fitzgerald, died 1905, vol. I
Gregg, James Reali, 1899–1978, vol. VII
Gregg, Most Rev. John Allen Fitzgerald, 1873–1961, vol. VI
Gregg, John Frank, 1912–1960, vol. V
Gregg, Milton Fowler, 1892–1978, vol. VII
Gregg, Sir Norman McAlister, died 1966, vol. VI
Gregge-Hopwood, Major Edward Byng George, 1880–1917, vol. II
Gregge-Hopwood, Edward Robert, 1846–1942, vol. IV
Grego, Joseph, died 1908, vol. I

Gregor, James Wyllie, 1900–1980, vol. VII (AII)
Gregorie, Maj.-Gen. Charles Frederick, 1834–1918, vol. II
Gregorowski, Hon. Reinhold, 1856–1922, vol. II
Gregory, Hon. Alexander Frederick, 1843–1927, vol. II
Gregory, Arnold, 1924–1976, vol. VII
Gregory, Augusta, (Lady Gregory), *died* 1932, vol. III
Gregory, Hon. Sir Augustus Charles, 1819–1905, vol. I
Gregory, Rev. Benjamin, 1875–1950, vol. IV
Gregory, Charles, *died* 1920, vol. II
Gregory, Sir Charles Hutton, 1817–1898, vol. I
Gregory, Maj.-Gen. Charles Levinge, 1870–1944, vol. IV
Gregory, Vice-Adm. Sir David; *see* Gregory, Vice-Adm. Sir G. D. A.
Gregory, Rev. Edmund Ironside, 1835–1912, vol. I
Gregory, Edward John, 1850–1909, vol. I
Gregory, Eric Craven, 1887–1959, vol. V
Gregory, Captain Ernest Foster, 1873–1940, vol. III
Gregory, Rt Rev. Francis Ambrose, 1848–1927, vol. II
Gregory, Lt-Col Francis Brooke, 1862–1936, vol. III
Gregory, Frederick, 1831–1919, vol. II
Gregory, Frederick Gugenheim, 1893–1961, vol. VI
Gregory, Captain George, 1872–1929, vol. III
Gregory, Vice-Adm. Sir (George) David (Archibald), 1909–1975, vol. VII
Gregory, George Frederick, *born* 1839, vol. II
Gregory, Hon. Henry, 1860–1940, vol. III
Gregory, Sir Henry Stanley, 1890–1959, vol. V
Gregory, Sir Holman, 1864–1947, vol. IV
Gregory, Jackson, 1882–1943, vol. IV
Gregory, John Duncan, 1878–1951, vol. V
Gregory, Sir (John) Roger Burrow, 1861–1938, vol. III
Gregory, John Water, 1864–1932, vol. III
Gregory, Joshua C., 1875–1964, vol. VI
Gregory, Padraic, 1886–1962, vol. VI
Gregory, Sir Philip Spencer, 1851–1918, vol. II
Gregory, Reginald Philip, 1879–1918, vol. II
Gregory, Sir Richard Arman, 1st Bt, 1864–1952, vol. V
Gregory, Very Rev. Robert, 1819–1911, vol. I
Gregory, Sir Roger; *see* Gregory, Sir J. R. B.
Gregory, Sir Theodore, 1890–1970, vol. VI
Gregory, Theophilus Stephen, 1897–1975, vol. VII
Gregory, Thomas Sherwin P.; *see* Pearson-Gregory.
Gregory, William King, 1876–1970, vol. VI (AII)
Gregory Smith, George, 1865–1932, vol. III
Gregson, Edward Gelson, 1877–1942, vol. IV
Gregson, Ven. Francis Sitwell Knight, *died* 1926, vol. II
Gregson, Col Henry Guy Fulljames Savage, 1872–1949, vol. IV
Gregson-Ellis, Maj.-Gen. Philip George Saxon, 1898–1956, vol. V
Greiffenhagen, Maurice, 1862–1931, vol. III
Greig, Sir Alexander, 1878–1950, vol. IV
Greig, Alexander Rodger, 1872–1947, vol. IV

Greig, Charles Alexis, 1880–1958, vol. V
Greig, David Middleton, *died* 1936, vol. III
Greig, Lt-Col Edward David Wilson, 1874–1950, vol. IV
Greig, Edward Hagerup, 1843–1907, vol. I
Greig, Col Frederick James, 1863–1931, vol. III
Greig, Sir James, *died* 1934, vol. III
Greig, James, 1861–1941, vol. IV
Greig, Rev. Lt-Col John Glennie, 1871–1958, vol. V
Greig, Rt Rev. John Harold, 1865–1938, vol. III
Greig, John Russell, 1889–1963, vol. VI
Greig, John Young Thomson, 1891–1963, vol. VI
Greig, Gp Captain Sir Louis, 1880–1953, vol. V
Greig, Maysie, (Mrs Jan Sopoushek), *died* 1971, vol. VII
Greig, Rear-Adm. Morice Gordon, 1914–1980, vol. VII
Greig, Sir Robert Blyth, 1874–1947, vol. IV
Greig, Captain Ronald Henry, 1876–1916, vol. II
Grein, J. T., 1862–1935, vol. III
Grenfell, 1st Baron, 1841–1925, vol. II
Grenfell, 2nd Baron, 1905–1976, vol. VII
Grenfell, Bernard Pyne, 1869–1926, vol. II
Grenfell, Lt-Col Cecil A., *died* 1924, vol. II
Grenfell, Charles Seymour, 1839–1924, vol. II
Grenfell, Rt Hon. David Rhys, 1881–1968, vol. VI
Grenfell, Rev. George, 1849–1906, vol. I
Grenfell, Col Harold Maxwell, 1870–1929, vol. III
Grenfell, Vice-Adm. Harry Tremenheere, 1845–1906, vol. I
Grenfell, Henry Riversdale, 1824–1902, vol. I
Grenfell, Joyce Irene, 1910–1979, vol. VII
Grenfell, Hon. Julian Henry Francis, 1888–1915, vol. I
Grenfell, Sir Wilfred Thomason, 1865–1940, vol. III
Grenier, Gerard, *died* 1917, vol. II
Grenier, Gustave, *born* 1847, vol. II
Grenier, Joseph Richard, 1852–1926, vol. II
Grenside, Rev. William Bent, 1821–1913, vol. I
Grensted, Rev. Frederic Finnis, 1857–1919, vol. II
Grensted, Rev. Canon Laurence William, 1884–1964, vol. VI
Grente, HE Cardinal George, 1872–1959, vol. V
Grenville, Lt-Col Hon. Thomas George Breadalbane M.; *see* Morgan-Grenville.
Gresley, Sir Herbert Nigel, 1876–1941, vol. IV
Gresley, Sir Nigel, 12th Bt, 1894–1974, vol. VII
Gresley, Rear-Adm. Richard Nigel, 1850–1928, vol. II
Gresley, Sir Robert, 11th Bt, 1866–1936, vol. III
Gresley, Rev. Roger St John, *died* 1935, vol. III
Gresley, Sir William Frances, 13th Bt, 1897–1976, vol. VII
Gresson, Rt. Hon. Sir Kenneth Macfarlane, 1891–1974, vol. VII
Gresson, Lt.-Col. Thomas Tinning, 1870–1921, vol. II
Gresson, William Jardine, *died* 1934, vol. III
Gresty, Hugh, 1899–1958, vol. V
Greswell, Richard Egerton, 1916–1979, vol. VII
Greswell, Rev. William Henry Parr, *died* 1923, vol. II

Greswolde-Williams, Francis Wigley Greswolde, 1873–1931, vol. III
Gretton, 1st Baron, 1867–1947, vol. IV
Gretton, Major Frederic, died 1928, vol. II
Gretton, Brig. John Cunliffe, 1880–1953, vol. V
Gretton, Mary Sturge, died 1961, vol. VI
Greville, 2nd Baron, 1841–1910, vol. I
Greville, 3rd Baron, 1871–1952, vol. V
Greville, Col Hon. Alwyn Henry Fulke, 1854–1929, vol. III
Greville, Major Charles Henry, 1889–1931, vol. III
Greville, Sir George, 1851–1937, vol. III
Greville, Hon. Louis George, 1856–1941, vol. IV
Greville, Dame Margaret Helen Anderson, (Hon. Mrs Ronald Greville), died 1942, vol. IV
Greville, Hon. Maynard, 1898–1960, vol. V
Greville, Hon. Mrs Ronald; see Greville, Dame M. H. A.
Greville, Hon. Sir Sidney Robert, 1866–1927, vol. II
Grew, Major Benjamin Dixon, 1892–1977, vol. VII
Grew, Edwin Sharpe, 1866–1950, vol. IV
Grew, Joseph Clark, 1880–1965, vol. VI
Grey, 4th Earl, 1851–1917, vol. II
Grey, 5th Earl, 1879–1963, vol. VI
Grey of Fallodon, 1st Viscount, 1862–1933, vol. III
Grey of Fallodon, Viscountess; (Pamela), died 1928, vol. II
Grey de Ruthyn, 23rd (shown as 24th) Baron, 1858–1912, vol. I
Grey de Ruthyn, 24th Baron, 1862–1934, vol. III
Grey de Ruthyn, 25th Baron, 1883–1963, vol. VI
Grey, Annie, vol. III
Grey, Arthur, 1840–1911, vol. I
Grey, Col Arthur, 1855–1924, vol. II
Grey, Sir Charles George, 4th Bt (cr 1814), 1880–1957, vol. V
Grey, Charles Grey, 1875–1953, vol. V
Grey, Clifford, 1887–1941, vol. IV
Grey, Egerton Spenser, 1863–1950, vol. IV
Grey, Francis Temple, 1886–1941, vol. IV
Grey, Rt Hon. Sir George, 1812–1898, vol. I
Grey, Captain George Charles, 1918–1944, vol. IV
Grey, Sir George Duncan, 1868–1937, vol. III
Grey, Rev. Harry George, 1851–1925, vol. II
Grey, Sir (Harry) Martin, 5th Bt (cr 1814), 1882–1960, vol. V
Grey, Sir Henry Foley, 7th Bt (cr 1710), 1861–1914, vol. I
Grey, Sir John Foley, 8th Bt (cr 1710), 1893–1938, vol. III
Grey, Sir John Howarth, 1875–1960, vol. V
Grey, Col Leopold John Herbert, born 1840, vol. II
Grey, Sir Martin; see Grey, Sir H. M.
Grey, Lt-Col Sir Raleigh, 1860–1936, vol. III
Grey, Major Robin, 1874–1922, vol. II
Grey, Sir Robin Edward Dysart, 6th Bt (cr 1814), 1886–1974, vol. VII
Grey, Rowland; see Brown, Lilian Kate Rowland.
Grey, Samuel John, 1878–1942, vol. IV
Grey, Comdr Spenser Douglas Adair, 1889–1937, vol. III
Grey, Lt-Col William George, 1866–1953, vol. V

Grey, Maj.-Gen. Wulff Henry, died 1961, vol. VI
Grey, Zane, 1875–1939, vol. III
Grey-Egerton, Rev. Sir Brooke de Malpas; see Egerton.
Grey-Egerton, Sir Philip Henry Brian; see Egerton.
Grey Egerton, Sir Philip Reginald le Belward, 14th Bt, 1885–1962, vol. VI
Grey-Smith, Sir Ross, 1901–1973, vol. VII
Grey Walter, William; see Walter.
Grey-Wilson, Sir William, 1852–1926, vol. II
Gribble, Bernard Finegan, 1872–1962, vol. VI
Gribble, Francis Henry, 1862–1946, vol. IV
Gribble, George James, 1846–1927, vol. II
Gribble, Col (Hon.) Howard Charles, 1886–1956, vol. V
Gribbon, Brig. Walter Harold, 1881–1944, vol. IV
Grice, Sir John, 1850–1935, vol. III
Grice, Col Walter Thomas, 1868–1926, vol. II
Grice-Hutchinson, George William, 1848–1906, vol. I
Gridley, 1st Baron, 1878–1965, vol. VI
Gridley, John Crandon, 1904–1968, vol. VI
Grier, Brig.-Gen. Harry Dixon, 1863–1942, vol. IV
Grier, John Arthur Bolton, 1882–1946, vol. IV
Grier, Louis Monro, 1864–1920, vol. II
Grier, Lynda, 1880–1967, vol. VI
Grier, Very Rev. Roy Macgregor, 1877–1940, vol. III
Grier, Sir Selwyn Macgregor, 1878–1946, vol. IV
Grier, Sydney C., 1868–1933, vol. III
Grierson, Sir Alexander Davidson, 9th Bt, 1858–1912, vol. I
Grierson, Sir Andrew, died 1936, vol. III
Grierson, Charles MacIver, 1864–1939, vol. III (A), vol. IV
Grierson, Rt Rev. Charles Thornton Primrose, 1857–1935, vol. III
Grierson, Edgar, 1884–1959, vol. V
Grierson, Francis, 1848–1927, vol. II
Grierson, Sir George Abraham, 1851–1941, vol. IV
Grierson, Sir Herbert John Clifford, 1866–1960, vol. V
Grierson, James Cullen, 1863–1919, vol. II
Grierson, Lt-Gen. Sir James Moncrieff, 1859–1914, vol. I
Grierson, John, 1898–1964, vol. VI
Grierson, John, 1898–1972, vol. VII
Grierson, Philip Francis H.; see Hamilton-Grierson.
Grierson, Sir Philip James Hamilton-, 1851–1927, vol. II
Grierson, Sir Robert Gilbert White, 10th Bt, 1883–1957, vol. V
Grierson, William Wylie, died 1935, vol. III
Griesbach, Charles Ludolf, 1847–1907, vol. I
Griesbach, Maj.-Gen. Hon. William Antrobus, 1878–1945, vol. IV
Grieve, Rev. Alexander James, 1874–1952, vol. V
Grieve, Lt-Col Angus Alexander M.; see Macfarlane-Grieve.
Grieve, Christopher Murray, 1892–1978, vol. VII
Grieve, Captain Edward Leonard, 1880–1936, vol. III

Grieve, Edward William Lawrence, 1902–1960, vol. V (A)
Grieve, Rev. Canon James Gavin, 1880–1937, vol. III
Grieve, Robert, 1839–1906, vol. I
Grieve, Robert G., 1881–1952, vol. V
Grieve, Hon. Walter Baine, 1850–1921, vol. II
Grieve, Walter Graham, died 1937, vol. III
Grieve, William, 1885–1967, vol. VI
Grieve, William Alexander M.; see Macfarlane-Grieve.
Grieves, Joseph Arthur, 1907–1976, vol. VII
Griffin, Alan Francis Rathbone, 1911–1965, vol. VI
Griffin, Alexander, 1883–1966, vol. VI
Griffin, Sir Arthur Cecil, 1888–1970, vol. VI
Griffin, Lt-Col Atholl Edwin, 1877–1956, vol. V
Griffin, His Eminence Cardinal Bernard W., 1899–1956, vol. V
Griffin, Sir Cecil; see Griffin, Sir L. C. L.
Griffin, Lt-Col Cecil Pender Griffith, 1864–1922, vol. II
Griffin, Sir Charles James, 1875–1962, vol. VI
Griffin, Air Vice-Marshal Charles Robert, 1919–1979, vol. VII
Griffin, Charles Thomas, died 1923, vol. II
Griffin, Brig.-Gen. Christopher Joseph, 1874–1957, vol. V
Griffin, Lt-Gen. Edward Christian, 1836–1917, vol. II
Griffin, Sir Elton Reginald, 1906–1975, vol. VII
Griffin, Ernest Harrison, 1877–1936, vol. III
Griffin, Sir Henry Daly, 1864–1936, vol. III
Griffin, Major Henry Lysaght, 1866–1930, vol. III
Griffin, Sir Herbert John Gordon, 1889–1969, vol. VI
Griffin, Hester Wolferstan, (Mrs R. L. Griffin); see Chapman, Mrs H. W.
Griffin, Maj.-Gen. John Arnold Atkinson, 1891–1972, vol. VII
Griffin, Sir (Lancelot) Cecil Lepel, 1900–1964, vol. VI
Griffin, Sir Lepel Henry, 1840–1908, vol. I
Griffin, Martin Joseph, 1847–1921, vol. II
Griffin, William Vincent, 1886–1958, vol. V
Griffis, Rev. William Elliot, 1843–1928, vol. II
Griffith, Alan Arnold, 1893–1963, vol. VI
Griffith, Arthur, 1872–1922, vol. II
Griffith, Hon. Arthur, died 1946, vol. IV
Griffith, Arthur Donald, 1882–1944, vol. IV
Griffith, Major Arthur Lefroy Pritchard, 1886–1932, vol. III
Griffith, Arthur Stanley, 1875–1941, vol. IV
Griffith, Very Rev. Charles Edward Thomas, 1857–1934, vol. III
Griffith, Brig.-Gen. Charles Richard Jebb, 1867–1948, vol. IV
Griffith, Cyril Cobham, 1891–1972, vol. VII
Griffith, Rev. David, vol. II
Griffith, Lt-Col Edward Hugh, 1858–1936, vol. III
Griffith, Lt-Col Edward Waldegrave, 1871–1937, vol. III
Griffith, Sir Elis Arundell Ellis-, 2nd Bt (cr 1918), 1896–1934, vol. III

Griffith, Ven. Ellis Hughes, died 1938, vol. III
Griffith, Rt Hon. Sir Ellis Jones Ellis-, 1st Bt (cr 1918), 1860–1926, vol. II
Griffith, Sir Francis Charles, 1878–1942, vol. IV
Griffith, Francis Llewellyn, 1862–1934, vol. III
Griffith, Frank Kingsley, 1889–1962, vol. VI
Griffith, George Chetwynd, died 1906, vol. I
Griffith, George Herbert, 1877–1947, vol. IV
Griffith, Lt-Col George Richard, 1857–1920, vol. II
Griffith, Rev. Henry Allday, 1875–1942, vol. IV
Griffith, Ven. Henry Wager, 1850–1932, vol. III
Griffith, Horace Major Brandford, 1863–1909, vol. I
Griffith, Hubert Freeling, 1896–1953, vol. V
Griffith, Hugh Emrys, 1912–1980, vol. VII
Griffith, Rev. James Shaw, 1875–1939, vol. III
Griffith, Sir John Purser, 1848–1938, vol. III
Griffith, (Llewelyn) Wyn, 1890–1977, vol. VII
Griffith, Patrick Waldron Cobham, 1925–1980, vol. VII
Griffith, Lt-Col Sir Ralph Edwin Hotchkin, 1882–1963, vol. VI
Griffith, Ralph Thomas Hotchkin, 1826–1906, vol. I
Griffith, Sir Richard (John) Waldie-, 3rd Bt (cr 1858), 1850–1933, vol. III
Griffith, Rt Hon. Sir Samuel Walker, 1845–1920, vol. II
Griffith, Thomas Wardrop, died 1946, vol. IV
Griffith, W. St Bodfan, 1876–1941, vol. IV
Griffith, Walter Spencer Anderson, 1854–1946, vol. IV
Griffith, William, 1868–1953, vol. V
Griffith, Sir William Brandford, 1858–1939, vol. III
Griffith, William Downes, died 1908, vol. I
Griffith, William L., 1864–1934, vol. III
Griffith, Wyn; see Griffith, L. W.
Griffith-Boscawen, Rt Hon. Sir Arthur Sackville Trevor, 1865–1946, vol. IV
Griffith-Jones, Ebenezer, 1860–1942, vol. IV
Griffith-Jones, Sir Eric Newton, 1913–1979, vol. VII
Griffith-Jones, (John) Mervyn (Guthrie), 1909–1979, vol. VII
Griffith-Jones, Mervyn; see Griffith-Jones, J. M. G.
Griffith-Jones, Morgan Phillips, 1876–1939, vol. III
Griffith-Jones, Rev. William, 1895–1961, vol. VI
Griffiths, Albert Edward, 1908–1970, vol. VI
Griffiths, Rev. Charles, 1847–1924, vol. II
Griffiths, Major Charles Du Plat R.; see Richardson-Griffiths.
Griffiths, Lt-Col Cyril Tracy, 1873–1934, vol. III
Griffiths, Surg. Rear-Adm. Cyril Verity, 1883–1959, vol. V
Griffiths, David, 1896–1977, vol. VII
Griffiths, Sir David Edward, died 1957, vol. V
Griffiths, Ven. David Henry, 1864–1926, vol. II
Griffiths, David Nathaniel, died 1961, vol. VI
Griffiths, Ernest Howard, 1851–1932, vol. III
Griffiths, Ezer, 1888–1962, vol. VI
Griffiths, Brig. Felix Alexander Vincent C.; see Copland-Griffiths.
Griffiths, Lt-Gen. Francis Home, 1877–1961, vol. VI

Griffiths, George Arthur, 1880–1945, vol. IV
Griffiths, Lt-Col George Cruickshank, 1884–1949, vol. IV
Griffiths, George Hollier, 1839–1911, vol. I, vol. I (A)
Griffiths, Gilbert, 1901–1979, vol. VII
Griffiths, Sir Hugh Ernest, 1891–1961, vol. VI
Griffiths, Rt Hon. James, 1890–1975, vol. VII
Griffiths, Ven. John, died 1897, vol. I
Griffiths, John, died 1947, vol. IV
Griffiths, John G., 1845–1922, vol. II
Griffiths, Lt-Col Sir John Norton-, 1st Bt, 1871 1930, vol. III
Griffiths, John Samuel, died 1933, vol. III
Griffiths, Air Cdre John Swire, 1894–1969, vol. VI
Griffiths, Col Joseph, died 1945, vol. IV
Griffiths, Engr Comdr Percy Frederick, 1873–1960, vol. V
Griffiths, Brig.-Gen. Thomas, 1865–1947, vol. IV
Griffiths, Thomas, 1867–1955, vol. V
Griffiths, Vincent, 1831–1917, vol. II
Griffiths, William, 1912–1973, vol. VII
Griffiths, William Russell, 1845–1910, vol. I
Griffiths, Sir William Thomas, 1895–1952, vol. V
Grigg, Rt Hon. Sir James; see Grigg, Rt Hon. Sir P. J.
Grigg, Rt Hon. Sir (Percy) James, 1890–1964, vol. VI
Grigg-Smith, Rev. Canon Thomas, died 1971, vol. VII
Griggs, Clare H., died 1950, vol. IV
Griggs, Frederick Landseer Maur, 1876–1938, vol. III
Griggs, Hon. John William, 1849–1927, vol. II (A), vol. III
Griggs, Sir Peter; see Griggs, Sir W. P.
Griggs, Sir (William) Peter, 1854–1920, vol. II
Grignard, Victor, 1871–1935, vol. III
Grigson, Air Cdre John William Boldero, 1893–1943, vol. IV
Grigson, Sir Wilfrid Vernon, 1896–1948, vol. IV
Grigson, Rev. William Shuckforth, 1845–1930, vol. III
Grille, Sir Frederick Louis, 1889–1958, vol. V
Grillo, Ernesto N. G., 1877–1946, vol. IV
Grimble, Sir Arthur Francis, 1888–1956, vol. V
Grimble, Augustus, 1840–1925, vol. II
Grime, Arthur, died 1938, vol. III
Grimes, Ven. (Cecil) John, 1881–1976, vol. VII
Grimes, Ven. John; see Grimes, Ven. C. J.
Grimes, Mary Katharine, 1861–1921, vol. II
Grimley, Bertram Griffiths, 1867–1952, vol. V
Grimm, Stanley, 1891–1966, vol. VI
Grimmer, Hon. W. C. Hazen, 1858–1945, vol. IV
Grimsdale, Harold Barr, 1866–1942, vol. IV
Grimsditch, Herbert Borthwick, 1898–1971, vol. VII
Grimshaw, Beatrice, died 1953, vol. V
Grimshaw, Captain Cecil Thomas Wrigley, 1875–1915, vol. I
Grimshaw, Most Rev. Francis Joseph, 1901–1965, vol. VI
Grimshaw, Thomas Wrigley, 1839–1900, vol. I
Grimshaw, Sir William Josiah, 1886–1958, vol. V

Grimshawe, Hellier Robert Hadsley G.; see Gosselin-Grimshawe.
Grimston of Westbury, 1st Baron, 1897–1979, vol. VII
Grimston, Col Lionel Augustus, 1868–1943, vol. IV
Grimston, Rev. Hon. Robert, 1860–1927, vol. V
Grimston, Brig.-Gen. Sir Rollo Estouteville, 1861–1916, vol. II
Grimston, Brig.-Gen. Sylvester Bertram, 1864–1928, vol. II
Grimston, William Hunter; see Kendal, W. H.
Grimthorpe, 1st Baron, 1816–1905, vol. I
Grimthorpe, 2nd Baron, 1856–1917, vol. II
Grimthorpe, 3rd Baron, 1891–1963, vol. VI
Grimwade, Hon. Frederick Sheppard, 1840–1910, vol. I
Grimwade, Geoffrey Holt, 1902–1961, vol. VI
Grimwade, Maj.-Gen. Harold William, 1869–1949, vol. IV
Grimwade, Sir Russell; see Grimwade, Sir W. R.
Grimwade, Sir (Wilfrid) Russell, 1879–1955, vol. V
Grimwood, Lt-Col James, 1873–1934, vol. III
Grindell-Matthews, Harry, 1880–1941, vol. IV
Grindle, Bernard Richard Theodore, 1879–1955, vol. V
Grindle, Sir Gilbert Edmund Augustine, 1869–1934, vol. III
Grinling, Charles Herbert, 1870–1906, vol. I
Grinling, Brig. Edward Johns, 1889–1963, vol. VI
Grinlinton, Frederick Henry, 1853–1938, vol. III
Grinlinton, Sir John Joseph, 1828–1912, vol. I
Grinsted, Harold, 1889–1955, vol. V
Gripenberg, Georg Achates, 1890–1975, vol. VII
Gripper, Col Hugh Thomas, 1867–1956, vol. V
Griscom, Sir Lloyd C., 1872–1959, vol. V
Grisdale, Rt Rev. John, born 1845, vol. II
Grisewood, Frederick Henry, 1888–1972, vol. VII
Grissell, Hartwell de la Garde, 1839–1907, vol. I
Grist, Frederic Edwin, 1883–1951, vol. V
Griswold, A(lfred) Whitney, 1906–1963, vol. VI
Griswold, Rev. H. D., 1860–1945, vol. IV
Griswold, Rt Rev. Sheldon M., 1861–1930, vol. III
Gritten, William George Howard, died 1943, vol. IV
Groener, Maria, 1883–1937, vol. III
Grogan, Brig.-Gen. Edward George, 1851–1944, vol. IV
Grogan, Col Sir Edward Ion Beresford, 2nd Bt, 1873–1927, vol. II
Grogan, Lt-Col George Meredyth, died 1942, vol. IV
Grogan, Brig.-Gen. George William St George, 1875–1962, vol. VI
Grogan, William Edward, 1863–1937, vol. III
Grohman, Vice-Adm. Harold Tom B.; see Baillie-Grohman.
Grohman, William A. B.; see Baillie-Grohman.
Gronchi, Giovanni, 1887–1978, vol. VII
Gronow, Albert George, 1878–1950, vol. IV
Groom, Gladys Laurence, (Mrs M. Cordellis), died 1948, vol. IV (A)
Groom, Hon. Sir Littleton Ernest, 1867–1936, vol. III
Groom, Percy, 1865–1931, vol. III

Groome, Francis Hindes, 1851–1902, vol. I
Groome, Adm. Robert Leonard, 1848–1917, vol. II
Gropper, William, 1897–1977, vol. VII
Gropius, Walter, 1883–1969, vol. VI
Grose, Frank Samuel, 1881–1941, vol. IV
Grose, Sir James Trevilly, 1872–1944, vol. IV
Grose-Hodge, Humfrey, 1891–1962, vol. VI
Gross, Edward John, 1844–1923, vol. II
Gross, Richard Oliver, 1882–1964, vol. VI
Grossmith, Caryll Archibald, 1895–1964, vol. VI
Grossmith, George, 1847–1912, vol. I
Grossmith, George, 1874–1935, vol. III
Grossmith, Weedon, *died* 1919, vol. II
Grosvenor, Earl; Edward George Hugh Grosvenor, 1904–1909, vol. I
Grosvenor, Countess; (Sibell Mary), 1855–1929, vol. III
Grosvenor, Lord Arthur Hugh, 1860–1929, vol. III
Grosvenor, Caroline, *died* 1940, vol. III
Grosvenor, Lord Edward Arthur, 1892–1929, vol. III
Grosvenor, Lord Gerald Richard, 1874–1940, vol. III
Grosvenor, Hon. Gilbert, 1881–1939, vol. III
Grosvenor, Gilbert Hovey, 1875–1966, vol. VI
Grosvenor, Lady Henry, (Rosamund Angharad), *died* 1941, vol. IV
Grosvenor, Lord Henry George, 1861–1914, vol. I
Grosvenor, Captain Lord Hugh William, 1884–1914, vol. II
Grosvenor, John Ernest, 1887–1963, vol. VI
Grosvenor, Hon. Richard Cecil, 1848–1919, vol. II
Grosvenor, Captain Robert Arthur, 1895–1953, vol. V
Grosvenor, Rosamund Angharad; *see* Grosvenor, Lady Henry.
Grosvenor, Vernon William, 1889–1961, vol. VI
Grotrian, Frederick Brent, *died* 1905, vol. I
Grotrian, Sir Herbert Brent, 1st Bt, *died* 1951, vol. V
Grouard, Rt Rev. Mgr Emile, 1840–1931, vol. III
Grousset, René, 1885–1952, vol. V
Grout, Rev. George W. G., 1837–1917, vol. II
Grout, Reginald George, 1901–1963, vol. VI
Grove, Agnes, (Lady Grove), 1864–1926, vol. II
Grove, Alfred John, 1888–1962, vol. VI
Grove, Archibald; *see* Grove, T. N. A.
Grove, Maj.-Gen. Sir Coleridge, 1839–1920, vol. II
Grove, Brig.-Gen. Edward Aickin William Stewart, 1852–1932, vol. III
Grove, Lt-Col Ernest William, 1870–1939, vol. III
Grove, Sir George, 1820–1900, vol. I
Grove, George Alexander, 1908–1971, vol. VII
Grove, Sir Gerald, 3rd Bt, 1886–1962, vol. VI
Grove, Henry Montgomery, 1867–1942, vol. IV
Grove, Col Reginald Parker, 1859–1942, vol. IV
Grove, (Thomas Newcomen) Archibald, *died* 1920, vol. II
Grove, Col Thomas Thackeray, 1879–1965, vol. VI
Grove, Sir Walter Felipe Philip, 4th Bt, 1927–1974, vol. VII
Grove, Sir Walter John, 2nd Bt, 1852–1932, vol. III

Grove-Hills, Col Edmond Herbert, 1864–1922, vol. II
Grove-White, Col James, 1852–1938, vol. III
Grove-White, Lt-Gen. Sir Maurice Fitzgibbon, 1887–1965, vol. VI
Grover, Maj.-Gen. John Malcolm Lawrence, 1897–1979, vol. VII
Grover, Gen. Sir Malcolm Henry Stanley, 1858–1945, vol. IV
Grover, Montague Macgregor, 1870–1943, vol. IV
Groves, Charles Nixon, 1871–1950, vol. IV
Groves, Ernest William Hey, 1872–1944, vol. IV
Groves, Herbert Austen, 1880–1943, vol. IV
Groves, James Grimble, 1854–1914, vol. I
Groves, Sir John, 1828–1905, vol. I
Groves, Col John Edward Grimble, 1863–1948, vol. IV
Groves, Brig.-Gen. Percy Robert Clifford, *died* 1959, vol. V
Groves, Thomas Edward, 1884–1958, vol. V
Groves-Raines, Lt-Col Ralph Gore Devereux; *see* Raines.
Grozier, Edwin Atkins, 1859–1924, vol. II
Grubb, Col Alexander Henry Watkins, 1873–1933, vol. III
Grubb, Edward, 1854–1939, vol. III
Grubb, Lt-Col Herbert Watkins, 1875–1934, vol. III
Grubb, Sir Howard, 1844–1931, vol. III
Grubb, Sir Kenneth George, 1900–1980, vol. VII
Grubbe, Adm. Sir Walter James H.; *see* Hunt-Grubbe.
Grubbe, Walter John, *died* 1926, vol. II
Gruber, Rudolph, 1868–1945, vol. IV
Grueber, Herbert Appold, 1846–1927, vol. II
Gruer, Harold George, 1886–1956, vol. V
Gruffydd, William John, 1881–1954, vol. V
Grumell, Ernest Sydney, 1885–1962, vol. VI
Grummitt, John Halliday, 1901–1979, vol. VII
Grundy, Cecil Reginald, 1870–1944, vol. III
Grundy, Sir Claude Herbert, 1891–1967, vol. VI
Grundy, Sir Cuthbert Cartwright, *died* 1946, vol. IV
Grundy, Eustace Beardoe, 1849–1938, vol. III
Grundy, Francis, 1882–1953, vol. V
Grundy, George Beardoe, *died* 1948, vol. IV
Grundy, Sydney, 1848–1914, vol. I
Grundy, Thomas Walter, 1864–1942, vol. IV
Grundy, Wilfred Walker, 1884–1936, vol. III
Grundy, William Mitchell, *died* 1960, vol. V
Gruning, John Frederick, 1870–1922, vol. II
Grutschnig, Karl, 1888–1965, vol. VI (AII)
Grylls, Charles John Tench Bedford, 1874–1946, vol. IV
Grylls, Rear-Adm. Henry John Bedford, 1903–1978, vol. VII
Gsell, Most Rev. Francis Xavier, 1872–1960, vol. V
Guard, Lt-Col Frederic Henry Wickham, *died* 1927, vol. II
Gubbay, Henri Abraham, 1883–1940, vol. III
Gubbay, Moses Mordecai Simeon, 1876–1947, vol. IV
Gubbins, Sir C. O'Grady, *died* 1911, vol. I

Gubbins, Maj.-Gen. Sir Colin McVean, 1896–1976, vol. VII
Gubbins, Frederick B., *died* 1902, vol. I
Gubbins, John Harington, 1852–1929, vol. III
Gubbins, John R., 1839–1906, vol. I
Gubbins, Nathaniel; *see* Mott, Edward Spencer.
Gubbins, Lt-Col Richard Rolls, 1868–1918, vol. II
Gubbins, Lt-Col Stamer, 1882–1940, vol. III
Gubbins, Lt-Gen. Sir W. Launcelotte, 1849–1925, vol. II
Gubbins, Major William John Mounsey, 1907–1979, vol. VII
Gudgeon, Stanley Herbert, 1896–1966, vol. VI
Guébhard, Madame; *see* Severine, Madame.
Guedalla, Philip, 1889–1944, vol. IV
Guedella, Mrs Herbert; *see* Hanbury, Lily.
Guerbel, Countess de; *see* Ward, Dame Genevieve.
Guerin, Hon. Edmund, 1858–1934, vol. III
Guerin, Hon. James John, 1856–1932, vol. III
Gueritz, Edward Peregrine, 1855–1938, vol. III
Guernsey, Lord; Heneage Greville Finch, 1883–1914, vol. I
Guess, George A., 1873–1954, vol. V
Guest, Air Marshal Sir Charles Edward Neville, 1900–1977, vol. VII
Guest, Lt-Col Hon. (Christian) Henry (Charles), 1874–1957, vol. V
Guest, Col Hon. Sir Ernest Lucas, 1882–1972, vol. VII
Guest, Captain Rt Hon. Frederick Edward, 1875–1937, vol. III
Guest, Lt-Col Hon. Henry; *see* Guest, Lt-Col. Hon. C. H. C.
Guest, John, 1867–1931, vol. III
Guest, Hon. Lionel George William, 1880–1935, vol. III
Guest, Montagu, 1839–1909, vol. I
Guest, Hon. Oscar Montague, 1888–1958, vol. V
Guest, Thomas Merthyr, 1838–1904, vol. I
Guest, William Campbell, 1864–1932, vol. III
Guest Williams, Rev. Samuel Blackwell, 1851–1920, vol. II
Gueterbock, Col Sir Paul Gottlieb Julius, 1886–1954, vol. V
Guggenheim, Edward Armand, 1901–1970, vol. VI
Guggisberg, Decima (Lady Guggisberg); *see* Moore Guggisberg.
Guggisberg, Brig.-Gen. Sir (Frederick) Gordon, 1869–1930, vol. III
Guggisberg, Brig.-Gen. Sir Gordon; *see* Guggisberg, Brig.-Gen. Sir F. G.
Gui, Vittorio, 1885–1975, vol. VII
Guibault, Joseph Alexandre, 1870–1940, vol. III (A), vol. IV
Guichard, Beatrice Catherine, (Beatrice Baskerville), 1878–1955, vol. V
Guider, James Adolphus, 1862–1943, vol. IV
Guilbert, Yvette, 1865–1944, vol. IV
Guild, David Alexander, 1884–1961, vol. VI
Guilford, 8th Earl of, 1876–1949, vol. IV
Guilford, Rev. Edward, 1853–1937, vol. III
Guillamore, 5th Viscount, 1841–1918, vol. II
Guillamore, 6th Viscount, 1847–1927, vol. II
Guillamore, 7th Viscount, 1860–1930, vol. III

Guillamore, 8th Viscount, 1867–1943, vol. IV
Guillamore, 9th Viscount, 1869–1955, vol. V
Guilland, Antoine, 1861–1938, vol. III
Guillaume, Rev. Alfred, 1888–1965, vol. VI
Guillaume, Charles Edouard, 1861–1938, vol. III
Guillebaud, Claude William, 1890–1971, vol. VII
Guillebaud, Walter Henry, 1890–1973, vol. VII
Guillemard, Francis Henry Hill, 1852–1933, vol. III
Guillemard, Hugh W.; *see* Wilkinson-Guillemard, W. H. J.
Guillemard, Sir Laurence Nunns, 1862–1951, vol. V
Guiney, John, 1868–1931, vol. III
Guiney, Louise Imogen, *died* 1920, vol. II
Guiney, Patrick, 1862–1913, vol. I
Guinness, Sir Algernon Arthur St Lawrence Lee, 3rd Bt, 1883–1954, vol. V
Guinness, Hon. (Arthur) Ernest, 1876–1949, vol. IV
Guinness, Arthur Eustace Seymour, 1867–1955, vol. V
Guinness, Hon. Sir Arthur Robert, *died* 1913, vol. I
Guinness, Sir Arthur Rundell, 1895–1951, vol. V
Guinness, Benjamin Lee, 1842–1900, vol. I
Guinness, Benjamin Seymour, 1868–1947, vol. IV
Guinness, Lt Eric Cecil, 1894–1920, vol. II
Guinness, Hon. Ernest; *see* Guinness, Hon. A. E.
Guinness, Rev. H. Grattan, 1835–1910, vol. I
Guinness, Henry Samuel Howard, 1888–1975, vol. VII
Guinness, Henry Seymour, 1858–1945, vol. IV
Guinness, Col Henry William Newton, 1854–1925, vol. II
Guinness, Sir Reginald Robert Bruce, 1842–1909, vol. I
Guinness, Robert Darley, 1858–1938, vol. III
Guise, Sir Anselm William Edward, 6th Bt, 1888–1970, vol. VI
Guise, Sir William Francis George, 5th Bt, 1851–1920, vol. II
Guise-Moores, Col Charles Frederick; *see* Moores.
Guise-Moores, Maj.-Gen. Sir Guise, 1863–1942, vol. IV
Guitry, Lucien, 1860–1925, vol. II
Guitry, Sacha, 1885–1957, vol. V
Gulbenkian, Calouste Sarkis, 1869–1955, vol. V
Gulbenkian, Nubar Sarkis, 1896–1972, vol. VII
Gull, Sir Cameron; *see* Gull, Sir W. C.
Gull, Cyril Arthur Edward Ranger, 1876–1923, vol. II
Gull, Captain Sir Richard Cameron, 3rd Bt, 1894–1960, vol. V
Gull, Sir (William) Cameron, 2nd Bt, 1860–1922, vol. II
Gullan, Marjorie Isabel Morton, *died* 1959, vol. V
Gulland, George Lovell, 1862–1941, vol. IV
Gulland, John Masson, 1898–1947, vol. IV
Gulland, Rt Hon. John William, 1864–1920, vol. II
Gullett, Hon. Sir Henry Somer, 1878–1940, vol. III
Gullick, Joseph William, *died* 1909, vol. I
Gullstrand, Alivar, 1862–1930, vol. III
Gully, Hon. Edward Walford Karslake, 1870–1931, vol. III
Gumbleton, Rt Rev. Maxwell Homfray M.; *see* Maxwell-Gumbleton.
Gumbley, Douglas William, 1880–1973, vol. VII

Gumley, Sir Louis Stewart, 1872–1941, vol. IV
Gun, William Townsend Jackson, 1876–1946, vol. IV
Gundry, Philip George, 1877–1929, vol. III
Gundry, Richard Simpson, 1838–1924, vol. II
Gunesekera, Sir Frank Arnold, 1887–1952, vol. V
Gunn, Major Alistair Dudley, 1884–1943, vol. IV
Gunn, Alistair Livingston, 1903–1970, vol. VI
Gunn, Battiscombe George, 1883–1950, vol. IV
Gunn, Air Marshal Sir George Roy, 1910–1974, vol. VII
Gunn, Herbert Smith, 1904–1962, vol. VI
Gunn, Hugh, 1870–1931, vol. III
Gunn, Sir James, 1893–1964, vol. VI
Gunn, James Andrew, 1882–1958, vol. V
Gunn, Sir John, 1837–1918, vol. II
Gunn, Col John Alexander, 1878–1960, vol. VI (AI)
Gunn, Maj.-Gen. John Alexander, 1873–1966, vol. VI
Gunn, John William Cormack, 1889–1941, vol. IV
Gunn, Neil M., 1891–1973, vol. VII
Gunn, Robert Marcus, 1850–1909, vol. I
Gunnarsson, Gunnar, 1889–1975, vol. VII
Gunning, Brig.-Gen. Sir Charles Vere, 7th Bt, 1859–1950, vol. IV
Gunning, Sir Frederick Digby, 6th Bt, 1853–1906, vol. I
Gunning, Col George Hamilton, 1876–1936, vol. III
Gunning, Sir George William, 5th Bt, 1828–1904, vol. I
Gunning, Col Orlando George, 1867–1917, vol. II
Gunning, Sir (Orlando) Peter, 1908–1964, vol. VI
Gunning, Sir Peter; see Gunning, Sir O. P.
Gunsaulus, Frank Wakeley, 1856–1921, vol. II
Gunsbourg, Raoul, 1859–1955, vol. V
Gunson, Sir James Henry, 1877–1963, vol. VI
Gunter, Archibald Clavering, 1847–1907, vol. I
Gunter, Eustace Edward, 1873–1935, vol. III
Gunter, Lt-Col Francis Ernest, 1869–1936, vol. III
Gunter, Sir Geoffrey Campbell, 1879–1961, vol. VI
Gunter, Maj.-Gen. James, 1833–1908, vol. I
Gunter, Rt Hon. Raymond Jones, 1909–1977, vol. VII
Gunter, Sir Robert, 1st Bt, 1831–1905, vol. I
Gunter, Col Sir Robert Benyon Nevill, 2nd Bt, 1871–1917, vol. II
Gunter, Sir Ronald Vernon, 3rd Bt, 1904–1980, vol. VII
Günther, Albert Charles Lewis Gotthilf, 1830–1914, vol. I
Gunther, Charles Eugene, 1863–1931, vol. III
Gunther, Eustace Rolfe, 1902–1940, vol. III
Gunther, John, 1901–1970, vol. VI
Gunther, Robert Theodore, 1869–1940, vol. III
Gunther, Ven. William James, 1839–1918, vol. II
Guppy, Henry, 1861–1948, vol. IV
Guppy, Henry Brougham, 1854–1926, vol. II
Guppy, Ronald James, 1916–1977, vol. VII
Gupta, Bihari Lal, 1849–1916, vol. II
Gupta, J. N., 1870–1947, vol. IV (A), vol. V
Gupta, Sir Krishna Govinda, 1851–1926, vol. II
Gupta, Satyendra Nath, 1895–1956, vol. V

Gurdon, Lt-Col Bertrand Evelyn Mellish, 1867–1949, vol. IV
Gurdon, Charles, 1855–1931, vol. III
Gurdon, Maj.-Gen. Edward Temple Leigh, 1896–1959, vol. V
Gurdon, Maj.-Gen. Evelyn Pulteney, 1833–1921, vol. II
Gurdon, Rt Rev. Francis, 1861–1929, vol. III
Gurdon, Lt-Col Philip Richard Thornhagh, 1863–1942, vol. IV
Gurdon, Rt Hon. Sir William Brampton, 1840–1901, vol. I
Gurion, David B.; see Ben-Gurion.
Gurnell, Engr Rear-Adm. Thompson, 1878–1965, vol. VI
Gurner, Sir (Cyril) Walter, 1888–1960, vol. V
Gurner, Henry Edward, 1853–1915, vol. I
Gurner, John Augustus, 1854–1937, vol. III
Gurner, Stanley Ronald Kershaw, 1890–1939, vol. III
Gurner, Vice-Adm. Victor Gallafent, 1869–1950, vol. IV
Gurner, Sir Walter; see Gurner, Sir C. W.
Gurney, (Ernest) Russell, 1879–1958, vol. V
Gurney, Sir Eustace, 1876–1927, vol. II
Gurney, Sir Henry Lovell Goldsworthy, 1898–1951, vol. V
Gurney, Rev. Henry Palin, 1841–1904, vol. I
Gurney, Sir Hugh, 1878–1968, vol. VI
Gurney, John Henry, 1848–1922, vol. II
Gurney, Martyn Pierre Cecil, 1861–1930, vol. III
Gurney, Norman William, 1880–1973, vol. VII
Gurney, Quintin Edward, 1883–1968, vol. VI
Gurney, Russell; see Gurney, E. R.
Gurney, Maj.-Gen. Russell, 1890–1947, vol. IV
Gurney, Sir Somerville Arthur, 1835–1917, vol. II
Gurney, Sir Walter Edwin, died 1924, vol. II
Gurney-Dixon, Sir Samuel, 1878–1970, vol. VI
Gurney-Salter, Emma, 1875–1967, vol. VI
Gurnhill, Rev. James, died 1928, vol. II
Gurowski, Major Count Dudley Beaumont, 1865–1939, vol. III
Guthrie, Hon. Lord; Charles John Guthrie, 1849–1920, vol. II
Guthrie, Hon. Lord; Henry Wallace Guthrie, 1903–1970, vol. VI
Guthrie, Charles, died 1953, vol. V
Guthrie, Charles John; see Guthrie, Hon. Lord.
Guthrie, Captain Sir Connop, 1st Bt, 1882–1945, vol. IV
Guthrie, David Charles, 1861–1918, vol. II
Guthrie, Douglas James, 1885–1975, vol. VII
Guthrie, Sir Giles Connop McEacharn, 2nd Bt, 1916–1979, vol. VII
Guthrie, Henry Wallace; see Guthrie, Hon. Lord.
Guthrie, Hon. Hugh, 1866–1939, vol. III
Guthrie, Sir James, 1859–1930, vol. III
Guthrie, John Douglas Maude, 1856–1928, vol. II
Guthrie, Leonard George, 1858–1918, vol. II
Guthrie, Malcolm, 1903–1972, vol. VII
Guthrie, Mrs Murray, died 1945, vol. IV
Guthrie, Ramsay; see Bowran, Rev. J. G.
Guthrie, Robert Lyall, 1867–1937, vol. III
Guthrie, Robin Craig, 1902–1971, vol. VII

Guthrie, Thomas Anstey, 1856–1934, vol. III
Guthrie, Thomas Maule, *died* 1943, vol. IV
Guthrie, Sir Tyrone; *see* Guthrie, Sir W. T.
Guthrie, Walter Murray, 1869–1911, vol. I
Guthrie, William, 1835–1908, vol. I
Guthrie, Sir (William) Tyrone, 1900–1971, vol. VII
Guthrie-Smith, William Herbert, 1861–1940, vol. III
Gutierrez-Ponce, Don Ignacio, *died* 1942, vol. IV
Gutt, Camille, 1884–1971, vol. VII
Gutteridge, Harold Cooke, 1876–1953, vol. V
Guttery, Rev. Arthur Thomas, 1862–1920, vol. II
Guttery, Sir Norman Arthur, 1889–1962, vol. VI
Guttmann, Sir Ludwig, 1899–1980, vol. VII
Guttridge, George Herbert, 1898–1969, vol. VI
Guy, Comdr Basil John Douglas, 1882–1956, vol. V
Guy, Rt Rev. Basil Tudor, 1910–1975, vol. VII
Guy, Ven. Cuthbert Arnold, 1884–1954, vol. V
Guy, Rev. Douglas Sherwood, 1855–1934, vol. III
Guy, Sir Henry Lewis, 1887–1956, vol. V
Guy, Hon. James Allan, 1890–1980, vol. VII
Guy, John Crawford, 1861–1928, vol. II
Guy, Oswald Vernon, 1890–1973, vol. VII
Guy, Lt-Col Philip Langstaffe Ord, 1885–1952, vol. V
Guy, Lt-Col Robert Francis, 1878–1927, vol. II
Guy, Sydney Slater, 1884–1971, vol. VII
Guy, William, 1859–1950, vol. IV
Guy, William Henry, *died* 1968, vol. VI
Guyomard, Rt Rev. John Alfred, 1884–1956, vol. V
Guyot, Y.; *see* Yves-Guyot.
Gwalior, HH Maharajah Sindhia of, 1876–1925, vol. II
Gwalior, Ruler of, 1916–1961, vol. VI
Gwatkin, Frank Trelawny Arthur A.; *see* Ashton-Gwatkin.
Gwatkin, Maj.-Gen. Sir Frederick, 1885–1969, vol. VI
Gwatkin, Col Frederick Stapleton, 1849–1940, vol. III
Gwatkin, Rev. Henry Melvill, *died* 1916, vol. II
Gwatkin, Brig. Sir Norman Wilmshurst, 1899–1971, vol. VII
Gwatkin, Rev. Walter Henry Trelawny Ashton-, 1861–1945, vol. IV
Gwatkin, Maj.-Gen. Sir Willoughby Garnons, 1859–1925, vol. II
Gwatkin-Williams, Captain Rupert Stanley, *died* 1949, vol. IV
Gwenn, Edmund, 1877–1959, vol. V
Gwillim, Calvert Merton, *died* 1972, vol. VII
Gwillim, John Cole, *died* 1920, vol. II
Gwilt, Richard Lloyd, 1901–1972, vol. VII
Gwydyr, 4th Baron, 1810–1909, vol. I
Gwydyr, 5th Baron, 1841–1915, vol. I
Gwyer, Barbara Elizabeth, *died* 1974, vol. VII
Gwyer, Rt Rev. Herbert Linford, *died* 1960, vol. V
Gwyer, Sir Maurice Linford, 1878–1952, vol. V
Gwyn, Tatham, 1839–1915, vol. I
Gwyn-Thomas, Brig.-Gen. Gwyn, 1871–1946, vol. IV
Gwynn, Maj.-Gen. Sir Charles William, 1870–1963, vol. VI

Gwynn, Denis Rolleston, 1893–1971, vol. VII
Gwynn, Edward John, 1868–1941, vol. IV
Gwynn, Rev. John, 1827–1917, vol. II (A), vol. III
Gwynn, John Tudor, 1881–1956, vol. V
Gwynn, Rev. Robert Malcolm, 1877–1962, vol. VI
Gwynn, Stephen Lucius, 1864–1950, vol. IV
Gwynn, Col William Purnell, *died* 1940, vol. III
Gwynne, Comdr Alban Lewis, 1880–1942, vol. IV
Gwynne, Brig. Alfred Howel E.; *see* Evans-Gwynne.
Gwynne, Clement Wansbrough, 1883–1939, vol. III
Gwynne, H. A., 1865–1950, vol. IV
Gwynne, James A., *died* 1902, vol. I
Gwynne, Rt Rev. Llewellyn Henry, 1863–1957, vol. V
Gwynne, Maj.-Gen. Nadolig Ximenes, 1832–1920, vol. II
Gwynne, Nevile Gwyn, 1868–1951, vol. V
Gwynne, Paul; *see* Slater, Ernest.
Gwynne, Brig.-Gen. Reginald John, 1863–1942, vol. IV
Gwynne, Lt-Col Sir Roland Vaughan, *died* 1971, vol. VII
Gwynne, Rupert Sackville, 1873–1924, vol. II
Gwynne-Evans, Sir Evan Gwynne, 2nd Bt, 1877–1959, vol. V
Gwynne-Evans, Sir William, 1st Bt, 1845–1927, vol. II
Gwynne-Hughes, John Williams; *see* Hughes.
Gwynne-James, Sir Arthur Gwynne; *see* James.
Gwynne-Jones, Howell, 1890–1946, vol. IV
Gwynne-Vaughan, David Thomas, 1871–1915, vol. I
Gwynne-Vaughan, Dame Helen Charlotte Isabella, 1879–1967, vol. VI
Gwyther, Ven. Arthur, *died* 1921, vol. II
Gwyther, Frank Edwin, *died* 1918, vol. II
Gwyther, Lt-Col Graham Howard, 1872–1934, vol. III
Gwyther, Reginald Duncan, 1887–1965, vol. VI
Gwyther, Very Rev. William Clements, 1866–1940, vol. III
Gye, Ernest Frederick, 1879–1955, vol. V
Gye, Percy, 1845–1916, vol. II
Gye, William Ewart, 1884–1952, vol. V
Gyee, Sir Maung, 1886–1971, vol. VII
Gyi, Sir Joseph Augustus Maung, 1872–1955, vol. V
Gyp, Sybille Gabrielle Marie Antoinette de Riquetti de Mirabeau, Comtesse de Martel, *died* 1932, vol. III
Gzowski, Sir Casimir Stanislas, 1813–1898, vol. I

H

Haag, Carl, 1820–1915, vol. I
Haag, Norman C., 1871–1950, vol. IV
Haagner, Alwin Karl, 1880–1962, vol. VI
Haarhoff, T. J., 1892–1971, vol. VII
Haas, Paul, 1877–1960, vol. V
Habberton, John, 1842–1921, vol. II
Habdank-Woynicz; *see* Voynich, Wilfrid Michael.

Häberlin, Henry, 1868–1947, vol. IV
Habershon, Samuel Herbert, 1857–1915, vol. I
Hackenley, Most Rev. John, 1877–1943, vol. IV
Hacker, Arthur, 1858–1919, vol. II
Hacket-Thompson, Brig.-Gen. Frederick; see Thompson.
Hackett, Most Rev. Bernard, died 1932, vol. III
Hackett, Felix E. W., 1882–1970, vol. VI (AII)
Hackett, Francis, 1883–1962, vol. VI
Hackett, Very Rev. Henry Monck Mason, 1849–1933, vol. III
Hackett, Hon. Sir John Winthrop, 1848–1916, vol. II
Hackett, Sir Maurice Frederick, 1905–1980, vol. VII
Hackett, Col Robert Isaac Dalby, 1857–1925, vol. II
Hackett, Very Rev. T. Aylmer P., 1854–1928, vol. II
Hackett, Walter, 1876–1944, vol. IV
Hackett, Walter William, 1874–1964, vol. VI
Hackett, William Henry, 1853–1926, vol. II
Hackforth, Edgar, died 1952, vol. V
Hackforth, Reginald, 1887–1957, vol. V
Hacking, 1st Baron, 1884–1950, vol. IV
Hacking, 2nd Baron, 1910–1971, vol. VII
Hacking, Ven. Egbert, 1854–1936, vol. III
Hacking, Sir James, 1850–1929, vol. III
Hacking, Sir John, 1888–1969, vol. VI
Hackney, Rev. Walter, 1852–1938, vol. III
Hadath, Gunby, died 1954, vol. V
Hadcock, Sir (Albert) George, 1861–1936, vol. III
Hadcock, Sir George; see Hadcock, Sir A. G.
Hadden, Sir Charles Frederick, 1854–1924, vol. II
Hadden, J. Cuthbert, 1816–1914, vol. I
Hadden, Rev. Robert Henry, 1854–1909, vol. I
Haddington, 11th Earl of, 1827–1917, vol. II
Haddock, Edgar Augustus, 1859–1926, vol. II
Haddock, George Bahr, 1863–1930, vol. III
Haddock, Captain Herbert James, 1861–1946, vol. IV
Haddock, Rev. Jeremiah William, died 1913, vol. I
Haddock, Maurice Robert, 1909–1974, vol. VII
Haddon, Alfred Cort, 1855–1940, vol. III
Haddon, Archibald, died 1942, vol. IV
Haddon, Frederick William, 1839–1906, vol. I
Haddon, Sir Richard Walker, 1893–1967, vol. VI
Haddon, Trevor, died 1941, vol. IV
Haddon-Smith, Sir George Basil, 1861–1931, vol. III
Haddow, Sir Alexander, 1907–1976, vol. VII
Haddow, Alexander John, 1912–1978, vol. VII
Haddow, Sir Renwick; see Haddow, Sir R. R.
Haddow, Sir (Robert) Renwick, 1891–1946, vol. IV
Haddy, Engr Rear-Adm. Frederick George, 1875–1950, vol. IV
Haden, Sir Francis Seymour, 1818–1910, vol. I
Haden, Francis Seymour, 1850–1918, vol. II
Haden-Guest, 1st Baron, 1877–1960, vol. V
Haden-Guest, 2nd Baron, 1902–1974, vol. VII
Hadfield, Maj.-Gen. Charles Arthur, 1852–1938, vol. III
Hadfield, Charles Frederick, 1875–1965, vol. VI
Hadfield, Sir Ernest, 1873–1947, vol. IV

Hadfield, Geoffrey, 1889–1968, vol. VI
Hadfield, James Arthur, 1882–1967, vol. VI
Hadfield, Rt Rev. Octavius, died 1904, vol. I
Hadfield, Sir Robert A., 1st Bt, 1858–1940, vol. III
Hadfield, Walton John, died 1944, vol. IV
Hadland, Rev. Richard Phipps, died 1934, vol. III
Hadley, Arthur Edward, 1870–1954, vol. V
Hadley, Arthur Twining, 1856–1930, vol. III
Hadley, Patrick Arthur Sheldon, 1899–1973, vol. VII
Hadley, Wilfred James, 1862–1944, vol. IV
Hadley, William Sheldon, died 1927, vol. II
Hadley, William Waite, died 1960, vol. V
Hadow, Lt-Col Arthur Lovell, 1877–1968, vol. VI
Hadow, Sir Austen; see Hadow, Sir F. A.
Hadow, Sir (Frederick) Austen, 1873–1932, vol. III
Hadow, Maj.-Gen. Frederick Edward, 1836–1915, vol. I
Hadow, Grace Eleanor, 1875–1940, vol. III
Hadow, Sir Henry; see Hadow, Sir W. H.
Hadow, Sir Raymond Patrick, 1879–1962, vol. VI
Hadow, Col Reginald Campbell, 1851–1919, vol. II
Hadow, Sir Robert Henry, 1895–1963, vol. VI
Hadow, Sir (William) Henry, 1859–1937, vol. III
Hadwen, Walter Robert, 1854–1932, vol. III
Hadwick, Sir William, 1891–1951, vol. V
Haffkine, Waldemar Mordecai Wolff, 1860–1930, vol. III
Hagan, Very Rev. Edward J., 1879–1956, vol. V
Hagan, Rt Rev. Mgr John, died 1930, vol. III
Hagart-Speirs, Alexander Archibald; see Speirs.
Hagarty, Hon. Sir John Hawkins, 1816–1900, vol. I
Hagarty, Parker, 1859–1934, vol. III
Hagenbeck, Carl, 1844–1913, vol. I
Hagestadt, Leonard, 1907–1974, vol. VII
Haggard, Lt-Col Andrew Charles Parker, 1854–1923, vol. II
Haggard, Lt-Col Claude Mason, died 1909, vol. I
Haggard, Major Edward Arthur, 1860–1925, vol. II
Haggard, Sir Godfrey Digby Napier, 1884–1969, vol. VI
Haggard, Sir (Henry) Rider, 1856–1925, vol. II
Haggard, Lilias Margitson Rider, 1892–1968, vol. VI
Haggard, Sir Rider; see Haggard, Sir H. R.
Haggard, Adm. Sir Vernon Harry Stuart, 1874–1960, vol. V
Haggard, Sir William Henry Doveton, 1846–1926, vol. II
Haggas, Sir James Ellison, 1849–1939, vol. III
Haggerston of Haggerston, Captain Sir Carnaby de Marie; see Haggerston of Haggerston, Captain Sir H. C. de M.
Haggerston of Haggerston, Sir Edward Charlton de Marie, 10th Bt, 1857–1925, vol. II
Haggerston of Haggerston, Captain Sir (Hugh) Carnaby de Marie, 11th Bt, 1906–1971, vol. VII
Haggerston of Haggerston, Sir John de Marie, 9th Bt, 1852–1918, vol. II
Haggerston, Sir Ralph Raphael Stanley de Marie, 12th Bt, 1912–1972, vol. VII

Haggitt, Very Rev. Percy Bolton, 1878–1957, vol. V

Hague, Anderson, *died* 1916, vol. II

Hague, Arnold, 1840–1918, vol. II

Hague, Bernard, 1893–1960, vol. VI (AI)

Hague, Sir (Charles) Kenneth (Felix), 1901–1974, vol. VII

Hague, Rev. Dyson, *died* 1935, vol. III

Hague, Sir Harry, *died* 1960, vol. V

Hague, Sir Kenneth; *see* Hague, Sir C. K. F.

Hahn, Kurt Matthias Robert Martin, 1886–1974, vol. VII

Hahn, Otto, 1879–1968, vol. VI

Haig, 1st Earl, 1861–1928, vol. II

Haig, Lt-Col Alan Gordon, 1877–1951, vol. V

Haig, Alexander, 1853–1924, vol. II

Haig, Captain Alexander Price, *died* 1940, vol. III

Haig, Lt-Col Arthur Balfour, 1840–1925, vol. II

Haig. Gen. Sir (Arthur) Brodie, 1886–1957, vol. V

Haig, Axel Herman, 1835–1921, vol. II

Haig, Gen. Sir Brodie; *see* Haig, Gen. Sir A. B.

Haig, Maj.-Gen. Charles Thomas, 1834–1907, vol. I

Haig, Col Claude Henry, 1874–1955, vol. V

Haig, Sir Harry Graham, 1881–1956, vol. V

Haig, Brig.-Gen. Neil Wolseley, 1868–1926, vol. II

Haig, Lt-Col Patrick Balfour, 1866–1949, vol. IV

Haig, Brig.-Gen. Roland Charles, 1873–1953, vol. V

Haig, Lt-Col Sir (Thomas) Wolseley, 1865–1938, vol. III

Haig, Lt-Col Sir Wolseley; *see* Haig, Lt-Col Sir T. W.

Haig, Lt-Col Wolseley de Haga, 1884–1960, vol. V

Haig-Brown, Rev. William, 1823–1907, vol. I

Haigh, Arthur Elam, 1855–1905, vol. I

Haigh, Hon. Col Bernard, 1876–1939, vol. III

Haigh, Bernard Parker, 1884–1941, vol. IV

Haigh, Charles, *died* 1913, vol. I

Haigh, Ernest Varley-, *died* 1948, vol. IV

Haigh, Engr Captain Francis Evans Percy, 1873–1934, vol. III

Haigh, Frank Fraser, 1891–1970, vol. VI

Haigh, Sir Fred, 1889–1954, vol. V

Haigh, Ven. Henry, 1837–1906, vol. I

Haigh, Rev. Henry, 1853–1917, vol. II

Haigh, Rt Rev. Mervyn George, 1887–1962, vol. VI

Haigh, Rev. William E., 1850–1932, vol. III

Haile Sellassie, 1892–1975, vol. VII

Hailes, 1st Baron, 1901–1974, vol. VII

Hailes, Clements David Grierson, 1860–1929, vol. III

Hailey, 1st Baron, 1872–1969, vol. VI

Hailey, Hammett Reginald Clode, *died* 1960, vol. V

Hailsham, 1st Viscount, 1872–1950, vol. IV

Hailwood, Augustine, 1875–1939, vol. III

Hain, Sir Edward, 1851–1917, vol. II

Hain, Henry William Theodore, 1899–1972, vol. VII

Haine, Paymaster-Comdr Alec Ernest, 1885–1953, vol. V

Haines, F(rederick) Merlin, 1898–1963, vol. VI

Haines, Field-Marshal Sir Frederick Paul, 1819–1909, vol. I

Haines, Air Cdre Harold Alfred, 1899–1955, vol. V

Haines, Henry Haselfoot, *died* 1945, vol. IV

Haines, James, 1868–1936, vol. III

Haines, Maj.-Gen. James Laurence Piggott, 1896–1974, vol. VII

Haining, Gen. Sir Robert Hadden, 1882–1959, vol. V

Hains, Charles Brazier, 1882–1962, vol. VI

Hair, Gilbert, 1899–1965, vol. VI

Haire of Whiteabbey, Baron (Life Peer); John Edwin Haire, 1908–1966, vol. VI

Haire, Very Rev. James, *died* 1959, vol. V

Haire, Norman, 1892–1952, vol. V

Haire, Rev. William John, *died* 1932, vol. III

Haire-Forster, Very Rev. Arthur Newburgh, *died* 1932, vol. III

Haite, George Charles, 1855–1924, vol. II

Hajibhoy, Sir Mahomedbhoy, *died* 1926, vol. II

Hajihafiz Hidayet Hosain, Khan Bahadur, 1881–1935, vol. III

Hake, Guy Donne Gordon, 1887–1964, vol. VI

Hake, Sir Henry M., 1892–1951, vol. V

Hake, Henry Wilson, 1851–1930, vol. III

Hake, Herbert Denys, 1894–1975, vol. VII

Hake, William Augustus Gordon, 1811–1914, vol. I

Haking, Gen. Sir Richard Cyril Byrne, 1862–1945, vol. IV

Halahan, Air Vice-Marshal Frederick Crosby, *died* 1965, vol. VI

Halahan, Very Rev. John, *died* 1920, vol. II

Halahan, Gp Captain John Crosby, 1878–1967, vol. VI

Halcrow, Sir William Thomson, 1883–1958, vol. V

Haldane, 1st Viscount, 1856–1928, vol. II

Haldane, Lt-Col Charles Levenax, 1866–1934, vol. III

Haldane, Elizabeth Sanderson, 1862–1937, vol. III

Haldane, Henry Chicheley, 1872–1957, vol. V

Haldane, Gen. Sir J. Aylmer L., 1862–1950, vol. IV

Haldane, James Brodrick C.; *see* Chinnery-Haldane.

Haldane, Rt Rev. James Robert Alexander C.; *see* Chinnery-Haldane.

Haldane, Very Rev. John Bernard, 1881–1938, vol. III

Haldane, John Burdon Sanderson, 1892–1964, vol. VI

Haldane, John Rodger, 1882–1967, vol. VI

Haldane, John Scott, 1860–1936, vol. III

Haldane, Sir William Stowell, 1864–1951, vol. V

Haldar, Hiralal, 1865–1942, vol. IV

Haldeman, Donald Carmichael, 1860–1930, vol. III

Haldin, Henry Hyman, 1863–1931, vol. III

Haldin, Sir Philip Edward, 1880–1953, vol. V

Haldin-Davis, H., *died* 1949, vol. IV

Haldon, 2nd Baron, 1846–1903, vol. I

Haldon, 3rd Baron, 1869–1933, vol. III

Haldon, 4th Baron, 1896–1938, vol. III

Haldon, 5th Baron, 1854–1939, vol. III (A), vol. IV

Hale, Arthur James, 1877–1970, vol. VI

Hale, Col Charles Henry, 1863–1921, vol. II

Hale, Col E. Matthew, *died* 1924, vol. II
Hale, Sir Edward, 1895–1978, vol. VII
Hale, Rev. Edward Everett, *died* 1909, vol. I
Hale, Frederick Marten, 1864–1931, vol. III
Hale, George Ellery, 1868–1938, vol. III
Hale, Lt-Col George Ernest, 1861–1933, vol. III
Hale, Herbert Edward John, 1927–1978, vol. VII
Hale, John Howard, 1863–1955, vol. V
Hale, Kathleen; *see* Burke, K.
Hale, Lionel Ramsay, 1909–1977, vol. VII
Hale, Col Sir Lonsdale Augustus, 1834–1914, vol. I
Hale, Maj.-Gen. Robert, 1834–1907, vol. I
Hale, Sarah J., *died* 1920, vol. II
Hale, Major Thomas Egerton, 1832–1909, vol. I
Hale, Brig.-Gen. Thomas Wyatt, 1864–1937, vol. III
Hale, W. Matthew, *died* 1929, vol. III
Hale, Sir William Edward, 1883–1967, vol. VI
Hale-White, Sir William, 1857–1949, vol. IV
Hales, A. G., 1870–1936, vol. III
Hales, Rev. Canon G. T. B.; *see* Brunwin-Hales.
Hales, Harold Keates, 1868–1942, vol. IV
Hales, Ven. John Percy, 1870–1952, vol. V
Hales, John Wesley, 1836–1914, vol. I
Halevy, Elie, 1870–1937, vol. III
Halevy, Ludovic, 1834–1908, vol. I
Haley, Francis Raymond, 1862–1931, vol. III
Halford, Frank Bernard, 1894–1955, vol. V
Halford, Frederic Michael, 1844–1914, vol. I
Halford, Rt Rev. George Dowglas, 1865–1948, vol. IV
Halford, Jeannette, *died* 1950, vol. IV
Halford, Rev. Sir John Frederick, 4th Bt, 1830–1897, vol. I
Haliburton, 1st Baron, 1832–1907, vol. I
Haliburton, Hugh; *see* Robertson, J. L.
Halifax, 1st Earl of, 1881–1959, vol. V
Halifax, 2nd Earl of, 1912–1980, vol. VII
Halifax, Dowager Countess of; (Dorothy Evelyn Augusta), 1885–1976, vol. VII
Halifax, 2nd Viscount, 1839–1934, vol. III
Halkett, Baron; Hugh Colin Gustave George, 1861–1904, vol. I
Halkett, George Roland, 1855–1918, vol. II
Halkett, Brig.-Gen. Hugh Marjoribanks Craigie, 1880–1952, vol. V
Halkett, Lt-Col John Cornelius Craigie, 1830–1912, vol. I
Halkett, John Gilbert Hay, 1863–1937, vol. III
Halkett, Sir Peter Arthur, 8th Bt, 1834–1904, vol. I
Halkyard, Col Alfred, 1892–1964, vol. VI
Hall, 1st Viscount, 1881–1965, vol. VI
Hall, Rev. Abraham Richard, 1851–1942, vol. IV
Hall, Alexander Cross, 1869–1920, vol. II
Hall, Alexander William, 1838–1919, vol. II
Hall, Alfred, 1873–1958, vol. V
Hall, Sir (Alfred) Daniel, 1864–1942, vol. IV
Hall, Rev. Alleyne Hall, 1845–1937, vol. III
Hall, Col Sir Angus William, 1834–1907, vol. I
Hall, Anmer; *see* Horne, A. B.
Hall, Rt Rev. Arthur Crawshay Alliston, 1847–1930, vol. III
Hall, Instr Rear-Adm. Sir Arthur Edward, 1885–1959, vol. V

Hall, Arthur Henry, 1876–1949, vol. IV
Hall, Sir Arthur John, 1866–1951, vol. V
Hall, Arthur Lewis, 1872–1955, vol. V
Hall, Surg. Vice-Adm. Sir Basil; *see* Hall, Surg. Vice-Adm. Sir R. W. B.
Hall, Sir Basil Francis, 7th Bt (*cr* 1687), 1832–1909, vol. I
Hall, Benjamin Tom, 1864–1931, vol. III
Hall, Rt Hon. Sir Charles, 1843–1900, vol. I
Hall, Rev. Charles Albert, 1872–1965, vol. VI
Hall, Sir Daniel; *see* Hall, Sir A. D.
Hall, Daniel George Edward, 1891–1979, vol. VII
Hall, Hon. David Robert, 1874–1945, vol. IV
Hall, Sir Douglas Bernard, 1st Bt (*cr* 1919), 1866–1923, vol. II
Hall, Maj.-Gen. Douglas Keith Elphinstone, 1869–1929, vol. III
Hall, Lt-Col Sir Douglas Montgomery Bernard, 2nd Bt (*cr* 1919), 1891–1962, vol. VI
Hall, Edna, (Lady Hall); *see* Clarke Hall, Edna.
Hall, Col Edward, 1872–1941, vol. IV
Hall, Brig. Edward George, 1882–1968, vol. VI
Hall, Edward Laret, 1864–1947, vol. IV
Hall, Sir Edward M.; *see* Marshall-Hall.
Hall, Edwin Geoffrey S.; *see* Sarsfield-Hall.
Hall, Edwin Stanley, 1881–1940, vol. III
Hall, Edwin Thomas, 1851–1923, vol. II
Hall, Col Ernest Frederic, 1865–1942, vol. IV
Hall, Ernest Thomas, 1871–1954, vol. V
Hall, Francis de Havilland, 1847–1929, vol. III
Hall, Brig.-Gen. Francis Henry, 1852–1919, vol. II
Hall, Francis J., 1857–1932, vol. III
Hall, Fred, 1855–1933, vol. III
Hall, Lt-Col Sir Frederick, 1st Bt (*cr* 1923), 1864–1932, vol. III
Hall, Frederick, 1860–1948, vol. IV
Hall, Sir Frederick Henry, 2nd Bt (*cr* 1923), 1899–1949, vol. IV
Hall, Frederick William, *died* 1933, vol. III
Hall, Col Frederick William George G.; *see* Gordon-Hall.
Hall, G. W. L. M.; *see* Marshall-Hall.
Hall, Captain Geoffrey Fowler, 1888–1970, vol. VI
Hall, Geoffrey William, 1906–1974, vol. VII
Hall, George, 1879–1955, vol. V
Hall, George A., *died* 1945, vol. IV
Hall, Lt-Col George Clifford Miller, 1872–1930, vol. III
Hall, George Derek Gordon, 1924–1975, vol. VII
Hall, George Edmund, 1925–1980, vol. VII
Hall, Adm. Sir George Fowler K.; *see* King-Hall.
Hall, Rt Rev. (George) Noel (Lankester), 1891–1962, vol. VI
Hall, George Thompson, 1865–1948, vol. IV
Hall, Lt-Col Gordon Charles William G.; *see* Gordon-Hall.
Hall, Grahame; *see* Muncaster, Claude.
Hall, Granville Stanley, 1846–1924, vol. II
Hall, Hammond, 1857–1940, vol. III
Hall, Harold F.; *see* Fielding-Hall.
Hall, Major Harold Wesley, 1888–1964, vol. VI
Hall, Harry Reginald Holland, 1873–1930, vol. III
Hall, Sir Henry, *died* 1928, vol. II
Hall, Sir Henry, 1845–1936, vol. III

Hall, Ven. Henry Armstrong, 1853–1921, vol. II
Hall, Sir Henry John, 8th Bt (*cr* 1687), 1835–1913, vol. I
Hall, Henry Noble, 1872–1949, vol. IV
Hall, Col Henry Samuel, *died* 1923, vol. II
Hall, Henry Sinclair, 1848–1934, vol. III
Hall, Rev. Herbert, 1845–1921, vol. II
Hall, Herbert Austen, 1881–1968, vol. VI
Hall, Adm. Sir Herbert Goodenough K.; *see* King-Hall.
Hall, Sir Herbert Hall, 1879–1964, vol. VI
Hall, Rt Rev. Herbert William, 1889–1955, vol. V
Hall, Hubert, 1857–1944, vol. IV
Hall, Sir Hugh, 1848–1940, vol. III
Hall, Paymaster Rear-Adm. Hugh Seymour, 1869–1940, vol. III
Hall, I. Walker, 1868–1953, vol. V
Hall, James Henry, 1877–1942, vol. IV
Hall, Hon. Sir John, 1824–1907, vol. I
Hall, John, 1915–1966, vol. VI
Hall, Sir John, 1911–1978, vol. VII
Hall, John Basil, 1866–1926, vol. II
Hall, John Carey, 1844–1921, vol. II
Hall, Surg. Rear-Adm. John Falconer, 1872–1946, vol. IV
Hall, Sir John Frederick, 1882–1959, vol. V
Hall, Brig.-Gen. John Hamilton, 1871–1953, vol. V
Hall, Sir John Hathorn, 1894–1979, vol. VII
Hall, Col Sir John Richard, 9th Bt (*cr* 1687), 1865–1928, vol. II
Hall, Rear-Adm. John Talbot Savignac, 1896–1964, vol. VI
Hall, John Thomas, 1896–1955, vol. V
Hall, Joseph, 1854–1927, vol. II
Hall, Joseph Compton, 1863–1937, vol. III
Hall, Lt-Gen. Julian, 1837–1911, vol. I
Hall, Julian Dudley, 1887–1961, vol. VI
Hall, Sir Julian Henry, 11th Bt (*cr* 1687), 1907–1974, vol. VII
Hall, Kenneth Lambert, 1887–1979, vol. VII
Hall, Kenneth Ronald Lambert, 1917–1965, vol. VI
Hall, Captain Leonard Joseph, 1879–1953, vol. V
Hall, Brig.-Gen. Lewis Montgomery Murray, 1855–1928, vol. II
Hall, Lindsay Bernard, 1859–1935, vol. III
Hall, Sir Lionel Reid, 12th Bt (*cr* 1687), 1898–1975, vol. VII
Hall, Magdalen K.; *see* King-Hall.
Hall, Marie, 1884–1956, vol. V
Hall, Sir Martin Julian, 10th Bt (*cr* 1687), 1874–1958, vol. V
Hall, Lt-Col Montagu Heath, 1856–1928, vol. II
Hall, Sir Neville Reynolds, 13th Bt (*cr* 1687), 1900–1978, vol. VII
Hall, Rev. Newman, 1816–1902, vol. I
Hall, Rt Rev. Noel; *see* Hall, Rt Rev. G. N. L.
Hall, Oliver, 1869–1957, vol. V
Hall, Owen, *died* 1907, vol. I
Hall, Percival Stanhope, 1879–1972, vol. VII
Hall, Percy, 1882–1955, vol. V
Hall, Col Philip de Havilland, 1885–1972, vol. VII
Hall, Miss Radclyffe, 1886–1943, vol. IV
Hall, Col Ralph Ellis Carr-, 1873–1963, vol. VI

Hall, Adm. Sir Reginald; *see* Hall, Adm. Sir W. R.
Hall, Richard James, *died* 1930, vol. III
Hall, Richard Nicklin, 1853–1914, vol. I
Hall, Robert, 1867–1949, vol. IV
Hall, Air Marshal Sir Robert Hamilton C.; *see* Clark-Hall.
Hall, Hon. Robert Newton, 1836–1917, vol. I
Hall, Surg. Vice-Adm. Sir (Robert William) Basil, 1876–1951, vol. V
Hall, Sir Roger Evans, 1883–1969, vol. VI
Hall, Roger Wilby, 1907–1973, vol. VII
Hall, Ronald, 1900–1975, vol. VII
Hall, Ronald Acott, 1892–1966, vol. VI
Hall, Rt Rev. Ronald Owen, *died* 1975, vol. VII
Hall, Sir Samuel, 1841–1907, vol. I
Hall, Stewart S.; *see* Scott Hall.
Hall, Sydney Prior, 1842–1922, vol. II
Hall, Adm. Sydney Stewart, 1872–1955, vol. V
Hall, T. Walter, 1862–1953, vol. V
Hall, Thomas Donald Horn, 1885–1970, vol. VI
Hall, Thomas Sergeant, *died* 1915, vol. I (A)
Hall, Lt-Col Walter D'Arcy, 1891–1980, vol. VII
Hall, Wilfrid John, 1892–1965, vol. VI
Hall, William Carby, 1864–1938, vol. III
Hall, Sir William Clarke, 1866–1932, vol. III
Hall, William Codrington Briggs, 1845–1914, vol. I
Hall, Rt Hon. William Glenvil, 1887–1962, vol. VI
Hall, Hon. William Lorimer, 1876–1958, vol. V
Hall, William M.; *see* Macalister-Hall.
Hall, Adm. Sir (William) Reginald, 1870–1943, vol. IV
Hall, William Thomas, 1855–1938, vol. III
Hall Caine, Gordon Ralph, 1884–1962, vol. VI
Hall-Dalwood, Lt-Col John, *died* 1954, vol. V
Hall-Dare, Robert Westley, 1866–1939, vol. III
Hall-Davis, Sir Alfred George Fletcher, 1924–1979, vol. VII
Hall-Dempster, Col Reginald Hawkins, 1854–1922, vol. II
Hall-Edwards, John Francis, 1858–1926, vol. II
Hall-Jones, Hon. Sir William, 1851–1936, vol. III
Hall-Patch, Sir Edmund Leo, 1896–1975, vol. VII
Hall-Thompson, Adm. Percival Henry, 1874–1950, vol. IV
Hall-Thompson, Lt-Col Rt Hon. S. H., 1885–1954, vol. V
Hallam, (Arthur) Rupert, 1877–1955, vol. V
Hallam, Sir Clement Thornton, *died* 1965, vol. VI
Hallam, Rupert; *see* Hallam, A. R.
Hallam, Rt Rev. William Thomas Thompson, 1878–1956, vol. V
Hallas, Eldred, 1870–1926, vol. II
Hallaran, Ven. Thomas Tuckey, *died* 1915, vol. I
Hallé, Charles E., 1846–1919, vol. II
Hallé, Wilma, (Lady Hallé; Madame Norman Neruda), 1839–1911, vol. I
Hallen, Vet. Lt-Col James Herbert Brockencote, 1829–1901, vol. I
Hallett, Rev. Canon Cyril, 1864–1942, vol. IV
Hallett, Sir Frederic G., 1860–1933, vol. III
Hallett, Harold Foster, 1886–1966, vol. VI
Hallett, Holt S., *died* 1911, vol. I
Hallett, Sir Hugh Imbert Periam, 1886–1967, vol. VI

Hallett, Col James Wyndham H.; *see* Hughes-Hallett.

Hallett, Vice-Adm. John H.; *see* Hughes-Hallett.

Hallett, Leslie Charles H.; *see* Hughes-Hallett.

Hallett, Sir Maurice Garnier, 1883–1969, vol. VI

Hallett, Rt Rev. Mgr Philip Edward, 1884–1948, vol. IV

Hallett, Vice-Adm. Sir Theodore John, 1878–1957, vol. V

Hallewell, Lt-Col Henry Lonsdale, 1852–1908, vol. I

Halliburton, Richard, 1900–1939, vol. III

Halliburton, William Dobinson, 1860–1931, vol. III

Halliday, Gen. Francis Edward, 1834–1911, vol. I

Halliday, Sir Frederick James, 1806–1901, vol. I

Halliday, Sir Frederick Loch, 1864–1937, vol. III

Halliday, Lt-Gen. George Thomas, 1841–1922, vol. II

Halliday, J., *died* 1962, vol. VI

Halliday, Gen. John Gustavus, 1822–1917, vol. II

Halliday, Gen. Sir Lewis Stratford Tollemache, 1870–1966, vol. VI

Halliday, Sir William Reginald, 1886–1966, vol. VI

Hallifax, Charles Joseph, *died* 1946, vol. IV

Hallifax, Edwin Richard, 1874–1950, vol. IV

Hallifax, Rear-Adm. Guy Waterhouse, 1884–1941, vol. IV

Hallifax, Mrs Joanne Mary, 1900–1972, vol. VII

Hallifax, Vice-Adm. Ronald Hamilton Curzon, 1885–1943, vol. IV

Hallilay, Lt-Col Herbert, *died* 1940, vol. III

Hallinan, Most Rev. Denis, 1849–1923, vol. II

Hallinan, Major Thomas John, 1886–1960, vol. V

Hallowes, Basil John Knight, 1884–1973, vol. VII

Hallowes, Col Francis William, 1866–1942, vol. IV

Hallowes, Frederick, 1907–1968, vol. VI

Hallowes, Maj.-Gen. Henry Jardine, 1838–1926, vol. II

Hallpike, Charles Skinner, 1900–1979, vol. VII

Halls, Arthur Norman, (Michael), 1915–1970, vol. VI

Halls, Michael; *see* Halls, Arthur Norman.

Halls, Walter, 1871–1953, vol. V

Hallstrom, Sir Edward John Lees, 1886–1970, vol. VI

Hallsworth, H. M., 1876–1953, vol. V

Hallsworth, Sir Joseph, 1884–1974, vol. VII

Hallward, Rev. Lancelot William, 1867–1951, vol. V

Hallward, Reginald, 1858–1948, vol. IV

Hallworth, Albert, 1898–1962, vol. VI

Halmos, Paul, 1911–1977, vol. VII

Halnon, Frederick James, 1881–1958, vol. V

Halpin, James, 1843–1909, vol. I

Halsall, Rt Rev. Joseph Formby, 1902–1958, vol. V

Halsbury, 1st Earl of, 1823–1921, vol. II

Halsbury, 2nd Earl of, 1880–1943, vol. IV

Halse, Most Rev. Reginald Charles, 1881–1962, vol. VI

Halse, Col Stanley Clarence, 1872–1961, vol. VI

Halsey, Captain Arthur, 1869–1957, vol. V

Halsey, Rt Hon. Sir Frederick; *see* Halsey, Rt Hon. Sir T. F.

Halsey, Sir Laurence Edward, 1871–1945, vol. IV

Halsey, Adm. Sir Lionel, 1872–1949, vol. IV

Halsey, Captain Sir Thomas Edgar, 3rd Bt, 1898–1970, vol. VI

Halsey, Rt Hon. Sir (Thomas) Frederick, 1st Bt, 1839–1927, vol. II

Halsey, Lt-Col Sir Walter Johnston, 2nd Bt, 1868–1950, vol. IV

Halsey-Bircham, Sir Bernard Edward, 1869–1945, vol. IV

Halstead, Albert, 1867–1949, vol. IV (A)

Halstead, Major David, 1861–1937, vol. III

Halsted, Maj.-Gen. John Gregson, 1890–1980, vol. VII

Halton, Herbert Welch, 1863–1919, vol. II

Halward, Rt Rev. (Nelson) Victor, 1897–1953, vol. V

Halward, Rt Rev. Victor; *see* Halward, Rt Rev. N. V.

Haly, Maj.-Gen. Richard Hebden O'G.; *see* O'Grady-Haly.

Ham, Very Rev. Herbert, *died* 1964, vol. VI

Ham, Engr-Rear-Adm. John William, 1863–1931, vol. III

Ham, Wilbur Lincoln, 1883–1948, vol. IV

Hamber, Col Hon. Eric W., 1879–1960, vol. V

Hambidge, Jay, 1867–1924, vol. II

Hambleden, Viscountess (1st in line), 1828–1913, vol. I

Hambleden, 2nd Viscount, 1868–1928, vol. II

Hambleden, 3rd Viscount, 1903–1948, vol. IV

Hambling, Captain Sir Guy; *see* Hambling, Captain Sir H. G. M.

Hambling, Sir Herbert, 1st Bt, 1857–1932, vol. III

Hambling, Captain Sir (Herbert) Guy (Musgrave), 2nd Bt, 1883–1966, vol. VI

Hambly, Wilfrid Dyson, 1886–1962, vol. VI

Hambourg, Mark, 1879–1960, vol. V

Hambro, Captain Angus Valdemar, 1883–1957, vol. V

Hambro, Sir Charles Jocelyn, 1897–1963, vol. VI

Hambro, Sir Eric, 1872–1947, vol. IV

Hambro, Sir Everard Alexander, 1842–1925, vol. II

Hambro, Lt-Col Harold Everard, 1876–1952, vol. V

Hambro, John Henry, 1904–1965, vol. VI

Hambro, Maj.-Gen. Sir Percy, 1870–1931, vol. III

Hambro, Ronald Olaf, 1885–1961, vol. VI

Hamburger, H. J., 1859–1924, vol. II

Hamel, Auguste Charles, 1854–1923, vol. II

Hamel, Gustav, 1861–1922, vol. II

Hamer, Rev. Charles John, 1856–1943, vol. IV

Hamer, Sir George Frederick, 1885–1965, vol. VI

Hamer, Jean; *see* Rhys, J.

Hamer, Captain Richard Lloyd, 1884–1951, vol. V

Hamer, Sam Hield, *died* 1941, vol. IV

Hamer, Sir William Heaton, *died* 1936, vol. III

Hamersley, Alfred St George, 1848–1929, vol. III

Hamerton, Bt Col Albert Ernest, 1873–1955, vol. V

Hames, Sir George Colvile H.; *see* Hayter Hames.

Hamill, John Molyneux, 1880–1960, vol. V

Hamill, Rev. Thomas Macafee, *died* 1919, vol. II

Hamilton, 13th Duke of, **and Brandon**, 10th Duke of, 1862–1940, vol. III

Hamilton, 14th Duke of, and Brandon, 11th Duke of, 1903–1973, vol. VII

Hamilton and Brandon, Duchess of; (Mary Louise Elizabeth), 1854–1934, vol. III

Hamilton, Marquess of; Captain James Albert Edward Hamilton, 1869–1913, vol. I

Hamilton of Dalzell, 1st Baron, 1829–1900, vol. I

Hamilton of Dalzell, 2nd Baron, 1872–1952, vol. V

Hamilton, Hon. Adam, 1880–1952, vol. V

Hamilton, Hon. Brig.-Gen. Alexander Beamish, 1860–1918, vol. II

Hamilton, Alexander Michell, 1872–1959, vol. V

Hamilton, Allan M'Lane, died 1919, vol. II

Hamilton, Allister McNicoll, 1895–1973, vol. VII

Hamilton, Andrew, 1862–1934, vol. III

Hamilton, Col Andrew Lorne, 1871–1951, vol. V

Hamilton, (Anthony Walter) Patrick, 1904–1962, vol. VI

Hamilton, Sir Archibald; see Hamilton, Sir C. E. A. W.

Hamilton, Archibald, 1895–1974, vol. VII

Hamilton, (Arthur Douglas) Bruce, 1900–1974, vol. VII

Hamilton, Lt-Col Arthur Francis, 1880–1965, vol. VI

Hamilton, Arthur Plumptre Faunce, 1895–1977, vol. VII

Hamilton, Bruce; see Hamilton, A. D. B.

Hamilton, Gen. Sir Bruce Meade, 1857–1936, vol. III

Hamilton, Charles Boughton, 1850–1927, vol. II

Hamilton, Sir Charles Edward, 1st Bt (cr 1892), 1845–1928, vol. II

Hamilton, Sir (Charles Edward) Archibald Watkin, 5th Bt (cr 1776) and 3rd Bt (cr 1819), 1876–1939, vol. III

Hamilton, Charles Gipps, 1857–1955, vol. V

Hamilton, Charles Harold St John; see Richards, Frank.

Hamilton, Rev. Charles James, 1840–1917, vol. II

Hamilton, Charles Keith Johnstone, 1890–1978, vol. VII

Hamilton, Hon. Charles William B.; see Baillie-Hamilton.

Hamilton, Sir (Charles) William (Feilden), 1899–1978, vol. VII

Hamilton, Cicely, 1872–1952, vol. V

Hamilton, Rev. Clarence Haselwood, 1877–1940, vol. III

Hamilton, Lt-Col Claud George Cole-, 1869–1957, vol. V

Hamilton, Rt Hon. Lord Claud John, 1843–1925, vol. II

Hamilton, Col Claud Lorn Campbell, 1874–1954, vol. V

Hamilton, Captain Lord Claud Nigel, 1889–1975, vol. VII

Hamilton, Col Claude de Courcy, 1861–1910, vol. I

Hamilton, Cosmo, died 1942, vol. IV

Hamilton, Sir Daniel Mackinnon, 1860–1939, vol. III

Hamilton, David James, 1849–1909, vol. I

Hamilton, Captain David Monteith, 1874–1942, vol. IV

Hamilton, Col Douglas James; see Proby, Col D. J.

Hamilton, Sir Edward Archibald, 4th Bt (cr 1776) and 2nd Bt (cr 1819), 1843–1915, vol. I (A)

Hamilton, Maj.-Gen. Sir Edward Owen Fisher, 1854–1944, vol. IV

Hamilton, Sir Edward Walter, 1847–1908, vol. I

Hamilton, Edwin, died 1919, vol. II

Hamilton, Edwin J., 1852–1946, vol. IV

Hamilton, Emily Moore, died 1972, vol. VII

Hamilton, Rt Rev. Eric Knightley Chetwode, 1890–1962, vol. VI

Hamilton, Eric Ronald, 1893–1967, vol. VI

Hamilton, Col Ernest Graham, died 1950, vol. IV

Hamilton, Lord Ernest William, 1858–1939, vol. III

Hamilton, Eugene L.; see Lee-Hamilton.

Hamilton, Rev. Francis Cole Lowry, died 1936, vol. III

Hamilton, Sir Frederic Harding Anson, 7th Bt (cr 1647), 1836–1919, vol. II

Hamilton, Lord Frederic Spencer, 1856–1928, vol. II

Hamilton, Sir Frederic Howard, 1865–1956, vol. V

Hamilton, Adm. Sir Frederick Hew George D.; see Dalrymple-Hamilton.

Hamilton, Adm. Sir Frederick Tower, 1856–1917, vol. II

Hamilton, G. E., vol. II

Hamilton, Gavin Macaulay, 1880–1941, vol. IV

Hamilton, Brig. Gawaine Basil R.; see Rowan-Hamilton.

Hamilton, Col Gawin William Rowan-, 1844–1930, vol. III

Hamilton, Sir George Clements, 1st Bt (cr 1937), 1877–1947, vol. IV

Hamilton, George Douglas F.; see Findlay-Hamilton.

Hamilton, Rt Hon. Lord George Francis, 1845–1927, vol. II

Hamilton, Ven. George Hans, died 1905, vol. I

Hamilton, Sir George Rostrevor, 1888–1967, vol. VI

Hamilton, Lt-Col George Vaughan, 1851–1911, vol. I

Hamilton, Col Gilbert Claud, 1879–1943, vol. IV

Hamilton, Col Gilbert Henry Claude, 1853–1933, vol. III

Hamilton, Rev. Hamilton Anne D.; see Douglas-Hamilton.

Hamilton, Rt Rev. Heber James, 1862–1952, vol. V

Hamilton, Henry, died 1918, vol. II

Hamilton, Surg.-Gen. Sir Henry, 1851–1932, vol. III

Hamilton, Henry, 1896–1964, vol. VI

Hamilton, Col Henry Best Hans, 1850–1935, vol. III

Hamilton, Col Henry Blackburne, 1841–1920, vol. II

Hamilton, Rev. Herbert Alfred, 1897–1977, vol. VII

Hamilton, Sir Horace Perkins, 1880–1971, vol. VII

Hamilton, Maj.-Gen. Hubert Ion Wetherall, 1861–1914, vol. I

Hamilton, Hugh Brown, 1892–1960, vol. V
Hamilton, Rear-Adm. Hugh Dundas, 1882–1963, vol. VI
Hamilton, Brig. Hugh William Roberts, 1892–1959, vol. V
Hamilton, Gen. Sir Ian Standish Monteith, 1853–1947, vol. IV
Hamilton, Rev. J. M'Curdy, 1834–1915, vol. I
Hamilton, Very Rev. James, *died* 1925, vol. II
Hamilton, Sir James, 1857–1935, vol. III
Hamilton, Surg. Rear-Adm. James, 1899–1964, vol. VI
Hamilton, Rear-Adm. James de Courcy, 1860–1936, vol. III
Hamilton, James Fetherstonhaugh, 1850–1915, vol. II
Hamilton, James Gilbert Murdoch, 1907–1972, vol. VII
Hamilton, Brig. James Melvill, 1886–1972, vol. VII
Hamilton, Lt-Col James S.; *see* Stevenson-Hamilton.
Hamilton, James Whitelaw, 1860–1932, vol. III
Hamilton, James Winterbottom, 1849–1899, vol. I
Hamilton, John, 1851–1939, vol. III
Hamilton, John Almeric de Courcy, 1896–1973, vol. VII
Hamilton, John Angus Lushington Moore, *died* 1913, vol. I
Hamilton, Col John Archibald, 1869–1931, vol. III
Hamilton, Air Vice-Marshal John Beresford C.; *see* Cole-Hamilton.
Hamilton, John Gardiner, *died* 1912, vol. I
Hamilton, Brig.-Gen. John George Harry, 1869–1945, vol. IV
Hamilton, John McLure, 1853–1936, vol. III
Hamilton, Captain Keith Randolph, 1871–1918, vol. II
Hamilton, Kismet Leland Brewer, 1883–1966, vol. VI
Hamilton, Hon. Leslie d'Henin, 1873–1914, vol. I
Hamilton, Lillias, *died* 1925, vol. II
Hamilton, Adm. Sir Louis Henry Keppel, 1890–1957, vol. V
Hamilton, Lord Malcolm Avendale D.; *see* Douglas-Hamilton.
Hamilton, Mary Agnes, *died* 1966, vol. VI
Hamilton, Col Hon. North de Coigny D.; *see* Dalrymple-Hamilton.
Hamilton, Col Sir North Victor Cecil D.; *see* Dalrymple-Hamilton.
Hamilton, Sir Orme R.; *see* Rowan-Hamilton.
Hamilton, Patrick; *see* Hamilton, A. W. P.
Hamilton, Brig.-Gen. Percy Douglas, 1867–1936, vol. III
Hamilton, Percy Seymour D.; *see* Douglas-Hamilton.
Hamilton, Pryce Bowman, 1844–1918, vol. II
Hamilton, Adm. Sir Richard Vesey, 1829–1912, vol. I
Hamilton, Sir Robert Caradoc, 8th Bt (*cr* 1647), 1877–1959, vol. V
Hamilton, Very Rev. Robert James S.; *see* Shaw-Hamilton.

Hamilton, Very Rev. Robert Smyly Greer, 1861–1928, vol. II
Hamilton, Brig. Robert Sydney, 1871–1945, vol. IV
Hamilton, Sir Robert William, 1867–1944, vol. IV
Hamilton, Lt-Col Roland, 1886–1953, vol. V
Hamilton, Sir Sydney; *see* Hamilton, Sir T. S. P.
Hamilton, Maj.-Gen. T. de Courcy, 1825–1908, vol. I
Hamilton, Rt Hon. and Rev. Thomas, 1842–1925, vol. II
Hamilton, Sir (Thomas) Sydney (Percival), 6th Bt (*cr* 1776) and 4th Bt (*cr* 1819), 1881–1966, vol. VI
Hamilton, Col Thomas William O'Hara, 1860–1918, vol. II
Hamilton, Walter, 1844–1899, vol. I
Hamilton, Sir William; *see* Hamilton, Sir C. W. F.
Hamilton, Sir William Alexander B.; *see* Baillie-Hamilton.
Hamilton, Rear-Adm. William Des Vœux, 1852–1907, vol. I
Hamilton, William Frederick, 1848–1922, vol. II
Hamilton, Brig.-Gen. William George, 1860–1940, vol. III
Hamilton, Rev. William Hamilton, 1886–1958, vol. V
Hamilton, Maj.-Gen. William Haywood, *died* 1955, vol. V
Hamilton, William James, 1903–1975, vol. VII
Hamilton, Maj.-Gen. William Ralston Duncan, 1895–1969, vol. VI
Hamilton, Sir William Stirling, 10th Bt (*cr* 1673), 1830–1913, vol. I
Hamilton, Sir William Stirling-, 11th Bt (*cr* 1673), 1868–1946, vol. IV
Hamilton-Dalrymple, Sir Hew Clifford; *see* Dalrymple.
Hamilton-Dalrymple, Sir Walter; *see* Dalrymple.
Hamilton-Gordon, Hon. and Rev. Douglas, 1824–1901, vol. I
Hamilton-Gordon, Lt-Col Edward Hyde; *see* Gordon.
Hamilton-Grace, Col Sheffield; *see* Grace.
Hamilton-Grierson, Philip Francis, 1883–1963, vol. VI
Hamilton-Grierson, Sir Philip James; *see* Grierson.
Hamilton Harding, George Trevor, 1895–1967, vol. VI
Hamilton-Hoare, Henry William, 1844–1931, vol. III
Hamilton-King, Mrs Grace M., *died* 1980, vol. VII
Hamilton-Montgomery, Sir Basil Purvis-Russell; *see* Montgomery.
Hamilton-Russell, Hon. Claud Eustace, 1871–1948, vol. IV
Hamilton-Russell, Hon. Frederick Gustavus, 1867–1941, vol. IV
Hamilton-Russell, Hon. Gustavus Lascelles, 1907–1940, vol. III
Hamilton-Spencer-Smith, Sir Drummond Cospatric; *see* Spencer-Smith.
Hamilton-Spencer-Smith, Sir Thomas Cospatric; *see* Spencer-Smith.
Hamley, Edmund Gilbert, 1818–1902, vol. I

Hamley, Col Francis Gilbert, 1851–1918, vol. II
Hamley, Herbert Russell, 1883–1949, vol. IV
Hamley, Joseph Osbertus, 1820–1911, vol. I
Hamling, William, 1912–1975, vol. VII
Hamlyn, Mrs Christine Louisa, 1855–1936, vol. III
Hamlyn, Frederick, 1846–1904, vol. I
Hamlyn, Rt Rev. N. Temple, 1864–1929, vol. III
Hamman, Lt-Col Jacob L., 1876–1948, vol. IV
Hammarskjöld, Dag Hjalmar Agne Carl, 1905–1961, vol. VI
Hammersley, Maj.-Gen. Frederick, 1858–1924, vol. II
Hammersley, Samuel Schofield, 1892–1965, vol. VI
Hammersley-Smith, Ralph Henry, 1880–1964, vol. VI
Hammerstein, Oscar, 1847–1919, vol. II
Hammerstein, Oscar, 2nd, 1895–1960, vol. V
Hammerton, Col George Herbert Leonard, 1875–1961, vol. VI
Hammerton, Sir John Alexander, 1871–1949, vol. IV
Hammet, Rear-Adm. James Lacon, 1849–1905, vol. I
Hammett, Dashiell; see Hammett, S. D.
Hammett, Richard C., 1880–1952, vol. V
Hammett, (Samuel) Dashiell, 1894–1961, vol. VI
Hammick, Dalziel Llewellyn, 1887–1966, vol. VI
Hammick, Ven. Ernest Austen, 1850–1920, vol. II
Hammick, Sir George Frederick, 4th Bt, 1885–1964, vol. VI
Hammick, Sir Murray, 1854–1936, vol. III
Hammick, Vice-Adm. Robert Frederick, 1843–1922, vol. II
Hammick, Brig. Robert Townsend, 1882–1947, vol. IV
Hammick, Sir St Vincent Alexander, 3rd Bt, 1839–1927, vol. II
Hammill, Captain Charles Ford, 1891–1980, vol. IV
Hammill, Captain John Schomberg, 1890–1959, vol. V
Hammond, Col Sir Arthur George, 1843–1919, vol. II
Hammond, Arthur Henry K.; see Knighton-Hammond.
Hammond, Aubrey Lindsay, 1893–1940, vol. III
Hammond, Basil Edward, 1842–1916, vol. II
Hammond, Rev. Charles Edward, 1837–1914, vol. I
Hammond, Chris, died 1900, vol. I
Hammond, Brig.-Gen. Dayrell Talbot, 1856–1942, vol. IV
Hammond, Dennis, 1913–1969, vol. VI
Hammond, Sir (Egbert) Laurie Lucas, 1873–1939, vol. III
Hammond, Brig.-Gen. Frederick Dawson, 1881–1952, vol. V
Hammond, Gertrude Demain, died 1952, vol. V
Hammond, John, died 1907, vol. I
Hammond, Sir John, 1889–1964, vol. VI
Hammond, John Harold, died 1932, vol. III
Hammond, John Hays, 1855–1936, vol. III
Hammond, John Lawrence Le Breton, 1872–1949, vol. IV
Hammond, Rev. Joseph, 1839–1912, vol. I

Hammond, Kay, (Dorothy Katharine), 1909–1980, vol. VII
Hammond, Sir Laurie; see Hammond, Sir E. L. L.
Hammond, Rt Rev. Lempriere Durell, 1881–1965, vol. VI
Hammond, Captain Leslie Jennings Lucas, 1877–1943, vol. IV
Hammond, Lucy Barbara, 1873–1961, vol. VI
Hammond, Col Peter Henry, 1848–1933, vol. III
Hammond, Ven. Thomas Chatterton, 1877–1961, vol. VI
Hammond, Thomas Edwin, 1888–1943, vol. IV
Hammond, Walter R., 1903–1965, vol. VI
Hammond, Rev. William A., 1853–1931, vol. III
Hammond-Chambers, Robert Sharp Borgnis, 1855–1907, vol. I
Hammonds, Rev. Edwin, died 1933, vol. III
Hamnett, Baron (Life Peer); Cyril Hamnett, 1906–1980, vol. VII
Hamnett, George, 1826–1904, vol. I
Hamon, Count Louis, 1866–1936, vol. III
Hamond, Sir Charles Frederick, 1817–1905, vol. I
Hamond-Graeme, Sir Egerton Hood Murray, 5th Bt, 1877–1969, vol. VI
Hamond-Graeme, Sir Graham Eden William, 4th Bt, 1845–1920, vol. II
Hamp, Arthur Edward, 1886–1951, vol. V
Hampden, 2nd Viscount, 1841–1906, vol. I
Hampden, 3rd Viscount, 1869–1958, vol. V
Hampden, 4th Viscount, 1900–1965, vol. VI
Hampden, 5th Viscount, 1902–1975, vol. VII
Hampden, Hon. Charles Edward H.; see Hobart-Hampden.
Hampden, Ernest Miles H.; see Hobart-Hampden.
Hampden, John, 1898–1974, vol. VII
Hampshire, Charles Herbert, 1885–1955, vol. V
Hampshire, Dugan Homfray, died 1942, vol. IV
Hampshire, Frederick William, 1863–1941, vol. IV
Hampson, Arthur Cecil, 1894–1972, vol. VII
Hampson, Sir Cyril Aubrey Charles, 12th Bt, 1909–1969, vol. VI
Hampson, Sir Dennys Francis, 11th Bt, 1897–1939, vol. III
Hampson, Sir George Francis, 10th Bt, 1860–1936, vol. III
Hampson, Sir Robert Alfred, 1852–1919, vol. II
Hampson, William, died 1926, vol. II
Hampton, 3rd Baron, 1848–1906, vol. I
Hampton, 4th Baron, 1883–1962, vol. VI
Hampton, 5th Baron, 1888–1974, vol. VII
Hampton, Lt-Col Bertie Cunynghame D.; see Dwyer-Hampton.
Hampton, Frederick, 1889–1958, vol. V
Hampton, Herbert, 1862–1929, vol. III
Hamson, Vincent Everard, 1888–1975, vol. VII
Hamsun, Knut, 1859–1952, vol. V
Hanafin, Lt-Col John Berchmans, 1882–1970, vol. VI
Hanauer, Rev. Canon James Edward, 1850–1938, vol. III
Hanbury, Rev. Hon. Arthur Allen B.; see Bateman-Hanbury.
Hanbury, Sir Cecil, 1871–1937, vol. III

Hanbury, Captain Hon. Charles Stanhope Melville B.; see Bateman-Hanbury.

Hanbury, Daniel, 1876–1948, vol. IV

Hanbury, Major Edward Reginald B.; see Bateman-Hanbury.

Hanbury, Evan, 1854–1918, vol. II

Hanbury, Frederick Janson, 1851–1938, vol. III

Hanbury, Sir James Arthur, 1832–1908, vol. I

Hanbury, Lily, died 1908, vol. I

Hanbury, Lt-Col Lionel Henry, 1864–1954, vol. V

Hanbury, Noel, 1881–1935, vol. III

Hanbury, Brig.-Gen. Philip Lewis, 1879–1966, vol. VI

Hanbury, Brig. Richard Nigel, 1911–1971, vol. VII

Hanbury, Rt Hon. Robert William, 1845–1903, vol. I

Hanbury, Sir Thomas, 1832–1907, vol. I

Hanbury-Tracy, Major Hon. Algernon Henry Charles, 1871–1915, vol. I (A)

Hanbury-Tracy, Hon. Frederick Stephen Archibald, 1848–1906, vol. I

Hanbury-Williams, Maj.-Gen. Sir John, 1859–1946, vol. IV

Hanbury-Williams, Sir John Coldbrook, 1892–1965, vol. VI

Hance, Lt-Gen. Sir Bennett; see Hance, Lt-Gen. Sir J. B.

Hance, Lt-Gen. Sir (James) Bennett, 1887–1958, vol. V

Hancock, Anthony Ilbert, 1906–1955, vol. V

Hancock, Anthony John, (Tony Hancock), 1924–1968, vol. VI

Hancock, Ernest, 1887–1950, vol. IV

Hancock, Ernest Legassicke, 1862–1932, vol. III

Hancock, Dame Florence May, 1893–1974, vol. VII

Hancock, Rev. Frederick, 1848–1920, vol. II

Hancock, George Charles, 1868–1938, vol. III

Hancock, Sir Henry Drummond, 1895–1965, vol. VI

Hancock, Sir Henry T., 1877–1957, vol. V

Hancock, John George, 1857–1940, vol. III

Hancock, Kingsley Montague, 1899–1969, vol. VI

Hancock, Col Mortimer Pawson, 1870–1939, vol. III

Hancock, Sir Patrick Francis, 1914–1980, vol. VII

Hancock, Comdr Reginald L., 1880–1919, vol. II

Hancock, Tony; see Hancock, A. J.

Hancock, Rev. William Edward, died 1927, vol. II

Hancock, William Ilbert, 1873–1910, vol. I

Hancox, Leslie Pascoe, 1906–1975, vol. VII

Hand, Rt Rev. George Sumner, died 1945, vol. IV

Hand, John Pierce, 1883–1933, vol. III

Hand, Hon. Learned, 1872–1961, vol. VI

Handfield-Jones, Montagu, 1855–1920, vol. II

Handfield-Jones, Ranald Montagu, 1892–1978, vol. VII

Handford, Sir John James William, 1881–1959, vol. V

Handford, Stanley Alexander, 1898–1978, vol. VII

Handley, Lt-Col Arthur, 1861–1927, vol. II

Handley, Tommy, 1896–1949, vol. IV

Handley, William Sampson, died 1962, vol. VI

Handley-Derry, Henry Forster, 1879–1966, vol. VI

Handley Page, Sir Frederick; see Page, Sir F. H.

Handley-Read, Edward Harry, died 1935, vol. III

Handman, Frederick William Adolph, 1876–1948, vol. IV

Handover, Lt-Col Sir Harry George, 1868–1948, vol. IV

Hands, C. E., died 1937, vol. III

Hands, Sir Harry, 1860–1948, vol. IV

Hands, Rev. John Compton, 1842–1928, vol. II (A), vol. III

Hands, Rev. Thomas, 1856–1926, vol. II

Hands, William Joseph, died 1947, vol. IV

Handyside, Surg. Rear-Adm. Sir Patrick Brodie, 1860–1939, vol. III

Hanford, Col John Compton, 1849–1911, vol. I

Hanforth, Thomas William, 1867–1948, vol. IV

Hanger, Sir Mostyn, 1908–1980, vol. VII

Hanham, Sir Henry Phelips, 11th Bt, 1901–1973, vol. VII

Hanham, Sir John Alexander, 9th Bt, 1854–1911 (this entry was not transferred to Who was Who).

Hanham, John Castleman S.; see Swinburne-Hanham.

Hanham, Sir John Ludlow, 10th Bt, 1898–1955, vol. V

Hanington, Rev. Edward A. W., died 1917, vol. II

Hanitsch, Karl Richard, 1860–1940, vol. III

Hankey, 1st Baron, 1877–1963, vol. VI

Hankey, Basil Howard Alers, died 1948, vol. IV

Hankey, Lt-Col Cyril, died 1945, vol. IV

Hankey, Very Rev. Cyril Patrick, 1886–1973, vol. VII

Hankey, Brig.-Gen. Edward Barnard, 1875–1959, vol. V

Hankey, Mabel, died 1943, vol. IV

Hankey, Richard Lyons A.; see Alers Hankey.

Hankey, W. L.; see Lee-Hankey.

Hankin, Mrs Agnes Mary; see Field, M.

Hankin, Arthur Crommelin, 1859–1930, vol. III

Hankin, Arthur Maxwell, 1905–1972, vol. VII

Hankin, Ernest Hanbury, 1865–1939, vol. III

Hankin, Gen. George Crommelin, died 1902, vol. I

Hankin, St John, 1869–1909, vol. I

Hankins, George Alexander, 1895–1950, vol. IV

Hankinson, Charles James; see Holland, Clive.

Hanley, Allan Hastings, 1863–1921, vol. II

Hanley, Denis Augustine, 1903–1980, vol. VII

Hanley, James Alec, 1886–1960, vol. V

Hanlon, Rt Rev. Henry, 1862–1937, vol. III

Hanlon, Air Vice-Marshal Thomas James, 1916–1977, vol. VII

Hanmer, Lt-Col Sir Edward; see Hanmer, Lt-Col Sir G. W. E.

Hanmer, Lt-Col Sir (Griffin Wyndham) Edward, 7th Bt, 1893–1977, vol. VII

Hanmer, Adm. John Graham Job, 1836–1919, vol. II

Hanmer, Marguerite Frances, 1895–1975, vol. VII

Hanmer, Sir Wyndham Charles Henry, 6th Bt, 1867–1922, vol. II

Hann, Edmund Lawrence, 1881–1968, vol. VI

Hanna, George Boyle, 1877–1938, vol. III

Hanna, Hon. Henry, 1871–1946, vol. IV

Hanna, Marcus Alonzo, 1837–1904, vol. I
Hanna, Very Rev. Robert K., 1872–1947, vol. IV
Hanna, Hon. William John, 1862–1919, vol. II
Hannaford, Charles Arthur, 1887–1972, vol. VII
Hannaford, Charles E., 1863–1955, vol. V
Hannaford, Guy George, 1901–1976, vol. VII
Hannah, Air Marshal Sir Colin Thomas, 1914–1978, vol. VII
Hannah, Ian Campbell, 1874–1944, vol. IV
Hannah, Flt-Sgt John, 1921–1947, vol. IV
Hannah, Very Rev. John Julius, 1843–1931, vol. III
Hannah, Rev. Joseph Addison, 1867–1928, vol. II
Hannah, William George, 1868–1945, vol. IV
Hannan, Albert James, 1887–1965, vol. VI
Hannay, Alexander Howard, 1889–1955, vol. V
Hannay, David, 1853–1934, vol. III
Hannay, Brig.-Gen. Frederick R.; see Rainsford-Hannay.
Hannay, Col Frederick R.; see Rainsford-Hannay.
Hannay, Sir Hugh Augustus Macnish, 1878–1962, vol. VI
Hannay, James, 1842–1910, vol. I
Hannay, James Lennox, 1826–1903, vol. I
Hannay, Rev. James Owen, 1865–1950, vol. IV
Hannay, Mrs Jane Ewing, 1868–1938, vol. III
Hannay, Col Ramsay William R.; see Rainsford-Hannay.
Hannay, Robert Kerr, 1867–1940, vol. III
Hannay, Maj.-Gen. Robert Strickland, 1871–1948, vol. IV
Hannay, Samuel Beveridge A.; see Armour-Hannay.
Hannay, Rt Rev. Thomas, 1887–1970, vol. VI
Hannay, Sir Walter Fergusson Leisrinck, 1904–1961, vol. VI
Hannay, Captain Walter Maxwell, 1873–1952, vol. V
Hannays, Sir Courtenay; see Hannays, Sir L. C.
Hannays, Sir (Leonard) Courtenay, 1892–1964, vol. VI
Hannen, Lancelot, 1866–1942, vol. IV
Hannen, Nicholas James, 1881–1972, vol. VII
Hannen, Sir Nicholas John, 1842–1900, vol. I
Hannon, Ven. Arthur Gordon, 1891–1978, vol. VII
Hannon, Rt Rev. Daniel Joseph, 1884–1946, vol. IV
Hannon, Sir Patrick Joseph Henry, died 1963, vol. VI
Hannyngton, Col John Arthur, 1868–1918, vol. II
Hanotaux, Gabriel, 1853–1944, vol. IV
Hansard, Col Arthur Clifton, 1855–1927, vol. II
Hansell, Rev. Arthur Lloyd, 1865–1948, vol. IV
Hansell, Sir (Edward) William, 1856–1937, vol. III
Hansell, Henry Peter, 1863–1935, vol. III
Hansell, Sir William; see Hansell, Sir E. W.
Hansen, Alvin H., 1887–1975, vol. VII
Hansen, David Ernest, 1884–1972, vol. VII
Hansen, Hans, died 1947, vol. IV
Hansen, Harry, 1884–1977, vol. VII
Hansen, Brig. Percy Howard, 1890–1951, vol. V
Hansen, Sir Sven Wohlford, 1st Bt, 1876–1958, vol. V
Hansford, Col Sir Benjamin, 1863–1954, vol. V
Hansford, S(idney) Howard, 1899–1973, vol. VII

Hansi, (Jacques Walz), died 1951, vol. V
Hanson, Albert Henry, 1913–1971, vol. VII
Hanson, Sir Charles Augustin, 1st Bt, 1846–1922, vol. II
Hanson, Major Sir Charles Edwin Bourne, 2nd Bt, 1874–1958, vol. V
Hanson, Daniel, 1892–1953, vol. V
Hanson, (Emmeline) Jean, 1919–1973, vol. VII
Hanson, Sir Francis Stanhope, 1868–1910, vol. I
Hanson, Frederick Horowhenua Melrose, 1896–1979, vol. VII
Hanson, Sir Gerald Stanhope, 2nd Bt, 1867–1946, vol. IV
Hanson, Lt-Col Harry Ernest, 1873–1934, vol. III
Hanson, Jean; see Hanson, E. J.
Hanson, Sir Philip, 1871–1955, vol. V
Hanson, Sir Reginald, 1st Bt, 1840–1905, vol. I
Hanson, Rev. Preb. Richard, 1880–1963, vol. VI
Hanson, Hon. Richard Burpee, 1879–1948, vol. IV
Hanson, Sir Richard Leslie Reginald, 3rd Bt, 1905–1951, vol. V
Hanson, Rev. Robert Edward Vernon, 1866–1947, vol. IV
Hanson, Rupert Willoughby, 1873–1936, vol. III
Hanworth, 1st Viscount, 1861–1936, vol. III
Hapgood, Henry James, 1855–1931, vol. III
Hapgood, Norman, 1868–1937, vol. III
Happell, Sir Alexander John, 1887–1968, vol. VI
Happell, Sir Arthur Comyn, 1891–1975, vol. VII
Happell, Brig. William Horatio, 1890–1971, vol. VII
Happold, Frederick Crossfield, 1893–1971, vol. VII
Harada, Rev. Tasuku, 1863–1940, vol. III
Haran, James Augustine, died 1940, vol. III (A), vol. IV
Haran, Timotheus, died 1904, vol. I
Harari, Sir Victor Pasha, 1857–1945, vol. IV
Harbach, Otto A., 1873–1963, vol. VI
Harben, Guy Philip, 1881–1949, vol. IV
Harben, Sir Henry, 1823–1911, vol. I
Harben, William Nathaniel, 1858–1919, vol. II
Harberton, 6th Viscount, 1836–1912, vol. I
Harberton, 7th Viscount, 1867–1944, vol. IV
Harberton, 8th Viscount, 1869–1956, vol. V
Harberton, 9th Viscount, 1908–1980, vol. VII
Harbison, Thomas James Stanislaus, 1864–1930, vol. III
Harbord, Sir Arthur, 1865–1941, vol. IV
Harbord, Brig.-Gen. Cyril Rodney, 1873–1958, vol. V
Harbord, Captain Eric Walter, 1879–1952, vol. V
Harbord, Frank William, died 1942, vol. IV
Harbord, Captain Maurice Assheton, 1874–1954, vol. V
Harbottle, Col Colin Clark, 1875–1933, vol. III
Harbottle, Frank, 1872–1923, vol. II
Harbottle, Sir John George, 1858–1920, vol. II
Harbour, Brian Hugo, 1899–1974, vol. VII
Harby, Sir Frank Neville, 1888–1952, vol. V
Harcourt, 1st Viscount, 1863–1922, vol. II
Harcourt, 2nd Viscount, 1908–1979, vol. VII
Harcourt, Alfred, 1881–1954, vol. V
Harcourt, Aubrey, 1852–1904, vol. I

Harcourt, Augustus George V.; *see* Vernon Harcourt.

Harcourt, Adm. Sir Cecil Halliday Jepson, 1892–1959, vol. V

Harcourt, Evelyn, (Lady Harcourt); *see* Suart, Evelyn.

Harcourt, George, 1868–1947, vol. IV

Harcourt, Captain Guy Elliot, 1869–1936, vol. III

Harcourt, Henry, 1873–1933, vol. III

Harcourt, Sir John; *see* Harcourt, Sir R. J. R.

Harcourt, Leveson Francis V.; *see* Vernon-Harcourt.

Harcourt, Hon. Richard, 1849–1932, vol. III

Harcourt, Sir (Robert) John (Rolston), *died* 1969, vol. VI

Harcourt, Robert Vernon, 1878–1962, vol. VI

Harcourt, Rt Hon. Sir William George Granville Venables Vernon-, 1827–1904, vol. I (A)

Harcourt-Smith, Sir Cecil; *see* Smith.

Harcourt-Smith, Air Vice-Marshal Gilbert, 1901–1968, vol. VI

Harcourt Williams, E. G.; *see* Williams.

Harcus, Rev. A(ndrew) Drummond, 1885–1964, vol. VI

Hardaker, Alan, 1912–1980, vol. VII

Hardaker, Benjamin Rigby, 1890–1961, vol. VI

Hardcastle, Captain Alexander, 1872–1933, vol. III

Hardcastle, Edward, 1826–1905, vol. I

Hardcastle, Ven. Edward Hoare, 1862–1945, vol. IV

Hardcastle, Joseph Alfred, 1868–1917, vol. II

Hardcastle, Mary, 1901–1964, vol. VI

Hardcastle, Monica Alice, 1904–1966, vol. VI

Hardcastle, Engr-Captain Sydney Undercliffe, 1875–1960, vol. V

Harden, Sir Arthur, 1865–1940, vol. III

Harden, Rt Rev. John Mason, *died* 1931, vol. III

Hardie, Agnes; *see* Hardie, Mrs G. D.

Hardie, Archibald William, 1911–1980, vol. VII

Hardie, Charles Martin, 1858–1916, vol. II

Hardie, David, *died* 1939, vol. III

Hardie, Sir David, 1856–1945, vol. IV

Hardie, Mrs George Downie, (Agnes Hardie), *died* 1951, vol. V

Hardie, George Downie Blyth Crookston, *died* 1937, vol. III

Hardie, James Keir, 1856–1915, vol. I

Hardie, Maj.-Gen. John Leslie, 1882–1956, vol. V

Hardie, Martin, 1875–1952, vol. V

Hardie, Captain Maurice Linton, 1909–1972, vol. VII

Hardie, Robert Purves, 1864–1942, vol. IV

Hardie, Steven James Lindsay, 1885–1969, vol. VI

Hardie, Rt Rev. William Auchterlonie, 1904–1980, vol. VII

Hardie, Most Rev. William George, 1878–1950, vol. IV

Hardie, William Ross, 1862–1916, vol. II

Hardie Neil, James, 1875–1955, vol. V

Hardiman, Alfred Frank, 1891–1949, vol. IV

Hardiman, John Percy, 1874–1964, vol. VI

Harding, Rt Rev. Alfred, 1852–1923, vol. II

Harding, Sir (Alfred) John, 1878–1953, vol. V

Harding, Sir Charles O'Brien, 1859–1929, vol. III

Harding, Col Colin, 1863–1939, vol. III

Harding, Rev. E. E., *died* 1909, vol. I

Harding, Edward Archibald Fraser, 1903–1953, vol. V

Harding, Sir Edward John, 1880–1954, vol. V

Harding, Francis Egerton, 1856–1937, vol. III

Harding, George Frederick Morris, 1874–1964, vol. VI

Harding, George Richardson, 1884–1976, vol. VII

Harding, George Trevor H.; *see* Hamilton Harding.

Harding, Gerald William Lankester, 1901–1979, vol. VII

Harding, Gilbert Charles, 1907–1960, vol. V

Harding, Harold Ivan, 1883–1943, vol. IV

Harding, Sir John; *see* Harding, Sir A. J.

Harding, Rev. John Taylor, 1835–1928, vol. II

Harding, Most Rev. Malcolm Taylor McAdam, *died* 1949, vol. IV

Harding, Lt-Col Maynard Ffolliott, *died* 1961, vol. VI

Harding, Sidnie M.; *see* Manton, S. M.

Harding, Col T. Walter, 1843–1927, vol. II

Harding, Walter Ambrose Heath, 1870–1942, vol. IV

Harding, Warren Gamaliel, 1865–1923, vol. II

Harding, Lt-Col William, *died* 1945, vol. IV

Harding-Newman, Brig.-Gen. Edward; *see* Newman.

Harding-Newman, Maj.-Gen. John Cartwright, 1874–1935, vol. III

Hardinge, 3rd Viscount, 1857–1924, vol. II

Hardinge, 4th Viscount, 1905–1979, vol. VII

Hardinge of Penshurst, 1st Baron, 1858–1944, vol. IV

Hardinge of Penshurst, 2nd Baron, 1894–1960, vol. V

Hardinge, Rt Hon. Sir Arthur Henry, 1859–1933, vol. III

Hardinge, Sir Charles Edmund, 5th Bt, 1878–1968, vol. VI

Hardinge, Sir Edmund Stracey, 4th Bt, 1833–1924, vol. II

Hardinge, Hon. Henry Ralph, 1895–1915, vol. I

Hardinge, Sir Robert, 6th Bt, 1887–1973, vol. VII

Hardisty, Charles William, 1893–1973, vol. VII

Hardman, Rev. Oscar, 1880–1964, vol. VI

Hardman, Lt-Col Reginald Stanley, 1870–1936, vol. III

Hardman-Jones, Vice-Adm. Everard John, 1881–1962, vol. VI

Hardwick, Donald Ross, 1895–1977, vol. VII

Hardwick, Francis William, 1861–1934, vol. III

Hardwick, Rev. John Charlton, 1885–1953, vol. V

Hardwick, John Jessop, 1831–1917, vol. II

Hardwick, Lt-Col Philip Edward, 1875–1919, vol. II

Hardwicke, 5th Earl of, 1836–1897, vol. I

Hardwicke, 6th Earl of, 1867–1904, vol. I

Hardwicke, 7th Earl of, 1840–1909, vol. I

Hardwicke, 8th Earl of, 1869–1936, vol. III

Hardwicke, 9th Earl of, 1906–1974, vol. VII

Hardwicke, Sir Cedric Webster, 1893–1964, vol. VI

Hardwicke, Herbert Junius, *died* 1921, vol. II

Hardy, Rt Rev. Alexander Ogilvy,1891–1970, vol. VI

Hardy, Hon. Alfred Erskine G.; see Gathorne-Hardy.

Hardy, Archibald C.; see Cozens-Hardy.

Hardy, Hon. Arthur Charles, 1872–1962, vol. VI

Hardy, Rev. Arthur Octavius, 1838–1910, vol. I

Hardy, Arthur Sherburne, 1847–1930, vol. III

Hardy, Rev. Canon Basil Augustus, 1901–1973, vol. VII

Hardy, Major Sir Bertram, 3rd Bt, 1877–1953, vol. V

Hardy, Charles, 1874–1940, vol. III

Hardy, Col Hon. Charles Gathorne G.; see Gathorne-Hardy.

Hardy, Charles Stewart, 1842–1914, vol. I

Hardy, Vice-Adm. Charles Talbot, 1877–1935, vol. III

Hardy, Dudley, 1867–1922, vol. II

Hardy, Rev. E. J., 1849–1920, vol. II

Hardy, Edgar Wrigley C.; see Cozens-Hardy.

Hardy, Sir Edward, 1887–1975, vol. VII

Hardy, Edward Arthur, 1884–1960, vol. V

Hardy, Col Edwin Greenwood, 1867–1944, vol. IV

Hardy, Major Eric John, 1884–1965, vol. VI

Hardy, Ernest George, 1852–1925, vol. II

Hardy, Evan A., 1890–1963, vol. VI

Hardy, Lt-Col Francis, 1875–1929, vol. III

Hardy, Francis, 1879–1977, vol. VII

Hardy, Maj.-Gen. Frederick, 1830–1916, vol. II

Hardy, Geoffrey Malcolm G.; see Gathorne-Hardy.

Hardy, George Alexander, 1851–1920, vol. II

Hardy, Sir George Francis, died 1914, vol. I

Hardy, Gerald Holbech, 1852–1929, vol. III

Hardy, Godfrey Harold, 1877–1947, vol. IV

Hardy, Gordon Sidey, 1884–1936, vol. III

Hardy, Henry Harrison, 1882–1958, vol. V

Hardy, Herbert Ronald, 1900–1954, vol. V

Hardy, Lady Isobel G.; see Gathorne-Hardy.

Hardy, Iza Duffus, died 1922, vol. II

Hardy, Major Jocelyn Lee, 1894–1958, vol. V

Hardy, Sir (John) Francis G.; see Gathorne-Hardy.

Hardy, Rt Hon. Laurence, 1854–1933, vol. III

Hardy, Lt-Col Leonard Henry, 1882–1954, vol. V

Hardy, Oswald Henry, died 1940, vol. III

Hardy, Sir Reginald, 2nd Bt, 1848–1938, vol. III

Hardy, Richard Gillies, 1852–1923, vol. II

Hardy, Hon. Robert G.; see Gathorne-Hardy.

Hardy, Air Cdre Stephen Haistwell, 1905–1945, vol. IV

Hardy, Rev. Theodore Bayley, 1866–1918, vol. II

Hardy, Thomas, 1840–1928, vol. II

Hardy, Maj.-Gen. Thomas Henry, 1863–1938, vol. III

Hardy, Thomas Lionel, 1887–1969, vol. VI

Hardy, Lt-Gen. William, 1822–1901, vol. I

Hardy, Sir William Bate, 1864–1934, vol. III

Hardy, William John, 1857–1919, vol. II

Hare, Alfred Thomas, 1855–1945, vol. IV

Hare, Amy, died 1939, vol. III

Hare, Augustus John Cuthbert, 1834–1903, vol. I

Hare, Bt Lt-Col Charles Tristram Melville, 1879 1950, vol. IV

Hare, Christopher, died 1929, vol. III

Hare, Cyril; see Gordon Clark, Alfred Alexander.

Hare, Dorothy Christian, died 1967, vol. VI

Hare, Edgar James, 1884–1969, vol. VI

Hare, Francis, 1858–1928, vol. II (A), vol. III

Hare, Col Frederick Stephen Christian, 1857–1931, vol. III

Hare, Brig. George Ambrose, 1880–1948, vol. IV

Hare, Sir (George) Ralph Leigh, 3rd Bt (cr 1818), 1866–1933, vol. III

Hare, George Thompson, 1863–1906, vol. I

Hare, Henry Thomas, died 1921, vol. II

Hare, Rev. Hugh James, 1829–1909, vol. I

Hare, Maj.-Gen. James Francis, 1897–1970, vol. VI

Hare, Sir John, 1844–1921, vol. II

Hare, John Gilbert, 1869–1951, vol. V

Hare, John Hugh Montague, died 1935, vol. III

Hare, Rt Rev. John Tyrrell Holmes, 1912–1976, vol. VII

Hare, Julius, 1859–1932, vol. III

Hare, Kenneth, 1888–1962, vol. VI

Hare, Sir Lancelot, 1851–1922, vol. II

Hare, Sir Ralph; see Hare, Sir G. R. L.

Hare, Major Sir Ralph Leigh, 4th Bt (cr 1818), 1903–1976, vol. VII

Hare, Reginald Charles, died 1933, vol. III

Hare, Rear-Adm. Hon. Richard, 1836–1903, vol. I (A)

Hare, Col Richard Charles, 1844–1917, vol. II

Hare, Hon. Richard Gilbert, 1907–1966, vol. VI

Hare, Robert Douglas, 1848–1929, vol. III

Hare, Brig.-Gen. Robert Hugh, 1867–1950, vol. IV

Hare, Brig.-Gen. Robert William, 1872–1953, vol. V

Hare, Robertson, 1891–1979, vol. VII

Hare, St George, 1857–1933, vol. III

Hare, Maj.-Gen. Sir Steuart Welwood, 1867–1952, vol. V

Hare, Theodore Julius, 1839–1907, vol. I

Hare, Sir Thomas Leigh, 1st Bt (cr 1905), 1859–1941, vol. IV

Hare, Thomas Leman, died 1935, vol. III

Hare, Tom, 1895–1959, vol. V

Hare, William Loftus, 1868–1943, vol. IV

Hares, Ven. Archdeacon Walter P., 1877–1962, vol. VI

Harewood, 5th Earl of, 1846–1929, vol. III

Harewood, 6th Earl of, 1882–1947, vol. IV

Harford, Sir Arthur; see Harford, Sir G. A.

Harford, Charles Forbes, died 1925, vol. II

Harford, Rev. Edward John, died 1917, vol. II

Harford, Frederic Dundas, 1862–1931, vol. III

Harford, Rev. George, 1860–1921, vol. II

Harford, Sir (George) Arthur, 2nd Bt, 1897–1967, vol. VI

Harford, Col Henry Charles, 1850–1937, vol. III

Harford, Rev. John Battersby, 1857–1937, vol. III

Harford, Major Sir John Charles, 1st Bt, 1860–1934, vol. III

Hargest, Brig. James, 1891–1944, vol. IV

Hargreaves, Anthony Dalzell, 1904–1959, vol. V

Hargreaves, George Ronald, 1908–1962, vol. VI
Hargreaves, Sir Gerald de la Pryme, *died* 1972, vol. VII
Hargreaves, John, 1864–1926, vol. II
Hargreaves, John Henry, 1856–1934, vol. III
Hargreaves, Lionel Stanley, 1882–1954, vol. V
Hargreaves, Sir Thomas, 1889–1966, vol. VI
Hargreaves, Sir Walter Ernest, 1865–1954, vol. V
Hargrove, Rev. Joseph, 1843–1914, vol. I
Hari Kishan Kaul, Raja Pandit, 1869–1942, vol. IV
Hari Singhji Raja, Rao Bahadur, 1877–1933, vol. III
Harington, Gen. Sir Charles Harington, 1872–1940, vol. III
Harington, Sir Charles Robert, 1897–1972, vol. VII
Harington, Edward, 1863–1937, vol. III
Harington, Brig.-Gen. John, 1873–1943, vol. IV
Harington, John Charles Dundas, 1903–1980, vol. VII
Harington, Sir Richard, 11th Bt, 1835–1911, vol. I
Harington, Sir Richard, 12th Bt, 1861–1931, vol. III
Harisinghji, Lt-Gen. Shri Sir, 1895–1961, vol. VI
Harker, Alfred, 1859–1939, vol. III
Harker, Mrs Allen, (Lizzie Harker), *died* 1933, vol. III
Harker, Brig. Arthur William Allen, 1890–1960, vol. V
Harker, Ven. Ernest Gardner, *died* 1928, vol. II
Harker, Gordon, 1885–1967, vol. VI
Harker, John Allen, 1870–1923, vol. II
Harker, Joseph Cunningham, 1855–1927, vol. II
Harker, Lizzie; *see* Harker, Mrs A.
Harker, Rowand, 1879–1946, vol. IV
Harkness, Sir Douglas Alexander Earsman, 1902–1980, vol. VII
Harkness, Edward Burns, 1874–1957, vol. V
Harkness, Rev. Canon Edward Law, 1874–1931, vol. III
Harkness, Edward S., 1874–1940, vol. III
Harkness, Col Henry D'Alton, 1859–1934, vol. III
Harkness, James, 1864–1923, vol. II
Harkness, Sir Joseph Welsh Park, 1890–1962, vol. VI
Harlan, John M., 1899–1971, vol. VII
Harland, Albert, 1869–1957, vol. V
Harland, Henry, 1861–1905, vol. I
Harland, Henry Peirson, 1876–1945, vol. IV
Harland, Ven. Lawrence Winston, 1905–1977, vol. VII
Harlech, 2nd Baron, 1819–1904, vol. I
Harlech, 3rd Baron, 1855–1938, vol. III
Harlech, 4th Baron, 1885–1964, vol. VI
Harlech, Lady; (Beatrice Mildred Edith), 1891–1980, vol. VII
Harley, Alexander Hamilton, 1882–1951, vol. V
Harley, Rev. Alfred W. M., 1862–1941, vol. IV
Harley, Col George Ernest, 1844–1907, vol. I
Harley, Sir Harry, (Herbert Henry), 1877–1951, vol. V
Harley, Lt-Col Henry Kellett, 1868–1920, vol. II
Harley, Sir Herbert Henry; *see* Harley, Sir Harry.
Harley, John Hunter, 1865–1947, vol. IV
Harley, Rev. Robert, 1828–1910, vol. I

Harley, Sir Stanley Jaffa, 1905–1979, vol. VII
Harley, Lt-Col Thomas William, 1876–1950, vol. IV
Harley, Vaughan, 1863–1923, vol. II
Harlow, Christopher Millward, 1889–1972, vol. VII
Harlow, Frederick James, *died* 1965, vol. VI
Harlow, Vincent Todd, 1898–1961, vol. VI
Harman, Brig.-Gen. Alexander Ramsay, 1877–1954, vol. V
Harman, Lt-Gen. Sir (Antony Ernest) Wentworth, 1872–1961, vol. VI
Harman, Sir Charles Anthony K.; *see* King-Harman.
Harman, Rt Hon. Sir Charles Eustace, 1894–1970, vol. VI
Harman, Sir (Clement) James, 1894–1975, vol. VII
Harman, Captain Douglas K.; *see* King-Harman.
Harman, Edward George, 1862–1921, vol. II
Harman, Major George Malcolm Nixon, 1872–1914, vol. I
Harman, Sir James; *see* Harman, Sir C. J.
Harman, N. Bishop, 1869–1945, vol. IV
Harman, Lt-Col Richard, *died* 1905, vol. I
Harman, Captain (Robert) Douglas K.; *see* King-Harman.
Harman, Lt-Gen. Sir Wentworth; *see* Harman, Lt-Gen. Sir A. E. W.
Harman, Col Wentworth Henry K.; *see* King-Harman.
Harmar, Fairlie, *died* 1945, vol. IV
Harmer, Florence Elizabeth, *died* 1967, vol. VI
Harmer, Frederic William, 1835–1923, vol. II
Harmer, Rt Rev. John Reginald, 1857–1944, vol. IV
Harmer, Lewis Charles, 1902–1975, vol. VII
Harmer, Sir Sidney Frederic, 1862–1950, vol. IV
Harmer, William Douglas, 1873–1962, vol. VI
Harmood-Banner, Major Sir Harmood, 2nd Bt, 1876–1950, vol. IV
Harmood-Banner, Sir John Sutherland, 1st Bt, 1847–1929, vol. II
Harmsworth, 1st Baron, 1869–1948, vol. IV
Harmsworth, Sir Alfred Leicester St Barbe, 2nd Bt (*cr* 1918), 1892–1962, vol. VI
Harmsworth, Anthony; *see* Harmsworth, P. A. T. H.
Harmsworth, Sir (Arthur) Geoffrey (Annesley), 3rd Bt (*cr* 1918), 1904–1980, vol. VII
Harmsworth, Sir Geoffrey; *see* Harmsworth, Sir A. G. A.
Harmsworth, Sir Harold Cecil Aubrey, 1897–1952, vol. V
Harmsworth, Sir Hildebrand Alfred Beresford, 2nd Bt (*cr* 1922), 1901–1977, vol. VII
Harmsworth, Sir Hildebrand Aubrey, 1st Bt (*cr* 1922), *died* 1929, vol. III
Harmsworth, Sir Leicester; *see* Harmsworth, Sir R. L.
Harmsworth, (Perceval) Anthony (Thomas Hildebrand), 1907–1968, vol. VI
Harmsworth, Sir (Robert) Leicester, 1st Bt (*cr* 1918), 1870–1937, vol. III
Harmsworth, Vyvyan George, 1881–1957, vol. V

298

Harnack, Adolf von, 1851–1930, vol. III
Harnam Singh, Hon. Raja Sir, 1851–1930, vol. III
Harness, Maj.-Gen. Arthur, 1838–1927, vol. II
Harnett, Air Cdre Edward St Clair, 1881–1964, vol. VI
Harnett, Walter Lidwell, 1879–1957, vol. V
Harnett, Rev. William Lee, 1864–1937, vol. III
Harney, Edward Augustine St Aubyn, died 1929, vol. III
Harold, Bt Lt-Col Charles Henry Hasler, 1885–1938, vol. III
Harold, Eileen, 1909–1974, vol. VII
Harold, John, died 1916, vol. II
Haroon, Seth Haji Sir Abdoola, 1872–1942, vol. IV
Harper, Charles G., 1863–1943, vol. IV
Harper, Sir Charles Henry, 1876–1950, vol. IV
Harper, Sir Edgar, 1860–1934, vol. III
Harper, Sir George, 1843–1937, vol. III
Harper, George MacGowan, 1899–1976, vol. VII
Harper, George McLean, 1863–1947, vol. IV
Harper, George Milne, 1882–1943, vol. IV
Harper, Lt-Gen. Sir George Montague, 1865–1922, vol. II
Harper, Gerald, died 1929, vol. III
Harper, Harry, 1880–1960, vol. V
Harper, Ven. Henry William, died 1922, vol. II
Harper, Very Rev. James Walker, 1859–1938, vol. III
Harper, Vice-Adm. John Ernest Troyte, 1874–1949, vol. IV
Harper, Lt-Col John Robinson, 1867–1947, vol. IV
Harper, Joseph, 1914–1978, vol. VII
Harper, Sir Kenneth Brand, 1891–1961, vol. VI
Harper, Norman, 1904–1967, vol. VI
Harper, Lt-Col Reginald Tristram, 1876–1958, vol. V
Harper, Sir Richard Stephenson, 1902–1973, vol. VII
Harper, Very Rev. Walter, 1848–1930, vol. III
Harper, William Rainey, 1856–1906, vol. I
Harpignies, Henri Joseph, 1819–1916, vol. II
Harpole, James; see Abraham, J. J.
Harraden, Beatrice, 1864–1936, vol. III
Harragin, Alfred Ernest Albert, 1877–1941, vol. IV
Harragin, Sir Walter, 1890–1966, vol. VI
Harrap, George Godfrey, 1867–1938, vol. III
Harrap, Walter Godfrey, 1894–1967, vol. VI
Harrel, Rt Hon. Sir David, 1841–1939, vol. III
Harrel, William Vesey, 1866–1956, vol. V
Harrey, Cyril Ogden W.; see Wakefield-Harrey.
Harries, Arthur John, 1856–1922, vol. II
Harries, Sir Arthur Trevor, 1892–1959, vol. V
Harries, Rear-Adm. David Hugh, 1903–1980, vol. VII
Harries, Air Vice-Marshal Sir Douglas, 1893–1972, vol. VII
Harries, Frederick James, died 1934, vol. III
Harries, Robert Henry, 1859–1918, vol. II
Harries, Victor Percy, 1907–1977, vol. VII
Harriman, Edward Henry, died 1909, vol. I
Harriman, Sir George, died 1973, vol. VII
Harrington, 8th Earl of, 1844–1917, vol. II
Harrington, 9th Earl of, 1859–1928, vol. II
Harrington, 10th Earl of, 1887–1929, vol. III

Harrington, Charles, died 1943, vol. IV
Harrington, Ernest John, 1864–1944, vol. IV
Harrington, Col Hon. Gordon Sidney, 1883–1943, vol. IV
Harrington, Vice-Adm. Sir Hastings; see Harrington, Vice-Adm. Sir W. H.
Harrington, Sir John Lane, 1865–1927, vol. II
Harrington, Rt Hon. Sir Stanley, 1856–1949, vol. IV
Harrington, Thomas Joseph, 1875–1953, vol. V
Harrington, Timothy Charles, 1851–1910, vol. I
Harrington, Vice-Adm. Sir (Wilfred) Hastings, 1906–1965, vol. VI
Harriott, George Moss, 1858–1943, vol. IV
Harris, 4th Baron, 1851–1932, vol. III
Harris, Hon. Addison C., 1840–1916, vol. II
Harris, Albert Henry, 1885–1945, vol. IV
Harris, Sir Alexander; see Harris, Sir C. A.
Harris, Lt-Col Alexander Sutherland S.; see Sutherland-Harris.
Harris, Sir Archibald, 1883–1971, vol. VII
Harris, Sir Arthur Ambrose Hall, 1854–1939, vol. III
Harris, Sir Austin Edward, 1870–1958, vol. V
Harris, Ven. Charles, died 1934, vol. III
Harris, Rev. Charles, 1865–1936, vol. III
Harris, Sir Charles, 1864–1943, vol. IV
Harris, Sir (Charles) Alexander, 1855–1947, vol. IV
Harris, Lt-Col Charles Beresford Maule, 1866–1932, vol. III
Harris, Sir Charles Felix, 1900–1974, vol. VII
Harris, Rear-Adm. Charles Frederick, 1887–1957, vol. V
Harris, Charles Reginald Schiller, 1896–1979, vol. VII
Harris, Col Sir David, 1852–1942, vol. IV
Harris, David Fraser F.; see Fraser-Harris.
Harris, David R., died 1958, vol. V
Harris, Sir Douglas Gordon, 1883–1967, vol. VI
Harris, Edward, 1849–1933, vol. III
Harris, (Emanuel) Vincent, died 1971, vol. VII
Harris, Frank, 1856–1931, vol. III
Harris, Captain Hon. Frank Ernest, 1877–1951, vol. V
Harris, Frederic Walter, 1915–1979, vol. VII
Harris, Lt-Gen. Sir Frederick, 1891–1976, vol. VII
Harris, Rt Hon. Frederick Leverton, 1864–1926, vol. II
Harris, Frederick Rutheroord, 1856–1920, vol. II
Harris, Frederick William, 1833–1917, vol. II
Harris, Geoffrey Wingfield, 1913–1971, vol. VII
Harris, George, 1844–1922, vol. II
Harris, Major George Arthur, 1879–1935, vol. III
Harris, Sir George David, 1827–1902, vol. I
Harris, Maj.-Gen. George Francis Angelo, 1856–1931, vol. III
Harris, Rev. Canon George Herbert, 1885–1968, vol. VI
Harris, George Montagu, 1868–1951, vol. V
Harris, Col Gerald Noel Anstice, 1866–1952, vol. V
Harris, Henry, died 1950, vol. IV
Harris, Henry Albert, 1886–1968, vol. VI
Harris, Sir Henry Percy, 1856–1941, vol. IV

Harris, (Henry) Wilson, 1883–1955, vol. V
Harris, Rev. Preb. Herbert, 1884–1971, vol. VII
Harris, Col Herbert Sextus, 1884–1932, vol. III
Harris, Air Vice-Marshal Jack Harris, 1903–1963, vol. VI
Harris, Sir James Charles, 1831–1904, vol. I
Harris, James Rendel, 1852–1941, vol. IV
Harris, Maj.-Gen. James Thomas, died 1914, vol. I
Harris, Joel Chandler, 1848–1908, vol. I
Harris, John Edward, 1910–1968, vol. VI
Harris, Sir John H., 1874–1940, vol. III
Harris, John Henry, 1875–1962, vol. VI
Harris, John Mitchell, 1856–1927, vol. II
Harris, John Redford Oberlin, 1877–1960, vol. VI (AI)
Harris, Hon. Sir John Richards, 1868–1946, vol. IV
Harris, Hon. John William, 1849–1932, vol. III
Harris, Brig. Lawrence Anstie, 1896–1970, vol. VI
Harris, Leonard Charles, 1873–1953, vol. V
Harris, Leonard Tatham, died 1960, vol. V
Harris, Leslie J., 1898–1973, vol. VII
Harris, Brig. Sir Lionel Herbert, 1897–1971, vol. VII
Harris, Lloyd, 1867–1925, vol. II
Harris, Mary Kathleen, 1885–1968, vol. VI
Harris, Sir Matthew, 1840–1917, vol. II
Harris, Noel Gordon, 1897–1963, vol. VI
Harris, Norman Charles, 1887–1963, vol. VI
Harris, Rt Hon. Sir Percy Alfred, 1st Bt, 1876–1952, vol. V
Harris, Percy Graham, 1894–1945, vol. IV
Harris, Sir Percy W.; see Wyn-Harris.
Harris, Gen. Philip Henry Farrell, 1833–1913, vol. I
Harris, Reader, 1847–1909, vol. I
Harris, Richard, died 1906, vol. I
Harris, Richard Hancock William Henry, 1851–1927, vol. II
Harris, Sir Richard Olver, 1894–1955, vol. V
Harris, Robert, died 1919, vol. II
Harris, Adm. Sir Robert Hastings, 1843–1926, vol. II
Harris, Robert John Cecil, 1922–1980, vol. VII
Harris, Robert Thornhill, 1865–1934, vol. III
Harris, Rev. Samuel Collard, 1869–1940, vol. III (A), vol. IV
Harris, Sidney, 1903–1976, vol. VII
Harris, Sir Sidney West, 1876–1962, vol. VI
Harris, Thomas Emlyn, 1894–1955, vol. V
Harris, Vincent; see Harris, E. V.
Harris, Walter B., 1866–1933, vol. III
Harris, Sir Walter Henry, 1851–1922, vol. II
Harris, Wilfred John, 1869–1960, vol. V
Harris, William, 1864–1923, vol. II
Harris, Sir William Henry, 1883–1973, vol. VII
Harris, William James, 1835–1911, vol. I
Harris, Ven. William Stuart, died 1935, vol. III
Harris, Wilson; see Harris, H. W.
Harris-Burland, John Burland, 1870–1926, vol. II
Harrison, Albert John, 1862–1941, vol. IV
Harrison, Alfred Bayford, 1845–1918, vol. II
Harrison, Alick Robin Walsham, 1900–1969, vol. VI

Harrison, Sir Archibald Frederick, died 1976, vol. VII
Harrison, Archibald Walter, 1882–1946, vol. IV
Harrison, Brig.-Gen. Arthur Howarth Pryce, 1871–1949, vol. IV
Harrison, Arthur Neville John, 1881–1973, vol. VII
Harrison, Austin, 1873–1928, vol. II
Harrison, Beatrice, died 1965, vol. VI
Harrison, Benjamin, 1833–1901, vol. I
Harrison, Sir (Bernard) Guy, 1885–1978, vol. VII
Harrison, Major Cecil Pryce, 1880–1938, vol. III
Harrison, Sir Cecil Reeves, 1856–1940, vol. III
Harrison, Cecil Stanley, 1902–1962, vol. VI
Harrison, Charles, 1835–1897, vol. I
Harrison, Charles, died 1943, vol. IV
Harrison, Charles Custis, 1844–1929, vol. III
Harrison, Col Charles Edward, 1852–1944, vol. IV
Harrison, Sir Charlton Scott Cholmeley, 1881–1951, vol. V
Harrison, Col Cholmeley Edward Carl Branfill, 1857–1937, vol. III
Harrison, Constance Cary, died 1920, vol. II
Harrison, Sir Cyril Ernest, 1901–1980, vol. VII
Harrison, Very Rev. Douglas Ernest William, 1903–1974, vol. VII
Harrison, Lt-Col Edgar Garston, 1863–1947, vol. IV
Harrison, Sir Edward Richard, 1872–1960, vol. V
Harrison, Ven. Edward Stanley, 1889–1948, vol. IV
Harrison, Rt Hon. Sir Eric John, 1892–1974, vol. VII
Harrison, Ernest, 1877–1943, vol. IV
Harrison, Major Esme Stuart Erskine, 1864–1902, vol. I
Harrison, Sir Fowler; see Harrison, Sir J. F.
Harrison, Francis Capel, 1863–1938, vol. III
Harrison, Fred, 1865–1954, vol. V
Harrison, Frederic, 1831–1923, vol. II
Harrison, Frederic James, died 1915, vol. I
Harrison, Lt-Col Sir Frederick, 1844–1914, vol. I
Harrison, Frederick, died 1926, vol. II
Harrison, Rev. Frederick, 1884–1958, vol. V
Harrison, Gabriel Harold, 1921–1974, vol. VII
Harrison, Major George, 1885–1961, vol. VI
Harrison, Major George Arthur, 1876–1939, vol. III
Harrison, Brig.-Gen. George Hyde, 1877–1965, vol. VI
Harrison, George Leslie, 1887–1958, vol. V
Harrison, Gerald Joseph Cuthbert, 1895–1954, vol. V
Harrison, Brig.-Gen. Gilbert Harwood, 1866–1930, vol. III
Harrison, Sir Guy; see Harrison, Sir B. G.
Harrison, Brig. Harold Cecil, died 1940, vol. III
Harrison, Sir Harwood; see Harrison, Sir J. H.
Harrison, Sir Heath, 1st Bt (cr 1917), 1857–1934, vol. III
Harrison, Henry, 1867–1954, vol. V
Harrison, Captain Henry Neville Baskcomb-, 1879–1915, vol. I
Harrison, James, 1899–1959, vol. V
Harrison, James Fraser, 1890–1971, vol. VII

Harrison, Sir (James) Harwood, 1st Bt (*cr* 1961), 1907–1980, vol. VII
Harrison, Sir James Humphreys, 1848–1933, vol. III
Harrison, James J., *died* 1923, vol. II
Harrison, Maj.-Gen. James Murray Robert, 1880–1957, vol. V
Harrison, Maj.-Gen. Sir James William, 1912–1971, vol. VII
Harrison, Jane Ellen, 1850–1928, vol. II
Harrison, John, 1847–1922, vol. II
Harrison, Sir John, 1st Bt (*cr* 1922), 1856–1936, vol. III
Harrison, Sir John, 1866–1944, vol. IV
Harrison, Sir John Burchmore, 1856–1926, vol. II
Harrison, Sir (John) Fowler, 2nd Bt (*cr* 1922), 1899–1947, vol. IV
Harrison, John Vernon, 1892–1972, vol. VII
Harrison, John William H.; *see* Heslop-Harrison.
Harrison, Sir (John) Wyndham, 3rd Bt (*cr* 1922), 1933–1955, vol. V
Harrison, Joseph Richard, 1888–1957, vol. V
Harrison, Julius Allan Greenway, 1885–1963, vol. VI
Harrison, Lawrence Alexander, *died* 1937, vol. III
Harrison, Col Lawrence Whitaker, 1876–1964, vol. VI
Harrison, Bt Col Louis Kenneth, 1871–1951, vol. V
Harrison, Mary St Leger, 1852–1931, vol. III
Harrison, May, *died* 1959, vol. V
Harrison, Michael, 1876–1935, vol. III
Harrison, Lt-Col Norman, *died* 1949, vol. IV
Harrison, Philip, *died* 1933, vol. III
Harrison, Reginald, 1837–1908, vol. I
Harrison, Gen. Sir Richard, 1837–1931, vol. III
Harrison, Air Vice-Marshal Richard, 1893–1974, vol. VII
Harrison, Rev. Robert, 1841–1927, vol. II
Harrison, Brig.-Gen. Robert Arthur Gwynne, 1855–1943, vol. IV
Harrison, Robert Francis, 1858–1927, vol. II
Harrison, Robert Hichens Camden, *died* 1924, vol. II
Harrison, Robert Tullis, 1876–1950, vol. IV
Harrison, Rosamond Mary, *died* 1948, vol. IV
Harrison, Ross G., 1870–1959, vol. V
Harrison, Ven. Talbot D.; *see* Dilworth-Harrison.
Harrison, Col Thomas Aylet, 1865–1935, vol. III
Harrison, Brig. Thomas Carleton, 1896–1962, vol. VI
Harrison, Sir Thomas Dalkin, 1885–1954, vol. V
Harrison, Lt-Col Thomas Elliot, 1862–1939, vol. III
Harrison, Thomas Fenwick, 1852–1916, vol. II
Harrison, Captain Walter Gordon, 1888–1951, vol. V
Harrison, Lt-Col Walter Lewis, *died* 1938, vol. III
Harrison, Wilfrid, 1909–1980, vol. VII
Harrison, William, *died* 1940, vol. III
Harrison, William English, *died* 1933, vol. III
Harrison, William Henry, 1880–1955, vol. V
Harrison, William Herbert, 1909–1975, vol. VII
Harrison, William Jerome, 1845–1909, vol. I

Harrison, William John, *died* 1943, vol. IV
Harrison, Sir William Montagu G.; *see* Graham-Harrison.
Harrison, Rt Rev. William Thomas, 1837–1920, vol. II
Harrison, Sir Wyndham; *see* Harrison, Sir J. W.
Harrison-Broadley, Henry Broadley; *see* Broadley.
Harrison-Smith, Sir Francis, *died* 1927, vol. II
Harrison-Topham, Lt-Col Thomas, 1864–1939, vol. III
Harrison-Wallace, Captain Henry Steuart Macnaghten, *died* 1963, vol. VI
Harriss, Charles Albert Edwin, 1862–1929, vol. III
Harrisson, Damer, 1852–1918, vol. II
Harrisson, Geoffry Harnett, *died* 1939, vol. III
Harrisson, Sydney Thirlwall, 1865–1953, vol. V
Harrisson, Tom, 1911–1976, vol. VII
Harrod, Frances M. D., 1866–1956, vol. V
Harrod, Sir Roy Forbes, 1900–1978, vol. VII
Harrop, Angus John, 1900–1963, vol. VI
Harrop, Wilfrid Orrell, 1893–1969, vol. VI
Harrop, William Edward Montagu H.; *see* Hulton-Harrop.
Harrop, Maj.-Gen. William Harrington H.; *see* Hulton-Harrop.
Harrowby, 3rd Earl of, 1831–1900, vol. I
Harrowby, 4th Earl of, 1836–1900, vol. I
Harrowby, 5th Earl of, 1864–1956, vol. V
Harrower, John, 1857–1933, vol. III
Harrower, John Gordon, 1890–1936, vol. III
Harrowing, Sir John H., 1859–1937, vol. III
Harrowing, Lt-Col Wilkinson Wilberforce, 1898–1967, vol. VI
Harry, Philip A., *died* 1953, vol. V
Harsant, Maj.-Gen. Arnold Guy, 1893–1977, vol. VII
Harston, Major Sir Ernest Sirdefield, 1891–1975, vol. VII
Hart, Albert Bushnell, 1854–1943, vol. IV
Hart, Alfred H., *died* 1953, vol. V
Hart, Arthur W.; *see* Woolley-Hart.
Hart, Sir Basil Henry L.; *see* Liddell Hart.
Hart, Bernard, 1879–1966, vol. VI
Hart, Bernard John W.; *see* Wilden-Hart.
Hart, Sir Bruce; *see* Hart, Sir E. B.
Hart, Cecil Augustus, 1902–1970, vol. VI
Hart, Charles Henry, 1847–1917, vol. II
Hart, Col Charles Joseph, *died* 1925, vol. II
Hart, Sir (Edgar) Bruce, 2nd Bt, 1873–1963, vol. VI
Hart, Lt-Col Eric George, 1878–1946, vol. IV
Hart, Ernest, 1836–1898, vol. I
Hart, Sir Ernest Sidney Walter, 1870–1957, vol. V
Hart, Frank, 1878–1959, vol. V
Hart, Sir George Sankey, 1866–1937, vol. III
Hart, George Vaughan, 1841–1912, vol. I
Hart, Heber Leonidas, *died* 1948, vol. IV
Hart, Henry George, 1843–1921, vol. II
Hart, Lt-Col Henry Travers, *died* 1948, vol. IV
Hart, Brig.-Gen. Sir Herbert Ernest, 1882–1968, vol. VI
Hart, Sir Israel, 1835–1911, vol. I
Hart, Ivor Blashka, 1889–1962, vol. VI
Hart, Rt Rev. John Stephen, 1866–1952, vol. V
Hart, Moss, 1904–1961, vol. VI

Hart, Air Marshal Sir Raymund George, 1899–1960, vol. V
Hart, Gen. Sir Reginald Clare, 1848–1931, vol. III
Hart, Sir Robert, 1st Bt, 1835–1911, vol. I
Hart, Sir Robert, 3rd Bt, 1918–1970, vol. VI
Hart, Siriol; see Hugh-Jones, S. M. A.
Hart, Thomas Wheeler, 1875–1958, vol. V
Hart, Vincent, 1881–1939, vol. III
Hart, Sir William Edward, 1866–1942, vol. IV
Hart, Sir William Ogden, 1903–1977, vol. VII
Hart, Rev. William Roland R.; see Raven-Hart.
Hart-Davies, Thomas, died 1920, vol. II
Hart-Davis, Charles Henry, 1874–1958, vol. V
Hart-Synnot, Maj.-Gen. Arthur FitzRoy, 1844–1910, vol. I
Hart-Synnot, Brig.-Gen. Arthur Henry Seton, 1870–1942, vol. IV
Hart-Synnot, Ronald Victor Okes, 1879–1976, vol. VII
Harte, Bret; see Harte, F. B.
Harte, (Francis) Bret, 1839–1902, vol. I
Harte, Walter James, 1866–1954, vol. V
Harte, Wilma, 1916–1976, vol. VII
Harter, Maj.-Gen. James Francis, 1888–1960, vol. V
Harter, James Francis Hatfeild, 1854–1910, vol. I
Hartert, Ernst, 1859–1933, vol. III
Hartford, Captain George Bibby, 1883–1941, vol. IV
Hartford, Rev. Canon Richard Randall, 1904–1962, vol. VI
Hartgill, Maj.-Gen. William Clavering, 1888–1968, vol. VI
Hartigan, Lt-Gen. Sir James Andrew, 1876–1962, vol. VI
Hartill, Ven. Percy, 1892–1964, vol. VI
Harting, James Edmund, 1841–1928, vol. II
Harting, Pieter, 1892–1970, vol. VI
Hartington, Marquess of; William John Robert Cavendish, 1917–1944, vol. IV
Hartland, Edwin Sidney, 1848–1927, vol. II
Hartland, Sir Frederick Dixon D.; see Dixon-Hartland.
Hartland, George Albert, 1884–1944, vol. IV
Hartland, William John, 1909–1972, vol. VII
Hartland-Swann, Louis Herbert, 1878–1947, vol. IV
Hartley, Gen. Sir Alan Fleming, 1882–1954, vol. V
Hartley, Alfred, 1855–1933, vol. III
Hartley, Arthur Clifford, 1889–1960, vol. V
Hartley, Col Bernard Charles, 1879–1960, vol. V
Hartley, C. Gasquoine, (Mrs Arthur D. Lewis), 1869–1928, vol. II
Hartley, Sir Charles Augustus, 1825–1915, vol. I
Hartley, Christiana, died 1948, vol. IV
Hartley, Lt-Col Donald Reginald Cavendish, 1893–1970, vol. VI
Hartley, Edmund Baron, 1847–1919, vol. II
Hartley, Frederic St Aubyn, 1896–1969, vol. VI
Hartley, Brig.-Gen. Sir Harold, 1878–1972, vol. VII
Hartley, Harold T., 1851–1943, vol. IV
Hartley, Rev. John Thorneycroft, 1849–1935, vol. III
Hartley, Leslie Poles, 1895–1972, vol. VII
Hartley, Lewis Wynne, 1867–1931, vol. III

Hartley, Rev. Marshall, 1846–1928, vol. II
Hartley, Sir Percival, 1881–1957, vol. V
Hartley, Sir Percival Horton-Smith-, 1867–1952, vol. V
Hartley, Percival Hubert Graham Horton-Smith, 1896–1977, vol. VII
Hartley, Sir Walter Noel, died 1913, vol. I
Hartley, Sir William Pickles, 1846–1922, vol. II
Hartmann, Karl Robert Eduard von, 1842–1906, vol. I
Hartmann, William, 1844–1926, vol. II
Hartnell, Sir Norman, 1901–1979, vol. VII
Hartnoll, Comdr Henry James, 1890–1940, vol. III
Hartnoll, Sir Henry Sulivan, 1862–1935, vol. III
Hartog, Marcus, died 1923, vol. II
Hartog, Sir Philip Joseph, 1864–1947, vol. IV
Harton, Very Rev. Frederic Percy, 1889–1958, vol. V
Hartopp, Sir Charles Edward Cradock-, 5th Bt, 1858–1929, vol. III
Hartopp, Sir Charles (William Everard) Cradock-, 6th Bt, 1893–1930, vol. III
Hartopp, Sir Frederick Cradock-, 7th Bt, 1869–1937, vol. III
Hartopp, Sir George Francis Fleetwood Cradock-, 8th Bt, 1870–1949, vol. IV
Hartree, Douglas Rayner, 1897–1958, vol. V
Hartrick, Archibald Standish, 1864–1950, vol. IV
Hartridge, Gustavus, died 1923, vol. II
Hartridge, Hamilton, 1886–1976, vol. VII
Hartshorn, Rt Hon. Vernon, 1872–1931, vol. III
Hartshorne, Albert, 1839–1910, vol. I
Hartung, Ernst Johannes, 1893–1979, vol. VII
Hartvigson, Frits, 1841–1919, vol. II
Hartwell, Sir Brodrick Cecil Denham Arkwright, 4th Bt, 1876–1948, vol. IV
Hartwell, Charles Leonard, 1873–1951, vol. V
Hartwell, Sir Francis Houlton, 3rd Bt, 1835–1900, vol. I
Hartwell, Maj.-Gen. John Redmond, 1887–1970, vol. VI
Harty, Agnes Helen, (Lady Harty), 1877–1959, vol. V
Harty, Maj.-Gen. Arthur Henry, 1890–1977, vol. VII
Harty, Sir Hamilton; see Harty, Sir Herbert H.
Harty, Sir Henry Lockington, 3rd Bt, 1826–1913 (this entry was not transferred to Who was Who).
Harty, Sir (Herbert) Hamilton, 1880–1941, vol. IV
Harty, Most Rev. J. M., 1867–1946, vol. IV
Harty, Sir Lionel Lockington, 4th Bt, 1864–1939, vol. III
Harty, Sir Robert, 2nd Bt, 1815–1902, vol. I
Harty, Hon. William, died 1929, vol. III
Hartzell, Joseph Crane, 1842–1928, vol. II
Harvey of Tasburgh, 1st Baron, 1893–1968, vol. VI
Harvey, Alexander Gordon Cummins, 1858–1922, vol. II
Harvey, Maj.-Gen. Alexander William Montgomery, 1881–1942, vol. IV
Harvey, Lt-Col Cecil Walter Lewery, 1897–1958, vol. V

Harvey, Sir Charles, 2nd Bt (*cr* 1868, of Crown Point), 1849–1928, vol. II
Harvey, Lt-Col Charles Darley, 1881–1929, vol. III
Harvey, Sir (Charles) Malcolm B.; *see* Barclay-Harvey.
Harvey, Maj.-Gen. Sir Charles Offley, 1888–1969, vol. VI
Harvey, Sir Charles Robert Lambart Edward, 3rd Bt (*cr* 1868, of Crown Point), 1871–1954, vol. V
Harvey, Rev. Clement Fox, 1847–1917, vol. II
Harvey, Conway, 1880–1943, vol. IV
Harvey, Cyril Pearce, 1900–1968, vol. VI
Harvey, Maj.-Gen. David, 1871–1958, vol. V
Harvey, Captain Edward M.; *see* Murray-Harvey.
Harvey, Sir Ernest Maes, 1872–1926, vol. II
Harvey, Sir Ernest Musgrave, 1st Bt (*cr* 1933), 1867–1955, vol. V
Harvey, Rev. Francis Clyde, *died* 1922, vol. II
Harvey, Col Francis George, 1872–1944, vol. IV
Harvey, Lt-Col Francis Henry, 1878–1960, vol. V
Harvey, Frederick William, *died* 1915, vol. I
Harvey, Col George, 1864–1928, vol. II
Harvey, Sir George, 1870–1939, vol. III
Harvey, Maj.-Gen. George Alfred Duncan, *died* 1957, vol. V
Harvey, Air Vice-Marshal Sir George David, 1905–1969, vol. VI
Harvey, Col Sir George Samuel Abercrombie, 1854–1930, vol. III
Harvey, Harold, *died* 1941, vol. IV
Harvey, Rear-Adm. Harold Lane, 1884–1960, vol. V
Harvey, Henry, 1899–1965, vol. VI
Harvey, Sir (Henry) Paul, 1869–1948, vol. IV
Harvey, Herbert Frost, 1875–1959, vol. V
Harvey, Hildebrand Wolfe, 1887–1970, vol. VI
Harvey, Hon. Horace, 1863–1949, vol. IV
Harvey, Rev. James, 1859–1950, vol. IV
Harvey, James Graham, 1869–1950, vol. IV (A), vol. V
Harvey, John, 1841–1915, vol. I (A)
Harvey, John Edmund Audley, 1851–1927, vol. II
Harvey, Sir John Martin-, 1863–1944, vol. IV
Harvey, Hon. Sir John Musgrave, 1865–1940, vol. III
Harvey, Lt-Col John Robert, 1861–1921, vol. II
Harvey, John Wilfred, 1889–1967, vol. VI
Harvey, Laurence, (Larushka Mischa Skikne), 1929–1973, vol. VII
Harvey, Air Marshal Sir Leslie Gordon, 1896–1972, vol. VI
Harvey, Rev. Moses, 1820–1901, vol. I
Harvey, Sir Paul; *see* Harvey, Sir H. P.
Harvey, Sir Percy Norman, 1887–1946, vol. IV
Harvey, Ven. Richard Charles Musgrave, 1864–1944, vol. IV
Harvey, Sir Richard Musgrave, 2nd Bt (*cr* 1933), 1898–1978, vol. VII
Harvey, Surg.-Gen. Robert, 1842–1901, vol. I
Harvey, Sir Robert, 1847–1930, vol. III
Harvey, Sir Robert Grenville, 2nd Bt (*cr* 1868, of Langley Park), 1856–1931, vol. III

Harvey, Sir Robert James Paterson, 1904–1965, vol. VI
Harvey, Maj.-Gen. Robert Napier, 1868–1937, vol. III
Harvey, Major Sir Samuel Emile, 1885–1959, vol. V
Harvey, Thomas, 1864–1940, vol. III
Harvey, Rt Rev. Thomas Arnold, 1878–1966, vol. VI
Harvey, Thomas Edmund, 1875–1955, vol. V
Harvey, Rev. Canon Treffry, 1853–1932, vol. III
Harvey, Lt-Col Valentine Vivyan, 1885–1930, vol. III
Harvey, Wilfred John, 1895–1971, vol. VII
Harvey, William, 1859–1927, vol. II
Harvey, William, 1874–1936, vol. III
Harvey, William Alfred, 1883–1946, vol. IV
Harvey, William Edwin, 1852–1914, vol. I
Harvey, Lt-Col William Frederick, 1873–1948, vol. IV
Harvey, William Leathem, *died* 1910, vol. I
Harvey, Lt-Col William Lueg, 1858–1937, vol. III
Harvey Evers, Henry; *see* Evers.
Harvey-Gibson, Robert John, 1860–1929, vol. III
Harvey-Kelly, Captain Hubert Dunsterville; *see* Kelly.
Harvie Anderson, Margaret Betty; *see* Baroness Skrimshire.
Harvie-Brown, John A., 1844–1916, vol. II
Harward, Col Arthur John Netherton, 1867–1938, vol. III
Harward, Charles Cuthbert, 1866–1933, vol. III
Harward, Lt-Gen. Thomas Netherton, 1829–1908, vol. I
Harwood, Basil, 1859–1949, vol. IV
Harwood, Charles Auguste de Lotbinière-, 1869–1954, vol. V
Harwood, Sir Edmund George, *died* 1964, vol. VI
Harwood, George, 1845–1912, vol. I
Harwood, Harold Marsh, *died* 1959, vol. V
Harwood, Henry Cecil, 1893–1964, vol. VI
Harwood, Adm. Sir Henry Harwood, 1888–1950, vol. IV
Harwood, Henry William Forsyth, 1856–1923, vol. II
Harwood, John Augustus, 1845–1929, vol. III
Harwood, Sir John James, 1832–1906, vol. I
Harwood, Sir Ralph Endersby, 1883–1951, vol. V
Hasan, Saiyid Ahmad, 1873–1936, vol. III
Haselden, Rev. John, 1854–1937, vol. III
Haselden, William Kerridge, 1872–1953, vol. V
Haselfoot, Captain Francis Edmund Blechynden, 1885–1938, vol. III
Hasell, Edward William, 1888–1972, vol. VII
Hasell, Rev. George Edmund, 1847–1932, vol. III
Haseltine, Herbert, 1877–1962, vol. VI
Haskard, Brig.-Gen. John McDougall, 1877–1967, vol. VI
Haskell, Arnold Lionel, 1903–1980, vol. VII
Haskell, Harold Noad, 1887–1955, vol. V
Haskell, Jacob Silas, 1857–1939, vol. III
Haskett-Smith, W. P.; *see* Smith.
Haskins, Charles Homer, 1870–1937, vol. III
Haskins, M. Louise, 1875–1957, vol. V

Haslam, Sir Alfred Seale, 1844–1927, vol. II
Haslam, Henry Cobden, 1870–1948, vol. IV
Haslam, Hon. Lt-Col Sir Humphrey; *see* Haslam, Hon. Lt-Col Sir R. H.
Haslam, J., 1842–1913, vol. I
Haslam, James, *died* 1937, vol. III
Haslam, Sir John, 1878–1940, vol. III
Haslam, John Fearby Campbell, 1888–1955, vol. V
Haslam, Lewis, 1856–1922, vol. II
Haslam, Robert Heywood, 1878–1954, vol. V
Haslam, Hon. Lt-Col Sir (Robert) Humphrey, 1882–1962, vol. VI
Haslam, Rev. Samuel Holker, *died* 1922, vol. II
Haslam, William Frederick, *died* 1932, vol. III
Haslegrave, Lt-Col Henry John, 1871–1956, vol. V
Haslegrave, John Ramsden, 1913–1980, vol. VII
Haslehust, Ernest William, *died* 1949, vol. IV
Haslett, Dame Caroline, *died* 1957, vol. V
Haslett, Sir James Horner, 1832–1905, vol. I
Haslett, Very Rev. Thomas, *died* 1947, vol. IV
Haslett, Sir William John Handfield, 1866–1954, vol. V
Hasluck, Paul Nooncree, 1854–1931, vol. III
Hassall, Arthur, 1853–1930, vol. III
Hassall, Christopher Vernon, 1912–1963, vol. VI
Hassall, John, 1868–1948, vol. IV
Hassam, Childe, 1859–1935, vol. III
Hassanein, Sir Ahmed Mohamed Pasha, 1889–1946, vol. IV
Hassard, Sir John, 1831–1900, vol. I
Hassard, Rev. Richard Samuel, 1848–1921, vol. II
Hassard-Short, Adrian Hugh, 1879–1956, vol. V
Hassard-Short, Rev. Canon Frederick Winning, 1873–1953, vol. V
Hassé, Henry Ronald, 1884–1955, vol. V
Hasselkus, John William, 1874–1951, vol. V
Hasted, Col Arthur Walter, 1864–1937, vol. III
Hasted, Lt-Col John Ord Cobbold, 1890–1942, vol. IV
Hasted, Maj.-Gen. William Freke, 1897–1977, vol. VII
Hastie, Edward, 1876–1947, vol. IV
Hastie, William, 1842–1903, vol. I
Hastilow, Cyril Alexander Frederick, 1895–1975, vol. VII
Hastings, 20th Baron, 1857–1904, vol. I
Hastings, 21st Baron, 1882–1956, vol. V
Hastings, Marchioness of; (Florence Cecilia), 1842–1907, vol. I
Hastings, Adm. Alexander Plantagenet, 1843–1925, vol. II
Hastings, Anne Wilson, *died* 1975, vol. VII
Hastings, Basil Macdonald, 1881–1928, vol. II
Hastings, Charles Godolphin William, 1854–1920, vol. II
Hastings, Rev. Edward, 1890–1980, vol. VII
Hastings, Maj.-Gen. Edward Spence, 1856–1932, vol. III
Hastings, Maj.-Gen. Francis Eddowes, 1843–1915, vol. I
Hastings, Lt-Gen. Francis William, 1825–1914, vol. I
Hastings, Frank, 1869–1940, vol. III (A), vol. IV
Hastings, Rev. Frederick, 1838–1937, vol. III

Hastings, Col Sir George, 1853–1943, vol. IV
Hastings, Graham, 1830–1922, vol. II
Hastings, Rev. James, 1852–1922, vol. II
Hastings, Col John Henry, 1858–1940, vol. III
Hastings, Hon. Osmond William Toone Westenra, 1873–1933, vol. III
Hastings, Sir Patrick, 1880–1952, vol. V
Hastings, Paulyn Charles James Reginald Rawdon-, 1889–1915, vol. I (A)
Hastings, Hon. Paulyn Francis Cuthbert R.; *see* Rawdon-Hastings.
Hastings, Somerville, 1878–1967, vol. VI
Hastings, Thomas, 1860–1929, vol. III
Hastings, Lt-Col Wilfred Charles Norrington, 1873–1925, vol. II
Hastings, Col William Holland, 1884–1930, vol. III
Haston, Dougal, 1940–1977, vol. VII
Haswell, Brig. Chetwynd Henry, 1879–1956, vol. V
Haswell, Col John Francis, 1864–1949, vol. IV
Haswell, William A., 1854–1925, vol. II
Haszard, Col Gerald Fenwick, 1894–1967, vol. VI
Hatch, Sir Ernest Frederick George, 1st Bt, 1859–1927, vol. II
Hatch, Frederick Henry, 1864–1932, vol. III
Hatch, Lt-Col George Pelham, 1855–1923, vol. II
Hatch, George Washington, 1872–1963, vol. VI
Hatchard, Caroline, (Caroline Langford), 1883–1970, vol. VI
Hatchell, Maj.-Gen. George, 1838–1912, vol. I
Hatchell, Col Henry Melville, 1852–1933, vol. III
Hatchell, John, 1825–1902, vol. I
Hatcher, Captain James Olden, 1867–1936, vol. III
Hatfield, Rev. Cyril Northcote, 1882–1940, vol. III
Hatfield, Henry, 1854–1926, vol. II
Hatfield, William Herbert, 1882–1943, vol. IV
Hathaway, Frank John, *died* 1942, vol. IV
Hathaway, Maj.-Gen. Harold George, 1860–1942, vol. IV
Hathaway, Dame Sibyl Mary, *died* 1974, vol. VII
Hatherell, William, 1855–1928, vol. II
Hatherton, 3rd Baron, 1842–1930, vol. III
Hatherton, 4th Baron, 1868–1944, vol. IV
Hatherton, 5th Baron, 1900–1969, vol. VI
Hatherton, 6th Baron, 1906–1973, vol. VII
Hatt, Sir Harry Thomas, 1858–1934, vol. III
Hatten, Rev. Preb. John Charles Le Pelley, 1875–1943, vol. IV
Hattersley, Alan Frederick, 1893–1976, vol. VII
Hatton, Brig.-Gen. Edward Heneage F.; *see* Finch Hatton.
Hatton, Edwin Fullarton, 1858–1940, vol. III
Hatton, Frank, 1921–1978, vol. VII
Hatton, George, 1849–1933, vol. III
Hatton, Maj.-Gen. George Seton, 1899–1974, vol. VII
Hatton, Hon. Harold F.; *see* Finch-Hatton.
Hatton, John Leigh Smeathman, 1865–1933, vol. III
Hatton, Joseph, 1841–1907, vol. I
Hatton, Richard George, 1864–1926, vol. II
Hatton, Sir Ronald George, 1886–1965, vol. VI
Hatton, Maj.-Gen. Villiers, 1852–1914, vol. I
Hatzfeldt, Prince Francis (Edmond Joseph Gabriel Vit), 1853–1910, vol. I

Hatzfeldt-Wildenburg, Count Paul von, 1831–1901, vol. I
Hauff, Mrs Janet Alderson, 1913–1973, vol. VII
Haugh, Hon. Kevin O'Hanrahan, 1901–1969, vol. VI
Haughton, Benjamin, 1865–1924, vol. II
Haughton, Maj.-Gen. Henry Lawrence, 1883–1955, vol. V
Haughton, Lt-Col Henry Wilfred, 1862–1931, vol. III
Haughton, Col Samuel George Steele, 1883–1956, vol. V
Haughton, Col Samuel Gillmor, 1889–1959, vol. V
Haulfryn Williams, John; see Williams.
Haultain, Hon. Sir Frederick William Gordon, 1857–1942, vol. IV
Haultain, Herbert Edward Terrick, 1869–1961, vol. VI
Haupt, Paul, 1858–1926, vol. II
Hauptmann, Gerhart, 1862–1946, vol. IV
Haussonville, Othenin Bernard Gabrielle de Cleron, Comte d', died 1924, vol. II
Havard, Sir Godfrey Thomas, 1885–1952, vol. V
Havard, Rt Rev. William Thomas, 1889–1956, vol. V
Havell, Ernest B., 1861–1934, vol. III
Havelock, Sir Arthur Elibank, 1844–1908, vol. I
Havelock, Eric Henry Edwardes, 1891–1974, vol. VII
Havelock, Sir Thomas Henry, 1877–1968, vol. VI
Havelock-Allan, Sir Henry Marshman, 1st Bt, 1830–1897, vol. I
Havelock-Allan, Sir Henry Ralph Moreton, 3rd Bt, 1899–1975, vol. VII
Havelock-Allan, Sir Henry Spencer Moreton, 2nd Bt, 1872–1953, vol. V
Havenga, Hon. Nicolaas Christiaan, died 1957, vol. V
Haverfield, Francis John, 1860–1919, vol. II
Havers, Sir Cecil Robert, 1889–1977, vol. VII
Havers, Air Vice-Marshal Sir E. William, 1887–1979, vol. VII
Havers, Air Vice-Marshal Sir William; see Havers, Air Vice-Marshal Sir E. W.
Haversham, 1st Baron, 1835–1917, vol. II
Haviland, Rev. Edmund Arthur, 1874–1966, vol. VI
Haviland, Ven. Francis Ernest, died 1945, vol. IV
Havinden, Ashley Eldrid, 1903–1973, vol. VII
Haward, Edwin, 1884–1961, vol. VI
Haward, Sir Harry Edwin, 1863–1953, vol. V
Haward, J. Warrington, 1841–1921, vol. II
Haward, Lawrence, 1878–1957, vol. V
Haward, Sir Walter, 1882–1959, vol. VI
Hawarden, 5th Viscount, 1842–1908, vol. I
Hawarden, 6th Viscount, 1890–1914, vol. I
Hawarden, 7th Viscount, 1877–1958, vol. V
Haweis, Rev. Hugh Reginald, 1838–1901, vol. I
Hawes, Albert G. S., died 1897, vol. I
Hawes, Alexander Travers, 1851–1924, vol. II
Hawes, Col Benjamin Reddie, 1854–1941, vol. IV
Hawes, Charles George, 1890–1963, vol. VI
Hawes, Sir Richard Brunel, 1893–1964, vol. VI
Hawes, Sir Ronald N.; see Nesbitt-Hawes.

Hawgood, John Arkas, 1905–1971, vol. VII
Hawk, William, 1851–1944, vol. IV
Hawke, 7th Baron, 1860–1938, vol. III
Hawke, 8th Baron, 1873–1939, vol. III
Hawke, Sir Anthony; see Hawke, Sir E. A.
Hawke, Sir Anthony; see Hawke, Sir J. A.
Hawke, Sir (Edward) Anthony, 1895–1964, vol. VI
Hawke, John, 1846–1932, vol. III
Hawke, Sir (John) Anthony, 1869–1941, vol. IV
Hawke, Adm. Hon. Stanhope, 1863–1936, vol. III
Hawke-Genn, Captain Otto Hermann, 1875–1955, vol. V
Hawken, Rev. Charles Sydney, 1862–1930, vol. III
Hawken, Roger William Hercules, 1878–1947, vol. IV
Hawker, Brig.-Gen. Claude Julian, 1867–1936, vol. III
Hawker, Sqdn Comdr Lanoe George, 1890–1916, vol. II
Hawker, Mary Elizabeth, 1848–1908, vol. I
Hawkes, Arthur John, 1885–1952, vol. V
Hawkes, Charles John, 1880–1953, vol. V
Hawkes, Lt-Col Charles Pascoe, 1877–1956, vol. V
Hawkes, Lt-Col Corlis St Leger Gillman, 1871–1963, vol. VI
Hawkes, Frederic Clare, 1892–1974, vol. VII
Hawkes, Rt Rev. Frederick Ochterloney Taylor, 1878–1966, vol. VI
Hawkes, Maj.-Gen. Sir Henry Montague Pakington, 1855–1946, vol. IV
Hawkes, Lt-Gen. Henry Philip, 1834–1900, vol. I
Hawkes, Ven. Leonard Stephen, 1907–1969, vol. VI
Hawkes, Captain William Arthur, 1881–1962, vol. VI
Hawkesworth, Sir (Edward) Gerald, died 1949, vol. IV
Hawkesworth, Geoffrey, 1904–1969, vol. VI
Hawkesworth, Sir Gerald; see Hawkesworth, Sir E. G.
Hawkesworth, Lt-Gen. Sir John Ledlie Inglis, 1893–1945, vol. IV
Hawkesworth, Rear-Adm. Richard Arthur, 1890–1968, vol. VI
Hawkey, Sir (Alfred) James, 1st Bt, 1877–1952, vol. V
Hawkey, Sir James; see Hawkey, Sir A. J.
Hawkey, Sir Roger Pryce, 2nd Bt, 1905–1975, vol. VII
Hawkins, Maj.-Gen. Alexander Caesar, 1823–1916, vol. II
Hawkins, Sir Anthony Hope, 1863–1933, vol. III
Hawkins, Arthur Vernon, died 1933, vol. III
Hawkins, Sir Benjamin, 1867–1930, vol. III
Hawkins, Brian Charles Keith, 1900–1962, vol. VI
Hawkins, Charles Caesar, 1864–1938, vol. III
Hawkins, Maj.-Gen. Edward Brian Barkley, died 1966, vol. VI
Hawkins, Rev. Edwards Comerford, 1827–1906, vol. I
Hawkins, Francis Henry, 1863–1936, vol. III
Hawkins, Adm. Sir Geoffrey Alan Brooke, 1895–1980, vol. VII

Hawkins, Maj.-Gen. George Ledsam Seymour, 1898–1978, vol. VII
Hawkins, Major Henry, 1876–1930, vol. III
Hawkins, Herbert Leader, 1887–1968, vol. VI
Hawkins, Herbert Pennell, 1859–1940, vol. III
Hawkins, Jack, 1910–1973, vol. VII
Hawkins, Rev. Sir John Caesar, 4th Bt, 1837–1929, vol. III
Hawkins, Sir John Scott Caesar, 5th Bt, 1875–1939, vol. III
Hawkins, Ven. John Stanley, 1903–1965, vol. VI
Hawkins, Leonard Cecil, 1897–1974, vol. VII
Hawkins, Sir Michael Babington Charles, 1914–1977, vol. VII
Hawkins, Percy, 1870–1949, vol. IV
Hawkins, Reginald Thomas, 1888–1978, vol. VII
Hawkins, Col Thomas Henry, 1873–1944, vol. IV
Hawkins, Sir Villiers Geoffry Caesar, 6th Bt, 1890–1955, vol. V
Hawkins, Col Walter Francis, 1856–1936, vol. III
Hawkins, Lt-Col William, 1861–1932, vol. III
Hawkins, William Francis Spencer, 1896–1979, vol. VII
Hawks, Ellison, 1889–1971, vol. VII
Hawkshaw, J. C., 1841–1921, vol. II
Hawksley, Dorothy Webster, 1884–1970, vol. VI
Hawksley, Ernest B., died 1931, vol. III
Hawksley, Vice-Adm. James Rose Price, died 1955, vol. V
Hawksley, Brig.-Gen. Randal Plunkett Taylor, 1870–1961, vol. VI
Hawksley, Richard Walter Benson, 1915–1976, vol. VII
Hawksworth, Frederick William, 1884–1976, vol. VII
Hawksworth, William Thomas Martin, died 1935, vol. III
Hawley, Arthur, 1870–1952, vol. V
Hawley, Rev. Charles Cusac, 1851–1914, vol. I
Hawley, Sir Henry Cusack Wingfield, 6th Bt, 1876–1923, vol. II
Hawley, Sir Henry James, 4th Bt, 1815–1898, vol. I
Hawley, Sir Henry Michael, 5th Bt, 1848–1909, vol. I
Hawley, Maj.-Gen. William Hanbury, 1829–1917, vol. II
Hawley, Willis Chatman, 1864–1941, vol. IV
Haworth, Sir Arthur Adlington, 1st Bt, 1865–1944, vol. IV
Haworth, Rev. James, 1853–1942, vol. IV
Haworth, James, 1896–1976, vol. VII
Haworth, Lt-Col Sir Lionel Berkeley Holt, 1873–1951, vol. V
Haworth, Sir Norman; see Haworth, Sir W. N.
Haworth, Peter, 1891–1956, vol. V
Haworth, Sir (Walter) Norman, 1883–1950, vol. IV
Haworth, Very Rev. William, 1880–1960, vol. V
Haworth-Booth, Rear-Adm. Sir Francis Fitzgerald, 1864–1935, vol. III
Hawtayne, George Hammond, 1832–1902, vol. I
Hawtayne, Lionel Edward, died 1920, vol. II
Hawthorn, Maj.-Gen. Douglas Cyril, 1897–1974, vol. VII

Hawthorn, Bt-Col Frank, died 1931, vol. III
Hawthorn, Brig.-Gen. George Montague Philip, 1873–1945, vol. IV
Hawthorne, Julian, 1846–1934, vol. III
Hawtrey, Sir Charles, 1858–1923, vol. II
Hawtrey, Brig. Henry Courtenay, 1882–1961, vol. VI
Hawtrey, Air Vice-Marshal John Gosset, 1901–1954, vol. V
Hawtrey, Sir Ralph George, 1879–1975, vol. VII
Hay, Alfred, 1866–1932, vol. III
Hay, Hon. Alistair George, 1861–1929, vol. III
Hay, Major Hon. Arthur, 1855–1932, vol. III
Hay, Maj.-Gen. Arthur Kenneth, died 1949, vol. IV
Hay, Lt-Col Arthur Sidney, 1879–1940, vol. III
Hay, Athole S., 1861–1933, vol. III
Hay, Sir Bache McEvers Athole, 11th Bt (cr 1635), 1892–1966, vol. VI
Hay, Charles Edward Norman L.; see Leith-Hay.
Hay, Maj.-Gen. Charles John Bruce, 1877–1940, vol. III
Hay, Sir Charles John D.; see Dalrymple Hay.
Hay, Hon. Claude George Drummond, died 1920, vol. II
Hay, Clifford Henderson, 1878–1949, vol. IV
Hay, Sir David Allan, 1878–1957, vol. V
Hay, Douglas, died 1949, vol. IV
Hay, Sir Duncan Edwyn, 10th Bt (cr 1635), 1882–1965, vol. VI
Hay, Ven. Edgar, 1863–1949, vol. IV
Hay, Sir Edward, 9th Bt (cr 1703), 1870–1936, did not prove his succession or use the title, and did not have an entry in Who's Who.
Hay, Lord Edward Douglas John, 1888–1944, vol. IV
Hay, Maj.-Gen. Edward Owen, 1846–1946, vol. IV
Hay, Francis Edward Drummond-, 1868–1943, vol. IV
Hay, Sir Francis Ringler Drummond-, 1830–1905, vol. I
Hay, Francis Stuart, 1863–1928, vol. II
Hay, George, died 1912, vol. I
Hay, Col Sir George Jackson, 1840–1921, vol. II
Hay, Col George Lennox, 1873–1946, vol. IV
Hay, Sir Harley Hugh D.; see Dalrymple-Hay.
Hay, Sir Hector Maclean, 7th Bt (cr 1703), 1821–1916, vol. II
Hay, Henry Hanby, 1849–1940, vol. III
Hay, Ian; see Beith, Maj.-Gen. J. H.
Hay, Col James, 1842–1915, vol. I (A)
Hay, Col James Adam Gordon Richardson-Drummond-, 1863–1928, vol. II
Hay, Col James Charles Edward, 1889–1975, vol. VII
Hay, Sir James Lawrence, 1888–1971, vol. VII
Hay, James Paterson, 1863–1925, vol. II
Hay, Brig.-Gen. James Reginald Maitland Dalrymple, 1858–1924, vol. II
Hay, Sir James Shaw, 1839–1924, vol. II
Hay, Hon. Col John, 1838–1905, vol. I
Hay, Rt Hon. Lord John, 1827–1916, vol. II
Hay, John, 1873–1959, vol. V
Hay, John Arthur Machray, 1887–1960, vol. V

Hay, John Binny, 1870–1939, vol. III
Hay, Rt Hon. Sir John Charles Dalrymple, 3rd Bt (cr 1798), 1821–1912, vol. I
Hay, Sir John George, 1883–1964, vol. VI
Hay, Captain John Primrose, 1878–1949, vol. IV
Hay, Paymaster Rear-Adm. Kenneth Sydney, 1872–1932, vol. III
Hay, Col Leith, 1818–1900, vol. I
Hay, Sir Lewis John Erroll, 9th Bt (cr 1663), 1866–1923, vol. II
Hay of Seaton, Major Malcolm Vivian, 1881–1962, vol. VI
Hay, Lady Margaret Katharine, 1918–1975, vol. VII
Hay, Marie, 1873–1938, vol. III
Hay, Mrs Mary Verena Campbell, 1875–1940, vol. III
Hay, Matthew, 1855–1932, vol. III
Hay, Noel Grant, 1910–1974, vol. VII
Hay, Peter Alexander, 1866–1952, vol. V
Hay, Lt-Gen. Sir Robert, 1889–1980, vol. VII
Hay, Sir Robert Hay-Drummond-, 1846–1926, vol. II
Hay, Lt-Gen. Sir Robert John, 1828–1910, vol. I
Hay, Rt Rev. Robert Milton, 1884–1973, vol. VII
Hay, Rt Rev. Robert Snowdon, 1867–1943, vol. IV
Hay, Brig. Ronald Bruce, 1887–1961, vol. VI
Hay, Lt-Col Sir Rupert; see Hay, Lt-Col Sir W. R.
Hay, Stephen Moffatt, 1857–1943, vol. IV
Hay, Thomas, died 1953, vol. V
Hay, Lt-Col Thomas William, 1882–1956, vol. V
Hay, Col Westwood Norman, 1871–1946, vol. IV
Hay, Will, 1888–1949, vol. IV
Hay, Sir William Archibald Dalrymple, 4th Bt (cr 1798), 1851–1929, vol. III
Hay, William Gosse, 1875–1945, vol. IV
Hay, Sir William Henry, 8th Bt (cr 1703), 1867–1927, vol. II (A), vol. IV
Hay, Lt-Col Sir (William) Rupert, 1893–1962, vol. VI
Hay-Dinwoody, Very Rev. Leofric Matthews, 1868–1936, vol. III
Hay-Drummond, Arthur William Henry, 1862–1953, vol. V
Hay-Drummond, Col Hon. Charles Rowley, 1836–1918, vol. II
Hay-Drummond-Hay, Sir Robert; see Hay.
Hay-Newton, Francis John Stuart, 1843–1913, vol. I
Hayashi, Gonsuke, 1861–1939, vol. III
Hayashi, Count Tadasu, 1850–1913, vol. I
Haycock, Alexander Wilkinson, 1882–1970, vol. VI
Haycock, Rev. Trevitt Reginald H.; see Hine-Haycock.
Haycock, Col Vaughan Randolph H.; see Hine-Haycock.
Haycraft, John Berry, died 1922, vol. II
Haycraft, John Berry, 1888–1969, vol. VI
Haycraft, Sir Thomas Wagstaffe, died 1936, vol. III
Hayday, Arthur, 1869–1956, vol. V
Hayden, Arthur, 1868–1946, vol. IV
Hayden, Sir Henry Hubert, 1869–1923, vol. II
Hayden, John Patrick, 1863–1954, vol. V
Hayden, Luke Patrick, 1850–1897, vol. I

Hayden, Mary Teresa, died 1942, vol. IV
Hayden, Most Rev. William, 1868–1936, vol. III
Haydn Williams, Benjamin, 1902–1965, vol. VI
Haydon, Dame Anne, 1892–1966, vol. VI
Haydon, Arthur Lincoln, 1872–1954, vol. V
Haydon, Maj.-Gen. Joseph Charles, 1899–1970, vol. VI
Haydon, Thomas Edmett, died 1952, vol. V
Haydon-Lewis, Jack; see Lewis.
Hayes, Alfred, 1857–1936, vol. III
Hayes, Rev. Arthur Herbert, 1850–1933, vol. III
Hayes, Surg.-Lt-Col Aylmer Ellis, 1850–1900, vol. I
Hayes, Cdre Sir Bertram Fox, 1864–1941, vol. IV
Hayes, Carlton Joseph Huntley, 1882–1964, vol. VI
Hayes, Claude, vol. II
Hayes, Sir Edmund Francis, 5th Bt, 1850–1912, vol. I
Hayes, Edwin, died 1904, vol. I
Hayes, Lt-Col Edwin Charles, 1868–1942, vol. IV
Hayes, Maj.-Gen. Eric Charles, 1896–1951, vol. V
Hayes, Rev. Francis Carlile, died 1931, vol. III
Hayes, Frederick William, 1848–1918, vol. II
Hayes, Gerald Ravenscourt, 1889–1955, vol. V
Hayes, Gertrude, (Mrs E. M. Betts), 1872–1956, vol. V
Hayes, Hugh, died 1928, vol. II (A), vol. III
Hayes, Rt Rev. James Thomas, 1847–1904, vol. I
Hayes, John, vol. II
Hayes, Hon. John Blyth, 1868–1956, vol. V
Hayes, John Henry, 1889–1941, vol. IV
Hayes, Lt-Col Joseph, 1864–1944, vol. IV
Hayes, Maurice Richard Joseph, died 1930, vol. III
Hayes, Michael, 1889–1976, vol. VII
Hayes, His Eminence Patrick Cardinal, 1867–1938, vol. III
Hayes, Very Rev. Richard, 1854–1938, vol. III
Hayes, Robert Edward, 1869–1931, vol. III
Hayes, Lt-Col Robert Hall, 1867–1946, vol. IV
Hayes, Rt Rev. Romuald, 1892–1945, vol. IV
Hayes, Thomas Crawford, died 1909, vol. I
Hayes, Brig.-Gen. Wade Hampton, 1879–1956, vol. V
Hayes, Captain William, 1891–1918, vol. II
Hayes, William, 1855–1940, vol. III
Hayford, John Fillmore, 1868–1925, vol. II (A), vol. III
Haygarth, Col Sir Joseph Henry, 1892–1969, vol. VI
Haygarth Jackson, Harold; see Jackson.
Hayhurst, William Hosken France-, 1873–1947, vol. IV
Hayhurst-France, Captain George Frederick Hayhurst, 1895–1940, vol. III
Hayler, Guy, 1850–1943, vol. IV
Hayley, Frederic Austin, 1881–1968, vol. VI
Hayman, Sir (Cecil George) Graham, 1893–1966, vol. VI
Hayman, Frank Harold, 1894–1966, vol. VI
Hayman, Sir Graham; see Hayman, Sir C. G. G.
Hayman, Rev. Henry, 1823–1904, vol. I
Hayman, Rev. Canon Henry Telford, 1853–1941, vol. IV

Hayman, Perceval Mills Cobham, 1883–1974, vol. VII
Hayman, Ven. Reginald John Edward, 1861–1927, vol. II
Hayman-Joyce, Maj.-Gen. Hayman John, 1897–1958, vol. V
Haymes, Lt-Col Robert Leycester, 1870–1942, vol. IV
Hayne, Louis Brightwell, 1869–1926, vol. II
Haynes, Col Alleyne, 1859–1938, vol. III
Haynes, Alwyn Sidney, 1878–1963, vol. VI
Haynes, Col Charles Edward, 1855–1935, vol. III
Haynes, Edmund Sidney Pollock, 1877–1949, vol. IV
Haynes, Brig.-Gen. Kenneth Edward, 1871–1944, vol. IV
Haynes, Richard Septimus, 1857–1922, vol. II
Haynes, Robert, 1920–1976, vol. VII
Haynes, Hon. Samuel Johnson, 1852–1932, vol. III
Haynes-Rudge, Mrs Florence, died 1934, vol. III
Haynes-Williams, John, died 1908, vol. I
Hays, Arthur Garfield, 1881–1954, vol. V
Hays, Very Rev. Francis, 1870–1943, vol. IV
Hays, Sir Marshall, 1872–1948, vol. IV
Hays, Will H., 1879–1954, vol. V
Haysom, Sir George, 1862–1924, vol. II
Hayter, 1st Baron, 1848–1946, vol. IV
Hayter, 2nd Baron, 1871–1967, vol. VI
Hayter, Harrison, 1825–1898, vol. I
Hayter, Rev. Harrison Goodenough, 1855–1934, vol. III
Hayter, Brig. Ross John Finnis, 1875–1929, vol. III
Hayter, Sir William Goodenough, 1869–1924, vol. II
Hayter, Rev. William Thomas Baring, 1858–1935, vol. III
Hayter Hames, Sir George Colvile, 1898–1968, vol. VI
Haythornthwaite, Rev. John Parker, 1862–1928, vol. II
Hayward, Alfred Robert, 1875–1971, vol. VII
Hayward, Arthur Canler, 1870–1945, vol. IV
Hayward, Arthur Lawrence, 1885–1967, vol. VI
Hayward, Rev. Edward, 1884–1974, vol. VII
Hayward, Sir Edwin James, 1868–1929, vol. III
Hayward, Lt-Col Edwyn Walton, died 1933, vol. III
Hayward, Evan, 1876–1958, vol. V
Hayward, Sir Fred, 1876–1944, vol. IV
Hayward, Frederick Edward Godfrey, 1893–1961, vol. VI
Hayward, Graham William, 1911–1976, vol. VII
Hayward, Maj.-Gen. Henry Blakeney, 1838–1930, vol. III
Hayward, Ven. Henry Rudge, died 1912, vol. I
Hayward, Ian Dudley, 1899–1964, vol. VI
Hayward, Sir Isaac James, 1884–1976, vol. VII
Hayward, John Davy, 1905–1965, vol. VI
Hayward, Marjorie Olive, 1885–1953, vol. V
Hayward, Sir Maurice Henry Weston, 1868–1964, vol. VI
Hayward, Lt-Col Reginald Frederick Johnson, died 1970, vol. VI
Hayward, Richard Frederick, 1879–1962, vol. VI

Hayward, Robert Baldwin, 1829–1903, vol. I
Hayward, Sidney Pascoe, 1896–1961, vol. VI
Hayward, Tom Christopher, 1904–1975, vol. VII
Hayward, William Thornborough, 1854–1928, vol. II
Hayward, Sir William Webb, 1818–1899, vol. I
Haywood, Col Austin Hubert Wightwick, died 1965, vol. VI
Haywood, Horace Mason, died 1942, vol. IV
Hazel, Alfred Ernest William, died 1944, vol. IV
Hazeldine, Evelyn Lilian; see Martinengo-Cesaresco, Countess.
Hazell, W. Howard, 1869–1929, vol. III
Hazell, Walter, died 1919, vol. II
Hazell, Captain William, 1857–1927, vol. II
Hazeltine, Harold Dexter, 1871–1960, vol. V
Hazelton, Maj.-Gen. Percy Orr, 1871–1952, vol. V
Hazen, Hon. Sir Douglas; see Hazen, Hon. Sir J. D.
Hazen, Hon. Sir (John) Douglas, 1860–1937, vol. III
Hazlehurst, Rev. George Arthur, 1873–1940, vol. III
Hazlehurst, Thomas Francis, died 1918, vol. II
Hazlerigg, 1st Baron, 1878–1949, vol. IV
Hazlerigg, Lt-Col Thomas, 1877–1935, vol. III
Hazlerigg, Maj.-Gen. Thomas Maynard, 1840–1915, vol. I (A)
Hazleton, Richard, 1880–1943, vol. IV
Hazlitt, William Carew, 1834–1913, vol. I
Head, Lt-Col Alfred Searle, 1874–1952, vol. V
Head, Lt-Col Arthur Edward Maxwell, 1876–1921, vol. II
Head, Barclay Vincent, 1844–1914, vol. I
Head, Lt-Col Charles Octavius, 1869–1952, vol. V
Head, Ernest, 1871–1923, vol. II
Head, Francis Somerville Cameron C.; see Cameron-Head.
Head, Most Rev. Frederick Waldegrave, 1874–1941, vol. IV
Head, Rev. Canon George Frederick, 1836–1912, vol. I
Head, George Herbert, died 1927, vol. II
Head, Sir Henry, 1861–1940, vol. III
Head, James C.; see Cameron-Head.
Head, John Joshua, 1838–1925, vol. II
Head, Leslie Charles B.; see Broughton-Head.
Head, Robert, died 1957, vol. V
Head, Sir Robert Garnett, 3rd Bt, 1845–1907, vol. I
Head, Sir (Robert Pollock) Somerville, 4th Bt, 1884–1924, vol. II
Head, Sir Somerville; see Head, Sir R. P. S.
Headfort, 4th Marquess of, 1878–1943, vol. IV
Headfort, 5th Marquess of, 1902–1960, vol. V
Heading, Sir James Alfred, 1884–1969, vol. VI (AII)
Headington, Arthur Hutton, 1878–1917, vol. II
Headington, Kenneth George John, 1898–1960, vol. V
Headlam, Rt Rev. Arthur Cayley, 1862–1947, vol. IV
Headlam, Rev. Arthur William, 1826–1909, vol. I
Headlam, Cecil, 1872–1934, vol. III

Headlam, Lt-Col Rt Hon. Sir Cuthbert Morley, 1st Bt, 1876–1964, vol. VI

Headlam, Captain Sir Edward James, 1873–1943, vol. IV

Headlam, Francis John, 1829–1908, vol. I

Headlam, Air Vice-Marshal Frank, 1914–1976, vol. VII

Headlam, Gerald Erskine, 1877–1954, vol. V

Headlam, Brig.-Gen. Hugh Roger, 1877–1955, vol. V

Headlam, Maj.-Gen. Sir John Emerson Wharton, 1864–1946, vol. IV

Headlam, Maurice Francis, 1873–1956, vol. V

Headlam, Rev. Canon Morley Lewis Caulfield, 1868–1953, vol. V

Headlam, Rev. Stewart Duckworth, died 1924, vol. II

Headlam, Walter George, 1866–1908, vol. I

Headlam-Morley, Sir James Wycliffe, 1863–1929, vol. III

Headland, Isaac Taylor, 1859–1942, vol. IV

Headland, John, 1840–1927, vol. II

Headley, 4th Baron, 1845–1913, vol. I

Headley, 5th Baron, 1855–1935, vol. III

Headley, 6th Baron, 1901–1969, vol. VI

Headley, Ven. Charles Theophilus, 1870–1930, vol. III

Headridge, David, 1869–1938, vol. III

Heaf, Frederick Roland George, 1894–1973, vol. VII

Heal, Sir Ambrose, 1872–1959, vol. V

Heald, Sir Benjamin Herbert, 1874–1940, vol. III

Heald, Charles Brehmer, 1882–1974, vol. VII

Heald, Edith Shackleton, died 1976, vol. VII

Heald, Henry Townley, 1904–1975, vol. VII

Heald, Nora Shackleton, died 1961, vol. VI

Heald, William, 1910–1980, vol. VII

Heale, Lt-Col Robert John Wingfield, 1876–1962, vol. VI

Healey, Col Charles, 1856–1939, vol. III

Healey, Sir Charles Edward Heley C.; see Chadwyck-Healey.

Healey, Col Coryndon William Rutherford, 1864–1953, vol. V

Healey, Sir Edward Randal C.; see Chadwyck-Healey.

Healey, Sir Gerald Edward C.; see Chadwyck-Healey.

Healey, Oliver Nowell C.; see Chadwyck-Healey.

Healy, Cahir, 1877–1970, vol. VI

Healy, Daniel, 1884–1962, vol. VI

Healy, Rev. George White, died 1943, vol. IV

Healy, Most Rev. John, 1841–1918, vol. II

Healy, Ven. John, 1850–1942, vol. IV

Healy, John Edward, died 1934, vol. III

Healy, Rt Rev. John F., 1900–1973, vol. VII

Healy, Maurice, 1859–1923, vol. II

Healy, Maurice, 1887–1943, vol. IV

Healy, Thomas Joseph, 1854–1925, vol. II

Healy, Timothy Michael, 1855–1931, vol. III

Hean, Hon. Alexander, 1859–1927, vol. II

Heane, Brig.-Gen. James, 1874–1954, vol. V

Heape, Walter, 1855–1929, vol. III

Heape, William Leslie, 1896–1972, vol. VII

Heard, Gerald; see Heard, H. F. G.

Heard, Henry Fitz Gerald, 1889–1971, vol. VII

Heard, Rev. Henry James, 1856–1931, vol. III

Heard, Adm. Hugh Lindsay Patrick, 1869–1954, vol. V

Heard, Brig. Leonard Ferguson, 1903–1976, vol. VII

Heard, Maj.-Gen. Richard, 1870–1950, vol. IV

Heard, Rev. Richard Grenville, died 1952, vol. V

Heard, Rev. William Augustus, 1847–1921, vol. II

Heard, His Eminence Cardinal William Theodore, 1884–1973, vol. VII

Hearle, Col Arthur Basset, 1884–1935, vol. III

Hearle, Francis Trounson, 1886–1965, vol. VI

Hearn, Sir Arthur Charles, 1877–1952, vol. V

Hearn, Col George William Richard, 1893–1973, vol. VII

Hearn, Col Sir Gordon Risley, 1871–1953, vol. V

Hearn, John Whitcombe, 1885–1968, vol. VI

Hearn, Lafcadio, 1850–1904, vol. I

Hearn, Rt Rev. Robert Thomas, died 1952, vol. V

Hearn, Sir Walter Risley, 1853–1930, vol. III

Hearne, Sir Hector, 1892–1962, vol. VI

Hearnshaw, Fossey John Cobb, 1869–1946, vol. IV

Hearson, Air Cdre John Glanville, 1883–1964, vol. VI

Hearst, Hon. Sir William Howard, 1864–1941, vol. IV

Hearst, William Randolph, 1863–1951, vol. V

Heartz, Hon. Frank Richard, 1871–1955, vol. V

Heaslett, Rt Rev. Samuel, 1875–1947, vol. IV

Heath, Albert Edward, 1887–1956, vol. V

Heath, Ambrose, 1891–1969, vol. VI

Heath, Archie Edward, 1887–1961, vol. VI

Heath, Arthur Douglas, died 1937, vol. III

Heath, Arthur Howard, 1856–1930, vol. III

Heath, Arthur Raymond, died 1943, vol. IV

Heath, Maj.-Gen. Sir Charles Ernest, 1854–1936, vol. III

Heath, Charles Joseph, 1856–1934, vol. III

Heath, Christopher, 1835–1905, vol. I

Heath, Cuthbert Eden, died 1939, vol. III

Heath, Col Edward, 1854–1927, vol. II

Heath, Col Edward Charles, 1873–1946, vol. IV

Heath, Francis George, 1843–1913, vol. I

Heath, Lt-Col Francis William, 1865–1936, vol. III

Heath, Sir Frank; see Heath, Sir H. F.

Heath, Col George Noah, 1881–1967, vol. VI

Heath, Maj.-Gen. Sir Gerard Moore, 1863–1929, vol. III

Heath, Maj.-Gen. Gerard William Egerton, 1897–1980, vol. VII

Heath, Harry Cecil, 1898–1972, vol. VII

Heath, Col Harry Heptinstall Rose, 1850–1922, vol. II

Heath, Sir (Henry) Frank, 1863–1946, vol. IV

Heath, Maj.-Gen. Henry Newport Charles, 1860–1915, vol. I

Heath, Adm. Sir Herbert Leopold, 1861–1954, vol. V

Heath, Sir James, 1st Bt, 1852–1942, vol. IV

Heath, Lt-Col John Macclesfield, 1843–1911, vol. I

Heath, Adm. Sir Leopold George, 1817–1907, vol. I

Heath, Lt-Gen. Sir Lewis Macclesfield, 1885–1954, vol. V

Heath, Robert Samuel, 1858–1931, vol. III

Heath, Brig.-Gen. Ronald Macclesfield, 1876–1942, vol. IV

Heath, Sir Thomas Little, 1861–1940, vol. III

Heath, Rear-Adm. William Andrew James, 1820–1903, vol. I

Heath-Caldwell, Maj.-Gen. Frederick Crofton, 1858–1945, vol. IV

Heath-Jones, Edgar, *died* 1949, vol. IV

Heathcoat-Amory, Sir Ian Murray Heathcoat, 2nd Bt; *see* Amory.

Heathcoat-Amory, Major Sir John, 3rd Bt; *see* Amory.

Heathcoat-Amory, Sir John Heathcoat, 1st Bt, 1829–1914, vol. I

Heathcote, Lt Alfred Spencer, *died* 1912, vol. I

Heathcote, Brig.-Gen. Charles Edensor, 1875–1947, vol. IV

Heathcote, Rt Rev. Sir Francis Cooke Caulfeild, 9th Bt, 1868–1961, vol. VI

Heathcote, Lt-Col Sir Gilbert Redvers, 8th Bt, 1854–1937, vol. III

Heathcote, John Norman, 1863–1946, vol. IV

Heathcote, Justinian Heathcote Edwards-, 1843–1928, vol. II

Heathcote, Sir Leonard Vyvyan, 10th Bt, 1885–1963, vol. VI

Heathcote, Reginald St Alban, 1888–1951, vol. V

Heathcote, Robert Evelyn Manners, 1884–1970, vol. VI

Heathcote, Rev. Sir William Arthur, 7th Bt, 1853–1924, vol. II

Heathcote, Sir William Perceval, 6th Bt, 1826–1903, vol. I

Heathcote-Drummond-Willoughby, Brig.-Gen. Hon. Charles Strathavon; *see* Willoughby.

Heathcote-Smith, Sir Clifford Edward, 1883–1963, vol. VI

Heathcote-Williams, Harold, 1896–1964, vol. VI

Heather, Very Rev. George Abraham, *died* 1907, vol. I

Heather, Henry James Shedlock, 1863–1939, vol. III (A), vol. IV

Heathershaw, James Thomas, 1871–1943, vol. IV

Heatley, David Playfair, 1867–1944, vol. IV

Heatly-Spencer, Col John, 1880–1946, vol. IV

Heaton, Sir Frederick; *see* Heaton, Sir J. F.

Heaton, Gwenllian Margaret, 1897–1979, vol. VII

Heaton, Herbert, 1890–1973, vol. VII

Heaton, Sir Herbert Henniker, 1880–1961, vol. VI

Heaton, Sir (John) Frederick, 1880–1949, vol. IV

Heaton, Sir John Henniker, 1st Bt, 1848–1914, vol. I

Heaton, Sir John Henniker, 2nd Bt, 1877–1963, vol. VI

Heaton, Sir (John Victor) Peregrine Henniker-, 3rd Bt, 1903–1971, vol. VII

Heaton, Sir Joseph John, 1860–1934, vol. III

Heaton, Joseph Rowland, 1881–1951, vol. V

Heaton, Sir Peregrine Henniker; *see* Heaton, Sir J. V. P. H.

Heaton, Raymond H.; *see* Henniker-Heaton.

Heaton, Rose Henniker, (Mrs Adrian Porter), 1884–1975, vol. VII

Heaton, Trevor Braby, 1886–1972, vol. VII

Heaton, William Haslam, *died* 1941, vol. IV

Heaton-Armstrong, Sir John Dunamace, 1888–1967, vol. VI

Heaton-Armstrong, William Charles, 1853–1917, vol. II

Heaton-Ellis, Lt-Col Sir Charles Henry Brabazon, 1864–1945, vol. IV

Heaton-Ellis, Vice-Adm. Sir Edward Henry Fitzhardinge, 1868–1943, vol. IV

Heaven, Rev. Hudson Grosett, 1826–1916, vol. II

Heaven, Joseph Robert, 1840–1911, vol. I

Heaviside, Arthur West, 1844–1923, vol. II

Heaviside, Oliver, *died* 1925, vol. II

Heawood, Edward, 1863–1949, vol. IV

Heawood, Percy John, 1861–1955, vol. V

Hebb, Rev. Harry Arthur, 1850–1934, vol. III

Hebb, Sir John Harry, 1878–1942, vol. IV

Hebb, R. G., *died* 1918, vol. II

Hebblethwaite, Percival, 1849–1922, vol. II

Hebden, George Brentnall, 1886–1968, vol. VI

Hebel, John William, 1891–1934, vol. III

Heber-Percy, Algernon; *see* Percy.

Heberden, Charles Buller, 1849–1921, vol. II

Heberden, Surg. Captain George Alfred, 1860–1916, vol. II

Heberden, William Buller, 1838–1922, vol. II

Hebert, Godfrey Taunton, *died* 1957, vol. V

Hebert, Louis Philippe, 1850–1917, vol. II

Hebrard, Emile A., 1862–1927, vol. II

Hechle, James Herbert, 1864–1935, vol. III

Heckstall-Smith, Major Brooke, 1869–1944, vol. IV

Heckstall-Smith, Hugh William, 1896–1973, vol. VII

Hector, Annie, (Mrs Alexander), 1825–1902, vol. I

Hector, Sir James, 1834–1907, vol. I

Hedderwick, Arthur Stuart, 1885–1939, vol. III

Hedderwick, Edwin Charles, 1850–1935, vol. III

Hedderwick, Thomas Charles Hunter, 1850–1918, vol. II

Hedgcock, Frank Arthur, 1875–1954, vol. V

Hedgcock, Walter W., *died* 1932, vol. III

Hedgeland, Rev. Philip, 1825–1911, vol. I

Hedges, Alfred Paget, 1867–1929, vol. III

Hedges, Frederick Albert M.; *see* Mitchell-Hedges.

Hedges, John, 1847–1934, vol. III

Hedges, Killingworth, *died* 1945, vol. IV

Hedges, Brig. Killingworth Michael Fentham, 1890–1969, vol. VI

Hedges, Robert Yorke, 1903–1963, vol. VI

Hedges, Sidney George, 1897–1974, vol. VII

Hedin, Sven Anders, 1865–1952, vol. V

Hedley, Col Sir Coote; *see* Hedley, Col Sir W. C.

Hedley, John, 1834–1916, vol. II

Hedley, Rt Rev. John Cuthbert, 1837–1915, vol. I (A)

Hedley, John Prescott, 1876–1957, vol. V

Hedley, Lt-Col John Ralph, 1871–1917, vol. II

Hedley, Ralph, 1851–1913, vol. I

Hedley, Maj.-Gen. Robert Cecil Osborne, 1900–1973, vol. VII

Hedley, Walter, 1879–1951, vol. V
Hedley, Col Sir (Walter) Coote, 1865–1937, vol. III
Hedley-Whyte, Angus, 1897–1971, vol. VII
Hedstrom, Sir (John) Maynard, 1872–1951, vol. V
Hedstrom, Sir Maynard; see Hedstrom, Sir J. M.
Hedworth, Rev. Thomas, died 1950, vol. IV
Heelis, Frederick, 1868–1930, vol. III
Heenan, His Eminence Cardinal John Carmel, 1905–1975, vol. VII
Heenan, Sir Joseph William Allan, 1888–1951, vol. V
Heenan, Hon. Peter, 1875–1948, vol. IV
Heeney, Arnold Danford Patrick, 1902–1970, vol. VI
Heffernan, Sir John Harold, 1834–1921, vol. II
Heffernan, Col Nesbitt Breillat, 1861–1930, vol. III
Hegan, Col Edward, 1855–1922, vol. II
Hegarty, Sir Daniel, 1849–1914, vol. I
Hegedus, Ferencz, 1881–1944, vol. IV
Heger, Paul, 1846–1925, vol. II
Heger, Robert, 1886–1978, vol. VII
Heggs, Gordon Barrett M.; see Mitchell-Heggs.
Hehir, Maj.-Gen. Sir Patrick, 1859–1937, vol. III
Heidegger, Martin, 1889–1976, vol. VII
Heidenstam, Karl Gustaf Verner von, 1859–1940, vol. III
Heilbron, Sir Ian, 1886–1959, vol. V
Heilbronn, Hans Arnold, 1908–1975, vol. VII
Heilbuth, George Henry, died 1942, vol. IV
Heilgers, Lt-Col Frank Frederick Alexander, 1892–1944, vol. IV
Heilpern, Godfrey, 1911–1973, vol. VII
Heinemann, William, 1863–1920, vol. II
Heinz, Howard, 1877–1941, vol. IV
Heisenberg, Werner, 1901–1976, vol. VII
Heiser, Rev. Canon F. B., died 1952, vol. V
Heiser, Victor George, 1873–1972, vol. VII
Heitland, M. (Margaret), 1860–1938, vol. III
Heitner, H. Jesse, 1893–1965, vol. VI
Hektoen, Ludvig, 1863–1951, vol. V
Helbert, Lt-Col Geoffrey Gladstone, died 1934, vol. III
Helder, Augustus, 1827–1906, vol. I
Hele, Thomas Shirley, 1881–1953, vol. V
Hele-Shaw, Henry Selby, 1854–1941, vol. IV
Helfrich, Adm. Conrad Emile Lambert, 1886–1962, vol. VI
Hellard, Frederick, 1850–1925, vol. II
Hellard, Col Robert Charles, 1851–1929, vol. III
Heller, Hans, 1905–1974, vol. VII
Heller, J. H. S.; see Heller, Hans.
Helleu, Paul-César, 1859–1927, vol. II
Hellier, John Banjamin, died 1924, vol. II
Hellings, Robert Bailey, 1863–1947, vol. IV
Hellins, Rev. Edgar William James, 1872–1946, vol. IV
Helliwell, Maj.-Gen. John Percival, 1884–1948, vol. IV
Hellmuth, Rt Rev. Isaac, 1820–1901, vol. I
Helm, Sir (Alexander) Knox, 1893–1964, vol. VI
Helm, Rev. George Francis, 1882–1958, vol. V
Helm, Henry James, 1839–1918, vol. II
Helm, Sir Knox; see Helm, Sir A. K.
Helm, William Henry, 1860–1936, vol. III

Helme, Sir Norval Watson, 1849–1932, vol. III
Helmer, Col Richard Alexis, 1864–1920, vol. II
Helmore, Sir James Reginald Carroll, 1906–1972, vol. VII
Helmore, Hon. Air Cdre William, 1894–1964, vol. VI
Helmsley, Viscountess; (Muriel), died 1925, vol. II
Helps, Rev. Canon Arthur Leonard, 1872–1960, vol. V
Helsby, Baron (Life Peer); Laurence Norman Helsby, 1908–1978, vol. VII
Helsham, Rev. Edward, 1891–1955, vol. V
Hely, Air Vice-Marshal William Lloyd, 1909–1970, vol. VI (AII)
Hely-Hutchinson, Christopher Douglas, 1885–1958, vol. V
Hely-Hutchinson, Maurice Robert, 1887–1961, vol. VI
Hely-Hutchinson, May, (Hon. Lady Hely-Hutchinson), died 1938, vol. III
Hely-Hutchinson, Victor, 1901–1947, vol. IV
Hely-Hutchinson, Rt Hon. Sir Walter Francis, 1849–1913, vol. I
Helyar, Brig.-Gen. Arthur Beaumont, 1858–1933, vol. III
Helyar, Lt-Comdr Kenneth Cary, 1887–1941, vol. IV
Hembry, Henry William McQuitty, 1903–1961, vol. VI
Hemeon, Clarence Reid, 1897–1953, vol. V
Heming, George Booth, 1858–1938, vol. III
Heming, Captain Thomas Henry, 1856–1932, vol. III
Hemingford, 1st Baron, 1869–1947, vol. IV
Hemingway, Charles Robert, 1860–1947, vol. IV
Hemingway, Ernest, 1898–1961, vol. VI
Hemingway, Sir William, 1880–1967, vol. VI
Hemmant, George, 1880–1964, vol. VI
Hemmerde, Edward George, 1871–1948, vol. IV
Hemming, (Arthur) Francis, 1893–1964, vol. VI
Hemming, Sir Augustus William Lawson, 1841–1907, vol. I
Hemming, Gen. Edward Hughes, 1860–1943, vol. IV
Hemming, Francis; see Hemming, A. F.
Hemming, Maj.-Gen. Frederick Wilson, 1850–1934, vol. III
Hemming, G. W., 1821–1905, vol. I
Hemming, Rev. George, 1859–1931, vol. III
Hemming, Lt-Col Henry Harold, 1893–1976, vol. VII
Hemming, Col Norman Mackenzie, 1868–1950, vol. IV
Hemming, Maj.-Gen. William Edward Gordon, 1899–1953, vol. V
Hempel, Frieda, died 1955, vol. V
Hemphill, 1st Baron, 1821–1908, vol. I
Hemphill, 2nd Baron, 1853–1919, vol. II
Hemphill, 3rd Baron, 1860–1930, vol. III
Hemphill, 4th Baron, 1901–1957, vol. III
Hemphill, Major Robert, 1888–1935, vol. III
Hemphill, Ven. Samuel, 1859–1927, vol. II
Hemsley, William, 1817–1906, vol. I

Hemsley, William Botting, 1843–1924, vol. II
Hemsted, Captain John Rustat, 1881–1953, vol. V
Hemsted, Rupert William, 1876–1952, vol. V
Hemy, Charles Napier, 1841–1917, vol. II
Hench, Philip Showalter, 1896–1965, vol. VI
Henchley, Lt-Col Albert Richard, died 1938, vol. III
Henchmen, Hereward Humfry, 1874–1939, vol. III
Henderson of Ardwick, 1st Baron, died 1950, vol. IV
Henderson, Acheson Thompson, died 1909, vol. I
Henderson, Sir Alan Gerald Russell, 1886–1963, vol. VI
Henderson, Rev. Alexander, died 1937, vol. III
Henderson, Alexander, 1914–1954, vol. V
Henderson, Alexander Edward, 1844–1906, vol. I
Henderson, Rev. Alexander Roy, 1862–1950, vol. IV
Henderson, Amos, 1864–1922, vol. II
Henderson, Col Andrew, 1867–1951, vol. V
Henderson, Andrew Graham, 1882–1963, vol. VI
Henderson, Ann, 1921–1976, vol. VII
Henderson, Rev. Archibald, 1837–1927, vol. II
Henderson, Archibald, 1886–1962, vol. VI
Henderson, Archibald, 1877–1963, vol. VI
Henderson, Arthur; see Baron Rowley.
Henderson, Rt Hon. Arthur, 1863–1935, vol. III
Henderson, Arthur Edward, 1870–1956, vol. V
Henderson, Bernard William, 1871–1929, vol. III
Henderson, Brig.-Gen. Sir Brodie Haldane, 1869–1936, vol. III
Henderson, Charles Alexander, 1882–1956, vol. V
Henderson, Sir Charles James, 1882–1974, vol. VII
Henderson, Charles Lamond, 1896–1966, vol. VI
Henderson, Lt-Gen. Sir David, 1862–1921, vol. II
Henderson, Sir David Kennedy, 1884–1965, vol. VI
Henderson, David Patrick, 1865–1931, vol. III
Henderson, David Willis Wilson, 1903–1968, vol. VI
Henderson, Duncan, 1870–1934, vol. III
Henderson, Very Rev. Edward Lowry, 1873–1947, vol. IV
Henderson, Effie; see Albanesi, Mme.
Henderson, Hon. Eric Brand B.; see Butler-Henderson.
Henderson, Comdr Francis Barkley, 1859–1934, vol. III
Henderson, Vice-Adm. Frank Hannam, 1850–1918, vol. II
Henderson, Frank Young, 1894–1966, vol. VI
Henderson, Sir Frederick Ness, 1862–1944, vol. IV
Henderson, Col George Burton, 1890–1940, vol. III
Henderson, George Cockburn, 1870–1944, vol. II
Henderson, Very Rev. George David, 1888–1957, vol. V
Henderson, Col George Frances Robert, died 1903, vol. I
Henderson, George Gerald, 1862–1942, vol. IV
Henderson, Sir George Henry, 1889–1958, vol. V
Henderson, George Hugh, 1892–1949, vol. IV
Henderson, Adm. George Morris, died 1915, vol. I
Henderson, George William, 1854–1934, vol. III
Henderson, Lt-Col Hon. Harold Greenwood, 1875–1922, vol. II

Henderson, Col Harry Dalton, 1858–1945, vol. IV
Henderson, Hector Bruce, 1895–1962, vol. VI
Henderson, Dame Henrietta Caroline, (Lady Henderson), died 1959, vol. V
Henderson, Lt-Col Henry Cockcroft P.; see Page-Henderson.
Henderson, Henry Ludwig, 1880–1963, vol. VI
Henderson, Herbert Stephen, 1870–1942, vol. IV
Henderson, Sir Hubert Douglas, 1890–1952, vol. V
Henderson, Rev. Ian, 1910–1969, vol. VI
Henderson, Sir Ian Leslie, 1901–1971, vol. VII
Henderson, Sir James, 1848–1914, vol. I
Henderson, Ven. James, 1840–1935, vol. III
Henderson, James, 1868–1945, vol. IV
Henderson, James, 1889–1963, vol. VI
Henderson, Sir James, 1882–1967, vol. VI
Henderson, James Bell, 1883–1975, vol. VII
Henderson, Sir James Blacklock, 1871–1950, vol. IV
Henderson, John, 1862–1938, vol. III
Henderson, John, 1876–1949, vol. IV
Henderson, John, 1883–1965, vol. VI
Henderson, Sir John, 1888–1975, vol. VII
Henderson, John Cochrane, 1881–1946, vol. IV
Henderson, Sir John Craik, 1890–1971, vol. VII
Henderson, John M'Donald, 1846–1922, vol. II
Henderson, John Robertson, 1863–1925, vol. II
Henderson, John Scott, 1895–1964, vol. VI
Henderson, Joseph Morris, 1863–1936, vol. III
Henderson, Maj.-Gen. Kennett Gregg, 1836–1902, vol. I
Henderson, Kingsley Anketell, 1883–1942, vol. IV
Henderson, Lt-Col Malcolm, died 1923, vol. II
Henderson, Air Vice-Marshal Malcolm, 1891–1978, vol. VII
Henderson, Rt Hon. Sir Nevile Meyrick, died 1942, vol. IV
Henderson, Comdr Oscar, 1891–1969, vol. VI
Henderson, Rev. Patrick Arkley W.; see Wright-Henderson.
Henderson, Maj.-Gen. Patrick Hagart, 1876–1968, vol. VI
Henderson, Maj.-Gen. Philip Durham, 1840–1918, vol. II
Henderson, Philip Prichard, 1906–1977, vol. VII
Henderson, R. B., 1880–1958, vol. V
Henderson, Ralph, 1897–1979, vol. VII
Henderson, Adm. Sir Reginald Friend Hannam, 1846–1932, vol. III
Henderson, Adm. Sir Reginald Guy Hannam, 1881–1939, vol. III
Henderson, Richard, 1854–1945, vol. IV
Henderson, Richard McNeil, 1886–1972, vol. VII
Henderson, Robert, 1842–1925, vol. II
Henderson, Robert Candlish, 1874–1964, vol. VI
Henderson, Sir Robert Herriot, died 1932, vol. III
Henderson, Hon. Robert Hugh, 1862–1956, vol. V
Henderson, Captain Robert Ronald, 1876–1932, vol. III
Henderson, Maj.-Gen. Sir Robert Samuel Findlay, 1858–1924, vol. II
Henderson, T. F., 1844–1923, vol. II
Henderson, Thomas, 1870–1945, vol. IV
Henderson, Sir Thomas, 1874–1951, vol. V

Henderson, Thomas, 1867–1960, vol. V
Henderson, Captain Thomas Maxwell Stuart M.; see Milne-Henderson.
Henderson, Thomson, died 1960, vol. V
Henderson, Sir Trevor, 1862–1930, vol. III
Henderson, Velyien Ewart, 1877–1945, vol. IV
Henderson, Lt-Col Sir Vivian Leonard, 1884–1965, vol. VI
Henderson, Rev. W. J., 1843–1929, vol. III
Henderson, Vice-Adm. Wilfred, 1873–1930, vol. III
Henderson, Sir William, 1826–1904, vol. I
Henderson, Sir William, 1863–1940, vol. III
Henderson, Brig. William Alexander, 1882–1949, vol. IV, vol. V
Henderson, William Craig, 1873–1959, vol. V
Henderson, Very Rev. William George, 1819–1905, vol. I
Henderson, Adm. Sir William Hannam, 1845–1931, vol. III
Henderson, William James, 1855–1937, vol. III
Henderson, William Walker, 1886–1960, vol. V
Henderson-Begg, Rev. Canon William, 1877–1934, vol. III
Henderson-Howat, Very Rev. Rudolph, 1896–1957, vol. V
Henderson-Scott, Lt-Col Archibald Malcolm, 1882–1967, vol. VI
Henderson-Smith, Mrs; see Klickmann, F.
Henderson-Stewart, Sir James, 1st Bt, 1897–1961, vol. VI
Hendley, Brig.-Gen. Charles Edward, 1863–1920, vol. II
Hendley, Maj.-Gen. Harold, 1861–1932, vol. III
Hendley, Col Thomas Holbein, 1847–1917, vol. II
Hendrey, Eiluned, (Mrs Graeme Hendrey); see Lewis, Eiluned.
Hendrick, James, 1867–1949, vol. IV
Hendrie, Donald Stewart, 1909–1965, vol. VI
Hendrie, Herbert, 1887–1946, vol. IV
Hendrie, Col Sir John Strathearn, 1857–1923, vol. II
Hendriks, Sir Charles, (C. A. C. J. Hendriks), 1883–1960, vol. V
Hendry, Sir Alexander, 1867–1932, vol. III
Hendry, (Alexander) Forbes, 1908–1980, vol. VII
Hendry, Charles, 1870–1952, vol. V
Hendry, Forbes; see Hendry, A. F.
Hendry, James, 1885–1945, vol. IV
Hendry, Brig.-Gen. Patrick William, 1861–1952, vol. V
Hendry, Robert, 1876–1951, vol. V
Hendry, William Edward Russell, 1911–1965, vol. VI
Hendy, Arthur, 1874–1953, vol. V
Hendy, Frederick James Roberts, 1858–1933, vol. III
Hendy, Sir Philip, 1900–1980, vol. VII
Hendy, Roy, 1890–1959, vol. V
Heneage, 1st Baron, 1840–1922, vol. II
Heneage, 2nd Baron, 1866–1954, vol. V
Heneage, 3rd Baron, 1877–1967, vol. VI
Heneage, Sir Algernon Charles Fiesché, 1834–1915, vol. I

Heneage, Lt-Col Sir Arthur Pelham, 1881–1971, vol. VII
Heneage, Major Godfrey Clement Walker, 1868–1939, vol. III
Heneage, Lt-Col Hon. Henry Granville, 1868–1947, vol. IV
Henegan, Lt-Col John, 1865–1920, vol. II
Heneker, Gen. Sir William Charles Giffard, 1867–1939, vol. III
Heney, Thomas William, 1862–1928, vol. II
Henig, Sir Mark, 1911–1979, vol. VII
Henley, 3rd Baron, 1825–1899, vol. I
Henley, 4th Baron, 1849–1923, vol. II
Henley, 5th Baron, 1858–1925, vol. II
Henley, 6th Baron, 1877–1962, vol. VI
Henley, 7th Baron, 1914–1977, vol. VII
Henley, Brig.-Gen. Hon. Anthony Morton, died 1925, vol. II
Henley, Col Frank Le Leu, 1888–1941, vol. IV
Henley, Herbert James, 1882–1937, vol. III
Henley, Vice-Adm. Joseph Charles Walrond, 1879–1968, vol. VI
Henley, Joseph John, 1821–1910, vol. I
Henley, Sir Thomas, 1860–1935, vol. III
Henley, William Ernest, 1849–1903, vol. I
Henn, Rt Rev. Henry, 1858–1931, vol. III
Henn, Sir Sydney Herbert Holcroft, 1861–1936, vol. III
Henn, Thomas Rice, 1814–1901, vol. I
Henn, Thomas Rice, 1901–1974, vol. VII
Henn, Col William Francis, 1892–1964, vol. VI
Henn-Collins, Hon. Sir Stephen Ogle, died 1958, vol. V
Hennell, Col Sir Reginald, 1844–1925, vol. II
Henner, Jean Jacques, 1829–1905, vol. I
Hennessey, John Baboneau Nicklerlien, 1829–1910, vol. I
Hennessy, Hon. Sir Alfred Theodore, 1875–1963, vol. VI
Hennessy, Rt Hon. Sir David Valentine, 1855–1923, vol. II
Hennessy, Maj.-Gen. Sir George Robertson, died 1905, vol. I
Hennessy, James P.; see Pope-Hennessy.
Hennessy, Lt-Col John, 1867–1954, vol. V
Hennessy, Col John Patrick Cumberlege, 1867–1933, vol. III
Hennessy, Maj.-Gen. Ladislaus Herbert Richard P.; see Pope-Hennessy.
Hennessy, Captain Richard, 1876–1953, vol. V
Hennessy, Richard M., 1854–1926, vol. II
Hennessy, Dame Una P.; see Pope-Hennessy.
Hennessy, William John, vol. II
Henniker, 5th Baron, 1842–1902, vol. I
Henniker, 6th Baron, 1872–1956, vol. V
Henniker, 7th Baron, 1883–1980, vol. VII
Henniker, Col Alan Major, 1870–1949, vol. IV
Henniker, Hon. Mrs Arthur, died 1923, vol. II
Henniker, Sir Brydges Powell, 4th Bt, 1835–1906, vol. I
Henniker, Sir Frederick Brydges Major, 5th Bt, 1862–1908, vol. I
Henniker, Lt-Col Sir Robert John Aldborough, 7th Bt, 1888–1958, vol. V

Henniker-Gotley, George Rainald, 1893–1974, vol. VII
Henniker-Heaton, Sir (John Victor) Peregrine; see Heaton.
Henniker-Heaton, Raymond, 1874–1963, vol. VI
Henniker-Hughan, Adm. Sir Arthur John, 6th Bt, 1866–1925, vol. II
Henniker-Major, Maj.-Gen. Hon. Arthur Henry, 1855–1912, vol. I
Henniker-Major, Hon. Edward Minet, 1848–1924, vol. II
Henniker-Major, Hon. Gerald Arthur George, 1872–1955, vol. V
Henning, Walter Bruno, 1908–1967, vol. VI
Henri, Robert, 1865–1929, vol. III
Henrici, Olaus M. F. E., 1840–1918, vol. II
Henriot, Emile, 1889–1961, vol. VI
Henriques, Sir Basil L. Q., 1890–1961, vol. VI
Henriques, Henry Straus Quixano, 1866–1925, vol. II
Henriques, Louis Fernando, 1916–1976, vol. VII
Henriques, Sir Philip Gutterez, 1867–1950, vol. IV
Henriques, Col Robert David Quixano, 1905–1967, vol. VI
Henry, Alexander, died 1904, vol. I
Henry, Augustine, 1857–1930, vol. III
Henry, Sir Charles Solomon, 1st Bt (cr 1911), 1860–1919, vol. II
Henry, Sir David, 1888–1963, vol. IV
Henry, Rt Hon. Sir Denis Stanislaus, 1st Bt (cr 1922), 1864–1925, vol. II
Henry, Sir Edward Richard, 1st Bt (cr 1918), 1850–1931, vol. III
Henry, Lt-Gen. George, 1846–1922, vol. II
Henry, George, 1858–1943, vol. IV
Henry, Hon. George Stewart, 1871–1958, vol. V
Henry, Rt Rev. Henry, died 1908, vol. I
Henry, Rev. J. Edgar, 1841–1911, vol. I
Henry, Major James D.; see Douglas-Henry.
Henry, James Macintyre, 1852–1929, vol. III
Henry, Sir John, 1858–1930, vol. III
Henry, Mitchell, 1826–1910, vol. I
Henry, Paul, died 1958, vol. V
Henry, Robert Francis Jack, 1902–1970, vol. VI
Henry, Robert Mitchell, 1873–1950, vol. IV
Henry, Maj.-Gen. St George Charles Henry, 1860–1909, vol. I
Henry, Seaghan P.; see Mac Enri, Seaghan P.
Henry, Col Vivian, 1868–1929, vol. III
Henry, William Alexander, 1863–1927, vol. II
Henry, Sir William Daniel, 1855–1934, vol. III
Henschel, Sir George, 1850–1934, vol. III
Henshall, John Henry, 1856–1928, vol. II
Henshaw, Rt Rev. Thomas, 1873–1938, vol. III
Hensley, Rev. Lewis, 1824–1905, vol. I
Hensley, Sir Robert Mitton, 1840–1912, vol. I
Henslow, Rev. George, 1835–1925, vol. II
Hensman, Col Henry Frank, 1839–1911, vol. I
Hensman, Howard, died 1916, vol. II
Henson, Rt Rev. Herbert Hensley, 1863–1947, vol. IV
Henson, John, 1879–1969, vol. VI
Henson, John James, 1868–1948, vol. IV
Henson, Leslie Lincoln, 1891–1957, vol. V

Hentschel, Carl, 1864–1930, vol. III
Henty, Hon. Sir Denham; see Henly, Hon. Sir N. H. D.
Henty, George Alfred, 1832–1902, vol. I
Henty, Hon. Sir (Norman Henry) Denham, 1903–1978, vol. VII
Henvey, Col Ralph, 1876–1945, vol. IV
Hepburn, Sir Archibald B.; see Buchan-Hepburn.
Hepburn, Col Bernard Richard, 1876–1939, vol. III
Hepburn, Lt-Col David, died 1931, vol. III
Hepburn, Sir Harry Frankland, 1867–1931, vol. III
Hepburn, Sir John Karslake Thomas B.; see Buchan-Hepburn.
Hepburn, Malcolm Langton, 1866–1942, vol. IV
Hepburn, Hon. Mitchell F., 1896–1953, vol. V
Hepburn, Sir Thomas Henry, 1840–1917, vol. II
Hepburn, Thomas Nicoll Gabriel Setoun, 1861–1930, vol. III
Hepburn, William Andrew Hardie, 1898–1965, vol. VI
Hepburn-Stuart-Forbes-Trefusis, Major Hon. John Frederick; see Trefusis.
Hepburne-Scott, Hon. Henry Robert, 1847–1914, vol. I
Hepburne-Scott, James Cospatrick; see Scott.
Hepenstal, Major Lambert John D.; see Dopping-Hepenstal.
Hepenstal, Col Maxwell Edward D.; see Dopping-Hepenstal.
Hepher, Rev. Canon Cyril, 1872–1931, vol. III
Heppell, Ralph Gordon, 1910–1976, vol. VII
Hepper, Col Albert James, 1839–1915, vol. I
Hepper, Sir Lawless, 1870–1935, vol. III
Hepple, Anne; see Dickinson, A. H.
Hepworth, Dame Barbara, 1903–1975, vol. VII
Hepworth, Joseph, died 1945, vol. IV
Hepworth, Captain Melville Willis Campbell, 1849–1919, vol. II
Herapath, Lt-Col Edgar, 1853–1933, vol. III
Herapath, Col Lionel, 1880–1934, vol. III
Herbage, Julian Livingston-, 1904–1976, vol. VII
Herbert, Agnes, died 1960, vol. V
Herbert, Sir Alan Patrick, 1890–1971, vol. VII
Herbert, Hon. Alan Percy Harty Molyneux, died 1907, vol. I
Herbert, Sir Alfred, 1866–1957, vol. V
Herbert, Arnold; see Herbert, T. A.
Herbert, Sir Arthur James, 1820–1897, vol. I
Herbert, Sir Arthur James, 1855–1921, vol. II
Herbert, Hon. Auberon E. W. M., 1838–1906, vol. I
Herbert, Hon. Aubrey Nigel Henry Molyneux, 1880–1923, vol. II
Herbert, Lt-Col Charles, 1854–1919, vol. II
Herbert, Sir Charles Gordon, 1893–1970, vol. VI
Herbert, Lt-Col Claude, 1862–1937, vol. III
Herbert, Desmond Andrew, 1898–1976, vol. VII
Herbert, Brig.-Gen. Edmund Arthur, 1866–1946, vol. IV
Herbert, Sir Edward Dave Asher, 1892–1963, vol. VI
Herbert, Edward Maxwell K.; see Kenney-Herbert.

Herbert, Brig.-Gen. Edward Sidney, 1866–1936, vol. III
Herbert, Col Edward William, 1855–1924, vol. II
Herbert, Edwin Savory; see Baron Tangley.
Herbert of Lea, Lady; (Elizabeth), died 1911, vol. I
Herbert, Col Hon. Sir George Sidney, 1st Bt (cr 1937), 1886–1942, vol. IV
Herbert, Lt-Col Herbert, 1865–1942, vol. IV
Herbert, Hilary A., died 1919, vol. II (A), vol. III
Herbert, Sir Jesse, 1851–1916, vol. II
Herbert, Jesse Basil, 1899–1972, vol. VII
Herbert, John Alexander, 1862–1948, vol. IV
Herbert, Lt-Col Sir John Arthur, 1895–1943, vol. IV
Herbert, Maj.-Gen. Lionel, 1860–1929, vol. III
Herbert, Hon. Mervyn Robert Howard Molyneux, 1882–1929, vol. III
Herbert, Hon. Sir Michael Henry, 1857–1903, vol. I
Herbert, Brig.-Gen. Otway Charles, 1877–1955, vol. V
Herbert, Rt Rev. Percy Mark, 1885–1968, vol. VI
Herbert, Air Cdre Philip Lee William, 1882–1936, vol. III
Herbert, Rt Hon. Sir Robert George Wyndham, 1831–1905, vol. I
Herbert, Roscoe, 1895–1975, vol. VII
Herbert, Captain Sir Sidney, 1st Bt (cr 1936), 1890–1939, vol. III
Herbert, Solomon, 1874–1940, vol. III
Herbert, Sydney, 1886–1967, vol. VI
Herbert, (Thomas) Arnold, died 1940, vol. III
Herbert, Violet Ida Evelyn; see Baroness Darcy de Knayth.
Herbert, Walter Elmes, 1902–1980, vol. VII
Herbert, William de Bracy, 1872–1928, vol. II
Herbert, Maj.-Gen. Hon. William Henry, 1834–1909, vol. I
Herbert, Maj.-Gen. William Norman, 1880–1949, vol. IV
Herbert-Smith, Charles, 1862–1944, vol. IV
Herbertson, Andrew John, died 1914, vol. I
Herbertson, James John William, 1883–1974, vol. VII
Herbst, Major John Frederick, 1873–1961, vol. VI
Herchenroder, Sir Furcy Alfred, 1865–1932, vol. III
Herchenroder, (Marie Ferdinand) Philippe, 1893–1968, vol. VI
Herchenroder, Philippe; see Herchenroder, M. F. P.
Hercus, Sir Charles Ernest, 1888–1971, vol. VII
Hercy, Sir Francis Hugh George, 1868–1947, vol. IV
Herd, Harold, 1893–1976, vol. VII
Herdman, Hon. Sir Alexander Lawrence, 1869–1953, vol. V
Herdman, Major Sir Emerson Crawford, 1869–1949, vol. IV
Herdman, Sir Ernest, 1856–1952, vol. V
Herdman, Robert Duddingstone, 1863–1922, vol. II
Herdman, Sir William Abbott, 1858–1924, vol. II
Herdon, Maj.-Gen. Hugh Edward, died 1958, vol. V

Herdt, Louis A., 1872–1926, vol. II
Hereford, 16th Viscount, 1843–1930, vol. III
Hereford, 17th Viscount, 1865–1952, vol. V
Herford, Charles Harold, died 1931, vol. III
Herford, Ethilda B. Meakin, 1872–1956, vol. V
Hergesheimer, Joseph, 1880–1954, vol. V
Heriot, Maj.-Gen. Mackay A. H. J., 1839–1918, vol. II
Heriot, Sir William M.; see Maitland-Heriot.
Heriot-Maitland, Brig.-Gen. James Dalgleish, 1874–1958, vol. V
Heriot-Maitland, Maj.-Gen. Sir James Makgill; see Maitland.
Heritage, Brig. Francis Bede, 1877–1934, vol. III
Heritage, James Edgar, 1880–1957, vol. V
Heritage, Stanley James, died 1980, vol. VII
Heriz, Captain Reginald Yorke, 1851–1910, vol. I
Herkless, Very Rev. Sir John, 1855–1920, vol. II
Herklots, Rev. Hugh Gerard Gibson, 1903–1971, vol. VII
Herkomer, Sir Hubert von, 1849–1914, vol. I
Herman, Mrs E., died 1923, vol. II
Herman, George Ernest, 1849–1914, vol. I
Herman-Hodge, Rear-Adm. Hon. Claude Preston, 1888–1952, vol. V
Hermon-Hodge, Major Hon. Robert Edward Udny, 1882–1937, vol. III
Hern, William, died 1939, vol. III
Hernaman-Johnson, Francis, 1879–1949, vol. IV
Herne-Soame, Sir Charles Buckworth; see Soame.
Herne-Soame, Sir Charles Burnett Buckworth-; see Soame.
Heron, Hon. Col Alexander Robert, 1888–1949, vol. IV
Heron, (Cuthbert) George, 1911–1979, vol. VII
Heron, Lt-Col Davis, 1878–1941, vol. IV
Heron, Edward Thomas, 1867–1949, vol. IV
Heron, George; see Heron, C. G.
Heron, George Allan, 1845–1915, vol. I (A)
Heron, Col Sir George Wykeham, 1880–1963, vol. VI
Heron, Rev. James, 1836–1918, vol. II
Heron, Brig.-Gen. Sir Thomas, 1857–1931, vol. III
Heron-Allen, Edward, 1861–1943, vol. IV
Heron-Maxwell, Mrs Beatrice, died 1927, vol. II
Heron-Maxwell, Captain Sir Ivor Walter, 8th Bt, 1871–1928, vol. II
Heron-Maxwell, Sir John Robert, 7th Bt, 1836–1910, vol. I
Heron-Maxwell, Robert Charles, 1848–1938, vol. III
Herrera, Senator Luis Alberto de, 1873–1959, vol. V
Herreshoff, Nathanael Greene, 1848–1938, vol. III
Herrick, Frederick Charles, 1887–1970, vol. VI
Herrick, Col Henry, 1872–1928, vol. II
Herrick, Myron T., 1854–1929, vol. III
Herrick, Robert, 1868–1938, vol. III
Herrick, Major Robert Lysle Warren, 1895–1936, vol. III
Herridge, Major Hon. William Duncan, 1888–1961, vol. VI
Herries, 11th Lord, 1837–1908, vol. I
Herries, Lady (12th in line), 1877–1945, vol. IV

Herries, Edward, 1821–1911, vol. I
Herries, Hon. Sir William Herbert, 1859–1923, vol. II
Herring, Major Alfred Cecil, 1888–1966, vol. VI
Herring, George, *died* 1906, vol. I
Herring, Percy Theodore, 1872–1967, vol. VI
Herring, Robert, 1903–1975, vol. VII
Herring, Brig.-Gen. Sydney Charles Edgar, 1882–1951, vol. V
Herring, Lt-Col William, 1839–1917, vol. II
Herring-Cooper, Lt-Col William Weldon, 1873–1953, vol. V
Herringham, Sir Wilmot Parker, 1855–1936, vol. III
Herrington, Hugh Geoffrey, 1900–1980, vol. VII
Herriot, Edonard, 1872–1957, vol. V
Herriotts, John, *died* 1935, vol. III
Herron, Very Rev. David Craig, 1882–1955, vol. V
Herron, Hon. Sir Leslie James, 1902–1973, vol. VII
Herron, Sir Robert, 1836–1900, vol. I (A), vol. III
Herschel, Alexander Stewart, *died* 1907, vol. I
Herschel, Col John, 1837–1921, vol. II
Herschel, Rev. Sir John Charles William, 3rd Bt, 1869–1950, vol. IV
Herschel, Sir William James, 2nd Bt, 1833–1917, vol. II
Herschell, 1st Baron, 1837–1899, vol. I
Herschell, 2nd Baron, 1878–1929, vol. III
Herschell, Charles Richard, 1877–1962, vol. VI
Herschell, George, 1856–1914, vol. I
Herter, Christian Archibald, 1895–1966, vol. VI
Hertford, 7th Marquess of, 1871–1940, vol. III
Hertslet, Sir Cecil, 1850–1934, vol. III
Hertslet, Sir Edward, 1824–1902, vol. I
Hertslet, Rev. Canon Edward Lewis Augustine, 1878–1936, vol. III
Hertslet, George Thomas, 1822–1906, vol. I
Hertslet, Harry Lester, 1856–1925, vol. II
Hertz, Alfred, 1872–1942, vol. IV
Hertz, Henry Felix, 1863–1932, vol. III
Hertz, Very Rev. Joseph Herman, 1872–1946, vol. IV
Hertz, William Axel, 1859–1950, vol. IV
Hertzberg, Maj.-Gen. Charles Sumner Lund, 1886–1944, vol. IV
Hertzberg, Maj.-Gen. Halfdan Fenton Harbo, 1884–1959, vol. V
Hertzog, Gen. Hon. James Barry Munnik, 1866–1942, vol. IV
Hervey, Arthur, 1855–1922, vol. II
Hervey, Gen. Charles Robert West, 1818–1903, vol. I
Hervey, Dudley Francis Amelius, 1849–1911, vol. I
Hervey, Lord Francis, 1846–1931, vol. III
Hervey, Rev. Frederick Alfred John, 1846–1910, vol. I
Hervey, Sir George William, 1845–1915, vol. I
Hervey, Henry Arthur William, 1832–1908, vol. I (A)
Hervey, Lord Walter John, 1865–1948, vol. IV
Hervey-Bathurst, Major Sir Frederick Edward William; *see* Bathurst.
Hervieu, Paul Ernest, 1857–1915, vol. I (A)
Herzfeld, Ernst Emil, 1879–1948, vol. IV

Herzog, Rt Rev. Edward, 1841–1924, vol. II
Herzog, Chief Rabbi Isaac, 1888–1959, vol. V
Heseltine, Lt-Col Christopher, 1869–1944, vol. IV
Heseltine, Major Godfrey, 1871–1932, vol. III
Heseltine, Harry Nelson, *died* 1935, vol. III
Heseltine, John Postle, 1843–1929, vol. III
Heseltine, Michael, 1886–1952, vol. V
Hesilrige, Arthur George Maynard, 1863–1953, vol. V
Hesketh, 1st Baron, 1881–1944, vol. IV
Hesketh, 2nd Baron, 1916–1955, vol. V
Hesketh, Air Vice-Marshal Allan, *died* 1973, vol. VII
Hesketh, Charles Hesketh Fleetwood-, 1871–1947, vol. IV
Hesketh, Lt-Col George, 1878–1929, vol. III
Hesketh, Lt-Col James Arthur, 1863–1923, vol. II
Hesketh, Col Rawdon John Isherwood, 1872–1959, vol. V
Hesketh, Sir Thomas George Fermor-, 7th Bt, 1849–1924, vol. II
Heslop, Major Alfred Herbert, 1880–1929, vol. III
Heslop, Air Vice-Marshal Herbert William, 1898–1976, vol. VII
Heslop, Richard Oliver, 1842–1916, vol. II
Heslop, Major Thomas Bernard, 1891–1938, vol. III
Heslop-Harrison, John William, 1881–1967, vol. VI
Hespeler, Hon. Wilhelm, *born* 1850, vol. II
Hess, Dame Myra, *died* 1965, vol. VI
Hess, Victor Francis, 1883–1964, vol. VI
Hess, Walter R., 1881–1973, vol. VII
Hess, Willy, 1859–1939, vol. III
Hesse, Hermann, 1877–1962, vol. VI
Hessey, Rev. Robert Falkner, 1826–1911, vol. I
Hessey, Brig.-Gen. William Francis, 1868–1939, vol. III
Hetherington, Arthur Lonsdale, 1881–1960, vol. V
Hetherington, Sir Hector James Wright, 1888–1965, vol. VI
Hetherington, Ivystan, *died* 1917, vol. II
Hetherington, Sir Roger Gaskell, 1876–1952, vol. V
Hetherington, Gp Captain Thomas Gerard, 1886–1951, vol. V
Hetherington, William Lonsdale, 1845–1911, vol. I
Hetherwick, Rev. Alexander, 1860–1939, vol. III
Hett, Major Francis Paget, *died* 1966, vol. VI
Hett, Geoffrey Seccombe, 1878–1949, vol. IV
Hett, Walter Stanley, 1882–1948, vol. IV
Heugh, Comdr John George, 1856–1915, vol. I
Heuston, Lt-Col Frederick Samuel, 1857–1914, vol. I
Heuvel, Frederick V.; *see* Vanden Heuvel.
Hevesy, George de, 1885–1966, vol. VI
Heward, Leslie Hays, 1897–1943, vol. IV
Hewart, 1st Viscount, 1870–1943, vol. IV
Hewart, 2nd Viscount, 1896–1964, vol. VI
Hewat, Aubrey Middleton, 1884–1976, vol. VII
Hewat, Air Cdre Harry Aitken, 1888–1970, vol. VI
Hewat, Col Sir John, 1863–1928, vol. II
Hewby, Louis John, 1871–1925, vol. II
Hewby, William Petch, 1866–1946, vol. IV
Hewer, Humphrey Robert, 1903–1974, vol. VII

Hewer, Maj.-Gen. Reginald Kingscote, 1892–1970, vol. VI

Hewetson, John T., 1872–1936, vol. III

Hewett, Edbert Ansgar, 1860–1915, vol. I (A)

Hewett, Edward Osborne, 1835–1897, vol. I

Hewett, Lt-Col Edward Vincent Osborne, 1867–1953, vol. V

Hewett, Sir (Frederick) Stanley, 1880–1954, vol. V

Hewett, Rear-Adm. George Hayley, 1855–1930, vol. III

Hewett, Captain George Stuart, 1863–1937, vol. III

Hewett, Captain Gilbert George Pearse, 1880–1966, vol. VI

Hewett, Sir Harold George, 4th Bt, 1858–1949, vol. IV

Hewett, Sir John Prescott, 1854–1941, vol. IV

Hewett, Col Murray Selwood, 1881–1939, vol. III

Hewett, Captain Robert Roy Scott, 1886–1967, vol. VI

Hewett, Sir Stanley; see Hewett, Sir F. S.

Hewins, Harold Preece, 1877–1956, vol. V

Hewins, Maurice Gravenor, 1897–1953, vol. V

Hewins, William Albert Samuel, 1865–1931, vol. III

Hewison, Robert, 1876–1959, vol. V

Hewit, Forrest, died 1956, vol. V

Hewitson, Captain Mark, 1897–1973, vol. VII

Hewitson, Rev. William, died 1932, vol. III

Hewitt, Abram S., 1822–1903, vol. I

Hewitt, Surg. Rear-Adm. Alfred James, died 1947, vol. IV

Hewitt, Captain Hon. Archibald Rodney, 1883–1915, vol. I (A)

Hewitt, Brig. Charles Caulfield, 1883–1949, vol. IV

Hewitt, Surg.-Rear-Adm. David Walker, 1870–1940, vol. III

Hewitt, Lt-Col Dudley Riddiford, 1877–1971, vol. VII

Hewitt, Edgar Percy, died 1928, vol. II

Hewitt, Air Chief Marshal Sir Edgar Rainey L.; see Ludlow-Hewitt.

Hewitt, Hon. Edward, 1848–1931, vol. III

Hewitt, Sir Frederic William, 1857–1916, vol. II

Hewitt, Adm. H. Kent, 1887–1972, vol. VII

Hewitt, Sir John Francis, 1910–1979, vol. VII

Hewitt, John Theodore, died 1954, vol. V

Hewitt, Lt-Col Sir Joseph, 1st Bt, 1865–1923, vol. II

Hewitt, Sir Joseph, 2nd Bt, 1907–1973, vol. VII

Hewitt, Sir Thomas, died 1923, vol. II

Hewitt, William Graily, 1864–1952, vol. V

Hewlett, Baron (Life Peer); Thomas Clyde Hewlett, 1923–1979, vol. VII

Hewlett, Brig.-Gen. Ernest, 1879–1965, vol. VI

Hewlett, Paymaster Captain Graham, 1864–1937, vol. III

Hewlett, Maurice Henry, 1861–1923, vol. II

Hewlett, Sir Meyrick; see Hewlett, Sir W. M.

Hewlett, Richard Tanner, 1865–1940, vol. III

Hewlett, Thomas Henry, 1882–1956, vol. V

Hewlett, Sir (William) Meyrick, died 1944, vol. IV

Hewlett, William Oxenham, 1845–1912, vol. I

Hewson, Hon. Mrs Anne Elizabeth Mary Llywelyn, 1902–1963, vol. VI

Hewson, Sir Bushby; see Hewson, Sir J. B.

Hewson, George Henry Phillips, 1881–1972, vol. VII

Hewson, Sir (Joseph) Bushby, 1902–1976, vol. VII

Hext, Rear-Adm. Sir John, 1842–1924, vol. II

Hext, Brig.-Gen. Lyonel John, 1871–1934, vol. III

Heycock, Charles Thomas, 1858–1931, vol. III

Heydeman, Maj.-Gen. C. A., 1889–1967, vol. VI

Heydon, Charles Gilbert, 1845–1932, vol. III

Heydon, Hon. Louis Francis, 1848–1918, vol. I, vol. II

Heydon, Sir Peter Richard, 1913–1971, vol. VII

Heyer, Georgette, 1902–1974, vol. VII

Heyes, Morris, died 1940, vol. III

Heygate, Rev. Ambrose, 1852–1941, vol. IV

Heygate, Arthur Conolly Gage, 1862–1935, vol. III

Heygate, Sir Frederick Gage, 3rd Bt, 1854–1940, vol. III

Heygate, Sir John Edward Nourse, 4th Bt, 1903–1976, vol. VII

Heygate, Captain Richard Lionel, 1859–1926, vol. II

Heygate, Col Robert Henry Gage, 1859–1923, vol. II

Heygate, Rev. William Augustine, 1847–1941, vol. IV

Heygate, William Unwin, 1825–1902, vol. I

Heyman, Lt-Col Arthur Augustus Inglis, 1864–1931, vol. III

Heyman, Maj.-Gen. George Douglas Gordon Dufferin, 1905–1965, vol. VI

Heyman, Lt-Col Sir (Herman) Melville, 1859–1938, vol. III

Heyman, Lt-Col Sir Melville; see Heyman, Lt-Col Sir H. M.

Heyner, Herbert, 1881–1954, vol. V

Heyrovský, Jaroslav, 1890–1967, vol. VI

Heys, John, 1899–1963, vol. VI

Heyse, Paul Johann Ludwig, 1830–1914, vol. I

Heysen, Sir Hans, 1877–1968, vol. VI

Heytesbury, 3rd Baron, 1862–1903, vol. I

Heytesbury, 4th Baron, 1863–1949, vol. IV

Heytesbury, 5th Baron, 1906–1971, vol. VII

Heyward, DuBose, 1885–1940, vol. III (A), vol. IV

Heywood, Sir Arthur Percival, 3rd Bt, 1849–1916, vol. II

Heywood, Rt Rev. Bernard O. F., 1871–1960, vol. V

Heywood, Bertram Charles Percival, 1864–1914, vol. II

Heywood, Maj.-Gen. Cecil Percival, 1880–1936, vol. III

Heywood, Charles Christopher, 1865–1948, vol. IV

Heywood, Sir (Graham) Percival, 4th Bt, 1878–1946, vol. IV

Heywood, James Barnes, died 1924, vol. II

Heywood, Sir Percival; see Heywood, Sir G. P.

Heywood, Rt Rev. Richard Stanley, 1867–1955, vol. V

Heywood, Maj.-Gen. Thomas George Gordon, 1886–1943, vol. IV

Heywood, Sir Thomas Percival, 2nd Bt, 1823–1897, vol. I
Heywood, Valentine, 1891–1963, vol. VI
Heywood, Wilfred Lanceley, 1900–1977, vol. VII
Heywood-Lonsdale, Lt-Col Arthur, 1900–1976, vol. VII
Heywood-Lonsdale, Arthur Pemberton, 1835–1897, vol. I
Heywood-Lonsdale, Lt-Col Henry Heywood, 1864–1930, vol. III
Heywood-Lonsdale, John Pemberton Heywood, 1869–1944, vol. IV
Heyworth, 1st Baron, 1894–1974, vol. VII
Heyworth, Brig.-Gen. Frederic James, 1863–1916, vol. II
Hezlet, Lt-Col Charles Owen, 1891–1965, vol. VI
Hezlet, Maj.-Gen. Robert Knox, 1879–1963, vol. VI
Hezlett, James, 1875–1963, vol. VI
Hiam, Sir Frederick, 1871–1938, vol. III
Hibben, John Grier, 1861–1933, vol. III
Hibberd, Charles M.; see Maxwell-Hibberd.
Hibbert, Denys Heseltine, 1905–1977, vol. VII
Hibbert, Rev. Preb. Francis Aidan, 1866–1933, vol. III
Hibbert, Francis Dennis, 1906–1975, vol. VII
Hibbert, Col Godfrey Leicester, 1864–1924, vol. II
Hibbert, Sir Henry Flemming, 1st Bt, 1850–1927, vol. II
Hibbert, Adm. Hugh Thomas, 1863–1951, vol. V
Hibbert, John Geoffrey, 1890–1968, vol. VI
Hibbert, Rt Hon. Sir John Tomlinson, 1824–1908, vol. I
Hibbert, Brig. Oswald Yates, 1882–1966, vol. VI
Hibbert, Paul Edgar Tichborne, 1846–1929, vol. III
Hibbert, Walter, 1852–1935, vol. III
Hibbert, Hon. Wilfrid H.; see Holland-Hibbert.
Hibbert, William Nembhard, 1873–1936, vol. III
Hichens, Rev. Frederick Harrison, 1836–1921, vol. II
Hichens, John Knill Jope, 1836–1908, vol. I
Hichens, Lionel; see Hichens, W. L.
Hichens, Robert Smythe, 1864–1950, vol. IV
Hichens, Rev. Thomas Sikes, died 1916, vol. II
Hichens, (William) Lionel, 1874–1940, vol. III
Hickes, Maj.-Gen. Lancelot Daryl, 1884–1965, vol. VI
Hickey, Captain Daniel, 1851–1935, vol. III
Hickey, Emily Henrietta, 1845–1924, vol. II
Hickford, Lawrence David, 1904–1978, vol. VII
Hickie, Brig.-Gen. Carlos Joseph, died 1959, vol. V
Hickie, Brig. George William Clement, 1897–1972, vol. VII
Hickie, Maj.-Gen. Sir William Bernard, 1865–1950, vol. IV
Hickin, Rev. Canon Henry Arthur, 1859–1938, vol. III
Hickin, Welton, 1876–1968, vol. VI
Hicking, Sir William Norton, 1st Bt, 1865–1947, vol. IV
Hickley, Adm. Cecil Spencer, 1865–1941, vol. IV
Hickley, Victor North, 1858–1923, vol. II
Hickling, Charles Frederick, 1902–1977, vol. VII
Hickling, Vice-Adm. Harold, 1892–1969, vol. VI

Hickling, Henry George Albert, 1883–1954, vol. V
Hickling, Lt-Col Horace Cyril Benjamin, 1879–1948, vol. IV
Hickman, Hon. Albert Edgar, 1875–1943, vol. IV
Hickman, Sir Alfred, 1st Bt, 1830–1910, vol. I
Hickman, Major Sir Alfred Edward, 2nd Bt, 1885–1947, vol. IV
Hickman, Sir (Alfred) Howard (Whitby), 3rd Bt, 1920–1979, vol. VII
Hickman, Captain Charlie Steward, 1868–1941, vol. IV
Hickman, Brig.-Gen. Harry Otho Devereux, 1860–1946, vol. IV
Hickman, Maj.-Gen. Henry Temple Devereux, 1888–1960, vol. V
Hickman, Sir Howard; see Hickman, Sir A. H. W.
Hickman, Maj.-Gen. Hugh Palliser, 1856–1930, vol. III
Hickman, Robert St John, 1867–1947, vol. IV
Hickman, Brig.-Gen. Thomas Edgecumbe, 1859–1930, vol. III
Hicks, Beatrice Janie, (Mrs Philip Hicks); see Whitby, B. J.
Hicks, Brig. Sir (Cedric) Stanton, 1892–1976, vol. VII
Hicks, Rev. Canon Edward Barry, 1858–1939, vol. III
Hicks, Rt Rev. Edward Lee, 1843–1919, vol. II
Hicks, Sir (Edward) Seymour, 1871–1949, vol. IV
Hicks, (Ernest) George, 1879–1954, vol. V
Hicks, Rt Rev. (Frederick Cyril) Nugent, 1872–1942, vol. IV
Hicks, George; see Hicks, E. G.
Hicks, Rt Rev. George Bruno, 1878–1954, vol. V
Hicks, George Dawes, 1862–1941, vol. IV
Hicks, Henry, 1837–1899, vol. I
Hicks, Brig.-Gen. Henry T.; see Tempest-Hicks.
Hicks, Rev. Herbert S., died 1928, vol. II
Hicks, John Donald, 1890–1972, vol. VII
Hicks, Rt Rev. John Wale, 1840–1899, vol. I
Hicks, Lt-Col Sir Maxwell, 1878–1959, vol. V
Hicks, Rt Rev. Nugent; see Hicks, Rt Rev. F. C. N.
Hicks, Brig. Philip Hugh Whitby, 1895–1967, vol. VI
Hicks, Reginald Jack, 1922–1980, vol. VII
Hicks, Robert Drew, 1850–1929, vol. III
Hicks, Sir Seymour; see Hicks, Sir E. S.
Hicks, Shadrach, died 1936, vol. III
Hicks, Brig. Sir Stanton; see Hicks, Brig. Sir C. S.
Hicks, Rev. Walter, 1868–1937, vol. III
Hicks, William Edward, 1852–1921, vol. II
Hicks, William Mitchinson, 1850–1934, vol. III
Hicks-Beach, Lady Victoria Alexandrina, 1879–1963, vol. VI
Hicks Beach, William Frederick, 1841–1923, vol. II
Hicks Beach, Major William Whitehead, 1907–1975, vol. VII
Hicks-Beach, William Wither Bramston, 1826–1901, vol. I
Hickson, Geoffrey Fletcher, 1900–1978, vol. VII
Hickson, Lt-Gen. Sir Gerald Robert Stedall, 1879–1957, vol. V
Hickson, Sir Joseph, 1830–1897, vol. I

Hickson, Joseph William Andrew, *died* 1956, vol. V

Hickson, Mrs Murray; *see* Kitcat, M.

Hickson, Oswald Squire, 1877–1944, vol. IV

Hickson, Brig.-Gen. Robert Albert, 1848–1934, vol. III

Hickson, Robert Rowan Purdon, 1842–1923, vol. II

Hickson, Maj.-Gen. Sir Samuel, 1859–1928, vol. II

Hickson, Hon. Brig.-Gen. Samuel Arthur Einem, 1853–1932, vol. III

Hickson, Sydney John, 1859–1940, vol. III

Hidayat Hosain, M., 1887–1941, vol. IV

Hidayatallah, Hon. Khan Bahadur Shaikh (Sir) Ghulam Husain, *died* 1948, vol. IV

Hide, Percy, 1874–1938, vol. III

Hiern, William Philip, 1839–1925, vol. II

Higgens, Charles, *died* 1920, vol. II

Higgin, Walter Wynnefield, 1889–1971, vol. VII

Higginbottom, Frederick James, 1859–1943, vol. IV

Higginbottom, S. W., *died* 1902, vol. I

Higgins, A., *died* 1903, vol. I

Higgins, Alexander Pearce, 1865–1935, vol. III

Higgins, Brig.-Gen. Charles Graeme, 1879–1961, vol. VI

Higgins, Clement, 1844–1916, vol. II

Higgins, Edward John, 1864–1947, vol. IV

Higgins, Ellen C., *died* 1951, vol. V

Higgins, Frederick P.; *see* Platt-Higgins,

Higgins, Frederick Robert, 1896–1941, vol. IV

Higgins, Sir George; *see* Higgins, Sir S. G.

Higgins, George Herbert, 1878–1937, vol. III

Higgins, Gen. Sir George Wentworth Alexander, 1826–1927, vol. II

Higgins, Maj.-Gen. Harold John, 1894–1951, vol. V

Higgins, Hon. Henry Bournes, *died* 1929, vol. III

Higgins, Henry Vincent, 1855–1928, vol. II

Higgins, John Comyn, 1882–1952, vol. V

Higgins, Air Marshal Sir John Frederick Andrews, 1875–1948, vol. IV

Higgins, Sir John Michael, 1862–1937, vol. III

Higgins, Rt Rev. Joseph, 1838–1915, vol. I

Higgins, Rt Rev. Michael, 1863–1918, vol. II

Higgins, Reginald Edward, 1877–1933, vol. III

Higgins, Sir (Sydney) George, 1867–1947, vol. IV

Higgins, Air Cdre Thomas Charles Reginald, 1880–1953, vol. V

Higgins, Thomas Twistington, 1887–1966, vol. VI

Higgins, Rev. Canon Walter Norman, 1880–1957, vol. V

Higgins Bernard, Lt-Col Francis Tyringham, *died* 1935, vol. III

Higginson, Captain Archibald Bertram Watson, *died* 1950, vol. IV

Higginson, Brig.-Gen. Cecil Pickford, 1866–1951, vol. V

Higginson, Charles James, 1871–1964, vol. VI

Higginson, Brig. Sir Frank, 1890–1958, vol. V

Higginson, Maj.-Gen. Harold Whitla, 1873–1954, vol. V

Higginson, Col Theophilus, 1839–1903, vol. I

Higginson, Thomas Wentworth, 1823–1911, vol. I

Higgs, Col Frederick William, 1881–1924, vol. II

Higgs, Henry, 1864–1940, vol. III

Higgs, Captain Michael Arnold, 1927–1978, vol. VII

Higgs, Sydney Limbrey, 1892–1977, vol. VII

Higgs, Walter Frank, 1886–1961, vol. VI

Higgs, Hon. William Guy, 1862–1951, vol. V

Higgs-Walker, James Arthur, 1892–1979, vol. VII

High, Sir William, 1857–1934, vol. III

Higham, Anthony Richard Charles, 1907–1975, vol. VII

Higham, Lt-Col Bernard, 1880–1944, vol. IV

Higham, Charles Daniel, 1849–1935, vol. III

Higham, Sir Charles Frederick, 1876–1938, vol. III

Higham, John Sharp, 1857–1932, vol. III

Higham, Sir Thomas, 1847–1910, vol. I

Higham, Sir Thomas, 1866–1947, vol. IV

Higham, Thomas Farrant, 1890–1975, vol. VII

Highet, Gilbert Arthur, 1906–1978, vol. VII

Highet, Hugh Campbell, 1868–1929, vol. III

Highet, Sir Robert Swan, 1859–1934, vol. III

Highfield, John Somerville, 1871–1945, vol. IV

Highmore, Sir Nathaniel Joseph, 1844–1924, vol. II

Hight, Sir James, 1870–1958, vol. V

Highton, John Elborn, 1884–1937, vol. III

Highton, Mark Edward, 1888–1966, vol. VI

Higinbotham, Major George Mowat, 1866–1915, vol. I

Hignell, Harold, 1879–1943, vol. IV

Hignell, Sidney Robert, 1873–1939, vol. III

Hignett, Mrs Dorothy Eleanor Augusta, *died* 1946, vol. IV

Hilbers, Ven. George Christopher, *died* 1918, vol. II

Hilbery, Rt Hon. Sir Malcolm, 1883–1965, vol. VI

Hilborne, Rev. Frederick Wilfred, 1901–1980, vol. VII

Hildebrand, Brig.-Gen. Arthur Blois Ross, 1870–1937, vol. III

Hildebrand, Arthur Hedding, 1843–1918, vol. II

Hilder, Lt-Col Frank, 1864–1951, vol. V

Hildesley, Alfred, 1873–1958, vol. V

Hilditch, Clarence Clifford, 1912–1974, vol. VII

Hilditch, Thomas Percy, 1886–1965, vol. VI

Hildreth, Lt-Col Harold Crossley, 1876–1937, vol. III

Hildyard, Gerard Moresby Thoroton, 1874–1956, vol. V

Hildyard, Brig.-Gen. Harold Charles Thoroton, 1872–1956, vol. V

Hildyard, Gen. Sir Henry John Thoroton, 1846–1916, vol. II

Hildyard, John Arundell, 1861–1935, vol. III

Hildyard, Gen. Sir Reginald John Thoroton, 1876–1965, vol. VI

Hiles, Sir Herbert, 1881–1968, vol. VI

Hiley, Sir (Ernest) Haviland, *died* 1943, vol. IV

Hiley, Sir Ernest Varvill, 1868–1949, vol. IV

Hiley, Sir Haviland; *see* Hiley, Sir E. H.

Hilken, Captain Thomas John Norman, 1901–1969, vol. VI

Hill, 4th Viscount, 1863–1923, vol. II

Hill, 5th Viscount, 1866–1924, vol. II

Hill, 6th Viscount, 1876–1957, vol. V

Hill, 7th Viscount, 1904–1974, vol. VII

Hill of Wivenhoe, Baron (Life Peer); Edward James Hill, 1899–1969, vol. VI

Hill, Adrian Keith Graham, 1895–1977, vol. VII

Hill, Sir Albert, 2nd Bt (*cr* 1917), 1877–1946, vol. IV

Hill, Alex, 1856–1929, vol. III

Hill, Sir Alexander Galloway E.; *see* Erskine-Hill.

Hill, Rt Hon. Alexander Staveley, 1825–1905, vol. I

Hill, Alfred, *died* 1945, vol. IV

Hill, Alfred Bostock, 1854–1932, vol. III

Hill, Alfred Francis, 1870–1960, vol. V

Hill, Alfred John, 1862–1927, vol. II

Hill, Rt Rev. Alfred Thomas, 1901–1969, vol. VI

Hill, Annie; *see* Hill, Lady Arthur.

Hill, Rev. Canon Archdall, *died* 1936, vol. III

Hill, Archibald Vivian, 1886–1977, vol. VII

Hill, Captain Arthur, 1873–1913, vol. I

Hill, Arthur, 1854–1927, vol. II

Hill, Arthur, 1858–1927, vol. II

Hill, Lady Arthur, (Annie), *died* 1944, vol. IV

Hill, Captain Arthur Blundell George Sandys, 1837–1923, vol. II

Hill, Lord (Arthur) Francis (Henry), 1895–1953, vol. V

Hill, Arthur George, 1857–1923, vol. II

Hill, Lt-Col Arthur Hardie, 1887–1963, vol. VI

Hill, Sir Arthur Norman, 1st Bt (*cr* 1919), 1863–1944, vol. IV

Hill, Rt Hon. Lord Arthur William, 1846–1931, vol. III

Hill, Sir Arthur William, 1875–1941, vol. IV

Hill, Ven. Arundel Charles, 1845–1921, vol. II

Hill, Brig.-Gen. Augustus West, 1853–1922, vol. II

Hill, Maj.-Gen. Sir Basil Alexander, 1880–1960, vol. V

Hill, Brig.-Gen. Cecil, 1861–1942, vol. IV

Hill, Charles Alexander, 1874–1948, vol. IV

Hill, Major Charles Glencairn, 1872–1915, vol. I

Hill, Charles Loraine, 1891–1976, vol. VII

Hill, Rev. Charles N.; *see* Noel-Hill.

Hill, Sir Claude Hamilton Archer, 1866–1934, vol. III

Hill, Sir Clement Lloyd, 1845–1913, vol. I

Hill, Clifford Francis, 1930–1979, vol. VII

Hill, Constance, *died* 1929, vol. III

Hill, Sir Cyril Rowley; *see* Hill, Sir G. C. R.

Hill, Hon. David Jayne, 1850–1932, vol. III

Hill, Col David John Jackson, 1874–1938, vol. III

Hill, Rev. Canon Douglas George, 1912–1980, vol. VII

Hill, Douglas Rowland Holdsworth, 1904–1966, vol. VI

Hill, Captain Duncan C., 1900–1977, vol. VII

Hill, Edward Bernard Lewin, 1834–1915, vol. I

Hill, Rev. Edward F., 1858–1931, vol. III

Hill, Edward John, 1897–1965, vol. VI

Hill, Sir Edward Stock, 1834–1902, vol. I

Hill, Rev. Canon Edwin, 1843–1933, vol. III

Hill, Sir Enoch, 1865–1942, vol. IV

Hill, Brig. Ernest Frederick John, 1879–1962, vol. VI

Hill, Ernest George, 1872–1917, vol. II

Hill, Ernest Saphir, 1891–1967, vol. VI

Hill, Col Eustace, 1869–1946, vol. IV

Hill, Eveline, (Mrs J. S. Hill), 1898–1973, vol. VII

Hill, Brig.-Gen. Felix Frederic, 1860–1940, vol. III

Hill, Lord Francis; *see* Hill, Lord A. F. H.

Hill, Sir Francis; *see* Hill, Sir J. W. F.

Hill, Lt-Col Francis Robert, 1873–1956, vol. V

Hill, Major Francis Rowley, 1872–1939, vol. III

Hill, Lt-Col Frank William Rowland, 1875–1942, vol. IV

Hill, Brig.-Gen. Frederic William, 1866–1954, vol. IV

Hill, Frederick George, 1865–1936, vol. III

Hill, Sir G. Rowland, 1855–1928, vol. II

Hill, George Birkbeck, 1835–1903, vol. I

Hill, Sir (George) Cyril Rowley, 8th Bt (*cr* 1779), 1890–1980, vol. VII

Hill, Sir George Francis, 1867–1948, vol. IV

Hill, Sir George Rowley, 7th Bt (*cr* 1779), 1864–1954, vol. V

Hill, Col Gerald Victor Wilmot, 1887–1958, vol. V

Hill, Gerard Robert, 1872–1946, vol. IV

Hill, Grace Livingston, (Mrs Thomas Franklin Hill), 1865–1947, vol. IV

Hill, Graham, 1929–1975, vol. VII

Hill, H. Lancelot H., 1883–1944, vol. IV

Hill, Headon, (F. Grainger), *died* 1927, vol. II

Hill, Sir Henry Blyth, 6th Bt (*cr* 1779), 1867–1929, vol. III

Hill, Col Henry Cecil de la Montague, 1864–1931, vol. III

Hill, Rev. Henry Erskine, 1864–1939, vol. III

Hill, Henry Staveley S.; *see* Staveley-Hill.

Hill, Col Henry Warburton, 1877–1951, vol. V

Hill, Henry William, 1850–1926, vol. II

Hill, Lt-Col Hugh, 1875–1916, vol. II

Hill, J. Arthur, 1872–1951, vol. V

Hill, J. Smith, 1866–1944, vol. IV

Hill, Sir James, 1st Bt (*cr* 1917), 1849–1936, vol. III

Hill, Sir James, 3rd Bt (*cr* 1917), 1905–1976, vol. VII

Hill, James Bastian, 1861–1927, vol. II

Hill, James J., 1838–1916, vol. II

Hill, James Meechan, 1899–1966, vol. VI

Hill, James Peter, 1873–1954, vol. V

Hill, James S., *died* 1921, vol. II

Hill, Sir (James William) Francis, 1899–1980, vol. VII

Hill, Maj.-Gen. John, 1866–1935, vol. III

Hill, Rt Rev. John Charles, 1862–1943, vol. IV

Hill, Sir John Edward Gray, 1839–1914, vol. I

Hill, John Gibson, 1910–1975, vol. VII

Hill, Mrs John Stanley; *see* Hill, Eveline.

Hill, Col Joseph, 1850–1918, vol. II

Hill, Joseph, 1888–1947, vol. IV

Hill, Kenneth Robson, 1911–1973, vol. VII

Hill, Laurence Carr, 1890–1959, vol. V

Hill, Sir Leonard Erskine, 1866–1952, vol. V

Hill, Leonard R.; *see* Raven-Hill.

Hill, Maj.-Gen. Leslie Rowley, 1884–1975, vol. VII

Hill, Levi Clement, 1883–1961, vol. VI

Hill, Martin; *see* Hill, W. M.

Hill, Martin Spencer, 1893–1968, vol. VI

Hill, Matthew Davenport, 1872–1958, vol. V

320

Hill, Maurice; see Hill, P. M.
Hill, Sir Maurice, 1862–1934, vol. III
Hill, Maurice Neville, 1919–1966, vol. VI
Hill, Micaiah John Muller, 1856–1929, vol. III
Hill, Montague, died 1929, vol. III
Hill, Lt-Col Sir Norman Gray, 2nd Bt (cr 1919), 1894–1944, vol. IV
Hill, Octavia, died 1912, vol. I
Hill, Oliver, 1887–1968, vol. VI
Hill, Osman; see Hill, W. C. O.
Hill, Col Peter Edward, 1834–1919, vol. II
Hill, Philip Ernest, died 1944, vol. IV
Hill, (Philip) Maurice, 1892–1952, vol. V
Hill, Sir Quintin; see Hill, Sir T. St Q.
Hill, Ralph William, 1893–1966, vol. VI
Hill, Reginald Duke, 1866–1922, vol. II
Hill, Reginald Dykers Richardson, 1902–1973, vol. VII
Hill, Reginald Harrison, 1894–1976, vol. VII
Hill, Sir Reginald Herbert, 1888–1971, vol. VII
Hill, Reginald John James, 1905–1977, vol. VII
Hill, Vice-Adm. Hon. Sir Richard A. S., 1880–1954, vol. V
Hill, Surg. Vice-Adm. Sir Robert, 1865–1938, vol. III
Hill, Maj.-Gen. Robert Charles C.; see Cottrell-Hill.
Hill, Robert Hughes, 1892–1963, vol. VI
Hill, Lt-Col Robert Montagu, 1872–1934, vol. III
Hill, Air Chief Marshal Sir Roderic Maxwell, 1894–1954, vol. V
Hill, Rowland, 1883–1962, vol. VI
Hill, Brig. Rowland Clement Ridley, 1879–1967, vol. VI
Hill, Gen. Sir Rowley Sale S.; see Sale-Hill.
Hill, Sir Sidney Pearson, 1900–1968, vol. VI
Hill, Sydney, 1902–1968, vol. VI
Hill, Thomas Arthur, 1854–1931, vol. III
Hill, Sir Thomas Eustace, died 1931, vol. III
Hill, Thomas George, 1876–1954, vol. V
Hill, Major Thomas Henry, 1844–1930, vol. III
Hill, Thomas Rowland, 1903–1967, vol. VI
Hill, Sir (Thomas St) Quintin, 1889–1963, vol. VI
Hill, Thomas William, 1866–1953, vol. V
Hill, Thomson; see Hill, W. T.
Hill, Vincent Walker, died 1913, vol. I
Hill, Lt-Col Walter de Marchot, 1877–1927, vol. II
Hill, Maj.-Gen. Walter Pitts Hendy, 1877–1942, vol. IV
Hill, Engr Rear-Adm. Walter S.; see Scott-Hill.
Hill, Maj.-Gen. William, 1846–1903, vol. I
Hill, William, died 1928, vol. II
Hill, Col Sir William Alexander, 1846–1931, vol. III
Hill, Hon. William Caldwell, 1866–1939, vol. III
Hill, William Charles Osman, 1901–1975, vol. VII
Hill, William George John, 1876–1933, vol. III
Hill, William Henry, 1872–1957, vol. IV
Hill, William Kirkpatrick, 1862–1944, vol. IV
Hill, (William) Martin, 1905–1976, vol. VII
Hill, (William) Thomson, 1875–1959, vol. V
Hill, William Wills, 1881–1974, vol. VII
Hill-Trevor, Hon. George Edwyn; see Trevor.

Hill-Walker, Major Alan Richard, 1859–1944, vol. IV
Hill Watson, Hon. Lord; Laurence Hill Watson, 1895–1957, vol. V
Hill Watson, Laurence; see Hill Watson, Hon. Lord.
Hill-Wood, Captain Sir Basil Samuel Hill, 2nd Bt, 1900–1954, vol. V
Hill-Wood, Major Sir Samuel Hill, 1st Bt, 1872–1949, vol. IV
Hill-Wood, Sir Wilfred William Hill, 1901–1980, vol. VII
Hillard, Rev. Albert Ernest, 1865–1935, vol. III
Hillard, Frederick Arthur, 1868–1937, vol. III
Hillard, Ronald Johnstone, 1903–1971, vol. VII
Hillary, Albert Ernest, 1868–1954, vol. V
Hillary, Michael, 1886–1976, vol. VII
Hiller, George François, 1916–1972, vol. VII
Hillgarth, Captain Alan Hugh, 1899–1978, vol. VII
Hillhouse, Percy Archibald, 1869–1942, vol. IV
Hillhouse, William, 1850–1910, vol. I
Hilliam, Maj.-Gen. Edward, 1863–1949, vol. IV
Hilliar, Harry William, died 1941, vol. IV
Hilliard, Edward, 1867–1940, vol. III
Hilliard, Harvey, died 1956, vol. V
Hilliard, Captain Maurice Alfred, 1863–1907, vol. I
Hilliard, Rt Rev. William George, died 1960, vol. V
Hillier, Alfred Peter, 1858–1911, vol. I
Hillier, Edward Guy, 1857–1924, vol. II
Hillier, Frank Norton, 1894–1959, vol. V
Hillier, Frederick James, 1869–1920, vol. II
Hillier, George Lacy, 1856–1941, vol. IV
Hillier, Joseph H., vol. II
Hillier, Sir Walter Caine, 1849–1927, vol. II
Hillingdon, 1st Baron, 1830–1898, vol. I
Hillingdon, 2nd Baron, 1855–1919, vol. II
Hillingdon, 3rd Baron, 1891–1952, vol. V
Hillingdon, 4th Baron, 1922–1978, vol. VII
Hillis, Rev. Newell Dwight, 1858–1929, vol. III
Hillman, G. B., 1867–1932, vol. III
Hills, Adam, 1880–1941, vol. IV
Hills, Sir Andrew Ashton Waller, 1st Bt, 1933–1955, vol. V
Hills, Col Edmond Herbert G.; see Grove-Hills.
Hills, Eustace Gilbert, died 1934, vol. III
Hills, Maj.-Gen. Sir John, 1834–1902, vol. I
Hills, Lt-Col John David, 1895–1975, vol. VII
Hills, Rt Hon. John Waller, 1867–1938, vol. III
Hills, Sir Reginald Playfair, 1877–1967, vol. VI
Hills-Johnes, Lt-Gen. Sir James, 1833–1919, vol. II
Hillyard, Comdr George Whiteside, 1864–1943, vol. IV
Hilston, Sir Duncan, 1837–1913, vol. I
Hilton of Upton, Baron (Life Peer); Albert Victor Hilton, 1908–1977, vol. VII
Hilton, Cecil, 1884–1931, vol. III
Hilton, Conrad Nicholson, 1887–1979, vol. VII
Hilton, Gwen, 1898–1971, vol. VII
Hilton, Harold Horsfall, 1869–1942, vol. IV
Hilton, James, 1900–1954, vol. V
Hilton, John, 1880–1943, vol. IV
Hilton, Reginald, 1895–1969, vol. VI
Hilton, Maj.-Gen. Richard, 1894–1978, vol. VII

Hilton, Sir Robert Stuart, 1870–1943, vol. IV
Hilton, Roger, 1911–1975, vol. VII
Hilton-Sergeant, Maj.-Gen. Frederick Cavendish, 1898–1978, vol. VII
Hilton-Simpson, Melville William, 1881–1938, vol. III
Himbury, Sir William Henry, died 1955, vol. V
Hime, Lt-Col Rt Hon. Sir Albert Henry, 1842–1919, vol. II
Hime, Maj.-Gen. Henry Charles Rupert, 1877–1945, vol. IV
Hime, Lt-Col Henry William Lovett, 1840–1929, vol. III
Hinchcliff, William Fryer, died 1931, vol. III
Hinchcliffe, Hon. Albert, 1860–1935, vol. III
Hinchcliffe, Sir (George) Raymond, 1900–1973, vol. VII
Hinchcliffe, Brig. John William, 1893–1975, vol. VII
Hinchcliffe, Sir Raymond; see Hinchcliffe, Sir G. R
Hinchcliffe, Richard George, died 1942, vol. IV
Hinchley, John William, 1871–1931, vol. III
Hinchliffe, Sir (Albert) Henry (Stanley), 1893–1980, vol. VII
Hinchliffe, (Frank) Philip (Rideal), 1923–1976, vol. VII
Hinchliffe, Sir Henry; see Hinchliffe, Sir A. H. S.
Hinchliffe, Sir James Peace, 1861–1933, vol. III
Hinchliffe, Philip; see Hinchliffe, F. P. R.
Hinchliffe, William Algernon S.; see Simpson-Hinchliffe.
Hincks, Hon. Sir Cecil Stephen, 1894–1963, vol. VI
Hincks, Rev. Thomas, 1818–1899, vol. I
Hind, Arthur Mayger, 1880–1957, vol. V
Hind, C. Lewis, 1862–1927, vol. II
Hind, Sir Jesse William, 1866–1946, vol. IV
Hind, Rt Rev. John, 1879–1958, vol. V
Hind, Maj.-Gen. Neville Godfray, 1892–1973, vol. VII
Hind, Richard Dacre A.; see Archer-Hind.
Hinde, Brig.-Gen. Alan, 1876–1950, vol. IV
Hinde, George Jennings, died 1918, vol. II
Hinde, George Langford, 1832–1910, vol. I
Hinde, Brig. Harold Montague, 1895–1965, vol. VI
Hinde, Rev. Herbert William, 1877–1955, vol. V
Hinde, Col John Henry Edward, 1847–1931, vol. III
Hinde, Lt-Col Reginald Graham, 1887–1971, vol. VII
Hinde, Sidney Langford, 1863–1930, vol. III
Hindemith, Paul, 1895–1963, vol. VI
Hindenburg, Frau Herbert von; see Hay, Marie.
Hindenburg, Field-Marshal Paul von Beneckendorff und von, 1847–1934, vol. III
Hindle, Edward, 1886–1973, vol. VII
Hindle, Sir Frederick, 1877–1953, vol. V
Hindle, Frederick George, 1848–1925, vol. II
Hindle, Wilfrid Hope, 1903–1967, vol. VI
Hindley, Sir Clement D. M., 1874–1944, vol. IV
Hindley, Brig. Geoffrey Bernard Sylvester, 1902–1980, vol. VII
Hindley, Ven. William George, died 1936, vol. III
Hindley-Smith, James Dury, 1894–1974, vol. VII
Hindlip, 2nd Baron, 1842–1897, vol. I

Hindlip, 3rd Baron, 1877–1931, vol. III
Hindlip, 4th Baron, 1906–1966, vol. VI
Hindmarsh, W(illiam) Russell, 1929–1973, vol. VII
Hinds, Benjamin, 1882–1952, vol. V
Hinds, John, 1862–1928, vol. II
Hindus, Maurice Gerschon, 1891–1969, vol. VI
Hine, George T., 1841–1916, vol. II
Hine, Harry, 1845–1941, vol. IV
Hine, Rt Rev. John Edward, 1857–1934, vol. III
Hine, Montague Leonard, 1883–1967, vol. VI
Hine, Reginald Leslie, 1883–1949, vol. IV
Hine-Haycock, Rev. Trevitt Reginald, 1861–1953, vol. V
Hine-Haycock, Col Vaughan Randolph, 1871–1937, vol. III
Hinge, Maj.-Gen. Harry Alexander, 1868–1948, vol. IV
Hingeston-Randolph, Rev. Francis Charles, 1833–1910, vol. I
Hingley, Sir Benjamin, 1st Bt, 1830–1905, vol. I
Hingley, Sir George Benjamin, 2nd Bt, 1850–1918, vol. II
Hingston, Lt-Col Clayton Alexander Francis, 1877–1969, vol. VI
Hingston, George, died 1925, vol. II
Hingston, Major Richard William George, 1887–1966, vol. VI
Hingston, Hon. Sir William Hales, 1829–1907, vol. I
Hingston, Surg. Captain William Percival, 1879–1950, vol. IV
Hinks, Arthur Robert, 1873–1945, vol. IV
Hinkson, Henry Albert, 1865–1919, vol. II
Hinkson, Mrs Katharine Tynan; see Tynan, Katharine.
Hinshelwood, Sir Cyril Norman, 1897–1967, vol. VI
Hinsley, His Eminence Cardinal Arthur, 1865–1943, vol. IV
Hinton, A. Horsley, 1863–1908, vol. I
Hinton, Arthur, 1869–1941, vol. IV
Hinton, Mrs Arthur; see Goodson, K.
Hinton, Captain Eric Perceval, 1902–1970, vol. VI
Hinton, Geoffrey Thomas Searle, 1918–1980, vol. VII
Hinton, Lt-Col Godfrey Bingham, 1871–1918, vol. II
Hinton, Howard Everest, 1912–1977, vol. VII
Hinton, Martin Alister Campbell, 1883–1961, vol. VI
Hinton, Wilfred John, 1887–1949, vol. IV
Hinton-Cooper, Harold, 1891–1980, vol. VII
Hinwood, George Yorke, 1894–1960, vol. V
Hinxman, Lionel Wordsworth, 1855–1936, vol. III
Hiorns, Frederick Robert, 1876–1961, vol. VI
Hipkins, Alfred James, 1826–1903, vol. I
Hippisley, John, died 1898, vol. I
Hippisley, Richard John Bayntun, died 1956, vol. V
Hippisley, Col Richard Lionel, 1853–1936, vol. III
Hipwell, Col Alfred George, 1853–1939, vol. III
Hipwell, Ven. Richard Senior, 1881–1962, vol. VI
Hipwood, Sir Charles, 1869–1946, vol. IV
Hirachand, Walchand, 1882–1953, vol. V
Hird, Rev. Arthur, 1883–1932, vol. III

Hird, Norman Leslie, 1886–1946, vol. IV
Hirsch, Maj.-Gen. Charles Ernest Rickards, 1903–1975, vol. VII
Hirsch, Emil G., 1851–1923, vol. II
Hirsch, Lt-Col Leonard, 1879–1942, vol. IV
Hirsch, Paul Adolf, 1881–1951, vol. V
Hirst, 1st Baron, 1863–1943, vol. IV
Hirst, Sir Amos Brook, 1878–1955, vol. V
Hirst, Sir Edmund Langley, 1898–1975, vol. VII
Hirst, Col Edward Audus, 1872–1937, vol. III
Hirst, Francis W., 1873–1953, vol. V
Hirst, Sir (Frank) Wyndham, died 1972, vol. VII
Hirst, George Henry, 1869–1933, vol. III
Hirst, George S. S., 1871–1912, vol. I
Hirst, Reginald John, 1880–1959, vol. V
Hirst, William, 1873–1946, vol. IV
Hirst, William Alfred, 1870–1948, vol. IV
Hirst, Sir Wyndham; see Hirst, Sir F. W.
Hirtzel, Sir Arthur, 1870–1937, vol. III
Hiscock, Alfred James, died 1930, vol. III
Hiscocks, Edward Stanley, 1903–1973, vol. VII
Hiscox, Ralph, 1907–1970, vol. VI
Hislop, James, 1870–1932, vol. III
Hislop, Joseph, died 1977, vol. VII
Hislop, Margaret Ross, 1894–1972, vol. VII
Hislop, Thomas Charles Atkinson, 1888–1965, vol. VI
Hislop, Hon. Thomas William, 1850–1925, vol. II
Hissey, James John, died 1921, vol. II
Hitch, Frederick Brook, 1877–1957, vol. V
Hitchcock, Sir Alfred Joseph, 1899–1980, vol. VII
Hitchcock, Lt-Gen. Sir Basil Ferguson Burnett-, 1877–1938, vol. III
Hitchcock, Sir Eldred Frederick, 1887–1959, vol. V
Hitchcock, Ethan Allen, 1835–1909, vol. I
Hitchcock, Rev. Francis Ryan Montgomery, 1867–1951, vol. V
Hitchcock, Rev. George Edward, 1862–1939, vol. III
Hitchcock, Howard, 1866–1932, vol. III
Hitchcock, Rev. William Maunder, 1835–1921, vol. II
Hitchens, Harry Butler, 1910–1963, vol. VI
Hitchens, Ivon; see Hitchens, S. I.
Hitchens, (Sydney) Ivon, 1893–1979, vol. VII
Hitching, Sir Thomas Henry B.; see Brooke-Hitching.
Hitching, Gp Captain John Phelp, 1899–1979, vol. VII
Hitchins, Col Charles Faunce, died 1959, vol. V
Hitchins, Col Charles Henry Macintire, 1860–1931, vol. III
Hitchins, Brig. Edward Norman Fortescue, 1884–1959, vol. V
Hitchins, Captain Henry Luxmoore, 1885–1961, vol. VI
Hitchman, Sir Alan; see Hitchman, Sir E. A.
Hitchman, Sir (Edwin) Alan, 1903–1980, vol. VII
Hitler, Adolph, 1889–1945, vol. IV
Hives, 1st Baron, 1886–1965, vol. VI
Hives, Rt Rev. Harry Ernest, 1901–1974, vol. VII
Hjelt, Edvard Immanuel, 1855–1921, vol. II
Hjort, Johan, 1869–1948, vol. IV
Ho Tung, Sir Robert, 1862–1956, vol. V

Hoad, Maj.-Gen. Sir John Charles, 1856–1911, vol. I
Hoadley, Charles Archibald, 1887–1947, vol. IV
Hoadley, Jane, died 1946, vol. IV
Hoar, Arthur Stanley George, 1903–1972, vol. VII
Hoar, Hon. Ernest Knight, 1898–1979, vol. VII
Hoar, George F., 1826–1904, vol. I
Hoare, Alfred, 1850–1938, vol. III
Hoare, Sir Archer, 1876–1973, vol. VII
Hoare, Lt-Col Arthur Fanshawe, 1854–1925, vol. II
Hoare, Arthur Hervey, 1877–1953, vol. V
Hoare, Charles Richard, 1868–1933, vol. III
Hoare, Christopher Gurney, 1882–1973, vol. VII
Hoare, Brig.-Gen. Cuthbert Gurney, 1883–1969, vol. VI
Hoare, Rear-Adm. Dennis John, 1891–1979, vol. VII
Hoare, Douglas, 1875–1947, vol. IV
Hoare, Edward Brodie, 1841–1911, vol. I
Hoare, Sir Edward O'Bryen, 7th Bt (cr 1784), 1898–1969, vol. VI
Hoare, Edward Ralphe Douro, 1894–1936, vol. III
Hoare, Edward Wallis, 1863–1920, vol. II (A), vol. III
Hoare, Maj.-Gen. Francis Richard Gurney, 1879–1959, vol. V
Hoare, Lt-Col Geoffrey Lennard, 1879–1960, vol. V
Hoare, Henry, 1866–1956, vol. V
Hoare, Sir Henry Hugh Arthur, 6th Bt (cr 1786), 1865–1947, vol. IV
Hoare, Henry Noel, 1877–1962, vol. VI
Hoare, Henry William H.; see Hamilton-Hoare.
Hoare, Hugh Edward, 1854–1929, vol. III
Hoare, Rev. John Gurney, 1847–1923, vol. II
Hoare, Rt Rev. Joseph, 1842–1927, vol. II
Hoare, Rt Rev. Joseph Charles, 1851–1906, vol. I
Hoare, Sir Joseph Wallis O'Bryen, 5th Bt (cr 1784), 1828–1904, vol. I
Hoare, Maj.-Gen. Lionel Lennard, 1881–1975, vol. VII
Hoare, Michael Richard, 1903–1970, vol. VI
Hoare, Oliver Vaughan Gurney, 1882–1957, vol. V
Hoare, Peter Arthur Marsham, 1869–1939, vol. III
Hoare, Sir Peter William, 7th Bt (cr 1786), 1898–1973, vol. VII
Hoare, Brig.-Gen. Reginald, 1865–1947, vol. IV
Hoare, Sir Reginald Hervey, died 1954, vol. V
Hoare, Rev. Richard Whitehead, 1840–1924, vol. II
Hoare, Major Robert Basil, 1870–1931, vol. III
Hoare, Col Robert Rawdon, 1897–1977, vol. VII
Hoare, Sir Samuel, 1st Bt (cr 1899), 1841–1915, vol. I
Hoare, Sir Samuel, 1896–1976, vol. VII
Hoare, Sir Sydney James O'Bryen, 6th Bt (cr 1784), 1860–1933, vol. III
Hoare, William Douro, 1862–1928, vol. II
Hobart, Lt-Col Sir (Claud) Vere Cavendish, 2nd Bt, 1870–1949, vol. IV
Hobart, Henry Metcalf, 1868–1946, vol. IV
Hobart, Brig. James Wilfred Lang Stanley, 1890–1970, vol. VI

Hobart, Maj.-Gen. Sir Percy Cleghorn Stanley, 1885–1957, vol. V

Hobart, Robert Charles Arthur Stanley, 1881–1955, vol. V

Hobart, Sir Robert Henry, 1st Bt, 1836–1928, vol. II

Hobart, Lt-Col Sir Vere; see Hobart, Sir C. V. C.

Hobart-Hampden, Hon. Charles Edward, 1825–1913, vol. I

Hobart-Hampden, Ernest Miles, 1864–1949, vol. IV

Hobbes, John Oliver, 1867–1906, vol. I

Hobbins, Robert, died 1922, vol. II

Hobbins, Thomas Phillips, 1877–1959, vol. V

Hobbs, Lt-Col George Radley, 1853–1907, vol. I

Hobbs, Harold William, 1903–1976, vol. VII

Hobbs, Captain Horace Edwin, 1896–1935, vol. III

Hobbs, Jack; see Hobbs, Sir John B.

Hobbs, Sir John (Berry), (Jack), 1882–1963, vol. VI

Hobbs, Lt-Gen. Sir (Joseph John) Talbot, 1864–1938, vol. III

Hobbs, Maj.-Gen. Percy Eyre Francis, 1865–1939, vol. III

Hobbs, Brig.-Gen. Reginald Francis Arthur, 1878–1953, vol. V

Hobbs, Maj.-Gen. Reginald Geoffrey Stirling, 1908–1977, vol. VII

Hobbs, Lt-Gen. Sir Talbot; see Hobbs, Lt-Gen. Sir J. J. T

Hobday, Alfred, 1870–1942, vol. IV

Hobday, Col Edmund Arthur Ponsonby, 1859–1931, vol. III

Hobday, Sir Frederick T. G., died 1939, vol. III

Hobday, Maj.-Gen. Thomas Francis, 1847–1938, vol. III

Hobhouse, 1st Baron, 1819–1904, vol. I

Hobhouse, Sir Arthur Lawrence, 1886–1965, vol. VI

Hobhouse, Rt Hon. Sir Charles Edward Henry, 4th Bt, 1862–1941, vol. IV

Hobhouse, Sir Charles Parry, 3rd Bt, 1825–1916, vol. II

Hobhouse, Rt Rev. Edmund, 1817–1904, vol. I

Hobhouse, Edmund, 1860–1933, vol. III

Hobhouse, Edmund W. Neill, 1888–1973, vol. VII

Hobhouse, Rt Hon. Henry, 1854–1937, vol. III

Hobhouse, Sir John Richard, 1893–1961, vol. VI

Hobhouse, Leonard Trelawney, 1864–1929, vol. III

Hobhouse, Sir Reginald Arthur, 5th Bt, 1878–1947, vol. IV

Hobhouse, Rev. Walter, 1862–1928, vol. II

Hobkirk, Brig.-Gen. Clarence John, 1869–1949, vol. IV

Hobley, Charles William, 1867–1947, vol. IV

Hobman, Joseph Burton, 1872–1953, vol. V

Hobson, Baron (Life Peer); Charles Rider Hobson, 1904–1966, vol. VI

Hobson, Sir Albert John, died 1923, vol. II

Hobson, Alfred Dennis, 1901–1974, vol. VII

Hobson, Alice Mary, 1860–1954, vol. V

Hobson, Clement, 1877–1952, vol. V

Hobson, Ven. Edward Waller, 1851–1924, vol. II

Hobson, Rev. Edwin, 1847–1936, vol. III

Hobson, Ernest William, 1856–1933, vol. III

Hobson, Maj.-Gen. Frederic Taylor, 1840–1909, vol. I

Hobson, Frederick Greig, died 1961, vol. VI

Hobson, Geoffrey Dudley, 1882–1949, vol. IV

Hobson, Lt-Col Gerald Walton, 1873–1962, vol. VI

Hobson, Harold, 1891–1973, vol. VII

Hobson, Harry Roy, died 1965, vol. VI

Hobson, Sir Henry Arthur, 1893–1968, vol. VI

Hobson, John Atkinson, 1858–1940, vol. III

Hobson, Rt Hon. Sir John Gardiner Sumner, 1912–1967, vol. VI

Hobson, John Lombard, died 1932, vol. III

Hobson, Neville, 1886–1975, vol. VII

Hobson, Sir Oscar Rudolf, 1886–1961, vol. VI

Hobson, Sir Patrick, 1909–1970, vol. VI

Hobson, Rev. R., died 1914, vol. I

Hobson, Robert Lockhart, 1872–1941, vol. IV

Hobson, Sidney, 1887–1970, vol. VI

Hoby, Major John Charles James, died 1938, vol. III

Hockaday, William Thomas, 1858–1933, vol. III

Hocken, Col Charles Augustus Frederick, 1870–1958, vol. V

Hocken, Hon. Horatio Clarence, 1857–1937, vol. III

Hocking, Sir Henry Hicks, 1842–1907, vol. I

Hocking, Joseph, died 1937, vol. III

Hocking, Silas Kitto, 1850–1935, vol. III

Hocking, William John, 1864–1953, vol. V

Hockley, Ven. Guy Wittenoom, 1869–1946, vol. IV

Hockliffe, Ernest, 1863–1944, vol. IV

Hodd, Ven. Henry Norman, 1905–1973, vol. VII

Hodder, Lt-Col Andrew Edward, died 1938, vol. III

Hodder, Edwin, 1837–1904, vol. I

Hodder-Williams, Sir Ernest; see Hodder-Williams, Sir J. E.

Hodder-Williams, Sir (John) Ernest, 1876–1927, vol. II

Hodder-Williams, Ralph Wilfred, 1890–1961, vol. VI

Hodder-Williams, Robert Percy, 1880–1958, vol. V

Hodding, Col John, 1854–1919, vol. II

Hodge, Alan, 1915–1979, vol. VII

Hodge, Albert H., 1875–1918, vol. II

Hodge, Rear-Adm. Hon. Claude Preston H.; see Herman-Hodge.

Hodge, Rev. Canon Edward Grose, died 1928, vol. II

Hodge, Lt-Col Edward Humfrey Vere, 1883–1968, vol. VI

Hodge, Francis Edwin, 1883–1949, vol. IV

Hodge, Frederick Webb, 1864–1956, vol. V

Hodge, Harold, 1862–1937, vol. III

Hodge, Harry, 1872–1947, vol. IV

Hodge, Horace Emerton, 1904–1958, vol. V

Hodge, Humfrey G.; see Grose-Hodge.

Hodge, Lt-Col James Philip, 1879–1946, vol. IV

Hodge, Rt Hon. John, 1855–1937, vol. III

Hodge, John Douglass Vere, 1887–1973, vol. VII

Hodge, Merton; see Hodge, H. E.

Hodge, Major Hon. Robert Edward Udny H.; see Hermon-Hodge.

Hodge, Sir Rowland Frederic William, 1st Bt, 1859–1950, vol. IV
Hodge, Stephen Oswald Vere, 1891–1979, vol. VII
Hodge, Sir William Vallance Douglas, 1903–1975, vol. VII
Hodgen, Maj.-Gen. Gordon West, 1894–1968, vol. VI
Hodges, Rev. Alfred, 1853–1909, vol. I
Hodges, Arthur Harris, 1884–1941, vol. IV
Hodges, Lt-Col Aubrey Dallas Percival, 1861–1946, vol. IV
Hodges, Barbara K., 1893–1949, vol. IV
Hodges, Rt Rev. Edward Noel, 1849–1928, vol. II
Hodges, Rt Rev. Evelyn Charles, 1887–1980, vol. VII
Hodges, Frank, 1887–1947, vol. IV
Hodges, Ven. George, 1851–1922, vol. II
Hodges, Hon. Sir Henry Edward Agincourt, 1844–1919, vol. II
Hodges, Herbert Arthur, 1905–1976, vol. VII
Hodges, Kenneth Henry, 1915–1961, vol. VI
Hodges, Captain Michael, 1904–1977, vol. VII
Hodges, Adm. Sir Michael Henry, 1874–1951, vol. V
Hodges, Sir Reginald John, 1889–1973, vol. VII
Hodges, Rev. William Herbert, 1873–1948, vol. IV
Hodgett, Rev. Richard, 1884–1927, vol. II
Hodgetts, Charles Alfred, 1859–1952, vol. V
Hodgetts, Edward Arthur Brayley, 1859–1932, vol. III
Hodgins, Frank Egerton, died 1932, vol. III
Hodgins, Lt-Col Frederick Owen, 1887–1924, vol. II
Hodgins, Rev. Joseph Rogerson Edmond Cotter, died 1919, vol. II
Hodgins, Thomas, 1828–1910, vol. I
Hodgins, Maj.-Gen. William Egerton, 1850–1930, vol. III
Hodgkin, Lt-Col Harry Sidney, 1879–1943, vol. IV
Hodgkin, Henry Theodore, 1877–1933, vol. III
Hodgkin, Jonathan Edward, 1875–1953, vol. V
Hodgkin, Lucy Violet, (Mrs John Holdsworth), 1869–1954, vol. V
Hodgkin, Robert Howard, 1877–1951, vol. V
Hodgkin, Thomas, 1831–1913, vol. I
Hodgkins, T., died 1909, vol. I
Hodgkinson, Col Charles, 1870–1939, vol. III
Hodgkinson, Rev. George Langton, 1837–1915, vol. I
Hodgkinson, Jonathan, 1886–1940, vol. III
Hodgkinson, William Richard, 1851–1935, vol. III
Hodgson, Sir Arthur, 1818–1902, vol. I
Hodgson, Arthur John, 1887–1971, vol. VII
Hodgson, Lt-Col Barnard Thornton, 1863–1939, vol. III
Hodgson, Sir Edward Highton, 1880–1955, vol. V
Hodgson, Sir Edward M., died 1904, vol. I
Hodgson, Ernest Atkinson, 1886–1975, vol. VII
Hodgson, Rev. Francis Greaves, 1840–1920, vol. II
Hodgson, Rev. Francis Henry, 1848–1930, vol. III
Hodgson, Francis Henry Birkett, 1879–1935, vol. III
Hodgson, Rev. Francis Roger, died 1920, vol. II
Hodgson, Sir Frederic Mitchell, 1851–1925, vol. II

Hodgson, George Bryan, 1863–1926, vol. II
Hodgson, Sir Gerald Hassall, 1891–1971, vol. VII
Hodgson, Geraldine E., 1865–1937, vol. III
Hodgson, Lt-Col Greenwood, 1875–1950, vol. IV
Hodgson, Sir Harold (Kingston) Graham-, died 1960, vol. V
Hodgson, Rt Rev. Henry Bernard, 1856–1921, vol. II
Hodgson, Maj.-Gen. Sir Henry West, 1868–1930, vol. III
Hodgson, Herbert Henry, 1883–1967, vol. VI
Hodgson, Rev. James Muscutt, died 1923, vol. II
Hodgson, Rear-Adm. John Coombe, 1881–1936, vol. III
Hodgson, (John) Stuart, 1877–1950, vol. IV
Hodgson, Rev. Leonard, 1889–1969, vol. VI
Hodgson, Sir Mark, 1880–1967, vol. VI
Hodgson, Norman, 1891–1963, vol. VI
Hodgson, Patrick Kirkman, 1884–1963, vol. VI
Hodgson, Ralph, 1871–1962, vol. VI
Hodgson, Ven. Robert, 1844–1917, vol. II
Hodgson, Robert Kirkman, 1850–1924, vol. II
Hodgson, Sir Robert MacLeod, 1874–1956, vol. V
Hodgson, Shadworth Hollway, 1832–1912, vol. I
Hodgson, Stuart; see Hodgson, J. S.
Hodgson, Ven. Thomas, died 1921, vol. II
Hodgson, Brig. Walter Thornton, 1880–1957, vol. V
Hodgson, Rev. William, died 1919, vol. II
Hodgson, Sir William, 1854–1940, vol. III
Hodgson, Sir William, died 1945, vol. IV
Hodgson, William Archer, 1887–1965, vol. VI
Hodgson, William Earl, died 1910, vol. I
Hodgson, William Hope, 1877–1918, vol. II
Hodgson, Lt-Col William Roy, 1892–1958, vol. V
Hodgson, Mrs Willoughby, died 1949, vol. IV
Hodsdon, Sir James W. B., 1858–1928, vol. II
Hodsoll, Wing Comdr Sir (Eric) John, 1894–1971, vol. VII
Hodsoll, Wing Comdr Sir John; see Hodsoll, Wing Comdr Sir E. J.
Hodson, Sir Arnold Wienholt, 1881–1944, vol. IV
Hodson, Rt Rev. Augustine John, 1879–1961, vol. VI
Hodson, Charles William, died 1910, vol. I
Hodson, Major Sir Edmond Adair, 5th Bt, 1893–1972, vol. VII
Hodson, Col Frederic Arthur, 1866–1925, vol. II
Hodson, Col George Benjamin, 1863–1916, vol. II
Hodson, Air Vice-Marshal George Stacey, 1899–1976, vol. VII
Hodson, James Lansdale, 1891–1956, vol. V
Hodson, Sir Robert Adair, 4th Bt, 1853–1921, vol. II
Hodson, Rt Rev. Robert Leighton, 1885–1960, vol. V
Hodson, Samuel John, died 1908, vol. I
Hodson, Thomas Callan, died 1953, vol. V
Hoehne, Most Rev. John, 1910–1978, vol. VII
Hoenig, Rose, died 1966, vol. VI
Hoernle, Augustus Frederic Rudolf, 1841–1918, vol. II
Hoernlé, R. F. Alfred, died 1943, vol. IV

Hoesch, Leopold Gustav Alexander von, 1881–1936, vol. III

Hoey, Frances Sarah, (Mrs Cashel Hoey), 1830–1908, vol. I

Hoey, Robert Alexander, 1883–1965, vol. VI

Hoey, William, 1849–1919, vol. II

Hoffding, Harold, 1843–1931, vol. III

Hoffe, Monckton, 1881–1951, vol. V

Hoffert, Hermann H., *born* 1860, vol. II

Hoffman, Paul Gray, 1891–1974, vol. VII

Hoffman, Philip Christopher, 1878–1959, vol. V

Hoffmann, Prof.; *see* Lewis, Angelo.

Hoffmeister, William, 1843–1910, vol. I

Hoffnung, Gerard, 1925–1959, vol. V

Hofmann, Josef, 1876–1957, vol. V

Hofmeyr, George Morgan, 1867–1928, vol. II (A), vol. III

Hofmeyr, Hon. Gysbert Reitz, 1871–1942, vol. IV

Hofmeyr, Hon. J. H., 1845–1909, vol. I

Hofmeyr, Rt Hon. Jan Hendrik, 1894–1948, vol. IV

Hofstadter, Richard, 1916–1970, vol. VI

Hog, Major Roger Thomas Alexander, 1893–1979, vol. VII

Hog, Steuart Bayley, 1864–1944, vol. IV

Hogan, Hon. Edmond John, 1884–1964, vol. VI

Hogan, Lt-Col Edward Vincent, 1874–1933, vol. III

Hogan, Henry Charles, 1860–1924, vol. II

Hogan, James Francis, 1855–1924, vol. II

Hogan, James H., 1883–1948, vol. IV

Hogan, Rt Rev. Mgr John F., 1858–1918, vol. II

Hogan, Patrick, 1891–1936, vol. III

Hogarth, Alfred Moore, 1876–1947, vol. IV

Hogarth, David George, 1862–1927, vol. II

Hogarth, Maj.-Gen. Donald Macdonald, 1879–1950, vol. IV (A), vol. V

Hogarth, Margaret Cameron, 1885–1980, vol. VII

Hogarth, Mary H. U., *died* 1935, vol. III

Hogarth, Robert George, 1868–1953, vol. V

Hogarth, William David, 1901–1965, vol. VI

Hogben, George, 1853–1920, vol. II

Hogben, Lancelot, 1895–1975, vol. VII

Hogbin, Ven. George Henry, 1869–1937, vol. III

Hogbin, Henry Cairn, 1880–1966, vol. VI

Hogg, Lt-Gen. Sir Adam George Forbes, 1836–1908, vol. I

Hogg, Adam Spencer, 1870–1937, vol. III

Hogg, Hon. Alan, *died* 1934, vol. III

Hogg, Rev. Andrew Albert Victor, 1864–1927, vol. II

Hogg, Sir Anthony Henry L.; *see* Lindsay-Hogg.

Hogg, Sir Cecil; *see* Hogg, Sir J. C.

Hogg, Col Conrad Charles Henry, 1875–1950, vol. IV

Hogg, Cuthbert Stuart, 1911–1973, vol. VII

Hogg, David C., 1840–1914, vol. I

Hogg, Maj.-Gen. Douglas McArthur, 1888–1965, vol. VI

Hogg, Edward Gascoigne, 1882–1971, vol. VII

Hogg, Sir Frederick Russell, 1836–1923, vol. II

Hogg, Maj.-Gen. George Crawford, 1842–1921, vol. II

Hogg, George Robert Disraeli, 1894–1977, vol. VII

Hogg, Sir Gilbert Pitcairn, 1884–1950, vol. IV

Hogg, Guy Weir, 1861–1943, vol. IV

Hogg, Wing Comdr Henry Robert William, 1886–1942, vol. IV

Hogg, Hope W., 1863–1912, vol. I

Hogg, Lt-Col Ian Graham, 1875–1914, vol. I

Hogg, Jabez, 1817–1899, vol. I

Hogg, Sir (James) Cecil, 1900–1973, vol. VII

Hogg, John Drummond, 1886–1937, vol. III

Hogg, Rt Hon. Jonathan, 1847–1930, vol. III

Hogg, Sir Lindsay L.; *see* Lindsay-Hogg.

Hogg, Sir Malcolm Nicholson, 1883–1948, vol. IV

Hogg, Margaret, *died* 1975, vol. VII

Hogg, Norman, 1907–1975, vol. VII

Hogg, Brig. Oliver Frederick Gillilan, 1887–1979, vol. VII

Hogg, Percy Herbertson, 1898–1978, vol. VII

Hogg, Quintin, 1845–1903, vol. I

Hogg, Robert Henry, *died* 1949, vol. IV

Hogg, Brig.-Gen. Rudolph Edward Trower, 1877–1955, vol. V

Hogg, Sir Stuart Saunders, 1833–1921, vol. II

Hogg, William Edward, 1880–1968, vol. VI

Hogg, Lt-Col Willoughby Lugard, 1881–1969, vol. VI

Hoggan, Maj.-Gen. John William, 1833–1900, vol. I

Hoggarth, Arthur Henry Graham, 1882–1964, vol. VI

Hoggatt, William, 1880–1961, vol. VI

Hogge, Col Charles, 1851–1911, vol. I

Hogge, James Myles, 1873–1928, vol. II

Hogge, Col John William, 1852–1910, vol. I

Hogshaw, Brig. John Harold, 1896–1968, vol. VI

Hogue, Hon. James Alexander, 1846–1920, vol. II

Hohenlohe-Langenburg, Prince of; Ernest William Frederic Charles Maximilian, *died* 1913, vol. I

Hohler, Sir Gerald Fitzroy, 1862–1934, vol. III

Hohler, Henry Booth, 1835–1916, vol. II

Hohler, Sir Thomas Beaumont, 1871–1946, vol. IV

Holbech, Rev. Charles William, 1816–1901, vol. I

Holbech, Lt-Col Laurence, 1888–1963, vol. VI

Holbech, Ronald Herbert Acland, 1887–1956, vol. V

Holbech, Rt Rev. William Arthur, 1850–1930, vol. III

Holbein, Arthur Montague, 1897–1970, vol. VI

Holberton, Sir Edgar Joseph, 1874–1949, vol. IV

Holborow, Col William Hillier, 1841–1917, vol. II (A), vol. III

Holbrook, Col Sir Arthur Richard, 1850–1946, vol. IV

Holbrook, Col Sir Claude Vivian, 1886–1979, vol. VII

Holbrook, Rear-Adm. Leonard Stanley, 1882–1974, vol. VII

Holbrook, Comdr Norman Douglas, 1888–1976, vol. VII

Holbrooke, Josef, 1878–1958, vol. V

Holbrooke, Maj.-Gen. Philip Lancelot, 1872–1958, vol. V

Holburn, John Goundry, 1843–1899, vol. I

Holcroft, Sir Charles, 1st Bt (*cr* 1905), 1831–1917, vol. II

Holcroft, Sir George Harry, 1st Bt (cr 1921), 1856–1951, vol. V

Holcroft, Sir Reginald Culcheth, 2nd Bt (cr 1921), 1899–1978, vol. VII

Holden, 1st Baron, 1833–1912 (this entry was not transferred to Who was Who).

Holden, 2nd Baron, 1867–1937, vol. III

Holden, 3rd Baron, 1898–1951, vol. V

Holden, Rev. Albert Thomas, 1866–1935, vol. III

Holden, Arthur, 1881–1964, vol. VI

Holden, Brig.-Gen. Sir Capel Lofft; see Holden, Brig.-Gen. Sir H. C. L.

Holden, Charles, 1875–1960, vol. V

Holden, Col Charles Walter, died 1939, vol. III

Holden, Captain Edward Charles Shuttleworth, 1865–1916, vol. II

Holden, Sir Edward Hopkinson, 1st Bt (cr 1909), 1848–1919, vol. II

Holden, Sir Edward Thomas, 1831–1926, vol. II

Holden, Hon. Sir Edward Wheewall, 1885–1947, vol. IV

Holden, Sir George, 2nd Bt (cr 1919), 1890–1937, vol. III

Holden, Sir George, 3rd Bt (cr 1919), 1914–1976, vol. VII

Holden, Harold H., 1885–1977, vol. VII

Holden, Sir Harry Cassie, 2nd Bt (cr 1909), 1877–1965, vol. VI

Holden, Rev. Henry, 1814–1909, vol. I

Holden, Brig.-Gen. Sir (Henry) Capel Lofft, 1856–1937, vol. III

Holden, Henry Smith, 1887–1963, vol. VI

Holden, Sir Isaac, 1st Bt (cr 1893), 1807–1897, vol. I

Holden, Sir Isaac Holden, 5th Bt (cr 1893), 1867–1962, vol. VI

Holden, Sir James Robert, 1903–1977, vol. VII

Holden, Rt Rev. John, 1882–1949, vol. IV

Holden, Sir John Henry, 1st Bt (cr 1919), 1862–1926, vol. II

Holden, Rev. John Stuart, died 1934, vol. III

Holden, Luther, died 1905, vol. I

Holden, Norman Edward, 1879–1946, vol. IV

Holden, Rev. Robert, 1853–1926, vol. II

Holden, Maj.-Gen. William Corson, 1893–1955, vol. V

Holder, Douglas William, 1923–1977, vol. VII

Holder, Sir Frank Wilfred, 1897–1967, vol. VI

Holder, Hon. Sir Frederick William, 1850–1909, vol. I

Holder, Sir Henry Charles, 2nd Bt, 1874–1945, vol. IV

Holder, Rear-Adm. Henry Lowe, 1832–1924, vol. II

Holder, Sir John Charles, 1st Bt, 1838–1923, vol. II

Holder, Rt Rev. Mgr Joseph, 1845–1917, vol. II

Holderness, Sir Ernest William Elsmie, 2nd Bt, 1890–1968, vol. VI

Holderness, Sir Thomas William, 1st Bt, 1849–1924, vol. II

Holdgate, Rev. William Wyatt, 1872–1949, vol. IV

Holdich, Gen. Sir Edward Alan, 1822–1909, vol. I

Holdich, Lt-Col Godfrey William Vanrennen, 1882–1921, vol. II

Holdich, Brig.-Gen. Harold Adrian, 1874–1964, vol. VI

Holdich, Col Sir Thomas Hungerford, 1843–1929, vol. III

Holding, Edgar Thomas, 1870–1952, vol. V

Holdsworth, Hon. Col Albert Amrytage, died 1932, vol. III

Holdsworth, Benjamin George, 1892–1943, vol. IV

Holdsworth, Sir Charles, 1863–1935, vol. III

Holdsworth, David, 1918–1978, vol. VII

Holdsworth, Sir Frank Wild, 1904–1969, vol. VI

Holdsworth, Brig.-Gen. George Lewis, 1862–1942, vol. IV

Holdsworth, Sir Herbert, 1890–1949, vol. IV

Holdsworth, Lt-Col John Joseph, 1844–1920, vol. II

Holdsworth, Lucy Violet; see Hodgkin, L. V.

Holdsworth, Mary, 1908–1978, vol. VII

Holdsworth, Sir William Searle, 1871–1944, vol. IV

Hole, Edwyn Cecil, died 1976, vol. VII

Hole, Francis George, 1904–1973, vol. VII

Hole, Lt-Col Hugh Marshall, 1865–1941, vol. IV

Hole, Robert Selby, 1875–1938, vol. III

Hole, S. Hugh F., 1862–1948, vol. IV

Hole, Very Rev. S. Reynolds, 1819–1904, vol. I

Hole, William, 1846–1917, vol. II

Holford, Baron (Life Peer); William Graham Holford, 1907–1975, vol. VII

Holford, Lt-Col Cecil Francis Lovell, 1900–1963, vol. VI

Holford, Lt-Col Sir George Lindsay, 1860–1926, vol. II

Holford, Mrs Gwynne, (Mary Eleanor), died 1947, vol. IV

Holford, Lt-Col James Henry Edward, 1873–1936, vol. III

Holford, James Price William Gwynne, 1833–1916, vol. II

Holford, Mary Eleanor; see Holford, Mrs Gwynne.

Holiday, Sir Frederick Charles, 1843–1930, vol. III

Holiday, Henry, 1839–1927, vol. II

Hollams, Frederick William, 1848–1941, vol. IV

Hollams, Sir John, 1820–1910, vol. I

Holland, Alfred, 1900–1936, vol. III

Holland, Sir Alfred Herbert, 1878–1968, vol. VI

Holland, Sir Arthur, 1842–1928, vol. II

Holland, Lt-Gen. Sir Arthur Edward Aveling, 1862–1927, vol. II

Holland, Bernard Henry, 1856–1926, vol. II

Holland, Vice-Adm. Cedric Swinton, 1889–1950, vol. IV

Holland, Charles Thurstan, died 1941, vol. IV

Holland, Clive, (Charles James Hankinson), 1866–1959, vol. V

Holland, Sir Eardley Lancelot, 1879–1967, vol. VI

Holland, Edgar William, 1899–1973, vol. VII

Holland, Sir Edward John, 1865–1939, vol. III

Holland, Sir (Edward) Milner, 1902–1969, vol. VI

Holland, Sir Erskine; see Holland, Sir T. E.

Holland, Fanny, (Mrs William Arthur Law), 1847–1931, vol. III

Holland, Rev. Francis James, 1828–1907, vol. I

Holland, Frank, 1899–1972, vol. VII

Holland, Frank William C.; see Crossley-Holland.

Holland, Sir George William Frederick, 1897–1962, vol. VI
Holland, Comdr Gerald Edward, 1860–1917, vol. II
Holland, Lt-Col Guy Lushington, *born* 1861, vol. II
Holland, Henry, 1859–1944, vol. IV
Holland, Henry Edmund, 1868–1933, vol. III
Holland, Rev. Henry Scott, 1847–1918, vol. II
Holland, Sir Henry Tristram, 1875–1965, vol. VI
Holland, Maj.-Gen. Henry William, 1825–1920, vol. II
Holland, Captain Herbert Christian, 1858–1916, vol. II
Holland, Rt Rev. Herbert St Barbe, 1882–1966, vol. VI
Holland, Hetty L.; *see* Lee-Holland.
Holland, Instr Captain Horace Herbert, *died* 1952, vol. V
Holland, Rear-Adm. Hubert Henry, 1873–1957, vol. V
Holland, Major Hugh, 1884–1922, vol. II
Holland, Maj.-Gen. John Charles Francis, 1897–1956, vol. V
Holland, Major John Vincent, 1889–1975, vol. VII
Holland, Col Lancelot, 1876–1943, vol. IV
Holland, Vice-Adm. Lancelot Ernest, 1887–1941, vol. IV
Holland, Leonard Duncan, 1874–1964, vol. VI
Holland, Hon. Lionel Raleigh, 1865–1936, vol. III
Holland, Sir Milner; *see* Holland, Sir E. M.
Holland, Sir (Reginald) Sothern, 1st Bt, 1876–1948, vol. IV
Holland, Richard, *died* 1942, vol. IV
Holland, Sir Robert Erskine, 1873–1965, vol. VI
Holland, Robert Henry Code, 1904–1974, vol. VII
Holland, Robert Wolstenholme, 1880–1962, vol. VI
Holland, Rt Hon. Sir Sidney George, 1893–1961, vol. VI
Holland, Sir Sothern; *see* Holland, Sir R. S.
Holland, Adm. Swinton Colthurst, 1844–1922, vol. II
Holland, Theodore, 1878–1947, vol. IV
Holland, Sir (Thomas) Erskine, 1835–1926, vol. II
Holland, Sir Thomas Henry, 1868–1947, vol. IV
Holland, Col Trevenen James, 1836–1910, vol. I
Holland, Vyvyan Beresford, 1886–1967, vol. VI
Holland, Rev. Preb. William Edward Sladen, 1873–1951, vol. V
Holland, William Jacob, 1848–1932, vol. III
Holland, Rev. William Lyall, 1846–1934, vol. III
Holland-Hibbert, Hon. Wilfrid, 1893–1961, vol. VI
Holland-Martin, Christopher John, 1910–1960, vol. V
Holland-Martin, Adm. Sir Deric Douglas Eric, 1906–1977, vol. VII
Holland-Pryor, Maj.-Gen. Sir Pomeroy; *see* Pryor.
Hollander, Bernard, 1864–1934, vol. III
Hollely, Sir Arthur Newton, *died* 1961, vol. VI
Hollenden, 1st Baron, 1845–1929, vol. III
Hollenden, 2nd Baron, 1885–1977, vol. VII
Holley, Maj.-Gen. Edmund Hunt, 1842–1919, vol. II
Holliday, Clifford, 1897–1960, vol. V

Holliday, Gilbert Leonard Gibson, 1910–1980, vol. VII
Holliday, Major Lionel Brook, 1880–1965, vol. VI
Holliman, John William, 1861–1937, vol. III
Hollingdrake, Sir Henry, 1872–1923, vol. II
Hollinghurst, Air Chief Marshal Sir Leslie Norman, 1895–1971, vol. VII
Hollings, Herbert John Butler, 1855–1922, vol. II
Hollingshead, John, 1827–1904, vol. I
Hollingsworth, Howard, 1871–1938, vol. III
Hollingsworth, John Ernest, 1916–1963, vol. VI
Hollington, Alfred Jordan, 1845–1926, vol. II
Hollingworth, Rev. Henry, 1841–1930, vol. III
Hollingworth, John, 1885–1976, vol. VII
Hollingworth, Sydney Ewart, 1899–1966, vol. VI
Hollins, Alfred, 1865–1942, vol. IV
Hollins, Arthur, 1876–1962, vol. VI
Hollins, Sir (Arthur) Meyrick, 2nd Bt, 1876–1938, vol. III
Hollins, Lt-Col Charles Ernest, 1875–1939, vol. III
Hollins, Sir Frank, 1st Bt, 1843–1924, vol. II
Hollins, Frank, 1907–1967, vol. VI
Hollins, Sir Frank Hubert, 3rd Bt, 1877–1963, vol. VI
Hollins, James Henry, *died* 1954, vol. V
Hollins, Sir Meyrick; *see* Hollins, Sir A. M.
Hollins, Samuel Thomas, 1881–1965, vol. VI
Hollinshead-Blundell, Henry B.; *see* Blundell-Hollinshead-Blundell.
Hollinshead-Blundell, Maj.-Gen. Richard B.; *see* Blundell-Hollinshead-Blundell.
Hollis, Sir (Alfred) Claud, 1874–1961, vol. VI
Hollis, Christopher; *see* Hollis, M. C.
Hollis, Sir Claud; *see* Hollis, Sir A. C.
Hollis, Rt Rev. Francis Septimus, 1884–1955, vol. V
Hollis, Rt Rev. George Arthur, 1868–1944, vol. IV
Hollis, Henry Park, 1858–1939, vol. III
Hollis, Sir Leslie Chasemore, 1897–1963, vol. VI
Hollis, (Maurice) Christopher, 1902–1977, vol. VII
Hollis, Sir Roger Henry, 1905–1973, vol. VII
Hollis, William Ainslie, 1839–1922, vol. II
Hollond, Henry Arthur, 1884–1974, vol. VII
Hollond, Maj.-Gen. Spencer Edmund, 1874–1950, vol. IV
Holloway, Baliol, 1883–1967, vol. VI
Holloway, Basil Edward, *died* 1947, vol. IV
Holloway, Maj.-Gen. Benjamin, 1861–1922, vol. II
Holloway, Rt Hon. Edward James, 1880–1967, vol. VI
Holloway, Sir Ernest, 1887–1961, vol. VI
Holloway, Frederick William, 1873–1954, vol. V
Holloway, Sir Henry, 1857–1923, vol. II
Holloway, Sir Henry Thomas, 1876–1951, vol. V
Holloway, Rev. John Ernest, 1881–1945, vol. IV
Holloway, Leonard Cloudesley, 1885–1966, vol. VI
Holm, Alexander, 1878–1943, vol. IV
Holman, Sir Adrian, 1895–1974, vol. VII
Holman, Arthur Treve, 1893–1959, vol. V
Holman, Bernard Welpton, *died* 1964, vol. VI
Holman, Sir Constantine, 1829–1910, vol. I
Holman, Lt-Gen. Sir Herbert Campbell, 1869–1949, vol. IV
Holman, James Frederick, 1916–1974, vol. VII

Holman, Percy, 1891–1978, vol. VII
Holman, Col Richard Charles, 1861–1933, vol. III
Holman, Hon. William Arthur, 1871–1934, vol. III
Holman-Hunt, Hilary Lushington Holman, 1879–1949, vol. IV
Holman-Hunt, William, 1827–1910, vol. I
Holmden, Major Frank Alfred Amphlett, 1861–1935, vol. III
Holmden, Sir Osborn George, 1869–1945, vol. IV
Holme, Alan Thomas, 1872–1931, vol. III
Holme, Charles, 1848–1923, vol. II
Holme, C(harles) Geoffrey, 1887–1954, vol. V
Holme, Charles Henry, 1853–1928, vol. II
Holme, Constance, (Mrs Punchard), 1880–1955, vol. V
Holme, Ernest Rudolph, died 1952, vol. V
Holme, George A., 1848–1917, vol. II
Holme, Major Harold L., 1879–1931, vol. III
Holme, Sir Randle Fynes Wilson, 1864–1957, vol. V
Holme-Sumner, Captain Berkeley, 1872–1943, vol. IV
Holmes, Albert Edward, died 1953, vol. V
Holmes, Arthur, 1890–1965, vol. VI
Holmes, Arthur Bromley, 1849–1927, vol. II
Holmes, Sir Arthur William, 1877–1960, vol. V
Holmes, Ven. Bernard Edgar, 1860–1928, vol. II
Holmes, Burton, 1870–1958, vol. V
Holmes, Rev. Cecil Frederick Joy, 1877–1938, vol. III
Holmes, Sir Charles John, 1868–1936, vol. III
Holmes, Daniel Turner, 1863–1955, vol. V
Holmes, Edmond Gore Alexander, 1850–1936, vol. III
Holmes, Edward Morell, 1843–1930, vol. III
Holmes, Eric Gordon, 1897–1972, vol. VII
Holmes, Ven. Ernest Edward, 1854–1931, vol. III
Holmes, Ernest Hamilton, 1876–1957, vol. V
Holmes, Florence Mary, (Lady Holmes); see Rivington, Mme Hill.
Holmes, Rt Rev. George, 1858–1912, vol. I
Holmes, George Augustus, 1861–1943, vol. IV
Holmes, Sir George Charles Vincent, 1848–1926, vol. II
Holmes, Rev. Canon George Edward Wilmot, 1869–1937, vol. III
Holmes, Ven. George Hedley, 1883–1972, vol. VII
Holmes, George John, 1874–1937, vol. III
Holmes, Comdr Gerard Robert Addison, 1881–1963, vol. VI
Holmes, Sir Gordon Morgan, died 1965, vol. VI
Holmes, Brig.-Gen. Hardress Gilbert, 1862–1922, vol. II
Holmes, Harold Kennard, 1875–1942, vol. IV
Holmes, Haywood Temple, 1865–1959, vol. V
Holmes, Lt-Col Henry, 1863–1933, vol. III
Holmes, Rev. Henry Comber, died 1920, vol. II
Holmes, Sir Henry Nicholas, 1868–1940, vol. III
Holmes, Sir Horace Edwin, 1888–1971, vol. VII
Holmes, Rt Hon. Hugh, 1840–1916, vol. II
Holmes, Sir Hugh Oliver, 1886–1955, vol. V
Holmes, James Macdonald, 1896–1966, vol. VI
Holmes, Paymaster Rear-Adm. John Dickonson, 1875–1947, vol. IV

Holmes, Rt Rev. John Garraway, died 1904, vol. I
Holmes, Rev. John Haynes, 1879–1964, vol. VI
Holmes, Rev. Joseph, 1820–1911, vol. I
Holmes, Hon. Julius Cecil, 1899–1968, vol. VI
Holmes, Sir Leonard Stanistreet, 1884–1961, vol. VI
Holmes, Sir Maurice Gerald, 1885–1964, vol. VI
Holmes, Hon. Oliver Wendell, 1841–1935, vol. III
Holmes, Air Vice-Marshal Peter Hamilton, 1912–1977, vol. VII
Holmes, Sir Richard Rivington, 1835–1911, vol. I
Holmes, Robert, 1861–1930, vol. III
Holmes, Col Robert Heuston, 1870–1952, vol. V
Holmes, Sir Robert William Arbuthnot, 1843–1910, vol. I
Holmes, Sir Stephen Lewis, 1896–1980, vol. VII
Holmes, Thomas, 1846–1918, vol. II
Holmes, Thomas Rice Edward, 1855–1933, vol. III
Holmes, Rev. Thomas Scott, 1852–1918, vol. II
Holmes, Sir Valentine, 1888–1956, vol. V
Holmes, Col William, 1862–1917, vol. II
Holmes, Lt-Gen. Sir William George, 1892–1969, vol. VI
Holmes, Rt Rev. William Hardy, 1873–1951, vol. VI
Holmes-à-Court, Hon. Edward Alexander, 1845–1923, vol. II
Holmes à Court, Vice-Adm. Hon. Herbert Edward, 1869–1934, vol. III
Holmes à Court, Col Rupert Edward, 1882–1958, vol. V
Holm-Patrick, 1st Baron, 1839–1898, vol. I
Holmpatrick, 2nd Baron, 1886–1942, vol. IV
Holms, John Mitchell, 1863–1948, vol. IV
Holms, William Frederick, 1866–1950, vol. IV
Holmwood, Sir Herbert, 1856–1930, vol. III
Holmyard, Eric John, 1891–1959, vol. V
Holness, Col Harold James, 1882–1941, vol. IV
Holroyd, Sir Charles, 1861–1917, vol. II
Holroyd, Hon. Sir Edward Dundas, 1828–1916, vol. II
Holroyd, Michael, 1892–1953, vol. V
Holroyd, Sir Ronald, 1904–1973, vol. VII
Holroyd-Reece, John, 1897–1969, vol. VI
Holst, Axel, 1860–1931, vol. III
Holst, Gustav, 1874–1934, vol. III
Holt, Lt-Col Alwyn Vesey, 1887–1956, vol. V
Holt, Charles, 1899–1966, vol. VI
Holt, Sir Edward, 1st Bt (cr 1916), 1849–1928, vol. II
Holt, Sir Edward, 2nd Bt (cr 1916), 1883–1968, vol. VI
Holt, Very Rev. Edward John, 1867–1948, vol. IV (A), vol. V
Holt, Ernest James Henry, 1883–1972, vol. VII
Holt, Air Vice-Marshal Felton Vesey, 1886–1931, vol. III
Holt, Sir Follett, 1865–1944, vol. IV
Holt, Rt Hon. Harold Edward, 1908–1968, vol. VI
Holt, Harold Edward Sherwin, 1862–1932, vol. III
Holt, Henry, 1840–1926, vol. II
Holt, Sir Henry Gisborne, 1864–1944, vol. IV
Holt, Herbert, 1894–1978, vol. VII
Holt, Major Herbert Paton, 1890–1971, vol. VII

Holt, Sir Herbert S., 1856–1941, vol. IV
Holt, James, 1899–1965, vol. VI
Holt, James Maden, 1829–1911, vol. I
Holt, John Alphonse, 1906–1968, vol. VI
Holt, L. Emmett, *died* 1924, vol. II
Holt, Lawrence During, 1882–1961, vol. VI
Holt, Martin Drummond Vesey, *died* 1956, vol. V
Holt, Maj.-Gen. Sir Maurice Percy Cue, 1862–1954, vol. V
Holt, Rev. Raymond Vincent, 1885–1957, vol. V
Holt, Vice-Adm. Reginald Vesey, 1884–1957, vol. V
Holt, Sir Richard Durning, 1st Bt (*cr* 1935), 1868–1941, vol. IV
Holt, Sir Stanley Silverwood, 1892–1973, vol. VII
Holt, Sir Vesey George Mackenzie, 1854–1923, vol. II
Holt, Sir Vyvyan, 1896–1960, vol. V
Holt, Col William John, 1839–1913, vol. I
Holt, William R., *born* 1870, vol. II
Holt-Thomas, George, 1869–1929, vol. III
Holt-Wilson, Brig. Sir Eric Edward Boketon, 1875–1950, vol. IV
Holtby, Winifred, 1898–1935, vol. III
Holthouse, Edwin Hermus, 1855–1949, vol. IV
Holtz, Alfred Christian Carlsen, 1874–1948, vol. IV
Holtze, Maurice, 1840–1923, vol. II
Holwell, Captain Raymond Vernon Doherty-, 1882–1917, vol. II
Holyman, Sir Ivan Nello, 1896–1957, vol. V
Holyoake, George Jacob, 1817–1906, vol. I
Holzmann, Sir Maurice, 1835–1909, vol. I
Hombersley, Ven. Arthur, 1855–1941, vol. IV
Homburg, Robert, 1848–1912, vol. I
Home, 12th Earl of, 1834–1918, vol. II
Home, 13th Earl of, 1873–1951, vol. V
Home, Sir Anthony Dickson, 1826–1914, vol. I
Home, Brig.-Gen. Sir Archibald Fraser, 1874–1953, vol. V
Home, David William M.; *see* Milne-Home.
Home, Ethel, *died* 1954, vol. V
Home, Col Frederick Jervis, 1839–1919, vol. II
Home, Lt-Col George, 1870–1956, vol. V
Home, Major George John Ninian L.; *see* Logan-Home.
Home, Gordon Cochrane, 1878–1969, vol. VI
Home, Sir James, 11th Bt, 1861–1931, vol. III
Home, Hon. James Archibald, 1837–1909, vol. I
Home, Col James Murray, 1866–1946, vol. IV
Home, Sir John, 12th Bt, 1872–1938, vol. III
Home, Sir John Hepburn Milne, 1876–1963, vol. VI
Home, Col Robert Elton, 1869–1943, vol. IV
Home, Walter, 1855–1936, vol. III
Home, Maj.-Gen. Hon. William Sholto, 1842–1916, vol. II
Home Drummond, Lt-Col Henry E. S.; *see* Stirling Home Drummond.
Home-Drummond, Lt-Col Henry Edward S.; *see* Drummond.
Homer, John Twigg, 1865–1934, vol. III
Homer, Louise, *died* 1947, vol. IV
Homer, Sidney, 1864–1953, vol. V

Homer, Winslow, 1836–1910, vol. I
Homfray, Herbert Richards, 1864–1940, vol. III
Homfray, Captain John Glynne Richards, 1861–1934, vol. III
Homfray, Lt-Col John Robert Henry, 1868–1944, vol. IV
Homolle, Jean Théophile, 1848–1925, vol. II
Hone, Sir Brian William, 1907–1978, vol. VII
Hone, Rt Rev. Campbell Richard, 1873–1967, vol. VI
Hone, Sir Evelyn Dennison, 1911–1979, vol. VII
Hone, Evie S., 1894–1955, vol. V
Hone, Frank Sandland, *died* 1951, vol. V
Hone, Joseph Maunsell, 1882–1959, vol. V
Hone, Nathaniel, *died* 1917, vol. II
Hone, Lt-Col Percy Frederick, 1878–1940, vol. III
Honegger, Arthur, 1892–1955, vol. V
Honey, Sir de Symons Montagu George, 1872–1945, vol. IV
Honey, John William, 1862–1932, vol. III
Honey, William Bowyer, 1889–1956, vol. V
Honeyball, Mrs Olympia Lœtitia, 1876–1956, vol. V
Honeyman, Sir George Gordon, 1898–1972, vol. VII
Honeyman, John, 1831–1914, vol. I
Honeyman, Tom John, 1891–1971, vol. VII
Honner, Joseph, 1859–1940, vol. III
Honoré, Bertha; *see* Palmer, Mrs Potter.
Honour, Benjamin, 1888–1961, vol. VI
Honyman, Sir William Macdonald, 5th Bt, 1820–1911, vol. I
Honywood, Constance Mary, (Lady Honywood), *died* 1956, vol. V
Honywood, Sir Courtenay John, 9th Bt, 1880–1944, vol. IV
Honywood, Sir John William, 8th Bt, 1857–1907 (this entry was not transferred to Who was Who).
Hood, 4th Viscount, 1838–1907, vol. I
Hood, 5th Viscount, 1868–1933, vol. III
Hood of Avalon, 1st Baron, 1824–1901, vol. I
Hood, Lt-Gen. Sir Alexander, 1888–1980, vol. VII
Hood, Sir (Alexander) Jarvie, 1860–1934, vol. III
Hood, Hon. Sir Alexander Nelson, 1854–1937, vol. III
Hood, Rev. Canon (Archibald) Frederic, 1895–1975, vol. VII
Hood, Captain Basil, 1864–1917, vol. II
Hood, Paymaster-Captain Basil Frederick, 1886–1941, vol. IV
Hood, Clifford Firoved, 1894–1978, vol. VII
Hood, David Wilson, 1874–1924, vol. II
Hood, Donald William Charles, 1847–1924, vol. II
Hood, Hon. Dorothy Violet, 1877–1965, vol. VI
Hood, Francis Campbell, 1895–1971, vol. VII
Hood, Rev. Canon Frederic; *see* Hood, Rev. Canon A. F.
Hood, George Percy J.; *see* Jacomb-Hood.
Hood, Rear-Adm. Hon. Horace Lambert Alexander, 1870–1916, vol. II
Hood, Sir Hugh Meggison, 1885–1952, vol. V
Hood, James Reaney, 1888–1968, vol. VI
Hood, Sir Jarvie; *see* Hood, Sir A. J.

Hood, Rev. John Charles Fulton, 1884–1964, vol. VI
Hood, Gen. John Cockburn, *died* 1901, vol. I
Hood, Sir Joseph, 1st Bt, 1863–1931, vol. III
Hood, Hon. Sir Joseph Henry, 1846–1922, vol. II
Hood, Hon. Maurice Henry Nelson, 1881–1915, vol. I
Hood, Lt-Col Hon. Neville Albert, 1872–1948, vol. IV
Hood, Sydney Walter, 1886–1960, vol. V
Hood, Thomas, 1870–1949, vol. IV
Hood, Hon. Victor Albert Nelson, 1862–1929, vol. III
Hood, William Francis, 1902–1980, vol. VII
Hook, Rt Rev. Cecil, 1844–1938, vol. III
Hook, Frederick Arthur, 1864–1935, vol. III
Hook, Henry, *died* 1905, vol. I
Hook, James Clarke, 1819–1907, vol. I
Hook, Very Rev. Norman, 1898–1976, vol. VII
Hooke, Rev. Daniel Burford, 1847–1933, vol. III
Hooke, Sir Lionel George Alfred, 1895–1974, vol. VII
Hooke, Samuel Henry, *died* 1968, vol. VI
Hooker, Sir Joseph Dalton, 1817–1911, vol. I
Hooker, Sir Leslie Joseph, 1903–1976, vol. VII
Hookey, James, 1839–1903, vol. I
Hookins, Rev. William, 1845–1917, vol. II
Hoole, Lt-Col James, 1850–1917, vol. II
Hooley, Samuel Cutler, 1848–1929, vol. III
Hooley, Lt-Col Vernon Vavasour, 1862–1952, vol. V
Hooper, Arthur George, 1857–1940, vol. III
Hooper, Col Arthur Winsmore, 1869–1945, vol. IV
Hooper, Barrington, 1885–1960, vol. V
Hooper, Charles Arthur, 1889–1960, vol. V
Hooper, Cyril Noel, 1884–1952, vol. V
Hooper, David, 1858–1947, vol. IV
Hooper, Edmund Huntly, 1845–1931, vol. III
Hooper, Sir Frederic Collins, 1st Bt, 1892–1963, vol. VI
Hooper, Rev. George, *born* 1866, vol. III
Hooper, Lt-Col Harry Uppington, *died* 1940, vol. III
Hooper, Howard Owen, 1911–1980, vol. VII
Hooper, Ian Mackay, 1902–1958, vol. V
Hooper, John, *died* 1907, vol. I
Hooper, John Robert Thomas, 1914–1975, vol. VII
Hooper, Reginald Stewart, 1889–1945, vol. IV
Hooper, Major Richard Grenside, 1873–1940, vol. III
Hooper, Lt-Col Stuart Huntly, 1867–1915, vol. I
Hooper, Sydney Ernest, 1880–1966, vol. VI
Hooper, Rev. William, 1837–1922, vol. II
Hooper, William Henry, 1876–1946, vol. IV
Hooper, Col Sir William Roe, 1837–1921, vol. II
Hooper, Wynnard, 1853–1935, vol. III
Hoops, Albert Launcelot, 1876–1940, vol. III (A), vol. IV
Hooton, Maj.-Gen. Alfred, 1870–1967, vol. VI
Hooton, John Charles, 1912–1980, vol. VII
Hoover, Calvin Bryce, 1897–1974, vol. VII
Hoover, Herbert, 1874–1964, vol. VI
Hoover, Herbert Clark, Jr, 1903–1969, vol. VI
Hoover, John Edgar, 1895–1972, vol. VII

Hope, Adrian Elias, 1845–1919, vol. II
Hope, Adrian James Robert, 1874–1963, vol. VI
Hope, Col Adrian Victor Webley, 1873–1960, vol. V
Hope, Sir Alexander, 15th Bt (*cr* 1628), 1824–1918, vol. II
Hope, Anthony; *see* Hawkins, Sir A. H.
Hope, Col Charles, 1850–1930, vol. III
Hope, Lord Charles Melbourne, 1892–1962, vol. VI
Hope, Collingwood, 1858–1949, vol. IV
Hope, Sir Edward Stanley, 1846–1921, vol. II
Hope, Edward William, 1854–1950, vol. IV
Hope, George Everard, 1886–1917, vol. II
Hope, Adm. Sir George Price Webley, 1869–1959, vol. V
Hope, Graham, *died* 1920, vol. II
Hope, Sir Harry, 1st Bt (*cr* 1932), 1865–1959, vol. V
Hope, Henry Walter, 1839–1913, vol. I
Hope, Sir Herbert James, 1851–1930, vol. III
Hope, Adm. Herbert Willes Webley, 1878–1968, vol. VI
Hope, Sir James, 2nd Bt (*cr* 1932), 1898–1979, vol. VII
Hope, Jasper Edward, 1852–1917, vol. II
Hope, Captain John, 1843–1915, vol. I
Hope, Col John Andrew, 1890–1954, vol. V
Hope, Lt-Col Sir John Augustus, 16th Bt (*cr* 1628), 1869–1924, vol. II
Hope, John Deans, 1860–1949, vol. IV
Hope, Brig.-Gen. John Frederic Roundell, 1883–1970, vol. VI
Hope, John Owen Webley, 1875–1927, vol. II
Hope, Lt-Col John William, 1876–1942, vol. IV
Hope, John Wilson, 1856–1938, vol. III
Hope, Laura Elizabeth Rachel, *died* 1929, vol. III
Hope, Captain Laurence Nugent, 1890–1973, vol. VII
Hope, Col Lewis Anstruther, 1855–1929, vol. III
Hope, Lt-Col Sir Percy Mirehouse, 1886–1972, vol. VII
Hope, Hon. Richard Frederick, 1901–1964, vol. VI
Hope, Robert, *died* 1936, vol. III
Hope, Robert Charles, 1855–1926, vol. II
Hope, Sydney, 1905–1959, vol. V
Hope, Sir Theodore Cracraft, 1831–1915, vol. I
Hope, Col Thomas, 1848–1925, vol. II
Hope, Sir William, 14th Bt (*cr* 1628), 1819–1898, vol. I
Hope, Sir William Henry St John, 1854–1919, vol. II
Hope, Lt-Col William Henry Webley, 1871–1919, vol. II
Hope-Dunbar, Sir Basil Douglas, 7th Bt, 1907–1961, vol. VI
Hope-Dunbar, Sir Charles Dunbar, 6th Bt, 1873–1958, vol. V
Hope-Johnstone, John James, 1842–1912, vol. I
Hope-Morley, Captain Hon. Claude Hope, 1887–1968, vol. VI
Hope-Vere, James Charles, 1858–1933, vol. III
Hope-Wallace, Philip Adrian, 1911–1979, vol. VII
Hopewell, Alan Francis John, 1892–1957, vol. V
Hopewell-Ash, Edwin Lancelot; *see* Ash.

Hopewell-Smith, Arthur, 1865–1931, vol. III
Hopkin, Major Daniel, 1886–1951, vol. V
Hopkin-James, Rev. Lemuel John, 1874–1937, vol. III
Hopkins, Major Adrian Edmund, 1894–1967, vol. VI
Hopkins, Arthur, 1848–1930, vol. III
Hopkins, Arthur Antwis, 1855–1916, vol. II
Hopkins, Rev. Charles, 1834–1908, vol. I
Hopkins, Charles James William, 1887–1954, vol. V
Hopkins, Paymaster-in-Chief David Bertie Lyndsay, died 1925, vol. II
Hopkins, Edward John, 1818–1901, vol. I
Hopkins, Everard, 1860–1928, vol. II
Hopkins, Rt Rev. Frederick C., 1844–1923, vol. II
Hopkins, Sir Frederick Gowland, 1861–1947, vol. IV
Hopkins, Gerard Walter Sturgis, 1892–1961, vol. VI
Hopkins, Harry L., 1890–1946, vol. IV
Hopkins, Harry Sinclair, 1870–1953, vol. V
Hopkins, Henry Mayne Reid, 1867–1956, vol. V
Hopkins, John Castell, 1864–1923, vol. II
Hopkins, Sir John Ommanney, 1834–1916, vol. II
Hopkins, Sir John Wells Wainwright, 1st Bt, 1863–1946, vol. IV
Hopkins, Lt-Col Lewis Egerton, 1873–1945, vol. IV
Hopkins, Lionel Charles, 1854–1952, vol. V
Hopkins, Livingston, 1846–1927, vol. II
Hopkins, Very Rev. Noel Thomas, 1892–1969, vol. VI
Hopkins, Reginald Haydn, 1891–1965, vol. VI
Hopkins, Rt Hon. Sir Richard Valentine Nind, 1880–1955, vol. V
Hopkins, Robert Thurston, died 1958, vol. V
Hopkins, Tighe, 1856–1919, vol. II
Hopkins, William Joseph, 1863–1927, vol. II
Hopkinson, Sir Alfred, 1851–1939, vol. III
Hopkinson, Rev. Arthur John, 1894–1953, vol. V
Hopkinson, Austin, 1879–1962, vol. VI
Hopkinson, Bertram, 1874–1918, vol. II
Hopkinson, Edward, 1859–1922, vol. II
Hopkinson, Emilius, 1869–1951, vol. V
Hopkinson, Sir Frederick Thomas, 1863–1947, vol. IV
Hopkinson, Gen. Henry, 1820–1899, vol. I
Hopkinson, Col Henry Charles Barwick Pasha, 1867–1946, vol. IV
Hopkinson, Sir Henry L., 1855–1936, vol. III
Hopkinson, John, 1849–1898, vol. I
Hopkinson, John, 1844–1919, vol. II
Hopkinson, Rev. John Henry, died 1957, vol. V
Hopley, Hon. William Musgrove, 1853–1919, vol. II
Hoppé, E. O., 1878–1972, vol. VII
Hopper, Nora, 1871–1906, vol. I
Hopps, Air Vice-Marshal Frank Linden, died 1976, vol. VII
Hopps, John Page, 1834–1911, vol. I
Hopson, Sir Donald Charles, 1915–1974, vol. VII
Hopton, Ven. Charles Ernest, 1861–1946, vol. IV
Hopton, Lt-Gen. Sir Edward, 1837–1912, vol. I
Hopton, Col John Dutton, 1858–1934, vol. III
Hopton, Rev. Preb. Michael, 1838–1928, vol. II

Hopwood, Brig. Alfred Henry, died 1956, vol. V
Hopwood, Aubrey, 1863–1917, vol. II
Hopwood, Avery, died 1928, vol. II
Hopwood, Charles Augustus, 1847–1922, vol. II
Hopwood, Major Edward Byng George G.; see Gregge-Hopwood.
Hopwood, Edward Robert G.; see Gregge-Hopwood.
Hopwood, Frank Lloyd, 1884–1954, vol. V
Hopwood, Vice-Adm. Geoffrey, 1877–1947, vol. IV
Hopwood, Henry Silkstone, 1860–1914, vol. I
Hopwood, Brig.-Gen. Herbert Reginald, 1871–1938, vol. III
Hopwood, Adm. Ronald Arthur, 1868–1949, vol. IV
Hopwood, Sir William, 1862–1936, vol. III
Horabin, Thomas Lewis, 1896–1956, vol. V
Horan, Rev. Charles Trevor, 1863–1932, vol. III
Horan, Gerald, 1879–1949, vol. IV
Horan, Henry Edward, 1890–1961, vol. VI
Horder, 1st Baron, 1871–1955, vol. V
Hordern, Anthony, 1889–1970, vol. VI (AII)
Hordern, Sir Archibald Frederick, 1889–1950, vol. IV
Hordern, Rev. Arthur Venables Calveley, 1866–1946, vol. IV
Hordern, Captain Edward Joseph Calveley, 1867–1944, vol. IV
Hordern, Brig.-Gen. Gwyn Venables, 1870–1945, vol. IV
Hordern, Rt Rev. Hugh Maudslay, 1868–1949, vol. IV
Hordern, Sir Samuel, 1876–1956, vol. V
Hordern, Samuel, 1909–1960, vol. V
Hore, Sir Adair; see Hore, Sir C. F. A.
Hore, Sir (Charles Fraser) Adair, 1874–1950, vol. IV
Hore, Col Charles Owen, 1860–1916, vol. II
Hore, Engr-Rear-Adm. Fred, 1863–1932, vol. III
Hore, Maj.-Gen. Walter Stuart, 1843–1918, vol. II
Hore-Belisha, 1st Baron, died 1957, vol. V
Hore-Ruthven, Col Hon. Malise; see Ruthven.
Horenstein, Jascha, 1899–1973, vol. VII
Horgan, John Joseph, 1881–1967, vol. VI
Horler, Sydney, 1888–1954, vol. V
Horlick, Sir Ernest Burford, 2nd Bt, 1880–1934, vol. III
Horlick, Sir James, 1st Bt, 1844–1921, vol. II
Horlick, Lt-Col Sir James Nockells, 4th Bt, died 1972, vol. VII
Horlick, Sir Peter James Cunliffe, 3rd Bt, 1908–1958, vol. V
Hormasji Bhiwandiwalla, Khan Bahadur Sir Dosabhai, died 1940, vol. III (A), vol. IV
Horn, Sir Arthur Edwin, died 1943, vol. IV
Horn, David Bayne, 1851–1927, vol. II
Horn, David Bayne, 1901–1969, vol. VI
Horn, Gunnar, 1894–1946, vol. IV
Horn, Brig. Robert Victor Galbraith, 1886–1959, vol. V
Horn, William Austin, 1841–1922, vol. II
Horn-Elphinstone, Sir Graeme Hepburn D.; see Elphinstone.

Hornabrook, Ven. Charles Soward, *died* 1922, vol. II

Hornabrook, Rev. John, 1848–1937, vol. III

Hornaday, William Temple, 1854–1937, vol. III

Hornby, Maj.-Gen. Alan Hugh, 1894–1958, vol. V

Hornby, Albert Neilson, 1847–1925, vol. II

Hornby, C. H. St John, 1867–1946, vol. IV

Hornby, Charles Windham Leycester P.; *see* Penrhyn-Hornby.

Hornby, Brig.-Gen. Edmund John Phipps, 1857–1947, vol. IV

Hornby, Frank, 1863–1936, vol. III

Hornby, Sir Henry; *see* Hornby, Sir W. H.

Hornby, Sir (Henry) Russell, 2nd Bt, 1888–1971, vol. VII

Hornby, Rt Rev. Hugh Leycester, 1888–1965, vol. VI

Hornby, Rev. James John, 1826–1909, vol. I

Hornby, Brig.-Gen. Montague Leyland, 1870–1948, vol. IV

Hornby, Ven. Phipps John, 1853–1936, vol. III

Hornby, Adm. Robert Stewart Phipps, 1866–1956, vol. V

Hornby, Sir Russell; *see* Hornby, Sir H. R.

Hornby, Rt Hon. Wilfrid Bird, 1851–1935, vol. III

Hornby, Ven. William, 1810–1899, vol. I

Hornby, Sir (William) Henry, 1st Bt, 1841–1928, vol. II

Hornby, Sir Windham, 1812–1899, vol. I

Horncastle, Walter Radcliffe, 1850–1908, vol. I

Horndon, David, 1863–1938, vol. III

Horne, 1st Baron, 1861–1929, vol. III

Horne of Slamannan, 1st Viscount, 1871–1940, vol. III

Horne, Alderson Burrell, 1863–1953, vol. V

Horne, Sir Allan; *see* Horne, Sir J. A.

Horne, Sir Andrew John, 1856–1924, vol. II

Horne, Rev. C. Silvester, 1865–1914, vol. I

Horne, (Charles) Kenneth, 1907–1969, vol. VI

Horne, Sir Edgar; *see* Horne, Sir W. E.

Horne, Edward Butler, 1881–1947, vol. IV

Horne, Col Edward William, 1857–1941, vol. IV

Horne, Frank Robert, 1904–1975, vol. VII

Horne, Frederic, 1863–1927, vol. II

Horne, Frederick Newman, 1863–1946, vol. IV

Horne, Maj.-Gen. Gerald Tom Warlters, 1898–1978, vol. VII

Horne, Herbert P., *died* 1916, vol. II

Horne, Sir (James) Allan, 1876–1944, vol. IV

Horne, Jobson; *see* Horne, W. J.

Horne, John, 1848–1928, vol. II

Horne, Kenneth; *see* Horne, C. K.

Horne, Lancelot Worthy, 1875–1924, vol. II

Horne, Leonard Thomas, 1860–1934, vol. III

Horne, Maynard, 1870–1944, vol. IV

Horne, (Walter) Jobson, 1865–1953, vol. V

Horne, Sir (William) Edgar, 1st Bt, 1856–1941, vol. IV

Horne, Major William Guy, 1889–1974, vol. VII

Horne, Sir William Kenneth, 1883–1959, vol. V

Horne, William Ogilvie, *died* 1943, vol. IV

Hornel, Edward Atkinson, 1864–1933, vol. III

Hornell, Vice-Adm. Sir Robert Arthur, 1877–1949, vol. IV

Hornell, Sir William Woodward, 1878–1950, vol. IV

Horner, Andrew L., 1863–1916, vol. II

Horner, Arthur Lewis, 1894–1968, vol. VI

Horner, Rev. Bernard, 1873–1960, vol. V

Horner, Egbert Foster, 1864–1928, vol. II

Horner, Sir John Francis Fortescue, 1842–1927, vol. II

Horner, Norman Gerald, 1882–1954, vol. V

Horner, Mrs Sibyl Gertrude, 1895–1978, vol. VII

Horniblow, Brig.-Gen. Frank Herbert, 1860–1931, vol. III

Horniblow, Col Frederick, 1862–1945, vol. IV

Hornibrook, Sir Manuel Richard, 1893–1970, vol. VI (AII)

Horniman, Annie Elizabeth Fredericka, 1860–1937, vol. III

Horniman, Benjamin Guy, 1873–1948, vol. IV

Horniman, Emslie John, 1863–1932, vol. III

Horniman, Frederick John, 1835–1906, vol. I

Horniman, Rear-Adm. Henry, *died* 1956, vol. V

Horniman, Laurence Ivan, 1893–1963, vol. VI

Horniman, Roy, *died* 1930, vol. III

Horning, Eric Stephen Gurney, 1900–1959, vol. V

Horning, Lewis Emerson, 1858–1925, vol. II

Hornsby, Sir Bertram, *died* 1943, vol. IV

Hornsby, Frederick Middleton, 1874–1931, vol. III

Hornsby, Harker William, 1912–1971, vol. VII

Hornsby, Captain James Arthur, 1891–1972, vol. VII

Hornsby-Wright, Lt-Col Guy Jefferys, 1872–1941, vol. IV

Hornung, Ernest William, 1866–1921, vol. II

Hornung, Lt-Col Sir John Derek, 1915–1978, vol. VII

Hornung, John Peter, 1861–1940, vol. III

Hornyold-Strickland, Henry, 1890–1975, vol. VII

Hornyold-Strickland, Hon. Mary Constance Elizabeth Christina, 1896–1970, vol. VI

Horobin, Sir Ian Macdonald, 1899–1976, vol. VII

Horobin, Norah Maud, 1898–1976, vol. VII

Horrabin, James Francis, 1884–1962, vol. VI

Horridge, John, 1893–1951, vol. V

Horridge, Sir Thomas Gardner, 1857–1938, vol. III

Horrobin, Walter, 1894–1967, vol. VI (AII)

Horrocks, Peter, *died* 1909, vol. I

Horrocks, Walter James Hodgson, 1897–1946, vol. IV

Horrocks, Col Sir William Heaton, 1859–1941, vol. IV

Horrox, Lewis, 1898–1975, vol. VII

Horsbrugh, Baroness (Life Peer); Florence Horsbrugh, *died* 1969, vol. VI

Horsbrugh-Porter, Sir John Scott; *see* Porter.

Horsburgh, Benjamin, 1868–1935, vol. III (A), vol. IV

Horsefield, Rev. Frederic John, 1859–1933, vol. III

Horsey, Captain Frank Lankester, 1884–1956, vol. V

Horsfall, Sir Donald; *see* Horsfall, Sir J. D.

Horsfall, Jeremiah Garnett, 1840–1920, vol. II

Horsfall, Sir John Cousin, 1st Bt, 1846–1920, vol. II
Horsfall, Sir (John) Donald, 2nd Bt, 1891–1975, vol. VII
Horsfall, Thomas Coglan, 1841–1932, vol. III
Horsfield, George, 1882–1956, vol. V
Horsfield, Lt-Col Richard Marshall, died 1940, vol. III
Horsford, Cyril Arthur Bennett, 1876–1953, vol. V
Horsley, Major Bernard Hill, died 1940, vol. III
Horsley, Rt Rev. Cecil Douglas, 1903–1953, vol. V
Horsley, Gerald Callcott, 1862–1917, vol. II
Horsley, John Callcott, 1817–1903, vol. I
Horsley, Rev. John William, 1845–1921, vol. II
Horsley, Reginald Ernest, 1863–1926, vol. II
Horsley, Terence Beresford, 1904–1949, vol. IV
Horsley, Sir Victor Alexander Haden, 1857–1916, vol. II
Horsley, Col Walter Charles, 1855–1934, vol. III
Horsman, Sir Henry, 1887–1966, vol. VI
Horsnell, Horace, 1882–1949, vol. IV
Hort, Sir Arthur Fenton, 6th Bt, 1864–1935, vol. III
Hort, Edward Collett, 1868–1922, vol. II
Hort, Sir Fenton George, 7th Bt, 1896–1960, vol. V
Hort, Sir Fenton Josiah, 5th Bt, 1836–1902, vol. I
Hort, Greta, 1903–1967, vol. VI
Horthy de Nagybanya, Adm. Nicholas Vitéz, 1868–1957, vol. V
Horton, Frank, 1878–1957, vol. V
Horton, Sir Henry, 1870–1943, vol. IV
Horton, Major James, 1845–1925, vol. II
Horton, Lt-Col James H., 1871–1917, vol. II
Horton, Adm. Sir Max Kennedy, 1883–1951, vol. V
Horton, Percy Frederick, 1897–1970, vol. VI
Horton, Ralph Albert, 1885–1969, vol. VI
Horton, Rev. Reginald, 1852–1914, vol. I
Horton, Rev. Robert Forman, 1855–1934, vol. III
Horton, William, 1854–1944, vol. IV
Horton, Brig.-Gen. William Edward, 1868–1935, vol. III
Horton, Lt-Col W(illiam) Gray, 1897–1974, vol. VII
Horton-Smith, Lionel Graham Horton, 1871–1953, vol. V
Horton-Smith, Richard Horton, 1831–1919, vol. II
Horton-Smith-Hartley, Sir Percival; see Hartley.
Horton-Smith-Hartley, Percival Hubert Graham; see Hartley.
Horton-Starkie, Rev. Preb. Le Gendre George, 1859–1943, vol. IV
Horwill, Herbert William, 1864–1952, vol. V
Horwill, Sir Lionel Clifford, 1890–1972, vol. VII
Horwood, Hon. Sir William Henry, 1862–1945, vol. IV
Horwood, Brig.-Gen. Sir William Thomas Francis, 1868–1943, vol. IV
Hose, Charles, 1863–1929, vol. III
Hose, Edward Shaw, 1871–1946, vol. IV
Hose, Rt Rev. George Frederick, 1838–1922, vol. II
Hose, Sir (John) Walter, 1865–1958, vol. V
Hose, Robert John, 1863–1935, vol. III

Hose, Sir Walter; see Hose, Sir J. W.
Hosie, Sir Alexander, 1853–1925, vol. II
Hosie, Lt-Col Andrew, 1860–1931, vol. III
Hosie, Dorothea, (Lady Hosie), 1885–1959, vol. V
Hosie, Ian, 1905–1970, vol. VI
Hosier, Arthur Julius, 1877–1963, vol. VI
Hosken, Clifford; see Keverne, Richard.
Hosken, Ernest Charles Heath, died 1934, vol. III
Hosker, Sir James Atkinson, 1857–1929, vol. III
Hoskin, Alan Simson, 1886–1945, vol. IV
Hoskin, John, 1836–1921, vol. II
Hoskin, Theo. Jenner Hooper, 1888–1954, vol. V
Hosking, Ethelbert Bernard, 1890–1960, vol. V
Hosking, Hon. Sir John Henry, 1854–1928, vol. II
Hosking, Paymaster Rear-Adm. Richard Bosustow, 1869–1962, vol. VI
Hoskins, Sir Anthony Hiley, 1828–1901, vol. I
Hoskins, Maj.-Gen. Sir (Arthur) Reginald, 1871–1942, vol. IV
Hoskins, Sir Cecil Harold, 1899–1971, vol. VII
Hoskins, Maj.-Gen. Sir Reginald; see Hoskins, Maj.-Gen. Sir A. R.
Hoskins, William, died 1928, vol. II
Hoskyn, Col John Cunningham Moore, 1875–1941, vol. IV
Hoskyns, Ven. Benedict George, 1856–1935, vol. III
Hoskyns, Col Sir Chandos, 10th Bt, 1848–1914, vol. I
Hoskyns, Sir Chandos Wren, 14th Bt, 1923–1945, vol. IV
Hoskyns, Rt Rev. Sir Edwyn, 12th Bt, 1851–1925, vol. II
Hoskyns, Rev. Canon Sir Edwyn Clement, 13th Bt, 1884–1937, vol. III
Hoskyns, Sir John Chevallier, 15th Bt, 1926–1956, vol. V
Hoskyns, Rev. Sir John Leigh, 9th Bt, 1817–1911, vol. I
Hoskyns, Sir Leigh, 11th Bt, 1850–1923, vol. II
Hoskyns, Rear–Adm. Peyton, 1852–1919, vol. II
Hoskyns-Abrahall, Bennet, 1858–1951, vol. V
Hoskyns-Abrahall, Sir Chandos; see Hoskyns-Abrahall, Sir T. C.
Hoskyns-Abrahall, Sir (Theo) Chandos, 1896–1975, vol. VII
Hoskyns-Festing, Major Arthur; see Festing.
Hosmer, James Kendall, 1834–1927, vol. II
Hossie, Major David Neil, 1890–1962, vol. VI
Hoste, Maj.-Gen. Dixon Edward, 1827–1905, vol. I
Hoste, Dixon Edward, 1861–1946, vol. IV
Hoste, Sir William Graham, 4th Bt, 1895–1915, vol. II
Hoste, Sir William Henry Charles, 3rd Bt, 1860–1902, vol. I
Hoster, Mrs Albert, 1864–1939, vol. III
Hotblack, Maj.-Gen. Frederick Elliot, 1887–1979, vol. VII
Hotblack, George Finch, 1883–1951, vol. V
Hotchin, Sir Claude, 1898–1977, vol. VII
Hotchkin, Stafford Vere, 1876–1953, vol. V
Hotham, 5th Baron, 1838–1907, vol. I
Hotham, 6th Baron, 1863–1923, vol. II

Hotham, 7th Baron, 1899–1967, vol. VI
Hotham, Adm. Sir Alan Geoffrey, 1876–1965, vol. VI
Hotham, Sir Charles Frederick, 1843–1925, vol. II
Hotham, Captain Henry Edward, 1855–1912, vol. I
Hotham, Brig.-Gen. John, 1851–1932, vol. III
Hotham, Rev. John Hallett, 1811–1901, vol. I
Hothfield, 1st Baron, 1844–1926, vol. II
Hothfield, 2nd Baron, 1873–1952, vol. V
Hothfield, 3rd Baron, 1897–1961, vol. VI
Hotine, Brig. Martin, 1898–1968, vol. VI
Hotson, Sir Ernest; see Hotson, Sir J. E. B.
Hotson, Sir (John) Ernest (Buttery), 1877–1944, vol. IV
Houblon, Mrs Doreen A.; see Archer Houblon.
Houblon, Col George Bramston Archer-, 1843–1913, vol. I
Houblon, Rev. Thomas Henry Archer, 1849–1933, vol. III
Houde, Camillien, 1889–1958, vol. V
Houfton, Sir John Plowright, 1857–1929, vol. III
Hough, Edwin Leadam, 1852–1928, vol. II
Hough, James Fisher, 1878–1960, vol. V
Hough, John Stanley, 1856–1928, vol. II
Hough, Rev. Lynn Harold, 1877–1971, vol. VII
Hough, Sydney Samuel, 1870–1923, vol. II
Hough, William, 1884–1962, vol. VI
Hough, Rt Rev. William Woodcock, 1859–1934, vol. III
Houghton, Alanson Bigelow, 1863–1941, vol. IV
Houghton, Charles Thomas, 1892–1975, vol. VII
Houghton, Claude; see Oldfield, C. H.
Houghton, Rev. Edward James, 1838–1919, vol. II
Houghton, Rev. Edward John Walford, 1867–1955, vol. V
Houghton, Rt Rev. Frank, died 1972, vol. VII
Houghton, Sir William Frederick, 1909–1971, vol. VII
Houghton, William Stanley, 1881–1913, vol. I
Houghton-Gastrell, Sir William; see Gastrell.
Houlden, George Houldsworth, 1902–1972, vol. VII
Houlder, Howard, 1858–1932, vol. III
Houldsworth, Sir Henry Hamilton, 2nd Bt (cr 1887), 1867–1947, vol. IV
Houldsworth, Brig. Sir Henry Walter, 1896–1963, vol. VI
Houldsworth, Sir Hubert Stanley, 1st Bt (cr 1956), 1889–1956, vol. V
Houldsworth, J. H., died 1910, vol. I
Houldsworth, J. Hamilton, 1867–1941, vol. IV
Houldsworth, Sir William Henry, 1st Bt (cr 1887), 1834–1917, vol. II
Houldsworth, Col Sir William Thomas Reginald, 3rd Bt (cr 1887), 1874–1960, vol. V
Hoult, Joseph, 1847–1917, vol. II
Houlton, Charlotte Leighton, 1882–1956, vol. V
Houlton, Sir Edward Victor Lewis, 1823–1899, vol. I
Houlton, Sir John Wardle, 1892–1973, vol. VII
Houndle, Henry Charles Herman Hawker, 1851–1919, vol. II

Hounsell, Maj.-Gen. Harold Arthur, 1897–1970, vol. VI
Hourigan, Thomas, 1904–1975, vol. VII
House, (Arthur) Humphry, 1908–1955, vol. V
House, Edward Mandell, 1858–1938, vol. III
House, George, 1892–1949, vol. IV
House, Humphry; see House, A. H.
Housman, Alfred Edward, 1859–1936, vol. III
Housman, Laurence, 1865–1959, vol. V
Houssay, Bernardo Alberto, 1887–1971, vol. VII
Houssaye, Henry, 1848–1911, vol. I
Houssemayne Du Boulay, Brig.-Gen. Noel Wilmot, 1861–1949, vol. IV
Houston, Sir Alexander Cruikshank, 1865–1933, vol. III
Houston, Arthur, 1833–1914, vol. I
Houston, Major Charles B.; see Blakiston-Houston.
Houston, Major Charles Elrington Duncan D.; see Davidson-Houston.
Houston, Dame Fanny Lucy, 1857–1936, vol. III
Houston, George, died 1947, vol. IV
Houston, John B.; see Blakiston-Houston.
Houston, Maj.-Gen. John B.; see Blakiston-Houston.
Houston, John R., 1856–1932, vol. III
Houston, Sir Robert Paterson, 1st Bt, 1853–1926, vol. II
Houston, Sir Thomas, died 1949, vol. IV
Houston, Lt-Col Wilfred Bennett D.; see Davidson-Houston.
Houston, William, 1846–1932, vol. III
Houston-Boswall-Preston, Thomas Alford, 1850–1918, vol. II
Houstoun, Robert Alexander, 1883–1975, vol. VII
Houstoun-Boswall, Sir George Lauderdale, 3rd Bt, 1847–1908, vol. I
Houstoun-Boswall, Sir George Reginald, 4th Bt, 1877–1915, vol. I (A)
Houstoun-Boswall, Major Sir Gordon, 6th Bt, 1887–1961, vol. VI
Houstoun-Boswall, Sir Randolph; see Houstoun-Boswall, Sir T. R.
Houstoun-Boswall, Sir (Thomas) Randolph, 5th Bt, 1882–1953, vol. V
Houstoun-Boswall, Sir William Evelyn, 1892–1960, vol. V
Houthuesen, Albert Antony John, 1903–1979, vol. VII
Hovell, Very Rev. De Berdt, 1850–1905, vol. I
Hovell, Lt-Col Hugh De Berdt, 1863–1923, vol. II
Hovell, T. Mark, died 1925, vol. II
Hovil, Major Richard, died 1931, vol. III
How, Ven. Henry Walsham, 1856–1923, vol. II
How, Rt Rev. John Charles Halland, died 1961, vol. VI
How, Rev. John Hall, 1871–1938, vol. III
How, Walter Wybergh, 1861–1932, vol. III
How, Rt Rev. William Walsham, 1823–1897, vol. I
Howard de Walden, 7th Baron, 1830–1899, vol. I
Howard de Walden, 8th Baron, 1880–1946, vol. IV
Howard of Glossop, 2nd Baron, 1859–1924, vol. II
Howard of Glossop, 3rd Baron, 1885–1972, vol. VII

Howard of Glossop, Lady; (Winifred), *died* 1909, vol. I

Howard of Penrith, 1st Baron, 1863–1939, vol. III

Howard, Captain Alan Frederic William, 1883–1971, vol. VII

Howard, Sir Albert, 1873–1947, vol. IV

Howard, Sir Algar Henry Stafford, 1880–1970, vol. VI

Howard, Andrée, 1910–1968, vol. VI

Howard, Hon. Sir Arthur Jared Palmer, 1896–1971, vol. VII

Howard, Bronson, 1842–1908, vol. I

Howard, Sir Charles, *died* 1909, vol. I

Howard, Brig. Sir Charles Alfred, 1878–1958, vol. V

Howard, Sir Ebenezer, 1850–1928, vol. II

Howard, Major Edmund, 1881–1960, vol. V

Howard, Sir (Edward) Stafford, 1851–1916, vol. II

Howard, Edwin Johnston, 1901–1971, vol. VII

Howard, Maj.-Gen. Sir Francis, 1848–1930, vol. III

Howard, Francis, 1874–1954, vol. V

Howard, Col Francis James Leigh, 1870–1942, vol. IV

Howard, Major Frederic George, 1872–1915, vol. I (A)

Howard, Sir Frederick, 1827–1915, vol. I

Howard, Frederick Richard, 1894–1977, vol. VII

Howard, Geoffrey, 1889–1973, vol. VII

Howard, Lt-Gen. Sir Geoffrey Weston, 1876–1966, vol. VI

Howard, Hon. Geoffrey William Algernon, 1877–1935, vol. III

Howard, Captain George Augustus Hotham, 1853–1931, vol. III

Howard, G(eorge) Wren, 1893–1968, vol. VI

Howard, Sir Gerald; *see* Howard, Sir S. G.

Howard, Maj.-Gen. Gordon Byron, 1895–1976, vol. VII

Howard, Captain Guy Robert, 1886–1918, vol. II

Howard, Sir (Harold Walter) Seymour, 1st Bt, 1888–1967, vol. VI

Howard, Sir Harry, (Henry Rudolph Howard), 1890–1970, vol. VI

Howard, Sir Henry, 1843–1921, vol. II

Howard, Rev. Henry, 1859–1933, vol. III

Howard, Lt-Col Hon. Henry Anthony Camillo, 1913–1977, vol. VII

Howard, Col Henry Cecil Lloyd, 1882–1950, vol. IV

Howard, Henry Charles, 1850–1914, vol. I

Howard, Sir Henry Francis, 1809–1898, vol. I

Howard, Sir Henry Fraser, 1874–1943, vol. IV

Howard, Major Sir Henry George, 1883–1968, vol. VI

Howard, Henry Newman, 1861–1929, vol. III

Howard, Col Henry Richard Lloyd, 1853–1922, vol. II

Howard, Henry Rudolph; *see* Howard, Sir Harry.

Howard, Sir Herbert; *see* Howard, Sir S. H.

Howard, Hon. Hugh Melville, 1883–1919, vol. II

Howard, John, *died* 1911, vol. I

Howard, John, *died* 1929, vol. III

Howard, Sir John Curtois, 1887–1970, vol. VI

Howard, Joseph, 1834–1923, vol. II

Howard, Keble; *see* Bell, John Keble.

Howard, Leon Alexander L.; *see* Lee Howard.

Howard, Leslie, 1893–1943, vol. IV

Howard, Lady Mabel, 1878–1942, vol. IV

Howard, Hon. Mabel Bowden, *died* 1972, vol. VII

Howard, Hon. Oliver, 1875–1908, vol. I

Howard, Peter D., 1908–1965, vol. VI

Howard, Philip John Canning, 1853–1934, vol. III

Howard, Sir Richard Nicholas, 1832–1905, vol. I

Howard, Robert Jared Bliss, *died* 1921, vol. II

Howard, Robert Mowbray, 1854–1928, vol. II

Howard, Rev. Robert Wilmot, 1887–1960, vol. V

Howard, Roy Wilson, 1883–1964, vol. VI

Howard, Russell John, 1875–1942, vol. IV

Howard, Lt-Col Samuel Lloyd, 1827–1901, vol. I

Howard, Sir Seymour; *see* Howard, Sir H. W. S.

Howard, Sir Stafford; *see* Howard, Sir E. S.

Howard, Sir (Stanley) Herbert, 1888–1968, vol. VI

Howard, Sir (Stephen) Gerald, 1896–1973, vol. VII

Howard, Major Stephen Goodwin, 1867–1934, vol. III

Howard, T. Henry, 1849–1923, vol. II

Howard, Rev. Thomas Henry, *died* 1931, vol. III

Howard, Brig.-Gen. Thomas Nairne Scott Moncrieff, *died* 1960, vol. V

Howard, Tom Forrest, 1888–1953, vol. V

Howard, Walter, 1866–1922, vol. II

Howard, Rev. Wilbert Francis, 1880–1952, vol. V

Howard, Captain William Gilbert, 1877–1960, vol. V

Howard, William Reginald, 1879–1966, vol. VI

Howard, Captain William Van Sittart, 1859–1937, vol. III

Howard-Brooke, Col Richard Edward Frederic, 1847–1918, vol. II

Howard-Vyse, Lt-Gen. Edward, 1826–1909, vol. I

Howard-Vyse, Howard Henry, 1858–1927, vol. II

Howard-Vyse, Maj.-Gen. Sir Richard Granville Hylton, 1883–1962, vol. VI

Howard-Williams, W., 1879–1962, vol. VI

Howarth, Sir Alfred, 1867–1937, vol. III

Howarth, Sir Edward, *died* 1953, vol. V

Howarth, Elijah, *died* 1938, vol. III

Howarth, Harry, 1916–1969, vol. VI

Howarth, Herbert Lomax, 1900–1974, vol. VII

Howarth, Osbert John Radclyffe, 1877–1954, vol. V

Howarth, Walter Goldie, 1879–1962, vol. VI

Howarth, William James, *died* 1928, vol. II

Howat, Very Rev. Rudolph H.; *see* Henderson-Howat.

Howden, Charles Robert Andrew, 1862–1936, vol. III

Howden, Captain Harry Leslie, 1896–1969, vol. VI

Howden, Robert, 1856–1940, vol. III

Howe, 3rd Earl, 1822–1900, vol. I

Howe, 4th Earl, 1861–1929, vol. III

Howe, 5th Earl, 1884–1964, vol. VI

Howe, Adm. Hon. Sir Assheton Gore C.; *see* Curzon-Howe.

Howe, Rt Hon. Clarence Decatur, 1886–1960, vol. V

Howe, George Frederick, 1856–1937, vol. III

Howe, George William Osborn, 1875–1960, vol. V

Howe, Sir Gerard Lewis, 1899–1955, vol. V

Howe, Hon. James Henderson, 1839–1920, vol. II
Howe, John Allen, 1869–1952, vol. V
Howe, Julia Ward, 1819–1910, vol. I
Howe, Captain Leicester Charles Assheton St John C.; see Curzon-Howe.
Howe, Col Randall Charles Annesley, 1858–1930, vol. III
Howe, Sir Ronald Martin, 1896–1977, vol. VII
Howe, Air Cdre Thomas Edward Barham, 1886–1970, vol. VI
Howel-Jones, Lt-Col Walter, 1868–1948, vol. IV
Howell, Col Arthur Anthony, 1862–1918, vol. II
Howell, Charles Alfred, 1905–1974, vol. VII
Howell, Hon. Clark, 1863–1936, vol. III
Howell, Conrad Meredyth Hinds, 1877–1960, vol. V
Howell, Very Rev. David, 1831–1903, vol. I
Howell, David Arnold, 1890–1953, vol. V
Howell, Sir Evelyn Berkeley, 1877–1971, vol. VII
Howell, Maj.-Gen. Frederick Duke Gwynne, 1881–1967, vol. VI
Howell, Rev. G., died 1918, vol. II
Howell, Lt-Col Geoffrey Llewellyn Hinds, 1875–1948, vol. IV
Howell, Col Harry Arthur Leonard, 1867–1937, vol. III
Howell, Hon. Hector Mansfield, 1842–1918, vol. II
Howell, Lt-Col Herbert Gwynne, 1879–1925, vol. II
Howell, John, 1871–1945, vol. IV
Howell, John Aldersey, 1888–1928, vol. II
Howell, Mortimer Sloper, 1841–1925, vol. II
Howell, Brig.-Gen. Philip, 1877–1916, vol. II
Howell, Sir Walter J., died 1913, vol. I
Howell, Col Wilfrid Russell, 1865–1930, vol. III
Howell, William Gough, 1922–1974, vol. VII
Howell, William Gruffydd Rhys, 1904–1956, vol. V
Howell, William H., 1860–1945, vol. IV
Howell, Rev. Canon Willoughby John, died 1938, vol. III
Howell-Jones, Col John Hyndman, 1877–1941, vol. IV
Howell-Price, Lt-Col Owen Glendower, vol. II
Howells, Rt Rev. Adelakun Williamson, 1905–1963, vol. VI
Howells, Rt Rev. Adolphus Williamson, 1866–1938, vol. III
Howells, George, 1871–1955, vol. V
Howells, William Dean, 1837–1920, vol. II
Howes, Lt-Gen. Albert Joseph, 1837–1914, vol. I
Howes, Arthur Burnaby, 1879–1963, vol. VI
Howes, Bobby, died 1972, vol. VII
Howes, Ernest James, 1895–1974, vol. VII
Howes, Frank Stewart, 1891–1974, vol. VII
Howes, George Bond, 1853–1905, vol. I
Howes, Henry William, 1896–1978, vol. VII
Howes, Brig. Sidney Gerald, died 1961, vol. VI
Howey, Maj.-Gen. William, 1838–1924, vol. II
Howgill, Richard John Frederick, 1895–1975, vol. VII
Howgrave-Graham, Hamilton Maurice, 1882–1963, vol. VI
Howick of Glendale, 1st Baron, 1903–1973, vol. VII
Howie, Hon. Sir Archibald, 1879–1943, vol. IV

Howie, Rev. Robert, 1836–1918, vol. II
Howison, George Holmes, 1834–1916, vol. II
Howitt, Sir Alfred Bakewell, 1879–1954, vol. V
Howitt, Alfred William, 1830–1908, vol. I
Howitt, Cecil; see Howitt, T. C.
Howitt, Charles Roberts, 1894–1969, vol. VI
Howitt, Frank Dutch, 1894–1954, vol. V
Howitt, Sir Harold Gibson, 1886–1969, vol. VI
Howitt, (Thomas) Cecil, 1889–1968, vol. VI
Howkins, Col Cyril Henry, 1876–1947, vol. IV
Howland, Hewitt Hanson, 1863–1944, vol. IV
Howland, Oliver Aiken, 1847–1904, vol. I
Howland, William Bailey, 1849–1917, vol. II
Howland, Hon. Sir William Pierce, 1811–1907, vol. I
Howles, Leonard, 1896–1957, vol. V
Howlett, Charles Edgar, 1854–1939, vol. III
Howlett, Edmund Henry, 1854–1930, vol. III
Howlett, Rt Rev. Mgr Martin, 1863–1949, vol. IV
Howlett, Brig. Reginald, 1882–1942, vol. IV
Howlett, Reginald, 1908–1969, vol. VI
Howlett, Richard, 1841–1917, vol. II
Howley, Major Jasper Joseph, 1868–1915, vol. I
Howley, John F. W., 1866–1941, vol. IV
Howley, Most Rev. Michael Francis, 1843–1914, vol. I
Howley, Richard Joseph, died 1955, vol. V
Howley, William John Joseph, 1865–1948, vol. IV
Howley, William Richard, 1875–1941, vol. IV
Howman, Brig. Ross Cosens, 1899–1976, vol. VII
Howorth, Col Henry Godfrey, 1870–1947, vol. IV
Howorth, Sir Henry Hoyle, 1842–1923, vol. II
Howorth, Sir Rupert Beswicke, 1880–1964, vol. VI
Howse, Francis, 1851–1925, vol. II
Howse, Sir Henry Greenway, 1841–1914, vol. I
Howse, Maj.-Gen. Hon. Sir Neville Reginald, 1863–1930, vol. III
Howson, G. W. S., died 1919, vol. II
Howson, Brig. Geoffrey, 1883–1961, vol. VI
Howson, Ven. George John, 1854–1943, vol. IV
Howson, Ven. James Francis, 1856–1934, vol. III
Howson, Hon. Comdr John, 1829–1907, vol. I
Howson, Captain John, 1871–1948, vol. IV
Howson, Captain John Montagu, 1893–1959, vol. V
Howth, 4th Earl of, 1827–1909, vol. I
Hoy, Baron (Life Peer); James Hutchison Hoy, 1909–1976, vol. VII
Hoy, Col Sir William Wilson, 1868–1930, vol. III
Hoyland, Harold Allan Dilke, 1885–1959, vol. V
Hoyland, John S., 1887–1957, vol. V
Hoyle, Arthur, born 1857, vol. III
Hoyle, Lt-Col Sir Emmanuel, 1st Bt, 1866–1939, vol. III
Hoyle, George, 1900–1979, vol. VII
Hoyle, Hon. Henry Clement, 1852–1926, vol. II
Hoyle, J. Rossiter, 1856–1926, vol. II
Hoyle, John Clifford, 1901–1976, vol. VII
Hoyle, William Evans, died 1926, vol. II
Hoyles, Newman Wright, 1844–1928, vol. II
Hoysted, Col Desmond Murree Fitzgerald, 1874–1945, vol. IV
Hozier, Col Sir Henry Montague, died 1907, vol. I

Hozumi, Baron Nobushige, 1855–1926, vol. II (A), vol. III

Hrdlička, Aleš, 1869–1943, vol. IV

Hsu Chen-Ping, Rt Rev. Francis, 1920–1974, vol. VII

Huban, Maj.-Gen. John Patrick, 1891–1957, vol. V

Hubback, Brig.-Gen. Arthur Benison, 1871–1948, vol. IV

Hubback, Vice-Adm. Sir (Arthur) Gordon Voules, 1902–1970, vol. VI

Hubback, Mrs Eva M., 1886–1949, vol. IV

Hubback, Most Rev. George Clay, 1882–1955, vol. V

Hubback, Vice-Adm. Sir Gordon Voules; see Hubback, Vice-Adm. Sir A. G. V.

Hubback, Sir John Austen, 1878–1968, vol. VI

Hubbard, Charles Edward, 1900–1980, vol. VII

Hubbard, Elbert, 1859–1915, vol. I

Hubbard, (Eric) Hesketh, 1892–1957, vol. V

Hubbard, Hon. Evelyn, 1852–1934, vol. III

Hubbard, George, 1859–1936, vol. III

Hubbard, George William, 1870–1939, vol. III

Hubbard, Rt Rev. Harold Evelyn, 1883–1953, vol. V

Hubbard, Hesketh; see Hubbard, E. H.

Hubbard, Cdre Lancelot Fortescue; see Hubbard, Cdre R. L. F.

Hubbard, Louisa M., 1836–1906, vol. I

Hubbard, Percival Cyril, 1902–1961, vol. VI

Hubbard, Cdre (Robert) Lancelot Fortescue, 1887–1972, vol. VII

Hubbard, Bey Robert Richard, 1843–1926, vol. II (A), vol. III

Hubbard, Thomas Frederick, 1898–1961, vol. VI

Hubbard, William Egerton, died 1918, vol. II

Hubble, Edwin Powell, 1889–1953, vol. V

Huberman, Bronislaw, 1882–1947, vol. IV

Hubrecht, J. B., 1883–1978, vol. VII

Huckin, Victor Henry St John, 1880–1943, vol. IV

Hudd, Hon. Sir Herbert Sydney, 1881–1948, vol. IV

Hudd, Walter, 1898–1963, vol. VI

Huddleston, Sir Arthur James Croft, 1880–1948, vol. IV

Huddleston, Lady Diana De Vere, died 1905, vol. I

Huddleston, Captain Sir Ernest Whiteside, 1874–1959, vol. V

Huddleston, George, 1862–1944, vol. IV

Huddleston, Maj.-Gen. Sir Hubert Jervoise, 1880–1950, vol. IV

Huddleston, Sisley, 1883–1952, vol. V

Huddleston, Tristram Frederick Croft, 1848–1936, vol. III

Huddleston, Captain Willoughby Baynes, 1866–1953, vol. V

Hudleston, Ven. Cuthbert, died 1944, vol. IV

Hudleston, Lt-Gen. John Wallace, 1880–1961, vol. VI

Hudleston, Wilfred H., 1828–1909, vol. I

Hudleston, Col Wilfrid Edward, 1872–1952, vol. V

Hudon, Lt-Col Joseph Alfred George, 1858–1918, vol. II (A), vol. III

Hudson, 1st Viscount, 1886–1957, vol. V

Hudson, 2nd Viscount, 1924–1963 (this entry was not transferred to Who was Who).

Hudson, Albert Blellock, 1875–1947, vol. IV

Hudson, Alfred Arthur, died 1930, vol. III

Hudson, Arthur, 1861–1948, vol. IV

Hudson, Arthur Cyril, 1875–1962, vol. VI

Hudson, Col Arthur Ross, 1876–1963, vol. VI

Hudson, Sir Austin Uvedale Morgan, 1st Bt, 1897–1956, vol. V

Hudson, Bernard, 1877–1957, vol. V

Hudson, Brig. Charles Edward, 1892–1959, vol. V

Hudson, Charles Thomas, 1828–1903, vol. I

Hudson, Lt-Col Charles Tilson, 1865–1948, vol. IV

Hudson, Maj.-Gen. Corrie, 1874–1958, vol. V

Hudson, Rev. Canon Cyril Edward, 1888–1960, vol. V

Hudson, Sir Edmund Peder, 1903–1978, vol. VII

Hudson, Edward, died 1936, vol. III

Hudson, Sir Edward Herbert, 1898–1966, vol. VI

Hudson, Sir Frank; see Hudson, Sir W. F.

Hudson, George Bickersteth, 1845–1912, vol. I

Hudson, Engr Rear-Adm. George William, 1861–1941, vol. IV

Hudson, Harry Kynoch, 1867–1958, vol. V

Hudson, Gen. Sir Havelock, 1862–1944, vol. IV

Hudson, Lt-Col Henry Cecil Harland, 1885–1929, vol. III

Hudson, James Frank, 1872–1949, vol. IV

Hudson, James Hindle, 1881–1962, vol. VI

Hudson, Rev. Joseph, 1834–1919, vol. II

Hudson, Sir Leslie S., 1872–1946, vol. IV

Hudson, Manley Ottmer, 1886–1960, vol. V

Hudson, Mary Elizabeth, (Lady Hudson), died 1963, vol. VI

Hudson, Rt Rev. Noel Baring, 1893–1970, vol. VI

Hudson, Col Percy, 1876–1955, vol. V

Hudson, Lt-Col Ralph Charles D.; see Donaldson-Hudson.

Hudson, Ralph Milbanke, 1849–1938, vol. III

Hudson, Rev. Robert, 1862–1936, vol. III

Hudson, Major Robert Arthur, 1880–1917, vol. II

Hudson, Sir Robert Arundell, 1864–1927, vol. II

Hudson, Robert George Spencer, 1895–1965, vol. VI

Hudson, Hon. Sir Robert James, 1885–1963, vol. VI

Hudson, Rowland Skeffington, 1900–1980, vol. VII

Hudson, R(upert) Vaughan, 1895–1967, vol. VI

Hudson, Sidney Rowland, 1897–1966, vol. VI

Hudson, Brig. Stanley Grey, 1902–1960, vol. V

Hudson, Stephen, died 1944, vol. IV

Hudson, Brig.-Gen. Thomas Roe Christopher, 1866–1940, vol. III

Hudson, Rev. Thomas William, 1861–1929, vol. III

Hudson, W. H., 1841–1922, vol. II

Hudson, Walter, 1852–1935, vol. III

Hudson, Sir (Walter) Frank, 1875–1958, vol. V

Hudson, Walter Richard Austen, 1894–1970, vol. VI

Hudson, Lt-Col William, 1880–1967, vol. VI

Hudson, Sir William, 1896–1978, vol. VII

Hudson, Sir William Brereton, 1843–1914, vol. I

Hudson, William Henry, 1862–1918, vol. II

Hudson, William Henry Hoar, 1838–1915, vol. I

Hudson-Davies, Sir Alan Meredyth, 1901–1975, vol. VII

Hudson-Kinahan, Sir Edward Hudson; see Kinahan.

Hudson-Kinahan, Lt-Col George Frederick, 1879–1939, vol. III

Hudson-Kinahan, Sir Robert Henry; see Kinahan.

Hudson-Williams, Thomas, 1873–1961, vol. VI

Hudspeth, Major Henry Moore, 1886–1971, vol. VII

Hueffer, Oliver Madox, died 1931, vol. III

Huffam, Major James Palmer, 1897–1968, vol. VI

Hufton, Philip Arthur, 1911–1974, vol. VII

Hügel, Anatole, Baron von, 1854–1928, vol. II

Hügel, Friedrich, Baron von, 1852–1925, vol. II

Hugessen, Adrian Norton K.; see Knatchbull-Hugessen.

Hugessen, Herbert Thomas K.; see Knatchbull-Hugessen.

Hugessen, Sir Hughe Montgomery K.; see Knatchbull-Hugessen.

Huggard, Sir Walter Clarence, died 1957, vol. V

Huggett, Arthur St George Joseph McCarthy, 1897–1968, vol. VI

Huggett, Esther Margaret; see Killick, E. M.

Huggill, Henry Percy, 1886–1957, vol. V

Huggins, Brig.-Gen. Alfred, 1884–1959, vol. V

Huggins, Sir George Frederick, died 1941, vol. IV

Huggins, Lt-Col Henry William, 1891–1965, vol. VI

Huggins, Sir John, 1891–1971, vol. VII

Huggins, Margaret Lindsay, (Lady Huggins), 1849–1915, vol. I

Huggins, Lt-Col Ponsonby Glenn, 1857–1925, vol. II

Huggins, Sir William, 1824–1910, vol. I

Hugh-Jones, Evan Bonnor, 1890–1978, vol. VII

Hugh-Jones, Llewelyn Arthur, 1888–1970, vol. VI

Hugh-Jones, Siriol (Mary Aprille), (Siriol Hart), 1924–1964, vol. VI

Hughan, Adm. Sir Arthur John H.; see Henniker-Hughan.

Hughes, Rt Rev. Albert Edward, 1878–1954, vol. V

Hughes, Sir Alfred, 9th Bt (cr 1773), 1825–1898, vol. I

Hughes, Alfred, 1860–1940, vol. III

Hughes, Alfred James, died 1947, vol. IV

Hughes, Col Arbuthnott James, 1856–1945, vol. IV

Hughes, Brig. Archibald Cecil, 1886–1961, vol. VI

Hughes, Captain Arthur Beckett, 1873–1925, vol. II

Hughes, Arthur John, 1843–1910, vol. I

Hughes, Arthur Montague D'Urban, 1873–1974, vol. VII

Hughes, Major Basil, 1878–1953, vol. V

Hughes, Cecil Hugh Myddleton, died 1960, vol. V

Hughes, Charles Evans, 1862–1948, vol. IV

Hughes, Maj.-Gen. Charles Frederick, 1844–1932, vol. III

Hughes, Sir Collingwood, 10th Bt (cr 1773), 1854–1932, vol. III

Hughes, Collingwood, 1872–1963, vol. VI

Hughes, Col Cyril E., 1890–1958, vol. V

Hughes, David Arthur, 1905–1968, vol. VI

Hughes, David Edward, 1831–1900, vol. I

Hughes, Donald Wynn, 1911–1967, vol. VI

Hughes, Col Edmund Locock, 1880–1945, vol. IV

Hughes, Rev. Edward, died 1910, vol. I

Hughes, Edward, 1899–1965, vol. VI

Hughes, Edward David, 1906–1963, vol. VI

Hughes, Captain Edward Glyn de Styrap J.; see Jukes Hughes.

Hughes, Captain Edward Llewellyn, 1875–1955, vol. V

Hughes, Edward R., died 1908, vol. I

Hughes, Col Edward Talfourd, 1855–1943, vol. IV (A), vol. V

Hughes, Col Sir Edwin, 1832–1904, vol. I

Hughes, Elizabeth Phillipps, 1851–1925, vol. II

Hughes, Col Emilius, 1844–1926, vol. II

Hughes, Emrys, 1894–1969, vol. VI

Hughes, Rev. Ernest Richard, 1883–1956, vol. V

Hughes, Rev. Ernest Selwyn, 1860–1942, vol. IV

Hughes, Evan, 1882–1951, vol. V

Hughes, Maj.-Gen. Frederick Godfrey, 1857–1944, vol. IV

Hughes, Very Rev. Frederick Llewelyn, 1894–1967, vol. VI

Hughes, G. Bernard, died 1975, vol. VII

Hughes, Maj.-Gen. Garnet Burk, 1880–1937, vol. III

Hughes, Col George Arthur, 1851–1926, vol. II

Hughes, Hon. George Edward, 1854–1937, vol. III

Hughes, George Lewis Hollingsworth, 1876–1932, vol. III

Hughes, Gerald Stephen, 1878–1959, vol. V

Hughes, Captain Guy D'O.; see D'Oyly-Hughes.

Hughes, Guy Erskine, 1904–1980, vol. VII

Hughes, Rev. Harold, 1884–1950, vol. IV

Hughes, Hector, died 1970, vol. VI

Hughes, Maj.-Gen. Henry Bernard Wylde, 1887–1953, vol. V

Hughes, Henry Harold, died 1940, vol. III

Hughes, Rev. Henry Maldwyn, 1875–1940, vol. III

Hughes, Brig.-Gen. Henry Thoresby, 1873–1947, vol. IV

Hughes, Herbert, 1853–1917, vol. II

Hughes, Major Herbert Francis, died 1939, vol. III

Hughes, H(ugh) L(lewelyn) Glyn, 1892–1973, vol. VII

Hughes, Rev. Hugh Price, 1847–1902, vol. I

Hughes, Hugh Robert, 1827–1911, vol. I

Hughes, Maj.-Gen. Ivor Thomas Percival, 1897–1962, vol. VI

Hughes, James John, 1874–1952, vol. V

Hughes, John, 1850–1932, vol. III

Hughes, Col John Arthur, 1860–1938, vol. III

Hughes, John David Ivor, 1885–1969, vol. VI

Hughes, Col John Gethin, 1866–1954, vol. V

Hughes, Captain John Grant Duncan-, 1882–1962, vol. VI

Hughes, John Rowland, 1856–1937, vol. III

Hughes, John Turnbull, 1919–1977, vol. VII

Hughes, John Williams Gwynne-, 1858–1917, vol. II

Hughes, Joseph John, 1928–1976, vol. VII

Hughes, Rt Rev. Joshua Pritchard, 1847–1938, vol. III

Hughes, Katherine, *died* 1931, vol. III

Hughes, Rev. Levi Gethin, 1885–1953, vol. V

Hughes, Rev. Llewelyn Robert, *died* 1925, vol. II

Hughes, M. K., *died* 1918, vol. II

Hughes, Dame Mary Ethel, *died* 1958, vol. V

Hughes, Mary Katherine H. P.; *see* Price Hughes.

Hughes, Rev. Nathaniel Thomas, 1834–1913, vol. I

Hughes, Sir Reginald Johnasson, 11th Bt (*cr* 1773), 1882–1945, vol. IV

Hughes, Reginald Richard M.; *see* Meyric Hughes.

Hughes, Ven. Richard, 1881–1962, vol. VI

Hughes, Richard Arthur Warren, 1900–1976, vol. VII

Hughes, Sir Richard Edgar, 13th Bt (*cr* 1773), 1897–1970, vol. VI

Hughes, Captain Robert Herbert Wilfrid, 1872–1936, vol. III

Hughes, Sir Robert Heywood, 12th Bt (*cr* 1773), 1865–1951, vol. V

Hughes, Sir Robert John, 1822–1904, vol. I

Hughes, Ronw Moelwyn, 1897–1955, vol. V

Hughes, Hon. Lt-Gen. Hon. Sir Sam, 1853–1921, vol. II

Hughes, Rev. Samuel William, 1874–1954, vol. V

Hughes, Spencer Leigh, *died* 1920, vol. II

Hughes, Sydney Herbert George, 1879–1962, vol. VI

Hughes, Talbot, 1869–1942, vol. IV

Hughes, Sir Thomas, 1838–1923, vol. II

Hughes, Hon. Sir Thomas, 1863–1930, vol. III

Hughes, Sir Thomas, 1863–1942, vol. IV

Hughes, Thomas Cann, 1860–1948, vol. IV

Hughes, Mrs Thomas H. R., *died* 1930, vol. III

Hughes, Sir Thomas Harrison, 1st Bt (*cr* 1942), 1881–1958, vol. V

Hughes, Thomas Lewis, 1897–1980, vol. VII

Hughes, Thomas M'Kenny, *died* 1917, vol. II

Hughes, Sir Thomas Raffles, 1856–1938, vol. III

Hughes, Rev. W. Worthington P.; *see* Poole-Hughes.

Hughes, Sir Walter Charleton, 1850–1922, vol. II

Hughes, Rev. Walter Octavius Marsh, *died* 1931, vol. III

Hughes, Walter Tatham, *died* 1917, vol. II

Hughes, Hon. Sir Wilfrid (Selwyn) Kent, 1895–1970, vol. VI

Hughes, Bt Col William Hesketh, 1872–1940, vol. III

Hughes, Rt Rev. William James, *died* 1979, vol. VII

Hughes, Rt Hon. William Morris, 1864–1952, vol .V

Hughes, Sir William Templer, 1822–1897, vol. I

Hughes-Buller, Ralph Buller, 1871–1949, vol. IV

Hughes D'Aeth, Rear-Adm. Arthur Cloudesley Shovel, 1875–1956, vol. V

Hughes-Games, Ven. Joshua, 1831–1904, vol. I

Hughes-Hallett, Col James Wyndham, 1852–1927, vol. II

Hughes-Hallett, Vice-Adm. John, 1901–1972, vol. VII

Hughes-Hallett, Leslie Charles, 1887–1966, vol. VI

Hughes-Hunter, Sir Charles, 1st Bt (*cr* 1906), 1844–1907, did not have an entry in Who's Who.

Hughes-Hunter, Sir William Bulkeley Hughes, 2nd Bt, 1880–1951, vol. V

Hughes-Morgan, Major Sir David, 1st Bt; *see* Morgan.

Hughes-Morgan, Sir John Vernon, 2nd Bt, 1900–1969, vol. VI

Hughes-Onslow, Sir Geoffrey Henry, 1893–1971, vol. VII

Hughes-Onslow, Henry, 1871–1932, vol. III

Hughes-Roberts, John Gwyndeg, 1894–1949, vol. IV

Hughes-Stanton, Sir Herbert, 1870–1937, vol. III

Hughman, Sir (Ernest) Montague, 1876–1956, vol. V

Hughman, Sir Montague; *see* Hughman, Sir E. M.

Hugill, Rear-Adm. René Charles, 1883–1962, vol. VI

Hugo, Lt-Col Edward Victor, 1865–1951, vol. V

Hugo, Lt-Col James Henry, 1870–1943, vol. IV

Huguenet, A. P., *died* 1910, vol. I

Huish, Marcus Bourne, *died* 1921, vol. II

Huish, Sir Raymond Douglas, 1898–1970, vol. VI

Hulbert, Sir Charles, *died* 1932, vol. III

Hulbert, Rev. Charles Augustus, 1838–1919, vol. II

Hulbert, Dame Cicely; *see* Courtneidge, Dame Cicely.

Hulbert, Claude Noel, 1900–1964, vol. VI

Hulbert, Jack, 1892–1978, vol. VII

Hulbert, Wing Comdr Sir Norman John, 1903–1972, vol. VII

Hulett, Hon. Sir (James) Liege, 1838–1928, vol. II

Hulett, Hon. Sir Liege; *see* Hulett, Hon. Sir J. L.

Hulin de Loo, Georges Charles Nicolas Marie, 1862–1946, vol. IV

Hull, Arthur Eaglefield, 1876–1928, vol. II

Hull, Maj.-Gen. Sir Charles Patrick Amyatt, 1865–1920, vol. II

Hull, Cordell, 1871–1955, vol. V

Hull, Edward, 1829–1917, vol. II

Hull, Eleanor H., 1860–1935, vol. III

Hull, Hon. Henry Charles, 1860–1932, vol. III

Hull, Henry Mitchell, 1861–1946, vol. IV

Hull, Surg. Rear-Adm. Herbert Richard Barnes, 1886–1970, vol. VI

Hull, Sir Hubert, 1887–1976, vol. VII

Hull, Lt-Col Hubert Charles Edward, 1891–1939, vol. III

Hull, Sir Percy Clarke, *died* 1968, vol. VI

Hull, Comdr Thomas A., *died* 1904, vol. I

Hullah, John, 1876–1955, vol. V

Hullah-Brown, J., 1875–1973, vol. VII

Hulme, Edward Maslin, 1869–1951, vol. V

Hulme, Frederick Edward, 1841–1909, vol. I

Hulme, Rev. Thomas Ferrier, 1856–1942, vol. IV

Hulme-Moir, Rt Rev. Francis Oag, 1910–1979, vol. VII

Hulme Taylor, Col Jack, 1894–1970, vol. VI

Hulse, Sir Edward, 5th Bt, 1809–1899, vol. I

Hulse, Sir Edward Hamilton Westrow, 7th Bt, 1889–1915, vol. I

Hulse, Sir Edward Henry, 6th Bt, 1859–1903, vol. I

Hulse, Sir Hamilton, 8th Bt, 1864–1931, vol. III

Hulton, Sir Edward, 1st Bt (*cr* 1921), 1869–1925, vol. II

Hulton, Col Frederick Courtenay Longuet, 1864–1940, vol. III (A), vol. IV

Hulton, Rev. Henry Edward, 1839–1922, vol. II

Hulton, Lt-Col Henry Horne, 1882–1941, vol. IV

Hulton, Col John Meredith, 1882–1942, vol. IV

Hulton, Sir Roger Braddyll, 3rd Bt (*cr* 1905), 1891–1956, vol. V

Hulton, Sir William Rothwell, 2nd Bt (*cr* 1905), 1868–1943, vol. IV

Hulton, Sir William Wilbraham Blethyn, 1st Bt (*cr* 1905), 1844–1907, vol. I

Hulton-Harrop, William Edward Montagu, 1848–1916, vol. II

Hulton-Harrop, Maj.-Gen. William Harrington, 1906–1979, vol. VII

Humble, Joseph Graeme, 1913–1980, vol. VII

Humble-Burkitt, Col Bernard Maynard, 1864–1945, vol. IV

Humble-Crofts, Rev. William John, 1846–1924, vol. II

Humby, Lt-Col James Frederick, 1860–1943, vol. IV

Hume, Alexander Williamson, 1850–1925, vol. II (A), vol. III

Hume, Allan Octavian, 1829–1912, vol. I

Hume, Basil; *see* Hume, J. B.

Hume, Col Charles Vernon, 1860–1915, vol. I

Hume, Fergus, 1859–1932, vol. III

Hume, George Alexander, 1860–1905, vol. I

Hume, George Haliburton, 1845–1923, vol. II

Hume, Sir George Hopwood, 1866–1946, vol. IV

Hume, Sir (Hubert) Nutcombe, 1893–1967, vol. VI

Hume, James Gibson, 1860–1949, vol. IV, vol. V

Hume, John Basil, 1893–1974, vol. VII

Hume, Col John Edward, 1866–1939, vol. III

Hume, Brig.-Gen. John James Francis, 1858–1935, vol. III

Hume, Maj.-Gen. John Richard, 1831–1906, vol. I

Hume, Major Martin Andrew Sharp, 1847–1910, vol. I

Hume, Sir Nutcombe; *see* Hume, Sir H. N.

Hume, Brig. Reginald Vernon, 1898–1960, vol. V

Hume, Sir Robert, 1828–1909, vol. I

Hume, Sir William Errington, 1879–1960, vol. V

Hume, William Fraser, 1867–1949, vol. IV

Hume, Lt-Col William James Parke, 1866–1952, vol. V

Hume-Campbell, Sir John Home-Purves; *see* Campbell.

Hume-Cook, Hon. James, 1866–1942, vol. IV

Hume-Rothery, William, 1899–1968, vol. VI

Hume-Spry, Lt-Col Leighton; *see* Spry.

Hume-Williams, Rt Hon. Sir Ellis, 1st Bt, 1863–1947, vol. IV

Hume-Williams, Sir Roy Ellis, 2nd Bt, 1887–1980, vol. VII

Humfrey, Rev. John B.; *see* Blake-Humfrey.

Humfrey, Lt-Col Richard Edmond, 1881–1962, vol. VI

Hummel, Rt Rev. Francis Ignatius, 1870–1924, vol. II

Humphery, Lt-Col Sir John, 1872–1938, vol. III

Humphery, John Edward, 1873–1946, vol. IV

Humphery, Sir William Henry, 1st Bt, 1827–1909, vol. I

Humphrey, Marshal of the Royal Air Force Sir Andrew Henry, 1921–1977, vol. VII

Humphrey, Douglas, 1880–1945, vol. IV

Humphrey, George, 1889–1966, vol. VI

Humphrey, George Magoffin, 1890–1970, vol. VI

Humphrey, Herbert Alfred, 1868–1951, vol. V

Humphrey, Hubert Horatio, Jr, 1911–1978, vol. VII

Humphrey, John, 1862–1933, vol. III

Humphrey, John, 1879–1956, vol. V

Humphrey, Rev. John Henry, 1860–1934, vol. III

Humphrey-Davy, Francis Herbert Mountjoy Nelson, *died* 1953, vol. V

Humphreys, Rev. Alfred Edward, 1843–1922, vol. II

Humphreys, Arthur L., 1865–1946, vol. IV

Humphreys, Cecil Lee Howard, 1893–1941, vol. IV

Humphreys, Major Dashwood William Harrington, 1872–1917, vol. II

Humphreys, Lt-Gen. Sir (Edward) Thomas, 1878–1955, vol. V

Humphreys, Brig.-Gen. Gardiner, 1865–1942, vol. IV

Humphreys, George Alfred, *died* 1948, vol. IV

Humphreys, Sir George William, 1863–1945, vol. IV

Humphreys, Gordon Noel, *died* 1966, vol. VI

Humphreys, Engr Rear-Adm. Sir Henry, *died* 1924, vol. II

Humphreys, Hubert, 1878–1967, vol. VI

Humphreys, Humphrey Francis, 1885–1977, vol. VII

Humphreys, John Lisseter, *died* 1929, vol. III

Humphreys, Captain Kenneth Noel, 1881–1955, vol. V

Humphreys, Noel Algernon, 1837–1923, vol. II

Humphreys, Very Rev. Robert, *died* 1917, vol. II

Humphreys, Lt-Gen. Sir Thomas; *see* Humphreys, Lt-Gen. Sir E. T.

Humphreys, Rt Hon. Sir Travers, 1867–1956, vol. V

Humphreys, Mrs W. Desmond; *see* Rita.

Humphreys-Davies, Brian, 1917–1971, vol. VII

Humphreys-Owen, Arthur Charles, 1836–1905, vol. I

Humphries, Albert, 1872–1951, vol. V

Humphries, Sir Albert Edward, *died* 1935, vol. III

Humphries, Sir Herbert Henry, *died* 1938, vol. III

Humphries, Rev. Canon James Henry, 1890–1962, vol. VI

Humphries, Sir Sidney Richard White, 1857–1941, vol. IV

Humphries, Sydney S.; *see* Sidney-Humphries.

Humphris, Francis Howard, 1866–1947, vol. IV

Humphry, Alfred Paget, 1850–1916, vol. II

Humphry, Mrs C. E., *died* 1925, vol. II

Humphry, Laurence, 1856–1920, vol. II

Humphry, Maj.-Gen. Lawrence, 1875–1931, vol. III

Humphrys, Brig.-Gen. Charles Vesey, 1862–1944, vol. IV

Humphrys, Lt-Col Sir Francis Henry, 1879–1971, vol. VII

Huneker, James Gibbons, 1860–1921, vol. II

Hungarton, 1st Baron, 1890–1966, vol. VI

Hungerford, Sir (Alexander) Wilson, *died* 1969, vol. VI

Hungerford, Margaret Wolfe, *died* 1897, vol. I

Hungerford, Samuel James, 1872–1955, vol. V

Hungerford, Sir Wilson; *see* Hungerford, Sir A. W.

Hunkin, Rt Rev. Joseph Wellington, 1887–1950, vol. IV

Hunloke, Henry Philip, 1906–1978, vol. VII

Hunloke, Major Sir Philip, 1868–1947, vol. IV

Hunn, Major Sydney Arthur, 1889–1942, vol. IV

Hunsdon of Hunsdon, 1st Baron, 1854–1935, vol. III

Hunsdon of Hunsdon, 2nd Baron; *see* Aldenham, 4th Baron.

Hunt, Dame Agnes Gwendoline, 1866–1948, vol. IV

Hunt, Alan Henderson, 1908–1970, vol. VI

Hunt, Albert, 1863–1957, vol. V

Hunt, Rev. Canon Alfred, 1862–1937, vol. III

Hunt, Adm. Sir (Allen) Thomas, 1866–1943, vol. IV

Hunt, Arthur Surridge, 1871–1934, vol. III

Hunt, Atlee Arthur, 1864–1935, vol. III

Hunt, Cecil Arthur, 1873–1965, vol. VI

Hunt, Rev. David J. Stather, 1856–1929, vol. III

Hunt, Edmund Langley, 1868–1925, vol. II

Hunt, Major Edwin Watkin, 1869–1945, vol. IV

Hunt, Frank William, 1870–1955, vol. V

Hunt, Surg. Rear-Adm. Frederick George, 1894–1975, vol. VII

Hunt, Sir Frederick Seager, 1st Bt, 1837-1904, vol. I

Hunt, Brig. Frederick Welsley, 1871–1944, vol. IV

Hunt, Rear-Adm. Geoffrey Harry C.; *see* Carew Hunt.

Hunt, George Henry, 1853–1940, vol. III

Hunt, Captain George Percy Edward, *died* 1917, vol. II

Hunt, Col (George) Vivian, 1905–1979, vol. VII

Hunt, Major Gerald Ponsonby Sneyd, 1877–1918, vol. II

Hunt, Gerard L.; *see* Leigh-Hunt.

Hunt, Rev. H. G. Bonavia, 1847–1917, vol. II

Hunt, Henry Ambrose, 1866–1946, vol. IV

Hunt, Rev. Henry de Vere, 1856–1919, vol. II

Hunt, Herbert James, 1899–1973, vol. VII

Hunt, Hilary Lushington Holman H.; *see* Holman-Hunt.

Hunt, Hubert Walter, 1865–1945, vol. IV

Hunt, Sir John, 1859–1945, vol. IV

Hunt, John Francis, 1906–1979, vol. VII

Hunt, Sir John Joseph, *died* 1933, vol. III

Hunt, John Middlemass, 1858–1932, vol. III

Hunt, Lt-Col John Patrick, 1875–1938, vol. III

Hunt, Col John Philip, 1907–1970, vol. VI

Hunt, Joseph, 1854–1936, vol. III

Hunt, Margaret, 1831–1912, vol. I

Hunt, Martita, 1900–1969, vol. VI

Hunt, Lt-Col Reginald Seager, 1874–1942, vol. IV

Hunt, Sir Reuben James, 1888–1970, vol. VI

Hunt, Richard William, 1908–1979, vol. VII

Hunt, Maj.-Gen. Robert Augustus Carew, 1838–1935, vol. III

Hunt, Comdr Robert Gregory Maze Durrant, 1886–1937, vol. III

Hunt, Captain Roland Cecil C.; *see* Carew Hunt.

Hunt, Rowland, 1858–1943, vol. IV

Hunt, Stanley Herbert, *died* 1934, vol. III

Hunt, Adm. Sir Thomas; *see* Hunt, Adm. Sir A. T.

Hunt, Thomas, 1854–1929, vol. III

Hunt, Thomas Cecil, 1901–1980, vol. VII

Hunt, Lt-Col Thomas Edward C.; *see* Carew-Hunt.

Hunt, Rev. Thomas Hankey, 1842–1921, vol. II

Hunt, Rev. Thomas Henry, 1865–1941, vol. IV

Hunt, Violet, *died* 1942, vol. IV

Hunt, Violet B.; *see* Brooke-Hunt.

Hunt, Col Vivian; *see* Hunt, Col G. V.

Hunt, Rev. William, 1842–1931, vol. III

Hunt, Sir William Duffus, 1867–1939, vol. III

Hunt, Sir William Edgar, 1883–1969, vol. VI

Hunt, William H.; *see* Holman-Hunt.

Hunt, Major William Morgan, 1881–1925, vol. II

Hunt-Grubbe, Adm. Sir Walter James, 1833–1922, vol. II

Hunter, Hon. Lord; William Hunter, 1865–1957, vol. V

Hunter, Maj.-Gen. Sir Alan John, 1881–1942, vol. IV

Hunter, Albert Edward, 1900–1969, vol. VI

Hunter, Andrew, 1876–1969, vol. VI

Hunter, Rev. Andrew Johnston, 1844–1914, vol. I

Hunter, Rev. Archer George, 1850–1939, vol. III

Hunter, Gen. Sir Archibald, 1856–1936, vol. III

Hunter, Sir Bernard; *see* Hunter, Sir W. B.

Hunter, Lt-Col Cecil Stuart, 1882–1935, vol. III

Hunter, Brig.-Gen. Charles George Woodburn, 1871–1932, vol. III

Hunter, Sir Charles Roderick, 3rd Bt, 1858–1924, vol. II

Hunter, Colin, 1841–1904, vol. I

Hunter, Adm. Cuthbert, 1866–1952, vol. V

Hunter, Sir David, 1841–1914, vol. I

Hunter, Donald, 1898–1978, vol. VII

Hunter, Captain Douglas William, *died* 1918, vol. II

Hunter, Sir Ellis, 1892–1961, vol. VI

Hunter, Col Evan Austin, 1887–1954, vol. V

Hunter, G. Sherwood, *died* 1920, vol. II

Hunter, Sir George, 1860–1930, vol. III

Hunter, Sir George Burton, 1845–1937, vol. III

Hunter, Maj.-Gen. George Douglas, 1860–1922, vol. II

Hunter, Brig.-Gen. George Gillett, 1864–1930, vol. III

Hunter, Gordon, 1863–1929, vol. III

Hunter, Hamilton, 1845–1923, vol. II

Hunter, Henry Charles Vicars, 1861–1934, vol. III

Hunter, Henry Hamilton, 1875–1944, vol. IV

Hunter, Air Cdre Henry John Francis, 1893–1966, vol. VI

Hunter, Brig. Henry Noel Alexander, 1881–1964, vol. VI

Hunter, Sir Herbert; *see* Hunter, Sir J. H.

Hunter, Col Sir Herbert Patrick, 1880–1968, vol. VI

Hunter, Ian Basil, 1900–1975, vol. VII
Hunter, James de Graaff, 1881–1967, vol. VI
Hunter, Captain James Edward, 1834–1932, vol. III
Hunter, John, 1833–1914, vol. II
Hunter, Rev. John, 1849–1917, vol. II
Hunter, Sir John, 1863–1936, vol. III
Hunter, Rt Rev. John, 1897–1965, vol. VI
Hunter, Sir John Adams, 1890–1962, vol. VI
Hunter, John B., 1890–1951, vol. V
Hunter, John George, 1888–1964, vol. VI
Hunter, Maj.-Gen. John Gunning, 1859–1926, vol. II
Hunter, Sir (John) Herbert, 1864–1930, vol. III
Hunter, Hon. John McEwan, 1863–1940, vol. III (A), vol. IV
Hunter, Sir (John) Mark (Somers), 1865–1932, vol. III
Hunter, Lt-Col John Muir, 1844–1920, vol. II
Hunter, Joseph, 1875–1935, vol. III
Hunter, Louis Lucien, 1889–1959, vol. V
Hunter, Sir Mark; see Hunter, Sir J. M. S.
Hunter, Matthew, died 1941, vol. IV
Hunter, Captain Michael John, 1891–1951, vol. V
Hunter, Norman Charles, 1908–1971, vol. VII
Hunter, Rev. Peter Hay, 1854–1909, vol. I
Hunter, Peter Sinclair, 1883–1954, vol. V
Hunter, Philip Vassar, 1883–1956, vol. V
Hunter, Sir Robert, 1844–1913, vol. I
Hunter, Robert Lewin, 1852–1942, vol. IV
Hunter, Samuel Robert, 1877–1948, vol. IV
Hunter, Summers, 1856–1940, vol. III
Hunter, Sir Summers, 1890–1963, vol. VI
Hunter, Sir Thomas, 1850–1919, vol. II
Hunter, Sir Thomas, 1872–1953, vol. V
Hunter, Lt-Col Thomas, 1873–1965, vol. VI
Hunter, Sir Thomas Alexander, 1876–1953, vol. V
Hunter, Sir Thomas Anderson, died 1958, vol. V
Hunter, Thomas Briggs, died 1957, vol. V
Hunter, Trevor Havard, died 1960, vol. V
Hunter, Walter King, 1867–1947, vol. IV
Hunter, William; see Hunter, Hon. Lord.
Hunter, William, 1861–1937, vol. III
Hunter, William, died 1967, vol. VI
Hunter, William Alexander, 1844–1898, vol. I
Hunter, Sir (William) Bernard, 1868–1924, vol. II
Hunter, Sir William Bulkeley Hughes H.; see Hughes-Hunter.
Hunter, William George, 1869–1950, vol. IV (A)
Hunter, Sir William Guyer, 1829–1902, vol. I
Hunter, William Henry, 1849–1917, vol. II
Hunter, Sir William Wilson, 1840–1900, vol. I
Hunter-Blair, Rt Rev. Sir David, 5th Bt, 1853–1939, vol. III
Hunter-Blair, Captain Sir Edward, 6th Bt, 1858–1945, vol. IV
Hunter-Blair, Maj.-Gen. Walter Charles, 1860–1938, vol. III
Hunter-Rodwell, Sir Cecil; see Rodwell.
Hunter-Weston, Lt-Gen. Sir Aylmer, 1864–1940, vol. III
Hunter-Weston, Lt-Col Gould, 1823–1904, vol. I
Hunting, (Gerald) Lindsay, 1891–1966, vol. VI
Hunting, Lindsay; see Hunting, G. L.
Hunting, Sir Percy Llewellyn, 1885–1973, vol. VII

Huntingdon, 14th Earl of, 1868–1939, vol. III
Huntingfield, 3rd Baron, 1818–1897, vol. I
Huntingfield, 4th Baron, 1842–1915, vol. I
Huntingfield, 5th Baron, 1883–1969, vol. VI
Huntingford, Lt-Col Walter Legh, 1882–1933, vol. III
Huntington, Archer Milton, 1870–1955, vol. V
Huntington, Major Arthur William, 1871–1933, vol. III
Huntington, Sir Charles Philip, 1st Bt, 1833–1906, vol. I
Huntington, Sir Charles Philip, 3rd Bt, 1888–1928, vol. II
Huntington, Emily Mabel, died 1948, vol. IV
Huntington, Henry Edwards, 1850–1927, vol. II
Huntington, Sir Henry Leslie, 2nd Bt, 1885–1907, vol. I
Huntington-Whiteley, Sir Herbert; see Whiteley.
Huntington-Whiteley, Captain Sir (Herbert) Maurice, 2nd Bt, 1896–1975, vol. VII
Huntington-Whiteley, Captain Sir Maurice; see Huntington-Whiteley, Captain Sir H. M.
Huntley, Arthur Geoffrey, 1897–1980, vol. VII (AII)
Huntly, 11th Marquess of, 1847–1937, vol. III
Huntly, Frances E.; see Mayne, Ethel Colburn.
Hunton, Sidney W., died 1941, vol. IV
Hunton, Gen. Sir Thomas Lionel, 1885–1970, vol. VI
Hurcomb, 1st Baron, 1883–1975, vol. VII
Hurd, Baron (Life Peer); Anthony Richard Hurd, 1901–1966, vol. VI
Hurd, Sir Archibald, died 1959, vol. V
Hurd, Sir Percy Angier, died 1950, vol. IV
Hurdon, Elizabeth, died 1941, vol. IV
Hurlbatt, Ethel, died 1934, vol. III
Hurle, Col Edward Forbes Cooke-, 1866–1923, vol. II
Hurle, John A. Cooke-, 1863–1941, vol. IV
Hurley, Captain Frank, (James Francis Hurley), 1890–1962, vol. VI
Hurley, James Francis; see Hurley, Captain Frank.
Hurley, Col Lionel James, 1879–1955, vol. V
Hurley, Sir (Thomas Ernest) Victor, 1888–1958, vol. V
Hurley, Sir Victor; see Hurley, Sir T. E. V.
Hurndall, Brig. Frank Brereton, 1883–1968, vol. VI
Hurok, Sol, 1888–1974, vol. VII
Hurrell, Ven. William Philip, 1860–1952, vol. V
Hurren, Samuel, 1875–1953, vol. V
Hurry, Jamieson Boyd, 1857–1930, vol. III
Hurry, Leslie, 1909–1978, vol. VII
Hurst, Sir Alfred William, 1884–1975, vol. VII
Hurst, Sir Arthur Frederick, 1879–1944, vol. IV
Hurst, Bertram Lawrance, 1875–1943, vol. IV
Hurst, Sir Cecil James Barrington, 1870–1963, vol. VI
Hurst, Charles Chamberlain, 1870–1947, vol. IV
Hurst, Christopher Salkeld, 1886–1963, vol. VI
Hurst, Sir Donald; see Hurst, Sir J. H. D.
Hurst, Edward Weston, 1900–1980, vol. VII
Hurst, Fannie, died 1968, vol. VI
Hurst, Frank Arnold, 1883–1967, vol. VI
Hurst, Sir Gerald Berkeley, 1877–1957, vol. V

Hurst, Gilbert Harrison John, 1872–1930, vol. III
Hurst, Hal, 1865–1938, vol. III
Hurst, Harold Edwin, 1880–1978, vol. VII
Hurst, Col Herbert Clarence, 1884–1951, vol. V
Hurst, James Edgar, 1893–1959, vol. V
Hurst, Sir (James Henry) Donald, 1895–1980, vol. VII
Hurst, John Gibbard, died 1931, vol. III
Hurst, Robert H., died 1905, vol. I
Hurst, William M.; see Martin-Hurst.
Hurstfield, Joel, 1911–1980, vol. VII
Hurt, Francis Cecil Albert, 1878–1930, vol. III
Hurt, Captain Henry Albert le Fowne, 1881–1969, vol. VI
Hurth, Peter Joseph, 1857–1935, vol. III
Hurwitz, Alter Max, 1899–1970, vol. VI
Husain, Hon. Mian Sir, Fazl-i-, 1877–1936, vol. III
Husain, Zakir, 1897–1969, vol. VI
Husband, Rev. John, 1841–1909, vol. I
Husband, Thomas Fair, 1862–1921, vol. II
Huskinson, Edward, 1877–1941, vol. IV
Huskinson, Air Cdre Patrick, 1897–1966, vol. VI
Huskinson, Richard King; see King, Richard.
Huskisson, Col Samuel George, 1837–1911, vol. I (A)
Huskisson, Maj.-Gen. William, 1859–1946, vol. IV
Huskisson, Lt-Col William Gordon, 1877–1949, vol. IV
Huson, Thomas, 1844–1920, vol. II
Hussain, Wajahat, 1894–1945, vol. IV
Hussey, Col Arthur Herbert, 1863–1923, vol. II
Hussey, Christopher Edward Clive, 1899–1970, vol. VI
Hussey, Dyneley, 1893–1972, vol. VII
Hussey, Edward Windsor, 1855–1952, vol. V
Hussey, Eric Robert James, 1855–1958, vol. V
Hussey, Sir George Alfred Ernest, 1864–1950, vol. IV
Hussey, Captain Thomas Edgar Cyril, 1884–1958, vol. V
Hussey, Major William Clive, died 1929, vol. III
Hussey-Walsh, Valentine John; see Walsh.
Hussey-Walsh, Lt-Col William, 1863–1925, vol. II
Huston, Major Desmond Wellesley William Desmond Mountjoy C.; see Chapman-Huston.
Huston, Maj.-Gen. John, 1901–1969, vol. VI
Hutber, Patrick, 1928–1980, vol. VII
Hutchen, Frank, 1870–1942, vol. IV
Hutchen, Lt-Col James William, 1880–1943, vol. IV
Hutcheon, Sir Alexander Byres, 1891–1956, vol. V
Hutcheson, Captain Bellenden Seymour, 1883–1954, vol. V
Hutcheson, John, 1870–1959, vol. V
Hutchings, Sir Alan, 1880–1951, vol. V
Hutchings, Charles Henry, 1869–1946, vol. IV
Hutchings, Harold Varlo, 1885–1948, vol. IV
Hutchings, Hugh Houston, 1869–1937, vol. III
Hutchings, Captain John Fenwick, 1885–1968, vol. VI
Hutchings, Norman Edwin, 1899–1960, vol. V
Hutchings, Sir Robert Howell, 1897–1976, vol. VII
Hutchings, Ven. William Henry, 1835–1912, vol. I
Hutchins, Sir David Ernest, 1850–1920, vol. II
Hutchins, George D'Oyly, 1866–1949, vol. IV

Hutchins, Ven. George Francis, 1909–1977, vol. VII
Hutchins, Harry Burns, 1847–1930, vol. III
Hutchins, Horace Albert, died 1923, vol. III
Hutchins, Sir Philip Perceval, 1838–1928, vol. II
Hutchins, Robert Maynard, 1899–1977, vol. VII
Hutchinson, Brig. Alan George Caldwell, 1879–1947, vol. IV
Hutchinson, Arthur, 1866–1937, vol. III
Hutchinson, Arthur Cyril William, 1889–1969, vol. VI
Hutchinson, Arthur Stuart Menteth, 1879–1971, vol. VII
Hutchinson, Col Charles Alexander Robert, 1872–1928, vol. II
Hutchinson, Sir Charles Fred., 1850–1907, vol. I
Hutchinson, Maj.-Gen. Charles Scrope, 1826–1912, vol. I
Hutchinson, Rev. Christopher Blick, 1828–1910, vol. I
Hutchinson, Christopher Clarke, 1854–1914, vol. I
Hutchinson, Christopher Douglas H.; see Hely-Hutchinson.
Hutchinson, Claude Mackenzie, 1869–1941, vol. IV
Hutchinson, Rev. Canon Deryck Reeves, 1911–1971, vol. VII
Hutchinson, Col Edward Douglas B. S.; see Browne-Synge-Hutchinson.
Hutchinson, Sir Edward Synge-, 4th Bt, 1830–1906, vol. I
Hutchinson, Rev. Francis Ernest, 1871–1947, vol. IV
Hutchinson, Maj.-Gen. Francis Hope Grant, 1870–1931, vol. III
Hutchinson, Col Francis Patrick, 1858–1944, vol. IV
Hutchinson, Frederick Heap, 1892–1975, vol. VII
Hutchinson, Rev. Canon Frederick William, 1870–1964, vol. VI
Hutchinson, Geoffrey Clegg; see Baron Ilford.
Hutchinson, Lt-Col George Higginson F.; see Ford-Hutchinson.
Hutchinson, George Thomas, 1880–1948, vol. IV
Hutchinson, Sir George Thompson, 1857–1931, vol. III
Hutchinson, George William G.; see Grice-Hutchinson.
Hutchinson, Lt-Gen. Henry Doveton, 1847–1924, vol. II
Hutchinson, Rev. Henry Neville, 1856–1927, vol. II
Hutchinson, Sir Herbert John, 1889–1971, vol. VII
Hutchinson, Horatio Gordon, 1859–1932, vol. III
Hutchinson, Lt-Col Hugh Moore, 1874–1924, vol. II
Hutchinson, Col James Bird, 1844–1921, vol. II
Hutchinson, John, died 1916, vol. II
Hutchinson, John, 1884–1972, vol. VII
Hutchinson, Sir Jonathan, 1828–1913, vol. I
Hutchinson, Jonathan, 1859–1933, vol. III
Hutchinson, Hon. Sir Joseph Turner, 1850–1924, vol. II
Hutchinson, Sir Lewis Bede, 1899–1975, vol. VII
Hutchinson, Maurice Robert H.; see Hely-Hutchinson.

Hutchinson, May H., (Hon. Lady Hutchinson); *see* Hely-Hutchinson.
Hutchinson, Ormond, 1896–1979, vol. VII
Hutchinson, Ray Coryton, 1907–1975, vol. VII
Hutchinson, St John, 1884–1942, vol. IV
Hutchinson, Sir Sydney Hutton Cooper, 1852–1929, vol. III
Hutchinson, Teasdale H., 1837–1928, vol. II
Hutchinson, Col Thomas Massie, 1877–1952, vol. V
Hutchinson, Vere Stuart Menteth, 1891–1932, vol. III
Hutchinson, Victor H.; *see* Hely-Hutchinson.
Hutchinson, Rt Hon. Sir Walter Francis H.; *see* Hely-Hutchinson.
Hutchinson, Walter Victor, 1887–1950, vol. IV
Hutchinson, Maj.-Gen. William Francis Moore, 1841–1917, vol. II
Hutchinson, William H., *died* 1965, vol. VI
Hutchinson, Rev. William P. H., 1810–1910, vol. I
Hutchison of Montrose, 1st Baron, 1873–1950, vol. IV
Hutchison, Gen. Sir Alexander Richard Hamilton, 1871–1930, vol. III
Hutchison, Lt-Gen. Sir Balfour Oliphant, 1889–1967, vol. VI
Hutchison, Brig. Colin Ross Marshall, 1893–1943, vol. IV
Hutchison, Brig. Sir Eric Alexander Ogilvy, 2nd Bt (*cr* 1923), 1897–1972, vol. VII
Hutchison, Sir George Aitken Clark, 1873–1928, vol. II
Hutchison, George Andrew, 1841–1913, vol. I
Hutchison, George William, 1882–1947, vol. IV
Hutchison, Lt-Col Graham Seton, 1890–1946, vol. IV
Hutchison, Col Henry Oliphant, 1883–1935, vol. III
Hutchison, Sir James, 1867–1946, vol. IV
Hutchison, Sir James Riley Holt, 1st Bt (*cr* 1956), 1893–1979, vol. VII
Hutchison, John, *died* 1910, vol. I
Hutchison, Sir John Colville, 1890–1965, vol. VI
Hutchison, Adm. John de Mestre, 1862–1932, vol. III
Hutchison, Very Rev. Michael Balfour, *born* 1844, vol. II
Hutchison, Sir Robert, 1st Bt (*cr* 1939), 1871–1960, vol. V
Hutchison, Robert Gemmell, *died* 1936, vol. III
Hutchison, Sir Thomas, 1st Bt (*cr* 1923), 1866–1925, vol. II
Hutchison, William, *died* 1924, vol. II
Hutchison, William, 1926–1976, vol. VII
Hutchison, William Gordon Douglas, 1904–1975, vol. VII
Hutchison, Sir William Oliphant, 1889–1970, vol. VI
Huth, Alfred Henry, 1850–1910, vol. I
Huth, Edward, 1847–1935, vol. III
Huth, Louis, 1821–1905, vol. I
Hutin, Marcel, 1869–1950, vol. IV
Hutson, Most Rev. Edward, *died* 1936, vol. III
Hutson, Ven. Eyre, *born* 1830, vol. II
Hutson, Sir Eyre, 1864–1936, vol. III
Hutson, Sir John, 1859–1950, vol. IV

Hutson, Thomas, 1896–1952, vol. V
Hutt, Sir (Alexander McDonald) Bruce, 1904–1978, vol. VII
Hutt, Sir Bruce; *see* Hutt, Sir A. McD. B.
Hutt, Rev. Henry Robert Mackenzie, 1870–1933, vol. III
Hutten, Baroness von, 1874–1957, vol. V
Hutton, Captain Alfred, 1840–1910, vol. I
Hutton, Alfred Eddison, 1865–1947, vol. IV
Hutton, Air Vice-Marshal Arthur Francis, 1900–1979, vol. VII
Hutton, Arthur Hill, 1859–1922, vol. II
Hutton, Rev. Arthur Wollaston, 1848–1912, vol. I
Hutton, Edward, 1875–1969, vol. VI
Hutton, Lt-Gen. Sir Edward Thomas Henry, 1848–1923, vol. II
Hutton, Rear-Adm. FitzRoy Evelyn Patrick, 1894–1975, vol. VII
Hutton, Captain Frederick Wollaston, 1836–1905, vol. I
Hutton, Rev. George Clark, 1825–1908, vol. I
Hutton, Major Gilbert Montgomerie, 1865–1911, vol. I
Hutton, Rev. Henry Wollaston, 1835–1916, vol. I
Hutton, Isabel Emslie, (Lady Hutton), *died* 1960, vol. V
Hutton, James Arthur, 1862–1955, vol. V
Hutton, Sir John, 1842–1903, vol. I
Hutton, John, 1847–1921, vol. II
Hutton, Rev. John Alexander, 1868–1947, vol. IV
Hutton, John Campbell, 1906–1978, vol. VII
Hutton, John Henry, 1885–1968, vol. VI
Hutton, John Morland, *died* 1901, vol. I
Hutton, Maurice, 1856–1940, vol. III
Hutton, Sir Maurice Inglis, 1904–1970, vol. VI
Hutton, Rear-Adm. Reginald Maurice James, 1899–1973, vol. VII
Hutton, Richard Holt, 1826–1897, vol. I
Hutton, Robert Crompton, 1897–1978, vol. VII
Hutton, Robert Salmon, 1876–1970, vol. VI
Hutton, Samuel King, 1877–1961, vol. VI
Hutton, Stamford, 1866–1941, vol. IV
Hutton, Thomas Winter, 1887–1973, vol. VII
Hutton, William, 1871–1933, vol. III
Hutton, Very Rev. William Holden, 1860–1930, vol. III
Hutton, William Kilpatrick, 1870–1937, vol. III
Hutton-Wilson, Col Arthur Harry, 1873–1955, vol. V
Hutty, Sir Fred Harvey, 1903–1974, vol. VII
Huxham, Harold James, 1889–1961, vol. VI
Huxham, Hon. John, *died* 1949, vol. IV
Huxley, Aldous Leonard, 1894–1963, vol. VI
Huxley, Gervas, 1894–1971, vol. VII
Huxley, Sir Julian Sorell, 1887–1975, vol. VII
Huxley, Leonard, 1860–1933, vol. III
Huxley, Mrs Lindsey Kathleen, 1894–1945, vol. IV
Huxley, Michael Heathorn, 1899–1979, vol. VII
Huxtable, Lt-Col Robert Beveridge, 1867–1920, vol. II
Huybers, Jessie; *see* Couvreur, Mme Jessie.
Huyshe-Eliot, Hon. Reginald Huyshe, 1868–1920, vol. II
Huysmans, Joris Karl, 1848–1907, vol. I

Hyams, Edward, 1910–1975, vol. VII
Hyamson, Albert Montefiore, 1875–1954, vol. V
Hyamson, Derek Joseph, 1914–1971, vol. VII
Hyamson, Moses, 1862–1949, vol. IV
Hyat-Khan, Hon. Lt-Col Sirdar Sir Sikander, 1892–1942, vol. IV
Hyatt, Stanley Portal, 1877–1914, vol. I
Hyatt-Woolf, Charles, 1863–1938, vol. III
Hydari, Rt Hon. Sir Akbar, 1869–1942, vol. IV
Hydari, Sir Muhammad Saleh Akbar, 1894–1948, vol. IV
Hyde, Lord; ·George Herbert Arthur Edward Hyde Villiers, 1906–1935, vol. III
Hyde, Lady; (Marion Féoderovna Louise), 1900–1970, vol. VI
Hyde, Sir Charles, 1st Bt, 1876–1942, vol. IV
Hyde, Sir Clarendon Golding, 1858–1934, vol. III
Hyde, Lt-Col Dermot Owen, 1877–1928, vol. II
Hyde, Donald Frizell, 1909–1966, vol. VI
Hyde, Douglas, 1860–1949, vol. IV
Hyde, Edward Wyllys, 1843–1930, vol. III
Hyde, Adm. Sir Francis; see Hyde, Adm. Sir G. F.
Hyde, Francis Edwin, 1908–1978, vol. VII
Hyde, Frederick, 1870–1939, vol. III
Hyde, Adm. Sir (George) Francis, 1877–1937, vol. III
Hyde, Sir Harry, died 1957, vol. V
Hyde, Henry Armroid, 1885–1976, vol. VII
Hyde, Rev. Henry Barry, 1854–1932, vol. III
Hyde, Rev. Canon Henry Edward, 1884–1941, vol. IV
Hyde, James Hazen, 1876–1959, vol. VI (AI)
Hyde, James Wilson, 1841–1918, vol. II
Hyde, Lt-Col John Irvine L.; see Lang-Hyde.
Hyde, Vice-Adm. Richard, 1872–1931, vol. III
Hyde, Sir Robert Robertson, 1878–1967, vol. VI
Hyde, Walter, died 1951, vol. V
Hyde, Walter Henry, 1864–1953, vol. V
Hyde, William, 1889–1945, vol. IV
Hyde, William De Witt, 1858–1917, vol. II
Hyde-Clarke, (Ernest) Meredyth, 1905–1972, vol. VII
Hyde-Clarke, Meredyth; see Hyde-Clarke, E. M.
Hyde-Lees, Rev. Harold Montagu, 1890–1963, vol. VI
Hyde-Page, Lt-Gen. George, 1823–1908, vol. I
Hyde Parker, Sir William Stephen; see Parker.
Hyderabad (Deccan), HH the Nizam of, 1866–1911, vol. I
Hyderabad, Nizam of, 1886–1967, vol. VI
Hyett, Sir Francis Adams, 1844–1941, vol. IV
Hyett, John Edward, died 1936, vol. III
Hyland, Maj.-Gen. Frederick Gordon, 1888–1962, vol. VI
Hyland, Hon. Sir Herbert John Thornhill, died 1970, vol. VI
Hylton, 2nd Baron, 1829–1899, vol. I
Hylton, 3rd Baron, 1862–1945, vol. IV
Hylton, 4th Baron, 1898–1967, vol. VI
Hylton, Jack, 1892–1965, vol. VI
Hylton-Foster, Rt Hon. Sir Harry Braustyn Hylton, 1905–1965, vol. VI
Hyman, Hon. Charles Smith, 1854–1926, vol. II

Hymans, Paul, 1865–1941, vol. IV
Hynard, Sir William George, 1881–1953, vol. V
Hynd, John Burns, 1902–1971, vol. VII
Hyndley, 1st Viscount, 1883–1963, vol. VI
Hyndman, Henry Mayers, 1842–1921, vol. II
Hyndman-Jones, Sir William Henry, 1847–1926, vol. II
Hyne, Engr-Rear-Adm. Arthur Edward, 1874–1956, vol. V
Hyne, Charles John Cutcliffe Wright, 1865–1944, vol. IV
Hyne, Sir Ragnar, 1893–1966, vol. VI
Hynes, Arthur Cecil, 1873–1940, vol. III
Hynes, Group Captain George Bayard, 1887–1938, vol. III
Hynes, John William, died 1930, vol. III
Hynes, Sir Lincoln Carruthers, 1912–1977, vol. VII
Hynes, Captain William Bayard, 1889–1968, vol. VI
Hyslop, Rev. Archibald Richard Frith, 1866–1926, vol. II
Hyslop, Lt-Col Francis, died 1944, vol. IV
Hyslop, Brig.-Gen. Henry Hugh Gordon, 1873–1932, vol. III
Hyslop, Col James, 1856–1917, vol. II
Hyslop, Sir Murray; see Hyslop, Sir R. M.
Hyslop, Sir (Robert) Murray, died 1935, vol. III
Hyslop, Theo Bulkeley, died 1933, vol. III
Hyslop, Sir Thomas, 1859–1919, vol. II
Hyslop, Lt-Col William Campbell, 1860–1915, vol. I
Hytten, Torleiv, 1890–1980, vol. VII

I

Iago-Trelawny, Maj.-Gen. John, died 1909, vol. I
Ibanez, Vicente Blasco, 1867–1928, vol. II
Ibberson, Dora, 1890–1962, vol. VI
Ibbetson, Hon. Sir Denzil Charles Jelf, 1847–1908, vol. I
Ibbotson, Sir William, 1886–1956, vol. V
Ibert, Jacques, 1890–1962, vol. VI
Ibsen, Henrik, 1828–1906, vol. I
Idar, Maharaja of, died 1931, vol. III
Iddesleigh, 2nd Earl of, 1845–1927, vol. II
Iddesleigh, 3rd Earl of, 1901–1970, vol. VI
Idelson, Vladimir Robert, died 1954, vol. V
Idington, Hon. John, 1840–1928, vol. II
Idris; see Mee, Arthur.
Idris, Thomas Howell Williams, 1842–1925, vol. II
Idun, Sir Samuel Okai Q.; see Quashie-Idun.
Ievers, Maj.-Gen. Osburne, died 1963, vol. VI
Ievers, Robert Wilson, died 1905, vol. I
Ife, HH Aderemi I, The Oni of Ife; Sir Titus Martins Adesoji Tadeniawo Aderemi, 1889–1980, vol. VII
Iftikhar-Ud-Din, died 1914, vol. I (A), vol. II
Igglesden, Sir Charles, 1861–1949, vol. IV
Iggulden, Sir Douglas Percy, 1907–1977, vol. VII
Iggulden, Brig.-Gen. Herbert Augustus, 1861–1937, vol. III

Ignatius, Father, (Joseph Leycester Lyne), 1837–1908, vol. I

Ikramullah, Mohammad, 1903–1963, vol. VI

Ilbert, Sir Courtenay Peregrine, 1841–1924, vol. II

Ilchester, 5th Earl of, 1847–1905, vol. I (A)

Ilchester, 6th Earl of, 1874–1959, vol. V

Ilchester, 7th Earl of, 1905–1964, vol. VI

Ilchester, 8th Earl of, 1887–1970, vol. VI

Ilderton, Col Charles Edward, 1841–1905, vol. I

Iles, Col Frederic Arthur, 1874–1966, vol. VI

Iles, John Henry, *died* 1951, vol. V

Iles, Air Vice-Marshal Leslie Millington, 1894–1974, vol. VII

Ilford, Baron (Life Peer); Geoffrey Clegg Hutchinson, 1893–1974, vol. VII

Iliff, Rt Rev. Geoffrey Durnford, 1867–1946, vol. IV

Iliff, Neil Atkinson, 1916–1973, vol. VII

Iliff, Sir William Angus Boyd, 1898–1972, vol. VII

Iliffe, 1st Baron, 1877–1960, vol. V

Iliffe, Frederick, *died* 1928, vol. II

Ilkeston, 1st Baron, 1840–1913, vol. I

Ilkeston, 2nd Baron, 1867–1952, vol. V

Illing, Vincent C., *died* 1969, vol. VI

Illingworth, 1st Baron, 1865–1942, vol. IV

Illingworth, Alfred, 1827–1907, vol. I

Illingworth, Captain Sir (Cyril) Gordon, *died* 1959, vol. V

Illingworth, Dudley Holden, 1876–1958, vol. V

Illingworth, Captain Sir Gordon; *see* Illingworth, Captain Sir C. G.

Illingworth, Rev. John Richardson, *died* 1915, vol. I

Illingworth, Leslie Gilbert, 1902–1979, vol. VII

Illingworth, Percy Holden, 1869–1915, vol. I

Ilott, Sir John Moody Albert, 1884–1973, vol. VII

Ilsley, Most Rev. Edward, 1838–1926, vol. II

Ilsley, Rt Hon. James Lorimer, 1894–1967, vol. VI

Ilyushin, Sergei Vladimirovich, 1894–1977, vol. VII

Image, Selwyn, 1849–1930, vol. III

Imam, Bahksh Khan, Mazari Sir, Mir Nawab, *died* 1903, vol. I

Imbert-Terry, Lt-Col Claude Henry Maxwell, 1880–1942, vol. IV

Imbert-Terry, Major Sir Edward Henry Bouhier, 3rd Bt, 1920–1978, vol. VII

Imbert-Terry, Captain Frederic Bouhier; *see* Terry.

Imbert-Terry, Lt-Col Sir Henry Bouhier, 2nd Bt, 1885–1962, vol. VI

Imbert-Terry, Sir Henry Machu, 1st Bt, 1854–1938, vol. III

Imms, Augustus Daniel, 1880–1949, vol. IV

Imperiali, Marquis Guglielmo, 1858–1944, vol. IV

Impey, Col Eugene Clutterbuck, 1830–1904, vol. I

Impey, Lt-Col Lawrence, 1862–1944, vol. IV

Impey, W. H. L., 1856–1905, vol. I

Imrie, Lt-Col Hew Francis Blair, 1873–1942, vol. IV

im Thurn, Sir Everard, 1852–1932, vol. III

Im Thurn, Vice-Adm. John Knowles, 1881–1956, vol. V

Inayat-Khan, Pir-o-Murshid, 1882–1927, vol. II

Inayat Masih, Rt Rev.; *see* Masih.

Ince, Charles Percy, 1875–1952, vol. V

Ince, Edward Lindsay, 1891–1941, vol. IV

Ince, Captain Edward Watkins W.; *see* Whittington-Ince.

Ince, Evelyn Grace, *died* 1941, vol. IV

Ince, Sir Godfrey Herbert, 1891–1960, vol. VI (AI)

Ince, Rev. William, 1825–1910, vol. I

Inch, Rev. Alex. S., 1863–1932, vol. III

Inchcape, 1st Earl of, 1852–1932, vol. III

Inchcape, 2nd Earl of, 1887–1939, vol. III

Inches, Cyrus Fiske, 1883–1956, vol. V

Inches, Lt-Col Edward James, 1877–1934, vol. III

Inches, Sir Robert Kirk, 1840–1918, vol. II

Inchiquin, 14th Baron, 1839–1900, vol. I

Inchiquin, 15th Baron, 1864–1929, vol. III

Inchiquin, 16th Baron, 1897–1968, vol. VI

Incledon-Webber, Brig.-Gen. Adrian Beare, 1876–1946, vol. IV

Incze, Jenö, 1901–1969, vol. VI

Ind, Charles Francis, 1905–1940, vol. III

Ind, Edward Murray, 1853–1915, vol. I

Inderwick, Frederic Andrew, 1836–1904, vol. I

Indore, HH Maharaja Holkar Tukaji Rao, Maharaja, of, 1899–1908, vol. I

Indore, Maj.-Gen. HH Maharaja of, 1908–1961, vol. VI

Indore, Ex-Maharaja of; HH Tukoji Rao Holkar, 1890–1978, vol. VII

Infield, Henry John, *died* 1921, vol. II

Ing, Col George Harold Absell, 1880–1957, vol. V

Ing, Harry Raymond, 1899–1974, vol. VII

Ingall, Douglas Heber, 1891–1968, vol. VI

Ingalls, John James, 1833–1900, vol. I

Inge, Mary Caroline, (Mrs W. F. Inge), *died* 1961, vol. VI

Inge, Mrs W. F.; *see* Inge, Mary Caroline.

Inge, William, 1829–1903, vol. I

Inge, Very Rev. William Ralph, 1860–1954, vol. V

Ingelow, Jean, 1820–1897, vol. I

Ingestre, Viscount; Charles John Alton Chetwynd Chetwynd-Talbot, 1882–1915, vol. I

Ingham, Albert Edward, 1900–1967, vol. VI

Ingham, Brig.-Gen. Charles St Maur, *died* 1936, vol. III

Ingham, Rt Rev. Ernest Graham, 1851–1926, vol. II

Ingham, Robert Wood, 1846–1928, vol. II

Ingham, Major Samuel, 1893–1950, vol. IV

Ingilby, Sir Henry Day, 2nd Bt, 1826–1911, vol. I

Ingilby, Sir Joslan William Vivian, 5th Bt, 1907–1974, vol. VII

Ingilby, Sir William, 3rd Bt, 1829–1918, vol. II

Ingilby, Sir William Henry, 4th Bt, 1874–1950, vol. IV

Ingle, Rt Rev. George Ernest, 1895–1964, vol. VI

Ingle-Finch, Peter; *see* Finch.

Ingleby, 1st Viscount, 1897–1966, vol. VI

Ingleby, Holcombe, 1854–1926, vol. II

Ingleby Mackenzie, Surg. Vice-Adm. Sir Alexander; *see* Ingleby Mackenzie, Surg. Vice-Adm. Sir K. A.

Ingleby Mackenzie, Surg. Vice-Adm. Sir (Kenneth) Alexander, 1892–1961, vol. VI

Inglefield, Rear-Adm. Sir Edward Fitzmaurice, 1861–1945, vol. IV

Inglefield, Maj.-Gen. Francis Seymour, 1855–1930, vol. III

Inglefield, Adm. Sir Frederick Samuel, 1854–1921, vol. II

Inglefield, Brig. Lionel Dalton, 1881–1953, vol. V

Inglefield, Brig.-Gen. Norman Bruce, 1855–1912, vol. I

Ingles, Ven. Charles Leycester, 1856–1930, vol. III

Ingles, Rev. Charles William Chamberlayne, 1869–1954, vol. V

Ingles, Rev. David, 1836–1921, vol. II

Ingles, Brig.-Gen. John Darnley, 1872–1957, vol. V

Inglis, Sir (Albemarle) Percy, 1841–1932, vol. III

Inglis, Captain Arthur McCulloch, 1884–1919, vol. II

Inglis, Sir Charles Edward, 1875–1952, vol. V

Inglis, Lt-Col Charles Elliot, 1878–1936, vol. III

Inglis, Sir Claude Cavendish, 1883–1974, vol. VII

Inglis, Air Vice-Marshal Francis Frederic, 1899–1969, vol. VI

Inglis, Maj.-Gen. George Henry, 1902–1979, vol. VII

Inglis, Rev. George John, 1900–1965, vol. VI

Inglis, Col Henry Alves, 1859–1924, vol. II

Inglis, Sir Hugh Arbuthnot, 1890–1948, vol. IV

Inglis, Hon. James, 1845–1908, vol. I

Inglis, Sir James Charles, 1851–1911, vol. I

Inglis, Rev. James W., 1861–1943, vol. IV

Inglis, Lt-Col John, 1882–1967, vol. VI

Inglis, John Alexander, 1873–1941, vol. IV

Inglis, Vice-Adm. Sir John Gilchrist Thesiger, 1906–1972, vol. VII

Inglis, John Kenneth Harold, 1877–1935, vol. III

Inglis, Lindsay Merritt, 1894–1966, vol. VI

Inglis of Glencorse, Sir Maxwell Ian Hector, 9th Bt, 1903–1974, vol. VII

Inglis, Sir Percy; see Inglis, Sir A. P.

Inglis, Sir Robert John Mathison, 1881–1962, vol. VI

Inglis, Lt-Col Sir Robert William, 1843–1923, vol. II

Inglis, Col Russell Tracy-, 1875–1937, vol. III

Inglis, William Arbuthnot, 1853–1936, vol. III

Ingold, Sir Christopher Kelk, 1893–1970, vol. VI

Ingpen, Arthur Robert, died 1917, vol. II

Ingpen, Lt-Col Percy Leigh, 1874–1930, vol. III

Ingpen, Roger, died 1936, vol. III

Ingram, Captain Alexander Gordon, 1883–1929, vol. III

Ingram, Archibald Kenneth, 1882–1965, vol. VI

Ingram, Rt Rev. and Rt Hon. Arthur Foley Winnington, 1858–1946, vol. IV

Ingram, Rev. Arthur John, died 1931, vol. III

Ingram, Ven. Arthur John W.; see Winnington-Ingram.

Ingram, Sir Bruce Stirling, 1877–1963, vol. VI

Ingram, Rev. Edward Henry Winnington-, 1849–1930, vol. III

Ingram, Edward Maurice Berkeley, 1890–1941, vol. IV

Ingram, Sir Herbert, 2nd Bt, 1875–1958, vol. V

Ingram, Sir Herbert, 3rd Bt, 1912–1980, vol. VII

Ingram, John H., 1849–1916, vol. II

Ingram, John Kells, 1823–1907, vol. I

Ingram, Lt-Col John O'Donnell, 1870–1939, vol. III

Ingram, John Thornton, 1899–1972, vol. VII

Ingram, Hon. Mrs Meynell, (Emily Charlotte), 1840–1904, vol. I

Ingram, Thomas Allan, 1870–1922, vol. II

Ingram, Captain Thomas Lewis, 1875–1916, vol. II

Ingram, W. Ayerst, 1855–1913, vol. I

Ingram, William, 1865–1943, vol. IV

Ingram, Very Rev. William Clavell, 1834–1901, vol. I

Ingram, Sir William James, 1st Bt, 1847–1924, vol. II

Ingram-Johnson, Rev. Rowland Theodore, 1877–1964, vol. VI

Ingrams, Leonard St Clair, 1900–1953, vol. V

Ingrams, William Harold, 1897–1973, vol. VII

Ingrem, Rev. Charles, 1854–1937, vol. III

Inigo-Jones, Captain Henry Richmund, 1899–1978, vol. VII

Inkson, Col Edgar Thomas, 1872–1947, vol. IV

Inman, 1st Baron, 1892–1979, vol. VII

Inman, Arnold, 1867–1951, vol. V

Inman, Arthur Conyers, 1879–1926, vol. II

Inman, Rev. Canon Edward, died 1924, vol. II

Innes, Alexander Taylor, 1833–1912, vol. I

Innes, Alfred M.; see Mitchell-Innes.

Innes, Sir Andrew Lockhart, 1898–1960, vol. V

Innes, Arthur Donald, died 1938, vol. III

Innes, Captain Cecil M.; see Mitchell-Innes.

Innes, Sir Charles Alexander, 1874–1959, vol. V

Innes, Sir Charles Alexander, 1902–1963, vol. VI

Innes, Donald Esme, 1888–1961, vol. VI

Innes, Edward Alfred M.; see Mitchell-Innes.

Innes, Guy Edward Mitchell, 1882–1953, vol. V

Innes, Sir James, 13th Bt, 1846–1919, vol. II

Innes, Lt-Col James Archibald, 1875–1948, vol. III

Innes, Sir James Bourchier, 14th Bt, 1883–1950, vol. IV

Innes, James John M'Leod, 1830–1907, vol. I

Innes, Rt Hon. Sir James R.; see Rose-Innes.

Innes, Captain James William Guy, 1873–1939, vol. III

Innes, Sir John, 12th Bt, 1840–1912, vol. II

Innes, John, 1888–1961, vol. VI

Innes, Surg.-Gen. Sir John Harry Ker, 1820–1907, vol. I

Innes, John Robert, 1863–1948, vol. IV

Innes, Sir Patrick R.; see Rose-Innes.

Innes, Sir Peter David, 1881–1961, vol. VI

Innes, Hon. Reginald Heath L.; see Long Innes.

Innes, Rev. Reginald John Simpson M.; see Mitchell-Innes.

Innes, Robert T. A., 1861–1933, vol. III

Innes, Col Thomas, 1814–1912, vol. I

Innes of Learney, Sir Thomas, 1893–1971, vol. VII

Innes, Sir Walter James, 15th Bt, 1903–1978, vol. VII

Innes, William Arnold, 1902–1973, vol. VII

Innes-Ker, Lord Alastair Robert, 1880–1936, vol. III

Innes-Ker, Major Lord Robert Edward, 1885–1958, vol. V

Innes-Noad, Sidney Reginald, died 1931, vol. III

Innes-Wilson, Col Campbell Aubrey Kenneth, 1905–1978, vol. VII
Inness, George, 1854–1926, vol. II
Inness, William James Deacon, 1877–1948, vol. IV
Innis, Harold Adams, 1894–1952, vol. V
Inonu, Gen. Ismet, 1884–1973, vol. VII
Inouyé, Marquis Kaoru, 1835–1915, vol. I
Inouyé, Marquis Katsunoske, 1861–1929, vol. III
Insall, Gp Captain Gilbert Stuart Martin, 1894–1972, vol. VII
Insh, George Pratt, 1883–1956, vol. VI (AI)
Inskip, Sir Arthur Cecil, 1894–1951, vol. V
Inskip, J. Henry, died 1947, vol. IV
Inskip, Rt Rev. James Theodore, 1868–1949, vol. IV
Inskip, Sir John Hampden, 1879–1960, vol. V
Inskip, Rev. Oliver Digby, died 1934, vol. III
Inskip, Maj.-Gen. Roland Debenham, 1885–1971, vol. VII
Instone, Sir Samuel, 1878–1937, vol. III
Insull, Samuel, 1859–1938, vol. III
Inverchapel, 1st Baron, died 1951, vol. V
Inverclyde, 1st Baron, 1829–1901, vol. I
Inverclyde, 2nd Baron, 1861–1905, vol. I
Inverclyde, 3rd Baron, 1864–1919, vol. II
Inverclyde, 4th Baron, 1897–1957, vol. V
Inverforth, 1st Baron, 1865–1955, vol. V
Inverforth, 2nd Baron, 1897–1975, vol. VII
Invernairn, 1st Baron, 1856–1936, vol. III
Inverurie, Lord; Ian Douglas Montagu Keith Falconer, 1877–1897, vol. I
Inwards, Richard, 1840–1937, vol. III
Ionides, Basil, 1884–1950, vol. IV
Ipswich, Viscount; William Henry Alfred Fitzroy, 1884–1918, vol. II
Irby, Hon. Cecil Saumarez, 1862–1935, vol. III
Iredell, Air Vice-Marshal Sir Alfred William, 1879–1967, vol. V
Iredell, Charles Edward, 1877–1961, vol. VI
Iredell, Lt-Gen. Francis Shrubb, 1837–1924, vol. II
Ireland, Alleyne; see Ireland, W. A.
Ireland, Arthur Joseph, 1874–1931, vol. III
Ireland, Most Rev. John, 1838–1918, vol. II
Ireland, John, 1879–1962, vol. VI
Ireland, Col Sir Robert Megaw, 1849–1919, vol. II
Ireland, (Walter) Alleyne, died 1951, vol. V
Iremonger, Col Edgar Assheton, 1862–1953, vol. V
Iremonger, Very Rev. Frederic Athelwold, 1878–1952, vol. V
Iremonger, Major Harold Edward William, died 1937, vol. III
Irgens, Johannes, 1869–1939, vol. III
Iron, Ralph; see Schreiner, Olive.
Ironside, 1st Baron, 1880–1959, vol. V
Ironside, Sir Henry George Outram B.; see Bax-Ironside.
Ironside, Redvers Nowell, 1899–1968, vol. VI
Ironside, Robin, 1912–1965, vol. VI
Irvin, Sir John Hannell, 1874–1952, vol. V
Irvin, Captain William Dion, 1870–1956, vol. V
Irvine, Lt-Col Acheson Gosford, born 1837, vol. II
Irvine, Alexander, 1836–1941, vol. IV
Irvine, Alexander Forbes, 1881–1922, vol. II
Irvine, Brig.-Gen. Alfred Ernest, 1876–1962, vol. VI

Irvine, Lt-Col Andrew Alexander, 1871–1939, vol. III
Irvine, Rt Hon. Sir Arthur James, 1909–1978, vol. VII
Irvine, Captain Charles Alexander Lindsay, 1876–1965, vol. VI
Irvine, Col Francis Stephen, 1873–1962, vol. VI
Irvine, Rt Rev. Gerard Addington D'A.; see D'Arcy-Irvine.
Irvine, Lt-Col Gerard Beatty, 1863–1947, vol. IV
Irvine, Sir James Colquhoun, 1877–1952, vol. V
Irvine, James Mercer, died 1945, vol. IV
Irvine, Lt-Col Richard Abercrombie, died 1946, vol. IV
Irvine, Adm. Sir St George Caufield D'Arcy-, 1833–1916, vol. II
Irvine, William Fergusson, 1869–1962, vol. VI
Irvine, Hon. Sir William Hill, 1858–1943, vol. IV
Irvine, William Tait, 1925–1980, vol. VII
Irvine-Fortescue, Col Archer, 1880–1959, vol. V
Irvine-Jones, Douglas Vivian, 1904–1974, vol. VII
Irving, Sir Æmilius, 1823–1913, vol. I
Irving, Lt-Col Andrew B.; see Bell-Irving.
Irving, Captain Charles Edward, 1871–1955, vol. V
Irving, Charles John, 1831–1917, vol. II
Irving, Dan, 1854–1924, vol. II
Irving, David Jarvis M.; see Mill Irving.
Irving, Dorothea, (Mrs Henry Irving), died 1933, vol. III
Irving, Ven. Edward Arthur, 1850–1943, vol. IV
Irving, Mrs H. B.; see Irving, Dorothea.
Irving, Sir Henry, 1838–1905, vol. I
Irving, Henry Brodribb, 1870–1919, vol. II
Irving, Sir Henry Turner, 1833–1923, vol. II
Irving, Herbert Cavan, 1854–1930, vol. III
Irving, James Jardine B.; see Bell-Irving.
Irving, John B.; see Bell-Irving.
Irving, Kelville Ernest, 1877–1953, vol. V
Irving, Laurence Sydney Brodribb, died 1914, vol. I
Irving, Martin Howy, 1831–1912, vol. I
Irving, Sir Miles, 1876–1962, vol. VI
Irving, Hon. Paulus Æmilius, 1857–1916, vol. II
Irving, Rev. Robert, 1840–1922, vol. II
Irving, Captain Sir Robert Beaufin, 1877–1954, vol. V
Irving, Robert Lock Graham, 1877–1969, vol. VI
Irving, Sir Stanley Gordon, 1886–1970, vol. VI
Irving, Rev. Thomas Henry, 1856–1926, vol. II
Irving, William John, 1892–1967, vol. VI
Irwin, Alfred, 1865–1951, vol. V
Irwin, Sir Alfred Macdonald Bulteel, 1853–1921, vol. II
Irwin, Ven. Charles King, 1837–1915, vol. I
Irwin, Rt Rev. Charles King, 1874–1960, vol. V
Irwin, Rev. Clarke Huston, 1858–1934, vol. III
Irwin, Cyril James, 1881–1962, vol. VI
Irwin, Col De la Cherois Thomas, 1843–1928, vol. II
Irwin, Sir George, 1832–1899, vol. I
Irwin, George Robert, 1855–1933, vol. III
Irwin, Henry, 1841–1922, vol. II
Irwin, Henry Raikes Alexander, 1858–1937, vol. III
Irwin, Col Sir (James) Murray, 1858–1938, vol. III
Irwin, Sir John, 1857–1935, vol. III

Irwin, Rev. John, *died* 1932, vol. III
Irwin, Lt-Gen. John Staples, 1846–1917, vol. II
Irwin, Joseph Boyd, 1895–1968, vol. VI
Irwin, Leighton Francis, 1892–1962, vol. VI
Irwin, Margaret, *died* 1967, vol. VI
Irwin, Margaret Hardinge, *died* 1940, vol. III
Irwin, Col Sir Murray; *see* Irwin, Col Sir J. M.
Irwin, Lt-Gen. Noel Mackintosh Stuart, 1892–1972, vol. VII
Irwin, Raymond, 1902–1976, vol. VII
Irwin, Robert, *died* 1941, vol. IV
Irwin, Robert Christopher, 1865–1937, vol. III
Irwin, Ven. Ronald John Beresford, 1880–1930, vol. III
Irwin, Sir Samuel Thompson, 1877–1961, vol. VI
Irwin, Maj.-Gen. Stephen Fenemore, 1895–1964, vol. VI
Irwin, Thomas Lennox, 1846–1918, vol. II
Irwin, William Henry, 1907–1974, vol. VII
Irwin, William Knox, 1883–1973, vol. VII
Isaac, Very Rev. Abraham, *died* 1906, vol. I
Isaac, Charles Leonard, *died* 1944, vol. IV
Isaac, Rev. Gerald Moore, *died* 1940, vol. III
Isaac, Joseph Charles, 1859–1939, vol. III
Isaac, Lt-Col Thomas William Talbot, 1880–1930, vol. III
Isaacs, Alick, 1921–1967, vol. VI
Isaacs, Edward Maurice, 1881–1953, vol. V
Isaacs, Rev. Frederick Walter, 1858–1935, vol. III
Isaacs, Rt Hon. George Alfred, 1883–1979, vol. VII
Isaacs, Godfrey Charles, *died* 1925, vol. II
Isaacs, Sir Henry Aaron, 1830–1909, vol. I
Isaacs, Rt Hon. Sir Isaac Alfred, 1855–1948, vol. IV
Isaacs, Jacob, 1896–1973, vol. VII
Isaacs, Susan Sutherland, 1885–1948, vol. IV
Isaacson, Frederick Wootton, 1836–1898, vol. I
Isaacson, Sir Robert Spencer, 1907–1972, vol. VII
Isacke, Maj.-Gen. Hubert, 1872–1943, vol. IV
Isbister, William James, 1866–1950, vol. IV
Iselin, Charles Oliver, *died* 1932, vol. III
Isemonger, Frederick Charles, 1876–1960, vol. V
Isham, Sir Charles Edmund, 10th Bt, 1819–1903 (this entry was not transferred to Who was Who).
Isham, Sir Gyles, 12th Bt, 1903–1976, vol. VII
Isham, Lt–Col Ralph Heyward, 1890–1955, vol. V
Isham, Sir Vere, 11th Bt, 1862–1941, vol. IV
Isherwood, Albert Arthur Mangnall, 1889–1957, vol. V
Isherwood, Col Charles Edward Ramsbottom, 1849–1934, vol. III
Isherwood, Lt-Col James, *died* 1929, vol. III
Isherwood, John Henry Bradshaw-, 1841–1924, vol. II
Isherwood, Sir Joseph William, 1st Bt, 1870–1937, vol. III
Isherwood, Sir William, 2nd Bt, 1898–1946, vol. IV
Ishibashi, Kazunori, *died* 1928, vol. II
Isitt, Dame Adeline G.; *see* Genée-Isitt.
Isitt, Air Vice-Marshal Sir Leonard Monk, 1891–1976, vol. VII
Isle, William Herbert Mosley, 1896–1973, vol. VII
Isles, Keith Sydney, 1902–1977, vol. VII

Islington, 1st Baron, 1866–1936, vol. III
Ismail, Sir Miras M., 1883–1959, vol. V
Ismail Sait, Khan Bahadur Fukhr-ut-tujjar Sir Hajee, 1859–1934, vol. III
Ismay, 1st Baron, 1887–1965, vol. VI
Ismay, James Hainsworth, 1867–1930, vol. III
Ismay, Joseph Bruce, 1862–1937, vol. III
Ismay, Sir Stanley, 1848–1914, vol. I
Ismay, Thomas Henry, 1837–1899, vol. I
Ismay, Rev. William, 1846–1922, vol. II
Isola; *see* Teeling, Mrs Bartle.
Israel, John William, 1850–1926, vol. II
Israels, Joseph, 1824–1911, vol. I
Israr, Hon. Sir Maulvi Mohammad Israr Hasan Khan, 1865–1934, vol. III
Isserstedt, Hans S.; *see* Schmidt-Isserstedt.
Ithel Jones, Rev. John; *see* Jones.
Ito, Prince Hirobumi, 1838–1909, vol. I
Ito, Admiral of the Fleet Count Yuko, 1843–1914, vol. I
Iturbi, José, 1895–1980, vol. VII
Ivatt, Henry George, 1886–1972, vol. VII
Iveagh, 1st Earl of, 1847–1927, vol. II
Iveagh, 2nd Earl of, 1874–1967, vol. VI
Iveagh, Countess of; (Gwendolen), *died* 1966, vol. VI
Ivelaw-Chapman, Air Chief Marshal Sir Ronald, 1899–1978, vol. VII
Ivens, Rev. Charles Llewelyn, 1854–1931, vol. III
Ivens, Richard, *died* 1931, vol. III
Ivens, Rev. William Edmunds, 1845–1910, vol. I
Iverach, Rev. James, 1839–1922, vol. II
Iversen, Johannes, 1904–1971, vol. VII
Ives, George Cecil, 1867–1950, vol. IV
Ives, Col Gordon Maynard G.; *see* Gordon-Ives.
Ives, Harry William Maclean, 1867–1941, vol. IV
Ivimey, John William, 1868–1961, vol. VI
Ivimey, Julia B., (Mrs Fairfax Ivimey); *see* Matthews, J. B.
Iwi, Edward Frank, 1904–1966, vol. VI
Iyengar, S. Kasturi Ranga, 1859–1923, vol. II
Izard, Ven. Herbert Crawford, 1869–1934, vol. III
Izat, Alexander, 1844–1920, vol. II
Izat, Sir (James) Rennie, 1886–1962, vol. VI
Izat, John, 1879–1966, vol. VI
Izat, Sir Rennie; *see* Izat, Sir J. R.
Izycki de Notto, Sir Matthew, 1899–1952, vol. V

J

Jack, A. G. Mackenzie, 1851–1927, vol. II
Jack, Adolphus Alfred, 1868–1946, vol. IV
Jack, Brig.-Gen. Archibald, 1874–1939, vol. III
Jack, Brig. Evan Maclean, 1873–1951, vol. V
Jack, Col Herbert Rowett Henry, 1863–1932, vol. III
Jack, Brig.-Gen. James Lochhead, 1880–1962, vol. VI
Jack, John Louttit, 1878–1954, vol. V
Jack, Mackenzie; *see* Jack, A. G. M.
Jack, Richard, 1866–1952, vol. V
Jack, Sir Robert Ernest, *died* 1962, vol. VI

Jack, Robert Logan, 1845–1921, vol. II
Jack, Hon. Sir Roy Emile, 1914–1977, vol. VII
Jack, William, 1834–1924, vol. II
Jack, William Robert, 1866–1927, vol. II
Jacklin, Air Vice-Marshal Edward Ward
Seymour, 1917–1969, vol. VI
Jackman, Mgr Canon Arthur, 1878–1945, vol. IV
Jackman, William T., 1871–1951, vol. V
Jacks, Graham Vernon, 1901–1977, vol. VII
Jacks, Lawrence Pearsall, 1860–1955, vol. V
Jacks, Maurice Leonard, 1894–1964, vol. VI
Jacks, Thomas Lavington, 1884–1966, vol. VI
Jacks, William, 1841–1907, vol. I
Jackson, 1st Baron, 1893–1954, vol. V
Jackson of Burnley, Baron (Life Peer); Willis
Jackson, 1904–1970, vol. VI
Jackson, Abraham Valentine Williams, 1862–1937,
vol. III
Jackson, Albert Edward, 1865–1930, vol. III
Jackson, Alexander Young, 1882–1974, vol. VII
Jackson, Col Arnold Nugent Strode S.; see
Strode-Jackson.
Jackson, Arthur, 1853–1938, vol. III
Jackson, Sir Arthur, died 1940, vol. III
Jackson, B. Leslie, born 1866, vol. III
Jackson, Sir Barry Vincent, 1879–1961, vol. VI
Jackson, Lt-Col Basil A.; see Archer-Jackson.
Jackson, Basil Rawdon, 1892–1957, vol. V
Jackson, Benjamin Daydon, 1846–1927, vol. II
Jackson, Rev. Blomfield, 1839–1905, vol. I
Jackson, Rev. Brice Lee, 1864–1941, vol. IV
Jackson, Hon. Cecil Gower, 1872–1920, vol. II
Jackson, Brig. Cecil Vivian Staveley, 1887–1964,
vol. VI
Jackson, Charles d'Orville Pilkington, 1887–1973,
vol. VII
Jackson, Sir Charles James, 1849–1923, vol. II
Jackson, Major Charles Lionel Atkins W.; see
Ward-Jackson.
Jackson, Sir Christopher Mather M., 5th Bt
(cr 1869); see Mather-Jackson, Sir G. C. M.
Jackson, Sir Cyril, 1863–1924, vol. II
Jackson, Rev. Canon Cyril, 1897–1969, vol. VI
Jackson, Daniel, 1858–1931, vol. III
Jackson, Sir Edward Arthur Mather-, 4th Bt
(cr 1869), 1899–1956, vol. V
Jackson, Sir Edward St John, 1886–1961, vol. VI
Jackson, Rev. Canon Edwin B.; see Brook-
Jackson.
Jackson, Egbert Joseph William, died 1975,
vol. VII
Jackson, Sir Ernest; see Jackson, Sir J. E.
Jackson, Lt-Col Ernest Somerville, 1872–1943,
vol. IV
Jackson, F. Ernest, died 1945, vol. IV
Jackson, Rt Rev. Fabian Menteath Elliot, 1902–
1978, vol. VII
Jackson, Rev. Forbes, died 1913, vol. I
Jackson, Col Sir Francis (James) Gidlow, 1889–
1979, vol. VII
Jackson, Rt Hon. Sir (Francis) Stanley, 1870–
1947, vol. IV
Jackson, Major Sir Francis Walter Fitton, 1881–
1936, vol. III

Jackson, Rev. Canon Frank Hilton, 1870–1960,
vol. V
Jackson, Col Frank Lawson John, 1919–1976,
vol. VII
Jackson, Frank Stather, 1853–1922, vol. II
Jackson, Major Frank Whitford, 1886–1955, vol. V
Jackson, Major Frederick George, died 1938,
vol. III
Jackson, Frederick Hamilton, 1848–1923, vol. II
Jackson, Rt Hon. Frederick Huth, 1863–1921,
vol. II
Jackson, Sir Frederick John, 1860–1929, vol. III
Jackson, Frederick John F.; see Foakes-Jackson.
Jackson, Brig.-Gen. Geoffrey Meinertzhagen,
1869–1946, vol. IV
Jackson, George, 1843–1931, vol. III
Jackson, Rev. George, 1864–1945, vol. IV
Jackson, Maj.-Gen. George Hanbury, 1876–1958,
vol. V
Jackson, Major Sir George Julius, 3rd Bt (cr 1902),
1883–1956, vol. V
Jackson, Lt-Col George Scott, died 1946, vol. IV
Jackson, Sir Gilbert Hollinshead Blomfield, 1875–
1956, vol. V
Jackson, Lt-Col Guy, 1903–1960, vol. V
Jackson, Harold Gordon, 1888–1950, vol. IV
Jackson, Captain Harold Gordon, died 1950,
vol. IV
Jackson, H(arold) Haygarth, 1896–1972, vol. VII
Jackson, Sir Harold Warters, 1883–1972, vol. VII
Jackson, Harry, 1892–1976, vol. VII
Jackson, Harry W., 1855–1930, vol. III
Jackson, Henry, 1839–1921, vol. II
Jackson, Sir Henry, 1st Bt (cr 1935), 1875–1937,
vol. III
Jackson, Admiral of the Fleet Sir Henry
Bradwardine, 1855–1929, vol. III
Jackson, Gen. Sir Henry Cholmondeley, 1879–
1972, vol. VII
Jackson, Rev. Henry Latimer, 1851–1926, vol. II
Jackson, Captain Henry Leigh, 1886–1956, vol. V
Jackson, Captain Henry Mather-, 1894–1928,
vol. II
Jackson, Sir Henry Mather-, 3rd Bt (cr 1869),
1855–1942, vol. IV
Jackson, Sir Henry Moore, 1849–1908, vol. I
Jackson, Sir Herbert, 1863–1936, vol. III
Jackson, Brig.-Gen. Herbert Kendall, 1859–1938,
vol. III
Jackson, Maj.-Gen. Sir Herbert William, 1861–
1931, vol. III
Jackson, Maj.-Gen. Herbert William, 1872–1940,
vol. III
Jackson, Holbrook, 1874–1948, vol. IV
Jackson, Hugh Marrison Gower, 1870–1934,
vol. III
Jackson, Col Hugh Milbourne, 1858–1940, vol. III
Jackson, Sir Hugh Nicholas, 2nd Bt (cr 1913),
1881–1979, vol. VII
Jackson, Maj.-Gen. James, 1866–1957, vol. V
Jackson, Ven. James M'Creight, 1841–1913, vol. I
Jackson, Sir John, 1851–1919, vol. II
Jackson, Sir John, 1865–1933, vol. III
Jackson, John, 1887–1958, vol. V

Jackson, John Arthur, 1862–1937, vol. III
Jackson, John Brinckerhoff, 1862–1920, vol. II
Jackson, Sir (John) Ernest, 1876–1941, vol. IV
Jackson, John Hughlings, *died* 1911, vol. I
Jackson, Sir John Montrésor, 6th Bt (*cr* 1815), 1914–1980, vol. VII
Jackson, Sir John Peter Todd, 1868–1945, vol. IV
Jackson, John Whitfield-, 1847–1910, vol. I
Jackson, Joseph Cooksey, 1879–1938, vol. III
Jackson, Sir Keith George, 4th Bt (*cr* 1815), 1842–1916, vol. II
Jackson, Col Lambert Cameron, 1875–1953, vol. V
Jackson, Lawrence Colvile, *died* 1905, vol. I
Jackson, Brig.-Gen. Lionel Warren de Vere S.; *see* Sadleir-Jackson.
Jackson, Maj.-Gen. Sir Louis Charles, 1856–1946, vol. IV
Jackson, Maunsell Bowers, *died* 1922, vol. II
Jackson, Morton Strode, 1848–1913, vol. I
Jackson, Nicholas L.; *see* Lane-Jackson.
Jackson, Rev. Percival, 1845–1929, vol. III
Jackson, Sir Percy Richard, 1869–1941, vol. IV
Jackson, Sir Ralph, 1872–1943, vol. IV
Jackson, Reginald Nevill, 1887–1937, vol. III
Jackson, Sir Richard Hoyle, 1869–1944, vol. IV
Jackson, Sir Richard Leofric, 1902–1975, vol. VII
Jackson, Lt-Col Richard Rolt Brash, 1874–1943, vol. IV
Jackson, Richard Stephens, 1850–1938, vol. III
Jackson, Maj.-Gen. Robert Edward, 1886–1948, vol. IV
Jackson, Robert Edwin, 1826–1909, vol. I
Jackson, Robert Frederick, 1880–1951, vol. V
Jackson, Robert H., 1892–1954, vol. V
Jackson, Sir Robert Montrésor, 5th Bt (*cr* 1815), 1876–1940, vol. III
Jackson, Col Sir Robert Whyte Melville, 1860–1928, vol. II
Jackson, Sir Robert William, 1826–1921, vol. II
Jackson, Rt Rev. Robert Wyse, 1908–1976, vol. VII
Jackson, Sir Russell; *see* Jackson, Sir W. D. R.
Jackson, S. P., *died* 1904, vol. I
Jackson, Col Samuel, 1845–1911, vol. I
Jackson, Samuel Macauley, 1851–1912, vol. I
Jackson, Rt Hon. Sir Stanley; *see* Jackson, Sir F. S.
Jackson, Col Sydney Charles Fishburn, 1863–1928, vol. II
Jackson, Sir Thomas, 1st Bt (*cr* 1902), 1841–1915, vol. I (A)
Jackson, Adm. Sir Thomas, 1868–1945, vol. IV
Jackson, Brig.-Gen. Sir Thomas Dare, 2nd Bt (*cr* 1902), 1876–1954, vol. V
Jackson, Sir Thomas Graham, 1st Bt (*cr* 1913), 1835–1924, vol. II
Jackson, Adm. Sir Thomas Sturges, 1842–1934, vol. III
Jackson, Thomas Vincent, *died* 1901, vol. I
Jackson, Rt Rev. Vibert, 1874–1963, vol. VI
Jackson, Lt-Col Vivian Archer, 1882–1943, vol. IV
Jackson, Sir (Walter David) Russell, 4th Bt (*cr* 1902), 1890–1956, vol. V
Jackson, Sir Wilfrid Edward Francis, 1883–1971, vol. VII

Jackson, Maj.-Gen. William, 1830–1912, vol. I
Jackson, William Alexander, 1905–1964, vol. VI
Jackson, William Henry, *died* 1920, vol. II
Jackson, Rear-Adm. William Lindsay, 1889–1962, vol. VI
Jackson, Rev. William V.; *see* Vincent-Jackson.
Jackson, Rev. William Walrond, 1838–1931, vol. III
Jacob, Albert Edward, 1858–1929, vol. III
Jacob, Mrs Arthur, (Violet Jacob), *died* 1946, vol. IV
Jacob, Maj.-Gen. Arthur Le Grand, 1867–1942, vol. IV
Jacob, Lt-Col Arthur Leslie, 1870–1944, vol. IV
Jacob, Field-Marshal Sir Claud William, 1863–1948, vol. IV
Jacob, Rt Rev. Edgar, 1844–1920, vol. II
Jacob, Edward Fountaine, 1852–1912, vol. I
Jacob, Ernest Fraser, 1894–1971, vol. VII
Jacob, Sir George Harold L.; *see* Lloyd-Jacob.
Jacob, Lt-Col Harold Fenton, 1866–1936, vol. III
Jacob, John Hier, 1884–1964, vol. VI
Jacob, Sir Lionel Montague, 1853–1934, vol. III
Jacob, Naomi, 1884–1964, vol. VI
Jacob, Rhoda Hannah, 1900–1979, vol. VII
Jacob, Sir (Samuel) Swinton, 1841–1917, vol. II
Jacob, Sir Swinton; *see* Jacob, Sir S. S.
Jacob, Col Sydney Long, 1845–1911, vol. I
Jacob, Violet; *see* Jacob, Mrs Arthur.
Jacob, Lt-Col Walter Henry Bell, 1871–1925, vol. II
Jacob, Maj.-Gen. William, 1837–1917, vol. II
Jacob, Rev. William, *died* 1940, vol. III
Jacobi, G., 1840–1906, vol. I
Jacobs, Joseph, 1854–1916, vol. II
Jacobs, William Wymark, 1863–1943, vol. IV
Jacobs-Bond, Carrie; *see* Bond.
Jacobsen, Arne, 1902–1971, vol. VII
Jacobsen, Thomas Owen, 1864–1941, vol. IV
Jacobson, Ernest Nathaniel Joseph, 1877–1947, vol. IV
Jacobsson, Per, 1894–1963, vol. VI
Jacobsthal, Paul Ferdinand, 1880–1957, vol. V
Jacoby, Felix, 1876–1959, vol. V
Jacoby, Sir James Alfred, 1852–1909, vol. I
Jacomb, Rear-Adm. Humphrey Benson, 1891–1969, vol. VI
Jacomb-Hood, George Percy, 1857–1929, vol. III
Jacques, Rev. Kinton, 1837–1915, vol. I
Jacques, Brig. Leslie Innes, 1897–1959, vol. V
Jacques, Reginald; *see* Jacques, T. R.
Jacques, (Thomas) Reginald, 1894–1969, vol. VI
Jacson, Rev. Owen Fitzherbert, 1861–1935, vol. III
Jadunath Mazoomdar, Rai Bahadur, Vedanta Bachaspati, 1859–1932, vol. III
Jaeger, John Conrad, 1907–1979, vol. VII
Jaeger, Werner W., 1888–1961, vol. VI
Jafar, Raja Sir Saiyid Abu, *died* 1927, vol. II
Ja'far El Askeri, General, 1885–1936, vol. III
Jaffe, Sir Otto, 1846–1929, vol. III
Jaffer, Sir Ebrahim Haroon, 1881–1930, vol. III
Jaffray, Sir John, 1st Bt, 1818–1901, vol. I
Jaffray, Sir John Henry, 3rd Bt, 1893–1916, vol. II
Jaffray, Hon. Robert, 1832–1914, vol. I
Jaffray, Sir William, 2nd Bt, 1852–1914, vol. I

Jaffray, Sir William Edmund, 4th Bt, 1895–1953, vol. V

Jaffray, Rev. William Stevenson, 1867–1941, vol. IV

Jaffrey, Francis, 1861–1919, vol. II

Jaffrey, Sir Thomas, 1st Bt, 1861–1953, vol. V

Jaggard, Captain William, died 1947, vol. IV

Jagger, Charles Sargeant, 1885–1934, vol. III

Jagger, David, died 1958, vol. V

Jagger, Rev. James Edwin, died 1937, vol. III

Jagger, John, 1872–1942, vol. IV

Jago, Thomas Sampson, 1835–1915, vol. I

Jago, William, 1854–1938, vol. III

Jagoe, Rt Rev. John Arthur, 1889–1962, vol. VI

Jahn, Gunnar, 1883–1971, vol. VII

Jahn, Hermann Arthur, 1907–1979, vol. VII

Jaipur, Maharaja of, 1861–1922, vol. II

Jaipur, Maharaja of, 1911–1970, vol. VI

Jaisalmer, Maharajahdhiraj of, 1882–1949, vol. IV (A), vol. V

Jalland, Arthur Edgar, 1889–1958, vol. V

Jalland, Rev. Trevor Gervase, 1896–1975, vol. VII

Jamal, Sir Abdul Karim Abdul Shakur, 1862–1924, vol. II

Jamer, Herman Watson, 1904–1972, vol. VII

James of Hereford, 1st Baron, 1828–1911, vol. I

James, Abraham Thomas, 1883–1940, vol. III

James, Alexander, 1850–1932, vol. III

James, Alfred Henry, 1868–1941, vol. IV

James, Brig.-Gen. Alfred Henry Cotes, 1873–1947, vol. IV

James, Wing Comdr Sir Archibald William Henry, 1893–1980, vol. VII

James, Arthur, 1871–1959, vol. V

James, Rev. Canon Arthur Dyfrig, 1902–1980, vol. VII

James, Rt Hon. Sir Arthur Evan, 1916–1976, vol. VII

James, Arthur Godfrey, 1876–1959, vol. V

James, Sir Arthur Gwynne Gwynne-, 1885–1936, vol. III

James, Captain Arthur Keedwell Harvey; see Craven, Arthur Scott.

James, Arthur L.; see Lloyd James.

James, Rev. Arthur Oswel, 1849–1932, vol. III

James, Maj.-Gen. Sir Bernard; see James, Maj.-Gen. Sir W. B.

James, Col Bernard Ramsden, 1864–1938, vol. III

James, Lt-Col Boucher Charlewood, 1882–1930, vol. III

James, Col Cecil Polglase, 1879–1943, vol. IV

James, Charles Ashworth, died 1937, vol. III

James, Charles Canniff, 1863–1916, vol. II

James, Lt-Col Charles Henry, 1863–1944, vol. IV

James, Charles Holloway, 1893–1953, vol. V

James, Engr Rear-Adm. Charles John, 1862–1943, vol. IV

James, Hon. Sir Claude Ernest Weymouth, died 1961, vol. VI

James, Lt-Col Hon. Cuthbert, 1872–1930, vol. III

James, Brig.-Gen. Cyril Henry Leigh, died 1946, vol. IV

James, David Gwilym, 1905–1968, vol. VI

James, Sir David John, 1887–1967, vol. VI

James, Ven. Denis, 1895–1965, vol. VI

James, Lt-Col Edmund Henry Salt, 1874–1952, vol. V

James, Edmund Janes, 1855–1925, vol. II

James, Rev. Edward, 1828–1913, vol. I

James, Edward, 1885–1971, vol. VII

James, Sir Edward Albert, 5th Bt, 1862–1942, vol. IV

James, Sir Edward Burnet, 1857–1927, vol. II

James, Rev. Edwin Oliver, 1888–1972, vol. VII

James, Florence, 1857–1929, vol. III

James, Sir Francis; see James, Sir J. F. W.

James, Francis Edward, died 1920, vol. II

James, F(rank) Cyril, 1903–1973, vol. VII

James, Sir Frederick Ernest, 1891–1971, vol. VII

James, Sir Frederick Seton, 1870–1934, vol. III

James, Captain Sir Fullarton, 6th Bt, 1864–1955, vol. V

James, Sir Gavin Fullarton, 4th Bt, 1859–1937, vol. III

James, George William Blomfield, died 1968, vol. VI

James, Mrs Helena Constance R; see Romanne-James.

James, Henry, 1843–1916, vol. II

James, Sir Henry Evan Murchison, 1846–1923, vol. II

James, Very Rev. Henry Lewis, 1864–1949, vol. IV

James, Henry Rosher, 1862–1931, vol. III

James, Col Herbert, 1859–1943, vol. IV

James, Rev. Herbert Armitage, 1844–1931, vol. III

James, Lt-Col Herbert Ellison Rhodes, died 1939, vol. III

James, Lt-Col Herbert Lionel, 1863–1946, vol. IV

James, Ivor Benjamin Hugh, 1882–1963, vol. VI

James, Sir Jack; see James, Sir John H.

James, Gen. Sir John, 1832–1901, vol. I

James, John Arthur, 1853–1917, vol. II

James, Ven. John D., 1862–1938, vol. III

James, John Egbert, 1876–1965, vol. VI

James, Sir John Ernest, died 1963, vol. VI

James, Sir (John) Francis (William), 1879–1950, vol. IV

James, Very Rev. John Gwynno, 1912–1967, vol. VI

James, Sir John Hastings, (Sir Jack), 1906–1980, vol. VII

James, Sir John Kingston Fullarton, 3rd Bt, 1852–1933, vol. III

James, John Richings, 1912–1980, vol. VII

James, John William, 1907–1975, vol. VII

James, Rev. Lemuel John H.; see Hopkin-James.

James, Lewis Cairns, 1865–1946, vol. IV

James, Lionel, 1868–1948, vol. IV

James, Col Lionel, 1871–1955, vol. V

James, Brig. Manley Angell, 1896–1975, vol. VII

James, Rt Rev. Melville Charles, 1877–1957, vol. V

James, Montague Rhodes, 1862–1936, vol. III

James, Col Murray Ray de Bruyne, 1870–1939, vol. III

James, Norah C., 1901–1979, vol. VII

James, Philip Brutton, 1901–1974, vol. VII

James, Philip Gaved, 1904–1978, vol. VII

James, Lt-Col Ralph Ernest Haweis, 1875–1964, vol. VI

James, Reginald Hugh Lloyd L.; see Langford-James.

James, Reginald William, 1891–1964, vol. VI

James, Richard Bush, 1889–1970, vol. VI

James, Richard Lewis Malcolm, 1897–1972, vol. VII

James, Hon. Robert, 1873–1960, vol. V

James, Rolfe Arnold S.; see Scott-James.

James, Lt-Col Sydney Price, died 1946, vol. IV

James, Ven. Sydney Rhodes, 1855–1934, vol. III

James, Thomas David, 1871–1955, vol. V

James, Thomas Maurice, 1890–1962, vol. VI

James, Vice-Adm. Thomas Norman, 1878–1965, vol. VI

James, Thurstan Trewartha, 1903–1975, vol. VII

James, Lt-Col Tristram Bernard Wordsworth, 1883–1939, vol. III

James, Hon. Sir Walter Hartwell, 1863–1943, vol. IV

James, Lt-Col Walter Haweis, 1847–1927, vol. II

James, Rev. Walter Hill, 1828–1910, vol. I

James, William, 1842–1 910, vol. I

James, Maj.–Gen. Sir (William) Bernard, 1865–1940, vol. III

James, William Dodge, 1854–1912, vol. I

James, William Garnet, 1895–1977, vol. VII

James, Adm. Sir William Milbourne, 1881–1973, vol. VII

James, William Owen, 1900–1978, vol. VII

James, Col William Reginald Wallwyn, 1860–1925, vol. II

James, William Warwick, 1874–1965, vol. VI

James, Winifred Lewellin, (Mrs Henry de Jan), died 1941, vol. IV

Jameson, Adam, 1860–1907, vol. I

Jameson, Alexander Hope, 1874–1952, vol. V

Jameson, Rt Hon. Andrew, 1855–1941, vol. IV

Jameson, Andrew; see Ardwall, Hon. Lord.

Jameson, Cecil Stuart, born 1883, vol. VI

Jameson, Ven. Francis Bernard, 1889–1960, vol. VI (AI)

Jameson, Brig. Frank Robert Wordsworth, 1893–1965, vol. VI

Jameson, Surgeon-Gen. James, 1837–1904, vol. I

Jameson, James Alexander, 1885–1961, vol. VI

Jameson, John, died 1920, vol. II

Jameson, Lt-Col John Bland, died 1954, vol. V

Jameson, Lt-Col John Eustace-, 1853–1919, vol. II

Jameson, John Franklin, 1859–1937, vol. III

Jameson, John Gordon, 1878–1955, vol. V

Jameson, Rt Hon. Sir Leander Starr, 1st Bt, 1853–1917, vol. II

Jameson, Noel Rutherford, 1892–1971, vol. VII

Jameson, Surg.-Captain Robert Dundonald, 1869–1938, vol. III

Jameson, William George, 1851–1939, vol. III

Jameson, Rear-Adm. Sir William Scarlett, 1899–1966, vol. VI

Jameson, Sir (William) Wilson, 1885–1962, vol. VI

Jameson, Sir Wilson; see Jameson, Sir W. W.

Jamiat Rai, Diwan, Rai Bahadur, Diwan Bahadur, 1861–1941, vol. IV

Jamieson, Rt Hon. Lord; Douglas Jamieson, 1880–1952, vol. V

Jamieson, Alexander, 1873–1937, vol. III

Jamieson, Sir Archibald Auldjo, 1884–1959, vol. V

Jamieson, Douglas; see Jamieson, Rt Hon. Lord.

Jamieson, Vice-Adm. Douglas Y.; see Young-Jamieson.

Jamieson, Edgar George, 1882–1958, vol. V

Jamieson, George, 1843–1920, vol. II

Jamieson, Sir James William, 1867–1946, vol. IV

Jamieson, John Kay, 1873–1948, vol. IV

Jamieson, R. Kirkland, 1881–1950, vol. IV

Jamieson, Stanley Wyndham, 1885–1970, vol. VI

Jamieson, William Allan, 1839–1916, vol. II

Jamison, Evelyn Mary, 1877–1972, vol. VII

Jan, Winifred Lewellin de; see James, W. L.

Jane, Frank William, 1901–1963, vol. VI

Jane, Fred. T., 1870–1916, vol. II

Janes, Emily, died 1928, vol. II

Janes, Sir Herbert Charles, 1884–1977, vol. VII

Janes, Norman Thomas, 1892–1980, vol. VII

Janet, Pierre, 1859–1947, vol. IV

Janion, Edwin Manifold, 1863–1952, vol. V

Janisch, Noel, died 1930, vol. III

Janjira, HH Nawab, 1862–1922, vol. II

Jannaris, Anthony, 1852–1909, vol. I

Jansen, Ernest George, 1881–1959, vol. V

Janson, Stanley Eric, 1908–1974, vol. VII

Jansz, Sir Eric; see Jansz, Sir H. E.

Jansz, Sir (Herbert) Eric, 1890–1976, vol. VII

Janvrin, Rev. William Langston Benest, 1853–1927, vol. II

Jaora State, Lt-Col HH Fakhr-ud-Daulah Nawab Sir Mohammad Iftikhar Ali Khan Bahadur Saulat Jang, 1883–1947, vol. IV

Japp, Francis Robert, 1848–1925, vol. II

Japp, Sir Henry, 1869–1939, vol. III

Jaques-Dalcroze, Emile, 1865–1950, vol. IV

Jaquet, Sir Robert Glover, 1856–1937, vol. III

Jardine, Sir Alexander, 10th Bt (cr 1672), 1868–1942, vol. IV

Jardine, Brig. Christian West B.; see Bayne-Jardine.

Jardine, Maj.-Gen. Sir Colin Arthur, 3rd Bt (cr 1916), 1892–1957, vol. V

Jardine, David Jardine, died 1922, vol. II

Jardine, Sir Douglas James, 1888–1946, vol. IV

Jardine, Douglas Robert, 1900–1958, vol. V

Jardine, Sir Ernest, 1st Bt (cr 1919), 1859–1947, vol. IV

Jardine, James, 1846–1909, vol. I

Jardine, Brig.-Gen. James Bruce, 1870–1955, vol. V

Jardine, James Willoughby, 1879–1945, vol. IV

Jardine, Sir John, 1st Bt (cr 1916), 1844–1919, vol. II

Jardine, Sir John, 2nd Bt (cr 1919), 1884–1965, vol. VI

Jardine, John, 1881–1974, vol. VII

Jardine, Major Sir John Eric Birdwood, 2nd Bt (cr 1916), 1890–1924, vol. II

Jardine, Captain Sir John William Buchanan-, 3rd Bt (cr 1885), 1900–1969, vol. VI

Jardine, Lionel Westropp, 1895–1980, vol. VII

Jardine, Malcolm Robert, 1869–1947, vol. IV

Jardine, Sir Robert, 1st Bt (*cr* 1885), 1825–1905, vol. I
Jardine, Robert, 1862–1932, vol. III
Jardine, Sir Robert William Buchanan, 2nd Bt (*cr* 1885), 1868–1927, vol. II
Jardine, Sir William, 9th Bt (*cr* 1672), 1865–1915, vol. I (A)
Jardine, William Ellis, 1867–1944, vol. IV
Jardine-Brown, Robert, 1905–1972, vol. VII
Jarman, Charles, 1893–1947, vol. IV
Jarman, Rev. Canon Cyril Edgar, 1892–1978, vol. VII
Jarman, John Robert, 1844–1922, vol. II
Jarmay, Sir John Gustav, 1856–1944, vol. IV
Jarrad, Sir Vivian Everard Donne, *died* 1938, vol. III
Jarratt, Sir Arthur William, 1894–1958, vol. V
Jarratt, Sir William Smith, 1871–1966, vol. VI
Jarrell, Randall, 1914–1965, vol. VI
Jarrett, Sir Francis Moncreiff K.; *see* Kerr-Jarrett.
Jarrett, George William Symonds, 1880–1960, vol. V
Jarrett, Col Henry Sullivan, 1839–1919, vol. II
Jarrett, James Henry, 1895–1943, vol. IV
Jarrold, (Herbert) John, 1906–1979, vol. VII
Jarrold, John; *see* Jarrold, H. J.
Jarvie, John Gibson, 1883–1964, vol. VI
Jarvis, Sir Adrian; *see* Jarvis, Sir A. A.
Jarvis, Alan Hepburn, 1915–1972, vol. VII
Jarvis, Very Rev. Alfred Charles Eustace, 1876–1957, vol. V
Jarvis, Sir (Arnold) Adrian, 2nd Bt, 1904–1965, vol. VI
Jarvis, Lt-Col Arthur Leonard Fitzgerald, 1852–1927, vol. II
Jarvis, Lt-Col Arthur Murray, 1863–1930, vol. III
Jarvis, Lt-Col Charles Francis Cracroft, *died* 1957, vol. V
Jarvis, Major Claude Scudamore, 1879–1953, vol. V
Jarvis, Edward Blackwell, 1873–1950, vol. IV
Jarvis, Very Rev. Ernest David, 1888–1964, vol. VI
Jarvis, Rev. Francis Amcotts, *died* 1937, vol. III
Jarvis, Sir John, 1st Bt, 1876–1950, vol. IV
Jarvis, Sir John Layton, 1887–1968, vol. VI
Jarvis, Maj.–Gen. Samuel Peters, 1820–1905, vol. I
Jarvis, Col Sir Weston, 1855–1939, vol. III
Jarvis, William Rose, 1885–1943, vol. IV
Jaspar, Henri, 1870–1939, vol. III
Jaspers, Karl, 1883–1969, vol. VI
Jast, L. Stanley, 1868–1944, vol. IV
Jastrow, Morris, Jr, 1861–1921, vol. II
Jatia, Sir Onkar Mull, 1882–1938, vol. III
Jaujard, Jacques, 1895–1967, vol. VI (AII)
Jaurès, Jean Léon, 1859–1914, vol. I
Javal, Paul C.; *see* Cremieu-Javal.
Jawahir Singh, Sardar Bahadur Sir Sardar, *died* 1947, vol. IV
Jay, Major Charles Douglas, *died* 1941, vol. IV
Jay, Edith Katharine Spicer; *see* Prescott, E. Livingston.
Jay, Harriett, 1863–1932, vol. III
Jay, Thomas, 1887–1962, vol. VI

Jay, William Samuel, *died* 1933, vol. III
Jayakar, Rt Hon. Mukund R., *died* 1959, vol. V
Jayasundera, Sir Ukwatte, 1896–1962, vol. VI
Jayatilaka, Sir Don Baron, 1868–1944, vol. IV
Jayetileke, Sir Edward George Perera, 1888–1975, vol. VII
Jayewardene, E. W., *died* 1932, vol. III
Jayne, Col Arthur Alfred, 1878–1934, vol. III
Jayne, Rt Rev. Francis John, 1845–1921, vol. II
Jayne, Ronald Garland, 1877–1951, vol. V
Jays, Tom, 1868–1947, vol. IV
Jeaffreson, John Cordy, 1831–1901, vol. I
Jeakes, Rev. James, 1829–1915, vol. I
Jeanneret, Charles-Edouard; *see* Le Corbusier.
Jeanneret, François Charles Archile, 1890–1967, vol. VI
Jeanniot, Pierre Georges, 1848–1934, vol. III
Jeans, Sir Alexander Grigor, 1849–1924, vol. II
Jeans, Sir Alick, (Alexander Grigor), 1912–1972, vol. VII
Jeans, Allan, 1877–1961, vol. VI
Jeans, Hon. Maj.-Gen. Charles Gilchrist, 1854–1920, vol. II
Jeans, Frank, 1878–1933, vol. III
Jeans, J. Stephen, 1846–1913, vol. I
Jeans, Sir James Hopwood, 1877–1946, vol. IV
Jeans, Sir Richard Walter, 1846–1924, vol. II
Jeans, Ronald, *died* 1973, vol. VII
Jeans, Major Thomas Kilvington, 1885–1962, vol. VI
Jeans, Surg. Rear-Adm. Thomas Tendron, *died* 1938, vol. III
Jeans, Ursula, *died* 1973, vol. VII
Jeans, William, *died* 1916, vol. II
Jebb, Eglantyne Mary, 1889–1978, vol. VII
Jebb, Geraldine Emma May, *died* 1959, vol. V
Jebb, Brig.-Gen. Gladwyn Dundas, 1877–1947, vol. IV
Jebb, Col (Joshua Henry) Miles, 1875–1935, vol. III
Jebb, Col Miles; *see* Jebb, Col J. H. M.
Jebb, Richard, 1874–1953, vol. V
Jebb, Sir Richard Claverhouse, 1841–1905, vol. I
Jeckell, George Allen, 1880–1950, vol. IV (A), vol. V
Jee, Joseph, *died* 1899, vol. I
Jeejeebhoy, Sir Byramjee, 1881–1946, vol. IV
Jeeves, William John, *died* 1932, vol. III
Jeffcoat, Col Algernon Cautley, 1877–1963, vol. VI
Jeffcoat, Captain Henry Jamieson Powell, *died* 1901, vol. I
Jeffcott, Henry Homan, *died* 1937, vol. III
Jefferis, Maj.-Gen. Sir Millis Rowland, 1899–1963, vol. VI
Jeffers, Le Roy, 1878–1926, vol. II
Jeffers, William Martin, 1876–1953, vol. V
Jefferson, Frederick Thomas, *died* 1920, vol. II
Jefferson, Sir Geoffrey, 1886–1961, vol. VI
Jefferson, Captain Henry, 1865–1937, vol. III
Jefferson, Lt-Col Sir John Alexander D.; *see* Dunnington-Jefferson.
Jefferson, Joseph, 1829–1905, vol. I
Jefferson, Rt Rev. Robert, 1881–1968, vol. VI
Jefferson, Wood G., *died* 1912, vol. I
Jeffery, Cecil Albert, 1888–1970, vol. VI (AII)

Jeffery, Edward Turner, 1843–1927, vol. II (A), vol. III
Jeffery, George Barker, 1891–1957, vol. V
Jeffery, George H. Everett, died 1935, vol. III
Jeffery, Rev. Samuel, died 1934, vol. III
Jeffery, Walter, 1861–1922, vol. II
Jeffery, Col Walter Hugh, 1878–1957, vol. V
Jefferys, Charles William, 1869–1951, vol. V
Jeffes, Maurice, died 1954, vol. V
Jefford, Vice-Adm. James Wilfred, 1901–1980, vol. VII
Jeffrey, Very Rev. George Johnstone, 1881–1961, vol. VI
Jeffrey, Maj.-Gen. Hugh Crozier, 1914–1976, vol. VII
Jeffrey, Sir John, 1871–1947, vol. IV
Jeffrey, Rev. Norman Stuart, died 1919, vol. II
Jeffrey, Robert, 1884–1956, vol. V
Jeffrey, William, 1896–1946, vol. IV
Jeffrey-Waddell, John, 1876–1941, vol. IV
Jeffreys, 1st Baron, 1878–1960, vol. V
Jeffreys, Rt Hon. Arthur Frederick, 1848–1906, vol. I
Jeffreys, Adm. Edmund Frederick, 1846–1925, vol. II
Jeffreys, Maj.-Gen. Henry Byron, 1854–1949, vol. IV
Jeffreys, Brig.-Gen. Patrick Douglas, 1848–1922, vol. II
Jeffreys, Rev. Tom Reginald Frederic, 1871–1938, vol. III
Jeffreys, W. Rees, 1871–1954, vol. V
Jeffries, Charles H., 1864–1936, vol. III
Jeffries, Sir Charles Joseph, 1896–1972, vol. VII
Jeffries, Hon. Sir Shirley Williams, 1886–1963, vol. VI
Jeffries, Brig. William Francis, 1891–1969, vol. VI
Jeffs, Ernest Harry, 1885–1973, vol. VII
Jeffs, Harry, 1860–1938, vol. III
Jeger, George, 1903–1971, vol. VII
Jeger, Santo Wayburn, 1898–1953, vol. V
Jehanghir, Sir Cowasjee, 1st Bt, 1853–1934, vol. III
Jehanghir, Sir Cowasjee, 2nd Bt, 1879–1962, vol. VI
Jehangir, Vakil Hon. Khan Bahadur Sardar Sir Rustom, died 1933, vol. III
Jehu, Ivor Stewart, 1908–1960, vol. V
Jehu, Thomas John, 1871–1943, vol. IV
Jejeebhoy, Sir (Cowasjee Cursetjee) Jamsetjee, 4th Bt, 1852–1908 (this entry was not transferred to Who was Who).
Jejeebhoy, Sir Jamsetjee, 3rd Bt, 1851–1898, vol. I
Jejeebhoy, Sir Jamsetjee, 6th Bt, 1909–1968, vol. VI
Jejeebhoy, Sir Jamsetjee; see Jejeebhoy, Sir R. C. C. J.
Jejeebhoy, Sir (Rustomjee Cowasjee Cursetjee) Jamsetjee, 5th Bt, 1878–1931, vol. III
Jekyll, Agnes, (Lady Jekyll), 1861–1937, vol. III
Jekyll, Gertrude, 1843–1932, vol. III
Jekyll, Col Sir Herbert, 1846–1932, vol. III
Jelf, Sir Arthur Richard, 1837–1917, vol. II
Jelf, Sir Arthur Selborne, 1876–1947, vol. IV

Jelf, Sir Ernest Arthur, 1868–1949, vol. IV
Jelf, Rev. George Edward, 1834–1908, vol. I
Jelf, Herbert William, 1882–1943, vol. IV
Jelf, Col Richard Henry, 1844–1913, vol. I
Jelf, Brig.-Gen. Rudolf George, 1873–1958, vol. V
Jelf, Col Wilfrid Wykeham, 1880–1933, vol. III
Jellett, Very Rev. Henry, died 1901, vol. I
Jellett, Henry, 1872–1948, vol. IV
Jellett, Col John Hewitt, 1859–1938, vol. III
Jellett, John Holmes, 1905–1971, vol. VII
Jellett, William Morgan, died 1936, vol. III
Jellicoe, 1st Earl, 1859–1935, vol. III
Jellicoe, Rear-Adm. Christopher Theodore, 1903–1977, vol. VII
Jellicoe, Brig.-Gen. Richard Carey, 1875–1962, vol. VI
Jellicorse, Rev. William, died 1920, vol. II
Jellinek, Lionel, 1898–1979, vol. VII
Jencken, Maj.-Gen. Francis John, 1858–1943, vol. IV
Jenkin, Mrs Bernard, (Margaret M. Giles), 1868–1949, vol. IV
Jenkin, Charles Frewen, 1865–1940, vol. III
Jenkin, Henry Archibald Tregarthen, 1886–1951, vol. V
Jenkin, Engr Rear-Adm. John Harry, 1866–1933, vol. III
Jenkin, Mary Elizabeth, 1892–1979, vol. VII
Jenkin, Thomas James, 1885–1965, vol. VI
Jenkin-Jones, Charles Mark, 1885–1971, vol. VII
Jenkin Pugh, Rev. Canon Thomas; see Pugh.
Jenkings, Adm. Albert Baldwin, 1846–1942, vol. IV
Jenkins, Baron (Life Peer); David Llewelyn Jenkins, 1899–1969, vol. VI
Jenkins, Rev. Canon Alfred Thomas, 1893–1960, vol. V
Jenkins, Arthur, died 1946, vol. IV
Jenkins, Charles Elliott Edward, 1859–1946, vol. IV
Jenkins, Rev. Canon Claude, 1877–1959, vol. V
Jenkins, David, 1848–1915, vol. I (A)
Jenkins, Rev. David, died 1926, vol. II
Jenkins, Ven. David, 1876–1960, vol. V
Jenkins, Rev. David Erwyd, died 1937, vol. III
Jenkins, Douglas, 1880–1961, vol. VI
Jenkins, Edward, 1838–1910, vol. I
Jenkins, Sir (Edward) Enoch, 1895–1960, vol. IV
Jenkins, Major Edward Vaughan, 1879–1941, vol. IV
Jenkins, Sir Enoch; see Jenkins, Sir E. E.
Jenkins, Evan David Thomas, 1882–1960, vol. V
Jenkins, Lt-Col Francis, 1877–1927, vol. II
Jenkins, Brig.-Gen. Francis Conway, 1888–1933, vol. III
Jenkins, Col Sir Francis Howell, 1832–1906, vol. I
Jenkins, Frank L.; see Lynn-Jenkins.
Jenkins, Sir George Frederick, 1878–1957, vol. V
Jenkins, Sir George Henry, 1843–1911, vol. I
Jenkins, George Kirkhouse, died 1957, vol. V
Jenkins, Gilbert Henry, 1875–1957, vol. V
Jenkins, Herbert, died 1923, vol. II
Jenkins, Lt-Col Herbert Harold, 1877–1932, vol. III
Jenkins, Herbert Riches, 1880–1944, vol. IV
Jenkins, Huntly E., died 1923, vol. II

Jenkins, Sir James, 1818–1912, vol. I
Jenkins, John, *born* 1852, vol. III
Jenkins, Hon. John Greeley, 1851–1923, vol. II
Jenkins, John Lewis, *died* 1912, vol. I
Jenkins, Joseph Barclay, 1870–1950, vol. IV
Jenkins, Rt Hon. Sir Lawrence Hugh, 1858–1928, vol. II
Jenkins, Leslie Augustus Westover, 1910–1978, vol. VII
Jenkins, Brig.-Gen. Noble Fleming, 1860–1927, vol. II
Jenkins, Robert Christmas Dewar, 1900–1978, vol. VII
Jenkins, Robert Thomas, 1881–1969, vol. VI
Jenkins, Romilly James Heald, 1907–1969, vol. VI
Jenkins, Walter Allen, 1891–1958, vol. V
Jenkins, Sir Walter St David, 1874–1951, vol. V
Jenkins, Sir William, 1871–1944, vol. IV
Jenkins, Sir William Albert, *died* 1968, vol. VI
Jenkins, William Frank, 1889–1980, vol. VII
Jenkins, William Henry Philips, 1842–1916, vol. II
Jenkins, Sir William John, 1892–1957, vol. V
Jenkins, Rev. William Owen, 1863–1919, vol. II
Jenkinson, Sir (Charles) Hilary, *died* 1961, vol. VI
Jenkinson, Sir Edward George, 1835–1919, vol. II
Jenkinson, Francis B. G., *died* 1902, vol. I
Jenkinson, Francis John Henry, 1853–1923, vol. II
Jenkinson, Sir George Banks, 12th Bt, 1851–1915, vol. I
Jenkinson, Major George Seymour Charles, 1858–1907, vol. I
Jenkinson, Sir Hilary; *see* Jenkinson, Sir C. H.
Jenkinson, John Edward, 1858–1937, vol. III (A), vol. IV
Jenkinson, Sir Mark Webster, *died* 1935, vol. III
Jenks, Clarence Wilfred, 1909–1973, vol. VII
Jenks, Rev. David, 1866–1935, vol. III
Jenks, Edward, 1861–1939, vol. III
Jenks, Sir Maurice, 1st Bt, 1872–1946, vol. IV
Jenks, Very Rev. Walter, 1864–1935, vol. III
Jenkyns, Sir Henry, 1838–1899, vol. I
Jenner, Lt-Col Sir Albert Victor, 3rd Bt, 1862–1954, vol. V
Jenner, George Francis Birt, *born* 1840, vol. II
Jenner, Rt Rev. Henry Lascelles, 1820–1898, vol. I
Jenner, Katherine Lee, *died* 1936, vol. III
Jenner, Lt-Col Leopold Christian Duncan, 1869–1953, vol. V
Jenner, Sir Walter Kentish William, 2nd Bt, 1860–1948, vol. IV
Jenner, Sir William, 1st Bt, 1815–1898, vol. I
Jenner-Fust, Herbert, 1806–1904, vol. I
Jenney, Col Archibald Offley, 1864–1946, vol. IV
Jenney, Brig. Reginald Charles Napier, 1906–1960, vol. V
Jennings, Sir Arthur Oldham, 1855–1934, vol. III
Jennings, Arthur Seymour, *born* 1860, vol. II
Jennings, Edward Charles, 1877–1955, vol. V
Jennings, Col Edward Lawrence Frederick, 1850–1931, vol. III
Jennings, Rev. Edward Linck, *died* 1940, vol. III
Jennings, Gertrude E., *died* 1958, vol. V

Jennings, Brig.-Gen. Herbert Alexander Kaye, 1862–1921, vol. II
Jennings, Herbert Spencer, 1868–1947, vol. IV
Jennings, Sir Ivor; *see* Jennings, Sir W. I.
Jennings, James George, 1866–1921, vol. II
Jennings, James George, 1866–1941, vol. IV
Jennings, Lt-Col James Willes, 1866–1954, vol. V
Jennings, Rev. Canon John Andrew, 1855–1923, vol. II
Jennings, Sir John Rogers, 1820–1897, vol. I
Jennings, Leonard, *died* 1956, vol. V
Jennings, Hon. Sir Patrick Alfred, 1831–1897, vol. I
Jennings, Col Richard, 1856–1935, vol. III
Jennings, Col Robert Henry, 1852–1918, vol. II
Jennings, Gen. Sir Robert Melvill, 1841–1922, vol. II
Jennings, Sir Roland, 1894–1968, vol. VI
Jennings, Sir (William) Ivor, 1903–1965, vol. VI
Jennings, William Thomas, 1854–1923, vol. II
Jenour, Brig.-Gen. Arthur Stawell, 1867–1938, vol. III
Jensen, Ernest T., 1873–1950, vol. IV
Jensen, Johannes Daniel, 1906–1973, vol. VII
Jensen, Sir John Klunder, 1884–1970, vol. VI
Jephcott, Alfred Roger, 1853–1932, vol. III
Jephcott, Sir Harry, 1st Bt, 1891–1978, vol. VII
Jephson, Sir Alfred, 1841–1900, vol. I
Jephson, Arthur Jermy Mounteney, *died* 1908, vol. I
Jephson, Rev. Arthur W., 1853–1935, vol. III
Jephson, Harriet Julia, (Lady Jephson), *died* 1930, vol. III
Jephson, Brig. Maurice Denham, 1890–1968, vol. VI
Jephson, Sir Stanhope William, 4th Bt, 1810–1900, vol. I
Jeppe, Sir Julius, 1859–1929, vol. III
Jepson, Edgar, 1863–1938, vol. III
Jepson, Richard Pomfret, 1918–1980, vol. VII
Jepson, Captain Rowland Walter, 1888–1954, vol. V
Jepson, Stanley, 1894–1976, vol. VII
Jerdan, Rev. Charles, 1843–1926, vol. II
Jerichow, Herbert Peter Andreas, 1889–1967, vol. VI
Jermyn, Sir Alfred, 1845–1921, vol. II
Jermyn, Rt Rev. Hugh Willoughby, 1820–1903, vol. I
Jerningham, Charles Edward Wynne, 1854–1921, vol. II
Jerningham, Sir Henry William Stafford, 11th Bt, 1867–1935, vol. III
Jerningham, Sir Hubert Edward Henry, 1842–1914, vol. I
Jerome, Maj.-Gen. Henry Edward, 1830–1901, vol. I
Jerome, Col Henry Joseph Walker, 1854–1943, vol. IV
Jerome, Jerome Klapka, 1859–1927, vol. II
Jerome, Lucien Joseph, 1870–1943, vol. IV
Jerome, Thomas Stroud, *died* 1917, vol. II
Jerome, William J. Smith, 1839–1929, vol. III
Jerram, Rev. Arnold Escombe, *died* 1934, vol. III

Jerram, Sir Bertrand; *see* Jerram, Sir C. B.
Jerram, Sir (Cecil) Bertrand, 1891–1971, vol. VII
Jerram, Lt-Col Charles Frederic, 1882–1969, vol. VI
Jerram, Adm. Sir Martyn; *see* Jerram, Adm. Sir T. H. M.
Jerram, Brig. Roy Martyn, 1895–1974, vol. VII
Jerram, Adm. Sir (Thomas Henry) Martyn, 1858–1933, vol. III
Jerrard, Brig. Charles Ian, 1900–1977, vol. VII
Jerred, Sir Walter Tapper, 1864–1918, vol. II
Jerrold, Douglas, 1893–1964, vol. VI
Jerrold, Laurence, 1873–1918, vol. II
Jerrold, Mary, 1877–1955, vol. V
Jerrold, Walter Copeland, 1865–1929, vol. III
Jersey, 7th Earl of, 1845–1915, vol. I
Jersey, 8th Earl of, 1873–1923, vol. II
Jersey, Dowager Countess of; (Margaret Elizabeth), 1849–1945, vol. IV
Jervis, Sir Henry (Felix) Jervis-White-, 5th Bt, 1859–1947, vol. IV
Jervis, Col Herbert Swynfen, 1878–1965, vol. VI
Jervis, Captain Hon. John Cyril Carnegie, 1898–1929, vol. III
Jervis, Col Sir John Henry Jervis-White-, 4th Bt, 1857–1943, vol. IV
Jervis, John Johnstone, 1882–1969, vol. VI
Jervis, Col Nicholas Gordon Mainwaring, 1881–1943, vol. IV
Jervis, Lt-Col Hon. St Leger Henry, 1863–1952, vol. V
Jervis, Hon. William Monk, 1827–1909, vol. I
Jervis, Lt-Col William Swynfen Whitehall P.; *see* Parker-Jervis.
Jervis-Smith, Rev. Frederick J., 1848–1911, vol. I
Jervis-White-Jervis, Sir Henry; *see* Jervis, Sir H. F. J. W.
Jervis-White-Jervis, Col Sir John Henry; *see* Jervis.
Jervois, Sir William Francis Drummond, 1821–1897, vol. I
Jervoise, Sir Arthur Henry Clarke-, 3rd Bt, 1856–1902, vol. I
Jervoise, Sir Dudley Alan Lestock Clarke-, 7th Bt, 1876–1933, vol. III
Jervoise, Rear-Adm. Edmund Purefoy Ellis, 1861–1950, vol. IV
Jervoise, Sir Eustace James Clarke, 6th Bt, 1870–1916, vol. II
Jervoise, Francis Henry Tristram, 1872–1959, vol. V
Jervoise, Sir Harry Samuel Cumming Clarke, 5th Bt, 1832–1911, vol. I
Jervoise, Sir Henry, 4th Bt, 1831–1908, vol. I
Jerwood, Rev. Thomas Frederick, *died* 1926, vol. II
Jesper, Col Norman McKay, 1896–1968, vol. VI
Jesperson, Otto, 1860–1943, vol. IV
Jess, Lt-Gen. Sir Carl Herman, 1884–1948, vol. IV
Jesse, F. Tennyson, *died* 1958, vol. V
Jesse, Col John Leonard, 1876–1944, vol. IV
Jesse, Richard Henry, 1853–1921, vol. II (A), vol. III
Jesse, William, 1870–1945, vol. IV

Jessel, 1st Baron, 1866–1950, vol. IV
Jessel, Albert Henry, 1864–1917, vol. VII
Jessel, Sir Charles James, 1st Bt, 1860–1928, vol. II
Jessel, Sir George, 2nd Bt, 1891–1977, vol. VII
Jessel, Sir Richard Hugh, 1896–1979, vol. VII
Jesson, Charles, *born* 1862, vol. II
Jesson, Major Thomas Edward, 1883–1958, vol. V
Jessop, Col Charles Thorp, 1858–1915, vol. I
Jessop, Frederic Hubert, 1882–1969, vol. VI
Jessop, Gilbert Laird, 1874–1955, vol. V
Jessop, Lt-Comdr John de Burgh, 1885–1924, vol. II
Jessop, Joseph Chasser, 1892–1972, vol. VII
Jessop, Thomas Edmund, 1896–1980, vol. VII
Jessop, Thomas Richard, 1837–1903, vol. I
Jessop, Walter Hamilton Hylton, 1853–1917, vol. II
Jessopp, Rev. Augustus, 1823–1914, vol. I
Jette, Sir Louis Amable, 1836–1920, vol. II
Jeudwine, Rev. George Wynne, 1849–1933, vol. III
Jeudwine, Lt-Gen. Sir Hugh Sandham, 1862–1942, vol. IV
Jeudwine, Lt-Col Wilfrid Wynne, 1877–1943, vol. IV
Jeune, John Frederic Symons-, 1849–1925, vol. II
Jevons, Frank Byron, 1858–1936, vol. III
Jevons, Herbert Stanley, 1875–1955, vol. V
Jevons, Shirley Byron, *died* 1928, vol. II
Jewell, Maurice Frederick Stewart, 1885–1978, vol. VII
Jewesbury, Reginald Charles, 1878–1971, vol. VII
Jewett, Sarah Orne, 1849–1909, vol. I
Jewson, Dorothy, 1884–1964, vol. VI
Jewson, Percy William, 1881–1962, vol. VI
Jex-Blake, Arthur John, *died* 1957, vol. V
Jex-Blake, Henrietta, *died* 1953, vol. V
Jex-Blake, Katharine, 1860–1951, vol. V
Jex-Blake, Sophia, 1840–1912, vol. I
Jex-Blake, Very Rev. Thomas William, 1832–1915, vol. I
Jeyes, Samuel Henry, *died* 1911, vol. I
Jeypore, Samasthanam, Maharaja Sri Sri Sri Ramachendra Deo of, 1893–1931, vol. III
Jha, Sir Mahamahopadhyaya Ganganath, *born* 1871, vol. V
Jhalawar, HH Maharaj Rana Sir Bhawani Singh Bahadur of, 1874–1929, vol. III
Jhalawar, Lieut HH Maharaj Rana Sir Shri Rajendra Singh Ji Dev Bahadur of, 1900–1943, vol. IV
Jibowu, Hon. Sir Olumuyiwa, 1899–1959, vol. V
Jiménez (Mantacon), Juan Ramón, 1881–1958, vol. V
Jind, Brig. HH Farzand-i-Dilband Rasikh-ul-Itikad Daulat-i-Inglishia, Raja-i-Rajgan Maharaja Sir Ranbir Singh Rajendra Bahadur, 1879–1948, vol. IV
Jinkin, Paymaster Rear-Adm. Robert Alfred, 1876–1944, vol. IV
Jinnah, Mahomed Ali, 1876–1948, vol. IV
Jivanjee, Sir Yusufali Alibhal Karimjee, 1882–1966, vol. VI

Joachim, Harold Henry, 1868–1938, vol. III
Joachim, Joseph, 1831–1907, vol. I
Joad, Cyril Edwin Mitchinson, 1891–1953, vol. V
Job, William Carson, 1864–1943, vol. IV
Jobberns, Very Rev. Jospeh Brewer, 1868–1936, vol. III
Jobling, Geoffrey Lionel, 1889–1965, vol. VI
Jobson, Brig.-Gen. Alexander, 1875–1933, vol. III
Jocelyn, Ada Maria; see Roden, Dowager Countess of.
Jocelyn, Captain Arthur Cecil, 1880–1959, vol. V
Jocelyn, Col Julian Robert John, 1852–1929, vol. III
Jodhpur, Maharaja of, 1880–1911, vol. I
Jodhpur, Maharaja of, 1898–1918, vol. II
Jodhpur, Maharaja of, 1903–1947, vol. IV
Jodhpur, Maharaja of, 1923–1952, vol. V
Jodl, Friedrich, 1849–1914, vol. I
Jodrell, Sir Alfred, 4th Bt, 1847–1929, vol. III
Jodrell, Dorothy Lynch R.; see Ramsden-Jodrell.
Jodrell, Col Sir Edward Thomas Davenant C.; see Cotton-Jodrell.
Jodrell, Lt-Col Henry Ramsden, died 1950, vol. IV
Jodrell, Sir Neville Paul, 1858–1932, vol. III
Joel, Dudley Jack Barnato, 1904–1941, vol. IV
Joel, Jack Barnato, 1862–1940, vol. III
Joel, Lt-Col Solomon Barnato, died 1931, vol. III
Joel, Woolf, died 1898, vol. I
Joelson, Ferdinand Stephen, 1893–1979, vol. VII
Joffre, Marshal Joseph Jacques Césaire, 1852–1931, vol. III
Jogendra Singh, Sir Sardar, 1877–1946, vol. IV
Joglekar, Rao Bahadur Ramchandra Narayan, 1858–1928, vol. II (A), vol. III
Johannson, Arwid, 1862–1935, vol. III
John XXIII, His Holiness Pope, (Angelo Giuseppe Roncalli), 1881–1963, vol. VI
John, Augustus E., 1878–1961, vol. VI
John, Edward Thomas, 1857–1931, vol. III
John, Sir Edwin, 1856–1935, vol. III
John, Sir Goscombe; see John, Sir W. G.
John, Rev. Griffith, 1831–1912, vol. I
John, Robert Michael, 1924–1980, vol. VII
John, Rt Rev. Thomas Charles, 1871–1936, vol. III
John, William, 1878–1955, vol. V
John, Sir (William) Goscombe, 1860–1952, vol. V
John O'London; see Whitten, Wilfred.
John Paul I, His Holiness Pope, (Albino Luciani), 1912–1978, vol. VII
Johnes, Lt-Gen. Sir James H.; see Hills-Johnes.
Johns, Sir Arthur William, 1873–1937, vol. III
Johns, Charles Rowland, 1882–1961, vol. VI
Johns, Rev. Claude Hermann Walter, 1857–1920, vol. II
Johns, Fred, 1868–1932, vol. III
Johns, Horace John, 1890–1961, vol. VI
Johns, John Francis, 1885–1967, vol. VI
Johns, Richard Henry, 1878–1960, vol. V
Johns, Rev. Thomas, died 1915, vol. I
Johns, Lt-Col Whitfield Glanville, 1877–1941, vol. IV
Johns, Col Sir William Arthur, died 1918, vol. II
Johns, Captain William Earl, 1893–1968, vol. VI
Johnson, Amy, died 1941, vol. IV

Johnson, Alexander, died 1913, vol. I
Johnson, Alice Neville Vowe, died 1938, vol. III
Johnson, Gen. Sir Allen Bayard, 1829–1907, vol. I
Johnson, Col Allen Victor, 1871–1939, vol. III
Johnson, Alvin Saunders, 1874–1971, vol. VII
Johnson, (Arthur) Basil (Noel), 1861–1950, vol. IV
Johnson, Rev. Arthur Henry, 1845–1927, vol. II
Johnson, Col Arthur Morrell, 1887–1946, vol. IV
Johnson, Sir Arthur Palmer, 1865–1944, vol. IV
Johnson, B. S., (Bryan Stanley William Johnson), 1933–1973, vol. VII
Johnson, Basil; see Johnson, A. B. N.
Johnson, Sir Benjamin Sands, 1865–1937, vol. III
Johnson, Bernard, 1868–1935, vol. III
Johnson, Bernard Richard Millar, 1905–1959, vol. V
Johnson, Bertha Jane, 1846–1927, vol. II
Johnson, Borough; see Johnson, E. B.
Johnson, Bryan Stanley William; see Johnson, B. S.
Johnson, Cecil W.; see Webb-Johnson.
Johnson, Ven. Charles, 1850–1927, vol. II
Johnson, Charles, 1870–1961, vol. VI
Johnson, Gen. Sir Charles Cooper, 1827–1905, vol. I
Johnson, Adm. Charles Duncan, 1869–1930, vol. III
Johnson, Charles Edward, 1832–1913, vol. I
Johnson, Charles Plumptre, 1853–1938, vol. III
Johnson, Brig. Charles Reginald, 1876–1953, vol. V
Johnson, Charles William Heaton, 1896–1964, vol. VI
Johnson, Christopher Hollis, 1904–1978, vol. VII
Johnson, Claude Goodman, died 1926, vol. II
Johnson, Maj.-Gen. Cyril Maxwell R.; see Ross-Johnson.
Johnson, Rear-Adm. (S) Cyril Sheldon, 1882–1954, vol. V
Johnson, Cyrus, 1848–1925, vol. II
Johnson, Daniel Cowan, 1915–1969, vol. VI
Johnson, Dennis R.; see Ross-Johnson.
Johnson, Donald McIntosh, 1903–1978, vol. VII
Johnson, Dorothy, 1890–1977, vol. VII
Johnson, Maj.-Gen. Dudley Graham, 1884–1975, vol. VII
Johnson, Sir (Edward) Gordon, 5th Bt (cr 1755), 1867–1957, vol. V
Johnson, Rt Rev. Edward Ralph, died 1911, vol. I
Johnson, Hon. Sir Elliot; see Johnson, Hon. Sir W. E.
Johnson, Eric Seymour Thewlis, 1897–1978, vol. VII
Johnson, Eric Townsend, 1875–1942, vol. IV
Johnson, (Ernest) Borough, died 1949, vol. IV
Johnson, Sir Ernest James, 1881–1962, vol. VI
Johnson, Eyvind, 1900–1976, vol. VII
Johnson, Francis H.; see Hernaman–Johnson.
Johnson, Rev. Frank, died 1927, vol. II
Johnson, Maj.-Gen. Frank Ernest, 1861–1945, vol. IV
Johnson, Lt-Col Sir Frank William Frederick, 1866–1943, vol. IV
Johnson, Sir Frederic Charles, 1890–1972, vol. VII

Johnson, Lt-Col Frederic L.; *see* Luttman-Johnson.

Johnson, Major Frederick Colpoys Ormsby, 1858–1932, vol. III

Johnson, Maj.-Gen. Frederick Francis, 1852–1931, vol. III

Johnson, Major Frederick Henry, 1890–1917, vol. II

Johnson, Very Rev. Frederick Wells, vol. III

Johnson, Sir George, 1867–1947, vol. IV

Johnson, George Arthur, 1903–1972, vol. VII

Johnson, Maj.-Gen. Sir George Frederick, 1903–1980, vol. VII

Johnson, George H., *died* 1933, vol. III

Johnson, Hon. Sir George H., 1872–1936, vol. III

Johnson, George Lindsay, 1853–1943, vol. IV

Johnson, George Macness, 1853–1935, vol. III

Johnson, Air Marshal George Owen, 1896–1980, vol. VII

Johnson, George William, 1857–1926, vol. II

Johnson, Sir Gordon; *see* Johnson, Sir E. G.

Johnson, Sir Gordon; *see* Johnson, Sir J. N. G.

Johnson, Brig. Guy Allen Colpoys Ormsby, 1886–1957, vol. V

Johnson, Guy Francis, *died* 1969, vol. VI

Johnson, H. C. Brooke, 1873–1949, vol. IV

Johnson, Harold Cottam, 1903–1973, vol. VII

Johnson, Harold Daintree, 1910–1980, vol. VII

Johnson, Captain Harry Cecil, 1877–1915, vol. I

Johnson, Harry Gordon, 1923–1977, vol. VII

Johnson, Col Harry Hall, 1892–1973, vol. VII

Johnson, Engr Rear-Adm. Harry Herbert, 1875–1961, vol. VI

Johnson, Sir Henry Allen Beaumont, 5th Bt (*cr* 1818), 1887–1965, vol. VI

Johnson, Brig.-Gen. Sir Henry Allen William, 4th Bt (*cr* 1818), 1855–1944, vol. IV

Johnson, Rt Rev. Henry Frank, 1834–1908, vol. I

Johnson, Henry Harrold, 1869–1940, vol. III (A), vol. IV

Johnson, Sir Henry James, 1851–1917, vol. II

Johnson, Henry Langhorne, 1874–1945, vol. IV

Johnson, Herbert, 1856–1949, vol. IV

Johnson, Herschel V., 1894–1966, vol. VI

Johnson, Very Rev. Hewlett, 1874–1966, vol. VI

Johnson, Hiram Warren, 1866–1945, vol. IV

Johnson, Major Hugh Spencer, *died* 1962, vol. VI

Johnson, Rev. James, *died* 1911, vol. I

Johnson, Rt Rev. James, *died* 1917, vol. II

Johnson, John, 1850–1910, vol. I

Johnson, John, 1882–1956, vol. V

Johnson, John Charles S.; *see* Sperrin-Johnson.

Johnson, Sir John Henry, 1826–1909, vol. I

Johnson, Sir (John Nesbitt) Gordon, 1885–1955, vol. V

Johnson, Sir John Paley, 6th Bt (*cr* 1755), 1907–1975, vol. VII

Johnson, Hon. John W. Fordham, 1866–1938, vol. III

Johnson, Rt Rev. Joseph Horsfall, 1847–1928, vol. II (A), vol. III

Johnson, Lionel, 1867–1902, vol. I

Johnson, Louis Arthur, 1891–1966, vol. VI

Johnson, Sir (Louis) Stanley, 1869–1937, vol. III

Johnson, Lyndon Baines, 1908–1973, vol. VII

Johnson, Most Rev. Martin Michael, 1899–1975, vol. VII

Johnson, Lt-Col Maurice Eustace Stanley, 1879–1937, vol. III

Johnson, Sir Nelson King, 1892–1954, vol. V

Johnson, Owen, 1878–1952, vol. V

Johnson, Lt-Col Pelham; *see* Johnson, Lt-Col T. P.

Johnson, Sir Philip Bulmer, 1887–1964, vol. VI

Johnson, R. Brimley, 1867–1932, vol. III

Johnson, Raymond, *died* 1944, vol. IV

Johnson, Hon. Sir Reginald Powell C.; *see* Croom-Johnson.

Johnson, Brig.-Gen. Richard Francis, 1852–1938, vol. III

Johnson, Sir Robert Arthur, 1874–1938, vol. III

Johnson, Sir Robert Stewart, 1872–1951, vol. V

Johnson, Robert Underwood, 1853–1937, vol. III

Johnson, Brig.-Gen. Ronald Marr, 1873–1925, vol. II

Johnson, Rev. Rowland Theodore I.; *see* Ingram-Johnson.

Johnson, Sir Samuel George, 1831–1909, vol. I

Johnson, Samuel Waite, *died* 1912, vol. I

Johnson, Seymour Shepherd, 1875–1962, vol. VI

Johnson, Sir Sidney Midlane, 1885–1960, vol. V

Johnson, Sir Stanley; *see* Johnson, Sir L. S.

Johnson, Stanley W.; *see* Webb-Johnson.

Johnson, Stephen Keymer, 1899–1936, vol. III

Johnson, Lt-Col T. Pelham, 1871–1918, vol. II

Johnson, Thomas, 1863–1954, vol. V

Johnson, Thomas Frank, *died* 1972, vol. VII

Johnson, Lt-Col Thomas Gordon Blois-, 1867–1918, vol. II

Johnson, Rt Rev. Thomas Sylvester Claudius, 1873–1955, vol. V

Johnson, Tom Loftin, 1854–1911, vol. I

Johnson, Tom Richard, *died* 1935, vol. III

Johnson, Sir Walter, 1845–1912, vol. I

Johnson, Sir Walter Burford, 1885–1951, vol. V

Johnson, Lt-Col Walter R.; *see* Russell-Johnson.

Johnson, Wilfrid A.; *see* Athelstan-Johnson.

Johnson, Rev. Wilfrid Harry Cowper, 1879–1967, vol. VI

Johnson, William, 1849–1919, vol. II

Johnson, Rt Rev. William Anthony, 1832–1909, vol. I

Johnson, Rev. William Cowper, *died* 1916, vol. II

Johnson, Hon. William Dartnell, 1872–1948, vol. IV

Johnson, Hon. Sir (William) Elliot, 1862–1932, vol. III

Johnson, William Evelyn Patrick, 1902–1976, vol. VII

Johnson, Sir William George, 4th Bt (*cr* 1755), 1830–1908 (this entry was not transferred to Who was Who).

Johnson, Rt Rev. William Herbert, 1889–1960, vol. V

Johnson, William Joseph, 1892–1971, vol. VII

Johnson, Rt Hon. Sir William Moore, 1st Bt (*cr* 1909), 1828–1918, vol. II

Johnson, Ven. William Percival, *died* 1928, vol. II

Johnson-Ferguson, Sir Edward; *see* Johnson-Ferguson, Sir J. E.

Johnson-Ferguson, Sir Edward Alexander James, 2nd Bt, 1875–1953, vol. V

Johnson-Ferguson, Sir (Jabez) Edward, 1st Bt, 1849–1929, vol. III

Johnson-Gilbert, Sir Ian Anderson, 1891–1974, vol. VII

Johnson-Walsh, Sir Hunt Henry Allen; *see* Walsh.

Johnston, Hon. Lord; Henry Johnston, 1844–1931, vol. III

Johnston, Alexander, 1867–1951, vol. V

Johnston, Alice Crawford, 1902–1976, vol. VII

Johnston, Andrew, 1835–1922, vol. II

Johnston, A(nthony) G(ordon) Knox, 1909–1972, vol. VII

Johnston, Carruthers Melvill, 1909–1970, vol. VI

Johnston, Sir Charles, 1st Bt (*cr* 1916), 1848–1933, vol. III

Johnston, Col Charles Arthur, 1867–1926, vol. II

Johnston, Lt-Col Charles Evelyn, 1878–1922, vol. II

Johnston, Ven. Charles Francis Harding, 1842–1925, vol. II

Johnston, Christopher Nicholson; *see* Sands, Hon. Lord.

Johnston, David, 1836–1899, vol. I

Johnston, Col David Seton, 1886–1960, vol. V

Johnston, Col Sir Duncan Alexander, 1847–1931, vol. III

Johnston, Edward, 1872–1944, vol. IV

Johnston, Edward Hamilton, 1885–1942, vol. IV

Johnston, Wing Comdr Ernest Henry, 1885–1938, vol. III

Johnston, Francis Alexander, 1864–1958, vol. V

Johnston, Brig.-Gen. Francis Earl, *died* 1917, vol. II

Johnston, Rt Rev. Francis Featherstonhaugh, 1891–1963, vol. VI

Johnston, Lt-Col Francis Gawen Dillon, 1875–1945, vol. IV

Johnston, Frederick, 1859–1937, vol. III

Johnston, Frederick Mair, 1903–1973, vol. VII

Johnston, Sir Frederick William, 1872–1947, vol. IV

Johnston, Sir Gaston, 1874–1965, vol. VI (AII)

Johnston, Sir George, 10th Bt, 1845–1921 (this entry was not transferred to Who was Who).

Johnston, George Douglas, 1886–1971, vol. VII

Johnston, George Francis, 1860–1943, vol. IV

Johnston, George Jameson, 1866–1926, vol. II

Johnston, Maj-Gen. George Jameson, 1868–1949, vol. IV

Johnston, Brig.-Gen. George Napier, 1867–1947, vol. IV

Johnston, Grace L. Keith, *died* 1929, vol. III

Johnston, Sir Harold Featherston, 1875–1959, vol. V

Johnston, Sir Harry Hamilton, 1858–1927, vol. II

Johnston, Henry; *see* Johnston, Hon. Lord.

Johnston, Col Henry Halcro, 1856–1939, vol. III

Johnston, Henry Joseph, 1858–1906, vol. I

Johnston, Hugh Anthony Stephen, 1913–1967, vol. VI

Johnston, Rev. Hugh William, *died* 1918, vol. II

Johnston, Rt Hon. Sir James, 1849–1924, vol. II

Johnston, Rev. James B., 1862–1953, vol. V

Johnston, James Osborne, 1921–1978, vol. VII

Johnston, Rt Rev. James Steptoe, 1843–1924, vol. II (A), vol. III

Johnston, Maj.-Gen. James Thomason, 1860–1938, vol. III

Johnston, James Wellwood, 1900–1958, vol. V

Johnston, Sir John, 1873–1952, vol. V

Johnston, John Alexander Hope, 1871–1938, vol. III

Johnston, Major John Alexander Weir, 1879–1957, vol. V

Johnston, Sir John Barr, 1843–1919, vol. II

Johnston, John Lawson, 1839–1900, vol. I

Johnston, Rev. John Octavius, 1852–1925, vol. II

Johnston, Joseph, 1890–1972, vol. VII

Johnston, Joseph Wilson-, 1876–1933, vol. III

Johnston, Malcolm Campbell-; *see* Campbell-Johnston.

Johnston, Mary, 1870–1936, vol. III

Johnston, Col Osmond Moncreiff, 1848–1934, vol. III

Johnston, Col Percy Herbert, 1851–1932, vol. III

Johnston, Philip Mainwaring, 1865–1936, vol. III

Johnston, R. M'Kenzie, 1856–1930, vol. III

Johnston, Reginald Eden, 1847–1922, vol. II

Johnston, Sir Reginald Fleming, 1874–1938, vol. III

Johnston, Major Robert, 1872–1950, vol. IV

Johnston, Brig. Robert, 1879–1956, vol. V

Johnston, Major Robert Douglas, 1882–1959, vol. V

Johnston, Robert Mackenzie, *died* 1918, vol. II

Johnston, Robert Matteson, 1867–1920, vol. II

Johnston, Samuel, *born* 1835, vol. II

Johnston, Rev. Samuel Alfred, 1864–1940, vol. III

Johnston, Rt Hon. Thomas, 1881–1965, vol. V

Johnston, Sir Thomas Alexander, 11th Bt, 1857–1950, vol. IV

Johnston, Sir Thomas Alexander, 12th Bt, 1888–1959, vol. V

Johnston, Thomas Baillie, 1883–1960, vol. V

Johnston, Thomas Harvey, 1881–1951, vol. V

Johnston, Brig.-Gen. Thomas Kelly Evans, 1860–1936, vol. III

Johnston, Thomas Kenneth, 1878–1953, vol. V

Johnston, Maj.-Gen. Walter Edward Wilson-, 1878–1948, vol. IV

Johnston, William, 1829–1902, vol. I

Johnston, Col William, 1843–1914, vol. I

Johnston, Sir William, 9th Bt, 1849–1917, vol. II

Johnston, William, 1890–1976, vol. VII

Johnston, Sir William Campbell, 1860–1938, vol. III

Johnston, Sir William Ernest George, 1884–1951, vol. V

Johnston, Lt-Col William Hamilton Hall, *died* 1952, vol. V

Johnston, Lt-Col William James, 1870–1937, vol. III

Johnston, William John, 1869–1940, vol. III (A), vol. IV

Johnston, Rev. William Murdoch, 1847–1905, vol. I

Johnston, Sir William Wallace Stewart, 1887–1962, vol. VI

Johnston-Saint, Captain Peter Johnston, *died* 1974, vol. VII

Johnston-Stewart of Physgill, Adm. Robert Hathorn, 1858–1940, vol. III

Johnstone, Hon. Sir Alan Vanden-Bempde-, 1858–1932, vol. III

Johnstone, Sir Alexander Howat, 1876–1956, vol. V

Johnstone, Alfred; *see* Johnstone, J. A.

Johnstone, Lt-Col Bede, 1877–1942, vol. IV

Johnstone, Vice-Adm. Charles, 1843–1927, vol. II

Johnstone, Major David Patrick, 1876–1951, vol. V

Johnstone, Sir Donald Campbell, 1857–1920, vol. II

Johnstone, Brig.-Gen. Francis Buchanan, 1863–1947, vol. IV

Johnstone, Sir Frederic John William, 8th Bt, 1841–1913 (this entry was not transferred to Who was Who).

Johnstone, Frederick John, 1841–1934, vol. III

Johnstone, Rev. George Alexander, 1868–1932, vol. III

Johnstone, Lt-Col George Charles Keppel, 1841–1912, vol. I

Johnstone, Sir George Frederic Thomas Tankerville, 9th Bt, 1876–1952, vol. V

Johnstone, Gerald Ewart, 1906–1973, vol. VII

Johnstone, Rt Hon. Harcourt, 1895–1945, vol. IV

Johnstone, Hilda, 1882–1961, vol. VI

Johnstone, Col Hope, 1868–1939, vol. III

Johnstone, J. Alfred, 1861–1941, vol. IV

Johnstone, Major James H. L'E., 1865–1906, vol. I

Johnstone, Maj.-Gen. James Robert, 1859–1932, vol. III

Johnstone, James William Douglas, 1855–1925, vol. II

Johnstone, John Andrew, 1893–1918, vol. II

Johnstone, John Heywood, 1850–1904, vol. I

Johnstone, John James H.; *see* Hope-Johnstone.

Johnstone, Joseph, 1860–1931, vol. III

Johnstone, Kenneth Roy, 1902–1978, vol. VII

Johnstone, Lewis Martin, 1870–1960, vol. V

Johnstone, Col Montague George, 1848–1928, vol. II

Johnstone, Morris Mackintosh O.; *see* Ord Johnstone.

Johnstone, Ralph William, *died* 1915, vol. I

Johnstone, Maj.-Gen. Reginald Forster, 1904–1976, vol. VII

Johnstone, Robert, 1861–1944, vol. IV

Johnstone, Rev. Robert Cuthbert, 1857–1934, vol. III

Johnstone, Sir Robert J., 1872–1938, vol. III

Johnstone, Sir Robert Stewart, 1855–1936, vol. III

Johnstone, Robert William, 1879–1969, vol. VI

Johnstone, Very Rev. Thomas McGimpsey, 1876–1961, vol. VI

Johnstone, Lt-Col Sir Walter E.; *see* Edgeworth-Johnstone.

Johnstone-Burt, Charles Kingsley, 1891–1973, vol. VII

Johnstone-Douglas, Arthur Henry; *see* Douglas.

Johnstone-Wallace, Denis Bowes, 1894–1960, vol. V

Johore, Sultan of, 1873–1959, vol. V

Joicey, 1st Baron, 1846–1936, vol. III

Joicey, 2nd Baron, 1880–1940, vol. III

Joicey, 3rd Baron, 1881–1966, vol. VI

Joicey, Major James, 1836–1912, vol. I

Joicey, James John, 1870–1932, vol. III

Joicey-Cecil, Lord John Packenham; *see* Cecil.

Jokai, Maurus, 1825–1904, vol. I

Joliot-Curie, Jean Frédéric, 1900–1958, vol. V

Joll, Cecil Augustus, *died* 1945, vol. IV

Jolley, Maj.-Gen. Norman Kempe, 1894–1951, vol. V

Jollie, Ethel M.; *see* Colquhoun, E. M.

Jollie, Mrs Tawse; *see* Colquhoun, Ethel M.

Jolliffe, Arthur Ernest, 1871–1944, vol. IV

Jolliffe, John Edward Austin, 1891–1964, vol. VI

Jolliffe, Richard Orlando, 1876–1932, vol. III

Jolliffe, Lt.-Col Thomas William, 1873–1944, vol. IV

Jolliffe, Captain Hon. William Sydney Hylton, 1841–1912, vol. I

Jolly, Gen. Sir Alan, 1910–1977, vol. VII

Jolly, Lt-Gen. Sir Gordon Gray, *died* 1962, vol. VI

Jolly, James, 1902–1968, vol. VI

Jolly, James Hornby, 1887–1972, vol. VII

Jolly, John Catterall, 1887–1950, vol. IV

Jolly, Rev. Canon Reginald Bradley, 1885–1972, vol. VII

Jolly, Thomas Riley, 1849–1929, vol. III

Jolly, William Adam, *died* 1939, vol. III

Jolly, William Alfred, *died* 1955, vol. IV

Jolly, Rear-Adm. Sir William E. H., 1887–1961, vol. VI

Jolowicz, Herbert Felix, 1890–1954, vol. V

Joly, Charles Jasper, 1864–1906, vol. I

Joly, John, *died* 1933, vol. III

Joly, John Swift, *died* 1943, vol. IV

Joly de Lotbinière, Maj.-Gen. Alain Chartier, 1862–1944, vol. IV

Joly de Lotbinière, Hon. Sir Henry Gustave, 1829–1908, vol. I

Joly de Lotbinière, Brig.-Gen. Henri Gustave, 1868–1960, vol. V

Jonas, Harry Marshall, 1866–1939, vol. III

Jones, Abel John, *died* 1949, vol. IV

Jones, Captain Adrian, 1845–1938, vol. III

Jones, Brig. Alan Harvey, 1910–1975, vol. VII

Jones, Alan Trevor, 1901–1979, vol. VII

Jones, Rev. Sir Albert E.; *see* Evans-Jones.

Jones, Alfred; *see* Jones, E. A.

Jones, (Alfred) Ernest, *died* 1958, vol. V

Jones, Alfred Gilpin, 1824–1906, vol. I

Jones, Sir Alfred Lewis, 1846–1909, vol. I

Jones, Lt-Col Alfred Stowell, 1832–1920, vol. II

Jones, Sir Andrew; *see* Jones, Sir W. J. A.

Jones, Arnold Hugh Martin, 1904–1970, vol. VI

Jones, Rt Hon. Arthur Creech, 1891–1964, vol. VI

Jones, Lt-Col Arthur Daniel D.; *see* Derviche-Jones.

Jones, Arthur Davies, 1897–1980, vol. VII

Jones, Arthur Griffith M.; *see* Maitland-Jones.

Jones, Sir Arthur Probyn P.; *see* Probyn-Jones.

Jones, Arthur R.; *see* Rocyn-Jones.
Jones, Very Rev. Arthur Stuart D.; *see* Duncan-Jones.
Jones, Brig. Arthur Thomas C.; *see* Cornwall-Jones.
Jones, Hon. Sir Austin Ellis Lloyd, 1884–1967, vol. VI
Jones, Austin Ernest D.; *see* Duncan-Jones.
Jones, Sir Barry; *see* Jones, Sir T. B.
Jones, Rev. Basil M., *died* 1925, vol. II
Jones, Rev. Canon Benjamin, 1865–1955, vol. V
Jones, Captain Benjamin Henry, *died* 1949, vol. IV
Jones, Benjamin Howell, *died* 1913, vol. I
Jones, Benjamin Rowland R.; *see* Rice-Jones.
Jones, Sir (Bennett) Melvill, 1887–1975, vol. VII
Jones, Bernard Mouat, 1882–1953, vol. V
Jones, Sir Bertram Hyde, 1879–1961, vol. VI
Jones, Bobby; *see* Jones, Robert Tyre.
Jones, Major Bryan John, 1874–1918, vol. II
Jones, Rev. Bulkeley Owen, 1824–1914, vol. I
Jones, Sir Cadwaladr Bryner, 1872–1954, vol. V
Jones, Cecil Artimus E.; *see* Evan-Jones.
Jones, Cecil Charles, 1872–1943, vol. IV
Jones, Chapman; *see* Jones, H. C.
Jones, Charles Alfred, 1848–1934, vol. III
Jones, Charles Edward, 1852–1932, vol. III
Jones, Charles Edward Irvine, 1899–1951, vol. V
Jones, Sir Charles Ernest, 1892–1953, vol. V
Jones, Charles Evan William, 1879–1951, vol. V
Jones, Charles Henry, 1857–1936, vol. III
Jones, Lt-Col Charles Herbert, 1865–1953, vol. V
Jones, Charles Hugh LePailleur, *died* 1949, vol. IV
Jones, Charles Jerome, 1847–1929, vol. III
Jones, Major Charles Llewelyn W.; *see* Wynne-Jones.
Jones, Sir Charles Lloyd, 1878–1958, vol. V
Jones, Charles Mark J.; *see* Jenkin-Jones.
Jones, Sir (Charles) Sydney, 1872–1947, vol. IV
Jones, Chester, 1854–1922, vol. II
Jones, Sir Clement Wakefield, 1880–1963, vol. VI
Jones, Clifford T., 1873–1948, vol. IV
Jones, Clinton; *see* Jones, J. C.
Jones, Constance; *see* Jones, E. E. C.
Jones, Col Conwyn M.; *see* Mansel-Jones.
Jones, Sir Crawford Douglas D.; *see* Douglas-Jones.
Jones, Sir Cyril Edgar, 1891–1970, vol. VI
Jones, Rev. Cyril L.; *see* Leslie-Jones.
Jones, Lt-Col Sir Cyril Vivian, 1882–1961, vol. VI
Jones, Rev. Daniel, *died* 1934, vol. III
Jones, Daniel, 1881–1967, vol. VI
Jones, Rev. David, 1848–1909, vol. I
Jones, David, 1895–1974, vol. VII
Jones, Rev. Canon David A.; *see* Akrill-Jones.
Jones, Rt Hon. Sir David Brynmor, 1852–1921, vol. II
Jones, Sir (David) Fletcher, 1895–1977, vol. VII
Jones, Very Rev. David John, 1870–1949, vol. IV
Jones, David Lewis, 1889–1953, vol. V
Jones, Ven. David Morgan, 1874–1950, vol. IV
Jones, David Thomas, 1866–1931, vol. III
Jones, David Thomas, *died* 1963, vol. VI
Jones, Sir David Thomas R.; *see* Rocyn-Jones.
Jones, Rev. Donald, 1857–1925, vol. II

Jones, Douglas Vivian I.; *see* Irvine-Jones.
Jones, Dudley William Carmalt, 1874–1957, vol. V
Jones, E. Alfred, 1872–1943, vol. IV
Jones, E. E. Constance, *died* 1922, vol. II
Jones, Sir E. Wynne C.; *see* Cemlyn-Jones.
Jones, Ebenezer G.; *see* Griffith-Jones.
Jones, Edgar H.; *see* Heath-Jones.
Jones, Edgar Montague, 1866–1938, vol. III
Jones, Sir Edgar Rees, 1878–1962, vol. VI
Jones, Sir Edmund Britten, 1888–1953, vol. V
Jones, Rev. Edmund Osborne, 1858–1931, vol. III
Jones, Sir Edward Coley B.; *see* Burne-Jones.
Jones, Col Sir Edward P.; *see* Pryce-Jones.
Jones, Rear-Adm. Edward Pitcairn, 1850–1908, vol. I
Jones, Sir Edward R.; *see* Redmayne-Jones.
Jones, Edward Taylor, 1872–1961, vol. VI
Jones, Edward William M.; *see* Milner-Jones.
Jones, Edwin, 1841–1900, vol. I
Jones, Eli Stanley, 1884–1973, vol. VII
Jones, Eric Kyffin, 1896–1977, vol. VII
Jones, Sir Eric Newton G.; *see* Griffith-Jones.
Jones, Ernest; *see* Jones, A. E.
Jones, Ernest; *see* Jones, W. E.
Jones, Ernest L.; *see* Lancaster-Jones.
Jones, Ernest W.; *see* Whitley-Jones.
Jones, Captain Sir Evan, *died* 1949, vol. IV
Jones, Evan Bonnor H.; *see* Hugh-Jones.
Jones, Evan Bowen, 1869–1940, vol. III
Jones, Sir Evan Davies, 1st Bt (*cr* 1917), 1859–1949, vol. IV
Jones, Major Evan Rowland, *died* 1920, vol. II
Jones, Vice-Adm. Everard John H.; *see* Hardman-Jones.
Jones, F. W. D.; *see* Doyle-Jones.
Jones, Sir Felix E. A.; *see* Aylmer-Jones.
Jones, Sir Fletcher; *see* Jones, Sir D. F.
Jones, Francis, 1845–1925, vol. II
Jones, Sir Francis Adolphus, 1861–1947, vol. IV
Jones, Frank, 1873–1961, vol. VI
Jones, Lt-Col Frank Aubrey, 1873–1916, vol. II
Jones, Ven. Frank Emlyn, *died* 1935, vol. III
Jones, Frank Ernest, *died* 1974, vol. VII
Jones, Rt Rev. Frank Melville, 1866–1941, vol. IV
Jones, Frank Newling, *died* 1942, vol. IV
Jones, (Frederic) Wood, 1879–1954, vol. V
Jones, Hon. Frederick, 1884–1966, vol. VI
Jones, Frederick Archibald L.; *see* Leslie-Jones.
Jones, Frederick Herbert P.; *see* Page-Jones.
Jones, Frederick James, 1874–1943, vol. IV
Jones, Sir Frederick John, 1st Bt (*cr* 1919), 1854–1936, vol. III
Jones, Frederick L.; *see* Llewellyn-Jones.
Jones, Frederick Theodore, 1885–1968, vol. VI
Jones, Col Frederick William C.; *see* Caton-Jones.
Jones, Frederick William F.; *see* Farey-Jones.
Jones, George, 1844–1921, vol. II
Jones, George Arthur, 1889–1962, vol. VI
Jones, George Basil Harris, 1896–1946, vol. IV
Jones, Sir (George) Basil T.; *see* Todd-Jones.
Jones, Vice-Adm. George Clarence, 1895–1946, vol. IV
Jones, Sir George L.; *see* Legh-Jones.

363

Jones, George Lewis, 1907–1971, vol. VII
Jones, George Mallory, 1873–1940, vol. III
Jones, George Morgan Edwardes, 1858–1936, vol. III
Jones, George William, 1860–1942, vol. IV
Jones, Sir George William Henry, *died* 1956, vol. V
Jones, Cdre Gerald N., 1885–1958, vol. V
Jones, Rev. Gilbert Basil, 1894–1958, vol. VI (AI)
Jones, Rev. Gustavus John, 1848–1929, vol. III
Jones, Maj.-Gen. Guy Carleton, 1864–1950, vol. IV
Jones, Gwilym Arthur, 1887–1957, vol. V
Jones, Gwilym Peredur, 1892–1975, vol. VII
Jones, H. Chapman, 1854–1932, vol. III
Jones, Sir Harold Spencer, 1890–1960, vol. V
Jones, Harry, 1866–1925, vol. II
Jones, Col Harry Balfour, 1866–1952, vol. V
Jones, Harry Davies Campbell, 1863–1935, vol. III
Jones, Harry O.; *see* Orton-Jones.
Jones, Henry, (Cavendish) 1831–1899, vol. I
Jones, Sir Henry, 1852–1922, vol. II
Jones, Sir Henry, 1862–1926, vol. II
Jones, Henry Albert, *died* 1945, vol. IV
Jones, Lt-Gen. Henry Albert H., *died* 1944, vol. IV
Jones, Henry Arthur, 1851–1929, vol. III
Jones, Rev. Henry David, 1842–1925, vol. II
Jones, Very Rev. Henry Donald Maurice S.; *see* Spence-Jones.
Jones, Henry Festing, 1851–1928, vol. II
Jones, Sir Henry Haydn, 1863–1950, vol. IV
Jones, Ven. Henry James Church, 1870–1941, vol. IV
Jones, Henry Lewis, 1857–1915, vol. I
Jones, Henry M.; *see* Macnaughton-Jones.
Jones, Sir Henry M.; *see* Morris-Jones, Sir J. H.
Jones, Captain Henry Michael, *died* 1916, vol. II
Jones, Bt Col Henry Morris P.; *see* Pryce-Jones.
Jones, Captain Henry Richmund I.; *see* Inigo-Jones.
Jones, Sir Henry S.; *see* Stuart-Jones.
Jones, Brig.-Gen. Herbert Arthur, *died* 1955, vol. V
Jones, Very Rev. Herbert Arthur, *died* 1969, vol. VI
Jones, Rt Rev. Herbert Edward, 1861–1920, vol. II
Jones, Air Cdre Herbert George, 1884–1979, vol. VII
Jones, Rt Rev. Herbert Gresford, 1870–1958, vol. V
Jones, Herbert Lee Jackson, 1870–1936, vol. III
Jones, Herbert Riversdale M.; *see* Mansel-Jones.
Jones, Sir Hildreth G.; *see* Glyn-Jones.
Jones, Howard Parker, 1863–1924, vol. II
Jones, Gen. Sir Howard Sutton, 1835–1912, vol. I
Jones, Rev. Howard W.; *see* Watkin-Jones.
Jones, Howell G.; *see* Gwynne-Jones.
Jones, Ven. Hugh, 1815–1897, vol. I
Jones, Hugh E.; *see* Emlyn-Jones.
Jones, Hugh Ferguson, 1913–1979, vol. VII
Jones, Humphrey Stanley Herbert, *died* 1902, vol. I
Jones, Ven. Humphrey Tudor Morrey, *died* 1936, vol. III
Jones, Idris Deane, 1899–1947, vol. IV
Jones, Ifano, 1865–1955, vol. V

Jones, Maj.-Gen. Inigo Richmund, 1848–1914, vol. I
Jones, Isaac, 1883–1968, vol. VI
Jones, J. Clinton, 1848–1936, vol. III
Jones, J. Morgan, 1873–1946, vol. IV
Jones, Jack, 1884–1970, vol. VI
Jones, Sir James, 1895–1962, vol. VI
Jones, James, 1921–1977, vol. VII
Jones, James Edmund, 1866–1939, vol. III
Jones, Sir James Edward, 1843–1922, vol. II
Jones, James Ilston, 1911–1976, vol. VII
Jones, Gp Captain James Ira Thomas, 1896–1960, vol. V
Jones, Lt-Col James Walker, 1887–1933, vol. III
Jones, Ven. James William Percy, 1881–1980, vol. VII
Jones, James William W.; *see* Webb-Jones.
Jones, John Arthur, 1867–1939, vol. III
Jones, Sir John Bowen Bowen-, 1st Bt (*cr* 1911), 1840–1925, vol. II
Jones, Rt Rev. John Charles, 1904–1956, vol. V
Jones, Rev. John Daniel, 1865–1942, vol. IV
Jones, John David Rheinallt, 1884–1953, vol. V
Jones, Paymaster Rear-Adm. John Edward, 1866–1948, vol. VI
Jones, Sir John Edward L.; *see* Lennard-Jones.
Jones, John Emlyn E.; *see* Emlyn-Jones.
Jones, John Harry, 1881–1973, vol. VII
Jones, John Henry, 1894–1962, vol. VI
Jones, Sir (John) Henry M.; *see* Morris-Jones.
Jones, Rev. John Hugh Watkins, 1862–1937, vol. III
Jones, Col John Hyndman H.; *see* Howell-Jones.
Jones, Rev. J(ohn) Ithel, 1911–1980, vol. VII (AII)
Jones, Rev. John James, *died* 1934, vol. III
Jones, Col Sir John James, 1845–1938, vol. III
Jones, John Joseph, 1873–1941, vol. IV
Jones, John Joseph Casimer, 1839–1929, vol. III
Jones, John Kenyon Netherton, 1912–1977, vol. VII
Jones, John L.; *see* Lees-Jones.
Jones, Ven. John Lloyd-, 1848–1934, vol. III
Jones, (John) Mervyn (Guthrie) G.; *see* Griffith-Jones.
Jones, Sir John Morris-, 1864–1929, vol. III
Jones, Sir John P.; *see* Prichard-Jones.
Jones, John Richard, 1881–1955, vol. V
Jones, (John) Share, *died* 1950, vol. IV
Jones, John Viriamu, 1856–1901, vol. I
Jones, John Walter, 1892–1973, vol. VII
Jones, Joseph, *died* 1948, vol. IV
Jones, Joseph, 1890–1979, vol. VII
Jones, Josiah Towyn, 1858–1925, vol. II
Jones, Dame Katharine Henrietta, 1888–1967, vol. VI
Jones, Keith M.; *see* Miller Jones.
Jones, Kennedy, 1865–1921, vol. II
Jones, Captain Kingsmill Williams, 1875–1918, vol. II
Jones, Lawrence, *died* 1949, vol. IV
Jones, Sir Lawrence Evelyn, 5th Bt (*cr* 1831), 1885–1969, vol. VI
Jones, Sir Lawrence John, 4th Bt (*cr* 1831), 1857–1954, vol. V

Jones, Maj.-Gen. Leslie Cockburn, 1870–1960, vol. V
Jones, Rev. Lewis, 1842–1928, vol. II
Jones, Maj.-Gen. Lewis, 1862–1935, vol. III
Jones, Sir Lewis, 1884–1968, vol. VI
Jones, Lewis; see Jones, G. L.
Jones, Lewis; see Jones, W. L.
Jones, Leycester Hudson L.; see Leslie-Jones.
Jones, Lionel P.; see Powys-Jones.
Jones, Rt Rev. Llewellyn, 1840–1918, vol. II
Jones, Llewellyn Archer A.; see Atherley-Jones.
Jones, Col Llewellyn Murray, 1871–1946, vol. IV
Jones, Llewellyn Rodwell, 1881–1947, vol. IV
Jones, Llewelyn Arthur H.; see Hugh-Jones.
Jones, Maj.-Gen. Llewelyn W.; see Wansbrough-Jones.
Jones, Very Rev. Llewelyn W.; see Wynne-Jones.
Jones, Rev. Lloyd Timothy, died 1920, vol. II
Jones, Brig.-Gen. Lumley Owen Williames, 1876–1918, vol. II
Jones, Sir Lyman Melvin, 1843–1917, vol. II
Jones, Mrs Mabel Mary Cheveley; see Rayner, M. M. C.
Jones, Martin, 1897–1979, vol. VII
Jones, Marvin, died 1976, vol. VII
Jones, Dame Mary Latchford Kingsmill, died 1968, vol. VI
Jones, Rev. Maurice, 1863–1957, vol. V
Jones, Maurice; see Jones, S. M.
Jones, Sir Melvill; see Jones, Sir B. M.
Jones, Lt-Col Michael Durwas Goring-, 1866–1919, vol. II
Jones, Montagu H.; see Handfield-Jones.
Jones, Brig.-Gen. Morey Q.; see Quayle-Jones.
Jones, Morgan, 1885–1939, vol. III
Jones, Morgan; see Jones, J. M.
Jones, Morgan Philips G.; see Griffith-Jones.
Jones, Norman Edward, 1904–1972, vol. VII
Jones, Rt Rev. Norman Sherwood, 1911–1951, vol. V
Jones, Captain Oscar Philip, 1898–1980, vol. VII
Jones, Captain Owen, 1866–1941, vol. IV
Jones, Owen Daniel, 1861–1951, vol. V
Jones, Owen Thomas, 1878–1967, vol. VI
Jones, Parry William John, 1891–1963, vol. VI
Jones, Patrick Nicholas Hill, 1864–1934, vol. III
Jones, Sir Pendrill Charles V.; see Varrier-Jones.
Jones, Penrhyn Grant, 1878–1945, vol. IV
Jones, Major Percy Arnold Lloyd-, 1876–1916, vol. II
Jones, Maj.-Gen. Percy George C.; see Calvert-Jones.
Jones, Rev. Percy Herbert, 1864–1941, vol. IV
Jones, Percy Mansell, 1889–1968, vol. VI
Jones, Hon. Percy Sydney T.; see Twentyman-Jones.
Jones, Sir Peter (Fawcett) Benton, 3rd Bt (cr 1919), 1911–1972, vol. VII
Jones, Peter Howard, 1911–1975, vol. VII
Jones, Philip Asterley, 1914–1978, vol. VII
Jones, Sir Philip B.; see Burne-Jones.
Jones, Col Philip Reginald B.; see Bence-Jones.
Jones, Sir Philip Sydney, 1836–1918, vol. II
Jones, Sir Pryce P.; see Pryce-Jones.

Jones, Sir Pryce Victor P.; see Pryce-Jones.
Jones, Ranald Montagu H.; see Handfield-Jones.
Jones, Raymond R.; see Ray-Jones.
Jones, Reginald Trevor, 1888–1974, vol. VII
Jones, Sir Reginald W.; see Watson-Jones.
Jones, Rev. Richard Charles Stuart, died 1941, vol. IV
Jones, Rev. Canon Richard E.; see Evan-Jones.
Jones, Richard Francis L.; see Lloyd Jones.
Jones, Lt-Col Richard Godfrey, 1855–1934, vol. III
Jones, Rev. Richard Thomas, died 1917, vol. II
Jones, Rt Rev. Richard William, died 1953, vol. V
Jones, Sir Robert, 1st Bt (cr 1926), 1858–1933, vol. III
Jones, Sir Robert Armstrong-, 1857–1943, vol. IV
Jones, Robert Edmond, 1887–1954, vol. V
Jones, Robert Noble, 1864–1942, vol. IV
Jones, Maj.-Gen. Robert Owen, 1837–1926, vol. II
Jones, Air Marshal Sir R(obert) Owen, 1901–1972, vol. VII
Jones, Robert Thomas, died 1940, vol. III
Jones, Robert Tyre, (Bobby), 1902–1971, vol. VII
Jones, Robert Walter, 1890–1951, vol. V
Jones, Sir Roderick, 1877–1962, vol. VI
Jones, Maj.-Gen. Roderick Idrisyn, 1895–1970, vol. VI
Jones, Comdr Ronald L.; see Langton-Jones.
Jones, Ronald Owen Lloyd A.; see Armstrong-Jones.
Jones, Royston Oscar, 1925–1974, col. VII
Jones, Rufus M., 1863–1948, vol. IV
Jones, Rev. S. M.; see Martin-Jones.
Jones, S. Maurice, died 1932, vol. III
Jones, Share; see Jones, J. S.
Jones, Siriol (Mary Aprille) H.; see Hugh-Jones.
Jones, Rev. Spencer John, 1857–1943, vol. IV
Jones, Stanley Wilson, 1888–1962, vol. VI
Jones, Sir Sydney; see Jones, Sir C. S.
Jones, Hon. Sydney Twentyman, 1849–1913, vol. I
Jones, Sir T. Barry, 2nd Bt (cr 1917), 1888–1952, vol. V
Jones, Col Theophilus Percy, 1866–1934, vol. III
Jones, Rev. Thomas, 1839–1927, vol. II
Jones, Sir Thomas, 1870–1945, vol. IV
Jones, Thomas, 1870–1955, vol. V
Jones, Captain Thomas Alban, 1869–1945, vol. IV
Jones, Sir Thomas Artemus, died 1943, vol. IV
Jones, Thomas Boughton B.; see Bovell-Jones.
Jones, Rt Rev. Thomas Edward, 1903–1972, vol. VII
Jones, Sir Thomas George, 1881–1948, vol. IV
Jones, Thomas Gwynn, 1871–1949, vol. IV
Jones, Thomas Isaac M.; see Mardy Jones.
Jones, Rev. Thomas Jesse, died 1930, vol. III
Jones, Sir Thomas M.; see Miller-Jones.
Jones, Thomas Rees, 1863–1938, vol. III
Jones, Thomas Ridge, 1840–1924, vol. II
Jones, Thomas Rupert, 1819–1911, vol. I
Jones, Rt Rev. Thomas Sherwood, 1872–1972, vol. VII
Jones, Sir Tom Barry; see Jones, Sir T. Barry.
Jones, Tom Neville W.; see Wynne-Jones.
Jones, Sir Tracy French Gavin, 1872–1953, vol. V

Jones, Vernon Stanley V.; see Vernon-Jones.
Jones, Sir Vincent Strickland, 1874–1967, vol. VI
Jones, W. Lewis, 1866–1922, vol. II
Jones, Walter, 1846–1924, vol. II
Jones, Sir Walter Benton, 2nd Bt (cr 1919), 1880–1967, vol. VI
Jones, Lt-Col Walter Dally, 1855–1926, vol. II
Jones, Lt-Col Walter H.; see Howel-Jones.
Jones, Walter L.; see Lindley-Jones.
Jones, Captain Walter Henry Clulee, 1899–1932, vol. III
Jones, W(alter) Idris, 1900–1971, vol. VII
Jones, Lt-Col Walter Thomas Cresswell, 1874–1923, vol. II
Jones, Wendell Phillips, 1866–1944, vol. IV
Jones, William, died 1915, vol. I
Jones, Sir William, 1888–1961, vol. VI
Jones, William Brittain, 1834–1912, vol. I
Jones, Rev. William David, 1909–1976, vol. VII
Jones, Very Rev. William Edward, 1897–1974, vol. VII
Jones, William Ernest, 1867–1957, vol. V (A)
Jones, (William) Ernest, 1895–1973, vol. VII
Jones, William Everard Tyldesley, 1874–1938, vol. III
Jones, Rev. William G.; see Griffith-Jones.
Jones, William Garmon, 1884–1937, vol. III
Jones, Hon. Sir William H.; see Hall-Jones.
Jones, William Henry, 1873–1944, vol. IV
Jones, Sir William Henry H.; see Hyndman-Jones.
Jones, William Henry Samuel, 1876–1963, vol. VI
Jones, Sir William Hollingworth Quayle, 1854–1925, vol. II
Jones, Rev. William Hudson M.; see Macnaughton-Jones.
Jones, William Hugh, 1866–1960, vol. V
Jones, William Jenkyn, 1867–1934, vol. III
Jones, Sir William John, 1866–1938, vol. III
Jones, Sir (William John) Andrew, 1889–1971, vol. VII
Jones, William Llewellyn, 1881–1950, vol. IV
Jones, William Morris, 1889–1963, vol. VI
Jones, Lt-Col William Nathaniel, 1858–1934, vol. III
Jones, William Neilson, 1883–1974, vol. VII
Jones, William Richard, 1880–1970, vol. VI
Jones, Rt Rev. William S.; see Stanton-Jones.
Jones, Sir William Samuel G.; see Glyn-Jones.
Jones, William Sydney, 1888–1959, vol. V
Jones, William Thorpe, 1864–1932, vol. III
Jones, William Tudor, 1865–1946, vol. IV
Jones, Most Rev. William West, died 1908, vol. I
Jones, Rt Rev. William Wynn, 1900–1950, vol. IV
Jones, Sir William Y.; see Yarworth-Jones.
Jones, Wood; see Jones, F. W.
Jones-Davies, Henry, 1870–1955, vol. V
Jones Mitton, Col George, 1860–1949, vol. IV
Jones-Parry, Rear-Adm. John Parry, 1829–1920, vol. II
Jones-Roberts, Kate Winifred, 1889–1971, vol. VII
Jones-Vaughan, Maj.-Gen. Hugh Thomas, 1841–1916, vol. II
Jonnart, Celestin Auguste, 1857–1927, vol. II

Jonsson, Einar, 1874–1954, vol. V
Jopling, Louise, 1843–1933, vol. III
Jopling-Rowe, Louise; see Jopling, Louise.
Jopp, Col John, 1940–1923, vol. II
Jopson, Sir Keith; see Jopson, Sir R. K.
Jopson, Norman Brooke, 1890–1969, vol. VI
Jopson, Sir (Reginald) Keith, 1898–1957, vol. V
Jordan, Alfred Charles, 1872–1956, vol. V
Jordan, David Starr, 1851–1931, vol. III
Jordan, Edwin Oakes, 1866–1926, vol. II (A), vol. III
Jordan, Elizabeth, died 1947, vol. IV
Jordan, Sir Frederick Richard, 1881–1949, vol. IV
Jordan, Rev. George, 1876–1936, vol. III
Jordan, H. E. Karl, 1861–1959, vol. V
Jordan, Helen; see Ashton, H.
Jordan, Herbert William, 1874–1947, vol. IV
Jordan, Humfrey Robertson, 1885–1963, vol. VI
Jordan, Rev. Canon James Henry, 1882–1959, vol. V
Jordan, Jeremiah, died 1911, vol. I
Jordan, Rt Hon. Sir John Newell, 1852–1925, vol. II
Jordan, Maj.-Gen. Joseph, 1826–1899, vol. I
Jordan, Karl; see Jordan, H. E. K.
Jordan, Louis Arnold, 1892–1964, vol. VI
Jordan, Rev. Louis Henry, 1855–1923, vol. II
Jordan, Philip Furneaux, 1902–1951, vol. V
Jordan, Lt-Col Richard Price, 1869–1963, vol. VI
Jordan, Sara M., (Mrs Penfield Mower), 1884–1959, vol. V
Jordan, Rev. W. G., 1852–1939, vol. III
Jordan, Wilbur Kitchener, 1902–1980, vol. VII
Jordan, William Edward, 1869–1938, vol. III
Jordan, William George, 1864–1928, vol. II
Jordan, Rt Hon. Sir William Joseph, died 1959, vol. V
Jordan Lloyd, Dorothy, 1889–1946, vol. IV
Jordan Malkin, Harold; see Malkin.
Jorden, John, died 1907, vol. I
Jory, Norman Adams, 1896–1965, vol. VI
Jory, Philip John, 1892–1973, vol. VII
Josa, Ven. Fortunato Pietro Luigi, 1851–1922, vol. II
Joscelyne, Rt Rev. Albert Ernest, 1866–1945, vol. IV
Jose, Captain Arthur Wilberforce, 1863–1934, vol. III
Jose, Very Rev. George Herbert, 1868–1956, vol. V
Jose, Sir Ivan Bede, 1893–1969, vol. VI (AII)
Joseph, Delissa, 1859–1927, vol. II
Joseph, Sir Francis L'Estrange, 1st Bt, 1870–1951, vol. V
Joseph, Horace William Brindley, 1867–1943, vol. IV
Joseph, Michael, 1897–1958, vol. V
Joseph, Rev. Morris, 1848–1930, vol. III
Joseph, Sir Norman; see Joseph, Sir S. N.
Joseph, Sir Samuel George, 1888–1944, vol. IV
Joseph, Sir (Samuel) Norman, 1908–1974, vol. VII
Joshi, Rev. Canon D. L., 1864–1923, vol. II
Joshi, Narayan Malhar, 1879–1955, vol. V
Joslin, David Maelgwyn, 1925–1970, vol. VI

Josselyn, Col John, 1872–1943, vol. IV
Joubert de la Ferte, Air Chief Marshal Sir Philip Bennet, *died* 1965, vol. VI
Jouhaux, Léon, 1879–1954, vol. V
Joulain, Rt Rev. Henry, 1852–1919, vol. II
Joules, Horace, 1902–1977, vol. VII
Jourdain, Lt-Col Charles Edward Arthur, 1869–1918, vol. II
Jourdain, Eleanor Frances, *died* 1924, vol. II
Jourdain, Rev. Francis C. R., *died* 1940, vol. III
Jourdain, Lt-Col Henry Francis Newdigate, 1872–1968, vol. VI
Jourdain, Sir Henry John, 1835–1901, vol. I
Jourdan, Rev. George Viviliers, *died* 1955, vol. V
Jowers, Reginald Francis, 1861–1937, vol. III
Jowett, Edmund, 1858–1936, vol. III
Jowett, Rt Hon. Frederick William, 1864–1944, vol. IV
Jowett, Rev. John Henry, 1864–1923, vol. II
Jowett, Percy Hague, 1882–1955, vol. V
Jowitt, 1st Earl, 1885–1957, vol. V
Jowitt, Frederick McCulloch, 1868–1919, vol. II
Jowitt, Harold, 1893–1963, vol. VI
Jowsey, Col Thomas, 1853–1934, vol. III
Joy, Albert B.; *see* Bruce-Joy.
Joy, David, *died* 1903, vol. I
Joy, Edith Katharine Spicer; *see* Prescott, E. Livingston.
Joy, Sir George Andrew, 1896–1974, vol. VII
Joy, George William, 1844–1925, vol. II
Joy, Henry Holmes, *died* 1934, vol. III
Joyce, Archibald, 1873–1963, vol. VI
Joyce, Rt Rev. Edward Michael, 1907–1964, vol. VI
Joyce, Rev. Frederick Wayland, 1852–1934, vol. III
Joyce, Rt Rev. Gilbert Cunningham, 1866–1942, vol. IV
Joyce, Maj.-Gen. Hayman John H.; *see* Hayman-Joyce.
Joyce, James, 1882–1941, vol. IV
Joyce, Rev. James Barclay, *died* 1934, vol. III
Joyce, Rt Hon. Sir Matthew Ingle, 1839–1930, vol. III
Joyce, Patrick Weston, 1827–1914, vol. I
Joyce, Lt-Col Pierce Charles, *died* 1965, vol. VI
Joyce, Rt Rev. Mgr T. J., *died* 1947, vol. IV
Joyce, Thomas Athol, 1878–1942, vol. IV
Joyce, Thomas Heath, 1850–1925, vol. II
Joyner, Robert Batson, 1844–1919, vol. II
Joynt, John William, 1852–1933, vol. III
Joynt, Rev. Robert Charles, 1856–1938, vol. III
Jubb, Edwin Charles, 1883–1978, vol. VII
Juda, Hans Peter, 1904–1975, vol. VII
Judd, Alfred, *died* 1932, vol. III
Judd, Charles Wilfred, 1896–1974, vol. VII
Judd, Sir George, 1840–1909, vol. I
Judd, George William, *born* 1854, vol. II
Judd, Harold Godfrey, 1878–1961, vol. VI
Judd, John Wesley, 1840–1916, vol. II
Judd, Thomas Langley, 1880–1945, vol. IV
Judd, Walter Albert, 1861–1931, vol. III
Jude, Sir Norman Lane, 1905–1975, vol. VII
Judge, Mark Hayler, 1847–1927, vol. II

Judge, Captain Spencer Francis, 1861–1911, vol. I
Judges, Arthur Valentine, 1898–1973, vol. VII
Judkins, Rev. Eimer, 1855–1940, vol. III
Judson, Harry Pratt, 1849–1927, vol. II
Jugmohandas Varjivandas, Sir, 1869–1934, vol. III
Juin, Alphonse Pierre, 1888–1967, vol. VI
Jukes, John Edwin Clapham, 1878–1955, vol. V
Jukes-Browne, Alfred John, 1851–1914, vol. I
Jukes Hughes, Captain Edward Glyn de Styrap, 1883–1966, vol. VI
Juler, Frank Anderson, 1880–1962, vol. VI
Juler, Henry Edward, *died* 1921, vol. II
Julian, Ernest Laurence, *died* 1915, vol. I (A)
Julian, Sir Ivor; *see* Julian, Sir K. I.
Julian, Rev. John, 1839–1913, vol. I
Julian, Sir (Kenneth) Ivor, 1895–1971, vol. VII
Julian, Maj.-Gen. Sir Oliver Richard Archer, 1863–1925, vol. II
Julius, Most Rev. Churchill, 1847–1938, vol. III
Julius, Sir George Alfred, 1873–1946, vol. IV
Julius, Very Rev. John Awdry, 1874–1956, vol. V
Jullian, Camille, 1859–1933, vol. III
Julyan, Sir Penrose Goodchild, 1816–1907, vol. I
Julyan, Lt-Col William Leopold, 1888–1972, vol. VII
Junagadh, Nawab Saheb of, 1900–1959, vol. V
Junagarh, HH Sir Rasul Khanji Muhabat Khanji, Nawab of, *died* 1911, vol. I
Jung, Carl Gustav, 1875–1961, vol. VI
Jupp, Rev. Canon, *died* 1911, vol. I
Jury, Col Edward Cotton, 1881–1966, vol. VI
Jury, Sir William Frederick, 1870–1944, vol. IV
Jusserand, Jean Adrien Antoine Jules, 1855–1932, vol. III
Just, Sir Hartmann, 1854–1929, vol. III
Justice, Maj.-Gen. Henry Annesley, 1832–1908, vol. I
Justice, James Norval Harald R.; *see* Robertson-Justice.
Justice, Maj.-Gen. William Clive, 1835–1908, vol. I
Juta, Sir Henry Hubert, 1857–1930, vol. III

K

Kadoorie, Sir Ellis, 1865–1922, vol. II
Kadoorie, Sir Elly, 1867–1944, vol. IV
Kagwa, Sir Apolo, *died* 1927, vol. II
Kahle, Paul Ernest, 1875–1964, vol. VI
Khan, Otto Hermann, 1867–1934, vol. III
Kahn-Freund, Sir Otto, 1900–1979, vol. VII
Kaine, Hon. John Charles, 1854–1921, vol. II
Kaiser, Henry J., 1882–1967, vol. VI
Kaiser Shamsher Jang Bahadur Rana, HH Commanding-Gen. Sir, 1892–1964, vol. VI
Kalat, Wali of, *died* 1931, vol. III
Kalat, HH Sir Beglar Begi Nawab Bahadur Mir Azam Jan, *died* 1933, vol. III
Kalergi, Richard N. C.; *see* Coudenhove-Kalergi.
Kalinin, Mikhail Ivanovich, 1875–1946, vol. IV
Kalisch, Alfred, 1863–1933, vol. III

Kallas, Madame Aino Julia Maria, *died* 1956, vol. V

Kallas, Oskar Philipp, 1868–1946, vol. IV

Kalmus, Herbert Thomas, 1881–1963, vol. VI

Kamâl, Gazi Mustafa; *see* Atatürk, K.

Kamal-ud-Din, Khwaja, 1870–1932, vol. III

Kamat, B. S., 1871–1945, vol. IV

Kambal, Miralai (Col) Beshir Bey, 1855–1919, vol. II

Kamphausen, Adolf Hermann Heinrich, 1829–1909, vol. I

Kandathil, Most Rev. Augustine, 1874–1956, vol. V

Kandel, Isaac Leon, 1881–1965, vol. VI

Kane, Albert Edmond, 1867–1949, vol. IV

Kane, Edward William, *died* 1934, vol. III

Kane, Adm. Sir Henry Coey, 1843–1917, vol. II

Kane, Robert Romney, 1842–1902, vol. I

Kane, Captain Robert Romney Godred, 1888–1918, vol. II

Kane, William Francis de Vismes, 1840–1918, vol. II

Kania, Hon. Sir Harilal Jekisundas, 1890–1951, vol. V

Kanika, Raja of, 1881–1948, vol. IV

Kantaraj Urs, Sir M., 1870–1923, vol. II

Kanthack, Alfred Antunes, 1863–1898, vol. I

Kanthack, Francis Edgar, 1872–1961, vol. VI

Kantorowicz, Hermann, 1877–1940, vol. III

Kapadia, Shaporji Aspaniarji, 1857–1941, vol. IV

Kapp, Edmond X., 1890–1978, vol. VII

Kapp, Gisbert, *died* 1922, vol. II

Kapp, Helen, 1907–1978, vol. VII

Kapp, Reginald Otto, 1885–1966, vol. VI

Kapurthala, HH Maharajah Raja-i-Rajgan of, 1872–1949, vol. IV

Karanjia, Sir Behram Narosji, 1876–1957, vol. V

Karauli, HH Maharaja Dhiraj Sir Bhanwar Pal, Deo Bahadur, Yadukul Chandra Bhal, 1864–1927, vol. II

Karauli, Maharaja of, HH Maharaja Sir Bhom Pal Deo Bahadur Yadukul Chandra Bhal, 1866–1947, vol. IV

Karkaria, R. P., 1869–1919, vol. II

Karloff, Boris, (William Henry Pratt), 1887–1969, vol. VI

Karminski, Rt Hon. Sir Seymour Edward, 1902–1974, vol. VII

Karn, Frederick James, 1862–1940, vol. III

Karney, Rt Rev. Arthur Baillie Lumsdaine, 1874–1963, vol. VI

Karr, Sir Henry S.; *see* Seton-Karr.

Karr, Heywood Walter S.; *see* Seton-Karr.

Karrer, Paul, 1889–1971, vol. VII

Karsavina, Tamara, (Mrs H. J. Bruce), 1885–1978, vol. VII

Karslake, Lt-Gen. Sir Henry, 1879–1942, vol. IV

Karslake, Lt-Col John Burgess Preston, 1868–1942, vol. IV

Karslake, Sir William Wollaston, 1834–1913, vol. I

Karve, Dattatreya Gopal, 1898–1967, vol. VI

Kashmir and Jammu, Lt-Gen. HH Maharaja of, 1850–1925, vol. II

Kasimbazar, Maharaja of, 1860–1929, vol. III

Kästner, Erich, 1899–1974, vol. VII

Kastner, L. E., *died* 1940, vol. III

Katchen, Julius, 1926–1969, vol. VI

Katenga, Bridger Winston, 1926–1975, vol. VII

Kater, Sir Gregory Blaxland, 1912–1978, vol. VII

Kater, Hon. Sir Norman William, 1874–1965, vol. VI

Kato, Viscount Takaaki, 1860–1926, vol. II

Kato, Adm. Baron Tomosaburo, 1859–1923, vol. II

Katrak, Khan Bahadur Sir Kavasji Hormusji, *died* 1946, vol. IV

Katsura, Gen. Marquess Taro, 1847–1913, vol. I

Katz, Mindru, 1925–1978, vol. VII

Kauffer, Edward McKnight, *died* 1954, vol. V

Kaufman, George S., 1889–1961, vol. VI

Kaufmann, Rev. Moritz, 1839–1920, vol. II

Kaula, Sir Ganga, 1877–1970, vol. VI

Kaulbach, Ven. James Albert, 1839–1913, vol. II

Kauntze, William Henry, 1887–1947, vol. IV

Kautsky, Karl, 1854–1938, vol. III

Kavan, Anna, *died* 1968, vol. VI

Kavanagh, Lt-Gen. Sir Charles Toler McMurrough, 1864–1950, vol. IV

Kavanagh, Col Sir Dermot M.; *see* McMorrough Kavanagh.

Kavanagh, Lt-Col Edward James, 1881–1940, vol. III

Kavanagh, Patrick, 1905–1967, vol. VI

Kavanagh, Rt Hon. Walter MacMurrough, 1856–1922, vol. II

Kay, Archibald, 1860–1935, vol. III

Kay, Arthur, *died* 1939, vol. III

Kay, Arthur William, 1904–1970, vol. VI

Kay, Sir Brook, 4th Bt, 1820–1907, vol. I

Kay, Rev. D. Miller, *died* 1930, vol. III

Kay, Rt Hon. Sir Edward Ebenezer, 1822–1897, vol. I

Kay, Harold Isherwood, 1893–1938, vol. III

Kay, Sir Herbert, 1879–1957, vol. V

Kay, Herbert Davenport, 1893–1976, vol. VII

Kay, James, 1858–1942, vol. IV

Kay, Sir James Reid, 1885–1965, vol. VI

Kay, Sir Joseph Aspden, 1884–1958, vol. V

Kay, Katharine Cameron, *died* 1965, vol. VI

Kay, Ven. Kenneth, 1902–1958, vol. V

Kay, Sir Robert Newbald, 1869–1947, vol. IV

Kay, Sydney Entwisle, 1888–1978, vol. VII

Kay, Thomas, *died* 1938, vol. III

Kay, Sir William, 1868–1955, vol. V

Kay, Very Rev. William, 1894–1980, vol. VII

Kay, Sir William Algernon, 5th Bt, 1837–1914, vol. I

Kay, Lt-Col Sir William Algernon Ireland, 6th Bt, 1876–1918, vol. II

Kay, Maj.-Gen. William Heape, 1871–1929, vol. III

Kay, Col William Martin, 1871–1948, vol. IV (A), vol. V

Kay-Mouat, John Richard, 1881–1952, vol. V

Kay-Shuttleworth, Edward James, 1890–1917, vol. II

Kay-Shuttleworth, Hon. Lawrence Ughtred, 1887–1917, vol. II

Kaye, Lt-Col Sir Cecil, 1868–1935, vol. III

Kaye, Sir Cecil Edmund L.; see Lister-Kaye.
Kaye, Cecil William 1865–1941, vol. IV
Kaye, George William Clarkson, 1880–1941, vol. IV
Kaye, Captain and Flt Comdr Sir Henry Gordon, 2nd Bt, 1889–1956, vol. V
Kaye, Lt-Col James Levett, 1861–1917, vol. II
Kaye, Sir John Pepys L.; see Lister-Kaye.
Kaye, Sir Joseph H., 1st Bt, 1856–1923, vol. II
Kaye, Sir Kenelm Arthur L.; see Lister-Kaye.
Kaye, Levett Mackenzie, 1869–1941, vol. IV
Kaye, Sir Lister L.; see Lister-Kaye.
Kaye, Ven. Martin, 1919–1977, vol. VII
Kaye, Col Ralph Arthur, 1863–1933, vol. III
Kaye, Robert Walter, 1871–1957, vol. V
Kaye, Ven. William Frederick John, died 1913, vol. I
Kaye, Sir William Squire Barker, 1831–1901, vol. I
Kaye-Smith, Sheila, died 1956, vol. V
Kays, Brig.-Gen. Horace Francis, 1861–1945, vol. IV
Kays, Brig.-Gen. Walpole Swinton, 1858–1941, vol. IV
Kayser, Charles William, 1870–1947, vol. IV
Kazanjian, Varaztad Hovhannes, 1879–1974, vol. VII
Keable, Robert, 1887–1927, vol. II
Kealy, Sir (Edward) Herbert, 1873–1953, vol. V
Kealy, Sir Herbert; see Kealy, Sir E. H.
Kean, Captain Abraham, 1855–1945, vol. IV
Kean, Oscar, 1875–1961, vol. VI
Kean, Thomas Alban, 1894–1968, vol. VI (AII)
Keane, Augustus Henry, 1833–1912, vol. I
Keane, Charles Alexander, died 1931, vol. III
Keane, Most Rev. David, 1871–1945, vol. IV
Keane, Major Gerald Joseph, 1880–1943, vol. IV
Keane, Lt-Col Sir John, 5th Bt, 1873–1956, vol. V
Keane, John Fryer Thomas, 1854–1937, vol. III
Keane, Sir Michael, 1874–1937, vol. III
Keane, Lt-Col Richard Henry, 1881–1925, vol. II
Kearney, Very Rev. Alexander Major, died 1912, vol. I
Kearney, Count Cecil; see Kearney, R. C. J. P.
Kearney, Elfric Wells Chalmers, 1881–1966, vol. VI
Kearney, Sir Francis Edgar, 1870–1938, vol. III
Kearney, Robert Cecil Joseph Patrick, (Count Cecil Kearney), died 1911, vol. I
Kearns, Sir (Henry Ward) Lionel, 1891–1962, vol. VI
Kearns, Sir Lionel; see Kearns, Sir H. W. L.
Kearns, Rev. John Willis, died 1962, vol. VI
Kearns, Major Reginald Arthur Ernest Holmes, died 1918, vol. II
Kearns, Col Thomas Joseph, 1861–1920, vol. II
Kearsley, Brig.-Gen. Sir Harvey; see Kearsley, Brig.-Gen. Sir R. H.
Kearsley, Brig.-Gen. Sir (Robert) Harvey, 1880–1956, vol. V
Kearton, Cherry, 1871–1940, vol. III
Kearton, Richard, 1862–1928, vol. II
Kearton, William Johnston, 1893–1978, vol. VII
Keary, Charles F., died 1917, vol. II
Keary, Lt-Gen. Sir Henry D'Urban, 1857–1937, vol. III

Keary, Peter, 1865–1915, vol. I
Keating, Most Rev. Frederick William, 1859–1928, vol. II
Keating, Brig. Harold John Buckler, 1893–1970, vol. VI (AII)
Keating, John, (Seán Céitinn), 1889–1977, vol. VII
Keating, Rev. John Fitzstephen, 1850–1911, vol. I
Keating, Hon. John Henry, 1872–1940, vol. III
Keating, Joseph, 1871–1934, vol. III
Keating, Rev. Joseph Ignatius, 1865–1939, vol. III
Keating, Matthew, 1869–1937, vol. III
Keating, Paul John Geoffrey, 1924–1980, vol. VII
Keatinge, Gerald Francis, 1872–1965, vol. VI
Keatinge, Henry Pottinger, 1860–1928, vol. II
Keatinge, Maurice Walter, 1868–1935, vol. III
Keatinge, Gen. Richard Harte, 1825–1904, vol. I
Keatinge, Richard Herbert, 1911–1968, vol. VI
Keatinge, Rt Rev. William Lewis, 1869–1934, vol. III
Keay, Herbert O., 1875–1958, vol. V
Keay, James Donald, died 1933, vol. III
Keay, Lt-Col John, died 1943, vol. IV
Keay, Sir John, 1894–1964, vol. VI
Keay, John Seymour, 1839–1909, vol. I
Keay, Sir Lancelot Herman, 1883–1974, vol. VII
Keble, Col Alfred Ernest Conquer, 1869–1940, vol. III
Kebty-Fletcher, J., 1868–1918, vol. II
Keck, Thomas Charles Leycester P.; see Powys-Keck.
Kedarnath Das, Sir, 1867–1936, vol. III
Keddie, Henrietta, (Sarah Tytler), 1827–1914, vol. I
Keddie, Col Herbert William Graham, 1873–1943, vol. IV
Kedward, Rev. Roderick Morris, 1881–1937, vol. III
Keeble, Sir Frederick William, 1870–1952, vol. V
Keeble, Lillah, (Lady Keeble); see McCarthy, L.
Keefe, Sir Ronald Barry, 1901–1967, vol. VI
Keefer, Thomas Coltrin, 1821–1915, vol. I
Keegan, Lt-Col Herbert Leo, 1888–1937, vol. III
Keel, James Frederick, 1871–1954, vol. V
Keel, Jonathan Edgar, 1895–1979, vol. VII
Keelan, Percival Stanley, 1875–1950, vol. IV(A)
Keeling, (Cyril) Desmond (Evans), 1921–1979, vol. VII
Keeling, Desmond; see Keeling, C. D. E.
Keeling, Edward Allis, 1885–1975, vol. VII
Keeling, Sir Edward Herbert, died 1954, vol. V
Keeling, Sir Hugh Trowbridge, died 1955, vol. V
Keeling, Sir John Henry, 1895–1978, vol. VII
Keeling, Thomas, 1882–1963, vol. VI
Keeling, Rev. William Hulton, 1840–1916, vol. II
Keeling, Rev. William Theodore, 1871–1946, vol. IV
Keen, Archibald, 1860–1932, vol. III
Keen, Arthur, died 1915, vol. I
Keen, Austin, died 1922, vol. II
Keen, Frank Noel, 1869–1957, vol. V
Keen, Frederick Grinham; see Kerr, Frederick.
Keen, Col Sir Frederick John, 1834–1902, vol. I
Keen, Col Frederick Stewart, 1874–1949, vol. IV
Keen, Gregory Bernard, 1844–1930, vol. III

Keen, Col John Fred, 1881–1949, vol. IV
Keen, Brig. Patrick Houston, 1877–1954, vol. V
Keen, Col Sidney, 1868–1941, vol. IV
Keen, Lt-Col William John, died 1958, vol. V
Keen, William Williams, 1837–1932, vol. III
Keenan, Margaret Helen, 1869–1939, vol. III
Keenan, Hon. Sir Norbert, 1866–1954, vol. V
Keenan, William, died 1955, vol. V
Keene, Col Alfred, 1855–1918, vol. II
Keene, Charles James, 1850–1917, vol. II
Keene, Sir Charles Robert, 1891–1977, vol. VII
Keene, Henry George, 1825–1915, vol. I
Keene, Most Rev. James Bennett, 1849–1919, vol. II
Keene, James Robert, 1838–1913, vol. I
Keene, Mary Frances Lucas, died 1977, vol. VII
Keene, Vice-Adm. Philip R.; see Ruck Keene.
Keene, William, 1851–1920, vol. II
Keene, Adm. William George Elmhirst Ruck, 1867–1935, vol. III
Keens, Sir Thomas, 1870–1953, vol. V
Keep, Arthur Corrie, 1861–1940, vol. III
Keesey, Walter Monckton, 1887–1970, vol. VI
Keesing, Felix Maxwell, 1902–1961, vol. VI
Keetley, Charles Robert Bell, died 1909, vol. I
Keeton, George Haydn, 1878–1949, vol. IV
Keeton, Haydn, 1847–1921, vol. II
Keevil, Col Sir Ambrose, 1893–1973, vol. VII
Kefauver, Estes, 1903–1963, vol. VI
Keflegzi, Gabre-Mascal, 1917–1969, vol. VI
Kehoe, Miles, died 1907, vol. I
Keighley, Col Charles Marsh, 1847–1911, vol. I
Keighley, Lt-Col Vernon Aubrey Scott, 1874–1939, vol. III
Keighly-Peach, Adm. Charles William, 1865–1943, vol. IV
Keightley, Gen. Sir Charles Frederic, 1901–1974, vol. VII
Keightley, Sir Samuel Robert, 1859–1949, vol. IV
Keigwin, Richard Prescott, 1883–1972, vol. VII
Keilin, David, died 1963, vol. VI
Keiller, Brian Edwin, 1901–1977, vol. VII
Keily, Maj.-Gen. Frederick Peter Charles, 1870–1938, vol. III
Keily, Rt Rev. John, 1854–1928, vol. II
Keir, Sir David Lindsay, 1895–1973, vol. VII
Keir, Lt-Gen. Sir John Lindesay, 1856–1937, vol. III
Keir, Surg. Rear-Adm. William Wallace, 1876–1949, vol. IV
Keirstead, Burton Seely, 1907–1973, vol. VII
Keirstead, Wilfred Currier, 1871–1944, vol. IV
Keith of Avonholm, Baron (Life Peer); James Keith, 1886–1964, vol. VI
Keith, Alexander Milne, 1886–1967, vol. VI
Keith, Rev. Canon Archibald Leslie, 1871–1956, vol. V
Keith, Sir Arthur, 1866–1955, vol. V
Keith, Arthur Berriedale, 1879–1944, vol. IV
Keith, Edward John, 1908–1968, vol. VI
Keith, George Skene, 1819–1910, vol. I
Keith, Sir Henry Shanks, 1852–1944, vol. IV
Keith, Col James, 1842–1919, vol. II
Keith, James, 1879–1953, vol. V

Keith, Leslie; see Johnston, Grace L. Keith.
Keith, Skene, 1858–1919, vol. II
Keith, Sir William John, 1873–1937, vol. III
Keith-Roach, Edward, 1885–1954, vol. V
Kekewich, Rt Hon. Sir Arthur, 1832–1907, vol. I
Kekewich, Sir George William, 1841–1921, vol. II
Kekewich, Rear-Adm. Piers Keane, 1889–1967, vol. VI
Kekewich, Maj.-Gen. Robert George, 1854–1914, vol. I
Kekewich, Sir Trehawke Herbert, 1st Bt, 1851–1932, vol. III
Kekwick, Alan, 1909–1974, vol. VII
Kelcey, Air Vice-Marshal Alick F.; see Foord-Kelcey.
Kelham, Brig.-Gen. Henry Robert, 1853–1931, vol. III
Kelk, Sir John William, 2nd Bt, 1851–1923, vol. II
Kell, Maj.-Gen. Sir Vernon George Waldegrave, 1873–1942, vol. IV
Kelland, Sir John; see Kelland, Sir P. J. L.
Kelland, Sir (Percy) John (Luxton), died 1958, vol. V
Kellar, Robert James, died 1980, vol. VII
Kellas, A. M., died 1921, vol. II
Kellaway, Charles Halliley, 1889–1952, vol. V
Kellaway, Rt Hon. Frederick George, 1870–1933, vol. III
Kelleher, Stephen B., 1875–1917, vol. II
Keller, Adolf, 1872–1963, vol. VI
Keller, Helen Adams, 1880–1968, vol. VI
Keller, Hon. John; see Keller, Hon. L. J. W.
Keller, Hon. (Laurence) John Walter, 1885–1959, vol. V
Keller, Maj.-Gen. Rodney Frederick Leopold, 1900–1954, vol. V
Kellett, Adelaide Maud, died 1945, vol. IV
Kellett, Lt-Col Edward Orlando, 1902–1943, vol. IV
Kellett, Ernest Edward, 1864–1950, vol. IV
Kellett, Maj.-Gen. Gerald, 1905–1973, vol. VII
Kellett, Sir Henry de Castres, 3rd Bt, 1851–1924, vol. II
Kellett, Sir Henry de Castres, 4th Bt, 1882–1966, vol. VI
Kellett, Sir Henry de Castres, 5th Bt, 1914–1966, vol. VI
Kellett, Col John Philip, 1890–1959, vol. V
Kellett, Maj.-Gen. Richard Orlando, 1864–1931, vol. III
Kelley, Major Sir Frederic Arthur, 1863–1926, vol. II
Kelley, Howard G., 1858–1928, vol. II
Kellie, Lawrence, 1862–1932, vol. III
Kellock, Hon. Roy Lindsay, 1893–1975, vol. VII
Kellock, Thomas Herbert, 1863–1922, vol. II
Kellogg, Frank Billings, 1856–1937, vol. III
Kelly, Annie Elizabeth, died 1946, vol. IV
Kelly, Major Arthur Dillon Denis, The O'Kelly, 1853–1936, vol. III
Kelly, Brig.-Gen. Arthur James, 1857–1930, vol. III
Kelly, Charles, 1815–1905, vol. I
Kelly, Rev. Charles H., 1833–1911, vol. I

Kelly, Col Courtenay Russell, 1872–1945, vol. IV
Kelly, Sir Dalziel; see Kelly, Sir G. D.
Kelly, Sir David Victor, 1891–1959, vol. V
Kelly, Rt Rev. Denis, 1852–1924, vol. II
Kelly, Edward Festus, 1854–1939, vol. III
Kelly, Brig. Edward Henry, 1883–1963, vol. VI
Kelly, Dame Elisabeth Hariott, died 1962, vol. VI
Kelly, Francis, 1868–1939, vol. III
Kelly, Maj.-Gen. Francis Henry, 1859–1937, vol. III
Kelly, Francis Michael, 1879–1945, vol. IV
Kelly, Frederick Septimus, 1881–1916, vol. II
Kelly, Brig. George Alexander, 1888–1973, vol. VII
Kelly, Maj.-Gen. George Charles, 1880–1938, vol. III
Kelly, Sir (George) Dalziel, 1891–1953, vol. V
Kelly, Sir Gerald Festus, 1879–1972, vol. VII
Kelly, Major Henry, died 1960, vol. V
Kelly, Brig.-Gen. Henry Edward Theodore, 1870–1932, vol. III
Kelly, Sir Henry G.; see Greene Kelly.
Kelly, Rev. Herbert Hamilton, 1860–1950, vol. IV
Kelly, Adm. Sir Howard; see Kelly, Adm. Sir W. A. H.
Kelly, Howard Atwood, 1858–1943, vol. IV
Kelly, Captain Hubert Dunsterville Harvey-, 1891–1917, vol. II
Kelly, Hon. Hugh Thomas, 1858–1945, vol. IV
Kelly, Captain James Alphonse Mari Joseph Patrick, 1875–1909, vol. I
Kelly, Rev. James Davenport, 1828–1912, vol. I
Kelly, James Gerald, 1897–1942, vol. IV
Kelly, Col James Graves, 1843–1923, vol. II
Kelly, John, vol. II
Kelly, Admiral of the Fleet Sir John Donald, 1871–1936, vol. III
Kelly, Lt-Col John Sherwood-, 1880–1931, vol. III
Kelly, Major John Upton, 1882–1943, vol. IV
Kelly, John William, 1885–1966, vol. VI
Kelly, Sir Malachy, 1850–1916, vol. II
Kelly, Mark Jamestown, 1848–1916, vol. II
Kelly, Mervin J., 1894–1971, vol. VII
Kelly, Most Rev. Michael, 1850–1940, vol. III
Kelly, Sir Patrick Aloysius, 1880–1966, vol. VI
Kelly, Lt-Surg. Peter Burrowes, 1888–1920, vol. II
Kelly, Brig.-Gen. Philip James Vandeleur, died 1948, vol. IV
Kelly, Hon. Sir Raymond; see Kelly, Hon. Sir W. R.
Kelly, Richard Barrett Talbot, 1896–1971, vol. VII
Kelly, Sir Richard Denis, (The O'Kelly Mor), 1815–1897, vol. I
Kelly, Richard John, died 1931, vol. III
Kelly, Brig.-Gen. Richard Makdougall Brisbane Francis, 1857–1915, vol. I
Kelly, R. Talbot, 1861–1934, vol. III
Kelly, Robert Alsop, 1881–1950, vol. IV
Kelly, Sir Robert Ernest, 1879–1944, vol. IV
Kelly, Sir Robert McErlean, 1902–1971, vol. VII
Kelly, Sir Samuel, died 1937, vol. III
Kelly, Sir Stanley Anthony Hill, 1869–1949, vol. IV
Kelly, Rev. Thomas, died 1926, vol. II
Kelly, Sir Thomas, 1862–1947, vol. IV

Kelly, Thomas Dwyer, 1880–1949, vol. IV
Kelly, Lt-Col Thomas Francis Henry, 1899–1940, vol. III
Kelly, Air Vice-Marshal Thomas James, 1890–1967, vol. VI
Kelly, Col Tom, 1869–1965, vol. VI
Kelly, William, died 1944, vol. IV
Kelly, Adm. Sir (William Archibald) Howard, 1873–1952, vol. V
Kelly, Rt Rev. William Bernard, 1855–1921, vol. II
Kelly, Lt-Gen. Sir William Freeman, 1847–1914, vol. I
Kelly, Captain William Henry, 1873–1941, vol. IV
Kelly, Hon. Sir (William) Raymond, 1898–1956, vol. V
Kelly, William Thomas, 1874–1944, vol. IV
Kelly-Kenny, Gen. Sir Thomas, 1840–1914, vol. I
Kelman, Rev. John, 1864–1929, vol. III
Kelsey, Vice-Adm. Marcel Harcourt Attwood, 1894–1964, vol. VI
Kelso, Maj.-Gen. John Edward U.; see Utterson-Kelso.
Kelson, William Henry, 1862–1940, vol. III
Keltie, Sir John Scott, 1840–1927, vol. II
Kelvin, 1st Baron, 1824–1907, vol. I
Kelway, Albert Clifton, 1865–1952, vol. V
Kelynack, Theo. N., 1866–1944, vol. IV
Kemball, Gen. Sir Arnold Burrowes, 1820–1908, vol. I
Kemball, Col Arnold Henry Grant, 1861–1917, vol. II
Kemball, Lt-Col Charles Arnold, 1860–1943, vol. IV
Kemball, Christopher Gurdon, 1899–1969, vol. VI
Kemball, Maj.-Gen. Sir George Vero, 1859–1941, vol. IV
Kemball-Cook, Sir Basil Alfred; see Cook.
Kemmis, Lt-Col William, 1861–1932, vol. III
Kemmis Betty, Vice-Adm. Arthur, 1877–1961, vol. VI
Kemmis Betty, Lt-Col Paget, 1876–1948, vol. IV
Kemnal, Sir James, 1864–1927, vol. II
Kemp, Hon. Sir (Albert) Edward, 1858–1929, vol. III
Kemp, Dixon, 1839–1899, vol. I
Kemp, Hon. Sir Edward; see Kemp, Hon. Sir A. E.
Kemp, Sir Ernest, 1870–1938, vol. III
Kemp, Rev. Frederick James, 1885–1943, vol. IV
Kemp, Brig.-Gen. Geoffrey Chicheley, 1868–1936, vol. III
Kemp, Maj.-Gen. Geoffrey Chicheley, 1890–1976, vol. VII
Kemp, Henry Thomas, 1852–1943, vol. IV
Kemp, Sir John, 1883–1955, vol. V
Kemp, Sir Joseph Horsford, 1874–1950, vol. IV
Kemp, Sir Kenneth Hagar, 12th Bt, 1853–1936, vol. III
Kemp, Sir Kenneth McIntrye, 1883–1949, vol. IV
Kemp, Sir Norman Wright, died 1937, vol. III
Kemp, Stanley Wells, 1882–1945, vol. IV
Kemp, Stephen, 1849–1918, vol. II
Kemp, Thomas R., 1836–1905, vol. I
Kemp, Adm. Thomas Webster, died 1928, vol. II

Kemp-Welch, Lucy Elizabeth, *died* 1958, vol. V
Kemp-Welch, Margaret, *died* 1968, vol. VI
Kemp-Welch, Brig.-Gen. Martin, 1885–1951, vol. V
Kempe, Sir Alfred Bray, 1849–1922, vol. II
Kempe, Charles Eamer, 1837–1907, vol. I
Kempe, Rev. Edward Wood, 1844–1918, vol. II
Kempe, Lt-Col Frederick Hawke, *died* 1954, vol. V
Kempe, Harry Robert, 1852–1935, vol. III
Kempe, Sir John Arrow, 1846–1928, vol. II
Kempe, Rev. John Edward, 1810–1907, vol. I
Kempe, Rudolf, 1910–1976, vol. VII
Kempling, William Bailey, *died* 1941, vol. IV
Kempson, Rt Rev. Edwin Hone, 1862–1931, vol. III
Kempson, Eric William Edward, *died* 1948, vol. IV
Kempster, Christopher Richard, 1869–1948, vol. IV
Kempster, Col Francis James, 1855–1925, vol. II
Kempster, Lt-Col Herbert William, *died* 1944, vol. IV
Kempster, John Westbeech, 1864–1947, vol. IV
Kempthorne, Lt-Col Gerard Ainslie, 1876–1939, vol. III
Kempthorne, Rt Rev. John Augustine, 1864–1946, vol. IV
Kempthorne, Rt Rev. Leonard Stanley, 1886–1963, vol. VI
Kempton, Charles Leslie, *died* 1965, vol. VI
Kemsley, 1st Viscount, 1883–1968, vol. VI
Kemsley, Col Sir Colin Norman T.; *see* Thornton-Kemsley.
Kenchington, Brig. Arthur George, 1890–1966, vol. VI
Kendal, Dame Madge Grimston, 1849–1935, vol. III
Kendal, Sir Norman, 1880–1966, vol. VI
Kendal, William Hunter, 1843–1917, vol. II
Kendall, Anthony Colin, 1898–1967, vol. VI
Kendall, Arthur Wallis, 1904–1975, vol. VII
Kendall, Sir Charles Henry Bayley, 1878–1935, vol. III
Kendall, Captain Charles James Cope, 1864–1943, vol. IV
Kendall, Edward Calvin, 1886–1972, vol. VII
Kendall, Col Ernest Arthur, 1876–1938, vol. III
Kendall, Guy, 1876–1960, vo V
Kendall, H. Bickerstaffe, 1844–1919, vol. II
Kendall, Henry, 1897–1962, vol. VI
Kendall, Rev. Henry Ewing, 1888–1963, vol. VI
Kendall, James, 1889–1978, vol. VII
Kendall, John David, 1893–1936, vol. III
Kendall, Rev. John Francis, 1862–1931, vol. III
Kendall, Major John Kaye, *died* 1952, vol. V
Kendall, Katherine Githa; *see* Sowerby, K.G.
Kendall, Percy Fry, 1856–1936, vol. III
Kendall, Maj.-Gen. Roy, 1897–1963, vol. VI
Kendall, Lt-Col Sydney Robert Gordon, 1879–1959, vol. V
Kendall, William Henry, *died* 1951, vol. V
Kenderdine, Sir Charles Halstaff, 1866–1936, vol. III
Kendon, Frank, 1893–1959, vol. V
Kendrew, Hubert, 1894–1966, vol. VI

Kendrew, Wilfrid George, *died* 1962, vol. VI
Kendrick, Albert Frank, 1872–1954, vol. V
Kendrick, Sydney Percy, 1874–1955, vol. V
Kendrick, Sir Thomas Downing, 1895–1979, vol. VII
Kenealy, Alexander, 1864–1915, vol. I
Kenealy, Most Rev. Anselm E. J., 1864–1943 vol. IV
Kenealy, Arabella, *died* 1938, vol. III
Kenealy, Noel Byron, *died* 1918, vol. II
Kenilworth, 1st Baron, 1866–1953, vol. V
Kenilworth, 2nd Baron, 1894–1971, vol. VII
Kenmare, 4th Earl of, 1825–1905, vol. I
Kenmare, 5th Earl of 1860–1941, vol. IV
Kenmare, 6th Earl of, 1891–1943, vol. IV
Kenmare, 7th Earl of, 1896–1952, vol. V
Kenna, Col Paul Aloysius, 1862–1915, vol. I
Kennan, George, 1845–1924, vol. II
Kennan, John Melville, 1904–1960, vol. V
Kennan, Thomas Brereton, 1891–1965, vol. VI
Kennard, Adam Steinmetz, 1833–1915, vol. I
Kennard, Major Arthur Molloy, 1867–1917, vol. II
Kennard, Rt Rev. Mgr Charles H., 1840–1920, vol. II
Kennard, Sir Coleridge Arthur Fitzroy, 1st Bt, 1885–1948, vol. IV
Kennard, Col Edmund Hegan, *died* 1912, vol. I
Kennard, Col Henry Gerard, *died* 1946, vol. IV
Kennard, Sir Howard William, 1878–1955, vol. V
Kennard, Sir Lawrence Ury Charles, 2nd Bt, 1912–1967, vol. VI
Kennard, Martyn Thomas, 1859–1920, vol. II
Kennard, Captain Willoughby Arthur, 1881–1918, vol. II
Kennaway, Sir Ernest Laurence, 1881–1958, vol. V
Kennaway, Sir John, 4th Bt, 1879–1956, vol. V
Kennaway, Rt Hon. Sir John Henry, 3rd Bt, 1837–1919, vol. II
Kennaway, Sir Walter, 1835–1920, vol. II
Kennedy, Hon. Lord; Neil J. D. Kennedy, 1855–1918, vol. II
Kennedy, Alex. Mills, *died* 1960, vol. V
Kennedy, Alexander, 1909–1960, vol. V
Kennedy, Sir Alexander Blackie William, 1847–1928, vol. II
Kennedy, Sir Alexander McAusland, 1860–1939, vol. III
Kennedy, Maj.-Gen. Alfred Alexander, 1870–1926, vol. II
Kennedy, Alfred Ravenscroft, 1879–1943, vol. IV
Kennedy, Lt-Col Andrew Campbell, 1872–1941, vol. IV
Kennedy, Rev. Archibald Cowan, 1892–1966, vol. VI
Kennedy, Rev. Archibald Robert Stirling, 1859–1938, vol. III
Kennedy, Aubrey Leo, 1885–1965, vol. VI
Kennedy, Bart, 1861–1930, vol. III
Kennedy, Brig.-Gen. Charles Henry, *died* 1916, vol. II
Kennedy, Sir Charles Malcolm, 1831–1908, vol. I
Kennedy, Charles Rann, 1871–1950, vol. IV
Kennedy, Sir Derrick Edward de Vere, 6th Bt, 1904–1976, vol. VII

Kennedy, Sir Donald; *see* Mackenzie-Kennedy, Sir H. C. D. C.

Kennedy, Maj.-Gen. Sir Edward Charles William M.; *see* Mackenzie-Kennedy.

Kennedy, Major Francis Malcolm Evory, 1869–1945, vol. IV

Kennedy, Adm. Francis William, 1862–1939, vol. III

Kennedy, Frank Robert, 1895–1971, vol. VII

Kennedy, Frederick Charles, 1849–1916, vol. II

Kennedy, Rev. Geoffrey Anketell Studdert, *died* 1929, vol. III

Kennedy, George, 1838–1916, vol. II (A), vol. III

Kennedy, Gilbert George, 1844–1909, vol. I

Kennedy, Rev. Harry Angus Alexander, 1866–1934, vol. III

Kennedy, Hartley, 1852–1938, vol. III

Kennedy, Henry Albert, 1877–1965, vol. VI

Kennedy, Brig.-Gen. Henry Brewster Percy Lion, *died* 1953, vol. V

Kennedy, Sir (Henry Charles) Donald (Cleveland) M.; *see* Mackenzie-Kennedy.

Kennedy, Very Rev. Herbert Brownlow, 1863–1939, vol. III

Kennedy, Howard Angus, 1861–1938, vol. III

Kennedy, Brig.-Gen. Hugh, 1864–1930, vol. III

Kennedy, Hugh, 1879–1936, vol. III

Kennedy, Hon. Sir James Arthur, 1882–1954, vol. V

Kennedy, Col. James Crawford, 1879–1944, vol. IV

Kennedy, Sir James Edward, 5th Bt, 1898–1974, vol. VII

Kennedy, Rev. James Houghton, *died* 1924, vol. II

Kennedy, Rev. John, 1813–1900, vol. I

Kennedy, Brig.-Gen. John, 1878–1921, vol. II

Kennedy, Rev. John, *died* 1931, vol. III

Kennedy, Maj.-Gen. Sir John, 1878–1948, vol. IV

Kennedy, Sir John Charles, 3rd Bt, 1856–1923, vol. II

Kennedy, John Fitzgerald, 1917–1963, vol. VI

Kennedy, Sir John Gordon, 1836–1912, vol. I

Kennedy, Rev. John Joseph, *born* 1882, vol. III

Kennedy, Sir John Macfarlane, 1879–1954, vol. V

Kennedy, Col John Murray, 1841–1928, vol. II

Kennedy, Maj.-Gen. Sir John Noble, 1893–1970, vol. VI

Kennedy, Sir John Ralph Bayly, 4th Bt, 1896–1968, vol. VI

Kennedy, John Robert, 1871–1956, vol. V

Kennedy, Lt-Col John Ross, 1905–1942, vol. IV

Kennedy, John William James Clark-, 1875–1939, vol. III

Kennedy, Jospeh Patrick, 1888–1969, vol. VI

Kennedy, Rt Rev. Kenneth William Stewart, *died* 1943, vol. IV

Kennedy, Captain Macdougall Ralston, 1878–1924, vol. II

Kennedy, Margaret, (Lady Davies), *died* 1967, vol. VI

Kennedy, Michael, 1859–1932, vol. III

Kennedy, Sir Michael Kavanagh, 1824–1898, vol. I

Kennedy, Milward; *see* Burge, M. R. K.

Kennedy, Rev. Mortimer Egerton, 1853–1929, vol. III

Kennedy, Myles, 1862–1928, vol. II

Kennedy, Captain Myles Arthur Claude, 1885–1918, vol. II

Kennedy, Myles Burton, 1861–1914, vol. I

Kennedy, Myles Storr Nigel, 1889–1964, vol. VI

Kennedy, Neil J. D.; *see* Kennedy, Hon. Lord.

Kennedy, Bt-Col Norman, 1881–1960, vol. V

Kennedy, Patrick James, 1864–1947, vol. IV

Kennedy, Robert, 1865–1913, vol. I

Kennedy, Robert, 1865–1924, vol. II

Kennedy, Hon. Sir Robert, 1887–1974, vol. VII

Kennedy, Robert Francis, 1925–1968, vol. VI

Kennedy, Robert Gregg, 1851–1920, vol. II

Kennedy, Sir Robert John, 1851–1936, vol. III

Kennedy, Vice-Adm. Theobald Walter, 1871–1934, vol. III

Kennedy, Rev. Thomas, 1828–1913, vol. I

Kennedy, Rt Hon. Thomas, 1876–1954, vol. V

Kennedy, Lt-Col Thomas Francis Archibald W.; *see* Watson-Kennedy.

Kennedy, Sir Thomas Sinclair, 1884–1951, vol. V

Kennedy, Vincent, 1876–1943, vol. IV

Kennedy, William, 1866–1936, vol. III

Kennedy of Knockgray, Lt-Col William Hew Clark-, 1879–1961, vol. VI

Kennedy, Lt-Col William Magill, 1868–1923, vol. II

Kennedy, William Paul McClure, 1879–1963, vol. VI

Kennedy, William Quarrier, 1903–1979, vol. VII

Kennedy, Rt Hon. Sir William Rann, 1846–1915, vol. I

Kennedy, Adm. Sir William Robert, 1838–1916, vol. II

Kennedy, Lt-Col Willoughby Pitcairn, 1850–1928, vol. II

Kennedy-Cooke, Brian, 1894–1963, vol. VI

Kennedy-Cox, Sir Reginald Kennedy, *died* 1966, vol. VI

Kennedy-Craufurd-Stuart, Lt-Col Charles; *see* Stuart.

Kennedy-Purvis, Adm. Sir Charles Edward, *died* 1946, vol. IV

Kenner, George Wallace, 1922–1978, vol. VII

Kenner, James, 1885–1974, vol. VII

Kennet, 1st Baron, 1879–1960, vol. V

Kennet, Lady; (Kathleen), *died* 1947, vol. IV

Kennett, Lt-Col Brackley Herbert Barrington B.; *see* Barrington-Kennett.

Kennett, Rev. Robert Hatch, 1864–1932, vol. III

Kennett-Barrington, Sir Vincent Hunter Barrington, 1844–1903, vol. I

Kenney, Col Arthur Herbert, 1855–1923, vol. II

Kenney, James C. F.; *see* Fitzgerald-Kenney.

Kenney-Herbert, Edward Maxwell, 1845–1916, vol. II

Kenning, Sir George, 1880–1956, vol. V

Kennington, Eric Henri, *died* 1960, vol. V

Kennington, T. B., *died* 1916, vol. II

Kennion, Rt Rev. George Wyndham, 1845–1922, vol. II

Kennion, Lt-Col Roger Lloyd, 1866–1942, vol. IV

Kenny, Augustus Leo, 1863–1946, vol. IV

Kenny, Courtney Stanhope, 1847–1930, vol. III
Kenny, Elizabeth, 1886–1952, vol. V
Kenny, Joseph Edward, 1845–1900, vol. I
Kenny, Matthew J., 1861–1942, vol. IV
Kenny, Sean, 1932–1973, vol. VII
Kenny, Gen. Sir Thomas K.; *see* Kelly-Kenny.
Kenny, Brig. Vincent Raymond, 1882–1966, vol. VI
Kenny, Rt Hon. William, 1846–1921, vol. II
Kenny, Maj.-Gen. William Wallace, 1854–1929, vol. III
Kenrick, Frank Boteler, 1874–1951, vol. V
Kenrick, Sir George Cranmer, 1863–1939, vol. III
Kenrick, Brig.-Gen. George Edmund Reginald, 1871–1935, vol. III
Kenrick, Sir George Hamilton, 1850–1939, vol. III
Kenrick, George Harry Blair, *died* 1952, vol. V
Kenrick, Brig. Harry Selwyn, 1898–1979, vol. VII
Kenrick, John Arthur, 1829–1926, vol. II
Kenrick, Rt Hon. William, 1831–1919, vol. II
Kensington, 5th Baron, 1863–1900, vol. I
Kensington, 6th Baron, 1873–1938, vol. III
Kensington, Sir Alfred, 1855–1918, vol. II
Kensington, Brig. Edgar Claude, 1879–1967, vol. VI
Kensington, William Charles, 1845–1922, vol. II
Kenswood, 1st Baron, 1887–1963, vol. VI
Kent, Albert Frank Stanley, 1863–1958, vol. V
Kent, Charles, 1823–1902, vol. I
Kent, Rev. Charles, 1857–1929, vol. III
Kent, Charles Kenneth Stafford, 1892–1963, vol. VI
Kent, Charles Weller, 1864–1952, vol. V
Kent, Chris Shotter, 1887–1954, vol. V
Kent, Rev. Harry Arnold, 1880–1962, vol. VI
Kent, Lt-Gen. Henry, 1825–1921, vol. II
Kent, Col Herbert Vaughan, 1863–1944, vol. IV
Kent, Hon. James M., 1872–1939, vol. III
Kent, Col Sir John; *see* Kent, Col Sir W. J.
Kent, Keneth; *see* Kent, C. K. S.
Kent, Percy Horace Braund, 1876–1963, vol. VI
Kent, Rockwell, 1882–1971, vol. VII
Kent, Sir Stephenson Hamilton, 1873–1954, vol. V
Kent, Thomas Parkes, *died* 1923, vol. II
Kent, Sir Walter George, 1858–1938, vol. III
Kent, Col Sir (William) John, 1877–1960, vol. V
Kent, William Richard Gladstone, 1884–1963, vol. VI
Kent-Lemon, Brig. Arthur Leslie, 1889–1970, vol. VI
Kentish, Brig.-Gen. Reginald John, 1876–1956, vol. V
Kenward, Rev. Herbert, *died* 1954, vol. V
Kenwood, Lt-Col Henry Richard, 1862–1945, vol. IV
Kenworthy, John Dalzell, 1858–1954, vol. V
Kenyatta, Hon. Mzee Jomo, 1889–1978, vol. VII
Kenyon, 4th Baron, 1864–1927, vol. II
Kenyon, Arthur William, *died* 1969, vol. VI
Kenyon, Barnet, 1853–1930, vol. III
Kenyon, Sir Bernard, 1904–1977, vol. VII
Kenyon, Edith C., *died* 1925, vol. II
Kenyon, Maj.-Gen. Edward Ranulph, 1854–1937, vol. III
Kenyon, Sir Frederic George, 1863–1952, vol. V
Kenyon, Hon. George Thomas, 1840–1908, vol. I
Kenyon, Sir Harold Vaughan, 1875–1959, vol. V

Kenyon, James, 1846–1924, vol. II
Kenyon, John George, 1843–1914, vol. I
Kenyon, Joseph, 1885–1961, vol. VI
Kenyon, Dame Kathleen Mary, 1906–1978, vol. VII
Kenyon, Maj.-Gen. Lionel Richard, 1867–1952, vol. V
Kenyon, Myles Noel, 1886–1960, vol. V
Kenyon, Sir Norris Vaughan, 1903–1958, vol. V
Kenyon, Robert Lloyd, 1848–1931, vol. III
Kenyon, Hon. and Rev. William Trevor, 1847–1930, vol. III
Kenyon-Slaney, Col Francis Gerald, 1858–1938, vol. III
Kenyon-Slaney, Major Philip Percy, 1896–1928, vol. II
Kenyon-Slaney, Major Robert Orlando Rodolph, 1892–1965, vol. VI
Kenyon-Slaney, Sybil Agnes, 1888–1970, vol. VI
Kenyon-Slaney, Maj.-Gen. Walter Rupert, 1851–1936, vol. III
Kenyon-Slaney, Rt Hon. William Slaney, 1847–1908, vol. I
Keogh, Lt-Gen. Sir Alfred, 1857–1936, vol. III
Keogh, Col James Blair, 1871–1944, vol. IV
Keogh, Joseph Wiseman, *died* 1947, vol. IV
Keogh, Martin Jerome, 1855–1928, vol. II (A), vol. III
Keogh, Michael Frederick, 1866–1940, vol. III
Keogh, Most Rev. Thomas, 1884–1969, vol. VI
Keown, Anna Gordon, *died* 1957, vol. V
Keown, Eric Oliver Dilworth, 1904–1963, vol. VI
Keown-Boyd, Sir Alexander William, 1884–1954, vol. V
Keppel, Adm. Sir Colin Richard, 1862–1947, vol. IV
Keppel, Hon. Sir Derek, 1863–1944, vol. IV
Keppel, Col Edward George, 1847–1934, vol. III
Keppel, Frederick Paul, 1875–1943, vol. IV
Keppel, Lt-Col Hon. George, 1865–1947, vol. IV
Keppel, Sir George Roos-, 1866–1921, vol. II
Keppel, Hon. Sir Henry, 1809–1904, vol. I
Keppel, Rear-Adm. Leicester Chantrey, *died* 1917, vol. II
Keppel, Cpatain Hon. Rupert Oswald Derek, 1886–1964, vol. VI
Keppie, John, 1862–1945, vol. IV
Ker, Lord Alastair Robert I.; *see* Innes-Ker.
Ker, Major Allan Ebenezer, *died* 1958, vol. V
Ker, Sir Arthur Milford, 1853–1915, vol. I
Ker, Charles, 1860–1940, vol. III
Ker, Maj.-Gen. Charles Arthur, 1875–1962, vol. VI
Ker, Lt-Col Douglas Rous E.; *see* Edwardes-Ker.
Ker, Frederick Innes, *died* 1977, vol. VII
Ker, James Campbell, 1878–1961, vol. VI
Ker, James Inglis, *died* 1936, vol. III
Ker, Ven. John, 1848–1913, vol. I
Ker, Hon. John Errington, 1860–1918, vol. II
Ker, Mrs Phyllis de Burgh; *see* Lett, Phyllis.
Ker, Richard William Blackwood, 1850–1942, vol. IV
Ker, Major Lord Robert Edward I.; *see* Innes-Ker.
Ker, William Paton, 1855–1923, vol. II
Ker, William Pollock, 1864–1945, vol. IV

Kerby, Air Vice-Marshal Harold Spencer, 1893–1963, vol. VI

Kerby, Captain Henry Briton, 1914–1971, vol. VII

Kerin, Col Michael William, 1856–1912, vol. I

Kerley, Sir Peter James, 1900–1979, vol. VII

Kerly, Sir Duncan Mackenzie, 1863–1938, vol. III

Kermack, William Ogilvy, 1898–1970, vol. VI

Kermode, Air Vice-Marshal Alfred Cotterill, 1897–1973, vol. VII

Kermode, Rev. Sir Derwent William, 1898–1960, vol. V

Kern, Jerome, 1885–1945, vol. IV

Kernahan, Coulson, 1858–1943, vol. IV

Kernahan, Mrs Coulson, died 1941, vol. IV

Kernoff, Harry, 1900–1974, vol. VII

Kernot, W. C., 1845–1909, vol. I

Kerouac, Jack, (Jean-Louis), 1922–1969, vol. VI

Kerr, Col Alex. Ferrier K.; see Kidston-Kerr.

Kerr, Mrs Anne Patricia, (Mrs R. W. Kerr), 1925–1973, vol. VII

Kerr, Douglas James Acworth, 1894–1960, vol. V

Kerr, Rev. F. W., 1881–1945, vol. IV

Kerr, Captain Frank Robison, 1889–1977, vol. VII

Kerr, Col Frederic Walter, 1867–1914, vol. I

Kerr, Frederick, 1858–1933, vol. III

Kerr, Sir Hamilton William, 1st Bt, 1903–1974, vol. VII

Kerr, Maj.-Gen. Sir (Harold) Reginald, 1897–1974, vol. VII

Kerr, Henry W., 1857–1936, vol. III

Kerr, Lt-Col Sir Howard, died 1977, vol. VII

Kerr, James, died 1941, vol. IV

Kerr, Hon. James Kirkpatrick, 1841–1916, vol. II

Kerr, James Lennox, 1899–1963, vol. VI

Kerr, James Rutherford, 1878–1942, vol. IV

Kerr, Rev. John, died 1907, vol. I

Kerr, John, 1830–1916, vol. II

Kerr, John, born 1852, vol. II

Kerr, Rev. John, 1852–1920, vol. II

Kerr, Sir John Graham, 1869–1957, vol. V

Kerr, Sir John Henry, 1871–1934, vol. III

Kerr, (John Martin) Munro, 1868–1960, vol. V

Kerr, Lt-Col Mark Ancrum, 1859–1941, vol. IV

Kerr, Adm. Mark Edward Frederic, 1864–1944, vol. IV

Kerr, Gen. Lord Mark Ralph George, 1817–1900, vol. I

Kerr, Munro; see Kerr, J. M. M.

Kerr, Philip Walter, died 1941, vol. IV

Kerr, Lord Ralph Drury, 1837–1916, vol. II

Kerr, Rev. Ralph Francis, 1874–1932, vol. III

Kerr, Maj.-Gen. Sir Reginald; see Kerr, Maj.-Gen. Sir H. R.

Kerr, Robert, 1823–1904, vol. I

Kerr, Robert Bird, 1867–1951, vol. V

Kerr, Robert Malcolm, 1821–1902, vol. I

Kerr, Brig.-Gen. Robert S.; see Scott-Kerr.

Kerr, Col Rowan Scrope R.; see Rait Kerr.

Kerr, Sir Russell James, 1863–1952, vol. V

Kerr, Thomas, 1818–1907, vol. I

Kerr, Admiral of the Fleet Lord Walter Talbot, 1839–1927, vol. II

Kerr, Captain William, 1877–1918, vol. II

Kerr, Sir William, 1895–1959, vol. V

Kerr, Captain William Alexander, died 1919, vol. II

Kerr, Rev. William Goodwin, 1862–1934, vol. III

Kerr, Adm. Sir William Munro, 1876–1959, vol. V

Kerr, William Richard, 1853–1943, vol. IV

Kerr, Rt Rev. William Shaw, 1873–1960, vol. V

Kerr, William Warren, 1864–1949, vol. IV

Kerr-Jarrett, Sir Francis Moncreiff, 1885–1968, vol. VI

Kerr-Muir, Ronald John, 1910–1974, vol. VII

Kerr-Pearse, Major Beauchamp Albert Thomas, 1871–1934, vol. III

Kerr-Smiley, Peter Kerr, 1879–1943, vol. IV

Kerrich, Lt-Col Walter Edmund, 1860–1938, vol. III

Kerridge, Sir Robert James, 1901–1979, vol. VII

Kerrigan, Daniel Patrick, 1909–1971, vol. VII

Kerrison, Lt-Col Edmund Roger Allday, 1855–1944, vol. IV

Kerrison, Roger, 1842–1924, vol. II

Kerry, Earl of; Henry Maurice John Petty-Fitzmaurice, 1913–1933, vol. III

Kersey, Major Henry Maitland, 1859–1941, vol. IV

Kersh, Gerald, 1911–1968, vol. VI

Kershaw, 1st Baron, 1881–1961, vol. VI

Kershaw, 2nd Baron, 1904–1961, vol. VI

Kershaw, 3rd Baron, 1906–1962, vol. VI

Kershaw, Harold Slaney, 1882–1969, vol. VI

Kershaw, John Felix, 1873–1927, vol. II

Kershaw, Rev. John Frederick, 1853–1935, vol. III

Kershaw, Sir Leonard William, 1864–1949, vol. IV

Kershaw, Sir Lewis Addin, 1845–1899, vol. I

Kershaw, Sir Louis James, 1869–1947, vol. IV

Kershaw, Sir Noel Thomas, 1863–1930, vol. III

Kershaw, S. Wayland, died 1914, vol. I

Kershaw, Thomas Herbert, 1851–1913, vol. I

Kertesz, Istvan, 1929–1973, vol. VII

Kerwin, Hon. Patrick, 1899–1963, vol. VI

Kessell, Ernest, 1868–1948, vol. IV

Kestell-Cornish, Rt Rev. George Kestell, 1856–1925, vol. II

Kestell-Cornish, Rt Rev. Rober Kestell, 1824–1909, vol. I

Kesteven, 2nd Baron, 1851–1915, vol. I

Kesteven, 3rd Baron, 1891–1915, vol. I (A)

Kesteven, Sir Charles Henry, died 1923, vol. II

Keswick, David Johnston, 1901–1976, vol. VII

Keswick, Major Henry, 1870–1928, vol. II

Keswick, William, 1835–1912, vol. I

Ketchen, Maj.-Gen. Huntly Douglas Brodie, 1872–1959, vol. V

Ketchen, Maj.-Gen. Isaac, 1839–1920, vol. II

Ketchum, Philip A. C., 1899–1964, vol. VI

Kethley, Andrew Horace Victor P.; see Pitt-Kethley.

Kettering, Charles Franklin, 1876–1958, vol. V

Kettle, Edgar Hartley, 1882–1936, vol. III

Kettle, Marguerite Henrietta, 1887–1939, vol. III

Kettle, Rupert Edward Cooke, 1854–1908, vol. I

Kettle, Sir Russell, 1887–1968, vol. VI

Kettle, Thomas Michael, 1880–1916, vol. II

Kettlewell, Arthur Bradley, 1871–1945, vol. IV

Kettlewell, Bernard; see Kettlewell, H. B. D.

Kettlewell, (Henry) Bernard (Davis), 1907–1979, vol. VII
Kettlewell, Rev. Percy W. H., 1868–1950, vol. IV
Ketton-Cremer, Robert Wyndham, 1906–1969, vol. VI
Kevenhoerster, Most Rev. John Bernard, 1869–1949, vol. IV
Keverne, Richard, 1882–1950, vol. IV
Kewley, Rev. James William, 1846–1935, vol. III
Kewley, Ven. John, 1860–1941, vol. IV
Key, Major Sir Aston C.; see Cooper-Key.
Key, Rt Rev. Bransby Lewis, 1838–1901, vol. I
Key, Carl Axel Helmer, 1864–1938, vol. III (A), vol. IV
Key, Sir Charles Edward, 1900–1978, vol. VII
Key, Rt. Hon. Charles William, died 1964, vol. VI
Key, Captain Edmund Moore Cooper C.; see Cooper-Key.
Key, Edward Emmerson, 1917–1976, vol. VII
Key, Ellen, 1849–1926, vol. II
Key, Rev. Sir John Kingsmill Causton, 3rd Bt, 1853–1926, vol. II
Key, Sir Kingsmill Grove, 2nd Bt, 1815–1899, vol. I
Key, Sir Kingsmill James, 4th Bt, 1864–1932, vol. III
Keyes, 1st Baron, 1872–1945, vol. IV
Keyes, Comdr Adrian St Vincent, 1882–1926, vol. II
Keyes, Frances Parkinson, (Mrs Henry Wilder Keyes), 1885–1970, vol. VI
Keyes, Brig.-Gen. Sir Terence Humphrey, 1877–1939, vol. III
Keymer, Sir Daniel Thomas, 1857–1933, vol. III
Keymer, Rev. Nathaniel, 1844–1922, vol. II
Keynes, 1st Baron, 1883–1946, vol. IV
Keynes, John Neville, 1852–1949, vol. IV
Keys, David Reid, 1856–1939, vol. III
Keys, Rear-Adm. (S) John Anthony, 1863–1955, vol. V
Keyser, Agnes, (Sister Agnes), died 1941, vol. IV
Keyser, Arthur Louis, died 1924, vol. II
Keyser, Charles Edward, 1847–1929, vol. III
Keyser, Col Frederick Charles, 1841–1920, vol. II
Keyser, Lionel Edward, 1878–1955, vol. V
Keyserling, Count Hermann, 1880–1946, vol. IV
Khachaturyan, Aram Ilych, 1903–1978, vol. VII
Khairpur, HH Mir Sir Faiz Mohammad Khan Talpur, Mir of, died 1909, vol. I
Khairpur State, HH Mir Imam Baksh Khan, Ruler of, died 1921, vol. II
Khairpur State, HH Mir Ali Nawaz Khan, Ruler of, died 1935, vol. III
Khalil, Mohammed Bey, 1895–1950, vol. IV (A), vol. V
Khama, Sir Seretse M., 1921–1980, vol. VII
Khan, Gen. Agha Muhammad Y.; see Yahya Khan.
Khan, Brig. Fazalur Rahman, 1914–1980, vol. VII
Khan, Ghaanfar Ali, 1875–1959, vol. V
Khan, Major Sir Khan Hashmatullah, died 1936, vol. III (A), vol. IV
Khan, Nawab Sir Khan-i-Zaman, died 1936, vol. III
Khan, Liaquat Ali, 1895–1951, vol. V

Khan, Field-Marshal Mohammad Ayub, died 1974, vol. VII
Khan, Sir Mohammed Y.; see Yamin Khan.
Khan, Raja Sir Muhammud Nazim, died 1938, vol. III
Khan, Pir-o-Murshid I.; see Inayat-Khan.
Khan, Sir Shafa'at Ahmad, 1893–1947, vol. IV
Kher, Shri Bal Gangadhar, 1888–1957, vol. V
Khrushchev, Nikita Sergeyevich, 1894–1971, vol. VII
Khundkar, Sir Nurul Azeem, 1890–1947, vol. IV
Khurshid Jah, Bahadur Sir, Nawab, died 1902, vol. I
Kibblewhite, Ebenezer Job, 1846–1924, vol. II
Kidd, Beatrice Ethel, 1867–1958, vol. V
Kidd, Benjamin, 1858–1916, vol. II
Kidd, Rev. Beresford James, 1864–1948, vol. IV
Kidd, Lt-Col Bertram Graham Balfour, 1875–1943, vol. IV
Kidd, Frank S., 1878–1934, vol. III
Kidd, Franklin, 1890–1974, vol. VII
Kidd, Frederic William, 1890–1971, vol. VII
Kidd, Henry, 1862–1923, vol. II
Kidd, James, 1872–1928, vol. II
Kidd, John, 1821–1910, vol. I
Kidd, Lt-Col John Franklin, died 1933, vol. III
Kidd, Rt Rev. John Thomas, 1868–1950, vol. IV (A), vol. V
Kidd, Rev. Joseph Henry, 1877–1930, vol. III
Kidd, Percy M., 1851–1942, vol. IV
Kiddle, Adm. Sir Edward Buxton, 1866–1933, vol. III
Kiddle, Col Frederick, 1871–1936, vol. III
Kiddle, Captain Kerrison, 1876–1949, vol. IV
Kiddy, Arthur William, 1868–1950, vol. IV
Kidman, Sir Sidney, 1857–1935, vol. III
Kidner, Brig. William Elworthy, 1884–1969, vol. VI
Kidson, Edward, 1882–1939, vol. III
Kidson, Fenn, 1874–1965, vol. VI
Kidson, Harold Percy, 1887–1971, vol. VII
Kidston, George Jardine, 1873–1954, vol. V
Kidston, Robert, died 1924, vol. II
Kidston, Hon. William, 1849–1919, vol. II
Kidston-Kerr, Col Alex. Ferrier, 1840–1926, vol. II
Kiek, Rev. Edward S., 1883–1959, vol. V
Kielberg, Sir Michael K.; see Kroyer-Kielberg.
Kielhorn, Franz, 1840–1908, vol. I
Kierkels, Most Rev. Leo Peter, 1882–1957, vol. V
Kiggell, Lt-Gen. Sir Launcelot Edward, 1862–1954, vol. V
Kikuchi, Baron Dairoku, 1855–1917, vol. II
Kilbracken, 1st Baron, 1847–1932, vol. III
Kilbracken, 2nd Baron, 1877–1950, vol. IV
Kilbride, Dennis, 1848–1924, vol. II
Kilburn, Bertram Edward D.; see Dunbar Kilburn.
Kilburn, John Maurice, 1885–1965, vol. VI
Kilburne, George Goodwin, 1839–1924, vol. II
Kilby, Reginald George, died 1949, vol. IV
Kiley, James Daniel, 1865–1953, vol. V
Kilgour, Rev. Robert, 1867–1942, vol. IV
Kilham Roberts, Denys, 1903–1976, vol. VII
Kilkelly, Surg.-Lt-Col Charles Randolph, 1861–1953, vol. V

Killam, Albert Clements, 1849–1908, vol. I
Killanin, 1st Baron; see Morris and Killanin.
Killanin, 2nd Baron, 1867–1927, vol. II
Killby, Leonard Gibbs, 1883–1975, vol. VII
Killearn, 1st Baron, 1880–1964, vol. VI
Killen, Rev. William D., died 1902, vol. I
Killey, Homer Charles, 1915–1976, vol. VII
Killian, Most Rev. Andrew, 1872–1939, vol. III
Killick, Brig. Sir Alexander Herbert, 1894–1975, vol. VII
Killick, Sir Anthony Bernard, 1901–1966, vol. VI
Killick, Esther Margaret, (Mrs A. St G. Huggett), 1902–1960, vol. V
Killick, John Spencer, 1878–1952, vol. V
Killik, Sir Stephen Henry Molyneux, 1961–1938, vol. III
Killin, Robert, 1870–1943, vol. IV
Kilmaine, 4th Baron, 1843–1907, vol. I
Kilmaine, 5th Baron, 1878–1946, vol. IV
Kilmaine, 6th Baron, 1902–1978, vol. VII
Kilmarnock, 6th Baron, 1903–1975, vol. VII
Kilmorey, 3rd Earl of, 1842–1915, vol. I
Kilmorey, 4th Earl of, 1883–1961, vol. VI
Kilmorey, 5th Earl of, 1915–1977, vol. VII
Kilmuir, 1st Earl of, 1900–1967, vol. VI
Kilner, Group Captain Cecil Francis, 1883–1925, vol. II
Kilner, Lt-Col Charles Harold, 1864–1936, vol. III
Kilner, Rt Rev. Francis Charles, died 1921, vol. II
Kilner, Major Sir Hew Ross, 1892–1953, vol. V
Kilner, T(homas) Pomfret, 1890–1964, vol. VI
Kilpatrick, Florence Antoinette, died 1968, vol. VI
Kilpatrick, George Gordon Dinwiddie, 1888–1975, vol. VII
Kilpatrick, Sir James MacConnell, 1902–1960, vol. V
Kilpin, Sir Ernest Fuller, 1854–1931, vol. III
Kilvert, Sir Harry Vernon, 1862–1924, vol. II
Kim, Tan Jiak, died 1917, vol. II
Kimalel, Shadrack Kiptenai, 1930–1980, vol. VII
Kimball, Katharine, 1866–1949, vol. IV
Kimball, Major Lawrence, 1900–1971, vol. VII
Kimball, LeRoy Elwood, 1888–1962, vol. VI
Kimbell, Rev. Ralph Raymond, 1884–1964, vol. VI
Kimber, Augustus Charles Edmund, died 1930, vol. III
Kimber, Lt-Col Edmund Gibbs, 1870–1954, vol. V
Kimber, Gurth, 1906–1978, vol. VII
Kimber, Sir Henry, 1st Bt, 1834–1923, vol. II
Kimber, Sir Henry Dixon, 2nd Bt, 1862–1950, vol. IV
Kimber, Sir Sidney Guy, 1873–1949, vol. IV
Kimberley, 1st Earl of, 1826–1902, vol. I
Kimberley, 2nd Earl of, 1848–1932, vol. III
Kimberley, 3rd Earl of, 1883–1941, vol. IV
Kimberley, Paul, died 1964, vol. VI
Kimens, Richard Edward, 1872–1950, vol. IV
Kimmins, Captain Anthony, 1901–1964, vol. VI
Kimmins, Lt-Gen. Sir Brian Charles Hannam, 1899–1979, vol. VII
Kimmins, Charles William, died 1948, vol. IV
Kimmins, Dame Grace Thyrza, died 1954, vol. V
Kimpton, Lawrence Alpheus, 1910–1977, vol. VII

Kinahan, Sir Edward Hudson Hudson-, 2nd Bt, 1865–1938, vol. III
Kinahan, Lt-Col George Frederick H.; see Hudson-Kinahan.
Kinahan, Adm. Sir Harold Richard George, 1893–1980, vol. VII
Kinahan, Sir Robert Henry Hudson-, 3rd Bt, 1872–1949, vol. IV
Kinane, Most Rev. Jeremiah, 1884–1959, vol. V
Kincaid, Charles Augustus, 1870–1954, vol. V
Kincaid, Maj.-Gen. William, 1831–1909, vol. I
Kincaid, Col William Francis Henry Style, 1861–1945, vol. IV
Kincaid-Lennox, Charles Spencer Bateman-Hanbury, 1827–1912, vol. I
Kincaid-Smith, Brig.-Gen. Kenneth John, 1871–1949, vol. IV
Kincaid-Smith, Lt-Col Malcolm, 1874–1938, vol. III
Kincairney, Hon. Lord; William Ellis Gloag, 1828–1909, vol. I
Kinch, Edward, 1848–1920, vol. II
Kinder, Claude William, 1852–1936, vol. III
Kindersley, 1st Baron, 1871–1954, vol. V
Kindersley, 2nd Baron, 1899–1976, vol. VII
Kindersley, Lt-Col Archibald Ogilvie Lyttelton, 1869–1955, vol. V
Kindersley, Rt Rev. George Aelred, 1860–1934, vol. III
Kindersley, Major Guy Molesworth, 1877–1956, vol. V
Kindersley, Major James Benjamin, 1893–1939, vol. III
King, Maj.-Gen. A. H., 1831–1899, vol. I
King, Very Rev. Albert Edward, 1865–1938, vol. III
King, Albert Theodore, 1885–1939, vol. III
King, Sir Alexander Boyne, 1888–1973, vol. VII
King, Sir Alexander Freeman, 1851–1942, vol. IV
King, Lt-Col Alexander James, 1863–1943, vol. IV
King, Sir Alexander William, 6th Bt (cr 1815), 1892–1969, vol. VI
King, Alfred Hazell, 1896–1956, vol. V
King, Alfred John, 1859–1920, vol. II
King, Brig.-Gen. Algernon D'Aguilar, 1862–1945, vol. IV
King, Sir Anthony Highmore, 1890–1977, vol. VII
King, Sir Archibald John, 1887–1961, vol. VI
King, Sir (Arthur) Henry (William), 1889–1966, vol. VI
King, Arthur Thomas, 1845–1922, vol. II
King, Sir Carleton Moss, 1878–1954, vol. V
King, Cecil, 1881–1942, vol. IV
King, Maj.-Gen. Charles, 1844–1933, vol. III
King, Charles A., died 1936, vol. III
King, Sir Charles Albert, 1853–1922, vol. II
King, Col Charles Dickson, 1860–1933, vol. III
King, Major Charles Edward Stuart, 1869–1934, vol. III
King, Lt-Gen. Sir Charles John Stuart, 1890–1967, vol. VI
King, Charles Macintosh, 1836–1920, vol. II
King, Charles Montague, 1872–1956, vol. V

King, Sir Charles Simeon, 3rd Bt (*cr* 1821), 1840–1921, vol. II

King, Charles Thomas, *died* 1932, vol. III

King, Brig.-Gen. Sir Charles Wallis, 1861–1943, vol. IV

King, Sir (Clifford) Robertson, 1895–1976, vol. VII

King, Colin Henry Harmsworth, 1931–1977, vol. VII

King, Cyril Lander, *died* 1972, vol. VII

King, David Wylie, *died* 1945, vol. IV

King, Col Sir Dudley Gordon Alan D.; *see* Duckworth-King.

King, Earl Judson, 1901–1962, vol. VI

King, Rt Rev. Edward, 1829–1910, vol. I

King, E(dward) J(ohn) Boswell, *died* 1975, vol. VII

King, Adm. Edward Leigh Stuart, 1889–1971, vol. VII

King, Col Sir Edwin James, 1877–1952, vol. V

King, Ernest Gerald, *died* 1955, vol. V

King, Fleet Admiral Ernest Joseph, 1878–1956, vol. V

King, Dame Ethel Locke, *died* 1956, vol. V

King, Engr Rear-Adm. Frank Victor, 1889–1961, vol. VI

King, Frederic, 1853–1933, vol. III

King, Sir (Frederic) Truby, 1858–1938, vol. III

King, Lt-Col Sir George, 1840–1909, vol. I

King, Mrs George, (Sister Janet Wells), *died* 1911, vol. I

King, George, *died* 1922, vol. II

King, Sir George Adolphus, 5th Bt (*cr* 1815), 1864–1954, vol. V

King, Sir George Anthony, 1858–1928, vol. II

King, George Edward Fenton, 1887–1962, vol. VI

King, George Falconer, *died* 1929, vol. III

King, Sir George Henry James D.; *see* Duckworth-King.

King, George Kemp, 1880–1920, vol. II

King, Rt Rev. George Lanchester, 1860–1941, vol. IV

King, Major Gerald Hartley, 1882–1940, vol. III

King, Lt-Col Giffard Hamilton Macarthur, 1885–1956, vol. VI (AI)

King, Sir Gilbert, 4th Bt (*cr* 1815), 1846–1920, vol. II

King, Gilbert Walter, 1871–1937, vol. III

King, Mrs Grace M. H.; *see* Hamilton-King.

King, Harold, 1887–1956, vol. V

King, Maj.-Gen. Harold Francis Sylvester, 1895–1974, vol. VII

King, Lt-Col Harold Holmes, 1884–1961, vol. VI

King, Mrs Harriet Eleanor Baillie Hamilton, *died* 1920, vol. II

King, Haynes, 1831–1904, vol. I

King, Sir Henry; *see* King, Sir A. H. W.

King, Sir Henry Clark, 1857–1920, vol. II

King, Cdre Rt Hon. Henry Douglas, 1877–1930, vol. III

King, Rev. Henry Hugh, 1869–1918, vol. II

King, Sir (Henry) Seymour, 1st Bt (*cr* 1932), 1852–1933, vol. III

King, Hugh Charles, 1872–1937, vol. III

King, Humphrey Hastings, 1880–1950, vol. IV

King, Rev. J. Harper, *died* 1933, vol. III

King, Sir James, 1st Bt (*cr* 1888), 1830–1911, vol. I

King, James Edward, *died* 1933, vol. III

King, James Foster, 1862–1947, vol. IV

King, Brig.-Gen. James Gurwood K.; *see* King-King.

King, James H., 1873–1955, vol. V

King, Janet; *see* King, Mrs George.

King, John Baragwanath, *died* 1939, vol. III

King, John Charles, 1847–1918, vol. II

King, John Hampden, 1865–1945, vol. IV

King, Most Rev. John Henry, 1880–1965, vol. VI

King, Rev. John Richard, 1835–1907, vol. I

King, Sir John Richard D.; *see* Duckworth-King.

King, Sir John Westall, 2nd Bt (*cr* 1888), 1863–1940, vol. III

King, Joseph, 1860–1943, vol. IV

King, Sir Kelso, 1853–1943, vol. IV

King, Kenneth Charles, 1911–1970, vol. VI

King, Lt-Col Lancelot Noel Friedrick Irving, 1878–1947, vol. IV

King, Leonard William, 1869–1919, vol. II

King, Sir Louis, 1904–1972, vol. VII

King, Louis Vessot, 1886–1956, vol. V

King, Sir Lucas White, 1856–1925, vol. II

King, Martin Luther, Jr, 1929–1968, vol. VI

King, Maurice John, 1880–1952, vol. V

King, Merton, *died* 1939, vol. III

King, Sir Norman, 1880–1963, vol. VI

King, Bt Col Norman Carew, 1871–1953, vol. V

King, Oliver, 1855–1923, vol. II (A), vol. III

King, Sir Peter Alexander, 7th Bt (*cr* 1815), 1928–1973, vol. VII

King, Philip, 1904–1979, vol. VII

King, Preston, 1862–1943, vol. IV

King, Richard, (Richard King Huskinson), 1879–1947, vol. IV

King, Richard Ashe, 1839–1932, vol. III

King, Very Rev. Richard George Salmon, *died* 1958, vol. V

King, Rear-Adm. Richard Matthew, 1883–1969, vol. VI

King, Sir Robertson; *see* King, Sir C. R.

King, Sir Seymour; *see* King, Sir H. S.

King, Thomas, 1842–1903, vol. I

King, Thomas Mulhall, 1842–1914, vol. II

King, Thomas William, 1881–1936, vol. III

King, Sir Truby; *see* King, Sir F. T.

King, Col Walter Gawen, 1851–1935, vol. III

King, Sir Wilfred Creyke, *died* 1943, vol. IV

King, William Benjamin Basil, 1859–1928, vol. II

King, William Bernard Robinson, 1889–1963, vol. VI

King, Maj.-Gen. William Birchall Macaulay, 1878–1950, vol. IV

King, William Charles Holland, 1884–1973, vol. VII

King, William Cyril Campbell, 1891–1963, vol. VI

King, William Frederick, 1854–1916, vol. II

King, William Joseph Harding, 1869–1933, vol. III

King, Rt Hon. W(illiam) L(yon) Mackenzie, 1874–1950, vol. IV

King, Sir William Oliver Evelyn M.; *see* Meade-King.

King, Rev. William Templeton, 1849–1933, vol. III

King, Yeend, 1855–1924, vol. II
King-Farlow, Sir Sydney Nettleton, 1864–1957, vol. V
King-Hall, Baron (Life Peer); William Stephen Richard King-Hall, 1893–1966, vol. VI
King-Hall, Adm. Sir George Fowler, 1850–1939, vol. III
King-Hall, Adm. Sir Herbert Goodenough, 1862–1936, vol. III
King-Hall, Magdalen, (Mrs Patrick Perceval-Maxwell), 1904–1971, vol. VII
King-Harman, Sir Charles Anthony, 1851–1939, vol. III
King-Harman, Captain (Robert) Douglas, 1891–1978, vol. VII
King-Harman, Col Wentworth Henry, 1840–1919, vol. II
King-King, Brig.-Gen. James Gurwood, 1863–1939, vol. III
King-Wood, William, 1867–1921, vol. II
Kingan, William Sinclair, 1876–1946, vol. IV
Kingcome, Engr Vice-Adm. Sir John, 1890–1950, vol. IV
Kingdom, Thomas, 1881–1957, vol. V
Kingdon, Sir Donald, 1883–1961, vol. VI
Kingdon, Rt Rev. Hollingworth Tully, 1835–1907, vol. I
Kingdon-Ward, F., 1885–1958, vol. V
Kingham, Sir Robert Dixon, 1883–1966, vol. VI
Kinghorn, Col Harry Jackson, 1867–1947, vol. IV
Kinglake, Robert Alexander, 1843–1915, vol. I
Kingsale, 33rd Baron, 1855–1931, vol. III
Kingsale, 34th Baron, 1882–1969, vol. VI
Kingsburgh, Rt Hon. Lord; see Macdonald, Rt Hon. John Hay Athole.
Kingsbury, Allan Neave, 1888–1965, vol. VI
Kingscote, Lady Emily Marie, 1836–1910, vol. I
Kingscote, Mrs Howard; see Cleeve, Lucas.
Kingscote, Col Sir Robert Nigel FitzHardinge, 1830–1908, vol. I
Kingscote, Thomas Arthur Fitzhardinge, 1845–1935, vol. III
Kingsford, A. Beresford, died 1944, vol. IV
Kingsford, Charles Lethbridge, 1862–1926, vol. II
Kingsford, Adm. Henry Coare, 1858–1941, vol. IV
Kingsford, Reginald John Lethbridge, 1900–1978, vol. VII
Kingsford-Smith, Air Cdre Sir Charles Edward, 1897–1935, vol. III
Kingsley, Brig. Harold Evelyn William Bell, 1885–1970, vol. VI
Kingsley, Hyman Herbert, 1897–1956, vol. V
Kingsley, J(ohn) Donald, 1908–1972, vol. VII
Kingsley, Col William Henry Bell, 1835–1901, vol. I
Kingsmill, Lt-Col Andrew de Portal, 1881–1956, vol. V
Kingsmill, Adm. Sir Charles Edmund, 1855–1935, vol. III
Kingsmill, Hugh, (Hugh Kingsmill Lunn), 1889–1949, vol. IV
Kingsmill, Sir Walter, 1864–1935, vol. III
Kingsmill, Lt-Col Walter B., 1876–1957, vol. V

Kingsmill, Lt-Col William Henry, 1905–1971, vol. VII
Kingsnorth, Engr Rear-Adm. Sir Arthur Frederick, 1864–1947, vol. IV
Kingston, 9th Earl of, 1874–1946, vol. IV
Kingston, 10th Earl of, 1897–1948, vol. IV
Kingston, Rt Hon. Charles Cameron, 1850–1908, vol. I
Kingston, Most Rev. George Frederick, 1889–1950, vol. IV
Kingston, George Henry, 1866–1933, vol. III
Kingston, Gertrude, died 1937, vol. III
Kingston-McCloughry, Air Vice-Marshal Edgar James, 1896–1972, vol. VII
Kingstone, Arthur Courtney, 1874–1938, vol. III
Kingstone, Brig. James Jospeh, died 1966, vol. VI
Kington, Captain William Miles, 1876–1914, vol. I
Kington-Blair-Oliphant, Lt-Col Philip Lawrence, 1867–1918, vol. II
Kingzett, Charles Thomas, 1852–1935, vol. III
Kinkead, Richard John, died 1928, vol. II
Kinley, John, died 1957, vol. V
Kinloch, Sir Alexander, 10th Bt (cr 1686), 1830–1912, vol. I
Kinloch, Maj.-Gen. Alexander Angus Airlie, 1838–1919, vol. II
Kinloch, Brig.-Gen. Sir David Alexander, 11th Bt (cr 1686), 1856–1944, vol. IV
Kinloch, Sir George, 3rd Bt (cr 1873), 1880–1948, vol. IV
Kinloch, J. Parlane, died 1932, vol. III
Kinloch, James Laird, 1878–1952, vol. V
Kinloch, Sir John George Smyth, 2nd Bt (cr 1873), 1849–1910, vol. I
Kinloch-Cooke, Sir Clement, 1st Bt, died 1944, vol. IV
Kinloss, Lady (11th in line, styled 8th), 1852–1944, vol. IV
Kinloss, Master of; Rev. Hon. Luis Chandos Francis Temple Morgan-Grenville, 1889–1944, vol. IV
Kinnaird, 11th Lord, 1847–1923, vol. II
Kinnaird, 12th Lord, 1880–1972, vol. VII
Kinnaird, Master of; Hon. Douglas Arthur Kinnaird, 1879–1914, vol. I
Kinnaird, Hon. Emily, died 1947, vol. IV
Kinnaird, Hon. Patrick, 1898–1948, vol. IV
Kinnear, 1st Baron, 1833–1917, vol. II
Kinnear, Alfred, died 1912, vol. I
Kinnear, Hon. Helen Alice, 1894–1970, vol. VI
Kinnear, John Boyd, 1828–1920, vol. II
Kinnear, Sir Norman Boyd, 1882–1957, vol. V
Kinnear, Sir Walter Samuel, 1872–1953, vol. V
Kinnell, Rev. Gordon, 1891–1971, vol. VII
Kinnoull, 13th (shown as 12th) Earl of, 1855–1916, vol. II
Kinnoull, 14th Earl of, 1902–1938, vol. III
Kino, Major Algernon Roderick, 1880–1924, vol. II
Kinross, 1st Baron, 1837–1905, vol. I
Kinross, 2nd Baron, 1870–1939, vol. III
Kinross, 3rd Baron, 1904–1976, vol. VII
Kinross, Albert, 1870–1929, vol. III
Kinross, John, died 1931, vol. III
Kinsey, Sir Joseph James, 1852–1936, vol. III

Kinsley, Albert, 1852–1945, vol. IV
Kinsman, Frederick Joseph, 1868–1944, vol. IV
Kinsman, Col Gerald Richard Vivian, 1876–1963, vol. VI
Kintore, 10th Earl of, 1852–1930, vol. III
Kintore, 11th Earl of, 1879–1966, vol. VI
Kintore, Countess of (12th in line), 1874–1974, vol. VII
Kinvig, Robert Henry, 1893–1969, vol. VI
Kipling, John Lockwood, 1837–1911, vol. I
Kipling, Rudyard, 1865–1936, vol. III
Kippen, William James, died 1928, vol. II
Kippenberger, Maj.-Gen. Sir Howard Karl, 1897–1957, vol. V
Kipping, Frederic Stanley, 1863–1949, vol. IV
Kipping, Sir Norman Victor, 1901–1979, vol. VII
Kipps, William John, 1866–1938, vol. III
Kiralfy, Imre, died 1919, vol. II
Kirby, Sir Alfred, 1840–1900, vol. I
Kirby, Brig.-Gen. Arthur Durham, 1867–1948, vol. IV
Kirby, Bertie Victor, 1887–1953, vol. V
Kirby, Adm. Francis George, 1854–1951, vol. V
Kirby, Gp Captain Frank Howard, 1871–1956, vol. V
Kirby, George, 1845–1937, vol. III
Kirby, Sir (Horace) Woodburn, 1853–1932, vol. III
Kirby, Sir James Norman, 1899–1971, vol. VII
Kirby, Air Cdre John Lawrence, 1899–1980, vol. VII
Kirby, Col Norborne, 1863–1922, vol. II
Kirby, Maj.-Gen. Stanley Woodburn, 1895–1968, vol. VI
Kirby, Brig.-Gen. Stuart Rodger, 1873–1959, vol. V
Kirby, William Forsell, 1844–1912, vol. I
Kirby, Sir Woodburn; see Kirby, Sir H. W.
Kirchhoffer, Hon. John Nesbitt, 1848–1914, vol. I
Kirk, Adam Kennedy, 1893–1975, vol. VII
Kirk, Adm. Alan Goodrich, 1888–1963, vol. VI
Kirk, Alexander Comstock, 1888–1979, vol. VII
Kirk, Sir Amos Child, 1856–1928, vol. II
Kirk, Geoffrey William, 1907–1975, vol. VII
Kirk, Harry B., died 1948, vol. IV
Kirk, Sir Henry Alexander, 1847–1929, vol. III
Kirk, Sir John, 1832–1922, vol. II
Kirk, Sir John, 1847–1922, vol. II
Kirk, John, 1881–1959, vol. V
Kirk, Rt Rev. Kenneth Escott, 1886–1954, vol. V
Kirk, Lucy Phoebe, 1890–1961, vol. VI
Kirk, Rt Hon. Norman Eric, 1923–1974, vol. VII
Kirk, Rev. Paul Thomas Radford-Rowe, died 1962, vol. VI
Kirk, Sir Peter Michael, 1928–1977, vol. VII
Kirk, Thomas Sinclair, 1869–1940, vol. III
Kirkaldy, Adam Willis, 1867–1931, vol. III
Kirkaldy, Harold Stewart, 1902–1976, vol. VII
Kirkbride, Sir Alec Seath, 1897–1978, vol. VII
Kirkby, Lt-Col Henry McKenzie, 1877–1952, vol. V
Kirkby, Rt Rev. Sydney James, 1879–1935, vol. III
Kirkconnell, Watson, 1895–1977, vol. VII
Kirke, Claud Cecil Augustus, 1875–1959, vol. V
Kirke, Henry, 1842–1925, vol. II

Kirke, Percy St George, died 1966, vol. VI
Kirke, Gen. Sir Walter Mervyn St George, 1877–1949, vol. IV
Kirkhope, Lt-Col Kenneth Macleay, 1877–1950, vol. IV
Kirkland, Edward Chase, 1894–1975, vol. VII
Kirkland, James Hampton, 1859–1939, vol. III
Kirkland, Rev. Canon Thomas James, 1884–1965, vol. VI
Kirkley, 1st Baron, 1863–1935, vol. III
Kirkman, Frederick Bernulf Beever, 1869–1945, vol. IV
Kirkman, Maj.-Gen. John Mather, 1898–1964, vol. VI
Kirkman, Hon. Thomas, 1843–1919, vol. II
Kirkness, Lewis Hawker, 1881–1950, vol. IV
Kirkpatrick, Very Rev. Alexander Francis, 1849–1940, vol. III
Kirkpatrick, Lt-Col Alexander Ronald Yvone, 1868–1950, vol. IV
Kirkpatrick, Hon. Andrew Alexander, 1848–1928, vol. II
Kirkpatrick, Maj.-Gen. Charles, 1879–1955, vol. V
Kirkpatrick, Sir Charles Sharpe, 9th Bt, 1874–1937, vol. III
Kirkpatrick, Sir Cyril Reginald Sutton, 1872–1957, vol. V
Kirkpatrick, Francis, 1840–1921, vol. II
Kirkpatrick, Frederick Alex., 1861–1953, vol. V
Kirkpatrick, Hon. Sir George Airey, 1841–1899, vol. I
Kirkpatrick, Gen. Sir George Macaulay, 1866–1950, vol. IV
Kirkpatrick, Lt-Col Henry, 1871–1958, vol. V
Kirkpatrick, Lt-Col Henry Pownall, 1862–1919, vol. II
Kirkpatrick, Rev. Canon Herbert Francis, 1888–1971, vol. VII
Kirkpatrick, Air Vice-Marshal Herbert James, 1910–1977, vol. VII
Kirkpatrick, Col Ivone, 1860–1936, vol. III
Kirkpatrick, Sir Ivone Augustine, died 1964, vol. VI
Kirkpatrick, Sir James, 8th Bt, 1841–1899, vol. I
Kirkpatrick, Sir James Alexander, 10th Bt, 1918–1954, vol. V
Kirkpatrick, John, 1835–1926, vol. II
Kirkpatrick, Col Roger, 1859–1933, vol. III
Kirkpatrick, T. Percy C., 1869–1954, vol. V
Kirkpatrick, Major William, 1863–1941, vol. IV
Kirkpatrick, William, 1886–1947, vol. IV
Kirkpatrick, William MacColin, 1878–1953, vol. V
Kirkpatrick, Brig.-Gen. William Johnston, 1851–1931, vol. III
Kirkpatrick-Caldecot, Ivone, 1867–1951, vol. V
Kirkup, Brig. Philip, 1893–1959, vol. V
Kirkup, Thomas, 1844–1912, vol. I
Kirkup, Thomas Henry, 1864–1951, vol. V
Kirkwood, 1st Baron, 1872–1955, vol. V
Kirkwood, 2nd Baron, 1903–1970, vol. VI
Kirkwood, Col Carleton Hooper Morrison, 1860–1937, vol. III
Kirkwood, Lt-Col James George, 1872–1955, vol. V

Kirkwood, Major John Hendley Morrison, 1877–1924, vol. II
Kirkwood, Sir Walter Guy Coffin, 1856–1935, vol. III
Kirkwood, William Montague Hammett, 1850–1926, vol. II
Kirwan, Lt-Gen. Sir Bertram Richard, 1871–1960, vol. V
Kirwan, Rev. Ernest Cecil, 1867–1936, vol. III
Kirwan, Lt-Col Ernest William O'Gorman, 1887–1965, vol. VI
Kirwan, Geoffrey Dugdale, 1896–1970, vol. VI
Kirwan, Hon. Sir John Waters, 1866–1949, vol. IV
Kirwan, Lionel M.; see Maitland-Kirwan.
Kisch, Barthold Schlesinger, 1882–1961, vol. VI
Kisch, Sir Cecil, 1884–1961, vol. VI
Kisch, Brig. Frederick Hermann, 1888–1943, vol. IV
Kisch, Harold, died 1959, vol. V
Kisch, Hermann Michael, 1850–1942, vol. IV
Kishangarh, Lt-Col HH Umdai Rajhae Buland Makan Maharajadhiraj Maharaj Sir Madan Singh Bahadur, 1884–1926, vol. II
Kishun Pershad, Raja-i-Rajayan Maharajah Bahadur, Yamin-us-Saltanat, Sir, 1864–1940, vol. III
Kissan, Edgar Duguid, died 1932, vol. III
Kitcat, Mabel, (Mrs S. A. P. Kitcat), died 1922, vol. II
Kitchen, Sir Geoffrey, 1906–1978, vol. VII
Kitchen, Percy Inman, 1883–1963, vol. VI
Kitchener of Khartoum, 1st Earl, 1850–1916, vol. II
Kitchener of Khartoum, 2nd Earl, 1846–1937, vol. III
Kitchener, Francis Elliott, 1838–1915, vol. I
Kitchener, Lt-Gen. Sir Frederick Walter, 1858–1912, vol. I
Kitchin, Ven. Arthur, 1855–1928, vol. II
Kitchin, Arthur James Warburton, 1870–1957, vol. V
Kitchin, Clifford Henry Benn, 1895–1967, vol. VI
Kitchin, Darcy Butterworth, 1863–1939, vol. III
Kitchin, Finlay Lorimer, died 1934, vol. III
Kitchin, Frederick Harcourt, 1867–1932, vol. III
Kitchin, Very Rev. George William, 1827–1912, vol. I
Kitchin, John, 1869–1951, vol. V
Kitchin, Shepherd Braithwaite, died 1944, vol. IV
Kitching, Rt Rev. Arthur Leonard, 1875–1960, vol. V
Kitching, Elsie, 1870–1955, vol. V
Kitching, Theodore Hopkins, 1866–1930, vol. III
Kitching, Wilfred, 1893–1977, vol. VII
Kite, Frederick William, 1856–1940, vol. III
Kite, Rev. Joseph Bertram, 1857–1939, vol. III
Kitiyakara, Prince Nakkhatra Mangala, 1898–1953, vol. V
Kitson, Sir Albert Ernest, 1868–1937, vol. III
Kitson, Col Charles Edward, 1874–1928, vol. II
Kitson, Charles Herbert, 1874–1944, vol. IV
Kitson, Geoffrey Herbert, 1896–1974, vol. VII
Kitson, Sir George Vernon, 1899–1980, vol. VII
Kitson, Maj.-Gen. Sir Gerald Charles, 1856–1950, vol. IV

Kitson, Vice-Adm. Sir Henry Karslake, 1877–1952, vol. V
Kitson, Captain James Buller, 1883–1976, vol. VII
Kitson, Hon. James Clifford, 1864–1942, vol. IV
Kitson, Col James Edward, 1848–1912, vol. I
Kitson, Sydney Decimus, 1871–1937, vol. III
Kitson, William Henry, 1886–1952, vol. V
Kitson Clark, George Sidney Roberts, 1900–1975, vol. VII
Kittermaster, F. R., 1899–1972, vol. VII
Kittermaster, Sir Harold Baxter, 1879–1939, vol. III
Kitto, John Vivian, 1875–1953, vol. V
Kittoe, Lt-Col Montagu Francis Markham Sloane, died 1967, vol. VI
Kitton, Frederic George, 1856–1903, vol. I
Kitts, Sir Francis Joseph, 1914–1979, vol. VII
Kittson, Rev. Henry, 1848–1925, vol. II (A), vol. III
Klaestad, Helge, 1885–1965, vol. VI
Klecki, Paul; see Kletzi, P.
Kleczkowski, Alfred Alexander Peter, 1908–1970, vol. VI
Kleiber, Erich, 1890–1956, vol. V
Klein, Edward Emanuel, 1844–1925, vol. II
Klein, Abbé Felix, 1862–1954, vol. V
Klein, Herman, 1856–1934, vol. III
Klein, Sydney Turner, 1853–1934, vol. III
Kleinwort, Sir Alexander Drake, 1st Bt, 1858–1935, vol. III
Kleinwort, Sir Cyril Hugh, 1905–1980, vol. VII
Kleinwort, Ernest Greverus, 1901–1977, vol. VII
Kleinwort, Herman Greverus, 1856–1942, vol. IV
Klemperer, Otto, 1885–1973, vol. VII
Kletzi, Paul, (Paul Klecki), 1900–1973, vol. VII
Klickmann, Flora, (Mrs Henderson-Smith), died 1958, vol. V
Klijnstra, Gerrit Dirk Ale, 1912–1976, vol. VII
Klinck, Leonard Sylvanus, 1877–1969, vol. VI
Klinghoffer, Clara, 1900–1970, vol. VI
Klopsch, Louis, died 1910, vol. I
Klotz, Otto, 1852–1923, vol. II
Klugh, Ven. Leonard, 1859–1943, vol. IV
Klyne, William, 1913–1977, vol. VII
Knaggs, Col Henry Thomas, 1863–1946, vol. IV
Knaggs, Col Morton Herbert, 1871–1948, vol. IV
Knaggs, Robert Lawford, died 1945, vol. IV
Knaggs, Sir Samuel William, 1856–1924, vol. II
Knapp, Sir Arthur Rowland, died 1954, vol. V
Knapp, Charles Welbourne, 1848–1916, vol. II
Knapp, Brig.-Gen. Kempster Kenmure, 1866–1948, vol. IV
Knapp, Marion Domville, 1870–1963, vol. VI
Knapp, Valentine, 1861–1935, vol. III
Knapp, William Ireland, 1835–1908, vol. I
Knapp-Fisher, Arthur Bedford, 1888–1965, vol. VI
Knapp-Fisher, Sir Edward Francis, 1864–1940, vol. III
Knaresborough, 1st Baron, 1845–1929, vol. III
Knatchbull, Brig.-Gen. George Wyndham Chichester, 1862–1943, vol. IV
Knatchbull, Major Reginald Norton, 1872–1917, vol. II

Knatchbull, Sir Wyndham, 12th Bt, 1844–1917, vol. II

Knatchbull-Hugessen, Hon. Adrian Norton, 1891–1976, vol. VII

Knatchbull-Hugessen, Herbert Thomas, 1835–1922, vol. II

Knatchbull-Hugessen, Sir Hughe Montgomery, 1886–1971, vol. VII

Kneale, Sydney James, 1895–1975, vol. VII

Knebworth, Viscount; Edward Anthony James Lytton, 1903–1933, vol. III

Knebworth, Viscount; Alexander Edward John Lytton, 1910–1942, vol. IV

Knecht, Edmund, 1861–1925, vol. II

Kneeland, Abner W., 1853–1928, vol. II

Kneen, John Joseph, 1873–1938, vol. III

Kneen, Thomas, died 1916, vol. II

Kneen, William, 1862–1921, vol. II

Knibbs, Sir George Handley, 1858–1929, vol. III

Knight, A. Charles, died 1958, vol. V

Knight, Most Rev. Alan John, 1902–1979, vol. VII

Knight, Rt Rev. Albion Williamson, 1859–1936, vol. III

Knight, Alfred Ernest, 1861–1934, vol. III

Knight, Rev. Angus Clifton, 1873–1931, vol. III

Knight, Archibald Patterson, died 1935, vol. III

Knight, Arthur Harold John, 1903–1963, vol. VI

Knight, Rt Rev. Arthur Mesac, 1864–1939, vol. III

Knight, (Arthur) Rex, 1903–1963, vol. VI

Knight, Charles, 1863–1941, vol. IV

Knight, Charles Andrew R. B.; see Rouse-Boughton-Knight.

Knight, Charles Joseph, 1863–1950, vol. IV

Knight, Captain Charles William Robert, 1884–1957, vol. V

Knight, Clara Millicent, died 1950, vol. IV

Knight, Clifford, 1909–1959, vol. V

Knight, Edward Frederick, 1852–1925, vol. II

Knight, Eric, 1897–1943, vol. IV

Knight, Eric Ayshford, 1863–1944, vol. IV

Knight, Sir Frederic Winn, 1812–1897, vol. I

Knight, Sir George, 1874–1951, vol. V

Knight, Gerald Hocken, 1908–1979, vol. VII

Knight, Gilfred Norman, 1891–1978, vol. VII

Knight, Harold, 1874–1961, vol. VI

Knight, Sir Henry Edmund, 1833–1917, vol. II

Knight, Sir Henry Foley, 1886–1960, vol. V

Knight, Rev. Henry Joseph Corbett, died 1920, vol. II

Knight, Brig.-Gen. Henry Lewkenor, 1874–1945, vol. IV

Knight, Rev. Herbert Theodore, 1869–1934, vol. III

Knight, Holford, 1877–1936, vol. III

Knight, Jasper Frederick, 1909–1972, vol. VII

Knight, John Broughton, 1863–1937, vol. III

Knight, John Buxton, 1842–1908, vol. I (A)

Knight, Captain John Peake, 1890–1916, vol. II

Knight, Joseph, 1829–1907, vol. I

Knight, Joseph, 1838–1909, vol. I

Knight, Dame Laura, 1877–1970, vol. VI

Knight, Rt Rev. Leslie Albert, 1890–1950, vol. IV (A), vol. V

Knight, Nicholas, 1861–1942, vol. IV

Knight, Percy, 1891–1968, vol. VI

Knight, Rex; see Knight, A. R.

Knight, Rt Rev. Samuel Kirshbaum, 1868–1932, vol. III

Knight, Chief Engr T. H., died 1918, vol. II

Knight, William Anderson, 1861–1915, vol. I (A), vol. III

Knight, William Angus, 1836–1916, vol. II

Knight, William Francis Jackson, 1895–1964, vol. VI

Knight, William George, died 1938, vol. III

Knight, William George, 1858–1943, vol. IV

Knight, William Lowry Craig, 1889–1955, vol. V

Knight, William Stanley Macbean, 1869–1950, vol. IV

Knight, Maj.-Gen. Sir Wyndham Charles, 1863–1942, vol. IV

Knight-Adkin, Harry Kenrick, 1851–1927, vol. II

Knight-Adkin, Rev. Walter Kenrick, 1880–1957, vol. V

Knight Dix, Dorothy; see Waddy, D. K.

Knightley, Lady; (Louisa Mary), 1842–1913, vol. I

Knightley, Sir Charles Valentine, 5th Bt, 1853–1932, vol. III

Knightley, Rev. Sir Henry Francis, 6th Bt, 1854–1938, vol. III

Knightley, Captain Percy Frank, 1874–1942, vol. IV

Knightley, Rev. Sir Valentine, 4th Bt, 1812–1898, vol. I

Knighton, William, died 1900, vol. I

Knighton-Hammond, Arthur Henry, 1875–1970, vol. VI

Knights, Henry Newton, died 1959, vol. V

Knights, Maj.-Gen. Robert William, 1912–1975, vol. VII

Knill, Sir Ian S.; see Stuart-Knill.

Knill, Sir John, 2nd Bt, 1856–1934, vol. III

Knill, Sir Stuart, 1st Bt, 1824–1898, vol. I

Knittel, John Herman Emanuel, 1891–1970, vol. VI

Knobel, Edward Ball, 1841–1930, vol. III

Knoblock, Edward, 1874–1945, vol. IV

Knocker, Sir Edward Wollaston Nadir, 1838–1907, vol. I

Knollys, 1st Viscount, 1837–1924, vol. II

Knollys, 2nd Viscount, 1895–1966, vol. VI

Knollys, Rev. Archibald A., 1851–1940, vol. III

Knollys, Hon. Charlotte, died 1930, vol. III

Knollys, Sir Courtenay, 1849–1905, vol. I

Knollys, Rev. Erskine William, 1842–1923, vol. II

Knollys, Col Sir Henry, 1840–1930, vol. III

Knollys, Major Louis Frederic, 1847–1922, vol. II

Knollys, William Edward, 1843–1910, vol. I

Knoop, Douglas, 1883–1948, vol. IV

Knott, Rev. Alfred Ernest, 1869–1951, vol. V

Knott, Cargill Gilston, 1856–1922, vol. II

Knott, Frank Alexander, 1889–1962, vol. VI

Knott, Lt-Gen. Sir Harold Edwin, 1903–1974, vol. VII

Knott, Sir James, 1st Bt, 1855–1934, vol. III

Knott, John, 1853–1921, vol. II

Knott, John Espenett, died 1959, vol. V

Knott, Ralph, 1878–1929, vol. III

Knott, Stratton Collings, 1856–1904, vol. I

Knott, Sir Thomas Garbutt, 2nd Bt, 1879–1949, vol. IV

Knottesford-Fortescue, Laurence; *see* Fortescue.

Knowland, William Fife, 1908–1974, vol. VII

Knowles, Arthur, 1858–1929, vol. III

Knowles, Arthur Richard, 1899–1960, vol. V

Knowles, Maj.-Gen. Sir Charles Benjamin, 1835–1924, vol. II

Knowles, Sir Charles George Frederick, 4th Bt, 1832–1918, vol. II

Knowles, Rev. David; *see* Knowles, Rev. Michael Clive.

Knowles, Rt Rev. Donald Rowland, 1898–1977, vol. VII

Knowles, Air Vice-Marshal Edgar, 1907–1977, vol. VII

Knowles, Rt Rev. Edwin Hubert, 1874–1962, vol. VI

Knowles, Frances Ivens; *see* Knowles, M. H. F. I.

Knowles, Rev. Francis, 1830–1916, vol. II

Knowles, Sir Francis Gerald William, 6th Bt, 1915–1974, vol. VII

Knowles, Sir Francis Howe Seymour, 5th Bt, 1886–1953, vol. V

Knowles, Frank, 1865–1934, vol. III

Knowles, Frederick Arthur, 1872–1922, vol. II

Knowles, Rear-Adm. George Herbert, 1881–1961, vol. VI

Knowles, Sir George Shaw, 1882–1947, vol. IV

Knowles, George Sheridan, 1863–1931, vol. III

Knowles, John, 1898–1977, vol. VII

Knowles, Lt-Col John George, *died* 1919, vol. II

Knowles, Joshua Kenneth, 1903–1974, vol. VII

Knowles, Ven. Kenneth Davenport, 1874–1944, vol. IV

Knowles, Sir Lees, 1st Bt (*cr* 1903), 1857–1928, vol. II

Knowles, Lilian Charlotte Anne, *died* 1926, vol. II

Knowles, Mabel Winifred, (May Wynne), 1875–1949, vol. IV

Knowles, (Mary Hannah) Frances Ivens, *died* 1944, vol. IV

Knowles, Rev. Michael Clive, (Rev. David Knowles), 1896–1974, vol. VII

Knowles, Lt-Col Robert, 1883–1936, vol. III

Knowles, Robert Millington, 1843–1924, vol. II

Knowles, William Henry, 1857–1943, vol. IV

Knowling, Hon. George, 1841–1923, vol. II

Knowling, Rev. Richard John, 1851–1919, vol. II

Knowlson, Thomas Sharper, 1867–1947, vol. IV

Knox, Rt Hon. Sir Adrian, 1863–1932, vol. III

Knox, Alfred Dilwyn, *died* 1943, vol. IV

Knox, Maj.-Gen. Sir Alfred William Fortescue, 1870–1964, vol. VI

Knox, Rev. Andrew, 1849–1915, vol. I

Knox, Col Arthur Francis Gore P.K.G.; *see* Pery-Knox-Gore.

Knox, Major Arthur Rice, 1863–1917, vol. II

Knox, Lt-Gen. Sir Charles Edmond, 1846–1938, vol. III

Knox, Collie, *died* 1977, vol. VII

Knox, Rt Rev. Edmund Arbuthnott, 1847–1937, vol. III

Knox, (Edmund Francis) Vesey, 1865–1921, vol. II

Knox, Edmund George Valpy, 1881–1971, vol. VII

Knox, Sir Edward, 1819–1901, vol. I

Knox, Sir Edward Ritchie, 1889–1973, vol. VII

Knox, Brig. Sir Errol Galbraith, 1889–1949, vol. IV

Knox, Sir Geoffrey George, 1884–1958, vol. V

Knox, Sir George Edward, *died* 1922, vol. II

Knox, Brig. Hon. Sir George Hodges, 1885–1960, vol. V

Knox, Lt-Col George Stuart, 1871–1945, vol. IV

Knox, Lt-Col Sir Hamish James Stuart, *died* 1940, vol. III

Knox, Gen. Sir Harry Hugh Sidney, 1873–1971, vol. VII

Knox, Brig.-Gen. Henry Owen, 1874–1955, vol. V

Knox, Sir James, 1850–1926, vol. II

Knox, Sir James, 1862–1938, vol. III

Knox, John Crawford, 1891–1964, vol. VI

Knox, Sir Malcolm; *see* Knox, Sir T. M.

Knox, Rt Hon. Sir Ralph Henry, 1836–1913, vol. I

Knox, Lt-Col Richard, 1848–1918, vol. II

Knox, Robert, *died* 1928, vol. II

Knox, Sir Robert Uchtred Eyre, 1889–1965, vol. VI

Knox, Sir Robert Wilson, 1890–1973, vol. VII

Knox, Rt Rev. Mgr Ronald Arbuthnott, 1888–1957, vol. V

Knox, Lt-Col Stuart George, 1869–1956, vol. V

Knox, Sir (Thomas) Malcolm, 1900–1980, vol. VII

Knox, Vesey; *see* Knox, E. F. V.

Knox, Walter Ernest, 1894–1970, vol. VI

Knox, Rev. Wilfred Lawrence, *died* 1950, vol. IV

Knox, Hon. William, 1850–1913, vol. I

Knox, Maj.-Gen. Sir William George, 1847–1916, vol. II

Knox Johnston, Anthony Gordon; *see* Johnston.

Knox Little, Rev. William John, 1839–1918, vol. II

Knox-Shaw, Charles Thomas, 1854–1939, vol. III

Knox-Shaw, Harold, 1885–1970, vol. VI

Knox-Shaw, Thomas, 1886–1972, vol. VII

Knubley, Rev. Edward Ponsonby, 1850–1931, vol. III

Knudsen, Sir Karl Fredrik, 1872–1937, vol. III

Knudsen, Martin, 1871–1949, vol. IV

Knuthsen, Sir Louis Francis Roebuck, *died* 1957, vol. V

Knutsford, 1st Viscount, 1825–1914, vol. I

Knutsford, 2nd Viscount, 1855–1931, vol. III

Knutsford, 3rd Viscount, 1855–1935, vol. III

Knutsford, 4th Viscount, 1888–1976, vol. VII

Knyvett, Alexander Vansittart, 1848–1911, vol. I

Knyvett, Rt Rev. Carey Frederick, 1885–1967, vol. VI

Knyvett, Seymour Henry, 1849–1915, vol. I

Koch, Lauge, 1892–1964, vol. VI

Koch, Ludwig, 1881–1974, vol. VII

Koch, Robert, 1843–1910, vol. I

Kodàly, Zoltán, 1882–1967, vol. VI

Kodama, Lt-Gen. Baron Gentaro, 1855–1906, vol. I

Koe, Maj.-Gen. Frederick William Brooke, 1862–1935, vol. III

Koe, Brig.-Gen. Lancelot Charles, *died* 1941, vol. IV

Koebel, Major Frederick Ernest, 1881–1940, vol. III

Koebel, W. H., 1872–1923, vol. II

Koechlin, Raymond, 1860–1931, vol. III

Koelle, Vice-Adm. Sir Harry Philpot, 1901–1980, vol. VII

Koenig, Gén. d'Armée Marie-Pierre, 1898–1970, vol. VI

Koenigsberger, Franz, 1907–1979, vol. VII

Koeppler, Sir Henry, (Sir Heinz), 1912–1979, vol. VII

Kohan, Major Charles Mendel, 1884–1974, vol. VII

Kohan, Robert Mendel, 1883–1967, vol. VI

Kohler, Kaufmann, 1843–1926, vol. II

Kohlsaat, Herman H., 1853–1924, vol. II (A), vol. III

Kokkinakis, Theodoros G.; see Athenagoras, T.

Kokoschka, Oskar, 1886–1980, vol. VII

Kole, Nene Sir Emmanuel Mate, 1860–1939, vol. III

Kolhapur, Maharaja of, 1874–1922, vol. II

Kolhapur, Maharaja of, 1897–1940, vol. III

Kollengode, Raja Sir Vengarad of, 1873–1940, vol. III

Koller, Pius Charles, 1904–1979, vol. VII

Komisarjevsky, Theodore, died 1954, vol. V

Komura, Marquis Jutaro, 1855–1911, vol. I

Kon, George Armand Robert, 1892–1951, vol. V

Konig, Frederick Adolphus, 1867–1940, vol. III

Konody, Paul G., 1872–1933, vol. III

Konstam, Edwin Max., 1870–1956, vol. V

Konstam, Geoffrey Lawrence Samuel, 1899–1962, vol. VI

Koop, Albert James, 1877–1945, vol. IV

Koppel, Percy Alexander, 1876–1932, vol. III

Korda, Sir Alexander, 1893–1956, vol. V

Korngold, Erich Wolfgang, 1897–1957, vol. V

Korsah, Sir Arku; see Korsah, Sir K. A.

Korsah, Sir (Kobina) Arku, 1894–1967, vol. VI

Kortright, Sir Cornelius Hendrichsen, 1817–1897, vol. I

Kortright, Henry Somers, 1870–1942, vol. IV

Kossuth, Francis, 1841–1914, vol. I

Kostelanetz, André, died 1980, vol. VII

Kosygin, Alexei Nikolaevich, 1904–1980, vol. VII

Kotah, Lt-Col HH Maharajahdiraj Maharaj Mahimahendra Maharaorajaji Shri Sir Umed Singh Bahadur, 1873–1941, vol. III

Kotelawala, Col Rt Hon. Sir John Lionel, 1897–1980, vol. VII

Kotewall, Sir Robert Hormus, 1880–1949, vol. IV

Kothari, Sir Jehangir Hormasji, died 1934, vol. III

Kothavala, Tehmasp Tehmul, 1893–1977, vol. VII

Kotval, Peshotan Sohrabji, 1868–1949, vol. IV (A)

Kotze, Sir John Gilbert, 1849–1940, vol. III

Kotzé, Sir Robert Nelson, 1870–1953, vol. V

Kouropatkin, Alexei Nicholaevitch, 1848–1921, vol. II

Koussevitzky, Serge, 1874–1951, vol. V

Kozygin, Alexei Nikolaevich; see Kosygin, A. N.

Krabbé, Paymaster-Rear-Adm. Frederick James, 1860–1933, vol. III

Kratovil, Bohuslav G., 1901–1972, vol. VII

Kraus, Adolf, 1849–1928, vol. II (A), vol. III

Kraus, Otakar, 1909–1980, vol. VII

Krause, Frederick Edward Traugott, 1868–1959, vol. V

Krause, Lotte, (Madame Otto Krause); see Lehmann, Lotte.

Krausse, Alexis Sidney, 1859–1904, vol. I

Kreisler, Fritz, 1875–1962, vol. VI

Kretser, Edward de, 1854–1925, vol. II

Kreuger, Ivar, 1880–1932, vol. III

Kreyer, Brig. Hubert Stanley, 1890–1949, vol. IV

Krips, Josef, 1902–1974, vol. VII

Krishna Menon, Vengalil Krishnan, 1896–1974, vol. VII

Krishna Rau, Sir Mysore Nanjundiah, 1877–1958, vol. V

Krishna Shumshere, Jung Bahadur Rana, General, 1900–1977, vol. VII

Krishnama Chariar, Sir Vangal Thiruvenkatachari, 1881–1964, vol. VI

Krishnan, Cheruvari, 1868–1927, vol. II

Krishnan, Sir Kariamanikkam Srinivasa, 1898–1961, vol. VI

Krishnan Nair, Dewan Bahadur Sir M., 1870–1938, vol. III

Krishnaswami Ayyar, Diwan Bahadur Sir Alladi, 1883–1953, vol. V

Krogh, August, 1874–1949, vol. IV

Kroll, Wilhelm, 1869–1939, vol. III

Kronberger, Hans, 1920–1970, vol. VI

Kropotkin, Prince Peter Alexeievitch, 1842–1921, vol. II

Kroyer-Kielberg, Sir (F.) Michael, 1882–1958, vol. V

Krug, Julius A., 1907–1970, vol. VI

Kruger, Stephen J. Paul, 1825–1904, vol. I

Kubelik, Jan, 1880–1940, vol. III

Küchemann, Dietrich, 1911–1976, vol. VII

Kuenen, Johannes Petrus, 1866–1922, vol. II

Kuhe, William, 1823–1912, vol. I

Kuhn, Richard, 1900–1967, vol. VI

Kuiper, Gerard Peter, 1905–1973, vol. VII

Kukday, Col Sir Krishnaji Vishnoo, 1870–1958, vol. VI (AI)

Kuklos; see Wray, W. Fitzwater.

Kuprin, Aleksandr Ivonovich, 1870–1938, vol. III

Kuroki, General Count, 1844–1923, vol. II

Kurz, Otto, 1908–1975, vol. VII

Kusel, Baron de, 1848–1917, vol. II

Küssner, Amalia, died 1932, vol. III

Kutch, Maharao of; Lt-Col HH Maharaja Dhiraj Mirza Maharao Shri Sir Vijayaraji, Savai Bahadur, 1885–1948, vol. IV

Kutch, HH Maharaja Dhiraj Mirzan Maharao Shri Khengarji Sawai Bahadur Maharao of, 1866–1942, vol. IV

Kutlehr, Raja Ram Pal of, 1849–1927, vol. II (A), vol. III

Kuwait, Emir of, 1895–1965, vol. VI

Kuyper, A., 1837–1920, vol. II

Kwan, Sir Cho-Yiu, 1907–1971, vol. VII

Kyd, Sir David Hope, 1862–1933, vol. III

Kyd, James Gray, 1882–1968, vol. VI

Kyd, John Normansell, 1864–1931, vol. III

Kydd, Ronald Robertson, 1920–1972, vol. VII

Kyffin-Taylor, Brig.-Gen. Gerald; see Taylor.

Kyle, Emily Escher, died 1958, vol. V

Kyle, Henry Greville, died 1956, vol. V

Kyle, Lt-Col Robert, 1862–1942, vol. IV
Kyle, William Galloway, 1875–1967, vol. VI
Kyllachy, Hon. Lord; William Mackintosh, 1842–1918, vol. II
Kylsant, 1st Baron, 1863–1937, vol. III
Kynaston, George Henry, 1850–1906, vol. I
Kynaston, Rev. Herbert, 1835–1910, vol. I
Kynaston, Walter Roger Owen, 1874–1935, vol. III
Kyne, Most Rev. John Anthony, 1904–1966, vol. VI
Kynnaird, Viscount; Sigismondo Maria Giuseppe Rospigliosi, 1886–1918, vol. II
Kynnersley, Charles Walter Sneyd-, 1849–1904, vol. I
Kynoch, John Alexander, *died* 1931, vol. III
Kynoch, Sir John Wheen, 1878–1946, vol. IV
Kynsey, Sir William Raymond, 1840–1904, vol. I
Kyrke, Lt-Col Henry Vernon Venables, 1881–1933, vol. III
Kyrle, Ven. Rowland Tracy Ashe M.; *see* Money-Kyrle.
Kyte, George William, 1864–1940, vol. III (A), vol. IV

L

Labarthe, André, 1902–1967, vol. VI
Labia, Princess Ida, *died* 1961, vol. VI
La Billois, Hon. Charles H., 1856–1928, vol. II
Laborde, Edward Daniel, 1863–1928, vol. II
Labori, Fernand, 1860–1917, vol. II
Labouchere, Rt Hon. Henry, 1831–1912, vol. I
La Brooy, Justin Theodore, 1857–1944, vol. IV
Laby, Thomas Howell, 1880–1946, vol. IV
Lacaita, Charles Carmichael, 1853–1933, vol. III
Lace, John Henry, *died* 1918, vol. II
Lacey, Alfred Travers, 1892–1966, vol. VI
Lacey, Sir Francis Eden, 1859–1946, vol. IV
Lacey, Gerald, 1887–1979, vol. VII
Lacey, Sir Ralph Wilfred, 1900–1965, vol. VI
Lacey, Rev. Thomas Alexander, 1853–1931, vol. III
Lacey, Walter Graham, 1894–1974, vol. VII
Lachaise, Gaston, 1882–1935, vol. III
Lachance, Arthur, 1868–1945, vol. IV
Lachman, Harry, 1886–1975, vol. VII
Lack, David, 1910–1973, vol. VII
Lack, Harry Lambert, 1867–1943, vol. IV
Lack, Henry Martyn, 1909–1979, vol. VII
Lack, Sir Henry Reader, 1832–1908, vol. I
Lackey, Hon. Sir John, 1830–1903, vol. I
Lackie, William Walter, 1869–1945, vol. IV
Lacon, Sir Edmund Beecroft Francis Heathcote, 5th Bt, 1878–1911, vol. I
Lacon, Sir Edmund Broughton Knowles, 4th Bt, 1842–1899, vol. I
Lacon, Sir George Haworth Ussher, 6th Bt, 1881–1950, vol. IV
Lacon, Sir George Vere Francis, 7th Bt, 1909–1980, vol. VII
Lacon, Captain Henry Edmund 1849–1924, vol. II
Lacoste, Hon. Sir Alexandre, 1842–1923, vol. II

Lacy, Captain Ernest Edward, 1865–1946, vol. IV
Lacy, Francis Brandon, 1872–1954, vol. V
Lacy, Frederick St John, 1862–1935, vol. III
Lacy, Sir Maurice John Pierce, 2nd Bt, 1900–1965, vol. VI
Lacy, Sir Pierce Thomas, 1st Bt, 1872–1956, vol. V
Lacy, Rt Rev. Richard, 1841–1929, vol. III
Ladd, George Trumbull, 1842–1921, vol. II
Lade, Hon. Henry Augustus M.; *see* Milles-Lade.
La Dell, Edwin, 1914–1970, vol. VI
Laemmle, Carl, 1867–1939, vol. III
La Fárge, John, 1835–1910, vol. I
La Farge, Oliver, 1901–1963, vol. VI
Laferla, Albert Victor, 1887–1943, vol. IV
Laferté, Hon. Hector, 1885–1971, vol. VII
Laffan, Bertha Jane; *see* Laffan, Mrs Robert Stuart de Courcy.
Laffan, Col Henry David, 1858–1931, vol. III
Laffan, Robert George Dalrymple, 1887–1972, vol. VII
Laffan, Mrs Robert Stuart de Courcy, (Bertha Jane Laffan), *died* 1912, vol. I
Laffan, Rev. Robert Stuart de Courcy, 1853–1927, vol. II
Laffan, William M., 1848–1909, vol. I
Lafleche, Maj.-Gen. Léo-Richer, *died* 1956, vol. V
Lafleur, Paul Theodore, *died* 1924, vol. II
La Follette, Robert M., jun., 1895–1953, vol. V
La Follette, Robert Marion, 1855–1925, vol. II
Lafone, Rear-Adm. Albert Sumner, 1863–1933, vol. III
Lafone, Alfred, 1821–1911, vol. I
Lafone, Major Edgar Mortimore, *died* 1938, vol. III
Lafone, Harold Carlisle, 1879–1938, vol. III
Lafone, Ven. Henry Pownall Malins, 1867–1955, vol. V
Lafont, Rev. Eugene, 1837–1908, vol. I
Lafontaine, Henri, 1854–1943, vol. IV
La Fontaine, Lt-Col Sydney Hubert, 1885–1964, vol. VI
La Force, Auguste de Caumont, Duc de, 1878–1961, vol. VI
Lagden, Sir Godfrey Yeatman, 1851–1934, vol. III
Lagerkvist, Pär Fabian, 1891–1974, vol. VII
Lagerlof, Selma, 1858–1940, vol. III
Lagos, Oba of, *died* 1964, vol. VI
LaGuardia, Fiorello Henry, 1882–1947, vol. IV
Lahej, Sultan of, Sir Abdul Karim Fadthli Bin Ali, *died* 1947, vol. IV
Laidlaw, Sir George, 1883–1969, vol. VI
Laidlaw, James, 1847–1913, vol. I
Laidlaw, Rev. John, 1832–1906, vol. I
Laidlaw, Sir Patrick Playfair, 1881–1940, vol. III
Laidlaw, Sir Robert, 1856–1915, vol. I (A)
Laidlaw, Robert, 1897–1964, vol. VI
Laidlaw, Rt Hon. Thomas Kennedy, 1864–1943, vol. IV
Laidlay, William James, 1846–1912, vol. I
Lailey, Barnard, *died* 1944, vol. IV
Lailey, Guy Patrick Barnard, 1888–1946, vol. IV
Lailey, John Raymond N.; *see* Nicholson-Lailey.
Laine, Sir Abraham James, 1876–1948, vol. IV
Laing, Alfred Martin, 1875–1949, vol. IV

Laing, Andrew, *died* 1931, vol. III
Laing, Bertram Mitchell, *died* 1960, vol. V
Laing, Frederick Ninian Robert, 1856–1931, vol. III
Laing, Air Vice-Marshal Sir George, 1884–1956, vol. V
Laing, Sir James, 1823–1901, vol. I
Laing, Sir John William, 1879–1978, vol. VII
Laing, Malcolm Alfred, 1846–1917, vol. II
Laing, Malcolm Buchanan, 1890–1974, vol. VII
Laing, Percy Lyndon, 1909–1979, vol. VII
Laing, Samuel, 1812–1897, vol. I
Laing, Col Stanley van Buren, 1884–1962, vol. VI
Lainson, Major Alexander John, 1869–1931, vol. III
Laird, David, 1833–1914, vol. I
Laird, John, 1887–1946, vol. IV
Laird, Brig. Kenneth Macgregor, 1880–1954, vol. V
Laird, Sir Patrick Ramsay, 1888–1967, vol. VI
Laird, Thomas Patrick, 1860–1927, vol. II
Laird, Sir William, *died* 1901, vol. I
Laird, William, 1881–1962, vol. VI
Laistner, Max Ludwig Wolfram, 1890–1959, vol. V
Lake, Sir Arthur Johnstone, 8th Bt, 1849–1924, vol. II
Lake, Captain Sir Atwell Henry, 9th Bt, 1891–1972, vol. VII
Lake, Sir Atwell King, 6th Bt, 1834–1897, vol. I
Lake, Adm. Atwell Peregrine Macleod, 1842–1915, vol. I
Lake, Col Ernest Atwell Winter, 1886–1945, vol. IV
Lake, Col Harry William, *died* 1940, vol. III
Lake, Rev. Henry Ashton, 1847–1929, vol. III
Lake, Kirsopp, 1872–1946, vol. IV
Lake, Lt-Col Morice Challoner, 1885–1943, vol. IV
Lake, Brig.-Gen. Noel Montagu, 1852–1932, vol. III
Lake, Norman C., 1888–1966, vol. VI
Lake, Lt-Gen. Sir Percy Henry Noel, 1855–1940, vol. III
Lake, Richard, 1861–1949, vol. IV
Lake, Sir Richard Stuart, 1860–1950, vol. IV
Lake, Sir St Vincent Atwell, 7th Bt, 1862–1916, vol. II
Laker, Albert, 1875–1948, vol. IV
Lakin, Charles Ernest, 1878–1972, vol. VII
Lakin, Cyril Harry Alfred, 1893–1948, vol. IV
Lakin, Sir Henry, 3rd Bt, 1904–1979, vol. VII
Lakin, John Edmund Douglas, 1920–1977, vol. VII
Lakin, Maj.-Gen. John Henry Foster, 1878–1943, vol. IV
Lakin, Sir Michael Henry, 1st Bt, 1846–1931, vol. III
Lakin, Sir Richard, 2nd Bt, 1873–1955, vol. V
Laking, Sir Francis Henry, 1st Bt, 1847–1914, vol. I
Laking, Sir Guy Francis, 2nd Bt, 1875–1919, vol. II
Laking, Sir Guy Francis William, 3rd Bt, 1904–1930, vol. III
Lal, Kanhaiya Lal, 1866–1945, vol. IV
Lalaing, Count de, 1856–1919, vol. II

Lalique, René, 1860–1945, vol. IV (A), vol. V
Lall, I. C., 1863–1922, vol. II
Lall, Panna; *see* Panna Lall.
Lall, Sir Shankar, 1901–1951, vol. V
Lally, Miss Gwen, *died* 1963, vol. VI
Lamarche, Rt Rev. Charles, 1870–1940, vol. III
Lamarque, Walter Geoffrey, 1913–1979, vol. VII
Lamb, Major Algernon Joseph Rutherfurd, 1891–1941, vol. IV
Lamb, Sir Archibald, 3rd Bt, 1845–1921, vol. II
Lamb, Arthur Moore, 1873–1946, vol. IV
Lamb, Rev. Benjamin, *died* 1925, vol. II
Lamb, Col Sir Charles Anthony, 4th Bt, 1857–1948, vol. IV
Lamb, David C., 1866–1951, vol. V
Lamb, Col David Ogilvy Wight, 1885–1942, vol. IV
Lamb, Edmund, 1863–1925, vol. II
Lamb, Ernest Horace, 1878–1946, vol. IV
Lamb, Frank de Villiers, 1880–1962, vol. VI
Lamb, Sir Harry Harling, 1857–1948, vol. IV
Lamb, Henry, 1883–1960, vol. V
Lamb, Sir Horace, 1849–1934, vol. III
Lamb, Sir John, 1871–1952, vol. V
Lamb, Rev. John, 1886–1974, vol. VII
Lamb, Sir John Cameron, 1845–1915, vol. I
Lamb, Sir John Edward Stewart, 1892–1954, vol. V
Lamb, Sir Joseph Quinton, 1873–1949, vol. IV
Lamb, Lynton Harold, 1907–1977, vol. VII
Lamb, Percy, 1896–1973, vol. VII
Lamb, Sir Richard Amphlett, 1858–1923, vol. II (A)
Lamb, Lt-Col Roger Montague Radcliffe, 1881–1937, vol. III
Lamb, Sir Thomas, *died* 1943, vol. IV
Lamb, Sir Walter Rangeley Maitland, 1882–1961, vol. VI
Lambarde, Brig.-Gen. Francis Fane, 1868–1948, vol. IV
Lambart, Brig.-Gen. Edgar Alan, 1857–1930, vol. III
Lambart, Lt-Col Sir Gustavus Francis, 1st Bt, 1848–1926, vol. II
Lambart, Hon. Lionel John Olive, 1873–1940, vol. III
Lambart, Richard, 1875–1924, vol. II
Lambe, Adm. of the Fleet Sir Charles Edward, 1900–1960, vol. V
Lambe, Air Vice-Marshal Sir Charles Laverock, *died* 1953, vol. V
Lambe, Philip Agnew, 1897–1968, vol. VI
Lambert, 1st Viscount, 1866–1958, vol. V
Lambert, Agnes, *died* 1917, vol. II
Lambert, Alfred Uvedale Miller, *died* 1928, vol. II
Lambert, Arthur Bradley, 1858–1929, vol. III
Lambert, Sir Arthur William, 1876–1948, vol. IV
Lambert, Bertram, 1881–1963, vol. VI
Lambert, Rev. Brooke, 1834–1901, vol. I
Lambert, Adm. Sir Cecil Foley, 1864–1928, vol. II
Lambert, Ven. Charles Edmund, 1872–1954, vol. V
Lambert, Charles Ernest, 1900–1974, vol. VII
Lambert, Engr. Rear-Adm. Charles William, 1891–1961, vol. VI
Lambert, Constant, 1905–1951, vol. V

Lambert, Rear-Adm. Sir David Sidney, 1885–1966, vol. VI

Lambert, Brig.-Gen. Edward Parry, 1865–1932, vol. III

Lambert, Ernest, 1874–1951, vol. V

Lambert, Dame Florence Barrie, died 1957, vol. V

Lambert, Francis Henry, 1867–1929, vol. III

Lambert, Francis L., 1838–1925, vol. II

Lambert, Frank, 1884–1973, vol. VII

Lambert, Rev. Frederick Fox, died 1920, vol. II

Lambert, Sir George Bancroft, 1873–1945, vol. IV

Lambert, Sir George Thomas, 1837–1918, vol. II

Lambert, George Washington, 1873–1930, vol. III

Lambert, Col Guy Lenox B.; see Bence-Lambert.

Lambert, Maj.-Gen. Harold Roger, 1896–1980, vol. VII

Lambert, Sir Henry Charles Miller, 1868–1935, vol. III

Lambert, Vet.-Col James Drummond, 1835–1905, vol. I

Lambert, Sir John, 1838–1916, vol. II

Lambert, Ven. Joseph Malet, 1853–1931, vol. III

Lambert, Maurice, 1901–1964, vol. VI

Lambert, Richard Cornthwaite, died 1939, vol. III

Lambert, Robert, 1908–1971, vol. VII

Lambert, Rear-Adm. Robert Cathcart Kemble, 1874–1950, vol. IV

Lambert, Col Thomas Stanton, 1871–1921, vol. II

Lambert, Victor Albert George, 1897–1971, vol. VII

Lambert, Brig.-Gen. Walter John, 1876–1944, vol. IV

Lambert, Lt-Col Walter Miller, 1843–1924, vol. II

Lambert, Maj.-Gen. William, 1836–1907, vol. I

Lambert, Maj.-Gen. William Harold, 1905–1978, vol. VII

Lambert, Rev. William Henry, 1833–1924, vol. II

Lambie, Charles George, 1891–1961, vol. VI

Lambkin, Col Francis, 1858–1912, vol. I

Lamble, Ven. George Edwin, 1877–1939, vol. III

Lambooy, Maj.-Gen. Albert Percy, 1899–1976, vol. VII

Lamborn, Edmund Arnold Greening, 1877–1950, vol. IV

Lambotte, Paul, 1862–1939, vol. III

Lambourne, 1st Baron, 1847–1928, vol. II

Lambton, Viscount; John Roderick Geoffrey Francis Edward Lambton, 1920–1941, vol. IV

Lambton, Lt-Gen. Arthur, 1836–1908, vol. I

Lambton, Arthur, 1869–1935, vol. III

Lambton, Brig.-Gen. Hon. Charles, 1857–1949, vol. IV

Lambton, Lt-Col Francis W., 1834–1921, vol. II

Lambton, Hon. George, 1860–1945, vol. IV

Lambton, Lt-Col George Charles, 1872–1927, vol. II

Lambton, Maj.-Gen. Hon. Sir William, 1863–1936, vol. III

Lamburn, Richmal Crompton, 1890–1969, vol VI

Lambury, 1st Baron, 1896–1967, vol. VI

Lamert, Sidney Streatfield, 1875–1963, vol. VI

Laming, Major Henry Thornton, 1863–1934, vol. III

Laming, Richard Valentine, 1887–1959, vol. V

Lamington, 2nd Baron, 1860–1940, vol. III

Lamington, 3rd Baron, 1896–1951, vol. V

Lammie, Col George, 1891–1946, vol. IV

Lamonby, Isaac Wannop, 1886–1938, vol. III

Lamond, Frederic, 1868–1948, vol. IV

Lamond, Henry, 1869–1934, vol. III

Lamond, Sir William, 1887–1974, vol. VII

Lamont, Very Rev. Daniel, died 1950, vol. IV

Lamont, Daniel Scott, 1851–1905, vol. I

Lamont, Sir James, 1st Bt, 1828–1913, vol. I

Lamont, Lt-Col John Charles, 1864–1945, vol. IV

Lamont, Hon. John Henderson, 1865–1936, vol. III

Lamont, Brig.-Gen. John William Fraser, 1872–1956, vol. V

Lamont, Sir Norman, 2nd Bt, 1869–1949, vol. IV

Lamont, Thomas William, 1870–1948, vol. IV

La Mothe, Frederick Malcolm, 1864–1947, vol. IV

Lamotte, Brig.-Gen. Frank Grimshaw Lagier, 1864–1938, vol. III

Lamotte, Major George Moorsom Lagier, 1869–1935, vol. III

Lampard-Vachell, Benjamin Garnet, 1892–1965, vol. VI

Lampe, Rev. Geoffrey William Hugo, 1912–1980, vol. VII

Lampen, Rev. Charles Dudley, 1859–1943, vol. IV

Lampen, Graham Dudley, 1899–1960, vol. V

Lampen, Rev. Canon Herbert Dudley, 1868–1941, vol. IV

Lampen, Lt-Gen. Lewis Charles, 1878–1946, vol. IV

Lampitt, Leslie Herbert, 1887–1957, vol. V

Lamplough, Augustus Osborne, 1877–1930, vol. III

Lamplugh, George William, 1859–1926, vol. II

Lamplugh, Rt Rev. Kenneth Edward Norman, 1901–1979, vol. VII

Lampson, Sir Curtis George, 3rd Bt, 1890–1971, vol. VII

Lampson, Curtis Walter, 1875–1952, vol. V

Lampson, Sir George Curtis, 2nd Bt, 1833–1899, vol. I

Lampson, Rt Hon. Godfrey Lampson Tennyson L.; see Locker-Lampson.

Lampson, Jane L.; see Locker-Lampson.

Lampson, Comdr Oliver Stillingfleet L.; see Locker-Lampson.

Lamrock, Brig.-Gen. John, 1859–1935, vol. III

Lamsdorff, Count Wladimir, 1844–1907, vol. I

Lamy, Etienne Marie Victor, 1845–1919, vol. II

Lancashire, George Herbert, 1866–1945, vol. IV

Lancaster, Col Claude Granville, 1899–1977, vol. VII

Lancaster, Brig. Edmund Henry, 1881–1975, vol. VII

Lancaster, John Roy, 1871–1951, vol. V

Lancaster, Joseph Torry, 1892–1966, vol. VI

Lancaster, Percy, 1878–1950, vol. IV

Lancaster, Sir Robert Fisher, 1885–1945, vol. IV

Lancaster, Sir William John, 1841–1929, vol. III

Lancaster, William Joseph Cosens, 1851–1922, vol. II

Lancaster-Jones, Ernest, 1891–1945, vol. IV

Lancaster-Ranking, Maj.-Gen. Robert Philip; see Ranking.

Lancastre, Countess of; (Adeline Louise Maria); *see* Cardigan and Lancastre.
Lance, Rev. Edwin Mildred, 1862–1935, vol. III
Lance, Lt-Gen. Sir Frederick, 1837–1913, vol. I
Lancelot, Rev. John Bennett, 1864–1944, vol. IV
Lanchester, Frank, 1870–1960, vol. IV
Lanchester, Frederick William, 1868–1946, vol. IV
Lanchester, Henry Vaughan, 1863–1953, vol. V
Lanciani, Commendatore Rodolfo, 1846–1929, vol. III
Lanctot, Charles, 1863–1946, vol. IV
Landale, David, 1868–1935, vol. III
Landale, David Fortune, 1905–1970, vol. VI
Landau, Dorothea, (Mrs C. Da Fano), *died* 1941, vol. IV
Landau, Lev Davidovich, 1908–1968, vol. VI
Landau, Muriel Elsie, (Mrs Samuel Sacks), 1895–1972, vol. VII
Landau, Rom, 1899–1974, vol. VII
Lander, Cecil Howard, 1881–1949, vol. IV
Lander, Rt Rev. Gerard Heath, 1861–1934, vol. III
Lander, Rt Rev. Richard Brook, *died* 1937, vol. III
Landey, Very Rev. Theophilus Patrick, *died* 1935, vol. III
Landis, James McCauley, 1899–1964, vol. VI
Landon, Lt-Col Charles Richard Henry Palmer, 1879–1940, vol. III
Landon, Maj.-Gen. Sir Frederick William Bainbridge, 1860–1937, vol. III
Landon, Maj.-Gen. Herman James Shelley, 1859–1948, vol. IV
Landon, Col James William Bainbridge, 1890–1966, vol. VI
Landon, Gp Captain Joseph Herbert Arthur, *died* 1935, vol. III
Landon, Perceval, 1869–1927, vol. II
Landon, Philip Aislabie, 1888–1961, vol. VI
Landor, A. Henry Savage, *died* 1924, vol. II
Landouzy, Louis Joseph, *died* 1917, vol. II
Landowski, Paul, 1875–1961, vol. VI
Landry, Col Hon. Auguste Charles Philippe Robert, 1846–1919, vol. II
Landry, Hon. David V., 1866–1929, vol. III
Landry, Maj.-Gen. Joseph Phillippe, 1870–1926, vol. II
Landry, Hon. Sir Pierre Armand, 1846–1916, vol. II
Landsteiner, Karl, 1868–1943, vol. IV
Lane, Sir Allen Lane Williams, 1902–1970, vol. VI
Lane, Annie E.; *see* Lane, Mrs John.
Lane, Sir Arbuthnot; *see* Lane, Sir W. A.
Lane, Charles Macdonald, 1882–1956, vol. V
Lane, Maj.-Gen. Sir Charles Reginald Cambridge, 1890–1964, vol. VI
Lane, Maj.-Gen. Charles Stuart, 1831–1913, vol. I
Lane, Sir Charlton Adelbert Gustavus, 1890–1962, vol. VI
Lane, Col Clayton Turner, 1842–1920, vol. II
Lane, Edward Arthur, 1909–1963, vol. VI
Lane, Very Rev. Ernald, 1836–1913, vol. I
Lane, Ernest Frederick Cambridge, 1882–1958, vol. V
Lane, Ernest Olaf, 1916–1976, vol. VII
Lane, Brig. Frank, 1888–1963, vol. VI

Lane, Col George Howard M.; *see* Moore-Lane.
Lane, Harry George, 1881–1957, vol. V
Lane, Sir Harry Philip Parnell, 1870–1927, vol. II
Lane, Brig.-Gen. Henry Arthur, 1868–1930, vol. III
Lane, Rear-Adm. Henry Gerald Elliot, 1875–1946, vol. IV
Lane, H(enry) J(errold) Randall, 1898–1975, vol. VII
Lane, Henry Murray, 1833–1913, vol. I
Lane, Rev. Henry Tydd, 1846–1939, vol. III
Lane, Herbert Allardyce, 1883–1959, vol. V
Lane, Brig.-Gen. Herbert Edward Bruce, 1862–1950, vol. IV
Lane, Sir Hugh Percy, 1875–1915, vol. I
Lane, Brig. Hugh Robert Charles, 1885–1953, vol. V
Lane, James Ernest, *died* 1926, vol. II
Lane, Jane, (Mrs Andrew Dakers), *died* 1978, vol. VII
Lane, John, 1854–1925, vol. II
Lane, Mrs John, (Annie E. Lane), *died* 1927, vol. II
Lane, John Henry Hervey Vincent, 1867–1917, vol. II
Lane, John Macdonald, 1840–1927, vol. II
Lane, Lupino, *died* 1959, vol. V
Lane, Col Maitland Moore-, 1841–1915, vol. I
Lane, Rhona Arbuthnot, *died* 1953, vol. V
Lane, Richard Ouseley Blake, 1842–1914, vol. I
Lane, Maj.-Gen. Sir Ronald Bertram, 1847–1937, vol. III
Lane, Col Samuel Willington, 1860–1948, vol. IV
Lane, Sir (William) Arbuthnot, 1st Bt, 1856–1943, vol. IV
Lane, Sir William Arbuthnot, 2nd Bt, 1897–1972, vol. VII
Lane, Lt-Col William Byam, 1866–1945, vol. IV
Lane-Jackson, Nicholas, 1849–1937, vol. III
Lane-Notter, Col J.; *see* Notter.
Lane Poole, Charles Edward, 1885–1970, vol. VI (AII)
Lane-Poole, Vice-Adm. Sir Richard Hayden Owen, 1883–1971, vol. VII
Lane-Poole, Stanley, 1854–1931, vol. III
Lane-Roberts, Cedric Sydney, *died* 1959, vol. V
Lanesborough, 6th Earl of, 1839–1905, vol. I
Lanesborough, 7th Earl of, 1865–1929, vol. III
Lanesborough, 8th Earl of, 1868–1950, vol. IV
Lang of Lambeth, 1st Baron, 1864–1945, vol. IV
Lang, Air Vice-Marshal Albert Frank, 1895–1977, vol. VII
Lang, Alexander, 1848–1930, vol. III
Lang, (Alexander) Matheson, *died* 1948, vol. IV
Lang, Andrew, 1844–1912, vol. I
Lang, Archibald Orr, 1880–1957, vol. V
Lang, Col Arthur Moffatt, 1832–1916, vol. II
Lang, Col Bertram John, 1878–1975, vol. VII
Lang, Charles Dowson, 1845–1930, vol. III
Lang, Charles Russell, 1862–1940, vol. III
Lang, Col Elliott Brownlow, 1862–1955, vol. V
Lang, Hon. Sir Frederic William, 1852–1937, vol. III
Lang, Lt-Col Godfrey George, 1867–1923, vol. II
Lang, Very Rev. John Marshall, 1834–1909, vol. I

Lang, Hon. John Thomas, 1876–1975, vol. VII
Lang, Rt Rev. Leslie Hamilton, 1889–1974, vol. VII
Lang, Lt-Col Lionel Edward, 1885–1956, vol. V
Lang, Very Rev. Marshall B., 1868–1954, vol. V
Lang, Matheson; see Lang, A. M.
Lang, Rt Rev. Norman Macleod, 1875–1956, vol. V
Lang, Patrick Keith, 1863–1961, vol. VI
Lang, Sir Peter Redford Scott, 1850–1926, vol. II
Lang, Robert Buntin, 1906–1970, vol. VI
Lang, Sir Robert Hamilton, 1836–1913, vol. I
Lang, William, 1852–1937, vol. III
Lang, Sir William Biggart, 1868–1942, vol. IV
Lang, William Dickson, 1878–1966, vol. VI
Lang, William Henry, died 1960, vol. V
Lang, William Lindsay Holmes, 1888–1928, vol. II
Lang, Col William Robert, died 1925, vol. II
Lang-Coath, Howell Lang, 1878–1949, vol. IV
Lang-Hyde, Lt-Col John Irvine, 1859–1940, vol. III
Langbridge, Rev. Frederick, 1849–1922, vol. II
Langbridge, Rosamond Grant, died 1964, vol. VI
Langdale, Henry Joseph, died 1923, vol. II
Langdale, Lt-Col Philip Joseph, died 1950, vol. IV
Langdon, Adolph Max, died 1949, vol. IV
Langdon, Rev. Alfred, died 1925, vol. II
Langdon, George, 1867–1957, vol. V
Langdon, Col Harry, 1855–1925, vol. II
Langdon, Stephen Herbert, 1876–1937, vol. III
Langdon, Hon. Thomas, 1832–1914, vol. I (A)
Langdon, Air Cdre William Frederick, 1898–1976, vol. VII
Langdon-Brown, Sir Walter, 1870–1946, vol. IV
Langdon-Davies, Bernard Noël, 1876–1952, vol. V
Langdon-Davies, John, 1897–1971, vol. VII
Lange, Christian Lous, 1869–1938, vol. III
Langelier, Hon. Charles, 1852–1920, vol. II
Langelier, Sir François Charles Stanislas, 1838–1915, vol. I
Langerman, Sir Jan Willem Stuckeris, 1853–1931, vol. III
Langevin, Hon. Sir Hector Louis, 1826–1906, vol. I
Langevin, Most Rev. Louis Philip Adelard, 1855–1915, vol. I
Langford, 4th Baron, 1848–1919, vol. II
Langford, 5th Baron, 1894–1922, vol. II
Langford, 6th Baron, 1849–1931, vol. III
Langford, 7th Baron, 1885–1952, vol. V
Langford, 8th Baron, 1870–1953, vol. V
Langford, Caroline; see Hatchard, C.
Langford, John Alfred, 1823–1903, vol. I
Langford, Surgeon Martyn Henry, died 1918, vol. II
Langford-James, Reginald Hugh Lloyd, 1876–1961, vol. VI
Langford-Sainsbury, Air Vice-Marshal Thomas Audley, 1897–1972, vol. VII
Langham, Sir Charles Arthur; see Langham, Sir H. C. A.
Langham, Sir Cyril Leigh Macrae, 1885–1950, vol. IV
Langham, Col Frederick George, 1863–1946, vol. IV

Langham, Sir (Herbert) Charles Arthur, 13th Bt, 1870–1951, vol. V
Langham, Sir Herbert Hay, 12th Bt, 1840–1909, vol. I
Langham, Sir John Charles Patrick, 14th Bt, 1894–1972, vol. VII
Langhorne, Maj.-Gen. Algernon Philip Yorke, 1882–1945, vol. IV
Langhorne, Brig.-Gen. Harold Stephen, 1866–1932, vol. III
Langhorne, Brig. James Archibald Dunboyne, 1879–1950, vol. IV
Langler, Sir Alfred, 1865–1928, vol. II
Langley, Alexander, 1871–1952, vol. V
Langley, Comdr Arthur Sydney, 1881–1964, vol. VI
Langley, Batty, 1834–1914, vol. I
Langley, Beatrice, (Mrs Basil Tozer), 1872–1958, vol. V
Langley, Sir Carleton George, 1885–1963, vol. VI
Langley, Frederick Oswald, 1883–1947, vol. IV
Langley, Brig. George Furner, 1891–1971, vol. VII
Langley, George Harry, 1881–1951, vol. V
Langley, Adm. Gerald Charles, 1848–1914, vol. I
Langley, Vice-Adm. Gerald Maxwell Bradshaw, 1895–1971, vol. VII
Langley, Rt Rev. Henry Archdall, died 1906, vol. I
Langley, Very Rev. Henry Thomas, 1877–1968, vol. VI
Langley, Rt Rev. John Douse, 1836–1930, vol. III
Langley, John Newport, 1852–1925, vol. II
Langley, Col John Penrice, 1860–1933, vol. III
Langley, Noel A., 1911–1980, vol. VII
Langley, Samuel Pierpont, 1834–1906, vol. I
Langley, Walter, 1852–1922, vol. II (A), vol. III
Langley, Sir Walter Louis Frederick Goltz, 1855–1918, vol. II
Langley, William Henry, died 1913, vol. I
Langley, William Kenneth Macaulay, 1883–1965, vol. VI
Langley-Taylor, Sir George, 1888–1968, vol. VI
Langlois, Hippolyte, 1839–1912, vol. I
Langlois, Most Rev. Mgr J. Alfred, 1876–1966, vol. VI
Langmaid, Lt-Comdr Rowland John Robb, 1897–1956, vol. V
Langmaid, Brig. Thomas John Robert, 1887–1965, vol. VI
Langman, Sir Archibald Lawrence, 2nd Bt, 1872–1949, vol. IV
Langman, Sir John Lawrence, 1st Bt, 1846–1928, vol. II
Langman, Thomas Witheridge, 1882–1960, vol. V
Langmead, Frederick, 1879–1969, vol. VI
Langmore, Col Edward Ham, died 1913, vol. I
Langmuir, Irving, 1881–1957, vol. V
Langrishe, Comdr Sir Hercules Robert, 5th Bt, 1859–1943, vol. IV
Langrishe, Sir James, 4th Bt, 1823–1910, vol. I
Langrishe, Captain Sir Terence Hume, 6th Bt, 1895–1973, vol. VII
Langton, Bennet, 1870–1955, vol. V
Langton, Hon. Chandos Graham T. G.; see Temple-Gore-Langton.

Langton, Comdr Hon. Evelyn Arthur Grenville T. G.; see Temple-Gore-Langton.
Langton, Sir George Philip, 1881–1942, vol. IV
Langton, Major Gerald Wentworth G.; see Gore-Langton.
Langton, Hon. Henry Powell G.; see Gore-Langton.
Langton, John, died 1910, vol. I
Langton, Joseph L., 1877–1961, vol. VI
Langton-Jones, Comdr Ronald, 1884–1967, vol. VI
Lankester, Edward Forbes, 1855–1934, vol. III
Lankester, Sir Edwin Ray, 1847–1929, vol. III
Lankester, Herbert, 1862–1947, vol. IV
Lanktree, Col Charles Joseph Dane, 1895–1951, vol. V
Lanman, Charles Rockwell, 1850–1941, vol. IV
Lannowe, Brig.-Gen. Edmund Byam Mathew-, 1875–1940, vol. III
Lansbury, Rt Hon. George, 1859–1940, vol. III
Lansdell, Rev. Henry, 1841–1919, vol. II
Lansdowne, 5th Marquess, of, 1845–1927, vol. II
Lansdowne, 6th Marquess of, 1872–1936, vol. III
Lansdowne, 7th Marquess of, 1917–1944, vol. IV
Lansell, Col Hon. Sir George Victor, 1883–1959, vol. V
Lansing, Robert, 1864–1928, vol. II
Lanson, Gustave, 1857–1934, vol. III
Lanteri, Edward, died 1917, vol. II
Lanyon, (George) Peter, 1918–1964, vol. VI
Lanyon, Peter; see Lanyon, G. P.
Lapage, Charles Paget, 1879–1947, vol. IV
Lapointe, Rt Hon. Ernest, 1876–1941, vol. IV
Laporte, Hon. Sir Hormisdas, 1850–1934, vol. III
Laprimaudaye, Comdr Clement, died 1910, vol. I
Lapworth, Arthur, died 1941, vol. IV
Lapworth, Charles, 1842–1920, vol. II
Larcom, Arthur, 1847–1924, vol. II
Larcom, Sir Philip, 4th Bt, 1887–1967, vol. VI
Larcom, Sir Thomas Perceval, 3rd Bt, 1882–1950, vol. IV
Larcombe, Dudley Thomas Reynolds, 1879–1944, vol. IV
Larcombe, Thomas, 1842–1916, vol. II
Lardner, James Carrige Rushe, 1879–1925, vol. II
Lardner-Clarke, Col J. de W., 1858–1951, vol. V
Large, Captain Edwin Ryder, 1878–1928, vol. II
Large, Stanley Dermott, 1889–1965, vol. VI
Large, Tennyson J. D., 1879–1959, vol. V
Larivière, Hon. Alphonse Alfred Clément, 1842–1925, vol. II (A), vol. III
Lark, Rev. William Blake, 1838–1913, vol. I
Larke, Sir William James, died 1959, vol. V
Larken, Lt-Col Edmund, 1876–1951, vol. IV
Larken, Rear-Adm. Edmund Thomas, 1907–1965, vol. VI
Larken, Adm. Sir Frank, 1875–1953, vol. V
Larken, Rev. Preb. Hubert, died 1964, vol. VI
Larkin, Herbert Benjamin George, 1872–1944, vol. IV
Larkin, Hon. Peter Charles, 1856–1930, vol. III
Larking, Captain Albert, 1857–1932, vol. III
Larking, Lt-Col Sir (Charles) Gordon, 1893–1978, vol. VII
Larking, Col Cuthbert, 1842–1910, vol. I

Larking, Captain Dennis Augustus Hugo, 1876–1970, vol. VI
Larking, Lt-Col Sir Gordon; see Larking, Lt-Col Sir C. G.
Larking, Sir John, 1857–1931, vol. III
Larking, Lt-Col Reginald Nesbitt Wingfield, 1868–1943, vol. IV
Larkins, Laurence Brouncker Southey, 1891–1953, vol. V
Larkworthy, Falconer, 1833–1928, vol. II
Larminie, Margaret Rivers, (Mrs M. R. Tragett), 1885–1964, vol. VI
Larmor, Alexander, died 1936, vol. III
Larmor, Sir Graham; see Larmor, Sir J. G.
Larmor, Sir (John) Graham, 1897–1968, vol. VI
Larmor, Sir Joseph, 1857–1942, vol. IV
Larnach, James Walker, 1849–1919, vol. II
Larnder, Col Eugene William, 1864–1941, vol. IV
La Rochelle, Michel Gautron, 1868–1934, vol. III
La Rocque, Rt Rev. Paul, 1846–1926, vol. II
Larpent, Sir George Albert de Hochepied, 3rd Bt, 1846–1899, vol. I
Larpent, Maj.-Gen. Lionel Henry Planta de H.; see de Hochepied Larpent.
Larsen, Roy Edward, 1899–1979, vol. VII
Lartigue, Alexander Raphael C.; see Cools-Lartigue.
Larue, Rt Rev. Stephen, 1865–1935, vol. III
Larymore, Major Henry Douglas, 1867–1946, vol. IV
Lasbrey, Rt Rev. Bertram, died 1976, vol. VII
Lascelles, Sir Alfred George, 1857–1952, vol. V
Lascelles, Sir Daniel William, 1902–1967, vol. VI
Lascelles, Bt Major Hon. Edward Cecil, 1887–1935, vol. III
Lascelles, Edward Charles Ponsonby, 1884–1956, vol. V
Lascelles, Lt-Col Edward ffrancis Ward, died 1959, vol. V
Lascelles, Sir Francis William, 1890–1979, vol. VII
Lascelles, Frank, died 1934, vol. III
Lascelles, Rt Hon. Sir Frank Cavendish, 1841–1920, vol. II
Lascelles, Hon. Frederick Canning, 1848–1928, vol. II
Lascelles, Hon. George Edwin, 1826–1911, vol. I (A)
Lascelles, Lt-Col George Reginald, 1864–1939, vol. III
Lascelles, Hon. Gerald William, 1849–1928, vol. II
Lascelles, Rev. Hon. James Walter, 1831–1901, vol. I
Lascelles, Rev. Maurice G., 1860–1940, vol. III
Lascelles, Captain Walter Charles, 1867–1911, vol. I
Lash, Zebulun Aiton, 1846–1920, vol. II
Lashmore, Engr Rear-Adm. Harry, 1868–1945, vol. IV
Lasker, Emanuel, 1868–1941, vol. IV
Laskey, Francis Seward, 1886–1972, vol. VII
Laski, Harold J., 1893–1950, vol. IV
Laski, Nathan, 1863–1941, vol. IV
Laski, Neville Jonas, 1890–1969, vol. VI
Lasky, Jesse L., 1880–1958, vol. V

Laslett, Henry James, 1844–1914, vol. I
Lassalle, Jean, 1859–1909, vol. I
Lassetter, Brig.-Gen. Harry Beauchamp, 1860–1926, vol. II
Last, Hugh Macilwain, died 1957, vol. V
Last, William Isaac, 1857–1911, vol. I
Laszlo de Lombos, Philip Alexius, 1869–1937, vol. III
Latchford, Francis Robert, 1854–1938, vol. III
Latey, John, 1842–1902, vol. I
Latey, William, 1885–1976, vol. VII
Latham, 1st Baron, 1888–1970, vol. VI
Latham, Albert George, 1864–1940, vol. III
Latham, Alexander Mere, 1862–1934, vol. III
Latham, Charles, 1868–1917, vol. II
Latham, Hon. Sir Charles George, 1882–1968, vol. VI
Latham, Edward Bryan, 1895–1980, vol. VII
Latham, Brig. Francis, 1883–1958, vol. V
Latham, Gustavus Henry, 1888–1975, vol. VII
Latham, Rev. Henry, 1821–1902, vol. I
Latham, Sir (Herbert) Paul, 2nd Bt, 1905–1955, vol. V
Latham, Ven. James King, 1847–1932, vol. III
Latham, Rt Hon. Sir John Greig, 1877–1964, vol. VI
Latham, Sir Paul; see Latham, Sir H. P.
Latham, Peter Wallwork, 1832–1923, vol. II
Latham, Russell, 1896–1964, vol. VI
Latham, Sir Thomas Paul, 1st Bt, 1855–1931, vol. III
Latham, William, died 1915, vol. I
Lathan, George, 1875–1942, vol. IV
La Thangue, H. H., died 1929, vol. III
Lathbury, Daniel Conner, 1831–1922, vol. II
Lathbury, Gen. Sir Gerald William, 1906–1978, vol. VII
Lathlain, Sir William Francis, 1862–1936, vol. III
Lathom, 1st Earl of, 1837–1898, vol. I
Lathom, 2nd Earl of, 1864–1910, vol. I
Lathom, 3rd Earl of, 1895–1930, vol. III
Lathrop, Lorin Andrews, died 1929, vol. III
Lathrop, Mother Mary Alphonsa; see Lathrop, R. H.
Lathrop, Rose Hawthorne, (Mother Mary Alphonsa Lathrop), 1851–1926, vol. II (A), vol. III
Latifi, Almá, 1879–1959, vol. V
Latimer, Sir Courtenay, 1880–1944, vol. IV
Latimer, Frederick William, 1845–1910, vol. I
Latimer, Rev. William Thomas, died 1919, vol. II
Laton, Col Stephen F.; see Frewen-Laton.
La Touche, Sir James John Digges, 1844–1921, vol. II
Latouche, John; see Crawfurd, Oswald.
La Touche, Robert Percy O'Connor, 1846–1921, vol. II
Latourette, Kenneth Scott, 1884–1968, vol. VI
Latrobe, William Sanderson, 1870–1943, vol. IV
La Trobe-Bateman, Rev. William Fairbairn; see Bateman.
Latta, Sir Andrew Gibson, died 1953, vol. V
Latta, Sir John, 1st Bt, 1867–1946, vol. IV
Latta, Robert, 1865–1932, vol. III
Latta, Hon. Samuel John, 1866–1946, vol. IV

Latter, Algernon, 1870–1944, vol. IV
Latter, Arthur Malcolm, 1875–1961, vol. VI
Latter, Maj.-Gen. John Cecil, 1896–1972, vol. VII
Latter, Oswald Hawkins, 1864–1948, vol. IV
Lattey, Rev. Cuthbert Charles, 1877–1954, vol. V
Lattimer, Robert Binney, 1863–1929, vol. III
Latulipe, Rt Rev. E. A., 1859–1922, vol. II
Latymer, 5th Baron, 1852–1923 (this entry was not transferred to Who was Who).
Latymer, 6th Baron, 1876–1949, vol. IV
Laudenbach, Pierre; see Fresnay, P.
Lauder, Charles James, died 1920, vol. II
Lauder, Sir George William Dalrymple Dick-, 10th Bt, 1852–1936, vol. III
Lauder, Sir Harry MacLennan, 1870–1950, vol. IV
Lauder, Major James La Fayette, 1889–1934, vol. III
Lauder, Lt-Col Sir John North Dalrymple Dick-, 11th Bt, 1883–1958, vol. V
Lauder, Sir Thomas North Dick-, 9th Bt, 1846–1919, vol. II
Lauderdale, 13th Earl of, 1840–1924, vol. II
Lauderdale, 14th Earl of, 1868–1931, vol. III
Lauderdale, 15th Earl of, 1891–1953, vol. V
Lauderdale, 16th Earl of, 1904–1968, vol. VI
Laughlin, Irwin, 1871–1941, vol. IV
Laughton, Col Arthur Frederick, 1840–1915, vol. I
Laughton, Charles, 1899–1962, vol. VI
Laughton, Lt-Gen. George Arnold, 1830–1912, vol. I
Laughton, George Christian, 1887–1952, vol. V
Laughton, Very Rev. John George, 1891–1965, vol. VI
Laughton, Sir John Knox, 1830–1915, vol. I
Laughton, Major Joseph Vinters, 1862–1948, vol. IV
Laughton-Scott, Edward Hey, 1926–1978, vol. VII
Laurence, Frederick Andrew, 1843–1912, vol. I (A)
Laurence, Adm. Sir Noel Frank, died 1970, vol. VI
Laurence, Sir Perceval Maitland, 1854–1930, vol. III
Laurence, Reginald Vere, 1876–1934, vol. III
Laurie, Rev. Albert Ernest, 1866–1937, vol. III
Laurie, Arthur Pillans, 1861–1949, vol. IV
Laurie, Col Sir Claude Villiers Emilius, 4th Bt (cr 1834), 1855–1930, vol. III
Laurie, Rev. Sir Emilius; see Laurie, Rev. Sir J. R. L. E.
Laurie, James S., 1831–1904, vol. I
Laurie, John B., 1865–1934, vol. III
Laurie, Lt-Col Sir John Dawson, 1st Bt (cr 1942), 1872–1954, vol. V
Laurie, Rev. Sir (John Robert Laurie) Emilius, 3rd Bt (cr 1834), 1823–1917, vol. II
Laurie, Lt-Gen. John Wimburn, 1835–1912, vol. I
Laurie, Malcolm Vyvyan, 1901–1973, vol. VII
Laurie, Brig. Sir Percy Robert, 1880–1962, vol. VI
Laurie, Ranald Macdonald, 1869–1927, vol. II
Laurie, Robert Douglas, 1874–1953, vol. V
Laurie, Col Robert Peter, 1835–1905, vol. I
Laurie, Maj.-Gen. Rufus Henry, 1892–1961, vol. VI
Laurie, Simon Somerville, 1829–1909, vol. I

Laurie, Sir Wilfrid Emilius, 5th Bt (*cr* 1834), 1859–1936, vol. III

Laurier, Rt Hon. Sir Wilfrid, 1841–1919, vol. II

Laurvig, Count Preben Ferdinand A.; *see* Ahlefeldt-Laurvig.

Lauterpacht, Sir Hersch, 1897–1960, vol. V

Laval, Pierre, 1883–1945, vol. IV

Lavarack, Lt-Gen. Sir John Dudley, 1885–1957, vol. V

Lavedan, Henri, 1859–1940, vol. III

Lavelle, Rev. Canon Alexander Bannerman, 1899–1964, vol. VI

Laver, James, 1899–1975, vol. VII

Laver, William Adolphus, 1866–1940, vol. III (A), vol. IV

Laverack, Frederick Joseph, *died* 1928, vol. II

Lavergne, Joseph, 1847–1922, vol. II

Lavergne, Hon. Louis, 1845–1931, vol. III

Lavers, Sydney Charles Robert, 1898–1972, vol. VII

Lavery, Cecil, 1894–1967, vol. VI

Lavery, Sir John, 1856–1941, vol. IV

Lavington Evans, Leonard Glyde; *see* Evans.

Lavis, Rt Rev. Sidney Warren, *died* 1965, vol. VI

Lavisse, Ernest, 1842–1922, vol. II

Law, Albert, 1872–1956, vol. V

Law, Lt-Col Alfred, 1871–1928, vol. II

Law, Sir Alfred Joseph, 1860–1939, vol. III

Law, Sir Algernon, 1856–1943, vol. IV

Law, Anastasia, (Mrs Nigel Law), *died* 1976, vol. VII

Law, Rt Hon. Andrew Bonar, 1858–1923, vol. II

Law, Sir Archibald Fitzgerald, 1853–1921, vol. II

Law, Arthur, 1876–1933, vol. III

Law, Sir Charles Ewan, 1884–1974, vol. VII

Law, Edward, 1853–1930, vol. III

Law, Major Sir Edward FitzGerald, 1846–1908, vol. I

Law, Ernest, 1854–1930, vol. III

Law, Francis Towry Adeane, 1835–1901, vol. I

Law, Henry Duncan Graves, 1883–1964, vol. VI

Law, Herbert Henry, 1862–1943, vol. IV

Law, Hugh Alexander, *died* 1943, vol. IV

Law, Margaret Dorothy, *died* 1980, vol. VII

Law, Mary, 1889–1919, vol. II

Law, Ralph Hamilton, 1915–1967, vol. VI

Law, Raja Reshee Case, 1852–1935, vol. III

Law, Rev. Robert, 1860–1919, vol. II

Law, Brig.-Gen. Robert Theophilus Hewitt, 1855–1949, vol. IV

Law, Samuel Horace, 1873–1940, vol. III (A), vol. IV

Law, Sir Sydney, 1861–1949, vol. IV

Law, Rev. Thomas, 1854–1910, vol. I

Law, Thomas Pakenham, 1834–1905, vol. I

Law, Maj.-Gen. Victor Edward, 1842–1910, vol. I

Law, William Arthur, 1844–1913, vol. I

Law, Mrs William Arthur; *see* Holland, Fanny.

Law, Rev. William Smalley, 1865–1937, vol. III

Lawes, Edward Thornton Hill, 1869–1921, vol. II

Lawes, Sir John Bennet, 1st Bt, 1814–1899, vol. I

Lawes, Sir John Claud Bennet, 4th Bt, 1898–1979, vol. VII

Lawes-Wittewronge, Sir Charles, 2nd Bt, 1843–1911, vol. I

Lawes-Wittewronge, Sir John Bennet, 3rd Bt, 1872–1931, vol. III

Lawford, John Bowring, 1858–1934, vol. III

Lawford, Lt-Gen. Sir Sydney Turing Barlow, 1865–1953, vol. V

Lawford, Captain (S) Vincent Adrian, 1871–1959, vol. V

Lawler, Wallace Leslie, 1912–1972, vol. VII

Lawless, Col Hon. Edward, 1841–1921, vol. II

Lawless, Hon. Emily, *died* 1913, vol. I

Lawless, Henry Hamilton, *died* 1913, vol. I

Lawless, Surg. Lt-Col Sir Warren Roland Crooke-, 1863–1931, vol. III

Lawley, Hon. Alethea Jane Wiel, *died* 1929, vol. III

Lawley, Edgar Ernest, *died* 1977, vol. VII

Lawlor, Very Rev. Hugh Jackson, 1860–1938, vol. III

Lawlor, John, 1906–1975, vol. VII

Lawn, James Gunson, 1868–1952, vol. V

Lawrance, Major. Sir Arthur Salisbury, 1880–1965, vol. VI

Lawrance, Rt Hon. Sir John Compton, 1832–1912, vol. I

Lawrance, Very Rev. Walter John, 1840–1914, vol. I

Lawrance, William Thomas, *died* 1932, vol. III

Lawrence, 2nd Baron, 1846–1913, vol. I

Lawrence, 3rd Baron, 1878–1947, vol. IV

Lawrence, 4th Baron, 1908–1968, vol. VI

Lawrence of Kingsgate, 1st Baron, 1855–1927, vol. II

Lawrence, Albert, 1893–1961, vol. VI

Lawrence, Alexander John, 1837–1905, vol. I

Lawrence, Sir Alexander Waldemar, 4th Bt (*cr* 1858), 1874–1939, vol. III

Lawrence, Hon. (Alfred) Clive, 1876–1926, vol. II

Lawrence, Alfred Kingsley, *died* 1975, vol. VII

Lawrence, (Arabella) Susan, 1871–1947, vol. IV

Lawrence, Rev. Arthur Evelyn B.; *see* Barnes-Lawrence.

Lawrence, Aubrey Trevor, 1875–1930, vol. III

Lawrence, Lt-Col Bryan Turner Tom, 1873–1949, vol. IV

Lawrence, C. E., 1870–1940, vol. III

Lawrence, Ven. Charles D'Aguilar, 1847–1935, vol. III

Lawrence, Hon. Clive; *see* Lawrence, Hon. A. C.

Lawrence, David Herbert, 1885–1930, vol. III

Lawrence, Sir Edward, 1825–1909, vol. I

Lawrence, Sir Edwin D.; *see* Durning-Lawrence.

Lawrence, Ernest O., 1901–1958, vol. V

Lawrence, Sir (Frederick) Geoffrey, 1902–1967, vol. VI

Lawrence, Major Freeling Ross, 1872–1914, vol. I

Lawrence, Sir Geoffrey; *see* Lawrence, Sir F. G.

Lawrence, Lt-Col George Henniker, 1868–1932, vol. III

Lawrence, Gertrude, (Mrs Richard Stoddard Aldrich), 1898–1952, vol. V

Lawrence, Sir Henry Eustace Waldemar, 5th Bt (*cr* 1858), 1905–1967, vol. VI

Lawrence, Sir Henry Hayes, 2nd Bt (*cr* 1858), 1864–1898, vol. I

Lawrence, Lt-Col Henry Rundle, 1878–1949, vol. IV

Lawrence, Sir Henry Staveley, 1870–1949, vol. IV

Lawrence, Sir Henry Waldemar, 3rd Bt (*cr* 1858), 1845–1908, vol. I

Lawrence, Captain Henry Walter Neville, 1891–1959, vol. V

Lawrence, Gen. Hon. Sir Herbert Alexander, 1861–1943, vol. IV

Lawrence, Herbert Cecil B.; *see* Barnes-Lawrence.

Lawrence, Col Hugh Duncan, 1862–1946, vol. IV

Lawrence, Sir James Clarke, 1st Bt (*cr* 1869), 1820–1897, vol. I

Lawrence, Sir James John Trevor, 2nd Bt (*cr* 1867), 1831–1913, vol. I

Lawrence, Sir (James) Taylor, 1888–1944, vol. IV

Lawrence, Sir Joseph, 1st Bt (*cr* 1918), 1848–1919, vol. II

Lawrence, Margery, (Mrs Arthur Towle), *died* 1969, vol. VI

Lawrence, Marjorie Florence, *died* 1979, vol. VII

Lawrence, Hon. Dame Maude Agnes, 1864–1933, vol. III

Lawrence, Rt Hon. Sir Paul Ogden, 1861–1952, vol. V

Lawrence, Penelope, *died* 1932, vol. III

Lawrence, Lt-Col Sir (Percy) Roland (Bradford), 2nd Bt (*cr* 1906), 1886–1950, vol. IV

Lawrence, Peter Frederick, 1937–1976, vol. VII

Lawrence, Lt-Col Richard Travers, 1890–1973, vol. VII

Lawrence, Robert Daniel, 1892–1968, vol. VI

Lawrence, Roger Bernard, *died* 1925, vol. II

Lawrence, Lt-Col Sir Roland; *see* Lawrence, Lt-Col Sir P. R. B.

Lawrence, Sir Russell; *see* Lawrence, Sir W. R.

Lawrence, Samuel Chave, 1894–1980, vol. VII

Lawrence, Susan; *see* Lawrence, A. S.

Lawrence, Sydney, 1905–1976, vol. VII

Lawrence, Sydney Boyle, *died* 1951, vol. V

Lawrence, Sir Taylor; *see* Lawrence, Sir J. T.

Lawrence, Thomas Edward; *see* Shaw, T. E.

Lawrence, Rev. Thomas Joseph, 1849–1919, vol. II

Lawrence, Vernon, 1899–1971, vol. VII

Lawrence, Sir Walter, 1872–1939, vol. III

Lawrence, Sir Walter Roper, 1st Bt (*cr* 1906), 1857–1940, vol. III

Lawrence, Sir William, 1818–1897, vol. I

Lawrence, Rt Rev. William, 1850–1941, vol. IV

Lawrence, Maj.-Gen. William Alexander, 1843–1924, vol. II

Lawrence, William Frederic, 1844–1935, vol. III

Lawrence, William John, 1862–1940, vol. III

Lawrence, Sir William Matthew Trevor, 3rd Bt (*cr* 1867), 1870–1934, vol. III

Lawrence, Sir (William) Russell, 1903–1976, vol. VII

Lawrence-Archer, Col James Henry, 1871–1948, vol. IV

Lawrie, Allan James, 1873–1926, vol. II

Lawrie, Sir Archibald Campbell, 1837–1914, vol. I

Lawrie, Maj.-Gen. Charles Edward, 1864–1953, vol. V

Lawrie, Captain Edward McConnell Wyndham, 1882–1933, vol. III

Lawrie, James Haldane, 1907–1979, vol. VII

Lawrie, John, 1861–1935, vol. III

Laws, Bernard Courtney, *died* 1947, vol. IV

Laws, Gp Captain Frederick Charles Victor, 1887–1975, vol. VII

Laws, Rev. George Edward, *died* 1923, vol. II

Laws, Lt-Col Henry William, 1876–1954, vol. V

Laws, Robert, 1851–1934, vol. III

Laws, Samuel Charles, 1879–1963, vol. VI

Lawson, 1st Baron, 1881–1965, vol. VI

Lawson, Abercrombie Anstruther, *died* 1927, vol. II

Lawson, Alexander, 1852–1921, vol. II

Lawson, Brig.-Gen. Algernon, 1869–1929, vol. III

Lawson, Andrew Sherlock, 1855–1914, vol. I

Lawson, Sir Arnold, 1867–1947, vol. IV

Lawson, Arthur Ernest, 1863–1933, vol. III

Lawson, Sir Arthur Tredgold, 1st Bt (*cr* 1900), 1844–1915, vol. I

Lawson, Sir Charles Allen, 1838–1915, vol. I

Lawson, Sir Digby, 2nd Bt (*cr* 1900), 1880–1959, vol. V

Lawson, Rev. Frederick Pike, *died* 1920, vol. II

Lawson, Major Frederick Washington, 1869–1924, vol. II

Lawson, Sir George, 1838–1898, vol. I

Lawson, George McArthur, 1906–1978, vol. VII

Lawson, H. S., 1876–1918, vol. II

Lawson, Sir Harry Sutherland Wightman, 1875–1952, vol. V

Lawson, Sir Henry Brailsford, 1898–1978, vol. VII

Lawson, Henry Hertzberg, 1867–1922, vol. II

Lawson, Sir Henry Joseph, 3rd Bt (*cr* 1841), 1877–1947, vol. IV

Lawson, Lt-Gen. Sir Henry Merrick, 1859–1933, vol. III

Lawson, Major Sir Hilton, 4th Bt (*cr* 1831), 1895–1959, vol. V

Lawson, Hon. James Earl, 1891–1950, vol. IV

Lawson, Sir John, 2nd Bt (*cr* 1841), 1829–1910, vol. I

Lawson, John, 1893–1977, vol. VII

Lawson, Sir John Grant, 1st Bt (*cr* 1905), 1856–1919, vol. II

Lawson, Col Sir Peter Grant, 2nd Bt (*cr* 1905), 1903–1973, vol. VII

Lawson, Sir Ralph Henry, 4th Bt (*cr* 1841), 1905–1975, vol. VII

Lawson, Rear-Adm. Robert Neale, 1873–1945, vol. IV

Lawson, Thomas William, 1857–1925, vol. II

Lawson, Victor F., 1850–1925, vol. II

Lawson, Sir Wilfrid, 2nd Bt (*cr* 1831), 1829–1906, vol. I

Lawson, Sir Wilfrid, 3rd Bt (*cr* 1831), 1862–1937, vol. III

Lawson, Sir William Halford, 1899–1971, vol. VII

Lawson, William Norton, 1830–1911, vol. I

Lawson, Rev. William Thomas, *died* 1937, vol. III

Lawson-Tancred, Major Sir Thomas Selby, 9th Bt, 1870–1945, vol. IV

Lawther, Barry Charles Alfred, 1888–1974, vol. VII
Lawther, Sir William, 1889–1976, vol. VII
Lawton, Frank, 1904–1969, vol. VI
Lawton, Frank Warburton, 1881–1966, vol. VI
Lay, Arthur Hyde, 1865–1934, vol. III
Lay, Brig. William Oswald, 1892–1952, vol. V
Layard, Austen Havelock, 1895–1956, vol. V
Layard, Sir Charles Peter, 1849–1915, vol. I
Layard, Edgar Leopold, 1824–1900, vol. I
Layard, George Somes, 1857–1925, vol. II
Layard, Raymond de Burgh Money, 1859–1941 vol. IV
Laybourne, Rear-Adm. Alan Watson, 1898–1977, vol. VII
Laybourne-Smith, Louis, 1880–1965, vol. VI
Laycock, Brig.-Gen. Sir Joseph Frederick, 1867–1952, vol. V
Laycock, Maj.-Gen. Sir Robert Edward, 1907–1968, vol. VI
Laye, Maj.-Gen. Joseph Henry, 1849–1938, vol. III
Layh, Lt-Col Herbert Thomas Christoph, 1885–1964, vol. VI
Layland-Barratt, Sir Francis; see Barratt.
Layland-Barratt, Captain Sir Francis Henry Godolphin, 2nd Bt, 1896–1968, vol. VI
Layng, Rev. Thomas Malcolm, 1892–1958, vol. V
Layng, Rev. William Wright, 1845–1936, vol. III
Layton, 1st Baron, 1884–1966, vol. VI
Layton, Major Edward, 1857–1913, vol. I
Layton, Edwin J., 1850–1929, vol. III
Layton, Adm. Sir Geoffrey, 1884–1964, vol. VI
Layton, Captain Perceval Norman, 1872–1943, vol. IV
Layton, Thomas Bramley, 1882–1964, vol. VI
Layton, William Grazebrook, 1868–1949, vol. IV
Lazarovich-Hrebelianovich, HH Princess, (Eleanor Calhoun), died 1957, vol. V
Lazarus-Barlow, Walter Sydney, died 1950, vol. IV
Lazenby, Frederick George, 1876–1943, vol. IV
Lazier, Stephen Franklin, 1841–1916, vol. II
Lea, Rt Rev. Arthur, 1868–1958, vol. V
Lea, Arthur Sheridan, died 1915, vol. I
Lea, Edward Thomas, 1852–1938, vol. III
Lea, Frederick Charles, died 1952, vol. V
Lea, George Harris, 1843–1915, vol. I
Lea, Lt-Col Harold Futvoye, 1867–1940, vol. III
Lea, Henry Charles, 1825–1909, vol. I
Lea, Hugh Cecil, died 1926, vol. II
Lea, John, 1871–1958, vol. V
Lea, Measham, 1869–1963, vol. VI
Lea, Lt-Col Percy Gerald Parker, 1875–1945, vol. IV
Lea, Col Samuel Job, 1851–1919, vol. II
Lea, Sir Sydney; see Lea, Sir T. S.
Lea, Sir Thomas, 1st Bt, 1841–1902, vol. I
Lea, Sir (Thomas) Sydney, 2nd Bt, 1867–1946, vol. IV
Lea-Cox, Maj.-Gen. Maurice, 1898–1974, vol. VII
Leach, Rt Hon. Sir (Alfred Henry) Lionel, 1883–1960, vol. V
Leach, Arthur Francis, 1851–1915, vol. I
Leach, Arthur Gordon, 1885–1978, vol. VII
Leach, Bernard Howell, 1887–1979, vol. VII
Leach, Charles, 1847–1919, vol. II

Leach, Charles Harold, 1901–1975, vol. VII
Leach, Maj.-Gen. Sir Edmund, 1836–1923, vol. II
Leach, Rev. Edmund Foxcroft, 1851–1939, vol. III
Leach, Gen. Sir Edward Pemberton, 1847–1913, vol. I
Leach, Frank Burton, 1881–1961, vol. VI
Leach, Frederick, 1843–1916, vol. II
Leach, Lt-Col Sir George Archibald, 1820–1913, vol. I
Leach, Brig.-Gen. Harold Pemberton, 1851–1930, vol. III
Leach, Rev. Henry, died 1921, vol. II
Leach, Henry, 1874–1942, vol. IV
Leach, Brig.-Gen. Henry Edmund Burleigh, 1870–1936, vol. III
Leach, Sir John, 1848–1927, vol. II
Leach, Captain John Catterall, 1894–1941, vol. IV
Leach, Rt Hon. Sir Lionel; see Leach, Rt Hon. Sir A. H. L.
Leach, Col Reginald Pemberton, 1855–1929, vol. III
Leach, Rear-Adm. Robert Owen, 1832–1920, vol. II
Leach, Thomas Stephen, 1896–1973, vol. VII
Leach, William, 1870–1949, vol. IV
Leachman, Col Gerard Evelyn, 1880–1920, vol. II
Leacock, Sir Dudley Gordon, 1880–1954, vol. V
Leacock, Stephen Butler, 1869–1944, vol. IV
Lead, Major Sir William Chollerton, died 1942, vol. IV
Leadam, Isaac Saunders, died 1913, vol. I
Leadbetter, James Stevenson, 1867–1939, vol. III
Leadbitter, Sir Eric Cyril Egerton, 1891–1971, vol. VII
Leader, Maj.-Gen. Henry Peregrine, 1865–1934, vol. III
Leader, William Nicholas, 1851–1931, vol. III
Leaf, Cecil Huntington, 1864–1910, vol. I
Leaf, Major Henry Meredith, 1862–1931, vol. III
Leaf, Walter, 1852–1927, vol. II
Leah, Samuel Dawson, 1844–1916, vol. II
Leahy, Arthur Herbert, 1857–1928, vol. II
Leahy, Engr Rear-Adm. James Palmer, 1871–1940, vol. III
Leahy, Lt-Col John Patrick Daunt, 1869–1935, vol. III
Leahy, Brig. Thomas Bernard Arthur, 1878–1947, vol. IV
Leahy, Major Thomas Joseph Carroll, 1889–1942, vol. IV
Leahy, Fleet Adm. William D., 1875–1959, vol. V
Leak, Hector, 1887–1976, vol. VII
Leake, Lt-Col Arthur Martin-, 1874–1953, vol. V
Leake, Vice-Adm. Francis M.; see Martin-Leake.
Leake, George, 1856–1902, vol. I
Leake, Henry Dashwood Stucley, 1876–1970, vol. VI
Leake, Hugh Martin-, 1878–1977, vol. VII
Leake, Col Jonas William, 1873–1934, vol. III
Leake, Percy Dewe, died 1949, vol. IV
Leake, Sidney Henry, 1892–1973, vol. VII
Leakey, Louis Seymour Bazett, 1903–1972, vol. VII
Leale, Rev. Sir John, 1892–1969, vol. VI
Leamy, Edmund, 1848–1904, vol. I

Lean, (Edward) Tangye, 1911–1974, vol. VII
Lean, Florence; see Marryat, F.
Lean, Captain John Trevor, 1903–1961, vol. VI
Lean, Maj.-Gen. Kenneth Edward, 1859–1921, vol. II
Lean, Tangye; see Lean, E. T.
Leane, Col Edwin Thomas, 1867–1928, vol. II
Leane, Brig.-Gen. Sir Raymond Lionel, 1878–1962, vol. VI
Lear, Ven. Francis, 1823–1914, vol. I
Learmonth, Agnes Moore L.; see Livingstone-Learmonth.
Learmonth, Lt-Col (Francis) Leger (Christian) Livingstone-, 1875–1930, vol. III
Learmonth, Adm. Sir Frederick Charles, 1866–1941, vol. IV
Learmonth, Frederick Valiant Cotton L.; see Livingstone-Learmonth.
Learmonth, Sir James Rögnvald, 1895–1967, vol. VI
Learmonth, Brig.-Gen. John Eric Christian L.; see Livingstone-Learmonth.
Learmonth, Lt-Col Leger Livingstone-; see Learmonth, Lt-Col F. L. C. L.
Learoyd-Cockburn, Col Charles Douglas, 1859–1946, vol. IV
Leask, George Alfred, 1878–1950, vol. IV (A)
Leask, Air Vice-Marshal Kenneth Malise St Clair Graeme, 1896–1974, vol. VII
Leatham, Major Bertram Henry, 1881–1915, vol. I
Leatham, Vice-Adm. Eustace La Trobe, 1870–1935, vol. III
Leatham, Adm. Sir Ralph, 1886–1954, vol. V
Leathem, Walter Henry, 1894–1967, vol. VI
Leather, Col Francis Holdsworth, 1864–1929, vol. III
Leather, John Walter, 1860–1934, vol. III
Leather, Lt-Col Kenneth John Walters, 1878–1963, vol. VI
Leathers, 1st Viscount, 1883–1965, vol. VI
Leathes, John Beresford, 1864–1956, vol. V
Leathes, Rev. Stanley, 1830–1900, vol. I
Leathes, Sir Stanley Mordaunt, 1861–1938, vol. III
Leaver, Noel Harry, 1889–1951, vol. V
Leavis, Frank Raymond, 1895–1978, vol. VII
Le Bargy, Charles Gustave, 1858–1936, vol. III
Le Bas, Edward, 1904–1966, vol. VI
Le Bas, Sir Hedley Francis, 1868–1926, vol. II
Le Blanc, Rt Rev. Edouard, 1870–1935, vol. III
Le Blanc, Sir Pierre Evariste, 1854–1918, vol. II
Le Blond, Elizabeth Alice Frances, (Mrs Aubrey Le Blond), died 1934, vol. III
Lebour, George Alexander Louis, 1847–1918, vol. II
Le Braz, Anatole, 1859–1926, vol. II
Le Breton, Clement Martin, 1852–1927, vol. II
Le Breton, Col Sir Edward Philip, 1883–1961, vol. VI
Le Breton-Simmons, Col Geroge Francis Henry, 1864–1930, vol. III
Lebrun, Albert, 1871–1950, vol. IV
Le Brun, Paymaster Captain William Henry, died 1942, vol. IV
Leburn, Gilmour; see Leburn, W. G.

Leburn, (William) Gilmour, 1913–1963, vol. VI
Lebus, Sir Herman Andrew Harris, 1884–1957, vol. V
Le Chatelier, Henry Louis, 1850–1936, vol. III
Leche, Sir John Hurleston, 1889–1960, vol. V
Lechmere, Sir Edmund Arthur, 4th Bt, 1865–1937, vol. III
Lechmere, Captain Sir Ronald Berwick Hungerford, 5th Bt, 1886–1965, vol. VI
Leck, David Calder, 1857–1927, vol. II
Leckie, Col John Edwards, 1872–1950, vol. IV
Leckie, Joseph Alexander, 1866–1938, vol. III
Leckie, Joseph Hannay, 1865–1935, vol. III
Leckie, Air Marshal Robert, 1890–1975, vol. VII
Lecky, Captain Arthur Macaulay, 1881–1933, vol. III
Lecky, Col Frederick Beauchamp, 1858–1928, vol. II
Lecky, Captain Halton Stirling, 1878–1940, vol. III
Lecky, Maj.-Gen. Robert St Clair, 1863–1940, vol. III
Lecky, Sir Thomas, 1828–1907, vol. I
Lecky, Rt Hon. William Edward Hartpole, 1838–1903, vol. I
Leclercq, Auguste B.; see Bouche-Leclercq.
Leclezio, Sir Eugene Pierre Jules, 1832–1915, vol. II
Leclezio, Hon. Sir Henry, died 1929, vol. III
Leclézio, Sir Jules, 1877–1951, vol. V
Lecocq, Charles, 1832–1918, vol. II
Lecomte, Georges, 1867–1958, vol. V
Leconfield, 2nd Baron, 1830–1901, vol. I
Leconfield, 3rd Baron, 1872–1952, vol. V
Leconfield, 4th Baron, 1877–1963, vol. VI
Leconfield, 5th Baron, 1883–1967, vol. VI
Le Corbusier, (Charles-Edouard Jeanneret), 1887–1965, vol. VI
Le Cornu, Col Charles Philip, 1829–1911, vol. I
le Couteur, Frank, died 1950, vol. IV
Ledeboer, John Henry, 1853–1930, vol. III
Ledgard, Sir Henry, 1853–1946, vol. IV
Ledgard, Rev. Ralph Gilbert, died 1939, vol. III
Ledgard, Reginald Armitage, 1883–1949, vol. IV
Ledger, Air Vice-Marshal Arthur Percy, 1897–1970, vol. VI
Ledger, Claude Kirwood, 1888–1974, vol. VII
Ledger, Edward, died 1921, vol. II
Ledingham, Col George Alexander, 1890–1978, vol. VII
Ledingham, Sir John C. G., 1875–1944, vol. IV
Ledingham, Mrs Una Christina, 1900–1965, vol. VI
Ledlie, James Crawford, 1860–1928, vol. II
Ledlie, Reginald Cyril Bell, 1898–1966, vol. VI
Ledóchowski, Wlodimir Halka, Count, 1866–1942, vol. IV
Leduc, Paul, 1889–1971, vol. VII
Ledward, Gilbert, 1888–1960, vol. V
Ledward, Richard Thomas Davenport, 1915–1963, vol. VI
Lee of Fareham, 1st Viscount, 1868–1947, vol. IV
Lee, Rev. Albert, 1852–1935, vol. III
Lee, Lt-Col Sir (Albert) George, 1879–1967, vol. VI
Lee, Maj.-Gen. Alec Wilfred, 1896–1973, vol. VII
Lee, Alfred Morgan, 1901–1975, vol. VII

Lee, Lt-Col Arthur Neale, 1877–1954, vol. V
Lee, Air Vice-Marshal Arthur Stanley Gould, 1894–1975, vol. VII
Lee, Col Arthur Vaughan Hanning V.; *see* Vaughan-Lee.
Lee, Mrs Asher; *see* Lee, Mollie Carpenter.
Lee, Auriol, 1880–1941, vol. IV
Lee, Bremner Patrick, 1864–1937, vol. III
Lee, Hon. Charles Alfred, 1842–1926, vol. II
Lee, Adm. Sir Charles Lionel V.; *see* Vaughan-Lee.
Lee, Edgar, 1851–1908, vol. I
Lee, Sir Edward, 1833–1909, vol. I
Lee, Edward Owen, 1891–1950, vol. IV
Lee, Rev. Canon Edwin Maywood O'Hara, 1859–1942, vol. IV
Lee, Ernest Markham, 1874–1956, vol. V
Lee, Fitzhugh, *died* 1905, vol. I
Lee, Brig.-Gen. Francis, 1866–1932, vol. III
Lee, Frank, 1867–1941, vol. IV
Lee, Rt Hon. Sir Frank Godbould, 1903–1971, vol. VII
Lee, Frank Herbert, *born* 1869, vol. V.
Lee, Rev. Frederick George, 1832–1902, vol. I
Lee, Lt-Col Sir George; *see* Lee, Lt-Col Sir A. G.
Lee, Lt-Gen. George Leonard, 1860–1939, vol. III
Lee, Gordon Ambrose de Lisle, 1864–1927, vol. II
Lee, Lt-Col H. R.; *see* Romer-Lee.
Lee, Harry Wilmot, 1848–1914, vol. I
Lee, Sir Henry Austin, 1847–1918, vol. II
Lee, Maj.-Gen. Henry Herbert, 1838–1920, vol. II
Lee, Henry William, 1865–1932, vol. III
Lee, Herbert William, 1865–1940, vol. III
Lee, Ivy Ledbetter, 1877–1934, vol. III
Lee, James Paris, 1831–1904, vol. I
Lee, Rev. James Wideman, 1849–1919, vol. II
Lee, John, 1867–1928, vol. II
Lee, Joseph Johnston, 1876–1954, vol. V (A)
Lee, Sir Kenneth, 1st Bt, *died* 1967, vol. VI
Lee, Lawford Y.; *see* Yate-Lee.
Lee, Lennox B., 1864–1949, vol. IV
Lee, Manfred B., *died* 1971, vol. VII
Lee, May B.; *see* Stott, May, (Lady Stott).
Lee, Mollie Carpenter, (Mrs Asher Lee), *died* 1973, vol. VII
Lee, Col Reginald Tilson, 1878–1940, vol. III
Lee, Rev. Richard, *died* 1922, vol. II
Lee, Richard Henry, *died* 1923, vol. II
Lee, Maj.-Gen. Sir Richard Phillips, 1865–1953, vol. V
Lee, Robert Warden, 1868–1958, vol. V
Lee, Roger Malcolm, 1902–1972, vol. VII
Lee, S. Richmond, (Mrs John W. Richmond Lee); *see* Yorke, Curtis.
Lee, Sir Sidney, 1859–1926, vol. II
Lee, Brig. Stanlake Swinton, 1890–1952, vol. V
Lee, Sydney, 1866–1949, vol. IV
Lee, Vernon; *see* Paget, Violet.
Lee, Hon. Sir Walter Henry, 1874–1963, vol. VI
Lee, Rt Rev. William, 1875–1948, vol. IV
Lee, William Alexander, 1886–1971, vol. VII
Lee, William Frederick, 1857–1930, vol. III
Lee, William Stevens, 1871–1965, vol. VI
Lee, Rev. William Walker, 1909–1979, vol. VII

Lee-Dillon, Hon. Harry Lee Stanton, 1874–1923, vol. II
Lee-Elliott, David Lee, 1869–1956, vol. V
Lee-Hamilton, Eugene, 1845–1907, vol. I
Lee-Hankey, W., 1869–1952, vol. V
Lee-Holland, Hetty, *died* 1954, vol. V
Lee Howard, Leon Alexander, 1914–1978, vol. VII
Lee Steere, Sir Ernest Augustus, 1866–1957, vol. V
Lee-Warner, Lt-Col Harry Granville, 1883–1932, vol. III
Lee Warner, Philip Henry, 1877–1925, vol. II
Lee-Warner, Sir William, 1846–1914, vol. I
Leebody, John R., 1840–1927, vol. II
Leece, Rev. Charles Henry, *died* 1930, vol. III
Leech, Arthur John, 1873–1940, vol. III
Leech, Sir Bosdin Thomas, 1836–1912, vol. I
Leech, Clifford, 1909–1977, vol. VII
Leech, Ernest Bosdin, 1875–1950, vol. IV
Leech, George William, 1894–1966, vol. VI
Leech, Henry Brougham, 1843–1921, vol. II
Leech, John, 1857–1942, vol. IV
Leech, Sir Joseph William, 1865–1940, vol. III
Leech, Priestley, *died* 1936, vol. III
Leech, Samuel Chetwynd, 1872–1931, vol. III
Leech, Sir Stephen, 1864–1925, vol. II
Leech, William John, 1881–1968, vol. VI
Leech, William Thomas, 1869–1953, vol. V
Leech-Porter, Maj.-Gen. John Edmund, 1896–1979, vol. VII
Leeder, S. H., *died* 1930, vol. III
Leedham, Air Cdre Hugh, 1889–1947, vol. IV
Leedham-Green, Charles, *died* 1931, vol. III
Leeds, 10th Duke of, 1862–1927, vol. II
Leeds, 11th Duke of, 1901–1963, vol. VI
Leeds, 12th Duke of, 1884–1964, vol. VI
Leeds, Duchess of; (Katherine), *died* 1952, vol. V
Leeds, Sir Edward Templer, 5th Bt, 1859–1924, vol. II
Leeds, Edward Thurlow, 1877–1955, vol. V
Leeds, Comdr Sir Reginald Arthur St John, 6th Bt, 1899–1970, vol. VI
Leeds, Lt-Col Thomas Louis, 1869–1926, vol. II
Leeds, William Henry Arthur St John, 1864–1917, vol. II
Leefe, Gen. John Beckwith, 1849–1922, vol. II
Leek, James, 1892–1978, vol. VII
Leeke, Rev. Edward Tucker, 1841–1925, vol. II
Leeke, George, *died* 1939, vol. III
Leeke, Rt Rev. John Cox, 1843–1919, vol. II
Leeke, Col Ralph, 1849–1943, vol. IV
Leeke, Ven. Thomas Newton, 1854–1933, vol. III
Leen, Very Rev. Edward, 1885–1944, vol. IV
Leen, Rt Rev. James, 1888–1949, vol. IV
Leeper, Alexander, 1848–1934, vol. III
Leeper, Alexander Wigram Allen, 1887–1935, vol. III
Leeper, Rev. Canon Arthur Lindsay, 1883–1942, vol. IV
Leeper, Sir Reginald Wildig Allen, 1888–1968, vol. VI
Lees, Air Marshal Sir Alan, 1895–1973, vol. VII
Lees, Sir Arthur Henry James, 5th Bt (*cr* 1804), 1863–1949, vol. IV
Lees, Arthur John, 1867–1956, vol. V

Lees, Mrs Charles; see Lees, Sarah Anne.
Lees, Charles Archibald, 1869–1943, vol. IV
Lees, Sir Charles Archibald Edward Ivor, 7th Bt (cr 1804), 1902–1963, vol. VI
Lees, Sir Charles Cameron, 1837–1898, vol. I
Lees, Col Charles Henry Brownlow, 1871–1941, vol. IV
Lees, Charles Herbert, 1864–1952, vol. V
Lees, Sir Clare; see Lees, Sir W. C.
Lees, David, died 1934, vol. III
Lees, David Bridge, died 1915, vol. I
Lees, Rear-Adm. Dennis Marescaux, 1900–1973, vol. VII
Lees, Donald Hector, died 1953, vol. V
Lees, Edith Mabel Lucy, 1878–1956, vol. V
Lees, Sir Elliott, 1st Bt (cr 1897), 1860–1908, vol. I
Lees, George Martin, 1898–1955, vol. V
Lees, Rev. George Robinson, 1860–1944, vol. IV
Lees, Sir Harcourt James, 4th Bt (cr 1804), 1840–1917, vol. II
Lees, Rev. Harold Montagu H.; see Hyde-Lees.
Lees, Most Rev. Harrington Clare, 1870–1929, vol. III
Lees, Sir Hereward; see Lees, Sir W. H. C.
Lees, Jack, died 1941, vol. IV
Lees, Very Rev. Sir James Cameron, 1834–1913, vol. I
Lees, James Ferguson, 1872–1935, vol. III
Lees, Sir Jean Marie Ivor, 6th Bt (cr 1804), 1875–1957, vol. V
Lees, Sir John M'Kie, 1843–1926, vol. II
Lees, Col Sir John Victor Elliott, 3rd Bt (cr 1897), 1887–1955, vol. V
Lees, Lt-Col Lawrence Werner Wyld, 1887–1976, vol. VII
Lees, Oswald Campbell, 1857–1945, vol. IV
Lees, Col Roderick Livingstone, 1864–1936, vol. III
Lees, Samuel, 1885–1940, vol. III
Lees, Sarah Anne, 1842–1935, vol. III
Lees, Stanley Lawrence, 1911–1980, vol. VII
Lees, Sir Thomas Evans Keith, 2nd Bt (cr 1897), 1886–1915, vol. I
Lees, Thomas Orde Hastings, 1846–1924, vol. II
Lees, Walter Kinnear P.; see Pyke-Lees.
Lees, Sir (William) Clare, 1st Bt (cr 1937), 1874–1951, vol. V
Lees, Sir (William) Hereward (Clare), 2nd Bt (cr 1937), 1904–1976, vol. VII
Lees-Jones, John, 1887–1966, vol. VI
Lees Read, Bertie, 1903–1960, vol. V
Lees-Smith, Rt Hon. Hastings Bertrand, 1878–1941, vol. IV
Leese, Sir Alexander William, 4th Bt, 1909–1979, vol. VII
Leese, Charles William, 1876–1969, vol. VI
Leese, Sir Joseph Francis, 1st Bt, 1845–1914, vol. I
Leese, Lt-Gen. Sir Oliver William Hargreaves, 3rd Bt, 1894–1978, vol. VII
Leese, Sir William Hargreaves, 2nd Bt, 1868–1937, vol. III
Leeson, Rt Rev. Spencer, 1892–1956, vol. V
Leeson-Marshall, Markham Richard, 1859–1939, vol. III

Leete, Alfred Chew, 1882–1933, vol. III
Leete, Frederick Alexander, died 1941, vol. IV
Leete, Leslie William Thomas, 1909–1976, vol. VII
Leetham, Lt-Col Sir Arthur, 1859–1933, vol. III
Le Fanu, George Ernest Hugh, 1874–1965, vol. VI
Le Fanu, Most Rev. Henry Frewen, 1870–1946, vol. IV
Le Fanu, Adm. Sir Michael, 1913–1970, vol. VI
Le Fanu, Thomas Philip, 1858–1945, vol. IV
Le Fanu, William Richard, 1861–1925, vol. II
Lefeaux, Leslie, 1886–1962, vol. VI
Le Feuvre, Amy, died 1929, vol. III
Leffingwell, Russell Cornell, 1878–1960, vol. V
Leffler, Gösta M.; see Mittag-Leffler.
le Fleming, Sir Andrew Fleming Hudleston; see Fleming.
Le Fleming, Sir (Ernest) Kaye, 1872–1946, vol. IV
le Fleming, Sir Frank Thomas, 10th Bt, 1887–1971, vol. VII
Le Fleming, Sir Kaye; see Le Fleming, Sir E. K.
Le Fleming, Maj.-Gen. Roger Eustace, 1895–1962, vol. VI
Le Fleming, Stanley Hughes, 1855–1939, vol. III
Le Fleming, Sir William Hudleston, 9th Bt, 1861–1945, vol. IV
Lefroy, A. H. F., 1852–1919, vol. II
Lefroy, Sir Anthony Langlois Bruce, 1881–1958, vol. V
Lefroy, Bt Major Bertram Perceval, 1878–1915, vol. I
Lefroy, Captain Cecil Maxwell-, 1876–1931, vol. III
Lefroy, Rev. Charles Edward Cotterell, died 1940, vol. III
Lefroy, Sir Edward Henry Bruce, 1887–1966, vol. VI
Lefroy, Rev. Frederick Anthony, 1846–1920, vol. II
Lefroy, Rt Rev. George Alfred, 1854–1919, vol. II
Lefroy, Major H., died 1935, vol. III
Lefroy, Harold Maxwell-, 1877–1925, vol. II
Lefroy, Hon. Sir Henry Bruce, 1854–1930, vol. III
Lefroy, Walter John Magrath, 1870–1955, vol. V
Lefroy, Very Rev. William, 1836–1909, vol. I
Lefroy, William Chambers, 1849–1915, vol. I (A)
Lefschetz, Solomon, 1884–1972, vol. VII
Le Gallais, Theodore, 1852–1903, vol. I
Le Gallienne, Richard, 1866–1947, vol. IV
Legard, Albert George, 1845–1922, vol. II
Legard, Bt-Col Alfred Digby, 1878–1939, vol. III
Legard, Sir Algernon Willoughby, 12th Bt, 1842–1923, vol. II
Legard, Rev. Cecil Henry, 1843–1918, vol. II
Legard, Sir Charles, 11th Bt, 1846–1901, vol. I
Legard, Brig.-Gen. D'Arcy, 1873–1953, vol. V
Legard, Sir Digby Algernon Hall, 13th Bt, 1876–1961, vol. VI
Legard, Col Sir James Digby, 1846–1935, vol. III
Legat, Charles Edward, 1876–1966, vol. VI
Legat, Harold, died 1960, vol. V
Legentilhomme, Général Paul Louis, 1884–1975, vol. VII
Leger, Alexis, see Leger, M.-R. A. St-L.
Léger, Rt Hon. Jules, 1913–1980, vol. VII

Leger, (Marie-René) Alexis Saint-Leger, 1887–1975, vol. VII

Le Geyt, Maj.-Gen. Philip Harrison, 1834–1922, vol. II

Legg, Captain Sir George Edward Wickham, 1870–1927, vol. II

Legg, John Wickham, 1843–1921, vol. II

Legg, Leopold George Wickham, 1877–1962, vol. VI

Legg, Ven. Richard Wickham, 1867–1952, vol. V

Legg, Thomas Percy, 1872–1930, vol. III

Leggate, Hon. William Muter, 1879–1955, vol. V

Leggatt, Charles Ashley Scott, 1861–1935, vol. III

Leggatt, Maj.-Gen. Charles St Quentin Outen Fullbrook-, 1889–1972, vol. VII

Leggatt, Captain Charles William Stares, 1864–1954, vol. V

Leggatt, Col Hon. Sir William Watt, 1894–1968, vol. VI

Legge, Rt Rev. Hon. Augustus, 1839–1913, vol. I

Legge, Hon. Charles Gounter, 1842–1907, vol. I

Legge, Francis Cecil, 1873–1940, vol. III

Legge, Col Hon. Sir Harry Charles, 1852–1924, vol. II

Legge, Col Hon. Heneage, 1845–1911, vol. I

Legge, Rev. James, 1815–1897, vol. I

Legge, Lt-Gen. James Gordon, 1863–1947, vol. IV

Legge, James Granville, 1861–1940, vol. III

Legge, Rear-Adm. Montague George Bentinck, 1883–1951, vol. V

Legge, Lt-Col Norton, died 1900, vol. I

Legge, Brig.-Gen. Reginald Francis, died 1955, vol. V

Legge, Robin Humphrey, 1862–1933, vol. III

Legge, Maj.-Gen. Stanley Ferguson, 1900–1977, vol. VII

Legge, Sir Thomas Morison, 1863–1932, vol. III

Legge, Brig.-Gen. William Kaye, 1869–1946, vol. IV

Legge-Bourke, Major Sir (Edward Alexander) Henry, (Sir Harry), 1914–1973, vol. VII

Legge-Bourke, Major Sir Harry; see Legge-Bourke, Major Sir E. A. H.

Leggett, Col Archibald Herbert, 1877–1936, vol. III

Leggett, B. J., 1890–1968, vol. VI (AII)

Leggett, Major Sir Edward Humphrey Manisty, 1871–1947, vol. IV

Leggett, Major Eric Henry Goodwin, 1880–1916, vol. II

Leggett, Henry Aufrere, 1874–1950, vol. IV

Leggett, Vice-Adm. Oliver Elles, 1876–1946, vol. IV

Legh, Edmund Willoughby, 1874–1943, vol. IV

Legh, Major Hon. Gilbert, 1858–1939, vol. III

Legh, Col Harry Shuldham S.; see Shuldham-Legh.

Legh, Lt-Col Hon. Sir Piers Walter, 1890–1955, vol. V

Legh-Jones, Sir George, 1890–1960, vol. V

Legouis, Emile, 1861–1937, vol. III

Le Grand, Gen. Frederick Gasper, 1836–1905, vol. I

Legrand, Rt Rev. Joseph, 1853–1937, vol. III

Le Grave, Rev. William, 1843–1922, vol. II

Le Grice, Charles Henry, 1870–1942, vol. IV

Legris, Hon. Joseph Hormidas, 1850–1932, vol. III

Legros, Alphonse, 1837–1911, vol. I

Lehar, Franz, 1870–1948, vol. IV

Lehfeldt, Robert Alfred, 1868–1927, vol. II

Lehman, Hon. Herbert H., 1878–1963, vol. VI

Lehmann, Adolf Ludwig Ferdinand, 1863–1937, vol. III

Lehmann, Beatrix, 1903–1979, vol. VII

Lehmann, Liza, died 1918, vol. II

Lehmann, Lotte, 1888–1976, vol. VII

Lehmann, Rudolf, 1819–1905, vol. I

Lehmann, Rudolf Chambers, 1856–1929, vol. III

Le Hunte, Sir George Ruthven, 1852–1925, vol. II

Lei Wang-Kee, Most Rev. Peter, 1922–1974, vol. VII

Leicester, 2nd Earl of, 1822–1909, vol. I

Leicester, 3rd Earl of, 1848–1941, vol. IV

Leicester, 4th Earl of, 1880–1949, vol. IV

Leicester, 5th Earl of, 1908–1976, vol. VII

Leicester, Sir Charles Byrne Warren, 9th Bt, 1896–1968, vol. VI

Leicester, James, 1915–1976, vol. VII

Leicester, Lt-Col John Cyril Holdich, 1872–1949, vol. IV

Leicester, Sir Peter Fleming Frederic, 8th Bt, 1863–1945, vol. IV

Leicester-Warren, Cuthbert, 1877–1954, vol. V

Leicester-Warren, Lt-Col John Leighton Byrne, 1907–1975, vol. VII

Leigh, 2nd Baron, 1824–1905 (this entry was not transferred to Who was Who).

Leigh, 3rd Baron, 1855–1938, vol. III

Leigh, 4th Baron, 1908–1979, vol. VII

Leigh, Alan de Verd, 1891–1961, vol. VI

Leigh, Arthur George, 1909–1968, vol. VI

Leigh, Major Chandos, 1873–1915, vol. I

Leigh, Charles Edward A.; see Austen-Leigh.

Leigh, Christopher Thomas Bowes, 1905–1971, vol. VII

Leigh, Hon. Sir Edward Chandos, 1832–1915, vol. I

Leigh, Egerton, 1843–1928, vol. II

Leigh, Lt-Col Henry Percy Poingdestre, 1851–1928, vol. II

Leigh, Hon. and Very Rev. James Wentworth, 1838–1923, vol. II

Leigh, Sir John, 1st Bt, 1884–1959, vol. V

Leigh, John Blundell, 1858–1931, vol. III

Leigh, Lt-Col John Cecil Gerard, 1889–1965, vol. VI

Leigh, Sir Joseph, 1841–1908, vol. I

Leigh, Rev. Neville Egerton, 1852–1929, vol. III

Leigh, Col Oswald Mosley, 1864–1949, vol. IV

Leigh, Reginald Gerard, 1880–1962, vol. VI

Leigh, Richard Arthur A., see Austen-Leigh.

Leigh, Roger, 1840–1924, vol. II

Leigh, Hon. Rupert, 1856–1919, vol. II

Leigh, Thomas Bowes, 1867–1947, vol. IV

Leigh, Vivien, 1913–1967, vol. VI

Leigh-Bennett, Henry Currie, 1852–1903, vol. I

Leigh-Bennett, Percy Raymond, 1887–1964, vol. VI

Leigh-Hunt, Gerard, 1873–1945, vol. IV

Leigh-Mallory, Rev. Herbert Leigh, 1856–1943, vol. IV
Leigh-Mallory, Air Chief Marshal Sir Trafford Leigh, 1892–1944, vol. IV
Leigh-Pemberton, Sir Edward, 1823–1910, vol. I
Leigh-Wood, Lt-Col Sir James, *died* 1949, vol. IV
Leighton of St Mellons, 1st Baron, 1896–1963, vol. VI
Leighton, Arthur Edgar, 1873–1961, vol. VI
Leighton, Major Bertie Edward Parker, 1875–1952, vol. V
Leighton, Major Sir Bryan Baldwin Mawddwy, 9th Bt, 1868–1919, vol. II
Leighton, Edmund Blair, 1853–1922, vol. II
Leighton, Gerald, 1868–1953, vol. V
Leighton, John, 1822–1912, vol. I
Leighton, Captain John Albert, 1881–1945, vol. IV
Leighton, Margaret, 1922–1976, vol. VII
Leighton, Marie Connor, *died* 1941, vol. IV
Leighton, Bt Col Sir Richard Tihel, 10th Bt, 1893–1957, vol. V
Leighton, Robert, *died* 1934, vol. III
Leighton, Sir Robert, 1884–1959, vol. V
Leighton, Stanley, 1837–1901, vol. I
Leiningen, HSH Prince Ernest Leopold Victor Charles Auguste Enrich, 1830–1904, vol. I
Leinster, 6th Duke of, 1887–1922, vol. II
Leinster, 7th Duke of, 1892–1976, vol. VII
Leiper, Robert Thomson, 1881–1969, vol. VI
Leiper, William, 1839–1916, vol. II
Leir, Rear-Adm. Ernest W., 1883–1971, vol. VII
Leir-Carleton, Maj.-Gen. Richard Langford, 1841–1933, vol. III
Leishman, Alan Ross, *died* 1937, vol. III
Leishman, Sir James, *died* 1939, vol. III
Leishman, James Blair, 1902–1963, vol. VI
Leishman, John G. A., 1857–1924, vol. II
Leishman, Maj.-Gen. John Thomas, 1835–1920, vol. II
Leishman, Rev. Thomas, 1825–1904, vol. I
Leishman, Lt-Gen. Sir William Boog, 1865–1926, vol. II
Leisk, James Rankine, 1876–1948, vol. IV
Leitch, Archibald, 1878–1931, vol. III
Leitch, Hon. James, *born* 1850, vol. II
Leitch, Lt-Col John Wilson, 1873–1935, vol. III
Leitch, Rev. Matthew, *died* 1922, vol. II
Leitch, Sir Walter, 1867–1945, vol. IV
Leitch, Sir William, 1880–1965, vol. VI
Leiter, Joseph, 1868–1932, vol. III
Leiter, Levi Zeigler, 1834–1904, vol. I
Leith of Fyvie, 1st Baron, 1847–1925, vol. II
Leith, Lt-Col Sir Alexander, 1st Bt, 1869–1956, vol. V
Leith, Captain George Piercy, 1877–1945, vol. IV
Leith, Gordon, 1879–1941, vol. IV
Leith of Fyvie, Sir Ian F.; *see* Forbes-Leith of Fyvie, Sir R. I. A.
Leith, Captain Lockhart, 1876–1940, vol. III
Leith, Robert Fraser Calder, 1854–1936, vol. III
Leith, Major Thomas, 1830–1920, vol. II
Leith-Buchanan, Sir Alexander Wellesley George Thomas, 5th Bt, 1866–1925, vol. II

Leith-Buchanan, Sir George Hector, 4th Bt, 1833–1903, vol. I
Leith-Buchanan, Sir George Hector Macdonald, 6th Bt, 1889–1973, vol. VII
Leith-Hay, Charles Edward Norman, 1858–1939, vol. III
Leith-Ross, Sir Frederick William, 1887–1968, vol. VI
Leitrim, 5th Earl of, 1879–1952, vol. V
Lejeune, C. A., (Mrs E. Roffe Thompson), *died* 1973, vol. VII
Le Jeune, Henry, 1819–1904, vol. I
Leland, Charles Godfrey, 1824–1903, vol. I
Leland, Col Francis William George, 1877–1943, vol. IV
Leland, Captain Herbert John Collett, 1873–1931, vol. III
Lelean, Percy Samuel, 1871–1956, vol. V
Leleux, Sydney Wallis, 1862–1941, vol. IV
Lelong, Lucien, 1889–1958, vol. V
Lely, Sir Frederic Styles Philpin, 1846–1934, vol. III
Lely, John Mountney, 1839–1907, vol. I
Lemaire, Ernest Joseph, 1874–1945, vol. IV
Le Maistre, Charles, *died* 1953, vol. V
Le Maitre, Sir Alfred Sutherland, 1896–1959, vol. V
Le Maitre, Ella Katharine Irving, 1896–1960, vol. V
Lemaitre, François Elie Jules, 1853–1915, vol. I
Leman, Count Georges, 1851–1920, vol. II
Le Marchant, Sir Denis, 3rd Bt, 1870–1922, vol. II
Le Marchant, Brig.-Gen. Sir Edward Thomas, 4th Bt, 1871–1953, vol. V
Le Marchant, Adm. Evelyn Robert, *died* 1949, vol. IV
Le Marchant, Sir Henry Denis, 2nd Bt, 1839–1915, vol. I
Le Marchant, Lt-Col Louis St Gratien, 1866–1914, vol. I
Lemare, Edwin H., 1866–1934, vol. III
Le Marinel, Very Rev. Matthew, 1883–1963, vol. VI
Lemass, Edwin Stephen, 1890–1970, vol. VI
Lemass, Peter Edmund, 1850–1928, vol. II (A), vol. III
Lemass, Seán Francis, 1899–1971, vol. VII
le May, Reginald Stuart, 1885–1972, vol. VII
Le May, Gp Captain William Kent, 1911–1978, vol. VII
Lemberg, (Max) Rudolf, 1896–1975, vol. VII
Lemberg, Rudolf; *see* Lemberg, M. R.
Le Messurier, Col Augustus, 1837–1916, vol. II
Le Messurier, Henry William, 1848–1931, vol. III
Le Mesurier, Col Cecil Brooke, 1831–1913, vol. I
Le Mesurier, Captain Charles Edward, *died* 1917, vol. II
Le Mesurier, Captain Edward Kirby, 1903–1980, vol. VII
Le Mesurier, Wing Comdr Eric Clive, 1915–1943, vol. IV
Le Mesurier, Col Frederick Augustus, 1839–1926, vol. II
Le Mesurier, Sir Havilland, 1866–1931, vol. III

Le Mesurier, Lt-Col Herbert Grenville, 1873–1940, vol. III

Lemieux, Auguste, 1874–1956, vol. V

Lemieux, Sir François Xavier, 1851–1933, vol. III

Lemieux, Louis Joseph, *born* 1870, vol. IV

Lemieux, Rodolphe, 1866–1937, vol. III

Lemmon, Col Sir Thomas Warne, 1838–1928, vol. II

Le Moine, J. de St Denis, 1850–1922, vol. II

Le Moine, Sir James MacPherson, 1825–1912, vol. I

Lemon, Arthur Henry, 1864–1933, vol. III

Lemon, Brig. Arthur Leslie K.; *see* Kent-Lemon.

Lemon, Sir Ernest John Hutchings, 1884–1954, vol. V

Lemon, Lt-Col Frederick Joseph, 1879–1952, vol. V

Lemon, Sir James, 1833–1923, vol. II

Lemonius, Lt-Col Gerard Maclean, *died* 1950, vol. IV

Lemonnier, Adm. André Georges, 1896–1963, vol. VI

Lempfert, Rudolph Gustave Karl, 1875–1957, vol. V

Lempriere, Lt-Col Henry Anderson, 1867–1914, vol. I

Lempriere, Rev. Philip Charles, 1890–1949, vol. IV (A), vol. V

Lempriere, Reginald Raoul, 1851–1931, vol. III

Lenanton, Carola Mary Anima, (Lady Lenanton); *see* Oman, C. M. A.

Lenanton, Sir Gerald, 1896–1952, vol. V

Lenbach, T. von, *died* 1904, vol. I

Lendon, Alfred Austin, 1856–1935, vol. III

Lendon, Penry Bruce, 1882–1914, vol. I

Le Neve Foster, Fermian; *see* Foster.

Lenfestey, Giffard Hocart, 1872–1943, vol. IV

Lenfestey, Col Leopold d'Estreville, 1875–1948, vol. IV

Leng, Christopher David, 1861–1921, vol. II

Leng, Sir Hilary Howard, 1862–1936, vol. III

Leng, Sir John, 1828–1906, vol. I

Leng, Sir William Christopher, 1825–1902, vol. I

Lenglen, Suzanne, *died* 1938, vol. III

Lenman, Rt Rev. Thomas, 1883–1959, vol. V

Lenn, Paymaster Captain Frank, 1868–1932, vol. III

Lennard, Sir Fiennes B.; *see* Barrett-Lennard.

Lennard, Lt-Col Sir Henry Arthur Hallam Farnaby, 2nd Bt (*cr* 1880), 1859–1928, vol. II

Lennard, Lt-Col John B.; *see* Barrett-Lennard.

Lennard, Sir John Farnaby, 1st Bt (*cr* 1880), 1816–1899, vol. I

Lennard, Reginald Vivian, 1885–1967, vol. VI

Lennard, Sir Richard Barrett-; *see* Lennard, Sir T. R. F. B.

Lennard, Sir Richard Fiennes Barrett-, 4th Bt (*cr* 1801), 1861–1934, vol. III

Lennard, Lt-Col Sir Stephen Arthur Hallam Farnaby, 3rd Bt (*cr* 1880), 1899–1980, vol. VII

Lennard, Sir Thomas Barrett-, 2nd Bt (*cr* 1801), 1826–1919, vol. II

Lennard, Sir Thomas Barrett-, 3rd Bt (*cr* 1801), 1853–1923, vol. II

Lennard, Sir Thomas J., 1861–1938, vol. III

Lennard, Sir (Thomas) Richard (Fiennes) Barrett-, 5th Bt (*cr* 1801), 1898–1977, vol. VII

Lennard-Jones, Sir John Edward, 1894–1954, vol. V

Lennie, Robert Aim, 1889–1961, vol. VI

Lennon, Hon. William, 1849–1938, vol. III

Lennox, Col Lord Algernon Charles G.; *see* Gordon-Lennox.

Lennox, Lady Algernon G.; *see* Gordon-Lennox.

Lennox, Lord Bernard Charles G.; *see* Gordon-Lennox.

Lennox, Charles Spencer Bateman-Hanbury K.; *see* Kincaid-Lennox.

Lennox, Cosmo Charles G.; *see* Gordon-Lennox.

Lennox, Lord Esme Charles G.; *see* Gordon-Lennox.

Lennox, Rt Hon. Lord Walter Charles G.; *see* Gordon-Lennox.

Lennox, Sir Wilbraham Oates, 1830–1897, vol. I

Lenotre, G., 1857–1935, vol. III

Lenox-Conyngham, Col Sir Gerald Ponsonby, 1866–1956, vol. V

Lenox-Conyngham, Sir William Fitzwilliam, 1824–1906, vol. I

Lenski, Lois, 1893–1974, vol. VII

Lentaigne, Sir John, *died* 1915, vol. I

Lentaigne, Maj.-Gen. Walter David Alexander, 1899–1955, vol. V

Lenton, Rev. Charles H., 1873–1951, vol. V

Lenton, Jessie; *see* Pope, J.

Leny, Bt Lt-Col R. L. Macalpine-, 1870–1941, vol. IV

Leo XIII, His Holiness Pope, (Vincent Joachim Pecci), 1810–1903, vol. I

Leon, Sir George Edward, 2nd Bt, 1875–1947, vol. IV

Leon, Henri Marcel, 1855–1932, vol. III

Leon, Henry Cecil, 1902–1976, vol. VII

Leon, Sir Herbert Samuel, 1st Bt, 1850–1926, vol. II

Leon, Paul, 1874–1962, vol. VI

Leon, Philip, 1895–1974, vol. VII

Leon, Sir Ronald George, 3rd Bt, 1902–1964, vol. VI

Leon, Samuel, 1848–1933, vol. III

Leonard, George Hare, 1863–1941, vol. IV

Leonard, James W., *died* 1909, vol. I

Leonard, John William, *died* 1910, vol. I

Leonard, Rt Rev. Martin Patrick Grainge, 1889–1963, vol. VI

Leonard, Patrick Marcellinus, 1821–1901, vol. I

Leonard, Lt-Col Reuben Wells, 1860–1930, vol. III

Leonard, Robert Galloway Louis, 1878–1957, vol. V

Leonard, Samuel Henry, 1854–1929, vol. III

Leonard, William, 1887–1969, vol. VI

Leonard, Rt Rev. William Andrew, 1848–1930, vol. III

Leonard, Col William Hugh, 1876–1960, vol. V

Leoncavallo, Ruggiero, 1858–1919, vol. II

Leoni, Franco, 1864–1949, vol. IV

Le Page, Engr-Rear-Adm. George Wilfred, 1883–1940, vol. III

Lepailleur, Rt Rev. Alfred, 1886–1952, vol. V

le Patourel, Herbert Augustus, 1875–1934, vol. III
Le Patourel, Brig. Herbert Wallace, 1916–1979, vol. VII
Le Pelley, Lt-Col Edward Carey, 1870–1942, vol. IV
Lepicier, Cardinal Alexis Henry Marie, 1863–1936, vol. III
Lepine, Louis, 1846–1933, vol. III
Le Poer Trench, Hon. Frederick, 1835–1913, vol. I
Le Poer Trench, Lt-Col Frederick Amelius, 1857–1942, vol. IV
Le-Poer-Trench, Col Hon. William, 1837–1920, vol. II
Le Quesne, Charles Thomas, 1885–1954, vol. V
Le Quesne, Ferdinand Simeon, 1863–1950, vol. IV
Le Queux, William Tufnell, 1864–1927, vol. II
Leray, Mgr Joseph M. M., 1854–1929, vol. III
Le Rossignol, Col Alfred Ernest, 1869–1951, vol. V
Le Rossignol, James Edward, 1866–1959, vol. V
Le Rossignol, Walter Aubin, died 1945, vol. IV
Le Rougetel, Sir John Helier, 1894–1975, vol. VII
Le Roy, Édouard Louis Emmanuel Julien, 1870–1954, vol. V
Le Roy-Lewis, Col Herman, 1860–1931, vol. III
Le Sage, Sir John Merry, 1837–1926, vol. II
Lescaze, William, 1896–1969, vol. VI
Lescher, Joseph Francis, 1842–1923, vol. II
Lescher, Thomas Edward, 1877–1938, vol. III
Leschititzky, Theodore, 1830–1915, vol. I (A)
Leslie, Lt-Col Archibald Stewart, 1873–1928, vol. II
Leslie, Col Archibald Young, died 1913, vol. I
Leslie, Sir Bradford, 1831–1926, vol. II
Leslie, Lt-Col Sir Bradford, 1867–1936, vol. III
Leslie, Lt-Col Charles, died 1930, vol. III
Leslie, Sir Charles Henry, 7th Bt (cr 1625), 1848–1905, vol. I
Leslie, Edward Henry John, 1880–1966, vol. VI
Leslie, Sir Francis Galloway, 1902–1971, vol. VII
Leslie, Frank, (Miriam Florence Folline, Baroness de Bazus), 1851–1914, vol. I
Leslie, Maj.-Gen. George Arthur James, 1867–1936, vol. III
Leslie, George Dunlop, 1835–1921, vol. II
Leslie, Hon. George Waldegrave-, 1825–1904, vol. I
Leslie, Henrietta, (Mrs Harrie Schütze), died 1946, vol. IV
Leslie, Sir (Henry John) Lindores, 9th Bt (cr 1625), 1920–1967, vol. VI
Leslie, James Campbell, died 1974, vol. VII
Leslie, Rt Hon. James Graham, 1868–1949, vol. IV
Leslie, Sir John, 1st Bt (cr 1876), 1822–1916, vol. II
Leslie, Col Sir John, 2nd Bt (cr 1876), 1857–1944, vol. IV
Leslie, Lt-Col John, 1888–1965, vol. VI
Leslie, John D.; see Dean-Leslie.
Leslie, Lt-Col John Henry, 1858–1943, vol. IV
Leslie, Very Rev. John Herbert, 1867–1934, vol. III
Leslie, Sir (John Randolph) Shane, 3rd Bt (cr 1876), 1885–1971, vol. VII
Leslie, John Robert, 1873–1955, vol. V
Leslie, Col John Robert Sloan, 1871–1943, vol. IV

Leslie, Lt-Col John Tasman Waddell, 1861–1911, vol. I
Leslie, John William St Lawrance, died 1934, vol. III
Leslie, Sir Lindores; see Leslie, Sir H. J. L.
Leslie, Miriam Florence Folline; see Leslie, Frank.
Leslie, Sir Norman Alexander, 1870–1945, vol. IV
Leslie, Wing Comdr Sir Norman Roderick Alexander David, 8th Bt (cr 1625), 1889–1937, vol. III
Leslie, Robert, 1885–1951, vol. V
Leslie, Robert Murray, 1866–1921, vol. II
Leslie, Maj.-Gen. Robert Walter Dickson, 1883–1957, vol. V
Leslie, Samuel Clement, 1898–1980, vol. VII
Leslie, Seymour Argent Sandford, 1902–1953, vol. V
Leslie, Sir Shane; see Leslie, Sir J. R. S.
Leslie, Gen. Sir Walter Stewart, 1876–1947, vol. IV
Leslie of Warthill, William A.; see Arbuthnot-Leslie.
Leslie-Ellis, Lt-Col Henry, died 1919, vol. II
Leslie-Jones, Rev. Cyril, 1873–1932, vol. III
Leslie-Jones, Frederick Archibald, 1874–1946, vol. IV
Leslie-Jones, Leycester Hudson, died 1935, vol. III
Leslie Melville, Lt-Col Hon. Ian, 1894–1967, vol. VI
Leslie-Roberts, H(ugh); see Roberts.
Le Souef, Albert Sherbourne, 1877–1951, vol. V
Le Souëf, W. H. Dudley, died 1924, vol. II
Lessard, Maj.-Gen. François Louis, 1860–1927, vol. II
Lesser, Henry, died 1966, vol. VI
Lessing, Edward Albert, 1890–1964, vol. VI
Lessing, Rudolf, 1878–1964, vol. VI
Lesslie, Brig.-Gen. William Breck, 1868–1942, vol. IV
Lessore, Frederick, 1879–1951, vol. V
Lessore, Thérèse, died 1945, vol. IV
Lester, Engr-Rear-Adm. Arthur Ellis, 1878–1956, vol. V
Lester, Rev. Henry Arthur, died 1922, vol. II
Lester, Sean, 1888–1959, vol. V
Lester, Rev. T. Major, died 1903, vol. I
Lester-Garland, Lester V., died 1944, vol. IV
Lestrade, Gérard Paul, 1897–1962, vol. VI
Le Strange, Charles Alfred, 1892–1933, vol. III
L'Estrange, Mrs Constance; see Collier, C.
Le Strange, Guy, 1854–1933, vol. III
Le Strange, Hamon, 1840–1918, vol. II
Le Strange, Roland, 1869–1919, vol. II
Lesueur, Daniel, died 1921, vol. II
Letch, Sir Robert, 1899–1962, vol. VI
Letchworth, Rev. Arnold, 1840–1923, vol. II
Letchworth, Sir Edward, 1833–1917, vol. II
Letchworth, Rev. Henry Howard, 1836–1921, vol. II
Letchworth, Thomas Edwin, 1906–1973, vol. VII
Lethaby, William Richard, 1857–1931, vol. III
Letham, James, 1907–1972, vol. VII
Lethbridge, Alan Bourchier, 1878–1923, vol. II
Lethbridge, Col Alfred, 1884–1968, vol. VI

Lethbridge, Lt-Col Sir Alfred Swaine, 1844–1917, vol. II

Lethbridge, Col Ernest Astley Edmund, 1864–1943, vol. IV

Lethbridge, Lt-Col Francis Washington, 1867–1939, vol. III

Lethbridge, Captain Sir Hector Wroth, 6th Bt, 1898–1978, vol. VII

Lethbridge, Maj.-Gen. John Sydney, 1897–1961, vol. VI

Lethbridge, Marion Eva, 1879–1959, vol. V

Lethbridge, Sir Roper, 1840–1919, vol. II

Lethbridge, Thomas Charles, 1901–1971, vol. VII

Lethbridge, Sir Wroth Acland, 4th Bt, 1831–1902, vol. I

Lethbridge, Sir Wroth Periam Christopher, 5th Bt, 1863–1950, vol. IV

Lethem, Sir Gordon James, 1886–1962, vol. VI

Letourneau, Séverin, 1871–1949, vol. IV

Lett, Eva, died 1945, vol. IV

Lett, Rev. Henry William, 1838–1920, vol. II

Lett, Sir Hugh, 1st Bt, 1876–1964, vol. VI

Lett, Phyllis, (Mrs Phyllis de Burgh Ker), died 1962, vol. VI

Letton, Charles Thomas, 1878–1949, vol. IV

Letts, Edmund Albert, 1852–1918, vol. II

Letts, Malcolm Henry Ikin, 1882–1957, vol. V

Letts, Rev. Reginald, 1857–1940, vol. III

Letts, Sir William Malesbury, 1873–1957, vol. V

Letts, Winifred M., 1882–1972, vol. VII

Leuba, James Henri, 1868–1946, vol. IV

Leuchars, Col Hon, Sir George, 1868–1924, vol. II

Leudesdorf, Charles, 1853–1924, vol. II

Leuty, Thomas Richmond, 1853–1911, vol. I

Levame, Mgr Albert, 1881–1958, vol. V

Levander, F. W., died 1916, vol. II

Leveen, Jacob, 1891–1980, vol. VII

Leven, 11th Earl of, and Melville, 10th Earl of, 1835–1906, vol. I

Leven, 12th Earl of, and Melville, 11th Earl of, 1886–1913 (this entry was not transferred to Who was Who).

Leven, 13th Earl of, and Melville, 12th Earl of, 1890–1947, vol. IV

Lever, Baron (Life Peer); Leslie Maurice Lever, 1905–1977, vol. VII

Lever, Col Sir Arthur Levy, 1st Bt (cr 1911), 1860–1924, vol. II

Lever, Sir Ernest Harry, 1890–1970, vol. VI

Lever, Sir Hardman; see Lever, Sir S. H.

Lever, Richard Hayley, 1876–1958, vol. VI (AI)

Lever, Sir (Samuel) Hardman, 1st Bt (cr 1920), 1869–1947, vol. IV

Lever, Sir Tresham Joseph Philip, 2nd Bt (cr 1911), 1900–1975, vol. VII

Leverhulme, 1st Viscount, 1851–1925, vol. II

Leverhulme, 2nd Viscount, 1888–1949, vol. IV

Leverson, Col George Francis, died 1938, vol. III

Leverson, Lt-Col George Riland Francis, 1886–1936, vol. III

Leverson, Col Julian John, 1853–1941, vol. IV

Levertoff, Rev. Paul Philip, 1878–1954, vol. V

Leveson, Adm. Sir Arthur Cavenagh, 1868–1929, vol. III

Leveson Gower, Major Lord Alastair St Clair Sutherland-, 1890–1921, vol. II

Leveson Gower, Arthur Francis Gresham, 1851–1922, vol. II

Leveson-Gower, Col Charles Cameron, 1866–1951, vol. V

Leveson Gower, Frederick Neville Sutherland, 1874–1959, vol. V

Leveson Gower, Sir George Granville, 1858–1951, vol. V

Leveson Gower, Granville Charles Gresham, 1865–1948, vol. IV

Leveson Gower, Sir Henry Dudley Gresham, 1873–1954, vol. V

Leveson Gower, Col Philip, died 1939, vol. III

Levett, Major Berkeley John Talbot, 1863–1941, vol. IV

Levett, Ernest Laurence, died 1916, vol. II

Levett, Theophilus Basil Percy, 1856–1929, vol. III

Levett-Yeats, Gerald Aylmer, 1863–1938, vol. III

Levey, Charles Joseph, 1846–1920, vol. II

Levey, George Collins, 1835–1919, vol. II

Levi, Sylvain, 1863–1935, vol. III

Levi, T. Arthur, 1874–1954, vol. V

Levick, Claude Blaxland, 1896–1953, vol. V

Levick, Surg.-Comdr G. Murray, died 1956, vol. V

Levick, Sir Hugh Gwynne, 1870–1937, vol. III

Levick, Thomas Henry Carlton, 1867–1957, vol. V

Levien, Jerome William John, 1893–1961, vol. VI

Levien, John Mewburn, 1863–1953, vol. V

Levin, Nyman, 1906–1965, vol. VI

Levine, Abraham, 1870–1949, vol. IV

Levinge, Sir Edward Vere, 1867–1954, vol. V

Levinge, Sir Richard William, 10th Bt, 1878–1914, vol. I

Levinstein, Herbert, died 1956, vol. V

Levison, Sir Leon, 1881–1936, vol. III

Levita, Lt-Col Sir Cecil Bingham, 1867–1953, vol. V

Levy, Aaron Harold, died 1977, vol. VII

Levy, Sir Albert, died 1937, vol. III

Levy, Sir Arthur, 1855–1938, vol. III

Levy, Benn Wolfe, 1900–1973, vol. VII

Levy, Hon. Sir Daniel, 1873–1937, vol. III

Levy, Hermann, 1881–1949, vol. IV

Levy, Hyman, 1889–1975, vol. VII

Levy, J. Langley, 1870–1945, vol. IV

Levy, Joseph Hiam, 1838–1913, vol. I

Levy, Joshua Moses, 1854–1922, vol. II

Levy, Sir Maurice, 1st Bt, 1859–1933, vol. III

Levy, Reuben, 1891–1966, vol. VI

Levy, Richard Francis, 1892–1968, vol. VI

Levy, Stanley Isaac, 1890–1968, vol. VI

Levy, Thomas, died 1953, vol. V

Levy, Major Walter Henry, 1876–1923, vol. II

Lewanika III, Sir Mwanawina; see Barotseland, Litunga of.

Lewenhaupt, Count Carl, 1835–1906, vol. I

Lewer, Ethel, 1861–1946, vol. IV

Lewer, Surg.-Maj.-Gen. Robert, died 1914, vol. I

Lewers, Arthur Hamilton Nicholson, died 1934, vol. III

Lewes, Earl of; Henry John Montacute Nevill, 1948–1965, vol. VI

Lewes, Brig.-Gen. Charles George, 1869–1938, vol. III
Lewes, Maj.-Gen. H. C., 1838–1907, vol. I
Lewes, Col Price Kinnear, 1870–1943, vol. IV
Lewes, Captain Price Vaughan, 1865–1914, vol. I
Lewes, Sir Samuel William Sayer, 1824–1907, vol. I
Lewes, Captain Thomas Powell, 1860–1940, vol. III
Lewes, Vivian Byam, 1852–1915, vol. I (A)
Lewey, Sir Arthur Werner, 1894–1973, vol. VII
Lewin, Brig.-Gen. Arthur Corrie, 1874–1952, vol. V
Lewin, Maj.-Gen. Ernest Ord, 1879–1950, vol. IV
Lewin, George Arthur, 1867–1941, vol. IV
Lewin, Rev. George Harrison R.; see Ross-Lewin.
Lewin, Brig.-Gen. Henry Frederick Elliott, 1872–1946, vol. IV
Lewin, Octavia Margaret Sophia, died 1955, vol. V
Lewin, Percy Evans, 1876–1955, vol. V
Lewin, Ven. Richard S. R.; see Ross-Lewin.
Lewin, Rev. Robert O'Donelan R.; see Ross-Lewin.
Lewin, Lt-Col Thomas Herbert, 1839–1916, vol. II
Lewin, Walpole Sinclair, 1915–1980, vol. VII
Lewin, William Charles James; see Terriss, William.
Lewis, Ada Travers, died 1931, vol. III
Lewis, Mrs Agnes Smith, 1843–1926, vol. II
Lewis, Sir Alfred Edward, 1868–1940, vol. III
Lewis, A(lfred) Neville; see Lewis, Neville.
Lewis, Sir Andrew Jopp Williams, 1875–1952, vol. V
Lewis, Angelo, 1839–1919, vol. II
Lewis, Arthur Cyril Wentworth, 1885–1928, vol. II
Lewis, Lt-Col Arthur Francis O.; see Owen-Lewis.
Lewis, Arthur Griffith Poyer, 1848–1909, vol. I
Lewis, Arthur Hornby, 1843–1926, vol. II
Lewis, Arthur King, 1867–1954, vol. V
Lewis, Sir Aubrey Julian, 1900–1975, vol. VII
Lewis, B. Roland, 1884–1959, vol. V
Lewis, Barnet, died 1929, vol. III
Lewis, Brig.-Gen. Bridges George, 1857–1925, vol. II
Lewis, Bunnell, 1824–1908, vol. I
Lewis, C. Gasquoine; see Hartley, C. G.
Lewis, Cecil D.; see Day-Lewis.
Lewis, Ven. Charles Gerwyn Rice, died 1964, vol. VI
Lewis, Ven. Christopher Gwynne, 1895–1963, vol. VI
Lewis, Brig. Sir Clinton Gresham, 1885–1978, vol. VII
Lewis, Clive Staples, 1898–1963, vol. VI
Lewis, Cyril Alexander O.; see Owen-Lewis.
Lewis, Cyril Arthur Liddon, 1873–1943, vol. IV
Lewis, D. Morgan, 1851–1937, vol. III
Lewis, David, 1849–1897, vol. I
Lewis, Col David Francis, 1855–1927, vol. II
Lewis, Dominic Bevan Wyndham, died 1969, vol. VI
Lewis, Lt Donald Swain, 1886–1916, vol. II
Lewis, Mrs Dorothy; see Lewis, Mrs M. D.
Lewis, Sir Duncan O.; see Orr-Lewis.

Lewis, Edgar Samuel, 1853–1922, vol. II
Lewis, E(dward) Daly, 1908–1977, vol. VII
Lewis, Rev. Edward Lincoln, 1865–1939, vol. III
Lewis, Maj.-Gen. Edward Mann, 1863–1949, vol. IV
Lewis, Sir Edward Roberts, 1900–1980, vol. VII
Lewis, Eiluned, died 1979, vol. VII
Lewis, Hon. Sir Elliott; see Lewis, Hon. Sir N. E.
Lewis, Emily Catherine, died 1965, vol. VI
Lewis, Major Ernest Albert, 1873–1937, vol. III
Lewis, Ernest Harry, 1877–1951, vol. V
Lewis, Essington, 1881–1961, vol. VI
Lewis, Very Rev. Evan, 1818–1901, vol. I
Lewis, Francis John, 1875–1955, vol. V
Lewis, Rev. Frank Ernest, died 1929, vol. III
Lewis, Frederic Henry, 1865–1940, vol. III
Lewis, Brig.-Gen. Frederick Gustav, 1873–1967, vol. VI
Lewis, Sir Frederick Orr O.; see Orr-Lewis.
Lewis, Lt-Col George Alfred, 1869–1961, vol. VI
Lewis, Sir George Henry, 1st Bt, 1833–1911, vol. I
Lewis, Sir George James Ernest, 3rd Bt, 1910–1945, vol. IV
Lewis, Sir George James Graham, 2nd Bt, 1868–1927, vol. II
Lewis, George P.; see Pitt-Lewis.
Lewis, Gerald Champion, 1863–1939, vol. III
Lewis, Gilbert Newton, 1875–1946, vol. IV
Lewis, Harold, 1856–1924, vol. II
Lewis, Maj.-Gen. Harold Victor, 1887–1945, vol. IV
Lewis, Sir Hawthorne; see Lewis, Sir W. H.
Lewis, Rev. Henry, 1857–1914, vol. I
Lewis, Sir Henry, 1847–1923, vol. III
Lewis, Col Henry, 1847–1925, vol. II
Lewis, Henry, 1889–1968, vol. VI
Lewis, Maj.-Gen. Henry Augustus, 1879–1966, vol. VI
Lewis, Henry David, 1875–1936, vol. III
Lewis, Captain Henry Edward, 1889–1979, vol. VII
Lewis, Rt Hon. Sir Herbert; see Lewis, Rt Hon. Sir J. H.
Lewis, Sir Herbert David William, 1872–1931, vol. III
Lewis, Col Herman Le R.; see Le Roy-Lewis.
Lewis, Howell Elvet, 1860–1953, vol. V
Lewis, Hugh, died 1937, vol. III
Lewis, Isaac, 1849–1927, vol. II
Lewis, Ivor Evan Gerwyn, 1904–1977, vol. VII
Lewis, J(ack) Haydon, 1904–1971, vol. VII
Lewis, Rev. Canon James Abraham, 1874–1946, vol. IV
Lewis, Brig. James Charles W.; see Windsor Lewis.
Lewis, Rev. James Dawson, 1845–1905, vol. I
Lewis, James Hamilton, died 1939, vol. III
Lewis, James Henry, 1856–1924, vol. II
Lewis, Jane, (Lady Lewis), died 1939, vol. III
Lewis, Hon. John, 1842–1923, vol. II
Lewis, Lt-Col John, 1859–1937, vol. III
Lewis, John, 1851–1943, vol. IV
Lewis, John, 1912–1969, vol. VI
Lewis, John Christopher, 1842–1918, vol. II
Lewis, Sir (John) Duncan O.; see Orr-Lewis.

Lewis, John F., 1876–1963, vol. VI
Lewis, John Hardwicke, 1840–1927, vol. II
Lewis, Rt Hon. Sir (John) Herbert, 1858–1933, vol. III
Lewis, John Llewellyn, 1880–1969, vol. VI
Lewis, John Penry, 1854–1923, vol. II
Lewis, Rev. John Price, 1857–1930, vol. III
Lewis, John Spedan, 1885–1963, vol. VI
Lewis, Sir John Todd, 1901–1977, vol. VII
Lewis, Most Rev. John Travers, 1825–1901, vol. I
Lewis, Very Rev. Julius, *died* 1920, vol. II
Lewis, Rt Rev. Lewis, 1821–1905, vol. I
Lewis, Lucas Reginald, 1883–1931, vol. III
Lewis, Mabel Terry, (Mrs R. C. Batley), *died* 1957, vol. V
Lewis, Malcolm Meredith, 1891–1955, vol. V
Lewis, Mary; *see* Milne, Mrs Leslie.
Lewis, Mrs (Mary) Dorothy, 1894–1975, vol. VII
Lewis, Mary W.; *see* Wolseley-Lewis.
Lewis, Michael Arthur, 1890–1970, vol. VI
Lewis, Morris Michael, 1898–1971, vol. VII
Lewis, Hon. Sir (Neil) Elliott, 1858–1935, vol. III
Lewis, Neville, 1895–1972, vol. VII
Lewis, Oswald, 1887–1966, vol. VI
Lewis, Percy G., 1862–1935, vol. III
Lewis, Col Percy John Tonson, 1861–1910, vol. I
Lewis, Peter Edwin, 1912–1976, vol. VII
Lewis, Lt-Col Richard Charles, *died* 1914, vol. I
Lewis, Maj.-Gen. Sir Richard George, 1895–1965, vol. VI
Lewis, Sir Samuel, 1843–1903, vol. I
Lewis, Sinclair, 1885–1951, vol. V
Lewis, Col Somers Reginald, 1843–1931, vol. III
Lewis, Stanley Radcliffe, 1878–1964, vol. VI
Lewis, Thomas, *died* 1928, vol. II
Lewis, Sir Thomas, 1881–1945, vol. IV
Lewis, Thomas, 1868–1953, vol. V
Lewis, Thomas, 1873–1962, vol. VI
Lewis, Thomas Arthur, 1881–1923, vol. II
Lewis, Col Thomas Lewis Hampton, 1834–1912, vol. I
Lewis, Sir Thomas William, 1852–1926, vol. II
Lewis, Vernon Arthur, *died* 1950, vol. IV
Lewis, Sir Walter Llewellyn, 1849–1930, vol. III
Lewis, Walter Samuel, 1894–1962, vol. VI
Lewis, Sir Wilfrid Hubert Poyer, 1881–1950, vol. IV
Lewis, Rev. Canon William, *died* 1922, vol. II
Lewis, William B.; *see* Bevan-Lewis.
Lewis, William Cudmore McCullagh, *died* 1956, vol. V
Lewis, William George, 1844–1926, vol. II
Lewis, Sir (William) Hawthorne, 1888–1970, vol. VI
Lewis, William Henry, 1866–1948, vol. IV
Lewis, William Henry, 1869–1963, vol. VI
Lewis, William James, 1847–1926, vol. II
Lewis, Sir Willmott Harsant, 1877–1950, vol. IV
Lewis, Wilmarth Sheldon, 1895–1979, vol. VII
Lewis, Wyndham, 1884–1957, vol. V
Lewis-Crosby, Very Rev. Ernest Henry, *died* 1961, vol. VI
Lewis-Dale, Henry Angley, 1876–1938, vol. III
Lewisham, Viscount; William Legge, 1913–1942, vol. IV

Lewisohn, Frederick, 1878–1951, vol. V
Lewtas, Lt-Col John, *died* 1920, vol. II
Lewthwaite, Raymond, 1894–1972, vol. VII
Lewthwaite, Sir William, 1st Bt, 1853–1927, vol. II
Lewthwaite, Sir William, 2nd Bt, 1882–1933, vol. III
Lewton-Brian, Lawrence, 1879–1922, vol. II
Ley, Arthur Herbert, 1879–1938, vol. III
Ley, Sir Francis, 1st Bt, 1846–1916, vol. II
Ley, Sir Gerald Gordon, 3rd Bt, 1902–1980, vol. VII
Ley, Sir Gordon; *see* Ley, Sir H. G.
Ley, Henry George, 1887–1962, vol. VI
Ley, Sir (Henry) Gordon, 2nd Bt, 1874–1944, vol. IV
Ley, Adm. James Clement, 1869–1946, vol. IV
Ley, James William Thomas, *died* 1943, vol. IV
Ley, William Henry, 1847–1919, vol. II
Leyborne-Popham, Francis William, 1862–1907, vol. I
Leycester, William Hamilton, 1864–1925, vol. II
Leyds, Willem Johannes, 1859–1940, vol. III
Leyel, Mrs C. F., (Hilda Winifred), *died* 1957, vol. V
Leyland, Christopher John, 1849–1926, vol. II
Leyland, Sir Edward N.; *see* Naylor-Leyland.
Leyland, Captain Sir Herbert Scarisbrick N.; *see* Naylor-Leyland.
Leyland, John, *died* 1924, vol. II
Leyland, Peter; *see* Pyke-Lees, W. K.
Leys, Sir Cecil; *see* Leys, Sir W. C.
Leys, John Kirkwood, 1847–1909, vol. I
Leys, Sir (William) Cecil, 1877–1950, vol. IV
Leyton, Albert Sidney Frankau, 1869–1921, vol. II
Leyton, Otto, 1873–1938, vol. III
Li Ching Fong, 1854–1934, vol. III
Liakat Ali, Sir Syed, 1878–1947, vol. IV
Liaqat Hyat Khan, Nawab Sir, 1887–1948, vol. IV
Liardet, Maj.-Gen. Sir Claude Francis, 1881–1966, vol. VI
Lias, Rev. John James, 1834–1923, vol. II
Lias, William John, *died* 1941, vol. IV
Libby, Willard Frank, 1908–1980, vol. VII
Liberty, Sir Arthur Lasenby, 1843–1917, vol. II
Liberty, Captain Ivor Stewart-, 1887–1952, vol. V
Lichfield, 3rd Earl of, 1856–1918, vol. II
Lichfield, 4th Earl of, 1883–1960, vol. V
Lichine, David, 1910–1972, vol. VII
Lichnowsky, Princess Mechtilde, 1879–1958, vol. V
Lichtenberger, Rt Rev. Arthur Carl, 1900–1968, vol. VI
Lichtenburg, Captain John Wills, 1872–1912, vol. I
Lidbury, Sir Charles, 1880–1978, vol. VII
Lidbury, Sir David John, 1884–1973, vol. VII
Lidbury, Ernest Alan, 1862–1948, vol. IV
Liddall, Sir Walter Sydney, 1884–1963, vol. VI
Liddell, Adolphus George Charles, 1846–1920, vol. II
Liddell, Lt-Col Arthur Robert, 1872–1966, vol. VI
Liddell, Charles, 1856–1922, vol. II
Liddell, Gen. Sir Clive Gerard, 1883–1956, vol. V
Liddell, Colin, 1862–1916, vol. II (A), vol. III
Liddell, Rev. Edward, *died* 1914, vol. I

Liddell, Sir Frederick Francis, 1865–1950, vol. IV
Liddell, Guy Maynard, 1892–1958, vol. V
Liddell, Harry, *died* 1931, vol. III
Liddell, Very Rev. Henry George, 1811–1898, vol. I
Liddell, Major John Stewart, *died* 1934, vol. III
Liddell, Lionel Charles, 1868–1942, vol. IV
Liddell, Mark Harvey, 1866–1936, vol. III
Liddell, Maximilian Friedrich, 1887–1968, vol. VI
Liddell, Peter John, 1921–1979, vol. VII
Liddell, Sir Robert Morris, 1870–1928, vol. II
Liddell, T. Hodgson, 1860–1925, vol. II
Liddell, Maj.-Gen. Sir William Andrew, 1865–1949, vol. IV
Liddell Hart, Sir Basil Henry, 1895–1970, vol. VI
Lidderdale, Rt Hon. William, 1832–1902, vol. I
Liddiard, Mabel, 1882–1962, vol. VI
Liddle, Henry Weddell, 1885–1956, vol. V
Liddle, R. W., 1864–1917, vol. II
Lidgett, Rev. John Scott, 1854–1953, vol. V
Lidiard, Sir Herbert, 1864–1941, vol. IV
Lidstone, George James, 1870–1952, vol. V
Lie, Jonas, 1833–1908, vol. I
Lie, Trygve Halvdan, 1896–1968, vol. VI
Lieber, B. Franklin, *died* 1915, vol. I (A)
Liebling, George, *died* 1946, vol. IV
Lienhop, Sir John, 1898–1967, vol. VI (AII)
Liesching, Sir Percivale, 1895–1973, vol. VII
Lifford, 5th Viscount, 1837–1913, vol. I
Lifford, 6th Viscount, 1844–1925, vol. II
Lifford, 7th Viscount, 1880–1954, vol. V
Ligertwood, Sir George Coutts, 1888–1967, vol. VI
Light, Sir Edgar William, 1885–1969, vol. VI
Lightbody, Philip Frazer, 1880–1936, vol. III
Lightbody, William Paterson Hay, 1893–1962, vol. VI
Lightbound, Rt Rev. Aloysius Anselm, *died* 1973, vol. VII
Lightfoot, Ben, 1888–1966, vol. VI
Lightfoot, Rev. John, 1853–1917, vol. II
Lightfoot, Rev. John Alfred, 1861–1928, vol. II
Lightfoot, Nicholas Morpeth Hutchinson, 1902–1962, vol. VI
Lightfoot, Ven. Reginald Prideaux, 1836–1906, vol. I
Lightfoot, Robert Henry, 1883–1953, vol. V
Lightfoot, Ven. Thomas Fothergill, 1831–1904, vol. I
Lightfoot Boston, Sir Henry Josiah; *see* Boston.
Lighthall, William Douw, 1857–1954, vol. V
Lightley, Rev. John W., 1867–1948, vol. IV
Lighton, Sir (Christopher) Robert, 7th Bt, 1848–1929, vol. III
Lighton, Sir Robert; *see* Lighton, Sir C. R.
Lightstone, Herbert, 1878–1942, vol. IV
Lilford, 5th Baron, 1863–1945, vol. IV
Lilford, 6th Baron, 1869–1949, vol. IV
Lilley, Rev. Canon Alfred Leslie, 1860–1948, vol. IV
Lilley, Cecil William, 1878–1953, vol. V
Lilley, Sir Charles, 1830–1897, vol. I
Lilley, Ernest Lewis, 1876–1948, vol. IV
Lilley, Francis James Patrick, 1907–1971, vol. VII
Lilley, Captain James Lindsay, 1871–1923, vol. II

Lilley, Thomas, 1902–1959, vol. V
Lillico, Hon. Sir Alexander, 1872–1966, vol. VI
Lillico, William Lionel James, 1880–1948, vol. IV
Lillicrap, Sir Charles Swift, 1887–1966, vol. VI
Lillie, Rev. Handley William Russell, 1902–1967, vol. VI
Lillingston, Rev. Canon Arthur Blackwell Goulburn, 1864–1943, vol. IV
Lilly, Walter Elsworthy, 1867–1940, vol. III
Lilly, William Samuel, 1840–1919, vol. II
Lima, Sir Bertram Lewis, *died* 1919, vol. II
Lima, Most Rev. Mgr Joaquim Rodriques, 1875–1936, vol. III
Limbdi, Thakore Saheb Shri Daulatsinhji Jaswantsinhji Bahadur, 1868–1940, vol. III
Limbert, Roy, *died* 1954, vol. V
Limerick, 4th Earl of, 1863–1929, vol. III
Limerick, 5th Earl of, 1888–1967, vol. VI
Limerick, Countess of; (Mary Imelda Josephine), *died* 1943, vol. IV
Limpenny, Engr-Rear-Adm. Charles Joseph, 1881–1952, vol. V
Limpus, Adm. Sir Arthur Henry, 1863–1931, vol. III
Limri, Thakur Saheb Sir, 1859–1907, vol. I
Lin Yutang, 1895–1976, vol. VII
Lincoln, Joseph, 1870–1944, vol. IV
Lincolnshire, 1st Marquess of, 1843–1928, vol. II
Lind, Hon. Sir Albert Eli, 1878–1964, vol. VI
Lind-af-Hageby, Emelie Augusta Louise, 1878–1963, vol. VI
Lindbergh, Col Charles Augustus, 1902–1974, vol. VII
Lindell, John Henry Stockton, 1908–1973, vol. VII
Lindemann, Lt-Col Charles Lionel, 1885–1970, vol. VI
Lindgren, Baron (Life Peer); George Samuel Lindgren, 1900–1971, vol. VII
Lindley, Baron (Life Peer); Nathaniel Lindley, 1828–1921, vol. II
Lindley, Charles Gustaf, 1865–1957, vol. V
Lindley, Rt Hon. Sir Francis Oswald, 1872–1950, vol. IV
Lindley, Sir Frank; *see* Lindley, Sir M. F.
Lindley, Rear-Adm. George Robert, 1850–1918, vol. II
Lindley, James Bryant, 1851–1940, vol. III
Lindley, Maj.-Gen. Hon. John Edward, 1860–1925, vol. II
Lindley, Sir (Mark) Frank, 1881–1951, vol. V
Lindley, Hon. Walter Barry, 1861–1944, vol. IV
Lindley, Sir William Heerlein, 1853–1917, vol. II
Lindley-Jones, Walter, 1863–1930, vol. III
Lindner, Doris Lexey Margaret, 1896–1979, vol. VII
Lindner, Ingram Joseph, *died* 1959, vol. V
Lindner, Peter Moffat, 1852–1949, vol. IV
Lindo, Sir (Henry) Laurence, 1911–1980, vol. VII
Lindo, Sir Laurence; *see* Lindo, Sir H. L.
Lindon, John Benjamin, 1884–1960, vol. V
Lindon, Sir Leonard Charles Edward, 1896–1978, vol. VII
Lindop, Col Carl Arthur Boys, 1899–1968, vol. VI

Lindow, Lt-Col Isaac William B.; *see* Burns-Lindow.
Lindrum, Walter, 1898–1960, vol. V
Lindsay, 11th Earl of, 1832–1917, vol. II
Lindsay, 12th Earl of, 1867–1939, vol. III
Lindsay, 13th Earl of, 1872–1943, vol. IV
Lindsay of Birker, 1st Baron, 1879–1952, vol. V
Lindsay, Alexander Martin, 1844–1906, vol. I
Lindsay, Sir Benjamin, *died* 1939, vol. III
Lindsay, Caroline Blanche Elizabeth, (Lady Lindsay), *died* 1912, vol. I
Lindsay, Sir Charles William, 1856–1939, vol. III
Lindsay, Sir Coutts, 2nd Bt, 1824–1913, vol. I
Lindsay, Col Creighton Hutchinson, 1877–1941, vol. IV
Lindsay, Sir Darcy, 1865–1941, vol. IV
Lindsay, Sir Daryl; *see* Lindsay, Sir E. D.
Lindsay, David, 1856–1922, vol. II
Lindsay, Ernest Charles, 1883–1943, vol. IV
Lindsay, Sir (Ernest) Daryl, 1889–1976, vol. VII
Lindsay, Maj.-Gen. George Mackintosh, 1880–1956, vol. V
Lindsay, Sir Harry Alexander Fanshawe, 1881–1963, vol. VI
Lindsay, Col Henry Arthur Peyton, 1868–1926, vol. II
Lindsay, Col Henry Edzell Morgan, 1857–1935, vol. III
Lindsay, Lt-Col Henry Gore, 1830–1914, vol. I
Lindsay, Howard, 1889–1968, vol. VI
Lindsay, Major Sir Humphrey B.; *see* Broun Lindsay.
Lindsay, Ian Gordon, 1906–1966, vol. VI
Lindsay, Rev. James, *died* 1923, vol. II
Lindsay, James Alexander, 1856–1931, vol. III
Lindsay, Lt-Col James Howard, *died* 1940, vol. III
Lindsay, Sir John, 1860–1927, vol. II
Lindsay, John Allan, 1865–1942, vol. IV
Lindsay, Leonard Cecil Colin, 1857–1941, vol. IV
Lindsay, Lionel Arthur, 1861–1945, vol. IV
Lindsay, Sir Lionel Arthur, 1874–1961, vol. VI
Lindsay, Nicholas Vachel; *see* Lindsay, Vachel.
Lindsay, Norman Alfred William, 1879–1969, vol. VI
Lindsay, Philip, 1906–1958, vol. V
Lindsay, Rt Hon. Sir Ronald Charles, 1877–1945, vol. IV
Lindsay, Ven. Thomas Enraght, *died* 1947, vol. IV
Lindsay, Thomas M., 1843–1914, vol. I
Lindsay, Ven. Thomas Somerville, 1854–1933, vol. III
Lindsay, Vachel, 1879–1931, vol. III
Lindsay, Wallace M., 1858–1937, vol. III
Lindsay, Walter Charles, 1866–1929, vol. III
Lindsay, Maj.-Gen. Sir Walter Fullerton Lodovic, 1855–1930, vol. III
Lindsay, William Alexander, 1846–1926, vol. II
Lindsay, William Arthur, 1866–1936, vol. III
Lindsay, Maj.-Gen. William Bethune, 1880–1933, vol. III
Lindsay, Sir William O'Brien, 1909–1975, vol. VII
Lindsay-Hogg, Sir Anthony Henry, 2nd Bt, 1908–1968, vol. VI

Lindsay-Hogg, Sir Lindsay, 1st Bt, 1853–1923, vol. II
Lindsay-Rea, Robert; *see* Rea.
Lindsell, Henry Martin, 1846–1925, vol. II
Lindsell, Herbert George, 1903–1973, vol. VII
Lindsell, Col Robert Frederick, 1856–1914, vol. I
Lindsell, Lt-Gen. Sir Wilfrid Gordon, 1884–1973, vol. VII
Lindsey, 11th Earl of, 1815–1899, vol. I
Lindsey, 12th Earl of, 1861–1938, vol. III
Lindsey, 13th Earl of, and Abingdon, 8th Earl of, 1887–1963, vol. VI
Line, Ven. Henry, *died* 1938, vol. III
Lineham, Joseph, 1869–1952, vol. V
Linehan, John, 1865–1935, vol. III
Linehan, Patrick Aloysius, 1904–1973, vol. VII
Linehan, William, 1892–1955, vol. V
Lines, Albert Walter, 1914–1976, vol. VII
Lines, Rt Rev. Edwin S., 1845–1927, vol. II
Lines, Vincent, 1909–1968, vol. VI
Lines, Walter, 1882–1972, vol. VII
Linfield, Frederick Caesar, *died* 1939, vol. III
Ling, Arthur Robert, 1861–1937, vol. III
Ling, Brig. Christopher George, 1880–1953, vol. V
Ling, George Herbert, 1874–1942, vol. IV
Lingeman, Eric Ralph, 1898–1966, vol. VI
Lingen, 1st Baron, 1819–1905, vol. I
Lingham, Brig. John, 1897–1976, vol. VII
Linklater, Eric, 1899–1974, vol. VII
Linklater, John Edmund, 1848–1917, vol. II
Linklater, Rev. Robert, 1839–1915, vol. I
Linlithgow, 1st Marquess of, 1860–1908, vol. I
Linlithgow, 2nd Marquess of, 1887–1952, vol. V
Linnell, Air Marshal Sir Francis John, 1892–1944, vol. IV
Linnell, John Wycliffe, 1878–1967, vol. VI
Linnett, John Wilfrid, 1913–1975, vol. VII
Linsley, Ven. Stanley Frederick, 1903–1974, vol. VII
Linstead, Sir Patrick; *see* Linstead, Sir R. P.
Linstead, Sir (Reginald) Patrick, 1902–1966, vol. VI
Lintern, Bernard Francis, 1908–1979, vol. VII
Lintern, Reep, 1902–1967, vol. VI
Linthorne, Sir Richard Roope, 1864–1935, vol. III
Linton, Sir Andrew, 1893–1971, vol. VII
Linton, David Leslie, 1906–1971, vol. VII
Linton, Elizabeth Lynn, 1822–1898, vol. I
Linton, Sir James Dromgole, 1840–1916, vol. II
Linton, Rt Rev. James Henry, 1879–1958, vol. V
Linton, Ralph, 1893–1953, vol. V
Linton, Sir Richard, 1879–1959, vol. V
Linton, Robert George, 1882–1960, vol. V
Lintott, Major Alfred Lord, *died* 1940, vol. III
Lintott, Henry John, 1877–1965, vol. VI
Linzee, Captain Robert Gordon Hood, 1900–1973, vol. VII
Lion, Flora, *died* 1958, vol. V
Lion, Leon M., 1879–1947, vol. IV
Lipatti, Dinu, 1917–1950, vol. IV
Lipinsky, Sigmund, 1873–1940, vol. III
Lippincott, Craige, 1846–1911, vol. I
Lippmann, Walter, 1889–1974, vol. VII
Lipsett, Maj.-Gen. Louis James, 1874–1918, vol. II
Lipson, Daniel Leopold, 1886–1963, vol. VI

Lipson, Ephraim, 1888–1960, vol. V
Lipton, Marcus, 1900–1978, vol. VII
Lipton, Sir Thomas Johnstone, 1st Bt, 1850–1931, vol. III
Lisburne, 6th Earl of, 1862–1899, vol. I
Lisburne, 7th Earl of, 1892–1965, vol. VI
Lish, Joseph J., died 1923, vol. II
Lisle, 5th Baron, 1811–1898, vol. I
Lisle, 6th Baron, 1840–1919, vol. II
Lismer, Arthur, 1885–1969, vol. VI
Lismore, 2nd Viscount, 1815–1898, vol. I
Lister, 1st Baron, 1827–1912, vol. I
Lister, Arthur, 1905–1975, vol. VII
Lister, Sir Ashton, 1845–1929, vol. III
Lister, Hon. Charles Alfred, 1887–1915, vol. I
Lister, Charles Ashton, 1871–1965, vol. VI
Lister, Sir Frederick; see Lister, Sir T. F.
Lister, Lt-Col Frederick Hamilton, 1880–1971, vol. VII
Lister, Sir (Frederick) Spencer, 1876–1939, vol. III
Lister, Col James Fraser, died 1944, vol. IV
Lister, Joseph Jackson, died 1927, vol. II
Lister, Hon. Sir Reginald, 1865–1912, vol. I
Lister, Sir Spencer; see Lister, Sir F. S.
Lister, Hon. Thomas, 1878–1904, vol. I
Lister, Thomas, 1892–1967, vol. VI
Lister, Thomas David, 1869–1924, vol. II
Lister, Sir (Thomas) Frederick, died 1966, vol. VI
Lister, Rev. Thomas Llewellyn, died 1926, vol. II
Lister, Sir Thomas Villiers, 1832–1902, vol. I
Lister, Tom, 1887–1945, vol. IV
Lister, Sir William Tindall, 1868–1944, vol. IV
Lister-Kaye, Sir Cecil Edmund, 4th Bt, 1854–1931, vol. III
Lister-Kaye, Sir John Pepys, 3rd Bt, 1853–1924, vol. II
Lister-Kaye, Sir Kenelm Arthur, 5th Bt, 1892–1955, vol. V
Lister-Kaye, Sir Lister, 6th Bt, 1873–1962, vol. VI
Liston, Most Rev. James Michael, 1881–1976, vol. VII
Liston, Lt-Col William Glen, 1873–1950, vol. IV
Liston-Foulis, Sir Archibald Charles; see Foulis.
Liston-Foulis, Sir William; see Foulis.
Listowel, 3rd Earl of, 1833–1924, vol. II
Listowel, 4th Earl of, 1866–1931, vol. III
Litauer, Stefan, 1892–1959, vol. V
Litchfield, Captain F. Shirley; see Speer, Rear-Adm. F. Shirley L.
Litchfield, Frederick, 1850–1930, vol. III
Litchfield-Speer, Rear-Adm. F. Shirley; see Speer.
Lithgow, Sir James, 1st Bt, 1883–1952, vol. V
Lithgow, Michael John, 1920–1963, vol. VI
Lithgow, Samuel, 1860–1937, vol. III
Lithiby, Sir John, 1852–1936, vol. III
Litster, William James, 1869–1930, vol. III
Litten, Maurice Sidney, 1919–1979, vol. VII
Little, Sir Alexander; see Little, Sir R. A.
Little, Andrew George, 1863–1945, vol. IV
Little, Mrs Archibald, died 1926, vol. II
Little, Archibald John, 1838–1908, vol. I
Little, Gen. Arthur Greenway, 1875–1948, vol. IV
Little, Rev. Arthur Wentworth Roberts, 1880–1932, vol. III

Little, Col Charles Blakeway, 1859–1929, vol. III
Little, Adm. Sir Charles James Colebrooke, 1882–1973, vol. VII
Little, David, 1867–1947, vol. IV
Little, Sir Ernest Gordon Graham-, died 1950, vol. IV
Little, Ernest Muirhead, 1854–1935, vol. III
Little, George Jerningham Knightley, 1886–1966, vol. VI
Little, George Leon, died 1941, vol. IV
Little, Lt-Gen. Henry Alexander, 1837–1908, vol. I
Little, Engr-Rear-Adm. Henry Augustus, 1883–1954, vol. V
Little, James, died 1916, vol. II
Little, Rev. James, 1868–1946, vol. IV
Little, James Stanley, 1856–1940, vol. III
Little, John Carruthers, 1874–1957, vol. V
Little, Sir Joseph Ignatius, died 1902, vol. I
Little, Brig.-Gen. Malcolm Orme, 1857–1931, vol. III
Little, Robert, died 1944, vol. IV
Little, Sir (Rudolf) Alexander, 1895–1977, vol. VII
Little, Rev. William John K.; see Knox Little.
Littleboy, Col Charles Norman, 1894–1966, vol. VI
Littledale, Harold, 1853–1930, vol. III
Littlehailes, Richard, 1878–1950, vol. IV
Littlejohn, Harvey, died 1927, vol. II
Littlejohn, Sir Henry Duncan, 1828–1914, vol. I
Littlejohn, Robert, died 1920, vol. II
Littlejohn, William Still, 1859–1933, vol. III
Littlejohns, Captain Astle Scott, 1875–1939, vol. III
Littler, Captain Charles Augustus, died 1916, vol. II
Littler, Rev. Harold Davies, 1887–1948, vol. IV
Littler, Prince, 1901–1973, vol. VII
Littler, Sir Ralph Daniel Makinson, 1835–1908, vol. I
Littleton, Alfred Henry, 1845–1914, vol. I
Littleton, Rev. Hon. Cecil James, 1850–1912, vol. I
Littleton, Hon. Charles Christopher Josceline, 1872–1950, vol. IV
Littlewood, Bt-Col Harry, 1861–1921, vol. II
Littlewood, James, 1885–1968, vol. VI
Littlewood, John Edensor, 1885–1977, vol. VII
Littlewood, Samuel Robinson, 1875–1963, vol. VI
Littlewood, Sir Sydney Charles Thomas, 1895–1967, vol. VI
Litvinov, Maxim, 1876–1951, vol. V
Liveing, Lt-Col Charles Hawker, 1872–1934, vol. III
Liveing, Edward, 1832–1919, vol. II
Liveing, Edward George Downing, 1895–1963, vol. VI
Liveing, George Downing, 1827–1924, vol. II
Liveing, Robert, 1834–1919, vol. II
Livens, Horace Mann, 1862–1936, vol. III
Liverpool, 1st Earl of (cr 1905, 2nd creation), 1846–1907, vol. I
Liverpool, 2nd Earl of, 1870–1941, vol. IV
Liverpool, 3rd Earl of, 1878–1962, vol. VI
Liverpool, 4th Earl of, 1887–1969, vol. VI
Liversidge, Archibald, 1847–1927, vol. II

Livesay, Brig.-Gen. Robert O'Hara, 1876–1946, vol. IV
Livesey, Sir Harry, 1860–1932, vol. III
Livesey, Rev. Herbert, 1892–1970, vol. VI
Livesey, James, 1831–1925, vol. II
Livesey, Roger, 1906–1976, vol. VII
Livingston, Charles, 1857–1937, vol. III
Livingston, Brig.-Gen. Guy, 1881–1950, vol. IV
Livingston, Henry Brockholst, 1895–1968, vol. VI
Livingston, Sir Noel Brooks, 1882–1954, vol. V
Livingston-Herbage, Julian; see Herbage.
Livingstone, Dame Adelaide Lord, died 1970, vol. VI
Livingstone, Sir Alexander Mackenzie, 1880–1950, vol. IV
Livingstone, Archibald Macdonald, died 1972, vol. VII
Livingstone, Ven. Arthur Guinness, 1840–1902, vol. I
Livingstone, Maj.-Gen. Sir Hubert Armine Anson, 1865–1940, vol. III
Livingstone, Matthew, 1837–1917, vol. II
Livingstone, Rev. Richard John, 1828–1907, vol. I
Livingstone, Sir Richard Winn, 1880–1960, vol. V
Livingstone, Rev. Robert George, 1838–1935, vol. III
Livingstone, Stuart Moodie, died 1902, vol. I
Livingstone, William P., died 1950, vol. IV (A)
Livingstone-Learmonth, Agnes Moore, 1877–1936, vol. III
Livingstone-Learmonth, Lt-Col (Francis) Leger (Christian); see Learmonth.
Livingstone-Learmonth, Frederick Valiant Cotton, 1862–1945, vol. IV
Livingstone-Learmonth, Brig.-Gen. John Eric Christian, 1876–1936, vol. III
Ljungberg, Göta, died 1955, vol. V
Llandaff, 1st Viscount, 1826–1913, vol. I
Llangattock, 1st Baron, 1837–1912, vol. I
Llangattock, 2nd Baron, 1870–1916, vol. II
Llewellin, 1st Baron, 1893–1957, vol. V
Llewellin, George Herbert, 1871–1946, vol. IV
Llewellyn, Sir David Richard, 1st Bt, 1879–1940, vol. III
Llewellyn, Col Evan Henry, 1847–1914, vol. I
Llewellyn, Brig.-Gen. Evan Henry, 1871–1948, vol. IV
Llewellyn, Col Sir Hoel, 1871–1945, vol. IV
Llewellyn, Lt-Col John Malet, died 1945, vol. IV
Llewellyn, Captain Llewellyn Evan Hugh, 1879–1970, vol. VI
Llewellyn, Lt-Col Sir Rhys, 2nd Bt, 1910–1978, vol. VII
Llewellyn, Richard Llewelyn Jones, died 1934, vol. III
Llewellyn, Robert William, 1848–1910, vol. I
Llewellyn, Sir William, 1863–1941, vol. IV
Llewellyn-Jones, Frederick, 1866–1941, vol. IV
Llewelyn, Sir John Talbot Dillwyn-, 1st Bt, 1836–1927, vol. II
Llewelyn, Sir Leonard Wilkinson, 1874–1924, vol. II
Llewelyn, Brig. Sir Michael Dillwyn- V.; see Venables-Llewelyn.

Llewelyn, Sir Robert Baxter, 1845–1919, vol. II
Llewelyn, W. Craven, died 1966, vol. VI
Llewelyn-Williams, David, 1870–1949, vol. IV
Llewhellin, Col George Elliot, 1874–1940, vol. III
Lloyd, 1st Baron, 1879–1941, vol. IV
Lloyd, Sir Alan Hubert, 1883–1948, vol. IV
Lloyd, Rev. Albert Henry, died 1941, vol. IV
Lloyd, Rev. Arthur, 1852–1911, vol. I
Lloyd, Captain Arthur Athelwold, 1864–1940, vol. III
Lloyd, Rev. Arthur Gittins, 1865–1931, vol. III
Lloyd, Brig.-Gen. Arthur Henry Orlando, 1864–1944, vol. IV
Lloyd, Rt Rev. Arthur Selden, 1857–1936, vol. III
Lloyd, Rt Rev. Arthur Thomas, died 1907, vol. I
Lloyd, Captain Arthur Wynell, 1883–1967, vol. VI
Lloyd, Bertram Arthur, 1884–1948, vol. IV
Lloyd, Charles Ellis, died 1939, vol. III
Lloyd, Lt-Col Charles Geoffrey, 1884–1953, vol. V
Lloyd, Charles Harford, 1849–1919, vol. II
Lloyd, Col Charles Robert, 1882–1930, vol. III
Lloyd, Cyril Edward, 1876–1963, vol. VI
Lloyd, Rt Rev. Daniel Lewis, 1843–1899, vol. I
Lloyd, David John, 1886–1951, vol. V
Lloyd, Dorothy J.; see Jordan Lloyd.
Lloyd, Edward, 1845–1927, vol. II
Lloyd, Edward Honoratus, 1860–1930, vol. III
Lloyd, Edward Mayow Hastings, 1889–1968, vol. VI
Lloyd, Col Edward Prince, 1887–1970, vol. VI
Lloyd, Comdr Edward William, 1855–1945, vol. IV
Lloyd, Eric Ivan, 1892–1954, vol. V
Lloyd, Ernest Sampson, 1870–1945, vol. IV
Lloyd, Lt-Col Fitzwarren, 1859–1923, vol. II
Lloyd, Lt-Gen. Sir Francis, 1853–1926, vol. II
Lloyd, Francis Ernest, 1868–1947, vol. IV
Lloyd, Francis Nelson, 1907–1974, vol. VII
Lloyd, Maj.-Gen. Francis Thomas, 1838–1912, vol. I
Lloyd, Col Frederic Percy L.; see Lousada Lloyd.
Lloyd, Brig.-Gen. Frederick Charles, 1860–1957, vol. V
Lloyd, Col Frederick Lindsay, 1866–1940, vol. III
Lloyd, George Butler, 1854–1930, vol. III
Lloyd, Col George Evan, 1855–1900, vol. I
Lloyd, Rt Rev. George Exton, 1861–1940, vol. III
Lloyd, George Whitelocke, 1830–1910, vol. I
Lloyd, Guy Vaughan, 1901–1975, vol. VII
Lloyd, Maj.-Gen. Herbert William, 1883–1957, vol. V
Lloyd, Brig.-Gen. Horace Giesler, 1872–1936, vol. III
Lloyd, Sir Horatio, 1829–1920, vol. II
Lloyd, Howard, 1837–1920, vol. II
Lloyd, Sir Howard Watson, 1868–1955, vol. V
Lloyd, Captain Sir Humphrey Clifford, 1893–1966, vol. VI
Lloyd, Huw Ifor, 1893–1977, vol. VII
Lloyd, Sir Idwal Geoffrey, 1878–1946, vol. IV
Lloyd, Rev. Iorwerth Grey, 1844–1920, vol. II
Lloyd, Air Cdre Ivor Thomas, 1896–1966, vol. VI
Lloyd, J. A. T., died 1956, vol. V
Lloyd, Rt Rev. John, 1847–1915, vol. I
Lloyd, Sir John Buck, 1874–1952, vol. V

Lloyd, Lt-Col Sir John Conway, 1878–1954, vol. V
Lloyd, John Davies Knatchbull, 1900–1978, vol. VII
Lloyd, Sir John Edward, 1861–1947, vol. IV
Lloyd, Col John Edward, 1894–1965, vol. VI
Lloyd, Sir John Hall S.; see Seymour-Lloyd.
Lloyd, Brig.-Gen. John Hardress, 1874–1952, vol. V
Lloyd, Brig.-Gen. John Henry, 1872–1941, vol. IV
Lloyd, (John) Selwyn (Brooke); see Baron Selwyn-Lloyd.
Lloyd, Ven. John Walter, 1879–1951, vol. V
Lloyd, Jordan, died 1913, vol. I
Lloyd, Rev. Joseph, died 1938, vol. III
Lloyd, Air Vice-Marshal Kenneth Buchanan, 1897–1973, vol. VII
Lloyd, Col Langford Newman, 1873–1956, vol. V
Lloyd, Llewelyn Southworth, 1876–1956, vol. V
Lloyd, Sir Marteine Owen Mowbray, 2nd Bt, 1851–1933, vol. III
Lloyd, Col Sir Morgan George, 1843–1917, vol. II
Lloyd, Nathaniel, 1867–1933, vol. III
Lloyd, Maj.-Gen. Sir Owen Edward Pennefather, 1854–1941, vol. IV
Lloyd, Col Pen; see Lloyd, Col Philip H.
Lloyd, Col Philip Henry, (Pen), 1905–1979, vol. VII
Lloyd, Lt-Col Reginald Broughton, 1881–1975, vol. VII
Lloyd, Major Richard Ernest, 1875–1935, vol. III
Lloyd, Rickard William, 1859–1933, vol. III
Lloyd, Col Robert Oliver, 1849–1921, vol. II
Lloyd, Sir Robert Owen, 1894–1970, vol. VI
Lloyd, Adm. Rodney Maclaine, 1841–1911, vol. I
Lloyd, Rev. Canon Roger Bradshaigh, died 1966, vol. VI
Lloyd, Samuel Cook, 1854–1929, vol. III
Lloyd, Brig.-Gen. Samuel Eyre Massy, 1867–1952, vol. V
Lloyd, Selwyn; see Baron Selwyn-Lloyd.
Lloyd, Stuart, vol. III
Lloyd, T. Alwyn, 1881–1960, vol. V
Lloyd, Theodore Howard, 1872–1959, vol. V
Lloyd, Col Thomas, 1853–1916, vol. II
Lloyd, Rt Rev. Thomas, 1857–1935, vol. III
Lloyd, Col Thomas Edward John, 1856–1937, vol. III
Lloyd, Maj.-Gen. Thomas Francis, 1839–1921, vol. II
Lloyd, Sir Thomas Ingram Kynaston, 1896–1968, vol. VI
Lloyd, Lt-Col Thomas Owen, 1866–1945, vol. IV
Lloyd, Tom, died 1910, vol. I
Lloyd, Col Wilford Neville, 1855–1935, vol. III
Lloyd, Maj.-Gen. Wilfrid Lewis, 1896–1944, vol. IV
Lloyd, William, 1874–1948, vol. IV
Lloyd, William Ernest, died 1975, vol. VII
Lloyd, Rt Hon. Sir William Frederick, 1864–1937, vol. III
Lloyd, William Harris, 1836–1923, vol. II
Lloyd, Wilson, 1835–1908, vol. I
Lloyd, Wynne Llewelyn, 1910–1973, vol. VII
Lloyd-Anstruther, Lt-Col Robert Hamilton; see Anstruther.

Lloyd-Baker, Granville Edwin Lloyd, 1841–1924, vol. II
Lloyd-Baker, Olive Katherine Lloyd, 1902–1975, vol. VII
Lloyd-Blood, Lancelot Ivan Neptune; see Blood.
Lloyd-Evans, Annie; see Evans.
Lloyd George of Dwyfor, 1st Earl, 1863–1945, vol. IV
Lloyd George of Dwyfor, 2nd Earl, 1889–1968, vol. VI
Lloyd George of Dwyfor, Countess; (Frances Louise), died 1972, vol. VII
Lloyd George, Lady Megan, died 1966, vol. VI
Lloyd-Jacob, Sir George Harold, 1897–1969, vol. VI
Lloyd James, Arthur, 1884–1943, vol. IV
Lloyd-Jones, Ven. John; see Jones.
Lloyd-Jones, Major Percy Arnold; see Jones.
Lloyd Jones, Richard Francis, 1908–1975, vol. VII
Lloyd-Mostyn, Hon. Henry Richard Howel, 1857–1938, vol. III
Lloyd-Mostyn, Maj.-Gen. Hon. Sir Savage, 1835–1914, vol. I
Lloyd Owen, David Charles, died 1925, vol. II
Lloyd-Roberts, Sir Richard, 1885–1956, vol. V
Lloyd-Williams, Dorothy Sylvia, 1901–1977, vol. VII
Lloyd-Williams, Hugh, 1889–1968, vol. VI
Lloyd-Williams, Comdr Hugh, 1900–1977, vol. VII
Lloyd-Williams, Captain James Evan, 1888–1969, vol. VI
Lloyd-Williams, Katharine Georgina, 1896–1973, vol. VII
Llubera, Ignacio Miguel G.; see Gonzalez-Llubera.
Llucen; see Cullen, Rev. John.
Llwyd, Very Rev. John Plummer Derwent, 1861–1933, vol. III
Lo, Hon. Sir Man-kam, 1893–1959, vol. V
Lo Feng-Luh, Sir Chih Chen, 1850–1903, vol. I
Loane, Miss M., died 1922, vol. II
Lobb, John, 1840–1921, vol. II
Lobban, Charles Henry, 1881–1963, vol. VI
Lobjoit, Sir William George, 1859–1939, vol. III
Lobnitz, Sir Frederick, 1863–1932, vol. III
Loch, 1st Baron, 1827–1900, vol. I
Loch, 2nd Baron, 1873–1942, vol. IV
Loch, Sir Charles Stewart, 1849–1923, vol. II
Loch, Maj.-Gen. Granville George, 1870–1950, vol. IV
Loch, Lt-Col Granville Henry, 1859–1929, vol. III
Loch, Col John Carysfort, 1877–1974, vol. VII
Loch, Lt-Gen. Sir Kenneth Morley, 1890–1961, vol. VI
Loch, Maj.-Gen. Stewart Gordon, 1873–1952, vol. V
Loch, Lt-Col William, 1845–1912, vol. I
Lochee of Gowrie, 1st Baron, 1845–1911, vol. I
Lochhead, James, died 1940, vol. III
Lochhead, John, died 1921, vol. II
Lochhead, William, 1864–1927, vol. II
Lochore, Sir James, 1874–1953, vol. V
Lock, B. Fossett, 1847–1922, vol. II
Lock, Flt Lt Eric Stanley, 1919–1942, vol. IV

Lock, Brig.-Gen. Frederic Robert Edward, 1867–1945, vol. IV

Lock, Rev. John Bascombe, 1849–1921, vol. II

Lock, Maj.-Gen. Sir Robert Ferguson, 1879–1957, vol. V

Lock, Robert Heath, 1879–1915, vol. I

Lock, Rev. Walter, 1846–1933, vol. III

Locke, Arthur, 1872–1932, vol. III

Locke, George Herbert, 1870–1937, vol. III

Locke, George T., 1872–1968, vol. VI

Locke, William John, 1863–1930, vol. III

Locke King, Dame Ethel; see King, Dame E. L.

Locker, William Algernon, 1863–1930, vol. III

Locker-Lampson, Rt Hon. Godfrey Lampson Tennyson, 1875–1946, vol. IV

Locker-Lampson, Jane, died 1915, vol. I

Locker-Lampson, Comdr Oliver Stillingfleet, 1880–1954, vol. V

Lockett, Air Cdre Charles Edward Stuart, 1910–1966, vol. VI

Lockett, Richard Jeffery, 1907–1980, vol. VII

Lockhart, Sir Allan Robert E.; see Eliott Lockhart.

Lockhart, Sir Charles Ramsdale, 1892–1954, vol. V

Lockhart, Sir Graeme Alexander Sinclair, 10th Bt (cr 1636), 1820–1904, vol. I

Lockhart, Sir Graeme Duncan Power S.; see Sinclair-Lockhart.

Lockhart, Sir James Haldane Stewart, 1858–1937, vol. III

Lockhart, Sir John Beresford S.; see Sinclair-Lockhart.

Lockhart, John Gilbert, 1891–1960, vol. V

Lockhart, John Harold Bruce, 1889–1956, vol. V

Lockhart, Maj.-Gen. Leslie Keith, 1897–1966, vol. VI

Lockhart, Lt-Col Percy Clare E.; see Eliott-Lockhart.

Lockhart, Sir Robert Cook, 1861–1943, vol. IV

Lockhart, Sir Robert Duncan S.; see Sinclair-Lockhart.

Lockhart, Sir Robert Hamilton B.; see Bruce Lockhart.

Lockhart, Sidney Alexander, 1914–1969, vol. VI

Lockhart, Sir Simon Macdonald, 5th Bt (cr 1806), 1849–1919, vol. II

Lockhart, W. E., died 1900, vol. I

Lockhart-Mummery, John Percy, 1875–1957, vol. V

Lockie, John, 1863–1906, vol. I

Lockitt, Charles Henry, 1877–1964, vol. VI

Lockroy, Edouard, 1838–1913, vol. I

Lockroy, Etienne Auguste Edouard Simon; see Lockroy, Edouard.

Lockton, Charles Langton, 1856–1932, vol. III

Lockwood, Charles Barrett, died 1914, vol. I

Lockwood, Sir Francis, 1847–1897, vol. I

Lockwood, Francis William, 1908–1955, vol. V

Lockwood, James Horace, 1888–1972, vol. VII

Lockwood, Sir John Francis, 1903–1965, vol. VI

Lockyer, Air Vice-Marshal Clarence Edward Williams, 1892–1963, vol. VI

Lockyer, Cuthbert H. J., 1867–1957, vol. V

Lockyer, Captain Hughes Campbell, 1866–1941, vol. IV

Lockyer, Sir (Joseph) Norman, 1836–1920, vol. II

Lockyer, Sir Nicholas Colston, 1855–1933, vol. III

Lockyer, Sir Norman; see Lockyer, Sir J. N.

Lockyer, William James Stewart, 1868–1936, vol. III

Locmaria, Marquis du P.; see Parc-Locmaria.

Locock, Sir Charles Bird, 3rd Bt, 1878–1965, vol. VI

Locock, Sir Guy Harold, 1883–1958, vol. V

Locock, Col Herbert, 1847–1910, vol. I

Loder, Sir Edmund Giles, 2nd Bt, 1849–1920, vol. II

Loder, Major Eustace, 1867–1914, vol. I

Loder, Lt-Col Giles Harold, 1884–1966, vol. VI

Loder, Sir Louis Francis, 1896–1972, vol. VII

Loder, Reginald Bernhard, 1864–1931, vol. III

Loder-Symonds, Captain F. C.; see Symonds.

Loder-Symonds, Vice-Adm. Frederick Parland; see Symonds.

Lodge, Alfred, 1854–1937, vol. III

Lodge, Alfred, 1893–1957, vol. V

Lodge, Eleanor Constance, 1869–1936, vol. III

Lodge, Lt-Col Francis Cecil, 1868–1951, vol. V

Lodge, Frank Adrian, 1861–1947, vol. IV

Lodge, Henry Cabot, 1850–1924, vol. II

Lodge, John, 1890–1954, vol. V

Lodge, Sir Oliver Joseph, 1851–1940, vol. III

Lodge, Oliver William Foster, 1878–1955, vol. V

Lodge, Sir Richard, 1855–1936, vol. III

Lodge, Sir Ronald Francis, 1889–1960, vol. V

Lodge, Rupert Clendon, 1886–1961, vol. VI

Lodge, Thomas, 1882–1958, vol. V

Lodge, Thomas Arthur, 1888–1967, vol. VI

Lodwick, John Alan Patrick, 1916–1959, vol. V

Lodwick, Captain John Thornton, 1882–1915, vol. I (A)

Loeb, Jacques, 1859–1924, vol. II

Loeb, James, 1867–1933, vol. III

Loewe, Herbert Martin James, 1882–1940, vol. III

Loewenstein-Wertheim, HSH Princess, 1866–1927, vol. II

Loewenthal, Sir John, 1914–1979, vol. VII

Loewi, Otto, 1873–1961, vol. VI

Lofthouse, Rt Rev. Joseph, 1855–1933, vol. III

Lofthouse, Rt Rev. Joseph, 1880–1962, vol. VI

Lofthouse, Samuel Hill Smith, 1843–1915, vol. I (A)

Lofthouse, Rev. William Frederick, 1871–1965, vol. VI

Loftie, Rev. Arthur Gershom, 1843–1922, vol. II

Loftie, Rev. William J., 1839–1911, vol. I

Lofting, Hugh John, 1886–1947, vol. IV

Loftus, Rt Hon. Lord Augustus William Frederick Spencer, 1817–1904, vol. I

Loftus, Cissie; see M'Carthy, Marie Cecilia.

Loftus, Montagu Egerton, 1860–1934, vol. III

Loftus, Pierse Creagh, 1877–1956, vol. V

Logan, Sir Charles Bowman, 1837–1907, vol. I

Logan, Brig.-Gen. David Finlay Hosken, 1862–1923, vol. II

Logan, David Gilbert, 1871–1964, vol. VI

Logan, Lt-Col Edward Townshend, died 1915, vol. I

Logan, Sir Ewen Reginald, 1868–1945, vol. IV

Logan, Brig.-Gen. Francis Douglas, 1875–1947, vol. IV

Logan, Hon. Hance James, 1869–1944, vol. IV

Logan, Lt-Col Harry Tremaine, 1887–1971, vol. VII

Logan, John William, 1845–1925, vol. II

Logan, Col Robert, 1863–1935, vol. III

Logan, Sir William Marston, 1889–1968, vol. VI

Logan-Home, Major George John Ninian, 1855–1936, vol. III

Loggin, George Nicholas, 1882–1955, vol. V

Logie, William Alexander, 1866–1933, vol. III

Login, Rear-Adm. Spencer Henry Metcalfe Login, 1851–1909, vol. I

Logsdail, William, 1859–1944, vol. IV

Logue, Lionel, 1880–1953, vol. V

Logue, His Eminence Cardinal Michael, 1840–1924, vol. II

Loharu, Hon. Nawab Sir Amir-ud-Din Ahmed Khan Bahadur, 1860–1937, vol. III

Lohr, Hervey, 1856–1927, vol. II

Löhr, Marie, 1890–1975, vol. VII

Loisy, Alfred, 1857–1940, vol. III

Lomas, Surg.-Captain Ernest Courtney, 1864–1921, vol. II

Lomas, Ernest Gabriel, 1878–1947, vol. IV

Lomas, Harry, 1916–1980, vol. VII

Lomas, Herbert, 1887–1961, vol. VI

Lomas, John, 1846–1927, vol. II

Lomas, Sophie Crawford, died 1929, vol. III

Lomas-Walker, Sir G. Bernard, 1881–1960, vol. V

Lomax, Maj.-Gen. Cyril Ernest Napier, 1893–1973, vol. VII

Lomax, Sir John, 1864–1936, vol. III

Lomax, John A., 1857–1923, vol. II

Lomax, Michael Roger T.; see Trappes-Lomax.

Lomax, Maj.-Gen. Samuel Holt, 1855–1915, vol. I

Lomax, Brig. Thomas Byrnand T.; see Trappes-Lomax.

Lombe, Vice-Adm. Sir Edward Malcolm E.; see Evans-Lombe.

Lombroso, Cesare, 1836–1909, vol. I

Londesborough, 1st Earl of, 1834–1900, vol. I

Londesborough, 2nd Earl of, 1864–1917, vol. II

Londesborough, 3rd Earl of, 1892–1920, vol. II

Londesborough, 4th Earl of, 1894–1937, vol. III

Londesborough, 6th Baron, 1876–1963, vol. VI

Londesborough, 7th Baron, 1885–1967, vol. VI

Londesborough, 8th Baron, 1901–1968, vol. VI

London, Sir (Edgar) Stanford, 1861–1943, vol. IV

London, Sir George Ernest, 1889–1957, vol. V

London, Heinz, 1907–1970, vol. VI

London, Hugh Stanford, 1884–1959, vol. V

London, Jack, 1876–1916, vol. II

London, Sir Stanford; see London, Sir E. S.

Londonderry, 6th Marquess of, 1852–1915, vol. I

Londonderry, 7th Marquess of, 1878–1949, vol. IV

Londonderry, 8th Marquess of, 1902–1955, vol. V

Londonderry, Dowager Marchioness of; (Edith Helen), 1879–1959, vol. V

Loney, Sidney Luxton, 1860–1939, vol. III

Long, 1st Viscount, 1854–1924, voll II

Long, 2nd Viscount, 1911–1944, vol. IV

Long, 3rd Viscount, 1892–1967, vol. VI

Long, Lt-Col Albert de Lande, 1880–1956, vol. V

Long, Alfred James, 1890–1952, vol. V

Long, Brig.-Gen. Sir Arthur, 1866–1941, vol. IV

Long, Arthur Tilney, 1871–1946, vol. IV

Long, Basil Kellett, 1878–1944, vol. IV

Long, Basil Somerset, 1881–1937, vol. III

Long, Sir Bertram, 1889–1975, vol. VII

Long, Charles Wigram, 1842–1911, vol. I

Long, Edward Charles, 1860–1940, vol. III

Long, Edward Ernest, died 1956, vol. V

Long, Captain Eustace Ruffel Drake, 1883–1941, vol. IV

Long, Gabrielle; see Long, M. G.

Long, Gavin Merrick, 1901–1968, vol. VI

Long, George Bathurst, 1855–1917, vol. II

Long, Sir George Henry, 1818–1900, vol. I

Long, Rt Rev. George Merrick, 1874–1930, vol. III

Long, Sir James, 1862–1928, vol. II

Long, John Luther, 1861–1927, vol. II

Long, Kathleen Ida, 1896–1968, vol. VI

Long, (Margaret) Gabrielle, 1888–1952, vol. V

Long, Ven. Robert, died 1907, vol. I

Long, Robert Edward Crozier, 1872–1938, vol. III

Long, Maj.-Gen. Sidney Selden, 1863–1940, vol. III

Long, Sydney, (Sid Long), 1878–1955, vol. V

Long, Sydney Herbert, 1870–1939, vol. III

Long, Lt-Col Walter, 1879–1917, vol. II

Long, Col Walter Edward Lionel, 1884–1960, vol. V

Long, Lt-Col Wilfred James, 1871–1954, vol. V

Long, Lt-Col William, 1843–1926, vol. II

Long, William Henry, 1900–1969, vol. VI

Long, Lt-Col William Hoare Bourchier, 1868–1943, vol. IV

Long, Rev. William Joseph, 1866–1952, vol. V

Long Innes, Hon. Reginald Heath, 1869–1947, vol. IV

Longard de Longgarde, Dorothea, 1855–1915, vol. I (A)

Longbotham, Hugh Ashley, 1880–1938, vol. III

Longbottom, Arthur William, 1883–1943, vol. IV

Longbottom, Sir Benjamin, 1876–1930, vol. III

Longbourne, Brig.-Gen. Francis Cecil M. M.; see More-Molyneux-Longbourne.

Longcroft, Air Vice-Marshal Sir Charles Alexander Holcombe, 1883–1958, vol. V

Longden, Major Alfred Appleby, died 1954, vol. V

Longden, Clifford; see Longden, H. C.

Longden, Fred, 1894–1952, vol. V

Longden, (Harry) Clifford, 1869–1953, vol. V

Longden, Vice-Adm. Horace Walker, 1877–1953, vol. V

Longden, Robert Paton, 1903–1940, vol. III

Longe, Col Francis Bacon, 1856–1922, vol. II

Longfellow, Ernest Wadsworth, 1845–1921, vol. II

Longfield, Captain John Percival, 1885–1915, vol. I

Longford, 5th Earl of, 1864–1915, vol. I (A)

Longford, 6th Earl of, 1902–1961, vol. VI

Longford, Joseph Henry, 1849–1925, vol. II

Longford, Rev. William Wingfield, 1882–1964, vol. VI

Longhurst, Col Arthur Lyster, 1872–1952, vol. V

Longhurst, Cyril, 1879–1948, vol. IV

Longhurst, Sir Henry Bell, 1835–1926, vol. II
Longhurst, Henry Carpenter, 1909–1978, vol. VII
Longhurst, Margaret Helen, 1882–1958, vol. V
Longhurst, Ven. William Belsey, 1847–1939, vol. III
Longhurst, William Henry, 1819–1904, vol. I
Longhurst, Rev. William Henry Roberts, died 1943, vol. IV
Longland, Austin Charles, 1888–1972, vol. VII
Longland, Rev. Sydney Ernest, 1873–1957, vol. V
Longley, Sir Henry, 1833–1899, vol. I
Longley, James Wilberforce, 1849–1922, vol. II
Longley, Maj.-Gen. Sir John Raynsford, 1867–1953, vol. V
Longley, Stanislaus Soutten, 1894–1966, vol. VI
Longman, Charles James, 1852–1934, vol. III
Longman, Sir Hubert Harry, 1st Bt, 1856–1940, vol. III
Longman, Mark Frederic Kerr, 1916–1972, vol. VII
Longman, Thomas Norton, 1849–1930, vol. III
Longman, William, 1882–1967, vol. VI
Longmore, Air Chief Marshal Sir Arthur Murray, 1885–1970, vol. VI
Longmore, Col Sir Charles Elton, 1855–1930, vol. III
Longmore, Lt-Col Charles Moorsom, 1882–1933, vol. III
Longmore, Brig. John Alexander, 1899–1973, vol. VII
Longmore, Brig.-Gen. John Constantine Gordon, 1870–1958, vol. V
Longmore, Philip Elton, 1884–1954, vol. V
Longmuir, Very Rev. James Boyd, 1907–1973, vol. VII
Longmuir, Robert Findlay, 1864–1942, vol. IV
Longridge, Rev. George, 1857–1936, vol. III
Longridge, Lt-Col Theodore, 1860–1940, vol. III
Longrigg, Brig. Stephen Hemsley, 1893–1979, vol. VII
Longson, Edward Harold, 1872–1941, vol. IV
Longstaff, Cedric Llewellyn, 1876–1950, vol. IV
Longstaff, George Blundell, 1849–1921, vol. II
Longstaff, Mrs George Blundell; see Longstaff, M. J.
Longstaff, Gilbert Conrad, 1884–1964, vol. VI
Longstaff, Sir John, 1862–1941, vol. IV
Longstaff, Llewellyn Wood, 1841–1918, vol. II
Longstaff, Mary Jane, (Mrs George Longstaff), died 1935, vol. III
Longstaff, Tom George, 1875–1964, vol. VI
Longstaffe, Amyas Philip, 1868–1914, vol. I
Longstreth-Thompson, Francis, 1890–1973, vol. VII
Longueville, Thomas, 1844–1922, vol. II
Longworth, Francis Travus Dames, 1834–1898, vol. I
Longworth, Sir Fred, 1890–1973, vol. VII
Longworth, Nicholas, 1869–1931, vol. III
Longworth, Rt Rev. Tom, 1891–1977, vol. VII
Lonsdale, 5th Earl of, 1857–1944, vol. IV
Lonsdale, 6th Earl of, 1867–1953, vol. V
Lonsdale, Allister, 1926–1977, vol. VII
Lonsdale, Lt-Col Arthur H.; see Heywood-Lonsdale.
Lonsdale, Arthur Pemberton H.; see Heywood-Lonsdale.

Lonsdale, Frederick, 1881–1954, vol. V
Lonsdale, Rev. Henry, died 1926, vol. II
Lonsdale, Lt-Col Henry Heywood H.; see Heywood-Lonsdale.
Lonsdale, James Rolston, 1865–1921, vol. II
Lonsdale, Rev. John Gylby, 1818–1907, vol. I
Lonsdale, John Pemberton Heywood H.; see Heywood-Lonsdale.
Lonsdale, Dame Kathleen, 1903–1971, vol. VII
Looker, Herbert William, 1871–1951, vol. V
Loombe, Claude Evan, 1905–1978, vol. VII
Loomis, Maj.-Gen. Sir Frederick Oscar Warren, 1870–1937, vol. III
Loomis, Roger Sherman, 1887–1966, vol. VI
Lopes, George, 1857–1910, vol. I
Lopes, Rt Hon. Sir Massey, 3rd Bt, 1818–1908, vol. I
Loraine, Sir Lambton, 11th Bt, 1838–1917, vol. II
Loraine, Rev. Nevison, died 1917, vol. II
Loraine, Rt Hon. Sir Percy Lyham, 12th Bt, 1880–1961, vol. VI
Loraine, Robert, 1876–1935, vol. III
Loram, Charles Templeman, 1879–1940, vol. III (A), vol. IV
Lord, Sir Frank, 1894–1974, vol. VII
Lord, Rev. Fred Townley, 1893–1962, vol. VI
Lord, Herbert Owen, 1854–1928, vol. II
Lord, Col John Ernest Cecil, 1870–1949, vol. IV
Lord, John King, 1848–1926, vol. II
Lord, John Robert, 1874–1931, vol. III
Lord, Sir Percy, 1903–1968, vol. VI
Lord, Sir Riley, 1838–1920, vol. II
Lord, Captain S(ydney) Riley, 1884–1959, vol. V
Lord, Sir Walter G.; see Greaves-Lord.
Lorden, Sir John William, 1862–1944, vol. IV
Loreburn, 1st Earl, 1846–1923, vol. II
Lorimer, Lt-Col David Lockhart Robertson, 1876–1962, vol. VI
Lorimer, Emily Overend, (Mrs D. L. R. Lorimer), 1881–1949, vol. IV
Lorimer, George Horace, 1868–1937, vol. III
Lorimer, Henry Dubs, 1879–1933, vol. III
Lorimer, John Campbell, died 1922, vol. II
Lorimer, John Gordon, 1870–1914, vol. I
Lorimer, John Henry, 1856–1936, vol. III
Lorimer, Norma, died 1948, vol. IV
Lorimer, Sir Robert Stodart, 1864–1929, vol. III
Lorimer, Sir William, 1844–1922, vol. II
Lorimer, William Laughton, 1885–1967, vol. VI
Loring, Andrew; see Lathrop, L. A.
Loring, Vice-Adm. Ernest Kindersley, 1869–1945, vol. IV
Loring, Frederick George, 1869–1951, vol. V
Loring, Sir (John) Nigel, 1896–1979, vol. VII
Loring, Sir Nigel; see Loring, Sir J. N.
Loring, William, 1865–1915, vol. I (A)
Loring, Col William, 1872–1935, vol. III
Lorne, Marion, 1888–1968, vol. VI
Lornie, James, 1876–1959, vol. V
Lorrain, Rt Rev. Narcisse Zephyrin, 1842–1915, vol. I (A)
Lort Phillips, Lt-Col John Frederick, 1854–1926, vol. II

Lort-Williams, Sir John Rolleston, 1881–1966, vol. VI

Lory, Frederic Burton Pendarves, 1875–1954, vol. V

Lote, Thomas Alfred, born 1863, vol. II

Loten, Harold Ivens, 1887–1980, vol. VII

Lothian, 9th Marquess of, 1833–1900, vol. I

Lothian, 10th Marquess of, 1874–1930, vol. III

Lothian, 11th Marquess of, 1882–1940, vol. III

Lothian, Sir Arthur Cunningham, 1887–1962, vol. VI

Loti, Pierre, 1850–1923, vol. II

Loton, Sir Ernest Thorley, 1895–1973, vol. VII

Loton, Sir William Thorley, 1839–1924, vol. II

Loubet, Emile, 1838–1929, vol. III

Louch, Ven. Thomas, 1848–1927, vol. II

Loucks, Rev. Edwin, 1829–1919, vol. II

Loud, Arthur Bertram, 1863–1931, vol. III

Loudan, Mouat, 1868–1925, vol. II

Loudon, James, 1841–1916, vol. II

Loudon, Sir John, 1881–1948, vol. IV

Loudon, John, died 1966, vol. VI

Loudoun, 11th Earl of, 1855–1920, vol. II

Loudoun, Countess of (12th in line), 1883–1960, vol. V

Loudoun, Donaldson, 1909–1980, vol. VII

Lough, Brig. John Robertson Stewart, 1887–1970, vol. VI

Lough, Lt-Gen. Reginald Dawson Hopcraft, 1885–1958, vol. V

Lough, Rt Hon. Thomas, 1850–1922, vol. II

Loughborough, Lord; Francis Edward Scudamore St Clair Erskine, 1892–1929, vol. III

Loughborough, Maj.-Gen. Arthur Harold, 1883–1967, vol. VI

Lougheed, Hon. Sir James Alexander, 1854–1925, vol. II

Lougheed, Lt-Col Samuel Forster, 1860–1932, vol. III

Lougher, Sir Lewis, 1871–1955, vol. V

Loughlin, Dame Anne, 1894–1979, vol. VII

Loughnane, Farquhar McGillivray, 1885–1948, vol. IV

Loughnane, Norman Gerald, 1883–1955, vol. V

Louis, Sir Charles, 4th Bt, 1818–1900, vol. I

Louis, Sir Charles, 5th Bt, 1859–1949, vol. IV

Louis, Henry, 1855–1939, vol. III

Louisson, Hon. Charles, 1842–1924, vol. II

Lounsbury, Thomas Raynesford, 1838–1915, vol. I (A)

Lousada, Duc de; Comdr Francis Clifford de Lousada, 1842–1916, vol. II

Lousada Lloyd, Col Frederic Percy, 1853–1930, vol. III

Louth, 14th Baron, 1868–1941, vol. IV

Louth, 15th Baron, 1892–1950, vol. IV

Louw, Hon. Eric Hendrik, 1890–1968, vol. VI

Louys, Pierre, 1870–1925, vol. II

Lovat, 14th Baron, 1871–1933, vol. III

Lovat-Fraser, James Alexander, 1868–1938, vol. III

Love, Augustus Edward Hough, 1863–1940, vol. III

Love, Sir Clifton; see Love, Sir J. C.

Love, Enid Rosamond, (Mrs G. C. F. Whitaker), 1911–1979, vol. VII

Love, James Kerr, 1858–1942, vol. IV

Love, Sir (Joseph) Clifton, 1868–1951, vol. V

Love, Richard Archibald, 1873–1941, vol. IV

Love, Robert, 1867–1934, vol. III

Love, Robert John McNeill, 1891–1974, vol. VII

Loveday, Alexander, 1888–1962, vol. VI

Loveday, Arthur Frederic, 1878–1968, vol. VI

Loveday, Rev. Eric Stephen, 1904–1947, vol. IV

Loveday, Thomas, 1875–1966, vol. VI

Lovegrove, Edwin William, 1868–1956, vol. V

Lovejoy, Arthur Oncken, 1873–1962, vol. VI

Lovel, Raymond William, 1912–1969, vol. VI

Lovelace, 2nd Earl of, 1839–1906, vol. I

Lovelace, 3rd Earl of, 1865–1929, vol. III

Lovelace, 4th Earl of, 1905–1964, vol. VI

Lovelace, Countess of; (Mary Caroline), died 1941, vol. IV

Loveland, Richard Loveland, 1841–1923, vol. II

Lovell, Sir Francis Henry, died 1916, vol. II

Lovell, Henry Willoughby, 1866–1939, vol. III

Lovell, Reginald, 1897–1972, vol. VII

Lovell, William George, 1868–1944, vol. IV

Lovely, Percy Thomas, 1894–1975, vol. VII

Lovemore, Wing Comdr Robert Baillie, died 1978, vol. VII

Loveridge, Arthur John, 1904–1975, vol. VII

Loveridge, Charles William, 1869–1957, vol. V

Loveridge, Walter David, 1867–1940, vol. III (A), vol. IV

Loverseed, John Frederick, 1881–1928, vol. II

Lovett, Col Alfred Crowdy, 1862–1919, vol. II

Lovett, Maj.-Gen. Beresford, 1839–1926, vol. II

Lovett, Rt Rev. Ernest Neville, 1869–1951, vol. V

Lovett, Sir (Harrington) Verney, 1864–1945, vol. IV

Lovett, Rev. Canon John Percival Willoughby, 1880–1968, vol. VI

Lovett, Rev. Richard, 1851–1904, vol. I

Lovett, Sir Verney; see Lovett, Sir H. V.

Lovett-Cameron, Rev. Charles Leslie, 1843–1927, vol. II

Loveys, Walter Harris, 1920–1969, vol. VI

Lovibond, Joseph Williams, 1833–1918, vol. II

Low, Hon. Lord; Alexander Low, 1845–1910, vol. I

Low, A. M., 1888–1956, vol. V

Low, Sir A. Maurice, 1860–1929, vol. III

Low, Gen. Alexander, 1817–1904, vol. I

Low, Alexander, 1868–1950, vol. IV

Low, Alexander; see Low, Hon. Lord.

Low, Sir Austin, 1862–1956, vol. V

Low, Sir Charles Ernest, 1869–1941, vol. IV

Low, Charles Rathbone, 1837–1918, vol. II

Low, Sir David Alexander Cecil, 1891–1963, vol. VI

Low, David Allan, 1857–1937, vol. III

Low, David Morrice, 1890–1972, vol. VII

Low, Sir Francis, 1893–1972, vol. VII

Low, Frank Harrison, 1854–1912, vol. II

Low, Sir Frederick, 1856–1917, vol. II

Low, George Carmichael, 1872–1952, vol. V

Low, George Macritchie, 1849–1922, vol. II

Low, Harold, 1863–1932, vol. III

Low, Sir Henry Telfer, 1880–1964, vol. VI

Low, Sir Hugh, 1824–1905, vol. I

Low, Sir James, 1st Bt, 1849–1923, vol. II

Low, John Laing, 1869–1929, vol. III
Low, Mabel Bruce, *died* 1972, vol. VII
Low, Lt-Col Robert Balmain, 1864–1927, vol. II
Low, Robert Bruce, 1846–1922, vol. II
Low, Robert Cranston, 1879–1949, vol. IV
Low, Gen. Sir Robert Cunliffe, 1838–1911, vol. I
Low, Hon. Seth, 1850–1916, vol. II
Low, Sir Sidney, 1857–1932, vol. III
Low, Sir Stephen Philpot, 1883–1955, vol. V
Low, Col Stuart, 1888–1942, vol. IV
Low, Vincent Warren, *died* 1942, vol. IV
Low, Sir Walter John Morrison-, 2nd Bt, 1899–1955, vol. V
Low, Ven. Walter Percival, 1876–1960, vol. V
Low, Will Hicok, 1853–1932, vol. III
Low, William Alexander, *died* 1970, vol. VI
Low, Rev. William Leslie, 1840–1929, vol. III
Low, William Malcolm, 1835–1923, vol. II
Low, William S.; *see* Stuart-Low.
Lowdon, Andrew Gilchrist Ross, 1911–1965, vol. VI
Lowdon, John, 1881–1963, vol. VI
Lowe, Sir (Albert) George, 1901–1967, vol. VI
Lowe, Alexander Francis, 1861–1929, vol. III
Lowe, Lt-Col Arthur Cecil, 1868–1917, vol. II
Lowe, Arthur Labron, 1861–1928, vol. II
Lowe, Charles, *died* 1931, vol. III
Lowe, Sir Charles John, 1880–1969, vol. VI
Lowe, David, 1868–1947, vol. IV
Lowe, Sir David, 1899–1980, vol. VII
Lowe, Sir Drury Curzon D., *see* Drury-Lowe.
Lowe, Rev. Edward Clarke, 1823–1912, vol. I
Lowe, Edward Cronin, 1880–1958, vol. V
Lowe, Edwin Ernest, 1877–1958, vol. V
Lowe, Elias Avery, 1879–1969, vol. VI
Lowe, Mrs Eveline M., *died* 1956, vol. V
Lowe, Sir (Francis) Gordon, 2nd Bt, 1884–1972, vol. VII
Lowe, Major Francis Manley, 1859–1934, vol. III
Lowe, Rt Hon. Sir Francis William, 1st Bt, 1852–1929, vol. III
Lowe, Sir George; *see* Lowe, Sir A. G.
Lowe, Sir Gordon; *see* Lowe, Sir F. G.
Lowe, Rev. Herbert Hampson, 1865–1945, vol. IV
Lowe, Herbert John, 1892–1960, vol. V
Lowe, Rear-Adm. John, 1838–1930, vol. III
Lowe, Rev. John, 1899–1960, vol. V
Lowe, Rev. Joseph, *died* 1920, vol. II
Lowe, Sir Lionel Harold Harvey, 1897–1960, vol. V
Lowe, Percy Roycroft, 1870–1948, vol. IV
Lowe, Rouxville Mark, 1881–1957, vol. V
Lowe, Ven. Sidney Edward, 1882–1968, vol. VI
Lowe, Vice-Adm. Sidney Robert D.; *see* Drury-Lowe.
Lowe, Lt-Col Thomas Alfred, 1888–1967, vol. VI
Lowe, Maj.-Gen. William Henry Muir, 1861–1944, vol. IV
Lowe, Very Rev. William James, 1853–1931, vol. III
Lowe-Brown, William Lowe, 1876–1956, vol. V
Lowell, Abbott Lawrence, 1856–1943, vol. IV
Lowell, Amy, 1874–1925, vol. II
Lowell, Percival, 1855–1916, vol. II
Lowell, Robert Traill Spence, Jr, 1917–1977, vol. VII

Lowenfeld, Margaret Frances Jane, 1890–1973, vol. VII
Lowenthal, Charles Frederick, *died* 1933, vol. III
Lowery, Harry, 1896–1967, vol. VI
Lowes, John Livingston, 1867–1945, vol. IV
Loweth, Sidney Harold, 1893–1977, vol. VII
Loweth, Walter Ernest, 1892–1968, vol. VI
Lowinger, Victor Alexander, 1879–1957, vol. V
Lowinsky, Thomas Esmond, 1892–1947, vol. IV
Lowis, Cecil Champain, 1866–1948, vol. IV
Lowis, Frank Currie, 1872–1963, vol. VI
Lowis, Lt-Col Penton Shakspear, 1870–1931, vol. III
Lowles, Sir Geoffrey; *see* Lowles, Sir J. G. N.
Lowles, Sir (John) Geoffrey (Nelson), 1898–1962, vol. VI
Lowman, Rev. Canon Edward Sydney Charles, 1908–1974, vol. VII
Lowndes, Alan, 1921–1978, vol. VII
Lowndes, Frederic Sawrey Archibald, *died* 1940, vol. III
Lowndes, Rt Hon. Sir George Rivers, 1862–1943, vol. IV
Lowndes, Marie; *see* Belloc, Marie Adelaide.
Lowndes, Mary E., 1863–1947, vol. IV
Lowndes, Brig. Montacute William Worrall S.; *see* Selby-Lowndes.
Lowndes, Maj.-Gen. Thomas, *died* 1927, vol. II
Lowndes, William Selby-, 1836–1920, vol. II
Lowndes, Col William Selby-, 1871–1951, vol. V
Lowrey, Sir Joseph, 1859–1936, vol. III
Lowrie, Rev. Walter, 1868–1959, vol. V
Lowry, Sir Arthur, 1868–1938, vol. III
Lowry, Charles, 1857–1922, vol. II
Lowry, Charles Gibson, 1880–1951, vol. V
Lowry, Henry Dawson, 1869–1906, vol. I
Lowry, Col James, 1856–1937, vol. III
Lowry, Laurence Stephen, 1887–1976, vol. VII
Lowry, Adm. Sir Robert Swinburne, 1854–1920, vol. II
Lowry, Lt-Gen. Robert William, 1824–1905, vol. I
Lowry, Thomas Martin, 1874–1936, vol. III
Lowry, Rt Hon. William, *died* 1949, vol. IV
Lowry-Corry, Adm. Hon. Armar, 1836–1919, vol. II
Lowry-Corry, Lt-Col Sir Henry Charles, 1887–1973, vol. VII
Lowry-Corry, Col Hon. Henry William, 1845–1927, vol. II
Lowry-Corry, Brig.-Gen. Noel Armar, 1867–1935, vol. III
Lowsley, Col Herbert de Lisle P.; *see* Pollard-Lowsley.
Lowsley-Williams, George, 1869–1937, vol. III
Lowson, Sir Denys Colquhoun Flowerdew, 1st Bt, 1906–1975, vol. VII
Lowson, James Gray Flowerdew, 1860–1942, vol. IV
Lowth, Lt-Col Frank Robert, 1850–1931, vol. III
Lowth, Thomas, 1858–1931, vol. III
Lowther, Viscount; Anthony Edward Lowther, 1896–1949, vol. IV
Lowther, Maj.-Gen. Sir Cecil; *see* Lowther, Maj.-Gen. Sir H. C.

Lowther, Lt-Col Sir Charles Bingham, 4th Bt (cr 1824), 1880–1949, vol. IV
Lowther, Major Hon. Christopher William, 1887–1935, vol. III
Lowther, Claude, 1872–1929, vol. III
Lowther, Rt Hon. Sir Gerard Augustus, 1st Bt (cr 1914), 1858–1916, vol. II
Lowther, Maj.-Gen. Sir (Henry) Cecil, 1869–1940, vol. III
Lowther, Sir Henry Crofton, 1858–1939, vol. III
Lowther, Rt Hon. James, 1840–1904, vol. I
Lowther, John Arthur, 1910–1942, vol. IV
Lowther, Col John George, 1885–1977, vol. VII
Lowther, Hon. William, 1821–1912, vol. I
Lowther-Crofton, Vice-Adm. Edward George, 1873–1942, vol. IV
Lowthian, Caroline; see Prescott, C.
Loyd, Archie Kirkman, 1847–1922, vol. II
Loyd, Arthur Thomas, 1882–1944, vol. IV
Loyd, Gen. Sir Charles; see Loyd, Gen. Sir H. C.
Loyd, Edward Henry, 1861–1938, vol. III
Loyd, Gen. Sir (Henry) Charles, 1891–1973, vol. VII
Loyd, Lewis Vivian, 1852–1908, vol. I
Loyd, Llewellyn Foster, 1861–1939, vol. III
Loyd, Lady Mary, died 1936, vol. III
Loyd, Rt Rev. Philip Henry, 1884–1952, vol. V
Luard, Maj.-Gen. Charles Camac, 1867–1947, vol. IV
Luard, Lt-Col Charles Eckford, 1869–1927, vol. II
Luard, Maj.-Gen. Charles Edward, 1839–1908, vol. I
Luard, Major Edward Bourryau, 1870–1916, vol. II
Luard, Adm. John Scott, 1865–1936, vol. III
Luard, Lowes Dalbiac, died 1944, vol. IV
Luard, Comdr William Blaine, 1897–1979, vol. VII
Luard, Adm. Sir William Garnham, 1820–1910, vol. I
Lubbock, Arthur Nevile, 1869–1939, vol. III
Lubbock, Basil, 1876–1944, vol. IV
Lubbock, Cecil, 1872–1956, vol. V
Lubbock, Edgar, 1847–1907, vol. I
Lubbock, Frederic, 1844–1927, vol. II
Lubbock, Geoffrey, 1873–1932, vol. III
Lubbock, Brig.-Gen. Guy, 1870–1956, vol. V
Lubbock, Hon. Harold Fox-Pitt, 1888–1918, vol. II
Lubbock, Henry James, 1838–1910, vol. I
Lubbock, Hon. Maurice Fox Pitt, 1900–1957, vol. V
Lubbock, Montagu, 1842–1925, vol. II
Lubbock, Sir Nevile, 1839–1914, vol. I
Lubbock, Hon. Norman, 1861–1926, vol. II
Lubbock, Percy, 1879–1965, vol. VI
Lubbock, Samuel Gurney, died 1958, vol. V
Lubbock, Lady Sybil Marjorie, 1879–1943, vol. IV
Lubienski, Count Louis B.; see Bodenham-Lubienski.
Lubitsch, Ernst, 1892–1947, vol. IV
Lucan, 4th Earl of, 1830–1914, vol. I
Lucan, 5th Earl of, 1860–1949, vol. IV
Lucan, 6th Earl of, 1898–1964, vol. VI
Lucas of Chilworth, 1st Baron, 1896–1967, vol. VI

Lucas of Crudwell, 8th Baron, and Dingwall, 5th Lord, 1876–1916, vol. II
Lucas of Crudwell, Baroness (9th in line), and Dingwall, Lady (6th in line), 1880–1958, vol. V
Lucas, Col Alfred George, 1854–1941, vol. IV
Lucas, Captain Armytage Anthony, died 1950, vol. IV
Lucas, Sir Arthur, 2nd Bt, 1853–1915, vol. I
Lucas, Rev. Arthur, 1851–1921, vol. II
Lucas, Sir Arthur, 1845–1922, vol. II
Lucas, Arthur, 1863–1932, vol. III
Lucas, Brig.-Gen. Cecil Courtenay, 1883–1957, vol. V
Lucas, Rear-Adm. Charles Davis, 1834–1914, vol. I
Lucas, Charles James, 1853–1928, vol. II
Lucas, Sir Charles Prestwood, 1853–1931, vol. III
Lucas, Claude Arthur, 1894–1974, vol. VII
Lucas, Maj.-Gen. Cuthbert Henry Tindall, 1879–1958, vol. V
Lucas, Hon. Sir Edward, 1857–1950, vol. IV
Lucas, Sir Edward Lingard, 3rd Bt, 1860–1936, vol. III
Lucas, Edward Verrall, 1868–1938, vol. III
Lucas, Edward William, 1864–1940, vol. III
Lucas, Rev. Egbert de Grey, 1878–1958, vol. V
Lucas, Col Francis Alfred, 1850–1918, vol. II
Lucas, Francis Herman, 1878–1920, vol. II
Lucas, Hon. Frank Archibald William, 1881–1959, vol. V
Lucas, Frank Laurence, 1894–1967, vol. VI
Lucas, Brig.-Gen. Frederic George, 1866–1922, vol. II
Lucas, Henry Frederick Lucas, died 1943, vol. IV
Lucas, Hon. Isaac Benson, 1867–1940, vol. III
Lucas, Rt Rev. James Richard, 1867–1938, vol. III
Lucas, Major Sir Jocelyn Morton, 4th Bt, 1889–1980, vol. VII
Lucas, John Seymour, 1849–1923, vol. II
Lucas, Keith, 1879–1916, vol. I
Lucas, Marie Elizabeth Seymour, 1855–1921, vol. II
Lucas, Brig. Reginald Hutchinson, 1888–1956, vol. V
Lucas, Reginald Jaffray, 1865–1914, vol. I
Lucas, Richard Clement, died 1915, vol. I
Lucas, St John Welles, 1879–1934, vol. III
Lucas, Sir Thomas, 1st Bt, 1822–1902, vol. I
Lucas, Col Thomas John Rashleigh, 1858–1929, vol. III
Lucas, Wilfrid Irvine, 1905–1973, vol. VII
Lucas, William Henry, 1867–1937, vol. III
Lucas, Rt Rev. William Vincent, 1883–1945, vol. IV
Lucas-Shadwell, William, 1852–1915, vol. I
Lucas-Tooth, Sir (Archibald) Leonard (Lucas), 2nd Bt, 1884–1918, vol. II
Lucas-Tooth, Sir Leonard; see Lucas-Tooth, Sir A. L. L.
Lucas-Tooth, Sir Robert Lucas, 1st Bt, 1844–1915, vol. I
Lucchesi, Andrea Carlo, 1860–1925, vol. II
Luce, Rev. Arthur Aston, 1882–1977, vol. VII
Luce, Adm. Sir David; see Luce, Adm. Sir J. D.

Luce, Rev. Edward, 1851–1917, vol. II
Luce, Rev. Canon Harry Kenneth, 1897–1972, vol. VII
Luce, Henry Robinson, 1898–1967, vol. VI
Luce, Adm. John, 1870–1932, vol. III
Luce, Adm. Sir (John) David, 1906–1971, vol. VII
Luce, Morton, 1849–1943, vol. IV
Luce, Reginald William, 1893–1971, vol. VII
Luce, Maj.-Gen. Sir Richard Harman, 1867–1952, vol. V
Luce, Sir William Henry Tucker, 1907–1977, vol. VII
Lucey, Col Walter Francis, 1880–1962, vol. VI
Luciani, Albino; see John Paul I.
Lucie-Smith, Sir Alfred van W., 1854–1947, vol. IV
Lucie-Smith, Sir John Alfred, 1888–1969, vol. VI
Luck, Col Brian John Michael, 1874–1948, vol. IV
Luck, Captain Cyril Montagu, 1872–1944, vol. IV
Luck, Gen. Sir George, 1840–1916, vol. II
Luck, Richard, 1847–1920, vol. II
Lucker, Sydney Charles, 1897–1977, vol. VII
Luckes, Eva C. E., died 1919, vol. II
Luckham, Major Arthur Albert, 1883–1957, vol. V
Luckman, Ven. William Arthur Grant, 1857–1921, vol. II
Luckner, Felix, Count, 1881–1966, vol. VI
Luckock, Maj.-Gen. Russell Mortimer, 1877–1950, vol. IV
Lucy, Major Sir Brian Fulke Cameron-Ramsay-F.; see Fairfax-Lucy.
Lucy, Sir Henry, 1845–1924, vol. II
Lucy, Sir Henry William Cameron-Ramsay-F.; see Fairfax-Lucy.
Lucy, Captain Sir Montgomerie F.; see Fairfax-Lucy, Captain Sir H. M. R.
Ludbrook, Samuel Lawrence, 1895–1976, vol. VII
Ludby, Max, 1858–1943, vol. IV
Luddington, James Little, 1853–1935, vol. III
Ludlow, 1st Baron, 1827–1899, vol. I
Ludlow, 2nd Baron, 1865–1922, vol. II
Ludlow, Lady; (Alice Sedgwick), died 1945, vol. IV
Ludlow, Brig.-Gen. Edmund Ranald Owen, 1864–1929, vol. III
Ludlow, Col Edmund Samuel, 1840–1906, vol. I
Ludlow, Sir Henry, 1834–1903, vol. I
Ludlow, John Malcolm, 1821–1911, vol. I
Ludlow, Sir Richard Robert, 1882–1956, vol. V
Ludlow, Brig.-Gen. Sir Walter Robert, 1857–1941, vol. IV
Ludlow-Hewitt, Air Chief Marshal Sir Edgar Rainey, 1886–1973, vol. VII
Ludovici, Captain Anthony M., 1882–1971, vol. VII
Ludwig, Emil, 1881–1948, vol. IV
Lueger, Karl, 1844–1910, vol. I
Luff, Arthur Pearson, 1855–1938, vol. III
Luff, Richard Edmund Reife, 1887–1969, vol. VI
Lugard, 1st Baron, 1858–1945, vol. IV
Lugard, Lady; (Flora), died 1929, vol. III
Lugard, Rt Hon. Sir Edward, 1810–1898, vol. I
Lugard, Major Edward James, 1865–1957, vol. V
Lugard, Col Edward John, 1845–1911, vol. I
Lugg, Gp Captain Sidney, 1906–1972, vol. VII
Luhrs, Lt-Col Henry Gordon-, 1880–1954, vol. V

Luke, 1st Baron, 1873–1943, vol. IV
Luke, Sir Charles Manley, 1857–1941, vol. IV
Luke, Lt-Col Edward Vyvyan, 1861–1908, vol. I
Luke, Sir Harry Charles, 1884–1969, vol. VI
Luke, Sir John Pearce, 1858–1931, vol. III
Luke, Sir Kenneth George, 1898–1971, vol. VII
Luke, Stephen Paget Walter Vyvyan, 1845–1929, vol. III
Luke, Brig.-Gen. Thomas Mawe, 1872–1952, vol. V
Luke, William Joseph, 1862–1934, vol. III
Luker, Col Roland, 1878–1947, vol. IV
Lukin, Maj.-Gen. Sir Henry Timson, 1860–1925, vol. II
Lukin, Hon. Lionel Oscar, 1868–1944, vol. IV
Lukin, Brig.-Gen. Robert Clarence Wellesley, 1870–1955, vol. V
Lukis, Surg.-Gen. Hon. Sir Charles Pardey, 1857–1918, vol. II
Lukis, Maj.-Gen. Wilfrid Boyd Fellowes, 1896–1969, vol. VI
Luling, Sylvia; see Thompson, S.
Lumb, Sir Charles F., died 1911, vol. I
Lumb, Col Frederick George Edward, 1877–1958, vol. V
Lumby, Lt-Col Arthur Friedrich Rawson, 1890–1943, vol. IV
Lumby, John Henry, died 1948, vol. IV
Lumholtz, Carl, 1851–1922, vol. II
Lumière, Louis, 1864–1948, vol. IV
Lumley, Sir Dudley Owen, 1895–1964, vol. VI
Lumley, Air Cdre Eric Alfred, 1891–1979, vol. VII
Lumley, Col Francis Douglas, 1857–1925, vol. II
Lumley, Lyulph, died 1944, vol. IV
Lumley, Brig.-Gen. Hon. Osbert Victor George Atheling, 1862–1923, vol. II
Lumley, Theodore, died 1922, vol. II
Lumley-Smith, Major Sir Thomas Gabriel Lumley, 1879–1961, vol. VI
Lumsdaine, Edwin Robert John S.; see Sandys-Lumsdaine.
Lumsden, Col Bruce John David, 1907–1965, vol. VI
Lumsden, Col Dugald M'Tavish, 1851–1915, vol. I
Lumsden, E. S., 1883–1948, vol. IV
Lumsden, Maj.-Gen. Herbert, 1897–1945, vol. IV
Lumsden, Sir James Robert, 1884–1970, vol. IV
Lumsden, Sir John, 1869–1944, vol. IV
Lumsden, Dame Louisa Innes, 1840–1935, vol. III
Lumsden, Gen. Sir Peter Stark, 1829–1918, vol. II
Lumsden, Thomas William, 1874–1953, vol. V
Lumsden, Rear-Adm. Walter, 1865–1947, vol. IV
Lunawada, Rajah of, 1860–1929, vol. III
Lund, Henrik, 1879–1935, vol. III
Lund, Niels M., 1863–1916, vol. II
Lund, Lt-Gen. Sir Otto Marling, 1891–1956, vol. V
Lundgren, Captain Albert Edvin, 1878–1942, vol. IV
Lundon, Thomas, 1883–1951, vol. V
Lunham, Col Sir Ainslie, died 1930, vol. III
Lunn, Sir Arnold, 1888–1974, vol. VII
Lunn, Sir George, 1861–1939, vol. III
Lunn, Sir Henry Simpson, 1859–1939, vol. III
Lunn, Hugh Kingsmill; see Kingsmill, Hugh.

Lunn, Louise Kirkby, 1873–1930, vol. III
Lunn, William, 1872–1942, vol. IV
Lunt, Alfred, 1892–1977, vol. VII
Lunt, Rt Rev. Geoffrey Charles Lester, *died* 1948, vol. IV
Lupton, Arnold, *died* 1930, vol. III
Lupton, Arthur Sinclair, 1877–1949, vol. IV
Lupton, Charles, 1855–1935, vol. III
Lupton, John, 1869–1946, vol. IV
Lurgan, 3rd Baron, 1858–1937, vol. III
Luscombe, Sir John Henry, 1848–1937, vol. III
Luscombe, Norman Percival, 1902–1976, vol. VII
Luscombe, Ven. Popham Street, *died* 1927, vol. II
Lush, Sir Archibald James, 1900–1976, vol. VII
Lush, Rt Hon. Sir Charles Montague, 1853–1930, vol. III
Lush-Wilson, Sir Herbert W., 1850–1941, vol. IV
Lushington, Alfred Wyndham, *died* 1920, vol. II
Lushington, Major Sir Arthur Patrick Douglas, 5th Bt, 1861–1937, vol. III
Lushington, Rev. Franklyn de Winton, 1868–1941, vol. IV
Lushington, Sir Godfrey, 1832–1907, vol. I
Lushington, Maj.-Gen. Godfrey Edward W.; *see* Wildman-Lushington.
Lushington, Sir Henry, 3rd Bt, 1802–1897, vol. I
Lushington, Sir Henry, 4th Bt, 1826–1898, vol. I
Lushington, Sir Herbert Castleman, 6th Bt, 1879–1968, vol. VI
Lushington, Brig.-Gen. Stephen, 1864–1940, vol. III
Lushington, Sydney George, 1859–1909, vol. I
Lushington, Vernon, 1832–1912, vol. I
Lusk, Sir Andrew, 1st Bt, 1810–1909, vol. I
Lusk, William C., 1875–1944, vol. IV
Lustgarten, Edgar, 1907–1978, vol. VII
Luther, Col Anthony John, 1864–1937, vol. III
Luther, Rev. George Minchin, *died* 1911, vol. I
Luthuli, Albert John, 1899–1967, vol. VI
Lutosławski, Wincenty, 1863–1955, vol. V
Luttig, Hendrik Gerhardus, 1907–1975, vol. VII
Luttman, Willie Lewis, 1874–1930, vol. III
Luttman-Johnson, Lt-Col Frederic, 1845–1917, vol. II
Luttrell, Alexander Fownes, 1855–1944, vol. IV
Luttrell, George Fownes, 1826–1910, vol. I
Luttrell, Hugh Courtenay Fownes, 1857–1918, vol. II
Lutwyche, Hudson Latham, 1856–1925, vol. II
Lutyens, Sir Edwin Landseer, 1869–1944, vol. IV
Lutyens, Lady Emily, 1874–1964, vol. VI
Lützow, Count, *died* 1916, vol. II
Luwum, Most Rev. Janani, 1924–1977, vol. VII
Luxford, Major Rev. John Aldred, *died* 1921, vol. II
Luxford, John Hector, 1890–1971, vol. VII
Luxmoore, Rt Hon. Sir (Arthur) Fairfax (Charles Coryndon), 1876–1944, vol. IV
Luxmoore, Rt Hon. Sir Fairfax; *see* Luxmoore, Rt Hon. Sir A. F. C. C.
Luxmoore, Henry Elford, *died* 1926, vol. II
Luxton, Brig. Daniel Aston, 1891–1960, vol. V (A)
Luxton, Rt Rev. George Nasmith, 1901–1970, vol. VI

Luxton, Sir Harold, 1888–1957, vol. V
Luzzatti, Luigi, 1841–1927, vol. II
Lyal, David Hume, 1892–1965, vol. VI
Lyall, Rt Hon. Sir Alfred Comyn, 1835–1911, vol. I
Lyall, Archibald Laurence, 1904–1964, vol. VI
Lyall, Dame Beatrix Margaret, *died* 1948, vol. IV
Lyall, Charles Elliott, 1877–1942, vol. IV
Lyall, Sir Charles James, 1845–1920, vol. II
Lyall, David Robert, 1841–1917, vol. II
Lyall, Edna; *see* Bayly, Ada Ellen.
Lyall, Major Edward, 1869–1929, vol. III
Lyall, Frank Frederick 1872–1950, vol. IV
Lyall, George, 1883–1959, vol. V
Lyall, Col Graham Thomson, 1892–1941, vol. IV
Lyall, Sir James Broadwood, 1838–1916, vol. II
Lyall, Lt-Col Robert Adolphus, 1876–1948, vol. IV
Lyall Grant, Sir Robert William, 1875–1955, vol. V
Lyautey, Marshal Hubert, 1854–1934, vol. III
Lycett, Brig. Cyril Vernon Lechmere, 1894–1978, vol. VII
Lyddon, Vice-Adm. Sir Horace Collier, 1912–1968, vol. VI
Lyddon, Col William George, 1871–1944, vol. IV
Lyde, Lionel William, 1863–1947, vol. IV
Lydekker, Richard, 1849–1915, vol. I
Lydford, Air Marshal Sir Harold Thomas, 1898–1979, vol. VII
Lye, Lt-Col Robert Cobbe, 1865–1917, vol. II
Lyell, 1st Baron, 1850–1926, vol. II
Lyell, 2nd Baron, 1913–1943, vol. IV
Lyell, Hon. Charles Henry, 1875–1918, vol. II
Lyell, Col David, 1866–1940, vol. III
Lyell, Denis David, 1871–1946, vol. IV
Lyell, Sir Maurice Legat, 1901–1975, vol. VII
Lyell, William Darling, 1860–1925, vol. II
Lygon, Major Hon. Henry, 1884–1936, vol. III
Lygon, Lt-Col Hon. Robert, 1879–1952, vol. V
Lyle of Westbourne, 1st Baron, 1882–1954, vol. V
Lyle of Westbourne, 2nd Baron, 1905–1976, vol. VII
Lyle, Sir Alexander Park, 1st Bt (*cr* 1929), 1849–1933, vol. III
Lyle, Sir Archibald Moir Park, 2nd Bt (*cr* 1929), 1884–1946, vol. IV
Lyle, Charles, 1851–1929, vol. III
Lyle, Col George Samuel Bateson, 1865–1943, vol. IV (A)
Lyle, Sir Harold, 1873–1927, vol. II
Lyle, Henry Samuel, 1857–1916, vol. II
Lyle, Herbert Willoughby, *died* 1956, vol. V
Lyle, Col Hugh Thomas, 1858–1942, vol. IV
Lyle, Sir Ian D., 1907–1978, vol. VII
Lyle, James Duncan, 1887–1972, vol. VII
Lyle, John Cromie, 1862–1947, vol. IV
Lyle, Sir Oliver, 1890–1961, vol. VI
Lyle, Robert, 1905–1966, vol. VI
Lyle, Robert Charles, 1887–1943, vol. IV
Lyle, Sir Robert Park, 1st Bt (*cr* 1915), 1859–1923, vol. II
Lyle, Robert Patton Ranken, 1870–1950, vol. IV
Lyle, Samuel, *died* 1941, vol. IV
Lyle, Thomas McElderry, 1886–1962, vol. VI
Lyle, Sir Thomas Ranken, 1860–1944, vol. IV

417

Lyle, William, 1871–1949, vol. IV
Lyle-Samuel, Alexander, 1883–1942, vol. IV
Lymer, Brig. Rymel Watts, 1909–1972, vol. VII
Lynam, Alfred Edmund, 1873–1956, vol. V
Lynam, Edward William O'Flaherty, *died* 1950, vol. IV
Lynam, Jocelyn Humphrey Rickman, 1902–1978, vol. VII
Lynch, Col Arthur, 1861–1934, vol. III
Lynch, Col Charles Joseph, *born* 1878, vol. III
Lynch, Col David A., 1880–1944, vol. IV
Lynch, Finian, 1889–1966, vol. VI
Lynch, Francis Joseph, 1909–1980, vol. VII
Lynch, George, 1868–1928, vol. II
Lynch, George William Augustus, *died* 1940, vol. III
Lynch, G(erald) Roche, 1889–1957, vol. V
Lynch, Hannah, *died* 1904, vol. I
Lynch, Henry Finnis Blosse, 1862–1913, vol. I
Lynch, Sir Henry Joseph, 1878–1958, vol. V
Lynch, John Gilbert Bohun, 1884–1928, vol. II
Lynch, Sir John Patrick, 1858–1921, vol. II
Lynch, Patrick, *died* 1947, vol. IV
Lynch, Hon. Patrick Joseph, 1867–1944, vol. IV
Lynch, Richard Irwin, 1850–1924, vol. II
Lynch, Captain Vincent James, 1892–1961, vol. VI
Lynch, William Joseph, 1853–1937, vol. III
Lynch-Blosse, Sir David Edward, 16th Bt, 1925–1971, vol. VII
Lynch-Blosse, Sir Henry, 15th Bt, 1884–1969, vol. VI
Lynch-Blosse, Sir Robert Cyril; *see* Blosse.
Lynch-Blosse, Sir Robert Geoffrey; *see* Blosse.
Lynch-Robinson, Sir Christopher Henry, 2nd Bt, 1884–1958, vol. V
Lynch-White, Lt-Col Robert, 1875–1940, vol. III
Lynd, Robert, 1879–1949, vol. IV
Lynd, Sylvia, 1888–1952, vol. V
Lynde, Carleton J., 1872–1971, vol. VII
Lynden-Bell, Maj.-Gen. Sir Arthur Lynden, 1867–1943, vol. IV
Lynden-Bell, Col Edward Horace Lynden, 1858–1922, vol. II
Lyndhurst, Lady; (Georgina), *died* 1901, vol. I
Lyne, Arthur W., 1884–1971, vol. VII
Lyne, Joseph Leycester; *see* Ignatius, Father.
Lyne, Rev. Leonard Augustus, *died* 1919, vol. II
Lyne, Maj.-Gen. Lewis Owen, 1899–1970, vol. VI
Lyne, Robert Francis, 1885–1957, vol. V
Lyne, Robert Nunez, 1864–1961, vol. VI
Lyne, Rear-Adm. Sir Thomas John Spence, 1870–1955, vol. V
Lyne, Hon. Sir William John, 1844–1913, vol. I
Lynen, Feodor, 1911–1979, vol. VII
Lynes, Rear-Adm. Charles Edward, 1875–1977, vol. VII
Lynes, Rear-Adm. Hubert, 1874–1942, vol. IV
Lynham, John E. A., 1882–1946, vol. IV
Lynn, Col Graham Rigby, *died* 1966, vol. VI
Lynn, Rev. Joseph, 1887–1956, vol. V
Lynn, Ralph, 1882–1962, vol. VI
Lynn, Sir Robert, 1873–1945, vol. IV
Lynn, William H., *died* 1915, vol. I
Lynn-Jenkins, Frank, 1870–1927, vol. II

Lynn-Thomas, Sir John, 1861–1939, vol. III
Lynskey, Sir George Justin, 1888–1957, vol. V
Lynx, Larry; *see* Sarl, Arthur J.
Lyon, Sir Alexander, 1850–1927, vol. II
Lyon, Lt-Col Charles, 1865–1944, vol. IV
Lyon, Brig.-Gen. Charles Harry, 1878–1959, vol. V
Lyon, Brig. Cyril Arthur, 1880–1955, vol. V
Lyon, Hon. Sir David B.; *see* Bowes-Lyon.
Lyon, David Murray, 1888–1956, vol. V
Lyon, Brig.-Gen. Francis, 1867–1953, vol. V
Lyon, Hon. Francis B.; *see* Bowes-Lyon.
Lyon, Maj.-Gen. Sir Francis James Cecil B.; *see* Bowes-Lyon.
Lyon, Captain Geoffrey Francis B.; *see* Bowes-Lyon.
Lyon, Adm. Sir George Hamilton D'Oyly, 1883–1947, vol. IV
Lyon, Adm. Herbert, 1856–1919, vol. II
Lyon, Brig. Surg. Lt-Col Isidore Bernadotte, 1839–1911, vol. I
Lyon, Kenneth, 1886–1956, vol. V
Lyon, Laurance, 1875–1932, vol. III
Lyon, Malcolm Douglas, 1898–1964, vol. VI
Lyon, Hon. Michael Claude Hamilton B.; *see* Bowes-Lyon.
Lyon, Percy Comyn, 1862–1952, vol. V
Lyon, Lt-Col Ralph Edward, 1865–1930, vol. III
Lyon, Rev. Ralph John, *died* 1914, vol. I
Lyon, Robert, 1894–1978, vol. VII
Lyon, Captain Ronald George B.; *see* Bowes Lyon.
Lyon, Thomas Glover, 1855–1915, vol. I (A)
Lyon, Thomas Henry, 1825–1914, vol. I
Lyon, Thomas Stewart, 1866–1946, vol. IV
Lyon, Ursula Mary, *died* 1961, vol. VI
Lyon, Ven. William John, 1883–1961, vol. VI
Lyons of Brighton, Baron (Life Peer); Braham Jack Dennis Lyons, 1918–1978, vol. VII
Lyons, A. Neil, 1880–1940, vol. III
Lyons, Abraham Montagu, 1894–1961, vol. VI
Lyons, Sir Algernon M'Lennan, 1833–1908, vol. I
Lyons, Eric Alfred, 1912–1980, vol. VII
Lyons, Col Sir Henry George, 1864–1944, vol. IV
Lyons, Most Rev. John, 1878–1958, vol. V
Lyons, Sir Joseph, *died* 1917, vol. II
Lyons, Rt Hon. Joseph Aloysius, 1879–1939, vol. III
Lyons, Mrs Miriam Isabel, 1880–1968, vol. VI
Lyons, Most Rev. Patrick, 1875–1949, vol. IV
Lyons, Most Rev. Patrick Francis, 1903–1967, vol. VI
Lyons, Rt Hon. William Henry Holmes, 1843–1924, vol. II
Lyons-Montgomery, Col Hugh Frederick, 1856–1931, vol. III
Lys, Christian; *see* Brebner, P. J.
Lys, Rev. Francis John, 1863–1947, vol. IV
Lysaght, Desmond Royse, 1903–1970, vol. VI
Lysaght, Gerald Stuart, 1869–1951, vol. V
Lysaght, Hon. Horace George, 1873–1918, vol. II
Lysaght, Sidney Royse, *died* 1941, vol. IV
Lysaght, William Royse, 1858–1945, vol. IV
Lysons, Sir Daniel, 1816–1898, vol. I
Lyster, Anthony St George, 1888–1971, vol. VII

Lyster, Adm. Sir (Arthur) Lumley (St George), 1888–1957, vol. V
Lyster, Cecil Rupert Chaworth, 1859–1920, vol. II
Lyster, Lt-Gen. Harry Hammon, 1830–1922, vol. II
Lyster, Very Rev. Henry Cameron, 1862–1932, vol. III
Lyster, Rt Rev. John, 1850–1911, vol. I
Lyster, Adm. Sir Lumley; *see* Lyster, Adm. Sir A. L. St G.
Lyster, Robert Arthur, *died* 1955, vol. V
Lyster, Thomas William, 1855–1922, vol. II
Lyte, Sir Henry Churchill Maxwell-, 1848–1940, vol. III
Lythgoe, Sir James, 1891–1972, vol. VII
Lythgoe, Richard James, 1896–1940, vol. III
Lyttelton, Rt Hon. Alfred, 1857–1913, vol. I
Lyttelton, Hon. Mrs Alfred, (Dame Edith Lyttelton), *died* 1948, vol. IV
Lyttelton, Rev. Hon. Charles Frederick, 1887–1931, vol. III
Lyttelton, Dame Edith; *see* Lyttelton, Hon. Mrs Alfred.
Lyttelton, Rev. Hon. Edward, 1855–1942, vol. IV
Lyttelton, Hon. George William, 1883–1962, vol. VI
Lyttelton, Hon. George William Spencer, 1847–1913, vol. I
Lyttelton, Gen. Rt Hon. Sir Neville Gerald, 1845–1931, vol. III
Lyttelton, Hon. Robert Henry, 1854–1939, vol. III
Lyttelton, Comdr Stephen Clive, 1887–1959, vol. V
Lyttelton-Annesley, Lt-Gen. Sir Arthur Lyttelton, 1837–1926, vol. II
Lytton, 2nd Earl of, 1876–1947, vol. IV
Lytton, 3rd Earl of, 1879–1951, vol. V
Lytton, Countess of; (Edith), 1841–1936, vol. III
Lytton, Lady Constance Georgina, 1869–1923, vol. II
Lytton, Sir Henry Alfred, 1867–1936, vol. III
Lytton Sells, Arthur Lytton, 1895–1978, vol. VII
Lyveden, 2nd Baron, 1824–1900, vol. I
Lyveden, 3rd Baron, 1857–1926, vol. II
Lyveden, 4th Baron, 1892–1969, vol. VI
Lyveden, 5th Baron, 1888–1973, vol. VII
Lywood, Air Vice-Marshal Oswyn George William Gifford, 1895–1957, vol. V

M

Maartens, Maarten, 1858–1915, vol. I
Maas, Paul, 1880–1964, vol. VI
Maasdorp, Hon. Sir Andries Ferdinand Stockenström, 1847–1931, vol. III
Maasdorp, Christian George, 1848–1926, vol. II
Maass, Otto, 1890–1961, vol. VI
Mabane, 1st Baron, 1895–1969, vol. VI
Maberly, Col Charles Evan, 1854–1920, vol. II
Mabie, Hamilton Wright, *died* 1917, vol. II
Mabson, Richard Rous, 1846–1933, vol. III
Maby, Sir Charles George, 1888–1967, vol. VI

Macadam, Sir Ivison Stevenson, 1894–1974, vol. VII
McAdam, Robert, 1906–1978, vol. VII
Macadam, Col Walter, 1865–1930, vol. III
M'Adam, Walter, 1866–1935, vol. III
McAdam, William, 1886–1952, vol. V
MacAdam, William, 1885–1976, vol. VII
McAdam, William Alexander, 1889–1961, vol. VI
McAdden, Sir Stephen James, 1907–1979, vol. VII
McAdoo, William Gibbs, 1863–1941, vol. IV
Macafee, Charles Horner Greer, 1898–1978, vol. VII
Macafee, Col John Leeper Anketell, 1915–1974, vol. VII
McAleer, Hugh K., *died* 1941, vol. IV
Macaleese, Daniel, 1840–1900, vol. I
MacAlevey, Maj.-Gen. Gerald Esmond, 1894–1969, vol. VI
Macalister, Alexander, 1844–1919, vol. II
Macalister, Charles John, *died* 1943, vol. IV
MacAlister, Sir Donald, 1st Bt, 1854–1934, vol. III
Macalister, George Hugh Kidd, 1879–1930, vol. III
MacAlister, Sir Ian, 1878–1957, vol. V
MacAlister, Sir John Young Walker, 1856–1925, vol. II
McAlister, Mary A., (Mrs J. Alexander McAlister), *died* 1976, vol. VII
Macalister, Robert Alexander Stewart, 1870–1950, vol. IV
Macalister, Sir Robert Lachlan, 1890–1967, vol. VI
McAlister, Samuel, 1896–1971, vol. VII
McAlister, William James, 1877–1937, vol. III
Macalister-Hall, William, 1872–1938, vol. III
McAllen, Captain Thomas Wilfred, 1888–1957, vol. V
McAllister, Alister; *see* Wharton, Anthony.
McAllister, Gilbert, 1906–1964, vol. VI
Macallum, Archibald Byron, 1858–1934, vol. III
McAlpin, Malcolm Caird, 1876–1930, vol. III
McAlpine, Sir Alfred David, 1881–1944, vol. IV
McAlpine, Sir (Alfred) Robert, 3rd Bt, 1907–1968, vol. VI
Macalpine, Sir George Watson, 1850–1920, vol. II
MacAlpine, J(ohn) Warren, *died* 1956, vol. V
McAlpine, Sir Malcolm; *see* McAlpine, Sir T. M.
McAlpine, Sir Robert; *see* McAlpine, Sir A. R.
McAlpine, Sir Robert, 1st Bt, 1847–1934, vol. III
McAlpine, Sir Robert, 2nd Bt, 1868–1934, vol. III
McAlpine, Sir (Thomas) Malcolm, 1877–1967, vol. VI
Macalpine-Leny, Bt Lt-Col R. L.; *see* Leny.
Macan, Sir Arthur Vernon, 1843–1908, vol. I
Macan, Reginald Walter, 1848–1941, vol. IV
Macan, Col Thomas Townley, 1860–1934, vol. III
Macan-Markar, Hadji Sir Mohamed, 1879–1952, vol. VI (AI)
McAnally, Rev. Charles Mortimer, 1854–1938, vol. III
McAnally, Sir Henry William Watson, 1870–1952, vol. V
Macandie, George Lionel, 1877–1968, vol. VI
MacAndrew, 1st Baron, 1888–1979, vol. VII
Macandrew, Sir Henry Cockburn, 1832–1898, vol. I

Macandrew, Maj.-Gen. Henry John Milnes, 1866–1919, vol. II

MacAndrew, Lt-Col James Orr, 1899–1979, vol. VII

Macann, Lt-Col Arthur Ernest Henry, 1898–1944, vol. IV

Macara, Sir Charles Wright, 1st Bt, 1845–1929, vol. III

McAra, Sir Thomas W., 1864–1942, vol. IV

Macara, Sir William Cowper, 2nd Bt, 1875–1931, vol. III

M'Ardle, John Stephen, 1859–1928, vol. II

Macardle, Sir Thomas Callan, 1856–1925, vol. II

M'Arthur, Alexander, 1814–1909, vol. I

M'Arthur, Charles, 1844–1910, vol. I

McArthur, Donald Neil, 1892–1965, vol. VI

MacArthur, General of the Army Douglas, 1880–1964, vol. VI

McArthur, Hon. Sir Gordon Stewart, 1896–1965, vol. VI

Macarthur, Sir Ian Hannay, 1906–1975, vol. VII

Macarthur, Rt Rev. James, 1848–1922, vol. II

Macarthur, Mary Reid, 1880–1921, vol. II

MacArthur, Neil, 1886–1973, vol. VII

MacArthur, Sir Oliphant; see MacArthur, Sir W. O.

McArthur, Hon. Sir Stewart; see McArthur, Hon. Sir W. G. S.

M'Arthur, William Alexander, born 1857, vol. II

McArthur, Hon. Sir (William Gilbert) Stewart, 1861–1935, vol. III

McArthur, William Lyon, 1870–1946, vol. IV

MacArthur, Sir (William) Oliphant, 1871–1953, vol. V

MacArthur, Lt-Gen. Sir William Porter, 1884–1964, vol. VI

Macarthur Onslow, Brig.-Gen. George Macleay, 1875–1931, vol. III

Macarthur-Onslow, Maj.-Gen. Hon James William, 1867–1946, vol. IV

Macartney, Sir Alexander Miller, 5th Bt, 1869–1960, vol. V

Macartney, Carlile Aylmer, 1895–1978, vol. VII

Macartney, Sir Edward Henry, 1863–1956, vol. V

Macartney, Sir George, 1867–1945, vol. IV

Macartney, Sir Halliday, 1833–1906, vol. I

Macartney, Lt-Col Henry Dundas Keith, 1880–1932, vol. III

Macartney, Sir John, 3rd Bt, 1832–1911, vol. I (A)

Macartney, John William Ellison-, 1818–1904, vol. I

Macartney, John William Merton, 1850–1925, vol. II

Macartney, Sir Mervyn Edmund, died 1932, vol. III

Macartney, Rt Hon. Sir William Grey Ellison-, 1852–1924, vol. II

Macartney, Sir William Isaac, 4th Bt, 1867–1942, vol. IV

Macartney-Filgate, John Victor Opynschae, 1897–1964, vol. VI

Macaskie, Charles Frederick Cunningham, 1888–1969, vol. VI

Macaskie, Nicholas Lechmere Cunningham, 1881–1967, vol. VI

Macaskie, Stuart Cunningham, 1853–1903, vol. I

Macassey, Rev. Ernest Livingston, died 1947, vol. IV

Macassey, Sir Lynden Livingston, 1876–1963, vol. VI

M'Aulay, Alexander, 1863–1931, vol. III

Macaulay, Rev. Alexander Beith, 1871–1950, vol. IV

Macaulay, Sir Alfred Newton, 1864–1939, vol. III

McAulay, Allan; see Stewart, Charlotte.

Macaulay, Francis Sowerby, 1862–1937, vol. III

Macaulay, Frederic Julius, 1830–1912, vol. I

Macaulay, G. C., 1852–1915, vol. I

Macaulay, James, 1817–1902, vol. I

Macaulay, Very Rev. James J., 1870–1951, vol. V

Macaulay, James Morison, 1889–1955, vol. V

Macaulay, Rev. John Heyrick, died 1914, vol. I

Macaulay, Hon. Leopold, 1887–1979, vol. VII

Macaulay, Dame Rose, died 1958, vol. V

Macaulay, Thomas Bassett, 1860–1942, vol. IV

Macaulay, William Herrick, 1853–1936, vol. III

Macaulay, William J. B., 1892–1964, vol. VI

Macaulay-Owen, Peter, 1906–1962, vol. VI

Macauley, Brig.-Gen. Sir George Bohun, 1869–1940, vol. III

McAuliffe, Gen. Anthony Clement, 1898–1975, vol. VII

McAuliffe, Sir Henry T., 1867–1951, vol. V

McAvity, Lt-Col Thomas Malcolm, 1889–1944, vol. IV

Macbain, Alexander, 1855–1907, vol. I

McBain, Alexander Richardson, 1887–1971, vol. VII

M'Bain, James Anderson Dickson, 1869–1938, vol. III

McBain, James William, 1882–1953, vol. V

McBain, Rev. John, 1871–1936, vol. III

McBarnet, Alexander Cockburn, 1867–1934, vol. III

M'Barnet, Lt-Col Alexander Edward, 1865–1932, vol. III

McBean, Col Alexander, 1854–1937, vol. III

Macbean, Maj.-Gen. Forbes, 1857–1919, vol. II

Macbean, Gen. George Scougal, died 1903, vol. I

Macbean, Captain John Albert Emmanuel, 1865–1900, vol. I

Macbean, Reginald Gambier, 1859–1942, vol. IV

Macbeath, Alexander, 1888–1964, vol. VI

Macbeath, Rev. John, died 1967, vol. VI

McBeath, Sir William George, 1865–1931, vol. III

McBee, Silas, 1853–1924, vol. II

Macbeth, Alexander Killen, 1889–1957, vol. V

Macbeth, Rev. John, 1841–1924, vol. II

Macbeth, Percy, 1877–1938, vol. III

Macbeth, Robert Walker, 1848–1910, vol. I

Macbeth-Raeburn, Henry Raeburn; see Raeburn.

McBey, James, 1883–1959, vol. V

MacBride, Alexander, 1859–1955, vol. V

MacBride, Ernest William, 1866–1940, vol. III

MacBride, Geoffrey Ernest Derek, 1917–1975, vol. VII

McBride, Neil, 1910–1974, vol. VII

M'Bride, Hon. Sir Peter, 1867–1923, vol. II

M'Bride, Peter, 1854–1946, vol. IV

M'Bride, Sir Richard, 1870–1917, vol. II

McBride, Robert, *died* 1934, vol. III

Macbride, Robert Knox, 1844–1905, vol. I

McBride, Wilbert George, 1879–1943, vol. IV

McBride, Vice-Adm. Sir William, 1895–1959, vol. V

MacBrien, Maj.-Gen. Sir James Howden, 1878–1938, vol. III

McBryde, Hon. Duncan Elphinstone, 1853–1920, vol. II

McBurney, Charles Brian Montagu, 1914–1979, vol. VII

McCabe, Alasdair, *died* 1972, vol. VII

M'Cabe, Sir Daniel, 1852–1919, vol. II

MacCabe, Sir Francis Xavier Frederick, 1833–1914, vol. I

McCabe, Joseph, 1867–1955, vol. V

Maccaffrey, Rt Rev. Mgr James, 1875–1935, vol. III

McCahearty, Ven. Reginald George Henry, *died* 1966, vol. VI

McCall, Sir Alexander, *died* 1973, vol. VII

McCall, Charles William Home, 1877–1958, vol. V

Maccall, Hon. Maj.-Gen. Henry Blackwood, 1845–1921, vol. II

McCall, Adm. Sir Henry William Urquhart, 1895–1980, vol. VII

McCall, Lt-Col Hugh William, 1878–1957, vol. V

M'Call, Hon. Sir John, 1860–1919, vol. II

M'Call, Brig.-Gen. John P.; *see* Pollok-M'Call.

McCall, Sir Robert Alfred, 1849–1934, vol. III

McCall, Robert Clark, 1906–1970, vol. VI

McCall, Rt Rev. Theodore Bruce, 1911–1969, vol. VI

McCall, William, 1851–1929, vol. III

MacCallan, Arthur Ferguson, *died* 1955, vol. V

McCallum, Colin Whitton; *see* Coborn, Charles.

McCallum, Major Sir Duncan, 1888–1958, vol. V

McCallum, Col Sir Henry Edward, 1852–1919, vol. II

MacCallum, James Dalgleish Kellie, 1845–1932, vol. III

McCallum, Rev. John Donaldson, 1856–1930, vol. III

McCallum, Major John Dunwoodie Martin, 1883–1967, vol. VI

M'Callum, Sir John Mills, 1847–1920, vol. II

MacCallum, Sir Mungo William, 1854–1942, vol. IV

MacCallum, Sir Peter, 1885–1975, vol. VII

McCallum, Ronald Buchanan, 1898–1973, vol. VII

McCallum, Sir William Alexander, 1883–1959, vol. V

MacCalman, Douglas Robert, 1903–1957, vol. V

M'Calmont, Col Barklie Cairns, 1860–1929, vol. III

M'Calmont, Harry Leslie Blundell, 1861–1902, vol. I

McCalmont, Maj.-Gen. Sir Hugh, 1845–1924, vol. II

M'Calmont, James Martin, 1847–1913, vol. I

McCalmont, Brig.-Gen. Sir Robert Chaine Alexander, 1881–1953, vol. V

M'Cammond, Sir William, 1831–1898, vol. I

McCandlish, Douglas, 1883–1954, vol. V

McCandlish, Maj.-Gen. John Edward Chalmers, 1901–1974, vol. VII

McCandlish, Lt-Col Patrick Dalmahoy, 1871–1942, vol. IV

McCann, Sir Charles Francis Gerald, 1880–1951, vol. V

McCann, Frederick John, *died* 1941, vol. IV

M'Cann, James, *died* 1904, vol. I

McCann, John, 1910–1972, vol. VII

McCann, P., *died* 1920, vol. II

McCann, Rt Rev. Philip Justin, 1882–1959, vol. V

M'Cann, Thomas S., 1868–1942, vol. IV

McCannell, Otway, 1883–1969, vol. VI

McCardie, Sir Henry Alfred, 1869–1933, vol. III

McCarrison, Maj.-Gen. Sir Robert, 1878–1960, vol. V

McCarroll, James Joseph, 1889–1937, vol. III

McCarroll, Col James Neil, 1873–1951, vol. V

McCarron, Edward Patrick, *died* 1970, vol. VI

M'Cartan, Michael, 1851–1902, vol. I

McCartan, Patrick, 1878–1963, vol. VI

MacCarthy, Sir Desmond, 1877–1952, vol. V

McCarthy, Adm. Sir Desmond; *see* McCarthy, Adm. Sir E. D. B.

McCarthy, Adm. Sir (Edward) Desmond (Bewley), 1893–1966, vol. VI

McCarthy, Most Rev. Edward Joseph, 1850–1931, vol. III

McCarthy, Sir Edwin, 1896–1980, vol. VII

McCarthy, Sir Frank, *died* 1924, vol. II

M'Carthy, James Desmond, *died* 1923, vol. II

McCarthy, Rt Rev. James W., 1853–1943, vol. IV

M'Carthy, Jeremiah, *died* 1924, vol. II

McCarthy, Most Rev. John, 1858–1950, vol. IV

McCarthy, John William, 1854–1935, vol. III

McCarthy, Joseph R., 1909–1957, vol. V

M'Carthy, Justin, 1830–1912, vol. I (A)

M'Carthy, Justin Huntly, 1861–1936, vol. III

McCarthy, Hon. Leighton Goldie, 1869–1952, vol. V

McCarthy, Sir Leslie Ernest Vivian, 1885–1970, vol. VI

McCarthy, Lillah, (Lady Keeble), 1875–1960, vol. V

M'Carthy, Marie Cecilia, 1876–1943, vol. IV

McCarthy, Dame Maud, 1858–1949, vol. IV

McCarthy, Michael John Fitzgerald, *died* 1928, vol. II

MacCarthy, Brig.-Gen. Morgan John, 1867–1939, vol. III

McCarthy, Sir Mortimer Eugene, 1890–1967, vol. VI

McCarthy, Ralph, 1906–1976, vol. VII

M'Carthy, Robert Henry, *died* 1927, vol. II

McCarthy, Tim, *died* 1928, vol. II

McCarthy, Lt-Col W. H. Leslie, 1885–1962, vol. VI

Maccarthy, Rt Rev. Welbore, *died* 1925, vol. II

MacCarthy-Morrogh, Lt-Col Donald Florence, 1869–1932, vol. III

McCarthy-O'Leary, Brig. Heffernan William Denis; *see* O'Leary.

Maccartie, Lt-Col Frederick Fitzgerald, 1851–1916, vol. II

McCartney, James Elvins, 1891–1969, vol. VI
McCaughey, Sir (David) Roy, 1898–1971, vol. VII
McCaughey, Sir Roy; see McCaughey, Sir D. R.
M'Caughey, Hon. Sir Samuel, died 1919, vol. II
McCaul, Ethel Rosalie Ferrier, 1867–1931, vol. III
McCauley, Ven. George James, died 1917, vol. II
M'Causland, Lt-Gen. Edwin Loftus, died 1923, vol. II
McCausland, Rt Hon. Maurice Marcus, 1872–1938, vol. III
M'Causland, Sir Richard Bolton, 1810–1900, vol. I
McCausland, Maj.Gen. William Henry, 1836–1916, vol. II
McCaw, George Tyrrell, 1870–1942, vol. IV
MacCaw, Sir Vivian, 1883–1936, vol. III
MacCaw, William John MacGeagh, died 1928, vol. II
McCawley, Thomas William, 1881–1925, vol. II
McCay, Lt-Col David, 1873–1948, vol. IV
M'Cay, Lt-Gen. Hon. Sir James Whiteside, 1864–1930, vol. III
McCay, L.-Gen. (Hon.) Sir Ross Cairns, 1895–1969, vol. VI
McCheane, Col Montague William Hiley, 1872–1955, vol. V
MacChesney, Brig.-Gen. Nathan William, 1878–1954, vol. V
McClaughry, Air Vice-Marshal Wilfred Ashton, 1894–1943, vol. IV
McClean, (Donald Francis) Stuart, 1909–1960, vol. V
McClean, Sir Francis Kennedy, 1876–1955, vol. V
M'Clean, Frank, 1837–1904, vol. I
McClean, Rt Rev. Gerard; see McClean, Rt Rev. J. G.
McClean, Rt Rev. (John) Gerard, 1914–1978, vol. VII
McClean, Rev. Richard Arthur, 1862–1948, vol. IV
McClean, Stuart; see McClean, D. F. S.
McCleary, George Frederick, 1867–1962, vol. VI
McCleary, Robert, 1869–1936, vol. III
McCleery, Rt Hon. Sir William Victor, 1887–1957, vol. V
M'Clelan, Hon. Abner Reid, 1831–1917, vol. II
McClellan, Frank Campbell, 1871–1957, vol. V
McClellan, George B., 1865–1940, vol. III
M'Clellan, Rev. John B., died 1916, vol. II
McClellan, John William Tyndale, 1865–1948, vol. IV
McClelland, Rev. Henry Simpson, 1882–1961, vol. VI
McClelland, Hugh Charles, 1893–1966, vol. VI
M'Clelland, John Alexander, 1870–1920, vol. II
McClelland, Sir Peter Hannay, 1856–1924, vol. II
McClelland, William, 1889–1968 (this entry was not transferred to Who was Who).
McClelland, William, 1873–1971, vol. VII
McClemens, John Henry, 1905–1975, vol. VII
Macclement, William Thomas, 1861–1938, vol. III
McClenaghan, Ven. Henry St George, 1865–1950, vol. IV
McClenaghan, Herbert Eric St George, 1896–1955, vol. V

Macclesfield, 7th Earl of, 1888–1975, vol. VII
McClintic, Katharine, (Mrs Guthrie McClintic); see Cornell, K.
M'Clintock, Lt-Col Arthur George, 1878–1936, vol. III
M'Clintock, Arthur George Florence, 1856–1930, vol. III
M'Clintock, Major Augustus, 1866–1912, vol. I
McClintock, Very Rev. Francis George le Poer, died 1924, vol. II
M'Clintock, Sir Francis Leopold, 1819–1907, vol. I
McClintock, Bt Col John Knox, 1864–1936, vol. III
McClintock, Vice-Adm. John William Leopold, 1874–1929, vol. III
McClintock, Lt-Col Robert Lyle, 1874–1943, vol. IV
McClintock, Brig.-Gen. William Kerr, 1858–1940, vol. III
McCloughry, Air Vice-Marshal Edgar James K.; see Kingston-McCloughry.
McCloy, John Moorcroft, 1874–1943, vol. IV
M'Clure, Alexander Logan, 1860–1932, vol. III
M'Clure, Rev. Edmund, died 1922, vol. II
McClure, George Buchanan, 1887–1955, vol. V
McClure, J. Campbell, 1873–1934, vol. III
M'Clure, James Gore King, 1848–1932, vol. III
McClure, Sir John David, 1860–1922, vol. II
McClure, Samuel S., 1857–1949, vol. IV
MacClure, Victor, 1887–1963, vol. VI
McClure, Sir William Kidston, 1877–1939, vol. III
McClure-Smith, Hugh Alexander, 1902–1961, vol. VI
McCluskey, Alexander, 1908–1959, vol. V
M'Clymont, Rt Rev. James A., 1848–1927, vol. II
McClymont, Lt-Col Robert Arthur, 1874–1949, vol. IV
MacColl, Sir Albert Edward, 1882–1951, vol. V
McColl, Sir Alexander Lowe, 1878–1962, vol. VI
McColl, Angus John, 1854–1902, vol. I
MacColl, Dugald Sutherland, 1859–1948, vol. IV
McColl, Col George Guthrie, 1858–1938, vol. III
MacColl, James Eugene, 1908–1971, vol. VII
M'Coll, Hon. James Hiers, 1844–1929, vol. III
MacColl, Rev. Malcolm, 1831–1907, vol. I
MacColl, Norman, 1843–1905, vol. I
MacColl, René, 1905–1971, vol. VII
McCollum, Elmer Verner, 1879–1967, vol. VI
McColvin, Lionel Roy, 1896–1976, vol. VII
McComas, Robert Bond, 1862–1938, vol. III
McComb, Col Robert Brophy, 1855–1925, vol. II (A), vol. III
McComb, Rev. Samuel, 1864–1938, vol. III
McCombe, Francis William Walker, 1894–1969, vol. VI
McCombe, Lt-Col Gault, 1885–1970, vol. VI (AII)
McCombe, Brig. John Smith, 1885–1959, vol. V
McCombie, Major Hamilton, 1880–1962, vol. VI
McCombie, Col William McCombie D.; see Duguid-McCombie.
McConachie, George William Grant, 1909–1965, vol. VI
M'Conaghey, Lt-Col Allen, 1864–1925, vol. II

McConaghy, Hugh, 1877–1943, vol. IV
McConaghy, Col John Gerald, 1879–1942, vol. IV
McConnach, James, 1896–1955, vol. V
McConnan, Sir Leslie James, 1887–1954, vol. V
McConnel, Maj.-Gen. Douglas Fitzgerald, 1893–1961, vol. VI
McConnel, John Wanklyn, 1855–1922, vol. II
McConnell, Adams Andrew, 1884–1973, vol. VII
McConnell, Sir Joseph, 2nd Bt, 1877–1942, vol. IV
M'Connell, Robert, died 1942, vol. IV
M'Connell, Sir Robert John, 1st Bt, 1853–1927, vol. II
McConnell, Sir Thomas Edward, 1868–1938, vol. III
M'Connell, W. R., 1837–1906, vol. I
McCorkell, Sir Dudley Evelyn Bruce, 1883–1960, vol. V
McCorkill, Hon. John Charles, 1854–1920, vol. II
MacCormac, Henry, died 1950, vol. IV
Mac Cormac, Sir William, 1st Bt, 1836–1901, vol. I
McCormack, Arthur John, 1866–1936, vol. III
MacCormack, Charles Joseph, 1861–1952, vol. V
Maccormack, Rt Rev. Francis Joseph, 1833–1909, vol. I
McCormack, John, Count, 1884–1945, vol. IV
McCormack, John William, 1891–1980, vol. VII
McCormack, Rt Rev. Joseph, 1887–1958, vol. V
McCormack, Percy Hicks, 1890–1980, vol. VII
McCormack, Hon. William, 1879–1947, vol. IV
MacCormick, Sir Alexander, 1856–1947, vol. IV
McCormick, Lt-Col Andrew Louis Charles, 1869–1943, vol. IV
McCormick, Anne O'Hare, died 1954, vol. V
M'Cormick, Arthur David, 1860–1943, vol. IV
McCormick, Ven. George Fitzherbert, died 1935, vol. III
McCormick, Gerald Bernard, died 1966, vol. VI
McCormick, Rev. James, died 1921, vol. II
McCormick, Major James Hanna, 1875–1955, vol. V
MacCormick, John MacDonald, 1904–1961, vol. VI
McCormick, Rt Rev. John Newton, 1863–1939, vol. III (A), vol. IV
McCormick, Rev. Joseph, 1834–1914, vol. I
McCormick, Very Rev. Joseph Gough, 1874–1924, vol. II
MacCormick, Brig. Kenneth, 1891–1963, vol. VI
McCormick, Adm. Lynde Dupuy, 1895–1956, vol. V
M'Cormick, Robert, died 1919, vol. II
McCormick, Robert Rutherford, 1880–1955, vol. V
McCormick, Rev. William Patrick Glyn, 1877–1940, vol. III
M'Cormick, Sir William Symington, 1859–1930, vol. III
McCormick-Goodhart, Leander, 1884–1965, vol. VI
McCorquodale of Newton, 1st Baron, 1901–1971, vol. VII
McCosh, Andrew Kirkwood, 1880–1967, vol. VI
McCosh, Robert, 1885–1959, vol. V
McCourt, Hon. William, died 1913, vol. I (A)
McCourt, William Rupert, 1884–1947, vol. IV

McCowan, Sir David, 1st Bt, 1860–1937, vol. III
McCowan, Sir David James Cargill, 2nd Bt, 1897–1965, vol. VI
McCowan, Lt-Col William Hew, 1878–1958, vol. V
McCowen, Oliver Hill, 1870–1942, vol. IV
M'Coy, Sir Frederick, 1823–1899, vol. I
McCoy, Captain James Abernethy, 1900–1955, vol. V
Maccoy, Sir John, 1843–1935, vol. III
McCoy, William Frederick, died 1976, vol. VII
McCoy, William Taylor, 1866–1929, vol. III
McCracken, Esther Helen, 1902–1971, vol. VII
McCracken, Lt-Gen. Sir Frederick William Nicholas, 1859–1949, vol. IV
Maccracken, Henry Mitchell, 1840–1919, vol. II
MacCracken, Henry Noble, 1880–1970, vol. VI
McCracken, William, died 1948, vol. IV
M'Crae, Sir George, 1860–1928, vol. II
McCraith, Sir Douglas, 1878–1952, vol. V
McCraith, Sir James William, 1853–1928, vol. II
M'Craith, Sir John Tom, 1847–1919, vol. II
McCraken, Sir Robert, 1846–1924, vol. II
McCrea, Rev. Alexander, 1879–1963, vol. VI
McCrea, Brig.-Gen. Alfred Coryton, 1864–1942, vol. IV
McCrea, Charles, 1877–1952, vol. V
McCrea, Major Frederick Bradford, 1833–1914, vol. I
McCrea, Hugh Moreland, died 1941, vol. IV
McCready, Hugh Latimer, 1876–1950, vol. IV
McCreery, Gen. Sir Richard Loudon, 1898–1967, vol. VI
M'Crie, Charles Greig, 1836–1910, vol. I
McCrie, John Gibb, 1902–1977, vol. VII
McCrindle, Major John Ronald, 1894–1977, vol. VII
McCrossan, Mary, died 1934, vol. III
McCrostie, Hugh Cecil, 1897–1970, vol. VI
McCuaig, Maj.-Gen. George Eric, 1885–1958, vol. V
McCubbin, Frederick, 1855–1917, vol. II
McCubbin, Lt-Col Thomas, died 1925, vol. II (A), vol. III
McCullagh, Rt Hon. Sir Crawford, 1st Bt, 1868–1948, vol. IV
McCullagh, Sir Crawford; see McCullagh, Sir J. C.
M'Cullagh, Francis, 1874–1956, vol. V
MacCullagh, Sir James Acheson, 1854–1918, vol. II
McCullagh, Sir (Joseph) Crawford, 2nd Bt, 1907–1974, vol. VII
McCullagh, McKim; see McCullagh, W.McK.H.
McCullagh, (William) McKim (Herbert), 1889–1964, vol. VI
McCullers, Carson, (Mrs Carson Smith McCullers), 1917–1967, vol. VI
McCulloch, Allan Riverstone, 1885–1925, vol. II
McCulloch, Maj.-Gen. Sir Andrew Jameson, 1876–1960, vol. V
McCulloch, Derek Ivor Breashur, 1897–1967, vol. VI
M'Culloch, George, 1848–1907, vol. I
M'Culloch, Rev. James Duff, 1836–1926, vol. II

423

MacCulloch, Rev. Canon John Arnott, 1868–1950, vol. IV
McCulloch, Joseph, 1893–1961, vol. VI
McCulloch, Sir Malcolm McLeod, 1894–1969, vol. VI
McCulloch, Norman George, 1882–1965, vol. VI
McCulloch, Brig.-Gen. Robert Henry Frederick, 1869–1946, vol. IV
M'Culloch, Hon. William, died 1909, vol. I
McCulluch, William Edward, 1896–1963, vol. VI
McCulloogh, Donald; see McCullough, W. D. H.
McCullough, (William) Donald (Hamilton), 1901–1978, vol. VII
MacCunn, Captain Fergus, 1890–1941, vol. IV
MacCunn, Hamish, 1868–1916, vol. II
McCunn, Major James, 1894–1967, vol. VI
MacCunn, John, 1846–1929, vol. III
McCurdy, Rt Hon. Charles Albert, 1870–1941, vol. IV
MacCurdy, Edward Alexander Coles, 1871–1957, vol. V
McCurdy, Hon. Fleming Blanchard, 1875–1952, vol. V
M'Curdy, J. F., 1847–1935, vol. III
MacCurdy, John Thomson, 1886–1947, vol. IV
M'Cutcheon, George Barr, 1866–1928, vol. II
McCutcheon, Katharine Howard, 1875–1956, vol. V
McCutcheon, Hon. (Malcolm) Wallace, 1906–1969, vol. VI
McCutcheon, Hon. Wallace; see McCutcheon, Hon. M. W.
McDavid, Sir Edwin Frank, 1895–1980, vol. VII
McDavid, Sir Herbert Gladstone, 1898–1966, vol. VI
McDavid, James Wallace, 1887–1964, vol. VI
MacDermot, The, (Charles Edward), 1862–1947, vol. IV
MacDermot, The, (Charles John), 1899–1979, vol. VII
MacDermot, The, (Rt Hon. Hugh Hyacinth O'Rorke), 1834–1904, vol. I
MacDermot, Charles Edward; see MacDermot, The.
MacDermot, Charles John; see MacDermot, The.
MacDermot, Captain Ffrench, died 1917, vol. II
MacDermot, Rev. Henry Myles Fleetwood, 1837–1918, vol. II
MacDermot, Rt Hon. Hugh Hyacinth O'Rorke; see MacDermot, The.
MacDermot, Terence, W. L., 1896–1966, vol. VI
MacDermot-Roe, The; see MacDermot, Captain Ffrench.
MacDermott, Baron (Life Peer); John Clarke MacDermott, 1896–1979, vol. VII
M'Dermott, Edward R., 1847–1932, vol. III
McDermott, Geoffrey Lyster, 1912–1978, vol. VII
Mac Dermott, Rev. George Martius, 1863–1939, vol. III
McDermott, John Frederick, 1906–1958, vol. V
Macdermott, Patrick, 1859–1942, vol. IV
M'Dermott, Peter Joseph, died 1922, vol. II
Macdiarmid, Sir Allan Campbell, 1880–1945, vol. IV

Macdiarmid, Duncan Stewart, 1873–1954, vol. V
Macdiarmid, Hon. Finlay George, 1869–1933, vol. III
McDiarmid, Hugh; see Grieve, C. M.
Macdiarmid, Niall Campbell, 1919–1978, vol. VII
Macdona, Brian Fraser, 1901–1971, vol. VII
Macdona, John Cumming, 1836–1907, vol. I
McDonagh, James Eustace Radclyffe, 1881–1965, vol. VI
Macdonagh, Michael, 1860–1946, vol. VI
Macdonald, 6th Baron, 1853–1947, vol. IV
Macdonald, 7th Baron, died 1970, vol. VI
Macdonald of Earnscliffe, Baroness (1st in line), 1836–1920, vol. II
Macdonald of Gwaenysgor, 1st Baron, 1888–1966, vol. VI
Macdonald, Adam Davidson, 1895–1978, vol. VII
Macdonald, Lt-Gen. Alastair M'Ian, 1830–1910, vol. I
Macdonald, Alexander, died 1921, vol. II
Macdonald, Alexander, 1878–1939, vol. III
Macdonald, Most Rev. Alexander, 1858–1941, vol. IV
MacDonald, Alexander, 1894–1954, vol. V
McDonald, Alexander, 1903–1968, vol. VI
McDonald, Alexander Hugh, 1908–1979, vol. VII
Macdonald of Sleat, Sir (Alexander) Somerled (Angus Bosville), 16th Bt (cr 1625), 1917–1958, vol. V
Macdonald of the Isles, Sir Alexander Wentworth Macdonald Bosville, 14th Bt (cr 1625), 1865–1933, vol. III
Macdonald, Rev. Allan John Macdonald, 1887–1959, vol. V
M'Donald, Sir Andrew, 1836–1919, vol. II
Macdonald, Hon. Andrew Archibald, 1829–1912, vol. I
Macdonald, Most Rev. Andrew Joseph, 1871–1950, vol. IV
Macdonald, Most Rev. Angus, 1844–1900, vol. I
Macdonald, Angus Alexander, 1904–1965, vol. VI
Macdonald, Hon. Angus Lewis, died 1954, vol. V
Macdonald, Angus Roderick, 1858–1944, vol. IV
McDonald, Air Comdt Ann Smith, 1914–1972, vol. VII
Macdonald, Anne, died 1958, vol. V
MacDonald, Anne Elizabeth Campbell Bard, (Betty MacDonald), 1908–1958, vol. V
Macdonald, Sir Archibald John, 4th Bt (cr 1813), 1871–1919, vol. II
Macdonald, Sir Archibald Keppel, 3rd Bt (cr 1813), 1820–1901, vol. I
Macdonald, Col Archibald William, 1869–1939, vol. III
Macdonald, Sir Arthur, 1887–1953, vol. V
Macdonald, Lt-Col Arthur Cameron, died 1940, vol. III
Macdonald, Augustine Colin, 1837–1919, vol. II
MacDonald, Betty; see MacDonald, A. E. C. B.
McDonald, Bouverie Francis Primrose, 1861–1931, vol. III
Macdonald of Sleat, Miss Celia Violet Bosville, 1889–1976, vol. VII
M'Donald, Hon. Charles, died 1925, vol. II

424

Macdonald, Charles Blair, 1855–1939, vol. III
McDonald, Sir Charles George, 1892–1970, vol. VI
Macdonald, Charles James Black, 1864–1930, vol. III
MacDonald, Col Charles Joseph, 1862–1947, vol. IV
Macdonald, Lt-Col Charles Leslie, 1881–1939, vol. III
Macdonald, Col Clarence Reginald, 1876–1962, vol. VI
Macdonald, Rt Hon. Sir Claude Maxwell, 1852–1915, vol. I
Macdonald, Daniel Alexander, 1858–1937, vol. III
MacDonald, David Keith Chalmers, 1920–1963, vol. VI
Macdonald, Adm. David R.; see Robertson-Macdonald.
Macdonald, Donald, died 1932, vol. III
McDonald, Sir Donald, 1849–1934, vol. III
McDonald, Hon. Donald, born 1865, vol. III
Macdonald, Maj.-Gen. Sir Donald Alexander, 1845–1920, vol. II
Macdonald, Rev. Donald Bruce, 1872–1962, vol. VI
Macdonald, Major Donald R., 1884–1934, vol. III
MacDonald, Rev. Duncan, 1885–1941, vol. IV
Macdonald, Rev. Duncan Black, 1863–1943, vol. IV
Macdonald, Edward Mortimer, 1865–1940, vol. III
Macdonald, Dame Ethel, died 1941, vol. IV
Macdonald, Rev. Frederic William, 1842–1928, vol. II
Macdonald, Rev. Frederick Charles, died 1936, vol. III
Macdonald, Rev. Frederick William, 1848–1928, vol. II
Macdonald, George, 1824–1905, vol. I
Macdonald, Sir George, 1862–1940, vol. III
Macdonald, George, 1903–1967, vol. VI
Macdonald, Hon. Godfrey Evan Hugh, 1879–1915, vol. I
Macdonald of the Isles, Sir Godfrey Middleton Bosville, 15th Bt (cr 1625), 1887–1951, vol. V
MacDonald, Greville, 1856–1944, vol. IV
McDonald, Brig.-Gen. Harold French, 1885–1943, vol. IV
Macdonald, Maj.-Gen. Harry, 1886–1976, vol. VII
Macdonald, Maj.-Gen. Sir Hector Archibald, 1853–1903, vol. I
Macdonald, Hector Munro, 1865–1935, vol. III
Macdonald, Hugh, 1885–1958, vol. V
M'Donald, Hugh Campbell, 1869–1921, vol. II
Macdonald, Hon. Sir Hugh John, 1850–1929, vol. III
Macdonald, James, 1852–1913, vol. I
Macdonald, James, 1877–1954, vol. IV
Macdonald, James, 1898–1963, vol. VI
Macdonald, James Alexander, 1862–1923, vol. II
Macdonald, Hon. James Alexander, 1858–1939, vol. III (A), vol. IV
Macdonald, Maj.-Gen. James Balfour, 1898–1959, vol. V
MacDonald, James E. H., died 1932, vol. III
McDonald, Sir James Gordon, 1867–1942, vol. IV
Macdonald, James Harold, 1878–1955, vol. V

MacDonald, Rt Hon. James Ramsay, 1866–1937, vol. III
Macdonald, Maj.-Gen. Sir James Ronald Leslie, 1862–1927, vol. II
Macdonald, James Smith, 1873–1923, vol. II
MacDonald, James Stuart, 1878–1952, vol. V
MacDonald, John, 1843–1928, vol. II
Macdonald, John, died 1940, vol. III
McDonald, Sir John, 1874–1964, vol. VI
Macdonald, Col John Andrew, 1837–1916, vol. II
Macdonald, Rt Hon. John Archibald Murray, 1854–1939, vol. III
Macdonald, John Blake, 1829–1902, vol. I
Macdonald, Sir John Denis, 1826–1908, vol. I
Macdonald, Maj.-Gen. John Frederick Matheson, 1907–1979, vol. VII
McDonald, Hon. Sir John Gladstone Black, 1898–1977, vol. VII
Macdonald, Rt Hon. Sir John Hay Athole, 1836–1919, vol. II
MacDonald, Most Rev. John Hugh, 1881–1965, vol. VI
Macdonald, John Robert, 1879–1965, vol. VI
Macdonald, John Ronald Moreton, 1873–1921, vol. II
Macdonald, John Smyth, 1867–1941, vol. IV
Macdonald, Rev. John Somerled, 1871–1956, vol. V
Macdonald, John William, 1882–1934, vol. III
Macdonald, Lt-Col Kenneth Lachlan, 1867–1938, vol. III
MacDonald, Sir Kenneth Mackenzie, 1879–1954, vol. V
Macdonald, Mrs L. M., (L. M. Montgomery), 1874–1942, vol. IV
Macdonald, Sir Murdoch, 1866–1957, vol. V
McDonald, Niel, 1886–1968, vol. VI
Macdonald, Col Norman, 1890–1948, vol. IV
Macdonald, Sir Percy, died 1957, vol. V
Macdonald, Percy Stuart, 1890–1945, vol. IV
Macdonald, Captain Sir Peter Drummond, 1895–1961, vol. VI
MacDonald, Pirie, 1867–1942, vol. IV
MacDonald, Ranald, 1868–1931, vol. III
Macdonald, Ranald Mackintosh, 1860–1928, vol. II
Macdonald, Sir Reginald John, 1820–1899, vol. I
Macdonald, Lt-Col Reginald Percy, born 1856, vol. II
MacDonald, Robert, died 1971, vol. VII
McDonald, Sir (Robert) Ross, 1888–1964, vol. VI
Macdonald, Lt-Col Roderick William, 1881–1959, vol. V
MacDonald, Ronald, 1860–1933, vol. III
McDonald, Sir Ross; see McDonald, Sir Robert R.
McDonald, Samuel, 1877–1957, vol. V
Macdonald of Sleat, Sir Somerled; see Macdonald of Sleat, Sir A. S. A. B.
Macdonald, Air Vice-Marshal Somerled Douglas, 1899–1979, vol. VII
Macdonald, Maj.-Gen. Stuart, 1861–1939, vol. III
MacDonald, Sydney Gray, 1879–1946, vol. IV
Macdonald, Hon. Sir Thomas Lachlan, 1898–1980, vol. VII
McDonald, Thomas Pringle, 1901–1969, vol. VI

M'Donald, Rev. Walter, 1854–1920, vol. II
McDonald, Sir Warren D'Arcy, 1901–1965, vol. VI
Macdonald, William, 1875–1935, vol. III
Macdonald, Captain William Balfour, 1870–1937, vol. III
Macdonald, Sir William Christopher, 1831–1917, vol. II
Macdonald, William Marshall, 1872–1956, vol. V
Macdonald, William Rae, 1843–1923, vol. II
Macdonald-Tyler, Sir Henry Hewey Francis, 1877–1962, vol. VI
McDonell, Æneas Ranald, 1875–1941, vol. IV
Macdonell, Angus Claude, 1861–1924, vol. II
Macdonell, Lt-Gen. Sir Archibald Cameron, 1864–1941, vol. IV
Macdonell, Archibald Gordon, 1895–1941, vol. IV
Macdonell, Maj.-Gen. Hon. Archibald Hayes, 1868–1939, vol. III
Macdonell, Arthur Anthony, 1854–1930, vol. III
MacDonell, Edgar Errol Napier, 1874–1928, vol. II
Macdonell, Rt Hon. Sir Hugh Guion, 1832–1904, vol. I
Macdonell, Sir John, 1846–1921, vol. II
Macdonell, Rt Hon. Sir Philip James, 1873–1940, vol. III
Macdonnell, 1st Baron, 1844–1925, vol. II
McDonnell, Col Hon. Angus, 1881–1966, vol. VI
M'Donnell, Col Francis, 1828–1904, vol. I
Macdonnell, Henry, 1839–1922, vol. II
McDonnell, Col John, 1851–1928, vol. II
Macdonnell, Very Rev. John Cotter, died 1902, vol. I
MacDonnell, John de Courcy, 1869–1915, vol. I (A)
MacDonnell, Mark Antony, 1854–1906, vol. I
MacDonnell, Mervyn Sorley, 1880–1949, vol. IV
McDonnell, Sir Michael Francis Joseph, 1882–1956, vol. V
Macdonnell, Hon. Norman Scarth, 1886–1938, vol. III
M'Donnell, Richard Grant Peter Purcell, died 1927, vol. II
McDonnell, Hon. Sir Schomberg Kerr, 1861–1915, vol. I (A)
Macdonnell, Col William, 1831–1919, vol. II (A), vol. III
Macdonnell, Rt Rev. William Andrew, 1853–1920, vol. II
Macdonogh, Lt-Gen. Sir George Mark Watson, 1865–1942, vol. IV
McDouall, John Crichton, 1912–1979, vol. VII
McDouall, Brig.-Gen. Robert, 1871–1941, vol. IV
M'Douall, William, 1855–1924, vol. II
McDougal, Thomas William Houldsworth, 1885–1931, vol. III
M'Dougald, John, 1848–1919, vol. II
Macdougall, Maj.-Gen. Alastair Ian, 1888–1972, vol. VII
MacDougall, Brig.-Gen. Alexander, 1878–1927, vol. II
MacDougall, Alexander James, 1872–1953, vol. V
MacDougall, Sir Alexander Maclean, 1878–1953, vol. V
McDougall, Alexander Patrick, died 1959, vol. V
McDougall, Dugald Gordon, 1867–1944, vol. IV

M'Dougall, Ernest Hugh, 1877–1908, vol. I
McDougall, Frank Lidgett, 1884–1958, vol. V
Macdougall, Gordon Walters, died 1947, vol. IV
MacDougall, Maj.-Gen. James Charles, 1863–1927, vol. II
McDougall, James Currie, 1890–1957, vol. V
MacDougall, Sir James Patten, 1849–1919, vol. II
M'Dougall, Sir John, 1844–1917, vol. II
McDougall, John Bowes, 1890–1967, vol. VI
McDougall, John Henry Gordon, 1889–1969, vol. VI
M'Dougall, John Lorn, 1838–1909, vol. I
MacDougall, Leslie Grahame, 1896–1974, vol. VII
McDougall, Sir Malcolm, 1899–1970, vol. VI
Macdougall, Margaret, died 1943, vol IV
MacDougall, Sir Raibeart MacIntyre, 1892–1949, vol. IV
McDougall, Sir Robert, 1871–1938, vol. III
Macdougall, Robert Stewart, 1862–1947, vol. IV
MacDougall, Lt-Col Stewart, 1854–1916, vol. II
Macdougall, Hon. William, 1822–1905, vol. I
McDougall, William, 1871–1938, vol. III
Macdougall, William Brown, died 1936, vol. III
M'Dowall, Rev. Charles Robert Loraine, 1872–1950, vol. IV
McDowall, Roger Gordon, 1886–1972, vol. VII
McDowall, Rev. Stewart Andrew, 1882–1935, vol. III
M'Dowall, Thomas William, died 1936, vol. III
McDowell, Lt-Col Arnott Edward Connell, 1883–1944, vol. IV
MacDowell, Col Charles Carlyle, died 1959, vol. V
McDowell, Donald Keith, 1867–1940, vol. III
M'Dowell, Surg.-Col Edmund Greswold, 1831–1907, vol. I
Macdowell, Edward, 1861–1908, vol. I
McDowell, John, 1874–1936, vol. III
MacDowell, Lt-Col Thain Wendell, 1890–1960, vol. V
McDowell, William Fraser, 1858–1937, vol. III
MacDuff, John Levy, 1905–1963, vol. VI
Mace, Cecil Alec, 1894–1971, vol. VII
Mace, Comdr Frederick William, 1872–1960, vol. V
MacEacharn, Hon. Sir Malcolm Donald, 1852–1910, vol. I
McEachern, Malcolm, died 1945, vol. IV
M'Eachran, Duncan, 1841–1926, vol. II (A), vol. II
M'Elderry, Robert Knox, 1869–1949, vol. IV
McElheran, Robert Benjamin, died 1939, vol. III
McElligott, Edward John, died 1946, vol. IV
McElligott, James, 1893–1974, vol. VII
McElroy, Neil H., 1904–1972, vol. VII
McElroy, Robert, 1872–1959, vol. V
McElwaine, Sir Percy Alexander, 1884–1969, vol. VI
Mac Enri, (Henry), Seaghan P., died 1930, vol. III
McEntee, 1st Baron, 1871–1953, vol. V
McEntegart, Air Vice-Marshal Bernard, 1891–1954, vol. V
MacEoin, Lt-Gen. Seán, 1893–1973, vol. VII
M'Evay, Most Rev. Fergus Patrick, 1852–1911, vol. I

MacEvilly, Most Rev. John, 1817–1902, vol. I
McEvoy, Ambrose, 1878–1927, vol. II
M'Evoy, Charles, 1879–1929, vol. III
McEvoy, John Alexander, 1882–1935, vol. III
MacEwan, David, 1830–1910, vol. I
MacEwan, David, 1846–1927, vol. II
MacEwan, Very Rev. James, died 1911, vol. I
MacEwan, Peter, 1856–1917, vol. II
M'Ewan, Rt Hon. William, 1827–1913, vol. I
MacEwen, Sir Alexander Malcolm, 1875–1941, vol. IV
MacEwen, Alexander R., 1851–1916, vol. II
MacEwen, Alexander Robert, 1894–1946, vol. IV
MacEwen, Brig.-Gen. Douglas Lilburn, 1867–1941, vol. IV
McEwen, Sir James Napier Finnie, 2nd Bt, 1924–1971, vol. VII
McEwen, Rt Hon. Sir John, 1900–1980, vol. VII
MacEwen, John A. C., died 1944, vol. IV
McEwen, Sir John Blackwood, 1868–1948, vol. IV
McEwen, Sir John Helias Finnie, 1st Bt, 1894–1962, vol. VI
MacEwen, Brig.-Gen. Maurice Lilburn, 1869–1943, vol. IV
Macewen, Air Vice-Marshal Sir Norman Duckworth Kerr, 1881–1953, vol. V
McEwen, Robert Finnie, 1861–1926, vol. II
McEwen, Sir Robert Lindley, 3rd Bt, 1926–1980, vol. VII
MacEwen, Sir William, 1848–1924, vol. II
MacFadden, Arthur William James, 1869–1933, vol. III
McFadden, Hon. David Henry, 1856–1935, vol. III
M'Fadden, Edward, born 1862, vol. III
McFadden, Gertrude Violet, died 1963, vol. VI
McFadyean, Sir Andrew, 1887–1974, vol. VII
McFadyean, Sir John, 1853–1941, vol. IV
Macfadyen, Allan, 1860–1907, vol. I
Macfadyen, Air Marshal Sir Douglas, 1902–1968, vol. VI
Macfadyen, Rev. Dugald, 1867–1936, vol. III
Macfadyen, Sir Eric, 1879–1966, vol. VI
M'Fadyen, John Edgar, 1870–1933, vol. III
Macfadyen, William Allison, 1865–1924, vol. II
Macfall, Haldane, 1860–1928, vol. II
Macfall, John Edward Whitley, 1873–1938, vol. III
Macfarlan, Brig.-Gen. Frederic Alexander, 1866–1954, vol. V
Macfarlan, Hon. Sir James Ross, 1872–1955, vol. V
McFarland, Arthur, 1893–1966, vol. VI
McFarland, Bryan Leslie, 1900–1963, vol. VI
MacFarland, Sir John Henry, 1851–1935, vol. III
MacFarland, Robert Arthur Henry, died 1922, vol. II
Macfarlane, Rt Rev. Angus, 1843–1912, vol. I
McFarlane, Sir Charles Stuart, 1895–1958, vol. V
Macfarlane, Col David Mason, 1862–1930, vol. III
Macfarlane, Donald, 1882–1946, vol. IV
Macfarlane, Sir Donald Horne, 1830–1904, vol. I
Macfarlane, Very Rev. Dugald, 1869–1956, vol. V
Macfarlane, Brig.-Gen. Duncan Alwyn, 1857–1941, vol. IV
MacFarlane, Lt-Gen. Sir (Frank) Noel Mason-, 1889–1953, vol. V

Macfarlane, George James, 1855–1933, vol. III
Macfarlane, George Lewis; see Ormidale, Hon. Lord.
Macfarlane, Hon. James, 1844–1914, vol. I
Macfarlane, Sir James, 1857–1944, vol. IV
Macfarlane, James Waddell, 1877–1952, vol. V
Macfarlane, Janet Alston, died 1980, vol. VII
Macfarlane, Lt-Gen. Sir Noel Mason-; see Macfarlane, Lt-Gen. Sir F. N. M.
McFarlane, Brig. Percy Muir, 1880–1946, vol. IV
Macfarlane, Robert Campbell, 1892–1963, vol. VI
McFarlane, Major Ronald, 1860–1915, vol. I
McFarlane, Stuart Gordon, 1885–1970, vol. VI
Macfarlane, Thomas, 1834–1907, vol. I
Macfarlane, William Dove, died 1932, vol. III
Macfarlane-Grieve, Lt-Col Angus Alexander, 1891–1970, vol. VI
Macfarlane-Grieve, William Alexander, 1844–1917, vol. II
Macfarren, Walter Cecil, 1826–1905, vol. I
McFee, William, 1881–1966, vol. VI
McFerran, Lt-Col Edwin Millar Gilliland, 1873–1962, vol. VI
Macfetridge, Ven. Charles, died 1920, vol. II
Macfetridge, William C., 1878–1957, vol. V
Macfie, Alec Lawrence, 1898–1980, vol. VII
Macfie, Brig.-Gen. Andrew Laurie, 1860–1936, vol. III
Macfie, John William Scott, 1879–1948, vol. IV
Macfie, Ronald Campbell, died 1931, vol. III
Macfie, Col William, 1840–1912, vol. I
McGann, Lt-Col H. H., died 1943, vol. IV
McGarry, Hon. Thomas William, 1871–1935, vol. III
McGarvey, Daniel, 1919–1977, vol. VII
McGavin, Maj.-Gen. Sir Donald Johnstone, 1876–1960, vol. V
McGavin, Lawrie Hugh, 1868–1932, vol. III
McGaw, Andrew Kidd, 1873–1956, vol. V
McGaw, Rev. Joseph Thoburn, 1836–1905, vol. I
McGaw, William Rankin, 1900–1974, vol. VII
MacGeagh, Col Sir Henry Davies Foster, 1883–1962, vol. VI
McGeer, Gerald Grattan, 1888–1947, vol. IV
Macgeorge, Col Henry King, 1865–1940, vol. III
Macgeorge, W. S., died 1931, vol. III
McGeough, Most Rev. Joseph F., 1903–1970, vol. VI
Macgeough Bond, Sir Walter Adrian, 1857–1945, vol. IV
McGhee, Henry George, 1898–1959, vol. V
MacGibbon, Rev. James, 1865–1922, vol. II
McGibbon, John E. G., died 1959, vol. V
M'Giffert, Arthur Cushman, 1861–1933, vol. III
MacGill, Major Campbell Gerald Hertslet, 1876–1922, vol. II
MacGill, Adm. Thomas, 1850–1926, vol. II
MacGillivray, Hon. Angus, 1842–1918, vol. II
MacGillivray of MacGillivray, Angus, 1865–1947, vol. IV
MacGillivray of MacGillivray, Angus Robertson, 1892–1955, vol. V
MacGillivray, Charles Watson, 1851–1932, vol. III
MacGillivray, Donald, 1862–1931, vol. III

MacGillivray, Sir Donald Charles, 1906–1966, vol. VI
MacGillivray, Evan James, 1873–1955, vol. V
Macgillivray, James Pittendrigh, 1856–1938, vol. III
Macgillivray, John, 1855–1930, vol. III
Macgillivray, John Walker, 1884–1961, vol. VI
MacGillivray, William, 1823–1917, vol. II
McGillycuddy, Denis Donough Charles, (The McGillycuddy of the Reeks), 1852–1921, vol. II
McGillycuddy, John Patrick, (The McGillycuddy of the Reeks), 1909–1959, vol. V
McGillycuddy, Lt-Col Ross Kinloch, (The McGillycuddy of the Reeks), 1882–1950, vol. IV
M'Gilp, Major Clyde, 1885–1918, vol. II
McGilvray, Sir William, 1887–1956, vol. V
M'Ginness, Brig.-Gen. John R., 1840–1918, vol. II
McGinnety, Frank Edward, 1907–1973, vol. VII
McGirr, John Joseph Gregory, 1879–1949, vol. IV
McGivern, Cecil, 1907–1963, vol. VI
Macgivern, Rt Rev. Thomas, died 1900, vol. I
McGlashan, Rear-Adm. Sir Alexander Davidson, 1901–1976, vol. VII
McGlashan, Archibald A., 1888–1980, vol. VII
McGlashan, Sir George Tait, 1885–1968, vol. VI
MacGlashan, John, 1874–1948, vol. IV
McGlinn, Brig.-Gen. John Patrick, 1869–1946, vol. IV
McGonigal, Rt Hon. Sir Ambrose Joseph, 1917–1979, vol. VII
McGonigal, John, 1870–1943, vol. IV
MacGonigal, Maurice, 1900–1979, vol. VII
M'Gonigle, Rev. William Alexander, 1849–1939, vol. III
McGougan, Malcolm, 1905–1976, vol. VII
M'Goun, Archibald, 1853–1921, vol. II
McGovern, John, 1887–1968, vol. VI
McGovern, Sir Patrick Silvesta, 1895–1975, vol. VII
M'Govern, Thomas, died 1904, vol. I
McGovern, William Montgomery, 1897–1964, vol. VI
McGowan, 1st Baron, 1874–1961, vol. VI
McGowan, 2nd Baron, 1906–1966, vol. VI
McGowan, Ven. Frank, 1895–1968, vol. VI
Macgowan, Gault, 1894–1970, vol. VI
McGowan, Rt Rev. Henry, 1891–1948, vol. IV
Macgowan, Rev. William Stuart, 1864–1939, vol. III
McGowen, Hon. James Sinclair Taylor, 1855–1922, vol. IV
MacGranahan, Very Rev. James, 1855–1940, vol. III (A), vol. IV
McGrath, Sir Charles; see McGrath, Sir J. C.
M'Grath, Sir Joseph, 1858–1923, vol. II
McGrath, Sir (Joseph) Charles, 1875–1951, vol. V
McGrath, Most Rev. Michael Joseph, 1882–1961, vol. VI
McGrath, Hon. Sir Patrick Thomas, 1868–1929, vol. III
McGrath, Raymond, 1903–1977, vol. VII
McGrath, Rosita, (Mrs Arthur T. McGrath); see Forbes, Joan R.
McGrath, Captain William, 1917–1942, vol. IV
M'Grath, William Martin, died 1912, vol. I

McGraw, Curtis Whittlesey, 1895–1953, vol. V
MacGregor, Alasdair Alpin, 1899–1970, vol. VI
MacGregor, Sir (Alasdair Duncan) Atholl, 1883–1945, vol. IV
Macgregor, Alastair Goold, 1919–1972, vol. VII
MacGregor, Alexander Brittan, 1909–1965, vol. VI
McGregor, Hon. Alexander John, 1864–1946, vol. IV
Macgregor, Sir Alexander S. M., 1881–1967, vol. VI
MacGregor, Alexander Stewart, 1848–1906, vol. I
MacGregor, Sir Atholl; see MacGregor, Sir Alasdair D. A.
Macgregor, Col Charles Reginald, 1847–1902, vol. I (A)
Macgregor, Sir Cyril Patrick M'Connell, 5th Bt (cr 1828), 1887–1958, vol. V
MacGregor, David Hutchison, 1877–1953, vol. V
MacGregor, David Sliman, 1864–1952, vol. V
Macgregor, Rev. Duncan Campbell, 1858–1943, vol. IV
Macgregor, Eric Dickson, 1886–1950, vol. IV
MacGregor, Sir Evan, 1842–1926, vol. II
Macgregor, Rev. George Hogarth Carnaby, 1892–1963, vol. VI
McGregor, Sir George Innes, 1899–1976, vol. VII
M'Gregor, Hon. Gregor, 1848–1913, vol. I
MacGregor, Gregor, 1869–1919, vol. II
MacGregor of MacGregor, Gylla Constance Susan, (Hon. Lady MacGregor of MacGregor), died 1980, vol. VII
McGregor, Air Marshal Sir Hector Douglas, 1910–1973, vol. VII
Macgregor, Col Henry Grey, 1838–1925, vol. II
MacGregor, Very Rev. James, 1832–1910, vol. I
M'Gregor, Rt Rev. Mgr James, 1860–1928, vol. II
Macgregor, James, 1889–1953, vol. V
Macgregor, James Cochran Stevenson, 1897–1949, vol. IV
Macgregor, Sir James Comyn, 1861–1935, vol. III
McGregor, James Drummond, 1838–1919, vol. II
McGregor, Hon. James Duncan, 1860–1935, vol. III
Macgregor, James Gordon, 1852–1913, vol. I
McGregor, Sir James Robert, 1889–1973, vol. VII
MacGregor, Lt-Col John, died 1932, vol. III
Macgregor, John, died 1967, vol. VI
Macgregor, John Julius, 1869–1948, vol. IV
MacGregor, John Marshall, 1879–1936, vol. III
Macgregor, Lewis Richard, 1886–1973, vol. VI
MacGregor of MacGregor, Sir Malcolm, 5th Bt (cr 1795), 1873–1958, vol. V
MacGregor, Malcolm Evan, 1889–1933, vol. III
Macgregor, Maj.-Gen. Malcolm John Robert, 1840–1914, vol. I
Macgregor, Lt-Col Philip Arthur, 1877–1934, vol. III
Macgregor, Robert, 1847–1922, vol. II
MacGregor, Robert Anderson, 1888–1953, vol. V
MacGregor, Robert Barr, 1896–1979, vol. VII
MacGregor, Lt-Col Robert Forrester Douglas, 1885–1960, vol. V
Macgregor, Sir Robert James McConnell, 6th Bt (cr 1828), 1890–1963, vol. VI

MacGregor, Hon. Robert Malcolm, 1876–1924, vol. II
MacGregor, Robert Menzies, 1882–1946, vol. IV
MacGregor, Robert Roy, 1847–1922, vol. II
Macgregor, W. Y., 1855–1923, vol. II
MacGregor, Rt Hon. Sir William, 1847–1919, vol. II
MacGregor, William Cunningham, 1862–1934, vol. III
MacGregor, William Duncan, 1878–1974, vol. VII
Macgregor, Sir William Gordon, 4th Bt (cr 1828), 1846–1905, vol. I
Macgregor, Very Rev. William Malcolm, 1861–1944, vol. IV
Macgregor Mitchell, Hon. Lord; Robert Macgregor Mitchell, died 1938, vol. III
Macgregor-Morris, John Turner, 1872–1959, vol. V
McGrigor, Lt-Col Sir Charles Colquhoun, 4th Bt, 1893–1946, vol. IV
M'Grigor, Brig.-Gen. Charles Roderic Robert, 1860–1927, vol. II
M'Grigor, Captain Sir James Rhoderick Duff, 3rd Bt, 1857–1924, vol. II
McGrigor, Adm. of the Fleet Sir Rhoderick Robert, 1893–1959, vol. V
M'Guckin, Barton, 1853–1913, vol. I
MacGuckin, Charles John Graham, died 1934, vol. III
McGuffie, Kenneth Cunningham, 1913–1972, vol. VII
McGuffin, Samuel, 1863–1952, vol. V
McGuigan, His Eminence Cardinal James Charles, 1894–1974, vol. VII
M'Guinness, Bingham, vol. III
McGuinness, Brig. Edward, 1883–1958, vol. V
McGuinness, Joseph, died 1922, vol. II
McGuinness, Norah Allison, died 1980, vol. VII (AII)
McGuire, Most Rev. Terence Bernard, 1881–1957, vol. V
McGuire, Thomas Horace, 1849–1923, vol. II
MccGwire, Maj.-Gen. Edward Thomas St Lawrance, 1830–1917, vol. II (p. 720)
MccGwire, Lt-Col John Edward, died 1950, vol. IV
Machain, Monsieur, 1839–1910, vol. I
McHardy, Maj.-Gen. Alexander Anderson, 1868–1958, vol. V
McHardy, Lt-Col Sir Alexander Burness, 1842–1917, vol. II
McHardy, Rev. Archibald, 1890–1973, vol. VII
M'Hardy, Malcolm Macdonald, 1852–1913, vol. I
Macharg, Sir Andrew Simpson, 1871–1959, vol. V
Machell, James Octavius, 1837–1902, vol. I
Machell, Percy Wilfrid, 1862–1916, vol. II
Machell, Lady Valda, 1868–1951, vol. V
Machen, Arthur, 1863–1947, vol. IV
Machin, Sir Stanley, 1861–1939, vol. III
Machray, Most Rev. Robert, 1831–1904, vol. I
Machray, Robert, 1857–1946, vol. IV
Machray, Robert, 1906–1968, vol. VI
Machtig, Sir Eric Gustav, 1889–1973, vol. VII
Machugh, Rt Rev. Charles, 1855–1926, vol. II
M'Hugh, Edward, died 1900, vol. I
M'Hugh, Patrick Aloysius, 1858–1909, vol. I

Machugh, Lt-Col Robert Joseph, died 1925, vol. II
McIllree, John Henry, 1849–1925, vol. II
McIlquham, Sir Gilbert, 1863–1953, vol. V
MacIlreith, R. T., died 1943, vol. IV
McIlroy, Dame (Anne) Louise, died 1968, vol. VI
McIlroy, Dame Louise; see McIlroy, Dame A. L.
McIlroy, Robert, died 1911, vol. I
McIlroy, William Ewart Clarke, 1893–1963, vol. VI
McIlwain, Charles Howard, 1871–1968, vol. VI (AII)
MacIlwaine, Alexander Gillilan Johnson, 1887–1942, vol. IV
MacIlwaine, John Bedell Stanford, 1857–1945, vol. IV
MacIlwaine, John Elder, 1874–1930, vol. III
McIlwaine, Hon. Sir Robert, 1871–1943, vol. IV
M'Ilwraith, Jean N., died 1938, vol. III
McIlwraith, Sir Malcolm, 1865–1941, vol. IV
M'Ilwraith, Hon. Sir Thomas, 1835–1900, vol. I
McIlwraith, William, 1924–1968, vol. VI
McIndoe, Sir Archibald Hector, 1900–1960, vol. V
Macinerney, Michael Chartres, 1850–1929, vol. III
M'Inerney, Lt-Col Timothy Marcus, 1869–1929, vol. III
MacInnes, Rev. Alexander M. F., 1866–1934, vol. III
MacInnes, Rt Rev. Angus Campbell, 1901–1977, vol. VII
MacInnes, Charles Malcolm, 1891–1971, vol. VII
MacInnes, Charles Stephen, 1872–1952, vol. V
MacInnes, Colin, 1914–1976, vol. VII
MacInnes, Rt Rev. Duncan, died 1970, vol. VI
Macinnes, Lt-Col Duncan Sayre, 1870–1918, vol. II
McInnes, James, 1901–1974, vol. VII
MacInnes, Miles, 1830–1909, vol. I
MacInnes, Rt Rev. Rennie, 1870–1931, vol. III
MacInnes, Robert Ian Aonas, 1902–1972, vol. VII
MacInnes, William Alexander, 1892–1977, vol. VII
MacInnes Shaw, Sir Douglas; see Shaw, Sir A. D. M.
McInnis, Lt-Col Edward Bowater, 1846–1927, vol. II
M'Inroy, Col Charles, 1838–1919, vol. II
McIntosh, Alastair James, 1913–1973, vol. VII
McIntosh, Alexander Morrison, 1877–1944, vol. IV
McIntosh, Sir Alister Donald, 1906–1978, vol. VII
McIntosh, Annie, 1871–1951, vol. V
McIntosh, Arthur Johnston, 1890–1956, vol. V
Macintosh, Douglas Clyde, 1877–1948, vol. IV (A), vol. V
MacIntosh, Duncan William, 1904–1966, vol. VI
Macintosh, Edward Hyde, 1895–1970, vol. VI
McIntosh, George, 1889–1949, vol. IV
McIntosh, Hon. Hugh Donald, 1876–1942, vol. IV
McIntosh, Ian Donald, 1908–1975, vol. VII
Macintosh, John Macintosh, died 1913, vol. I
McIntosh, Hon. Sir Malcolm, 1888–1960, vol. V
McIntosh, Robert, 1894–1972, vol. VII
Macintosh, Sir William, 1863–1929, vol. III
M'Intosh, William Carmichael, 1838–1931, vol. III
MacIntyre, Sir Alexander, 1879–1952, vol. V
Macintyre, David Lowe, 1895–1967, vol. VI
McIntyre, Rev. David Martin, 1859–1938, vol. III

Macintyre, Maj.-Gen. Donald, 1831–1903, vol. I
McIntyre, Donald, 1891–1954, vol. V
Macintyre, Sir Donald, 1891–1978, vol. VII
Macintyre, Maj.-Gen. Donald Charles Frederick, 1859–1938, vol. III
MacIntyre, Ian, 1869–1946, vol. IV
Macintyre, Captain Ian Agnew Patteson, 1893–1967, vol. VI
McIntyre, Rev. Canon James, 1888–1978, vol. VII
M'Intyre, Hon. Sir John, 1832–1904, vol. I
Macintyre, John, 1859–1928, vol. II
M'Intyre, Most Rev. John, 1855–1934, vol. III
McIntyre, Air Vice-Marshal Sir John, died 1950, vol. IV
M'Intyre, John M'Intyre, 1842–1930, vol. III
Macintyre, Margaret, died 1943, vol. IV
McIntyre, Raymond, died 1933, vol. III
Macintyre, Very Rev. Ronald George, 1863–1954, vol. V
McIntyre, William Keverall, 1882–1969, vol. VI
MacIver, Alan Squarey, 1894–1975, vol. VII
MacIver, Arthur Milne, 1905–1972, vol. VII
MacIver, Major Sir Charles, 1866–1935, vol. III
MacIver, David, 1840–1907, vol. I
MacIver, David R.; see Randall-MacIver.
M'Iver, Sir Lewis, 1st Bt, 1846–1920, vol. II
MacIver, Robert Morrison, 1882–1970, vol. VI
McIver, William, 1871–1930, vol. III
Mack, Rear-Adm. Frederick Robert Joseph, 1897–1959, vol. V
Mack, Sir Henry; see Mack, Sir W. H. B.
Mack, Sir Hugh, 1832–1920, vol. II
Mack, Hon. Jason Miller, 1843–1927, vol. II
Mack, John David, died 1957, vol. V
Mack, Rear-Adm. Philip John, 1892–1943, vol. IV
Mack, Hon. Sir Ronald William, 1904–1968, vol. VI
Mack, Sir William George, 1904–1979, vol. VII
Mack, Sir (William) Henry (Bradshaw), 1894–1974, vol. VII
McKaig, Col Sir John Bickerton, 1883–1962, vol. VI
Mackail, Denis George, 1892–1971, vol. VII
Mackail, John William, 1859–1945, vol. IV
Mackain of Ardnamurchan, Rev. William James, 1854–1936, vol. III
Mackarness, Ven. Charles Coleridge, 1850–1918, vol. II
Mackarness, Cuthbert George Milford, 1890–1962, vol. VI
Mackarness, Frederic Coleridge, 1854–1920, vol. II
Mackawee, Khan Bahadur Sir Mahomed Abdul Kader, 1875–1954, vol. V (A)
Mackay, Hon. Lord; Alexander Morrice Mackay, 1875–1955, vol. V
Mackay, Æneas James George, 1839–1911, vol. I
Mackay, Alexander Grant, 1860–1920, vol. II
Mackay, Hon. Col Alexander Howard, 1848–1929, vol. III
Mackay, Alexander Morrice; see Mackay, Hon. Lord.
McKay, Andrew Foggo, 1923–1979, vol. VII
McKay, Sir Charles Holly, 1896–1972, vol. VII

MacKay, Donald G., 1870–1958, vol. V
Mackay, Ebenezer, 1864–1920, vol. II
Mackay, Edward Fairbairn, 1868–1953, vol. V
Mackay, Eric, 1851–1898, vol. I
Mackay, Ernest John Henry, 1880–1943, vol. IV
Mackay, George, died 1949, vol. IV
Mackay, Hon. George Hugh, 1872–1961, vol. VI
McKay, Sir George Mills, 1869–1937, vol. III
Mackay, Helen M. M., 1891–1965, vol. VI
Mackay, Rev. Henry Falconar Barclay, died 1936, vol. III
McKay, Col Henry Kellock, 1850–1930, vol. III
Mackay, Henry Martyn, 1868–1930, vol. III
MacKay, Ira Allen, 1875–1934, vol. III
Mackay, Lt-Gen. Sir Iven Giffard, 1882–1966, vol. VI
M'Kay, James, 1862–1931, vol. III
Mackay, Maj.-Gen. Hon. James Alexander Kenneth, 1859–1935, vol. III
Mackay, James Francis, 1855–1933, vol. III
Mackay, Jessie, 1864–1938, vol. III
Mackay, John, 1839–1914, vol. II
Mackay, Rev. John, died 1938, vol. III
McKay, Ven. John, 1870–1942, vol. IV
McKay, John, died 1964, vol. VI
Mackay, Ven. John Alexander, 1838–1923, vol. II
Mackay, Lt-Col John F., died 1930, vol. III
Mackay, Hon. John Keiller, 1888–1970, vol. VI
Mackay, John Martin, 1899–1970, vol. VI
Mackay, Rev. John Robertson, 1865–1939, vol. III
Mackay, John Sturgeon, 1843–1914, vol. I
Mackay, John William, 1831–1902, vol. I
McKay, John William, 1883–1936, vol. III
Mackay, John Yule, 1860–1930, vol. III
Mackay, Brig. Kenneth, 1901–1974, vol. VII
Mackay, Rev. Canon Malcolm, 1873–1953, vol. V
Mackay, Mary; see Corelli, Marie.
Mackay, Hon. Robert, 1840–1916, vol. II
Mackay, Robert John, 1859–1935, vol. III
Mackay, Very Rev. Roderick John, 1874–1956, vol. V
Mackay, Ronald William Gordon, 1902–1960, vol. V
M'Kay, Hon. Thomas, 1839–1912, vol. II
Mackay, William Æneas, 1871–1929, vol. III
Mackay, Lt-Col William Bertie, 1863–1938, vol. III
M'Kay, William D., 1844–1924, vol. II
McKeag, Major William, 1897–1972, vol. VII
M'Kean, Col Alexander Chalmers, 1852–1933, vol. III
M'Kean, Captain George Burdon, 1890–1926, vol. II
McKean, Air Vice-Marshal Sir Lionel Douglas Dalzell, 1886–1963, vol. VI
Mackean, Rev. Canon William Herbert, 1877–1960, vol. V
M'Kechnie, Alexander Balfour, 1860–1930, vol. III
M'Kechnie, Dugald, 1845–1912, vol. I
McKechnie, Hector, 1899–1966, vol. VI
McKechnie, Sir James, died 1931, vol. III
McKechnie, James, 1911–1964, vol. VI
McKechnie, William Sharp, 1863–1930, vol. III
McKechnie, Sir William Wallace, died 1947, vol. IV
McKee, Sir Dermot St Oswald, 1904–1980, vol. VII

McKee, Major Hugh Kennedy, 1896–1957, vol. V
McKee, Captain James, 1886–1934, vol. III
McKee, J(ohn) Ritchie, 1900–1964, vol. VI
McKee, Rev. Robert Alexander, 1847–1926, vol. II
McKee, Col Samuel Hanford, 1875–1942, vol. IV
McKee, William Henry, 1881–1956, vol. V
McKeefry, His Eminence Cardinal Peter Thomas Bertram, 1899–1973, vol. VII
Mackeen, Hon. David, 1839–1916, vol. II
Mackeith, Malcolm Henry, 1895–1942, vol. IV
Mac Keith, Ronald Charles, 1908–1977, vol. VII
Mackellar, Hon. Sir Charles Kinnaird, 1844–1926, vol. II
McKelvey, Sir John Lawrance, 1881–1939, vol. III
MacKelvie, Col Maxwell, 1877–1933, vol. III
Mackelvie, Col Thomas, 1867–1952, vol. V
McKendrick, Archibald, 1876–1960, vol. VI (AI)
M'Kendrick, John Gray, 1841–1926, vol. II
McKenna, Harold, 1879–1946, vol. IV
MacKenna, Sir James, 1872–1940, vol. III
McKenna, Brig. James Charles, 1879–1943, vol. IV
M'Kenna, Sir Joseph Neale, 1819–1906, vol. I
McKenna, Rt Rev. Patrick, 1869–1942, vol. IV
McKenna, Rt Hon. Reginald, 1863–1943, vol. IV
Mackenna, Robert William, 1874–1930, vol. III
McKenna, Stephen, 1888–1967, vol. VI
Mackennal, Rev. Alexander, 1835–1904, vol. I
Mackennal, Sir Bertram, 1863–1931, vol. III
Mackennal, Ven. William Leavers, 1881–1947, vol. IV
Mackenzie, Hon. Lord; Charles Kincaid Mackenzie, 1857–1938, vol. III
MacKenzie, Agnes Mure, 1891–1955, vol. V
MacKenzie, Alasdair Francis, 1910–1971, vol. VII
Mackenzie, Alasdair Roderick, 1903–1970, vol. VI
Mackenzie, Alastair Oswald Morison, 1858–1949, vol. IV
McKenzie, Alex., 1869–1951, vol. V
Mackenzie, Sir Alexander, 1842–1902, vol. I
Mackenzie, Sir Alexander, 1860–1943, vol. IV
Mackenzie, Sir Alexander Campbell, 1847–1935, vol. III
Mackenzie, Lt-Col Alexander Dalziel; see Mackenzie, Lt-Col D. W. A. D.
Mackenzie, Col Alexander Francis, 1861–1935, vol. III
Mackenzie, Alexander George Robertson, 1879–1963, vol. VI
Mackenzie, Alexander Herbert, 1867–1952, vol. V
Mackenzie, Sir Alexander M.; see Muir-Mackenzie.
Mackenzie, Alexander Marshall, 1848–1933, vol. III
Mackenzie, Col Sir Alfred Robert Davidson, 1835–1921, vol. II
Mackenzie, Sir Allan Russell, 2nd Bt (cr 1890), 1850–1906, vol. I
M'Kenzie, Lt-Col Archibald Ernest Graham, 1878–1918, vol. II
Mackenzie, Sir Arthur George Ramsay, 11th Bt (cr 1673), 1865–1935, vol. III
Mackenzie, Arthur Henderson, 1880–1936, vol. III
Mackenzie, Arthur Stanley, 1865–1938, vol. III
Mackenzie, Austin, 1856–1935, vol. III

Mackenzie, Captain Cecil James Granville, 1889–1959, vol. V
Mackenzie, Lt-Col Charles, 1869–1953, vol. V
Mackenzie, Major Charles Fraser, died 1955, vol. V
Mackenzie, Charles Kincaid; see Mackenzie, Hon. Lord.
Mackenzie, Sir Clutha Nantes, 1895–1966, vol. VI
MacKenzie, Sir Colin, 1877–1938, vol. III
Mackenzie, Rear-Adm. Colin, 1872–1968, vol. VI
Mackenzie, Maj.-Gen. Sir Colin John, 1861–1956, vol. V
Mackenzie, Sir Compton, 1883–1972, vol. VII
M'Kenzie, Dan, died 1935, vol. III
Mackenzie, Brig. David Alexander Laurance, 1897–1976, vol. VII
Mackenzie, David James, 1855–1925, vol. II
Mackenzie, Donald Alexander, 1873–1936, vol. III
M'Kenzie, Donald Duncan, 1859–1927, vol. II
Mackenzie, Lt-Col (Douglas William) Alexander Dalziel, 1889–1955, vol. V
Mackenzie, Brig.-Gen. Sir Duncan, 1859–1932, vol. III
Mackenzie, Sir Duncan George, 1883–1965, vol. VI
Mackenzie, Col Edward Leslie, 1870–1947, vol. IV
Mackenzie, Sir Edward Montague Compton; see Mackenzie, Sir C.
Mackenzie, Col Edward Philippe, 1842–1929, vol. III
Mackenzie, Col Eric Dighton, 1891–1972, vol. VII
Mackenzie, Faith Compton, (Lady Mackenzie), died 1960, vol. V
Mackenzie, Col Sir Felix Calvert, 1826–1902, vol. I
Mackenzie, Rev. Francis Scott, 1884–1970, vol. VI
MacKenzie, Fraser, 1905–1978, vol. VII
Mackenzie, Frederick A., 1869–1931, vol. III
Mackenzie, Lt-Col Frederick Finch, 1849–1934, vol. III
Mackenzie, Ven. Gaden Crawford, died 1920, vol. II
Mackenzie, George, 1881–1950, vol. IV
Mackenzie, Brig.-Gen. George Birnie, 1872–1952, vol. V
Mackenzie, Col George Frederick Campbell, 1855–1909, vol. I
Mackenzie, Sir George Sutherland, 1844–1910, vol. I
Mackenzie, H. Millicent, 1863–1942, vol. IV
Mackenzie, Col Harry Malcolm, died 1947, vol. IV
M'Kenzie, Rev. Harry Ward, 1850–1941, vol. IV
Mackenzie, Sir Hector David, 8th Bt (cr 1703, of Gairloch), 1893–1958, vol. V
Mackenzie, Lt-Col Hector G. Gordon, 1869–1930, vol. III
Mackenzie, Sir Hector William Gavin, 1856–1929, vol. III
Mackenzie, Helen Margaret, died 1966, vol. VI
Mackenzie, Lt-Col Herbert John, 1878–1941, vol. IV
Mackenzie, Hugh, 1861–1940, vol. III
M'Kenzie, Hon. Hugh, 1853–1942, vol. IV
Mackenzie, Sir Hugh, 1888–1959, vol. V
Mackenzie, Rt Hon. Ian Alistair, 1890–1949, vol. IV

Mackenzie, J. Hamilton, 1875–1926, vol. II
Mackenzie, J. J., 1865–1922, vol. II
Mackenzie, Sir James, 1853–1925, vol. II
Mackenzie, Rev. James Cameron, *died* 1931, vol. III
Mackenzie, Sir James Dixon, 7th Bt (*cr* 1703, of Scatwell), 1830–1900, vol. I
MacKenzie, Brig. James Dunbar, 1889–1947, vol. IV
Mackenzie, Sir (James) Kenneth Douglas, 8th Bt (*cr* 1703, of Scatwell), 1859–1930, vol. III
Mackenzie, Sir (James) Moir, 1886–1963, vol. VI
Mackenzie, James Young, 1914–1971, vol. VII
Mackenzie, Lt-Col John, 1876–1949, vol. IV
McKenzie, Very Rev. John, 1883–1955, vol. V
MacKenzie, Lt-Col John Alexander, 1881–1960, vol. V
Mackenzie, John Alexander S.; *see* Shaw-Mackenzie.
McKenzie, John Grant, 1882–1963, vol. VI
Mackenzie, John Gurney, 1907–1975, vol. VII
Mackenzie, Col John Hugh, 1876–1963, vol. VI
MacKenzie, Maj.-Gen. John Percival, 1884–1961, vol. VI
McKenzie, Sir John Robert, 1876–1955, vol. V
Mackenzie, John Stuart, 1860–1935, vol. III
Mackenzie, Sir John William Pitt M.; *see* Muir-Mackenzie.
Mackenzie, Rt Rev. Kenneth, 1863–1945, vol. IV
Mackenzie, Surg. Vice-Adm. Sir (Kenneth) Alexander I.; *see* Ingleby Mackenzie.
Mackenzie, Rt Rev. Kenneth Donald, 1876–1966, vol. VI
Mackenzie, Sir Kenneth Douglas; *see* Mackenzie, Sir J. K. D.
Mackenzie, Rear-Adm. Kenneth Harry Litton, 1889–1970, vol. VI
Mackenzie, Kenneth James Joseph, 1867–1924, vol. II
Mackenzie, Col Kenneth James Loch, *died* 1903, vol. I
Mackenzie, Kenneth James M.; *see* Muir Mackenzie.
Mackenzie, Sir Kenneth John, 7th Bt (*cr* 1703, of Gairloch), 1861–1929, vol. III
Mackenzie, Sir Kenneth Smith, 6th Bt (*rc* 1703, of Gairloch), 1832–1900, vol. I
Mackenzie, Sir Leslie, 1862–1935, vol. III
Mackenzie, Sir (Lewis) Roderick Kenneth, 9th Bt (*cr* 1703, of Scatwell), 1902–1972, vol. VII
McKenzie, Malcolm George, 1917–1979, vol. VII
McKenzie, Marian, *died* 1927, vol. II
Mackenzie, Melville Douglas, 1889–1972, vol. VII
Mackenzie, Michael Alexander, 1866–1949, vol. IV
Mackenzie, Sir Moir; *see* Mackenzie, Sir J. M.
Mackenzie, Montague M.; *see* Muir-Mackenzie.
MacKenzie, Nicol Finlayson, 1857–1943, vol. IV
Mackenzie, Peter Alexander Cameron; *see* Count de Serra Largo.
Mackenzie, Col Sir Robert Campbell, 1856–1945, vol. IV
Mackenzie, Sir Robert Cecil M.; *see* Muir-Mackenzie.
McKenzie, Hon. Robert Donald, 1865–1928, vol. II (A), vol. III

Mackenzie, Sir Robert Henry M.; *see* Muir Mackenzie.
Mackenzie, Col Robert Holden, vol. II
Mackenzie, Robert Jameson, 1857–1912, vol. I
Mackenzie, Lt-Col Sir Robert Smythe M.; *see* Muir-Mackenzie.
McKenzie, (Robert) Tait, 1867–1938, vol. III
Mackenzie, Maj.-Gen. Roderick, 1830–1916, vol. II
Mackenzie, Sir Roderick; *see* Mackenzie, Sir L. R. K.
Mackenzie, Ronald Pierson, 1864–1930, vol. III
McKenzie, Tait; *see* McKenzie, R. T.
Mackenzie, Hon. Sir Thomas, 1854–1930, vol. III
McKenzie, Thomas, 1891–1954, vol. V
Mackenzie, Thomas William, 1875–1939, vol. III
Mackenzie, Col Sir Victor Audley Falconer, 3rd Bt (*cr* 1890), 1882–1944, vol. IV
Mackenzie, W. G., vol. II
Mackenzie, Sir William, 1849–1923, vol. II
Mackenzie, William Andrew, 1870–1942, vol. IV
Mackenzie, William Cook, 1862–1952, vol. V
Mackenzie, William Dalziel, 1840–1928, vol. II
Mackenzie, William Douglas, 1859–1936, vol. III
MacKenzie, William Forbes, 1907–1980, vol. VII
Mackenzie, William Lyon, *died* 1938, vol. III
Mackenzie, William Mackay, 1871–1952, vol. V
Mackenzie, Major William Roderick Dalziel, 1864–1952, vol. V
Mackenzie, Lt-Col William Scobie, *died* 1926, vol. II
Mackenzie, Col William Shand, 1876–1944, vol. IV
Mackenzie-Kennedy, Sir Donald; *see* Mackenzie-Kennedy, Sir H. C. D. C.
Mackenzie-Kennedy, Maj.-Gen. Sir Edward Charles William, *died* 1932, vol. III
Mackenzie-Kennedy, Sir (Henry Charles) Donald (Cleveland), 1889–1965, vol. VI
Mackenzie King, Rt Hon. William Lyon; *see* King.
Mackenzie-Rogan, Lt-Col John, 1855–1932, vol. III
M'Keown, Hon. Harrison Andrew, 1863–1932, vol. III
McKeown, Robert John, 1869–1925, vol. II
McKeown, Walter, 1866–1925, vol. II
McKercher, Sir William Gourley, *died* 1937, vol. III
MacKereth, Sir Gilbert, 1893–1962, vol. VI
McKergow, Lt-Col Robert Wilson, 1866–1947, vol. IV
McKerihan, Sir (Clarence) Roy, 1896–1969, vol. VI
McKerihan, Sir Roy; *see* McKerihan, Sir C. R.
M'Kerlie, Sir John Graham, 1814–1900, vol. I
McKerral, Andrew, 1876–1967, vol. VI
McKerrell, Brig.-Comdr Augustus de Ségur, 1863–1916, vol. II
McKerron, Sir Patrick Alexander Bruce, 1896–1964, vol. VI
McKerron, Robert Gordon, 1862–1937, vol. III
McKerron, Robert Gordon, 1900–1973, vol. VII
McKerrow, Ronald Brunlees, 1872–1940, vol. III
Mackeson, Brig. Sir Harry Ripley, 1st Bt, 1905–1964, vol. VI
Mackessack, George Ross, 1851–1935, vol. III
Mackesy, Col Charles Ernest Randolph, 1861–1925, vol. II

Mackesy, Maj.-Gen. Pierse Joseph, 1883–1956, vol. V
Mackesy, Lt-Gen. William Henry, 1837–1914, vol. I
Mackeurtan, Harold Graham, 1884–1942, vol. IV
McKew, Rev. Robert, died 1944, vol. IV
Mackey, Archibald John, 1844–1936, vol. III
Mackey, Brig.-Gen. Hugh James Alexander, 1876–1927, vol. II
Mackey, Hon. Sir John Emanuel, 1865–1924, vol. II
McKibbin, Col Alan John, 1892–1958, vol. V
McKibbin, Major Thomas, 1879–1943, vol. IV
Mackichan, Rev. D., 1851–1932, vol. III
Mackie, Alexander, 1876–1955, vol. V
Mackie, Alfred William White, 1877–1951, vol. V
Mackie, Brig. Andrew Hugh, 1897–1968, vol. VI
Mackie, Charles, died 1940, vol. III (A), vol. IV
Mackie, Charles H., 1862–1920, vol. II
McKie, Douglas, 1896–1967, vol. VI
Mackie, Edwin Gordon, 1896–1980, vol. VII
Mackie, Bt Col F. Percival, 1875–1944, vol. IV
Mackie, Rev. George M., 1854–1922, vol. II
McKie, Helen Madeleine, died 1957, vol. V
Mackie, Sir Horatio George Arthur, 1868–1940, vol. III
Mackie, Sir James, 1838–1898, vol. I
McKie, Lt-Col John, 1857–1934, vol. III
Mackie, John, 1862–1939, vol. III
Mackie, John Beveridge, 1848–1919, vol. II
Mackie, John Duncan, 1887–1978, vol. VII
Mackie, John Hamilton, 1898–1958, vol. V
Mackie, John Lindsay, 1864–1956, vol. V
Mackie, Sir Peter Jeffrey, 1st Bt, 1855–1924, vol. II
Mackie, Peter Robert McLeod, died 1959, vol. V
Mackie, Sir Richard, 1851–1923, vol. II
Mackie, Thomas Jones, 1888–1955, vol. V
Mackie, Col Tom Darke, 1883–1941, vol. IV
McKie, William Murray, 1866–1932, vol. III
McKie Reid, Col Andrew; see Reid.
Mackilligin, Robert Springett, 1890–1972, vol. VII
MacKillop, Douglas, 1891–1959, vol. V
McKillop, James, 1844–1913, vol. I
M'Killop, William, died 1909, vol. I
McKim, Ven. Charles W., 1867–1934, vol. III
McKim, Rt Rev. John, 1852–1936, vol. III
Mackinder, Rt Hon. Sir Halford John, 1861–1947, vol. IV
Mackinder, William, 1880–1930, vol. III
McKinlay, Adam Storey, died 1950, vol. IV
Mackinlay, Antoinette, (Mrs John Mackinlay); see Sterling, A.
Mackinlay, Lt-Col George, 1847–1928, vol. II
Mackinlay, Sir George Mason, 1906–1973, vol. VII
Mackinlay, Jean Sterling, died 1958, vol. V
Mackinlay, Malcolm Sterling, 1876–1952, vol. V
M'Kinley, William, 1843–1901, vol. I
McKinnell, James Jesse, 1869–1950, vol. IV
Mackinney, Frederick Walker, 1871–1950, vol. IV
McKinney, Sir William, 1897–1979, vol. VII
Mackinnon, Rev. Albert Glenthorne Tait, 1871–1939, vol. III
Mackinnon, Lt-Col Alexander Charles Broughton, 1878–1942, vol. IV

Mackinnon, Archibald Donald, 1864–1937, vol. III
Mackinnon of Mackinnon, Comdr Arthur Avalon, 1893–1964, vol. VI
Mackinnon, Donald, died 1914, vol. I
Mackinnon, Hon. Donald, 1859–1932, vol. III
Mackinnon, Hon. Donald Alexander, 1863–1928, vol. II
Mackinnon, Doris Livingston, died 1956, vol. V
Mackinnon, Rear-Adm. Edmund Julius Gordon, 1880–1940, vol. III
MacKinnon of MacKinnon, Francis Alexander, 1848–1947, vol. IV
MacKinnon, Rt Hon. Sir Frank Douglas, 1871–1946, vol. IV
MacKinnon, Gena; see MacKinnon, Georgina R. D.
MacKinnon, Georgina Russell Davidson, (Gena MacKinnon), 1885–1973, vol. VII
MacKinnon, Gen. Sir Henry; see MacKinnon, Gen. Sir W. H.
Mackinnon, Lt-Col Henry William Alexander, 1842–1905, vol. I
Mackinnon, James, 1860–1945, vol. IV
McKinnon, Sir James, 1894–1971, vol. VII
MacKinnon, James Alexander Rudolf, 1888–1955, vol. V
Mackinnon, John, 1886–1958, vol. V
Mackinnon, Kenneth Wulsten, 1906–1964, vol. VI
Mackinnon, Col Lachlan, 1886–1973, vol. VII
MacKinnon, Vice-Adm. Lachlan Donald Ian, 1882–1948, vol. IV
Mackinnon, Sir Lauchlan Charles, 1848–1925, vol. II
Mackinnon, Murdoch, 1865–1944, vol. IV
Mackinnon, Sir Percy Graham, 1872–1956, vol. V
M'Kinnon, Rev. W., 1843–1925, vol. II (A), vol. III
Mackinnon, Sir William Alexander, 1830–1897, vol. I
MacKinnon, Gen. Sir (William) Henry, 1852–1929, vol. III
Mackinnon, Lt-Col William Thomas Morris, died 1957, vol. V
McKinstry, Sir Archibald, 1877–1952, vol. V
McKinstry, Captain Edward Robert, 1861–1943, vol. IV
Mackintosh, Hon. Lord; Charles Mackintosh, 1888–1978, vol. VII
Mackintosh of Halifax, 1st Viscount, 1891–1964, vol. VI
Mackintosh of Halifax, 2nd Viscount, 1921–1980, vol. VII
Mackintosh, The; Alfred Donald Mackintosh, 1851–1938, vol. III
Mackintosh, The; see Mackintosh of Mackintosh, Vice-Adm. L. D.
Mackintosh, Rt Rev. Mgr Alexander, 1854–1922, vol. II
Mackintosh, Sir Alexander, 1858–1948, vol. IV
Mackintosh, Alfred Donald; see Mackintosh, The.
Mackintosh, Sir Ashley Watson, 1868–1937, vol. III
Mackintosh, Charles; see Mackintosh, Hon. Lord.
Mackintosh, (Charles Ernest Whistler) Christopher, 1903–1974, vol. VII

433

Mackintosh, Charles Rennie, 1869–1928, vol. II
Mackintosh, Christopher; see Mackintosh, Charles E. W. C.
Mackintosh, Most Rev. Donald, died 1943, vol. IV
Mackintosh, Most Rev. Donald A., 1845–1919, vol. II
Mackintosh, Donald James, 1862–1947, vol. IV
Mackintosh, Eric Donald, 1906–1978, vol. VII
Mackintosh, Col Ernest Elliot Buckland, 1880–1957, vol. V
Mackintosh, Col George, 1860–1954, vol. V
Mackintosh, Rev. Hugh Ross, 1870–1936, vol. III
Mackintosh, James, 1858–1944, vol. IV
Mackintosh, James M., 1891–1966, vol. VI
Mackintosh, John, 1833–1907, vol. I
Mackintosh, John Pitcairn, 1929–1978, vol. VII
Mackintosh, Captain Sir Kenneth Lachlan, 1902–1979, vol. VII
Mackintosh of Mackintosh, Vice-Adm. Lachlan Donald, (The Mackintosh), 1896–1957, vol. V
Mackintosh, Rev. Robert, 1858–1933, vol. III
Mackintosh, Stanley Hugh, 1883–1967, vol. VI
Mackintosh, William; see Kyllachy, Hon. Lord.
Mackintosh, William Archibald, 1895–1970, vol. VI (AII)
Mackintosh, Rev. William Lachlan, 1859–1926, vol. II
McKisack, Sir Audley, 1903–1966, vol. VI
M'Kisack, Henry Lawrence, 1859–1928, vol. II
McKittrick, Thomas Harrington, 1889–1970, vol. VI
Macklin, Sir (Albert) Noel (Campbell), died 1946, vol. IV
Macklin, Albert Romer, 1863–1921, vol. II
Macklin, Sir (Albert) Sortain (Romer), 1890–1976, vol. VII
Macklin, Sir James, 1864–1944, vol. IV
Macklin, Sir Noel; see Macklin, Sir A. N. C.
Macklin, Sir Sortain; see Macklin, Sir A. S. R.
Macklin, T. Eyre, 1867–1943, vol. IV
Mackness, Rev. George, 1834–1914, vol. I (p. 463)
Mackness, Lt-Comdr George John, 1892–1970, vol. VI
Mackness, William Robert, 1879–1963, vol. VI
Macknight, Dodge, 1860–1950, vol. IV (A)
Macknight, Lt-Col John James Thow, died 1965, vol. VI
Macknight, Thomas, 1829–1899, vol. I (p. 463)
Mackworth, Sir Arthur William, 6th Bt, 1842–1914, vol. I
Mackworth, Vice-Adm. Geoffrey, 1879–1952, vol. V
Mackworth, Col Sir Harry Llewellyn, 8th Bt, 1878–1952, vol. V
Mackworth, Sir Humphrey, 7th Bt, 1871–1948, vol. IV
Mackworth, John Dolben, 1887–1939, vol. III
Mackworth, Air Vice-Marshal Philip Herbert, 1897–1958, vol. V
Mackworth-Praed, Sir Herbert Bulkley; see Praed.
Mackworth-Young, Gerard; see Young.
Maclachlan, Alan Bruce, 1874–1955, vol. V
Maclachlan, Lt-Col Alexander Fraser Campbell, 1875–1918, vol. II

Maclachlan, Adm. Crawford, 1867–1952, vol. V
McLachlan, Donald Harvey, 1908–1971, vol. VII
McLachlan, Duncan Clark, 1853–1929, vol. III
McLachlan, Herbert, 1876–1958, vol. V
McLachlan, Maj.-Gen. James Douglas, 1869–1937, vol. III
Maclachlan of Maclachlan, John, 1859–1942, vol. IV
M'Lachlan, Robert, 1837–1904, vol. I
MacLachlan, Robert Boyd, 1880–1975, vol. VII
Maclachlan, Brig.-Gen. Ronald Campbell, 1872–1917, vol. II
Maclachlan, Sir T. J. Leigh, 1864–1946, vol. IV
Maclachlan, Thomas Banks, died 1952, vol. V
Maclachlan, Thomas Kay, 1895–1972, vol. VII
Maclachlan, Col Thomas Robertson, 1870–1921, vol. II
McLagan, Archibald Gibson, 1853–1928, vol. II
Maclagan, Sir Douglas, 1812–1900, vol. I
Maclagan, Sir Edward Douglas, 1864–1952, vol. V
Maclagan, Sir Eric Robert Dalrymple, 1879–1951, vol. V
Maclagan, Maj.-Gen. Ewen George S; see Sinclair-Maclagan.
Maclagan, John, 1846–1929, vol. III
Maclagan, Col Robert Smeiton, 1860–1931, vol. III
Maclagan, Most Rev. William Dalrymple, 1826–1910, vol. I
Maclagan, William Gauld, 1903–1972, vol. VII
McLaggan, Sir Douglas; see McLaggan, Sir J. D.
McLaggan, Sir (John) Douglas, 1893–1967, vol. VI
McLaglen, Victor, died 1959, vol. V
Maclaine of Lochbuie, Kenneth Douglas Lorne, 1880–1935, vol. III
Maclaine of Lochbuie, Murdoch Gillian, 1845–1909, vol. I
M'Laren, Hon. Lord; John M'Laren, 1831–1910, vol. I
M'Laren, Rev. Alexander, 1826–1910, vol. I
MacLaren, Andrew, 1883–1975, vol. VII
Maclaren, Archibald Campbell, 1871–1944, vol. IV
MacLaren, Brig.-Gen. Charles Henry, 1878–1962, vol. VI
McLaren, Sir Charles Northrop, 1898–1955, vol. V
MacLaren of MacLaren, Donald, 1910–1966, vol. VI
M'Laren, Rev. Douglas, 1866–1956, vol. V
M'Laren, Hon. Francis Walter Stafford, died 1917, vol. II
McLaren, Henry, 1883–1943, vol. IV
Maclaren, Ian; see Watson, Rev. John.
McLaren, Jack, 1887–1954, vol. V
Maclaren, James Anderson, 1866–1926, vol. II
McLaren, Sir John, 1850–1920, vol. II
M'Laren, John; see M'Laren, Hon. Lord.
McLaren, Sir John Gilbert, 1871–1958, vol. V
Maclaren, John James, died 1926, vol. II
Maclaren, Major Kenneth, 1860–1924, vol. II
McLaren, Martin, 1914–1979, vol. VII
McLaren, Moray, 1901–1971, vol. VII
MacLaren, Col Murray, 1861–1942, vol. IV
McLaren, Robert, 1856–1940, vol. III
McLaren, Ross Scott, 1906–1975, vol. VII
M'Laren, Walter Stowe Bright, 1853–1912, vol. I

McLaren, Rev. William David, 1856–1921, vol. II
McLarty, Hon. Sir (Duncan) Ross, 1891–1962, vol. VI
McLarty, Hon. Norman Alexander, 1889–1945, vol. IV
McLarty, Hon. Sir Ross; see McLarty, Hon. Sir D. R.
Maclauchlan, Hugh Simon, died 1899, vol. I
MacLaughlin, Lt-Col Alexander John Maunsell, 1854–1932, vol. III
M'Laughlin, Andrew Cunningham, 1861–1947, vol. IV
MacLaughlin, Col Arthur Maunsell, died 1954, vol. V
McLaughlin, Charles Redmond, 1909–1979, vol. VII
McLaughlin, Sir Henry, 1876–1927, vol. II
M'Laughlin, Lt-Col Hubert James, 1860–1915, vol. I
McLaughlin, Rev. John Fletcher, 1863–1933, vol. III
McLaughlin, Rear-Adm. Patrick Vivian, 1901–1969, vol. VI
M'Laurin, Duncan, 1848–1921, vol. II
MacLaurin, Hon. Sir Henry Normand, 1835–1914, vol. I
McLaurin, Engr-Rear-Adm. John, died 1955, vol. V
Maclaurin, Richard Cockburn, 1870–1920, vol. II
Maclaverty, Edward Hyde East, 1847–1922, vol. II
Maclay, 1st Baron, 1857–1951, vol. V
Maclay, 2nd Baron, 1899–1969, vol. VI
Maclay, Hon. Walter Symington, 1901–1964, vol. VI
McLean, Major Sir Alan, 1875–1959, vol. V
Maclean, Alexander, 1867–1940, vol. III
Maclean, Surg. Rear-Adm. Alexander, 1868–1945, vol. IV
Maclean, Sir Alexander, 1872–1948, vol. IV
Maclean of Ardgour, Alexander John Hew, 1880–1930, vol. III
Maclean, Rev. Alexander Miller, 1865–1925, vol. II
Maclean, Alexander Morvaren, 1872–1936, vol. III
Maclean, Alick; see Maclean, Alexander Morvaren.
M'Lean, Hon. Allan, 1840–1911, vol. I
Maclean, Allan, 1858–1918, vol. II
MacLean, Angus, 1863–1948, vol. IV
Maclean, Angus Alexander, 1854–1943, vol. IV
MacLean, Col Archibald Campbell Holms, 1883–1970, vol. VI
Maclean, Most Rev. Arthur John, 1858–1943, vol. IV
McLean, Calvin Stowe, 1888–1970, vol. VI
Maclean, Catherine Macdonald, died 1960, vol. V
Maclean, Brig.-Gen. Charles Alexander Hugh, 1874–1947, vol. IV
MacLean, Col Charles Allan, 1892–1978, vol. VII
Maclean, Charles Donald, 1843–1916, vol. II
McLean, Lt-Col Charles Herbert, 1877–1940, vol. III (A), vol. IV
Maclean, Maj.-Gen. Charles Smith, 1836–1921, vol. II

McLean, Col Charles Wesley Weldon, 1882–1962, vol. VI
Maclean, Vice-Adm. Colin Kenneth, died 1935, vol. III
MacLean, Air Vice-Marshal Cuthbert Trelawder, 1886–1969, vol. VI
M'Lean, Donald, died 1915, vol. I
Maclean, Rt Hon. Sir Donald, 1864–1932, vol. III
Maclean, Captain Donald Charles Hugh, 1875–1909, vol. I
Maclean, Sir Douglas; see Maclean, Sir R. D. D.
McLean, Edward B., died 1941, vol. IV
Maclean, Sir Ewen John, died 1953, vol. V
Maclean, Sir Fitzroy Donald, 10th Bt, 1835–1936, vol. III
Maclean, Sir Francis William, 1844–1913, vol. I
Maclean, Frederick Gurr, 1848–1915, vol. I (A)
M'Lean, Hon. Sir George, 1834–1917, vol. II
Maclean, George Edwin, 1850–1938, vol. III
Maclean, Gordon Thompson, 1884–1943, vol. IV
Maclean, Kaid, Gen. Sir Harry Aubrey deVere, 1848–1920, vol. II
Maclean, Lt-Col Henry Donald Neil, 1872–1926, vol. II
McLean, Lt-Col Henry John, 1868–1931, vol. III
MacLean, Hugh, 1879–1957, vol. V
McLean, Maj.-Gen. Hon. Hugh Havelock, 1854–1938, vol. III
MacLean, Ida Smedley, died 1944, vol. IV
MacLean, James A., 1868–1945, vol. IV
Maclean, James Borrowman, 1881–1940, vol. III
Maclean, James Mackenzie, 1835–1906, vol. I
McLean, Col James Reynolds, 1872–1921, vol. II
McLean, John, 1893–1978, vol. VII
Maclean, Lt-Col John Bayne, 1862–1950, vol. IV
Maclean, John Cassilis Birkmyre, 1849–1925, vol. II
MacLean, Hon. John Duncan, 1873–1948, vol. IV
Maclean, John Kennedy, 1874–1933, vol. III
McLean, John Reid, 1856–1935, vol. III
McLean, John Roll, 1848–1916, vol. II
Maclean, Lachlan Frederick Copeland, 1885–1957, vol. V
Maclean, Magnus, died 1937, vol. III
McLean, Miss Mary, died 1949, vol. IV
Maclean, Neil, died 1953, vol. V
MacLean, Neil Adam, 1885–1944, vol. IV
M'Lean, Norman, 1865–1947, vol. IV
Maclean, Very Rev. Norman, 1869–1952, vol. V
McLean, Sir Robert, 1884–1964, vol. VI
Maclean, Sir (Robert Donald) Douglas, 1852–1929, vol. III
M'Lean, Simon James, 1871–1946, vol. IV
Maclean, William Campbell, died 1898, vol. I
Maclean, William Findlay, 1854–1929, vol. III
McLean, Sir William Hannah, 1877–1967, vol. VI
McLean, Rev. Col William Richard James, 1858–1932, vol. III
McLean, Sir William Ross, 1901–1965, vol. VI
Macleane, Rev. Douglas, 1856–1925, vol. II
Maclear, Rev. George Frederick, 1833–1902, vol. I
Maclear, Lt-Col Harry, 1872–1916, vol. II
Maclear, Adm. John Pearse, 1838–1907, vol. I
McLearn, Sir William, 1837–1918, vol. II

McLeavy, Baron (Life Peer); Frank McLeavy, 1899–1976, vol. VII
Macleay, Col Alexander Caldcleugh, 1843–1907, vol. I
McLeay, Hon. George, 1892–1955, vol. V
Macleay, Sir (James William) Ronald, 1870–1943, vol. IV
Macleay, John Thomson, 1870–1955, vol. V
Macleay, Sir Ronald; see Macleay, Sir J. W. R.
Maclehose, James, 1857–1943, vol. IV
Maclehose, Norman M., 1859–1931, vol. III
McLeish, Donald Alexander Stewart, 1893–1958, vol. V (A)
M'Leish, Col Duncan, 1851–1920, vol. II
M'Lellan, Alexander Matheson, 1872–1957, vol. V
MacLellan, Alexander Stephen, 1886–1966, vol. VI
M'Lellan, C. M. S., 1865–1916, vol. II
McLellan, Lt-Col William, died 1934, vol. III
MacLellan, William Turner, died 1945, vol. IV
MacLennan, Alexander, 1872–1953, vol. V
M'Lennan, Lt-Col Bartlett, 1868–1918, vol. II
Maclennan, Farquhar Stuart, died 1925, vol. II
MacLennan, Sir Hector, 1905–1978, vol. VII
M'Lennan, Sir John Cunningham, 1867–1935, vol. III
M'Lennan, John Ferguson, 1855–1917, vol. II
McLennan, John Stewart, 1853–1939, vol. III
Maclennan, Kenneth, 1872–1952, vol. V
MacLennan, Sir Robert Laing, 1888–1977, vol. VII
M'Lennan, William, 1856–1904, vol. I
MacLeod, Alexander Cameron, 1899–1971, vol. VII
McLeod, Hon. Alexander Donald, 1872–1938, vol. III
Macleod, Allan, 1887–1955, vol. V
Macleod, Adm. Angus, 1847–1920, vol. II
MacLeod, Cameron; see MacLeod, A. C.
McLeod, Sir Charles Campbell, 1st Bt (cr 1925), 1858–1936, vol. III
Macleod, Maj.-Gen. Charles William, 1881–1944, vol. IV
M'Leod, Clement Henry, died 1917, vol. II
Macleod, Very Rev. Donald, died 1916, vol. II
M'Leod, Hon. Donald, died 1918, vol. II (A), vol. III
M'Leod, Gen. Sir Donald James Sim, 1845–1922, vol. II
McLeod, Lt-Gen. Sir (Donald) Kenneth, 1885–1958, vol. V
MacLeod, Douglas Hamilton, 1901–1970, vol. VI
MacLeod, Duncan, 1876–1949, vol. IV
McLeod, Sir Ezekiel, 1840–1920, vol. II
Macleod, Fiona; see Sharp, William.
MacLeod of MacLeod, Dame Flora, 1878–1976, vol. VII
Macleod, Frederick Henry, died 1938, vol. III
MacLeod, Sir Frederick Larkins, 1858–1936, vol. III
McLeod, George William Buckham, 1868–1947, vol. IV
M'Leod, Hon. Harry Fulton, 1871–1920, vol. II
M'Leod, Herbert, 1841–1923, vol. II
Macleod, Rt Hon. Iain Norman, 1913–1970, vol. VI

MacLeod, Captain Sir Ian Francis Norman, 3rd Bt (cr 1924), 1921–1944, vol. IV
Macleod, James John, 1841–1919, vol. II
MacLeod, Sir James MacIver, 1866–1944, vol. IV
McLeod, (James) Walter, 1887–1978, vol. VII
Macleod, Rev. John, 1840–1898, vol. I
Macleod, John, 1839–1927, vol. II
Macleod, John, 1891–1969, vol. VI (AII)
Macleod, John James Rickard, 1876–1935, vol. III
MacLeod, Sir John Lorne, 1873–1946, vol. IV
MacLeod, Sir John Mackintosh, 1st Bt (cr 1924), 1857–1934, vol. III
MacLeod, Sir (John Mackintosh) Norman, 2nd Bt (cr 1924), 1891–1939, vol. III
MacLeod, John MacLeod Hendrie, 1870–1954, vol. V
MacLeod, Col John Norman, 1865–1932, vol. III
Macleod, Col Kenneth, 1840–1922, vol. II
McLeod, Lt-Gen. Sir Kenneth; see McLeod, Lt-Gen. Sir D. K.
Macleod, Lewis Rose, 1875–1941, vol. IV
MacLeod, Maj.-Gen. Malcolm Neynoe, 1882–1969, vol. VI
McLeod, Sir Murdoch Campbell, 2nd Bt (cr 1925), 1893–1950, vol. IV
Macleod, Rev. Norman, 1838–1911, vol. I
Macleod, Lt-Col Norman, 1872–1960, vol. V
MacLeod, Sir Norman; see MacLeod, Sir J. M. N.
Macleod, Sir Norman Cranstoun, 1866–1945, vol. IV
M'Leod, Norman F., 1856–1921, vol. II
Macleod of Macleod, Norman Magnus, 1839–1929, vol. III
Macleod of Macleod, Sir Reginald, 1847–1935, vol. III
McLeod, Lt-Col Reginald George M'Queen, 1859–1910, vol. I
Macleod, Robert Duncan, died 1973, vol. VII
Macleod, Col Robert Lockhart Ross, 1863–1943, vol. IV
Macleod, Rev. Roderick Charles, 1852–1934, vol. III
Macleod, Col Roderick William, 1851–1932, vol. III
McLeod, Gen. Sir Roderick William, 1905–1980, vol. VII
Macleod, Roderick Willoughby, 1858–1931, vol. III
Macleod, Simon John Fraser, 1857–1938, vol. III
McLeod, Walter; see McLeod, J. W.
Macleod, Inspector-Gen. William, died 1904, vol. I
Macleod, Very Rev. William Arthur, 1867–1932, vol. III
McLeod, Brig.-Gen. William Kelty, 1862–1928, vol. II
Macleod, Captain William Simon Fraser, 1888–1940, vol. III
McLetchie, James Leslie, 1909–1965, vol. VI
Mac Liammóir, Micheál, 1899–1978, vol. VII
McLintock, Sir Thomson, 2nd Bt, 1905–1953, vol. V
McLintock, Sir William, 1st Bt, 1873–1947, vol. IV
McLintock, William Francis Porter, 1887–1960, vol. V
Macloone, James, died 1934, vol. III

McLoughlin, Edward Patrick, *died* 1956, vol. V

McLoughlin, Maj.-Gen. George Somers, 1867–1943, vol. IV

McLuhan, (Herbert) Marshall, 1911–1980, vol. VII

McLuhan, Marshall; *see* McLuhan, H. M.

Maclure, Lt-Col Alan Francis, 1873–1929, vol. III

Maclure, Very Rev. Edward Craig, 1833–1906, vol. I

Maclure, Sir John Edward Stanley, 2nd Bt, 1869–1938, vol. III

Maclure, Sir John William, 1st Bt, 1835–1901, vol. I

Maclure, Lt-Col Sir John William Spencer, 3rd Bt, 1899–1980, vol. VII

McMahon, Col Sir (Arthur) Henry, 1862–1949, vol. IV

McMahon, Col Bernard William Lynedoch, 1865–1928, vol. II

McMahon, Gen. Charles Alexander, 1830–1904, vol. I

Macmahon, Cortlandt, *died* 1954, vol. V

MacMahon, Ella, *died* 1956, vol. V

McMahon, Gregan, 1874–1941, vol. IV

McMahon, Lt-Col Sir Eyre, 6th Bt, 1860–1935, vol. III

McMahon, Col Sir Henry; *see* McMahon, Col Sir A. H.

M'Mahon, Major Sir Horace Westropp, 5th Bt, 1863–1932, vol. III

Macmahon, Hugh, 1836–1911, vol. I

MacMahon, Maj.-Gen. Hugh Francis Edward, 1880–1939, vol. III

Macmahon, Rt Hon. James, 1865–1954, vol. V

McMahon, Rt Rev. Mgr John, 1844–1932, vol. III

M'Mahon, Sir Lionel, 4th Bt, 1856–1926, vol. II

McMahon, Lt-Col Norman Reginald, 1866–1914, vol. I

McMahon, Sir Patrick; *see* McMahon, Sir W. P.

Macmahon, Lt-Gen. Peadar, 1893–1975, vol. VII

MacMahon, Percy Alexander, 1854–1929, vol. III

McMahon, Sir (William) Patrick, 7th Bt, 1900–1977, vol. VII

M'Mahon, Sir William Samuel, 3rd Bt, 1839–1905, vol. I

Macmanaway, Rt Rev. James, *died* 1947, vol. IV

MacManaway, Rev. James Godfrey, 1898–1951, vol. V

MacManus, Emily Elvira Primrose, 1886–1978, vol. VII

Macmanus, Joseph Edward, *died* 1921, vol. II

MacManus, Seumas, *died* 1960, vol. V

McMaster, Hon. Andrew R., 1876–1937, vol. III

Macmaster, Sir Donald, 1st Bt, 1846–1922, vol. II

McMaster, Sir Fergus, 1879–1950, vol. IV (A), vol. V

McMaster, Sir Frederick Duncan, 1873–1954, vol. V

McMaster, Ian, 1898–1978, vol. VII

Macmaster, James, *died* 1933, vol. III

McMaster, John Bach, 1852–1932, vol. III

McMaster, Col John Maxwell, 1855–1937, vol. III

McMaster, Robert Maxwell, 1892–1936, vol. III

M'Means, Lt-Col Hon. Lendrum, 1859–1941, vol. IV (A), vol. V

MacMechan, Archibald M'Kellar, 1862–1933, vol. III

McMenemey, William Henry, 1905–1977, vol. VII

MacMichael, Sir Harold Alfred, 1882–1969, vol. VI

Macmichael, Neil, 1871–1949, vol. IV

McMichael, Robert Clark, 1878–1957, vol. V

M'Michael, Solon William, 1848–1923, vol. II

McMicking, Major Gilbert, 1862–1942, vol. IV

McMicking, Col Harry, 1867–1944, vol. IV

McMicking, Maj.-Gen. Neil, 1894–1963, vol. VI

Macmillan, Baron (Life Peer); Hugh Pattison Macmillan, 1873–1952, vol. V

McMillan, Alec, *died* 1919, vol. II

Macmillan, Lt-Col Alexander, 1871–1929, vol. III

Macmillan, Archibald Morven, 1880–1954, vol. V

McMillan, Rev. Charles D. H., *died* 1919, vol. II

Macmillan, Chrystal, *died* 1937, vol. III

Macmillan, Daniel, 1886–1965, vol. VI

Macmillan, Sir Daniel Hunter, 1846–1933, vol. III

M'Millan, Hon. Donald, 1835–1914, vol. I

Macmillan, Rev. Donald, 1855–1927, vol. II

MacMillan, Donald Baxter, 1874–1970, vol. VI

Macmillan, Very Rev. Ebenezer, 1881–1944, vol. IV

MacMillan, Sir Ernest Campbell, 1893–1973, vol. VII

Macmillan, Sir Frederick, 1851–1936, vol. III

Macmillan, George A., 1855–1936, vol. III

MacMillan, Harvey Reginald, 1885–1976, vol. VII

Macmillan, Rev. Hugh, 1833–1903, vol. I

McMillan, James Athole, 1896–1977, vol. VII

McMillan, John, 1873–1939, vol. III

Macmillan, Rt Rev. Mgr John, 1899–1957, vol. V

Macmillan, Rt Rev. John Victor, 1877–1956, vol. V

Macmillan, Malcolm K., 1913–1978, vol. VII

McMillan, Margaret, 1860–1931, vol. III

Macmillan, Maurice Crawford, 1853–1936, vol. III

Macmillan, Michael, 1853–1925, vol. II

Macmillan, Norman, 1892–1976, vol. VII

Macmillan, Rev. Robert Alexander Cameron, 1883–1917, vol. II

McMillan, Sir Robert Furse, 1858–1931, vol. III

McMillan, Thomas McLellan, 1919–1980, vol. VII

McMillan, W. H., *died* 1947, vol. IV

MacMillan, W. J. P., 1881–1957, vol. V

M'Millan, Hon. Sir William, 1850–1926, vol. II

McMillan, William, 1887–1977, vol. VII

McMillan, William Bentley, 1871–1922, vol. II

Macmillan, William Miller, 1885–1974, vol. VII

McMillan, Sir William Northrup, 1872–1925, vol. II

MacMonnies, Frederick William, 1863–1937, vol. III

McMordie, Mrs Julia, *died* 1942, vol. IV

M'Mordie, Robert James, 1849–1914, vol. I

M'Morine, Ven. John Ker, *died* 1912, vol. I

Macmorran, Alexander, 1852–1933, vol. III

McMorran, Donald Hanks, 1904–1965, vol. VI

Macmorran, Kenneth Mead, 1883–1973, vol. VII

McMorrough Kavanagh, Col Sir Dermot, 1890–1958, vol. V

MacMullan, Charles W. Kirkpatrick, 1889–1973, vol. VII

McMullan, Sir Thomas Wallace, 1864–1945, vol. IV

McMullen, Alexander Percy, 1875–1961, vol. VI

Macmullen, Gen. Sir (Cyril) Norman, 1877–1944, vol. IV

McMullen, Col Denis, 1902–1973, vol. VII

McMullen, Maj.-Gen. Sir Donald Jay, 1891–1967, vol. VI

MacMullen, Maj.-Gen. Hugh Tennent, 1892–1946, vol. IV

Macmullen, Gen. Sir Norman; see Macmullen, Gen. Sir C. N.

McMullen, Lt-Col Osmond Robert, died 1946, vol. IV

M'Mullen, William Halliburton, 1876–1958, vol. V

MacMunn, Charles Alexander, 1852–1911, vol. I

MacMunn, Lt-Gen. Sir George Fletcher, 1869–1952, vol. V

McMunn, Maj.-Gen. James Robert, 1866–1945, vol. IV

MacMurchy, Helen, 1862–1953, vol. V

McMurdo, Captain Arthur Montagu, 1861–1914, vol. I

McMurray, Hon. Edward James, 1878–1969, vol. VI

McMurray, James Hamish, died 1950, vol. IV

Macmurray, John, 1891–1976, vol. VII

McMurray, Thomas Porter, 1887–1949, vol. IV

M'Murrich, James Playfair, 1859–1939, vol. III

McMurtrie, Francis Edwin, 1884–1949, vol. IV

M'Murtrie, Very Rev. John, 1831–1912, vol. I

Macnab, Col Allan James, 1864–1947, vol. IV

Macnab of Macnab, Archibald Corrie, 1886–1970, vol. VI

McNab, Hon. Archibald Peter, 1864–1945, vol. IV

Macnab, Brig.-Gen. Colin Lawrance, 1870–1918, vol. II

Macnab, George Henderson, 1904–1967, vol. VI

Macnab of Barachastlain, Iain, 1890–1967, vol. VI

Macnab, Brig. John Francis, 1906–1980, vol. VII

M'Nab, Hon. Robert, 1864–1917, vol. II

Macnab, William, 1858–1941, vol. IV

McNabb, Surg.-Rear-Adm. Sir Daniel Joseph Patrick, 1862–1937, vol. III

Macnabb, Sir Donald Campbell, 1832–1913, vol. I

Macnabb, Lt-Col Donald John Campbell, 1864–1936, vol. III

MacNachtan, Col Neil F., 1850–1928, vol. II

Macnaghten, Baron (Life Peer); Edward Macnaughten, 1830–1913, vol. I

Macnaghten, Sir Antony, 10th Bt, 1899–1972, vol. VII

Macnaghten, Sir Arthur Douglas, 7th Bt, 1897–1916, did not have an entry in Who's Who.

Macnaghten, Col Charles Melville, 1879–1931, vol. III

Macnaghten, Hon. Sir Edward Charles, 5th Bt, 1859–1914, vol. I

Macnaghten, Sir Edward Henry, 6th Bt, 1896–1916 (this entry was not transferred to Who was Who).

Macnaghten, Brig.-Gen. Ernest Brander, 1872–1948, vol. IV

Macnaghten, Hon. Sir Francis Alexander, 8th Bt, 1863–1951, vol. V

Macnaghten, Rt Hon. Sir Francis Edmund Workman-, 3rd Bt, 1828–1911, vol. I

Macnaghten, Hon. Sir Frederic Fergus, 9th Bt, 1867–1955, vol. V

Macnaghten, Sir Henry, 1880–1949, vol. IV

Macnaghten, Rev. Henry Alexander, 1850–1928, vol. II

Macnaghten, Hugh Vibart, died 1929, vol. III

Macnaghten, Rt Hon. Sir Malcolm, 1869–1955, vol. V

Macnaghten, Sir Melville Leslie, 1853–1921, vol. II

Macnaghten, Steuart, 1873–1952, vol. V

Macnaghten, Terence Charles, 1872–1944, vol. IV

McNair, 1st Baron, 1885–1975, vol. VII

McNair, Arthur James, 1887–1964, vol. VI

McNair, Arthur Wyndham, 1872–1965, vol. VI

McNair, Sir Douglas; see McNair, Sir G. D.

M'Nair, Lt-Gen. Edward John, 1838–1921, vol. II

McNair, Captain Eric Archibald, died 1918, vol. II

McNair, Sir (George) Douglas, 1887–1967, vol. VI

McNair, John, 1887–1968, vol. VI

M'Nair, Major John Frederick Adolphus, 1828–1910, vol. I

McNair, Brig. John Kirkland, 1893–1973, vol. VII

Macnair, Peter, 1868–1929, vol. III

Macnair, Sir Robert Hill, 1877–1959, vol. V

McNair, Sir William Lennox, 1892–1979, vol. VII

McNairn, Edward Somerville, 1907–1975, vol. VII

McNally, Most Rev. John Thomas, 1871–1952, vol. V

McNalty, Brig.-Gen. Arthur George Preston, 1871–1958, vol. V

MacNalty, Sir Arthur Salusbury, 1880–1969, vol. VI

M'Nalty, Lt-Col George William, 1837–1912, vol. I

Macnamara, Arthur, 1829–1906, vol. I

McNamara, Lt-Gen. Sir Arthur Edward, 1877–1949, vol. IV

MacNamara, Arthur James, 1885–1962, vol. VI

Macnamara, Eric Danvers, died 1934, vol. III

McNamara, Air Vice-Marshal Frank Hubert, 1894–1961, vol. VI

McNamara, George, 1881–1953, vol. V

Macnamara, Col John Robert Jermain, 1905–1944, vol. IV

Macnamara, N. C., died 1918, vol. II

Macnamara, Neil Cameron, 1891–1968, vol. VI

Macnamara, Rear-Adm. Sir Patrick, 1886–1957, vol. V

Macnamara, Rt Hon. Thomas James, 1861–1931, vol. III

Macnamara, Walter Henry, 1851–1920, vol. II

M'Namara, Surg.-Gen. William Henry, 1846–1915, vol. I

McNamara Ryan, Patrick John; see Ryan.

Mac-Namee, Rt Rev. James Joseph, 1876–1966, vol. VI

McNarney, Gen. Joseph T., 1893–1972, vol. VII

M'Naught, W. G., 1849–1918, vol. II

McNaught, William, 1883–1953, vol. V

McNaught, William Kirkpatrick, 1845–1919, vol. II

Macnaughtan, S., *died* 1916, vol. II
Macnaughton, Allan Wight, 1859–1937, vol. III
McNaughton, Gen. Hon. Andrew George Latta, 1887–1966, vol. VI
McNaughton, Brig. Forbes Lankester, 1891–1959, vol. V
McNaughton, Sir George Matthew, *died* 1966, vol. VI
Macnaughton, Rev. John, 1858–1943, vol. IV
Macnaughton-Jones, Henry, *died* 1918, vol. II
Macnaughton-Jones, Rev. William Hudson, *died* 1941, vol. IV
Macneal, Sir Hector Murray, 1879–1966, vol. VI
MacNeece, Maj.-Gen. James Gaussen, 1856–1919, vol. II
MacNeece, William Foster; *see* Foster, Air Vice-Marshal W. F. MacN.
McNeely, Most Rev. William, 1888–1963, vol. VI
McNeice, Rt Rev. John Frederick, *died* 1942, vol. IV
Macneice, Louis, 1907–1963, vol. VI
McNeil, Charles, 1881–1964, vol. VI
M'Neil, Daniel, 1853–1918, vol. II
McNeil, Rt Hon. Hector, 1907–1955, vol. V
McNeil, Sir Hector, 1904–1978, vol. VII
MacNeil, Hermon Atkins, 1866–1947, vol. IV (A)
McNeil, Kenneth Gordon, 1902–1970, vol. VI
M'Neil, Most Rev. Neil, 1851–1934, vol. III
McNeil Engr Rear-Adm. Percival Edwin, 1883–1951, vol. V
Macneil of Barra, Robert Lister, (The Macneil of Barra), 1889–1970, vol. VI
M'Neile, Rev. Alan Hugh, 1871–1933, vol. III
McNeile, Lt-Col Cyril, 1888–1937, vol. III
McNeill, Maj.-Gen. Alister Argyll Campbell, 1884–1971, vol. VII
M'Neill, Brig.-Gen. Angus John, 1874–1950, vol. IV
Macneill, Eoin; *see* Macneill, John.
McNeill, Florence Marian, 1885–1973, vol. VII
McNeill, Sir Hector, 1892–1952, vol. V
McNeill, James, 1869–1938, vol. III
MacNeill, Maj.-Gen. James Graham Robert Douglas, 1842–1904, vol. I
McNeill, Sir James McFadyen, 1892–1964, vol. VI
M'Neill, Rev. John, 1854–1933, vol. III
Macneill, Rev. John, 1874–1937, vol. III
Macneill, John, (Eoin Macneill), 1867–1945, vol. IV
M'Neill, Maj.-Gen. Sir John Carstairs, 1831–1904, vol. I
Macneill, John Gordon Swift, 1849–1926, vol. II
M'Neill, Captain Malcolm, 1866–1917, vol. II
McNeill, Sir Malcolm, 1839–1919, vol. II
Macneill, Murray, 1877–1951, vol. V
McNeill, Robert Norman, *died* 1956, vol. V
McNeill-Moss, Major Geoffrey, *died* 1954, vol. V
McNerney, Joshua William, 1872–1944, vol. IV
McNess, Sir Charles, 1853–1938, vol. III
Macnicol, Nicol, 1870–1952, vol. V
McNicoll, Brig.-Gen. Sir Walter Ramsay, 1877–1947, vol. IV
McNish, Col George, 1866–1943, vol. IV
McNulty, Rev. C. T. Bernard, 1875–1939, vol. III

McNulty, Rt Rev. John, 1879–1943, vol. IV
Macnutt, Ernest Augustus, 1876–1955, vol. V
Macnutt, Rev. Canon Frederick Brodie, 1873–1949, vol. IV
McNutt, Hon. Peter, 1834–1919, vol. II
MacNutt, Hon. Thomas, 1850–1927, vol. II
Maconachie, Sir Richard Roy, 1885–1962, vol. VI
Maconchy, Brig.-Gen. Ernest William Stuart King, 1860–1945, vol. IV
Maconchy, Captain Frederick Campbell, 1868–1943, vol. IV
Maconochie, A. White, 1855–1926, vol. II
Maconochie, Charles Cornelius, 1852–1930, vol. III
Maconochie, Sir Evan, 1868–1927, vol. II
Maconochie, Sir Robert Henry, 1883–1962, vol. VI
MacOrlan, Pierre, 1882–1970, vol. VI
Macoun, James Melville, 1862–1920, vol. II
Macoun, John, 1831–1921, vol. II
McOwan, George, 1894–1972, vol. VII
M'Owan, Islay, 1871–1948, vol. IV
MacOwan, Michael Charles Henry, 1906–1980, vol. VII
M'Peake, James Young, 1868–1924, vol. II
Macphail, Alexander, 1872–1938, vol. III
Macphail, Col Alexander, 1870–1949, vol. IV
Macphail, Sir Andrew, 1864–1938, vol. III
Macphail, Rev. Earle Monteith, 1861–1937, vol. III
Macphail, James Robert Nicolson, *died* 1933, vol. III
McPhail, Walter, *died* 1941, vol. IV
Macphail, Rev. William Merry, 1857–1916, vol. II
M'Phedran, Alexander, *died* 1934, vol. III
McPhee, Hon. Sir John Cameron, 1878–1952, vol. V
Macpherson of Drumochter, 1st Baron, 1888–1965, vol. VI
Macpherson, Alan, 1857–1930, vol. III
McPherson, Brig. Alan Bruce, 1887–1978, vol. VII
Macpherson, Brig. Alan David, (Cluny Macpherson), 1887–1969, vol. VI
Macpherson, Albert Cameron, (Cluny Macpherson), 1854–1932, vol. III
Macpherson, Brig.-Gen. Alexander Duncan, 1877–1944, vol. IV
Macpherson of Pitmain, Lt-Col Alexander Kilgour, 1888–1974, vol. VII
Macpherson, Lt-Col Archibald Duncan, 1872–1928, vol. II
Macpherson, Sir Arthur George, 1828–1921, vol. II
Macpherson, Arthur George Holdsworth, 1873–1942, vol. IV
Macpherson, Arthur Holte, 1867–1953, vol. V
Macpherson, Hon. Campbell Leonard, 1907–1973, vol. VII
Macpherson, Charles, 1870–1927, vol. II
Macpherson, Charles Gordon Welland, 1846–1910, vol. I (A)
McPherson, Sir Clive, 1884–1958, vol. V
Macpherson, Lt-Col Cluny, 1879–1966, vol. VI
Macpherson, Colin Francis, 1884–1970, vol. VI
McPherson, Col David William, 1869–1923, vol. II
McPherson, Donald George, 1914–1973, vol. VII
Macpherson, Sir Duncan James, 1855–1936, vol. III
Macpherson, Ewan Francis, *died* 1941, vol. IV

Macpherson, Ewen, 1872–1962, vol. VI
McPherson, Ewen Alexander, 1879–1954, vol. V
Macpherson, Rev. Ewen George Fitzroy, 1863–1926, vol. II
Macpherson, Brig.-Gen. Ewen Henry Davidson, (Cluny Macpherson), 1836–1900, vol. I
Macpherson, George, died 1924, vol. II
Macpherson, Hector, died 1924, vol. II
Macpherson, Rev. Hector, 1888–1956, vol. V
McPherson, Henry Alexander, 1855–1939, vol. III
M'Pherson, Sir Hugh, 1870–1960, vol. V, vol. VI
Macpherson, Lt-Col James, 1876–1938, vol. III
McPherson, Bt Col James, 1876–1963, vol. VI
Macpherson, James Simpson, 1863–1935, vol. III
Macpherson, Sir John, 1857–1942, vol. IV
Macpherson, Sir John Molesworth, 1853–1914, vol. I
Macpherson, Sir John Stuart, 1898–1971, vol. VII
Macpherson, Rear-Adm. Kenneth Douglas Worsley, 1883–1962, vol. VI
MacPherson, Malcolm, 1904–1971, vol. VII
MacPherson, Major Hon. Murdoch Alexander, 1891–1966, vol. VI
Macpherson, Sir Norman Macgregor, died 1947, vol. IV
Macpherson, Stewart, died 1941, vol. IV
Macpherson, Sir Stewart; see Macpherson, Sir T. S.
McPherson, Sir Thomas, died 1947, vol. IV
Macpherson, Sir (Thomas) Stewart, 1876–1949, vol. IV
Macpherson, Rev. Thomas William, 1863–1936, vol. III
Macpherson, Sir William, 1836–1909, vol. I
Macpherson, William Charles, 1855–1936, vol. III
Macpherson, Maj.-Gen. Sir William Grant, 1858–1927, vol. II
McPherson, Hon. Sir William Murray, 1865–1932, vol. III
Macpherson, Very Rev. William Stuart, 1901–1978, vol. VII
Macpherson-Grant, Sir George, 5th Bt, 1890–1951, vol. V
Macpherson-Grant, Captain George Bertram, died 1932, vol. III
Macpherson-Grant, Sir John, 4th Bt, 1863–1914, vol. I
McPhillips, Captain Hon. Albert Edward, 1861–1938, vol. III
McQuaid, Most Rev. John Charles, 1895–1973, vol. VII
Macquaker, Sir Thomas, 1851–1938, vol. III
MacQuarrie, Josiah H., 1897–1971, vol. VII
McQuarrie, William Garland, 1876–1943, vol. IV
Macqueen, James, 1853–1936, vol. III
MacQueen, Maj.-Gen. John Henry, 1893–1980, vol. VII
M'Queen, Lt-Gen. Sir John Withers, 1836–1909, vol. I
Macqueen-Pope, Walter James, 1888–1960, vol. V
McQuesten, Hon. Thomas Baker, 1882–1948, vol. IV
M'Quhae, Captain John Mackenzie, 1847–1901, vol. I
McQuibban, Lewis, 1866–1944, vol. IV

Macquisten, Frederick Alexander, 1870–1940, vol. III
Macquoid, Brig.-Gen. Charles Edward Every Francis Kirwan, 1869–1945, vol. III
Macquoid, Gilbert Samuel, 1854–1940, vol. III
Macquoid, Katharine Sarah, 1824–1917, vol. II
Macquoid, Percy, died 1925, vol. II
Macquoid, Thomas Robert, 1820–1912, vol. I
Macrae, Maj.-Gen. Albert Edward, 1886–1958, vol. V
McRae, Maj.-Gen. Hon. Alexander Duncan, 1874–1946, vol. IV
Macrae, Col Alexander William, 1858–1920, vol. II
Macrae, Angus, 1893–1975, vol. VII
Macrae, Charles Colin, 1843–1922, vol. II
Macrae, Sir Colin George, 1844–1925, vol. II
MacRae of Feoirlinn, Col Sir Colin William, 1869–1952, vol. V
MacRae, Donald Mackenzie, 1869–1955, vol. V
McRae, Col Henry Napier, 1851–1915, vol. I
Macrae, Herbert Alexander, 1886–1967, vol. VI
Macrae, Hugh, 1880–1965, vol. VI
Macrae, Maj.-Gen. Ian Macpherson, 1882–1956, vol. V
Macrae, Col John Cecil, 1881–1940, vol. III
MacRae, Very Rev. John Eric, 1870–1947, vol. IV
Macrae, Robert Scarth Farquhar, 1877–1926, vol. II
Macrae, Col Roderick, died 1915, vol. I (A)
Macrae, Russell Duncan, 1888–1956, vol. V
McRae, William, 1878–1952, vol. V
MacRae-Gilstrap, Lt-Col John, 1861–1937, vol. III
Macran, Henry Stewart, died 1937, vol. III
Macray, Rev. William Dunn, 1826–1916, vol. II
McRea, Sir Charles James Hugh, 1874–1951, vol. V
Macready, Gen. Rt Hon. Sir (Cecil Frederick) Nevil, 1st Bt, 1862–1946, vol. IV
Macready, Lt-Gen. Sir Gordon Nevil, 2nd Bt, 1891–1956, vol. V
Macready, Brig. John, 1887–1957, vol. V
Macready, Gen. Rt Hon. Sir Nevil; see Macready, Gen. Rt Hon. Sir C. F. N.
MacRedmond, Rt Rev. Thomas, 1838–1904, vol. I
MacRitchie, David, 1851–1925, vol. II
MacRobert, Sir Alasdair Workman, 2nd Bt, 1912–1938, vol. III
M'Robert, Sir Alexander, 1st Bt, 1854–1922, vol. II
MacRobert, Rt Hon. Alexander Munro, 1873–1930, vol. III
McRobert, Sir George Reid, 1895–1976, vol. VII
MacRobert, Sir Iain Workman, 4th Bt, 1917–1941, vol. IV
MacRobert, Norman Murie, 1899–1972, vol. VII
MacRobert, Rachel W., (Lady MacRobert), died 1954, vol. V
MacRobert, Sir Roderic Alan, 3rd Bt, 1915–1941, vol. IV
MacRobert, Thomas Murrary, 1884–1962, vol. VI
Macrorie, Vice-Adm. Arthur Kenneth, 1874–1947, vol. IV
Macrorie, Rt Rev. William Kenneth, 1831–1905, vol. I
Macrory, Edmund, died 1904, vol. I

MacRory, His Eminence Cardinal Joseph, 1861–1945, vol. IV

Macrossan, Hugh Denis, 1881–1940, vol. III

Macrossan, Hon. Neal William, 1889–1955, vol. V

McShane, John J., 1882–1972, vol. VII

McSheehy, Maj.-Gen. Oswald William, 1884–1975, vol. VII

Mac-Sherry, Most Rev. Hugh, 1852–1940, vol. III

McSparran, James, 1892–1970, vol. VI

MacSweeney, Rev. Patrick M., 1873–1935, vol. III

McSweeny, George, 1865–1923, vol. II (A), vol. III

McSwiney, Bryan Austin, 1894–1947, vol. IV

McSwiney, Col Edward Frederick Henry, 1858–1907, vol. I

McSwiney, Col Herbert Frederick Cyril, 1886–1963, vol. VI

MacSwiney, Terence Joseph, died 1920, vol. II

MacTaggart, Sir Andrew McCormick, 1888–1978, vol. VII

Mactaggart, Col Charles, 1861–1930, vol. III

Mactaggart, Sir John Auld, 1st Bt, 1867–1956, vol. V

Mactaggart, Sir John Auld, 2nd Bt, 1898–1960, vol. V

M'Taggart, John M'Taggart Ellis, 1866–1925, vol. II

McTaggart, Lt-Col Maxwell Fielding, 1874–1936, vol. III

McTaggart, Captain W. B., died 1919, vol. II

M'Taggart, William, 1835–1910, vol. I

MacTaggart-Stewart, Sir Edward Orde; see Stewart.

M'Turk, Michael, 1843–1915, vol. I (A)

M'Vail, Sir David Caldwell, 1845–1917, vol. II

McVail, John Christie, 1849–1926, vol. II

Macveagh, Jeremiah, 1870–1932, vol. III

M'Vean, Col Donald Archibald Dugald, 1870–1937, vol. III

McVeigh, Rt Hon. Sir Herbert Andrew, 1908–1977, vol. VII

McVey, Arthur Michael, 1879–1964, vol. VI

McVey, Sir Daniel, 1892–1972, vol. VII

MacVicar, Hon. John, 1859–1928, vol. II (A), vol. III

M'Vicker, Sir Robert, 1822–1897, vol. I

McVie, John, 1888–1967, vol. VI

M'Vittie, Surg.-Gen. Charles Edwin, died 1916, vol. II

McVittie, Lt-Col Charles Edwin, 1870–1933, vol. III

McVittie, Col Robert Henry, 1872–1949, vol. IV

McVittie, Wilfrid Wolters, 1906–1980, vol. VII

Macwatt, Maj.-Gen. Sir Charles; see Macwatt, Maj.-Gen. Sir R. C.

MacWatt, Hay, 1855–1920, vol. II

Macwatt, John, 1857–1938, vol. III

Macwatt, Maj.-Gen. Sir (Robert) Charles, 1865–1945, vol. IV

McWatters, Sir Arthur Cecil, 1880–1965, vol. VI

McWeeney, Edmond J., 1864–1925, vol. II (A), vol. III

McWeeney, Henry Charles, 1867–1935, vol. III

McWhae, Brig. Douglas Murray, 1884–1969, vol. VI

M'Whae, Hon. Sir John, 1858–1927, vol. II

McWhan, John, 1885–1943, vol. IV

McWhinnie, Hugh, died 1923, vol. II

McWhirter, (Alan) Ross, 1925–1975, vol. VII

Macwhirter, Clara Elizabeth Littlewort, died 1971, vol. VII

MacWhirter, John, 1839–1911, vol. I

McWhirter, Ross; see McWhirter, A. R.

McWhirter, William Allan, died 1955, vol. V

MacWhite, Michael, 1883–1958, vol. V

M'William, Andrew, died 1922, vol. II

McWilliam, Sir John, 1910–1974, vol. VII

MacWilliam, John Alexander, 1857–1937, vol. III

Macy, George, 1900–1956, vol. V

Madan, Falconer, 1851–1935, vol. III

Madan, Rev. Nigel, 1840–1915, vol. I

Madariaga, Don Salvador de, 1886–1978, vol. VII

Maddan, James Gracie, 1873–1966, vol. VI

Maddan, Martin, 1920–1973, vol. VII

Madden, Adm. Sir Alexander Cumming Gordon, 1895–1964, vol. VI

Madden, Archibald Maclean, 1864–1928, vol. II

Madden, Charles Dodgson, 1833–1910, vol. I

Madden, Admiral of the Fleet Sir Charles Edward, 1st Bt, 1862–1935, vol. III

Madden, Rt Hon. Dodgson Hamilton, 1840–1928, vol. II

Madden, Hon. Sir Frank, 1847–1921, vol. II

Madden, Frank Cole, 1873–1929, vol. III

Madden, Frederic William, 1839–1904, vol. I

Madden, Lt-Col George Colquhoun, 1856–1912, vol. I

Madden, Hon. Sir John, 1844–1918, vol. II

Madden, Lt-Col John Clements Waterhouse, 1870–1935, vol. III

Madden, Samuel Fitzgerald, 1878–1934, vol. III

Madden, Ven. T. J., 1853–1915, vol. I (A)

Madden, Thomas More, 1844–1902, vol. I

Madden, Hon. Walter, 1848–1925, vol. II

Madden, William Thomas, 1877–1967, vol. VI

Madden, Wyndham D'Arcy, 1885–1968, vol. VI

Maddick, Edmund Distin, died 1939, vol. III

Maddick, George John, 1849–1942, vol. IV

Maddison, Rev. Arthur Roland, 1843–1912, vol. I

Maddison, Fred, 1856–1937, vol. III

Maddison, Rev. William, 1853–1920, vol. II

Maddock, Lt-Col Edward Cecil Gordon, 1876–1952, vol. V

Maddock, Sir Simon, 1869–1927, vol. II

Maddocks, George, 1896–1980, vol. VII

Maddocks, Sir Henry, 1871–1931, vol. III

Maddocks, Henry Hollingdrake, 1898–1969, vol. VI

Maddox, Ernest Edmund, 1860–1933, vol. III

Maddox, Lt-Col Ralph Henry, 1864–1935, vol. III

Maddox, Samuel, 1930–1979, vol. VII

Maddox, Stuart Lockwood, 1866–1942, vol. IV

Maddrell, Rev. Thomas Fisher, 1861–1932, vol. III

Maddy, Rev. H. W., 1829–1909, vol. I

Madeley, Earl of; Richard George Archibald John Lucien Hungerford Crew-Milnes, 1911–1922, vol. II

Maden, Henry, 1892–1960, vol. V

Maden, Sir John Henry, 1862–1920, vol. II

Madgavkar, Sir Govind Dinanath, 1871–1948, vol. IV

Madge, Rev. Francis Thomas, 1849–1933, vol. III

Madge, Captain Sir Frank William, 2nd Bt, 1897–1962, vol. VI

Madge, Sidney Joseph, 1874–1961, vol. VI

Madge, Sir William Thomas, 1st Bt, 1845–1927, vol. II

Madhava, Rao, V. P., died 1934, vol. III (A), vol. IV

Madigan, Cecil Thomas, 1889–1947, vol. IV

Madill, Surg. Rear-Adm. Thomas, 1895–1962, vol. VI

Madoc, Lt-Col Henry William, died 1937, vol. III

Madocks, Brig.-Gen. William Robarts Napier, 1871–1946, vol. IV

Madrid, Duke of; see Carlos, Don.

Madsen, Sir John Percival Vissing, 1879–1969, vol. VI

Maenan, 1st Baron, 1854–1951, vol. V

Maeterlinck, Count Maurice, 1862–1949, vol. IV

Maflin, Major George Hamilton, vol. II

Magan, Lt-Col Arthur Tilson Shaen, 1880–1965, vol. VI

Magauran, Wilfrid Henry Bertram, 1898–1964, vol. VI

Magee, Allan Angus, 1881–1961, vol. VI

Magee, Sir Cuthbert Gaulter, died 1963, vol. VI

Magee, Hon. James, born 1846, vol. III

Mageean, Most Rev. Daniel, 1882–1962, vol. VI

Magenis, Maj-Gen. Henry Cole, 1838–1906, vol. I

Magennis, Rt Rev. Edward, died 1906, vol. I

Magennis, Edward, died 1938, vol. III

Magennis, William, 1869–1946, vol. IV

Mager, Sydney, 1877–1952, vol. V

Maggs, Joseph Herbert, 1875–1964, vol. VI

Magheramorne, 2nd Baron, 1861–1903, vol. I

Magheramorne, 3rd Baron, 1863–1946, vol. IV

Magheramorne, 4th Baron, 1865–1957, vol. V

Magian, Anthony John Capper, 1878–1956, vol. V

Magill, Andrew Philip, died 1941, vol. IV

Magill, Col Sir James, 1850–1936, vol. III

Magill, Walter Alexander, 1879–1950, vol. IV

Maginess, Rt Hon. William Brian, 1901–1967, vol. VI

Maginness, Edmund John, 1857–1938, vol. III

Maginness, Sir Greville Simpson, 1888–1961, vol. VI

Maglione, His Eminence Cardinal Luigi, 1877–1944, vol. IV

Magnani, Anna, 1918–1973, vol. VII

Magnay, Brig. Arthur Douglas, 1893–1964, vol. VI

Magnay, Major Sir Christopher Boyd William, 3rd Bt, 1884–1960, vol. V

Magnay, Harold Swindale, 1904–1971, vol. VII

Magnay, Thomas, 1876–1949, vol. IV

Magnay, Sir William, 2nd Bt, 1855–1917, vol. II

Magner, Jeremiah John, 1891–1973, vol. VII

Magnes, Judah Leon, 1877–1948, vol. IV

Magniac, Brig.-Gen. Sir Charles Lane, 1873–1953, vol. V

Magniac, Major Hubert, died 1909, vol. I

Magniac, Oswald Cecil, died 1939, vol. III

Magnus, Henry Adolph, 1909–1967, vol. VI

Magnus, Katie, (Lady Magnus), 1844–1924, vol. II

Magnus, Laurie, 1872–1933, vol. III

Magnus, Sir Philip, 1st Bt, 1842–1933, vol. III

Magowan, Sir John Hall, 1893–1951, vol. V

Magowan, Joseph Irvine, 1901–1977, vol. VII

Magrane, Col John Plunkett, 1896–1963, vol. VI

Magrath, Maj.-Gen. Beauchamp Henry Whittingham, 1832–1920, vol. II

Magrath, Charles Alexander, 1860–1949, vol. IV

Magrath, Harry William, died 1969, vol. VI

Magrath, Rev. John Richard, 1839–1930, vol. III

Maguiness, Rev. John Thomas, died 1920, vol. II

Maguire, Sir Alexander Herbert, 1876–1947, vol. IV

Maguire, Conor A., 1889–1971, vol. VII

Maguire, Very Rev. Edward, 1822–1913, vol. I

Maguire, Maj.-Gen. Frederick Arthur, 1888–1953, vol. V (A)

Maguire, James Rochfort, 1855–1925, vol. II

Maguire, Most Rev. John A., 1851–1920, vol. II

Maguire, Robert, 1857–1915, vol. I (A)

Maguire, William Joseph, died 1934, vol. III

Mahadeva, Sir Arunachalam, born 1885, vol. VI

Mahaffy, Alexander Francis, 1891–1962, vol. VI

Mahaffy, Arthur William, 1869–1919, vol. II

Mahaffy, Rev. Gilbert, died 1916, vol. II

Mahaffy, Sir John Pentland, 1839–1919, vol. II

Mahaffy, Robert Pentland, 1871–1943, vol. IV

Mahaim, Ernest A. J., 1865–1938, vol. III (A), vol. IV

Mahalanobis, Prasanta Chandra, 1893–1972, vol. VII

Mahalanobis, S. C., 1867–1953, vol. V

Mahan, Rear Adm. Alfred T., 1840–1914, vol. I

Mahdi Husain, Khan, Wahud-ud-Daula, Azod-ul-Mulk, Nawab Mirza, Khan Bahadur, born 1834, vol. II

Maher, Charles Ernest, 1896–1961, vol. VI

Maher, Maj.-Gen. Sir James, 1858–1928, vol. II

Maheshwari, Panchanan, 1904–1966, vol. VI

Maheu, René G., 1905–1975, vol. VII

Mahir, Thomas Edward, 1915–1970, vol. VI

Mahmudabad, Maharaja of, 1877–1931, vol. III

Mahon, Lt-Col Bryan MacMahon, 1890–1949, vol. IV

Mahon, Gen. Rt Hon. Sir Bryan Thomas, 1862–1930, vol. III

Mahon, Edward Elphinstone, 1851–1912, vol. I

Mahon, Harold J. D., 1873–1938, vol. III

Mahon, Captain Henry P.; see Pakenham-Mahon.

Mahon, Hon. Hugh, 1858–1931, vol. III

Mahon, John FitzGerald, 1858–1942, vol. IV

Mahon, Ralph Bodkin, 1862–1943, vol. IV (A)

Mahon, Maj.-Gen. Reginald Henry, 1859–1929, vol. III

Mahon, Sir William Henry, 5th Bt, 1856–1926, vol. II

Mahoney, Charles, 1903–1968, vol. VI

Mahoney, Sir John Andrew, 1883–1966, vol. VI

Mahoney, Merchant Michael, 1886–1946, vol. IV

Mahony, Rt Rev. Mgr John Mathew, 1862–1918, vol. II

Mahony, Major Michael Joseph, died 1927, vol. II

Mahony, Peirce Gun, 1878–1914, vol. I

Mahood, James, 1876–1950, vol. IV

Maiden, Joseph Henry, 1859–1925, vol. II

Maillard, Staff Surgeon William J., died 1903, vol. I

Maillol, Aristide, 1861–1944, vol. IV

Main, Rev. Archibald, 1876–1947, vol. IV

Main, David, 1861–1941, vol. IV

Main, David Duncan, 1856–1934, vol. III

Main, Lt-Comdr Frank Morgan, died 1924, vol. II

Main, Henry, 1888–1949, vol. IV

Main, Brig. John Walter, 1900–1971, vol. VII

Main, Col Thomas Ryder, 1850–1934, vol. III

Maindron, Maurice Georges Rene, 1857–1911, vol. I

Mainds, Allan Douglass, 1881–1945, vol. IV

Maine, Rev. Basil Stephen, 1894–1972, vol. VII

Maine, Henry Cecil Sumner, 1886–1968, vol. VI

Mainprise, Maj.-Gen. Cecil Wilmot, 1873–1951, vol. V

Mainprise, Captain William Thomas, died 1902, vol. I

Mainstone, Madeleine Françoise, 1925–1979, vol. VII

Mainwaring, Albert James, 1891–1941, vol. IV

Mainwaring, Charles Francis Kynaston, 1877–1949, vol. IV

Mainwaring, Col Charles Salusbury, 1845–1920, vol. II

Mainwaring, Brig. Guy Rowland, 1885–1956, vol. V

Mainwaring, Sir Harry Stapleton, 5th Bt, 1878–1934, vol. III

Mainwaring, Brig. Hugh Salusbury Kynaston, 1906–1976, vol. VII

Mainwaring, Sir Philip Tatton, 4th Bt, 1838–1906, vol. I

Mainwaring, Hon. Maj.-Gen. Rowland Broughton, 1850–1926, vol. II

Mainwaring, Col Sir Watkin Randle Kynaston, 1875–1944, vol. IV

Mainwaring, Hon. William Frederick Barton Massey-, 1845–1907, vol. I

Mainwaring, Gen. William George, 1823–1905, vol. I

Mainwaring, William Henry, 1884–1971, vol. VII

Mainwaring-Bowen, Arthur Charles, 1922–1980, vol. VII

Mair, Alexander, 1870–1927, vol. II

Mair, Alexander W., died 1928, vol. II

Mair, Charles, 1838–1927, vol. II

Mair, George Herbert, 1887–1926, vol. II

Mair, Brig.-Gen. George Tagore, 1873–1941, vol. IV

Mair, Rev. John, 1822–1902, vol. I

Mair, John Bagrie, 1857–1927, vol. II

Mair, Col Robert John Byford, 1868–1940, vol. III

Mair, Dame Sarah Elizabeth Siddons, 1846–1941, vol. IV

Mair, Very Rev. William, 1830–1920, vol. II

Mairet, Ethel, 1872–1952, vol. V

Mairis, Gen. Geoffrey, 1834–1917, vol. II

Mais, Stuart Petre Brodie, 1885–1975, vol. VII

Maisky, Ivan Mikhailovich, 1884–1975, vol. VII

Maistre, Le Roy de, (Roy de Maistre), 1894–1968, vol. VI

Maitland, Viscount; Ivor Colin James Maitland, 1915–1943, vol. IV

Maitland, Sir Adam, 1885–1949, vol. IV

Maitland, Rev. Adam Gray, died 1928, vol. II

Maitland, Agnes Catherine, 1849–1906, vol. I

Maitland, Sir Alexander, 1877–1965, vol. VI

Maitland, Sir Alexander Keith, 8th Bt, 1920–1963, vol. VI

Maitland, Rt Hon. Sir Arthur Herbert Drummond Ramsay S.; see Steel-Maitland.

Maitland, Dalrymple, 1848–1919, vol. II

Maitland, Maj.-Gen. David M. C.; see Makgill-Crichton-Maitland.

Maitland, Col Eardley, 1833–1911, vol. I

Maitland, Air-Cdre Edward Maitland, 1880–1921, vol. II

Maitland, Frederic William, 1850–1906, vol. I

Maitland, Lt-Col Sir (George) Ramsay, 7th Bt, 1882–1960, vol. V

Maitland, Lt-Col Hon. George Thomas, 1841–1910, vol. I

Maitland, Sir Herbert Lethington, 1868–1923, vol. II

Maitland, Hugh Bethune, 1895–1972, vol. VII

Maitland, J. A. F.; see Fuller-Maitland.

Maitland, Brig.-Gen. James Dalgleish H.; see Heriot-Maitland.

Maitland, Maj.-Gen. Sir James Makgill Heriot-, 1837–1902, vol. I

Maitland, Sir James S.; see Steel-Maitland.

Maitland, Sir John, 6th Bt, 1879–1949, vol. IV

Maitland, Comdr Sir John Francis Whitaker, 1903–1977, vol. VII

Maitland, Sir John Nisbet, 5th Bt, 1850–1936, vol. III

Maitland, Sir Keith Richard Felix Ramsay-Steel; see Steel-Maitland.

Maitland, Col Mark Edward Makgill Crichton, 1882–1972, vol. VII

Maitland, Maj.-Gen. Pelham James, 1847–1935, vol. III

Maitland, Lt-Col Sir Ramsay; see Maitland, Lt-Col Sir G. R.

Maitland, Lt-Col Reginald Charles Frederick, 1882–1939, vol. III

Maitland, Thomas Gwynne, died 1948, vol. IV

Maitland, Victor Kennard, 1897–1950, vol. IV

Maitland, William F.; see Fuller-Maitland.

Maitland, William James, 1847–1919, vol. II

Maitland, William Whitaker, 1864–1926, vol. II

Maitland-Gordon, James Charles; see Gordon.

Maitland-Heriot, Sir William, 1856–1939, vol. III

Maitland-Jones, Arthur Griffith, 1890–1957, vol. V

Maitland-Kirwan, Lionel, 1849–1927, vol. II

Maitland-Makgill-Crichton, Brig. Henry Coventry; see Crichton.

Maizels, Montague, 1899–1976, vol. VII

Majdalany, Fred, 1913–1967, vol. VI

Majendie, Brig.-Gen. Bernard J., 1875–1959, vol. V

Majendie, James Henry Alexander, 1871–1932, vol. III

Majendie, Sir Vivian Dering, 1836–1898, vol. I

Majendie, Maj.-Gen. Vivian Henry Bruce, 1886–1960, vol. V

Majendie, Rev. William Richard Stuart, 1869–1932, vol. III

Major, Albany Featherstonehaugh, 1858–1925, vol. II

Major, Sir Alfred, died 1907, vol. I

Major, Alfred George, 1879–1940, vol. III (A), vol. IV

Major, Maj.-Gen. Hon. Arthur Henry H.; see Henniker-Major.

Major, Charles, 1856–1913, vol. I

Major, Sir Charles Henry, 1860–1933, vol. III

Major, Charles Immanuel Forsyth, 1843–1923, vol. II

Major, Col Charles Thomas, 1869–1938, vol. III

Major, Edith Helen, 1867–1951, vol. V

Major, Hon. Edward Minet H.; see Henniker-Major.

Major, Ernest Harry, 1876–1941, vol. IV

Major, Francis William, 1863–1923, vol. II

Major, Hon. Gerald Arthur George H.; see Henniker-Major.

Major, Rev. Henry Dewsbury Alves, 1871–1961, vol. VI

Major, James Perrins, 1878–1964, vol. VI (AII)

Makarios III, Archbishop, 1913–1977, vol. VII

Makdougall, Hugh James Elibank S.; see Scott Makdougall.

Makgill, Sir George, 11th Bt, 1868–1926, vol. II

Makgill, Robert Haldane, 1870–1946, vol. IV

Makgill-Crichton-Maitland, Maj.-Gen. David, 1841–1907, vol. I

Makino, Nobuaki, Count, 1861–1949, vol. IV

Makins, Sir (Alfred) John (Ware), 1894–1972, vol. VII

Makins, Brig.-Gen. Sir Ernest, 1869–1959, vol. V

Makins, Captain Geoffry, 1877–1915, vol. I

Makins, Sir George Henry, 1853–1933, vol. III

Makins, Sir John; see Makins, Sir A. J. W.

Makins, Sir Paul Augustine, 2nd Bt, 1871–1939, vol. III

Makins, Col Sir William Thomas, 1st Bt, 1840–1906 (this entry was not transferred to Who was Who).

Makins, Lt-Col Sir William Vivian, 3rd Bt, 1903–1969, vol. VI

Makinson, Joseph, 1836–1914, vol. I

Makower, Ernest Samuel, 1876–1946, vol. IV

Makower, Walter, 1879–1945, vol. IV

Malabari, Behramji Merwanji, 1854–1912, vol. I

Malalasekera, Gunapala Piyasena, 1899–1973, vol. VII

Malan, Gp Captain Adolph Gysbert, 1910–1963, vol. VI

Malan, Hon. Daniel François, 1874–1959, vol. V

Malan, Rt Hon. François Stephanus, 1871–1941, vol. IV

Malaviya, Pandit Madan Mohan, 1861–1946, vol. IV

Malbrán, Manuel E., 1876–1942, vol. IV

Malcolm of Poltalloch, 1st Baron, 1833–1902, vol. I

Malcolm, Angus Christian Edward, 1908–1971, vol. VII

Malcolm, Charles Adolf, 1879–1948, vol. IV

Malcolm, Sir Dougal Orme, 1877–1955, vol. V

Malcolm, Col Edward Donald, 1837–1930, vol. III

Malcolm, Sir George, 1818–1897, vol. I

Malcolm, George, 1876–1941, vol. IV

Malcolm, Col George Alexander, 1872–1933, vol. III

Malcolm of Poltalloch, Lt-Col George Ian, 1903–1976, vol. VII

Malcolm, Hon. George John Huntly, 1865–1930, vol. III

Malcolm, George William, 1870–1933, vol. III

Malcolm, Harcourt Gladstone, 1875–1936, vol. III

Malcolm, Brig.-Gen. Henry Huntly Leith, 1860–1938, vol. III

Malcolm, Sir Ian Zachary, 1868–1944, vol. IV

Malcolm, Sir James, 8th Bt, 1823–1901, vol. I

Malcolm, Hon. James, 1880–1935, vol. III

Malcolm, Sir James William, 9th Bt, 1862–1927, vol. II

Malcolm, John, 1873–1954, vol. V

Malcolm, John D., 1857–1937, vol. III

Malcolm, Sir Michael Albert James, 1898–1976, vol. VII

Malcolm, Maj.-Gen. Sir Neill, 1869–1953, vol. V

Malcolm, Lt-Col Pulteney, 1861–1940, vol. III

Malcolm, Robert Carmichael, 1868–1941, vol. IV

Malcolm, Ronald, died 1949, vol. IV

Malcolmson, John Grant, died 1902, vol. I

Malcolmson, Maj.-Gen. John Henry Porter, 1832–1920, vol. II

Malcolmson, Vernon Austen, 1872–1947, vol. IV

Malden, Charles Edward, 1845–1926, vol. II

Malden, Edmund Claud, 1890–1962, vol. VI

Malden, Very Rev. Richard Henry, 1879–1951, vol. V

Male, Emile, 1862–1954, vol. V

Maler Kotla, Nawab of, 1881–1947, vol. IV

Malet, Sir Charles St Lo, 6th Bt, 1906–1918, vol. II

Malet, Rt Hon. Sir Edward Baldwin, 4th Bt, 1837–1908, vol. I

Malet, Sir Edward St Lo, 5th Bt, 1872–1909, vol. I

Malet, Guilbert Edward Wyndham, 1839–1918, vol. II

Malet, Sir Harry Charles, 7th Bt, 1873–1931, vol. III

Malet, Sir Henry Charles Eden, 3rd Bt, 1835–1904, vol. I

Malet, John C., died 1901, vol. I

Malet, Lucas; see Harrison, Mary St Leger.

Malet de Carteret, Captain Charles Edward, died 1942, vol. IV

Malet de Carteret, Lt-Col E. C., 1838–1914, vol. I

Malet de Carteret, Reginald, 1865–1935, vol. III

Malik Khuda Bakhsh Khan Tiwana, Nawab Sir, died 1930, vol. III

Malik Mohammed Umar Hayat Khan (Tiwana), Maj.-Gen. Hon. Sir, 1874–1944, vol. IV

Malik, Sardar Bahadur Sir Teja Singh, died 1953, vol. V

Malik, Yakov Alexandrovich, 1906–1980, vol. VII

Malim, Frederic Blagden, 1872–1966, vol. VI

444

Maling, George Allan, 1889–1929, vol. III
Maling, Captain Irwin Charles, 1841–1918, vol. II
Malinovsky, Marshal Rodion Yakovlevich, 1898–1967, vol. VI
Malinowski, Bronislaw, 1884–1942, vol. IV
Malins, Sir Edward, 1841–1922, vol. II
Malipiero, G. Francesco, 1882–1973, vol. VII
Malkin, Harold Jordan, 1898–1978, vol. VII
Malkin, Herbert Charles, 1836–1913, vol. I
Malkin, Sir (Herbert) William, 1883–1945, vol. IV
Malkin, Sir William; see Malkin, Sir H. W.
Malko, Nicolai, 1888–1961, vol. VI
Mallabar, Herbert John, 1871–1956, vol. V
Mallaby, Col Aubertin Walter Sothern, 1899–1945, vol. IV
Mallaby, Sir George; see Mallaby, Sir H. G. C.
Mallaby, Sir (Howard) George (Charles), 1902–1978, vol. VII
Mallaby, Rev. John Jackson, died 1929, vol. III
Mallaby-Deeley, Sir Anthony Meyrick, 3rd Bt, 1923–1962, vol. VI
Mallaby-Deeley, Sir Guy Meyrick Mallaby, 2nd Bt, 1897–1946, vol. IV
Mallaby-Deeley, Sir Harry Mallaby, 1st Bt, 1863–1937, vol. III
Malladra, Alessandro, 1868–1944, vol. IV
Mallalieu, Sir Edward Lancelot, (Sir Lance), 1905–1979, vol. VII
Mallalieu, Frederick William, 1860–1932, vol. III
Mallalieu, Sir Joseph Percival William, 1908–1980, vol. VII
Mallalieu, Sir Lance; see Mallalieu, Sir E. L.
Mallalieu, Sir William; see Mallalieu, Sir J. P. W.
Mallam, Lt-Col Rev. George Leslie, 1895–1978, vol. VII
Mallarmé, Stéphane, 1842–1898, vol. I
Malleson, Lady Constance, (Colette O'Niel), 1895–1975, vol. VI
Malleson, Col George Bruce, 1825–1898, vol. I
Malleson, Herbert Cecil, died 1935, vol. III
Malleson, Miles; see Malleson, W. M.
Malleson, Maj.-Gen. Sir Wilfrid, 1866–1946, vol. IV
Malleson, Comdr Wilfrid St Aubyn, died 1975, vol. VII
Malleson, (William) Miles, 1888–1969, vol. VI
Mallet, Sir Bernard, 1859–1932, vol. III
Mallet, Sir Charles Edward, 1862–1947, vol. IV
Mallet, Sir Claude Coventry, 1860–1941, vol. IV
Mallet, John William, 1832–1912, vol. I, vol I (A)
Mallet, Rt Hon. Sir Louis du Pan, 1864–1936, vol. III
Mallet, Matilde de Obarrio, (Lady Mallet), 1872–1964, vol. VI
Mallet, Sir Victor Alexander Louis, 1893–1969, vol. VI
Mallett, Edward, 1888–1950, vol. IV
Mallett, Richard, 1910–1972, vol. VII
Mallett, Sir Rowland, 1869–1947, vol. IV
Malley, William Bernard, 1889–1966, vol. VI
Mallik, Devendra Nath, 1866–1941, vol. IV
Mallik, Manmath C., born 1853, vol. III
Mallinson, Albert, 1870–1946, vol. IV
Mallinson, Sir Dyson, 1852–1929, vol. III

Mallinson, Lt-Col Henry, 1879–1940, vol. III
Mallinson, Sir William, 1st Bt, died 1936, vol. III
Mallinson, Sir William James, 2nd Bt, 1879–1944, vol. IV
Malloch, George Reston, died 1953, vol. V
Malloch, James, 1860–1932, vol. III
Mallock, Brig. Arthur Richard Ogilvie, 1885–1972, vol. VII
Mallock, Major Charles Herbert, 1878–1917, vol. II
Mallock, Henry Reginald A., died 1933, vol. III
Mallock, Richard, 1843–1900, vol. I
Mallock, Lt-Col Thomas Raymond, died 1934, vol. III
Mallock, William Hurrell, 1849–1923, vol. II
Mallon, James Joseph, 1875–1961, vol. VI
Mallory, Rev. Herbert Leigh L.; see Leigh-Mallory.
Mallory, Air Chief Marshal Sir Trafford Leigh L.; see Leigh-Mallory.
Mallowan, Dame Agatha; see Christie, Dame A. M. C.
Mallowan, Sir Max Edgar Lucien, 1904–1978, vol. VII
Malmesbury, 4th Earl of, 1842–1899, vol. I
Malmesbury, 5th Earl of, 1872–1950, vol. IV
Malone, Surg. Rear-Adm. Albert Edward, died 1970, vol. VI
Malone, Lt-Col Cecil L'Estrange, died 1965, vol. VI
Malone, Sir Clement, died 1967, vol. VI
Malone, Herbert, died 1962, vol. VI
Malone, Leah, (Mrs L'Estrange Malone), died 1951, vol. V
Malone, Major Sir Patrick Bernard, 1857–1939, vol. III
Malory, Shaun; see Russell, Reginald James Kingston.
Malouin, Arthur Cyrille Albert, 1857–1930, vol. III
Malraux, André, 1901–1976, vol. VII
Maltby, Maj.-Gen. (Christopher) Michael, 1891–1980, vol. VII
Maltby, Lt-Comdr Gerald Rivers, 1851–1922, vol. II
Maltby, Henry Francis, 1880–1963, vol. VI
Maltby, Maj.-Gen. Michael; see Maltby, Maj.-Gen. C. M.
Maltby, Air Vice-Marshal Sir Paul Copeland, 1892–1971, vol. VII
Maltby, Sir Thomas Karran, died 1976, vol. VII
Malthus, Col Sydenham, 1831–1916, vol. II
Maltwood, Mrs Katharine, died 1961, vol. VI
Malvern, 1st Viscount, 1883–1971, vol. VII
Malvern, 2nd Viscount, 1922–1978, vol. VII
Mamhead, 1st Baron, 1871–1945, vol. IV
Man, Edward Garnet, 1837–1920, vol. II
Man, Edward Horace, 1846–1929, vol. III
Man, Col Hubert William, died 1956, vol. V
Man, Col John Alexander; see Stuart, Col J. A. M.
Man, Captain Joseph, 1867–1951, vol. V
Man, Maj.-Gen. Patrick Holberton, 1913–1979, vol. VII
Manby, Sir Alan Reeve, 1848–1925, vol. II
Manby, Percy Alan Farrer, 1877–1940, vol. III
Mance, Brig.-Gen. Sir H. Osborne, 1875–1966, vol. VI

Mance, Sir Henry Christopher, 1840–1926, vol. II
Manchester, 9th Duke of, 1877–1947, vol. IV
Manchester, 10th Duke of, 1902–1977, vol. VII
Manchester, Sir William Edwin, 1869–1956, vol. V
Mancinelli, Luigi, 1848–1921, vol. II
Mancroft, 1st Baron, 1872–1942, vol. IV
Mander, Sir Charles Arthur, 2nd Bt, 1884–1951, vol. V
Mander, Sir Charles Tertius, 1st Bt, 1852–1929, vol. III
Mander, Sir Frederick, 1883–1964, vol. VI
Mander, Maj.-Gen. Frederick Day, 1842–1939, vol. III
Mander, Sir Geoffrey Le Mesurier, 1882–1962, vol. VI
Mander, Captain John Harold, 1869–1927, vol. II
Mander, Lionel Henry Miles, 1888–1946, vol. IV
Manders, Horace Craigie, 1882–1963, vol. VI
Manders, Richard, 1854–1931, vol. III
Manderson, Maj.-Gen. George Rennie, 1834–1918, vol. II
Mandeville, Rt Rev. Gay Lisle Griffith, 1894–1969, vol. VI
Mandleberg, Sir G. Charles, 1860–1932, vol. III
Mandleberg, J. Harold, 1885–1973, vol. VII
Mandleberg, Brig. Lennard Charles, 1893–1975, vol. VII
Mandlik, Sir Narayan Vishvanath, 1870–1948, vol. IV
Manfield, Harry, died 1923, vol. II
Manfield, Sir Philip, 1819–1899, vol. I
Mangan, Rt Rev. John, 1852–1917, vol. II
Mangham, Sydney, 1886–1962, vol. VI
Mangiagalli, Riccardo P.; see Pick-Mangiagalli.
Mangin, Ven. Robert Rattray, 1863–1944, vol. IV
Mangin, Sir Thorleif Rattray Orde, 1896–1950, vol. IV
Mangles, Maj.-Gen. Cecil, 1842–1906, vol. I
Mangles, Brig.-Gen. Roland Henry, 1874–1948, vol. IV
Mangles, Ross Lowis, 1833–1905, vol. I
Mangles, Major Walter James, 1862–1929, vol. III
Manifold, Hon. Sir Chester; see Manifold, Hon. Sir T. C.
Manifold, Maj.-Gen. Sir Courtenay Clarke, 1864–1957, vol. V
Manifold, Maj.-Gen. Sir Graham; see Manifold, Maj.-Gen. Sir M. G. E. B.
Manifold, Maj.-Gen. John Alexander, 1884–1960, vol. V
Manifold, Lt-Col John Forster, 1857–1933, vol. III
Manifold, Maj.-Gen. Sir (Michael) Graham Egerton Bowman-, 1871–1940, vol. III
Manifold, Hon. Sir (Thomas) Chester, 1897–1979, vol. VII
Manifold, Hon. Sir Walter Synnot, 1849–1928, vol. II
Manion, Hon. Robert James, 1881–1943, vol. IV
Manipur, HH Sir Chura Chand Singh Maharajah of, 1886–1941, vol. IV
Manisty, Rear-Adm. Sir Eldon; see Manisty, Rear-Adm. Sir H. W. E.
Manisty, Rear-Adm. Sir (Henry Wilfred) Eldon, 1876–1960, vol. V

Manisty, Herbert Francis, 1853–1939, vol. III
Manktelow, Sir (Arthur) Richard, 1899–1977, vol. VII
Manktelow, Sir Richard; see Manktelow, Sir A. R.
Manley, Edgar Booth, 1897–1959, vol. V
Manley, Gordon, 1902–1980, vol. VII
Manley, Norman Washington, 1893–1969, vol. VI
Mann, Sir Alan Harbury, 1914–1970, vol. VI (AII)
Mann, Alexander, died 1908, vol. I
Mann, Arthur Henry, 1876–1972, vol. VII
Mann, Rt Rev. Cameron, 1851–1932, vol. III
Mann, Cathleen (Mrs J. R. Follett), died 1959, vol. V
Mann, Sir Donald, 1853–1934, vol. III
Mann, Sir Duncombe; see Mann, Sir T. D.
Mann, Sir Edward, 1st Bt, 1854–1943, vol. IV
Mann, Sir (Edward) John, 2nd Bt, 1883–1971, vol. VII
Mann, Mrs Fairman; see Mann, Mary E.
Mann, Hon. Sir Frederick Wollaston, 1869–1958, vol. V
Mann, Harold Hart, 1872–1961, vol. VI
Mann, Harrington, 1864–1937, vol. III
Mann, Heinrich, 1871–1950, vol. IV
Mann, Rt Rev. Mgr Horace K., 1859–1928, vol. II
Mann, J. Dixon, died 1912, vol. I
Mann, Jacob, 1888–1940, vol. III (A), vol. IV
Mann, Sir James Gow, 1897–1962, vol. VI
Mann, Maj.-Gen. James Robert, 1823–1915, vol. I
Mann, James Scrimgeour, 1883–1946, vol. IV
Mann, Mrs Jean, died 1964, vol. VI
Mann, Sir John, 1863–1955, vol. V
Mann, Sir John, died 1957, vol. V
Mann, Sir John; see Mann, Sir E. J.
Mann, Rt Rev. John Charles, 1880–1967, vol. VI
Mann, Keith Cranston, 1903–1972, vol. VII
Mann, Ludovic MacLellan, died 1955, vol. V
Mann, Mary E., died 1929, vol. III
Mann, Thomas, 1875–1955, vol. V
Mann, Sir (Thomas) Duncombe, 1857–1949, vol. IV
Mann, Tom, 1856–1941, vol. IV
Mann, Major William Edgar, 1885–1969, vol. VI
Mann, Air Cdre William Edward George, 1899–1966, vol. VI
Mannering, Rev. Ernest, 1882–1977, vol. VII
Mannering, Rev. Canon Leslie George, 1883–1974, vol. VII
Manners, 3rd Baron, 1852–1927, vol. II
Manners, 4th Baron, 1897–1972, vol. VII
Manners, Lord Cecil Reginald John, 1868–1945, vol. IV
Manners, Charles, 1857–1935, vol. III
Manners, Brig. Charles Molyneux Sandys, 1885–1954, vol. V
Manners, Lord Edward William John, 1864–1903, vol. I
Manners, Ernest John, 1877–1944, vol. IV
Manners, Rear-Adm. Sir Errol, 1883–1953, vol. V
Manners, Sir George Espec John, 1860–1939, vol. III
Manners, J. Hartley, 1870–1928, vol. II
Manners, Major Lord Robert William Orlando 1870–1917, vol. II

Manners-Smith, Francis St George, *died* 1941, vol. IV

Manners-Sutton, Francis Henry Astley, 1869–1916, vol. II

Mannheim, Hermann, 1889–1974, vol. VII

Mannheim, Karl, 1893–1947, vol. IV

Mannheim, Lucie, 1905–1976, vol. VII

Manning, Miss, *died* 1905, vol. I

Manning, Bernard Lord, 1892–1941, vol. IV

Manning, Brian O'Donoghue, 1891–1964, vol. VI

Manning, Charles Anthony Woodward, 1894–1978, vol. VII

Manning, Air Cdre Edye Rolleston, 1889–1957, vol. V

Manning, Dame (Elizabeth) Leah, *died* 1977, vol. VII

Manning, Sir George, 1887–1976, vol. VII

Manning, Sir Henry Edward, 1877–1963, vol. VI

Manning, Sir (James) Kenneth, 1907–1976, vol. VII

Manning, John Westley, 1866–1954, vol. V

Manning, Sir Kenneth; *see* Manning, Sir J. K.

Manning, Dame Leah; *see* Manning, Dame E. L.

Manning, Olivia Mary, (Mrs R. D. Smith), 1915–1980, vol. VII

Manning, Richard Joseph, 1883–1979, vol. VII

Manning, W. Westley, *died* 1954, vol. V

Manning, Brig.-Gen. Sir William Henry, 1863–1932, vol. III

Manning, Sir William Patrick, 1845–1915, vol. I

Manning, Rt Rev. William Thomas, 1866–1949, vol. IV

Manningham-Buller, Lt-Col Sir Mervyn Edward, 3rd Bt, 1876–1956, vol. V

Manningham-Buller, Sir Morton Edward; *see* Buller.

Mannix, Most Rev. Daniel, 1864–1963, vol. VI

Mannooch, Geoffrey Herbert, 1890–1959, vol. V

Manns, Sir August, 1825–1907, vol. I

Manohar Lal, Hon. Sir, 1880–1949, vol. IV

Mansbridge, Albert, 1876–1952, vol. V

Mansbridge, Very Rev. Harold Chad, 1917–1980, vol. VII

Mansel, Col Alfred, 1852–1918, vol. II

Mansel, Sir Courtenay Cecil, 13th Bt (shown as 11th Bt), 1880–1933, vol. III (the 12th and 13th Bts are wrongly numbered in their entries).

Mansel, Sir Edward Berkeley, 12th Bt (shown as 10th Bt), 1839–1908, vol. I

Mansel, George, *died* 1914, vol. I

Mansel, Col George Clavell, 1861–1910, vol. I

Mansel, Sir John Philip Ferdinand, 14th Bt, 1910–1947, vol. IV

Mansel, Major Rhys Clavell, 1891–1969, vol. VI

Mansel-Jones, Col Conwyn, 1871–1942, vol. IV

Mansel-Jones, Herbert Riversdale, 1836–1907, vol. I

Mansel-Pleydell, Lt-Col Edmund Morton, *died* 1914, vol. I

Mansel-Pleydell, John Clavell, 1817–1902, vol. I

Mansel-Pleydell, Rev. John Colvile Morton, 1851–1938, vol. III

Mansell, Vice-Adm. Sir (George) Robert, 1868–1936, vol. III

Mansell, Lt-Col Sir John Herbert, 1864–1933, vol. III

Mansell, Air Vice-Marshal Reginald Baynes, 1896–1945, vol. IV

Mansell, Vice-Adm. Sir Robert; *see* Mansell, Vice-Adm. Sir G. R.

Mansell-Moullin, Charles William, 1851–1940, vol. III

Mansergh, Cornewall Lewis, 1863–1935, vol. III

Mansergh, Gen. Sir (E. C.) Robert, 1900–1970, vol. VI

Mansergh, Fanny; *see* Moody, F.

Mansergh, James, 1834–1905, vol. I

Mansergh, Adm. Sir Maurice James, 1896–1966, vol. VI

Mansergh, Gen. Sir Robert; *see* Mansergh, Gen. Sir E. C. R.

Mansergh, Southcote; *see* Manners, Charles.

Mansfield and Mansfield, 4th Earl of, 1806–1898, vol. I

Mansfield and Mansfield, 5th Earl of, 1860–1906, vol. I

Mansfield and Mansfield, 6th Earl of, 1864–1935, vol. III

Mansfield and Mansfield, 7th Earl of, 1900–1971, vol. VII

Mansfield, Sir Alfred, 1870–1940, vol. III

Mansfield, Sir Charles Edward, 1828–1907, vol. I

Mansfield, Cyril James, *died* 1916, vol. II

Mansfield, F. J., 1872–1946, vol. IV

Mansfield, Henry, 1914–1979, vol. VII

Mansfield, Maj.-Gen. Sir Herbert, 1855–1939, vol. III

Mansfield, Horace Rendall, 1863–1914, vol. I

Mansfield, Vice-Adm. Sir John Maurice, 1893–1949, vol. IV

Mansfield, Orlando Augustine, 1863–1936, vol. III

Mansfield, Philip Theodore, 1892–1975, vol. VII

Mansfield, Purcell James, 1889–1968, vol. VI

Mansfield, Richard, 1857–1907, vol. I

Mansfield, Robert William, 1850–1911, vol. I

Mansfield, Walter, 1870–1916, vol. II

Mansfield, Wilfrid Stephen, 1894–1968, vol. VI

Mansfield, William Thomas, *died* 1939, vol. III (A), vol. IV

Manship, Paul, 1885–1966, vol. VI

Mansion, John Edmond, 1870–1942, vol. IV

Manson, Edward, 1849–1919, vol. II

Manson, Henry James, 1869–1952, vol. V

Manson, James Alexander, 1851–1921, vol. II

Manson, James Bolivar, 1879–1945, vol. IV

Manson, John, 1842–1923, vol. II

Manson, Sir Patrick, 1844–1922, vol. II

Manson, Robert George, 1893–1969, vol. VI

Manson, Rev. Thomas Walter, 1893–1958, vol. V

Manson, Rev. William, 1882–1958, vol. V

Manson-Bahr, Sir Philip, 1881–1966, vol. VI

Mant, Sir Reginald Arthur, 1870–1942, vol. IV

Mantegazza, Paul, 1831–1910, vol. I

Mantell, Col Patrick Riners, 1862–1936, vol. III

Mantle, Lee, 1851–1934, vol. III

Manton, 1st Baron (*cr* 1922), 1873–1922, did not have an entry in Who's Who.

Manton, 2nd Baron, 1899–1968, vol. VI

Manton, G. Grenville, *died* 1932, vol. III
Manton, Sir Henry, 1835–1924, vol. II
Manton, Brig. Lionel, 1887–1961, vol. VI
Manton, Sidnie M., (Mrs J. P. Harding), 1902–1979, vol. VII
Mantoux, Paul Joseph, 1877–1956, vol. V
Manuel, Archibald Clark, 1901–1976, vol. VII
Manuel, Stephen, 1880–1954, vol. V
Manuwa, Chief Hon. Sir Samuel Layinka Ayodeji, 1903–1975, vol. VII
Manvell, Rev. Arnold Edward William, 1868–1927, vol. II
Manvers, 3rd Earl, 1825–1900 (this entry was not transferred to Who was Who).
Manvers, 4th Earl, 1854–1926, vol. II
Manvers, 5th Earl, 1888–1940, vol. III
Manvers, 6th Earl, 1881–1955, vol. V
Manville, Sir Edward, 1862–1933, vol. III
Manwaring, George Ernest, 1882–1939, vol. III
Manzoni, Sir Herbert John Baptista, 1899–1972, vol. VII
Maple, Sir John Blundell, 1st Bt, 1845–1903, vol. I
Maplesden, Rev. Arthur William, 1864–1932, vol. III
Mapleson, Henry, 1851–1927, vol. II
Maplestone, Philip Alan, *died* 1969, vol. VI
Mapother, Edward, 1881–1940, vol. III
Mapother, Edward Dillon, 1835–1908, vol. I
Mapp, Charles, 1903–1978, vol. VII
Mapp, Henry William, 1871–1955, vol. V
Mappin, Sir Charles Thomas Hewitt, 4th Bt, 1909–1941, vol. IV
Mappin, Sir Frank, 2nd Bt, 1846–1920, vol. II
Mappin, Sir Frank Crossley, 6th Bt, 1884–1975, vol. VII
Mappin, Sir Frederick Thorpe, 1st Bt, 1821–1910, vol. I
Mappin, Sir Samuel Wilson, 5th Bt, 1854–1942, vol. IV
Mappin, Sir Wilson, 3rd Bt, 1848–1925, vol. II
Mapson, Leslie William, 1907–1970, vol. VI
Mar, 27th (styled 33rd) Earl of, 1836–1930, vol. III
Mar, 28th (styled 34th) Earl of, 1868–1932, vol. III
Mar, 29th Earl of, 1891–1965, vol. VI
Mar, 30th Earl of, 1914–1975, vol. VII
Mar, Master of; *see* Garioch, Lord.
Mar, 12th Earl of, **and** Kellie, 14th Earl of, 1865–1955, vol. V
Mar, Helen, *died* 1940, vol. III (A), vol. IV
Marais, Colin B.; *see* Bain-Marais.
Marais, Rev. Johannes Izak, 1848–1919, vol. II
Maratib Ali, Sir Syed, 1883–1961, vol. VI
Marcel, Gabriel, 1889–1973, vol. VII
Marcet, William, *died* 1900, vol. I
March, George Edward, 1834–1922, vol. II
March, Rt Rev. John, 1863–1940, vol. III
March, Gen. Payton C., 1864–1955, vol. V
March, Samuel, 1861–1935, vol. III
Marchamley, 1st Baron, 1855–1925, vol. II
Marchamley, 2nd Baron, 1886–1949, vol. IV
Marchand, Geoffrey Isidore Charles, *died* 1965, vol. VI
Marchand, Gen. Jean Baptiste, 1863–1934, vol. III

Marchant, Maj.-Gen. Alfred Edmund, 1863–1924, vol. II
Marchant, Bessie, (Mrs J. A. Comfort), 1862–1941, vol. IV
Marchant, Edgar Cardew, 1864–1960, vol. V
Marchant, Edgar Walford, 1876–1962, vol. VI
Marchant, Ernest Cecil, 1902–1979, vol. VII
Marchant, Sir James, 1867–1956, vol. V
Marchant, James Robert Vernam, 1853–1936, vol. III
Marchant, Sir Stanley, 1883–1949, vol. IV
Marchant, Brig.-Gen. Thomas Harry Saunders, 1875–1952, vol. V
Marchant, William Sydney, 1894–1953, vol. V
Marchbank, John, 1883–1946, vol. IV
Marchbanks, James, 1862–1947, vol. IV
Marchesi, Blanche, 1863–1940, vol. III
Marchesi, Mathilde, 1826–1913, vol. I
Marchmont, Arthur Williams, 1852–1923, vol. II
Marchwood, 1st Viscount, 1876–1955, vol. V
Marchwood, 2nd Viscount, 1912–1979, vol. VII
Marcil, Hon. Charles, 1860–1937, vol. III
Marcks, Violet Olivia C.; *see* Cressy-Marcks.
Marcon,, Rev. Walter Hubert, *died* 1937, vol. III
Marconi, Marchese; Guglielmo Marconi, 1874–1937, vol. III
Marcosson, Isaac Frederick, 1876–1961, vol. VI
Marcotte, Rev. F. X., 1883–1967, vol. VI
Marcus, Michael, 1894–1960, vol. VI (AI)
Marcuse, Herbert, 1898–1979, vol. VII
Marden, Orison Swett, 1850–1924, vol. II
Marden, Maj.-Gen. Sir Thomas Owen, 1866–1951, vol. V
Marder, Arthur Jacob, 1910–1980, vol. VII
Mardy Jones, Thomas Isaac, *died* 1970, vol. VI
Mare, Captain Philip Armitage, 1891–1951, vol. V
Marek, Kurt W., 1915–1972, vol. VII
Marescaux, Captain Alfred Edward Hay, *died* 1942, vol. IV
Marescaux, Vice-Adm. Gerald Charles Adolphe, 1860–1920, vol. II
Marett, Robert Ranulph, 1866–1943, vol. IV
Margai, Sir Albert Michael, 1910–1980, vol. VII
Margai, Rt Hon. Sir Milton Augustus Strieby, 1895–1964, vol. VI
Margerison, Sir Lawrence, 1872–1958, vol. V
Margesson, 1st Viscount, 1890–1965, vol. VI
Margesson, Col Evelyn William, 1865–1944, vol. IV
Margesson, Sir Mortimer R., 1861–1947, vol. IV
Margesson, Captain Wentworth Henry Davies, 1869–1950, vol. IV
Margesson, Lt-Col William George, 1821–1911, vol. I
Margetson, Alfred James, 1877–1944, vol. IV
Margetson, W. H., 1861–1940, vol. III
Margetson, Very Rev. William James, 1874–1946, vol. IV
Margoliouth, David Samuel, 1858–1940, vol. III
Margoliouth, Rev. G., 1853–1924, vol. II
Margoliouth, Herschel Maurice, 1887–1959, vol. V
Margrett, Charles Henry, 1863–1941, vol. IV
Marillier, Frank William, 1855–1928, vol. II
Marillier, Henry Currie, 1865–1951, vol. V

Marin, John C., 1870–1953, vol. V
Marindin, Maj.-Gen. Arthur Henry, 1868–1947, vol. IV
Marindin, Col Cecil Colvile, 1879–1932, vol. III
Marindin, Sir Francis Arthur, 1838–1900, vol. I
Marion, Léo Edmond, 1899–1979, vol. VII
Maris, Matthew, 1839–1917, vol. II
Maritain, Jacques, 1882–1973, vol. VII
Marix, Air Vice-Marshal Reginald Lennox George, 1889–1966, vol. VI
Marjoribanks, Hon. Coutts, 1860–1924, vol. II
Marjoribanks, Dudley Sinclair, 1858–1929, vol. III
Marjoribanks, Edward, 1900–1932, vol. III
Marjoribanks, Sir George John, 1856–1931, vol. III
Marjoribanks, Sir Norman Edward, 1872–1939, vol. III
Mark, J. M., died 1948, vol. IV
Mark, Sir John, 1832–1909, vol. I
Mark-Wardlaw, Rear-Adm. Alexander Livingston Penrose, 1891–1975, vol. VII
Mark-Wardlaw, Rear-Adm. William Penrose, 1887–1952, vol. V
Markar, Hadji Sir Mohamed M.; see Macan-Markar.
Markby, Sir William, 1829–1914, vol. I
Markelius, Sven Gottfrid, 1889–1972, vol. VII
Marker, Edwin Henry Simon, 1888–1973, vol. VII
Marker, Col Raymond John, 1867–1914, vol. I
Marker, Richard, 1835–1916, vol. II
Markham, Adm. Sir Albert Hastings, 1841–1918, vol. II
Markham, Rt Rev. Algernon A., 1869–1949, vol. IV
Markham, Sir Arthur Basil, 1st Bt, 1866–1916, vol. II
Markham, Sir Charles, 2nd Bt, 1899–1952, vol. V
Markham, Brig.-Gen. Charles John, 1862–1927, vol. II
Markham, Sir Clements Robert, 1830–1916, vol. II
Markham, Lt-Gen. Sir Edwin, 1833–1918, vol. II
Markham, Edwin, 1852–1940, vol. III
Markham, Sir Frank; see Markham, Sir S. F.
Markham, Sir Henry Vaughan, 1897–1946, vol. IV
Markham, Roy, 1916–1979, vol. VII
Markham, Sir (Sydney) Frank, 1897–1975, vol. VII
Markham, Violet Rosa, (Mrs J. Carruthers), died 1959, vol. V
Markievicz, Constance Georgine, died 1927, vol. II
Marklew, Ernest, 1874–1939, vol. III
Marks, 1st Baron, 1858–1938, vol. III
Marks of Broughton, 1st Baron, 1888–1964, vol. VI
Marks, Alexander Hammett, 1880–1954, vol. V
Marks, B. S., 1827–1916, vol. II
Marks, Major Claud Laurie, 1863–1910, vol. I
Marks, David Woolf, 1811–1909, vol. I
Marks, Derek John, 1921–1975, vol. VII
Marks, Eric Astor David; see Marshall, Eric.
Marks, Ernest Samuel, 1872–1947, vol. IV
Marks, Frederick William, 1886–1942, vol. IV
Marks, Geoffrey, 1864–1938, vol. III
Marks, Harry Hananel, 1855–1916, vol. II
Marks, Hon. Sir Henry, 1861–1938, vol. III
Marks, Henry Stacy, 1829–1898, vol. I
Marks, Leslie, 1889–1956, vol. V

Marks, Oliver, 1866–1940, vol. III
Marks, Captain Percy D'Evelyn, 1883–1968, vol. VI
Markwick, Col Ernest Elliott, 1853–1925, vol. II
Marlar, Edward Alfred Geoffrey, 1901–1978, vol. VII
Marlay, Charles Brinsley, 1831–1912, vol. I
Marlborough, 9th Duke of, 1871–1934, vol. III
Marlborough, 10th Duke of, 1897–1972, vol. VII
Marler, Hon. Sir Herbert, 1876–1940, vol. III
Marler, William de Montmollin, 1849–1929, vol. III
Marley, 1st Baron, 1884–1952, vol. V
Marley, Brig. Cuthbert David, 1897–1960, vol. V
Marley, James, 1893–1954, vol. V
Marling, Sir Charles Murray, 1862–1933, vol. III
Marling, Lt-Col Sir John Stanley Vincent, 4th Bt, 1910–1977, vol. VII
Marling, Col Sir Percival Scrope, 3rd Bt, 1861–1936, vol. III
Marling, Sir William Henry, 2nd Bt, 1835–1919, vol. II
Marlow, Arthur Herbert, 1893–1964, vol. VI
Marlow, Col Benjamin William, 1863–1943, vol. IV
Marlow, Ewart, 1895–1965, vol. VI
Marlow, Frederick William, 1877–1936, vol. III
Marlow, Louis; see Wilkinson, L. U.
Marlow, Sydney Raymond, 1896–1945, vol. IV
Marlowe, Anthony Alfred Harmsworth, 1904–1965, vol. VI
Marlowe, Thomas, 1868–1935, vol. III
Marnham, Francis John, 1853–1941, vol. IV
Marnoch, Col Sir John, 1867–1936, vol. III
Marochetti, Baron, 1894–1952, vol. V
Marples, Baron (Life Peer); Alfred Ernest Marples, 1907–1978, vol. VII
Marples, George, 1869–1939, vol. III
Marquand, Rt Hon. Hilary Adair, 1901–1972, vol. VII
Marquand, John Phillips, 1893–1960, vol. V
Marquand, Reginald, 1874–1931, vol. III
Marr, Alexander, 1876–1938, vol. III
Marr, Sir Charles William Clanan, 1880–1960, vol. V
Marr, Francis Alleyne, 1894–1942, vol. IV
Marr, Hamilton Clelland, 1870–1936, vol. III
Marr, Sir James, 1st Bt, 1854–1932, vol. III
Marr, James William Slesser, 1902–1965, vol. VI
Marr, John Edward, 1857–1933, vol. III
Marr, Col John Lynn, 1877–1931, vol. III
Marrable, Brig.-Gen. Arthur George, 1863–1925, vol. II
Marrable, Mrs, died 1916, vol. II
Marrack, Rear-Adm. Hugh Richard, 1888–1972, vol. VII
Marrack, John Richardson, 1886–1976, vol. VII
Marriage, Herbert James, 1872–1946, vol. IV
Marric, J. J.; see Creasey, John.
Marrinan, Patrick Aloysius, 1877–1940, vol. III
Marriner, Lt-Col Bryan Lister, 1888–1943, vol. IV
Marriott, Col Alfred Sinclair, 1876–1943, vol. IV
Marriott, Charles, 1869–1957, vol. V
Marriott, Charles Bertrand, 1868–1946, vol. IV

Marriott, Sir Charles Hayes, 1834–1910, vol. I
Marriott, Captain Charles John Bruce, 1861–1936, vol. III
Marriott, Cyril Herbert Alfred, 1897–1977, vol. VII
Marriott, Eric Llewellyn, 1888–1945, vol. IV
Marriott, Ernest, 1882–1918, vol. II
Marriott, Francis, 1876–1957, vol. V
Marriott, Frederick, 1860–1941, vol. IV
Marriott, Sir Hayes, 1873–1929, vol. III
Marriott, Ven. Henry, 1870–1952, vol. V
Marriott, Herbert, 1865–1935, vol. III
Marriott, Rev. Sir Hugh Randolph Cavendish S.; see Smith-Marriott.
Marriott, James William, 1884–1953, vol. V
Marriott, Brig.-Gen. John, 1861–1953, vol. V
Marriott, Sir John Arthur Ransome, 1859–1945, vol. IV
Marriott, Maj.-Gen. Sir John Charles Oakes, 1895–1978, vol. VII
Marriott, Captain John Peter Ralph, 1879–1938, vol. III
Marriott, Sir John Richard Wyldbore S.; see Smith-Marriott.
Marriott, Very Rev. John Thomas, died 1924, vol. II
Marriott, Patrick Arthur, 1899–1980, vol. VII
Marriott, Major Reginald Adams, 1857–1930, vol. III
Marriott, Major Richard George Armine, 1867–1924, vol. II
Marriott, Richard Michael Harris, 1926–1975, vol. VII
Marriott, Rev. Stephen Jack, 1886–1964, vol. VI
Marriott, William, 1848–1916, vol. II
Marriott, Sir William Henry S.; see Smith-Marriott.
Marriott, Sir William John S.; see Smith-Marriott.
Marriott, William Mason, 1889–1960, vol. V
Marriott, Sir William S.; see Smith-Marriott.
Marriott, Rt Hon. Sir William Thackeray, 1834–1903, vol. I
Marriott-Dodington, Brig.-Gen. Wilfred; see Dodington.
Marris, Eric Denyer, 1891–1976, vol. VII
Marris, Rev. Nisbet Colquhoun, died 1937, vol. III
Marris, Sir William Sinclair, 1873–1945, vol. IV
Marrs, Robert, 1884–1951, vol. IV
Marryat, Very Rev. Charles, 1827–1907, vol. I
Marryat, Florence, (Mrs Francis Lean), 1838–1899, vol. I
Marryshow, Hon. Theophilus Albert, 1887–1958, vol. V
Marsden, Alexander Edwin, 1832–1902, vol. I
Marsden, Captain Arthur, 1883–1960, vol. V
Marsden, Ven. E(dwyn) Lisle, 1886–1960, vol. V
Marsden, Col Sir Ernest, 1889–1970, vol. VI
Marsden, Captain George, 1874–1916, vol. II
Marsden, Sir John Denton, 1st Bt, 1873–1944, vol. IV
Marsden, Percy, 1888–1955, vol. V
Marsden, R. Sydney, 1856–1919, vol. II
Marsden, Rt Rev. Samuel Edward, 1832–1912, vol. I
Marsden, Sir Thomas Rogerson, died 1927, vol. II

Marsden, Wilfred Alexander, 1878–1949, vol. IV
Marsden, Lt-Col William, 1841–1925, vol. II
Marsh, Col Cunliffe Hebbert, 1878–1938, vol. III
Marsh, Rt Rev. Donald Ben, 1903–1973, vol. VII
Marsh, Maj.-Gen. Edward Bertram, 1890–1976, vol. VII
Marsh, Sir Edward Howard, 1872–1953, vol. V
Marsh, Col Frank, 1855–1943, vol. IV
Marsh, Frank Burr, 1880–1940, vol. III (A), vol. IV
Marsh, Brig.-Gen. Frank Graham, 1875–1957, vol. V
Marsh, Maj.-Gen. Frank Hale Berwick, 1841–1923, vol. II
Marsh, Rev. Fred Shipley, 1886–1953, vol. V
Marsh, Henry, 1850–1939, vol. III
Marsh, Howard, 1839–1915, vol. I
Marsh, James Ernest, 1860–1938, vol. III
Marsh, Lt-Col Jeremy-Taylor, 1872–1944, vol. IV
Marsh, Margaret Munnerlyn Mitchell, (Mrs John Robert Marsh), died 1949, vol. IV
Marsh, Othniel Charles, 1831–1899, vol. I
Marsh, Sir Percy William, 1881–1969, vol. VI
Marsh, Richard, died 1915, vol. I
Marsh, Richard, 1851–1933, vol. III
Marsh, Rev. Sidney Frank, 1860–1936, vol. III
Marsh, Thomas Robertson, 1847–1929, vol. III
Marsh, Sir William Henry, 1827–1906, vol. I
Marsh, William Waller, 1877–1959, vol. V
Marsh Smith, Reginald Norman, 1891–1975, vol. VII
Marshall, 1st Baron, 1865–1936, vol. III
Marshall, Alfred, 1842–1924, vol. II
Marshall, Sir Anthony, 1826–1911, vol. I
Marshall, Archibald, 1866–1934, voll III
Marshall, Archibald Cook, 1890–1959, vol. V
Marshall, Sir Archie Pellow, 1899–1966, vol. VI
Marshall, Arthur, 1873–1968, vol. VI
Marshall, Sir Arthur Harold, 1870–1956, vol. V
Marshall, Col Sir Arthur Wellington, 1841–1918, vol. II
Marshall, Charles Devereux, 1867–1918, vol. II
Marshall, Charles Frederic, 1864–1940, vol. III
Marshall, Brig. Charles Frederick Keilk, 1888–1953, vol. V
Marshall, Charles Jennings, 1890–1954, vol. V
Marshall, Charles Robertshaw, 1869–1952, vol. V
Marshall, D. H., 1848–1932, vol. III
Marshall, (Davis) Edward, 1869–1933, vol. III
Marshall, Comdr Sir Douglas, 1906–1976, vol. VII
Marshall, Hon. Duncan M'Lean, 1872–1946, vol. IV
Marshall, Edward, see Marshall, D. E.
Marshall, Rev. Edward Thory, 1842–1933, vol. III
Marshall, Elizabeth Middleton O.; see Ord Marshall.
Marshall, Emma, 1828–1899, vol. I
Marshall, Eric, (Eric Astor David Marks), 1891–1961, vol. VI
Marshall, Eric Stewart, 1879–1963, vol. VI
Marshall, Frances; see St Aubyn, Alan.
Marshall, Francis Hugh Adam, 1878–1949, vol. IV
Marshall, Maj.-Gen. Francis James, 1876–1942, vol. IV

Marshall, Frank, 1886–1952, vol. V
Marshall, Frank James, 1877–1944, vol. IV
Marshall, Fred, 1883–1962, vol. VI
Marshall, Frederic, died 1910, vol. I
Marshall, Lt-Gen. Sir Frederick, 1829–1900, vol. I
Marshall, Frederick Henry, 1878–1955, vol. V
Marshall, Engr-Adm. Frederick William, 1870–1956, vol. V
Marshall, George Balfour, 1863–1928, vol. II
Marshall, Hon. George Catlett, 1880–1959, vol. V
Marshall, Maj.-Gen. George Frederick Leycester, 1843–1934, vol. III
Marshall, Maj.-Gen. Sir George Henry, 1843–1909, vol. I
Marshall, George Leslie, died 1964, vol. VI
Marshall, George William, 1839–1905, vol. I
Marshall, Major George William, 1867–1940, vol. III
Marshall, Rt Rev. Guy, 1909–1978, vol. VII
Marshall, Sir Guy Anstruther Knox, 1871–1959, vol. V
Marshall, Col Hannath Douglas, 1872–1944, vol. IV
Marshall, Henry D., died 1906, vol. I
Marshall, Major Henry Seymour, 1879–1937, vol. III
Marshall, Rt Rev. Henry Vincent, 1884–1955, vol. V
Marshall, Sir Herbert, 1851–1918, vol. II
Marshall, Herbert Brough Falcon, 1890–1966, vol. VI
Marshall, Herbert Menzies, 1841–1913, vol. I
Marshall, Horace, died 1944, vol. IV
Marshall, Howard Percival, 1900–1973, vol. VII
Marshall, Hugh, 1868–1913, vol. I
Marshall, Hugh John Cole, 1873–1947, vol. IV
Marshall, Brig.-Gen. Hugh John Miles, 1867–1946, vol. IV
Marshall, J. Fitz, 1859–1932, vol. III
Marshall, Sir James, 1894–1979, vol. VII
Marshall, Sir James Brown, 1853–1922, vol. II
Marshall, James Cole, 1876–1952, vol. V
Marshall, Rev. James M'Call, 1838–1926, vol. II
Marshall, James Rissik, 1886–1959, vol. V
Marshall, John, 1845–1915, vol. I (A)
Marshall, John, 1860–1951, vol. V
Marshall, John, 1895–1970, vol. VI
Marshall, Captain John Dodds, 1878–1931, vol. III
Marshall, John Edwin, 1864–1937, vol. III
Marshall, John Frederick, 1874–1949, vol. IV
Marshall, Sir John Hubert, 1876–1958, vol. V
Marshall, Maj.-Gen. John Stuart, 1883–1944, vol. IV
Marshall, Rev. John Turner, 1850–1923, vol. II
Marshall, Brig.-Gen. John Willoughby Astell, 1854–1921, vol. II
Marshall, John Wilson, died 1923, vol. II
Marshall, Rev. Joseph William, 1835–1915, vol. I
Marshall, Kenneth McLean, 1874–1954, vol. V
Marshall, Rev. Laurence Henry, 1882–1953, vol. V
Marshall, Lumley Arnold, 1852–1942, vol. IV
Marshall, Markham Richard L.; see Leeson-Marshall.

Marshall, Lt-Col Noel George Lambert, 1852–1926, vol. II
Marshall, Brig. Norman, 1886–1942, vol. IV
Marshall, Norman, 1901–1980, vol. VII
Marshall, Captain Oswald Percival, 1857–1939, vol. III
Marshall, Patrick, 1869–1950, vol. IV (A)
Marshall, Captain Robert, 1863–1910, vol. I
Marshall, Robert, 1889–1975, vol. VII
Marshall, Sir Robert C.; see Calder-Marshall.
Marshall, Robert Ian, 1899–1970, vol. VI
Marshall, Robert Smith, 1902–1976, vol. VII
Marshall, Septimus, 1876–1962, vol. VI
Marshall, Sheina Macalister, 1896–1977, vol. VII
Marshall, Sir Sidney, 1882–1973, vol. VII
Marshall, Brig.-Gen. Thomas Edward, 1865–1946, vol. IV
Marshall, Col Sir Thomas Horatio, 1833–1917, vol. II
Marshall, Thomas Riley, 1854–1925, vol. II
Marshall, Major W. R., died 1916, vol. II
Marshall, Cdre William, 1873–1930, vol. III
Marshall, Rev. William, 1875–1955, vol. V
Marshall, William Hibbert, 1866–1929, vol. III
Marshall, William Lawrence Wright, died 1939, vol. III
Marshall, Sir William Marchbank, 1875–1967, vol. VI
Marshall, Lt-Gen. Sir William Raine, 1865–1939, vol. III
Marshall, Lt-Col William Thomas, 1854–1920, vol. II
Marshall, William Thomas, 1907–1975, vol. VII
Marshall-Hall, Sir Edward, 1858–1927, vol. II
Marshall-Hall, G. W. L., 1862–1915, vol. I
Marshall-Reynolds, Clyde Albert, 1898–1977, vol. VII
Marsham, Brig. Francis William Bullock-, 1883–1971, vol. VII
Marsham, George, 1849–1927, vol. II
Marsham, Dame Joan; see Marsham, Hon. Mrs S.
Marsham, Rev. Hon. John, 1842–1926, vol. II
Marsham, Robert H. Bullock-, 1833–1913, vol. I
Marsham, Hon. Mrs Sydney, died 1972, vol. VII
Marsham-Townshend, Hon. Robert, 1834–1914, vol. I
Marsillac, Jacques J. B. de, 1879–1962, vol. VI
Marston, Archibald Daniel, 1891–1962, vol. VI
Marston, Sir Charles, 1867–1946, vol. IV
Marston, Edward, 1825–1914, vol. I
Marston, Freda, 1895–1949, vol. IV
Marston, Hedley Ralph, 1900–1965, vol. VI
Marston, Surg.-Gen. Jeffery Allen, 1831–1911, vol. I
Marston, Reginald St Clair, 1886–1943, vol. IV
Marston, Robert Bright, 1853–1927, vol. II
Martel, Comtesse de; see Gyp, Sybille.
Martel, Brig.-Gen. Sir Charles Philip, 1861–1945, vol. IV
Martel, Lt-Gen. Sir Giffard Le Quesne, 1889–1958, vol. V
Martelli, Ernest Wynne, died 1917, vol. II
Martelli, Maj.-Gen. Sir Horace de Courcy, 1877–1959, vol. V

Martello Tower; *see* Norman, Comdr F. M.
Marten, Hon. Sir Alfred George, 1839–1906, vol. I
Marten, Sir Amberson Barrington, 1870–1962, vol. VI
Marten, Sir (Clarence) Henry (Kennett), 1872–1948, vol. IV
Marten, Eric Charles, 1899–1948, vol. IV
Marten, Vice-Adm. Sir Francis Arthur, 1879–1950, vol. IV
Marten, Ven. George Henry, 1876–1966, vol. VI
Marten, Sir Henry; *see* Marten, Sir C. H. K.
Marten, John Thomas, 1872–1929, vol. III
Marti, Karl, 1855–1925, vol. II
Martin, Sir Albert, *died* 1943, vol. IV
Martin, Col Albert Edward, 1876–1936, vol. III
Martin, Sir Albert Victor, 1897–1968, vol. VI
Martin, Sir Alec, 1884–1971, vol. VII
Martin, Very Rev. Alexander, 1857–1946, vol. IV
Martin, Alfred James, 1875–1959, vol. V
Martin, Lt-Gen. Sir Alfred Robert, 1853–1926, vol. II
Martin, Hon. Archer, 1865–1941, vol. IV
Martin, Arthur Anderson, *died* 1916, vol. II
Martin, Arthur Campbell, 1875–1963, vol. VI
Martin, Arthur John, 1883–1942, vol. IV
Martin, Arthur Patchett, 1851–1902, vol. I
Martin, (Basil) Kingsley, 1897–1969, vol. VI
Martin, Vice-Adm. Sir Benjamin Charles Stanley, 1891–1957, vol. V
Martin, Bradley, 1841–1913, vol. I
Martin, Sir Charles Carnegie, 1901–1969, vol. VI
Martin, Charles Emanuel, 1891–1977, vol. VII
Martin, Charles F., 1868–1953, vol. V
Martin, Sir Charles James, 1866–1955, vol. V
Martin, Chester, 1882–1958, vol. V
Martin, Christopher, 1866–1933, vol. III
Martin, Christopher John H.; *see* Holland-Martin.
Martin, Col Claude Buist, 1869–1950, vol. IV
Martin, Rt Rev. Clifford Arthur, 1895–1977, vol. VII
Martin, Cornwallis Philip Wykeham-, 1855–1924, vol. II
Martin, Col Cunliffe, 1834–1917, vol. II
Martin, Brig. Cyril Gordon, 1891–1980, vol. VII
Martin, Cyril Hubert, 1867–1940, vol. III (A), vol. IV
Martin, Daisy Maud, *died* 1964, vol. VI
Martin, Sir David Christie, 1914–1976, vol. VII
Martin, Adm. Sir Deric Douglas Eric H.; *see* Holland-Martin.
Martin, Rt Rev. Donald, 1873–1938, vol. III
Martin, Lt-Col Edward Cuthbert De R.; *see* De Renzy-Martin.
Martin, Brig.-Gen. Edward Fowell, 1875–1950, vol. IV
Martin, Captain Edward Harington, *died* 1921, vol. II
Martin, Edward Kenneth, 1883–1980, vol. VII
Martin, Edward Pritchard, 1844–1910, vol. I
Martin, Brig. Edwyn Sandys Dawes, 1894–1954, vol. V
Martin, Emma; *see* Marshall, E.
Martin, Sir Ernest, 1872–1957, vol. V

Martin, Col Ernest Edmund, 1869–1925, vol. II
Martin, Frank, 1890–1974, vol. VII
Martin, Frederick, 1882–1950, vol. IV
Martin, Frederick John, 1891–1964, vol. VI
Martin, Frederick Townsend, 1849–1914, vol. I
Martin, Col George Blake Napier, 1847–1917, vol. II
Martin, Sir George Clement, 1844–1916, vol. II
Martin, Rev. George Currie, 1865–1937, vol. III
Martin, George Peter, 1823–1910, vol. I
Martin, Sir George William, 1884–1976, vol. VII
Martin, Col Gerald Hamilton, 1879–1952, vol. V
Martin, Glenn L., 1886–1955, vol. V
Martin, Granville Edward B.; *see* Bromley-Martin.
Martin, Captain Harry Cutfield, 1852–1932, vol. III
Martin, Helen, (Lady Martin); *see* Faucit, H.
Martin, Rev. Henry, 1844–1919, vol. II
Martin, Rev. Henry, 1844–1923, vol. II
Martin, Henry, 1889–1964, vol. VI
Martin, Rt Rev. Henry David, 1889–1971, vol. VII
Martin, Col Henry Graham, 1872–1955, vol. V
Martin, Henry Robert Charles, 1889–1942, vol. IV
Martin, Brig.-Gen. Herbert, 1857–1931, vol. III
Martin, Howard, *died* 1924, vol. II
Martin, Hubert, *died* 1938, vol. III
Martin, Rev. Hugh, 1890–1964, vol. VI
Martin, Lt-Gen. Hugh Gray, 1887–1969, vol. VI
Martin, Humphrey Trice, *died* 1931, vol. III
Martin, Sir James, 1861–1935, vol. III
Martin, Major James Evans Baillie, 1859–1931, vol. III
Martin, Maj.-Gen. James Fitzgerald, 1876–1958, vol. V
Martin, James Hamilton, 1841–1937, vol. III
Martin, James Rea, 1877–1951, vol. V
Martin, John, 1847–1944, vol. IV
Martin, John, 1884–1949, vol. IV
Martin, Brig. John Crawford, 1896–1963, vol. VI
Martin, Maj.-Gen. John Simson Stuart, 1888–1973, vol. VII
Martin, Hon. Joseph, 1852–1923, vol. II
Martin, Joseph Samuel, 1845–1911, vol. I
Martin, Maj.-Gen. Kevin John, 1890–1958, vol. V
Martin, Kingsley; *see* Martin, B. K.
Martin, Leonard Cyril, 1886–1976, vol. VII
Martin, Hon. Maurice, 1872–1937, vol. III
Martin, Hon. Sir Norman Angus, 1893–1978, vol. VII
Martin, Olive F., 1887–1967, vol. VI
Martin, Percy F., 1861–1941, vol. IV
Martin, Reginald James, 1892–1970, vol. VI
Martin, Col Reginald Victor, 1889–1973, vol. VII
Martin, Rt Hon. Sir Richard, 1st Bt (*cr* 1885), 1831–1901, vol. I
Martin, Sir Richard, *died* 1922, vol. II
Martin, Rev. Richard, 1836–1927, vol. II
Martin, Sir Richard Biddulph, 1st Bt (*cr* 1905), 1838–1916, vol. II
Martin, Sir Richard Byam, 5th Bt (*cr* 1791), 1841–1910, vol. I
Martin, Sir Richard Edward Rowley, 1847–1907, vol. I
Martin, Lt-Col Sir Robert Edmund, 1874–1961, vol. VI

Martin, Robert M. Holland, 1872–1944, vol. IV
Martin, Col Rowland Hill, 1848–1919, vol. II
Martin, Sidney, 1860–1927, vol. II
Martin, Stapleton, 1846–1922, vol. II
Martin, Sir T. Carlaw, died 1920, vol. II
Martin, Sir Theodore, 1816–1909, vol. I
Martin, Very Rev. Thomas, 1856–1942, vol. IV
Martin, Thomas, 1893–1971, vol. VII
Martin, Sir Thomas Acquin, 1850–1906, vol. I
Martin, Col Thomas Morgan, 1854–1928, vol. II
Martin, Thomas Shannon, 1891–1954, vol. V
Martin, Victoria Claflin Woodhull, 1838–1927, vol. II
Martin, Violet, died 1915, vol. I (A)
Martin, W. A. P., 1827–1916, vol. II
Martin, Captain W. R., died 1913, vol. I
Martin, Willem, 1876–1954, vol. V
Martin, Sir William, 1856–1924, vol. II
Martin, Paymaster Rear-Adm. William Ernest Russell, 1867–1946, vol. IV
Martin, William Gregory W.; see Wood-Martin.
Martin, William Henry Blyth, 1862–1946, vol. IV
Martin, William Henry Porteous, 1886–1939, vol. III
Martin, Hon. William Lee, 1870–1950, vol. IV
Martin, William Pethebridge, 1859–1933, vol. III
Martin du Gard, Roger, 1881–1958, vol. V
Martin-Harvey, Sir John; see Harvey.
Martin-Hurst, William, 1876–1941, vol. IV
Martin-Jones, Rev. S., 1872–1941, vol. IV
Martin-Leake, Lt-Col Arthur; see Leake.
Martin-Leake, Vice-Adm. Francis, 1869–1928, vol. II
Martin-Leake, Hugh; see Leake.
Martindale, Sir Arthur Henry Temple, 1854–1942, vol. IV
Martindale, Col Ben. Hay, 1824–1904, vol. I
Martindale, Rev. Cyril Charlie, 1879–1963, vol. VI
Martindale, Ven. Henry, 1879–1946, vol. IV
Martindale, Hilda, 1875–1952, vol. V
Martindale, Louisa, died 1966, vol. VI
Martindell, Herbert Edward West, 1866–1933, vol. III
Martineau, Alfred, died 1903, vol. I
Martineau, Edith, 1842–1909, vol. I
Martineau, Lt-Col Ernest, 1861–1951, vol. V
Martineau, George, 1835–1919, vol. II
Martineau, Rev. Canon George Edward, 1905–1969, vol. VI
Martineau, James, 1805–1900, vol. I
Martineau, Paul Gideon, 1858–1934, vol. III
Martineau, Sir Philip Hubert, 1862–1944, vol. IV
Martineau, Sir Wilfrid, 1889–1964, vol. VI
Martineau, Sir William, 1865–1950, vol. IV
Martinengo-Cesaresco, Countess; Evelyn Lilian Hazeldine, died 1931, vol. III
Martino, Commendatore Eduardo de, died 1912, vol. I
Martinson, Rt Rev. Ezra Douglas, 1885–1968, vol. VI
Martinson, Harry E., 1904–1978, vol. VII
Marton, Col George Blucher Heneage, 1839–1905, vol. I (A)
Marton, Lt-Col Richard Oliver, 1872–1945, vol. IV

Martyn, Col Anthony Wood, 1864–1955, vol. V
Martyn, Brig.-Gen. Arundel, 1868–1945, vol. IV
Martyn, Brig. Athelstan Markham, 1881–1956, vol. V
Martyn, David Forbes, 1906–1970, vol. VI
Martyn, Edward, 1859–1923, vol. II
Martyn, Sir Henry Linnington, 1888–1947, vol. IV
Martyn, Rev. Richard James, 1846–1913, vol. I
Martyn, Selwyn Rawlings, 1892–1956, vol. V
Martyr, Lt-Col Cyril Godfrey, 1860–1936, vol. III
Martyr, (Joseph) Weston, 1885–1966, vol. VI
Martyr, Richard Edward, 1857–1940, vol. III
Marvin, Francis Sydney, 1863–1943, vol. IV
Marwick, Hugh, 1881–1965, vol. VI
Marwick, Sir James David, 1826–1908, vol. I
Marwood, Sir William Francis, 1863–1935, vol. III
Marwood-Elton, Lt-Col William, 1865–1931, vol. III
Marx, Adm. John Locke, 1852–1939, vol. III
Maryon, Herbert, 1874–1965, vol. VI
Maryon-Wilson, George Maryon; see Wilson.
Maryon-Wilson, Rev. Canon Sir (George) Percy (Maryon), 12th Bt, 1898–1965, vol. VI
Maryon-Wilson, Sir Hubert Guy Maryon, 13th Bt, 1888–1978, vol. VII
Maryon-Wilson, Rev. Canon Sir Percy; see Maryon-Wilson, Rev. Canon Sir G. P. M.
Maryon-Wilson, Sir Spencer Pocklington Maryon; see Wilson.
Marzban, Jehangier B., 1848–1928, vol. II
Marzban, Pherozeshah Jehangir, 1876–1933, vol. III
Marzials, Sir Frank Thomas, 1840–1912, vol. I
Masani, Sir Rustom Pestonji, 1876–1966, vol. VI
Masaryk, Jan Garrigue, 1886–1948, vol. IV
Masaryk, Thomas Garrigue, 1850–1937, vol. III
Mascagni, Pietro, 1863–1945, vol. IV
Mascall, Col Maurice Edward, 1882–1958, vol. V
Maschwitz, Eric, 1901–1969, vol. VI
Masefield, John, died 1967, vol. VI
Masefield, Col Robert Taylor, 1839–1922, vol. II
Masey, Albert, died 1910, vol. I
Masham, 1st Baron, 1815–1906, vol. I
Masham, 2nd Baron, 1857–1917, vol. II
Masham, 3rd Baron, 1867–1924, vol. II
Masham, William George, 1843–1916, vol. II
Mashiter, Col Sir George Coope, 1843–1927, vol. II
Masih, Rt Rev. Inayat, 1918–1980, vol. VII
Maskell, Alfred Ogle, died 1912, vol. I
Maskell, Ernest John, 1895–1958, vol. V
Maskelyne, John Nevil, 1839–1917, vol. II
Maskelyne, Mervyn Herbert Nevil Story, 1823–1911, vol. I
Maskew, Rev. Arthur Fairclough 1854–1938, vol. III
Mason, Alfred Edward Woodley, 1865–1948, vol. IV
Mason, Alfred John, 1853–1918, vol. II
Mason, Arnold Henry, 1885–1963, vol. VI
Mason, Rev. Arthur James, 1851–1928, vol. II
Mason, Sir Arthur Wier, 1860–1924, vol. II
Mason, Charlotte Maria Shaw, 1842–1923, vol. II
Mason, Sir David, 1862–1940, vol. III

Mason, David Marshall, 1865–1945, vol. IV
Mason, Rev. Edmund Robert, *died* 1922, vol. II
Mason, Eudo Colecestra, 1901–1969, vol. VI
Mason, Frank H., 1876–1965, vol. VI
Mason, Sir George Charles, 1855–1904, vol. I
Mason, Rev. George Edward, 1847–1928, vol. II
Mason, Maj.-Gen. Harry Macan, 1850–1929, vol. III
Mason, Rev. Henry Alfred, 1851–1939, vol. III
Mason, Hon. Henry Greathead Rex, 1885–1975, vol. VII
Mason, Col Hubert Oliver Browne B.; *see* Browne-Mason.
Mason, Rev. James, 1840–1912, vol. I
Mason, Lt-Col James Cooper, 1875–1923, vol. II
Mason, James Francis, 1861–1929, vol. III
Mason, John H., 1875–1951, vol. V
Mason, Joseph, 1866–1933, vol. III
Mason, Lt-Col Kenneth, 1887–1976, vol. VII
Mason, Sir Laurence, 1886–1970, vol. VI
Mason, Leonard Ralph, 1910–1974, vol. VII
Mason, Marianne Harriet, *died* 1932, vol. III
Mason, Michael; *see* Mason, R. M.
Mason, Sir Paul, 1904–1978, vol. VII
Mason, Lt-Col Percival Lawrence, 1857–1938, vol. III
Mason, Major Philip Granville, 1872–1915, vol. I
Mason, (Richard) Michael, 1917–1977, vol. VII
Mason, Rev. Richard Swann S.; *see* Swann-Mason.
Mason, Robert, 1857–1927, vol. II
Mason, Robert Heath, 1918–1969, vol. VI
Mason, Brig. Searle Dwyer, 1892–1953, vol. V
Mason, Sir Thomas, *died* 1924, vol. II
Mason, Thomas Godfrey, 1890–1959, vol. V (A)
Mason, Adm. Thomas Henry, 1811–1900, vol. I
Mason, Walt, 1862–1939, vol. III
Mason, Lt-Col Walter, 1863–1937, vol. III
Mason, William, 1872–1961, vol. VI
Mason-Macfarlane, Lt-Gen. Sir Noel; *see* Macfarlane.
Masood, Sir Syed Ross, 1889–1937, vol. III
Maspero, Sir Gaston Camille Charles, 1846–1916, vol. II
Massenet, Jules Emile Frédéric, 1842–1912, vol. I
Massereene, 11th Viscount, **and Ferrard**, 4th Viscount, 1842–1905, vol. I
Massereene, 12th Viscount, **and Ferrard**, 5th Viscount, 1873–1956, vol. V
Massey, Sir Arthur, 1894–1980, vol. VII
Massey, Dame Christina Allen, *died* 1932, vol. III
Massey, Rev. Edwyn Reynolds, 1847–1923, vol. II
Massey, Gerald, 1828–1907, vol. I
Massey, Mrs Gertrude, 1868–1957, vol. V
Massey, Rev. John Cooke, 1842–1928, vol. II
Massey, Rt Hon. Vincent, 1887–1967, vol. VI
Massey, Rt Hon. William Ferguson, 1856–1925, vol. II
Massey, William Henry, *died* 1940, vol. III
Massey-Mainwaring, Hon. William Frederick Barton; *see* Mainwaring.
Massiah, Sir Grey; *see* Massiah, Sir H. G.
Massiah, Sir (Hallam) Grey, 1888–1972, vol. VII
Massie, Grant, 1896–1964, vol. VI
Massie, John, 1842–1925, vol. II

Massie, Major John Hamon, 1872–1914, vol. I
Massie, Lt-Col Robert John Allwright, 1890–1966, vol. VI
Massie, Brig.-Gen. Roger Henry, 1869–1927, vol. II
Massie, Adm. Thomas Leeke, 1802–1898, vol. I
Massine, Léonide, 1896–1979, vol. VII
Massingberd, Mrs, *died* 1897, vol. I
Massingberd, Field-Marshal Sir Archibald Armar M.; *see* Montgomery-Massingberd.
Massingberd, Stephen Langton, 1869–1925, vol. II
Massingham, Harold John, 1888–1952, vol. V
Massingham, Henry William, 1860–1924, vol. II
Masson, David, 1822–1907, vol. I
Masson, Sir David Orme, 1858–1937, vol. III
Masson, Hon. Col Sir David Parkes, 1847–1915, vol. I (A)
Masson, Flora, *died* 1937, vol. III
Masson, Frederic, 1847–1923, vol. II
Masson, Sir Irvine; *see* Masson, Sir J. I. O.
Masson, Sir (James) Irvine (Orme), 1887–1962, vol. VI
Masson, John, *died* 1927, vol. II
Masson, Sir John Robertson, 1898–1965, vol. VI
Masson, Rosaline, *died* 1949, vol. IV
Massy, 6th Baron, 1835–1915, vol. I (A)
Massy, 7th Baron, 1864–1926, vol. II
Massy, 8th Baron, 1894–1958, vol. V
Massy, Brig. Charles Walter, 1887–1973, vol. VII
Massy, Brig.-Gen. Edward Charles, 1868–1946, vol. IV
Massy, Col Godfrey, 1863–1944, vol. IV
Massy, Col Harry Stanley, 1855–1920, vol. II
Massy, Lt-Gen. Hugh Royds Stokes, 1884–1965, vol. VI
Massy, Col Percy Hugh Hamon, 1857–1939, vol. III
Massy, Col William George, 1857–1941, vol. IV
Massy, Lt-Gen. William Godfrey Dunham, 1838–1906, vol. I
Massy-Beresford, John George, 1856–1923, vol. II
Massy-Dawson, Captain Francis Evelyn, 1872–1939, vol. III
Massy-Greene, Hon. Sir Walter, 1874–1952, vol. V
Massy-Westropp, Col John, 1860–1951, vol. V
Master, Alfred, 1883–1978, vol. VII
Master, Lt-Col Arthur Gilbert, 1867–1942, vol. IV
Master, Captain Charles Edward Hoskins, 1878–1960, vol. V
Master, Charles Gilbert, *died* 1903, vol. I
Master, Rev. Harold C.; *see* Chester-Master.
Master, Lt-Col Richard C.; *see* Chester-Master.
Master, Thomas William Chester C.; *see* Chester-Master.
Master, Col William Alfred C.; *see* Chester-Master.
Masterman, Arthur Thomas, 1869–1941, vol. IV
Masterman, Rt Hon. Charles Frederick Gurney, 1873–1927, vol. III
Masterman, Air Cdre Edward Alexander Dimsdale, 1880–1957, vol. V
Masterman, Sir John Cecil, 1891–1977, vol. VII
Masterman, Rt Rev. John Howard Bertram, 1867–1933, vol. III

Masterman, William, 1846–1903, vol. I
Masters, Albert Edward Hefford, 1902–1968, vol. VI
Masters, Col Alexander, 1848–1936, vol. III
Masters, C. H., 1852–1931, vol. III
Masters, David, died 1965, vol. VI
Masters, Edgar Lee, 1869–1950, vol. IV
Masters, Sir Frederick, 1872–1947, vol. IV
Masters, Rev. Canon James Herbert, 1863–1942, vol. IV
Masters, Rev. James Hoare, died 1918, vol. II
Masters, Maxwell T., 1833–1907, vol. I
Masters, Hon. Robert, 1879–1967, vol. VI
Masters, Very Rev. Thomas Heywood, 1865–1939, vol. III
Masters, Rev. William Caldwall, 1843–1924, vol. II
Masterson, Major James Edward I., 1862–1935, vol. III
Masterson, Most Rev. Mgr Joseph, 1899–1953, vol. V
Masterton, William, 1913–1971, vol. VII
Masterton-Smith, Sir James Edward, 1878–1938, vol. III
Mastin, John, 1865–1932, vol. III
Matania, Chevalier Fortunino, 1881–1963, vol. VI
Matcham, Col William Eyre E.; see Eyre-William.
Mather, Arthur Stanley, 1842–1929, vol. III
Mather, Rev. Frederic Vaughan, 1824–1914, vol. I
Mather, Rt Rev. Herbert, 1840–1922, vol. II
Mather, James Marshall, 1851–1916, vol. II
Mather, John Chadwick, 1904–1961, vol. VI
Mather, Loris Emerson, 1886–1976, vol. VII
Mather, Richard, 1886–1964, vol. VI
Mather, Thomas, died 1937, vol. III
Mather, Rt Hon. Sir William, 1838–1920, vol. II
Mather, Col William, 1888–1966, vol. VI
Mather, William Allan, 1885–1961, vol. VI
Mather-Jackson, Sir Christopher; see Mather-Jackson, Sir G. C. M.
Mather-Jackson, Sir Edward Arthur; see Jackson.
Mather-Jackson, Sir (George) Christopher (Mather), 5th Bt, 1896–1976, vol. VII
Mather-Jackson, Sir Henry; see Jackson.
Mathers, 1st Baron, 1886–1965, vol. VI
Mathers, Edward P., 1850–1924, vol. II
Mathers, Edward Powys, 1892–1939, vol. III
Mathers, Frederick Francis, 1871–1947, vol. IV
Mathers, Helen, 1853–1920, vol. II
Mathers, Thomas Graham, 1859–1927, vol. II
Matheson, Captain Alexander Francis, 1905–1976, vol. VII
Matheson, Sir Alexander Perceval, 3rd Bt, 1861–1929, vol. III
Matheson, Angus, 1912–1962, vol. VI
Matheson, Annie, 1853–1924, vol. II
Matheson, Lt-Col Archibald, 1876–1936, vol. III
Matheson, Lt-Col Hon. Arthur James, 1845–1913, vol. I
Matheson, Cdre Sir Charles George, 1876–1948, vol. IV
Matheson, Charles Louis, 1851–1921, vol. II
Matheson, Sir Donald, 1832–1901, vol. I
Matheson, Donald, died 1901, vol. I
Matheson, Donald Alexander, 1860–1935, vol. III

Matheson, Donald Capell, 1880–1948, vol. IV
Matheson, Donald Macleod, 1896–1979, vol. VII
Matheson, Lt-Col Duncan, 1850–1930, vol. III
Matheson, Very Rev. Frederick William, 1882–1942, vol. IV
Matheson, Rev. George, 1842–1906, vol. I
Matheson, John, 1873–1944, vol. IV
Matheson, Rt Rev. John A., 1901–1950, vol. IV
Matheson, Sir Kenneth James, 2nd Bt, 1854–1920, vol. II
Matheson, M. Cecile, died 1950, vol. IV
Matheson, Percy Ewing, 1859–1946, vol. IV
Matheson, Rt Hon. Sir Robert Edwin, 1845–1926, vol. II
Matheson, Sir Roderick Mackenzie Chisholm, 4th Bt, 1861–1944, vol. IV
Matheson, Most Rev. Samuel Pritchard, 1852–1942, vol. IV
Matheson, Gen. Sir Torquhil George, 5th Bt, 1871–1963, vol. VI
Mathew, Rev. Anthony Gervase, 1905–1976, vol. VII
Mathew, Sir Charles, 1903–1968, vol. VI
Mathew, Charles James, 1872–1923, vol. II
Mathew, Maj.-Gen. Sir Charles Massy, 1866–1932, vol. III
Mathew, Most Rev. David, 1902–1975, vol. VII
Mathew, Francis, 1907–1965, vol. VI
Mathew, Frank, 1865–1924, vol. II
Mathew, Lt-Gen. George, 1879–1958, vol. V
Mathew, George Felton, 1846–1931, vol. III
Mathew, Rt Hon. Sir James Charles, 1830–1908, vol. I
Mathew, Rev. John, died 1929, vol. III
Mathew, Robert, 1911–1966, vol. VI
Mathew, Theobald, 1866–1939, vol. III
Mathew, Sir Theobald, 1898–1964, vol. VI
Mathew-Lannowe, Brig.-Gen. Edmund Byam; see Lannowe.
Mathews, Basil Joseph, 1879–1951, vol. V
Mathews, Sir Charles, 1st Bt, 1850–1920, vol. II
Mathews, Ernest, 1847–1930, vol. III
Mathews, George Ballard, 1861–1922, vol. II
Mathews, Gregory Macalister, 1876–1949, vol. IV
Mathews, Henry Edmund, 1868–1947, vol. IV
Mathews, Henry Montague Segundo, 1860–1941, vol. IV
Mathews, Sir Lloyd William, 1850–1901, vol. I
Mathews, Shailer, 1863–1941, vol. IV
Mathews, Dame Vera Laughton, died 1959, vol. V
Mathews, Rev. William Arnold, 1839–1925, vol. II
Mathewson, Sir Alexander Robert, 1907–1968, vol. VI
Mathias, Alfred Ernest, 1880–1963, vol. VI
Mathias, Charles Ronald, 1877–1949, vol. IV
Mathias, Col Henry Harding, 1850–1914, vol. I
Mathias, Brig. Leonard William Henry, 1890–1972, vol. VII
Mathias, Lewis James, 1864–1945, vol. IV
Mathias, Most Rev. Louis, 1887–1965, vol. VI
Mathias, Sir Richard, 1st Bt, 1863–1942, vol. IV
Mathias, Ronald Cavill, 1912–1968, vol. VI
Mathias, William Delamotte, 1877–1940, vol. III
Mathieson, Hon. John A., 1863–1947, vol. IV

Mathieson, William Law, 1868–1938, vol. III
Mathieu, Most Rev. Mgr Olivier Elzear, 1853–1929, vol. III
Mathieu-Perez, Sir Joseph Leon; see Perez.
Mathys, Sir (Herbert) Reginald, 1908–1977, vol. VII
Mathys, Sir Reginald; see Mathys, Sir H. R.
Matisse, Henri, 1869–1954, vol. V
Matley, Charles Alfred, 1866–1947, vol. IV
Matsudaira, Tsuneo, 1877–1949, vol. IV
Matsui, Rt Rev. Peter Yonetaro, 1869–1946, vol. IV
Matsumura, Jinzo, 1856–1928, vol. II (A), vol. III
Matt, Albert E., 1864–1941, vol. IV
Mattei, Marchese Alfred, 1853–1930, vol. III
Mattei, Tito, 1841–1914, vol. I
Matters, Sir Francis; see Matters, Sir R. F.
Matters, Leonard Warburton, 1881–1951, vol. V
Matters, Sir (Reginald) Francis, 1895–1975, vol. VII
Matthai, George, 1887–1947, vol. IV
Matthai, John, 1886–1959, vol. V
Matthay, Tobias, 1858–1945, vol. IV
Matthew, Edwin, died 1950, vol. IV
Matthew, Frederic David, 1838–1918, vol. II
Matthew, John Godfrey, 1881–1947, vol. IV
Matthew, Col John Smart, 1864–1935, vol. III
Matthew, Reginald Walter, 1879–1928, vol. II
Matthew, Sir Robert Hogg, 1906–1975, vol. VII
Matthew, Thomas Urquhart, 1909–1962, vol. VI
Matthews, Alfred Edward, 1869–1960, vol. V
Matthews, Sir (Alfred) Herbert (Henry), 1870–1958, vol. V
Matthews, Sir Arthur, 1886–1971, vol. VII
Matthews, Arthur Ratcliff, 1866–1932, vol. III
Matthews, Brander, 1852–1929, vol. III
Matthews, Sir Bromhead; see Matthews, Sir J. B.
Matthews, Ven. Cecil Lloyd, 1881–1962, vol. VI
Matthews, David, 1868–1960, vol. V
Matthews, Major Durham, 1876–1950, vol. IV
Matthews, Edith Marcia, 1883–1946, vol. IV
Matthews, Rev. Edward Walter, 1846–1933, vol. III
Matthews, Ernest Lewis, 1871–1941, vol. IV
Matthews, Ernest Romney, 1873–1930, vol. III
Matthews, Maj.-Gen. Francis Raymond Gage, 1903–1976, vol. VII
Matthews, Brig.-Gen. Frank Broadwood, 1857–1940, vol. III
Matthews, Frank Herbert, 1861–1909, vol. I (A)
Matthews, Gilbert, died 1969, vol. VI
Matthews, Col Godfrey Estcourt, 1866–1917, vol. II
Matthews, Maj.-Gen. Harold Halford, 1877–1940, vol. III
Matthews, Harry G.; see Grindell-Matthews.
Matthews, Sir Herbert; see Matthews, Sir A. H. H.
Matthews, Ven. Hubert John, 1889–1971, vol. VII
Matthews, Rt Rev. James Joseph Edmund, 1871–1939, vol. III
Matthews, James Robert, 1889–1978, vol. VII
Matthews, Sir (John) Bromhead, 1864–1934, vol. III
Matthews, John Charles, 1872–1946, vol. IV
Matthews, Joseph Bridges, died 1928, vol. II

Matthews, Julia B., (Mrs Fairfax Ivimey), died 1948, vol. IV
Matthews, Norman Derek, 1922–1976, vol. VII
Matthews, Rev. Norman Gregory, 1904–1964, vol. VI
Matthews, Percy John, 1895–1964, vol. VI
Matthews, Hon. Robert Charles, 1871–1952, vol. V
Matthews, Robert Lee, 1876–1950, vol. IV
Matthews, Sir Ronald Wilfred, 1885–1959, vol. V
Matthews, Rt Rev. Seering John, 1900–1978, vol. VII
Matthews, Sir Thomas, 1849–1930, vol. III
Matthews, Sir Trevor Jocelyn, 1882–1954, vol. V
Matthews, Col Valentine, 1855–1921, vol. II
Matthews, Lt-Col Walter Hudson, 1864–1929, vol. III
Matthews, Very Rev. Walter Robert, 1881–1973, vol. VII
Matthews, Sir William, 1844–1922, vol. II
Matthews, William, 1905–1975, vol. VII
Matthews, William E., 1862–1938, vol. III
Matthews, William Kleesmann, 1901–1958, vol. V
Matthews, Sir William Thomas, 1888–1968, vol. VI
Matthey, Col Edward, 1836–1918, vol. II
Matthey, George, died 1913, vol. I
Matthiessen, Francis Otto, 1902–1950, vol. IV (A), vol. V
Mattingly, Garrett, 1900–1962, vol. VI
Mattingly, Harold, 1884–1964, vol. VI
Mattinson, Sir Miles, 1854–1944, vol. IV
Maturin, Father Basil William, 1847–1915, vol. I
Matz, Bertram Waldrom, 1865–1925, vol. II
Maubert, Louis, 1875–1949, vol. IV
Mauchline, Lord; Ian Huddleston Abney-Hastings, 1918–1944, vol. IV
Maud, Captain Charles Carus, 1875–1914, vol. I
Maud, Constance Elizabeth, died 1929, vol. III
Maud, Col Harry, 1867–1948, vol. IV
Maud, Rt Rev. John Primatt, 1860–1932, vol. III
Maud, Brig.-Gen. Philip, 1870–1947, vol. IV
Maud, W. T., died 1903, vol. I
Maud, Lt-Col William Hartley, 1868–1948, vol. IV
Maude, Col Alan Hamer, 1885–1979, vol. VII
Maude, Aylmer, 1858–1938, vol. III
Maude, Ven. Charles Bulmer, 1848–1927, vol. II
Maude, Charles John, 1847–1910, vol. I
Maude, Brig. Christian George, 1884–1971, vol. VII
Maude, Cyril, 1862–1951, vol. V
Maude, Edith Caroline, 1865–1922, vol. II
Maude, Evan Walter, 1919–1980, vol. VII
Maude, Sir (Evelyn) John, 1883–1963, vol. VI
Maude, Col Francis Cornwallis, 1828–1900, vol. I
Maude, Col Frederic Natusch, 1854–1933, vol. III
Maude, Sir Frederick Francis, 1821–1897, vol. I
Maude, Lt-Gen. Sir Frederick Stanley, 1864–1917, vol. II
Maude, Isabel Winifred Maud Emery; see Emery, Winifred.
Maude, Sir John; see Maude, Sir E. J.
Maude, Major Ralph Walter, 1873–1922, vol. II
Maude, Sir Walter, 1862–1943, vol. IV
Maudling, Rt Hon. Reginald, 1917–1979, vol. VII
Maudslay, Alfred Percival, 1850–1931, vol. III
Maudslay, Algernon, 1873–1948, vol. IV

Maudslay, Cecil Winton, 1880–1969, vol. VI
Maudslay, Walter Henry, 1844–1927, vol. II
Maudsley, Henry, 1835–1918, vol. II
Maudsley, Sir Henry Carr, 1859–1944, vol. IV
Maufe, Sir Edward, 1883–1974, vol. VII
Maufe, Herbert Brantwood, 1879–1946, vol. IV
Maufe, Captain T. Harold Broadbent, 1898–1942, vol. IV
Mauger, Hon. Samuel, 1857–1936, vol. III
Maugham, 1st Viscount, 1866–1958, vol. V
Maugham, Reginald Charles Fulke, 1866–1956, vol. V
Maugham, Somerst; see Maugham, W. S.
Maugham, (William) Somerset, 1874–1965, vol. VI
Maughan, Sir David, 1873–1955, vol. V
Maughan, Janet Leith; see Story, J. L.
Maughan, Lt-Col Francis Gilfrid, died 1938, vol. III
Maul, Rev. John Frederic, 1849–1915, vol. I
Maula Bakhsh, Nawab Maula Bakhsh Khan Bahadur of Batala, 1862–1949, vol. IV
Maule, Col Henry Noel St John, 1873–1953, vol. V
Maule, Major Hugh Patrick Guarin, 1873–1940, vol. III
Maule, Sir Robert, 1852–1931, vol. III
Maulvi Haji, Sir Rahim Bakhsh, died 1935, vol. III
Maund, Air Vice-Marshal Arthur Clinton, 1891–1942, vol. IV
Maund, Rear-Adm. Loben Edward Harold, 1892–1957, vol. V
Maunder, Annie Scott Dill, (Mrs Walter Maunder), 1868–1947, vol. IV
Maunder, Edward Walter, 1851–1928, vol. II
Maundrell, Captain Arthur Goodall, 1884–1972, vol. VII
Maung Kin, Hon. Sir, 1872–1924, vol. II
Maung Me, 1871–1952, vol. V
Maung Pe, 1858–1924, vol. II
Maunsell, Lt-Col Francis Richard, 1861–1936, vol. III
Maunsell, Brig.-Gen. Frederick Guy, 1864–1929, vol. III
Maunsell, Gen. Sir Frederick Richard, 1828–1916, vol. II
Maunsell, Col George William, 1859–1937, vol. III
Maunsell, Mark Stuart Ker, 1910–1980, vol. VII
Maunsell, Brig. Raymund John, 1903–1976, vol. VII
Maunsell, Richard Edward Lloyd, died 1944, vol. IV
Maunsell, Robert Charles Butler, 1872–1930, vol. III
Maunsell, Maj.-Gen. Sir Thomas, 1822–1908, vol. I
Maunsell, Surg.-Gen. Thomas, 1839–1937, vol. III
Mauny-Talvande, Countess de; (Lady Mary Elizabeth Agnes Byng), died 1946, vol. IV
Maurault, Rt Rev. Mgr Olivier, 1886–1968, vol. VI
Maurel, Victor, 1848–1923, vol. II
Mauriac, François, 1885–1970, vol. VI
Maurice, Lt-Col Albert Jafa, 1864–1943, vol. IV
Maurice, Lt-Col David Blake, 1866–1925, vol. II
Maurice, Maj.-Gen. Sir Frederick; see Maurice, Maj.-Gen. Sir J. F.

Maurice, Maj.-Gen. Sir Frederick Barton, 1871–1951, vol. V
Maurice, Col George Thelwall Kindersley, 1867–1950, vol. IV
Maurice, Col Godfrey Kindersley, 1887–1949, vol. IV
Maurice, Henry Gascoyen, 1874–1950, vol. IV
Maurice, Maj.-Gen. Sir (John) Frederick, 1841–1912, vol. I
Maurois, André, 1885–1967, vol. VI
Maurras, Charles, 1868–1952, vol. V
Maury, Amy-Gaston B.; see Bonet Maury.
Mavor, James, 1854–1925, vol. II
Mavor, O. H.; see Bridie, James.
Mavrogordato, John Nicolas, 1882–1970, vol. VI
Maw, William Henry, 1838–1924, vol. II
Maw, William Nawton, 1869–1946, vol. IV
Mawbey, Adm. Henry Lancelot, 1870–1933, vol. III
Mawby, Sir Maurice Alan Edgar, 1904–1977, vol. VII
Mawer, Sir Allen, 1879–1942, vol. IV
Mawhinny, Col Robert John Watt, died 1953, vol. V
Mawhood, Mrs Mary; see Clare, M.
Mawson, Cecil Allerton Greville, 1876–1950, vol. IV
Mawson, Sir Douglas, 1882–1958, vol. V
Mawson, Thomas H., died 1933, vol. III
Max-Müller, Rt Hon. Friedrich, 1823–1900, vol. I
Max-Muller, Sir William Grenfell, 1867–1945, vol. IV
Maxim, Sir Hiram Stevens, 1840–1916, vol. II
Maxse, Ernest George Berkeley, 1863–1943, vol. IV
Maxse, Adm. Frederick A., 1833–1900, vol. I
Maxse, Gen. Sir Ivor, 1862–1958, vol. V
Maxse, Leopold James, 1864–1932, vol. III
Maxse, Dame Marjorie, 1891–1975, vol. VII
Maxton, James, 1885–1946, vol. IV
Maxtone-Graham, Anthony George, 1854–1930, vol. III
Maxtone Graham, James, 1863–1940, vol. III
Maxwell, Sir Alexander, 1880–1963, vol. VI
Maxwell, Alexander Hyslop, 1864–1957, vol. V
Maxwell, Sir Alexander Hyslop, 1896–1971, vol. VII
Maxwell, Allan Victor, 1887–1975, vol. VII
Maxwell, Col Sir Arthur, 1875–1935, vol. III
Maxwell, Arthur Crawford, 1909–1964, vol. VI
Maxwell, Maj.-Gen. Sir Aymer, 1891–1971, vol. VII
Maxwell, Mrs Beatrice H.; see Heron-Maxwell.
Maxwell, Hon. Bernard Constable, 1848–1938, vol. III
Maxwell, Bertram Wayburn, 1891–1972, vol. VII
Maxwell, Constantia Elizabeth, died 1962, vol. VI
Maxwell, Vice-Adm. Hon. Sir Denis Crichton, 1892–1970, vol. VII
Maxwell, Denis Oliver, 1906–1971, vol. VII
Maxwell, Donald, 1877–1936, vol. III
Maxwell, Douglas Rider, 1885–1967, vol. VI
Maxwell, Lt-Col F. D., 1862–1910, vol. I
Maxwell, Col Francis Aylmer, 1871–1917, vol. II

Maxwell, Sir Frederic Mackenzie, 1860–1931, vol. III
Maxwell, Gavin, 1914–1969, vol. VI
Maxwell, Col Geoffrey Archibald Prentice, 1885–1953, vol. V
Maxwell, Sir George; see Maxwell, Sir W. G.
Maxwell, George Arnot, died 1935, vol. III
Maxwell, Wing-Comdr Gerald Constable, 1895–1959, vol. V
Maxwell, Gerald Verner, 1877–1965, vol. VI
Maxwell, Hamilton, 1830–1923, vol. II
Maxwell, Rt Rev. Harold Alexander, 1897–1975, vol. VII
Maxwell, Col Hon. Henry Edward, 1857–1919, vol. II
Maxwell, Lt-Col Henry St Patrick, 1850–1928, vol. II
Maxwell, Rt Hon. Sir Herbert Eustace, 7th Bt (cr 1681), 1845–1937, vol. III
Maxwell, Herbert William, 1888–1979, vol. VII
Maxwell, Sir Ivor Walter H.; see Heron-Maxwell.
Maxwell, James, 1905–1956, vol. V
Maxwell, Major James Andrew Colvile W.; see Wedderburn-Maxwell.
Maxwell, Sir James Crawford, 1869–1932, vol. III
Maxwell, James Laidlaw, 1873–1951, vol. V
Maxwell, Brig.-Gen. James McCall, 1865–1945, vol. IV
Maxwell, James Robert, 1902–1970, vol. VI
Maxwell, Sir John, 1875–1946, vol. IV
Maxwell, John, 1905–1962, vol. VI
Maxwell, Sir John, 1882–1968, vol. VI
Maxwell, Gen. Rt Hon. Sir John Grenfell, 1859–1929, vol. III
Maxwell, Sir John Maxwell Stirling-, 10th Bt (cr 1682), 1866–1956, vol. V
Maxwell, Sir John Robert H.; see Heron-Maxwell.
Maxwell, Joseph, died 1967, vol. VI
Maxwell, Surgeon Rear-Adm. Joseph Archibald, 1890–1980, vol. VII
Maxwell, Brig.-Gen. Laurence Lockhart, 1868–1954, vol. V
Maxwell, Lawrence, 1853–1927, vol. II (A), vol. III
Maxwell, Magdalen Perceval, (Mrs Patrick Perceval-Maxwell); see King-Hall, M.
Maxwell, Mary Elizabeth; see Braddon, M. E.
Maxwell, Maxwell Hyslop, died 1937, vol. III
Maxwell, Perriton, died 1947, vol. IV (A)
Maxwell, Sir Reginald Maitland, 1882–1967, vol. VI
Maxwell, Brig. Richard Hobson, 1899–1965, vol. VI
Maxwell, Richard Ponsonby, 1853–1928, vol. II
Maxwell, Robert Charles H.; see Heron-Maxwell.
Maxwell, Col Rt Hon. Robert David Perceval, 1870–1932, vol. III
Maxwell, Lt-Gen. Sir Ronald Charles, 1852–1924, vol. II
Maxwell, Hon. Somerset Arthur, 1905–1942, vol. IV
Maxwell, Thomas Doveton, died 1946, vol. IV
Maxwell, Wellwood, 1857–1933, vol. III
Maxwell, Rear-Adm. Sir Wellwood George Courtenay, 1882–1965, vol. VI

Maxwell, Captain Sir William, died 1928, vol. II
Maxwell, Sir William, 1841–1929, vol. III
Maxwell, Sir William, 1870–1947, vol. IV
Maxwell, Sir William, died 1947, vol. IV
Maxwell, William, 1873–1957, vol. V
Maxwell, Captain William Babington, 1866–1938, vol. III
Maxwell, Sir William Edward, 1846–1897, vol. I
Maxwell, Lt-Col William Ernest, 1898–1951, vol. V
Maxwell, Sir William Francis, 4th Bt (cr 1804), 1844–1924, vol. II
Maxwell, Lt-Col William Frederick, 1878–1940, vol. III
Maxwell, Sir (William) George, 1871–1959, vol. V
Maxwell, Rev. William Gilchrist C.; see Clark-Maxwell.
Maxwell, Adm. William Henry, 1840–1920, vol. II
Maxwell, William Henry, 1852–1921, vol. II
Maxwell, William Jardine Herries, 1852–1933, vol. III
Maxwell-Anderson, Captain Sir Maxwell Hendry; see Anderson.
Maxwell-Carpendale, Major Frederic; see Carpendale.
Maxwell-Gumbleton, Rt Rev. Maxwell Homfray, 1872–1952, vol. V
Maxwell-Hibberd, Charles, 1853–1935, vol. III
Maxwell-Lefroy, Captain Cecil; see Lefroy.
Maxwell-Lefroy, Harold; see Lefroy.
Maxwell-Lyte, Sir Henry Churchill; see Lyte.
Maxwell-Scott, Rear-Adm. Malcolm; see Scott.
Maxwell-Scott, Maj.-Gen. Sir Walter Joseph Constable, 1st Bt, 1875–1954, vol. V
Maxwell Stuart, Arthur Constable, 1845–1942, vol. IV
Maxwell-Stuart, Herbert Constable, 1842–1921, vol. II
Maxwell-Willshire, Sir Arthur Reginald Thomas; see Willshire.
Maxwell-Willshire, Sir Gerard Arthur; see Willshire.
May, 1st Baron, 1871–1946, vol. IV
May, 2nd Baron, 1904–1950, vol. IV
May, Rt Rev. Alston James Weller, 1869–1940, vol. III
May, Captain Arthur Dekewer Livius, 1875–1943, vol. IV
May, Sir Arthur William, 1854–1925, vol. II
May, Aylmer William, 1874–1950, vol. IV
May, Barry, 1869–1948, vol. IV
May, Bennett, 1846–1937, vol. III
May, Surgeon Vice-Adm. Sir Cyril; see May, Surgeon Vice-Adm. Sir R. C.
May, Edward Hooper, 1831–1914, vol. I
May, Maj.-Gen. Sir Edward Sinclair, 1856–1936, vol. III
May, Sir Francis Henry, 1860–1922, vol. II
May, Major Frederick, (Fred May), 1891–1976, vol. VII
May, Sir Gould, died 1944, vol. IV
May, Col Henry Allan Roughton, 1863–1930, vol. III
May, Rear-Adm. Henry John, 1853–1904, vol. I

May, Maj.-Gen. James, 1837–1903, vol. I
May, James Lewis, 1873–1961, vol. VI
May, John Cecil, 1890–1959, vol. V
May, Lt-Col John Cyril, 1874–1943, vol. IV
May, Otto, died 1946, vol. IV
May, Percy, 1886–1974, vol. VII
May, Phil, 1864–1903, vol. I
May, Gen. Sir Reginald Seaburne, 1879–1958, vol. V
May, Richard William Legerton, 1902–1967, vol. VI
May, Surgeon Vice-Adm. Sir (Robert) Cyril, 1897–1979, vol. VII
May, Rev. Thomas Henry, 1851–1932, vol. III
May, Major Thomas James, 1864–1952, vol. V
May, W. Charles, 1853–1931, vol. III
May, William, 1863–1932, vol. III
May, Col William Allan, 1850–1937, vol. III
May, Admiral of the Fleet Sir William Henry, 1849–1930, vol. III
May, Rt Hon. William Morrison, 1909–1962, vol. VI
May, Major William Southall Reid, 1864–1937, vol. III
Mayall, Robert Cecil, 1893–1962, vol. VI
Maybin, Sir Alexander, 1889–1941, vol. IV
Maybrick, Michael, 1844–1913, vol. I
Maybury, Bernard Constable, 1888–1953, vol. V
Maybury, Brig.-Gen. Sir Henry Percy, 1864–1943, vol. IV
Maycock, Alan Lawson, 1898–1968, vol. VI
Maycock, Rev. Francis Hugh, 1903–1980, vol. VII
Maycock, Rev. Herbert William, 1863–1939, vol. III
Maycock, Sir Willoughby Robert Dottin, 1849–1922, vol. II
Maydon, Hon. John George, 1857–1919, vol. II
Maydon, Lt-Comdr Stephen Lynch Conway, 1913–1971, vol. VII
Mayeda, Marquis Toshinari, 1885–1942, vol. IV
Mayer, Col Edward Rudolph, 1902–1973, vol. VII
Mayer, John, 1904–1967, vol. VI
Mayer, Maria Goeppert, 1906–1972, vol. VII
Mayer, René, 1895–1972, vol. VII
Mayer, Sylvain, 1863–1948, vol. IV
Mayers, Very Rev. George Samuel, died 1952, vol. V
Mayers, Thomas Henry, 1907–1970, vol. VI
Mayes, William, 1874–1960, vol. V
Mayfield, Ven. Guy, 1905–1976, vol. VII
Maygar, Lt-Col Leslie Cecil, 1871–1917, vol. II
Mayhew, Rev. Arnold, 1873–1939, vol. III
Mayhew, Arthur Innes, 1878–1948, vol. IV
Mayhew, Sir Basil Edgar, 1883–1966, vol. VI
Mayhew, Captain George Henry, 1901–1973, vol. VII
Mayhew, Lt-Col Sir John, 1884–1954, vol. V
Mayle, Norman Leslie, 1899–1980, vol. VII
Maynard, Maj.-Gen. Sir Charles Clarkson Martin, 1870–1945, vol. IV
Maynard, Charles Gordon, 1889–1970, vol. VI
Maynard, Constance Louisa, 1849–1935, vol. III
Maynard, Dudley Christopher, 1874–1941, vol. IV
Maynard, Air Vice-Marshal Forster Herbert Martin, 1893–1976, vol. VII

Maynard, Brig.-Gen. Francis Herbert, 1881–1979, vol. VII
Maynard, Lt-Col Frederic P., died 1921, vol. II
Maynard, Harry Russell, 1873–1954, vol. V
Maynard, Rev. Henry Langston, 1865–1940, vol. III
Maynard, Sir (Herbert) John, 1865–1943, vol. IV
Maynard, Sir John; see Maynard, Sir H. J.
Maynard, John Percy Gordon, died 1918, vol. II
Maynard, Richard de Kirklevington, 1892–1969, vol. III
Mayne, Arthur Brinley, 1893–1948, vol. IV
Mayne, Gen. Sir (Ashton Gerard Oswald) Mosley, 1889–1955, vol. V
Mayne, Brig.-Gen. Charles Robert Graham, 1874–1944, vol. IV
Mayne, Cuthbert Joseph, 1902–1972, vol. VII
Mayne, Ethel Colburn, died 1941, vol. IV
Mayne, Very Rev. Frank, died 1929, vol. III
Mayne, Lt-Col George Nisbet, 1854–1932, vol. III
Mayne, Gerald Outram, 1919–1980, vol. VII
Mayne, Horace Ardran, 1876–1958, vol. V
Mayne, Captain Jasper Graham, 1859–1936, vol. III
Mayne, Rev. Jonathan, 1838–1912, vol. I
Mayne, Jonathan Webster Coryton, 1868–1940, vol. III
Mayne, Ven. Joseph, 1843–1927, vol. II
Mayne, Gen. Sir Mosley; see Mayne, Gen. Sir A. G. O. M.
Mayne, Major Otway, 1855–1939, vol. III
Mayne, Col Richard Charles Graham, 1852–1939, vol. III
Mayne, Very Rev. William Cyril, 1877–1962, vol. VI
Mayo, 7th Earl of, 1851–1927, vol. II
Mayo, 8th Earl of, 1859–1939, vol. III
Mayo, 9th Earl of, 1890–1962, vol. VI
Mayo, Arthur, 1840–1920, vol. II
Mayo, Rev. Charles Herbert, 1845–1929, vol. III
Mayo, Charles Horace, 1865–1939, vol. III
Mayo, Charles William, 1898–1968, vol. VI
Mayo, Rev. Cuthbert Edward, 1860–1934, vol. III
Mayo, Sir Herbert, 1885–1972, vol. VII
Mayo, Isabella, (Mrs John Mayo), 1843–1914, vol. I
Mayo, Rev. John Augustus, died 1941, vol. IV
Mayo, Katherine, 1868–1940, vol. III
Mayo, Robert Hobart, 1890–1957, vol. V
Mayo, William James, 1861–1939, vol. III
Mayo-Robson, Sir Arthur William; see Robson.
Mayor, John Eyton Bickersteth, 1825–1910, vol. I
Mayor, Rev. Joseph Bickersteth, 1828–1916, vol. II
Mayor, Robert John Grote, 1869–1947, vol. IV
Mayou, M. Stephen, 1876–1934, vol. III
Mayrs, Edward Brice Cooper, 1891–1964, vol. VI
Mays-Smith, Sir Alfred, 1861–1931, vol. III
Mayston, Very Rev. Richard John Forrester, 1907–1963, vol. VI
Mayston, Engr Rear-Adm. Robert, 1851–1936, vol. III
Mayurbhanj, Maharaja of, born 1901, vol. VI
Maze, Sir Frederick William, died 1959, vol. V
Maze, Paul Lucien, 1887–1979, vol. VII
Mbanefo, Sir Louis Nwachukwu, 1911–1977, vol. VII

Mboya, Tom, (Thomas Joseph), 1930–1969, vol. VI
Meaby, Kenneth Tweedale, 1883–1965, vol. VI
Meachen, George Norman, 1876–1955, vol. V
Mead, Sir Cecil, 1900–1979, vol. VII
Mead, Frederick, 1847–1945, vol. IV
Mead, George Edward, 1849–1932, vol. III
Mead, George Robert Stow, 1863–1933, vol. III
Mead, John Phillips, 1886–1951, vol. V
Mead, Margaret, 1901–1978, vol. VII
Mead, Maj.-Gen. Owen Herbert, 1892–1942, vol. IV
Mead, Percy James, 1871–1923, vol. II
Mead, Rev. Richard Gawler, 1833–1909, vol. I
Mead, Brig. Stephen, 1882–1972, vol. VII
Meade, Elizabeth Thomasina; see Meade, L. T.
Meade, Major Harry Edward, 1884–1952, vol. V
Meade, Gen. John Michael de Courcy, 1831–1909, vol. I
Meade, Rt Hon. Joseph Michael, 1839–1900, vol. I
Meade, L. T., died 1914, vol. I
Meade, Lt-Col Malcolm John, 1854–1933, vol. III
Meade, Hon. Sir Robert Henry, 1835–1898, vol. I
Meade, Rev. Hon. Sidney, 1839–1917, vol. II
Meade, Rt Rev. William Edward, 1832–1912, vol. I
Meade-Fetherstonhaugh, Adm. Hon. Sir Herbert, 1875–1964, vol. VI
Meade-King, Sir William Oliver Evelyn, 1858–1940, vol. III
Meaden, Lt-Col Alban Anderson, 1876–1934, vol. III
Meaden, Surg.-Captain Edward Henry, 1864–1943, vol. IV
Meadon, Ernest John, 1911–1970, vol. VI
Meadon, Sir Percival Edward, 1878–1959, vol. V
Meadowcroft, Lancelot Vernon, 1884–1952, vol. V
Meadows, Alice Maud, died 1913, vol. I
Meadows, Surg.-Maj.-Gen. Robert Wyatt, 1832–1911, vol. I
Meadus, Engr-Captain Harry Howard, 1856–1934, vol. III
Meadus, Engr-Captain William Henry, 1862–1947, vol. IV
Meagher, Michael, 1846–1927, vol. II
Meagher, Hon. Nicholas Hogan, 1842–1932, vol. III
Meagher, Hon. Richard Denis, 1866–1931, vol. III
Meagher, Sir Thomas, 1902–1979, vol. VII
Meakin, Annette M. B., died 1959, vol. V
Meakin, Budgett, 1866–1906, vol. I
Meakin, Henry William, 1847–1939, vol. III
Meakin, Walter, 1878–1940, vol. III
Meakins, Brig. Jonathan Campbell, 1882–1959, vol. V
Meale, Arthur; see Meale, J. A.
Meale, (John) Arthur, 1880–1932, vol. III
Mealing, Sir Kenneth William, 1895–1968, vol. VI
Meany, George, 1894–1980, vol. VII
Meara, Rev. Henry George Jephson, died 1921, vol. II
Meares, John Willoughby, 1871–1946, vol. IV
Meares, Lt-Col Mervyn, 1880–1930, vol. III
Meares, Maj.-Gen. William Lewis D.; see Devenish-Meares.
Mearns, Andrew Daniel, 1857–1925, vol. II

Mears, Sir Frank Charles, 1880–1953, vol. V
Mears, Brig. Gerald Grimwood, 1896–1979, vol. VII
Mears, Sir Grimwood, 1869–1963, vol. VI
Mears, Thomas Lambert, died 1918, vol. II (A), vol. III
Mears, Lt-Col Trevor Irvine Nevitt, 1875–1937, vol. III
Mease, Very Rev. Charles William O'Hara, 1856–1922, vol. II
Measham, Paymaster Rear-Adm. Herbert Stanley, 1875–1954, vol. V
Measham, Richard John Rupert, 1885–1976, vol. VII
Measom, Sir George Samuel, 1818–1901, vol. I
Measures, Wing Comdr Arthur Harold, 1882–1969, vol. VI
Measures, Harry Bell, 1862–1940, vol. III
Measures, Sir Philip Herbert, 1893–1961, vol. VI
Meath, 12th Earl of, 1841–1929, vol. III
Meath, 13th Earl of, 1869–1949, vol. IV
Mechan, Sir Henry, died 1943, vol. IV
Mecredy, Sir James, 1854–1938, vol. III
Mecredy, Richard James, 1861–1924, vol. II
Medd, Rev. Peter Goldsmith, 1829–1908, vol. I
Medd, Wilfrid, 1877–1956, vol. V
Medforth, Marguerite Elizabeth, 1879–1966, vol. VI
Medhurst, Air Chief Marshal Sir Charles Edward Hastings, 1896–1954, vol. V
Medill, Brig. Percy Montgomery, 1882–1963, vol. VI
Medland, Hubert Moses, 1881–1964, vol. VI
Medley, Charles Douglas, 1870–1963, vol. VI
Medley, Dudley Julius, 1861–1953, vol. V
Medley, Brig. Edgar J., 1893–1972, vol. VII
Medley, Sir John Dudley Gibbs, 1891–1962, vol. VI
Medlicott, Sir Frank, 1903–1972, vol. VII
Medlicott, Henry Benedict, 1829–1905, vol. I
Medlicott, Col Henry Edward, 1882–1948, vol. IV
Medlicott, Rev. Canon Robert Sumner, died 1941, vol. IV
Medlicott, William Norton, died 1923, vol. II
Medlycott, Sir Edward Bradford, 4th Bt, 1832–1902, vol. I
Medlycott, Rev. Sir Hubert James, 6th Bt, 1841–1920, vol. II
Medlycott, Sir Hubert Mervyn, 7th Bt, 1874–1964, vol. VI
Medlycott, Sir Mervyn Bradford, 5th Bt, 1837–1908, vol. I
Medtner, Nicholas, 1879–1951, vol. V
Mee, Arthur, 1860–1926, vol. II
Mee, Arthur, 1875–1943, vol. IV
Meech, Sir John Valentine, 1907–1971, vol. VII
Meech, Thomas Cox, died 1940, vol. III
Meecham, Bert, 1886–1964, vol. VI
Meehan, Francis Edward, 1868–1946, vol. IV
Meehan, Patrick Aloysius, 1852–1913, vol. I
Meek, Alexander, 1865–1949, vol. IV
Meek, Lt-Col Arthur Stanley, 1883–1955, vol. V
Meek, Charles Kingsley, 1885–1965, vol. VI
Meek, Sir David Burnett, 1885–1964, vol. VI
Meek, Col James, 1861–1939, vol. III

Meek, William Alfred, 1850–1929, vol. III
Meeking, Lt-Col Charles, 1839–1912, vol. I
Meeks, Hon. Sir Alfred William, 1849–1932, vol. III
Meenan, James Nahor, 1879–1950, vol. IV (A), vol. V
Meeres, Col Charles Stuart, 1861–1935, vol. III
Meers, James Blackader, 1850–1933, vol. III
Mees, Charles Edward Kenneth, 1882–1960, vol. V
Meeson, Dora, (Mrs George J. Coates), died 1955, vol. V
Meeson, Engr-Comdr Edward Hickman Tucker, 1877–1916, vol. II
Meff, Sir William, 1861–1935, vol. III
Megaw, Arthur Stanley, diéd 1961, vol. VI
Megaw, Maj.-Gen. Sir John Wallace Dick, 1874–1958, vol. V
Megaw, Robert Dick, died 1947, vol. IV
Meghnad Saha, 1893–1956, vol. V
Mégroz, Rodolphe Louis, 1891–1968, vol. VI
Meharry, Rev. J. B., died 1916, vol. II
Mehta, Khan Bahadur, Sir Bezonji Dalabhoy, died 1927, vol. II
Mehta, Hon. Sir Homi, 1871–1948, vol. IV
Mehta, Jivraj Narayan, 1887–1978, vol. VII
Mehta, Sir Mangaldas Vijbhukandas, died 1945, vol. IV
Mehta, Sir Manubhai Nandshankar, 1868–1946, vol. IV
Mehta, Sir Phirozshah Merwanji, died 1915, vol. I (A)
Mehta, Roostumjee Dhunjeebhoy, 1849–1930, vol. III
Mehta Shuja-ul-Mulk, Sir, died 1936, vol. III (A), vol. IV
Mehta, Sir Sorabji Bezonji, died 1938, vol. III
Meier, Frederic Alfred, 1887–1954, vol. V
Meighen, Rt Hon. Arthur, 1874–1960, vol. V
Meighen, Maj.-Gen. Frank Stephen, 1870–1946, vol. IV
Meikle, Alexander, 1905–1980, vol. VII
Meikle, Andrew, 1847–1922, vol. II
Meikle, Captain Archibald Robert, 1886–1958, vol. V
Meikle, Henry William, 1880–1958, vol. V
Meikle, Lt-Col James Hamilton, 1876–1941, vol. IV
Meiklejohn, Col John Forbes, 1889–1966, vol. VI
Meiklejohn, John Miller Dow, 1836–1902, vol. I
Meiklejohn, Major Matthew Fontaine Maury, 1870–1913, vol. I
Meiklejohn, Surg. Rear-Adm. Norman Sinclair, 1879–1961, vol. VI
Meiklejohn, Ven. Robert, 1889–1974, vol. VII
Meiklejohn, Sir Roderick Sinclair, 1876–1962, vol. VI
Meiklejohn, Maj.-Gen. Sir William Hope, 1845–1909, vol. I
Meiklereid, Sir (Ernest) William, 1899–1965, vol. VI
Meiklereid, Sir William; see Meiklereid, Sir E. W.
Meillet, Paul Jules Antoine, 1866–1936, vol. III
Mein, Major Desbrisay Blundell, 1889–1937, vol. III

Meinertzhagen, Sir Ernest Louis, 1854–1933, vol. III
Meinertzhagen, Col Richard, 1878–1967, vol. VI
Meir, Golda, 1898–1978, vol. VII
Meiss, Millard, 1904–1975, vol. VII
Meissas, Gaston, vol. II
Mekie, Eoin Cameron, 1906–1977, vol. VII
Melas, Michael Constantine, 1902–1967, vol. VI
Melba, Dame Nellie, 1861–1931, vol. III
Melcher, Frederic Gershom, 1879–1963, vol. VI
Melchett, 1st Baron, 1868–1930, vol. III
Melchett, 2nd Baron, 1898–1949, vol. IV
Melchett, 3rd Baron, 1925–1973, vol. VII
Melchett, Lady; (Violet), died 1945, vol. IV
Melchior, Lauritz L. H., 1890–1973, vol. VII
Meldola, Raphael, 1849–1915, vol. I (A)
Meldon, Sir Albert, 1845–1924, vol. II
Meldon, Lt-Col James Austin, 1869–1931, vol. III
Meldon, Lt-Col Philip Albert, 1874–1942, vol. IV
Meldrum, Charles, 1821–1901, vol. I
Meldrum, David Storrar, 1864–1940, vol. III
Meldrum, Sir Peter Lowrie, 1910–1965, vol. VI
Meldrum, Brig.-Gen. William, 1865–1964, vol. VI
Melhado, Carlos, 1852–1922, vol. II
Melhuish, Sir Charles W., 1860–1946, vol. IV
Meline, Felix Jules, 1838–1925, vol. II
Melitus, Paul Gregory, 1858–1924, vol. II
Mellanby, Alexander Lawson, 1871–1951, vol. V
Mellanby, Sir Edward, 1884–1955, vol. V
Mellanby, John, 1878–1939, vol. III
Mellanby, May, (Lady Mellanby), 1882–1978, vol. VII
Mellanby, Molly, 1893–1962, vol. VI
Melland, Charles Herbert, 1872–1953, vol. V
Melland, Norman, 1865–1933, vol. III
Meller, Grahame Temple, 1905–1965, vol. VI
Meller, Sir Richard James, 1872–1940, vol. III
Mellersh, Arthur, 1857–1938, vol. III
Mellersh, Air Vice-Marshal Sir Francis John Williamson, 1898–1955, vol. V
Melles, Major William Eugene, 1883–1953, vol. V
Mellis, Rev. James, 1843–1925, vol. II
Mellis, Col William Andrew, died 1925, vol. II
Mellish, Rev. Edward Noel, 1880–1962, vol. VI
Mellish, Lt-Col Henry, 1856–1927, vol. II
Mellish, Humphrey, 1862–1937, vol. III
Mellish, Robert Walter, 1869–1938, vol. III
Melliss, Maj.-Gen. Sir Charles John, 1862–1936, vol. III
Melliss, Col Sir Howard, 1847–1921, vol. II
Mellon, Andrew William, 1855–1937, vol. III
Mellon, Rt Rev. William H., 1877–1952, vol. V
Mellone, Sydney Herbert, died 1956, vol. V
Mellor, Lt-Col Abel, 1880–1967, vol. VI
Mellor, Francis Hamilton, 1854–1925, vol. II
Mellor, Sir Frank, 1863–1941, vol. IV
Mellor, Sir George, died 1947, vol. IV
Mellor, Brig.-Gen. Sir Gilbert, 1872–1947, vol. IV
Mellor, Wing-Comdr Harry Manners, 1903–1941, vol. IV
Mellor, Sir James Robert, 1839–1926, vol. II
Mellor, John Edward, died 1925, vol. II
Mellor, John James, 1830–1916, vol. II
Mellor, Sir John Paget, 1st Bt, 1862–1929, vol. III

Mellor, Brig. John Seymour, 1883–1962, vol. VI
Mellor, Rt Hon. John William, 1835–1911, vol. I
Mellor, Joseph William, *died* 1938, vol. III
Mellor, Col Robert Ramsden, 1870–1951, vol. V
Mellor, Captain William, 1874–1928, vol. II
Mellor, William, 1888–1942, vol. IV
Mellowes, William Joseph, *died* 1923, vol. II
Melly, George Henry, 1860–1927, vol. II
Melrose, James, 1841–1922, vol. II
Melrose, James, 1828–1929, vol. III
Melrose, John, 1853–1927, vol. II
Melrose, Sir John, 1860–1938, vol. III
Melvill, Maj.-Gen. Charles William, 1878–1925, vol. II
Melvill, Philip Sandys, 1827–1906, vol. I
Melvill, Sir William Henry, 1827–1911, vol. I
Melville, 5th Viscount, 1835–1904, vol. I
Melville, 6th Viscount, 1843–1926, vol. II
Melville, 7th Viscount, 1873–1935, vol. III
Melville, 8th Viscount, 1909–1971, vol. VII
Melville, Arthur, 1855–1904, vol. I
Melville, Beresford Valentine, 1857–1931, vol. III
Melville, Col Charles Henderson, 1863–1943, vol. IV
Melville, Maj.-Gen. Charles William Francis, 1877–1949, vol. IV
Melville, Rev. David, 1813–1904, vol. I
Melville, Lt-Col Edward Patrick Alexander, 1880–1936, vol. III
Melville, Frances Helen, 1873–1962, vol. VI
Melville, Sir George, 1842–1924, vol. II
Melville, Lt-Col Harry George, 1869–1918, vol. II
Melville, Henry Edward, 1883–1976, vol. VII
Melville, Lt-Col Hon. Ian L.; *see* Leslie Melville.
Melville, Sir James Benjamin, 1885–1931, vol. III
Melville, Rev. Leslie, 1838–1908, vol. I
Melville, Leslie Melville B.; *see* Balfour-Melville.
Melville, Lewis; *see* Benjamin, L. S.
Melville, Robert Dundonald, 1872–1927, vol. II
Melville, William, 1852–1918, vol. II
Melville, Rev. William Gardner, 1863–1939, vol. III
Melvin, George Spencer, 1887–1949, vol. IV
Melvin, Sir Martin John, 1st Bt, 1879–1952, vol. V
Menardos, Simos, 1872–1933, vol. III
Menary, Surg.-Captain John, 1865–1941, vol. IV
Mencken, H. L., 1880–1956, vol. V
Mendel, William, 1854–1917, vol. II
Mendelsohn, Eric, 1887–1953, vol. V
Mendelson, John Jakob, 1917–1978, vol. VII
Mendelssohn, Kurt Alfred Georg, 1906–1980, vol. VII
Mendes, Catulle, 1841–1909, vol. I
Mendl, Sir Charles, 1871–1958, vol. V
Mendl, Sir Sigismund Ferdinand, 1866–1945, vol. IV
Mends, Hon. Brig.-Gen. Horatio Reginald, 1851–1933, vol. III
Mends, Sir William Robert, 1812–1897, vol. I
Meneces, Maj.-Gen. Ambrose Neponucene Trelawny, 1904–1979, vol. VII
Menendez, Sir (Manuel) Raymond, 1864–1952, vol. V
Menéndez y Pelayo, Marcelino, 1856–1912, vol. I

Menendez, Sir Raymond; *see* Menendez, Sir M. R.
Mengelberg, Rudolf, 1892–1959, vol. V
Menges, Herbert, 1902–1972, vol. VII
Menges, Isolde, 1893–1976, vol. VII
Meninsky, Bernard, 1891–1950, vol. IV
Mennell, George Gillies, 1878–1959, vol. V
Mennell, James Beaver, 1880–1957, vol. V
Mennell, Zebulon, 1876–1959, vol. V
Menninger, William C., 1899–1966, vol. VI
Menon, Sir Konkoth R.; *see* Ramunni Menon.
Menon, Rao Bahadur Vapal Pangunni, 1894–1966, vol. VI
Menon, Vengalil Krishnan K.; *see* Krishna Menon.
Menpes, Mortimer, *died* 1938, vol. III
Mensforth, Sir Holberry, 1871–1951, vol. V
Menson, Sir Charles William T.; *see* Tachie-Menson.
Menteth, Lt-Col Sir James Frederick Stuart-, 4th Bt, 1846–1926, vol. II
Menteth, Sir James Stuart-, 3rd Bt, 1841–1918, vol. II
Menteth, Sir William Frederick Stuart-, 5th Bt, 1874–1952, vol. V
Menzies, Alexander John Pople, 1863–1943, vol. IV
Menzies, Rev. Allan, 1845–1916, vol. II
Menzies, Captain Arthur John Alexander, *died* 1918, vol. II
Menzies, Col Charles T., 1858–1943, vol. IV
Menzies, Rt Hon. Sir Douglas Ian, 1907–1974, vol. VII
Menzies, Sir Frederick Norton Kay, 1875–1949, vol. IV
Menzies, George Kenneth, 1869–1954, vol. V
Menzies, James Acworth, *died* 1921, vol. II
Menzies, Sir Neil James, 8th Bt, 1855–1910, vol. I
Menzies, Sir Robert, 7th Bt, 1817–1903, vol. I
Menzies, Sir Robert, 1891–1967, vol. VI
Menzies, Rt Hon. Sir Robert Gordon, 1894–1978, vol. VII
Menzies of Menzies, Ronald Steuart, 1884–1961, vol. VI
Menzies, Maj.-Gen. Sir Stewart Graham, 1890–1968, vol. VI
Menzies, Maj.-Gen. Thomas, 1893–1969, vol. VI
Menzies, Thomas Graham, 1869–1958, vol. V
Menzies, Tom Alexander, 1877–1950, vol. IV (A)
Menzies, Sir Walter, 1856–1913, vol. I
Menzies, William George S.; *see* Steuart-Menzies.
Menzies, William Gladstone, 1879–1938, vol. III
Menzies Anderson, Sir Gilmour, 1914–1977, vol. VII
Menzler, Frederick August Andrew, 1888–1968, vol. VI
Mercadier, Elie, 1844–1916, vol. II
Mercer, Alexander Warren, 1871–1943, vol. IV
Mercer, Major Cecil William, 1885–1960, vol. V
Mercer, Maj.-Gen. Sir David, 1864–1920, vol. II
Mercer, David, 1928–1980, vol. VII
Mercer, Col Edward Gilbert, *died* 1926, vol. II
Mercer, Maj.-Gen. Sir Frederic; *see* Mercer, Maj.-Gen. Sir H. F.
Mercer, George Gibson, 1873–1964, vol. VI
Mercer, Maj.-Gen. Sir (Harvey) Frederic, 1858–1936, vol. III

Mercer, Col Herbert, 1862–1944, vol. IV
Mercer, Howard, 1896–1973, vol. VII
Mercer, James, 1883–1932, vol. III
Mercer, Rt Rev. John Edward, died 1922, vol. II
Mercer, John Swan, 1867–1947, vol. IV
Mercer, Laurence, 1863–1932, vol. III
Mercer, Rev. Samuel Alfred Browne, 1879–1969, vol. VI
Mercer, Stephen Pascal, 1891–1944, vol. IV
Mercer, Sir Walter, 1890–1971, vol. VII
Mercer, Sir William Hepworth, 1855–1932, vol. III
Mercer, Rev. William Marsden, 1858–1939, vol. III
Mercer-Nairne, Major Lord Charles George Francis, 1874–1914, vol. I
Merchant, Livingston Tallmadge, 1903–1976, vol. VII
Merchant, Wilfred, 1912–1965, vol. VI
Mercie, Jean Marius Antonin, 1845–1916, vol. II
Mercieca, Hon. Sir Arturo, 1878–1969, vol. VI
Mercier, Charles Arthur, 1852–1919, vol. II
Mercier, His Eminence Cardinal Desiré, 1851–1926, vol. II
Mercier, Hon. Honoré, 1875–1937, vol. III
Mercier, Winifred Louise, 1878–1934, vol. III
Meredith, Arthur, 1856–1915, vol. I
Meredith, Arthur C., died 1938, vol. III (A)
Meredith, Air Vice-Marshal Sir Charles Warburton, 1896–1977, vol. VII
Meredith, George, 1828–1909, vol. I
Meredith, George Patrick, 1904–1978, vol. VII
Meredith, George Thomas, 1907–1959, vol. V
Meredith, Sir Herbert Ribton, 1890–1959, vol. V
Meredith, Hubert Angelo, 1884–1965, vol. VI
Meredith, Hugh Owen, 1878–1964, vol. VI
Meredith, Sir James Creed, 1842–1912, vol. I
Meredith, James Creed, died 1942, vol. IV
Meredith, Leonard Arthur De Lacy, 1888–1971, vol. VII
Meredith, Rt Rev. Lewis Evan, 1900–1968, vol. VI
Meredith, Margaret, died 1964, vol. VI (AII)
Meredith, Rev. Canon Ralph Creed, 1887–1970, vol. VI
Meredith, Rev. Richard, died 1928, vol. II (A), vol. III
Meredith, Richard, 1867–1957, vol. V
Meredith, Rt Hon. Richard Edmund, 1855–1916, vol. II
Meredith, Richard Martin, 1847–1934, vol. III
Meredith, Sir Vincent, 1st Bt, 1850–1929, vol. III
Meredith, Sir Vincent Robert Sissons, 1877–1965, vol. VI
Meredith, William Appleton, 1848–1916, vol. II
Meredith, Rev. William Macdonald, 1848–1931, vol. III
Meredith, William Maxse, 1865–1937, vol. III
Meredith, Hon. Sir William Ralph, 1840–1923, vol. II
Meredith, Col William Rice, 1882–1964, vol. VI
Meredyth, Captain Arthur Gwynn Moreton, 1862–1955, vol. V
Meredyth, Paymaster Rear-Adm. Charles Edward Hughes, 1861–1949, vol. IV
Meredyth, Sir Edward Henry John, 10th Bt (cr 1660), 1828–1904, vol. I

Meredyth, Sir Henry Bayly, 5th Bt (cr 1795), 1863–1923, vol. II
Merer, Air Vice-Marshal John William Frederick, 1899–1964, vol. VI
Merewether, Sir Edward Marsh, 1858–1938, vol. III
Merewether, Edward Rowland Alworth, 1892–1970, vol. VI
Merewether, Lt-Col John Walter Beresford, 1867–1942, vol. IV
Merewether, Rev. Wyndham Arthur Scinde, 1852–1928, vol. II
Merezhkovski, Dmitri Sergeievich, 1865–1941, vol. IV (A), vol. V
Merivale, Dame Gladys; see Cooper, Dame Gladys.
Merivale, Herman Charles, 1839–1906, vol. I
Merk, William Rudolph Henry, 1852–1925, vol. II
Merrett, Sir Charles Edward, 1863–1948, vol. IV
Merrett, Sir Herbert, 1886–1959, vol. V
Merriam, John Campbell, 1869–1945, vol. IV
Merriam, Sir Laurence Pierce Brooke, 1894–1966, vol. VI
Merrick, Major George Charleton, 1872–1913, vol. I
Merrick, Sir John Edward-Siegfried, 1888–1968, vol. VI
Merrick, Leonard, 1864–1939, vol. III
Merricks, Frank, 1866–1936, vol. III
Merrifield, Leonard Stanford, 1880–1943, vol. IV
Merrill, Elmer Truesdell, 1860–1936, vol. III
Merriman, 1st Baron, 1880–1962, vol. VI
Merriman, Gen. Charles James, 1881–1906, vol. I
Merriman, Rev. Charles Victor, died 1931, vol. III
Merriman, Henry Seton, 1862–1903, vol. I
Merriman, Rt Hon. John Xavier, 1841–1926, vol. II
Merriman, P. J., 1877–1943, vol. IV
Merriman, Lt-Col Reginald Gordon, 1866–1938, vol. III
Merriman, Roger Bigelow, 1876–1945, vol. IV
Merriman, Sir Walter Thomas, 1882–1972, vol. VII
Merriman, Col William, 1838–1917, vol. II
Merrington, Rev. Ernest Northcroft, 1876–1953, vol. V
Merritt, Anna Lea, 1844–1930, vol. III
Merrivale, 1st Baron, 1855–1939, vol. III
Merrivale, 2nd Baron, 1883–1951, vol. V
Merry, Archibald William, died 1933, vol. III
Merry, Rev. William Walter, 1835–1918, vol. II
Merry Del Val, Marquis de, 1864–1943, vol. IV
Merry del Val, His Eminence Cardinal Raphael, 1865–1930, vol. III
Mersey, 1st Viscount, 1840–1929, vol. III
Mersey, 2nd Viscount, 1872–1956, vol. V
Mersey, 3rd Viscount, 1906–1979, vol. VII
Merthyr, 1st Baron, 1837–1914, vol. I
Merthyr, 2nd Baron, 1866–1932, vol. III
Merthyr, 3rd Baron, 1901–1977, vol. VII
Merton, Sir Thomas Ralph, 1888–1969, vol. VI
Merz, Charles, 1893–1977, vol. VII
Merz, Charles Hesterman, 1874–1940, vol. III
Merz, John Theodore, 1840–1922, vol. II
Mess, Henry Adolphus, 1884–1944, vol. IV

Messager, André, 1853–1929, vol. III
Messager, Hope, (Mme André Messager); see Temple, Hope.
Messel, Oliver Hilary Sambourne, 1904–1978, vol. VII
Messel, Rudolph, 1848–1920, vol. II
Messent, Philip Glynn, 1862–1925, vol. II
Messent, Sir Philip Santo, 1895–1976, vol. VII
Messer, Adam Brunton, died 1919, vol. II
Messer, Allan Ernest, 1865–1954, vol. V
Messer, Lt-Col Arthur Albert, 1863–1934, vol. III
Messer, Sir Frederick, 1886–1971, vol. VII
Messervy, Gen. Sir Frank Walter, 1893–1974, vol. VII
Messina, Count, Don Francesco (di Paola), born 1848, vol. III
Messiter, Lt-Col Charles Bayard, 1870–1940, vol. III
Meston, 1st Baron, 1865–1943, vol. IV
Meston, Rev. William, 1871–1933, vol. III
Mestrovic, Ivan, 1883–1962, vol. VI
Metalious, Grace, 1924–1964, vol. VI
Metaxa, Count Andrea, 1844–1921, vol. II
Metaxa, Vice-Adm. Count Frederick Cosmeto, 1847–1910, vol. I
Metaxas, Sir D. G., died 1928, vol. II
Metcalf, Maurice Rupert, 1905–1972, vol. VII
Metcalfe, Sir Aubrey; see Metcalfe, Sir H. A. F.
Metcalfe, Sir Charles Herbert Theophilus, 6th Bt, 1853–1928, vol. II
Metcalfe, Maj.-Gen. Charles Theophilus Evelyn, 1856–1912, vol. I
Metcalfe, Captain Christopher Powell, 1873–1935, vol. III
Metcalfe, Rev. Edmund Lionel, died 1941, vol. IV
Metcalfe, Major Edward Dudley, died 1957, vol. V
Metcalfe, Brig.-Gen. Francis Edward, 1878–1934, vol. III
Metcalfe, Sir Frederic William, 1886–1965, vol. VI
Metcalfe, Sir George, 1848–1931, vol. III
Metcalfe, Henry Wray, 1864–1937, vol. III
Metcalfe, Herbert, 1887–1940, vol. III
Metcalfe, Sir (Herbert) Aubrey (Francis), 1883–1957, vol. V
Metcalfe, Lt-Col Herbert Charles, 1864–1940, vol. III
Metcalfe, James, 1863–1930, vol. III
Metcalfe, Maj.-Gen. John Francis, 1908–1975, vol. VII
Metcalfe, Percy, 1895–1970, vol. VI
Metcalfe, Sir Ralph Ismay, 1896–1977, vol. VII
Metcalfe, Brig.-Gen. Sydney Fortescue, 1870–1948, vol. IV
Metcalfe, Sir Theophilus John, 8th Bt, 1916–1979, vol. VII
Metcalfe, Sir Theophilus John Massie, 7th Bt, 1866–1950, vol. IV
Metcalfe, Thomas Llewellyn, 1870–1922, vol. II
Metcalfe, Rev. W. M., 1840–1916, vol. II
Metcalfe-Smith, Lt-Col Bertram, 1863–1944, vol. IV
Metchnikoff, Elie, died 1916, vol. II
Metford, Col Sir Francis Killigrew Seymour, 1863–1946, vol. IV

Methold, Sir Henry Tindal, 1869–1952, vol. V
Methuen, 3rd Baron, 1845–1932, vol. III
Methuen, 4th Baron, 1886–1974, vol. VII
Methuen, 5th Baron, 1891–1975, vol. VII
Methuen, Sir Algernon Methuen Marshall, 1st Bt, 1856–1924, vol. II
Methven, Sir Harry Finlayson, 1886–1968, vol. VI
Methven, Sir John; see Methven, Sir M. J.
Methven, John Cecil Wilson, 1885–1968, vol. VI
Methven, Sir (Malcolm) John, 1926–1980, vol. VII
Mettam, A. E., died 1917, vol. II
Meuleman, Most Rev. Brice, 1862–1924, vol. II
Meux, Admiral of the Fleet Hon. Sir Hedworth, 1856–1929, vol. III
Mewburn, Maj.-Gen. Hon. Sydney Chilton, 1863–1956, vol. V
Mews, Arthur, 1864–1947, vol. IV
Mexborough, 4th Earl of, 1810–1899, vol. I
Mexborough, 5th Earl of, 1843–1916, vol. II
Mexborough, 6th Earl of, 1868–1945, vol. IV
Mexborough, 7th Earl of, 1906–1980, vol. VII
Mexborough, Countess of; (Anne), died 1943, vol. IV
Meyendorff, Alexander, 1869–1964, vol. VI
Meyer, Arthur, 1845–1924, vol. II
Meyer, Sir Carl, 1st Bt, 1851–1922, vol. II
Meyer, Lt-Col Charles Hardwick Louw, 1859–1942, vol. IV
Meyer, Eugene, 1875–1959, vol. V
Meyer, Sir Frank Cecil, 2nd Bt, 1886–1935, vol. III
Meyer, Rev. Frederick Brotherton, 1847–1929, vol. III
Meyer, George von Lengerke, 1858–1918, vol. II
Meyer, Heinerich Carl, 1896–1972, vol. VII
Meyer, John Mount Montague, 1915–1979, vol. VII
Meyer, Kuno, 1859–1919, vol. II (A), vol. III
Meyer, Louis, 1871–1915, vol. I
Meyer, Sir Manasseh, 1831–1930, vol. III
Meyer, Paul, 1840–1917, vol. II
Meyer, Sir Robert, 1858–1935, vol. III
Meyer, Sir William Stevenson, 1860–1922, vol. II
Meyerheim, Robert Gustav, died 1920, vol. II
Meyerhof, Otto, 1884–1951, vol. V
Meyerstein, Edward Harry William, 1889–1952, vol. V
Meyerstein, Sir Edward William, 1863–1942, vol. IV
Meyjes, Anthony Cornelius, died 1929, vol. III
Meyler, Lt-Col Hugh Mowbray, 1875–1929, vol. III
Meynell, Alice, 1847–1922, vol. II
Meynell, Edgar, 1859–1923, vol. II
Meynell, Edgar John, 1825–1901, vol. I
Meynell, Esther Hallam, (E. Hallam Moorhouse), died 1955, vol. V
Meynell, Everard, 1882–1926, vol. II
Meynell, Sir Everard Charles, 1885–1956, vol. V
Meynell, Sir Francis, 1891–1975, vol. VII
Meynell, Francis Hugo Lindley, 1880–1941, vol. IV
Meynell, Rev. Francis William, 1851–1932, vol. III
Meynell, Hon. Frederick George Lindley, 1846–1910, vol. I
Meynell, Brig.-Gen. Godfrey, 1870–1943, vol. IV

Meynell, Viola, *died* 1956, vol. V
Meynell, Wilfrid, 1852–1948, vol. IV
Meynink, John Fitzsimmons, 1887–1972, vol. VII
Meyric Hughes, Reginald Richard, 1915–1962, vol. VI
Meyrick, Edward, 1854–1938, vol. III
Meyrick, Brig.-Gen. Sir Frederick Charlton, 2nd Bt (*cr* 1880), 1862–1932, vol. III
Meyrick, Rev. Frederick J., 1871–1945, vol. IV
Meyrick, Sir George Augustus Eliott Tapps-Gervis-, 4th Bt (*cr* 1791), 1855–1928, vol. II
Meyrick, Major Sir George Llewelyn Tapps-Gervis-, 5th Bt (*cr* 1791), 1885–1960, vol. V
Meyrick, James Joseph, 1834–1925, vol. II
Meyrick, Adm. Sir Sidney Julius, 1879–1973, vol. VII
Meyrick, Col Sir Thomas C.; *see* Charlton-Meyrick.
Meyrick, Walter Henry, 1880–1950, vol. IV
Meysey-Thompson, Captain Sir Algar de Clifford Charles, 3rd Bt, 1885–1967, vol. VI
Meysey-Thompson, Captain Hon. Claude Henry, 1887–1915, vol. I
Meysey-Thompson, Ernest Claude, 1859–1944, vol. IV
Meysey-Thompson, Hubert Charles, 1883–1956, vol. V
Meysey-Thompson, Col Richard Frederick, 1847–1926, vol. II
Mézières, Alfred Jean François, *died* 1915, vol. I (A)
Miall, Louis Compton, 1842–1921, vol. II
Micallef, Sir Richard, 1846–1933, vol. III
Michael, Albert Davidson, 1836–1927, vol. II
Michael, Rev. J. Hugh, 1878–1959, vol. V
Michael, Gen. James, 1828–1907, vol. I
Michaelis, Sir Archie, 1889–1975, vol. VII
Michaelis, Sir Maximillian, *died* 1932, vol. III
Michel, Louise, 1830–1905, vol. I
Michelham, 1st Baron, 1851–1919, vol. II
Michelham, Lady; (Aimée Geraldine), *died* 1927, vol. II
Michelin, William Plunkett, 1872–1943, vol. IV
Michell, Anthony George Maldon, *died* 1959, vol. V
Michell, Eveline Louisa; *see* Forbes, Hon. Mrs Walter R. D.
Michell, Rev. Francis Rodon, 1839–1920, vol. II
Michell, George Babington, 1864–1936, vol. III
Michell, Rev. Gilbert Arthur, 1883–1960, vol. V
Michell, Harry Denis, 1923–1971, vol. VII
Michell, Humphrey, 1883–1970, vol. VI
Michell, John, 1836–1921, vol. II
Michell, John Henry, *died* 1940, vol. III
Michell, Comdr Kenneth, 1887–1967, vol. VI
Michell, Hon. Sir Lewis Loyd, 1842–1928, vol. II
Michell, Sir Robert Carminowe, 1876–1956, vol. V
Michell, Roland Lyons Nosworthy, 1847–1931, vol. III
Michell, Walter Cecil, 1864–1939, vol. III
Michelli, Sir James, 1853–1935, vol. III
Michelson, Albert Abraham, 1852–1931, vol. III
Michelson, Christian, 1857–1925, vol. II
Michie, Alexander, 1833–1902, vol. I

Michie, Sir Archibald, 1810–1899, vol. I
Michie, J. Coutts, 1861–1919, vol. II
Michie, James, 1867–1943, vol. IV
Michie, James Kilgour, 1887–1967, vol. VI
Michie, John, 1853–1934, vol. III
Michie, John Lundie, 1882–1946, vol. IV
Michie, Robert James, 1856–1928, vol. II
Micholls, E. Montefiore, 1852–1926, vol. II
Micklem, Major Charles, 1882–1955, vol. V
Micklem, Maj.-Gen. Edward, 1840–1934, vol. III
Micklem, Comdr Sir (Edward) Robert, 1891–1952, vol. V
Micklem, Col Henry Andrew, 1872–1963, vol. VI
Micklem, Brig.-Gen. John, 1889–1952, vol. V
Micklem, Nathaniel, 1853–1954, vol. V
Micklem, Rev. Nathaniel, 1888–1976, vol. VII
Micklem, Very Rev. Philip Arthur, 1876–1965, vol. VI
Micklem, Brig. Ralph, 1884–1977, vol. VII
Micklem, Comdr Sir Robert; *see* Micklem, Comdr Sir E. R.
Micklethwait, Frances Mary Gore, 1867–1950, vol. IV
Micklethwait, Hon Ivy Mary, (Hon. Mrs Micklethwait), 1895–1967, vol. IV
Micklethwait, Rear-Adm. St John Aldrich, 1901–1977, vol. VII
Micklethwait, St John Gore, 1870–1951, vol. V
Micks, Sir Robert, 1825–1902, vol. I
Micks, Robert Henry, 1895–1970, vol. VI
Micks, William Lawson, 1851–1928, vol. II
Middlebro, William Sora, 1868–1948, vol. IV
Middlebrook, Sir Harold, 2nd Bt, 1887–1971, vol. VII
Middlebrook, Sir William, 1st Bt, 1851–1936, vol. III
Middlemas, Noel Allan, 1892–1967, vol. VI
Middlemiss, Charles Stewart, 1859–1945, vol. IV
Middlemore, Sir John Throgmorton, 1st Bt, 1844–1925, vol. II
Middleton, 9th Baron, 1844–1922, vol. II
Middleton, 10th Baron, 1847–1924, vol. II
Middleton, 11th Baron, 1887–1970, vol. VI
Middleton, A. Safroni, *died* 1950, vol. IV
Middleton, Sir Arthur Edward, 7th Bt, 1838–1933, vol. III
Middleton, Sir Arthur Edward, 1891–1953, vol. V
Middleton, Sir Charles Arthur, 8th Bt, 1873–1942, vol. IV
Middleton, Edgar, 1894–1939, vol. III
Middleton, Sir Frederick D., 1825–1898, vol. I
Middleton, Sir George, 1876–1938, vol. III
Middleton, George Walker, 1898–1971, vol. VII
Middleton, Adm. Gervase Boswell, 1893–1961, vol. VI
Middleton, Hubert Stanley, 1890–1959, vol. V
Middleton, Sir John, 1870–1954, vol. V
Middleton, Sir John Page, 1851–1932, vol. III
Middleton, Lambert William, 1877–1941, vol. IV
Middleton, Noel, 1875–1955, vol. V
Middleton, Mrs Peggy Arline, 1916–1974, vol. VII
Middleton, Reginald Empson, 1844–1925, vol. II
Middleton, Richard William Evelyn, 1846–1905, vol. I

Middleton, Sir Thomas, 1863–1943, vol. IV
Middleton, William Aberdein, 1876–1940, vol. III
Midgley, Rt Hon. Harry, *died* 1957, vol. V
Midgley, Lt-Col Stephen, 1871–1954, vol. V
Midgley, Wilson, 1887–1954, vol. V
Midlane, Albert, 1825–1909, vol. I
Midleton, 1st Earl of, 1856–1942, vol. IV
Midleton, 2nd Earl of, 1888–1979, vol. VII
Midleton, 8th Viscount, 1830–1907, vol. I
Midwinter, Captain Sir Edward Colpoys, 1872–1947, vol. IV
Midwood, Lt-Col Harrison, 1857–1944, vol. IV
Miers, Sir Henry Alexander, 1858–1942, vol. IV
Mies van der Rohe, Ludwig, 1886–1969, vol. VI
Mieville, Arthur Leonard, 1879–1976, vol. VII
Mieville, Sir Eric Charles, 1896–1971, vol. VII
Miéville, Sir Walter Frederick, 1855–1929, vol. III
Mifflin, Lloyd, 1846–1921, vol. II
Mifsud, Edward Robert, 1875–1970, vol. VI
Mifsud, Hon. Sir Ugo Pasquale, 1889–1942, vol. IV
Migeod, Frederick William Hugh, 1872–1952, vol. V
Mighell, Sir Norman Rupert, 1894–1955, vol. V
Mignault, Pierre Basile, 1854–1945, vol. IV
Mignot, Rev. Peter Thomas, 1863–1935, vol. III
Mijatovich, Chedomille, 1842–1932, vol. III
Mikkelsen, Captain Ejnar, 1880–1971, vol. VII
Mikoyan, Anastas Ivanovich, 1895–1978, vol. VII
Milbank, Sir Frederick Acclom, 1st Bt, 1820–1898, vol. I
Milbank, Major Sir Frederick Richard Powlett, 3rd Bt, 1881–1964, vol. VI
Milbank, Sir Powlett Charles John, 2nd Bt, 1852–1918, vol. II
Milbanke, Sir John Charles Peniston, 11th Bt, 1902–1947, vol. IV
Milbanke, Sir John Peniston, 10th Bt, 1872–1915, vol. I
Milbanke, Sir Peniston, 9th Bt, 1847–1899, vol. I
Milbanke, Ralph, 1852–1903, vol. I
Milbanke, Sir Ralph Mark, 12th Bt, 1907–1949, vol. IV
Milborne-Swinnerton-Pilkington, Major Sir Arthur William; *see* Pilkington.
Milborne-Swinnerton-Pilkington, Sir Thomas Edward; *see* Pilkington.
Milburn, Captain Booker, 1888–1941, vol. IV
Milburn, Charles Henry, 1860–1948, vol. IV
Milburn, Sir Charles Stamp, 2nd Bt, 1878–1917, vol. II
Milburn, James Booth, 1860–1923, vol. II
Milburn, Sir John Davison, 1st Bt, 1851–1907, vol. I
Milburn, Sir Leonard John, 3rd Bt, 1884–1957, vol. V
Mildmay of Flete, 1st Baron, 1861–1947, vol. IV
Mildmay of Flete, 2nd Baron, 1909–1950, vol. IV
Mildmay, Sir Anthony St John-, 8th Bt, 1894–1947, vol. IV
Mildmay, Rev. Sir (Aubrey) Neville St John-, 10th Bt, 1865–1955, vol. V
Mildmay, Sir Gerald Anthony Shaw-Lefevre St John-, 7th Bt, 1860–1929, vol. III
Mildmay, Sir Henry Bouverie Paulet St John-, 5th Bt, 1810–1902, vol. I

Mildmay, Sir Henry Gerald St John-, 9th Bt, 1926–1949, vol. IV
Mildmay, Major Sir Henry Paulet St John, 6th Bt, 1853–1916, vol. II
Mildmay, Lt-Col Herbert Alexander St John-, 1836–1922, vol. II
Mildmay, Rev. Sir Neville St John-; *see* Mildmay, Rev. Sir A. N. St J.
Mildmay, Major Wyndham Paulet St John-, 1855–1934, vol. III
Mildren, Col William Frederick, 1874–1948, vol. IV
Miles, Alexander, 1865–1953, vol. V
Miles, Alfred Henry, 1848–1929, vol. III
Miles, Alfred Henry, 1855–1933, vol. III
Miles, Major Arthur Tremayne, 1889–1934, vol. III
Miles, Sir Cecil Leopold, 3rd Bt, 1873–1898, vol. I
Miles, Lt-Gen. Charles George Norman, 1884–1958, vol. V
Miles, Col Charles Napier, 1854–1918, vol. II
Miles, Sir Charles Watt, 1901–1970, vol. VI
Miles, Sir Charles William, 5th Bt, 1883–1966, vol. VI
Miles, Maj.-Gen. Eric Grant, 1891–1977, vol. VII
Miles, Eustace, 1868–1948, vol. IV
Miles, Rev. Frederic James, 1869–1962, vol. VI
Miles, Frederick George, 1903–1976, vol. VII
Miles, George Edward, 1852–1942, vol. IV
Miles, George Herbert, 1880–1955, vol. V
Miles, Gordon, 1891–1959, vol. V
Miles, Sir Henry Robert William, 4th Bt, 1843–1915, vol. I
Miles, Lt-Gen. Sir Herbert Scott Gould, 1850–1926, vol. II
Miles, Sir John Charles, 1870–1963, vol. VI
Miles, Rev. Joseph Henry, *died* 1935, vol. III
Miles, Lt-Gen. Nelson Appleton, 1839–1925, vol. II
Miles, Brig.-Gen. Philip John, 1864–1948, vol. IV
Miles, Philip Napier, 1865–1935, vol. III
Miles, Brig. Reginald, 1892–1943, vol. IV
Miles, Richard, 1893–1976, vol. VII
Miles, Captain Wilfrid, 1885–1962, vol. VI
Miles, William Ernest, 1869–1947, vol. IV
Miley, Col James, 1846–1919, vol. II
Milford, 1st Baron, 1874–1962, vol. VI
Milford, Maj.-Gen. Edward James, *died* 1972, vol. VII
Milford, Brig. Ernest William, 1898–1944, vol. IV
Milford, Sir Humphrey Sumner, 1877–1952, vol. V
Milford Haven, 1st Marquess of, 1854–1921, vol. II
Milford Haven, 2nd Marquess of, 1892–1938, vol. III
Milford Haven, 3rd Marquess of, 1919–1970, vol. VI
Milhaud, Darius, 1892–1974, vol. VII
Mill, Hugh Robert, 1861–1950, vol. IV
Mill, Thomas, 1878–1941, vol. IV
Mill, William Allin, 1902–1968, vol. VI
Mill, William Claude Frederick V. B.; *see* Vaudrey-Barker-Mill.
Mill Irving, David Jarvis, 1904–1978, vol. VII
Millais, Sir Everett, 2nd Bt, 1856–1897, vol. I

Millais, Sir Geoffroy William, 4th Bt, 1863–1941, vol. IV
Millais, Sir John Everett, 3rd Bt, 1888–1920, vol. II
Millais, John Guille, 1865–1931, vol. III
Millar, A. H., 1847–1927, vol. II
Millar, Alexander, 1867–1944, vol. IV
Millar, Edric William Hoyer, 1880–1963, vol. VI
Millar, Eric George, 1887–1966, vol. VI
Millar, Frederick Charles James, died 1899, vol. I
Millar, Henry James, 1878–1960, vol. V
Millar, Sir Jackson, 1888–1958, vol. V
Millar, Sir James Duncan, 1871–1932, vol. III
Millar, James Gardner, 1855–1917, vol. II
Millar, John, 1905–1978, vol. VII
Millar, John Alexander Stevenson, 1854–1938, vol. III
Millar, John Hepburn, 1864–1929, vol. III
Millar, Robert, 1850–1908, vol. I
Millard, Charles Killick, 1870–1952, vol. V
Millard, Ven. Ernest Norman, 1899–1969, vol. VI
Millard, Evelyn, died 1941, vol. IV
Millard, Col Reginald Jeffery, 1868–1943, vol. IV
Millard, Thomas, 1884–1935, vol. III
Millay, Edna St Vincent, 1892–1950, vol. IV
Millbourn, Rev. Arthur Russell, 1892–1973, vol. VII
Millbourn, Sir Ralph, 1862–1942, vol. IV
Miller, Sir Alastair George Lionel Joseph, 6th Bt (cr 1788), 1893–1964, vol. VI
Miller, Sir Alexander Edward, 1828–1903, vol. I
Miller, Alexander Gordon, 1843–1929, vol. III
Miller, Alexander James Nicol, 1911–1974, vol. VII
Miller, Alexander Thomas, 1875–1942, vol. IV
Miller, Brig.-Gen. Alfred Douglas, 1864–1933, vol. III
Miller, Archibald Elliot Haswell, 1887–1979, vol. VII
Miller, A(rthur) Austin, 1900–1968, vol. VI
Miller, Arthur Hallowes, 1880–1956, vol. V
Miller, Arthur William Kaye, 1849–1914, vol. I
Miller, Maj.-Gen. Austin T., 1888–1947, vol. IV
Miller, Charles A. Duff, 1854–1909, vol. I
Miller, Vice-Adm. Charles Blois, 1867–1926, vol. II
Miller, Lt-Col Charles Darley, 1868–1951, vol. V
Miller, Maj.-Gen. Charles Harvey, 1894–1974, vol. VII
Miller, Charles Hewitt, 1875–1939, vol. III
Miller, Sir (Charles John) Hubert, 8th Bt (cr 1705), 1858–1940, vol. III
Miller, Cincinnatus Heine; see Miller, Joaquin.
Miller, Brig.-Gen. David, 1857–1934, vol. III
Miller, Sir Dawson, 1867–1942, vol. IV
Miller, Sir Denison Samuel King, 1860–1923, vol. II
Miller, Douglas Gordon, 1881–1956, vol. V
Miller, Edmund Morris, 1881–1964, vol. VI
Miller, Hon. Sir Edward, 1848–1932, vol. III
Miller, Lt-Col Edward Darley, 1865–1930, vol. III
Miller, Emanuel, 1894–1970, vol. VI
Miller, Sir Eric; see Miller, Sir H. E.
Miller, Sir Ernest, 1879–1939, vol. III
Miller, Sir Ernest Henry John, 10th Bt (cr 1705), 1897–1960, vol. V

Miller, Florence Fenwick, 1854–1935, vol. III
Miller, Rev. Francis Broughton Anson, 1855–1934, vol. III
Miller, Sir (Francis) Henry, 1865–1936, vol. III
Miller, Sir Francis N.; see Norie-Miller.
Miller, Adm. Francis Spurstow, 1863–1954, vol. V
Miller, Fred, 1863–1924, vol. II
Miller, Frederick Robert, died 1967, vol. VI
Miller, Col Sir Geoffry C.; see Christie-Miller.
Miller, George, 1833–1909, vol. I
Miller, George, 1842–1923, vol. II
Miller, Maj.-Gen. George Murray, 1829–1911, vol. I
Miller, George Waterston, 1874–1955, vol. V
Miller, Gilbert Heron, 1884–1969, vol. VI
Miller, Sir Gordon William, 1844–1906, vol. I
Miller, Gray, 1885–1947, vol. IV
Miller, Captain Grenville Acton, died 1951, vol. V
Miller, Sir (Hans) Eric, 1882–1958, vol. V
Miller, Harold Tibbatts, 1873–1948, vol. IV
Miller, Henry, 1859–1927, vol. II
Miller, Sir Henry; see Miller, Sir F. H.
Miller, Henry George, 1913–1976, vol. VII
Miller, Sir Henry Holmes, 9th Bt (cr 1705), 1865–1952, vol. V
Miller, Hon. Sir Henry John, 1830–1918, vol. II
Miller, Henry Valentine, 1891–1980, vol. VII
Miller, Sir Hubert; see Miller, Sir C. J. H.
Miller, Rear-Adm. Hugh, 1880–1972, vol. VII
Miller, Hugh C.; see Crichton-Miller.
Miller, Brig. Hugh de Burgh, 1874–1951, vol. V
Miller, Hugh Rodolph, 1875–1953, vol. V
Miller, Maj.-Gen. James, 1835–1929, vol. III
Miller, James, died 1947, vol. IV
Miller, James, 1875–1958, vol. V
Miller, Sir James, 1905–1977, vol. VII
Miller, James Gordon, 1874–1950, vol. IV
Miller, Bt Col Sir James MacBride, 1896–1977, vol. VII
Miller, Sir James Percy, 2nd Bt (cr 1874), 1864–1906, vol. I
Miller, Joaquin, 1842–1913, vol. I
Miller, John, 1911–1975, vol. VII
Miller, Sir John Alexander, 3rd Bt (cr 1874), 1867–1918, vol. II
Miller, John Duncan, 1902–1977, vol. VII
Miller, Very Rev. John Harry, 1869–1940, vol. III
Miller, Sir John Ontario, 1857–1943, vol. IV
Miller, Sir John Wilson Edington, 1894–1957, vol. V
Miller, Brig. Laurence Walter, 1882–1958, vol. V
Miller, Leonard; see Merrick, L.
Miller, Sir Leslie Creery, 1862–1925, vol. II
Miller, Dame Mabel, died 1978, vol. VII
Miller, Mrs Millie, 1923–1977, vol. VII
Miller, Rev. Norman, died 1980, vol. VII
Miller, Rev. Norman James, died 1932, vol. III
Miller, Rev. Peter Watters, 1890–1976, vol. VII
Miller, Philip Homan, died 1928, vol. II
Miller, Ralph William Richardson, 1892–1958, vol. V
Miller, Reginald Henry, died 1948, vol. IV
Miller, René F.; see Fülop-Miller.
Miller, Rt Rev. Robert, 1866–1931, vol. III

Miller, Robert Brown, 1905–1963, vol. VI
Miller, Sir Roderick William, 1911–1971, vol. VII
Miller, Samuel Vandeleur C.; see Christie-Miller.
Miller, Sinclair, 1885–1961, vol. VI
Miller, Sir Stanley N.; see Norie-Miller.
Miller, Stearnhall, 1813–1897, vol. I
Miller, Sydney Richardson C.; see Christie-Miller.
Miller, Thomas Butt, 1859–1915, vol. I
Miller, Willet G., died 1925, vol. II
Miller, Sir William, 1828–1900, vol. I
Miller, Rt Hon. William, 1834–1912, vol. I
Miller, Rev. William, 1838–1923, vol. II
Miller, William, 1864–1945, vol. IV
Miller, Major William Archibald, died 1925, vol. II
Miller, William Christopher, 1898–1976, vol. VII
Miller, Sir William Frederic, 5th Bt (cr 1788), 1868–1948, vol. IV
Miller, William Lash, 1866–1940, vol. III
Miller, Col William Miles, 1891–1946, vol. IV
Miller, William Thomas, 1865–1930, vol. III
Miller, William Thomas, 1880–1963, vol. VI
Miller-Cunningham, Sir George, 1867–1945, vol. IV
Miller Jones, Keith, 1899–1978, vol. VII
Miller-Jones, Sir Thomas, 1874–1944, vol. IV
Millerand, Alexandre, 1859–1943, vol. IV
Millers, Harold Cuthbert Townley, 1903–1968, vol. VI
Milles, Carl, 1875–1955, vol. V
Milles-Lade, Hon. Henry Augustus, 1867–1937, vol. III
Millet, Francis Davis, 1846–1912, vol. I
Millett, George Prideaux, 1863–1950, vol. IV
Millevoye, Lucien, 1850–1918, vol. II
Milligan, Rt Hon. Lord; William Rankine Milligan, 1898–1975, vol. VII
Milligan, Very Rev. George, 1860–1934, vol. III
Milligan, John Williamson, 1875–1965, vol. VI
Milligan, Patrick Ward, 1910–1978, vol. VII
Milligan, Samuel, 1874–1954, vol. V
Milligan, Lt-Col Stanley Lyndall, 1887–1968, vol. VI
Milligan, Sir William, 1864–1929, vol. III
Milligan, Rt Hon. William Rankine; see Milligan, Rt Hon. Lord.
Millikan, Robert Andrews, 1868–1953, vol. V
Milliken, Alexander, 1841–1914, vol. I
Milliken, Brig. Robert Cecil, 1883–1959, vol. V
Millin, Albert, 1893–1964, vol. VI
Millin, Sarah Gertrude, died 1968, vol. VI
Millingen, Alexander van, 1840–1915, vol. I
Millington, Powell; see Synge, Major Mark.
Millington-Drake, Sir Eugen John Henry Vanderstegen, 1889–1972, vol. VII
Milln, Rear-Adm. William Bryan Scott, 1915-1979, vol. VII
Mills, 1st Viscount, 1890–1968, vol. VI
Mills, Hon. Algernon Henry, 1856–1922, vol. II
Mills, Arthur, 1887–1955, vol. V
Mills, Rev. Arthur Everard, 1863–1929, vol. III
Mills, Arthur John, 1868–1956, vol. V
Mills, Maj.-Gen. Sir Arthur Mordaunt, 1879–1964, vol. VI
Mills, Arthur Stewart Hunt, 1897–1968, vol. VI
Mills, Bertram Wagstaff, 1873–1938, vol. III

Mills, Charles A., vol. II
Mills, Hon. Charles Houghton, 1844–1923, vol. II
Mills, Darius Ogden, 1825–1910, vol. I
Mills, David, 1831–1903, vol. I
Mills, Lady Dorothy R. M., died 1959, vol. V
Mills, Edmund James, 1840–1921 ,vol. II
Mills, Edward, 1849–1933, vol. III
Mills, Eric, 1892–1961, vol. VI
Mills, Sir Ernest Arnold, died 1949, vol. IV
Mills, Sir Frederick, 1st Bt, 1865–1953, vol. V
Mills, Major Sir (Frederick Leighton) Victor, 2nd Bt, 1893–1955, vol. V
Mills, Captain Hon. Geoffrey Edward, 1875–1917, vol. II
Mills, Brig.-Gen. George Arthur, 1855–1927, vol. II
Mills, Air Chief Marshal Sir George Holroyd, 1902–1971, vol. VII
Mills, George Percival, 1883–1952, vol. V
Mills, Harry Woosnam, 1873–1925, vol. II
Mills, Rev. Canon Henry Holroyd, 1860–1947, vol. IV
Mills, Col Herbert James, 1836–1927, vol. II
Mills, J. Saxon, died 1929, vol. III
Mills, James, 1840–1924, vol. II
Mills, Sir James, 1847–1936, vol. III
Mills, Col James Edgar, 1878–1937, vol. III
Mills, James Philip, 1890–1960, vol. V
Mills, Col Sir John Digby, 1879–1972, vol. VII
Mills, John Edmund, died 1951, vol. V
Mills, John Frobisher, 1859–1929, vol. III
Mills, John Norton, 1914–1977, vol. VII
Mills, John Spencer, 1817–1976, vol. VII
Mills, Joseph Trueman, 1836–1924, vol. II
Mills, Lawrence Heyworth, born 1837, vol. II
Mills, Hon. Ogden L., 1884–1937, vol. III
Mills, Maj.-Gen. Percy Strickland, died 1973, vol. VII
Mills, Air Vice-Marshal Reginald Percy, 1885–1968, vol. VI
Mills, Sir Richard, 1830–1906, vol. I
Mills, Richard Charles, 1886–1952, vol. V
Mills, Robert Watkin, 1856–1930, vol. III
Mills, Stephen, 1857–1948, vol. IV
Mills, T. Wesley, died 1915, vol. I
Mills, Major Sir Victor; see Mills, Major Sir F. L. V.
Mills, Rev. William, died 1922, vol. II
Mills, Sir William, 1856–1932, vol. III
Mills, William Haslam, 1874–1930, vol. III
Mills, William Hobson, 1873–1959, vol. V
Mills, Rt Rev. William Lennox, died 1917, vol. II
Mills-Roberts, Robert Herbert, 1862–1935, vol. III
Millspaugh, Arthur Chester, 1883–1955, vol. V
Millspaugh, Rt Rev. Frank Rosebrook, 1848–1916, vol. II
Milman, Archibald John Scott, died 1902, vol. I
Milman, Sir Francis, 5th Bt, 1872–1946, vol. IV
Milman, Sir Francis John, 4th Bt, 1842–1922, vol. II
Milman, Lt-Gen. Sir George Bryan, 1822–1915, vol. I
Milman, Brig.-Gen. Sir Lionel Charles Patrick, 7th Bt, 1877–1962, vol. VI

Milman, Lt-Col Octavius Rodney Everard, 1882–1971, vol. VII

Milman, Sir William Ernest, 6th Bt, 1875–1962, vol. VI

Miln, Mrs George Chichton, 1864–1933, vol. III

Miln, Louise Jordan; see Miln, Mrs George Crichton.

Milne, 1st Baron, 1866–1948, vol. IV

Milne, Alan Alexander, 1882–1956, vol. V

Milne, Alan Hay, 1869–1919, vol. II

Milne, Alexander, died 1903, vol. I

Milne, Alexander Boland, 1842–1904, vol. I

Milne, Rt Rev. Andrew Jamieson, 1831–1906, vol. I

Milne, Sir (Archibald) Berkeley, 2nd Bt, 1855–1938, vol. III

Milne, Archibald George, 1910–1980, vol. VII

Milne, Arthur; see Milne, E. A.

Milne, Arthur Dawson, 1867–1932, vol. III

Milne, Sir Berkeley; see Milne, Sir A. B.

Milne, Charles, died 1960, vol. V

Milne, Christian Hoyer Millar, 1870–1945, vol. IV

Milne, David, 1876–1954, vol. V

Milne, Sir David, 1896–1972, vol. VII

Milne, Rev. Edgar Astley, 1862–1945, vol. IV

Milne, (Edward) Arthur, 1896–1950, vol. IV

Milne, Lt-Col George, 1857–1939, vol. III

Milne, George Torrance, 1862–1943, vol. IV

Milne, J. Maclauchlan, died 1957, vol. V

Milne, James, 1865–1951, vol. V

Milne, Sir James, 1883–1958, vol. V

Milne, Sir James Allan, 1896–1966, vol. VI

Milne, James Mathewson, 1883–1959, vol. V

Milne, John, 1850–1913, vol. I

Milne, John Alexander, 1872–1955, vol. V

Milne, Sir John Sydney W.; see Wardlaw-Milne.

Milne, Joseph Grafton, 1867–1951, vol. V

Milne, Kenneth John, 1880–1929, vol. III

Milne, Mrs Leslie, (Mary Lewis), 1860–1952, vol. V

Milne, Oswald Partridge, 1881–1968, vol. VI

Milne, Lt-Col Richard Lewis, 1832–1906, vol. I

Milne, Col Thomas, 1882–1959, vol. V

Milne, William Proctor, 1881–1967, vol. VI

Milne, Sir William Robertson, died 1959, vol. V

Milne-Bailey, Walter, died 1935, vol. III

Milne Henderson, Captain Thomas Maxwell Stuart, 1888–1968, vol. VI

Milne-Home, David William, 1873–1918, vol. II

Milne-Redhead, Lt-Col Richard Henry, 1862–1944, vol. IV

Milne-Thomson, Col Alexander, died 1944, vol. IV

Milne-Thomson, Louis Melville, 1891–1974, vol. VII

Milne-Watson, Sir David, 1st Bt, died 1945, vol. IV

Milner, 1st Viscount, 1854–1925, vol. II

Milner, Viscountess; (Violet Georgina), died 1958, vol. V

Milner of Leeds, 1st Baron, 1889–1967, vol. VI

Milner, Elizabeth Eleanor, died 1953, vol. V

Milner, Frank, 1875–1944, vol. IV

Milner, Frank Leopold, 1870–1946, vol. IV

Milner, Fred, died 1939, vol. III

Milner, Frederic, 1905–1957, vol. V

Milner, Rt Hon. Sir Frederick George, 7th Bt, 1849–1931, vol. III

Milner, George, 1829–1914, vol. I

Milner, Brig.-Gen. George Francis, 1862–1921, vol. II

Milner, James Donald, 1874–1927, vol. II

Milner, Engr-Rear-Adm. John William, died 1953, vol. V

Milner, Marcus Henry, 1864–1939, vol. III

Milner, Samuel Roslington, 1875–1958, vol. V

Milner, Thomas Stuart, 1909–1969, vol. VI

Milner, William Aldam, 1854–1931, vol. III

Milner, Sir William Frederick Victor Mordaunt, 8th Bt, 1893–1960, vol. V

Milner-Barry, E. L., died 1917, vol. II

Milner-Jones, Edward William, 1853–1942, vol. IV

Milner-White, Very Rev. Eric, 1884–1963, vol. VI

Milner-White, Sir Henry, 1854–1922, vol. II

Milnes, Alfred, 1849–1921, vol. II

Milnes, Nora, 1882–1972, vol. VII

Milnes, W. H., 1865–1957, vol. V

Milnes-Coates, Captain Sir Clive; see Coates.

Milnes Gaskell, Lady Constance, 1885–1964, vol. VI

Milroy, Hugh, 1840–1919, vol. II

Milroy, John Alexander, died 1934, vol. III

Milroy, Thomas Hugh, 1869–1950, vol. IV

Milsom, Hilda Maud, died 1972, vol. VII

Milton, Ernest, 1890–1974, vol. VII

Milton, Sir Frank, 1906–1976, vol. VII

Milton, Sir William Henry, 1854–1930, vol. III

Milvain, Sir Thomas, 1844–1916, vol. II

Milverton, 1st Baron, 1885–1978, vol. VII

Milward, Sir Christopher Annakin, 1834–1906, vol. I

Milward, Maj.-Gen. Sir Clement Arthur, 1877–1951, vol. V

Milward, Col Victor, died 1901, vol. I

Minchin, Lt-Col Alfred Beckett, 1870–1939, vol. III

Minchin, Lt-Col Charles Frederick, 1862–1943, vol. IV

Minchin, Charles Owen, 1844–1930, vol. III

Minchin, E. A., 1866–1915, vol. I

Minchin, Maj.-Gen. Frederick Falkiner, 1860–1922, vol. II

Minchin, George M., died 1914, vol. I

Minchin, Harry Christopher, 1861—1941, vol. IV

Minchin, James George Cotton, died 1933, vol. III

Minchin, Col William Cyril, 1856–1924, vol. II

Mines, George Ralph, 1886–1914, vol. I

Minett, Francis Colin, 1890–1953, vol. V

Minford, Hugh, died 1950, vol. IV

Minford, Rt Hon. Nathaniel Owens, 1912–1975, vol. VII

Mingana, Alphonse, 1881–1937, vol. III

Minney, Rubeigh James, 1895–1979, vol. VII

Minnis, Samuel Ellison, 1882–1971, vol. VII

Minns, Captain Allan Noel, 1891–1921, vol. II

Minns, Sir Ellis Hovell, 1874–1953, vol. V

Minoprio, Frank Charles, 1870–1951, vol. V

Minor, Clark Haynes, 1878–1967, vol. VI

Minorsky, Vladimir, 1877–1966, vol. VI

Minot, Charles Sedgwick, 1852–1914, vol. I

Minot, George Richards, 1885–1950, vol. IV

Minshull-Ford, Maj.-Gen. John Randle; *see* Ford.

Minter, Sir Frederick Albert, 1887–1976, vol. VII

Minter, Percy, 1866–1955, vol. V

Minto, 4th Earl of, 1847–1914, vol. I

Minto, 5th Earl of, 1891–1975, vol. VII

Minto, John, 1863–1935, vol. III

Minton, (Francis) John, 1917–1957, vol. V

Minton, John; *see* Minton, F. J.

Miraj (Junior), Chief of; Sir Shrimant Madhavrao Harihar, *alias* Baba Saheb Patwardhan, *died* 1950, vol. IV (A), vol. V

Mirbeau, Octave, 1850–1917, vol. II

Mirehouse, Lt-Col Richard Walter Byrd, 1849–1914, vol. I

Mirehouse, William Edward, 1844–1925, vol. II

Mirrielees, Sir Frederick James, *died* 1914, vol. I

Mirrlees, Maj.-Gen. William Henry Buchanan, 1892–1964, vol. VI

Mirza Ali Akbar Khan, 1880–1934, vol. III

Mirza, Maj.-Gen. Iskander, 1899–1969, vol. VI

Misa, Brig. Lawrence Edward, 1896–1968, vol. VI

Misra, Sir Lakshmipati, 1888–1964, vol. VI

Missenden, Sir Eustace James, 1886–1973, vol. VII

Mistinguett, (Jeanne Bourgeois), 1875–1956, vol. V

Mistral, Frederic, 1830–1914, vol. I

Mitchell, Alan Alexander McCaskill, 1882–1941, vol. IV

Mitchell, Alexander, 1871–1934, vol. III

Mitchell, Alexander Ferrier, 1822–1899, vol. I

Mitchell, Andrew, 1843–1915, vol. I

Mitchell, Andrew Park, 1894–1975, vol. VII

Mitchell, Sir Angus Sinclair, 1884–1961, vol. VI

Mitchell, Rt Rev. Anthony, 1868–1917, vol. II

Mitchell, Arnold, *died* 1944, vol. IV

Mitchell, Sir Arthur, 1826–1909, vol. I

Mitchell, Arthur Brownlow, 1865–1942, vol. IV

Mitchell, Arthur James, 1893–1967, vol. VI

Mitchell, Bertram, 1898–1978, vol. VII

Mitchell, Charles, *died* 1957, vol. V

Mitchell, Charles Ainsworth, 1867–1948, vol. IV

Mitchell, Sir Charles Bullen Hugh, *died* 1899, vol. I

Mitchell, Brig.-Gen. Charles Hamilton, 1872–1941, vol. IV

Mitchell, Major Charles Johnstone, 1879–1918, vol. II

Mitchell, Hon. Charles Richmond, 1872–1942, vol. IV

Mitchell, Charles W., *died* 1903, vol. I

Mitchell, Craig, 1896–1975, vol. VII

Mitchell, Sir David George, 1879–1963, vol. VI

Mitchell, Edmund, 1861–1917, vol. II

Mitchell, Edward Card, 1853–1914, vol. I

Mitchell, Sir Edward Fancourt, 1855–1941, vol. IV

Mitchell, Edward Rosslyn, 1879–1965, vol. VI

Mitchell, Edwin Laurence, 1883–1960, vol. V

Mitchell, Adm. Francis Herbert, 1876–1946, vol. IV

Mitchell, Maj.-Gen. Francis Neville, 1904–1954, vol. V

Mitchell, Sir Frank Herbert, 1878–1951, vol. V

Mitchell, Frank William Drew, 1845–1936, vol. III

Mitchell, Air Vice-Marshal Frederick George Stewart, 1901–1974, vol. VII

Mitchell, Rt Rev. Frederick Julian, 1901–1979, vol. VII

Mitchell, George, 1867–1937, vol. III

Mitchell, Sir George Arthur, 1860–1948, vol. IV

Mitchell, George Hoole, 1902–1976, vol. VII

Mitchell, Sir George Irvine, 1911–1978, vol. VII

Mitchell, Mrs George J., (Maggie Richardson), *died* 1953, vol. V

Mitchell, George Winter, 1865–1935, vol. III

Mitchell, Harold John, 1877–1941, vol. IV

Mitchell, Rev. Harry, 1847–1935, vol. III

Mitchell, Helen Porter; *see* Melba, Dame Nellie.

Mitchell, Sir Henry, 1823–1898, vol. I

Mitchell, Henry McCormick, 1870–1935, vol. III

Mitchell, Henry Tai, 1877–1944, vol. IV

Mitchell, Henry Thomas, 1870–1946, vol. IV

Mitchell, Sir Herbert Edward, 1861–1936, vol. III

Mitchell, J. Campbell, 1865–1922, vol. II

Mitchell, Very Rev. James, 1830–1911, vol. I

Mitchell, Hon. Sir James, 1866–1951, vol. V

Mitchell, Sir James, 1905–1968, vol. VI

Mitchell, James Alexander, 1849–1905, vol. I

Mitchell, James Leslie, 1901–1935, vol. III

Mitchell, Very Rev. James Robert Mitford, 1843–1914, vol. I

Mitchell, John, 1860–1923, vol. II

Mitchell, Sir John, *died* 1934, vol. III

Mitchell, John Ames, 1845–1918, vol. II

Mitchell, John David Bawden, 1917–1980, vol. VII

Mitchell, Lt-Col John Douglas, 1881–1955, vol. V

Mitchell, Sir John Edwin, 1865–1931, vol. III

Mitchell, John Malcolm, 1879–1940, vol. III

Mitchell, Rev. John Thomas, *died* 1947, vol. IV

Mitchell, Rt Rev. Joseph, 1859–1931, vol. III

Mitchell, Sir Kenneth Grant, 1885–1966, vol. VI

Mitchell, Margaret; *see* Marsh, Margaret Munnerlyn Mitchell.

Mitchell, Sir Mark Ledingham, 1902–1977, vol. VII

Mitchell, Sir Miles Ewart, 1875–1955, vol. V

Mitchell, Norman Frederick, 1900–1972, vol. VII

Mitchell, Oliver Worden, 1898–1963, vol. VI

Mitchell, Sir Peter Chalmers, 1864–1945, vol. IV

Mitchell, Maj.-Gen. Sir Philip Euen, 1890–1964, vol. VI

Mitchell, Philip George Myine, 1875–1954, vol. V

Mitchell, Richard Arthur Henry, 1843–1905, vol. I

Mitchell, Major Robert, 1855–1933, vol. III

Mitchell, Major Robert, 1873–1939, vol. III

Mitchell, Very Rev. Robert Andrew, *died* 1949, vol. IV

Mitchell, Robert Macgregor; *see* Macgregor Mitchell, Hon. Lord.

Mitchell, Robert William Span, 1840–1909, vol. I

Mitchell, Silas Weir, 1829–1914, vol. I

Mitchell, Stephen, 1884–1951, vol. V

Mitchell, Sir Thomas, 1844–1919, vol. II

Mitchell, Col Thomas, 1839–1921, vol. II

Mitchell, Sir Thomas, 1869–1959, vol. V

Mitchell, Col Thomas John, 1882–1966, vol. VI

Mitchell, Thomas Walker, 1869–1944, vol. IV

Mitchell, Victor Evelyn, 1865–1932, vol. III

Mitchell, Col Wilfrid James, 1871–1953, vol. V

Mitchell, William, 1838–1914, vol. I

Mitchell, William, *died* 1937, vol. III
Mitchell, Sir William, 1861–1962, vol. VI
Mitchell, Captain William Edward Clifton, *born* 1875, vol. III
Mitchell, Sir William Foot, 1859–1947, vol. IV
Mitchell, Air Chief Marshal Sir William Gore Sutherland, 1888–1944, vol. IV
Mitchell, William H., 1853–1929, vol. III
Mitchell, Sir William Lane, 1861–1940, vol. III
Mitchell, Sir William Wilson, 1840–1915, vol. I (A)
Mitchell, Yvonne, *died* 1979, vol. VII
Mitchell-Cotts, Sir Campbell; *see* Cotts, Sir W. C. M.
Mitchell-Gill, Andrew John; *see* Gill.
Mitchell-Hedges, Frederick Albert, 1882–1959, vol. V
Mitchell-Heggs, Gordon Barrett, 1904–1975, vol. VII
Mitchell-Innes, Alfred, 1864–1950, vol. IV
Mitchell-Innes, Captain Cecil, 1866–1949, vol. IV
Mitchell-Innes, Edward Alfred, 1863–1932, vol. III
Mitchell-Innes, Rev. Reginald John Simpson, 1848–1930, vol. III
Mitchell-Thomson, Sir Mitchell, 1st Bt, 1846–1918, vol. II
Mitchelson, Sir Archibald, 1st Bt, 1878–1945, vol. IV
Mitchelson, Hon. Sir Edwin, 1846–1934, vol. III
Mitcheson, Sir George Gibson, 1883–1955, vol. V
Mitcheson, James Cecil, 1898–1979, vol. VII
Mitcheson, John Moncaster Ley, 1893–1966, vol. VI
Mitchiner, Philip Henry, 1888–1952, vol. V
Mitchinson, Rt Rev. John, 1833–1918, vol. II
Mitchison, Baron (Life Peer); Gilbert Richard Mitchison, 1890–1970, vol. VI
Mitchison, Rev. Richard Stovin, 1850–1936, vol. III
Mitford, Bertram, *died* 1914, vol. I
Mitford, Maj.-Gen. Bertram Reveley, 1863–1936, vol. III
Mitford, Hon. Clement Bertram Ogilvy F.; *see* Freeman-Mitford.
Mitford, Nancy, (Hon. Mrs Peter Rodd), 1904–1973, vol. VII
Mitford, Maj.-Gen. Reginald C. W. Reveley, 1839–1925, vol. II
Mitford, Captain Robert Osbaldeston-, 1846–1924, vol. II
Mitford, Robert Sidney, 1849–1931, vol. III
Mitford, Terence Bruce, 1905–1978, vol. VII
Mitford, Major Hon. Thomas David Freeman-, 1909–1945, vol. IV
Mitford, Col William Kenyon, 1857–1943, vol. IV
Mitford-Barberton, Ivan Graham; *see* Barberton.
Mitha, Hon. Sardar Sir Suleman Cassum, vol. VII
Mitra, Sir Bhupendra Nath, 1875–1937, vol. III
Mitra, Sir Dhirendra Nath, 1891–1966, vol. VI
Mitra, S. M., 1856–1925, vol. II
Mitra, Sisir Kumar, 1890–1963, vol. VI
Mitrany, David, 1888–1975, vol. VII
Mitropoulos, Dimitri, 1896–1960, vol. V
Mittag-Leffler, Gösta, 1846–1927, vol. II
Mittelholzer, Edgar Austin, 1909–1965, vol. VI

Mitter, Rt Hon. Sir Binod Chandra, 1872–1930, vol. III
Mitter, Sir Brojendra Lal, 1875–1950, vol. IV
Mitter, Sir Provash Chandra, 1875–1934, vol. III
Mitton, Geraldine Edith, (Lady Scott), *died* 1955, vol. V
Mitton, Col George J.; *see* Jones Mitton.
Mitton, H. Eustace, 1871–1946, vol. IV
Mitton, Rev. Henry Arthur, 1837–1918, vol. II
Mitton, Rev. Welbury Theodore, 1862–1933, vol. III
Mivart, Frederick St George, *died* 1925, vol. II
Mivart, St George, 1827–1900, vol. I
Mobbs, Sir (Arthur) Noel, 1880–1959, vol. V
Mobbs, Sir Noel; *see* Mobbs, Sir A. N.
Moberly, Brig. Archibald Henry, 1879–1960, vol. V
Moberly, Sir Arthur Norman, 1873–1934, vol. III
Moberly, Lt-Gen. Sir Bertrand Richard, 1877–1963, vol. III
Moberly, Charles Noel, 1880–1969, vol. VI
Moberly, Charlotte Anne Elizabeth, 1846–1937, vol. III
Moberly, Brig.-Gen. Frederick James, 1867–1952, vol. V
Moberly, Brig. Hugh Stephenson, 1873–1947, vol. IV
Moberly, Rev. Robert Campbell, 1845–1903, vol. I
Moberly, Rt Rev. Robert Hamilton, 1884–1978, vol. VII
Moberly, Sir Walter Hamilton, 1881–1974, vcl. VII
Moberly, Winifred Horsbrugh, 1875–1928, vol. II
Mockett, Sir Vere, 1885–1977, vol. VII
Mockford, Julian, 1898–1950, vol. IV
Mockler, Col Percy Rice, 1860–1927, vol. II
Mockler-Ferryman, Lt-Col Augustus Ferryman, 1856–1930, vol. III
Mockler-Ferryman, Col Eric Edward, 1896–1978, vol. VII
Modi, Sir Jivanji Jamshedji, 1854–1933, vol. III
Modjeska-Chlapowska, Helena, 1844–1909, vol. I
Mody, Sir Homi, 1881–1969, vol. VI
Moe, Henry Allen, 1894–1975, vol. VII
Moens, Gen. Sir Arthur William Hamilton May, 1879–1939, vol. III
Moens, Hon. Lt-Col Seaburne Godfrey Arthur May, 1876–1956, vol. V
Moeran, Ernest John, 1894–1950, vol. IV
Moffat, Alfred, 1868–1950, vol. IV
Moffat, David H., 1839–1911, vol. I (A)
Moffat, Graham, 1866–1951, vol. V
Moffat, Hon. Howard Unwin, 1869–1951, vol. V
Moffat, John, 1879–1966, vol. VI (AII), vol. VII
Moffat, John, 1891–1973, vol. VII
Moffat, Rev. John Smith, 1835–1918, vol. II
Moffat, Rennie John, 1891–1978, vol. VII
Moffat, Robert Unwin, 1866–1947, vol. IV
Moffatt, Alexander, 1863–1921, vol. II
Moffatt, Rev. James, 1870–1944, vol. IV
Moffatt, Paul McGregor, *died* 1963, vol. VI
Moffet, Stanley Ormerod, 1886–1960, vol. V
Moffett, John Perry, 1909–1972, vol. VII
Moffett, Sir Thomas William, *died* 1908, vol. I
Mogg, Lt-Col Graham Beauchamp Coxeter R.; *see* Rees-Mogg.

Mogg, Rev. Henry Herbert, 1850–1929, vol. III
Mogg, Rev. Canon Joseph William, 1882–1970, vol. VI (AII)
Mogg, Engr Rear-Adm. William George, 1860–1929, vol. III
Moggridge, Adm. Arthur Yerbury, 1858–1946, vol. IV
Moggridge, Ernest Grant, 1863–1925, vol. II
Moggridge, Lt-Col Harry Weston, 1879–1960, vol. V
Mohamed, Hon. Sir Abdool Razack, 1906–1978, vol. VII
Mohamed Akbar Khan, Lt-Col Nawab Sir, 1885–1952, vol. V
Mohan Singh, Sardar Bahadur Sardar, 1897–1961, vol. VI
Mohsin-ul-Mulk, Nawab, 1837–1907, vol. I
Moinet, Rev. Charles, 1842–1913, vol. I
Moir, Brig.-Gen. Alan James Gordon, 1873–1940, vol. III
Moir, Captain Sir Arrol, 2nd Bt, 1894–1957, vol. V
Moir, Byres, 1853–1928, vol. II
Moir, Vice-Adm. Dashwood Fowler, 1880–1942, vol. IV
Moir, Sir Ernest William, 1st Bt, 1862–1933, vol. III
Moir, Rt Rev. Francis Oag H.; see Hulme-Moir.
Moir, James, died 1915, vol. I (A)
Moir, Col James Philip, 1872–1934, vol. III
Moir, James Reid, 1879–1944, vol. IV
Moir, John Chassar, 1900–1977, vol. VII
Moir, John William, died 1940, vol. III
Moir, Percival John, 1893–1980, vol. VII
Moir, Sir Thomas Eyebron, 1874–1932, vol. III
Moir, Rear-Adm. William Mitchell, 1873–1942, vol. IV
Moira, Gerald, died 1959, vol. V
Moiseiwitsch, Benno, 1890–1963, vol. VI
Mok, Rt Rev. Shau Tsang, 1866–1943, vol. IV
Molamure, Sir (Alexander) Francis, 1886–1951, vol. V
Molamure, Sir Francis; see Molamure, Sir A. F.
Mold, Brig. Gilbert Leslie, 1893–1963, vol. VI
Mole, Sir Charles Johns, 1886–1962, vol. VI
Mole, Brig. Gerard Herbert Leo, 1897–1944, vol. IV
Mole, Harold Frederic, 1866–1917, vol. II
Moles, Rt Hon. Thomas, 1871–1937, vol. III
Molesworth, 8th Viscount, 1829–1906, vol. I
Molesworth, 9th Viscount, 1867–1947, vol. IV
Molesworth, 10th Viscount, 1869–1961, vol. VI
Molesworth, Brig. Alec Lindsay Mortimer, 1881–1939, vol. III
Molesworth, Col Arthur Ludovic, 1860–1939, vol. III
Molesworth, Major Edward Algernon, died 1939, vol. III
Molesworth, Brig.-Gen. Edward Hogarth, 1854–1943, vol. IV
Molesworth, Lt-Gen. George Noble, 1890–1968, vol. VI
Molesworth, Sir Guilford Lindsey, 1828–1925, vol. II
Molesworth, Hender Delves, 1907–1978, vol. VII

Molesworth, Col Herbert Ellicombe, 1872–1941, vol. IV
Molesworth, Hickman, 1842–1907, vol. I
Molesworth, Hugh Wilson, 1870–1959, vol. V
Molesworth, Mrs Mary Louisa, 1839–1921, vol. II
Molesworth, Col Richard Pigot, 1868–1946, vol. IV
Molesworth, Col William, 1865–1951, vol. V
Molesworth-St Aubyn, Sir Hugh, 13th Bt, 1865–1942, vol. IV
Molesworth-St Aubyn, Rev. Sir St A. Hender, 12th Bt, 1833–1913, vol. I
Molin, C. Hjalmar V., 1868–1954, vol. V
Moline, Rev. Robert Percy, died 1935, vol. III
Moline, Most Rev. Robert William Haines, 1889–1979, vol. VII
Molineux, Rev. Arthur Ellison, died 1919, vol. II
Molineux, Rev. Charles Hurlock, died 1927, vol. II
Moll, Rev. William Edmund, 1856–1932, vol. III
Mollan, Lt-Col William Campbell, 1820–1910, vol. I
Mollett, Sir John, 1892–1952, vol. V
Mollison, James Allan, 1905–1959, vol. V
Mollison, James W., died 1927, vol. II
Mollison, William Loudon, 1851–1929, vol. III
Mollison, William Mayhew, 1878–1967, vol. VI
Molloy, Bernard Charles, 1842–1916, vol. II
Molloy, Col Edward, died 1905, vol. I
Molloy, Rt Rev. Mgr Gerald, 1834–1906, vol. I
Molloy, Ven. John, died 1915, vol. I
Molloy, Joseph Fitzgerald, 1858–1908, vol. I
Molloy, Leonard Greenham Star, died 1937, vol. III
Molohan, Michael John Brew, 1906–1980, vol. VII
Moloney, Sir Cornelius Alfred, 1848–1913, vol. I
Moloney, Henry J., 1887–1965, vol. VI
Molony, Rev. Brian Charles, 1892–1963, vol. VI
Molony, Col Charles Mills, 1836–1901, vol. I
Molony, Edmund Alexander, 1866–1942, vol. IV
Molony, Rev. Henry William Eliott, died 1919, vol. II
Molony, Rt Rev. Herbert James, 1865–1939, vol. III
Molony, Sir Hugh Francis, 2nd Bt, 1900–1976, vol. VII
Molony, Sir Joseph Thomas, 1907–1978, vol. VII
Molony, Rt Hon. Sir Thomas Francis, 1st Bt, 1865–1949, vol. IV
Molson, Lt-Col Herbert, 1875–1938, vol. III
Molson, Major John Elsdale, 1863–1925, vol. II
Molteno, Hon. Sir James Tennant, 1865–1936, vol. III
Molteno, Percy Alport, 1861–1937, vol. III
Molteno, Vice-Adm. Vincent Barkly, 1872–1952, vol. V
Molyneux, Major Edward Mary Joseph, 1866–1913, vol. I
Molyneux, Sir Ernest, 10th Bt, 1865–1940, vol. III
Molyneux, Rt Rev. Frederick Merivale, 1885–1948, vol. IV
Molyneux, Maj-Gen. George Hand M.; see More-Molyneux.
Molyneux, Rev. Sir John Charles, 9th Bt, 1843–1928, vol. II
Molyneux, Sir John Harry, 1882–1968, vol. VI
Molyneux, Sir Percy, 1870–1937, vol. III

Molyneux, Major Philip Lucas, 1893–1939, vol. III

Molyneux, Major Hon. Sir Richard F., 1873–1954, vol. V

Molyneux, Adm. Sir Robert Henry M.; see More-Molyneux.

Molyneux-Seel, Major Edward, 1862–1939, vol. III

Momber, Captain Edward Marie Felix, died 1917, vol. II

Momerie, Rev. Alfred Williams, 1848–1900, vol. I

Momin, Khan Bahadur Mohammad Abdul, 1876–1946, vol. IV

Mommsen, Theodor, 1817–1903, vol. I

Monaco, Prince of, Albert Honoré Charles, 1848–1922, vol. II

Monahan, Rt Rev. Alfred Edwin, 1877–1945, vol. IV

Monahan, George Henry, 1873–1944, vol. IV

Monahan, Most Rev. Peter Joseph, 1882–1947, vol. IV

Monahan, Hon. Sir Robert Vincent, 1898–1975, vol. VII

Monash, Gen. Sir John, 1865–1931, vol. III

Moncheur, Ludovic, 2nd Baron, 1857–1940, vol. III

Monck, 5th Viscount, 1849–1927, vol. II

Monck, Hon. Charles Henry Stanley, 1876–1914, vol. I

Monck, Sir John Berkeley, 1883–1964, vol VI

Monck, Nugent; see Monck, W. N. B.

Monck, Lt-Gen. Hon. Richard, 1829–1904, vol. V

Monck, (Walter) Nugent (Bligh), 1878–1958, vol. I

Monckton of Brenchley, 1st Viscount, 1891–1965, vol. VI

Monckton, Arthur, 1845–1917, vol. II

Monckton, Edward Philip, 1840–1916, vol. II

Monckton, Francis, 1844–1926, vol. II

Monckton, Col Hon. Horace Manners, 1824–1904, vol. I

Monckton, Sir John Braddick, 1832–1902, vol. I

Monckton, Lionel, 1862–1924, vol. II

Monckton, Reginald Francis Percy, 1896–1975, vol. VII

Moncreiff, 2nd Baron, 1840–1909, vol. I

Moncreiff, 3rd Baron, 1843–1913, vol. I

Moncreiff, 4th Baron, 1872–1942, vol. IV

Moncreiff, Hon. Frederick Charles, 1847–1929, vol. III

Moncreiff, Hon. James William, 1845–1920, vol. II

Moncreiffe of that Ilk, Sir David Gerald, 10th Bt, 1922–1957, vol. V

Moncreiffe, Comdr Sir John Robert Guy, 9th Bt, 1884–1934, vol. III

Moncreiffe, Sir Robert Drummond, 8th Bt, 1856–1931, vol. III

Moncrief, Rev. Archibald, 1845–1938, vol. III

Moncrieff, Rt. Hon. Lord; Alexander Moncrieff, died 1949, vol. IV

Moncrieff, Sir Alan Aird, 1901–1971, vol. VII

Moncrieff, Adm. Sir Alan Kenneth S.; see Scott-Moncrieff.

Moncrieff, Col Sir Alexander, 1829–1906, vol. I

Moncrieff, Rt Hon. Alexander; see Moncrieff, Rt Hon. Lord

Moncrieff, Alexander Bain, 1845–1928, vol. II

Moncrieff, Charles Kenneth S.; see Scott Moncrieff.

Moncrieff, Sir Colin Campbell S.; see Scott-Moncrieff.

Moncrieff, Lt-Gen. George Hay, 1836–1918, vol. II

Moncrieff, Maj.-Gen. Sir George Kenneth S.; see Scott-Moncrieff.

Moncrieff, William George S.; see Scott-Moncrieff.

Moncrieff, Joanna Constance S.; see Scott-Moncrieff.

Moncrieff, Lt-Col John Mitchell, 1865–1931, vol. III

Moncrieff, Robert Hope, 1846–1927, vol. II

Moncur, George, 1868–1946, vol. IV

Mond, Ludwig, 1839–1909, vol. I

Mond, Sir Robert Ludwig, 1867–1938, vol. III

Mondor, Henri Jean, 1885–1962, vol. VI

Monet, Claude, 1840–1926, vol. II

Monet, Dominique, 1865–1923, vol. II

Moneta, Ernesto Teodoro, 1833–1918, vol. II

Money, Sir Alonzo, died 1900, vol. I

Money, Maj.-Gen. Sir Arthur Wigram, 1866–1951, vol. V

Money, Vice-Adm. Brien Michael, 1880–1939, vol. III

Money, Col Charles Gilbert Colvin, 1852–1928, vol. II

Money, Brig.-Gen. Ernest Douglas, 1866–1952, vol. V

Money, Rev. Canon Frank Reginald, 1905–1968, vol. VI

Money, Brig.-Gen. Gordon Lorn Campbell, 1848–1929, vol. III

Money, Brig. Harold Douglas Kyrie, 1896–1965, vol. VI

Money, Maj.-Gen. Herbert Cecil, 1857–1939, vol. III

Money, Sir Leo (George) Chiozza, 1870–1944, vol. IV

Money, Brig.-Gen. Noel Ernest, 1867–1941, vol. IV

Money, Col Robert Cotton, 1861–1954, vol. V

Money, Walter, 1836–1926, vol. II

Money, William James, died 1910, vol. I

Money-Kyrle, Ven. Rowland Tracy Ashe, died 1928, vol. II

Moneypenny, Frederick William, 1859–1912, vol. I

Moneypenny, Sir Frederick William, 1859–1932, vol. III

Monie, Rev. Peter William, 1877–1946, vol. IV

Monier-Williams, Clarence Faithfull, 1893–1974, vol. VII

Monier-Williams, Major Craufurd Victor, 1888–1922, vol. II

Monier-Williams, Sir Monier, 1819–1899, vol. I

Monier-Williams, Monier Faithfull, 1849–1928, vol. II

Monier-Williams, Montagu Sneade Faithfull, 1860–1931, vol. III

Moniz, Egas Antonio Caetano de Abren Freire, 1874–1955, vol. V

Monk, Albert Ernest, 1900–1975, vol. VII

Monk, Beatrice Marsh; see Monk, M. B. M.

Monk, Charles James, 1824–1900, vol. I

Monk, Hon. Frederick Debartzch, 1856–1914, vol. I

473

Monk, Mark James, 1858–1929, vol. III
Monk, (Mary) Beatrice Marsh, *died* 1962, vol. VI
Monk Bretton, 1st Baron, 1825–1897, vol. I
Monk Bretton, 2nd Baron, 1869–1933, vol. III
Monkhouse, Allan Noble, 1858–1936, vol. III
Monkhouse, Sir Edward Bertram, 1890–1959, vol. V
Monkhouse, Francis John, 1914–1975, vol. VII
Monkhouse, John Parry, 1899–1968, vol. VI
Monkhouse, Brig.-Gen. William Percival, 1871–1935, vol. III
Monks, Air Vice-Marshal Alfred Thomas, 1908–1972, vol. VII
Monkswell, 2nd Baron, 1845–1909, vol. I
Monkswell, 3rd Baron, 1875–1964, vol. VI
Monnet, Jean, 1888–1979, vol. VII
Mönnig, Hermann Otto, 1897–1978, vol. VII
Monnington, Sir Thomas; *see* Monnington, Sir W. T.
Monnington, Rev. Thomas Pateshall, *died* 1937, vol. III
Monnington, Sir (Walter) Thomas, 1902–1976, vol. VII
Monod, Gustave Jean Philippe, 1878–1932, vol. III
Monod, Jacques Lucien, 1910–1976, vol. VII
Monod, Théodore, 1836–1921, vol. II
Monod, Wilfred, 1867–1943, vol. IV
Monro, Alexander, 1847–1916, vol. II
Monro, Alexander, 1890–1953, vol. V
Monro, Alexander William, 1875–1960, vol. V
Monro, Gen. Sir Charles Carmichael, 1st Bt, 1860–1929, vol. III
Monro, David Binning, 1836–1905, vol. I
Monro, Maj.-Gen. David Carmichael, 1886–1960, vol. V, vol. VI
Monro, Edwin George, 1875–1954, vol. V
Monro, George, 1876–1951, vol. V
Monro, Harold Edward, 1879–1932, vol. III
Monro, Sir Horace Cecil, 1861–1949, vol. IV
Monro, James, 1838–1920, vol. II
Monro, Hon. Mary Caroline, (Hon. Lady Monro), *died* 1972, vol. VII
Monro, Col Seymour Charles Hale, 1856–1906, vol. I
Monro, Thomas Kirkpatrick, 1865–1958, vol. V
Monroe, Rev. Horace Granville, 1872–1933, vol. III
Monroe, Vice-Adm. Hubert Seeds, 1877–1966, vol. VI
Monroe, James Harvey, 1884–1944, vol. IV
Monroe, Rt Hon. John, 1839–1899, vol. I
Monroe, Paul, 1869–1947, vol. IV
Monroe, Hon. Walter S., 1871–1952, vol. V
Monroe, Will S., 1863–1939, vol. III (A), vol. IV
Monsarrat, Keith Waldegrave, 1872–1968, vol. VI
Monsarrat, Nicholas John Turney, 1910–1979, vol. VII
Monsell, 1st Viscount, *died* 1969, vol. VI
Monsey, Yvonne, (Mrs Derek Monsey); *see* Mitchell, Yvonne.
Monslow, Baron (Life Peer); Walter Monslow, *died* 1966, vol. VI
Monson, 8th Baron, 1830–1900, vol. I
Monson, 9th Baron, 1868–1940, vol. III
Monson, 10th Baron, 1907–1958, vol. V

Monson, Rt Hon. Sir Edmund John, 1st Bt, 1834–1909, vol. I
Monson, Sir Edmund St John Debonnaire John, 3rd Bt, 1883–1969, vol. VI
Monson, Sir George Louis Esmé John, 4th Bt, 1888–1969, vol. VI
Monson, Sir Maxwell William Edmund John, 2nd Bt, 1882–1936, vol. III
Montagu of Beaulieu, 1st Baron, 1832–1905, vol. I
Montagu of Beaulieu, 2nd Baron, 1866–1929, vol. III
Montagu, Ainsley Marshall Rendall, 1891–1977, vol. VII
Montagu, Lord Charles William Augustus, 1860–1939, vol. III
Montagu, Col Edward, 1861–1941, vol. IV
Montagu, Rt Hon. Edwin Samuel, 1879–1924, vol. II
Montagu, Sir Ernest William Sanders, 1862–1952, vol. V
Montagu, Captain Frederick James Osbaldeston, 1878–1957, vol. V
Montagu, Gen. Sir Horace William, 1823–1916, vol. II
Montagu, James Drogo, *died* 1958, vol. V
Montagu, Hon. Lilian Helen, 1873–1963, vol. VI
Montagu, Rt Hon. Lord Robert, 1825–1902, vol. I
Montagu, Hon. Robert Henry D. S.; *see* Douglas-Scott-Montagu.
Montagu, Rear-Adm. Hon. Victor Alexander, 1841–1915, vol. I
Montagu-Douglas-Scott, Lord Charles Thomas; *see* Scott.
Montagu-Douglas-Scott, Lt-Col Lord Francis George; *see* Scott.
Montagu-Douglas-Scott, Lord George William; *see* Scott.
Montagu-Douglas-Scott, Col Lord Henry Francis; *see* Scott.
Montagu-Douglas-Scott, Lord Herbert Andrew; *see* Scott.
Montagu-Douglas-Scott, Lt-Col Lord William Walter; *see* Scott.
Montagu-Pollock, Sir Montagu Frederick; *see* Pollock.
Montagu-Stuart-Wortley, Maj.-Gen. Hon. Edward James; *see* Stuart-Wortley.
Montagu-Stuart-Wortley, Lt-Gen. Hon. Sir Richard; *see* Stuart-Wortley.
Montague, Charles Edward, 1867–1928, vol. II
Montague, Francis Charles, 1858–1935, vol. III
Montague, Major Furry Ferguson, 1884–1950, vol. IV (A)
Montague, Lt-Gen. Hon. Percival John, 1882–1966, vol. VI
Montague, Maj.-Gen. William Edward, 1838–1906, vol. I
Montague-Barlow, Rt Hon. Sir Anderson; *see* Montague-Barlow, Rt Hon. Sir C. A.
Montague-Barlow, Rt Hon. Sir (Clement) Anderson, 1868–1951, vol. V
Montalba, Clara, *died* 1929, vol. III
Montanaro, Col Arthur Forbes, 1862–1914, vol. I

Montanaro, Brig. Gerald Charles Stokes, 1916–1979, vol. VII

Monteagle of Brandon, 2nd Baron, 1849–1926, vol. II

Monteagle of Brandon, 3rd Baron, 1883–1934, vol. III

Monteagle of Brandon, 4th Baron, 1852–1937, vol. III

Monteagle of Brandon, 5th Baron, 1887–1946, vol. IV

Monteath, Alexander McLaurin, 1859–1933, vol. III

Monteath, Sir David Taylor, 1887–1961, vol. VI

Monteath, Harry Henderson, 1885–1962, vol. VI

Monteath, Sir James, 1847–1929, vol. III

Monteath, John, 1878–1955, vol. V

Monteath, Sir Ruthven Grey, 1864–1949, vol. IV

Montefiore, Claude Joseph Goldsmid-, 1858–1938, vol. III

Montefiore, Edmund Sebag-, 1869–1929, vol. III

Montefiore, Sir Francis Abraham, 1st Bt, 1860–1935, vol. III

Montefiore, Sir Joseph Sebag-, 1822–1903, vol. I

Monteith, Col John, 1852–1928, vol. II

Monteith, Jos. D., 1865–1934, vol. III

Monteith, Nelson, 1862–1949, vol. IV

Montessori, Maria, 1870–1952, vol. V

Monteux, Pierre, 1875–1964, vol. VI

Montford, Paul Raphael, 1868–1938, vol. III

Montgomerie, Lt-Col Alexander, 1882–1932, vol. III

Montgomerie, Alexander, 1879–1958, vol. V

Montgomerie, Harvey Hugh, 1888–1965, vol. VI

Montgomerie, James, 1873–1962, vol. VI

Montgomerie, Adm. John Eglinton, 1825–1902, vol. I

Montgomerie, Rear-Adm. Robert Archibald James, 1855–1908, vol. I

Montgomerie, Samuel Hynman, 1856–1915, vol. I

Montgomery of Alamein, 1st Viscount, 1887–1976, vol. VII

Montgomery, Sir Alexander, 5th Bt (cr 1808), 1859–1939, vol. III

Mongomery, Sir Basil Purvis-Russell Hamilton-, 8th Bt (cr 1801), 1884–1964, vol. VI

Montgomery, Sir Basil Templer Graham-, 5th Bt (cr 1801), 1852–1928, vol. II

Montgomery, Bo Gabriel de, Count, 1894–1969, vol. VI

Montgomery, Sir (Charles) Hubert, 1876–1942, vol. IV

Montgomery, Rev. Sir Charles Percy Graham-, 6th Bt (cr 1801), 1855–1930, vol. III

Montgomery, Brig. Ernest John, 1901–1972, vol. VII

Montgomery, Florence, 1843–1923, vol. II

Montgomery, Sir Frank Percival, 1892–1972, vol. VII

Montgomery, George Allison, 1898–1969, vol. VI

Montgomery, George H. A., 1874–1951, vol. V

Montgomery, Sir Graham Graham, 3rd Bt (cr 1801), 1823–1901, vol. I

Montgomery, Harold Robert, 1884–1958, vol. V

Montgomery, Henry Greville, 1864–1951, vol. V

Montgomery, Rt Rev. Henry Hutchinson, 1847–1932, vol. III

Montgomery, Sir Henry James Purvis-Russell-Hamilton, 7th Bt (cr 1801), 1859–1947, vol. IV

Montgomery, Lt-Col Henry Keith Purvis-Russell-, 1896–1954, vol. V

Montgomery, Sir Hubert; see Montgomery, Sir C. H.

Montgomery, Sir Hugh Conyngham Gaston, 4th Bt (cr 1808), 1847–1915, vol. I (A)

Montgomery, Rt Hon. Hugh de Fellenberg, died 1924, vol. II

Montgomery, Col Hugh Frederick L.; see Lyons-Montgomery.

Montgomery, Maj.-Gen. Hugh Maude de Fellenberg, 1870–1954, vol. V

Montgomery, Ian, 1913–1971, vol. VII

Montgomery, Col James Alexander Lawrence, 1849–1940, vol. III

Montgomery, Sir James Graham, 4th Bt (cr 1801), 1850–1902, vol. I

Montgomery, John, 1858–1937, vol. III

Montgomery, Col John Willoughby Verner, 1867–1968, vol. VI

Montgomery, K. L.; see Montgomery, Kathleen, and Montgomery, Letitia.

Montgomery, Kathleen, died 1960, vol. V

Montgomery, L. M.; see Macdonald, Mrs L. M.

Montgomery, Leslie Alexander; see Doyle, Lynn.

Montgomery, Letitia, died 1930, vol. III

Montgomery, Sir Matthew Walker, 1859–1933, vol. III

Montgomery, Maj.-Gen. Robert Arthur, 1848–1931, vol. III

Montgomery, Maj.-Gen. Sir Robert Arundel Kerr, 1862–1951, vol. V

Montgomery, Robert Ernest, 1878–1962, vol. VI

Montgomery, Robert Eustace, 1880–1932, vol. III

Montgomery, Robert Mortimer, died 1948, vol. IV

Montgomery, Walter Basil Graham, 1881–1928, vol. II

Montgomery, Major William Alexander, died 1932, vol. III

Montgomery, William Barr, 1865–1936, vol. III

Montgomery, Maj.-Gen. William Edward, 1847–1927, vol. II

Montgomery, William Hugh, 1866–1958, vol. V

Montgomery Campbell, Rt Rev. and Rt Hon. Henry Colville, 1887–1970, vol. VI

Montgomery-Campbell, Brig.-Gen. Herbert, 1861–1937, vol. III

Montgomery-Cuninghame, Sir Andrew; see Cuninghame, Sir W. A. M. M. O. M.

Montgomery-Cuninghame, Sir Thomas Andrew Alexander; see Cuninghame.

Montgomery-Cuninghame, Sir William James; see Cuninghame.

Montgomery-Massingberd, Field Marshal Sir Archibald Armar, 1871–1947, vol. IV

Montgomery-Moore, Gen. Sir Alexander George, 1833–1919, vol. II

Montgomery-Smith, Col Edwin Charles, 1869–1963, vol. VI

Montgomery White, Cyril; see White.

Montgorge, Alexis Jean; *see* Gabin, J.
Montherlant, Henry de, 1896–1972, vol. VII
Montini, Giovanni Battista; *see* Paul VI.
Montizambert, Frederick, 1843–1929, vol. III
Montresor, Miss F. F., *died* 1934, vol. III
Montrose, 5th Duke of, 1852–1925, vol. II
Montrose, 6th Duke of, 1878–1954, vol. V
Monty, Hon. Rodolphe, 1874–1928, vol. II
Moodie, Alexander Reid, 1886–1968, vol. VI
Moodie, Donald, 1892–1963, vol. VI
Moodie, William, 1886–1960, vol. V
Moody, Lt-Col Arthur Hatfield, 1875–1926, vol. II
Moody, Arthur Seymour, 1891–1976, vol. VII
Moody, Charles Harry, 1874–1965, vol. VI
Moody, Adm. Sir Clement, 1891–1960, vol. V
Moody, Madame Fanny, (Mrs Southcote Mansergh), 1866–1945, vol. IV
Moody, Sir George Edward James, 1859–1939, vol. III
Moody, Sir James Matthew, *died* 1915, vol. I
Moody, John C., 1884–1962, vol. VI
Moody, Maj.-Gen. Sir John Macdonald, 1839–1921, vol. II
Moody, Col Richard Stanley Hawks, 1854–1930, vol. III
Moody, Robert Ley, 1909–1970, vol. VI
Moody, Sydney, 1889–1979, vol. VII
Moody, William H., 1853–1917, vol. II
Moody-Stuart, Sir Alexander, 1899–1971, vol. VII
Mookerjee, Sir Asutosh, 1864–1924, vol. II
Mookerjee, Sir Rajendra Nath, 1854–1936, vol. III
Mookerji, Radha Kumud, 1884–1963, vol. VI
Moon, Col Alfred, 1861–1943, vol. IV
Moon, Arthur, 1882–1961, vol. VI
Moon, Sir (Arthur) Wilfred Graham-, 4th Bt (*cr* 1855), 1905–1954, vol. V
Moon, Sir Cecil Ernest, 2nd Bt (*cr* 1887), 1867–1951, vol. V
Moon, Rev. Sir Edward Graham, 2nd Bt (*cr* 1855), 1825–1904, vol. I
Moon, Edward Robert Pacy, 1858–1949, vol. IV
Moon, Sir Ernest Robert, 1854–1930, vol. III
Moon, Sir Francis Sidney Graham, 3rd Bt (*cr* 1855), 1855–1911, vol. I
Moon, George Washington, 1823–1909, vol. I
Moon, Henry E., *died* 1920, vol. II
Moon, Sir John Arthur, 4th Bt (*cr* 1887), 1905–1979, vol. VII
Moon, Sir Richard, 1st Bt (*cr* 1887), 1815–1899, vol. I
Moon, Sir Richard, 3rd Bt (*cr* 1887), 1901–1961, vol. VI
Moon, Robert Oswald, 1865–1953, vol. V
Moon, Walter, 1871–1954, vol. V
Moon, Sir Wilfred Graham-; *see* Moon, Sir A. W. G.
Mooney, His Eminence Cardinal Edward, 1882–1958, vol. V
Mooney, George Stuart, 1900–1965, vol. VI (AII)
Mooney, Herbert C., *died* 1948, vol. IV
Mooney, Herbert Francis, 1897–1964, vol. VI
Mooney, Sir John, 1874–1934, vol. III
Moor, Rev. Edward, 1880–1953, vol. V

Moor, Rt Hon. Sir Frederick Robert, 1853–1927, vol. II
Moor, George Raymond Dallas, *died* 1918, vol. II
Moor, Sir Ralph Denham Rayment. 1860–1909, vol. I
Moor, Samuel Albert, *died* 1944, vol. IV
Moorcroft, William, 1872–1945, vol. IV
Moore, Sir Alan Hilary, 2nd Bt (*cr* 1919), 1882–1959, vol. V
Moore, Ven. Alexander Duff, 1872–1942, vol. IV
Moore, Gen. Sir Alexander George M.; *see* Montgomery-Moore.
Moore, Rev. Alfred Edgar, *died* 1924, vol. II
Moore, Captain Alldin Usborne, 1878–1942, vol. IV
Moore, Adm. Sir Archibald Gordon Henry Wilson, 1862–1934, vol. III
Moore, Archie Murrell Acheson, 1904–1979, vol. VII
Moore, Arthur Collin, 1866–1952, vol. V
Moore, Ven. Arthur Crompton, *died* 1954, vol. V
Moore, Arthur Edward, 1872–1951, vol. V
Moore, Hon. Arthur Edward, 1876–1963, vol. VI
Moore, Count Arthur John, 1849–1904, vol. I
Moore, Rev. Arthur John, 1853–1919, vol. II
Moore, Maj.-Gen. Arthur Thomas, 1830–1913, vol. I
Moore, Col Arthur Trevelyan, *died* 1948, vol. IV
Moore, Arthur William, 1853–1909, vol. I
Moore, Adm. Sir Arthur William, 1847–1934, vol. III
Moore, Col Athelstan, 1879–1918, vol. II
Moore, Mrs Beatrice Esther, *died* 1953, vol. V
Moore, Benjamin, *died* 1922, vol. II
Moore, Maj.-Gen. Charles Alfred, 1839–1925, vol. II
Moore, Charles Gordon, 1884–1957, vol. V
Moore, Adm. Charles Henry Hodgson, 1858–1920, vol. II
Moore, Col Charles Hesketh Grant, 1868–1942, vol. IV
Moore, Sir Charles James S.; *see* Stevenson-Moore.
Moore, Charles Joseph Henry O'Hara, 1880–1965, vol. VI
Moore, Charles Thomas John, 1827–1900, vol. I
Moore, Clarence L., 1869–1953, vol. V
Moore, Maj.-Gen. Claude Douglas Hamilton, 1875–1928, vol. II
Moore, Rev. Mgr Clement Harington, 1845–1905, vol. I
Moore, Rev. Courtenay, 1840–1922, vol. II
Moore, Rev. Daniel, 1809–1899, vol. I
Moore, Rev. David Keys, 1854–1935, vol. III
Moore, Dorothea Mary, *died* 1933, vol. III
Moore, Rev. Edward, *died* 1916, vol. II
Moore, Rt Rev. Edward Alfred Livingstone, 1870–1944, vol. IV
Moore, Sir Edward Cecil, 1st Bt (*cr* 1923), 1851–1923, vol. II
Moore, Col Edward James, 1862–1925, vol. II
Moore, Ven. Edward Marsham, *died* 1921, vol. II
Moore, Eldon, 1901–1954, vol. V
Moore, Eric Olawolu, 1878–1944, vol. IV

Moore, Eva, (Mrs Henry V. Esmond), *died* 1955, vol. V

Moore, Evelyn, (Mrs Stuart Moore); *see* Underhill, E.

Moore, Col Francis, 1879–1938, vol. III

Moore, Lt-Col Francis Hamilton, 1876–1952, vol. V

Moore, Maj.-Gen. Francis Malcolm, 1897–1974, vol. VII

Moore, Francis William, 1849–1927, vol. II

Moore, Frank Frankfort, 1855–1931, vol. III

Moore, Sir Fred Denby, 1863–1951, vol. V

Moore, Frederick Craven, 1871–1943, vol. IV

Moore, Lt-Col Frederick Grattan, 1877–1955, vol. V

Moore, Sir Frederick William, 1857–1949, vol. IV

Moore, Col George A., 1869–1955, vol. V

Moore, George Arbuthnot, 1857–1923, vol. II

Moore, George Augustus, 1852–1933, vol. III

Moore, Rear-Adm. George Dunbar, 1893–1979, vol. VII

Moore, George Edward, 1873–1958, vol. V

Moore, George Foot, 1851–1931, vol. III

Moore, Lt-Col Sir George Montgomery John, 1844–1911, vol. I

Moore, Grace; *see* Parera, G. M.

Moore, Harold, 1878–1972, vol. VII

Moore, Col Harold Arthur, 1880–1945, vol. IV

Moore, Brig. Harold Edward, 1888–1968, vol. VI

Moore, Sir Harold John de Courcy, 1877–1976, vol. VII

Moore, Sir Harrison; *see* Moore, Sir W. H.

Moore, Harry, 1887–1960, vol. V

Moore, Captain Hartley Russell Gwennap, 1881–1953, vol. V

Moore, Lt-Gen. Sir Henry, 1829–1915, vol. I (A)

Moore, Henry Charles, 1862–1933, vol. III

Moore, Rev. Henry Dodwell, 1838–1919, vol. II

Moore, Henry F., 1887–1954, vol. V

Moore, Henry Ian, 1905–1976, vol. VII

Moore, Henry John, 1872–1950, vol. V

Moore, Rev. Henry Kingsmill, *died* 1943, vol. IV

Moore, Sir Henry Monck-Mason, 1887–1964, vol. VI

Moore, Adm. Sir Henry Ruthven, 1886–1978, vol. VII

Moore, Rev. Herbert Augustine, *died* 1937, vol. III

Moore, Col Herbert Tregosse Gwennap, 1875–1958, vol. V

Moore, James Lennox Irwin, 1866–1953, vol. V

Moore, James M., 1871–1932, vol. III

Moore, Jocelyn A. M., (Mrs David Symon), 1904–1979, vol. VII

Moore, Maj.-Gen. Sir John, 1864–1940, vol. III

Moore, John Bassett, 1860–1947, vol. IV

Moore, John Cecil, 1907–1967, vol. VI

Moore, Sir John Samuel, 1831–1916, vol. II

Moore, Sir John Voce, 1826–1904, vol. I

Moore, Rev. John Walter Barnwell, 1886–1969, vol. VI

Moore, Rev. John Walter Brady, *died* 1938, vol. III

Moore, Sir John William, 1845–1937, vol. III

Moore, Joseph Henry Hamilton, 1852–1933, vol. III

Moore, Kathleen Ella, 1874–1969, vol. VI

Moore, Kenneth Alfred Edgar, 1894–1976, vol. VII

Moore, Sir Leopold Frank, 1868–1945, vol. IV

Moore, Louis Herbert, 1860–1918, vol. II

Moore, Marianne Craig, 1887–1972, vol. VII

Moore, Mary, 1861–1931, vol. III

Moore, Mary Emily MacLeod; *see* Rees, Mrs Leonard.

Moore, Col Maurice George, 1854–1939, vol. III

Moore, Col Maxtone, 1876–1950, vol. IV

Moore, Major Montagu Seymour, 1896–1966, vol. VI

Moore, Maj.-Gen. Hon. Sir Newton James, 1870–1936, vol. III

Moore, Noel Temple, 1833–1903, vol. I

Moore, Sir Norman, 1st Bt (*cr* 1919), 1847–1922, vol. II

Moore, Rev. Obadiah, 1848–1923, vol. II

Moore, Percival, 1886–1964, vol. VI

Moore, Pierce Langrishe, 1873–1944, vol. IV

Moore, Ralph Westwood, 1906–1953, vol. V

Moore, Ramsey Bignall, 1880–1969, vol. VI

Moore, Reginald, 1910–1968, vol. VI

Moore, Sir Richard Greenslade, 1878–1966, vol. VI

Moore, Lt-Col Richard St Leger, 1848–1921, vol. II

Moore, Rev. Robert, 1863–1935, vol. III

Moore, Rev. and Rt Hon. Robert, 1886–1960, vol. V

Moore, Robert Ernest, 1863–1934, vol. III

Moore, Robert Foster, 1877–1963, vol. V

Moore, Very Rev. Robert Henry, 1872–1964, vol. VI

Moore, Col Robert Reginald Heber, 1858–1942, vol. IV

Moore, Hon. Samuel Wilkinson, 1854–1935, vol. III

Moore, Vice-Adm. Stephen St Leger, 1884–1955, vol. V

Moore, Thomas, 1858–1920, vol. II

Moore, Lt-Col Sir Thomas Cecil Russell, 1st Bt (*cr* 1956), 1886–1971, vol. VII

Moore, Sir Thomas O'Connor, 11th Bt (*cr* 1681), 1845–1926, vol. II

Moore, Thomas Sturge, 1870–1944, vol. IV

Moore, Thomas Warren, 1872–1937, vol. III

Moore, Tom Sidney, 1881–1966, vol. VI

Moore, Vice-Adm. W. Usborne, 1849–1918, vol. II

Moore, Hon. William, 1817–1914, vol. II

Moore, Rev. Canon William, *died* 1943, vol. IV

Moore, Rt Hon. Sir William, 1st Bt (*cr* 1932), 1864–1944, vol. II

Moore, W(illiam) Arthur, 1880–1962, vol. VI

Moore, Rev. William B.; *see* Bramley-Moore.

Moore, William H., 1848–1923, vol. II

Moore, Sir (William) Harrison, 1867–1935, vol. III

Moore, William Harvey, 1891–1961, vol. VI

Moore, William Monro, 1880–1936, vol. III

Moore, Rt Rev. William Richard, 1858–1930, vol. III

Moore, Sir William Samson, 2nd Bt (*cr* 1932), 1891–1978, vol. VII

Moore Darling, Rev. Canon Edward, 1884–1968, vol. VI

Moore-Guggisberg, Decima, (Lady Moore-Guggisberg), *died* 1964, vol. VI

Moore-Lane, Col George Howard, 1844–1905, vol. I

Moore-Lane, Col Maitland; *see* Lane.

Moore-Park, Carton, 1877–1956, vol. V

Moores, Col Charles Frederick Guise-, 1873–1938, vol. III

Moores, Maj.-Gen. Sir Guise G.; *see* Guise-Moores.

Moorhead, Maj.-Gen. Charles Dawson, 1894–1965, vol. VI

Moorhead, Thomas Gillman, 1878–1960, vol. V

Moorhouse, E. Hallam; *see* Meynell, Esther H.

Moorhouse, Lt-Col Sir Harry Claude, 1872–1934, vol. III

Moorhouse, Rt Rev. James, 1826–1915, vol. I

Mooring, Sir (Arthur) George (Rixson), 1908–1969, vol. VI

Mooring, Sir George; *see* Mooring, Sir A. G. R.

Moorman, Frederic William, 1872–1919, vol. II

Moorshead, Engr-Rear-Adm. Herbert Brooks, 1870–1955, vol. V

Moorsom, Maj.-Gen. Charles John, 1837–1908, vol. I

Moorsom, Lt-Col Henry Martin, 1839–1921, vol. II

Moorsom, James Marshall, *died* 1918, vol. II

Moos, Sorab Nanabhoy, 1890–1974, vol. VII

Moran, 1st Baron, 1882–1977, vol. VII

Moran, Frances Elizabeth, 1893–1977, vol. VII

Moran, Joseph Michael, 1925–1978, vol. VII

Moran, His Eminence Cardinal Patrick Francis, 1830–1911, vol. I

Moran, Rev. Canon Walter Isidore, 1865–1958, vol. V

Morand, Paul, 1889–1975, vol. VII

Morant, Captain Edgar Robert, 1874–1931, vol. III

Morant, Adm. Sir George Digby, 1837–1921, vol. II

Morant, Brig.-Gen. Hubert Horatio Shirley, 1870–1946, vol. IV

Morant, Sir Robert Laurie, 1863–1920, vol. II

Moraud, Hon. Lucien, *died* 1951, vol. V

Moray, 15th Earl of, 1840–1901, vol. I

Moray, 16th Earl of, 1842–1909, vol. I

Moray, 17th Earl of, 1855–1930, vol. III

Moray, 18th Earl of, 1892–1943, vol. IV

Moray, 19th Earl of, 1894–1974, vol. VII

Moray, Captain William Augustus Stirling Home Drummond, 1852–1939, vol. III

Moray Williams, Barbara, (Frú Barbara Arnason), 1911–1975, vol. VII

Morcom, Lt-Col Reginald Keble, *died* 1961, vol. VI

Morcom, William Boase, 1846–1910, vol. I

Morcom, Sir William John, 1859–1934, vol. III

Mordaunt, Sir Charles, 10th Bt, 1836–1897, vol. I

Mordaunt, Elinor, *died* 1942, vol. IV

Mordaunt, Sir Henry, 12th Bt, 1867–1939, vol. III

Mordaunt, Lt-Col Sir Nigel John, 13th Bt, 1907–1979, vol. VII

Mordaunt, Sir Osbert L'Estrange, 11th Bt, 1884–1934, vol. III

Mordell, Louis Joel, 1888–1972, vol. VII

Morden, Lt-Col Walter Grant, 1880–1932, vol. III

Mordey, William M., 1856–1938, vol. III

More, Lt-Col James Carmichael, 1883–1959, vol. V

More, John William, 1879–1959, vol. V

More, Paul Elmer, 1864–1937, vol. III

More, Richard Edwardes, 1879–1936, vol. III

More, Brig.-Gen. Robert Henry, *died* 1951, vol. V

More, Robert Jasper, *died* 1903, vol. I

More-Molyneux, Maj.-Gen. George Hand, 1851–1903, vol. I

More-Molyneux, Adm. Sir Robert Henry, 1838–1904, vol. I

More-Molyneux-Longbourne, Brig.-Gen. Francis Cecil, 1883–1963, vol. VI

More-O'Ferrall, Dominic; *see* O'Ferrall.

Moreau, Emile Edouard, 1856–1937, vol. III

Moreing, Adrian Charles, 1892–1940, vol. III

Moreing, Captain Algernon Henry, 1889–1974, vol. VII

Morel, Edmund D., 1873–1924, vol. II

Morel, Sir Thomas, 1847–1903, vol. I

Moreland, Rt Rev. William Hall, 1861–1946, vol. IV

Moreland, William Harrison, 1868–1938, vol. III

Morell, Sir Stephen Joseph, 1869–1944, vol. IV

Moresby, Adm. John, 1830–1922, vol. II

Moresby, Walter Halliday, *died* 1951, vol. V

Moreton, Lord; Henry Haughton Reynolds-Moreton, 1857–1920, vol. II

Moreton, Hon. Algernon Howard, 1880–1951, vol. V

Moreton, Rev. Arthur Cyprian, 1866–1936, vol. III

Moreton, Rev. Canon H. A. V., 1889–1966, vol. VI

Moreton, Hon. Sir Richard Charles, 1846–1928, vol. II

Morfill, William Richard, 1834–1909, vol. I

Morford, Maj.-Gen. Albert Clarence St C.; *see* St Clair-Morford.

Morford, Howard Frederick, 1894–1963, vol. VI

Morgan, Alexander, 1860–1946, vol. IV

Morgan, Col Alexander Braithwaite, 1866–1930, vol. III

Morgan, Col Sir Alexander Brooke, 1837–1911, vol. I

Morgan, Alfred Kedington, 1868–1928, vol. II

Morgan, Angela, *died* 1957, vol. V

Morgan, Lt-Col Anthony Hickman, 1858–1924, vol. II

Morgan, Hon. Sir Arthur, 1856–1916, vol. II

Morgan, Sir Arthur Croke, *died* 1955, vol. V

Morgan, Sir Arthur E., 1886–1956, vol. V

Morgan, Arthur Eustace, 1886–1972, vol. VII

Morgan, Sir Benjamin Howell, *died* 1937, vol. III

Morgan, Major Cecil Buckley, 1860–1918, vol. II

Morgan, Cecil Lloyd, 1882–1965, vol. VI

Morgan, Adm. Sir Charles Eric, 1889–1951, vol. V

Morgan, Sir Charles Langbridge, 1855–1940, vol. III

Morgan, Charles Langbridge, 1894–1958, vol. V

Morgan, Col Claude Kyd, 1871–1934, vol. III

Morgan, Clement Yorke, 1903–1960, vol. V

Morgan, Conwy Lloyd, 1852–1936, vol. III

Morgan, D. J., 1844–1918, vol. II

Morgan, Major Sir David Hughes-, 1st Bt (*cr* 1925), 1871–1941, vol. IV
Morgan, David Loftus, 1904–1976, vol. VII
Morgan, Very Rev. David Watcyn, *died* 1940, vol. III
Morgan, Lt-Col David Watts, 1867–1933, vol. III
Morgan, Rt Rev. Edmund Robert, 1888–1979, vol. VII
Morgan, Hon. Sir Edward James Ranembe, 1900–1977, vol. VII
Morgan, Col Emmanuel Maria, 1853–1929, vol. III
Morgan, Col Farrar Robert Horton, 1893–1978, vol. VII
Morgan, Sir Frank William, 1887–1974, vol. VII
Morgan, Hon. Frederic Courtenay, 1834–1909, vol. I
Morgan, Lt-Gen. Sir Frederick Edgworth, 1894–1967, vol. VI
Morgan, Col Frederick James, 1862–1931, vol. III
Morgan, Rear-Adm. Frederick Robert William, 1861–1910, vol. I
Morgan, Captain Frederick Thomas de Mallet, 1889–1959, vol. V
Morgan, Rev. G. Campbell, 1863–1945, vol. IV
Morgan, Engr Rear-Adm. Geoffrey, 1889–1956, vol. V
Morgan, George, 1853–1943, vol. IV
Morgan, George, 1867–1957, vol. V
Morgan, George Ernest, 1861–1934, vol. III
Morgan, George Hay, 1866–1931, vol. III
Morgan, Rt Hon. Sir George Osborne, 1st Bt (*cr* 1892), 1826–1897, vol. I
Morgan, Sir Gilbert Thomas, 1872–1940, vol. III
Morgan, Gladys Mary, *died* 1957, vol. V
Morgan, Harington, *died* 1914, vol. I
Morgan, Maj.-Gen. Harold de Riemer, 1888–1964, vol. VI
Morgan, Rev. Harold Dunbar, *died* 1945, vol. IV
Morgan, Col Harrison Ross Lewin, 1842–1914, vol. I
Morgan, Ven. Harry J., 1871–1947, vol. IV
Morgan, Heaton Andrew Kenneth, 1889–1962, vol. VI
Morgan, Henry, 1875–1944, vol. IV
Morgan, Rev. Henry Arthur, 1830–1912, vol. I
Morgan, Henry James, 1842–1913, vol. I
Morgan, Sir Herbert Edward, 1880–1951, vol. V
Morgan, Brig.-Gen. Sir Hill Godfrey, 1862–1923, vol. II
Morgan, Hopkin, 1849–1933, vol. III
Morgan, H(opkin) Trevor; *see* Morgan, Trevor.
Morgan, Captain Horace Leslie, 1888–1973, vol. VII
Morgan, Hyacinth Bernard Wenceslaus, 1885–1956, vol. V
Morgan, Hywel Glyn, 1899–1966, vol. VI
Morgan, Very Rev. J., *died* 1904, vol. I
Morgan, James, 1882–1968, vol. VI
Morgan, James Conwy, 1910–1977, vol. VII
Morgan, Rev. John, *died* 1924, vol. II
Morgan, John, *died* 1938, vol. III
Morgan, John, 1892–1940, vol. III
Morgan, Most Rev. John, 1886–1957, vol. V
Morgan, Sir John David, 1874–1939, vol. III

Morgan, John Hammond, 1847–1924, vol. II
Morgan, Brig.-Gen. John Hartman, 1876–1955, vol. V
Morgan, John Lloyd, 1861–1944, vol. IV
Morgan, John Pierpont, 1837–1913, vol. I
Morgan, John Pierpont, 1867–1943, vol. IV
Morgan, John T., 1824–1907, vol. I
Morgan, Sir John Vernon H.; *see* Hughes-Morgan.
Morgan, Sir Kenyon Pascoe V.; *see* Vaughan-Morgan.
Morgan, Col Kevern Ivor, 1894–1971, vol. VII
Morgan, Montagu Travers, 1889–1974, vol. VII
Morgan, Brig. Morgan Cyril, 1891–1960, vol. V
Morgan, Sir Morien Bedford, 1912–1978, vol. VII
Morgan, Paul Robert James, 1898–1974, vol. VII
Morgan, Lt-Gen. Reginald Hallward, 1871–1948, vol. IV
Morgan, Richard Cope, 1827–1908, vol. I
Morgan, Rev. Richard James Basil P.; *see* Paterson-Morgan.
Morgan, Robert Harry, 1880–1960, vol. V
Morgan, R(obert) Orlando, 1865–1956, vol. V
Morgan, Brig.-Gen. Rosslewin Westropp, 1879–1947, vol. IV
Morgan, Lt-Col Stuart Williams, 1867–1922, vol. II
Morgan, Sydney Cope, 1887–1967, vol. VI
Morgan, Thomas Hunt, 1866–1945, vol. IV
Morgan, Trevor, 1892–1976, vol. VII
Morgan, Adm. Sir Vaughan, 1891–1969, vol. VI
Morgan, Sir Walter, 1821–1906, vol. I
Morgan, Walter, 1886–1960, vol. V
Morgan, Walter J., *died* 1924, vol. II
Morgan, Sir Walter Vaughan, 1st Bt (*cr* 1906), 1831–1916, vol. II
Morgan, Air Cdre Wilfred W.; *see* Wynter-Morgan.
Morgan, Rev. William, 1862–1928, vol. II
Morgan, William, 1870–1945, vol. IV
Morgan, Gen. Sir William Duthie, 1891–1977, vol. VII
Morgan, Rev. Preb. William Edgar, 1888–1968, vol. VI
Morgan, Major William Henry, 1883–1966, vol. VI
Morgan, William Matheson, 1906–1972, vol. VII
Morgan, William Pritchard, 1844–1924, vol. II
Morgan-Brown, Rev. Nigel Mackenzie, 1859–1932, vol. III
Morgan-Grenville, Lt-Col Hon. Thomas George Breadalbane, 1891–1965, vol. VI
Morgan-Owen, Maj.-Gen. Llewellyn Isaac Gethin, 1879–1960, vol. V
Morgan-Powell, Samuel, 1878–1962, vol. VI
Morgenthau, Henry, 1856–1946, vol. IV
Morgenthau, Henry, Jr, 1891–1967, vol. VI
Moriarty, Rt Rev. Ambrose James, 1870–1949, vol. IV
Moriarty, Cecil Charles Hudson, 1877–1958, vol. V
Moriarty, Captain Henry Augustus, 1815–1906, vol. I
Moriarty, Rt Hon. John Francis, *died* 1915, vol. I
Morice, Beaumont, *died* 1937, vol. III
Morice, Sir George, Pasha, *died* 1904, vol. I
Morin, Leopold Frédéric Germain, 1861–1946, vol. IV

Morine, Sir Alfred Bishop, 1857–1944, vol. IV
Morison, Rt Hon. Lord; Thomas Brash Morison, died 1945, vol. IV
Morison, Alexander Blackhall, 1850–1927, vol. II
Morison, Cecil Graham Traquair, 1881–1965, vol. VI
Morison, Donald, 1857–1924, vol. II
Morison, Hector, 1850–1939, vol. III
Morison, Sir John, 1893–1958, vol. V
Morison, Lt-Col John, 1879–1971, vol. VII
Morison, John Lyle, 1875–1952, vol. V
Morison, John Miller Woodburn, 1875–1951, vol. V
Morison, Engr-Rear-Adm. Richard Barns, 1871–1932, vol. III
Morison, Sir Ronald Peter, 1900–1976, vol. VII
Morison, Rutherford, 1853–1939, vol. III
Morison, Samuel Eliot, 1887–1976, vol. VII
Morison, Stanley, 1889–1967, vol. VI
Morison, Sir Theodore, 1863–1936, vol. III
Morison, Rt Hon. Thomas Brash; see Morison, Rt Hon. Lord.
Morison, Sir William Thomson, 1860–1931, vol. III
Moritz, Rudolph, 1878–1940, vol. III
Moritz, Siegmund, 1855–1932, vol. III
Morkill, William Lucius, 1858–1936, vol. III
Morland, Andrew John, 1896–1957, vol. V
Morland, Egbert Coleby, 1874–1955, vol. V
Morland, Captain Henry, 1876–1966, vol. VI (AII)
Morland, Sir Oscar Charles, 1904–1980, vol. VII
Morland, Gen. Sir Thomas Lethbridge Napier, 1865–1925, vol. II
Morland, William Vane, 1884–1962, vol. VI
Morle, Philip Bartlett, 1876–1956, vol. V
Morley, 3rd Earl of, 1843–1905, vol. I
Morley, 4th Earl of, 1877–1951, vol. V
Morley, 5th Earl of, 1878–1962, vol. VI
Morley of Blackburn, 1st Viscount, 1838–1923, vol. II
Morley, Sir Alexander Francis, 1908–1971, vol. VII
Morley, Rt Hon. Arnold, 1849–1916, vol. II
Morley, Arthur, 1881–1946, vol. IV
Morley, Arthur, 1876–1962, vol. VI
Morley, Austin, 1898–1970, vol. VI
Morley, Charles, died 1916, vol. II
Morley, Charles, 1847–1917, vol. II
Morley, Charles, 1885–1955, vol. V
Morley, Christopher, 1890–1957, vol. V
Morley, Captain Hon. Claude Hope H.; see Hope-Morley.
Morley, Edith Julia, 1875–1964, vol. VI
Morley, Edward Williams, 1838–1923, vol. II
Morley, Sir George, 1873–1942, vol. IV
Morley, Air Vice-Marshal George Henry, 1907–1971, vol. VII
Morley, Harry, 1881–1943, vol. IV
Morley, Henry Forster, 1855–1943, vol. IV
Morley, Henry Seaward, 1897–1960, vol. V
Morley, Sir James Wycliffe H.; see Headlam-Morley.
Morley, John, died 1974, vol. VII
Morley, Lt-Col Lyddon Charteris, 1877–1954, vol. V

Morley, Ralph, 1882–1955, vol. V
Morley, Robert, 1857–1941, vol. IV
Morley, Rt Rev. Samuel, 1841–1923, vol. II
Mornement, Bt Col Edward, 1867–1956, vol. V
Moro, Aldo, 1916–1978, vol. VII
Morony, Thomas Henry, died 1961, vol. VI
Morphett, Lt-Col George Charles, 1878–1968, vol. VI
Morphew, Col Edward Maudsley, 1867–1947, vol. IV
Morphy, Hugh Boulton, 1860–1932, vol. III
Morrah, Dermot Michael Macgregor, 1896–1974, vol. VII
Morrah, Herbert Arthur, died 1939, vol. III
Morrell, Rear-Adm. Arthur, died 1915, vol. I
Morrell, Arthur Claude, 1894–1978, vol. VII
Morrell, Captain Sir Arthur Routley Hutson, 1878–1968, vol. VI
Morrell, Charles, 1842–1913, vol. I
Morrell, Mrs G. Herbert, (Emily Alicia Morrell), died 1938, vol. III
Morrell, George Herbert, 1845–1906, vol. I
Morrell, Philip, 1870–1943, vol. IV
Morrell, R. M., died 1912, vol. I
Morren, Sir William Booth Rennie, 1890–1972, vol. VII
Morrice, Humphrey Alan Walter, 1906–1959, vol. V
Morrice, Rev. James Cornelius, 1874–1953, vol. V
Morrice, Rev. John David, 1849–1938, vol. III
Morrice, Lt-Col Lewis Edward, 1862–1933, vol. III
Morrill, Thomas James, 1886–1969, vol. VI
Morris, 1st Baron, 1858–1935, vol. III
Morris, 2nd Baron, 1903–1975, vol. VII
Morris and Killanin, 1st Baron, 1827–1901, vol. I
Morris of Borth-y-Gest, Baron (Life Peer); John William Morris, 1896–1979, vol. VII
Morris of Kenwood, 1st Baron, 1893–1954, vol. V
Morris, Alfred, 1874–1945, vol. IV
Morris, Air Cdre Alfred Drummond W.; see Warrington-Morris.
Morris, Most Rev. (Alfred) Edwin, 1894–1971, vol. VII
Morris, Air Vice-Marshal Sir (Alfred) Samuel, 1889–1964, vol. VI
Morris, Brig. Arthur de Burgh, 1902–1978, vol. VII
Morris, Rt Rev. Arthur Harold, 1898–1977, vol. VII
Morris, Col Arthur Henry, 1861–1939, vol. III
Morris, Brig. Arthur Henry Musgrave, 1904–1972, vol. VII
Morris, Col Arthur Hugh, 1872–1941, vol. IV
Morris, Col Augustus William, 1845–1906, vol. I
Morris, C. J., see Morris, John.
Morris, Charles, died 1929, vol. III
Morris, Charles Arthur, died 1942, vol. IV
Morris, Lt-Col Charles Reade Monroe, 1882–1936, vol. III
Morris, Charles Sculthorpe, 1875–1949, vol. IV
Morris, Col Charles Temple, 1876–1956, vol. V
Morris, Major Cyril Clarke Boville, 1882–1950, vol. IV
Morris, Sir Daniel, 1844–1933, vol. III
Morris, Edmund Montague 1871–1913, vol. II

Morris, Brig.-Gen. Edmund Merritt, 1868–1939, vol. III
Morris, Commissary-Gen. Sir Edward, 1833–1923, vol. II
Morris, Edward Ellis, 1843–1902, vol. I
Morris, Edward Gilbert, 1884–1943, vol. IV
Morris, Edward Robert, 1862–1934, vol. III
Morris, Most Rev. Edwin; see Morris, Most Rev. A. E.
Morris, Gen. Sir Edwin Logie, 1889–1970, vol. VI
Morris, Rev. Ernest Edwin, 1856–1924, vol. II
Morris, Sir Ernest William, died 1937, vol. III
Morris, Sir Francis, 1859–1944, vol. IV
Morris, Geoffrey Grant, 1888–1938, vol. III
Morris, Geoffrey O'C.; see O'Connor-Morris.
Morris, Sir George, 1833–1912, vol. I
Morris, Col George Abbott, 1879–1957, vol. V
Morris, Sir George Cecil, 6th Bt (cr 1806), 1852–1940, vol. IV
Morris, Lt-Col Hon. George Henry, 1872–1915, vol. I
Morris, Captain George Horace Guy, 1897–1979, vol. VII
Morris, Sir George Lockwood, 8th Bt (cr 1806), 1859–1947, vol. IV
Morris, Brig.-Gen. George Mortimer, 1868–1954, vol. V
Morris, Sir George Parker; see Morris, Sir Parker.
Morris, Greville, died 1922, vol. II
Morris, Guy Wilfrid, 1884–1956, vol. V
Morris, Gwilym Ivor, 1911–1965, vol. VI
Morris, Sir Harold, 1876–1967, vol. VI
Morris, Harrison Smith, 1856–1948, vol. IV
Morris, Sir Henry, 1st Bt (cr 1909), 1844–1926, vol. II
Morris, Sir Herbert Edward, 7th Bt (cr 1806), 1884–1947, vol. IV
Morris, Brig. Herbert Edwin Abrahall, 1894–1969, vol. VI
Morris, Herbert Picton, 1856–1946, vol. IV
Morris, Ira Nelson, died 1942, vol. IV
Morris, Rt Rev. James, 1876–1957, vol. V
Morris, James Archibald, 1857–1942, vol. IV
Morris, John, (C. J. Morris), 1895–1980, vol. VII
Morris, Rev. John C., 1870–1940, vol. III
Morris, John David, 1895–1972, vol. VII
Morris, Hon. Sir John Demetrius, 1902–1956, vol. V
Morris, Sir John Henry, 1828–1912, vol. I
Morris, Maj.-Gen. John Ignatius, 1842–1902, vol. I
Morris, Sir John N.; see Newman-Morris.
Morris, Major John Patrick, 1894–1962, vol. VI
Morris, Brig. John Sidney, 1890–1961, vol. VI
Morris, John Turner M.; see Macgregor-Morris.
Morris, Hon. Sir Kenneth James, 1903–1978, vol. VII
Morris, Lawrence Henry, 1902–1969, vol. VI
Morris, Air Marshal Sir Leslie D.; see Dalton-Morris.
Morris, Sir Lewis, 1833–1907, vol. I
Morris, Sir Malcolm, died 1924, vol. II
Morris, Malcolm John, 1913–1972, vol. VII
Morris, May, died 1938, vol. III
Morris, Noah, died 1947, vol. IV

Morris, Sir Parker, 1891–1972, vol. VII
Morris, Percy, 1893–1967, vol. VI
Morris, Philip Richard, 1833–1902, vol. I
Morris, Sir Philip Robert, 1901–1979, vol. VII
Morris, Ralph Clarence, 1889–1959, vol. V
Morris, Reginald Owen, 1886–1948, vol. IV
Morris, Sir Rhys Hopkin, 1888–1956, vol. V
Morris, Rev. Richard, died 1923, vol. II
Morris, Richard John, 1860–1936, vol. III
Morris, Richard Murchison, 1898–1979, vol. VII
Morris, Maj.-Gen. Robert, 1840–1914, vol. I
Morris, Sir Robert Armine, 4th Bt (cr 1806), 1848–1927, vol. II
Morris, R(obert) Schofield, 1898–1964, vol. VI
Morris, Rev. Rupert Hugh, 1844–1918, vol. II
Morris, Samuel, 1846–1920, vol. II
Morris, Air Vice-Marshal Sir Samuel; see Morris, Air Vice-Marshal Sir A. S.
Morris, Sir Samuel Meeson, 1857–1937, vol. III
Morris, Rev. Silas, 1862–1923, vol. II
Morris, Captain Sir Tankerville Robert Armine, 5th Bt (cr 1806), 1892–1937, vol. III
Morris, Lt-Col Thomas Henry, 1848–1927, vol. II
Morris, Thomas Joseph, 1876–1953, vol. V
Morris, Rev. Canon Walter Edmund Harston, 1872–1968, vol. VI
Morris, William Alexander, 1905–1979, vol. VII
Morris, William Alfred, 1912–1973, vol. VII
Morris, Col Sir William George, 1847–1935, vol. III
Morris, William O'Connor, 1824–1904, vol. I
Morris, Col William P.; see Pollok Morris.
Morris, William Russell, 1853–1936, vol. III
Morris-Airey, Harold, 1880–1927, vol. II
Morris-Eyton, Lt-Col Charles Reginald, 1890–1961, vol. VI
Morris-Jones, Sir Henry; see Morris-Jones, Sir J. H.
Morris-Jones, Sir John; see Jones.
Morris-Jones, Sir (John) Henry, 1884–1972, vol. VII
Morrisby, Major Hon. Arthur, 1847–1925, vol. II
Morrish, Arthur Gabriel, 1869–1936, vol. III
Morrish, Rev. Francis, 1852–1937, vol. III
Morrish, Rear-Adm. William Douglas Travers, 1882–1958, vol. V
Morrison, 1st Baron, 1881–1953, vol. V
Morrison of Lambeth, Baron (Life Peer); Herbert Stanley Morrison, 1888–1965, vol. VI
Morrison, Agnes Brysson, 1867–1934, vol. III
Morrison, Alexander, 1868–1941, vol. IV
Morrison, Alexander Thomas, 1886–1954, vol. V
Morrison, Archibald Cameron, 1870–1948, vol. IV
Morrison, Arthur, 1863–1945, vol. III
Morrison, Arthur Andrew, 1858–1934, vol. III
Morrison, Arthur Cecil Lockwood, 1881–1960, vol. V
Morrison, Hon. Aulay MacAulay, 1863–1942, vol. IV
Morrison, Brig.-Gen. Colquhoun Grant, 1860–1916, vol. II
Morrison, David, died 1936, vol. III
Morrison, Maj.-Gen. Sir Edward Whipple Bancroft, 1867–1925, vol. II
Morrison, Col F. L., 1863–1917, vol. II

Morrison, Col Frank Stanley, 1881–1969, vol. VI
Morrison, George Alexander, 1869–1956, vol. V
Morrison, George Ernest, 1862–1920, vol. II
Morrison, Very Rev. George Herbert, 1866–1928, vol. II
Morrison, Herbert Needham, 1891–1963, vol. VI
Morrison, Hugh, 1868–1931, vol. III
Morrison, Hugh Smith, 1858–1929, vol. III
Morrison, Most Rev. James, 1861–1950, vol. IV
Morrison, Major James Archibald, 1873–1934, vol. III
Morrison, Rt Rev. James Dow, 1844–1934, vol. III
Morrison, James Thomas Jackman, died 1933, vol. III
Morrison, Col John, died 1919, vol. II
Morrison, Joseph Albert Colquhoun, 1882–1964, vol. VI
Morrison, Mrs Julia Minnie, died 1942, vol. IV
Morrison, Sir Murray; see Morrison, Sir W. M.
Morrison, R. E., born 1851, vol. II
Morrison, Walter, 1836–1921, vol. II
Morrison, Sir William, 1877–1951, vol. V
Morrison, Rev. William Douglas, 1852–1943, vol. IV
Morrison, Sir (William) Murray, 1873–1948, vol. IV
Morrison-Bell, Sir (Arthur) Clive, 1st Bt (cr 1923), 1871–1956, vol. V
Morrison-Bell, Sir Charles Reginald Francis, 3rd Bt (cr 1905), 1915–1967, vol. VI
Morrison-Bell, Sir Charles William, 1st Bt (cr 1905), 1833–1914, vol. I
Morrison-Bell, Sir Claude William Hedley, 2nd Bt (cr 1905), 1867–1943, vol. IV
Morrison-Bell, Sir Clive; see Morrison-Bell, Sir A. C.
Morrison-Bell, Lt-Col Ernest FitzRoy, 1871–1960, vol. V
Morrison-Bell, Lt-Col Eustace Widdrington, 1874–1947, vol. IV
Morrison-Low, Sir Walter John; see Low.
Morrisroe, Rt Rev. Patrick, 1869–1946, vol. IV
Morrogh, Lt-Col Donald Florence MacC.; see MacCarthy-Morrogh.
Morrogh, Brig. Walter Francis, 1891–1954, vol. V
Morrogh Bernard, Rt Rev. Mgr Canon Eustace Anthony, 1893–1972, vol. VII
Morrow, Albert, 1863–1927, vol. II
Morrow, Sir (Arthur) William, 1903–1977, vol. VII
Morrow, Dwight Whitney, 1873–1931, vol. III
Morrow, Forbes St John, 1860–1949, vol. IV
Morrow, George, 1870–1955, vol. V
Morrow, Cdre James Cairns, 1905–1963, vol. VI
Morrow, Very Rev. John Love, died 1940, vol. III
Morrow, Sir William; see Morrow, Sir A. W.
Morrow, Very Rev. William Edward Reginald, 1869–1950, vol. IV
Morse, Vice-Adm. Sir Anthony; see Morse, Vice-Adm. Sir J. A. V.
Morse, Sir Arthur, 1892–1967, vol. VI
Morse, Charles, 1860–1945, vol. IV
Morse, Sir George Henry, 1857–1931, vol. III
Morse, Hosea Ballou, 1855–1934, vol. III

Morse, Vice-Adm. Sir (John) Anthony (Vere), 1892–1960, vol. V
Morse, L. Lapper, 1853–1913, vol. I
Morse, Rev. Wallace Ransom, 1860–1932, vol. III
Morse, William Ewart, 1878–1952, vol. V
Morse, Withrow, 1880–1951, vol. V
Morse-Boycott, Rev. Desmond, 1892–1979, vol. VII
Morshead, Edmund Doidge Anderson, died 1912, vol. I
Morshead, Lt-Col Henry Treise, 1882–1931, vol. III
Morshead, Leonard Frederick, 1868–1936, vol. III
Morshead, Lt-Gen. Sir Leslie James, 1889–1959, vol. V
Morshead, Sir Owen Frederick, 1893–1977, vol. VII
Morshead, Lt-Col Rupert Henry A.; see Anderson-Morshead.
Morshead, Sir Warwick Charles, 3rd Bt, 1824–1905, vol. I
Morson, A(lbert) Clifford, died 1975, vol. VII
Morson, Walter Augustus Ormsby, 1851–1921, vol. II
Mort, David Llewellyn, 1888–1963, vol. VI
Morten, Edward, 1845–1929, vol. III
Morten, Frederick Joseph, 1888–1960, vol. V
Morten, Honnor, died 1913, vol. I
Mortensen, Theodor, 1868–1952, vol. V
Morter, Col Sidney Pelham, 1869–1933, vol. III
Mortimer, Sir Charles Edward, 1886–1974, vol. VII
Mortimer, Rev. Christian, died 1916, vol. II
Mortimer, Emile Samuel, 1853–1935, vol. III
Mortimer, Francis James, 1875–1944, vol. IV
Mortimer, George Frederick Lloyd, 1866–1928, vol. II
Mortimer, Lt-Col James, died 1916, vol. II
Mortimer, John Desmond, died 1942, vol. IV
Mortimer, Brig. Philip, 1882–1963, vol. VI
Mortimer, Sir Ralph George Elphinstone, 1869–1955, vol. V
Mortimer, Raymond, 1895–1980, vol. VII
Mortimer, Rt Rev. Robert Cecil, 1902–1976, vol. VII
Mortimer, William Egerton, 1878–1940, vol. III
Mortimer, Col Sir William Hugh, 1846–1921, vol. II
Mortimore, Lt-Col Claude Alick, 1875–1927, vol. II
Mortimore, Frederick William, 1858–1928, vol. II
Mortished, Ronald James Patrick, 1891–1957, vol. V
Mortlock, Rev. Canon Charles Bernard, 1888–1967, vol. VI
Mortlock, Rev. Canon E., 1859–1945, vol. IV
Morton, 20th Earl of, 1844–1935, vol. III
Morton, 21st Earl of, 1907–1976, vol. VII
Morton of Henryton, Baron (Life Peer); Fergus Dunlop Morton, 1887–1973, vol. VII
Morton, Sir Alpheus Cleophas, died 1923, vol. II
Morton, Anthony; see Creasey, John.
Morton, Arthur Henry Aylmer, 1836–1913, vol. I
Morton, Gen. Boyce William Dunlop, 1829–1919, vol. II
Morton, Charles, 1819–1904, vol. I

Morton, Charles Alexander, 1860–1929, vol. III
Morton, Sir Charles Henry, 1852–1939, vol. III
Morton, Lt-Col David Simson, *died* 1937, vol. III
Morton, Major Sir Desmond John Falkiner, 1891–1971, vol. VII
Morton, Edward, *died* 1922, vol. II
Morton, Brig.-Gen. Edward, 1871–1949, vol. IV
Morton, Edward John Chalmers, 1856–1902, vol. I
Morton, Edward Reginald, 1867–1944, vol. IV
Morton, G. F., 1882–1975, vol. VII
Morton, Sir George, 1870–1953, vol. V
Morton, Sir George Bond, 1893–1954, vol. V
Morton, Lt-Gen. Sir Gerald de Courcy, 1845–1906, vol. I
Morton, Guy Mainwaring, 1896–1968, vol. VI
Morton, Major Harold Trestrail, 1894–1972, vol. VII
Morton, Henry Vollam, 1892–1979, vol. VII
Morton, Hugh, 1883–1941, vol. IV
Morton, Col Hugh Murray, 1873–1946, vol. IV
Morton, J. B.; *see* Morton, J. C. A. B. M.
Morton, Sir James, 1867–1943, vol. IV
Morton, James Elliot Vowler, 1861–1924, vol. II
Morton, James H., 1881–1918, vol. II
Morton, John Cameron Andrieu Bingham Michael, (J. B. Morton), 1893–1979, vol. VII
Morton, Levi Parsons, 1824–1920, vol. II
Morton, Michael, *died* 1931, vol. III
Morton, Richard Alan, 1899–1977, vol. VII
Morton, Rev. Robert, 1847–1932, vol. III
Morton, Sir Stanley William Gibson, 1911–1975, vol. VII
Morton, Air Vice-Marshal Terence Charles St Clessie, 1893–1968, vol. VI
Morton, Thomas Corsan, 1859–1928, vol. II
Morton, William Blair, 1868–1949, vol. IV
Morton, William Cuthbert, 1875–1971, vol. VII
Morvi, HH Thakur Saheb Sir Waghji Ravaji, 1858–1922, vol. II
Morvi State, ex-Ruler of, 1876–1957, vol. V
Moscheles, Felix, 1833–1917, vol. II
Moseley, Charles Herbert Harley, 1857–1933, vol. III
Moseley, Geoffrey, 1882–1953, vol. V
Moseley, Herbert Harvey, 1873–1959, vol. V
Moseley, Sydney Alexander, 1888–1961, vol. VI
Mosely, Alfred, 1855–1917, vol. II
Mosely, Sir Archie Gerard, 1883–1951, vol. V
Moser, Oswald, 1874–1916, vol. II
Moser, Robert Oswald, *died* 1953, vol. V
Moses, James J. H., 1873–1946, vol. IV
Moshier, H. H., 1889–1918, vol. II
Mosley, Sir Alexander, 1847–1927, vol. II
Mosley, Lady Cynthia Blanche, *died* 1933, vol. III
Mosley, Rt Rev. Henry, 1868–1948, vol. IV
Mosley, Brig. Henry Samuel, 1879–1975, vol. VII
Mosley, Sir Oswald, 4th Bt, 1848–1915, vol. I
Mosley, Sir Oswald, 5th Bt, 1873–1928, vol. II
Mosley, Sir Oswald Ernald, 6th Bt, 1896–1980, vol. VII
Moss, Abraham, 1899–1964, vol. VI
Moss, Sir Charles, 1840–1912, vol. I
Moss, Charles Edward, 1872–1930, vol. III

Moss, Col Edward Lawton, 1880–1975, vol. VII
Moss, Captain Ernest William, 1876–1915, vol. I
Moss, Geoffrey; *see* McNeill-Moss, Major G.
Moss, Sir George Sinclair, 1882–1959, vol. V
Moss, Sir H. Edward, *died* 1912, vol. I
Moss, Rev. Henry Whitehead, 1841–1917, vol. II
Moss, John, 1890–1976, vol. VII
Moss, Sir John Edwards E.; *see* Edwards-Moss.
Moss, Kenneth Neville, 1891–1942, vol. IV
Moss, Lewis S., *died* 1903, vol. I
Moss, Brig.-Gen. Lionel Boyd B.; *see* Boyd-Moss.
Moss, Hon. Matthew Lewis, 1863–1946, vol. IV
Moss, Rev. Richard Waddy, 1850–1935, vol. III
Moss, Robert, *died* 1973, vol. VII
Moss, Samuel, 1858–1918, vol. II
Moss, Sir Thomas E.; *see* Edwards-Moss.
Moss, Wilfred, 1867–1938, vol. III
Moss-Blundell, Lt-Col Bryan Seymour; *see* Blundell.
Moss-Blundell, Henry Seymour; *see* Blundell.
Mosscockle, Rita Francis, *died* 1943, vol. IV
Mosse, Lt-Col Arthur Henry Eyre, 1877–1943, vol. IV
Mosse, Charles Benjamin, 1830–1912, vol. I
Mosse, Robert Lee, 1877–1963, vol. VI
Mosse, Rev. William George, 1859–1929, vol. III
Mosses, William, 1858–1943, vol. IV
Mossman, Robert Cockburn, 1870–1940, vol. III
Mossop, Major Albert Isaac, *died* 1936, vol. III
Mossop, Sir Allan George, 1887–1965, vol. VI
Mossop, Joseph Upjohn, 1872–1928, vol. II (A), vol. III
Mossop, Leonard, 1869–1933, vol. III
Moston, Henry E., 1881–1962, vol. VI
Mostyn, 3rd Baron, 1856–1929, vol. III
Mostyn, 4th Baron, 1885–1965, vol. VI
Mostyn, Sir Basil Antony Trevor, 13th Bt, 1902–1956, vol. V
Mostyn, Most Rev. Francis, 1860–1939, vol. III
Mostyn, Hon. Henry Richard Howel L.; *see* Lloyd-Mostyn.
Mostyn, Rev. Hon. Hugh Wynne, 1838–1930, vol. III
Mostyn, Sir Pyers Charles, 10th Bt, 1895–1917, vol. II
Mostyn, Sir Pyers Edward, 12th Bt, 1928–1955, vol. V
Mostyn, Captain Sir Pyers George Joseph, 11th Bt, 1893–1937, vol. III
Mostyn, Sir Pyers William, 9th Bt, 1846–1912, vol. I
Mostyn, Maj.-Gen. Hon. Sir Savage L.; *see* Lloyd-Mostyn.
Mostyn, Tom, 1864–1930, vol. III
Mostyn-Owen, Lt-Col Roger Arthur; *see* Owen.
Moten, Brig. Murray John, 1899–1953, vol. V
Motherwell, Hon. William Richard, 1860–1943, vol. IV
Moti Chand, Raja Sir, *died* 1934, vol. III
Motilal, Raja Bahadur Sir Bansilal, *died* 1935, vol. IV
Motion, Andrew Richard, 1857–1933, vol. III
Motion, Robert Russa, 1867–1940, vol. III (A), vol. IV

Motion, Major Thomas Augustus, *died* 1942, vol. IV

Mott, Sir Adrian Spear, 2nd Bt, 1889–1964, vol. VI

Mott, Sir Basil, 1st Bt, 1859–1938, vol. III

Mott, Edward Spencer, 1844–1910, vol. I

Mott, Sir Frederick Walker, 1853–1926, vol. II

Mott, John R., 1865–1955, vol. V

Mott, Hon. Maj.-Gen. Stanley Fielder, 1873–1959, vol. V

Mottistone, 1st Baron, 1868–1947, vol. IV

Mottistone, 2nd Baron, 1899–1963, vol. VI

Mottistone, 3rd Baron, 1905–1966, vol. VI

Mottl, Felix, 1856–1911, vol. I

Motton, Paymaster-Rear-Adm. Frederick George, *died* 1935, vol. III

Mottram, James Cecil, 1880–1945, vol. IV

Mottram, Ralph Hale, 1883–1971, vol. VII

Mottram, Sir Richard, 1848–1914, vol. I

Mottram, Sir Thomas Harry, 1859–1937, vol. III

Mottram, Vernon Henry, 1882–1976, vol. VII

Mottram, Rev. William, 1836–1921, vol. II

Mouat, Sir James, 1815–1899, vol. I

Mouat, John Richard K.; *see* Kay-Mouat.

Moubray, John James, 1857–1928, vol. II

Mould, James, 1893–1958, vol. V

Mould, John, 1890–1964, vol. VI

Mould, Percy, *died* 1923, vol. II

Mould, Sam Carter, 1880–1963, vol. VI

Mould, Col William Thomas, 1865–1935, vol. III

Mould-Graham, Col Robert, 1895–1979, vol. VII

Moulden, Sir Frank Beaumont, 1876–1932, vol. III

Moule, Rev. Arthur Christopher, 1873–1957, vol. V

Moule, Ven. Arthur Evans, 1836–1918, vol. II

Moule, Charles Walter, 1834–1921, vol. II

Moule, Edward Christopher, 1902–1945, vol. IV

Moule, Rt Rev. George Evans, 1828–1912, vol. I

Moule, Rt Rev. Handley Carr Glyn, 1841–1920, vol. II

Moule, Horace D'Oyly, 1843–1925, vol. II

Moule, Ven. Walter Stephen, *died* 1949, vol. IV

Moullin, Charles William M.; *see* Mansell-Moullin.

Moullin, Eric Balliol, 1893–1963, vol. VI

Moulsdale, Rev. Stephen Richard Platt, 1872–1944, vol. IV

Moult, Thomas, *died* 1974, vol. VII

Moulton, Baron (Life Peer); John Fletcher Moulton, 1844–1921, vol. II

Moulton, Hon. Hugh Fletcher, *died* 1962, vol. VI

Moulton, Rev. James Hope, 1863–1917, vol. II

Moulton, Louise Chandler, *died* 1908, vol. I

Moulton, Richard Green, 1849–1924, vol. II

Moulton, Rev. William Fiddian, 1835–1898, vol. I

Moulton-Barrett, Brig.-Gen. Edward Alfred, 1859–1932, vol. III

Mounet, Jean Sully, 1841–1916, vol. II

Mounsey, Sir George Augustus, 1879–1966, vol. VI

Mounsey, John Edward, 1879–1929, vol. III

Mounsey, John Little, 1852–1933, vol. III

Mounsey, Rt Rev. William Robert Rupert, 1867–1952, vol. V

Mount, Lt-Col Sir Alan Henry Lawrence, 1881–1955, vol. V

Mount, Ven. Francis John, 1831–1903, vol. I

Mount, Sir William Arthur, 1st Bt, 1866–1930, vol. III

Mount, William George, 1824–1906, vol. I

Mount Edgcumbe, 4th Earl of, 1832–1917, vol. II

Mount Edgcumbe, 5th Earl of, 1865–1944, vol. IV

Mount Edgcumbe, 6th Earl of, *died* 1965, vol. VI

Mount Stephen, 1st Baron, 1829–1921, vol. II

Mount Stephen, Lady; (Gian), *died* 1933, vol. III

Mount Temple, 1st Baron, 1867–1939, vol. III

Mountain, Arthur Reginald, 1877–1940, vol. III

Mountain, Lt-Col Sir Brian Edward Stanley, 2nd Bt, 1899–1977, vol. VII

Mountain, Sir Edward Mortimer, 1st Bt, 1872–1948, vol. IV

Mountain, John Francis, 1895–1965, vol. VI

Mountain, Surgeon Rear-Adm. (D) William Leonard, 1908–1980, vol. VII

Mountbatten of Burma, 1st Earl, 1900–1979, vol. VII

Mountbatten of Burma, Countess; (Edwina Cynthia Annette), 1901–1960, vol. V

Mountbatten, Major Lord; Leopold Arthur Louis, 1889–1922, vol. II

Mountcashell, 5th Earl, 1826–1898, vol. I

Mountcashell, 6th Earl, 1829–1915, vol. I

Mountevans, 1st Baron, 1881–1957, vol. V

Mountevans, 2nd Baron, 1918–1974, vol. VII

Mountford, Edward William, 1855–1908, vol. I

Mountford, Sir James Frederick, 1897–1979, vol. VII

Mountford, Lewis James, 1871–1944, vol. IV

Mountgarret, 13th Viscount, 1816–1900, vol. I

Mountgarret, 14th Viscount, 1844–1912, vol. I

Mountgarret, 15th Viscount, 1875–1918, vol. II

Mountgarret, 16th Viscount, 1903–1966, vol. VI

Mountifield, Engr Rear-Adm. James, 1871–1957, vol. V

Mountmorres, 6th Viscount, 1872–1936, vol. III

Mountmorres, 7th Viscount, 1879–1951, vol. V

Mountstephen, Sir William H., 1868–1946, vol. IV

Mountsteven, Col Francis Hender, 1844–1935, vol. III

Mousley, Edward Opotiki, 1886–1965, vol. VI

Mowat, Col Sir Alfred Law, 2nd Bt, 1890–1968, vol. VI

Mowat, Rev. Canon John Dickson, *died* 1955, vol. V

Mowat, Sir John Gunn, 1st Bt, 1859–1935, vol. III

Mowat, Brig.-Gen. Magnus, 1875–1953, vol. V

Mowat, Hon. Sir Oliver, 1820–1903, vol. I

Mowat, Robert Anderson, 1843–1925, vol. II

Mowat, Robert Balmain, 1883–1941, vol. IV

Mowatt, Lt-Col Charles Ryder John, 1872–1943, vol. IV

Mowatt, Rt Hon. Sir Francis, 1837–1919, vol. II

Mowbray, 24th Baron, **Segrave**, 25th Baron, **and** Stourton, 21st Baron, 1867–1936, vol. III

Mowbray, 25th Baron, **Segrave**, 26th Baron, **and** Stourton, 22nd Baron, 1895–1965, vol. VI

Mowbray, Rev. Sir Edmund George Lionel, 4th Bt, 1859–1919, vol. II

Mowbray, Sir George Robert, 5th Bt, 1899–1969, vol. VI

Mowbray, Major John Leslie, 1875–1916, vol. II

Mowbray, Rt Hon. Sir John Robert, 1st Bt, 1815–1899, vol. I

Mowbray, Sir Reginald Ambrose, 3rd Bt, 1852–1916, vol. II

Mowbray, Robert, 1877–1947, vol. IV

Mowbray, Sir Robert Gray Cornish, 2nd Bt, 1850–1916, vol. II

Mower, Sara M.; see Jordan, S. M.

Mowle, William Stewart, 1867–1935, vol. III

Mowll, Rt Rev. Edward Worsfold, 1881–1964, vol. VI

Mowll, Most Rev. Howard West Kilvinton, 1890–1958, vol. V

Mowrer, Edgar Ansel, 1892–1977, vol. VII

Moxham, Sir Harry Cuthbertson, died 1965, vol. VI

Moxon, Col Charles Carter, 1866–1924, vol. II

Moxon, Sir John, died 1943, vol. IV

Moxon, Rev. Canon Reginald Stewart, died 1950, vol. IV

Moxon, Ven. Robert Julius, vol. II

Moxon, Rev. Preb. Thomas Allen, 1877–1943, vol. IV

Moyer, L. Clare, 1887–1958, vol. V

Moyers, Sir George, 1836–1916, vol. II

Moyes, Rt Rev. John Stoward, 1884–1972, vol. VII

Moyes, William Henry, died 1926, vol. II

Moylan, Sir John Fitzgerald, 1882–1967, vol. VI

Moyle, Baron (Life Peer); Arthur Moyle, 1894–1974, vol. VII

Moynan, R. T., 1856–1906, vol. I

Moyne, 1st Baron, 1880–1944, vol. IV

Moynihan, 1st Baron, 1865–1936, vol. III

Moynihan, 2nd Baron, 1906–1965, vol. VI

Moynihan, Most Rev. Denis, 1885–1975, vol. VII

Moyse, Charles E., 1852–1924, vol. II

Moysey, Maj.-Gen. Charles John, 1840–1922, vol. II

Moysey, Edward Luttrell, died 1970, vol. VI

Moysey, Henry Luttrell, 1849–1918, vol. II

Mozley, Lt-Col Edward Newman, 1875–1950, vol. IV

Mozley, Rev. John Kenneth, 1883–1946, vol. IV

Muchmore, Alfred, 1893–1962, vol. VI

Mucklow, Graham Fernie, 1894–1973, vol. VII

Mudaliar, Diwan Bahadur Sir Arcot Lakshmanaswami, 1887–1974, vol. VII

Mudaliar, Diwan Bahadur Sir Arcot Ramaswami, 1877–1976, vol. VII

Mudaliar, Dewan Bahadur V. Shanmuga, 1874–1953, vol. V

Mudaliyar, Rao Bahadur C. Jumbulingam, died 1906, vol. I

Muddiman, Sir Alexander Phillips, 1875–1928, vol. II

Muddock, J. E. Preston, died 1934, vol. III

Mudford, W. H., 1839–1916, vol. II

Mudge, Brig.-Gen. Arthur, 1871–1958, vol. V

Mudhol, Lt Meherban Raja Sir Malojirao Vyankatrao Raje Ghorpade, 1884–1937, vol. III

Mudholkar, Hon. Rao Bahadur Rangnath Narsinh, 1857–1921, vol. II

Mudie, Sir Francis; see Mudie, Sir R. F.

Mudie, Sir (Robert) Francis, 1890–1976, vol. VII

Mudie, Brig. Thomas Couper, 1880–1948, vol. IV

Mudie-Smith, Richard, 1877–1916, vol. II

Muecke, Francis Frederick, 1879–1945, vol. IV

Mueller, Sir Ferdinand von, 1825–1897, vol. I

Muggeridge, Henry Thomas, 1864–1942, vol. IV

Mugliston, Francis Hugh, 1886–1932, vol. III

Muhammad Amir Hasan Khan, 1849–1903, vol. I

Muhammad Fakhr-ud-Din, Khan Bahadur Sir Saiyed, died 1933, vol. III

Muhammad Iqbal, Sheikh Sir, 1876–1938, vol. III

Muhammad Rafiq, Sir, died 1929, vol. III

Muhammed Aslam Khan, Hon. Col Nawab, died 1914, vol. I

Muhrman, Henry, 1854–1916, vol. II

Muir, Sir (Alexander) Kay, 2nd Bt, 1868–1951, vol. V

Muir, Col Archibald Huleatt Huntly, 1886–1948, vol. IV

Muir, Col Charles Wemyss, 1850–1920, vol. II

Muir, Sir Edward Francis, 1905–1979, vol. VII

Muir, Sir Edward Grainger, 1906–1973, vol. VII

Muir, Edwin, 1887–1959, vol. V

Muir, Ernest, 1880–1974, vol. VII

Muir, James, 1875–1945, vol. IV

Muir, James, died 1960, vol. V

Muir, Sir John, 1st Bt, 1828–1903, vol. I

Muir, John, 1838–1914, vol. I

Muir, Lt-Col John Balderstone, died 1955, vol. V

Muir, John William, 1879–1931, vol. III

Muir, Sir Kay; see Muir, Sir A. K.

Muir, Matthew Moncrieff Pattison, 1848–1931, vol. III

Muir, Rt Rev. Pearson M'Adam, 1846–1924, vol. II

Muir, Percival Horace, 1894–1979, vol. VII

Muir, Ramsay, 1872–1941, vol. IV

Muir, Sir Richard David, 1857–1924, vol. II

Muir, Sir Robert, 1864–1959, vol. V

Muir, Ronald James Samuel, 1899–1960, vol. V

Muir, Ronald John K.; see Kerr-Muir.

Muir, Sir Thomas, 1844–1934, vol. III

Muir, Ward, 1878–1927, vol. II

Muir, Sir William, 1819–1905, vol. I

Muir, William, 1844–1929, vol. III

Muir, Lt-Col Wingate Wemyss, 1879–1966, vol. VI

Muir-Mackenzie, 1st Baron, 1845–1930, vol. III

Muir-Mackenzie, Sir Alexander, 3rd Bt, 1840–1909, vol. I

Muir-Mackenzie, Sir John William Pitt, 1854–1916, vol. II

Muir Mackenzie, Kenneth James, 1882–1931, vol. III

Muir-Mackenzie, Montague, 1847–1919, vol. II

Muir-Mackenzie, Sir Robert Cecil, 5th Bt, 1891–1918, vol. II

Muir Mackenzie, Sir Robert Henry, 6th Bt, 1917–1970, vol. VI

Muir-Mackenzie, Lt-Col Sir Robert Smythe, 4th Bt, 1841–1918, vol. II

Muirhead, Alexander, died 1920, vol. III

Muirhead, Alexander, 1859–1935, vol. III

Muirhead, Lt-Col Anthony John, 1890–1939, vol. III

Muirhead, Charles Alexander, 1888–1967, vol. VI

Muirhead, David, died 1930, vol. III

Muirhead, Findlay, 1860–1935, vol. III

Muirhead, James Fullarton, 1853–1934, vol. III
Muirhead, Lt-Col James Ingram, 1893–1964, vol. VI
Muirhead, John, 1863–1927, vol. II
Muirhead, John Henry, 1855–1940, vol. III
Muirhead, Sir John Spencer, 1889–1972, vol. VII
Muirhead, (Litellus) Russell, 1896–1976, vol. VII
Muirhead, Peter Haig, died 1958, vol. V
Muirhead, Russell; see Muirhead, L. R.
Mukerjee, Most Rev. Arabinda Nath, 1892–1970, vol. VI (AII)
Mukerjee, Radhakamal, 1889–1968, vol. VI
Mukerjee, Air Marshal Subroto, 1911–1960, vol. V
Mukerji, Sir Lal Gopal, 1874–1942, vol. IV
Mukerji, Sir Manmatha Nath, 1874–1942, vol. IV
Mukerji, Rai Bahadur P. N., 1882–1965, vol. VI
Mukle, May, 1880–1963, vol. VI
Mulcahy, Hon. Edward, 1850–1927, vol. II
Mulcahy, Maj.-Gen. Sir Francis Edward, 1857–1940, vol. III
Mulcahy, Gen. Richard, 1886–1971, vol. VII
Muldoon, John, 1865–1938, vol. III
Mules, Sir Charles; see Mules, Sir H. C.
Mules, Rt Rev. Charles Oliver, 1837–1927, vol. II
Mules, Sir (Horace) Charles, 1856–1939, vol. III
Mulford, Clarence Edward, 1883–1956, vol. V
Mulhall, John Archibald, 1899–1971, vol. VII
Mulhall, Michael G., 1836–1900, vol. I
Mulhern, Most Rev. Edward C., 1863–1943, vol. IV
Mulholland, Hon. Alfred John, 1856–1938, vol. III
Mulholland, Hon. (Andrew) Edward (Somerset), 1882–1914, vol. I
Mulholland, Gp Captain Denis Osmond, 1891–1949, vol. IV
Mulholland, Hon. Edward; see Mulholland, Hon. A. E. S.
Mulholland, Hon. (Godfrey) John (Arthur Murray Lyle), 1892–1948, vol. IV
Mulholland, Rt Hon. Sir Henry George Hill, 1st Bt, 1888–1971, vol. VII
Mulholland, Hon. John; see Mulholland, Hon. G. J. A. M. L.
Mulholland, Rosa; see Gilbert, Rosa, (Lady Gilbert).
Mulholland, W., 1843–1907, vol. I
Mulholland, Sir Walter; see Mulholland, Sir W. W.
Mulholland, Sir (William) Walter, 1887–1971, vol. VII
Mulji, Rao Sahib Sir Vasanji Trikamji, 1866–1925, vol. II (A), vol. III
Mulla, Rt Hon. Sir Dinshah Fardunji, 1868–1934, vol. III
Mullally, Gerald Thomas, 1887–1969, vol. VI
Mullaly, Maj.-Gen. Sir Herbert, 1860–1932, vol. III
Mullaly, Joseph John, 1853–1936, vol. III
Mullan, Charles Seymour, 1893–1969, vol. VI
Mullen, Benjamin Henry, 1862–1925, vol. II
Mullen, Lt-Col John Lawrence William F.; see Ffrench-Mullen.
Mullen, Lt-Col Leslie Miltiades, 1882–1943, vol. IV
Mulleneux, Captain Hugh Bowring, 1878–1947, vol. IV
Mulleneux-Grayson, Louise Mary, (Lady Mulleneux-Grayson); see Dale, Louise.

Mullens, Sir Harold Hill, 1900–1980, vol. VII
Mullens, Sir John Ashley, 1869–1937, vol. III
Mullens, Maj.-Gen. Richard Lucas, 1871–1952, vol. V
Mullens, Sir William John Herbert de Wette, 1909–1975, vol. VII
Müller, Rt Hon. Friedrich M.; see Max-Müller.
Muller, Col George Herbert, 1856–1932, vol. III
Muller, Hermann Joseph, 1890–1967, vol. VI
Müller, Hugo, died 1915, vol. I
Muller, J. P., 1866–1938, vol. III
Muller, Lt-Col John, 1883–1942, vol. IV
Muller, Oswald Valdemar, 1868–1900, vol. I
Müller, W. Max, 1862–1919, vol. II
Muller, Walter Angus, 1898–1970, vol. VI
Muller, Sir William Grenfell M.; see Max-Muller.
Mullick, Sir Basanta Kumar, 1868–1931, vol. III
Mulligan, James, 1847–1937, vol. III
Mullin, Daniel, born 1860, vol. III
Mulliner, Ven. Harold George, 1897–1946, vol. IV
Mullinger, James Bass, died 1917, vol. II
Mullings, Sir Clement Tudway, 1874–1962, vol. VI
Mullings, Frank Coningsby, 1881–1953, vol. V
Mullins, Arthur, 1895–1963, vol. VI
Mullins, Major Charles Herbert, died 1916, vol. II
Mullins, Claud, 1887–1968, vol. VI
Mullins, Gen. George James Herbert, died 1943, vol. IV
Mullins, Lt-Col George Lane, 1862–1918, vol. II
Mullins, Hon. John Lane, 1857–1939, vol. III
Mulock, Air Cdre Redford Henry, 1886–1961, vol. IV
Mulock, Rt Hon. Sir William, 1844–1944, vol. IV
Mulvany, Charles Mathew, 1867–1945, vol. IV
Mulvany, T. R., 1839–1907, vol. I
Mulvany, Most Rev. Thomas, died 1943, vol. IV
Mulvey, Anthony, 1882–1957, vol. V
Mulvey, Thomas, 1863–1935, vol. III
Mumford, A. Harold, 1864–1939, vol. III
Mumford, Henry Plevy, 1862–1941, vol. IV
Mummery, John Howard, 1847–1926, vol. II
Mummery, John Percy L.; see Lockhart-Mummery.
Mumtazud Dowlah Muhammad Faiyaz Ali Khan; see Faiyaz Ali Khan.
Mun, Adrien Albert Marie, Comte de, 1841–1914, vol. I
Munby, Alan Noel Latimer, 1913–1974, vol. VII
Munby, Lt-Col Aldwin Montgomery, 1882–1939, vol. III
Munby, Lt-Col Joseph Ernest, 1881–1962, vol. VI
Muncaster, 5th Baron, 1834–1917, vol. II
Muncaster, Claude, 1903–1974, vol. VII
Muncey, Rev. Edward Howard Parker, 1886–1954, vol. V
Munch, Charles, 1891–1968, vol. VI
Mundahl, Henry Smethurst, 1865–1938, vol. III
Munday, Charles Frederick, 1868–1948, vol. IV
Munday, John A., 1863–1932, vol. III
Munday, Luther, 1857–1922, vol. II
Munday, Maj.-Gen. Richard Cleveland, 1867–1952, vol. V
Munday, Sir William Luscombe, 1865–1952, vol. V

Mundelein, Cardinal George William, 1872–1939, vol. III

Mundella, Rt Hon. Anthony John, 1825–1897, vol. I

Mundy, Alfred Edward Miller, 1849–1920, vol. II

Mundy, Adm. Godfrey Harry Brydges, 1860–1928, vol. II

Mundy, John Cloudesley, 1900–1971, vol. VII

Mundy, Sir Otto, 1887–1958, vol. V

Mundy, Talbot, 1879–1940, vol. III

Munford, James, 1852–1932, vol. III

Muni, Paul, 1895–1967, vol. VI

Munir Bey, Sir Mehmed, 1890–1957, vol. V

Munn, Rt Rev. Eric George, 1903–1968, vol. VI

Munn, Mrs Marguerite; see Bryant, M.

Munn, Lt-Col Reginald George, died 1947, vol. IV

Munnings, Sir Alfred J., 1878–1959, vol. V

Munro, Sir Alan Whiteside, 1898–1968, vol. VI

Munro, Maj.-Gen. Archibald Campbell, 1886–1961, vol. VI

Munro, Sir Arthur Herman, 14th Bt (cr 1634), 1893–1972, vol. VII

Munro, Sir Arthur Talbot, 13th Bt (cr 1634), 1866–1953, vol. V

Munro, Sir Campbell, 3rd Bt (cr 1825), 1823–1913 (this entry was not transferred to Who was Who).

Munro, C(harles) K.; see MacMullan, C. W. K.

Munro, Air Vice-Marshal Sir David, 1878–1952, vol. V

Munro, Lt-Col David Campbell Duncan, 1885–1974, vol. VII

Munro, Captain Donald John, 1865–1952, vol. V

Munro, Sir George Hamilton, 12th Bt (cr 1634), 1864–1945, vol. IV

Munro, Sir Gordon; see Munro, Sir R. G.

Munro, Lt-Gen. Gustavus Francis, 1835–1908, vol. I

Munro, Sir Hector, 11th Bt (cr 1634), 1849–1935, vol. III

Munro, Sir Henry, 1842–1921, vol. II

Munro, Sir Hugh Thomas, 4th Bt (cr 1825), 1856–1919, vol. II

Munro, John, died 1930, vol. III

Munro, John Arthur Ruskin, 1864–1944, vol. IV

Munro, Leo, 1878–1957, vol. V

Munro, Sir Leslie Knox, 1901–1974, vol. VII

Munro, Col Lewis, 1859–1927, vol. II

Munro, Neil, 1864–1930, vol. III

Munro, Patrick, 1883–1942, vol. IV

Munro, Sir (Richard) Gordon, 1895–1967, vol. VI

Munro, Robert, 1835–1920, vol. II

Munro, Sir Thomas, 2nd Bt (cr 1825), 1819–1901, vol. I

Munro, Sir Thomas, 1866–1923, vol. II

Munro, Thomas Arthur Howard, 1905–1966, vol. VI

Munro, William Bennett, 1875–1957, vol. V

Munro, William Thow, 1884–1948, vol. IV

Munroe, Sir Harry C.; see Courthope-Munroe.

Munroe, Lt-Col Hon. Hugh Edwin, 1879–1947, vol. IV

Munrow, David John, 1942–1976, vol. VII

Munsey, Frank Andrew, 1854–1925, vol. II

Munster, 2nd Earl of, 1824–1901, vol. I

Munster, 3rd Earl of, 1859–1902, vol. I

Munster, 4th Earl of, 1862–1928, vol. II

Munster, 5th Earl of, 1906–1975, vol. VII

Munster, Countess; (Wilhelmina), 1830–1906, vol. I

Münster Derneburg, Prince, 1820–1902, vol. I

Münsterberg, Hugo, 1863–1916, vol. II

Munthe, Axel, 1857–1949, vol. IV

Muntz, Frederick Ernest, 1845–1920, vol. II

Muntz, Sir Gerard Albert, 2nd Bt, 1864–1927, vol. II

Muntz, Sir Gerard Philip Graves, 3rd Bt, 1917–1940, vol. III (A), vol. IV

Muntz, Sir Philip Albert, 1st Bt, 1839–1908, vol. I

Murchie, Lt-Gen. John Carl, 1895–1966, vol. VI

Murchison, Sir (Charles) Kenneth, 1872–1952, vol. V

Murchison, Sir Kenneth; see Murchison, Sir C. K.

Murdoch, Charles, 1902–1962, vol. VI (AII)

Murdoch, Charles, 1925–1979, vol. VII

Murdoch, Charles Stewart, 1838–1908, vol. I

Murdoch, Charles Townshend, 1837–1898, vol. I

Murdoch, Hector B.; see Burn-Murdoch.

Murdoch, James, 1856–1921, vol. II

Murdoch, Lt-Col Sir James Anderson, 1867–1939, vol. III

Murdoch, Rev. Canon James McGibbon B.; see Burn-Murdoch.

Murdoch, Maj.-Gen. Sir John Francis B.; see Burn-Murdoch.

Murdoch, John Smith, 1863–1945, vol. IV

Murdoch, Sir Keith Arthur, 1886–1952, vol. V

Murdoch, Hon. Thomas, 1868–1946, vol. IV

Murdoch, W. G. Blaikie, 1880–1934, vol. III

Murdoch, W. G. Burn; see Burn-Murdoch.

Murdoch, Sir Walter, 1874–1970, vol. VI

Murdoch, William, 1888–1942, vol. IV

Murdoch, William Lloyd, 1855–1911, vol. I

Murdock, Kenneth Ballard, 1895–1975, vol. VII

Mure, Geoffrey Reginald Gilchrist, 1893–1979, vol. VII

Mure, William, 1898–1977, vol. VII

Mure, William John, 1845–1924, vol. II

Murfree, Mary Noailles, died 1922, vol. II (A), vol. III

Murie, James, died 1925, vol. II

Muriel, Rev. Herbert Claude, 1867–1939, vol. III

Murison, Alexander Falconer, 1847–1934, vol. III

Murison, Alfred Ross, 1891–1968, vol. VI

Murison, Sir (James) William, 1872–1945, vol. IV

Murison, Sir William; see Murison, Sir J. M.

Murland, William, died 1926, vol. II

Murnaghan, Francis Dominic, 1893–1976, vol. VII

Murnaghan, George, 1847–1929, vol. III

Murnaghan, James Augustine, 1881–1973, vol. VII

Murphy, Sir Alexander Paterson, 1892–1976, vol. VII

Murphy, Alfred John, 1901–1980, vol. VII

Murphy, Hon. Charles, 1863–1935, vol. III

Murphy, Brig.-Gen. Cyril Francis de Sales, 1882–1961, vol. VI

Murphy, Hon. Denis, 1870–1947, vol. IV

Murphy, Sir Dermod Art Pelly, 1914–1975, vol. VII

Murphy, Rt Hon. Edward Sullivan, 1880–1945, vol. IV
Murphy, Emily F., *died* 1933, vol. III
Murphy, Emmett Patrick, 1887–1960, vol. V
Murphy, Hon. Frank, 1890–1949, vol. IV
Murphy, Air Vice-Marshal Frederick John, 1892–1969, vol. VI
Murphy, George Fitzgerald, 1850–1920, vol. II
Murphy, Col George Francis, 1883–1962, vol. VI
Murphy, Sir George Francis, 2nd Bt (*cr* 1912), 1881–1963, vol. VI
Murphy, Col George Patterson, 1883–1938, vol. III
Murphy, Lt-Col Gerald Patrick, 1888–1978, vol. VII
Murphy, Harold Lawson, 1882–1942, vol. IV
Murphy, Most Rev. Henry, 1912–1973, vol. VII
Murphy, Rev. Hugh Davis, 1849–1927, vol. II
Murphy, Rt Hon. James, 1826–1901, vol. I
Murphy, James Francis, 1893–1949, vol. IV
Murphy, Sir James Joseph, 1st Bt (*cr* 1903), 1843–1922, vol. II
Murphy, James Keogh, 1869–1916, vol. II
Murphy, Very Rev. Jeremiah Matthias, *died* 1955, vol. V
Murphy, Very Rev. John, vol. II
Murphy, John, 1871–1930, vol. III (A), vol. IV
Murphy, Rev. John, 1876–1949, vol. IV
Murphy, Rt Rev. John Baptist Tuohill, 1854–1926, vol. II
Murphy, John Harvey, 1862–1924, vol. II
Murphy, John Patrick, 1831–1907, vol. I
Murphy, (John) Pelly, 1909–1979, vol. VII
Murphy, Martin, 1832–1926, vol. II
Murphy, Martin Joseph, *died* 1919, vol. II
Murphy, Sir Michael, 1st Bt (*cr* 1912), 1845–1925, vol. II
Murphy, Neville Richard, 1890–1971, vol. VII
Murphy, Patrick Charles, 1868–1925, vol. II
Murphy, Pelly; *see* Murphy, J. P.
Murphy, Maj.-Gen. Richard, 1896–1971, vol. VII
Murphy, Robert Daniel, 1894–1978, vol. VII
Murphy, Sir Shirley Forster, *died* 1923, vol. II
Murphy, Sir Stephen James, *died* 1950, vol. IV
Murphy, Rev. William, 1872–1943, vol. IV
Murphy, Sir William Lindsay, 1887–1965, vol. VI
Murphy, William Lombard, *died* 1943, vol. IV
Murphy, William Martin, 1844–1919, vol. II
Murphy, Col William Reed, 1849–1927, vol. II
Murrant, Sir Ernest Henry, 1889–1974, vol. VII
Murray, Rt Hon. Lord; Charles David Murray, 1866–1936, vol. III
Murray of Elibank, 1st Baron, 1870–1920, vol. II
Murray of Gravesend, Baron (Life Peer); Albert James Murray, 1930–1980, vol. VII
Murray, Abijah, *died* 1912, vol. I
Murray, Adam George, 1893–1966, vol. VI
Murray, Alan James Ruthven-, 1900–1959, vol. V
Murray of Blackbarony, Sir Alan John Digby, 14th Bt (*cr* 1628), 1909–1978, vol. VII
Murray, Alastair Campbell, 1895–1957, vol. V
Murray, Albert E., 1849–1924, vol. II
Murray, Albert Victor, 1890–1967, vol. VI
Murray, Col Alexander, 1850–1910, vol. I
Murray, Alexander Davidson, 1840–1907, vol. I

Murray, Alexander Henry Hallam, 1854–1934, vol. III
Murray, Major Alexander Penrose, 1863–1926, vol. II
Murray, Sir Alexander Robertson, 1872–1956, vol. V
Murray, Alexander Stuart, 1841–1904, vol. I
Murray, Sir Alistair; *see* Murray, Sir R. A.
Murray, Alma, 1854–1945, vol. IV
Murray, Col Andrew, 1837–1915, vol. I
Murray, Hon. Andrew David, 1863–1901, vol. I
Murray, Sir Andrew Hunter Arbuthnot, 1903–1977, vol. VII
Murray, Sir Angus Johnston, *died* 1968, vol. VI
Murray, Maj.-Gen. Anthony Hepburn, 1840–1917, vol. II
Murray, Gen. Sir Archibald James, 1860–1945, vol. IV
Murray, Lt-Col Arthur Alexander W.; *see* Wolfe-Murray.
Murray, Lt-Col Arthur E.; *see* Erskine-Murray.
Murray, Adm. Arthur John Layard, 1886–1959, vol. V
Murray, Col Arthur Mordaunt, 1852–1920, vol. II
Murray, Catherine Joan Suzette; *see* Gauvain, C. J. S.
Murray, Charles, 1864–1941, vol. IV
Murray, Lt-Col Charles Crawford, 1863–1939, vol. III
Murray, Rt Hon. Charles David; *see* Murray, Rt Hon. Lord.
Murray, Charles de Bois, 1891–1974, vol. VII
Murray, Gp-Captain Charles Geoffrey, 1880–1962, vol. VI
Murray, Rt Rev. Charles Herbert, 1899–1950, vol. IV
Murray, Charles James, 1851–1929, vol. III
Murray, Charles Oliver, *died* 1924, vol. II
Murray, Charles Stewart, 1858–1903, vol. I
Murray, Charles Wadsworth, 1894–1945, vol. IV
Murray, Colin Alexander, 1847–1913, vol. I
Murray, Colin Robert Baillie, 1892–1979, vol. VII
Murray, Lt-Col Cyril Francis Tyrell, 1863–1929, vol. III
Murray, David, 1842–1928, vol. II
Murray, Sir David, 1849–1933, vol. III
Murray, David Christie, 1847–1907, vol. I
Murray, Col David Keith, 1865–1952, vol. V
Murray, David King; *see* Birnam, Hon. Lord.
Murray, David Leslie, 1888–1962, vol. VI
Murray of Blackbarony, Sir Digby, 11th Bt (*cr* 1628), 1829–1906, vol. I
Murray, Donald, 1862–1923, vol. II
Murray, Col Donald Norman Watson, 1876–1945, vol. IV
Murray, Rev. Canon Edmund Theodore, 1877–1969, vol. VI
Murray, Edward C.; *see* Croft-Murray.
Murray, Paymaster Rear-Adm. Edward F., 1877–1933, vol. III
Murray, Lt-Col Sir Edward Robert, 13th Bt (*cr* 1626), 1875–1958, vol. V
Murray, Sir Evelyn; *see* Murray, Sir G. E. P.

Murray, Everitt George Dunne, 1890–1964, vol. VI

Murray, Brig. Francis Mackenzie, 1880–1958, vol. V

Murray, Col Frank, 1864–1917, vol. II

Murray, Ven. Frederic Richardson, 1845–1925, vol. II

Murray, Rev. Frederick William, *died* 1913, vol. I

Murray, Sir George, 1865–1942, vol. IV

Murray, Brig. Sir (George David) Keith, 1898–1965, vol. VI

Murray, Sir (George) Evelyn (Pemberton), 1880–1947, vol. IV

Murray, (George) Gilbert (Aimé), 1866–1957, vol. V

Murray, Hon. George Henry, 1861–1929, vol. III

Murray, Rt Hon. Sir George Herbert, 1849–1936, vol. III

Murray, Hon. Sir George John Robert, 1863–1942, vol. IV

Murray, George McIntosh, 1900–1970, vol. VI

Murray, George Redmayne, *died* 1939, vol. III

Murray, George Robert Milne, 1858–1911, vol. I

Murray, Sir George Sheppard, 1851–1928, vol. II

Murray, George William Welsh, 1885–1966, vol. VI

Murray, Most Rev. Gerald, *died* 1951, vol. V

Murray, Gilbert; *see* Murray, G. G. A.

Murray, Gladstone; *see* Murray, W. E. G.

Murray, Lt-Col Henry William, 1883–1966, vol. VI

Murray, Lt-Col Herbert Edward, 1889–1951, vol. V

Murray, Sir Herbert Harley, 1829–1904, vol. I

Murray, Herbert Leith, 1880–1932, vol. III

Murray, Rear-Adm. Herbert Patrick William George, 1880–1958, vol. V

Murray, Howard, 1859–1930, vol. III

Murray, Lt-Col Howard, 1876–1934, vol. III

Murray, Sir Hubert; *see* Murray, Sir J. H. P.

Murray, Hubert Leonard, 1886–1963, vol. VI

Murray, Hubert Montague, 1855–1907, vol. I

Murray, Sir Hugh, 1861–1941, vol. IV

Murray, Ian, 1899–1974, vol. VII

Murray, Sir (Jack) Keith, 1889–1979, vol. VII

Murray, Rt Rev. James, 1828–1909, vol. I

Murray, James, 1865–1914, vol. I (A)

Murray, Sir James, 1850–1932, vol. III

Murray, James Alexander, 1873–1950, vol. IV

Murray, Sir James Augustus Henry, 1837–1915, vol. I

Murray, James Dixon, 1887–1965, vol. VI

Murray, James Whiteford, *died* 1941, vol. IV

Murray, Lt-Gen. Sir James Wolfe, 1853–1919, vol. II

Murray, Captain James Wolfe, 1880–1930, vol. III

Murray, Sir John, 1841–1914, vol. I

Murray, Sir John, 1851–1928, vol. II

Murray, John, 1883–1937, vol. III

Murray, John, 1863–1943, vol. IV

Murray, John, 1871–1954, vol. V

Murray, John, 1879–1964, vol. VI

Murray, Sir John, 1884–1967, vol. VI

Murray, Engr Captain John Adam, 1860–1948, vol. IV

Murray of Blackbarony, Sir John Digby, 12th Bt (*cr* 1628), 1867–1938, vol. III

Murray, John George, 1864–1953, vol. V

Murray, Lt-Col John Hanna, *died* 1959, vol. V

Murray, Sir (John) Hubert (Plunkett), 1861–1940, vol. III

Murray, Gen. Sir John Irvine, 1826–1902, vol. I

Murray, Sir John Murray, 1888–1976, vol. VII

Murray, Rev. John Oswald, 1869–1943, vol. IV

Murray, Rev. John Owen Farquhar, 1858–1944, vol. IV

Murray, John Pears, 1866–1947, vol. IV (A), vol V

Murray, Sir (John) Stanley, 1884–1971, vol. VII

Murray, Brig. Sir Keith; *see* Murray, Brig. Sir G. D. K.

Murray, Sir Keith; *see* Murray, Sir J. K.

Murray, Keith William, 1860–1922, vol. II

Murray of Blackbarony, Sir Kenelm Bold, 13th Bt (*cr* 1628), 1898–1959, vol. V

Murray, Col Kenelm Digby, 1839–1915, vol. I

Murray, Col Kenelm Digby Bold, 1879–1947, vol. IV

Murray, Sir Kenneth, 1891–1979, vol. VII

Murray, Rear-Adm. Leonard Warren, 1896–1971, vol. VII

Murray, Lt-Col Sir Malcolm Donald, 1867–1938, vol. III

Murray, (Malcolm) Patrick, 1905–1979, vol. VII

Murray, Margaret Alice, 1863–1963, vol. VI

Murray, Margaret Mary Alberta, *died* 1974, vol. VII

Murray, Sir Norman McIver, *died* 1934, vol. III

Murray, Sir Oswyn Alexander Ruthven, 1873–1936, vol. III

Murray, Patrick; *see* Murray, M. P.

Murray, Sir Patrick Ian Keith, 10th Bt (*cr* 1673), 1904–1962, vol. VI

Murray, Sir Patrick Keith, 8th Bt (*cr* 1673), 1835–1921, vol. II

Murray, Philip, 1886–1952, vol. V

Murray, Richard, 1865–1925, vol. II

Murray, Sir Robert, 1846–1924, vol. II

Murray, Robert, 1870–1950, vol. IV

Murray, Sir (Robert) Alistair, 1896–1973, vol. VII

Murray, Col Robert Davidson, 1851–1920, vol. II

Murray, Rev. Canon Robert Henry, *died* 1947, vol. IV

Murray, Robert Howson, 1882–1960, vol. V

Murray, Maj.-Gen. Robert Hunter, 1847–1925, vol. II

Murray, Rear-Adm. Ronald Gordon, 1898–1975, vol. VII

Murray, Major Hon. Ronald Thomas Graham, 1875–1934, vol. III

Murray, Col Shadwell John, 1867–1940, vol. III

Murray, Sir Stanley; *see* Murray, Sir J. S.

Murray, Lt-Col Stewart George Cromartie, 1884–1932, vol. III

Murray, T. C., 1873–1959, vol. V

Murray, T. Douglas, 1841–1911, vol. I

Murray, Brig. Terence Desmond, 1891–1961, vol. VI

Murray, Thomas J., 1880–1936, vol. III

Murray, Hon. Sir Thomas Keir, 1854–1936, vol. III
Murray, Brig.-Gen. Sir Valentine, 1867–1942, vol. IV
Murray, Violet Cecil, 1885–1961, vol. VI
Murray, Rev. W. Rigby, *died* 1914, vol. I
Murray, Walter Charles, 1866–1946, vol. IV
Murray, Lt-Col Walter Graham, 1868–1937, vol. III
Murray, Major William, 1865–1923, vol. II
Murray, William Alexander, 1889–1935, vol. III
Murray, Lt-Col William Atholl, 1879–1953, vol. V
Murray, (William Ewart) Gladstone, 1893–1970, vol. VI
Murray, Rev. William Hill, 1843–1911, vol. I
Murray, Brig.-Gen. William Hugh Eric, 1858–1915, vol. I
Murray, Sir William Keith, 9th Bt (*cr* 1673), 1872–1956, vol. V
Murray, Sir William Patrick Keith, 11th Bt (*cr* 1673), 1939–1977, vol. VII
Murray, Sir William Robert, 12th Bt (*cr* 1626), 1840–1904, vol. I
Murray, William Staite, 1881–1962, vol. VI
Murray, Col Sir Wyndham, 1844–1928, vol. II
Murray-Aynsley, Sir Charles Murray, 1893–1967, vol. VI
Murray Baillie, Lt-Col Frederick David, 1862–1924, vol. II
Murray-Harvey, Captain Edward, 1886–1967, vol. VI
Murray-Philipson, Hylton Ralph; *see* Philipson.
Murray-Smith, Lt-Col Arthur, 1868–1943, vol. IV
Murray-Threipland, Col William, 1866–1942, vol. IV
Murray-White, Col Richard Stephen; *see* White.
Murrell, Frank Edric Joseph, 1874–1931, vol. III
Murrell, William, 1853–1912, vol. I
Murrell, William Lee, 1893–1971, vol. VII
Murrill, Herbert Henry John, 1909–1952, vol. V
Murrough, John Patrick, 1822–1901, vol. I
Murrow, Edward R., 1908–1965, vol. VI
Murry, John Middleton, 1889–1957, vol. V
Murshedabad, Nawab Bahadur of, 1846–1906, vol. I
Murshidabad, Nawab Bahadur of, 1875–1959, vol. V (A)
Murton, Sir Walter, 1836–1927, vol. II
Muscat, HH The Sultan of, *died* 1913, vol. I
Muschamp, Sidney, *died* 1929, vol. III
Muscio, Bernard, 1887–1926, vol. III
Muselier, Vice-Am. d'Escadre Emile Henry, 1882–1965, vol. VI
Musgrave, Hon. Anthony, 1849–1912, vol. I
Musgrave, Brig.-Gen. Arthur David, 1874–1931, vol. III
Musgrave, Sir Charles, 14th Bt (*cr* 1611), 1913–1970, vol. VI
Musgrave, Charles Edwin, 1861–1923, vol. II
Musgrave, Sir Christopher George, 1855–1929, vol. III
Musgrave, Lt-Col Sir Christopher Norman, 6th Bt (*cr* 1782), 1892–1956, vol. V
Musgrave, Sir Courtenay; *see* Musgrave, Sir N. C.

Musgrave, Ernest Illingworth, 1901–1957, vol. V
Musgrave, Major Herbert, 1876–1918, vol. II
Musgrave, Herbert Wenman W.; *see* Wykeham-Musgrave.
Musgrave, Sir James, 1st Bt (*cr* 1897), 1829–1904, vol. I
Musgrave, Sir (Nigel) Courtenay, 13th Bt (*cr* 1611), 1896–1957, vol. V
Musgrave, Noel Henry, 1903–1971, vol. VII
Musgrave, Sir Richard George, 12th Bt (*cr* 1611), 1872–1926, vol. II
Musgrave, Sir Richard John, 5th Bt (*cr* 1782), 1850–1930, vol. III
Musgrave, Rev. Vernon, *died* 1906, vol. I
Musgrove, James, 1862–1935, vol. III
Muskerry, 4th Baron, 1854–1929, vol. III
Muskerry, 5th Baron, 1874–1952, vol. V
Muskerry, 6th Baron, 1875–1954, vol. V
Muskerry, 7th Baron, 1874–1966, vol. VI
Muspratt, Edmund K., 1833–1923, vol. II
Muspratt, Brig.-Gen. Francis Clifton, 1864–1944, vol. IV
Muspratt, Sir Max, 1st Bt, 1872–1934, vol. III
Muspratt, Gen. Sir Sydney Frederick, 1878–1972, vol. VII
Muspratt-Williams, Lt-Col Charles Augustus, 1861–1925, vol. II
Musselwhite, Ven. William Ralph, 1887–1956, vol. V
Mussen, Sir Gerald, 1872–1960, vol. V
Mussenden, Maj.-Gen. William, 1836–1910, vol. I
Mussolini, Benito, 1883–1945, vol. IV
Musson, Maj.-Gen. Arthur Ingram, 1877–1961, vol. VI
Musson, Dame Ellen Mary, *died* 1960, vol. V
Musson, Francis William, 1894–1962, vol. VI
Musters, Col John Nevile C.; *see* Chaworth-Musters.
Musters, John Patricius Chaworth, 1860–1921, vol. II
Musto, Sir Arnold Albert, 1883–1977, vol. VII
Mustoe, Nelson Edwin, *died* 1976, vol. VII
Musurus Pasha, Stephen, 1841–1907, vol. I
Mutch, Air Cdre James Richard, 1905–1973, vol. VII
Muther, Richard, 1860–1909, vol. I
Muthiah Chettiar, Sir M. C. T., 1887–1929, vol. III
Mutter, Rev. Cecil G., 1876–1942, vol. IV
Muzammilullah Khan, Khan Bahadur Nawab Sir Muhammad, *died* 1938, vol. III
Myburgh, Brig. Philip Stafford, 1893–1963, vol. VI
Myddelton, Robert Edward, 1866–1949, vol. IV
Myer, Lt-Col George Val., 1883–1959, vol. V
Myer, Horatio, 1850–1916, vol. II
Myer, Sir Norman, 1897–1956, vol. V
Myers, Hon. Sir Arthur, 1867–1926, vol. II
Myers, Arthur Wallis, 1878–1939, vol. III
Myers, Asher Isaac, 1848–1902, vol. I
Myers, Bernard, 1872–1957, vol. V
Myers, Rev. Canon Charles, 1856–1948, vol. IV
Myers, Charles Samuel, 1873–1946, vol. IV
Myers, Sir Dudley Borron, 1861–1944, vol. IV
Myers, Most Rev. Edward, 1875–1956, vol. V
Myers, Frederic W. H., 1843–1901, vol. I

Myers, Sir James Eckersley, 1890–1958, vol. V
Myers, Leo Hamilton, 1881–1944, vol. IV
Myers, Leonard William, *died* 1962, vol. VI
Myers, Rt Hon. Sir Michael, 1873–1950, vol. IV
Myers, Tom, 1872–1949, vol. IV
Myers, William Henry, 1854–1933, vol. III
Myles, Captain Edgar Kinghorn, 1894–1977, vol. VII
Myles, Sir Thomas, 1857–1937, vol. III
Myles, Surg.-Captain Thomas William, 1878–1933, vol. III
Mylks, Gordon Wright, 1874–1957, vol. V
Mylne, Rev. Alan Moultrie, 1886–1944, vol. IV
Mylne, Rt Rev. Louis George, 1843–1921, vol. II
Mynors, Rev. Aubrey Baskerville, 1865–1937, vol. III
Myrander; *see* Stevenson, James Alexander.
Myrddin-Evans, Sir Guildhaume, 1894–1964, vol. VI
Myres, Sir John Linton, 1869–1954, vol. V
Mysore, HH Maharaja of, 1884–1940, vol. III
Mysore, HH Maharaja of, 1919–1974, vol. VII
Mysore, Yuvaraja of, 1888–1940, vol. III
Mytton, Sir Thomas Henry, 1878–1966, vol. VI

N

Nabarro, David Nunes, 1874–1958, vol. V
Nabarro, Sir Gerald David Nunes, 1913–1973, vol. VII
Nabha, HH Rajah, 1843–1911, vol. I
Nabokov, Vladimir, 1899–1977, vol. VII
Nadia, Maharaja of, 1890–1928, vol. II
Naef, Sir Conrad James, 1871–1954, vol. V
Naegeli, Otto, *died* 1938, vol. III (A), vol. IV
Naesmith, Sir Andrew, 1888–1961, vol. VI
Naesmyth, Sir Douglas Arthur Bradley, 8th Bt, 1905–1928, vol. II
Naesmyth, Sir James Tolmé, 7th Bt, 1864–1922, vol. II
Naesmyth, Sir Michael George, 6th Bt, 1828–1907 (this entry was not transferred to Who was Who)
Nagar, Raja Sir Sikander Khan of, *died* 1940, vol. III
Nahum, Jack Messoud Eric di Victor, 1906–1959, vol. V
Naidu, Mme Sarojini, *died* 1949, vol. IV
Nair, Rt Hon. Sir C. Madhavan, 1879–1970, vol. VI (AII)
Nair, Sir Chettur S.; *see* Sankaran Nair.
Nairac, Sir Edouard; *see* Nairac, Sir G. E.
Nairac, Sir (George) Edouard, 1876–1960, vol. VI (AI)
Nairn, Bryce James Miller, 1903–1978, vol. VII
Nairn, Sir Douglas Leslie Spencer-, 2nd Bt, 1906–1970, vol. VI
Nairn, George Alexander Stokes, 1889–1974, vol. VII
Nairn, Rev. John Arbuthnot, 1874–1957, vol. V
Nairn, Sir Michael, 2nd Bt, 1874–1952, vol. V

Nairn, Sir Michael Barker, 1st Bt, 1838–1915, vol. I (A)
Nairn, Major Sir Robert S.; *see* Spencer-Nairn.
Nairn, Walter Maxwell, *died* 1958, vol. V
Nairne, Rev. Alexander, 1863–1936, vol. III
Nairne, Gen. Sir Charles Edward, 1836–1899, vol. I
Nairne, Major Lord Charles George Francis M.; *see* Mercer-Nairne.
Nairne, Brig.-Gen. Edward Spencer Hoare, 1869–1958, vol. V
Nairne, Sir Gordon; *see* Nairne, Sir J. G.
Nairne, Rev. John Domett, 1846–1929, vol. III
Nairne, Sir (John) Gordon, 1st Bt, 1861–1945, vol. IV
Nairne, Sir Perceval Alleyn, 1841–1921, vol. II
Naish, Albert Ernest, 1871–1964, vol. VI
Naish, Rear-Adm. George Oswald, 1904–1960, vol. V
Naish, Lt-Comdr George Prideaux Brabant, 1909–1977, vol. VII
Naish, John Paull, *died* 1964, vol. VI
Naish, Redmond, *born* 1848, vol. II
Naismith, Lt-Col William John, 1847–1926, vol. II
Nalder, Leonard Fielding, 1888–1958, vol. V
Nalder, Maj.-Gen. Reginald Francis Heaton, 1895–1978, vol. VII
Naldrett, Edward James, *died* 1930, vol. III
Nall, J(ohn) Spencer, 1887–1970, vol. VI
Nall, Col Sir Joseph, 1st Bt, 1887–1958, vol. V
Nally, Will, 1914–1965, vol. VI
Namier, Sir Lewis Bernstein, 1888–1960, vol. V
Nan Kivell, Sir Rex de Charambac, 1899–1977, vol. VII
Nanak Chand, Masheerud-dowal Rai Bahadur, 1860–1920, vol. II (A), vol. III
Nanavati, Sir Manilal B., 1877–1967, vol. VI
Nanavatty, Col Sir Byramji Hormasji, 1861–1937, vol. III
Nance, Surg.-Captain Sir Arthur Stanley, 1860–1938, vol. III
Nance, Rev. James Trengove, 1852–1942, vol. IV
Nand Lal, Diwan Bahadur Pandit, 1857–1926, vol. II
Nandris, Grigore, 1895–1968, vol. VI
Nanjundayya, H. Velpanuru, 1860–1920, vol. II
NanKivell, Sir Rex de Charambac; *see* Nan Kivell.
Nannetti, Joseph Patrick, 1851–1915, vol. I
Nansen, Fridtjof, 1861–1930, vol. III
Nanson, Edward John, 1850–1936, vol. III
Nanson, Group Captain Eric Roper-Curzon, 1883–1960, vol. V
Nanson, Hon. John Leighton, 1863–1916, vol. II
Nantel, Hon. Wilfrid Bruno, 1857–1940, vol. III (A), vol. IV
Nanton, Sir Augustus Meredith, 1860–1925, vol. II
Nanton, Brig.-Gen. Herbert Colbourne, 1863–1935, vol. III
Naoroji, Dadabhai, 1825–1917, vol. II
Naper, Captain William Lenox, 1879–1942, vol. IV
Napier, 10th Lord, **and Ettrick**, 1st Baron, 1819–1898, vol. I
Napier, 11th Lord, **and Ettrick**, 2nd Baron, 1846–1913, vol. I

Napier, 12th Lord, **and Ettrick,** 3rd Baron, 1876–1941, vol. IV

Napier, 13th Lord, **and Ettrick,** 4th Baron, 1900–1954, vol. V

Napier of Magdala, 2nd Baron, 1845–1921, vol. II

Napier of Magdala, 3rd Baron, 1849–1935, vol. III

Napier of Magdala, 4th Baron, 1861–1948, vol. IV

Napier, Hon. Sir Albert Edward Alexander, 1881–1973, vol. VII

Napier, Albert Napier Williamson, 1894–1969, vol. VI

Napier, Col Alexander, 1851–1928, vol. II

Napier, Captain Sir Alexander Lennox Milliken, 11th Bt (*cr* 1627), 1882–1954, vol. V

Napier, Sir Archibald Lennox Milliken, 10th Bt (*cr* 1627), 1855–1907, vol. I

Napier, Arthur Sampson, 1853–1916, vol. II

Napier, Charles Frederick, 1862–1932, vol. III

Napier, Charles Goddard, 1889–1978, vol. VII

Napier, Adm. Charles Lionel, 1861–1934, vol. III

Napier, Col Charles Scott, 1899–1946, vol. IV

Napier, Major Egbert, 1867–1916, vol. II

Napier, Lt-Col Hon. George Campbell, 1845–1914, vol. I

Napier, Lt-Col Hon. Henry Dundas, 1864–1941, vol. IV

Napier, Ian Patrick Robert, 1895–1977, vol. VII

Napier, Brig. John Lenox Clavering, 1898–1966, vol. VI

Napier, Hon. Sir (John) Mellis, 1882–1976, vol. VII

Napier, Col Hon. John Scott, 1848–1938, vol. III

Napier, Lionel Everard, 1888–1957, vol. V

Napier, Hon. Mark Francis, 1852–1919, vol. II

Napier, Hon. Sir Mellis; *see* Napier, Hon. Sir J. M.

Napier, Sir Robert Archibald, 12th Bt (*cr* 1627), 1889–1965, vol. VI

Napier, Thomas Bateman, 1854–1933, vol. III

Napier, Vice-Adm. Sir Trevylyan Dacres Willes, 1867–1920, vol. II

Napier, Brig. Vernon Monro Colquhoun, 1881–1957, vol. V

Napier, Sir Walter John, 1857–1945, vol. IV

Napier, Col William, 1861–1920, vol. II (A), vol. III

Napier, William Heathcote Unwin, *died* 1959, vol. V

Napier, Maj.-Gen. William John, 1863–1925, vol. II

Napier, Sir William Lennox, 3rd Bt (*cr* 1867), 1867–1915, vol. I

Napier, Adm. William Rawdon, 1877–1951, vol. V

Napier-Clavering, Col Charles Warren, 1858–1931, vol. III

Napier-Clavering, Maj.-Gen. Noel Warren, 1888–1964, vol. VI

Napoleon, Prince Louis, 1864–1932, vol. III

Napoleon, HIH Prince (Victor Jerome Frederic), 1862–1926, vol. II

Napper, Jack Hollingworth, 1904–1978, vol. VII

Narang, Sir Gokul Chand, 1878–1970, vol. VI

Narasimha Gopalaswami Ayyangar, Sir, 1882–1953, vol. V

Narasimha Sarma, Rao Bahadur Sir Bayya, 1867–1932, vol. III

Naratomdas, Sir Harkisandas, 1849–1908, vol. I

Narayan Kissen Sen, 1861–1935, vol. III

Narbeth, John Harper, 1863–1944, vol. IV

Narborough, Rt Rev. Dudley Vaughan; *see* Narborough, Rt Rev. F. D. V.

Narborough, Rt Rev. (Frederick) Dudley Vaughan, 1895–1966, vol. VI

Narendra, Krishna, Sir, Maharajah Bahadur, 1822–1903, vol. I

Nares, Maj.-Gen. Eric Paytherus, 1892–1947, vol. IV

Nares, Sir George Strong, 1831–1915, vol. I

Nares, Vice-Adm. John Dodd, 1877–1957, vol. V

Nares, Owen Ramsay, *died* 1943, vol. IV

Nariman, Sir Temulji Bhicaji, 1848–1940, vol. III

Narracott, Arthur Henson, 1905–1967, vol. VI

Narsingarh, Sahib Bahadur of, 1887–1924, vol. II

Nash, Rev. Adam James Glendinning, *died* 1920, vol. II

Nash, Rev. Alexander, 1845–1924, vol. II

Nash, Alfred William, 1886–1942, vol. IV

Nash, Eveleigh, 1873–1956, vol. V

Nash, Captain Geoffrey Stewart Fleetwood, 1883–1936, vol. III

Nash, George Howard, 1881–1950, vol. IV

Nash, Gilbert John, 1905–1974, vol. VII

Nash, Rev. Glendinning, *died* 1915, vol. I

Nash, Brig.-Gen. Henry Edmund Palmer, 1869–1949, vol. IV

Nash, Rt Rev. James Okey, 1862–1943, vol. IV

Nash, Rev. James Palmer, 1842–1915, vol. I (A)

Nash, John Brady, *born* 1857, vol. II

Nash, John Northcote, 1893–1977, vol. VII

Nash, Joseph, *died* 1922, vol. II

Nash, Col Llewellyn Thomas Manly, 1861–1928, vol. II

Nash, Norman E. Keown, 1885–1966, vol. VI

Nash, Ogden, 1902–1971, vol. VII

Nash, Paul, 1889–1946, vol. IV

Nash, Maj.-Gen. Sir Philip Arthur Manley, 1875–1936, vol. III

Nash, Rev. Robert Seymour, 1822–1904, vol. I

Nash, Vaughan, 1861–1932, vol. III

Nash, Sir Vincent, 1865–1942, vol. IV

Nash, Rt Hon. Sir Walter, 1882–1968, vol. VI

Nash, Major William Fleetwood, 1861–1915, vol. I (A)

Nash, William Harry, 1848–1929, vol. III

Nash-Williams, Victor Erle, 1897–1955, vol. V

Nashimoto, Morimasa, Prince, 1874–1951, vol. V

Nasim Ali, Sir Syed, *died* 1946, vol. IV

Nasir-El-Mulk, Abdul Kassim Khan, 1858–1927, vol. II

Nasmith, Adm. Sir Martin Eric Dunbar-, *died* 1965, vol. VI

Nasmyth, Thomas Goodall, *died* 1937, vol. III

Nason, Col Fortescue John, 1859–1952, vol. V

Nason, Rev. George Stephen, 1901–1975, vol. VII

Nason, Lt-Col Henry Hyde Williamson, 1857–1929, vol. III

Nasser, President Gamal Abdel, 1918–1970, vol. VI

Nath, Rao Bahadur Bhagavatula V.; *see* Viswa Nath.

Nathan, 1st Baron, 1889–1963, vol. VI

Nathan, Lady; (Eleanor Joan Clara), 1892–1972, vol. VII
Nathan, Charles, 1891–1949, vol. IV
Nathan, Sir Charles Samuel, 1870–1936, vol. III
Nathan, Col Sir Frederic Lewis, 1861–1933, vol. III
Nathan, George Jean, 1882–1958, vol. V
Nathan, Sir Gustavus, 1835–1902, vol. I
Nathan, Manfred, 1875–1945, vol. IV
Nathan, Lt-Col Rt Hon. Sir Matthew, 1862–1939, vol. III
Nathan, Sir Nathaniel, 1843–1916, vol. II
Nathan, Sir Robert, died 1921, vol. II
Nathan, Major Walter Simeon, 1867–1940, vol. III
Nathubhai, Tribhovandas Mangaldas, 1856–1920, vol. II
Nation, Brig.-Gen. John James Henry, 1874–1946, vol. IV
Nation, Sir John Louis, 1825–1906, vol. I
Nation, William Hamilton Codrington, 1843–1914, vol. I
Natta, Giulio, 1903–1979, vol. VII
Nattrass, Frederick John, 1891–1979, vol. VII
Naughton, Most Rev. James, 1864–1950, vol. IV
Navarro, Mary Anderson de, 1859–1940, vol. III
Naville, Henri Edouard, 1844–1926, vol. II
Nawanagar, Maharaja Jamsaheb of, 1872–1933, vol. III
Nawanagar, Maharaja Jam Saheb of, 1895–1966, vol. VI
Naylor, Very Rev. Alfred Thomas Arthur, 1889–1966, vol. VI
Naylor, Henry Darnley, 1872–1945, vol. IV
Naylor, James Richard, 1842–1922, vol. II
Naylor, Margaret Ailsa; see Naylor, Margot.
Naylor, Margot, (Margaret Ailsa), 1907–1972, vol. VII
Naylor, Maj.-Gen. Robert Francis Brydges, 1889–1971, vol. VII
Naylor, Thomas Ellis, 1868–1958, vol. V
Naylor, Thomas Humphrey, 1890–1966, vol. VI
Naylor, Ven. William Herbert, 1846–1918, vol. II
Naylor-Leyland, Sir (Albert) Edward (Herbert), 2nd Bt, 1890–1952, vol. V
Naylor-Leyland, Sir Edward; see Naylor-Leyland, Sir A. E. H.
Naylor-Leyland, Captain Sir Herbert Scarisbrick, 1st Bt, 1864–1899, vol. I
Naz, Sir Virgile, 1825–1901, vol. I
Nazimuddin, (Sir) Al-Haj Khwaja, 1894–1964, vol. VI
Neal, Arthur, 1862–1933, vol. III
Neal, Harold, 1897–1972, vol. VII
Neal, John, 1889–1962, vol. VI
Neal, Mary C. S., died 1944, vol. IV
Neal, Sir Phené; see Neal, Sir W. P.
Neal, Sir (William) Phené, 1st Bt, 1860–1942, vol. IV
Neale, Rev. Edgar, 1872–1937, vol. III
Neale, Edward A., 1858–1943, vol. IV
Neale, Folliott Sandford, 1901–1972, vol. VII
Neale, Lt-Col Sir Gordon; see Neale, Lt-Col Sir W. G.
Neale, Sir Henry James Vansittart-, 1842–1923, vol. II

Neale, Sir John Ernest, 1890–1975, vol. VII
Neale, Lt-Col Sir (Walter) Gordon, 1880–1966, vol. VI
Neales, Very Rev. Scovil, 1864–1936, vol. III
Neame, Lt-Col Arthur Laurence Cecil, 1883–1948, vol. IV
Neame, Gwendolyn Mary, (Lady Neame); see Desmond, Astra.
Neame, Humphrey, died 1968, vol. VI
Neame, Lawrence Elwin, died 1964, vol. VI
Neame, Lt-Gen. Sir Philip, 1888–1978, vol. VII
Neame, Sir Thomas, 1885–1973, vol. VII
Neat, Captain (S) Edward Hugh, 1864–1948, vol. IV
Neatby, Edwin Awdas, 1858–1933, vol. III
Neate, Horace Richard, 1891–1966, vol. VI
Neathercoat, Ernest Tom, 1880–1950, vol. IV
Neave, Airey Middleton Sheffield, 1916–1979, vol. VII
Neave, James Stephen, 1898–1970, vol. VI
Neave, Sheffield, 1853–1936, vol. III
Neave, Sheffield Airey, 1879–1961, vol. VI
Neave, Major Sir Thomas Lewis Hughes, 5th Bt, 1874–1940, vol. III
Neden, Sir Wilfred John, 1893–1978, vol. VII
Needham, Col Alfred Owen, 1883–1951, vol. V
Needham, Alicia Adelaide, died 1945, vol. IV
Needham, Col Charles, 1844–1934, vol. III
Needham, Sir Christopher Thomas, 1866–1944, vol. IV
Needham, Major Hon. Francis Edward, 1886–1955, vol. V
Needham, Sir Frederick, died 1924, vol. II
Needham, Sir George William, 1843–1928, vol. II
Needham, Maj.-Gen. Henry, 1876–1965, vol. VI
Needham, Jack Francis, 1842–1924, vol. II
Needham, James Ernest, died 1937, vol. III
Needham, Rev. Canon John Stafford, 1875–1942, vol. IV
Needham, Joseph, 1853–1920, vol. II
Needham, Col Joseph George, died 1939, vol. III
Needham, Sir Raymond Walter, died 1965, vol. VI
Needham, Bt Col Sir Richard Arthur, 1877–1949, vol. IV
Neef, Walter, 1857–1905, vol. I
Neel, Edmund, 1841–1933, vol. III
Neelands, Abram Rupert, died 1971, vol. VII
Neeld, Sir Algernon William, 2nd Bt, 1846–1900, vol. I
Neeld, Lt-Col Sir Audley Dallas, 3rd Bt, 1849–1941, vol. IV
Neeld, Rear-Adm. Reginald Rundell, 1850–1939, vol. III
Neely, Major George Henry, 1885–1934, vol. III
Neep, Edward John Cecil, 1900–1980, vol. VII
Neerunjun, Sir Rampersad, 1906–1967, vol. VI
Neff, Erroll Aubrey, 1887–1942, vol. IV
Negus, Sir Victor Ewings, 1887–1974, vol. VII
Nehru, Shri Jawaharial, 1889–1964, vol. VI
Nehru, Pandit Motilal, 1861–1931, vol. III
Neil, Albert Michael; see Lyons, A. Neil.
Neil, Edwin Lee, 1872–1934, vol. III
Neil, James H.; see Hardie Neil.
Neil, Rev. John, 1853–1928, vol. II

Neil, Robert Alexander, 1852–1901, vol. I
Neil, Rev. William, 1909–1979, vol. VII
Neilans, Alison R. N., 1884–1942, vol. IV
Neild, Rev. Canon Alfred, 1865–1941, vol. IV
Neill, Alexander Sutherland, 1883–1973, vol. VII
Neill, Charles Ernest, 1873–1931, vol. III
Neill, Col Duncan Ferguson Dempster, 1868–1938, vol. III
Neill, Col Sir Frederick Austin, 1891–1967, vol. VI
Neill, James Scott, 1889–1958, vol. V
Neill, Col James William S.; see Smith-Neill.
Neill, Sir Thomas, 1856–1937, vol. III
Neill, Sir William Frederick, 1889–1960, vol. V
Neilson, Alexander, 1868–1929, vol. III
Neilson, Francis, 1867–1961, vol. VI
Neilson, George, 1858–1923, vol. II
Neilson, Henry John, 1862–1949, vol. IV
Neilson, Col James, died 1903, vol. I
Neilson, Lt-Col John Beaumont, 1885–1957, vol. V
Neilson, Lt-Col John Fraser, 1884–1962, vol. VI
Neilson, John Shaw, 1872–1942, vol. IV
Neilson, Julia, (Mrs Fred Terry), died 1957, vol. V
Neilson, Richard Gillies, 1876–1956, vol. V
Neilson, Col Walter Gordon, 1876–1927, vol. II
Neilson, William Allan, 1869–1946, vol. IV
Neilson-Gray, Norah; see Gray.
Neilson-Terry, Phyllis, 1892–1977, vol. VII
Neish, Arthur Charles, 1916–1973, vol. VII
Neish, Sir Charles Henry Lawrence, 1857–1934, vol. III
Neish, Edward William, died 1938, vol. III
Neitenstein, Frederick William, 1850–1921, vol. II
Neligan, Rt Rev. Moore Richard, died 1922, vol. II
Nelke, Paul, 1860–1925, vol. II
Nell, Sir Harry, 1882–1958, vol. V
Nelles, Brig.-Gen. Charles Macklem, 1863–1936, vol. III
Nelles, Adm. Percy Walker, 1892–1951, vol. V
Nelson, 3rd Earl, 1823–1913, vol. I
Nelson, 4th Earl, 1857–1947, vol. IV
Nelson, 5th Earl, 1860–1951, vol. V
Nelson, 6th Earl, 1890–1957, vol. V
Nelson, 7th Earl, 1894–1972, vol. VII
Nelson of Stafford, 1st Baron, 1887–1962, vol. VI
Nelson, Sir Amos, 1860–1947, vol. IV
Nelson, Sir Arthur Edward, 1875–1950, vol. IV
Nelson, Charles Gilbert, 1880–1962, vol. VI
Nelson, Rev. Canon Charles Moseley, 1843–1919, vol. II
Nelson, Rt Rev. Cleland Kinloch, 1852–1917, vol. II
Nelson, Lieut David, 1886–1918, vol. II
Nelson, Donald Marr, 1888–1959, vol. V
Nelson, Brig.-Gen. Edgar F., 1859–1933, vol. III
Nelson, Edward Milles, died 1938, vol. III
Nelson, Sir Edward Montague, 1841–1919, vol. II
Nelson, Sir Frank, 1883–1966, vol. VI
Nelson, Gp Captain Hugh, 1890–1948, vol. IV
Nelson, Rt Hon. Sir Hugh Muir, 1835–1906, vol. I
Nelson, Sir James Hope, 2nd Bt, 1883–1960, vol. V
Nelson, John Howard, 1925–1979, vol. VII
Nelson, Col John Joseph Harper, 1882–1961, vol. VI
Nelson, Major John Weddall, 1878–1935, vol. III

Nelson, Captain Maurice Henry Horatio, 1864–1942, vol. IV
Nelson, Rear-Adm. Hon. Maurice Horatio, 1832–1914, vol. I
Nelson, Col Percy Reginald, 1884–1939, vol. III
Nelson, Rt Rev. Richard Henry, 1859–1931, vol. III
Nelson, Rt Rev. Robert, 1913–1959, vol. V
Nelson, Robert Frederick William Robertson, 1888–1932, vol. III
Nelson, Sir William, 1st Bt, 1851–1922, vol. II
Nelson, William Henry, 1880–1948, vol. IV
Nelson-Ward, Adm. Philip, 1866–1937, vol. III
Nelthorpe, Col Oliver S.; see Sutton Nelthorpe.
Nelthorpe, Robert Nassau S.; see Sutton-Nelthorpe.
Nenk, David Moerel, 1916–1960, vol. V
Nepal, Maharaja Chandra Shum Shere Jung Bahadur Rana, 1863–1929, vol. III
Nepal, Maharaja Bhim Shum Shere Jung Bahadur Rana, 1865–1932, vol. III
Nepal, Ex-Maharaja of, 1875–1952, vol. V
Nepal, Maharaja Mohan Shamsher Jang Bahadur Rana, 1885–1967, vol. VI
Nepean, Sir Charles Evan Molyneux Yorke, 5th Bt, 1867–1953, vol. V
Nepean, Edith, died 1960, vol. V
Nepean, Sir Evan Colville, 1836–1908, vol. I
Nepean, Rev. Sir Evan Yorke, 4th Bt, 1825–1903, vol. I
Nepean, Col Herbert Dryden Home Yorke, 1893–1956, vol. V
Nepean, Brig.-Gen. Herbert Evan Charles, 1865–1951, vol. V
Nepean, Comdr St Vincent, 1844–1915, vol. I
Neruda, Pablo, 1904–1973, vol. VII
Nervi, Pier Luigi, 1891–1979, vol. VII
Nesbit, E., (Mrs Hubert Bland), 1858–1924, vol. II
Nesbit, Paris, 1852–1927, vol. II
Nesbitt, Rev. Allan James, died 1918, vol. II
Nesbitt, Maj.-Gen. Frederick George B.; see Beaumont-Nesbitt.
Nesbitt, Major Randolph Cosby, 1867–1956, vol. V
Nesbitt, Lt-Col Richard Atholl, died 1905, vol. I
Nesbitt, Robert Chancellor, died 1944, vol. IV
Nesbitt, Hon. Wallace, 1858–1930, vol. III
Nesbitt-Hawes, Sir Ronald, 1895–1969, vol. VI
Ness, E. Wilhelmina; see Ness, Mrs P.
Ness, J. A., died 1931, vol. III
Ness, Mrs Patrick, (E. Wilhelmina Ness), died 1962, vol. VI
Ness, Robert Barclay, died 1954, vol. V
Nessi, Pio B.; see Baroja Nessi.
Nestle, (Christof) Eberhard, 1851–1913, vol. I
Nestle, Eberhard; see Nestle, C. E.
Nethersole, Lt-Col Frederick Ralph, died 1933, vol. III
Nethersole, Sir Michael, 1859–1920, vol. II
Nethersole, Sir Michael Henry Braddon, 1891–1965, vol. VI
Nethersole, Olga, 1870–1951, vol. V
Netherthorpe, 1st Baron, 1908–1980, vol. VII
Netherwood, A., died 1930, vol. III
Nettlefold, Sir Thomas Sydney, 1879–1956, vol. V
Nettleship, Edward, 1845–1913, vol. I

Nettleship, John Trivett, 1841–1902, vol. I
Nettleton, Wing Comdr John Dering, 1917–1943, vol. IV
Nettleton, Martin Barnes, 1911–1964, vol. VI
Neubauer, Adolf, 1832–1907, vol. I
Neumann, Sir Cecil Gustavus Jacques; see Newman.
Neumann, Sir Sigmund, 1st Bt, 1857–1916, vol. II
Nevada, Mignon, died 1971, vol. VII
Nevares, Celso, born 1850, vol. II
Neve, Arthur, 1858–1919, vol. II
Neve, Eric Read, 1887–1958, vol. V
Neve, Ernest Frederic, 1861–1946, vol. IV
Neven-Spence, Col Sir Basil Hamilton Hebden, 1888–1974, vol. VII
Nevile, Christopher, 1891–1962, vol. VI
Nevile, Sir Sydney Oswald, 1873–1969, vol. VI
Nevill, Col Charles William, 1907–1973, vol. VII
Nevill, Lady Dorothy, died 1913, vol. I
Nevill, Edmund Neville, died 1940, vol. III
Nevill, Rev. Edmund Robert, 1862–1933, vol. III
Nevill, Lord George Montacute, 1856–1920, vol. II
Nevill, Ven. Henry Ralph, 1821–1900, vol. I
Nevill, Henry Rivers, 1876–1939, vol. III
Nevill, Captain Hugh Lewis, 1877–1915, vol. I
Nevill, Ralph Henry, 1865–1930, vol. III
Nevill, Hon. Ralph Pelham, 1832–1914, vol. I
Nevill, Lord Richard Plantagenet, 1864–1939, vol. III
Nevill, Most Rev. Samuel Tarratt, born 1837, vol. II
Nevill, Rev. Thomas Seymour, 1901–1980, vol. VII
Nevill, Rev. Valentine Paul, 1882–1954, vol. V
Nevill, Comdr Walter Howard, 1887–1956, vol. V
Nevill, Sir Walter Palmer, 1854–1929, vol. III
Neville, Brig. Alfred Geoffrey, 1891–1955, vol. V
Neville, Arthur William, 1884–1948, vol. IV
Neville, Bertie Aylmer Crampton, 1882–1973, vol. VII
Neville, Edith, 1874–1951, vol. V
Neville, Eric Harold, 1889–1961, vol. VI
Neville, Francis Henry, 1847–1915, vol. I
Neville, Adm. Sir George, 1850–1923, vol. II
Neville, Rev. Hon. Grey, 1857–1920, vol. II
Neville, Henry, 1837–1910, vol. I
Neville, Henry Allen Dugdale, 1880–1952, vol. V
Neville, Kenneth Percival Rutherford, 1876–1957, vol. V
Neville, Nigel Charles Alfred, 1849–1923, vol. II
Neville, Captain Philip Lloyd, 1888–1976, vol. VII
Neville, Sir Ralph, died 1918, vol. II
Neville, Sir Reginald James Neville, 1st Bt, 1863–1950, vol. IV
Neville, Col William Candler, 1859–1926, vol. II
Neville-Rolfe, Eustace, 1845–1908, vol. I
Nevin, Robert Wallace, 1907–1980, vol. VII
Nevin, Samuel, died 1979, vol. VII
Nevins, Allan, 1890–1971, vol. VII
Nevinson, Christopher Richard Wynne, 1889–1946, vol. IV
Nevinson, Henry Woodd, 1856–1941, vol. IV
Nevinson, Margaret Wynne, died 1932, vol. III
New, Charles George Morley, 1879–1957, vol. V
New, Edmund Hort, 1871–1931, vol. III
New, Sir Henry Francis, 1859–1931, vol. III

New, Rev. James Marr, 1855–1931, vol. III
Newall, 1st Baron, 1886–1963, vol. VI
Newall, Dame Bertha Surtees, 1877–1932, vol. III
Newall, Hugh Frank, 1857–1944, vol. IV
Newall, Norman Dakeyne, 1888–1952, vol. V
Newall, Col Stuart, 1843–1920, vol. II
Newark, Francis Headon, 1907–1976, vol. VII
Newberry, Percy Edward, 1869–1949, vol. IV
Newbery, Arthur, died 1930, vol. III
Newbery, Francis H., died 1946, vol. IV
Newbigging, Brig.-Gen. William Patrick Eric, 1871–1940, vol. III
Newbigin, Marion I., died 1934, vol. III
Newbold, Lt-Col Charles Joseph, died 1946, vol. IV
Newbold, Sir Douglas, 1894–1945, vol. IV
Newbold, John Turner Walton, 1888–1943, vol. IV
Newbolt, Captain (Arthur) Francis, 1893–1966, vol. VI
Newbolt, Captain Francis; see Newbolt, Captain A. F.
Newbolt, Sir Francis George, 1863–1940, vol. III
Newbolt, Sir Henry John, 1862–1938, vol. III
Newbolt, Rev. Michael Robert, 1874–1956, vol. V
Newbolt, Rev. William Charles Edmund, 1844–1930, vol. III
Newborough, 4th Baron, 1873–1916, vol. II
Newborough, 5th Baron, 1878–1957, vol. V
Newborough, 6th Baron, 1877–1965, vol. VI
Newbould, Alfred Ernest, 1873–1952, vol. V
Newbould, Sir (Babington) Bennett, 1867–1937, vol. III
Newbould, Sir Bennett; see Newbould, Sir Babington B.
Newboult, Sir Alexander Theodore, 1896–1964, vol. VI
Newburgh, 8th (shown as 9th) Earl of, 1818–1908 (this entry was not transferred to Who was Who).
Newburgh, 9th (shown as 10th) Earl of, 1862–1941, vol. IV
Newburgh, Countess of (10th in line), 1889–1977, vol. VII
Newcastle, 7th Duke of, 1864–1928, vol. II
Newcastle, 8th Duke of, 1866–1941, vol. IV
Newcastle, Duchess of; (Kathleen Florence May), died 1955, vol. V
Newcomb, Lt-Col Clive, 1882–1968, vol. VI
Newcomb, Simon, 1835–1909, vol. I
Newcomb, Wilfrid Davison, 1889–1971, vol. VII
Newcombe, Edmund Leslie, 1859–1931, vol. III
Newcombe, Major Edward Osborn Armstrong, 1874–1941, vol. IV
Newcombe, Luxmoore, 1880–1952, vol. V
Newcombe, Col Stewart Francis, 1878–1956, vol. V
Newcombe, Maj.-Gen. Henry William, 1875–1963, vol. VI
Newcomen, Col Arthur Hills G.; see Gleadowe-Newcomen.
Newcomen, Gleadowe Henry Turner, 1877–1932, vol. III
Newdegate, A. E. Newdigate-, (Lady Newdigate-Newdegate), died 1924, vol. II

495

Newdegate, Sir Edward Newdigate, 1825–1902, vol. I

Newdegate, Sir Francis Alexander Newdigate, 1862–1936, vol. III

Newdigate, Bernard Henry, 1869–1944, vol. IV

Newdigate, Lt-Gen. Sir Henry Richard Legge, 1832–1908, vol. I

Newdigate-Newdegate, A. E.; see Newdegate.

Newell, Arthur Franklin, 1885–1976, vol. VII

Newell, Gordon Ewart, 1908–1968, vol. VI

Newell, Harold, died 1937, vol. III

Newell, Lt-Col Herbert Andrews, 1869–1934, vol. III

Newell, Hugh Hamilton, 1878–1941, vol. IV

Newell, Rev. Canon John Philip Peter, 1911–1980, vol. VII

Newell, William Homan, 1819–1901, vol. I

Newenham, Brig.-Gen. Henry Edward Berkeley, 1866–1934, vol. III

Newham, Lt-Col Hugh Basil Greaves, 1874–1959, vol. V

Newhouse, Rev. Robert Perceval, died 1933, vol. III

Newill, Ven. Edward Joseph, 1877–1954, vol. V

Newitt, Dudley Maurice, 1894–1980, vol. VII

Newland, Col Edmund Walcott, 1858–1937, vol. III

Newland, Maj.-Gen. Sir Foster Reuss, 1862–1943, vol. IV

Newland, Captain H. Osman, died 1920, vol. II

Newland, Sir Henry Simpson, 1873–1969, vol. VI

Newland-Pedley, Frederick, died 1944, vol. IV

Newlands, 1st Baron, 1825–1906, vol. I

Newlands, 2nd Baron, 1851–1929, vol. III

Newlands, Alexander, 1870–1938, vol. III

Newlands, Harry Scott, 1884–1933, vol. III

Newlands, Hon. Sir John, 1864–1932, vol. III

Newlands, John, 1857–1937, vol. III

Newling, (Alfred) John, 1896–1957, vol. V

Newling, John; see Newling, A. J.

Newman, Albert Gordon, 1894–1956, vol. V

Newman, Lt-Col (Augustus) Charles, 1904–1972, vol. VII

Newman, Bernard, 1897–1968, vol. VI

Newman, Bertram, 1886–1962, vol. VI

Newman, Sir Cecil Gustavus Jacques, 2nd Bt (cr 1912), 1891–1955, vol. V

Newman, Lt-Col Charles; see Newman, Lt-Col A. C.

Newman, Maj.-Gen. Charles Richard, 1875–1954, vol. V

Newman, David, 1853–1924, vol. II

Newman, Edward, 1858–1946, vol. IV

Newman, Edward Braxton, 1842–1916, vol. II

Newman, Brig.-Gen. Edward Harding-, 1872–1955, vol. V

Newman, Captain Edward John Kendall, 1860–1941, vol. IV

Newman, Major Edward William Polson, 1887–1967, vol. VI

Newman, Ernest, 1868–1959, vol. V

Newman, Lt-Col Ernest Alan Robert, 1867–1943, vol. IV

Newman, Ven. Ernest Frederick, 1859–1928, vol. II

Newman, Francis William, 1805–1897, vol. I

Newman, Frank Herbert, 1875–1948, vol. IV

Newman, Sir George, 1870–1948, vol. IV

Newman, Harold Lancelot, 1878–1949, vol. IV

Newman, Maj.-Gen. Hubert Thomas, 1895–1965, vol. VI

Newman, Maj.-Gen. John Cartwright H.; see Harding-Newman.

Newman, Sir John Robert Pretyman, 1871–1947, vol. IV

Newman, Philip Harry, 1840–1927, vol. II

Newman, Sir Ralph Alured, 5th Bt (cr 1836), 1902–1968, vol. VI

Newman, Rev. Canon Richard ,1871–1961, vol. VI

Newman, Col Richard Ernest Upton, 1883–1956, vol. V

Newman, Robert Lydston, 1865–1937, vol. III

Newman, Sidney Thomas Mayow, 1906–1971, vol. VII

Newman, Thomas Prichard, 1846–1915, vol. I (A)

Newman, Trevor Clyde, 1882–1955, vol. V

Newman, William Henry, 1865–1947, vol. IV

Newman-Morris, Sir John, 1879–1957, vol. V

Newmarch, Alexander, 1869–1935, vol. III

Newmarch, Bernard James, 1856–1929, vol. III

Newmarch, Francis Welles, 1853–1918, vol. II

Newmarch, Maj.-Gen. George, 1833–1912, vol. I

Newmarch, Sir Oliver Richardson, 1834–1920, vol. II

Newmarch, Rosa Harriet, 1857–1940, vol. III

Newnes, Sir Frank Hillyard, 2nd Bt, 1876–1955, vol. V

Newnes, Sir George, 1st Bt, 1851–1910, vol. I

Newnham, Ernest Percy, 1870–1943, vol. IV

Newnham, Hubert Ernest, 1886–1970, vol. VI

Newnham, Rt Rev. Jervois Arthur, 1852–1941, vol. IV

Newnham, Ven. Obadiah Samuel, 1848–1932, vol. III

Newnham, William Harry Christopher, 1859–1941, vol. IV

Newnham-Davis, Lt-Col Nathaniel, 1854–1917, vol. II

Newport, Surg. Captain Alexander Charles William, 1874–1948, vol. IV

Newsam, Sir Frank Aubrey, 1893–1964, vol. VI

Newsholme, Sir Arthur, 1857–1943, vol. IV

Newsom, Col Augustus Charles, 1866–1936, vol. III

Newsom, Rev. George Ernest, 1871–1934, vol. III

Newsom, Rear-Adm. John Bertram, 1902–1971, vol. VII

Newsom, Sir John Hubert, 1910–1971, vol. VII

Newson, Sir Percy Wilson, 1st Bt, 1874–1950, vol. IV

Newson-Smith, Sir Frank Edwin, 1st Bt, 1879–1971, vol. VII

Newstead, Robert, 1859–1947, vol. IV

Newsum, Sir Clement Henry, 1865–1947, vol. IV

Newte, Horace Wykeham Can, died 1949, vol. IV

Newth, Brig. Arthur Leslie Walter, 1897–1978, vol. VII

Newton, 1st Baron, 1828–1898, vol. I

Newton, 2nd Baron, 1857–1942, vol. IV

Newton, 3rd Baron, 1888–1960, vol. V

Newton, Sir Alan, 1887–1949, vol. IV

Newton, Alfred, 1829–1907, vol. I
Newton, Sir Alfred James, 1st Bt (*cr* 1900), 1849–1921, vol. II
Newton, Algernon, 1880–1968, vol. VI
Newton, Arthur, 1858–1942, vol. IV
Newton, Arthur Percival, 1873–1942, vol. IV
Newton, Sir Basil Cochrane, 1889–1965, vol. VI
Newton, Bernard St John, 1890–1977, vol. VII
Newton, Charles Edmund, 1831–1908, vol. I
Newton, Sir Charles Henry, 1882–1973, vol. VII
Newton, Captain Denzil Onslow Cochrane, 1880–1915, vol. I
Newton, Sir Edgar Henry, 2nd Bt (*cr* 1924), 1893–1971, vol. VII
Newton, Sir Edward, 1832–1897, vol. I
Newton, Edwin Tulley, 1840–1930, vol. III
Newton, Eric, 1893–1965, vol. VI
Newton, Ernest, 1856–1922, vol. II
Newton, Sir Francis James, 1857–1948, vol. IV
Newton, Francis John Stuart H.; *see* Hay-Newton.
Newton, Lt-Col Frank Graham, 1877–1962, vol. VI
Newton, George Percival, 1868–1951, vol. V
Newton, Giles Fendall, 1891–1974, vol. VII
Newton, Sir Harry Kottingham, 2nd Bt (*cr* 1900), 1875–1951, vol. V
Newton, Rt Rev. Henry, 1866–1947, vol. IV
Newton, Lt-Col Henry, 1880–1959, vol. V
Newton, Henry Chance, 1854–1931, vol. III
Newton, Sir Henry William, 1842–1914, vol. I
Newton, Sir Hibbert Alan Stephen; *see* Newton, Sir Alan.
Newton, Hibbert Henry, 1861–1927, vol. II
Newton, Rev. Horace, 1841–1920, vol. II
Newton, John, 1864–1916, vol. II
Newton, Rev. Joseph Fort, 1880–1950, vol. IV
Newton, Col Sir Louis Arthur, 1st Bt (*cr* 1924), 1867–1945, vol. IV
Newton, Rev. Richard Heber, 1840–1914, vol. I
Newton, Robert, 1905–1956, vol. V
Newton, Robert Henry, *died* 1943, vol. IV
Newton, Robert Milnes, 1821–1900, vol. I
Newton, Maj.-Gen. Thomas Cochrane, 1885–1976, vol. VII
Newton, Sir Wilberforce Stephen, 1890–1956, vol. V
Newton, Sir William, *died* 1915, vol. II
Newton, William George, 1859–1920, vol. II
Newton, William Godfrey, 1885–1949, vol. IV
Newton, William Henry, 1904–1949, vol. IV
Newton, William James Oliver, 1884–1952, vol. V
Newton-Brady, Sir Andrew, 1849–1918, vol. II
Newton-Robinson, Charles Edmund, 1853–1913, vol. I
Newton-Butler, Lord; John Brinsley Danvers, 1893–1912, vol. I
Neylan, Sir Daniel, 1866–1943, vol. IV
Neylan, Lt-Col John Nolan, *died* 1936, vol. III
Ngata, Hon. Sir Apirana Turupa, 1874–1950, vol. IV
Niblack, Rear-Adm. Albert P., 1859–1929, vol. III
Niblett, Adm. Harry Seawell Frank, 1852–1939, vol. III
Niblett, Robert Henry, 1859–1918, vol. II
Nichol, Col Charles Edward, 1859–1939, vol. III

Nichol, R., 1890–1925, vol. II
Nichol, Robert John, *died* 1946, vol. IV
Nichol, Hon. Walter Cameron, 1866–1928, vol. II
Nicholas, Captain John, 1851–1920, vol. II
Nicholas, Montagu Richmond, 1905–1964, vol. VI
Nicholas, Col Stephen Henry Edmund, 1870–1948, vol. IV
Nicholas, Sir Walter Powell, 1868–1926, vol. II
Nicholas, Rev. William, 1838–1912, vol. I
Nicholl, Sir Allan Hume, *died* 1941, vol. IV
Nicholl, Rear-Adm. Angus Dacres, 1896–1977, vol. VII
Nicholl, Maj.-Gen. Sir Christopher Rice Havard, 1836–1928, vol. II
Nicholl, Sir Edward, 1862–1939, vol. III
Nicholl, George Frederick, *died* 1913, vol. I
Nicholl, Air Vice-Marshal Sir Hazelton Robson, 1882–1956, vol. V
Nicholl, John Storer, 1888–1958, vol. V
Nicholls, Agnes; *see* Harty, A. H.
Nicholls, Albert George, 1870–1946, vol. IV
Nicholls, Arthur, 1880–1974, vol. VII
Nicholls, Rev. Arthur Bell, 1816–1906, vol. I
Nicholls, Bertram, 1883–1974, vol. VII
Nicholls, Frederick, 1871–1952, vol. V
Nicholls, George, 1864–1943, vol. IV
Nicholls, Rt Hon. George Heaton, 1876–1959, vol. V
Nicholls, Harry, 1852–1926, vol. II
Nicholls, Harry, 1915–1975, vol. VII
Nicholls, Hon. Sir Henry Alfred Alford, 1851–1926, vol. II
Nicholls, Hon. Sir Herbert, 1868–1940, vol. III
Nicholls, John Ralph, 1889–1970, vol. VI
Nicholls, Sir John Walter, 1909–1970, vol. VI
Nicholls, Maj.-Gen. Sir Leslie, (Burtonshaw), 1895–1975, vol. VII
Nicholls, Lucius, 1885–1969, vol. VI
Nicholls, Sir Marriott Fawckner, 1898–1969, vol. VI
Nicholls, Surg. Vice-Adm. Sir Percival Thomas, 1877–1959, vol. V
Nicholls, Richard Howell, 1868–1946, vol. IV
Nicholls, Sir Robert Dove, 1889–1970, vol. VI
Nicholls, Col Stephen Charles Phillips, 1883–1959, vol. V
Nicholls, William, 1882–1970, vol. VI
Nicholls, Lt-Col William Ashley, 1883–1941, vol. IV
Nicholls, Gen. Sir William Charles, 1854–1935, vol. III
Nicholls, Sir William Edgar, 1858–1932, vol. III
Nicholls, Arthur Eastwood, 1891–1959, vol. V
Nichols, Catherine Maude, *died* 1923, vol. II
Nichols, Edward Leamington, 1854–1937, vol. III
Nichols, George Herbert Fosdike, *died* 1933, vol. III
Nichols, Herbert John, 1895–1959, vol. V
Nichols, Joseph Cowie, *died* 1954, vol. V
Nichols, Sir Philip Bouverie Bowyer, 1894–1962, vol. VI
Nichols, Robert Malise Bowyer, 1893–1944, vol. IV
Nichols, Roy Franklin, 1896–1973, vol. VII
Nichols, Rt Rev. William Ford, 1849–1924, vol. II

Nicholson, 1st Baron, 1845–1918, vol. II
Nicholson, Sir Arthur, 1842–1929, vol. III
Nicholson, Bt Col Arthur Falkner, 1885–1954, vol. V
Nicholson, Arthur Pole, 1869–1940, vol. III
Nicholson, Sir Arthur William, 1852–1932, vol. III
Nicholson, Bertram, 1875–1943, vol. IV
Nicholson, Captain Bertram William Lothian, 1879–1958, vol. V
Nicholson, Gen. Sir Cameron Gordon Graham, 1898–1979, vol. VII
Nicholson, Maj.-Gen. Sir Cecil Lothian, 1865–1933, vol. III
Nicholson, Sir Charles, 1st Bt (cr 1859), 1808–1903, vol. I
Nicholson, Sir Charles, 2nd Bt (cr 1859), 1867–1949, vol. IV
Nicholson, Charles Ernest, 1868–1954, vol. V
Nicholson, Rear-Adm. Charles Hepworth, 1891–1966, vol. VI
Nicholson, Sir Charles Norris, 1st Bt (cr 1912), 1857–1918, vol. II
Nicholson, Adm. Sir Douglas Romilly Lothian, 1867–1946, vol. IV
Nicholson, Lt-Col Edmund James Houghton, 1870–1955, vol. V
Nicholson, Comdr Edward Hugh Meredith, 1876–1956, vol. V
Nicholson, Edward Williams Byron, 1849–1912, vol. I
Nicholson, Maj.-Gen. Francis Lothian, 1884–1953, vol. V
Nicholson, Sir Frank, 1875–1952, vol. V
Nicholson, Frank Carr, died 1962, vol. VI
Nicholson, Sir Frederick Augustus, 1846–1936, vol. III
Nicholson, Major Geoffrey, 1894–1976, vol. VII
Nicholson, George Crosfield Norris, 1884–1915, vol. I (A)
Nicholson, George Gibb, 1875–1948, vol. IV
Nicholson, Brig.-Gen. George Harvey, 1862–1942, vol. IV
Nicholson, Brig.-Gen. Graham Henry Whalley, 1869–1946, vol. IV
Nicholson, Adm. Sir Gresham; see Nicholson, Adm. Sir R. S. G.
Nicholson, Harold, 1883–1949, vol. IV
Nicholson, Harry Oliphant, 1870–1941, vol. IV
Nicholson, Henry Alleyne, 1844–1899, vol. I
Nicholson, Adm. Sir Henry Frederick, 1835–1914, vol. I
Nicholson, Horace Watson, 1883–1935, vol. III
Nicholson, Major Hugh Blomfield, died 1957, vol. V
Nicholson, Ivor Percy, died 1937, vol. III
Nicholson, Brig. John Gerald, 1906–1979, vol. VII
Nicholson, Sir John Gibb, 1879–1959, vol. V
Nicholson, John Henry, 1889–1972, vol. VII
Nicholson, Sir John Rumney, 1866–1939, vol. III
Nicholson, Brig.-Gen. John Sanctuary, 1863–1924, vol. II
Nicholson, John Wilfred, 1893–1949, vol. IV
Nicholson, John William, died 1955, vol. V
Nicholson, Joseph Shield, 1850–1927, vol. II

Nicholson, Joseph Sinclair, 1882–1968, vol. VI
Nicholson, Lt-Col Mark Alleyne, 1885–1952, vol. V
Nicholson, Meredith, 1866–1947, vol. IV
Nicholson, Maj.-Gen. Octavius Henry Lothian, 1877–1938, vol. III
Nicholson, Otho William, 1891–1978, vol. VII
Nicholson, Rev. Ralph, 1856–1930, vol. III
Nicholson, Major Randolph, 1894–1928, vol. II
Nicholson, Adm. Sir (Randolph Stewart) Gresham, 1892–1975, vol. VII
Nicholson, Reginald, 1869–1946, vol. IV
Nicholson, Reginald Popham, 1874–1950, vol. IV
Nicholson, Reynold Alleyne, 1868–1945, vol. IV
Nicholson, Sir Richard, 1828–1913, vol. I
Nicholson, Captain Richard Lindsay, 1882–1940, vol. III
Nicholson, Adm. Stuart, 1865–1936, vol. III
Nicholson, Maj.-Gen. Stuart James, 1836–1917, vol. II
Nicholson, Sir Sydney Hugo, 1875–1947, vol. IV
Nicholson, Sir Walter Frederic, 1876–1946, vol. IV
Nicholson, Col Walter Norris, 1877–1964, vol. VI
Nicholson, Sir William, 1865–1944, vol. IV
Nicholson, Adm. Sir William Coldingham Masters, 1863–1932, vol. III
Nicholson, Rt Hon. William Graham, 1862–1942, vol. IV
Nicholson, Gen. Sir William Gustavus, 1845–1909, vol. I
Nicholson, Sir William Newzam Prior, 1872–1949, vol. IV
Nicholson, Adm. Wilmot Stuart, 1872–1947, vol. IV
Nicholson-Lailey, John Raymond, 1900–1979, vol. VII
Nickalls, Captain Guy, died 1935, vol. III
Nickalls, Guy Oliver, 1899–1974, vol. VII
Nickalls, Sir Patteson, 1836–1910, vol. I
Nickerson, Maj.-Gen. William Henry Snyder, 1875–1954, vol. V
Nicklin, Hon. Sir Francis; see Nicklin, Hon. Sir G. F. R.
Nicklin, Hon. Sir (George) Francis (Reuben), 1895–1978, vol. VII
Nicklin, Robert Shenstone, 1901–1975, vol. VII
Nickolls, Lewis Charles, 1899–1970, vol. VI
Nickson, Rt Rev. George, 1864–1949, vol. IV
Nickson, Col John Edgar, 1899–1969, vol. VI
Nicol, Rev. Anderson, 1906–1972, vol. VII
Nicol, Brig. Cameron Macdonald, 1891–1965, vol. VI
Nicol, Donald Ninian, 1843–1903, vol. I
Nicol, Erskine, 1825–1904, vol. I
Nicol, Henry, 1821–1905, vol. I
Nicol, Jacob, died 1958, vol. V
Nicol, James Lauder, 1889–1971, vol. VII
Nicol, John, 1838–1920, vol. II
Nicol, Hon. Brig.-Gen. Lewis Loyd, 1858–1935, vol. III
Nicol, Rev. Thomas, 1846–1916, vol. II
Nicol, Sir Thomas Drysdale, 1878–1961, vol. VI
Nicolas, Nicholas Harris, 1830–1905, vol. I
Nicolay, Col Bernard Underwood, 1873–1960, vol. V, vol. VI

Nicolet, Gabriel, 1856–1921, vol. II
Nicoll, Allardyce; see Nicoll, J. R. A.
Nicoll, Gordon, died 1959, vol. V
Nicoll, Gen. Henry, 1816–1907, vol. I
Nicoll, James Gibson, 1870–1949, vol. IV
Nicoll, James H., 1865–1921, vol. II
Nicoll, John Ramsay Allardyce, 1894–1976, vol. VII
Nicoll, Maurice, 1884–1953, vol. V
Nicoll, Lt-Col Peter Strachan, 1864–1942, vol. IV
Nicoll, Sir William, 1860–1908, vol. I
Nicoll, Sir William Robertson, 1851–1923, vol. II
Nicolle, Edmund Toulmin, 1868–1929, vol. III
Nicolle, John Macarthur, 1885–1964, vol. VI
Nicolle, Maurice, 1862–1932, vol. III
Nicolls, Arthur Edward Jefferys, died 1963, vol. VI
Nicolls, Sir Basil Edward, 1893–1965, vol. VI
Nicolls, Brig.-Gen. Edmund Gustavus, 1858–1932, vol. III
Nicolls, Edward Hugh Dyneley, 1871–1963, vol. VI
Nicolls, Ven. Gerald Edward, 1862–1937, vol. III
Nicolls, Maj.-Gen. Oliver Henry Atkins, 1834–1920, vol. II
Nicolson, Sir Arthur John Frederick William, 11th Bt, 1882–1952, vol. V
Nicolson, Sir Arthur Thomas Bennet Robert, 9th Bt, 1842–1917, vol. II
Nicolson, David, 1844–1932, vol. III
Nicolson, Sir Frederick William Erskine, 10th Bt, 1815–1899, vol. I
Nicolson, Hon. Sir Harold George, 1886–1968, vol. VI
Nicolson, Sir (Harold) Stanley, 12th Bt, 1883–1961, vol. VI
Nicolson, Wing Comdr James Brindley, 1917–1945, vol. IV
Nicolson, Sir John William, 1895–1965, vol. VI
Nicolson, Sir Kenneth, 1891–1964, vol. VI
Nicolson, Lionel Benedict, 1914–1978, vol. VII
Nicolson, Lt-Gen. Malcolm Hassels, 1843–1904, vol. I
Nicolson, Sir Stanley; see Nicolson, Sir H. S.
Nicoresti, Carol Adolph C.; see Cofman-Nicoresti.
Niebuhr, Reinhold, 1892–1971, vol. VII
Niecks, Frederick, 1845–1924, vol. II
Niehaus, Charles Henry, 1855–1935, vol. III
Nield, Rt Hon. Sir Herbert, 1862–1932, vol. III
Nielson, Hon. Niel, 1869–1930, vol. III
Niemeyer, Sir Otto Ernst, 1883–1971, vol. VII
Nietzsche, Friedrich, 1844–1900, vol. I
Nightingale, Sir Charles Athelstan, 16th Bt, 1902–1977, vol. VII
Nightingale, Sir Edward Manners, 14th Bt, 1888–1953, vol. V
Nightingale, Florence, 1820–1910, vol. I
Nightingale, Sir Geoffrey Slingsby, 15th Bt, 1904–1972, vol. VII
Nightingale, Sir Henry Dickonson, 13th (styled 9th) Bt, 1830–1911, vol. I
Nightingale, Maj.-Gen. Manners Ralph Willmot, 1871–1956, vol. V
Nightingale, Thomas Slingsby, 1866–1918, vol. II
Nihalsingh, Rev. Canon Solomon, 1852–1916, vol. II

Nihill, Sir Barclay; see Nihill, Sir J. H. B.
Nihill, Sir (John Harry) Barclay, 1892–1975, vol. VII
Nijland, Albertus Antonie, 1868–1936, vol. III
Niland, D'Arcy Francis, died 1967, vol. VI
Niles, Emory Hamilton, 1892–1976, vol. VII
Nilkanth, Rao Bahadur Sir Ramanbhai Mahipatram, died 1928, vol. II
Nilsson, Mme Christine, (Comtesse de Miranda), 1843–1921, vol. II
Nimitz, Fleet Adm. Chester W., 1885–1966, vol. VI
Nimmo, Sir Adam, died 1939, vol. III
Nimmo, Surg. Rear-Adm. Frank Hutton, 1872–1954, vol. V
Nimmo, Henry, 1885–1954, vol. V
Nimmo, Sir Robert, 1894–1979, vol. VII
Nimmo, Maj.-Gen. Thomas Rose, 1831–1904, vol. I
Nimptsch, Uli, 1897–1977, vol. VII
Nind, William Walker, 1882–1964, vol. VI
Ninis, Rev. Richard Duncan, 1867–1940, vol. III
Ninnes, Bernard, 1899–1971, vol. VII
Ninnis, Insp.-Gen. Belgrave, died 1922, vol. II
Nipher, Francis Eugene, 1847–1926, vol. II
Nisbet, Brig.-Gen. Francis Courtenay, 1869–1953, vol. V
Nisbet, Hugh Bryan, 1902–1969, vol. VI
Nisbet, Hume, born 1849, vol. II
Nisbet, James Wilkie, 1903–1974, vol. VII
Nisbet, John, 1853–1914, vol. I
Nisbet, John Ferguson, 1851–1899, vol. I
Nisbet, Rev. Matthew Alexander, 1838–1919, vol. II
Nisbet, Noel L., 1887–1956, vol. V
Nisbet, Pollok Sinclair, born 1848, vol. II
Nisbet, Robert Buchan, 1857–1942, vol. IV
Nisbet, Col Robert Parry, died 1916, vol. II
Nisbet, Col Thomas, 1882–1956, vol. V
Nisbet-Hamilton Ogilvy, Mrs; see Ogilvy.
Nisbett, Lt-Col George Dalrymple More, 1850–1922, vol. II
Nisbett, George Hinde, 1866–1940, vol. III
Nisse, Bertram Sydney, died 1946, vol. IV
Nissen, Lt-Col Peter Norman, 1871–1930, vol. III
Nissim, Charles, 1845–1918, vol. II
Nitch, Cyril Alfred Rankin, died 1969, vol. VI
Niven, Charles, died 1923, vol. II
Niven, Frederick John, 1878–1944, vol. IV
Niven, James, 1851–1925, vol. II
Niven, Sir John, 1877–1947, vol. IV
Niven, Very Rev. T. B. W., 1834–1914, vol. I
Niven, William, died 1921, vol. II
Niven, Sir William Davidson, 1842–1917, vol. II
Niven, William Dickie, 1874–1965, vol. VI
Nixon, Alfred, 1858–1928, vol. II
Nixon, Maj.-Gen. Arundel James, 1849–1925, vol. II
Nixon, Sir (Charles) Norman, 1891–1978, vol. VII
Nixon, Sir Christopher John, 1st Bt, 1849–1914, vol. I
Nixon, Major Sir Christopher John Louis Joseph, 3rd Bt, 1918–1978, vol. VII
Nixon, Sir Christopher William, 2nd Bt, 1877–1945, vol. IV

Nixon, Sir Edwin Vandervord, 1876–1955, vol. V
Nixon, Sir Frank Horsfall, 1890–1966, vol. VI
Nixon, Ven. George Robinson, *died* 1963, vol. VI
Nixon, Henry, 1874–1939, vol. III
Nixon, Rev. Howard, *died* 1936, vol. III
Nixon, Job, 1891–1938, vol. III
Nixon, John Alexander, 1874–1951, vol. V
Nixon, Sir John Carson, 1887–1958, vol. V
Nixon, Gen. Sir John Eccles, 1857–1921, vol. II
Nixon, John William, *died* 1949, vol. IV
Nixon, Rev. Leigh Hunter, 1871–1941, vol. IV
Nixon, Sir Norman; *see* Nixon, Sir C. N.
Nixon, Rev. Robin Ernest, 1931–1978, vol. VII
Nixon, Wilfrid Ernest, 1892–1970, vol. VI
Nixon, William Charles Wallace, 1903–1966, vol. VI
Nizamat Jung; *see* Ahmad, Maulvi Sir N.
Nkrumah, Kwame, 1909–1972, vol. VII
Noad, Lewis, 1865–1950, vol. IV
Noad, Sidney Reginald I.; *see* Innes-Noad.
Noakes, Ven. Edward Spencer, *died* 1944, vol. IV
Noal, Comdr Richard John, 1870–1950, vol. IV
Nobbs, Percy Erskine, 1875–1966, vol. VI
Noble, Sir Andrew, 1st Bt (*cr* 1902), 1831–1915, vol. I (A)
Noble, Dennis, 1898–1966, vol. VI
Noble, Edward, 1857–1941, vol. IV
Noble, Frederick Arnold W.; *see* Williamson-Noble.
Noble, Sir George John William, 2nd Bt (*cr* 1902), 1859–1937, vol. III
Noble, Sir Humphrey Brunel, 4th Bt (*cr* 1902), 1892–1968, vol. VI
Noble, J. Campbell, 1846–1913, vol. I
Noble, John, 1837–1898, vol. I
Noble, Sir John Henry Brunel, 1st Bt (*cr* 1923), 1865–1938, vol. III
Noble, Adm. Sir Percy Lockhart Harnam, 1880–1955, vol. V
Noble, Philip Ernest, *died* 1931, vol. III
Noble, Robert, 1857–1917, vol. II
Noble, Sir Saxton William Armstrong, 3rd Bt (*cr* 1902), 1863–1942, vol. IV
Noble, T. Tertius, 1867–1953, vol. V
Noble, Thomas Paterson, 1887–1959, vol. V
Noble, Rev. Walter James, 1879–1962, vol. VI
Noble, Sir William, 1861–1943, vol. IV
Noble, William James, 1855–1914, vol. I
Noble, Rev. William Mackreth, 1845–1929, vol. III
Noble, Wilson, 1854–1917, vol. II
Noblett, Bt Lt-Col Louis Hemington, 1869–1948, vol. IV
Nock, Arthur Darby, 1902–1963, vol. VI
Nodzu, Michitsura, Marshal Marquess, 1841–1908, vol. I
Noel, Andre Espitalier-, 1898–1950, vol. IV (A), vol. V
Noel, Lady Augusta, 1838–1902, vol. I
Noel, Hon. Charles Hubert Francis, 1885–1947, vol. IV
Noel, Rev. Conrad le Despenser Roden, 1869–1942, vol. IV
Noel, Lt-Col Hon. Edward, 1852–1917, vol. II
Noel-Walker, Sir Edward; *see* Walker.

Noel, Ernest, 1831–1931, vol. III
Noel, Evan Baillie, 1879–1928, vol. II
Noel, Adm. Francis Charles Methuen, 1852–1925, vol. II
Noel, Admiral of the Fleet Sir Gerard Henry Uctred, 1845–1918, vol. II
Noel, Rt Hon. Gerard James, 1823–1911, vol. I
Noel, Bt Col Harold Ernest, 1884–1941, vol. IV
Noel, Rev. Canon John Monk, 1840–1921, vol. II
Noel-Buxton, 1st Baron, 1869–1948, vol. IV
Noel-Buxton, 2nd Baron, 1917–1980, vol. VII
Noel-Buxton, Lady, (Lucy Edith), *died* 1960, vol. V
Noel-Hill, Rev. Charles, 1848–1911, vol. I
Noghi, Gen. Count Mare-Suke, 1849–1912, vol. I
Nokes, George Augustus; *see* Sekon, G. A.
Nokes, Gerald Dacre, 1899–1971, vol. VII
Nolan, Lt-Col Andrew Bellew, 1867–1932, vol. III
Nolan, Very Rev. Mgr Edmond, 1857–1931, vol. III
Nolan, James Joseph, 1869–1939, vol. III
Nolan, John J., 1888–1952, vol. V
Nolan, Col John Philip, *died* 1912, vol. I
Nolan, Michael James, 1859–1944, vol. IV
Nolan, Sir Robert Howard, *died* 1923, vol. II
Nöldeke, Theodor, 1836–1930, vol. III
Nolhac, Pierre de, 1859–1936, vol. III
Nollet, Edouard, 1865–1941, vol. IV
Nolloth, Rev. Charles Frederick, 1850–1932, vol. III
Nolloth, Rev. Henry Edward, 1846–1929, vol. III
Nonweiler, Maj.-Gen. Wilfrid Ivan, 1900–1953, vol. V
Noon, Firoz Khan, 1893–1970, vol. VI
Noon, Nawab Sir Malik Mohamed Hayat, 1875–1941, vol. IV
Noott, Col Cuthbert Cecil, 1870–1933, vol. III
Nops, Walter, 1850–1918, vol. II
Nops, Sir Wilfrid Walter, 1884–1948, vol. IV
Norbury, 4th Earl of, 1862–1943, vol. IV
Norbury, 5th Earl of, 1893–1955, vol. V
Norbury, Edwin Arthur, 1849–1918, vol. II
Norbury, Insp.-Gen. Sir Henry Frederick, 1839–1925, vol. II
Norbury, Sir Henry Frederick Oswald, 1880–1948, vol. IV
Norbury, Captain Herbert Reginald, 1876–1967, vol. IV
Norbury, Lionel Edward Close, 1882–1967, vol. VI
Norbury, Col Thomas Coningsby, 1829–1899, vol. I
Norcock, Vice-Adm. Charles James, 1847–1933, vol. III
Norcott, Col Charles Hawtrey Bruce, 1849–1931, vol. III
Nordau, Max Simon, 1849–1923, vol. II
Nordenskiold, Baron Adolphe Eric, 1832–1901, vol. I
Nordenskjöld, Otto, 1869–1928, vol. II
Nordhoff, Heinrich, 1899–1968, vol. VI
Nordica, Lillian, 1859–1914, vol. I
Norfolk, 15th Duke of, 1847–1917, vol. II
Norfolk, 16th Duke of, 1908–1975, vol. VII
Norfolk, Rear-Adm. George Anthony Francis, 1907–1966, vol. VI
Norie, Maj.-Gen. Charles Edward Manley, 1866–1929, vol. III

Norie, Maj.-Gen. Evelyn Medows, 1833–1913, vol. I

Norie-Miller, Sir Francis, 1st Bt, 1859–1947, vol. IV

Norie-Miller, Sir Stanley, 2nd Bt, 1888–1973, vol. VII

Norman, 1st Baron, 1871–1950, vol. IV

Norman, Vice-Adm. Alfred Headley, 1881–1973, vol. VII

Norman, Rev. Alfred Merle, 1831–1918, vol. II

Norman, Arthur William, 1850–1928, vol. II

Norman, Sir Charles, 1892–1976, vol. VII

Norman, Rev. Charles Frederick, 1829–1913, vol. I

Norman, Charles Kensit, 1857–1937, vol. III

Norman, Maj.-Gen. Charles Wake, 1891–1974, vol. VII

Norman, Brig.-Gen. Claude Lumsden, 1876–1967, vol. VI

Norman, Brig. Compton Cardew, 1877–1955, vol. V

Norman, Duncan Thomas, 1889–1972, vol. VII

Norman, Edward, 1847–1923, vol. II

Norman, Comdr F. M., 1833–1918, vol. II

Norman, Sir Francis Booth, 1830–1901, vol. I

Norman, Sir Frederick, 1857–1936, vol. III

Norman, Frederick, 1897–1968, vol. VI

Norman, Col Harold Hugh, 1875–1933, vol. III

Norman, Rt Hon. Sir Henry, 1st Bt, 1858–1939, vol. III

Norman, Henry Gordon, 1890–1967, vol. VI

Norman, Sir (Henry) Nigel St Valery, 2nd Bt, 1897–1943, vol. IV

Norman, Lt-Gen. Sir Henry Radford, 1818–1899, vol. I

Norman, Sir Henry Wylie, 1826–1904, vol. I

Norman, Herman Cameron, 1872–1955, vol. V

Norman, Brig. Hugh Ronald, 1905–1979, vol. VII

Norman, Sir Nigel; see Norman, Sir H. N. St V.

Norman, Philip, died 1931, vol. III

Norman, Ronald Collet, 1873–1963, vol. VI

Norman, Surg.-Vice-Adm. Sir William Henry, 1855–1934, vol. III

Norman, Col William Wylie, 1860–1935, vol. III

Norman Barnett, Lt-Col Henry, died 1952, vol. V

Norman-Walker, Col John Norman, 1872–1951, vol. V

Normanbrook, 1st Baron, 1902–1967, vol. VI

Normanby, 3rd Marquess of, 1846–1932, vol. III

Normand, Baron (Life Peer); Wilfrid Guild Normand, 1884–1962, vol. VI

Normand, Alexander Robert, 1880–1958, vol. V

Normand, Mrs Ernest, (Henrietta Rae), 1859–1928, vol. II

Normand, Captain Patrick Hill, 1876–1943, vol. IV

Normand, Robert Casley, 1897–1962, vol. VI

Normanton, 4th Earl of, 1865–1933, vol. III

Normanton, 5th Earl of, 1910–1967, vol. VI

Normanton, Helena Florence, died 1957, vol. V

Norreys, Lord; Montague Edmund Henry Cecil Towneley-Bertie, 1887–1919, vol. II

Norrie, 1st Baron, 1893–1977, vol. VII

Norrie, Mrs Beatrice, died 1933, vol. III

Norrie, Col Edward Creer, 1885–1958, vol. V

Norrington, Lt-Col Reginald Lewis, died 1960, vol. V

Norris, Arthur Gilbert, 1889–1962, vol. VI

Norris, Arthur Herbert, 1875–1953, vol. V

Norris, Charles Arthur, 1874–1941, vol. IV

Norris, Charles Gilman, died 1945, vol. IV

Norris, Adm. David Thomas, 1875–1937, vol. III

Norris, Donald Craig, died 1968, vol. VI

Norris, Rev. Edward John, 1860–1940, vol. III

Norris, Edward Samuel, 1832–1908, vol. I

Norris, Francis Edward Boshear, died 1966, vol. VI

Norris, Rt Rev. Francis Lushington, 1864–1945, vol. IV

Norris, George Michael, 1841–1922, vol. II

Norris, Henry, 1852–1954, vol. V

Norris, Col Henry Crawley, 1841–1914, vol. I

Norris, Lt-Col Henry Everard DuCane, 1869–1960, vol. V

Norris, Col Sir Henry George, 1865–1934, vol. III

Norris, Herbert, died 1950, vol. IV

Norris, Rt Rev. Ivor Arthur, 1901–1969, vol. VI

Norris, Very Rev. John, 1843–1911, vol. I

Norris, John Alexander, 1872–1962, vol. VI

Norris, John Freeman, 1842–1904, vol. I

Norris, Kathleen, 1880–1966, vol. VI

Norris, Oswald Thomas, 1883–1973, vol. VII

Norris, Richard Hill, 1886–1970, vol. VI

Norris, Lt-Col Richard Joseph, 1854–1935, vol. III

Norris, Captain Stephen Hugh, 1903–1944, vol. IV

Norris, Rev. Canon Walter Edward, 1905–1971, vol. VII

Norris, William Edward, died 1925, vol. II

Norris, Very Rev. William Foxley, 1859–1937, vol. III

Norrish, Ronald George Wreyford, 1897–1978, vol. VII

Norritt, Sir James Henry, 1889–1963, vol. VI

North, 11th Baron, 1836–1932, vol. III

North, 12th Baron, 1860–1938, vol. III

North, 13th Baron, 1917–1941, vol. IV

North, Lord; Francis George North, 1902–1940, vol. III

North, Brig.-Gen. Bordrigge North, 1862–1936, vol. III

North, Rev. Christopher Richard, 1888–1975, vol. VII

North, Col Dudley, 1840–1917, vol. II

North, Adm. Sir Dudley Burton Napier, 1881–1961, vol. VI

North, Hon. Dudley William John, 1891–1936, vol. III

North, Col Edward, 1856–1927, vol. II

North, Lt-Col Edward Bunbury, 1869–1944, vol. IV

North, Major Edward Tempest Tunstall, 1900–1942, vol. IV

North, Rt Hon. Sir Ford, 1830–1913, vol. I

North, Brig. Francis Roger, 1894–1978, vol. VII

North, Frederic Dudley, 1866–1921, vol. II

North, Frederick Keppel, 1860–1948, vol. IV

North, Sir George Cecil, 1895–1971, vol. VII

North, Brig. Harold Napier, 1883–1957, vol. V

North, Sir Harry, 1866–1920, vol. II

North, Herbert L., 1871–1941, vol. IV

North, Major John, 1894–1973, vol. VII
North, John Dudley, 1893–1968, vol. VI
North, John W., *died* 1924, vol. II
North, Lt-Col Sir Jonathan, 1855–1939, vol. III
North, North, 1824–1910, vol. I
North, Roland Arthur Charles, 1889–1961, vol. VI
North, Walter Meyrick, *died* 1900, vol. I
North, William Albert, 1881–1946, vol. IV
Northam, Sir Reginald, *died* 1967, vol. VI
Northampton, 4th Marquess of, 1818–1897, vol. I
Northampton, 5th Marquess of, 1851–1913, vol. I
Northampton, 6th Marquess of, 1885–1978, vol. VII
Northbourne, 2nd Baron, 1846–1923, vol. II
Northbourne, 3rd Baron, 1869–1932, vol. III
Northbrook, 1st Earl of, 1826–1904, vol. I
Northbrook, 2nd Earl of, 1850–1929, vol. III
Northbrook, Countess of; (Florence Anita Eyre), *died* 1946, vol. IV
Northbrook, 4th Baron, 1882–1947, vol. IV
Northcliffe, 1st Viscount, 1865–1922, vol. II
Northcote, 1st Baron, 1846–1911, vol. I
Northcote, Lady; (Alice), *died* 1934, vol. III
Northcote, Rev. Hon. Arthur Francis, 1852–1943, vol. IV
Northcote, Sir Ernest Augustus, 1850–1915, vol. I
Northcote, Sir Geoffry Alexander Stafford, 1881–1948, vol. IV
Northcote, Rev. Hon. John Stafford, 1850–1920, vol. II
Northcote, Lady Rosalind Lucy Stafford, *died* 1950, vol. IV
Northcott, Gen. Sir John, 1890–1966, vol. VI
Northcott, Captain Ralph William Frank, 1907–1976, vol. VII
Northcott, Richard A., 1871–1931, vol. III
Northcott, Rev. William, 1854–1924, vol. II
Northcroft, Sir Erima Harvey, 1884–1953, vol. V
Northcroft, Ernest George Drennan, 1896–1976, vol. VII
Northen, Lt-Col Arthur, 1873–1964, vol. VI
Northesk, 10th Earl of, 1865–1921, vol. II
Northesk, 11th Earl of, 1901–1963, vol. VI
Northesk, 12th Earl of, 1895–1975, vol. VII
Northey, Sir Armand Hunter Kennedy Wilbraham, 1897–1964, vol. VI
Northey, Maj.-Gen. Sir Edward, 1868–1953, vol. V
Northey, Lt-Col Herbert Hamilton, 1870–1938, vol. III
Northey, Captain William, 1876–1914, vol. I
Northfield, Douglas William Claridge, *died* 1976, vol. VII
Northland, Viscount; Thomas Uchter Caulfield Knox, 1882–1915, vol. I
Northmore, Sir John Alfred, 1865–1958, vol. V
Northrop, Cyrus, 1834–1922, vol. II
Northrup, William Barton, *died* 1925, vol. II
Northumberland, 6th Duke of, 1810–1899, vol. I
Northumberland, 7th Duke of, 1846–1918, vol. II
Northumberland, 8th Duke of, 1880–1930, vol. III
Northumberland, 9th Duke of, 1912–1940, vol. IV
Northumberland, Duchess of; (Helen Magdalen), *died* 1965, vol. VI
Northwick, Lady; (Elizabeth Augusta), 1832–1912, vol. I

Norton, 1st Baron, 1814–1905, vol. I
Norton, 2nd Baron, 1846–1926, vol. II
Norton, 3rd Baron, 1872–1933, vol. III
Norton, 4th Baron, 1885–1944, vol. IV
Norton, 5th Baron, 1854–1945, vol. IV
Norton, 6th Baron, 1886–1961, vol. VI
Norton, Major Alfred Edward Marston, 1869–1922, vol. II
Norton, Arthur Trehern, 1841–1912, vol. I
Norton, Brig.-Gen. Cecil Burrington, 1868–1953, vol. V
Norton, Sir Charles; *see* Norton, Sir W. C.
Norton, Lt-Col Charles Edward, 1861–1931, vol. III
Norton, Charles Eliot, 1827–1908, vol. I
Norton, Brig.-Gen. Charles Ernest Graham, 1869–1953, vol. V
Norton, Charles William, 1870–1946, vol. IV
Norton, David, 1851–1929, vol. III
Norton, David Evans, 1863–1946, vol. IV
Norton, Edward, 1841–1923, vol. II
Norton, Lt-Gen. Edward Felix, 1884–1954, vol. V
Norton, Sir Evan Augustus, 1901–1967, vol. VI
Norton, George Frederic, *died* 1946, vol. IV
Norton, Col Gilbert Paul, 1882–1962, vol. VI
Norton, Ven. Hugh Ross, 1890–1969, vol. VI
Norton, Rt Rev. John F., 1891–1963, vol. VI
Norton, Ven. John George, 1840–1924, vol. II
Norton, Rt Rev. John Henry, 1855–1923, vol. II
Norton, Richard, 1872–1918, vol. II
Norton, Robert, 1838–1926, vol. II
Norton, Robert Frederick, 1854–1929, vol. III
Norton, Roger Edward, 1897–1978, vol. VII
Norton, Thomas, 1845–1935, vol. III
Norton, Sir (Walter) Charles, 1896–1974, vol. VII
Norton, Wilfrid, *died* 1973, vol. VII
Norton, William, *died* 1963, vol. VI
Norton-Griffiths, Lt-Col Sir John; *see* Griffiths.
Norval, Sir James, 1862–1936, vol. III
Norway, Arthur Hamilton, 1859–1938, vol. III
Norway, Nevil Shute, 1899–1960, vol. V
Norwich, 1st Viscount, 1890–1954, vol. V
Norwood, Sir Charles John Boyd, 1871–1966, vol. VI
Norwood, Christopher Bonnewell Burton, 1932–1972, vol. VII
Norwood, Sir Cyril, 1875–1956, vol. V
Norwood, Rev. Frederick William, *died* 1958, vol. V
Norwood, Gilbert, 1880–1954, vol. V
Norwood, Captain John, 1876–1914, vol. I
Norwood, Rev. Reginald, 1874–1928, vol. II (A), vol. III
Norwood, William Stuart, *died* 1944, vol. IV
Nosworthy, Lt-Gen. Sir Francis Poitiers, 1887–1971, vol. VII
Nosworthy, Richard, 1860–1946, vol. IV
Nosworthy, Sir Richard Lysle, 1885–1966, vol. VI
Nosworthy, Hon. Sir William, 1867–1946, vol. IV
Notcutt, Henry Clement, 1865–1935, vol. III
Notestein, Wallace, 1878–1969, vol. VI
Notley, Captain Sir Franke Bartlett Stuart, 1865–1939, vol. III
Nott, Frederic Trevor, 1885–1950, vol. IV

Nott, Comdr Sir James Grenvile P.; see Pyke-Nott.
Nott-Bower, Sir Edmund Ernest, 1853–1933, vol. III
Nott-Bower, Sir Guy; see Nott-Bower, Sir W. G.
Nott-Bower, Sir John Reginald Hornby, 1892–1972, vol. VII
Nott-Bower, Captain Sir (John) William, 1849–1939, vol. III
Nott-Bower, Captain Sir William; see Nott-Bower, Captain Sir J. W.
Nott-Bower, Sir (William) Guy, 1890–1977, vol. VII
Notten-Pole, Sir Cecil Pery Van; see Pole.
Notter, Col J. Lane-, died 1923, vol. II
Nottidge, Sir William Rolfe, 1889–1966, vol. VI
Nottingham, Rev. Edward Emil, 1866–1921, vol. II
Nougués, Jean, died 1932, vol. III
Nourse, William John Chichele, died 1937, vol. III
Novar, 1st Viscount, 1860–1934, vol. III
Novar, Viscountess; (Helen Hermione), 1865–1941, vol. IV
Novello, Ivor, 1893–1951, vol. V
Novikoff, Mme Olga, 1848–1925, vol. II
Novy, Frederick G., 1864–1957, vol. V
Nowell, Arthur T., 1861–1940, vol. III
Nowell, Charles, 1890–1954, vol. V
Nowell, Air Cdre Henry Edward, 1903–1967, vol. VI
Nowell, Ralph Machattie, 1903–1973, vol. VII
Nowell, William, 1880–1968, vol. VI
Nowell, Rev. William Edward, died 1929, vol. III
Nowell-Rostron, Rev. Sydney, 1883–1948, vol. IV
Noxon, William Courtland, died 1943, vol. IV
Noyce, Sir Frank, 1878–1948, vol. IV
Noyes, Alfred, 1880–1958, vol. V
Noyes, Gen. Sir Cyril Dupré, 1885–1946, vol. IV
Nuffield, 1st Viscount, 1877–1963, vol. VI
Nugee, Rev. Francis Edward, died 1930, vol. III
Nugee, Francis John, 1891–1966, vol. VI
Nugent, 1st Baron, 1895–1973, vol. VII
Nugent, Albert Beauchamp, died 1938, vol. III
Nugent, Algernon John FitzRoy, 1865–1922, vol. II
Nugent, Sir Charles, 5th Bt (cr 1795), 1847–1927, vol. II
Nugent, Sir Charles Butler Peter Hodges, 1827–1899, vol. I
Nugent, Col Charles Hugh Hodges, 1868–1924, vol. II
Nugent, Sir Edmund Charles, 3rd Bt (cr 1806), 1839–1928, vol. II
Nugent, Brig.-Gen. Frank B.; see Burnell-Nugent.
Nugent, Col George Colborne, 1864–1915, vol. I
Nugent, Sir (George) Guy (Bulwer), 4th Bt (cr 1806), 1892–1970, vol. VI
Nugent, Sir Guy; see Nugent, Sir G. G. B.
Nugent of Clonlost, Guy Patrick Douglas John, 1915–1944, vol. IV
Nugent, Sir Horace Dickinson, 1858–1924, vol. II
Nugent, Hon. John, 1843–1900, vol. I
Nugent, John Dillon, died 1940, vol. III
Nugent, Maj.-Gen. John Fagan Henslowe, 1889–1975, vol. VII
Nugent, Sir John Nugent, 3rd Bt (cr 1831 of Cloncoskoran), 1849–1929, vol. III

Nugent, Maj.-Gen. Sir Oliver Stewart Wood, 1860–1926, vol. II
Nugent, Vice-Adm. Raymond Andrew, 1870–1959, vol. V
Nugent, Hon. Richard Anthony, 1842–1912, vol. I
Nugent, Col Robert Arthur, 1853–1926, vol. II
Nugent, Rt Hon. Sir Roland Thomas, 1st Bt (cr 1961), 1886–1962, vol. VI
Nugent, Sir Walter Richard, 4th Bt (cr 1831 of Donore), 1865–1955, vol. V
Nugent, Col Walter Vyvian, 1880–1963, vol. VI
Nugent, Captain Hon. William Andrew, 1876–1915, vol. I
Nulty, Rt Rev. Thomas, died 1898, vol. I
Nunan, Sir Joseph, 1873–1934, vol. III
Nunan, William, 1880–1955, vol. V
Nunburnholme, 1st Baron, 1833–1907, vol. I
Nunburnholme, 2nd Baron, 1875–1924, vol. II
Nunburnholme, 3rd Baron, 1904–1974, vol. VII
Nunn, Rev. Henry Drury Cust, died 1922, vol. II
Nunn, Col Joshua Arthur, 1853–1908, vol. I
Nunn, Sir Percy, 1870–1944, vol. IV
Nunn, Thomas William, 1825–1909, vol. I
Nunn, Vice-Adm. Wilfrid, died 1956, vol. V
Nunn, William, 1879–1971, vol. VII
Nunns, Hector Matthew, 1905–1979, vol. VII
Nurse, George Edward, 1873–1945, vol. IV
Nussey, Col Albert Henry Mortimer, 1880–1944, vol. IV
Nussey, Sir Thomas Moore, 2nd Bt, 1898–1971, vol. VII
Nussey, Sir Willans, 1st Bt, 1868–1947, vol. IV
Nuthall, Brig.-Gen. Charles Edwin, 1862–1943, vol. IV
Nuthall, Col Henry John, died 1914, vol. I
Nutt, Albert Boswell, 1898–1978, vol. VII
Nutt, Alfred Trubner, 1856–1910, vol. I
Nutt, Alfred Young, 1847–1924, vol. II
Nutt, Arthur Edgar W.; see Woodward-Nutt.
Nutt, Francis George, 1878–1954, vol. V
Nutt, Maj.-Gen. Harold Rothery, 1876–1953, vol. V
Nutt, Col Herbert John, 1861–1940, vol. III
Nutt, Col James Anson Francis, died 1924, vol. II
Nuttall, Sir Edmund, 1st Bt, 1870–1923, vol. II
Nuttall, Lt-Col Sir (Edmund) Keith, 2nd Bt, 1901–1941, vol. IV
Nuttall, Ellis, 1890–1951, vol. V
Nuttall, Most Rev. Enos, 1842–1916, vol. II
Nuttall, Rev. Frank, 1870–1943, vol. IV
Nuttall, George Henry Falkiner, 1862–1937, vol. III
Nuttall, Harry, 1849–1924, vol. II
Nuttall, Sir James, 1891–1962, vol. VI
Nuttall, Sir James Mansfield, 1827–1897, vol. I
Nuttall, Lt-Col Sir Keith; see Nuttall, Sir E. K.
Nuttall, Thomas Downham, 1877–1934, vol. III
Nuttall, Captain William Ewart, 1876–1939, vol. III
Nutting, Arthur Ronald Stansmore, 1888–1964, vol. VI
Nutting, Air Vice-Marshal Charles William, 1889–1964, vol. VI
Nutting, Sir Harold Stansmore, 2nd Bt, 1882–1972, vol. VII

Nutting, Sir John Gardiner, 1st Bt, 1852–1918, vol. II
Nye, Engr Captain Alfred John, 1855–1932, vol. III
Nye, Lt-Gen. Sir Archibald Edward, 1895–1967, vol. VI
Nye, Sir Geoffrey Walter, 1902–1976, vol. VII
Nygaardsvold, John, 1879–1952, vol. V
Nyholm, Sir Ronald Sydney, 1917–1971, vol. VII
Nys, Ernest, 1851–1920, vol. II
Nystrom, Anton, 1842–1931, vol. III

O

Oak-Rhind, Edwin Scoby, 1883–1963, vol. VI
Oakden, Sir Ralph, 1871–1953, vol. V
Oake, George Robert, 1903–1969, vol. VI
Oakeley, Sir Charles John, 5th Bt, 1862–1938, vol. III
Oakeley, Sir Charles Richard Andrew, 6th Bt, 1900–1959, vol. V
Oakeley, Sir Charles William Atholl, 4th Bt, 1828–1915, vol. I (A)
Oakeley, Sir Herbert Stanley, 1830–1903, vol. I
Oakeley, Hilda Diana, 1867–1950, vol. IV
Oakes, Sir Augustus Henry, 1839–1919, vol. II
Oakes, Sir Cecil, 1884–1959, vol. V
Oakes, Hon. Charles William, 1861–1928, vol. II
Oakes, Ven. George Spencer, 1855–1932, vol. III
Oakes, Sir Harry, 1st Bt (cr 1939), 1874–1943, vol. IV
Oakes, Sir Reginald Louis, 4th Bt (cr 1815), 1847–1927, vol. II
Oakes, Col Richard, 1876–1944, vol. IV
Oakes, Sir Sydney, 2nd Bt (cr 1939), 1927–1966, vol. VI
Oakeshott, Maj.-Gen. John Field Fraser, 1899–1957, vol. V
Oakeshott, Keith Robertson, 1920–1974, vol. VII
Oakey, John Martin, 1888–1963, vol. VI
Oakley, Alfred James, 1880–1959, vol. V
Oakley, Rev. Austin, 1890–1977, vol. VII
Oakley, Cyril Leslie, 1907–1975, vol. VII
Oakley, Harry Ekermans, 1866–1943, vol. IV
Oakley, Sir Henry, 1823–1912, vol. I
Oakley, Lt-Col Henry John Percy, 1878–1942, vol. IV
Oakley, John, died 1945, vol. IV
Oakley, Sir John Hubert, 1867–1946, vol. IV
Oakley, Philip Douglas, 1883–1958, vol. V
Oakley, Thomas, 1879–1936, vol. III
Oaksey, 1st Baron; see under Trevethin, 3rd Baron and Oaksey, 1st Baron.
Oakshott, Baron (Life Peer); Hendrie Dudley Oakshott, 1904–1975, vol. VII
Oaten, Edward Farley, 1884–1973, vol. VII
Oates, Francis Hamer, died 1923, vol. II
Oates, Frederick Arthur Harman, died 1928, vol. II
Oates, Lt-Col William Coape, 1862–1942, vol. IV
Oatley, Sir George Herbert, 1863–1950, vol. IV
Obaidulla Khan, Nowabzada Hafiz Mohamad Bahadur, 1878–1924, vol. II

O'Beirne, Hugh James, 1866–1916, vol. II
Oberg, Olof David August, 1893–1975, vol. VII
Oberon, Merle, (Estelle Merle O'Brien Thompson), 1911–1979, vol. VII
Obert de Thieusies, Vicomte Alain, 1888–1979, vol. VII
Obey, André, 1892–1975, vol. VII
Obeyesekere, Sir James Peter, 1879–1968, vol. VI
Obeyesekere, Hon. Sir Solomon Christoffel, 1848–1926, vol. II (A), vol. III
Obre, Henry, died 1922, vol. II
O'Briain, Art Patrick, 1872–1949, vol. IV
O'Brien, 1st Baron, 1842–1914, vol. I
O'Brien, Arthur John Rushton, 1883–1940, vol. III
O'Brien, Lt-Col Aubrey John, 1870–1930, vol. III
O'Brien, Brian, died 1973, vol. VII
O'Brien, Brig. Brian Palliser Tiegue, 1898–1966, vol. VI
O'Brien, Bryan Justin, 1902–1978, vol. VII
O'Brien, Lt-Col Sir Charles Richard Mackey, 1859–1935, vol. III
O'Brien, Christopher Michael, 1861–1935, vol. III
O'Brien, Most Rev. Cornelius, 1843–1906, vol. I
O'Brien, Daniel Joseph, died 1949, vol. IV
O'Brien, Dermod, 1865–1945, vol. IV
O'Brien, Hon. Donough, 1879–1953, vol. V
O'Brien, Brig.-Gen. Edmund Donough John, 1858–1945, vol. IV
O'Brien, Lt-Col Edward, 1872–1965, vol. VI
O'Brien, Edward Joseph Harrington, 1890–1941, vol. IV
O'Brien, Ernest Edward, 1869–1932, vol. III
O'Brien, Sir (Frederick) Lucius, 1896–1974, vol. VII
O'Brien, George, 1892–1973, vol. VII
O'Brien, Sir George Thomas Michael, 1844–1906, vol. I
O'Brien, Henry, born 1836, vol. III
O'Brien, Lt-Col Hon. Henry Barnaby, 1887–1969, vol. VI
O'Brien, James Francis Xavier, died 1905, vol. I
O'Brien, John, 1895–1947, vol. V
O'Brien, Sir John Edmond Noel, 5th Bt, 1899–1969, vol. VI
O'Brien, Sir John Terence Nicolls, 1830–1903, vol. I
O'Brien, Kate, 1897–1974, vol. VII
O'Brien, Kendal Edmund, 1849–1909, vol. I
O'Brien, Sir Lucius; see O'Brien, Sir F. L.
O'Brien, Very Rev. Lucius H., 1842–1913, vol. I
O'Brien, Most Rev. Michael, 1877–1952, vol. V
O'Brien, Michael, 1883–1958, vol. V
O'Brien, Rt Rev. Mgr Michael Joseph, 1913–1978, vol. VII
O'Brien, Lt-Col Hon. Murrough, 1866–1934, vol. III
O'Brien, Patrick, died 1917, vol. II
O'Brien, Patrick Joseph, died 1911, vol. I
O'Brien, Richard Alfred, 1878–1970, vol. VI
O'Brien, Richard Barry, 1847–1918, vol. II
O'Brien, Sir Robert Rollo Gillespie, 4th Bt, 1901–1952, vol. IV
O'Brien, Sir Timothy Carew, 3rd Bt, 1861–1948, vol. IV
O'Brien, Sir Tom, 1900–1970, vol. VI

O'Brien, Rt Hon. William, 1832–1899, vol. I

O'Brien, William, 1852–1928, vol. II

O'Brien-Butler, Pierce Essex, 1858–1954, vol. V

O'Brien Twohig, Brig. Joseph Patrick, 1905–1973, vol. VII

O'Brien-Twohig, Col Michael Joseph, 1893–1971, vol. VII

O'Bryan, Sir Norman, 1894–1968, vol. VI

O'Byrne, Count John, 1834–1905, vol. I

O'Byrne, John, 1884–1954, vol. V

O'Callagham, The; *see* O'Callaghan-Westropp, Col George.

O'Callaghan, Col Denis Moriarty, 1861–1926, vol. II

O'Callaghan, Maj.-Gen. Sir Desmond Dykes Tynte, 1843–1931, vol. III

O'Callaghan, Most Rev. Eugene, 1888–1973, vol. VII

O'Callaghan, Sir Francis Langford, 1839–1909, vol. I

O'Callaghan, Adm. George William Douglass, *died* 1900, vol. I

O'Callaghan, Adm. Michael Pelham, 1850–1937, vol. III

O'Callaghan, Robert Alexander, *died* 1903, vol. I

O'Callaghan, Most Rev. Thomas Alphonsus, 1839–1916, vol. II

O'Callaghan, Timothy Patrick Moriarty, 1886–1961, vol. VI

O'Callaghan-Westropp, Col George, (The O'Callaghan), 1864–1944, vol. IV

O'Carroll, Joseph Francis, 1855–1942, vol. IV

O'Carroll Scott, Maj.-Gen. Anthony Gerald; *see* Scott.

O'Casey, Sean, 1880–1964, vol. VI

Ochs, Adolph S., 1858–1935, vol. III

Ochterlony, Sir Charles Francis, 5th Bt, 1891–1964, vol. VI

Ochterlony, Sir David Ferguson, 3rd Bt, 1848–1931, vol. III

Ochterlony, Sir Matthew Montgomerie, 4th Bt, 1880–1946, vol. IV

O'Clery, Count, (The O'Clery), 1849–1913, vol. I

O'Connell, Daniel Patrick, 1924–1979, vol. VII

O'Connell, Sir Daniel Ross, 3rd Bt, 1861–1905, vol. I

O'Connell, Captain Donal Bernard, 1893–1971, vol. VII

O'Connell, Rev. Frederick William, 1876–1929, vol. III

O'Connell, Captain James Ross, 1863–1925, vol. II

O'Connell, Rev. Sir John Robert, 1868–1943, vol. IV

O'Connell, Captain Sir Maurice James Arthur, 5th Bt, 1889–1949, vol. IV

O'Connell, Sir Morgan Ross, 4th Bt, 1862–1919, vol. II

O'Connell, Sir Peter Reilly, *died* 1927, vol. II

O'Connell, Thomas J., 1882–1969, vol. VI

O'Connell, Hon. W. B., *died* 1903, vol. I

O'Connell, His Eminence Cardinal William Henry, 1859–1944, vol IV

O'Connor, Arthur, 1844–1923, vol. II

O'Connor, Arthur John, 1888–1950, vol. IV (A), vol. V

O'Connor, Col Arthur Patrick, 1856–1920, vol. II

O'Connor, Rt Hon. Charles Andrew, 1854–1928, vol. II

O'Connor, Charles Gerald, 1890–1949, vol. IV (A)

O'Connor, Charles Yelverton, 1843–1902, vol. I

O'Connor, Most Rev. Denis, *died* 1911, vol. I

O'Connor, Rev. Edward Dominic, 1874–1954, vol. V

O'Connor, Frank, 1903–1966, vol. VI

O'Connor, Lt-Col Sir Frederick; *see* O'Connor, Lt-Col Sir W. F. T.

O'Connor, George Bligh, 1883–1957, vol. V

O'Connor, Col Henry Willis-, 1886–1957, vol. V

O'Connor, James, 1836–1910, vol. I

O'Connor, Rt Hon. Sir James, 1872–1931, vol. III

O'Connor, James Malachy, 1886–1974, vol. VII

O'Connor, John, 1850–1928, vol. II

O'Connor, Maj.-Gen. Sir Luke, 1832–1915, vol. I

O'Connor, Lt-Col Patrick Fenelon, 1850–1939, vol. III

O'Connor, Rt Rev. Patrick Joseph, *died* 1932, vol. III

O'Connor, Richard Edward, 1851–1912, vol. I

O'Connor, Sir Terence James, 1891–1940, vol. III

O'Connor, Thomas Arthur Leslie S.; *see* Scott O'Connor.

O'Connor, Rt Hon. Thomas Power, 1848–1929, vol. III

O'Connor, Vincent Clarence Scott, *died* 1945, vol. IV

O'Connor, Lt-Col Sir (William) Frederick (Travers), 1870–1943, vol. IV

O'Connor-Morris, Geoffrey, 1886–1964, vol. VI

O'Conor, Rt Hon. Charles Owen, (The O'Conor Don), 1838–1906, vol. I

O'Conor, Rt Hon. Denis Charles Joseph, (The O'Conor Don), 1869–1917, vol. II

O'Conor, James Edward, *died* 1917, vol. II

O'Conor, Sir John, 1863–1927, vol. II

O'Conor, Norreys Jephson, 1885–1958, vol. V

O'Conor, Owen Phelim, (The O'Conor Don), 1870–1943, vol. IV

O'Conor Don, The; *see* O'Conor, Rt Hon. C. O.

O'Conor Don, The; *see* O'Conor, Rt Hon. D. C. J.

O'Conor Don, The; *see* O'Conor, O. P.

O'Conor-Eccles, Miss, *died* 1911, vol. I

Ó Dálaigh, Cearbhall, 1911–1978, vol. VII

Oddie, John William, *died* 1923, vol. II

Oddin-Taylor, Harry Willoughby, 1886–1967, vol. VI

Oddy, Sir John James, 1867–1921, vol. II

O'Dea, Rt Rev. Thomas, 1858–1923, vol. II

O'Dea, William, 1870–1936, vol. III (A), vol. V

O'Deirg, Tomás, (Thomas Derrig), 1897–1956, vol. V

O'Dell, Andrew Charles, 1909–1966, vol. VI

Odell, Thomas Alexander, 1847–1909, vol. I

Odets, Clifford, 1906–1963, vol. VI

Odgers, Sir Charles Edwin, 1870–1964, vol. VI

Odgers, Lindsey Noel Blake, 1892–1979, vol. VII

Odgers, Walter Blake, 1880–1969, vol. VI

Odgers, William Blake, 1849–1924, vol. II

Odhams, Ernest Lynch, 1880–1947, vol. IV
Odle, Dorothy M.; see Richardson, D. M.
Odling, Charles William, 1847–1932, vol. III
Odling, Thomas Francis, died 1906, vol. I
Odling, William, 1829–1921, vol. II
Odlum, Maj.-Gen. Victor Wentworth, 1880–1971, vol. VII
O'Dogherty, Engr-Rear-Adm. Francis Blake, died 1952, vol. V
O'Doherty, Most Rev. Eugene, 1896–1979, vol. VII
O'Doherty, Rt Rev. J. Keys, died 1907, vol. I
O'Doherty, Philip, 1871–1926, vol. II
O'Doherty, Rt Rev. Thomas, 1877–1936, vol. III
O'Doherty, William, 1868–1905, vol. I
Odom, Rev. William, 1846–1933, vol. III
O'Donnell, Charles James, 1850–1934, vol. III
O'Donnell, Elliott, died 1965, vol. VI
O'Donnell, Maj.-Gen. Eric Hugh, 1893–1950, vol. IV
O'Donnell, Frank Hugh Macdonald, 1848–1916, vol. II
O'Donnell, Maj.-Gen. Hugh, 1858–1917, vol. II
O'Donnell, Rev. Michael J., 1881–1944, vol. IV
O'Donnell, His Eminence Cardinal Patrick, 1856–1927, vol. II
O'Donnell, Sir Samuel Perry, 1874–1946, vol. IV
O'Donnell, Thomas, 1872–1943, vol. IV
O'Donnell, Maj.-Gen. Sir Thomas Joseph, 1858–1947, vol. IV
O'Donoghue, Charles Henry, 1885–1961, vol. VI
O'Donoghue, David J., 1866–1917, vol. II (A), vol. III
O'Donoghue, Geoffrey Charles Patrick, (The O'Donoghue of the Glens), 1859–1935, vol. III
O'Donoghue, Geoffrey Charles Patrick Randal, (The O'Donoghue of the Glens), 1896–1974, vol. VII
O'Donoghue, John Kingston, 1894–1976, vol. VII
O'Donoghue, Col Montague Ernest, 1859–1943, vol. IV
O'Donoghue, Richard John Langford, 1889–1972, vol. VII
O'Donoghue, Thomas Henry, 1886–1957, vol. V
O'Donoghue of the Glens, The; see O'Donoghue, G. C. P.
O'Donoghue of the Glens, The; see O'Donoghue, G. C. P. R.
O'Donohoe, Sir James, died 1933, vol. III
O'Donovan, The; see O'Donovan, Brig. M. J. W.
O'Donovan, The; see O'Donovan, M. W.
O'Donovan, John, 1858–1927, vol. II
O'Donovan, Michael; see O'Connor, Frank.
O'Donovan, Brig. Morgan John Winthrop, (The O'Donovan), 1893–1969, vol. VI
O'Donovan, Morgan William, (The O'Donovan), 1861–1940, vol. III
O'Donovan, William James, died 1955, vol. V
O'Dowd, Sir James Cornelius, 1829–1903, vol. I
O'Dowda, Lt-Gen. Sir James Wilton, 1871–1961, vol. VI
O'Driscoll, Florence, died 1939, vol. III
O'Duffy, Eimar Ultan, 1893–1935, vol. III
O'Duffy, Gen. Eoin, 1892–1944, vol. IV

O'Dwyer, Rt Rev. Edward Thomas, 1842–1917, vol. II
O'Dwyer, Sir Michael Francis, 1864–1940, vol. III
O'Dwyer, Robert, 1862–1949, vol. IV
O'Dwyer, Surg.-Gen. Thomas Francis, died 1919, vol. II
O'Dwyer, Una, (Lady O'Dwyer), 1872–1956, vol. V
O'Dwyer, William, 1890–1964, vol. VI
Oehlers, Sir George Edward Noel, 1908–1968, vol. VI
Oelrichs, Hermann, 1850–1906, vol. I
Oelsner, Herman, 1871–1923, vol. II
Oesterley, Rev. William O. E., 1866–1950, vol. IV
O'Farrell, Sir Edward, 1856–1926, vol. II
O'Farrell, Sir George Plunkett, 1845–1911, vol. I
O'Farrell, Rt Rev. Michael, 1865–1928, vol. II
O'Feeney, Sean; see Ford, John.
O'Ferrall, Dominic More-, 1854–1942, vol. IV
O'Ferrall, Rt Rev. Ronald Stanhope More-, 1890–1973, vol. VII
Officer, Sir (Frank) Keith, 1889–1969, vol. VI
Officer, Sir Keith; see Officer, Sir F. K.
Offner, Richard, 1889–1965, vol. VI
Offor, Richard, 1882–1964, vol. VI
O'Flynn, Surg. Rear-Adm. Joseph Aloysius, 1889–1976, vol. VII
Ogden, Charles Kay, 1889–1957, vol. V
Ogden, Fred, 1871–1933, vol. III
Ogden, George Washington, 1871–1966, vol. VI
Ogg, David, 1887–1965, vol. VI
Ogg, Col George Sim, 1866–1935, vol. III
Ogg, Sir William Gammie, 1891–1979, vol. VII
Ogg, Col William Mortimer, 1873–1958, vol. V
Ogilby, Col Robert James Leslie, 1880–1964, vol. VI
Ogilvie, Alan Grant, 1887–1954, vol. V
Ogilvie, Hon. Albert George, 1891–1939, vol. III
Ogilvie, Alexander, 1882–1962, vol. VI
Ogilvie, Sir Andrew Muter John, 1858–1924, vol. II
Ogilvie, Sir Charles MacIvor Grant, 1891–1967, vol. VI
Ogilvie, Lt-Col Duncan, 1873–1941, vol. IV
Ogilvie, Col Edward Collingwood, 1867–1950, vol. IV
Ogilvie, Sir Francis Grant, 1858–1930, vol. III
Ogilvie, Sir Frederick Wolff, 1893–1949, vol. IV
Ogilvie, George, 1852–1918, vol. II
Ogilvie, Lt-Col Sir George Drummond, 1882–1966, vol. VI
Ogilvie, Glencairn Stuart, 1858–1932, vol. III
Ogilvie, Lt-Col Gordon, 1878–1958, vol. V
Ogilvie, Sir Heneage; see Ogilvie, Sir W. H.
Ogilvie, Rt Rev. James Nicoll, 1860–1926, vol. II
Ogilvie, Lt-Col Sholto Stuart, 1884–1961, vol. VI
Ogilvie, Col Thomas, 1871–1944, vol. IV
Ogilvie, Maj.-Gen. Sir Walter Holland, 1869–1936, vol. III
Ogilvie, Sir (William) Heneage, 1887–1971, vol. VII
Ogilvie, William Henry, 1869–1963, vol. VI
Ogilvie-Farquharson, Mrs; see Farquharson.
Ogilvie-Forbes, Sir George Arthur D.; see Forbes.
Ogilvie Gordon, Dame Maria M., died 1939, vol. III

Ogilvie-Grant, William Robert, 1863–1924, vol. II
Ogilvy, Major Angus Howard Reginald, 1860–1906, vol. I
Ogilvy, Brig. David, 1881–1949, vol. IV
Ogilvy, Gilbert Francis Molyneux, 1868–1953, vol. V
Ogilvy, Sir Gilchrist Nevill, 11th Bt, 1892–1914, vol. I
Ogilvy, Henry Thomas Nisbet Hamilton, 1837–1909, vol. I
Ogilvy, Sir Herbert Kinnaird, 12th Bt, 1865–1956, vol. V
Ogilvy, Captain J. H. C., 1872–1901, vol. I
Ogilvy, Mary Georgina Constance Nisbet-Hamilton; see Ogilvy, Mrs N.-H.
Ogilvy, Mrs Nisbet-Hamilton, (Mary Georgiana Constance), died 1920, vol. II
Ogilvy, Sir Reginald Howard Alexander, 10th Bt, 1832–1910, vol. I
Ogilvy, Col William Lewis Kinloch, 1840–1900, vol. I
Ogilvy-Dalgleish, Wing Comdr James William, 1888–1969, vol. VI
Ogilvy-Wedderburn, Sir John Andrew, 11th and 5th Bt, 1866–1956, vol. V
Ogilvy-Wedderburn, Comdr Sir (John) Peter, 12th and 6th Bt, 1917–1977, vol. VII
Ogilvy-Wedderburn, Comdr Sir Peter; see Ogilvy-Wedderburn, Comdr Sir J. P.
Oglander, Brig.-Gen. Cecil Faber A.; see Aspinall-Oglander.
Ogle, Col Sir Edmund Ashton, 8th Bt, 1857–1940, vol. III
Ogle, Lt-Col Edmund Chaloner, 1878–1935, vol. III
Ogle, Maj.-Gen. Frederic Amelius, 1841–1931, vol. III
Ogle, Sir Henry Asgill, 7th Bt, 1850–1921, vol. II
Ogle, Newton Charles, 1850–1912, vol. I
Ogle, William, 1827–1905, vol. I
Ogmore, 1st Baron, 1903–1976, vol. VII
O'Gorman, The; see O'Gorman, Col N. P.
O'Gorman, Col Charles John, 1872–1930, vol. III
O'Gorman, Rt Rev. John A., 1866–1935, vol. III
O'Gorman, Mervyn, 1871–1958, vol. V
O'Gorman, Col Nicholas Purcell, (The O'Gorman), 1845–1935, vol. III
O'Gorman, Lt-Col Patrick Wilkins, 1860–1950, vol. IV
O'Gowan, Maj.-Gen. Robert W.; see Wanless-O'Gowan.
O'Grady, The; see O'Grady, W. de R.
O'Grady, Donald de Courcy, 1881–1943, vol. IV
O'Grady, Guillamore, 1879–1952, vol. V
O'Grady, Brig.-Gen. Henry de Courcy, 1873–1949, vol. IV
O'Grady, Sir James, 1866–1934, vol. III
O'Grady, Lt-Col John de Courcy, 1856–1920, vol. II
O'Grady, Standish, 1846–1928, vol. II
O'Grady, Lt-Col Standish de Courcy, 1872–1920, vol. II
O'Grady, William de Rienzi, (The O'Grady), 1852–1932, vol. III

O'Grady, Rev. William Waller, 1844–1921, vol. II
O'Grady-Haly, Maj.-Gen. Richard Hebden, 1841–1911, vol. I
Ogston, Sir Alexander, 1844–1929, vol. III
Ogston, Brig.-Gen. Charles, 1877–1944, vol. IV
Ogston, Frank, 1846–1917, vol. II
Ogundipe, Brig. Babafemi Olatunde, 1924–1971, vol. VII
O'Hagan, 2nd Baron, 1878–1900, vol. I
O'Hagan, 3rd Baron, 1882–1961, vol. VI
O'Hagan, Thomas, 1855–1939, vol. III
O'Halloran, Cornelius Hawkins, 1890–1963, vol. VI
O'Halloran, George Finley, 1862–1937, vol. III
O'Halloran, Joseph Sylvester, 1842–1920, vol. II
O'Halloran, Rev. Richard, died 1925, vol. II
O'Hanlon, Rt Rev. Mgr James, 1840–1921, vol. II
O'Hara, Major Charles Kean, 1860–1947, vol. IV
O'Hara, Col Errill Robert, died 1956, vol. V
O'Hara, Francis Charles Trench, 1870–1954, vol. V
O'Hara, Most Rev. Gerald Patrick, 1895–1963, vol. VI
O'Hara, Rt Rev. Henry Stewart, 1843–1923, vol. II
O'Hara, Col James, 1865–1928, vol. II
O'Hara, John Bernard, 1862–1927, vol. II
O'Hara, John Henry, 1905–1970, vol. VI
O'Hara, Valentine J., 1875–1941, vol. IV
O'Hare, P., died 1917, vol. II
O'Hare, Patrick Joseph, 1883–1961, vol. VI
O'Hegarty, Patrick Sarsfield, 1879–1955, vol. V
O'Higgins, Kevin Christopher, 1892–1927, vol. II
Ohlenschlager, Comdr Norman Albert Gustave, 1890–1938, vol. III
Ohlin, Bertil Gotthard, 1899–1979, vol. VII
Ohlson, Sir Erik, 1st Bt, 1873–1934, vol. III
Ohnet, Georges, 1848–1918, vol. II
Oistrakh, David Fyodorovich, 1908–1974, vol. VII
Ojukwu, Sir Odumegwu, 1909–1966, vol. VI
O'Kane, Rt Rev. Bernard, died 1939, vol. III
Oke, Harris Rendell, 1891–1940, vol. III
Okeden, Richard Godfrey Christian P.; see Parry-Okeden.
Okeden, William Edward P.; see Parry-Okeden.
O'Keefe, Hon. David John, 1864–1943, vol. IV
O'Keefe, Hon. Michael, 1865–1926, vol. II
O'Keeffe, Francis Arthur, 1856–1909, vol. I
O'Keeffe, James George, died 1937, vol. III
O'Keeffe, Maj.-Gen. Sir Menus William, 1859–1944, vol. IV
O'Keeffe, Stephen Martin Lanigan, 1878–1948, vol. IV
Okell, Charles Cyril, 1888–1939, vol. III
Okell, Rt Rev. Frank Jackson, 1887–1950, vol. IV
O'Kelly, The; see Kelly, Major A. D. D.
O'Kelly, The; see Kelly, Sir R. D.
O'Kelly, Edward Peter, died 1914, vol. I
O'Kelly, James, 1845–1916, vol. II
O'Kelly, John Joseph, died 1957, vol. V
O'Kelly, Sean Thomas, 1882–1966, vol. VI
O'Kelly de Gallagh et Tycooly, Count Gerald Edward, 1890–1968, vol. VI
Okeover, Haughton Charles, 1825–1912, vol. I

Okey, Thomas, 1852–1935, vol. III
O'Kinealy, Lt-Col Frederick, 1865–1940, vol. III
Okoro, Godfrey; see Benin, Oba of.
Oku, Field-Marshal Count Yasukata, 1845–1930, vol. III
Okuma, Prince Shigenobu, 1838–1922, vol. II
Okyar, Bay Fethi, died 1943, vol. IV
Olcott, Col Henry Steel, died 1907, vol. I
Oldcastle, John; see Meynell, Wilfred.
Oldershaw, John, 1850–1938, vol. III
Oldershaw, William James Norman, 1856–1926, vol. II
Oldfield, Col Arthur Radulphus, 1872–1940, vol. III
Oldfield, Rev. Charles, died 1908, vol. I
Oldfield, Col Christopher George, 1863–1944, vol. IV
Oldfield, Claude Houghton, died 1961, vol. VI
Oldfield, Sir Francis Du Pre, 1869–1928, vol. II
Oldfield, Rev. George Biscoe, 1840–1932, vol. III
Oldfield, Maj.-Gen. John Rawdon Hodge, died 1940, vol. III
Oldfield, Major John William, 1886–1955, vol. V
Oldfield, Josiah, died 1953, vol. V
Oldfield, Maj.-Gen. Sir Louis, 1872–1949, vol. IV
Oldfield, Sir Richard Charles, 1828–1918, vol. II
Oldfield, Richard Charles, 1909–1972, vol. VII
Oldfield, Bt Lt-Col Richard William, 1891–1933, vol. III
Oldfield, William Henry, died 1961, vol. VI
Oldfield, Rev. William John, 1857–1934, vol. III
Oldham, Alan Trevor, 1904–1971, vol. VII
Oldham, Ven. Algernon Langston, died 1916, vol. II
Oldham, Charles Evelyn Arbuthnot William, 1869–1949, vol. IV
Oldham, Charles H., died 1926, vol. II
Oldham, Sir Ernest Fitzjohn, 1870–1926, vol. II
Oldham, Col Sir Henry Hugh, 1840–1922, vol. II
Oldham, Henry Yule, 1862–1951, vol. V
Oldham, James Bagot, 1899–1977, vol. VII
Oldham, Joseph Houldsworth, 1874–1969, vol. VI
Oldham, Richard Dixon, 1858–1936, vol. III
Oldham, William Benjamin, 1845–1916, vol. II
Oldman, Cecil Bernard, 1894–1969, vol. VI
Oldman, Maj.-Gen. Richard Deare Furley, 1877–1943, vol. IV
Oldmeadow, Ernest James, 1867–1949, vol. IV
Oldrieve, William Thomas, 1853–1922, vol. II
Oldroyd, George, 1886–1951, vol. V
Oldroyd, Sir Mark, 1843–1927, vol. II
Olds, Irving Sands, 1887–1963, vol. VI
O'Leary, Daniel, 1878–1954, vol. V
O'Leary, Rev. De Lacy Evans, 1872–1957, vol. V
O'Leary, Brig. Heffernan William Denis McCarthy-, 1885–1948, vol. IV
O'Leary, Most Rev. Henry Joseph, 1879–1938, vol. III
O'Leary, Rt Hon. Sir Humphrey Francis, 1886–1953, vol. V
O'Leary, John, 1830–1907, vol. I
O'Leary, Rt Rev. Louis James, 1877–1930, vol. III
O'Leary, Major Michael J., 1888–1961, vol. VI
O'Leary, Brig.-Gen. Tom Evelyn, 1862–1924, vol. II

Oliphant, Ernest Henry Clark, 1862–1936, vol. III
Oliphant, Captain Henry Gerard Laurence, 1879–1955, vol. V
Oliphant, John Ninian, 1887–1960, vol. V
Oliphant, Sir Lancelot, 1881–1965, vol. VI
Oliphant, Mrs Laurence, 1846–1937, vol. III
Oliphant, Gen. Sir Laurence James, 1846–1914, vol. I
Oliphant, Margaret Oliphant Wilson, 1828–1897, vol. I
Oliphant, Patrick James, 1914–1979, vol. VII
Oliphant, Lt-Col Philip Lawrence K. B.; see Kington-Blair-Oliphant.
Oliphant, Rosamond; see Oliphant, Mrs Laurence.
Oliphant-Sheffield, Robert Stoney, 1864–1937, vol. III
Olive, George William, died 1963, vol. VI
Olive, Sir James William, 1856–1942, vol. IV
Oliveira, Mrs A. J. E.; see Tubb, Carrie.
Oliveira, Francisco Regis de, died 1916, vol. II
Oliver, Major Alfred Alexander, 1874–1965, vol. VI
Oliver, Sir Arthur Maule, 1871–1937, vol. III
Oliver, Rev. Arthur West, 1858–1941, vol. IV
Oliver, Dame Beryl, 1882–1972, vol. VII
Oliver, Charles A., 1861–1945, vol. IV
Oliver, Lt-Col Sir (Charles) Frederick, died 1939, vol. III
Oliver, Charles Nicholson Jewel, 1848–1920, vol. II (A), vol. III
Oliver, Charles Pye, 1861–1951, vol. V
Oliver, Daniel, 1830–1916, vol. II
Oliver, Wing-Comdr Douglas Austin, 1887–1939, vol. III
Oliver, Very Rev. Edmund Henry, 1882–1935, vol. III
Oliver, Edwin, died 1950, vol. IV
Oliver, Hon. Dame Florence C.; see Cardell-Oliver, Hon. Dame A. F. G.
Oliver, Francis Alfred, 1866–1944, vol. IV
Oliver, Francis Wall, 1864–1951, vol. V
Oliver, Hon. Frank, 1853–1933, vol. III
Oliver, Lt-Col Sir Frederick; see Oliver, Lt-Col Sir C. F.
Oliver, Frederick Scott, 1864–1934, vol. III
Oliver, Adm. Sir Geoffrey Nigel, 1898–1980, vol. VII
Oliver, George, 1841–1915, vol. I (A)
Oliver, Rev. George, 1848–1920, vol. II
Oliver, Henry Alfred, 1854–1935, vol. III
Oliver, Admiral of the Fleet Sir Henry Francis, 1865–1965, vol. VI
Oliver, Henry John Callard, 1915–1978, vol. VII
Oliver, James, 1857–1941, vol. IV
Oliver, John Orlando Hercules Norman, 1822–1901, vol. I
Oliver, John Rathbone, 1872–1943, vol. IV
Oliver, Maj.-Gen. John Ryder, 1834–1909, vol. I
Oliver, Sir John William Lambton, 1873–1952, vol. V
Oliver, Laurence Herbert, 1881–1962, vol. VI
Oliver, Col Lionel Grant, 1858–1936, vol. III
Oliver, Mary Louise, (Lady Oliver), 1868–1950, vol. IV

Oliver, Matthew W. B., *died* 1926, vol. II
Oliver, Philip Milner, 1884–1954, vol. V
Oliver, Raymond, 1921–1976, vol. VII
Oliver, Rev. Richard John Deane, *died* 1942, vol. IV
Oliver, Vice-Adm. Robert Don, 1895–1980, vol. VII
Oliver, Sir Roland Giffard, 1882–1967, vol. VI
Oliver, Sir Thomas, 1853–1942, vol. IV
Oliver, Thomas, 1871–1946, vol. IV
Oliver, Victor, 1898–1964, vol. VI
Oliver, Walter Reginald Brook, 1883–1957, vol. V
Oliver, William, *died* 1917, vol. II
Oliver, William, *died* 1962, vol. VI
Oliver, Col William James, 1860–1937, vol. III
Oliver-Bellasis, Captain Richard, 1900–1964, vol. VI
Olivey, Sir Walter Rice, 1831–1922, vol. II
Olivier, 1st Baron, 1859–1943, vol. IV
Olivier, C. F., *died* 1940, vol. III (A), vol. IV
Olivier, Rev. Dacres, 1831–1919, vol. II
Olivier, Edith, *died* 1948, vol. IV
Olivier, George B.; *see* Borg Olivier.
Olivier, Rev. Henry Eden, 1866–1936, vol. III
Olivier, Herbert Arnould, 1861–1952, vol. V
Olivier, Martin John, 1900–1959, vol. V
Olivier, Captain Sidney Richard, 1870–1932, vol. III
Ollard, Lt-Col John William Arthur, 1893–1961, vol. VI
Ollard, Rev. Sidney Leslie, 1875–1949, vol. IV
Ollerenshaw, Robert, 1882–1948, vol. IV
Ollivant, Alfred, 1874–1927, vol. II
Ollivant, Brig.-Gen. Alfred Henry, 1871–1919, vol. II
Ollivant, Sir Charles; *see* Ollivant, Sir E. C. K.
Ollivant, Sir (Edward) Charles (Kyall), 1846–1928, vol. II
Ollivant, Col John Spencer, 1872–1937, vol. III
Ollivier, Olivier Emile, 1825–1913, vol. I
Olmsted, Rt Rev. Charles Sanford, 1853–1918, vol. II
Olmsted, Rt Rev. Charles Tyler, 1842–1924, vol. II
Olney, Hon. Sir Herbert Horace, 1875–1957, vol. V
Olney, Richard, 1835–1917, vol. II
O'Loghlen, Hon. Sir Bryan, 3rd Bt, 1828–1905, vol. I
O'Loghlen, Sir Charles Hugh Ross, 5th Bt, 1881–1951, vol. V
O'Loghlen, Sir Michael, 4th Bt, 1866–1934, vol. III
O'Loghlin, Hon. James Vincent, 1852–1925, vol. II
Olorenshaw, Leslie, 1912–1972, vol. VII
O'Loughlin, Hon. Laurence, 1854–1927, vol. II
O'Loughlin, Very Rev. Robert Stuart, 1852–1925, vol. II
Olphert, Sir John, 1844–1917, vol. II
Olphert, Captain Wybrants, 1879–1938, vol. III
Olpherts, Sir William, 1822–1902, vol. I
Olsen, Björn Magnusson, 1850–1919, vol. II
Olson, Sven Olof, 1916–1977, vol. VII
Olsson, Julius, 1864–1942, vol. IV
Oluwole, Rt Rev. Isaac, *died* 1932, vol. III
Olver, Col Sir Arthur, 1875–1961, vol. VI

O'Mahony, The; *see* O'Mahony, P. C. de L.
O'Mahony, John, (Sean), *died* 1934, vol. III
O'Mahony, Pierce Charles de Lacy, (The O'Mahony), 1850–1930, vol. III
Omáille, Tomás, *died* 1938, vol. III
O'Malley, Rt Hon. Brian Kevin, 1930–1976, vol. VII
O'Malley, Maj.-Gen. David Vincent, 1891–1955, vol. V
O'Malley, Sir Edward Loughlin, 1842–1932, vol. III
O'Malley, Hon. King, *died* 1953, vol. V
O'Malley, Lewis Sydney Steward, 1874–1941, vol. IV
O'Malley, Mary Dolling, (Lady O'Malley); *see* Bridge, Ann.
O'Malley, Sir Owen St Clair, 1887–1974, vol. VII
O'Malley, William, 1853–1939, vol. III
O'Malley, Col William Arthur D'Oyly, 1853–1925, vol. II
Oman, Carola Mary Anima, (Lady Lenanton), 1897–1978, vol. VII
Oman, Sir Charles William Chadwick, 1860–1946, vol. IV
Oman, John Campbell, 1841–1911, vol. I
Oman, John Wood, 1860–1939, vol. III
O'Mara, Joseph, *died* 1927, vol. II
O'Meagher, Col John Kevin, 1866–1946, vol. IV
O'Meara, Captain Bulkeley Ernest Adolphus, 1867–1916, vol. II
O'Meara, Lt-Col Charles Albert Edmond, 1868–1923, vol. II
O'Meara, Rev. Daniel, 1877–1929, vol. III
O'Meara, Francis, 1886–1941, vol. IV
O'Meara, Maj.-Gen. Francis Joseph, 1900–1967, vol. VI
O'Meara, Stephen, 1854–1918, vol. III
O'Meara, Rev. Thomas Robert, 1864–1930, vol. III
O'Meara, Lt-Col Walter Alfred John, 1863–1939, vol. III
Ommanney, Brig.-Gen. Albert Edward, 1849–1930, vol. III
Ommanney, Charles Henry, 1852–1915, vol. I
Ommanney, Lt-Col Charles Vernon, 1872–1952, vol. V
Ommanney, Col Edward Lacon, 1834–1914, vol. I
Ommanney, Adm. Sir Erasmus, 1814–1904, vol. I
Ommanney, Francis Downes, 1903–1980, vol. VII
Ommanney, Sir Montagu Frederick, 1842–1925, vol. II
Ommanney, Adm. Sir Nelson, 1854–1938, vol. III
Omololu, Olumide Olusanya, 1925–1967, vol. VI
Omond, George William Thomson, 1846–1929, vol. III
Omond, Robert Traill, 1858–1914, vol. I
Omont, Henri, 1857–1940, vol. III (A), vol. IV
O'Morchoe, Captain Arthur Donel MacMurrogh, (The O'Morchoe), 1892–1966, vol. VI
O'Morchoe, Rev. Thomas Arthur, (The O'Morchoe), 1865–1921, vol. II
Onassis, Aristotle Socrates, 1906–1975, vol. VII
O'Neil, Bryan Hugh St John, 1905–1954, vol. V
O'Neil, Rt Rev. Henry, 1843–1915, vol. I (A)

O'Neill, 2nd Baron, 1839–1928, vol. II
O'Neill, 3rd Baron, 1907–1944, vol. IV
O'Neill, Hon. Arthur Edward Bruce, 1876–1914, vol. I
O'Neill, Sir Arthur Eugene, 1877–1950, vol. IV
O'Neill, Charles, 1849–1918, vol. II
O'Neill, Eugene Gladstone, 1888–1953, vol. V
O'Neill, Col Eugene Joseph, 1875–1962, vol. VI
O'Neill, Rev. George, 1863–1947, vol. IV
O'Neill, Herbert Charles, died 1953, vol. V
O'Neill, Most Rev. Hugh John, 1898–1955, vol. V
O'Neill, Rev. John, 1880–1947, vol. IV
O'Neill, Sir John; see O'Neill, Sir M. J.
O'Neill, Joseph, 1886–1953, vol. V
O'Neill, Sir (Matthew) John, 1914–1976, vol. VII
O'Neill, Michael, 1909–1976, vol. VII
O'Neill, Norman, 1875–1934, vol. III
O'Neill, Patrick, died 1938, vol. III
O'Neill, Most Rev. Patrick, 1891–1958, vol. V
O'Neill, Col Patrick Laurence, 1876–1962, vol. VI
O'Neill, Rt Rev. Peter Austin, 1841–1911, vol. I
O'Neill, Hon. Robert T., 1845–1910, vol. I
O'Neill, Col William Henry Slingsby, 1854–1931, vol. III
O'Nial, Surg.-Gen. John, 1827–1919, vol. II (A), vol. III
O'Niel, Colette; see Malleson, Lady Constance.
Onions, Alfred, 1858–1921, vol. II
Onions, Berta, (Mrs Oliver Onions); see Ruck, B.
Onions, Charles Talbut, 1873–1965, vol. VI
Onions, Oliver, 1873–1961, vol. VI
Onkar Singh, Maj.-Gen. Sir Apji, 1872–1951, vol. V
Onnes, H. Kamerlingh, 1853–1926, vol. II
Onraet, Rene Henry de S., 1887–1952, vol. V
Onsager, Lars, 1903–1976, vol. VII
Onslow, 4th Earl of, 1853–1911, vol. I (A)
Onslow, 5th Earl of, 1876–1945, vol. IV
Onslow, 6th Earl of, 1913–1971, vol. VII
Onslow, Sir Alexander Campbell, 1842–1908, vol. I
Onslow, Brig.-Gen. Cranley Charlton, 1869–1940, vol. III
Onslow, Denzil Roberts, 1839–1908, vol. I
Onslow, Sir Geoffrey Henry H.; see Hughes-Onslow.
Onslow, Brig.-Gen. George Macleay M.; see Macarthur Onslow.
Onslow, Maj.-Gen. George Thorp, 1858–1921, vol. II
Onslow, Henry H.; see Hughes-Onslow.
Onslow, Hon. Mrs Huia, died 1932, vol. III
Onslow, Maj.-Gen. Hon. James William M.; see Macarthur-Onslow.
Onslow, Muriel Wheldale; see Onslow, Hon. Mrs Huia.
Onslow, Captain Richard Francis John, died 1942, vol. IV
Onslow, Adm. Sir Richard George, 1904–1975, vol. VII
Onslow, Sir Richard Wilmot, 7th Bt, 1906–1963, vol. VI
Onslow, Sir Roger Warin Beaconsfield, 6th Bt, 1880–1931, vol. III

Onslow, Sibella Macarthur, 1871–1943, vol. IV
Onslow, Maj.-Gen. Sir William Henry, 1863–1929, vol. III
Onslow, Sir William Wallace Rhoderic, 5th Bt, 1845–1916, vol. II
Onyon, Engr-Captain William, 1862–1953, vol. V
Oonvala, Mancherahaw Framji, 1851–1914, vol. I
Openshaw, Sir James, 1871–1935, vol. III
Openshaw, Thomas Horrocks, 1856–1929, vol. III
Opie, Air Vice-Marshal William Alfred, 1901–1977, vol. VII
Oppé, Adolph Paul, 1878–1957, vol. V
Oppenheim, E(dward) Phillips, 1866–1946, vol. IV
Oppenheim, Ernest Ferdinand, 1875–1939, vol. III
Oppenheim, Henry, 1835–1912, vol. I
Oppenheim, Lassa Francis Lawrence, 1858–1919, vol. II
Oppenheim, Lt-Col Lawrie, 1871–1923, vol. II
Oppenheimer, Albert Martin, 1872–1945, vol. IV
Oppenheimer, Sir Bernard, 1st Bt, 1866–1921, vol. II
Oppenheimer, Sir Charles, 1836–1900, vol. I
Oppenheimer, Charles, 1875–1961, vol. VI
Oppenheimer, Sir Ernest, 1880–1957, vol. V
Oppenheimer, Sir Francis Charles, 1870–1961, vol. VI
Oppenheimer, J. Robert, 1904–1967, vol. VI
Oppenheimer, Joseph, born 1876, vol. VI
Oppenheimer, Sir Michael, 2nd Bt, 1892–1933, vol. III
Opper, Frederick Burr, 1857–1937, vol. III (A), vol. IV
Orage, Alfred Richard, 1873–1934, vol. III
Oram, Dame Elizabeth; see Oram, Dame S. E.
Oram, Engr Vice-Adm. Sir Henry John, 1858–1939, vol. III
Oram, Sir Matthew Henry, 1885–1969, vol. VI
Oram, Richard Edward Sprague, 1830–1909, vol. I
Oram, Dame (Sarah) Elizabeth, 1860–1946, vol. IV
Orange, Beatrice, died 1955, vol. V
Orange, George James, died 1925, vol. II
Orange, Sir Hugh William, 1866–1956, vol. V
Orange, William, 1833–1916, vol. II
Oranmore and Browne, 2nd Baron, 1819–1900, vol. I
Oranmore and Browne, 3rd Baron, 1861–1927, vol. II
Orbach, Maurice, 1902–1979, vol. VII
Orchard, Henry Ben, died 1937, vol. III
Orchard, Jonathan, 1853–1938, vol. III
Orchard, Hon. Richard Beaumont, 1871–1942, vol. IV
Orchard, W(illiam) Arundel, died 1961, vol. VI
Orchard, Rev. William Edwin, 1877–1955, vol. V
Orchardson, Sir William Quiller, 1835–1910, vol. I
Orchha, Maharaja, Sir Pratap Singh Bahadur, 1854–1930, vol. III
Orchin, Frederick Joseph, 1885–1971, vol. VII
Orczy, Baroness, (Mrs Montague Barstow), died 1947, vol. IV
Ord, Bernhard Boris, died 1961, vol. VI
Ord, Ven. Charles Edward B.; see Blackett Ord.
Ord, Col Frederick Cusac, 1851–1938, vol. III
Ord, William Miller, 1834–1902, vol. I

Ord Johnstone, Morris Mackintosh, 1907–1978, vol. VII
Ord Marshall, Elizabeth Middleton, *died* 1931, vol. III
Orde, Sir Arthur John Campbell-Orde, 4th Bt, 1865–1933, vol. III
Orde, Sir Charles William, 1884–1980, vol. VII
Orde, John Fosbery, 1870–1932, vol. III
Orde, Sir John William Powlett Campbell-, 3rd Bt, 1827–1897, vol. I
Orde, Sir Julian Walter, 1861–1929, vol. III
Orde, Sir Percy Lancelot, 1888–1975, vol. VII
Orde, Brig. Reginald John, 1893–1975, vol. VII
Orde, Roden Horace Powlett, 1867–1941, vol. IV
Orde, Major Sir Simon Arthur Campbell-, 5th Bt, 1907–1969, vol. VI
Orde Browne, Sir Granville St John, 1883–1947, vol. IV
Ordish, Thomas Fairman, 1855–1924, vol. II
O'Reilly, The; *see* O'Reilly, M. G.
O'Reilly, Rt Rev. James, 1856–1928, vol. II
O'Reilly, Sir Lennox Arthur Patrick, 1880–1949, vol. IV
O'Reilly, Myles George, (The O'Reilly), 1830–1911, vol. I
O'Reilly, William Edmund, 1873–1934, vol. III
O'Reily, Most Rev. John, 1846–1915, vol. I
O'Rell, Max, 1848–1903, vol. I
Orenstein, Maj.-Gen. Alexander Jeremiah, 1879–1972, vol. VI
Orford, 5th Earl of, 1854–1931, vol. III
Orgill, Tyrrell Churton, 1884–1975, vol. VII
O'Riain, 'Liam P.; *see* Ryan, William Patrick.
Oriel, George Harold, 1894–1939, vol. III (A), vol. IV
Oriel, John Augustus, 1896–1968, vol. VI
O'Riordan, Conal Holmes O'Connell, 1874–1948, vol. IV
O'Riordan, Rt Rev. Mgr Michael, 1857–1919, vol. II
Orkney, 7th Earl of, 1867–1951, vol. V
Orleans, Duc d'; Louis Philippe Robert, 1869–1926, vol. II
Orloff, Nicholas, *died* 1915, vol. I (A)
Ormandy, William Reginald, 1870–1941, vol. IV
Ormathwaite, 2nd Baron, 1827–1920, vol. II
Ormathwaite, 3rd Baron, 1859–1937, vol. III
Ormathwaite, 4th Baron, 1863–1943, vol. IV
Ormathwaite, 5th Baron, 1868–1944, vol. IV
Orme, Edith Temple, *died* 1960, vol. V
Orme, Lt-Col Frank Leslie, 1898–1968, vol. VI
Orme, Frederick George, *died* 1954, vol. V
Orme, Gilbert Edward, 1874–1945, vol. IV
Orme, William Bryce, 1871–1962, vol. VI
Ormerod, Rt Hon. Sir Benjamin, 1890–1974, vol. VII
Ormerod, Eleanor Anne, 1828–1901, vol. I
Ormerod, Frank Cunliffe, 1894–1967, vol. VI
Ormerod, George Milner, 1879–1936, vol. III
Ormerod, Henry Arderne, 1886–1964, vol. VI
Ormerod, Herbert Eliot, 1831–1911, vol. I
Ormerod, Joseph Arderne, 1848–1925, vol. II
Ormidale, Hon. Lord; George Lewis Macfarlane, 1854–1941, vol. IV

Ormiston, Thomas, 1878–1937, vol. III
Ormiston, Lt-Col Thomas Lane, 1867–1954, vol. V
Ormond, Arthur William, 1871–1964, vol. VI
Ormond, Maj.-Gen. Daniel Mowat, 1885–1974, vol. VII
Ormond, E. W., 1863–1930, vol. III
Ormond, Ernest Charles, 1896–1962, vol. VI
Ormond, Sir Herbert John, 1867–1934, vol. III
Ormonde, 3rd Marquess of, 1844–1919, vol. II
Ormonde, 4th Marquess of, 1849–1943, vol. IV
Ormonde, 5th Marquess of, 1890–1949, vol. IV
Ormonde, 6th Marquess of, 1893–1971, vol. VII
Ormrod, Peter, 1869–1923, vol. II
Ormsby, Rev. Edwin Robert, 1845–1915, vol. I (A)
Ormsby, Rt Rev. George Albert, 1843–1924, vol. II
Ormsby, Sir Lambert Hepenstal, 1850–1923, vol. II
Ormsby, Lt-Gen. Robert Daly, 1879–1946, vol. IV
Ormsby, Rev. Thomas, 1871–1942, vol. IV
Ormsby, Lt-Col Vincent Alexander, 1865–1917, vol. II
Ormsby-Gore, Hon. Seymour Fitzroy, 1863–1950, vol. IV
Ornstein, John Isidore Maurice, 1854–1919, vol. II
O'Rorke, Rev. Benjamin Garniss, 1875–1918, vol. II
O'Rorke, E. Brian, 1901–1974, vol. VII
O'Rorke, Lt-Col Frederick Charles, *died* 1976, vol. VII
O'Rorke, Lt-Col George Mackenzie, 1883–1958, vol. V
O'Rorke, Hon. Sir George Maurice, 1830–1916, vol. II
O'Rorke, Rt Rev. Mowbray Stephen, 1869–1953, vol. V
Orpen, R. Caulfeild, 1863–1938, vol. III
Orpen, Rt Rev. Raymond d'Audemar, 1837–1930, vol. III
Orpen, Major Redmond Newenham Morris, 1864–1940, vol. III (A), vol. IV
Orpen, Richard Theodore, 1869–1926, vol. II
Orpen, Major Sir William, 1878–1931, vol. III
Orpen-Palmer, Brig.-Gen. Harold Bland Herbert, 1876–1941, vol. IV
Orpen-Palmer, Col Reginald Arthur Herbert, 1877–1943, vol. IV
Orphoot, Burnett Napier Henderson, 1880–1964, vol. VI
Orr, Col Alexander Stewart, 1861–1914, vol. I
Orr, Arthur A., *died* 1949, vol. IV
Orr, Charles Roger, *died* 1938, vol. III
Orr, Sir Charles William James, 1870–1945, vol. IV
Orr, Christine Grant Millar, *died* 1963, vol. VI
Orr, Major Frank George, 1881–1945, vol. IV
Orr, Col Gerald Maxwell, 1876–1934, vol. III
Orr, James, 1844–1913, vol. I
Orr, James, 1841–1920, vol. II
Orr, James Peter, 1867–1949, vol. IV
Orr, Most Rev. John, 1874–1938, vol. III
Orr, John, 1885–1966, vol. VI
Orr, Major John Boyd, 1871–1915, vol. I
Orr, John Boyd; *see* Baron Boyd Orr.
Orr, John Charles, 1858–1941, vol. IV
Orr, John Wellesley, 1878–1956, vol. V
Orr, Maj.-Gen. John William, 1829–1916, vol. II

Orr, Major Michael Harrison, 1859–1926, vol. II
Orr, Robert Low, 1854–1944, vol. IV
Orr, Sir Samuel, 1886–1972, vol. VII
Orr, Thomas, 1857–1937, vol. III
Orr, William James, 1873–1963, vol. VI
Orr, William M'Fadden, 1866–1934, vol. III
Orr-Ewing, Sir Archibald Ernest, 3rd Bt, 1853–1919, vol. II
Orr-Ewing, Charles Lindsay, 1860–1903, vol. I
Orr Ewing, Sir Ian Leslie, 1893–1958, vol. V
Orr-Ewing, Major James Alexander, 1857–1900, vol. I
Orr Ewing, Brig.-Gen. Sir Norman Archibald, 4th Bt, 1880–1960, vol. V
Orr-Ewing, Sir William, 2nd Bt, 1848–1903, vol. I
Orr-Lewis, Sir Duncan; see Orr-Lewis, Sir J. D.
Orr-Lewis, Sir Frederick Orr, 1st Bt, 1866–1921, vol. II
Orr-Lewis, Sir (John) Duncan, 2nd Bt, 1898–1980, vol. VII
Orrin, Herbert Charles, 1878–1963, vol. VI
Orrock, James, 1829–1913, vol. I
Orsborn, Albert William Thomas, 1886–1967, vol. VI
Orsman, W. J., 1838–1923, vol. II
Ortcheson, Sir John, 1905–1977, vol. VII
Orton, Charles William P.; see Previté-Orton.
Orton, Maj.-Gen. Sir Ernest Frederick, 1874–1960, vol. V
Orton, George Harrison, 1873–1947, vol. IV
Orton, Harold, 1898–1975, vol. VII
Orton, James Herbert, 1884–1953, vol. V
Orton, Kennedy Joseph Previté, 1872–1930, vol. III
Orton, Brig. Sidney Bernard, 1881–1933, vol. III
Orton-Jones, Harry, 1894–1976, vol. VII
Orwell, George, (Eric Blair), died 1950, vol. IV
Orwin, Charles Stewart, 1876–1955, vol. V
Osbaldeston-Mitford, Captain Robert; see Mitford.
Osborn, Sir Algernon Kerr Butler, 7th Bt, 1870–1948, vol. IV
Osborn, E. B., died 1938, vol. III
Osborn, Sir Francis; see Osborn, Sir N. F. B.
Osborn, Sir Frederic James, 1885–1978, vol. VII
Osborn, Henry Fairfield, 1857–1935, vol. III
Osborn, Sir Melmoth, 1833–1899, vol. I
Osborn, Sir (N.) Francis (B.), 1872–1954, vol. V
Osborn, Major Philip Barlow, died 1909, vol. I
Osborn, Samuel, 1848–1936, vol. III
Osborn, Sir Samuel, 1864–1952, vol. V
Osborn, Theodore George Bentley, 1887–1973, vol. VII
Osborn, Brig.-Gen. William Lushington, 1871–1951, vol. V
Osborne, Col Arthur de Vere-W.; see Willoughby-Osborne.
Osborne, Rev. Charles Edward, 1856–1936, vol. III
Osborne, Sir Cyril, 1898–1969, vol. VI
Osborne, Lt-Gen. Edmund Archibald, 1885–1969, vol. VI
Osborne, Edward, 1861–1939, vol. III
Osborne, Vice-Adm. Edward Oliver Brudenell Seymour, 1883–1956, vol. V
Osborne, Rt Rev. Edward William, 1845–1926, vol. II

Osborne, Captain F. Creagh-, died 1943, vol. IV
Osborne, Sir Francis, 15th Bt, 1856–1948, vol. IV
Osborne, Lord Francis Granville Godolphin, 1864–1924, vol. II
Osborne, Sir George Francis, 16th Bt, 1894–1960, vol. V
Osborne, Col Henry Campbell, 1874–1949, vol. IV
Osborne, Rev. (Henry James) Reginald, died 1952, vol. V
Osborne, Rev. James Denham, 1854–1934, vol. III
Osborne, Captain John Warde, 1851–1936, vol. III
Osborne, Lithgow, 1892–1980, vol. VII
Osborne, Malcolm, 1880–1963, vol. VI
Osborne, Maj.-Gen. Osborne Herbert D.; see Delano-Osborne.
Osborne, Rev. Reginald; see Osborne, Rev. H. J. R.
Osborne, Robert Ernest, 1861–1939, vol. III
Osborne, Rosabelle, died 1958, vol. V
Osborne, William Alexander, 1873–1967, vol. VI
Osborne-Gibbes, Sir Edward; see Gibbes.
Osborne-Gibbes, Sir Philip Arthur; see Gibbes.
Osbourne, Brig.-Gen. George Nowell Thomas S.; see Smyth-Osbourne.
Osbourne, Air Cdre Sir Henry Percy S.; see Smyth-Osbourne.
Osbourne, Lloyd, 1868–1947, vol. IV
Osburn, Lt-Col Arthur, died 1952, vol. V
Osburn, Comdr Francis, 1834–1917, vol. II
Osgood, Sir (Frederic) Stanley, 1872–1952, vol. V
Osgood, Sir Stanley; see Osgood, Sir F. S.
O'Shaughnessy, Patrick Joseph, 1872–1920, vol. II
O'Shaughnessy, Richard, 1842–1918, vol. II
O'Shaughnessy, Rt Hon. Sir Thomas Lopdell, 1850–1933, vol. III
O'Shea, Sir Henry, 1858–1926, vol. II (A), vol. III
O'Shea, Henry George, 1838–1905, vol. I
O'Shea, Lucius Trant, died 1920, vol. II
O'Shea, Most Rev. Thomas, 1870–1954, vol. V
O'Shea, Lt-Col Timothy, 1856–1921, vol. II
O'Shee, James John, 1866–1946, vol. IV
O'Shee, Lt-Col Richard Alfred Poer, 1867–1942, vol. IV
Osler, Sir Edmund Boyd, 1845–1924, vol. II
Osler, Featherston, 1838–1924, vol. II
Osler, Col Stratton Harry, 1882–1930, vol. III
Osler, Sir William, 1st Bt, 1849–1919, vol. II
Osmaston, Bertram Beresford, 1868–1961, vol. VI
Osmaston, Col Cecil Alvend FitzHerbert, 1866–1949, vol. IV
Osmond, Wing-Comdr Edward, 1890–1946, vol. IV
Osmond, Brig. William Robert Fiddes, 1890–1952, vol. V
Ossiannilsson, Karl Gustav, 1875–1970, vol. VI (AII)
Ossit; see Deslandes, Baronne M.
Ostberg, Ragnar, 1866–1945, vol. IV
Ostenso, Martha, 1900–1963, vol. VI
Ostler, Hon. Sir Henry Hubert, 1876–1944, vol. IV
Ostrer, Isidore, died 1975, vol. VII
Ostrorog, Count Leon, 1867–1932, vol. III
O'Sullevan, Col John Joseph, 1879–1936, vol. III
O'Sullivan, Most Rev. Charles, 1862–1927, vol. II
O'Sullivan, Cornelius, 1841–1907, vol. I
O'Sullivan, Col Daniel, 1853–1946, vol. IV (A)

O'Sullivan, Dennis Neil, 1899–1973, vol. VII
O'Sullivan, Hon. Edward William, 1846–1910, vol. I
O'Sullivan, Eugene, 1879–1942, vol. IV
O'Sullivan, Maj.-Gen. Hugh Dermod Evan, 1874–1958, vol. V
O'Sullivan, John M., 1881–1948, vol. IV
O'Sullivan, Most Rev. Joseph Anthony, 1886–1972, vol. VII
O'Sullivan, Ven. Leopold, *died* 1919, vol. II
O'Sullivan, Sir Neil, 1900–1968, vol. VI
O'Sullivan, Richard, 1888–1963, vol. VI
O'Sullivan, Seumas, (James Sullivan Starkey), 1879–1958, vol. V
O'Sullivan, Hon. Thomas, 1856–1953, vol. V
O'Sullivan, Timothy, *died* 1950, vol. IV
O'Sullivan-Beare, Daniel Robert, 1865–1921, vol. II
Oswald, Arthur Louis, 1858–1931, vol. III
Oswald, Col Christopher Percy, 1875–1966, vol. VI
Oswald, Eugene, *died* 1912, vol. I
Oswald, Felix, 1866–1958, vol. V
Oswald, Henry Robert, *died* 1940, vol. III
Oswald, James Francis, 1838–1908, vol. I
Oswald, Brig.-Gen. Oswald Charles Williamson, 1863–1938, vol. III
Oswald, Richard Alexander, 1841–1921, vol. II
Oswald, Col St Clair, 1858–1938, vol. III
Oswald, William Digby, 1880–1916, vol. II
Ottaway, Christopher Wyndham, 1910–1978, vol. VII
Ottaway, Eric Carlton, 1904–1967, vol. VI
Otter, Sir John Lonsdale, 1852–1932, vol. III
Otter, Robert Edward, *died* 1932, vol. III
Otter, Gen. Sir William Dillon, 1843–1929, vol .III
Otter-Barry, Rt Rev. Hugh Van Lynden, 1887–1971, vol. VII
Otter-Barry, William Whitmore, 1878–1973, vol. VII
Otterson, Henry, 1846–1929, vol. III
Ottley, Rear-Adm. Sir Charles Langdale, 1858–1932, vol. III
Ottley, Rev. Edward Bickersteth, 1853–1910, vol. I
Ottley, Rev. Feilding Hay, 1877–1958, vol. V
Ottley, Rev. Henry Bickersteth, *died* 1932, vol. III
Ottley, Col Sir John Walter, 1841–1931, vol. III
Ottley, Rev. Robert Lawrence, 1856–1933, vol. III
Ottley, Warner Herbert Taylor, 1889–1980, vol. VII (AII)
Otto, Rudolf, 1869–1937, vol. III
Otway, Rt Hon. Sir Arthur John, 3rd Bt, 1822–1912, vol. I
Oudendyk, Dame Margaret, 1876–1971, vol. VII
Oudendyk, William J., 1874–1953, vol. V
Ouida, 1839–1908, vol. I
Ouimet, Hon. Joseph Alderic, 1848–1916, vol. II (A), vol. III
Ould, Hermon, 1885–1951, vol. V
Ould, Robert F.; *see* Fielding-Ould.
Ouless, Walter William, 1848–1933, vol. III
Oulsnam, Sir Harrison; *see* Oulsnam, Sir S. H. Y.
Oulsnam, Sir (Samuel) Harrison (Yardley), 1898–1972, vol. VII
Oulton, George N., *died* 1928, vol. II

Oulton, Rev. John Ernest Leonard, 1886–1957, vol. V
Oulton, William Harold Stowe, 1869–1941, vol. IV
Oury, Libert, 1868–1939, vol. III
Ouseley, Brig.-Gen. Ralph Glynn, 1866–1931, vol. III
Outcault, Richard Felton, 1863–1928, vol. II
Outen, Roland Thomas, 1900–1957, vol. V
Outerbridge, Sir Joseph, 1843–1933, vol. III
Outhwaite, Ernest, 1875–1931, vol. III
Outhwaite, R. L., 1868–1930, vol. III
Outram, Comdr Edmund, 1858–1937, vol. III
Outram, Sir Francis Boyd, 2nd Bt, 1836–1912, vol. I
Outram, Major Sir Francis Davidson, 4th Bt, 1867–1945, vol. IV
Outram, Lt-Col Harold William Sydney, *died* 1944, vol. IV
Outram, Sir James, 3rd Bt, 1864–1925, vol. II
Outtrim, Hon. Alfred Richard, 1845–1925, vol. II
Outtrim, Frank Leon, 1847–1917, vol. II
Ouvry, Ernest Carrington, 1866–1951, vol. V
Ovans, Major Hugh Lambert, 1881–1946, vol. IV
Ovenden, Very Rev. Charles T., 1846–1924, vol. II
Ovenden, Harry, 1876–1974, vol. VII
Ovens, Hon. Brig.-Gen. Gerald Hedley, 1856–1933, vol. III
Ovens, Col Robert Montgomery, 1868–1950, vol. IV
Overbury, Sir Robert Leslie, 1887–1955, vol. V
Overend, Thomas George, 1846–1915, vol. I
Overend, Walker, *died* 1926, vol. II (A), vol. III
Overman, Henry Jacob, 1862–1933, vol. III
Overstreet, Harry Allen, 1875–1970, vol. VI
Overton, Sir Arnold Edersheim, 1893–1975, vol. VII
Overton, Charles Ernest, 1865–1933, vol. III
Overton, Rev. Frederick Arnold, 1862–1935, vol. III
Overton, George Leonard, 1875–1948, vol. IV
Overton, Rev. John Henry, 1835–1903, vol. I
Overtoun, Robert, 1859–1924, vol. II
Overtoun, 1st Baron, 1843–1908, vol. I
Overy, Sir Thomas Stuart, 1893–1973, vol. VII
Ovey, Sir Esmond, 1879–1963, vol. VI
Ovey, Lt-Col Richard Lockhart, 1878–1946, vol. IV
Owen, Sir Alfred George Beech, 1908–1975, vol. VII
Owen, Col Arthur Allen, 1842–1917, vol. II
Owen, Arthur Charles H.; *see* Humphreys-Owen.
Owen, Sir (Arthur) David Kemp, 1904–1970, vol. VI
Owen, Sir (Arthur) Douglas, 1904–1977, vol. VII
Owen, Col Arthur Lewis S.; *see* Scott-Owen.
Owen, Basil Wilberforce Longmore, *died* 1943, vol. IV
Owen, Sir Cecil; *see* Owen, Sir W. C.
Owen, Brig.-Gen. Charles C.; *see* Cunliffe-Owen.
Owen, Lt-Col Charles Harold Wells, 1872–1936, vol. III
Owen, Maj.-Gen. Charles Henry, 1830–1921, vol. II

Owen, Very Rev. Charles Mansfield, 1852–1940, vol. III
Owen, Col Charles Richard Blackstone, 1870–1954, vol. V
Owen, Brig.-Gen. Charles Samuel, 1879–1959, vol. V
Owen, Lt-Col Charles William, 1853–1922, vol. II
Owen, Collinson, 1882–1956, vol. V
Owen, David Charles L.; see Lloyd Owen.
Owen, Sir David John, 1874–1941, vol. IV
Owen, Sir David Kemp; see Owen, Sir A. D. K.
Owen, Most Rev. Derwyn Trevor, 1876–1947, vol. IV
Owen, Sir Douglas, 1850–1920, vol. II
Owen, Sir Douglas; see Owen, Sir A. D.
Owen, Edmund, died 1915, vol. I
Owen, Edward Cunliffe, 1857–1918, vol. II
Owen, Rev. Edward Cunliffe, died 1937, vol. III
Owen, Edwin Augustine, 1887–1973, vol. VII
Owen, Evan Roger, died 1930, vol. III
Owen, Lt-Col F. C.; see Cunliffe-Owen.
Owen, Frank, 1905–1979, vol. VII
Owen, Rev. G., died 1914, vol. I
Owen, George Douglas, 1887–1965, vol. VI
Owen, George Elmslie, 1899–1964, vol. VI
Owen, George Sherard, 1892–1976, vol. VII
Owen, Rev. George Vale, 1869–1931, vol. III
Owen, Lt-Col Sir Goronwy, 1881–1963, vol. VI
Owen, Grace, 1873–1965, vol. VI
Owen, Gwilym, 1880–1940, vol. III (A), vol. IV
Owen, H. F.; see Owen, F.
Owen, Harold, 1872–1930, vol. III
Owen, Harrison, 1890–1966, vol. VI (AII)
Owen, Henry, died 1919, vol. II
Owen, Col Henry Mostyn, 1858–1927, vol. II
Owen, Captain Hilary Dorsett, 1894–1980, vol. VII
Owen, Sir Hugh, 1835–1916, vol. II
Owen, Sir Hugh Charles, 3rd Bt, 1826–1909, vol. I
Owen, Sir Hugo C.; see Cunliffe-Owen.
Owen, Sir Isambard, 1850–1927, vol. II
Owen, Rev. Ithel George, 1863–1941, vol. IV
Owen, Sir James George, 1869–1939, vol. III
Owen, Jean A., (Mrs Owen Visger), died 1922, vol. II
Owen, Rt Rev. John, 1854–1926, vol. II
Owen, John, died 1949, vol. IV
Owen, Sir John Arthur, 4th Bt, 1892–1973, vol. VII
Owen, Gen. Sir John Fletcher, 1839–1924, vol. II
Owen, John Glendwr, 1914–1977, vol. VII
Owen, Rev. John Smith, died 1922, vol. II
Owen, Sir Langer Meade Loftus, 1862–1935, vol. III
Owen, Leonard, 1890–1965, vol. VI
Owen, Sir Leonard; see Owen, Sir W. L.
Owen, Leonard Victor Davies, 1888–1952, vol. V
Owen, Rt Rev. Leslie, 1886–1947, vol. II
Owen, Lt-Col Lindsay Cunliffe, died 1941, vol. IV
Owen, Maj.-Gen. Llewellyn Isaac Gethin M.; see Morgan-Owen.
Owen, Lloyd, 1903–1966, vol. VI
Owen, Mary Alicia, 1858–1935, vol. III
Owen, O. Morgan, died 1930, vol. III
Owen, Owen William, 1863–1930, vol. III

Owen, Col Percy Thomas, 1864–1936, vol. III
Owen, Peter M.; see Macaulay-Owen.
Owen, Most Rev. Reginald Herbert, 1887–1961, vol. VI
Owen, Lt-Col Robert Haylock, died 1927, vol. II
Owen, Lt-Col Roger Arthur Mostyn-, 1888–1947, vol. IV
Owen, Lt-Col Roger Carmichael Robert, 1866–1941, vol. IV
Owen, Rosamond Dale; see Oliphant, Mrs Laurence.
Owen, Sackville Herbert Edward Gregg, 1880–1960, vol. V
Owen, Sidney George, 1858–1940, vol. III
Owen, Sidney James, 1827–1912, vol. I
Owen, Lt-Col Sydney Lloyd, born 1872, vol. II
Owen, Thomas, 1840–1898, vol. I
Owen, Sir Thomas David, 1854–1921, vol. II
Owen, Rev. Thomas M. Bulkeley B.; see Bulkeley-Owen.
Owen, Cdre Trevor Lewis, 1895–1980, vol. VII
Owen, Ven. Walter Edwin, 1879–1945, vol. IV
Owen, Will, 1869–1957, vol. V
Owen, Sir William, 1834–1912, vol. I
Owen, William, 1837–1918, vol. II
Owen, Sir (William) Cecil, 1872–1959, vol. V
Owen, Rt Hon. Sir William Francis Langer, 1899–1972, vol. VII
Owen, Captain William Henry, 1857–1931, vol. III
Owen, William Hugh, 1886–1957, vol. V
Owen, Sir (William) Leonard, 1897–1971, vol. VII
Owen, William Stevenson, 1834–1909, vol. I
Owen-Lewis, Lt-Col Arthur Francis, 1868–1926, vol. II
Owen-Lewis, Cyril Alexander, 1871–1905, vol. I
Owen-Smyth, Charles Edward, 1851–1925, vol. II
Owens, Captain Sir Arthur Lewis, died 1967, vol. VI
Owens, Sir Charles John, 1845–1933, vol. III
Owens, Most Rev. Richard, died 1909, vol. I
Owens, Col Robert Leonce, 1862–1937, vol. III
Owens, Tom Paterson, 1888–1968, vol. VI
Owens, Hon. William, 1840–1917, vol. II
Owles, Captain Garth Henry Fyson, 1896–1975, vol. VII
Owles, Thomas Arthur, 1890–1966, vol. VI
Owsley, John William, 1840–1929, vol. III
Owst, Gerald Robert, 1894–1962, vol. VI
Oxborrow, Brig. Claud Catton, 1898–1972, vol. VII
Oxenbridge, 1st Viscount, 1829–1898, vol. I
Oxenden, Sir Percy Dixwell Nowell Dixwell-, 10th Bt, 1838–1924, vol. II
Oxenham, Elsie Jeannette, died 1960, vol. V
Oxenham, John, died 1941, vol. IV
Oxford and Asquith, 1st Earl of, 1852–1928, vol. II
Oxford and Asquith, Countess of; (Emma Alice Margaret) (Margot), 1864–1945, vol. IV
Oxland, Air Vice-Marshal Robert Dickinson, 1889–1959, vol. V
Oxley, Sir Alfred James R.; see Rice-Oxley.
Oxley, Adm. Charles Lister, 1841–1920, vol. II
Oxley, Douglas George R.; see Rice-Oxley.
Oxley, John Stewart, 1861–1935, vol. III
Oxley, Brig.-Gen. Reginald Stewart, 1863–1951, vol. V

Oxley, Maj.-Gen. Walter Hayes, 1891–1978, vol. VII

Oyama, Iwao, Field-Marshal Prince, 1842–1916, vol. II

Oyebode, Rt Rev. David Richard, 1898–1960, vol. V

Ozanne, Sir Edward Chepmell, 1852–1929, vol. III

Ozanne, James William, died 1931, vol. III

Ozanne, John Henry, 1850–1902, vol. I

Ozanne, Maj.-Gen. William Maingay, 1891–1966, vol. VI

P

Pace, Rev. Edward George, 1881–1953, vol. V

Pace, George Gaze, 1915–1975, vol. VII

Pace, Most Rev. Pietro, 1831–1914, vol. I

Pacelli, Eugene; see Pius XII.

Pachmann, Vladimir de, 1848–1933, vol. III

Pack, Arthur Denis Henry Heber R.; see Reynell-Pack.

Pack, Captain Stanley Walter Croucher, 1904–1977, vol. VII

Pack-Beresford, Denis R., 1864–1942, vol. IV

Packard, Sir Edward, 1843–1932, vol. III

Packard, Lt-Col Henry Norrington, 1870–1916, vol. II

Packe, Sir Edward Hussey, 1878–1946, vol. IV

Packe, Lt-Col Frederick Edward, 1879–1953, vol. V

Packe, Hussey, 1846–1908, vol. I

Packer, Sir (Douglas) Frank (Hewson), 1906–1974, vol. VII

Packer, Sir Frank; see Packer, Sir D. F. H.

Packer, Col Harry Dixon, 1872–1947, vol. IV

Packer, Adm. Sir Herbert Annesley, 1894–1962, vol. VI

Packer, Joy, (Lady Packer), 1905–1977, vol. VII

Packman, Lt-Col Kenneth Chalmers, 1899–1969, vol. VI

Paddison, Sir George Frederick, died 1927, vol. II

Paddock, Rt Rev. Robert L., vol. III

Paddon, Lt John Frederick, 1856–1913, vol. I

Paddon, Lt-Col Sir Stanley Somerset Wreford, 1881–1963, vol. VI

Paddon, Rev. William Francis Locke, died 1922, vol. II

Padel, Charles Frederick Christian, 1872–1958, vol. V

Paderewski, Ignace Jean, 1860–1941, vol. IV

Padfield, Rev. William Herbert Greenland, 1875–1936, vol. III

Padley, Wilfred, 1910–1968, vol. VI

Padwick, Francis Herbert, 1856–1945, vol. IV

Padwick, Surgeon-Captain Harold Boultbee, 1889–1972, vol. VII

Padwick, Philip Hugh, 1876–1958, vol. V

Pae, David, 1864–1948, vol. IV

Pagan, Brig.-Gen. Alexander William, 1878–1949, vol. IV

Pagan, Very Rev. John, 1830–1909, vol. I

Pagden, Arthur Sampson, 1858–1942, vol. IV

Page, Sir Archibald, 1875–1949, vol. IV

Page, Very Rev. Arnold Henry, 1851–1943, vol. IV

Page, Sir Arthur, 1876–1958, vol. V

Page, Sir (Charles) Max, 1882–1963, vol. VI

Page, Lt-Col Cuthbert Frederick Graham, 1880–1919, vol. II

Page, Sir Denys Lionel, 1908–1978, vol. VII

Page, Rt Hon. Sir Earle Christmas Grafton, 1880–1961, vol. VI

Page, Edward, 1877–1937, vol. III

Page, Ernest, 1848–1930, vol. III

Page, Lt-Col F., died 1917, vol. II

Page, Frederick, died 1919, vol. II

Page, Sir Frederick Handley, 1885–1962, vol. VI

Page, Lt-Gen. George H.; see Hyde-Page.

Page, Gertrude, (Mrs Dobbin), died 1922, vol. II

Page, Major Harold Hillis, 1888–1942, vol. IV

Page, Harold James, 1890–1972, vol. VII

Page, Harry Marmaduke, 1860–1942, vol. IV

Page, Herbert William, 1845–1926, vol. II

Page, Hon. James, 1860–1921, vol. II

Page, John Lloyd Warden, 1858–1916, vol. II

Page, Sir Leo Francis, 1890–1951, vol. V

Page, Maj.-Gen. Lionel Frank, 1884–1944, vol. IV

Page, Sir Max; see Page, Sir C. M.

Page, Robert Palgrave, 1867–1947, vol. IV

Page, Sidney John, 1892–1973, vol. VII

Page, Lt-Col Stanley Hatch, 1874–1962, vol. VI

Page, Thomas Ethelbert, 1850–1936, vol. III

Page, Thomas Nelson, 1853–1922, vol. II

Page, Sir Thomas Spurgeon, 1879–1958, vol. V

Page, Thomas Walker, 1866–1937, vol. III

Page, Walter Hines, 1855–1918, vol. II

Page, William, 1861–1934, vol. III

Page, William Frank, 1894–1980, vol. VII

Page, William Morton, 1883–1950, vol. IV

Page, William Walter Keightley, 1878–1962, vol. VI

Page-Henderson, Lt-Col Henry Cockcroft, 1856–1942, vol. IV

Page-Jones, Frederick Herbert, 1903–1972, vol. VII

Page-Roberts, Very Rev. William; see Roberts.

Page Wood, Sir David John Hatherley, 7th Bt, 1921–1955, vol. V

Pagenstecher, Hermann, 1844–1932, vol. III

Paget, Lt-Col Albert Edward Sydney Louis, 1879–1917, vol. II

Paget, Adm. Sir Alfred Wyndham, 1852–1918, vol. II

Paget, Gen. Rt Hon. Sir Arthur Henry Fitzroy, 1851–1928, vol. II

Paget, Gen. Sir Bernard Charles Tolver, 1887–1961, vol. VI

Paget, Lt-Col Sir Cecil Walter, 2nd Bt (cr 1897), 1874–1936, vol. III

Paget, Major Eden Wilberforce, 1865–1955, vol. V

Paget, Very Rev. Edward Clarence, 1851–1927, vol. II

Paget, Most Rev. Edward Francis, 1886–1971, vol. VII

Paget, Sir Ernest; see Paget, Sir G. E.

Paget, Rt Rev. Francis, 1851–1911, vol. I

Paget, Sir (George) Ernest, 1st Bt (cr 1897), 1841–1923, vol. II

Paget, Major George Thomas Cavendish, 1853–1939, vol. III
Paget, Col Harold, 1849–1933, vol. III
Paget, Lt-Comdr Henry Edward Clarence, 1860–1940, vol. III
Paget, Rt Rev. Henry Luke, 1853–1937, vol. III
Paget, Henry Marriott, 1856–1936, vol. III
Paget, Captain J. Otho, 1860–1934, vol. III
Paget, Sir James, 1st Bt (cr 1871), 1814–1899, vol. I
Paget, Captain Sir James Francis, 3rd Bt (cr 1871), 1890–1972, vol. VII
Paget, John, 1811–1898, vol. I
Paget, Sir John Rahere, 2nd Bt (cr 1871), 1848–1938, vol. III
Paget, Dame Leila; see Paget, Dame L. M. L. W.
Paget, Dame (Louise Margaret) Leila (Wemyss), died 1958, vol. V
Paget, Mary, (Lady Paget), died 1919, vol. II
Paget, Rt Hon. Sir Ralph Spencer, 1864–1940, vol. III
Paget, Sir Richard Arthur Surtees, 2nd Bt (cr 1886), 1869–1955, vol. V
Paget, Rt Hon. Sir Richard Horner, 1st Bt (cr 1886), 1832–1908, vol. I
Paget, Dame Rosalind, 1855–1948, vol. IV
Paget, Sidney Edward, 1860–1908, vol. I
Paget, Stephen, 1855–1926, vol. II
Paget, Major Thomas Guy Frederick, 1886–1952, vol. V
Paget, Lord Victor William, 1889–1952, vol. V
Paget, Violet, 1856–1935, vol. III
Paget, Walburga, (Lady Paget), 1839–1929, vol. III
Paget, Brig.-Gen. Wellesley L. H., 1858–1918, vol. II
Paget, William Edmund, 1879–1928, vol. II
Paget-Cooke, Sir Henry, 1861–1923, vol. II
Paget-Cooke, Oliver Dayrell Paget, 1891–1954, vol. V
Pagnol, Marcel, 1895–1974, vol. VII
Paice, Rev. Arthur, 1857–1923, vol. II
Paige, Lt-Col Cyril Penrose, 1882–1958, vol. V
Paige, Col Douglas, 1886–1958, vol. V
Pain, Arthur Bernard, 1904–1973, vol. VII
Pain, Rt Rev. Arthur Wellesley, 1841–1920, vol. II
Pain, Barry, died 1928, vol. II
Pain, Sir Charles John, 1873–1961, vol. VI
Pain, Brig.-Gen. Sir William Hacket, 1855–1924, vol. II
Paine, Lt-Col Albert Ingraham, 1874–1949, vol. IV
Paine, Brig. Douglas Duke, 1892–1960, vol. V (A)
Paine, Rear-Adm. Sir Godfrey Marshall, 1871–1932, vol. III
Paine, Sir (Herbert) Kingsley, 1883–1972, vol. VII
Paine, Hubert S.; see Scott-Paine.
Paine, Major James Henry, 1870–1918, vol. II
Paine, Brig.-Gen. John Jackson, 1864–1936, vol. III
Paine, Sir Kingsley; see Paine, Sir H. K.
Paine, Sir Thomas, 1822–1908, vol. I
Paine, William Worship, 1861–1946, vol. IV
Paine, Wyatt W.; see Wyatt-Paine.
Painleve, Paul, 1863–1933, vol. III
Painter, Brig.-Gen. Arnaud Clarke, 1863–1945, vol. IV
Painter, Sir Frederic George, 1844–1926, vol. II

Painter, Brig. Gordon Whistler Arnaud, 1893–1960, vol. V
Painter, Robert John, 1927–1972, vol. VII
Paish, Sir George, 1867–1957, vol. V
Pakeman, Sir John, 1860–1946, vol. IV
Pakeman, Robert J., died 1906, vol. I
Pakenham, Hon. Sir Francis John, 1832–1905, vol. I
Pakenham, Col George de la Poer Beresford, 1875–1960, vol. V
Pakenham, Col Hercules Arthur, died 1937, vol. III
Pakenham, Lt-Gen. Thomas Henry, 1826–1913, vol. I
Pakenham, Adm. Sir William Christopher, 1861–1933, vol. III
Pakenham-Mahon, Captain Henry, 1851–1922, vol. II
Pakenham-Walsh, Ernst, 1875–1964, vol. VI
Pakenham-Walsh, Rt Rev. Herbert Pakenham, 1871–1959, vol. V (A)
Pakenham-Walsh, Maj.-Gen. Ridley P., 1888–1966, vol. VI
Palacio Valdés, Armando, 1853–1938, vol. III
Paladini, Carlo, 1864–1922, vol. II (A), vol. III
Palairet, Lionel Charles Hamilton, 1870–1933, vol. III
Palairet, Sir Michael, 1882–1956, vol. V
Palanpur, Nawab of, 1852–1918, vol. II
Palanpur, Nawab of, 1883–1957, vol. V
Paléologue, Maurice, 1859–1944, vol. IV
Paley, Col Alan Thomas, 1876–1950, vol. IV
Paley, Maj.-Gen. Sir (Alexander George) Victor, 1903–1976, vol. VII
Paley, Frederick John, 1859–1924, vol. II
Paley, Maj.-Gen. Sir Victor; see Paley, Maj.-Gen. Sir A. G. V.
Palfrey, William John Henry, 1906–1979, vol. VII
Palgrave, Francis Turner, 1824–1897, vol. I
Palgrave, Sir Reginald Francis Douce, 1829–1904, vol. I
Palgrave, Sir Robert Harry Inglis, 1827–1919, vol. II
Palin, Col Gilbert Walter, 1862–1946, vol. IV
Palin, John Henry, vol. III
Palin, Maj.-Gen. Sir Philip Charles, 1864–1937, vol. III
Palin, Lt-Col Randle Harry, 1873–1950, vol. IV
Palin, Ven William, 1893–1967, vol. VI
Palin, William Mainwaring, 1862–1947, vol. IV
Paling, Gerald Richard, 1895–1966, vol. VI
Paling, Rt Hon. Wilfred, 1883–1971, vol. VII
Palit, Sir Tarak Nath, died 1914, vol. I
Palitana, Thakur Saheb Sir, Mansinghji Sursinghji, 1863–1905, vol. I
Palk, Major Hon. Lawrence Charles Walter, 1870–1916, vol. II
Palles, Rt Hon. Christopher, 1831–1920, vol. II
Pallin, Lt-Col Samuel Farrer Godfrey, 1878–1930, vol. III
Pallin, Col William Alfred, 1873–1956, vol. V
Pallis, Alex., 1851–1935, vol. III
Palliser, Adm. Sir Arthur Francis Eric, died 1956, vol. V

Palliser, Charles Frederick Wray Bury, 1854–1934, vol. III
Palliser, Adm. Henry St Leger Bury, 1839–1907, vol. I
Palliser, Herbert William, 1883–1963, vol. VI
Pallot, Rev. Elias George, 1876–1954, vol. V
Palmella, 5th Duke of, 1897–1969, vol. VI
Palmer, 1st Baron, 1858–1948, vol. IV
Palmer, 2nd Baron, 1882–1950, vol. IV
Palmer, Col Albert John, died 1940, vol. III
Palmer, Alexander Croydon, 1887–1963, vol. VI
Palmer, Captain Alexander Edward Guy, 1886–1926, vol. II
Palmer, Alexander Mitchell, 1872–1936, vol. III
Palmer, Col Aleyn Zouch, 1882–1934, vol. III
Palmer, Alfred, 1852–1936, vol. III
Palmer, Sir Alfred Molyneux, 3rd Bt (cr 1886), 1853–1935, vol. III
Palmer, Sir Anthony Frederick Mark, 4th Bt (cr 1886), 1914–1941, vol. IV
Palmer, Sir Archdale Robert, 4th Bt (cr 1791), 1838–1905, vol. I
Palmer, Arthur, 1841–1897, vol. I
Palmer, Sir Arthur Hunter, 1819–1898, vol. I
Palmer, Captain Arthur Percy, 1872–1915, vol. I
Palmer, Gen. Sir Arthur Power, 1840–1904, vol. I
Palmer, Charles, 1869–1920, vol. II
Palmer, Sir (Charles) Eric, died 1948, vol. IV
Palmer, Charles Felix, died 1919, vol. II
Palmer, Charles George, 1847–1940, vol. III
Palmer, Col Charles Henry Dayrell, 1872–1939, vol. III
Palmer, Ven. Charles Jasper, 1863–1931, vol. III
Palmer, Sir Charles Mark, 1st Bt (cr 1886), 1822–1907, vol. I
Palmer, Rev. Charles Samuel, 1830–1921, vol. II
Palmer, Lt-Col Claude Bowes, 1868–1949, vol. IV
Palmer, Clement Charlton, 1871–1944, vol. IV
Palmer, Brig.-Gen. Cyril Eustace, 1870–1939, vol. III
Palmer, Sir Edward Geoffrey Broadley, 10th Bt (cr 1660), 1864–1925, vol. II
Palmer, Edward Timothy, 1878–1947, vol. IV
Palmer, Rt Rev. Edwin James, 1869–1954, vol. V
Palmer, Sir Elwin Mitford, 1852–1906, vol. I
Palmer, Sir Eric; see Palmer, Sir C. E.
Palmer, Eustace Exall, 1878–1931, vol. III
Palmer, Sir Francis Beaufort, 1845–1917, vol. II
Palmer, Francis Noel, died 1961, vol. VI
Palmer, Sir Frederick, 1862–1934, vol. III
Palmer, Frederick, 1873–1958, vol. V
Palmer, Sir Frederick Archdale, 6th Bt (cr 1791), 1857–1933, vol. III
Palmer, Frederick Bernard, 1862–1947, vol. IV
Palmer, Lt-Col Frederick Carey Stuckley S.; see Samborne-Palmer.
Palmer, Frederick Stephen, died 1926, vol. II
Palmer, Frederick William, 1891–1955, vol. V
Palmer, Lt-Col Sir Geoffrey Frederick Neill, 11th Bt (cr 1660), 1893–1951, vol. V
Palmer, Maj.-Gen. Geoffrey Woodroffe, 1891–1952, vol. V
Palmer, Rear-Adm. George, 1829–1917, vol. II

Palmer, Maj.-Gen. George Erroll P.; see Prior-Palmer.
Palmer, George Henry, 1871–1945, vol. IV
Palmer, Rev. George Herbert, 1846–1926, vol. II
Palmer, Sir George Hudson, 5th Bt (cr 1791), 1841–1919, vol. II
Palmer, Brig.-Gen. George Llewellen, 1856–1932, vol. III
Palmer, Sir George Robson, 2nd Bt (cr 1886), 1849–1910, vol. I
Palmer, Rev. George Thomas, died 1908, vol. I
Palmer, Rt Hon. George William, 1851–1913, vol. I
Palmer, Godfrey Mark, 1878–1933, vol. III
Palmer, Brig.-Gen. Harold Bland Herbert O.; see Orpen-Palmer.
Palmer, Rev. Henry, 1835–1931, vol. III
Palmer, Henry Alleyn, 1893–1965, vol. VI
Palmer, Col Henry Ingham Evered, 1862–1943, vol. IV
Palmer, Henry John, 1853–1903, vol. I
Palmer, Rev. Henry John, 1861–1936, vol. III
Palmer, Herbert Edward, 1880–1961, vol. VI
Palmer, Sir (Herbert) Richmond, 1877–1958, vol. V
Palmer, Horace Stanley, 1904–1968, vol. VI
Palmer, James L., died 1961, vol. VI
Palmer, James Lynwood, died 1941, vol. IV
Palmer, Rev. James Nelson, died 1908, vol. I
Palmer, Sir John Archdale, 7th Bt (cr 1791), 1894–1963, vol. VI
Palmer, John Leslie, 1885–1944, vol. IV
Palmer, Rev. Joseph Blades, 1849–1930, vol. III
Palmer, Ven. Joseph John Beauchamp, 1866–1942, vol. IV
Palmer, Hon. Lewis; see Palmer, Hon. W. J. L.
Palmer, Rev. Sir Lewis Henry, 9th Bt (cr 1660), 1818–1909, vol. I
Palmer, Adm. Norman Craig, 1866–1926, vol. II
Palmer, Maj.-Gen. Peter Garwood, 1914–1979, vol. VII
Palmer, Philip, 1867–1940, vol. III
Palmer, Mrs Potter, (Bertha Honoré), died 1918, vol. II
Palmer, Ralph Charlton, 1839–1923, vol. II
Palmer, Col Reginald Arthur Herbert O.; see Orpen-Palmer.
Palmer, Reginald Howard Reed, 1898–1970, vol. VI
Palmer, Sir Richmond; see Palmer, Sir H. R.
Palmer, Maj.-Gen. Robert John, 1891–1957, vol. V
Palmer, Lt-Col Roderick George F.; see Fenwick-Palmer.
Palmer, Sir Roger William Henry, 5th Bt (cr 1777), 1832–1910, vol. I
Palmer, Sutton, 1854–1933, vol. III
Palmer, Sir Sydney Bacon, 1890–1954, vol. V
Palmer, W. Howard, 1865–1923, vol. II
Palmer, Sir Walter, 1st Bt (cr 1904), 1858–1910, vol. I
Palmer, Sir William, 1883–1964, vol. VI
Palmer, Hon. (William Jocelyn) Lewis, 1894–1971, vol. VII
Palmer, Lt-Col William Legh, 1868–1955, vol. V
Palmer, Col William Llewellen, 1883–1954, vol. V

Palmes, Rev. George, 1851–1927, vol. II
Palmes, Col Philip, 1856–1914, vol. I
Palmgren, Selim, 1878–1951, vol. V
Palmour, Sir Charles John Geoffrey, 1877–1948, vol. IV
Palmstierna, Baron Erik Kule, 1877–1959, vol. V
Paltridge, Sir Shane Dunne, 1910–1966, vol. VI
Pam, Major Albert, 1875–1955, vol. V
Pamphlett, Engr Rear-Adm. William Frederic, died 1940, vol. III
Panagal, Rajah of, 1866–1928, vol. II
Panapa, Rt Rev. Wiremu Netana, 1898–1970, vol. VI
Panckridge, Sir Hugh Rahere, 1885–1942, vol. IV
Pandya, Jagannath Bhavanishanker, 1891–1942, vol. IV
Panet, Brig.-Gen. Alphonse Eugene, 1867–1950, vol. IV
Panet, Maj.-Gen. Henri Alexandre, 1869–1951, vol. V
Paneth, Friedrich Adolf, 1887–1958, vol. V
Panikkar, Kavalam Madhava, 1895–1963, vol. VI
Pank, Col Cecil Henry, 1876–1957, vol. V
Pank, Sir John Lovell, 1846–1922, vol. II
Pankhurst, Albert Stanley, 1897–1975, vol. VII
Pankhurst, Dame Christabel, 1880–1958, vol. V
Pankhurst, Emmeline, 1857–1928, vol. II
Pankhurst, (Estelle) Sylvia, 1882–1960, vol. V
Pankhurst, Sylvia; see Pankhurst, E. S.
Panna Lall, 1883–1967, vol. VI (AII)
Pannall, Major J. Charles, 1879–1960, vol. V
Pannell, Baron (Life Peer); Thomas Charles Pannell, 1902–1980, vol. VII
Pannell, Norman Alfred, 1901–1976, vol. VII
Pannett, Charles Aubrey, 1884–1969, vol. VI
Pannirselvam, Sir Arogyaswami Thamaraiselvam, Avargal, died 1940, vol. III
Panofsky, Erwin, 1892–1968, vol. VI
Panter, Air Vice-Marshal Arthur Edward, 1889–1969, vol. VI
Pantin, Carl Frederick Abel, 1899–1967, vol. VI
Pantin, William Abel, 1902–1973, vol. VII
Panton, Alexander Hugh, 1877–1951, vol. V
Panton, Edward Brooks Henderson, 1873–1929, vol. III
Panton, Mrs J. E., 1848–1923, vol. II
Panton, Col John Gerald, 1861–1915, vol. I (A)
Panton, Sir Philip Noel, died 1950, vol. IV
Panzera, Lt-Col Francis William, 1851–1917, vol. II
Papalexopoulo, Rear-Adm. Dimitri, died 1959, vol. V
Pape, Archibald Gabriel, 1876–1927, vol. II
Papillon, Lt-Col Pelham Rawstorn, 1864–1940, vol. III
Papillon, Rev. Thomas Leslie, 1841–1926, vol. II
Papini, Giovanni, 1881–1956, vol. V
Papprill, Rev. Frederick, 1859–1924, vol. II
Papworth, Rev. Sir Harold Charles, 1888–1967, vol. VI
Paradis, Hon. Philippe, 1868–1933, vol. III
Paramore, Richard Horace, 1876–1965, vol. VI
Paranjpye, Sir Raghunath Purushottam, 1876–1966, vol. VI

Parc-Locmaria, Marquis du, Alain, 1892–1973, vol. VII
Pardo-Bazan, Countess Emilia, 1852–1921, vol. II
Pardoe, Col Frank Lionel, 1880–1948, vol. IV
Pardoe, John George, 1871–1965, vol. VI
Pardoe-Thomas, Bertie, 1866–1937, vol. III
Pare, Rev. Canon Clive Frederick, 1908–1973, vol. VII
Parekh, Sir Gokuldas Kahandas, 1847–1925, vol. II
Parent, Hon. George, 1879–1942, vol. IV
Parent, Hon. Simon Napoleon, 1855–1920, vol. II
Pareparambil, Rt Rev. Aloysius, 1847–1919, vol. II
Parera, Grace Moore, died 1947, vol. IV
Pares, Surg. Lt-Col Basil, 1869–1943, vol. IV
Pares, Sir Bernard, 1867–1949, vol. IV
Pares, Rev. Canon Norman, 1857–1936, vol. III
Pares, Richard, 1902–1958, vol. V
Paret, Bishop William, 1826–1911, vol. I
Parfit, Rev. Joseph Thomas, 1870–1953, vol. V
Parfitt, James John, 1857–1926, vol. II
Pargiter, Frederick Eden, 1852–1927, vol. II
Parham, Rt Rev. Arthur Groom, 1883–1961, vol. VI
Parham, Hedley John, 1892–1978, vol. VII
Parham, Maj.-Gen. Hetman Jack, 1895–1974, vol. VII
Paris, Maj.-Gen. Sir Archibald, 1861–1937, vol. III
Paris, Gaston Bruno Paulin, 1839–1903, vol. I
Pariser, Sir Maurice Philip, 1906–1968, vol. VI
Pariset, Georges, 1865–1927, vol. II
Parish, Arthur John, 1861–1942, vol. IV
Parish, Frank, 1824–1906, vol. I
Parish, Rev. John William, 1857–1937, vol. III
Parish, Ven. William Okes, 1859–1940, vol. III
Parish, Lt-Col Woodbine, 1862–1938, vol. III
Park, Alexander Dallas, 1882–1971, vol. VII
Park, Sir Archibald Richard, 1888–1959, vol. V
Park, Carton M.; see Moore-Park.
Park, Maj.-Gen. Cecil William, 1856–1913, vol. I
Park, James, 1857–1946, vol. IV
Park, Col James Smith, 1854–1921, vol. II
Park, John, died 1913, vol. I
Park, Air Chief Marshal Sir Keith Rodney, 1892–1975, vol. VII
Park, Sir Maitland Hall, 1862–1921, vol. II
Park, Rev. Philip Lees, 1860–1925, vol. II
Park, Rev. William, 1844–1925, vol. II
Park, William H., 1863–1939, vol. III
Park, Rev. William Robert, 1880–1961, vol. VI
Park, Col William Urquhart, 1846–1917, vol. II
Parke, Ernest, 1860–1944, vol. IV
Parke, Lt-Col Roger Kennedy, 1848–1911, vol. I
Parke, Sir William, 1822–1897, vol. I
Parker of Waddington, Baron (Life Peer); Robert John Parker, 1857–1918, vol. II
Parker of Waddington, Baron (Life Peer); Hubert Lister Parker, 1900–1972, vol. VII
Parker, Albert, 1892–1980, vol. VII
Parker, Hon. Alexander Edward, 1864–1958, vol. V
Parker, Lt-Col Alfred Chevallier, 1874–1935, vol. III
Parker, Sir Alfred Livingston, 1875–1935, vol. III

Parker, Rear-Adm. (S) Alfred Ramsay, *died* 1951, vol. V

Parker, Alwyn, 1877–1951, vol. V

Parker, Dom Anselm Edward Stanislaus, 1880–1962, vol. VI

Parker, Brig.-Gen. Arthur, 1867–1941, vol. IV

Parker, Bertie Patterson, 1871–1930, vol. III

Parker, Cecil, 1897–1971, vol. VII

Parker, Hon. Cecil Thomas, 1845–1931, vol. III

Parker, Charles Arthur, 1863–1938, vol. III

Parker, Charles Sandbach, 1864–1920, vol. II

Parker, Rt Hon. Charles Stuart, 1829–1910, vol. I

Parker, Charles Thomas, 1859–1944, vol. IV

Parker, Christopher John, 1859–1932, vol. III

Parker, Rt Rev. Clement George St Michael, 1900–1980, vol. VII

Parker, Rt Hon. Dame Dehra, *died* 1963, vol. VI

Parker, Dorothy, (Mrs Alan Campbell), 1893–1967, vol. VI

Parker, Adm. Edmond Hyde, 1868–1951, vol. V

Parker, Hon. Edmund William, 1857–1943, vol. IV

Parker, Edward Harper, 1849–1926, vol. II

Parker, Rt Rev. Edward Melville, 1855–1925, vol. II (A), vol. III

Parker, Eric, 1870–1955, vol. V

Parker, Rev. Ernest Julius, 1872–1942, vol. IV

Parker, Hon. Francis, 1851–1931, vol. III

Parker, Captain Francis Maitland Wyborn, 1876–1915, vol. I

Parker, Col Frederic James, 1861–1944, vol. IV

Parker, Geoffrey Edward, 1902–1973, vol. VII

Parker, Adm. George, 1827–1904, vol. I

Parker, George, 1853–1937, vol. III

Parker, Sir George Arthur, 1843–1900, vol. I

Parker, George Howard, 1864–1955, vol. V

Parker, Sir George Phillips, 1863–1943, vol. IV

Parker, Rt Hon. Sir Gilbert, 1st Bt (*cr* 1915), 1862–1932, vol. III

Parker, Gordon; *see* Parker, H. G.

Parker, Hampton Wildman, 1897–1968, vol. VI

Parker, Col Harold, 1881–1939, vol. III

Parker, Harold, 1873–1962, vol. VI

Parker, Sir Harold, 1895–1980, vol. VII

Parker, Harper, 1864–1929, vol. III

Parker, Sir Henry, 1846–1927, vol. II

Parker, (Henry) Gordon, 1892–1980, vol. VII

Parker, Henry Michael Denne, 1894–1971, vol. VII

Parker, Col Henry William Manwaring, *died* 1948, vol. IV

Parker, Adm. Henry Wise, 1875–1940, vol. III

Parker, Horatio William, 1863–1919, vol. II

Parker, Lt-Col Hon. Hubert Stanley Wyborn, 1883–1966, vol. VI

Parker, James, 1863–1948, vol. IV

Parker, James Gordon, 1869–1948, vol. IV

Parker, John, 1875–1952, vol. V

Parker, Hon. John Holford, 1886–1955, vol. V

Parker, Lt-Col John Oxley, 1886–1979, vol. VII

Parker, Col John William Robinson, 1857–1938, vol. III

Parker, John Williams, 1885–1961, vol. VI

Parker, Rev. Joseph, 1830–1902, vol. I

Parker, Joseph, 1831–1924, vol. II

Parker, Louis N., 1852–1944, vol. IV

Parker, Matthew Archibald, 1871–1953, vol. V

Parker, Sir Melville, 6th Bt (*cr* 1797), 1824–1903, vol. I

Parker, Rt Rev. Michael; *see* Parker, Rt Rev. C. G. St M.

Parker, Maj.-Gen. Neville Fraser, 1841–1916, vol. II

Parker, Owen, 1860–1936, vol. III

Parker, Vice-Adm. Patrick Edward, 1881–1941, vol. IV

Parker, Percy Livingstone, 1867–1925, vol. II

Parker, Hon. Reginald, 1854–1942, vol. IV

Parker, Captain Reginald Francis, 1871–1946, vol. IV

Parker, Richard Barry, *died* 1947, vol. IV

Parker, Col Richard Cecil Oxley, 1894–1959, vol. V

Parker, Robert, 1847–1937, vol. III

Parker, Brig.-Gen. Robert Gabbett, 1875–1927, vol. II

Parker, Robert Lewis, 1862–1948, vol. IV

Parker, Roger Henry, 1889–1973, vol. VII

Parker, Rushton, 1847–1932, vol. III

Parker, Brig.-Gen. St John William Topp, *died* 1943, vol. IV

Parker, Rt Rev. T. Leo, 1887–1975, vol. VII

Parker, Captain Walter Henry, 1869–1935, vol. III

Parker, Brig.-Gen. Walter Mansel, 1875–1962, vol. VI

Parker, Wilfred Henry, 1888–1938, vol. III

Parker, Rt Rev. Wilfrid, 1883–1966, vol. VI

Parker, Rev. Canon William, 1871–1952, vol. V

Parker, Sir William Biddulph, 2nd Bt (*cr* 1844), 1824–1902, vol. I

Parker, William Frye, *born* 1855, vol. II

Parker, Rev. William Hasell, *died* 1935, vol. III

Parker, Rev. Sir William Hyde, 10th Bt (*cr* 1681), 1863–1931, vol. III

Parker, Sir William Lorenzo, 3rd Bt (*cr* 1844), 1889–1971, vol. VII

Parker, William Newton, *died* 1923, vol. II

Parker, Engr-Captain William Ramsey, 1862–1943, vol. IV

Parker, Sir William Stephen Hyde, 11th Bt (*cr* 1681), 1892–1951, vol. V

Parker-Jervis, Lt-Col William Swynfen Whitehall, 1879–1936, vol. III

Parkes, Edward, 1890–1953, vol. V

Parkes, Sir Edward E., 1848–1919, vol. II

Parkes, Ernest William, 1873–1941, vol. IV

Parkes, Sir Fred, 1881–1962, vol. VI

Parkes, Major Harry Reeves, 1873–1949, vol. IV (A), vol. V

Parkes, Kineton, 1865–1938, vol. III

Parkes, Louis C., *died* 1942, vol. IV

Parkes, Oscar, 1885–1958, vol. V

Parkes, Sir Roderick Wallis, 1909–1972, vol. VII

Parkes, Sir Sydney, 1879–1961, vol. VI

Parkes, Col William Henry, 1864–1933, vol. III

Parkhill, Hon. Sir Archdale; *see* Parkhill, Hon. Sir R. A.

Parkhill, Hon. Sir (Robert) Archdale, 1879–1947, vol. IV

Parkin, Benjamin Theaker, 1906–1969, vol. VI

Parkin, Rev. George, 1846–1933, vol. III
Parkin, Sir George Robert, 1846–1922, vol. II
Parkin, Lt-Col Henry, 1858–1937, vol. III
Parkin, Sir Ian Stanley Colston, 1896–1971, vol. VII
Parkington, Sir John Roper, 1845–1924, vol. II
Parkington, Thomas Robert, 1866–1942, vol. IV
Parkinson, Sir (Albert) Lindsay, 1870–1936, vol. III
Parkinson, Sir (Arthur Charles) Cosmo, 1884–1967, vol. VI
Parkinson, Rev. Charles Meredith Octavius, 1852–1936, vol. III
Parkinson, Sir Cosmo; see Parkinson, Sir A. C. C.
Parkinson, Frank, 1887–1946, vol. IV
Parkinson, Brig. George Singleton, 1880–1953, vol. V
Parkinson, Maj.-Gen. Graham Beresford, 1896–1979, vol. VII
Parkinson, Hargreaves, 1896–1950, vol. IV
Parkinson, Sir Harold, 1894–1974, vol. VII
Parkinson, Rt Rev. Mgr Henry, 1852–1924, vol. II
Parkinson, John, 1872–1947, vol. IV
Parkinson, Sir John, 1885–1976, vol. VII
Parkinson, John Allen, 1870–1941, vol. IV
Parkinson, John Porter, 1863–1930, vol. III
Parkinson, John Wilson Henry, 1877–1923, vol. II
Parkinson, Joseph Ernest, 1883–1962, vol. VI
Parkinson, Sir Lindsay; see Parkinson, Sir A. L.
Parkinson, Dame Nancy, died 1974, vol. VII
Parkinson, Sir Thomas Wright, 1863–1935, vol. III
Parkinson, Wilfrid, 1887–1965, vol. VI
Parkinson, William Edward, 1871–1927, vol. II
Parks, Mrs Elizabeth; see Robins, E.
Parks, Sir John, 1844–1919, vol. II
Parks, Rev. Leighton, 1852–1938, vol. III
Parks, William Arthur, 1868–1936, vol. III
Parkyn, Very Rev. Nathaniel Lindon, died 1931, vol. III
Parkyn, William Samuel, 1875–1949, vol. IV
Parkyns, Sir Thomas Mansfield Forbes, 7th Bt, 1853–1926, vol. II
Parlby, Joshua, 1889–1975, vol. VII
Parlett, Sir Harold George, 1869–1945, vol. IV
Parlett, Harry Edgar, died 1931, vol. III
Parmar, Rt Rev. Philip, 1909–1970, vol. VI
Parmelee, James Grannis, 1875–1953, vol. V
Parmelee, William Grannis, 1833–1921, vol. II
Parminter, Brig. Reginald Horace Roger, 1893–1967, vol. VI
Parmoor, 1st Baron, 1852–1941, vol. IV
Parmoor, 2nd Baron, 1882–1977, vol. VII
Parmoor, 3rd Baron, 1885–1977, vol. VII
Parnall, Robert Boyd Cochrane, 1912–1976, vol. VII
Parnall, Engr-Rear-Adm. Walter Rudolph, died 1954, vol. V
Parnell, Col Hon. Arthur, 1841–1914, vol. I
Parnell, Ven. Arthur Henry, died 1935, vol. III
Parnell, John Howard, 1843–1923, vol. II
Parnell, Lt-Gen. John William, 1860–1931, vol. III
Parnell, Valentine Charles, 1894–1972, vol. VII
Parnwell, Sidney Arthur, 1880–1944, vol. IV
Parodi, Ernest Victor, 1870–1944, vol. IV
Parr, Adm. Alfred Arthur Chase, 1849–1914, vol. I

Parr, Cecil Francis, 1847–1928, vol. II
Parr, Cecil William Chase, died 1943, vol. IV
Parr, Hon. Sir (Christopher) James, 1869–1941, vol. IV
Parr, Col Clements, 1865–1935, vol. III
Parr, George Herbert Edmeston, 1890–1969, vol. VI
Parr, Maj.-Gen. Sir Harington Owen, died 1928, vol. II
Parr, Maj.-Gen. Sir Henry Hallam, 1847–1914, vol. I
Parr, Hon. Sir James; see Parr, Hon. Sir C. J.
Parr, Rev. John, died 1935, vol. III
Parr, Joseph Charlton, 1837–1920, vol. II
Parr, Louisa, died 1903, vol. I
Parr, Olive Katharine, (Beatrice Chase), 1874–1955, vol. V
Parr, Raymond Cecil, 1884–1965, vol. VI
Parr, Sir Robert, 1894–1979, vol. VII
Parr, Sir Robert John, 1862–1931, vol. III
Parr, Roger Charlton, 1874–1958, vol. V
Parr, Thomas Henning, 1864–1937, vol. III
Parratt, Sir Walter, 1841–1924, vol. II
Parrish, Anne, (Mrs Josiah Titzell), died 1957, vol. V
Parrish, Maxfield, 1870–1966, vol. VI
Parrock, Richard Arthur, 1869–1938, vol. III
Parrott, Sir Edward; see Parrott, Sir J. E.
Parrott, Sir (James) Edward, 1863–1921, vol. II
Parrott, William, 1843–1905, vol. I
Parry, Very Rev. Albert William, died 1950, vol. IV
Parry, Rear-Adm. Cecil Ramsden Langworthy, 1901–1977, vol. VII
Parry, Charles de Courcy, 1869–1948, vol. IV
Parry, Claude Frederick, 1896–1980, vol. VII
Parry, Captain Cuthbert Morris, 1907–1980, vol. VII
Parry, Sir David Hughes, 1893–1973, vol. VII
Parry, Adm. Sir Edward; see Parry, Adm. Sir W. E.
Parry, Sir Edward Abbott, 1863–1943, vol. IV
Parry, Most Rev. Edward Archibald, died 1943, vol. IV
Parry, Major Ernest G.; see Gambier-Parry.
Parry, Sir (Frederick) Sydney, 1861–1941, vol. IV
Parry, Lt-Col Henry Jules, 1867–1944, vol. IV
Parry, Hon. Sir Henry W.; see Wynn Parry.
Parry, Engr Rear-Adm. Herbert Lyell, 1875–1963, vol. VI
Parry, Ven. Herbert Thomas, 1869–1940, vol. III
Parry, Sir Hubert Hastings, 1st Bt, 1848–1918, vol. II
Parry, Adm. Sir John Franklin, 1863–1926, vol. II
Parry, Rear-Adm. John Parry J.; see Jones-Parry.
Parry, Joseph, 1841–1903, vol. I
Parry, Rev. Kenneth Loyd, 1884–1962, vol. VI
Parry, Lt-Col Llewelyn England Sidney, 1856–1929, vol. III
Parry, Maj.-Gen. Michael Denman G.; see Gambier-Parry.
Parry, Rt Rev. Oswald Hutton, 1868–1936, vol. III
Parry, Rev. Reginald St John, 1858–1935, vol. III
Parry, Vice-Adm. Reginald St Pierre, 1879–1939, vol. III

Parry, Air Vice-Marshal Rey Griffith, 1889–1969, vol. VI

Parry, Brig. Sir Richard G.; *see* Gambier-Parry.

Parry, Sir Sydney; *see* Parry, Sir F. S.

Parry, Lt-Col Thomas Henry, 1881–1939, vol. III

Parry, Thomas Robert G.; *see* Gambier-Parry.

Parry, Col William, 1867–1935, vol. III

Parry, Hon. William Edward, 1878–1952, vol. V

Parry, Adm. Sir (William) Edward, 1893–1972, vol. VII

Parry, William John, 1842–1927, vol. II

Parry-Evans, Rev. Joseph David Samuel, 1876–1936, vol. III

Parry-Okeden, Richard Godfrey Christian, 1900–1978, vol. VII

Parry-Okeden, William Edward, 1840–1926, vol. II

Parry Pryce, Ven. Thomas, *died* 1953, vol. V

Parry-Williams, Sir Thomas Herbert, *died* 1975, vol. VII

Parselle, Air Vice-Marshal Thomas Alford Boyd, 1911–1979, vol. VII

Parsey, Edward Moreland, 1900–1976, vol. VII

Parshall, Horace Field, 1865–1932, vol. III

Parson, Col George, 1879–1950, vol. IV (A)

Parsons, Sir Alan Lethbridge; *see* Parsons, Sir Alfred A. L.

Parsons, Albert, 1865–1938, vol. III

Parsons, Alfred, 1847–1920, vol. II

Parsons, Sir (Alfred) Alan Lethbridge, 1882–1964, vol. VI

Parsons, Lt-Col Alfred Woodis, 1878–1954, vol. V

Parsons, Hon. Sir Angas; *see* Parsons, Hon. Sir H. A.

Parsons, Maj.-Gen. Sir Arthur Edward Broadbent, 1884–1966, vol. VI

Parsons, Beatrice, *died* 1955, vol. V

Parsons, Lt-Col Cecil, 1870–1935, vol. III

Parsons, Maj.-Gen. Sir Charles, 1855–1923, vol. II

Parsons, Hon. Sir Charles Algernon, 1854–1931, vol. III

Parsons, Mrs Clement, (Florence Mary Parsons), 1864–1934, vol. III

Parsons, Lt-Gen. Cunliffe McNeile, 1865–1923, vol. II

Parsons, Lt-Col Durie, 1872–1945, vol. IV

Parsons, Major Edward Howard Thornbrough, 1868–1946, vol. IV

Parsons, Rt Rev. Edward Lambe, 1868–1960, vol. V (A)

Parsons, Florence Mary; *see* Parsons, Mrs Clement.

Parsons, Frank Bett, 1902–1948, vol. IV

Parsons, Major Frederick George, *died* 1904, vol. I

Parsons, Col Frederick George, 1856–1933, vol. III

Parsons, Frederick Gymer, 1863–1943, vol. IV

Parsons, Hon. Geoffry Lawrence, 1874–1956, vol. V

Parsons, George Richard, 1898–1961, vol. VI

Parsons, Godfrey Valentine Hope, 1894–1948, vol. IV

Parsons, Maj.-Gen. Sir Harold Daniel Edmund, 1863–1925, vol. II

Parsons, Harold George, *died* 1905, vol. I

Parsons, Henry Franklin, 1846–1913, vol. I

Parsons, Hon Sir (Herbert) Angas, 1872–1945, vol. IV

Parsons, Sir Herbert James Francis, 1st Bt, 1870–1940, vol. III

Parsons, Ian Macnaghten, 1906–1980, vol. VII

Parsons, J. W., 1859–1937, vol. III

Parsons, Col Sir John; *see* Parsons, Col Sir P. J.

Parsons, Sir John Herbert, *died* 1957, vol. V

Parsons, John Inglis, 1857–1928, vol. II

Parsons, John Randal, 1884–1967, vol. VI

Parsons, Brig. Johnston Lindsey Rowlett, 1876–1935, vol. III

Parsons, Rev. Canon Laurence Edmund, 1883–1972, vol. VII

Parsons, Lt-Gen. Sir Lawrence Worthington, 1850–1923, vol. II

Parsons, Sir Leonard Gregory, 1879–1950, vol. IV

Parsons, Sir Maurice Henry, 1910–1978, vol. VII

Parsons, Col Sir (Percy) John, 1881–1954, vol. V

Parsons, Philip Harry, *died* 1920, vol. II

Parsons, Rev. Hon. Randal, 1848–1936, vol. III

Parsons, Hon. Richard Clere, 1851–1923, vol. II

Parsons, Rev. Canon Richard Edward, 1888–1971, vol. VII

Parsons, Rt Rev. Richard Godfrey, 1882–1948, vol. IV

Parsons, William Barclay, 1859–1932, vol. III

Parsons, Col William Forster, 1879–1959, vol. V

Parsons, Engr Rear-Adm. William Roskilly, 1865–1954, vol. V

Parsons-Smith, Basil Thomas, 1882–1954, vol. V

Part, Lt-Col Sir Dealtry Charles, *died* 1961, vol. VI

Partabgarh, Maharawat of, 1857–1929, vol. III

Partington, Rev. Canon Ellis Foster E.; *see* Edge-Partington.

Partington, James Riddick, 1886–1965, vol. VI

Partington, Wilfred, 1888–1955, vol. V

Parton, Cyril John, 1880–1953, vol. V

Parton, Ernest, *died* 1933, vol. III

Partridge, Ann St John, *died* 1936, vol. III

Partridge, Sir Bernard, 1861–1945, vol. IV

Partridge, Sir Cecil, 1873–1937, vol. III

Partridge, Edward Hincks, 1901–1962, vol. VI

Partridge, Eric Honeywood, 1894–1979, vol. VII

Partridge, Ernest, 1895–1974, vol. VII

Partridge, Francis, 1846–1906, vol. I

Partridge, Rt Rev. Frank, 1877–1941, vol. IV

Partridge, Maurice William, 1913–1973, vol. VII

Partridge, Col Sydney George, 1881–1957, vol. V

Partridge, William Ordway, 1861–1930, vol. III

Pascal, Rt Rev. Albert, 1848–1920, vol. II

Pascal, Gabriel, 1894–1954, vol. V

Pascal, Jean Louis, 1837–1920, vol. II (A), vol. III

Pascal, Roy, 1904–1980, vol. VII

Pascall, Charles, 1853–1931, vol. III

Paschalis, Neoptolemus, 1880–1946, vol. V

Pascoe, Sir Edwin Hall, 1878–1949, vol. IV

Pascoe, Sir (Frederick) John, 1893–1963, vol. VI

Pascoe, Sir John; *see* Pascoe, Sir F. J.

Pask, Edgar Alexander, 1912–1966, vol. VI

Paske-Smith, Montague Bentley Talbot, *died* 1946, vol. IV

Paskin, Sir (Jesse) John, 1892–1972, vol. VII

Paskin, Sir John; see Paskin, Sir J. J.
Pasley, Maj.-Gen. Gilbert James, 1834–1910, vol. I
Pasley, Maj.-Gen. Joseph Montagu Sabine, 1898–1978, vol. VII
Pasley, Major Sir Thomas Edward Sabine, 3rd Bt, 1863–1947, vol. IV
Pasley, Thomas Hamilton Sabine, 1861–1927, vol. II
Pasolini, Pierpaolo, 1922–1975, vol. VII
Pass, (Alfred) Douglas, 1885–1970, vol. VI
Pass, Douglas; see Pass, A. D.
Pass, Rev. Herman Leonard, 1875–1938, vol. III
Passant, Ernest James, 1890–1959, vol. V
Passey, Richard Douglas, 1888–1971, vol. VII
Passfield, 1st Baron, 1859–1947, vol. IV
Passfield, Lady; (Beatrice); see Webb, Mrs Sidney.
Passingham, Col Augustus Mervyn Owen A.; see Anwyl-Passingham.
Passmore, John Reginald Jutsum, 1878–1965, vol. VI
Passmore, Rt Rev. Nicholas Wilfrid, 1907–1976, vol. VII
Pasternak, Boris, 1890–1960, vol. V
Pasteur, Louis V.-R.; see Vallery-Radot Pasteur.
Pasteur, William, died 1943, vol. IV
Paston-Bedingfeld, Sir Henry Edward, 8th Bt, 1860–1941, vol. IV
Paston-Bedingfeld, Sir Henry George, 7th Bt, 1830–1902, vol. I
Paston-Cooper, Sir Astley Paston, 3rd Bt, 1824–1904, vol. I
Paston-Cooper, Sir Charles Naunton Paston, 4th Bt, 1867–1941, vol. IV
Pastor, Antonio Ricardo, 1894–1971, vol. VII
Pasture, 4th Marquis de la, 1836–1916, vol. II
Pasture, 5th Marquis de la, 1886–1962, vol. VI
Patch, Lt-Gen. Alexander McCarrell, 1889–1945, vol. IV
Patch, Sir Edmund Leo H.; see Hall-Patch.
Patch, Brig.-Gen. Francis Robert, 1868–1947, vol. IV
Patch, Col Robert, 1842–1927, vol. II
Patchell, William Henry, 1862–1932, vol. III
Patchett, William, died 1915, vol. I
Pate, Henry Reginald, 1880–1942, vol. IV
Patel, Khan Bahadur Burjorji D., died 1931, vol. III
Patenaude, Esioff Léon, 1875–1963, vol. VI
Paterson, A., 1865–1944, vol. IV
Paterson, Col Adrian Gordon, 1888–1940, vol. III
Paterson, Albert Rutherford, 1885–1959, vol. V
Paterson, Sir Alexander, 1884–1947, vol. IV
Paterson, Alexander Brown, 1917–1980, vol. VII
Paterson, Alexander Nisbet, 1862–1947, vol. IV
Paterson, Sir (Alexander) Swinton, 1893–1980, vol. VII
Paterson, Alfred Croom, 1875–1933, vol. III
Paterson, Andrew Barton, 1864–1941, vol. IV
Paterson, Andrew Melville, 1862–1919, vol. II
Paterson, Rev. Archibald, died 1932, vol. III
Paterson, Arthur Henry, 1862–1928, vol. II
Paterson, Lt-Col Arthur William Sibbald, 1878–1937, vol. III
Paterson, Aylmer John Noel, 1902–1977, vol. VII
Paterson, Sir Clifford Copland, 1879–1948, vol. IV

Paterson, Donald Hugh, 1890–1968, vol. VI
Paterson, Emily Murray, died 1934, vol. III
Paterson, Brig.-Gen. Ewing, 1873–1950, vol. IV
Paterson, Col George Fredrick Joseph, 1885–1949, vol. IV
Paterson, George McLeod, 1891–1953, vol. V
Paterson, Graham, died 1938, vol. III
Paterson, Surg.-Maj.-Gen. Henry Foljambe, 1836–1920, vol. II
Paterson, Lt-Col Henry Francis William, 1880–1943, vol. IV
Paterson, Herbert John, 1868–1940, vol. III
Paterson, Maj.-Gen. Herbert MacGregor, 1898–1979, vol. VII
Paterson, James, 1854–1932, vol. III
Paterson, Rev. James Alexander, 1851–1915, vol. I (A)
Paterson, James Veitch, 1866–1943, vol. IV
Paterson, John Sidney, 1899–1965, vol. VI
Paterson, John Waugh, 1869–1958, vol. V
Paterson, John Wilson, 1887–1970, vol. VI
Paterson, Marcus, 1870–1932, vol. III
Paterson, Mary Muirhead, died 1941, vol. IV
Paterson, Nicholas Julian, died 1934, vol. III
Paterson, Lt-Col Norman Fitzherbert, 1843–1925, vol. II
Paterson, Col Philip Joseph, 1874–1930, vol. III
Paterson, Captain Quentin Hunter, 1888–1975, vol. VII
Paterson, Sir Reginald G. C., 1875–1939, vol. III
Paterson, Gen. Robert Ormiston, 1878–1941, vol. IV
Paterson, Brig.-Gen. Robert Walter, 1876–1936, vol. III
Paterson, Col Stanley, 1860–1950, vol. IV
Paterson, Stronach, 1886–1957, vol. V
Paterson, Sir Swinton; see Paterson, Sir A. S.
Paterson, Maj.-Gen. Thomas George Ferguson, 1876–1942, vol. IV
Paterson, Thomas Wilson, born 1851, vol. II
Paterson, William, 1815–1903, vol. I
Paterson, Sir William, 1874–1956, vol. V
Paterson, William Bromfield, died 1924, vol. II
Paterson, William G. R., 1878–1954, vol. V
Paterson, William James Macdonald, 1911–1976, vol. VII
Paterson, Very Rev. William Paterson, 1860–1939, vol. III
Paterson-Morgan, Rev. Richard James Basil, 1879–1966, vol. VI
Pateshall, Col Henry Evan Pateshall, 1879–1948, vol. IV
Patey, David Howard, 1899–1977, vol. VII
Patey, Adm. Sir George Edwin, 1859–1935, vol. III
Patiala, Lt-Gen. HH Maharaja Dhiraj of, 1891–1938, vol. III
Patiala, Lt-Gen. HH Maharajadhiraj of, 1913–1974, vol. VII
Patna, HH Maharaja of, 1912–1975, vol. VII
Paton, Alexander Allan, died 1934, vol. III
Paton, Sir Alfred Vaughan, 1861–1930, vol. III
Paton, Brig. Charles Morgan, 1896–1979, vol. VII
Paton, Diarmid Noel, 1859–1928, vol. II
Paton, Florence Beatrice, died 1976, vol. VII

Paton, Frederick Noel, 1861–1914, vol. I
Paton, G., *died* 1906, vol. I
Paton, Maj.-Gen. George, 1841–1931, vol. III
Paton, George Pearson, 1882–1975, vol. VII
Paton, Sir George William, 1859–1934, vol. III
Paton, Herbert James, 1887–1969, vol. VI
Paton, Hugh, 1853–1927, vol. II
Paton, James, 1843–1921, vol. II
Paton, James Bowie, *died* 1940, vol. III (A), vol. IV
Paton, Sir James Wallace, 1863–1948, vol. IV
Paton, Maj.-Gen. John, 1867–1943, vol. IV
Paton, John, 1886–1976, vol. VII
Paton, John Brown, 1830–1911, vol. I
Paton, John Gibson, 1824–1907, vol. I
Paton, John Lewis, 1863–1946, vol. IV
Paton, Sir Joseph Noël, 1821–1901, vol. I
Paton, Leslie, 1872–1943, vol. IV
Paton, Rev. Lewis Bayles, 1864–1932, vol. III
Paton, Robert Thomson, 1856–1929, vol. III
Paton, Robert Young, 1894–1973, vol. VII
Paton, Rev. William, 1886–1943, vol. IV
Paton, William Calder, 1886–1979, vol. VII
Paton, Vice-Adm. William Douglas, 1874–1952, vol. V
Patrick, Rt Hon. Lord; William Donald Patrick, 1889–1967, vol. VI
Patrick, Adam, 1883–1970, vol. VI
Patrick, Major Charles Kennedy Cochran-, 1896–1933, vol. III
Patrick, (Colin) Mark, 1893–1942, vol. IV
Patrick, David, 1849–1914, vol. I
Patrick, Rev. John, 1850–1933, vol. III
Patrick, Mark; *see* Patrick, C. M.
Patrick, Mary Mills, 1850–1940, vol. III
Patrick, Sir Neil James Kennedy C.; *see* Cochran-Patrick.
Patrick, Sir Paul Joseph, 1888–1975, vol. VII
Patrick, Rt Hon. William Donald; *see* Patrick, Rt Hon. Lord.
Patro Garu, Rao Bahadur Sir Annepu Parasuramadas, 1875–1946, vol. IV
Patron, Joseph Armand, 1856–1922, vol. II
Patry, Edward, *died* 1940, vol. III
Pattani, Sir Prabhashanker Dalpatram, 1862–1938, vol. III
Patten, Charles J., 1870–1948, vol. IV
Patten, Rev. John Alexander, 1883–1952, vol. V
Pattenson, Arthur Eric Tylden, 1888–1955, vol. V
Pattenson, Major Arthur Henry T.; *see* Tylden-Pattenson.
Pattenson, Lt-Col Edwin Cooke Tylden-, 1871–1940, vol. III
Patterson, Alexander Blakeley, 1842–1919, vol. II
Patterson, Rev. Alexander Hamilton, 1851–1943, vol. IV
Patterson, Annie W., *died* 1934, vol. III
Patterson, Daniel Wells, 1871–1932, vol. III
Patterson, David Clarke, 1879–1948, vol. IV
Patterson, Eric James, 1891–1972, vol. VII
Patterson, George, 1846–1925, vol. II (A), vol. III
Patterson, Hon. James Colebrooke, 1839–1929, vol. III
Patterson, James Kennedy, 1833–1922, vol. II
Patterson, Rt Rev. James Laird, 1822–1902, vol. I

Patterson, Jocelyn, 1900–1965, vol. VI
Patterson, John Edward, *died* 1919, vol. II
Patterson, Sir John Robert, 1892–1976, vol. VII
Patterson, Rear-Adm. Julian Francis Chichester, 1884–1972, vol. VII
Patterson, Rev. Melville Watson, 1873–1944, vol. IV
Patterson, Norman, 1879–1909, vol. I
Patterson, Norman, 1877–1950, vol. IV
Patterson, Sir Reginald Stewart, 1878–1930, vol. III
Patterson, Sir Robert Lloyd, 1836–1906, vol. I
Patterson, Robert Porter, 1891–1952, vol. V
Patterson, Lt-Col Sir Stewart Blakeley Agnew, 1872–1942, vol. IV
Patterson, Thomas Redden, 1898–1972, vol. VII
Patterson, Thomas Stewart, 1872–1949, vol. IV
Patterson, Lt-Col Thomas W., 1844–1902, vol. I
Patterson, Adm. Sir Wilfrid Rupert, 1893–1954, vol. V
Patteson, John Coleridge, 1896–1954, vol. V
Patti, Mme Adelina, (Baroness Rolf Cederström), 1843–1919, vol. II
Pattinson, Arthur Edward, 1868–1939, vol. III
Pattinson, George Norman, 1887–1966, vol. VI
Pattinson, Rev. Canon Joseph Alfred, 1861–1919, vol. II
Pattinson, Air Marshal Sir Lawrence Arthur, 1890–1955, vol. V
Pattinson, Sir Robert, 1872–1954, vol. V
Pattinson, Samuel, 1870–1942, vol. IV
Pattison, Andrew Seth Pringle; *see* Seth, Andrew.
Pattison, Harold Arthur Langston, 1897–1966, vol. VI
Pattisson, Jacob Luard, 1841–1915, vol. I
Pattisson, Adm. John Robert Ebenezer, 1844–1928, vol. II
Patton, Arnold Gordon, 1892–1960, vol. V
Patton, Rev. Francis Landey, 1843–1932, vol. III
Patton, Gen. George S., 1885–1945, vol. IV
Patton, Col Henry Bethune, 1835–1915, vol. I
Patton, Rt Rev. Henry Edmund, 1867–1943, vol. IV
Patton, Walter Scott, 1876–1960, vol. V
Pattrick, Michael; *see* Pattrick, W. M. T.
Pattrick, (William) Michael (Thomas), 1913–1980, vol. VII
Pattullo, Hon. Thomas Dufferin, 1873–1956, vol. V
Pattullo, William Ogilvy, 1924–1975, vol. VII
Patwardhan, Baba Saheb; *see* Miraj (Junior), Chief of.
Pau, Gen. Paul Mary Cæsar Gerald, 1848–1932, vol. III
Pauer, Max, 1866–1945, vol. IV
Paul VI, His Holiness Pope, (Giovanni Battista Montini), 1897–1978, vol. VII
Paul, Alfred Wallis, 1847–1912, vol. I
Paul, Sir Aubrey Edward Henry Dean, 5th Bt (*cr* 1821), 1869–1961, vol. VI
Paul, Sir Brian Kenneth, 6th Bt (*cr* 1821), 1904–1972, vol. VII
Paul, Cedar, *died* 1972, vol. VII
Paul, Charles Kegan, 1828–1902, vol. I
Paul, Sir (Charles) Norman, 1883–1959, vol. V

Paul, Very Rev. David, 1845–1929, vol. III
Paul, Col Denis, 1865–1944, vol. IV
Paul, Elliot Harold, 1891–1958, vol. V
Paul, Eric Barlow, 1919–1968, vol. VI
Paul, Rev. F. J., *died* 1941, vol. IV
Paul, Francis Kinnier, 1911–1965, vol. VI
Paul, Frank Thomas, 1851–1941, vol. IV
Paul, Rev. G. W., 1820–1911, vol. I
Paul, Sir (George) Graham, 1887–1960, vol. V
Paul, Sir George Morison, 1839–1926, vol. II
Paul, Brig.-Gen. Gerard Robert Clark, 1861–1913, vol. I
Paul, Sir Graham; *see* Paul, Sir George G.
Paul, Sir Gregory Charles, 1830–1900, vol. I
Paul, Sir Harisankar, 1888–1951, vol. V
Paul, Herbert Woodfield, 1853–1935, vol. III
Paul, Sir James Balfour, 1846–1931, vol. III
Paul, Rev. Sir Jeffrey; *see* Paul, Rev. Sir W. E. J.
Paul, Lt-Col John William Balfour, 1873–1957, vol. V
Paul, Leslie Douglas, 1903–1970, vol. VI
Paul, Maurice Eden, 1865–1944, vol. IV
Paul, Sir Norman; *see* Paul, Sir C. N.
Paul, Engr-Rear-Adm. Oliver Richard, 1868–1955, vol. V
Paul, Paul, 1865–1937, vol. III
Paul, Sir Robert Joshua, 3rd Bt (*cr* 1794), 1820–1898, vol. I
Paul, Captain Sir Robert Joshua, 5th Bt (*cr* 1794), 1883–1955, vol. V
Paul, Stuart, 1879–1961, vol. VI
Paul, Maj.-Gen. Walter Reginald, 1882–1953, vol. V
Paul, Rev. Sir (William Edmund) Jeffrey, 6th Bt (*cr* 1794), 1885–1961, vol. VI
Paul, Sir William Joshua, 4th Bt (*cr* 1794), 1851–1912, vol. I
Paul-Boncour, Joseph, 1873–1972, vol. VII
Paulet, Major Charles Standish, 1873–1953, vol. V
Paulin, Sir David, 1847–1930, vol. III
Paulin, George Henry, 1888–1962, vol. VI
Paulin, Sir William Thomas, 1848–1931, vol. III
Pauline, Sister; *see* Young, Hilda Beatrice.
Paull, Harry Major, 1854–1934, vol. III
Paull, Richard James, 1862–1937, vol. III
Paulton, James Mellor, 1857–1923, vol. II
Pauncefort-Duncombe, Sir Everard; *see* Duncombe, Sir E. P. D. P.
Pauncefote, 1st Baron, 1828–1902, vol. I
Paur, Emil, 1855–1932, vol. III
Paus, Christopher L., 1881–1963, vol. VI
Pavière, Sydney Herbert, 1891–1971, vol. VII
Pavlides, Sir Paul George, 1897–1977, vol. VII
Pavlides, Stelios, 1892–1968, vol. VI (AII)
Pavry, Faredun Cursetji, 1877–1943, vol. IV
Pavy, Emily Dorothea, *died* 1967, vol. VI
Pavy, Frederick William, 1829–1911, vol. I
Pawan, Joseph Lennox, 1887–1957, vol. V
Pawel-Rammingen, Baron Luitbert Alexander George Lionel Alphons, 1843–1932, vol. III
Pawle, Brig. Hanbury, 1886–1972, vol. VII
Pawsey, Sir Charles Ridley, 1894–1972, vol. VII
Pawsey, Joseph Lade, 1908–1962, vol. VI
Pawson, Henry Cecil, 1897–1978, vol. VII

Pawson, Ven. Wilfrid Denys, 1905–1959, vol. V
Paxton, Air Vice-Marshal Sir Anthony Lauderdale, 1896–1957, vol. V
Paxton, Sir Thomas, 1st Bt, *died* 1930, vol. III
Payen-Payne, de Vincheles, 1866–1945, vol. IV
Payn, James, 1830–1898, vol. I
Payne, Col Alexander Vaughan, 1857–1943, vol. IV
Payne, Arthur Robert, 1926–1976, vol. VII
Payne, Ben Iden, 1881–1976, vol. VII
Payne, Charles, 1871–1948, vol. IV
Payne, Charles Frederick, 1875–1966, vol. VI
Payne, Charles Robert Salusbury, 1859–1942, vol. IV
Payne, Vice-Adm. Christopher Russell, 1874–1952, vol. V
Payne, Rev. David Bruce, 1827–1913, vol. I
Payne, de Vincheles P.; *see* Payen-Payne,
Payne, Col. Edward Henry, 1868–1941, vol. IV
Payne, Edward John, 1844–1904, vol. I
Payne, Rev. Ernest Alexander, 1902–1980, vol. VII
Payne, Rev. Francis Reginald Chassereau, 1876–1961, vol. VI
Payne, Henry, 1871–1945, vol. IV
Payne, Henry A., 1868–1940, vol. III
Payne, Sir Henry Arthur, 1873–1931, vol. III
Payne, Col Herbert Chidgey Brine, 1862–1945, vol. IV
Payne, Hon. Herbert James Mockford, 1866–1944, vol. IV
Payne, Humfry Gilbert Garth, 1902–1936, vol. III
Payne, John Bruce, *died* 1928, vol. II
Payne, John Horne, 1837–1920, vol. II
Payne, Joseph Frank, 1840–1910, vol. I
Payne, Lt-Col Leslie Herbert, 1888–1942, vol. IV
Payne, Sir Reginald Withers, 1904–1980, vol. VII
Payne, Maj.-Gen. Richard Lloyd, 1854–1921, vol. II
Payne, Major Robert Leslie, 1880–1942, vol. IV
Payne, Sylvia May, 1880–1976, vol. VII
Payne, Walter, *died* 1949, vol. IV
Payne, Sir William Labatt, 1890–1962, vol. VI
Payne-Gallwey, Sir Ralph William Frankland; *see* Gallwey.
Payne-Gallwey, Sir Reginald Frankland; *see* Gallwey.
Payne-Gallwey, Captain William Thomas Frankland; *see* Gallwey.
Paynter, Col Camborne Haweis, 1864–1949, vol. IV
Paynter, Brig.-Gen. Sir George Camborne Beauclerk, 1880–1950, vol. IV
Payton, Sir Charles Alfred, 1843–1926, vol. II
Payton, Wilfrid Hugh, 1892–1965, vol. VI
Peabody, George Foster, 1852–1938, vol. III
Peace, Albert Lister, 1844–1912, vol. I
Peace, Captain Alfred Geoffrey, 1885–1940, vol. III
Peace, Sir Walter, 1840–1917, vol. II
Peacey, Rt Rev. Basil William, 1889–1969, vol. VI
Peacey, Rev. J. R., 1896–1971, vol. VII
Peach, Benjamin Neeve, 1842–1926, vol. II
Peach, Adm. Charles William K.; *see* Keighly-Peach.
Peach, Major Edmund, 1865–1902, vol. I

Peach, Lawrence du Garde, 1890–1974, vol. VII
Peachey, Captain Allan Thomas George Cumberland, 1896–1967, vol. VI
Peacock, Alexander David, died 1976, vol. VII
Peacock, Hon. Sir Alexander James, 1861–1933, vol. III
Peacock, Rev. Charles Alfred, 1868–1944, vol. IV
Peacock, David Henry, 1889–1978, vol. VII
Peacock, Edward Eden, 1850–1909, vol. I
Peacock, Sir Edward Robert, 1871–1962, vol. VI
Peacock, Major Ferdinand Mansel, 1861–1908, vol. I
Peacock, Frederick Hood, 1886–1969, vol. VI
Peacock, Major Frederick William, died 1924, vol. II
Peacock, Sir Kenneth Swift, 1902–1968, vol. VI
Peacock, Matthew Henry, 1856–1929, vol. III
Peacock, Millie, (Lady Peacock), died 1948, vol. IV
Peacock, Sir Peter, 1872–1948, vol. IV
Peacock, Col Pryce, 1868–1956, vol. V
Peacock, Ralph, died 1946, vol. IV
Peacock, Sir Robert, 1859–1926, vol. II
Peacock, Sir Thomas, died 1959, vol. V
Peacock, Rev. W. Arthur, 1905–1968, vol. VI
Peacock, Sir Walter, 1871–1956, vol. V
Peacock, Rev. Canon Wilfrid Morgan, 1890–1970, vol. VI
Peacock, William Henry, 1881–1946, vol. IV
Peacocke, Emilie Hawkes, 1883–1964, vol. VI
Peacocke, Most Rev. Joseph Ferguson, 1835–1916, vol. II
Peacocke, Rt Rev. Joseph Irvine, 1866–1962, vol. VI
Peacocke, Col Thomas George, 1865–1939, vol. III
Peacocke, Col William, 1848–1931, vol. III
Peake, Hon. Archibald Henry, 1859–1920, vol. II
Peake, Sir Arthur Copson, 1854–1934, vol. III
Peake, Arthur Samuel, 1865–1929, vol. III
Peake, Sir Charles Brinsley Pemberton, 1897–1958, vol. V
Peake, Brig. Edward Robert Luxmoore, 1894–1964, vol. VI
Peake, Frederick Gerard, 1886–1970, vol. VI
Peake, George Herbert, 1859–1950, vol. IV
Peake, Sir Harald, 1899–1978, vol. VIII
Peake, Harold John Edward, 1867–1946, vol. IV
Peake, Brig.-Gen. Malcolm, 1865–1917, vol. II
Peake, Mervyn, 1911–1968, vol. VI
Peake, Thomas, 1868–1945, vol. IV
Peaker, Alfred Pearson, 1896–1973, vol. VII
Peaker, Frederick, 1867–1942, vol. IV
Peal, Lt-Col Edward Raymond, 1884–1967, vol. VI
Pear, Tom Hatherley, 1886–1972, vol. VII
Pearce, C. Maresco, 1874–1964, vol. VI
Pearce, Charles E., died 1924, vol. II
Pearce, Sir (Charles) Frederick (Byrde), 1892–1964, vol. VI
Pearce, Charles William, 1856–1928, vol. II
Pearce, Col Cyril Harvey, 1878–1943, vol. IV
Pearce, Rt Rev. Edmund Courtenay, 1870–1935, vol. III
Pearce, Sir Edward Charles, 1862–1928, vol. II
Pearce, E(dward) Ewart, 1898–1963, vol. VI
Pearce, Ernest Alfred John, 1868–1943, vol. IV

Pearce, Rt Rev. Ernest Harold, 1865–1930, vol. III
Pearce, Major Francis Barrow, 1866–1926, vol. II
Pearce, Sir Frank James, 1878–1946, vol. IV
Pearce, Sir Frederick; see Pearce, Sir C. F. B.
Pearce, Air Cdre Frederick Laurence, 1898–1975, vol. VII
Pearce, Sir George Alfred, 1894–1971, vol. VII
Pearce, Rt Hon. Sir George Foster, 1870–1952, vol. V
Pearce, Harold Seward, 1880–1961, vol. VI
Pearce, Henry, 1869–1925, vol. II
Pearce, Sir Leonard; see Pearce, Sir S. L.
Pearce, Sir Robert, 1840–1922, vol. II
Pearce, Rev. Robert John, 1841–1920, vol. II
Pearce, Seward, 1866–1951, vol. V
Pearce, Sir (Standen) Leonard, 1873–1947, vol. IV
Pearce, Thomas Ernest, 1883–1941, vol. IV
Pearce, Sir William, 1853–1932, vol. III
Pearce, Rev. William Fletcher, 1869–1935, vol. III
Pearce, Sir William George, 2nd Bt, 1861–1907, vol. I
Pearce-Serocold, Brig.-Gen. Eric, 1870–1926, vol. II
Pearce-Serocold, Oswald, 1865–1951, vol. V
Peard, Frances Mary, died 1923, vol. II
Pearl, Amy Lea, (Mrs F. Warren Pearl), 1880–1964, vol. VI
Pearl, Mrs F. Warren; see Pearl, Amy Lea.
Pearl, Raymond, 1879–1940, vol. III (A), vol. IV
Pearless, Brig.-Gen. Charles William, 1872–1940, vol. III
Pearman, Rev. Augustus John, died 1909, vol. I
Pearman-Smith, Sir William Joseph, 1863–1939, vol. III
Pears, Charles, 1873–1958, vol. V
Pears, Adm. Sir Edmund Radcliffe, 1862–1941, vol. IV
Pears, Sir Edwin, 1835–1919, vol. II
Pears, Major M. L., died 1916, vol. II
Pears, Sidney John, 1900–1972, vol. VII
Pears, Rear-Adm. Steuart Arnold, 1894–1978, vol. VII
Pears, Sir Steuart Edmund, 1875–1931, vol. III
Pearsall, William Booth, 1845–1913, vol. I
Pearsall, William Harold, 1891–1964, vol. VI
Pearse, Albert William, 1857–1951, vol. V
Pearse, Captain Alfred, died 1933, vol. III
Pearse, Major Beauchamp Albert Thomas K.; see Kerr-Pearse.
Pearse, Gen. George Godfrey, 1827–1905, vol. I
Pearse, H. H. S., died 1905, vol. I
Pearse, Col Hugh Wodehouse, 1855–1919, vol. II
Pearse, James, 1871–1962, vol. VI
Pearse, Sir John Slocombe, 1870–1949, vol. IV
Pearse, Rev. Mark Guy, 1842–1930, vol. III
Pearse, Ronald Livian, 1880–1960, vol. V
Pearse, Lt-Col Sydney Arthur, died 1937, vol. III
Pearse, Thomas Lawrence S.; see Smith-Pearse.
Pearse, Rev. Thomas Northmore Hart S.; see Smith-Pearse.
Pearse, Brig.-Gen. Tom Harry Finch, 1864–1947, vol. IV
Pearson, Baron (Life Peer); Colin Hargreaves Pearson, 1899–1980, vol. VII

Pearson, Hon. Lord; Charles John Pearson, 1843–1910, vol. I

Pearson, Rt Rev. Alfred, 1848–1909, vol. I

Pearson, Gen. Sir Alfred Astley, 1850–1937, vol. III

Pearson, Alfred Chilton, 1861–1935, vol. III

Pearson, Rev. Andrew Forret Scott, 1886–1952, vol. V

Pearson, Andrew Russell; see Pearson, Drew.

Pearson, Sir Arthur, 1866–1921, vol. II

Pearson, Arthur, 1897–1980, vol. VII

Pearson, Arthur Ashley, 1847–1933, vol. III

Pearson, Aylmer Cavendish, 1876–1926, vol. II

Pearson, Hon. (Bernard) Clive, 1887–1965, vol. VI

Pearson, Burton, 1872–1937, vol. III

Pearson, Charles Child, 1875–1955, vol. V

Pearson, Charles John; see Pearson, Hon. Lord.

Pearson, Sir Charles Knight, 1834–1909, vol. I

Pearson, Charles Yelverton, 1857–1947, vol. IV

Pearson, Claude Edmund, 1903–1971, vol. VII

Pearson, Hon. Clive; see Pearson, Hon. B. C.

Pearson, Colin Bateman, 1889–1974, vol. VII

Pearson, Drew, (Andrew Russell Pearson), 1897–1969, vol. VI

Pearson, Sir Edward Ernest, 1874–1925, vol. II

Pearson, Egon Sharpe, 1895–1980, vol. VII

Pearson, Ethel, (Lady Pearson), died 1959, vol. V

Pearson, Frederick John, 1866–1932, vol. III

Pearson, George Sherwin Hooke, 1875–1941, vol. IV

Pearson, Col George Thomson, 1876–1946, vol. IV

Pearson, Gerald Lionel, 1918–1978, vol. VII

Pearson, Sir Glen Gardner, 1907–1976, vol. VII

Pearson, Henry Harold Welch, 1870–1916, vol. II

Pearson, Sir Herbert Grayhurst, 1878–1958, vol. V

Pearson, Hesketh, 1887–1964, vol. VI

Pearson, Hugh Drummond, 1873–1922, vol. II

Pearson, Adm. Sir Hugo Lewis, 1843–1912, vol. I

Pearson, James Rae, 1871–1951, vol. V

Pearson, Vice-Adm. John Lewis, 1879–1965, vol. VI

Pearson, John Loughborough, 1817–1897, vol. I

Pearson, Joseph, 1881–1971, vol. VII

Pearson, Karl, 1857–1936, vol. III

Pearson, Rt Hon. Lester Bowles, 1897–1972, vol. VII

Pearson, Lionel Godfrey, 1879–1953, vol. V

Pearson, Sir Louis Frederick, 1863–1943, vol. IV

Pearson, Louise Kirkby; see Lunn, L. K.

Pearson, Rev. Marchant, 1871–1956, vol. V

Pearson, Col Michael Brown, 1840–1923, vol. II

Pearson, Lt-Col Noel Gervis, 1884–1958, vol. V

Pearson, Octavius Henry, 1839–1914, vol. I

Pearson, Sir Ralph Sneyd, 1874–1958, vol. V

Pearson, Richard Francis Malachy, 1872–1956, vol. V

Pearson, Sir Robert Barclay, 1871–1954, vol. V

Pearson, Robert Hooper, 1866–1918, vol. II

Pearson, Rupert Samuel Bruce, 1904–1974, vol. VII

Pearson, Sidney Vere, 1875–1950, vol. IV

Pearson, Thomas Bailey, 1864–1927, vol. II

Pearson, Thomas William, 1872–1957, vol. V

Pearson, Rt Rev. Thomas Wulstan, 1870–1938, vol. III

Pearson, Brig.-Gen. Vere Lorraine Nuttall, 1880–1939, vol. III

Pearson, Col Walter Bagot, 1872–1954, vol. V

Pearson, Major Wilfred John, 1884–1957, vol. V

Pearson, William, died 1907, vol. I

Pearson, William, 1882–1976, vol. VII

Pearson, William George, died 1963, vol. VI

Pearson-Gregory, Thomas Sherwin, 1851–1935, vol. III

Peart, Col Charles Lubé, 1876–1957, vol. V

Peart, Joseph Norriss, 1900–1942, vol. IV

Peary, Robert Edwin, 1856–1920, vol. II

Pease, Sir Alfred Edward, 2nd Bt (cr 1882), 1857–1939, vol. III

Pease, Arthur, 1837–1898, vol. I

Pease, Sir Arthur Francis, 1st Bt (cr 1920), 1866–1927, vol. II

Pease, Sir Edward, 3rd Bt (cr 1882), 1880–1963, vol. VI

Pease, Edward R., 1857–1955, vol. V

Pease, Col Henry Thomas, 1862–1943, vol. IV

Pease, Joseph Gerald, 1863–1928, vol. II

Pease, Sir Joseph Whitwell, 1st Bt (cr 1882), 1828–1903, vol. I

Pease, Lt-Gen. Leonard Thales, 1857–1936, vol. III

Pease, Sir Richard Arthur, 2nd Bt (cr 1920), 1890–1969, vol. VI

Pease, Col Sir Thales, 1835–1919, vol. II

Pease, William Edwin, 1865–1926, vol. II

Peasgood, Osborne Harold, 1902–1962, vol. VI

Peat, Charles Urie, 1892–1979, vol. VII

Peat, Sir George, 1893–1945, vol. IV

Peat, Sir Harry William Henry, 1878–1959, vol. V

Peat, Lt-Comdr Percy Sutcliffe, 1889–1936, vol. III

Peat, Stanley, 1902–1969, vol. VI

Peat, Sir William Barclay, 1852–1936, vol. III

Pecci, Vincent Joachim; see Leo XIII.

Pechell, Sir Alexander B., 7th Bt; see Brooke-Pechell, Sir Augustus A.

Pechell, Sir George Samuel Brooke-, 5th Bt, 1819–1897, vol. I

Pechell, Lt-Col Sir Paul, 8th Bt, 1889–1972, vol. VII

Pechell, Sir Samuel George Brooke-, 6th Bt, 1852–1904, vol. I

Pechey, Archibald Thomas, 1876–1961, vol. VI

Peck, Vice-Adm. Ambrose Maynard, died 1963, vol. VI

Peck, Arthur Leslie, 1902–1974, vol. VII

Peck, Maj.-Gen. Arthur Wharton, 1869–1948, vol. IV

Peck, Col Cyrus Wesley, 1871–1956, vol. V

Peck, Lt-Col Edward George, died 1939, vol. III

Peck, Maj.-Gen. Henry Richardson, 1874–1965, vol. VI

Peck, Sir James Wallace, 1875–1964, vol. VI

Peck, Jasper Augustine, 1905–1980, vol. VII

Peck, Very Rev. Michael David Saville, 1914–1968, vol. VI

Peck, Air-Marshal Sir Richard Hallam, 1893–1952, vol. V

Peck, Maj.-Gen. Sydney Capel, 1871–1949, vol. IV

Peck, Sir William, 1862–1925, vol. II

Peck, Winifred Frances, (Lady Peck), *died* 1962, vol. VI
Peckitt, Reginald Godfrey, *died* 1937, vol. III
Peckover, 1st Baron, 1830–1919, vol. II
Pedder, John, 1850–1929, vol. III
Pedder, Sir John, 1869–1956, vol. V
Peddie, Baron (Life Peer); James Mortimer Peddie, 1907–1978, vol. VII
Peddie, Coventry Dick, 1863–1950, vol. IV
Peddie, John Ronald, 1887–1979, vol. VII
Peddie, John Taylor, 1879–1947, vol. IV
Peddie, William, 1861–1946, vol. IV
Peddie-Waddell, Alexander; *see* Waddell.
Peden, Hon. Sir John Beverley, 1871–1946, vol. IV
Pedler, Sir Alexander, 1849–1918, vol. II
Pedler, Margaret, *died* 1948, vol. IV
Pedley, Arthur Charles, 1859–1943, vol. IV
Pedley, Frederick N.; *see* Newland-Pedley.
Pedley, John Edward, 1891–1972, vol. VII
Pedley, Richard Rodman, 1912–1973, vol. VII
Pedley, Brig.-Gen. Stanhope Humphrey, 1865–1938, vol. III
Peebles, Allan Charles Chiappini, 1907–1974, vol. VII
Peebles, Lt-Col Arthur Stansfield, 1872–1933, vol. III
Peebles, Brig.-Gen. Evelyn Chiappini, 1865–1937, vol. III
Peebles, Major Herbert Walter, 1877–1955, vol. V
Peebles, James Ross, 1909–1967, vol. VI
Peech, James, 1878–1935, vol. III
Peek, Sir Cuthbert Edgar, 2nd Bt, 1855–1901, vol. I
Peek, Sir Henry William, 1st Bt, 1825–1898, vol. I
Peek, Sir Wilfrid, 3rd Bt, 1884–1927, vol. II
Peel, 1st Earl, 1867–1937, vol. III
Peel, 2nd Earl, 1901–1969, vol. VI
Peel, 1st Viscount, 1829–1913, vol. I
Peel, Rev. Albert, 1887–1949, vol. IV
Peel, Algernon Robert, *died* 1920, vol. II
Peel, Lt-Col Arthur, 1882–1938, vol. III
Peel, Hon. (Arthur) George (Villiers), 1868–1956, vol. V
Peel, Sir Arthur Robert, 1861–1952, vol. V
Peel, Lt-Col Basil Gerard, 1881–1954, vol. V
Peel, Charles Lawrence Kinloch, 1883–1954, vol. V
Peel, Sir Charles Lennox, 1823–1899, vol. I
Peel, Mrs Charles S., *died* 1934, vol. III
Peel, Brig.-Gen. Edward John Russell, 1869–1939, vol. III
Peel, Sir Edward Townley, 1884–1961, vol. VI
Peel, Captain Sir (Francis Richard) Jonathan, 1897–1979, vol. VII
Peel, Rt Hon. Sir Frederick, 1823–1906, vol. I
Peel, Hon. George; *see* Peel, Hon. A. G. V.
Peel, (Gerald) Graham, 1877–1937, vol. III
Peel, Graham; *see* Peel, Gerald G.
Peel, Col Herbert Haworth, 1866–1956, vol. V
Peel, Horace, 1857–1940, vol. III
Peel, Major Hugh Edmund Ethelston, 1871–1950, vol. IV
Peel, James, 1811–1906, vol. I
Peel, Sir Jonathan; *see* Peel, Sir F. R. J.

Peel, Rev. Hon. Maurice Berkeley, 1873–1917, vol. II
Peel, Sir Mervyn Lloyd, 1856–1929, vol. III
Peel, Sir Robert, 4th Bt (*cr* 1800), 1867–1925, vol. II
Peel, Sir Robert, 5th Bt (*cr* 1800), 1898–1934, vol. III
Peel, Sir Robert, 6th Bt (*cr* 1800), 1920–1942, vol. IV
Peel, Robert, 1881–1969, vol. VI
Peel, Col Robert Francis, 1874–1924, vol. II
Peel, Roland Tennyson, 1892–1945, vol. IV
Peel, Col Hon. Sir Sidney Cornwallis, 1st Bt (*cr* 1936), 1870–1938, vol. III
Peel, Sir Theophilus, 1st Bt (*cr* 1897), *died* 1911, vol. I
Peel, Walter, 1868–1949, vol. IV
Peel, Sir William, 1875–1945, vol. IV
Peel, William Croughton, 1870–1957, vol. V
Peel, Rt Rev. William George, 1854–1916, vol. II
Peel Yates, Lt-Gen. Sir David, 1911–1978, vol. VII
Peers, Sir Charles Reed, 1868–1952, vol. V
Peers, Edgar Allison, *died* 1952, vol. V
Peers, Robert, 1888–1972, vol. VII
Peers, Roger Ernest, 1906–1968, vol. VI
Peet, Hubert William, 1886–1951, vol. V
Peet, Thomas Eric, 1882–1934, vol. III
Pegasus; *see* Lawrence, B. T. T.
Pegg, Arthur John, 1906–1978, vol. VII
Pegg, Rev. Canon Henry F.; *see* Foster Pegg.
Pegler, Louis Hemington, 1852–1927, vol. II
Pegram, A. Bertram, 1873–1941, vol. IV
Pegram, Vice-Adm. Frank Henderson, 1890–1944, vol. IV
Pegram, Frederick, 1870–1937, vol. III
Pegram, Henry, 1862–1937, vol. III
Peile, Rev. A. L. B., 1830–1911, vol. I
Peile, Henry, *died* 1935, vol. III
Peile, Sir James Braithwaite, 1833–1906, vol. I
Peile, Ven. James Hamilton Francis, 1863–1940, vol. III
Peile, John, 1838–1910, vol. I
Peile, Col Schofield Patten, 1859–1940, vol. III
Peile, Col Solomon Charles Frederick, 1855–1932, vol. III
Peirce, Lt-Col Harold Ernest, 1892–1979, vol. VII
Peiris, Hon. Sir James, 1856–1930, vol. III
Peirs, Hugh John Chevallier, 1886–1943, vol. IV
Peirse, Sir Henry Bernard de la Poer B.; *see* Beresford-Peirse.
Peirse, Sir Henry Campbell de la Poer B.; *see* Beresford-Peirse.
Peirse, Sir Henry Monson de la Poer B.; *see* Beresford-Peirse.
Peirse, Lt-Gen. Sir Noel Monson de la Poer B. *see* Beresford-Peirse.
Peirse, Air Chief Marshal Sir Richard Edmund Charles, 1892–1970, vol. VI
Peirse, Adm. Sir Richard H., 1860–1940, vol. III
Peirse, Rev. Richard Windham de la Poer B.; *see* Beresford-Peirse.
Peirse, Rev. Canon Windham de la Poer B.; *see* Beresford-Peirse.

Peirson, David Edward Herbert, 1915–1976, vol. VII

Peirson, Garnet Frank, 1911–1963, vol. VI

Pelham, Major Hon. Dudley Roger Hugh, 1872–1953, vol. V

Pelham, Sir (Edward) Henry, 1876–1949, vol. IV

Pelham, Adm. Frederick Sidney, 1854–1931, vol. III

Pelham, Sir Henry; see Pelham, Sir E. H.

Pelham, Henry Francis, 1846–1907, vol. I

Pelham, Rt Rev. Herbert S., 1881–1944, vol. IV

Pelham, James T.; see Thursby-Pelham.

Pelham, Rev. John Barrington, 1848–1941, vol. IV

Pelham, Rev. Sidney, 1849–1926, vol. II

Pelham, Hon. Thomas Henry William, 1847–1916, vol. II

Pelham Browne, Cynthia; see Stockley, C.

Pelham Burn, Brig.-Gen. Henry; see Burn.

Pelham-Clinton, Lord Edward William; see Clinton.

Pelham Welby, Charles Cornwallis Anderson, 1876–1959, vol. V

Pell, Albert, 1820–1907, vol. I

Pell, Major Albert Julian, 1863–1916, vol. II

Pell, Major Beauchamp Tyndall, 1866–1914, vol. I

Pellatt, Sir Henry Mill, 1860–1939, vol. III

Pelletier, Sir Charles Alphonse Pantaleon, 1837–1911, vol. I

Pelletier, Hector Rooney, 1911–1976, vol. VII

Pelletier, Lt-Col J. M. J. Pantaleon, 1860–1924, vol. II

Pelletier, Hon. Louis Philippe, 1857–1921, vol. II

Pellew, Lancelot Vivian, 1899–1970, vol. VI

Pelliot, Paul, 1878–1945, vol. IV

Pelly, Air Chief Marshal Sir Claude Bernard Raymond, 1902–1972, vol. VII

Pelly, Rev. Douglas Raymond, 1865–1943, vol. IV

Pelly, Lt-Col Edmund Godfrey, 1889–1939, vol. III

Pelly, Sir Harold, 4th Bt, 1863–1950, vol. IV

Pelly, Adm. Sir Henry Bertram, 1867–1942, vol. IV

Pelly, Captain John Noel, 1888–1945, vol. IV

Pelly, Lt-Col John Stannus, 1859–1938, vol. III

Pelly, Sir Kenneth Raymond, 1893–1973, vol. VII

Pelly, Rear-Adm. Peter Douglas Herbert Raymond, 1904–1980, vol. VII

Pelly, Rev. Raymond P., 1841–1911, vol. I

Pelly, Brig.-Gen. Raymond Theodore, 1881–1952, vol. V

Pelly, Rev. Canon Richard Lawrence, 1886–1976, vol. VII

Pember, Edward Henry, 1833–1911, vol. I

Pember, Francis William, 1862–1954, vol. V

Pemberton, Sir Edward Leigh, 1823–1910, vol. I

Pemberton, Horatio Nelson, 1902–1967, vol. VI

Pemberton, John Stapylton Grey, 1860–1940, vol. III

Pemberton, Sir Max, 1863–1950, vol. IV

Pemberton, Maj.-Gen. Robert Charles Boileau, 1834–1914, vol. I

Pemberton, T. Edgar, 1849–1905, vol. I

Pemberton, Rev. Thomas Percy, died 1921, vol. II

Pemberton, William Shakespear C.; see Childe-Pemberton.

Pemberton, Maj.-Gen. Sir Wykeham Leigh, 1833–1918, vol. II

Pemberton-Pigott, Alan Desmond Frederick, 1916–1972, vol. VII

Pembleton, Edgar Stanley, 1888–1968, vol. VI

Pembrey, John Cripps, 1831–1918, vol. II

Pembrey, Marcus Seymour, 1868–1934, vol. III

Pembroke, 14th Earl of, and Montgomery, 11th Earl of, 1853–1913, vol. I

Pembroke, 15th Earl of, and Montgomery, 12th Earl of, 1880–1960, vol. V

Pembroke, 16th Earl of, and Montgomery, 13th Earl of, 1906–1969, vol. VI

Penberthy, John, 1858–1927, vol. II

Pendarves, William Cole, 1841–1929, vol. III

Pendavis, Ven. Whylock, died 1924, vol. II

Pendenys, Arthur; see Humphreys, Arthur L.

Pender, 1st Baron, 1882–1949, vol. IV

Pender, 2nd Baron, 1907–1965, vol. VI

Pender, Major Henry Denison Denison, 1884–1967, vol. VI

Pender, Sir James, 1st Bt, 1841–1921, vol. II

Pender, Major James, 1860–1936, vol. III

Pender, Sir John Denison Denison-, 1855–1929, vol. III

Pender, Bt Col William Stanhope, 1889–1948, vol. IV

Pendered, Mary Lucy, 1858–1940, vol. III (A), vol. IV

Penderel-Brodhurst, James George Joseph, 1859–1934, vol. III

Pendlebury, Charles, 1854–1941, vol. IV

Pendlebury, Herbert Stringfellow, 1870–1953, vol. V

Pendlebury, John Devitt Stringfellow, 1904–1941, vol. IV

Pendleton, Alan O'Bryan George William, 1837–1916, vol. II

Pendred, Loughnan St Lawrence, 1870–1953, vol. V

Penfield, Wilder Graves, 1891–1976, vol. VII

Penfold, Surg. Rear-Adm. Ernest Alfred, 1866–1956, vol. V

Penfold, Very Rev. John Brookes Vernon, 1864–1922, vol. II

Penfold, Captain Marchant Hubert, 1873–1961, vol. VI

Penfold, Lt-Col Sir Stephen, 1842–1925, vol. II

Pengelley, Gen. George Farquharson, 1843–1929, vol. III

Pengelly, Herbert Staddon, 1892–1963, vol. VI

Pengilly, Sir Alexander, 1868–1965, vol. VI

Peniakoff, Lt-Col Vladimir, 1897–1951, vol. V

Penlake, Richard; see Salmon, Percy R.

Penley, Belville S., 1861–1940, vol. III

Penley, William Sydney, 1851–1912, vol. I

Penman, David, died 1961, vol. VI

Penn, Sir Arthur Horace, 1886–1960, vol. V

Penn, John, 1848–1903, vol. I

Penn, Will C., died 1968, vol. VI

Pennant, Hon. Alan George Sholto D.; see Douglas-Pennant.

Pennant, Hon. Charles D.; see Douglas-Pennant.

Pennant, Adm. Hon. Sir Cyril Eustace D.; see Douglas-Pennant.

Pennant, Captain Hon. George Henry D.; see Douglas-Pennant.

Pennant, Hon. Violet Blanche D.; see Douglas-Pennant.

Pennefather, Sir (Alfred) Richard, 1845–1918 vol. II

Pennefather, Harold Wilfrid Armine F.; see Freese-Pennefather.

Pennefather, Sir John de Fonblanque, 1st Bt, 1856–1933, vol. III

Pennefather, Sir Richard; see Pennefather, Sir A. R.

Pennefather, Rev. Preb. Somerset Edward, 1848–1917, vol. II

Pennefather-Evans, Brig. Brian, 1897–1954, vol. V

Pennefather-Evans, Lt-Col Granville, died 1963, vol. VI

Pennell, Arthur, 1852–1926, vol. II

Pennell, Sir Charles Henry, 1805–1898, vol. I

Pennell, Charles Henry, born 1848, vol. III

Pennell, Elizabeth Robins, died 1936, vol. III

Pennell, Henry Cholmondeley-, 1837–1915, vol. I

Pennell, Captain Henry Singleton, 1874–1907, vol. I

Pennell, Joseph, died 1926, vol. II

Pennell, Kenneth Eustace Lee, 1890–1948, vol. IV

Pennell, Lt-Col Richard, 1885–1963, vol. VI

Pennell, Vernon Charles, 1889–1976, vol. VII

Pennethorne, Rev. Gregory Walton, 1837–1915, vol. I

Penney, Air Cdre Howard Wright, 1903–1970, vol. VI

Penney, José Campbell, 1893–1976, vol. VII

Penney, Maj.-Gen. Sir Ronald Campbell; see Penney, Maj.-Gen. Sir W. R. C.

Penney, Scott Moncrieff, 1857–1932, vol. III

Penney, Rev. William Campbell, died 1945, vol. IV

Penney, Maj.-Gen. Sir (William) Ronald Campbell, 1896–1964, vol. VI

Pennington, Hon. Alan Joseph, 1837–1913, vol. I

Pennington, Brig.-Gen. Arthur Watson, 1867–1927, vol. II

Pennington, Lt-Gen. Sir Charles Richard, 1838–1910, vol. I

Pennington, Frederick, 1819–1914, vol. I

Pennington, Lt-Col Hubert Stanley Whitmore, died 1949, vol. IV

Pennington, Hon. John Warburton, 1870–1945, vol. IV

Pennington, Sydney Content Boeth, 1869–1937, vol. III

Pennoyer, Richard Edmands, 1885–1968, vol. VI

Penny, Rev. Alfred, 1845–1935, vol. III

Penny, Major Arthur Taylor, 1871–1915, vol. I

Penny, Edmund, 1852–1919, vol. II

Penny, Fanny Emily, died 1939, vol. III

Penny, Col Frederick Septimus, 1869–1955, vol. V

Penny, Sir James Downing, 1886–1978, vol. VII

Pennycuick, Hon. Alexander, 1844–1906, vol. I

Pennycuick, Charles Edward Ducat, died 1903, vol. I

Pennycuick, Brig. James Alexander Charles, 1890–1966, vol. VI

Pennycuick, Col John, 1841–1911, vol. I

Pennyman, Rev. Preb. William Geoffrey, died 1942, vol. IV

Pennymore, Lt-Col Percy George, 1869–1940, vol. III (A), vol. IV

Penoyre, John, 1870–1954, vol. V

Penrhyn, 2nd Baron, 1836–1907, vol. I

Penrhyn, 3rd Baron, 1864–1927, vol. II

Penrhyn, 4th Baron, 1894–1949, vol. IV

Penrhyn, 5th Baron, 1865–1967, vol. VI

Penrhyn, Rev. Oswald Henry Leycester, 1828–1918, vol. II

Penrhyn-Hornby, Charles Windham Leycester, 1873–1966, vol. VI

Penrose, Brig.-Gen. Cooper, 1855–1927, vol. II

Penrose, Dame Emily, 1858–1942, vol. IV

Penrose, Francis Cranmer, 1817–1903, vol. I

Penrose, Francis George, 1857–1932, vol. III

Penrose, J. Doyle, 1862–1932, vol. III

Penrose, James Edward, 1850–1936, vol. III

Penrose, Lionel Sharples, 1898–1972, vol. VII

Penrose, Sir Penrose Charles, 1822–1902, vol. I

Penrose-Welsted, Col Reginald Hugh, 1891–1966, vol. VI

Penson, Sir Henry; see Penson, Sir T. H.

Penson, John Hubert, 1893–1979, vol. VII

Penson, Dame Lillian Margery, 1896–1963, vol. VI

Penson, Sir (Thomas) Henry, 1864–1955, vol. V

Penston, Norah Lillian, 1903–1974, vol. VII

Pentecost, Rev. George F., 1841–1920, vol. II

Pentin, Rev. Herbert, 1873–1965, vol. VI

Pentland, 1st Baron, 1860–1925, vol. II

Pentland, Norman, 1912–1972, vol. VII

Penton, Maj.-Gen. Arthur Pole, 1854–1920, vol. II

Penton, Brig. Bertie Cyril, 1880–1962, vol. VI

Penton, Cyril Frederick, 1886–1960, vol. V

Penton, Sir Edward, 1875–1967, vol. VI

Penton, Frederick Thomas, 1851–1929, vol. III

Penton, Col Richard Hugh, 1863–1934, vol. III

Pentreath, Ven. Edwyn Sandys Wetmore, 1846–1913, vol. I

Penzance, 1st Baron, 1816–1899, vol. I

Penzer, Norman Mosley, 1892–1960, vol. V

Pepler, Sir George Lionel, 1882–1959, vol. V

Peploe, Rev. Hanmer William W.; see Webb-Peploe.

Peploe, Mrs J. R.; see Stevenson, D. E.

Peploe, S. J., died 1935, vol. III

Pepper, Augustus Joseph, died 1935, vol. III

Pepper, Sir Francis Henry, died 1936, vol. III

Pepper, George Wharton, 1867–1961, vol. VI

Pepperell, Elizabeth Maud, (E. M. Brewin), 1914–1971, vol. VII

Peppiatt, Sir Leslie Ernest, 1891–1968, vol. VI

Pepys, Rev. Charles Sidney, 1875–1927, vol. II

Pepys, Rt Rev. George Christopher Cutts, 1914–1974, vol. VII

Pepys, George Digby, 1868–1957, vol. V

Pepys, Col Gerald Leslie, 1879–1936, vol. III

Pepys, Rev. Herbert George, 1830–1918, vol. II

Pepys, Walter Evelyn, 1885–1966, vol. VI

Perak, HH Sultan of, died 1916, vol. II

Perak, HH Sultan of, 1887–1948, vol. IV

Perceval, Col Charles C., 1866–1937, vol. III

Perceval, Col Christopher Peter Westby, 1890–1967, vol. VI

Perceval, Brig.-Gen. Claude John, 1864–1932, vol. III

Perceval, Maj.-Gen. Sir Edward Maxwell, 1861–1955, vol. V

Perceval, Sir Westby Brook, 1854–1928, vol. II

Perceval-Maxwell, Magdalen, (Mrs Patrick Perceval-Maxwell); *see* King-Hall, M.

Percival, Archibald Stanley, 1862–1935, vol. III

Percival, Lt-Gen. Arthur Ernest, 1887–1966, vol. VI

Percival, Major Arthur Jex-Blake, 1870–1914, vol. I

Percival, Francis William, *died* 1929, vol. III

Percival, Col Sir Harold Franz Passawer, 1876–1944, vol. IV

Percival, Harold Stanley, 1868–1914, vol. I

Percival, Rt Rev. John, 1834–1918, vol. II

Percival, John, *died* 1949, vol. IV

Percival, Sir John Hope, 1870–1954, vol. V

Percival, Rev. Preb. Launcelot Jefferson, 1869–1941, vol. IV

Percival, Philip Edward, 1872–1939, vol. III

Percival, Sir Tom, 1877–1933, vol. III

Percival, Rev. Wilfred Ernest Holtzendorff, 1861–1935, vol. III

Percy, Earl; Henry Algernon George, 1871–1909, vol. I

Percy of Newcastle, 1st Baron, 1887–1958, vol. V

Percy, Algernon Heber-, 1845–1911, vol. I

Percy, Lord Algernon Malcolm Arthur, 1851–1933, vol. III

Percy, Charles, *died* 1929, vol. III

Percy, Esmé; *see* Percy, S. E.

Percy, Sir James Campbell, 1869–1928, vol. II

Percy, Maj.-Gen. Sir Jocelyn, 1871–1952, vol. V

Percy, (Saville) Esmé, 1887–1957, vol. V

Percy, Col Lord William Richard, 1882–1963, vol. VI

Percy-Chapman, Major William, 1850–1932, vol. III

Perdue, Hon. William Egerton, 1850–1933, vol. III

Peregrine, Rev. David Wilkie, 1859–1940, vol. III

Pereira, Adeodato Anthony, 1889–1965, vol. VI

Pereira, Maj.-Gen. Sir Cecil Edward, 1869–1942, vol. IV

Pereira, Fredrick Linwood Clinton, 1880–1958, vol. V

Pereira, Brig.-Gen. George Edward, 1865–1923, vol. II

Pereira, Rt Rev. Henry Horace, 1845–1926, vol. II

Pereira, Sir Horace Alvarez de Courcy, 1879–1963, vol. VI

Pereira, Pedro T.; *see* Theotonio Pereira.

Pereira, Richard Lionel, 1880–1960, vol. V

Perelman, Sidney Joseph, 1904–1979, vol. VII

Peren, Sir Geoffrey Sylvester, 1892–1980, vol. VII

Perez, Sir Joseph Leon Mathieu-, 1896–1967, vol. VI

Perfect, Captain Herbert Mosley, 1867–1928, vol. II

Perier, Jean Paul Pierre C.; *see* Casimir-Perier.

Peries, Sir Albert; *see* Peries, Sir P. P. A. F.

Peries, Sir (Pattiya Pathirannahalgae) Albert (Frederick), 1900–1967, vol. VI

Perini, Rt Rev. Paul, 1867–1932, vol. III

Peritz, Rev. Ismar J., 1863–1950, vol. IV (A), vol. V

Perkin, Arthur George, 1861–1937, vol. III

Perkin, Sir Athol; *see* Perkin, Sir E. A. O.

Perkin, (Edwin) Graham, 1929–1975, vol. VII

Perkin, Sir (Emil) Athol (Owen), 1889–1951, vol. V

Perkin, Frederick Mollwo, *died* 1928, vol. II

Perkin, Graham; *see* Perkin, E. G.

Perkin, Sir William Henry, 1838–1907, vol. I

Perkin, William Henry, 1860–1929, vol. III

Perkins, Gen. Sir Æneas, 1834–1901, vol. I

Perkins, Alan Hubert Banbury, 1898–1977, vol. VII

Perkins, Sir (Albert) Edward, 1908–1977, vol. VII

Perkins, Lt-Col Alfred Edward, *born* 1863, vol. II

Perkins, Col Alfred Thrale, 1843–1934, vol. III

Perkins, Major Alfred Thrale, 1869–1935, vol. III

Perkins, Brig.-Gen. Arthur Ernest John, *died* 1921, vol. II

Perkins, Sir Edward; *see* Perkins, Sir A. E.

Perkins, Col Sir Edwin King, 1855–1937, vol. III

Perkins, Rev. E(rnest) Benson, 1881–1974, vol. VII

Perkins, Frances, *died* 1965, vol. VI

Perkins, Rev. Francis Leonard, 1865–1932, vol. III

Perkins, Sir Frederick, 1826–1902, vol. I

Perkins, Rev. Canon Frederick Howard, *died* 1977, vol. VII

Perkins, Frederick William, *died* 1938, vol. III

Perkins, George, *died* 1979, vol. VII

Perkins, Col George Forder, 1884–1972, vol. VII

Perkins, George Walbridge, 1862–1920, vol. II

Perkins, Harry Innes, *died* 1924, vol. II

Perkins, J. H. Raymond R.; *see* Roze, Raymond.

Perkins, Rev. Jocelyn Henry Temple, 1870–1962, vol. VI

Perkins, Lt-Col John Charles Campbell, 1866–1916, vol. II

Perkins, Joseph John, *died* 1928, vol. II

Perkins, Norman Stuart, 1904–1972, vol. VII

Perkins, Surg.-Captain Robert Clerk, *died* 1916, vol. I, vol. II

Perkins, Robert Cyril Layton, 1866–1955, vol. V

Perkins, Robert George, 1850–1922, vol. II

Perkins, Thomas Luff, 1867–1940, vol. III

Perkins, Walter Frank, 1865–1946, vol. IV

Perkins, Rev. William, 1843–1922, vol. II

Perkins, William Jackson, *died* 1939, vol. III

Perkins, William Turner, *died* 1927, vol. II

Perks, Sir Malcolm; *see* Perks, Sir R. M. M.

Perks, Sir (Robert) Malcolm (Mewburn), 2nd Bt, 1892–1979, vol. VII

Perks, Sir Robert William, 1st Bt, 1849–1934, vol. III

Perks, Sydney, *died* 1944, vol. IV

Perley, Rt Hon. Sir George Halsey, 1857–1938, vol. III

Perlo, Rt Rev. G. O. Filippo, 1873–1948, vol. IV

Perlo, Rt Rev. P. G. Gabriele, 1879–1948, vol. IV

Pernet, George, 1861–1940, vol. III

Perodeau, Hon. Narcisse, 1851–1932, vol. III

Perowne, Rt Rev. Arthur William Thomson, 1867–1948, vol. IV

Perowne, Rev. Edward Henry, 1826–1906, vol. I
Perowne, Rt Rev. John James Stewart, 1823–1904, vol. I (A)
Perowne, Sir John Victor Thomas Woolrych Tait, 1897–1951, vol. V
Perowne, Ven. Thomas John, 1868–1954, vol. V
Perowne, Ven. Thomas Thomason, *died* 1913, vol. I
Perram, George James, 1848–1939, vol. III
Perrault, Hon. Joseph Edouard, 1874–1948, vol. IV
Perreau, Brig.-Gen. Arthur Montagu, 1870–1953, vol. V
Perreau, Col Charles Noel, 1874–1952, vol. V
Perree, Walter Francis, 1871–1950, vol. IV
Perren, Edward Arthur, 1900–1978, vol. VII
Perrier, Edmond, 1844–1921, vol. II
Perrin, Alice, 1867–1934, vol. III
Perrin, Harold Ernest, 1877–1948, vol. IV
Perrin, Harry Crane, 1865–1953, vol. V
Perrin, William Gordon, 1874–1931, vol. III
Perrin, Rt Rev. William Willcox, 1848–1934, vol. III
Perring, Engr Rear-Adm. Harold Hepworth, 1885–1949, vol. IV
Perring, Col Sir John, 1870–1948, vol. IV
Perring, Rev. Sir Philip, 4th Bt, 1828–1920, vol. II
Perring, Sir William, 1866–1937, vol. III
Perring, William George Arthur, 1898–1951, vol. V
Perrins, Charles William Dyson, 1864–1958, vol. V
Perris, Ernest A., *died* 1961, vol. VI
Perris, George Herbert, 1866–1920, vol. II
Perron, Hon. Joseph Léonide, 1872–1930, vol. III
Perrott, Arthur Finch, 1892–1969, vol. VI
Perrott, Sir Herbert Charles, 6th Bt, 1849–1922, vol. II
Perrott, Samuel Wright, 1870–1964, vol. VI
Perrott, Maj.-Gen. Sir Thomas, 1851–1919, vol. II
Perry, 1st Baron, 1878–1956, vol. V
Perry, Alan Cecil, 1892–1971, vol. VII
Perry, Sir Allan, 1860–1929, vol. III
Perry, Rev. Arthur John, *died* 1926, vol. II
Perry, Maj.-Gen. Aylesworth Bowen, 1860–1956, vol. V
Perry, Bliss, 1860–1954, vol. V
Perry, Sir Cooper; *see* Perry, Sir E. C.
Perry, Edward William, 1891–1971, vol. VII
Perry, Sir (Edwin) Cooper, 1856–1938, vol. III
Perry, Lt-Col Ernest Middleton, 1878–1963, vol. VI
Perry, Lt-Col Francis Frederic, 1854–1940, vol. III
Perry, Sir Frank Tennyson, 1887–1946, vol. VI
Perry, Ven. George Gresley, 1820–1897, vol. I
Perry, Rev. George Henry, 1854–1935, vol. III
Perry, Sir Gerald Raoul de C.; *see* de Courcy-Perry.
Perry, Maj.-Gen. Henry Marrian, 1884–1955, vol. V
Perry, Maj.-Gen. Sir Hugh Whitchurch, 1861–1938, vol. III
Perry, Rt Rev. James De Wolf, 1871–1947, vol. IV
Perry, John, 1850–1920, vol. II
Perry, Hon. John, 1845–1922, vol. II
Perry, Rear-Adm. John Laisné, *died* 1917, vol. II
Perry, John Tavenor, 1842–1915, vol. II

Perry, Rev. Nathaniel Irwin, 1867–1931, vol. III
Perry, Ralph Barton, 1876–1957, vol. V
Perry, Robert Grosvenor, 1873–1949, vol. IV
Perry, Samuel Frederick, 1877–1954, vol. V
Perry, Rev. Stephen Nugent, 1861–1941, vol. IV
Perry, Sir (Thomas) Wilfred, 1899–1979, vol. VII
Perry, Sir Wilfred; *see* Perry, Sir T. W.
Perry, Rev. William, *died* 1948, vol. IV
Perry, Sir William, 1863–1956, vol. V
Perry, Sir William, 1885–1968, vol. VI
Perry, William James, *died* 1949, vol. IV
Perry, Sir William Payne, 1858–1931, vol. III
Perse, St John; *see* Léger, M.-R. A. St-L.
Pershing, Gen. John Joseph, 1860–1948, vol. IV
Persse, Burton Walter, 1854–1935, vol. III
Pertab Singhji, Gen. Sir, 1845–1922, vol. II
Perth, 14th Earl of, **and Melfort,** 6th Earl of, 1807–1902, vol. I
Perth, 15th Earl of, 1871–1937, vol. III
Perth, 16th Earl of, 1876–1951, vol. V
Pertinax; *see* Géraud, C. J. A.
Pertwee, Rev. Arthur, *died* 1919, vol. II
Pertwee, Captain Herbert Guy, 1893–1978, vol. VII
Pertwee, Roland, *died* 1963, vol. VI
Perugini, Charles Edward, *died* 1918, vol. II
Perugini, Kate, *died* 1929, vol. III
Perugini, Mark Edward, *died* 1948, vol. IV
Pery-Knox-Gore, Col Arthur Francis Gore, 1880–1954, vol. V
Peshall, Rev. Charles John Eyre, 1881–1957, vol. V
Peshall, Samuel Frederick, 1882–1977, vol. VII
Pestangi, Jehangir Khan Bahadur, *died* 1914, vol. I
Pétain, Philippe, 1856–1951, vol. V
Petavel, James William, 1870–1945, vol. IV
Petavel, Sir Joseph Ernest, 1873–1936, vol. III
Peter, Bernard Hartley, 1885–1970, vol. VI
Peter, Sir John Charles, 1863–1939, vol. III
Peterkin, Col Alfred, 1854–1929, vol. III
Peterkin, Lt-Col Charles Duncan, 1887–1962, vol. VI
Peterkin, Rt Rev. George William, 1841–1916, vol. II
Peters, Hon. Arthur, 1854–1908, vol. I
Peters, Arthur, *died* 1956, vol. V
Peters, Rev. Canon Arthur E. G., 1866–1943, vol. IV
Peters, Adm. Sir Arthur Malcolm, 1888–1979, vol. VII
Peters, Augustus Dudley, 1892–1973, vol. VII
Peters, Bernard George, 1903–1967, vol. VI
Peters, Sir Byron; *see* Peters, Sir L. B.
Peters, Edwin Arthur, *died* 1945, vol. IV
Peters, Captain Frederic Thornton, *died* 1942, vol. IV
Peters, Sir George Henry, 1853–1931, vol. III
Peters, Major John Weston Parsons, 1864–1924, vol. II, and vol. III
Peters, Sir (Lindsley) Byron, 1867–1939, vol. III
Peters, Sidney John, 1885–1976, vol. VII
Peters, Sir William, 1889–1964, vol. VI
Peters, Maj.-Gen. William Henry Brooke, 1842–1913, vol. I
Petersen, Sir William, 1856–1925, vol. II

Peterson, Sir Arthur Frederick, 1859–1922, vol. II
Peterson, Brig.-Gen. Frederick Hopewell, 1864–1925, vol. II
Peterson, John Carlos Kennedy, 1876–1955, vol. V
Peterson, John Magnus, 1902–1978, vol. VII
Peterson, Margaret, 1883–1933, vol. III
Peterson, Sir Maurice Drummond, 1889–1952, vol. V
Peterson, Sir William, 1856–1921, vol. II
Peterson, Lt-Col William Gordon, 1888–1930, vol. III
Petfield, Sir Arthur Henry, 1912–1974, vol. VII
Pethebridge, Col Sir Samuel Augustus, 1862–1918, vol. II
Petheram, Sir William Comer, 1835–1922, vol. II
Petherick, Captain Cyril Hamley, 1893–1944, vol. IV
Pethick-Lawrence, 1st Baron, 1871–1961, vol. VI
Petigara, Khan Bahadur Kavasji Jamshedji, 1877–1941, vol. IV
Petit, Sir Dinshaw Manockjee, 1st Bt, 1823–1901, vol. I
Petit, Sir Dinshaw Manockjee, 2nd Bt, 1873–1933, vol. III
Petit, Rt Rev. John Edward, 1895–1973, vol. VII
Petit, Rev. Paul, 1856–1941, vol. IV
Petley, Eaton Wallace, 1850–1913, vol. I
Petman, Charles Earle Bevan, 1866–1939, vol. III
Peto, Sir Basil, 1st Bt (cr 1927), 1862–1945, vol. IV
Peto, Major (Basil Arthur) John, 1900–1954, vol. V
Peto, Brig. Sir Christopher Henry Maxwell, 3rd Bt (cr 1927), 1897–1980, vol. VII
Peto, Dorothy Olivia Georgiana, 1886–1974, vol. VII
Peto, Comdr Sir Francis; see Peto, Comdr Sir H. F. M.
Peto, Sir Geoffrey Kelsall, 1878–1956, vol. V
Peto, Gladys Emma, 1890–1977, vol. VII
Peto, Sir Henry, 2nd Bt (cr 1855), 1840–1938, vol. III
Peto, Comdr Sir (Henry) Francis (Morton), 3rd Bt (cr 1855), 1889–1978, vol. VII
Peto, Lt-Col Sir (James) Michael, 2nd Bt (cr 1927), 1894–1971, vol. VII
Peto, Major John; see Peto, Major B. A. J.
Peto, Mrs Mechtilde; see Lichnowsky, Princess Mechtilde.
Peto, Lt-Col Sir Michael; see Peto, Lt-Col Sir J. M.
Petre, 14th Baron, 1858–1908, vol. I
Petre, 15th Baron, 1864–1908, vol. I
Petre, 16th Baron, 1890–1914, vol. I
Petre, Hon. Albert Henry, 1832–1917, vol. II
Petre, Major Edward Henry, 1881–1941, vol. IV
Petre, Edward Oswald Gabriel T.; see Turville-Petre.
Petre, Francis Loraine, 1852–1925, vol. II
Petre, Francis William, 1847–1918, vol. II
Petre, Sir George Glynn, 1822–1905, vol. I
Petre, Major Henry Aloysius, 1884–1962, vol. VI
Petre, Col Henry Cecil, 1861–1939, vol. III
Petre, Maud D. M., died 1942, vol. IV
Petre, Lt-Col Oswald Henry Philip T.; see Turville-Petre.

Petre, Maj.-Gen. Roderic Loraine, 1887–1971, vol. VII
Petre, Rear-Adm. Walter Reginald Glynn, 1873–1942, vol. IV
Petri, Egon, 1881–1962, vol. VI
Petrides, Sir Philip Bertie, 1881–1956, vol. V
Petrie, Ven. Alan Julian, 1888–1947, vol. IV
Petrie, Alfred Alexander Webster, 1884–1962, vol. VI
Petrie, Sir Charles, 1st Bt, 1853–1920, vol. II
Petrie, Sir Charles Alexander, 3rd Bt, 1895–1977, vol. VII
Petrie, Lt-Col Charles Louis Rowe, 1866–1922, vol. II
Petrie, Sir David, 1879–1961, vol. VI
Petrie, Sir Edward Lindsay Haddon, 2nd Bt, 1881–1927, vol. II
Petrie, Sir Flinders; see Petrie, Sir W. M. F.
Petrie, Ven. Frederick Herbert, 1875–1948, vol. IV
Petrie, Graham, 1859–1940, vol. III
Petrie, Col Ricardo Dartnel, 1861–1925, vol. II
Petrie, Sir (William Matthew) Flinders, 1853–1942, vol. IV
Petter, Sir Ernest Willoughby, 1873–1954, vol. V
Petticrew, Rev. Francis, died 1909, vol. I
Pettigrew, Sir Andrew Hislop, 1857–1942, vol. IV
Pettigrew, James Bell, 1834–1908, vol. I
Peyton, Sir Algernon, 7th Bt, 1889–1962, vol. VI
Peyton, Sir Algernon Francis, 6th Bt, 1855–1916, vol. II
Peyton, Francis, 1823–1905, vol. I
Peyton, Guy Wynne Alfred, 1862–1950, vol. IV
Peyton, Rev. Thomas Thornhill, 1856–1927, vol. II
Peyton, Gen. Sir William Eliot, 1866–1931, vol. III
Pfeiffer, Rudolf, 1889–1979, vol. VII
Pfeil, Leonard Bessemer, 1898–1969, vol. VI
Phair, Rev. Ernest Edward Maxwell, 1870–1915, vol. I
Phair, Rt Rev. John Percy, 1876–1967, vol. VI
Phayre, Lt-Gen. Sir Arthur, 1856–1940, vol. III
Phear, Arthur George, 1867–1959, vol. V
Phear, Sir John Budd, 1825–1905, vol. I
Phear, Rev. Samuel George, 1829–1918, vol. II
Phelan, Edward Joseph, 1888–1967, vol. VI
Phelan, Major Ernest Cyril, vol. II
Phelan, Maj.-Gen. Frederick Ross, 1885–1970, vol. VI (AII)
Phelan, Rt Rev. Patrick, 1860–1925, vol. II
Phelips, William Robert, 1846–1919, vol. II
Phelps, Lt-Gen. Arthur, 1837–1920, vol. II
Phelps, Brig.-Gen. Arthur, 1867–1940, vol. III
Phelps, Most Rev. Francis Robinson, 1863–1938, vol. III
Phelps, Rev. Lancelot Ridley, 1853–1936, vol. III
Phelps, William Lyon, 1865–1943, vol. IV
Phelps, William Peyton, 1865–1942, vol. IV
Phibbs, Sir Charles, 1878–1964, vol. VI
Philbrick, Arthur James, 1866–1941, vol. IV
Philbrick, Frederick Adolphus, 1836–1910, vol. I
Philby, Harry St John Bridger, 1885–1960, vol. V
Philby, Captain Ralph Montague, 1884–1969, vol. VI
Philip, Very Rev. Adam, 1856–1945, vol. IV
Philip, Alexander, 1911–1979, vol. VII

532

Philip, Anne Glenday, 1878–1952, vol. V
Philip, Charles Lyall, 1881–1951, vol. V
Philip, James Charles, 1873–1941, vol. IV
Philip, Sir (James) Randall, 1900–1957, vol. V
Philip, Sir Randall; see Philip, Sir J. R.
Philip, Sir Robert William, 1857–1939, vol. III
Philip, William Marshall, 1872–1932, vol. III
Philipe, Maj.-Gen. Arthur Terence de R.; see de Rhé- Philipe.
Philipp, John, 1869–1938, vol. III (A), vol. III
Philipps, Sir Charles Edward Gregg, 1st Bt (cr 1887), 1840–1928, vol. II
Philipps, Lt-Col Sir Grismond Picton, 1898–1967, vol. VI
Philipps, Captain Sir Henry Erasmus Edward, 2nd Bt (cr 1887), 1871–1938, vol. III
Philipps, Maj.-Gen. Sir Ivor, 1861–1940, vol. III
Philipps, Rev. Sir James Erasmus, 12th Bt (cr 1621), 1824–1912, vol. I
Philipps, Sir John Erasmus Gwynne Alexander, 3rd Bt (cr 1887), 1915–1948, vol. IV
Philipps, Sir Richard Foley F., 4th Bt (cr 1887); see Foley-Philipps.
Philipps, Tracy, 1890–1959, vol. V
Philips, Austin; see Philips, J. A. D.
Philips, Lt-Col Burton Henry, 1858–1927, vol. II
Philips, F. C., 1849–1921, vol. II
Philips, John Austin Drury, 1875–1947, vol. IV
Philips, Lt-Col John Lionel, 1878–1975, vol. VII
Philips, Brig.-Gen. Lewis Francis, 1870–1935, vol. III
Philipson, Sir George Hare, 1836–1918, vol. II
Philipson, Hilton, 1892–1941, vol. IV
Philipson, Mrs Hilton, (Mabel Russell), 1887–1951, vol. V
Philipson, Hylton, 1866–1935, vol. III
Philipson, Hylton Ralph Murray-, 1902–1934, vol. III
Philipson, Robert, 1860–1916, vol. II
Philipson-Stow, Sir Elliot Philipson; see Stow.
Philipson-Stow, Sir Frederic Lawrence; see Stow.
Philipson-Stow, Sir Frederic Samuel; see Stow.
Philipson-Stow, Robert Frederic; see Stow.
Phillimore, 1st Baron, 1845–1929, vol. III
Phillimore, 2nd Baron, 1879–1947, vol. IV
Phillimore, Sir Augustus, 1822–1897, vol. I
Phillimore, Rt Hon. Sir Henry Josceline, 1910–1974, vol. VII
Phillimore, John Swinnerton, 1873–1926, vol. II
Phillimore, Col Reginald Henry, 1879–1964, vol. VI
Phillimore, Adm. Sir Richard Fortescue, 1864–1940, vol. III
Phillimore, Ven. Hon. Stephen Henry, 1881–1956, vol. V
Phillimore, Captain Valentine Egerton Bagot, 1875–1945, vol. IV
Phillimore, William P. W., 1853–1913, vol. I
Phillip, Colin Bent, 1855–1932, vol. III
Phillipps, Maj.-Gen. Henry Pye, 1836–1927, vol. II
Phillipps, Henry Vivian, died 1955, vol. V
Phillipps, Sir Herbert; see Phillipps, Sir W. H.
Phillipps, Lt-Gen. Picton, 1869–1928, vol. II
Phillipps, William Douglas, died 1932, vol. III

Phillipps, Sir (William) Herbert, 1847–1935, vol. III
Phillipps-Wolley, Sir Clive, 1854–1918, vol. II
Phillips, Col Alan Andrew, 1889–1972, vol. VII
Phillips, Alban William Housego, 1914–1975, vol. VII
Phillips, Alison; see Phillips, W. A.
Phillips, Sir Beaumont; see Phillips, Sir F. B.
Phillips, Sir Benjamin Samuel F.; see Faudel-Phillips.
Phillips, Rt Rev. Charles, 1847–1906, vol. I
Phillips, Sir Charles; see Phillips, Sir E. C.
Phillips, Charles James, 1852–1930, vol. III
Phillips, Sir Claude, died 1924, vol. II
Phillips, Maj.-Gen. Sir Edward, 1889–1973, vol. VII
Phillips, Sir (Edward) Charles, 1888–1974, vol. VII
Phillips, Major Edward Hawtin, 1876–1914, vol. I
Phillips, Eleanor Addison, 1874–1952, vol. V
Phillips, Col Eric Charles Malcolm, 1883–1957, vol. V
Phillips, Ernest, 1870–1956, vol. V
Phillips, Rear-Adm. Esmonde; see Phillips, Rear-Adm. P. E.
Phillips, Very Rev. Evan Owen, died 1897, vol. I
Phillips, Maj.-Gen. Sir Farndale, 1905–1961, vol. VI
Phillips, Rev. Forbes Alexander, 1866–1917, vol. II
Phillips, Francis, 1835–1925, vol. II
Phillips, Sir Frederick, 1884–1943, vol. IV
Phillips, Sir (Frederick) Beaumont, 1890–1957, vol. V
Phillips, Frederick William, 1879–1956, vol. V
Phillips, Col Geoffrey Francis, 1880–1968, vol. VI
Phillips, George, 1876–1948, vol. IV
Phillips, Surg. Rear-Adm. George, 1902–1980, vol. VII
Phillips, Major George Edward, died 1902, vol. I
Phillips, Sir George Faudel F.; see Faudel-Phillips.
Phillips, Brig.-Gen. George Fraser, 1863–1921, vol. II
Phillips, George Godfrey, 1900–1965, vol. VI
Phillips, Bt Lt-Col George Ingleton, 1866–1936, vol. III
Phillips, Rev. Godfrey Edward, 1878–1963, vol. VI
Phillips, Gordon, 1890–1952, vol. V
Phillips, Captain H. C. B., died 1906, vol. I
Phillips, Harold Ernest, 1877–1941, vol. IV
Phillips, Henry Bettesworth, 1866–1950, vol. IV
Phillips, Vice-Adm. Sir Henry Clarmont, died 1968, vol. VI
Phillips, Rev. Henry Frederick, died 1914, vol. I
Phillips, Major Henry Jacob Vaughan, died 1914, vol. I
Phillips, Sir Herbert, 1878–1957, vol. V
Phillips, Brig.-Gen. Herbert de Touffreville, 1862–1933, vol. III
Phillips, Hubert, 1891–1964, vol. VI
Phillips, Hugh Richard, 1873–1932, vol. III
Phillips, Ven. Hugh Stowell, 1865–1940, vol. III
Phillips, J. S. Ragland, 1850–1919, vol. II
Phillips, James Falkner, died 1933, vol. III
Phillips, John, died 1917, vol. II
Phillips, Sir John, 1855–1928, vol. II
Phillips, Col John Alfred Steele, 1882–1960, vol. V

Phillips, Major John Charles S.; *see* Spencer-Phillips.
Phillips, Rev. John Francis, 1860–1934, vol. III
Phillips, Lt-Col John Frederick L.; *see* Lort Phillips.
Phillips, John George P.; *see* Porter-Phillips.
Phillips, John Henry Hood, 1902–1977, vol. VII
Phillips, Very Rev. John Leoline, 1879–1947, vol. IV
Phillips, Sir John Randal, 1857–1945, vol. IV
Phillips, Rev. Lawrence Arthur, 1870–1949, vol. IV
Phillips, Lawrence Barnett, 1842–1922, vol. II
Phillips, Leonard George, 1890–1975, vol. VII
Phillips, Maj.-Gen. Sir Leslie Gordon, 1892–1966, vol. VI
Phillips, Sir Lionel, 1st Bt, 1855–1936, vol. III
Phillips, Captain Sir Lionel Francis, 2nd Bt, 1914–1944, vol. IV
Phillips, Sir Lionel Lawson Faudel F.; *see* Faudel-Phillips.
Phillips, Llewellyn Powell, 1871–1927, vol. II
Phillips, Mrs McGrigor, (Dorothy Una Ratcliffe), *died* 1967, vol. VI
Phillips, Mandeville Blackwood, 1848–1929, vol. III
Phillips, Marion, 1881–1932, vol. III
Phillips, Montague Fawcett, 1885–1969, vol. VI
Phillips, Morgan Hector, 1885–1953, vol. V
Phillips, Morgan Walter, 1902–1963, vol. VI
Phillips, Lt-Col Noel Clive, 1883–1961, vol. VI
Phillips, Father Oliver Rodie V.; *see* Vassall-Phillips.
Phillips, Maj.-Gen. Owen Forbes, 1882–1966, vol. VI
Phillips, Patrick Edward, 1907–1976, vol. VII
Phillips, Patrick Laurence, 1912–1980, vol. VII
Phillips, Sir Percival, 1877–1937, vol. III
Phillips, Sir Philip David, 1897–1970, vol. VI
Phillips, Rear-Adm. (Philip) Esmonde, 1888–1960, vol. V
Phillips, Reginald William, 1854–1926, vol. II
Phillips, Robert Randal, 1878–1967, vol. VI
Phillips, Air Cdre Ronald Lancelot, 1909–1956, vol. V
Phillips, Sir Rowland Ricketts, 1904–1976, vol. VII
Phillips, Rt Rev. Samuel Charles, 1881–1974, vol. VII
Phillips, Rev. Sidney, 1840–1917, vol. II
Phillips, Sidney, *died* 1951, vol. V
Phillips, Sidney Hill, 1882–1962, vol. VI
Phillips, Stephen, *died* 1915, vol. I (A)
Phillips, Rev. Stephen, *died* 1919, vol. II
Phillips, Rev. Theodore Evelyn Reece, 1868–1942, vol. IV
Phillips, Maj.-Gen. Thomas, 1837–1913, vol. I
Phillips, Rev. Thomas, 1868–1936, vol. III
Phillips, Lt-Col Thomas Richmond, 1866–1963, vol. VI
Phillips, Rear-Adm. Thomas Tyacke, 1832–1920, vol. II
Phillips, Sir Thomas Williams, 1883–1966, vol. VI
Phillips, Ven. Thompson, *died* 1909, vol. I
Phillips, Adm. Sir Tom Spencer Vaughan, 1888–1941, vol. IV

Phillips, Wallace Banta, 1886–1952, vol. V
Phillips, (Walter) Alison, 1864–1950, vol. IV
Phillips, Bt-Col Walter Ernest, 1858–1911, vol. I
Phillips, Walter R., 1855–1930, vol. III
Phillips, William, 1867–1941, vol. IV
Phillips, William, 1878–1968, vol. VI
Phillips, Lt-Col William Eric, 1893–1964, vol. VI
Phillips, William James, *died* 1963, vol. VI
Phillips, William Lambert Collyer, 1858–1924, vol. II
Phillips, Sir William Watkin, 1870–1933, vol. III
Phillips Brocklehurst, Charles Douglas Fergusson, 1904–1977, vol. VII
Phillipson, Andrew Tindal, 1910–1977, vol. VII
Phillipson, Coleman, 1875–1958, vol. V
Phillipson, John Tindal, 1865–1929, vol. III
Phillipson, Sir Sydney, 1892–1966, vol. VI
Phillott, Constance, *died* 1931, vol. III
Phillott, Lt-Col Douglas Craven, 1860–1930, vol. III
Phillpotts, Arthur Stephens, 1844–1920, vol. II
Phillpotts, Dame Bertha Surtees; *see* Newall, Dame B. S.
Phillpotts, Eden, 1862–1960, vol. V
Phillpotts, Adm. Edward Montgomery, 1871–1952, vol. V
Phillpotts, James Surtees, 1839–1930, vol. III
Phillpotts, Lt-Col Louis Murray, 1870–1916, vol. II
Phillpotts, Owen Surtees, 1870–1932, vol. III
Phillpotts, Sir Ralegh Buller, 1871–1950, vol. IV
Philp, Hon. Sir Robert, 1851–1922, vol. II
Philp, Lt-Col Robert, 1896–1980, vol. VII
Philp, Sir Roslyn Foster Bowie, 1895–1965, vol. VI
Philpot, Frederick Freeman, *died* 1916, vol. II
Philpot, Glyn Warren, 1884–1937, vol. III
Philpot, Joseph Henry, 1850–1939, vol. III
Philpot, Robert, 1849–1913, vol. I
Philpott, Rev. John Nigel, 1859–1932, vol. III
Philps, (Alan) Seymour, 1906–1956, vol. V
Philps, Seymour; *see* Philps, A. S.
Phimister, Rev. Alexander, *died* 1921, vol. II
Phin, Sir John, 1881–1955, vol. V
Phippen, Hon. Frank Hedley, 1862–1932, vol. III
Phipps, Brig. Charles Constantine, 1889–1958, vol. V
Phipps, Lt-Col Charles Edward, 1864–1946, vol. IV
Phipps, Col Charles Foskett, 1871–1931, vol. III
Phipps, Charles Nicholas Paul, 1845–1913, vol. I
Phipps, Rev. Constantine Osborne, 1861–1921, vol. II
Phipps, Sir Edmund Bampfylde, 1869–1947, vol. IV
Phipps, Sir Edmund Constantine Henry, 1840–1911, vol. I
Phipps, Rt Hon. Sir Eric Clare Edmund, 1875–1945, vol. IV
Phipps, Rev. Frederick, 1858–1934, vol. III
Phipps, Gerald Hastings, 1882–1973, vol. VII
Phipps, Hon. Harriet Lepel, *died* 1922, vol. II
Phipps, Henry, 1839–1930, vol. III
Phipps, Maj.-Gen. Herbert Clive, 1898–1975, vol. VII
Phipps, Dame Jessie Wilton, 1855–1934, vol. III
Phipps, Col John Hare, 1871–1936, vol. III
Phipps, Paul, 1880–1953, vol. V

Phipps, Ven. Richard, 1865–1934, vol. III
Phipps, Captain William Duncan, 1882–1967, vol. VI
Phipson, Col Edward Selby, 1884–1973, vol. VII
Phoenix, George, 1863–1935, vol. III
Phythian, John Ernest, 1858–1935, vol. III
Phythian-Adams, Rev. Canon William John Telia Phythian, 1888–1967, vol. VI
Piaget, Jean, 1896–1980, vol. VII
Piaggio, Henry Thomas Herbert, 1884–1967, vol. VI
Piatigorsky, Gregor, 1903–1976, vol. VII
Piatti, Alfredo, 1822–1901, vol. I
Pibworth, Charles James, 1878–1958, vol. V
Picard, Émile, 1856–1941, vol. IV
Picasso, Pablo Ruiz, 1881–1973, vol. VII
Piccard, Auguste, 1884–1962, vol. VI
Piccaver, Alfred, 1889–1958, vol. V
Picciotto, Cyril Moses, 1888–1940, vol. III
Pick, Surg. Rear-Adm. Bryan Pickering, 1879–1959, vol. V
Pick, Frank, 1878–1941, vol. IV
Pick, Thomas Pickering, 1841–1919, vol. II
Pick-Mangiagalli, Riccardo, 1882–1949, vol. IV
Pickard, Alexander, 1897–1972, vol. VII
Pickard, Benjamin, 1842–1904, vol. I
Pickard, Lt-Col Jocelyn Arthur Adair, 1885–1962, vol. VI
Pickard, Gp Captain Percy Charles, 1915–1944, vol. IV
Pickard, Col Ransom, 1867–1953, vol. V
Pickard, Sir Robert Howson, 1874–1949, vol. IV
Pickard-Cambridge, Sir Arthur Wallace, 1873–1952, vol. V
Pickard-Cambridge, Rev. Octavius, 1828–1917, vol. II
Pickard-Cambridge, William Adair, 1879–1957, vol. V
Picken, Andrew, 1886–1938, vol. III
Picken, David Kennedy, 1879–1956, vol. V
Picken, Ralph Montgomery Fullarton, 1884–1955, vol. V
Pickerill, Henry Percy, died 1956, vol. V
Pickering, Col Charles James, 1880–1951, vol. V
Pickering, Edward Charles, 1846–1919, vol. II
Pickering, Bt Col Emil William, 1882–1942, vol. IV
Pickering, Sir George Hunter, 1877–1971, vol. VII
Pickering, Sir George White, 1904–1980, vol. VII
Pickering, J. L., died 1912, vol. I
Pickering, Loring, 1888–1959, vol. V (A)
Pickering, Percival Spencer Umfreville, 1858–1920, vol. II
Pickering, Brig. Ralph Emerson, 1898–1962, vol. VI
Pickering, Wilfred Francis, 1915–1980, vol. VII
Pickering, Captain William, 1856–1933, vol. III
Pickering, William Alexander, 1840–1907, vol. I
Pickering, William Henry, 1858–1912, vol. I
Pickersgill, Frederick Richard, 1820–1900, vol. I
Pickersgill, William Clayton, 1846–1901, vol. I
Pickett, Rev. Henry John, died 1931, vol. III
Pickett, Jacob, 1835–1922, vol. II
Pickett, Rev. James, 1853–1918, vol. II
Pickford, Sir Alfred Donald, 1872–1947, vol. IV

Pickford, Sir Anthony Frederick Ingham, 1885–1970, vol. VI
Pickford, Mary, 1893–1979, vol. VII
Pickford, Hon. Mary Ada, died 1934, vol. III
Pickles, Edward Llewellyn, 1884–1949, vol. IV
Pickles, Sir John Sydney, 1898–1972, vol. VII
Pickles, Wilfred, 1904–1978, vol. VII
Pickles, William Norman, 1885–1969, vol. VI
Pickmere, Edward Ralph, died 1941, vol. IV
Pickop, Rev. James, 1847–1919, vol. II
Pickthall, Marmaduke William, 1875–1936, vol. III
Pickthall, Col Wallace Edward Colin, 1891–1948, vol. IV
Pickthorn, Rt Hon. Sir Kenneth William Murray, 1st Bt, 1892–1975, vol. VII
Pickup, Sir Arthur, 1878–1960, vol. V
Pickwoad, Col Edwin Hay, 1853–1932, vol. III
Pickworth, Sir Frederick, 1890–1959, vol. V
Picot, Francis Raymond, 1893–1971, vol. VII
Picot, Lt-Col Francis Slater, 1859–1939, vol. III
Picot, Lt-Col Henry Philip, 1857–1937, vol. III
Picton, Ven. Arnold Stanley, 1899–1962, vol. VI
Picton, James Allanson, 1832–1910, vol. I
Picton, Col Reginald Ernest, 1863–1932, vol. III
Picton-Turbervill, Edith, died 1960, vol. V
Pidcock, Air Vice-Marshal Geoffrey Arthur Henzell, 1897–1976, vol. VII
Piddington, Albert Bathurst, 1862–1945, vol. IV
Pidduck, Frederick Bernard, 1885–1952, vol. V
Pidsley, Brig. Wilfrid Gould, 1892–1967, vol. VI
Pielou, Douglas Percival, 1887–1927, vol. II
Pienaar, Maj.-Gen. Daniel Hermanus, 1893–1942, vol. IV
Pierce, Bedford, 1861–1932, vol. III
Pierce, Rev. Charles Frederick, 1877–1936, vol. III
Pierce, Rev. Francis Dormer, died 1923, vol. II
Pierce, Sir John, 1863–1949, vol. IV
Pierce, Robert, 1884–1968, vol. VI
Pierce, Stephen Rowland, 1896–1966, vol. VI
Piercy, 1st Baron, 1886–1966, vol. VI
Piercy, Benjamin Herbert, 1870–1941, vol. IV
Piercy, Norman Augustus Victor, 1891–1953, vol. V
Pieris, Sir Paulus Edward Deraniyagala, 1874–1959, vol. V
Pierpoint, Robert, 1845–1932, vol. III
Pierre, Hon. Charles Henry, 1878–1937, vol. III
Piers, Sir Charles Pigott, 9th Bt, 1870–1945, vol. IV
Piers, Sir Eustace Fitz-Maurice, 8th Bt, 1840–1913, vol. I
Pierse, Rev. Garrett, 1882–1932, vol. III
Pierson, Reginald Kirshaw, 1891–1948, vol. IV
Pierson, Warren Lee, 1896–1978, vol. VII
Pierssené, Sir Stephen Herbert, 1899–1966, vol. VI
Pieshkov, Alexei Maximovitch; see Gorky, Maxim.
Piggott, Maj.-Gen. Francis Stewart Gilderoy, 1883–1966, vol. VI
Piggott, Sir Francis Taylor, 1852–1925, vol. II
Piggott, Sir George Bettesworth, 1867–1952, vol. V
Piggott, Sir Henry Howard, 1871–1951, vol. V
Piggott, Col Joseph Clive, 1892–1975, vol. VII
Piggott, Julian Ito, 1888–1965, vol. VI
Piggott, Sir Theodore Caro, 1867–1944, vol. IV

Piggott, Rev. William Charter, *died* 1943, vol. IV
Pigot, Sir George, 5th Bt, 1850–1934, vol. III
Pigot, John H., 1863–1928, vol. II
Pigot, Brig.-Gen. Sir Robert, 6th Bt, 1882–1977, vol. VII
Pigot, Rev. William Melville, 1842–1916, vol. II
Pigott, Alan Desmond Frederick P.; *see* Pemberton-Pigott.
Pigott, Maj.-Gen. Alan John Keefe, 1892–1969, vol. VI
Pigott, Sir Charles Robert, 3rd Bt, 1835–1911, vol. I
Pigott, Sir Digby; *see* Pigott, Sir T. D.
Pigott, Brig. Frank Borkman, 1894–1971, vol. VII
Pigott, Lt-Col Grenville Edmund, 1870–1942, vol. IV
Pigott, Rt Rev. Harold Grant, 1894–1979, vol. VII
Pigott, Harry, *died* 1974, vol. VII
Pigott, John Robert Wilson, 1850–1928, vol. II
Pigott, Gp Captain (Joseph) Ruscombe (Wadham) S.; *see* Smyth-Pigott.
Pigott, Montague Horatio Mostyn Turtle, 1865–1927, vol. II
Pigott, Sir Paynton, 1840–1915, vol. I (A)
Pigott, Richard, 1861–1931, vol. III
Pigott, Col Robert Edward Pemberton, 1866–1943, vol. IV
Pigott, Gp Captain Ruscombe S.; *see* Smyth-Pigott.
Pigott, Sir Stephen J., 1880–1955, vol. V
Pigott, Sir (Thomas) Digby, 1840–1927, vol. II
Pigott, William; *see* Wales, Hubert.
Pigott, Vice-Adm. William Harvey, 1848–1924, vol. II
Pigott-Brown, Captain Sir John Hargreaves, 2nd Bt, 1913–1942, vol. IV
Pigou, Arthur Cecil, 1877–1959, vol. V
Pigou, Very Rev. Francis, 1832–1916, vol. II
Pike, Cecil Frederick, 1898–1968, vol. VI
Pike, Lt-Col Cuthbert Joseph, 1868–1947, vol. IV
Pike, Douglas Henry, 1908–1974, vol. VII
Pike, Col Ebenezer John Lecky, 1884–1965, vol. VI
Pike, Edmund William, 1838–1910, vol. I
Pike, Vice-Adm. Frederick Owen, 1851–1921, vol. II
Pike, John Milton, 1872–1940, vol. III (A), vol. IV
Pike, Joseph, *died* 1929, vol. III
Pike, Leonard Henry, 1885–1961, vol. VI
Pike, Most Rev. Robert Bonsall, 1905–1973, vol. VII
Pike, Maj.-Gen. Sir William Watson, 1860–1941, vol. IV
Pilcher, Lt-Col Alan Humphrey, 1898–1957, vol. V
Pilcher, Vice-Adm. Cecil Horace, 1877–1953, vol. V
Pilcher, Rt Rev. Charles Venn, 1879–1961, vol. VI
Pilcher, Maj.-Gen. Edgar Montagu, 1865–1947, vol. IV
Pilcher, George, 1882–1962, vol. VI
Pilcher, Sir Gonne St Clair, 1890–1966, vol. VI
Pilcher, Robert Stuart, 1882–1961, vol. VI
Pilcher, Maj.-Gen. Thomas David, 1858–1928, vol. II
Pilditch, Sir Denys, 1891–1975, vol. VII

Pilditch, Sir Philip Edward, 1st Bt, 1861–1948, vol. IV
Pilditch, Sir Philip Harold, 2nd Bt, 1890–1949, vol. IV
Pilditch, Sir Philip John Frederick, 3rd Bt, 1919–1954, vol. V
Pile, Gen. Sir Frederick Alfred, 2nd Bt, 1884–1976, vol. VII
Pile, Sir George Clarke, 1821–1906, vol. I
Pile, Sir George Laurie, 1857–1948, vol. IV
Pile, Sir Thomas Devereux, 1st Bt, 1856–1931, vol. III
Pilgrim, David; *see* Saunders, H. A. St G.
Pilgrim, Guy Ellcock, 1875–1943, vol. IV
Pilkington, Major Sir Arthur William Milborne-Swinnerton-, 13th Bt, 1898–1952, vol. V
Pilkington, Lt-Col Charles Raymond, 1875–1938, vol. III
Pilkington, Sir George Augustus, 1848–1916, vol. II
Pilkington, Harry Seymour Hoyle, 1869–1954, vol. V
Pilkington, Major Sir Henry, 1849–1930, vol. III
Pilkington, Col Henry Lionel, 1857–1914, vol. I
Pilkington, Col Herbert Edward, 1877–1956, vol. V
Pilkington, Col Lionel Edward, *died* 1952, vol. V
Pilkington, Sir Lionel Milborne Swinnerton, 11th Bt, 1835–1901, vol. I
Pilkington, M. Evelyn, 1879–1955, vol. V
Pilkington, Margaret, 1891–1974, vol. VII
Pilkington, Captain Sir Richard Antony, 1908–1976, vol. VII
Pilkington, Robert Rivington, *died* 1942, vol. IV
Pilkington, Sir Thomas Edward Milborne-Swinnerton-, 12th Bt, 1857–1944, vol. IV
Pilkington, Sir William Handcock, 1859–1905, vol. I
Pilkington, Col William Norman, 1877–1935, vol. III
Pilkington Jackson, Charles d'Orville; *see* Jackson.
Pillans, Charles Eustace, 1850–1919, vol. II (A), vol. III
Pilleau, Maj.-Gen. Gerald Arthur, 1896–1964, vol. VI
Pilleau, Major Henry Charles, 1866–1914, vol. I
Pilley, Charles, 1885–1937, vol. III
Pilley, John Gustave, 1899–1968, vol. VI
Pilling, Sir Guy; *see* Pilling, Sir H. G.
Pilling, Sir (Henry) Guy, 1886–1953, vol. V
Pilling, Tom Sharpley, 1921–1977, vol. VII
Pillsbury, Harry N., 1872–1906, vol. I
Pilot, Rev. William, 1841–1913, vol. I (A)
Pilson, Major Arthur Forde, 1865–1929, vol. III
Pilsudski, Joseph Clemens, 1867–1935, vol. III
Pilter, Sir John George, 1848–1935, vol. III
Pilter, Col William Frederick, 1831–1915, vol. I
Pim, Sir Alan William, *died* 1958, vol. V
Pim, Frederic William, 1839–1925, vol. II
Pim, Brig. George Adrien, 1888–1965, vol. VI
Pim, Howard, *died* 1934, vol. III
Pim, Rev. John, *died* 1932, vol. III
Pim, Rt Hon. Jonathan, 1858–1949, vol. IV
Pimlott, John Alfred Ralph, 1909–1969, vol. VI
Pinault, Col Louis Felix, 1852–1906, vol. I

Pinchard, Rev. Arnold Theophilus Biddulph, *died* 1934, vol. III
Pinches, Theophilus Goldridge, 1856–1934, vol. III
Pinchin, Arthur John Scott, *died* 1936, vol. III
Pinchin, Ernest Alfred, 1874–1929, vol. III
Pinching, Sir Horace Henderson, 1857–1935, vol. III
Pinchot, Gifford, 1865–1946, vol. IV
Pinckard, George Henry, *died* 1950, vol. IV
Pinckney, John Robert Hugh, 1876–1964, vol. VI
Pine-Coffin, Major John Edward, 1866–1919, vol. II
Pine-Coffin, Gen. Roger, 1847–1921, vol. II
Pinero, Sir Arthur Wing, 1855–1934, vol. III
Piney, Alfred, 1896–1965, vol. VI
Ping, Aubrey Charles, 1905–1978, vol. VII
Pinhey, Lt-Col Sir Alexander Fleetwood, 1861–1916, vol. II
Pinhorn, Col Henry Quinten, 1862–1929, vol. III
Pininfarina, Battista, 1895–1966, vol. VI
Pink, Col Francis John, 1857–1934, vol. III
Pink, Sir Harold Rufus, 1858–1952, vol. V
Pink, Ven. Hubert Arthur Stanley, 1905–1976, vol. VII
Pink, Sir Ivor Thomas Montague, 1910–1966, vol. VI
Pink, Air Cdre Richard Charles Montagu, 1888–1932, vol. III
Pink, Sir Thomas, 1855–1926, vol. II
Pink, Sir William, 1829–1906, vol. I
Pinkerton, John, 1845–1908, vol. I
Pinkerton, Robert Hamilton, 1855–1938, vol. III
Pinkham, Lt-Col Sir Charles, 1853–1938, vol. III
Pinkham, Rt Rev. William Cyprian, 1844–1928, vol. II
Pinkney, Col Edmund Walker Renny, 1876–1940, vol. III
Pinnell, Leonard George, 1896–1979, vol. VII
Pinney, Charles Robert, 1883–1945, vol. IV
Pinney, Maj.-Gen. Sir Reginald John, 1863–1943, vol. IV
Pinnock, Frank Frewin, 1902–1977, vol. VII
Pinsent, Dame Ellen Frances, 1866–1949, vol. IV
Pinsent, Gerald Hume Saverie, 1888–1976, vol. VII
Pinsent, Col John Ryland, 1888–1957, vol. V
Pinsent, Sir Richard Alfred, 1st Bt, 1852–1948, vol. IV
Pinsent, Sir Roy, 2nd Bt, 1883–1978, vol. VII
Pinto, Vivian de Sola, 1895–1969, vol. VI
Piper, Arthur William, 1865–1936, vol. III
Piper, Harold Bayard, 1894–1953, vol. V
Piper, Henry Mansell, 1890–1949, vol. IV
Piper, John Edwin, 1854–1938, vol. III
Piper, Stephen Harvey, 1887–1963, vol. VI
Piper, Air Marshal Sir Thomas William; *see* Piper, Air Marshal Sir Tim.
Piper, Air Marshal Sir Tim, (Thomas William), 1911–1978, vol. VII
Pipes, Hon. William Thomas, 1850–1908, vol. I
Pipon, Maj.-Gen. Henry, 1843–1924, vol. II
Pipon, Vice-Adm. Sir James Murray, 1882–1971, vol. VII
Pipon, John Pakenham, 1849–1899, vol. I
Pipon, Gen. Philip Gosset, 1824–1905, vol. I

Pipon, Philip James Griffiths, 1874–1960, vol. V
Pippard, Alfred John Sutton, 1891–1969, vol. VI
Pippett, Roger Samuel, 1895–1962, vol. VI
Pirandello, Luigi, 1867–1936, vol. III
Pirbright, 1st Baron, 1840–1903, vol. I
Pire, Rev. Père Dominique-Georges, 1910–1969, vol. VI
Pirenne, Henri, 1862–1935, vol. III
Pirie, Alexander Howard, 1875–1944, vol. IV
Pirie, Major Arthur Murray, 1869–1917, vol. II
Pirie, Maj.-Gen. Charles Patrick William, 1859–1933, vol. III
Pirie, Duncan Vernon, 1858–1931, vol. III
Pirie, Rev. George, 1843–1904, vol. I
Pirie, Sir George, 1863–1946, vol. IV
Pirie, Air Chief Marshal Sir George Clark, 1896–1980, vol. VII
Pirie-Gordon of Buthlaw, Christopher Martin, 1911–1980, vol. VII
Pirow, Hon. Oswald, *died* 1959, vol. V
Pirquet, Clemens, Freiherr von, 1874–1929, vol. III
Pirrie, 1st Viscount, 1847–1924, vol. II
Pirrie, Viscountess; (Margaret), *died* 1935, vol. III
Pirrie, Col Francis William, 1867–1948, vol. IV
Pisani, Salvator Aloysius, 1828–1908, vol. I
Pissarro, Lucien, 1863–1944, vol. IV
Piston, Walter, 1894–1976, vol. VII
Pitcher; *see* Binstead, A. M.
Pitcher, Col Duncan George, *born* 1839, vol. II
Pitcher, Air Cdre Duncan le Geyt, 1877–1944, vol. IV
Pitcher, William J. C., 1858–1925, vol. II
Pitchford, Lt-Col Herbert W.; *see* Watkins-Pitchford.
Pite, Arthur Beresford, 1861–1934, vol. III
Pite, Arthur Goodhart, 1896–1938, vol. III
Pite, William Alfred, 1860–1949, vol. IV
Pithie, Michael, 1846–1915, vol. I
Pitkeathly, Sir James Scott, 1882–1949, vol. IV
Pitman, Hon. Lord; James Campbell Pitman, 1864–1941, vol. IV
Pitman, Alfred, 1862–1952, vol. V
Pitman, Charles Edward, 1845–1933, vol. III
Pitman, Charles Murray, 1872–1948, vol. IV
Pitman, Captain Charles Robert Senhouse, 1890–1975, vol. VII
Pitman, Clement Fothergill, 1894–1973, vol. VII
Pitman, Frederick Islay, 1863–1942, vol. IV
Pitman, Sir Henry Alfred, 1808–1908, vol. I
Pitman, James Campbell; *see* Pitman, Hon. Lord.
Pitman, John Sitwell, 1860–1938, vol. III
Pitman, Captain Robert, 1836–1921, vol. II
Pitman, Maj.-Gen. Thomas Tait, 1868–1941, vol. IV
Pitt, Douglas F.; *see* Fox-Pitt.
Pitt, Dame Edith Maud, 1906–1966, vol. VI
Pitt, Frances, 1888–1964, vol. VI
Pitt, Captain Francis Joseph, 1840–1929, vol. III
Pitt, George Newton, 1853–1929, vol. III
Pitt, Henry Arthur, 1872–1955, vol. V
Pitt, Percy, 1870–1932, vol. III
Pitt, Col Robert Brindley, 1888–1974, vol. VII
Pitt, Captain Stanley Talbot Dean, 1853–1936, vol. III
Pitt, Col William, *died* 1933, vol. III

Pitt-Kethley, Andrew Horace Victor, 1879–1955, vol. V

Pitt-Lewis, George, 1845–1906, vol. I

Pitt-Pitts, Ven. W. A., 1890–1940, vol. III

Pitt-Rivers, Augustus Henry Lane F.; see Fox-Pitt-Rivers.

Pitt-Rivers, George Henry Lane Fox, 1890–1966, vol. VI

Pitt-Taylor, Gen. Sir Walter William, 1878–1950, vol. IV

Pitt-Watson, Very Rev. James, 1893–1962, vol. VI

Pittar, Barry, 1880–1948, vol. IV

Pittar, Sir Thomas John, 1846–1924, vol. II

Pittendrigh, Rev. George, 1857–1930, vol. III

Pitti, Sir Thyagaraya Chetti Garum, Diwan Bahadur, died 1925, vol. II (A), vol. III

Pittman, Osmund, 1874–1958, vol. V

Pitts, Arthur Thomas, 1881–1939, vol. III

Pitts, Hon. James Stewart, 1847–1914, vol. I

Pitts, Captain Percy, 1876–1937, vol. III

Pitts, Thomas, 1857–1919, vol. II

Pitts, Rev. Thomas, died 1929, vol. III

Pitts, Ven. W. A. P.; see Pitt-Pitts.

Pitts, William Ewart, 1900–1980, vol. VII

Pitts-Chambers, Sir Newman; see Chambers.

Pius X, His Holiness Pope, (Giuseppe Sarto), 1835–1914, vol. I

Pius XI, His Holiness Pope, (Achille Ambrogio Damiano Ratti), 1857–1939, vol. III

Pius XII, His Holiness Pope, (Eugene Pacelli), 1876–1958, vol. V

Pixley, Col Francis W., 1852–1933, vol. III

Place, Major (Charles) Godfrey (Morris), 1886–1931, vol. III

Place, Col Charles Otley, 1875–1955, vol. V

Place, Major Godfrey; see Place, Major C. G. M.

Placzek, Mrs A. K.; see Struther, Jan.

Plamenatz, John Petrov, 1912–1975, vol. VII

Planck, Max, 1858–1947, vol. IV

Plant, Sir Arnold, 1898–1978, vol. VII

Plant, Edmund Carter, 1842–1902, vol. I

Plant, Maj.-Gen. Eric Clive Pegus, 1890–1950, vol. IV

Plant, George Frederick, 1877–1954, vol. V

Plant, Morton F., died 1918, vol. II

Plante, Mgr J. Omer, 1867–1948, vol. IV

Plarr, Victor Gustave, 1863–1929, vol. III

Plaskett, Harry Hemley, 1893–1980, vol. VII

Plaskett, John Stanley, 1865–1941, vol. IV

Platnauer, Maurice, 1887–1974, vol. VII

Platt, Baron (Life Peer); Robert Platt, 1900–1978, vol. VII

Platt, Benjamin Stanley, 1903–1969, vol. VI

Platt, Major Eric James Walter, 1871–1946, vol. IV

Platt, Comdr Francis Cuthbert, 1885–1941, vol. IV

Platt, Sir Frank, 1890–1955, vol. V

Platt, Rev. Frederic, 1859–1955, vol. V

Platt, Col Henry, 1842–1914, vol. I

Platt, J. Arthur, 1860–1925, vol. II

Platt, James Westlake, 1897–1972, vol. VI

Platt, Samuel R., died 1902, vol. I

Platt, Sir Thomas Comyn-, 1875–1961, vol. VI

Platt, Gen. Sir William, 1885–1975, vol. VII

Platt-Higgins, Frederick, 1840–1910, vol. I

Platts, Frederick William, 1865–1941, vol. IV

Platts, Col Matthew George, 1886–1969, vol. VI

Platts, Thomas, 1843–1919, vol. II

Platts, W. Carter, 1864–1944, vol. IV

Playfair, 1st Baron, 1818–1898, vol. I

Playfair, 2nd Baron, 1849–1939, vol. III

Playfair, Maj.-Gen. Archibald Lewis, 1838–1915, vol. I

Playfair, Arthur Lambert, died 1939, vol. III

Playfair, Arthur Wyndham, 1869–1918, vol. II

Playfair, George Macdonald Home, 1850–1917, vol. II

Playfair, Maj.-Gen. Ian Stanley Ord, 1894–1972, vol. VII

Playfair, Hon. Lyon George Henry Lyon, 1888–1915, vol. I

Playfair, Sir Nigel, 1874–1934, vol. III

Playfair, Sir Patrick, 1852–1915, vol. I (A)

Playfair, Air Marshal Sir Patrick Henry Lyon, 1889–1974, vol. VII

Playfair, Rev. Patrick M., 1858–1924, vol. II

Playfair, Sir R. Lambert, 1828–1899, vol. I

Playfair, William Smoult, 1836–1903, vol. I

Playford, Hon. Thomas, 1837–1915, vol. I

Playne, Air Cdre Basil Alfred, 1885–1944, vol. IV

Pledge, Henry, died 1949, vol. IV (A), vol. V

Pledge, Humphrey Thomas, 1903–1960, vol. V, vol. VI

Plender, 1st Baron, 1861–1946, vol. IV

Plender, Lady; (Mabel Agnes), died 1970, vol. VI

Plenderleath, Captain Claude William Manners, 1863–1937, vol. III

Plenderleith, Air Vice-Marshal Brian William, 1927–1978, vol. VII

Pless, HSH Daisy, (Mary Theresa Olivia), Princess of, died 1943, vol. IV

Pleydell, Lt-Col Edmund Morton M.; see Mansel-Pleydell.

Pleydell, John Clavell M.; see Mansel-Pleydell.

Pleydell, Rev. John Colvile Morton M.; see Mansel-Pleydell.

Pleydell-Bouverie, Rev. Hon. Bertrand, 1845–1926, vol. II

Pleydell-Bouverie, Hon. Duncombe, 1842–1909, vol. I

Pleydell-Bouverie, Col Hon. Stuart, 1877–1947, vol. IV

Pleydell-Railston, Lt-Col Henry George Moreton, 1885–1936, vol. III

Plimmer, Henry George, died 1918, vol. II

Plimmer, Robert Henry Aders, 1877–1955, vol. V

Plomer, William Charles Franklyn, 1903–1973, vol. VII

Plomer, Col William Harry Percival, 1861–1937, vol. III

Plowden, Alfred Chichele, 1844–1914, vol. I

Plowden, Brig. Bryan Edward Chicheley, 1892–1965, vol. VI

Plowden, Cecil Ward Chicheley, 1864–1944, vol. IV

Plowden, Lt-Col Charles Terence Chichele, 1883–1956, vol. V

Plowden, Sir Henry Meredyth, 1840–1920, vol. II

Plowden, Rear-Adm. Richard Anthony Aston, died 1941, vol. IV

Plowden, Roger Edmund Joseph, 1879–1946, vol. IV

Plowden, Sir Trevor John Chichele C.; see Chichele-Plowden.

Plowden, Sir William Chichele, 1832–1915, vol. I

Plowden, William Francis, 1853–1914, vol. I

Plowden-Wardlaw, Rev. James Tait, 1873–1963, vol. VI

Plowman, Sir Claude, 1895–1954, vol. V

Plowman, Clifford Henry Fitzherbert, 1889–1948, vol. IV

Plowman, Sir George Thomas, 1858–1943, vol. IV

Plowman, Mark, (Max Plowman), 1883–1941, vol. IV

Plowman, Max; see Plowman, Mark.

Plucknett, Theodore Frank Thomas, 1897–1965, vol. VI

Plugge, Lt-Col Arthur, 1878–1934, vol. III

Plumb, Rt Rev. C. E., 1864–1930, vol. III

Plumbe, William John Conway, 1910–1979, vol. VII

Plume, William Thomas, 1869–1962, vol. VI

Plumer, 1st Viscount, 1857–1932, vol. III

Plumer, 2nd Viscount, 1890–1944, vol. IV

Plumer, Hon. Eleanor Mary, 1885–1967, vol. VI

Plummer, Baroness (Life Peer); Beatrice Plummer, 1903–1972, vol. VII

Plummer, Rev. Alfred, 1841–1926, vol. II

Plummer, Alfred, 1896–1978, vol. VII

Plummer, Rev. Charles, 1851–1927, vol. II

Plummer, Charles Henry Scott, 1859–1948, vol. IV

Plummer, Sir Edgar Stroud, 1873–1940, vol. III

Plummer, Rev. Francis Bowes, 1851–1932, vol. III

Plummer, Henry Crozier, 1875–1946, vol. IV

Plummer, John Archibald Temple, 1877–1943, vol. IV

Plummer, Sir Leslie Arthur, 1901–1963, vol. VI

Plummer, Norman Swift, 1907–1978, vol. VII

Plummer, Sir Walter Richard, 1858–1917, vol. II

Plummer, William Edward, 1849–1928, vol. II

Plumptre, Adelaide M., (Mrs H. P. Plumptre), died 1948, vol. IV

Plumptre, Mrs H. P.; see Plumptre, A. M.

Plumptre, Reginald Charles Edward, 1848–1929, vol. III

Plunket, 5th Baron, 1864–1920, vol. II

Plunket, 6th Baron, 1899–1938, vol. III

Plunket, 7th Baron, 1923–1975, vol. VII

Plunket, Hon. and Most Rev. Benjamin J., 1870–1947, vol. IV

Plunket, Hon. Emmeline Mary, 1835–1924, vol. II

Plunkett, Brig.-Gen. Edward Abadie, 1870–1926, vol. II

Plunkett, Rt Hon. Sir Francis Richard, 1835–1907, vol. I

Plunkett, George Noble, Count, 1851–1948, vol. IV

Plunkett, Lt-Col George Tindall, 1842–1922, vol. II

Plunkett, Rt Hon. Sir Horace Curzon, 1854–1932, vol. III

Plunkett-Ernle-Erle-Drax, Adm. Hon Sir Reginald Aylmer Ranfurly, 1880–1967, vol. VI

Plurenden, Baron (Life Peer); Rudy Sternberg, 1917–1978, vol. VII

Plymen, Francis Joseph, 1879–1960, vol. V

Plymouth, 1st Earl of, 1857–1923, vol. II

Plymouth, 2nd Earl of, 1889–1943, vol. IV

Po, Sir San Crombie, 1870–1946, vol. IV

Poate, Sir Hugh Raymond Guy, 1884–1961, vol. VI

Pobedonosteff, Constantini Petrovitch, 1827–1907, vol. I

Pochin, Horace Wilmer, 1903–1961, vol. VI

Pochin, Victor Robert, 1879–1972, vol. VII

Pochkhanawala, Sir Sorabji Nusserwanji, 1881–1937, vol. III

Pockley, Francis Antill, 1857–1941, vol. IV

Pocklington, Geoffrey Richard, 1879–1958, vol. V

Pocklington, Henry Cabourn, 1870–1952, vol. V

Pocock, Carmichael Charles Peter, (Michael Pocock), 1920–1979, vol. VII

Pocock, Sir Charles Guy Coventry, 4th Bt, 1863–1921, vol. II

Pocock, Childe, 1854–1934, vol. III

Pocock, Sir George Francis Coventry, 3rd Bt, 1830–1915, vol. I (A)

Pocock, Guy Noël, 1880–1955, vol. V

Pocock, Col Herbert Innes, 1861–1947, vol. IV

Pocock, Michael; see Pocock, C. C. P.

Pocock, Brig. Philip Frederick, 1871–1941, vol. IV

Pocock, Reginald Innes, 1863–1947, vol. IV

Pocock, Captain Roger, 1865–1941, vol. IV

Pocock, Sir Sidney Job, 1855–1931, vol. III

Pode, Sir (Edward) Julian, 1902–1968, vol. VI

Pode, Sir Julian; see Pode, Sir E. J.

Podmore, Edward Boyce, 1860–1928, vol. II

Podmore, Frank, 1856–1910, vol. I

Poe, Adm. Sir Edmund Samuel, 1849–1921, vol. II

Poe, Lt-Col Sir Hutcheson; see Poe, Lt-Col Sir W. H.

Poe, Col John, 1873–1941, vol. IV

Poe, Lt-Col Sir (William) Hutcheson, 1st Bt, 1848–1934, vol. III

Poë, Col William Skeffington, 1878–1958, vol. V

Poë Domvile, Sir Hugo Compton Domvile, 2nd Bt, 1889–1959, vol. V

Poel, William, 1852–1934, vol. III

Poett, Maj.-Gen. Joseph Howard, 1858–1929, vol. III

Pogany, Willy, (William Andrew), 1882–1955, vol. V

Poincaré, Jules Henri, 1854–1912, vol. I

Poincaré, Raymond, 1860–1934, vol. III

Pointer, Joseph, 1875–1914, vol. I

Poire, Emmanuel; see D'Ache, Caran.

Poiret, Paul, 1879–1944, vol. IV

Poirier, Hon. Pascal, 1852–1932, vol. III

Polack, Rudolph, 1842–1917, vol. II

Poland, Vice-Adm. Sir Albert Lawrence, 1895–1967, vol. VI

Poland, Sir Harry Bodkin, 1829–1928, vol. II

Poland, Vice-Adm. James Augustus, 1832–1918, vol. II

Poland, John, 1855–1937, vol. III

Poland, Comdr John Roberts, 1893–1961, vol. VI

Polanyi, Michael, 1891–1976, vol. VII

Pole, Alexander Edward, 1848–1909, vol. I

Pole, Sir Cecil Pery Van Notten-, 4th Bt (cr 1791), 1863–1948, vol. IV

Pole, Major David Graham, *died* 1952, vol. V

Pole, Sir Edmund Reginald Talbot de la, 10th Bt (*cr* 1628), 1844–1912, vol. I

Pole, Sir Felix John Clewett, 1877–1956, vol. V

Pole, Sir Frederick Arundell de la, 11th Bt (*cr* 1628), 1850–1926, vol. II

Pole, Brig.-Gen. Harry Anthony C.; *see* Chandos-Pole.

Pole, William, 1814–1900, vol. I

Pole-Evans, Illtyd Buller, 1879–1968, vol. VI

Poley, Thomas W.; *see* Weller-Poley.

Polhill, Rev. Arthur Twisleton, *died* 1935, vol. III

Polignano, 6th Duke of, *died* 1920, vol. II

Poling, Daniel Alfred, 1884–1968, vol. VI

Polk, Hon. Frank L., 1871–1943, vol. IV

Pollard, Alan Faraday Campbell, 1877–1948, vol. IV

Pollard, Albert Frederick, 1869–1948, vol. IV

Pollard, Captain Alfred Oliver, 1893–1960, vol. VI (AI)

Pollard, Alfred William, 1859–1944, vol. IV

Pollard, Arthur Tempest, 1854–1934, vol. III

Pollard, Rt Rev. Benjamin, 1890–1967, vol. VI

Pollard, Bilton, 1855–1931, vol. III

Pollard, Lt.-Gen. Charles, 1826–1911, vol. I

Pollard, Paymaster Rear-Adm. Sir Charles Fleetwood, 1868–1938, vol. III

Pollard, Claude, *died* 1957, vol. V

Pollard, Rear-Adm. Edwin John, 1833–1909, vol. I

Pollard, Lt-Col George Chambers, *died* 1954, vol. V

Pollard, Sir George Herbert, 1864–1937, vol. III

Pollard, Rear-Adm. George Northmore Arthur, 1847–1920, vol. II

Pollard, Graham; *see* Pollard, H. G.

Pollard, (Henry) Graham, 1903–1976, vol. VII

Pollard, Major Hugh B. C., *died* 1966, vol. VI

Pollard, Maj.-Gen. James Hawkins-Whitshed, 1866–1942, vol. IV

Pollard, Lt-Gen. Sir Reginald George, 1903–1978, vol. VII

Pollard-Lowsley, Col Herbert de Lisle, 1877–1936, vol. III

Pollard-Urquhart, Lt-Col Francis Edward Romulus, 1848–1915, vol. I

Pollen, Arthur Joseph Hungerford, 1866–1937, vol. III

Pollen, Captain Francis Gabriel Hungerford, 1862–1944, vol. IV

Pollen, Henry Court W.; *see* Willock-Pollen.

Pollen, John, 1848–1923, vol. II

Pollen, John Hungerford, 1820–1902, vol. I

Pollen, Rev. John Hungerford, 1858–1925, vol. II

Pollen, Sir John Launcelot Hungerford, 6th Bt, 1884–1959, vol. V

Pollen, Sir Richard, 5th Bt, 1878–1930, vol. III

Pollen, Sir Richard Hungerford, 4th Bt, 1846–1918, vol. II

Pollen, Lt-Col Stephen Hungerford, *died* 1935, vol. III

Pollen, Sir Walter Michael Hungerford, 1894–1968, vol. VI

Pollitt, George Paton, 1878–1964, vol. VI

Pollitt, Gerald Paton, 1877–1943, vol. IV

Pollitt, Harry, 1890–1960, vol. V

Pollitt, Col Sir William, 1842–1908, vol. I

Pollitzer, Sir Frank Joseph Coleman, 1869–1944, vol. IV

Pollock, Sir Adrian Donald Wilde, 1867–1943, vol. IV

Pollock, Maj.-Gen. Arthur Jocelyn Coleman, 1891–1968, vol. VI

Pollock, Lt-Col Arthur Williamson Alsager, 1853–1923, vol. II

Pollock, Rt Rev. Bertram, 1863–1943, vol. IV

Pollock, Rev. Charles Archibald Edmund, 1858–1944, vol. IV

Pollock, Hon. Sir Charles Edward, 1823–1897, vol. I

Pollock, Maj.-Gen. Charles Edward, *died* 1929, vol. III

Pollock, Courtenay Edward Maxwell, *died* 1943, vol. IV

Pollock, Hon. Surg. Comdr Sir Donald; *see* Pollock, Hon. Surg. Comdr Sir J. D.

Pollock, Sir Edward James, 1841–1930, vol. III

Pollock, Rt Hon. Sir (Frederick), 3rd Bt (*cr* 1866), 1845–1937, vol. III

Pollock, Sir (Frederick) John, 4th Bt (*cr* 1866), 1878–1963, vol. VI

Pollock, Sir Frederick Richard, 1827–1899, vol. I

Pollock, George Frederick, 1821–1915, vol. I

Pollock, Guy Cameron, 1878–1957, vol. V

Pollock, Harry Frederick, 1857–1901, vol. I

Pollock, Henry Brodhurst, 1883–1958, vol. V

Pollock, Hon. Sir Henry Edward, 1864–1953, vol. V

Pollock, Rev. Herbert Charles, 1852–1910, vol. I

Pollock, Rt Hon. Hugh McDowell, 1852–1937, vol. III

Pollock, J. Arthur, *died* 1922, vol. II

Pollock, James Edward, 1819–1910, vol. I

Pollock, Rev. Jeremy Taylor, 1850–1916, vol. II

Pollock, Sir John; *see* Pollock, Sir F. J.

Pollock, Lt-Col John Alsager, 1882–1941, vol. IV

Pollock, Maj.-Gen. John Archibald Henry, 1856–1949, vol. IV

Pollock, Hon. Surg. Comdr Sir (John) Donald, 1st Bt (*cr* 1939), 1868–1962, vol. VI

Pollock, Sir Montagu Frederick Montagu-, 3rd Bt (*cr* 1872), 1864–1938, vol. III

Pollock, Robert Erskine, 1849–1915, vol. I

Pollock, Sir Ronald Evelyn, 1891–1974, vol. VII

Pollock, W. Rivers, 1859–1909, vol. I

Pollock, Walter Herries, 1850–1926, vol. II

Pollock, William Barr Inglis, 1878–1953, vol. V

Pollok, Rev. Allan, 1829–1918, vol. II

Pollok, Maj.-Gen. Robert Valentine, 1884–1979, vol. VII

Pollok-M'Call, Brig.-Gen. John Buchanan, 1870–1951, vol. V

Pollok Morris, Col William, 1867–1936, vol. III

Polo de Bernabe, Don Luis, 1854–1929, vol. III

Polson, Milson George, 1917–1977, vol. VII

Polson, Col Sir Thomas Andrew, 1865–1946, vol. IV

Polson, Hon. Sir William John, 1875–1960, vol. V

Poltimore, 2nd Baron, 1837–1908, vol. I

Poltimore, 3rd Baron, 1859–1918, vol. II
Poltimore, 4th Baron, 1882–1965, vol. VI
Poltimore, 5th Baron, 1883–1967, vol. VI
Poltimore, 6th Baron, 1888–1978, vol. VII
Polwarth, 8th (styled 6th) Lord, 1838–1920, vol. II
Polwarth, 9th Lord, 1864–1944, vol. IV
Polwarth, Master of; Hon. Walter Thomas Hepburne-Scott, 1890–1942, vol. IV
Polybe; see Reinach, Joseph.
Pomare, Hon. Sir Maui, 1876–1930, vol. III
Pomeroy, F. W., died 1924, vol. II
Pompidou, Georges Jean Raymond, 1911–1974, vol. VII
Ponce, Don Ignacio G.; see Gutierrez-Ponce.
Poncet, André F.; see François-Poncet.
Pond, James Burton, 1838–1903, vol. I
Poniatowski, Prince Louis Leopold Charles Marie André, 1864–1954, vol. V
Pons, Lily, died 1976, vol. VII
Ponsonby of Shulbrede, 1st Baron, 1871–1946, vol. IV
Ponsonby of Shulbrede, 2nd Baron, 1904–1976, vol. VII
Ponsonby, Arthur Gordon, 1892–1978, vol. VII
Ponsonby, Hon. Bertie Brabazon, 1885–1967, vol. VI
Ponsonby, Col Sir Charles Edward, 1st Bt, 1879–1976, vol. VII
Ponsonby, Hon. Cyril Myles Brabazon, 1881–1915, vol. I
Ponsonby, Hon. Edwin Charles William, 1851–1939, vol. III
Ponsonby, Sir George Arthur, 1878–1969, vol. VI
Ponsonby, Hon. Gerald, 1829–1908, vol. I
Ponsonby, Rev. Gordon; see Ponsonby, Rev. S. G.
Ponsonby, Brig. Henry Chambré, 1883–1953, vol. V
Ponsonby, Maj.-Gen. Sir John, 1866–1952, vol. V
Ponsonby, Col Justinian Gordon, died 1929, vol. III
Ponsonby, Rev. Maurice George Jesser, 1880–1943, vol. IV
Ponsonby, Noel Edward, 1891–1928, vol. II
Ponsonby, Rev. (Stewart) Gordon, died 1938, vol. III
Ponsonby, Thomas Brabazon, died 1946, vol. IV
Ponsonby, Captain William Rundall, 1874–1919, vol. II
Ponsonby-Fane, Rt Hon. Sir Spencer Cecil Brabazon, 1824–1915, vol. I (A)
Pontifex, Sir Charles, 1831–1912, vol. I
Ponting, Herbert George, died 1935, vol. III
Ponting, Brig. Theophilus John, 1886–1972, vol. VII
Pontoppidan, Henrik, 1857–1943, vol. IV
Pontypridd, 1st Baron, 1840–1927, vol. II
Pool, Arthur George, 1905–1963, vol. VI
Pool, Augustus Frank, 1872–1955, vol. V
Pool, Bernard Frank, 1896–1977, vol. VII
Pool, William Arthur, 1889–1969, vol. VI
Poole, Brig.-Gen. Arthur James, 1872–1956, vol. V
Poole, Austin Lane, 1889–1963, vol. VI
Poole, Major Cecil Charles, 1902–1956, vol. V
Poole, Charles Edward L.; see Lane Poole.
Poole, Edgar Girard Croker, 1891–1940, vol. III

Poole, Ernest, 1880–1950, vol. IV (A), vol. V
Poole, Rev. Frederic John, 1852–1923, vol. II
Poole, Maj.-Gen. Sir Frederick Cuthbert, 1869–1936, vol. III
Poole, Lt-Gen. Gerald Robert, 1868–1937, vol. III
Poole, Granville, 1885–1962, vol. VI
Poole, Henry, 1873–1928, vol. II
Poole, Brig. Ivan Maxwell Conway, 1878–1963, vol. VI
Poole, Sir James, 1827–1903, vol. I
Poole, John Hewitt Jellett, 1893–1976, vol. VII
Poole, Maj.-Gen. Leopold Thomas, 1888–1965, vol. VI
Poole, Sir Lionel Pinnock, 1894–1967, vol. VI
Poole, Reginald Lane, 1857–1939, vol. III
Poole, Sir Reginald Ward Edward Lane, 1864–1941, vol. IV
Poole, Vice-Adm. Sir Richard Hayden Owen L.; see Lane-Poole.
Poole, Stanley L.; see Lane-Poole.
Poole, Lt-Col Sir Thomas G., 1859–1937, vol. III
Poole, Hon. Thomas Slaney, 1873–1927, vol. II
Poole, Maj.-Gen. William Henry Evered, 1902–1969, vol. VI
Poole, Wordsworth, 1868–1902, vol. I
Poole-Hughes, Rev. W. Worthington, 1865–1928, vol. II
Pooler, Ven. Lewis Arthur, 1858–1924, vol. II
Pooley, Charles Blois, 1881–1938, vol. III
Pooley, Sir Ernest Henry, 1st Bt, 1876–1966, vol. VI
Poore, Sir Edward, 5th Bt, 1894–1938, vol. III
Poore, Maj.-Gen. Francis Harwood, 1841–1928, vol. II
Poore, George Vivian, 1843–1904, vol. I
Poore, Adm. Sir Richard, 4th Bt, 1853–1930, vol. III
Poore, Brig.-Gen. Robert Montagu, 1866–1938, vol. III
Poore, Major Roger Alvin, 1870–1917, vol. II
Pope, Col Albert Augustus, 1843–1909, vol. I
Pope, Alfred, 1842–1934, vol. III
Pope, Arthur Upham, 1881–1969, vol. VI
Pope, Arthur William Uglow, 1858–1927, vol. II
Pope, Lt-Col Edward Alexander, 1875–1919, vol. II
Pope, Frank Aubrey, 1893–1962, vol. VI
Pope, Rev. George Uglow, 1820–1908, vol. I
Pope, Col Harold, 1873–1938, vol. III
Pope, Rev. Henry John, 1836–1912, vol. I
Pope, Rev. Hugh, 1869–1946, vol. IV
Pope, James Alister, 1883–1954, vol. V
Pope, Jessie, (Mrs Babington Lenton), died 1941, vol. IV
Pope, John van Someren, 1850–1932, vol. III
Pope, Sir Joseph, 1854–1926, vol. II
Pope, Lt-Gen. Maurice Arthur, 1889–1978, vol. VII
Pope, Mildred Katherine, 1872–1956, vol. V
Pope, Col Philip Edward, 1842–1916, vol. II
Pope, Rev. Richard William Massy, 1849–1923, vol. II
Pope, Brig. Ronald James, 1924–1976, vol. VII
Pope, Samuel, 1826–1901, vol. I
Pope, Samuel, died 1935, vol. III
Pope, Maj.-Gen. Sydney Buxton, 1879–1955, vol. V
Pope, Thomas Michael, 1875–1930, vol. III

Pope, Maj.-Gen. Vyvyan Vavasour, 1891–1941, vol. IV
Pope, Walter James M.; see Macqueen-Pope.
Pope, Sir William Jackson, 1870–1939, vol. III
Pope, Lt-Col William Wippell, died 1926, vol. II
Pope, Wilson, 1866–1953, vol. V
Pope-Hennessy, James, 1916–1974, vol. VII
Pope-Hennessy, Maj.-Gen. Ladislaus Herbert Richard, 1875–1942, vol. IV
Pope-Hennessy, Dame Una, died 1949, vol. IV
Popham, Arthur Ewart, 1889–1970, vol. VI
Popham, Francis William L.; see Leyborne-Popham.
Popham, Sir Henry Bradshaw, 1881–1947, vol. IV
Popham, Air Chief Marshal Sir (Henry) Robert (Moore) Brooke-, 1878–1953, vol. V
Popham, Air Chief Marshal Sir Robert Brooke-; see Popham, Air Chief Marshal Sir H. R. M. B.
Popham, Col Robert Stewart, 1876–1949, vol. IV
Popkess, Captain Athelstan, 1893–1967, vol. VI
Popplewell, Baron (Life Peer); Ernest Popplewell, 1899–1977, vol. VII
Porcelli, Col Baron Alfred, 1849–1937, vol. III
Porcelli, Lt-Col Baron Ernest George Macdonald di S Andrea, 1886–1965, vol. VI
Porch, Col Edward Albert, 1879–1937, vol. III
Porges, Waldo William, 1899–1976, vol. VII
Porral, Albert, 1846–1918, vol. II
Porritt, Arthur, 1872–1947, vol. IV
Porritt, Lt-Col Austin Townsend, 1875–1956, vol. V
Porritt, Benjamin Dawson, 1884–1940, vol. III
Porritt, Edward, 1860–1921, vol. II
Porritt, Captain Richard W., 1910–1940, vol. III
Portal, 1st Viscount, 1885–1949, vol. IV
Portal of Hungerford, 1st Viscount, 1893–1971, vol. VII
Portal, Brig.-Gen. Sir Bertram Percy, 1866–1949, vol. IV
Portal, Melville, 1819–1904, vol. I
Portal, Sir Spencer John, 4th Bt, 1864–1955, vol. V
Portal, Sir William Wyndham, 2nd Bt, 1850–1931, vol. III
Portal, Sir Wyndham Spencer, 1st Bt, 1822–1905, vol. I
Portarlington, 5th Earl of, 1858–1900, vol. I
Portarlington, 6th Earl of, 1883–1959, vol. V
Portelli, Rt Rev. Angelo, born 1852, vol. II
Porteous, Alexander, 1855–1932, vol. III
Porteous, Col Charles Arkcoll, 1839–1929, vol. III
Porteous, Douglas Archibald, 1891–1974, vol. VII
Porteous, Lt-Col John James, 1857–1948, vol. IV
Porteous, Norman, 1881–1940, vol. III
Porter, Baron (Life Peer); Samuel Lowry Porter, 1877–1956, vol. V
Porter, Surg.-Col Alex., 1841–1918, vol. II
Porter, Sir Alexander, 1853–1926, vol. II
Porter, Sir Alfred de Bock, 1840–1908, vol. I
Porter, Rev. Alfred Stephenson, 1841–1914, vol. I
Porter, Alfred William, 1863–1939, vol. III
Porter, Rt Hon. Sir Andrew Marshall, 1st Bt (cr 1902), 1837–1919, vol. II
Porter, Annie, (Mrs H. B. Fantham), died 1963, vol. VI

Porter, Cecil George, 1887–1938, vol. III
Porter, Air Vice-Marshal Cedric Ernest Victor, 1893–1975, vol. VII
Porter, Charles, 1873–1952, vol. V
Porter, Rev. Charles Fleetwood, 1830–1914, vol. I
Porter, Cole, 1893–1964, vol. VI
Porter, Brig.-Gen. Cyril Lachlan, 1872–1951, vol. V
Porter, Edward, 1880–1960, vol. V
Porter, Edward Guss, 1859–1929, vol. III
Porter, Frederick, 1871–1949, vol. IV (A)
Porter, Gene Stratton-, 1868–1924, vol. II
Porter, Col Geoffrey M., 1854–1944, vol. IV
Porter, George, 1884–1973, vol. VII
Porter, Sir George Swinburne, 3rd Bt (cr 1889), 1908–1974, vol. VII
Porter, Sir Haldane; see Porter, Sir W. H.
Porter, Harold, 1879–1938, vol. III
Porter, Sir Harry Edwin Bruce B.; see Bruce-Porter
Porter, Major Herbert Alfred, 1872–1939, vol. III (A), vol. IV
Porter, Rev. James, died 1900, vol. I
Porter, Sir James, died 1935, vol. III
Porter, John, 1838–1922, vol. II
Porter, John Bonsall, 1861–1944, vol. IV
Porter, Maj.-Gen. John Edmund L.; see Leech-Porter.
Porter, John Fletcher, 1873–1927, vol. II
Porter, Captain John Grey Archdale, 1886–1917, vol. II
Porter, John Porter, 1855–1939, vol. III
Porter, Sir John Scott Horsbrugh-, 2nd Bt (cr 1902), 1871–1953, vol. V
Porter, Katherine Anne, 1890–1980, vol. VII
Porter, Keith Ridley Douglas, 1913–1977, vol. VII
Porter, Sir Leslie Alexander Selim, 1854–1932, vol. III
Porter, Sir Ludovic Charles, 1869–1928, vol. II
Porter, Sir Neale, died 1905, vol. I
Porter, Major Reginald Whitworth, died 1902, vol. I
Porter, Maj.-Gen. Sir Robert, 1858–1928, vol. II
Porter, Robert P., 1852–1917, vol. II
Porter, Rev. Robert Waltham, died 1927, vol. II
Porter, Rose Henniker, (Mrs Adrian Porter); see Heaton, R. H.
Porter, Rt Hon. Samuel Clarke, 1875–1956, vol. V
Porter, Brig.-Gen. Thomas Cole, 1851–1938, vol. III
Porter, Thomas Cunningham, 1860–1933, vol. III
Porter, Col Thomas William, 1844–1920, vol. II
Porter, Sir (William) Haldane, 1867–1944, vol. IV
Porter, Sir William Henry, 2nd Bt (cr 1889), 1862–1935, vol. III
Porter, William Ninnis, died 1929, vol. III
Porter, William Smith, 1855–1927, vol. II
Porter, Hon. William Thomas, 1877–1928, vol. III
Porter-Phillips, John George, died 1946, vol. IV
Porteus, Rev. Canon Thomas Cruddas, 1876–1948, vol. IV
Portland, 6th Duke of, 1857–1943, vol. IV
Portland, 7th Duke of, 1893–1977, vol. VII
Portland, 8th Duke of, 1889–1980, vol. VII

Portman, 2nd Viscount, 1829–1919, vol. II
Portman, 3rd Viscount, 1860–1923, vol. II
Portman, 4th Viscount, 1864–1929, vol. III
Portman, 5th Viscount, 1898–1942, vol. IV
Portman, 6th Viscount, 1868–1946, vol. IV
Portman, 7th Viscount, 1875–1948, vol. IV
Portman, 8th Viscount, 1903–1967, vol. VI
Portman, Hon. Edward William Berkeley, 1856–1911, vol. I
Portman, Hon. Edwin Berkeley, 1830–1921, vol. II
Portman, Eric, 1903–1969, vol. VI
Portman, Guy Maurice Berkeley, 1890–1961, vol. VI
Portman-Dalton, Seymour Berkeley, 1838–1912, vol. I
Porto-Riche, Georges de, 1849–1930, vol. III
Portsea, 1st Baron, 1860–1948, vol. IV
Portsmouth, 6th Earl of, 1856–1917, vol. II
Portsmouth, 7th Earl of, 1859–1925, vol. II
Portsmouth, 8th Earl of, 1861–1943, vol. IV
Portsmouth, Percy, 1874–1953, vol. V
Portway, Col Donald, 1887–1979, vol. VII
Poskitt, Rt Rev. Henry John, 1888–1950, vol. IV
Post, Emily, (Mrs Price Post), died 1960, vol. V
Post, Mrs Price; see Post, Emily.
Post, Rear-Adm. Simon Edward, 1910–1965, vol. VI
Postgate, John Percival, 1853–1926, vol. II
Postgate, Raymond William, 1896–1971, vol. VII
Postill, Ronald, 1907–1980, vol. VII
Postlethwaite, John Rutherfoord Parkin, 1883–1956, vol. V
Potez, Andrew Louis, 1920–1977, vol. VII
Po Tha, Sir Maung, died 1933, vol. III
Pothecary, Major Walter Frank, 1882–1958, vol. V
Potier, Gilbert George, 1915–1969, vol. VI
Pott, Anthony Percivall, 1904–1963, vol. VI
Pott, Col Douglas, 1888–1974, vol. VII
Pott, Francis Lister Hawks, 1864–1947, vol. IV
Pott, Sir (George) Stanley, 1870–1951, vol. V
Pott, Gladys Sydney, 1867–1961, vol. VI
Pott, H(enry) Percivall, 1908–1964, vol. VI
Pott, Rear-Adm. Herbert, 1886–1945, vol. IV
Pott, Sir Stanley; see Pott, Sir G. S.
Potter, Sir Alan Graeme, 1891–1969, vol. VI
Potter, Albert Knight, 1864–1948, vol. IV
Potter, Beatrice; see Webb, Mrs Sidney.
Potter, Ven. Beresford, 1853–1931, vol. III
Potter, Carlyle Thornton, died 1962, vol. VI
Potter, Lt-Col Claud Furniss, 1881–1965, vol. VI
Potter, Col Colin Kynaston, 1877–1964, vol. VI
Potter, Cora Urquhart, died 1936, vol. III
Potter, Cyril H., 1877–1941, vol. IV
Potter, David Morris, 1910–1971, vol. VII
Potter, Frank, died 1919, vol. II
Potter, Frederick Felix, 1882–1955, vol. V
Potter, Harold, 1896–1951, vol. V
Potter, Rt Rev. Henry Codman, 1834–1908, vol. I
Potter, Sir Henry Steven, 1904–1976, vol. VII
Potter, Brig.-Gen. Herbert Cecil, 1875–1964, vol. VI
Potter, Howard Vincent, 1888–1970, vol. VI (AII)
Potter, Mrs J. Brown; see Potter, Cora Urquhart.
Potter, Lt-Col James Archer, 1875–1962, vol. VI

Potter, John, 1873–1940, vol. III
Potter, John Alexander, 1851–1929, vol. III
Potter, Rev. John Hasloch, 1847–1935, vol. III
Potter, Rev. Michael Cressé, 1858–1948, vol. IV
Potter, Rev. Reginald Joseph William Henry, 1877–1941, vol. IV
Potter, Ven. Richard Harry, 1861–1931, vol. III
Potter, Rupert Barnadiston, 1899–1970, vol. VI
Potter, Simeon, 1898–1976, vol. VII
Potter, Stephen, 1900–1969, vol. VI
Potter, Thomas Bayley, 1817–1898, vol. I
Potter, Col William Allen, died 1953, vol. V
Pottinger, Lt-Gen. Brabazon Henry, 1840–1913, vol. I
Pottinger, David, 1843–1938, vol. III
Pottinger, Lt-Col Eldred Thomas, 1840–1905, vol. I
Pottinger, Sir Henry, 3rd Bt, 1834–1909, vol. I
Pottinger, Lt-Col Robert Southey, 1870–1943, vol. IV
Potts, Lt-Col Edmund Thurlow, 1878–1948, vol. IV
Potts, Brig.-Gen. Frederick, 1866–1945, vol. IV
Potts, George, 1877–1948, vol. IV
Potts, John, died 1938, vol. III
Potts, William Alexander, 1866–1939, vol. III
Pouishnoff, Leff, 1891–1959, vol. V
Poulenc, Francis, 1899–1963, vol. VI
Poulett, 6th Earl, 1827–1899, vol. I
Poulett, 7th Earl, 1883–1918, vol. II
Poulett, 8th Earl, 1909–1973, vol. VII
Pouliot, Joseph Camille, 1865–1935, vol. III
Poultney, Alfred Henry, died 1906, vol. I
Poulton, Lt-Col Arthur Faulconer, 1858–1935, vol. III
Poulton, Sir Edward Bagnall, 1856–1943, vol. IV
Poulton, Edward Lawrence, 1865–1937, vol. III
Poulton, Edward Palmer, 1883–1939, vol. III
Poulton, Elgan Nathaniel George, 1881–1944, vol. IV
Poulton, Lt-Col Henry Mortimer, 1898–1973, vol. VII
Pound, Admiral of the Fleet Sir (Alfred) Dudley (Pickman Rogers), 1877–1943, vol. IV
Pound, Sir Allen Leslie, 3rd Bt, 1888–1952, vol. V
Pound, Sir Derek Allen, 4th Bt, 1920–1980, vol. VII
Pound, Admiral of the Fleet Sir Dudley; see Pound, Admiral of the Fleet Sir A. D. P. R.
Pound, Ezra, 1885–1972, vol. VII
Pound, Sir John, 1st Bt, 1829–1915, vol. I
Pound, Sir (John) Lulham, 2nd Bt, 1862–1937, vol. III
Pound, Sir Lulham; see Pound, Sir J. L.
Pound, Roscoe, 1870–1964, vol. VI
Pounds, Charles Courtice, 1862–1927, vol. II
Pounsett, Clement Aubrey, 1900–1968, vol. VI
Pountney, Arthur Meek, 1873–1940, vol. III
Povah, Rev. John Walter, 1883–1961, vol. VI
Powel, Thomas, 1845–1922, vol. II
Powell, Agnes B.; see Baden-Powell.
Powell, Alan Richard, 1894–1975, vol. VII
Powell, Sir Allan; see Powell, Sir G. A.
Powell, Rev. Canon Arnold Cecil, 1882–1963, vol. VI
Powell, Arthur, 1864–1926, vol. II

Powell, Arthur, 1853–1930, vol. III
Powell, Rev. Astell Drayner, 1851–1934, vol. III
Powell, Col Atherton Ffolliott, 1858–1941, vol. IV
Powell, Major Baden Fletcher Smyth B.; *see* Baden-Powell.
Powell, Baden Henry B.; *see* Baden-Powell.
Powell, Cecil Frank, 1903–1969, vol. VI
Powell, Maj.-Gen. Sir Charles Herbert, 1857–1943, vol. IV
Powell, Ven. Dacre Hamilton, 1843–1912, vol. I
Powell, Lt-Col David Watson, 1878–1935, vol. III
Powell, Brig. Donald, 1896–1942, vol. IV
Powell, Lt-Col Sir Douglas, 2nd Bt (*cr* 1897), 1874–1932, vol. III
Powell, E. Alexander, 1879–1957, vol. V
Powell, Rt Rev. Edmund Nathanael, 1859–1928, vol. II
Powell, Brig.-Gen. Edward Weyland Martin, 1869–1954, vol. V
Powell, Ellis Thomas, 1869–1922, vol. II
Powell, Lt-Col Evelyn George Harcourt, 1883–1961, vol. VI
Powell, F. York, 1850–1904, vol. I
Powell, Sir Francis, 1833–1914, vol. I
Powell, Adm. Sir Francis, 1849–1927, vol. II
Powell, Francis Edward, *died* 1938, vol. III
Powell, Sir Francis Sharp, 1st Bt (*cr* 1892), 1827–1911, vol. I
Powell, Frank John, 1891–1971, vol. VII
Powell, Frank Smyth B.; *see* Baden-Powell.
Powell, Sir (George) Allan, *died* 1948, vol. IV
Powell, Vice-Adm. George Bingham, 1871–1952, vol. V
Powell, George Herbert, 1856–1924, vol. II
Powell, Sir George Smyth B.; *see* Baden-Powell.
Powell, Rt Rev. Grandage Edwards, 1882–1948, vol. IV
Powell, Helena Langhorne, 1862–1942, vol. IV
Powell, Henry Arthur, 1868–1944, vol. IV
Powell, Col Henry Lloyd, 1866–1941, vol. IV
Powell, Rear-Adm. James, 1887–1971, vol. VII
Powell, Col James Leslie Grove, 1853–1925, vol. II
Powell, Col John, 1876–1936, vol. III
Powell, Lt-Col John, 1856–1938, vol. III
Powell, Gp-Captain John Alexander, 1909–1944, vol. IV
Powell, Rt Hon. John Blake, *died* 1923, vol. II
Powell, Lawrence Fitzroy, 1881–1975, vol. VII
Powell, Sir Leonard; *see* Powell, Sir R. L.
Powell, Llewelyn, 1870–1934, vol. III
Powell, Rev. Morgan Jones, 1863–1947, vol. IV
Powell, Dame Muriel, 1914–1978, vol. VII
Powell, Percival Herbert, *died* 1958, vol. V
Powell, Lt-Col Philip Lionel William, 1882–1959, vol. V
Powell, Raphael, 1904–1965, vol. VI
Powell, Ray Edwin, 1887–1973, vol. VII
Powell, Richard, 1889–1961, vol. VI
Powell, Richard Albert Brakell, 1892–1957, vol. V
Powell, Sir Richard Douglas, 1st Bt (*cr* 1897), 1842–1925, vol. II
Powell, Major Sir Richard George Douglas, 3rd Bt (*cr* 1897), 1909–1980, vol. VII
Powell, Sir (Robert) Leonard, 1853–1938, vol. III

Powell, Ronald Arthur, 1888–1966, vol. VI
Powell, Samuel M.; *see* Morgan-Powell.
Powell, Sidney, 1894–1964, vol. VI
Powell, Maj.-Gen. Sidney Henry, 1866–1945, vol. IV
Powell, Warington B.; *see* Baden-Powell.
Powell, Lt-Col William Bowen, 1868–1940, vol. III
Powell, Rev. William Hawkshaw, 1842–1930, vol. III
Powell, Col William Jackson, 1881–1961, vol. VI
Powell-Cotton, Percy Horace Gordon, 1866–1940, vol. III
Powell-Price, John Cadwgan, 1888–1964, vol. VI
Power, Sir Adam Clayton, 6th Bt (*cr* 1836), 1844–1903 (this entry was not transferred to Who was Who).
Power, Albert G., 1883–1945, vol. IV
Power, Admiral of the Fleet Sir Arthur John, 1889–1960, vol. V
Power, Beryl Millicent le Poer, 1891–1974, vol. VII
Power, Charles Gavan, 1888–1968, vol. VI
Power, Sir D'Arcy, 1855–1941, vol. IV
Power, Air Vice-Marshal D'Arcy, 1889–1958, vol. V
Power, Eileen, 1889–1940, vol. III
Power, Sir Elliott Derrick le Poer, 5th Bt (*cr* 1836), 1872–1902, vol. I
Power, Sir George, 7th Bt (*cr* 1836), 1846–1928, vol. II
Power, Ven. George Edmund, *died* 1950, vol. IV (A), vol. V
Power, Gerald, 1891–1967, vol. VI
Power, Lt-Col Gervase Bushe, 1883–1974, vol. VII
Power, Harold Septimus, *died* 1951, vol. V
Power, Henry, *died* 1911, vol. I
Power, Hubert, *born* 1860, vol. II
Power, Sir Ivan McLannahan Cecil, 2nd Bt (*cr* 1924), 1903–1954, vol. V
Power, Sir James Douglas Talbot, 4th Bt (*cr* 1841), 1884–1914, vol. I
Power, Sir James Talbot, 5th Bt (*cr* 1841), 1851–1916, vol. II
Power, Sir John Cecil, 1st Bt (*cr* 1924), 1870–1950, vol. IV
Power, John Danvers, 1858–1927, vol. II
Power, Sir John Elliott Cecil, 4th Bt (*cr* 1836), 1870–1900, vol. I
Power, Sir John Talbot, 3rd Bt (*cr* 1841), 1845–1901, vol. I
Power, Mrs (John) Wyse, *died* 1941, vol. IV
Power, Adm. Sir Laurence Eliot, 1864–1927, vol. II
Power, Hon. Lawrence Geoffrey, 1841–1921, vol. II
Power, Rev. Patrick, 1862–1951, vol. V
Power, Patrick Joseph, 1850–1913, vol. I
Power, Patrick Joseph Mahon, 1826–1913, vol. I
Power, Sir Samuel Murray, 1863–1933, vol. III
Power, Gen. Thomas Sarsfield, 1905–1970, vol. VI
Power, Sir Thomas Talbot, 6th Bt (*cr* 1841), 1863–1930, vol. III
Power, William, 1873–1951, vol. V
Power, Sir William Henry, 1842–1916, vol. II
Power, Sir William Richard, 1861–1945, vol. IV
Power, Major William Sayer, 1859–1940, vol. III
Power, Mrs Wyse; *see* Power, Mrs John W.

Powers, Hon. Sir Charles, 1853–1939, vol. III
Powers, George Wightman, 1864–1932, vol. III
Powerscourt, 7th Viscount, 1836–1904, vol. I
Powerscourt, 8th Viscount, 1880–1947, vol. IV
Powerscourt, 9th Viscount, 1905–1973, vol. VII
Powicke, Frederick James, 1854–1935, vol. III
Powicke, Sir (Frederick) Maurice, 1879–1963, vol. VI
Powicke, Sir Maurice; see Powicke, Sir F. M.
Powis, 4th Earl of, 1862–1952, vol. V
Powis, 5th Earl of, 1889–1974, vol. VII
Powles, Col (Charles) Guy, 1872–1951, vol. V
Powles, Col Guy; see Powles, Col C. G.
Powles, Lewis Charles, 1860–1942, vol. IV
Powlett, Adm. Armund Temple, 1841–1925, vol. II
Powlett, Vice-Adm. Frederick Armand, 1873–1963, vol. VI
Powlett, Col Percy William, 1837–1910, vol. I
Powley, Albert E., 1868–1937, vol. III
Powley, Edward B., 1887–1968, vol. VI
Pownall, Lt-Col Sir Assheton, 1877–1953, vol. V
Pownall, Adm. Charles Pipon B.; see Beaty-Pownall.
Pownall, George Henry, 1850–1916, vol. II
Pownall, Lt-Gen. Sir Henry Royds, 1887–1961, vol. VI
Pownall, John Cecil Glossop, 1891–1967, vol. VI
Pownall, Mary, died 1937, vol. III
Powter, John, 1881–1930, vol. III
Powys, Albert Reginad, 1881–1936, vol. III
Powys, John Cowper, 1872–1963, vol. VI
Powys, Llewelyn, 1884–1939, vol. III
Powys, Theodore Francis, died 1953, vol. V
Powys-Jones, Lionel, 1894–1966, vol. VI
Powys-Keck, Thomas Charles Leycester, 1871–1931, vol. III
Poy; see Fearon, Percy Hutton.
Poynder, Lt-Col Frederic Sinclair, 1893–1943, vol. IV
Poynter, Sir Ambrose Macdonald, 2nd Bt, 1867–1923, vol. II
Poynter, Sir Edward John, 1st Bt, 1836–1919, vol. II
Poynter, (Frederick) Noel (Lawrence), 1908–1979, vol. VII
Poynter, Sir Hugh Edward, 3rd Bt, 1882–1968, vol. VI
Poynter, Noel; see Poynter, F. N. L.
Poynting, John Henry, 1852–1914, vol. I
Poynter, Hon. Alexander, 1853–1935, vol. III
Poynton, Arthur Blackburne, 1867–1944, vol. IV
Poynton, Frederic John, 1869–1943, vol. IV
Poyntz, Rev. Newdigate, 1842–1931, vol. III
Poyser, Sir (Arthur Hampden) Ronald (Wastell), 1884–1957, vol. V
Poyser, Arthur Horatio, 1849–1923, vol. II
Poyser, Sir Kenneth Elliston, died 1943, vol. IV
Poyser, Col Richard, 1842–1919, vol. II
Poyser, Sir Ronald; see Poyser, Sir A. H. R. W.
Pozzi, Jean Samuel, 1849–1918, vol. II
Pozzoni, Mgr Dominico, 1861–1924, vol. II
Pradhan, Sir Govindrao Balwantrao, 1874–1943, vol. IV
Praed, Sir Herbert Bulkley Mackworth-, 1st Bt, 1841–1921, vol. II

Praed, Rosa Caroline Mackworth, 1851–1935, vol. III
Praeger, Robert Lloyd, 1865–1953, vol. V
Praeger, S. Rosamond, died 1954, vol. V
Praga, Alfred, died 1949, vol. IV
Pragnell, Sir George, 1863–1916, vol. II
Pragnell, Col Thomas Wykeham, 1883–1957, vol. V
Prain, Lt-Col Sir David, 1857–1944, vol. IV
Prance, Basil Camden, 1884–1948, vol. IV
Prance, Brig. Robert Courtenay, 1882–1966, vol. VI
Prang, Louis, 1824–1909, vol. I
Prasad, Ganesh, 1876–1935, vol. III
Prasad, Jagat, 1879–1957, vol. V
Prasad, Sir Jwala, 1875–1933, vol. III
Prasad, Rajendra, 1884–1963, vol. VI
Prater, Stanley Henry, 1890–1960, vol. V
Pratt, Col (Arthur) Spencer, 1855–1933, vol. III
Pratt, Sir Bernard; see Pratt, Sir E. B.
Pratt, Rear-Adm. Charles Bernard, 1907–1973, vol. VII
Pratt, David Doig, 1894–1962, vol. VI
Pratt, Maj.-Gen. Douglas Henry, 1892–1958, vol. V
Pratt, Sir (E.) Bernard, 1889–1975, vol. VII
Pratt, Edward Millard, 1865–1949, vol. IV
Pratt, Edward Roger, 1847–1921, vol. II
Pratt, Edwin John, 1883–1964, vol. VI
Pratt, Brig.-Gen. (Ernest) St George, 1863–1918, vol. II
Pratt, Col Fendall William Harvey, 1892–1960, vol. V
Pratt, Rev. Canon Francis William, 1900–1971, vol. VII
Pratt, Frederick Greville, 1869–1949, vol. IV
Pratt, Col Henry Marsh, 1838–1919, vol. II
Pratt, Sir Henry Sheldon, 1873–1954, vol. V
Pratt, John, 1880–1935, vol. III
Pratt, John Lhind, 1885–1960, vol. V
Pratt, Sir John Thomas, 1876–1970, vol. VI
Pratt, Sir John William, 1873–1952, vol. V
Pratt, Joseph, 1843–1929, vol. III
Pratt, Brig. Reginald S.; see Sutton-Pratt.
Pratt, Brig.-Gen. St George; see Pratt, Brig.-Gen. E. St G.
Pratt, Col Spencer; see Pratt, Col A. S.
Pratt, William Henry; see Karloff, Boris.
Pratt, Surg.-Gen. William Simson, 1849–1917, vol. II
Pratt-Tynte, Fortescue Joseph; see Tynte.
Pratten, Herbert Edward, 1865–1928, vol. II
Pratz, Claire de, died 1934, vol. III
Prausnitz Giles, Carl, 1876–1963, vol. VI
Prebensen, Per Preben, 1896–1961, vol. VI
Preece, Sir Arthur Henry, 1867–1951, vol. V
Preece, Engr Vice-Adm. Sir George, died 1945, vol. IV
Preece, John Richard, 1843–1917, vol. II
Preece, Sir William Henry, 1834–1913, vol. I
Preedy, Rev. Arthur, died 1929, vol. III
Preedy, Digby C.; see Cotes-Preedy.
Preedy, George R.; see Long, M. G.
Preedy, Kenelm, died 1945, vol. IV

Preeston, Lt-Col Noel Percival Richard, 1880–1937, vol. III

Préfontaine, Hon. Joseph Raymond Fournier, 1850–1905, vol. I

Preller, Charles S. Du Riche, 1844–1929, vol. III

Prelooker, Jaakoff, 1860–1935, vol. III

Prem, Dhani Ram, 1904–1979, vol. VII

Premchand, Sir Kikabhai, 1883–1953, vol. V

Prempeh II, Otumfuo Sir Osei Agyeman, 1892–1970, vol. VI

Prendergast, Brig.-Gen. Charles Gordon, 1864–1930, vol. III

Prendergast, Brig.-Gen. Donald Guy, 1861–1938, vol. III

Prendergast, Hon. George Michael, 1854–1937, vol. III

Prendergast, Maj.-Gen. Guy Annesley, 1834–1919, vol. II

Prendergast, Gen. Sir Harry North Dalrymple, 1834–1913, vol. I

Prendergast, Hon. Sir James, 1828–1921, vol. II

Prendergast, Hon. James Emile Pierre, 1858–1945, vol. IV

Prendergast, Adm. Sir Robert John, 1864–1946, vol. IV

Prendergast, W. Dowling, 1862–1933, vol. III

Prendergast, William, 1868–1933, vol. III

Prenderville, Arthur de, died 1919, vol. II

Prendiville, Most Rev. Redmond, 1900–1968, vol. VI

Prentice, Bertram, 1867–1938, vol. III

Prentice, Frank Douglas, 1898–1962, vol. VI

Prentice, Brig.-Gen. Robert Emile Shepherd, 1872–1953, vol. V

Prentice, Sir William David Russell, died 1933, vol. III

Prescott, Caroline, (Mrs Cyril Prescott), died 1943, vol. IV

Prescott, Charles Barrow Clarke, 1870–1932, vol. III

Prescott, Charles John, 1857–1946, vol. IV

Prescott, Sir Charles William Beeston, 6th Bt (cr 1794), 1877–1955, vol. V

Prescott, Mrs Cyril; see Prescott, Caroline.

Prescott, E. Livingston, died 1901, vol. I

Prescott, Sir George Lionel Lawson Bagot, 5th Bt (cr 1794), 1875–1942, vol. IV

Prescott, Lt-Col Henry Cecil, 1882–1960, vol. V

Prescott, Hilda F. M., 1896–1972, vol. VII

Prescott, James C., 1894–1964, vol. VI

Prescott, Ven. John Eustace, died 1920, vol. II

Prescott, Richard Gordon Bathgate, 1896–1963, vol. VI

Prescott, Sir Richard Stanley, 2nd Bt (cr 1938), 1899–1965, vol. VI

Prescott, Stanley; see Prescott, W. R. S.

Prescott, Sir Stanley Lewis, 1910–1978, vol. VII

Prescott, Col Sir William Henry, 1st Bt (cr 1938), 1874–1945, vol. IV

Prescott, (William Robert) Stanley, 1912–1962, vol. VI

Prescott-Davies, N., 1862–1915, vol. I

Prescott-Decie, Brig.-Gen. Cyril; see Decie.

Prescott-Westcar, Lt-Col Sir William Villiers Leonard, 7th Bt (cr 1794), 1882–1959, vol. V

Presgrave, Col Edward Robert John, 1855–1919, vol. II

Presland, John, (Gladys Bendit), died 1975, vol. VII

Pressly, David Leith, 1855–1922, vol. II

Prest, Major Edward Papillon, 1864–1932, vol. III

Prest, Stanley Faber, 1858–1931, vol. III

Prestage, Edgar, 1869–1951, vol. V

Prestige, Rev. Canon George Leonard, 1889–1955, vol. V

Prestige, Major Sir John Theodore, 1884–1962, vol. VI

Preston, Arthur, 1864–1948, vol. IV

Preston, Major Arthur John, 1842–1930, vol. III

Preston, Rt Rev. Arthur Llewellyn, died 1936, vol. III

Preston, Bryan Wentworth, 1905–1965, vol VI

Preston, Col D'Arcy Brownlow, 1860–1932, vol. III

Preston, Lt-Col Sir Edward Hulton, 5th Bt, 1888–1963, vol. VI

Preston, Francis Noel Dykes, 1888–1957, vol. V

Preston, Frank Sansome, 1875–1970, vol. VI

Preston, Sir Frederick George Panizzi, died 1949, vol. IV

Preston, Rev. George, 1840–1913, vol. I

Preston, George Dawson, 1896–1972, vol. VII

Preston, George Frederic, died 1939, vol. III

Preston, Sir Harry John, 1860–1936, vol. III

Preston, Henry Edward, 1857–1924, vol. II

Preston, Herbert Sansome, died 1935, vol. III

Preston, Sir Jacob, 4th Bt, 1887–1918, vol. II

Preston, Lt-Col Jenico Edward, 1855–1940, vol. III

Preston, Kerrison, 1884–1974, vol. VII

Preston, Adm. Sir Lionel George, 1875–1971, vol. VII

Preston, Lt-Col Hon. Richard Martin Peter, 1884–1965, vol. VI

Preston, Sidney, 1850–1938, vol. III

Preston, Thomas, 1860–1900, vol. I

Preston, Thomas, 1834–1901, vol. I

Preston, Col Thomas, 1886–1966, vol. VI

Preston, Thomas Alford H. B.; see Houston-Boswall-Preston.

Preston, Sir Thomas Hildebrand, 6th Bt, 1886–1976, vol. VII

Preston, Sir Walter Reuben, 1875–1946, vol. IV

Preston, William, 1874–1941, vol. IV

Preston, Sir William Edward, 1865–1939, vol. III

Preston, Lt-Col William John Phaelim, 1873–1943, vol. IV

Preston-Thomas, Herbert, died 1909, vol. I

Pretorius, Major Philip Jacobus, died 1945, vol. IV

Pretty, Eric Ernest Falk, 1891–1967, vol. VI

Pretty, Air Marshal Sir Walter Philip George, 1909–1975, vol. VII

Pretyman, Rt Hon. Ernest George, 1860–1931, vol. III

Pretyman, Frederic Henry, 1875–1939, vol. III

Pretyman, Wing-Comdr George Frederick, 1891–1937, vol. III

Pretyman, Maj.-Gen. Sir George Tindal, 1845–1917, vol. II

Prevett, Comdr Harry, 1900–1972, vol. VII

Previté-Orton, Charles William, 1877–1947, vol. IV
Prevost, Sir Augustus, 1st Bt (*cr* 1903), 1837–1913, vol. I
Prevost, Sir Charles, 3rd Bt (*cr* 1805), 1831–1902, vol. I
Prevost, Sir Charles Thomas Keble, 4th Bt (*cr* 1805), 1866–1939, vol. III
Prevost, Francis; *see* Battersby, H. F. P.
Prevost, Marcel, 1862–1941, vol. IV
Preziosi, Count Luigi, *died* 1965, vol. VI
Price, Col Adolphus James, 1846–1937, vol. III
Price, Albert Thomas, 1903–1978, vol. VII
Price, Allen, 1905–1970, vol. VI
Price, Sir Archibald Grenfell, 1892–1977, vol. VII
Price, Aubrey Joseph, 1899–1978, vol. VII
Price, Bartholomew, 1818–1898, vol. I
Price, Hon. Brig.-Gen. Bartholomew George, 1870–1947, vol. IV
Price, Maj.-Gen. Charles Basil, 1889–1975, vol. VII
Price, Charles Edward, *died* 1934, vol. III
Price, Sir Charles Frederick Rugge-, 7th Bt (*cr* 1804), 1868–1953, vol. V
Price, Brig.-Gen. Charles Henry Uvedale, 1862–1942, vol. IV
Price, Lt-Col Sir Charles James Napier Rugge-, 8th Bt (*cr* 1804), 1902–1966, vol. VI
Price, Captain Charles Lempriere, 1877–1914, vol. I
Price, Sir (Charles) Roy, 1893–1976, vol. VII
Price, Sir Charles Rugge-, 6th Bt (*cr* 1804), 1841–1927, vol. II
Price, Major Sir Charles William Mackay, 1872–1954, vol. V
Price, Rev. Clement, 1858–1937, vol. III
Price, Rev. Cyril, *died* 1943, vol. IV
Price, Col Cyril Uvedale, 1868–1956, vol. V
Price, Maj.-Gen. Denis Walter, 1908–1966, vol. VI
Price, Dennis, 1915–1973, vol. VII
Price, Dorothy Stopford, 1890–1954, vol. V
Price, Rt Rev. Dudley William Mackay, 1899–1971, vol. VII
Price, (Edith) Mary, 1897–1980, vol. VII
Price, Rev. Canon Edward Hyde B.; *see* Blackwood-Price.
Price, Edwin Lessware, 1874–1935, vol. III
Price, Ernest Griffith, 1870–1962, vol. VI
Price, Rev. Ernest Jones, 1882–1952, vol. V
Price, Sir Francis Caradoc Rose, 5th Bt (*cr* 1815), 1880–1949, vol. IV
Price, Frank Corbyn, *born* 1862, vol. III
Price, Sir Frederick; *see* Price, Sir J. F.
Price, Frederick George Hilton, 1842–1909, vol. I
Price, Frederick William, *died* 1957, vol. V
Price, G. Ward, *died* 1961, vol. VI
Price, Gabriel, 1879–1934, vol. III
Price, George Basil, *died* 1939, vol. III
Price, Brig.-Gen. George Dominic, 1867–1943, vol. IV
Price, Comdr George Edward, 1842–1926, vol. II
Price, H. L., 1899–1943, vol. IV
Price, Harry, 1881–1948, vol. IV
Price, Sir Henry Philip, 1st Bt (*cr* 1953), 1877–1963, vol. VI

Price, Captain Henry Talbot, 1839–1915, vol. I
Price, Herbert Spencer, 1892–1976, vol. VII
Price, Rt Rev. Hetley; *see* Price, Rt Rev. S. H.
Price, Rt Rev. Horace MacCartie Eyre, 1863–1941, vol. IV
Price, Major Hubert Davenport, 1890–1958, vol. V
Price, Sir James Frederick George, 1873–1957, vol. V
Price, John Cadwgan P.; *see* Powell-Price.
Price, Sir (John) Frederick, 1839–1927, vol. II
Price, Sir John G.; *see* Green-Price.
Price, John Lloyd, 1882–1941, vol. IV
Price, Rev. John Willis, 1872–1940, vol. III
Price, (Joseph) Thomas, 1902–1973, vol. VII
Price, Julius Mendes, *died* 1924, vol. II
Price, Sir Keith, 1879–1956, vol. V
Price, Langford Lovell F. R., 1862–1950, vol. IV
Price, (Lilian) Nancy (Bache), 1880–1970, vol. VI
Price, Marjorie Muriel, 1907–1946, vol. IV
Price, Mary; *see* Price, E. M.
Price, Morgan Philips, 1885–1973, vol. VII
Price, Nancy; *see* Price, L. N. B.
Price, Lt-Col Owen Glendower H.; *see* Howell-Price.
Price, Col Sir Rhys Howell, 1872–1943, vol. IV
Price, Sir Richard Dansey G.; *see* Green-Price.
Price, Richard John Lloyd, 1843–1923, vol. II
Price, Major Sir Robert Henry G.; *see* Green-Price.
Price, Sir Robert John, 1854–1926, vol. II
Price, Sir Rose, 4th Bt (*cr* 1815), 1878–1901, vol. I
Price, Sir Rose Francis, 6th Bt (*cr* 1815), 1910–1979, vol. VII
Price, Sir Rose Lambart, 3rd Bt (*cr* 1815), 1837–1899, vol. I
Price, Sir Roy; *see* Price, Sir C. R.
Price, S. Warren, *died* 1944, vol. IV
Price, Seymour James, 1886–1959, vol. V
Price, Rt Rev. (Stuart) Hetley, 1922–1977, vol. VII
Price, Hon. Thomas, 1852–1909, vol. I
Price, Col Thomas, 1842–1911, vol. I
Price, Thomas; *see* Price, J. T.
Price, Brig.-Gen. Thomas Herbert Francis, 1869–1945, vol. IV
Price, Thomas Phillips, 1844–1932, vol. III
Price, Sir Thomas Rees, 1848–1916, vol. II
Price, Brig. Thomas Reginald, 1894–1978, vol. VII
Price, Brig.-Gen. Thomas Rose Caradoc, 1875–1949, vol. IV
Price, Thomas Slater, 1875–1949, vol. IV
Price, Major Vincent Walter, 1890–1976, vol. VII
Price, Walter Harrington C.; *see* Crawfurd-Price.
Price, Wilfrid, 1879–1961, vol. VI
Price, Sir William, 1867–1924, vol. II
Price, Sir William, *died* 1938, vol. III
Price, Hon. Brig.-Gen. William, 1864–1952, vol. V
Price, Lt-Col William Herbert, 1877–1963, vol. VI
Price, Rev. William James, *died* 1928, vol. II
Price, William James, 1884–1973, vol. VII
Price-Davies, Brig. Charles Stafford, 1892–1959, vol. V
Price-Davies, Maj.-Gen. Llewelyn Alberic Emilius, 1878–1965, vol. VI

Price Hughes, Mary Katherine H., 1853–1948, vol. IV
Price Thomas, Sir Clement, 1893–1973, vol. VII
Price-White, Lt-Col David Archibald, 1906–1978, vol. VII
Prichard, Rev. Alfred George, 1869–1945, vol. IV
Prichard, Arthur William, *died* 1926, vol. II
Prichard, Brig.-Gen. Charles Stewart, 1861–1942, vol. IV
Prichard, Major H. Hesketh, 1876–1922, vol. II
Prichard, Harold Arthur, 1871–1947, vol. IV
Prichard, Herbert William, 1873–1951, vol. V
Prichard, Lt-Col Hubert Cecil, 1865–1942, vol. IV
Prichard, Sir John, 1887–1971, vol. VII
Prichard, Katharine Susannah, *died* 1969, vol. VI
Prichard, Sir Norman George Mollett, 1895–1972, vol. VII
Prichard, Rev. Canon Thomas Estlin, 1910–1975, vol. VII
Prichard, Brig. Walter Clavel Herbert, 1883–1965, vol. VI
Prichard-Jones, Sir John, 1st Bt, 1845–1917, vol. II
Prickard, Arthur Octavius, 1843–1939, vol. III
Prickard, Thomas Francis Vaughan, 1879–1973, vol. VII
Prickett, Brig. Charles Henry, 1881–1958, vol. V
Prideaux, Sir Francis; *see* Prideaux, Sir J. F. E.
Prideaux, Lt-Col Francis Beville, 1871–1938, vol. III
Prideaux, Sir (Joseph) Francis (Engledue), 1884–1959, vol. V
Prideaux, Rev. Canon Walter Archibald, 1882–1965, vol. VI
Prideaux, Rev. Walter Cross, 1845–1912, vol. I
Prideaux, Sir Walter Sherburne, 1846–1928, vol. II
Prideaux, Col William Francis, 1840–1914, vol. I
Prideaux-Brune, Charles Glynn, 1821–1907, vol. I
Prideaux-Brune, Col Charles Robert, 1848–1936, vol. III
Prideaux-Brune, Sir Humphrey Ingelram, 1886–1979, vol. VII
Pridham, Vice-Adm. Sir (Arthur) Francis, 1886–1975, vol. VII
Pridham, Vice-Adm. Sir Francis; *see* Pridham, Vice-Adm. Sir A. F.
Pridham, Col Geoffrey Robert, 1872–1951, vol. V
Pridham-Wippell, Adm. Sir Henry Daniel, 1885–1952, vol. V
Pridie, Sir Eric Denholm, 1896–1978, vol. VII
Pridmore, Albert Edward, 1864–1927, vol. II
Pridmore, Walter George, 1864–1943, vol. IV
Priebsch, Robert, 1866–1935, vol. III
Priest, Alfred, 1874–1929, vol. III
Priest, Maj.-Gen. Robert Cecil, *died* 1966, vol. VI
Priestley, Sir Arthur, 1864–1933, vol. III
Priestley, Briggs, 1832–1907, vol. I
Priestley, Sir Gerald William, 1888–1978, vol. VII
Priestley, Lt-Col Harold Edgar, *died* 1941, vol. IV
Priestley, Henry, 1884–1961, vol. VI
Priestley, Henry James, 1883–1932, vol. III
Priestley, Herbert Ingram, 1875–1944, vol. IV
Priestley, Sir Joseph Child, 1862–1941, vol. IV
Priestley, Joseph Hubert, 1883–1944, vol. IV

Priestley, Sir Raymond Edward, 1886–1974, vol. VII
Priestley, Sir William Edwin Briggs, 1859–1932, vol. III
Priestman, Bertram, 1868–1951, vol. V
Priestman, Harold Eddey, 1888–1956, vol. V
Priestman, Howard, 1865–1931, vol. III
Priestman, Sir John, 1st Bt, *died* 1941, vol. IV
Priestman, Maj.-Gen. John Hedley Thornton, 1885–1964, vol. VI
Prime-Stevenson, Edward Irenaeus; *see* Stevenson.
Primo de Rivera, Duke of, *died* 1964, vol. VI
Primrose, Alexander, 1861–1944, vol. IV
Primrose, Vice-Adm. George Anson, 1849–1930, vol. III
Primrose, Rt Hon. Sir Henry, 1846–1923, vol. II
Primrose, Sir John Ure, 1st Bt, 1847–1924, vol. II
Primrose, Sir John Ure, 1900–1974, vol. VII
Primrose, Rt Hon. Neil James Archibald, 1882–1917, vol. II
Primrose, Sir William Louis, 2nd Bt, 1880–1953, vol. V
Prince, Sir Alexander William, 1870–1933, vol. III
Prince, Edward Ernest, 1858–1936, vol. III
Prince, J.-E., 1851–1923, vol. II (A), vol. III
Prince, John Dyneley, 1868–1945, vol. IV
Prince, Lt-Col Peregrine, 1882–1935, vol. III
Prince, Lt-Col Robert, *died* 1945, vol. IV
Prince-Smith, Sir Prince, 2nd Bt, 1869–1940, vol. III
Prince-Smith, Sir William, 3rd Bt, 1898–1964, vol. VI
Prinetti, Marchese Giulio, 1851–1908, vol. I
Pring, Hon. Robert Darlow, 1853–1922, vol. II
Pringle, Rev. Arthur, 1866–1933, vol. III
Pringle, Lt-Col David, *died* 1936, vol. III (A), vol. IV
Pringle, G. L. Kerr, *died* 1961, vol. VI
Pringle, Sir George, 1825–1911, vol. I
Pringle, George Taylor, 1890–1955, vol. V
Pringle, Brig. Hall Grant, 1876–1942, vol. IV
Pringle, Harold, *died* 1935, vol. III
Pringle, James Alexander, 1874–1935, vol. III
Pringle, James Hogarth, *died* 1941, vol. IV
Pringle, Sir James Scott, 1876–1951, vol. V
Pringle, Sir John, 1848–1923, vol. II
Pringle, Rev. John Christian, 1872–1938, vol. III
Pringle, John James, *died* 1922, vol. II
Pringle, John Mackay, 1888–1955, vol. V
Pringle, J(ohn) Seton Michael, 1909–1975, vol. VII
Pringle, Col Sir John Wallace, 1863–1938, vol. III
Pringle, Captain Lionel Graham, 1880–1915, vol. I
Pringle, Sir Norman Hamilton, 9th Bt, 1903–1961, vol. VI
Pringle, Sir Norman Robert, 8th Bt, 1871–1919, vol. II
Pringle, Maj.-Gen. Sir Robert, 1855–1926, vol. II
Pringle, Seton Sidney, 1879–1955, vol. V
Pringle, William Henderson, 1877–1967, vol. VI
Pringle, William Mather Rutherford, 1874–1928, vol. II
Pringle-Pattison, Andrew Seth; *see* Seth, Andrew.
Prinsep, Anthony Leyland, 1888–1942, vol. IV

Prinsep, Lt-Gen. Arthur Haldimand, 1840–1915, vol. I

Prinsep, Col Evelyn Siegfried MacLeod, 1892–1973, vol. VII

Prinsep, Hon. Sir Henry Thoby, 1836–1914, vol. I

Prinsep, Valentine Cameron, 1838–1904, vol. I

Prioleau, John Randolph Hamilton, 1882–1954, vol. V

Prior, A. C. Vincent, 1881–1954, vol. V

Prior, Rev. Alfred Hall, *died* 1937, vol. III

Prior, Arthur Norman, 1914–1969, vol. VI

Prior, Sir (Charles) Geoffrey, *died* 1972, vol. VII

Prior, Col Hon. Edward Gawler, 1853–1920, vol. II

Prior, Edward Schroder, 1852–1932, vol. III

Prior, Sir Geoffrey; *see* Prior, Sir C. G.

Prior, George Thurland, 1862–1936, vol. III

Prior, Maj.-Gen. George Upton, 1843–1919, vol. II

Prior, Sir Henry Carlos, 1890–1967, vol. VI

Prior, Melton, 1845–1910, vol. I

Prior, Oliver Herbert Phelps, 1871–1934, vol. III

Prior, Comdr Redvers Michael, *died* 1964, vol. VI

Prior, Samuel Henry, 1869–1933, vol. III

Prior, Ven. William Henry, 1883–1969, vol. VI

Prior-Palmer, Maj.-Gen. George Erroll, 1903–1977, vol. VII

Priston, Rev. Stewart Browne, 1880–1960, vol. V

Pritchard, Sir Albert Edward, 1859–1937, vol. III

Pritchard, Brig.-Gen. Aubrey Gordon, 1869–1943, vol. IV

Pritchard, Sir Charles Bradley, 1837–1903, vol. I

Pritchard, Brig. Charles Hilary Vaughan; *see* Vaughan, Brig. C. H. V.

Pritchard, Brig.-Gen. Clive Gordon, 1871–1948, vol. IV

Pritchard, Sir Edward Evan E.; *see* Evans-Pritchard.

Pritchard, Eric; *see* Pritchard, G. E. C.

Pritchard, Eric Alfred Blake, 1889–1962, vol. VI

Pritchard, (George) Eric (Campbell), *died* 1943, vol. IV

Pritchard, Maj.-Gen. Gordon Arthur Thomas, 1902–1957, vol. V

Pritchard, Lt-Gen. Sir Gordon Douglas, 1835–1912, vol. I

Pritchard, Sir Harry Goring, 1868–1962, vol. VI

Pritchard, Maj.-Gen. Harry Lionel, 1871–1953, vol. V

Pritchard, Lt-Col Hugh Robert Norman, 1879–1967, vol. VI

Pritchard, Col Hurlock Galloway, 1836–1909, vol. I

Pritchard, Ivor Mervyn, *died* 1948, vol. IV (A), vol. V

Pritchard, John Joseph, 1916–1979, vol. VII

Pritchard, Captain John Laurence, 1885–1968, vol. VI

Pritchard, Leslie Francis Gordon, 1918–1977, vol. VII

Pritchard, Robert Albion, *died* 1916, vol. II

Pritchard, Urban, 1845–1925, vol. II

Pritchard, Rev. William Charles, 1856–1931, vol. III

Pritchett, John Suckling, *died* 1941, vol. IV

Pritchett, Sir Theodore Beal, 1890–1969, vol. VI

Pritt, Denis Nowell, 1887–1972, vol. VII

Privett, Frank John, 1874–1937, vol. III

Probert, Arthur Reginald, 1909–1975, vol. VII

Probert, Rev. Lewis, 1841–1908, vol. I

Probert, Rhys Price, 1921–1980, vol. VII

Proby, Col Douglas James, 1856–1931, vol. III

Proby, Granville, 1883–1947, vol. IV

Proby, Major Sir Richard George, 1st Bt, 1886–1979, vol. VII

Probyn, Rt Hon. Sir Dighton Macnaghten, 1833–1924, vol. II

Probyn, Sir Lesley Charles, 1834–1916, vol. II

Probyn, Sir Leslie, 1862–1938, vol. III

Probyn, Lt-Col Percy John, *died* 1940, vol. III

Probyn-Jones, Sir Arthur Probyn, 2nd Bt, 1892–1951, vol. V

Probyn-Williams, Robert James, 1866–1952, vol. V

Procter, Rev. Arthur Herbert, 1890–1973, vol. VII

Procter, Rev. Charles James, *died* 1925, vol. II

Procter, Dod, *died* 1972, vol. VII

Procter, Ernest, *died* 1935, vol. III

Procter, Evelyn Emma Stefanos, 1897–1980, vol. VII

Procter, Henry Adam, 1883–1955, vol. V

Procter, Sir Henry Edward Edleston, 1866–1928, vol. II

Procter, Henry Richardson, 1848–1927, vol. II

Procter, Lt-Col James, 1884–1955, vol. V

Procter, Joan Beauchamp, 1897–1931, vol. III

Procter, Very Rev. John, 1849–1911, vol. I

Procter, Rev. John Mathias, 1835–1917, vol. II

Procter, Sir William, 1871–1951, vol. V

Procter-Gregg, Humphrey, 1895–1980, vol. VII

Proctor, Adam E., 1864–1913, vol. I

Proctor, Alexander Phimister, 1862–1950, vol. IV (A), vol. V

Proctor, Col Alfred Henry, *died* 1950, vol. IV

Proctor, Captain Andrew Weatherley Beauchamp, *died* 1921, vol. II

Proctor, Rev. Henry, *died* 1940, vol. III

Proctor, Mary, *died* 1957, vol. V

Proctor, Sir Philip Bridger, 1870–1940, vol. III

Proctor, Surg. Rear-Adm. Richard Louis Gibbon, 1900–1969, vol. VI

Proctor, William Thomas, 1896–1967, vol. VI

Proctor-Beauchamp, Col Sir Horace George; *see* Beauchamp.

Proctor-Beauchamp, Rev. Sir Ivor Cuthbert; *see* Beauchamp.

Proctor-Beauchamp, Rev. Sir Montagu Harry; *see* Beauchamp.

Proctor-Beauchamp, Sir Reginald William; *see* Beauchamp.

Proctor-Sims, Ernest William; *see* Sims.

Proe, Thomas, 1852–1922, vol. II

Proes, Lt-Col Ernest Marinus, 1871–1940, vol. III

Profeit, Col Charles William, 1870–1937, vol. III

Profumo, Albert, 1879–1940, vol. III

Prokofieff, Serge Sergeyevich, 1891–1953, vol. V

Propert, Rev. P. S. G., 1861–1940, vol. III

Propsting, Hon. William Bispham, 1861–1937, vol. III

Prosser, Rt Rev. Charles Keith Kipling, 1897–1954, vol. V

Prosser, Rt Rev. David Lewis, *died* 1950, vol. IV
Prosser, David Russell, 1889–1974, vol. VII
Prosser, Ernest Albert, *died* 1933, vol. III
Prosser, Francis Richard W.; *see* Wegg-Prosser.
Prosser, Rev. Henry Paul, *died* 1932, vol. III
Prosser, Sir John, 1857–1945, vol. IV
Prosser, Seward, 1871–1942, vol. IV
Prothero, Adm. Arthur William Edward, 1850–1931, vol. III
Prothero, Sir George Walter, 1848–1922, vol. II
Prothero, Vice-Adm. Reginald Charles, 1849–1927, vol. II
Protheroe, Ven. James Havard, *died* 1903, vol. I
Protheroe, Maj.-Gen. Montagu, 1841–1905, vol. I
Protheroe-Beynon, Major Godfrey Evan Schaw, 1872–1958, vol. V
Protheroe-Smith, Lt-Col Sir Hugh Bateman, 1872–1961, vol. VI
Proud, Sir George, 1910–1976, vol. VII
Proudfoot, Alexander, 1878–1957, vol. V
Proudfoot, Col Frank Grégoire, 1869–1940, vol. III
Proudfoot, James, 1908–1971, vol. VII
Proudman, Joseph, 1888–1975, vol. VII
Prout, Ebenezer, 1835–1909, vol. I
Prout, Henry Goslee, *died* 1927, vol. II (A), vol. III
Prout, Margaret F.; *see* Fisher Prout.
Prout, Sir William Thomas, *died* 1939, vol. III
Provand, Andrew Dryburgh, 1839–1915, vol. I
Provis, Edward, 1849–1941, vol. IV
Provis, Sir Samuel Butler, 1845–1926, vol. II
Prowde, Oswald Longstaff, 1882–1949, vol. IV
Prower, Brig. John Mervyn, 1885–1968, vol. VI
Prowse, Arthur Bancks, 1856–1925, vol. II
Prowse, Daniel Woodley, 1834–1914, vol. I
Prowse, Richard Orton, 1862–1949, vol. IV
Prowse, Richard Thomas, 1835–1921, vol. II
Prudden, T. Mitchell, 1849–1924, vol. II
Pruden, Arthur George, 1860–1936, vol. III
Prunty, Francis Thomas Garnet, 1910–1979, vol. VII
Prunty, Garnet; *see* Prunty, F. T. G.
Pryce, Daniel Merlin, 1902–1976, vol. VII
Pryce, Edward Calcott, 1885–1972, vol. VII
Pryce, Frederick Norman, 1888–1953, vol. V
Pryce, Howard Lloyd, *died* 1932, vol. III
Pryce, Very Rev. John, *died* 1903, vol. I
Pryce, Ven. Lewis Hugh Oswald, 1873–1930, vol. III
Pryce, Rev. R. Vaughan, 1834–1917, vol. II
Pryce, Richard, *died* 1942, vol. IV
Pryce, Very Rev. Shadrach, *died* 1914, vol. I
Pryce, Ven. Thomas P.; *see* Parry Pryce.
Pryce-Jones, Col Sir Edward, 1st Bt, 1861–1926, vol. II
Pryce-Jones, Bt Col Henry Morris, 1878–1952, vol. V
Pryce-Jones, Sir Pryce, 1834–1920, vol. II
Pryce-Jones, Sir Pryce Victor, 2nd Bt, 1887–1963, vol. VI
Pryde, David Johnstone, 1890–1959, vol. V
Pryde, George Smith, 1899–1961, vol. VI
Pryde, James, 1869–1941, vol. IV
Pryde, James Richmond Northridge, 1894–1980, vol. VII

Pryer, Major Alfred Amos, 1891–1943, vol. IV
Pryke, Sir Dudley; *see* Pryke, Sir W. R. D.
Pryke, Rev. William Emmanuel, 1843–1920, vol. II
Pryke, Sir William Robert, 1st Bt, 1847–1932, vol. III
Pryke, Sir (William Robert) Dudley, 2nd Bt, 1882–1959, vol. V
Pryn, Surg. Rear-Adm. Sir William Wenmoth, 1859–1942, vol. IV
Prynne, E. A. Fellowes, 1854–1921, vol. II
Prynne, Rev. George Rundle, 1818–1903, vol. I
Prynne, Brig. Harold Gordon Lusby, 1899–1976, vol. VII
Prynne, Col Harold Vernon, *died* 1954, vol. V
Prynne, Maj.-Gen. Michael Whitworth, 1912–1977, vol. VII
Pryor, Arthur Vickris, 1846–1927, vol. II
Pryor, Grafton Deen, 1883–1947, vol. IV
Pryor, Maurice Arthur, 1911–1969, vol. VI
Pryor, Rev. Michael, 1857–1929, vol. III
Pryor, Maj.-Gen. Sir Pomeroy Holland-, 1866–1955, vol. V
Pryor, Robert Nelson, 1921–1979, vol. VII
Pryor, S. J., 1865–1924, vol. II
Pryor, Lt-Col Walter Marlborough, 1880–1962, vol. VI
Prys, Rev. Owen, 1857–1934, vol. III
Pryse, Sir Edward John Webley-Parry-, 2nd Bt, 1862–1918, vol. II
Pryse, Gerald Spencer, 1882–1956, vol. V
Pryse, Sir Lewes Thomas Loveden, 3rd Bt, 1864–1946, vol. IV
Pryse, Sir Pryse, 1st Bt, 1838–1906, vol. I
Pryse, Sir Pryse Loveden S.; *see* Saunders-Pryse.
Pryse-Rice, Dame Margaret Ker, *died* 1948, vol. IV
Pryse-Saunders, Sir George Rice, 4th Bt, 1870–1948, vol. IV
Ptolemy, William John, 1850–1920, vol. II
Puccino, Giacomo, 1858–1924, vol. II
Puckle, Sir Frederick Hale, 1889–1966, vol. VI
Puckle, Lt-Col Frederick Kaye, 1880–1959, vol. V
Puckle, Lt-Col John, 1869–1917, vol. II
Puckle, Richard Kaye, 1830–1917, vol. II
Puckridge, Geoffrey Martin, 1895–1974, vol. VII
Puddester, Sir John Charles, 1881–1947, vol. IV
Puddicombe, Anne Adalisa, (Mrs Beynon Puddicombe); *see* Raine, Allen.
Pudner, Anthony Serle, 1917–1980, vol. VII
Pudney, John Sleigh, 1909–1977, vol. VII
Pudsey, Lt-Col Denison, 1876–1940, vol. III (A), vol. IV
Pudukota, Raja of, 1875–1928, vol. II
Pudumjee, Nowrojee, 1841–1930, vol. III
Puech, Albert G., 1859–1929, vol. III
Puech, Denys, 1854–1942, vol. IV
Pugh, Sir Alun; *see* Pugh, Sir J. A.
Pugh, Sir Arthur, 1870–1955, vol. V
Pugh, Lt-Col David Charles, 1859–1929, vol. III
Pugh, Ven. Edward William Wynn, *died* 1950, vol. IV
Pugh, Edwin William, 1874–1930, vol. III
Pugh, Sir (John) Alun, 1894–1971, vol. VII
Pugh, Rev. Canon John Richards, 1885–1961, vol. VI

Pugh, Leslie Mervyn, 1905–1978, vol. VII
Pugh, Lewis Pugh, 1837–1908, vol. I
Pugh, Lewis Pugh Evans, 1865–1940, vol. III
Pugh, Rev. Canon T(homas) Jenkin, 1903–1980, vol. VII
Pugh, Sir William John, 1892–1974, vol. VII
Pugh, William Thomas Gordon, died 1945, vol. IV
Pugno, Raoul, 1852–1914, vol. I
Pugsley, Sir Reuben James, 1886–1975, vol. VII
Pugsley, Hon. William, 1850–1925, vol. II
Pulbrook, Sir Eustace Ralph, 1881–1953, vol. V
Puleston, Sir John Henry, 1830–1908, vol. I
Pulford, Air Vice-Marshal Conway Walter Heath, died 1942, vol. IV
Pulford, Col Russell Richard, 1845–1920, vol. II
Pulitzer, Joseph, 1847–1911, vol. I
Pulitzer, Ralph, 1879–1939, vol. III
Pullan, Ayrton George Popplewell, 1879–1973, vol. VII
Pullan, Ayrton John Seaton, 1906–1967, vol. VI
Pullan, Rev. Leighton, 1865–1940, vol. III
Pullar, Sir Robert, 1828–1912, vol. I
Pullar, Rufus D., 1861–1917, vol. II
Pullein, John, died 1948, vol. IV
Pullein-Thompson, Mrs Joanna; see Cannan, J.
Pulleine, Rt Rev. John James, 1841–1913, vol. I
Pullen, Rev. Henry William, 1836–1903, vol. I
Pullen, William le Geyt, 1855–1922, vol. II
Pullen-Burry, Bessie, 1858–1937, vol. III
Puller, Rev. Frederick William, 1843–1938, vol. III
Pulley, Col Charles, 1851–1925, vol. II
Pulley, Sir Charles Thornton, 1864–1947, vol. IV
Pulley, Sir Joseph, 1st Bt, 1822–1901, vol. I
Pulliblank, Engr-Rear-Adm. John Blackler, 1879–1951, vol. V
Pullicino, Sir Philip, 1885–1960, vol. V
Pullin, Victor Edward, died 1956, vol. V
Pulling, Alexander, 1857–1942, vol. IV
Pulling, Rev. Edward Herbert, 1859–1928, vol. II
Pullinger, Frank, 1866–1920, vol. II
Pullinger, Henry Robert, 1884–1970, vol. VI
Pullinger, Thomas Charles Willis, 1867–1945, vol. IV
Pullman, Major Alfred Hopewell, died 1942, vol. IV
Pulsford, Rev. Edward John, 1878–1952, vol. V
Pulteney, Lt-Gen. Sir William Pulteney, 1861–1941, vol. IV
Pumpelly, Raphael, 1837–1923, vol. II
Pumphrey, Richard Julius, 1906–1967, vol. VI
Punch, Arthur Lisle, died 1964, vol. VI
Punchard, Constance, (Mrs F. B. Punchard); see Holme, C.
Punchard, Rev. Elgood George, 1844–1917, vol. II
Punnett, Reginald Crundall, 1875–1967, vol. VI
Pupin, Michael Idvorsky, 1858–1935, vol. III
Purbrick, Reginald, 1877–1950, vol. IV
Purcell, Albert Arthur, 1872–1935, vol. III
Purcell, Sir Gilbert Kenelm Treffry, 1867–1934, vol. III
Purcell, Rev. Handfield Noel, died 1925, vol. II
Purcell, Hubert Kennett, 1884–1962, vol. VI
Purcell, Sir John, 1839–1924, vol. II
Purcell, Pierce Francis, 1881–1968, vol. VI

Purcell, Major Raymond John Hugo, 1885–1928, vol. II
Purcell, Ronald Herbert, 1904–1969, vol. VI
Purcell, Victor, 1896–1965, vol. VI
Purcell-Buret, Captain Theobald John Claud, 1879–1974, vol. VII
Purchas, Rev. Canon Alban Charles Theodore, 1890–1976, vol. VII
Purchase, Sir Bentley; see Purchase, Sir W. B.
Purchase, Edward James, died 1924, vol. II
Purchase, Henry George, 1873–1945, vol. IV
Purchase, Sir (William) Bentley, 1890–1961, vol. VI
Purchase, Sir William Henry, 1860–1924, vol. II
Purchon, William Sydney, 1879–1942, vol. IV
Purdie, Rev. Albert B., 1888–1976, vol. VII
Purdie, Edna, 1894–1968, vol. VI
Purdie, Thomas, 1843–1916, vol. II
Purdom, Charles Benjamin, 1883–1965, vol. VI
Purdom, Thomas Hunter, 1853–1923, vol. II
Purdon, Lt-Col David William, 1853–1948, vol. IV (A), vol. V
Purdon, Maj.-Gen. William Brooke, died 1950, vol. IV
Purdy, Lt-Col John Smith, 1872–1936, vol. III
Purefoy, Richard Dancer, died 1919, vol. II
Purefoy, Adm. Richard Purefoy FitzGerald, 1862–1943, vol. IV
Purefoy, Wilfred Bagwell, 1862–1930, vol. III
Purey-Cust, Very Rev. Arthur Perceval; see Cust.
Purey-Cust, Adm. Sir Herbert Edward; see Cust.
Purey-Cust, Brig. Richard Brownlow, 1888–1958, vol. V
Purey Cust, Rev. Canon William Arthur; see Cust.
Purnell, Charlotte, died 1944, vol. IV
Purnell, Christopher James, 1878–1959, vol. V
Purnell, David Cuthbert, 1932–1979, vol. VII
Purohit, Sir Gopinath Sahitya Bhusan, 1863–1935, vol. III
Purse, Benjamin Ormond, 1876–1950, vol. IV
Purser, Maj.-Gen. Arthur William, 1884–1953, vol. V
Purser, Frederick, 1840–1910, vol. I
Purser, John Mallet, 1839–1929, vol. III
Purser, Louis Claude, 1854–1932, vol. III
Pursey, Comdr Harry, 1891–1980, vol. VII
Purssell, Richard Stanley, 1882–1954, vol. V
Purucker, Gottfried von; see Purucker, H. L. G. von.
Purucker, (Hobart Lorenz) Gottfried von, 1874–1942, vol. IV
Purves, James Liddell, 1843–1910, vol. I
Purves, Laidlaw; see Purves, W. L.
Purves, Sir Raymond Edgar, 1910–1973, vol. VII
Purves, Robert Egerton, 1859–1943, vol. IV
Purves, Col Sir Thomas Fortune, 1871–1950, vol. IV
Purves, William Donald Campbell Laidlaw, 1888–1964, vol. VI
Purves, (William) Laidlaw, died 1917, vol. II
Purves-Stewart, Sir James; see Stewart.
Purvis, Brig.-Gen. Alexander Burridge, 1854–1928, vol. II
Purvis, Rt Hon. Arthur Blaikie, 1890–1941, vol. IV

Purvis, Adm. Sir Charles Edward K.; *see* Kennedy-Purvis.
Purvis, Sir Robert, 1844–1920, vol. II
Purvis, Tom, *died* 1959, vol. V
Purvis-Russell-Montgomery, Lt-Col Henry Keith; *see* Montgomery.
Pusey, Philip Francis B.; *see* Bouverie-Pusey.
Putnam, George Haven, 1844–1930, vol. III
Putnam, Herbert, 1861–1955, vol. V
Putnam, Sir Thomas, 1862–1936, vol. III
Puttanna Chetty, Sir Krishnarajapur Palligondé, 1856–1938, vol. III
Puttick, Lt-Gen. Sir Edward, 1890–1976, vol. VII
Puxley, Henry Lavallin, *died* 1909, vol. I
Pybus, Sir John; *see* Pybus, Sir P. J.
Pybus, Sir (Percy) John, 1st Bt, *died* 1935, vol. III
Pycraft, W. P., 1868–1942, vol. IV
Pye, Sir David Randall, 1886–1960, vol. V
Pye, Joseph Patrick, *died* 1920, vol. II
Pye, Col William Edmund, 1872–1949, vol. IV
Pye-Smith, Arnold, 1847–1933, vol. III
Pye-Smith, Philip Henry, *died* 1914, vol. I
Pye-Smith, Rutherfoord John, 1848–1921, vol. II
Pyke, Air Cdre Alan, 1911–1977, vol. VII
Pyke, Cyril John, 1892–1976, vol. VII
Pyke, Joseph, 1884–1955, vol. V
Pyke, Lionel Edward, 1854–1899, vol. I
Pyke, Rev. R., 1873–1965, vol. VI
Pyke-Lees, Walter Kinnear, 1909–1978, vol. VII
Pyke-Nott, Comdr Sir James Grenvile, 1897–1972, vol. VII
Pyle, Howard, 1853–1912, vol. I
Pym, Barbara Mary Crampton, 1913–1980, vol. VII
Pym, Sir Charles Evelyn, 1879–1971, vol. VII
Pym, Charles Guy, 1841–1918, vol. II
Pym, Francis, 1849–1927, vol. II
Pym, Col Frederick Harry Norris, 1868–1944, vol. IV
Pym, Leslie Ruthven, 1884–1945, vol. IV
Pym, Rev. Thomas Wentworth, 1885–1945, vol. IV
Pyman, Frank Lee, 1882–1944, vol. IV
Pyman, Gen. Sir Harold English, 1908–1971, vol. VII
Pyne, Brig. Henry George, 1887–1945, vol. IV
Pyne, James Kendrick, 1852–1938, vol. III
Pyne, Hon. Robert Allan, 1855–1931, vol. III
Pyne, Sir Salter; *see* Pyne, Sir T. S.
Pyne, Thomas, 1843–1935, vol. III
Pyne, Sir (Thomas) Salter, 1860–1921, vol. II

Q

Qadir, Khan Bahadur Sheikh Sir Abdul, 1874–1951, vol. V
Quail, Jesse, *died* 1939, vol. III
Quain, Sir Richard, 1st Bt, 1816–1898, vol. I
Qualtrough, Sir Joseph Davidson, 1885–1960, vol. V
Quaranta di San Severino, Baron Bernardo, 1870–1934, vol. III

Quarles, Donald Aubrey, 1894–1959, vol. V
Quarmby, Sir John, 1868–1943, vol. IV
Quaroni, Pietro, 1898–1971, vol. VII
Quarrington, Rev. Edwin Fowler, *died* 1922, vol. II
Quartermaine, Sir Allan Stephen, 1888–1978, vol. VII
Quartermaine, Leon, 1876–1967, vol. VI
Quashie-Idun, Sir Samuel Okai, 1902–1966, vol. VI
Quasimodo, Salvatore, 1901–1968, vol. VI
Quass, Phineas, *died* 1961, vol. VI
Quayle, Richard William, 1901–1973, vol. VII
Quayle, Thomas, 1884–1963, vol. VI
Quayle-Jones, Brig.-Gen. Morey, 1855–1946, vol. IV
Queen, Rt Rev. Carman John, 1912–1974, vol. VII
Queenborough, 1st Baron, 1861–1949, vol. IV
Queensberry, 9th Marquess of, 1844–1900, vol. I (A)
Queensberry, 10th Marquess of, 1868–1920, vol. II
Queensberry, 11th Marquess of, 1896–1954, vol. V
Quekett, Sir Arthur Scott, 1881–1945, vol. IV
Quenington, Viscount; Michael Hugh Hicks-Beach, 1877–1916, vol. II
Quennell, Charles Henry Bourne, 1872–1935, vol. III
Quennell, Marjorie, *died* 1972, vol. VII
Quennell, Rev. William, 1839–1908, vol. I
Querido, Israël, 1874–1932, vol. III
Queripel, Hon. Col Alfred Ernest, 1870–1921, vol. II
Queripel, Col Leslie Herbert, 1881–1962, vol. VI
Quex; *see* Nichols, George Herbert Fosdike.
Quibell, 1st Baron, 1879–1962, vol. VI
Quick, Hon. Sir John, 1852–1932, vol. III
Quick, Rev. Oliver Chase, 1885–1944, vol. IV
Quick, Richard, *died* 1939, vol. III
Quicke, Captain Noel Arthur Godolphin, 1888–1943, vol. IV
Quickswood, 1st Baron, 1869–1956, vol. V
Quidde, Ludwig, 1858–1941, vol. IV
Quig, Alexander Johnstone, 1892–1962, vol. VI
Quigley, Arthur Grainger, *died* 1945, vol. IV
Quigley, Hugh, 1895–1979, vol. VII
Quigley, Most Rev. James Edward, 1854–1916, vol. II
Quill, Albert William, *died* 1908, vol. I
Quill, Lt-Col Berkeley Crosbie, 1852–1932, vol. III
Quill, Maj.-Gen. Richard Henry, 1848–1924, vol. II
Quiller-Couch, Sir Arthur Thomas, 1863–1944, vol. IV
Quilter, Sir Cuthbert; *see* Quilter, Sir W. C.
Quilter, Sir Cuthbert; *see* Quilter, Sir W. E. C.
Quilter, Harry, 1851–1907, vol. I
Quilter, Sir (John) Raymond (Cuthbert), 3rd Bt, 1902–1959, vol. V
Quilter, Sir Raymond; *see* Quilter, Sir J. R. C.
Quilter, Roger, 1877–1953, vol. V
Quilter, Sir (William) Cuthbert, 1st Bt, 1841–1911, vol. I
Quilter, Sir (William Eley) Cuthbert, 2nd Bt, 1873–1952, vol. V

Quin, Sir Stephen, 1860–1944, vol. IV
Quin, Maj.-Gen. Thomas James, 1842–1919, vol. II
Quinan, Gen. Sir Edward Pellew, 1885–1960, vol. V
Quinan, Kenneth Bingham, 1878–1948, vol. IV
Quine, Rev. John, 1857–1940, vol. III
Quinlan, Hon. Timothy Francis, 1861–1927, vol. II
Quinn, Most Rev. Austin, 1892–1974, vol. VII
Quinn, Harley; see Thorley, Wilfrid.
Quinn, James, 1870–1951, vol. V
Quinn, John, 1870–1924, vol. II (A), vol. III
Quinn, Sir Patrick, 1855–1936, vol. III
Quinnell, Cecil Watson, 1868–1932, vol. III
Quinton, Hon. Herman William, 1896–1952, vol. V
Quinton, Richard Frith, 1849–1934, vol. III
Quirk, Lt-Col Douglas, 1887–1941, vol. IV
Quirk, Rev. James Francis, 1850–1927, vol. II
Quirk, Rt Rev. Canon John Nathaniel, 1849–1924, vol. II
Quirk, Col John Owen, 1847–1928, vol. II
Quirk, Rev. Canon Robert, 1883–1949, vol. IV
Quirk, Roger Nathaniel, 1909–1964, vol. VI
Quirk, Ronald Charles, 1908–1973, vol. VII
Quist, Sir Emmanuel Charles, died 1959, vol. V
Quraishi, Khan Bahadur Nawab, born 1878, vol. VI

R

Rabagliati, Andrea Carlo Francisco, 1843–1930, vol. III
Rabagliati, Herman Victor, 1883–1962, vol. VI
Raban, Brig.-Gen. Sir Edward, 1850–1927, vol. II
Rabett, Brig. Reginald Lee Rex, 1887–1966, vol. VI
Rabino, H. Louis, 1877–1950, vol. IV, vol. V
Raby, Frederic James Edward, 1888–1966, vol. VI
Raby, Henry James, 1827–1907, vol. I
Raby, Joseph Thomas, 1853–1916, vol. II
Rachmaninoff, Sergei Vassilievitch, 1873–1943, vol. IV
Rackham, Arthur, 1867–1939, vol. III
Rackham, Bernard, 1876–1964, vol. VI
Rackham, Clara Dorothea, died 1966, vol. VI
Rackham, Harris, 1868–1944, vol. IV
Radcliffe, 1st Viscount, 1899–1977, vol. VII
Radcliffe, Alexander Nelson, 1856–1944, vol. IV
Radcliffe, Very Rev. Bennett Samuel, died 1943, vol. IV
Radcliffe, Brig.-Gen. Sir Charles D.; see Delme-Radcliffe.
Radcliffe, Sir Clifford Walter, 1888–1965, vol. VI
Radcliffe, Sir David, 1834–1907, vol. I
Radcliffe, Sir Everard; see Radcliffe, Sir J. B. E. H.
Radcliffe, Sir Everard Joseph, 5th Bt, 1884–1969, vol. VI
Radcliffe, Francis Reynolds Yonge, 1851–1924, vol. II
Radcliffe, Sir Frederick Morton, 1861–1953, vol. V
Radcliffe, Brig.-Gen. Frederick Walter, 1873–1934, vol. III

Radcliffe, Geoffrey Reynolds Yonge, 1886–1959, vol. V
Radcliffe, Ven. Harry Sydney, 1867–1949, vol. IV
Radcliffe, Henry, died 1921, vol. II
Radcliffe, Major Jasper Fitzgerald, 1867–1916, vol. II
Radcliffe, John Ed., 1846–1919, vol. II
Radcliffe, Sir (Joseph Benedict) Everard (Henry), 6th Bt, 1910–1975, vol. VII
Radcliffe, Sir Joseph Edward, 4th Bt, 1858–1949, vol. IV
Radcliffe, Sir Joseph Percival Pickford, 3rd Bt, 1824–1908, vol. I
Radcliffe, Col Nathaniel Robert, 1870–1930, vol. III
Radcliffe, Gen. Sir Percy Pollexfen de Blaquiere, 1874–1934, vol. III
Radcliffe, Col Philip John Joseph, 1863–1943, vol. IV
Radcliffe, Sir Ralph Hubert John D.; see Delme-Radcliffe.
Radcliffe, Lt-Gen. Robert Parker, 1819–1907, vol. I
Radcliffe, Vice-Adm. Stephen Herbert, 1874–1939, vol. III
Radcliffe, Sir W. Pollexfen, 1822–1897, vol. I
Radcliffe, William, 1856–1938, vol. III
Radcliffe, Wyndham Ivor, died 1927, vol. II
Radcliffe-Brown, Alfred Reginald, 1881–1955, vol. V
Radcliffe-Cooke, Charles Wallwyn; see Cooke.
Radclyffe, Lt-Col Charles Edward, 1864–1915, vol. I (A)
Radclyffe, Major (Charles Robert) Eustace, 1873–1953, vol. V
Radclyffe, Major Eustace; see Radclyffe, Major C. R. E.
Radden, Horace Gray, 1903–1966, vol. VI
Radford, Arthur, 1888–1963, vol. VI
Radford, Adm. Arthur William, 1896–1973, vol. VII
Radford, Basil, 1897–1952, vol. V
Radford, Sir Charles Horace, 1854–1916, vol. II
Radford, Edmund Ashworth, 1881–1944, vol. IV
Radford, Edward, 1831–1920, vol. II
Radford, Sir George Heynes, 1851–1917, vol. II
Radford, Rt Rev. Lewis Bostock, 1869–1937, vol. III
Radford, Col Oswald Claude, 1850–1924, vol. II
Radford, Robert, 1874–1933, vol. III
Radhakrishnan, Sir Sarvepalli, 1888–1975, vol. VII
Radhanpur, Nawab Sahib of, 1889–1936, vol. III
Radice, Mrs A. H., (Sheila Radice), died 1960, vol. V
Radice, Evasio Hampden, 1866–1909, vol. I
Radice, Sheila; see Radice, Mrs A. H.
Radin, Max, 1880–1950, vol. IV (A), vol. V
Radley, Sir Gordon; see Radley, Sir W. G.
Radley, Brig. Hugh Poynton, 1891–1943, vol. IV
Radley, Oswald Alfred, 1887–1977, vol. VII
Radley, Sir (William) Gordon, 1898–1970, vol. VI
Radnor, 5th Earl of, 1841–1900, vol. I
Radnor, 6th Earl of, 1868–1930, vol. III
Radnor, 7th Earl of, 1895–1968, vol. VI

Radstock, 3rd Baron, 1833–1913, vol. I
Radstock, 4th Baron, 1859–1937, vol. III
Radstock, 5th Baron, 1867–1953, vol. V
Rae, Sir Alexander, *died* 1924, vol. II
Rae, Sir Alexander (Montgomery) Wilson, 1896–1978, vol. VII
Rae, Lt-Col Cecil, 1880–1945, vol. IV
Rae, Brig. Cecil Alexander, 1889–1966, vol. VI
Rae, Cecil Douglas, 1882–1942, vol. IV
Rae, Duncan McFadyen, 1888–1964, vol. VI
Rae, George Bentham Leathart, 1884–1958, vol. V
Rae, Henrietta; *see* Normand, Mrs Ernest.
Rae, Sir (Henry) Norman, 1860–1928, vol. II
Rae, Sir James, 1879–1957, vol. V
Rae, Captain Sir James Robert, *died* 1928, vol. II
Rae, Sir James Stanley, 1881–1956, vol. V
Rae, John, 1845–1915, vol. I
Rae, Sir Norman; *see* Rae, Sir H. N.
Rae, Sir Robert, 1894–1971, vol. VII
Rae, W. Fraser, 1835–1905, vol. I
Rae, William, 1840–1907, vol. I
Rae, Lt-Col William, 1883–1973, vol. VII
Rae Smith, Sir Alan, 1885–1961, vol. VI
Raeburn, Agnes M., *died* 1955, vol. V
Raeburn, Sir Colin, 1894–1970, vol. VI
Raeburn, Sir Edward Alfred, 3rd Bt, 1919–1977, vol. VII
Raeburn, Sir Ernest Manifold, 1878–1922, vol. II
Raeburn, Henry Raeburn Macbeth-, 1860–1947, vol. IV
Raeburn, Walter Augustus Leopold, 1897–1972, vol. VII
Raeburn, Sir William Hannay, 1st Bt, 1850–1934, vol. III
Raeburn, Sir William Norman, 2nd Bt, 1877–1947, vol. IV
Raemaekers, Louis, 1869–1956, vol. V
Raffaelli, J. F., 1850–1924, vol. II
Raffan, Peter Wilson, 1863–1940, vol. III
Rafferty, Michael Harvey, 1877–1953, vol. V
Raffety, Frank Walter, 1875–1946, vol. IV
Raffles, Harold Vezey, 1873–1948, vol. IV
Raffles, Rev. Thomas Stamford, 1853–1926, vol. II
Raffles-Flint, Ven. Stamford R., 1847–1925, vol. II
Raffray, Sir Philippe, 1888–1975, vol. VII
Rafter, Sir Charles Haughton, *died* 1935, vol. III
Ragg, Rt Rev. Harry Richard, 1889–1967, vol. VI
Ragg, Sir Hugh Hall, 1882–1963, vol. VI
Ragg, Ven. Lonsdale, 1866–1945, vol. IV
Ragg, Air Vice-Marshal Robert Linton, 1901–1973, vol. VII
Ragg, Rev. William Henry Murray, 1861–1944, vol. IV
Raggatt, Sir Harold George, 1900–1968, vol. VI
Raghava Rau, G. Pantulu, 1862–1921, vol. II
Raghavendra Rao, E., *died* 1942, vol. IV
Raghunath Das Rai Bahadur, Diwan Bahadur Sir Chaube, 1849–1923, vol. II
Raghunath Rao Dinkar, Rao Raja, Mashir-i-Khas Bahadur, Madar-ul-Moham, *born* 1858, vol. II
Raglan, 3rd Baron, 1857–1921, vol. II
Raglan, 4th Baron, 1885–1964, vol. VI
Rahilly, Captain Denis Edward, 1887–1966, vol. VI
Rahim, Sir Abdur, 1867–1952, vol. V

Rahimtoola, Sir Fazal Ibrahim, 1895–1977, vol. VII
Rahimtoola, Sir Ibrahim, 1862–1942, vol. IV
Rahman, Shaikh Abdur, 1903–1979, vol. VII
Rahman, Sir Ahmed Fazlur, *died* 1945, vol. IV (A), vol. V
Rahman, Sheikh Mujibur, 1920–1975, vol. VII
Raikes, Captain Arthur E. H., 1867–1915, vol. I
Raikes, Arthur Stewart, 1856–1925, vol. II
Raikes, Vice-Adm. Cecil Dacre Staveley, 1874–1947, vol. IV
Raikes, Maj.-Gen. Charles Lewis, 1837–1919, vol. II
Raikes, Col David Taunton, 1897–1966, vol. VI
Raikes, Ernest Barkley, 1863–1931, vol. III
Raikes, Francis Edward, 1870–1922, vol. II
Raikes, Francis William, *died* 1906, vol. I
Raikes, Lt-Col Frederick Duncan, 1848–1915, vol. I
Raikes, Maj.-Gen. Sir Geoffrey Taunton, 1884–1975, vol. VII
Raikes, Maj.-Gen. George Leonard, 1878–1949, vol. IV
Raikes, Henry St John Digby, 1863–1943, vol. IV
Raikes, Humphrey Rivaz, *died* 1955, vol. V
Raikes, Col Lawrence Taunton, 1882–1932, vol. III
Raikes, Adm. Sir Robert Henry Taunton, 1885–1953, vol. V
Raikes, Gen. Robert Napier, 1813–1909, vol. I
Raikes, Rev. Walter Allan, 1852–1928, vol. II
Railing, Sir Harry, 1878–1963, vol. VI
Railing, Max John, 1868–1942, vol. IV
Railston, Lt-Col Henry George Moreton P.; *see* Pleydell-Railston.
Railton, Herbert, 1857–1911, vol. I
Railton, James, 1863–1949, vol. IV
Railton, Ven. Nathaniel Gerard, 1886–1948, vol. IV
Railton, Reid Antony, 1895–1977, vol. VII
Raimond, C. E.; *see* Robins, Elizabeth.
Rainals, Sir Harry Thomas Alfred, 1816–1899, vol. I
Raine, Allen, 1836–1908, vol. I
Raine, Sir Walter, 1874–1938, vol. III
Raines, Gen. Sir Julius Augustus Robert, 1827–1909, vol. I
Raines, Lt-Col Ralph Gore Devereux Groves-, 1877–1953, vol. V
Rainey, Lt-Col John Wakefield, 1881–1967, vol. VI
Rainey, William, 1852–1936, vol. III
Rainey-Robinson, Col Robert Maximilian, 1861–1932, vol. III
Rainier, Adm. John Harvey, 1847–1915, vol. I (A)
Rains, Claude, 1889–1967, vol. VI
Rainsford, Col Marcus Edward Read, 1853–1933, vol. III
Rainsford, Col Stephen Dickson, 1853–1920, vol. II
Rainsford, Col William John Read, 1852–1932, vol. III
Rainsford-Hannay, Brig.-Gen. Frederick, 1854–1950, vol. IV
Rainsford-Hannay, Col Frederick, 1878–1959, vol. V
Rainsford-Hannay, Col Ramsay William, 1844–1933, vol. III
Rainville, Hon. Henri B., 1852–1937, vol. III

Rainy, Adam Rolland, 1862–1911, vol. I
Rainy, Sir George, 1875–1946, vol. IV
Rainy, Rev. Robert, 1826–1906, vol. I
Raisman, Sir (Abraham) Jeremy, 1892–1978, vol. VII
Raisman, Sir Jeremy; see Raisman, Sir A. J.
Raison, Rev. Herbert Chaplin, 1889–1952, vol. V
Raistrick, Harold, 1890–1971, vol. VII
Rait, Lt-Col Arthur John, 1839–1902, vol. I
Rait, Miss Helen Anna Macdonald, died 1955, vol. V
Rait, Sir Robert Sangster, 1874–1936, vol. III
Rait Kerr, Col Rowan Scrope, 1891–1961, vol. VI
Raitt, Maj.-Gen. Sir Herbert Aveling, 1858–1935, vol. III
Rajadhyaksha, Ganpat Sakharam, 1896–1955, vol. V
Rajagopala, Sir Chariyar, Perungavur, 1862–1927, vol. II
Rajagopalachari, Sir Shrinivas Prasonna, 1883–1963, vol. VI
Rajagopalacharya, Chakravarti, 1878–1972, vol. VII
Rajapakse, Sir Lalita Abhaya, 1900–1976, vol. VII
Rajgarh, HH Rajah Bir Indra of, died 1936, vol. III
Rajkot, Thakore Saheb Shri Dharmendrasinhji Lakhaji Raj, 1910–1940, vol. III
Rajkot, Thakore Saheb Sir Lakhaji Raj Bawaji Raj, 1885–1930, vol. III
Rajpipla, Raja of, 1862–1915, vol. I
Rajpipla, Maharaja of, died 1951, vol. V
Rajwade, Maj.-Gen. Ganpatrao Raghunath Raja, Mushir-i-Khas Bahadur, Shaukat-Jung, 1884–1945, vol. IV
Rake, Alfred Mordey, 1906–1978, vol. VII
Raleigh, Cecil, died 1914, vol. I
Raleigh, Hon. Sir Thomas, 1850–1920, vol. II
Raleigh, Sir Walter, 1861–1922, vol. II
Ralfs, Maj.-Gen. Bertram George, 1905–1977, vol. VII
Ralli, Augustus John, 1875–1954, vol. V
Ralli, Constantine S.; see Scaramanga-Ralli.
Ralli, Sir Lucas Eustratio, 1st Bt, 1846–1931, vol. III
Ralli, Pandeli, 1845–1928, vol. II
Ralli, Sir Strati, 2nd Bt, 1876–1964, vol. VI
Ralph, Col Alfred Colyer, 1869–1932, vol. III
Ralph, Annabella, 1884–1962, vol. VI
Ralph, Helen Douglas Guest, 1892–1961, vol. VI
Ralph, Herbert Walter, 1885–1955, vol. V
Ralph, William, died 1928, vol. II (A), vol. III
Ralphs, Sir (Frederick) Lincoln, 1909–1978, vol. VII
Ralphs, Sir Lincoln; see Ralphs, Sir F. L.
Ralston, Alexander Gerard, 1860–1932, vol. III
Ralston, Col Alexander Windeyer, 1885–1971, vol. VII
Ralston, Col Hon. James Layton, 1881–1948, vol. IV
Ralston, Maj.-Gen. William Henry, 1837–1914, vol. I
Ram, Abel John, 1842–1920, vol. II
Ram, Sir Granville; see Ram, Sir L. A. J. G.
Ram, Rai Bahadur Sir Lala G.; see Ganga Ram.

Ram, Sir (Lucius Abel John) Granville, 1885–1952, vol. V
Ram, Rev. Robert Digby, 1844–1925, vol. II
Ram, Sir Shri, 1884–1963, vol. VI
Ram, Rev. Stephen Adye Scott, 1864–1928, vol. II
Ram, William Francis Willett, 1907–1968, vol. VI
Ramachandra Rao, Dewan Bahadur Sir M., 1868–1936, vol. III
Ramaciotti, Maj.-Gen. Gustave, 1861–1927, vol. II
Ramage, Sir Richard Ogilvy, 1896–1971, vol. VII
Ramakrishna, T., born 1854, vol. II
Raman, Sir (Chandrasekhara) Venkata, 1888–1970, vol. VI
Raman, Sir Venkata; see Raman, Sir C. V.
Ramanathan, Sir Ponnambalam, 1851–1930, vol. III
Ramasany Mudaliyar, Raja Sir Savalai, 1840–1911, vol. I
Ramaswami Aiyar, Sir C. P., 1879–1966, vol. VI
Rambaut, Arthur Alcock, 1859–1923, vol. II
Ramée, Louise de la; see Ouida.
Rammingen, Baron Luitbert Alexander George Lionel Alphons P.; see Pawel-Rammingen.
Rampal Singh, Raja, 1867–1909, vol. I
Rampolla, His Eminence Cardinal Mariano, 1843–1913, vol. I
Rampur, Nawab Sir Sayed Mohammad Hamid Ali Khan Bahadur, 1875–1930, vol. III
Rampur, Maj.-Gen. HH the Nawab, 1906–1966, vol. VI
Ramsay, Maj.-Gen. Sir Alan Hollick, 1895–1973, vol. VII
Ramsay, Alexander, 1822–1909, vol. I
Ramsay, Rev. Alexander, 1857–1935, vol. III
Ramsay, Sir Alexander, 1887–1969, vol. VI
Ramsay, Sir Alexander Burnett, 6th Bt (cr 1806), 1903–1965, vol. VI
Ramsay, Sir Alexander Entwisle, 4th Bt (cr 1806), 1837–1902 (this entry was not transferred to Who was Who).
Ramsay, Adm. Hon. Sir Alexander Robert Maule, 1881–1972, vol. VII
Ramsay, Allen Beville, 1872–1955, vol. V
Ramsay, Andrew Maitland, 1859–1946, vol. IV
Ramsay, Captain Archibald Henry Maule, died 1955, vol. V
Ramsay, Lt-Col Arthur Dennys Gilbert, 1872–1939, vol. III
Ramsay, Adm. Sir Bertram Home, 1883–1945, vol. IV
Ramsay, Hon. Charles Maule, 1859–1936, vol. III
Ramsay, Clyde Archibald, 1914–1974, vol. VII
Ramsay, Maj.-Gen. Frank William, 1875–1954, vol. V
Ramsay, Rev. Frederick Ernest, died 1913, vol. I
Ramsay, Sir George Dalhousie, 1828–1920, vol. II
Ramsay, George Gilbert, 1839–1921, vol. II
Ramsay, Gilbert Anderson, 1880–1915, vol. I
Ramsay, Graham Colville, 1889–1959, vol. V
Ramsay, Henry Havelock, 1863–1929, vol. III
Ramsay, Sir Herbert, 5th Bt (cr 1806), 1868–1924, vol. II
Ramsay, Maj.-Gen. Herbert Maynard, 1843–1917, vol. II

Ramsay, Comdr Hugh Malcolm, 1884–1975, vol. VII
Ramsay, Rev. Ivor Erskine St Clair, 1902–1956, vol. V
Ramsay, J. Grant, 1856–1940, vol. III
Ramsay, James, 1905–1959, vol. V
Ramsay, Sir James Douglas, 11th Bt (*cr* 1666), 1878–1959, vol. V
Ramsay, Lt-Col James Gordon, 1880–1952, vol. V
Ramsay, Sir James Henry, 10th Bt (*cr* 1666), 1832–1925, vol. II
Ramsay, Lt-Col Sir John, 1862–1942, vol. IV
Ramsay, Sir John, 1872–1944, vol. IV
Ramsay, Maj.-Gen. Sir John George, 1856–1920, vol. II
Ramsay, Dom Leander; *see* Ramsay, H. H.
Ramsay, Louis Eveleigh Bawtree C.; *see* Cobden-Ramsay.
Ramsay, Mabel Lieda, *died* 1954, vol. V
Ramsay, Sir Malcolm Graham, 1871–1946, vol. IV
Ramsay, The Lady Patricia, (Victoria Patricia Helena Elizabeth), 1886–1974, vol. VII
Ramsay, Hon. Sir Patrick William Maule, 1879–1962, vol. VI
Ramsay, Robert Anstruther, 1887–1975, vol. VII
Ramsay, Rt Rev. Ronald Erskine, 1882–1954, vol. V
Ramsay, Thomas Bridgehill Wilson, 1887–1956, vol. V
Ramsay, Sir William, 1852–1916, vol. II
Ramsay, Sir William Clark, 1901–1973, vol. VII
Ramsay, Sir William Mitchell, 1851–1939, vol. III
Ramsay-Fairfax, Lt-Col William George Astell, 1876–1946, vol. IV
Ramsay-Fairfax, Sir William George Herbert Taylor; *see* Fairfax.
Ramsay-Fairfax-Lucy, Major Sir Brian Fulke Cameron; *see* Fairfax-Lucy.
Ramsay-Fairfax-Lucy, Sir Henry William Cameron; *see* Fairfax-Lucy.
Ramsay-Steel-Maitland, Sir Keith Richard Felix; *see* Steel-Maitland.
Ramsbottom, Edmund Cecil, 1881–1959, vol. V
Ramsbottom, John, 1885–1974, vol. VII
Ramsbottom, John William, 1883–1966. vol. VI
Ramsden, 1st Baron, 1883–1955, vol. V
Ramsden, Brig. Sir Arthur Maxwell, 1894–1957, vol. V
Ramsden, Charles Frederick Ingram, 1888–1958, vol. V
Ramsden, George Taylor, 1879–1936, vol. III
Ramsden, Lady Guendolen; *see* Ramsden, Lady H. G.
Ramsden, Lady (Helen) Guendolen, 1846–1910, vol. I
Ramsden, Col Herbert Frecheville Smyth, 1856–1931, vol. III
Ramsden, John Charles Francis, 1835–1910, vol. I
Ramsden, Sir John Frecheville, 6th Bt, 1877–1958, vol. V
Ramsden, John Watkinson, 1880–1943, vol. IV
Ramsden, Sir John William, 5th Bt, 1831–1914, vol. I
Ramsden, Lt-Col Josslyn Vere, 1876–1952, vol. V

Ramsden, Omar, 1873–1939, vol. III
Ramsden, Lt-Col Vincent Basil, 1888–1936, vol. III
Ramsden, Walter, *died* 1947, vol. IV
Ramsden, Sir William, 1857–1928, vol. II
Ramsden, Maj.-Gen. William Havelock, 1888–1969, vol. VI
Ramsden-Jodrell, Dorothy Lynch, *died* 1958, vol. V
Ramsey, Alicia, *died* 1933, vol. III
Ramsey, Arthur Stanley, 1867–1954, vol. V
Ramsey, Adm. Sir Charles Gordon, 1882–1966, vol. VI
Ramsey, Col Colin Worthington Pope, 1883–1926, vol. II
Ramsey, Rt Rev. Ian Thomas, 1915–1972, vol. VII
Ramsey, Stanley Churchill, 1882–1968, vol. VI
Ramson, Ven. John Luce, 1870–1944, vol. IV
Ramunni Menon, Sir Konkoth, 1872–1949, vol. IV
Ranalow, Frederick Baring, 1873–1953, vol. V
Ranbir Singh, Raja Sir, *died* 1916, vol. II
Rance, Maj.-Gen. Sir Hubert Elvin, 1898–1974, vol. VII
Rand, Benjamin, 1856–1934, vol. III
Rand, Ivan Cleveland, 1884–1969, vol. VI
Randall, Sir Alec Walter George, 1892–1977. vol. VII
Randall, Gp Captain Charles Russell Jekyl, 1879–1956, vol. V
Randall, Harry, 1860–1932, vol. III
Randall, Harry Enos, 1899–1976, vol. VII
Randall, Sir Henry Edward, 1847–1930, vol. III
Randall, Henry John, 1877–1964, vol. VI
Randall, Henry John, 1894–1967, vol. VI
Randall, J(ames) G(arfield), 1881–1953, vol. V
Randall, Rt Rev. James Leslie, *died* 1922, vol. II
Randall, John, 1810–1910, vol. I
Randall, John William, 1891–1979, vol. VII
Randall, Very Rev. Richard William, 1824–1906, vol. I
Randall, Terence George, 1904–1979, vol. VII
Randall Lane, Henry Jerrold; *see* Lane.
Randall-MacIver, David, 1873–1945, vol. IV
Randegger, Alberto, 1832–1911, vol. I
Randell, Major Charles Edmund, 1893–1961, vol. VI
Randell, David, 1854–1912, vol. I
Randell, Hon. George, 1830–1912, vol. I
Randell, Wilfrid L., 1874–1952, vol. V
Randle, Herbert Niel, 1880–1973, vol. VII
Randles, Sir John Scurrah, 1857–1945, vol. IV
Randles, Rev. Marshall, 1826–1904, vol. I
Randolph, Lt-Col Algernon Forbes, 1865–1953, vol. V
Randolph, Rev. Berkeley William, 1858–1925, vol. II
Randolph, Mrs Evelyn St L.; *see* St Leger, E.
Randolph, Rev. Francis Charles H.; *see* Hingeston-Randolph.
Randolph, George Boscawen, 1864–1951, vol. V
Randolph, Adm. Sir George Granville, 1818–1907, vol. I
Randolph, Rt Rev. John Hugh Granville, 1866–1936, vol. III
Randolph, Joseph Randolph, 1867–1936, vol. III

Randolph, Peter, 1920–1971, vol. VII
Randolph-Rose, Walter Clerk, 1884–1938, vol. III
Ranfurly, 5th Earl of, 1856–1933, vol. III
Ranganathan, Shiyali Ramamrita, 1892–1972, vol. VII
Ranger, James, 1889–1975, vol. VII
Ranger, Sir Washington, 1848–1929, vol. III
Rangnekar, Hon. Sir Saiba Shankar, 1878–1949, vol. IV
Ranjitsinhji, Kumar Shri; see Nawanagar, Maharaja Jamsaheb of.
Rank, 1st Baron, 1888–1972, vol. VII
Rank, James Voase, 1881–1952, vol. V
Rank, Joseph, died 1943, vol. IV
Rankeillour, 1st Baron, 1870–1949, vol. IV
Rankeillour, 2nd Baron, 1897–1958, vol. V
Rankeillour, 3rd Baron, 1899–1967, vol. VI
Ranken, William Bruce Ellis, 1881–1941, vol. IV
Rankin, Lt-Col Allan Coats, 1877–1959, vol. V
Rankin, Archibald Aloysius, 1871–1951, vol. V
Rankin, Lt-Col (Arthur) Niall (Talbot), 1904–1965, vol. VI
Rankin, Brig.-Gen. Charles Herbert, 1873–1946, vol. IV
Rankin, Ethel Mary, 1893–1956, vol. V
Rankin, Rt Hon. Sir George Claus, 1877–1946, vol. IV
Rankin, Guthrie, 1854–1919, vol. II
Rankin, Maj.-Gen. Henry Charles Deans, 1888–1965, vol. VI
Rankin, Sir James, 1st Bt (cr 1898), 1842–1915, vol. I
Rankin, James Stuart, died 1960, vol. V
Rankin, John, 1845–1928, vol. II
Rankin, John, died 1973, vol. VII
Rankin, John Elliott, 1882–1960, vol. V
Rankin, John Eric, 1905–1976, vol. VII
Rankin, John Mitchell, 1924–1980, vol. VII
Rankin, Lt-Col Niall; see Rankin, Lt-Col A. N. T.
Rankin, Rev. Oliver Shaw, 1885–1954, vol. V
Rankin, Lt-Col Sir Reginald, 2nd Bt (cr 1898), 1871–1931, vol. III
Rankin, Sir Robert, 1st Bt (cr 1937), 1877–1960, vol. V
Rankin, Thomas, 1884–1959, vol. V
Rankin, William Brian, 1915–1976, vol. VII
Rankine, Alexander Oliver, 1881–1956, vol. V
Rankine, Sir John, 1846–1922, vol. II
Rankine, Sir Richard Sims Donkin, died 1961, vol. VI
Rankine, Col Robert, 1868–1941, vol. IV
Ranking, Lt-Col George Speirs Alexander, 1852–1934, vol. III
Ranking, Maj.-Gen. Robert Philip Lancaster-, 1896–1961, vol. VI
Rankl, Karl, 1898–1968, vol. VI
Ranksborough, 1st Baron, 1852–1921, vol. II
Ransford, Col Sir Alister John, 1895–1974, vol. VII
Ransford, Ella, died 1968, vol. IV
Ransford, Rev. Robert Bolton, 1840–1914, vol. I
Ransom, Hon. Sir Alfred; see Ransom, Hon. Sir E. A.
Ransom, Rear-Adm. (S) Alfred Charles, 1871–1953, vol. V

Ransom, Hon. Sir (Ethelbert) Alfred, 1868–1943, vol. IV
Ransom, Herbert Charles, 1881–1960, vol. V
Ransom, William Henry, 1824–1907, vol. I
Ransome, Maj.-Gen. Algernon Lee, 1883–1969, vol. VI
Ransome, Arthur, 1834–1922, vol. II (A)
Ransome, Arthur, 1884–1967, vol. VI
Ransome, Edward Coleby, 1864–1939, vol. III
Ransome, Sir Gordon Arthur, 1910–1978, vol. VII
Ransome, James, 1865–1944, vol. IV
Ransome, Stafford, 1860–1931, vol. III
Ranson, Col Wilson, 1870–1937, vol. III
Raper, Agnes Madeline, died 1948, vol. IV
Raper, Alfred Baldwin, 1889–1941, vol. IV
Raper, Maj.-Gen. Allan Graeme, 1843–1906, vol. I
Raper, Henry Stanley, died 1951, vol. V
Raper, Sir John Hugh Francis, 1889–1955, vol. V
Raper, Sir Robert George, 1827–1901, vol. I
Raper, Robert William, 1842–1915, vol. I
Raphael, Francis Charles, 1871–1945, vol. IV
Raphael, Geoffrey G., 1893–1969, vol. VI
Raphael, Sir Herbert Henry, 1st Bt, 1859–1924, vol. II
Raphael, John N. (Percival), 1868–1917, vol. II
Rappoport, Angelo Solomon, 1871–1950, vol. IV
Rapson, Edward James, 1861–1937, vol. III
Ras Mekonen, Sir, 1852–1906, vol. I
Rasch, Sir Carne; see Rasch, Sir F. C.
Rasch, Sir Frederic Carne, 1st Bt, 1847–1914, vol. I
Rasch, Sir (Frederic) Carne, 2nd Bt, 1880–1963, vol. VI
Rasch, Brig. Guy Elland Carne, 1885–1955, vol. V
Raschen, George H., 1889–1964, vol. VI
Rashbrook, Engr Rear-Adm. Henry Samuel, 1856–1942, vol. IV
Rashdall, Very Rev. Hastings, 1858–1924, vol. II
Rashleigh, Sir Colman Battie, 3rd Bt, 1846–1907, vol. I
Rashleigh, Sir Colman Battie Walpole, 4th Bt, 1873–1951, vol. V
Rashleigh, Rev. John Kendall, 1847–1933, vol. III
Rashleigh, Major Philip, 1881–1949, vol. IV
Rashleigh, Captain Vernon Stanhope, 1879–1946, vol. IV
Rashleigh, Rev. William, 1867–1937, vol. III
Rasmussen, Knud, 1879–1933, vol. III
Rason, Hon. Sir Cornthwaite Hector, 1858–1927, vol. II
Rason, Ernest Goldfinch, vol. II
Rassam, Hormuzd, 1826–1910, vol. I
Rastall, Robert Heron, 1871–1950, vol. IV
Ratcliff, Rev. Canon Edward Craddock, 1896–1967, vol. VI
Ratcliff, Robert Frederick, died 1943, vol. IV
Ratcliffe, Arthur, 1882–1963, vol. VI
Ratcliffe, Dorothy Una; see Phillips, Mrs McGrigor.
Ratcliffe, Henry Butler, died 1929, vol. III
Ratcliffe, Samuel Kerkham, 1868–1958, vol. V
Ratcliffe-Ellis, Sir Thomas Ratcliffe, 1842–1925, vol. II
Rathbone, Basil, 1892–1967, vol. VI

Rathbone, Eleanor, *died* 1946, vol. IV
Rathbone, Hugh Reynolds, *died* 1940, vol. III
Rathbone, John Rankin, 1910–1940, vol. III
Rathbone, Monroe Jackson, 1900–1976, vol. VII
Rathbone, William Gair, 1849–1919, vol. II
Rathborne, Air Cdre Charles Edward Harry, *died* 1943, vol. IV
Rathcreedan, 1st Baron, *died* 1930, vol. III
Rathdonnell, 2nd Baron, 1848–1929, vol. III
Rathdonnell, 3rd Baron, 1881–1937, vol. III
Rathdonnell, 4th Baron, 1914–1959, vol. V
Rathmore, 1st Baron, 1838–1919, vol. II
Rathom, John Revelstoke, 1868–1923, vol. II
Ratlam, Maj.-Gen. HH Maharaja Sir Sajjan Singhji, 1880–1947, vol. IV
Ratsey, Col Harold Edward, 1861–1953, vol. V
Ratten, Victor Richard, 1878–1962, vol. VI
Rattenbury, John Ernest, 1870–1963, vol. VI
Rattenbury, Robert Mantle, 1901–1970, vol. VI
Ratteray, Hon. Sir George Oswald, 1903–1980, vol. VII
Rattey, Engr-Rear-Adm. William, 1871–1939, vol. III
Ratti, Achille Ambrogio Damiano; *see* Pius XI.
Rattigan, Frank; *see* Rattigan, W. F. A.
Rattigan, Sir Henry Adolphus Byden, 1864–1920, vol. II
Rattigan, Sir Terence Mervyn, 1911–1977, vol. VII
Rattigan, (William) Frank (Arthur), 1879–1952, vol. V
Rattigan, Sir William Henry, 1842–1904, vol. I
Rattray, Rear-Adm. Sir Arthur Rullion, 1891–1966, vol. VI
Rattray, Brig.-Gen. Charles, 1868–1943, vol. IV
Rattray, Lt-Col Haldane Burney, 1870–1917 vol. II
Rattray, Lt-Gen. Sir James C.; *see* Clerk-Rattray.
Rattray, Col John Grant, 1867–1944, vol. IV
Rattray, Col Paul Robert Burn Clerk, 1859–1937, vol. III
Rattray, Robert Fleming, *died* 1967, vol. VI
Rattray, Captain Robert Sutherland, 1881–1938, vol. III
Rattray, Wellwood, 1849–1902, vol. I
Ratwatte, Sir Jayatilaka Cudah, *died* 1940, vol. III (A), vol. V
Rau, Sir Benegal Rama, 1889–1969, vol. VI
Rau, Bhimanakunté Hanumanta, 1855–1922, vol. II
Rau, Sir Narsing, 1887–1953, vol. V
Rau, Sir Raghavendra, 1889–1942, vol. IV
Ravel, Maurice, 1875–1937, vol. III
Raven, Rev. Berney Wodehouse, *died* 1911, vol. I
Raven, Rev. Charles Earle, 1885–1964, vol. VI
Raven, Edward, 1874–1952, vol. V
Raven, Rev. Edward Earle, 1889–1951, vol. V
Raven, Rev. John James, 1833–1906, vol. I
Raven, Martin Owen, 1888–1976, vol. VII
Raven, Sir Vincent Litchfield, 1859–1934, vol. III
Raven-Hart, Rev. William Roland, *died* 1919, vol. II
Raven-Hill, Leonard, 1867–1942, vol. IV
Ravenel, Mazyck P., *died* 1946, vol. IV
Ravenhill, Lt-Col Edgar Evelyn, 1859–1907, vol. I

Ravenhill, Brig.-Gen. Frederick Thornhill, 1865–1935, vol. III
Ravenhill, Col Harry Stuart, 1872–1930, vol. III
Ravenhill, Rev. Henry Everett, 1831–1913, vol. I
Ravenscroft, Edward William, 1831–1911, vol. I
Ravensdale, Baroness (2nd in line), 1896–1966, vol. VI
Ravenshaw, Lt-Col Charles Withers, 1851–1935, vol. III
Ravenshaw, Maj.-Gen. Hurdis Secundus Lalande, 1869–1920, vol. II
Ravenshear, Ewart Watson, 1893–1959, vol. V
Ravenstein, Ernest George, 1834–1913, vol. I
Ravensworth, 2nd Earl, 1821–1903, vol. I
Ravensworth, 3rd Earl, 1833–1904, vol. I
Ravensworth, 5th Baron, 1837–1919, vol. II
Ravensworth, 6th Baron, 1869–1932, vol. III
Ravensworth, 7th Baron, 1902–1950, vol. IV
Raverat, Gwendolen Mary, 1885–1957, vol. V
Ravilious, Eric, *died* 1942, vol. IV
Raw, Brig. Cecil Whitfield, 1900–1969, vol. VI
Raw, Lt-Col Nathan, 1866–1940, vol. III
Raw, Vice-Adm. Sir Sydney Moffatt, 1898–1967, vol. VI
Rawcliffe, Gordon Hindle, 1910–1979, vol. VII
Rawdon, Rev. J. Hamer, *died* 1916, vol. II
Rawdon-Hastings, Paulyn Charles James Reginald; *see* Hastings.
Rawdon-Hastings, Hon. Paulyn Francis Cuthbert, 1856–1907, vol. I
Rawdon Smith, Edward Rawdon, 1890–1957, vol. V
Rawle, Francis, 1846–1930, vol. III
Rawling, Brig.-Gen. Cecil Godfrey, 1870–1917, vol. II
Rawling, Ven. John, 1869–1955, vol. V
Rawlings, Adm. Sir Bernard; *see* Rawlings, Adm. Sir H. B. H.
Rawlings, Edmund Charles, 1854–1917, vol. II
Rawlings, Francis Ian Gregory, 1895–1969, vol. VI
Rawlings, Gertrude Burford, *died* 1939, vol. III
Rawlings, Adm. Sir (Henry) Bernard (Hughes), 1889–1962, vol. VI
Rawlings, Rear-Adm. Henry Clive, 1883–1965, vol. VI
Rawlings, Justly John Gabriel, 1868–1950, vol. IV
Rawlings, Marjorie Kinnan, 1896–1953, vol. V
Rawlins, Maj.-Gen. Alexander Macdonell, 1838–1916, vol. II
Rawlins, Lt-Col Arthur Kennedy, 1868–1943, vol. IV
Rawlins, Evelyn Charles Donaldson, 1884–1971, vol. VII
Rawlins, Francis Hay, 1850–1920, vol. II
Rawlins, Morna Lloyd, 1882–1969, vol. VI
Rawlins, Percy Lionel Edwin, 1902–1977, vol. VII
Rawlins, Maj.-Gen. Stuart Blundell, 1897–1955, vol. V
Rawlins, Col Stuart William Hughes, 1880–1927, vol. II
Rawlins, William Donaldson, 1846–1920, vol. II
Rawlinson, 1st Baron, 1864–1925, vol. II
Rawlinson, Lt-Col Sir Alfred, 3rd Bt, 1867–1934, vol. III

Rawlinson, Rt Rev. Alfred Edward John, 1884–1960, vol. V

Rawlinson, Sir (Alfred) Frederick, 4th Bt, 1900–1969, vol. VI

Rawlinson, Rev. Bernard Stephen, 1865–1953, vol. V

Rawlinson, Lt-Col Charles Brooke, 1866–1919, vol. II

Rawlinson, Charles William, died 1910, vol. I

Rawlinson, Francis William, 1856–1944, vol. IV

Rawlinson, Sir Frederick; see Rawlinson, Sir A. F.

Rawlinson, Rev. Canon George, 1812–1902, vol. I

Rawlinson, Hugh George, 1880–1957, vol. V

Rawlinson, Rt Hon. John Frederick Peel, 1860–1926, vol. II

Rawlinson, Sir Joseph, 1897–1971, vol. VII

Rawlinson, Sir Robert, 1810–1898, vol. I

Rawlinson, Lt-Col Spencer R., 1848–1903, vol. I

Rawnsley, Col Claude, 1862–1944, vol. IV

Rawnsley, Edward Preston, 1851–1934, vol. III

Rawnsley, Col Gerald Thomas, 1865–1942, vol. IV

Rawnsley, Rev. Hardwicke Drummond, 1851–1920, vol. II

Raworth, Benjamin Alfred, 1849–1919, vol. II

Raws, Lt-Col Sir Lennon; see Raws, Lt-Col Sir W. L.

Raws, Lt-Col Sir (William) Lennon, 1878–1958, vol. V

Rawson, Sir Cooper, 1876–1946, vol. IV

Rawson, Brig. Creswell Duffield, 1883–1964, vol. VI

Rawson, Frank, 1856–1928, vol. II

Rawson, Maj.-Gen. Geoffrey Grahame, 1887–1979, vol. VII

Rawson, Harry, 1862–1930, vol. III

Rawson, Adm. Sir Harry Holdsworth, 1843–1910, vol. I

Rawson, Col Herbert Edward, 1852–1924, vol. II

Rawson, Sir Rawson William, 1812–1899, vol. I

Rawson, Col Richard Hamilton, 1863–1918, vol. III

Rawson, Sir Stanley Walter, 1891–1973, vol. VII

Rawson-Shaw, William, 1860–1932, vol. III

Rawsthorne, Alan, 1905–1971, vol. VII

Rawstorne, Rt Rev. Atherton Gwillym, 1855–1936, vol. III

Rawstorne, Brig. George Streynsham, 1895–1962, vol. VI

Rawstorne, Lawrence, 1842–1938, vol. III

Rawstorne, Ven. Robert Atherton, 1824–1902, vol. I

Ray, Maharaja Rao Sir Jogendra Narayan, died 1946, vol. IV

Ray, Maj.-Gen. Kenneth, 1894–1956, vol. V

Ray, Major MacCarthy Emmet, 1867–1906, vol. I

Ray, Mahendranath, 1862–1925, vol. II

Ray, Matthew Burrow, died 1950, vol. IV

Ray, Sir Prafulla Chandra, 1861–1944, vol. IV

Ray, Prithwis Chandra, 1870–1927, vol. II

Ray, Reginald Edwin Anthony, 1891–1972, vol. VII

Ray, Sidney Herbert, 1858–1939, vol. III

Ray, Ted, 1905–1977, vol. VII

Ray, Sir William, 1876–1937, vol. III

Ray-Jones, Raymond, 1886–1942, vol. IV

Raybould, Clarence, 1886–1972, vol. VII

Raybould, Sidney Griffith, 1903–1977, vol. VII

Rayburn, Sam, 1882–1961, vol. VI

Rayleigh, 3rd Baron, 1842–1919, vol. II

Rayleigh, 4th Baron, 1875–1947, vol. IV

Rayment, Instr Captain Guy Varley, 1878–1951, vol. V

Raymer, Rev. Robert Richmond, 1870–1948, vol. IV

Raymond, Air Vice-Marshal Adélard, 1889–1962, vol. VI

Raymond, E. T.; see Thompson, Edward Raymond.

Raymond, Ernest, 1888–1974, vol. VII

Raymond, Col Francis, 1854–1945, vol. IV

Raymond, George, died 1929, vol. III

Raymond, George Lansing, 1839–1929, vol. III

Raymond, Harold, 1887–1975, vol. VII

Raymond, Lt-Col Maurice Claud, 1884–1959, vol. V

Raymond, Walter, 1852–1931, vol. III

Raymont, John Edwin George, 1915–1979, vol. VII

Raymont, Thomas, 1864–1953, vol. V

Rayner, Frank, 1866–1945, vol. IV

Rayner, Henry, 1841–1926, vol. II

Rayner, Vice-Adm. Herbert Sharples, 1911–1976, vol. VII

Rayner, Mabel Mary Cheveley, (Mrs W. N. Jones), died 1948, vol. IV

Rayner, Brig. Sir Ralph, died 1977, vol. VII

Rayner, Sir Thomas Crossley, 1860–1914, vol. I

Raynes, Harold Ernest, 1882–1964, vol. VI

Raynes, John Richard, 1881–1944, vol. IV

Raynes, Rev. Raymond Richard Elliott, 1903–1958, vol. V

Raynes, William Robert, 1871–1966, vol. VI

Raynham, Eustace Frederick, died 1939, vol. III

Raynor, Rev. Philip Edwin, 1857–1930, vol. III

Raynor, Sir William Pick, 1854–1927, vol. II

Raynsford, Lt-Col Richard Montague, 1877–1965, vol. VI

Raza Ali, Sir Syed, 1882–1949, vol. IV

Razak bin Hussein, Hon. Tun Haji Abdul; see Abdul Razak.

Rea, 1st Baron, 1873–1948, vol. IV

Rea, Lady; (Lorna), 1897–1978, vol. VII

Rea, Alec Lionel, 1878–1953, vol. V

Rea, Cecil W., died 1935, vol. III

Rea, Edward Hugh, died 1901, vol. I

Rea, George Grey, 1858–1931, vol. III

Rea, Major John George Grey, 1886–1955, vol. V

Rea, Robert Lindsay-, 1881–1971, vol. VII

Rea, Rt Hon. Russell, 1846–1916, vol. II

Read, Alexander Llewellyn, 1877–1942, vol. IV

Read, Alfred Burgess, 1899–1973, vol. VII

Read, Sir Alfred Henry, 1871–1955, vol. V

Read, Col Alfred Howard, 1893–1977, vol. VII

Read, Arthur Avery, 1868–1943, vol. IV

Read, Vice-Adm. Arthur Duncan, 1889–1976, vol. VII

Read, Bertie L.; see Lees Read.

Read, Carveth, 1848–1931, vol. III

Read, Sir Charles David, 1902–1957, vol. V

Read, Sir (Charles) Hercules, 1857–1929, vol. III

Read, Clare Sewell, 1826–1905, vol. I

Read, Conyers, Read 1881–1959, vol. V
Read, Edward Harry H.; see Handley-Read.
Read, Ernest, 1879–1965, vol. VI
Read, Francis Charles Jennings, 1875–1958, vol. V
Read, Grantly Dick-, 1890–1959, vol. V
Read, Brig.-Gen. Hastings, 1852–1928, vol. II
Read, Rt Rev. Henry Cecil, 1890–1963, vol. VI
Read, Sir Herbert, 1893–1968, vol. VI
Read, Herbert Harold, 1889–1970, vol. VI
Read, Sir Herbert James, 1863–1949, vol. IV
Read, Sir Hercules; see Read, Sir C. H.
Read, John, 1884–1963, vol. VI
Read, (Sir) John Cecil, (styled 9th Bt cr 1641), 1820–1899, vol. I
Read, John Erskine, 1888–1973, vol. VII
Read, John Gordon, 1886–1958, vol. V
Read, Opie, 1852–1939, vol. III (A), vol. IV
Read, Col Randulph Offley C.; see Crewe-Read.
Read, Col Richard Valentine, 1892–1964, vol. VI
Read, Thomas Talmage, 1893–1974, vol. VII
Read, Walter William, 1855–1907, vol. I
Read, William Henry McLeod, 1819–1909, vol. I
Read, (Sir) William Vero, (styled 10th Bt cr 1641), born 1839 (this entry was not transferred to Who was Who).
Reade, Aleyn Lyell, 1876–1953, vol. V
Reade, Lt-Col Charles James, 1863–1912, vol. I (A), vol. III
Reade, Sir George Compton, 9th Bt, 1845–1908 (this entry was not transferred to Who was Who).
Reade, Rev. George Edwin Pearsall, 1841–1937, vol. III
Reade, Sir George Franklin, 10th Bt, 1869–1923, vol. II
Reade, Herbert Taylor, 1828–1897, vol. I
Reade, Herbert Vincent, 1870–1929, vol. III
Reade, John, 1837–1919, vol. II
Reade, Surg. Maj.-Gen. Sir John By Cole, 1832–1914, vol. I
Reade, Sir John Stanhope, 11th Bt, 1896–1958, vol. V
Reade, Maj.-Gen. Raymond Northland Revell, 1861–1943, vol. IV
Reade, Robert Henry, died 1913, vol. I
Readett-Bayley, Sir H. Dennis, 1878–1940, vol. III
Readhead, Sir James, 1st Bt, died 1930, vol. III
Readhead, Sir James Halder, 2nd Bt, 1879–1940, vol. III
Reading, 1st Marquess of, 1860–1935, vol. III
Reading, 2nd Marquess of, 1889–1960, vol. V
Reading, 3rd Marquess of, 1916–1980, vol. VII
Reading, Marchioness of; (Stella); Baroness Swanborough (Life Peer), 1894–1971, vol. VII
Reading, Marchioness of; (Eva Violet), 1895–1973, vol. VII
Reading, Maj.-Gen. Arnold Hughes Eagleton, 1896–1975, vol. VII
Reading, Sir Claude Hill, 1874–1946, vol. IV
Reading, Joseph Lewis, 1907–1980, vol. VII
Reading, Martin Luther, 1869–1943, vol. IV
Readman, Maj.-Gen. Edgar Platt, 1893–1980, vol. VII
Ready Gen. Sir Felix Fordati, 1872–1940, vol. III

Reakes, Charles John, 1865–1943, vol. IV
Reakes, George Leonard, 1889–1961, vol. VI
Real, Patrick, 1847–1928, vol. II
Reardon-Smith, Sir Willie; see Smith.
Reaume, Hon. Joseph Octave, 1856–1933, vol. III
Reavell, Arthur; see Reavell, J. A.
Reavell, (James) Arthur, 1872–1973, vol. VII
Reavell, Sir William, 1866–1948, vol. IV
Reay, 11th Lord, 1839–1921, vol. II
Reay, 12th Lord, 1870–1921, vol. II
Reay, 13th Lord, 1905–1963, vol. VI
Reay, Hon. Brig.-Gen. Charles Tom, 1857–1933, vol. III
Reay, George Adam, 1901–1971, vol. VII
Reay, Margaret Edith, 1876–1959, vol. V
Reay, Rev. Thomas Osmotherley, 1834–1914, vol. I
Rebbeck, Sir Frederick Ernest, died 1964, vol. VI
Rébora, Piero, 1889–1963, vol. VI
Rebsch, Brig. William Knowles, 1885–1940, vol. III
Reckitt, Sir Harold James, 2nd Bt, 1868–1930, vol. III
Reckitt, Sir James, 1st Bt, 1833–1924, vol. II
Reckitt, Sir Philip Bealby, 3rd Bt, 1873–1944, vol. IV
Recknell, George Hugh, 1893–1975, vol. VII
Reclus, Jacques Elisée, 1830–1905, vol. I
Record, Edgar W., 1873–1943, vol. IV
Reddaway, William Fiddian, 1872–1949, vol. IV
Reddick, Ven. Percy George, 1896–1978, vol. VII
Reddie, Brig.-Gen. Anthony Julian, 1873–1960, vol. V
Reddie, Cecil, 1858–1932, vol. III
Reddie, Charles Frederick, died 1931, vol. III
Reddie, Lt-Col Sir John Murray, 1872–1954, vol. V
Redding, Rt Rev. Donald Llewellyn, 1898–1969, vol. VI
Redding, John Magnus, 1889–1930, vol. III
Reddish, Sir Halford Walter Lupton, 1898–1978, vol. VII
Reddy, Sir C. Ramalinga, 1880–1951, vol. V
Reddy, Michael, died 1919, vol. II
Rede, Captain Roger L'Estrange Murray, died 1930, vol. III
Redesdale, 1st Baron, 1837–1916, vol. II
Redesdale, 2nd Baron, 1878–1958, vol. V
Redesdale, 3rd Baron, died 1962, vol. VI
Redesdale, 4th Baron, 1885–1963, vol. VI
Redfern, Rev. Thomas, 1853–1924, vol. II
Redfern, Thomas William, died 1924, vol. II
Redford, Arthur, 1896–1961, vol. VI
Redford, Sir Edward Pigott William, 1850–1933, vol. III
Redford, George Alexander, died 1916, vol. II
Redhead, Edward Charles, 1902–1967, vol. VI
Redhead, Captain Mahon, 1871–1940, vol. III
Redhead, Lt-Col Richard Henry M.; see Milne-Redhead.
Redington, Rt Hon. Christopher Talbot, 1847–1899, vol. I
Redl, Lt-Col Ernest Arthur Frederick, 1869–1954, vol. V
Redlich, Rev. Canon Edwin Basil, 1878–1960, vol. V

Redlich, Hans Ferdinand, 1903–1968, vol. VI
Redman, Rev. Alfred, *died* 1927, vol. II
Redman, Brig. Arthur Stanley, 1879–1963, vol. VI
Redman, George Herbert, 1882–1959, vol. V
Redman, Sir (Herbert) Vere, 1901–1975, vol. VII
Redman, Roderick Oliver, 1905–1975, vol. VII
Redman, Sir Vere; *see* Redman, Sir H. V.
Redmayne, Sir Richard Augustine Studdert, 1865–1955, vol. V
Redmayne-Jones, Sir Edward, 1877–1963, vol. VI
Redmond, John Edward, 1851–1918, vol. II
Redmond, Lt-Gen. John Patrick Sutton, *died* 1902, vol. I
Redmond, Sir Joseph Michael, *died* 1921, vol. II
Redmond, Captain William Archer, 1886–1932, vol. III
Redmond, Major William Hoey Kearney, 1861–1917, vol. II
Redpath, Anne, 1895–1965, vol. VI
Redpath, Rev. Henry A., 1848–1908, vol. I
Redpath, Robert, 1871–1960, vol. V
Redwood, Sir Boverton, 1st Bt, 1846–1919, vol. II
Redwood, Most Rev. Francis Mary, 1839–1935, vol. III
Redwood, Rev. Canon Frederick Arthur, 1891–1964, vol. VI
Redwood, Hugh; *see* Redwood, W. A. H.
Redwood, Sir Thomas Boverton, 2nd Bt, 1906–1974, vol. VII
Redwood, (William Arthur) Hugh, 1883–1963, vol. V
Ree, Sir Frank, *died* 1914, vol. I
Reece, B(razilla) Carroll, 1889–1961, vol. VI
Reece, Francis Bertram, 1888–1971, vol. VII
Reece, John H.; *see* Holroyd-Reece.
Reece, Surg.-Col Richard James, 1862–1924, vol. II
Reed, Sir (Albert) Ralph, 1884–1958, vol. V
Reed, Sir Alfred Hamish, 1875–1975, vol. VII
Reed, Sir Andrew, 1837–1914, vol. I
Reed, Sir Arthur Conrad, *died* 1961, vol. VI
Reed, Arthur William, 1873–1957, vol. V
Reed, Austin Leonard, 1873–1954, vol. V
Reed, Bellamy Alexander C.; *see* Cash-Reed.
Reed, Sir Carol, 1906–1976, vol. VII
Reed, Col Charles, 1879–1958, vol. V
Reed, Clinton Austin, 1876–1954, vol. V
Reed, Douglas, 1895–1976, vol. VII
Reed, Edward, 1902–1953, vol. V
Reed, Sir Edward James, 1830–1906, vol. I
Reed, Edward Tennyson, 1860–1933, vol. III
Reed, Rt Rev. Ernest Samuel, *died* 1970, vol. VI
Reed, Hon. Sir Geoffrey Sandford, 1892–1970, vol. VI (AII)
Reed, Maj.-Gen. Hamilton Lyster, 1869–1931, vol. III
Reed, Haythorne, 1873–1934, vol. III
Reed, Henry Ashman, 1866–1935, vol. III
Reed, Col Henry Robert Baynes, 1880–1939, vol. III
Reed, Herbert Langford, 1889–1954, vol. V
Reed, Herbert Parker, *died* 1920, vol. II
Reed, Sir (Herbert) Stanley, 1872–1969, vol. VI
Reed, Lt-Col John Arthur Wemyss, 1864–1939, vol. III

Reed, Hon. Sir John Ranken, 1864–1955, vol. V
Reed, Sir John Seymour B.; *see* Blake-Reed.
Reed, Col Sir Joseph, 1867–1942, vol. IV
Reed, Joseph Martin, 1857–1932, vol. III
Reed, Langford; *see* Reed, H. L.
Reed, Rev. Martin, 1856–1926, vol. II
Reed, Maurice Ernest, 1908–1975, vol. VII
Reed, Sir Ralph; *see* Reed, Sir A. R.
Reed, Rev. Samuel, 1844–1932, vol. III
Reed, Sir Stanley; *see* Reed, Sir H. S.
Reed, Thomas Brackett, 1839–1902, vol. I
Reed, William Henry, 1877–1942, vol. IV
Rees, Arthur J., *died* 1942, vol. IV
Rees, Sir Beddoe, *died* 1931, vol. III
Rees, Ven. David John, 1862–1924, vol. II
Rees, David Morgan, 1904–1980, vol. VII
Rees, E(dgar) Philip, 1896–1964, vol. VI
Rees, Lt-Col Evan Thomas, 1883–1955, vol. V
Rees, Sir Frederick; *see* Rees, Sir J. F.
Rees, Sir Frederick Tavinor, 1890–1976, vol. VII
Rees, Goronwy; *see* Rees, M. G.
Rees, Griffith Caradoc, 1868–1924, vol. II
Rees, Rev. Henry, 1844–1924, vol. II
Rees, Howell, 1847–1933, vol. III
Rees, Brig.-Gen. Hubert Conway, 1882–1948, vol. IV
Rees, Sir Hugh E.; *see* Ellis-Rees.
Rees, Sir (James) Frederick, 1883–1967, vol. VI
Rees, Sir John David, 1st Bt, 1854–1922, vol. II
Rees, Engr-Captain John David, 1861–1951, vol. V
Rees, Lt-Col John Gordon, 1884–1963, vol. VI
Rees, John Rawlings, 1890–1969, vol. VI
Rees, (John) Tudor, *died* 1956, vol. V
Rees, Sir Josiah, 1821–1899, vol. I
Rees, Leonard, 1856–1932, vol. III
Rees, Mrs Leonard, (Mary Emily MacLeod Moore), *died* 1960, vol. V
Rees, Gp Captain Lionel Wilmot Brabazon, 1884–1955, vol. V
Rees, Sir Milsom, 1866–1952, vol. V
Rees, (Morgan) Goronwy, 1909–1979, vol. VII
Rees, Sir Richard Lodowick Edward Montagu, 2nd Bt, 1900–1970, vol. VI
Rees, Rev. Thomas, 1869–1926, vol. II
Rees, Thomas Ifor, 1890–1977, vol. VII
Rees, Thomas James, 1875–1957, vol. V
Rees, Rev. Thomas Morgan, 1850–1937, vol. III
Rees, Maj.-Gen. Thomas Wynford, *died* 1959, vol. V
Rees, Rt Rev. Timothy, 1874–1939, vol. III
Rees, Tudor; *see* Rees, J. T.
Rees, Ven. Vaughan William Treharne, 1879–1948, vol. IV
Rees, William, 1887–1978, vol. VII
Rees, Rev. William Goodman Edwards, *died* 1936, vol. III
Rees, Adm. William Stokes, 1853–1929, vol. III
Rees-Davies, Sir Colin, 1867–1933, vol. III
Rees-Davies, Sir William; *see* Davies.
Rees-Mogg, Lt-Col Graham Beauchamp Coxeter, 1881–1949, vol. IV
Rees-Thomas, Ruth, (Mrs William Rees-Thomas); *see* Darwin, R.
Rees-Thomas, William, 1887–1978, vol. VII

Reese, Frederick Focke, 1854–1924, vol. II
Reeve, Ada, 1874–1966, vol. VI
Reeve, Charles Arthur, 1857–1936, vol. III
Reeve, Charles William, 1879–1965, vol. VI
Reeve, Rev. Edward Henry Lisle, *died* 1936, vol. III
Reeve, Henry Fenwick, 1854–1920, vol. II
Reeve, Raymond Roope, 1875–1952, vol. V
Reeve, Russell, 1895–1970, vol. VI
Reeve, Simms, 1826–1919, vol. II
Reeve, Rt Rev. William Day, 1844–1925, vol. II
Reeves, Rt Rev. Ambrose; *see* Reeves, Rt. Rev. R. A.
Reeves, Vice-Adm. Edward, 1869–1954, vol. V
Reeves, Edward Ayearst, 1862–1945, vol. IV
Reeves, Helen, (Mrs Henry Reeves); *see* Mathers, Helen.
Reeves, Henry Albert, *died* 1914, vol. I
Reeves, Col Henry Spencer Edward, 1843–1914, vol. I
Reeves, James, 1909–1978, vol. VII
Reeves, Col John, 1854–1904, vol. I
Reeves, John Sims, 1822–1900, vol. I
Reeves, Joseph, 1888–1969, vol. VI
Reeves, Rt Rev. (Richard) Ambrose, 1899–1980, vol. VII
Reeves, Hon. Sir William Conrad, 1838–1902, vol. I
Reeves, Hon. William Pember, 1857–1932, vol. III
Reeves-Smith, Sir George, *died* 1941, vol. IV
Refalo, Sir Michelangelo, 1876–1923, vol. II
Reford, John Hope, 1873–1957, vol. V
Regan, Charles Tate, 1878–1943, vol. IV
Regan, Col James Louis, 1888–1948, vol. IV
Regener, Erich, 1881–1955, vol. V
Regester, William, 1848–1929, vol. III
Regg, Ven. Thomas Richard, *died* 1930, vol. III
Regis de Oliveira, Raul, *died* 1942, vol. IV
Regnart, Sir Horace Grece, 1841–1912, vol. I
Regnier, Henri François Joseph de, 1864–1936, vol. III
Rehan, Ada, 1860–1916, vol. II
Reiach, Herbert, 1873–1921, vol. II
Reich, Emil, 1854–1910, vol. I
Reichardt, Charles Henry, 1851–1903, vol. I
Reichel, Sir Harry Rudolf, 1856–1931, vol. III
Reichel, Rev. Oswald Joseph, 1840–1923, vol. II
Reid, Baron (Life Peer); James Scott Cumberland Reid, 1890–1975, vol. VII
Reid, Surg.-Gen. Sir Adam Scott, 1848–1918, vol. II
Reid, Captain Alec Stratford C.; *see* Cunningham-Reid.
Reid, Alexander, 1843–1919, vol. II
Reid, Lt-Col Alexander, 1863–1927, vol. II
Reid, Sir Alexander James, 1889–1968, vol. VI
Reid, Maj.-Gen. Sir Alexander John Forsyth, 1846–1913, vol. I
Reid, Col Alexander Kirkwood, 1884–1948, vol. IV
Reid, Alfred Henry, 1845–1931, vol. III
Reid, Col A(ndrew) McKie, 1893–1973, vol. VII
Reid, Sir Archdall; *see* Reid, Sir G. A. O'B.
Reid, Archibald D., 1844–1908, vol. I
Reid, Sir Archibald Douglas, 1871–1924, vol. II
Reid, Arthur Beatson, 1888–1965, vol. VI
Reid, Sir Arthur Hay Stewart, 1851–1930, vol. III

Reid, Sir Charles, 1819–1901, vol. I
Reid, Charles, 1892–1961, vol. VI
Reid, Sir Charles Carlow, 1879–1961, vol. VI
Reid, Dame Clarissa Guthrie, *died* 1933, vol. III
Reid, Clement, *died* 1916, vol. II
Reid, Sir David Douglas, 1st Bt (*cr* 1936), 1872–1939, vol. III
Reid, Lt-Col David Elder, 1864–1930, vol. III
Reid, Maj.-Gen. Denys Whitehorn, 1897–1970, vol. VI
Reid, Donald Darnley, 1914–1977, vol. VII
Reid, Sir Douglas Neilson, 2nd Bt (*cr* 1922), 1898–1971, vol. VII
Reid, Sir Edward, 1819–1912, vol. I
Reid, Edward Douglas Whitehead, 1883–1930, vol. III
Reid, Sir Edward James, 2nd Bt (*cr* 1897), 1901–1972, vol. VII
Reid, Rt Rev. Edward Thomas Scott, 1871–1938, vol. III
Reid, Edward Waymouth, 1862–1948, vol. IV
Reid, Col Ellis Ramsay, 1850–1918, vol. II
Reid, Ven. Ernest Gordon, *died* 1966, vol. VI
Reid, Forrest, 1876–1947, vol. IV
Reid, Col Francis Maude, 1849–1922, vol. II
Reid, Brig. Sir Francis Smith, 1900–1970, vol. VI
Reid, Frank Aspinall, 1875–1961, vol. VI
Reid, Very Rev. G. R. S., 1871–1964, vol. VI
Reid, Sir George, 1841–1913, vol. I
Reid, George, *died* 1925, vol. II
Reid, George Agnew, 1860–1947, vol. IV
Reid, Sir (George) Archdall O'Brien, 1860–1929, vol. III
Reid, Col George Eric, *died* 1938, vol. III
Reid, Rt Hon. Sir George Houstoun, 1845–1918, vol. II
Reid, George Ogilvy, *died* 1928, vol. II (A)
Reid, Sir George Thomas, 1881–1966, vol. VI
Reid, Harold Alexander, 1891–1974, vol. VII
Reid, Lt-Col Harry Avery, 1877–1947, vol. IV
Reid, Rt Rev. Harry Seymour, *died* 1943, vol. IV
Reid, Col Hector Gowans, 1881–1966, vol. VI
Reid, Helen Richmond Young, 1869–1941, vol. IV
Reid, Helen Rogers, (Mrs Ogden Reid), 1882–1970, vol. VI
Reid, Rev. Henry M. B., 1856–1927, vol. II
Reid, Sir Henry Valentine Rae, 4th Bt (*cr* 1823), 1845–1903, vol. I
Reid, Lt-Col Herbert Cartwright, 1864–1950, vol. IV
Reid, Vice-Adm. Howard Emerson, 1897–1962, vol. VI
Reid, Sir Hugh, 1st Bt (*cr* 1922), 1860–1935, vol. III
Reid, Sir Hugh Gilzean-, 1836–1911, vol. I
Reid, James, 1839–1908, vol. I
Reid, Sir James, 1st Bt (*cr* 1897), 1849–1923, vol. II
Reid, Rev. James, 1877–1963, vol. VI
Reid, James Robert, 1838–1908, vol. I
Reid, James Smith, 1846–1926, vol. II
Reid, Very Rev. James Watson, *died* 1904, vol. I
Reid, Sir John, 1861–1933, vol. III
Reid, John, 1874–1934, vol. III
Reid, John Alexander, 1895–1969, vol. VI
Reid, Hon. John Dowsley, 1859–1929, vol. III

Reid, Lt-Col John Garnet, 1878–1939, vol. III
Reid, Adm. Sir (John) Peter (Lorne), 1903–1973, vol. VII
Reid, John R., *died* 1926, vol. II
Reid, Sir John Watt, 1823–1909, vol. I
Reid, Rev. Kenneth Lyle, 1873–1937, vol. III
Reid, Col Lestock Hamilton, 1857–1936, vol. III
Reid, Sir Marshall Frederick, 1864–1925, vol. II
Reid, May, 1882–1980, vol. VII
Reid, Ogden, 1882–1947, vol. IV
Reid, Mrs Ogden; *see* Reid, Helen Rogers.
Reid, Col Percy Lester, 1882–1968, vol. VI
Reid, Adm. Sir Peter; *see* Reid, Adm. Sir J. P. L.
Reid, Rachel Robertson, 1876–1952, vol. V
Reid, Lt-Col Richard, *died* 1918, vol. II
Reid, Robert, 1922–1980, vol. VII
Reid, Robert Lawrence, 1858–1916, vol. II
Reid, Sir Robert Niel, 1883–1964, vol. VI
Reid, Robert Payton, 1859–1945, vol. IV
Reid, Robert Whyte, 1885–1929, vol. III
Reid, Robert William, *died* 1939, vol. III
Reid, Samuel, *born* 1854, vol. II
Reid, Stephen, 1873–1948, vol. IV
Reid, Stuart J., *died* 1927, vol. II
Reid, Thomas, 1881–1963, vol. VI
Reid, Sir (Thomas) Wemyss, 1842–1905, vol. I
Reid, Walter, *died* 1917, vol. II
Reid, Col Walter Richard, 1880–1959, vol. V
Reid, Sir Wemyss; *see* Reid, Sir T. W.
Reid, Hon. Whitelaw, 1837–1912, vol. I
Reid, Major Sir William, *died* 1934, vol. III
Reid, William, *died* 1965, vol. VI
Reid, William Allan, 1865–1952, vol. V
Reid, Rev. William Cawley, *died* 1933, vol. III
Reid, William Clarke, 1909–1956, vol. V
Reid, William David, 1883–1964, vol. VI
Reid, Sir William Duff, 1869–1924, vol. II
Reid, William Edwin Charles, 1870–1947, vol. IV
Reid, Sir William James, 1871–1939, vol. III
Reid, William Paton, 1854–1932, vol. III
Reid, William Sydney, 1880–1960, vol. V
Reid Dick, Sir W(illiam), 1879–1961, vol. VI
Reilly, Lt-Col Sir Bernard Rawdon, 1882–1966, vol. VI
Reilly, Col Charles Cooper, 1862–1926, vol. II
Reilly, Sir Charles Herbert, 1874–1948, vol. IV
Reilly, Sir D'Arcy; *see* Reilly, Sir H. D. C.
Reilly, E. Albert, 1868–1943, vol. IV
Reilly, Sir (Henry) D'Arcy (Cornelius), 1876–1948, vol. IV
Reilly, Joseph, 1889–1965, vol. VI
Reilly, Very Rev. Thomas, *died* 1921, vol. II
Reinach, Joseph, 1856–1921, vol. II
Reinach, Salomon, 1858–1932, vol. III
Reinhardt, Max, 1873–1943, vol. IV
Reinold, Arnold William, 1843–1921, vol. II
Reinold, Vice-Adm. Harold Owen, 1877–1962, vol. VI
Reisner, George Andrew, 1867–1942, vol. IV
Reiss, Lt-Col Alec, 1871–1932, vol. III
Reiss, Charles, 1873–1949, vol. IV
Reiss, Richard Leopold, 1883–1959, vol. V
Reith, 1st Baron, 1889–1971, vol. VII
Reith, Rev. David, 1842–1909, vol. I

Reitlinger, Gerald Roberts, 1900–1978, vol. VII
Reitz, Col Deneys, 1882–1944, vol. IV
Reitz, Hon. Francis William, 1844–1934, vol. III
Réjane, Madame, (Gabrielle Réju), 1857–1920, vol. II
Relf, Ernest Frederick, 1888–1970, vol. VI
Relph, George, 1888–1960, vol. V
Relton, Arthur John, 1856–1946, vol. IV
Relton, Frederick Ernest, 1883–1963, vol. VI
Relton, Rev. Herbert Maurice, 1882–1971, vol. VII
Remarque, Erich Maria, 1898–1970, vol. VI
Remer, John Rumney, 1883–1948, vol. IV
Remington, Geoffrey Cochrane, 1897–1968, vol. VI
Remizov, Alexei, 1877–1957, vol. V
Remnant, 1st Baron, 1863–1933, vol. III
Remnant, 2nd Baron, 1895–1967, vol. VI
Remnant, Ernest, 1872–1941, vol. IV
Remnant, Hon. Peter Farquharson, 1897–1968, vol. VI
Remsen, Ira, 1846–1927, vol. II
Renals, Sir Herbert, 3rd Bt, 1919–1961, vol. VI
Renals, Sir James Herbert, 2nd Bt, 1870–1927, vol. II (A), vol. III
Renals, Sir Joseph, 1st Bt, 1843–1908, vol. I
Renard, Samuel, *died* 1924, vol. II
Renaud, Maj.-Gen. Ernest James, *died* 1967, vol. VI
Renault, Louis, 1843–1918, vol. II
Rendall, Athelstan, 1871–1948, vol. IV
Rendall, Rev. Gerald Henry, 1851–1945, vol. IV
Rendall, Montague John, 1862–1950, vol. IV
Rendall, Richard Antony, 1907–1957, vol. V
Rendall, Vernon Horace, 1869–1960, vol. V
Rendel, 1st Baron, 1834–1913, vol. I
Rendel, Sir Alexander Meadows, 1829–1918, vol. II
Rendel, George Wightwick, 1833–1902, vol. I
Rendel, Sir George William, 1889–1979, vol. VII
Rendel, Harry Stuart G.; *see* Goodhart-Rendel.
Rendell, Rev. Arthur Medland, 1842–1918, vol. II
Rendell, Rev. James Robson, 1850–1926, vol. II
Rendell, Col Walter Frederic, 1888–1951, vol. V
Rendell, William Reginald, 1868–1948, vol. IV
Rendle, Alfred Barton, 1865–1938, vol. III
Rendlesham, 5th Baron, 1840–1911 (this entry was not transferred to Who was Who).
Rendlesham, 6th Baron, 1868–1938, vol. III
Rendlesham, 7th Baron, 1874–1943, vol. IV
Renfrew, Thomas, 1901–1975, vol. VII
Renier, Gustaaf Johannes, 1892–1962, vol. VI
Renison, Sir Patrick Muir, 1911–1965, vol. VI
Renison, Most Rev. Robert John, 1875–1957, vol. V
Rennell, 1st Baron, 1858–1941, vol. IV
Rennell, 2nd Baron, 1895–1978, vol. VII
Rennenkampff, Gen.-Lt Paul Charles von, 1854–1918, vol. II
Rennert, Guenther, 1911–1978, vol. VII
Rennie, Charles Robert, 1880–1969, vol. VI
Rennie, Edward Henry, 1852–1927, vol. II
Rennie, Sir Ernest Amelius, 1868–1935, vol. III
Rennie, Francis Pepys, 1872–1946, vol. IV
Rennie, Col George Arthur Paget, 1872–1951, vol. V
Rennie, Col. George Septimus, *died* 1930, vol. III
Rennie, Lt-Col Horace Watt, *died* 1943, vol. IV

Rennie, James, 1814–1903, vol. I
Rennie, John, *died* 1960, vol. V (A)
Rennie, Major John George, 1865–1920, vol. II
Rennie, Sir Richard Temple, 1839–1905, vol. I
Rennie, Maj.-Gen. Robert, 1862–1949, vol. IV
Rennie, Col Samuel James, 1855–1935, vol. III
Rennie, Maj.-Gen. Tom Gordon, 1900–1945, vol. IV
Rennie, William, *died* 1957, vol. V
Renny, Brig. George Douglas, 1908–1971, vol. VII
Renny, Gen. Henry, 1815–1900, vol. I
Renny, Col Lewis Frederick, 1877–1955, vol. V
Renny, Maj.-Gen. Sidney Mercer, 1861–1921, vol. II
Renny-Tailyour, Col Thomas Francis Bruce, 1863–1937, vol. III
Renoir, Jean, 1894–1979, vol. VII
Renold, Sir Charles Garonne, 1883–1967, vol. VI
Renouf, Vice-Adm. Edward de Faye, 1888–1972, vol. VII
Renouf, Sir Peter le Page, 1822–1897, vol. I
Renouf, Winter Charles, 1868–1954, vol. V
Renouvin, Pierre, 1893–1974, vol. VII
Renshaw, Arthur Henry, *died* 1918, vol. II
Renshaw, Sir Charles Bine, 1st Bt, 1848–1918, vol. II
Renshaw, Sir (Charles) Stephen (Bine), 2nd Bt, 1883–1976, vol. VII
Renshaw, John W., 1877–1955, vol. V
Renshaw, Sir Stephen; *see* Renshaw, Sir C. S. B.
Renshaw, Walter Charles, 1840–1922, vol. II
Rentell, Henry William Sidney, 1864–1927, vol. II (A), vol. III
Renton, Major (Alexander) Leslie, 1868–1947, vol. IV
Renton, Sir Alexander Wood, 1861–1933, vol. III
Renton, James Crawford, *died* 1919, vol. II
Renton, Brig. James Malcolm Leslie, 1898–1972, vol. VII
Renton, Major Leslie; *see* Renton, Major A. L.
Rentoul, Sir Gervais, 1884–1946, vol. IV
Rentoul, James Alexander, *died* 1919, vol. II
Rentoul, Rt Rev. John Laurence, 1846–1926, vol. II
Renwick, 1st Baron, 1904–1973, vol. VII
Renwick, Hon. Sir Arthur, 1837–1910, vol. I (A)
Renwick, Sir Eustace Deuchar, 3rd Bt (*cr* 1921), 1902–1973, vol. VII
Renwick, Sir George, 1st Bt (*cr* 1921), 1850–1931, vol. III
Renwick, Major Gustav Adolph, 1883–1956, vol. V
Renwick, Sir Harry Benedetto, 1st Bt, 1861–1932, vol. III
Renwick, Sir John Robert, 2nd Bt (*cr* 1921), 1877–1946, vol. IV
Renwick, William Lindsay, 1889–1970, vol. VI
Renzis, Francesco de, Baron, *died* 1900, vol. I
Repington, Lt-Col Charles A'Court-, 1858–1925, vol. II
Repington, Charles Henry Wyndham A'C.; *see* A'Court-Repington.
Repplier, Agnes, 1858–1950, vol. IV
Restler, Sir James William, *died* 1918, vol. II
Reston, Clifford Arthur, 1928–1979, vol. VII
Reszke, Jean de, 1853–1925, vol. II

Rettie, Middleton, *died* 1910, vol. I
Rettie, Lt-Col William John Kerr, 1868–1939, vol. III
Retzius, Magnus Gustaf, 1842–1919, vol. II
Reuter, Baron de; Paul Julius, 1816–1899, vol. I
Reuter, Baron de; Auguste Julius Clemens Herbert, 1852–1915, vol. I
Reuther, Walter Philip, 1907–1970, vol. VI
Revel, John Daniel, 1884–1967, vol. VI
Revell, Alfred Edgar, 1877–1932, vol. III
Revell, Daniel Graisberry, 1869–1954, vol. V
Revell-Smith, Maj.-Gen. William Revell, 1894–1956, vol. V
Revelstoke, 1st Baron, 1828–1897, vol. I
Revelstoke, 2nd Baron, 1863–1929, vol. III
Revelstoke, 3rd Baron, 1864–1934, vol. III
Reventlow, Count Eduard, 1883–1963, vol. VI
Reville, Rt Rev. Mgr Stephen, 1844–1916, vol. II
Rew, Lt-Col Horace Edward, 1899–1967, vol. VI
Rew, Sir (R.) Henry, 1858–1929, vol. III
Rewa, Bandhvesh Ex-Maharaja of, Sir Gulab Singh Bahadur, 1903–1950, vol. IV
Rewah, HH Maharaja Venkat Raman Singh Bahadur, 1876–1918, vol. II
Rewcastle, Cuthbert Snowball, 1888–1962, vol. VI
Rewse, Rev. Gilbert Flesher S.; *see* Smith-Rewse.
Rewse, Col Henry Whistler, S.; *see* Smith-Rewse
Rex, Marcus, 1886–1971, vol. VII
Rey, Lt-Col Sir Charles Fernand, 1877–1968, vol. VI
Reymont, Wladislaw, 1868–1925, vol. II
Reynard, Helene, 1875–1947, vol. IV
Reynard, Matthew Andrew, 1878–1946, vol. IV
Reynard, Robert Froding, 1857–1926, vol. II
Reynardson, Col Charles Birch-, 1845–1919, vol. II
Reynardson, Lt-Col Henry T. Birch, 1892–1972, vol. VII
Reynaud, Paul, 1878–1966, vol. VI
Reyne, Rear-Adm. Sir Cecil Nugent, 1881–1958, vol. V
Reyne, Lt-Col Gerard van Rossum, 1886–1940, vol. III
Reynell, Douglas, 1877–1949, vol. IV
Reynell, Walter Rupert, 1885–1948, vol. IV
Reynell-Pack, Arthur Denis Henry Heber, 1860–1937, vol. III
Reynolds, Lt-Col Alan Boyd, 1879–1940, vol. III
Reynolds, Alan Lowe, 1897–1977, vol. VII
Reynolds, Sir Alfred, 1850–1931, vol. III
Reynolds, Alfred Charles, 1884–1969, vol. VI
Reynolds, Mrs Alice; *see* Cullen, Mrs A.
Reynolds, Rev. Bernard, 1850–1930, vol. III
Reynolds, Air Marshal Sir Bryan Vernon, 1902–1965, vol. VI
Reynolds, Cedric Lawton, 1888–1958, vol. V
Reynolds, Charles Henry, 1844–1908, vol. I
Reynolds, Clyde Albert M.; *see* Marshall-Reynolds.
Reynolds, Lt-Col Denys Walter, 1884–1940, vol. III
Reynolds, Major Douglas, 1881–1916, vol. II
Reynolds, Edward, 1874–1944, vol. IV
Reynolds, Ernest Septimus, 1861–1926, vol. II
Reynolds, Sir Francis Jubal, 1857–1924, vol. II
Reynolds, Frank, 1876–1953, vol. V

Reynolds, Frank Neon, 1895–1952, vol. V
Reynolds, Sir Frank Umhlali, 1852–1930, vol. III
Reynolds, George McClelland, 1865–1940, vol. III
Reynolds, Rt Hon. Gerald William, 1927–1969, vol. VI
Reynolds, Adm. Harry Campbell, 1853–1949, vol. IV
Reynolds, Captain Henry, 1881–1948, vol. IV
Reynolds, Henry Osborne, 1883–1947, vol. IV
Reynolds, Herbert John, 1832–1916, vol. II
Reynolds, J. H., 1842–1927, vol. II
Reynolds, James Emerson, 1844–1920, vol. II
Reynolds, Lt-Col James Henry, 1844–1932, vol. III
Reynolds, Col Sir James Philip, 1st Bt, 1865–1932, vol. III
Reynolds, Sir Jeffrey Fellowes Crofts, 1893–1966, vol. VI
Reynolds, Lt-Col Sir John Francis Roskell, 2nd Bt, 1899–1956, vol. V
Reynolds, John Henry, 1874–1949, vol. IV
Reynolds, John Richardson, 1873–1934, vol. III
Reynolds, Sir Leonard William, 1874–1946, vol. IV
Reynolds, Mrs Louis Baillie, died 1939, vol. III
Reynolds, Louis George Stanley, died 1945, vol. IV
Reynolds, Osborne, 1842–1912, vol. I
Reynolds, Paul Kenneth Baillie, 1896–1973, vol. VII
Reynolds, Major Sir Percival Reuben, 1876–1965, vol. VI
Reynolds, Major Philip Guy, 1871–1936, vol. III
Reynolds, Quentin James, 1902–1965, vol. VI
Reynolds, Reginald Francis, died 1936, vol. III
Reynolds, Reginald Philip Neri, 1867–1936, vol. III
Reynolds, Richard Samuel, Jr, 1908–1980, vol. VII
Reynolds, Russell John, 1880–1964, vol. VI
Reynolds, Sidney Hugh, 1867–1949, vol. IV
Reynolds, Stephen, 1881–1919, vol. II
Reynolds, Warwick, 1880–1926, vol. II
Reynolds, William George Waterhouse, 1860–1928, vol. II
Reynolds-Ball, Eustace Alfred, died 1928, vol. II
Reynolds-Stephens, Sir William, 1862–1943, vol. IV
Rhayader, 1st Baron, 1862–1939, vol. III
Rhead, George Woolliscroft, died 1920, vol. II
Rheam, Henry Meynell, 1859–1920, vol. II
Rhigini, Madame de; see Russell, Ella.
Rhind, Lt-Col Sir Duncan; see Rhind, Lt-Col Sir T. D.
Rhind, Edwin Scoby O.; see Oak-Rhind.
Rhind, John Massey, 1868–1936, vol. III
Rhind, Lt-Col Sir (Thomas) Duncan, 1871–1927, vol. II
Rhind, William Birnie, died 1933, vol. III
Rhine, Joseph Banks, 1895–1980, vol. VII
Rhoades, James, 1841–1923, vol. II
Rhoads, Cornelius Packard, 1898–1959, vol. V
Rhodes, Sir Campbell, 1874–1941, vol. IV
Rhodes, Rt Hon. Cecil John, 1853–1902, vol. I
Rhodes, Charles Kenneth, 1889–1941, vol. IV
Rhodes, Sir Christopher George, 3rd Bt, 1914–1964, vol. VI
Rhodes, Hon. Edgar Nelson, 1877–1942, vol. IV
Rhodes, Sir Edward, 1870–1959, vol. V
Rhodes, Major Elmhirst, 1858–1931, vol. III

Rhodes, Col Francis William, 1851–1905, vol. I
Rhodes, Sir Frederick Edward, 4th Bt, 1843–1911, vol. I
Rhodes, Geoffrey William, 1928–1974, vol. VII
Rhodes, George, 1851–1924, vol. II
Rhodes, Sir George, 1st Bt, 1860–1924, vol. II
Rhodes, Brig.-Gen. Sir Godfrey Dean, 1886–1971, vol. VII
Rhodes, Harold, 1885–1964, vol. VI
Rhodes, Harold Vale, died 1970, vol. VI
Rhodes, Harold William, 1889–1956, vol. V
Rhodes, Col Hon. Sir Heaton; see Rhodes, Col Hon. Sir R. H.
Rhodes, Helen, died 1936, vol. III
Rhodes, Rev. Herbert A., 1869–1956, vol. V
Rhodes, James Ford, 1848–1927, vol. II
Rhodes, Lt-Col Sir John Phillips, 2nd Bt, 1884–1955, vol. V
Rhodes, Kathyln, died 1962, vol. VI
Rhodes, Col Hon. Sir (Robert) Heaton, 1861–1956, vol. V
Rhodes, Col Stephen, died 1966, vol. VI
Rhodes, Walter Harpham, 1888–1962, vol. VI
Rhondda, 1st Viscount, 1856–1918, vol. II
Rhondda, Viscountess (2nd in line), died 1958, vol. V
Rhondda, Viscountess; (Sybil), died 1941, vol. IV
Rhydderch, Sir William Edmund Hodges, 1890–1961, vol. VI
Rhys, Ernest, 1859–1946, vol. IV
Rhys, Jean, (Mrs Jean Hamer), 1894–1979, vol. VII
Rhys, Rt Hon. Sir John, 1840–1915, vol. I (A)
Rhys-Roberts, Thomas Esmôr Rhys, 1910–1975, vol. VII
Rhys Williams, Juliet Evangeline, (Lady Rhys Williams), 1898–1964, vol. VI
Rhys-Williams, Lt-Col Sir Rhys; see Williams.
Riach, Col William, 1873–1942, vol. IV
Ribbentrop, Joachim von, 1893–1946, vol. IV
Ribblesdale, 4th Baron, 1854–1925, vol. II
Riberi, His Eminence Cardinal Antonio, 1897–1967, vol. VI
Ribot, Alexandre F., 1842–1923, vol. II
Ribton, Sir George, 4th Bt, 1842–1901, vol. I
Ricardo, Lt-Col Ambrose St Quintin, 1866–1923 vol. II
Ricardo, Adm. Arthur David, 1861–1931, vol. III
Ricardo, Col Francis Cecil, 1852–1924, vol. II
Ricardo, Halsey Ralph, 1854–1928, vol. II
Ricardo, Sir Harry Ralph, 1885–1974, vol. VII
Ricardo, Major Harry William Ralph, 1860–1945, vol. IV
Ricardo, Lt-Col Henry George, 1860–1940, vol. III
Ricardo, Col Horace, 1850–1935, vol. III
Ricardo, Col Percy Ralph, 1855–1907, vol. I
Ricci, Luigi, died 1915, vol. I
Rice, Alexander Hamilton, 1875–1956, vol. V
Rice, Mrs Alice Hegan, died 1942, vol. IV
Rice, B. Lewis, 1837–1927, vol. II
Rice, Cale Young, 1872–1943, vol. IV (A), vol. V
Rice, Rt Hon. Sir Cecil Arthur S.; see Spring-Rice.
Rice, David Talbot, 1903–1972, vol. VII
Rice, Dominick S.; see Spring-Rice.

Rice, Air Vice-Marshal Sir Edward Arthur Beckton, 1893–1948, vol. IV
Rice, Sir Edward Bridges, 1819–1902, vol. I
Rice, Elmer, 1892–1967, vol. VI
Rice, Adm. Sir Ernest, 1840–1927, vol. II
Rice, Sir Frederick Gill, 1866–1935, vol. III
Rice, George Samuel, 1866–1950, vol. IV
Rice, Col Henry James, 1894–1964, vol. VI
Rice, James, 1874–1936, vol. III
Rice, Joseph M., 1857–1934, vol. III
Rice, Dame Margaret Ker P.; see Pryse-Rice.
Rice, Percy Christopher, 1877–1963, vol. VI
Rice, Lt-Col Sidney Mervyn, 1873–1959, vol. V
Rice, Maj.-Gen. Sir Spring Robert, 1858–1929, vol. III
Rice, Stephen Edward S.; see Spring-Rice.
Rice, Thomas Edmund, died 1941, vol. IV
Rice, Walter Francis, died 1941, vol. IV
Rice, Wilfred Eric, 1898–1979, vol. VII
Rice, Sir William George, 1861–1936, vol. III
Rice, Rev. William Ignatius, 1883–1955, vol. V
Rice, Hon. and Rev. William Talbot, 1861–1945, vol. IV
Rice, Comdr William Victor, died 1932, vol. III
Rice-Jones, Benjamin Rowland, 1888–1978, vol. VII
Rice-Oxley, Sir Alfred James, 1856–1941, vol. IV
Rice-Oxley, Douglas George, 1885–1972, vol. VII
Rich, Adena M., (Mrs Kenneth F. Rich), died 1967, vol. VI
Rich, Alfred William, 1856–1922, vol. II
Rich, Sir Almeric Edmund Frederic, 5th Bt, 1859–1948, vol. IV
Rich, Sir Charles Henry Stuart, 4th Bt, 1859–1913, vol. I
Rich, Charles T., 1869–1940, vol. III
Rich, Edmund Milton, 1875–1954, vol. V
Rich, Col Edmund Tillotson, 1874–1937, vol. III
Rich, Edward Charles, 1895–1959, vol. V
Rich, Edwin Ernest, 1904–1979, vol. VII
Rich, Vice-Adm. Frederick St George, 1852–1914, vol. I
Rich, Rt Hon. Sir George Edward, 1863–1956, vol. V
Rich, Maj.-Gen. Henry Hampden, 1891–1976, vol. VII
Rich, Rev. John, 1826–1913, vol. I
Rich, Mrs Kenneth F.; see Rich, Adena M.
Rich, Rev. Leonard James, died 1920, vol. II
Rich, Roy, 1912–1970, vol. VI
Richard, Ven. Robert Henry, 1869–1929, vol. III
Richard, Timothy, 1845–1919, vol. II
Richards, Albert Edwin George, 1856–1942, vol. IV
Richards, Albert Elswood, 1848–1918, vol. II
Richards, Alfred Newton, 1876–1966, vol. VI
Richards, Ceri Giraldus, 1903–1971, vol. VII
Richards, Brig. Collen Edward Melville, died 1971, vol. VII
Richards, Dickinson W., 1895–1973, vol. VII
Richards, Sir Edmund Charles, 1889–1955, vol. V
Richards, Edward Windsor, died 1921, vol. II
Richards, Major Francis Howe, 1890–1937, vol. III
Richards, Francis John, 1901–1965, vol. VI
Richards, Frank, 1875–1961, vol. VI

Richards, Frank Roydon, 1899–1978, vol. VII
Richards, Franklin Thomas Grant, 1872–1948, vol. IV
Richards, Fred C., died 1932, vol. III
Richards, Sir Frederick William, 1833–1912, vol. I
Richards, Hon. Sir Frederick William, 1869–1957, vol. V
Richards, Rear-Adm. G. E., 1852–1927, vol. II
Richards, Rev. George Chatterton, 1867–1951, vol. V
Richards, George Edward Fugl, 1891–1974, vol. VII
Richards, Maj.-Gen. George Warren, 1898–1978, vol. VII
Richards, Miss Gertrude Mary, died 1944, vol. IV
Richards, Gilbert Stanley Nowell, 1912–1980, vol. VII
Richards, Lt-Col Harold Arthur David, 1874–1947, vol. IV
Richards, Harold Meredith, died 1942, vol. IV
Richards, Henry Caselli, 1884–1947, vol. IV
Richards, Henry Charles, 1851–1905, vol. I
Richards, Sir Henry Erle, 1861–1922, vol. II
Richards, Sir Henry George, 1860–1928, vol. II
Richards, Sir Henry Maunsell, 1869–1957, vol. V
Richards, Henry William, 1865–1956, vol. V
Richards, Herbert Arthur, 1866–1957, vol. V
Richards, Herbert Paul, 1848–1916, vol. II
Richards, Hugh Augustine, 1884–1949, vol. IV
Richards, Rt Rev. Isaac, 1859–1936, vol. III
Richards, Ivor Armstrong, 1893–1979, vol. VII
Richards, Engr-Captain John Arthur, 1865–1949, vol. IV
Richards, John Eugene, 1885–1951, vol. V
Richards, John Gower Meredith, 1900–1968, vol. VI
Richards, Very Rev. John Harold, 1869–1952, vol. V
Richards, John Henry, 1818–1901, vol. I
Richards, John Morgan, 1841–1918, vol. II
Richards, Sir Joseph, 1888–1968, vol. VI
Richards, Rev. Leyton, 1879–1948, vol. IV
Richards, Maurice John, 1894–1969, vol. VI
Richards, Hon. Mrs Noel Olivier, 1892–1969, vol. VI (AII)
Richards, Sir Norman Grantham Lewis, 1905–1977, vol. VII
Richards, Owen, 1873–1949, vol. IV
Richards, Percy Andrew Ellis, 1868–1937, vol. III
Richards, Raymond, 1906–1978, vol. VII
Richards, Reginald James, died 1950, vol. IV
Richards, Robert, 1884–1954, vol. V
Richards, Rupert Peel, 1872–1941, vol. IV
Richards, Col Samuel Smith Crosland, 1841–1918, vol. II
Richards, Major Sidney, vol. III
Richards, Stephen Elswood, 1878–1950, vol. IV (A), vol. V
Richards, Theodore William, 1868–1928, vol. II (A), vol. III
Richards, Rt Hon. Thomas, 1859–1931, vol. III
Richards, Thomas Frederick, 1863–1942, vol. IV
Richards, Whitmore Lionel, 1869–1954, vol. V
Richards, William, 1863–1939, vol. III

Richards, Air Cdre William Edward Victor, 1897–1964, vol. VI

Richards, William James, 1915–1978, vol. VII

Richards, William John, 1903–1976, vol. VII

Richards, Maj.-Gen. William Watson, 1892–1961, vol. VI

Richardson, Very Rev. Alan, 1905–1975, vol. VII

Richardson, Sir Albert Edward, 1880–1964, vol. VI

Richardson, Air Marshal Sir (Albert) Victor (John), 1884–1960, vol. V

Richardson, Sir Albion Henry Herbert, *died* 1950, vol. IV

Richardson, Sir Alexander, 1864–1928, vol. II

Richardson, Maj.-Gen. Alexander Whitmore Colquhoun, 1887–1964, vol. VI

Richardson, Alfred, *died* 1934, vol. III

Richardson, Arnold Edwin Victor, 1883–1949, vol. IV

Richardson, Arthur, 1860–1936, vol. III

Richardson, Arthur Johnstone, 1862–1940, vol. III

Richardson, Charles Arthur, 1918–1972, vol. VII

Richardson, Lt-Gen. Sir Charles William Grant, 1868–1929, vol. III

Richardson, Cyril Albert, 1891–1966, vol. VI

Richardson, Maj.-Gen. David Turnbull, 1886–1957, vol. V

Richardson, Dorothy M., (Mrs Alan Odle), *died* 1957, vol. V

Richardson, Sir Edward Austin Stewart-, 15th Bt (*cr* 1630), 1872–1914, vol. I

Richardson, Edward Gick, 1896–1960, vol. V

Richardson, E(dward) Ryder, 1901–1961, vol. VI

Richardson, Ven. Edward Shaw, 1862–1921, vol. II

Richardson, Lt-Col Edwin Hautonville, 1863–1948, vol. IV

Richardson, Emily Moore; *see* Hamilton, E. M.

Richardson, Foster, *died* 1942, vol. IV

Richardson, Major Francis James, 1866–1917, vol. II

Richardson, Frank, 1870–1917, vol. II

Richardson, Frederic Stuart, 1855–1934, vol. III

Richardson, Rev. Canon Frederick, 1885–1967, vol. VI

Richardson, Rev. George Leyburn, 1867–1934, vol. III

Richardson, Lt-Gen. Sir George Lloyd Reily, 1847–1931, vol. III

Richardson, Maj.-Gen. Sir George Spafford, 1868–1938, vol. III

Richardson, Col Gerald, 1907–1974, vol. VII

Richardson, Major Guy; *see* Richardson, Major T. G. F.

Richardson, Harry, 1891–1966, vol. VI

Richardson, Harry Linley, 1878–1947, vol. IV

Richardson, Sir Henry; *see* Richardson, Sir J. H. S.

Richardson, Henry Gerald, *died* 1974, vol. VII

Richardson, Henry Handel, *died* 1946, vol. IV

Richardson, Henry Marriott, 1876–1936, vol. III

Richardson, Lt-Col Henry Sacheverell Carleton, 1883–1958, vol. III

Richardson, Hon. Horace Frank, 1854–1935, vol. III

Richardson, Major Sir Ian Rorie Hay S.; *see* Stewart-Richardson.

Richardson, Ven. James Banning, 1843–1923, vol. II

Richardson, Col James Jardine, 1873–1942, vol. IV

Richardson, James Nicholson, 1846–1921, vol. II

Richardson, Ven. John, 1817–1904, vol. I

Richardson, Engr-Rear-Adm. John, 1862–1928, vol. II

Richardson, Major John, 1859–1935, vol. III

Richardson, Rt Rev. John, *died* 1978, vol. VII

Richardson, Most Rev. John Andrew, 1868–1938, vol. III

Richardson, Maj.-Gen. John Booth, 1838–1923, vol. II

Richardson, Maj.-Gen. John Dalyell, 1880–1954, vol. V

Richardson, Ven. John Gray, 1849–1924, vol. II

Richardson, John Henry, 1890–1970, vol. VI

Richardson, Sir (John) Henry (Swain), 1889–1980, vol. VII

Richardson, John I., 1836–1913, vol. I

Richardson, Very Rev. John Macdonald, 1880–1964, vol. VI

Richardson, Joseph, 1830–1902, vol. I

Richardson, Maj.-Gen. Joseph Fletcher, 1822–1900, vol. I

Richardson, Joseph Hall, 1857–1945, vol. IV

Richardson, Josephus Hargreaves, 1856–1932. vol. III

Richardson, Leopold John Dixon, 1893–1979, vol. VII

Richardson, Captain Leslie, 1885–1934, vol. III

Richardson, Sir Lewis, 1st Bt (*cr* 1924), 1873–1934, vol. III

Richardson, Lewis Fry, 1881–1953, vol. V

Richardson, Linetta de Castelvecchio, *died* 1975, vol. VII

Richardson, Maggie; *see* Mitchell, Mrs G. J.

Richardson, Maurice Robert, 1884–1950, vol. IV

Richardson, Brig.-Gen. Morris Ernald, 1878–1929, vol. III

Richardson, Lt-Col Neil Graham Stewart-, 1881–1934, vol. III

Richardson, Sir Owen Willans, 1879–1959, vol. V

Richardson, Philip John Sampey, 1875–1963, vol. VI

Richardson, Lt-Col Sir Philip Wigham, 1st Bt (*cr* 1929), 1865–1953, vol. V

Richardson, Ralph, 1845–1933, vol. III

Richardson, Rev. Raymond William, 1909–1968, vol. VI

Richardson, Robert, 1862–1943, vol. IV

Richardson, Bt Lt-Col Robert Airth, 1864–1936, vol. III

Richardson, Maj.-Gen. Roland, 1896–1973, vol. VII

Richardson, Spencer William, 1869–1927, vol. II

Richardson, Sir Thomas, 1846–1906, vol. I

Richardson, Thomas, 1868–1928, vol. II

Richardson, Thomas, *died* 1956, vol. V

Richardson, Major (Thomas) Guy (Fenton), 1885–1966, vol. VI

Richardson, Sir Thomas William, 1865–1947, vol. IV

Richardson, Maj.-Gen. Thomas William, 1895–1968, vol. VI

Richardson, Air Marshal Sir Victor; *see* Richardson, Air Marshal Sir A. V. J.

Richardson, Violet Roberta S.; *see* Stewart-Richardson.

Richardson, Rt Rev. William Moore, 1844–1915, vol. I

Richardson, William Rowson, 1892–1978, vol. VII

Richardson, Maj.-Gen. William Stewart, *died* 1901, vol. I

Richardson, Sir William Wigham, 2nd Bt (*cr* 1929), 1893–1973, vol. VII

Richardson, Col Sir Wodehouse Dillon, 1854–1929, vol. III

Richardson-Bunbury, Sir Mervyn William; *see* Bunbury.

Richardson-Cox, Major Eustace, 1862–1935, vol. III

Richardson-Drummond-Hay, Col James Adam Gordon; *see* Hay.

Richardson-Griffiths, Major Charles Du Plat, 1855–1925, vol. II

Riche, Georges de P.; *see* Porto-Riche.

Richepin, Jean, 1849–1926, vol. II

Riches, Lindsay Gordon, 1904–1972, vol. VII

Riches, Tom Hurry, 1846–1911, vol. I

Richet, Charles, 1850–1935, vol. III

Richey, Lt-Col George Henry Mills, 1867–1949, vol. IV

Richey, James Alexander, 1874–1931, vol. III

Richey, Sir James Bellett, 1834–1902, vol. I

Richey, James Ernest, 1886–1968, vol. VI

Richmond, 7th Duke of, **and Gordon,** 2nd Duke of, 1845–1928, vol. II

Richmond, 8th Duke of, **and Gordon,** 3rd Duke of, 1870–1935, vol. III

Richmond and Gordon, Duchess of; (Hilda Madeleine), *died* 1971, vol. VII

Richmond, Sir Arthur Cyril, 1879–1968, vol. VI

Richmond, Brig. Arthur Eaton, 1892–1961, vol. VI

Richmond, Sir Bruce Lyttelton, *died* 1964, vol. VI

Richmond, Sir Daniel; *see* Richmond, Sir R. D.

Richmond, Sir David, 1843–1908, vol. I

Richmond, Douglas Close, 1839–1930, vol. III

Richmond, Sir Frederick Henry, 1st Bt, 1873–1953, vol. V

Richmond, Rev. George Edward, 1859–1935, vol. III

Richmond, Adm. Sir Herbert W., 1871–1946, vol. IV

Richmond, Herbert William, 1863–1948, vol. IV

Richmond, Sir Ian, 1902–1965, vol. VI

Richmond, James, 1849–1914, vol. I

Richmond, Sir John Ritchie, 1869–1963, vol. VI

Richmond, Lawrence, 1885–1968, vol. VI

Richmond, Leonard, *died* 1965, vol. VI

Richmond, Maurice Wilson, 1860–1919, vol. II

Richmond, Oliffe Legh, 1881–1977, vol. VII

Richmond, Sir (Robert) Daniel, 1878–1948, vol. IV

Richmond, Rev. Thomas Knyvett, *died* 1901, vol. I

Richmond, Rev. Wilfrid John, 1848–1938, vol. III

Richmond, Col Wilfrid Stanley, 1881–1962, vol. VI

Richmond, Sir William Blake, 1842–1921, vol. II

Richter, Eugen, 1838–1906, vol. I

Richter, Gisela M. A., 1882–1972, vol. VII

Richter, Hans, 1843–1916, vol. II

Richter, Hon. Sir Harold, 1906–1979, vol. VII

Richter, Herbert Davis, 1874–1955, vol. V

Richter, Jean Paul, 1847–1937, vol. III

Richter, Mrs Jean Paul; *see* Richter, Louise Marie.

Richter, Louise Marie, *died* 1938, vol. III

Rickaby, Father Joseph, 1845–1932, vol. III

Rickard, Sir Arthur, 1868–1948, vol. IV

Rickard, Charles Ernest, 1880–1961, vol. VI

Rickard, Rev. Herbert, *died* 1926, vol. II

Rickard, Jessie Louisa; *see* Rickard, Mrs Victor.

Rickard, Thomas Arthur, 1864–1953, vol. V

Rickard, Mrs Victor, (Jessie Louisa), *died* 1963, vol. VI

Rickards, Arthur George, 1848–1924, vol. II

Rickards, David Ayscough, 1912–1973, vol. VII

Rickards, George William, 1877–1943, vol. IV

Rickards, Maj.-Gen. Gerald Arthur, 1886–1972, vol. VII

Rickards, Rev. Marcus Samuel Cam, 1840–1928, vol. II

Rickenbacker, Edward Vernon, 1890–1973, vol. VII

Ricketson, Staniforth, 1891–1967, vol. VI

Rickett, Arthur C.; *see* Compton-Rickett.

Rickett, Harold Robert Norman, 1909–1969, vol. VI

Rickett, Rt Hon. Sir Joseph C.; *see* Compton-Rickett.

Ricketts, Major Arthur, 1874–1968, vol. VI

Ricketts, Charles, 1866–1931, vol. III

Ricketts, Sir Claude Albert Frederick, 6th Bt, 1880–1937, vol. III

Ricketts, Rt Rev. Clement Mallory, 1885–1961, vol. VI

Ricketts, Sir Frederick William Rodney, 5th Bt, 1857–1925, vol. II

Ricketts, George Henry Mildmay, 1827–1914, vol. I

Ricketts, George William, 1864–1927, vol. II

Ricketts, Gordon Randolph, 1918–1968, vol. VI

Ricketts, Lt-Col Percy Edward, 1868–1940, vol. III

Rickman, Lt-Col Arthur Wilmot, 1874–1925, vol. II

Rickman, Captain William Edward, 1855–1927, vol. II

Rickmers, W. Rickmer, 1873–1965, vol. VI

Riddel, Vice-Adm. Daniel MacNab, *died* 1941, vol. IV

Riddel, James, 1857–1928, vol. II

Riddell, 1st Baron, 1865–1934, vol. III

Riddell, Sir Alexander Oliver, 1844–1918, vol. II

Riddell, Rt Rev. Arthur, 1836–1907, vol. I

Riddell, Athol George, 1917–1974, vol. VII

Riddell, Maj.-Gen. Charles James Buchanan, 1817–1903, vol. I

Riddell, Charlotte Eliza Lawson; *see* Riddell, Mrs J. H.

Riddell, Cuthbert David Giffard, 1868–1937, vol. III

Riddell, Brig.-Gen. Sir Edward Pius Arthur, 1875–1957, vol. V

Riddell, Col Edward Vansittart Dick, 1873–1942, vol. IV

Riddell, Florence, *died* 1960, vol. V
Riddell, Captain George Hutton, 1878–1915, vol. I
Riddell, Mrs J. H., (Charlotte Eliza Lawson Riddell), 1832–1906, vol. I
Riddell, Rev. John Gervase, 1896–1955, vol. V
Riddell, John Robertson, 1874–1941, vol. IV
Riddell, Col John Scott, 1864–1929, vol. III
Riddell, Sir John Walter Buchanan-, 11th Bt (*cr* 1628), 1849–1924, vol. II
Riddell, Sir Rodney Stuart, 4th Bt (*cr* 1778), 1838–1907, vol. I
Riddell, Victor Horsley, *died* 1976, vol. VII
Riddell, Walter Alexander, 1881–1963, vol. VI
Riddell, Sir Walter Robert Buchanan-, 12th Bt (*cr* 1628), 1879–1934, vol. III
Riddell, William John Brownlow, 1899–1976, vol. VII
Riddell, William Renwick, 1852–1945, vol. IV
Riddell-Blount, Edward Francis; *see* Blount.
Riddell-Webster, Gen. Sir Thomas Sheridan, 1886–1974, vol. VII
Riddet, William, 1896–1958, vol. V
Riddick, Col John Galloway, 1879–1964, vol. VI
Ridding, Rt Rev. George, 1828–1904, vol. I
Riddle, Sir Ernest Cooper, 1873–1939, vol. III
Riddle, Sir George, 1875–1944, vol. IV
Riddle, John Wallace, 1864–1941, vol. IV
Riddoch, George, 1888–1947, vol. IV
Riddoch, John William, 1893–1969, vol. VI
Riddoch, William, 1862–1942, vol. IV
Ride, Sir Lindsay Tasman, 1898–1977, vol. VII
Rideal, Sir Eric Keightley, 1890–1974, vol. VII
Rideal, Samuel, *died* 1929, vol. III
Ridehalgh, Arthur, 1907–1971, vol. VII
Rideing, William Henry, 1853–1919, vol. II
Rideout, Maj.-Gen. Arthur Kennedy, 1835–1913, vol. I
Rideout, Maj.-Gen. Francis Goring, 1839–1913, vol. I
Rideout, Percy Rodney, 1868–1956, vol. V
Rider, Engr Rear-Adm. Sydney, *died* 1943, vol. IV
Rider, Thomas Francis, 1843–1922, vol. II
Ridge, Pett; *see* Ridge, W. P.
Ridge, (William) Pett, 1857–1930, vol. III
Ridgeway, Rt Rev. Charles John, 1841–1927, vol. II
Ridgeway, Rev. Charles Spencer-Churchill FitzGerald, (F. Gerald Ridgeway), 1872–1958, vol. V
Ridgeway, Brig. David Graeme, 1879–1950, vol. IV
Ridgeway, Major Edward William Crawfurd, *died* 1917, vol. II
Ridgeway, F. Gerald; *see* Ridgeway, Rev. C. S.-C. F.
Ridgeway, Rt Rev. Frederick Edward, 1848–1921, vol. II
Ridgeway, Rt Hon. Sir (Joseph) West, 1844–1930, vol. III
Ridgeway, Col Richard Kirby, 1848–1924, vol. II
Ridgeway, Ven. S., 1872–1951, vol. V
Ridgeway, Rt Hon. Sir West; *see* Ridgeway, Rt Hon. Sir J. W.
Ridgeway, Sir William, 1853–1926, vol. II

Ridgway, Brig.-Gen. Richard Thomas Incledon, 1868–1939, vol. III
Ridley, 1st Viscount, 1842–1904, vol. I (A)
Ridley, 2nd Viscount, 1874–1916, vol. II
Ridley, 3rd Viscount, 1902–1964, vol. VI
Ridley, Alice, (Lady Ridley), *died* 1945, vol. IV
Ridley, Brig.-Gen. Charles Parker, 1855–1937, vol. III
Ridley, Wing Comdr Claude Alward, 1896–1942, vol. IV
Ridley, Rt Hon. Sir Edward, 1843–1928, vol. II
Ridley, Col Edward Davenport, 1883–1934, vol. III
Ridley, Frederick Thomas, 1903–1977, vol. VII
Ridley, George, 1886–1944, vol. IV
Ridley, Guy, 1885–1947, vol. IV
Ridley, Henry Nicholas, 1855–1956, vol. V
Ridley, Hon. Sir Jasper Nicholas, 1887–1951, vol. V
Ridley, Maurice Roy, 1890–1969, vol. VI
Ridley, Nicholas Charles, 1863–1937, vol. III
Ridley, Samuel Forde, 1864–1944, vol. IV
Ridley, Rt Rev. William, 1836–1911, vol. I
Ridout, Maj.-Gen. Sir Dudley Howard, 1866–1941, vol. IV
Ridpath, Sir Henry, 1873–1950, vol. IV
Ridsdale, Arthur Francis, *died* 1935, vol. III
Ridsdale, Rt Rev. Charles Henry, 1873–1952, vol. V
Ridsdale, Sir Edward Aurelian, 1864–1923, vol. II
Ridsdale, Sir William, 1890–1957, vol. V
Riefler, Winfield William, 1897–1974, vol. VII
Rieger, Sir Clarence Oscar Ferrero, 1897–1978, vol. VII
Riesenfeld, Hugo, 1884–1939, vol. III (A), vol. IV
Rietchel, Julius, *died* 1963, vol. VI
Rieu, Charles Pierre Henri, 1820–1902, vol. I
Rieu, Emile Victor, 1887–1972, vol. VII
Rieu, Sir (Jean) Louis, 1872–1964, vol. VI
Rieu, Sir Louis; *see* Rieu, Sir J. L.
Rifaat, Kamal Eldin Mahmoud, 1921–1977, vol. VII
Rigby, Cuthbert, 1850–1935, vol. III
Rigby, Col Sir Hugh Mallinson, 1st Bt, 1870–1944, vol. IV
Rigby, Rt Hon. Sir John, 1834–1903, vol. I
Rigby, Brig. Thomas, 1897–1969, vol. VI
Rigg, Caroline E., *died* 1929, vol. III
Rigg, Sir Edward, 1850–1933, vol. III
Rigg, Harry Sibson Leslie, 1915–1976, vol. VII
Rigg, Herbert Addington, *died* 1924, vol. II
Rigg, James Harrison, 1821–1909, vol. I
Rigg, John, 1858–1943, vol. IV
Rigg, Major Richard, 1877–1942, vol. IV
Rigg, Sir Theodore, 1888–1972, vol. VII
Rigg, Ven. William Harrison, 1877–1966, vol. VI
Riggall, Major Arthur Horton, 1867–1929, vol. III
Riggall, Lt-Col Harold William, 1882–1930, vol. III
Riggall, Robert Marmaduke, 1881–1970, vol. VI
Riggs, Kate Douglas, (Mrs George Christopher Riggs); *see* Wiggin, K. D.
Righton, Thomas Edward Corrie Burns, *died* 1899, vol. I
Rignold, Hugo Henry, 1905–1976, vol. VII

Riis, Jacob A., *died* 1914, vol. I
Riley, Athelstan, 1858–1945, vol. IV
Riley, Ben, 1866–1946, vol. IV
Riley, Rt Rev. Charles Lawrence, 1888–1971, vol. VII
Riley, Most Rev. Charles Owen Leaver, 1854–1929, vol. III
Riley, Frederick Fox, *died* 1934, vol. III
Riley, Maj.-Gen. Sir Guy; *see* Riley, Maj-Gen. Sir H. G.
Riley, Lt-Col Hamlet Lewthwaite, 1882–1932, vol. II
Riley, Maj.-Gen. Sir (Henry) Guy, 1884–1964, vol. VI
Riley, James Whitcomb, 1849–1916, vol. II
Riley, Norman Denbigh, 1890–1979, vol. VII
Riley, Brig. Rupert Farquhar, 1873–1941, vol. IV
Riley, William, 1866–1961, vol. VI
Riley, William Edward, 1852–1937, vol. III
Riley, Engr Rear-Adm. William Henry, *died* 1926, vol. II
Rilot, Charles Frederick, 1864–1942, vol. IV
Rimington, A. Wallace, *died* 1918, vol. II
Rimington, Maj.-Gen. Joseph Cameron, 1864–1942, vol. IV
Rimington, Maj.-Gen. Sir Michael Frederic, 1858–1928, vol. II
Rimington-Wilson, Reginald Henry Rimington; *see* Wilson.
Rimmer, Edward Johnson, 1883–1962, vol. VI
Rind, Col Alexander Thomas Seton Abercromby, 1847–1925, vol. II
Rind, Lt-Col George Burnet Abercrombie, 1880–1958, vol. V
Rinder, Frank, 1863–1937, vol. III
Rinehart, Mary Roberts, *died* 1958, vol. V
Rinfret, Rt Hon. Thibaudeau, 1879–1962, vol. VI
Ring, George Alfred, *died* 1927, vol. II
Ring, Rev. Timothy J., 1858–1941, vol. IV
Ringer, Sydney, 1835–1910, vol. I
Ringham, Reginald, 1894–1973, vol. VII
Riordan, Very Rev. Father James John, 1896–1959, vol. V
Riordan, Most Rev. Patrick William, 1841–1914, vol. I
Rios Urruti, Fernando de los, *born* 1879, vol. IV
Ripley, Lt-Col B., 1880–1958, vol. V
Ripley, Sir Edward, 2nd Bt (*cr* 1880), 1840–1903, vol. I
Ripley, Sir Frederick, 1st Bt (*cr* 1897), 1846–1907, vol. I
Ripley, Sir Frederick Hugh, 2nd Bt (*cr* 1897), 1878–1945, vol. IV
Ripley, Sir Geoffrey Arnold, 3rd Bt (*cr* 1897), 1883–1954, vol. V
Ripley, Gladys, (Mrs E. A. Dick), 1908–1955, vol. V
Ripley, Sir Henry William Alfred, 3rd Bt (*cr* 1880), 1879–1956, vol. V
Ripley, Rev. William Nottidge, *died* 1912, vol. I
Ripman, Walter, 1869–1947, vol. IV
Ripon, 1st Marquess of, 1827–1909, vol. I (A)
Ripon, 2nd Marquess of, 1852–1923, vol. II
Ripper, Walter Eugene, 1908–1965, vol. VI

Ripper, William, 1853–1937, vol. III
Riquetti de Mirabeau, Sybille Gabrielle Marie Antoinette de; *see* Gyp, Sybille.
Riseley, George, 1845–1932, vol. III
Rishworth, Frank Sharman, 1876–1960, vol. V
Risk, Captain Richard Henry Litle, 1857–1933, vol. III
Risley, Sir Herbert Hope, 1851–1911, vol. I
Risley, Sir John Shuckburgh, 1867–1957, vol. V
Rissik, Hon. Johann Friedrich Bernhardt, *died* 1925, vol. II
Ristori, Madame, 1822–1906, vol. I
Rita, (Mrs W. Desmond Humphreys), *died* 1938, vol. III
Ritchard, Cyril, 1898–1977, vol. VII
Ritchie of Dundee, 1st Baron, 1838–1906, vol. I
Ritchie of Dundee, 2nd Baron, 1866–1948, vol. IV
Ritchie of Dundee, 3rd Baron, 1902–1975, vol. VII
Ritchie of Dundee, 4th Baron, 1908–1978, vol. VII
Ritchie, Sir Adam Beattie, 1881–1957, vol. V
Ritchie, Alexander Brown, 1865–1936, vol. III
Ritchie, Ven. Andrew Binny, 1880–1956, vol. V
Ritchie, Anne Isabella, (Lady Ritchie), 1837–1919, vol. II
Ritchie, Maj.-Gen. Sir Archibald Buchanan, 1869–1955, vol. V
Ritchie, Arthur David, 1891–1967, vol. VI
Ritchie, Rev. Canon Charles Henry, 1887–1958, vol. V
Ritchie, Charles John, 1871–1950, vol. IV
Ritchie, David George, 1853–1903, vol. I
Ritchie, Rev. David Lakie, 1864–1951, vol. V
Ritchie, Douglas Ernest, 1905–1967, vol. VI
Ritchie, Sir George, 1849–1921, vol. II
Ritchie, Hon. Sir George, 1864–1944, vol. IV
Ritchie, Major Hon. Harold, 1876–1918, vol. II
Ritchie, Captain Henry Peel, 1876–1958, vol. V
Ritchie, Hugh, 1864–1948, vol. IV
Ritchie, James, 1864–1923, vol. II
Ritchie, James, 1882–1958, vol. V
Ritchie, Sir James Martin, 1874–1951, vol. V
Ritchie, Rear-Adm. James Stuart McLaren, 1884–1955, vol. V
Ritchie, Sir James Thomson, 1st Bt (*cr* 1903), 1835–1912, vol. I
Ritchie, Sir James William, 1st Bt *cr* 1918 (styled 2nd Bt), 1868–1937, vol. III
Ritchie, Maj.-Gen. John, 1834–1919, vol. II
Ritchie, Sir John, *died* 1947, vol. IV
Ritchie, John, 1882–1959, vol. V
Ritchie, Sir John Neish, 1904–1977, vol. VII
Ritchie, Captain Sir Lewis Anselmo, 1886–1967, vol. VI
Ritchie, R. L. Græme, 1880–1954, vol. V
Ritchie, Sir Richmond Thackeray, 1854–1912, vol. I
Ritchie, Lt-Col Thomas Fraser, 1875–1931, vol. III
Ritchie, Sir Thomas Malcolm, 1894–1971, vol. VII
Ritchie, William, 1854–1910, vol. III
Ritchie, Col William Buchanan, 1877–1937, vol. III
Ritchie, William George Brookfield, 1875–1949, vol. IV
Ritchie, William Thomas, 1873–1945, vol. IV
Ritchie-Scott, A., 1874–1962, vol. VI

Ritson, Lt-Col John Anthony Sydney, 1887–1957, vol. V
Ritson, Rev. John Holland, 1868–1953, vol. V
Ritson, Joshua, 1874–1955, vol. V
Ritson, Lady Kitty, 1887–1969, vol. VI
Ritson, Muriel, 1885–1980, vol. VII
Ritson, Col William Henry, 1867–1942, vol. IV
Ritter, Gustave Albert, died 1914, vol. I
Ritter, His Eminence Cardinal Joseph Elmer, 1892–1967, vol. VI
Rivalland, Sir Michel Jean Joseph Laval, 1910–1970, vol. VI
Rivard, Adjutor, 1868–1945, vol. IV
Rivaz, Hon. Sir Charles Montgomery, 1845–1926, vol. II
Rivaz, Col Vincent, 1842–1924, vol. II
Riverdale, 1st Baron, 1873–1957, vol. V
Rivers, Lady; (Emmeline Laura), died 1918, vol. II
Rivers, Alfred Peter, 1906–1979, vol. VII
Rivers, Very Rev. Arthur Richard, 1857–1940, vol. III (A), vol. IV
Rivers, Augustus Henry Lane F. P.; see Fox-Pitt-Rivers.
Rivers, George Henry Lane Fox P.; see Pitt-Rivers.
Rivers, William Halse R., 1864–1922, vol. II
Rives, Amélie, (Princess Pierre Troubetskoy), 1863–1945, vol. IV
Rivet, Raoul, 1896–1957, vol. V
Rivett, Sir (Albert Cherbury) David, 1885–1961, vol. VI
Rivett, Sir David; see Rivett, Sir A. C. D.
Rivett, Louis Carnac, 1888–1947, vol. IV
Rivett-Carnac, Charles James, 1853–1935, vol. III
Rivett-Carnac, Sir Claud James, 4th Bt, 1877–1909, vol. I (A)
Rivett-Carnac, Rev. Sir George, 6th Bt, 1850–1932, vol. III
Rivett-Carnac, Sir Henry George Crabbe, 7th Bt, 1889–1972, vol. VII
Rivett-Carnac, Vice-Adm. James William, 1891–1970, vol. VI
Rivett-Carnac, Col John Henry, 1838–1923, vol. II
Rivett-Carnac, Col Percy Temple, 1852–1932, vol. III
Rivett-Carnac, Sir William Percival, 5th Bt, 1847–1924, vol. II
Rivière, A. Joseph, 1859–1946, vol. IV
Riviere, Briton, 1840–1920, vol. II
Riviere, Clive, 1872–1929, vol. III
Riviere, Hugh Goldwin, 1869–1956, vol. V
Rivington, Albert Gibson, 1883–1950, vol. IV
Rivington, Rev. Cecil Stansfeld, 1853–1934, vol. III
Rivington, Charles Robert, 1846–1928, vol. II
Rivington, Mme Hill, (Lady Holmes), died 1957, vol. V
Rivington, Gerald Chippindale, 1893–1977, vol. VII
Rivington, Rev. Thurston, 1848–1929, vol. III
Rivington, William John, 1845–1914, vol. I
Rix, Rt Rev. George Alexander, died 1945, vol. IV
Roach, Alfred Thomas, 1899–1946, vol. IV
Roach, Edward K.; see Keith-Roach.
Roach, Rt Rev. Frederick, 1856–1922, vol. II

Roach, Air Vice-Marshal Harold Jace, 1896–1977, vol. VII
Roach, Harry Robert, 1906–1979, vol. VII
Road, Sir Alfred, 1891–1972, vol. VII
Roaf, Herbert Eldon, 1881–1952, vol. V
Rob, John Vernon, 1915–1971, vol. VII
Robartes, Hon. Thomas Charles Reginald A.; see Agar-Robartes.
Robarts, Abraham John, 1838–1926, vol. II
Robarts, John, 1872–1954, vol. V
Robb, Alexander, died 1934, vol. III
Robb, Alfred Arthur, 1873–1936, vol. III
Robb, Andrew McCance, 1887–1968, vol. VI
Robb, Sir Douglas; see Robb, Sir G. D.
Robb, Maj.-Gen. Sir Frederick Spencer, 1858–1948, vol. IV
Robb, Sir (George) Douglas, 1899–1974, vol. VI
Robb, Hon. James Alexander, 1859–1929, vol. III
Robb, Air Chief Marshal Sir James Milne, died 1968, vol. VI
Robb, Rt Hon. John Hanna, 1873–1956, vol. V
Robb, Hon. John Morrow, 1876–1942, vol. IV
Robb, Leonard Arthur, 1891–1964, vol. VII
Robb, Michael Antony Moyse, 1914–1977, vol. VII
Robb, Nesca Adeline, 1905–1976, vol. VII
Robb, Ven. Percy Douglas, 1902–1976, vol. VII
Robb, William George, 1872–1940, vol. III
Robberds, Rt Rev. Walter John Forbes, 1863–1944, vol. IV
Robbins, Alan Pitt, 1888–1967, vol. VI
Robbins, Sir Alfred Farthing, 1856–1931, vol. III
Robbins, Alfred Gordon, 1883–1944, vol. IV
Robbins, Sir Edmund, 1847–1922, vol. II
Robbins, Rowland Richard, died 1960, vol. V
Roberson, Rev. Henry, 1858–1934, vol. III
Robert, Henri, 1863–1936, vol. III
Roberton, Sir Hugh S., 1874–1952, vol. V
Roberton, Rev. Ivor Johnstone, 1865–1948, vol. IV
Roberton, Violet Mary Craig, 1888–1954, vol. V
Roberts, 1st Earl, 1832–1914, vol. I
Roberts, Countess (2nd in line), 1870–1944, vol. IV
Roberts, Countess (3rd in line), 1875–1955, vol. V
Roberts, Aled Owen, 1889–1949, vol. IV
Roberts, Rev. Alexander, 1826–1901, vol. I
Roberts, Lt-Col Sir Alexander Fowler, 1882–1961, vol. VI
Roberts, Hon. Alexander William, 1857–1938, vol. III
Roberts, Sir Alfred, 1823–1899, vol. I
Roberts, Ven. Alfred, 1853–1937, vol. III
Roberts, Sir Alfred, 1897–1963, vol. VI
Roberts, Allan Arbuthnot Lane, 1884–1967, vol. VI
Roberts, Angus, 1893–1937, vol. III
Roberts, Arthur, 1852–1933, vol. III
Roberts, Rev. Arthur Betton, 1880–1961, vol. VI
Roberts, Sir Arthur Cornelius, 1869–1946, vol. IV
Roberts, Arthur James Rooker, 1882–1943, vol. IV
Roberts, Rt Rev. Basil Coleby, 1887–1957, vol. V
Roberts, Rev. Bleddyn Jones, 1906–1977, vol. VII
Roberts, Brian Birley, 1912–1978, vol. VII
Roberts, Bryn, 1897–1964, vol. VI
Roberts, Carl Eric Bechhofer, 1894–1949, vol. IV

Roberts, Cecil Edric Mornington, 1892–1976, vol. VII
Roberts, Cedric Sydney L.; see Lane-Roberts.
Roberts, Chalmers; see Roberts, H. C.
Roberts, Ven. Charles Frederic, died 1942, vol. IV
Roberts, Col Charles Fyshe, 1837–1914, vol. I
Roberts, Sir Charles George Douglas, 1860–1943, vol. IV
Roberts, Charles Henry, 1865–1959, vol. V
Roberts, Charles Hubert, died 1929, vol. III
Roberts, Hon. Charles James, 1846–1925, vol. II
Roberts, Rev. Charles Philip, 1842–1918, vol. II
Roberts, Cyril, 1871–1949, vol. IV
Roberts, Sir David Charles, 1859–1940, vol. III
Roberts, Ven. David Egryn, died 1935, vol. III
Roberts, David Lloyd, died 1920, vol. II
Roberts, David Thomas, died 1903, vol. I
Roberts, Denys K.; see Kilham-Roberts.
Roberts, Rev. E. Berwyn, 1869–1951, vol. V
Roberts, Col Edward, 1841–1904, vol. I
Roberts, Very Rev. Edward Albert Trevillian, 1877–1968, vol. VI
Roberts, Rev. Edward Dale, 1848–1927, vol. II
Roberts, Edward E.; see Emrys-Roberts.
Roberts, Ellis, 1860–1930, vol. III
Roberts, Sir Ernest Handforth Goodman, 1890–1969, vol. VI
Roberts, Rev. Ernest Marling, 1873–1929, vol. III
Roberts, Rev. Ernest Stewart, 1847–1912, vol. I
Roberts, Francis Noel, 1893–1969, vol. VI
Roberts, Rt Hon. Frederick Owen, 1876–1941, vol. IV
Roberts, Frederick Thomas, died 1918, vol. II
Roberts, Geoffrey Dorling, 1886–1967, vol. VI
Roberts, Sir George, 1st Bt (cr 1930), 1859–1950, vol. IV
Roberts, George Augustus, 1875–1962, vol. VI
Roberts, Col Sir George Fossett, 1870–1954, vol. V
Roberts, Rt Hon. George Henry, 1869–1928, vol. II
Roberts, George Lawrence, 1904–1967, vol. VI
Roberts, George Quinlan, 1860–1943, vol. IV
Roberts, Sir George William Kelly, 1907–1964, vol. VI
Roberts, Gervase Henry, died 1944, vol. IV
Roberts, Sir Gilbert, 1899–1978, vol. VII
Roberts, Very Rev. Griffith, 1845–1943, vol. IV
Roberts, Harold, 1884–1950, vol. IV
Roberts, Harold, 1879–1959, vol. V
Roberts, Harry, 1871–1946, vol. IV
Roberts, (Henry) Chalmers, died 1949, vol. IV
Roberts, Henry David, 1870–1951, vol. V
Roberts, Lt-Col Henry Roger Crompton-, 1863–1925, vol. II
Roberts, Herbert Ainslie, 1864–1932, vol. III
Roberts, Brig.-Gen. Hereward Llewelyn, 1864–1947, vol. IV
Roberts, Sir Howard; see Roberts, Sir J. R. H.
Roberts, Col Sir Howland, 5th Bt (cr 1809), 1845–1917, vol. II
Roberts, Hugh Douglas, 1869–1942, vol. IV
Roberts, Hugh Gordon, 1885–1961, vol. VI
Roberts, Hugh Leslie-, 1860–1949, vol. IV
Roberts, Hugh Lloyd, died 1906, vol. I

Roberts, Isaac, 1829–1904, vol. I
Roberts, Rev. J. J., 1840–1914, vol. I
Roberts, Sir James, 1st Bt (cr 1909), 1848–1935, vol. III
Roberts, Hon. James, 1881–1967, vol. VI
Roberts, James Alexander, 1876–1945, vol. IV
Roberts, Sir James Denby, 2nd Bt (cr 1909), 1904–1973, vol. VII
Roberts, James Ernest Helme, died 1948, vol. IV
Roberts, James Frederick, 1847–1911, vol. II
Roberts, Sir (James Reginald) Howard, 1891–1975, vol. VII
Roberts, Lt-Col Sir James Reid, 1861–1941, vol. IV
Roberts, Sir John, 1861–1917, vol. II
Roberts, Sir John, 1845–1934, vol. III
Roberts, Captain John, 1867–1943, vol. IV
Roberts, Sir John, 1876–1966, vol. VI
Roberts, John Bryn, 1843–1931, vol. III
Roberts, Rev. John Edward, 1866–1929, vol. III
Roberts, John Gwyndeg H.; see Hughes-Roberts.
Roberts, Maj.-Gen. John Hamilton, 1891–1962, vol. VI
Roberts, John Keith, 1897–1944, vol. IV
Roberts, John Reginald, 1893–1971, vol. VII
Roberts, Sir John Reynolds, 1834–1917, vol. II
Roberts, John Varley, 1841–1920, vol. II
Roberts, Kate Winifred J.; see Jones-Roberts.
Roberts, Kenneth, 1885–1957, vol. V
Roberts, Lancelot, died 1950, vol. IV (A), vol. V
Roberts, Sir Leslie, died 1976, vol. VII
Roberts, Llewelyn, 1881–1939, vol. III
Roberts, Major Marmaduke Torin Cramer-, 1880–1939, vol. III
Roberts, Captain Marshall Owen, 1878–1931, vol. III
Roberts, Martin, 1853–1926, vol. II (A), vol. III
Roberts, Michael, 1902–1948, vol. IV
Roberts, Brig. Michael Rookherst, 1894–1977, vol. VII
Roberts, Morley, 1857–1942, vol. IV
Roberts, Sir Norman Stanley, 1893–1972, vol. VII
Roberts, Sir Owen, 1835–1915, vol. I
Roberts, Owen Glynne, 1880–1947, vol. IV
Roberts, Owen Josephus, 1875–1955, vol. V
Roberts, Patrick Maxwell, 1895–1937, vol. III
Roberts, Paul Ernest, 1873–1949, vol. IV
Roberts, Peter Burman Moir, 1874–1956, vol. V
Roberts, Lt-Comdr Peter Scawen Watkinson, 1917–1979, vol. VII
Roberts, Rachel, 1927–1980, vol. VII
Roberts, Sir Randal Howland, 4th Bt (cr 1809), 1837–1899, vol. I
Roberts, Reginald Arthur, 1874–1940, vol. III
Roberts, Reginald Hugh, 1883–1955, vol. V
Roberts, Very Rev. Richard, 1874–1945, vol. IV
Roberts, Richard Arthur, 1851–1943, vol. IV
Roberts, Richard Ellis, 1879–1953, vol. V
Roberts, Rev. Richard Gwylfa, 1871–1935, vol. III
Roberts, Ven. Richard Henry, died 1970, vol. VI
Roberts, Sir Richard L.; see Lloyd-Roberts.
Roberts, Richard Owen, 1876–1929, vol. III
Roberts, Robert A.; see Alun Roberts.
Roberts, Robert David Valpo, 1906–1973, vol. VII

Roberts, Robert Davies, 1851–1911, vol. I
Roberts, Rev. Canon Robert Edwin, 1878–1940, vol. III
Roberts, Robert Herbert M.; see Mills-Roberts.
Roberts, Robert Lewis, 1875–1956, vol. V
Roberts, Robert Silyn, died 1930, vol. III
Roberts, Rev. Canon Roland Harry William, 1894–1951, vol. V
Roberts, Samuel, 1852–1913, vol. I
Roberts, Rt Hon. Sir Samuel, 1st Bt (cr 1919), 1852–1926, vol. II
Roberts, Sir Samuel, 2nd Bt (cr 1919), 1882–1955, vol. V
Roberts, Sidney Morton Pearson, 1860–1930, vol. III
Roberts, Sir Stephen Henry, 1901–1971, vol. VII
Roberts, Lt-Col Stephen Richard Harricks, 1874–1943, vol. IV
Roberts, Sir Sydney Castle, 1887–1966, vol. VI
Roberts, T. Stanley, died 1935, vol. III
Roberts, Most Rev. Thomas d'Esterre, 1893–1976, vol. VII
Roberts, Sir Thomas Edwards, 1851–1926, vol. II
Roberts, Thomas Esmôr Rhys R.; see Rhys-Roberts.
Roberts, Thomas Francis, 1860–1919, vol. II
Roberts, Col Sir Thomas Langdon Howland, 6th Bt (cr 1809), 1898–1979, vol. VII
Roberts, Sir Thomas Lee, 1848–1924, vol. II
Roberts, Tom, 1856–1931, vol. III
Roberts, W. J., died 1943, vol. IV
Roberts, Sir Walter St Clair Howland, 1893–1978, vol. VII
Roberts, Walter Stewart S.; see Stewart-Roberts.
Roberts, Sir Walworth Howland, 1855–1924, vol. II
Roberts, Sir William, 1830–1899, vol. I
Roberts, William, 1862–1940, vol. III
Roberts, Sir William, 1884–1971, vol. VII
Roberts, William, 1895–1980, vol. VII
Roberts, Rev. William Corbett, 1873–1953, vol. V
Roberts, Rev. William Henry, 1844–1921, vol. II
Roberts, Col William Henry, 1848–1926, vol. II
Roberts, Brig. William Henry, 1882–1954, vol. V
Roberts, William Lee Henry, 1871–1928, vol. II
Roberts, Rev. William Masfen, died 1927, vol. II
Roberts, Very Rev. William Page-, 1836–1928, vol. II
Roberts, William Poulter, 1874–1937, vol. III
Roberts, Col William Quincey, 1912–1980, vol. VII
Roberts, Rev. William Ralph Westropp, 1850–1935, vol. III
Roberts, William Rhys, 1858–1929, vol. III
Roberts, Col William Richter, 1888–1975, vol. VII
Roberts, William Stewart, died 1937, vol. III
Roberts, Ven. Windsor, 1898–1962, vol. VI
Roberts-Austen, Sir William Chandler, 1843–1902, vol. I
Roberts-Wray, Captain Thomas Henry; see Wray.
Robertshaw, Vice-Adm. Sir Ballin Illingworth, 1902–1971, vol. VII
Robertshaw, Sir Charles, 1874–1960, vol. V
Robertshaw, Wilfrid, 1893–1974, vol. VII

Robertson, Baron (Life Peer); James Patrick Bannerman Robertson, 1845–1909, vol. I
Robertson, Hon. Lord; Thomas Graham Robertson, 1881–1944, vol. IV
Robertson of Oakridge, 1st Baron, 1896–1974, vol. VII
Robertson, Alasdair Stewart Struan-Robertson, 1863–1910, vol. I
Robertson, Rear-Adm. Albert John, 1884–1954, vol. V
Robertson, Rev. Alaxander, 1846–1933, vol. III
Robertson, Alexander, died 1970, vol. VI
Robertson, Brig.-Gen. Alexander Brown, 1878–1951, vol. V
Robertson, Algar Ronald Ward, 1902–1975, vol. VII
Robertson, Andrew, died 1977, vol. VII
Robertson, Rt Rev. Archibald, 1853–1931, vol. III
Robertson, Archibald Wallace, 1895–1966, vol. VI
Robertson, Cdre A(rthur) Ian, 1898–1961, vol. VI
Robertson, Sir Benjamin, 1864–1953, vol. V
Robertson, Sir Carrick Hey, died 1963, vol. VI
Robertson, Maj.-Gen. Cecil Bruce, 1897–1977, vol. VII
Robertson, Rev. Charles, died 1921, vol. II
Robertson, Charles, 1874–1968, vol. VI
Robertson, Sir Charles Grant, 1869–1948, vol. IV
Robertson, Adm. Charles Hope, 1856–1942, vol. IV
Robertson, Lt-Col Charles Lonsdale, 1867–1943, vol. IV
Robertson, Very Rev. Charles R., 1873–1946, vol. IV
Robertson, Col Colin MacLeod, 1870–1951, vol. V
Robertson, Maj.-Gen. David, died 1913, vol. I
Robertson, Rev. David, 1838–1916, vol. II
Robertson, David, died 1925, vol. II
Robertson, David, 1875–1941, vol. IV
Robertson, David, died 1952, vol. V
Robertson, Sir David, 1890–1970, vol. VI
Robertson, Sir Dennis Holme, 1890–1963, vol. VI
Robertson, Lt-Col Sir Donald, 1847–1930, vol. III
Robertson, Maj.-Gen. Donald Elphinston, 1879–1953, vol. V
Robertson, Donald James, 1926–1970, vol. VI
Robertson, Col Donald Murdoch, 1859–1938, vol. III
Robertson, Donald Struan, 1885–1961, vol. VI
Robertson, Douglas Argyll, 1837–1909, vol. I
Robertson, E. Arnot, (Lady Turner), died 1961, vol. VI
Robertson, Edith Anne, 1883–1973, vol. VII
Robertson, Air Cdre Edmund Digby Maxwell, 1887–1956, vol. V
Robertson, Edward, died 1964, vol. VI
Robertson, Sir Frederick Alexander, 1854–1918, vol. II
Robertson, Frederick Ewart, 1847–1912, vol. I
Robertson, Sir Frederick Wynne, 1885–1964, vol. VI
Robertson, George, 1883–1956, vol. V
Robertson, George Matthew, 1864–1932, vol. III
Robertson, Sir George Scott, 1852–1916, vol. II

Robertson, George Scott, 1893–1948, vol. IV
Robertson, Sir George Stuart, 1872–1967, vol. VI
Robertson, Hon. Gideon Decker, 1874–1933, vol. III
Robertson, Lt-Col Gordon McMahon, 1891–1932, vol. III
Robertson, Lt-Col Graham; see Robertson, Lt-Col J. H. G.
Robertson, Granville Douglas, 1891–1951, vol. V
Robertson, Sir Helenus Robert, 1841–1919, vol. II
Robertson, Sir Henry Beyer, 1862–1948, vol. IV
Robertson, Henry Robert, 1839–1921, vol. II
Robertson, Herbert, 1849–1916, vol. II
Robertson, Lt-Gen. Sir Horace Clement Hugh, 1894–1960, vol. V
Robertson, Sir Howard Morley, 1888–1963, vol. VI
Robertson, Engr-Comdr Hugh, died 1940, vol. III (A)
Robertson, Very Rev. James, 1837–1920, vol. II
Robertson, Rev. James, 1840–1920, vol. II
Robertson, Rev. James, 1855–1929, vol. III
Robertson, James, died 1938, vol. III
Robertson, Rev. James Alex., 1880–1955, vol. V
Robertson, Lt-Col James Archibald St George Fitzwarenne D.; see Despencer-Robertson.
Robertson, Brig.-Gen. James Campbell, 1878–1951, vol. V
Robertson, James Cassels, 1921–1978, vol. VII
Robertson, Lt-Col James Currie, died 1923, vol. II
Robertson, James Edwin, 1840–1915, vol. II
Robertson, Col James F.; see Forbes-Robertson.
Robertson, Lt-Col (James Herbert) Graham, died 1956, vol. V
Robertson, Sir James Jackson, 1893–1970, vol. VI
Robertson, Group Captain James Leask, 1882–1945, vol. IV
Robertson, James Logie, died 1922, vol. II
Robertson, Col James Peter, died 1916, vol. II
Robertson, James Wilson, 1857–1930, vol. III
Robertson, Jean F.; see Forbes-Robertson.
Robertson, Rev. John, 1852–1913, vol. I
Robertson, Col John, 1837–1915, vol. I
Robertson, Rev. John, died 1925, vol. II
Robertson, John, 1867–1926, vol. II
Robertson, Sir John, 1862–1936, vol. III
Robertson, John, died 1937, vol. III
Robertson, Col John, 1878–1951, vol. V
Robertson, John Archibald Campbell, 1912–1962, vol. VI
Robertson, John Arthur Thomas, 1873–1942, vol. IV
Robertson, Rev. John Charles, 1868–1931, vol. III
Robertson, John Charles, 1864–1956, vol. V
Robertson, John F.; see Forbes-Robertson.
Robertson, John G., 1867–1933, vol. III
Robertson, John Henry; see Connell, John.
Robertson, Captain John Hercules, 1864–1943, vol. IV
Robertson, John James, 1898–1955, vol. V
Robertson, John McKellar, 1883–1939, vol. III
Robertson, Rt Hon. John Mackinnon, 1856–1933, vol. III
Robertson, Col John Richard Hugh, 1912–1977, vol. VII
Robertson, John Williamson, 1900–1969, vol. VI

Robertson, Sir Johnston F.; see Forbes-Robertson.
Robertson, Laurence, died 1945, vol. IV
Robertson, Lindesay John, 1861–1929, vol. III
Robertson, Sir MacPherson, 1860–1945, vol. IV
Robertson, Rt Hon. Sir Malcolm Arnold, 1877–1951, vol. V
Robertson, Margaret Ethel, 1861–1943, vol. IV
Robertson, Muriel, 1883–1973, vol. VII
Robertson, Norman Alexander, 1904–1968, vol. VI
Robertson, Norman Charles, 1908–1956, vol. V
Robertson, Maj.-Gen. Sir Philip Rynd, 1866–1936, vol. III
Robertson, Rae, 1893–1956, vol. V
Robertson, Sir Robert, 1869–1949, vol. IV
Robertson, Robert Burns, 1861–1938, vol. III
Robertson, Robert Spelman, 1870–1955, vol. V
Robertson, Robin Haskew, 1898–1952, vol. V
Robertson, Stuart, died 1958, vol. V
Robertson, Thomas, died 1906, vol. I
Robertson, Thomas, 1842–1925, vol. II
Robertson, Thomas Atholl, died 1955, vol. V
Robertson, Thomas Dixon Marr Trotter, 1856–1913, vol. I
Robertson, Thomas Graham; see Robertson, Hon. Lord.
Robertson, Thomas Logan, 1901–1969, vol. VI
Robertson, Thorburn Brailsford, 1884–1930, vol. III
Robertson, Tom, 1850–1947, vol. IV
Robertson, Vernon Alec Murray, 1890–1971, vol. VII
Robertson, W. Graham, 1866–1948, vol. IV
Robertson, Major W. M., died 1902, vol. I
Robertson, Walter James, 1869–1942, vol. IV
Robertson, Watson A.; see Askew-Robertson.
Robertson, Wheatley Alexander, 1885–1964, vol. VI
Robertson, Sir William, 1856–1923, vol. II
Robertson, Rev. William, 1847–1936, vol. III
Robertson, Lt-Col William, 1865–1949, vol. IV
Robertson, William Albert, 1885–1942, vol. IV
Robertson, Sir William Charles Fleming, died 1937, vol. III
Robertson, William Chrystal, died 1922, vol. II
Robertson, William Francis, 1882–1939, vol. III
Robertson, William Haggerston A.; see Askew Robertson.
Robertson, Rev. William Lewis, 1860–1947, vol. IV
Robertson, William Nathaniel, died 1938, vol. III
Robertson, Field-Marshal Sir William Robert, 1st Bt, 1860–1933, vol. III
Robertson-Aikman, Col Thomas S. G. H.; see Aikman.
Robertson-Eustace, Major Charles Legge Eustace, 1867–1908, vol. I
Robertson-Eustace, Mrs Marjory Edith, died 1957, vol. V
Robertson-Eustace, Robert William Barrington, 1870–1935, vol. III
Robertson-Glasgow, Raymond Charles, 1901–1965, vol. VI
Robertson-Justice, James Norval Harald, 1905–1975, vol. VII

Robertson-Macdonald, Adm. David, 1817–1910, vol. I

Robertson Scott, John William, 1866–1962, vol. VI

Robeson, Ven. Hemming, *died* 1912, vol. I

Robeson, Paul Le Roy, 1898–1976, vol. VII

Robey, Sir George, 1869–1954, vol. V

Robidoux, Joseph Emery, 1843–1929, vol. III

Robieson, Sir William, 1890–1977, vol. VII

Robin, Maj.-Gen. Sir Alfred William, 1860–1935, vol. III

Robin, Rt Rev. Bryan Percival, 1887–1969, vol. VI

Robins, 1st Baron, 1884–1962, vol. VI

Robins, Rev. Arthur, 1834–1899, vol. I

Robins, Rt Rev. Edwin Frederick, 1870–1951, vol. V

Robins, Elizabeth, (Mrs George Richmond Parks; C. E. Raimond), 1862–1952, vol. V

Robins, G. M.; *see* Reynolds, Mrs Louis Baillie.

Robins, Very Rev. Henry Charles, 1882–1960, vol. V

Robins, Sir Reginald Edwin, 1891–1971, vol. VII

Robins, Ven. William Aubrey, 1868–1949, vol. IV

Robins, Rev. William Henry, 1847–1923, vol. II

Robins, William Palmer, 1882–1959, vol. V

Robinson, 1st Baron, 1883–1952, vol. V

Robinson, Albert, 1878–1943, vol. IV

Robinson, Rev. Canon Albert Gossage, 1863–1948, vol. IV

Robinson, Maj.-Gen. Alfred Eryk, 1894–1978, vol. VII

Robinson, Sir Alfred Theodore Vaughan, 1879–1945, vol. IV

Robinson, Andrew, 1858–1929, vol. III

Robinson, Rev. Archibald, *died* 1902, vol. I

Robinson, Sir Arnet, 1898–1975, vol. VII

Robinson, Sir Arnold Percy, 1879–1960, vol. V

Robinson, Hon. Sir Arthur, 1872–1945, vol. IV

Robinson, Arthur, 1862–1948, vol. IV

Robinson, Arthur, 1864–1948, vol. IV

Robinson, Sir Arthur; *see* Robinson, Sir W. A.

Robinson, Sir (Arthur) Douglas, 1878–1939, vol. III

Robinson, Arthur Hildyard, 1859–1939, vol. III

Robinson, Arthur Leyland, 1887–1959, vol. V

Robinson, Rev. Arthur William, 1856–1928, vol. II

Robinson, Rev. Cecil Lowes, 1869–1936, vol. III

Robinson, Charles, 1870–1937, vol. III

Robinson, Charles Edmund N.; *see* Newton-Robinson.

Robinson, Adm. Charles Grey, 1850–1934, vol. III

Robinson, Rev. Charles Henry, 1861–1925, vol. II

Robinson, Rev. Charles Kirkby, 1826–1909, vol. I

Robinson, Charles Napier, 1849–1936, vol. III

Robinson, Charles Stanley, 1887–1969, vol. VI

Robinson, Maj.-Gen. Sir Charles Walker, 1836–1924, vol. II

Robinson, Sir Christopher Henry L.; *see* Lynch-Robinson.

Robinson, Hon. Clifford William, 1866–1944, vol. IV

Robinson, Sir Clifton, 1849–1910, vol. I

Robinson, Rear-Adm. Sir Cloudesley Varyl, 1883–1959, vol. V

Robinson, Courtenay Denis Carew, 1887–1958, vol. V

Robinson, Rt Rev. Cuthbert Cooper, 1893–1971, vol. VII

Robinson, Captain David Lubbock, 1882–1943, vol. IV

Robinson, David Moore, 1880–1958, vol. V

Robinson, David Morrant, 1910–1977, vol. VII

Robinson, Cdre David Samuel, 1888–1972, vol. VII

Robinson, Sir Douglas; *see* Robinson, Sir A. D.

Robinson, Sir Douglas Innes, 6th Bt (*cr* 1823), 1863–1944, vol. IV

Robinson, Rev. Edward Colles, 1877–1956, vol. V

Robinson, Edward G., 1893–1973, vol. VII

Robinson, Edward Kay, 1857–1928, vol. II

Robinson, Sir Edward Stanley Gotch, *died* 1976, vol. VII

Robinson, Edwin Arlington, 1869–1935, vol. III

Robinson, Eric, 1908–1974, vol. VII

Robinson, Rear-Adm. Eric Gascoigne, 1882–1965, vol. VI

Robinson, Col Ernest, 1877–1935, vol. III

Robinson, Sir (Ernest) Stanley, 1905–1977, vol. VII

Robinson, Sir Ernest William, 5th Bt (*cr* 1823), 1862–1924, vol. II

Robinson, (Esmé Stuart) Lennox, 1886–1958, vol. V

Robinson, Sir Foster Gotch, 1880–1967, vol. VI

Robinson, Frederic Cayley-, 1862–1927, vol. II

Robinson, Sir Frederic Lacy, 1840–1911, vol. I

Robinson, Sir Frederick Arnold, 3rd Bt (*cr* 1854), 1855–1901, vol. I

Robinson, Sir (Frederick) Percival, 1887–1949, vol. IV

Robinson, Major Sir Frederick Villiers Laud, 10th Bt (*cr* 1660), 1880–1975, vol. VII

Robinson, Frederick William, 1830–1901, vol. I

Robinson, George Drummond, 1864–1950, vol. IV

Robinson, Surg.-Gen. George Winsor, 1854–1929, vol. III

Robinson, Gerald Philip, 1858–1942, vol. IV

Robinson, Sir Gerald William Collingwood, 4th Bt (*cr* 1819), 1857–1903, vol. I

Robinson, Gilbert Wooding, 1888–1950, vol. IV

Robinson, Gleeson Edward, *died* 1978, vol. VII

Robinson, Godfrey, 1897–1961, vol. VI

Robinson, Lt-Col Godfrey Walker, 1863–1930, vol. III

Robinson, Maj.-Gen. Guy St George, 1887–1973, vol. VII

Robinson, Sir Harold Ernest, 1905–1979, vol. VII

Robinson, Sir Harold Francis C.; *see* Cartmel-Robinson.

Robinson, Harold Roper, 1889–1955, vol. V

Robinson, Sir Harry Perry, 1859–1930, vol. III

Robinson, Lt-Col Sir Heaton Forbes, 1873–1946, vol. IV

Robinson, Rt Rev. Hector Gordon, 1899–1965, vol. VI

Robinson, Henry, *died* 1901, vol. I

Robinson, Rev. Henry, 1849–1918, vol. II

Robinson, Rt Hon. Sir Henry Augustus, 1st Bt (*cr* 1920), 1857–1927, vol. II

Robinson, Henry Betham, 1860–1918, vol. II

Robinson, Henry Goland, 1896–1960, vol. V
Robinson, Captain Henry Harold, *died* 1919, vol. II
Robinson, Henry Morton, 1898–1961, vol. VI
Robinson, Maj.-Gen. Henry R.; *see* Rowan-Robinson.
Robinson, Rear-Adm. Sir Henry Russell, 1856–1942, vol. IV
Robinson, Rev. Henry Wheeler, 1872–1945, vol. IV
Robinson, Hon. Hercules Edward Joseph, 1895–1915, vol. I
Robinson, Sir (Hugh) Malcolm, 1857–1933, vol. III
Robinson, James, 1884–1956, vol. V
Robinson, Hon. Sir John, 1839–1903, vol. I
Robinson, Sir John, 1839–1929, vol. III
Robinson, Hon. John Alexander, 1862–1929, vol. III
Robinson, Sir John Beverley, 4th Bt (*cr* 1854), 1848–1933, vol. III
Robinson, Sir John Beverley, 6th Bt (*cr* 1854), 1885–1954, vol. V
Robinson, Sir John Beverley Beverley, 5th Bt (*cr* 1854), 1895–1948, vol. IV
Robinson, Sir John Charles, 1824–1913, vol. I
Robinson, Sir John Edgar, 1895–1978, vol. VII
Robinson, John George, 1856–1943, vol. IV
Robinson, Sir John Holdsworth, 1855–1927, vol. II
Robinson, Rev. John J., *died* 1916, vol. II
Robinson, John Lovell, 1849–1939, vol. III
Robinson, Col John Poole Bowring, 1881–1966, vol. VI
Robinson, John Robert, 1850–1910, vol. I
Robinson, John William Dudley, 1886–1967, vol. VI
Robinson, Joseph, 1905–1970, vol. VI
Robinson, Very Rev. Joseph Armitage, 1858–1933, vol. III
Robinson, Sir Joseph Benjamin, 1st Bt (*cr* 1908), 1840–1929, vol. III
Robinson, Sir Joseph Benjamin, 2nd Bt (*cr* 1908), 1887–1954, vol. V
Robinson, Joseph John, 1858–1939, vol. III
Robinson, Laurence Milner, 1885–1957, vol. V
Robinson, Lennox; *see* Robinson, E. S. L.
Robinson, Leonard Nicholas, 1869–1955, vol. V
Robinson, Sir Leslie Harold, 1903–1974, vol. VII
Robinson, Rev. Ludovick Stewart, 1864–1923, vol. II
Robinson, Lt-Col Macleod Bawtree, 1858–1935, vol. III
Robinson, Sir Malcolm; *see* Robinson, Sir H. M.
Robinson, Air Cdre Maurice Wilbraham Sandford, 1910–1977, vol. VII
Robinson, Sir Montague Arnet; *see* Robinson, Sir Arnet.
Robinson, Very Rev. Norman, 1905–1973, vol. VII
Robinson, Sir Norman De Winton, 1890–1972, vol. VII
Robinson, Rev. Norman Hamilton Galloway, 1912–1978, vol. VII
Robinson, Maj.-Gen. Oliver Long, 1867–1947, vol. IV
Robinson, Most Rev. Mgr Paschal, 1870–1948, vol. IV

Robinson, Sir Percival; *see* Robinson, Sir F. P.
Robinson, Percival James, 1879–1944, vol. IV
Robinson, Brig.-Gen. Percy Morris, 1873–1949, vol. IV
Robinson, Rev. Canon Reginald Henry, 1881–1970, vol. VI
Robinson, Sir Richard Atkinson, 1849–1928, vol. II
Robinson, Sir Richard Harcourt, 5th Bt (*cr* 1819), 1828–1910, vol. I
Robinson, Sir Robert, 1886–1975, vol. VII
Robinson, Col Robert Maximilian R.; *see* Rainey-Robinson.
Robinson, Robert Thomson, 1867–1926, vol. II
Robinson, Ronald Henry Ottywell Betham, 1896–1973, vol. VII
Robinson, Samuel, 1870–1958, vol. V
Robinson, Samuel, 1893–1967, vol. VI
Robinson, Sidney, 1863–1956, vol. V
Robinson, Sir Stanley; *see* Robinson, Sir E. S.
Robinson, Col Stapylton Chapman Bates, 1855–1927, vol. II
Robinson, Brig.-Gen. Stratford Watson, 1871–1962, vol. VI
Robinson, Sydney Allen, 1905–1978, vol. VII
Robinson, Sir Sydney Maddock, 1865–1948, vol. IV
Robinson, Sir Sydney Walter, 1876–1950, vol. IV
Robinson, Theodore Henry, 1881–1964, vol. VI
Robinson, Sir Thomas, 1827–1897, vol. I
Robinson, Sir Thomas, 1855–1927, vol. II
Robinson, Sir Thomas, *died* 1953, vol. V
Robinson, Lt-Col Sir Thomas Bilbe, 1853–1939, vol. III
Robinson, Sir Thomas William, 1864–1946, vol. IV
Robinson, Tom, *died* 1916, vol. II
Robinson, Sir Victor Lloyd, 1899–1966, vol. VI
Robinson, Vincent Joseph, 1829–1910, vol. I
Robinson, Rt Rev. Mgr Walter Croke, 1839–1914, vol. I
Robinson, Rt Rev. Walter Wade, 1919–1975, vol. VII
Robinson, Maj.-Gen. Wellesley Gordon Walker, 1839–1908, vol. I
Robinson, Sir William, 1836–1912, vol. I
Robinson, Sir William, *died* 1932, vol. III
Robinson, William, 1838–1935, vol. III
Robinson, Sir William, 1879–1961, vol. VI
Robinson, William Albert, *died* 1949, vol. IV
Robinson, Brig.-Gen. William Arthur, 1864–1929, vol. III
Robinson, Sir (William) Arthur, 1874–1950, vol. IV
Robinson, Sir William C. F., 1835–1897, vol. I
Robinson, William Cornforth, 1861–1931, vol. III
Robinson, William Edward, 1863–1927, vol. II
Robinson, Rev. W(illiam) Gordon, 1903–1977, vol. VII
Robinson, William Heath, 1872–1944, vol. IV
Robinson, Sir William Henry, *died* 1940, vol. III
Robinson, Sir William Henry, 1874–1964, vol. VI
Robinson, Maj.-Gen. William Henry Banner, 1863–1922, vol. II
Robinson, William Leefe, 1895–1918, vol. II
Robinson, William Oscar James, 1909–1968, vol. VI
Robinson, William Sugden, *died* 1968, vol. VI

Robinson-Douglas, William Douglas; see Douglas.
Robiquet, Jean, 1874–1960, vol. VI (AI)
Robison, Lionel MacDowall, 1886–1967, vol. VI
Robison, Robert, 1883–1941, vol. IV
Robjent, Frederick Pring, 1859–1938, vol. III
Robjohns, Sydney, 1878–1954, vol. V
Robley, Maj.-Gen. Horatio Gordon, 1840–1930, vol. III
Roblin, Hon. Sir Rodmond Palen, 1853–1937, vol. III
Roborough, 1st Baron, 1859–1938, vol. III
Robson, Baron (Life Peer); William Snowdon Robson, 1852–1918, vol. II
Robson, Air Vice-Marshal Adam Henry, 1892–1980, vol. VII
Robson, Albert Henry, died 1939, vol. III
Robson, Sir Arthur William Mayo-, 1853–1933, vol. III
Robson, Edward Robert, 1835–1917, vol. II
Robson, George, 1842–1911, vol. I
Robson, Hon. Harold Burge, 1888–1964, vol. VI
Robson, Sir Henry, 1848–1911, vol. I
Robson, Henry Naunton, 1861–1925, vol. II
Robson, Lt-Col Henry William Cumine, 1886–1942, vol. IV
Robson, Sir Herbert Thomas, 1874–1935, vol. III
Robson, Hugh Amos, 1871–1945, vol. IV
Robson, Sir Hugh Norwood, 1917–1977, vol. VII
Robson, Captain Humphrey Maurice, 1889–1940, vol. III
Robson, Rev. John, 1836–1908, vol. I
Robson, John Henry Matthews, 1870–1945, vol. IV
Robson, Sir Kenneth, 1909–1978, vol. VII
Robson, Col Lancelot, 1855–1936, vol. III
Robson, Leonard Charles, 1894–1964, vol. VI
Robson, Philip Appleby, 1871–1951, vol. V
Robson, Robert, 1845–1928, vol. II
Robson, William, 1893–1975, vol. VII
Robson, William Alexander, 1895–1980, vol. VII
Robson, Rev. William Henry Fairfax, 1834–1913, vol. I
Robson Brown, Sir William, died 1975, vol. VII
Robson-Scott, William Douglas, 1901–1980, vol. VII
Roby, Arthur Godfrey, 1862–1944, vol. IV
Roby, Henry John, 1830–1915, vol. I
Roch, Col Horace Sampson, 1876–1960, vol. V
Roch, Walter Francis, 1880–1965, vol. VI
Rochdale, 1st Baron, 1866–1945, vol. IV
Roche, Baron (Life Peer); Alexander Adair Roche, 1871–1956, vol. V
Roche, Alexander, 1861–1921, vol. II
Roche, Alexander Ernest, 1896–1963, vol. VI
Roche, Hon. Alexis Charles Burke, 1853–1914, vol. I (A)
Roche, Augustine, died 1915, vol. I (A)
Roche, Sir David Vandeleur, 2nd Bt, 1833–1908, vol. I
Roche, Most Rev. Edward Patrick, 1874–1950, vol. IV (A)
Roche, Sir George, 1850–1932, vol. III
Roche, Col Henry John, 1864–1944, vol. IV
Roche, Most Rev. James J., 1870–1956, vol. V
Roche, John, 1848–1914, vol. I

Roche, Sir Standish, 3rd Bt, 1845–1914, vol. I
Roche, Sir Standish O'Grady, 4th Bt, 1911–1977, vol. VII
Roche, Col Hon. Ulick de Rupe Burke, 1856–1919, vol. II
Roche, Hon. William, 1842–1925, vol. II
Roche, William, 1880–1942, vol. IV
Roche, Hon. William James, 1860–1937, vol. III
Rochefort, Henri, 1831–1913, vol. I
Rochefort-Lucay, Marquis de, Victor Henri; see Rochefort, Henri.
Rochester, 1st Baron, 1876–1955, vol. V
Rochfort, Maj.-Gen. Sir Alexander Nelson, 1850–1916, vol. II
Rochfort, Captain George Arthur B.; see Boyd-Rochfort.
Rochfort-Boyd, Col Charles Augustus, 1850–1940, vol. III
Rochfort-Boyd, Lt-Col Henry Charles, 1877–1917, vol. II
Rocke, Col Cyril Edmund Alan, 1876–1968, vol. VI
Rocke, Maj.-Gen. James Harwood, 1829–1913, vol. I
Rocke, Col Walter Leslie, 1862–1932, vol. III
Rockefeller, John Davison, 1839–1937, vol. III
Rockefeller, John Davison, Jr, 1874–1960, vol. V
Rockefeller, John Davison, 3rd, 1906–1978, vol. VII
Rockefeller, Nelson Aldrich, 1908–1979, vol. VII
Rockhill, William Woodville, 1854–1914, vol. I
Rockley, 1st Baron, 1865–1941, vol. IV
Rockley, 2nd Baron, 1901–1976, vol. VII
Rockley, Lady; (Alicia-Margaret), died 1941, vol. IV
Rockliff, Percy, 1869–1958, vol. V
Rocyn-Jones, Arthur, died 1972, vol. VII
Rocyn-Jones, Sir David Thomas, 1872–1953, vol. V
Rod, Edouard, 1857–1910, vol. I
Rodd, Hon. Nancy, (Hon. Mrs Peter Rodd); see Mitford, N.
Rodda, Diwan Bahadur Shrinivas Konher, 1851–1929, vol. III
Roddick, Sir Thomas George, 1846–1923, vol. II
Roddie, Lt-Col William Stewart, 1878–1961, vol. VI
Roddy, Col Henry Hugh, 1866–1932, vol. III
Roden, 5th Earl of, 1823–1897, vol. I
Roden, 6th Earl of, 1842–1910, vol. I
Roden, 7th Earl of, 1845–1915, vol. I (A)
Roden, 8th Earl of, 1883–1956, vol. V
Roden, Countess of; (Ada Maria), 1860–1931, vol. III
Roden, Sir Robert Blair, 1860–1939, vol. III
Rodenberg, Julius, 1831–1914, vol. I
Rodes Green, Brig.-Gen. Henry Clifford; see Green.
Rodger, Adam Keir, 1855–1946, vol. IV
Rodger, Sir Alexander, died 1950, vol. IV
Rodger, Sir John Pickersgill, 1851–1910, vol. I
Rodger, Thomas Ferguson, 1907–1978, vol. VII
Rodger, T(homas) Ritchie, 1878–1968, vol. VI

Rodgers, Air Cdre Alexander Mitchell, 1906–1973, vol. VII

Rodgers, David John, 1890–1975, vol. VII

Rodgers, Rt Rev. Harold Nickinson, *died* 1947, vol. IV

Rodgers, Richard, 1902–1979, vol. VII

Rodgers, William Robert, 1909–1969, vol. VI

Rodham, Brig. Cuthbert Harold Boyd, 1900–1973, vol. VII

Rodham, Rear-Adm. (S) Harold, 1873–1947, vol. IV

Rodin, Auguste, 1840–1917, vol. II

Rodman, Adm. Hugh, 1859–1940, vol. III

Rodney, 7th Baron, 1857–1909, vol. I

Rodney, 8th Baron, 1891–1973, vol. VII

Rodney, Hon. James Henry Bartie, 1893–1933, vol. III

Rodocanachi, Emmanuel Michel, 1855–1932, vol. III

Rodrigo, Joseph Lionel Christie, *born* 1895, vol. VII

Rodrigo, Sir Philip; *see* Rodrigo, Sir S. T. P.

Rodrigo, Sir (Senapathige Theobald) Philip, *born* 1899, vol. VII

Rodway, James, 1848–1926, vol. II

Rodway, Leonard, 1853–1936, vol. III

Rodwell, Sir Cecil Hunter-, 1874–1953, vol. V

Rodwell, Brig.-Gen. Ernest Hunter, 1858–1937, vol. III

Rodwell, Air Cdre Robert John, 1897–1970, vol. VI

Rodzianko, Col Paul, *died* 1965, vol. VI

Rodzinski, Artur, 1894–1958, vol. V

Roe, 1st Baron, 1832–1923, vol. II

Roe, Sir Alliott Verdon-, 1877–1958, vol. V

Roe, Sir Charles, 1841–1927, vol. II

Roe, Brig.-Gen. Cyril Harcourt, 1864–1928, vol. II

Roe, Francis Reginald, 1869–1942, vol. IV

Roe, Fred, *died* 1947, vol. IV

Roe, Frederick Charles, 1894–1958, vol. V

Roe, Harold Riley, 1883–1963, vol. VI

Roe, Humphrey Verdon, 1878–1949, vol. IV

Roe, Rev. Robert Gordon, 1860–1927, vol. II

Roe, Rev. Robert James, *died* 1921, vol. II

Roe, Brig. William C.; *see* Carden Roe.

Roe, Dep. Surg.-Gen. William Carden, 1834–1922, vol. II

Roe, Lt-Col William Francis, 1871–1925, vol. II

Roe, Maj.-Gen. Sir William Gordon, 1904–1969, vol. VI

Roe-Thompson, Edwin Reginald, 1894–1970, vol. VI

Roebuck, Alfred, 1889–1962, vol. VI

Roerich, Nicholas K., 1874–1947, vol. IV

Roff, William George, 1858–1926, vol. II

Roffey, Edgar Stuart, 1875–1957, vol. V

Roffey, Sir (George) Walter, 1870–1940, vol. III

Roffey, Sir James, *died* 1912, vol. I

Roffey, Sir Walter; *see* Roffey, Sir G. W.

Rogan, Lt-Col John M.; *see* Mackenzie-Rogan.

Roger, Alastair Forbes, 1916–1980, vol. VII

Roger, Sir Alexander, 1878–1961, vol. VI

Roger, Captain Archibald, *born* 1842, vol. II

Rogers, Arthur Kenyon, 1868–1936, vol. III

Rogers, Sir Arthur Stanley, 1883–1953, vol. V

Rogers, Arthur William, 1872–1946, vol. IV

Rogers, Benjamin, 1837–1923, vol. II

Rogers, Bertram Mitford Heron, 1860–1953, vol. V

Rogers, Bruce, 1870–1957, vol. V

Rogers, Charles Coltman Coltman, 1854–1929, vol. III

Rogers, Rev. Charles Fursdon, 1848–1928, vol. II

Rogers, Charles Gilbert, *died* 1937, vol. III

Rogers, Claude Maurice, 1907–1979, vol. VII

Rogers, Rev. Clement Francis, 1866–1949, vol. IV

Rogers, Brig. Edgar William, 1892–1973, vol. VII

Rogers, Edmund Dawson, 1823–1910, vol. I

Rogers, Edwin John, 1858–1951, vol. V

Rogers, Captain Francis Caryer Campbell, 1883–1915, vol. I

Rogers, Francis Edward Newman, 1868–1925, vol. II

Rogers, Frederick, 1846–1915, vol. I (A)

Rogers, Rev. Frederick Arundel, 1876–1944, vol. IV

Rogers, Ven. George Herbert, *died* 1926, vol. II

Rogers, Col George William, 1843–1917, vol. II

Rogers, Graham, 1907–1973, vol. VII

Rogers, Rev. Guy; *see* Rogers, Rev. T. G.

Rogers, Sir Hallewell, 1864–1931, vol. III

Rogers, Lt-Col Henry, 1876–1931, vol. III

Rogers, Sir Henry Montagu, 1855–1931, vol. III

Rogers, Lt-Col Henry Schofield, 1869–1955, vol. V

Rogers, Henry Wade, 1853–1926, vol. II

Rogers, Herbert Lionel, 1871–1950, vol. IV

Rogers, Lt-Col Hugh Henry, 1858–1932, vol. III

Rogers, Rear-Adm. Hugh Hext, 1883–1955, vol. V

Rogers, Brig.-Gen. Hugh Stuart, 1878–1952, vol. V

Rogers, Rev. James Guinness, 1822–1911, vol. I

Rogers, John, *died* 1945, vol. IV

Rogers, John, 1878–1975, vol. VII

Rogers, Lt-Col Sir John Godfrey, 1850–1922, vol. II

Rogers, Lt-Col John Middleton, 1864–1945, vol. IV

Rogers, Brig. Joseph Bartlett, *died* 1940, vol. III

Rogers, Lambert Charles, 1897–1961, vol. VI

Rogers, Maj.-Gen. Sir Leonard, 1868–1962, vol. VI

Rogers, Leonard James, 1862–1933, vol. III

Rogers, Lindsay, 1891–1970, vol. VI (AII)

Rogers, Mark, 1848–1933, vol. III

Rogers, Muriel Augusta Gillian C.; *see* Coltman-Rogers.

Rogers, Hon. Norman McLeod, 1894–1940, vol. III

Rogers, Sir Percival Halse, 1883–1945, vol. IV

Rogers, Rev. Percy, 1826–1910, vol. I

Rogers, Philip Graham, *died* 1958, vol. V

Rogers, Hon. Robert, 1864–1936, vol. III

Rogers, Lt-Gen. Sir Robert Gordon, 1832–1906, vol. I

Rogers, Sir Robert Hargreaves, 1850–1924, vol. II

Rogers, Robert Vashon, 1843–1911, vol. I

Rogers, Robert William, 1864–1930, vol. III

Rogers, Roland, 1847–1927, vol. II

Rogers, Thomas Arthur, 1897–1965, vol. VI

Rogers, Thomas Englesby, 1817–1912, vol. I
Rogers, Rev. (Travers) Guy, died 1967, vol. VI
Rogers, Major Vivian Barry, 1887–1965, vol. VI
Rogers, William Penn Adair, 1879–1935, vol. III
Rogerson, Captain John Edwin, 1865–1925, vol. II
Rogerson, Col Sidney, 1894–1968, vol. VI
Roget, F. F., 1859–1938, vol. III
Rogosinski, Werner Wolfgang, 1894–1964, vol. VI
Rohan, Duchess de, (dowager); Herminie de Verteillac, died 1926, vol. II
Rohde, Eleanour Sinclair, died 1950, vol. IV
Rohlfs, Mrs Charles, (Anna Katharine Rohlfs), 1846–1935, vol. III
Rohmer, Sax, died 1959, vol. V
Roles, Francis Crosbie, 1867–1931, vol. III
Rolfe, Douglass Horace B.; see Boggis-Rolfe.
Rolfe, Eustace N.; see Neville-Rolfe.
Rolfe, Rev. Harry Roger, 1851–1924, vol. II
Rolfe, Captain Herbert Neville, 1854–1942, vol. IV
Rolfe, William James, 1827–1910, vol. I
Roll, Sir Cecil Ernest, 3rd Bt, 1878–1938, vol. III
Roll, Sir Frederick James, 2nd Bt, 1873–1933, vol. III
Roll, Grahame Winfield, died 1942, vol. IV
Roll, Sir James, 1st Bt, 1846–1927, vol. II
Rolland, Brig.-Gen. Alexander, 1871–1939, vol. III
Rolland, Very Rev. Sir Francis William, 1878–1965, vol. VI
Rolland, Major George Murray, 1869–1910, vol. I
Rolland, Romain, 1866–1944, vol. IV
Rolland, Brig.-Gen. Stewart Erskine, 1846–1927, vol. II
Rolland, Vice-Adm. W. R., 1817–1904, vol. I
Rollason, Ernest Clarence, 1908–1972, vol. VII
Rolle, Hon. Mark George Kerr, 1835–1907, vol. I
Roller, Major George C., 1856–1941, vol. IV
Rolleston, Charles Ffranck, 1833–1913, vol. I
Rolleston, Francis Joseph, 1873–1946, vol. IV
Rolleston, Sir Humphry Davy, 1st Bt, 1862–1944, vol. IV
Rolleston, Mrs Iris Brenda, 1880–1948, vol. IV
Rolleston, John Davy, 1873–1946, vol. IV
Rolleston, Sir John Fowke Lancelot, 1848–1919, vol. II
Rolleston, Adm. John Philip, 1859–1936, vol. III
Rolleston, Col Sir Lancelot, 1847–1941, vol. IV
Rolleston, Thomas William, 1857–1920, vol. II
Rolleston, Sir William Gustavus Stanhope, 1862–1944, vol. IV
Rolleston, Col William Lancelot, 1905–1974 vol. VII
Rollett, Herbert, 1872–1932, vol. III
Rolling, Col Bernard Ismay, 1883–1937, vol. III
Rollins, John Wenlock, died 1940, vol. III
Rollit, Sir Albert Kaye, 1842–1922, vol. II
Rollo, 10th Lord, 1835–1916, vol. II
Rollo, 11th Lord, 1860–1946, vol. IV
Rollo, 12th Lord, 1889–1947, vol. IV
Rollo, Hon. Bernard Francis, 1868–1935, vol. III
Rollo, Hon. Eric Norman, 1861–1930, vol. III
Rollo, Lt-Col George, 1881–1944, vol. IV
Rollo, Gen. Hon. Sir Robert, 1814–1907, vol. I
Rollo, Rev. William, 1859–1949, vol. IV

Rolls, Hon. Charles Stewart, 1877–1910, vol. I
Rolls, Captain Sir John Courtown Edward S.; see Shelley-Rolls.
Rolo, Sir Robert, 1869–1944, vol. IV
Rolph, Sir Gordon Burns, 1893–1959, vol. V
Rolt, Bernard, 1874–1937, vol. III
Rolt, Very Rev. Cecil Henry, 1865–1926, vol. II
Rolt, James, 1860–1938, vol. III
Rolt, Lionel Thomas Caswall, 1910–1974, vol. VII
Rolt, Brig.-Gen. Stuart Peter, 1862–1933, vol. III
Rolt, Vivian, 1874–1933, vol. III
Romains, Jules, 1885–1972, vol. VII
Romanes, Ethel, died 1927, vol. II
Romanes, Mrs George; see Romanes, Ethel.
Romanis, William Hugh Cowie, 1889–1972, vol. VII
Romanne-James, Mrs Helena Constance, (Mrs H. C. Aylen), died 1966, vol. VI
Romanos, Athos, 1858–1940, vol. III
Rome, Brig. Charles Leslie, 1878–1936, vol. III
Rome, Brig.-Gen. Claude Stuart, 1875–1956, vol. V
Rome, Thomas, 1852–1938, vol. III
Romer, Baron (Life Peer); Mark Lemon Romer, 1866–1944, vol. IV
Romer, Carrol, 1883–1951, vol. V
Romer, Gen. Sir Cecil Francis, 1869–1962, vol. VI
Romer, Rt Hon. Sir Charles Robert Ritchie, 1897–1969, vol. VI
Romer, Frank, 1871–1939, vol. III
Romer, Lt-Col Frederick Charles, 1854–1915, vol. I
Romer, Rt Hon. Sir Robert, 1840–1918, vol. II
Romer, Thomas Ansdell, 1848–1917, vol. II
Romer-Lee, Lt-Col H., 1874–1955, vol. V
Romeril, Herbert George, 1881–1963, vol. VI
Romilly, 3rd Baron, 1866–1905, vol. I
Romilly, Col Bertram Henry Samuel, 1878–1940, vol. III
Romilly, Eric Carnegie, (Frederic Carnegie Romilly), 1886–1953, vol. V
Romilly, Frederic Carnegie; see Romilly, E. C.
Romilly, Col Frederick William, 1854–1935, vol. III
Romilly, George, died 1933, vol. III
Romilly, Samuel Henry, 1849–1940, vol. III
Romiti, William, 1850–1936, vol. III
Romney, 4th Earl of, 1841–1905, vol. I
Romney, 5th Earl of, 1864–1933, vol. III
Romney, 6th Earl of, 1892–1975, vol. VII
Ronald, E. B.; see Barker, Ronald Ernest.
Ronald, Sir Landon, 1873–1938, vol. III
Ronald, Sir Nigel Bruce, 1894–1973, vol. VII
Ronalds, Andrew John, 1897–1978, vol. VII
Ronaldson, James Bruce, 1886–1952, vol. V
Ronaldson, Brig.-Gen. Robert William Hawthorn, 1864–1946, vol. IV
Ronaldson, Thomas Martine, 1881–1942, vol. IV
Ronan, Very Rev. Myles V., 1877–1959, vol. V (A)
Ronan, Rt Hon. Stephen, 1848–1925, vol. II
Ronayne, Thomas, 1848–1925, vol. II
Roncalli, Angelo Giuseppe; see John XXIII.
Roney, Sir Ernest, 1871–1952, vol. V
Roocroft, Col William Mitchell, 1859–1943, vol. IV
Rood, Felix Stephen, 1883–1933, vol. III

Rook, Air Vice-Marshal Sir Alan Filmer, *died* 1960, vol. V

Rook, Sir William James, 1885–1958, vol. V

Rooke, Charles Eustace, 1892–1947, vol. IV

Rooke, Lt-Col Everard Home, 1875–1936, vol. III

Rooke, Col Harry William, 1842–1921, vol. II

Rooke, Ven. Henry, 1829–1926, vol. II

Rooke, Herbert K., 1872–1944, vol. IV

Rooke, Thomas Matthews, 1842–1942, vol. IV

Rooke, Maj.-Gen. William, 1836–1919, vol. II

Rooker, John Kingsley, 1887–1951, vol. V

Rooks, Maj.-Gen. Lowell W., 1893–1973, vol. VII

Rookwood, 1st Baron, 1826–1902, vol. I

Roome, Gen. Frederick, 1829–1907, vol. I

Roome, Engr-Rear-Adm. George W., 1865–1945, vol. IV

Roome, Henry Delacombe, 1882–1930, vol. III

Roome, Maj.-Gen. Sir Horace Eckford, 1887–1964, vol. VI

Rooney, Rt Rev. John, *died* 1927, vol. II

Rooney, Maj.-Gen. Sir Owen Patrick James, 1900–1972, vol. VII

Roos, Gustaf Ehrenreich, 1838–1928, vol. II

Roos-Keppel, Sir George; *see* Keppel.

Roose, Robson, 1848–1905, vol. I

Roosevelt, (Anna) Eleanor, (Mrs F. D. Roosevelt), 1884–1962, vol. VI

Roosevelt, Eleanor; *see* Roosevelt, A. E.

Roosevelt, Franklin Delano, 1882–1945, vol. IV

Roosevelt, Col Kermit, *died* 1943, vol. IV

Roosevelt, Robert Barnewell, 1829–1906, vol. I

Roosevelt, Col Theodore, 1858–1919, vol. II

Roosevelt, Theodore, 1887–1944, vol. IV

Root, Hon. Elihu, 1845–1937, vol. III

Rootes, 1st Baron, 1894–1964, vol. VI

Rootes, Sir Reginald Claud, 1896–1977, vol. VII

Rooth, Henry Goodwin, 1861–1928, vol. II

Rooth, Ivar, 1888–1972, vol. VII

Rooth, John, 1864–1930, vol. III

Rootham, Cyril Bradley, 1875–1938, vol. III

Roots, Rt Rev. Logan Herbert, 1870–1945, vol. IV

Roots, William Lloyd, 1911–1971, vol. VII

Rope, Ellen Mary, *died* 1934, vol. III

Roper, Brig.-Gen. Alexander William, 1862–1940, vol. III

Roper, Edgar Stanley, 1878–1953, vol. V

Roper, Edward Ridgill, 1885–1974, vol. VII

Roper, Freeman, 1862–1925, vol. II

Roper, Garnham, 1862–1940, vol. III

Roper, Sir Harold, 1891–1971, vol. VII

Roper, Henry Basil, *died* 1918, vol. II

Roper, Most Rev. John Charles, 1858–1940, vol. III

Roper, Philip Hampden, 1906–1956, vol. V

Ropes, Arthur Reed, 1859–1933, vol. III

Ropner, Sir (Emil Hugo Oscar) Robert, 3rd Bt (*cr* 1904), 1893–1962, vol. VI

Ropner, Sir Guy; *see* Ropner, Sir W. G.

Ropner, Sir John Henry, 2nd Bt (*cr* 1904), 1860–1936, vol. III

Ropner, Leonard, 1873–1937, vol. III

Ropner, Col Sir Leonard, 1st Bt (*cr* 1952), 1895–1977, vol. VII

Ropner, Col Sir Robert, 1st Bt (*cr* 1904), 1838–1924, vol. II

Ropner, Sir Robert; *see* Ropner, Sir E. H. O. R.

Ropner, Sir Robert Desmond, 1908–1977, vol. VII

Ropner, Sir (William) Guy, 1896–1971, vol. VII

Rops, Henry D.; *see* Daniel-Rops.

Roques, Frederick William, 1898–1964, vol. VI

Roques, Mario Louis Guillaume, 1875–1961, vol. VI

Rorie, Col David, 1867–1946, vol. IV

Rorie, James, 1838–1911, vol. I

Rorimer, James J., 1905–1966, vol. VI

Rorison, Very Rev. Vincent Lewis, 1851–1910, vol. I

Rorke, Rev. Joseph, *died* 1932, vol. III

Rorke, Kate, (Mrs Douglas Cree), *died* 1945, vol. IV

Rosa, John Nogueira, 1903–1977, vol. VII

Rosay, Françoise, 1891–1974, vol. VII

Rosbotham, Sir Samuel Thomas, 1864–1950, vol. IV

Roscoe, Edward Stanley, 1849–1932, vol. III

Roscoe, Frank, 1870–1942, vol. IV

Roscoe, Rt Hon. Sir Henry Enfield, 1833–1915, vol. I (A)

Roscoe, Rev. John, 1861–1932, vol. III

Roscoe, Kenneth Harry, 1914–1970, vol. VI

Rose, Sir Alan Edward Percival, 1899–1975, vol. VII

Rose, Rt Rev. Alfred Carey Wollaston, *died* 1971, vol. VII

Rose, Algernon Sidney, *died* 1934, vol. III

Rose, Archibald; *see* Rose, C. A. W.

Rose, Hon. Lt-Col Sir Arthur; *see* Rose, Hon. Lt-Col Sir H. A.

Rose, (Charles) Archibald (Walker), 1879–1961, vol. VI

Rose, Sir Charles Day, 1st Bt (*cr* 1909), 1847–1913, vol. I

Rose, Sir Charles Henry, 3rd Bt (*cr* 1909), 1912–1966, vol. VI

Rose, Sir Cyril Stanley, 3rd Bt (*cr* 1872), 1874–1915, vol. I

Rose, Sir David James Gardiner, 1923–1969, vol. VI

Rose, Edward, 1849–1904, vol. I

Rose, Edward, 1845–1910, vol. I

Rose, Gen. Edward Lee, 1841–1903, vol. I

Rose, Lt-Col Ernest Albert, 1879–1976, vol. VII

Rose, Sir Francis Cyril, 4th Bt (*cr* 1872), 1909–1979, vol. VII

Rose, Frank Atcherley, 1873–1935, vol. III

Rose, Vice-Adm. Sir Frank Forrester, 1878–1955, vol. V

Rose, Frank Herbert, 1857–1928, vol. II

Rose, Sir Frank Stanley, 2nd Bt (*cr* 1909), 1877–1914, vol. I

Rose, Frederick, *died* 1932, vol. III

Rose, Frederick Campbell, 1865–1946, vol. IV

Ross, Sir Frederick William L.; *see* Leith-Ross.

Rose, Geoffrey Keith, 1889–1959, vol. V

Rose, George Pringle, 1855–1918, vol. II

Rose, Herbert Jennings, 1883–1961, vol. VI

Rose, Horace Arthur, 1867–1933, vol. III

Rose, Lt-Col Hugh, 1863–1946, vol. IV

Rose, Sir Hugh, 2nd Bt (*cr* 1935) 1902–1976, vol. VII

Rose, Major Hugh Alexander Leslie, *died* 1918, vol. II

Rose, Hon. Lt-Col Sir (Hugh) Arthur, 1st Bt (*cr* 1935), 1875–1937, vol. III

Rose, Hugh Edward, 1869–1945, vol. IV

Rose, Major James, 1820–1909, vol. I

Rose, John, 1841–1926, vol. II

Rose, John Donald, 1911–1976, vol. VII

Rose, John Holland, 1855–1942, vol. IV

Rose, Brig.-Gen. John Latham, 1867–1931, vol. III

Rose, Col John Markham, 1865–1942, vol. IV

Rose, Percy Jesse, 1878–1959, vol. V

Rose, Sir Philip Frederick, 2nd Bt (*cr* 1874), 1843–1919, vol. II

Rose, Reginald Leslie S.; *see* Smith-Rose.

Rose, Col Richard Aubrey De Burgh, 1877–1962, vol. VI

Rose, Captain Thomas Allen, 1874–1914, vol. I (A)

Rose, Sir Thomas Kirke, 1865–1953, vol. V

Rose, Walter Clerk R.; *see* Randolph-Rose.

Rose, Sir William, 2nd Bt (*cr* 1872), 1846–1902, vol. I

Rose, William, 1847–1910, vol. I

Rose, William, 1894–1961, vol. VI

Rose, William John, 1885–1968, vol. VI

Rose-Innes, Rt Hon. Sir James, 1855–1942, vol. IV

Rose-Innes, Sir Patrick, 1853–1924, vol. II

Rosebery, 5th Earl of, 1847–1929, vol. III

Rosebery, 6th Earl of, 1882–1974, vol. VII

Rosedale, Captain Rev. Honyel Gough, 1863–1928, vol. II

Rosenbach, Abraham S. Wolf, 1876–1952, vol. V

Rosenfeld, Léon, 1904–1974, vol. VII

Rosenhain, Walter, 1875–1934, vol. III

Rosenheim, Baron (Life Peer); Max Leonard Rosenheim, 1908–1972, vol. VII

Rosenheim, Otto, 1871–1955, vol. V

Rosenman, Samuel Irving, 1896–1973, vol. VII

Rosenthal, Maj.-Gen. Sir Charles, 1875–1954, vol. V

Rosenthal, Moriz, 1862–1946, vol. IV

Roseveare, Rt Rev. Reginald Richard, 1902–1972, vol. VII

Roseveare, Rev. Richard Polgreen, 1865–1924, vol. II

Roseveare, Richard Victor Harley, 1897–1968, vol. VI

Roseveare, William Nicholas, 1864–1948, vol. IV

Rosewater, Hon. Edward, 1841–1906, vol. I

Rosewater, Victor, 1871–1940, vol. III (A), vol. IV

Roseway, Sir David; *see* Roseway, Sir G. D.

Roseway, Sir (George) David, 1890–1969, vol. VI

Rosing, Vladimir, *died* 1963, vol. VI

Roskill, John, *died* 1940, vol. III

Rosling, Sir Edward, 1863–1946, vol. IV

Roslyn, Louis Frederick, 1878–1940, vol. III

Rosman, Alice Grant, *died* 1961, vol. VI

Rosmead, 1st Baron, 1824–1897, vol. I

Rosmead, 2nd Baron, 1866–1933, vol. III

Rosmer, Milton, 1882–1971, vol. VII

Ross, Adrian; *see* Ropes, A. R.

Ross, Brig. Alan Campbell, 1878–1937, vol. III

Ross, Alan Strode Campbell, 1907–1980, vol. VII

Ross, Alexander, 1845–1923, vol. II

Ross, Rev. Alexander, 1888–1965, vol. VI

Ross, Brig.-Gen. Alexander, 1880–1973, vol. VII

Ross, Alexander Carnegie, 1859–1940, vol. III (A), vol. IV

Ross, Alexander David, 1883–1966, vol. VI

Ross, Lt-Gen. Sir Alexander George, 1840–1910, vol. I

Ross, Rev. Alexander George Gordon, *died* 1938, vol. III

Ross, Alexander Howard, 1880–1965, vol. VI

Ross, Andrew, 1849–1925, vol. II

Ross, Archibald Hugh Houstoun, 1896–1969, vol. VI

Ross, Sir Archibald John Campbell, 1867–1931, vol. III

Ross, Brig.-Gen. Arthur Edward, 1870–1952, vol. V

Ross, Rt Rev. Arthur Edwin, 1869–1923, vol. II

Ross, Lt-Col Arthur Murray, 1879–1933, vol. III

Ross, Maj.-Gen. Charles, 1864–1930, vol. III

Ross of that Ilk, Charles Campbell, yr, 1901–1966, vol. VI

Ross, Charles Griffith, 1885–1950, vol. IV

Ross, Sir Charles Henry Augustus Frederick Lockhart, 9th Bt (*cr* 1672), 1872–1942, vol. IV

Ross, Sir David; *see* Ross, Sir W. D.

Ross, Rev. David Morison, 1852–1927, vol. II

Ross, Sir David Palmer, 1842–1904, vol. I

Ross, Sir Denison; *see* Ross, Sir E. D.

Ross, Edward Alsworth, 1866–1951, vol. V

Ross, Sir Edward Charles, 1836–1913, vol. I

Ross, Sir (Edward) Denison, 1871–1940, vol. III

Ross, Edward Rowlandson, 1868–1941, vol. IV

Ross, Rt Rev. Mgr Canon Francis, 1873–1945, vol. IV

Ross, Hon. Frank Mackenzie, 1891–1971, vol. VII

Ross, Col George, 1853–1926, vol. II

Ross, Rev. George Alexander Johnston, 1865–1937, vol. III

Ross, George Edward Aubert, 1847–1931, vol. III

Ross, George Mabyn, 1883–1954, vol. V

Ross, Rear-Adm. George Parish, 1875–1942, vol. IV

Ross, George Robert Thomson, 1874–1959, vol. V

Ross, Col George Whitehill, 1878–1952, vol. V

Ross, Hon. Sir George William, 1841–1914, vol. I

Ross, Hon. Dame (Grace) Hilda, 1884–1959, vol. V

Ross, Col Harry, 1869–1938, vol. III

Ross, Lt-Col Henry, 1877–1958, vol. V

Ross, Sir Henry James, 1893–1973, vol. VII

Ross, Hon. Dame Hilda; *see* Ross, Hon. Dame G. H.

Ross, Howard Salter, 1872–1955, vol. V

Ross, Major Hugh Alexander, 1880–1918, vol. II

Ross, Lt-Col Hugh Cairns Edward, 1884–1940, vol. III

Ross, Hugh Campbell, 1875–1926, vol. II

Ross, Captain Hugo Donald, 1880–1960, vol. V

Ross, Sir Ian C.; *see* Clunies-Ross.

Ross, James, 1836–1902, vol. I

Ross, James, 1848–1913, vol. I
Ross, James, *died* 1953, vol. V
Ross, Maj.-Gen. James George, 1861–1956, vol. V
Ross, Sir James Paterson, 1st Bt (*cr* 1960), 1895–1980, vol. VII
Ross, Sir James Stirling, 1877–1961, vol. VI
Ross, James Stiven, 1892–1975, vol. VII
Ross, Janet Anne, 1842–1927, vol. II
Ross, Gen. Sir John, 1829–1905, vol. I
Ross, Rev. John, 1842–1915, vol. I
Ross, Sir John, 1834–1927, vol. II
Ross, Sir John, 1838–1931, vol. III
Ross, Rt Hon. Sir John, 1st Bt (*cr* 1919), 1854–1935, vol. III
Ross, John, 1893–1967, vol. VI
Ross, Major John Alexander, 1893–1917, vol. II
Ross, Brig. John Ellis, 1893–1965, vol. VI
Ross, Sir John Foster George; *see* Ross-of-Bladensburg.
Ross, John Kenneth Murray, 1856–1939, vol. III
Ross, John M. E., 1870–1925, vol. II
Ross, Maj.-Gen. John Munro, 1877–1959, vol. V
Ross, Sir John Sutherland, 1877–1959, vol. V
Ross, Rev. John Trelawny T.; *see* Trelawny-Ross.
Ross, Joseph Thorburn, 1849–1903, vol. I
Ross, Kenneth Brebner, 1901–1973, vol. VII
Ross, Rev. Kenneth Needham, 1908–1970, vol. VI
Ross, Rev. Neil, 1871–1943, vol. IV
Ross, Mrs Norah Cecil; *see* Runge, N. C.
Ross, Peter McGregor, 1919–1974, vol. VII
Ross, Philip Dansken, 1858–1949, vol. IV
Ross, Reginald James Blair, *born* 1871, vol. II
Ross, Robert, 1893–1969, vol. VI
Ross, Robert Baldwin, 1869–1918, vol. II
Ross, Brig.-Gen. Robert James, 1865–1943, vol. IV
Ross, Maj.-Gen. Robert Knox, 1893–1951, vol. V
Ross, Air Cdre Robert Peel, *died* 1963, vol. VI
Ross, Roderick, 1863–1943, vol. IV
Ross, Col Sir Ronald, 1857–1932, vol. III
Ross, Lt-Col Sir Ronald Deane, 2nd Bt (*cr* 1919), 1888–1958, vol. V
Ross, Rev. Spence, 1843–1929, vol. III
Ross, Stanley Graham, 1888–1980, vol. VII
Ross, Thomas Arthur, 1875–1941, vol. IV
Ross, Rev. Thomas Harry, 1863–1943, vol. IV
Ross, Sir Thomas Mackenzie, *died* 1927, vol. II
Ross of Cromarty, Brig.-Gen. Sir Walter Charteris, 1857–1928, vol. II
Ross, Hon. William, 1825–1912, vol. I
Ross, Hon. William, 1850–1925, vol. II
Ross, William Alexander, 1891–1977, vol. VII
Ross, Captain William Alston, 1875–1944, vol. IV
Ross, Hon. William Benjamin, 1854–1929, vol. III
Ross, Sir (William) David, 1877–1971, vol. VII
Ross, Hon. William Donald, 1869–1947, vol. IV
Ross, William Henry, 1862–1944, vol. IV
Ross, William Munro, 1858–1914, vol. I (A), vol. III
Ross, Hon. William Roderick, 1869–1928, vol. II (A), vol. III
Ross-Brown, James William, *died* 1938, vol. III
Ross-Frames, Col Percival, 1863–1947, vol. IV

Ross-Johnson, Maj.-Gen. Cyril Maxwell, 1868–1934, vol. III
Ross-Johnson, Dennis, 1860–1941, vol. IV
Ross-Lewin, Rev. George Harrison, 1846–1913, vol. I
Ross-Lewin, Ven. Richard S., 1848–1921, vol. II
Ross-Lewin, Rev. Robert O'Donelan, 1850–1922, vol. II
Ross-of-Bladensburg, Sir John Foster George, 1848–1926, vol. III
Ross Skinner, Lt-Col Harry Crawley, 1896–1972, vol. VII
Ross-Taylor, Sir Joshua, 1878–1959, vol. V
Ross Taylor, Walter, 1877–1958, vol. V
Ross Williamson, Hugh, 1901–1978, vol. VII
Ross Williamson, Reginald Pole, 1907–1966, vol. VI
Rosse, 4th Earl of, 1840–1908 (this entry was not transferred to Who was Who).
Rosse, 5th Earl of, 1873–1918, vol. II
Rosse, 6th Earl of, 1906–1979, vol. VII
Rosselli, (Ignace Adolphe) Jacques, 1907–1974, vol. VII
Rosselli, Jacques; *see* Rosselli, I. A. J.
Rossetti, William Michael, 1829–1919, vol. II
Rossillon, Rt Rev. Peter, 1874–1947, vol. IV
Rossiter, James Leonard, 1887–1963, vol. VI
Rosslyn, 5th Earl of, 1869–1939, vol. III
Rosslyn, 6th Earl of, 1917–1977, vol. VII
Rossmore, 5th Baron, 1853–1921, vol. II
Rossmore, 6th Baron, 1892–1958, vol. V
Rostand, Edmond, 1868–1918, vol. II
Rostand, Jean, 1894–1977, vol. VII
Rostern, Joseph, 1862–1930, vol. III
Rostovtzeff, Michael I., 1870–1952, vol. V
Rostron, Captain Sir Arthur Henry, 1869–1940, vol. III
Rostron, Rev. Sydney N.; *see* Nowell-Rostron.
Rotch, Abbott Lawrence, 1861–1912, vol. I
Roth, Cecil, 1899–1970, vol. VI
Roth, George Kingsley, 1903–1960, vol. V
Roth, Leon, 1896–1963, vol. VI
Roth, Paul Bernard, 1882–1962, vol. VI
Roth, Brig.-Gen. Reuter Emerich, 1858–1924, vol. II
Roth, Air Cdre Victor Henry Batten, 1904–1979, vol. VII
Rothband, Sir Henry Lesser, 1st Bt, *died* 1940 vol. III (A), vol. IV
Rothenstein, Sir William, 1872–1945, vol. IV
Rothera, Sir Percy, 1877–1940, vol. III
Rotherham, 1st Baron, 1849–1927, vol. II
Rotherham, 2nd Baron, 1876–1950, vol. IV
Rotherham, Arthur, *died* 1946, vol. IV
Rothermere, 1st Viscount, 1868–1940, vol. III
Rothermere, 2nd Viscount, 1898–1978, vol. VII
Rotherwick, 1st Baron, 1881–1958, vol. V
Rothery, Guy Cadogan, 1863–1940, vol. III (A), vol. IV
Rothery, William Gurney, 1858–1930, vol. III
Rothery, William H.; *see* Hume-Rothery.
Rothes, 19th Earl of, 1877–1927, vol. II
Rothes, 20th Earl of, 1902–1975, vol. VII
Rothko, Mark, 1903–1970, vol. VI
Rothschild, 1st Baron, 1840–1915, vol. I

Rothschild, 2nd Baron, 1868–1937, vol. III
Rothschild, Alfred Charles de, 1842–1918, vol. II
Rothschild, Anthony Gustav de, 1887–1961, vol. VI
Rothschild, Baron Ferdinand James de, 1839–1898, vol. I
Rothschild, Baron Henri de, 1872–1947, vol. IV
Rothschild, James A. de, died 1957, vol. V
Rothschild, Leopold de, 1845–1917, vol. II
Rothschild, Lionel Nathan de, 1882–1942, vol. IV
Rothschild, Hon. Nathaniel Charles, 1877–1923, vol. II
Rothwell, Harry, 1902–1980, vol. VII
Rothwell, James Herbert, 1881–1944, vol. IV
Rothwell, Brig. Richard Sutton, 1882–1962, vol. VI
Rothwell, Lt-Col William Edward, 1879–1937, vol. III
Rotter, Rear-Adm. (S) Charles John Ehrhardt, 1871–1948, vol. IV
Rotter, Godfrey, 1879–1969, vol. VI
Rotton, Sir John Francis, 1837–1926, vol. II
Rotton, Brig.-Gen. John Guy, 1867–1940, vol. III
Rouault, Georges, 1871–1958, vol. V
Roughead, William, 1870–1952, vol. V
Roughton, Edmund W., 1861–1913, vol. I
Roughton, Francis John Worsley, 1899–1972, vol. VII
Roughton, Noel James, 1885–1953, vol. V
Rougier, George Ronald, 1900–1976, vol. VII
Rouillard, Frederic Melchoir Louis, 1866–1933, vol. III
Rouleau, His Eminence Cardinal Raymond Marie, 1866–1931, vol III
Roullier, Jean Georges, 1898–1974, vol. VII
Roulston, Air Cdre Jack Fendick, 1913–1973, vol. VII
Roumania, Queen Elizabeth of; see Sylva, Carmen.
Round, Charles James, 1885–1945, vol. IV
Round, Francis Richard, 1845–1920, vol. II
Round, Rt Hon. James, 1842–1916, vol. II
Round, John Horace, 1854–1928, vol. II
Round-Turner, Vice-Adm. Charles Wolfran, died 1953, vol. V
Roundell, Charles Savile, 1827–1906, vol. I
Roundell, Christopher Foulis, 1876–1958, vol. V
Roundell, Richard Foulis, 1872–1940, vol. III
Roundway, 1st Baron, 1854–1925, vol. II
Roundway, 2nd Baron, 1880–1944, vol. IV
Rounsevell, Hon. William Benjamin, 1842–1923, vol. II
Rountree, Gilbert Harry, 1907–1962, vol. VI
Rountree, Harry, 1878–1950, vol. IV
Rountree, Rev. James Peter, 1846–1929, vol. III
Roupell, Lt-Col Ernest Percy Stuart, 1870–1938, vol. III
Roupell, Brig. George Rowland Patrick, 1892–1974, vol. VII
Rous, (Francis) Peyton, 1879–1970, vol. VI
Rous, Peyton; see Rous, F. P.
Rous, William John, 1833–1914, vol. I
Rouse, Sir Alexander Macdonald, 1878–1966, vol. VI
Rouse, Harold Lindsay, 1887–1959, vol. V
Rouse, Col Hubert, 1864–1945, vol. IV

Rouse, William Henry Denham, 1863–1950, vol. IV
Rouse-Boughton, Sir Charles Henry; see Boughton.
Rouse-Boughton, Sir Edward Hotham; see Boughton.
Rouse-Boughton, Sir William St Andrew; see Boughton.
Rouse-Boughton-Knight, Charles Andrew, 1859–1947, vol. IV
Rousseau, Arthur, 1871–1934, vol. III
Rousseau, Pierre Marie W.; see Waldeck-Rousseau.
Roussin, Leander Gaspard, 1870–1936, vol. III
Routh, Amand J. McC., 1853–1927, vol. II
Routh, Edward John, 1831–1907, vol. I
Routh, Col Guy Montgomery, 1882–1963, vol. VI
Routh, Harold Victor, 1878–1951, vol. V
Routh, Vice-Adm. Henry Peter, 1851–1944, vol. IV
Routh, Robert Gordon, 1869–1964, vol. VI
Routhier, Hon. Sir Adolphe Basile, 1839–1919, vol. II
Routledge, Rev. C. F., 1838–1904, vol. I
Routledge, Robert M., died 1907, vol. I
Routledge, Scoresby, 1859–1939, vol. III
Routley, Frederick William, 1879–1951, vol. V
Routley, Thomas Clarence, 1889–1963, vol. VI
Roux, François C.; see Charles-Roux.
Row, Canchi Sarvothama, born 1856, vol. II
Row, Kodikal S.; see Sanjiva Row.
Row, Paymaster Rear-Adm. Philip John Hawkins Lander, 1870–1932, vol. III
Row, Brig. Robert Amos, 1888–1959, vol. V (A)
Rowallan, 1st Baron, 1856–1933, vol. III
Rowallan, 2nd Baron, 1895–1977, vol. VII
Rowan, John, died 1948, vol. IV
Rowan, Sir Leslie; see Rowan, Sir T. L.
Rowan, Lt-Col Percy Stewart, 1882–1931, vol. III
Rowan, Ven. Robert Philip, 1870–1946, vol. IV
Rowan, Sir (Thomas) Leslie, 1908–1972, vol. VII
Rowan-Hamilton, Brig. Gawaine Basil, 1884–1947, vol. IV
Rowan-Hamilton, Col Gawin William; see Hamilton.
Rowan-Hamilton, Sir Orme, 1877–1949, vol. IV
Rowan-Robinson, Maj.-Gen. Henry, 1873–1947, vol. IV
Rowan-Thomson, Sir William, 1867–1929, vol. III
Rowand, Alexander, 1868–1936, vol. III
Rowatt, Hugh Howard, 1861–1938, vol. III
Rowatt, Thomas, 1879–1950, vol. IV
Rowbotham, Edgar Stanley, 1890–1979, vol. VII
Rowbotham, Sir Hanson; see Rowbotham, Sir S. H.
Rowbotham, Rev. John Frederick, 1859–1925, vol. II
Rowbotham, Sir (Samuel) Hanson, 1880–1946, vol. IV
Rowbotham, Sir Thomas, 1851–1939, vol. III
Rowcroft, Maj.-Gen. Sir Bertram; see Rowcroft, Maj.-Gen. Sir E. B.
Rowcroft, Maj.-Gen. Sir (Eric) Bertram, 1891–1963, vol. VI
Rowcroft, Major Ernest Cave, 1866–1916, vol. II
Rowcroft, Maj.-Gen. George Cleland, 1831–1922, vol. II

Rowden, Aldred William, *died* 1919, vol. II
Rowe, Albert Percival, *died* 1976, vol. VII
Rowe, Rev. Alfred William, *died* 1921, vol. II
Rowe, Charles Henry, 1869–1925, vol. II
Rowe, Charles Henry, *died* 1943, vol. IV
Rowe, Charles William Dell, 1893–1954, vol. V
Rowe, Edward Rowe F.; *see* Fisher-Rowe.
Rowe, Frederick Maurice, 1891–1946, vol. IV
Rowe, Col Herbert Mayow F.; *see* Fisher-Rowe.
Rowe, John Clifford, 1872–1944, vol. IV
Rowe, Ven. John Tetley, *died* 1915, vol. I
Rowe, Louise J.; *see* Jopling, Louise.
Rowe, Sir Michael Edward, 1901–1978, vol. VII
Rowe, Rt Rev. Peter Trimble, 1856–1942, vol. IV
Rowe, Sir Reginald P. P., *died* 1945, vol. IV
Rowe, Lt-Col Richard Herbert, 1883–1933, vol. III
Rowe, S. Grant, 1861–1928, vol. II
Rowe, Chief Engr William, *died* 1924, vol. II
Rowe, William Hugh Cecil, *died* 1939, vol. III (A), vol. IV
Rowe-Dutton, Sir Ernest, 1891–1965, vol. VI
Rowell, Sir Andrew Herrick, 1890–1973, vol. VII
Rowell, Sir Herbert Babington, 1860–1921, vol. II
Rowell, Col James, 1851–1940, vol. III
Rowell, John Soulsby, 1846–1916, vol. II
Rowell, Hon. Newton Wesley, 1867–1941, vol. IV
Rowell, Percy Fitz-Patrick, 1874–1940, vol. III
Rowell, Sir Reginald Kaye, 1888–1964, vol. VI
Rowell, Lt-Gen. Sir Sydney Fairbairn, 1894–1975, vol. VII
Rowell, Thomas Irvine, 1840–1932, vol. III
Rowett, John Quiller, 1876–1924, vol. II
Rowland, Rev. Alfred, 1840–1925, vol. II
Rowland, Christopher John Salter, 1929–1967, vol. VI
Rowland, Ernest Daniel, 1858–1933, vol. III
Rowland, Francis George, 1883–1957, vol. V
Rowland, Frank Mortimer, 1866–1932, vol. III
Rowland, Sir Frederick, 1st Bt, 1874–1959, vol. V
Rowland, Sir John, 1877–1941, vol. IV
Rowland, Sir John Edward Maurice, 1882–1969, vol. VI
Rowland, Sir John Thomas Podger, 1878–1933, vol. III
Rowland, John William, 1852–1925, vol. II
Rowland, Sir Leonard Bromfield, 1862–1939, vol. III
Rowland, Col Michael Carmichael, 1862–1947, vol. IV
Rowland, Col Thomas, 1831–1914, vol. I
Rowland, Sir Wentworth Lowe, 2nd Bt, 1909–1970, vol. VI
Rowland, Sir William, 1858–1945, vol. IV
Rowland-Brown, Lilian Kate; *see* Brown.
Rowlands, Sir Alun; *see* Rowlands, Sir R. A.
Rowlands, Sir Archibald, 1892–1953, vol. V
Rowlands, Rev. David, 1836–1907, vol. I
Rowlands, Ernest Brown B.; *see* Bowen-Rowlands.
Rowlands, Sir Gwilym, 1878–1949, vol. IV
Rowlands, Horace, 1869–1954, vol. V
Rowlands, Gen. Sir Hugh, 1829–1909, vol. I
Rowlands, James, 1851–1920, vol. II
Rowlands, John Wilfred, 1869–1948, vol. IV
Rowlands, Moses John, 1876–1932, vol. III

Rowlands, Sir (Richard) Alun, 1885–1977, vol. VII
Rowlands, Robert Pugh, 1874–1933, vol. III
Rowlands, Rowland, *died* 1935, vol. III
Rowlands, W. Bowen, *died* 1906, vol. I
Rowlands, W. S., *died* 1939, vol. III
Rowlandson, Edmund James, 1882–1962, vol. VI
Rowlatt, Charles James, 1894–1959, vol. V
Rowlatt, Sir Frederick Terry, 1865–1950, vol. IV
Rowlatt, Sir John, 1898–1956, vol. V
Rowlatt, Rt Hon. Sir Sidney Arthur Taylor, 1862–1945, vol. IV
Rowledge, A. J., *died* 1957, vol. V
Rowlette, Robert James, 1873–1944, vol. IV
Rowley, Baron (Life Peer); Arthur Henderson, 1893–1968, vol. VI
Rowley, Alec, 1892–1958, vol. V
Rowley, Adm. Charles John, 1832–1919, vol. II
Rowley, Lt-Col Sir Charles Samuel, 6th Bt (*cr* 1786), 1891–1962, vol. VI
Rowley, Brig.-Gen. Frank George Mathias, 1866–1949, vol. IV
Rowley, Rev. Sir George Charles Augustus, 4th Bt (*cr* 1836), 1869–1924, vol. II
Rowley, Sir George Charles Erskine, 3rd Bt (*cr* 1836), 1844–1922, vol. II
Rowley, George Fydell, 1851–1933, vol. III
Rowley, Captain Sir George William, 5th Bt (*cr* 1836), 1896–1953, vol. V
Rowley, Rev. Harold Henry, 1890–1969, vol. VI
Rowley, Hercules Douglas Edward, 1859–1945, vol. IV
Rowley, Hon. Hercules Langford, 1828–1904, vol. I
Rowley, Captain Howard Fiennes Julius, 1868–1948, vol. IV
Rowley, Hon. Hugh, 1833–1908, vol. I
Rowley, Ven. Hugh Edward, *died* 1938, vol. III
Rowley, Sir Joshua Thellusson, 5th Bt (*cr* 1786), 1838–1931, vol. III
Rowley, Sir William Joshua, 6th Bt (*cr* 1836), 1891–1971, vol. VII
Rowley, Rev. William Walter, 1812–1907, vol. I
Rowley-Conwy, Rear-Adm. Rafe Grenville; *see* Conwy.
Rowntree, Arnold Stephenson, 1872–1951, vol. V
Rowntree, Arthur, 1861–1949, vol. IV
Rowntree, B. Seebohm, 1871–1954, vol. V
Rowntree, Cecil, *died* 1943, vol. IV
Rowntree, Ernest William, 1877–1936, vol. III
Rowntree, Joseph, 1836–1925, vol. II
Roworth, Edward, 1880–1964, vol. VI
Rowse, Herbert James, *died* 1963, vol. VI
Rowse, William Crapo, 1883–1961, vol. VI
Rowsell, Mary Catharine, vol. II
Rowsell, Philip Foale, 1864–1946, vol. IV
Rowsell, Rev. Walter Frederick, 1837–1924, vol. II
Rowson, Edmund, *died* 1951, vol. V
Rowson, Guy, *died* 1937, vol. III
Rowton, 1st Baron, 1838–1903, vol. I
Roxburgh, Alexander Bruce, *died* 1953, vol. V
Roxburgh, Archibald Cathcart, 1886–1954, vol. V
Roxburgh, Eleanor Mary Ann, (Lady Roxburgh), *died* 1929, vol. III

Roxburgh, Francis, 1850–1935, vol. III
Roxburgh, Sir James; see Roxburgh, Sir T. J. Y.
Roxburgh, Sir John Archibald, 1854–1937, vol. III
Roxburgh, John Fergusson, 1888–1954, vol. V
Roxburgh, Sir (Thomas) James (Young), 1892–1974, vol. VII
Roxburgh, Sir Thomas Laurence, 1853–1945, vol. IV
Roxburghe, 8th Duke of, 1876–1932, vol. III
Roxburghe, 9th Duke of, 1913–1974, vol. VII
Roxburghe, Duchess of; (Anne Emily), died 1923, vol. II
Roxby, Rev. Edmund Lally, 1844–1912, vol. I
Roxby, Captain Herbert, 1848–1905, vol. I
Roxby, Percy Maude, 1880–1947, vol. IV
Roy, Sir Bijoy Prosad S.; see Singh Roy.
Roy, Camille, 1870–1943, vol. IV
Roy, Catherine Murray, died 1976, vol. VII
Roy, Charles T., 1854–1897, vol. I
Roy, Donald Whatley, 1881–1960, vol. V
Roy, Ferdinand, 1873–1948, vol. IV
Roy, Sir Ganen, 1872–1943, vol. IV
Roy, James Alexander, died 1973, vol. VII
Roy, Brig.-Gen. John William Gascoigne, 1863–1941, vol. IV
Roy, Lt-Col Joseph Edensor Gascoigne, 1872–1935, vol. III
Roy, Most Rev. Paul Eugene, 1859–1926, vol. II
Roy, Comdr Robert Stewart, 1878–1924, vol. II
Roy, Sir Satyendra Nath, 1888–1955, vol. V
Royall, Kenneth Claiborne, 1894–1971, vol. VII
Royce, Sir (Frederick) Henry, 1st Bt, 1863–1933, vol. III
Royce, Sir Henry; see Royce, Sir F. H.
Royce, William Stapleton, 1857–1924, vol. II
Royde Smith, Naomi Gwladys, died 1964, vol. VI
Royden, 1st Baron, 1871–1950, vol. IV
Royden, (Agnes) Maude, (Mrs G. W. H. Shaw), 1876–1956, vol. V
Royden, Sir Ernest Bland, 3rd Bt, 1873–1960, vol. V
Royden, Sir John Ledward, 4th Bt, 1907–1976, vol. VII
Royden, Maude; see Royden, A. M.
Royden, Sir Thomas Bland, 1st Bt, 1831–1917, vol. II
Royds, Vice-Adm. Sir Charles William Rawson, 1876–1931, vol. III
Royds, Col Sir Clement Molyneux, 1842–1916, vol. II
Royds, Sir Edmund, 1860–1946, vol. IV
Royds, Rev. F. C., 1825–1913, vol. I
Royds, Rev. Gilbert Twemlow, 1845–1933, vol. III
Royds, Adm. Sir Percy Molyneux Rawson, 1874–1955, vol. V
Royds, William Massy, 1879–1951, vol. V
Roylance, Robert Walker, 1882–1962, vol. VI
Royle, Baron (Life Peer); Charles Royle, 1896–1975, vol. VII
Royle, Arnold, 1837–1919, vol. II
Royle, Rev. Canon Arthur, 1895–1973, vol. VII
Royle, Charles, 1872–1963, vol. VI
Royle, Sir George, 1861–1949, vol. IV

Royle, Adm. Sir Guy Charles Cecil, 1885–1954, vol. V
Royle, Rear-Adm. Henry Lucius Fanshawe, 1849–1906, vol. I
Royle, Joseph Ralph Edward John, 1844–1929, vol. III
Royle, Sir Lancelot Carrington, 1898–1978, vol. VII
Royle, Col Reginald George, 1887–1938, vol. III
Royle, Thomas Wright, 1882–1969, vol. VI
Royle, Rev. Vernon Peter Fanshawe Archer, 1854–1929, vol. III
Royston, Viscount; Philip Simon Prospero Lindley Rupert Yorke, 1938–1973, vol. VII
Royston, Brig.-Gen. John Robinson, 1860–1942, vol. IV
Royston, Rt Rev. Peter Sorenson, 1830–1915, vol. I
Roze, Marie, 1846–1926, vol. II
Roze, Raymond, 1875–1920, vol. II
Roze-Perkins, J. H. Raymond; see Roze, Raymond.
Rube, Charles, 1852–1914, vol. I
Rubens, Paul Alfred, 1875–1917, vol. II
Rubie, Rev. Alfred Edward, 1863–1948, vol. IV
Rubie, Lt-Col Claude Blake, 1888–1939, vol. III
Rubie, John Fonthill, died 1907, vol. I
Rubinstein, Harold Frederick, 1891–1975, vol. VII
Rubinstein, Helena, (Princess Gourielli), 1871–1965, vol. VI
Rubra, Edward John, 1902–1974, vol. VII
Ruck, Berta, (Mrs Oliver Onions), 1878–1978, vol. VII
Ruck, Maj.-Gen. Sir Richard Matthews, 1851–1935, vol. III
Ruck Keene, Vice-Adm. Philip, 1897–1977, vol. VII
Ruck Keene, Adm. William George Elmhirst, 1867–1935, vol. III
Rücker, Sir Arthur William, 1848–1915, vol. I (A)
Ruckstull, Frederick Wellington, 1853–1942, vol. IV
Rudd, Surg. Rear-Adm. Eric Thomas Sutherland, 1902–1977, vol. VII
Rudd, G(eoffrey) Burkitt (Whitcomb), 1908–1975, vol. VII
Rudd, Col Thomas William, 1869–1943, vol. IV
Ruddell, Ven. Joseph, 1866–1941, vol. IV
Rudderham, Rt Rev. Joseph Edward, 1899–1979, vol. VII
Ruddle, Lt-Col Sir (George) Kenneth (Fordham), 1903–1979, vol. VII
Ruddle, Lt-Col Sir Kenneth; see Ruddle, Lt-Col Sir G. K. F.
Ruddock, Ven. David, died 1920, vol. II
Ruddock, Richard, 1837–1908, vol. I
Ruddock, Thomas Emerson, 1873–1932, vol. III
Rudgard, Rev. R. W., died 1933, vol. III
Rudge, Mrs Florence H.; see Haynes-Rudge.
Rudini, Antonio Starrabba, Marquis di, 1839–1908, vol. I
Rudkin, Brig.-Gen. Charles Mark Clement, 1872–1957, vol. V
Rudkin, George Drury, 1879–1929, vol. III
Rudkin, Brig.-Gen. William Charles Eric, 1875–1930, vol. III

Rudler, Frederick William, 1840–1915, vol. I
Rudler, Gustave, 1872–1957, vol. V
Rudmose-Brown, Robert Neal, 1879–1957, vol. V
Rudmose-Brown, Thomas Brown, 1878–1942, vol. IV
Rudolf, Rev. Edward de Montjoie, 1852–1933, vol. III
Rudolf, Robert Dawson, 1865–1941, vol. IV
Rudolf, Robert de Montjoie, 1856–1932, vol. III
Rudolph, Felix; see Scatcherd, F. R.
Rueff, Jacques, 1896–1978, vol. VII
Ruegg, Alfred Henry, died 1941, vol. IV
Ruff, Howard, died 1928, vol. II
Ruffer, Sir Marc Armand, 1859–1917, vol. II
Ruffside, 1st Viscount, 1879–1958, vol. V
Rugby, 1st Baron, 1877–1969, vol. VI
Rugge-Price, Sir Charles; see Price.
Rugge-Price, Sir Charles Frederick; see Price.
Rugge-Price, Lt-Col Sir Charles James Napier; see Price.
Ruggeri, Vincenzo G.; see Giuffrida-Ruggeri.
Ruggles, Maj.-Gen. John, 1827–1919, vol. II
Ruggles-Brise, Archibald Weyland, 1853–1939, vol. III
Ruggles-Brise, Col Sir Edward Archibald, 1st Bt, 1882–1942, vol. IV
Ruggles-Brise, Sir Evelyn John, 1857–1935, vol. III
Ruggles-Brise, Maj.-Gen. Sir Harold Goodeve, 1864–1927, vol. II
Ruggles Brise, Col Sir Samuel; see Brise.
Rugman, Sir Francis Dudley, 1894–1946, vol. IV
Rukidi III, HH Sir George David Kamurasi, 1906–1966, vol. VI
Rule, Frank Gordon, 1882–1965, vol. VI
Rule, Mrs Mollie, 1899–1965, vol. VI
Rumball, Air Vice-Marshal Sir Aubrey; see Rumball, Air Vice-Marshal Sir C. A.
Rumball, Air Vice-Marshal Sir (Campion) Aubrey, 1904–1975, vol. VII
Rumble, Sir Bertram Thomas, 1875–1949, vol. IV
Rumbold, Captain Charles E. A. L., 1872–1943, vol. IV
Rumbold, Rev. Canon Charles Robert, died 1973, vol. VII
Rumbold, Etheldred, (Lady Rumbold), 1879–1964, vol. VI
Rumbold, Rt Hon. Sir Horace, 8th Bt, 1829–1913, vol. I
Rumbold, Rt Hon. Sir Horace George Montagu, 9th Bt, 1869–1941, vol. IV
Rumbold, Col William Edwin, 1870–1947, vol. IV
Rumboll, Arthur Charles, 1869–1935, vol. III
Rumford, R. Kennerley, 1870–1957, vol. V
Ruml, Beardsley, 1894–1960, vol. V
Rumney, Abraham Wren, 1863–1942, vol. IV
Rumsey, Almaric, 1825–1899, vol. I
Rumsey, Harry Victor, 1898–1971, vol. VII
Rumsey, Robert Murray, 1849–1922, vol. II
Runciman, 1st Baron, 1847–1937, vol. III
Runciman of Doxford, 1st Viscount, 1870–1949, vol. IV
Runciman of Doxford, Viscountess, (Hilda), died 1956, vol. V
Runciman, Philip, died 1953, vol. V

Runcorn, Baron (Life Peer); Dennis Forwood Vosper, 1916–1968, vol. VI
Rundall, Lt-Col Charles Frank, 1871–1951, vol. V
Rundall, Gen. Francis Hornblow, 1823–1908, vol. I
Rundall, Col Frank Montagu, 1851–1930, vol. III
Rundell, Matthew Adkins, 1856–1935, vol. III
Rundle, Col George Richard Tyrrell, 1860–1947, vol. IV
Rundle, Gen. Sir (Henry Macleod) Leslie, 1856–1934, vol. III
Rundle, Gen. Sir Leslie; see Rundle, Gen. Sir H. M. L.
Rundle, Rear-Adm. Mark, 1871–1958, vol. V
Runge, Rev. Charles Herman Schmettau, 1889–1970, vol. VI
Runge, Norah Cecil, (Mrs Thomas A. Ross), 1884–1978, vol. VII
Runge, Sir Peter Francis, 1909–1970, vol. VI
Runnett, Henry Brian, 1935–1970, vol. VI
Runtz, Sir John Johnson, 1842–1922, vol. II
Ruse, Harold Stanley, 1905–1974, vol. VII
Rushbrook Williams, Laurence Frederick; see Williams.
Rushbrooke, Vice-Adm. Edmund Gerard Noel, 1892–1972, vol. VII
Rushbrooke, Rev. James Henry, 1870–1947, vol. IV
Rushbrooke, William George, 1849–1926, vol. II
Rushbury, Sir Henry George, 1889–1968, vol. VI
Rushcliffe, 1st Baron, 1872–1949, vol. IV
Rushmore, Frederick Margetson, 1869–1933, vol. III
Rusholme, 1st Baron, 1890–1977, vol. VII
Rushout, Sir Charles Hamilton, 4th Bt, 1868–1931, vol. III
Rushton, Sir Arnold, 1870–1930, vol. III
Rushton, Vice-Adm. Edward Astley Astley-, 1879–1935, vol. III
Rushton, George R., died 1948, vol. IV
Rushton, Major Harold P., 1895–1968, vol. VI
Rushton, Martin Amsler, 1903–1970, vol. VI
Rushton, Sir Reginald Fielding, died 1979, vol. VII
Rushton, William Albert Hugh, 1901–1980, vol. VII
Rushton, William S., 1850–1924, vol. II
Rushworth, Geoffrey Harrington, 1899–1969, vol. VI
Rusk, Robert Robertson, 1879–1972, vol. VII
Ruskin, John, 1819–1900, vol. I
Russ, Sidney, 1879–1963, vol. VI
Russel, James, 1858–1939, vol. III
Russell, 2nd Earl, 1865–1931, vol. III
Russell, 3rd Earl, 1872–1970, vol. VI
Russell, Countess; (Elizabeth Mary), died 1941, vol. IV
Russell, Baron (Life Peer); Charles Russell, 1832–1900, vol. I
Russell, 1st Baron, 1834–1920, vol. II
Russell, Hon. Lord; Albert Russell, 1884–1975, vol. VII
Russell of Killowen, Baron (Life Peer); Frank Russell, 1867–1946, vol. IV
Russell, Albert; see Russell, Hon. Lord.

Russell, Captain Sir Alec Charles, 2nd Bt (*cr* 1916), 1894–1938, vol. III
Russell, Alexander, 1861–1943, vol. IV
Russell, Alexander David, 1864–1934, vol. III
Russell, Col Alexander Fraser, 1856–1938, vol. III
Russell, Hon. Sir (Alexander) Fraser, 1876–1952, vol. V
Russell, Lord Alexander George, 1821–1907, vol. I
Russell, Col Sir Alexander James Hutchison, 1882–1958, vol. V
Russell, Alexander Smith, 1888–1972, vol. VII
Russell, Brig.-Gen. Hon. Alexander Victor Frederick Villiers, 1874–1965, vol. VI
Russell, Sir Alexander West, 1879–1961, vol. VI
Russell, Alfred Ernest, 1870–1944, vol. IV
Russell, Rev. Alfred Francis, *died* 1936, vol. III
Russell, Sir Alison, 1875–1948, vol. IV
Russell, Maj.-Gen. Sir Andrew Hamilton, 1868–1960, vol. V
Russell, Archibald George Blomefield, 1879–1955, vol. V
Russell, Hon. Arthur, 1861–1907, vol. I
Russell, Sir Arthur Edward Ian Montagu, 6th Bt (*cr* 1812), 1878–1964, vol. VI
Russell, Gen. Sir Baker Creed, 1837–1911, vol. I
Russell, Ben Harold, 1891–1979, vol. VII
Russell, Hon. Benjamin, 1849–1935, vol. III
Russell, Hon. Sir Charles, 1st Bt (*cr* 1916), 1863–1928, vol. II
Russell, Charles Alfred, 1855–1926, vol. II
Russell, Charles Barrett, 1823–1911, vol. I
Russell, Rev. Charles Dickenson, *died* 1915, vol. II
Russell, Rev. Charles Frank, 1882–1951, vol. V
Russell, Charles Gilchrist, 1840–1916, vol. II
Russell, Sir (Charles) Lennox (Somerville), 1872 1960, vol. V
Russell, Charles Pearce, 1887–1961, vol. VI
Russell, Charles Scott, 1912–1971, vol. VII
Russell, Charles Taze, (Pastor Russell), 1852–1916, vol. II
Russell, Hon. Claud Eustace H.; *see* Hamilton-Russell.
Russell, Sir Claud Frederick William, 1871–1959, vol. V
Russell, Hon. Cyril, 1866–1920, vol. II
Russell, Sir David, 1872–1956, vol. V
Russell, Lt-Gen. Sir Dudley, 1896–1978, vol. VII
Russell, Lt-Col Edmund Stuart Eardley Wilmot E.; *see* Eardley-Russell.
Russell, Rev. Edward Francis, 1844–1925, vol. II
Russell, Hon. Edward John, 1879–1925, vol. II
Russell, Sir (Edward) John, 1872–1965, vol. VI
Russell, Sir Edward Lechmere, 1818–1904, vol. I
Russell, Edward Stuart, 1887–1954, vol. V
Russell, Madame Ella, 1864–1935, vol. III
Russell, Hon. (Francis Albert) Rollo, 1849–1914, vol. I
Russell, Maj.-Gen. Frank Shirley, 1840–1912, vol. I
Russell, Hon. Sir Fraser; *see* Russell, Hon. Sir A. F.
Russell, Hon. Frederick Gustavus H.; *see* Hamilton-Russell.

Russell, Frederick Vernon, 1870–1942, vol. IV
Russell, Sir George, 4th Bt, 1828–1898, vol. I
Russell, Sir George Arthur Charles, 5th Bt (*cr* 1812), 1868–1944, vol. IV
Russell, George Clifford Dowsett, 1901–1970, vol. VI
Russell, Maj.-Gen. George Neville, 1899–1971, vol. VII
Russell, Rev. George Stanley, *died* 1957, vol. V
Russell, George William, 1867–1935, vol. III
Russell, Rt Hon. George William Erskine, 1853–1919, vol. II
Russell, Adm. Gerald Walter, 1850–1928, vol. II
Russell, Sir Gordon; *see* Russell, Sir S. G.
Russell, Hon. Frederick Gustavus H.; *see* Hamilton-Russell.
Russell, Sir Guthrie; *see* Russell, Sir T. G.
Russell, Col Guy Hamilton, 1882–1958, vol. V
Russell, Adm. Hon. Sir Guy Herbrand Edward, 1898–1977, vol. VII
Russell, Gyrth, 1892–1970, vol. VI
Russell, Hamer, *died* 1941, vol. IV
Russell, Harold G. Bedford, 1886–1957, vol. V
Russell, Harold John Hastings, 1868–1926, vol. II
Russell, Henry, 1813–1900, vol. I
Russell, Henry Blythe Westrap, 1868–1912, vol. I
Russell, Henry Chamberlain, 1836–1907, vol. I
Russell, Henry Norris, 1877–1957, vol. V
Russell, Rear-Adm. Sir (Henshaw) Robert, 1875–1957, vol. V
Russell, Air Vice-Marshal Herbert Bainbrigge, 1895–1963, vol. VI
Russell, Herbert John, 1890–1949, vol. IV
Russell, Sir Herbert William Henry, 1869–1944, vol. IV
Russell, Lt-Col Horatio Douglas, 1874–1931, vol. III
Russell, James, 1839–1923, vol. II
Russell, Sir James Alexander, 1846–1918, vol. II
Russell, James Burn, 1837–1905, vol. I
Russell, Rt Rev. James Curdie, 1830–1925, vol. II
Russell, James George, 1848–1918, vol. II
Russell, Captain James Reginald, 1893–1920, vol. II
Russell, James Samuel Risien, *died* 1939, vol. III
Russell, Sir John; *see* Russell, Sir E. J.
Russell, John Archibald, 1816–1899, vol. I
Russell, Air Vice-Marshal John Bernard, 1916–1978, vol. VII
Russell, Air Cdre John Cannan, 1896–1956, vol. V
Russell, Maj.-Gen. John Cecil, 1839–1909, vol. I
Russell, John Eaton Nevill, 1911–1970, vol. VI
Russell, John Francis Robert V.; *see* Vaughan-Russell.
Russell, Maj.-Gen. John Joshua, 1862–1941, vol. IV
Russell, Rt Rev. John Keith, 1916–1979, vol. VII
Russell, Sir John Weir, 1893–1978, vol. VII
Russell, Sir Lennox; *see* Russell, Sir C. L. S.
Russell, Leonard, 1906–1974, vol. VII
Russell, Leonard James, 1884–1971, vol. VII
Russell, Mrs Lilian M., 1875–1949, vol. IV
Russell, Louis Pitman, 1850–1914, vol. I
Russell, Mabel; *see* Philipson, Mrs H.
Russell, Rev. Matthew, 1834–1912, vol. I

Russell, Maj.-Gen. Sir Michael William, 1860–1949, vol. IV

Russell, Brig. Nelson, 1897–1971, vol. VII

Russell, Hon. Sir Odo William Theophilus Villiers, 1870–1951, vol. V

Russell, Patrick Wimberley D.; see Dill-Russell.

Russell, Sir Peter Nicol, died 1905, vol. I

Russell, Col Reginald Edmund Maghlin, 1879–1950, vol. IV

Russell, Reginald James Kingston, 1883–1943, vol. IV

Russell, Reginald Pemberton, 1860–1917, vol. II

Russell, Richard John, 1872–1943, vol. IV

Russell, Col Richard Tyler, 1875–1940, vol. III

Russell, Ritchie; see Russell, W. R.

Russell, Robert, 1843–1910, vol. I

Russell, Rear-Adm. Sir Robert; see Russell, Rear-Adm. Sir H. R.

Russell, Sir Robert Edwin, 1890–1972, vol. VII

Russell, Robert Tor, 1888–1972, vol. VII

Russell, Hon. Rollo; see Russell, Hon. F. A. R.

Russell, Sir Ronald Stanley, 1904–1974, vol. VII

Russell, Rosalind, (Mrs F. Brisson), 1911–1976, vol. VII

Russell, Captain Stuart Hugh Minto, 1909–1943, vol. IV

Russell, Sir (Sydney) Gordon, 1892–1980, vol. VII

Russell, Thomas, 1830–1904, vol. I

Russell, Sir (Thomas) Guthrie, 1887–1963, vol. VI

Russell, Rt Hon. Sir Thomas Wallace, 1st Bt, 1841–1920, vol. II

Russell, Sir Thomas Wentworth, 1879–1954, vol. V

Russell, Col Valentine Cubitt, 1896–1976, vol. VII

Russell, Rev. Vernon William, 1861–1953, vol. V

Russell, Hon. Victor Alexander Frederick Villiers, 1874–1965, vol. VI

Russell, Sir Walter Westley, 1867–1949, vol. IV

Russell, Sir William, 3rd Bt (cr 1832), 1865–1915, vol. I (A)

Russell, William, 1868–1931, vol. III

Russell, William, 1859–1937, vol. III (A), vol. IV

Russell, William, 1852–1940, vol. III

Russell, William Clark, 1844–1911, vol. I

Russell, Sir William Fleming, died 1925, vol. II

Russell, Sir William Howard, 1820–1907, vol. I

Russell, William James, 1830–1910, vol. I

Russell, Col William Kelson, 1873–1949, vol. IV

Russell, (William) Ritchie, 1903–1980, vol. VII

Russell, Captain Sir William Russell, 1838–1913, vol. I

Russell, Captain Wilmot Peregrine Maitland, 1874–1950, vol. IV

Russell-Astley, Bertram Frankland F.; see Astley.

Russell-Astley, Henry Jacob Delaval F.; see Astley.

Russell-Brown, Col Claude, 1873–1939, vol. III

Russell-Johnson, Lt-Col Walter, 1888–1940, vol. III

Russell-Wells, Sir Sydney, 1869–1924, vol. II

Russia, Grand Duke Michael of, 1861–1929, vol. III

Russon, Sir Clayton; see Russon, Sir W. C.

Russon, Sir (William) Clayton, 1895–1968, vol. VI

Rust, William, 1903–1949, vol. IV

Rust, William Thomas Cutler, 1874–1937, vol. III

Rustomjee, Heerjeebhoy Manackjee, died 1904, vol. I

Ruston, Lt-Col Joseph Seward, 1869–1939, vol. III

Ruston, Col Reginald Seward, 1867–1963, vol. VI

Ruth, Rev. Thomas E., 1875–1956, vol. V

Ruthen, Sir Charles Tamlin, 1871–1926, vol. II

Rutherfoord, Captain J. B., born 1864, vol. II

Rutherford, 1st Baron, 1871–1937, vol. III

Rutherford, Hon. Alexander Cameron, 1857–1941, vol. IV

Rutherford, Col Charles, 1858–1922, vol. II

Rutherford, Very Rev. Claude Anselm, 1886–1952, vol. V

Rutherford, Sir David Carter, 1868–1948, vol. IV

Rutherford, Sir Ernest Victor Buckley, died 1929, vol. III

Rutherford, George, 1818–1904, vol. I

Rutherford, Gideon Campbell, 1888–1971, vol. VII

Rutherford, James Rankin, 1882–1967, vol. VI

Rutherford, Sir John, 1st Bt (cr 1916), 1854–1932, vol. III

Rutherford, Sir John George, 1886–1967, vol. VI

Rutherford, John Gunion, 1857–1923, vol. II

Rutherford, Sir John Hugo, 2nd Bt (cr 1923), 1887–1942, vol. IV

Rutherford, John Rutherford, 1904–1957, vol. V

Rutherford, Dame Margaret, 1892–1972, vol. VII

Rutherford, Mark; see White, William Hale.

Rutherford, Sir Robert, 1854–1930, vol. III

Rutherford, Sir Thomas George, 1886–1957, vol. V

Rutherford, Brig.-Gen. Thomas John, 1893–1975, vol. VII

Rutherford, Vickerman Henzell, 1860–1934, vol. III

Rutherford, Sir Watson; see Rutherford, Sir William W.

Rutherford, William, 1839–1899, vol. I

Rutherford, Rev. William Gunion, 1853–1907, vol. I

Rutherford, William John, 1868–1930, vol. III

Rutherford, Sir (William) Watson, 1st Bt (cr 1923), 1853–1927, vol. II

Rutherfurd, Andrew, 1835–1906, vol. I

Rutherfurd, James Hunter, 1864–1927, vol. II

Rutherfurd, Maj.-Gen. Thomas Walter, 1832–1918, vol. II

Rutherston, Albert Daniel, 1881–1953, vol. V

Ruths, Johannes, 1879–1935, vol. III

Ruthven of Freeland, 8th Lord, 1838–1921, vol. II

Ruthven of Freeland, 9th Lord, 1870–1956, vol. V

Ruthven, Col Hon. (Christian) Malise Hore, 1880–1969, vol. VI

Ruthven, Col Hon. Malise Hore-; see Ruthven, Col Hon. C. M. H.

Ruthven-Murray, Alan James; see Murray.

Rutkowski, Sir Miecislas de, 1853–1941, vol. IV

Rutland, 7th Duke of, 1818–1906, vol. I

Rutland, 8th Duke of, 1852–1925, vol. II

Rutland, 9th Duke of, 1886–1940, vol. III

Rutland, Duchess of; (Violet), died 1937, vol. III

Rutland, Charles, 1858–1943, vol. IV

Rutledge, Hon. Sir Arthur, 1843–1917, vol. II

Rutledge, Sir Guy; see Rutledge, Sir J. G.
Rutledge, Sir (John) Guy, 1872–1930, vol. III
Rutledge, Wiley, 1894–1949, vol. IV
Ruttan, Robert F., 1856–1930, vol. III
Rutter, Frank V. P., 1876–1937, vol. III
Rutter, Sir Frederick William Pascoe, 1859–1949, vol. IV
Rutter, Herbert Hugh, 1905–1975, vol. VII
Rutter, Owen, 1889–1944, vol. IV
Rutter, W(illiam) Arthur, 1890–1980, vol. VII
Ruttledge, David Knox, 1865–1931, vol. III
Ruttledge, Hugh, 1884–1961, vol. VI
Ruttledge, Lt-Col Thomas Geoffrey, 1882–1958, vol. V
Ruvigny and Raineval, 9th Marquis of, 1868–1921, vol. II
Ruvigny and Raineval, 10th Marquis of, 1903–1941, vol. IV
Ruxton, Major U. FitzHerbert, 1873–1954, vol. V
Ryall, Sir Charles, died 1922, vol. II
Ryalls, Hon. Captain Harry Douglas, 1887–1964, vol. VI
Ryan, Alfred Patrick, 1900–1972, vol. VII
Ryan, Sir Andrew, 1876–1949, vol. IV
Ryan, Sir Charles Lister, 1831–1920, vol. II
Ryan, Brig.-Gen. Charles Montgomerie, 1867–1935, vol. III
Ryan, Maj.-Gen. Sir Charles Snodgrass, 1853–1926, vol. II
Ryan, Cornelius John, 1920–1974, vol. VII
Ryan, Curteis Norwood, 1891–1969, vol. VI
Ryan, Captain Cyril Percy, 1875–1940, vol. III
Ryan, Major Denis George Jocelyn, 1885–1927, vol. II
Ryan, Edward Joseph, 1845–1923, vol. II
Ryan, Col Eugene, 1873–1951, vol. V
Ryan, Most Rev. Finbar, 1882–1975, vol. VII
Ryan, Adm. Frank Edward Cavendish, 1865–1945, vol. IV
Ryan, Bt Major George Julian, 1878–1915, vol. I
Ryan, Sir Gerald Ellis, 2nd Bt, 1888–1947, vol. IV
Ryan, Sir Gerald Hemmington, 1st Bt, died 1937, vol. III
Ryan, Hugh, 1873–1931, vol. III
Ryan, Most Rev. Hugh Edward, 1888–1977, vol. VII
Ryan, James, 1892–1970, vol. VI
Ryan, John, 1894–1975, vol. VII
Ryan, Rt Rev. John A., 1869–1945, vol. IV
Ryan, John Francis, 1894–1978, vol. VII
Ryan, Mary, died 1961, vol. VI
Ryan, Mervyn Frederick, died 1952, vol. V
Ryan, Patrick Francis William, 1873–1939, vol. III
Ryan, Patrick John McNamara, 1919–1978, vol. VII
Ryan, Most Rev. Richard, 1881–1957, vol. V
Ryan, Lt-Col Rupert Sumner, 1884–1952, vol. V
Ryan, Sir Thomas, 1879–1934, vol. III
Ryan, Thomas Joseph, 1876–1921, vol. II
Ryan, Wing-Comdr William John, 1883–1959, vol. V
Ryan, William Patrick, died 1942, vol. IV
Ryckman, Hon. Edmond Baird, 1866–1934, vol. III

Rycroft, Sir Benjamin William, 1902–1967, vol. VI
Rycroft, Bt Major Julian Neil Oscar, 1892–1928, vol. II
Rycroft, Sir Nelson Edward Oliver, 6th Bt, 1886–1958, vol. V
Rycroft, Sir Richard Nelson, 5th Bt, 1859–1925, vol. II
Rycroft, Maj.-Gen. Sir William Henry, 1861–1925, vol. II
Ryde, John Walter, 1898–1961, vol. VI
Ryde, Walter Cranley, 1856–1938, vol. III
Ryder, Rev. Alexander Roderick, 1852–1919, vol. II
Ryder, Charles Foster, died 1942, vol. IV
Ryder, Col Charles Henry Dudley, 1868–1945, vol. IV
Ryder, Lady Frances, 1888–1965, vol. VI
Ryder, Col Francis John, 1866–1920, vol. II
Ryder, Sir Gerard, 1909–1973, vol. VII
Rydge, Sir Norman Bede, 1900–1980, vol. VII
Rye, Frank Gibbs, 1874–1948, vol. IV
Rye, Reginald Arthur, 1876–1945, vol. IV
Rye, Walter, 1843–1929, vol. III
Ryerson, Maj.-Gen. George Sterling, 1854–1926, vol. II
Rylah, Hon. Sir Arthur Gordon, 1909–1974, vol. VII
Ryland, Charles Ivor Phipson Smith, 1898–1929, vol. III
Ryland, Edward Charles, 1864–1941, vol. IV
Ryland, Frederick, 1854–1902, vol. I
Ryland, Henry, died 1924, vol. II
Rylands, Louis Gordon, 1862–1942, vol. IV
Rylands, Sir Peter; see Rylands, Sir W. P.
Rylands, Sir (William) Peter, 1st Bt, 1868–1948, vol. IV
Ryle, Arthur Johnston, 1857–1915, vol. I
Ryle, George Bodley, 1902–1978, vol. VII
Ryle, Gilbert, 1900–1976, vol. VII
Ryle, Herbert, 1881–1966, vol. VI
Ryle, Rt Rev. Herbert Edward, 1856–1925, vol. II
Ryle, John Alfred, 1889–1950, vol. IV
Ryle, Rt Rev. John Charles, 1816–1900, vol. I
Ryle, Reginald John, 1854–1922, vol. II
Rylett, Rev. Harold, 1851–1936, vol. III
Ryley, Madeleine Lucette, 1868–1934, vol. III
Rymer, Sir Joseph Sykes, 1841–1923, vol. II
Rymill, John Riddoch, 1905–1968, vol. VI
Ryner, Harry, 1872–1964, vol. VI
Ryrie, Maj.-Gen. Hon. Sir Granville de Laune, 1865–1937, vol. III

S

Sabatier, Paul, 1858–1928, vol. II
Sabatier, Paul, died 1941, vol. IV (A), vol. V
Sabatini, Rafael, 1875–1950, vol. IV
Sabelli, Humbert Anthony, 1878–1961, vol. VI
Sabin, Arthur Knowles, 1879–1959, vol. V
Sacher, Harry, 1881–1971, vol. VII
Sachin, Nawab of, 1886–1930, vol. III
Sachs, Maj.-Gen. Albert, 1904–1976, vol. VII

Sachs, Edwin O., 1870–1919, vol. II
Sachs, Rt Hon. Sir Eric, 1898–1979, vol. VII
Sachs, Nelly Leonie, 1891–1970, vol. VI
Sachse, Sir Frederic Alexander, 1878–1957, vol. V
Sackett, Alfred Barrett, 1895–1977, vol. VII
Sacks, Muriel Elsie, (Mrs Samuel Sacks); see Landau, M. E.
Sackville, 2nd Baron, 1827–1908, vol. I
Sackville, 3rd Baron, 1867–1928, vol. II
Sackville, 4th Baron, 1870–1962, vol. VI
Sackville, 5th Baron, 1901–1965, vol. VI
Sackville, Major Lionel Charles Stopford, 1891–1920, vol. II
Sackville, Lady Margaret, died 1963, vol. VI
Sackville, Col Nigel Victor S.; see Stopford Sackville.
Sackville, Sackville George Stopford, 1840–1926, vol. II
Sackville-West, Hon. V., (Victoria Mary), 1892–1962, vol. VI
Sacre, Rev. Arthur Joseph, 1862–1931, vol. III
Sadasiva Aiyar, Sir Theagaraja Aiyar, died 1927, vol. II
Sadd, Sir Clarence Thomas Albert, 1883–1962, vol. VI
Sadhu, Rai Tarak Nath, 1875–1937, vol. III
Sadleir, Michael, 1888–1957, vol. V
Sadleir-Jackson, Brig.-Gen. Lionel Warren de Vere, 1876–1932, vol. III
Sadler, Adm. Arthur Hayes, 1863–1952, vol. V
Sadler, Arthur Lindsay, 1882–1970, vol. VI
Sadler, Herbert Charles, 1872–1948, vol. IV
Sadler, Lt-Col Sir James Hayes, 1851–1922, vol. II
Sadler, Sir Michael Ernest, 1861–1943, vol. IV
Sadler, Col Sir Samuel Alexander, 1842–1911, vol. I
Sadler, Walter Dendy, 1854–1923, vol. II
Sadlier, Rt Rev. William Charles, 1867–1935, vol. III
Sadul Singh, Col Rao Bahadur, Thakur, Sir, 1881–1937, vol. III
Safford, Sir Archibald, 1892–1961, vol. VI
Safford, Col Arthur Hunt, 1873–1933, vol. III
Safford, Frank, died 1929, vol. III
Safonoff, Wassily, 1852–1918, vol. II
Sagrada, Rt Rev. V. Emanuel, 1860–1939, vol. III
Sahni, Birbal, 1891–1949, vol. IV
Sahni, Rai Bahadur Daya Ram, 1879–1939, vol. III
Sailana, Raja of, 1864–1919, vol. II
Sailana, Raja of, 1891–1961, vol. VI
Sainsbury, Rev. Charles, 1837–1915, vol. I
Sainsbury, Air Vice-Marshal Thomas Audley L.; see Langford-Sainsbury.
Saint, Charles Frederick Morris, 1886–1973, vol. VII
Saint, Lawrence Bradford, 1885–1961, vol. VI
Saint, Captain Peter Johnston J.; see Johnston-Saint.
Saint, Sir Thomas Wakelin, 1861–1928, vol. II
St Albans, 10th Duke of, 1840–1898, vol. I
St Albans, 11th Duke of, 1870–1934, vol. III
St Albans, 12th Duke of, 1874–1964, vol. VI
St Albans, Duchess of; (Grace), died 1926, vol. II
St Aldwyn, 1st Earl, 1837–1916, vol. II

St Aubyn, Alan, died 1920, vol. II
St Aubyn, Hon. Edward Stuart, 1858–1915, vol. I (A)
St Aubyn, Geoffrey Peter, born 1858, vol. II
St Aubyn, Sir Hugh M.; see Molesworth-St Aubyn.
St Aubyn, Captain Hon. Lionel Michael, 1878–1965, vol. VI
St Aubyn, Rev. Sir St A. Hender M.; see Molesworth-St Aubyn.
St Audries, 1st Baron, 1853–1917, vol. II
St Audries, 2nd Baron, 1893–1971, vol. VII
Saint Aulaire, Comte de, 1866–1954, vol. V
Saint-Clair, George; see Coudurier de Chassaigne, Joseph.
St Clair, Maj.-Gen. George James Paul, 1885–1955, vol. V
St Clair, Col James Latimer Crawshay, 1850–1940, vol. III
St Clair, Hon. Lockhart Matthew, 1855–1930, vol. III
St Clair, William; see Ford, William.
St Clair, Lt-Col William Augustus Edmond, 1854–1923, vol. II
St Clair, William Graeme, 1849–1930, vol. III
St Clair, Adm. William Home Chisholme, 1841–1905, vol. I
St Clair, Major William Lockhart, 1883–1920, vol. II
St Clair-Morford, Maj.-Gen. Albert Clarence, 1893–1945, vol. IV
St Cyres, Viscount; Stafford Harry Northcote, 1869–1926, vol. II
St Davids, 1st Viscount, 1860–1938, vol. III
St Davids, Viscountess; (Elizabeth Frances), 1884–1974, vol. VII
Saint-Denis, Michel Jacques, 1897–1971, vol. VII
St George, 6th Marquis of, born 1875, vol. III
St George, Frederick Ferris Bligh, 1908–1970, vol. VI
Saint-George, Henry, 1866–1917, vol. II
St George, Sir John, 5th Bt, 1851–1938, vol. III
St George, Sir Theophilus John, 6th Bt, 1856–1943, vol. IV
St Germans, 5th Earl of, 1835–1911, vol. I
St Germans, 6th Earl of, 1890–1922, vol. II
St Germans, 7th Earl of, 1867–1942, vol. IV
St Germans, 8th Earl of, 1870–1960, vol. V
St Helens, 1st Baron, 1912–1980, vol. VII
St Helier, Lady; (Mary), died 1931, vol. III
St John of Bletso, 17th Baron, 1876–1920, vol. II
St John of Bletso, 18th Baron, 1877–1934, vol. III
St John of Bletso, 19th Baron, 1917–1976, vol. VII
St John of Bletso, 20th Baron, 1918–1978, vol. VII
St John, Alfred, 1857–1939, vol. III
St John, Lt-Col Sir Beauchamp; see St John, Lt-Col Sir H. B.
St John, Charles Edward, 1857–1935, vol. III
St John, Col Edmund Farquhar, 1879–1945, vol. IV
St John, Vice-Adm. Francis Gerald, 1869–1947, vol. IV
St John, Sir Frederick Robert, 1831–1923, vol. II
St John, Geoffrey Robert, 1889–1972, vol. VII

St John, Brig.-Gen. George Francis William, 1861–1937, vol. III
St John, Lt-Col Sir (Henry) Beauchamp, 1874–1954, vol. V
St John, Adm. Henry Craven, died 1909, vol. I
St John, Henry Percy, 1854–1921, vol. II
St John, Hon. Joseph Wesley, 1854–1907, vol. I
St John, Rev. Maurice William Ferdinand, 1827–1914, vol. I
St John, Lt-Col Oliver Charles Beauchamp, 1907–1976, vol. VII
St John, Maj.-Gen. Richard Stukeley, 1876–1959, vol. V
St John, Hon. Rowland Tudor, 1882–1948, vol. IV
St John, Sir Spenser, 1825–1910, vol. I
St John-Brooks, Ralph Terence, 1884–1963, vol. VI
St John-Mildmay, Sir Anthony; see Mildmay.
St John-Mildmay, Sir Gerald Anthony Shaw-Lefevre; see Mildmay.
St John-Mildmay, Sir Henry Bouverie Paulet; see Mildmay.
St John-Mildmay, Sir Henry Gerald; see Mildmay.
St John-Mildmay, Major Wyndham Paulet; see Mildmay.
St John-Mildmay, Rev. Sir Neville; see Mildmay.
St John-Mildmay, Major. Wyndham Paulet; see Mildmay.
St John Perse; see Léger, Marie-René Alexis Saint-Léger.
St Johnston, Sir Reginald, 1881–1950, vol. IV
St Just, 1st Baron, 1870–1941, vol. IV
St Laurent, Rt Hon. Louis Stephen, 1882–1973, vol. VII
St Lawrence, Julian Charles G.; see Gaisford-St Lawrence.
St Leger, Evelyn, died 1944, vol. IV
St Leger, Col Henry Hungerford, 1833–1925, vol. II
St Leger, Col Stratford Edward, 1878–1935, vol. III
St Leonards, 2nd Baron, 1847–1908, vol. I
St Leonards, 3rd Baron, 1890–1972, vol. VII
St Levan, 1st Baron, 1829–1908 (this entry was not transferred to Who was Who).
St Levan, 2nd Baron, 1857–1940, vol. III
St Levan, 3rd Baron, 1895–1978, vol. VII
St Maur, Lord Ernest, 1847–1922, vol. II
St Maur, Lord Percy, 1847–1907, vol. I
St Oswald, 2nd Baron, 1857–1919, vol. II
St Oswald, 3rd Baron, 1893–1957, vol. V
St Quintin, William Herbert, 1851–1933, vol. III
Saint-Saens, Camille, 1835–1921, vol. II
St Vigeans, Hon. Lord; David Anderson, 1862–1948, vol. IV
St Vincent, 5th Viscount, 1855–1908, vol. I
St Vincent, 6th Viscount, 1859–1940, vol. III
St Vincent Ferreri, 7th Marquis of, 1880–1945, vol. IV
Sainthill, Loudon, 1919–1969, vol. VI
Sainton, Charles Prosper, 1861–1914, vol. I
Saintsbury, George Edward Bateman, 1845–1933, vol. III

Saionji, Prince, died 1940, vol. III
Sait, Edward M'Chesney, 1881–1943, vol. IV
Saiyid, Fazl Ali, Sir, 1886–1959, vol. V
Saklatvala, Sir Nowroji, 1875–1938, vol. III
Saklatvala, Shapurji, 1874–1936, vol. III
Saklatvala, Sir Sorabji Dorabji, died 1948, vol. IV (A), vol. V
Sala, Antoni, 1893–1945, vol. IV
Salaman, Charles Kensington, 1814–1901, vol. I
Salaman, Malcolm Charles, 1855–1940, vol. III
Salaman, Redcliffe Nathan, 1874–1955, vol. V
Salandra, Antonio, 1853–1931, vol. III
Salazar, Antonio de Oliveira, 1889–1970, vol. VI
Salberg, Major Frank James, 1884–1964, vol. VI
Sale, Charles Vincent, 1868–1943, vol. IV
Sale, George S., 1831–1922, vol. II
Sale, John Lewis, 1885–1973, vol. VII
Sale, Col Matthew Townsend, 1841–1913, vol. I
Sale, Sir Stephen George, 1852–1934, vol. III
Sale, Stephen Leonard, 1889–1958, vol. V
Sale, Ven. Thomas Rawlinson, 1865–1939, vol. III
Sale, Brig. Walter Morley, 1903–1976, vol. VII
Sale-Hill, Gen. Sir Rowley Sale, 1839–1916, vol. II
Saleeby, Caleb Williams, 1878–1940, vol. III
Salis-Schwabe, Maj.-Gen. George, 1843–1907, vol. I
Salisbury, 3rd Marquess of, 1830–1903, vol. I (A)
Salisbury, 4th Marquess of, 1861–1947, vol. IV
Salisbury, 5th Marquess of, 1893–1972, vol. VII
Salisbury, Lt-Col Alfred George Grazier, 1885–1942, vol. IV
Salisbury, Sir Edward James, 1886–1978, vol. VII
Salisbury, Francis, 1850–1922, vol. II
Salisbury, Frank O., 1874–1962, vol. VI
Salles, Georges Adolphe, 1889–1966, vol. VI
Salmon, Alfred, 1868–1928, vol. II
Salmon, Amedee Victor, 1857–1919, vol. II
Salmon, Balliol, 1868–1953, vol. V
Salmon, Barnett Alfred, 1895–1965, vol. VI
Salmon, Lt-Col Hon. Charles Carty, died 1917, vol. II
Salmon, Edward, 1865–1955, vol. V
Salmon, Ven. Edwin Arthur, 1832–1899, vol. I
Salmon, Sir Eric Cecil Heygate, 1896–1946, vol. IV
Salmon, Frederick John, 1882–1964, vol. VI
Salmon, Col Geoffrey Nowell, 1871–1954, vol. V
Salmon, Rev. George, 1819–1904, vol. I
Salmon, Rev. Preb. Harold Bryant, 1891–1965, vol. VI
Salmon, Harry, 1881–1950, vol. IV
Salmon, Sir Isidore, 1876–1941, vol. IV
Salmon, John Cuthbert, 1844–1917, vol. II
Salmon, Sir Julian, 1903–1978, vol. VII
Salmon, Admiral of the Fleet Sir Nowell, 1835–1912, vol. I
Salmon, Percy R., 1872–1959, vol. V
Salmon, Sir Samuel Isidore, 1900–1980, vol. VII
Salmond, Air Chief Marshal Sir Geoffrey; see Salmond, Air Chief Marshal Sir W. G. H.
Salmond, Hubert George, 1889–1946, vol. IV

Salmond, Captain Hubert Mackenzie, 1874–1947, vol. IV

Salmond, Marshal of the Royal Air Force Sir John Maitland, 1881–1968, vol. VI

Salmond, Sir John William, 1862–1924, vol. II

Salmond, Robert Williamson Asher, 1883–1953, vol. V

Salmond, Rev. Stewart Dingwall Fordyce, 1838–1905, vol. I

Salmond, Rev. William, 1835–1917, vol. II

Salmond, Maj.-Gen. Sir William, 1840–1933, vol. III

Salmond, Air Chief Marshal Sir (William) Geoffrey (Hanson), 1878–1933, vol. III

Salmone, H. Anthony, 1860–1904, vol. I

Salomons, Sir David Lionel Goldsmid-Stern-, 2nd Bt, 1851–1925, vol. II

Salomons, Hon. Sir Julian Emanuel, 1836–1909, vol. I

Saloway, Sir Reginald Harry, 1905–1959, vol. V

Salt, Dame Barbara, 1904–1975, vol. VII

Salt, Sir David Shirley, 5th Bt (cr 1869), 1930–1978, vol. VII

Salt, Sir Edward William, 1881–1970, vol. VI

Salt, Rev. Enoch, 1845–1919, vol. II

Salt, Maj.-Gen. Harold Francis, 1879–1971, vol. VII

Salt, Henry Edwin, died 1970, vol. VI

Salt, Henry Stephens, 1851–1939, vol. III

Salt, Sir John William Titus, 4th Bt (cr 1869), 1884–1953, vol. V

Salt, Sir Shirley Harris, 3rd Bt (cr 1869), 1857–1920, vol. II

Salt, Sir Thomas, 1st Bt (cr 1899), 1830–1904, vol. I

Salt, Sir Thomas Anderdon, 2nd Bt (cr 1899), 1863–1940, vol. III

Salt, Lt-Col Sir Thomas Henry, 3rd Bt (cr 1899), 1905–1965, vol. VI

Salter, 1st Baron, 1881–1975, vol. VII

Salter, Alfred, 1873–1945, vol. IV

Salter, Sir Arthur Clavell, 1859–1928, vol. II

Salter, Emma G.; see Gurney-Salter.

Salter, Frank Reyner, 1887–1967, vol. VI

Salter, Rev. Herbert Edward, 1863–1951, vol. V

Salter, Mortyn de Carle Sowerby, 1880–1923, vol. II

Salter Davies, Ernest, 1872–1955, vol. V

Saltmarsh, Sir (Edward) George, 1869–1931, vol. III

Saltmarsh, Sir George; see Saltmarsh, Sir E. G.

Saltmarsh, John, 1848–1916, vol. II

Saltmarshe, Col Philip, 1853–1941, vol. IV

Saltoun, 18th Lord, 1851–1933, vol. III

Saltoun, 19th Lord, 1886–1979, vol. VII

Saltoun, Master of; Hon. Alexander Simon Fraser, 1921–1944, vol. IV

Saltus, Edgar Evertson, 1858–1921, vol. II

Salusbury, Charles Vanne, 1887–1969, vol. VI

Salusbury, Frederic George Hamilton Piozzi, 1895–1957, vol. V

Salusbury-Trelawny, Sir John William; see Trelawny.

Salusbury-Trelawny, Sir John William Robin Maurice; see Trelawny.

Salusbury-Trelawny, Sir William Lewis; see Trelawny.

Salvage, Sir Samuel Agar, 1876–1946, vol. IV

Salvemini, Gaetano, 1873–1957, vol. V

Salvesen, Rt Hon. Lord; Edward Theodore Salvesen, 1857–1942, vol. IV

Salvesen, Edward Theodore; see Rt Hon. Lord Salvesen.

Salvidge, Rt Hon. Sir Archibald Tutton James, 1863–1928, vol. II

Salvin, Gerard Thornton, 1878–1921, vol. II

Salvin, Henry; see Salvin, M. H.

Salvin, (Marmaduke) Henry, 1849–1924, vol. II

Salvin, Osbert, 1835–1898, vol. I

Salvini, Comdr Tommaso, died 1915, vol. I (A)

Salwey, Rev. Herbert, 1842–1929, vol. III

Salwey, Rev. John, 1867–1943, vol. IV

Salzman, Louis Francis, 1878–1971, vol. VII

Samaldas, Sir Lalubhai, 1863–1936, vol. III

Samarth, Narayan Madhav, died 1926, vol. II

Sambell, Most Rev. Geoffrey Tremayne, 1914–1980, vol. VII

Sambon, Louis Westenra, died 1931, vol. III

Samborne-Palmer, Lt-Col Frederick Carey Stuckley, 1868–1950, vol. IV

Sambourne, Edward Linley, 1845–1910, vol. I

Sambrook, Henry Fabian, 1886–1935, vol. III

Samman, Lt-Col Charles Thomas, 1865–1939, vol. III

Samman, Sir Henry, 1st Bt, 1849–1928, vol. II

Samman, Sir Henry, 2nd Bt, 1881–1960, vol. V

Sammarco, Giuseppe Mario, 1873–1930, vol. III

Sammons, Albert E., 1886–1957, vol. V

Sammons, Herbert, 1896–1967, vol. VI

Sammut, Oscar, 1879–1959, vol. V

Sampayo, Sir Thomas Edward de, 1855–1927, vol. II

Sampson, Alexander Whitehead, 1859–1932, vol. III

Sampson, Col Sir Aubrey W.; see Wools-Sampson.

Sampson, Charles Henry, 1859–1936, vol. III

Sampson, Rev. Canon Christopher Bolckow, 1903–1967, vol. VI

Sampson, George, 1873–1950, vol. IV

Sampson, Rev. Gerald Victor, 1864–1928, vol. II

Sampson, Hon. Henry William, 1872–1938, vol. III

Sampson, Herbert E., 1871–1962, vol. VI

Sampson, Jack; see Sampson, Jacob Albert.

Sampson, Jacob Albert, (Jack Sampson), 1905–1976 ,vol. VII

Sampson, John, 1859–1925, vol. II

Sampson, Major Patrick, 1881–1922, vol. II

Sampson, Ralph Allen, 1866–1939, vol. III

Sampson, Hon. Victor, 1855–1940, vol. II, vol. III

Sampson, William Thomas, 1840–1902, vol. I

Sampson-Way, Maj.-Gen. Nowell FitzUpton; see Way.

Sams, Sir Hubert Arthur, 1875–1957, vol. V

Samson, Col Arthur Oliver, 1888–1955, vol. V

Samson, Charles Leopold, 1853–1923, vol. II

Samson, Air Cdre Charles Rumney, 1883–1931, vol. III

Samson, Sir (Edward) Marlay, 1869–1949, vol. IV
Samson, Sir Frederick; *see* Samson, Sir W. F.
Samson, John, 1848–1905, vol. I
Samson, Lt-Col Louis Lort Rhys, 1866–1944, vol. IV
Samson, Sir Marlay; *see* Samson, Sir E. M.
Samson, Otto William, 1900–1976, vol. VII
Samson, Sir (William) Frederick, 1892–1974, vol. VII
Samthar, Maharaja of, 1865–1936, vol. III
Samuel, 1st Viscount, 1870–1963, vol. VI
Samuel, 2nd Viscount, 1898–1978, vol. VII
Samuel, Alexander L.; *see* Lyle-Samuel.
Samuel, Sir Edward Levien, 2nd Bt (*cr* 1898), 1862–1937, vol. III
Samuel, Sir Edward Louis, 3rd Bt (*cr* 1898), 1896–1961, vol. VI
Samuel, Col Frederick Dudley, 1877–1951, vol. V
Samuel, Harold, 1879–1937, vol. III
Samuel, Rt Hon. Sir Harry Simon, 1853–1934, vol. III
Samuel, Howel Walter, 1881–1953, vol. V
Samuel, John Augustus, 1887–1965, vol. VI
Samuel, Sir John Oliver Cecil, 4th Bt (*cr* 1898), 1916–1962, vol. VI
Samuel, Sir John Smith, 1870–1934, vol. III
Samuel, Jonathan, 1853–1917, vol. II
Samuel, Marcus, 1873–1942, vol. IV
Samuel, Rev. Richard W.; *see* Wood-Samuel.
Samuel, Samuel, 1855–1934, vol. III
Samuel, Hon. Sir Saul, 1st Bt (*cr* 1898), 1820–1900, vol. I
Samuel, Sir Stuart Montagu, 1st Bt (*cr* 1912), 1856–1926, vol. II
Samuels, Rt Hon. Arthur Warren, 1852–1925, vol. II
Samuels, Herbert David, 1880–1947, vol. IV
Samuels, Moss T.; *see* Turner-Samuels.
Samuelson, Berhard Martin, 1874–1921, vol. II
Samuelson, Rt Hon. Sir Bernhard, 1st Bt, 1820–1905, vol. I
Samuelson, Cecil Llewellyn, 1882–1950, vol. IV
Samuelson, Sir Francis, 3rd Bt, 1861–1946, vol. IV
Samuelson, Godfrey Blundell, 1863–1941, vol. IV
Samuelson, Sir Henry Bernhard, 2nd Bt, 1845–1937, vol. III
Samuelson, Sir Herbert, 1865–1952, vol. V
Samut, Lt-Col Achilles, 1859–1935, vol. III
Samwell, Ven. Frederick William, 1861–1925, vol. II
San Giovanni, 12th Baron, 1866–1934, vol. III
San Giuliano, Antonino Paterno Castello, Marquis of, 1852–1914, vol. I
Sanchez-Gavito, Vicente, 1910–1976, vol. VII
Sanctuary, Rev. Charles LLoyd, 1854–1934, vol. III
Sand, Alec, 1901–1945, vol. IV
Sandall, Ray St Clair, 1924–1980, vol. VII
Sandall, Col Thomas Edward, 1869–1930, vol. III
Sandars, Lt-Col Edward Carew, 1869–1944, vol. IV
Sandars, John Drysdale, 1860–1922, vol. II
Sandars, John Eric William Graves, 1906–1974, vol. VII

Sandars, Rt Hon. John Satterfield, 1853–1934, vol. III
Sandars, Vice-Adm. Sir (Reginald) Thomas, 1904–1975, vol. VII
Sandars, Vice-Adm. Sir Thomas; *see* Sandars, Vice-Adm. Sir R. T.
Sanday, Rev. William, 1843–1920, vol. II
Sandbach, Maj.-Gen. Arthur Edmund, 1859–1928, vol. II
Sandbach, Francis Edward, 1874–1946, vol. IV
Sandbach, John Brown, *died* 1951, vol. V
Sandberg, Christer Peter, 1876–1941, vol. IV
Sandberg, N. Percy Patrick, 1881–1934, vol. III
Sandbrook, John Arthur, 1876–1942, vol. IV
Sandburg, Carl, 1878–1967, vol. VI
Sandeman, Albert George, 1833–1923, vol. II
Sandeman, Christopher, 1882–1951, vol. V
Sandeman, Condie, 1866–1933, vol. III
Sandeman, Col Donald George, 1884–1965, vol. VI
Sandeman, Edward, 1862–1959, vol. V
Sandeman, Rear-Adm. Henry George Glas, 1868–1928, vol. II
Sandeman, John Glas, 1836–1921, vol. II
Sandeman, Sir Nairne Stewart, 1st Bt, 1876–1940, vol. III
Sanders, Alan, 1878–1969, vol. VI
Sanders, Air Chief Marshal Sir Arthur Penrose Martyn, 1898–1974, vol. VII
Sanders, Rev. Charles Evatt, 1846–1927, vol. II
Sanders, Sir Charles John Ough, 1865–1938, vol. III
Sanders, Sir Edgar Christian, 1871–1942, vol. IV
Sanders, Rev. Ernest Arthur Blackwell, 1858–1917, vol. II
Sanders, Ven. Frederick Arthur, 1856–1930, vol. III
Sanders, Brig. Geoffrey Percival, 1880–1952, vol. V
Sanders, Brig.-Gen. George Herbert, 1868–1935, vol. III
Sanders, Brig.-Gen. Gerard Arthur Fletcher, 1869–1941, vol. IV
Sanders, Col Gilbert Edward, 1863–1955, vol. V
Sanders, Henry Arthur, 1868–1956, vol. VI (AI)
Sanders, Rev. Henry Martyn, 1869–1963, vol. VI
Sanders, Rev. Canon Henry S., 1864–1920, vol. II
Sanders, Sir John Owen, 1892–1954, vol. V
Sanders, Sir Percy Alan, 1881–1962, vol. VI
Sanders, Rev. S. J. W., 1846–1915, vol. I (A)
Sanders, Thomas W., 1855–1926, vol. II
Sanders, Engr Rear-Adm. William Cory, 1868–1933, vol. III
Sanders, Captain William Stephen, 1871–1941, vol. IV
Sanderson, 1st Baron (*cr* 1905), 1841–1923, vol. II
Sanderson, 1st Baron (*cr* 1930), 1868–1939, vol. III
Sanderson of Ayot, 1st Baron, 1894–1971, vol. VII
Sanderson, Air Marshal Sir (Alfred) Clifford, 1898–1976, vol. VII
Sanderson, Lt-Col Aymor Eden, 1886–1932, vol. III
Sanderson, Sir Charles Claxton, 1864–1929, vol. III
Sanderson, Air Marshal Sir Clifford; *see* Sanderson, Air Marshal Sir A. C.

Sanderson, Rev. Edward, *died* 1930, vol. III
Sanderson, Rev. Edward Manners, 1847–1932, vol. III
Sanderson, Sir Frank Bernard, 1st Bt, 1880–1965, vol. VI
Sanderson, Frederick William, 1857–1922, vol. II
Sanderson, Harold Arthur, *died* 1932, vol. III
Sanderson, Sir Harold Leslie, 1890–1966, vol. VI
Sanderson, Col Henry Bristow, 1840–1915, vol. I
Sanderson, Sir John, 1868–1945, vol. IV
Sanderson, Sir John Scott B.; *see* Burdon-Sanderson.
Sanderson, Kenneth Francis Villiers, 1895–1973, vol. VII
Sanderson, Rt Hon. Sir Lancelot, 1863–1944, vol. IV
Sanderson, Oswald, 1863–1926, vol. II
Sanderson, Sir Percy, 1842–1919, vol. II
Sanderson, Robert, 1881–1943, vol. IV
Sanderson, Rev. Robert Edward, 1828–1913, vol. I
Sanderson, Sibyl, *died* 1903, vol. I
Sanderson, Wilfrid Ernest, 1878–1935, vol. III
Sanderson, William Allendale, 1913–1961, vol. VI
Sanderson, Col William Denziloe, 1868–1941, vol. IV
Sanderson, William Waite, 1868–1944, vol. IV
Sanderson-Wells, John Sanderson, 1872–1955, vol. V
Sanderson-Wells, Thomas Henry, 1871–1958, vol. V
Sandes, Alfred James Terence F.; *see* Fleming-Sandes.
Sandes, Lt-Col Edward Warren Caulfeild, 1880–1973, vol. VII
Sandes, Elise, 1851–1934, vol. III
Sandford, 1st Baron, 1887–1959, vol. V
Sandford, Arthur Wellesley, 1858–1939, vol. III
Sandford, Rt Rev. Charles Waldegrave, 1828–1903, vol. I
Sandford, Brig. Daniel Arthur, 1882–1972, vol. VII
Sandford, Ven. Ernest Grey, 1839–1910, vol. I
Sandford, Ven. Folliott George, 1861–1945, vol. IV
Sandford, Captain Francis Hugh, 1887–1926, vol. II
Sandford, Brig. Francis Rossall, 1898–1962, vol. VI
Sandford, Sir George Ritchie, 1892–1950, vol. IV
Sandford, Hon. Sir (James) Wallace, 1879–1958, vol. V
Sandford, Kenneth Stuart, 1899–1971, vol. VII
Sandford, Thomas Frederick, 1886–1963, vol. VI
Sandford, Hon. Sir Wallace; *see* Sandford, Hon. Sir J. W.
Sandham, E., *died* 1944, vol. IV
Sandham, Henry, 1842–1910, vol. I
Sandhurst, 1st Viscount, 1855–1921, vol. II
Sandhurst, 3rd Baron, 1857–1933, vol. III
Sandhurst, 4th Baron, 1892–1964, vol. VI
Sandie, Brig. John Grey, 1897–1975, vol. VII
Sandiford, Charles Thomas, 1840–1919, vol. II
Sandiford, Peter, 1882–1941, vol. IV
Sandilands, George Sommerville, 1889–1961, vol. VI
Sandilands, Brig. Harold Richard, 1876–1961, vol. VI

Sandilands, Brig.-Gen. Henry George, 1864–1930, vol. III
Sandilands, Maj.-Gen. James Walter, 1874–1959, vol. V
Sandison, Sir Alfred, *died* 1906, vol. I
Sandlands, Paul Ernest, 1878–1962, vol. VI
Sandon, Frank, 1890–1979, vol. VII
Sands, Hon. Lord; Christopher Nicholson Johnston, 1857–1934, vol. III
Sands, Ven. Havilland Hubert Allport, 1896–1970, vol. VI
Sands, Rev. Hubert, 1855–1922, vol. II
Sands, Sir James Patrick, 1859–1925, vol. II
Sands, Percy Cooper, 1883–1971, vol. VII
Sands, Sir Stafford Lofthouse, 1913–1972, vol. VII
Sands, William Southgate, 1853–1924, vol. II
Sandwich, 8th Earl of, 1839–1916, vol. II
Sandwich, 9th Earl of, 1874–1962, vol. VI
Sandwith, Fleming Mant, 1853–1918, vol. II
Sandwith, Major Ralph Leslie, 1859–1920, vol. II
Sandwith, Thomas Backhouse, 1831–1900, vol. I
Sandys, 4th Baron, 1840–1904, vol. I
Sandys, 5th Baron, 1855–1948, vol. IV
Sandys, 6th Baron, 1876–1961, vol. VI
Sandys, Hon. Edmund Arthur Marcus, 1860–1914, vol. I
Sandys, Lt-Col Edward Seton, 1872–1953, vol. V
Sandys, Frederick, 1832–1904, vol. I
Sandys, Captain George John, 1875–1937, vol. III
Sandys, George Owen, 1884–1973, vol. VII
Sandys, Sir John Edwin, 1844–1922, vol. II
Sandys, Oliver, *died* 1964, vol. VI
Sandys, Col Thomas Myles, 1837–1911, vol. I
Sandys, Brig.-Gen. William Bain Richardson, 1868–1946, vol. IV
Sandys-Lumsdaine, Edwin Robert John, 1864–1933, vol. III
Saner, Col John Arthur, 1864–1952, vol. V
Sanford, Col Edward Charles Ayshford, 1859–1923, vol. II
Sanford, Lt-Gen. George Edward Langham Somerset, 1840–1901, vol. I
Sangar, Owen Jermy, 1893–1972, vol. VII
Sanger, Sir Ernest, 1875–1939, vol. III
Sanger, William, 1873–1948, vol. IV
Sangster, Sir Donald Burns, 1911–1967, vol. VI
Sangster, John Young, 1896–1977, vol. VII
Sangster, Leith, *died* 1962, vol. VI
Sangster, Margaret Elizabeth, 1838–1912, vol. I (A)
Sangster, Maj.-Gen. Patrick Barclay, 1872–1951, vol. V
Sangster, Rev. William Edwin Robert, 1900–1960, vol. V
Sanguinetti, Frederick Shedden, 1847–1906, vol. I
Sanjiva Row, Kodikal, 1890–1951, vol. V
Sankaran Nair, Sir Chettur, 1857–1934, vol. III
Sankey, 1st Viscount, 1866–1948, vol. IV
Sankey, Col Harold Bantock, 1895–1954, vol. V
Sankey, Ira David, 1840–1908, vol. I
Sankey, Captain Matthew Henry Phineas Riall, 1853–1925, vol. II
Sankey, Sir Richard Hieram, 1829–1908, vol. I
Sankey, Col Sir Stuart, 1854–1940, vol. III

Sansar Chandra Sen, Rao Bahadur, 1846–1909, vol. I

Sansbury, Rev. Canon Graham Rogers, 1909–1980, vol. VII

Sansom, Arthur Ernest, 1838–1907, vol. I

Sansom, Col Charles Henry, 1886–1949, vol. IV

Sansom, Charles Lane, 1862–1951, vol. V

Sansom, Sir George Bailey, 1883–1965, vol. VI

Sansom, George Samuel, 1888–1980, vol. VII

Sansom, William, 1912–1976, vol. VII

Sant, Raja of, 1881–1946, vol. IV

Sant, James, 1820–1916, vol. II

Sant, Captain Mowbray Lees, 1863–1943, vol. IV

Sant-Cassia, 7th Count, 1889–1947, vol. IV

Santayana, George, 1863–1952, vol. V

Santi, Philip Robert William de, died 1942, vol. IV

Santley, Sir Charles, 1834–1922, vol. II

Santos-Dumont, Alberto, 1873–1932, vol. III

Sao, Sir Moung, 1847–1926, vol. II

Sao Kin Maung, 1883–1936, vol. III

Sapara-Williams, Hon. Christopher Alexander, 1854–1915, vol. II

Sapellnikoff, Wassily, 1868–1941, vol. IV (A), vol. V

Sapper; see McNeile, Lt-Col Cyril.

Sapru, Rt Hon. Sir Tej Bahadur, died 1949, vol. IV

Sapsworth, Captain Charles Howard, 1883–1958, vol. V

Sapte, Ven. John Henry, 1821–1906, vol. I

Sara, Rt Rev. Edmund Willoughby, 1891–1965, vol. VI

Sarasate, Pablo Martin Meliton de, 1844–1908, vol. I

Saravanamuttu, Sir Ratnajoti, died 1949, vol. IV

Sarawak, Rajah of, 1829–1917, vol. II

Sarawak, Rajah of; see Brooke, Sir C. V.

Sarawak, HH Ranee Margaret of, died 1936, vol. III

Sarbah, John Mensah, 1864–1910, vol. I

Sardou, Victorien, 1831–1908, vol. I

Sarel, Rear-Adm. Colin Alfred Molyneux, 1880–1954, vol. V

Sarel, Col George Benedict Molyneux, died 1953, vol. V

Sarel, Rev. Sydney Lancaster, died 1950, vol. IV

Sarel, William Samuel, 1861–1933, vol. III

Sarell, Philip Charles, 1866–1942, vol. IV

Sargant, Rt Hon. Sir Charles Henry, 1856–1942, vol. IV

Sargant, Ethel, 1863–1918, vol. II

Sargant, Walter Lee, died 1956, vol. V

Sargant-Florence, Mary, 1857–1954, vol. V

Sargeant, Sir Alfred Read, 1873–1949, vol. IV

Sargeaunt, Bertram Edward, 1877–1978, vol. VII

Sargeaunt, John, 1857–1922, vol. II

Sargeaunt, Margaret Joan, 1903–1978, vol. VII

Sargent, Arthur J., 1871–1947, vol. IV

Sargent, Sir Charles, 1821–1900, vol. I

Sargent, Rt Rev. Christopher Birdwood Roussel, 1906–1943, vol. IV

Sargent, Rt Rev. Douglas Noel, 1907–1979, vol. VII

Sargent, Sir Frank Leyden, 1871–1940, vol. III

Sargent, Sir (Harold) Malcolm (Watts), 1895–1967, vol. VI

Sargent, Maj.-Gen. Harry Neptune, 1866–1946, vol. IV

Sargent, Very Rev. John Paine, 1838–1919, vol. II

Sargent, Sir John Philip, 1888–1972, vol. VII

Sargent, John Singer, 1856–1925, vol. II

Sargent, Sir Malcolm; see Sargent, Sir H. M. W.

Sargent, Sir Orme, 1884–1962, vol. VI

Sargent, Sir Percy, 1873–1933, vol. III

Sargood, Hon. Lt-Col Sir Frederick Thomas, 1834–1903, vol. I

Sargood, Mrs Lilian Mary, 1879–1945, vol. IV

Sargood, Sir Percy Rolfe, 1865–1940, vol. III

Sargood, Richard, 1888–1979, vol. VII

Sarjant, Reginald Josiah, died 1965, vol. VI

Sarjeant, Frederick Arthur, 1861–1933, vol. III

Sarkar, Sir Jadunath, 1870–1958, vol. V

Sarkodee-Adoo, Julius, 1908–1971, vol. VII

Sarl, Arthur J., died 1946, vol. IV

Sarle, Sir Allen Lanyon, 1828–1903, vol. I

Sarle, Charles Spenser, died 1936, vol. III

Sarma, Rao Bahadur Sir Bayya N.; see Narasimha Sarma.

Sarma, Sir (Ramaswami) Srinivasa, 1890–1957, vol. V

Sarma, Sir Srinivasa; see Sarma, Sir R. S.

Sarnoff, David, 1891–1971, vol. VII

Sarolea, Charles, 1870–1953, vol. V

Sarrailh, Jean, 1891–1964, vol. VI

Sarsfield-Hall, Edwin Geoffrey, 1886–1975, vol. VII

Sarson, Col John Edward, 1844–1940, vol. III

Sarto, Giuseppe; see Pius X.

Sartoris, Alfred Urbain, 1826–1909, vol. I

Sartoris, Francis Charles, 1857–1923, vol. II

Sartorius, Maj.-Gen. Euston Henry, 1844–1925, vol. II

Sartorius, Col George, 1840–1912, vol. I

Sartorius, Maj.-Gen. Reginald William, 1841–1907, vol. I

Sartre, Jean-Paul, 1905–1980, vol. VII

Sarup, Anand, HH Sahabji Maharaj Sir, 1881–1937, vol. III

Sarvadhikary, Sir Deva Prasad, 1862–1935, vol. III

Sarzano, 11th Marquis of, 1847–1920, vol. II

Sasse, Captain Cecil Duncan, 1891–1934, vol. III

Sassoon, Arthur Abraham David, 1840–1912, vol. I

Sassoon, Sir Edward Albert, 2nd Bt (cr 1890), 1856–1912 (this entry was not transferred to Who was Who).

Sassoon, Sir Edward Elias, 2nd Bt (cr 1909), 1853–1924, vol. II

Sassoon, Sir (Ellice) Victor, 3rd Bt (cr 1909), 1881–1961, vol. VI

Sassoon, Eugenie Louise Judith, 1854–1943, vol. IV

Sassoon, Sir Jacob Elias, 1st Bt (cr 1909), 1844–1916, vol. II

Sassoon, Joseph S., 1855–1918, vol. II

Sassoon, Meyer Elias, 1855–1924, vol. II

Sassoon, Rt Hon. Sir Philip Albert Gustave David, 3rd Bt (cr 1890), 1888–1939, vol. III

Sassoon, Siegfried, 1886–1967, vol. VI

Sassoon, Sir Victor; see Sassoon, Sir E. V.

Sastri, Sir Calamur Viravalli Kumaraswami, 1870–1934, vol. III

Sastri, Rt Hon. Valangiman Sankaranarayana Srinivasa, 1869–1946, vol. IV

Satow, Rt Hon. Sir Ernest Mason, 1843–1929, vol. III

Satow, Sir Harold Eustace, 1876–1969, vol. VI

Satow, Hugh Ralph, 1877–1967, vol. VI

Satow, Captain Lawrence de W., 1865–1948, vol. IV

Satow, Samuel Augustus Mason, 1847–1925, vol. II

Satterlee, Rt Rev. Henry Yates, 1843–1908, vol. I

Satterly, John, 1879–1963, vol. VI

Satterthwaite, Rev. Charles James, 1834–1910, vol. I

Satterthwaite, Lt-Col Clement Richard, 1884–1953, vol. V

Satterthwaite, Col Edward, 1857–1932, vol. III

Sauber, Robert, 1868–1936, vol. III

Saudi Arabia, HM King of, 1905–1975, vol. VII

Sauer, Hon. J. W., died 1913, vol. I

Sauerwein, Jules Auguste, 1880–1967, vol. VI

Saugman, Christian Ditlev Trappaud, 1895–1976, vol. VII

Saul, Bazil Sylvester W.; see Wingate-Saul.

Saul, Sir Ernest Wingate W.; see Wingate-Saul.

Saul, Air Vice-Marshal Richard Ernest, died 1965, vol. VI

Saulles, G. W. de, died 1903, vol. I

Saumarez, Lt-Col Richard James, 1864–1943, vol. IV

Saundby, Robert, 1849–1918, vol. II

Saundby, Air Marshal Sir Robert Henry Magnus Spencer, 1896–1971, vol. VII

Saunders, Col Alan, 1886–1964, vol. VI

Saunders, Sir Alan Arthur, died 1957, vol. V

Saunders, Sir Alexander Morris C.; see Carr-Saunders.

Saunders, Arthur Leslie, 1862–1935, vol. III

Saunders, Benjamin James, 1856–1938, vol. III

Saunders, Lt-Col Cecil Howie, 1881–1954, vol. V

Saunders, Sir Charles Edward, 1867–1937, vol. III

Saunders, Sir Charles James Renault, 1857–1931, vol. III

Saunders, Rt Rev. Charles John Godfrey, 1888–1973, vol. VII

Saunders, Lt-Col Cyril, 1875–1935, vol. III

Saunders, Edward, 1848–1910, vol. I

Saunders, Captain Edward Aldbrough, 1873–1934, vol. III

Saunders, Edward Arthur, 1866–1947, vol. IV

Saunders, Sir Edwin, 1814–1901, vol. I

Saunders, Major Frederick John, 1876–1916, vol. II

Saunders, Sir Frederick Richard, 1838–1910, vol. I

Saunders, George, 1823–1913, vol. I

Saunders, George, 1859–1922, vol. II

Saunders, Major George Frederick Cullen, 1869–1934, vol. III

Saunders, Sir George Rice P.; see Pryse-Saunders.

Saunders, Captain Harold Cecil Rich, 1882–1919, vol. II

Saunders, Sir Harold Leonard, 1885–1965, vol. VI

Saunders, Ven. Harry Patrick, 1913–1967, vol. VI

Saunders, Hilary Aidan St George, 1898–1951, vol. V

Saunders, Howard, 1835–1907, vol. I

Saunders, John O'Brien, died 1903, vol. I

Saunders, John Tennant, 1888–1965, vol. VI

Saunders, Maj.-Gen. Macan, 1884–1956, vol. V

Saunders, Margaret B.; see Baillie-Saunders.

Saunders, Margaret Marshall, 1861–1947, vol. IV

Saunders, Reginald George Francis, 1882–1947, vol. IV

Saunders, Col Robert Joseph Pratt, 1841–1908, vol. I (A)

Saunders, Samuel Edgar, 1857–1933, vol. III

Saunders, Thomas Bailey, 1860–1928, vol. II

Saunders, Rev. Thomas Bekenn Avening, 1870–1950, vol. IV

Saunders, William, 1836–1914, vol. I

Saunders-Davies, Rt Rev. David Henry, 1894–1975, vol. VII

Saunders-Pryse, Sir Pryse Loveden, 5th Bt, 1896–1962, vol. VI

Saunderson, Col Rt Hon. Edward James, 1837–1906, vol. I

Saurat, Denis, 1890–1958, vol. V

Sausmarez, Sir Havilland Walter de, 1st Bt, 1861–1941, vol. IV

Sauter, George, 1866–1937, vol. III

Sauve, Hon. Arthur, 1875–1944, vol. IV

Sauveur, Albert, 1863–1939, vol. III

Sauzier, Anatole, 1849–1920, vol. II (A), vol. III

Savage, Sir Alfred William Lungley, 1903–1980, vol. VII

Savage, Col Arthur Johnson, 1874–1933, vol. III

Savage, Rev. Edwin Sidney, 1862–1947, vol. IV

Savage, Ernest A., 1877–1966, vol. VI

Savage, Rev. Ernest Bickersteth, 1849–1915, vol. I

Savage, Rev. Francis Forbes, died 1932, vol. III

Savage, Sir Geoffrey Herbert, 1893–1953, vol. V

Savage, Sir George Henry, 1842–1921, vol. II

Savage, Col George Robert Rollo, 1849–1930, vol. III

Savage, Henry, 1854–1912, vol. I

Savage, Very Rev. Henry Edwin, died 1939, vol. III

Savage, John Percival, 1895–1970, vol. VI

Savage, Rt Hon. Michael Joseph, 1872–1940, vol. III

Savage, Lt-Col Morris Boscawen, 1879–1958, vol. V

Savage, Raymond, died 1964, vol. VI

Savage, Rt Rev. Thomas Joseph, 1900–1966, vol. VI

Savage, Sir William George, 1872–1961, vol. VI

Savage, Col William Henry, 1863–1951, vol. V

Savage-Armstrong, Major Francis Savage Nesbitt, 1880–1917, vol. II

Savage-Armstrong, George Francis, 1845–1906, vol. I

Savary, Alfred William, 1831–1918, vol. II

Savary, Ven. T. W., 1878–1948, vol. IV

Savatard, Louis Charles Arthur, 1874–1962, vol. VI

Savery, Frank, 1883–1965, vol. VI

Savery, Sir S. Servington, died 1938, vol. III

Savi, Ethel Winifred, died 1954, vol. V

Savige, Lt-Gen. Sir Stanley George, 1890–1954, vol. V

Savile, 2nd Baron, 1853–1931, vol. III
Savile, Lady Anne; see Loewenstein-Wertheim, HSH Princess.
Savile, Brig. Clare Ruxton Uvedale, 1881–1949, vol. IV
Savile, Rev. E. S. Gordon, 1866–1937, vol. III
Savile, Hon. George, 1871–1937, vol. III
Savile, Bt Col George Walter Wrey, 1860–1936, vol. III
Savile, Col Henry Bourchier Osborne, 1819–1917, vol. II
Savile, Sir Leopold Halliday, 1870–1953, vol. V
Savile, Robert Stewart, 1863–1945, vol. IV
Savile, Lt-Col Robert Vesey, 1873–1947, vol. IV
Savile, Brig.-Gen. Walter Clare, 1857–1928, vol. II
Savill, Agnes F., 1875–1964, vol. VI
Savill, Lt-Col Alfred Cecil, 1897–1943, vol. IV
Savill, Sir Edwin, 1868–1947, vol. IV
Savill, Sir Eric Humphrey, 1895–1980, vol. VII
Savill, Ven. Leonard, 1869–1959, vol. V
Savill, Lt-Col Sydney Rowland, 1891–1967, vol. VI
Savill, Thomas Dixon, 1856–1910, vol. I
Savorgnan, Count de; see Brazza, P. P. F. C. de.
Savory, Rev. Sir Borradaile, 2nd Bt, 1855–1906, vol. I
Savory, Sir Douglas Lloyd, 1878–1969, vol. VI
Savory, Rev. Edmund, died 1912, vol. I
Savory, Vice-Adm. Herbert Whitmore, 1857–1918, vol. II
Savory, Sir Joseph, 1st Bt, 1843–1921, vol. II
Savory, Major Kenneth Stevens, 1894–1939, vol. III
Savory, Lt-Gen. Sir Reginald Arthur, 1894–1980, vol. VII
Savory, Sir William Borradaile, 3rd Bt, 1882–1961, vol. VI
Saw, Hon. Athelstan John Henton, 1868–1929, vol. III
Sawantwadi, Raja of, 1897–1937, vol. III
Saward, Maj.-Gen. Michael Henry, 1840–1928, vol. II
Saward, Sidney Carman, 1889–1967, vol. VI
Sawbridge, Rear-Adm. Henry Richard, 1885–1956, vol. V
Sawbridge, Rev. John Sikes, died 1925, vol. II
Sawkins, Harold, 1888–1957, vol. V
Sawle, Sir Charles Brune Graves, 2nd Bt, 1816–1903, vol. I
Sawle, Sir Charles John Graves–, 4th Bt, 1851–1932, vol. III
Sawle, Col Sir Francis Aylmer Graves, 3rd Bt, 1849–1903, vol. I
Sawrey-Cookson, Sydney Spencer, 1876–1933, vol. III
Sawyer, Charles, 1887–1979, vol. VII
Sawyer, Col Charles Edward, 1848–1931, vol. III
Sawyer, Ethel V.; see Vaughan-Sawyer.
Sawyer, George Alexander, died 1944, vol. IV
Sawyer, Rev. Harold Athelstane Parry, 1865–1939, vol. III
Sawyer, Maj.-Gen. Henry Thomas, 1871–1955, vol. V
Sawyer, Sir James, 1844–1919, vol. II

Sawyer, James Edward Hill, 1874–1953, vol. V
Sawyer, Maj.-Gen. Richard Henry Stewart, 1857–1926, vol. II
Sawyer, Robert Henry, 1832–1905, vol. I
Sawyer, Sir William Phillips, 1844–1908, vol. I
Saxby, Jessie Margaret Edmondston, 1842–1940, vol. III (A), vol. IV
Saxe-Weimar, HH Prince (William Augustus) Edward of, 1823–1902, vol. I
Saxl, Fritz, 1890–1948, vol. IV
Saxon Snell, Alfred Walter, 1860–1949, vol. IV
Saxton, John Arthur, 1914–1980, vol. VII
Saxton, Rev. William Isaac, 1891–1975, vol. VII
Sayce, Rev. Archibald Henry, 1845–1933, vol. III
Sayce, Col George Edward, 1857–1940, vol. III
Sayce, George Ethelbert, 1875–1953, vol. V
Saye and Sele, 17th (styled 14th) Baron, 1830–1907, vol. I
Saye and Sele, 18th Baron, 1858–1937, vol. III
Saye and Sele, 19th Baron, 1884–1949, vol. IV
Saye and Sele, 20th Baron, 1885–1968, vol. VI
Saye, Air Vice-Marshal Geoffrey Ivon Laurence, 1907–1959, vol. V
Sayer, Brig. Arthur Penrice, 1885–1962, vol. VI
Sayer, Ettie, died 1923, vol. II
Sayer, Captain Humphrey, 1889–1943, vol. IV
Sayer, Captain M. B., died 1928, vol. II
Sayers, Dorothy Leigh, 1893–1957, vol. V
Sayers, Sir Frederick, 1885–1977, vol. VII
Sayers, John Edward, 1911–1969, vol. VI
Sayers, Dame Lucile Newell, died 1959, vol. V
Sayers, William Charles Berwick, 1881–1960, vol. V
Sayle, Robert, 1889–1971, vol. VII
Saywell, Rev. Preb. George Frederick, 1882–1956, vol. V
Sbarretti, His Eminence Cardinal Donatus, 1856–1939, vol. III
Scaddan, Hon. John, 1876–1934, vol. III
Scadding, Rt Rev. Charles, 1861–1914, vol. I
Scafe, Gen. Charles, 1844–1918, vol. II
Scafe, Lt-Col William Ernest, 1878–1951, vol. V
Scales, Francis Shillington, died 1927, vol. II
Scallan, Eugene Kevin, 1893–1966, vol. VI
Scallon, Gen. Sir Robert Irvin, 1857–1939, vol. III
Scammell, Lt-Col Alfred George, 1878–1941, vol. IV
Scamp, Sir (Athelstan) Jack, 1913–1977, vol. VII
Scamp, Sir Jack; see Scamp, Sir A. J.
Scanlan, Most Rev. Mgr James Donald, 1899–1976, vol. VII
Scanlan, Thomas, died 1930, vol. III
Scanlen, Hon. Sir Thomas Charles, 1834–1912, vol. I
Scannell, Rev. Thomas Bartholomew, 1854–1917, vol. II
Scaramanga-Ralli, Constantine, 1854–1934, vol. III
Scarbrough, 10th Earl of, 1857–1945, vol. IV
Scarbrough, 11th Earl of, 1896–1969, vol. VI
Scarbrough, John Impey, 1846–1929, vol. III
Scarff, Robert Wilfred, 1899–1970, vol. VI
Scarfoglio, Carlo, 1887–1969, vol. VI
Scarisbrick, Sir Charles, 1839–1923, vol. II

Scarisbrick, Sir Everard Talbot, 2nd Bt, 1896–1955, vol. V

Scarisbrick, Sir Tom Talbot Leyland, 1st Bt, 1874–1933, vol. III

Scarles, Sir Edward John, 1871–1947, vol. IV

Scarlett, Air Vice-Marshal Francis Rowland, 1875–1934, vol. III

Scarlett, Maj.-Gen. Hon. Gerald, 1885–1957, vol. V

Scarlett, Lt-Col Henry A.; see Ashley-Scarlett.

Scarlett, Lt-Col James Alexander, 1877–1925, vol. II

Scarsdale, 2nd Viscount, 1898–1977, vol. VII

Scarsdale, 4th Baron, 1831–1916, vol. II

Scarth, Sir Charles, 1846–1921, vol. II

Scarth of Breckness, Col Henry William, 1899–1972, vol. VII

Scarth, Rev. John, 1826–1909, vol. I

Scarth, Lt-Col Robert, 1894–1966, vol. VI

Scatcherd, Felicia Rudolphina, died 1927, vol. II

Sceales, Col George Adinston M'Laren, 1878–1956, vol. V

Scebarras, Sir Fillipo, died 1928, vol. II

Scerri, Arthur J., 1921–1980, vol. VII

Schacht, Hjalmar Horace Greely, 1877–1970, vol. VI

Schacht, Joseph, 1902–1969, vol. VI

Schafer, Sir Edward Albert S.; see Sharpey-Schafer.

Schafer, Edward Peter S.; see Sharpey-Schafer.

Schalch, Col Vernon Ansdell, 1849–1935, vol. III

Schärf, Adolf, 1890–1965, vol. VI

Scharff, Robert Francis, 1858–1934, vol. III

Scharlieb, Dame Mary Ann Dacomb, 1845–1930, vol. III

Scharrer, Irene, died 1971, vol. VII

Schaw, Maj.-Gen. Henry, 1829–1902, vol. I

Schechter, Solomon, died 1915, vol. I (A)

Schelfhaut, Mgr Philip, 1850–1921, vol. II

Schelling, Ernest, died 1939, vol. III

Schermbrucker, Lt-Col Hon. Frederic, died 1904, vol. I

Schiaparelli, Mme Elsa, died 1975, vol. VII

Schick, Béla, 1877–1967, vol. VI

Schierwater, Harry Turner, 1876–1952, vol. V

Schiff, Sir Ernest Frederick, 1840–1918, vol. II

Schiller, Ferdinand Canning Scott, 1864–1937, vol. III

Schiller, Ferdinand Philip Maximilian, 1868–1946, vol. IV

Schilsky, Eric, 1898–1974, vol. VII

Schindler, Gen. Sir A. Houtum, died 1916, vol. II

Schipa, Tito, 1890–1965, vol. VI

Schlapp, Otto, 1859–1939, vol. III

Schlapp, Walter, 1898–1966, vol. VI

Schlesinger, Arthur Meier, 1888–1965, vol. VI

Schlesinger, Frank, 1871–1943, vol. IV

Schleswig-Holstein, HH Major Prince Christian Victor of, 1867–1900, vol. I

Schleswig-Holstein, HRH Gen. Prince Frederick Christian Charles Augustus of, 1831–1917, vol. II

Schletter, Col Percy, 1855–1922, vol. II

Schley, Rear-Adm. Winfield Scott, 1839–1911, vol. I

Schlich, Sir William, 1840–1925, vol. II

Schlink, Sir Herbert Henry, 1883–1962, vol. VI

Schloesser, C. W. Adolph, 1830–1913, vol. I

Schmidt, Carl Friedrich, 1875–1948, vol. IV

Schmidt, Nathaniel, 1862–1939, vol. III (A), vol. IV

Schmidt-Isserstedt, Hans, 1900–1973, vol. VII

Schmiedel, Paul Wilhelm, 1851–1935, vol. III

Schmitt, Marchese Albert Félix; see Della Torre Alta.

Schmitt, Bernadotte Everly, 1886–1969, vol. VI

Schnabel, Artur, 1882–1951, vol. V

Schnadhorst, Francis, 1840–1900, vol. I

Schneider, Charles Eugene, 1868–1942, vol. IV

Schneider, Sir Gualterus Stewart, 1864–1938, vol. III

Schneider, Sir John William, 1824–1903, vol. I

Schober, Johannes, 1874–1932, vol. III

Schoenberg, Arnold; see Schönberg, A.

Schofield, Alfred Norman, 1903–1973, vol. VII

Schofield, Alfred Taylor, 1846–1929, vol. III

Schofield, Rt Rev. Charles de Veber, 1871–1936, vol. III

Schofield, Lt-Col Frederick William, 1856–1949, vol. IV

Schofield, Lt-Col Harry Norton, 1865–1931, vol. III

Schofield, Herbert, 1883–1963, vol. VI

Schofield, Ivor Frederick Wentworth, 1904–1979, vol. VII

Schofield, J. W., died 1944, vol. IV

Schofield, W. Elmer, 1867–1944, vol. IV

Schofield, Wentworth, 1891–1957, vol. V

Scholder, Charles Albert, 1861–1918, vol. II

Scholderer, (Julius) Victor, 1880–1971, vol. VII

Scholderer, Victor; see Scholderer, J. V.

Scholefield, Arthur, 1853–1930, vol. III

Scholefield, Guy Hardy, 1877–1963, vol. VI

Scholefield, Sir Joshua, died 1950, vol. IV

Scholes, Frank Victor Gordon, 1885–1954, vol. V

Scholes, G. E., died 1968, vol. VI

Scholes, Percy Alfred, 1877–1958, vol. V

Scholey, Harry, 1872–1945, vol. IV

Scholfield, Alwyn Faber, 1884–1969, vol. VI

Scholfield, Brig.-Gen. George Peabody, 1868–1952, vol. V

Schomberg, Rev. Edward St George, 1882–1952, vol. V

Schomberg, Gen. Sir George Augustus, 1821–1907, vol. I

Schomberg, Brig. Harold St George, 1886–1954, vol. V

Schomberg, Lt-Gen. Herbert St George, 1845–1915, vol. I

Schomberg, Col Reginald Charles Francis, died 1958, vol. V

Schönberg, Arnold, 1874–1951, vol. V

Schonell, Sir Fred Joyce, 1900–1969, vol. VI

Schöner, Josef A., 1904–1978, vol. VII

Schonland, Sir Basil Ferdinand Jamieson, 1896–1972, vol. VII

Schonland, Selmar, 1860–1940, vol. III

Schooles, Sir Henry Pipon, died 1913, vol. I

Schooling, Frederick, 1851–1936, vol. III
Schooling, John Holt, 1859–1927, vol. II
Schooling, Sir William, 1860–1936, vol. III
Schorr, Friedrich, 1888–1953, vol. V
Schorstein, Gustave, died 1906, vol. I
Schott, George Adolphus, 1868–1937, vol. III
Schreiber, Col Acton Lemuel, 1865–1951, vol. V
Schrieber, Maj.-Gen. Brymer Francis, 1835–1907, vol. I
Schreiber, Sir Collingwood, 1831–1918, vol. II
Schreiber, Brig. Derek, 1904–1972, vol. VII
Schreiber, Lt-Gen. Sir Edmond Charles Acton, 1890–1972, vol. VII
Schreiber, Ricardo Rivera, 1892–1969, vol. VI
Schreiner, Olive Emilie Albertina, 1855–1920, vol. II
Schreiner, S. C. Cronwright; see Cronwright, S. C.
Schreiner, Rt Hon. William Philip, 1857–1919, vol. II
Schröder, Baron Bruno, 1867–1940, vol. III
Schroder, Helmut William Bruno, 1901–1969, vol. VI
Schröder, Sir John Henry William, 1st Bt, 1825–1910, vol. I
Schröder, Sir Walter, 1855–1942, vol. IV
Schroder, Captain William Henry, 1867–1945, vol. IV
Schrödinger, Erwin, 1887–1961, vol. VI
Schryver, Samuel Barnett, 1869–1929, vol. III
Schüddekopf, Albert Wilhelm, 1861–1916, vol. II
Schuler, Gottlieb Frederick Henry, 1854–1926, vol. II
Schumacher, Ernst F(riedrich), 1911–1977, vol. VII
Schuman, Robert, 1886–1963, vol. VI
Schumann, Elisabeth, 1885–1952, vol. V
Schunck, Henry Edward, 1820–1903, vol. I
Schurman, Jacob Gould, 1854–1942, vol. IV
Schuschnigg, Kurt von, 1897–1977, vol. VII
Schuster, 1st Baron, 1869–1956, vol. V
Schuster, Sir Arthur, 1851–1934, vol. III
Schuster, Ernest Joseph, 1850–1924, vol. II
Schuster, Sir Felix, 1st Bt, 1854–1936, vol. III
Schuster, Sir (Felix) Victor, 2nd Bt, 1885–1962, vol. VI
Schuster, Sir Victor; see Schuster, Sir F. V.
Schutt, William John, 1868–1933, vol. III
Schütze, Gladys Henrietta, (Mrs Harrie Schütze); see Leslie, Henrietta.
Schütze, Harrie Leslie Hugo, 1882–1946, vol. IV
Schütze, Henrietta; see Leslie, H.
Schwab, Charles M., 1862–1939, vol. III
Schwab, John Christopher, 1865–1916, vol. II
Schwabe, Maj.-Gen. George S.; see Salis-Schwabe.
Schwabe, Randolph, 1885–1948, vol. IV
Schwabe, Sir Walter George Salis, 1873–1931, vol. III
Schwarz, Ernest H. L., 1873–1928, vol. II
Schwarzenberg, Johannes Erkinger, 1903–1978, vol. VII
Schweinitz, E. A. de, died 1904, vol. I
Schweitzer, Albert, 1875–1965, vol. VI
Schwerdt, Captain Charles Max Richard, 1889–1968, vol. VI

Sciortino, Anthony, 1883–1947, vol. IV
Sclater, Charlotte Seymour, 1858–1942, vol. IV
Sclater, Edith Harriet, (Lady Sclater), died 1927, vol. II
Sclater, Gen. Sir Henry Crichton, 1855–1923, vol. II
Sclater, Very Rev. John Robert Paterson, 1876–1949, vol. IV
Sclater, Philip Lutley, 1829–1913, vol. I
Sclater, William Lutley, 1863–1944, vol. IV
Sclater-Booth, Hon. Charles Lutley, 1861–1931, vol. III
Sclater-Booth, Col Hon. Walter Dashwood, 1869–1953, vol. V
Scobell, Ven. Edward Chessall, 1850–1917, vol. II
Scobell, Maj.-Gen. Sir Henry Jenner, 1859–1912, vol. I
Scobell, Maj.-Gen. Sir John; see Scobell, Maj.-Gen. Sir S. J. P.
Scobell, Maj.-Gen. Sir (Sanford) John (Palairet), 1879–1955, vol. V
Scobie, Col Mackay John Graham, 1852–1930, vol. III
Scobie, Lt-Gen. Sir Ronald MacKenzie, 1893–1969, vol. VI
Scoble, Rt Hon. Sir Andrew Richard, 1831–1916, vol. II
Scoby-Smith, George, 1848–1929, vol. III
Scoggins, Air Vice-Marshal Roy, 1908–1970, vol. VI
Scogings, Very Rev. Frank, died 1976, vol. VII
Scollard, Clinton, 1860–1932, vol. III
Scollard, Rt Rev. David Joseph, 1862–1934, vol. III
Scoones, Gen. Sir Geoffry Allen Percival, 1893–1975, vol. VII
Scopes, Sir Frederick, 1892–1978, vol. VII
Scorgie, Sir Norman Gibb, 1884–1956, vol. V
Scorgie, Norman James, 1908–1958, vol. V
Scot-Skirving, Archibald Adam, 1868–1930, vol. III
Scothern, Col Albert Edward, 1882–1970, vol. VI
Scotland, Sir Colley Harman, 1818–1903, vol. I
Scotland, Rear-Adm. John Earl, 1911–1978, vol. VII
Scotson, Frederick Hector, 1900–1955, vol. V
Scott, A. R.; see Ritchie-Scott.
Scott, Adrian Gilbert, 1882–1963, vol. VI
Scott, Agnes Catharine, 1875–1955, vol. V
Scott, Vice-Adm. Albert Charles, 1872–1969, vol. VI
Scott, Alexander, 1853–1947, vol. IV
Scott, Alexander MacCallum, 1874–1928, vol. II
Scott, Alfred Henry, 1868–1939, vol. III
Scott, Sir Andrew, 1857–1939, vol. III
Scott, Lt-Col Angel; see Scott, Lt-Col W. A.
Scott, Sir Angus Newton, 1876–1958, vol. V
Scott, Maj.-Gen. Anthony Gerald O'Carroll, 1899–1980, vol. VII
Scott, Very Rev. Archibald, 1837–1909, vol. I
Scott, Archibald Gifford, 1889–1980, vol. VII
Scott, Lt-Col Archibald Malcolm H.; see Henderson-Scott.
Scott, Sir (Arleigh) Winston, 1900–1976, vol. VII
Scott, Arthur, 1881–1953, vol. V

Scott, Maj.-Gen. Sir Arthur Binny, 1862–1944, vol. IV

Scott, Sir (Arthur) Guillum, 1842–1909, vol. I

Scott, Arthur William, 1846–1927, vol. II

Scott, Ven. Avison Terry, 1848–1925, vol. II

Scott, Sir Basil, 1859–1926, vol. II

Scott, Sir Benjamin, 1841–1927, vol. II

Scott, Benjamin Charles George, 1846–1929, vol. III

Scott, Col Bertal Hopton, 1863–1926, vol. II

Scott, Col Sir Buchanan, 1850–1937, vol. III

Scott, Catharine Amy D.; see Dawson Scott.

Scott, Charles, 1851–1934, vol. III

Scott, Rev. Charles Anderson, 1859–1941, vol. IV

Scott, Charles Clare, 1850–1925, vol. II

Scott, Rev. Canon Charles Harold, 1871–1940, vol. III (A), vol. IV

Scott, Maj.-Gen. Sir Charles Henry, 1848–1919, vol. II

Scott, Col Charles Inglis, 1866–1941, vol. IV

Scott, Charles Norman Lindsay Tollemache, 1852–1938, vol. III

Scott, Charles Paley, 1881–1950, vol. IV

Scott, Rt Rev. Charles Perry, 1847–1927, vol. II

Scott, Charles Prestwich, 1846–1932, vol. III

Scott, Charles Russell, 1898–1979, vol. VII

Scott, Rt Hon. Sir Charles Stewart, 1838–1924, vol. II

Scott, Charles Thomas, 1868–1953, vol. V

Scott, Lord Charles Thomas Montagu-Douglas-, 1839–1911, vol. I

Scott, Maj.-Gen. Charles Walker, 1875–1929, vol. III

Scott, Christopher Fairfax, 1894–1958, vol. V

Scott, Clement, 1841–1904, vol. I

Scott, Cyril, 1879–1970, vol. VI

Scott, David Aylmer, 1892–1971, vol. VII

Scott, Hon. David Lynch, 1845–1924, vol. II

Scott, David Robert, died 1943, vol. IV

Scott, David Russell, died 1954, vol. V

Scott, Denis Herbert, 1899–1958, vol. V

Scott, Sir Donald; see Scott, Sir R. D.

Scott, Maj.-Gen. Douglas Alexander, 1848–1924, vol. II

Scott, Sir Douglas Edward, 7th Bt (cr 1806), 1863–1951, vol. V

Scott, Dukinfield Henry, 1854–1934, vol. III

Scott, Duncan Campbell, 1862–1947, vol. IV

Scott, Rev. Edward Anderson Seymour, 1865–1941, vol. IV

Scott, Edward B.; see Baliol Scott.

Scott, Sir Edward Dolman, 6th Bt (cr 1806), 1826–1905, vol. I

Scott, Edward Hey L.; see Laughton-Scott.

Scott, Edward John Long, 1840–1918, vol. II

Scott, Edward Taylor, 1883–1932, vol. III

Scott, Elisabeth Whitworth, 1898–1972, vol. VII

Scott, Sir Ernest, 1868–1939, vol. III

Scott, Ernest Findlay, 1868–1954, vol. V

Scott, Ernest Newey, died 1952, vol. V

Scott, Hon. Sir Ernest Stowell, 1872–1953, vol. V

Scott, Eustace Lindsay, 1885–1956, vol. V

Scott, Major Finlay Forbes, died 1949, vol. IV

Scott, Francis Clayton, 1881–1979, vol. VII

Scott, Maj.-Gen. Sir Francis Cunningham, 1834–1902, vol. I

Scott, Sir Francis David Sibbald, 4th Bt (cr 1806), 1851–1906, vol. I

Scott, Lt-Col Lord Francis George Montagu-Douglas-, 1879–1952, vol. V

Scott, Sir Francis Montagu Sibbald, 5th Bt (cr 1806), 1885–1945, vol. IV

Scott, Francis Reginald Fairfax, 1897–1969, vol. VI

Scott, Col Frederick Beaufort, died 1903, vol. I

Scott, Ven. Frederick George, 1861–1944, vol. IV

Scott, Gavin, 1876–1933, vol. III

Scott, Lt-Col George, 1859–1955, vol. V

Scott, Sir George; see Scott, Sir J. G.

Scott, George Alexander, 1862–1933, vol. III

Scott, George Batley, 1844–1932, vol. III

Scott, Lt-Col George John, 1858–1925, vol. II

Scott, George Walter, 1896–1963, vol. VI

Scott, Lord George William Montagu-Douglas-, 1866–1947, vol. IV

Scott, Col Gerald Bassett, 1875–1964, vol. VI

Scott, Geraldine Edith, (Lady Scott); see Mitton, G. E.

Scott, G(ilbert) Shaw, 1884–1969, vol. VI

Scott, Sir Giles Gilbert, 1880–1960, vol. V

Scott, Sir Guillum; see Scott, Sir A. G.

Scott, Guy Harden Guillum, 1874–1960, vol. V

Scott, Sir Harold; see Scott, Sir Henry H.

Scott, Sir Harold Richard, 1887–1969, vol. VI

Scott, Major Harvey, 1868–1912, vol. I

Scott, Henry Cooper, 1915–1977, vol. VII

Scott, Col Lord Henry Francis Montagu-Douglas-, 1868–1945, vol. IV

Scott, Henry George, 1875–1935, vol. III

Scott, Sir (Henry) Harold, 1874–1956, vol. V

Scott, Brig. Sir Henry Lawrence, 1882–1971, vol. VII

Scott, Sir (Henry) Maurice, 1910–1976, vol. VII

Scott, Sir Henry Milne, 1876–1956, vol. V

Scott, Hon. Henry Robert H.; see Hepburne-Scott.

Scott, Brig. Henry St George Stewart, 1880–1940, vol. III

Scott, Lord Herbert Andrew Montagu-Douglas-, 1872–1944, vol. IV

Scott, Sir Herbert Septimus, 1873–1952, vol. V

Scott, Hugh, 1885–1960, vol. V

Scott, Hugh Stowell; see Merriman, Henry Seton.

Scott, James, 1850–1920, vol. II

Scott, Sir James, 1838–1925, vol. II

Scott, James, died 1929, vol. III

Scott, James, 1876–1939, vol. III

Scott, Maj.-Gen. James Bruce, 1892–1974, vol. VII

Scott, James Cospatrick Hepburne-, 1882–1942, vol. IV

Scott, Sir (James) George, 1851–1935, vol. III

Scott, James Henderson, 1913–1970, vol. VI

Scott, Sir James William, 1st Bt (cr 1909), 1844–1913, vol. I

Scott, Maj.-Gen. James Woodward, 1838–1914, vol. I

Scott, Col Sir Jervoise Bolitho, 1st Bt (cr 1962), 1892–1965, vol. VI

Scott, Sir John, 1814–1898, vol. I
Scott, John, 1830–1903, vol. I
Scott, Hon. Sir John, 1841–1904, vol. I
Scott, Rev. John, 1836–1906, vol. I
Scott, John, *died* 1919, vol. II
Scott, Sir John, 2nd Bt (*cr* 1907), 1854–1922, vol. II
Scott, Sir John, 1878–1946, vol. IV
Scott, Brig. John, 1887–1971, vol. VII
Scott, John Alexander, 1900–1965, vol. VI
Scott, John Dick, 1917–1980, vol. VII
Scott, John Gordon Cameron, 1888–1946, vol. IV
Scott, John Halliday, *died* 1914, vol. I (A), vol. II
Scott, Sir John Harley, *died* 1931, vol. III
Scott, John Healey, 1843–1925, vol. II
Scott, John Russell, 1879–1949, vol. IV
Scott, Maj.-Gen. John Walter Lennox, 1883–1960, vol. V
Scott, John Waugh, 1878–1974, vol. VII
Scott, Comdr John Wilfred, 1881–1926, vol. II
Scott, John William R.; *see* Robertson Scott.
Scott, Rev. Canon Joseph John, *died* 1931, vol. III
Scott, Kathleen, (Lady Scott); *see* Kennet, Lady.
Scott, Kenneth, *died* 1918, vol. II
Scott, Rt Hon. Sir Leslie Frederic, 1869–1950, vol. IV
Scott, Sir Lindsay; *see* Scott, Sir W. L.
Scott, Lt-Col Lothian Kerr, 1841–1919, vol. II
Scott, Hon. Louis Guy, 1850–1900, vol. I
Scott, Mackay Hugh Baillie, 1865–1945, vol. IV
Scott, Rear-Adm. Malcolm Maxwell-, 1883–1943, vol. IV
Scott, Col Sir Malcolm S.; *see* Stoddart-Scott.
Scott, Margaret, 1841–1917, vol. II
Scott, Sir Maurice; *see* Scott, Sir H. M.
Scott, Hon. Mrs Maxwell, (Mary Monica), 1852–1920, vol. II
Scott, Rev. Melville, *died* 1929, vol. III
Scott, Ven. Melville Horne, 1827–1898, vol. I
Scott, Napier B.; *see* Baliol Scott.
Scott, Noel, 1890–1956, vol. V
Scott, Norman Carson, 1899–1975, vol. VII
Scott, Lt-Col Norman Emile Henry, 1875–1958, vol. V
Scott, Sir Oswald Arthur, 1893–1960, vol. V
Scott, Owen Stanley, 1852–1922, vol. II
Scott, Paul Mark, 1920–1978, vol. VII
Scott, Adm. Sir Percy, 1st Bt (*cr* 1913), 1853–1924, vol. II
Scott, Rev. Percy Richard, 1850–1906, vol. I
Scott, Peter, *died* 1972, vol. VII
Scott, Peter Duncan, 1914–1977, vol. VII
Scott, Peter Heathcote Guillum, 1913–1961, vol. VI
Scott, Brig.-Gen. Philip Clement J., 1871–1932, vol. III
Scott, Ralph Roylance, 1893–1978, vol. VII
Scott, Brig. Raymond S., *died* 1972, vol. VII
Scott, Rear-Adm. Richard James Rodney, 1887–1967, vol. VII
Scott, Hon. Sir Richard William, 1825–1913, vol. I
Scott, Sir Robert, 1903–1968, vol. VI
Scott, Sir Robert Claude, 7th Bt (*cr* 1821), 1886–1961, vol. VI
Scott, Sir (Robert) Donald, 1901–1974, vol. VII

Scott, Captain Robert Falcon, 1868–1912, vol. I
Scott, Very Rev. Robert Forrester Victor, 1897–1975, vol. VII
Scott, Sir Robert Forsyth, 1849–1933, vol. III
Scott, Robert George, 1857–1918, vol. II
Scott, Robert Henry, 1833–1916, vol. II
Scott, Robert Julian, 1861–1930, vol. III
Scott, Maj.-Gen. Robert Kellock, 1871–1942, vol. IV
Scott, Gen. Robert Nicholl D.; *see* Dawson-Scott.
Scott, Robert Pickett, 1856–1931, vol. III
Scott, Sir (Robert) Russell, 1877–1960, vol. V
Scott, Sir Robert Townley, 1841–1922, vol. II
Scott, Sir Russell; *see* Scott, Sir Robert R.
Scott, Rev. Samuel Cooper, 1838–1923, vol. II
Scott, Sir Samuel Edward, 6th Bt, (*cr* 1821), 1873–1943, vol. IV
Scott, Rev. Samuel Gilbert, 1847–1916, vol. II
Scott, Sir Samuel Haslam, 2nd Bt (*cr* 1909), 1875–1960, vol. V
Scott, Sebastian Gilbert, 1879–1941, vol. IV
Scott, Rev. Sidney; *see* Scott, Rev. W. S.
Scott, Sydney Richard, *died* 1966, vol. VI
Scott, Rev. Thomas, 1831–1914, vol. I
Scott, Maj.-Gen. Thomas, 1897–1968, vol. VI
Scott, Rt. Rev. Thomas Arnold, 1879–1956, vol. V
Scott, Thomas Bodley, *died* 1924, vol. II
Scott, Lt-Gen. Sir Thomas Edwin, 1867–1937, vol. III
Scott, Rev. Thomas Errington, *died* 1930, vol. III
Scott, Thomas Gilbert, 1874–1933, vol. III
Scott, Maj.-Gen. Thomas Patrick David, 1905–1976, vol. VII
Scott, Tom, 1854–1927, vol. II
Scott, Col Wallace Arthur, *died* 1949, vol. IV (A), vol. V
Scott, Sir Walter, 1st Bt (*cr* 1907), 1826–1910, vol. I
Scott, Hon. Walter, 1867–1938, vol. III
Scott, Sir Walter, 3rd Bt (*cr* 1907), 1895–1967, vol. VI
Scott, Rev. Walter Henry, 1842–1931, vol. III
Scott, Maj.-Gen. Sir Walter Joseph Constable M.; *see* Maxwell-Scott.
Scott, Sir Walter Lawrence, 1880–1951, vol. IV
Scott, Walter Montagu, 1867–1920, vol. II
Scott, Walter Samuel, 1870–1951, vol. V
Scott, Rev. (Walter) Sidney, 1900–1980, vol. VII
Scott, Sir (Warwick) Lindsay, 1892–1952, vol. V
Scott, Sir William, 1898–1965, vol. VI
Scott, William A., 1871–1918, vol. II
Scott, Lt-Col (William) Angel, 1857–1932, vol. III
Scott, Maj.-Gen. Sir William Arthur, 1899–1976, vol. VII
Scott, Col William Augustus, 1856–1930, vol. III
Scott, William Berryman, 1858–1947, vol. IV
Scott, William Coxon, 1895–1968, vol. VI
Scott, Sir William Dalgliesh, 1890–1966, vol. VI
Scott, Col Sir William Dishington, 1878–1952, vol. V
Scott, William Douglas R.; *see* Robson-Scott.
Scott, Ven. William Edward, *died* 1918, vol. II
Scott, Rev. William Major, 1879–1932, vol. III

Scott, Sir William Monteath, 7th Bt (*cr* 1671), 1829–1902, vol. I

Scott, Rev. William Morris FitzGerald, 1912–1959, vol. V

Scott, William Robert, 1868–1940, vol. III

Scott, Maj.–Gen. William Walter Hopton, 1843–1906, vol. I

Scott, Lt-Col Lord William Walter Montagu-Douglas-, 1896–1958, vol. V

Scott, Winifred Mary, (Pamela Wynne), *died* 1959, vol. V

Scott, Sir Winston; *see* Scott, Sir A. W.

Scott-Barrett, Rev. Hugh, 1887–1958, vol. V

Scott-Batey, Rowland William John, 1913–1980, vol. VII

Scott-Duff, Bt Lt-Col Arthur Abercromby, 1874–1951, vol. V

Scott-Elliot, Walter Travers, 1895–1977, vol. VII

Scott-Gatty, Sir Alfred Scott, 1847–1918, vol. II

Scott Hall, Stewart, 1905–1961, vol. VI

Scott-Hill, Engr Rear-Adm. Walter, 1873–1963, vol. VI

Scott-James, Rolfe Arnold, 1878–1959, vol. V

Scott-Kerr, Brig.-Gen. Robert, 1859–1942, vol. IV

Scott Makdougall, Hugh James Elibank, 1861–1934, vol. III

Scott-Moncrieff, Adm. Sir Alan Kenneth, *died* 1980, vol. VII

Scott Moncrieff, Charles Kenneth, 1889–1930, vol. III

Scott-Moncrieff, Sir Colin Campbell, 1836–1916, vol. II

Scott-Moncrieff, Maj.-Gen. Sir George Kenneth, 1855–1924, vol. II

Scott-Moncrieff, Joanna Constance, 1920–1978, vol. VII

Scott-Moncrieff, William George, 1846–1927, vol. II

Scott O'Connor, Thomas Arthur Leslie, 1878–1944, vol. IV

Scott-Owen, Col Arthur Lewis, 1885–1944, vol. IV

Scott-Paine, Hubert, 1891–1954, vol. V

Scott-Smith, Sir Henry, 1865–1950, vol. IV

Scott-Taggart, Wing Comdr John, 1897–1979, vol. VII

Scott Thomson, Gladys, *died* 1966, vol. VI

Scotter, Sir Charles, 1st Bt, 1835–1910, vol. I

Scotter, Sir Frederick Charles, 2nd Bt, 1868–1911, vol. I

Scotti, Antonio, 1866–1936, vol. III

Scougal, Andrew E., 1846–1916, vol. II

Scourfield, Sir Owen Henry Philipps, 2nd Bt, 1847–1921, vol. II

Scovell, Sir Augustus Charles, 1840–1924, vol. II

Scovell, Lt-Col George Julian Selwyn, *died* 1948, vol. IV

Scovell, Rowley Fielding, 1902–1972, vol. VII

Scrase-Dickins, Col Spencer William; *see* Dickins.

Scrase-Dickins, Maj.-Gen. William Drummond, 1832–1914, vol. I

Scratchley, Herbert Arthur, 1855–1920, vol. II

Scratchley, Lt-Col Victor Henry Sylvester, 1870–1936, vol. III

Scriabin, Alexander, 1872–1915, vol. I (A)

Scribner, Charles, 1890–1952, vol. V

Scrimgeour, H(ugh) Carron, 1883–1958, vol. V

Scrimgeour, John Stuart, 1887–1950, vol. IV

Scrimger, Lt-Col Francis Alexander Carron, 1880–1937, vol. III

Scriven, Ven. Augustine, *died* 1916, vol. II

Scrivener, Sir Patrick Stratford, 1897–1966, vol. VI

Scroggie, Rev. William Graham, 1877–1958, vol. V

Scroggie, Col William Reith John, 1876–1953, vol. V

Scroope, Arthur Edgar, *died* 1954, vol. V

Scrope, Henry Aloysius, 1862–1950, vol. IV

Scrutton, James Herbert, 1858–1938, vol. III

Scrutton, Sir Thomas Edward, 1856–1934, vol. III

Scrymgeour, Edwin, 1866–1947, vol. IV

Scrymgeour, Norval, 1870–1952, vol. V

Scrymsoure-Steuart-Fothringham, Walter Thomas James, 1862–1936, vol. III

Scudamore, Brig.-Gen. Charles Philip, 1861–1929, vol. III

Scudder, Horace Elisha, 1838–1902, vol. I

Scullard, Rev. Herbert Hayes, 1862–1926, vol. II

Scullin, Rt Hon. James Henry, 1876–1953, vol. V

Scully, Harry, *died* 1935, vol. III

Scully, James Aloysius, 1856–1929, vol. III

Scully, Major Vincent Joseph, 1876–1941, vol. IV

Scully, Lt-Col Vincent Marcus Barron, 1881–1941, vol. IV

Scully, Vincent William Thomas, 1900–1980, vol. VII

Scupham, Brig. Sir William Eric Halstead, 1893–1958, vol. V

Scurfield, Harold, 1863–1941, vol. IV

Scurr, John, 1876–1932, vol. III

Seabrook, William, 1886–1945, vol. IV

Seabrooke, Elliott, *died* 1950, vol. IV

Seabrooke, Sir James Herbert, 1852–1933, vol. III

Seaby, Allen W., 1867–1953, vol. V

Seafield, 11th Earl of, 1876–1915, vol. I (A)

Seafield, Countess of (12th in line), 1906–1969, vol. VI

Seafield, Countess of; (Caroline), *died* 1911, vol. I

Seaford, Sir Frederick Jacob, *died* 1968, vol. VI

Seaforth of Brahan, 1st Baron, 1847–1923, vol. II

Seaforth, Lady; (Mary Margaret), *died* 1933, vol. III

Seager, Basil William, 1898–1977, vol. VII

Seager, Most Rev. Charles Allen, 1872–1948, vol. IV

Seager, Captain John Elliot, 1891–1955, vol. V

Seager, Philip Samuel, 1845–1924, vol. II

Seager, Samuel Hurst, 1855–1933, vol. III

Seager, Sir William Henry, 1862–1941, vol. IV

Seago, Edward Brian, 1910–1974, vol. VII

Seagram, Brig.-Gen. Tom Ogle, 1872–1958, vol. V

Seal, Sir Brajendranath, 1864–1938, vol. III

Seal, Sir Eric Arthur, 1898–1972, vol. VII

Seale, A. Barney, *died* 1957, vol. V

Seale, Rev. E. G., 1870–1936, vol. III

Seale, Sir John Carteret Hyde, 4th Bt, 1881–1964, vol. VI

Seale, Sir John Henry, 3rd Bt, 1843–1914, vol. I

Sealy, Sir John, 1807–1899, vol. I

Sealy, Patrick Persse, 1853–1938, vol. III

Seaman, Clarence Milton Edwards, 1908–1974, vol. VII
Seaman, Col Edwin Charles, 1867–1919, vol. II
Seaman, Sir Owen, 1st Bt, 1861–1936, vol. III
Seaman, Paymaster-Captain Tom, *died* 1943, vol. IV
Seamer, Rev. Arthur John, *died* 1963, vol. VI
Searight, Major Hugh fforde, 1875–1942, vol. IV
Searle, Alfred Broadhead, 1877–1967, vol. VI
Searle, Maj.-Gen. Arthur Thaddeus, 1830–1925, vol. II
Searle, Rev. Charles Edward, 1828–1902, vol. I
Searle, Col Frank, *died* 1948, vol. IV
Searle, George Frederick Charles, 1864–1954, vol. V
Searle, Herbert Victor, 1892–1968, vol. VI
Searle, Sir Malcolm William, *died* 1926, vol. II
Searles-Wood, Herbert Duncan, 1853–1936, vol. III
Sears, Rear-Adm. Harold Baker, 1880–1959, vol. V
Sears, John Edward, 1857–1941, vol. IV
Sears, John Edward, 1883–1954, vol. V
Sears, William, *died* 1929, vol. III
Seath, Maj.-Gen. Gordon Hamilton, *died* 1952, vol. V
Seaton, 3rd Baron, 1854–1933, vol. III
Seaton, 4th Baron, 1863–1955, vol. V
Seaton, Albert Edward, 1848–1930, vol. III
Seaton, Rev. Douglas, 1839–1923, vol. II
Seaton, Edward Cox, 1847–1915, vol. I
Seaton, J. S., *died* 1929, vol. III
Seaton, Rt Rev. James Buchanan, 1868–1938, vol. III
Seaton, Reginald Ethelbert, 1899–1978, vol. VII
Seaver, Very Rev. Charles, 1820–1907, vol. I
Seaver, Very Rev. George, 1890–1976, vol. VII
Seaverns, Joel Herbert, 1860–1923, vol. II
Sebag-Montefiore, Edmund; *see* Montefiore.
Sebag-Montefiore, Sir Joseph; *see* Montefiore.
Sebastian, Erroll Graham, 1892–1978, vol. VII
Sebright, Sir Edgar Reginald Saunders, 11th Bt, 1854–1917, vol. II
Sebright, Sir Egbert Cecil Saunders, 10th Bt, 1871–1897, vol. I
Sebright, Lt-Col Sir Giles Edward, 13th Bt, 1896–1954, vol. V
Sebright, Sir Guy Thomas Saunders, 12th Bt, 1856–1933, vol. III
Seccombe, Brig.-Gen. Archibald Kennedy, 1868–1931, vol. III
Seccombe, Thomas, 1866–1923, vol. II
Seccombe, Sir Thomas Lawrence, 1812–1902, vol. I
Secker, Martin, 1882–1978, vol. VII
Seckham, Lt-Col Bassett Thorne, 1863–1925, vol. II
Seckham, Lt-Col Douglas Thorne, 1873–1937, vol. III
Secombe, Maj.-Gen. Victor Clarence, 1897–1962, vol. VI
Secretan, Hubert Arthur, 1891–1969, vol. VI
Secretan, Walter Bernard, 1875–1966, vol. VI
Seddon, Charles Norman, 1870–1950, vol. IV
Seddon, Sir Harold, 1881–1958, vol. V
Seddon, Harry Sterratt, 1881–1944, vol. IV

Seddon, Sir Herbert John, 1903–1977, vol. VII
Seddon, James Andrew, 1868–1939, vol. III
Seddon, John Pollard, 1827–1906, vol. I
Seddon, Rt Hon. Richard John, 1845–1906, vol. I
Seddon-Brown, Lt-Col Sir Norman Seddon, 1880–1971, vol. VII
Sedgefield, W. J., 1866–1945, vol. IV
Sedgewick, Hon. George Herbert, 1878–1939, vol. III
Sedgwick, Adam, 1854–1913, vol. I
Sedgwick, Anne Douglas, 1873–1935, vol. III
Sedgwick, Rear-Adm. Cyril Gordon, 1885–1948, vol. IV
Sedgwick, Ellery, 1872–1960, vol. V
Sedgwick, Lt-Col Francis Roger, 1876–1955, vol. V
Sedgwick, Rev. Gordon, 1840–1921, vol. II
Sedgwick, Henry Dwight, 1861–1957, vol. V
Sedgwick, Richard Romney, 1894–1972, vol. VII
Sedgwick, Rev. S. N., 1872–1941, vol. IV
Sedgwick, William Thompson, 1855–1921, vol. II
Sedgwick, Rt Rev. William Walmsley, 1858–1948, vol. IV
See, Hon. Sir John, 1845–1907, vol. I
Sée, Peter Henri, 1910–1963, VI
Seebohm, Frederic, 1833–1912, vol. I
Seebohm, Hugh Exton, 1867–1946, vol. IV
Seeds, Sir William, 1882–1973, vol. VII
Seel, Major Edward M.; *see* Molyneux-Seel.
Seel, Sir George Frederick, 1895–1976, vol. VII
Seeley, Edward Alexander, 1913–1979, vol. VII
Seeley, Ven. George Henry, *died* 1935, vol. III
Seeley, Harry Govier, 1839–1909, vol. I
Seely, Sir Charles, 1st Bt, 1833–1915, vol. I
Seely, Sir Charles Hilton, 2nd Bt, 1859–1926, vol. II
Seely, Sir Victor Basil John, 4th Bt, 1900–1980, vol. VII
Seferiades, George, 1900–1971, vol. VII
Seferis, George; *see* Seferiades, G.
Sefton, 4th Earl of, 1835–1897, vol. I
Sefton, 5th Earl of, 1867–1901, vol. I
Sefton, 6th Earl of, 1871–1930, vol. III
Sefton, 7th Earl of, 1898–1972, vol. VII
Sefton, Anne Harriet, (Mrs Walter Sefton); *see* Fish, A. H.
Sefton-Cohen, Arthur, 1879–1968, vol. VI (AII)
Segar, George Xavier, 1838–1901, vol. I
Segar, Hugh William, 1868–1954, vol. V
Segonzac, André D. de; *see* Dunoyer de Segonzac.
Segrave, Edmond, 1904–1971, vol. VII
Segrave, Brig.-Gen. Eric; *see* Segrave, Brig.-Gen. W. H. E.
Segrave, Major Sir Henry O'Neal Dehane, 1896–1930, vol. III
Segrave, Vice-Adm. John Roderick, 1871–1938, vol. III
Segrave, Captain Sir Thomas George, 1865–1941, vol. IV
Segrave, Brig.-Gen. (William Henry) Eric, 1875–1964, vol. VI
Séguel, George Gregory M., *died* 1954, vol. V
Segur, Marquis de; Pierre Marie Maurice Henri, 1853–1916, vol. II

Seigne, John Thomas, 1844–1922, vol. II
Seignobos, Charles, 1854–1942, vol. IV
Seillière, Baron Ernest, 1866–1955, vol. V
Seitz, John Arnold, 1883–1963, vol. VI
Sekers, Miki; see Sekers, Sir N. T.
Sekers, Sir Nicholas Thomas, (Miki Sekers), 1910–1972, vol. VII
Sekon, George Augustus, 1867–1948, vol. IV
Selbie, Rev. John A., 1856–1931, vol. III
Selbie, Robert Hope, 1868–1930, vol. III
Selbie, Rev. William Boothby, 1862–1944, vol. IV
Selborne, 2nd Earl of, 1859–1942, vol. IV
Selborne, 3rd Earl of, 1887–1971, vol. VII
Selby, 1st Viscount, 1835–1909, vol. I
Selby, 2nd Viscount, 1867–1923, vol. II
Selby, 3rd Viscount, 1911–1959, vol. V
Selby, Arthur Laidlaw, 1861–1942, vol. IV
Selby, Maj.-Gen. Arthur Roland, 1893–1966, vol. VI (AII)
Selby, Lt-Col Charles Westrope, 1883–1929, vol. III
Selby, Francis Guy, 1852–1927, vol. II
Selby, Francis James, 1867–1942, vol. IV
Selby, Percival Marchant, 1886–1955, vol. V
Selby, Rev. Thomas Gunn, 1846–1910, vol. I
Selby, Sir Walford Harmood Montague, 1881–1965, vol. VI
Selby, Lt-Col William, 1869–1916, vol. II
Selby, Rev. William John, 1858–1935, vol. III
Selby-Bigge, Sir Amherst; see Selby-Bigge, Sir L. A.
Selby-Bigge, Sir John Amherst, 2nd Bt, 1892–1973, vol. VII
Selby-Bigge, Sir (Lewis) Amherst, 1st Bt, 1860–1951, vol. V
Selby-Lowndes, Brig. Montacute William Worrall, 1896–1972, vol. VII
Selby-Lowndes, Col William; see Lowndes.
Self, Sir (Albert) Henry, 1890–1975, vol. VII
Self, Sir Henry; see Self, Sir A. H.
Selfe, Sir Robert Carr, 1840–1926, vol. II
Selfe, Sir William Lucius, 1845–1924, vol. II
Selfridge, Harry Gordon, 1858–1947, vol. IV
Seligman, Sir Charles David, 1869–1954, vol. V
Seligman, Charles Gabriel, 1873–1940, vol. III
Seligman, Edwin Robert Anderson, 1861–1939, vol. III
Seligman, Brig.-Gen. Herbert Spencer, 1872–1951, vol. V
Selincourt, Agnes de, 1872–1917, vol. II
Sélincourt, Anne de; see Sedgwick, Anne Douglas.
Selincourt, Ernest de, 1870–1943, vol. IV
Selincourt, Hugh de, 1878–1951, vol. V
Selkirk, Countess of; (Cecely Louisa), died 1920, vol. II
Sell, Rev. Edward, 1839–1932, vol. III
Sell, William James, died 1915, vol. I
Sellar, Harry Harpham, 1893–1966, vol. VI
Sellar, Robert Watson, 1894–1965, vol. VI
Sellar, Lt-Col Thomas Byrne, 1865–1924, vol. II
Selleck, Sir Francis Palmer, 1895–1976, vol. VII
Sellers, Rt Hon. Sir Frederic Aked, 1893–1979, vol. VII
Sellers, Peter Richard Henry, 1925–1980, vol. VII

Sellers, Rev. Robert Victor, 1894–1973, vol. VII
Selley, Sir Harry Ralph, 1871–1960, vol. V
Sellheim, Maj.-Gen. Victor Conradsdorf Morisset, 1866–1928, vol. II
Sellon, Hugh Gilbert René, 1901–1974, vol. VII
Sells, Arthur Lytton L.; see Lytton Sells.
Sells, Vice-Adm. William Fortescue, 1881–1966, vol. VI
Selous, Frederick Courteney, 1851–1917, vol. II
Selous, Gerald Holgate, 1887–1978, vol. VII
Selsdon, 1st Baron, 1877–1938, vol. III
Selsdon, 2nd Baron, 1913–1963, vol. VI
Seltman, Charles Theodore, 1886–1957, vol. V
Selway, Cornelius James, 1875–1948, vol. IV
Selwyn, Rev. Edward Carus, 1853–1918, vol. II
Selwyn, Very Rev. Edward Gordon, 1885–1959, vol. V
Selwyn, Rt Rev. George Theodore, 1887–1957, vol. V
Selwyn, Rt Rev. John Richardson, 1844–1898, vol. I
Selwyn, Rev. William, 1840–1914, vol. I
Selwyn, Rt Rev. William Marshall, 1880–1951, vol. V
Selwyn-Clarke, Sir Selwyn, 1893–1976, vol. VII
Selwyn-Lloyd, Baron (Life Peer); John Selwyn Brooke Selwyn-Lloyd, 1904–1978, vol. VII
Selznick, David Oliver, 1902–1965, vol. VI
Semon, Sir Felix, 1849–1921, vol. II
Semon, Henry, 1881–1971, vol. VII
Sempill, 17th Lord, 1836–1905, vol. I
Sempill, 18th Lord, 1863–1934, vol. III
Sempill, 19th Lord, 1893–1965, vol. VI
Sempill, Major Hon. Douglas F.; see Forbes-Sempill.
Semple, Lt-Col Sir David, 1856–1937, vol. III
Semple, Dugald, 1884–1964, vol. VI
Semple, John Edward, 1903–1969, vol. VI
Semple, Patrick, 1875–1954, vol. V
Semple, Hon. Robert, 1873–1955, vol. V
Sen, Jitendranath, 1875–1945, vol. IV
Sen, Nirmul Chunder, 1869–1936, vol. III
Sen, Susil C., died 1946, vol. IV
Sen, Sir Usha Nath, 1880–1959, vol. V
Senanayake, Rt. Hon. Don Stephen, 1884–1952, vol. V
Senanayake, Hon. Dudley Shelton, 1911–1973, vol. VII
Sencourt, Robert, 1890–1969, vol. VI
Sendall, Sir Walter Joseph, 1832–1904, vol. I
Senier, Alfred, 1853–1918, vol. II
Senier, Sir Frederic William, 1869–1951, vol. V
Senior, Albert, 1867–1929, vol. III
Senior, Bernard, 1865–1934, vol. III
Senior, Col Henry William Richard, 1866–1935, vol. III
Senior, Mark, 1863–1927, vol. II
Senior, William, died 1920, vol. II
Senior, William Goodwin, 1894–1969, vol. VI
Senior, Hon. William Sidney, 1888–1938, vol. III
Senn, Charles Herman, died 1934, vol. III
Sennett, Sir Richard, 1862–1947, vol. IV
Senter, George, 1874–1942, vol. IV
Senter, Sir John Watt, 1905–1966, vol. VI

Sequeira, James Harry, *died* 1948, vol. IV
Serao, Matilde, 1856–1927, vol. II
Serena, Arthur, *died* 1922, vol. II
Serena, Clara, *died* 1972, vol. VII
Sergeant, Adeline, 1851–1904, vol. I
Sergeant, Emily Frances Adeline; *see* Sergeant, Adeline.
Sergeant, Maj.-Gen. Frederick Cavendish H.; *see* Hilton-Sergeant.
Sergeant, Lewis, 1841–1902, vol. I
Sergison, Captain Charles Warden, 1867–1911, vol. I
Sergison-Brooke, Lt-Gen. Sir Bertram Norman; *see* Brooke.
Serjeant, Sir David Maurice, *died* 1929, vol. III
Serjeant, Col Sir William Charles Eldon, 1857–1930, vol. III
Serle, Rev. Samuel Edward Bayard, 1866–1939, vol. III
Serocold, Brig.-Gen. Eric P.; *see* Pearce-Serocold.
Serocold, Oswald P.; *see* Pearce-Serocold.
Serpell, Henry Oberlin, 1853–1943, vol. IV
Serra Largo, Count de; Peter Alexander Cameron Mackenzie, 1856–1931, vol. III
Servaes, Vice-Adm. Reginald Maxwell, 1893–1978, vol. VII
Service, Hon. James, 1823–1899, vol. I
Service, Robert William, 1874–1958, vol. V
Seshadri, Tiruvenkata Rajendra, 1900–1975, vol. VII
Setalvad, Sir Chimanlal Harilal, *died* 1947, vol. IV
Setchell, Herbert Leonard, 1892–1976, vol. VII
Seth, Andrew, 1856–1931, vol. III
Seth, Arathoon, 1852–1918, vol. II
Seth, James, 1860–1924, vol. II
Seth-Smith, David, 1875–1963, vol. VI
Seth-Smith, Brig. Hugh Garden, 1885–1958, vol. V
Seth-Smith, W. H., 1852–1928, vol. II
Sethna, Hon. Sir Phiroze, 1866–1938, vol. III
Seton, Sir Alexander Hay, 10th Bt (*cr* 1663), 1904–1963, vol. VI
Seton, Col Sir Bruce Gordon, 9th Bt (*cr* 1663), 1868–1932, vol. III
Seton, Sir Bruce Lovat, 11th Bt (*cr* 1663), 1909–1969, vol. VI
Seton, Sir Bruce Maxwell, 8th Bt (*cr* 1663), 1836–1915, vol. I
Seton, Ernest Thompson, 1860–1946, vol. IV
Seton, George, 1822–1908, vol. I
Seton, Mrs Grace Gallatin Thompson, *died* 1959, vol. V
Seton, Captain Sir John Hastings, 10th Bt (*cr* 1683), 1888–1956, vol. V
Seton, Sir Malcolm Cotter Cariston, 1872–1940, vol. III
Seton, Miles Charles Cariston, 1874–1919, vol. II
Seton, Robert George, 1860–1939, vol. III
Seton, Robert S., *died* 1942, vol. IV
Seton, Walter, 1882–1927, vol. II
Seton, Sir William Samuel, 9th Bt (*cr* 1683), 1837–1914 (this entry was not transferred to Who was Who).
Seton-Karr, Sir Henry, 1853–1914, vol. I
Seton-Karr, Heywood Walter, 1859–1938, vol. III

Seton Pringle, John; *see* Pringle, J. S. M.
Seton-Steuart, Sir Alan Henry; *see* Steuart.
Seton-Steuart, Sir Douglas Archibald; *see* Steuart.
Seton-Thompson; *see* Seton, E. T.
Seton-Watson, Robert William, 1879–1951, vol. V
Settle, Alison, *died* 1980, vol. VII
Settle, Charles Arthur, 1905–1979, vol. VII
Settle, Lt-Gen. Sir Henry Hamilton, 1847–1923, vol. II
Settrington, Lord; Frederick Charles Gordon-Lennox, 1904–1919, vol. II
Ševčík, Otakar, 1852–1934, vol. III
Severine, Madame, 1855–129, vol. III
Severn, Arthur, *died* 1931, vol. III
Severn, Sir Claud, 1869–1933, vol. III
Severn, Walter, 1830–1904, vol. I
Seversky, Major Alexander P. de, 1894–1974, vol. VII
Sevestre, Robert, 1868–1949, vol. IV
Sewall, May Wright, *died* 1920, vol. II
Seward, Sir Albert Charles, 1863–1941, vol. IV
Seward, Sir Conrad; *see* Seward, Sir S. C.
Seward, Edwin, 1853–1924, vol. II
Seward, Sir (Samuel) Conrad, 1908–1976, vol. VII
Seward, Air Vice-Marshal Walter John, 1898–1972, vol. VII
Sewell, Rev. Archibald Hankey, 1874–1943, vol. IV
Sewell, Arnold Edward, 1886–1969, vol. VI
Sewell, Brig. Edgar Patrick, 1905–1957, vol. V
Sewell, Elizabeth Missing, 1815–1906, vol. I
Sewell, Col Evelyn Pierce, *died* 1960, vol. V
Sewell, Rev. Henry, 1847–1943, vol. IV
Sewell, Brig.-Gen. Horace Somerville, 1881–1953, vol. V
Sewell, Rev. James Edwards, 1810–1903, vol. I
Sewell, John Thomas Beadsworth, 1858–1930, vol. III
Sewell, Brig.-Gen. Jonathan William Shirley, 1872–1941, vol. IV
Sewell, Lt-Col Robert Beresford Seymour, 1880–1964, vol. VI
Sewell, Sir Sidney Valentine, 1880–1949, vol. IV
Sewell, Col Thomas Davies, 1832–1916, vol. II
Sexton, Frederic Henry, 1879–1955, vol. V
Sexton, Most Rev. Harold Eustace, 1888–1972, vol. VII
Sexton, Sir James, 1856–1938, vol. III
Sexton, Col Michael John, 1860–1922, vol. II
Sexton, Sir Robert, 1814–1901, vol. I
Sexton, T. M., *died* 1946, vol. IV (A), vol. V
Sexton, Thomas, 1848–1932, vol. III
Sexton, Walter, 1877–1941, vol. IV
Seyler, Clarence Arthur, 1866–1959, vol. V
Seymour, Ven. Albert Eden, 1841–1908, vol. I
Seymour, Sir Albert Victor Francis, 2nd Bt (*cr* 1869), 1879–1949, vol. IV
Seymour, Alfred Wallace, 1881–1960, vol. V
Seymour, Very Rev. Algernon Giles, 1886–1933, vol. III
Seymour, Brig.-Gen. Archibald George, 1875–1933, vol. III
Seymour, Captain Arthur George, 1884–1935, vol. III
Seymour, Mrs Beatrice Kean, *died* 1955, vol. V

Seymour, Charles, 1885–1963, vol. VI
Seymour, Charles Derick, 1863–1935, vol. III
Seymour, Lt-Col Charles Hugh Napier, 1874–1933, vol. III
Seymour, Vice-Adm. Claude, 1876–1941, vol. IV
Seymour, Edgar William, 1868–1926, vol. II
Seymour, Major Sir Edward, 1877–1948, vol. IV
Seymour, Lord Edward Beauchamp, 1879–1917, vol. II
Seymour, Admiral of the Fleet Rt Hon. Sir Edward Hobart, 1840–1929, vol. III
Seymour, Lord Ernest James, 1850–1930, vol. III
Seymour, Sir George S.; see Seymour Seymour.
Seymour, Brig.-Gen. Lord Henry Charles, 1878–1939, vol. III
Seymour, Henry J., 1876–1954, vol. V
Seymour, Horace Alfred Damer, 1843–1902, vol. I
Seymour, Sir Horace James, 1885–1978, vol. VII
Seymour, Leslie George, 1900–1976, vol. VII
Seymour, Sir Michael Culme-, 3rd Bt (cr 1809), 1836–1920, vol. II
Seymour, Vice-Adm. Sir Michael Culme-, 4th Bt (cr 1809), 1867–1925, vol. II
Seymour, Michael Richard, 1880–1936, vol. III
Seymour, Comdr Ralph Frederick, 1886–1922, vol. II
Seymour, Lt-Col Sir Reginald Henry, 1878–1938, vol. III
Seymour, Richard Sturgis, 1875–1959, vol. V
Seymour, Rev. Lord Victor Alexander, 1859–1935, vol. III
Seymour, Gen. Lord William Frederick Ernest, 1838–1915, vol. I
Seymour, Gen. Sir William Henry, 1829–1921, vol. II
Seymour, William Kean, 1887–1975, vol. VII
Seymour-Lloyd, Sir John Hall, 1873–1939, vol. III
Seymour Seymour, Sir George, 1880–1962, vol. VI
Seys, Roland Alex. W.; see Wood-Seys.
Sforza, Count Carlo, 1873–1952, vol. V
Sgambati, Giovanni, 1843–1914, vol. I
Shackle, Major Ernest William, 1862–1938, vol. III
Shackle, Robert Jones, 1895–1950, vol. IV
Shackleton, Sir David James, 1863–1938, vol. III
Shackleton, Edith; see Heald, E. S.
Shackleton, Major Sir Ernest Henry, 1874–1922, vol. II
Shackleton, Sir Harry Bertram, 1878–1958, vol. V
Shackleton, William, 1872–1933, vol. III
Shadbolt, Ernest Ifill, 1851–1936, vol. III
Shadi Lal, Rt Hon. Sir, 1874–1945, vol. IV
Shadwell, Arthur, 1854–1936, vol. III
Shadwell, Charles Lancelot, 1840–1919, vol. II
Shadwell, Lionel Lancelot, 1845–1925, vol. II
Shadwell, William L.; see Lucas-Shadwell.
Shafi, Sir Muhammad, 1869–1932, vol. III
Shafter, William Rufus, 1835–1906, vol. I
Shaftesbury, 9th Earl of, 1869–1961, vol. VI
Shafto, Captain Arthur Duncombe, 1880–1914, vol. I
Shah, Hon. Sir Lallubhai Asharam, 1873–1926, vol. II
Shah, Khan Bahadur Sir Sayyid Mehdi, died 1927, vol. II (A), vol. III

Shahan, Rt Rev. Thomas Joseph, 1857–1932, vol. III
Shahpura, Raja Sir Nahar Singh Dhiraj, 1855–1932, vol. III
Shahub-ud-Din, Khan Bahadur Sir Chaudhri, died 1949, vol. IV (A), vol. V
Shaikh, Lt-Col Abdul Hamid, 1890–1963, vol. VI
Shairp, Lt-Col Alexander, 1873–1944, vol. IV
Shakerley, Sir Charles Watkin, 2nd Bt, 1833–1898, vol. I
Shakerley, Major Sir Cyril Holland, 5th Bt, 1897–1970, vol. VI
Shakerley, Major Geoffrey Charles, 1869–1915, vol. I
Shakerley, Sir George Herbert, 4th Bt, 1863–1945, vol. IV
Shakerley, Sir Walter Geoffrey, 3rd Bt, 1859–1943, vol. IV
Shakespear, Alexander Blake, 1873–1949, vol. IV
Shakespear, Brig. Arthur Talbot, 1884–1964, vol. VI
Shakespear, Dame Ethel Mary Reader, 1871–1946, vol. IV
Shakespear, Maj.-Gen. George Robert James, 1842–1926, vol. II
Shakespear, Lt-Col John, 1861–1942, vol. IV
Shakespear, Col Leslie Waterfield, 1860–1933, vol. III
Shakespeare, Rt Hon. Sir Geoffrey Hithersay, 1st Bt, 1893–1980, vol. VII
Shakespeare, Rev. John Howard, 1857–1928, vol. II
Shakespeare, William, 1849–1931, vol. III
Shams-ul-Huda, Nawab Sir Syed, 1864–1922, vol. II
Shamsher Singh, Sir Sardar, Sardar Bahadur, 1860–1920, vol. II (A), vol. III
Shanahan, Col Daniel Davis, 1863–1954, vol. V
Shanahan, Foss, 1910–1964, vol. VI
Shand, 1st Baron, 1828–1904, vol. I
Shand, Alexander Faulkner, 1858–1936, vol. III
Shand, Alexander Innes, 1832–1907, vol. I
Shand, Sir Charles Lister, 1846–1925, vol. II
Shand, Surg. Rear-Adm. Jonathan, 1865–1961, vol. VI
Shand, Philip Morton, 1888–1960, vol. V
Shand, Samuel James, 1882–1957, vol. V
Shand, Rev. Thomas Henry Rodie, 1827–1914, vol. I
Shandon, 1st Baron, 1857–1930, vol. III
Shanker Shamsher Jang Bahadur Rana, Gen., 1909–1976, vol. VII
Shanks, Edward, 1892–1953, vol. V
Shanks, S(eymour) Cochrane, 1893–1980, vol. VII
Shanks, W(illiam) Somerville, 1864–1951, vol. V
Shann, Edward Owen Giblin, 1884–1935, vol. III
Shann, Sir Thomas Thornhill, 1846–1923, vol. III
Shannan, A. M'F., died 1915, vol. I
Shannon, 6th Earl of, 1860–1906, vol. I
Shannon, 7th Earl of, 1897–1917 (this entry was not transferred to Who was Who).
Shannon, 8th Earl of, 1900–1963, vol. VI
Shannon, Charles, 1863–1937, vol. III
Shannon, Howard Huntley, 1892–1976, vol. VII

Shannon, Sir James Jebusa, 1862–1923, vol. II
Shannon, Brig.-Gen. Lewis William, 1859–1936, vol. III
Shansfield, William Newton, *died* 1925, vol. II
Shapcott, Brig. Sir Henry, 1888–1967, vol. VI
Shapcott, John Dufour, 1857–1923, vol. II
Shapcott, Louis Edward, 1877–1950, vol. IV
Shapland, Cyril Dee, 1899–1980, vol. VII
Shapland, Maj.-Gen. John Dee, 1897–1971, vol. VII
Shapland, Rev. Richard Henry Bowden, 1877–1937, vol. III
Shapley, Harlow, 1885–1972, vol. VII
Shapley, Rt Rev. Ronald Norman, 1890–1964, vol. VI
Shapurji, Sir Burjorji Broacha, *died* 1920, vol. II
Share, Sir Hamnet Holditch, 1864–1937, vol. III
Sharfuddin, Syed, *born* 1856, vol. II
Sharkey, Sir Seymour John, 1847–1929, vol. III
Sharman, Col Charles Henry Ludovic, 1881–1970, vol. VI
Sharman, Charlotte, 1832–1929, vol. III
Sharman-Crawford, Col Rt Hon. Robert Gordon, 1853–1934, vol. III
Sharp, Col Alexander Dunstan, 1870–1955, vol. V
Sharp, Air Vice-Marshal Alfred Charles Henry, 1904–1956, vol. V
Sharp, Alphonse, 1872–1942, vol. IV
Sharp, Rev. Arnold Mortimer, 1864–1938, vol. III
Sharp, Ven. Arthur Frederick, 1866–1960, vol. V
Sharp, Cecil James, 1859–1924, vol. II
Sharp, Clifford Dyce, 1883–1935, vol. III
Sharp, David, 1840–1922, vol. II
Sharp, Dorothea, *died* 1955, vol. V
Sharp, Sir Edward, 1st Bt (*cr* 1922), 1854–1931, vol. III
Sharp, Elizabeth Amelia, 1856–1932, vol. III
Sharp, Ernest Hamilton, *died* 1922, vol. II
Sharp, Evelyn, 1869–1955, vol. V
Sharp, Francis Everard, 1890–1972, vol. VII
Sharp, Lt-Col Frederick Leonard, 1867–1916, vol. II
Sharp, Geoffrey Newton, 1914–1974, vol. VII
Sharp, Most Rev. Gerald, 1865–1933, vol. III
Sharp, Gilbert Granville-, 1894–1968, vol. VI
Sharp, Harold Gregory, 1886–1972, vol. VII
Sharp, Sir Henry, 1869–1954, vol. V
Sharp, Sir Herbert Edward, 2nd Bt (*cr* 1922), 1879–1936, vol. III
Sharp, Janet A.; *see* Achurch, J.
Sharp, Rev. John, 1837–1917, vol. II
Sharp, Rev. John Alfred, 1856–1932, vol. III
Sharp, Gen. Sir John Aubrey Taylor, 1917–1977, vol. VII
Sharp, Rev. Canon John Herbert, 1887–1950, vol. IV
Sharp, Major John Reuben Philip, *died* 1922, vol. II
Sharp, Lauriston William, 1897–1959, vol. V
Sharp, Sir Milton, 2nd Bt (*cr* 1920), 1880–1941, vol. IV
Sharp, Sir Milton Sheridan, 1st Bt (*cr* 1920), 1856–1924, vol. II
Sharp, Noel Farquharson, 1905–1978, vol. VII
Sharp, Sir Percival, 1867–1953, vol. V
Sharp, Robert Farquharson, 1864–1945, vol. IV

Sharp, Thomas, 1901–1978, vol. VII
Sharp, Thomas Herbert, 1840–1918, vol. II
Sharp, W. H. Cartwright, 1883–1950, vol. IV
Sharp, William, 1856–1905, vol. I, vol. I (A)
Sharp, Mrs William; *see* Sharp, Elizabeth Amelia.
Sharp, Rev. Canon William Hey, 1845–1928, vol. II
Sharpe, Sir Alfred, 1853–1935, vol. III
Sharpe, Charles W., *died* 1955, vol. V
Sharpe, Ven. Ernest Newton, *died* 1949, vol. IV
Sharpe, Rev. Harold Stephen, 1886–1960, vol. V
Sharpe, Rev. Henry Edmund, 1859–1939, vol. III
Sharpe, Joseph, 1859–1930, vol. III
Sharpe, Sir Montagu, 1856–1942, vol. IV
Sharpe, Phoebe Elizabeth, 1888–1941, vol. IV
Sharpe, Reginald Robinson, 1848–1925, vol. II
Sharpe, Richard Bowdler, 1847–1909, vol. I
Sharpe, Major Robert William, 1886–1943, vol. IV
Sharpe, Rev. Thomas Wetherherd, 1829–1905, vol. I
Sharpe, Major Wilfred Stanley, 1860–1917, vol. II
Sharpe, William Edward Thompson, 1834–1909, vol. I
Sharpe, Sir William Rutton Searle, 1881–1968, vol. VI
Sharpey-Schafer, Sir Edward Albert, 1850–1935, vol. III
Sharpey-Schafer, Edward Peter, 1908–1963, vol. VI
Sharpin, Ven. Frederick Lloyd, *died* 1921, vol. II
Sharples, Charles Norman, 1906–1954, vol. V
Sharples, Sir Richard Christopher, 1916–1973, vol. VII
Sharples, William Johnson, 1865–1948, vol. IV
Sharpley, Forbes Wilmot, 1897–1965, vol. VI
Sharrock, Rev. John Alfred, 1853–1932, vol. III
Sharrock, Rev. Canon William R., *died* 1940, vol. III
Sharwood-Smith, Edward, 1865–1954, vol. V
Shastri, Shri Lal Bahadur, 1904–1966, vol. VI
Shastri, Prabhu Dutt, *born* 1885, vol. IV
Shatford, Rev. Canon Allan P., 1873–1935, vol. III
Shattock, Clement Edward, 1887–1969, vol. VI
Shattock, Samuel George, 1852–1924, vol. II
Shaughnessy, 1st Baron, 1853–1923, vol. II
Shaughnessy, 2nd Baron, 1883–1938, vol. III
Shaw, Albert, 1857–1947, vol. IV
Shaw, Alexander Malcolm, 1885–1974, vol. VII
Shaw, Sir Alexander William, 1847–1923, vol. II
Shaw, (Agnes) Maude; *see* Royden, A. M.
Shaw, Ven. Archibald, 1879–1956, vol. V
Shaw, Sir (Archibald) Douglas MacInnes, 1895–1957, vol. V
Shaw, Sir Archibald M'Innes, 1862–1931, vol. III
Shaw, Arthur, 1880–1939, vol. III
Shaw, Arthur Frederick Bernard, *died* 1947, vol. IV
Shaw, Arthur W.; *see* Winter-Shaw.
Shaw, Bernard; *see* Shaw, G. B.
Shaw, Sir Charles; *see* Shaw, Sir T. F. C. E.
Shaw, Rev. Sir Charles John Monson, 8th Bt (*cr* 1665), 1860–1922, vol. II
Shaw, Charles Thomas K.; *see* Knox-Shaw.
Shaw, Clarice McNab, *died* 1946, vol. IV
Shaw, Captain (E) Cyril Arthur, 1894–1946, vol. IV

Shaw, Maj.-Gen. David G. Levinge, 1860–1930, vol. III

Shaw, Sir Douglas MacInnes; see Shaw, Sir A. D. M.

Shaw, Sir Doyle Money, 1830–1918, vol. II

Shaw, Rt Rev. Edward Domett, 1860–1937, vol. III

Shaw, Edward Wingfield, 1895–1916, vol. II

Shaw, Sir Evelyn Campbell, 1882–1974, vol. VII

Shaw, Sir Eyre Massey, 1830–1908, vol. I

Shaw, Col Francis Stewart Kennedy, 1871–1964, vol. VI

Shaw, Lt-Gen. Rt Hon. Sir Frederick Charles, 1861–1942, vol. IV

Shaw, Frederick John Freshwater, 1885–1936, vol. III

Shaw, Sir Frederick William, 5th Bt (cr 1821), 1858–1927, vol. II

Shaw, Geoffrey Mackintosh, 1927–1978, vol. VII

Shaw, Geoffrey Reginald Devereux, 1896–1960, vol. V

Shaw, Geoffrey Turton, 1879–1943, vol. IV

Shaw, (George) Bernard, 1856–1950, vol. IV

Shaw, George Ernest, 1877–1958, vol. V

Shaw, George Ferdinand, 1821–1899, vol. I

Shaw, George Thomas, 1863–1938, vol. III

Shaw, Sir George Watson, 1858–1931, vol. III

Shaw, Rev. George William Hudson, died 1944, vol. IV

Shaw, Air Cdre Gerald Stanley, 1898–1976, vol. VII

Shaw, Harold Batty, 1867–1936, vol. III

Shaw, Harold K.; see Knox-Shaw.

Shaw, Harry Balmforth, 1899–1976, vol. VII

Shaw, Sir Havergal D.; see Downes-Shaw.

Shaw, Helen Brown, died 1964, vol. VI

Shaw, Henry Selby H.; see Hele-Shaw.

Shaw, Herman, 1891–1950, vol. IV

Shaw, J. Byam, 1872–1919, vol. II

Shaw, Sir James Dods, died 1916, vol. II

Shaw, James Johnston, 1845–1910, vol. I

Shaw, John C. Middleton, 1901–1961, vol. VI

Shaw, Sir John Charles Kenward, 7th Bt (cr 1665), 1829–1909, vol. I

Shaw, Sir John Houldsworth, 1874–1962, vol. VI

Shaw, Rev. John Mackintosh, 1879–1972, vol. VII

Shaw, John Woollands, 1875–1937, vol. III

Shaw, Joseph, 1856–1933, vol. III

Shaw, Kathleen Trousdell, 1870–1958, vol. V

Shaw, Lauriston Elgie, 1859–1923, vol. II

Shaw, Hon. Leslie Mortier, 1848–1932, vol. III

Shaw, Martin Fallas, 1875–1958, vol. V

Shaw, Mary, (Mrs Robert Shaw); see Ure, M.

Shaw, Maurice Elgie, 1894–1977, vol. VII

Shaw, Sir Napier; see Shaw, Sir W. N.

Shaw, Sir Patrick, 1913–1975, vol. VII

Shaw, Major Peter Stapleton-, 1888–1953, vol. V

Shaw, Philip Egerton, 1866–1949, vol. IV

Shaw, Reeves, 1886–1952, vol. V

Shaw, Richard James Herbert, 1885–1946, vol. IV

Shaw, Richard Norman, 1831–1912, vol. I

Shaw, Robert, 1927–1978, vol. VII

Shaw, Sir Robert de Vere, 6th Bt (cr 1821), 1890–1969, vol. VI

Shaw, Sir (Theodore Frederick) Charles (Edward), 1st Bt (cr 1908), 1859–1942, vol. IV

Shaw, Surg. Rear-Adm. Thomas Brown, 1879–1961, vol. VI

Shaw, Thomas Claye, 1841–1927, vol. II

Shaw, Thomas Edward, 1888–1935, vol. III

Shaw, Thomas K.; see Knox-Shaw.

Shaw, Rt Hon. Tom, 1872–1938, vol. III

Shaw, Trevor Ian, 1928–1972, vol. VII

Shaw, Sir Walter Sidney, 1863–1937, vol. III

Shaw, Captain Walter William, 1868–1927, vol. II

Shaw, Wilfred, 1897–1953, vol. V

Shaw, William Arthur, 1865–1943, vol. IV

Shaw, William Barbour, 1868–1930, vol. III

Shaw, William Boyd Kennedy, 1901–1979, vol. VII

Shaw, Sir William Fletcher, 1878–1961, vol. VI

Shaw, Rev. William Francis, died 1904, vol. I

Shaw, Rev. William Frederick, 1843–1931, vol. III

Shaw, Sir (William) Napier, 1854–1945, vol. IV

Shaw, William R.; see Rawson-Shaw.

Shaw, William Thomas, 1879–1965, vol. VI

Shaw-Hamilton, Very Rev. Robert James, 1840–1908, vol. I

Shaw-Mackenzie, John Alexander, 1857–1933, vol. III

Shaw-Stewart, Col Basil Heron, 1877–1939, vol. III

Shaw-Stewart, Sir Euan Guy, 10th Bt, 1928–1980, vol. VII

Shaw-Stewart, Lt-Col Sir Guy; see Shaw-Stewart, Lt-Col Sir W. G.

Shaw-Stewart, Sir Hugh; see Shaw-Stewart, Sir M. H.

Shaw-Stewart, Sir (Michael) Hugh, 8th Bt, 1854–1942, vol. IV

Shaw-Stewart, Sir Michael Robert, 7th Bt, 1826–1903, vol. I

Shaw-Stewart, Lt-Col Sir (Walter) Guy, 9th Bt, 1892–1976, vol. VII

Shaw-Stewart, Walter Richard, 1861–1934, vol. III

Shaw-Zambra, William Warren, 1898–1971, vol. VII

Shawcross, Christopher Nyholm, 1905–1973, vol. VII

Shawe, Lt-Col Charles, 1878–1951, vol. V

Shawe, Henry Benjamin, 1864–1943, vol. IV

Shawyer, Arthur Frederic, 1876–1954, vol. V

Shaylor, Joseph, 1844–1923, vol. II

Shea, Lt-Col Alexander Gallwey, 1880–1935, vol. III

Shea, Hon. Sir Edward Dalton, 1820–1913, vol. I

Shea, Gen. Sir John Stuart Mackenzie, 1869–1966, vol. VI

Shead, Sir Samuel George, 1871–1948, vol. IV

Shearburn, Rt Rev. Victor George, 1900–1975, vol. VII

Sheard, Thomas Frederick Mason, 1866–1921, vol. II

Shearer, Sir Bruce, 1888–1971, vol. VII

Shearer, Cresswell, 1874–1941, vol. IV

Shearer, E., died 1945, vol. IV

Shearer, Brig. Eric James, 1892–1980, vol. VII

Shearer, Sir James Greig, 1893–1966, vol. VI

Shearer, Sir John, 1843–1908, vol. I

Shearer, John Burt, 1904–1962, vol. VI
Shearer, Col Johnston, 1852–1917, vol. II
Shearer, Lt-Col Magnus, 1890–1961, vol. VI
Shearing, Joseph; see Long, M. G.
Shearman, Arthur T., 1866–1937, vol. III
Shearman, Brig. Charles Edward Gowran, 1889–1968, vol. VI
Shearman, Rt Hon. Sir Montague, 1857–1930, vol. III
Shearme, Edward, died 1920, vol. II
Shearme, Paymaster-Captain Edward Haweis, 1876–1925, vol. II
Shearme, Rev. John, 1842–1925, vol. II
Shears, Frederick Sidney, 1892–1932, vol. III
Shears, Maj.-Gen. Philip James, 1887–1972, vol. VII
Sheat, Sir Oliver; see Sheat, Sir W. J. O.
Sheat, Sir (William James) Oliver, 1864–1944, vol. IV
Shebbeare, Rev. Charles John, 1865–1945, vol. IV
Shebbeare, Edward Oswald, 1884–1964, vol. VI
Shedden, Sir Frederick Geoffrey, 1893–1971, vol. VII
Shedden, Sir George, 1856–1937, vol. III
Shedden, Sir Lewis, 1870–1941, vol. IV
Shedden, Rt Rev. Roscow George, 1882–1956, vol. V
Shedlock, John South, 1843–1919, vol. II
Shee, Sir George Richard Francis, 1869–1939, vol. III
Shee, Henry Gordon, 1847–1909, vol. I
Shee, Lt-Col Sir Martin A.; see Archer-Shee.
Sheean, (James) Vincent, 1899–1975, vol. VII
Sheean, Vincent; see Sheean, J. V.
Sheehan, Sir Henry John, 1883–1941, vol. IV
Sheehan, Most Rev. Michael, 1870–1945, vol. IV
Sheehan, Rev. Patrick Augustine, 1852–1913, vol. I
Sheehan, Most Rev. Richard Alphonsus, 1845–1915, vol. I
Sheehy, Sir Christopher, 1894–1960, vol. V
Sheehy, Sir John Francis, 1889–1949, vol. IV
Sheehy, Sir Joseph Aloysius, 1900–1971, vol. VII
Sheen, Alfred William, 1869–1945, vol. IV
Sheen, Engr-Rear-Adm. Charles C., 1871–1952, vol. V
Sheen, Most Rev. Fulton John, 1895–1979, vol. VII
Sheen, Air Vice-Marshal Walter Charles, 1907–1969, vol. VI (AII)
Sheepshanks, Rt Rev. John, 1834–1912, vol. I
Sheepshanks, Sir Thomas Herbert, 1895–1964, vol. VI
Sheepshanks, William, 1851–1928, vol. II
Sheffield, 3rd Earl of, 1832–1909, vol. I
Sheffield, 4th Baron, and Stanley of Alderley, 4th Baron, 1839–1925 (this entry was not transferred to Who was Who).
Sheffield, 6th Baron, and Stanley of Alderley, 6th Baron, 1907–1971, vol. VII
Sheffield, 7th Baron, and Stanley of Alderley, 7th Baron, 1915–1971, vol. VII
Sheffield, Sir Berkeley Digby George, 6th Bt, 1876–1946, vol. IV

Sheffield, Edmund Charles Reginald, 1908–1977, vol. VII
Sheffield, Sir Robert Arthur, 7th Bt, 1905–1977, vol. VII
Sheffield, Robert Stoney O.; see Oliphant-Sheffield.
Shehyn, Hon. Joseph, 1829–1918, vol. II
Sheil, Charles Leo, 1897–1968, vol. VI
Sheil, James, 1829–1908, vol. I
Sheil, John Devonshire, 1855–1935, vol. III
Sheild, Arthur Marmaduke, 1858–1922, vol. II
Sheilds, Francis Ernest W.; see Wentworth-Sheilds.
Sheilds, Rt Rev. Wentworth Francis W.; see Wentworth-Sheilds.
Sheils, George Kingsley, 1894–1953, vol. V
Shekleton, Brig.-Gen. Hugh Pentland, 1860–1938, vol. III
Sheldon, Charles Monroe, 1857–1946, vol. IV
Sheldon, Christine Mary, died 1970, vol. VI
Sheldon, John Prince, died 1913, vol. I
Sheldon, Sir Mark, 1871–1956, vol. V
Sheldon, Norman Lindsay, 1876–1946, vol. IV
Shelford, Frederic, 1871–1943, vol. IV
Shelford, Rev. Leonard Edmund, 1836–1914, vol. I
Shell, Rita, died 1950, vol. IV
Shelley, Col Bertram Arthur Graham, 1869–1947, vol. IV
Shelley, Sir Charles, 5th Bt (cr 1806), 1838–1902, vol. I
Shelley, Herbert John, 1895–1975, vol. VII
Shelley, Sir James, 1884–1961, vol. VI
Shelley, Sir John, 9th Bt (cr 1611), 1848–1931, vol. III
Shelley, Sir John Frederick, 10th Bt (cr 1611), 1884–1976, vol. VII
Shelley, Kew Edwin, 1894–1964, vol. VI
Shelley, Malcolm Bond, 1879–1968, vol. VI
Shelley, Sir Percy Bysshe, 7th Bt (cr 1806), 1872–1953, vol. V
Shelley, Sir Sidney Patrick, 8th Bt (cr 1806), 1880–1965, vol. VI
Shelley-Rolls, Captain Sir John Courtown Edward, 6th Bt (cr 1806), 1871–1951, vol. V
Shellshear, Joseph Lexden, 1885–1958, vol. V
Shelmerdine, Lt-Col Sir Francis Claude, 1881–1945, vol. IV
Shennan, Sir Alfred Ernest, 1887–1959, vol. V
Shennan, Hay, 1859–1937, vol. III
Shennan, Theodore, died 1948, vol. IV
Shenstone, Allen Goodrich, 1893–1980, vol. VII
Shenstone, William Ashwell, 1850–1908, vol. I
Shentall, Sir Ernest, 1861–1936, vol. III
Shenton, Edward Warren Hine, 1872–1955, vol. V
Shenton, Hon. Sir George, 1842–1909, vol. I
Shenton, Sir William Edward Leonard, 1885–1967, vol. VI
Shepard, Ernest Howard, 1879–1976, vol. VII
Shepard, Helen Gould, 1868–1938, vol. III (A), vol. IV
Shepardson, Whitney Hart, 1890–1966, vol. VI
Shephard, Cecil Yaxley, 1900–1959, vol. V
Shephard, Lt-Col Charles Sinclair, 1848–1930, vol. III

609

Shephard, Firth, 1891–1949, vol. IV
Shephard, Sir Horatio Hale, *died* 1921, vol. II
Shephard, Rev. John, 1837–1926, vol. II
Shephard, Sidney, 1894–1953, vol. V
Shepheard, Rex Beaumont, 1902–1980, vol. VII
Shepherd, 1st Baron, 1881–1954, vol. V
Shepherd, Rev. Ambrose, 1854–1915, vol. I
Shepherd, Arthur, 1884–1951, vol. V
Shepherd, Arthur Edmond, 1867–1942, vol. IV
Shepherd, Ven. Arthur Pearce, 1885–1968, vol. VI
Shepherd, Col Charles Herbert, 1846–1920, vol. II
Shepherd, Lt-Col Claude Innes, 1884–1960, vol. V
Shepherd, Sir (Edward Henry) Gerald, 1886–1967, vol. VI
Shepherd, E(dwin) Colston, 1891–1976, vol. VII
Shepherd, Eric Andres, *died* 1937, vol. III
Shepherd, F. H. S., *died* 1948, vol. IV
Shepherd, Francis John, 1851–1929, vol. III
Shepherd, Sir Francis Michie, 1893–1962, vol. VI
Shepherd, Sir Gerald; *see* Shepherd, Sir E. H. G.
Shepherd, Gilbert David, 1880–1958, vol. V
Shepherd, Brig. Gilbert John Victor, 1887–1969, vol. VI
Shepherd, Harold Richard Bowman A.; *see* Adie-Shepherd.
Shepherd, Sir (Harry) Percy, *died* 1946, vol. IV
Shepherd, Henry Bryan, 1917–1974, vol. VII
Shepherd, Very Rev. Henry Young, *died* 1947, vol. IV
Shepherd, James Affleck, 1867–1946, vol. IV
Shepherd, Joseph Wilfrid, 1885–1975, vol. VII
Shepherd, Sir Percy; *see* Shepherd, Sir H. P.
Shepherd, Very Rev. Robert Henry Wishart, 1888–1971, vol. VII
Shepherd, Sir Walker; *see* Shepherd, Sir William W. F.
Shepherd, William Kidd Ogilvy, 1888–1941, vol. IV
Shepherd, Rev. William Mutrie, 1832–1910, vol. I
Shepherd, Sir (William) Walker (Frederick), 1895–1959, vol. V
Shepherd-Barron, Wilfrid Philip, 1888–1979, vol. VII
Shepherd-Cross, Herbert, 1847–1916, vol. II
Shepherd-Folker, Horace, 1859–1938, vol. III
Sheppard, Alfred Tresidder, 1871–1947, vol. IV
Sheppard, Adm. Sir Dawson; *see* Sheppard, Adm. Sir T. D. L.
Sheppard, Rev. Canon Edgar, 1845–1921, vol. II
Sheppard, Col George Sidney, 1867–1936, vol. III
Sheppard, Brig.-Gen. Herbert Cecil, *died* 1953, vol. V
Sheppard, Very Rev. Hugh Richard Lawrie, 1880–1937, vol. III
Sheppard, Sir John Tresidder, 1881–1968, vol. VI
Sheppard, Oliver, *died* 1941, vol. IV
Sheppard, Percival Albert, (Peter), 1907–1977, vol. VII
Sheppard, Peter; *see* Sheppard, Percival A.
Sheppard, Philip Macdonald, 1921–1976, vol. VII
Sheppard, Major Samuel Gurney, 1865–1915, vol. I
Sheppard, Samuel Townsend, 1880–1951, vol. V
Sheppard, Maj.-Gen. Seymour Hulbert, 1869–1957, vol. V
Sheppard, Thomas, 1876–1945, vol. IV

Sheppard, Adm. Sir (Thomas) Dawson Lees, 1866–1953, vol. V
Sheppard, Vivian Lee Osborne, 1877–1963, vol. VI
Sheppard, Sir William Didsbury, 1865–1933, vol. III
Shepperson, Claude Allin, 1867–1921, vol. II
Shepperson, Sir Ernest Whittome, 1st Bt, 1874–1949, vol. IV
Shepstone, Arthur Jesse, 1852–1912, vol. I
Shepstone, John Wesley, 1827–1916, vol. II
Shepstone, Theophilus, 1843–1907, vol. I
Shera, Arthur Geoffrey, 1889–1971, vol. VII
Shera, Frank Henry, 1882–1956, vol. V
Sherard, 10th Baron, 1849–1902, vol. I
Sherard, 11th Baron, 1851–1924, vol. II
Sherard, 12th Baron, 1858–1931, vol. III
Sherard, Col Ralph Woodchurch, 1860–1922, vol. II
Sherard, Robert Harborough, 1861–1943, vol. IV
Sheraton, Rev. James Paterson, 1841–1906, vol. I
Sherborne, 4th Baron, 1831–1919, vol. II
Sherborne, 5th Baron, 1840–1920, vol. II
Sherborne, 6th Baron, 1873–1949, vol. IV
Sherbrooke, Captain Henry Graham, 1877–1940, vol. III
Sherbrooke, Rev. Henry Nevile, 1846–1916, vol. II
Sherbrooke, Col Nevile Hugh Cairns, 1880–1944, vol. IV
Sherbrooke, Rear-Adm. Robert St Vincent, 1901–1972, vol. VII
Sherburn, Sir John, 1851–1926, vol. II
Sherek, Major Henry, 1900–1967, vol. VI
Sherer, Brig.-Gen. James Donnelly, 1870–1959, vol. V
Sherer, John Walter, 1823–1911, vol. I
Sheridan, Algernon Thomas Brinsley, 1845–1931, vol. III
Sheridan, Charles Cahill, *died* 1941, vol. IV
Sheridan, Clare Consuelo, *died* 1970, vol. VI
Sheridan, Sir Dermot Joseph, 1914–1978, vol. VII
Sheridan, Edward, *died* 1949, vol. IV
Sheridan, Rear-Adm. Henry A., 1884–1959, vol. V
Sheridan, Sir Joseph, 1882–1964, vol. VI
Sheridan, Sir Philip Cahill, 1871–1949, vol. IV
Sheriff, Rev. Thomas Holmes, *died* 1923, vol. II
Sheringham, George, 1884–1937, vol. III
Sheringham, Rev. Harry Alsager, 1852–1907, vol. I
Sheringham, Hugh Tempest, 1876–1930, vol. III
Sheringham, Ven. John William, *died* 1904, vol. I
Sherlock, Sir Alfred Parker, 1876–1946, vol. IV
Sherlock, Col David John Christopher Eustace, 1879–1938, vol. III
Sherlock, David Thomas Joseph, 1881–1964, vol. VI
Sherlock, Frederick, 1853–1914, vol. I
Sherlock, Ven. William, *died* 1919, vol. II
Sherman, Gina, (Mrs Alec Sherman); *see* Bachauer, G.
Sherman, John, 1823–1900, vol. I
Sherman, Most Rev. Louis Ralph, 1886–1953, vol. V
Sherrard, Col James William, *died* 1926, vol. II
Sherren, James, *died* 1945, vol. IV

Sherriff, Lt-Gen. John Pringle, 1831–1911, vol. I
Sherriff, Robert Cedric, 1896–1975, vol. VII
Sherrill, Brig.-Gen. Charles H., 1867–1936, vol. III
Sherrill, Rt Rev. Henry Knox, 1890–1980, vol. VII
Sherrington, Sir Charles Scott, 1857–1952, vol. V
Sherston, Brig. John Reginald Vivian, 1888–1975, vol. VII
Sherston, Col William Maxwell, 1859–1925, vol. II
Sherston-Baker, Lt-Col Sir Dodington George Richard, 5th Bt, 1877–1944, vol. IV
Sherwell, Arthur, 1863–1942, vol. IV
Sherwen, Ven. William, died 1915, vol. I
Sherwill, Sir Ambrose James, 1890–1968, vol. VI
Sherwin, Amy, died 1935, vol. III
Sherwood, 1st Baron, 1898–1970, vol. VI
Sherwood, Col Sir Arthur Percy, 1854–1940, vol. III
Sherwood, Rev. Edward Charles, died 1947, vol. IV
Sherwood, Frederic William, 1864–1931, vol. III
Sherwood, George Henry, 1877–1935, vol. III
Sherwood, Harry Leslie, 1863–1946, vol. IV
Sherwood, Leslie Robert, 1889–1974, vol. VII
Sherwood, Robert Emmet, 1896–1955, vol. V
Sherwood, Will, 1871–1955, vol. V
Sherwood, William Albert, 1855–1919, vol. II
Sherwood, Rev. William Edward, 1851–1927, vol. II
Sherwood-Kelly, Lt-Col John; see Kelly.
Sheshadri Iyar, K., Sir, died 1901, vol. I
Shewell, Brig. Eden Francis, 1877–1964, vol. VI
Shiel, Rt Rev. Joseph, 1873–1931, vol. III
Shiel, Matthew Phipps, 1865–1947, vol. IV
Shield, George William, 1876–1935, vol. III
Shield, Hugh, 1831–1903, vol. I
Shields, Sir Douglas Andrew, 1878–1952, vol. V
Shields, Frederic James, 1833–1911, vol. I
Shields, Harry G., 1859–1935, vol. III
Shields, John Veysie Montgomery, 1914–1966, vol. VI
Shields, Hon. Tasman, 1872–1950, vol. IV
Shiels, Sir Drummond; see Shiels, Sir T. D.
Shiels, Sir (Thomas) Drummond, 1881–1953, vol. V
Shiffner, Rev. Sir George Croxton, 4th Bt, 1819–1906, vol. I
Shiffner, Major Sir Henry Burrows, 7th Bt, 1902–1941, vol. IV
Shiffner, Sir John, 5th Bt, 1857–1914, vol. I
Shiffner, Sir John Bridger, 6th Bt, 1899–1918, vol. II
Shigemitsu, Mamoru, 1887–1957, vol. V
Shillaker, James Frederick, 1870–1943, vol. IV
Shillidy, George Alexander, 1886–1968, vol. VI
Shillidy, John Armstrong, 1882–1952, vol. V
Shillington, Major Rt Hon. David Graham, 1872–1944, vol. IV
Shillito, Rev. Edward, 1872–1948, vol. IV
Shine, Eustace Beverley, 1873–1952, vol. V
Shine, Col James Mathew Forrest, 1861–1931, vol. III
Shine, Most Rev. Thomas, 1872–1955, vol. V
Shiner, Lt-Col Sir Herbert, 1890–1962, vol. VI
Shiner, Ronald Alfred, 1903–1966, vol. VI
Shingleton, Frederick, 1846–1938, vol. III
Shinkwin, Col Ion Richard Staveley, 1875–1961, vol. VI

Shinn, Frederick George, 1867–1950, vol. IV
Shinnie, Andrew James, 1886–1963, vol. VI
Shipley, Sir Arthur Everett, 1861–1927, vol. II
Shipley, Brig.-Gen. Charles Orby, 1867–1934, vol. III
Shipley, Col Charles Tyrell, 1863–1933, vol. III
Shipley, Hammond Smith, 1858–1930, vol. III
Shipley, Orby, 1832–1916, vol. II
Shipley, Lt-Col Reginald Burge, died 1924, vol. II
Shipley, Sir William Alexander, died 1922, vol. II
Shipman, Louis Evan, 1869–1933, vol. III
Shippard, Sir Sidney Godolphin Alexander, 1837–1902, vol. I
Shipstone, Sir Thomas, 1851–1940, vol. III
Shipton, Eric Earle, 1907–1977, vol. VII
Shipway, Sir Francis Edward, 1875–1968, vol. VI
Shipwright, Lottie Adelina de Lara; see de Lara, Adelina.
Shircore, John Owen, 1882–1953, vol. V
Shirlaw, John Fenton, 1896–1975, vol. VII
Shirlaw, Matthew, 1873–1961, vol. VI
Shirley; see Skelton, John.
Shirley, Evelyn Philip Sewallis, 1900–1978, vol. VII
Shirley, Rev. (Frederick) John, 1890–1967, vol. VI
Shirley, Herbert John, 1868–1943, vol. IV
Shirley, Rev. John; see Shirley, Rev. F. J.
Shirley, Hon. Ralph, 1865–1946, vol. IV
Shirley, Sewallis Evelyn, 1844–1904, vol. I
Shirley, William, 1866–1930, vol. III
Shirley-Fox, John Shirley, died 1939, vol. III
Shirras, George Findlay, 1885–1955, vol. V
Shirres, Major John Chivas, 1854–1899, vol. I
Shirtcliffe, Sir George, 1862–1941, vol. IV
Shoaib, Mohammad, 1905–1976, vol. VII
Shoenberg, Sir Isaac, 1880–1963, vol. VI
Shoesmith, Kenneth Denton, 1890–1939, vol. III
Sholl, Richard Adolphus, 1846–1919, vol. II
Shone, Rt Rev. Samuel, 1820–1897, vol. I
Shone, Sir Terence Allen, 1894–1965, vol. VI
Shone, Lt-Gen. Sir William Terence, 1850–1938, vol. III
Shoobert, Sir Harold; see Shoobert, Sir W. H.
Shoobert, Sir (Wilfred) Harold, 1896–1969, vol. VI
Shoobridge, Hon. Sir Rupert Oakley, 1883–1962, vol. VI
Shoolbred, Frederick Thomas, 1841–1922, vol. II
Shoolbred, Lt-Col Rupert, 1869–1946, vol. IV
Shoosmith, Maj.-Gen. Stephen Newton, 1900–1956, vol. V
Shoosmith, Thurston Laidlaw, 1865–1933, vol. III
Shore, Lewis Erle, 1863–1944, vol. IV
Shore, Brig.-Gen. Offley Bohun Stovin Fairless, 1863–1922, vol. II
Shore, Robert S., died 1931, vol. III
Shore, Rev. Thomas Teignmouth, 1841–1911, vol. I
Shore, Thomas William, 1861–1947, vol. IV
Shore, W. Teignmouth, died 1932, vol. III
Shores, John Wallis, 1851–1935, vol. III
Shorrock, William Gordon, 1879–1944, vol. IV
Short, Adrian Hugh H.; see Hassard-Short.
Short, Alfred, 1882–1938, vol. III
Short, Brig.-Gen. Anthony Holbeche, 1862–1940, vol. III

Short, Arthur Rendle, *died* 1953, vol. V
Short, Ernest Henry, 1875–1959, vol. V
Short, Lt-Col Ernest William George, 1877–1953, vol. V
Short, Sir Frank, 1857–1945, vol. IV
Short, Rev. Frank, 1895–1975, vol. VII
Short, Rev. Canon Frederick Winning H.; *see* Hassard-Short.
Short, Rev. Harry Lismer, 1906–1975, vol. VII
Short, Herbert Arthur, 1895–1967, vol. VI
Short, John, 1894–1967, vol. VI
Short, John Tregerthen, 1858–1933, vol. III
Short, Richard, 1841–1916, vol. II
Short, Thomas Sydney, *died* 1924, vol. II
Short, Vivian Augustus, 1883–1950, vol. IV
Short, Wilfrid Maurice, 1870–1947, vol. IV
Short, William, 1866–1929, vol. III
Short, Lt-Col William Ambrose, *died* 1917, vol. II
Shortall, Sir Patrick, 1872–1925, vol. II
Shorter, Clement King, 1857–1926, vol. II
Shorter, Dora, *died* 1918, vol. II
Shorthouse, Joseph Henry, 1834–1903, vol. I
Shortland, Adm. Edward George, 1855–1929, vol. III
Shortland, Captain Henry Vincent, *died* 1913, vol. I
Shorto, William Alfred Thomas, 1876–1951, vol. V
Shortt, Adam, 1859–1931, vol. III
Shortt, Rt Hon. Edward, 1862–1935, vol. III
Shortt, John, *died* 1932, vol. III
Shostakovich, Dmitry Dmitrievich, 1906–1975, vol. VII
Shott, Henry Hammond, 1877–1914, vol. I
Shotwell, James Thomson, 1874–1965, vol. VI
Shoubridge, Harry Oliver Baron, 1872–1934, vol. III
Shoubridge, Maj.-Gen. Herbert; *see* Shoubridge, Maj.-Gen. T. H.
Shoubridge, Maj.-Gen. (Thomas) Herbert, 1871–1923, vol. II
Shove, Gerald Frank, 1887–1947, vol. IV
Shove, Captain Herbert William, 1886–1943, vol. IV
Shove, Ralph Samuel, 1889–1966, vol. VI
Shovelton, Sydney Taverner, 1881–1967, vol. VI
Showers, Lt-Col Herbert Lionel, 1861–1916, vol. II
Shrapnell-Smith, Edward Shrapnell, 1875–1952, vol. V
Shreeve, George Harry, 1888–1960, vol. V
Shrewsbury and Waterford, 20th Earl of, 1860–1921, vol. II
Shrewsbury and Waterford, 21st Earl of, 1914–1980, vol. VII
Shrewsbury, J. F. D., 1898–1971, vol. VII
Shrubsall, Frank Charles, *died* 1935, vol. III
Shrubsole, Rear-Adm. Percy Joseph, 1875–1958, vol. V
Shuard, Amy, (Mrs Peter Asher), 1924–1975, vol. VII
Shuckburgh, Evelyn Shirley, 1843–1906, vol. I
Shuckburgh, Sir Gerald Francis Stewkley, 11th Bt, 1882–1939, vol. III
Shuckburgh, Sir John Evelyn, 1877–1953, vol. V
Shuckburgh, Robert Shirley, 1882–1954, vol. V

Shuckburgh, Sir Stewkley Frederick Draycott, 10th Bt, 1880–1917, vol. II
Shufeldt, Major Robert Wilson, 1850–1934, vol. III
Shufflebotham, Frank, *died* 1932, vol. III
Shuffrey, Paul, 1889–1955, vol. V
Shuffrey, Rev. William Arthur, 1851–1932, vol. III
Shuldham-Legh, Col Harry Shuldham, 1854–1915, vol. I
Shurmer, Percy Lionel Edward, *died* 1959, vol. V
Shute, Gen. Sir Cameron Deane, 1866–1936, vol. III
Shute, Gen. Sir Charles Cameron, 1816–1904, vol. I
Shute, Lt-Col Cyril Aveling, 1886–1950, vol. IV
Shute, Geoffrey Gay, 1892–1951, vol. V
Shute, Col Henry Gwynn Deane, 1860–1909, vol. I
Shute, Col Sir John Joseph, *died* 1948, vol. IV
Shute, Nevil; *see* Norway, N. S.
Shuter, Comdr Joseph Armand, 1876–1915, vol. I
Shuter, Brig.-Gen. Reginald Gauntlett, 1875–1957, vol. V
Shutt, Frank Thomas, 1859–1940, vol. III
Shuttleworth, 1st Baron, 1844–1939, vol. III
Shuttleworth, 2nd Baron, 1913–1940, vol. III
Shuttleworth, 3rd Baron, 1917–1942, vol. IV
Shuttleworth, 4th Baron, 1917–1975, vol. VII
Shuttleworth, Alfred, 1843–1925, vol. II
Shuttleworth, Brig. Betham Wilkins, 1880–1937, vol. III
Shuttleworth, Maj.-Gen. Sir Digby Inglis, 1876–1948, vol. IV
Shuttleworth, Edward Cheke Smalley, 1866–1943, vol. IV
Shuttleworth, Edward James K.; *see* Kay-Shuttleworth.
Shuttleworth, Col Frank, 1845–1913, vol. I
Shuttleworth, George Edward, 1842–1928, vol. II
Shuttleworth, Rev. Henry Cary, 1850–1900, vol. I
Shuttleworth, Hon. Lawrence Ughtred K.; *see* Kay-Shuttleworth.
Shvernik, Nikolai Mikhailovich, 1888–1970, vol. VI
Siam, HM King of, Rama VI, 1881–1925, vol. II
Sibbald, Sir John, 1833–1905, vol. I
Sibbald, Rev. Samuel James Ramsay, 1869–1950, vol. IV
Sibbett, Cecil James, *died* 1967, vol. VI
Sibelius, Jean Julius Christian, 1865–1957, vol. V
Sibley, Walter Knowsley, 1862–1944, vol. IV
Sibly, Sir Franklin; *see* Sibly, Sir T. F.
Sibly, Sir (Thomas) Franklin, 1883–1948, vol. IV
Sibly, William Arthur, 1883–1959, vol. V
Siborne, Maj.-Gen. Herbert Taylor, 1826–1902, vol. I
Sibree, Rev. James, 1836–1929, vol. III
Sibthorpe, Surg.-Gen. Charles, 1847–1906, vol. I
Sichel, Alan William Stuart, 1886–1966, vol. VI
Sichel, Edith, 1862–1914, vol. I
Sichel, Walter, 1855–1933, vol. III
Sickert, Walter Richard, 1860–1942, vol. IV
Sidaner, Henri Le, 1862–1939, vol. III
Siddall, Joseph Bower, 1840–1925, vol. II
Sidebotham, Herbert, 1872–1940, vol. III
Sidebotham, Joseph Watson, 1857–1925, vol. II
Sidebottom, Tom Harrop, *died* 1908, vol. I

Sidebottom, William, *died* 1933, vol. III
Sidey, Sir Thomas Kay, 1863–1933, vol. III
Sidgreaves, Sir Arthur Frederick, 1882–1948, vol. IV
Sidgreaves, Rev. Walter, 1837–1919, vol. II
Sidgwick, Alfred, 1850–1943, vol. IV
Sidgwick, Arthur, *died* 1920, vol. II
Sidgwick, Cecily, *died* 1934, vol. III
Sidgwick, Eleanor Mildred, 1845–1936, vol. III
Sidgwick, Ethel, 1877–1970, vol. VI
Sidgwick, Henry, 1838–1900, vol. I
Sidgwick, Mrs Henry; *see* Sidgwick, Eleanor Mildred.
Sidgwick, Nevil Vincent, 1873–1952, vol. V
Sidmouth, 3rd Viscount, 1824–1913, vol. I
Sidmouth, 4th Viscount, 1854–1915, vol. I
Sidmouth, 5th Viscount, 1882–1953, vol. V
Sidmouth, 6th Viscount, 1887–1976, vol. VII
Sidney, Herbert, *died* 1923, vol. II
Sidney, Thomas Stafford, 1863–1917, vol. II
Sidney-Humphries, Sydney, 1862–1941, vol. IV
Sidwell, Rt Rev. Henry Bindley, 1857–1936, vol. III
Sieff, Baron (Life Peer); Israel Moses Sieff, 1889–1972, vol. VII
Siegbahn, (Karl) Manne (Georg), 1886–1978, vol. VII
Siegbahn, Manne; *see* Siegbahn, K. M. G.
Siegfried, André, 1875–1959, vol. V
Siemens, Alexander, 1847–1928, vol. II
Sienkiewicz, Henryk, *died* 1916, vol. II
Siepmann, Harry Arthur, 1889–1963, vol. VI
Sieveking, Albert Forbes, 1857–1951, vol. V
Sieveking, Sir Edward Henry, 1816–1904, vol. I
Sieveking, Captain Lancelot de Giberne, 1896–1972, vol. VII
Sievier, Robert Standish, 1860–1939, vol. III
Sievwright, Andrew George Hume, 1885–1956, vol. V
Sievwright, J. D., 1863–1947, vol. IV
Sifton, Rt Hon. Arthur Lewis, 1858–1921, vol. II
Sifton, Hon. Sir Clifford, 1861–1929, vol. III
Sifton, Sir James David, 1878–1952, vol. V
Sifton, John William, 1925–1969, vol. VI
Sifton, Victor, 1897–1961, vol. VI
Sigerson, George, *died* 1925, vol. II
Siggers, Ven. William C.; *see* Curzon-Siggers.
Sigrist, Frederick, 1884–1956, vol. V
Sigsbee, Rear-Adm. Charles Dwight, 1845–1923, vol. II
Sigurdsson, Asgeir Thorsteinn, 1864–1935, vol. III
Sikes, Alfred Walter, 1869–1948, vol. IV
Sikes, Edward Ernest, 1867–1940, vol. III
Sikes, Francis Henry, 1862–1943, vol. IV
Sikes, Howard Lecky, 1881–1943, vol. IV
Sikkim, Maharaj Kumar Sidkeong Tulku of, 1879–1914, vol. I
Sikkim, Maharaj Sidkeong Tulku of, *died* 1914, vol. I
Sikkim, Maharaja of, 1893–1963, vol. VI
Sikorski, Gen. Wladyslaw, 1881–1943, vol. IV
Sikorsky, Igor Ivan, 1889–1972, vol. VII
Silberrad, Oswald John, 1878–1960, vol. V
Silberrad, Una L., 1872–1955, vol. V

Silburn, Col Percy Arthur Baxter, 1876–1929, vol. III
Silcock, Arnold, 1889–1953, vol. V
Silcock, Arthur Quarry, 1855–1904, vol. I
Silcock, Henry Thomas, 1882–1969, vol. VI
Silcock, Thomas Ball, 1854–1924, vol. II
Silcox, Albert Henry, 1895–1971, vol. VII
Silk, Paymaster Rear-Adm. Ernest Edwin, 1862–1940, vol. III
Silk, John Frederick William, 1858–1943, vol. IV
Silkin, 1st Baron, 1889–1972, vol. VII
Sillem, Maj.-Gen. Sir Arnold Frederick, 1865–1949, vol. IV
Sillery, Anthony, 1903–1976, vol. VII
Sillince, William Augustus, 1906–1974, vol. VII
Sillitoe, Sir Percy Joseph, 1888–1962, vol. VI
Sills, George, 1832–1905, vol. I
Silone, Ignazio, 1900–1978, vol. VII
Siloti, Alexander, 1863–1945, vol. IV
Silsoe, 1st Baron, 1894–1976, vol. VII
Silver, Albert Harlow, 1875–1954, vol. V
Silver, Alfred Jethro, 1870–1935, vol. III
Silver, Gertrude; *see* Kingston, G.
Silver, Lt-Col John Payzant, 1868–1957, vol. V
Silver, Vice-Adm. Mortimer L'E., 1869–1946, vol. IV
Silverman, (Samuel) Sydney, 1895–1968, vol. VI
Silverman, Sydney; *see* Silverman, S. S.
Silverstone, Arnold; *see* Baron Ashdown.
Silvester, Air Cdre James, 1898–1956, vol. V
Silvester, Norman Langton, 1894–1969, vol. VI (AII)
Silvester, Victor Marlborough, 1900–1978, vol. VII
Silvestri, Constantin, 1913–1969, vol. VI
Sim, Alastair, 1900–1976, vol. VII
Sim, Sir Alexander; *see* Sim, Sir G. A. S.
Sim, Sir (George) Alexander (Strachan), 1905–1980, vol. VII
Sim, Brig. George Edward Herman, 1886–1952, vol. V
Sim, George Gall, 1878–1930, vol. III
Sim, Col George Hamilton, 1852–1929, vol. III
Sim, Henry Alexander, 1856–1928, vol. II
Sim, James Duncan Stuart, 1849–1912, vol. I
Sim, Sir Wilfrid Joseph, 1890–1974, vol. VII
Sim, Sir William Alexander, 1858–1928, vol. II
Sime, John, 1842–1911, vol. I
Simeon, Vice-Adm. Sir Charles Edward Barrington, 1889–1955, vol. V
Simeon, Sir Edmund Charles, 5th Bt, 1855–1915, vol. I
Simeon, Sir John Stephen Barrington, 4th Bt, 1850–1909, vol. I
Simeon, Sir John Walter Barrington, 6th Bt, 1886–1957, vol. IV
Simeon, Stephen Louis, 1857–1937, vol. III
Simes, Charles Erskine Woollard, 1893–1978, vol. VII
Simey, Baron (Life Peer); Thomas Spensley Simey, 1906–1969, vol. VI
Simkin, Rt Rev. William John, 1883–1967, vol. VI
Simm, Matthew Turnbull, 1869–1928, vol. II
Simmonds, Arthur, 1892–1968, vol. VI
Simmonds, B(ernard) Sangster, 1886–1953, vol. V

Simmonds, Frederick, 1845–1921, vol. II
Simmonds, Herbert John, 1867–1950, vol. IV
Simmonds, Hugh Henry Dawes, 1886–1952, vol. V
Simmonds, Sidney, 1899–1977, vol. VII
Simmonds, William George, 1876–1968, vol. VI
Simmonds, William Henry, 1860–1934, vol. III
Simmons, Mrs Amy, died 1964, vol. VI
Simmons, Sir Anker, 1857–1927, vol. II
Simmons, Arthur Thomas, 1865–1921, vol. II
Simmons, Charles James, 1893–1975, vol. VII
Simmons, Ernest J., 1903–1972, vol. VII
Simmons, Maj.-Gen. Frank Keith, 1888–1952, vol. V
Simmons, Rev. Frederic Pearson Copland, 1902–1978, vol. VII
Simmons, Sir Frederick James, 1867–1955, vol. V
Simmons, Col George Francis Henry Le B.; see Le Breton-Simmons.
Simmons, Engr-Captain George Thomas, 1853–1933, vol. III
Simmons, George Thomas Wagstaffe, died 1954, vol. V
Simmons, Sir John Lintorn Arabin, 1821–1903, vol. I
Simmons, Major Sir Percy Coleman, 1875–1939, vol. III
Simms, Ven. Arthur Hennell, 1853–1921, vol. II
Simms, Captain Charles Edward, 1900–1963, vol. VI
Simms, Very Rev. John Morrow, 1854–1934, vol. III
Simms, Ven. William, 1845–1932, vol. III
Simner, Col Sir Percy Reginald Owen Abel, 1878–1963, vol. VI
Simnett, William Edward, 1880–1958, vol. V
Simon, 1st Viscount, 1873–1954, vol. V
Simon, Viscountess; (Kathleen), died 1955, vol. V
Simon of Wythenshawe, 1st Baron, 1879–1960, vol. V
Simon of Wythenshawe, Lady; (Shena Dorothy), 1883–1972, vol. VII
Simon, André Louis, 1877–1970, vol. VI
Simon, Rev. D. W., 1830–1909, vol. I
Simon, Sir Francis Eugene, 1893–1956, vol. V
Simon, George Percival, 1893–1963, vol. VI
Simon, Rt Rev. Glyn; see Simon, Rt Rev. W. G. H.
Simon, Sir John, 1818–1897, vol. I
Simon, Sir John, 1816–1904, vol. I
Simon, Rev. John Smith, 1843–1933, vol. III
Simon, Sir Leon, 1881–1965, vol. VI
Simon, Col Maximilian St Leger, 1876–1951, vol. V
Simon, Oliver, 1895–1956, vol. V
Simon, Sir Robert Michael, 1850–1914, vol. I
Simon, Walter, died 1967, vol. VI
Simon, Rt Rev. (William) Glyn (Hughes), 1903–1972, vol. VII
Simond, Charles François, died 1957, vol. V
Simonds, 1st Viscount, 1881–1971, vol. VII
Simonds, Frank H., 1878–1936, vol. III
Simonds, Frederick Adolphus, 1881–1953, vol. V
Simonds, Lt-Gen. Guy Granville, 1903–1974, vol. VII
Simonds, John Hayes, 1879–1946, vol. IV
Simonds, Most Rev. Justin Daniel, 1890–1967, vol. VI

Simonds, William Barrow, 1820–1911, vol. I
Simons, Adm. Ernest Alfred, 1856–1928, vol. II
Simons, Very Rev. William Charles, died 1921, vol. II
Simonsen, Sir John Lionel, 1884–1957, vol. V
Simonson, Lee, 1888–1967, vol. VI
Simopoulos, Charalambos John, 1874–1942, vol. IV
Simpkin, Sir Oswald Richard Arthur, 1879–1936, vol. III
Simpkinson, Henry Walrond, 1853–1934, vol. III
Simpson, Lt-Col Adrian Francis Hugh Sibbald, 1880–1960, vol. V
Simpson, Rev. Alan Haldane, 1875–1941, vol. IV
Simpson, Rev. Albert Edward, 1868–1947, vol. IV
Simpson, Sir Alexander Russell, 1835–1916, vol. II
Simpson, Alfred Allen, 1875–1939, vol. III
Simpson, Alfred Muller, 1843–1917, vol. II
Simpson, Archibald Henry, 1843–1918, vol. II
Simpson, Sir Basil Robert James, 2nd Bt (cr 1935), 1898–1968, vol. VI
Simpson, Bertie Soutar, 1896–1972, vol. VII
Simpson, Rt Rev. Bertram Fitzgerald, 1883–1971, vol. VII
Simpson, Bertram Lenox; see Weale, Putnam.
Simpson, Col Charles Napier, 1856–1933, vol. III
Simpson, Maj.-Gen. Charles Rudyerd, 1856–1948, vol. IV
Simpson, Charles Walter, 1885–1971, vol. VII
Simpson, Sir Clement Bell, 1866–1933, vol. III
Simpson, Rear-Adm. Cortland Herbert, 1856–1943, vol. IV
Simpson, Very Rev. Cuthbert Aikman, 1892–1969, vol. VI
Simpson, Rev. David Capell, 1883–1955, vol. V
Simpson, Edward Sydney, 1875–1939, vol. III
Simpson, Miss Evelyn Blantyre, 1856–1920, vol. II
Simpson, Dame Florence Edith Victoria, 1874–1956, vol. V
Simpson, Col Sir Frank Robert, 1st Bt (cr 1935), 1864–1949, vol. IV
Simpson, Fred Brown, 1886–1939, vol. III
Simpson, Rev. Frederick Arthur, 1883–1974, vol. VII
Simpson, Frederick Moore, died 1928, vol. II
Simpson, Maj.-Gen. George, 1845–1908, vol. I
Simpson, Sir George Bowen, 1838–1915, vol. I
Simpson, Sir George Clarke, 1878–1965, vol. VI
Simpson, Col George Selden, 1878–1971, vol. VII
Simpson, Rear-Adm. George Walter Gillow, 1901–1972, vol. VII
Simpson, Gerald Gordon, 1918–1979, vol. VII
Simpson, Harold, 1876–1974, vol. VII
Simpson, Harry Butler, 1861–1940, vol. III
Simpson, Helen de Guerry, 1897–1940, vol. III
Simpson, Col Henry Charles, 1879–1943, vol. IV
Simpson, Col Henry Cuthbert Connell Dunlop, 1854–1942, vol. IV
Simpson, Henry Fife Morland, 1859–1920, vol. II
Simpson, Sir Henry Lunnon, 1842–1900, vol. I
Simpson, Captain Henry Valentine, 1864–1937, vol. III
Simpson, Herbert Clayton, 1872–1947, vol. IV
Simpson, Sir James, 1858–1934, vol. III

Simpson, James, 1874–1939, vol. III
Simpson, Sir James Dyer, 1888–1979, vol. VII
Simpson, Sir James Fletcher, 1874–1967, vol. VI
Simpson, Very Rev. James Gilliland, 1865–1948, vol. IV
Simpson, Rev. James Harvey, 1825–1915, vol. I
Simpson, James Herbert, 1883–1959, vol. V
Simpson, Sir James Hope, 1864–1924, vol. II
Simpson, Sir James Walter Mackay, 3rd Bt (cr 1866), 1882–1924, vol. II
Simpson, James Young, 1873–1934, vol. III
Simpson, John Alexander, 1892–1977, vol. VII
Simpson, Rt Rev. John Basil, died 1942, vol. IV
Simpson, Rev. John E., 1905–1970, vol. VI
Simpson, Air Cdre John Herbert Thomas, 1907–1967, vol. VI
Simpson, Sir John Hope, 1868–1961, vol. VI
Simpson, Sir John Roughton, 1899–1976, vol. VII
Simpson, Sir John William, 1858–1933, vol. III
Simpson, Joseph, 1879–1939, vol. III
Simpson, Sir Joseph, 1909–1968, vol. VI
Simpson, Lightly Stapleton, died 1942, vol. IV
Simpson, Mary Goudie, died 1934, vol. III
Simpson, Sir Maurice George, 1866–1954, vol. V
Simpson, Maxwell, 1815–1902, vol. I
Simpson, Melville William H.; see Hilton-Simpson.
Simpson, Maj.-Gen. Noel William, 1907–1972, vol. VII
Simpson, Rev. Patrick Carnegie, 1865–1947, vol. IV
Simpson, Percy, 1865–1962, vol. VI
Simpson, Rev. Percy John, 1864–1944, vol. IV
Simpson, Pierce Adolphus, 1837–1900, vol. I
Simpson, Rayene Stewart, 1926–1978, vol. VII
Simpson, Richard Jefferson, 1874–1936, vol. III
Simpson, Rev. Robert, 1900–1977, vol. VII
Simpson, Robert Gordon, 1887–1958, vol. V
Simpson, Col Robert John Shaw, 1858–1931, vol. III
Simpson, Col Robert Mills, 1865–1945, vol. IV (A)
Simpson, Sir Robert Russell, 1840–1923, vol. II
Simpson, Samuel, 1876–1952, vol. V
Simpson, Air Vice-Marshal Sturley Philip, 1896–1966, vol. VI
Simpson, Thomas, 1877–1964, vol. VI
Simpson, Thomas Blantyre, 1892–1954, vol. V
Simpson, Rear-Adm. (E) Thomas Harold, 1896–1952, vol. V
Simpson, Col Thomas Thomson, 1836–1916, vol. II
Simpson, Thomas Young, died 1963, vol. VI
Simpson, Trevor Claude, 1877–1929, vol. III
Simpson, Rev. W. J. Sparrow, 1859–1952, vol. V
Simpson, Sir Walter Grindlay, 2nd Bt (cr 1866), 1843–1898, vol. I
Simpson, Wilfred L., 1862–1937, vol. III
Simpson, William, 1823–1899, vol. I
Simpson, William Douglas, 1896–1968, vol. VI
Simpson, Col William George, 1876–1961, vol. VI
Simpson, Sir William John Ritchie, 1855–1931, vol. III
Simpson, William Marshall, 1868–1951, vol. V
Simpson-Baikie, Brig.-Gen. Sir Hugh Archie Dundas; see Baikie.

Simpson-Hinchliffe, William Algernon, 1880–1963, vol. VI
Sims, Sir Alfred John, 1907–1977, vol. VII
Sims, Sir Arthur, 1877–1969, vol. VI
Sims, Arthur Mitford, 1889–1977, vol. VII
Sims, Charles, 1873–1928, vol. II
Sims, Ernest William Proctor-, 1868–1943, vol. IV
Sims, Francis John, 1856–1950, vol. IV
Sims, George Robert, 1847–1922, vol. II
Sims, Brig.-Gen. Reginald Frank Manley, 1878–1951, vol. V
Sims, Sir Thomas, 1858–1936, vol. III
Sims, Adm. William Sowden, 1858–1936, vol. III
Simson, Captain Sir Donald Petrie, died 1961, vol. VI
Simson, Harold F.; see Fraser-Simson.
Simson, Sir Henry John Forbes, 1872–1932, vol. III
Simson, Richard Arbuthnot, 1871–1958, vol. V
Simson, Col William Amor, 1872–1925, vol. II
Sinbad; see Dingle, Aylward Edward.
Sinclair, 15th Lord, 1831–1922, vol. II
Sinclair, 16th Lord, 1875–1957, vol. V
Sinclair of Cleeve, 1st Baron, 1893–1979, vol. VII
Sinclair, Alexander Garden, 1859–1930, vol. III
Sinclair, Lt-Col Alfred Law, 1853–1911, vol. I
Sinclair, Archibald, 1866–1922, vol. II
Sinclair, Arthur Henry Havens, 1868–1962, vol. VI
Sinclair, Rev. Hon. Charles Augustus, 1865–1944, vol. IV
Sinclair, Hon. Sir Colin Archibald, 1876–1956, vol. V
Sinclair, Surg.-Gen. David, 1847–1919, vol. II
Sinclair, Dep. Surg.-Gen. Edward M., 1832–1916, vol. II
Sinclair, Adm. Sir Edwyn Sinclair A.; see Alexander-Sinclair.
Sinclair, George Robertson, 1863–1917, vol. II
Sinclair, Adm. Sir Hugh Francis Paget, 1873–1939, vol. III
Sinclair, Col Hugh Montgomerie, 1855–1924, vol. II
Sinclair, James, 1832–1910, vol. I
Sinclair, John, 1860–1938, vol. III
Sinclair, John Alexander, 1885–1961, vol. VI
Sinclair, Maj.-Gen. Sir John Alexander, 1897–1977, vol. VII
Sinclair, Sir John George Tollemache, 3rd Bt (cr 1786), 1825–1899, vol. I
Sinclair, John Houston, 1871–1961, vol. VI
Sinclair, Rt Hon. John Maynard, 1896–1953, vol. V
Sinclair, Sir John Robert, 1850–1940, vol. III
Sinclair, Sir John Rose George, 7th Bt (cr 1704, shown as 8th Bt cr 1631), 1864–1926, vol. II
Sinclair, Ven. John Stewart, 1853–1919, vol. II
Sinclair, Captain Sir Kenneth Duncan Lecky, 1889–1973, vol. VII
Sinclair, Louis, 1861–1928, vol. II
Sinclair, Lt-Col Malcolm Cecil, 1899–1955, vol. V
Sinclair, May, 1870–1946, vol. IV
Sinclair, Meurice, 1878–1966, vol. VI
Sinclair, Sir Robert Charles, 9th Bt (cr 1636), 1820–1899, vol. I

Sinclair, Major Sir Ronald Norman John Charles Udny, 8th Bt (cr 1704, shown as 1631), 1899–1952, vol. V

Sinclair, Rev. Canon Ronald Sutherland Brook, 1894–1953, vol. V

Sinclair, Shapton Donald, 1923–1974, vol. VII

Sinclair, Rt Hon. Thomas, 1838–1914, vol. I

Sinclair, Col Thomas, died 1940, vol. III

Sinclair, T(homas) Alan, 1899–1961, vol. VI

Sinclair, Col Thomas Charles, 1879–1948, vol. IV

Sinclair, Upton, 1878–1968, vol. VI

Sinclair, Lt-Col Sir Walrond Arthur Frank, 1880–1952, vol. V

Sinclair, Sir William, 1895–1976, vol. VII

Sinclair, William Angus, 1905–1954, vol. V

Sinclair, Sir William Japp, 1846–1912, vol. I

Sinclair, Ven. William Macdonald, 1850–1917, vol. II

Sinclair-Burgess, Maj.-Gen. Sir William Livingstone Hatchwell, 1880–1964, vol. VI

Sinclair Lockhart, Sir Graeme Alexander, 10th Bt (cr 1636); see Lockhart.

Sinclair-Lockhart, Sir Graeme Duncan Power, 12th Bt (cr 1636), 1897–1959, vol. V

Sinclair-Lockhart, Sir John Beresford, 13th Bt (cr 1636), 1904–1970, vol. VI

Sinclair-Lockhart, Sir Robert Duncan, 11th Bt (cr 1636), 1856–1919, vol. II

Sinclair-Maclagan, Maj.-Gen. Ewen George, 1868–1948, vol. IV

Sinderson, Sir Harry Chapman, Pasha, 1891–1974 vol. VII

Sinding, Stephan, 1846–1922, vol. II

Sing, John Millington, 1863–1947, vol. IV

Sing, Roger Percy, 1865–1940, vol. III

Sing, Rt Rev. Tsae-Seng, 1861–1940, vol. III (A), vol. IV

Singer, Charles, 1876–1960, vol. V

Singer, Brig.-Gen. Charles William, 1870–1936, vol. III

Singer, Dorothea Waley, 1882–1964, vol. VI

Singer, Adm. Sir Morgan, 1864–1938, vol. III

Singer, Sir Mortimer, 1863–1929, vol. III

Singer, Rev. Simeon, 1848–1906, vol. I

Singer, Washington Merritt Grant, 1866–1934, vol. III

Singers-Davies, Rev. R. W. F., died 1936, vol. III

Singh, Sardar Bahadur Sir D.; see Datar Singh.

Singh, Prince Frederick D.; see Duleep Singh.

Singh, Sir Ganesh Dutta, 1868–1943, vol. IV

Singh, Kanwar Jasbir, 1889–1942, vol. IV

Singh, Raja Sir Maharaj, 1878–1959, vol. V

Singh, Raja Sir Padam, 1873–1947, vol. IV

Singh, Prince Victor Albert Jay D.; see Duleep Singh.

Singh Roy, Sir Bijoy Prosad, 1894–1961, vol. VI

Singleton, Esther, died 1930, vol. III

Singleton, Col Henry Townsend Corbet, 1874–1934, vol. III

Singleton, Rt Rev. Hugh, 1851–1934, vol. III

Singleton, Rt Hon. Sir John Edward, 1885–1957, vol. V

Singleton, Rev. John J., 1838–1917, vol. II

Singleton, Rear-Adm. Uvedale Corbet, 1838–1910, vol. I

Singleton, William Adam, 1916–1960, vol. V

Sington, Gerald Henry Adolphus, 1876–1946, vol. IV

Sinha, 1st Baron, 1864–1928, vol. II

Sinha, 2nd Baron, 1887–1967, vol. VI

Sinha, Narendra Prasanna, born 1858, vol. III

Sinha, Rajandhari, 1893–1976, vol. VII

Sinha, Sir Rajivaranjan Prashad, 1893–1948, vol. IV (A), vol. V

Sinker, Sir (Algernon) Paul, 1905–1977, vol. VII

Sinker, Rev. Canon Arthur, died 1940, vol. III

Sinker, Rev. Edmund, 1872–1941, vol. IV

Sinker, Very Rev. John, 1874–1936, vol. III

Sinker, Sir Paul; see Sinker, Sir A. P.

Sinker, Rev. Robert, 1838–1913, vol. I

Sinkinson, George, 1874–1939, vol. III

Sinnatt, Frank Sturdy, 1880–1943, vol. IV

Sinnatt, Oliver Sturdy, 1882–1965, vol. VI

Sinnett, Alfred Percy, 1840–1921, vol. II

Sinnot, Most Rev. Alfred A., 1877–1954, vol. V

Sinnott, Col Edward Stockley, 1868–1969, vol. VI

Sinnott, John Joseph, 1882–1943, vol. IV

Sinton, Lt-Col John Alexander, 1884–1956, vol. V

Siqueland, Col Tryggve Albert, 1888–1937, vol. III

Sircar, Sir Nilratan, 1861–1943, vol. IV

Sircar, Sir Nripendra Nath, died 1945, vol. IV

Sire, Henry Alphonse, 1864–1947, vol. IV

Siriwardena, N. D. A. Silva-Wijayasinghe; see Wijayasinghe Siriwardena.

Sirmur (Nahan), Raja of, 1867–1911, vol. I

Sirmur, Maharaja of, 1888–1933, vol. III

Sirohi, HH Maharajadhiraj, 1888–1946, vol. IV

Sisam, Kenneth, 1887–1971, vol. VII

Sisley, Charles Percival, 1867–1934, vol. III

Sisnett, Sir Herbert Kortright McDonnell, 1862–1937, vol. III

Sisson, Charles Jasper, 1885–1966, vol. VI

Sisson, Marshall Arnott, 1897–1978, vol. VII

Sissons, Charles B., 1879–1965, vol. VI

Sissons, Ven. Gilbert Holme, 1870–1940, vol. III

Sita Ram, Rai Bahadur Sir, 1885–1972, vol. VII

Sitwell, Dame Edith Louisa, 1887–1964, vol. VI

Sitwell, Sir George Reresby, 4th Bt, 1860–1943, vol. IV

Sitwell, Maj.-Gen. Hervey Degge Wilmot, 1896–1973, vol. VII

Sitwell, Sir Osbert, 5th Bt, 1892–1969, vol. VI

Sitwell, Sir Sidney Ashley Hurt, 1871–1956, vol. V

Sitwell, Brig.-Gen. William Henry, 1860–1932, vol. III

Sivagnanam Pillai, Diwan Bahadur Sir Tinnevelly Nelliappa Pillai, died 1936, vol. III

Sivell, Robert, 1888–1958, vol. V

Sivewright, Hon. Sir James, 1848–1916, vol. II

Skae, Victor Delvine Burnham, 1914–1979, vol. VII

Skaife, Brig. Sir Eric Ommanney, 1884–1956, vol. V

Skaug, Arne, 1906–1974, vol. VII

Skeaping, John Rattenbury, 1901–1980, vol. VII

Skeat, Rev. Walter William, 1835–1912, vol. I

Skeats, Ernest Willington, 1875–1953, vol. V

Skeen, Gen. Sir Andrew, 1873–1935, vol. III

Skeffington, Arthur Massey, 1909–1971, vol. VII
Skeffington, Hon. Oriel John Clotworthy Whyte-Melville Foster–, 1871–1905, vol. I
Skeffington Smyth, Lt-Col Geoffrey Henry Julian; see FitzPatrick, Lt-Col G. H. J.
Skeggs, Rev. Thomas Charles, died 1927, vol. II
Skelmersdale, 5th Baron, 1876–1969, vol. VI
Skelmersdale, 6th Baron, 1896–1973, vol. VII
Skelton, Archibald Noel, 1880–1935, vol. III
Skelton, Rev. Charles Arthur, died 1913, vol. I
Skelton, Sir Charles Thomas, 1833–1913, vol. I
Skelton, Maj.-Gen. Dudley Sheridan, 1878–1962, vol. VI
Skelton, Rt Rev. Henry Aylmer, 1884–1959, vol. V
Skelton, Sir John, 1831–1897, vol. I
Skelton, Oscar Douglas, 1878–1941, vol. IV
Skelton, Engr Vice-Adm. Sir Reginald William, 1872–1956, vol. V
Skelton, Robert Lumley, 1896–1973, vol. VII
Skelton, Rev. Canon Thomas, 1834–1915, vol. I
Skemp, Arthur Rowland, 1882–1918, vol. II
Skemp, Frank Whittingham, 1880–1971, vol. VII
Skene, Macgregor, 1889–1973, vol. VII
Skene, Hon. Thomas, died 1910, vol. I
Skene, W. B., 1838–1911, vol. I
Skerrett, Hon. Sir Charles Perrin, 1863–1929, vol. III
Skerrington, Hon. Lord; William Campbell, 1855–1927, vol. II
Sketch, Ralph Yeo, 1877–1952, vol. V
Sketchley, Major Ernest Frederick Powys, 1881–1916, vol. II
Skevington, Sir Joseph Oliver, 1873–1952, vol. V
Skewes-Cox, Sir Thomas, 1849–1913, vol. I
Skey, Rev. Oswald William Laurie, 1878–1954, vol. V
Skidmore, Charles, 1839–1908, vol. I
Skiffington, Sir Donald Maclean, 1880–1963, vol. VI
Skikne, Larushka Mischa; see Harvey, Laurence.
Skilbeck, William Wray, 1864–1919, vol. II
Skillicorn, Alice Havergal, 1894–1979, vol. VII
Skillicorn, William James Kinlay, 1883–1955, vol. V
Skimming, Ian Edward Bowring, 1920–1973, vol. VII
Skinner, Rev. Albert James, 1869–1949, vol. IV
Skinner, Allan Maclean, 1846–1901, vol. I
Skinner, Arthur Banks, 1861–1911, vol. I
Skinner, Maj.-Gen. Bruce Morland, 1858–1932, vol. III
Skinner, C(harles) William, 1895–1971, vol. VII
Skinner, Clarence Farringdon, 1900–1962, vol. VI
Skinner, Colin Marshall, 1882–1968, vol. VI
Skinner, Cornelia Otis, (Mrs A. S. Blodget), 1901–1979, vol. VII
Skinner, Maj.-Gen. Sir Cyriac; see Skinner, Maj.-Gen. Sir P. C. B.
Skinner, Col Edmund Grey, 1850–1917, vol. II
Skinner, Maj.-Gen. Frank Hollamby Jerry, 1897–1979, vol. VII
Skinner, Col Frederick St Duthus, 1859–1938, vol. III
Skinner, Col George John, 1841–1930, vol. III

Skinner, Sir Gordon; see Skinner, Sir T. G.
Skinner, Lt-Col Harry Crawley R.; see Ross Skinner.
Skinner, Sir Harry Ross, 1867–1943, vol. IV
Skinner, Herbert Wakefield Banks, 1900–1960, vol. V
Skinner, Sir Hewitt; see Skinner, Sir T. H.
Skinner, Horace Wilfrid, 1884–1955, vol. V
Skinner, Rev. James Henry, died 1913, vol. I
Skinner, Col James Tierney, 1845–1902, vol. I
Skinner, Rev. John, 1851–1925, vol. II
Skinner, John William, 1890–1955, vol. V
Skinner, Maj.-Gen. Sir (Percy) Cyriac Burrell, 1871–1955, vol. V
Skinner, Robert, 1877–1955, vol. V
Skinner, Robert Peet, 1866–1960, vol. V
Skinner, Robert Taylor, 1867–1946, vol. IV
Skinner, Sidney, 1863–1944, vol. IV
Skinner, Sir Sydney Martyn, 1864–1941, vol. IV
Skinner, Sir Thomas, 1st Bt, 1840–1926, vol. II
Skinner, Sir (Thomas) Gordon, 3rd Bt, 1899–1972, vol. VII
Skinner, Sir (Thomas) Hewitt, 2nd Bt, 1875–1968, vol. VI
Skinner, Waldo W., 1878–1943, vol. IV
Skinner, Walter Robert, 1851–1924, vol. II
Skinner, Rev. William, 1859–1942, vol. IV
Skinner, William Goudie, died 1935, vol. III
Skipton, Rev. Horace Pitt Kennedy, 1861–1943, vol. IV
Skipwith, Col Frederick George, 1870–1964, vol. VI
Skipwith, Sir Grey Humberston d'Estoteville, 11th Bt, 1884–1950, vol. IV
Skipwith, Vice-Adm. Harry Louis d'Estoteville, 1868–1955, vol. V
Skipworth, Frank Markham, 1854–1929, vol. III
Skira, Albert, 1904–1973, vol. VII
Skirmunt, Constantine, 1866–1939, vol. III
Skirrow, Major Arthur George Walker, 1862–1941, vol. IV
Skirving, Archibald Adam S.; see Scot-Skirving.
Sklodowska, Marie; see Curie Madame.
Skottowe, Britiffe Constable, 1857–1925, vol. II
Skouras, Spyros Panayiotis, 1893–1971, vol. VII
Skrimshire of Quarter, Baroness (Life Peer); Margaret Betty Harvie Anderson, 1915–1979, vol. VII
Skrine, Sir Clarmont Percival, 1888–1974, vol. VII
Skrine, Francis Henry, 1847–1933, vol. III
Skrine, Henry Mills, 1844–1915, vol. I
Skrine, Rev. John Huntley, 1848–1923, vol. II
Skues, George Edward Mackenzie, 1858–1949, vol. IV
Skyrm, Llewellyn Sidgwick M., died 1964, vol. VI
Slack, Captain Charles, died 1925, vol. II
Slack, Sir John B.; see Bamford-Slack.
Slack, Samuel Benjamin, 1859–1955, vol. V
Slacke, Francis Alexander, 1853–1940, vol. III
Slacke, Sir Owen Randal, 1837–1910, vol. I
Sladden, Sir Julius, 1847–1928, vol. II
Slade, Sir Alfred Fothringham, 5th Bt, 1898–1960, vol. V
Slade, Cecil William Paulet, 1863–1943, vol. IV
Slade, Sir Cuthbert, 4th Bt, 1863–1908, vol. I

Slade, Adm. Sir Edmond John Warre, 1859–1928, vol. II

Slade, Lt-Gen. Frederick George, 1851–1910, vol. I

Slade, George Penkivil, 1899–1942, vol. IV

Slade, Sir Gerald Osborne, 1891–1962, vol. VI

Slade, Sir James Benjamin, 1861–1950, vol. IV

Slade, Maj.-Gen. Sir John Ramsay, 1843–1913, vol. I

Slade, Mead, 1894–1954, vol. V

Slade, Sir Michael Nial, 6th Bt, 1900–1962, vol. VI

Slade, Roland Edgar, 1886–1968, vol. VI

Slade, William Ball, 1843–1938, vol. III

Slade, Wyndham, 1826–1910, vol. I

Slade, Wyndham Neave, 1867–1941, vol. IV

Sladen, Arthur French, 1866–1944, vol. IV

Sladen, Brig.-Gen. David Ramsay, 1869–1923, vol. II

Sladen, Douglas Brooke Wheelton, 1856–1947, vol. IV

Sladen, Francis Farquhar, 1875–1970, vol. VI

Sladen, Major Gerald Carew, 1881–1930, vol. III

Sladen, Hugh Alfred Lambart, 1878–1962, vol. VI

Sladen, Col Joseph, 1840–1930, vol. III

Sladen, Joseph Maurice, 1896–1956, vol. V

Sladen, Lt-Comdr Sir Sampson, 1868–1940, vol. III

Slaney, Col Francis Gerald K.; see Kenyon-Slaney.

Slaney, George Wilson, 1884–1978, vol. VII

Slaney, Major Philip Percy K.; see Kenyon-Slaney.

Slaney, Major Robert Orlando Rodolph K.; see Kenyon-Slaney.

Slaney, Sybil Anges, K.; see Kenyon-Slaney.

Slaney, Maj.-Gen. Walter Rupert K.; see Kenyon-Slaney.

Slaney, Rt Hon. William Slaney K.; see Kenyon-Slaney.

Slater, Baron (Life Peer); Joseph Slater, 1904–1977, vol. VII

Slater, Sir (Alexander) Ransford, 1874–1940, vol. III

Slater, Charles, 1856–1940, vol. III

Slater, David A., 1866–1938, vol. III

Slater, Ernest, died 1942, vol. IV

Slater, George, died 1941, vol. IV

Slater, George, 1874–1956, vol. V

Slater, Gilbert, 1864–1938, vol. III

Slater, Gordon Archbold, 1896–1979, vol. VII

Slater, Mrs Harriet, died 1976, vol. VII

Slater, John, 1847–1924, vol. II

Slater, John, 1889–1935, vol. III

Slater, Col John William, 1867–1936, vol. III

Slater, Col Owen, 1890–1976, vol. VII

Slater, Sir Ransford; see Slater, Sir A. R.

Slater, Samuel Henry, 1880–1967, vol. VI

Slater, Hon. William, 1890–1960, vol. V

Slater, Rev. William Fletcher, 1831–1924, vol. II

Slater, William Henry, 1896–1962, vol. VI

Slater, Sir William Kershaw, 1893–1970, vol. VI

Slatin Pacha, Baron Rudolf Carl, 1857–1932, vol. III

Slator, Instr Captain Thomas, died 1961, vol. VI

Slatter, Air Marshal Sir Leonard Horatio, 1894–1961, vol. VI

Slattery, Rt Rev. Charles Lewis, 1867–1930, vol. III

Slattery, John, 1886–1958, vol. V

Slaughter, Lt-Col Reginald Joseph, 1874–1968, vol. VI

Slaughter, Sir William Capel, 1857–1917, vol. II

Slayter, Col Edward Wheeler, 1869–1946, vol. IV

Slayter, Adm. William Firth, 1867–1936, vol. III

Slayter, Adm. Sir William Rudolph, 1896–1971, vol. VII

Sleator, James Sinton, died 1950, vol. IV

Slee, Frederick Abraham, 1882–1963, vol. VI

Slee, Comdr John Ambrose, 1878–1944, vol. IV

Slee, Col Percy Henry, 1861–1929, vol. III

Sleeman, Cyril Montagu, 1883–1971, vol. VII

Sleeman, Col Sir James Lewis, 1880–1963, vol. VI

Sleeman, John Herbert, 1880–1963, vol. VI

Sleep, Arthur, 1894–1959, vol. V

Sleigh, Charles William, 1863–1949, vol. IV

Sleigh, Sir Hamilton Morton Howard, 1896–1979, vol. VII

Sleigh, Sir William Lowrie, 1865–1945, vol. IV

Sleight, Major Sir Ernest, 2nd Bt, 1873–1946, vol. IV

Sleight, Sir George Frederick, 1st Bt, 1853–1921, vol. II

Slesinger, Edward G., died 1975, vol. VII

Slesser, Rt Hon. Sir Henry, 1883–1979, vol. VII

Slessor, Alexander Johnston, 1912–1954, vol. V

Slessor, Marshal of the Royal Air Force Sir John Cotesworth, 1897–1979, vol. VII

Sligo, 4th Marquess of, 1824–1903, vol. I

Sligo, 5th Marquess of, 1831–1913, vol. I

Sligo, 6th Marquess of, 1856–1935, vol. III

Sligo, 7th Marquess of, 1898–1941, vol. IV

Sligo, 8th Marquess of, 1867–1951, vol. V

Sligo, 9th Marquess of, 1873–1952, vol. V

Slim, 1st Viscount, 1891–1970, vol. VI

Slingo, Sir William, 1855–1935, vol. III

Sliwinski, Stanislaw, 1893–1940, vol. III (A), vol. IV

Sloan, Alexander, died 1945, vol. IV

Sloan, Alfred Pritchard, Jun., 1875–1966, vol. VI

Sloan, Hon. Gordon McGregor, 1898–1959, vol. V

Sloan, Maj.-Gen. John Macfarlane, 1872–1941, vol. IV

Sloan, John MacGavin, died 1926, vol. II

Sloan, Lawrence Gunn, 1859–1939, vol. III

Sloan, Robert Patrick, 1874–1947, vol. IV

Sloan, Sir Tennant, 1884–1972, vol. VII

Sloane, Mary Annie, died 1961, vol. VI

Sloane, William Milligan, 1850–1928, vol. II

Sloane-Stanley, Ronald Francis Assheton, 1867–1948, vol. IV

Slocock, Francis Samuel Alfred, died 1945, vol. IV

Slocombe, George Edward, 1894–1963, vol. VI

Slocum, William Frederick, 1851–1934, vol. III

Sloggett, Col Arthur John Henry, 1882–1950, vol. IV

Sloggett, Lt-Gen. Sir Arthur Thomas, 1857–1929, vol. III

Sloley, Sir Herbert Cecil, 1855–1937, vol. III

Sloman, Rev. Arthur, 1851–1919, vol. II

Sloman, Very Rev. Ernest, died 1918, vol. II

Sloman, Harold Newnham Penrose, 1885–1965, vol. VI

Sloman, Brig.-Gen. Henry Stanhope, 1861–1945, vol. IV
Slot, Gerald Maurice Joseph, *died* 1972, vol. VII
Slotki, Israel Wolf, 1884–1973, vol. VII
Sly, Sir Frank George, 1866–1928, vol. II
Sly, Henry Edward, 1876–1932, vol. III
Sly, Richard Meares, 1849–1929, vol. III
Slyne, Denis, *died* 1928, vol. II
Smail, James Cameron, 1880–1970, vol. VI
Smail, William Mitchell, 1885–1971, vol. VII
Smaldon, Catherine Agnes, 1903–1980, vol. VII
Smale, Morton Alfred, 1847–1916, vol. II
Small, Sir Alexander Sym, 1887–1944, vol. IV
Small, Sir Frank Augustus, 1903–1973, vol. VII
Small, James, 1889–1955, vol. V
Small, James, *died* 1968, vol. VI
Small, William, 1843–1929, vol. III
Small, Col William George, *died* 1931, vol. III
Small, William Watson, 1909–1978, vol. VII
Smallbones, Robert Townsend, 1884–1976, vol. VII
Smalley, George Washburn, 1833–1916, vol. II
Smalley, Sir Herbert, 1851–1945, vol. IV
Smalley-Baker, Charles Ernest, 1891–1972, vol. VII
Smallfield, F., *died* 1915, vol. I
Smallman, Lt-Col Arthur Briton, 1873–1950, vol. IV
Smallman, Sir George; *see* Smallman, Sir H. G.
Smallman, Sir (Henry) George, 1854–1923, vol. II
Smallwood, Arthur William, 1873–1938, vol. III
Smallwood, Edward, 1861–1939, vol. III
Smallwood, Lt-Col Frank Graham, 1867–1919, vol. II
Smallwood, Geoffrey Arthur John, 1900–1973, vol. VII
Smallwood, Maj.-Gen. Gerald Russell, 1889–1977, vol. VII
Smallwood, Henry Armstrong, 1869–1942, vol. IV
Smallwood, Oliver Daniel, 1889–1962, vol. VI
Smallwood, Richard Coningsby, *died* 1933, vol. III
Smart, Archibald Guelph Holdsworth, 1882–1964, vol. VI
Smart, Borlase, 1881–1947, vol. IV
Smart, Brig.-Gen. Charles Allan, 1868–1937, vol. III
Smart, D. I., *died* 1970, vol. VI (AII)
Smart ,E. Hodgson, *died* 1942, vol. IV
Smart, Lt-Gen. Edward Kenneth, 1891–1961, vol. VI
Smart, Sir Eric Fleming, 1911–1973, vol. VII
Smart, Sir Harold Nevil, 1883–1950, vol. IV
Smart, Henry C., 1878–1951, vol. V
Smart, John, 1838–1899, vol. I
Smart, Joseph McCaig, 1882–1953, vol. V
Smart, Leslie Masson, 1889–1972, vol. VII
Smart, Comdr Sir Morton, 1878–1956, vol. V
Smart, V. Irving, 1874–1940, vol. III
Smart, Sir Walter Alexander, 1883–1962, vol. VI
Smart, Wilfred Wilmot, 1876–1961, vol. VI
Smart, William, 1853–1915, vol. I
Smart, William Marshall, 1889–1975, vol. VII
Smart, William Wilkinson, *died* 1943, vol. IV
Smartt, Rt Hon. Sir Thomas William, 1858–1929, vol. III
Smartt, Rev. William Hanbury, 1854–1933, vol. III

Smeaton, Lt-Col (Charles) Oswald, 1862–1923, vol. II
Smeaton, Donald Mackenzie, 1848–1910, vol. I
Smeaton, Oliphant; *see* Smeaton, W. H. O.
Smeaton, Lt-Col Oswald; *see* Smeaton, Lt-Col C. O.
Smeaton, William Henry Oliphant, *died* 1914, vol. I
Smedley, Constance, *died* 1941, vol. IV
Smeed, Reuben Jacob, 1909–1976, vol. VII
Smeeton, Captain Samuel Page, 1842–1916, vol. II
Smele, William Samuel George, 1912–1976, vol. VII
Smellie, Alexander, 1857–1923, vol. II
Smellie, Elizabeth Lawrie, 1884–1968, vol. VI
Smellie, James Maclure, 1893–1961, vol. VI
Smeterlin, Jan, 1892–1967, vol. VI
Smethurst, Albert H., 1868–1935, vol. III
Smethurst, Rev. Canon Arthur Frederick, 1904–1957, vol. V
Smethurst, Sir Thomas, 1860–1935, vol. III
Smiddy, Timothy A., 1875–1962, vol. VI
Smijth, Sir William Bowyer-, 12th Bt (*cr* 1661), 1840–1916, vol. II
Smiles, Samuel, 1812–1904, vol. I
Smiles, Samuel, 1877–1953, vol. V
Smiles, Lt-Col Sir Walter Dorling, *died* 1953, vol. V
Smiles, William, 1824–1915, vol. I
Smiley, Sir Hugh Houston, 1st Bt, 1841–1909, vol. I
Smiley, Sir John, 2nd Bt, 1876–1930, vol. III
Smiley, Norman Bryce, 1909–1968, vol. VI
Smiley, Peter Kerr K.; *see* Kerr-Smiley.
Smillie, Robert, 1857–1940, vol. III
Smit, Hon. Jacob Hendrik, 1881–1959, vol. V
Smit, Jacobus Stephanus, 1878–1960, vol. V
Smith, A. Reginald, *died* 1934, vol. III
Smith, Abel, 1829–1898, vol. I
Smith, Abel Henry, 1862–1930, vol. III
Smith, Hon. Sir Abercrombie; *see* Smith, Hon. Sir C. A.
Smith, Adam, 1854–1920, vol. II
Smith, Sir Alan R.; *see* Rae Smith.
Smith, Albert, 1867–1942, vol. IV
Smith, Sir Albert, 1862–1944, vol. IV
Smith, Brig. Albert, 1896–1959, vol. V
Smith, Albert Hugh, 1903–1967, vol. VI
Smith, Albert William, 1863–1940, vol. III
Smith, Lt-Col Alexander Hugh Dickson, 1890–1960, vol. V
Smith, Alfred, *died* 1931, vol. III
Smith, Alfred Emanuel, 1873–1944, vol. IV
Smith, Alfred John, 1865–1925, vol. II (A), vol. III
Smith, Hon. Alfred Lee, *born* 1838, vol. II
Smith, Sir Alfred M.; *see* Mays-Smith.
Smith, Maj.-Gen. Alfred Travers Fairtlough, 1890–1965, vol. VI
Smith, Sir Alfred van W. L.; *see* Lucie-Smith.
Smith, Rt Rev. Alfred William, 1875–1958, vol. V
Smith, Lt-Col Algernon Fox Eric, 1857–1942, vol. IV
Smith, Alic Halford, 1883–1958, vol. V
Smith, Sir Allan Chalmers, 1893–1980, vol. VII
Smith, Allan Frith, 1857–1935, vol. III

Smith, Sir Allan Gordon G.; see Gordon-Smith.
Smith, Sir Allan Macgregor, died 1941, vol. IV
Smith, Allan Ramsay, 1875–1926, vol. II
Smith, Andrew, 1849–1914, vol. I
Smith, Sir Andrew, 1880–1967, vol. VI
Smith, Andrew Thomas, 1884–1943, vol. IV
Smith, Comdr Andrew W.; see Wilmot-Smith.
Smith, Dame Ann Beadsmore, died 1960, vol. V
Smith, Annie Shepherd; see Smith, Mrs Burnet.
Smith, Sir Anthony Paul G.; see Grafftey-Smith.
Smith, Rt Hon. Sir Archibald Levin, 1836–1901, vol. I
Smith, (Arnold) John Hugh, 1881–1964, vol. VI
Smith, Arnold P.; see Pye-Smith.
Smith, Arthur C.; see Corbett-Smith.
Smith, Arthur Croxton, 1865–1952, vol. V
Smith, Rev. Arthur Edward, 1871–1952, vol. V
Smith, Lt-Gen. Sir Arthur Francis, 1890–1977, vol. VII
Smith, Vice-Adm. Arthur Gordon, 1873–1953, vol. V
Smith, Arthur H.; see Hopewell-Smith.
Smith, Arthur Hamilton, 1860–1941, vol. IV
Smith, Rev. Arthur Henderson, 1845–1932, vol. III
Smith, Arthur Kirke, 1878–1937, vol. III
Smith, Arthur Lionel, 1850–1924, vol. II
Smith, Arthur Lionel Forster, 1880–1972, vol. VII
Smith, Arthur Llewellyn, 1903–1978, vol. VII
Smith, Lt-Col Arthur M.; see Murray-Smith.
Smith, Arthur William, 1880–1961, vol. VI
Smith, Sir Aubrey; see Smith, Sir Charles A.
Smith, Adm. Sir Aubrey Clare Hugh, 1872–1957, vol. V
Smith, Ven. Augustus Elder, died 1916, vol. II
Smith, Rev. Canon Basil Alec, 1908–1969, vol. VI
Smith, Basil Guy Oswald, 1861–1928, vol. II
Smith, Basil Thomas P.; see Parsons-Smith.
Smith, Gen. Bedell; see Smith, Gen. W. B.
Smith, Rt Hon. Sir Ben, 1879–1964, vol. VI
Smith, Benjamin Eli, 1857–1913, vol. I
Smith, Ven. Benjamin Frederick, died 1900, vol. I
Smith, Bernard, 1881–1936, vol. III
Smith, Bernard Joseph G.; see Gilliat-Smith.
Smith, Sir Berry C.; see Cusack-Smith.
Smith, Col Bertram Abel, 1879–1947, vol. IV
Smith, Captain Bertram Hornsby, 1874–1945, vol. IV
Smith, Lt-Col Bertram M.; see Metcalfe-Smith.
Smith, Sir Bracewell, 1st Bt (cr 1947), 1884–1966, vol. VI
Smith, Major Brooke H.; see Heckstall-Smith.
Smith, Hon. Bruce, 1851–1937, vol. III
Smith, Mrs Burnett, 1860–1943, vol. IV
Smith, Sir Carl Victor, 1897–1979, vol. VII
Smith, Carlton A., 1853–1946, vol. IV
Smith, Cecil Archibald, died 1948, vol. IV
Smith, Rt Hon. Sir Cecil Clementi, 1840–1916, vol. II
Smith, Sir Cecil F.; see Furness-Smith.
Smith, Sir Cecil Harcourt-, 1859–1944, vol. IV
Smith, Mrs Cecil W.; see Woodham-Smith.
Smith, Charles, 1844–1916, vol. II
Smith, Hon. Sir (Charles) Abercrombie, 1834–1919, vol. II

Smith, Lt-Col Charles Aitchison, 1871–1940, vol. III
Smith, Captain Charles Appleton, 1864–1928, vol. II
Smith, Sir (Charles) Aubrey, 1863–1948, vol. IV
Smith, Col Sir Charles Bean Euan-, 1842–1910, vol. I
Smith, Charles Bennett, 1870–1939, vol. III (A), vol. IV
Smith, Sir Charles Cunliffe, 3rd Bt (cr 1804), 1827–1905, vol. I
Smith, Air Cdre Sir Charles Edward K.; see Kingsford-Smith.
Smith, Charles Emory, 1842–1908, vol. I
Smith, Captain Charles Futcher, died 1925, vol. II
Smith, Air Cdre Charles Gainer, 1880–1948, vol. IV
Smith, Sir Charles Garden A.; see Assheton-Smith.
Smith, Hon. Sir Charles George, died 1941, vol. IV
Smith, Charles George Percy; see Baron Delacourt-Smith.
Smith, Charles H.; see Herbert-Smith.
Smith, Charles Henry C.; see Chichester Smith.
Smith, Sir (Charles) Herbert, 1871–1941, vol. IV
Smith, Maj.-Gen. Sir Charles Holled, 1846–1925, vol. II
Smith, Charles Howard, 1888–1942, vol. IV
Smith, Rev. Charles John, died 1940, vol. III
Smith, Charles Johnston, 1880–1943, vol. IV
Smith, Charles Michie, 1854–1922, vol. II
Smith, Very Rev. Charles Pressley, 1862–1935, vol. III
Smith, Sir (Charles) Robert, 1887–1959, vol. V
Smith, Rev. Charles Ryder, 1873–1956, vol. V
Smith, Charles Stewart, 1859–1934, vol. III
Smith, Captain Charles Valentine, 1854–1932, vol. III
Smith, Mgr Charles William, 1873–1954, vol. V
Smith, Charlotte F.; see Fell-Smith.
Smith, Chilton Lind A.; see Addison-Smith.
Smith, Cicely Fox, died 1954, vol. V
Smith, Sir Clarence, 1849–1941, vol. IV
Smith, Rev. Clement, 1845–1921, vol. II
Smith, Lt-Gen. Clement John, 1831–1910, vol. I
Smith, Brig.-Gen. Clement Leslie, died 1927, vol. II
Smith, Sir Clifford Edward H.; see Heathcote-Smith.
Smith, Clifford P., 1869–1945, vol. IV
Smith, Colin, 1881–1940, vol. III
Smith, Sir Colville; see Smith, Sir P. C.
Smith, Surg.-Gen. Sir Colvin C.; see Colvin-Smith.
Smith, Constance Isabella Stuart, died 1930, vol. III
Smith, Cyril James, 1909–1974, vol. VII
Smith, Rev. David, 1866–1932, vol. III
Smith, David B.; see Baird-Smith.
Smith, David Bonner-, 1890–1950, vol. IV
Smith, Hon. David John, 1907–1976, vol. VII
Smith, David Murray, died 1952, vol. V
Smith, David Nichol, 1875–1962, vol. VI
Smith, David S.; see Seth-Smith.
Smith, Sir David Wadsworth, 1883–1948, vol. IV
Smith, Dempster, died 1953, vol. V
Smith, Desmond A.; see Abel Smith.

Smith, Lt-Col Douglas Kirke, 1883–1923, vol. II
Smith, Sir Drummond Cospatric Hamilton-S., 5th Bt (cr 1804); see Spencer-Smith.
Smith, Sir Drummond Cuncliffe, 4th Bt (cr 1804), 1861–1947, vol. IV
Smith, Sir Dudley S.; see Stewart-Smith.
Smith, Maj.-Gen. E. Davidson-, died 1916, vol. II
Smith, E. W.; see Whitney-Smith.
Smith, Ean Kendal S.; see Stewart-Smith.
Smith, Edgar Albert, 1847–1916, vol. II
Smith, Adm. Edmund Hyde, 1865–1939, vol. III
Smith, Edmund Robinson, 1856–1942, vol. IV
Smith, Sir Edmund Wyldbore-, 1877–1938, vol. III
Smith, Edward, 1839–1919, vol. II
Smith, Sir Edward, 1857–1926, vol. II
Smith, Edward B.; see Barclay-Smith.
Smith, Col Edward Castleman C.; see Castleman-Smith.
Smith, Edward Orford, 1841–1915, vol. I (A)
Smith, Lt-Col Edward Osborne, 1864–1930, vol. III
Smith, Major Edward Pelham, 1868–1937, vol. III
Smith, Major Edward Pendarves D.; see Dorrien-Smith.
Smith, Edward Percy, 1891–1968, vol. VI
Smith, Edward Rawdon R.; see Rawdon Smith.
Smith, Edward S.; see Sharwood-Smith.
Smith, Edward Shrapnell S.; see Shrapnell-Smith.
Smith, Edwin, 1870–1937, vol. III
Smith, Col Edwin Charles M.; see Montgomery-Smith.
Smith, Hon. Sir Edwin Thomas, 1830–1919, vol. II
Smith, Rev. Edwin W., 1876–1957, vol. V
Smith, Lady Eleanor, died 1945, vol. IV
Smith, Ellis, 1896–1969, vol. VI
Smith, Captain Eric; see Smith, Captain Evan C. E.
Smith, Sir Eric Conran C.; see Conran-Smith.
Smith, Eric Martin, 1908–1951, vol. V
Smith, Eric Percival, 1890–1938, vol. III
Smith, Erik John, 1914–1972, vol. VII
Smith, Ernest, 1869–1945, vol. IV
Smith, Hon. Ernest D'Israeli, 1853–1948, vol. IV
Smith, Ernest Gardiner, died 1956, vol. V
Smith, Ernest T.; see Thornton-Smith.
Smith, Brig. Ernest Thomas Cobley, 1895–1977, vol. VII
Smith, Sir Ernest Woodhouse, 1884–1960, vol. V
Smith, Eustace, died 1914, vol. I
Smith, Col Sir Eustace; see Smith, Col Sir T. E.
Smith, Eustace Abel, 1862–1938, vol. III
Smith, Captain Evan Cadogan Eric, 1894–1950, vol. IV
Smith, Everard Reginald Martin, 1875–1938, vol. III
Smith, Florence Margaret; see Smith, Stevie.
Smith, Sir Francis Edward James, 1863–1950, vol. IV
Smith, Francis Edward Viney, 1902–1979, vol. VII
Smith, Sir Francis H.; see Harrison-Smith.
Smith, Francis Hopkinson, 1838–1915, vol. I
Smith, Francis Jagoe, 1873–1969, vol. VI
Smith, Francis St George M.; see Manners-Smith.
Smith, Sir Francis Villeneuve-, 1819–1909, vol. I

Smith, Sir Francis Whitmore, 1844–1931, vol. III
Smith, Francis William Head, 1886–1964, vol. VI
Smith, Hon. Sir Frank, died 1901, vol. I
Smith, Frank, 1854–1940, vol. III
Smith, Frank, 1882–1951, vol. V
Smith, Frank Braybrook, 1864–1950, vol. IV
Smith, Sir Frank Edward, 1879–1970, vol. VI
Smith, Sir Frank Edwin N.; see Newson-Smith.
Smith, Frank Guthrie, 1873–1932, vol. III
Smith, Frank Moffatt, 1872–1940, vol. III
Smith, Frederic G.; see Gordon-Smith.
Smith, Frederic Marlett B.; see Bell-Smith.
Smith, Maj.-Gen. Sir Frederick, 1857–1929, vol. III
Smith, Col Frederick, 1858–1933, vol. III
Smith, Sir Frederick, 1859–1945, vol. IV
Smith, Frederick A., 1887–1943, vol. IV
Smith, Frederick Bonham, born 1837, vol. II
Smith, Rev. Frederick J. J.; see Jervis-Smith.
Smith, Col Frederick John, 1866–1915, vol. I
Smith, Lt Col Frederick Lawrence C.; see Coldwell-Smith.
Smith, Fred, 1880–1940, vol. III
Smith, Fred John, 1857–1919, vol. II
Smith, Sir Frederick William, 1861–1926, vol. II
Smith, Garden Grant, 1860–1913, vol. I
Smith, Geoffrey, 1878–1910, vol. I
Smith, Geoffrey R. H., 1901–1964, vol. VI
Smith, Geoffrey Samuel A.; see Abel-Smith.
Smith, Ven. Geoffry Bertram, 1889–1957, vol. V
Smith, George, 1833–1919, vol. II
Smith, George, 1870–1934, vol. III
Smith, Sir George, 1858–1938, vol. III
Smith, George, 1867–1957, vol. V
Smith, George A.; see Armitage-Smith.
Smith, Very Rev. Sir George Adam, 1856–1942, vol. IV
Smith, George Barnett, 1841–1909, vol. I
Smith, Brig.-Gen. George Barton, 1860–1921, vol. II
Smith, Sir George Basil H.; see Haddon-Smith.
Smith, Sir George Bracewell, 2nd Bt (cr 1947), 1912–1976, vol. VII
Smith, George Charles Moore, 1858–1940, vol. III
Smith, George Douglas, 1865–1949, vol. IV
Smith, Brig.-Gen. George Edward, 1868–1944, vol. IV
Smith, Sir George Fenwick, 1914–1978, vol. VII
Smith, George Frederick Herbert, 1872–1953, vol. V
Smith, Rev. George Furness, 1849–1929, vol. III
Smith, George G.; see Gregory Smith.
Smith, George Geoffrey, 1885–1951, vol. V
Smith, Sir George Henry F.; see Fisher-Smith.
Smith, Rev. George Herbert, 1851–1923, vol. II
Smith, George Hill, 1833–1926, vol. III
Smith, Rt Rev. George John, 1840–1918, vol. II
Smith, Sir George John, 1845–1921, vol. II
Smith, Col George John, 1862–1946, vol. IV
Smith, George Lind A.; see Addison-Smith.
Smith, Rev. George Maberly, 1831–1917, vol. II
Smith, Lt-Col George Maciver Campbell, 1869–1946, vol. IV
Smith, Col George Moultrie B.; see Bullen-Smith.

Smith, George Munro, 1856–1917, vol. II
Smith, George Murray, 1859–1919, vol. II
Smith, Sir George R.; *see* Reeves-Smith.
Smith, George S.; *see* Scoby-Smith.
Smith, George Stuart G.; *see* Graham-Smith.
Smith, George Tulloch B.; *see* Bisset-Smith.
Smith, George W. Duff A.; *see* Assheton-Smith.
Smith, Major George Wilson, 1880–1940, vol. IV
Smith, Gerald Dudley, 1866–1936, vol. III
Smith, Lt-Col Sir Gerard, 1839–1920, vol. II
Smith, Brig.-Gen. Gilbert Boys, 1859–1937, vol. III
Smith, Rev. Gilbert Edward, *died* 1912, vol. I
Smith, Air Vice-Marshal Gilbert H.; *see* Harcourt-Smith.
Smith, Col Sir Gilbertson, 1867–1958, vol. V
Smith, Ven. Godfrey Scott, 1878–1944, vol. IV
Smith, Goldwin, 1823–1910, vol. I
Smith, Sir Grafton Elliot, 1871–1937, vol. III
Smith, Graham Burrell, 1880–1975, vol. VII
Smith, Granville, 1859–1925, vol. II
Smith, Col Granville Roland Francis, 1860–1917, vol. II
Smith, Rev. Granville V. V., 1838–1929, vol. III
Smith, Guy Basil G.; *see* Gilliat-Smith.
Smith, Guy Bellingham, 1865–1945, vol. IV
Smith, Rt Rev. Guy Vernon, 1880–1957, vol. V
Smith, Rev. Gwilym, 1881–1939, vol. III
Smith, H. Herbert, 1851–1913, vol. I
Smith, Sir Hamilton Pym F.; *see* Freer Smith.
Smith, Sir Harold, 1876–1924, vol. II
Smith, Col Sir Harold Charles T.; *see* Templar-Smith.
Smith, Harold Clifford, 1876–1960, vol. V
Smith, Harold Hamel, 1867–1944, vol. IV
Smith, Harold Octavius, 1882–1952, vol. V
Smith, Harold Ross, 1906–1956, vol. V
Smith, Harry, 1870–1940, vol. III
Smith, Rev. Harry, 1865–1942, vol. IV
Smith, Sir Harry, 1874–1949, vol. IV
Smith, Ven. (Harry Kingsley) Percival, 1898–1965, vol. VI
Smith, Maj.-Gen. Sir Harry Reginald Walter Marriott, 1875–1955, vol. V
Smith, Harry Worcester, 1865–1945, vol. IV
Smith, Harvey Hall, 1880–1958, vol. V
Smith, Rev. Haskett, 1847–1906, vol. I
Smith, Rt Hon. Hastings Bertrand L.; *see* Lees-Smith.
Smith, Helen Gregory, *died* 1956, vol. V
Smith, Hely, 1862–1941, vol. IV
Smith, Sir Henry, *died* 1919, vol. II
Smith, Lt-Col Sir Henry, 1835–1921, vol. II
Smith, Rev. Henry, 1857–1939, vol. III
Smith, Lt-Col Henry, 1862–1948, vol. IV
Smith, Henry B.; *see* Batty-Smith.
Smith, Sir Henry Babington, 1863–1923, vol. II
Smith, Henry Bompas, 1867–1953, vol. V
Smith, Maj.-Gen. Henry C.; *see* Coape-Smith.
Smith, Engr Rear-Adm. Henry Frank, 1875–1939, vol. III
Smith, Rev. Henry Gibson, *died* 1931, vol. III
Smith, Brig. Henry Gilbertson, 1896–1977, vol. VII
Smith, Lt-Col Henry Lockhart, 1859–1935, vol. III

Smith, Sir Henry Martin, 1907–1979, vol. VII
Smith, Sir Henry Moncrieff, 1873–1951, vol. V
Smith, H(enry) Norman, 1890–1962, vol. VI
Smith, Col Henry Robert, 1843–1917, vol. II
Smith, Henry Roy William, 1891–1971, vol. VII
Smith, Sir Henry S.; *see* Scott-Smith.
Smith, Sir Henry Sutcliffe, 1864–1938, vol. III
Smith, Henry W.; *see* Whitby-Smith.
Smith, Sir Henry W.; *see* White-Smith.
Smith, Sir Henry W.; *see* Wilson Smith.
Smith, Henry Wood, 1865–1906, vol. I
Smith, Sir Herbert; *see* Smith, Sir C. H.
Smith, Sir Herbert, 1st Bt (*cr* 1920), 1872–1943, vol. IV
Smith, Herbert, 1881–1953, vol. V
Smith, Sir Herbert, 2nd Bt (*cr* 1920), 1903–1961, vol. VI
Smith, Herbert Alexander, 1896–1976, vol. VII
Smith, Herbert Arthur, 1885–1961, vol. VI
Smith, Col Herbert Austen, 1866–1949, vol. IV
Smith, Col Herbert Francis, 1859–1948, vol. IV
Smith, Lt-Col Herbert Frederick Edgar, 1888–1940, vol. III
Smith, Herbert Greenhough, *died* 1935, vol. III
Smith, Maj.-Gen. Sir Herbert Guthrie, 1864–1930, vol. III
Smith, Rev. Herbert Maynard, 1869–1949, vol. IV
Smith, Herbert S.; *see* Somerville Smith.
Smith, Major Herbert Stoney-, 1868–1915, vol. I (A)
Smith, Horace, 1836–1922, vol. II
Smith, Howard; *see* Smith, P. H.
Smith, Col Howard William, 1858–1905, vol. I
Smith, Brig. Hubert Clementi, 1878–1958, vol. V
Smith, Sir Hubert Llewellyn, 1864–1945, vol. IV
Smith, Hon. Hugh Adeane Vivian, 1910–1978, vol. VII
Smith, Hugh Alexander McC.; *see* McClure-Smith.
Smith, Lt-Col Sir Hugh Bateman P.; *see* Protheroe-Smith.
Smith, Hugh Bellingham, 1866–1922, vol. II
Smith, Hugh Colin, 1836–1910, vol. I
Smith, Hugh Crawford, *died* 1907, vol. I
Smith, Brig. Hugh Garden S.; *see* Seth-Smith.
Smith, Hugh William H.; *see* Heckstall-Smith.
Smith, Vice-Adm. Humphrey Hugh, 1875–1940, vol. III
Smith, Ida Phyllis B.; *see* Barclay-Smith.
Smith, Rev. Irton, 1855–1933, vol. III
Smith, Rev. Isaac A., *died* 1940, vol. III
Smith, Rev. Isaac Gregory, 1826–1920, vol. II
Smith, J. Allister, 1866–1960, vol. V
Smith, J. T., *died* 1937, vol. III
Smith, Sir James, 1847–1932, vol. III
Smith, Most Rev. James A., 1841–1928, vol. II
Smith, James Alexander George, *died* 1942, vol. IV
Smith, Very Rev. James Allan, 1841–1918, vol. II
Smith, Col James Aubrey, 1877–1955, vol. V
Smith, Sir James B., 1845–1913, vol. I
Smith, Sir James Cowlishaw, 1873–1946, vol. IV
Smith, James Cruickshank, 1867–1946, vol. IV
Smith, James David Maxwell, 1895–1969, vol. VI

Smith, James Dury H.; *see* Hindley-Smith.
Smith, Sir James Edward M.; *see* Masterton-Smith.
Smith, James Hamblin, 1827–1901, vol. I
Smith, Hon. Sir (James) Joynton, 1855–1943, vol. IV
Smith, Surg.-Rear-Adm. James Lawrence, 1862–1945, vol. IV
Smith, James Lorrain, *died* 1931, vol. III
Smith, James Maclaren G.; *see* Gray-Smith.
Smith, Rt Hon. James Parker, 1854–1929, vol. III
Smith, Lt-Col Sir James Robert Dunlop, 1858–1921, vol. II
Smith, James Walter, 1868–1931, vol. III
Smith, Rev. John, 1844–1905, vol. I
Smith, John, 1825–1910, vol. I
Smith, John, 1837–1922, vol. II
Smith, Very Rev. John, 1854–1927, vol. II
Smith, John, 1883–1964, vol. VI
Smith, John Alexander, 1863–1939, vol. III
Smith, Sir John Alfred L.; *see* Lucie-Smith.
Smith, Maj.-Gen. John Blackburne, 1865–1928, vol. II
Smith, John F.; *see* Forest Smith.
Smith, John George, 1881–1968, vol. VI
Smith, Sir John George Lawley V.; *see* Vassar-Smith.
Smith, John Gerald, 1907–1979, vol. VII
Smith, Lt-Col John Grant, *died* 1942, vol. IV
Smith, J(ohn) G(uthrie) Spence, 1880–1951, vol. V
Smith, John Henry E.; *see* Etherington-Smith.
Smith, John Hugh; *see* Smith, A. J. H.
Smith, John Hughes W.; *see* Wardle-Smith.
Smith, Sir John James, 1875–1957, vol. V
Smith, John Keats C.; *see* Catterson-Smith.
Smith, Lt-Col John Manners, 1864–1920, vol. II
Smith, John Mitchell Aitken, 1902–1974, vol. VII
Smith, John Obed, 1864–1937, vol. III
Smith, Rev. John Reader, *died* 1923, vol. II
Smith, Sir John Smalman, 1847–1913, vol. I
Smith, Rt Rev. John Taylor, 1860–1938, vol. III
Smith, John William, 1864–1926, vol. II
Smith, Sir Jonah W.; *see* Walker-Smith.
Smith, Joseph, 1855–1939, vol. III
Smith, Maj.-Gen. Joseph Barnard, 1839–1925, vol. II
Smith, Sir Joseph Benjamin George, 1878–1950, vol. IV
Smith, Rt Rev. Joseph Oswald, 1854–1924, vol. II
Smith, Hon. Sir Joynton; *see* Smith, Hon. Sir James J.
Smith, K. W. A., 1899–1951, vol. V
Smith, Sir Keith Macpherson, 1890–1955, vol. V
Smith, Col Kenneth, 1885–1971, vol. VII
Smith, Kenneth Brooke Farley, 1913–1943, vol. IV
Smith, Brig.-Gen. Kenneth John K.; *see* Kincaid-Smith.
Smith, Lancelot Grey Hugh, 1870–1941, vol. IV
Smith, Launcelot Eustace, 1868–1948, vol. IV
Smith, Col Leonard Kirke, 1877–1941, vol. IV
Smith, Lewis, 1869–1944, vol. III
Smith, Captain Sir Lindsey, 1870–1960, vol. V
Smith, Brig.-Gen. Lionel A.; *see* Abel-Smith.

Smith, Col Lionel Fergus, 1869–1945, vol. IV
Smith, Lionel Graham Horton H.; *see* Horton-Smith.
Smith, Logan Pearsall, 1865–1949, vol. IV
Smith, Louis L.; *see* Laybourne-Smith.
Smith, Sir Louis W., *died* 1939, vol. III
Smith, Rt Rev. Lucius, 1860–1934, vol. III
Smith, Sir Lumley, 1834–1918, vol. II
Smith, Lyman Cornelius, *died* 1910, vol. II
Smith, Sir Malcolm, *died* 1935, vol. III
Smith, Lt-Col Malcolm K.; *see* Kincaid-Smith.
Smith, Marcella, *died* 1963, vol. VI
Smith, Maria Constance, *died* 1930, vol. III
Smith, Marshall King, 1867–1946, vol. IV
Smith, Rt Rev. Martin Linton, 1869–1950, vol. IV
Smith, Martin Ridley, 1833–1908, vol. I
Smith, Mary Isobel Barr, *died* 1941, vol. IV
Smith, Mary Sybil, *died* 1952, vol. V
Smith, Sir Matthew Arnold Bracy, 1879–1959, vol. V
Smith, May, 1879–1968, vol. VI
Smith, Maynard, 1875–1928, vol. II
Smith, Maj.-Gen. Merton B.; *see* Beckwith-Smith.
Smith, Michael Seymour S.; *see* Spencer-Smith.
Smith, Hon. Miles Staniforth Cater, 1869–1934, vol. III
Smith, Montague Bentley Talbot P.; *see* Paske-Smith.
Smith, Morton William, 1851–1925, vol. II
Smith, Naomi Gwladys R.; *see* Royde Smith.
Smith, Sir Nathaniel B.; *see* Bowden-Smith.
Smith, Nevil Digby B.; *see* Bosworth-Smith.
Smith, Noel James Gillies, *born* 1899, vol. VI
Smith, Norman, 1877–1963, vol. VI
Smith, Norman Kemp, 1872–1958, vol. V
Smith, Norman Lockhart, 1887–1968, vol. VI
Smith, Sir Norman Percival Arthur, 1892–1964, vol. VI
Smith, Captain Norman Wesley, 1900–1977, vol. VII
Smith, Nowell Charles, 1871–1961, vol. VI
Smith, Lt-Gen. Octavius Ludlow, 1828–1927, vol. II
Smith, Olivia Mary, (Mrs R. D. Smith); *see* Manning, O. M.
Smith, Lt-Col Osbert Walter Dudley, 1898–1973, vol. VII
Smith, Sir Osborne Arkell, 1876–1952, vol. V
Smith, Very Rev. Oswin Harvard G.; *see* Gibbs-Smith.
Smith, Owen Hugh, *died* 1958, vol. V
Smith, Owen Maurice, 1888–1957, vol. V
Smith, Patrick, 1858–1930, vol. III
Smith, Ven. Percival; *see* Smith, Ven. H. K. P.
Smith, Major Percy George D.; *see* Darvil-Smith.
Smith, Percy John Delf, *died* 1948, vol. IV
Smith, Surg.-Rear-Adm. Sir Percy W. B.; *see* Bassett-Smith.
Smith, Peter Caldwell, 1858–1923, vol. II
Smith, Philip, 1853–1922, vol. II
Smith, Sir (Philip) Colville, *died* 1937, vol. III
Smith, Philip H. Law, 1866–1920, vol. II
Smith, Philip Henry P.; *see* Pye-Smith.

Smith, (Philip) Howard, 1845–1919, vol. II
Smith, Rear-Adm. P(hilip) Sydney, 1899–1973, vol. VII
Smith, Rev. Philip Vernon, 1845–1929, vol. III
Smith, Brig. Philip William Lilian B.; see Broke-Smith.
Smith, Phyllis B.; see Barclay-Smith.
Smith, Priestley, died 1933, vol. III
Smith, Sir Prince, 1st Bt (cr 1911), 1840–1922, vol. II
Smith, Sir Prince P., 2nd Bt (cr 1911); see Prince-Smith.
Smith, Ralph Henry H.; see Hammersley-Smith.
Smith, Ralph Henry T.; see Tottenham-Smith.
Smith, Ravenscroft Elsey, 1859–1930, vol. III
Smith, Reginald, vol. II
Smith, Rev. Reginald, 1844–1936, vol. III
Smith, Reginald Allender, died 1940, vol. III
Smith, Reginald Eccles, 1887–1963, vol. VI
Smith, Reginald Henry Macaulay A.; see Abel Smith.
Smith, Col Rt Hon. Sir Reginald Hugh D.; see Dorman-Smith.
Smith, Reginald John, 1857–1916, vol. II
Smith, Reginald Montagu B.; see Bosworth-Smith.
Smith, Reginald Norman M.; see Marsh Smith.
Smith, Rennie, 1888–1962, vol. VI
Smith, Richard Edwin, 1910–1978, vol. VII
Smith, Richard G.; see Gordon-Smith.
Smith, Richard Horton H.; see Horton-Smith.
Smith, Richard M.; see Mudie-Smith.
Smith, Maj.-Gen. Richard Talbot S.; see Snowden-Smith.
Smith, Sir Richard Vassar V.; see Vassar-Smith.
Smith, Sir Robert; see Smith, Sir C. R.
Smith, Robert Addison, died 1925, vol. II
Smith, Robert Allan, 1909–1980, vol. VII
Smith, Robert Cooper, 1859–1917, vol. II
Smith, Robert John, 1866–1942, vol. IV
Smith, Robert Macaulay, 1859–1927, vol. II
Smith, Sir Robert Murdoch, 1835–1900, vol. I
Smith, Robert Murray, 1831–1921, vol. II
Smith, Robert Paterson, 1903–1971, vol. VII
Smith, Robert Percy, died 1941, vol. IV
Smith, Robert Shingleton, 1845–1922, vol. II
Smith, Sir Robert Workman, 1st Bt (cr 1945), 1880–1957, vol. V
Smith, Rt Rev. Rocksborough Remington, 1872–1955, vol. V
Smith, Gipsy Rodney, 1860–1947, vol. IV
Smith, Roger Thomas, 1863–1940, vol. III
Smith, Rev. Ronald Gregor, 1913–1968, vol. VI
Smith, Sir Ross G.; see Grey-Smith.
Smith, Sir Ross Macpherson, 1892–1922, vol. II
Smith, Sir Rudolph Hampden; see Smith, Sir T. R. H.
Smith, Rutherfoord John P.; see Pye-Smith.
Smith, S. Carterson, 1849–1912, vol. I
Smith, Samuel, 1836–1906, vol. I
Smith, Samuel, 1855–1921, vol. II
Smith, Samuel Harold, 1888–1971, vol. VII
Smith, Samuel Walter Johnson, 1871–1948, vol. IV
Smith, Sarah; see Stretton, Hesba.

Smith, Sheila K.; see Kaye-Smith.
Smith, Sidney, 1889–1979, vol. VII
Smith, Lt-Col Sidney Browning, died 1930, vol. III
Smith, Sidney Earle, 1897–1959, vol. V
Smith, Solomon Charles Kaines, died 1958, vol. V
Smith, Spence; see Smith, John G. S.
Smith, Stanley Alexander de; see de Smith.
Smith, Major Stanley Alwyn, 1882–1931, vol. III
Smith, Stanley Livingston, 1889–1958, vol. V
Smith, Stanley Parker, 1884–1953, vol. V
Smith, Stanley Wyatt-, 1887–1958, vol. V
Smith, Stephen Henry, 1865–1943, vol. IV
Smith, Col Steuart B.; see Bogle-Smith.
Smith, Stevie, (Florence Margaret Smith), 1902–1971, vol. VII
Smith, Stuart Hayne G.; see Granville-Smith.
Smith, Captain Sutton, died 1938, vol. III
Smith, Sir Swire, 1842–1918, vol. II
Smith, Maj.-Gen. Sir Sydenham Campbell Urquhart, 1859–1940, vol. III
Smith, Hon. Sydney, 1856–1934, vol. III
Smith, Sir Sydney Alfred, died 1969, vol. VI
Smith, Sir Sydney Armitage A.; see Armitage-Smith.
Smith, Sydney David, 1873–1936, vol. III
Smith, Col Sydney Ernest, 1881–1943, vol. IV
Smith, Rev. Sydney Fenn, 1843–1921, vol. II
Smith, Sydney Ure, 1887–1949, vol. IV
Smith, Sydney William, 1878–1963, vol. VI
Smith, T. Gilbert, died 1904, vol. I
Smith, Theobald, 1859–1934, vol. III
Smith, Theodore Clarke, 1870–1960, vol. VI (AI)
Smith, Thomas, 1817–1906, vol. I
Smith, Sir Thomas, 1st Bt (cr 1897), 1833–1909, vol. I
Smith, Sir Thomas, 1875–1963, vol. VI
Smith, Thomas, 1883–1969, vol. VI
Smith, Thomas Algernon D.; see Dorrien-Smith.
Smith, Major Thomas Close, 1878–1946, vol. IV
Smith, Sir Thomas Cospatric Hamilton-S., 6th Bt (cr 1804); see Spencer-Smith.
Smith, Sir Thomas D. S.; see Straker-Smith.
Smith, Col Sir (Thomas) Eustace, 1900–1971, vol. VII
Smith, Rev. Canon Thomas G.; see Grigg-Smith.
Smith, Major Sir Thomas Gabriel Lumley L.; see Lumley-Smith.
Smith, Sir Thomas James, died 1939, vol. III
Smith, Thomas James, 1905–1970, vol. VI
Smith, Thomas Roger, 1830–1903, vol. I
Smith, Sir (Thomas) Rudolph Hampden, 2nd Bt (cr 1897), 1869–1958, vol. V
Smith, Sir Thomas Turner, 3rd Bt (cr 1897), 1903–1961, vol. VI
Smith, (Thomas) Wareham, 1874–1938, vol. III
Smith, Thomas William, 1878–1946, vol. IV
Smith, Tom, 1886–1953, vol. V
Smith, Sir Tom Elder B.; see Barr Smith.
Smith, Mrs Toulmin; see Meade, L. T.
Smith, Trafford, 1912–1975, vol. VII
Smith, Vernon Russell, 1849–1921, vol. II
Smith, Victor, 1879–1931, vol. III
Smith, Vincent Arthur, 1848–1920, vol. II
Smith, Vivian Francis C.; see Crowther-Smith.

Smith, W. Harding, *died* 1922, vol. II
Smith, W. H. S.; *see* Seth-Smith.
Smith, W. P. Haskett-, *died* 1946, vol. IV
Smith, Sir Walter B.; *see* Buchanan-Smith.
Smith, Gen. (Walter) Bedell, 1895–1961, vol. VI
Smith, Rev. Walter Chalmers, 1824–1908, vol. I
Smith, Walter George, 1844–1932, vol. III
Smith, Rev. Walter Percy, 1848–1922, vol. II
Smith, Rev. Walter R., 1845–1921, vol. II
Smith, Walter Robert, 1872–1942, vol. IV
Smith, Walter Robert George, 1887–1966, vol. VI
Smith, Walter William Marriott, 1846–1944, vol. IV
Smith, Wareham; *see* Smith, T. W.
Smith, Watson, 1845–1920, vol. II
Smith, Wilfred, 1903–1955, vol. V
Smith, Maj.-Gen. Wilfrid Edward Bownas, 1867–1942, vol. IV
Smith, Sir William, 1843–1916, vol. II
Smith, Maj.-Gen. William, 1835–1922, vol. II
Smith, William, 1859–1932, vol. III
Smith, Sir William Alexander, 1854–1914, vol. I
Smith, Col William Apsley, 1856–1927, vol. II
Smith, Vice-Adm. William B.; *see* Bowden Smith.
Smith, William Benjamin, 1850–1934, vol. III (A), vol. IV
Smith, William Binns, 1837–1911, vol. I
Smith, William Brownhill, *died* 1948, vol IV
Smith, Sir William C.; *see* Cusack-Smith.
Smith, William Charles, 1849–1915, vol. I
Smith, William Charles Clifford, 1855–1931, vol. III
Smith, Maj.-Gen. Sir William Douglas, 1865–1939, vol. III
Smith, Maj.-Gen. William Dunlop, 1865–1940, vol. III
Smith, Sir William Edward, 1850–1930, vol. III
Smith, Hon. William Forgan, 1887–1953, vol. V
Smith, Sir William Frederick Haynes, 1839–1928, vol. II
Smith, Sir William George Verdon, 1876–1957, vol. V
Smith, William Henry, 1894–1968, vol. VI
Smith, William Herbert G.; *see* Guthrie-Smith.
Smith, Rev. William Hodson, 1856–1943, vol. IV
Smith, Brig.-Gen. William Hugh Usher, 1869–1940, vol. III
Smith, Captain William Humphrey, 1879–1942, vol. IV
Smith, Rev. William Isaac Carr, *died* 1930, vol. III
Smith, Sir William James, 1853–1912, vol. I
Smith, Sir William Joseph P.; *see* Pearman-Smith.
Smith, William Owen Lester, 1888–1976, vol. VII
Smith, Sir William P.; *see* Prince-Smith.
Smith, Sir William Proctor, 1891–1963, vol. VI
Smith, Sir William R., *died* 1932, vol. III
Smith, William Ramsay, 1859–1937, vol. III
Smith, Sir William Reardon, 1st Bt (*cr* 1920), 1856–1935, vol. III
Smith, Maj.-Gen. William Revell R.; *see* Revell-Smith.
Smith, Sir (William Robert) Dermot (Joshua) C.; *see* Cusack-Smith.

Smith, Sir William Rose, 1852–1934, vol. III
Smith, Most Rev. William Saumarez, 1836–1909, vol. I
Smith, William Sydney, 1866–1945, vol. IV
Smith, Sir William Sydney Winwood, 4th Bt (*cr* 1809), 1879–1953, vol. V
Smith, Sir William Wright, 1875–1956, vol. V
Smith, Sir Willie Reardon-, 2nd Bt (*cr* 1920), 1887–1950, vol. IV
Smith, Wilson, 1897–1965, vol. VI
Smith, Winifred L. B.; *see* Boys-Smith.
Smith-Bingham, Brig.-Gen. Oswald Buckley Bingham; *see* Bingham.
Smith-Bosanquet, Major George Richard Bosanquet, 1866–1939, vol. III
Smith-Carington, Herbert Hanbury; *see* Carington.
Smith-Carington, Neville Woodford, 1878–1933, vol. III
Smith-Dodsworth, Sir Claude Matthew, 7th Bt, 1888–1940, vol. III
Smith-Dorrien, Olive Crofton, (Lady Smith-Dorrien), *died* 1951, vol. V
Smith-Dorrien, Gen. Sir Horace Lockwood, 1858–1930, vol. III
Smith-Dorrien, Rev. Walter Montgomery, *died* 1924, vol. II
Smith-Gordon, Sir Lionel Eldred, 2nd Bt, 1833–1905, vol. I
Smith-Gordon, Sir Lionel Eldred Pottinger, 3rd Bt, 1857–1933, vol. III
Smith-Gordon, Sir Lionel Eldred Pottinger, 4th Bt, 1889–1976, vol. VII
Smith-Marriott, Rev. Sir Hugh Randolph Cavendish, 9th Bt, 1868–1944, vol. IV
Smith-Marriott, Sir John Richard Wyldbore, 7th Bt, 1875–1942, vol. IV
Smith-Marriott, Sir William, 8th Bt, 1865–1943, vol. IV
Smith-Marriott, Sir William Henry, 5th Bt, 1835–1924, vol. II
Smith-Marriott, Sir William John, 6th Bt, 1870–1941, vol. IV
Smith-Neill, Col James William, 1865–1935, vol. III
Smith-Pearse, Thomas Lawrence, 1893–1972, vol. VII
Smith-Pearse, Rev. Thomas Northmore Hart, 1854–1943, vol. IV
Smith-Rewse, Rev. Gilbert Flesher, *died* 1935, vol. III
Smith-Rewse, Col Henry Whistler, 1850–1930, vol. III
Smith-Rose, Reginald Leslie, 1894–1980, vol. VII
Smithard, Major Richard Glass, 1891–1939, vol. III
Smithe, Ida Elizabeth, *died* 1951, vol. V
Smithe, Major Percy Bourdillon, 1860–1912, vol. I
Smithells, Arthur, 1860–1939, vol. III
Smithers, Sir Alfred Waldron, 1850–1924, vol. II
Smithers, Sir Arthur Tennyson, 1894–1972, vol. VII
Smithers, Brig. Leonard Sueton Hirsch, 1879–1954, vol. V
Smithers, Sir Waldron, 1880–1954, vol. V
Smithson, Col Walter Charles, 1860–1938, vol. III

Smithwick, Rear-Adm. Algernon Robert, 1887–1948, vol. IV
Smithwick, John Francis, 1844–1913, vol. I
Smolka, H. P.; see Smollett, H. P.
Smollett, Maj.-Gen. Alexander Patrick Drummond T.; see Telfer-Smollett.
Smollett, Harry Peter, 1912–1980, vol. VII
Smollett, Captain James Drummond T.; see Telfer-Smollett.
Smoot, Reed, 1862–1941, vol. IV
Smout, Sir Arthur John Griffiths, 1888–1961, vol. VI
Smout, Charles Frederick Victor, 1895–1978, vol. VII
Smuts, Field Marshal Rt Hon. Jan Christian, 1870–1950, vol. IV
Smuts, Johannes, 1865–1937, vol. III
Smylie, Air Cdre Gilbert Formby, 1895–1965, vol. VI
Smyly, Col Dennis Douglas Pilkington, 1913–1979, vol. VII
Smyly, J. Gilbart, 1867–1948, vol. IV
Smyly, Sir Philip Crampton, 1838–1904, vol. I
Smyly, Sir Philip Crampton, 1896–1953, vol. V
Smyly, William Cecil, 1840—1921, vol. II
Smyly, Sir William Josiah, 1850–1941, vol. IV
Smyth, Sir Alfred John Bowyer-, 13th Bt (cr 1661), 1850–1927, vol. II
Smyth, Austin Edward Arthur Watt, 1877–1949, vol. IV
Smyth, Col Charles Coghlan, 1842–1920, vol. II
Smyth, Charles Edward O.; see Owen-Smyth.
Smyth, David Henry, 1908–1979, vol. VII
Smyth, Dame Ethel Mary, 1858–1944, vol. IV
Smyth, Col Etwall Walter, 1843–1929, vol. III
Smyth, Lt-Col Geoffrey Henry Julian Skeffington; see FitzPatrick, Lt-Col G. H. J.
Smyth, George Watson, 1838–1910, vol. I
Smyth, Captain Gerald Brice Ferguson, 1885–1920, vol. II
Smyth, Hon. Gilbert Neville, 1864–1940, vol. III
Smyth, Rear-Adm. Harry Hesketh, 1872–1926, vol. II
Smyth, Lt-Col Henry, 1866–1943, vol. IV
Smyth, Gen. Sir Henry Augustus, 1825–1906, vol. I
Smyth, (Herbert) Warington, died 1943, vol. IV
Smyth, Major Humphrey Etwall, 1884–1927, vol. II
Smyth, James Richard, 1895–1953, vol. V
Smyth, John, 1864–1927, vol. II
Smyth, Brig.-Gen. John Ambard B.; see Bell-Smyth.
Smyth, John Andrew, 1893–1971, vol. VII
Smyth, Lt-Col John Henry Graham Holroyd, 1846–1904, vol. I
Smyth, Sir John Henry Greville, 1st Bt, 1836–1901, vol. I
Smyth, Ven. John Paterson, died 1932, vol. III
Smyth, John William, 1880–1968, vol. VI
Smyth, Michael Joseph, died 1964, vol. VI
Smyth, Montague, 1863–1965, vol. VI
Smyth, Vice-Adm. Morris Henry, 1853–1940, vol. III

Smyth, Maj.-Gen. Sir Nevill Maskelyne, 1868–1941, vol. IV
Smyth, Col Owen Stuart, 1853–1923, vol. II
Smyth, Captain Sir Philip Weyland Bowyer-, 14th Bt, 1894–1978, vol. VII
Smyth, Sir Robert Middleton Watson, 1872–1939, vol. III
Smyth, Brig.-Gen. Robert Napier, 1868–1947, vol. IV
Smyth, Lt-Col Robert Riversdale, 1875–1946, vol. IV
Smyth, Sir Samuel Andrew, 1877–1953, vol. V
Smyth, Rev. Thomas Alexander, died 1936, vol. III
Smyth, Thomas Francis, 1875–1937, vol. III
Smyth, Warington; see Smyth, H. W.
Smyth, Rev. William A. B.; see Blood-Smyth.
Smyth, William Bates, 1874–1946, vol. IV
Smyth, Rt Rev. William Edmund, 1858–1950, vol. IV
Smyth, Col William Ross, 1857–1932, vol. III
Smyth-Osbourne, Brig.-Gen. George Nowell Thomas, 1877–1942, vol. IV
Smyth-Osbourne, Air Cdre Sir Henry Percy, 1879–1969, vol. VI
Smyth-Pigott, Gp Captain (Joseph) Ruscombe (Wadham), 1889–1971, vol. VII
Smyth-Pigott, Gp Captain Ruscombe; see Smyth-Pigott, Gp Captain J. R. W.
Smythe, Albert Charles B.; see Butler-Smythe.
Smythe, Charles John, 1852–1918, vol. II
Smythe, Col David Murray, 1850–1928, vol. II
Smythe, Sir Edward Walter Joseph Patrick Herbert, 9th Bt, 1869–1942, vol. IV
Smythe, Rev. Canon Francis Henry Dumville, 1873–1966, vol. VI
Smythe, Francis Sydney, 1900–1949, vol. IV
Smythe, Sir (John) Walter, 8th Bt, 1827–1919 vol. II
Smythe, Lionel Percy, 1840–1918, vol. II
Smythe, Very Rev. Patrick Murray, 1860–1935, vol. III
Smythe, Lt-Col Rupert Cæsar, 1879–1943, vol. IV
Smythe, Sir Walter; see Smythe, Sir J. W.
Smythies, Evelyn Arthur, 1885–1975, vol. VII
Snadden, Sir William McNair, 1st Bt, 1896–1959, vol. V
Snagge, Vice-Adm. Arthur Lionel, 1878–1955, vol. V
Snagge, Sir Harold Edward, 1872–1949, vol. IV
Snagge, Sir Mordaunt; see Snagge, Sir T. M.
Snagge, Sir (Thomas) Mordaunt, 1868–1955, vol. V
Snagge, Sir Thomas William, 1837–1914, vol. I
Snaith, John Collis, 1876–1936, vol. III
Snaith, Stanley, 1903–1976, vol. VII
Snape, Henry Lloyd, 1861–1933, vol. III
Snark, The; see Wood, Starr.
Snead-Cox, John, 1855–1939, vol. III
Snedden, Sir Richard, 1900–1970, vol. VI
Sneddon, Rev. James, 1871–1945, vol. IV
Snell, 1st Baron, 1865–1944, vol. IV
Snell, Alfred Walter S.; see Saxon-Snell.
Snell, Rev. Bernard J., 1856–1934, vol. III
Snell, Harvie Kennard, 1898–1969, vol. VI
Snell, Captain Ivan Edward, 1884–1958, vol. V

Snell, J. Herbert, 1861–1935, vol. III
Snell, Sir John Francis Cleverton, 1869–1938, vol. III
Snell, Simeon, *died* 1909, vol. I
Snell, William Thomas, *died* 1951, vol. V
Snelling, Maj.-Gen. Arthur Hugh Jay, 1897–1965, vol. VI
Snelus, George James, 1837–1906, vol. I
Sneyd, Ralph, 1863–1949, vol. IV
Sneyd, Vice-Adm. Ralph Stuart W.; *see* Wykes-Sneyd.
Sneyd, Maj.-Gen. Thomas William, 1837–1918, vol. II
Sneyd-Kynnersley, Charles Walter; *see* Kynnersley, C. W. S.
Snodgrass, William Robertson, 1890–1955, vol. V
Snow, Baron (Life Peer); Charles Percy Snow, 1905–1980, vol. VII
Snow, Rt Rev. George D'Oyly, 1903–1977, vol. VII
Snow, Edgar Parks, 1905–1972, vol. VII
Snow, Ernest Charles, 1886–1959, vol. V
Snow, Sir Frederick Sidney, 1899–1976, vol. VII
Snow, (George) Robert Sabine, 1897–1969, vol. VI
Snow, Sir Gordon Keith, 1898–1954, vol. V
Snow, Sir Harold Ernest, 1897–1971, vol. VII
Snow, Henry Martin, 1859–1931, vol. III
Snow, Herbert, 1847–1930, vol. III
Snow, Lt-Col Humphry Waugh, 1879–1969, vol. VI
Snow, Philip Chicheley Hyde, 1853–1931, vol. III
Snow, Robert Sabine; *see* Snow, G. R. S.
Snow, Sir Sydney, 1887–1958, vol. V
Snow, Lt-Gen. Sir Thomas D'Oyly, 1858–1940, vol. III
Snowden, 1st Viscount, 1864–1937, vol. III
Snowden, Viscountess; (Ethel), 1881–1951, vol. V
Snowden, Sir Arthur, 1829–1918, vol. II
Snowden, Arthur de Winton, 1872–1950, vol. IV
Snowden, Rev. Arthur Hillersdon, 1856–1940, vol. III
Snowden, Lt-Col Sir Eccles; *see* Snowden, Lt-Col Sir R. E.
Snowden, James; *see* Snowden, Keighley.
Snowden, Rev. John Hampden, 1828–1907, vol. I
Snowden, Joseph Stanley, 1901–1980, vol. VII
Snowden, Keighley, 1860–1947, vol. IV
Snowden, Lt-Col Sir (Robert) Eccles, 1880–1934, vol. III
Snowden, Tom, 1875–1949, vol. IV
Snowden-Smith, Maj.-Gen. Richard Talbot, 1887–1951, vol. V
Snoy, Baron Robert, 1879–1946, vol. IV
Soady, Brig.-Gen. George Joseph FitzMaurice, 1863–1940, vol. III
Soame, Sir Charles Buckworth-Herne-, 9th Bt, 1830–1906, vol. I
Soame, Sir Charles Buckworth-Herne-, 10th Bt, 1864–1931 (this entry was not transferred to Who was Who)
Soame, Sir Charles Burnett Buckworth-Herne-, 11th Bt, 1894–1977, vol. VII (inserted in error in vol. III)
Soames, Major Alfred, 1862–1915, vol. I
Soames, Arthur Gilstrap, 1854–1934, vol. III

Soames, Arthur Wellesley, 1852–1934, vol. III
Soames, Geoffrey Ewart, 1881–1952, vol. V
Soar, Joseph, 1878–1971, vol. VII
Soar, Leonard Charles, 1899–1969, vol. VI
Soares, Sir Ernest Joseph, 1864–1926, vol. II
Sobha Singh, Hon. Sardar Bahadur Sir Sardar, 1890–1978, vol. VII
Sobry, Henri, 1861–1937, vol. III
Soddy, Frederick, 1877–1956, vol. V
Soden, Freiherr Hermann von, 1852–1914, vol. I
Soden, Thomas Spooner, 1837–1920, vol. II
Soderblom, Nathan Lars Olof Jonathan, 1866–1931, vol. III
Soertsz, Sir Francis Joseph, 1886–1951, vol. V
Soheily, Ali, 1896–1958, vol. V
Sokhey, Maj.-Gen. Sir Sahib Singh, 1887–1971, vol. VII
Solberg, Thorvald, 1852–1949, vol. IV (A), vol. V
Soldene, Emily, *died* 1912, vol. I
Sole, Brig. Denis Mavesyn Anslow, 1883–1962, vol. VI
Sollas, William Johnson, 1849–1936, vol. III
Solley, Leslie Judah, 1905–1968, vol. VI
Solloway, Rev. John, 1860–1946, vol. IV (A)
Solly, S. Edwin, 1845–1906, vol. I
Solly-Flood, Maj.-Gen. Arthur, 1871–1940, vol. III
Solly-Flood, Maj.-Gen. Sir Frederick Richard, 1829–1909, vol. I
Solly-Flood, Brig.-Gen. Richard Elles, 1877–1954, vol. V
Sologub, Feodor, 1864–1927, vol. II
Solomon, Hon. Albert Edgar, 1876–1914, vol. I (A)
Solomon, Sir (Aubrey) Kenneth, 1884–1954, vol. V
Solomon, Hon. Sir Edward Philip, *died* 1914, vol. I
Solomon, Frank Oakley, 1867–1941, vol. IV
Solomon, Sir Kenneth; *see* Solomon, Sir A. K.
Solomon, Sir Richard, 1850–1913, vol. I
Solomon, Saul, 1875–1960, vol. VI
Solomon, Solomon Joseph, 1860–1927, vol. II
Solomon, Captain William Ewart Gladstone, 1880–1965, vol. VI
Solomon, Rt Hon. Sir William Henry, 1852–1930, vol. III
Solomons, Bethel, *died* 1965, vol. VI
Solomons, Estella Frances, *died* 1968, vol. VI
Solomons, Henry, 1902–1965, vol. VI
Soltau, Col Alfred Bertram, 1876–1930, vol. III
Soltau, Roger Henry, 1887–1953, vol. V
Soltau-Symons, Lt-Col George Algernon James, 1867–1947, vol. IV
Soltau-Symons, George William Culme, 1831–1916, vol. II
Soltykoff, HSH Prince Dimitri, *died* 1903, vol. I
Solvay, Ernest, 1839–1922, vol. II
Sombart, Werner, 1863–1941, vol. IV
Somerhough, Hon. Anthony George, 1906–1960, vol. V
Somerleyton, 1st Baron, 1857–1935, vol. III
Somerleyton, 2nd Baron, 1889–1959, vol. V
Somerleyton, Lady; (Phyllis), *died* 1948, vol. IV
Somers, 5th Baron, 1815–1899, vol. I
Somers, 6th Baron, 1887–1944, vol. IV

Somers, 7th Baron, 1864–1953, vol. V

Somers, Thomas Peter Miller, 1877–1965, vol. VI

Somers-Cocks, Rev. Henry Lawrence, 1862–1940, vol. III

Somers Cocks, John Sebastian, 1907–1964, vol. VI

Somerset, 15th Duke of, 1846–1923, vol. II

Somerset, 16th Duke of, 1860–1931, vol. III

Somerset, 17th Duke of, 1882–1954, vol. V

Somerset, Col Sir Alfred Plantagenet Frederick Charles, 1829–1915, vol. I

Somerset, Brig.-Gen. Charles Wyndham, 1862–1938, vol. III

Somerset, Lady Henry, (Isabel), 1851–1921, vol. II

Somerset, Henry Charles Somers Augustus, 1874–1945, vol. IV

Somerset, Rt Hon. Lord Henry Richard Charles, 1849–1932, vol. III

Somerset, Henry Robert Somers Fitzroy de Vere, 1898–1965, vol. VI

Somerset, John Henry William, 1848–1928, vol. II (A), vol. III

Somerset, Brig. Hon. Nigel FitzRoy, 1893–1979, vol. VII

Somerset, Richard Gay, 1848–1928, vol. III

Somerset, Raglan Horatio Edwyn Henry, 1885–1956, vol. V

Somerset, Sir Thomas, 1870–1947, vol. IV

Somerset-Thomas, William Edwin, 1867–1946, vol. IV

Somervell of Harrow, Baron (Life Peer); Donald Bradley Somervell, 1889–1960, vol. V

Somervell, Sir Arnold Colin, 1883–1957, vol. V

Somervell, Sir Arthur, 1863–1937, vol. III

Somervell, David Churchill, 1885–1965, vol. VI

Somervell, James, 1845–1924, vol. II

Somervell, Rupert Churchill Gelderd, 1892–1969, vol. VI

Somervell, Theodore Howard, 1890–1975, vol. VII

Somervell, William Henry, 1860–1934, vol. III

Somerville, Sir Annesley Ashworth, 1858–1942, vol. IV

Somerville, Arthur Fownes, 1850–1942, vol. IV

Somerville, Vice-Adm. Boyle; see Somerville, Vice-Adm. H. B. T.

Somerville, Daniel Gerald, 1879–1938, vol. III

Somerville, David Hughes, 1840–1918, vol. II

Somerville, Edith Œnone, 1858–1949, vol. IV

Somerville, Col George Cattell, 1878–1959, vol. V

Somerville, Vice-Adm. (Henry) Boyle (Townshend), 1863–1936, vol. III

Somerville, Howard, 1873–1952, vol. V

Somerville, Vice-Adm. Hugh Gaultier-Coghill, 1873–1950, vol. IV

Somerville, Lt-Col James Aubrey Henry Bellingham, 1884–1950, vol. IV

Somerville, Admiral of the Fleet Sir James Fownes, 1882–1949, vol. IV

Somerville, Col John Arthur Coghill, 1872–1955, vol. V

Somerville, Sir John Livingston, 1885–1964, vol. VI

Somerville, Mary, 1897–1963, vol. VI

Somerville, Comdr Philip, 1906–1942, vol. IV

Somerville, Rev. Richard Neville, 1864–1932, vol. III

Somerville, Col Thomas Cameron FitzGerald, 1860–1942, vol. IV

Somerville, Walter Harold, 1881–1959, vol .V

Somerville, Sir William, 1860–1932, vol. III

Somerville, Lt-Col William Arthur Tennison Bellingham, 1882–1951, vol. V

Somerville, William Dennistoun, 1842–1917, vol. II

Somerville Smith, Herbert, 1890–1967, vol. VI

Somjee, Mahomedbhoy Alladinbhoy, 1889–1942, vol. IV

Sommerlad, Hon. Ernest Christian, 1886–1952, vol. V

Sommerville, David, died 1937, vol. III

Sommerville, Duncan M'Laren Young, 1879–1934, vol. III

Sommerville, Vice-Adm. Frederick Avenel, 1883–1962, vol. VI

Sommerville, Norman, 1878–1941, vol. IV

Sonbarsa, Maharaja of, 1846–1907, vol. I

Sondes, 2nd Earl, 1861–1907, vol. I

Sondes, 3rd Earl, 1866–1941, vol. IV

Sondes, 4th Earl, 1914–1970, vol. VI

Song Ong Siang, Sir, died 1941, vol. IV

Sonnenschein, Edward Adolf, 1851–1929, vol. III

Sonnino, Baron Sidney, 1847–1922, vol. II

Sontag, Raymond James, 1897–1972, vol. VII

Soothill, Alfred, 1863–1926, vol. II

Soothill, Ronald Gray, 1898–1980, vol. VII

Soothill, Rev. William Edward, 1861–1935, vol. III

Soper, George, died 1942, vol. IV

Soper, Harry Tapley Tapley-, 1875–1951, vol. V

Sopoushek, Mrs Jan; see Greig, Maysie.

Sopwith, Douglas George, 1906–1970, vol. VI

Sopwith, Ven. Thomas Karl, 1873–1945, vol. IV

Sorabji, Cornelia, died 1954, vol. V

Sorby, Rev. Albert Ernest, 1859–1934, vol. III

Sorby, Henry Clifton, 1826–1908, vol. I

Sorel, Albert, 1842–1906, vol. I

Sorell-Cameron, George Cecil Minett; see Cameron.

Sorensen, Baron (Life Peer); Reginald William Sorensen, 1891–1971, vol. VII

Sorine, Savely, 1886–1953, vol. V

Sorley, Herbert Tower, 1892–1968, vol. VI

Sorley, Air Marshal Sir Ralph Squire, 1898–1974, vol. VII

Sorley, William Ritchie, 1855–1935, vol. III

Sorokin, Pitirim Alexandrovitch, 1889–1968, vol. VI

Sorrell, Alan, 1904–1974, vol. VII

Sorsbie, Brig.-Gen. Robert Fox, 1866–1948, vol. IV

Sorsby, Arnold, 1900–1980, vol. VII

Sorsby, Maurice, 1898–1949, vol. IV

Soskice, Frank; see Baron Stow Hill.

Sotheby, Sir Edward Southwell, 1813–1902, vol. I

Sotheby, Lt-Col Herbert George, 1871–1954, vol. V

Sothern, Edward H., 1859–1933, vol. III

Sotheron-Estcourt, Rev. Edmund Walter, 1850–1938, vol. III

Sotheron-Estcourt, Captain Thomas Edmund, 1881–1958, vol. V

Sothers, Donald Bevan, 1889–1979, vol. VII

Souchon, Sir (Hippolyte) Louis (Wiehe du Coudray), 1865–1957, vol. V

Souchon, Sir Louis; *see* Souchon, Sir H. L. W. du C.

Soulbury, 1st Viscount, 1887–1971, vol. VII

Soulby, Rev. Charles Frederick Hodgkinson, 1881–1952, vol. V

Soule, Malcolm H., 1896–1951, vol. V

Soulsby, Sir Llewellyn T. G., 1885–1966, vol. VI

Soulsby, Sir William Jameson, 1851–1937, vol. III

Soundy, Hon. Sir John, 1878–1960, vol. VI (AI)

Soundy, Sir John Thomas, 1851–1935, vol. III

Sousa, John Philip, 1854–1932, vol. III

Soutar, Andrew, 1879–1941, vol. IV

Soutar, Brig. John James Macfarlane, 1889–1956, vol. V

Soutar, William, 1898–1943, vol. IV

Souter, Alexander, 1873–1949, vol. IV

Souter, Sir Charles Alexander, 1877–1958, vol. V

Souter, Sir Edward Matheson, 1891–1959, vol. V

Souter, Col. Hugh Maurice Wellesley, 1873–1941, vol. IV

Souter, Sir William Alfred, 1879–1968, vol. VI

Souter, William Lochiel Berkeley, 1865–1945, vol. IV

South, Richard, *died* 1932, vol. III

Southall, Joseph Edward, 1861–1944, vol. IV

Southall, Reginald Bradbury, 1900–1965, vol. VI

Southall, Thomas Frederick, 1898–1965, vol. VI

Southam, Rev. Eric George, 1884–1952, vol. V

Southam, Frederick Armitage, *died* 1927, vol. II

Southam, Harry Stevenson, *died* 1954, vol. V

Southampton, 4th Baron, 1867–1958, vol. V

Southborough, 1st Baron, 1860–1947, vol. IV

Southborough, 2nd Baron, 1889–1960, vol. V

Southby, Comdr Sir Archibald Richard James, 1st Bt, 1886–1969, vol. VI

Southcott, Rev. Canon Ernest William, 1915–1976, vol. VII

Southee, Ethelbert Ambrook, 1890–1968, vol. VI

Southern, Sir James Wilson, 1840–1909, vol. I

Southern, Ralph Lang, 1893–1968, vol. VI (AII)

Southerton, Sydney James, 1874–1935, vol. III

Southesk, 9th Earl of, 1827–1905, vol. I

Southesk, 10th Earl of, 1854–1941, vol. IV

Southey, Hon. Charles William, 1832–1924, vol. II

Southey, Air Cdre Harold Frederic George, 1906–1979, vol. VII

Southey, Reginald, 1835–1899, vol. I

Southey, Sir Richard, 1808–1901, vol. I

Southey, Col Richard George, 1844–1909, vol. I

Southey, Maj.-Gen. William Melvill, 1866–1939, vol. III

Southgate, Bernard Alfred, 1904–1975, vol. VII

Southgate, Margaret Cecil Irene, 1918–1970, vol. VI

Southorn, Sir Thomas; *see* Southorn, Sir W. T.

Southorn, Sir (Wilfrid) Thomas, 1879–1957, vol. V

Southouse-Cheyney, Major Reginald Evelyn Peter; *see* Cheyney, Peter.

Southward, Rev. Walter Thomas, 1851–1919, vol. II

Southwark, 1st Baron, 1843–1929, vol. III

Southwell, 5th Viscount, 1872–1944, vol. IV

Southwell, 6th Viscount, 1898–1960, vol. V

Southwell, Rt Rev. Henry Kemble, *died* 1937, vol. III

Southwell, Rev. Herbert Burrows, *died* 1922, vol. II

Southwell, Sir Richard Vynne, 1888–1970, vol. VI

Southwood, 1st Viscount, 1873–1946, vol. IV

Southwood, Albert Ray, *died* 1973, vol. VII

Souttar, Sir Henry, 1875–1964, vol. VI

Souttar, Robinson, 1848–1912, vol. I

Soutter, Francis William, 1844–1932, vol. III

Sovereign, Rt Rev. Arthur Henry, 1881–1966, vol. VI (AII)

Soward, Sir Alfred Walter, 1856–1949, vol. IV

Sowby, Rev. Cedric Walter, 1902–1975, vol. VII

Sowden, Sir William John, 1858–1943, vol. IV

Sowerby, (Amy) Millicent, 1878–1967, vol. VI (AII)

Sowerby, Arthur de Carle, 1885–1954, vol. V

Sowerby, Lt-Col Harry John, 1867–1935, vol. III

Sowerby, Katherine Githa, (Mrs John Kendall), *died* 1970, vol. VI

Sowerby, Millicent; *see* Sowerby, A. M.

Sowler, Col Harry, *died* 1962, vol. VI

Sowman, Air Cdre John Edward Rudkin, 1902–1979, vol. VII

Sowrey, Gp Captain Frederick, 1893–1968, vol. VI

Sowrey, Air Cdre William, 1894–1968, vol. VI

Sowter, Ven. Francis Briggs, *died* 1928, vol. II

Sowton, Charles, 1865–1932, vol. III

Spaak, Paul-Henri, 1899–1972, vol. VII

Spaatz, Gen. Carl, 1891–1974, vol. VII

Spackman, Air Vice-Marshal Charles Basil Slater, 1895–1971, vol. VII

Spackman, Cyril Saunders, 1887–1963, vol. VI

Spahlinger, Henry, 1882–1965, vol. VI

Spaight, James Molony, 1877–1968, vol. VI

Spain, Lt-Col George Redesdale Booker, 1877–1961, vol. VI

Spain, John Edward D.; *see* Dixon-Spain.

Spain-Dunk, Susan, 1880–1962, vol. VI

Spalding, Franklin Spencer, 1865–1914, vol. I

Spalding, Henry Norman, 1877–1953, vol. V

Spalding, Kenneth Jay, 1879–1962, vol. VI

Spalding, Col Warner, 1844–1920, vol. II

Spalding, William F., 1879–1963, vol. VI

Spanton, Rev. Ernest Frederick, 1871–1936, vol. III

Spargo, John, 1876–1966, vol. VI

Sparke, George Archibald, 1871–1970, vol. VI

Sparkes, Henry, 1871–1950, vol. IV

Sparkes, Sir James; *see* Sparkes, Sir W. B. J. G.

Sparkes, Rear-Adm. Robert C.; *see* Copland-Sparkes.

Sparkes, Stanley Robert, 1910–1976, vol. VII

Sparkes, Sir (Walter Beresford) James (Gordon), 1889–1974, vol. VII

Sparkes, Col William Spottiswoode, 1862–1906, vol. I

Sparks, Sir Ashley, 1877–1964, vol. VI

Sparks, Beatrice M., *died* 1953, vol. V

Sparks, Charles Pratt, 1866–1940, vol. III
Sparks, Sir Frederick James, 1881–1953, vol. V
Sparks, Col Hubert Conrad, 1874–1933, vol. III
Sparks, Nathaniel, 1880–1957, vol. V
Sparrow, Col Richard, 1871–1953, vol. V
Sparrow, Walter Shaw, died 1940, vol. III
Sparshott, Margaret Elwin, 1870–1940, vol. III
Spater, Ernest George, 1886–1975, vol. VII
Spath, Leonard Frank, 1882–1957, vol. V
Spaul, Eric Arthur, 1895–1978, vol. VII
Speaight, Frederick William, 1869–1942, vol. IV
Speaight, Richard Langford, 1906–1976, vol. VII
Speaight, Richard Neville, 1875–1938, vol. III
Speaight, Robert William, 1904–1976, vol. VII
Speakman, Sir Harry, 1865–1946, vol. IV
Speakman, John Bamber, 1897–1969, vol. VI
Speakman, Lionel, died 1948, vol. IV
Spear, Lt-Col Christopher Ronald, 1897–1942, vol. IV
Spear, Sir John Ward, 1848–1921, vol. II
Speares, Denis James, 1922–1970, vol. VI
Spearman, Sir Alexander Bowyer, 4th Bt, 1917–1977, vol. VII
Spearman, Sir Alexander Young, 3rd Bt, 1881–1959, vol. V
Spearman, Charles E., 1863–1945, vol. IV
Spearman, Edmund Robert, 1837–1918, vol. II
Spearman, Sir Joseph Layton Elmes, 2nd Bt, 1857–1922, vol. II
Spears, Maj.-Gen. Sir Edward Louis, 1st Bt, 1886–1974, vol. VII
Spears, Mary, (Lady Spears); see Borden, Mary.
Speck, Rev. Jocelyn Henry, died 1922, vol. II
Spedding, Major Charles Rodney, 1871–1915, vol. I (A)
Spedding, Brig.-Gen. Edward Wilfrid, 1867–1939, vol. III
Speechly, Rt Rev. John Martindale, 1836–1898, vol. I
Speed, Sir Edwin Arney, 1869–1941, vol. IV
Speed, Sir Eric Bourne Bentinck, 1895–1971, vol. VII
Speed, Harold, 1872–1957, vol. V
Speed, James A.; see Andrews-Speed.
Speed, Lancelot, 1860–1931, vol. III
Speelman, Sir Cornelis Jacob, 7th Bt, 1881–1949, vol. IV
Speelman, Sir Cornelis Jacob Abraham, 5th Bt, 1823–1898, did not have an entry in Who's Who.
Speelman, Sir Helenus, 6th Bt, 1852–1907, did not have an entry in Who's Who.
Speer, Rear-Adm. F. Shirley Litchfield-, 1874–1922, vol. II
Speer, Robert Elliott, 1867–1947, vol. IV
Speight, Harold Edwin Balme, 1887–1975, vol. VII
Speight, Thomas Wilkinson, 1830–1915, vol. I (A), vol. II
Speir, Col Guy Thomas, 1875–1951, vol. V
Speir, Wing Comdr Robert Cecil Talbot, 1904–1980, vol. VII
Speir, Robert Thomas Napier, 1841–1922, vol. II
Speirs, Alexander Archibald Hagart-, 1869–1958, vol. V

Spellman, Cardinal Francis J., 1889–1967, vol. VI
Spence, Sir Alexander, 1866–1939, vol. III (A), vol. IV
Spence, Col Alexander Hierom Ogilvy, 1869–1936, vol. III
Spence, Col Sir Basil Hamilton Hebden N.; see Neven-Spence.
Spence, Sir Basil Urwin, 1907–1976, vol. VII
Spence, Catherine Helen, 1825–1910, vol. I
Spence, Edward Fordham, 1860–1932, vol. III
Spence, Sir George Hemming, 1888–1962, vol. VI
Spence, Col Gilbert Ormerod, 1879–1925, vol. II
Spence, Sir James Calvert, 1892–1954, vol. V
Spence, James Knox, 1844–1919, vol. II
Spence, (James) Lewis (Thomas Chalmers), 1874–1955, vol. V
Spence, Ven. John, died 1914, vol. I
Spence, John, 1878–1949, vol. IV
Spence, John Bowring, 1861–1918, vol. II
Spence, Lewis; see Spence, J. L. T. C.
Spence, Sir Reginald, 1880–1961, vol. VI
Spence, Robert, 1870–1964, vol. VI
Spence, Robert, 1879–1966, vol. VI
Spence, Robert, 1905–1976, vol. VII
Spence, Most Rev. Robert William, 1860–1934, vol. III
Spence, Thomas William Leisk, 1845–1923, vol. II
Spence, William Robert Locke, 1875–1954, vol. V
Spence-Colby, Col Cecil John Herbert, 1873–1954, vol. V
Spence-Jones, Very Rev. Henry Donald Maurice, 1836–1917, vol. II
Spencelayh, Charles, 1865–1958, vol. V
Spencer, 5th Earl, 1835–1910, vol. I
Spencer, 6th Earl, 1857–1922, vol. II
Spencer, 7th Earl, 1892–1975, vol. VII
Spencer, Countess; (Cynthia Ellinor Beatrix), 1897–1972, vol. VII
Spencer, Rev. Arthur John, 1850–1922, vol. II
Spencer, Lt-Col Aubrey Vere, 1886–1973, vol. VII
Spencer, Augustus, 1860–1924, vol. II
Spencer, Sir Baldwin; see Spencer, Sir W. B.
Spencer, Sir Charles Gordon Spencer, 1869–1934, vol. III
Spencer, Col Charles Louis, 1870–1948, vol. IV
Spencer, Dorothy, died 1969, vol. VI
Spencer, Sir Ernest, 1848–1937, vol. III
Spencer, Brig. Francis Elmhirst, 1881–1972, vol. VII
Spencer, Frederic, 1861–1942, vol. IV
Spencer, Air Vice-Marshal Geoffrey Roger Cole, 1901–1969, vol. VI
Spencer, Ven. George, died 1926, vol. II (A), vol. III
Spencer, George Alfred, 1872–1957, vol. V
Spencer, Gilbert, 1893–1979, vol. VII
Spencer, Sir Harris, 1863–1934, vol. III
Spencer, Sir Henry Francis, 1892–1964, vol. VI
Spencer, Herbert, 1820–1903, vol. I
Spencer, Major Herbert Eames, 1871–1945, vol. IV
Spencer, Herbert Ritchie, 1860–1941, vol. IV
Spencer, Hugh, 1867–1926, vol. II
Spencer, James Frederick, 1881–1950, vol. IV
Spencer, Brig.-Gen. John Almeric Walter, 1881–1952, vol. V

Spencer, Col John H.; see Heatly-Spencer.
Spencer, Leonard James, 1870–1959, vol. V
Spencer, Surg.-Gen. Sir Lionel Dixon, 1842–1915, vol. I
Spencer, Col Maurice, 1863–1940, vol. III
Spencer, Percival, 1864–1913, vol. I
Spencer, Rev. Percival L., 1845–1932, vol. III
Spencer, Captain Richard Austin, 1892–1956, vol. V
Spencer, Lt-Col Rowland Pickering, 1892–1965, vol. VI
Spencer, Sir Stanley, 1891–1959, vol. V
Spencer, Terence John Bew, 1915–1978, vol. VII
Spencer, Sir Thomas George, 1888–1976, vol. VII
Spencer, Sir (Walter) Baldwin, 1860–1929, vol. III
Spencer, Walter George, died 1940, vol. III
Spencer, William Kingdon, died 1955, vol. V
Spencer Chapman, Lt-Col Frederick, 1907–1971, vol. VII
Spencer-Churchill, Baroness (Life Peer); Clementine Ogilvy Spencer-Churchill, 1885–1977, vol. VII
Spencer-Churchill, Lord Edward; see Churchill.
Spencer-Churchill, Captain Edward George; see Churchill.
Spencer-Nairn, Sir Douglas Leslie; see Nairn.
Spencer-Nairn, Major Sir Robert, 1st Bt, 1880–1960, vol. V
Spencer-Phillips, Major John Charles, died 1937, vol. III
Spencer-Smith, Sir Drummond Cospatric Hamilton-, 5th Bt, 1876–1955, vol. V
Spencer-Smith, Michael Seymour, 1881–1928, vol. II
Spencer-Smith, Sir Thomas Cospatric Hamilton-, 6th Bt, 1917–1959, vol. V
Spender, A. F., died 1947, vol. IV
Spender, Arthur Edmund, 1871–1923, vol. II
Spender, E. Harold, 1864–1926, vol. II
Spender, Hugh Frederick, 1873–1930, vol. III
Spender, John Alfred, 1862–1942, vol. IV
Spender, Lt-Col Sir Wilfrid Bliss, 1876–1960, vol. V
Spender-Clay, Lt-Col Rt Hon. Herbert Henry, 1875–1937, vol. III
Spengler, Oswald, 1880–1936, vol. III
Spenlove-Spenlove, Frank, 1868–1933, vol. III
Spens, 1st Baron, died 1973, vol. VII
Spens, Ven. Andrew N. W., 1844–1932, vol. III
Spens, Col Hugh Baird, 1885–1958, vol. V
Spens, Maj.-Gen. James, 1853–1934, vol. III
Spens, Janet, 1876–1963, vol. VI
Spens, J(ohn) Ivan, 1890–1964, vol. VI
Spens, Nathaniel, 1850–1933, vol. III
Spens, Sir Will, 1882–1962, vol. VI
Spenser, Harry Joseph, 1866–1937, vol. III
Sperling, Sir Rowland Arthur Charles, 1874–1965, vol. VI
Sperrin-Johnson, John Charles, 1885–1948, vol. IV
Sperring, Digby, 1897–1969, vol. VI
Sperry, Willard Learoyd, 1882–1954, vol. V
Speyer, Sir Edgar, 1st Bt, 1862–1932, vol. III
Spicer, Rt Hon. Sir Albert, 1st Bt, 1847–1934, vol. III

Spicer, Sir (Albert) Dykes, 2nd Bt, 1880–1966, vol. VI
Spicer, Sir Dykes; see Spicer, Sir A. D.
Spicer, Sir Evan, 1849–1937, vol. III
Spicer, Gerald Sydney, 1874–1942, vol. IV
Spicer, Henry Gage, 1875–1944, vol. IV
Spicer, Holmes W. T., 1860–1935, vol. III
Spicer, Sir Howard, 1872–1926, vol. II
Spicer, James Leonard, 1873–1949, vol. IV
Spicer, Hon. Sir John Armstrong, 1899–1978, vol. VII
Spicer, John Edmund Philip, 1850–1928, vol. II
Spicer, Rev. Canon John Maurice, died 1920, vol. II
Spicer, Lancelot Dykes, 1893–1979, vol. VII
Spicer, Robert Henry Scanes, died 1925, vol. II
Spicer, Roy Godfrey Bullen, 1889–1946, vol. IV
Spicer, Captain Sir Stewart Dykes, 3rd Bt, 1888–1968, vol. VI
Spicer, W. T. H.; see Spicer, Holmes W. T.
Spicer-Jay, Edith Katharine; see Prescott, E. Livingston.
Spickernell, Sir Frank Todd, 1885–1956, vol. V
Spidle, Rev. Simeon, 1867–1954, vol. V
Spielman, Sir Meyer A., 1856–1936, vol. III
Spielmann, Sir Isidore, 1854–1925, vol. II
Spielmann, Mabel Henrietta, 1862–1938, vol. III
Spielmann, Marion Harry Alexander, 1858–1948, vol. IV
Spielmann, Percy Edwin, 1881–1964, vol. VI
Spiers, Harry Ratcliff, 1883–1956, vol. V
Spiers, Richard Phené, 1838–1916, vol. II
Spiers, Victor Julian Taylor, died 1937, vol. III
Spiller, John Wyatt, 1878–1949, vol. IV
Spilsbury, Alfred John, 1874–1940, vol. III
Spilsbury, Sir Bernard Henry, 1877–1947, vol. IV
Spingarn, J. E., 1875–1939, vol. III (A), vol. IV
Spinks, Maj.-Gen. Sir Charlton Watson, 1877–1959, vol. V
Spinks, Frederick Lowten, 1816–1899, vol. I
Spinks, Rev. George Stephens, 1903–1978, vol. VII
Spinks, Major John Thomas, 1889–1969, vol. VI
Spinner, Alice; see Fraser, Mrs Angela Zelia.
Spinney, George Franklin, 1852–1926, vol. II
Spinney, George Wilbur, 1889–1948, vol. IV
Spire, Frederick, 1863–1951, vol. V
Spitta, Edmund Johnson, 1853–1921, vol. II
Spitta, Harold Robert Dacre, 1877–1954, vol. V
Spittel, Richard Lionel, 1881–1969, vol. VI
Spitteler, Carl Friedrich Georg, 1845–1924, vol. II
Spoer, Mrs H. H.; see Goodrich-Freer, A. M.
Spofforth, Marknam, 1825–1907, vol. I
Spokes, Arthur Hewett, 1854–1922, vol. II
Spokes, Sir Peter, 1830–1910, vol. I
Spong, Major Charles Stuart, 1859–1925, vol. II
Spooner, Brig.-Gen. Arthur Hardwicke, 1879–1945, vol. IV
Spooner, Charles Edwin, 1853–1909, vol. I
Spooner, Edgar Clynton Ross, 1908–1976, vol. VII
Spooner, Very Rev. Edward, died 1899, vol. I
Spooner, Edwin George, 1898–1977, vol. VII
Spooner, Rear-Adm. Ernest John, 1887–1942, vol. IV

Spooner, Ven. George Hardwicke, *died* 1933, vol. III
Spooner, Henry John, 1856–1940, vol. III
Spooner, Rev. Henry Maxwell, *died* 1929, vol. III
Spooner, Rev. William Archibald, 1844–1930, vol. III
Spooner, Rt Hon. Sir William Henry, 1897–1966, vol. VI
Spoor, Rt Hon. Benjamin Charles, 1878–1928, vol. II
Spottiswoode, John Roderick Charles Herbert, 1882–1946, vol. IV
Spottiswoode, Col Robert Collinson D'Esterre, 1841–1936, vol. III
Spottiswoode, William Hugh, 1864–1915, vol. I
Spowers, Col Allan, 1892–1968, vol. VI
Spragge, Lt-Col Basil Edward, 1852–1926, vol. II
Spragge, Brig.-Gen. Charles Henry, 1842–1920, vol. II
Spraggett, Col Richard William, *died* 1976, vol. VII
Sprague, Oliver Mitchell Wentworth, 1873–1953, vol. V
Sprague, Thomas Bond, 1830–1920, vol. II
Sprankling, Rt Rev. Mgr James, 1860–1935, vol. III
Spratt, Most Rev. Michael J., 1854–1938, vol. III
Sprawson, Maj.-Gen. Sir Cuthbert Allan, 1877–1956, vol. V
Sprawson, Evelyn Charles, 1881–1955, vol. V
Spreckels, Claus, 1828–1908, vol. I
Spreckels, John Diedrich, 1853–1926, vol. II
Spreckley, Air Marshal Sir Herbert Dorman, 1904–1963, vol. VI
Spreckley, Herbert William, 1857–1950, vol. IV
Sprengel, Hermann Johann Philipp, 1834–1906, vol. I
Sprigg, Alfred Gordon, 1861–1921, vol. II
Sprigg, Rt Hon. Sir John Gordon, 1830–1913, vol. I
Sprigg, Stanhope William, *died* 1932, vol. III
Sprigge, Cecil Jackson Squire, 1896–1959, vol. V
Sprigge, Elizabeth Miriam Squire, 1900–1974, vol. VII
Sprigge, Sir Squire, 1860–1937, vol. III
Spriggs, Sir Edmund Ivens, *died* 1949, vol. IV
Spriggs, Sir Frank Spencer, 1895–1969, vol. VI
Spring, Sir Francis Joseph Edward, 1849–1933, vol. III
Spring, Brig.-Gen. Frederick Gordon, 1878–1963, vol. VI
Spring, Howard, 1889–1965, vol. VI
Spring-Rice, Rt Hon. Sir Cecil Arthur, 1859–1918, vol. II
Spring-Rice, Dominick, 1889–1940, vol. III
Spring-Rice, Stephen Edward, 1856–1902, vol. I
Springett, Rev. William Douglas, 1850–1928, vol. II
Springfield, George, 1861–1939, vol. III
Springfield, Lincoln, *died* 1950, vol. IV
Springhall, Brig. Robert John, 1900–1965, vol. VI
Sprot, Col Sir Alexander, 1st Bt, 1853–1929, vol. III
Sprot, Lt-Gen. John, 1830–1907, vol. I
Sprot, Major Mark, 1881–1946, vol. IV
Sprott, Sir Frederick Lawrence, 1863–1943, vol. IV
Sprott, Rt Rev. Thomas Henry, *died* 1942, vol. IV

Sprott, Walter John Herbert, 1897–1971, vol. VII
Sproul, Robert Gordon, 1891–1975, vol. VII
Sproule, Brig. James Chambers, 1887–1955, vol. V
Sproule, Percy Julian, 1873–1954, vol. V
Sproule, Hon. Robert, *died* 1948, vol. IV
Sproule, Thomas Simpson, 1843–1917, vol. II
Sproull, Maj.-Gen. Alexander Wallace, 1892–1961, vol. VI
Sprules, Dorothy Winifred, 1883–1972, vol. VII
Spry, Charles Gordon, 1872–1940, vol. III
Spry, Mrs Constance, *died* 1960, vol. V
Spry, Lt-Col Leighton Hume-, 1871–1934, vol. III
Spurgeon, Sir Arthur, 1861–1938, vol. III
Spurgeon, Caroline F. E., 1869–1942, vol. IV
Spurgeon, Christopher Edward, 1879–1951, vol. V
Spurgeon, Rev. John, 1810–1902, vol. 1
Spurgeon, Rev. Thomas, 1856–1917, vol. II
Spurgin, Sir John Blick, 1821–1903, vol. I
Spurling, Rev. Frederick William, 1844–1914, vol. I
Spurling, Maj.-Gen. John Michael Kane, 1906–1980, vol. VII
Spurling, Sir Stanley, 1879–1961, vol. VI
Spurr, Frederic Chambers, 1862–1942, vol. IV
Spurrell, Walter Roworth, 1897–1966, vol. VI
Spurrier, Alfred Henry, 1862–1935, vol. III
Spurrier, Sir Henry, 1898–1964, vol. VI
Spurrier, Rev. Horatio, 1832–1913, vol. I
Spurrier, John Marston, 1886–1973, vol. VII
Spurrier, Mabel Annie, *died* 1979, vol. VII
Spurrier, Steven, *died* 1961, vol. VI
Spyers, Roper, 1868–1961, vol. VI
Squair, John, 1850–1928, vol. II
Squire, Alice, *died* 1936, vol. III
Squire, Sir Giles Frederick, 1894–1959, vol. V
Squire, Herbert Brian, 1909–1961, vol. VI
Squire, Sir John Collings, 1884–1958, vol. V
Squire, John Edward, 1855–1917, vol. II
Squire, Rev. John Henry, *died* 1955, vol. V
Squire, John Rupert, 1915–1966, vol. VI
Squire, Sir Peter Wyatt, 1847–1919, vol. II
Squire, Ronald, 1886–1958, vol. V
Squire, Rose Elizabeth, 1861–1938, vol. III
Squire, William Barclay, 1855–1927, vol. II
Squire, William Henry, 1871–1963, vol. VI
Squires, Lt-Gen. Ernest Ker, 1882–1940, vol. III
Squires, Herbert Chavasse, 1880–1964, vol. VI
Squires, Rt Hon. Sir Richard Anderson, 1880–1940, vol. III
Squirrell, Leonard Russell, 1893–1979, vol. VII
Srámek, Mgr Jan, 1870–1956, vol. V
Srawley, Rev. James Herbert, 1868–1954, vol. V
Srivastava, Sir Bisheshwar Nath, 1881–1938, vol. III
Srivastava, Sir Jwala Prasad, 1889–1954, vol. V
Staal, Baron de, 1822–1907, vol. I
Stabb, Sir Newton John, 1868–1931, vol. III
Stable, Daniel Wintringham, 1856–1929, vol. III
Stable, J. Joseph, 1883–1953, vol. V
Stable, Rt Hon. Sir Wintringham Norton, 1888–1977, vol. VII
Stableforth, Arthur Wallace, 1902–1978, vol. VII
Stabler, Harold, 1872–1945, vol. IV
Stabler, Mrs Phœbe, *died* 1955, vol. V

Stables, William G.; see Gordon-Stables.
Stacey, Sir Ernest, 1896–1973, vol. VII
Stacey, Major Gerald Arthur, 1881–1916, vol. II
Stacey, Reginald Stephen, 1905–1974, vol. VII
Stack, Austin, 1880–1929, vol. III
Stack, Rt Rev. Charles Maurice, 1825–1914, vol. I
Stack, Lt-Col Charles Spottiswoode, 1868–1943, vol. IV
Stack, Maj.-Gen. Sir Lee Oliver Fitzmaurice, 1868–1924, vol. II
Stackhouse, J. Foster, died 1915, vol. I
Stacpole, Col John, 1849–1916, vol. II
Stacpoole, Florence, died 1942, vol. IV
Stacpoole, Frederic, 1813–1907, vol. I
Stacpoole, Lt-Col George William Robert, 1872–1939, vol. III
Stacpoole, Henry de Vere Stacpoole, 1863–1951, vol. V
Stacton, David Derek, 1925–1968, vol. VI
Stacy, Lt-Col Bertie Vandeleur, 1886–1971, vol. VII
Staddon, John Henry, died 1944, vol. IV
Stadler, Sir Sydney Martin, 1893–1976, vol. VII
Stafford, 11th Baron, 1833–1913, vol. I
Stafford, 12th Baron, 1859–1932, vol. III
Stafford, 13th Baron, 1864–1941, vol. IV
Stafford, Maj.-Gen. Boyle Torriano, 1828–1913, vol. I
Stafford, Hon. Sir Edward William, 1820–1901, vol. I
Stafford, James William, 1884–1945, vol. IV
Stafford, Rev. John T. Wardle, 1861–1944, vol. IV
Stafford, Rt Hon. Sir Thomas, 1st Bt, 1857–1935, vol. III
Stafford, Brig.-Gen. William Francis Howard, 1854–1942, vol. IV
Stagg, Cecil, died 1955, vol. V
Stagg, James Martin, 1900–1975, vol. VII
Stagni, Most Rev. Pellegrino Francesco, 1859–1918, vol. II
Staig, Sir Bertie Munro, 1892–1952, vol. V
Stainer, George Henry, died 1901, vol. I
Stainer, Sir John, 1840–1901, vol. I
Staines, Donald Victor, 1897–1960, vol. V
Staines, Herbert J., died 1958, vol. V
Staines, Michael, 1885–1955, vol. V
Stainforth, Lt-Col Herbert Graham, 1865–1916, vol. II
Stainton, Sir John Armitage, 1888–1957, vol. V
Stair, 10th Earl of, 1819–1903, vol. I
Stair, 11th Earl of, 1848–1914, vol. I
Stair, 12th Earl of, 1879–1961, vol. VI
Stair, Alfred, 1845–1914, vol. I
Stairs, Gilbert S., 1882–1947, vol. IV
Stairs, Major Henry Bertram, 1871–1940, vol. III (A), vol. IV
Stalbridge, 1st Baron, 1837–1912 (this entry was not transferred to Who was Who).
Stalbridge, 2nd Baron, 1880–1949, vol. IV
Staley, Rt Rev. Thomas N., 1823–1898, vol. I
Staley, Rev. Vernon, 1852–1933, vol. III
Stalin, Generalissimo Joseph Vissarionovich, 1879–1953, vol. V

Stalker, Alexander Mitchell, 1853–1932, vol. III
Stalker, Rev. James, 1848–1927, vol. II
Stallard, Col Hon. Charles Frampton, 1871–1971, vol. VII
Stallard, George, 1856–1912, vol. I
Stallard, Hyla Bristow, 1901–1973, vol. VII
Stallard, John Prince, 1857–1952, vol. V
Stallard, Lt-Col Sidney, 1870–1949, vol. IV
Stallard, Brig.-Gen. Stacy Frampton, 1873–1961, vol. VI
Stallwood, Frank, 1910–1978, vol. VII
Stallybrass, William Swan, 1855–1931, vol. III
Stallybrass, William Teulon Swan, 1883–1948, vol. IV
Stamer, Arthur Cowie, 1869–1944, vol. IV
Stamer, Sir Lovelace, 4th Bt, 1859–1941, vol. IV
Stamer, Rt Rev. Sir Lovelace Tomlinson, 3rd Bt, 1829–1908, vol. I
Stamer, Maj.-Gen. William Donovan, died 1963, vol. VI
Stamford, 9th Earl of, 1850–1910, vol. I
Stamford, 10th Earl of, 1896–1976, vol. VII
Stamford, Thomas William, 1882–1949, vol. IV
Stamfordham, 1st Baron, 1849–1931, vol. III
Stammers, Arthur Dighton, 1889–1971, vol. VII
Stamp, 1st Baron, 1880–1941, vol. IV
Stamp, 2nd Baron, 1904–1941 (died with 1st Baron and did not have an entry in Who's Who).
Stamp, Alfred Edward, 1870–1938, vol. III
Stamp, Sir Dudley; see Stamp, Sir L. D.
Stamp, Ernest, 1869–1942, vol. IV
Stamp, Sir (Laurence) Dudley, 1898–1966, vol. VI
Stampa, George Loraine, 1875–1951, vol. V
Stampe, Sir William Leonard, 1882–1951, vol. V
Stamper, James William, 1873–1947, vol. IV
Stamper, Thomas Henry Gilborn, 1884–1980, vol. VII
Stancomb, William, 1850–1941, vol. IV
Stancomb-Wills, Dame Janet Stancomb Graham, died 1932, vol. III
Standage, Lt-Col Robert Fraser, 1868–1927, vol. II
Standen, Rev. Canon Aubrey Owen, 1898–1961, vol. VI
Standen, Sir Bertram Prior, 1867–1947, vol. IV
Standen, Edward James, 1836–1921, vol. II
Standen, Rev. James Edward, 1865–1933, vol. III
Standford, Col William, died 1926, vol. II
Standing, Rev. George, 1875–1966, vol. VI
Standing, Comdr Sir Guy, 1873–1937, vol. III
Standing, Percy Cross, died 1931, vol. III
Standish, Henry Noailles Widdrington, 1847–1920, vol. II
Standish, Col Ivon Tatham, 1883–1967, vol. VI
Standish, Major William Pery, 1860–1922, vol. II
Standish-White, Robert, 1888–1961, vol. VI
Stanes, Sir Robert, 1841–1936, vol. III
Stanfield, Richard, 1863–1950, vol. IV (A), vol. V
Stanford, Gp-Captain C. E. C.; see Cortis-Stanford.
Stanford, Sir Charles T.; see Thomas-Stanford.

Stanford, Sir Charles Villiers, 1852–1924, vol. II
Stanford, Ernest, 1894–1966, vol. VI
Stanford, Rt Rev. Frederic, 1883–1964, vol. VI
Stanford, John Keith, 1892–1971, vol. VII
Stanford, Ven. Leonard John, 1896–1967, vol. VI
Stanford, Col Hon. Sir Walter Ernest Mortimer, 1850–1933, vol. III
Stanger, Henry Yorke, 1849–1929, vol. III
Stanham, Maj.-Gen. Sir Reginald George, 1893–1957, vol. V
Stanhope, 6th Earl, 1838–1905, vol. I
Stanhope, 7th Earl, 1880–1967, vol. VI
Stanhope, Ven. Hon. Berkeley Lionel Scudamore, 1824–1919, vol. II
Stanhope, Hon. Charles Hay Scudamore, 1864–1937, vol. III
Stanhope, Hon. Evelyn Theodore Scudamore, 1862–1925, vol. II
Stanhope, Hon. Henry Augustus, 1845–1933, vol. III
Stanhope, James Banks, 1821–1904, vol. I
Stanhope, Hon. Richard Philip, 1885–1916, vol. II
Stanhope, Col Sir Walter Thomas William Spencer, 1827–1911, vol. I
Stanier, Sir Beville, 1st Bt, 1867–1921, vol. II
Stanier, Robert Spenser, 1907–1980, vol. VII
Stanier, Sir William Arthur, 1876–1965, vol. VI
Staniforth, Joseph Morewood, 1863–1921, vol. II
Stanistreet, Maj.-Gen. Sir George Bradshaw, 1866–1941, vol. IV
Stanley of Alderley, 3rd Baron, 1827–1903, vol. I
Stanley of Alderley, 5th Baron, and Sheffield, 5th Baron, 1875–1931, vol. III
Stanley, Lord; Edward Montagu Cavendish Stanley, 1894–1938, vol. III
Stanley, Albert, 1863–1915, vol. I (A)
Stanley, Rt Rev. Mgr the Hon. Algernon Charles, 1843–1928, vol. II
Stanley, Col Hon. Algernon Francis, 1874–1962, vol. VI
Stanley, Hon. Sir Arthur, 1869–1947, vol. IV
Stanley, Arthur; see Megaw, Arthur Stanley.
Stanley, Carleton Wellesley, 1886–1971, vol. VII
Stanley, Charles Sidney Bowen W.; see Wentworth-Stanley.
Stanley, Captain Sir Charles Wentworth, 1860–1939, vol. III
Stanley, Dorothy, (Lady Stanley), died 1926, vol. II
Stanley, Edward Arthur Vesey, 1879–1941, vol. IV
Stanley, Edward James, 1826–1907, vol. I
Stanley, Brig.-Gen. Hon. Ferdinand Charles, 1871–1935, vol. III
Stanley, Lt-Col Hon. Frederick William, 1878–1942, vol. IV
Stanley, Col Geoffrey, 1855–1943, vol. IV
Stanley, Lt-Col Rt Hon. Sir George Frederick, 1872–1938, vol. III
Stanley, George J., 1852–1931, vol III
Stanley, Harry Merridew, 1865–1945, vol. IV
Stanley, Sir Henry Morton, 1841–1904, vol. I
Stanley, Sir Herbert James, 1872–1955, vol. V
Stanley, Rev. Howard Spencer, 1901–1975, vol. VII
Stanley, Sir John, 1846–1931, vol. III

Stanley, Lt-Col Joseph Henry, 1864–1937, vol. III
Stanley, Hon. Maude Alethea, 1833–1915, vol. I
Stanley, Rt Hon. Oliver Frederick George, 1896–1950, vol. IV
Stanley, Lt-Col Hon. Oliver Hugh, 1879–1952, vol. V
Stanley, Robert Crooks, 1876–1951, vol. V
Stanley, Ronald Francis Assheton S.; see Sloane-Stanley.
Stanley, Adm. Hon. Sir Victor Albert, 1867–1934, vol. III
Stanley, Wendell M., 1904–1971, vol. VII
Stanley, Captain William Blakeney, 1878–1935, vol. III
Stanley-Wrench, Mollie Louise, died 1966, vol. VI
Stanmore, 1st Baron, 1829–1912, vol. I
Stanmore, 2nd Baron, 1871–1957, vol. V
Stannard, Mrs Arthur, (Henrietta Eliza Vaughan Stannard), 1856–1911, vol. I
Stannard, H. Sylvester, 1870–1951, vol. V
Stannard, Henrietta Eliza Vaughan; see Stannard, Mrs Arthur.
Stannard, Henry, died 1920, vol. II
Stannard, Captain Richard Been, 1902–1977, vol. VII
Stannus, Hugh Stannus, 1877–1957, vol. V
Stansbury, Captain Hubert, 1873–1949, vol. IV
Stansfeld, Maj.-Gen. Henry Hamer, 1839–1914, vol. I
Stansfeld, Rt Hon. Sir James, 1820–1898, vol. I
Stansfeld, Col James Rawdon, 1866–1936, vol. III
Stansfeld, Captain John, 1840–1928, vol. II
Stansfeld, Captain John Raymond Evelyn, 1880–1915, vol. I
Stansfeld, Captain Logan Sutherland, 1859–1936, vol. III
Stansfeld, Miss Margaret, died 1951, vol. V
Stansfeld, Brig.-Gen. Thomas Wolryche, 1877–1935, vol. III
Stansfield, Alfred, died 1944, vol. IV
Stansfield, Sir Charles Henry Renn, 1856–1926, vol. II
Stansfield, Herbert, 1872–1960, vol. V
Stansfield, Knowles; see Stansfield, T. E. K.
Stansfield, (Thomas Edward) Knowles, 1862–1939, vol. III
Stansfield, Lt-Gen. Thomas Wolrich, 1829–1910, vol. I
Stansfield, William, 1877–1946, vol. IV
Stansgate, 1st Viscount, 1877–1960, vol. V
Stantiall, William, 1865–1947, vol. IV
Stanton, Sir (Ambrose) Thomas, 1875–1938, vol. III
Stanton, Rev. Arthur Henry, 1839–1913, vol. I
Stanton, Charles Butt, 1873–1946, vol. IV
Stanton, Sir Edward, 1827–1907, vol. I
Stanton, Col Edward Alexander, 1867–1947, vol. IV
Stanton, Brig.-Gen. Frederick William Starkey, 1863–1930, vol. III
Stanton, Rt Rev. George Henry, 1835–1905, vol. I
Stanton, Major Harold James Clifford, 1859–1927, vol. II

Stanton, Maj.-Gen. Sir Henry Ernest, 1861–1943, vol. IV

Stanton, Sir Herbert H.; see Hughes-Stanton.

Stanton, Rev. Herbert Udny Weitbrecht, 1851–1937, vol. III

Stanton, Lt-Col John Percy, 1899–1974, vol. VII

Stanton, Joseph, 1859–1935, vol. III

Stanton, Sir Joseph, 1884–1963, vol. VI

Stanton, Lionel William, 1843–1925, vol. II

Stanton, Sir Thomas, 1865–1931, vol. III

Stanton, Sir Thomas; see Stanton, Sir A. T.

Stanton, Rev. Vincent Henry, 1846–1924, vol. II

Stanton, Walter Kendall, 1891–1978, vol. VII

Stanton, Rev. William Henry, 1824–1910, vol. I

Stanton-Jones, Rt Rev. William, 1866–1951, vol. V

Stanuell, Lt-Col Herbert Stewart M'Cance, 1857–1930, vol. III

Stanyforth, Lt-Col Edwin Wilfrid, 1861–1939, vol. III

Stanyforth, Lt-Col Ronald Thomas, 1892–1964, vol. VI

Stanyon, Sir Henry John, 1857–1934, vol. III

Stapf, Otto, 1857–1933, vol. III

Stapledon, Sir George; see Stapledon, Sir R. G.

Stapledon, Sir (Reginald) George, 1882–1960, vol. V

Stapledon, Sir Robert de Stapledon, 1909–1975, vol. VII

Stapledon, William Olaf, 1886–1950, vol. IV

Staples, Irene E. Toye W.; see Warner-Staples.

Staples, Sir John Molesworth, 11th Bt, 1847–1933, vol. III

Staples, Sir Nathaniel Alexander, 10th (shown as 8th) Bt, 1817–1899, vol. I

Staples, Sir Robert George Alexander, 13th Bt, 1894–1970, vol. VI

Staples, Sir Robert Ponsonby, 12th Bt, 1853–1943, vol. IV

Stapleton, Sir Francis George, 8th Bt, 1831–1899, vol. I

Stapleton, Brig. Francis Harry, 1876–1956, vol. V

Stapleton, Air Vice-Marshal Frederick Snowden, 1912–1974, vol. VII

Stapleton, Henry Ernest, 1878–1962, vol. VI

Stapleton, Major Sir Miles Talbot, 9th Bt, 1893–1977, vol. VII

Stapleton-Bretherton, Frederick, 1841–1919, vol. II

Stapleton-Cotton, Adm. Richard Greville Arthur Wellington, 1873–1953, vol. V

Stapleton-Cotton, Col Hon. Richard Southwell George, 1849–1925, vol. II

Stapleton-Shaw, Major Peter; see Shaw.

Stapley, Sir Richard, 1842–1920, vol. II

Stapylton, Col Bryan Henry C.; see Chetwynd-Stapylton.

Stapylton, Granville Brian C.; see Chetwynd-Stapylton.

Stapylton, Lt-Gen. Granville George C.; see Chetwynd-Stapylton.

Stapylton, Rev. William C.; see Chetwynd-Stapylton.

Starey, Captain Stephen Helps, 1896–1972, vol. VII

Stark, Adm. Harold Raynsford, 1880–1972, vol. VII

Stark, Rev. James, 1838–1922, vol. II

Stark, John, 1865–1940, vol. III

Starke, Sir Hayden Erskine, 1871–1958, vol. V

Starkey, James Sullivan; see O'Sullivan, Seumas.

Starkey, Sir John Ralph, 1st Bt, 1859–1940, vol. III

Starkey, Lewis Randle, 1836–1910, vol. I

Starkey, Thomas Albert, 1872–1939, vol. III (A), vol. IV

Starkey, William Joseph Starkey B.; see Barber-Starkey.

Starkey, Lt-Col Sir William Randle, 2nd Bt, 1899–1977, vol. VII

Starkie, Enid Mary, died 1970, vol. VI

Starkie, Rev. Le Gendre George H.; see Horton-Starkie.

Starkie, Le Gendre Nicholas, 1828–1899, vol. I

Starkie, Robert Fitzwilliam, 1855–1934, vol. III

Starkie, Walter Fitzwilliam, 1894–1976, vol. VII

Starkie, Rt Hon. William Joseph Myles, 1860–1920, vol. II

Starling, Ernest Henry, 1866–1927, vol. II

Starling, Frederick Charles, 1886–1962, vol. VI

Starling, Hubert John, 1874–1950, vol. IV

Starling, John Henry, 1883–1966, vol. VI

Starmer, Sir Charles Walter, 1870–1933, vol. III

Starr, Clarence L., 1868–1928, vol. II

Starr, Frederic Newton Gisborne, 1867–1934, vol. III

Starr, Sir Kenneth William, 1908–1976, vol. VII

Starr, Col William Henderson, 1861–1947, vol. IV

Starte, Oliver Harold Baptist, 1882–1969, vol. VI

Startin, Adm. Sir James, 1855–1948, vol. IV

Statham, Hon. Sir Charles Ernest, 1875–1946, vol. IV

Statham, Rev. George Herbert, 1842–1922, vol. II

Statham, Heathcote Dicken, 1889–1973, vol. VII

Statham, Henry Heathcote, 1839–1924, vol. II

Statham, Ira Cyril Frank, 1886–1967, vol. VI

Statham, Col John Charles Barron, 1872–1933, vol. III

Statham, Sir Randulph Meverel, 1890–1944, vol. IV

Statham, Reginald Samuel Sherard, 1884–1959, vol. V

Staudinger, Hermann, 1881–1965, vol. VI

Staughton, Captain S. T., 1876–1903, vol. I

Staunton, Hugh Geoffrey, 1871–1951, vol. V

Staunton, Most Rev. James, 1889–1963, vol. VI

Staunton, Lt-Col Reginald Kirkpatrick Lynch, 1880–1918, vol. II

Staveley, Adm. Cecil Minet, 1874–1934, vol. III

Staveley, Brig. Robert, 1892–1968, vol. VI

Staveley, Brig.-Gen. William Cathcart, 1865–1939, vol. III

Staveley-Hill, Henry Staveley, 1865–1946, vol. IV

Stavert, Sir William Ewen, 1861–1937, vol. III

Stavert, Rev. William James, 1858–1932, vol. III

Stavridi, Sir John, 1867–1948, vol. IV

Stawell, Sir Richard Rawdon, 1864–1935, vol. III

Stawell, Mrs Rodolph, died 1949, vol. IV

Stayner, Brig. Gerrard Francis Hood, 1900–1980, vol. VII

Staynes, Percy Angelo, died 1953, vol. V

Steacie, Edgar William Richard, 1900–1962, vol. VI

Steacy, Rev. Richard Henry, 1869–1950, vol. IV

Stead, Alfred, 1877–1933, vol. III

Stead, Lt-Col Alfred James, 1845–1909, vol. I

Stead, Sir Charles, 1877–1961, vol. VI

Stead, Francis Bernard, 1873–1954, vol. V

Stead, Francis Herbert, 1857–1928, vol. II

Stead, Gilbert, 1888–1979, vol. VII

Stead, James Lister, 1864–1915, vol. I

Stead, John Edward, 1851–1923, vol. II

Stead, Kingsley Willans, 1883–1950, vol. IV

Stead, William Thomas, 1849–1912, vol. I

Steadman, Frank St J., 1880–1943, vol. IV

Steadman, W. C., 1851–1911, vol. I

Steane, Bruce Harry Dennis, 1866–1939, vol. III

Steavenson, Arthur Paget, 1872–1934, vol. III

Steavenson, Hon. Brig.-Gen. Charles John, 1867–1933, vol. III

Steavenson, David Fenwick, 1844–1920, vol. II

Steavenson, William Herbert, 1894–1975, vol. VII

Stebbing, Edward Percy, 1870–1960, vol. V

Stebbing, (Lizzie) Susan, 1885–1943, vol. IV

Stebbing, Susan; see Stebbing, L. S.

Stebbing, Rev. Thomas Roscoe Rede, 1835–1926, vol. II

Stebbing, William, died 1926, vol. II

Stedeford, Sir Ivan Arthur Rice, 1897–1975, vol. VII

Stedman, Edgar, 1890–1975, vol. VII

Stedman, Edmund Clarence, 1833–1908, vol. I

Stedman, Gen. Sir Edward, 1842–1914, vol. I

Stedman, Air Vice-Marshal Ernest W., 1888–1957, vol. V

Stedman, Sir Leonard Foster, 1871–1948, vol. IV

Stedman, Ralph Elliott, died 1964, vol. VI

Steed, Henry Wickham, 1871–1956, vol. V

Steeds-Bird, Elliott Beverley, 1881–1945, vol. IV

Steegman, John E. H., 1899–1966, vol. VI

Steel, Allan Gibson, 1858–1914, vol. I

Steel, Anthony Bedford, 1900–1973, vol. VII

Steel, Charles, 1847–1925, vol. II

Steel, Sir Christopher Eden, 1903–1973, vol. VII

Steel, Edward, 1906–1976, vol. VII

Steel, Major Edward Anthony, 1880–1919, vol. II

Steel, Flora Annie, 1847–1929, vol. III

Steel, Gerald, 1895–1957, vol. V

Steel, Gerald Arthur, died 1963, vol. VI

Steel, Sir James, 1st Bt (cr 1903), 1830–1904, vol. I

Steel, Air Chief Marshal Sir John Miles, 1877–1965, vol. III

Steel, Lt-Col Matthew Reginald, 1896–1941, vol. IV

Steel, Col Richard Alexander, died 1928, vol. II

Steel, Robert, 1839–1903, vol. I

Steel, Major Sir Samuel Strang, 1st Bt (cr 1938), 1882–1961, vol. VI

Steel, William Strang, 1832–1911, vol. I

Steel-Maitland, Rt Hon. Sir Arthur Herbert Drummond Ramsay, 1st Bt, 1876–1935, vol. III

Steel-Maitland, Sir (Arthur) James (Drummond Ramsay-), 2nd Bt, 1902–1960, vol. V

Steel-Maitland, Sir James; see Steel-Maitland, Sir A. J. D. R.

Steel-Maitland, Sir Keith Richard Felix Ramsay-, 3rd Bt, 1912–1965, vol. VI

Steele, Bertram Dillon, 1870–1934, vol. III

Steele, Col Charles Edward Beevor, 1876–1940, vol. III

Steele, Air Marshal Sir Charles Ronald, 1897–1973, vol. VII

Steele, Maj.-Gen. Sir Clive Selwyn, 1892–1955, vol. V

Steele, Fanny; see Steele, Francesca Maria.

Steele, Francesca Maria, died 1931, vol. III

Steele, Lt-Col Frederick William, 1858–1909, vol. I

Steele, Lt-Col Harwood Robert Elmes, 1897–1978, vol. VII

Steele, Sir Henry, 1879–1963, vol. VI

Steele, Gen. Sir James Stuart, 1894–1975, vol. VII

Steele, John, 1837–1922, vol. II

Steele, John Scott, 1870–1947, vol. IV

Steele, Maj.-Gen. Julian McCarty, 1870–1926, vol. II

Steele, Norman James, 1918–1977, vol. VII

Steele, Robert, 1860–1944, vol. IV

Steele, Col St George Loftus, 1859–1936, vol. III

Steele, Maj.-Gen. Sir Samuel Benfield, 1849–1919, vol. II

Steele, Thomas, 1905–1979, vol. VII

Steele, Col William Lawrence, 1878–1958, vol. V

Steell, David G., 1856–1930, vol. III

Steell, Graham, 1851–1942, vol. IV

Steen, Marguerite, 1894–1975, vol. VII

Steen, Robert Hunter, 1870–1926, vol. II

Steenbock, Harry, 1886–1967, vol. VI

Steenkamp, Major William, 1868–1935, vol. III

Steer, Edward Pemberton, 1881–1938, vol. III

Steer, Francis William, 1912–1978, vol. VII

Steer, George Lowther, 1909–1944, vol. IV

Steer, Henry Reynolds, 1858–1928, vol. II

Steer, P. Wilson, 1860–1942, vol. IV

Steer, Captain T. Bruce, died 1904, vol. I

Steer, William Bridgland, 1867–1939, vol. III (A), vol. IV

Steere, Sir Ernest Augustus L.; see Lee Steere.

Steere, Henry Charles Lee, 1859–1933, vol. III

Steere, Hon. Sir James George Lee, 1830–1903, vol. I

Steevens, Maj.-Gen. Sir John, 1855–1925, vol. II

Stefansson, Vilhjalmur, 1879–1962, vol. VI

Steggall, Charles, 1826–1905, vol. I

Steggall, John Edward Aloysius, 1855–1935, vol. III

Steggall, Reginald, 1867–1938, vol. III

Stein, Adolphe, 1878–1938, vol. III

Stein, Sir Aurel, 1862–1943, vol. IV

Stein, Gertrude, 1874–1946, vol. IV

Stein, Leonard Jacques, 1887–1973, vol. VII

Stein, William Howard, 1911–1980, vol. VII

Steinaecker, Lt-Col Francis Christian Ludwig, Baron von, born 1854, vol. II

Steinbeck, John Ernest, 1902–1968, vol. VI

Steinberg, Sigfrid Henry, 1899–1969, vol. VI

Steinberg, William, 1899–1978, vol. VII

Steinhardt, Laurence A., 1892–1950, vol. IV

Steinlen, Theophile Alexander, 1859–1923, vol. II

Stemp, Major Charles Hubert, 1871–1948, vol. IV
Stenbock, Count Otto, 1838–1915, vol. I
Stengel, Erwin, 1902–1973, vol. VII
Stenhouse, Maj.-Gen. William, 1840–1914, vol. I
Stennett, Col Harry March, 1877–1941, vol. IV
Stenning, Sir Alexander Rose, 1846–1928, vol. II
Stenning, Ven. Ernest Henry, 1885–1964, vol. VI
Stenning, Rev. George Covey, 1840–1915, vol. I (A)
Stenning, John Frederick, died 1959, vol. V
Stent, Percy John Hodsoll, 1888–1962, vol. VI
Stentiford, Charles Douglas, died 1920, vol. II
Stenton, Doris Mary, (Lady Stenton), 1894–1971, vol. VII
Stenton, Sir Frank Merry, 1880–1967, vol. VI
Step, Edward, 1855–1931, vol. III
Stephen, Captain Albert Alexander Leslie, 1879–1914, vol. I
Stephen, Sir Alexander Condie, 1850–1908, vol. I
Stephen, Sir Alexander Murray, 1892–1974, vol. VII
Stephen, Sir Andrew, 1906–1980, vol. VII
Stephen, Campbell, 1884–1947, vol. IV
Stephen, Col Charles Merton, 1874–1955, vol. V
Stephen, Sir Colin Campbell, 1872–1937, vol. III
Stephen, Edward Milner, 1870–1939, vol. III
Stephen, Col Fitzroy, 1835–1906, vol. I
Stephen, George, 1886–1972, vol. VII
Stephen, George Arthur, 1880–1934, vol. III
Stephen, Lt-Col Guy Neville, 1858–1932, vol. III
Stephen, Sir Harry Lushington, 3rd Bt, 1860–1945, vol. IV
Stephen, Sir Henry; see Stephen, Sir M. H.
Stephen, Sir Herbert, 2nd Bt, 1857–1932, vol. III
Stephen, Katharine, 1856–1924, vol. II
Stephen, Sir Leslie, 1832–1904, vol. I
Stephen, Sir (Matthew) Henry, 1828–1920, vol. II
Stephen, Norman Kenneth, 1865–1948, vol. IV
Stephen, Rt Rev. Reginald, 1860–1956, vol. V
Stephen, Brig.-Gen. Robert Campbell, 1867–1947, vol. IV
Stephens, Maj.-Gen. Adolphus Haggerston, 1835–1916, vol. II
Stephens, Sir Alfred, 1871–1938, vol. III
Stephens, Alfred George Gower, died 1933, vol. III
Stephens, Berkeley John Byng, 1871–1950, vol. IV
Stephens, Sir Edgar; see Stephens, Sir L. E.
Stephens, Brig. Frederick, 1906–1967, vol. VI
Stephens, Frederick James, 1903–1978, vol. VII
Stephens, George Arbour, 1870–1945, vol. IV
Stephens, George Henry, died 1927, vol. II
Stephens, Rear-Adm. George Leslie, 1889–1979, vol. VII
Stephens, George Washington, 1866–1942, vol. IV
Stephens, Henry Morse, 1857–1919, vol. II
Stephens, Herbert John, 1875–1957, vol. V
Stephens, Surg. Rear-Adm. Horace Elliott Rose, 1883–1959, vol. V
Stephens, James, died 1950, vol. IV
Stephens, James Brunton, 1835–1902, vol. I
Stephens, James Henry, 1862–1937, vol. III

Stephens, John Edward Robert, 1869–1941, vol. IV
Stephens, Rev. John Otter, 1832–1925, vol. II
Stephens, John William Watson, 1865–1946, vol. IV
Stephens, Sir (Leon) Edgar, 1901–1977, vol. VII
Stephens, Engr Rear-Adm. Lindsay James, 1868–1958, vol. V
Stephens, Lockhart, 1858–1940, vol. III
Stephens, Rear-Adm. (S) Montague, died 1950, vol. IV
Stephens, Pembroke Scott, died 1914, vol. I
Stephens, Gen. Sir Reginald Byng, 1869–1955, vol. V
Stephens, Captain Richard Markham Tyringham, 1875–1967, vol. VI
Stephens, Lt-Col Rupert, 1884–1970, vol. VI
Stephens, Sir William, 1848–1929, vol. III
Stephens, William Francis, 1869–1963, vol. VI
Stephens, Sir William R.; see Reynolds-Stephens.
Stephens, Very Rev. William Richard Wood, 1839–1902, vol. I
Stephens Spinks, Rev. George; see Spinks.
Stephenson, Sir (Albert) Edward, 1864–1928, vol. II
Stephenson, Sir Albert Frederick, 1854–1934, vol. III
Stephenson, Lt-Col Arthur, died 1950, vol. IV
Stephenson, Sir Arthur George, 1890–1967, vol. VI
Stephenson, Sir Augustus Frederick William Keppel, 1827–1904, vol. I
Stephenson, Basil Ernest, 1901–1977, vol. VII
Stephenson, Sir Edward; see Stephenson, Sir A. E.
Stephenson, Edward F., 1868–1948, vol. IV
Stephenson, Col Eric Lechmere, 1892–1978, vol. VII
Stephenson, Eric Seymour, 1879–1915, vol. I
Stephenson, Francis Lawrance, 1845–1920, vol. II
Stephenson, Rev. Frank, died 1936, vol. III
Stephenson, Gen. Sir Frederick Charles Arthur, 1821–1911, vol. I
Stephenson, George Robert, 1819–1905, vol. I
Stephenson, Vice-Adm. Sir Gilbert Owen, 1878–1972, vol. VII
Stephenson, Sir Guy, 1865–1930, vol. III
Stephenson, Sir Henry, 1826–1904, vol. I
Stephenson, Adm. Sir Henry Frederick, 1842–1919, vol. II
Stephenson, Lt-Col Sir Henry Kenyon, 1st Bt, 1865–1947, vol. IV
Stephenson, Rev. Henry Spencer, 1871–1957, vol. V
Stephenson, Sir Hugh Lansdown, 1871–1941, vol. IV
Stephenson, Sir Hugh Southern, 1906–1972, vol. VII
Stephenson, Rev. Jacob, 1844–1927, vol. II
Stephenson, Lt-Col John, 1871–1933, vol. III
Stephenson, Sir John Everard, 1893–1948, vol. IV
Stephenson, Sir John Walker, died 1960, vol. V
Stephenson, Joseph, 1882–1965, vol. VI
Stephenson, Katharine J., 1874–1953, vol. V
Stephenson, Marjory, 1885–1948, vol. IV
Stephenson, Rt Rev. Percival William, 1888–1962, vol. VI

Stephenson, Sir Percy, 1909–1979, vol. VII
Stephenson, Lt-Col Robert, 1876–1959, vol. V
Stephenson, Sydney, 1862–1923, vol. II
Stephenson, Rev. T. Bowman, 1839–1912, vol. I
Stephenson, Maj.-Gen. Theodore Edward, 1856–1928, vol. II
Stephenson, Thomas, 1864–1938, vol. III
Stephenson, Thomas, 1889–1974, vol. VII
Stephenson, Thomas Alan, died 1961, vol. VI
Stephenson, Rev. Thomas Wilkinson, died 1936, vol. III
Stephenson, William, 1837–1919, vol. II
Stephenson, Sir William Haswell, 1836–1918, vol. II
Stephenson, Sir William Henry, 1811–1898, vol. I
Stephenson, William Lawrence, 1880–1963, vol. VI
Stephenson, Willie, died 1938, vol. III (A), vol. IV
Stepney, Sir Emile Algernon Arthur Keppel C.; see Cowell-Stepney.
Steptoe, Harry Nathaniel, 1892–1949, vol. IV
Sterling, Antoinette, 1843–1904, vol. I
Sterling, Herbert Harry, 1886–1959, vol. V
Sterling, Maj.-Gen. John Barton, 1840–1926, vol. II
Sterling, Sir Louis Saul, died 1958, vol. V
Sterling, Thomas Smith, 1883–1970, vol. VI
Stern, Lt-Col Sir Albert, 1878–1966, vol. VI
Stern, Sir Edward David, 1st Bt, 1854–1933, vol. III
Stern, Sir Frederick Claude, 1884–1967, vol. VI
Stern, Gladys Bertha, 1890–1973, vol. VII
Stern, Rev. Joseph Frederick, 1865–1934, vol. III
Stern, Philip, died 1933 vol. III
Stern-Salomons, Sir David Lionel Goldsmid-; see Salomons.
Sternberg, Hon. Joseph, 1855–1928, vol. II
Sternberg, Rudy; see Baron Plurenden.
Sterndale, 1st Baron, 1849–1923, vol. II
Sterndale, Robert Armitage, 1839–1902, vol. I
Sterndale-Bennett, T. C., died 1944, vol. IV
Sterne, Maurice, 1877–1957, vol. V
Sterrett, John Robert Sitlington, 1851–1914, vol. I (A), vol. II
Sterry, Joseph A.; see Ashby-Sterry.
Sterry, Sir Wasey, 1866–1955, vol. V
Stettinius, Edward R., (Jr), 1900–1949, vol. IV
Steuart, Sir Alan Henry Seton-, 4th Bt, 1856–1913, vol. I
Steuart, Sir Douglas Archibald Seton-, 5th Bt, 1857–1930, vol. III
Steuart, Ethel Mary, died 1960, vol. V
Steuart, John Alexander, died 1932, vol. III
Steuart, Rev. Robert H. J., 1874–1948, vol. IV
Steuart-Fothringham, Walter Thomas James S.; see Scrymsoure-Steuart-Fothringham.
Steuart-Menzies, William George, 1858–1941, vol. IV
Steven, Temp. Captain Fraser; see Steven, Temp. Captain J. F.
Steven, Guy Savile, 1906–1980, vol. VII
Steven, Henry Marshall, 1893–1969, vol. VI
Steven, Temp. Captain (John) Fraser, died 1920, vol. II

Stevens, Col Arthur Borlase, 1881–1965, vol. VI
Stevens, Col Arthur Cornish Jeremie, 1875–1962, vol. VI
Stevens, Bertram, died 1922, vol. II
Stevens, Hon. Sir Bertram Sydney Barnsdale, 1889–1973, vol. VII
Stevens, Air Vice-Marshal Cecil Alfred, 1898–1958, vol. V
Stevens, Lt-Col Cecil Robert, 1867–1919, vol. II
Stevens, Engr-Rear-Adm. Charles, 1869–1933, vol. III
Stevens, Sir Charles Cecil, 1840–1909, vol. I
Stevens, Col Charles Frederick, 1866–1944, vol. IV
Stevens, Charles John, 1857–1917, vol. II
Stevens, Clement Henry, 1870–1959, vol. V
Stevens, Hon. E. J., 1845–1922, vol. II
Stevens, E. S.; see Drower, Ethel May Stefana (Lady Drower).
Stevens, Ernest Hamilton, 1864–1945, vol. IV
Stevens, Frank, 1850–1935, vol. III
Stevens, Lt-Col Sir Frank, 1877–1939, vol. III
Stevens, Frederick, 1840–1917, vol. II
Stevens, Frederick Guy, 1878–1944, vol. IV
Stevens, Frederick William, 1847–1900, vol. I
Stevens, Brig.-Gen. George Archibald, 1875–1951, vol. V
Stevens, George Bridges, 1882–1937, vol. III
Stevens, George Cooper, 1905–1975, vol. VII
Stevens, Col Harold Raphael Gaetano, 1883–1961, vol. VI
Stevens, Sir Harold Samuel Eaton, 1892–1969, vol. VI
Stevens, Henry, 1885–1963, vol. VI
Stevens, Rev. Henry Bingham, 1835–1924, vol. II
Stevens, Hon. Henry Herbert, 1878–1973, vol. VII
Stevens, Herbert Lawrence, 1892–1978, vol. VII
Stevens, Maj.-Gen. Sir Jack Edwin Stawell, 1896–1969, vol. VI
Stevens, James Algernon, 1873–1934, vol. III
Stevens, Sir John Foster, 1845–1925, vol. II
Stevens, Engr Captain John Greet, 1857–1943, vol. IV
Stevens, Sir John Melior, 1913–1973, vol. VII
Stevens, Sir Joseph W.; see Weston-Stevens.
Stevens, Marshall, 1852–1936, vol. III
Stevens, Lt-Col Nathaniel Melhuish Comins, 1868–1954, vol. V
Stevens, Rt Rev. Percy, 1882–1966, vol. VI
Stevens, Sir Roger Bentham, 1906–1980, vol. VII
Stevens, Rt Rev. Thomas, 1841–1920, vol. II
Stevens, Thomas George, 1869–1953, vol. V
Stevens, Lt-Col Thomas Harry Goldsworthy, 1883–1970, vol. VI
Stevens, Walter Charles, 1904–1954, vol. V
Stevens, Rt Rev. William Bertrand, 1884–1947, vol. IV
Stevens, William C.; see Cleveland-Stevens.
Stevens, William Charles, 1900–1973, vol. VII
Stevens, William George, 1883–1971, vol. VII
Stevens, Maj.-Gen. William George, 1893–1974, vol. VII
Stevens, William Mitchell, 1868–1944, vol. IV
Stevens, William Oswald, 1891–1972, vol. VII
Stevenson, 1st Baron, 1873–1926, vol. II

Stevenson, Hon. Lord; James Stevenson, *died* 1963, vol. VI

Stevenson, Adlai Ewing, 1900–1965, vol. VI

Stevenson, Alan; *see* Stevenson, D. A.

Stevenson, Sir Alexander, 1860–1936, vol. III

Stevenson, Maj.-Gen. Alexander Gavin, 1871–1939, vol. III

Stevenson, Alexander James, 1901–1970, vol. VI

Stevenson, Alexander Wight, 1886–1954, vol. V

Stevenson, Allan, 1878–1948, vol. IV

Stevenson, D. E., 1892–1973, vol. VII

Stevenson, Sir Daniel Macaulay, 1st Bt, 1851–1944, vol. IV

Stevenson, D(avid) Alan, 1891–1971, vol. VII

Stevenson, David Watson, 1842–1904, vol. I

Stevenson, Air Vice-Marshal Donald Fasken, 1895–1964, vol. VI

Stevenson, Sir Edmond Sinclair, 1850–1927, vol. II

Stevenson, Lt-Col Sir Edward Daymonde, 1895–1958, vol. V

Stevenson, Brig.-Gen. Edward Hall, 1872–1964, vol. VI

Stevenson, Edward Irenæus Prime-, 1868–1942, vol. IV

Stevenson, Edward Snead Boyd, 1849–1917, vol. II

Stevenson, Flora Clift, *died* 1905, vol. I

Stevenson, Frances; *see* Lloyd George of Dwyfor, Countess.

Stevenson, Col Francis, 1851–1922, vol. II

Stevenson, Francis Seymour, 1862–1938, vol. III

Stevenson, Sir George Augustus, 1856–1931, vol. III

Stevenson, George Hope, 1880–1952, vol. V

Stevenson, Col George Ingram, 1882–1958, vol. V

Stevenson, Surg.-Gen. Henry Wickham, 1857–1944, vol. IV

Stevenson, Sir Hubert Craddock, 1888–1971, vol. VII

Stevenson, Rev. J. Ross, 1866–1939, vol. III

Stevenson, Col James, 1838–1926, vol. II

Stevenson, James; *see* Stevenson, Hon. Lord.

Stevenson, James Alexander, 1881–1937, vol III

Stevenson, James Arthur Radford, *died* 1974, vol. VII

Stevenson, James Cochran, 1825–1905, vol. I

Stevenson, James Verdier, 1858–1933, vol. III

Stevenson, Lt-Col John, 1895–1952, vol. V

Stevenson, Rear-Adm. John Bryan, 1876–1957, vol. V

Stevenson, John Horne, 1855–1939, vol. III

Stevenson, John Lynn, 1927–1971, vol. VII

Stevenson, Rev. John Sinclair, 1868–1930, vol. III

Stevenson, Sir Malcolm, 1878–1927, vol. II

Stevenson, Margaret; *see* Stevenson, Mrs Sinclair.

Stevenson, Rev. Canon Morley, 1851–1930, vol. III

Stevenson, Gen. Nathaniel, 1840–1911, vol. I

Stevenson, R. Macaulay, *died* 1952, vol. V

Stevenson, Sir Ralph Clarmont Skrine, 1895–1977, vol. VII

Stevenson, Ralph Cornwallis, 1894–1967, vol. VI

Stevenson, Col Robert, 1845–1930, vol. III

Stevenson, Robert Alan Mowbray, 1847–1900, vol. I

Stevenson, Robert Scott, 1889–1967, vol. VI

Stevenson, Sir Roy Hunter, 1892–1963, vol. VI

Stevenson, Mrs Sinclair, (Margaret), 1875–1957, vol. V

Stevenson, Sir Thomas, 1838–1908, vol. I

Stevenson, Thomas Henry Craig, 1870–1932, vol. III

Stevenson, Maj.-Gen. Thomas Rennie, 1841–1923, vol. II

Stevenson, Walter Clegg, 1877–1931, vol. III

Stevenson, William Barron, 1869–1954, vol. V

Stevenson, Lt-Col William David Henderson, *died* 1945, vol. IV

Stevenson, Maj.-Gen. William Flack, 1844–1922, vol. II

Stevenson, William Grant, 1849–1919, vol. II

Stevenson, Rt Rev. William Henry Webster, 1878–1945, vol. IV

Stevenson-Hamilton, Lt-Col James, 1867–1957, vol. V

Stevenson-Moore, Sir Charles James, 1866–1947, vol. IV

Steward, Rev. Edward, 1851–1930, vol. III

Steward, Maj.-Gen. Edward Harding, 1835–1918, vol. II

Steward, Maj.-Gen. Edward Merivale, 1881–1947, vol. IV

Steward, Francis James, *died* 1940, vol. III

Steward, Lt-Col Sir George, 1866–1920, vol. II

Steward, George Frederick, 1884–1952, vol. V

Steward, Col Godfrey Robert Viveash, 1881–1969, vol. VI

Steward, Sir Harold Macdonald, 1904–1977, vol. VII

Steward, Sir Henry Allan Holden, 1865–1954, vol. V

Steward, Rt Rev. John Manwaring, 1874–1937, vol. III

Steward, Maj.-Gen. Reginald Herbert Ryrie, 1898–1975, vol. VII

Stewardson, Edward Alfred, 1904–1973, vol. VII

Stewart, Lt-Col Albert Fortescue, *died* 1925, vol. II

Stewart, Very Rev. Alexander, 1847–1915, vol. I

Stewart, Rev. Alexander, *died* 1916, vol. II

Stewart, Sir Alexander, 2nd Bt (*cr* 1920, of Balgownie), 1886–1934, vol. III

Stewart, Sir Alexander Anderson, 1877–1956, vol. V

Stewart, Alexander Bernard, 1908–1974, vol. VII

Stewart, Alexander Carmichael, 1865–1944, vol. IV

Stewart, Maj.-Gen. Alexander Charles Hector, 1838–1917, vol. II

Stewart, Lt-Col Alexander Dron, 1883–1969, vol. VI

Stewart, Brig.-Gen. Alexander Edward, 1867–1940, vol. III

Stewart, Alexander G.; *see* Graham-Stewart.

Stewart, Alexander MacKay, 1878–1952, vol. V

Stewart, Alfred Walter, *died* 1947, vol. IV

Stewart, Major Algernon Bingham Anstruther, 1869–1916, vol. II

Stewart, Allan, 1865–1951, vol. V

Stewart, Andrew, 1895–1972, vol. VII
Stewart, Andrew Charles, 1907–1979, vol. VII
Stewart, Andrew Graham, 1901–1964, vol. VI
Stewart, Lt-Col Archibald Campbell, 1872–1936, vol. III
Stewart, Comdr Archibald Thomas, 1876–1968, vol. VI
Stewart, Arthur, 1877–1941, vol. IV
Stewart, Captain Arthur Courtenay, 1871–1958, vol. V
Stewart, Col Basil Heron S.; see Shaw-Stewart.
Stewart, Sir Bruce Fraser, 2nd Bt (cr 1920, of Fingask), 1904–1979, vol. VII (A II)
Stewart, Col Bryce, 1857–1936, vol. III
Stewart, Charles, 1840–1907, vol. I
Stewart, Charles, 1840–1916, vol. II
Stewart, Hon. Charles, 1868–1946, vol. IV
Stewart, Col Charles Edward, 1836–1904, vol. I
Stewart, Lt-Col Charles Edward, 1868–1916, vol. II
Stewart, Rev. Charles Henry Hylton, died 1922, vol. II
Stewart, Charles Hunter, 1854–1924, vol. II
Stewart, Charles Hylton, 1884–1932, vol. III
Stewart, Sir Charles John, 1851–1932, vol. III
Stewart, Charles John, died 1954, vol. V
Stewart, Charlotte, 1863–1918, vol. II
Stewart, Brig.-Gen. Cosmo Gordon, 1869–1948, vol. IV
Stewart, Daniel, died 1912, vol. I
Stewart, Sir David, 1835–1919, vol. II
Stewart, Col David Brown Douglas, 1862–1935, vol. III
Stewart, David Macfarlane, 1878–1950, vol. IV
Stewart, David Mitchell, 1853–1924, vol. II
Stewart, Donald, 1894–1976, vol. VII
Stewart, Sir Donald Martin, 1st Bt (cr 1881), 1824–1900, vol. I
Stewart, Sir Donald William, 1860–1905, vol. I
Stewart, Lt-Col Douglas, 1875–1943, vol. IV
Stewart, Sir Douglas Law, 3rd Bt (cr 1881), 1878–1951, vol. V
Stewart, Douglas Roy, 1886–1939, vol. III
Stewart, Col Dudley Strathearn, 1859–1933, vol. III
Stewart, Duncan George, 1904–1949, vol. IV
Stewart, Edith Anne; see Robertson, E. A.
Stewart, Lt-Col Sir Edward, 1857–1948, vol. IV
Stewart, Sir Edward Orde MacTaggart-, 2nd Bt (cr 1892), 1883–1948, vol. IV
Stewart, Ellen Frances, died 1945, vol. IV
Stewart of Coll, Brig.-Gen. Ernest Moncrieff Paul, 1864–1942, vol. III
Stewart, Sir Evan Guy S.; see Shaw-Stewart.
Stewart, Sir Findlater; see Stewart, Sir S. F.
Stewart, Frances Henrietta, (Lady Stewart), 1883–1962, vol. VI
Stewart, Sir Francis Hugh, 1869–1921, vol. II
Stewart, Francis William, 1885–1963, vol. VI
Stewart, Francis William Sutton C.; see Cumbrae-Stewart.
Stewart, Frank Ogilvie, 1893–1964, vol. VI
Stewart, Rev. Frank White, 1867–1933, vol. III
Stewart, Col Sir Frederick Charles, died 1950, vol. IV

Stewart, Sir Frederick Harold, 1884–1961, vol. VI
Stewart, Maj.-Gen. George, 1839–1927, vol. II
Stewart, Rt Rev. George Craig, 1879–1940, vol. III
Stewart, Rt Hon. George Francis, 1851–1928, vol. II
Stewart, George Innes, 1896–1968, vol. VI
Stewart, Lt-Col Sir George Powell, 5th Bt (cr 1803), 1861–1945, vol. IV
Stewart, Sir Gershom, 1857–1929, vol. III
Stewart, Haldane Campbell, 1868–1942, vol. IV
Stewart, Sir Halley, 1838–1937, vol. III
Stewart, Sir Harry Jocelyn Urquhart, 11th Bt (cr 1623), 1871–1945, vol. IV
Stewart, Henrietta; see Shell, Rita.
Stewart, Henry Cockburn, 1844–1899, vol. I
Stewart, Ven. Henry John, 1873–1960, vol. V
Stewart, Lt-Col Henry King, 1861–1907, vol. I
Stewart, Maj.-Gen. Herbert William Vansittart, 1886–1975, vol. VII
Stewart, Howard Hilton, 1900–1961, vol. VI
Stewart, Lt-Col Hugh, 1872–1931, vol. III
Stewart, Hugh, 1884–1934, vol. III
Stewart, Rev. Hugh Fraser, 1863–1948, vol. IV
Stewart, Brig.-Gen. Sir Hugh Houghton, 4th Bt (cr 1803), 1858–1942, vol. IV
Stewart, Sir Hugh S.; see Shaw-Stewart.
Stewart, Brig.-Gen. Ian, 1874–1941, vol. IV
Stewart, Ian Struthers, 1876–1930, vol. III
Stewart, James, 1846–1906, vol. I
Stewart, James, 1863–1931, vol. III
Stewart, James, 1867–1943, vol. IV
Stewart, Maj.-Gen. James Calder, 1840–1930, vol. III
Stewart, Brig.-Gen. James Campbell, 1884–1947, vol. IV
Stewart, Hon. James Charles, 1850–1931, vol. III
Stewart, Brig. James Crossley, 1891–1972, vol. VII
Stewart, Hon. James D., 1874–1933, vol. III
Stewart, James Douglas, 1869–1955, vol. V
Stewart, Sir James H.; see Henderson-Stewart.
Stewart, James King, 1863–1938, vol. III
Stewart, Maj.-Gen. Sir James Marshall, 1861–1943, vol. IV
Stewart, Sir James Purves-, 1869–1949, vol. IV
Stewart, Sir James Watson, 1st Bt (cr 1920, of Balgownie), 1852–1922, vol. II
Stewart, Sir James Watson, 3rd Bt (cr 1920, of Balgownie), 1889–1955, vol. V
Stewart, Col John, 1833–1914, vol. I
Stewart, Sir John, 1st Bt (cr 1920, of Fingask), 1877–1924, vol. II
Stewart, Lt-Col John, 1869–1931, vol. III
Stewart, Col John, 1848–1933, vol. III
Stewart, Sir John, 1867–1947, vol. IV
Stewart, Sir John, 1887–1958, vol. V
Stewart, John Alexander, 1846–1933, vol. III
Stewart, John Alexander, 1882–1948, vol. IV
Stewart, John Alexander, 1915–1974, vol. VII
Stewart, Captain John Christie, 1888–1978, vol. VII
Stewart, John Graham, died 1917, vol. II
Stewart, Maj.-Gen. Sir (John Henry) Keith, 1872–1955, vol. V
Stewart, John McKellar, 1878–1953, vol. V

Stewart, Sir John Marcus, 3rd Bt (*cr* 1803), 1830–1905, vol. I

Stewart, Brig.-Gen. John Smith, 1877–1970, vol. VI

Stewart, Maj.-Gen. John William, 1862–1938, vol. III

Stewart, Rev. Joseph Atkinson, *died* 1913, vol. I

Stewart, Joseph Francis, 1889–1964, vol. VI

Stewart, Maj.-Gen. Sir Keith; *see* Stewart, Maj.-Gen. Sir J. H. K.

Stewart, Maj.-Gen. Sir Keith Lindsay, 1896–1972, vol. VII

Stewart, Sir Kenneth Dugald, 1st Bt (*cr* 1960), 1882–1972, vol. VII

Stewart, Louisa Mary, 1861–1943, vol. IV

Stewart, Sir Malcolm; *see* Stewart, Sir P. M.

Stewart, Sir Mark John MacTaggart, 1st Bt (*cr* 1892), 1834–1923, vol. II

Stewart, Very Rev. Matthew, 1881–1952, vol. V

Stewart, Matthew John, 1885–1956, vol. V

Stewart, Sir Michael Hugh S.; *see* Shaw-Stewart.

Stewart, Sir Michael Robert S.; *see* Shaw-Stewart.

Stewart, Major Noel St Vincent Ramsay, 1870–1940, vol. III

Stewart, Sir Norman Robert, 2nd Bt (*cr* 1881), 1851–1926, vol. II

Stewart, Major Oliver, 1895–1976, vol. VII

Stewart, Col Patrick Alexander Vansittart, 1875–1960, vol. V

Stewart, Rev. Percy, 1856–1934, vol. III

Stewart, Sir (Percy) Malcolm, 1st Bt (*cr* 1937), 1872–1951, vol. V

Stewart, Rev. Ravenscroft, 1845–1921, vol. II

Stewart, Sir Richard Campbell, 1836–1904, vol. I

Stewart, Sir Robert, 1858–1937, vol. III

Stewart, Robert Bruce, 1863–1948, vol. IV

Stewart, Maj.-Gen. Robert Crosse, 1825–1913, vol. I

Stewart of Physgill, Adm. Robert Hathorn J.; *see* Johnston-Stewart of Physgill.

Stewart, Col Sir Robert King, 1854–1930, vol. III

Stewart, Gen. Sir Robert Macgregor, 1842–1919, vol. II

Stewart, Sir Robert Sproul, 1874–1969, vol. VI

Stewart, Robert Strother-, 1878–1954, vol. V

Stewart, Lt-Col Rupert, 1864–1930, vol. III

Stewart, Sir (Samuel) Findlater, 1879–1960, vol. V

Stewart, Sir Thomas Alexander, 1888–1964, vol. VI

Stewart, Brig. Thomas G.; *see* Grainger-Stewart.

Stewart, Thomas Grainger, *died* 1957, vol. V

Stewart, Valentine Peter Beardmore, 1882–1933, vol. III

Stewart, Lt-Col Sir Walter Guy S.; *see* Shaw-Stewart.

Stewart, Walter Richard S.; *see* Shaw-Stewart.

Stewart, Walter W., 1885–1958, vol. V

Stewart, Rt Rev. Weston Henry, 1887–1969, vol. VI

Stewart, Major William, 1859–1918, vol. II

Stewart, William, 1835–1919, vol. II

Stewart, William, 1856–1947, vol. IV (A), vol. V

Stewart, William, 1879–1964, vol. VI

Stewart, William, 1916–1975, vol. VII

Stewart, Lt-Col William Burton, 1872–1936, vol. III

Stewart, Hon. William Downie, 1878–1949, vol. IV

Stewart, William James, 1889–1969, vol. VI

Stewart, William John, 1849–1908, vol. I

Stewart, William John, *died* 1946, vol. IV

Stewart, William Joseph, *died* 1960, vol. V

Stewart, Air Vice-Marshal William Kilpatrick, 1913–1967, vol. VI

Stewart, Lt-Col William Murray, 1875–1948, vol. IV

Stewart, Brig.-Gen. William Robert, 1862–1932, vol. III

Stewart, Maj.-Gen. William Ross, 1889–1966, vol. VI

Stewart, Hon. William Snodgrass, 1855–1938, vol. III (A), vol. IV

Stewart-Bam of Ards, Lt-Col Sir Pieter Canzius van Blommestein, 1869–1928, vol. II

Stewart-Brown, Ronald, 1872–1940, vol. III

Stewart-Brown, Ronald David, 1911–1963, vol. VI

Stewart-Clark, Sir John, 1st Bt, 1864–1924, vol. II

Stewart-Clark, Sir Stewart, 2nd Bt, 1904–1971, vol. VII

Stewart-Dick-Cunyngham, Sir William; *see* Cunyngham.

Stewart-Liberty, Captain Ivor; *see* Liberty.

Stewart-Richardson, Sir Edward Austin, 15th Bt; *see* Richardson.

Stewart-Richardson, Major Sir Ian Rorie Hay, 16th Bt, 1904–1969, vol. VI

Stewart-Richardson, Lt-Col Neil Graham; *see* Richardson.

Stewart-Richardson, Violet Roberta, 1882–1967, vol. VI

Stewart-Roberts, Walter Stewart, 1889–1975, vol. VII

Stewart-Smith, Sir Dudley, 1857–1919, vol. II

Stewart-Smith, Ean Kendal, 1907–1964, vol. VI

Stewart-Wallace, Sir John Stewart, *died* 1963, vol. VI

Stewart-Wilson, Sir Charles, 1864–1950, vol. IV

Steyn, Lucas Cornelius, 1903–1976, vol. VII

Steyn, Martinus Theunis, 1857–1916, vol. II

Sthamer, Friedrich, 1856–1931, vol. III

Stibbe, Edward Philip, 1884–1943, vol. IV

Stiebel, Sir Arthur, 1875–1949, vol. IV

Stiebel, Herbert Cecil, 1876–1941, vol. IV

Stiebel, Victor Frank, 1907–1976, vol. VII

Stiffe, Captain Arthur William, 1831–1912, vol. I

Stigand, Major Chauncey Hugh, *died* 1919, vol II

Stigand, William, 1825–1915, vol. I (A)

Stikeman, William Rucker, 1854–1927, vol. II

Stikker, Dirk Uipko, 1897–1979, vol. VII

Stileman, Rt Rev. Charles Harvey, 1863–1925, vol. II

Stileman, Rear-Adm. Sir Harry Hampson, 1860–1938, vol. III

Stileman, Maj.-Gen. William Coughton, *died* 1915, vol. I

Stiles, Charles Wardell, 1867–1941, vol. IV

Stiles, Lt-Col Sir Harold Jalland, 1863–1946, vol. IV

Stiles, Walter, 1886–1966, vol. VI

Stilgoe, Henry Edward, *died* 1943, vol. IV
Still, Alexander William, 1860–1931, vol. III
Still, Dame Alicia Frances Jane Lloyd, *died* 1944, vol. IV
Still, Andrew, 1866–1939, vol. III
Still, Charles, 1849–1930, vol. III
Still, Sir George Frederic, 1868–1941, vol. IV
Still, Rev. John, *died* 1914, vol. I
Still, William Chester, 1878–1928, vol. II
Stillman, William James, 1828–1901, vol. I
Stilwell, Gen. Joseph W., 1883–1946, vol. IV
Stimson, Henry Lewis, 1867–1950, vol. IV
Stinton, T., 1886–1957, vol. V
Stirling, Mrs A. M. W., *died* 1965, vol. VI
Stirling, Brig. Alexander Dickson, 1886–1961, vol. VI
Stirling, Adm. Anselan John Buchanan, 1875–1936, vol. III
Stirling, Brig.-Gen. Archibald, 1867–1931, vol. III
Stirling, Archibald William, *died* 1923, vol. II
Stirling, Carl Ludwig, 1890–1973, vol. VII
Stirling, Sir Charles Elphinstone Fleming, 8th Bt (*cr* 1666), 1831–1910, vol. I
Stirling, Edward, 1891–1948, vol. IV
Stirling, Sir Edward Charles, 1848–1919, vol. II
Stirling, Col Sir George; *see* Stirling, Col Sir W. G.
Stirling, George Claudius Beresford, 1861–1929, vol. III
Stirling, Col Sir George Murray Home, 9th Bt (*cr* 1666), 1869–1949, vol. IV
Stirling, Gilbert, 1843–1915, vol. I
Stirling, Hon. Grote, 1875–1953, vol. V
Stirling, Rt Hon. Sir James, 1836–1916, vol. II
Stirling, Sir James; *see* Stirling, Sir R. J. L.
Stirling, Brig. James Erskine, 1898–1968, vol. VI
Stirling, James Heron, 1867–1928, vol. II
Stirling, James Hutchison, 1820–1909, vol. I
Stirling, Hon. Brig.-Gen. James Wilfred, 1855–1926, vol. II
Stirling, Sir John, 1893–1975, vol. VII
Stirling, John Ashwell, 1891–1965, vol. VI
Stirling, Hon. Sir (John) Lancelot, 1849–1932, vol. III
Stirling, John W., 1859–1923, vol. II
Stirling, Hon. Sir Lancelot; *see* Stirling, Hon. Sir J. L.
Stirling, Sir (Robert) James (Lindsay), 1907–1974, vol. VII
Stirling, Rt Rev. Waite Hockin, 1829–1923, vol. II
Stirling, Brig. Walter Andrew, 1883–1972, vol. VII
Stirling, Lt-Col Walter Francis, 1880–1958, vol. V
Stirling, Col Sir (Walter) George, 3rd Bt (*cr* 1800), 1839–1934, vol. III
Stirling, Gen. Sir William, 1835–1906, vol. I
Stirling, William, 1851–1932, vol. III
Stirling, Brig.-Gen. William, 1878–1949, vol. IV
Stirling, Gen. Sir William Gurdon, 1907–1973, vol. VII
Stirling-Hamilton, Sir William; *see* Hamilton.
Stirling Home Drummond, Lt-Col Henry E., 1846–1911, vol. I
Stirling-Home-Drummond, Lt-Col Henry Edward; *see* Drummond.

Stirling-Maxwell, Sir John M.; *see* Maxwell.
Stirton, Rev. John, 1871–1944, vol. IV
Stitt, Rear-Adm. Edward Rhodes, 1867–1948, vol. IV
Stobart, Col George Herbert, 1873–1943, vol. IV
Stobart, Lt-Col Hugh Morton, 1883–1952, vol. V
Stobart, Mrs St Clair, (Mrs Stobart Greenhalgh), *died* 1954, vol. V
Stobie, Harry, 1882–1948, vol. IV
Stobie, William, 1886–1957, vol. V
Stock, Arthur Boy, *died* 1915, vol. I (A)
Stock, Eugene, 1836–1928, vol. II
Stock, Henry John, 1853–1930, vol. III
Stock, James Henry, 1855–1907, vol. I
Stock, Col Philip Graham, *died* 1975, vol. VII
Stock, Ralph, *died* 1962, vol. VI
Stockdale, Sir Frank Arthur, 1883–1949, vol. IV
Stockdale, Brig.-Gen. Herbert Edward, 1867–1953, vol. V
Stockdale, Herbert Fitton, 1868–1951, vol. V
Stockdale, Maj.-Gen. Reginald Booth, 1908–1979, vol. VII
Stockenström, Sir Anders Johan Booysen, 4th Bt, 1908–1957, vol. V
Stockenström, Sir Andries, 3rd Bt, 1868–1922, vol. II
Stockenström, Hon. Sir Gysbert Henry, 2nd Bt, 1841–1912 (this entry was not transferred to Who was Who).
Stocker, Edgar Percy, 1888–1959, vol. V
Stocker, Ven. Harry, *died* 1922, vol. II
Stocker, Richard Dimsdale, 1877–1935, vol. III
Stockings, Major Arthur Perry, 1880–1943, vol. IV
Stockley, Brig.-Gen. Arthur Uniacke, 1869–1939, vol. III
Stockley, Lt-Col Charles Hugh, 1882–1955, vol. V
Stockley, Col Charles More, 1845–1923, vol. II
Stockley, Cynthia, *died* 1936, vol. III
Stockley, David Dudgeon, 1900–1980, vol. VII
Stockley, Brig.-Gen. Ernest Norman, 1872–1946, vol. IV
Stockley, Major Sir Harry Hudson Fraser, 1878–1951, vol. V
Stockley, Brig.-Gen. Hugh Roderick, 1868–1935, vol. III
Stockley, Rev. Joseph John Gabbett, 1862–1949, vol. IV
Stockley, William F. P., 1859–1943, vol. IV
Stockman, Ralph, 1861–1946, vol. IV
Stockman, Sir Stewart, 1869–1926, vol. II
Stocks, Baroness (Life Peer); Mary Danvers Stocks, 1891–1975, vol. VII
Stocks, Sir (Andrew) Denys, 1884–1961, vol. VI
Stocks, Arthur Hudson, 1889–1940, vol. III
Stocks, Charles Lancelot, 1878–1975, vol. VII
Stocks, Sir Denys; *see* Stocks, Sir A. D.
Stocks, Francis W., 1873–1929, vol. III
Stocks, Harold Carpenter Lumb, 1884–1956, vol. V
Stocks, Rev. John Edward, 1843–1926, vol. II
Stocks, John Leofric, 1882–1937, vol. III
Stocks, Percy, 1889–1974, vol. VII

Stockton, Rear-Adm. Charles Herbert, 1845–1924, vol. II
Stockton, Sir Edwin Forsyth, 1873–1939, vol. III
Stockton, Francis Richard, 1834–1902, vol. I
Stockwell, Brig.-Gen. Clifton Inglis, 1879–1953, vol. V
Stockwell, Hon. Maj.-Gen. George Clifton Inglis, 1863–1936, vol. III
Stockwell, Captain Henry, 1875–1962, vol. VI
Stockwell, Col Ralph Frederick, 1885–1962, vol. VI
Stockwood, Ven. Charles Vincent, 1885–1958, vol. V
Stodart, Sqdn Ldr David Edmund, 1882–1938, vol. III
Stodart, James Carlyle, 1880–1956, vol. V
Stodart, Col Thomas, 1868–1934, vol. III
Stoddard, Charles Warren, 1843–1909, vol. I
Stoddard, Francis Hovey, 1847–1936, vol. III
Stoddard, Lothrop, 1883–1950, vol. IV (A)
Stoddart, Alexander Frederick Richard, 1904–1973, vol. VII
Stoddart, Andrew Ernest, 1863–1915, vol. I
Stoddart, Anna M., 1840–1911, vol. I
Stoddart, Adm. Archibald Peile, 1860–1939, vol. III
Stoddart, Sir Charles John, 1839–1913, vol. I
Stoddart, Jane T., died 1944, vol. IV
Stoddart, William Henry Butter, died 1950, vol. IV
Stoddart-Scott, Col Sir Malcolm, 1901–1973, vol. VII
Stogdon, Rev. Edgar, 1870–1951, vol. V
Stoker, Abraham; see Stoker, Bram.
Stoker, Bram, 1847–1912, vol. I
Stoker, Col Claude Bayfield, 1875–1948, vol. IV
Stoker, George, 1855–1920, vol. II (A), vol. III
Stoker, George Herbert, 1874–1935, vol. III
Stoker, Graves, 1864–1938, vol. III
Stoker, Captain Hew Gordon Dacre, 1885–1966, vol. VI
Stoker, Robert Burdon, died 1919, vol. II
Stoker, Thomas, 1849–1925, vol. II
Stoker, Sir Thornley; see Stoker, Sir W. T.
Stoker, William Henry, died 1944, vol. IV
Stoker, Sir (William) Thornley, 1st Bt, 1845–1912, vol. I
Stokes, A. G. Folliott, died 1939, vol. III
Stokes, Adrian, 1887–1927, vol. II
Stokes, Adrian, 1854–1935, vol. III
Stokes, Adrian Durham, 1902–1972, vol. VII
Stokes, Brig.-Gen. Alfred, 1860–1931, vol. III
Stokes, Rev. Anson Phelps, 1874–1958, vol. V
Stokes, Sir Arthur, 2nd Bt, 1858–1916, vol. II
Stokes, Rev. Augustus Sidney, died 1922, vol. II
Stokes, Edith, died 1936, vol. III
Stokes, Maj.-Gen. Sir Folliott Stuart Furneaux, 1849–1911, vol. I
Stokes, Sir (Frederick) Wilfrid Scott, 1860–1927, vol. II
Stokes, Sir Gabriel, 1849–1920, vol. II
Stokes, Sir George Gabriel, 1st Bt, 1819–1903, vol. I
Stokes, George Joseph, 1859–1935, vol. III
Stokes, Rev. George Thomas, 1843–1898, vol. I
Stokes, George Vernon, 1873–1954, vol. V

Stokes, Rear-Adm. Graham Henry, 1902–1969, vol. VI
Stokes, Haldane Day, 1885–1915, vol. I
Stokes, Sir Harold Frederick, 1899–1977, vol. VII
Stokes, Col Harold William Puzey, 1878–1949, vol. IV
Stokes, Sir Henry Edward, 1841–1926, vol. II
Stokes, Rev. Henry Paine, 1849–1931, vol. III
Stokes, Sir Hopetoun Gabriel, 1873–1951, vol. V
Stokes, Hugh, 1875–1932, vol. III
Stokes, Sir John, 1825–1902, vol. I
Stokes, Leonard Aloysius Scott, 1858–1925, vol. II
Stokes, Brig. Ralph Shelton Griffin, 1882–1979, vol. VII
Stokes, Rt Hon. Richard Rapier, 1897–1957, vol. V
Stokes, Sir Robert Baret, 1833–1899, vol. I
Stokes, Rear-Adm. Robert Henry Simpson, 1855–1914, vol. I
Stokes, Whitley, 1830–1909, vol. I
Stokes, Sir Wilfrid; see Stokes, Sir F. W. S.
Stokes, Sir William, 1839–1900, vol. I
Stokes, William Henry, 1894–1977, vol. VII
Stokowski, Leopold Boleslawowicz Stanislaw Antoni, 1887–1977, vol. VII
Stoll, Sir Oswald, 1866–1942, vol. IV
Stollery, Col John, 1852–1940, vol. III
Stone, Ven. Arthure Edward, 1852–1927, vol. II
Stone, Sir Benjamin; see Stone, Sir J. B.
Stone, Bertram Gilchrist, 1903–1978, vol. VII
Stone, Sir Charles, 1850–1931, vol. III
Stone, Christopher Reynolds, 1882–1965, vol. VI
Stone, Rev. Darwell, 1859–1941, vol. IV
Stone, Hon. Sir Edward Albert, 1844–1920, vol. II
Stone, Edward James, 1831–1897, vol. I
Stone, Brig.-Gen. Francis Gleadowe, 1857–1929, vol. III
Stone, George Frederick, 1855–1928, vol. II
Stone, Sir Gilbert, 1886–1967, vol. VI
Stone, Harlan F., 1872–1946, vol. IV
Stone, Rev. Henry Cecil Brough, died 1936, vol. III
Stone, Henry Walter James, 1877–1954, vol. V
Stone, Air Vice-Marshal James Ambrose, 1885–1966, vol. VI
Stone, Sir (John) Benjamin, 1838–1914, vol. I
Stone, Sir (John) Leonard, 1896–1978, vol. VII
Stone, John William, 1852–1936, vol. III
Stone, Sir Joseph Henry, 1858–1941, vol. IV
Stone, Sir Leonard; see Stone, Sir J. L.
Stone, Col Lionel George Tempest, 1874–1946, vol. IV
Stone, Marcus, 1840–1921, vol. II
Stone, Brig.-Gen. Percy Vere Powys, 1883–1959, vol. V
Stone, Reynolds, 1909–1979, vol. VII
Stone, Richard Evelyn, 1914–1980, vol. VII
Stone, Lt-Gen. Robert Graham William Hawkins, 1890–1974, vol. VII
Stone, Rev. Samuel John, 1839–1900, vol. I
Stone, Thomas Archibald, 1900–1965, vol. VI
Stone, Rev. W. H., 1860–1920, vol. II
Stone, William, 1857–1958, vol. V
Stone, William George Rush, 1855–1939, vol. III

Stone, Very Rev. William Henry, *died* 1912, vol. I
Stone-Wigg, Rt Rev. Montagu John, 1861–1918, vol. II
Stoneham, Sir Ralph Thompson, 1888–1965, vol. VI
Stoneham, Robert Thompson Douglas, 1883–1962, vol. VI
Stonehaven, 1st Viscount, 1874–1941, vol. IV
Stonehewer Bird, Sir Hugh, 1891–1973, vol. VII
Stonehouse, Sir Edmund, 1854–1938, vol. III
Stoneley, Robert, 1894–1976, vol. VII
Stoneman, Walter E., 1876–1958, vol. V
Stoner, Edmund Clifton, 1899–1968, vol. VI
Stones, Sir Frederick, 1886–1947, vol. IV
Stones, Hubert Horace, 1892–1965, vol. VI
Stones, James, *died* 1935, vol. III
Stones, William, 1904–1969, vol. VI
Stonestreet, George William, 1863–1940, vol. III
Stonex, Rev. Francis Tilney, 1857–1920, vol. II
Stoney, Bindon Blood, 1828–1909, vol. I
Stoney, Edith Anne, 1869–1938, vol. III
Stoney, Edward Waller, *died* 1931, vol. III
Stoney, Florence Ada, 1870–1932, vol. III
Stoney, George Gerald, 1863–1942, vol. IV
Stoney, George Johnstone, 1826–1911, vol. I
Stoney, Richard Atkinson, 1877–1966, vol. VI
Stoney-Smith, Major Herbert; *see* Smith.
Stonham, Baron (Life Peer); Victor John Collins, 1903–1971, vol. VII
Stonham, Charles, 1858–1916, vol. II
Stonham, Edwin Earle, 1867–1934, vol. III
Stonhouse, Sir Arthur Allan, 17th Bt, and 13th Bt, 1885–1967, vol. VI
Stonhouse, Sir Ernest Hay, 16th Bt, and 12th Bt, 1855–1937, vol. III
Stonor, Most Rev. Mgr Hon. Edmund, 1831–1912, vol. I
Stonor, Hon. Edward Alexander, 1867–1940, vol. III
Stonor, Hon. Sir Harry, 1859–1939, vol. III
Stonor, Henry James, 1820–1908, vol. I
Stonor, Oswald Francis Gerard, 1872–1940, vol. III
Stoodley, Edwin Edward, 1844–1922, vol. II
Stopes, Charlotte Carmichael, *died* 1929, vol. III
Stopes, Marie Carmichael, *died* 1958, vol. V
Stopford of Fallowfield, Baron (Life Peer); John Sebastian Bach Stopford, 1888–1961, vol. VI
Stopford, Vice-Adm. Hon. Arthur, 1879–1955, vol. V
Stopford, Francis Powys, 1861–1935, vol. III
Stopford, Lt-Gen. Hon. Sir Frederick William, 1854–1929, vol. III
Stopford, Captain Hon. Guy, 1884–1954, vol. V
Stopford, Hon. Horatia Charlotte Frances, 1835–1920, vol. II
Stopford, Rev. John Bird, 1859–1934, vol. III
Stopford, Maj.-Gen. Sir Lionel Arthur Montagu, 1860–1942, vol. IV
Stopford, Louise, *died* 1935, vol. III
Stopford, Gen. Sir Montagu George North, 1892–1971, vol. VII
Stopford, Robert Jemmett, 1895–1978, vol. VII
Stopford, Vice-Adm. Robert Wilbraham, 1844–1911, vol. I

Stopford, Rt Rev. and Rt Hon. Robert Wright, 1901–1976, vol. VII
Stopford Sackville, Col Nigel Victor, 1901–1972, vol. VII
Stopford-Taylor, Richard, 1884–1964, vol. VI
Stopp, Eric John Carl, 1894–1967, vol. VI
Stoppani, Rt Rev. Antonio, 1873–1940, vol. III (A), vol. IV
Stops, Col George, 1876–1940, vol. III
Storer, Bellamy, 1847–1922, vol. II
Storey, Charles Ambrose, 1888–1967, vol. VI
Storey, Major Charles Ernest, 1877–1943, vol. IV
Storey, Hon. Sir David, 1856–1924, vol. II
Storey, George Adolphus, 1834–1919, vol. II
Storey, Gladys; *see* Storey, M. G.
Storey, Harold Haydon, 1894–1969, vol. VI
Storey, Sir John Stanley, 1896–1955, vol. V
Storey, (Mary) Gladys, *died* 1978, vol. VII
Storey, Robert Holme, *died* 1956, vol. V
Storey, Samuel, 1840–1925, vol. II
Storey, Samuel; *see* Baron Buckton.
Storey, Sir Thomas, 1825–1898, vol. I
Storey, Sir Thomas James, 1851–1933, vol. III
Storke, Arthur Ditchfield, 1894–1949, vol. IV
Storkey, Percy Valentine, 1893–1969, vol. VI
Storm, Lesley, *died* 1975, vol. VII
Stormonth-Darling, Hon. Lord; Moir Tod Stormonth-Darling, 1844–1912, vol. I
Stormonth-Darling, Major John Collier, 1878–1916, vol. III
Stormonth-Darling, Moir Tod; *see* Hon. Lord Stormonth-Darling.
Storr, Francis, 1839–1919, vol. II
Storr, Lt-Col Lancelot, 1874–1944, vol. IV
Storr, Rev. Canon Vernon Faithfull, 1869–1940, vol. III
Storrar, Air Vice-Marshal Sydney Ernest, 1895–1969, vol. VI
Storrs, Rt Rev. Christopher E., 1889–1977, vol. VII
Storrs, Very Rev. John, *died* 1928, vol. II
Storrs, Rear-Adm. Robert Francis, 1906–1968, vol. VI
Storrs, Sir Ronald, 1881–1955, vol. V
Storrs, William Hargrave, 1880–1964, vol. VI
Story, A. B. Herbert, *died* 1910, vol. I
Story, Alfred Thomas, 1842–1934, vol. III
Story, Arthur John, 1864–1938, vol. III
Story, Douglas, 1872–1921, vol. II
Story, Janet Leith, 1828–1926, vol. II
Story, John Benjamin, *died* 1926, vol. II
Story, Lt-Gen. Philip, 1840–1916, vol. II
Story, Very Rev. Robert Herbert, 1835–1907, vol. I
Story, Col William Frederick, *died* 1939, vol. III
Story, Adm. William Oswald, 1859–1938, vol. III
Stothert, Sir Percy Kendall, 1863–1929, vol. III
Stott, Sir Arnold Walmsley, *died* 1958, vol. V
Stott, Edward, *died* 1918, vol. III
Stott, Sir George Edward, 2nd Bt, 1887–1957, vol. V
Stott, Maj.-Gen. Hugh, 1884–1966, vol. VI
Stott, May, (Lady Stott; May B. Lee), *died* 1977, vol. VII
Stott, Sir Philip Sidney, 1st Bt, 1858–1937, vol. III

Stott, Sir Philip Sidney, 3rd Bt, 1914–1979, vol. VII
Stott, Lt-Col William Henry, 1863–1930, vol. III
Stoughton, Rev. John, 1807–1897, vol. I
Stoughton, Raymond Henry, 1903–1979, vol. VII
Stourton, Col Hon. Edward Plantagenet Joseph Corbally, 1880–1966, vol. VI
Stourton, Rt Rev. Mgr Joseph, 1845–1921, vol. II
Stout, Sir Duncan; see Stout, Sir T. D. M.
Stout, George Frederick, 1860–1944, vol. IV
Stout, Percy Wyfold, 1875–1937, vol. III
Stout, Rt Hon. Sir Robert, 1844–1930, vol. III
Stout, Sir (Thomas) Duncan (Macgregor), 1885–1979, vol. VII
Stow, Sir Alexander Montague, 1873–1936, vol. III
Stow, Sir Elliot Philipson Philipson-, 2nd Bt, 1876–1954, vol. V
Stow, Sir Frederic Lawrence Philipson-, 3rd Bt, 1905–1976, vol. VII
Stow, Sir Frederic Samuel Philipson-, 1st Bt, 1849–1908, vol. I
Stow, Robert Frederic Philipson-, 1878–1949, vol. IV
Stow, Vincent Aubrey Stewart, 1883–1968, vol. VI
Stow Hill, Baron (Life Peer); Frank Soskice, 1902–1979, vol. VII
Stowe, Leonard, 1837–1920, vol. II
Stowell, Lt-Col Arthur Terence, 1873–1945, vol. IV
Stowell, Gordon William, 1898–1972, vol. VII
Stowell, Rev. Thomas Alfred, 1831–1916, vol. II
Stowell, Thomas Edmund Alexander, died 1970, vol. VI
Stowers, Arthur, 1897–1977, vol. VII
Strabolgi, 9th Baron, 1853–1934, vol. III
Strabolgi, 10th Baron, 1886–1953, vol. V
Stracey, Sir Edward Paulet, 7th Bt, 1871–1949, vol. IV
Stracey, Maj.-Gen. Henry, 1839–1930, vol. III
Stracey, Sir Michael George Motley, 8th Bt, 1911–1971, vol. VII
Stracey-Clitherow, Lt-Col John Bourchier, 1853–1931, vol. III
Strachan, Hon. Lord; James Frederick Strachan, 1894–1978, vol. VII
Strachan, Sir Andrew Henry, 1895–1976, vol. VII
Strachan, Douglas, 1875–1950, vol. IV
Strachan, Gilbert Innes, 1888–1963, vol. VI
Strachan, James, died 1917, vol. II
Strachan, James Frederick; see Strachan, Hon. Lord.
Strachan, John, 1838–1918, vol. II
Strachan, John, 1877–1934, vol. III
Strachan, Rev. Robert Harvey, 1873–1958, vol. V
Strachan, William Henry Williams, died 1921, vol. II
Strachan-Davidson, James Leigh, 1843–1916, vol. II
Strachey, Hon. Sir Arthur, 1858–1901, vol. I
Strachey, Sir Charles, 1862–1942, vol. IV
Strachey, Christopher, 1916–1975, vol. VII
Strachey, Sir Edward, 3rd Bt, 1812–1901, vol. I
Strachey, Rt Hon. (Evelyn) John (St Loe), 1901–1963, vol. VI
Strachey, (Giles) Lytton, 1880–1932, vol. III

Strachey, Jane Maria, (Lady Strachey), died 1928, vol. II
Strachey, Joan Pernel, 1876–1951, vol. V
Strachey, Sir John, 1823–1907, vol. I (A)
Strachey, Rt Hon. John; see Strachey, Rt Hon. E. J. St L.
Strachey, John St Loe, 1860–1927, vol. II
Strachey, Lytton; see Strachey, G. L.
Strachey, Oliver, 1874–1960, vol. V
Strachey, Mrs Oliver; see Strachey, Ray.
Strachey, Philippa, 1872–1968, vol. VI
Strachey, Ray, 1887–1940, vol. III
Strachey, Lt-Gen. Sir Richard, 1817–1908, vol. I
Strachey, Col Richard John, 1861–1935, vol. III
Strachie, 1st Baron, 1858–1936, vol. III
Strachie, 2nd Baron, 1882–1973, vol. VII
Stradbroke, 3rd Earl of, 1862–1947, vol. IV
Stradling, Sir Reginald Edward, died 1952, vol. V
Strafford, 3rd Earl of, 1830–1898, vol. I
Strafford, 4th Earl of, 1831–1899, vol. I
Strafford, 5th Earl of, 1835–1918, vol. II
Strafford, 6th Earl of, 1862–1951, vol. V
Strafford, Countess of; (Alice), 1830–1928, vol. II
Strafford, Air Marshal Stephen Charles, 1898–1966, vol. VI
Straghan, Col Abel, 1836–1914, vol. I
Strahan, Sir Aubrey, 1852–1928, vol. II
Strahan, Lt-Gen. Charles, 1843–1930, vol. III
Strahan, Frank, 1886–1976, vol. VII
Strahan, Lt-Col Geoffrey Carteret, 1886–1973, vol. VII
Strahan, Rev. James, 1863–1926, vol. II
Strahan, James Andrew, 1858–1930, vol. III
Straight, Sir Douglas, 1844–1914, vol. I
Straight, Major Douglas Marshall, 1869–1949, vol. IV
Straight, Whitney Willard, 1912–1979, vol. VII
Strain, Euphans H., died 1934, vol. III
Strain, Lt-Col Laurence Hugh, 1876–1952, vol. V
Straker, Herbert, 1856–1929, vol. III
Straker, John Coppin, 1847–1937, vol. III
Straker, William, 1855–1941, vol. IV
Straker-Smith, Sir Thomas D., 1890–1970, vol. VI
Strakosch, Sir Henry, 1871–1943, vol. IV
Stralia, Elsa, died 1945, vol. IV
Stranders, Michael O'Connell, 1911–1973, vol. VII
Strang, 1st Baron, 1893–1978, vol. VII
Strang, Alexander Ronald, 1848–1926, vol. II
Strang, Ian, 1886–1952, vol. V
Strang, John Martin, 1888–1970, vol. VI
Strang, William, 1859–1921, vol. II
Strang-Watkins, Watkin, 1869–1921, vol. II
Strange of Knokin, Baroness; see St Davids, Viscountess.
Strange, Rev. Cresswell, 1842–1905, vol. I
Strange, Lt-Col Edward Fairbrother, 1862–1929, vol. III
Strange, Lt-Col Louis Arbon, 1891–1966, vol. VI
Strange, Brig.-Gen. Robert George, 1861–1949, vol. IV
Strange, Maj.-Gen. Thomas Bland, 1831–1925, vol. II
Stranger, Innes Harold, 1879–1936, vol. III
Strangman, James Gonville, 1902–1977, vol. VII

Strangman, Sir Thomas Joseph, 1873–1971, vol. VII
Strangways, Arthur Henry Fox, 1859–1948, vol. IV
Strangways, Mary, died 1945, vol. IV
Strangways, Maurice Walter F.; see Fox-Strangways.
Stransham, Sir Anthony Blaxland, 1805–1900, vol. I
Strategicus; see O'Neill, H. C.
Stratford, Brig.-Gen. Cecil Vernon W.; see Wingfield-Stratford.
Stratford, Esmé Cecil W.; see Wingfield-Stratford.
Stratford, Rt Hon. James, 1869–1952, vol. V
Strath, Sir William, 1906–1975, vol. VII
Strathalmond, 1st Baron, 1888–1970, vol. VI
Strathalmond, 2nd Baron, 1916–1976, vol. VII
Strathcarron, 1st Baron, 1880–1937, vol. III
Strathclyde, 1st Baron, 1853–1928, vol. II
Strathcona and Mount Royal, 1st Baron, 1820–1914, vol. I
Strathcona and Mount Royal, Baroness (2nd in line), 1854–1926, vol. II
Strathcona and Mount Royal, 3rd Baron, 1891–1959, vol. V
Strathearn, Sir John Calderwood, 1878–1950, vol. IV
Stratheden, 3rd Baron, and Campbell, 3rd Baron, 1829–1918, vol. II
Stratheden and Campbell, Lady; (Jean Helen), died 1956, vol. V
Strathie, Sir (David) Norman, 1886–1959, vol. V
Strathie, Sir Norman; see Strathie, Sir D. N.
Strathmore and Kinghorne, 13th Earl of, 1824–1904, vol. I
Strathmore and Kinghorne, 14th Earl of, 1855–1944, vol. IV
Strathmore and Kinghorne, 15th Earl of, 1884–1949, vol. IV
Strathmore and Kinghorne, 16th Earl of, 1918–1972, vol. VII
Strathspey, 4th Baron, 1879–1948, vol. IV
Straton, Rt Rev. Norman Dumenil John, 1840–1918, vol. II
Stratten, Thomas Price, 1904–1980, vol. VII
Strattmann, HSH Edmund B.; see Batthyany-Strattmann.
Stratton, Arthur, died 1955, vol. V
Stratton, Sir (Francis) John, 1906–1976, vol. VII
Stratton, Frederick John Marrian, 1881–1960, vol. V
Stratton, Hon. J. R., 1858–1916, vol. II
Stratton, Sir John; see Stratton, Sir F. J.
Stratton, Rev. Joseph, 1839–1917, vol. II
Stratton, Lt-Col Wallace Christopher Ramsay, 1862–1942, vol. IV
Stratton-Porter, Gene; see Porter.
Strauchon, John, 1848–1934, vol. III
Straus, Bertram Stuart, 1867–1933, vol. III
Straus, Nathan, 1848–1931, vol. III
Straus, Oscar, 1870–1954, vol. V
Straus, Oscar S., 1850–1926, vol. II
Straus, Ralph, 1882–1950, vol. IV
Strauss, Arthur, 1847–1920, vol. II
Strauss, Edward Anthony, 1862–1939, vol. III

Strauss, Eric Benjamin, 1894–1961, vol. VI
Strauss, Adm. Joseph, 1861–1948, vol. IV
Strauss, Lewis L., 1896–1974, vol. VII
Strauss, Richard, 1864–1949, vol. IV
Stravinsky, Igor, 1882–1971, vol. VII
Streat, Sir (Edward) Raymond, 1897–1979, vol. VII
Streat, Sir Raymond; see Streat, Sir E. R.
Streatfeild, Frank Newton, 1843–1916, vol. II
Streatfeild, Sir Geoffrey Hugh Benbow, 1897–1979, vol. VII
Streatfeild, Mrs Granville, (Lucy Anne Evelyn Streatfeild), died 1950, vol. IV
Streatfeild, Col Sir Henry, 1857–1938, vol. III
Streatfeild, Rev. Henry Bertram, 1852–1922, vol. II
Streatfeild, Henry Cuthbert, 1866–1950, vol. IV
Streatfeild, Lucy Anne Evelyn; see Streatfeild, Mrs Granville.
Streatfeild, Richard Alexander, 1866–1919, vol. II
Streatfeild, Brig. Richard John, 1903–1952, vol. V
Streatfeild, Rt Rev. William Champion, 1865–1929, vol. III
Streatfield, Captain Eric, died 1902, vol. I
Street, Lt-Col Alfred William Frederick, 1852–1911, vol. I
Street, Arthur George, 1892–1966, vol. VI
Street, Sir Arthur William, 1892–1951, vol. V
Street, Lt-Col Ashton, 1864–1946, vol. IV
Street, Captain Edmund Rochfort, died 1916, vol. II
Street, Fanny, 1877–1962, vol. VI
Street, Brig. Hon. Geoffrey Austin, 1894–1940, vol. III
Street, George Slythe, 1867–1936, vol. III
Street, Col Harold Edward, died 1917, vol. II
Street, John Hugh, 1914–1977, vol. VII
Street, Hon. Sir Kenneth Whistler, 1890–1972, vol. VII
Street, Hon. Sir Philip Whistler, 1863–1938, vol. III
Street, Reginald Owen, 1890–1967, vol. VI
Street, Robert William, 1860–1954, vol. V
Street, Maj.-Gen. Vivian Wakefield, 1912–1970, vol. VI
Street, William P. R., 1841–1906, vol. I
Streeter, Rev. Burnett Hillman, 1874–1937, vol. III
Streeter, Wilfrid A., 1877–1962, vol. VI
Streeton, Sir Arthur, 1867–1943, vol. IV
Streicher, Most Rev. Henry, 1863–1944, vol. IV
Stresemann, Gustav, 1878–1929, vol. III
Stretch, Rt Rev. John Francis, 1855–1919, vol. II
Strettell, Maj.-Gen. Sir C. B. Dashwood, 1881–1958, vol. V
Stretten, Charles James Derrickson, 1830–1919, vol. II
Stretton, Lt-Col Arthur John, 1863–1947, vol. IV
Stretton, Hesba, 1832–1911, vol. I
Stretton, Leonard Edward Bishop, 1893–1967, vol. VI
Stribling, Thomas Sigismund, 1881–1965, vol. VI
Strick, Col John, 1838–1903, vol. I
Strick, Maj.-Gen. John Arkwright, 1870–1934, vol. III
Strickland, 1st Baron, 1861–1940, vol. III
Strickland, Algernon Henry Peter, 1863–1928, vol. II

Strickland, Algernon Walter, 1891–1938, vol. III
Strickland, Rear-Adm. Sir Arthur Foster, 1882–1955, vol. V
Strickland, Barbara, (Lady Strickland), 1884–1977, vol. VII
Strickland, Sir Charles William, 8th Bt, 1819–1909, vol. I
Strickland, Claude Francis, 1881–1962, vol. VI
Strickland, Gen. Sir (Edward) Peter, 1869–1951, vol. V
Strickland, Frederic, 1867–1934, vol. III
Strickland, Henry H.; see Hornyold-Strickland.
Strickland, Hon. Mary Constance Elizabeth Christina H.; see Hornyold-Strickland.
Strickland, Captain Paul Sebring, 1885–1964, vol. VI
Strickland, Gen. Sir Peter; see Strickland, Gen. Sir E. P.
Strickland, Walter G., 1850–1928, vol. II
Strickland, Sir Walter William, 9th Bt, 1851–1938, vol. III
Strickland, Captain William Frederick, 1880–1954, vol. V
Strickland-Constable, Sir Henry Marmaduke, 10th Bt, 1900–1975, vol. VII
Striedinger, Col Oscar, 1875–1938, vol. III
Strijdom, Hon. Johannes Gerhardus, 1893–1958, vol. V
Strindberg, Auguste, 1849–1912, vol. I
Stringer, Most Rev. Isaac O., 1866–1934, vol. III
Stringer, John Daniel, 1914–1971, vol. VII
Stringer, Sir (Thomas) Walter, 1855–1944, vol. IV
Stringer, Sir Walter; see Stringer, Sir T. W.
Stritch, His Eminence Cardinal Samuel Alphonsus, 1887–1958, vol. V
Strobl, Kisfalud Sigismund de, 1884–1975, vol. VII
Strode, Edward David C.; see Chetham-Strode.
Strode, Warren C.; see Chetham-Strode.
Strode-Jackson, Col Arnold Nugent Strode, died 1972, vol. VII
Strohmenger, Sir Ernest John, 1873–1967, vol. VI
Stromeyer, Charles E., 1856–1935, vol. III
Stronach, Catherine Geddes, died 1962, vol. VI
Stronach, John Clark, 1887–1967, vol. VI
Strong, Lt-Col Addington Dawsonne, 1875–1930, vol. III
Strong, Sir Archibald Thomas, 1876–1930, vol. III
Strong, Austin, 1881–1952, vol. V
Strong, Rev. Charles, 1844–1942, vol. IV
Strong, Maj.-Gen. Dawsonne Melancthon, died 1903, vol. I
Strong, Rev. Canon Edward Herbert, died 1960, vol. VI (AI)
Strong, Emilia Francis; see Dilke, E. F.
Strong, Eugénie, 1860–1943, vol. IV
Strong, Lt-Col Henry Stuart, 1873–1949, vol. IV
Strong, Herbert A., died 1918, vol. II
Strong, Hugh W., 1861–1920, vol. II
Strong, John, 1868–1945, vol. IV
Strong, John Alexander, 1844–1917, vol. II
Strong, Leonard Alfred George, 1896–1958, vol. V
Strong, Richard Pearson, 1872–1948, vol. IV
Strong, Rt Hon. Sir Samuel Henry, 1825–1909, vol. I

Strong, Sandford Arthur, 1863–1904, vol. I
Strong, Rt Rev. Thomas Banks, 1861–1944, vol. IV
Strong, Rt Hon. Sir Thomas Vezey, died 1920, vol. II
Strong, Brig.-Gen. William, 1870–1956, vol. V
Stronge, Sir Charles Edmond Sinclair, 7th Bt, 1862–1939, vol. III
Stronge, Sir Francis William, 1856–1924, vol. II
Stronge, Sir Herbert Cecil, 1875–1963, vol. VI
Stronge, Brig. Humphrey Cecil Travell, 1891–1977, vol. VII
Stronge, Rt Hon. Sir James Henry, 5th Bt, 1849–1928, vol. II
Stronge, Sir John Calvert, 4th Bt, 1813–1899, vol. I
Stronge, Sir Walter Lockhart, 6th Bt, 1860–1933, vol. III
Stross, Sir Barnett, 1899–1967, vol. VI
Strother-Stewart, Robert; see Stewart.
Stroud, Lt-Gen. Edward James, 1867–1935, vol. III
Stroud, Frederick, 1835–1912, vol. I
Stroud, Henry, 1861–1940, vol. III
Stroud, William, 1860–1938, vol. III
Stroyan, John, 1856–1941, vol. IV
Struben, William Charles Marinus, 1856–1928, vol. II (A), vol. III
Strudwick, Ethel, 1880–1954, vol. V
Strudwick, J. M., 1849–1937, vol. III
Strugnell, Surg. Rear-Adm. Lionel Frederick, 1892–1962, vol. VI
Struther, Jan, (Mrs A. K. Placzek), 1901–1953, vol. V
Struthers, Sir John, 1823–1899, vol. I
Struthers, Sir John, 1857–1925, vol. II
Strutt, Alfred William, died 1924, vol. II
Strutt, Vice-Adm. Hon. Arthur Charles, 1878–1973, vol. VII
Strutt, Sir Austin; see Strutt, Sir H. A.
Strutt, Hon. Charles Hedley, 1849–1926, vol. II
Strutt, Hon. Edward Gerald, 1854–1930, vol. III
Strutt, Lt-Col Edward Lisle, 1874–1948, vol. IV
Strutt, Geoffrey St John, 1888–1971, vol. VII
Strutt, George Herbert, 1854–1928, vol. II
Strutt, Sir (Henry) Austin, 1903–1979, vol. VII
Strutt, Maj.-Gen. J. R., 1831–1909, vol. I
Strutt, Hon. Richard, 1848–1927, vol. II
Strutt, William, died 1915, vol. I
Struve, Otto, 1897–1963, vol. VI
Stryker, M. Woolsey, 1851–1929, vol. III
Strzygowski, Josef, 1862–1941, vol. IV
Stuart, Viscount; David Andrew Noel Stuart, 1921–1942, vol. IV
Stuart, Viscount; Robert John Ochiltree Stuart, 1923–1944, vol. IV
Stuart of Findhorn, 1st Viscount, 1897–1971, vol. VII
Stuart of Wortley, 1st Baron, 1851–1926, vol. II
Stuart, Sir Alexander M.; see Moody-Stuart.
Stuart, Alexander Mackenzie, 1877–1935, vol. III
Stuart, Alexander Moody, died 1915, vol. I (A)
Stuart, Andrew Edmund Castlestuart, died 1936, vol. III

Stuart, Maj.-Gen. Sir Andrew Mitchell, 1861–1936, vol. III

Stuart, Arthur Constable M.; *see* Maxwell Stuart.

Stuart, Col Burleigh Francis Brownlow, 1868–1952, vol. V

Stuart, Sir Campbell, *died* 1972, vol. VII

Stuart, Charles Allan, 1864–1926, vol. II

Stuart, Rear-Adm. Charles Gage, 1887–1970, vol. VI

Stuart, Sir Charles James, 2nd Bt (*cr* 1840), 1824–1901, vol. I

Stuart, Lt-Col Charles Kennedy-Craufurd-, *died* 1942, vol. IV

Stuart, Charles Maddock, 1857–1932, vol. III

Stuart, Charles Russell, 1895–1975, vol. VII

Stuart, Lord Colum Edmund C.; *see* Crichton-Stuart.

Stuart, Brig.-Gen. Donald MacKenzie, 1864–1946, vol. IV

Stuart, Dorothy Margaret, *died* 1963, vol. VI

Stuart, Maj.-Gen. Douglas, 1894–1955, vol. V

Stuart, Dudley, 1861–1939, vol. III

Stuart, Rev. Edward Alexander, 1853–1917, vol. II

Stuart, Sir Edward Andrew, 3rd Bt (*cr* 1840), 1832–1903, vol. I

Stuart, Rt Rev. Edward Craig, 1827–1911, vol. I

Stuart, George Eustace B.; *see* Burnett-Stuart.

Stuart, George Moody, 1851–1940, vol. III

Stuart, Gerald Fitzgerald, 1897–1938, vol. III

Stuart, Major Godfrey Richard Conyngham, 1866–1955, vol. V

Stuart, Sir Harold Arthur, 1860–1923, vol. II

Stuart, Very Rev. Henry Venn, 1864–1933, vol. III

Stuart, Herbert Constable M.; *see* Maxwell-Stuart.

Stuart, Hilda Violet, *died* 1975, vol. VII

Stuart, Sir Houlton John, 8th Bt (*cr* 1660), 1863–1959, vol. V

Stuart, Ian Malcolm Bowen, 1902–1969, vol. VI

Stuart, Rev. James, 1841–1911, vol. I

Stuart, Rt Hon. James, 1843–1913, vol. I

Stuart, Rev. Sir James, 4th Bt (*cr* 1840), 1837–1915, vol. I

Stuart, John, 1836–1926, vol. II

Stuart, John, 1847–1931, vol. III

Stuart, Col John Alexander Man, *died* 1908, vol. I

Stuart, John Matthew Blackwood, 1882–1942, vol. IV

Stuart, Col John Patrick V.; *see* Villiers-Stuart.

Stuart, Gen. Sir John Theodosius B.; *see* Burnett-Stuart.

Stuart, John Windsor, *died* 1905, vol. I

Stuart, Lt-Gen. Kenneth, 1891–1945, vol. IV

Stuart, Leslie, 1866–1928, vol. II

Stuart, Rear-Adm. Leslie Creery, 1851–1908, vol. I

Stuart, Brig. Lionel Arthur, 1892–1959, vol. V

Stuart, Sir Louis, 1870–1949, vol. IV

Stuart, Captain Murray, 1882–1967, vol. VI

Stuart, Lord Ninian Edward C.; *see* Crichton-Stuart.

Stuart, Norman; *see* Teeling, Mrs Bartle.

Stuart, Maj.-Gen. Sir Robert Charles Ochiltree, 1861–1948, vol. IV

Stuart, Captain Hon. Robert Sheffield, 1886–1914, vol. I (A)

Stuart, Captain Ronald Niel, 1886–1954, vol. V

Stuart, Ruth M'Enery, *died* 1917, vol. II

Stuart, Sir Simeon Henry Lechmere, 7th Bt (*cr* 1660), 1864–1939, vol. III

Stuart, Sir Thomas Anderson, 1856–1920, vol. II

Stuart, William C. S.; *see* Crawfurd-Stirling-Stuart.

Stuart, Maj.-Gen. William James, 1831–1914, vol. I

Stuart, Brig.-Gen. William V.; *see* Villiers-Stuart.

Stuart-Clark, Arthur Campbell, 1906–1973, vol. VII

Stuart-Forbes of Pitsligo, Sir Hugh; *see* Forbes of Pitsligo.

Stuart-Forbes-Trefusis, Major Hon. John Frederick Hepburn; *see* Trefusis.

Stuart-Jones, Sir Henry, 1867–1939, vol. III

Stuart-Knill, Sir Ian, 3rd Bt, 1886–1973, vol. VII

Stuart-Low, William, 1857–1935, vol. III

Stuart-Menteth, Sir James; *see* Menteth.

Stuart-Menteth, Lt-Col Sir James Frederick; *see* Menteth.

Stuart-Menteth, Sir William Frederick; *see* Menteth.

Stuart Taylor, Sir Richard Laurence, 3rd Bt, 1925–1978, vol. VII

Stuart-Williams, Sir Charles; *see* Stuart-Williams, Sir S. C.

Stuart-Williams, Sir (Sydney) Charles, 1876–1960, vol. V

Stuart-Wortley, Lt-Gen. Hon. Sir (Alan) Richard Montagu-, 1868–1949, vol. IV

Stuart-Wortley, Hon. Clare Euphemia, 1889–1945, vol. IV

Stuart-Wortley, Maj.-Gen. Hon. Edward James Montagu-, 1857–1934, vol. III

Stuart-Wortley, Lt-Gen. Hon. Sir Richard; *see* Stuart-Wortley, Lt-Gen. Hon. Sir A. R. M.

Stuart Wortley, Violet, (Hon. Mrs Edward Stuart Wortley), *died* 1953, vol. V

Stubbs, Albert Ernest, 1877–1962, vol. VI

Stubbs, Rev. Arthur James, 1861–1945, vol. IV

Stubbs, Rt Rev. Charles William, 1845–1912, vol. I

Stubbs, Sir Edward; *see* Stubbs, Sir R. E.

Stubbs, George, 1864–1940, vol. III

Stubbs, Brig.-Gen. Guy Clifford, 1883–1939, vol. III

Stubbs, Lawrence Morley, 1874–1958, vol. V

Stubbs, Sir (Reginald) Edward, 1876–1947, vol. IV

Stubbs, Roy, 1897–1951, vol. V

Stubbs, Stanley, 1906–1976, vol. VII

Stubbs, Sydney, 1861–1953, vol. V

Stubbs, Rt Rev. William, 1825–1901, vol. I

Stubbs, William, 1911–1967, vol. VI

Stuck, Ven. Hudson, 1863–1920, vol. II

Stuckey, Reginald Robert, 1881–1948, vol. IV

Stucley, Sir Edward Arthur George, 3rd Bt, 1852–1927, vol. II

Stucley, Sir George Stucley, 1st Bt, 1812–1900, vol. I

Stucley, Sir Hugh Nicholas Granville, 4th Bt, 1873–1956, vol. V

Stucley, Sir Lewis; *see* Stucley, Sir W. L.

Stucley, Sir (William) Lewis, 2nd Bt, 1836–1911, vol. I

Studd, C. T., *died* 1931, vol. III

Studd, Sir Eric, 2nd Bt, 1887–1975, vol. VII

Studd, Brig.-Gen. Herbert William, 1870–1947, vol. IV

Studd, Sir (John Edward) Kynaston, 1st Bt, 1858–1944, vol. IV

Studd, Sir Kynaston; *see* Studd, Sir J. E. K.

Studd, Sir Kynaston; *see* Studd, Sir R. K.

Studd, Brig. Malden Augustus, 1887–1973, vol. VII

Studd, Sir (Robert) Kynaston, 3rd Bt, 1926–1977, vol. VII

Studdert, Ven. Augustine John de Clare, 1901–1972, vol. VII

Studdert, Maj.-Gen. Robert Hallam, 1890–1968, vol. VI

Studdy, Sir Henry, 1894–1975, vol. VII

Studer, Paul, 1879–1927, vol. II

Studholme, Lt-Col John, 1863–1934, vol. III

Studholme, Sir Richard Home, 1901–1963, vol. VI

Stupart, Sir Frederic; *see* Stupart, Sir R. F.

Stupart, Sir (Robert) Frederic, 1857–1940, vol. III

Sturdee, Col Alfred Hobart, 1863–1939, vol. III

Sturdee, Admiral of the Fleet Sir Doveton; *see* Sturdee, Admiral of the Fleet Sir F. C. D.

Sturdee, Admiral of the Fleet Sir (Frederick Charles) Doveton, 1st Bt, 1859–1925, vol. II

Sturdee, Rear-Adm. Sir Lionel Arthur Doveton, 2nd Bt, 1884–1970, vol. VI

Sturdee, Rev. Robert James, 1879–1932, vol. III

Sturdee, Lt-Gen. Sir Vernon Ashton Hobart, 1890–1966, vol. VI

Sturdy, William Arthur, 1877–1958, vol. V

Sturge, Arthur Lloyd, 1868–1942, vol. IV

Sturge, William Allen, 1850–1919, vol. II

Sturges, Hugh Murray, 1863–1952, vol. V

Sturges, Lt-Gen. Sir Robert Grice, 1891–1970, vol. VI

Sturgess, Paymaster Rear-Adm. Richard Ernest Stanley, *died* 1933, vol. III

Sturgis, Julian, 1848–1904, vol. I

Sturgis, Sir Mark Beresford Russell G.; *see* Grant-Sturgis.

Sturley, Major Albert Avern, 1887–1922, vol. II

Sturrock, Alick Riddell, 1885–1953, vol. V

Sturrock, Hon. Claud; *see* Sturrock, Hon. F. C.

Sturrock, Hon. (Frederick) Claud, 1882–1958, vol. V

Sturrock, Brig. George Colleymore, *died* 1935, vol. III

Sturrock, John, 1845–1926, vol. II

Sturrock, Sir John Christian Ramsay, 1875–1937, vol. III

Sturrock, John Leng, 1878–1943, vol. IV

Sturrock, William Duncan, 1880–1942, vol. IV

Sturt, Maj.-Gen. Charles Sheppey, 1838–1910, vol. I

Sturt, George, 1863–1927, vol. II

Sturt, Hon. Gerard Philip Montagu Napier, 1893–1918, vol. II

Sturt, Lt-Col Robert Ramsay Napier, 1852–1907, vol. I

Stutchbury, George Frederick, 1844–1934, vol. III

Stutfield, Hugh E. M., 1858–1929, vol. III

Stuttaford, Hon. Richard, 1870–1945, vol. IV

Style, Sir Frederick Montague, 10th Bt, 1857–1930, vol. III

Style, Rev. George, *died* 1922, vol. II

Style, Sir William Frederick, 11th Bt, 1887–1943, vol. IV

Style, Sir William Henry Marsham, 9th Bt, 1826–1904, vol. I

Styles, (Herbert) Walter, 1889–1965, vol. VI

Styles, Walter; *see* Styles, H. W.

Suárez, Eduardo, 1895–1976, vol. VII

Suart, Evelyn, (Lady Harcourt), *died* 1950, vol. IV

Suart, Brig.-Gen. William Hodgson, 1850–1923, vol. II

Suckling, Rev. Charles William B.; *see* Baron-Suckling.

Suckling, Rev. Robert Alfred J., *died* 1917, vol. II

Sudborough, John Joseph, 1869–1963, vol. VI

Sudeley, 4th Baron, 1840–1922, vol. II

Sudeley, 5th Baron, 1870–1932, vol. III

Sudeley, 6th Baron, 1911–1941, vol. IV

Sudermann, Hermann, 1857–1928, vol. II

Sudmerson, Frederick William, *died* 1953, vol. V

Sueter, Rear-Adm. Sir Murray Fraser, 1872–1960, vol. V

Suffield, 5th Baron, 1830–1914, vol. I

Suffield, 6th Baron, 1855–1924, vol. II

Suffield, 7th Baron, 1897–1943, vol. IV

Suffield, 8th Baron, 1907–1945, vol. IV

Suffield, 9th Baron, 1861–1946, vol. IV

Suffield, 10th Baron, 1865–1951, vol. V

Suffolk, 18th Earl of, **and Berkshire,** 11th Earl of, 1833–1898, vol. I

Suffolk, 19th Earl of, **and Berkshire,** 12th Earl of, 1877–1917, vol. II

Suffolk, 20th Earl of, **and Berkshire,** 13th Earl of, 1906–1941, vol. IV

Sugden, Alan Victor, 1877–1956, vol. V

Sugden, Sir Bernard, 1877–1954, vol. V

Sugden, General Sir Cecil Stanway, 1903–1963, vol. VI

Sugden, Charles, 1850–1921, vol. II

Sugden, Frank, 1852–1927, vol. II

Sugden, Maj.-Gen. Sir Henry Haskins Clapham, 1904–1977, vol. VII

Sugden, Kaye Aspinall Ramsden, 1880–1966, vol. VI

Sugden, Brig.-Gen. Richard Edgar, 1871–1951, vol. V

Sugden, Gp Captain Ronald Scott, 1896–1971, vol. VII

Sugden, Samuel, 1892–1950, vol. IV

Sugden, Sir Wilfrid Hart, *died* 1960, vol. V

Sugerman, Sir Bernard, 1904–1976, vol. VII

Suggia, Guilhermina, 1888–1950, vol. IV

Suhrawardy, Sir Abdulla Al-Mamun, *died* 1935, vol. III

Suhrawardy, Lt-Col Sir Hassan, 1884–1946, vol. IV

Suhrawardy, Huseyn Shaheed, 1893–1963, vol. VI

Suhrawardy, Sir Zahhadur Rahim Zahid, 1870–1949, vol. IV

Sukhdeo Prasad Kak, Rao Bahadur Pandit Sir, 1862–1935, vol. III

Sukuna, Sir Joseva Lalabalavu Vanaaliali, *died* 1958, vol. V

Sulaiman, Sir Shah Muhammad, 1886–1941, vol. IV

Sulivan, Col Ernest Frederic, 1860–1928, vol. II

Sulivan, Vice-Adm. Norton Allen, 1879–1964, vol. VI

Sullivan, Alexander Martin, 1871–1959, vol. V

Sullivan, Rev. Arnold Moon, 1878–1943, vol. IV

Sullivan, Sir Arthur Seymour, 1842–1900, vol. I

Sullivan, Basil Martin, 1882–1946, vol. IV

Sullivan, Bernard Ponsonby, 1891–1958, vol. V

Sullivan, Hon. Daniel Giles, 1882–1947, vol. IV

Sullivan, Donal, 1838–1907, vol. I

Sullivan, Edmund J., 1869–1933, vol. III

Sullivan, Rt Rev. Edward, *died* 1899, vol. I

Sullivan, Sir Edward, 2nd Bt (*cr* 1881), 1852–1928, vol. II

Sullivan, Brig.-Gen. Edward Langford, 1865–1949, vol. IV

Sullivan, Sir Edward Robert, 5th Bt (*cr* 1804), 1826–1899, vol. I

Sullivan, Francis Loftus, 1903–1956, vol. V

Sullivan, Sir Francis William, 6th Bt (*cr* 1804), 1834–1906, vol. I

Sullivan, Rev. Sir Frederick, 7th Bt (*cr* 1804), 1865–1954, vol. V

Sullivan, Henry Edward, 1830–1905, vol. I

Sullivan, James Frank, *died* 1936, vol. III

Sullivan, John William Navin, 1886–1937, vol. III

Sullivan, Joseph, 1866–1935, vol. III

Sullivan, Very Rev. Martin Gloster, 1910–1980, vol. VII

Sullivan, Sir Richard Benjamin Magniac, 8th Bt (*cr* 1804), 1906–1977, vol. VII

Sullivan, Timothy, 1874–1949, vol. IV

Sullivan, Timothy Daniel, 1827–1914, vol. I

Sullivan, Sir William, 3rd Bt (*cr* 1881), 1860–1937, vol. III

Sullivan, Sir William, 1891–1967, vol. VI

Sullivan, William Charles, *died* 1926, vol. II

Sullivan, Sir William John, 1895–1971, vol. VII

Sullivan, Sir William Wilfred, 1843–1923, vol. II

Sully, James, 1842–1923, vol. II

Sully, Air Vice-Marshal John Alfred, 1892–1968, vol. VI (AII)

Sulman, Sir John, 1849–1934, vol. III

Sulte, Benjamin, 1841–1923, vol. II

Sulzberger, Arthur Hays, 1891–1968, vol. VI

Sulzberger, Mayer, 1843–1923, vol. II

Sumichrast, Frederick C. de, 1845–1933, vol. III

Summerbell, Thomas, 1861–1910, vol. I

Summerford, Engr Rear-Adm. Horace George, 1872–1963, vol. VI

Summerhayes, Lt-Col John Orlando, 1869–1942, vol. IV

Summerhays, Reginald Sherriff, 1881–1976, vol. VII

Summers, Rev. Alphonsus Joseph-Mary Augustus Montague, 1880–1948, vol. IV

Summers, Sir Geoffrey, 1st Bt, 1891–1972, vol. VII

Summers, Bt-Lt-Col Sir Gerald Henry, 1885–1925, vol. II

Summers, Sir (Gerard) Spencer, 1902–1976, vol. VII

Summers, James Woolley, 1849–1913, vol. I

Summers, Captain Joseph J., *died* 1954, vol. V

Summers, Sir Richard Felix, 1902–1977, vol. VII

Summers, Sir Spencer; *see* Summers, Sir G. S.

Summers, Thomas, *died* 1944, vol. IV

Summers, Walter Coventry, 1869–1937, vol. III

Summersby, Charles Harold, 1882–1961, vol. VI

Summerscale, Sir John Percival, 1901–1980, vol. VII

Summerskill, Baroness (Life Peer); Edith Summerskill, 1901–1980, vol. VII

Summerville, Sir Alan; *see* Summerville, Sir W. A. T.

Summerville, Sir (William) Alan (Thompson), 1904–1980, vol. VII

Sumner, 1st Viscount, 1859–1934, vol. III

Sumner, Benedict Humphrey, 1893–1951, vol. V

Sumner, Captain Berkeley H.; *see* Holme-Sumner.

Sumner, Rt Rev. George Henry, 1824–1909, vol. I

Sumner, James Batcheller, 1887–1955, vol. V

Sumner, Sir John, 1856–1934, vol. III

Sumner, John Richard Hugh, 1886–1971, vol. VII

Sundar Singh Majithia, Sirdar Sir, 1872–1941, vol. IV

Sundarlal, Hon. Pandit, 1857–1918, vol. II

Sunday, Rev. William Ashley, 1863–1935, vol. III

Sunderland, Earl of; John David Ivor Spencer-Churchill, 1952–1955, vol. V

Sunderland, J. E., 1885–1956, vol. V

Sunderland, Col Marsden Samuel James, 1841–1929, vol. III

Sunderland, Septimus Philip, *died* 1950, vol. IV

Sunley, Bernard, 1910–1964, vol. VI

Sunlight, Joseph, 1889–1978, vol. VII

Supervia, Conchita, 1899–1936, vol. III

Supomo, Raden, 1903–1958, vol. V

Supple, Col James Francis, 1843–1922, vol. II

Surfaceman; *see* Anderson, Alexander.

Surplice, Reginald Alwyn, 1906–1977, vol. VII

Surtees, Col Charles Freville, 1823–1906, vol. I

Surtees, Brig.-Gen. Sir Conyers, 1858–1933, vol. III

Surtees, Maj.-Gen. George, 1895–1976, vol. VII

Surtees, Major (Henry) Siward (Balliol), 1873–1955, vol. V

Surtees, Major Siward; *see* Surtees, Major H. S. B.

Surtees, Rt Rev. William F., 1871–1956, vol. V

Surveyer, Hon. Edouard-Fabre, 1875–1957, vol. V

Susskind, (Jan) Walter, 1913–1980, vol. VII

Susskind, Walter; *see* Susskind, J. W.

Sutch, Ven. Ronald Huntley, 1890–1975, vol. VII

Sutcliffe, Halliwell, 1870–1932, vol. III

Sutcliffe, Sir Harold, 1897–1958, vol. V

Sutcliffe, Bt Col Richard Douglas, *died* 1941, vol. IV

Sutcliffe, Tom, 1865–1931, vol. III

Sutcliffe, Very Rev. William Ormond, 1856–1944, vol. IV

Suter, George Edward, 1869–1939, vol. III

Suter, Captain Roy Neville, 1884–1958, vol. V

Suther, Gen. Cuthbert Collingwood, 1839–1927, vol. II

Suther, Brig. Percival, 1873–1945, vol. IV

Sutherland, 4th Duke of, 1851–1913, vol. I
Sutherland, 5th Duke of, 1888–1963, vol. VI
Sutherland, Duchess of; (Millicent Fanny), 1867–1955, vol. V
Sutherland, Alexander Malcolm G.; see Græme-Sutherland.
Sutherland, Algernon Robert, 1854–1933, vol. III
Sutherland, Angus, 1848–1922, vol. II
Sutherland, Sir Arthur Munro, 1st Bt, 1867–1953, vol. V
Sutherland, Sir (Benjamin) Ivan, 2nd Bt, 1901–1980, vol. VII
Sutherland, Charles Leslie, 1839–1911, vol. I
Sutherland, D. M., died 1951, vol. V
Sutherland, David M., 1883–1973, vol. VII
Sutherland, Lt-Col David Waters, 1871–1939, vol. III
Sutherland, Lt-Col Hon. Donald Matheson, 1879–1949, vol. IV
Sutherland, Earl Wilbur, 1915–1974, vol. VII
Sutherland, Edward Davenport, 1853–1923, vol. II
Sutherland, George Alexander, died 1939, vol. III
Sutherland, George Arthur, 1891–1970, vol. VI
Sutherland, Sir George Henry, 1866–1937, vol. III
Sutherland, Sir Gordon Brims Black McIvor, 1907–1980, vol. VII
Sutherland, Graham Vivian, 1903–1980, vol. VII
Sutherland, Halliday Gibson, 1882–1960, vol. V
Sutherland, Lt-Col Henry Homes, 1871–1940, vol. III
Sutherland, Sir Ivan; see Sutherland, Sir B. I.
Sutherland, Hon. James, 1849–1905, vol. I
Sutherland, Joan, died 1947, vol. IV
Sutherland, Sir John Donald, 1865–1952, vol. V
Sutherland, John Ebenezer, died 1918, vol. II
Sutherland, Lewis Robertson, 1863–1933, vol. III
Sutherland, Dame Lucy Stuart, 1903–1980, vol. VII
Sutherland, Mary Elizabeth, died 1972, vol. VII
Sutherland, Rt Hon. Robert Franklin, 1859–1922, vol. II
Sutherland, Sir Thomas, 1834–1922, vol. II
Sutherland, Hon. William, 1857–1935, vol. III
Sutherland, William, died 1945, vol. IV
Sutherland, Rt Hon. Sir William, 1880–1949, vol. IV
Sutherland, Hon. William Charles, 1865–1940, vol. III
Sutherland-Dunbar, Sir George Cospatrick D.; see Duff-Sutherland-Dunbar.
Sutherland-Dunbar, Sir George D.; see Duff-Sutherland-Dunbar.
Sutherland-Gower, Rt Hon. Lord Ronald; see Gower.
Sutherland-Harris, Lt-Col Alexander Sutherland, 1865–1934, vol. III
Sutherland-Leveson Gower, Major Lord Alastair St Clair; see Leveson Gower.
Suthers, Rev. Canon George, 1908–1965, vol. VI
Sutro, Alfred, 1863–1933, vol. III
Suttie, Sir George Grant-, 7th Bt, 1870–1947, vol. IV
Suttie, Col Hubert Francis Grant-, 1884–1973, vol. VII

Suttner, Baroness Bertha von, 1843–1914, vol. I
Sutton, Sir Abraham, 1849–1921, vol. II
Sutton, Maj.-Gen. Alexander Arthur, 1861–1941, vol. IV
Sutton, Col Alfred, died 1922, vol. II
Sutton, Rev. Alfred, 1851–1938, vol. III
Sutton, Sir Arthur, 7th Bt (cr 1772), 1857–1948, vol. IV
Sutton, Rev. Arthur Frederick, died 1925, vol. II
Sutton, Arthur Warwick, 1854–1925, vol. II
Sutton, Air Marshal Sir Bertine Entwisle, 1886–1946, vol. IV
Sutton, Engr Rear-Adm. Charles Edwin, 1880–1968, vol. VI
Sutton, Charles William, 1848–1920, vol. II
Sutton, Surg.-Rear-Adm. Edward, 1870–1940, vol. III
Sutton, Maj.-Gen. Evelyn Alexander, 1891–1964, vol. VI
Sutton, Maj.-Gen. F. A., 1884–1944, vol. IV
Sutton, Francis Henry Astley M.; see Manners-Sutton.
Sutton, Sir George, 1st Bt (cr 1922), 1856–1934, vol. III
Sutton, Sir George Augustus, 1st Bt, 1869–1947, vol. IV
Sutton, George Lowe, 1872–1964, vol. VI
Sutton, Hon. Sir George Morris, 1834–1913, vol. I
Sutton, Brig. George William, 1893–1971, vol. VII
Sutton, Sir Graham; see Sutton, Sir O. G.
Sutton, Sir Henry, 1845–1920, vol. II
Sutton, Rev. Henry, 1833–1921, vol. II
Sutton, Henry Cecil, 1868–1936, vol. III
Sutton, Maj.-Gen. Hugh Clement, 1867–1928, vol. II
Sutton, John Edward, 1862–1945, vol. IV
Sutton, Sir John Smale, died 1942, vol. IV
Sutton, Leonard Goodhart, 1863–1932, vol. III
Sutton, Martin Hubert Foquett, 1875–1930, vol. III
Sutton, Martin John, 1850–1913, vol. I
Sutton, Sir (Oliver) Graham, 1903–1977, vol. VII
Sutton, Ralph, 1881–1960, vol. V
Sutton, Sir Richard Vincent, 6th Bt (cr 1772), 1891–1918, vol. II
Sutton, Ven. Robert, 1832–1910, vol. I
Sutton, Stanley Cecil, 1907–1977, vol. VII
Sutton, Brig. William Moxhay, 1885–1949, vol. IV
Sutton Nelthorpe, Col Oliver, 1888–1963, vol. VI
Sutton-Nelthorpe, Robert Nassau, 1850–1937, vol. III
Sutton-Pratt, Brig. Reginald, 1898–1962, vol. VI
Suttor, Hon. Sir Francis Bathurst, 1839–1915, vol. I
Suvorin, Alexis, 1834–1912, vol. I
Suyematsu, Viscount Kencho, 1855–1920, vol. II
Swabey, Christopher, 1906–1972, vol. VII
Swabey, Vice-Adm. Sir George Thomas Carlisle Parker, 1881–1952, vol. V
Swabey, Brig.-Gen. Wilfred Spedding, 1871–1939, vol. III
Swaby, Ven. J. A. R., died 1944, vol. IV
Swaby, Rt Rev. John Cyril Emerson, 1905–1975, vol. VII

Swaby, Rt Rev. William Proctor, 1844–1916, vol. II

Swaffer, Hannen, 1879–1962, vol. VI

Swain, Rt Rev. Edgar Priestley, 1881–1949, vol. IV

Swain, Rev. Edmund Gill, 1861–1938, vol. III

Swain, Very Rev. George Lill, 1870–1955, vol. V

Swain, Hon. Col George Llewellyn Douglas, 1858–1924, vol. II

Swain, James, died 1951, vol. V

Swain, Joseph, 1857–1927, vol. II

Swain, Percival Francis, 1888–1924, vol. II

Swain, Thomas Henry, 1911–1979, vol. VII

Swain, Walter, 1876–1945, vol. IV

Swaine, Col Charles Edward, 1844–1928, vol. II

Swaine, Maj.-Gen. Sir Leopold Victor, 1840–1931, vol. III

Swainson, Maj.-Gen. Frederick Joseph, 1911–1965, vol. VI

Swainson, Willan, died 1970, vol. VI

Swaish, Sir John, 1852–1931, vol. III

Swales, A. B., died 1952, vol. V

Swales, John Kirby, 1879–1956, vol. V

Swallow, Rev. Richard Dawson, 1847–1930, vol. III

Swamikannu Pillai, Louis Dominic, 1865–1925, vol. II

Swan, Sir Alexander Brown, 1869–1941, vol. IV

Swan, Alice Macallan, died 1939, vol. III

Swan, Annie Shepherd; see Smith, Mrs Burnett.

Swan, Col Charles Arthur, 1854–1941, vol. IV

Swan, Sir Charles Sheriton, 1870–1944, vol. IV

Swan, Captain Donald C.; see Cameron-Swan.

Swan, Rear-Adm. (S) Edgar Bocquet, 1874–1951, vol. V

Swan, Ernest William, 1883–1948, vol. IV

Swan, Harold Couch, 1890–1972, vol. VII

Swan, Henry Frederick, 1842–1908, vol. I

Swan, John Arthur Laing, 1877–1938, vol. III

Swan, John Edmund, 1877–1956, vol. V

Swan, John Macallan, 1847–1910, vol. I

Swan, Sir Joseph Wilson, 1828–1917, vol. I

Swan, Lt-Comdr Sir Kenneth Raydon, 1877–1973, vol. VII

Swan, Lionel Maynard, 1885–1969, vol. VI

Swan, Robert A., 1849–1937, vol. III

Swan, Robert Clayton, died 1929, vol. III

Swan, Russell Henry Jocelyn, 1876–1943, vol. IV

Swan, Maj.-Gen. William Travers, 1861–1949, vol. IV

Swanborough, Baroness (Life Peer); see Reading, Marchioness of.

Swann, Rev. Canon Alfred, died 1961, vol. VI

Swann, Rev. Cecil Gordon Aldersey, 1888–1969, vol. VI

Swann, Sir (Charles) Duncan, 2nd Bt, 1879–1962, vol. VI

Swann, Rt Hon. Sir Charles Ernest, 1st Bt, 1844–1929, vol. III

Swann, Sir Duncan; see Swann, Sir C. D.

Swann, Rev. Ernest Henry, 1869–1948, vol. IV

Swann, Frederick Samuel Philip, died 1921, vol. II

Swann, Harry Kirke, 1871–1926, vol. II (A), vol. III

Swann, Maj.-Gen. John Christopher, 1856–1939, vol. III

Swann, Louis Herbert H.; see Hartland-Swann.

Swann, Air Vice-Marshal Sir Oliver, 1878–1948, vol. IV

Swann, Rev. Sidney, 1862–1942, vol. IV

Swann, Rev. Canon Sidney Ernest, 1890–1976, vol. VII

Swann, William Francis Gray, 1884–1962, vol. VI

Swann-Mason, Rev. Richard Swann, died 1942, vol. IV

Swansea, 2nd Baron, 1848–1922, vol. II

Swansea, 3rd Baron, 1875–1934, vol. III

Swanson, John Leslie, 1892–1974, vol. VII

Swanson, Sir John Warren, 1865–1924, vol. II

Swanston, Lt-Col Charles Oliver, 1865–1914, vol. I

Swanston, John Francis Alexander, 1877–1958, vol. V

Swanwick, Anna, 1813–1899, vol. I

Swanwick, Harold, died 1929, vol. III

Swanwick, Helena Maria, 1864–1939, vol. III

Swanzy, Very Rev. Henry Biddall, 1873–1932, vol. III

Swanzy, Sir Henry Rosborough, died 1913, vol. I

Swanzy, Rev. Thomas Erskine, 1869–1950, vol. IV

Swarbrick, John, 1879–1964, vol. VI

Swarbrick, Thomas, 1900–1965, vol. VI

Swayne, Col Charles Henry, 1848–1925, vol. II

Swayne, Charles Richard, 1843–1921, vol. II

Swayne, Brig.-Gen. Sir Eric John Eagles, 1863–1929, vol. III

Swayne, Col. Harald George Carlos, 1860–1940, vol. III

Swayne, Maj.-Gen. James Dowell, 1827–1916, vol. II

Swayne, Lt-Gen. Sir John George des Réaux, 1890–1964, vol. VI

Swayne, Walter Carless, 1862–1925, vol. II

Swayne, Rt Rev. William Shuckburgh, 1862–1941, vol. IV

Swaythling, 1st Baron, 1832–1911, vol. I

Swaythling, 2nd Baron, 1869–1927, vol. II

Sweatman, Most Rev. Arthur, 1834–1909, vol. I

Sweeney, Hon. Francis J., 1862–1921, vol. II (A), vol. III

Sweeney, Very Rev. Canon Garrett Daniel, 1912–1979, vol. VII

Sweeney, James Augustine, 1883–1945, vol. IV

Sweeny, Most Rev. James Fielding, 1857–1940, vol. III

Sweeny, Lt-Col Roger Lewis Campbell, 1878–1926, vol. II

Sweet, Lt-Col Edward Herbert, 1871–1966, vol. VI

Sweet, Henry, 1845–1912, vol. I

Sweet, Ven. John Hales Sweet, 1849–1929, vol. III

Sweet-Escott, Sir Bickham; see Sweet-Escott, Sir E. B.

Sweet-Escott, Sir (Ernest) Bickham, 1857–1941, vol. IV

Sweeting, Richard Deane, 1856–1913, vol. I

Sweetman, Sir Henry, 1858–1944, vol. IV

Sweny, Captain William Halpin Paterson, 1871–1951, vol. V

Swete, Henry Barclay, 1835–1917, vol. II

Swetenham, Clement William, 1852–1927, vol. II

Swettenham, Sir Alexander, 1846–1933, vol. III

Swettenham, Sir Frank Athelstane, 1850–1946, vol. IV
Swettenham, Lt-Col George Kilner, 1866–1933, vol. III
Swettenham, Lt-Col William Alexander Whybault, 1870–1947, vol. IV
Swift, Brig.-Gen. Albert Edward, 1870–1948, vol. IV
Swift, Sir Brian Herbert, 1893–1969, vol. VI
Swift, Herbert Walker, 1894–1960, vol. V
Swift, Sir Rigby Philip Watson, 1874–1937, vol. III
Swifte, Sir Ernest Godwin, 1839–1927, vol. II
Swinburne, A. J., 1846–1915, vol. I
Swinburne, Algernon Charles, 1837–1909, vol. I
Swinburne, Hon. George, 1861–1928, vol. II
Swinburne, Sir Hubert, 8th Bt, 1867–1934, vol. III
Swinburne, Sir James, 9th Bt, 1858–1958, vol. V
Swinburne, Sir John, 7th Bt, 1831–1914, vol. I
Swinburne, Sir Spearman Charles, 10th Bt, 1893–1967, vol. VI
Swinburne, Lt-Col Thomas Robert, 1853–1921, vol. II
Swinburne-Hanham, John Castleman, 1860–1935, vol. III
Swinburne-Ward, Col Henry Charles, 1879–1966, vol. VI
Swindell, Rev. Frank Guthrie, 1874–1975, vol. VII
Swindell, Rev. Canon Frederic Smith, died 1941, vol. IV
Swindells, Rev. Bernard Guy, 1887–1977, vol. VII
Swindlehurst, Joseph Eric, 1890–1972, vol. VII
Swindley, Maj.-Gen. John Edward, 1831–1919, vol. II
Swiney, Brig.-Gen. Alexander John Henry, 1866–1933, vol. III
Swiney, Maj.-Gen. Sir (George Alexander) Neville, 1897–1970, vol. VI
Swiney, Maj.-Gen. John, 1832–1918, vol. II
Swiney, Maj.-Gen. Sir Neville; see Swiney, Maj.-Gen. Sir G. A. N.
Swinfen, 1st Baron, 1851–1919, vol. II
Swinfen, 2nd Baron, 1904–1977, vol. VII
Swing, Raymond, 1887–1968, vol. VI
Swingler, Rt Hon. Stephen Thomas, 1915–1969, vol. VI
Swinhoe, Lt-Gen. Frederick William, 1821–1907, vol. I
Swinley, Maj.-Gen. George, 1842–1924, vol. II
Swinnerton, Henry Hurd, 1875–1966, vol. VI
Swinnerton-Pilkington, Sir Thomas Edward Milborne-; see Pilkington.
Swinny, Shapland Hugh, 1857–1923, vol. II
Swinstead, Felix Gerald, 1880–1959, vol. V
Swinstead, Frank Hillyard, 1862–1937, vol. III
Swinstead, George Hillyard, died 1926, vol. II
Swinstead, Rev. John Howard, 1864–1924, vol. II
Swinton, 1st Earl of, 1884–1972, vol. VII
Swinton, Alan Archibald Campbell, 1863–1930, vol. III
Swinton, Brig. Alan Henry Campbell, 1896–1972, vol. VII
Swinton, Col Charles William, 1872–1935, vol. III
Swinton, Maj.-Gen. Sir Ernest Dunlop, 1868–1951, vol. V

Swinton, Lt-Col Francis Edward, died 1927, vol. II
Swinton, Captain George Herbert Tayler, 1852–1923, vol. II
Swinton, Captain George Sitwell Campbell, 1859–1937, vol. III
Swinton, John Edulf Blagrave, 1864–1941, vol. IV
Swinton, John Liulf Campbell, 1858–1920, vol. II
Swiny, Brig.-Gen. William Frederick, 1873–1950, vol. IV
Swire, John, 1861–1933, vol. III
Swire, Rev. S., 1866–1936, vol. III
Swire, William, 1862–1942, vol. IV
Swithinbank, Bernard Winthrop, 1884–1958, vol. V
Swithinbank, Harold William, 1858–1928, vol. II
Swords, William Francis, 1873–1964, vol. VI
Swynnerton, Annie Louisa, died 1933, vol. III
Swynnerton, Charles Francis Massy, 1877–1938, vol. III
Swynnerton, Maj.-Gen. Charles Roger Alan, 1901–1973, vol. VII
Sydenham of Combe, 1st Baron, 1848–1933, vol. III
Sydenham, Engr-Rear-Adm. Ernest Dickerson, 1875–1952, vol. V
Sydenham, Engr Rear-Adm. Frederick William, 1871–1946, vol. IV
Sydnor, Charles Sackett, 1898–1954, vol. V
Syed, Sir Ali Imam, 1869–1932, vol. III
Syed Sirdar Ali Khan, Nawab, 1879–1942, vol. IV
Syers, Rev. Henry S., 1838–1915, vol. I (A)
Syfret, Adm. Sir (Edward) Neville, 1889–1972, vol. VI
Syfret, Adm. Sir Neville; see Syfret, Adm. Sir E. N.
Sykes, Sir Alan John, 1st Bt (cr 1917), 1868–1950, vol. IV
Sykes, Vice-Adm. Alfred Charles, 1868–1933, vol. III
Sykes, Sir Arthur, 7th Bt (cr 1781), 1871–1934, vol. III
Sykes, Arthur Alkin, died 1939, vol. III
Sykes, Brig. Arthur Clifton, 1891–1967, vol. VI
Sykes, (Arthur) Frank (Seton), 1903–1980, vol. VII
Sykes, Sir (Benjamin) Hugh, 2nd Bt (cr 1921), 1893–1974, vol. VII
Sykes, Sir Charles, 1st Bt (cr 1921), 1867–1950, vol. IV
Sykes, Christopher, 1831–1898, vol. I
Sykes, Brig.-Gen. Clement Arthur, 1871–1938, vol. III
Sykes, Rev. Edward, 1862–1937, vol. III
Sykes, Ella Constance, died 1939, vol. III
Sykes, Ernest, 1870–1958, vol. V
Sykes, Frank; see Sykes, A. F. S.
Sykes, Rev. Canon Frank Morris, 1879–1939, vol. III
Sykes, Sir Frederic Henry, 5th Bt (cr 1781), 1826–1899, vol. I
Sykes, Rev. Sir Frederic John, 8th Bt (cr 1781), 1876–1956, vol. V
Sykes, Maj.-Gen. Rt Hon. Sir Frederick Hugh, died 1954, vol. V
Sykes, Sir Henry, 6th Bt (cr 1781), 1828–1916, vol. II
Sykes, Sir Hugh; see Sykes, Sir B. H.
Sykes, James, 1857–1929, vol. III

Sykes, Sir John Charles Gabriel, 1869–1952, vol. V
Sykes, John Frederick Joseph, *died* 1913, vol. I
Sykes, Joseph, 1899–1967, vol. VI
Sykes, Lt-Col Sir Mark, 6th Bt (*cr* 1783), 1879–1919, vol. II
Sykes, Sir (Mark Tatton) Richard T., 7th Bt (*cr* 1783); *see* Tatton-Sykes.
Sykes, Very Rev. Norman, 1897–1961, vol. VI
Sykes, Brig.-Gen. Sir Percy Molesworth, 1867–1945, vol. IV
Sykes, Comdr Percy Stanley, 1878–1966, vol. VI
Sykes, Lt-Col Peter Thomas Wellesley, 1903–1975, vol. VII
Sykes, Reginald James, 1869–1940, vol. III
Sykes, Sir Richard Adam, 1920–1979, vol. VII
Sykes, Rev. Simon Joseph, 1867–1941, vol. IV
Sykes, Sir Tatton, 5th Bt (*cr* 1783), 1826–1913, vol. I
Sykes, Lt-Col William Ainley, 1857–1940, vol. III
Sykes, Sir William Edmund, 1884–1961, vol. VI
Sykes, William Stanley, 1894–1961, vol. VI
Sylva, Carmen, 1843–1916, vol. II
Sylvaine, Vernon, 1897–1957, vol. V
Sylvester, Sir (Arthur) Edgar, 1891–1969, vol. VI
Sylvester, Sir Edgar; *see* Sylvester, Sir A. E.
Sylvester, George Oscar, 1898–1961, vol. VI
Sylvester, Asst Surgeon Henry Thomas, *died* 1920, vol. II
Sylvester, James Joseph, 1814–1897, vol. I
Sylvester, Rev. Samuel Augustus Kirwan, 1852–1928, vol. II
Sylvester-Bradley, Peter Colley, 1913–1978, vol. VII
Sym, John David, 1855–1931, vol. III
Sym, Maj.-Gen. Sir John Munro, 1839–1919, vol. II
Sym, William George, 1864–1938, vol. III
Syme, David, 1827–1908, vol. I
Syme, Sir Geoffrey, 1873–1942, vol. IV
Syme, Sir George Adlington, 1859–1929, vol. III
Symes, Sir Edward Spence, 1852–1901, vol. I
Symes, Lt-Col Sir (George) Stewart, 1882–1962, vol. VI
Symes, Maj.-Gen. George William, 1896–1980, vol. VII
Symes, Lt-Col Gustavus Phelps, 1857–1938, vol. III
Symes, Rev. John Elliotson, 1847–1921, vol. II
Symes, John Odery, 1867–1951, vol. V
Symes, Sir Robert Henry, 1837–1908, vol. I
Symes, Rev. Ronald, 1870–1935, vol. III
Symes, Lt-Col Sir Stewart; *see* Symes, Lt-Col Sir G.S.
Symes-Thompson, Edmund, 1837–1906, vol. I
Symes-Thompson, Henry Edmund, *died* 1952, vol. V
Symington, Herbert James, 1881–1965, vol. VI
Symington, John Alexander, 1887–1961, vol. VI
Symington, Johnson, 1851–1924, vol. II
Symmers, W. St Clair, 1863–1937, vol. III
Symmons, Israel Alexander, 1862–1923, vol. II
Symon, Sir Alexander Colin Burlington, 1902–1974, vol. VII
Symon, Rev. Dudley James, 1887–1961, vol. VI

Symon, Col Frank, 1879–1956, vol. V
Symon, Harold, 1896–1971, vol. VII
Symon, Jocelyn, (Mrs David Symon); *see* Moore, Miss J. A. M.
Symon, Hon. Sir Josiah Henry, 1846–1934, vol. III
Symon, Lt-Col Walter Conover, 1874–1949, vol. IV
Symonds, Sir Alfred Percival, *died* 1929, vol. III
Symonds, (Arthur) Leslie, 1910–1960, vol. V
Symonds, Sir Aubrey Vere, 1874–1931, vol. III
Symonds, Sir Charles Putnam, 1890–1978, vol. VII
Symonds, Sir Charters James, 1852–1932, vol. III
Symonds, Captain F. C. Loder-, 1846–1923, vol. II
Symonds, Vice-Adm. Frederick Parland Loder-, 1876–1952, vol. V
Symonds, Rev. Henry Herbert, 1885–1958, vol. V
Symonds, Leslie; *see* Symonds, A. L.
Symonds, Robert Wemyss, 1889–1958, vol. V
Symonds, Rev. William, 1832–1919, vol. II
Symonds-Tayler, Adm. Sir Richard Victor, 1897–1971, vol. VII
Symonette, Hon. Sir Roland Theodore, 1898–1980, vol. VII
Symons, Brig.-Gen. Adolphe, 1872–1954, vol. V
Symons, Albert James Alroy, 1900–1941, vol. IV
Symons, Arthur, 1865–1945, vol. IV
Symons, Col Charles Bertie Owen, 1874–1948, vol. IV
Symons, Rev. Charles Douglas, 1885–1949, vol. IV
Symons, Lt-Col Frank Albert, 1869–1917, vol. II
Symons, Lt-Col George Algernon James S.; *see* Soltau-Symons.
Symons, George James, 1838–1900, vol. I
Symons, George William Culme S.; *see* Soltau-Symons.
Symons, Maj.-Gen. Sir Henry; *see* Symons, Maj.-Gen. Sir T. H.
Symons, Hubert Wallace, 1890–1973, vol. VII
Symons, Sir Robert F.; *see* Fox-Symons.
Symons, Ronald Stuart, 1904–1977, vol. VII
Symons, Maj.-Gen. Sir (Thomas) Henry, 1872–1948, vol. IV
Symons, Captain Thomas Raymond, 1866–1922, vol. II
Symons-Jeune, John Frederic; *see* Jeune.
Sympson, Edward Mansel, 1860–1922, vol. II
Synge, Sir Francis Robert Millington, 6th Bt, 1851–1924, vol. II
Synge, John Millington, 1871–1909, vol. I
Synge, Major Mark, 1871–1921, vol. II
Synge, Sir Robert Follett, 1853–1920, vol. II
Synge, Sir Robert Millington, 7th Bt, 1877–1942, vol. IV
Synge, Victor Millington, 1893–1976, vol. VII
Synge-Hutchinson, Sir Edward; *see* Hutchinson, Sir E. S.
Synnot, Maj.-Gen. Arthur FitzRoy H.; *see* Hart-Synnot.
Synnot, Brig.-Gen. Arthur Henry Seton H.; *see* Hart-Synnot.
Synnot, Ronald Victor Okes H.; *see* Hart-Synnot.
Synnott, Nicholas Joseph, *died* 1920, vol. II
Synnott, Bt Lt-Col Wilfrid Thomas, 1877–1941, vol. IV
Syrett, Herbert Sutton, *died* 1959, vol. V

Syrett, Netta, *died* 1943, vol. IV
Sysonby, 1st Baron, 1867–1935, vol. III
Sysonby, 2nd Baron, 1903–1956, vol. V
Szarvasy, Frederick Alexander, *died* 1948, vol. IV
Szczepanski, Maj.-Gen. Henry Charles Antony, 1841–1923, vol. II
Szigeti, Joseph, 1892–1973, vol. VII
Szlumper, Alfred Weeks, 1858–1934, vol. III
Szlumper, Gilbert Savil, 1884–1969, vol. VI
Szlumper, Sir James Weeks, 1834–1926, vol. II

T

Taaffe, George Joseph, *died* 1923, vol. II
Tabor, James, 1869–1938, vol. III
Tabor, Margaret Emma, *died* 1954, vol. V
Tabor, Richard John, *died* 1958, vol. V
Tabrar, Joseph, 1857–1931, vol. III
Tabuteau, Maj.-Gen. George Grant, 1881–1940, vol. III
Tachie-Menson, Sir Charles William, 1889–1962, vol. VI
Tacon, Sir Thomas Henry, 1838–1922, vol. II
Tadema, Miss Anna A.; *see* Alma-Tadema.
Tadema, Laura Theresa A.; *see* Alma-Tadema.
Tadema, Miss Laurence A.; *see* Alma-Tadema.
Tadema, Sir Lawrence A.; *see* Alma-Tadema.
Tafawa Balewa, Alhaji Rt Hon. Sir Abubakar, 1912–1966, vol. VI
Taflia, 4th Marquis of, 1837–1921, vol. II
Taft, Lorado, 1860–1936, vol. III
Taft, Robert A., 1889–1953, vol. V
Taft, William Howard, 1857–1930, vol. III
Tagart, Edward Samuel Bourn, 1877–1956, vol. V
Tagart, Maj.-Gen. Sir Harold Arthur Lewis, 1870–1930, vol. III
Tagg, Sir Arundel; *see* Arundel, Sir A. T.
Taggart, Sir James, 1849–1929, vol. III
Taggart, Wing Comdr John S.; *see* Scott-Taggart.
Tagore, Abanindra Nath, 1871–1951, vol. V
Tagore, Maharaja Bahadur Sir Joteendro Mohun, 1831–1908, vol. I
Tagore, Hon. Maharaja Bahadur Sir Prodyot Coomar, 1873–1942, vol. IV
Tagore, Sir Rabindranath, 1861–1941, vol. IV
Tagore, Raja Sir Sourindro Mohun, 1840–1914, vol. I
Taillon, Hon. Sir Louis Olivier, 1840–1923, vol. II
Tailyour, Gen. Sir Norman Hastings, 1914–1979, vol. VII
Tailyour, Col Thomas Francis Bruce R.; *see* Renny-Tailyour.
Tainsh, Lt-Col Joseph Ramsay, 1874–1954, vol. V
Tait, Andrew Wilson, 1876–1930, vol. III
Tait, Rev. Arthur James, 1872–1944, vol. IV
Tait, Adm. Sir Campbell; *see* Tait, Adm. Sir W. E. C.
Tait, Ven. Donald, 1862–1932, vol. III
Tait, Sir Frank Samuel, 1883–1965, vol. VI
Tait, George Hope, 1861–1943, vol. IV
Tait, Hugh Nimmo, 1888–1960, vol. V

Tait, James, 1863–1944, vol. IV
Tait, John, 1878–1944, vol. IV
Tait, Sir John, *died* 1972, vol. VII
Tait, Lt-Col John Spottiswood, 1875–1951, vol. V
Tait, Lawson, 1845–1899, vol. I
Tait, Sir Melbourne McTaggart, 1842–1917, vol. II
Tait, Peter Guthrie, 1831–1901, vol. I
Tait, Sir Thomas, 1864–1940, vol. III (A), vol. IV
Tait, Thomas Smith, 1882–1954, vol. V
Tait, Adm. Sir (William Eric) Campbell, 1886–1946, vol. IV
Taite, Charles Davis, 1872–1948, vol. IV
Taitt, Rt Rev. Francis Marion, 1862–1943, vol. IV
Takamine, Jokichi, 1854–1923, vol. II
Talbot de Malahide, 5th Baron, 1846–1921, vol. II
Talbot de Malahide, 6th Baron, 1874–1948, vol. IV
Talbot de Malahide, 7th Baron, 1912–1973, vol. VII
Talbot of Malahide, 8th Baron, 1897–1975, vol. VII
Talbot, Lt-Col Sir Adelbert Cecil, 1845–1920, vol. II
Talbot, Very Rev. Albert Edward, 1877–1936, vol. III
Talbot, Vice-Adm. Arthur George, 1892–1960, vol. V
Talbot, Rev. Arthur Henry, 1855–1927, vol. II
Talbot, Benjamin, 1864–1947, vol. IV
Talbot, Bertram, 1865–1936, vol. III
Talbot, Bridget Elizabeth, *died* 1971, vol. VII
Talbot, Vice-Adm. Sir Cecil Ponsonby, 1884–1970, vol. VI
Talbot, Charles Henry, 1842–1916, vol. II
Talbot, Rev. Edward Keble, 1877–1949, vol. IV
Talbot, Rt Rev. Edward Stuart, 1844–1934, vol. III
Talbot, Emily Charlotte, *died* 1918, vol. II
Talbot, Rt Rev. Ethelbert, 1848–1928, vol. II
Talbot, George, 1823–1914, vol. I
Talbot, Lt-Col George James Francis, 1857–1941, vol. IV
Talbot, Rt Hon. Sir George John, 1861–1938, vol. III
Talbot, Sir Gerald Francis, 1881–1945, vol. IV
Talbot, Gustavus Arthur, 1848–1920, vol. II
Talbot, Howard, 1865–1928, vol. II
Talbot, John Ellis, 1906–1967, vol. VI
Talbot, Rt Hon. John Gilbert, 1835–1910, vol. I
Talbot, Matilda Theresa, 1871–1958, vol. V
Talbot, Dame Meriel, *died* 1956, vol. V
Talbot, Col Hon. Milo George, 1854–1931, vol. III
Talbot, Rt Rev. Neville Stuart, *died* 1943, vol. IV
Talbot, Lt-Gen. Sir Norman Graham Guy, 1914–1979, vol. VII
Talbot, Hon. Sir Patrick Wellington, 1817–1898, vol. I
Talbot, Percy Amaury, 1877–1945, vol. IV
Talbot, Maj.-Gen. Hon. Sir Reginald Arthur James, 1841–1929, vol. III
Talbot, Comdr Reginald George Chetwynd, 1881–1939, vol. III
Talbot, Hon. Reginald Gilbert Murray, 1849–1930, vol. III
Talbot, Very Rev. Reginald Thomas, 1862–1935, vol. III
Talbot, Sir Samuel Thomas, *died* 1931, vol. III

Talbot, Thomas, *died* 1929, vol. III
Talbot, Walter Stanley, 1869–1935, vol. III
Talbot, Sir William Henry, 1831–1919, vol. II
Talbot, Sir William J., 1872–1947, vol. IV
Talbot, William John, 1859–1923, vol. II
Talbot Rice, David; *see* Rice.
Tallberg, Axel, 1860–1928, vol. II
Tallents, George William, 1856–1924, vol. II
Tallents, Philip Cubitt, 1886–1962, vol. VI
Tallents, Sir Stephen George, 1884–1958, vol. V
Tallis, Sir George, 1869–1948, vol. IV
Talmage, Algernon, *died* 1939, vol. III
Tamagno, Francisco, 1851–1905, vol. I
Tamm, Igor Evgenievich, 1895–1971, vol. VII
Tamplin, Herbert Travers, 1853–1925, vol. II
Tan, Dato Sir Cheng-lock, 1883–1960, vol. V
Tancock, Lt-Col Alexander Charles, *died* 1966, vol. VI
Tancock, Rev. Charles Coverdale, 1851–1922, vol. II
Tancock, Col Osborne Kendall, 1866–1946, vol. IV
Tancock, Rev. Osborne William, 1839–1930, vol. III
Tancred, Vice-Adm. James Charles, 1864–1943, vol. IV
Tancred, Maj.-Gen. Thomas Angus, 1867–1944, vol. IV
Tancred, Sir Thomas Selby, 8th Bt, 1840–1910, vol. I
Tancred, Major Sir Thomas Selby L.; *see* Lawson-Tancred.
Tandy, Sir Arthur Harry, 1903–1964, vol. VI
Tandy, Brig. Sir Edward Aldborough, 1871–1950, vol. IV
Tandy, Brig.-Gen. Ernest Napper, 1879–1953, vol. V
Tandy, Col Maurice O'Connor, 1873–1942, vol. IV
Tangley, Baron (Life Peer); Edwin Savory Herbert, *died* 1973, vol. VII
Tangye, Captain Sir Basil Richard Gilzean, 2nd Bt, 1895–1969, vol. VI
Tangye, Claude Edward, 1877–1952, vol. V
Tangye, Sir (Harold) Lincoln, 1st Bt, 1866–1935, vol. III
Tangye, Sir Lincoln; *see* Tangye, Sir H. L.
Tangye, Sir Richard, 1833–1906, vol. I
Tangye, Lt-Col Richard Trevithick Gilbertstone, 1875–1944, vol. IV
Tankerville, 6th Earl of, 1810–1899, vol. I
Tankerville, 7th Earl of, 1852–1931, vol. III
Tankerville, 8th Earl of, 1897–1971, vol. VII
Tankerville, 9th Earl of, 1921–1980, vol. VII
Tanner, Archibald Gerard, 1895–1937, vol. III
Tanner, Charles Elliott, 1857–1946, vol. IV
Tanner, Sir Edgar Stephen, 1914–1979, vol. VII
Tanner, Maj.-Gen. Edward, 1839–1916, vol. II
Tanner, Dame Emmeline Mary, 1876–1955, vol. V
Tanner, Lt-Col Frederick Courtney, 1879–1965, vol. VI
Tanner, Frederick John Shirley; *see* Tanner, Jack.
Tanner, Col Sir Gilbert, 1877–1953, vol. V
Tanner, Sir Henry, 1849–1935, vol. III
Tanner, Henry, 1876–1947, vol. IV

Tanner, Henry William Lloyd, 1851–1915, vol. I
Tanner, Herbert George, 1882–1974, vol. VII
Tanner, Jack, (Frederick John Shirley Tanner), 1889–1965, vol. VI
Tanner, Brig.-Gen. John Arthur, 1858–1917, vol. II
Tanner, John Arthur Charles, 1854–1928, vol. II
Tanner, John Edward, 1834–1906, vol. I
Tanner, Joseph Robson, 1860–1931, vol. III
Tanner, Lawrence Edward, 1890–1979, vol. VII
Tanner, Lt-Gen. Sir Oriel Viveash, 1832–1911, vol. I
Tanner, Lt-Col Richard Morrison, 1871–1936, vol. III
Tanner, William Edward, 1889–1951, vol. V
Tanner, Maj.-Gen. William Ernest Collins, 1875–1943, vol. IV
Tanqueray, Rev. Truman, 1888–1960, vol. V
Tanquerey, F. J., *died* 1942, vol. IV
Tansley, Sir Arthur George, 1871–1955, vol. V
Tapley, Harold Livingstone, 1875–1932, vol. III
Tapley, Maj.-Gen. James John Bonifant, 1877–1958, vol. V
Tapley-Soper, Harry Tapley; *see* Soper.
Tapp, Norman Charles, 1925–1977, vol. VII
Tapp, Percy John Rutty, 1886–1964, vol. VI
Tapper, Sir Walter John, 1861–1935, vol. III
Tapps-Gervis-Meyrick, Sir George Augustus Eliott; *see* Meyrick.
Tapps-Gervis-Meyrick, Major Sir George Llewelyn; *see* Meyrick.
Tarbat, Sir John Allan, 1891–1977, vol. VII
Tarbet, Lt-Col Alexander Francis, 1860–1939, vol. III
Tarbet, Captain William Godfrey, 1878–1911, vol. I
Tarbolton, Harold Ogle, *died* 1947, vol. IV
Tardieu, André Pierre Gabriel Amedée, 1876–1945, vol. IV
Tardrew, Rev. Canon Thomas Hedley, 1889–1966, vol. VI
Targett, James Henry, *died* 1913, vol. I
Targett, Sir Robert William, 1891–1965, vol. VI
Tarkington, Booth, 1869–1946, vol. IV
Tarleton, Captain Alfred Henry, 1862–1921, vol. II
Tarleton, Francis Alexander, 1841–1920, vol. II
Tarn, Sir William Woodthorpe, 1869–1957, vol. V
Tarrant, Dorothy, 1885–1973, vol. VII
Tarrant, Surg.-Gen. Thomas, 1830–1909, vol. I
Tarrant, William Charles, 1881–1941, vol. IV
Tarrant, Rev. William George, 1853–1928, vol. II
Tarring, Sir Charles James, 1845–1923, vol. II
Tarry, Frederick Thomas, 1896–1976, vol. VII
Tarte, Hon. Joseph Israel, 1848–1907, vol. I
Tarver, Maj.-Gen. Alexander Leigh, 1871–1941, vol. IV
Tarver, J. C., *died* 1926, vol. II
Tarver, Maj.-Gen. William Knapp, 1872–1952, vol. IV
Tasadduk Rasul Khan, Raja Sir, *died* 1928, vol. II
Taschereau, His Eminence Cardinal Elzear Alexander, 1820–1898, vol. I
Taschereau, Rt Hon. Sir Henri Elzear, 1836–1911, vol. I

Taschereau, Sir Henri Thomas, 1841–1909, vol. I
Taschereau, Hon. Louis Alexandre, 1867–1952, vol. V
Taschereau, Rt Hon. Robert, 1896–1970, vol. VI
Tasker, Rev. Canon Derek Morris Phipps, 1916–1978, vol. VII
Tasker, Rev. John Greenwood, 1853–1936, vol. III
Tasker, Rev. Randolph Vincent Greenwood, 1895–1976, vol. VII
Tasker, Major Sir Robert Inigo, 1868–1959, vol. V
Tasma; see Couvreur, Jessie.
Tassell, Alick James, 1865–1932, vol. III
Tata, Sir Dorabji Jamsetji, 1859–1932, vol. III
Tata, Jamsetjee Nasarwanji, 1839–1904, vol. I
Tata, Sir Ratan, 1871–1918, vol. II
Tatchell, Sydney Joseph, 1887–1965, vol. VI
Tate, Col Alan Edmondson, 1859–1934, vol. III
Tate, Adm. Alban Giffard, 1853–1930, vol. III
Tate, Lt-Col Arthur Wignall, 1888–1939, vol. III
Tate, Charles James Gerrard, 1880–1951, vol. V
Tate, D'Arcy, 1866–1935, vol. III
Tate, Sir Ernest William, 3rd Bt, 1867–1939, vol. III
Tate, Frank, 1863–1939, vol. III
Tate, George Vernon, 1890–1955, vol. V
Tate, Col Gerard William, 1866–1937, vol. III
Tate, Maj.-Gen. Godfrey, 1873–1944, vol. IV
Tate, Harry, died 1940, vol. III
Tate, Sir Henry, 1st Bt, 1819–1899, vol. I
Tate, James William, 1875–1922, vol. II
Tate, Jonathan, 1899–1958, vol. V
Tate, Mavis Constance, died 1947, vol. IV
Tate, Col Robert Ward, 1864–1938, vol. III
Tate, Major Sir Robert William, 1872–1952, vol. V
Tate, Thomas Bailey, 1882–1957, vol. V
Tate, Walter William Hunt, 1865–1916, vol. II
Tate, Sir William Henry, 2nd Bt, 1842–1921, vol. II
Tatham, Brig.-Gen. Arthur Glanville, 1856–1933, vol. III
Tatham, Rev. Edward Henry Ralph, 1857–1938, vol. III
Tatham, Lt-Col Hon. Frederic Spence, 1865–1934, vol. III
Tatlock, Robert Rattray, 1889–1954, vol. V
Tatlow, Frank, 1861–1934, vol. III
Tatlow, Joseph, 1851–1929, vol. III
Tatlow, Hon. Robert Garnett, 1855–1910, vol. I
Tatlow, Rev. Canon Tissington, 1876–1957, vol. V
Tattersall, Creassey Edward Cecil, 1877–1957, vol. V
Tattersall, Lt-Col Edmund Harry, 1897–1968, vol. VI
Tattersall, John Lincoln, 1865–1942, vol. IV
Tattersall, Rev. Thomas Newell, 1879–1943, vol. IV
Tattersall, William, died 1914, vol. I
Tattersall, William Boothman, 1873–1943, vol. IV
Tatton-Sykes, Sir (Mark Tatton) Richard, 7th Bt, 1905–1978, vol. VII
Tatum, E(dward) L(awrie), 1909–1975, vol. VII
Tauber, Richard, 1892–1948, vol. IV
Taubman, Frank Mowbray, 1868–1946, vol. IV

Taubman, Sir John Senhouse G.; see Goldie-Taubman.
Taunton, Agnes, 1877–1941, vol. IV
Taunton, Sir Ivon Hope, 1890–1957, vol. V
Taussig, Francis William, 1859–1940, vol. III (A), vol. IV
Taveggia, Rt Rev. Santino, 1855–1928, vol. II (A), vol. III
Taverner, Hon. Sir John William, 1856–1923, vol. II
Taverner, William Burgoyne, 1879–1958, vol. V
Taw Sein Ko, 1864–1930, vol. III
Tawney, Charles Henry, 1837–1922, vol. II
Tawney, Richard Henry, 1880–1962, vol. VI
Tawse, Col Harry Storey, 1889–1959, vol. V
Tay, Waren, died 1927, vol. II
Tayler, Albert Chevallier, 1862–1925, vol. II
Tayler, Lt-Col Francis Lionel, 1883–1933, vol. III
Tayler, Maj.-Gen. John Charles, 1834–1913, vol. I
Tayler, Adm. Sir Richard Victor S.; see Symonds-Tayler.
Taylor, Alan Carey, 1905–1975, vol. VII
Taylor, Rt Hon. Sir Alan Russell, 1901–1969, vol. VI (AII)
Taylor, Albert Booth, 1896–1971, vol. VII
Taylor, Sir Alexander, 1826–1912, vol. I
Taylor, Alexander, 1872–1917, vol. II
Taylor, Alexander Burt, 1904–1972, vol. VII
Taylor, Sir Alexander Thomson, 1873–1953, vol. V
Taylor, Alfred Edward, 1869–1945, vol. IV
Taylor, Rear-Adm. Alfred Hugh, 1886–1972, vol. VII
Taylor, (Alfred) Maurice, 1903–1979, vol. VII
Taylor, Sir Allen, 1864–1940, vol. III
Taylor, Sir Andrew Thomas, 1850–1937, vol. III
Taylor, Brig.-Gen. Arthur Henry Mendle, 1870–1934, vol. III
Taylor, Lt-Col Arthur James, 1876–1949, vol. IV (A), vol. V
Taylor, Arthur John Ernest, 1913–1979, vol. VII
Taylor, Captain Arthur Lombe, 1882–1968, vol. VI
Taylor, Captain Arthur Trevelyan, 1864–1956, vol. V
Taylor, Lt-Col Arthur William Neufville, 1863–1930, vol. III
Taylor, Austin, died 1955, vol. V
Taylor, Col Bertie Harry Waters, died 1946, vol. IV
Taylor, Rear-Adm. Bertram Wilfrid, 1906–1970, vol. VI
Taylor, Maj.-Gen. Sir Brian; see Taylor, Maj.-Gen. Sir G. B. O.
Taylor, Rev. Charles, 1840–1908, vol. I
Taylor, Charles Allison, 1885–1965, vol. VI
Taylor, Charles Bell, 1829–1909, vol. I
Taylor, Charles Edward, 1853–1924, vol. II
Taylor, Lt-Col Charles Newton, 1866–1949, vol. IV
Taylor, Rev. Charles Reeve, 1845–1931, vol. III
Taylor, Charles William, 1878–1960, vol. V
Taylor, Very Rev. Charles William Gray, 1879–1950, vol. IV
Taylor, Claude, 1877–1957, vol. V

Taylor, Rev. Decimus A. G., 1871–1933, vol. III
Taylor, Desmond Maxwell, 1928–1978, vol. VII
Taylor, Dorothy Daisy C.; see Cottington-Taylor.
Taylor, Douglas, 1915–1971, vol. VII
Taylor, Col. Edward, 1860–1931, vol. III
Taylor, Lt-Col Edward Harrison Clough, 1849–1921, vol. II
Taylor, Edward Henry, died 1922, vol. II
Taylor, Edward R., 1838–1911, vol. I
Taylor, (Edward) Wilfred, 1891–1980, vol. VII
Taylor, Edwin, 1881–1972, vol. VII
Taylor, Edwin, 1905–1973, vol. VII
Taylor, Elizabeth, (Mrs J. W. K. Taylor), 1912–1975, vol. VII
Taylor, Sir Eric Stuart, 2nd Bt (cr 1917), 1889–1977, vol. VII
Taylor, Vice-Adm. Sir Ernest Augustus, 1876–1971, vol. VII
Taylor, Ernest Edward, 1897–1974, vol. VII
Taylor, Col Ernest Fitzwilliam, 1867–1944, vol. IV
Taylor, Lt-Col Eustace Trevor Neave, 1894–1971, vol. VII
Taylor, Eva Germaine Rimington, died 1966, vol. VI
Taylor, Fanny Isabel, died 1947, vol. IV
Taylor, Lt-Col Hon. Fawcett Gowler, 1878–1940, vol. III (A), vol. IV
Taylor, Francis, 1845–1915, vol. I
Taylor, Sir Francis Edward W.; see Worsley-Taylor.
Taylor, Francis Henry, 1903–1957, vol. V
Taylor, Rt Rev. Francis John, 1912–1971, vol. VII
Taylor, Francis Maurice Gustavus D. P.; see Du-Plat-Taylor.
Taylor, Col Francis Pitt Stewart, 1869–1924, vol. II
Taylor, Frank Alwyn, 1890–1960, vol. V
Taylor, Frank Herbert Graham, 1890–1971, vol. VII
Taylor, F(rank) Sherwood, 1897–1956, vol. V
Taylor, Franklin, 1843–1919, vol. II
Taylor, Fred, 1875–1963, vol. VI
Taylor, Ven. Frederic Norman, 1871–1960, vol. V
Taylor, Frederic Richard, 1876–1929, vol. III
Taylor, Sir Frederick, 1st Bt (cr 1917), 1847–1920, vol. II
Taylor, Rt Rev. Frederick Adrian, 1892–1961, vol. VI
Taylor, Sir Frederick W.; see Williams-Taylor.
Taylor, Sir Geoffrey Ingram, 1886–1975, vol. VII
Taylor, Hon. George, 1840–1919, vol. II
Taylor, Maj.-Gen. Sir (George) Brian (Ogilvie), died 1973, vol. VII
Taylor, George Francis, 1903–1979, vol. VII
Taylor, Sir George L.; see Langley-Taylor.
Taylor, George Paul, 1860–1917, vol. II
Taylor, George Reginald Thomas, 1876–1965, vol. VI
Taylor, George Simon Arthur W.; see Watson-Taylor.
Taylor, George William, 1864–1929, vol. III
Taylor, Rear-Adm. George William, 1883–1964, vol. VI

Taylor, Brig.-Gen. Gerald Kyffin-, 1863–1949, vol. IV
Taylor, Dame Gladys, 1890–1950, vol. IV
Taylor, Sir Gordon G.; see Gordon-Taylor.
Taylor, Griffith; see Taylor, T. G.
Taylor, Col H. Brooke, 1855–1923, vol. II
Taylor, H. Stanley, 1871–1959, vol. V
Taylor, Major Harold Blake, 1862–1936, vol. III
Taylor, Rev. Harold Milman Strickland, 1890–1966, vol. VI
Taylor, Harold Victor, died 1965, vol. VI
Taylor, Harry Ashworth, died 1907, vol. I
Taylor, Harry Mead, 1872–1928, vol. II
Taylor, Harry Willoughby O.; see Oddin-Taylor.
Taylor, Col Haydon D'Aubrey Potenger, 1860–1939, vol. III
Taylor, Henry Archibald, died 1980, vol. VII
Taylor, Henry G.; see Gawan Taylor.
Taylor, Rev. Henry James, died 1945, vol. IV
Taylor, Henry Martyn, 1842–1927, vol. II
Taylor, Henry Osborn, 1856–1941, vol. IV
Taylor, Sir Henry Wilson W.; see Worsley-Taylor.
Taylor, Herbert, 1885–1970, vol. VI (AII)
Taylor, Captain Herbert Bardsley, 1884–1947, vol. IV
Taylor, Col Herbert James Cox-, 1872–1936, vol. III
Taylor, Sir Herbert John, 1865–1943, vol. IV
Taylor, Hobart Chatfield C.; see Chatfield-Taylor.
Taylor, Horace, 1881–1934, vol. III
Taylor, Lt-Col Hugh Neufville, 1859–1931, vol. III
Taylor, Sir Hugh Stott, 1890–1974, vol. VII
Taylor, Rev. Isaac, 1829–1901, vol. I
Taylor, Col Jack H.; see Hulme Taylor.
Taylor, Rev. Jackson, died 1929, vol. III
Taylor, James, 1871–1944, vol. IV
Taylor, James, 1859–1946, vol. IV
Taylor, James Benjamin, 1860–1944, vol. IV
Taylor, Sir James Braid, 1891–1943, vol. IV
Taylor, Air Vice-Marshal James Clarke, 1910–1978, vol. VII
Taylor, James Haward, 1909–1968, vol. VI
Taylor, James Henry, 1861–1926, vol. II
Taylor, James Monroe, 1848–1916, vol. II
Taylor, Lt-Col Sir James W.; see Worsley-Taylor.
Taylor, Sir John, 1833–1912, vol. I
Taylor, John, 1834–1922, vol. II
Taylor, John, 1857–1936, vol. III
Taylor, John, 1861–1945, vol. IV
Taylor, Maj.-Gen. Sir John, 1884–1959, vol. V
Taylor, John, 1902–1962, vol. VI
Taylor, Sir John, 1876–1971, vol. VII
Taylor, Rev. John Edward, 1899–1966, vol. VI
Taylor, Captain Sir John Godfrey W.; see Worsley-Taylor.
Taylor, John Gray, 1890–1944, vol. IV
Taylor, John Idowu Conrad, 1917–1973, vol. VII
Taylor, Sir John James, 1859–1945, vol. IV
Taylor, Col John Lowther Du Plat, died 1904, vol. I
Taylor, John Norman, died 1945, vol. IV
Taylor, Rt Rev. John Ralph Strickland, 1883–1961, vol. VI
Taylor, John T., 1840–1908, vol. I

Taylor, Sir John W.; *see* Wilson-Taylor.
Taylor, John William, 1851–1910, vol. I
Taylor, Sir John William, 1895–1974, vol. VII
Taylor, Mrs John William Kendell; *see* Taylor, Elizabeth.
Taylor, Joseph Charlton, 1913–1971, vol. VII
Taylor, Sir Joshua R.; *see* Ross-Taylor.
Taylor, Julian, 1889–1961, vol. VI
Taylor, Most Rev. Leo Hale, 1889–1965, vol. VI
Taylor, Leonard Campbell, 1874–1969, vol. VI
Taylor, Leonard Whitworth, 1880–1979, vol. VII
Taylor, Sir Lionel Goodenough, 1871–1963, vol. VI
Taylor, Lionel Robert Stewart, 1915–1972, vol. VII
Taylor, Luke, 1876–1916, vol. II
Taylor, Rev. Malcolm Campbell, *died* 1922, vol. II
Taylor, Gen. Sir Malcolm Cartwright C.; *see* Cartwright-Taylor.
Taylor, Air Vice-Marshal Malcolm Lincoln, 1893–1970, vol. VI
Taylor, Hon. Mrs Margaret Sophia, 1877–1962, vol. VI
Taylor, Margerie Venables, 1881–1963, vol. VI
Taylor, Mark Ronald, *died* 1942, vol. IV
Taylor, Maurice; *see* Taylor, A. M.
Taylor, Gen. Sir Maurice Grove, 1881–1960, vol. V
Taylor, Myron C., 1874–1959, vol. V
Taylor, Captain Sir Patrick Gordon, *died* 1966, vol. VI
Taylor, Peter Athol, 1926–1976, vol. VII
Taylor, Col Philip Beauchamp, *died* 1939, vol. III
Taylor, Rear-Adm. Philip Cardwell, 1902–1965, vol. VI
Taylor, Rachel Annand, 1876–1960, vol. V
Taylor, Raymond Charles, 1926–1977, vol. VII
Taylor, Brig.-Gen. Reginald O'Bryen, 1872–1949, vol. IV
Taylor, Sir Reginald William, 1895–1971, vol. VII
Taylor, Brig.-Gen. Reynell Hamilton Baylay, 1858–1942, vol. IV
Taylor, Rev. Richard, *died* 1922, vol. II
Taylor, Sir Richard Chambré Hayes, 1819–1904, vol. I
Taylor, Sir Richard Laurence S.; *see* Stuart Taylor.
Taylor, Richard S.; *see* Stopford-Taylor.
Taylor, Richard Sanderson, *died* 1932, vol. III
Taylor, Sir Richard Stephens, 1842–1928, vol. II
Taylor, Richard Whately C.; *see* Cooke-Taylor.
Taylor, Sir Robert, 1855–1921, vol. II
Taylor, Robert, *died* 1969, vol. VI
Taylor, Robert Arthur, 1886–1934, vol. III
Taylor, Robert Bruce, 1869–1954, vol. V
Taylor, Rt Hon. Robert John, 1881–1954, vol. V
Taylor, Col Robert Lewis, 1822–1906, vol. I
Taylor, Very Rev. Robert Oswald Patrick, 1873–1944, vol. IV
Taylor, Robert Walter, 1883–1972, vol. VII
Taylor, Lt-Col St John Louis Hyde du Plat-, 1865–1936, vol. III
Taylor, Samuel C.; *see* Coleridge-Taylor.
Taylor, Rt Rev. Samuel Mumford, 1859–1929, vol. III
Taylor, Seymour, 1851–1931, vol. III
Taylor, Sidney Berald, 1900–1960, vol. V

Taylor, Stanley Grisewood, 1893–1980, vol. VII
Taylor, Stanley Shelbourne, 1875–1965, vol. VI
Taylor, Theodore Cooke, 1850–1952, vol. V
Taylor, Thomas, 1851–1916, vol. II
Taylor, Thomas, 1849–1938, vol. III
Taylor, Rev. Thomas, 1858–1938, vol. III
Taylor, Sir Thomas, 1876–1941, vol. IV
Taylor, (Thomas) Griffith, 1880–1963, vol. VI
Taylor, Sir Thomas Marris, 1871–1941, vol. IV
Taylor, Sir Thomas Murray, 1897–1962, vol. VI
Taylor, Rt Rev. Mgr Thomas N., *died* 1963, vol. VI
Taylor, Sir Thomas Wardlaw, 1833–1917, vol. II
Taylor, Sir Thomas Weston Johns, 1895–1953, vol. V
Taylor, Tom Lancelot, 1878–1960, vol. V
Taylor, Rev. Vincent, 1887–1968, vol. VI
Taylor, Walter R.; *see* Ross Taylor.
Taylor, Rev. Walter Ross, 1838–1907, vol. I
Taylor, Gen. Sir Walter William P.; *see* Pitt-Taylor.
Taylor, Wilfred; *see* Taylor, E. W.
Taylor, Surg.-Gen. Sir William, 1843–1917, vol. II
Taylor, Col Sir William, 1871–1933, vol. III
Taylor, William, 1865–1937, vol. III
Taylor, William, 1892–1977, vol. VII
Taylor, William Benjamin, 1875–1932, vol. III
Taylor, William Ernest, 1900–1965, vol. VI
Taylor, Ven. William Francis, *died* 1906, vol. I
Taylor, Lt-Col William Herbert, 1885–1959, vol. V
Taylor, Sir William Johnson, 1st Bt (*cr* 1963), 1902–1972, vol. VII
Taylor, Sir William Ling, 1882–1969, vol. VI
Taylor, William T., 1843–1933, vol. III
Taylor, Sir William Thomas, 1848–1931, vol. III
Tayside, Baron (Life Peer); David Lauchlan Urquhart, 1912–1975, vol. VII
Tchigorin, T., 1950–1908, vol. I
Teacher, Anthony Donald Macdonald, 1905–1969, vol. VI
Teacher, John Hammond, 1869–1930, vol. III
Teago, Frederick Jerrold, 1886–1964, vol. VI
Teague, Rev. John Jessop, 1856–1929, vol. III
Teakle, Laurence John Hartley, 1901–1979, vol. VII
Teale, Sir Edmund Oswald, 1874–1971, vol. VII
Teale, Sir Francis Hugo, *died* 1959, vol. V
Teale, Rear-Adm. Godfrey Benjamin, 1908–1978, vol. VII
Teale, Major Joseph William, 1876–1926, vol. II
Teale, Thomas Pridgin, 1831–1923, vol. II
Teall, Major George Harris, 1880–1939, vol. III
Teall, Sir Jethro Justinian Harris, 1849–1924, vol. II
Teare, Robert Donald, 1911–1979, vol. VII
Tearle, Sir Godfrey Seymour, 1884–1953, vol. V
Teasdale, Sir John Smith, 1881–1962, vol. VI
Tebb, William, 1830–1918, vol. II
Tebbitt, Sir Alfred St Valery, *died* 1941, vol. IV
Tebbs, Herbert Louis, 1868–1940, vol. III
Tebbutt, Edward G. F., *died* 1934, vol. III
Tebbutt, Rev. Henry Jemson, *died* 1915, vol. I
Teck, HH the Duke of; Francis Paul Louis Alexander, 1837–1900, vol. I

Teck, HSH Prince Francis Joseph Leopold Frederick of, 1870–1910, vol. I
Tedder, 1st Baron, 1890–1967, vol. VI
Tedder, Sir Arthur John, 1851–1931, vol. III
Tedder, Henry Richard, 1850–1924, vol. II
Tee, Lt-Col James Henry Stanley, 1876–1951, vol. V
Teed, Frank Litherland, 1858–1937, vol. III
Teeling, Bartholomew, 1848–1921, vol. II
Teeling, Mrs Bartle, *died* 1906, vol. I
Teeling, Charles Hamilton, *died* 1921, vol. II
Teeling, Luke Alexander, 1856–1943, vol. IV
Teeling, Sir (Luke) William (Burke), 1903–1975, vol. VII
Teeling, Sir William; *see* Teeling, Sir L. W. B.
Teesdale, Rev. Frederic Dobree, 1845–1935, vol. III
Teetzel, James Vernal, 1853–1926, vol. II
Teevan, Thomas Leslie, 1927–1954, vol. V
Tegart, Sir Charles Augustus, 1881–1946, vol. IV
Tegetmeier, William B., 1816–1912, vol. I
Tehri, HH Raja Sir Keerti Shah, 1874–1913, vol. I
Tehri-Garhwal, Maharaja of, 1898–1950, vol. IV (A), vol. V
Teichman, Sir Eric, 1884–1944, vol. IV
Teichman, Major Oskar, 1880–1959, vol. V
Teichman-Derville, Major Max, 1876–1963, vol. VI
Teignmouth, 3rd Baron, 1840–1915, vol. I
Teignmouth, 4th Baron, 1844–1916, vol. II
Teignmouth, 5th Baron, 1847–1926, vol. II
Teignmouth, 6th Baron, 1881–1964, vol. IV
Teixeira de Mattos, Alexander Louis, 1865–1921, vol. II
Tek Chand, Sir, 1883–1962, vol. VI
Telfer, Rev. Andrew Cecil, 1893–1978, vol. VII
Telfer, Rev. Canon William, 1886–1968, vol. VI
Telfer-Smollett, Maj.-Gen. Alexander Patrick Drummond, 1884–1954, vol. V
Telfer-Smollett, Captain James Drummond, 1824–1909, vol I
Telford, Evelyn Davison, 1876–1961, vol. VI
Telford, Rev. John, 1851–1936, vol. III
Tellier, Hon. Sir Joseph Mathias, 1861–1952, vol. V
Tellier, Louis, 1844–1935, vol. III
Telling, Harry George, 1880–1961, vol. VI
Tempany, Sir Harold Augustin, 1881–1955, vol. V
Tempel, Frederik Jan, 1900–1974, vol. VII
Temperley, Rev. Canon Arthur, 1850–1927, vol. II
Temperley, Maj.-Gen. Arthur Cecil, 1877–1940, vol. III
Temperley, Major Harold William Vazeille, 1879–1939, vol. III
Tempest, Major Adolphus V.; *see* Vane-Tempest.
Tempest, Lord Henry John V.; *see* Vane-Tempest.
Tempest, Lord Henry V.; *see* Vane-Tempest.
Tempest, Dame Mary Susan, 1866–1942, vol. IV
Tempest, Sir Percy Crosland, 1861–1924, vol. II
Tempest, Sir Robert Tempest, 3rd Bt, 1836–1901, vol. I
Tempest, Brig.-Gen. Roger Stephen, 1876–1948, vol. IV
Tempest, Sir Tristram Tempest, 4th Bt, 1865–1909, vol. I

Tempest-Hicks, Brig.-Gen. Henry, 1852–1922, vol. II
Templar-Smith, Col Sir Harold Charles, 1890–1970, vol. VI
Temple of Stowe, 5th Earl, 1871–1940, vol. III
Temple of Stowe, 6th Earl, 1909–1966, vol. VI
Temple, Sir Alfred George, 1848–1928, vol. II
Temple, Maj.-Gen. Bertram, 1896–1973, vol. VII
Temple, Charles Lindsay, 1871–1929, vol. III
Temple, Edwin, *died* 1932, vol. III
Temple, Col Frank Valiant, 1879–1937, vol. III
Temple, Most Rev. and Rt Hon. Frederick; *see* Canterbury, Archbishop of.
Temple, Frederick Charles, 1879–1957, vol. V
Temple, Comdr Grenville Mathias, 1897–1965, vol. VI
Temple, Rev. Henry, *died* 1906, vol. I
Temple, Lt-Col Henry Martindale, 1853–1905, vol. I
Temple, Hope, 1859–1938, vol. III
Temple, John, 1839–1922, vol. II
Temple, Lt-Gen. Reginald Cecil, 1877–1959, vol. V
Temple, Rt Hon. Sir Richard, 1st Bt, 1826–1902 (this entry was not transferred to Who was Who).
Temple, Lt-Col Sir Richard Carnac, 2nd Bt, 1850–1931, vol. III
Temple, Col Sir Richard Durand, 3rd Bt, 1880–1962, vol. VI
Temple, Lt-Col William, 1833–1919, vol. II
Temple, Most Rev. and Rt Hon. William, 1881–1944, vol. IV
Temple-Gore-Langton, Hon. Chandos Graham, 1873–1921, vol. II
Temple-Gore-Langton, Comdr Hon. Evelyn Arthur Grenville, 1884–1972, vol. VII
Templeman, Philip George, 1910–1972, vol. VII
Templeman, Hon. William, 1844–1914, vol. I
Templemore, 2nd Baron, 1821–1906, vol. I
Templemore, 3rd Baron, 1854–1924, vol. II
Templemore, 4th Baron, 1880–1953, vol. V
Templer, Brig.-Gen. Cyril Frank, 1869–1947, vol. IV
Templer, Frederic Gordon, 1849–1918, vol. II
Templer, Col J. L. B., 1846–1924, vol. II
Templer, Lt-Col Walter Francis, 1865–1942, vol. IV
Templeton, Archibald Angus, 1893–1969, vol. VI
Templeton, Charles Perry, 1884–1929, vol. III
Templeton, James Stanley, 1906–1977, vol. VII
Templeton, Col John Montgomery, 1840–1908, vol. I
Templeton, William Paterson, 1876–1938, vol. III
Templetown, 4th Viscount, 1853–1939, vol. III
Templewood, 1st Viscount, 1880–1959, vol. V
Tenby, 1st Viscount, 1894–1967, vol. VI
Tengbom, Ivar Justus, 1878–1968, vol. VI
Tennant, Sir Charles, 1st Bt, 1823–1906, vol. I
Tennant, Charles Coombe, 1852–1928, vol. II
Tennant, Hon. Sir David, 1829–1905, vol. I
Tennant, Francis John, 1861–1942, vol. IV
Tennant, Rev. Frederick Robert, 1866–1957, vol. V
Tennant, Rt Hon. Harold John, 1865–1935, vol. III
Tennant, Hercules, 1850–1925, vol. II
Tennant, Lt-Gen. James Francis, 1829–1915, vol. I

Tennant, Lt-Col John Edward, 1890–1941, vol. IV
Tennant, Major John Trenchard, *died* 1904, vol. I
Tennant, May, 1869–1946, vol. IV
Tennant, Robert Hugh, 1860–1936, vol. III
Tennant, Adm. Sir William George, 1890–1963, vol. VI
Tennant, Sir William Robert, 1892–1969, vol. VI
Tennent, Thomas, 1900–1962, vol. VI
Tenney, John, 1856–1944, vol. IV
Tenniel, Sir John, 1820–1914, vol. I
Tennyson, 2nd Baron, 1852–1928, vol. II
Tennyson, 3rd Baron, 1889–1951, vol. V
Tennyson, Sir Charles Bruce Locker, 1879–1977, vol. VII
Tennyson, Frederick, 1807–1898, vol. I
Tennyson-d'Eyncourt, Edmund Charles, 1855–1924, vol. II
Tennyson d'Eyncourt, Adm. Edwin Clayton; *see* d'Eyncourt.
Tennyson d'Eyncourt, Sir (Eustace) Gervais, 2nd Bt, 1902–1971, vol. VII
Tennyson-d'Eyncourt, Sir Eustace Henry William, 1st Bt, 1868–1951, vol. V
Tennyson d'Eyncourt, Sir Gervais; *see* Tennyson d'Eyncourt, Sir E. G.
Tenterden, 4th Baron, 1865–1939, vol. III
Ternan, Brig.-Gen. Trevor Patrick Breffney, 1860–1949, vol. IV
Terrell, Arthur Koberwein à Beckett, 1881–1956, vol. V
Terrell, Sir Courtney, 1881–1938, vol. III
Terrell, Edward, 1902–1979, vol. VII
Terrell, George, 1862–1952, vol. V
Terrell, Henry, 1856–1944, vol. IV
Terrell, Captain Sir Reginald, 1889–1979, vol. VII
Terrell, Thomas, *died* 1928, vol. II
Terrey, Henry, *died* 1954, vol. V
Terrington, 1st Baron, 1852–1921, vol. II
Terrington, 2nd Baron, 1877–1940, vol. III
Terrington, 3rd Baron, 1887–1961, vol. VI
Terriss, William, 1852–1897, vol. I
Terrot, Brig. Charles Russell, *died* 1944, vol. IV
Terry, Charles Sanford, 1864–1936, vol. III
Terry, Lt-Col Claude Henry Maxwell I.; *see* Imbert-Terry.
Terry, Major Sir Edward Henry Bouhier I.; *see* Imbert-Terry.
Terry, Edward O'Connor, 1844–1912, vol. I
Terry, Dame Ellen, 1848–1928, vol. II
Terry, Sir Francis William, 1877–1960, vol. V
Terry, Fred, 1863–1933, vol. III
Terry, Captain Frederic Bouhier Imbert-, 1887–1963, vol. VI
Terry, Rev. Canon George Frederick, 1864–1919, vol. II
Terry, George Percy Warner, 1867–1949, vol. IV
Terry, Harold; *see* Terry, J. E. H.
Terry, Lt-Col Sir Henry Bouhier I.; *see* Imbert-Terry.
Terry, Sir Henry Machu I.; *see* Imbert-Terry.
Terry, Captain Herbert Durell, 1847–1911, vol. I
Terry, Sir Joseph, 1827–1898, vol. I
Terry, (Joseph Edward) Harold, 1885–1939, vol. III
Terry, Joseph Pitches, 1880–1955, vol. V

Terry, Julia; *see* Neilson, J.
Terry, Marion, *died* 1930, vol. III
Terry, Phyllis N.; *see* Neilson-Terry.
Terry, Sir Richard Runciman, 1865–1938, vol. III
Terry, Major Robert Joseph Atkinson, 1869–1915, vol. I
Terry, Stephen Harding, 1853–1924, vol. II
Tertis, Lionel, 1876–1975, vol. VII
Teschemacher, Edward, 1876–1940, vol. III (A), vol. IV
Tesla, Nikola, 1857–1943, vol. IV
Tessier, Hon. Auguste, 1853–1938, vol. III
Tessier, Hon. Jules, 1852–1934, vol. III
Tester, Air Cdre John Andrews, 1907–1972, vol. VII
Tester, Leslie, 1891–1975, vol. VII
Teternikov, Feodor Kuzmich; *see* Sologub, Feodor.
Tetley, Rev. James George, 1843–1924, vol. II
Tetley, Brig. James Noel, 1898–1971, vol. VII
Tetrazzini, Luisa, 1871–1940, vol. III
Teunon, Sir William, 1863–1926, vol. II
Teversham, Brig. Mark Symonds, 1895–1973, vol. VII
Teversham, Col Richard Kinlock, 1856–1929, vol. III
Teviot, 1st Baron, 1874–1968, vol. VI
Tew, Lt-Col Harold Stuart, 1869–1945, vol. IV
Tew, Sir Mervyn Lawrence, 1876–1963, vol. VI
Tew, Percy, 1840–1921, vol. II
Tew, Thomas Percy, 1876–1953, vol. V
te Water, Charles Theodore, 1887–1964, vol. VI
Tewsley, Cyril Hocken, 1878–1950, vol. IV
Tey, Josephine; *see* Daviot, Gordon.
Teyen, Charles St Leger, 1877–1947, vol. IV
Teynham, 18th Baron, 1867–1936, vol. III
Teynham, 19th Baron, 1896–1972, vol. VII
Teyte, Dame Maggie, (Dame Margaret Cottingham), 1888–1976, vol. VII
Thacker, Maj.-Gen. Herbert Cyril, 1870–1953, vol. V
Thacker, Maj.-Gen. Percival Edward, 1873–1945, vol. IV
Thacker, Ransley Samuel, 1891–1965, vol. VI
Thackeray, Col Charles Bouverie, 1875–1938, vol. III
Thackeray, Col Edward Francis, 1870–1956, vol. V
Thackeray, Col Sir Edward Talbot, 1836–1927, vol. II
Thackeray, Rev. Francis St John, 1832–1919, vol. II
Thackeray, Brig.-Gen. Frank Staniford, 1880–1960, vol. V
Thackeray, Lance, *died* 1916, vol. II
Thackersey, Sir Vithaldas Damodher, 1873–1922, vol. II
Thackstone, Howard Harrison, 1905–1969, vol. VI
Thackwell, Major Charles Joseph, 1870–1933, vol. III
Thackwell, Col Colquhoun Grant Roche, 1857–1931, vol. III
Thackwell, Gen. Joseph Edwin, 1813–1900, vol. I
Thackwell, Maj.-Gen. William de Wilton Roche, 1834–1910, vol. I
Thaddeus, Henry Jones, 1860–1929, vol. III

Thaine, Robert Niemann, 1875–1943, vol. IV
Thakorram Kapilram, Diwan Bahadur, *born* 1868, vol. V
Thakurdas, Sir Purshotamdas, 1879–1961, vol. VI
Thane, Sir George Dancer, 1850–1930, vol. III
Thankerton, Baron (Life Peer); William Watson, 1873–1948, vol. IV
Thant, U, 1909–1974, vol. VII
Thapa, Hon. Captain Lalbahadur, 1907–1968, vol. VI
Tharp, Arthur Keane, 1848–1928, vol. II
Tharp, Philip Anthony, 1890–1958, vol. V
Thatcher, J. Wells, 1856–1946, vol. IV
Thatcher, Sir Reginald Sparshatt, 1888–1957, vol. V
Thatcher, William Sutherland, 1888–1966, vol. VI
Thavenot, Alexander Frank Noel, 1883–1947, vol. IV
Thayer, William Sydney, *died* 1932, vol. III
Theak, Air Vice-Marshal William Edward, 1898–1955, vol. V
Theaker, Harry G., 1873–1954, vol. V
Theiler, Sir Arnold, 1867–1936, vol. III
Theiler, Max, 1899–1972, vol. VII
Theis, Otto Frederick, 1881–1966, vol. VI
Thelwall, John Walter Francis, 1884–1934, vol. III
Thelwell, Sir Arthur Frederick, 1889–1966, vol. VI
Theobald, Rev. Charles, 1831–1930, vol. III
Theobald, Frederic Vincent, 1868–1930, vol. III
Theobold, Sir Henry Studdy, 1847–1934, vol. III
Theodore, Hon. Edward Granville, 1884–1950, vol. IV
Theotonio Pereira, Pedro, 1902–1972, vol. VII
Theron, Maj.-Gen. François Henri, 1891–1967, vol. VI
Thesiger, Arthur Lionel Bruce, 1872–1968, vol. VI
Thesiger, Adm. Sir Bertram Sackville, 1875–1966, vol. VI
Thesiger, Lt-Gen. Hon. Charles Wemyss, 1831–1903, vol. I
Thesiger, Hon. Sir Edward Peirson, 1842–1928, vol. II
Thesiger, Ernest, 1879–1961, vol. VI
Thesiger, Brig.-Gen. George Handcock, 1868–1915, vol. I
Thesiger, Captain Hon. Wilfred Gilbert, 1871–1920, vol. II
Theunis, Georges, 1873–1966, vol. VI
Theuriet, Claude André, *died* 1907, vol. I
Thew, Sir Edgar William, 1879–1942, vol. IV
Thibaudeau, Hon. Alfred Arthur, 1860–1926, vol. II
Thibaut, George Frederick William, 1848–1914, vol. I
Thicknesse, Very Rev. Cuthbert Carroll, 1887–1971, vol. VII
Thicknesse, Rt Rev. Francis Henry, 1829–1921, vol. II
Thicknesse, Ven. Francis Norman, 1858–1946, vol. IV
Thiman, Eric Harding, 1900–1975, vol. VII
Thin, Robert, 1861–1941, vol. IV
Thirkell, Angela Margaret, (Mrs G. L. Thirkell), 1890–1961, vol. VI

Thirkill, Sir Henry, 1886–1971, vol. VII
Thirlmere, Rowland, 1861–1932, vol. III
Thirtle, James William, 1854–1934, vol. III
Thiselton-Dyer, Sir William Turner, 1843–1928, vol. II
Thoday, David, 1883–1964, vol. VI
Thom, Donaldson Rose, *died* 1920, vol. II
Thom, Col George St Clair, *died* 1935, vol. III
Thom, Herbert James, 1895–1972, vol. VII
Thom, Lt-Col Sir John Gibb, 1891–1941, vol. IV
Thom, Sir William, *died* 1939, vol. III
Thomas, Baron (Life Peer); William Miles Webster Thomas, 1897–1980, vol. VII
Thomas, Abel, 1848–1912, vol. I
Thomas, Sir (Abraham) Garrod, 1853–1931, vol. III
Thomas, Alan Ernest Wentworth, 1896–1969, vol. VI
Thomas, Rev. Alexander, *died* 1918, vol. II
Thomas, Rev. Canon Alfred, *died* 1957, vol. V
Thomas, Sir (Alfred) Brumwell, 1868–1948, vol. IV
Thomas, Alfred Patten, 1860–1931, vol. III
Thomas, Sir Algernon Phillips Withiel, 1857–1937, vol. III
Thomas, Annie, *died* 1918, vol. II
Thomas, Col Arthur Havilland, 1860–1919, vol. II
Thomas, Arthur Hermann, 1877–1971, vol. VII
Thomas, Rt Rev. Arthur Nutter, 1869–1954, vol. V
Thomas, (Aubrey) Ralph, 1879–1957, vol. V
Thomas, Augustus, 1857–1934, vol. III
Thomas, Sir Ben Bowen, 1899–1977, vol. VII
Thomas, Bert, *died* 1966, vol. VI
Thomas, Bertie P.; *see* Pardoe-Thomas.
Thomas, Bertram Sidney, 1892–1950, vol. IV
Thomas, Brandon, 1849–1914, vol. I
Thomas, Sir Brumwell; *see* Thomas, Sir A. B.
Thomas, Carmichael, 1856–1942, vol. IV
Thomas, Cecil, 1885–1976, vol. VII
Thomas, Cecil James, 1902–1973, vol. VII
Thomas, Maj.-Gen. Charles Frederick, *died* 1922, vol. II
Thomas, Sir (Charles) Inigo, 1846–1929, vol. III
Thomas, Lt-Col Sir Charles John Howell, 1874–1943, vol. IV
Thomas, Captain Charles William, 1854–1935, vol. III
Thomas, Sir Clement P.; *see* Price Thomas.
Thomas, Daniel, 1880–1938, vol. III
Thomas, Sir Daniel Lleufer, 1863–1940, vol. III
Thomas, David Emlyn, 1892–1954, vol. V
Thomas, Rev. David John, 1862–1936, vol. III
Thomas, Ven. David Richard, *died* 1916, vol. II
Thomas, David Rowland, *died* 1955, vol. V
Thomas, Rev. David Walter, *died* 1905, vol. I
Thomas, Ven. David William, *died* 1951, vol. V
Thomas, David Winton, 1901–1970, vol. VI
Thomas, Rev. Canon Dennis Daven-, 1913–1973, vol. VII
Thomas, Dylan Marlais, 1914–1953, vol. V
Thomas, Ebenezer Rhys, 1885–1979, vol. VII
Thomas, Edgar, 1900–1979, vol. VII
Thomas, Edgar William, 1879–1963, vol. VI
Thomas, Edward, 1878–1917, vol. II

Thomas, Brig.-Gen. Edward Algernon D'Arcy, 1858–1937, vol. III
Thomas, Edward Francis, 1880–1954, vol. V
Thomas, Elbert Duncan, 1883–1953, vol. V
Thomas, Sir Eric; see Thomas, Hon. Sir W. E.
Thomas, Ethel Nancy Miles, died 1944, vol. IV
Thomas, Sir Eustace; see Thomas, Sir W. E. R.
Thomas, Evan Kyffin, 1866–1935, vol. III
Thomas, Evan Lewis, died 1935, vol. III
Thomas, Rev. Evan Lorimer, 1872–1953, vol. V
Thomas, Wing Comdr Forest Frederick Edward Y.; see Yeo-Thomas.
Thomas, Col Francis Herbert Sullivan, 1862–1944, vol. IV
Thomas, Gen. Sir Francis William, 1832–1925, vol. II
Thomas, Lt-Col Frank S. W.; see Williams-Thomas.
Thomas, Frederic George, 1872–1937, vol. III
Thomas, Frederic William W.; see Watkyn-Thomas.
Thomas, Frederick William, 1867–1956, vol. V
Thomas, Sir Garrod; see Thomas, Sir A. G.
Thomas, Sir George Alan, 7th Bt (cr 1766), 1881–1972, vol. VII
Thomas, George Arthur, 1877–1950, vol. IV
Thomas, George H.; see Holt-Thomas.
Thomas, Sir George Hector, 1884–1965, vol. VI
Thomas, George Ross, 1876–1955, vol. V
Thomas, Sir George Sidney Meade, 6th Bt (cr 1766), 1847–1918, vol. II
Thomas, Gerwyn Pascal, 1895–1956, vol. V
Thomas, Gilbert Oliver, 1891–1978, vol. VII
Thomas, Rt Hon. Sir Godfrey John Vignoles, 10th Bt (cr 1694), 1889–1968, vol. VI
Thomas, Brig.-Gen. Sir Godfrey Vignoles, 9th Bt (cr 1694), 1856–1919, vol. II
Thomas, Sir Griffith, died 1923, vol. II
Thomas, Grosvenor, 1856–1923, vol. II
Thomas, Gwilym Ewart A.; see Aeron-Thomas.
Thomas, Gen. Sir (Gwilym) Ivor, 1893–1972, vol. VII
Thomas, Brig.-Gen. Gwyn G.; see Gwyn-Thomas.
Thomas, Harold, 1847–1917, vol. II
Thomas, Rt Rev. Harry, 1897–1955, vol. V
Thomas, Sir Henry, 1878–1952, vol. V
Thomas, Henry Arnold, 1848–1924, vol. II
Thomas, Henry Hugh, 1904–1967, vol. VI
Thomas, Brig.-Gen. Henry Melville, 1870–1940, vol. III
Thomas, Herbert Henry, 1876–1935, vol. III
Thomas, Herbert J., 1892–1947, vol. IV
Thomas, Herbert James, 1882–1960, vol. V
Thomas, Herbert P.; see Preston-Thomas.
Thomas, Herbert Percival, 1879–1972, vol. VII
Thomas, Lt-Col Hubert St George, 1862–1936, vol. III
Thomas, Adm. Sir Hugh E.; see Evan-Thomas.
Thomas, Hugh Hamshaw, 1885–1962, vol. VI
Thomas, Major Sir Hugh James Protheroe, 1879–1924, vol. II
Thomas, Hugh Lloyd, 1888–1938, vol. III
Thomas, Hugh Whitelegge, died 1960, vol. V

Thomas, Sir Illtyd, 1864–1943, vol. IV
Thomas, Sir Inigo; see Thomas, Sir C. I.
Thomas, Iorwerth Rhys, 1895–1966, vol. VI
Thomas, Gen. Sir Ivor; see Thomas, Gen. Sir G. I.
Thomas, Sir Ivor Broadbent, 1890–1955, vol. V
Thomas, Ivor Cradock, 1861–1942, vol. IV
Thomas, J. Havard, 1854–1921, vol. II
Thomas, Rt Hon. James Henry, 1874–1949, vol. IV
Thomas, James Jonathan, 1850–1919, vol. II
Thomas, Sir (James William) Tudor, 1893–1976, vol. VII
Thomas, Sir John, 1834–1920, vol. II
Thomas, John Aeron, 1850–1935, vol. III
Thomas, John Herbert, 1895–1960, vol. V
Thomas, Sir John L.; see Lynn-Thomas.
Thomas, John Owen, 1862–1928, vol. II
Thomas, John Richard, 1897–1968, vol. VI
Thomas, Lt-Gen. Sir John Wellesley, 1822–1908, vol. I
Thomas, Rev. Joseph Llewelyn, died 1940, vol. III
Thomas, Joseph Silvers Williams-, 1848–1933, vol. III
Thomas, Hon. Josiah, 1863–1933, vol. III
Thomas, Ven. Lawrence, 1889–1960, vol. V
Thomas, Leonard Charles, 1879–1964, vol. VI
Thomas, Sir Leslie Montagu, 1906–1971, vol. VII
Thomas, Col Lionel B.; see Beaumont-Thomas.
Thomas, Llewelyn E.; see Evan-Thomas.
Thomas, Sir Lynn U.; see Ungoed-Thomas, Sir A. L.
Thomas, Margaret, died 1929, vol. III
Thomas, Meirion, 1894–1977, vol. VII
Thomas, Captain Mervyn Somerset, 1900–1947, vol. IV
Thomas, Rt Rev. Nathaniel Seymour, 1867–1937, vol. III
Thomas, Oldfield, 1858–1929, vol. III
Thomas, Percy, died 1922, vol. II
Thomas, Sir Percy Edward, 1883–1969, vol. VI
Thomas, Percy Goronwy, 1875–1954, vol. V
Thomas, Major Peter David, 1873–1952, vol. V
Thomas, Philip Henry, 1854–1920, vol. II
Thomas, Philip Martin, 1924–1968, vol. VI
Thomas, Ralph; see Thomas, A. R.
Thomas, Rees Griffith, 1870–1934, vol. III
Thomas, Lt-Col Sir Reginald Aneurin, 1879–1975, vol. VII
Thomas, Rt Rev. Richard, 1881–1958, vol. V
Thomas, Richard, 1890–1977, vol. VII
Thomas, Rev. Richard Albert, 1873–1943, vol. IV
Thomas, Richard Macaulay, 1857–1937, vol. III
Thomas, Ven. Richard Rice, died 1942, vol. IV
Thomas, Robert Clifford Lloyd, 1893–1969, vol. VI
Thomas, Brig. Robert Henry, 1877–1946, vol. IV
Thomas, Sir Robert John, 1st Bt (cr 1918), 1873–1951, vol. V
Thomas, Sir Robert Kyffin, 1851–1910, vol. I
Thomas, Sir Roger, 1886–1960, vol. V
Thomas, Ronald Hamilton Eliot, 1896–1977, vol. VII
Thomas, Ruth Rees-, (Mrs William Rees-Thomas); see Darwin, R.

Thomas, Salusbury Vaughan, 1856–1943, vol. IV
Thomas, Sir Samuel Joyce, *died* 1952, vol. V
Thomas, Sir Shenton; *see* Thomas, Sir T. S. W.
Thomas, Stephen Peter John Quao, *born* 1904, vol. VII
Thomas, Rev. Sutcliffe, *died* 1930, vol. III
Thomas, Terry, 1888–1978, vol. VII
Thomas, Theodore, 1835–1905, vol. I
Thomas, Sir Theodore Eastaway, 1882–1951, vol. V
Thomas, Theodore Lynam, 1900–1976, vol. VII
Thomas, Thomas Henry, 1839–1915, vol. I
Thomas, Sir Thomas Powell, *died* 1932, vol. III
Thomas, Sir (Thomas) Shenton (Whitelegge), 1879–1962, vol. VI
Thomas, Sir Tudor; *see* Thomas, Sir J. W. T.
Thomas, Sir (Walter) Eric, 1889–1963, vol. VI
Thomas, Rt Rev. Wilfrid William Henry, *died* 1953, vol. V
Thomas, William, 1891–1958, vol. V
Thomas, William, *died* 1974, vol. VII
Thomas, Sir William Beach, 1868–1957, vol. V
Thomas, Sir William Bruce, 1878–1952, vol. V
Thomas, Rev. William Ceidrych, 1850–1937, vol. III
Thomas, William Edwin S.; *see* Somerset-Thomas.
Thomas, Sir (William) Eustace (Rhyddlad), 2nd Bt (*cr* 1918), 1909–1957, vol. V
Thomas, Sir William Henry, 1859–1947, vol. IV
Thomas, Rev. William Henry Griffith, 1861–1924, vol. II
Thomas, William Herbert Evans, 1886–1979, vol. VII
Thomas, Sir William James, 1st Bt (*cr* 1919), 1867–1945, vol. IV
Thomas, William Luson, 1830–1900, vol. I
Thomas, William Moy, 1828–1910, vol. I
Thomas, William Norman, 1885–1960, vol. V
Thomas, William R.; *see* Rees-Thomas.
Thomas, William Stanley Russell, 1896–1957, vol. V
Thomas, William Thelwall, 1865–1927, vol. II
Thomas-Stanford, Sir Charles, 1st Bt, 1858–1932, vol. III
Thomason, Maj.-Gen. Charles Simson, 1833–1911, vol. I
Thomasson, Lt-Col Franklin, *died* 1941, vol. IV
Thomasson, John Pennington, *died* 1904, vol. I
Thomlinson, Lt-Col Sir William, 1854–1943, vol. IV
Thompson, Col Albert George, *died* 1940, vol. III
Thompson, Alexander Hamilton, 1873–1952, vol. V
Thompson, Alexander M., 1861–1948, vol. IV
Thompson, Alfred Corderoy, *died* 1928, vol. II
Thompson, Captain Sir Algar de Clifford Charles M.; *see* Meysey-Thompson.
Thompson, Lt-Gen. Arnold Bunbury, 1822–1917, vol. II
Thompson, Rev. Arthur Charles, 1868–1933, vol. III
Thompson, Arthur Hugh, *died* 1937, vol. III
Thompson, Ven. Arthur Huxley, 1872–1951, vol. V

Thompson, Rev. Arthur Wellington, *died* 1937, vol. III
Thompson, Rev. Austin Henry, 1870–1941, vol. IV
Thompson, Lt-Col Cecil Henry Farrer, 1882–1975, vol. VII
Thompson, Charles Henry, 1865–1948, vol. IV
Thompson, Charles John S., *died* 1943, vol. IV
Thompson, Comdr Charles Ralfe, 1894–1966, vol. VI
Thompson, Maj.-Gen. Charles William, 1859–1940, vol. III
Thompson, Captain Hon. Claude Henry M.; *see* Meysey-Thompson.
Thompson, Claude Metford, 1855–1933, vol. III
Thompson, Lt-Col Cyril Powney, 1864–1924, vol. II
Thompson, Daniel Varney, 1902–1980, vol. VII
Thompson, Sir D'Arcy Wentworth, 1860–1948, vol. IV
Thompson, Dorothy, 1894–1961, vol. VI
Thompson, Mrs E. Roffe; *see* Lejeune, C. A.
Thompson, Lt-Col Edgar Hynes, 1910–1976, vol. VII
Thompson, Edith Marie, *died* 1961, vol. VI
Thompson, Edmund S.; *see* Symes-Thompson.
Thompson, Edward, 1881–1954, vol. V
Thompson, Edward Charles, 1851–1933, vol. III
Thompson, Edward Herbert, 1860–1935, vol. III
Thompson, Edward John, 1886–1946, vol. IV
Thompson, Sir Edward Maunde, 1840–1929, vol. III
Thompson, Edward Raymond, 1872–1928, vol. II
Thompson, Edward Vincent, 1880–1976, vol. VII
Thompson, Edwin, 1881–1967, vol. VI
Thompson, Edwin Reginald R.; *see* Roe-Thompson.
Thompson, Eric, 1905–1969, vol. VI
Thompson, Sir Eric; *see* Thompson, Sir J. E. S.
Thompson, Sir Ernest, 1865–1941, vol. IV
Thompson, Ernest Claude M.; *see* Meysey-Thompson.
Thompson, E(rnest) Heber, 1891–1971, vol. VII
Thompson, Estelle Merle O'Brien; *see* Oberon, Merle.
Thompson, Francis, 1859–1907, vol. I
Thompson, Francis L.; *see* Longstreth-Thompson.
Thompson, Frank Charles, 1890–1977, vol. VII
Thompson, Fred, 1884–1949, vol. IV
Thompson, Fred, 1883–1951, vol. V
Thompson, Frederick Charles, *died* 1919, vol. II
Thompson, Brig.-Gen. Frederick Hacket-, 1858–1944, vol. IV
Thompson, Sir Geoffrey Harington, 1898–1967, vol. VI
Thompson, Rev. George, *died* 1941, vol. IV
Thompson, George Henry Main, 1882–1957, vol. V
Thompson, Rev. Gerald Alexander, 1868–1939, vol. III
Thompson, Gibson, *died* 1917, vol. II
Thompson, Gustav Weber, 1878–1944, vol. IV
Thompson, Captain Harold, 1881–1917, vol. II
Thompson, Maj.-Gen. Sir Harry Neville, 1861–1925, vol. II

Thompson, Harry Sydney, 1878–1966, vol. VI
Thompson, Sir Henry, 1st Bt (cr 1899), 1820–1904, vol. I
Thompson, Rev. Henry, died 1916, vol. II
Thompson, Henry Edmund S.; see Symes-Thompson.
Thompson, Sir (Henry Francis) Herbert, 2nd Bt (cr 1899), 1859–1944, vol. IV
Thompson, Rt Rev. Henry Gregory, 1871–1942, vol. IV
Thompson, Henry Nilus, died 1938, vol. III
Thompson, Rev. (Henry) Percy, 1858–1935, vol. III
Thompson, Henry Yates, 1838–1928, vol. II
Thompson, Herbert, 1856–1945, vol. IV
Thompson, Herbert, 1870–1949, vol. IV
Thompson, Sir Herbert; see Thompson, Sir Henry F. H.
Thompson, Herbert Marshall, died 1945, vol. IV
Thompson, Col Horace Cuthbert Rees, 1893–1975, vol. VII
Thompson, Hubert Charles M.; see Meysey-Thompson.
Thompson, Sir Ivan, 1894–1970, vol. VI
Thompson, J. Ashburton, 1846–1915, vol. I
Thompson, Sir James, 1835–1906, vol. I
Thompson, James Coulthred, died 1935, vol. III
Thompson, Rt Rev. James Denton, 1856–1924, vol. II
Thompson, Rev. James Matthew, 1878–1956, vol. V
Thompson, Maj.-Gen. John, 1830–1915, vol. I (A)
Thompson, John Baird, 1868–1948, vol. IV
Thompson, Sir (John) Eric (Sidney), 1898–1975, vol. VII
Thompson, John Fairfield, 1881–1968, vol. VI
Thompson, John McLean, 1887–1977, vol. VII
Thompson, John Ockelford, 1872–1940, vol. III
Thompson, Sir John Perronet, 1873–1935, vol. III
Thompson, John William Howard, died 1959, vol. V
Thompson, Rt Rev. Kenneth George, 1909–1975, vol. VII
Thompson, Llewellyn E., 1904–1972, vol. VII
Thompson, Sir Luke, 1867–1941, vol. IV
Thompson, Sir Matthew William, 3rd Bt (cr 1890), 1872–1956, vol. V
Thompson, Maurice, died 1901, vol. I
Thompson, Merrick Arnold Bardsley D.; see Denton-Thompson.
Thompson, Owen, 1868–1958, vol. V
Thompson, Rev. Sir Peile, 2nd Bt (cr 1890), 1844–1918, vol. II
Thompson, Sir Peile Beaumont, 4th Bt (cr 1890), 1874–1972, vol. VII
Thompson, Adm. Percival Henry H.; see Hall-Thompson.
Thompson, Sir Percy, 1872–1946, vol. IV
Thompson, Rev. Percy; see Thompson, Rev. H. P.
Thompson, Peter, 1871–1921, vol. II
Thompson, Piers Gilchrist, 1893–1969, vol. VI
Thompson, Rev. Ralph Wardlaw, died 1916, vol. II
Thompson, Rt Hon. Sir Ralph Wood, 1830–1902, vol. I
Thompson, Reginald Campbell, 1876–1941, vol. IV

Thompson, Reginald Edward, 1834–1912, vol. I
Thompson, Rev. Reginald William, died 1953, vol. V
Thompson, Col Richard, 1852–1932, vol. III
Thompson, Col Richard Frederick M.; see Meysey-Thompson.
Thompson, Lt-Col Richard James Campbell, 1880–1946, vol. IV
Thompson, Maj.-Gen. Richard Lovell Brereton, 1874–1957, vol. V
Thompson, Rt Hon. Robert, 1839–1918, vol. II
Thompson, Robert Cyril, 1907–1967, vol. VI
Thompson, Sir Robert James, 1845–1926, vol. II
Thompson, Robert John, 1867–1951, vol. V
Thompson, Sir Robert Norman, 1878–1951, vol. V
Thompson, Lt-Col Roland-Wycliffe, 1864–1940, vol. III
Thompson, Lt-Col Rt Hon. S. H. H.; see Hall-Thompson.
Thompson, Samuel Nock, 1851–1938, vol. III
Thompson, Silvanus Phillips, 1851–1916, vol. II
Thompson, Major Stephen John, 1875–1955, vol. V
Thompson, Sylvia, (Mrs Peter Luling), 1902–1968, vol. VI
Thompson, Theodore, 1878–1935, vol. III
Thompson, Hon. Thomas, vol. II
Thompson, Sir Thomas Raikes, 3rd Bt (cr 1806), 1852–1904, vol. I
Thompson, Lt-Col Sir Thomas Raikes Lovett, 4th Bt (cr 1806), 1881–1964, vol. VI
Thompson, Maj.-Gen. Sir Treffry Owen, 1888–1979, vol. VII
Thompson, Viginti Tertius, 1862–1946, vol. IV
Thompson, Sir Walter, 1875–1951, vol. V
Thompson, Walter Scott, 1885–1966, vol. VI
Thompson, Rev. William, died 1909, vol. I
Thompson, Brig.-Gen. William Arthur Murray, 1866–1938, vol. III
Thompson, William David James C.; see Cargill Thompson.
Thompson, William George, 1863–1953, vol. V
Thompson, Brig.-Gen. William George Hemsley, 1871–1944, vol. IV
Thompson, William Harding, 1887–1946, vol. IV
Thompson, Sir William Henry, died 1918, vol. II
Thompson, William Hugh, 1885–1966, vol. VI
Thompson, Rt Rev. William Jameson, 1885–1975, vol. VII
Thompson, Sir William John, 1861–1929, vol. III
Thompson, William John, 1871–1959, vol. V
Thompson, William John, died 1971, vol. VII
Thompson, William Marcus, 1857–1907, vol. I
Thompson, Lt-Col William Maxwell, 1869–1934, vol. III
Thompson, Col William Oliver, 1844–1917, vol. II
Thompson, William Robin, 1887–1972, vol. VII
Thompson, William Whitaker, 1857–1920, vol. II
Thompstone, Sir Eric Westbury, 1897–1974, vol. VII
Thompstone, Sydney Wilson, 1863–1935, vol. III
Thoms, Lt-Col Nathaniel William Benjamin Butler, 1880–1957, vol. V
Thomson, 1st Baron, 1875–1930, vol. III

Thomson, Hon. Lord; Alexander Thomson, 1914–1979, vol. VII

Thomson, Rt Hon. Lord; George Reid Thomson, 1893–1962, vol. VI

Thomson of Fleet, 1st Baron, 1894–1976, vol. VII

Thomson, A(dam) Bruce, 1885–1976, vol. VII

Thomson, Addison Yalden, 1863–1931, vol. III

Thomson, Brig. Alan Fortescue, 1880–1957, vol. V

Thomson, Engr Captain Alan Leslie, 1890–1970, vol. VI

Thomson, Alexander; see Thomson, Hon. Lord.

Thomson, Lt-Col Alexander Guthrie, 1873–1953, vol. V

Thomson, Col Alexander M.; see Milne-Thomson.

Thomson, Hon. Alexander Macdonald, 1863–1924, vol. II

Thomson, Alexander Stuart Duff, 1854–1927, vol. II

Thomson, Alfred Reginald, died 1979, vol. VII

Thomson, Rev. Andrew, 1814–1901, vol. I

Thomson, Brig.-Gen. Andrew Graham, 1858–1926, vol. II

Thomson, Captain Anthony Standidge, 1851–1925, vol. II

Thomson, Arthur, 1858–1935, vol. III

Thomson, Sir Arthur; see Thomson, Sir J. A.

Thomson, Sir (Arthur) Landsborough, 1890–1977, vol. VII

Thomson, Sir Arthur Peregrine, 1890–1977, vol. VII

Thomson, Sir Basil Home, 1861–1939, vol. III

Thomson, Benjamin, died 1934, vol. III

Thomson, César, 1856–1931, vol. III

Thomson, Rev. Canon Clement R., 1870–1953, vol. V

Thomson, Sir Daniel, 1912–1976, vol. VII

Thomson, David, 1912–1970, vol. VI

Thomson, David Alexander, 1872–1922, vol. II

Thomson, David Couper, 1861–1954, vol. V

Thomson, David Croal, 1855–1930, vol. III

Thomson, Lt-Col David George, 1856–1923, vol. II

Thomson, David Landsborough, 1901–1964, vol. VI

Thomson, Donald F., 1901–1970, vol. VI (AII)

Thomson, Sir Douglas; see Thomson, Sir J. D. W.

Thomson, Hon. Dugald, 1848–1922, vol. II

Thomson, Edward William, 1849–1924, vol. II

Thomson, Elihu, 1853–1937, vol. III

Thomson, Eric Hugh, 1909–1973, vol. VII

Thomson, Vice-Adm. Evelyn Claude Ogilvie, 1884–1941, vol. IV

Thomson, Sir (Francis) Vernon, 1st Bt (cr 1938), 1881–1953, vol. V

Thomson, Frank David, 1877–1934, vol. III

Thomson, Sir Frederick Charles, 1st Bt (cr 1929), 1875–1935, vol. III

Thomson, Sir Frederick Whitley W.; see Whitley-Thomson.

Thomson, Surg.-Col Sir George, 1843–1903, vol. I

Thomson, George, died 1939, vol. III

Thomson, Major George, 1889–1970, vol. VI

Thomson, George Malcolm, 1848–1933, vol. III

Thomson, Sir George Paget, 1892–1975, vol. VII

Thomson, Rear-Adm. Sir George Pirie, 1887–1965, vol. VI

Thomson, Rt Hon. George Reid; see Thomson, Rt Hon. Lord.

Thomson, Lt-Col George Ritchie, died 1946, vol. IV

Thomson, Rev. George Thomas, 1887–1958, vol. V

Thomson, George Walker, 1883–1949, vol. IV

Thomson, George William, 1845–1928, vol. II

Thomson, Gladys S.; see Scott Thomson.

Thomson, Sir Godfrey Hilton, 1881–1955, vol. V

Thomson, Sir Graeme, 1875–1933, vol. III

Thomson, Harry Redmond, 1860–1917, vol. II

Thomson, Harry Torrance, 1868–1944, vol. IV

Thomson, Henry, 1840–1916, vol. II

Thomson, Maj.-Gen. Henry, 1851–1932, vol. III

Thomson, Henry Alexis, 1863–1924, vol. II

Thomson, Henry John, died 1966, vol. VI

Thomson, Henry Wagstaffe, 1874–1941, vol. IV

Thomson, Herbert Campbell, 1870–1940, vol. III

Thomson, Hugh, 1860–1920, vol. II

Thomson, Col Sir Hugh Davie W.; see White-Thomson.

Thomson, Maj.-Gen. Hugh Gordon, 1830–1910, vol. I

Thomson, Sir James, 1848–1929, vol. III

Thomson, Maj.-Gen. James, 1862–1953, vol. V

Thomson, James, 1895–1959, vol. V

Thomson, James Alexander Kerr, 1879–1959, vol. V

Thomson, Sir (James) Douglas (Wishart), 2nd Bt (cr 1929), 1905–1972, vol. VII

Thomson, James Moffat, died 1953, vol. V

Thomson, Maj.-Gen. James Noel, 1888–1978, vol. VII

Thomson, James Oliver, 1889–1971, vol. VII

Thomson, James Park, 1854–1941, vol. IV

Thomson, Very Rev. James Sutherland, 1892–1972, vol. VII

Thomson, Lt-Col Sir James Wishart, 1871–1929, vol. III

Thomson, Captain Jocelyn Home, 1859–1908, vol. I

Thomson, John, 1856–1926, vol. II

Thomson, John, 1903–1974, vol. VII

Thomson, John A.; see Anstruther-Thomson.

Thomson, Sir (John) Arthur, 1861–1933, vol. III

Thomson, John Ebenezer Honeyman, 1841–1923, vol. II

Thomson, Lt-Col John Ferguson, 1880–1937, vol. III

Thomson, John Gordon, died 1937, vol. III

Thomson, Sir John Mackay, 1887–1974, vol. VII

Thomson, John Millar, 1849–1933, vol. III

Thomson, J(ohn) Murray, 1885–1974, vol. VII

Thomson, John Stuart, 1888–1973, vol. VII

Thomson, Sir Joseph John, 1856–1940, vol. III

Thomson, Sir Landsborough; see Thomson, Sir A. L.

Thomson, Rt Rev. Leonard Jauncey W.; see White-Thomson.

Thomson, Leslie, died 1929, vol. III

Thomson, Louis Melville M.; see Milne-Thomson.

Thomson, Mark Alméras, 1903–1962, vol. VI

Thomson, (Matthew) Sydney, 1894–1969, vol. VI

Thomson, Sir Mitchell M.; see Mitchell-Thomson.

Thomson, Gen. Sir Mowbray, 1832–1917, vol. II
Thomson, Brig.-Gen. Noel Arbuthnot, 1872–1959, vol. V
Thomson, Very Rev. P. D., 1872–1955, vol. V
Thomson, Col Sir Robert Thomas W.; see White-Thomson.
Thomson, Col Roger Gordon, 1878–1976, vol. VII
Thomson, Sir Ronald Jordan, 1895–1978, vol. VII
Thomson, Roy Harry Goodisson, 1891–1974, vol. VII
Thomson, Sir StClair, 1859–1943, vol. IV
Thomson, Col Samuel John, 1853–1936, vol. III
Thomson, Sydney; see Thomson, M. S.
Thomson, Theodore, died 1916, vol. II
Thomson, Rev. T(homas) B(entley) Stewart, 1889–1973, vol. VII
Thomson, Trevelyan, 1875–1928, vol. II
Thomson, Sir Vernon; see Thomson, Sir F. V.
Thomson, Walter Henry, 1856–1917, vol. II
Thomson, Sir Wilfrid Forbes Home, 1st Bt (cr 1925), 1858–1939, vol. III
Thomson, Sir William, 1843–1910, vol. I
Thomson, Sir William, 1856–1947, vol. IV
Thomson, Sir William, 1916–1971, vol. VII
Thomson, Sir William Brown, 1863–1937, vol. III
Thomson, Col William David, 1858–1941, vol. IV
Thomson, Sir William Gardner, 1874–1938, vol. III
Thomson, Sir William Johnston, 1881–1949, vol. IV
Thomson, Lt-Gen. Sir William Montgomerie, 1877–1963, vol. VI
Thomson, Sir William R.; see Rowan-Thomson.
Thomson, Sir William Willis Dalziel, died 1950, vol. IV
Thomson-Walker, Sir John William, died 1937, vol. III
Thorburn, Archibald, 1860–1935, vol. III
Thorburn, Col Harold Hay, 1882–1937, vol. III
Thorburn, J. Hay, 1848–1931, vol. III
Thorburn, James Jamieson, 1864–1929, vol. III
Thorburn, Sir Michael Grieve, 1851–1934, vol. III
Thorburn, Hon. Sir Robert, 1836–1906, vol. I
Thorburn, Septimus Smet, 1844–1924, vol. II
Thorburn, Thomas, died 1927, vol. II
Thorburn, Rev. Thomas James, 1858–1923, vol. II
Thorburn, Sir Walter, 1842–1908, vol. I
Thorburn, Sir William, died 1923, vol. II
Thorburn, Lt-Col William, 1881–1959, vol. V
Thorby, Hon. Harold Victor Campbell, 1888–1973, vol. VII
Thorley, George Earlam, 1830–1904, vol. I
Thorley, Wilfrid, 1878–1963, vol. VI
Thorman, Rt Rev. Joseph, 1871–1936, vol. III
Thorn, Sir Jules, 1899–1980, vol. VII
Thorn-Drury, George; see Drury.
Thorndike, (Arthur) Russell, 1885–1972, vol. VII
Thorndike, Russell; see Thorndike, A. R.
Thorndike, Dame Sybil, 1882–1976, vol. VII
Thorne, Alfred Charles, 1870–1952, vol. V
Thorne, Gen. Sir Andrew; see Thorne, Gen. Sir A. F. A. N.
Thorne, Atwood, 1867–1932, vol. III
Thorne, Gen. Sir (Augustus Francis) Andrew (Nicol), 1885–1970, vol. VI

Thorne, Charles, died 1933, vol. III
Thorne, Edward Henry, 1834–1916, vol. II
Thorne, George Rennie, 1853–1934, vol. III
Thorne, Gordon, 1912–1965, vol. VI
Thorne, Sir John Anderson, 1888–1964, vol. VI
Thorne, Sir Richard Thorne, 1841–1899, vol. I
Thorne, Air Vice-Marshal Walter, 1890–1960, vol. V
Thorne, Rt Hon. Will, 1857–1946, vol. IV
Thorne, Sir William, 1839–1917, vol. II
Thorne, Sir William Calthrop, 1864–1935, vol. III
Thorne, William Hobart Houghton, 1875–1931, vol. III
Thorne, William Huxtable, 1882–1951, vol. V
Thorne-Waite, Robert, 1842–1935, vol. III
Thorneloe, Most Rev. George, 1848–1935, vol. III
Thornely, Sir Arnold, 1870–1953, vol. V
Thornely, P. Wilfrid, 1879–1926, vol. II
Thornely, Thomas, 1855–1949, vol. IV
Thorneycroft, Maj.-Gen. Alexander Whitelaw, 1859–1931, vol. III
Thorneycroft, Major George Edward Mervyn, 1883–1943, vol. IV
Thorneycroft, Harry, 1892–1956, vol. V
Thorneycroft, Thomas Hamo, died 1970, vol. VI
Thorneycroft, Wallace, 1864–1954, vol. V
Thornhill, Sir Anthony John Compton-, 2nd Bt, 1868–1949, vol. IV
Thornhill, Arthur Horace, 1895–1970, vol. VI
Thornhill, Arthur John, 1850–1930, vol. III
Thornhill, Col Cudbert John Massy, 1883–1952, vol. V
Thornhill, George, died 1908, vol. I
Thornhill, Col George B.; see Badham-Thornhill.
Thornhill, Lt-Col Sir Henry Beaufoy, 1854–1942, vol. IV
Thornhill, Noel, 1881–1955, vol. V
Thornhill, Dame Rachel; see Crowdy, Dame R. E.
Thornhill, Sir Thomas, 1st Bt, 1837–1900, vol. I
Thornhill, Thomas Bryan C.; see Clarke-Thornhill.
Thornley, Sir Hubert Gordon, 1884–1962, vol. VI
Thornley, Reginald Ernest, 1872–1942, vol. IV
Thornley, Major Samuel Kerr, 1871–1947, vol. IV
Thornton, Alfred Henry Robinson, 1863–1939, vol. III
Thornton, Lt-Col Arthur Parry, 1848–1909, vol. I
Thornton, Rev. Augustus Vansittart, 1851–1913, vol. I
Thornton, Lt-Col Charles Edward, 1867–1946, vol. IV
Thornton, Charles Inglis, 1850–1929, vol. III
Thornton, Ven. Claude Cyprian, died 1939, vol. III
Thornton, Edna, died 1964, vol. VI
Thornton, Rt Hon. Sir Edward, 1817–1906, vol. I
Thornton, Brig. Sir Edward Newbury, 1878–1946, vol. IV
Thornton, Sir Ernest Hugh, 1884–1951, vol. V
Thornton, Rev. Frederick Ferdinand Martin S., died 1938, vol. III
Thornton, George Lestock, 1872–1951, vol. V

Thornton, Rev. George Ruthven, 1882–1964, vol. VI

Thornton, Sir Gerard; see Thornton, Sir H. G.

Thornton, Sir (Henry) Gerard, 1892–1977, vol. VII

Thornton, Air Vice-Marshal Henry Norman, 1896–1971, vol. VII

Thornton, Sir Henry Worth, 1871–1933, vol. III

Thornton, Rev. Herbert Parry, died 1923, vol. II

Thornton, Hugh Aylmer, 1872–1962, vol. VI

Thornton, Sir Hugh Cholmondeley, 1881–1962, vol. VI

Thornton, James Cholmondeley, 1906–1969, vol. VI

Thornton, Sir James Howard, 1834–1919, vol. II

Thornton, Col Leslie Heber, 1873–1937, vol. III

Thornton, Rev. Lionel Spencer, 1884–1960, vol. V

Thornton, Maxwell Ruthven, 1878–1950, vol. IV

Thornton, Percy Melville, 1841–1918, vol. II

Thornton, R. M., 1841–1913, vol. I

Thornton, Major Robert Lawrence, 1865–1947, vol. IV

Thornton, Hon. Robert Stirton, 1863–1936, vol. III

Thornton, Major Roland Hobhouse, 1892–1967, vol. VI

Thornton, Russel William, 1881–1966, vol. VI

Thornton, Rt Rev. Samuel, 1835–1917, vol. II

Thornton, Rev. Stephen Augustine Lawrence, 1871–1936, vol. III

Thornton, Swinford Leslie, 1853–1939, vol. III

Thornton, Sir Thomas, 1829–1903, vol. I

Thornton, Col Thomas Anson, 1887–1978, vol. VII

Thornton, Thomas Henry, 1832–1913, vol. I

Thornton, William Mundell, 1870–1944, vol. IV

Thornton-Berry, Trevor, 1895–1967, vol. VI

Thornton Cook, Mrs Elsie; see Cook.

Thornton-Duesbury, Rt Rev. Charles Leonard, 1867–1928, vol. II

Thornton-Kemsley, Col Sir Colin Norman, 1903–1977, vol. VII

Thornton-Smith, Ernest T., 1881–1971, vol. VII

Thornycroft, Lt-Col Charles Mytton, 1879–1948, vol. IV

Thornycroft, Sir Hamo; see Thornycroft, Sir W. H.

Thornycroft, Sir John Edward, 1872–1960, vol. V

Thornycroft, Sir John Isaac, 1843–1928, vol. II

Thornycroft, Oliver, 1885–1956, vol. V

Thornycroft, Sir (William) Hamo, 1850–1925, vol. II

Thoroddsen, Thorvald, 1855–1921, vol. II

Thorogood, Horace Walter, died 1962, vol. VI

Thorogood, Stanley, 1873–1953, vol. V

Thorold, Algar Labouchere, 1866–1936, vol. III

Thorold, Rev. Ernest Hayford, 1879–1940, vol. III

Thorold, Sir Guy Frederick, 1898–1970, vol. VI

Thorold, Col Hayford Douglas, 1859–1934, vol. III

Thorold, Air Vice-Marshal Henry Karslake, 1896–1966, vol. VI

Thorold, Sir James Ernest, 14th Bt, 1877–1965, vol. VI

Thorold, Sir John George, 13th Bt, 1870–1951, vol. V

Thorold, Sir John Henry, 12th Bt, 1842–1922, vol. II

Thorold, Montague George, 1844–1920, vol. II

Thorold, William James, 1871–1942, vol. IV (A), vol. V

Thoroton, Lt-Col Charles Julian, 1875–1939, vol. III

Thorp, Lt-Col Arthur Hugh, 1869–1955, vol. V

Thorp, Austin, 1873–1918, vol. II

Thorp, Adm. Charles Frederick, 1869–1954, vol. V

Thorp, Col Herbert Walter Beck, 1879–1934, vol. III

Thorp, J. Walter H., 1851–1912, vol. I

Thorp, Sir John Kingsmill Robert, 1912–1961, vol. VI

Thorp, Joseph Peter, 1873–1962, vol. VI

Thorp, Linton Theodore, 1884–1950, vol. IV

Thorp, Brig. Robert Allen Fenwick, 1900–1966, vol. VI

Thorp, William Henry, 1852–1944, vol. IV

Thorpe, A(rthur) Winton, 1865–1952, vol. V

Thorpe, Sir Edward, 1845–1925, vol. II

Thorpe, Brig.-Gen. Edward Ivan de Sausmarez, 1871–1942, vol. IV

Thorpe, Frank Gordon, 1885–1967, vol. VI

Thorpe, Col Sir Fred Garner, 1893–1970, vol. VI

Thorpe, Maj.-Gen. Gervase, 1877–1962, vol. VI

Thorpe, Harry, 1913–1977, vol. VII

Thorpe, James, 1876–1949, vol. IV

Thorpe, Sir Jocelyn Field, 1872–1940, vol. III

Thorpe, John Henry, 1887–1944, vol. IV

Thorpe, Ven. John Henry, died 1932, vol. III

Thorpe, Lewis Guy Melville, 1913–1977, vol. VII

Thorpe, Surg. Rear-Adm. Vidal Gunson, 1864–1948, vol. IV

Thorpe, William Geoffrey, 1909–1975, vol. VII

Thorson, Hon. Joseph T., 1889–1978, vol. VII

Thorvaldson, Gunnar S., 1901–1969, vol. VI

Thorvardsson, Stefan, 1900–1951, vol. V

Thoseby, William Martin, 1901–1959, vol. V

Threipland, Col William M.; see Murray-Threipland.

Threlfall, Sir Richard, 1861–1932, vol. III

Threlfall, Thomas, 1842–1907, vol. I

Threlford, Sir W. Lacon, died 1958, vol. V

Thresh, John Clough, 1850–1932, vol. III

Thresher, Lt-Col James Henville, 1870–1943, vol. IV

Thrift, Sir John Edward, 1845–1926, vol. II

Thrift, William Edward, 1870–1942, vol. IV

Thring, 1st Baron, 1818–1907, vol. I

Thring, Sir Arthur Theodore, 1860–1932, vol. III

Thring, Captain Ernest Walsham Charles, 1875–1970, vol. VI

Thring, George Herbert, 1859–1941, vol. IV

Thring, Captain Walter Hugh Charles Samuel, 1873–1949, vol. IV

Throckmorton, Geoffrey William Berkeley, 1883–1976, vol. VII

Throckmorton, Sir Nicholas William George, 9th Bt, 1838–1919, vol. II

Throckmorton, Sir Richard Charles Acton, 10th Bt, 1839–1927, vol. II

Throssell, Arthur Graham, 1881–1942, vol. IV

Throssell, Hon. George, 1840–1910, vol. I

Throssell, Hugo Vivian Hope, 1884–1933, vol. III

Thubron, John Brown Sydney, 1879–1949, vol. IV
Thuillier, Sir Henry Edward Landor, 1813–1906, vol. I
Thuillier, Maj.-Gen. Sir Henry Fleetwood, 1868–1953, vol. V
Thuillier, Sir Henry Ravenshaw, 1838–1922, vol. II
Thuillier, Brig.-Gen. Willoughby, 1860–1941, vol. IV
Thulrai, Taluqdar of, 1865–1920, vol. II (A), vol. III
Thumboo Chetty, Amatyasiromani Sir Bernard T., 1877–1952, vol. VI (AI)
Thunder, Lt-Col Stuart Harman Joseph, 1879–1948, vol. IV
Thurber, James Grover, 1894–1961, vol. VI
Thurburn, Edward Alexander, 1841–1915, vol. I (A)
Thurburn, Col James White, 1848–1930, vol. III
Thureau-Dangin, François, 1872–1944, vol. IV
Thureau-Dangin, Paul Marie Pierre, 1837–1913, vol. I
Thurles, Viscount; James Anthony Butler, 1916–1940, vol. III
Thurlow, 5th Baron, 1838–1916, vol. II
Thurlow, 6th Baron, 1869–1952, vol. V
Thurlow, 7th Baron, 1910–1971, vol. VII
Thurnam, Walter Digby, 1854–1934, vol. III
Thurnheer, Walter, 1884–1945, vol. IV
Thursby, Adm. Sir Cecil Fiennes, 1861–1936, vol. III
Thursby, Sir George James, 3rd Bt, 1869–1941, vol. IV
Thursby, Sir John Hardy, 1st Bt, 1826–1901, vol. I
Thursby, Sir John Ormerod Scarlett, 2nd Bt, 1861–1920, vol. II
Thursby-Pelham, James, 1869–1947, vol. IV
Thursfield, (Edward) Philip, 1876–1962, vol. VI
Thursfield, Rear-Adm. Henry George, 1882–1963, vol. VI
Thursfield, Hugh, died 1944, vol. IV
Thursfield, Sir James Richard, 1840–1923, vol. II
Thursfield, Philip; see Thursfield, E. P.
Thursfield, Captain (S) Raymond Spencer, 1882–1953, vol. V
Thurso, 1st Viscount, 1890–1970, vol. VI
Thurstan, Edward William Paget, 1880–1947, vol. IV
Thurstan, Violetta, died 1978, vol. VII
Thurston, Albert Peter, 1881–1964, vol. VI
Thurston, E. Temple, 1879–1933, vol. III
Thurston, Edgar, 1855–1935, vol. III
Thurston, Frederick John, 1901–1953, vol. V
Thurston, Gavin Leonard Bourdas, 1911–1980, vol. VII
Thurston, Sir George; see Thurston, Sir T. G. O.
Thurston, Rev. Herbert, 1856–1939, vol. III
Thurston, Col Hugh Champneys, 1862–1919, vol. II
Thurston, Col Hugh Stanley, 1869–1945, vol. IV
Thurston, Katherine Cecil, 1875–1911, vol. I
Thurston, Sir (T.) George (O.), died 1950, vol. IV
Thurtle, Ernest, 1884–1954, vol. V

Thwaite, Hartley, 1903–1978, vol. VII
Thwaites, Lt-Col Norman Graham, 1872–1956, vol. V
Thwaites, Gen. Sir William, 1868–1947, vol. IV
Thwing, Charles Franklin, 1853–1937, vol. III
Thyateira, Archbishop of; see Athenagoras, Archbishop.
Thyne, William, 1901–1978, vol. VII
Thynne, Lord Alexander George, 1873–1918, vol. II
Thynne, Major Algernon Carteret, 1868–1917, vol. II
Thynne, Col Hon. Andrew Joseph, 1847–1927, vol. II
Thynne, Rev. Arthur Barugh, 1840–1917, vol. II
Thynne, Rev. Arthur Christopher, 1832–1908, vol. II
Thynne, Captain Denis Granville, 1875–1955, vol. V
Thynne, Francis John, 1830–1910, vol. I
Thynne, Sir Henry, 1839–1915, vol. I (A)
Thynne, Rt Hon. Lord Henry Frederick, 1832–1904, vol. I
Thynne, Maj.-Gen. Sir Reginald Thomas, 1843–1926, vol. II
Thynne, Col Ulric Oliver, 1871–1957, vol. V
Tiarks, Frank Cyril, 1874–1952, vol. V
Tiarks, Rt Rev. John Gerhard, 1903–1974, vol. VII
Tibbits, Vice-Adm. Charles, 1872–1947, vol. IV
Tibbits, Charles John, 1861–1935, vol. III
Tibbits, Sir Cliff; see Tibbits, Sir J. C.
Tibbits, Sir (Jabez) Cliff, 1884–1974, vol. VII
Tibble, John William, 1901–1972, vol. VII
Tibbles, Sydney Granville, 1884–1960, vol. V
Tibbles, William, 1859–1928, vol. II
Tichborne, Sir Anthony Joseph Henry Doughty Doughty-, 14th Bt, 1914–1968, vol. VI
Tichborne, Charles Robert, died 1905, vol. I
Tichborne, Rt Rev. Ford, died 1940, vol. III
Tichborne, Sir Henry Alfred Joseph Doughty-, 12th Bt, 1866–1910, vol. I
Tichborne, Sir Joseph Henry Bernard Doughty-, 13th Bt, 1890–1930, vol. III
Tickell, Lt-Col Edward James, 1861–1942, vol. IV
Tickell, Maj.-Gen. Sir Eustace Francis, 1893–1972, vol. VII
Tickell, Rear-Adm. Frederick, 1857–1919, vol. II
Tickell, Richard Hugh, died 1948, vol. IV
Tickle, Ernest William, 1882–1947, vol. IV
Tickler, Thomas George, 1852–1938, vol. III
Tidbury-Beer, Sir Frederick Tidbury, 1892–1959, vol. V
Tiddeman, Lizzie Ellen, died 1937, vol. III
Tidswell, Brig.-Gen. Edward Cecil, 1862–1937, vol. III
Tidy, Sir Henry Letheby, 1877–1960, vol. V
Tiegs, Oscar Werner, 1897–1956, vol. V
Tierney, Michael, 1894–1975, vol. VII
Tiffany, Stanley, 1908–1971, vol. VII
Tiffin, Arthur Ernest, 1896–1955, vol. V
Tigar, Edward, 1851–1937, vol. III
Tighe, Edward Kenrick Banbury, 1862–1917, vol. II
Tighe, Henry, (Harry), 1877–1946, vol. IV

Tighe, Lt-Gen. Sir Michael Joseph, 1864–1925, vol. II

Tighe, Thomas, 1829–1914, vol. I (A)

Tighe, Major Vincent John, 1865–1919, vol. II

Tighe, Rear-Adm. Wilfred Geoffrey Stuart, 1905–1975, vol. VII

Tilby, A. Wyatt, 1880–1948, vol. IV

Tilden, Philip Armstrong, 1887–1956, vol. V

Tilden, Sir William Augustus, 1842–1926, vol. II

Tilden, William Tatem, 1893–1953, vol. V

Tilea, Viorel Virgil, 1896–1972, vol. VII

Tillard, Col Arthur Basil, 1870–1938, vol. III

Tillard, Rear-Adm. Sir Aubrey Thomas, 1881–1952, vol. V

Tillard, Maj.-Gen. John Arthur, 1837–1928, vol. II

Tillard, Adm. Philip Francis, 1852–1933, vol. III

Tillett, Benjamin, 1860–1943, vol. IV

Tillett, John Varnell, 1868–1931, vol. III

Tillett, Louis John, 1865–1929, vol. III

Tilley, Arthur Augustus, 1851–1942, vol. IV

Tilley, Cecil Edgar, 1894–1973, vol. VII

Tilley, Sir George, 1866–1948, vol. IV

Tilley, George Reginald Louis, 1904–1963, vol. VI

Tilley, Herbert, died 1941, vol. IV

Tilley, Sir John, 1813–1898, vol. I

Tilley, Rt Hon. Sir John Anthony Cecil, 1869–1952, vol. V

Tilley, Leonard Percy De Wolfe, 1870–1947, vol. IV

Tilley, Vesta, (Lady de Frece; Matilda Alice), 1864–1952, vol. V

Tillich, Paul, 1886–1965, vol. VI

Tillie, Lt-Col William Kingsley, died 1939, vol. III

Tilling, Richard Stephen, 1851–1929, vol. III

Tillotson, Geoffrey, 1905–1969, vol. VI

Tilly, Maj.-Gen. Justice Crosland, 1888–1941, vol. IV

Tillyard, Eustace Mandeville Wetenhall, 1889–1962, vol. VI

Tillyard, Sir Frank, 1865–1961, vol. VI

Tillyard, Henry Julius Wetenhall, 1881–1968, vol. VI

Tillyard, Robin John, 1881–1937, vol. III

Tilman, Harold William, 1898–1977/8, vol. VII

Tilney, Frederick Colin, 1870–1951, vol. V

Tilney, John Deane, 1841–1909, vol. I

Tilney, Lt-Col Norman Eccles, 1872–1950, vol. IV

Tilsley, Frank, 1904–1957, vol. V

Tiltman, H(ugh) Hessell, 1897–1976, vol. VII

Timins, Rev. Francis Charles, 1866–1941, vol. IV

Timmins, Samuel, died 1903, vol. I

Timmis, Col Reginald Symonds, 1884–1968, vol. VI

Timmis, Shirley Sutton, 1875–1957, vol. V

Timoshenko, Marshal Semyon Konstantinovich, 1895–1970, vol. VI

Timoshenko, Stephen, 1878–1972, vol. VII

Timpson, Sir John, 1863–1937, vol. III

Tims, Henry William Marett, 1863–1954, vol. V

Tims, Ven. John William, 1857–1945, vol. IV

Tinayre, Marcelle; see Tinayre, M. S. M.

Tinayre, (Marguerite Suzanne) Marcelle, died 1948, vol. IV

Tindal, Rev. William Strang, 1899–1965, vol. VI

Tindal-Carill-Worsley, Philip Ernest, 1881–1946, vol. IV

Tindall, Albert Alfred, 1840–1931, vol. III

Tindall, Benjamin Arthur, died 1963, vol. VI

Tindall, Christian, 1878–1951, vol. V

Tindall, Rt Rev. Gordon Leslie, died 1969, vol. VI

Tindall, Rev. Peter Francis, died 1931, vol. III

Tindall, William Edwin, 1863–1938, vol. III

Tindaro, Count del; see Rampolla, Cardinal Mariano.

Tingley, Katherine, 1852–1929, vol. III

Tinker, Brian, 1892–1977, vol. VII

Tinker, Chauncey Brewster, 1876–1963, vol. VI

Tinker, John Joseph, 1875–1957, vol. V

Tinkler, Charles Kenneth, 1881–1951, vol. V

Tinley, Col Gervase Francis Newport, 1857–1918, vol. II

Tinling, Rev. Edward Douglas, died 1898, vol. I

Tinne, John Abraham, 1877–1933, vol. III

Tinsley, Captain Richard Bolton, 1875–1944, vol. IV

Tinton, Major Ben Thomas, 1897–1966, vol. VI

Tinworth, George, 1843–1913, vol. I

Tipperah, Hill, Raja of, 1857–1909, vol. I

Tippet, Captain Arthur Grendon, 1885–1943, vol. IV

Tippetts, Sydney Atterbury, 1878–1946, vol. IV

Tipping, Col Robert Francis G.; see Gartside-Tipping.

Tippinge, Captain Leicester Francis Gartside, 1855–1938, vol. III

Tirard, Sir Nestor Isidore Charles, 1853–1928, vol. II

Tirebuck, William Edwards, died 1900, vol. I

Tireman, Henry Stainton, 1871–1951, vol. V

Tirikatene, Sir Eruera Tihema, 1895–1967, vol. VI

Tisdale, Lt-Col Hon. David, 1835–1913, vol. I

Tisdall, Col Arthur Lance, 1860–1927, vol. II

Tisdall, Rev. William St Clair, 1859–1928, vol. II

Tiselius, Arne Wilhelm Kaurin, 1902–1971, vol. VII

Tisserant, His Eminence Cardinal Eugène, 1884–1972, vol. VII

Titchmarsh, Edward Charles, 1899–1963, vol. VI

Titheradge, Madge, died 1961, vol. VI

Titheridge, Lieut Benjamin, died 1918, vol. II

Titman, Sir George Alfred, 1889–1980, vol. VII

Titmas, Air Cdre John Francis, 1898–1973, vol. VII

Titmuss, Richard Morris, 1907–1973, vol. VII

Tito, President (Josip Broz), 1892–1980, vol. VII

Tito, Pittore Ettore, 1860–1941, vol. IV

Titta, Commendatore Ruffo, 1877–1953, vol. V

Titterington, Meredith Farrar, 1886–1949, vol. IV

Titterton, Frank, 1882–1956, vol. V

Tittle, Walter Ernest, 1883–1966, vol. VI

Tittoni, Tommaso, 1855–1931, vol. III

Titulesco, Nicolas, 1883–1941, vol. IV

Titus, Rev. Murray Thurston, 1885–1964, vol. VI

Titzell, Mrs Anne; see Parrish, A.

Tivey, Maj.-Gen. Edwin, 1866–1947, vol. IV

Tivey, Sir John Proctor, 1882–1968, vol. VI

Tivy, Henry Lawrence, 1848–1929, vol. III

Tiwana, Al-Haj Lt-Col Nawab Sir Malik Khizar Hayat Khan, 1900–1975, vol. VII

Tizard, Sir Henry Thomas, 1885–1959, vol. V

Tizard, Jack, 1919–1979, vol. VII

Tizard, Captain Thomas Henry, 1839–1923, vol. II

Tobias, Rt Rev. George Wolfe Robert, 1882–1974, vol. VII

Tobin, Sir Alfred Aspinall, 1855–1939, vol. III

Tobin, Maurice J., 1901–1953, vol. V

Tobler, Adolf, 1835–1910, vol. I

Tocher, Rev. Forbes Scott, 1885–1973, vol. VII

Tocher, James Fowler, 1864–1945, vol. IV

Tocker, Albert Hamilton, 1884–1964, vol. VI

Tod, Sir Alan Cecil, 1887–1970, vol. VI

Tod, Hunter F., died 1923, vol. II

Tod, James Niebuhr, 1876–1947, vol. IV

Tod, Col John Kelso, died 1946, vol. IV

Tod, Marcus Niebuhr, 1878–1974, vol. VII

Tod, Murray Macpherson, 1909–1974, vol. VII

Todd, Adam Brown, 1822–1915, vol. I

Todd, Alan Livesey Stuart, 1900–1976, vol. VII

Todd, Lt-Col Alfred John Kennett, 1890–1970, vol. VI

Todd, Col Arthur George, died 1954, vol. V

Todd, Arthur Henry Ashworth, 1884–1938, vol. III

Todd, Arthur James Stewart, 1895–1978, vol. VII

Todd, Arthur Ralph Middleton, died 1966, vol. VI

Todd, Sir Charles, 1826–1910, vol. I

Todd, Charles, 1869–1957, vol. V

Todd, Col Charles Campbell, 1870–1956, vol. V

Todd, Sir Desmond Henry, 1897–1970, vol. VI

Todd, Frederick, died 1940, vol. III (A), vol. IV

Todd, Frederick Augustus, 1880–1944, vol. IV

Todd, George, 1844–1912, vol. I

Todd, George E.; see Eyre-Todd.

Todd, George William, 1886–1950, vol. IV

Todd, Guy M., 1883–1958, vol. V

Todd, Howard, 1855–1925, vol. II

Todd, James Eadie, died 1949, vol. IV

Todd, John Aiton, 1875–1954, vol. V

Todd, John L., 1876–1949, vol. IV

Todd, (John) Spencer Brydges, 1840–1921, vol. II

Todd, John William, 1882–1957, vol. V

Todd, Sir Joseph White, 1st Bt, 1846–1926, vol. II

Todd, Margaret; see Travers, Graham.

Todd, Ronald Ruskin, 1902–1980, vol. VII

Todd, Spencer Brydges; see Todd, J. S. B.

Todd, Thomas Robert Rushton, 1895–1975, vol. VII

Todd, W. J. Walker, 1884–1944, vol. IV

Todd, Sir William Alexander Forster, died 1946, vol. IV

Todd, Hon. William Frederic, 1854–1935, vol. III

Todd, Captain Sir William Henry W.; see Wilson-Todd.

Todd, Captain Sir William Pierrepoint W.; see Wilson-Todd.

Todd-Jones, Sir Basil; see Todd-Jones, Sir G. B.

Todd-Jones, Sir (George) Basil, 1898–1980, vol. VII

Todhunter, Sir Charles George, 1869–1949, vol. IV

Todhunter, Brig. Edward Joseph, 1900–1976, vol. VII

Todhunter, Col Herbert William, 1875–1936, vol. III

Todhunter, John, 1839–1916, vol. II

Toft, Albert, 1862–1949, vol. IV

Toft, Alfonso, died 1964, vol. VI

Togo, Adm. Marquis Heihachiro, 1847–1934, vol. III

Tohill, Rt Rev. John, 1855–1914, vol. I

Toker, Maj.-Gen. Sir Alliston Champion, 1843–1936, vol. III

Tolansky, Samuel, 1907–1973, vol. VII

Tole, Hon. Joseph Augustus, died 1920, vol. II

Toler, Hector Robert Graham, 1847–1899, vol. I

Toler, Otway Scarlett Graham, 1886–1941, vol. IV

Tolerton, Sir Robert Hill, 1887–1956, vol. V

Tolkien, John Ronald Reuel, 1892–1973, vol. VII

Tollemache, 2nd Baron, 1832–1904, vol. I

Tollemache, 3rd Baron, 1883–1955, vol. V

Tollemache, 4th Baron, 1910–1975, vol. VII

Tollemache, Arthur Frederick Churchill, 1860–1923, vol. II

Tollemache, Sir (Cecil) Lyonel (Newcomen), 5th Bt, 1886–1969, vol. VI

Tollemache, David, died 1918, vol. II

Tollemache, Lt-Col Hon. Denis Plantagenet, 1884–1942, vol. IV

Tollemache, Hon. Douglas Alfred, 1862–1944, vol. IV

Tollemache, Maj.-Gen. Edward Devereux Hamilton, 1885–1947, vol. IV

Tollemache, Henry James, 1846–1939, vol. III

Tollemache, Hon. Lionel Arthur, 1838–1919, vol. II

Tollemache, Sir Lyonel; see Tollemache, Sir C. L. N.

Tollemache, Sir Lyonel Felix Carteret Eugene, 4th Bt, 1854–1952, vol. V

Tollemache, Lyonulph De Oreliana, 1892–1966, vol. VI

Tollemache, Hon. Mortimer Granville, 1872–1950, vol. IV

Tollemache, Hon. Stratford, 1864–1937, vol. III

Toller, Arthur Thomas, 1857–1899, vol. I

Toller, Ernst, 1893–1939, vol. III

Toller, Brig. Hamlet Bush, 1871–1950, vol. IV

Toller, William Stark, 1884–1968, vol. VI

Tolley, Major Cyril James Hastings, 1895–1978, vol. VII

Tolley, Louis, died 1959, vol. V

Tollinton, Henry Phillips, 1870–1937, vol. III

Tollinton, Rev. Richard Bartram, 1866–1932, vol. III

Tollinton, Richard Bartram Boyd, 1903–1978, vol. VII

Tollit, Percy Kitto, 1863–1942, vol. IV

Tollner, Col Barrett Lennard, 1839–1918, vol. II

Tolmie, Hon. James, 1862–1939, vol. III (A), vol. IV

Tolmie, Hon. Simon Fraser, 1867–1937, vol. III

Tolstoy, Alexandra, 1884–1979, vol. VII

Tolstoy, Count Leo, 1828–1910, vol. I

Tom, Henry, 1881–1937, vol. III

Tomasson, Captain Sir William Hugh, 1858–1922, vol. II

Tomb, John Walker, 1882–1948, vol. IV
Tomblings, Douglas Griffith, 1889–1970, vol. VI
Tombs, Robert Charles, 1842–1923, vol. II
Tomes, Sir Charles Sissmore, 1846–1928, vol. II
Tomes, Brig. Clement Thurstan, 1882–1972, vol. VII
Tomkins, Ernest William, 1872–1925, vol. II
Tomkins, Lt-Col Harry Leith, 1870–1926, vol. II
Tomkins, Herbert Gerard, 1869–1934, vol. III
Tomkins, Sir Lionel Linton, 1871–1936, vol. III
Tomkins, Stanley Charles, *died* 1946, vol. IV
Tomkins, William Douglas, 1882–1959, vol. V
Tomkins, Gen. William Percival, 1841–1922, vol. II
Tomkinson, Charles, 1893–1976, vol. VII
Tomkinson, Sir Geoffrey Stewart, 1881–1963, vol. VI
Tomkinson, Brig. Henry Archdale, 1881–1937, vol. III
Tomkinson, Joseph Goodwin-, *died* 1940, vol. III
Tomkinson, Michael, 1841–1921, vol. II
Tomkinson, Vice-Adm. Wilfred, 1877–1971, vol. VII
Tomley, John Edward, 1874–1951, vol. V
Tomlin of Ash, Baron (Life Peer); Thomas James Chesshyre Tomlin, 1867–1935, vol. III
Tomlin, Vice-Adm. George Napier, 1875–1947, vol. IV
Tomlin, Rev. James William Sackett, 1871–1959, vol. V
Tomlin, Lt-Col Julian Latham, 1886–1960, vol. V
Tomlinson, Rev. Cyril Edric, 1886–1968, vol. VI
Tomlinson, Rt Hon. George, 1890–1952, vol. V
Tomlinson, Sir George John Frederick, 1876–1963, vol. VI
Tomlinson, H. M., 1873–1958, vol. V
Tomlinson, Harry, 1846–1938, vol. III
Tomlinson, Herbert, 1845–1931, vol. III
Tomlinson, Maj.-Gen. Sir Percy Stanley, 1884–1951, vol. V
Tomlinson, Reginald Robert, 1885–1978, vol. VII
Tomlinson, Robert Parkinson, *died* 1943, vol. IV
Tomlinson, Miss Ruth, *died* 1972, vol. VII
Tomlinson, Sir Thomas, 1877–1957, vol. V
Tomlinson, Sir Thomas Symonds, 1877–1965, vol. VI
Tomlinson, Sir William Edward Murray, 1st Bt, 1838–1912, vol. I
Tomonaga, Sin-itiro, 1906–1979, vol. VII
Tomory, Maj.-Gen. Kenneth Alexander Macdonald, 1891–1968, vol. VI
Tompkins, Engr Captain Albert Edward, 1863–1927, vol. II
Tompson, Col Hew Wakeman, 1870–1933, vol. III
Tompson, Rev. Reginald, 1845–1907, vol. I
Tompson, Maj.-Gen. Reginald Henry Dalrymple, 1879–1937, vol. III
Tompson, Maj.-Gen. William Dalrymple, 1833–1916, vol. II
Toms, Frederick, *died* 1900, vol. I
Tomson, Rev. John, *died* 1926, vol. II
Toner, Rt Rev. John, 1857–1949, vol. IV
Tong, Sir Walter Wharton, 1890–1978, vol. VII
Tonga, HM the Queen of; Queen Salote Tupou, 1900–1965, vol. VI

Tonge, Francis Henry, 1855–1936, vol. III
Tonge, George Edward, 1876–1956, vol. V
Tonge, George Edward, 1910–1979, vol. VII
Tonge, Col William Corrie, 1862–1943, vol. IV
Tonk, HH Amin-ud-Daula Wazir-ul Mulk Nawab Sir Hafiz Muhammad Ibrahim Ali Khan Bahadur, Saulat Jung, 1848–1930, vol. III
Tonk, HH Said-ud-Daulah Wazir-ul-Mulk Nawab Hafiz Sir Mohammed Saadat Ali Khan Bahadur Sowlat-i-Jung, 1879–1947, vol. IV
Tonkinson, Harry, 1880–1937, vol. III
Tonks, Ven. Charles Frederick, 1881–1957, vol. V
Tonks, Henry, 1862–1937, vol. III
Tonks, Rt Rev. Horace Norman Vincent, 1891–1959, vol. V
Tonnochy, Alec Bain, *died* 1963, vol. VI
Toogood, Col Cyril George, 1894–1962, vol. VI
Tookey, Geoffrey William, 1902–1976, vol. VII
Toole, John Lawrence, 1830–1906, vol. I
Toole, Joseph, 1887–1945, vol. IV
Tooley, Sarah A., *died* 1946, vol. IV
Toomer, Air Vice-Marshal Sydney Edward, 1895–1954, vol. V
Toone, Sir Frederick Charles, 1868–1930, vol. III
Toone, Rev. John, 1844–1934, vol. III
Toop, Engr-Rear-Adm. William, *died* 1950, vol. IV
Toosey, Sir Philip John Denton, 1904–1975, vol. VII
Tooth, Sir (Archibald) Leonard (Lucas) L.; *see* Lucas-Tooth.
Tooth, Sir Edwin Marsden, 1886–1957, vol. V
Tooth, Howard Henry, 1856–1925, vol. II
Tooth, Sir Robert Lucas L.; *see* Lucas-Tooth.
Tootill, Robert, 1850–1934, vol. III
Toovey, Maj.-Gen. Cecil Wotton, 1891–1954, vol. V
Toovey, Rev. Henry, 1843–1922, vol. II
Tope, Maj.-Gen. Wilfrid Shakespeare, 1892–1962, vol. VI
Topham, Alfred Frank, 1874–1952, vol. V
Topham, Frank W. W., 1838–1924, vol. II
Topham, Rev. John, 1863–1955, vol. V
Topham, Lt-Col Thomas H.; *see* Harrison-Topham.
Topley, William Whiteman Carlton, 1886–1944, vol. IV
Toplis, James, 1876–1961, vol. VI
Topp, Charles Alfred, 1847–1932, vol. III
Topp, Brig.-Gen. Charles Beresford, 1893–1976, vol. VII
Topp, Wilfred Bethridge, 1891–1978, vol. VII
Toppin, Aubrey John, 1881–1969, vol. VI
Topping, Andrew, 1890–1955, vol. V
Topping, Sir (Hugh) Robert, 1877–1952, vol. V
Topping, Sir Robert; *see* Topping, Sir H. R.
Topping, Col Thomas Edward, *died* 1926, vol. II
Topping, Rt Hon. Walter William Buchanan, 1908–1978, vol. VII
Torphichen, 12th Lord, 1846–1915, vol. I
Torphichen, 13th Lord, 1886–1973, vol. VII
Torphichen, 14th Lord, 1917–1975, vol. VII
Torphichen, Master of; Hon. James Archibald Douglas Sandilands, 1884–1909, vol. I

Torr, Cecil, 1857–1928, vol. II
Torr, James Fenning, *died* 1915, vol. I
Torr, Rev. William Edward, 1851–1924, vol. II
Torr, Brig. (William) Wyndham (Torre), 1890–1963, vol. VI
Torr, Brig. Wyndham; *see* Torr, Brig. W. W. T.
Torrance, Sir A. M., *died* 1909, vol. I
Torre-Diaz, Count de; Brodie Manuel de Zulueta, 1842–1918, vol. II
Torrens, James Aubrey, 1881–1954, vol. V
Torres Bodet, Jaime, 1902–1974, vol. VII
Torrey, Charles Cutler, 1863–1956, vol. V
Torrey, Reuben Archer, 1856–1928, vol. II
Torriano, Col Charles Edward, 1833–1908, vol. I
Torrie, Lt-Col Claud Jameson, 1879–1936, vol. III
Torrington, 9th Viscount, 1886–1944, vol. IV
Torrington, 10th Viscount, 1876–1961, vol. VI
Tortise, Col Herbert James, *died* 1954, vol. V
Tory, Henry Marshall, 1864–1947, vol. IV
Tory, Hon. James Cranswick, *died* 1944, vol. IV
Toscanini, Arturo, 1867–1957, vol. V
Toseland, Charles Stephen, 1894–1971, vol. VII
Tostevin, Engr-Captain Harold Bertram, 1884–1956, vol. V
Tosti, Sir F. Paolo, 1847–1916, vol. II
Tothill, Adm. Sir Hugh Henry Darby, 1865–1927, vol. II
Tothill, John Douglas, 1888–1969, vol. VI
Tottenham, Sir Alexander Robert Loftus, 1873–1946, vol. IV
Tottenham, Major Charles Bosvile, 1869–1911, vol. I
Tottenham, Col Charles George, 1835–1918, vol. II
Tottenham, Charles Gore Loftus, 1861–1929, vol. III
Tottenham, Rear-Adm. Edward Loftus, 1896–1974, vol. VII
Tottenham, Adm. Sir Francis Loftus, 1880–1967, vol. VI
Tottenham, Very Rev. George, 1825–1911, vol. I
Tottenham, Sir (George) Richard (Frederick), 1890–1977, vol. VII
Tottenham, Adm. Henry Loftus, 1860–1950, vol. IV
Tottenham, Percy Marmaduke, 1873–1975, vol. VII
Tottenham, Sir Richard; *see* Tottenham, Sir G. R. F.
Tottenham, Richard E., *died* 1971, vol. VII
Tottenham-Smith, Ralph Henry, 1893–1971, vol. VII
Totterdell, Sir Joseph, 1885–1959, vol. V
Touche, Sir George Alexander, 1st Bt (*cr* 1920), 1861–1935, vol. III
Touche, Rt Hon. Sir Gordon Cosmo, 1st Bt (*cr* 1962), 1895–1972, vol. VII
Touche, Sir Norman George, 2nd Bt (*cr* 1920), 1888–1977, vol. VII
Toulmin, Sir George, 1857–1923, vol. II
Toulmin Smith, Elizabeth Thomasina; *see* Meade, L. T.
Tours, Berthold George, 1871–1944, vol. IV
Tours, Frank E., 1877–1963, vol. VI
Tout, Sir Frederick Henry, *died* 1950, vol. IV
Tout, Thomas Frederick, 1855–1929, vol. III

Tout, W. J., 1870–1946, vol. IV
Tovell, Brig. Raymond Walter, 1890–1966, vol. VI
Tovey, 1st Baron, 1885–1971, vol. VII
Tovey, Sir Donald Francis, 1875–1940, vol. III
Tovey, Lt-Col George Strangways, 1875–1943, vol. IV
Towell, Brig. Rowland Henry, 1891–1973, vol. VII
Tower, Bernard Henry, *died* 1933, vol. III
Tower, Charlemagne, 1848–1923, vol. II
Tower, Christopher John Hume, 1841–1924, vol. II
Tower, Adm. Cyril Everard, 1861–1929, vol. III
Tower, Comdr Francis FitzPatrick, 1859–1944, vol. IV
Tower, Vice-Adm. Sir Francis Thomas Butler, 1885–1964, vol. VI
Tower, Rev. Henry, 1862–1948, vol. IV
Tower, Rev. Henry Bernard, 1882–1964, vol. VI
Tower, Sir Reginald Thomas, 1860–1939, vol. III
Towers, Graham Ford, 1897–1975, vol. VII
Towers, Samuel, 1863–1943, vol. IV
Towers-Clark, James, 1852–1926, vol. II
Towle, Arthur Edward, 1878–1948, vol. IV
Towle, Lt-Col Sir Francis William, 1876–1951, vol. V
Towle, Mrs Margery; *see* Lawrence, M.
Towle, Sir William, 1849–1929, vol. III
Town, Sir (Hugh) Stuart, 1893–1972, vol. VII
Town, Sir Stuart; *see* Town, Sir H. S.
Townend, Arnold Ernest, 1880–1970, vol. VI (AII)
Townend, Harry, 1872–1949, vol. IV
Townend, Sir Harry Douglas, 1891–1976, vol. VII
Townend, Herbert Patrick Victor, 1887–1950, vol. IV
Towner, Major Edgar Thomas, 1890–1972, vol. VII
Townesend, Air Cdre Ernest John Dennis, 1896–1975, vol. VII
Townesend, Stephen, *died* 1914, vol. I
Townley, Athol Gordon, 1907–1963, vol. VI
Townley, Rev. Charles Francis, 1856–1930, vol. III
Townley, Rev. Charles Gale, 1848–1942, vol. IV
Townley, Rt Rev. George Frederick, 1891–1977, vol. VII
Townley, Maximilian Gowran, 1864–1942, vol. IV
Townley, Sir Walter Beaupre, 1863–1945, vol. IV
Townroe, Bernard Stephen, 1885–1962, vol. VI
Townroe, Rev. James Weston, *died* 1934, vol. III
Townsend, Alexander Cockburn, 1905–1964, vol. VI
Townsend, Crewe Armand Hamilton, *died* 1954, vol. V
Townsend, Adm. Cyril Samuel, 1875–1949, vol. IV
Townsend, Surg.-Gen. Sir Edmond, 1845–1917, vol. II
Townsend, Major Edward Neville, 1871–1938, vol. III
Townsend, Brig. Edward Philip, 1909–1978, vol. VII
Townsend, Frederick Henry, 1868–1920, vol. II
Townsend, Rev. Henry, *died* 1955, vol. V
Townsend, Sir John Sealy Edward, 1868–1957, vol. V
Townsend, Sir Reginald, 1882–1938, vol. III
Townsend, Stephen Chapman, 1826–1901, vol. I
Townsend, Thomas Sutton, 1847–1918, vol. II

Townsend, Rev. William John, 1835–1915, vol. I
Townsend-Farquhar, Sir Robert; see Farquhar.
Townshend, 5th Marquess, 1831–1899, vol. I
Townshend, 6th Marquess, 1866–1921, vol. II
Townshend, Sir Charles James, 1844–1924, vol. II
Townshend, Maj.-Gen. Sir Charles Vere Ferrers, 1861–1924, vol. II
Townshend, Col Frederick Trench, 1838–1924, vol. II
Townshend, Captain Harry Leigh, 1842–1924, vol. II
Townshend, Hugh, 1890–1974, vol. VII
Townshend, James, died 1949, vol. IV
Townshend, Hon. Robert M.; see Marsham-Townshend.
Townshend, Samuel Nugent, 1844–1910, vol. I
Townshend, William Tower, 1855–1943, vol. IV
Towse, Captain Sir Beachcroft; see Towse, Captain Sir E. B. B.
Towse, Captain Sir (Ernest) Beachcroft Beckwith, 1864–1948, vol. IV
Towse, Sir (John) Wrench, 1848–1929, vol. III
Towse, Sir Wrench; see Towse, Sir J. W.
Towsey, Brig.-Gen. Francis William, died 1948, vol. IV
Toy, Crawford Howell, 1836–1919, vol. II
Toy, Sir Henry, 1862–1939, vol. III
Toye, Brig. Alfred Maurice, 1897–1955, vol. V
Toye, Dudley Bulmer, 1888–1968, vol. VI
Toye, Major Edward Geoffrey, 1889–1942, vol. IV
Toye, Francis; see Toye, J. F.
Toye, Herbert Graham Donovan, 1911–1969, vol. VI
Toye, (John) Francis, 1883–1964, vol. VI
Toynbee, Arnold Joseph, 1889–1975, vol. VII
Toynbee, Brig. Guy Elliston, 1884–1947, vol. IV
Toynbee, Paget, 1855–1932, vol. III
Toyne, Rev. Frederick Elijah, died 1927, vol. II
Toyne, Stanley Mease, died 1962, vol. VI
Tozer, Basil, 1896–1949, vol. IV
Tozer, Beatrice Cordelia Auchmuty, (Mrs Basil Tozer); see Langley, B.
Tozer, Rev. Henry Fanshawe, 1829–1916, vol. II
Tozer, Hon. Sir Horace, 1844–1916, vol. II
Tozer, Major Sir James Clifford, 1889–1970, vol. VI
Tozer, Col William, 1894–1971, vol. VII
Tozer, Rt Rev. William George, died 1899, vol. I
Tracey, Herbert Trevor, 1884–1955, vol. V
Tracey, Sir Richard, 1837–1907, vol. I
Tracy, Major Hon. Algernon Henry Charles H.; see Hanbury-Tracy.
Tracy, Frederick, 1862–1951, vol. V
Tracy, Hon. Frederick Stephen Archibald H.; see Hanbury-Tracy.
Tracy, Louis, 1863–1928, vol. II
Tracy, Spencer, 1900–1967, vol. VI
Tracy-Inglis, Col Russell; see Inglis.
Trafalgar, Viscount; Herbert Horatio Nelson, 1854–1905, vol. I
Trafford, Edward Southwell, 1838–1912, vol. I
Trafford, Marcus Antonius Johnston de L.; see de Lavis-Trafford.

Trafford, Rt Rev. Ralph Sigebert, 1886–1976, vol. VII
Tragett, Mrs Margaret Rivers; see Larminie, M. R.
Trahan, Hon. Arthur, 1877–1950, vol. IV(A), vol. V
Trail, James William Helenus, 1851–1919, vol. II
Trail, Richard Robertson, 1894–1971, vol. VII
Traill, Anthony, 1838–1914, vol. I
Traill, Major Cecil James, 1888–1968, vol. VI
Traill, Maj.-Gen. Geoge Balfour, 1833–1913, vol. I
Traill, Henry Duff, 1842–1900, vol. I
Traill, Lt-Col John Charles Merriman, 1881–1942, vol. IV
Traill, Peter; see Morton, Guy Mainwaring.
Traill, Major Thomas Balfour, 1881–1920, vol. II
Traill, Air Vice-Marshal Thomas Cathcart, 1899–1973, vol. VII
Traill, Lt-Col William Henry, 1871–1951, vol. V
Traill, Lt-Col William Stewart, 1868–1959, vol. V
Train, Arthur, 1875–1945, vol. IV
Train, G. F., 1829–1904, vol. I
Train, Sir John, 1873–1942, vol. IV
Train, Rev. John Gilkison, 1847–1920, vol. II
Train, Sir (John) Landale, 1888–1969, vol. VI
Train, Sir Landale; see Train, Sir J. L.
Transjordan, King of; HH Abdullah Ibn Hussein, died 1951, vol. V
Trant, John Philip, 1889–1953, vol. V
Trapani, Lt-Col Alfred, 1859–1928, vol. II (A), vol. III
Trapnell, John Graham, died 1949, vol. IV
Trappes-Lomax, Michael Roger, 1900–1972, vol. VII
Trappes-Lomax, Brig. Thomas Byrnand, 1895–1962, vol. VI
Traquair, Harry Moss, 1875–1954, vol. V
Traquair, Ramsay, 1874–1952, vol. V
Traquair, Ramsay Heatley, 1840–1912, vol. I
Trask, Katrina, died 1922, vol. II
Tratman, David William, died 1953, vol. IV
Tratman, Edgar Kingsley, 1899–1978, vol. VII
Travancore, Maharajah of, 1857–1924, vol. II
Travers, Ben, 1886–1980, vol. VII
Travers, Captain Francis Eaton, died 1953, vol. V
Travers, Lt-Col George Alfred, 1867–1950, vol. IV
Travers, Graham, 1859–1918, vol. II
Travers, Sir Guy Francis Travers Clarke-, 3rd Bt (cr 1804), 1842–1905, vol. I
Travers, Col Henry Cecil, died 1958, vol. V
Travers, Brig.-Gen. Jonas Hamilton du Boulay, 1861–1933, vol. III
Travers, Brig.-Gen. Joseph Oates, 1867–1936, vol. III
Travers, Sir Lancelot; see Travers, Sir W. L.
Travers, Morris William, 1872–1961, vol. VI
Travers, Sir (Walter) Lancelot, 1880–1937, vol. III
Travis, Comdr Sir Edward Wilfrid Harry, 1888–1956, vol. V
Travis, Harry, 1858–1927, vol. II
Travis, Rev. James, 1840–1919, vol. II
Travis, Rev. William Travis, died 1924, vol. II
Travis-Clegg, Sir James Travis, 1874–1942, vol. IV

Trayner, Hon. Lord; John Trayner, 1834–1929, vol. III

Trayner, John; see Hon. Lord Trayner.

Treacher, Rev. Preb. Hubert Harold, 1891–1964, vol. VI

Treacher, Sir William Hood, 1849–1919, vol. II

Treacy, Rt Rev. Eric, 1907–1978, vol. VII

Treadgold, Group Captain Henry A., 1883–1941, vol. IV

Treadwell, Brig. John William Ferguson, 1901–1968, vol. VI

Treanor, Ven. James, died 1926, vol. II

Treasure, William Houston, died 1916, vol. II

Treble, Rev. Edmund John, died 1924, vol. II

Treble, Col George Walker, 1865–1929, vol. III

Tredcroft, Lt-Col Charles Lennox, 1832–1917, vol. II

Tredegar, 1st Viscount (cr 1905), 1830–1913, vol. I

Tredegar, 1st Viscount (cr 1926), 1867–1934, vol. III

Tredegar, 2nd Viscount (cr 1926), 1893–1949, vol. IV

Tredegar, 5th Baron, 1873–1954, vol. V

Tredegar, 6th Baron, 1908–1962, vol. VI

Tredennick, Rev. George Nesbitt Haydon, 1860–1942, vol. IV

Tredennick, Rev. John Nesbitt Ernest, 1892–1976, vol. VII

Tredgold, Alfred Frank, 1870–1952, vol. V

Tredgold, Sir Clarkson Henry, 1865–1938, vol. III

Tredgold, Rt Hon. Sir Robert Clarkson, 1899–1977, vol. VII

Tredgold, Roger Francis, 1911–1975, vol. VII

Tree, Charles, died 1940, vol. III

Tree, Sir Herbert Beerbohm, 1853–1917, vol. II

Tree, Maud, (Lady Tree), 1864–1937, vol. III

Tree, Ronald, died 1976, vol. VII

Tree, Ven. Ronald James, 1914–1970, vol. VI

Treeby, Lt-Col Henry Paul, 1858–1935, vol. III

Treffry, Charles Ebenezer, 1842–1924, vol. II

Treffry, Col Edward, 1869–1942, vol. IV

Treffry, Mary Beatrice, 1865–1942, vol. IV

Trefgarne, 1st Baron, 1894–1960, vol. V

Trefle, Hon. John Louis, died 1915, vol. I

Trefusis, Hon. Henry Walter Hepburn-Stuart-Forbes-, 1864–1948, vol. IV

Trefusis, Major Hon. John Frederick Hepburn-Stuart-Forbes-, 1878–1915, vol. I (A)

Trefusis, Col Hon. John Schomberg, 1852–1932, vol. III

Trefusis, Lady Mary, died 1927, vol. II

Trefusis, Rt Rev. Robert Edward, 1843–1930, vol. III

Tregarthen, John Coulson, 1854–1933, vol. III

Tregear, Edward, 1846–1931, vol. III

Tregear, Maj.-Gen. Sir Vincent William, 1842–1925, vol. III

Tregoning, Wynn Harold, 1876–1930, vol. III

Treharne, Reginald Francis, 1901–1967, vol. VI

Trehearne, Alfred Frederick Aldridge, 1874–1962, vol. VI

Trehearne, Frank William, 1881–1956, vol. V

Treherne, Rev. Charles Albert, 1856–1919, vol. II

Treherne, Maj.-Gen. Sir Francis Harper, 1858–1955, vol. V

Trelawny, Horace Dormer, 1824–1906, vol. I

Trelawny, Maj.-Gen. John I.; see Iago-Trelawny.

Trelawny, Sir John William Robin Marurice Salusbury-, 12th Bt, 1908–1956, vol. V

Trelawny, Sir John William Salusbury-, 11th Bt, 1869–1944, vol. IV

Trelawny, Sir William Lewis Salusbury-, 10th Bt, 1844–1917, vol. II

Trelawny-Ross, Rev. John Trelawny, 1852–1935, vol. III

Treloar, Sir William Purdie, 1st Bt, 1843–1923, vol. II

Trematon, Viscount; Rupert Alexander George Augustus Cambridge, 1907–1928, vol. II

Tremayne, Lt-Col Arthur, 1827–1905, vol. I

Tremayne, Arthur, 1879–1954, vol. V

Tremayne, Harold, died 1908, vol. I

Tremayne, John, 1825–1901, vol. I

Tremayne, Air Marshal Sir John Tremayne, 1891–1979, vol. VII

Tremblay, Maj.-Gen. Thomas Louis, 1886–1951, vol. V

Tremellen, Norman Cleverton, 1895–1979, vol. VII

Tremlett, Charles Hugh, 1876–1939, vol. III

Tremlett, Col Colin Percy, 1880–1972, vol. VII

Trenam, E., 1843–1909, vol. I

Trench, Anthony C.; see Chenevix-Trench.

Trench, Col Arthur Henry C.; see Chenevix-Trench.

Trench, Charles Godfrey C.; see Chenevix-Trench.

Trench, Hon. Cosby Godolphin, 1844–1925, vol. II

Trench, Ernest Frederic Crosbie, 1869–1960, vol. V

Trench, Col Frederic John Arthur, 1857–1942, vol. IV

Trench, Hon. Frederic Sydney, 1894–1916, vol. II

Trench, Lt-Col Frederick Amelius Le P.; see Le Poer Trench.

Trench, Hon. Frederick Le P.; see Le Poer Trench.

Trench, Lt-Col George Frederick C.; see Chenevix-Trench.

Trench, Herbert, 1865–1923, vol. II

Trench, Col Lawrence C.; see Chenevix-Trench.

Trench, Brig. Ralph C.; see Chenevix-Trench.

Trench, Lt-Col Sir Richard Henry C.; see Chenevix-Trench.

Trench, Wilbraham Fitz-John, 1873–1939, vol. III

Trench, Hon. William Cosby, 1869–1944, vol. IV

Trench, William Launcelot Crosbie, died 1949, vol. IV

Trench, Col Hon. William Le-P.; see Le-Poer-Trench.

Trench, Rev. William Robert, 1838–1913, vol. I

Trenchard, 1st Viscount, 1873–1956, vol. V

Trend, John Brande, 1887–1958, vol. V

Trendell, Sir Arthur James Richens, 1836–1909, vol. I

Trendell, Herbert Arthur Previté, 1864–1929, vol. III

Trenholme, Norman William, 1837–1919, vol. II
Trent, 1st Baron, 1850–1931, vol. III
Trent, 2nd Baron, 1889–1956, vol. V
Trent, Col George Alexander, 1870–1930, vol. III
Trent, Newbury Abbot, 1885–1953, vol. V
Trentham, Everard Noel Rye, 1888–1963, vol. VI
Trentham, George Percy, died 1940, vol. III
Treowen, 1st Baron, 1851–1933, vol. III
Tresidder, Lt-Col Alfred Geddes, 1881–1970, vol. VI
Tresidder, Captain Tolmie John, 1850–1931, vol. III
Treston, Hubert Joseph, 1888–1959, vol. V
Treston, Col Maurice Lawrence, 1891–1970, vol. VI
Trestrail, Major Alfred Ernest Yates, 1876–1935, vol. III
Trethowan, Hon. Sir Arthur King, 1863–1937, vol. III
Trevail, Silvanus, 1851–1903, vol. I
Trevan, John William, 1887–1956, vol. V
Trevaskis, Rev. Hugh Kennedy, 1882–1962, vol. VI
Trevelyan, Rt Hon. Sir Charles Philips, 3rd Bt (cr 1874), 1870–1958, vol. V
Trevelyan, Edmond Fauriel, died 1911, vol. I
Trevelyan, Sir Ernest John, 1850–1924, vol. II
Trevelyan, George Macaulay, 1876–1962, vol. VI
Trevelyan, Rt Hon. Sir George Otto, 2nd Bt (cr 1874), 1838–1928, vol. II
Trevelyan, Hilda, died 1959, vol. V
Trevelyan, Janet Penrose, 1879–1956, vol. V
Trevelyan, Robert Calverley, 1872–1951, vol. V
Trevelyan, Sir Walter John, 8th Bt (cr 1662), 1866–1931, vol. III
Trevelyan, Rev. William Bouverie, 1853–1929, vol. III
Trevelyan, Sir Willoughby John, 9th Bt (cr 1662), 1902–1976, vol. VII
Treves, Sir Frederick, 1st Bt, 1853–1923, vol. II
Trevethin, 1st Baron, 1843–1936, vol. III
Trevethin, 2nd Baron, 1879–1959, vol. V
Trevethin, 3rd Baron, and Oaksey, 1st Baron, 1880–1971, vol. VII
Trevithick, Arthur Reginald, 1858–1939, vol. III
Trevor, 2nd Baron, 1852–1923, vol. II
Trevor, 3rd Baron, 1863–1950, vol. IV
Trevor, Lady; (Rosamond Catherine), 1857–1942, vol. IV
Trevor, Sir Arthur Charles, 1841–1920, vol. II
Trevor, Arthur Hill, 1858–1924, vol. II
Trevor, Lt-Col Arthur Prescott, 1872–1930, vol. III
Trevor, Sir Cecil; see Trevor, Sir Charles C.
Trevor, Sir Cecil Russell, 1899–1971, vol. VII
Trevor, Sir (Charles) Cecil, 1830–1921, vol. II
Trevor, Sir (Charles) Gerald, 1882–1959, vol. V
Trevor, Surg.-Gen. Sir Francis Woollaston, 1851–1922, vol. II
Trevor, Frederick George Brunton, 1838–1924, vol. II
Trevor, Hon. George Edwyn Hill-, 1859–1922, vol. II
Trevor, Col George Herbert, 1840–1927, vol. II
Trevor, Sir Gerald; see Trevor, Sir C. G.
Trevor, Brig.-Gen. Herbert Edward, 1871–1939, vol. III
Trevor, Col Philip Christian William, 1863–1932, vol. III
Trevor, Rev. Thomas Warren, 1839–1924, vol. II
Trevor, Col William Herbert, 1872–1936, vol. III
Trevor, Maj.-Gen. William Spottiswoode, 1831–1907, vol. I
Trevor-Battye, Aubyn Bernard Rochfort, died 1922, vol. II
Trevor Jones, Alan; see Jones.
Trew, Brig.-Gen. Edward Fynmore, 1879–1935, vol. III
Trewavas, Joseph, 1835–1905, vol. I
Trewby, Vice-Adm. George, 1874–1953, vol. V
Tribe, Sir Frank Newton, 1893–1958, vol. V
Trickett, Sir Henry Whittaker, 1857–1913, vol. I
Trickett, William, 1840–1928, vol. II (A), vol. III
Trickett, Hon. William Joseph, 1844–1916, vol. II
Triggs, H. Inigo, 1876–1923, vol. II
Triggs, William Henry, 1855–1934, vol. III
Trilling, Lionel, 1905–1975, vol. VII
Trimble, Charles Joseph, 1856–1944, vol. IV
Trimble, S. Delmege, 1857–1947, vol. IV
Trimble, William Copeland, 1851–1941, vol. IV
Trimen, Roland, 1840–1916, vol. II
Trimingham, Sir Eldon Harvey, 1889–1959, vol. V
Trimlestown, 18th Baron, 1862–1937, vol. III
Trimmer, Sir George William Arthur, 1882–1972, vol. VII
Trimnell, Col William Duncan Conabeare, 1874–1953, vol. V
Trine, Ralph Waldo, 1866–1958, vol. V
Trinkler, Emil, 1896–1931, vol. III
Tripp, Sir Alker; see Tripp, Sir H. A.
Tripp, Bernard Edward Howard, 1868–1940, vol. III (A), vol. IV
Tripp, George Henry, 1860–1922, vol. II
Tripp, Sir (Herbert) Alker, 1883–1954, vol. V
Tripp, Lt-Gen. William Henry Lainson, 1881–1959, vol. V
Trippel, Sir Francis, 1866–1930, vol. III
Tripura, Maharaja of, 1908–1947, vol. IV
Triscott, Col Charles Prideaux, 1857–1926, vol. II
Tristram, Ernest William, 1882–1952, vol. V
Tristram, Rev. Henry, 1881–1955, vol. V
Tristram, Rev. Henry Baker, 1822–1906, vol. I
Tristram, Henry Barrington, 1861–1946, vol. IV
Tristram, Rev. John William, died 1926, vol. II
Tristram, Katharine Alice Salvin, 1858–1948, vol. IV
Tristram, Thomas H., 1825–1912, vol. I
Tritton, Sir Alfred Ernest, 2nd Bt, 1873–1939, vol. III
Tritton, Arthur Henry, 1855–1936, vol. III
Tritton, Arthur Stanley, 1881–1973, vol. VII
Tritton, Sir (Charles) Ernest, 1st Bt, 1845–1918, vol. II
Tritton, Sir Ernest; see Tritton, Sir C. E.
Tritton, Major Sir Geoffrey Ernest, 3rd Bt, 1900–1976, vol. VII
Tritton, Herbert Leslie Melville, 1870–1940, vol. III

Tritton, Joseph Herbert, 1844–1923, vol. II
Tritton, Julian Seymour, 1889–1979, vol. VII
Tritton, Sir Seymour Biscoe, 1860–1937, vol. III
Tritton, Sir William Ashbee, 1876–1946, vol. IV
Trofimov, M. V., died 1948, vol. IV
Trollip, Arthur Stanley, 1888–1963, vol. VI
Trollope, Lt-Col Sir Arthur Grant, 13th Bt, 1866–1937, vol. III
Trollope, Fabian George, 1872–1960, vol. V
Trollope, Sir Frederic Farrand, 14th Bt, 1875–1957, vol. V
Trollope, Sir Gordon Clavering, 15th Bt, 1885–1958, vol. V
Trollope, Sir Henry Cracroft, 12th Bt, 1860–1935, vol. III
Trollope, Brig. Hugh Charles Napier, 1895–1953, vol. V
Trollope, Rt Rev. Mark Napier, 1862–1930, vol. III
Trollope, Hon. Robert Cranmer, 1852–1908, vol. I
Trollope, Sir Thomas Ernest, 11th Bt, 1858–1927, vol. II
Trollope, Sir William Henry, 10th Bt, 1858–1921, vol. II
Troop, Rev. G. Osborne, 1854–1932, vol. III
Trotman, Arthur Edwin, 1906–1961, vol. VI
Trotman, Gen. Sir Charles Newsham, 1864–1929, vol. III
Trotman, Rev. Edward Fiennes, 1828–1910, vol. I
Trotman-Dickenson, Rev. Lenthall Greville, 1864–1931, vol. III
Trotsky, Lev Davidovich, 1879–1940, vol. III
Trott, Alan Charles, 1895–1959, vol. V
Trott, George Henry, 1889–1972, vol. VII
Trott, Hon. Sir Howard; see Trott, Hon. Sir W. J. H.
Trott, Hon. Sir (William James) Howard, 1883–1971, vol. VII
Trotter, Alexander Cooper, 1902–1975, vol. VII
Trotter, Alexander Pelham, 1857–1947, vol. IV
Trotter, Col Charles William, 1865–1931, vol. III
Trotter, Edith, died 1962, vol. VI
Trotter, Rev. Canon Edward Bush, 1842–1920, vol. II
Trotter, Major Edward Henry, 1872–1916, vol. II
Trotter, Col Gerald Frederic, 1871–1945, vol. IV
Trotter, Maj.-Gen. Sir Henry, 1844–1905, vol. I
Trotter, Lt-Col Sir Henry, 1841–1919, vol. II
Trotter, Henry Alexander, 1869–1949, vol. IV
Trotter, Rev. Henry Eden, 1844–1922, vol. II
Trotter, Hugh, 1890–1965, vol. VI
Trotter, Maj.-Gen. Sir James Keith, 1849–1940, vol. III
Trotter, Rev. John Crawford, 1848–1942, vol. IV
Trotter, Rev. John George, died 1917, vol. II
Trotter, Lt-Col John Moubray, 1842–1924, vol. II
Trotter, Rev. Mowbray, 1848–1913, vol. I
Trotter, Col Sir Philip, 1844–1918, vol. II
Trotter, Reginald George, 1888–1951, vol. V
Trotter, Captain Richard Durant, 1887–1968, vol. VI
Trotter, Richard Stanley, 1903–1974, vol. VII
Trotter, Thomas, 1868–1944, vol. IV
Trotter, Thomas Henry Yorke, 1854–1934, vol. III

Trotter, Sir Victor Murray Coutts, 1874–1929, vol. III
Trotter, Wilfred, died 1939, vol. III
Trotter, William, 1839–1908, vol. I
Trotter, William Finlayson, 1871–1945, vol. IV
Troubetskoi, Prince, died 1915, vol. I
Troubetskoy, Princess Pierre; see Rives, Amélie.
Troubridge, Adm. Sir Ernest Charles Thomas, 1862–1926, vol. II
Troubridge, Laura, (Lady Troubridge), died 1946, vol. IV
Troubridge, Lt-Col Sir St Vincent; see Troubridge, Lt-Col T. St V. W.
Troubridge, Sir Thomas Herbert Cochrane, 4th Bt, 1860–1938, vol. III
Troubridge, Vice-Adm. Sir Thomas Hope, 1895–1949, vol. IV
Troubridge, Lt-Col Sir (Thomas) St Vincent (Wallace), 5th Bt, 1895–1963, vol. VI
Troughton, Rev. Arthur Perceval, 1858–1937, vol. III
Troughton, John Frederick George, 1902–1975, vol. VII
Trouncer, Cecil, 1898–1953, vol. V
Trouncer, Harold Moltke, 1871–1948, vol. IV
Troup, Lt-Col Alan Gordon, 1879–1931, vol. III
Troup, Sir (Charles) Edward, 1857–1941, vol. IV
Troup, Sir Edward; see Troup, Sir C. E.
Troup, Francis William, 1859–1941, vol. IV
Troup, Sir George Alexander, 1863–1941, vol. IV
Troup, James, 1840–1925, vol. II
Troup, Vice-Adm. Sir James Andrew Gardiner, 1883–1975, vol. VII
Troup, Robert Scott, 1874–1939, vol. III
Trousdale, Major Robert Cecil, 1876–1934, vol. III
Trout, Sir (Herbert) Leon, 1906–1978, vol. VII
Trout, Sir Leon; see Trout, Sir H. L.
Troutbeck, John, 1860–1912, vol. I
Troutbeck, Sir John Monro, 1894–1971, vol. VII
Trouton, Frederick Thomas, 1863–1922, vol. II
Trow, Albert Howard, died 1939, vol. III
Trowbridge, John Townsend, 1827–1916, vol. II
Trower, Col Courtney Vor, 1856–1947, vol. IV
Trower, Rt Rev. Gerard, 1860–1928, vol. II
Trower, John Henry Peter, 1913–1968, vol. VI
Trower, Sir Walter, 1853–1924, vol. II
Trower, Sir William Gosselin, 1889–1963, vol. VI
Troy, Hon. Michael Francis, 1877–1953, vol. V
Troyte, Sir Gilbert John A.; see Acland-Troyte.
Troyte-Bullock, Lt-Col Edward George, 1862–1942, vol. IV
Trubshaw, Dame Gwendoline Joyce, died 1954, vol. V
Trubshaw, Wilfred, 1870–1944, vol. III
Trudeau, E. L., 1848–1915, vol. I (A)
Truell, Maj.-Gen. Robert Holt, 1837–1900, vol. I
Trueman, Sir Arthur Elijah, 1894–1956, vol. V
Trueman, George Johnstone, 1872–1949, vol. IV
Trueta, Joseph, 1897–1977, vol. VII
Truman, Charles Edwin, died 1938, vol. III
Truman, Lt-Col Egerton Danford, died 1938, vol. III
Truman, Harry S., 1884–1972, vol. VII

Truman, Maj.-Gen. William Robinson, *died* 1905, vol. I

Trumble, Thomas, 1872–1954, vol. V

Trump, John, 1858–1941, vol. IV

Trumpler, Stephen Alfred Herman, 1879–1963, vol. VI

Truninger, Lionel, 1870–1961, vol. VI

Truro, 3rd Baron, 1856–1899, vol. I

Truscott, Sir Eric Homewood Stanham, 2nd Bt, 1898–1973, vol. VII

Truscott, Sir George Wyatt, 1st Bt, 1857–1941, vol. IV

Truscott, Samuel John, 1870–1950, vol. IV

Trust, Mrs Helen, *died* 1953, vol. V

Trustam, Sir Charles Frederick, 1900–1964, vol. VI

Trutch, Sir Joseph William, 1826–1904, vol. I

Truter, Sir Theodore Gustaff, 1873–1949, vol. IV

Trye, Captain John Henry, 1875–1959, vol. V

Tryhorn, Frederick Gerald, 1893–1972, vol. VII

Tryon, 1st Baron, 1871–1940, vol. III

Tryon, 2nd Baron, 1906–1976, vol. VII

Tschiffely, Aimé Felix, 1895–1954, vol. V

Tschudi, Hugo von, 1851–1911, vol. I

Tsen, Rt Rev. P(hilip) Lindel, *died* 1954, vol. V

Tubb, Carrie, (Mrs A. J. E. Oliveira), 1876–1976, vol. VII

Tubb, Captain Frederick Harold, *died* 1917, vol. II

Tubbs, Francis Ralph, 1907–1980, vol. VII

Tubbs, Rt Rev. Norman H., 1879–1965, vol. VI

Tubbs, Percy Burnell, 1868–1933, vol. III

Tubbs, Sir Stanley William, 1st Bt, 1871–1941, vol. IV

Tubby, Alfred Herbert, 1862–1930, vol. III

Tuck, Sir Adolph, 1st Bt, 1854–1926, vol. II

Tuck, Col Charles Harold Amys, 1880–1951, vol. V

Tuck, Col Gerald Louis Johnson, 1889–1966, vol. VI

Tuck, Gustave, 1857–1942, vol. IV

Tuck, Major Sir Reginald; *see* Tuck, Major Sir W. R.

Tuck, William Henry, 1840–1922, vol. II

Tuck, Major Sir (William) Reginald, 2nd Bt, 1883–1954, vol. V

Tucker, Baron (Life Peer); Frederick James Tucker, 1888–1975, vol. VII

Tucker, Alexander Lauzun Pendock, 1861–1941, vol. IV

Tucker, Alfred Brook, 1861–1945, vol. IV

Tucker, Rt Rev. Alfred Robert, 1849–1914, vol. I

Tucker, Archibald Norman, 1904–1980, vol. VII

Tucker, Arthur, 1864–1929, vol. III

Tucker, Col Aubrey Hervey, 1833–1907, vol. I

Tucker, Rt Rev. Beverley Dandridge, 1846–1930, vol. III

Tucker, Lt-Gen. Sir Charles, 1838–1935, vol. III

Tucker, Sir Edward George, 1896–1961, vol. VI

Tucker, Francis Ellis, 1844–1921, vol. II

Tucker, Frederick St George de Lautour B.; *see* Booth Tucker.

Tucker, Rev. George, 1835–1908, vol. I

Tucker, Howard Archibald, 1889–1963, vol. VI

Tucker, Sir James Millard, 1892–1963, vol. VI

Tucker, Rev. John Savile, 1866–1954, vol. V

Tucker, Keith Ravenscroft, 1890–1963, vol. VI

Tucker, Maj.-Gen. Louis Henry Emile, 1843–1925, vol. II

Tucker, Sir Norman Sanger, 1895–1965, vol. VI

Tucker, Norman Walter Gwynn, 1910–1978, vol. VII

Tucker, Captain S. N., 1876–1902, vol. I

Tucker, Thomas George, 1859–1946, vol. IV

Tucker, William, *died* 1909, vol. I

Tucker, Very Rev. William Frederic, 1856–1934, vol. III

Tucker, Maj.-Gen. William Guise, 1850–1906, vol. I

Tucker, William Kidger, 1857–1944, vol. IV

Tucker, Lt-Col William Kington, 1877–1956, vol. V

Tuckey, Rev. Canon James Grove White, 1864–1947, vol. IV

Tuckwell, Gertrude Mary, 1861–1951, vol. V

Tuckwell, Rev. W., 1829–1919, vol. II

Tudball, Sir William, 1866–1939, vol. III

Tudhope, George Ranken, 1893–1955, vol. V

Tudor, Sir Daniel Thomas, 1866–1928, vol. II

Tudor, Hon. Frank Gwynne, 1866–1922, vol. II

Tudor, Adm. Sir Frederick Charles Tudor, 1863–1946, vol. IV

Tudor, Maj.-Gen. Sir H. Hugh, 1871–1965, vol. VI

Tudor-Craig, Major Sir Algernon Tudor, 1873–1943, vol. IV

Tudor Davies, William; *see* Davies.

Tudor-Evans, Rev. George Simon, 1867–1935, vol. III

Tudsbery, Sir Francis Cannon Tudsbery, 1888–1968, vol. VI

Tudsbery, Col Henry Tudsbery, 1886–1946, vol. IV

Tudsbery, J. H. T., 1859–1939, vol. III

Tudway, Brig.-Gen. Robert John, 1859–1944, vol. IV

Tuer, Andrew White, 1838–1900, vol. I

Tuff, Charles, 1855–1929, vol. III

Tuff, Sir Charles, 1881–1961, vol. VI

Tuffier, Sir Theodore Martin, 1857–1929, vol. III

Tuffill, Comdr (S) Harold Birch, 1870–1950, vol. IV

Tufnell, Col Arthur Wyndham, *died* 1920, vol. II

Tufnell, Lt-Col Edward, 1848–1909, vol. I

Tufnell, Brig.-Gen. Lionel Charles Gostling, 1865–1941, vol. IV

Tufnell, Adm. Lionel Grant, 1857–1930, vol. III

Tufnell, Lt-Comdr Richard Lionel, 1896–1956, vol. V

Tufnell, Col W. Nevill, *died* 1922, vol. II

Tufton, Hon. Charles Henry, 1879–1923, vol. II

Tufts, J. F., *died* 1921, vol. II

Tufts, James Hayden, 1862–1942, vol. IV

Tugendhat, Georg, 1898–1973, vol. VII

Tugwell, Rt Rev. Herbert, *died* 1936, vol. III

Tugwell, Ven. Lewen Greenwood, *died* 1937, vol. III

Tuite, Sir Brian Hugh Morgan, 12th Bt, 1897–1970, vol. VI

Tuite, James, 1849–1916, vol. II

Tuite, Sir Mark Anthony Henry, 10th Bt, 1808–1898, vol. I

Tuite, Sir Morgan Harry Paulet, 11th Bt, 1861–1946, vol. IV

Tuke, Anthony William, 1897–1975, vol. VII

Tuke, Lt-Col George Francis Stratford, 1876–1948, vol. IV

Tuke, Captain Godfrey, 1871–1944, vol. IV

Tuke, Henry Scott, 1858–1929, vol. III

Tuke, Sir John Batty, 1835–1913, vol. I

Tuke, Col John Melville, 1885–1958, vol. V

Tuke, Dame Margaret Janson, 1862–1947, vol. IV

Tuke, William Favill, 1863–1940, vol. III

Tuker, Lt-Gen. Sir Francis Ivan Simms, 1894–1967, vol. VI

Tulloch, Maj.-Gen. Sir Alexander Bruce, 1838–1920, vol. I

Tulloch, Angus Alexander Gregorie, 1867–1932, vol. III

Tulloch, Maj.-Gen. Derek; see Tulloch, Maj.-Gen. Donald D. C.

Tulloch, Maj.-Gen. (Donald) Derek (Cuthbertson), 1903–1974, vol. VII

Tulloch, Major Hector, 1835–1922, vol. II

Tulloch, Brig.-Gen. James Bruce Gregorie, died 1946, vol. IV

Tulloch, Brig.-Gen. John Arthur Stamford, 1865–1946, vol. IV

Tulloch, Maj.-Gen. John Walter Graham, 1861–1934, vol. III

Tulloch, Rev. W. W., 1846–1920, vol. II

Tulloch, William John, 1887–1966, vol. VI

Tulloh, Maj.-Gen. John Stewart, 1827–1901, vol. I

Tully, Jasper, 1858–1938, vol. III

Tully, Kivas, 1820–1905, vol. I

Tully, Sydney Strickland, died 1911, vol. I

Tun, Hon. Sir Paw, died 1953, vol. V

Tunbridge, Brig.-Gen. Walter Howard, 1856–1943, vol. IV

Tunnard, John Samuel, 1900–1971, vol. VII

Tunnecliffe, Hon. Thomas, 1869–1948, vol. IV

Tunnicliffe, Charles Frederick, 1901–1979, vol. VII

Tunnicliffe, Francis Whittaker, died 1928, vol. II

Tunstall, Brian; see Tunstall, W. C. B.

Tunstall, (William Cuthbert) Brian, 1900–1970, vol. VI

Tuohy, James M., 1859–1923, vol. II

Tuohy, Patrick Joseph, 1894–1930, vol. III

Tuplin, William Alfred, died 1975, vol. VII

Tupolev, Andrei Nikolaevich, 1888–1972, vol. VII

Tupou, Queen Salote; see Tonga, HM the Queen of.

Tupp, Alfred Cotterell, 1840–1914, vol. I

Tupper, Rt Hon. Sir Charles, 1st Bt, 1821–1915, vol. I (A)

Tupper, Sir Charles, 3rd Bt, 1880–1962, vol. VI

Tupper, Hon. Sir Charles Hibbert, 1855–1927, vol. II

Tupper, Sir Charles Stewart, 2nd Bt, 1884–1960, vol. V

Tupper, Sir Daniel Alfred Anley, 1849–1922, vol. II

Tupper, Gen. Gaspard le Marchant, 1826–1906, vol. I

Tupper, J. Stewart, 1851–1915, vol. I

Tupper, Sir James Macdonald, 4th Bt, 1887–1967, vol. VI

Tupper, Sir Lewis, 1848–1910, vol. I

Tupper, Adm. Sir Reginald Godfrey Otway, 1859–1945, vol. IV

Tupper, William Johnston, 1862–1947, vol. IV

Tupper-Carey, Rev. Albert Darell, 1866–1943, vol. IV

Turbayne, Albert Angus, 1866–1940, vol. III

Turbervill, Edith P.; see Picton-Turbervill.

Turberville, Arthur Stanley, 1888–1945, vol. IV

Turck, Hermann, 1856–1933, vol. III

Turgeon, Hon. Adelard, 1863–1930, vol. III

Turgeon, Hon. William Ferdinand Alphonse, 1877–1969, vol. VI

Turing, Alan Mathison, 1912–1954, vol. V

Turing, Harvey Doria, 1877–1950, vol. IV

Turing, Henry, 1843–1922, vol. II

Turing, Sir James Walter, 9th Bt, 1862–1928, vol. II

Turing, Sir Robert Andrew Henry, 10th Bt, 1895–1970, vol. VI

Turing, Sir Robert Fraser, 8th Bt, 1827–1913, vol. I

Turle, Rear-Adm. Charles Edward, 1883–1966, vol. VI

Turle, Henry Bernard, 1885–1974, vol. VII

Turley, Henry, died 1929, vol. III

Turnbull, Col Alan William, 1893–1964, vol. VI

Turnbull, Sir Alfred Clarke, died 1962, vol. VI

Turnbull, Col Bruce, 1880–1952, vol. V

Turnbull, Dora Amy; see Turnbull, Mrs George.

Turnbull, Brig. Douglas John Tulloch, 1901–1973, vol. VII

Turnbull, Major Dudley Ralph, 1891–1917, vol. II

Turnbull, Edwin Laurence, 1888–1968, vol. VI

Turnbull, Mrs George, (Dora Amy), died 1961, vol. VI

Turnbull, George Henry, 1889–1961, vol. VI

Turnbull, Herbert Westren, 1885–1961, vol. VI

Turnbull, Hubert Maitland, 1875–1955, vol. V

Turnbull, Lt-Col Sir Hugh Stephenson, 1882–1973, vol. VII

Turnbull, Cdre James, 1874–1964, vol. VI

Turnbull, Jane Holland, died 1958, vol. V

Turnbull, Col John, 1864–1937, vol. III

Turnbull, Ven. John William, 1905–1979, vol. VII

Turnbull, Sir March; see Turnbull, Sir R. M. K.

Turnbull, Maj.-Gen. Peter Stephenson, 1836–1921, vol. II

Turnbull, Sir (Reginald) March Kesterson, 1878–1943, vol. IV

Turnbull, Robert, 1823–1901, vol. I

Turnbull, Sir Robert, 1852–1926, vol. II

Turnbull, Sir Roland Evelyn, 1905–1960, vol. V

Turnbull, Lt-Col Thomas, died 1929, vol. III

Turnbull, Sir Winston George, 1899–1980, vol. VII

Turner, Sir Adolphus Hilgrove, died 1911, vol. I

Turner, Alfred, 1874–1922, vol. II

Turner, Alfred, 1874–1940, vol. III

Turner, Sir Alfred Charles; see Turner, Sir V. A. C.
Turner, Maj.-Gen. Sir Alfred Edward, 1842–1918, vol. II
Turner, Rt Rev. Arthur Beresford, 1862–1910, vol. I
Turner, Arthur James, 1889–1971, vol. VII
Turner, Brig.-Gen. Arthur Jervois, 1878–1952, vol. V
Turner, Arthur Logan, 1865–1939, vol. III
Turner, Engr Rear-Adm. Arthur William, 1859–1928, vol. II
Turner, Col Augustus Henry, 1842–1925, vol. II
Turner, Miss Beatrice Ethel, 1891–1964, vol. VI
Turner, Sir Ben, 1863–1942, vol. IV
Turner, Captain Bingham Alexander, 1877–1914, vol. I
Turner, Maj.-Gen. Cecil Douglas Lovett, 1898–1976, vol. VII
Turner, Sir Charles Arthur, 1833–1907, vol. I
Turner, Major Charles Cyril, 1870–1952, vol. V
Turner, Col Charles Edward, 1876–1961, vol. VI
Turner, Charles George, 1838–1913, vol. I
Turner, Rt Rev. Charles Henry, 1842–1923, vol. II
Turner, Sir Charles William Aldis, 1879–1938, vol. III
Turner, Vice-Adm. Charles Wolfran R.; see Round-Turner.
Turner, Major Clarence Roy, 1891–1957, vol. V
Turner, Cuthbert Hamilton, 1860–1930, vol. III
Turner, Dawson, 1857–1928, vol. II
Turner, Douglas William, 1894–1977, vol. VII
Turner, Dudley Charles, 1885–1958, vol. V
Turner, E. A., (Lady Turner); see Robertson, E. Arnot.
Turner, E. L., died 1940, vol. III
Turner, Edmund Robert, 1826–1899, vol. I
Turner, Edward Beadon, 1854–1931, vol. III
Turner, Edward Raymond, 1881–1929, vol. III
Turner, Eric, 1918–1980, vol. VII
Turner, Ernest George, 1874–1932, vol. III
Turner, Ernest James, 1877–1966, vol. VI
Turner, Maj.-Gen. Ernest Vere, died 1949, vol. IV
Turner, Ethel, (Mrs H. R. Curlewis), 1872–1958, vol. V
Turner, Eustace Ebenezer, 1893–1966, vol. VI
Turner, Lt-Col Francis Charles, 1866–1942, vol. IV
Turner, Frank Douglas, 1871–1957, vol. V
Turner, Franklyn Lewis, 1866–1933, vol. III
Turner, Fred, 1852–1939, vol. III
Turner, Frederick Bancroft, died 1966, vol. VI
Turner, Frederick Charles, 1872–1950, vol. IV
Turner, Vice-Adm. Sir Frederick Richard Gordon, 1889–1976, vol. VII
Turner, Sir George, died 1915, vol. I
Turner, Rt Hon. Sir George, 1851–1916, vol. II
Turner, George Charlewood, 1891–1967, vol. VI
Turner, Col George Frederick Brown, 1876–1941, vol. IV
Turner, George Grey, 1877–1951, vol. V
Turner, George Henry, 1837–1903, vol. I
Turner, George James, died 1946, vol. IV
Turner, Sir George Robertson, 1855–1941, vol. IV
Turner, Sir George Wilfred, 1896–1974, vol. VII

Turner, Rt Rev. Gilbert Price Lloyd, 1888–1968, vol. VI
Turner, Maj.-Gen. Guy Roderick, 1889–1963, vol. VI
Turner, Captain Harry Gordon, born 1862, vol. III
Turner, Hawes Harison, 1851–1939, vol. III
Turner, Henry Blois Hawkins, 1839–1909, vol. I (A)
Turner, Sir Henry Ernest, died 1961, vol. VI
Turner, H(enry) F(rederic) Lawrence, 1908–1977, vol. VII
Turner, Col Henry Fyers, 1840–1909, vol. I
Turner, Sir Henry Samuel Edwin, 1887–1978, vol. VII
Turner, Herbert Arthur, 1912–1972, vol. VII
Turner, Herbert Hall, 1861–1930, vol. III
Turner, Rt Rev. Herbert Victor, 1888–1968, vol. VI
Turner, Rev. Herbert William, died 1922, vol. II
Turner, Maj.-Gen. James Gibbon, 1859–1950, vol. IV
Turner, Sir John, 1858–1931, vol. III
Turner, John Andrew, 1858–1922, vol. II
Turner, Ven. John Carpenter, 1867–1952, vol. V
Turner, Col John Eamer, 1880–1955, vol. V
Turner, Col Sir John Fisher, 1881–1958, vol. V
Turner, John Hastings, 1892–1956, vol. V
Turner, John Herbert, 1833–1923, vol. II
Turner, John Sidney, 1843–1920, vol. II
Turner, John William Aldren, 1911–1980, vol. VII
Turner, Sir Joseph, 1868–1939, vol. III
Turner, Joseph Harling, 1859–1942, vol. IV
Turner, Rear-Adm. Laurence, 1882–1963, vol. VI
Turner, Laurence Beddome, 1886–1963, vol. VI
Turner, Sir Llewelyn, 1823–1903, vol. I
Turner, Sir Mark; see Turner, Sir R. M. C.
Turner, Brig.-Gen. Martin Newman, 1865–1944, vol. IV
Turner, Maxwell Joseph Hall, 1907–1960, vol. V
Turner, Sir Michael William, 1905–1980, vol. VII
Turner, Sir Montagu Cornish, 1853–1934, vol. III
Turner, Brig.-Gen. Percy Alexander, 1868–1940, vol. III
Turner, Percy Frederick, 1878–1926, vol. II
Turner, Philip, 1873–1955, vol. V
Turner, Lt-Col Ralph Beresford, 1879–1972, vol. VII
Turner, Lt-Col Reginald, 1870–1953, vol. V
Turner, Col Reginald George, 1870–1953, vol V
Turner, Lt-Gen. Sir Richard Ernest William, 1871–1961, vol. VI
Turner, Richard Whitbourn, 1867–1932, vol. III
Turner, Vice-Adm. Sir Robert Ross, 1885–1977, vol. VII
Turner, Sir (Ronald) Mark (Cunliffe), 1906–1980, vol. VII
Turner, Sir Samuel, 1840–1924, vol. II
Turner, Sir Samuel, 1878–1955, vol. V
Turner, Maj.-Gen. Samuel Compton, died 1900, vol. I
Turner, Sir Sidney, 1882–1966, vol. VI
Turner, Sir Skinner, 1868–1935, vol. III
Turner, Sydney George, 1880–1967, vol. VI
Turner, Thomas, 1861–1951, vol. V
Turner, Sir Victor Alfred Charles, 1892–1974, vol. VII

Turner, Lt-Col Victor Buller, 1900–1972, vol. VII
Turner, Sir Walford Hollier, 1881–1962, vol. VI
Turner, Walter James Redfern, 1889–1946, vol. IV
Turner, Rt Rev. William, 1844–1914, vol. I
Turner, Sir William, 1832–1916, vol. II
Turner, William, 1856–1936, vol. III
Turner, Rt Hon. Sir William, 1872–1937, vol. III
Turner, Lt-Col William, 1859–1940, vol. III
Turner, William, died 1944, vol. IV
Turner, William Aldren, 1864–1945, vol. IV
Turner, William Ernest Stephen, 1881–1963, vol. VI
Turner, Sir William Henry, 1868–1923, vol. II
Turner, William Hovell, 1891–1979, vol. VII
Turner, William Percy Whitford, 1884–1962, vol. VI
Turner-Samuels, Moss, died 1957, vol. V
Turney, Sir John, 1839–1927, vol. II
Turnor, Algernon, 1845–1921, vol. II
Turnor, Christopher Hatton, 1873–1940, vol. III
Turnor, Edmund, 1838–1903, vol. I (A), vol. III
Turnor, Lady Mary Katherine, died 1930, vol. III
Turnour, Rear-Adm. Edward Winterton, 1821–1901, vol. I
Turnour-Fetherstonhaugh, Hon. Keith; see Fetherstonhaugh.
Turpin, Edmund Hart, 1885–1907, vol. I
Turpin, George Sherbrooke, died 1948, vol. IV
Turpin, Sir William Gibbs, 1854–1940, vol. III
Turpin, Ven. William Homan, died 1920, vol. II
Turquan, Joseph, died 1928, vol. II
Turquet, André, died 1940, vol. III
Turquet, Gladys, died 1977, vol. VII
Turrell, Charles, 1846–1932, vol. III
Turrell, Harry Joseph, 1863–1936, vol. III
Turrell, Walter John, 1865–1943, vol. IV
Turrill, William Bertram, 1890–1961, vol. VI
Turton, Sir Edmund Russborough, 1st Bt, 1857–1929, vol. III
Turton, Col Ralph Douglas, 1862–1936, vol. III
Turton, Lt-Col William Harry, 1856–1938, vol. III
Turvey, Isaiah, 1845–1934, vol. III
Turville-Petre, Edward Oswald Gabriel, 1908–1978, vol. VII
Turville-Petre, Lt-Col Oswald Henry Philip, 1862–1941, vol. IV
Tushingham, Sidney, died 1968, vol. VI
Tuson, Alan Arthur Lancelot, 1890–1968, vol. VI
Tuson, Brig.-Gen. Harry Denison, 1866–1958, vol. V
Tuson, Sir Henry Brasnell, 1836–1916, vol. II
Tussaud, John Theodore, 1858–1943, vol. IV
Tute, Sir Richard Clifford, 1874–1950, vol. IV
Tutt, James William, 1858–1911, vol. I
Tuttiett, M. G.; see Gray, Maxwell.
Tuttle, Rt Rev. Daniel Sylvester, 1837–1923, vol. II
Tuttle, Wilbur C., 1883–1969, vol. VI
Tutton, Alfred Edwin Howard, 1864–1938, vol. III
Tuxford, Brig.-Gen. George Stuart, 1870–1943, vol. IV
Twain, Mark, 1835–1910, vol. I
Tweed, Rev. Henry Earle, 1827–1910, vol. I
Tweed, John, 1869–1933, vol. III

Tweed, Lt-Col Thomas Frederic, 1890–1940, vol. III
Tweedale, Rev. Charles L., died 1944, vol. IV
Tweedale, Violet, died 1936, vol. III
Tweeddale, 10th Marquess of, 1826–1911 (this entry was not transferred to Who was Who).
Tweeddale, 11th Marquess of, 1884–1967, vol. VI
Tweeddale, 12th Marquis of, 1921–1979, vol. VII
Tweeddale, Marchioness of; (Julia), died 1937, vol. III
Tweedie, Mrs Alec, died 1940, vol. III
Tweedie, Lt-Col David Keltie, 1878–1941, vol. IV
Tweedie, Adm. Sir Hugh Justin, 1877–1951, vol. V
Tweedie, Col John Lannoy, 1842–1920, vol. II
Tweedie, Hon. Lemuel John, 1849–1917, vol. II
Tweedie, Mary, 1875–1961, vol. VI
Tweedie, Maj.-Gen. Michael, 1836–1917, vol. II
Tweedie, Maj.-Gen. William, 1836–1914, vol. I
Tweedie, Col William John Bell, 1869–1929, vol. III
Tweedmouth, 2nd Baron, 1849–1909, vol. I
Tweedmouth, 3rd Baron, 1874–1935, vol. III
Tweedsmuir, 1st Baron, 1875–1940, vol. III
Tweedsmuir, Lady; (Susan), died 1977, vol. VII
Tweedsmuir of Belhelvie, Baroness (Life Peer); Priscilla Jean Fortescue Buchan, 1915–1978, vol. VII
Tweedy, Ernest Hastings, 1862–1945, vol. IV
Tweedy, George Alfred, died 1934, vol. III
Tweedy, Sir John, 1849–1924, vol. II
Twells, Rt Rev. Edward, 1828–1898, vol. I
Twemlow, Col Francis Randle, 1852–1927, vol. II
Twemlow, George Fletcher Fletcher-, 1857–1935, vol. III
Twentyman, Col Augustus Charles, 1836–1913, vol. I
Twentyman-Jones, Hon. Percy Sydney, 1876–1954, vol. V
Twidale, Lt-Col Cecil; see Twidale, Lt-Col W. C. E.
Twidale, Lt-Col (William) Cecil Erasmus, 1877–1949, vol. IV
Twigg, Surg. Rear-Adm. Francis John Despard, 1888–1962, vol. VI
Twigg, Sir John, 1856–1935, vol. III
Twigg, John J., died 1920, vol. II
Twigg, Brig.-Gen. Robert Henry, 1860–1956, vol. V
Twinberrow, James Frederick, 1866–1931, vol. III
Twining, Baron (Life Peer); Edward Francis Twining, 1899–1967, vol. VI
Twining, Louisa, 1820–1911, vol. I
Twining, Maj.-Gen. Sir Philip Geoffrey, 1862–1920, vol. II
Twining, Richard Haynes, 1889–1979, vol. VII
Twinn, Frank Charles George, 1885–1972, vol. VII
Twisaday, Major C. E. J., 1850–1925, vol. II
Twisden, Rev. Sir John Francis, 11th Bt, 1825–1914, vol. I
Twisden, Sir John Ramskill, 12th Bt, 1856–1937, vol. III
Twisleton-Wykeham-Fiennes, Lt-Col Sir Ranulph; see Fiennes.
Twiss, Brig.-Gen. Francis Arthur, 1871–1952, vol. V
Twiss, Lt-Col George Edward, 1856–1921, vol. II

Twiss, Vice-Adm. Guy Ouchterlony, 1834–1918, vol. II

Twiss, Brig.-Gen. John Henry, 1867–1941, vol. IV

Twiss, Maj.-Gen. Sir William Louis Oberkirch, 1879–1962, vol. VI

Twist, Henry, 1870–1934, vol. III

Twitchell, Rt Rev. Thomas Clayton, 1864–1947, vol. IV

Twitchett, Ven. Cyril Frederick, 1890–1950, vol. IV

Twohig, Brig. Joseph Patrick O.; see O'Brien Twohig.

Twohig, Col Michael Joseph O.; see O'Brien-Twohig.

Twomey, Sir Daniel Harold Ryan, 1864–1935, vol. III

Twopeny, Richard Ernest Nowell, 1857–1915, vol. I (A)

Twort, Frederick William, 1877–1950, vol. IV

Twyford, Sir Harry Edward Augustus, 1870–1967, vol VI

Twyford, Thomas William, 1849–1921, vol. II

Twyman, Frank, died 1959, vol. V

Twynam, Sir Henry Joseph, 1887–1966, vol. VI

Twynam, Major Humphrey Martin, 1858–1913, vol. I

Twynam, Col Philip Alexander Anstruther, 1832–1920, vol. II

Twynam, Sir William Crofton, died 1922, vol. II

Twysden, Sir Anthony Roger Duncan, 11th Bt, 1918–1946, vol. IV

Twysden, Sir Louis John Francis, 9th Bt, 1831–1911, vol. I

Twysden, Sir Roger Thomas, 10th Bt, 1894–1934, vol. III

Twysden, Sir William Adam Duncan, 12th Bt, 1897–1970, vol. VI

Tyabji, Badruddin, 1844–1906, vol. I

Tylden, Brig.-Gen. William, died 1942, vol. IV

Tylden-Pattenson, Major Arthur Henry, 1856–1938, vol. III

Tylden-Pattenson, Lt-Col Edwin Cooke; see Pattenson.

Tylecote, Edward Ferdinando Sutton, 1849–1938, vol. III

Tylecote, Frank Edward, died 1965, vol. VI

Tyler, Sir Alfred, 1869–1936, vol. III

Tyler, Brig.-Gen. Arthur Malcolm, 1866–1950, vol. IV

Tyler, Sir Frederick Charles, 2nd Bt, 1865–1907, vol. I

Tyler, Sir George Robert, 1st Bt, 1835–1897, vol. I

Tyler, Rev. Henry Francis Macdonald, 1846–1929, vol. III

Tyler, Sir Henry Hewey Francis M.; see Macdonald-Tyler.

Tyler, Sir Henry Whatley, 1827–1908, vol. I

Tyler, Brig.-Gen. James Arbuthnot, 1867–1945, vol. IV

Tyler, Sir John William, 1839–1913, vol. I

Tyler, Maj.-Gen. Trevor Bruce, 1841–1923, vol. II

Tylor, Alfred, 1888–1958, vol. V

Tylor, Sir Edward Burnett, 1832–1917, vol. II

Tylor, Sir Theodore Henry, 1900–1968, vol. VI

Tymms, Rev. T. Vincent, 1842–1921, vol. II

Tynan, Katharine, 1861–1931, vol. III

Tynan, Kenneth Peacock, 1927–1980, vol. VII

Tyndale, Geoffrey Clifford, 1887–1966, vol. VI

Tyndale, Henry Edmund Guise, 1887–1948, vol. IV

Tyndale, Walter, 1855–1943, vol. IV

Tyndale, Lt-Col Wentworth Francis, 1874–1964, vol. VI

Tyndale-Biscoe, Rev. Cecil Earle, 1863–1949, vol. IV

Tyndale-Biscoe, Brig.-Gen. Julian Dallas Tyndale, 1867–1960, vol. V

Tyndall, Sir Arthur, 1891–1979, vol. VII

Tyndall, Arthur Mannering, 1881–1961, vol. VI

Tyndall, Rt Rev. Charles John, 1900–1971, vol. VII

Tyndall, Maj.-Gen. Henry, 1833–1912, vol. I

Tyndall, Lt-Col Henry Stuart, 1875–1942, vol. IV

Tyndall, Maj.-Gen. William Ernest, 1891–1975, vol. VII

Tyndall, Lt-Col William Ernest Marriott, 1875–1916, vol. II

Tyner, Rt Rev. Richard, died 1958, vol. V

Tynte, Fortescue Joseph Pratt-, 1841–1907, vol. I

Tyrer, Anderson; see Tyrer, F. A.

Tyrer, (Frank) Anderson, died 1962, vol. VI

Tyrer, William Henry, 1876–1947, vol. IV

Tyrrell, 1st Baron, 1866–1947, vol. IV

Tyrrell, Col Charles Robert, 1859–1934, vol. III

Tyrrell, Sir Francis Graeme, died 1964, vol. VI

Tyrrell, Rev. George, 1861–1909, vol. I

Tyrrell, George Walter, 1883–1961, vol. VI

Tyrrell, Lt-Col Gerald Ernest, 1871–1917, vol. II

Tyrrell, Lt-Col Jasper Robert Joly, died 1951, vol. V

Tyrrell, Col John Frederick, 1872–1944, vol. IV

Tyrrell, Robert Yelverton, 1844–1914, vol. I

Tyrrell, Thomas, 1857–1929, vol. III

Tyrrell, Air Vice-Marshal Sir William, 1885–1968, vol. VI

Tyrrell, Brig. William Grant, 1882–1961, vol. VI

Tyrrell-Green, Rev. Edmund; see Green.

Tyrwhitt, Hon. Clement, 1857–1938, vol. III

Tyrwhitt, Captain Hon. Hugh, 1856–1907, vol. I

Tyrwhitt, Rev. Hon. Leonard Francis, 1863–1921, vol. II

Tyrwhitt, Adm. of the Fleet Sir Reginald Yorke, 1st Bt, 1870–1951, vol. V

Tyrwhitt, Adm. Sir St John Reginald Joseph, 2nd Bt, 1905–1961, vol. VI

Tyrwhitt, Walter Spencer-Stanhope, 1859–1932, vol. III

Tyrwhitt-Drake, Sir Garrard; see Drake.

Tyrwhitt-Drake, Hon. Montague W.; see Drake.

Tyser, Sir Charles Robert, 1848–1926, vol. II

Tyser, Granville, 1884–1970, vol. VI

Tyson, Dorothy Estelle Esmé W.; see Wynne-Tyson.

Tyson, Geoffrey William, 1898–1971, vol. VII

Tyson, George Alfred, 1888–1972, vol. VII

Tyson, Sir John Dawson, 1893–1976, vol. VII

Tyson, Moses, 1897–1969, vol. VI

Tyson, William Joseph, 1851–1927, vol. II

Tyssen, Air Vice-Marshal John Hugh Samuel, 1889–1953, vol. V
Tytler, Adam Gillies, 1845–1929, vol. III
Tytler, Edward Grant F.; see Fraser-Tytler.
Tytler, Maj.-Gen. Sir Harry Christopher, 1867–1939, vol. III
Tytler, Sir James Macleod Bannatyne F.; see Fraser-Tytler.
Tytler, Bt Col Neil F.; see Fraser-Tytler.
Tytler, Maj.-Gen. Robert Francis Christopher Alexander, died 1916, vol. II
Tytler, Sarah; see Keddie, Henrietta.
Tytler, William Howard, 1885–1957, vol. V
Tytler, Lt-Col Sir William Kerr F.; see Fraser-Tytler.
Tyzack, Group Captain John Edward Valentine, 1904–1979, vol. VII

U

Udaipur, HH Maharajahdhiraja Maharana of, 1849–1930, vol. III
Udaipur, HH Maharana of, 1884–1955, vol. V
Udal, (Nicholas) Robin, 1883–1964, vol. VI
Udal, Robin; see Udal, N. R.
Udny, John Henry Fullarton, 1853–1934, vol. III
Udny, Sir Richard, 1847–1923, vol. II
Uhr, Sir Clive Wentworth, died 1974, vol. VII
Uhthoff, John Caldwell, 1856–1927, vol. II
Ullah, Rev. Ihsan, 1857–1929, vol. III
Ullman, Maj.-Gen. Peter Alfred, 1897–1972, vol. VII
Ullmann, Stephen, 1914–1976, vol. VII
Ullswater, 1st Viscount, 1855–1949, vol. IV
Ulrich, Ruy E.; see Ennes Ulrich.
Umfreville, Col Percy, 1868–1922, vol. II
Umfreville, Lt-Col Ralph Brunton, died 1937, vol. III
Umney, John Charles, 1868–1919, vol. II
Umpherston, Francis Albert, 1869–1940, vol. III
Unbegaun, Boris Ottokar, 1898–1973, vol. VII
Underdown, Emanuel Maguire, died 1913, vol. I
Underdown, Thomas H. J., 1872–1953, vol. V
Underhill, Sir Arthur, 1850–1939, vol. III
Underhill, Charles Edward, 1845–1908, vol. I
Underhill, Adm. Edwin Veale, 1868–1928, vol. II
Underhill, Evelyn, 1875–1941, vol. IV
Underhill, Rt Rev. Francis, 1878–1943, vol. IV
Underhill, Rev. Percy Cyril, 1883–1963, vol. VI
Underwood, Rev. Alfred Clair, 1885–1948, vol. IV
Underwood, Arthur Swayne, died 1916, vol. II
Underwood, Edgar Ashworth, 1899–1980, vol. VII
Underwood, Eric Gordon, died 1952, vol. V
Underwood, Eric John, 1905–1980, vol. VII
Underwood, John Ernest Alfred, 1886–1960, vol. V
Underwood, Brig. John Percy Delabene, 1882–1958, vol. V
Underwood, Leon, 1890–1975, vol. VII
Undset, Sigrid, 1882–1949, vol. IV
Unett, Captain John Alfred, 1868–1932, vol. III
Unger, Gladys Buchanan, died 1940, vol. III, vol. IV

Unger, Josef, 1912–1967, vol. VI
Ungoed-Thomas, Sir (Arwyn) Lynn, 1904–1972, vol. VII
Ungoed-Thomas, Sir Lynn; see Ungoed-Thomas, Sir A. L.
Uniacke, Lt-Gen. Sir Herbert Crofton Campbell, 1866–1934, vol. III
Uniacke-Penrose-Fitzgerald, Sir Robert; see Fitzgerald.
Unmack, Randall Carter, 1899–1978, vol. VII
Untermeyer, Louis, 1885–1977, vol. VII
Unwin, Edward, 1840–1933, vol. III
Unwin, Captain Edward, 1864–1950, vol. IV
Unwin, Francis Sydney, 1885–1925, vol. II
Unwin, Col Garton Bouverie, 1859–1928, vol. II
Unwin, Rear-Adm. John Harold, 1906–1970, vol. VI
Unwin, Joseph Daniel, 1895–1936, vol. III
Unwin, Sir Raymond, 1863–1940, vol. III
Unwin, Sir Stanley, 1884–1968, vol. VI
Unwin, Thomas Fisher, 1848–1935, vol. III
Unwin, William Cawthorne, 1838–1933, vol. III
Upcher, Rev. Abbot Roland, 1849–1929, vol. III
Upcher, Rev. Arthur Charles Wodehouse, 1846–1938, vol. III
Upcher, Sir Henry Edward Sparke, 1870–1954, vol. V
Upcher, Henry Morris, 1839–1921, vol. II
Upcher, Ven. James Hay, died 1931, vol. III
Upcher, Maj.-Gen. Russell, 1844–1936, vol. III
Upcott, Ven. Arthur William, 1857–1922, vol. II
Upcott, Sir Frederick Robert, 1847–1918, vol. II
Upcott, Sir Gilbert Charles, 1880–1967, vol. VI
Updike, Daniel Berkeley, 1860–1941, vol. IV
Upington, Sir Thomas, 1844–1898, vol. I
Upjohn, Baron (Life Peer); Gerald Ritchie Upjohn, 1903–1971, vol. VII
Upjohn, Howard Emlyn, 1925–1980, vol. VII
Upjohn, Sir William George Dismore, 1888–1980 vol. VII
Upjohn, William Henry, 1853–1941, vol. IV
Upperton, Maj.-Gen. John, 1838–1924, vol. II
Upson, Rt Rev. Dom Wilfrid, 1880–1963, vol. VI
Upton, Charles B., 1831–1920, vol. II
Upton, Captain Edward James Gott, died 1943, vol. IV
Upton, Hon. Eric Edward Montagu John, 1885–1915, vol. I
Upton, Sir Everard; see Upton, Sir T. E. T.
Upton, Florence, died 1922, vol. II
Upton, James Bryan, 1900–1976, vol. VII
Upton, John Herbert, 1865–1930, vol. III
Upton, Leslie William Stokes, 1900–1979, vol. VII
Upton, Sir (Thomas) Everard (Tichborne), 1871–1937, vol. III
Upton, Rev. William Clement, died 1922, vol. II
Upward, Allen, 1863–1926, vol. II
Upward, Herbert, died 1944, vol. IV
Urban, Wilbur Marshall, 1873–1952, vol. V
Ure, Alexander; see Baron Strathclyde.
Ure, Mary Eileen, (Mrs Robert Shaw), 1933–1975, vol. VII
Ure, Percy Neville, 1879–1950, vol. IV
Ure, Peter, 1919–1969, vol. VI

Uriburu, José Evaristo, *died* 1956, vol. V
Urich, John, 1849–1939, vol. III (A), vol. IV
Urling Clark, Sir Henry Laurence, 1883–1975, vol. VII
Urmson, George Harold, 1851–1907, vol. I
Urmson, Rev. Thomas, *died* 1926, vol. II
Urmston, Col Edward Brabazon, 1858–1920, vol. II
Urquhart, Alexander, 1867–1942, vol. IV
Urquhart, Lt-Col Francis Edward Romulus P.; *see* Pollard-Urquhart.
Urquhart, Francis Fortescue, 1868–1934, vol. III
Urquhart, Frederic Charles, 1858–1936, vol. III
Urquhart, George A., 1888–1951, vol. V
Urquhart, Sir James, 1864–1930, vol. III
Urquhart, John Leslie 1874–1933, vol. III
Urquhart, Col Robert, 1845–1922, vol. II
Urquhart, Maj.-Gen. Ronald Walton, 1906–1968, vol. VI
Urquhart, Rev. William Spence, 1877–1964, vol. VI
Urwick, Edward Johns, 1867–1945, vol. IV
Urwick, Col Frank Davidson, 1874–1936, vol. III
Urwick, Sir Henry, 1859–1931, vol. III
Urwick, Sir Thomas Hunter, 1865–1939, vol. III
Usborne, Vice-Adm. Cecil Vivian, 1880–1951, vol. V
Usborne, Thomas, 1840–1915, vol. I
Usher, Sir George Clemens, 1889–1963, vol. VI
Usher, Herbert Brough, 1892–1969, vol. VI
Usher, James Ward, *died* 1921, vol. II
Usher, Sir John, 1st Bt, 1828–1904, vol. I
Usher, Col Sir John Turnbull, 3rd Bt, 1891–1951, vol. V
Usher, Rev. Philip Charles Alexander, 1899–1941, vol. IV
Usher, Sir Robert, 2nd Bt, 1860–1933, vol. III
Usher, Sir (Robert) Stuart, 4th Bt, 1898–1962, vol. VI
Usher, Sir Stuart; *see* Usher, Sir R. S.
Usherwood, John F., *died* 1964, vol. VI
Usherwood, Ven. Thomas Edward, 1841–1939, vol. III
Usman, Sir Mahomed, 1884–1960, vol. V
Ussher, Col Allan Vesey, 1860–1941, vol. IV
Ussher, Captain Edward, *died* 1902, vol. I
Ussishkin, Menahem, *died* 1941, vol. IV
Uthwatt, Baron (Life Peer); Augustus Andrewes Uthwatt, 1879–1949, vol. IV
Uthwatt, Ven. William Andrewes, *died* 1952, vol. V
Utley, Clifton Maxwell, 1904–1978, vol. VII
Utrillo, Maurice, (Maurice Valadon), 1883–1955, vol. V
Utterson, Maj.-Gen. Archibald Hammond, 1836–1912, vol. I
Utterson-Kelso, Maj.-Gen. John Edward, 1893–1972, vol. VII
Utterton, Ven. Frank Ernest, *died* 1908, vol. I
Utting, Sir John, *died* 1927, vol. II
Uttley, Alison, 1884–1976, vol. VII
Uttley, George Harry, 1879–1960, vol. V
Uvarov, Sir Boris Petrovitch, 1889–1970, vol. VI
Uvedale of North End, 1st Baron, 1885–1974, vol. VII
Uwins, Cyril Frank, 1896–1972, vol. VII

Uzanne, Octave, 1852–1931, vol. III
Uzès, Duchesse d', 1848–1933, vol. III
Uzielli, Herbert Rex, 1890–1961, vol. VI
Uzielli, Col Theodore John, 1882–1934, vol. III

V

Vacaresco, Helen, *died* 1947, vol. IV
Vachell, Benjamin Garnet L.; *see* Lampard-Vachell.
Vachell, Charles Francis, 1854–1935, vol. III
Vachell, Horace Annesley, 1861–1955, vol. V
Vachon, Most Rev. Mgr Alexandre, 1885–1953, vol. V
Vade-Walpole, Henry Spencer, 1837–1913, vol. I
Vade-Walpole, Thomas Henry Bourke, 1879–1915, vol. I
Vaghjee, Sir Harilal Ranchhordas, 1912–1979, vol. VII
Vaillancourt, Hon. Cyrille, 1892–1969, vol. VII
Vailland, Roger, 1907–1965, vol. VI
Vaisey, Dame Dorothy May, *died* 1969, vol. VI
Vaisey, Sir Harry Bevir, 1877–1965, vol. VI
Vaithianathan, Sir Kanthiah, 1896–1965, vol. VI
Vaizey, Mrs G. de Horne, *died* 1927, vol. II
Vakil, Sardar Khan Bahadur Sir Rustom Jehangir, 1879–1933, vol. III
Valadier, Sir Auguste Charles, 1873–1931, vol. III
Valadon, Maurice; *see* Utrillo, M.
Valantine, Louis Francis, 1907–1977, vol. VII
Valdés, Armando P.; *see* Palacio Valdés.
Vale, Brig. Croxton Sillery, 1896–1975, vol. VII
Vale, Edmund; *see* Vale, H. E. T.
Vale, (Henry) Edmund (Theodoric), 1888–1969, vol. VI
Vale, Captain Seymour Douglas, 1865–1931, vol. III
Valentia, 11th Viscount, 1843–1927, vol. II
Valentia, 12th Viscount, 1883–1949, vol. IV
Valentia, 13th Viscount, 1875–1951, vol. V
Valentine; *see* Pechey, Archibald T.
Valentine, Sir Alec, (Alexander Balmain Bruce Valentine), 1899–1977, vol. VII
Valentine, Alfred Buyers, 1894–1970, vol. VI
Valentine, Charles Wilfrid, 1879–1964, vol. VI
Valentine, George Donald, 1877–1946, vol. IV
Valentine, Wing-Comdr George Engebret, 1909–1941, vol. IV
Valentine, William Alexander, 1869–1959, vol. V
Valéry, Paul, 1871–1945, vol. IV
Valintine, Thomas Harcourt Ambrose, 1865–1945, vol. IV
Vallance, Lt-Col Aylmer, (George Alexander Gerald Vallance), 1892–1955, vol. V
Vallance, David James, 1849–1915, vol. I
Vallance, George Alexander Gerald; *see* Vallance, Lt-Col Aylmer.
Vallance, William Fleming, 1827–1904, vol. I
Vallery-Radot Pasteur, Louis, 1886–1970, vol. VI
Valluy, Général d'Armée Jean Étienne, 1899–1970, vol. VI

Valon, Maj.-Gen. Albert Robert, 1885–1971, vol. VII

Valpy, Rev. Arthur Sutton, *died* 1909, vol. I

Valtorta, Rt Rev. Mgr Henry Paschal, 1883–1951, vol. V

Vambery, Arminius, 1832–1913, vol. I

van Allen, Rev. William Harman, 1870–1931, vol. III

van Anrooy, A., 1870–1949, vol. IV

Van Beinum, Eduard, 1900–1959, vol. V

Van Beneden, Edward, *died* 1910, vol. I (A), vol. III

van Boeschoten, Sir Johannes Gerard, 1862–1937, vol. III

van Broekhuizen, Herman Dirk, 1872–1953, vol. V

Vanbrugh, Dame Irene, 1872–1949, vol. IV

Vanbrugh, Violet, 1867–1942, vol. IV

Van Buren, Rt Rev. James Heartt, 1850–1917, vol. II

Vance, Very Rev. George Oakley, 1828–1910, vol. I

Vance, Rt Rev. John Gabriel, 1885–1968, vol. VI

Van Cuylenburg, Sir Hector, 1847–1915, vol. I (A)

Vandal, Louis Jules Albert, 1853–1910, vol. I

Vandam, Albert Dresden, 1843–1903, vol. I

Vandeleur, Lt-Col C. F. Seymour, 1869–1901, vol. I

Vandeleur, Captain Hector Stewart, 1836–1909, vol. I

Vandeleur, Brig. Henry Martley, 1875–1951, vol. V

Vandeleur, Maj.-Gen. John Ormsby, 1832–1908, vol. I

Vandeleur, Brig.-Gen. Robert Seymour, 1869–1956, vol. V

Vanden-Bempde-Johnstone, Hon. Sir Alan; *see* Johnstone.

Vandenberg, Arthur Hendrick, 1884–1951, vol. V

Van Den Berg, Frederick, 1893–1957, vol. V

Van den Bergh, Donald Stanley, 1888–1949, vol. IV

Van den Bergh, Henry, 1851–1937, vol. III

van den Heever, C. M., 1902–1957, vol. V

Vanden Heuvel, Frederick, 1885–1963, vol. VI

Vandepeer, Sir Donald Edward, 1890–1968, vol. VI

van der Bijl, Hendrik Johannes, 1887–1948, vol. IV

Vanderbilt, Alfred Gwynne, 1877–1915, vol. I

Vanderbilt, Brig.-Gen. Cornelius, 1873–1942, vol. IV

Vanderbilt, Cornelius, 1898–1974, vol. VII

Vanderbilt, Frederick William, 1856–1938, vol. III

Vanderbilt, George Washington, 1862–1914, vol. I

Vanderbilt, William Kissam, 1849–1920, vol. II

Van der Byl, Brig. John, 1878–1953, vol. V

van der Byl, Major Hon. Pieter Voltelyn Graham, 1889–1975, vol. VII

Vanderbyl, Captain P. B., 1867–1930, vol. III

Van Der Hoeve, Jan, 1878–1952, vol. V

Van der Kiste, Lt-Col Freegift William, 1875–1948, vol. IV

Vanderlip, Frank Arthur, 1864–1937, vol. III

Vanderlyn, Nathan, 1872–1946, vol. IV

Van der Meulen, Sir Frederick Alan, 1875–1935, vol. III

Vander-Meulen, Adm. Frederick Samuel, 1839–1913, vol. I

Vanderpant, Sir Harry Sheil Elster, 1866–1955, vol. V

Van der Poorten-Schwartz, Joost Marius Willem; *see* Maartens, Maarten.

Van der Riet, Frederick John Werndly, *died* 1929, vol. III

Van der Smissen, William Henry, 1844–1929, vol. III

Van der Veer, John Conrad, 1869–1928, vol. II

Vandervelde, Emile, *died* 1938, vol. III

Vandervell, Harry, 1870–1956, vol. V

Van der Vlugt, W., 1853–1928, vol. II

Van der Waals, J. D., *died* 1923, vol. II

Vanderzee, Maj.-Gen. Francis Henry, 1841–1909, vol. I

Van Deventer, Hon. Lt-Gen. Sir Louis Jacob, *died* 1922, vol. II

Van de Weyer, Victor William Bates, 1839–1915, vol. I (A)

Van de Weyer, Major William John Bates, 1870–1946, vol. IV

Van Dine, S. S.; *see* Wright, Willard Huntington.

Van Druten, John William, 1901–1957, vol. V

Vandry, Rt Rev. Mgr Ferdinand, 1887–1967, vol. VI (AII)

Van Dyck, Ernest Marie Hubert, 1861–1923, vol. II

Van Dyke, Rev. Henry, 1852–1933, vol. III

Vane, Major Sir Francis Patrick Fletcher, 5th Bt, 1861–1934, vol. III

Vane, Frederick William, 1852–1935, vol. III

Vane, Harry Tempest, *died* 1943, vol. IV

Vane, Captain Hon. Henry Cecil, 1882–1917, vol. II

Vane, Sir Henry Ralph Fletcher, 4th Bt, 1830–1908, vol. I

Vane, Hon. Ralph Frederick, 1891–1928, vol. II

Vane, Hon. William Lyonel, 1859–1920, vol. II

Vane-Tempest, Major Adolphus; *see* Vane-Tempest, Major F. A.

Vane-Tempest, Major (Francis) Adolphus, 1863–1932, vol. III

Vane-Tempest, Lord Henry; *see* Vane-Tempest, Lord Herbert L. H.

Vane-Tempest, Lord Henry John, 1854–1905, vol. I

Vane-Tempest, Lord (Herbert Lionel) Henry, 1862–1921, vol. II

van Geyzel, Lt-Col John Lawrence, 1857–1932, vol. III

Van Heerden, Hon. H. C., 1862–1933, vol. III

Van Horne, Sir William Cornelius, 1843–1915, vol. I

Van Hulsteyn, Sir Willem, 1865–1939, vol. III

Vanier, Gen. Rt Hon. Georges Philias, 1888–1967, vol. VI

Van Koughnet, Captain Edmund Barker, 1849–1905, vol. I

Van Lare, William Bedford, 1904–1969, vol. VI

van Loon, Hendrik Willem, *died* 1944, vol. IV

Van Miltenburg, Most Rev. Mgr Alcuin, 1909–1966, vol. VI

Vanneck, Hon. Andrew Nicolas Armstrong, 1890–1965, vol. VI

Van Neck, Captain Stephen Hugh, 1889–1963, vol. VI

Vanneck, Hon. William Arcedeckne, 1845–1912, vol. I

Van Notten-Pole, Sir Cecil Pery; see Pole.

van Raalte, Charles, 1857–1907, vol. I

Van Reeth, Rt Rev. Joseph, 1843–1923, vol. II

Van Rhyn, Albertus Johannes Roux, 1890–1971, vol. VII

Van Roey, His Eminence Cardinal Joseph Ernest, 1874–1961, vol. VI

Van Ryneveld, Gen. Sir Pierre, 1891–1972, vol. VII

Vans Agnew, Lt-Col John, 1859–1943, vol. IV

Van Scoy, Thomas, 1848–1901, vol. I

Vansittart, 1st Baron, 1881–1957, vol. V

Vansittart, Arthur George, 1854–1911, vol. I

Vansittart, Col Eden, 1856–1936, vol. III

Vansittart, Adm. Edward Westby, 1818–1904, vol. I

Vansittart, Ronald Arnold, 1851–1938, vol. III

Vansittart, Spencer Charles Patrick, 1860–1928, vol. II

Vansittart-Neale, Sir Henry James; see Neale.

Van Someren, William Taylor, 1855–1944, vol. IV

Van Someren, Major William Weymouth, 1876–1939, vol. III

Vanston, Sir George Thomas Barrett, 1853–1923, vol. II

van Straubenzee, Maj.-Gen. Sir Casimir Cartwright, 1867–1956, vol. V

van Straubenzee, Brig.-Gen. Casimir Henry Claude, 1864–1943, vol. IV

van Straubenzee, Maj.-Gen. Turner, 1838–1920, vol. II

Van Swinderen, Jonkheer Rene de Marees-, 1860–1955, vol. V

Van Vechten, Carl, 1880–1964, vol. VI

van Verduynen, (Edgar) Michiels, 1885–1952, vol. V

van Verduynen, Michiels; see van Verduynen, E. M.

Van Vleck, John Hasbrouck, 1899–1980, vol. VII

Van Wyck, Robert Anderson, 1849–1918, vol. II

van Zeeland, Paul, Vicomte, 1893–1973, vol. VII

Van Zyl, Rt Hon. Gideon Brand, 1873–1956, vol. V

Vapereau, Louis Gustave, 1819–1906, vol. I

Varcoe, Frederick Percy, 1889–1965, vol. VI

Vardon, Harry, 1870–1937, vol. III

Vardy, Rev. Albert Richard, 1841–1900, vol. I

Varin, René Louis, 1896–1976, vol. VII

Varjivandas, Sir Jugmohandas; see Jugmohandas Varjivandas.

Varley, Frank Bradley, died 1929, vol. III

Varley-Haigh, Ernest; see Haigh.

Varrier-Jones, Sir Pendrill Charles, 1883–1941, vol. IV

Vasey, Maj.-Gen. George Alan, 1895–1945, vol. IV

Vaskess, Henry Harrison, 1891–1969, vol. VI

Vassal, Gabrielle M., died 1959, vol. V

Vassall-Phillips, Father Oliver Rodie, died 1932, vol. III

Vassar-Smith, Sir John George Lawley, 2nd Bt, 1868–1942, vol. IV

Vassar-Smith, Sir Richard Vassar, 1st Bt, 1843–1922, vol. II

Vasse, Air Cdre Gordon Herbert, 1899–1965, vol. VI

Vatcher, Rev. James Raynold Morley, 1861–1931, vol. III

Vaucher, Paul, 1887–1966, vol. VI

Vaudin, William Marshall, 1866–1919, vol. II

Vaudrey, Sir William Henry, 1855–1926, vol. II

Vaudrey-Barker-Mill, William Claude Frederick, 1874–1916, vol. II

Vaughan, Rev. Bernard, 1847–1922, vol. II

Vaughan, Major Charles Davies, 1868–1915, vol. I

Vaughan, Charles Edwyn, 1854–1922, vol. II

Vaughan, Brig. (Charles) Hilary (Vaughan), 1905–1976, vol. VII

Vaughan, Col Charles Jerome, 1873–1948, vol. IV

Vaughan, Very Rev. Charles John, 1816–1897, vol. I

Vaughan, Hon. Crawford, 1874–1947, vol. IV

Vaughan, David, 1873–1938, vol. III

Vaughan, Rev. David James, 1825–1905, vol. I

Vaughan, David Thomas G.; see Gwynne-Vaughan.

Vaughan, Brig.-Gen. Edward, 1866–1956, vol. V

Vaughan, Brig.-Gen. Edward James Forrester, 1875–1957, vol. V

Vaughan, Brig. Edward William Drummond, 1894–1953, vol. V

Vaughan, Major Eugene Napoleon Ernest Mallet, 1878–1934, vol. III

Vaughan, Francis Baynham, 1844–1919, vol. II

Vaughan, Rt Rev. Francis John, 1877–1935, vol. III

Vaughan, Captain George Augustus, 1833–1914, vol. I

Vaughan, Dame Helen Charlotte Isabella G.; see Gwynne-Vaughan.

Vaughan, Rev. Henry, 1848–1920, vol. II

Vaughan, His Eminence Cardinal Herbert, 1832–1903, vol. I

Vaughan, Very Rev. Herbert, 1874–1936, vol. III

Vaughan, Herbert Millingchamp, 1870–1948, vol. IV

Vaughan, Col Herbert Radclyffe, 1864–1947, vol. IV

Vaughan, Brig. Hilary; see Vaughan, Brig. C. H. V.

Vaughan, Maj.-Gen. Hugh Thomas J.; see Jones-Vaughan.

Vaughan, Sir James, 1814–1906, vol. I

Vaughan, Rev. Canon John, 1841–1918, vol. II

Vaughan, Rev. Canon John, 1855–1922, vol. II

Vaughan, Maj.-Gen. John, 1871–1956, vol. V

Vaughan, Sir (John Charles) Tudor (St Andrew-), 1870–1929, vol. III

Vaughan, John Edwards, 1863–1929, vol. III

Vaughan, John Henry, 1892–1965, vol. VI

Vaughan, (John) Keith, 1912–1977, vol. VII

Vaughan, John Howard, 1879–1955, vol. V

Vaughan, Sir John Luther, 1820–1911, vol. I

Vaughan, Rt Rev. John Stephen, 1853–1925, vol. II

Vaughan, Keith; see Vaughan, J. K.

Vaughan, Lt-Col Joseph Charles Stoelke, 1862–1932, vol. III
Vaughan, Lt-Gen. Sir Louis Ridley, 1875–1942, vol. IV
Vaughan, Margaret; see Vaughan, Mrs William Wyamar.
Vaughan, Reginald Charles, 1874–1935, vol. III
Vaughan, Reginald Charles, 1896–1960, vol. V
Vaughan, Sir Robert, 1866–1941, vol. IV
Vaughan, Robert Charles, 1883–1966, vol. VI
Vaughan, Maj.-Gen. Robert Edward, 1866–1946, vol. IV
Vaughan, Sir Tudor; see Vaughan, Sir J. C. T. St A.
Vaughan, Victor C., 1851–1929, vol. III
Vaughan, Rt Rev. William, 1814–1902, vol. I
Vaughan, William Hubert, 1894–1959, vol. V
Vaughan, William Wyamar, 1865–1938, vol. III
Vaughan, Mrs William Wyamar, (Margaret Vaughan), 1869–1925, vol. II
Vaughan-Lee, Col Arthur Vaughan Hanning, 1862–1933, vol. III
Vaughan-Lee, Adm. Sir Charles Lionel, 1867–1928, vol. II
Vaughan-Morgan, Sir Kenyon Pascoe, 1873–1933, vol. III
Vaughan-Russell, John Francis Robert, 1895–1958, vol. V
Vaughan-Sawyer, Ethel, 1868–1949, vol. IV
Vaughan-Williams, Major Francis, 1856–1920, vol. II
Vaughan Williams, Ralph, 1872–1958, vol. V
Vaux of Harrowden, 7th Baron, 1860–1935, vol. III
Vaux of Harrowden, Baroness (8th in line), 1887–1958, vol. V
Vaux of Harrowden, 9th Baron, 1914–1977, vol. VII
Vaux, Lt-Col Ernest, 1865–1925, vol. II
Vaux, Lt-Col Henry George, 1883–1957, vol. V
Vaux, Sir Richard Augustus, 1869–1946, vol. IV
Vavasour, Sir Henry Mervin, 3rd Bt (cr 1801), 1814–1912, vol. I
Vavasour, Captain Sir Leonard Pius, 4th Bt (cr 1828), 1881–1961, vol. VI
Vavasour, Sir William Edward, 3rd Bt (cr 1828), 1846–1915, vol. I (A)
Vavasseur, Josiah, 1834–1908, vol. I
Vawdrey, Col George, 1872–1961, vol. VI
Vawdrey, Rev. John Cossham, died 1931, vol. III
Veale, Sir Douglas, 1891–1973, vol. VII
Veale, Sir Geoffrey, 1906–1971, vol. VII
Veblen, Oswald, 1880–1960, vol. V
Vecqueray, Rev. Gerard Cokayne, 1851–1933, vol. III
Vedder, Elihu, 1836–1923, vol. II
Vedrenne, John E., 1867–1930, vol. III
Veidt, Conrad, 1893–1943, vol. IV
Veitch, Allan, 1900–1971, vol. VII
Veitch, George Stead, 1885–1943, vol. IV
Veitch, Sir Harry James, 1840–1924, vol. II
Veitch, Marian, (Mrs Donald Barnie), 1913–1973, vol. VII
Veitch, William, 1885–1968, vol. VI
Veitch, Maj.-Gen. William Lionel Douglas, 1901–1969, vol. VI

Velázquez, Carlos María, 1918–1970, vol. VI
Veley, Lilian Jane, 1861–1936, vol. III
Veley, Victor Herbert, 1856–1933, vol. III
Vella, Hon. Tom, born 1849, vol. II
Vella, Col Victor George, 1901–1963, vol. VI
Vellacott, Paul Cairn, 1891–1954, vol. V
Venables, Major Charles John, 1865–1915, vol. I
Venables, Rev. Canon E(dward) Malcolm, 1884–1957, vol. V
Venables, Rev. George, 1821–1908, vol. I
Venables, Harry Archbutt, 1858–1944, vol. IV
Venables, Oswald Eric, 1891–1960, vol. V
Venables, Sir Peter Percy Frederick Ronald, 1904–1979, vol. VII
Venables-Llewelyn, Sir Charles Leyshon Dillwyn-, 2nd Bt, 1870–1951, vol. V
Venables-Llewelyn, Brig. Sir (Charles) Michael Dillwyn-, 3rd Bt, 1900–1976, vol. VII
Venables-Llewelyn, Brig. Sir Michael Dillwyn-; see Venables-Llewelyn, Brig. Sir C. M. D.
Venables-Vernon, Sir William Henry; see Vernon.
Venis, Arthur, died 1918, vol. II
Venizelos, Eleutherios, 1864–1936, vol. III
Venkata Reddi Naidu, Sir Kurma, 1875–1942, vol. IV
Venkatagiri, Rajah of, 1857–1916, vol. II
Venkatagiri, Maharajah of, died 1937, vol. III
Venkatanarayana Nayudu, Diwan Bahadur J., 1875–1958, vol. V
Venkataratnam Nayudu, Sir R., 1862–1939, vol. III
Venkatasweta Chalapati Runga-Rao Bahadur, Maharajah Sir Ravu, Maharajah of Bobbili, 1862–1920, vol. II
Venmore, Arthur, 1883–1961, vol. VI
Venn, Albert John, 1840–1919, vol. II
Venn, George William Cavendish, died 1933, vol. III
Venn, Rev. Henry, 1838–1923, vol. II
Venn, John, 1834–1923, vol. II
Venn, John Archibald, 1883–1958, vol. V
Venner, Sir Edwin John, 1871–1955, vol. V
Venner, John Franklyn, 1902–1955, vol. V
Venning, Alfred Reid, 1846–1927, vol. II
Venning, Sir Edgcombe, 1837–1920, vol. II
Venning, Brig. Francis Esmond Wingate, 1882–1970, vol. VI
Venning, Lieut Gordon Ralph, died 1902, vol. I
Venning, Gen. Sir Walter King, 1882–1964, vol. VI
Veno, Sir William Henry, 1866–1933, vol. III
Venour, Major Wilfred John, 1870–1914, vol. I
Venter, Gen. Christoffel Johannes, 1892–1977, vol. VII
Ventry, 4th Baron, 1828–1914, vol. I
Ventry, 5th Baron, 1861–1923, vol. II
Ventry, 6th Baron, 1864–1936, vol. III
Ventris, Maj.-Gen. Francis, 1857–1929, vol. III
Verco, Sir Joseph Cooke, 1851–1933, vol. III
Verdi, Giuseppe, 1813–1901, vol. I
Verdin, Sir Joseph, 1st Bt, 1838–1920, vol. II
Verdin, Lt-Col Sir Richard Bertram, 1912–1978, vol. VII
Verdin, William Henry, 1848–1929, vol. III
Verdon, Rt Rev. Michael, 1838–1918, vol. II

Verdon-Roe, Sir Alliott; *see* Roe.
Vere, James Charles H.; *see* Hope-Vere.
Vere, Very Rev. Langton George, 1844–1924, vol. II
Vere Hodge, John Douglass; *see* Hodge.
Vereker, Sir (George) Gordon (Medlicott), 1889–1976, vol. VII
Vereker, Sir Gordon; *see* Vereker, Sir G. G. M.
Vereker, Hon. Henry Prendergast, 1824–1904, vol. I
Veresmith, Daniel Albert, 1861–1932, vol. III
Veresmith, Emile, vol. III
Verestchagin, Vassili, 1842–1904, vol. I
Verey, Lt-Col Henry Edward, 1877–1968, vol. VI
Verey, Sir Henry William, 1836–1920, vol. II
Verey, Rev. Lewis, 1874–1961, vol. VI
Verhaeren, Emil, 1855–1916, vol. II
Verity, Sir Edgar William, 1891–1975, vol. VII
Verity, Francis Thomas, *died* 1937, vol. III
Verity, George, 1867–1936, vol. III
Verity, Rev. Heron Beresford, *died* 1940, vol. III (A), vol. IV
Verity, Sir John, 1892–1970, vol. VI
Verne, Adela, 1886–1952, vol. V
Verne, Jules, 1828–1905, vol. I
Verner, Sir Edward Derrick Wingfield, 6th Bt, 1907–1975, vol. VII
Verner, Sir Edward Wingfield, 4th Bt, 1830–1899, vol. I
Verner, Captain Sir Edward Wingfield, 5th Bt, 1865–1936, vol. III
Verner, Maj.-Gen. Thomas Edward, 1845–1931, vol. III
Verner, Col William Willoughby Cole, 1852–1922, vol. II
Verneuil, Louis, 1893–1952, vol. V
Verney, Sir Edmund Hope, 3rd Bt (*cr* 1818), 1838–1910, vol. I
Verney, Ernest Basil, 1894–1967, vol. VI
Verney, Frank Arthur, 1874–1952, vol. V
Verney, Frederick William, 1846–1913, vol. I
Verney, Maj.-Gen. Gerald Lloyd, 1900–1957, vol. V
Verney, Sir Harry Calvert Williams, 4th Bt (*cr* 1818), 1881–1974, vol. VII
Verney, Sir Harry Lloyd, 1872–1950, vol. IV
Verney, Margaret Maria, (Lady Verney), 1844–1930, vol. III
Verney, Lt-Col Sir Ralph, 1st Bt (*cr* 1946), 1879–1959, vol. V
Verney, Air Cdre Reynell Henry, 1886–1974, vol. VII
Vernham, John Edward, 1854–1921, vol. II
Vernon, 7th Baron, 1854–1898, vol. I
Vernon, 8th Baron, 1888–1915, vol. I (A)
Vernon, 9th Baron, 1889–1963, vol. VI
Vernon, Ambrose White, 1870–1951, vol. V
Vernon, Sir (Bowater) George (Hamilton), 2nd Bt (*cr* 1885), 1865–1940, vol. III
Vernon, Rev. Canon C. W., 1871–1934, vol. III
Vernon, Major Frank, 1875–1940, vol. III
Vernon, Air Cdre Frederick Edward, 1899–1963, vol. VI
Vernon, Sir George; *see* Vernon, Sir B. G. H.

Vernon, Rt Rev. Gerald Richard, 1899–1963, vol. VI
Vernon, Hon. Greville Richard, 1835–1909, vol. I
Vernon, Harold Anselm Bellamy, 1874–1945, vol. IV
Vernon, Sir Harry Foley, 1st Bt (*cr* 1885), 1834–1920, vol. II
Vernon, Brig.-Gen. Henry Albemarle, 1879–1943, vol. IV
Vernon, Sir Herbert; *see* Vernon, Sir J. H.
Vernon, Horace Middleton, 1870–1951, vol. V
Vernon, Captain Hubert Edward, 1867–1902, vol. I
Vernon, Rev. James Edmund, 1837–1928, vol. II
Vernon, Sir (John) Herbert, 2nd Bt (*cr* 1914), 1858–1933, vol. III
Vernon, Sir Norman; *see* Vernon, Sir W. N.
Vernon, Roland Venables, *died* 1942, vol. IV
Vernon, Rupert Robert, 1872–1940, vol. III
Vernon, Sir Sydney, 1876–1966, vol. VI
Vernon, Sir Wilfred Douglas, 1897–1973, vol. VII
Vernon, Major Wilfrid Foulston, 1882–1975, vol. VII
Vernon, Sir William, 1st Bt (*cr* 1914), 1835–1919, vol. II
Vernon, Sir William Henry Venables-, 1852–1934, vol. III
Vernon, Sir (William) Norman, 3rd Bt (*cr* 1914), 1890–1967, vol. VI
Vernon Harcourt, Augustus George, 1834–1919, vol. II
Vernon-Harcourt, Leveson Francis, 1839–1907, vol. I
Vernon-Harcourt, Rt Hon. Sir William George Granville Venables; *see* Harcourt.
Vernon-Jones, Vernon Stanley, 1875–1955, vol. V
Vernon-Wentworth, Captain Bruce Canning, 1862–1951, vol. V
Vernon-Wentworth, Captain Frederick Charles Ulick, 1866–1947, vol. IV
Veronese, Senator Giuseppe, *born* 1854, vol. II
Verpilleux, Antoine Emile, 1888–1964, vol. VI
Verrall, Arthur Woollgar, 1851–1912, vol. I
Verrall, George Henry, 1848–1911, vol. I
Verrall, Sir Jenner; *see* Verrall, Sir T. J.
Verrall, Paul Jenner, 1883–1951, vol. V
Verrall, Sir (Thomas) Jenner, 1852–1929, vol. III
Verrett, Lt-Col Hector Bacon, 1874–1926, vol. II
Verrieres, Albert Claude, 1871–1940, vol. III
Verrill, Alpheus Hyatt, 1871–1954, vol. V
Verschoyle, Arthur Robert, 1859–1937, vol. III
Verschoyle, Beresford St George, *died* 1962, vol. VI
Verschoyle, Derek Hugo, 1911–1973, vol. VII
Verschoyle, James Kynaston Edwards, 1858–1907, vol. I
Verschoyle-Campbell, Maj.-Gen. William Henry McNeile, 1884–1964, vol. VI
Verstone, Philip Eason, 1882–1973, vol. VII
Verteillac, Herminie de; *see* Rohan, Duchess de.
Vertue, Rt Rev. John, 1826–1900, vol. I
Verulam, 3rd Earl of, 1852–1924, vol. II
Verulam, 4th Earl of, 1880–1949, vol. IV
Verulam, 5th Earl of, 1910–1960, vol. V
Verulam, 6th Earl of, 1912–1973, vol. VII

Verwoerd, Hendrik Frensch, 1901–1966, vol. VI
Vesey, Captain Charles Nicholas C.; see Colthurst-Vesey.
Vesey, Ven. Francis Gerald, 1832–1915, vol. I
Vesey, Gen. Sir Ivo Lucius Beresford, 1876–1975, vol. VII
Vesey, Lt-Col Hon. Sir Osbert Eustace, 1884–1957, vol. V
Vesey, Sidney Philip Charles, 1873–1932, vol. III
Vesey, Col Hon. Thomas Eustace, 1885–1946, vol. IV
Vesey-Fitzgerald, James Foster-; see Fitzgerald.
Vesey-FitzGerald, John Foster, died 1932, vol. III
Vesey-FitzGerald, John Vesey, 1848–1929, vol. III
Vesey-Fitzgerald, Seymour Gonne, 1884–1954, vol. V
Vesnin, Victor, 1882–1950, vol. IV (A)
Vestal, Stanley; see Campbell, W. S.
Vestey, 1st Baron, 1859–1940, vol. III
Vestey, 2nd Baron, 1882–1954, vol. V
Vestey, Sir Edmund Hoyle, 1st Bt, 1866–1953, vol. V
Vetch, Col Robert Hamilton, 1841–1916, vol. II
Vetch, Maj.-Gen. William Francis, 1845–1910, vol. I
Vevers, Geoffrey Marr, 1890–1970, vol. VI
Vezin, Hermann, 1829–1910, vol. I
Vial, Rev. Frank Gifford, 1872–1948, vol. IV
Vialls, Lt-Col Harry George, 1859–1918, vol. II
Vian, Admiral of the Fleet Sir Philip, 1894–1968, vol. VI
Viant, Samuel Philip, 1882–1964, vol. VI
Viardot, Michelle Pauline, 1821–1910, vol. I
Viaud, Louis Marie Julien; see Loti, Pierre.
Vibart, Col Henry Meredith, 1839–1917, vol. II
Vibart, Captain John Fleming, 1877–1948, vol. IV (A), vol. V
Vibart, Bt Lt-Col Noel Meredith, 1893–1935, vol. III
Vibert, Captain Frederick William, 1859–1935, vol. III
Vicars, Sir Arthur Edward, 1864–1921, vol. II
Vicars, Edward Robert Eckersall, 1869–1949, vol. IV
Vicars, Sir John, 1857–1936, vol. III
Vicars, Sir William, 1859–1940, vol. III
Vicary, Col Alexander Craven, 1888–1975, vol. VII
Viccars, John Ellis, 1882–1940, vol. III
Vick, Sir Godfrey Russell, 1892–1958, vol. V
Vick, Reginald Martin, died 1971, vol. VII
Vickers, Albert, 1838–1919, vol. II
Vickers, Allan Robert Stanley, 1901–1967, vol. VI
Vickers, Douglas, 1861–1937, vol. III
Vickers, Harold James, 1895–1970, vol. VI
Vickers, Kenneth Hotham, 1881–1957, vol. V
Vickers, Col Thomas Edward, 1833–1915, vol. I
Vickers, Vincent Cartwright, 1879–1939, vol. III
Vickers, William John, 1898–1979, vol. VII
Vickery, Col Charles Edwin, 1881–1951, vol. V
Vicky; see Weisz, Victor.
Victor, Rt Rev. Dennis, 1882–1949, vol. IV
Vidal, Col Francis Peter, 1879–1952, vol. V
Vidal, Rt Rev. Julian, 1846–1922, vol. II

Viener, Rev. Harry Dan Leigh, 1868–1947, vol. IV
Vigne, Lt-Col Robert Austen, 1862–1940, vol. III
Vignoles, Charles Malcolm, 1901–1961, vol. VI
Vigors, Edward Cliffe, died 1945, vol. IV
Vigors, Captain Philip Urban, 1875–1917, vol. II
Vigors, Major Philip Urban Walter, 1863–1935, vol. III
Viljoen, Hon. Sir Antonie Gysbert, 1858–1918, vol. II
Viljoen, W. J., 1869–1929, vol. III
Villa-Urrutia, Marquis de, 1850–1933, vol. III
Villalobar, Marquis of, 1866–1926, vol. II
Villar, Captain George, 1887–1970, vol. VI
Villard, Oswald Garrison, 1872–1949, vol. IV
Villars, Henry G.; see Gauthier-Villars.
Villars, Paul, 1849–1935, vol. III
Villasante, Julian Martinez-Villasante y Navarro, 1876–1945, vol. IV
Villeneuve, Son Eminence le Cardinal J. M. Rodrigue, 1883–1947, vol. IV
Villeneuve-Smith, Sir Francis; see Smith.
Villiers, Hon. Arthur George Child, 1883–1969, vol. VI
Villiers, Lt-Col Charles Hyde, died 1947, vol. IV
Villiers, Rt Hon. Charles Pelham, 1802–1898, vol. I
Villiers, Lt-Col Charles Walter, 1873–1938, vol. III
Villiers, Sir Edward; see Villiers, Sir F. E. E.
Villiers, Rear-Adm. Edward Cecil, 1866–1939, vol. III
Villiers, Col Ernest, 1838–1921, vol. III
Villiers, Ernest Amherst, 1863–1923, vol. II
Villiers, Lt-Col Evelyn Fountaine, 1875–1955, vol. V
Villiers, Sir (Francis) Edward Earle, 1889–1967, vol. VI
Villiers, Rt Hon. Sir Francis Hyde, 1852–1925, vol. II
Villiers, Francis John, 1851–1925, vol. II
Villiers, Frederic, 1852–1922, vol. II
Villiers, Gerald Hyde, 1882–1953, vol. V
Villiers, Rev. Henry Montagu, died 1908, vol. I
Villiers, Maria Theresa; see Earle, Mrs C. W.
Villiers, Richard J., 1850–1913, vol. I
Villiers, Brig. Richard Montagu, 1905–1973, vol. VII
Villiers, Sir Thomas Lister, 1869–1959, vol. V
Villiers-Stuart, Col John Patrick, 1879–1958, vol. V
Villiers-Stuart, Brig.-Gen. William, 1872–1961, vol. VI
Vinall, Joseph William Topham, 1873–1953, vol. V
Vinaver, Eugène, 1899–1979, vol. VII
Vince, Charles Anthony, 1855–1929, vol. III
Vincent, Sir Alfred, 1891–1967, vol. VI
Vincent, Sir Anthony Francis, 14th Bt (cr 1620), 1894–1936, vol. III
Vincent, Col Arthur Craigie Fitz-Hardinge, 1857–1929, vol. III
Vincent, Arthur Rose, 1876–1956, vol. V
Vincent, Brig.-Gen. Sir Berkeley, 1871–1963, vol. VI
Vincent, Rt Rev. Boyd, 1845–1935, vol. III

Vincent, Sir (Charles Edward) Howard, 1849–1908, vol. I
Vincent, Air Vice-Marshal Claude McClean, 1896–1967, vol. VI
Vincent, Eric Reginald Pearce, 1894–1978, vol. VII
Vincent, Ethel Gwendoline, (Lady Vincent), 1861–1952, vol. V
Vincent, Sir Francis Erskine, 13th Bt (cr 1620), 1869–1935, vol. III
Vincent, Frank Arthur Money, 1875–1950, vol. IV
Vincent, Sir Frederick d'Abernon, 15th Bt (cr 1620), 1852–1936, vol. III
Vincent, George Edgar, 1864–1941, vol. IV
Vincent, Sir Harry, 1874–1952, vol. V
Vincent, Brig.-Gen. Henry Osman, 1863–1945, vol. IV
Vincent, Sir Howard; see Vincent, Sir C. E. H.
Vincent, Sir Hugh Corbet, died 1931, vol. III
Vincent, James Edmund, 1857–1909, vol. I
Vincent, Rt Rev. John Dacre, 1894–1960, vol. V
Vincent, John Lewis, 1845–1915, vol. I
Vincent, Very Rev. John Ranulph, died 1914, vol. I
Vincent, Lady Kitty; see Ritson, Lady K.
Vincent, Sir Lacey Eric, 2nd Bt (cr 1936), 1902–1963, vol. VI
Vincent, Marvin Richardson, 1834–1922, vol. II
Vincent, Sir Percy, 1st Bt (cr 1936), 1868–1943, vol. IV
Vincent, Ralph, 1870–1922, vol. II
Vincent, Robert William Edward Hampe, 1841–1914, vol. I
Vincent, Rev. Samuel, 1839–1910, vol. I
Vincent, Air Vice-Marshal Stanley Flamank, 1897–1976, vol. VII
Vincent, Swale, 1868–1933, vol. III
Vincent, Sir William, 12th Bt (cr 1620), 1834–1914, vol. I
Vincent, Sir William Henry Hoare, 1866–1941, vol. IV
Vincent, William James Nathaniel, 1867–1953, vol. V
Vincent, Sir William W., 1843–1916, vol. II
Vincent-Gompertz, Frank Priestly, died 1968, vol. VI
Vincent-Jackson, Rev. William, died 1919, vol. II
Vinden, Brig. Frederick Hubert, 1898–1977, vol. VII
Vine, Rev. Aubrey Russell, 1900–1973, vol. VII
Vine, Francis Seymour, 1904–1961, vol. VI
Vine, Sir John Richard Somers, 1847–1929, vol. III
Vine, Laurence Arthur, 1885–1954, vol. V
Vine, Rev. Marshall George, 1850–1918, vol. II
Viney, Lt-Col Horace George, 1885–1972, vol. VII
Vine, Norman Douglas, 1890–1966, vol. VI
Vines, Col Clement Erskine, 1878–1964, vol. VI
Vines, Sydney Howard, 1849–1934, vol. III
Vines, Rev. Thomas Hotchkin, died 1928, vol. II
Viney, Col Oscar Vaughan, 1886–1976, vol. VII
Vining, Most Rev. Leslie Gordon, 1885–1955, vol. V
Vinogradoff, Sir Paul, 1854–1925, vol. II
Vinson, Frederick Moore, 1890–1953, vol. V

Vintcent, Sir Joseph, 1861–1914, vol. I
Vintras, George Charles Louis Bartlett, 1864–1934, vol. III
Viollet, Paul, 1840–1914, vol. I (A)
Vipan, Alfred, 1884–1947, vol. IV
Vipan, Major Charles, 1849–1921, vol. II
Vipan, Captain John Alexander Maylin, 1849–1939, vol. III
Virchow, Rudolf, 1821–1902, vol. I
Virgo, Charles G., 1843–1907, vol. I
Virgo, John James, 1865–1956, vol. V
Virtanen, Artturi Ilmari, 1895–1973, vol. VII
Vischer, Sir Hanns, 1876–1945, vol. IV
Visconti, Luchino, 1906–1976, vol. VII
Visetti, Albert, 1846–1928, vol. II
Visger, Mrs Owen; see Owen, Jean A.
Vissanji, Sir Mathuradas, 1881–1949, vol. IV
Visvesvaraya, Sir Mokshagundam, 1861–1962, vol. VI
Viswa Nath, Rao Bahadur Bhagavatula, 1889–1964, vol. VI
Vivian, 4th Baron, 1878–1940, vol. III
Vivian, Adm. Algernon W. H.; see Walker-Heneage-Vivian.
Vivian, Captain Anthony Hamilton, 1880–1937, vol. III
Vivian, Sir Arthur Pendarves, 1834–1926, vol. II
Vivian, Hon. Claud Hamilton, 1849–1902, vol. I
Vivian, Captain Gerald William, 1869–1921, vol. II
Vivian, Graham Linsell, 1887–1978, vol. VII
Vivian, Henry, 1868–1930, vol. III
Vivian, Herbert, 1865–1940, vol. III
Vivian, Vice-Adm. John Guy Protheroe, 1887–1963, vol. VI
Vivian, Preston G.; see Graham-Vivian, R. P.
Vivian, Lt-Col Ralph, 1845–1924, vol. II
Vivian, Sir Sylvanus Percival, 1880–1958, vol. V
Vivian, Lt-Col Valentine, 1880–1948, vol. IV
Vivian, Lt-Col Valentine Patrick Terrel, 1886–1969, vol. VI
Vivian, William Graham, 1827–1912, vol. I
Vizard, Brig.-Gen. Robert Davenport, 1861–1941, vol. IV
Vizetelly, Ernest Alfred, 1853–1922, vol. II
Vizetelly, Francis Horace, (Frank), 1864–1938, vol. III
Vizianagram, Rajkumar of, 1905–1965, vol. VI
Vlasto, Michael, 1888–1979, vol. VII
Vlieland, Alice Edith, died 1944, vol. IV
Vodden, Rt Rev. Henry Townsend, 1887–1960, vol. V
Voelcker, Arthur Francis, 1861–1946, vol. IV
Voelcker, Francis William, 1896–1954, vol. V
Voelcker, John Augustus, 1854–1937, vol. III
Vogel, Harry Benjamin, 1868–1947, vol. IV
Vogel, Hon. Sir Julius, 1835–1899, vol. I (A)
Vogt, Alfred, 1879–1943, vol. IV
Vogt, Paul Benjamin, 1863–1947, vol. IV
Voguë, Marquis Charles Jean Melchior de, 1829–1916, vol. II
Voigt, F. A., 1892–1957, vol. V
Volkers, Robert Charle s Francis, died 1929, vol. III
von Anrep, Boris, 1883–1969, vol. VI

Von Arnheim, Edward Henry Silberstein; *see* Arnheim.

von Berg, Clement, 1853–1936, vol. III

von Bibra, Major Sir Eric Ernest, 1895–1958, vol. V

von Braun, Wernher, 1912–1977, vol. VII

von Bülow, Prince Bernhard Henry Martin Charles, 1849–1929, vol. III

Von der Heyde, Brig. John Leslie, 1896–1974, vol. VII

von Donop, Lt-Col Pelham George, 1851–1921, vol. II

von Donop, Maj.-Gen. Sir Stanley Brenton, 1860–1941, vol. IV

von Halle, Ernst, 1868–1909, vol. I

Vonier, Rt Rev. Dom Anscar, 1875–1938, vol. III

von Karman, Theodore, 1881–1963, vol. VI

von Laue, Max Theodor Felix, 1879–1960, vol. V

von Neumann, John, 1903–1957, vol. V

von Neurath, Freiherr Constantin, 1873–1956, vol. V

Vonnoh, Bessie Potter, 1872–1955, vol. V

Vonnoh, Robert, 1858–1933, vol. III

von Nordenwall, Oswald Hans Carl Maria; *see* von Stroheim, Erich.

von Purucker, (Hobart Lorenz) Gottfried; *see* Purucker.

von Ribbentrop, Joachim; *see* Ribbentrop.

von Sauer, Emil, 1862–1942, vol. IV

von Schroder, Baron William Henry, 1841–1912, vol. I

von Seeckt, Gen., 1866–1936, vol. III

von Stroheim, Erich, (Oswald Hans Carl Maria von Nordenwall), 1885–1957, vol. V

Vonwiller, Oscar Ulrich, 1882–1972, vol. VII

Vora, Sir Manmohandas Ramji, 1857–1934, vol. III (A), vol. V

Vorley, Lt-Col John Stuart, 1898–1953, vol. V

Voronoff, Serge, 1866–1951, vol. V

Voroshilov, Kliment Efremovich, 1881–1969, vol. VI

Vos, Philip, 1891–1948, vol. IV

Vosper, Dennis Forwood; *see* Baron Runcorn.

Vosper, Sydney Curnow, 1866–1942, vol. IV

Voules, Arthur Blennerhassett, 1870–1954, vol. V

Voules, Sir Francis Minchin, 1867–1947, vol. IV

Voules, Sir Gordon Blennerhassett, 1839–1924, vol. II

Voules, Horace St George, 1844–1909, vol. I

Vousden, William John, 1845–1902, vol. I

Voynich, Wilfrid Michael, 1865–1930, vol. III

Voysey, Rev. Charles, 1828–1912, vol. I

Voysey, Charles Francis Annesley, 1857–1941, vol. IV

Voysey, Violet Mary Annesley, 1880–1943, vol. IV

Vroom, Ven. Fenwick Williams, 1856–1944, vol. IV

Vulliamy, Colwyn Edward, 1886–1971, vol. VII

Vulliamy, Maj.-Gen. Colwyn Henry Hughes, 1894–1972, vol. VII

Vulliamy, Edward, 1876–1962, vol. VI

Vulliamy, Grace, 1878–1957, vol. V

Vyle, Sir Gilbert Christopher, 1870–1933, vol. III

Vyner, Robert Charles de Grey, 1842–1915, vol. I

Vynne, Nora, *died* 1914, vol. I

Vyse, Charles, 1882–1971, vol. VII

Vyse, Lt-Gen. Edward H.; *see* Howard-Vyse.

Vyse, Howard Henry H.; *see* Howard-Vyse.

Vyse, Maj.-Gen. Sir Richard Granville Hylton H.; *see* Howard-Vyse.

Vyshinsky, Andrei Yanuarievich, 1883–1954, vol. V

Vyvyan, Col Sir Courtenay Bourchier, 10th Bt, 1858–1941, vol. IV

Vyvyan, Captain Sir George Rawlinson, 1838–1914, vol. I

Vyvyan, Jennifer Brigit, 1925–1974, vol. VII

Vyvyan, Maj.-Gen. Ralph Ernest, 1891–1971, vol. VII

Vyvyan, Sir Richard Philip, 11th Bt, 1891–1978, vol. VII

Vyvyan, Major Richard Walter Comyn, 1859–1931, vol. III

Vyvyan, Air Vice-Marshal Sir Vyell, 1875–1935, vol. III

Vyvyan, Rev. Sir Vyell Donnithorne, 9th Bt, 1826–1917, vol. II

Vyvyan, Rt Rev. Wilmot Lushington, 1861–1937, vol. III

W

Waal, Hon. Sir Frederic de; *see* Waal, Hon. Sir N. F. de.

Waal, Hon. Sir (Nicholaas) Frederic de, 1853–1932, vol. III

Wace, Alan John Bayard, 1879–1957, vol. V

Wace, Sir Blyth; *see* Wace, Sir F. B.

Wace, Brig.-Gen. Edward Gurth, 1876–1962, vol. VI

Wace, Col Ernest Charles, 1850–1927, vol. II

Wace, Ernest William Cornish, 1894–1977, vol. VII

Wace, Sir (Ferdinand) Blyth, 1891–1964, vol. VI

Wace, Very Rev. Henry, 1836–1924, vol. II

Wace, Herbert, *died* 1906, vol. I

Wace, Maj.-Gen. Richard, 1842–1920, vol. II

Wacha, Sir Dinsha Edulji, 1844–1936, vol. III

Waddams, Rev. Canon Herbert Montague, 1911–1972, vol. VII

Wadel, William, 1868–1946, vol. IV

Waddell, Hon. (Charles) Graham, 1877–1960, vol. V (A)

Waddell, Gilbert, 1894–1967, vol. VI

Waddell, Hon. Sir Graham; *see* Waddell, Hon. Sir C. G.

Waddell, Helen, 1889–1965, vol. VI

Waddell, John J.; *see* Jeffrey-Waddell.

Waddell, Alexander Peddie-, 1832–1917, vol. II

Waddell, John, *died* 1923, vol. II

Waddell, John J.; *see* Jeffrey-Waddell.

Waddell, Lt-Col Laurence Austine, 1854–1938, vol. III

Waddell, Hon. Thomas, 1854–1940, vol. III

Waddell, William Gillan, 1884–1945, vol. IV

Waddilove, Douglas Edwin, 1918–1976, vol. VII

Waddilove, Sir Joshua Kelley, *died* 1920, vol. II

Waddington, Charles Willoughby, 1865–1946, vol. IV
Waddington, Conrad Hal, 1905–1975, vol. VII
Waddington, Sir (Eubule) John, 1890–1957, vol. V
Waddington, John, 1855–1935, vol. III
Waddington, Sir John; see Waddington, Sir E. J.
Waddington, Mary King, died 1923, vol. II
Waddington, Sir Robert, 1868–1941, vol. IV
Waddington, Samuel, 1844–1923, vol. II
Waddington, Maj.-Gen. Thomas, 1827–1921, vol. II
Waddington, Brig. Thomas Thelwall, 1888–1958, vol. V
Waddy, Bentley Herbert, 1893–1956, vol. V
Waddy, Dorothy Knight, 1909–1970, vol. VI
Waddy, Henry Turner, 1863–1926, vol. II
Waddy, Rev. Percival Stacy, 1875–1937, vol. III
Waddy, Samuel Danks, 1830–1902, vol. I
Wade, Sir Armigel de Vins, 1880–1966, vol. VI
Wade, Arthur Shepherd, died 1941, vol. IV
Wade, Hon. Sir Charles Gregory, 1863–1922, vol. II
Wade, Emlyn Capel Stewart, 1895–1978, vol. VII
Wade, Brig. Ernest Wentworth, 1889–1970, vol. VI
Wade, Hon. Frederick Coate, 1860–1924, vol. II
Wade, Surg.-Maj.-Gen. Frederick William, died 1906, vol. I
Wade, George Edward, 1853–1933, vol. III
Wade, Major George Frederick Dennis, 1899–1968, vol. VI
Wade, Rev. George Woosung, 1858–1941, vol. IV
Wade, Sir Henry, 1877–1955, vol. V
Wade, Col Henry Oswald, 1869–1941, vol. IV
Wade, Philip Harold, 1860–1930, vol. III
Wade, Sir Robert Blakeway, 1874–1954, vol. V
Wade, Rt Rev. (Sydney) Walter, 1909–1976, vol. VII
Wade, Sqdn Ldr Trevor Sidney, 1920–1951, vol. V
Wade, Rt Rev. Walter; see Wade, Rt Rev. S. W.
Wade, Sir William, 1849–1935, vol. III
Wade, Sir Willoughby Francis, 1827–1906, vol. I
Wade-Evans, Rev. Arthur Wade, 1875–1964, vol. VI
Wade-Gery, Henry Theodore, 1888–1972, vol. VII
Wadely, Frederick William, 1882–1970, vol. VI
Wadeson, Maj.-Gen. Frederick William George, 1860–1920, vol. II
Wadham, Arthur, 1852–1923, vol. II
Wadham, Sir Samuel MacMahon, 1891–1972, vol. VII
Wadia, Sir Bomanji Jamsetji, 1881–1947, vol. IV
Wadia, Sir Cusrow, 1869–1950, vol. IV
Wadia, D. N., 1883–1969, vol. VI
Wadia, Sir Hormasji Ardeshir, died 1928, vol. II
Wadia, Sir Ness Nowrosjee, 1873–1952, vol. V
Wadley, Lt-Col Edward John, 1880–1950, vol. IV
Wadsley, Olive, died 1959, vol. V
Wadson, Hon. Sir Thomas John, 1844–1921, vol. II
Wadsworth, Alfred Powell, 1891–1956, vol. V
Wadsworth, Edward Alexander, 1889–1949, vol. IV
Wadsworth, John, 1850–1921, vol. II
Wadsworth, Sir Sidney, 1888–1976, vol. VII
Waechter, Sir Harry, 1st Bt, 1871–1929, vol. III
Waechter, Sir Max Leonard, 1837–1924, vol. II

Wager, Harold, 1862–1929, vol. III
Wager, Lawrence Rickard, 1904–1965, vol. VI
Wagg, Alfred Ralph, 1877–1969, vol. VI
Waggett, Ernest Blechynden, 1866–1939, vol. III
Waggett, Rev. Philip Napier, 1862–1939, vol. III
Waghorn, Brig.-Gen. Sir William Danvers, died 1936, vol. III
Wagner, Wieland Adolf Gottfried, 1917–1966, vol. VI
Wagner, Very Rev. William Wolfe, died 1937, vol. III
Wagstaff, Maj.-Gen. Cyril Mosley, 1878–1934, vol. III
Wagstaff, John Edward Pretty, 1890–1963, vol. VI
Wagstaff, Lt-Col Lewis Cecil, 1882–1951, vol. V
Wagstaff, William George, 1837–1918, vol. II
Wahab, Col Robert Alexander; see Wauhope, Col R. A.
Wahba, Sheikh Hafiz, 1889–1967, vol. VI
Wahlstatt, Blucher von, 3rd Prince, 1836–1916, vol. II
Waight, Leonard, 1895–1970, vol. VI
Wain, Louis William, 1860–1939, vol. III
Wainewright, Brig.-Gen. Arthur Reginald, 1874–1970, vol. VI
Wainwright, Maj.-Gen. Charles Brian, 1893–1968, vol. VI
Wainwright, Desmond; see Wainwright, E. D.
Wainwright, (Edward) Desmond, 1902–1976, vol. VII
Wainwright, Elsie, died 1964, vol. VI
Wainwright, Rev. Frederick, died 1921, vol. II
Wainwright, Sir Gilbert Cochrane, 1871–1954, vol. V
Wainwright, Sir James Gadesden, 1837–1929, vol. III
Wainwright, William J., 1855–1931, vol. III
Waistell, Adm. Sir Arthur Kipling, 1873–1953, vol. V
Wait, Air Vice-Marshal George Enoch, 1895–1972, vol. VII
Wait, Col Hugh Godfrey Killigrew, 1871–1948, vol. IV
Wait, Walter Ernest, 1878–1961, vol. VI
Waite, Arthur Edward, 1857–1942, vol. IV
Waite, Clifford, 1896–1974, vol. VII
Waite, Col Hon. Fred, 1885–1952, vol. V
Waite, Herbert William, 1887–1967, vol. VI
Waite, Rev. Joseph, 1824–1908, vol. I
Waite, Air Cdre Reginald Newnham, 1901–1975, vol. VII
Waite, Robert T.; see Thorne-Waite.
Waithman, Robert W., 1828–1914, vol. I
Waithman, William Sharp, 1853–1922, vol. II
Wake, Major Charles St Aubyn, 1861–1938, vol. III
Wake, Adm. Sir Drury St Aubyn, 1863–1935, vol. III
Wake, Lt-Col Edward St Aubyn, 1862–1944, vol. IV
Wake, Sir Herewald, 12th Bt, 1852–1916, vol. II
Wake, Herewald Crawfurd, 1828–1901, vol. I
Wake, Maj.-Gen. Sir Hereward, 13th Bt, 1876–1963, vol. VI
Wake, Major Hugh St Aubyn, 1870–1914, vol. I

Wake, Joan, 1884–1974, vol. VII

Wake, Vice-Adm. Sir St Aubyn Baldwin, 1882–1951, vol. V

Wake, William St Aubyn, died 1900, vol. I

Wake-Walker, Adm. Sir William Frederic, 1888–1945, vol. IV

Wakefield, 1st Viscount, 1859–1941, vol. IV

Wakefield, Arthur John, 1900–1973, vol. VII

Wakefield, Sir Edward Birkbeck, 1st Bt, 1903–1969, vol. VI

Wakefield, George Edward Campbell, 1873–1944, vol. IV

Wakefield, Rt Rev. Henry Russell, 1854–1933, vol. III

Wakefield, Maj.-Gen. Hubert Stephen, 1883–1962, vol. VI

Wakefield, Lt-Col Thomas Montague, 1878–1936, vol. III

Wakefield-Harrey, Cyril Ogden, 1894–1971, vol. VII

Wakeford, Edward Felix, 1914–1973, vol. VII

Wakeford, Major Richard, 1921–1972, vol. VII

Wakeham, Rev. Charles Thomas, 1852–1931, vol. III

Wakehurst, 1st Baron, 1861–1936, vol. III

Wakehurst, 2nd Baron, 1895–1970, vol. VI

Wakelam, Lt-Col Henry Blythe Thornhill, 1893–1963, vol. VI

Wakely, Maj.-Gen. Arthur Victor Trocke, 1886–1959, vol. V

Wakely, Sir Cecil Pembrey Grey, 1st Bt, 1892–1979, vol. VII

Wakely, Sir Clifford Holland, 1891–1976, vol. VII

Wakely, John, 1861–1942, vol. IV

Wakely, Sir Leonard Day, 1880–1961, vol. VI

Wakeman, Henry Offley, 1852–1899, vol. I

Wakeman, Sir Offley, 3rd Bt, 1850–1929, vol. III

Wakeman, Captain Sir Offley, 4th Bt, 1887–1975, vol. VII

Wakerley, Rev. John E., 1858–1923, vol. II

Wakley, Thomas, 1851–1909, vol. I

Wakley, Thomas H., 1821–1907, vol. I

Waksman, Selman Abraham, 1888–1973, vol. VII

Walbrook, Anton, 1900–1967, vol. VI

Walbrook, Henry Mackinnon, died 1941, vol. IV

Walby, Herbert Charles, 1897–1966, vol. VI

Walch, Sir Geoffrey Archer, 1898–1971, vol. VII

Walcot, Lt-Col Basil, 1880–1918, vol. II

Walcot, William, 1874–1943, vol. IV

Walcott, Charles Doolittle, 1850–1927, vol. II

Walcott, Captain Colpoys Cleland, 1878–1961, vol. VI

Walcott, Col Edmund Scopoli, 1842–1923, vol. II

Walcott, Sir Henry Barclay, 1866–1931, vol. III

Walde, Ernest Herman Stewart, 1874–1958, vol. V

Waldeck-Rousseau, Pierre Marie, 1846–1904, vol. I

Waldegrave, 9th Earl, 1851–1930, vol. III

Waldegrave, 10th Earl, 1882–1933, vol. III

Waldegrave, 11th Earl, 1854–1936, vol. III

Waldegrave, Countess; (Mary), 1850–1933, vol. III

Waldegrave-Leslie, Hon. George; see Leslie.

Walden, Alfred Edward, 1893–1968, vol. VI

Walden, Sir Robert Woolley, died 1929, vol. III

Walden, Stanley Arthur, 1905–1980, vol. VII

Walden, Trevor Alfred, 1916–1979, vol. VII

Walder, (Alan) David, 1928–1978, vol. VII

Walder, David; see Walder, A. D.

Walder, Hon. Sir Samuel Robert, 1879–1946, vol. IV

Waldersee, Field-Marshal Count Von, 1832–1904, vol. I

Waldie-Griffith, Sir Richard John; see Griffith.

Waldman, Milton, 1895–1976, vol. VII

Waldman, Ronald Hartley, 1914–1978, vol. VII

Waldo, Frederick Joseph, 1852–1933, vol. III

Waldram, Percy John, 1869–1949, vol. IV

Waldron, Rev. Arthur John, 1868–1925, vol. II

Waldron, Brig.-Gen. Francis, 1853–1932, vol. III

Waldron, Rt Hon. Laurence Ambrose, 1858–1923, vol. II

Waldron, Sir John Lovegrove, 1909–1975, vol. VII

Waldron, Col Sir William James, 1876–1957, vol. V

Waldstein, Sir Charles; see Walston, Sir Charles.

Waldstein, Louis, 1853–1915, vol. I

Waldteufel, Emile, 1837–1915, vol. I

Waleran, 1st Baron, 1849–1925, vol. II

Waleran, 2nd Baron, 1905–1966, vol. VI

Wales, Sir (Alexander) George, 1885–1962, vol. VI

Wales, Rev. Arthur Philip, 1896–1964, vol. VI

Wales, Sir George; see Wales, Sir A. G.

Wales, Hubert, 1870–1943, vol. IV

Waley, Sir David; see Waley, Sir S. D.

Waley, Alfred Joseph, 1861–1953, vol. V

Waley, Arthur David, 1889–1966, vol. IV

Waley, Sir Frederick George, 1860–1933, vol. III

Waley, Sir (Sigismund) David, 1887–1962, vol. VI

Walford, Col J. A., died 1903, vol. I

Walford, Lucy Bethia, 1845–1915, vol. I

Walkden, 1st Baron, 1873–1951, vol. V

Walkden, Evelyn, 1893–1970, vol. VI

Walkem, Joseph B., 1842–1938, vol. III

Walker, Hon. Lord; James Walker, 1890–1972, vol. VII

Walker, Sir Alan, died 1978, vol. VII

Walker, Major Alan Richard H.; see Hill-Walker.

Walker, Maj.-Gen. Albert Lancelot, 1839–1918, vol. II

Walker, Maj.-Gen. Alexander, 1838–1905, vol. I

Walker, Alexander, 1866–1945, vol. IV

Walker, Sir Alexander, 1869–1950, vol. IV

Walker, Sir Alexander Arthur, 2nd Bt (cr 1906), 1857–1932, vol. III

Walker, Alexander Neilson Strachan, 1921–1980, vol. VII

Walker, Andrew Barclay, 1865–1930, vol. III

Walker, Archibald, 1858–1945, vol. IV

Walker, Archibald Stodart, 1869–1934, vol. III

Walker, Sir Arnold Learoyd, died 1968, vol. VI

Walker, Rev. Arthur, died 1918, vol. II

Walker, Arthur George, 1861–1939, vol. III

Walker, Rear-Adm. Arthur Horace, 1881–1947, vol. IV

Walker, Augustus Merrifield, 1880–1965, vol. VI

Walker, Sir Baldwin Wake, 2nd Bt (cr 1856), 1846–1905 (this entry was not transferred to Who was Who).

Walker, Bernard F.; *see* Fleetwood-Walker.

Walker, Bertram James, 1880–1947, vol. IV

Walker, Sir (Byron) Edmund, 1848–1924, vol. II

Walker, Major Sir Cecil Edward, 3rd Bt (*cr* 1906), 1882–1964, vol. VI

Walker, Sir Charles, 1871–1940, vol. III

Walker, Charles Alfred le Maistre, 1873–1961, vol. VI

Walker, Charles Clement, 1877–1968, vol. VI

Walker, Charles Edward, *died* 1953, vol. V

Walker, Rear-Adm. Charles Francis, 1836–1925, vol. II

Walker, Col Charles William Garne, 1882–1974, vol. VII

Walker, Lt-Col Claude Edward Forestier-, *died* 1932, vol. III

Walker, Cyril Herbert, 1888–1970, vol. VI

Walker, Cyril Hutchinson, 1861–1955, vol. V

Walker, David Esdaile, 1907–1968, vol. VI

Walker, Rev. Dawson D.; *see* Dawson-Walker.

Walker, Douglas Learoyd, 1894–1962, vol. VI

Walker, Dame Eadith Campbell, *died* 1937, vol. III

Walker, Sir Edmund; *see* Walker, Sir B. E.

Walker, Edmund W., 1832–1919, vol. II

Walker, Sir Edward Daniel, 1840–1919, vol. II

Walker, Rev. Edward Mewburn, 1857–1941, vol. IV

Walker, Sir Edward Noel-, 1842–1908, vol. I

Walker, Sir Emery, 1851–1933, vol. III

Walker, Eric Anderson, 1886–1976, vol. VII

Walker, Ernest, 1870–1949, vol. IV

Walker, Maj.-Gen. Sir Ernest Alexander, 1880–1944, vol. IV

Walker, Ernest Octavius, 1850–1919, vol. II

Walker, Ernest William A.; *see* Ainley-Walker.

Walker, Dame Ethel, 1861–1951, vol. V

Walker, Sir Francis Elliot, 3rd Bt (*cr* 1856), 1851–1928, vol. II

Walker, Francis John, *died* 1940, vol. III

Walker, Rev. Francis Joseph, 1876–1933, vol. III

Walker, Francis S., 1848–1916, vol. II

Walker, Lt-Col Francis Spring, 1876–1941, vol. IV

Walker, Sir Francis William, 1887–1968, vol. VI

Walker, Captain Frederic John, 1896–1944, vol. IV

Walker, Lt-Col Frederic William, 1870–1954, vol. V

Walker, Frederick James, 1835–1913, vol. I

Walker, Frederick William, 1830–1910, vol. I

Walker, Gen. Sir Frederick William Edward Forestier Forestier-, 1844–1910, vol. I

Walker, Sir G. Bernard L.; *see* Lomas-Walker.

Walker, Garrett William, 1856–1932, vol. III

Walker, Maj.-Gen. George, 1869–1936, vol. III

Walker, George Abram, 1879–1959, vol. V

Walker, Sir George Casson, 1854–1925, vol. II

Walker, George Edward Orr, 1909–1973, vol. VII

Walker, Sir George Ferdinand Forestier-, 3rd Bt (*cr* 1835), 1855–1933, vol. III

Walker, Major Sir George Ferdinand Forestier-, 4th Bt (*cr* 1835), 1899–1976, vol. VII

Walker, Major George Goold, *died* 1955, vol. V

Walker, Sir George Gustavus, 1831–1897, vol. I

Walker, Col George Gustavus, 1897–1972, vol. VII

Walker, George Henry, 1874–1954, vol. V

Walker, George Herbert Dacres, 1845–1929, vol. III

Walker, Col George Kemp, 1872–1942, vol. IV

Walker, Maj.-Gen. Sir George Townshend Forestier-, 1866–1939, vol. III

Walker, George Walker, 1874–1921, vol. II

Walker, Gen. George Warren, 1823–1920, vol. II

Walker, Rev. Gilbert George, 1858–1933, vol. III

Walker, Sir Gilbert Thomas, 1868–1958, vol. V

Walker, Lt-Gen. Sir Harold Bridgwood, 1862–1934, vol. III

Walker, Adm. Sir Harold Thomas Coulthard, 1891–1975, vol. VII

Walker, Sir Henry, 1873–1954, vol. V

Walker, Henry; *see* Walker, R. St J.

Walker, Brig.-Gen. Henry Alexander, 1874–1953, vol. V

Walker, Henry Claude, 1851–1939, vol. III

Walker, Henry de Rosenbach, 1867–1923, vol. II

Walker, Sir Herbert Ashcombe, 1868–1949, vol. IV

Walker, Lt-Col Herbert Sutherland, 1864–1932, vol. III

Walker, Hirst, 1868–1957, vol. V

Walker, Sir (Horace) Alan; *see* Walker, Sir Alan.

Walker, Sir Hubert Edmund, 1891–1969, vol. VI

Walker, Hugh, 1855–1939, vol. III

Walker, J. Wallace, *died* 1932, vol. III

Walker, Sir James, 1864–1933, vol. III

Walker, Sir James, 1863–1935, vol. III

Walker, Lt-Col James, *died* 1940, vol. III

Walker, James, *died* 1945, vol. IV

Walker, James; *see* Walker, Hon. Lord.

Walker, James Arthur H.; *see* Higgs-Walker.

Walker, James Atkinson, 1878–1954, vol. V

Walker, James Douglas, 1841–1920, vol. II

Walker, Maj.-Gen. James Grant Duff, 1842–1921, vol. II

Walker, Captain Sir James Heron, 3rd Bt (*cr* 1868), 1865–1900, vol. I

Walker, Sir James Lewis, 1845–1927, vol. II

Walker, Sir James Robert, 2nd Bt, 1829–1898, vol. I

Walker, Hon. James Thomas, 1841–1923, vol. II

Walker, Major James Thomas, *died* 1930, vol. III

Walker, Brig.-Gen. James Workman, 1873–1945, vol. IV

Walker, Jane Harriett, 1859–1938, vol. III

Walker, Rev. John, 1837–1910, vol. I

Walker, John, 1900–1964, vol. VI

Walker, John; *see* Thirlmere, Rowland.

Walker, John Bayldon, 1854–1927, vol. II

Walker, John Brisben, 1847–1931, vol. III

Walker, John Crampton, 1890–1942, vol. IV

Walker, John Henry, 1915–1974, vol. VII

Walker, Norman Macdonald Lockhart, 1889–1975, vol. VII

Walker, Col John Norman N.; *see* Norman-Walker.

Walker, John Reid, 1855–1934, vol. III

Walker, Sir John William T.; *see* Thomson-Walker.

Walker, Kenneth, 1874–1947, vol. IV
Walker, Kenneth Macfarlane, *died* 1966, vol. VI
Walker, Sir Leolin F.; *see* Forestier-Walker, Sir C. L.
Walker, Leonard, *died* 1964, vol. VI
Walker, Malcolm Thomas, 1915–1980, vol. VII
Walker, Sir Mark, *died* 1902, vol. I
Walker, Miles, *died* 1941, vol. IV
Walker, Sir Norman, 1862–1942, vol. IV
Walker, Norman, 1907–1963, vol. VI
Walker, Norman Marshall, 1882–1956, vol. V
Walker, Oliver Ormerod, 1833–1914, vol. I
Walker, Patrick Chrestien G.; *see* Baron Gordon-Walker.
Walker, Sir Peter Carlaw, 2nd Bt (*cr* 1886), 1854–1915, vol. I
Walker, Raymond St John, (Henry), 1917–1980, vol. VII
Walker, Paymr Captain Reginald Phelps, 1871–1958, vol. V
Walker, Major Reginald Selby, 1871–1918, vol. II
Walker, Richard Cornelius Critchett, 1841–1903, vol. I
Walker, Richard Johnson, 1868–1934, vol. III
Walker, Robert, *died* 1910, vol. I
Walker, Robert, 1842–1920, vol. II
Walker, Sir Robert Bryce, 1873–1956, vol. V
Walker, Ven. Robert Henry, 1857–1939, vol. III
Walker, Major Sir Robert James Milo, 4th Bt (*cr* 1868), 1890–1930, vol. III
Walker, Robert John, 1870–1936, vol. III
Walker, Lt-Col Robert Sandilands Frowd, 1850–1917, vol. II
Walker, Bt-Col Roland Stuart Forestier-, 1871–1938, vol. III
Walker, Sir Ronald Fitz-John, 1880–1971, vol. VII
Walker, Rt Hon. Sir Samuel, 1st Bt (*cr* 1906), 1832–1911, vol. I
Walker, Samuel, 1875–1945, vol. IV
Walker, Air Cdre Sidney George, 1911–1975, vol. VII
Walker, Rev. Thomas, *died* 1929, vol. III
Walker, Hon. Thomas, 1858–1932, vol. III
Walker, Rev. Thomas Alfred, 1862–1935, vol. III
Walker, Very Rev. Thomas Gordon, *died* 1916, vol. II
Walker, Sir Thomas Gordon, 1849–1917, vol. II
Walker, Lt-Col Thomas Henry, 1877–1955, vol. V
Walker, Thomas Hollis, 1860–1945, vol. IV
Walker, Thomas Kennedy, 1893–1970, vol. VI
Walker, Thomas Leonard, 1867–1942, vol. IV
Walker, Adm. Thomas Philip, *died* 1932, vol. III
Walker, Very Rev. William, *died* 1911, vol. I
Walker, Sir William, 1863–1930, vol. III
Walker, Sir William, *died* 1961, vol. VI
Walker, William Anderson Macpherson, 1891–1962, vol. VI
Walker, Hon. William Campbell, 1837–1904, vol. I
Walker, Col William Eric, 1885–1949, vol. IV
Walker, William Eyre, 1847–1930, vol. III
Walker, Adm. Sir William Frederic W.; *see* Wake-Walker.

Walker, Maj.-Gen. William George, 1863–1936, vol. III
Walker, William Gregory, 1848–1910, vol. I
Walker, William Henry, 1864–1933, vol. III
Walker, William James Dickson, 1854–1926, vol. II
Walker, William James Stirling, 1897–1958, vol. V
Walker, Rev. William Lowe, 1845–1930, vol. III
Walker, William Sylvester, 1846–1926, vol. II
Walker-Heneage-Vivian, Adm. Algernon, 1871–1952, vol. V
Walker Lee, Rev. William; *see* Lee.
Walker-Smith, Sir Jonah, 1874–1964, vol. VI
Walkey, Rear-Adm. Howarth Seymour, 1900–1970, vol. VI
Walkey, Rev. James Rowland, 1880–1960, vol. V
Walkinton, John James Gordon, 1895–1968, vol. VI
Walkley, Arthur Bingham, 1855–1926, vol. II
Walkley, Sir William Gaston, 1896–1976, vol. VII
Wall, Baron (Life Peer); John Edward Wall, 1913–1980, vol. VII
Wall, Arnold, *died* 1966, vol. VI
Wall, Arthur Joseph, *died* 1927, vol. II
Wall, Rt Rev. Bernard Patrick, 1894–1976, vol. VII
Wall, Col Edward Watkin, 1866–1954, vol. V
Wall, Rt Rev. Francis Joseph, 1866–1947, vol. IV
Wall, Col Frank, 1868–1950, vol. IV
Wall, Sir Frederick Joseph, 1858–1944, vol. IV
Wall, Sir (George) Rolande (Percival), 1898–1972, vol. VII
Wall, Engr Rear-Adm. Henry, 1867–1950, vol. IV
Wall, Reginald Cecil Bligh, 1869–1947, vol. IV
Wall, Sir Rolande; *see* Wall, Sir G. R. P.
Wallace, Abraham, *died* 1930, vol. III
Wallace, Maj-Gen. Sir Alexander, 1858–1922, vol. II
Wallace, Alexander Falconer, 1836–1925, vol. II
Wallace, Alfred Russel, 1823–1913, vol. I
Wallace, Sir Arthur Robert, 1837–1912, vol. I
Wallace, Rev. Charles Hill, 1833–1912, vol. I
Wallace, Maj.-Gen. Charles John, 1890–1943, vol. IV
Wallace, Charles Redwood Vachell, 1877–1944, vol. IV
Wallace, Rev. Charles Stebbing, *died* 1914, vol. I
Wallace, Charles William, 1865–1932, vol. III
Wallace, Sir Cuthbert Sidney, 1st Bt (*cr* 1937), 1867–1944, vol. IV
Wallace, Sir David, 1862–1952, vol. V
Wallace, Captain Rt Hon. (David) Euan, 1892–1941, vol. IV
Wallace, Major David Johnston, 1886–1965, vol. VI
Wallace, Denis Bowes J.; *see* Johnstone-Wallace.
Wallace, Sir Donald Mackenzie, 1841–1919, vol. II
Wallace, Edgar, 1875–1932, vol. III
Wallace, Sir Edward Hamilton, 1873–1943, vol. IV
Wallace, Edward Wilson, 1880–1941, vol. IV
Wallace, Captain Rt Hon. Euan; *see* Wallace, Captain Rt Hon. D. E.
Wallace, Rev. Francis Huston, 1851–1930, vol. III
Wallace, George, 1854–1927, vol. II

Wallace, Col George Smith, 1878–1951, vol. V
Wallace, George Williamson, 1862–1952, vol. V
Wallace, Harold Frank, 1881–1962, vol. VI
Wallace, Harry Wright, 1885–1973, vol. VII
Wallace, Henry Agard, 1888–1965, vol. VI
Wallace, Captain Henry Steuart Macnaghten H.;
see Harrison-Wallace.
Wallace, Maj.-Gen. Hill, 1823–1899, vol. I
Wallace, Hugh Campbell, 1863–1931, vol. III
Wallace, Lt-Col Hugh Robert, 1861–1924, vol. II
Wallace, Air Cdre James, 1918–1980, vol. VII
Wallace, James Sim, 1869–1951, vol. V
Wallace, Sir John, 1868–1949, vol. IV
Wallace, Air Vice-Marshal John Brown, 1907–
1980, vol. VII
Wallace, John Henry, 1903–1960, vol. V
Wallace, John Madder, 1887–1975, vol. VII
Wallace, Sir John Stewart S.; see Stewart-Wallace.
Wallace, Col Sir Johnstone, 1861–1922, vol. II
Wallace, Sir Lawrence Aubrey, 1857–1942, vol. IV
Wallace, Gen. Lew, (Lewis), 1827–1905, vol. I
Wallace, Malcolm William, 1873–1960, vol. V
Wallace, Sir Martin Kelso, 1898–1978, vol. VII
Wallace, Sir Matthew Gemmill, 1st Bt (cr 1922),
1854–1940, vol. III
Wallace, Hon. Nathaniel Clarke, 1844–1901, vol. I
Wallace, Col Nesbit Willoughby, 1839–1931,
vol. III
Wallace, O. C. S., 1856–1947, vol. IV
Wallace, Percy Maxwell, 1863–1943, vol. IV
Wallace, Rear-Adm. Richard Roy, 1895–1963,
vol. VI
Wallace, Robert, 1831–1899, vol. I (A)
Wallace, Robert, 1878–1931, vol. III
Wallace, Sir Robert, 1850–1939, vol. III
Wallace, Robert, 1853–1939, vol. III
Wallace, Robert Charles, 1881–1955, vol. V
Wallace of that Ilk, Col Robert Francis Hurter,
1880–1970, vol. VI
Wallace, Col Rt Hon. Robert Hugh, 1860–1929,
vol. III
Wallace, Robert John, 1846–1909, vol. I
Wallace, Robert Johnston, 1886–1967, vol. VI
Wallace, Sir Robert Strachan, 1882–1961, vol. VI
Wallace, Roger William, 1854–1926, vol. II
Wallace, Lt-Gen. Rowland Robert, 1830–1915,
vol. I
Wallace, S. Williamson, 1855–1932, vol. III
Wallace, Samuel Thomas Dickson, 1892–1968,
vol. VI
Wallace, Thomas, 1891–1965, vol. VI
Wallace, Thomas Brown, 1865–1951, vol. V
Wallace, Sir William, 1856–1916, vol. II
Wallace, William, 1843–1921, vol. II
Wallace, William, 1860–1922, vol. II
Wallace, William, 1860–1940, vol. III
Wallace, Sir William, 1881–1963, vol. VI
Wallace, William, 1891–1976, vol. VII
Wallace, Col William Arthur James, died 1902,
vol. I
Wallace, Lt-Col William Berkeley, died 1934,
vol. III
Wallace, William Kelly, 1883–1969, vol. VI

Wallace, William Reeve, 1873–1966, vol. VI
Wallace, William Stewart, 1884–1970, vol. VI
Wallace-Copland, Harold, 1893–1973, vol. VII
Wallach, Lewis Charles, 1871–1964, vol. VI
Wallack, Maj.-Gen. Ernest Townshend, 1857–
1932, vol. III
Wallas, Graham, 1858–1932, vol. III
Wallas, Katharine Talbot, 1864–1944, vol. IV
Waller, Alfred Rayney, 1867–1922, vol. II
Waller, Vice-Adm. Arthur Craig, 1872–1943,
vol. IV
Waller, Augustus Désiré, 1856–1922, vol. II
Waller, Rev. Bolton Charles, 1890–1936, vol. III
Waller, Sir Charles, 6th Bt (cr 1780), 1835–1912
(this entry was not transferred to Who was
Who).
Waller, Rev. Charles Cameron, 1869–1944, vol. IV
Waller, Very Rev. Charles Kempson, 1891–1951,
vol. V
Waller, Sir David Grierson, 1872–1949, vol. IV
Waller, Sir Edmund, 6th Bt (cr 1815), 1871–1954,
vol. V
Waller, Very Rev. Edward Hardress, 1859–1933,
vol. III
Waller, Rt Rev. Edward Harry Mansfield, 1871–
1942, vol. IV
Waller, Sir Francis Ernest, 4th Bt (cr 1815), 1880–
1914, vol. I
Waller, Maj.-Gen. John Edmund, 1841–1934,
vol. III
Waller, Captain John Hampden, 1839–1934,
vol. III
Waller, Vice-Adm. John William Ashley, 1892–
1975, vol. VII
Waller, Lewis, 1860–1915, vol. I (A)
Waller, Mary Lemon, died 1931, vol. III
Waller, Sir Maurice Lyndham, 1875–1932, vol. III
Waller, Mervyn Napier, 1893–1972, vol. VII
Waller, Brig.-Gen. Richard Lancelot, 1875–1961,
vol. VI
Waller, Sir Roland Edgar, 8th Bt (cr 1780), 1892–
1958, vol. V
Waller, Samuel Edmund, 1850–1903, vol. I
Waller, Col Stanier, 1844–1930, vol. III
Waller, Sir Wathen Arthur, 5th Bt (cr 1815),
1881–1947, vol. IV
Waller, Sir William Edgar, 7th Bt (cr 1780), 1863–
1943, vol. IV
Wallers, Sir Evelyn Ashley, 1876–1934, vol. III
Wallerston, Brig.-Gen. Francis Edward, 1856–
1926, vol. II
Wallhead, Richard Collingham, 1869–1934,
vol. III
Walling, Robert Alfred John, 1869–1949, vol. IV
Wallinger, Lt-Col Ernest Arnold, 1875–1934,
vol. III
Wallinger, Sir Geoffrey Arnold, 1903–1979,
vol. VII
Wallinger, Sir John Arnold, 1872–1931, vol. III
Wallingford, Air Cdre Sidney, 1898–1978, vol. VII
Wallington, Sir Edward William, 1854–1933,
vol. III
Wallington, Hon. Sir Hubert Joseph, died 1962,
vol. VI

Wallington, Col Sir John Williams, 1822–1910, vol. I
Wallis, Arthur Henry, 1847–1929, vol. III
Wallis, Sir Barnes Neville, 1887–1979, vol. VII
Wallis, Major Charles Braithwaite, died 1945, vol. IV
Wallis, Rev. Charles Steel, 1875–1959, vol. V
Wallis, Charles Edward, died 1927, vol. II
Wallis, Claude Edgar, 1886–1980, vol. VII
Wallis, Rt Rev. Frederic, 1853–1928, vol. II
Wallis, Sir Fred. C., 1859–1912, vol. I
Wallis, Frederick Samuel, 1857–1939, vol. III (A) vol. IV
Wallis, George Harry, died 1936, vol. III
Wallis, Harry Bernard, 1882–1956, vol. V
Wallis, Henry Aubrey Beaumont, died 1926, vol. II
Wallis, Henry Richard, 1866–1946, vol. IV
Wallis, Rt Hon. Sir John Edward Power, 1861–1946, vol. IV
Wallis, Rev. Canon John Eyre Winstanley, 1886–1957, vol. V
Wallis, Leonard George C.; see Coke Wallis.
Wallis, Mrs Ransome, 1858–1928, vol. II
Wallis, Sir Whitworth, 1855–1927, vol. II
Wallop, Hon. Frederick Henry Arthur, 1870–1953, vol. V
Walls, Rev. John W., 1858–1924, vol. II
Walls, Tom, 1883–1949, vol. IV
Walls, William, 1860–1942, vol. IV
Wallscourt, 4th Baron, 1841–1918, vol. II
Wallscourt, 5th Baron, 1876–1920, vol. II
Walmsley, Allan, 1889–1963, vol. VI
Walmsley, Ben, 1871–1960, vol. VI (AI)
Walmsley, Sir Hugh, 1871–1950, vol. IV
Walmsley, Rt Rev. John, died 1922, vol. II
Walmsley, Air Cdre John Banks, 1896–1976, vol. VII
Walmsley, Kenneth Maurice, 1914–1977, vol. VII
Walmsley, Leo, 1892–1966, vol. VI
Walmsley, Robert Mullineux, died 1924, vol. II
Walmsley, Thomas, died 1951, vol. V
Waln, Nora, 1895–1964, vol. VI
Walpole, Sir Charles George, 1848–1926, vol. II
Walpole, George Frederick, 1892–1975, vol. VII
Walpole, Rt Rev. George Henry Somerset, 1854–1929, vol. III
Walpole, Henry Spencer V.; see Vade-Walpole.
Walpole, Sir Horatio George, 1843–1923, vol. II
Walpole, Sir Hugh Seymour, 1884–1941, vol. IV
Walpole, Ralph Charles, 1844–1928, vol. II
Walpole, Sir Spencer, 1839–1907, vol. I
Walpole, Rt Hon. Spencer Horatio, 1806–1898, vol. I
Walpole, Thomas Henry Bourke V.; see Vade-Walpole.
Walrond, Arthur Melville Hood, 1861–1946, vol. IV
Walrond, Col Henry, 1841–1917, vol. II
Walrond, Main Swete Osmond, 1870–1927, vol. II
Walrond, Hon. W. Lionel Charles, 1876–1915, vol. I (A)
Walsh, Hon. Sir Albert Joseph, died 1958, vol. V
Walsh, Arthur Donald, 1916–1977, vol. VII
Walsh, Sir Cecil, 1869–1946, vol. IV

Walsh, Sir Charles Arthur, 1869–1949, vol. IV
Walsh, Rt Hon. Sir Cyril Ambrose, 1909–1973, vol. VII
Walsh, Ernest Herbert Cooper, 1865–1952, vol. V
Walsh, Ernst P.; see Pakenham-Walsh.
Walsh, Rt Rev. Francis, 1901–1974, vol. VII
Walsh, Geoffrey, 1884–1946, vol. IV
Walsh, Maj.-Gen. George Peregrine, 1899–1972, vol. VII
Walsh, Air Vice-Marshal George Victor, 1893–1960, vol. V
Walsh, Hon. Gerald, 1864–1925, vol. II
Walsh, Rt Rev. Gordon John, 1880–1971, vol. VII
Walsh, Col Henry Alfred, 1853–1918, vol. II
Walsh, Henry Francis Chester, 1891–1977, vol. VII
Walsh, Rt Rev. Herbert Pakenham P.; see Pakenham-Walsh.
Walsh, Sir Hunt Henry Allen Johnson-, 5th Bt, 1864–1953, vol. V
Walsh, Very Rev. James Hornidge, died 1919, vol. II
Walsh, James J., 1865–1942, vol. IV
Walsh, James Joseph, 1880–1948, vol. IV
Walsh, James Morgan, 1897–1952, vol. V
Walsh, John, 1856–1925, vol. II
Walsh, Most Rev. Joseph, 1888–1973, vol. VII
Walsh, Langton Prendergast, 1856–1927, vol. II
Walsh, Brig. Mainwaring Ravell, 1876–1940, vol. III
Walsh, Maurice, 1879–1964, vol. VI
Walsh, Hon. Nigel Christopher, 1867–1931, vol. III
Walsh, Hon. Patrick Joseph Stanislaus, 1872–1943, vol. IV
Walsh, Ven. Philip, 1843–1914, vol. II
Walsh, Brig.-Gen. Richard Knox, 1873–1960, vol. V
Walsh, Maj.-Gen. Ridley P. P.; see Pakenham-Walsh.
Walsh, Ven. Robert, died 1917, vol. II
Walsh, Col Robert Henry, 1884–1968, vol. VI
Walsh, Rt Hon. Stephen, 1859–1929, vol. III
Walsh, Lt-Col Theobald Alfred, 1882–1935, vol. III
Walsh, Valentine John Hussey-, 1862–1925, vol. II
Walsh, Walter, 1847–1912, vol. I
Walsh, Rev. Walter, 1857–1931, vol. III
Walsh, Rt Rev. William, 1836–1918, vol. II
Walsh, Lt-Col William H.; see Hussey-Walsh.
Walsh, Most Rev. William J., 1841–1921, vol. II
Walsh, William Joseph, 1919–1978, vol. VII
Walsh, Hon. William Legh, 1857–1938, vol. III
Walsh, Rt Rev. William Pakenham, 1820–1902, vol. I
Walsham, Hugh, died 1924, vol. II
Walsham, Sir John, 2nd Bt, 1830–1905, vol. I
Walsham, Sir John Scarlett, 3rd Bt, 1869–1940, vol. III
Walsham, William Johnson, 1847–1903, vol. I
Walshe, Sir Francis Martin Rouse, died 1973, vol. VII
Walshe, Brig.-Gen. Frederick William Henry, died 1931, vol. III
Walshe, Lt-Col Henry Ernest, 1866–1947, vol. IV

Walshe, Lt-Col Sarsfield James Ambrose Hall 1881–1959, vol. V

Walshe, Rt Rev. Mgr T. J., 1861–1938, vol. III

Walsingham, 6th Baron, 1843–1919, vol. II

Walsingham, 7th Baron, 1849–1929, vol. III

Walsingham, 8th Baron, 1884–1965, vol. VI

Walston, Sir Charles, 1856–1927, vol. II

Waltari, Mika, 1908–1979, vol. VII

Walter, Arthur, 1874–1921, vol. II

Walter, Arthur Fraser, 1846–1910, vol. I

Walter, Arthur James, *died* 1919, vol. II

Walter, Bruno, 1876–1962, vol. VI

Walter, Lt-Col Edmund, 1881–1951, vol. V

Walter, Sir Edward, 1823–1904, vol. I

Walter, Major Frederick Edward, 1848–1931, vol. III

Walter, Hubert, 1870–1933, vol. III

Walter, John, 1873–1968, vol. VI

Walter, Maj.-Gen. John McNeill, 1861–1951, vol. V

Walter, Rear-Adm. Keith McNeil C.; *see* Campbell-Walter.

Walter, Louis Heathcote, *died* 1922, vol. II

Walter, Madison Melville, 1897–1960, vol. V

Walter, Robert, *died* 1959, vol. V

Walter, William, 1852–1942, vol. IV

Walter, W(illiam) Grey, 1910–1977, vol. VII

Walters, Air Vice-Marshal Allan Leslie, 1905–1968, vol. VI

Walters, Arthur Melmoth, 1865–1941, vol. IV

Walters, Rev. Charles Ensor, 1872–1938, vol. III

Walters, Rev. David John, 1893–1979, vol. VII

Walters, Francis Paul, 1888–1976, vol. VII

Walters, Frank Bridgman, 1851–1899, vol. I

Walters, Rev. Harold Crawford, *died* 1958, vol. V

Walters, Henry Beauchamp, 1867–1944, vol. IV

Walters, Hubert Algernon, 1898–1969, vol. VI

Walters, Lt-Col Hubert de Lancey, 1868–1936, vol. III

Walters, John Cuming, *died* 1933, vol. III

Walters, Rt Hon. Sir (John) Tudor, 1868–1933, vol. III

Walters, Rt Hon. Sir Tudor; *see* Walters, Rt Hon. Sir J. T.

Walters, W. C. Flamstead, *died* 1927, vol. II

Walters, Rev. W. D., 1839–1913, vol. I

Walters, Ven. William, *died* 1912, vol. I

Walters, Col William Barker, 1839–1929, vol. III

Walters, Sir William Howell, 1857–1934, vol. III

Walters, William Melmoth, 1835–1925, vol. II

Walthall, Brig.-Gen. Edward Charles Walthall Delves, 1874–1961, vol. VI

Walther, David Philippe, 1909–1973, vol. VII

Walthew, Richard Henry, 1872–1951, vol. V

Walton, Allan, 1891–1948, vol. IV

Walton, Cecil Simpson, 1905–1955, vol. V

Walton, Col Sir Cusack, 1878–1966, vol. VI

Walton, Lt-Col Edgar Brocas, 1880–1964, vol. VI

Walton, Hon. Sir Edgar Harris, 1856–1942, vol. IV

Walton, Edward Arthur, 1860–1922, vol. II

Walton, Frank, 1840–1928, vol. II

Walton, Frederick Parker, 1858–1948, vol. IV

Walton, Frederick Thomas Granville, 1840–1925, vol. II

Walton, Brig. Sir George Hands, *died* 1976, vol. VII

Walton, Sir George O'Donnell, 1871–1950, vol. IV

Walton, Col Granville, 1888–1974, vol. VII

Walton, Henry George, 1876–1962, vol. VI

Walton, Rev. Herbert Arthur, *died* 1955, vol. V

Walton, Herbert Francis Raine, 1869–1929, vol. III

Walton, James, 1867–1924, vol. II

Walton, Sir James, 1881–1955, vol. V

Walton, James Ratcliffe, 1898–1973, vol. VII

Walton, John, 1895–1971, vol. VII

Walton, Sir John Charles, 1885–1957, vol. V

Walton, Sir John Lawson, 1852–1908, vol. I

Walton, Sir Joseph, 1845–1910, vol. I

Walton, Sir Joseph, 1st Bt, 1849–1923, vol. II

Walton, Kenneth, 1923–1979, vol. VII

Walton, Leslie Bannister, 1895–1960, vol. V

Walton, Norman Burdett, 1884–1950, vol. IV

Walton, Sir Richmond, 1888–1971, vol. VII

Walton, Sir Robert, 1843–1914, vol. I

Walton, Lt-Col Robert Henry, 1877–1959, vol. V (A)

Walton, Sydney, 1882–1964, vol. VI

Walton, Sir William, 1844–1929, vol. III

Walton, Brig.-Gen. William Crawford, 1864–1937, vol. III

Walton, William Stanley, 1901–1979, vol. VII

Waltz, Jacques; *see* Hansi.

Walwyn, Algernon Edward Vere, 1888–1970, vol. VI

Walwyn, Eileen Mary, (Lady Walwyn), *died* 1973, vol. VII

Walwyn, Vice-Adm. Sir Humphrey Thomas, 1879–1957, vol. V

Walzer, Richard Rudolf, 1900–1975, vol. VII

Wanamaker, John, 1838–1922, vol. II

Wanamaker, Rodman, *died* 1928, vol. II

Wand, Rt Rev. and Rt Hon. (John) William (Charles), 1885–1977, vol. VII

Wand, Rt Rev. and Rt Hon. William; *see* Wand, Rt Rev. and Rt Hon. J. W. C.

Wandsworth, 1st Baron, *died* 1912, vol. I

Wang, Chung-Yik, 1888–1930, vol. III

Wankaner, Maharana Raj Saheb of, 1879–1954, vol. V

Wanklyn, Lt-Comdr Malcolm David, 1911–1942, vol. IV

Wanless, Sir William James, 1865–1933, vol. III

Wanless-O'Gowan, Maj.-Gen. Robert, 1864–1947, vol. IV

Wanliss, Col David Sydney, 1864–1943, vol. IV

Wanliss, Captain Harold Boyd, 1891–1917, vol. II

Wannell, Lt-Col George Edward, 1882–1933, vol. III

Wannop, Rev. Thomas Nicholson, 1822–1910, vol. I

Wansbrough, George, 1904–1979, vol. VII

Wansbrough, Hon. Lt-Col Thomas Percival, 1875–1943, vol. IV

Wansbrough-Jones, Maj.-Gen. Llewelyn, 1900–1974, vol. VII

Wanstall, Rev. Walter, 1847–1918, vol. II

Wantage, 1st Baron, 1832–1901, vol. I

Wantage, Lady; (Harriet Sarah), 1837–1920, vol. II

Wapshare, Lt-Gen. Sir Richard, 1860–1932, vol. III
Warbey, William Noble, 1903–1980, vol. VII
Warburg, Sir Oscar Emanuel, 1876–1937, vol. III
Warburg, Otto Heinrich, 1883–1970, vol. VI
Warburton, A. Bannerman, 1852–1929, vol. III
Warburton, Geoffrey E.; *see* Egerton-Warburton.
Warburton, John E.; *see* Egerton-Warburton.
Warburton, John Paul, 1840–1919, vol. II
Warburton, Piers E.; *see* Egerton-Warburton.
Warburton, Col Sir Robert, *died* 1899, vol. I
Warburton, Lt-Col William Melvill, 1877–1952, vol. V
Warburton, Col William Pleace, 1843–1911, vol. I
Ward of North Tyneside, Baroness (Life Peer); Irene Mary Bewick Ward, 1895–1980, vol. VII
Ward, A. C., 1878–1914, vol. I
Ward, Sir Adolphus William, 1837–1924, vol. II
Ward, Col Sir (Albert) Lambert, 1st Bt (*cr* 1929), 1875–1956, vol. V
Ward, Ven. Algernon, 1869–1947, vol. IV
Ward, Anthony Edward Walter, 1905–1968, vol. VI
Ward, Arnold Sandwith, 1876–1950, vol. IV
Ward, Lt-Col Arthur, 1866–1935, vol. III
Ward, Lt-Col Arthur Blackwood, 1870–1950, vol. IV
Ward, Rev. Canon Arthur Evelyn, 1877–1944, vol. IV
Ward, Arthur Samuel, *died* 1952, vol. V
Ward, Arthur William, 1858–1919, vol. II
Ward, Sir Ashley Skelton, 1877–1959, vol. V
Ward, Basil Robert, 1902–1976, vol. VII
Ward, Rt Rev. Mgr Bernard, 1857–1920, vol. II
Ward, Lt-Gen. Hon. Bernard Matthew, 1831–1918, vol. II
Ward, Col Bernard Rowland, 1863–1933, vol. III
Ward, Rear-Adm. (S) Cecil Arthur, 1881–1954, vol. V
Ward, Charles James, *died* 1913, vol. I
Ward, Rev. Charles Triffit, *died* 1925, vol. II
Ward, Cyril, 1863–1935, vol. III
Ward, Captain Hon. Cyril Augustus, 1876–1930, vol. III
Ward, Sir Cyril Rupert Joseph, 2nd Bt (*cr* 1911), 1884–1940, vol. III
Ward, Dudley, 1885–1957, vol. V
Ward, Ebenezer Thomas, 1879–1942, vol. IV
Ward, Edward, *died* 1921, vol. II
Ward, Lt-Col Edward Francis, 1870–1935, vol. III
Ward, Captain Sir Edward Simons, 2nd Bt (*cr* 1914), 1882–1930, vol. III
Ward, Col Sir Edward Willis Duncan, 1st Bt (*cr* 1914), 1853–1928, vol. II
Ward, Edwin, 1880–1934, vol. III
Ward, Lt-Col Ellacott Leamon, 1873–1968, vol. VI
Ward, Enoch, 1859–1922, vol. II
Ward, F. K.; *see* Kingdon-Ward.
Ward, Maj.-Gen. Francis William, 1840–1919, vol. II
Ward, Rev. Frederick Hubert, 1858–1918, vol. II
Ward, Frederick Josiah, 1861–1941, vol. IV
Ward, Frederick Temple B.; *see* Barrington-Ward.
Ward, Rev. Frederick William Orde, 1843–1922, vol. II

Ward, Genevieve, Countess de Guerbel, 1837–1922, vol. II
Ward, George, 1878–1951, vol. V
Ward, George Edgar Septimus, 1888–1969, vol. VI
Ward, Ven. George Herbert, 1862–1946, vol. IV
Ward, Hon. Gerald Ernest Francis, 1877–1914, vol. I (A)
Ward, Lt-Col Guy Bernard Campbell, 1875–1933, vol. III
Ward, Col Harry, 1876–1939, vol. III
Ward, Harry Marshall, 1854–1905, vol. I
Ward, Henrietta Mary Ada, *died* 1924, vol. II
Ward, Col Henry Charles S.; *see* Swinburne-Ward.
Ward, Col Henry Constantine Evelyn, 1837–1907, vol. I
Ward, Maj.-Gen. Henry Dudley Ossulston, 1872–1947, vol. IV
Ward, Herbert, *died* 1919, vol. II
Ward, Herbert, 1866–1938, vol. III
Ward, Mrs Humphry, (Mary Augusta Ward), 1851–1920, vol. II
Ward, Ida Caroline, 1880–1949, vol. IV
Ward, James, 1851–1924, vol. II
Ward, James, 1843–1925, vol. II
Ward, Rt Rev. James, 1905–1973, vol. VII
Ward, Sir John, *died* 1908, vol. I
Ward, John, 1832–1912, vol. I
Ward, Lt-Col John, 1866–1934, vol. III
Ward, Col Sir John Chappell, 1877–1942, vol. IV
Ward, John Frederick, 1883–1954, vol. V
Ward, John Grosvenor B.; *see* Barrington-Ward.
Ward, Major Hon. Sir John Hubert, 1870–1938, vol. III
Ward, Captain John Richard Le Hunte, 1870–1953, vol. V
Ward, Engr-Captain John Tom Hickman, *died* 1939, vol. III
Ward, Rev. John William, 1874–1938, vol. III
Ward, Joseph, *died* 1963, vol. VI
Ward, Rt Hon. Sir Joseph George, 1st Bt (*cr* 1911), 1856–1930, vol. III
Ward, Sir Joseph George Davidson, 3rd Bt (*cr* 1911), 1909–1970, vol. VI
Ward, Col Sir Lambert; *see* Ward, Col Sir A. L.
Ward, Sir Lancelot Edward B.; *see* Barrington-Ward.
Ward, Lt-Col Lancelot Edward Seth, 1875–1929, vol. III
Ward, Sir Leslie, 1851–1922, vol. II
Ward, Leslie Moffat; *see* Ward, P. L. M.
Ward, Lester F., 1841–1913, vol. I (A)
Ward, Rev. Mark James B.; *see* Barrington-Ward.
Ward, Mary Augusta; *see* Ward, Mrs Humphry.
Ward, Comdr Sir Melvill Willis, 3rd Bt (*cr* 1914), 1885–1973, vol. VII
Ward, Sir Michael B.; *see* Barrington-Ward.
Ward, Philip, 1845–1916, vol. II
Ward, (Philip) Leslie Moffat, 1888–1978, vol. VII
Ward, Adm. Philip N.; *see* Nelson-Ward.
Ward, Captain Hon. Reginald, 1874–1904, vol. I
Ward, Richard Percyvale, 1894–1945, vol. IV
Ward, Hon. Robert Arthur, 1871–1942, vol. IV
Ward, Robert De Courcy, 1867–1931, vol. III

Ward, Robert M'Gowan B.; see Barrington-Ward.
Ward, Robert Percy, 1868–1936, vol. III
Ward, Ronald, 1909–1973, vol. VII
Ward, Ronald Ogier, 1886–1971, vol. VII
Ward, Sarah Adelaide, died 1969, vol. VI
Ward, Captain Hon. Somerset, 1833–1912, vol. I
Ward, Stacey George, 1906–1980, vol. VII
Ward, Brig.-Gen. Thomas, 1861–1949, vol. IV
Ward, Thomas Humphry, 1845–1926, vol. II
Ward, Adm. Thomas Le Hunte, 1830–1907, vol. I
Ward, Sir Thomas Robert John, 1863–1944, vol. IV
Ward, Sir (Victor) Michael B.; see Barrington-Ward.
Ward, Col Walter, died 1948, vol. IV
Ward, Brig.-Gen. Walter Reginald, 1869–1952, vol. V
Ward, Wilfrid Philip, 1856–1916, vol. II
Ward, Sir William, 1841–1927, vol. II
Ward, Rt Hon. William Dudley, 1877–1946, vol. IV
Ward, Sir William Erskine, 1838–1916, vol. II
Ward, Rev. William Hayes, 1835–1916, vol. II
Ward-Jackson, Major Charles Lionel Atkins, 1869–1930, vol. III
Wardale, Edith Elizabeth, 1863–1943, vol. IV
Wardale, John Dobson, died 1958, vol. V
Warde, Mrs Beatrice Lamberton, 1900–1969, vol. VI
Warde, Lt-Col Charles Arthur Madan, 1839–1912, vol. I
Warde, Col Sir Charles Edward, 1st Bt, 1845–1937, vol. III
Warde, Rt Rev. Geoffrey Hodgson, 1889–1972, vol. VII
Warde, Lt-Col Henry Murray Ashley, 1850–1940, vol. III
Warde, Engr Rear-Adm. Thomas Herbert, 1882–1960, vol. V
Warde-Aldam, Col William St Andrew, 1882–1958, vol. V
Wardell, Lt-Col Henry, died 1933, vol. III
Wardell, John Henry, 1878–1957, vol. V
Wardell-Yerburgh, Rev. Oswald Pryor, 1858–1913, vol. I
Warden, Archibald A., 1869–1943, vol. IV
Warden, Florence; see James, Florence.
Warden, Herbert Lawton, 1877–1946, vol. IV
Warden, William Luck, died 1942, vol. IV
Wardington, 1st Baron, 1869–1950, vol. IV
Wardlaw, Hon. Alan Lindsay, 1887–1938, vol. III
Wardlaw, Rear-Adm. Alexander Livingston Penrose M.; see Mark-Wardlaw.
Wardlaw, Sir Henry, 18th (shown as 15th) Bt, 1822–1897, vol. I
Wardlaw, Sir Henry, 19th Bt, 1867–1954, vol. V
Wardlaw, Rev. James Tait P.; see Plowden-Wardlaw.
Wardlaw, William, 1892–1958, vol. V
Wardlaw, Rear-Adm. William Penrose M.; see Mark-Wardlaw.
Wardlaw-Milne, Sir John Sydney, died 1967, vol. VI
Wardle, Arthur, 1864–1949, vol. IV

Wardle, Captain Ernest Vivian Livesey, 1878–1931, vol. III
Wardle, George James, 1865–1947, vol. IV
Wardle, Sir Thomas, 1831–1909, vol. I
Wardle, Vice-Adm. Thomas Erskine, 1877–1944, vol. IV
Wardle, Rev. William Lansdell, 1877–1946, vol. IV
Wardle-Smith, John Hughes, 1909–1968, vol. VI
Wardley, Donald Joule, 1893–1950, vol. IV
Wardrop, Maj.-Gen. Alexander, 1831–1908, vol. I
Wardrop, Gen. Sir Alexander, 1872–1961, vol. VI
Wardrop, Col Douglas, 1854–1937, vol. III
Wardrop, Col Frederick Meyer, 1847–1905, vol. I
Wardrop, Rev. James, died 1909, vol. I
Wardrop, Sir (John) Oliver, 1864–1948, vol. IV
Wardrop, Sir Oliver; see Wardrop, Sir J. O.
Wardrope, William Hugh, 1860–1947, vol. IV
Ware, Maj.-Gen. Sir Fabian Arthur Goulstone, 1869–1949, vol. IV
Ware, Sir Frank, 1886–1968, vol. VI
Ware, Lt-Col Frank Cooke W.; see Webb-Ware.
Ware, Lt-Col George William Webb, died 1943, vol. IV
Ware, Rev. Martin Stewart, died 1934, vol. III
Wareing, Alfred, 1876–1942, vol. IV
Wareing, Eustace Bernard Foley, 1890–1958, vol. V
Warfield, Benjamin Breckinridge, 1851–1921, vol. II
Wargrave, 1st Baron, 1862–1936, vol. III
Waring, 1st Baron, 1860–1940, vol. III
Waring, Col Anthony Henry, 1871–1941, vol. IV
Waring, Sir (Arthur) Bertram, 1893–1974, vol. VII
Waring, Captain Arthur Cunliffe Bernard C.; see Critchley-Waring.
Waring, Sir Bertram; see Waring, Sir A. B.
Waring, Lady Clementine; see Waring, Lady S. E. C.
Waring, Sir Douglas Tremayne, 1904–1980, vol. VII
Waring, Francis John, 1843–1924, vol. II
Waring, Sir Henry John, 1817–1903, vol. I
Waring, (Henry) William (Allen), 1906–1962, vol. VI
Waring, Herbert, 1857–1932, vol. III
Waring, Sir Holburt Jacob, 1st Bt, 1866–1953, vol. V
Waring, Rev. Canon John, 1890–1967, vol. VI
Waring, Mrs Margaret Alicia, 1887–1968, vol. VI
Waring, Lady (Susan Elizabeth) Clementine, died 1964, vol. VI
Waring, Col Thomas, died 1898, vol. I
Waring, Walter, 1876–1930, vol. III
Waring, William; see Waring, H. W. A.
Warington, Robert, 1838–1907, vol. I
Wark, Hon. Lord; John Lean Wark, 1877–1943, vol. IV
Wark, Anna Elisa, 1867–1944, vol. IV
Wark, Lt-Col Blair Anderson, 1894–1941, vol. IV
Wark, John Lean; see Wark, Hon. Lord.
Warleigh, Captain Percival H., 1873–1933, vol. III
Warlow, Ven. Edmund John, 1863–1937, vol. III
Warlow-Davies, Eric John, 1910–1964, vol. VI

Warman, Rt Rev. (Frederic Sumpter) Guy, 1872–1953, vol. V
Warman, Rt Rev. Guy; see Warman, Rt Rev. F. S. G.
Warmington, Sir Cornelius Marshall, 1st Bt, 1842–1908, vol. I
Warmington, Sir Marshall Denham, 2nd Bt, 1871–1935, vol. III
Warne, Rt Rev. Francis Wesley, 1854–1932, vol. III
Warne, George Henry, 1881–1928, vol. II
Warne-Browne, Air Marshal Sir Thomas Arthur, 1898–1962, vol. VI
Warner, Hon. Sir Arthur George, 1899–1966, vol. VI
Warner, Brodrick Ashton, 1888–1942, vol. IV
Warner, Charles Dudley, 1829–1900, vol. I
Warner, Rev. Canon Charles Edward, 1868–1945, vol. IV
Warner, Sir Christopher Frederick Ashton, 1895–1957, vol. V
Warner, Sir Courtenay; see Warner, Sir T. C. T.
Warner, Col Sir Edward Courtenay Thomas, 2nd Bt, 1886–1955, vol. V
Warner, Edward Handley, 1850–1925, vol. II
Warner, Edwin Charles, 1900–1968, vol. VI
Warner, Francis, 1847–1926, vol. II
Warner, Sir Frank, 1862–1930, vol. III
Warner, Sir George Frederic, 1845–1936, vol. III
Warner, Sir George Redston, 1879–1978, vol. VII
Warner, Lt-Col Harry Granville L.; see Lee-Warner.
Warner, Rev. John, 1860–1933, vol. III
Warner, Sir Joseph Henry, 1836–1897, vol. I
Warner, Leonard William, died 1959, vol. V
Warner, Sir Lionel Ashton Piers, 1875–1953, vol. V
Warner, Oliver, 1903–1976, vol. VII
Warner, Sir Pelham Francis, 1873–1963, vol. VI
Warner, Philip Henry L.; see Lee Warner.
Warner, Rev. Richard Edward, 1836–1910, vol. I
Warner, Robert Stewart Aucher, 1859–1944, vol. IV
Warner, Robert Townsend, 1868–1938, vol. III
Warner, Rev. Canon Stephen Mortimer, 1873–1947, vol. IV
Warner, Sydney Jeannetta, 1890–1979, vol. VII
Warner, Sylvia Townsend, 1893–1978, vol. VII
Warner, Sir (Thomas) Courtenay Theydon, 1st Bt, 1857–1934, vol. III
Warner, Sir William L.; see Lee-Warner.
Warner, Brig.-Gen. William Ward, 1867–1950, vol. IV
Warner-Staples, Irene E. Toye, died 1954, vol. V
Warnock, Rt Hon. Edmond, 1887–1971, vol. VII
Warnock, Frederick Victor, 1893–1976, vol. VII
Warnock, John, 1864–1942, vol. IV
Warnock, Rt Hon. (John) Edmond; see Warnock, Rt Hon. E.
Warnock, William Robertson Lyon, 1916–1971, vol. VII
Warr, Augustus Frederick, 1847–1908, vol. I
Warr, Very Rev. Charles Laing, 1892–1969, vol. VI
Warr, George Charles Winter, 1845–1901, vol. I
Warr, Sir George Godfrey, 1882–1943, vol. IV

Warrack, Grace Harriet, 1855–1932, vol. III
Warrack, Sir James Howard, 1855–1926, vol. II
Warrand, Maj.-Gen. William Edmund, 1831–1910, vol. I
Warre, Rev. Edmond, 1837–1920, vol. II
Warre, Felix Walter, 1879–1953, vol. V
Warre, Rev. Francis, died 1917, vol. II
Warre, Captain George Francis, 1876–1957, vol. V
Warre, Lt-Col Henry Charles, 1866–1934, vol. III
Warre, Sir Henry James, 1819–1898, vol. I
Warren, Albert Henry, 1830–1911, vol. I
Warren, Sir Alfred Haman, 1856–1927, vol. II
Warren, Arthur, 1860–1924, vol. II
Warren, Maj.-Gen. Sir Arthur Frederick, 1830–1913, vol. I
Warren, Arthur George, 1887–1967, vol. VI
Warren, Sir (Augustus George) Digby, 7th Bt, 1898–1958, vol. V
Warren, Sir Augustus Riversdale, 5th Bt, 1833–1914, vol. I
Warren, Sir Augustus Riversdale John Blennerhasset, 6th Bt, 1865–1914, did not have an entry in Who's Who.
Warren, Gen. Sir Charles, 1840–1927, vol. II
Warren, Charles, 1868–1954, vol. V
Warren, Clarence Henry, 1895–1966, vol. VI
Warren, Cuthbert L.; see Leicester-Warren.
Warren, Maj.-Gen. Dawson Stockley, 1830–1908, vol. I
Warren, Sir Digby; see Warren, Sir A. G. D.
Warren, Douglas Daintry, 1897–1972, vol. VII
Warren, Earl, 1891–1974, vol. VII
Warren, Brig. Edward Galwey, 1893–1975, vol. VII
Warren, Edward Prioleau, 1856–1937, vol. III
Warren, Ernest, 1871–1946, vol. IV
Warren, Falkland George Edgeworth, 1834–1908, vol. I
Warren, Rev. Frederick Edward, 1842–1930, vol. III
Warren, Frederick Samuel Edward Wright, 1878–1952, vol. V
Warren, Major George Ernest, 1871–1942, vol. IV
Warren, Rear-Adm. Guy Langton, 1888–1961, vol. VI
Warren, Rev. Henry George, 1851–1942, vol. IV,
Warren, Sir (Henry William) Hugh, 1891–1961 vol. VI
Warren, Sir Herbert; see Warren, Sir T. H.
Warren, Adm. Herbert Augustus, 1855–1926, vol. II
Warren, Howard Crosby, 1867–1934, vol. III
Warren, Sir Hugh; see Warren, Sir Henry W. H.
Warren, John, 1830–1919, vol. II
Warren, Vice-Adm. John Borlase, 1838–1919, vol. II
Warren, John Herbert, 1895–1960, vol. V
Warren, Lt-Col John Leighton Byrne L.; see Leicester-Warren.
Warren, Col John Raymond, 1888–1956, vol. V
Warren, Rev. John Shrapnel, died 1925, vol. II
Warren, Ven. Latham Coddington, died 1912, vol. I
Warren, Low, died 1941, vol. IV
Warren, Rev. Max Alexander Cunningham, 1904–1977, vol. VII

Warren, Sir Mortimer Langton, 1903–1972, vol. VII

Warren, Nigel Sebastian Sommerville, 1912–1967, vol. VI

Warren, Sir Norcot Hastings Yeeles, 1864–1947, vol. IV

Warren, Sir Pelham Laird, 1845–1923, vol. II

Warren, Col Peter, 1866–1952, vol. V

Warren, Philip David, 1851–1928, vol. II

Warren, Richard, 1876–1957, vol. V

Warren, Rt Hon. Robert Richard, 1817–1897, vol. I

Warren, Thomas Alfred, 1882–1968, vol. VI

Warren, Sir (Thomas) Herbert, 1853–1930, vol. III

Warren, Col Sir Thomas Richard Pennefather, 8th Bt, 1885–1961, vol. VI

Warren, Sir Victor Dunn, 1903–1953, vol. V

Warren, William Fairfield, 1833–1929, vol. III

Warren, William Henry, 1852–1926, vol. II

Warren, Hon. William Robertson, 1879–1927, vol. II

Warren, Col William Robinson, 1882–1969, vol. VI

Warrender, Sir George, 6th Bt, 1825–1901 (this entry was not transferred to Who was Who).

Warrender, Vice-Adm. Sir George John Scott, 7th Bt, 1860–1917, vol. II

Warrender, Lt-Col Hugh Valdave, 1868–1926, vol. II

Warrender, Lady Maud, 1870–1945, vol. IV

Warriner, John, 1860–1938, vol. III

Warrington of Clyffe, 1st Baron, 1851–1937, vol. III

Warrington-Morris, Air Cdre Alfred Drummond, 1883–1962, vol. VI

Warry, George Deedes, 1831–1904, vol. I

Warry, William Taylor, 1836–1906, vol. I

Warter, Sir Philip Allan, 1903–1971, vol. VII

Warton, Rear-Adm. John Fenwick, 1877–1950, vol. IV

Warwick, 5th Earl of, 1853–1924, vol. II

Warwick, 6th Earl of, 1882–1928, vol. II

Warwick, Countess of; (Frances), 1861–1938, vol. III

Warwick, Countess of; (Marjorie), 1887–1943, vol. IV

Warwick, Rt Rev. Mgr J. V., 1857–1939, vol. III

Warwick, Captain John Abraham, 1871–1937, vol. III

Warwick, Sir Norman Richard Combe, 1892–1962, vol. VI

Warwick, Walter Curry, 1877–1963, vol. VI

Warwick, Rev. William Geoffrey, 1898–1955, vol. V

Warwick, William Turner, 1888–1949, vol. IV

Washbourn, John Wichenford, 1863–1902, vol. I

Washbourn, William, 1862–1959, vol. V

Washington, Vice-Adm. Basil George, died 1940, vol. III

Washington, Booker T., died 1915, vol. I (A)

Washington, Horace Lee, 1864–1938, vol. III

Washington, Rev. Marmaduke, 1846–1935, vol. III

Wason, Rear-Adm. Cathcart Romer, 1874–1941, vol. IV

Wason, Rt Hon. Eugene, 1846–1927, vol. II

Wason, John Cathcart, 1848–1921, vol. II

Wason, Lt-Gen. Sydney Rigby, 1887–1969, vol. VI

Wass, Samuel Hall, 1907–1970, vol. VI

Wassermann, Jakob, 1873–1934, vol. III

Watchorn, Col Edwin Thomas, 1856–1940, vol. III (A), vol. V

Waterer, Sir Bernard; see Waterer, Sir R. B.

Waterer, Sir (Robert) Bernard, 1891–1971, vol. VII

Waterfall, Sir Charles Francis, 1888–1954, vol. V

Waterfall, William Duncan, 1889–1970, vol. VI

Waterfield, Sir (Alexander) Percival, 1888–1965, vol. VI

Waterfield, Bt-Col Arthur Charles Mallison, 1866–1943, vol. IV

Waterfield, Sir Henry, 1837–1913, vol. I

Waterfield, Maj.-Gen. Henry Gordon, died 1901, vol. I

Waterfield, Lina, 1874–1964, vol. VI

Waterfield, Sir Percival; see Waterfield, Sir A. P.

Waterfield, Very Rev. Reginald, 1867–1967, vol. VI

Waterford, 6th Marquess of, 1875–1911 (this entry was not transferred to Who was Who).

Waterford, 7th Marquess of, 1901–1934, vol. III

Waterhouse, Alfred, 1830–1905, vol. I

Waterhouse, Captain Rt Hon. Charles, 1893–1975, vol. VII

Waterhouse, Charles Owen, 1843–1917, vol. II

Waterhouse, Eben Gowrie, 1881–1977, vol. VII

Waterhouse, Edwin, 1841–1917, vol. II

Waterhouse, Rev. Eric Strickland, 1879–1964, vol. VI

Waterhouse, Maj.-Gen. George Guy, 1886–1975, vol. VII

Waterhouse, Gilbert, 1888–1977, vol. VII

Waterhouse, Sir Herbert Furnivall, 1864–1931, vol. III

Waterhouse, J. W., died 1917, vol. II

Waterhouse, Maj.-Gen. James, 1842–1922, vol. II

Waterhouse, Michael Theodore, 1888–1968, vol. VI

Waterhouse, Sir Nicholas Edwin, 1877–1964, vol. VI

Waterhouse, Osborn, 1881–1945, vol. IV

Waterhouse, Paul, 1861–1924, vol. II

Waterhouse, Lt-Col Sir Ronald, 1878–1942, vol. IV

Waterhouse, Rupert, 1873–1958, vol. V

Waterhouse, Thomas, 1878–1961, vol. VI

Waterhouse, Walter Lawry, 1887–1969, vol. VI

Waterloo, Stanley, 1846–1913, vol. I

Waterlow, David Sydney, 1857–1924, vol. II

Waterlow, Sir Edgar Lutwyche, 3rd Bt (cr 1873), 1870–1954, vol. V

Waterlow, Sir Ernest Albert, 1850–1919, vol. II

Waterlow, Col Sir James; see Waterlow, Col Sir W. J.

Waterlow, Col James Francis, 1869–1942, vol. IV

Waterlow, Sir Philip Alexander, 4th Bt (cr 1873), 1897–1973, vol. VII

Waterlow, Sir Philip Hickson, 2nd Bt (cr 1873), 1847–1931, vol. III

Waterlow, Sir Sydney Hedley, 1st Bt (cr 1873), 1822–1906, vol. I

Waterlow, Sir Sydney Philip, 1878–1944, vol. IV

Waterlow, Sir William Alfred, 1st Bt (cr 1930), 1871–1931, vol. III

Waterlow, Col Sir (William) James, 2nd Bt (cr 1930), 1905–1969, vol. VI
Watermeyer, Rt Hon. Ernest Frederick, 1880–1958, vol. V
Waterpark, 4th Baron, 1839–1912, vol. I
Waterpark, 5th Baron, 1883–1932, vol. III
Waterpark, 6th Baron, 1876–1948, vol. IV
Waters, Alfred Charles, died 1912, vol. I
Waters, Arthur George, 1888–1953, vol. V
Waters, Edwin George Ross, 1890–1930, vol. III
Waters, Rev. Francis Edward, 1847–1929, vol. III
Waters, Frank George, 1911–1974, vol. VII
Waters, Frank Henry, 1908–1954, vol. V
Waters, G., died 1905, vol. I
Waters, Sir George Alexander, 1880–1967, vol. VI
Waters, Sir Harry G., 1868–1946, vol. IV
Waters, James, died 1923, vol. II
Waters, John Dallas, 1889–1967, vol. VI
Waters, Lt-Col Robert, died 1927, vol. II
Waters, Rev. Thomas Brocas, died 1922, vol. II
Waters, Brig.-Gen. Wallscourt Hely-Hutchinson, 1855–1945, vol. IV
Waterson, David, died 1942, vol. IV
Waterson, David, 1870–1954, vol. V
Waterson, Hon. Sidney Frank, 1896–1976, vol. VII
Wates, George Leslie, 1884–1958, vol. V
Wathen, Gerald Anstruther, 1878–1958, vol. V
Watherston, Lt-Col Alan Edward Garrard, 1867–1909, vol. I
Watherston, Charles Fell, 1875–1940, vol. III
Watherston, Sir David Charles, 1907–1977, vol. VII
Watkin, Sir Alfred Meller, 2nd Bt, 1846–1914, vol. I
Watkin, Sir Edward William, 1st Bt, 1819–1901, vol. I
Watkin, Ernest Lucas, 1876–1951, vol. V
Watkin, Col Henry Samuel Spiller, 1843–1905, vol. I
Watkin, Sir Herbert George, died 1966, vol. VI
Watkin, Morgan, 1878–1970, vol. VI
Watkin, Thomas Morgan Joseph, 1856–1915, vol. I
Watkin-Davies, Rev. Francis Parry, 1862–1939, vol. III
Watkin-Jones, Rev. Howard, 1888–1953, vol. V
Watkin-Williams, Robert Thesiger, 1867–1953, vol. V
Watkins, Arthur Ernest, 1898–1967, vol. VI
Watkins, Brig. Bernard Springett, 1900–1977, vol. VII
Watkins, Col Charles Bell, 1859–1929, vol. III
Watkins, Ven. D. Glyn, 1844–1907, vol. I
Watkins, Frederick Charles, 1883–1954, vol. V
Watkins, Frederick Henry, 1859–1928, vol. II (A), vol. III
Watkins, Col Fredric Mostyn, 1873–1946, vol. IV
Watkins, Rear-Adm. Geoffrey Robert Sladen, 1885–1950, vol. IV
Watkins, Henry George, 1907–1932, vol. III
Watkins, Col Henry George, 1880–1935, vol. III
Watkins, Ven. Henry William, 1844–1922, vol. II
Watkins, Rt Rev. Ivor Stanley, 1896–1960, vol. V
Watkins, James William, 1890–1959, vol. V

Watkins, Rear-Adm. John Kingdon, 1913–1970, vol. VI
Watkins, Sir Metford, 1900–1950, vol. IV
Watkins, Michael John, 1875–1945, vol. IV
Watkins, Ven. Oscar Daniel, 1848–1926, vol. II
Watkins, Lt-Col Oscar Ferris, 1877–1943, vol. IV
Watkins, Rev. Owen Spencer, 1873–1957, vol. V
Watkins, Sir Percy E., 1871–1946, vol. IV
Watkins, Stanley Heath, died 1967, vol. VI
Watkins, Rev. Thomas Benjamin, 1856–1933, vol. III
Watkins, Vernon Phillips, 1906–1967, vol. VI
Watkins, Watkin S.; see Strang-Watkins.
Watkins, William Henry, 1877–1964, vol. VI
Watkins-Pitchford, Lt-Col Herbert, died 1951, vol. V
Watkinson, Arnold Edwards, 1893–1953, vol. V
Watkinson, Sir (George) Laurence, 1896–1974, vol. VII
Watkinson, Sir Laurence; see Watkinson, Sir G. L.
Watkinson, William Henry, 1860–1932, vol. III
Watkinson, Rev. William L., 1838–1925, vol. II
Watkis, Gen. Sir Henry Bulckley Burlton, 1860–1931, vol. III
Watkyn-Thomas, Frederic William, died 1963, vol. VI
Watling, Col Francis Wyatt, 1869–1953, vol. V
Watlington, Sir Henry William, 1866–1942, vol. IV
Watmough, John Edwin, 1860–1939, vol. III
Watney, Col Charles Norman, 1868–1956, vol. V
Watney, Dendy, 1865–1955, vol. V
Watney, Col Sir Frank Dormay, 1870–1965, vol. VI
Watney, Sir John, 1834–1923, vol. II
Watney, Oliver Vernon, 1902–1966, vol. VI
Watney, Vernon James, 1860–1928, vol. II
Watson, Baron (Life Peer); William Watson, 1828–1899, vol. I
Watson, Aaron, 1850–1926, vol. II
Watson, Very Rev. Alan Cameron, 1900–1976, vol. VII
Watson, Alexandra Mary Chalmers, 1873–1936, vol. III
Watson, Alfred Edward Thomas, 1849–1922, vol. II
Watson, Sir Alfred Henry, 1874–1967, vol. VI
Watson, Sir Alfred William, 1870–1936, vol. III
Watson, Col Andrew Alexander, died 1931, vol. III
Watson, A(ndrew) Aiken, 1897–1969, vol. VI
Watson, Andrew Gordon, died 1949, vol. IV
Watson, Sir Angus; see Watson, Sir J. A.
Watson, Archibald, 1849–1940, vol. III (A), vol. IV
Watson, Sir Arthur, 1873–1954, vol. V
Watson, Arthur E., 1880–1969, vol. VI
Watson, Sir Arthur Egerton, 1882–1967, vol. VI
Watson, Arthur George, 1829–1916, vol. II
Watson, Ven. Arthur Herbert, 1864–1952, vol. V
Watson, Arthur Kenelm, 1867–1947, vol. IV
Watson, Sir Arthur Townley, 2nd Bt (cr 1866), 1830–1907, vol. I
Watson, Arthur William, 1874–1925, vol. II
Watson, Basil Bernard, died 1941, vol. IV
Watson, Benjamin Philip, 1880–1976, vol. VII

Watson, Vice-Adm. Bertram Chalmers, 1887–1976, vol. VII
Watson, Sir Bertrand, 1878–1948, vol. IV
Watson, Rear-Adm. Burges, 1846–1902, vol. I
Watson, Most Rev. Campbell West W.; see West-Watson.
Watson, Chalmers, 1870–1946, vol. IV
Watson, Sir Charles Cuningham, 1874–1934, vol. III
Watson, Brig.-Gen. Charles Frederic, 1877–1948, vol. IV
Watson, Maj.-Gen. Sir Charles G.; see Gordon-Watson.
Watson, Col Sir Charles Moore, 1844–1916, vol. II
Watson, Sir Charles Rushworth, 3rd Bt (cr 1866), 1865–1922, vol. II
Watson, Gen. Sir Daril G., 1888–1967, vol. VI
Watson, Maj.-Gen. Sir David, 1871–1922, vol. II
Watson, David, died 1940, vol. III
Watson, David Archibald Beverley, 1905–1971, vol. VII
Watson, Hon. David John, 1911–1959, vol. V
Watson, Sir David M.; see Milne-Watson.
Watson, David Meredith Seares, 1886–1973, vol. VII
Watson, Dennis George, died 1977, vol. VII
Watson, Sir Duncan, 1873–1959, vol. V
Watson, Edith Margaret, died 1953, vol. V
Watson, Edmund Henry Lacon, 1865–1948, vol. IV
Watson, Rev. Edward William, 1859–1936, vol. III
Watson, Elliot Lovegood Grant, 1885–1970, vol. VI
Watson, Rear-Adm. Fischer Burges, 1884–1960, vol. V
Watson, Lt-Col Forrester Colvin, 1878–1951, vol. V
Watson, Foster, 1860–1929, vol. III
Watson, Sir Francis, 1864–1947, vol. IV
Watson, Col Francis William, 1893–1966, vol. VI
Watson, Sir Frank Pears, 1878–1941, vol. IV
Watson, Rev. Frederick, 1844–1906, vol. I
Watson, Frederick, 1885–1935, vol. III
Watson, Frederick, 1880–1947, vol. IV
Watson, Rev. Frederick Vincent, 1869–1954, vol. V
Watson, Sir Geoffrey Lewin, 3rd Bt (cr 1918), 1879–1959, vol. V
Watson, George, 1845–1927, vol. II
Watson, George, 1872–1937, vol. III
Watson, Sir George; see Watson, Sir W. G.
Watson, George Lennox, 1851–1904, vol. I
Watson, George Spencer, 1869–1934, vol. III
Watson, Ven. George Wade, 1838–1915, vol. I (A)
Watson, Sir George Willes, 1827–1897, vol. I
Watson, George William, 1877–1956, vol. V
Watson, Gilbert, died 1920, vol. II
Watson, Gilbert, 1864–1941, vol. IV
Watson, Maj.-Gen. Gilbert France, 1895–1976, vol. VII
Watson, G(ordon) G(raham) Gibbes, 1891–1971, vol. VII
Watson, Harold Argyle, 1884–1959, vol. V
Watson, Lt-Col Harold Farnell, 1876–1941, vol. IV
Watson, Harrison, 1864–1948, vol. IV

Watson, Harry, 1871–1936, vol. III
Watson, Maj.-Gen. Sir Harry Davis, 1866–1945, vol. IV
Watson, Henry Angus, 1863–1952, vol. V
Watson, Henry Brereton Marriott, 1863–1921, vol. II
Watson, Henry C.; see Cradock-Watson.
Watson, Sir Henry Edmund, 1815–1901, vol. I
Watson, Hon. Sir (Henry) Keith, 1900–1973, vol. VII
Watson, Rev. Henry Lacon, 1823–1903, vol. I
Watson, Brig. Henry Neville Grylls, 1885–1976, vol. VII
Watson, Rev. Henry William, 1827–1903, vol. I
Watson, Herbert Adolphus G.; see Grant Watson.
Watson, Rev. Herbert Armstrong, 1860–1937, vol. III
Watson, Herbert Edmeston, 1886–1980, vol. VII
Watson, Major Herbert Frazer, 1881–1937, vol. III
Watson, Homer, 1855–1936, vol. III
Watson, Captain Horace Cyril, 1876–1949, vol. IV
Watson, Hubert Digby, 1869–1947, vol. IV
Watson, Sir Hugh, 1897–1966, vol. VI
Watson, Adm. Sir Hugh Dudley Richards, 1872–1954, vol. V
Watson, Sir Hugh Wesley Allen, 1875–1953, vol. V
Watson, Maj.-Gen. Hugh Wharton Myddleton, 1881–1938, vol. III
Watson, Sir James Anderson Scott, 1889–1966, vol. VI
Watson, Sir (James) Angus, 1874–1961, vol. VI
Watson, Lt-Col James Kiero, 1865–1942, vol. IV
Watson, James Murray, 1888–1955, vol. V
Watson, Very Rev. James P.; see Pitt-Watson.
Watson, Sir John, 1st Bt (cr 1895), 1819–1898, vol. I
Watson, Sir John, 2nd Bt (cr 1895), 1860–1903 (this entry was not transferred to Who was Who).
Watson, Rev. John, 1850–1907, vol. I
Watson, John, died 1908, vol. I
Watson, Sir John, 3rd Bt (cr 1895), 1898–1918, vol. II
Watson, Gen. Sir John, 1829–1919, vol. II
Watson, John, died 1928, vol. II
Watson, Rev. John, 1843–1930, vol. III
Watson, John, died 1936, vol. III
Watson, John, 1847–1939, vol. III
Watson, John Alfred, died 1931, vol. III
Watson, John Arthur Fergus, 1903–1978, vol. VII
Watson, Sir John Ballingall Forbes, 1879–1952, vol. V
Watson, Sir John Charles, 1883–1944, vol. IV
Watson, Hon. John Christian, 1867–1941, vol. IV
Watson, John Duncan, 1860–1946, vol. IV
Watson, Brig.-Gen. John Edward, 1859–1951, vol. V
Watson, John Harry, 1875–1944, vol. IV
Watson, Sir John Mathewson, died 1942, vol. IV
Watson, Lt-Col John William, 1874–1962, vol. VI
Watson, Hon. Sir Keith; see Watson, Hon. Sir H. K.
Watson, Laurence H.; see Hill Watson, Hon. Lord

Watson, Engr Rear-Adm. Lewis Jones, 1871–1942, vol. IV
Watson, Sir Logie Pirie, 1864–1933, vol. III
Watson, Malcolm, 1853–1929, vol. III
Watson, Sir Malcolm, 1873–1955, vol. V
Watson, Maj.-Gen. Norman Vyvyan, 1898–1974, vol. VII
Watson, P. F.; see Fletcher-Watson.
Watson, Sir Patrick Heron, 1832–1907, vol. I
Watson, Reginald George, 1862–1926, vol. II
Watson, Captain Reginald James Newall, 1877–1930, vol. III
Watson, Sir Renny; see Watson, Sir W. R.
Watson, Hon. Robert, 1853–1929, vol. III
Watson, Hon. Robert, 1868–1930, vol. III
Watson, Robert, 1882–1948, vol. IV
Watson, Robert, 1894–1977, vol. VII
Watson, Rev. Robert A., 1845–1921, vol. II
Watson, Rt Hon. Robert Spence, 1837–1911, vol. I
Watson, Robert William S.; see Seton-Watson.
Watson, Col Ronald Macgregor, 1887–1936, vol. III
Watson, Samuel, 1898–1967, vol. VI
Watson, Lt-Col Stancliffe Wallace, 1889–1947, vol. IV
Watson, Sir Stephen John, 1898–1976, vol. VII
Watson, Lt-Col Sydney Twells, 1879–1936, vol. III
Watson, Thomas, 1844–1914, vol. I
Watson, Sir Thomas Aubrey, 4th Bt (cr 1866), 1911–1941, vol. IV
Watson, Lt-Col Thomas Colclough, 1867–1917, vol. II
Watson, Sir Thomas Edward, 1st Bt (cr 1918), 1851–1921, vol. II
Watson, Thomas J., 1847–1912, vol. I (A), vol. III
Watson, Thomas William, 1889–1957, vol. V
Watson, Ven. W. C., 1867–1916, vol. II (A), vol. III
Watson, Sir Wager Joseph, 5th Bt (cr 1760), 1837–1904, vol. I
Watson, Rev. Wentworth, 1848–1925, vol. II
Watson, Sir Wilfrid Hood, 2nd Bt (cr 1918), 1875–1922 (this entry was not transferred to Who was Who).
Watson, William, 1843–1909, vol. I
Watson, Sir William, 1842–1918, vol. II
Watson, William, 1868–1919, vol. II
Watson, Sir William, 1858–1935, vol. III
Watson, Major William, 1885–1942, vol. IV
Watson, William; see Baron Thankerton.
Watson, Maj.-Gen. William Arthur, 1860–1944, vol. IV
Watson, Sir (William) George, 1st Bt (cr 1912), 1861–1930, vol. III
Watson, William Henry Lowe, 1891–1932, vol. III
Watson, William John, 1865–1948, vol. IV
Watson, William Law, 1883–1958, vol. V
Watson, William Livingstone, 1835–1903, vol. I
Watson, William McLean, 1874–1962, vol. VI
Watson, William Peter, died 1932, vol. III
Watson, Sir (William) Renny, 1838–1900, vol. I
Watson, William Trevor, 1886–1943, vol. IV
Watson, Lt-Col William Walter Russell, 1875–1924, vol. II
Watson-Jones, Sir Reginald, 1902–1972, vol. VII

Watson-Kennedy, Lt-Col Thomas Francis Archibald, 1856–1935, vol. III
Watson-Taylor, George Simon Arthur, 1850–1942, vol. IV
Watson-Watt, Air Chief Comdt Dame Katherine Jane Trefusis, 1899–1971, vol. VII
Watson-Watt, Sir Robert Alexander, 1892–1973, vol. VII
Watson-Williams, Eric, 1890–1964, vol. VI
Watson-Williams, Patrick, 1863–1938, vol. III
Watt, Lt-Col Alexander Fitzgerald, 1871–1957, vol. V
Watt, Alexander Pollock, died 1914, vol. I
Watt, Alexander Strahan, died 1948, vol. IV
Watt, Brig-Gen. Donald Munro, 1871–1942, vol. IV
Watt, Lt-Col Edward William, 1877–1955, vol. V
Watt, Commissary-Gen. FitzJames Edward, 1822–1902, vol. I
Watt, Francis, 1849–1927, vol. II
Watt, Francis Clifford, 1896–1971, vol. VII
Watt, Sir George, 1851–1930, vol. III
Watt, George, 1854–1940, vol. III
Watt, George Fiddes, 1873–1960, vol. V
Watt, Harry Anderson, 1863–1929, vol. III
Watt, Henry J., 1879–1925, vol. II
Watt, Very Rev. Hugh, 1879–1968, vol. VI
Watt, Rt Hon. Hugh, 1912–1980, vol. VII
Watt, James, 1867–1929, vol. III
Watt, Sir James, died 1935, vol. III
Watt, James, 1863–1945, vol. IV
Watt, James, 1870–1945, vol. IV
Watt, James Crabb, 1853–1917, vol. II
Watt, James Cromar, 1862–1940, vol. III (A), vol. IV
Watt, Rev. John, 1862–1930, vol. III
Watt, John Mitchell, 1892–1980, vol. VII
Watt, Dame Katherine Christie, died 1963, vol. VI
Watt, Air Chief Comdt Dame Katherine Jane Trefusis W.; see Watson-Watt.
Watt, Langmuir; see Watt, W. L.
Watt, Very Rev. Lauchlan MacLean, died 1957, vol. V
Watt, Rev. Lewis, 1885–1965, vol. VI
Watt, Michael Herbert, 1887–1967, vol. VI
Watt, Sir Robert Alexander W.; see Watson-Watt.
Watt, Sir Robert Dickie, 1881–1965, vol. VI
Watt, Samuel, 1876–1927, vol. II
Watt, Captain Samuel Alexander, 1876–1950, vol. IV
Watt, Theodore, 1884–1946, vol. IV
Watt, Hon. Sir Thomas, 1857–1947, vol. IV
Watt, Sir Thomas, 1853–1955, vol. V
Watt, (Walter) Langmuir, 1876–1953, vol. V
Watt, Rt Hon. William Alexander, 1871–1946, vol. IV
Watt, William Robert, 1888–1949, vol. IV
Watt, William Warnock, 1890–1963, vol. VI
Watterson, Hon. Henry, 1840–1921, vol. II
Watterston, David, 1845–1931, vol. III
Wattie, Sir James, 1902–1974, vol. VII
Wattie, James MacPherson, 1862–1943, vol. IV
Watts, Arthur, died 1935, vol. III
Watts, Arthur Francis, 1916–1972, vol. VII

Watts, Arthur Frederick, 1897–1970, vol. VI (AII)
Watts, Rev. Arthur Herbert, 1886–1960, vol. V
Watts, Charles Albert, 1858–1946, vol. IV
Watts, Maj.-Gen. Charles Donald Raynsford, 1871–1943, vol. IV
Watts, Rt Rev. Christopher Charles, *died* 1958, vol. V
Watts, Sir (Fenwick) Shadforth, 1858–1926, vol. II
Watts, Sir Francis, 1859–1930, vol. III
Watts, George Frederick, 1817–1904, vol. I
Watts, Gordon Edward, 1902–1974, vol. VII
Watts, Henry Edward, 1832–1904, vol. I
Watts, Lt-Gen. Sir Herbert Edward, 1858–1934, vol. III
Watts, Rt Rev. Horace Godfrey, 1901–1959, vol. V
Watts, Sir Hugh Edmund, 1888–1958, vol. V
Watts, James, 1903–1961, vol. VI
Watts, James T., *died* 1930, vol. III
Watts, John Hylton, 1890–1972, vol. VII
Watts, Leonard, 1871–1951, vol. V
Watts, Maurice Emygdius, 1878–1933, vol. III
Watts, Col Sir Philip, 1846–1926, vol. II
Watts, Rev. Robert Rowley, *died* 1911, vol. I
Watts, Sir Shadforth; *see* Watts, Sir F. S.
Watts, Rev. Sidney Maurice, 1892–1979, vol. VII
Watts, Sir Thomas, 1868–1951, vol. V
Watts, Weldon Patrick Tyrone, 1897–1972, vol. VII
Watts, Col Sir William, 1858–1922, vol. II
Watts, William Marshall, 1844–1919, vol. II
Watts, William Walter, 1862–1948, vol. IV
Watts, William Whitehead, 1860–1947, vol. IV
Watts-Ditchfield, Rt Rev. John Edwin, 1861–1923, vol. II
Watts-Dunton, Walter Theodore, 1832–1914, vol. I
Wauchope, Gen. Sir Arthur Grenfell, 1874–1947, vol. IV
Wauchope, Lt-Col David Alexander, 1871–1929, vol. III
Wauchope, Mrs, (Jean Mary Wauchope), *died* 1942, vol. IV
Wauchope, Sir John Douglas Don-, 9th Bt, 1859–1951, vol. V
Waugh, Sir (Alexander) Telford, 1865–1950, vol. IV
Waugh, Arthur, 1866–1943, vol. IV
Waugh, Sir Arthur Allen, 1891–1968, vol. VI
Waugh, Ven. Arthur Thornhill, 1842–1922, vol. II
Waugh, Rev. Benjamin, 1839–1908, vol. I
Waugh, Evelyn Arthur St John, 1903–1966, vol. VI
Waugh, George Ernest, *died* 1940, vol. III
Waugh, Sir Telford; *see* Waugh, Sir A. T.
Waugh, William James, 1856–1931, vol. III
Waugh, William Templeton, 1884–1932, vol. III
Wauhope, Col Robert Alexander, 1855–1921, vol. II
Wauters, Emile, 1846–1933, vol. III
Wauton, Edric Brenton, 1883–1957, vol. V
Wavell, 1st Earl, 1883–1950, vol. IV
Wavell, 2nd Earl, 1916–1953, vol. V
Wavell, Maj.-Gen. Archibald Graham, 1843–1935, vol. III

Waverley, 1st Viscount, 1882–1958, vol. V
Waverley, Viscountess; (Ava), 1896–1974, vol. VII
Wavertree, 1st Baron, 1856–1933, vol. III
Wavertree, Lady; (Sophie Florence Lothrop), (Mrs F. M. B. Fisher), *died* 1952, vol. V
Way, Andrew Greville Parry, 1909–1974, vol. VII
Way, Arthur S., 1847–1930, vol. III
Way, Lt-Col Benjamin Irby, 1869–1932, vol. III
Way, Lt-Col Bromley George Vere, 1873–1940, vol. III
Way, Rev. Charles Parry, 1870–1949, vol. IV
Way, Christine Stella, 1895–1975, vol. VII
Way, Col George Augustus, 1837–1899, vol. I
Way, Gerald Oscar, 1875–1938, vol. III
Way, Rev. John Hugh, 1834–1912, vol. I
Way, Rev. John Pearce, 1850–1937, vol. III
Way, Maj.-Gen. Nowell FitzUpton Sampson-, 1838–1926, vol. II
Way, Rt Hon. Sir Samuel James, 1st Bt, 1836–1916, vol. II
Way, Captain William, 1847–1927, vol. II
Wayland, Edward James, 1888–1966, vol. VI
Wayland, Lt-Col Edward Robert, 1871–1939, vol. III
Wayland, Lt-Col Sir William Abraham, 1869–1950, vol. IV
Wayman, Lt-Col Harry Reginald Bland, 1877–1931, vol. III
Wayman, Lt-Col Sir Myers, 1890–1959, vol. V
Wayman, Thomas, 1833–1901, vol. I
Waymouth, Adm. Arthur William, 1863–1936, vol. III
Waymouth, Paymaster-Captain Frederick Richard, 1862–1927, vol. II
Wayne, Naunton, 1901–1970, vol. VI
Wayne, Richard St John Ormerod, 1904–1959, vol. V
Waynforth, Harry Morton, 1867–1916, vol. II
Wayte, Lt-Col Adrian Barclay, 1882–1934, vol. III
Wazir Hasan, Hon. Sir Saiyid, 1874–1947, vol. IV (A), vol. V
Weakley, Ernest, 1861–1923, vol. II
Weale, Putnam, 1877–1930, vol. III
Weale, W. H. James, 1832–1917, vol. II
Wear, Col Algernon Edward Luke, 1866–1941, vol. IV
Weardale, 1st Baron, 1847–1923, vol. II
Weare, Sir Henry Edwin, 1825–1898, vol. I
Wearing, John Frederick, 1922–1974, vol. VII
Weatherall, Col Henry Burgess, *died* 1917, vol. II
Weatherall, John Henry, 1868–1950, vol. IV
Weatherburn, Charles Ernest, 1884–1974, vol. VII
Weatherby, Sir Francis, 1885–1969, vol. VI
Weatherhead, Arthur Evelyn, 1880–1956, vol. V
Weatherhead, Rev. Arthur Swinton, 1866–1937, vol. III
Weatherhead, Rev. Herbert Thomas Candy, 1875–1930, vol. III
Weatherhead, Very Rev. James, 1863–1944, vol. IV
Weatherhead, Rev. Leslie Dixon, 1893–1976, vol. VII
Weatherhead, Rev. Robert Johnston, 1839–1912, vol. I
Weatherill, Charles, 1874–1944, vol. IV

Weatherill, Rev. Canon David, 1866–1933, vol. III
Weatherill, Henry, 1868–1943, vol. IV
Weatherly, Frederic Edward, 1848–1929, vol. III
Weatherstone, Sir Duncan Mackay, 1898–1972, vol. VII
Weaver, Mrs Baillie, (Gertrude Weaver), died 1926, vol. II
Weaver, Gertrude; see Weaver, Mrs Baillie.
Weaver, Herbert Parsons, 1872–1945, vol. IV
Weaver, John Reginald Homer, 1882–1965, vol. VI
Weaver, Sir Lawrence, 1876–1930, vol. III
Weaver, Percy William, 1882–1943, vol. IV
Weaver, Warren, 1894–1978, vol. VII
Web-Gilbert, Charles, 1869–1925, vol. II
Webb, Rt Rev. Allan Becher, 1839–1907, vol. I
Webb, Sir (Ambrose) Henry, 1882–1964, vol. VI
Webb, Lt-Col Andrew Henry, 1873–1949, vol. IV
Webb, Sir Arthur Lewis, 1860–1921, vol. II
Webb, Col Sir (Arthur) Lisle Ambrose, 1871–1945, vol. IV
Webb, Sir Aston, 1849–1930, vol. III
Webb, Augustus D., 1880–1953, vol. V
Webb, Beatrice; see Webb, Mrs Sidney.
Webb, C. Locock, 1822–1898, vol. I
Webb, Cecil Richard, 1887–1974, vol. VII
Webb, Sir Charles Morgan, 1872–1963, vol. VI
Webb, Clement Charles Julian, 1865–1954, vol. V
Webb, Clifford, 1895–1972, vol. VII
Webb, Hon. Sir Clifton; see Webb, Hon. Sir T. C.
Webb, Francis Gilbert, 1853–1941, vol. IV
Webb, Frederick William, 1837–1919, vol. II
Webb, Geoffrey Fairbank, 1898–1970, vol. VI
Webb, Lt-Col George Ambrose Congreve, 1869–1942, vol. IV
Webb, Brig. George Clifford, 1905–1945, vol. IV
Webb, Lt-Col Sir Henry, 1st Bt, 1866–1940, vol. III
Webb, Sir Henry; see Webb, Sir A. H.
Webb, Mrs Henry Bertram Law; see Webb, Mary.
Webb, Col James B.; see Baldwin-Webb.
Webb, John, 1885–1954, vol. V
Webb, John Curtis, 1868–1949, vol. IV
Webb, Katharine, (Katharine Adams), 1862–1952, vol. V
Webb, Col Sir Lisle; see Webb, Col Sir A. L. A.
Webb, Marion St John, died 1930, vol. III
Webb, Mary, 1881–1927, vol. II
Webb, Maurice, 1880–1946, vol. IV
Webb, Rt Hon. Maurice, 1904–1956, vol. V
Webb, Maurice Everett, 1880–1939, vol. III
Webb, Millicent Vere, 1878–1969, vol. VI
Webb, Sir Montagu de Pomeroy, 1869–1938, vol. III
Webb, Montague, 1847–1930, vol. III
Webb, Percy Henry, 1856–1937, vol. III
Webb, Philip George Lancelot, 1856–1937, vol. III
Webb, Adm. Sir Richard, 1870–1950, vol. IV
Webb, Robert Alexander, 1891–1978, vol. VII
Webb, Mrs Sidney, (Beatrice Webb), 1858–1943, vol. IV
Webb, Sir Sydney, 1816–1898, vol. I
Webb, Hon. Sir (Thomas) Clifton, 1889–1962, vol. VI
Webb, Thomas Ebenezer, 1827–1903, vol. I
Webb, Lt-Col Walter Edward, died 1934, vol. III

Webb, Col Walter George, 1838–1919, vol. II
Webb, Walter Prescott, 1888–1963, vol. VI
Webb, Lt-Col Wilfred Francis, 1897–1973, vol. VII
Webb, Wilfred Mark, 1868–1952, vol. V
Webb, William Flood, 1887–1972, vol. VII
Webb, William Harcourt, 1875–1968, vol. VI
Webb, William Seward, 1851–1926, vol. II
Webb, Rt Rev. William Walter, 1857–1934, vol. III
Webb-Bowen, Col Hildred Edward, 1882–1958, vol. V
Webb-Bowen, Air Vice-Marshal Sir Tom Ince, 1879–1956, vol. V
Webb-Johnson, 1st Baron, 1880–1958, vol. V
Webb-Johnson, Cecil, died 1930, vol. III
Webb-Johnson, Stanley, 1888–1965, vol. VI
Webb-Jones, James William, 1904–1965, vol. VI
Webb-Peploe, Rev. Hanmer William, 1837–1923, vol. II
Webb-Ware, Lt-Col Frank Cooke, 1866–1934, vol. III
Webbe, Alexander Josiah, 1855–1941, vol. IV
Webbe, Sir Harold, 1885–1965, vol. VI
Webber, Brig.-Gen. Adrian Beare I.; see Incledon-Webber.
Webber, Sir Arthur Frederick Clarence, 1873–1952, vol. V
Webber, Maj.-Gen. Charles Edmund, 1838–1904, vol. I
Webber, Harold Norris, 1881–1954, vol. V
Webber, Lt-Col Horace Armine William, 1880–1940, vol. III
Webber, Brig.-Gen. Norman William, 1881–1950, vol. IV
Webber, Robert Bryan, 1860–1934, vol. III
Webber, Sir Robert John, 1884–1962, vol. VI
Webber, William Downes, 1834–1924, vol. II
Webber, Rt Rev. William Thomas Thornhill, 1837–1903, vol. I
Weber, F. Parkes, 1863–1962, vol. VI
Weber, Sir Herman, 1823–1918, vol. II
Weber, Col William Hermann Frank, 1875–1936, vol. III
Weber-Brown, Lt-Col Arthur Miles, 1898–1965, vol. VI
Webley-Parry-Pryse, Sir Edward John; see Pryse.
Webster, Adam Blyth, 1882–1956, vol. VI
Webster, Mrs Amy Marjorie, 1901–1967, vol. VI
Webster, Col Arthur George, 1837–1916, vol. II
Webster, Hon. Arthur Harold, 1874–1902, vol. I
Webster, Sir Augustus Frederick Walpole Edward, 8th Bt, 1864–1923, vol. II
Webster, Benjamin, 1864–1947, vol. IV
Webster, Sir Charles Kingsley, 1886–1961, vol. VI
Webster, Sir David Lumsden, 1903–1971, vol. VII
Webster, David William Ernest, 1923–1969, vol. VI
Webster, Edmund Foster, died 1913, vol. I
Webster, Sir Francis, 1850–1924, vol. II
Webster, Rev. Francis Scott, died 1920, vol. II
Webster, George Frederick, 1889–1959, vol. V
Webster, George Henry, 1887–1955, vol. V
Webster, Rev. George Russell B.; see Bullock-Webster.
Webster, Rt Rev. Hedley, 1880–1954, vol. V
Webster, Herbert Cayley, died 1917, vol. II

Webster, Herman Armour, 1878–1970, vol. VII (A)

Webster, Sir Hugh Calthrop, 1869–1941, vol. IV

Webster, James Alexander, 1877–1964, vol. VI

Webster, James Mathewson, *died* 1973, vol. VII

Webster, John, 1891–1947, vol. IV

Webster, Captain John Alexander, 1874–1924, vol. II

Webster, John Clarence, 1863–1950, vol. IV

Webster, John Edward, 1870–1943, vol. IV

Webster, John Henry Douglas, 1882–1975, vol. VII

Webster, Sir Lonsdale; *see* Webster, Sir T. L.

Webster, Lorne C., 1871–1941, vol. IV

Webster, Margaret, 1905–1972, vol. VII

Webster, Dame May, 1865–1948, vol. IV

Webster, Very Rev. Reginald Godfrey Michael, 1860–1913, vol. I

Webster, Robert Grant, *died* 1925, vol. II

Webster, Thomas Bertram Lonsdale, 1905–1974, vol. VII

Webster, Lt-Gen. Thomas Edward, 1830–1909, vol. I

Webster, Sir (Thomas) Lonsdale, 1868–1930, vol. III

Webster, Gen. Sir Thomas Sheridan R.; *see* Riddell-Webster.

Webster, Tom, 1890–1962, vol. VI

Webster, Walter Ernest, 1878–1959, vol. V

Webster, Col William, 1865–1934, vol. III

Webster, William, 1866–1953, vol. V

Webster, Major William Henry Albert, 1884–1968, vol. VI

Wedd, Major Aubrey Pattisson Wallman, 1885–1945, vol. IV

Wedd, Nathaniel, *died* 1940, vol. III

Wedd, Brig. William Basil, 1890–1966, vol. VI

Weddell, Col John Murray, 1884–1966, vol. VI

Wedderburn, Alexander, 1854–1931, vol. III

Wedderburn, Alexander Henry Melvill, 1892–1968, vol. VI

Wedderburn, Sir Ernest Maclagan, 1884–1958, vol. V

Wedderburn, Henry Scrymgeour, 1840–1914, vol. I

Wedderburn, Lt-Col Henry Scrymgeour, 1872–1924, vol. II

Wedderburn, Sir John Andrew O.; *see* Ogilvy-Wedderburn.

Wedderburn, Comdr Sir (John) Peter O.; *see* Ogilvy-Wedderburn.

Wedderburn, Joseph Henry Maclagan, 1882–1948, vol. IV

Wedderburn, Sir Maxwell MacLagan, 1883–1953, vol. V

Wedderburn, Sir William, 10th and 4th Bt, 1838–1918, vol. II

Wedderburn-Maxwell, Major James Andrew Colvile, 1849–1917, vol. II

Wedgwood, 1st Baron, 1872–1943, vol. IV

Wedgwood, 2nd Baron, 1898–1959, vol. V

Wedgwood, 3rd Baron, 1921–1970, vol. VI

Wedgwood, Hon. Camilla Hildegarde, 1901–1955, vol. V

Wedgwood, Major Cecil, *died* 1916, vol. II

Wedgwood, Francis Hamilton, *died* 1930, vol. III

Wedgwood, Dame Ivy Evelyn, *died* 1975, vol. VII

Wedgwood, Hon. Josiah, 1899–1968, vol. VI

Wedgwood, Julia, *died* 1913, vol. I

Wedgwood, Sir Ralph Lewis, 1st Bt, 1874–1956, vol. V

Wedlake, John, 1892–1958, vol. V

Wedmore, Edmund Basil, 1876–1956, vol. V

Wedmore, Sir Frederick, 1844–1921, vol. II

Weech, William Nassau, 1878–1961, vol. VI

Weedon, Augustus Walford, *died* 1908, vol. I

Weedon, Air Marshal Sir Colin Winterbotham, 1901–1975, vol. VII

Weedon, Hon. Sir Henry, 1859–1921, vol. II

Weekes, Ven. Christian William Hampton, 1880–1948, vol. IV

Weekes, Rev. George Arthur, 1869–1953, vol. V

Weekes, Col Henry Wilson, 1870–1943, vol. IV

Weekes, Paymaster Rear-Adm. Victor Herbert Thomas, 1873–1937, vol. III

Weekes, Rev. William Haye, 1867–1945, vol. IV

Weekley, Ernest, *died* 1954, vol. V

Weeks, 1st Baron, 1890–1960, vol. V

Weeks, Engr Rear-Adm. Edward John, 1868–1954, vol. V

Wegg-Prosser, Francis Richard, 1824–1911, vo

Weguelin, Mrs Arthur, *died* 1931, vol. III

Weguelin, John Reinhard, 1849–1927, vol. II

Wei Yuk, Sir Boshan, 1849–1921, vol. II

Weigall, Albert Bythesea, *died* 1912, vol. I

Weigall, Lt-Col Sir Archibald; *see* Weigall, Lt-Col Sir W. E. G. A.

Weigall, Arthur Edward Pearse Brome, 1880–1934, vol. III

Weigall, Cecil Edward, 1870–1955, vol. V

Weigall, Henry, 1829–1925, vol. II

Weigall, Julian William Wellesley, 1868–1945, vol. IV

Weigall, Lady Rose Sophia Mary, 1834–1921, vol. II

Weigall, Theyre à Beckett, 1860–1926, vol. II

Weigall, Lt-Col Sir (William Ernest George) Archibald, 1st Bt, 1874–1952, vol. V

Weight, Rev. Thomas Joseph, 1845–1922, vol. II

Weightman, Sir Hugh, 1898–1949, vol. IV

Weightman, William Henry, 1887–1970, vol. VI

Weighton, Robert Lunan, 1851–1937, vol. III

Weill, David D.; *see* David-Weill.

Weinberger, Jaromir, 1896–1967, vol. VI

Weingartner, Felix, 1863–1942, vol. IV

Weinthal, Leo, 1865–1930, vol. III

Weir, 1st Viscount, 1877–1959, vol. V

Weir, 2nd Viscount, 1905–1975, vol. VII

Weir, Archibald A. E., 1859–1935, vol. III

Weir, Sir Cecil McAlpine, 1890–1960, vol. V

Weir, Air Vice-Marshal Cecil Thomas, 1913–1965, vol. VI

Weir, Lt-Col Donald Lord, 1885–1921, vol. II

Weir, Gen. Sir George Alexander, 1876–1951, vol. V

Weir, George Moir, 1885–1949, vol. IV

Weir, Harrison William, 1824–1906, vol. I

Weir, Miss Helen Stuart, *died* 1969, vol. VI

Weir, James Galloway, 1839–1911, vol. I

Weir, James George, 1887–1973, vol. VII

Weir, Lt-Col James Leslie Rose, 1883–1950, vol. IV
Weir, Sir John, 1879–1971, vol. VII
Weir, Sir John Charles, 1872–1936, vol. III
Weir, (Lauchlan) MacNeill, 1877–1939, vol. III
Weir, MacNeill; see Weir, L. MacN.
Weir, Neil Archibald Campbell, 1895–1967, vol. VI
Weir, Maj.-Gen. Sir Norman William McDonald, 1893–1961, vol. VI
Weir, Rt Rev. Mgr Peter John, 1831–1917, vol. II
Weir, Ralph Somerville, 1884–1962, vol. VI
Weir, Major Hon. Robert, 1882–1939, vol. III
Weir, Robert Fulton, 1838–1927, vol. II
Weir, Robert Stanley, 1856–1926, vol. II
Weir, Brig.-Gen. Stanley Price, 1866–1944, vol. IV
Weir, Maj.-Gen. Sir Stephen Cyril Ettrick, 1905–1969, vol. VI
Weir, Hon. William Alexander, 1858–1929, vol. III
Weir, Rev. Canon William Mortimer, 1868–1936, vol. III
Weirter, Louis, 1873–1932, vol. III
Weis-Fogh, Torkel, 1922–1975, vol. VII
Weisberg, Hyman, 1890–1976, vol. VII
Weismann, August, 1834–1914, vol. I
Weiss, Frederick Ernest, 1865–1953, vol. V
Weiss, Joseph J., 1907–1972, vol. VII
Weiss, Roberto, 1906–1969, vol. VI
Weisz, Victor, 1913–1966, vol. VI
Weizmann, Chaim, 1874–1952, vol. V
Welbourne, Edward, 1894–1966, vol. VI
Welby, 1st Baron, 1832–1915, vol. I (A)
Welby, Sir Alfred Cholmeley Earle, 1849–1937, vol. III
Welby, Charles Cornwallis Anderson P.; see Pelham Welby.
Welby, Sir Charles Glynne Earle, 5th Bt, 1865–1938, vol. III
Welby, Edward Montague Earle, 1836–1926, vol. II
Welby, Sir George Earle, 1851–1936, vol. III
Welby, Hugh Robert Everard Earle, 1885–1970, vol. VI
Welby, John Earle, 1820–1905, vol. I
Welby, Sir Oliver Charles Earle, 6th Bt, 1902–1977, vol. VII
Welby, Rt Rev. Thomas Earle, 1811–1899, vol. I
Welby, Thomas Earle, 1881–1933, vol. III
Welby-Everard, Edward Everard Earle, 1870–1951, vol. V
Welch, Rev. Adam Cleghorn, 1864–1943, vol. IV
Welch, Charles, 1848–1924, vol. II
Welch, Col Sir Cullum; see Welch, Col Sir G. J. C.
Welch, Sir David Nairne, 1820–1912, vol. I
Welch, Rev. Edward Ashurst, 1860–1932, vol. III
Welch, Surg.-Rear-Adm. Sir George, 1858–1947, vol. IV
Welch, Col Sir (George James) Cullum, 1st Bt, 1895–1980, vol. VII
Welch, Col George Osbaldeston, 1861–1935, vol. III
Welch, Sir Gordon; see Welch, Sir H. G. G.
Welch, Sir (Henry George) Gordon, 1890–1960, vol. V
Welch, Henry John, 1872–1958, vol. V
Welch, James, 1865–1917, vol. II

Welch, James William, 1900–1967, vol. VI
Welch, John Joseph, 1861–1950, vol. IV
Welch, Lucy Elizabeth K.; see Kemp-Welch.
Welch, Brig.-Gen. Malcolm Hammond Edward, 1872–1946, vol. IV
Welch, Margaret K.; see Kemp-Welch.
Welch, Brig.-Gen. Martin K.; see Kemp-Welch.
Welch, William Henry, 1850–1934, vol. III
Welch, William Tom, 1910–1979, vol. VII
Welchman, Col Edmund Walter St George, 1857–1933, vol. III
Welchman, Edward Theodore, 1881–1914, vol. I
Welchman, Ven. William, 1866–1954, vol. V
Weld, Brig. Charles Joseph, 1893–1962, vol. VI
Weld, Francis Joseph, 1873–1958, vol. V
Weld, Rt Rev. George, 1883–1959, vol. V
Weld, Harry Porter, 1877–1970, vol. VI (AII)
Weld, Herbert, died 1935, vol. III
Weld, Reginald Joseph, 1842–1923, vol. II
Weld, Rev. Walter Joseph, 1881–1969, vol. VI
Weld-Blundell, Charles Joseph, 1845–1927, vol. II
Weld-Forester, Hon. Charles Cecil Orlando; see Forester.
Weld-Forester, Major Hon. Edric Alfred Cecil; see Forester.
Weld-Forester, Lt-Comdr Wolstan Beaumont Charles, 1899–1961, vol. VI
Weldon, Col Sir Anthony Arthur, 6th Bt, 1863–1917, vol. II
Weldon, Sir Anthony Crosdill, 5th Bt, 1827–1900, vol. I
Weldon, Sir Anthony Edward Wolseley, 7th Bt, 1902–1971, vol. VII
Weldon, Lt-Col Ernest Steuart, 1877–1946, vol. IV
Weldon, Major Francis Harry, 1869–1920, vol. II
Weldon, George, 1908–1963, vol. VI
Weldon, Surg.-Rear-Adm. Gerald; see Weldon, Surg.-Rear-Adm. S. G.
Weldon, Surg.-Rear-Adm. (Samuel) Gerald, 1900–1958, vol. V
Weldon, Col Thomas, 1834–1905, vol. I
Weldon, Sir Thomas Brian, 8th Bt, 1905–1979, vol. VII
Weldon, Thomas Dewar, 1896–1958, vol. V
Weldon, Walter Frank Raphael, 1860–1906, vol. I
Weldon, Sir William Henry, 1837–1919, vol. II
Welford, Richard, 1836–1919, vol. II
Welland, Rt Rev. Thomas James, 1830–1907, vol. I
Wellborne, Lt-Col Cyril de Montfort, 1884–1965, vol. VI
Wellcome, Sir Henry, 1853–1936, vol. III
Welldon, Rt Rev. James Edward Cowell, 1854–1937, vol. III
Weller, Major Bernard George, 1881–1941, vol. IV
Weller, Bernard Williams, 1870–1943, vol. IV
Weller, Rt Rev. John Reginald, 1880–1969, vol. VI
Weller, Rt Rev. Reginald Heber, 1857–1935, vol. III
Weller-Poley, Thomas, 1850–1924, vol. II
Welles, Sumner, 1892–1961, vol. VI
Wellesley, Col Hon. Frederick Arthur, 1844–1931, vol. III
Wellesley, Lord George, 1889–1967, vol. VI

Wellesley, Sir George Greville, 1814–1901, vol. I
Wellesley, Lord Richard, 1879–1914, vol. I
Wellesley, Brig.-Gen. Richard Ashmore Colley, 1868–1939, vol. III
Wellesley, Sir Victor Alexander Augustus Henry, 1876–1954, vol. V
Wellesz, Egon Joseph, 1885–1974, vol. VII
Wellings, Milton, 1850–1929, vol. III
Wellington, 3rd Duke of, 1846–1900, vol. I
Wellington, 4th Duke of, 1849–1934, vol. III
Wellington, 5th Duke of, 1876–1941, vol. IV
Wellington, 6th Duke of, 1912–1943, vol. IV
Wellington, 7th Duke of, 1885–1972, vol. VII
Wellington, Arthur Robartes, 1877–1961, vol. VI
Wellington, Gilbert Trevor, 1882–1963, vol. VI
Wellington, Hubert Lindsay, 1879–1967, vol. VI
Wellington, Rt Rev. John, 1889–1976, vol. VII
Wellish, Edward Montague, 1882–1948, vol. IV
Wellock, Wilfred, 1879–1972, vol. VII
Wells, Arthur Collings, 1857–1922, vol. II
Wells, Arthur Quinton, 1896–1956, vol. V
Wells, Sir Arthur Spencer, 2nd Bt (cr 1883), 1866–1906, vol. I
Wells, Carveth; see Wells, G. C.
Wells, Charles, died 1917, vol. I
Wells, Charles, 1859–1932, vol. III
Wells, Cyril Mowbray, 1871–1963, vol. VI
Wells, Denys George, 1881–1973, vol. VII
Wells, Eugene, died 1925, vol. II
Wells, Frederick Arthur, 1901–1971, vol. VII
Wells, Sir Frederick Michael, 1st Bt (cr 1948), 1884–1966, vol. VI
Wells, Rt Rev. George Anderson, 1877–1964, vol. VI
Wells, Vice-Adm. Sir Gerard Aylmer, died 1943, vol. IV
Wells, (Grant) Carveth, died 1957, vol. V
Wells, Air Cdre Hardy Vesey, 1877–1956, vol. V
Wells, Lt-Gen. Sir Henry, 1898–1973, vol. VII
Wells, Henry Bensley, 1891–1967, vol. VI
Wells, Henry Tanworth, 1828–1903, vol. I
Wells, Sir Henry Weston, 1911–1971, vol. VII
Wells, Herbert George, 1866–1946, vol. IV
Wells, Rev. Herbert Methuen, 1862–1931, vol. III
Wells, Rev. James, 1838–1924, vol. II
Wells, Sister Janet; see King, Mrs George.
Wells, Brig.-Gen. John Bayford, 1881–1952, vol. V
Wells, John Sanderson S.; see Sanderson-Wells.
Wells, Captain John Stanhope Collings, 1880–1918, vol. II
Wells, Major John Stuart Kerr, 1873–1937, vol. III (A), vol. IV
Wells, Joseph, 1855–1929, vol. III
Wells, Rt Rev. Lemuel H., 1841–1936, vol. III
Wells, Captain Sir Lionel de Lautour, 1859–1929, vol. III
Wells, Adm. Sir Lionel Victor, 1884–1965, vol. VI
Wells, Madeline, died 1959, vol. V
Wells, Percy Lawrence, 1891–1964, vol. VI
Wells, Reginald F., 1877–1951, vol. V
Wells, Sir Richard; see Wells, Sir S. R.
Wells, Robert Douglas, 1875–1963, vol. VI
Wells, Sidney Herbert, 1865–1923, vol. II

Wells, Stanley Walter, 1887–1975, vol. VII
Wells, Sir Sydney R.; see Russell-Wells.
Wells, Sir (Sydney) Richard, 1st Bt (cr 1944), 1879–1956, vol. V
Wells, Thomas Bucklin, 1875–1944, vol. IV
Wells, Thomas Grantham, 1901–1943, vol. IV
Wells, Thomas Henry S.; see Sanderson-Wells.
Wells, Sir William Henry, 1871–1933, vol. III
Wells, William Page Atkinson, 1872–1923, vol. II
Wells-Cole, Lt-Col Henry, 1864–1914, vol. I
Wells-Durrant, Frederick Chester, 1864–1934, vol. III
Wellstood, Frederick Christian, 1884–1942, vol. IV
Wellwood, William, 1893–1971, vol. VII
Welman, Captain Arthur Eric Pole, 1893–1966, vol. VI
Welman, Maj.-Gen. William Henry Dowling Reeves, 1828–1906, vol. I
Welpton, William P., 1872–1939, vol. III
Welsford, Sir Robert Mills, 1861–1933, vol. III
Welsh, Hon. Sir Allan Ross, 1875–1957, vol. V
Welsh, David Arthur, died 1948, vol. IV
Welsh, Elizabeth, died 1921, vol. II
Welsh, James, 1881–1969, vol. VI
Welsh, James C., 1880–1954, vol. V
Welsh, John, 1887–1950, vol. IV
Welsh, John Aitken, 1871–1940, vol. III
Welsh, Rt Rev. John Francis, died 1916, vol. II
Welsh, Rev. Robert E., 1857–1935, vol. III
Welsh, Rev. Thomas, died 1920, vol. II (A), vol. III
Welsh, Air Marshal Sir William Lawrie, died 1962, vol. VI
Welsh, Brig. William Miles Moss O'Donnell, 1888–1965, vol. VI
Welsted, Col Reginald Hugh P.; see Penrose-Welsted.
Welton, James, 1854–1942, vol. IV
Welwood, John Allan Maconochie, died 1934, vol. III
Wemyss, 10th Earl of, and March, 6th Earl of, 1818–1914, vol. I
Wemyss, 11th Earl of, and March, 7th Earl of, 1857–1937, vol. III
Wemyss, Gen. Sir Colville; see Wemyss, Gen. Sir H. C. B.
Wemyss, Sir Francis C.; see Colchester-Wemyss.
Wemyss, Gen. Sir (Henry) Colville (Barclay), 1891–1959, vol. V
Wemyss, Maj.-Gen. Henry Manley, 1831–1915, vol. I (A)
Wemyss, Maynard Willoughby C.; see Colchester Wemyss.
Wemyss, Randolph Gordon Erskine, died 1908, vol. I
Wendell, Barrett, 1855–1921, vol. II
Wenden, Henry Charles Edward, died 1919, vol. II
Wendover, Viscount; Albert Edward Samuel Charles Robert Wynn-Carrington, 1895–1915, vol. I
Wendt, Henry Lorenz, 1858–1911, vol. I
Wenger, Adolph Henry Charles, 1877–1954, vol. V
Wenham, Edward Gordon, 1884–1956, vol. V
Wenham, Sir John Henry, 1891–1970, vol. VI
Wenley, Robert Mark, 1861–1929, vol. III

Wenlock, 3rd Baron, 1849–1912 (this entry was not transferred to Who was Who).

Wenlock, 4th Baron, 1856–1918, vol. II

Wenlock, 5th Baron, 1857–1931, vol. III

Wenlock, 6th Baron, 1860–1932, vol. III

Wenlock, Lady; (Annie), died 1944, vol. IV

Wensinck, Arent Jan, 1882–1939, vol. III (A), vol. IV

Went, Rev. James, 1845–1936, vol. III

Wentworth, Baroness (14th in line), 1871–1917, vol. II

Wentworth, Baroness (15th in line), 1837–1917, vol. II

Wentworth, Baroness (16th in line), died 1957, vol. V

Wentworth, Captain Bruce Canning V.; see Vernon-Wentworth.

Wentworth, Captain Frederick Charles Ulick V.; see Vernon-Wentworth.

Wentworth, Patricia; see Turnbull, Mrs George.

Wentworth-Fitzwilliam, George Charles; see Fitzwilliam.

Wentworth-Fitzwilliam, Captain Hon. Sir (William) Charles; see Fitzwilliam.

Wentworth-Fitzwilliam, Hon. William Henry; see Fitzwilliam.

Wentworth-Sheilds, Francis Ernest, 1869–1959, vol. V

Wentworth-Sheilds, Rt Rev. Wentworth Francis, 1867–1944, vol. IV

Wentworth-Stanley, Charles Sidney Bowen, 1892–1960, vol. V

Wenyon, Charles Morley, died 1948, vol. IV

Wenyon, Herbert John, 1888–1944, vol. IV

Were, Cecil Allan Walter, 1889–1977, vol. VII

Were, Rt Rev. Edward Ash, 1846–1915, vol. I

Were, Major Harry Harris, 1865–1925, vol. II

Werfel, Franz, 1890–1945, vol. IV

Werner, Alfred, 1866–1919, vol. II

Werner, Alice, 1859–1935, vol. III

Werner, E. A., died 1951, vol. V

Werner, Edward Theodore Chalmers, 1864–1954, vol. V

Werner, Louis, died 1936, vol. III

Wernher, Sir Derrick Julius, 2nd Bt, 1889–1948, vol. IV

Wernher, Hon. Maj.-Gen. Sir Harold Augustus, 3rd Bt, 1893–1973, vol. VII

Wernher, Sir Julius Charles, 1st Bt, 1850–1912, vol. I

Wertenbaker, Thomas Jefferson, 1879–1966, vol. VI

Werth, Albertus Johannes, 1888–1948, vol. IV

Werth, Alexander, 1901–1969, vol. VI

Wertheimer, Julius, died 1924, vol. II

Wesbrook, F. F., 1868–1918, vol. II

Wesselitsky, Gabriel de, 1841–1930, vol. III

Wessels, Hon. Sir Cornelius Hermanus, 1851–1924, vol. II

Wessels, Rt Hon. Sir Johannes Wilhelmus, 1862–1936, vol. III

West, Brig. Alexander Henry Delap, 1877–1959, vol. V

West, Alfred Slater, 1846–1932, vol. III

West, Rt Hon. Sir Algernon, 1832–1921, vol. II

West, Andrew F., 1853–1943, vol. IV

West, Rev. Arthur George Bainbridge, 1864–1952, vol. V

West, Cecil McLaren, 1893–1951, vol. V

West, Charles Ernest, died 1951, vol. V

West, Charles Henry, 1859–1923, vol. II

West, Christopher, 1915–1967, vol. VI

West, Maj.-Gen. Clement Arthur, 1892–1972, vol. VII

West, David, died 1936, vol. III

West, Rev. Edward Courtenay, 1872–1938, vol. III

West, Fielding Reginald, 1892–1935, vol. III

West, Sir Frederick John, 1897–1971, vol. VII

West, Sir Frederick Joseph, died 1959, vol. V

West, Rt Rev. George Algernon, 1893–1980, vol. VII

West, Major George F. M. C.; see Cornwallis-West.

West, George Stephen, 1876–1919, vol. II

West, Gladys; see Young, G.

West, Sir Glynn Hamilton, 1877–1945, vol. IV

West, Sir Harold Ernest Georges, 1895–1968, vol. VI

West, Sir James Grey, 1885–1951, vol. V

West, John Henry Rickard, 1846–1920, vol. II

West, Col John Milns, 1897–1973, vol. VII

West, Maj.-Gen. John Weir, 1875–1949, vol. IV

West, Joseph Walter, died 1933, vol. III

West, Sir Leonard Henry, 1864–1950, vol. IV

West, Leonard R., 1859–1910, vol. I

West, Gen. Sir Michael Montgomerie Alston Roberts, 1905–1978, vol. VII

West, Ralph Winton, 1895–1968, vol. VI

West, Sir Raymond, 1832–1911, vol. I

West, Samuel, 1848–1920, vol. II

West, Stewart Ellis Lawrence, 1890–1968, vol. VI

West, Hon. V. S.; see Sackville-West.

West, Sir Walter Wooll, 1861–1952, vol. V

West, William Cornwallis Cornwallis-, 1835–1917, vol. II

West, William Frederick, 1882–1954, vol. V

West-Watson, Most Rev. Campbell West, 1877–1953, vol. V

Westall, Bernard Clement, 1893–1970, vol. VI

Westall, William, 1834–1903, vol. I

Westaway, Katharine Mary, 1893–1973, vol. VII

Westbrook, Bernard Anson, 1884–1969, vol. VI

Westbrook, Trevor Cresswell Lawrence, 1901–1978, vol. VII

Westbury, 3rd Baron, 1852–1930, vol. III

Westbury, 4th Baron, 1914–1961, vol. VI

Westbury, Lt-Col Frederic Newell, 1877–1946, vol. IV

Westcar, Lt-Col Sir William Villiers Leonard P.; see Prescott-Westcar.

Westcott, Rt Rev. Brooke Foss, 1825–1901, vol. I

Westcott, Rt Rev. Foss, 1863–1949, vol. IV

Westcott, Ven. Frederick Brooke, 1857–1918, vol. II

Westcott, Rt Rev. George Herbert, died 1916, vol. II

Westcott, J. B., died 1907, vol. I

Westcott, Col Sinclair, 1859–1923, vol. II
Westcott, William Wynn, 1848–1925, vol. II
Westell, William Percival, 1874–1943, vol. IV
Wester Wemyss, 1st Baron, 1864–1933, vol. III
Westerman, Percy F., 1876–1959, vol. V
Westermann, Diedrich H., 1875–1956, vol. V
Westermarck, Edward Alexander, 1862–1939, vol. III
Western, Lt-Col Bertram Charles Maximilian, 1886–1942, vol. IV
Western, Col Charles Maximilian, died 1915, vol. I (A)
Western, Rt Rev. Frederick James, 1880–1951, vol. V
Western, George Trench, 1877–1948, vol. IV
Western, Lt-Col James Halifax, 1842–1917, vol. II
Western, Col John Sutton Edward, died 1931, vol. III
Western, Sir Thomas Charles Callis, 3rd Bt, 1850–1917, vol. II
Western, Maj.-Gen. Sir William George Balfour, 1861–1936, vol. III
Westhoven, Joseph Charles, 1876–1957, vol. V
Westinghouse, George, 1846–1914, vol. I
Westlake, Alan Robert Cecil, 1894–1978, vol. VII
Westlake, Col Almond Paul, 1858–1927, vol. II
Westlake, Sir Charles Redvers, 1900–1972, vol. VII
Westlake, Rev. Herbert Francis, 1879–1925, vol. II
Westlake, John, 1828–1913, vol. I
Westlake, Nathaniel Hubert John, 1833–1921, vol. II
Westland, Sir James, 1842–1903, vol. I
Westley, Lt-Col Joseph Harold Stops, 1882–1959, vol. V
Westmacott, Brig.-Gen. Claude Berners, 1865–1948, vol. IV
Westmacott, Frederic Hibbert, 1867–1935, vol. III
Westmacott, Percy Graham Buchanan, 1830–1917, vol. II
Westmacott, Maj.-Gen. Sir Richard, 1841–1925, vol. II
Westmacott, Rev. Walter, 1853–1939, vol. III
Westmeath, 11th Earl of, 1870–1933, vol. III
Westmeath, 12th Earl of, 1880–1971, vol. VI
Westminster, 1st Duke of, 1825–1899, vol. I
Westminster, 2nd Duke of, 1879–1953, vol. V
Westminster, 3rd Duke of, 1894–1963, vol. VI
Westminster, 4th Duke of, 1907–1967, vol. VI
Westminster, 5th Duke of, 1910–1979, vol. VII
Westmorland, 13th Earl of, 1859–1922, vol. II
Westmorland, 14th Earl of, 1893–1948, vol. IV
Westmorland, Brig.-Gen. Charles Henry, 1856–1916, vol. II
Westmorland, Lt-Col Percy Thuillier, 1863–1929, vol. III
Weston, Dame Agnes, 1840–1918, vol. II
Weston, Rev. Arthur Ernest, 1890–1971, vol. VII
Weston, Captain Arthur Fullam, 1879–1962, vol. VI
Weston, Sir Arthur Reginald Astley, 1892–1969, vol. VI
Weston, Lt-Gen. Sir Aylmer H.; see Hunter-Weston.
Weston, Col Claude Horace, 1879–1946, vol. IV

Weston, Sir Eric, 1892–1976, vol. VII
Weston, Lt-Gen. Eric Culpeper, 1888–1950, vol. IV
Weston, Lt-Col Ernest Arthur, 1880–1940, vol. III
Weston, Rt Rev. Frank, 1871–1924, vol. II
Weston, Garfield; see Weston, W. G.
Weston, George, 1878–1956, vol. V
Weston, Maj.-Gen. Gerald Patrick Linton, 1910–1977, vol. VII
Weston, Lt-Col Gould H.; see Hunter-Weston.
Weston, Jessie Laidlay, died 1928, vol. II
Weston, Air Vice-Marshal Sir John Gerard Willsley, 1908–1979, vol. VII
Weston, Hon. Brig. John Leslie, 1882–1963, vol. VI
Weston, Sir John Wakefield, 1st Bt, 1852–1926, vol. II
Weston, Kenneth Southwold, 1899–1971, vol. VII
Weston, Laurence, 1909–1972, vol. VII
Weston, Lt-Col Reginald Salter, 1867–1944, vol. IV
Weston, Brig.-Gen. Spencer Vaughan Percy, 1883–1973, vol. VII
Weston, Rev. Walter, 1861–1940, vol. III
Weston, (Willard) Garfield, 1898–1978, vol. VII
Weston, William Guy, 1907–1980, vol. VII
Weston-Stevens, Sir Joseph, 1861–1917, vol. II
Westphal, Bishop Augustus, 1864–1939, vol. III (A), vol. IV
Westrop, Brig. Sidney Albert, 1895–1979, vol. VII
Westropp, Col George O'C.; see O'Callaghan-Westropp.
Westropp, Col George Ralph Collier, 1859–1934, vol. III
Westropp, Col John M.; see Massy-Westropp.
Westropp, Maj.-Gen. Roberts Michael, 1824–1910, vol. I
Westropp, Maj.-Gen. Victor John Eric, 1897–1974, vol. VII
Westrup, Sir Jack Allan, 1904–1975, vol. VII
Westwood, 1st Baron, 1880–1953, vol. V
Westwood, Earle Cathers, 1909–1980, vol. VII (A)
Westwood, John David, 1881–1964, vol. VI
Westwood, Rt Hon. Joseph, 1884–1948, vol. IV
Wetherall, Lt-Gen. Sir Edward; see Wetherall, Lt-Gen. Sir H. E. de R.
Wetherall, Lt-Gen. Sir (Harry) Edward de Robillard, 1889–1979, vol. VII
Wetherall, Col William Alexander, 1847–1935, vol. III
Wetherbee, George, 1851–1920, vol. II
Wethered, Ernest Handel Cossham, 1878–1975, vol. VII
Wethered, Lt-Col Francis Owen, 1864–1922, vol. II
Wethered, Frank Joseph, 1860–1928, vol. II
Wethered, Brig. Herbert Lawrence, 1877–1953, vol. V
Wethered, Col Joseph Robert, 1873–1942, vol. IV
Wethered, Thomas Owen, 1832–1921, vol. II
Wethered, Vernon, 1865–1952, vol. V
Wetherell, Col Robert May, 1874–1960, vol. V
Wetherill, Henry Buswell, 1876–1959, vol. V
Wethey, Captain Edwin Howard, 1887–1963, vol. VI
Wetmore, Hon. Edward Ludlow, 1841–1922, vol. II

Wetton, Henry Davan, 1862–1928, vol. II
Weygand, Général Maxime, 1867–1965, vol. VI
Weyler y Nicolau, Valeriano, 1838–1930, vol. III
Weyman, Stanley John, 1855–1928, vol. II
Weymouth, Viscount; John Alexander Thynne, 1895–1916, vol. II
Whaite, Col Thomas du Bédat, 1862–1943, vol. IV
Whale, George, 1849–1925, vol. II
Whale, George Harold Lawson, 1876–1943, vol. IV
Whale, Philip Barrett, 1898–1950, vol. IV
Whale, Winifred Stephens, died 1944, vol. IV
Whalley, Frank Douglas, 1877–1932, vol. III
Whalley, Philip Guy Rothay, 1901–1950, vol. IV
Whalley, Major Richard Cyril Rae, 1896–1944, vol. IV
Wharhirst, Sir Robert William, 1885–1949, vol. IV
Wharncliffe, 1st Earl of, 1827–1899, vol. I
Wharncliffe, 2nd Earl of, 1856–1926, vol. II
Wharncliffe, 3rd Earl of, 1892–1953, vol. V
Wharry, Harry Mortimer, 1891–1933, vol. III
Wharton, 8th Baron, 1876–1934, vol. III
Wharton, 9th Baron, 1908–1969, vol. VI
Wharton, Baroness (10th in line), 1906–1974, vol. VII
Wharton, Anthony, 1877–1943, vol. IV
Wharton, Sir Anthony; see Wharton, Sir G. A.
Wharton, Rev. Edgar, died 1936, vol. III
Wharton, Edith, 1862–1937, vol. III
Wharton, Sir (George) Anthony, 1917–1980, vol. VII
Wharton, Rt Hon. John Lloyd, 1837–1912, vol. I
Wharton, William Henry Anthony, 1859–1938, vol. III
Wharton-Duff, John Wharton; see Duff.
Whately, Ven. Herbert Edward, 1876–1947, vol. IV
Whately, William, died 1937, vol. III
Whates, Harry Richard, died 1923, vol. II
Whatham, Rev. William Laurence T., 1866–1938, vol. III
Whatley, Norman, 1884–1965, vol. VI
Whatman, George Dunbar, 1846–1923, vol. II
Whatman, Col William Douglas, 1860–1929, vol. III
Whatmough, Joshua, 1897–1964, vol. VI
Whayman, Engr Rear-Adm. William Matthias, 1871–1955, vol. V
Wheare, Sir Kenneth Clinton, 1907–1979, vol. VII
Wheatcroft, Rev. Frank Elam, died 1930, vol. III
Wheatcroft, Harry, 1898–1977, vol. VII
Wheatley, Major Cyril Moreton, 1870–1942, vol. IV
Wheatley, Dennis Yates, 1897–1977, vol. VII
Wheatley, Edith Grace, died 1970, vol. VI
Wheatley, Frederick William, 1871–1955, vol. V
Wheatley, Henry Benjamin, died 1917, vol. II
Wheatley, Col Henry Spencer, 1851–1932, vol. III
Wheatley, Rt Hon. John, 1869–1930, vol. III
Wheatley, John, 1892–1955, vol. V
Wheatley, Joseph Larke, 1846–1932, vol. III
Wheatley, Brig.-Gen. Leonard Lane, 1876–1954, vol. V
Wheatley, Major Sir Mervyn James, 1880–1974, vol. VII

Wheatley, Maj.-Gen. Mervyn Savile, 1900–1979, vol. VII
Wheatley, Col Moreton John, 1837–1916, vol. II
Wheatley, Brig.-Gen. Philip, 1871–1935, vol. III
Wheatley, Robert Albert, 1873–1954, vol. V
Wheatley, Major William Prescott Ross, 1878–1925, vol. II
Wheatley, Sir Zachariah, 1865–1950, vol. IV
Wheeldon, Edward Christian, 1907–1980, vol. VII
Wheeldon, William Edwin, 1898–1960, vol. V
Wheeler, Rev. Alfred, died 1949, vol. IV
Wheeler, Sir Arthur, 1st Bt, 1860–1943, vol. IV
Wheeler, Sir Arthur F. P., 2nd Bt, 1900–1964, vol. VI
Wheeler, Arthur H., died 1935, vol. III
Wheeler, Rear-Adm. Aubrey John, 1894–1970, vol. VI
Wheeler, Burton Kendall, 1882–1975, vol. VII
Wheeler, Sir Charles Reginald, 1904–1975, vol. VII
Wheeler, Sir Charles Thomas, 1892–1974, vol. VII
Wheeler, Denis Edward, 1910–1977, vol. VII
Wheeler, Brig. Sir (Edward) Oliver, 1890–1962, vol. VI
Wheeler, Edwin Paul, 1874–1944, vol. IV
Wheeler, Sir Henry, 1870–1950, vol. IV
Wheeler, Major Henry Littelton, 1868–1924, vol. II
Wheeler, Rev. Hugh Trever, 1874–1949, vol. IV
Wheeler, Gen. Joseph, 1836–1906, vol. I
Wheeler, Sir Mortimer; see Wheeler, Sir R. E. M.
Wheeler, Dame Olive Annie, died 1963, vol. VI
Wheeler, Brig. Sir Oliver; see Wheeler, Brig. Sir E. O.
Wheeler, Brig. Ralph Pung, 1898–1977, vol. VII
Wheeler, Richard Vernon, 1883–1939, vol. III
Wheeler, Sir (Robert Eric) Mortimer, 1890–1976, vol. VII
Wheeler, Rev. Thomas Littleton, 1834–1910, vol. I
Wheeler, Thomas Sherlock, 1899–1962, vol. VI
Wheeler, Thomas Whittenbury, died 1923, vol. II
Wheeler, William, died 1926, vol. II
Wheeler, Sir William Ireland de Courcy, 1879–1943, vol. IV
Wheeler-Bennett, John Wheeler, died 1926, vol. II
Wheeler-Bennett, Sir John Wheeler, 1902–1975, vol. VII
Wheeler-Cuffe, Sir Charles Frederick Denny; see Cuffe.
Wheeler-Cuffe, Sir Otway Fortescue Luke; see Cuffe.
Wheelock, Frank E., 1877–1941, vol. IV
Wheelwright, Charles Apthorpe, 1873–1954, vol. V
Wheelwright, Rowland, 1870–1955, vol. V
Whelan, Leo, 1892–1956, vol. V
Wheldon, Robert William, 1893–1954, vol. V
Wheldon, Sir Wynn Powell, died 1961, vol. VI
Wheler, Sir Edward, 12th Bt (cr 1660), 1857–1903, vol. I
Wheler, Sir Granville Charles Hastings, 1st Bt (cr 1925), 1872–1927, vol. II
Wheler, Sir Trevor, 11th Bt (cr 1660), 1828–1900, vol. I
Whelpton, Rev. Henry Urling, 1860–1935, vol. III
Wherry, George Edward, 1852–1928, vol. II

Whetham, Rear-Adm. Edye Kington B.; *see* Boddam-Whetham.

Whetham, Major Sydney A. B.; *see* Boddam-Whetham.

Whettnall, Baron Edward Charles Stephen, 1840–1903, vol. I

Whetton, John Thomas, 1894–1979, vol. VII

Whewell, Herbert, 1863–1951, vol. V

Whibley, Charles, 1859–1930, vol. III

Whibley, Leonard, 1863–1941, vol. IV

Whichcote, Sir George, 9th Bt, 1870–1946, vol. IV

Whichcote, Sir Hugh Christopher, 10th Bt, 1874–1949, vol. IV

Whidden, Howard Primrose, 1871–1952, vol. V

Whiddington, Richard, 1885–1970, vol. VI

Whigham, Gen. Sir Robert Dundas, 1865–1950, vol. IV

Whigham, Walter Kennedy, 1878–1948, vol. IV

Whillis, James, 1900–1955, vol. V

Whinney, Sir Arthur, 1865–1927, vol. II

Whinney, Margaret Dickens, 1897–1975, vol. VII

Whipham, Thomas Rowland Charles, 1871–1945, vol. IV

Whipham, Thomas Tillyer, *died* 1917, vol. II

Whipple, Dorothy, *died* 1966, vol. VI

Whipple, Francis John Welsh, 1876–1943, vol. IV

Whipple, George Hoyt, 1878–1976, vol. VII

Whipple, Rt Rev. Henry Benjamin, 1823–1901, vol. I

Whipple, Robert Stewart, 1871–1953, vol. V

Whishaw, Sir Ralph, 1895–1976, vol. VII

Whiskard, Sir Geoffrey Granville, 1886–1957, vol. V

Whistler, Rev. Charles Watts, 1856–1913, vol. I

Whistler, Group Captain Harold Alfred, 1896–1940, vol. III

Whistler, James M'Neill, *died* 1903, vol. I

Whistler, Gen. Sir Lashmer Gordon, 1898–1963, vol. VI

Whitaker, Col Sir Albert Edward, 1st Bt, 1860–1945, vol. IV

Whitaker, Sir Arthur; *see* Whitaker, Sir F. A.

Whitaker, Sir Cuthbert Wilfrid, 1873–1950, vol. IV

Whitaker, Edgar, *died* 1903, vol. I

Whitaker, Enid Rosamond, (Mrs G. C. F. Whitaker); *see* Love, E. R.

Whitaker, Ernest Gillett, 1903–1975, vol. VII

Whitaker, Frank, *died* 1962, vol. VI

Whitaker, Sir (Frederick) Arthur, 1893–1968, vol. VI

Whitaker, Major George Cecil, 1880–1959, vol. V

Whitaker, George Herbert, 1862–1933, vol. III

Whitaker, James, 1863–1946, vol. IV

Whitaker, Sir James Smith, 1866–1936, vol. III

Whitaker, Maj.-Gen. Sir John Albert Charles, 2nd Bt, 1897–1957, vol. V

Whitaker, William, 1836–1925, vol. II

Whitaker, William Ingham, 1866–1936, vol. III

Whitamore, Charles Eric, 1890–1965, vol. VI

Whitbread, Francis Pelham, 1867–1941, vol. IV

Whitbread, Col Sir Howard, 1836–1908, vol. I

Whitbread, Samuel, 1830–1915, vol. I (A)

Whitbread, Samuel Howard, 1858–1944, vol. IV

Whitburgh, 1st Baron, 1874–1967, vol. VI

Whitby, Anthony Charles, 1929–1975, vol. VII

Whitby, Beatrice Janie, *died* 1931, vol. III

Whitby, Sir Bernard James, 1892–1973, vol. VII

Whitby, G. Stafford, 1887–1972, vol. VII

Whitby, Sir Lionel Ernest Howard, 1895–1956, vol. V

Whitby, Rev. Thomas, 1835–1918, vol. II

Whitby-Smith, Henry, 1858–1934, vol. III

Whitchurch, Major Harry Frederick, 1866–1907, vol. I

Whitcombe, Rt Rev. Robert Henry, 1862–1922, vol. II

White, Adam Seaton, *died* 1950, vol. IV

White, Hon. Albert Scott, 1855–1931, vol. III

White, Alexander Hay, 1898–1975, vol. VII

White, Sir (Alfred Edward) Rowden, 1876–1963, vol. VI

White, Alfred George Hastings, 1859–1945, vol. IV

White, Andrew Dickson, 1832–1918, vol. II

White, Anne Margaret Wilson, 1916–1976, vol. VII

White, Antonia, 1899–1980, vol. VII

White, Sir Archibald Woollaston, 4th Bt (*cr* 1802), 1877–1945, vol. IV

White, Col Archie Cecil Thomas, 1891–1971, vol. VII

White, Arnold, 1848–1925, vol. II

White, Sir Arnold; *see* White, Sir C. A.

White, Ven. Arthur, 1880–1961, vol. VI

White, Lt-Col Arthur Denham, 1879–1950, vol. IV

White, Arthur Silva, 1859–1932, vol. III

White, Maj.-Gen. Arthur Thomas, 1860–1947, vol. IV

White, Aubrey, *died* 1915, vol. II

White, Sir Bernard Kerr, 1888–1964, vol. VI

White, Gen. Sir Brudenell; *see* White, Gen. Sir C. B. B.

White, Sir (Charles) Arnold, 1858–1931, vol. III

White, Charles Francis, 1890–1966, vol. VI

White, Charles Frederick, 1863–1923, vol. II

White, Charles Frederick, 1891–1956, vol. V

White, Major Hon. Charles James, 1860–1930, vol. III

White, Major Charles James B.; *see* Brooman-White.

White, Charles Percival, *died* 1928, vol. II

White, Charles Powell, 1867–1930, vol. III

White, Claude G.; *see* Graham-White.

White, Clifford, 1881–1957, vol. V

White, Gen. Sir (Cyril) Brudenell (Bingham), 1876–1940, vol. III

White, Cyril Grove C.; *see* Costley-White.

White, Cyril Montgomery, 1897–1980, vol. VII

White, Lt-Col David Archibald P.; *see* Price-White.

White, Dudley, 1873–1930, vol. III

White, Sir Edward, 1847–1914, vol. I

White, Edward, *died* 1952, vol. V

White, Brig.-Gen. Edward Dalrymple, 1865–1929, vol. III

White, (Elizabeth) Evelyne (McIntosh), *died* 1972, vol. VII

White, Sir Eric Henry W.; *see* Wyndham White.

White, Very Rev. Eric M.; *see* Milner-White.

White, Sir (Eric) Richard Meadows, 2nd Bt (cr 1937), 1910–1972, vol. VII
White, Brig. Eric Stuart, 1888–1979, vol. VII
White, Sir Ernest, 1867–1949, vol. IV
White, Lt-Col Ernest William, 1851–1935, vol. III
White, Ethelbert, 1891–1972, vol. VII
White, Evelyne; see White, Elizabeth E. M.
White, Col Frank Augustin Kinder, 1873–1948, vol. IV
White, Frank Faulder, 1861–1939, vol. III
White, Lt-Col Frederick, 1847–1918, vol. II
White, Col Frederick, 1861–1924, vol. II
White, Major Frederick Alexander, 1872–1919, vol. II
White, Frederick Meadows, 1829–1898, vol. I
White, Major Frederick Norman, 1877–1964, vol. VI
White, Geoffrey Charles, 1912–1961, vol. VI
White, Geoffrey Henllan, 1873–1969, vol. VI
White, Maj.-Gen. Geoffrey Herbert Anthony, 1870–1959, vol. V
White, Sir George, 1840–1912, vol. I
White, Sir George, 1st Bt (cr 1904), 1854–1916, vol. II
White, Brig.-Gen. George Francis, died 1938, vol. III
White, Brig. George Frederick Charles, 1882–1953, vol. V
White, George Gilbert, 1857–1916, vol. II
White, Air Vice-Marshal George Holford, 1904–1965, vol. VI
White, George Rivers Blanco, 1883–1966, vol. VI
White, Sir (George) Stanley, 2nd Bt (cr 1904), 1882–1964, vol. VI
White, Field-Marshal Sir George Stuart, 1835–1912, vol. I
White, Col Hon. Gerald Verner, 1879–1948, vol. IV
White, Rt Rev. Gilbert, 1859–1933, vol. III
White, Gleeson, 1851–1898, vol. I
White, Lt-Col Sir Godfrey Dalrymple D.; see Dalrymple-White.
White, Ven. Graham, born 1884, vol. IV
White, Rt Hon. Graham; see White, Rt Hon. H. G.
White, Very Rev. Harold C.; see Costley-White.
White, Lt-Col Harold Fletcher, 1883–1971, vol. VII
White, Rt Rev. Harry Vere, 1853–1941, vol. IV
White, Sir Headley Dymoke, 3rd Bt (cr 1922), 1914–1971, vol. VII
White, Henrietta Margaret, died 1936, vol. III
White, Henry, 1850–1927, vol. II
White, Henry, 1890–1964, vol. VI
White, Sir Henry Arthur, 1849–1922, vol. II
White, Henry Bantry, died 1929, vol. III
White, Surg. Rear-Adm. Sir Henry Ellis Yeo, 1888–1976, vol. VII
White, Hon. Henry Frederic, 1859–1903, vol. I
White, Maj.-Gen. Henry George, 1835–1906, vol. I
White, Rt Hon. (Henry) Graham, died 1965, vol. VI
White, Lt-Col Henry Herbert Ronald, 1879–1939, vol. III
White, Henry James, 1898–1961, vol. VI

White, Very Rev. Henry Julian, 1859–1934, vol. III
White, Sir Henry M.; see Milner-White.
White, Herbert Arthur, 1876–1958, vol. V
White, Sir Herbert Edward, 1855–1947, vol. IV
White, Herbert Martyn Oliver, 1885–1963, vol. VI
White, Maj.-Gen. Herbert Southey Neville, 1862–1938, vol. III
White, Sir Herbert Thirkell, 1855–1931, vol. III
White, Horace, 1834–1916, vol. II
White, Horace Powell W.; see Winsbury-White.
White, Hugh Fortescue Moresby, 1891–1979, vol. VII
White, James, 1878–1927, vol. II
White, James, 1863–1928, vol. II
White, James Charles Napoleon, died 1923, vol. II
White, James Cobb, 1855–1927, vol. II
White, J(ames) Dundas, 1866–1951, vol. V
White, Col James G.; see Grove-White.
White, James Martin, 1857–1928, vol. II
White, James William, 1850–1916, vol. II
White, Jessie, 1865–1958, vol. V
White, John, 1839–1912, vol. I
White, Hon. John, 1852–1922, vol. II
White, John, 1851–1933, vol. III (A), vol. IV
White, Instr Captain John, 1870–1934, vol. III
White, Rt Rev. John, 1867–1951, vol. V
White, John B.; see Bazley-White.
White, John Bell, 1857–1934, vol. III
White, Maj.-Gen. John Burton, 1874–1945, vol. IV
White, John Claude, died 1918, vol. II
White, Lt-Col John Henry, 1868–1942, vol. IV
White, Maj.-Gen. John Hubbard, 1834–1910, vol. I
White, John W., died 1919, vol. II
White, John Williams, 1849–1917, vol. II
White, Joseph Henry Lachlan, 1859–1940, vol. III
White, Lt-Col Joshua Chaytor, 1864–1924, vol. II
White, Kenneth James Macarthur, 1894–1969, vol. VI
White, Leslie Gordon, 1889–1979, vol. VII
White, Sir Luke, 1845–1920, vol. II
White, Margaret B.; see Bourke-White.
White, Maude Valérie, 1855–1937, vol. III
White, Lt-Gen. Sir Maurice Fitzgibbon G.; see Grove-White.
White, Montagu, died 1916, vol. II
White, Rev. Newport John Davis, 1860–1936, vol. III
White, Norman Lewis, died 1978, vol. VII
White, Lt-Col Oliver Woodhouse, 1884–1940, vol. III
White, Oswald, 1884–1970, vol. VI
White, P. Bruce, died 1949, vol. IV
White, Paul Dudley, 1886–1973, vol. VII
White, Percy, 1852–1938, vol. III
White, Maj.-Gen. Percy C.; see Carr-White.
White, Philip Jacob, died 1929, vol. III
White, Col Reginald Strelley Moresby, 1893–1947, vol. IV
White, Sir Richard, died 1925, vol. II
White, Sir Richard; see White, Sir E. R. M.
White, Richard Charles B.; see Brooman-White.
White, Adm. Richard Dunning, 1813–1899, vol. I

White, Col Richard Stephen Murray, 1876–1942, vol. IV

White, Vice-Adm. Richard William, 1849–1924, vol. II

White, Sir Robert, 1827–1902, vol. I

White, Brig.-Gen. Hon. Robert, 1861–1936, vol. III

White, Robert, 1872–1959, vol. V

White, Sir Robert Eaton, 1st Bt (cr 1937), 1864–1940, vol. III

White, Robert George, 1885–1976, vol. VII

White, Lt-Col Robert L.; see Lynch-White.

White, Robert Prosser, 1855–1934, vol. III

White, Robert S.; see Standish-White.

White, Sir Rowden; see White, Sir A. E. R.

White, Sir Rudolph Dymoke, 2nd Bt (cr 1922), 1888–1968, vol. VI

White, Rt Rev. Russell Berridge, 1896–1978, vol. VII

White, Captain Samuel Albert, 1870–1954, vol. V

White, Lt-Col Samuel Robert Llewellyn, 1863–1925, vol. II

White, Sinclair, 1858–1920, vol. II

White, Stanford, 1853–1906, vol. I

White, Sir Stanley; see White, Sir G. S.

White, Stuart Arthur Frank, died 1951, vol. V

White, Sir Sydney Arthur, 1884–1958, vol. V

White, T. Charters, 1828–1916, vol. II

White, Terence Hanbury, 1906–1964, vol. VI

White, Sir Thomas, died 1938, vol. III

White, Rt Hon. Sir Thomas; see White, Rt Hon. Sir W. T.

White, Group Captain Hon. Sir Thomas Walter, 1888–1957, vol. V

White, Sir Thomas Woollaston, 3rd Bt (cr 1802), 1828–1907, vol. I

White, Wilbert Webster, 1863–1944, vol. IV

White, Brig.-Gen. Wilfred Arthur, 1870–1935, vol. III

White, William, died 1912, vol. I

White, Rt Rev. William Charles, 1865–1943, vol. IV

White, Rt Rev. William Charles, 1873–1960, vol. V

White, Sir William H.; see Hale-White.

White, William Hale, 1831–1913, vol. I

White, William Harry, died 1914, vol. I

White, Sir William Henry, 1845–1913, vol. I

White, Col William Lambert, 1849–1929, vol. III

White, Brig.-Gen. William Lewis, 1856–1931, vol. III

White, William Lindsay, 1900–1973, vol. VII

White, Brig. William Nicholas, 1879–1951, vol. V

White, William Rogerson, 1850–1913, vol. I

White, Rt Hon. Sir (William) Thomas, 1866–1955, vol. V

White, Col William Westropp, 1862–1927, vol. II

White, Rev. Wilson Woodhouse, 1864–1941, vol. IV

White, Sir Woolmer Rudolph Donati, 1st Bt (cr 1922), 1858–1931, vol. III

White-Jervis, Sir Henry Felix Jervis; see Jervis.

White-Jervis, Col Sir John Henry Jervis; see Jervis.

White-Smith, Sir Henry, 1878–1943, vol. IV

White-Thomson, Col Sir Hugh Davie, 1866–1922, vol. II

White-Thomson, Rt Rev. Leonard Jauncey, 1863–1933, vol. III

White-Thomson, Col Sir Robert Thomas, 1831–1918, vol. II

White-Winton, Meryon, died 1921, vol. II

Whiteaves, Joseph Frederick, 1835–1909, vol. I

Whitchurch, Rev. Victor Lorenzo, 1868–1933, vol. III

Whitefoord, Rev. Canon B., 1848–1911, vol. I

Whitefoord, Maj.-Gen. Philip Geoffrey, 1894–1975, vol. VII

Whitehead, Alfred North, 1861–1947, vol. IV

Whitehead, Arnold Sydney, 1895–1966, vol. VI

Whitehead, Arthur Longley, died 1930, vol. III

Whitehead, Sir Charles, 1834–1912, vol. I

Whitehead, Rt Rev. Cortlandt, 1842–1922, vol. II

Whitehead, Sir Edgar Cuthbert Fremantle, 1905–1971, vol. VII

Whitehead, Comdr Edward, 1908–1978, vol. VII

Whitehead, Vice-Adm. Frederic Aubrey, 1874–1958, vol. V

Whitehead, Frederick, died 1938, vol. III

Whitehead, Sir George Hugh, 2nd Bt, 1861–1931, vol. III

Whitehead, Maj.-Gen. Sir Hayward Reader, 1855–1925, vol. II

Whitehead, Henry, 1842–1921, vol. II

Whitehead, Sir Henry, 1859–1928, vol. II

Whitehead, Rt Rev. Henry, 1853–1947, vol. IV

Whitehead, Sir James, 1st Bt, 1834–1917, vol. II

Whitehead, James, died 1936, vol. III

Whitehead, Brig. James, 1880–1955, vol. V

Whitehead, Sir James Beethom, 1858–1928, vol. II

Whitehead, John Henry Constantine, 1904–1960, vol. V

Whitehead, Col John Herbert, 1869–1928, vol. II

Whitehead, Major Sir Philip Henry Rathbone, 4th Bt, 1897–1953, vol. V

Whitehead, Maj.-Gen. Robert Children, 1833–1905, vol. I

Whitehead, Sir Rowland Edward, 3rd Bt, 1863–1942, vol. IV

Whitehead, Rev. Silvester, 1841–1917, vol. II

Whitehead, Spencer, 1845–1922, vol. II

Whitehead, Thomas Alec, 1886–1959, vol. V

Whitehead, Thomas Henderson, 1851–1933, vol. III

Whitehead, Lt-Col Wilfred James, 1873–1934, vol. III

Whitehill, Clarence Eugene, 1871–1932, vol. III

Whitehorn, Joseph Hammond, 1861–1935, vol. III

Whitehorn, Rev. Roy Drummond, 1891–1976, vol. VII

Whitehorne, James Charles, died 1905, vol. I

Whitehouse, Arthur Wildman, 1865–1944, vol. IV

Whitehouse, Sir George, 1857–1938, vol. III

Whitehouse, Sir Harold Beckwith, 1882–1943, vol. IV

Whitehouse, John Howard, 1873–1955, vol. V

Whitehouse, Sir Julian Osborn, 1876–1942, vol. IV

Whitehouse, Rev. Owen Charles, 1849–1916, vol. II

Whitehouse, Wallace Edward, 1882–1963, vol. VI

Whitehouse, William Edward, 1859–1935, vol. III

Whitehouse, Major William Henry, 1873–1963, vol. VI
Whiteing, Richard, 1840–1928, vol. II
Whitelaw, Alexander, 1862–1938, vol. III
Whitelaw, Anne Watt, 1875–1966, vol. VI
Whitelaw, David, 1876–1971, vol. VII
Whitelaw, Græme Alexander Lockhart, 1863–1928, vol. II
Whitelaw, Maj.-Gen. John Stewart, 1894–1964, vol. VI
Whitelaw, Robert Pender, 1865–1934, vol. III
Whitelaw, Thomas, 1840–1917, vol. II
Whitelaw, William, 1868–1946, vol. IV
Whitelegge, Sir (B.) Arthur, 1852–1933, vol. III
Whiteley, Cecil, 1875–1942, vol. IV
Whiteley, Frank, 1856–1933, vol. III
Whiteley, Sir Gerald Charles, 1891–1958, vol. V
Whiteley, Sir Herbert Huntington-, 1st Bt, 1857–1936, vol. III
Whiteley, Captain Sir (Herbert) Maurice H.; see Huntington-Whiteley.
Whiteley, Gen. Sir John Francis Martin, 1896–1970, vol. VI
Whiteley, Brig. John Percival, died 1943, vol. IV
Whiteley, Martha Annie, 1866–1956, vol. V
Whiteley, Wilfrid, 1882–1970, vol. VI
Whiteley, Rt Hon. William, 1882–1955, vol. V
Whitelocke, R. Henry Anglin, 1861–1927, vol. II
Whiteman, George W., 1903–1974, vol. VII
Whiteside, Borras Noel Hamilton, 1903–1948, vol. IV
Whiteside, Sir Cuthbert William, 1880–1969, vol. VI (AII)
Whiteside, Surg. Rear-Adm. Henry Cadman, died 1949, vol. IV
Whiteside, Most Rev. Thomas, 1857–1921, vol. II
Whiteway, Ronald Harry Clift, 1885–1951, vol. V
Whiteway, Rt Hon. Sir William Vallance, 1828–1908, vol. I
Whitfeld, Hubert Edwin, 1875–1939, vol. III
Whitfield, Arthur, died 1947, vol. IV
Whitfield, Maj.-Gen. John Yeldham, 1899–1971, vol. VI
Whitfield-Jackson, John; see Jackson, J. W.
Whitford, Air Vice-Marshal Sir John, 1893–1966, vol. VI
Whitham, Rev. Arthur Richard, 1863–1930, vol. III
Whitham, Gilbert Shaw, 1889–1970, vol. VI
Whitham, Lt-Gen. John Lawrence, 1881–1952, vol. V
Whitham, Air Cdre Robert Parker Musgrave, 1895–1943, vol. IV
Whiting, Arthur John, died 1941, vol. IV
Whiting, Rev. Charles Edwin, 1871–1953, vol. V
Whiting, Frederic, died 1962, vol. VI
Whiting, John Robert, 1917–1963, vol. VI
Whiting, William Henry, 1854–1927, vol. II
Whiting, William Robert Gerald, 1884–1947, vol. IV
Whiting, Winifred Ada, 1898–1979, vol. VII
Whitington, Ven. Frederick Taylor, 1853–1938, vol. III
Whitla, Sir William, 1851–1933, vol. III

Whitley, Brig.-Gen. Sir Edward Nathan, 1873–1966, vol. VI
Whitley, Very Rev. Henry Charles, 1906–1976, vol. VII
Whitley, Rt Rev. Jabez Cornelius, 1837–1904, vol. I
Whitley, Rt Hon. John Henry, 1866–1935, vol. III
Whitley, John Robinson, 1843–1922, vol. II
Whitley, Kate Mary, died 1920, vol. II
Whitley, Sir Michael Henry, 1872–1959, vol. V
Whitley, Sir Norman Henry Pownall, 1883–1957, vol. V
Whitley, William Thomas, 1858–1942, vol. IV
Whitley, William Thomas, 1861–1947, vol. IV
Whitley-Jones, Ernest, 1890–1965, vol. VI
Whitley-Thomson, Sir Frederick Whitley, 1851–1925, vol. II
Whitlock, Brand, 1869–1934, vol. III
Whitlock, Col George Frederic Ashford, 1868–1936, vol. III
Whitman, Alfred, 1860–1910, vol. I
Whitman, Sidney, died 1925, vol. II
Whitmarsh, Rev. Robert Thomas, died 1921, vol. II
Whitmee, Harold James Conder, 1901–1954, vol. V
Whitmore, Charles Algernon, 1851–1908, vol. I
Whitmore, Francis, 1903–1975, vol. VII
Whitmore, Col Sir Francis Henry Douglas Charlton, 1st Bt, 1872–1962, vol. VI
Whitmore, Hon. Col Sir George Stoddart, 1830–1903, vol. I
Whitnall, S. E., 1876–1950, vol. IV
Whitney, Sir Benjamin, 1833–1916, vol. II
Whitney, Caspar, 1864–1929, vol. III
Whitney, Sir Cecil Arthur, 1862–1956, vol. V
Whitney, George, 1885–1963, vol. VI
Whitney, Harry Payne, 1872–1930, vol. III
Whitney, Henry Ernest William F.; see Fetherstonhaugh-Whitney.
Whitney, Hon. Sir James Pliny, 1843–1914, vol. I
Whitney, James Pounder, 1857–1939, vol. III
Whitney, William Collins, 1841–1904, vol. I
Whitney, William Dwight, 1899–1973, vol. VII
Whitney-Smith, E., 1880–1952, vol. V
Whitson, Sir Thomas Barnby, 1869–1948, vol. IV
Whittaker, Sir Edmund Taylor, 1873–1956, vol. V
Whittaker, Sir Meredith Thompson, 1841–1931, vol. III
Whittaker, Maj.-Gen. Robert Frederick Edward, 1894–1967, vol. VI
Whittaker, Thomas, 1856–1935, vol. III
Whittaker, Rt Hon. Sir Thomas Palmer, 1850–1919, vol. II
Whittaker, William Gillies, 1876–1944, vol. IV
Whittaker, William Joseph, 1868–1931, vol. III
Whittall, Sir (James) William, 1838–1910, vol. I
Whittall, Lionel Harry, 1907–1977, vol. VII
Whittall, Lt-Col Percival Frederick, 1877–1943, vol. IV
Whittall, Sir William; see Whittall, Sir J. W.
Whittard, Walter Frederick, 1902–1966, vol. VI
Whitten, Wilfred, died 1942, vol. IV
Whitten-Brown, Sir Arthur, 1886–1948, vol. IV
Whittick, Henry John, 1870–1937, vol. III
Whitting, Brig. Everard Le Grice, 1881–1953, vol. V

Whittingham, Col Charles Herbert, 1873–1932, vol. III

Whittingham, Rev. George Gustavus Napier, 1866–1941, vol. IV

Whittingham, Rt Rev. Walter Godfrey, *died* 1941, vol. IV

Whittingham, Engr-Rear-Adm. William, 1862–1940, vol. III

Whittingstall, Francis Herbert F.; *see* Fearnley-Whittingstall.

Whittingstall, William Arthur F.; *see* Fearnley-Whittingstall.

Whittington, Brig.-Gen. Cecil Henry, 1878–1934, vol. III

Whittington, Col George John Charles, 1836–1916, vol. II

Whittington, Rev. Richard, 1825–1900, vol. I

Whittington, Sir Richard, 1905–1975, vol. VII

Whittington-Ince, Captain Edward Watkins, 1886–1976, vol. VII

Whittle, Alfred Thomas, *died* 1913, vol. I

Whittle, Ven. John Tyler, 1889–1969, vol. VI

Whittome, Sir Maurice Gordon, 1902–1974, vol. VII

Whitton, Charlotte Elizabeth, 1896–1975, vol. VII

Whitton, Lt-Col Frederick Ernest, 1872–1940, vol. III

Whitton, James Reid, *died* 1919, vol. II

Whitty, Maj.-Gen. Henry Martin, 1896–1961, vol. VI

Whitty, Sir John Tarlton, 1876–1948, vol. IV

Whitty, Dame May; *see* Webster, Dame May.

Whitty, Brig. Noel Irwine, 1885–1964, vol. VI

Whitty, Sir Reginald Ramson, 1891–1960, vol. V

Whitwell, Edward Robson, 1843–1922, vol. II

Whitwell, Joseph Fry, 1869–1932, vol. III

Whitwell, William Fry, 1867–1942, vol. IV

Whitwill, Col Mark, 1889–1967, vol. VI

Whitworth, Arthur, 1875–1972, vol. VII

Whitworth, Charles Stanley, 1880–1963, vol. VI

Whitworth, Cyril, 1904–1968, vol. VI

Whitworth, Brig. Dysart Edward, 1890–1974, vol. VII

Whitworth, Eric Edward Allen, *died* 1971, vol. VII

Whitworth, Geoffrey Arundel, 1883–1951, vol. V

Whitworth, Harry, 1870–1930, vol. III

Whitworth, Air Cdre John Nicholas Haworth, 1912–1974, vol. VII

Whitworth, Thomas, 1917–1979, vol. VII

Whitworth, Rev. William Allen, 1840–1905, vol. I

Whitworth, William Hervey Allen, *died* 1960, vol. V

Whitworth, Adm. Sir William Jock, 1884–1973, vol. VII

Whorlow, Rev. Alfred, 1852–1937, vol. III

Whyatt, Sir John, 1905–1978, vol. VII

Whyham, William Henry, *born* 1848, vol. II

Whymper, Charles, 1853–1941, vol. IV

Whymper, Edward, 1840–1911, vol. I

Whymper, Josiah Wood, 1813–1903, vol. I

Whyte, Rev. Alexander, 1836–1921, vol. II

Whyte, Sir (Alexander) Frederick, 1883–1970, vol. VI

Whyte, Angus H.; *see* Hedley-Whyte.

Whyte, Frederic, 1867–1941, vol. IV

Whyte, Sir Frederick; *see* Whyte, Sir A. F.

Whyte, Ian, 1901–1960, vol. V

Whyte, J. Mackie, 1858–1930, vol. III

Whyte, James Wilkinson, 1852–1923, vol. II

Whyte, Jardine Bell, 1880–1954, vol. V

Whyte, Major John Nicholas, 1864–1906, vol. I

Whyte, Ven. Richard Athenry, *died* 1917, vol. II

Whyte, Air Comdt Dame Roberta Mary, 1897–1979, vol. VII

Whyte, Sir William, 1843–1914, vol. I

Whyte, Sir William, *died* 1945, vol. IV

Whyte, Sir William Edward, *died* 1950, vol. IV

Whyte, William Hamilton, 1885–1973, vol. VII

Whyte, Sir William Marcus Charles Beresford, 1863–1932, vol. III

Whytehead, Rev. Henry Robert, 1849–1937, vol. III

Whytehead, Rev. Canon Ralph Layard, 1883–1956, vol. V

Whytlaw-Gray, Robert Whytlaw, 1877–1958, vol. V

Wibberley, Charles, 1851–1929, vol. III

Wibberley, T., 1880–1930, vol. III

Wickens, Charles Henry, 1872–1939, vol. III

Wickham, Rev. Archdale Palmer, 1855–1935, vol. III

Wickham, Lt-Col Sir Charles George, 1879–1971, vol. VII

Wickham, Very Rev. Edward Charles, 1834–1910, vol. I

Wickham, Lt-Col Edward Thomas Ruscombe, 1890–1957, vol. V

Wickham, Rev. Gordon Bolles, 1850–1920, vol. II

Wickham, Sir Henry, 1846–1928, vol. II

Wickham, Lt-Col Henry, 1855–1933, vol. III

Wickham, Col Henry Francis, 1874–1931, vol. III

Wickham, Brig. John Charles, 1886–1970, vol. VI

Wickham, Major Thomas Edmund Palmer, 1879–1917, vol. II

Wickham, Captain Thomas Strange, 1878–1914, vol. I

Wickham, William, 1831–1897, vol. I

Wickham, Col William James Richard, 1860–1932, vol. III

Wickham, William Reginald Lamplugh, 1908–1956, vol. V

Wickham-Boynton, Captain Thomas Lamplugh, 1869–1942, vol. IV

Wickins, Bt-Col George Cradock, 1884–1973, vol. VII

Wickins, Ven. William John, *died* 1933, vol. III

Wicklow, 7th Earl of, 1877–1946, vol. IV

Wicklow, 8th Earl of, 1902–1978, vol. VII

Wickremasinghe, N. Don Martino de Zilva, 1865–1937, vol. III

Wickremesinghe, Cyril Leonard, 1890–1945, vol. IV

Wicks, Frederick, 1840–1910, vol. I

Wicks, Margaret Campbell Walker, 1893–1970, vol. VI

Wicks, Pembroke, 1882–1957, vol. V

Wicksteed, Joseph Hartley, 1842–1919, vol. II

Wicksteed, Rev. Philip Henry, 1844–1927, vol. II

Wicksteed, Thomas Frederic, 1848–1901, vol. I

Widdicombe, Lt-Col George Templer, 1867–1952, vol. V

Widdicombe, Rev. John, 1839–1927, vol. II

Widdows, Archibald Edwards, 1878–1942, vol. IV

Widdowson, Thomas William, 1877–1956, vol. V

Widdrington, Brig.-Gen. Bertram FitzHerbert, 1873–1942, vol. IV

Widdrington, Major Shallcross Fitzherbert, 1826–1917, vol. II

Widener, Joseph E., died 1943, vol. IV

Widener, Peter A. Brown, 1834–1915, vol. I (A)

Widgery, Alban Gregory, 1887–1968, vol. VI

Widor, Charles-Marie, 1847–1937, vol. III

Wieland, Heinrich, 1877–1957, vol. V

Wieler, Brig. Leslie Frederic Ethelbert, 1899–1965, vol. VI

Wiener, Leo, 1862–1939, vol. III (A), vol. IV

Wiener, Norbert, 1894–1964, vol. VI

Wigan, Alfred Edmund, 1855–1940, vol. III

Wigan, Charles, 1860–1937, vol. III

Wigan, Sir Frederick, 1st Bt, 1827–1907, vol. I

Wigan, Sir Frederick Adair, 4th Bt, 1911–1979, vol. VII

Wigan, Sir Frederick William, 2nd Bt, 1859–1907, did not have an entry in Who's Who.

Wigan, Brig.-Gen. John Tyson, 1877–1952, vol. V

Wigan, Sir Roderick Grey, 3rd Bt, 1886–1954, vol. V

Wigg, Rt Rev. Montagu John S.; see Stone-Wigg.

Wiggin, Alfred Harold, 1864–1933, vol. III

Wiggin, Arthur Francis Holme, 1892–1935, vol. III

Wiggin, Sir Charles Douglas, 1922–1977, vol. VII

Wiggin, Sir Charles Richard Henry, 3rd Bt, 1885–1972, vol. VII

Wiggin, Brig.-Gen. Edgar Askin, 1867–1939, vol. III

Wiggin, Sir Henry, 1st Bt, 1824–1905, vol. I

Wiggin, Sir Henry Arthur, 2nd Bt, 1852–1917, vol. II

Wiggin, Kate Douglas, 1856–1923, vol. II

Wiggin, Lt-Col Walter William, 1856–1936, vol. III

Wiggin, Lt-Col Sir William Henry, 1888–1951, vol. V

Wiggins, Rev. Clare Aveling, died 1965, vol. VI

Wiggins, Captain Joseph, 1832–1905, vol. I

Wiggins, William Denison Clare, 1905–1971, vol. VII

Wiggins, William Martin, 1870–1950, vol. IV

Wigglesworth, Air Cdre Cecil George, 1893–1961, vol. VI

Wigglesworth, Air Marshal Sir (Horace Ernest) Philip, 1896–1975, vol. VII

Wigglesworth, Air Marshal Sir Philip; see Wigglesworth, Air Marshal Sir H. E. P.

Wigglesworth, Walter Somerville, 1906–1972, vol. VII

Wigham, Joseph Theodore, 1874–1951, vol. V

Wight, Sir Gerald Robert, 1898–1962, vol. VI

Wight, Martin; see Wight, R. J. M.

Wight, (Robert James) Martin, 1913–1972, vol. VII

Wight-Boycott, Lt-Col T. A., 1872–1916, vol. II

Wightman, Sir Owen William, 1869–1948, vol. IV

Wightman, Ralph, 1901–1971, vol. VII

Wightwick, Humphrey Wolseley, 1889–1962, vol. VI

Wigley, Frederick George, 1855–1918, vol. II

Wigley, Sir George, 1837–1925, vol. II

Wigley, Rev. Henry Townsend, 1893–1970, vol. VI

Wigley, John Edwin Mackonochie, 1892–1962, vol. VI

Wigley, Sir Wilfrid Murray, 1876–1959, vol. V

Wigmore, John Henry, 1863–1943, vol. IV

Wignall, Frederick William, died 1939, vol. III

Wignall, James, 1856–1925, vol. II

Wignall, Joshua Jennings, 1859–1941, vol. IV

Wigram, 1st Baron, 1873–1960, vol. V

Wigram, Alfred Money, 1856–1899, vol. I

Wigram, Sir Charles Hampden, 1826–1903, vol. I

Wigram, Sir Edgar Thomas Ainger, 6th Bt, 1864–1935, vol. III

Wigram, Vice-Adm. Ernest, 1877–1944, vol. IV

Wigram, Maj.-Gen. Godfrey James, 1836–1908, vol. I

Wigram, Sir Henry Francis, 1857–1934, vol. III

Wigram, Gen. Sir Kenneth, 1875–1949, vol. IV

Wigram, Loftus Edward, 1877–1963, vol. VI

Wigram, Ralph Follet, 1890–1936, vol. III

Wigram, Rev. William Ainger, 1872–1953, vol. V

Wigram, Rev. Woolmore, 1831–1907, vol. I

Wijhe, J. W. van, 1856–1935, vol. III

Wijayasinghe Siriwardena, N. D. A. Silva-, 1888–1949, vol. IV (A)

Wijeyekoon, Sir Gerard, 1878–1952, vol. V

Wijeyeratne, Sir Edwin Aloysius Perera, 1890–1968, vol. VI

Wijeyewardene, Hon. Sir Arthur; see Wijeyewardene, Hon. Sir E. A. L.

Wijeyewardene, Hon. Sir (Edwin) Arthur (Lewis), 1887–1964, vol. VI

Wilberforce, Ven. Albert Basil Orme, 1841–1916, vol. II

Wilberforce, Edward, 1834–1914, vol. I

Wilberforce, Rt Rev. Ernest Roland, 1840–1907, vol. I

Wilberforce, Col Harold Hartley, 1881–1943, vol. IV

Wilberforce, Brig.-Gen. Sir Herbert William, 1866–1952, vol. V

Wilberforce, Sir Herbert William Wrangham, 1864–1941, vol. IV

Wilberforce, Lionel Robert, 1861–1944, vol. IV

Wilberforce, Samuel, 1874–1954, vol. V

Wilberforce-Bell, Lt-Col Sir Harold, 1885–1956, vol. V

Wilbraham, Lt-Col Bernard Hugh, died 1942, vol. IV

Wilbraham, Edward; see Lathom, 3rd Earl of.

Wilbraham, Sir George Barrington Baker-, 5th Bt, 1845–1912, vol. I

Wilbraham, Hugh Edward, 1857–1930, vol. III

Wilbraham, Sir Philip Wilbraham Baker, 6th Bt, 1875–1957, vol. V

Wilbraham, Sir Randle John Baker, 7th Bt, 1906–1980, vol. VII

Wilbraham, Sir Richard, 1811–1900, vol. I

Wilby, Col (Arthur William) Roger, 1875–1942, vol. IV

Wilby, Col Roger; see Wilby, Col A. W. R.

Wilcock, Alfred William, died 1953, vol. V

Wilcock, Gp Captain Clifford Arthur Bowman, died 1962, vol. VI
Wilcock, John Stewart, 1905–1951, vol. V
Wilcocks, Hon. Carl Theodorus Muller, 1861–1936, vol. III
Wilcocks, C(harles), 1896–1977, vol. VII
Wilcox, Rev. Arthur John, 1889–1960, vol. V
Wilcox, Bernard Herbert, 1917–1980, vol. VII
Wilcox, Ella Wheeler, 1855–1919, vol. II
Wilcox, Herbert, 1892–1977, vol. VII
Wild, Albert, 1899–1971, vol. VII
Wild, Maj.-Gen. Edward John, died 1914, vol. I
Wild, Sir Ernest Edward, 1869–1934, vol. III
Wild, F. Percy, died 1950, vol. IV
Wild, Frank, 1874–1939, vol. III
Wild, Rt Rev. Herbert Louis, 1865–1940, vol. III
Wild, Rt Hon. Sir (Herbert) Richard (Churton), 1912–1978, vol. VII
Wild, Ira, 1895–1974, vol. VII
Wild, James Anstey, 1853–1922, vol. II
Wild, Rev. Marshall, 1834–1916, vol. II
Wild, Ralph Bagnall B.; see Bagnall-Wild.
Wild, Brig.-Gen. Ralph Kirkby B.; see Bagnall-Wild.
Wild, Rt Hon. Sir Richard; see Wild, Rt Hon. Sir H. R. C.
Wild, Robert Briggs, 1862–1941, vol. IV
Wild, Lt-Col Wilfrid Hubert, 1874–1953, vol. V
Wilde, Henry, 1833–1919, vol. II
Wilde, Johannes, 1891–1970, vol. VI
Wilde, Percy, 1857–1929, vol. III
Wilden-Hart, Bernard John, 1881–1932, vol. III
Wildenburg, Count Paul von H.; see Hatzfeldt-Wildenburg.
Wilder, Thornton Niven, 1897–1975, vol. VII
Wildey, Alexander Gascoigne, 1860–1934, vol. III
Wilding, Anthony Frederick, 1883–1915, vol. I
Wilding, Brig.-Gen. Charles Arthur, 1868–1953, vol. V
Wilding, Edward, 1875–1939, vol. III
Wilding, Longworth Allen, 1902–1963, vol. VI
Wilding, Michael, 1912–1979, vol. VII
Wilding, Captain Michael Henry, 1875–1933, vol. III
Wildish, Engr Rear-Adm. Sir Henry William, 1884–1973, vol. VII
Wildman-Lushington, Maj.-Gen. Godfrey Edward, 1897–1970, vol. VI
Wile, Frederic William, 1873–1941, vol. IV
Wileman, Alfred Ernest, 1860–1929, vol. III
Wilenski, Reginald Howard, 1887–1975, vol. VII
Wiles, Sir Gilbert, 1880–1961, vol. VI
Wiles, Sir Harold Herbert, 1892–1965, vol. VI
Wiles, Philip, 1899–1967, vol. VI
Wiles, Reid, 1919–1975, vol. VII
Wiles, Rt Hon. Thomas, died 1951, vol. V
Wiley, Very Rev. C. Ormsby, 1839–1915, vol. I
Wiley, Charles Joseph, 1873–1939, vol. III
Wiley, Louis, 1869–1935, vol. III
Wilford, Rev. Canon John Russell, 1877–1954, vol. V
Wilford, Sir Thomas Mason, died 1939, vol. III
Wilgar, Lt-Col William Percy, 1877–1940, vol. III (A), vol. IV

Wilgress, Rev. George Frederick, 1868–1953, vol. V
Wilgress, L. Dana, 1892–1969, vol. VI
Wilkes, Richard Leslie Vaughan, 1904–1970, vol. VI
Wilkie, Alexander, 1850–1928, vol. II
Wilkie, Alexander Mair, 1917–1966, vol. VI
Wilkie, Rev. Arthur West, 1875–1958, vol. V
Wilkie, Daniel R., 1846–1914, vol. I
Wilkie, Sir David Percival Dalbreck, 1882–1938, vol. III
Wilkie, Hugh Graham, 1893–1969, vol. VI
Wilkie, James, 1890–1957, vol. V
Wilkie-Dalyell, Major Sir James Bruce; see Dalyell.
Wilkin, Sir Albert Scholick, 1883–1943, vol. IV
Wilkin, Vice-Adm. Henry Douglas, 1862–1931, vol. III
Wilkin, Sir Walter Henry, 1842–1922, vol. II
Wilkins, Augustus Samuel, 1843–1905, vol. I
Wilkins, Charles Timothy, 1905–1979, vol. VII
Wilkins, Major Cyril Francis, died 1935, vol. III
Wilkins, Rev. George, died 1920, vol. II
Wilkins, Sir (George) Hubert, 1888–1958, vol. V
Wilkins, Sir Henry John Arthur, died 1936, vol. III
Wilkins, Rev. Henry Russell, 1859–1924, vol. II
Wilkins, Sir Hubert; see Wilkins, Sir G. H.
Wilkins, Col James Sutherland, 1851–1916, vol. II
Wilkins, Mary E., died 1930, vol. III
Wilkins, Roland Field, 1872–1950, vol. IV
Wilkins, William Henry, 1860–1905, vol. I
Wilkins, William Vaughan, 1890–1959, vol. V
Wilkinson, Col Arthur Clement, 1870–1950, vol. IV
Wilkinson, Rev. Arthur Henry, 1885–1973, vol. VII
Wilkinson, Rev. Arthur Rupert B.; see Browne-Wilkinson.
Wilkinson, Engr Rear-Adm. Brian John Hamilton, died 1963, vol. VI
Wilkinson, Rt Rev. (Charles Robert) Heber, 1900–1979, vol. VII
Wilkinson, Ven. Charles Thomas, 1823–1910, vol. I
Wilkinson, Col Charles William, 1868–1954, vol. V
Wilkinson, Clennell Anstruther, 1883–1936, vol. III
Wilkinson, Clennell Frank Massy D.; see Drew-Wilkinson.
Wilkinson, Cyril Hackett, 1888–1960, vol. V
Wilkinson, Cyril Theodore Anstruther, 1884–1970, vol. VI
Wilkinson, Sir David; see Wilkinson, Sir L. D.
Wilkinson, Edgar Riley, 1898–1977, vol. VII
Wilkinson, Edward Sheldon, 1883–1950, vol. IV
Wilkinson, Rt Hon. Ellen Cicely, 1891–1947, vol. IV
Wilkinson, Fanny Rollo, died 1951, vol. V
Wilkinson, Most Rev. Francis Oliver G.; see Green-Wilkinson.
Wilkinson, Frank, 1900–1970, vol. VI
Wilkinson, Frank Clare, 1889–1979, vol. VII
Wilkinson, Frederick, 1891–1978, vol. VII
Wilkinson, Frederick Edgar, 1871–1950, vol. IV
Wilkinson, Lt-Gen. Frederick G.; see Green-Wilkinson.
Wilkinson, George, 1867–1956, vol. V

Wilkinson, Col George Alexander Eason, 1860–1941, vol. IV

Wilkinson, Maj.-Gen. George Allix, 1828–1919, vol. II

Wilkinson, Sir George Henry, 1st Bt, 1885–1967, vol. VI

Wilkinson, Rt Rev. George Howard, 1833–1907, vol. I

Wilkinson, Rt Rev. Heber; see Wilkinson, Rt Rev. C. R. H.

Wilkinson, Hector Russell, 1888–1972, vol. VII

Wilkinson, Lt-Col Henry Benfield Des Vœux, 1870–1943, vol. IV

Wilkinson, Lt-Gen. Sir Henry Clement, 1837–1908, vol. I

Wilkinson, (Henry) Spenser, 1853–1937, vol. III

Wilkinson, Hiram Parkes, 1866–1935, vol. III

Wilkinson, Sir Hiram Shaw, 1840–1926, vol. II

Wilkinson, Hon. James, 1854–1915, vol. I (A)

Wilkinson, Rev. John, 1856–1935, vol. III

Wilkinson, Brig. John Shann, 1884–1977, vol. VII

Wilkinson, Sir Joseph Loftus, 1845–1903, vol. I

Wilkinson, Vice-Adm. Julian Charles Allix, 1859–1917, vol. II

Wilkinson, Kenneth Douglas, 1886–1951, vol. V

Wilkinson, Lancelot Craven, died 1923, vol. II

Wilkinson, Sir (Leonard) David, 2nd Bt, 1920–1972, vol. VII

Wilkinson, Leslie, 1882–1973, vol. VII

Wilkinson, Brig.-Gen. Lewis Frederic G.; see Green-Wilkinson.

Wilkinson, Louis Umfreville, 1881–1966, vol. VI

Wilkinson, Dame Louisa Jane, 1889–1968, vol. VI

Wilkinson, Brig. Maurice Lean, 1873–1946, vol. IV

Wilkinson, Rev. Michael Marlow Umfreville, 1831–1916, vol. II

Wilkinson, Brig.-Gen. Montagu Grant, 1857–1943, vol. IV

Wilkinson, Major Sir Nevile Rodwell, 1869–1940, vol. III

Wilkinson, Norman, 1882–1934, vol. III

Wilkinson, Norman, 1878–1971, vol. VII

Wilkinson, Maj.-Gen. Osborn, 1822–1906, vol. I

Wilkinson, Maj.-Gen. Sir Percival Spearman, 1865–1953, vol. V

Wilkinson, Reginald Warren Hale, 1882–1973, vol. VII

Wilkinson, Richard Edward, 1901–1972, vol. VII

Wilkinson, Richard James, 1867–1941, vol. IV

Wilkinson, Sir Robert Pelham, 1883–1962, vol. VI

Wilkinson, Sir Russell Facey, 1888–1968, vol. VI

Wilkinson, Spenser; see Wilkinson, H. S.

Wilkinson, Stephen, 1876–1962, vol. VI

Wilkinson, Rt Rev. Thomas Edward, died 1914, vol. I

Wilkinson, Major Thomas Henry Des Vœux, 1858–1928, vol. II

Wilkinson, Rt Rev. Thomas W., 1825–1909, vol. I

Wilkinson, Walter Sutherland, 1875–1943, vol. IV

Wilkinson, William, 1882–1944, vol. IV

Wilkinson, William Dale, 1893–1973, vol. VII

Wilkinson, Rev. Canon William Evans, 1891–1967, vol. VI

Wilkinson, Sir William Henry, 1858–1930, vol. III

Wilkinson-Guillemard, Hugh; see Wilkinson-Guillemard, W. H. J.

Wilkinson-Guillemard, (Walter) Hugh (John), 1874–1939, vol. III

Wilks, Rev. William, 1843–1923, vol. II

Will, John Shiress, 1840–1910, vol. I

Will, Robert Ross, 1883–1968, vol. VI

Willan, Col Frank, 1846–1931, vol. III

Willan, Brig.-Gen. Frank Godfrey, 1878–1957, vol. V

Willan, Sir Harold Curwen, 1896–1971, vol. VII

Willan, Healey, 1880–1968, vol. VI

Willan, Col Henry Percy Douglas, 1848–1912, vol. I

Willan, Col Robert Hugh, 1882–1960, vol. V

Willan, Robert Joseph, 1878–1955, vol. V

Willans, Sir Frederic Jeune, died 1949, vol. IV

Willans, Maj.-Gen. Harry, 1892–1943, vol. IV

Willans, Lt-Col Thomas James, 1872–1922, vol. II

Willans, William Henry, 1833–1904, vol. I

Willar, Paul; see Villars, Paul.

Willard, E. S., died 1915, vol. I (A)

Willard, Frances Elizabeth, 1839–1898, vol. I

Willcock, Rev. John, 1853–1931, vol. III

Willcock, Hon. John Collings, 1879–1956, vol V

Willcock, Major Ralph, 1887–1969, vol. VI

Willcocks, G. Waller, died 1918, vol. II

Willcocks, Gen. Sir James, 1857–1926, vol. II

Willcocks, Sir William, 1852–1932, vol. III

Willcox, Arthur, 1909–1963, vol. VI

Willcox, Lt-Gen. Sir Henry Beresford Dennitts, 1889–1968, vol. VI

Willcox, Captain Howard James Lionel Walter Kox, died 1936, vol. III

Willcox, Lt-Col Walter Temple, 1869–1943, vol. IV

Willcox, Sir William Henry, 1870–1941, vol. IV

Willert, Sir Arthur, 1882–1973, vol. VII

Willert, Paul Ferdinand, 1844–1912, vol. I

Willes, Lt-Col Charles Edward, 1870–1952, vol. V

Willes, Adm. Sir George Lambart A.; see Atkinson-Willes.

Willes, Sir George Ommanney, 1823–1901, vol. I

Willes, Richard Augustus, 1881–1966, vol. VI

Willes, William, 1855–1924, vol. II

Willets, Lt-Col Charles Richard Edward, 1880–1931, vol. III

Willett, Alfred, 1837–1913, vol. I

Willett, Captain Basil Rupert, 1896–1966, vol. VI

Willett, John Eddowes, 1853–1937, vol. III

Willett, Comdr William Basil, 1919–1976, vol. VII

Willey, Arthur, 1867–1942, vol. IV

Willey, Basil, 1897–1978, vol. VII

Willey, Octavius George, 1886–1952, vol. V

Williams, 1st Baron, 1892–1966, vol. VI

Williams of Barnburgh, Baron (Life Peer); Thomas Williams, 1888–1967, vol. VI

Williams, A. Franklyn, 1907–1979, vol. VII

Williams, Rt Rev. Aidan; see Williams, Rt Rev. Augustine A.

Williams, Sir Alan Meredith, 1909–1972, vol. VII

Williams, Captain Albert, 1864–1926, vol. II

Williams, Maj.-Gen. Sir Albert Henry Wilmot, 1832–1919, vol. II

Williams, Ven. Aldred; see Williams, Ven. E. D. A.

Williams, Alexander, *died* 1930, vol. III
Williams, Alfred Cecil, 1899–1976, vol. VII
Williams, Col Alfred Ernest, 1871–1941, vol. IV
Williams, Alice Helena Alexandra, 1863–1957, vol. V
Williams, Rt Rev. Alwyn Terrell Petre, 1888–1968, vol. VI
Williams, Alyn, *died* 1941, vol. IV
Williams, Aneurin, 1859–1924, vol. II
Williams, Anna, *died* 1924, vol. II
Williams, Rt Rev. Anthony Lewis Elliott, 1892–1975, vol. VII
Williams, Arnold, 1890–1958, vol. V
Williams, Rt Rev. Arthur Acheson, *died* 1914, vol. I
Williams, Brig.-Gen. Arthur Blount Cuthbert, 1860–1918, vol. II
Williams, Lt-Col Arthur Cecil, 1871–1940, vol. III
Williams, Ven. Arthur Charles, 1899–1974, vol. VII
Williams, Arthur de Coetlogon, 1890–1973, vol. VII
Williams, A(rthur) Emlyn, 1910–1976, vol. VII
Williams, (Arthur Frederic) Basil, 1867–1950, vol. IV
Williams, Col Arthur Frederick Carlisle, 1876–1934, vol. III
Williams, Arthur James, 1880–1962, vol. VI
Williams, Arthur John, 1835–1911, vol. I (A)
Williams, Brig.-Gen. Sir Arthur John A.; *see* Allen-Williams.
Williams, Sir (Arthur) Leonard, 1904–1972, vol. VII
Williams, Rt Rev. Arthur Llewellyn, 1856–1919, vol. II
Williams, Rev. Arthur Lukyn, 1853–1943, vol. IV
Williams, Sir (Arthur) Osmond, 1st Bt (*cr* 1909), 1849–1927, vol. II
Williams, Captain Ashley Paget Wilmot, 1867–1913, vol. I
Williams, Maj.-Gen. Aubrey Ellis, 1888–1977, vol. VII
Williams, Rt Rev. (Augustine) Aidan, 1904–1965, vol. VI
Williams, Brig. Augustus John, 1876–1945, vol. IV
Williams, B. Francis, 1845–1914, vol. I
Williams, Barbara M.; *see* Moray Williams.
Williams, Basil; *see* Williams, A. F. B.
Williams, Sir Benjamin Allen, *died* 1968, vol. VI
Williams, Benjamin H.; *see* Haydn Williams.
Williams, Captain Berkeley Cole Wilmot, 1865–1938, vol. III
Williams, Bernard Warren, 1895–1970, vol. VI
Williams, Lt-Col Brian Robertson, 1909–1980, vol. VII
Williams, Sir Burton Robert, 6th Bt (*cr* 1866), 1889–1917, vol. II
Williams, C. F. Abdy, 1855–1923, vol. II
Williams, Brig. Cecil James, 1898–1948, vol. IV
Williams, Charles, 1834–1900, vol. I
Williams, Charles, 1838–1904, vol. I
Williams, Rt Hon. Charles, 1886–1955, vol. V
Williams, Lt-Col Charles Augustus M.; *see* Muspratt-Williams.
Williams, Rt Rev. Charles David, 1860–1923, vol. II

Williams, Major Charles Edward, 1873–1955, vol. V
Williams, Charles Garrett, 1901–1976, vol. VII
Williams, Charles Greville, 1829–1910, vol. I
Williams, Charles Riby, 1857–1924, vol. II
Williams, Sir Charles S.; *see* Stuart-Williams.
Williams, Captain Charles Shrine, 1895–1973, vol. VII
Williams, Charles Theodore, 1838–1912, vol. I
Williams, Charles Walter Stansby, 1886–1945, vol. IV
Williams, Charles Wodehouse, 1899–1957, vol. V
Williams, Chisholm, 1866–1928, vol. II
Williams, Christmas Price, *died* 1965, vol. VI
Williams, Christopher A.; *see* Addams Williams.
Williams, Hon. Christopher Alexander S.; *see* Sapara-Williams.
Williams, Christopher David, 1873–1934, vol. III
Williams, Clarence Faithfull M.; *see* Monier-Williams.
Williams, Conrad Veale, 1903–1969, vol. VI
Williams, Major Craufurd Victor M.; *see* Monier-Williams.
Williams, Daniel, 1876–1944, vol. IV
Williams, Sir (Daniel) Thomas, *died* 1973, vol. VII
Williams, David, 1877–1927, vol. II
Williams, Ven. David, 1841–1929, vol. III
Williams, Most Rev. David, 1859–1931, vol. III
Williams, Ven. David, 1862–1936, vol. III
Williams, David, 1865–1941, vol. IV
Williams, David, 1900–1978, vol. VII
Williams, David Davey, 1874–1954, vol. V (A)
Williams, Ven. David Edward, 1847–1920, vol. II
Williams, David Gwynne, 1886–1975, vol. VII
Williams, David James, 1897–1972, vol. VII
Williams, David L.; *see* Llewelyn-Williams.
Williams, David Parry, 1842–1909, vol. I
Williams, Sir David Philip, 3rd Bt (*cr* 1915), 1909–1970, vol. VI
Williams, Lt-Gen. David Walter, 1839–1909, vol. I
Williams, Sir Dawson, 1854–1928, vol. II
Williams, Dorothy Sylvia L.; *see* Lloyd-Williams.
Williams, Captain Douglas, 1892–1975, vol. VII
Williams, D(ouglas) Graeme, 1909–1970, vol. VI
Williams, Hon. Sir Dudley, 1889–1963, vol. VI
Williams, E. C., 1892–1973, vol. VII
Williams, E. G. Harcourt, 1880–1957, vol. V
Williams, Edith, *died* 1919, vol. II
Williams, Rev. Edward Adams, 1826–1913, vol. I
Williams, Edward Cecil, 1867–1939, vol. III
Williams, Maj.-Gen. Edward Charles Ingouville, 1861–1916, vol. II
Williams, Sir Edward Charles Sparshott, 1831–1907, vol. I
Williams, Major Edward Ernest, 1875–1915, vol. I
Williams, Edward Francis; *see* Baron Francis-Williams.
Williams, Brig.-Gen. Edward George, 1867–1941, vol. IV
Williams, Rt Hon. Sir Edward John, 1890–1963, vol. VI
Williams, Sir Edward Leader, 1828–1910, vol. I
Williams, Brig. Edward Stephen Bruce, 1892–1977, vol. VII

Williams, Edward Wilmot, 1826–1913, vol. I
Williams, Rev. Eleazar, *died* 1905, vol. I
Williams, Lt-Col Eliot C.; *see* Crawshay-Williams.
Williams, Rt Hon. Sir Ellis H.; *see* Hume-Williams.
Williams, Eric Charles, 1915–1980, vol. VII
Williams, Eric W.; *see* Watson-Williams.
Williams, Ernest Edwin, 1866–1935, vol. III
Williams, Sir Ernest H.; *see* Hodder-Williams, Sir J. E.
Williams, Sir Ernest Hillas, 1899–1965, vol. VI
Williams, (Ernest) Rohan, 1906–1963, vol. VI
Williams, Ethel Mary Nucella, 1863–1948, vol. IV
Williams, Sir Evan, 1st Bt (*cr* 1935), 1871–1959, vol. V
Williams, Ven. (Evan Daniel) Aldred, 1879–1951, vol. V
Williams, Evan James, 1903–1945, vol. IV
Williams, Sir (Evan) Owen, 1890–1969, vol. VI
Williams, Bt-Col Evelyn Hugh Watkin, 1884–1934, vol. III
Williams, F. Harald; *see* Ward, Rev. Frederick W. O.
Williams, Major Francis V.; *see* Vaughan-Williams.
Williams, Francis Wigley Greswolde G.; *see* Greswolde-Williams.
Williams, Surg. Rear-Adm. (D) Frank Reginald Parry, 1897–1965, vol. VI
Williams, Franklyn; *see* Williams, A. F.
Williams, Sir Frederic Calland, 1911–1977, vol. VII
Williams, Rev. Frederick Billingsley Ambrose, 1870–1932, vol. III
Williams, Brig. and Chief Paymaster Frederick Christian, 1891–1970, vol. VI
Williams, Rev. Frederick Farewell Sanigear, 1870–1956, vol. V
Williams, Sir Frederick Law, 7th Bt (*cr* 1866), 1862–1921, vol. II
Williams, Frederick Sims, 1855–1941, vol. IV
Williams, Sir Frederick William, 5th Bt (*cr* 1866), 1888–1913, vol. I
Williams, Brig.-Gen. G. Coventry, 1860–1947, vol. IV
Williams, Very Rev. Garfield Hodder, 1881–1960, vol. V
Williams, Geoffrey Sydney, 1871–1952, vol. V
Williams, Sir George, 1821–1905, vol. I
Williams, George, 1879–1951, vol. V
Williams, Sir George Clark, 1st Bt (*cr* 1955), 1878–1958, vol. V
Williams, Comdr George Davies, 1879–1947, vol. IV
Williams, Rev. George H., 1859–1926, vol. II
Williams, George L.; *see* Lowsley-Williams.
Williams, Brig.-Gen. George Mostyn, 1868–1943, vol. IV
Williams, Rt Rev. Gershom Mott, 1857–1923, vol. II
Williams, Gilbert Milner, 1898–1979, vol. VII
Williams, Maj.-Gen. Sir Godfrey, 1859–1940, vol. III
Williams, Godfrey Herbert, 1875–1956, vol. V

Williams, Sir Griffith Goodland, 1890–1974, vol. VII
Williams, Gen. Sir Guy Charles, 1881–1959, vol. V
Williams, Gwilym, 1839–1906, vol. I
Williams, Sir Gwilym Ffrangcon, 1902–1969, vol. VI
Williams, Gwyn, 1904–1955, vol. V
Williams, Gwynne Evan Owen, *died* 1958, vol. V
Williams, Harcourt; *see* Williams, E. G. H.
Williams, Harley; *see* Williams, J. H. H.
Williams, Lt-Gen. Sir Harold, 1897–1971, vol. VII
Williams, Harold Beck, 1889–1969, vol. VI
Williams, Harold H.; *see* Heathcote-Williams.
Williams, Sir Harold Herbert, 1880–1964, vol. VI
Williams, Hon. Sir Hartley, 1843–1929, vol. III
Williams, Henry, 1850–1933, vol. III
Williams, Col Henry David, 1854–1924, vol. II
Williams, Lt-Gen. Sir Henry Francis, 1825–1907, vol. I
Williams, Rt Rev. Henry Herbert, 1872–1961, vol. VI
Williams, Lt-Col Henry John, 1870–1935, vol. III
Williams, Henry Owen, 1855–1943, vol. IV
Williams, Herbert, 1862–1916, vol. II
Williams, Sir Herbert Geraint, 1st Bt (*cr* 1953), 1884–1954, vol. V
Williams, Rt Rev. Herbert William, *died* 1937, vol. III
Williams, Howard, 1837–1931, vol. III
Williams, Sir Howell Jones, *died* 1939, vol. III
Williams, Hubert Llewelyn, 1890–1964, vol. VI
Williams, Rev. Hugh, 1843–1911, vol. I
Williams, Hugh Anthony Glanmor, 1904–1969, vol. VI
Williams, Maj.-Gen. Sir Hugh Bruce Bruce-, 1865–1942, vol. IV
Williams, Rev. Hugh Cernyw, 1843–1937, vol. III
Williams, Sir Hugh Grenville, 6th Bt (*cr* 1798), 1889–1961, vol. VI
Williams, Comdr Hugh L.; *see* Lloyd-Williams.
Williams, Hugh Noel, 1870–1925, vol. II
Williams, Adm. Hugh Pigot, 1858–1934, vol. III
Williams, Sir (I.) Thomas, 1853–1941, vol. IV
Williams, Sir Ifor, 1881–1965, vol. VI
Williams, Iolo Aneurin, 1890–1962, vol. VI
Williams, Isaac John, 1875–1939, vol. III
Williams, Ivor Maredydd B.; *see* Bankes-Williams.
Williams, J. H., 1855–1942, vol. IV
Williams, J. Lloyd, *died* 1945, vol. IV
Williams, Jack F.; *see* Fox-Williams.
Williams, James, 1851–1911, vol. I
Williams, James Alexander, *born* 1856, vol. II
Williams, Ven. James Evan, *died* 1953, vol. V
Williams, Captain James Evan L.; *see* Lloyd-Williams.
Williams, James Howard, 1897–1958, vol. V
Williams, James Leslie, 1870–1949, vol. IV
Williams, Hon. James Rowland, 1860–1916, vol. II
Williams, John, 1861–1922, vol. II
Williams, Sir John, 1st Bt, 1840–1926, vol. II
Williams, Lt-Col John, 1874–1942, vol. IV
Williams, John, *died* 1951, vol. V
Williams, John Basil, 1906–1953, vol. V
Williams, John Carvell, 1821–1907, vol. I

Williams, John Charles, 1861–1939, vol. III
Williams, Sir John Coldbrook H.; *see* Hanbury-Williams.
Williams, John David, 1853–1923, vol. II
Williams, Sir John Fischer, 1870–1947, vol. IV
Williams, Maj.-Gen. Sir John H.; *see* Hanbury-Williams.
Williams, John H.; *see* Haynes-Williams.
Williams, (John Hargreaves) Harley, *died* 1974, vol. VII
Williams, John Haulfryn, 1908–1980, vol. VII
Williams, John Henry, 1870–1936, vol. III
Williams, Sir John Lias Cecil C.; *see* Cecil-Williams.
Williams, Sir (John Lloyd Vaughan) Seymour, 1868–1945, vol. IV
Williams, Rev. John Owen, 1853–1932, vol. III
Williams, Sir John Rolleston L.; *see* Lort-Williams.
Williams, Sir John William Collman, 1823–1911, vol. I
Williams, John Williams, 1885–1957, vol. V
Williams, Joseph Grout, 1848–1923, vol. II
Williams, Rt Hon. Joseph Powell, 1840–1904, vol. I
Williams, Rt Rev. Joseph Watkin, 1857–1934, vol. III
Williams, Rt Hon. Sir Joshua Strange, 1837–1915, vol. I (A)
Williams, Katharine Georgina L.; *see* Lloyd-Williams.
Williams, Lt-Col Kenneth Greville, 1892–1972, vol. VII
Williams, L. Gwendolen, *died* 1955, vol. V
Williams, Laurence Frederic Rushbrook, 1890–1978, vol. VII
Williams, Maj.-Gen. Lawrence Henry, 1834–1916, vol. II
Williams, Rt Rev. Lennox Waldron, 1859–1958, vol. V
Williams, Sir Leonard; *see* Williams, Sir A. L.
Williams, Leonard John, 1894–1975, vol. VII
Williams, Leonard Llewelyn Bulkeley, 1861–1939, vol. III
Williams, Col Leslie Gwatkin, 1878–1926, vol. II
Williams, Maj.-Gen. Sir Leslie Hamlyn, 1892–1965, vol. VI
Williams, Leslie Harry, 1909–1978, vol. VII
Williams, Leslie Herbert Whitby, 1893–1972, vol. VII
Williams, Leslie Thomas Douglas, 1905–1976, vol. VII
Williams, Lily, 1874–1940, vol. III
Williams, Llywelyn, 1911–1965, vol. VI
Williams, Margaret Lindsay, *died* 1960, vol. V
Williams, Mary, 1882–1977, vol. VII
Williams, Mary Atkinson, *died* 1949, vol. IV
Williams, Monier Faithfull M.; *see* Monier-Williams.
Williams, Sir Monier M.; *see* Monier-Williams.
Williams, Montagu Sneade Faithfull M.; *see* Monier-Williams.
Williams, Morgan Stuart, 1846–1909, vol. I
Williams, Neville John, 1924–1977, vol. VII
Williams, Rev. Norman Powell, 1883–1943, vol. IV

Williams, Brig.-Gen. Oliver de Lancey, 1875–1959, vol. V
Williams, Orlando Cyprian, (Orlo), 1883–1967, vol. VI
Williams, Sir Osmond; *see* Williams, Sir A. O.
Williams, Sir Owen; *see* Williams, Sir E. O.
Williams, Owen Gwyn Revell, 1886–1954, vol. V
Williams, Owen Herbert, 1884–1962, vol. VI
Williams, Owen J., 1850–1908, vol. I
Williams, Lt-Gen. Owen Lewis Cope, 1836–1904, vol. I
Williams, Owen Thomas, 1877–1913, vol. I
Williams, Patrick W.; *see* Watson-Williams.
Williams, Penry, 1866–1945, vol. IV
Williams, Rev. Philip, *died* 1933, vol. III
Williams, Sir Philip Francis Cunningham, 2nd Bt (*cr* 1915), 1884–1958, vol. V
Williams, Sir Ralph Champneys, 1848–1927, vol. II
Williams, Ralph Paul, 1874–1939, vol. III
Williams, Ralph V.; *see* Vaughan Williams.
Williams, Ralph Wilfred H.; *see* Hodder-Williams.
Williams, Brig.-Gen. Raymond Burlton, 1855–1929, vol. III
Williams, Sir Reginald Lawrence William, 7th Bt (*cr* 1798), 1900–1971, vol. VII
Williams, Lt-Col Sir Rhys Rhys-, 1st Bt (*cr* 1918), 1865–1955, vol. V
Williams, Air Marshal Sir Richard, 1890–1980, vol. VII
Williams, Richard James, 1876–1964, vol. VI
Williams, Sir Richard John, 1853–1941, vol. IV
Williams, Richard Tecwyn, 1909–1979, vol. VII
Williams, Robert, 1881–1936, vol. III
Williams, Sir Robert, 1st Bt (*cr* 1928), 1860–1938, vol. III
Williams, Ven. Robert, 1863–1938, vol. III
Williams, Col Sir Robert, 1st Bt (*cr* 1915), 1848–1943, vol. IV
Williams, Robert Allan, *died* 1951, vol. V
Williams, Rev. Robert C.; *see* Camber-Williams.
Williams, Lt-Col Robert Carlisle, 1880–1964, vol. VI
Williams, Maj.-Gen. Robert Ernest, 1855–1943, vol. IV
Williams, Sir Robert Ernest, 9th Bt (*cr* 1866), 1924–1976, vol. VII
Williams, Robert James P.; *see* Probyn-Williams.
Williams, Robert Percy H.; *see* Hodder-Williams.
Williams, Robert Stenhouse, 1871–1932, vol. III
Williams, Robert Thesiger W.; *see* Watkin-Williams.
Williams, Rohan; *see* Williams, E. R.
Williams, Roland Edmund Lomax Vaughan, 1866–1949, vol. IV
Williams, Rt Hon. Sir Roland Lomax Bowdler Vaughan, 1838–1916, vol. II
Williams, Romer, 1850–1942, vol. IV
Williams, Rt Rev. Ronald Ralph, 1906–1979, vol. VII
Williams, Major Ronald Samuel Ainslie, 1890–1971, vol. VII
Williams, Ronald Watkins, 1907–1958, vol. V
Williams, Sir Roy Ellis H.; *see* Hume-Williams.

Williams, Captain Rupert Stanley G.; *see* Gwatkin-Williams.

Williams, Ven. Samuel, 1822–1907, vol. I

Williams, Rev. Samuel Blackwell G.; *see* Guest Williams.

Williams, Samuel Charles Evans, 1842–1926, vol. II

Williams, Sir Seymour; *see* Williams, Sir J. L. V. S.

Williams, Lt-Col Stanley Price, 1885–1977, vol. VII

Williams, Brig.-Gen. Sydney Frederick, 1866–1942, vol. IV

Williams, Terrick, 1860–1936, vol. III

Williams, Theodore Rowland, 1889–1964, vol. VI

Williams, Rev. Thomas, *died* 1915, vol. I (A)

Williams, Sir Thomas, 1893–1967, vol. VI

Williams, Sir Thomas; *see* Williams, Sir D. T.

Williams, Sir Thomas; *see* Williams, Sir I. T.

Williams, Very Rev. Thomas Alfred, 1870–1941, vol. IV

Williams, Rev. Thomas Charles, *died* 1927, vol. II

Williams, Thomas Christopher, 1913–1972, vol. VII

Williams, Thomas H.; *see* Hudson-Williams.

Williams, Sir Thomas Herbert P.; *see* Parry-Williams.

Williams, Thomas Jeremiah, 1872–1919, vol. II

Williams, Ven. Thomas John, 1889–1956, vol. V

Williams, Most Rev. Thomas Leighton, 1877–1946, vol. IV

Williams, Sir Thomas Marchant, 1845–1914, vol. I

Williams, Air Marshal Sir Thomas Melling, 1899–1956, vol. V

Williams, Rev. Thomas Rhondda, 1860–1945, vol. IV

Williams, Maj.-Gen. Thomas Rhys, 1884–1950, vol. IV

Williams, Lt-Col Thomas Samuel Beauchamp, 1877–1927, vol. II

Williams, Valentine, 1883–1946, vol. IV

Williams, Victor Erle N.; *see* Nash-Williams.

Williams, W. H.; *see* Howard-Williams.

Williams, W. Llewelyn, 1867–1922, vol. II

Williams, W. Phillpotts, 1860–1916, vol. II

Williams, Engr-Comdr Waller Kent, *died* 1914, vol. I

Williams, Maj.-Gen. Walter David Abbott, 1897–1973, vol. VII

Williams, Walter Nalder, 1880–1966, vol. VI

Williams, Rt Rev. Watkin Herbert, 1845–1944, vol. IV

Williams, Rev. Watkin Wynn, 1859–1944, vol. IV

Williams, Maj.-Gen. Weir De Lancey, 1872–1961, vol. VI

Williams, Very Rev. William, *died* 1930, vol. III

Williams, Engr-Captain William Arthur, 1882–1953, vol. V

Williams, William Daniel, 1888–1970, vol. VI

Williams, Surg.-Gen. Sir William Daniel Campbell, 1856–1919, vol. II

Williams, Sir William Emrys, 1896–1977, vol. VII

Williams, Sir William Frederick, 4th Bt (*cr* 1866), 1886–1905, vol. I

Williams, Sir William Grenville, 4th Bt (*cr* 1798), 1844–1904, vol. I

Williams, William Henry, 1852–1941, vol. IV

Williams, Col William Hugh, 1857–1938 vol. III

Williams, Sir William John, 1828–1903, vol. I

Williams, William John, 1878–1952, vol. V

Williams, Lt-Col Sir William Jones, 1904–1976, vol. VII

Williams, Sir William Law, 8th Bt (*cr* 1866), 1907–1960, vol. V

Williams, Rt Rev. William Leonard, 1829–1916, vol. II

Williams, Hon. William Micah *died* 1924, vol. II

Williams, William Owen, 1860–1911, vol. I

Williams, Sir Wliliam Richard, 1879–1961, vol. VI

Williams, William Richard, 1895–1963, vol. VI

Williams, Sir William Robert, 3rd Bt (*cr* 1866), 1860–1903, vol. I

Williams, William St John F.; *see* Pranc's-Williams.

Williams, Sir William Willoughby, 5th Bt (*cr* 1798), 1888–1932, vol. III

Williams-Bulkeley, Sir Richard Henry; *see* Bulkeley.

Williams-Drummond, Sir James Hamlyn Williams; *see* Drummond.

Williams-Drummond, Sir William Hugh Dudley; *see* Drummond.

Williams-Ellis, Sir (Bertram) Clough, 1883–1978, vol. VII

Williams-Ellis, Sir Clough; *see* Williams-Ellis, Sir B. C.

Williams-Freeman, Comdr Frederick Arthur Peere, 1889–1939, vol. III

Williams-Taylor, Sir Frederick, 1863–1945, vol. IV

Williams-Thomas, Lt-Col Frank S., 1879–1942, vol. IV

Williams-Thomas, Joseph Silvers; *see* Thomas.

Williams Wynn, Frederick R., 1865–1940, vol. III

Williams-Wynn, Col Sir Herbert Lloyd Watkin, 7th Bt, 1860–1944, vol. III

Williams-Wynn, Col Sir Robert William Herbert Watkin, 9th Bt, 1862–1951, vol. V

Williams-Wynn, Sir Watkin, 8th Bt, 1891–1949, vol. IV

Williamson, Captain Adolphus Huddleston, 1869–1918, vol. II

Williamson, Alec, 1886–1975, vol. VII

Williamson, Sir Alexander, 1879–1971, vol. VII

Williamson, Alexander William, 1824–1904, vol. I

Williamson, Alice Muriel, 1869–1933, vol. III

Williamson, Andrew, *died* 1937, vol. III

Williamson, Rt Rev. Andrew Wallace, 1856–1926, vol. II

Williamson, Benjamin, 1827–1916, vol. II

Williamson, Mrs Catherine Ellis, 1896–1977, vol. VII

Williamson, Rev. Charles David Robertson, 1853–1943, vol. IV

Williamson, Sir Charles Hedworth, 10th Bt, 1903–1946, vol. IV

Williamson, Charles Norris, 1859–1920, vol. II

Williamson, Mrs Charles Norris; *see* Williamson, Alice Muriel.

Williamson, Colin Martin, 1887–1976, vol. VII

Williamson, David, 1868–1955, vol. V

Williamson, David, 1916–1980, vol. VII

Williamson, David Robertson, 1830–1913, vol. I

Williamson, Rt Rev. Edward William, 1892–1953, vol. V

Williamson, Francis John, 1833–1920, vol. II

Williamson, Brig.-Gen. Sir Frederic Herbert, 1876–1939, vol. III

Williamson, Frederick, 1891–1935, vol. III

Williamson, Sir George Alexander, 1898–1975, vol. VII

Williamson, George Charles, 1858–1942, vol. IV

Williamson, George Watkins, 1875–1957, vol. V

Williamson, Harold, 1872–1935, vol. III

Williamson, Sir Hedworth, 8th Bt, 1827–1900, vol. I

Williamson, Sir Hedworth, 9th Bt, 1867–1942, vol. IV

Williamson, Henry, 1895–1977, vol. VII

Williamson, Rev. Henry Drummond, 1854–1926, vol. II

Williamson, Rev. Henry Trevor, *died* 1940, vol. III

Williamson, Herbert, 1872–1924, vol. II

Williamson, Sir Horace, 1880–1965, vol. VI

Williamson, Gp Captain Hugh Alexander, 1885–1979, vol. VII

Williamson, Hugh R.; *see* Ross Williamson.

Williamson, Sir James, 1839–1932, vol. III

Williamson, Sir James, 1877–1959, vol. V

Williamson, James Alexander, 1886–1964, vol. VI

Williamson, Col John Francis, 1851–1930, vol. III

Williamson, John Thoburn, 1907–1958, vol. V

Williamson, Kenneth Bertram, 1875–1959, vol. V

Williamson, Lawrence Collingwood, 1886–1955, vol. V

Williamson, Ven. Montague Blamire, 1863–1939, vol. III

Williamson, Oliver Key, *died* 1941, vol. IV

Williamson, Reginald Pole R.; *see* Ross Williamson.

Williamson, Richard Harcourt, 1879–1941, vol. IV

Williamson, Richard Thomas, 1862–1937, vol. III

Williamson, Col Robert Frederic, 1843–1938, vol. III

Williamson, Robert Wood, 1856–1932, vol. III

Williamson, Samuel, *died* 1950, vol. IV

Williamson, Stephen, 1827–1903, vol. I

Williamson, Thomas Broadwood, 1911–1963, vol. VI

Williamson, Victor Alexander, 1838–1924, vol. II

Williamson, Sir Walter James Franklin, 1867–1954, vol. V

Williamson, Rev. William, 1851–1936, vol. III

Williamson-Noble, Frederick Arnold, 1889–1969, vol. VI

Willingdon, 1st Marquis of, 1866–1941, vol. IV

Willingdon, 2nd Marquess of, 1899–1979, vol. VII

Willingdon, Marchioness of; (Marie Adelaide), 1875–1960, vol. V

Willink, Rt Hon. Sir Henry Urmston, 1st Bt, 1894–1973, vol. VII

Willink, Very Rev. John Wakefield, 1858–1927, vol. II

Willis, Sir Addington; *see* Willis, Sir W. A.

Willis, Hon. Albert Charles, 1876–1954, vol. V

Willis, Rt Rev. Alfred, 1836–1920, vol. II

Willis, Admiral of the Fleet Sir Algernon Usborne, 1889–1976, vol. VII

Willis, Anthony Armstrong, 1897–1976, vol. VII

Willis, Arthur d'Anyers, 1879–1953, vol V

Willis, Charles Armine, 1881–1975, vol. VII

Willis, Col Charles Fancourt, 1854–1918, vol. II

Willis, Lt-Col Charles Hope, 1859–1940, vol. III

Willis, Maj.-Gen. Edward Henry, 1870–1961, vol. VI

Willis, Sir Edward William, 1849–1941, vol. IV

Willis, Ernest William, 1874–1939, vol. III

Willis, Frank, 1865–1932, vol. III

Willis, Sir Frank; *see* Willis, Sir Z. F.

Willis, Captain Frank Reginald, 1881–1964, vol. VI

Willis, Rev. Frederic Earle d'Anyers, 1869–1940, vol. III

Willis, Rev. Frederic William, 1842–1930, vol. III

Willis, Sir Frederick James, 1863–1946, vol. IV

Willis, Rt Rev. Frederick Roberts, 1900–1976, vol. VII

Willis, Sir George H. S., 1823–1900, vol. I

Willis, Col Sir George Henry, 1875–1940, vol. III

Willis, Paymaster Captain George Hughlings Armstrong, 1863–1934, vol. III

Willis, Hon. Henry, 1860–1950, vol. IV

Willis, John Christopher, 1868–1958, vol. V

Willis, Maj.-Gen. John Christopher Temple, 1900–1969, vol. VI

Willis, Rt Rev. John Jamieson, 1872–1954, vol. V

Willis, Joseph George, 1861–1924, vol. II

Willis, Col Richard ffolliott, 1875–1960, vol. V

Willis, Major Richard Raymond, 1876–1966, vol. VI

Willis, Rupert Allan, 1898–1980, vol. VII

Willis, Samuel William Ward, 1870–1948, vol. IV

Willis, Sir (Walter) Addington, 1862–1953, vol. V

Willis, Sir William, 1821–1906, vol. I

Willis, William, 1835–1911, vol. I

Willis, Ven. William Newcombe de Laval, 1846–1916, vol. II

Willis, William Outhwaite, 1870–1940, vol. III

Willis, Sir (Zwinglius) Frank, 1890–1974, vol. VII

Willis-Bund, John William, 1843–1928, vol. II

Willis-O'Connor, Col Henry; *see* O'Connor.

Willison, Brig. Arthur Cecil, 1896–1966, vol. VI

Willison, Herbert, *died* 1943, vol. IV

Willison, Sir John Stephen, 1856–1927, vol. II

Willkie, Wendell Lewis, 1892–1944, vol. IV

Willmore, Henry Horace Albert, 1871–1919, vol. II

Willmot, Joseph William, 1849–1929, vol. III

Willmot, Roger Boulton, 1892–1964, vol. VI

Willmott, Harry, 1851–1931, vol. III

Willmott, Sir Maurice Gordon, 1894–1977, vol. VII

Willock, Brig.-Gen. Frederick George, *died* 1955, vol. V

Willock, Air Vice-Marshal Robert Peel, 1893–1973, vol. VII

Willock-Pollen, Henry Court, 1860–1934, vol. III

Willoughby de Broke, 18th (shown as 10th) Baron, 1844–1902, vol. I

Willoughby de Broke, 19th Baron, 1869–1923, vol. II

Willoughby de Eresby, Lord; Timothy Gilbert Heathcote-Drummond-Willoughby, 1936–1963, vol. VI

Willoughby, Brig.-Gen. Hon. Charles Strathavon Heathcote-Drummond-, 1870–1949, vol. IV

Willoughby, Lt-Col Hon. Claud Heathcote-Drummond, 1872–1950, vol. IV

Willoughby, Col Hon. Claude Henry Comaraich, 1862–1932, vol. III

Willoughby, Col Douglas Vere, 1882–1949, vol. IV

Willoughby, Maj.-Gen. James Fortnom, 1844–1922, vol. II

Willoughby, Major Sir John Christopher, 5th Bt, 1859–1918, vol. II

Willoughby, Leonard Ashley, 1885–1977, vol. VII

Willoughby, Brig.-Gen. Michael Edward, 1864–1939, vol. III

Willoughby, Lt-Gen. Michael Weekes, 1833–1925, vol. II

Willoughby, Percival Robert Augustus, 1868–1913, vol. I

Willoughby, Wellington Bartley, 1859–1932, vol. III

Willoughby-Osborne, Col Arthur de Vere, 1869–1933, vol. III

Willox, Sir John Archibald, 1842–1905, vol. I

Wills, Rt Hon. Sir Alfred, 1828–1912, vol. I

Wills, Captain Arnold Stancomb, 1877–1961, vol. VI

Wills, Arthur Walters, 1868–1948, vol. IV

Wills, Lt-Col Caleb Shera, 1834–1906, vol. I

Wills, Cecil Upton, died 1954, vol. V

Wills, Charles James, 1842–1912, vol. I

Wills, Vice-Adm. Charles Samuel, died 1931, vol. III

Wills, Edith Agnes, 1892–1970, vol. VI

Wills, Sir Edward Chaning, 2nd Bt (cr 1904), 1861–1921, vol. II

Wills, Sir Edward Payson, 1st Bt (cr 1904), 1834–1910, vol. I

Wills, Sir Ernest Salter, 3rd Bt (cr 1904), 1869–1958, vol. V

Wills, Sir Frank William, 1852–1932, vol. III

Wills, Sir Frederick, 1st Bt (cr 1897), 1838–1909, vol. I

Wills, Rev. Freeman, died 1913, vol. I

Wills, Sir George Alfred, 1st Bt (cr 1923), 1854–1928, vol. II

Wills, Sir (George) Peter (Vernon), 3rd Bt (cr 1923), 1922–1945, vol. IV

Wills, Sir George Vernon Proctor, 2nd Bt (cr 1923), 1887–1931, vol. III

Wills, Sir Gerald, 1905–1969, vol. VI

Wills, Henry Herbert, 1856–1922, vol. II

Wills, Herbert W., died 1937, vol. III

Wills, Dame Janet Stancomb Graham S.; see Stancomb-Wills.

Wills, John Joseph, 1877–1971, vol. VII

Wills, Brig. Sir Kenneth Agnew, 1896–1977, vol. VII

Wills, Leonard Johnston, 1884–1979, vol. VII

Wills, Rev. Percival Banks, died 1936, vol. III

Wills, Sir Peter; see Wills, Sir G. P. V.

Wills, Philip Aubrey, 1907–1978, vol. VII

Wills, Richard Lloyd Joseph, 1914–1969, vol. VI

Wills, Dame Violet Edith, died 1964, vol. VI

Wills, Walter Kenneth, 1872–1968, vol. VI

Wills, Wilfrid Dewhurst, 1898–1954, vol. V

Wills, Major William Arthur, 1863–1937, vol. III

Willshire, Sir Arthur Reginald Thomas Maxwell-, 2nd Bt, 1850–1919, vol. II

Willshire, Sir Gerard Arthur Maxwell-, 3rd Bt, 1892–1947, vol. IV

Willson, Rev. Archdall Beaumont Wynne, died 1958, vol. V

Willson, Beckles, 1869–1942, vol. IV

Willson, Leslie, died 1924, vol. II

Willson, Maj.-Gen. Sir Mildmay Willson, 1847–1912, vol. I

Willson, Rt Rev. St J. Basil Wynne, 1868–1946, vol. IV

Willson, Rev. Thomas B., 1851–1932, vol. III

Willson, Thomas Olaf, 1880–1973, vol. VII

Willson, Sir Walter Stuart James, 1876–1952, vol. V

Willson, William Thomas C.; see Curtis-Willson.

Willway, Brig. Alfred Cedric Cowan, 1898–1980, vol. VII

Willway, Brig. Cedric; see Willway, Brig. A. C. C.

Willy; see Gauthier-Villars, Henry.

Willyams, Arthur Champion Phillips, 1837–1917, vol. II

Willyams, Edward Brydges, 1836–1916, vol. II

Willyams, Bt Col Edward Neynoe, 1891–1964, vol. VI

Wilmer, Brig. Eric Randal Gordon, 1882–1958, vol. V

Wilmer, Rev. John Kidd, died 1928, vol. II (A), vol. II

Wilmot of Selmeston, 1st Baron, 1895–1961, vol. VI

Wilmot, Hon. Alexander, 1836–1923, vol. II

Wilmot, Col Arthur E.; see Eardley-Wilmot.

Wilmot, Captain Sir Arthur Ralph, 7th Bt (cr 1759), 1909–1942, vol. IV

Wilmot, Chester, (Reginald William Winchester Wilmot), 1911–1954, vol. V

Wilmot, Sir Henry, 5th Bt (cr 1759), 1831–1901, vol. I

Wilmot, Captain Cecil F. E.; see Eardley-Wilmot.

Wilmot, Rev. Ernest Augustus E.; see Eardley-Wilmot.

Wilmot, Harold, 1895–1966, vol. VI

Wilmot, Hugh Eden E.; see Eardley-Wilmot.

Wilmot, Sir John E.; see Eardley-Wilmot.

Wilmot, May E.; see Eardley-Wilmot.

Wilmot, Sir Ralph Henry Sacheverel, 6th Bt (cr 1759), 1875–1918, vol. II

Wilmot, Reginald William Winchester; see Wilmot, C.

Wilmot, Maj.-Gen. Revell E.; see Eardley-Wilmot.

Wilmot, Sir Robert Arthur, 8th Bt, 1939–1974 (cr 1759), vol. VII

Wilmot, Sir Robert Rodney, 6th Bt (cr 1772), 1853–1931, vol. III

Wilmot, Sir Sainthill E.; *see* Eardley-Wilmot.

Wilmot, Rear-Adm. Sir Sydney Marow E.; *see* Eardley-Wilmot.

Wilmot-Smith, Comdr Andrew, *died* 1937, vol. III

Wilmott, Alfred James, 1888–1950, vol. IV

Wilmshurst, Thomas Percival, *died* 1950, vol. IV

Wilsden, Rev. Joseph Samuel, 1835–1914, vol. I

Wilsey, Maj.-Gen. John Harold Owen, 1904–1961, vol. VI

Wilshaw, Sir Edward, 1879–1968, vol. VI

Wilshere, Alfred Henry, 1854–1927, vol. II (A), vol. III

Wilshire, Frederick Allen, 1868–1944, vol. IV

Wilsmore, Norman T. M., 1868–1940, vol. III

Wilson, 1st Baron, 1881–1964, vol. VI

Wilson of High Wray, Baron (Life Peer); Paul Norman Wilson, 1908–1980, vol. VII

Wilson, Adam, 1882–1951, vol. V

Wilson, Alan, 1896–1959, vol. V

Wilson, Lt-Col Alban; *see* Wilson, Lt-Col J. A.

Wilson, Albert Edward, *died* 1960, vol. V

Wilson, Sir Alexander, 1st Bt (*cr* 1897), 1837–1907, vol. I

Wilson, Sir Alexander, 1843–1907, vol. I

Wilson, Maj.-Gen. Sir Alexander, 1858–1937, vol. III

Wilson, Alexander, 1917–1978, vol. VII

Wilson, Captain Alexander Guy Berners, 1890–1942, vol. IV

Wilson, Alexander Johnstone, 1841–1921, vol. II

Wilson, Alpheus Waters, 1834–1916, vol. II

Wilson, Rev. Ambrose John, 1853–1929, vol. III

Wilson, Andrew, 1852–1912, vol. I

Wilson, Andrew, 1909–1974, vol. VII

Wilson, Archibald Wayet, *died* 1950, vol. IV (A), vol. V

Wilson, Lt-Col Sir Arnold Talbot, 1884–1940, vol. III

Wilson, Arthur, 1836–1909, vol. I

Wilson, Rt Hon. Sir Arthur, 1837–1915, vol. I (A)

Wilson, Col Arthur Harry H.; *see* Hutton-Wilson.

Wilson, Adm. Sir Arthur Knyvet, 3rd Bt (*cr* 1857), 1842–1921, vol. II

Wilson, Arthur Stanley, 1868–1938, vol. III

Wilson, Sir Arton, 1893–1977, vol. VII

Wilson, Rev. Barton Worsley, *died* 1920, vol. II

Wilson, Rev. Bernard Robert, 1857–1909, vol. I

Wilson, Sir Bertram, 1893–1974, vol. VII

Wilson, Bertram Martin, 1896–1935, vol. III

Wilson, Beryl Charlotte Mary, *died* 1951, vol. V

Wilson, Maj.-Gen. Bevil Thomson, 1885–1975, vol. VII

Wilson, Col Campbell Aubrey Kenneth I.; *see* Innes-Wilson.

Wilson, Rt Rev. Cecil, 1860–1941, vol. IV

Wilson, Cecil Claude, 1885–1968, vol. VI

Wilson, Cecil Henry, 1862–1945, vol. IV

Wilson, Rt Rev. Cecil Wilfred, 1875–1937, vol. III

Wilson, Major Cecil William, 1870–1937, vol. III

Wilson, Charles Ashley C.; *see* Carus-Wilson.

Wilson, Mrs Charles Ashley C.; *see* Carus-Wilson.

Wilson, Captain Charles Benjamin, 1885–1957, vol. V

Wilson, Charles Edward, 1848–1938, vol. III (A), vol. IV

Wilson, Rev. Charles Edward, 1871–1956, vol. V

Wilson, Charles Edward, 1886–1972, vol. VII

Wilson, Charles Erwin, 1890–1961, vol. VI

Wilson, Sir Charles Henry, 1859–1930, vol. III

Wilson, Charles Henry, 1858–1937, vol. III

Wilson, Col Charles Henry Luttrell Fahie, 1858–1935, vol. III

Wilson, Charles Paul, 1900–1970, vol. VI

Wilson, Sir Charles Rivers, 1831–1916, vol. II

Wilson, Sir Charles S.; *see* Stewart-Wilson.

Wilson, Brig.-Gen. Charles Stuart, 1867–1933, vol. III

Wilson, Charles Thomson Rees, 1869–1959, vol. V

Wilson, Rev. Charles William Goodall, 1860–1948, vol. IV

Wilson, Christopher James, 1879–1956, vol. V

Wilson, Col Christopher Wyndham, 1844–1918, vol. II

Wilson, Claude, 1860–1937, vol. III

Wilson, Clive Henry Adolphus, 1876–1921, vol. II

Wilson, Clyde Tabor, 1889–1971, vol. VII

Wilson, Sir Courthope; *see* Wilson, Sir William C. T.

Wilson, Col Cyril Edward, 1873–1938, vol. III

Wilson, D. Forrester, *died* 1950, vol. IV

Wilson, Rev. Daniel Frederic, 1830–1918, vol. II

Wilson, Hon. Daniel Martin, 1862–1932, vol. III

Wilson, Sir David, 1838–1924, vol. II

Wilson, Sir David, 1st Bt (*cr* 1920), 1855–1930, vol. III

Wilson, David Alec, 1864–1933, vol. III

Wilson, Very Rev. David Frederick Ruddell, 1871–1957, vol. V

Wilson, David Mackay, 1863–1929, vol. III

Wilson, Rt Rev. Douglas John, 1903–1980, vol. VII

Wilson, Sir Duncan Randolph, 1875–1945, vol. IV

Wilson, Major Duncan William, 1881–1935, vol. III

Wilson, Lt-Col Edmond Munkhouse, 1855–1921, vol. II

Wilson, Edmund, 1895–1972, vol. VII

Wilson, Edmund Beecher, 1856–1939, vol. III

Wilson, Col Edward Hales, 1845–1917, vol. II

Wilson, Edward Meryon, 1906–1977, vol. VII

Wilson, Brig. Edward William Gravatt, 1888–1971, vol. VII

Wilson, Edwin John B.; *see* Boyd-Wilson.

Wilson, Eleanora Mary C.; *see* Carus-Wilson.

Wilson, Maj.-Gen. Erastus William, 1860–1922, vol. II

Wilson, Brig. Sir Eric Edward Boketon H.; *see* Holt-Wilson.

Wilson, Ernest, *died* 1932, vol. III

Wilson, Ernest Henry, 1876–1930, vol. III

Wilson, Florence Roma Muir; *see* Wilson, Romer.

Wilson, Forsyth James, 1880–1944, vol. IV

Wilson, Maj.-Gen. Francis Adrian, 1874–1954, vol. V

Wilson, Maj.-Gen. Francis Edward Edwards, 1839–1905, vol. I

Wilson, Hon. Frank, 1859–1918, vol. II

Wilson, Captain Sir Frank O'Brien, 1883–1962, vol. VI

Wilson, Frank Percy, 1889–1963, vol. VI
Wilson, Col Frank Walter, 1869–1953, vol. V
Wilson, Lt-Col Frederick Alfred, 1863–1932, vol. III
Wilson, Frederick James, 1858–1926, vol. II
Wilson, Maj.-Gen. Frederick Maurice, 1868–1956, vol. V
Wilson, Sir Frederick William, 1844–1924, vol. II
Wilson, Sir Garnet Douglas, 1885–1975, vol. VII
Wilson, Geoffrey; see Wilson, H. G. B.
Wilson, Captain George, 1849–1932, vol. III
Wilson, Lt-Col George, 1869–1935, vol. III
Wilson, George, 1862–1943, vol. IV
Wilson, Sir George, 1900–1979, vol. VII
Wilson, George Ambler, 1906–1977, vol. VII
Wilson, George Bailey, 1863–1952, vol. V
Wilson, George Frederick, 1886–1970, vol. VI
Wilson, George Hamilton Bracher, 1895–1963, vol. VI
Wilson, Sir George Henry, 1869–1939, vol. III
Wilson, Rev. Canon George Herbert, 1870–1952, vol. V
Wilson, George Heron, 1868–1959, vol. V
Wilson, George Maryon Maryon-, 1861–1941, vol. IV
Wilson, Rev. Canon Sir George Percy Maryon M.; see Maryon-Wilson.
Wilson, Lt-Col George Robert Stewart, 1896–1958, vol. V
Wilson, Gerald Sidney, 1880–1960, vol. V
Wilson, Godfrey Harold Alfred, 1871–1958, vol. V
Wilson, Maj.-Gen. Sir Gordon, 1887–1971, vol. VII
Wilson, Lt-Col Gordon Chesney, 1865–1914, vol. I
Wilson, Grace Margaret, (Mrs Bruce Campbell), died 1957, vol. V
Wilson, Graham Malcolm, 1917–1977, vol. VII
Wilson, Gregg, 1865–1951, vol. V
Wilson, Rt Hon. Sir Guy Douglas Arthur Fleetwood, 1850–1940, vol. III
Wilson, Col Hon. Guy Greville, 1877–1943, vol. IV
Wilson, Rev. Canon Harold, 1919–1975, vol. VII
Wilson, Harold Albert, 1874–1964, vol. VI
Wilson, Col Harold René, 1890–1941, vol. IV
Wilson, Harold William, died 1959, vol. V
Wilson, Harry, 1852–1928, vol. II
Wilson, Rear-Adm. (S) Harry George, 1874–1947, vol. IV
Wilson, Harry Leon, 1867–1939, vol. III
Wilson, Helen Russell, died 1924, vol. II
Wilson, Rt Rev. Henry Albert, 1876–1961, vol. VI
Wilson, Rev. Henry Austin, 1854–1927, vol. II
Wilson, Sir Henry Francis, (Harry), 1859–1937, vol. III
Wilson, Lt-Gen. Sir Henry Fuller Maitland, 1859–1941, vol. IV
Wilson, Field-Marshal Sir Henry Hughes, 1st Bt (cr 1919), 1864–1922, vol. II
Wilson, Henry Joseph, 1833–1914, vol. I
Wilson, Henry Leonard, 1897–1968, vol. VI
Wilson, Henry Wilcox, 1895–1974, vol. VII
Wilson, Herbert, 1862–1927, vol. III
Wilson, Captain Herbert Haydon, 1875–1917, vol. II

Wilson, Sir Herbert W. L.; see Lush-Wilson.
Wilson, Herbert Wrigley, 1866–1940, vol. III
Wilson, Sir Horace John, 1882–1972, vol. VII
Wilson, Sir Hubert Guy Maryon M.; see Maryon-Wilson.
Wilson, Hubert Wilberforce, 1867–1949, vol. IV
Wilson, (Hugh) Geoffrey (Birch), 1903–1975, vol. VII
Wilson, Hon. Sir Ian; see Wilson, Hon. Sir T. I. F.
Wilson, Sir Isaac Henry, died 1944, vol. IV
Wilson, Sir Jacob, 1836–1905, vol. I
Wilson, Rev. James, 1856–1923, vol. II
Wilson, James, 1847–1924, vol. II
Wilson, Sir James, 1853–1926, vol. II
Wilson, James, 1861–1941, vol. IV
Wilson, James, 1879–1943, vol. IV
Wilson, Lt-Col (James) Alban, 1865–1928, vol. II
Wilson, Rev. James Allen, 1827–1917, vol. II
Wilson, Sir James Arthur, 1877–1950, vol. IV
Wilson, Maj.-Gen. James Barnett, 1862–1936, vol. III
Wilson, Sir James Glenny, 1849–1929, vol. III
Wilson, Ven. James Maurice, 1836–1931, vol. III
Wilson, Sir James Robertson, 2nd Bt (cr 1906), 1883–1964, vol. VI
Wilson, Sir (James) Steuart, 1889–1966, vol. VI
Wilson, James Thomas, 1861–1945, vol. IV
Wilson, James Thomas Pither, 1884–1976, vol. VII
Wilson, Sir Jeremiah, died 1930, vol. III
Wilson, John, 1837–1915, vol. I
Wilson, Sir John, 1st Bt (cr 1906), 1844–1918, vol. II
Wilson, John, 1837–1928, vol. II
Wilson, John, 1860–1938, vol. III
Wilson, Rev. John, 1854–1939, vol. III
Wilson, John; see Ashmore, Hon. Lord.
Wilson, Sir John Carnegie Dove-, 1865–1935, vol. III
Wilson, John Dove, 1833–1908, vol. I
Wilson, John Dover, 1881–1969, vol. VI
Wilson, Col John George Yule, 1853–1935, vol. III
Wilson, Col John Gerald, 1841–1902, vol. I
Wilson, John Gideon, 1876–1963, vol. VI
Wilson, John Gray, 1915–1968, vol. VI
Wilson, John Henry, 1862–1932, vol. III
Wilson, Rev. John Kenneth, 1890–1949, vol. IV
Wilson, Rt Rev. John Leonard, 1897–1970, vol. VI
Wilson, Sir John Menzies, 3rd Bt (cr 1906), 1885–1968, vol. VI
Wilson, Sir John Mitchell Harvey, 2nd Bt (cr 1920), 1898–1975, vol. VII
Wilson, Very Rev. John Skinner, 1849–1926, vol. II
Wilson, Col John Skinner, 1888–1969, vol. VI
Wilson, John Thomson, 1855–1930, vol. III
Wilson, Rt Hon. John William, 1858–1932, vol. III
Wilson, Joseph Havelock, 1859–1929, vol. III
Wilson, Rev. Joseph Kershaw, 1854–1930, vol. III
Wilson, Joseph Maitland, 1868–1940, vol. III
Wilson, Hon. Joseph Marcellin, 1859–1940, vol. III (A), vol. IV
Wilson, Joseph Vivian, 1894–1977, vol. VII
Wilson, Joseph William, 1851–1930, vol. III
Wilson, Kenneth Henry, 1885–1969, vol. VI

Wilson, Brig.-Gen. Lachlan Chisholm, 1871–1947, vol. IV
Wilson, Col Lancelot Machell, 1873–1950, vol. IV
Wilson, Sir Leonard, 1888–1980, vol. VII
Wilson, Col Rt Hon. Sir Leslie Orme, 1876–1955, vol. V
Wilson, Sir Mark, 1896–1956, vol. V
Wilson, Sir Mathew Amcotts, 3rd Bt (cr 1874), 1853–1914, vol. I
Wilson, Lt-Col Sir Mathew Richard Henry, 4th Bt (cr 1874), 1875–1958, vol. V
Wilson, Sir Mathew Wharton, 2nd Bt (cr 1874), 1827–1909, vol. I
Wilson, Matthew, 1854–1920, vol. II
Wilson, Maurice, 1862–1936, vol. III
Wilson, Sir Maurice B.; see Bromley-Wilson.
Wilson, Mona, 1872–1954, vol. V
Wilson, Morris W., 1883–1946, vol. IV
Wilson, Lt-Col Sir Murrough John, 1875–1946, vol. IV
Wilson, Lt-Col Nathaniel, died 1944, vol. IV
Wilson, Captain Neville Frederick Jarvis, 1865–1947, vol. IV
Wilson, Maj.-Gen. Nigel Maitland, 1884–1950, vol. IV
Wilson, Maj.-Gen. Norman Methven, 1881–1961, vol. VI
Wilson, Oscar, 1867–1930, vol. III
Wilson, P. Macgregor, died 1928, vol. II (A), vol. III
Wilson, Lt-Col Patrick Hogarth, 1874–1939, vol. III
Wilson, Rev. Canon Sir Percy M.; see Maryon-Wilson.
Wilson, Lt-Col Percy Norton Whitestone, 1886–1933, vol. III
Wilson, Philip Duncan, 1886–1969, vol. VI
Wilson, Philip Whitwell, 1875–1956, vol. V
Wilson, Rt Rev. Piers Holt, died 1956, vol. V
Wilson, Ralph Darrell, 1892–1967, vol. VI
Wilson, Reginald Appleby, 1878–1955, vol. V
Wilson, Rev. Reginald Francis, 1873–1937, vol. III
Wilson, Reginald Henry Rimington Rimington-, 1852–1927, vol. II
Wilson, Reginald Page, died 1950, vol. IV
Wilson, Hon. Sir (Reginald) Victor, 1877–1957, vol. V
Wilson, Col Richard Henry, 1886–1969, vol. VI
Wilson, Lt-Col Richard Henry Francis Wharton, 1855–1936, vol. III
Wilson, Richard Henry George, 1874–1944, vol. IV
Wilson, Rev. Richard Mercer, 1887–1976, vol. VII
Wilson, Robert, 1871–1920, vol. II
Wilson, Sir Robert, 1865–1943, vol. IV
Wilson, Captain Robert Amcotts, 1882–1960, vol. V
Wilson, Hon. Sir Robert Christian, 1896–1973, vol. VII
Wilson, Lt-Col Robert Edward, 1884–1936, vol. III
Wilson, Rev. Robert James, died 1897, vol. I
Wilson, Robert John, 1865–1946, vol. IV
Wilson, Robert McNair, 1882–1963, vol. VI
Wilson, Sir (Roderick) Roy, 1876–1942, vol. IV

Wilson, Gen. Sir Roger Cochrane, 1882–1966, vol. VI
Wilson, Lt-Col Roger Parker, 1870–1943, vol. IV
Wilson, Sir Roland Knyvet, 2nd Bt (cr 1857), 1840–1919, vol. II
Wilson, Romer, 1891–1930, vol. III
Wilson, Sir Roy; see Wilson, Sir Roderick R.
Wilson, Sir Samuel, 1861–1937, vol. III
Wilson, Samuel Alexander Kinnier, 1874–1937, vol. III
Wilson, Brig.-Gen. Sir Samuel Herbert, 1873–1950, vol. IV
Wilson, Lady Sarah Isabella Augusta, 1865–1929, vol. III
Wilson, Sir Spencer Maryon Maryon, 10th Bt (cr 1661), 1829–1897, vol. I
Wilson, Sir Spencer Pocklington Maryon Maryon-, 11th Bt (cr 1661), 1859–1944, vol. IV
Wilson, Stanley Reginald, 1890–1973, vol. VII
Wilson, Sir Steuart; see Wilson, Sir J. S.
Wilson, Sydney Ernest, died 1973, vol. VII
Wilson, T. Henry, died 1941, vol. IV
Wilson, Theodora Wilson, died 1941, vol. IV
Wilson, Theodore Stacey, 1861–1949, vol. IV
Wilson, Col Thomas, 1831–1915, vol. I
Wilson, Sir Thomas, 1863–1930, vol. III
Wilson, Maj.-Gen. Thomas Arthur Atkinson, 1882–1958, vol. V
Wilson, Ven. Thomas Bowstead, 1882–1961, vol. VI
Wilson, Thomas Corby, died 1934, vol. III
Wilson, Rev. Thomas Erskine, 1874–1951, vol. V
Wilson, Sir Thomas Fleming, 1862–1929, vol. III
Wilson, Sir Thomas George, 1876–1958, vol. V
Wilson, Sir (Thomas) George; see Wilson, Sir G.
Wilson, Maj.-Gen. Thomas Needham Furnival, 1896–1961, vol. VI
Wilson, Hon. Sir (Tom) Ian (Findley), 1904–1971, vol. VII
Wilson, Hon. Sir Victor; see Wilson, Hon. Sir R. V.
Wilson, Gp Captain Walter Carandini, 1885–1968, vol. VI
Wilson, Walter Gordon, 1874–1957, vol. V
Wilson, Hon. Walter Horatio, 1839–1902, vol. I
Wilson, Sir Wemyss G.; see Grant-Wilson.
Wilson, William, 1884–1944, vol. IV
Wilson, William, 1875–1965, vol. VI
Wilson, William, 1920–1972, vol. VII
Wilson, Engr-Captain William Anderson, 1868–1957, vol. V
Wilson, William Combe, 1897–1974, vol. VII
Wilson, Sir (William) Courthope (Townshend), 1865–1944, vol. IV
Wilson, Surg.-Gen. Sir William Deane, 1843–1921, vol. II
Wilson, William Edward, 1851–1908, vol. I
Wilson, Sir William G.; see Grey-Wilson.
Wilson, Very Rev. William Hay, died 1925, vol. II
Wilson, Major William Herbert, died 1928, vol. II
Wilson, William James, 1879–1954, vol. V
Wilson, William Lyne, 1843–1900, vol. I
Wilson, Gp Captain William Proctor, 1902–1980, vol. VII
Wilson, William Robert, 1844–1928, vol. II
Wilson, Sir William Tweedley, 1882–1942, vol. IV

Wilson, William Tyson, 1855–1921, vol. II
Wilson, William Wright, 1843–1919, vol. II
Wilson, Woodrow, 1856–1924, vol. II
Wilson-Farquharson, Lt-Col David Lorraine; see Farquharson.
Wilson-Fox, Hon. Mrs Eleanor Birch, died 1963, vol. VI
Wilson-Fox, Henry; see Fox.
Wilson-Johnston, Joseph; see Johnston.
Wilson-Johnston, Maj.-Gen. Walter Edward; see Johnston.
Wilson Smith, Sir Henry, 1904–1978, vol. VII
Wilson Taylor, Sir John, died 1943, vol. IV
Wilson-Todd, Captain Sir William Henry, 1st Bt, 1828–1910, vol. I
Wilson-Todd, Captain Sir William Pierrepoint, 2nd Bt, 1857–1925, vol. II
Wilsone, Arthur Henry, 1860–1939, vol. III
Wilthew, Gerard Herbert Guy, 1876–1913, vol. I (A), vol. III
Wilton, 4th Earl of, 1839–1898, vol. I
Wilton, 5th Earl of, 1863–1915, vol. I
Wilton, 6th Earl of, 1896–1927, vol. II
Wilton, Sir Ernest Colville Collins, 1870–1952, vol. V
Wilton, George Wilton, 1862–1964, vol. VI
Wilton, Herbert George, 1882–1959, vol. V
Wilton, Captain Sir James M., died 1946, vol. IV
Wilton, John Raymond, 1884–1944, vol. IV
Wilton, Sir Thomas, 1861–1929, vol. III
Wiltshire, Aubrey Roy Liddon, 1891–1969, vol. VI
Wiltshire, Sir Frank H. C., 1881–1949, vol. IV
Wiltshire, Harold Waterlow, 1879–1937, vol. III
Wiltshire, Samuel Paul, 1891–1967, vol. VI
Wimberley, Col Charles Neil Campbell, 1867–1949, vol. IV
Wimble, Ernest Walter, 1887–1979, vol. VII
Wimble, Sir John Bowring, 1868–1927, vol. II
Wimborne, 1st Baron, 1835–1914, vol. I
Wimborne, 1st Viscount, 1873–1939, vol. III
Wimborne, 2nd Viscount, 1903–1967, vol. VI
Wimperis, Arthur Harold, 1874–1953, vol. V
Wimperis, Harry Egerton, 1876–1960, vol. V
Wimshurst, James, 1832–1903, vol. I
Winans, Walter, died 1920, vol. II
Winant, Hon. John Gilbert, 1889–1947, vol. IV
Winby, Lt-Col Lewis Phillips, 1874–1956, vol. V
Winchell, Walter, 1897–1972, vol. VII
Winchester, 15th Marquess of, 1858–1899, vol. I
Winchester, 16th Marquess of, 1862–1962, vol. VI
Winchester, 17th Marquess, of, 1905–1968, vol. VI
Winchester, Tarleton, 1895–1967, vol. VI
Winchilsea, 12th Earl of, and Nottingham, 7th Earl of, 1851–1898, vol. I
Winchilsea, 13th Earl of, and Nottingham, 8th Earl of, 1852–1927, vol. II
Winchilsea, 14th Earl of, and Nottingham, 9th Earl of, 1885–1939, vol. III
Winchilsea, 15th Earl of, and Nottingham, 10th Earl of, 1911–1950, vol. IV
Winckley, Rev. Canon Sidney Thorold, 1858–1937, vol. III
Winckworth, Chauncey P. Tietjens, 1896–1954, vol. V

Wincott, Harold Edward, 1906–1969, vol. VI
Wind, Edgar, 1900–1971, vol. VII
Windaus, Adolf Otto Reinhold, 1876–1959, vol. V
Winder, Sir Arthur Benedict, 1875–1953, vol. V
Winder, Lt-Col Maurice Guy, died 1932, vol. III
Winder, Captain Robert Cecil, died 1920, vol. II
Winder, Very Rev. Thomas Edward, died 1926, vol. II
Winder, Major William John C.; see Corbett-Winder.
Windeyer, John Cadell, 1875–1951, vol. V
Windeyer, Sir William Charles, 1834–1897, vol. I
Windham, Vice-Adm. Charles, 1851–1916, vol. II
Windham, Lt-Col Charles Joseph, 1867–1941, vol. IV
Windham, Sir Ralph, 1905–1980, vol. VII
Windham, Comdr Sir Walter George, 1868–1942, vol. IV
Windham, Sir William, 1864–1961, vol. VI
Windham, William Evan, 1904–1977, vol. VII
Windle, Sir Bertram Coghill Alan, 1858–1929, vol. III
Windlesham, 1st Baron, 1877–1953, vol. V
Windlesham, 2nd Baron, 1903–1962, vol. VI
Windley, Sir Edward Henry, 1909–1972, vol. VII
Windsor, Viscount; Other Robert Windsor-Clive, 1884–1908, vol. I
Windsor, Bt-Col Arthur Herbert, 1880–1972, vol. VII
Windsor, Lt-Col Frank Needham, 1868–1951, vol. V
Windsor, Robert, 1916–1980, vol. VII
Windsor, Walter, died 1945, vol. IV
Windsor-Clive, Lt-Col George, 1878–1968, vol. VI
Windsor-Clive, Lt-Col Hon. George Herbert Windsor, 1835–1918, vol. II
Windsor Lewis, Brig. James Charles, 1907–1964, vol. VI
Winegarten, Asher, 1922–1979, vol. VII
Winfield, Rev. Benjamin, died 1933, vol. III
Winfield, Sir Percy Henry, 1878–1953, vol. V
Winfrey, Sir Richard, 1858–1944, vol. IV
Wing, Brig.-Gen. Frederick Drummond Vincent, 1860–1915, vol. I
Wing, Thomas Edward, 1853–1935, vol. III
Wingate, Col Alfred Woodrow Stanley, 1861–1938, vol. III
Wingate, Sir Andrew, 1846–1937, vol. III
Wingate, Col Basil Fenton, died 1940, vol. III
Wingate, Gen. Sir (Francis) Reginald, 1st Bt, 1861–1953, vol. V
Wingate, Col George, 1852–1936, vol. III
Wingate, Sir J. Lawton, 1846–1924, vol. II
Wingate, Captain Malcolm Roy, 1893–1918, vol. II
Wingate, Maj.-Gen. Orde Charles, 1903–1944, vol. IV
Wingate, Gen. Sir Reginald; see Wingate, Gen. Sir F. G.
Wingate, Sir Ronald Evelyn Leslie, 2nd Bt, 1889–1978, vol. VII
Wingate-Saul, Bazil Sylvester, 1906–1975, vol. VII
Wingate-Saul, Sir Ernest Wingate, 1873–1944, vol. IV

Winge, Ojvind, 1886–1964, vol. VI
Wingfield, Sir Anthony H., 1857–1952, vol. V
Wingfield, Sir Charles John FitzRoy Rhys, 1877–1960, vol. V
Wingfield, Sir Edward, 1834–1910, vol. I
Wingfield, Lt-Col John Maurice, 1863–1931, vol. III
Wingfield, Maj.-Gen. Hon. Maurice Anthony, 1883–1956, vol. V
Wingfield, Maurice Edward, 1869–1937, vol. III
Wingfield, Mervyn Edward George Rhys, 1872–1952, vol. V
Wingfield, Major Walter Clopton, 1833–1912, vol. I
Wingfield, Rev. Lt-Col William Edward, 1867–1927, vol. II
Wingfield-Stratford, Brig.-Gen. Cecil Vernon, 1853–1939, vol. III
Wingfield-Stratford, Esmé Cecil, 1882–1971, vol. VII
Wingrave, Vitruvius Harold Wyatt, 1858–1938, vol. III
Winks, William Edward, 1842–1926, vol. II
Winlock, Herbert Eustis, 1884–1950, vol. IV
Winmill, Thomas Field, 1888–1953, vol. V
Winn, Rt Hon. Sir (Charles) Rodger (Noel), 1903–1972, vol. VII
Winn, Godfrey Herbert, 1908–1971, vol. VII
Winn, Rt Hon. Sir Rodger; see Winn, Rt Hon. Sir C. R. N.
Winn, Lt-Comdr Sydney Thornhill, died 1924, vol. II
Winnicott, Sir Frederick; see Winnicott, Sir J. F.
Winnicott, Sir (John) Frederick, 1855–1948, vol. IV
Winning, Theodore Norman, 1884–1946, vol. IV
Winnington, Sir Francis Salwey, 5th Bt, 1849–1931, vol. III
Winnington, Lt-Col John Francis Sartorius, 1876–1918, vol. II
Winnington Ingram, Rt Rev. and Rt Hon. Arthur Foley; see Ingram.
Winnington-Ingram, Ven. Arthur John, 1888–1965, vol. VI
Winnington-Ingram, Rev. Edward Henry; see Ingram.
Winsbury-White, Horace Powell, died 1962, vol. VI
Winser, Col Charles Rupert Peter, 1880–1961, vol. VI
Winsloe, Adm. Sir Alfred Leigh, 1852–1931, vol. III
Winsloe, Col Alfred Raynaud, 1868–1932, vol. III
Winsloe, Lt-Col Herbert Edward, 1873–1921, vol. II
Winsloe, Col Richard William Charles, 1835–1917, vol. II
Winslow, Rev. Forbes Edward, 1842–1913, vol. I
Winslow, L. Forbes, 1844–1913, vol. I
Winslow, Rev. William Copley, 1840–1925, vol. II
Winstanley, Denys Arthur, 1877–1947, vol. IV
Winstedt, Sir Richard Olaf, 1878–1966, vol. VI
Winster, 1st Baron, 1885–1961, vol. VI
Wint, Hon. Dunbar Theophilus, 1879–1938, vol. III
Winter, Carl, 1906–1966, vol. VI

Winter, Col Clifford Boardman, 1869–1930, vol. III
Winter, Rev. Edward George Adlington, 1853–1933, vol. III
Winter, Edwin, 1840–1915, vol. I
Winter, Lt-Col Ernest Arthur, died 1925, vol. II
Winter, Hon. Sir Francis Pratt, 1848–1919, vol. II
Winter, Rev. Canon George Percival Thomas Horden, 1885–1953, vol. V
Winter, Hon. Henry Daniel, 1851–1927, vol. II
Winter, James Alexander, 1886–1971, vol. VII
Winter, Sir James Spearman, 1845–1911, vol. I
Winter, John Strange; see Stannard, Mrs Arthur.
Winter, Hon. Sir Marmaduke George, 1857–1936, vol. III
Winter, Brig.-Gen. Sir Ormonde de l'Epée, died 1962, vol. VI
Winter, Reginald Keble, 1883–1955, vol. V
Winter, Robert Pearson, 1897–1973, vol. VII
Winter, Col Samuel Henry, 1854–1938, vol. III
Winter, Thomas, 1866–1912, vol. I
Winter, W. Tatton, died 1928, vol. II
Winter, William, 1836–1917, vol. II
Winter-Shaw, Arthur, died 1948, vol. IV
Winterbotham, Sir Geoffrey Leonard, died 1966, vol. VI
Winterbotham, Brig. Harold St John Lloyd, 1878–1946, vol. IV
Winterbotham, Sir Henry Martin, 1847–1932, vol. III
Winterbotham, Rev. Rayner, died 1924, vol. II
Winterbotham, Sir William Howard, 1843–1926, vol. II
Winterbottom, Lt-Col Archibald Dickson, 1885–1942, vol. IV
Winterbottom, Richard Emanuel, 1899–1968, vol. VI
Winters, Ellen Dorothea Margaret, 1894–1956, vol. V
Winterstoke, 1st Baron, 1830–1911, vol. I
Winterton, 5th Earl, 1837–1907, vol. I
Winterton, 6th Earl, 1883–1962, vol. VI
Winterton, George Ernest, 1873–1942, vol. IV
Wintle, Col Charles Edmund Hunter, died 1969, vol. VI
Wintle, Col Frank Graham, 1852–1907, vol. I
Winton, Meryon W.; see White-Winton.
Wintour, Maj.-Gen. Fitzgerald, 1860–1949, vol. IV
Wintour, Ulick Fitzgerald, 1877–1947, vol. IV
Wintringham, Col John Workman, 1894–1980, vol. VII
Wintringham, Margaret, died 1955, vol. V
Wintringham, T., died 1921, vol. II
Wintringham, Thomas Henry, 1898–1949, vol. IV
Wintz, Adm. Lewis Edmund, 1849–1933, vol. III
Wintz, Dame Sophia Gertrude, died 1929, vol. III
Winwood, Lt-Col William Quintyne, 1873–1954, vol. V
Wippell, Adm. Sir Henry Daniel P.; see Pridham-Wippell.
Wippell, Rev. Canon John Cecil, 1883–1978, vol. VII
Wirgman, Ven. Augustus Theodore, 1846–1917, vol. II

732

Wirgman, T. Blake, *died* 1925, vol. II
Wisdom, Brig.-Gen. Evan Alexander, 1869–1945, vol. IV
Wisdom, George Evan Cameron, 1899–1958, vol. V
Wise, 1st Baron, 1887–1968, vol. VI
Wise, Alfred Gascoyne, 1854–1923, vol. II
Wise, Lt-Col Alfred Roy, 1901–1974, vol. VII
Wise, Hon. Bernhard Ringrose, 1858–1916, vol. II
Wise, Edward Frank, 1885–1933, vol. III
Wise, Francis Hubert, 1869–1917, vol. II
Wise, Sir Fredric, 1871–1928, vol. II
Wise, Hon. George Henry, 1853–1950, vol. IV
Wise, Lt-Col Henry Edward Disbrowe Disbrowe-, 1868–1948, vol. IV
Wise, Sir Lloyd; *see* Wise, Sir W. L.
Wise, Gp Captain Percival Kinnear, 1885–1968, vol. VI
Wise, Rabbi Stephen S., 1874–1949, vol. IV
Wise, Thomas James, 1859–1937, vol. III
Wise, Sir (William) Lloyd, 1845–1910, vol. I
Wiseham, Sir Joseph Angus Lucien, 1906–1972, vol. VII
Wiseman, Arthur Maurice, 1893–1948, vol. IV
Wiseman, Rev. Frederick Luke, 1858–1944, vol. IV
Wiseman, Very Rev. James, *died* 1925, vol. II
Wiseman, Air Cdre Percy John, 1888–1948, vol. IV
Wiseman, Robert Arthur, 1886–1955, vol. V
Wiseman, Stephen, 1907–1971, vol. VII
Wiseman, Sir William George Eden, 10th Bt, 1885–1962, vol. VI
Wiseman-Clarke, Lt-Gen. Somerset Molyneux, 1830–1905, vol. I
Wishart, D. J. Gibb, 1859–1934, vol. III
Wishart, George Macfeat, 1895–1958, vol. V
Wishart, John, 1898–1956, vol. V
Wishart, John, 1879–1970, vol. VI
Wishart, Rear-Adm. John Webster, 1892–1968, vol. VI
Wishart, Captain Robert, 1875–1938, vol. III (A), vol. IV
Wishart, Col Sir Sidney, 1854–1935, vol. III
Wiskemann, Elizabeth, 1901–1971, vol. VII
Wissman, Major Herman von, 1853–1905, vol. I
Wister, Owen, 1860–1938, vol. III
Witham, Col James Kirkconnell Maxwell, 1848–1937, vol. III
Witham, Philip, *died* 1921, vol. II
Witherby, Harry Forbes, 1873–1943, vol. IV
Withers, Alfred, *died* 1932, vol. III
Withers, Col Charles M'Gregor, 1876–1958, vol. V
Withers, Captain Edgar Clements, 1883–1951, vol. V
Withers, Harry Livingston, 1864–1902, vol. I
Withers, Hartley, 1867–1950, vol. IV
Withers, Lt-Col Henry Hastings Cavendish, 1904–1948, vol. IV
Withers, Isobelle; *see* Dods-Withers.
Withers, Sir John James, 1863–1939, vol. III
Withers, Percy, 1867–1945, vol. IV
Withers, Lt-Col Samuel Henry, *died* 1942, vol. IV
Withycombe, Brig.-Gen. William Maunder, 1869–1951, vol. V
Witney, John Humphrey, 1879–1964, vol. VI

Witt, John George, *died* 1906, vol. I
Witt, Sir Robert Clermont, *died* 1952, vol. V
Witt, Tansley, *died* 1915, vol. I
Witte, Count Sergius, 1849–1915, vol. I
Wittenham, 1st Baron, 1852–1931, vol. III
Wittenoom, Hon. Sir Edward Horne, 1854–1936, vol. III
Wittet, John, 1868–1952, vol. V
Wittewronge, Sir Charles L.; *see* Lawes-Wittewronge.
Wittewronge, Sir John Bennet L.; *see* Lawes-Wittewronge.
Wittewronge, Sir John Claud Bennet Lawes; *see* Lawes, Sir J. C. B.
Wittgenstein, Ludwig, 1889–1951, vol. V
Wittkower, Rudolf, 1901–1971, vol. VII
Witts, Rev. Francis Edward Broome, 1840–1913, vol. I
Witts, Brig. Frank Hole, 1887–1941, vol. IV
Witts, Maj.-Gen. Frederick Vavasour Broome, 1889–1969, vol. VI
Woakes, Claud Edward, 1868–1936, vol. III
Wodehouse, Hon. Armine, 1860–1901, vol. I
Wodehouse, Rev. Armine, 1860–1938, vol. III
Wodehouse, Edmond Henry, 1837–1923, vol. II
Wodehouse, Rt Hon. Edmond Robert, 1835–1914, vol. I
Wodehouse, Major Sir (Edwin) Frederick, 1851–1934, vol. III
Wodehouse, Major Ernest Charles Forbes, 1871–1915, vol. I
Wodehouse, Lt-Col Frederic William, 1867–1961, vol. VI
Wodehouse, Major Sir Frederick; *see* Wodehouse, Major Sir E. F.
Wodehouse, Helen Marion, 1880–1964, vol. VI
Wodehouse, Henry Ernest, 1845–1929, vol. III
Wodehouse, Gen. Sir Josceline Heneage, 1852–1930, vol. III
Wodehouse, Vice-Adm. Norman Atherton, 1887–1941, vol. IV
Wodehouse, Sir Pelham Grenville, 1881–1975, vol. VII
Wodehouse, Rev. Philip John, 1836–1917, vol. II
Wodehouse, Philip Peveril John, 1877–1951, vol. V
Wodeman, Guy Stanley, 1886–1970, vol. VI
Woden, George; *see* Slaney, G. W.
Woelmont, Henry, Baron de, 1881–1931, vol. III
Wofinden, Robert Cavill, 1914–1975, vol. VII
Woinarski, Casimir Julius Z.; *see* Zichy-Woinarski.
Wolf, Abraham, 1876–1948, vol. IV
Wolf, Lucien, 1857–1930, vol. III
Wolf-Ferrari, Ermanno, 1876–1948, vol. IV
Wolfe, Rev. Clarence Albert Edward, 1892–1967, vol. VI
Wolfe, Frederick John, *died* 1962, vol. VI
Wolfe, George, 1859–1941, vol. IV
Wolfe, Herbert Robert Inglewood, 1907–1970, vol. VI
Wolfe, Humbert, 1886–1940, vol. III
Wolfe-Barry, Sir John Wolfe; *see* Barry.
Wolfe-Murray, Lt-Col Arthur Alexander, 1866–1918, vol. II
Wolff, Hon. Sir Albert Asher, 1899–1977, vol. VII

Wolff, Lt-Col Arnold Johnston, 1873–1941, vol. IV

Wolff, Edna; see Best, E.

Wolff, Ernest Charteris Holford, 1875–1946, vol. IV

Wolff, Eugene, 1896–1954, vol. V

Wolff, Gustav William, 1834–1913, vol. I

Wolff, Rt Hon. Sir Henry Drummond, 1830–1908, vol. I

Wolff, Henry William, 1840–1931, vol. III

Wolff, Johannes, born 1862, vol. IV

Wolff, Michael, 1930–1976, vol. VII

Wolfflin, Heinrich, 1864–1945, vol. IV

Wolffsohn, Sir Arthur Norman, 1888–1967, vol. VI

Wolfit, Sir Donald, 1902–1968, vol. VI

Wollaston, Alexander Frederick Richmond, 1875–1930, vol. III

Wollaston, Sir Arthur Naylor, 1842–1922, vol. II

Wollaston, Sir Gerald Woods, 1874–1957, vol. V

Wollaston, Sir Harry Newton Phillips, 1846–1921, vol. II

Wollaston, Vice-Adm. Herbert Arthur Buchanan-, 1878–1975, vol. VII

Wollen, William Barnes, 1857–1936, vol. III

Wolley, Sir Clive P.; see Phillipps-Wolley.

Wolley, Rev. Henry Francklyn, 1839–1915, vol. I (A)

Wolley-Dod, Brig.-Gen. Owen Cadogan, 1863–1942, vol. IV

Wolmark, Alfred Aaran, 1877–1961, vol. VI

Wolmer, Viscount; William Matthew Palmer, 1912–1942, vol. IV

Wolrige-Gordon, Henry, 1831–1906, vol. I (p. 780)

Wolrige-Gordon, Col John Gordon, 1859–1925, vol. II

Wolrige Gordon, Captain Robert, died 1939, vol. III

Wolseley, 1st Viscount, 1833–1913, vol. I

Wolseley, Viscountess (2nd in line), 1872–1936, vol. III

Wolseley, Sir Capel Charles, 9th Bt (cr 1744), 1870–1923, vol. II

Wolseley, Sir Charles Michael, 9th Bt (cr 1628), 1846–1931, vol. III

Wolseley, Sir Edric Charles Joseph, 10th Bt (cr 1628), 1886–1954, vol. V

Wolseley, Garnet Ruskin, 1884–1967, vol. VI

Wolseley, Gen. Sir George Benjamin, 1839–1921, vol. II

Wolseley, Sir Reginald Beatty, 10th Bt (cr 1744), 1872–1933, vol. III

Wolseley, Rev. Sir William Augustus, 11th Bt (cr 1744), 1865–1950, vol. IV

Wolseley-Lewis, Mary, 1865–1955, vol. V

Wolstencroft, Frank, 1882–1952, vol. V

Wolstenholme, William, 1865–1931, vol. III

Wolverhampton, 1st Viscount, 1830–1911, vol. I

Wolverhampton, 2nd Viscount, 1870–1943, vol. IV

Wolverson, William Alfred, 1905–1974, vol. VII

Wolverton, 4th Baron, 1861–1932, vol. III

Wolvin, Roy Mitchell, 1880–1945, vol. IV

Wombwell, Lt-Gen. Arthur, 1821–1914, vol. I

Wombwell, Sir (Frederick) Philip (Alfred William), 6th Bt, 1910–1977, vol. VII

Wombwell, Sir George Orby, 4th Bt, 1832–1913, vol. I

Wombwell, Captain Sir Henry Herbert, 5th Bt, 1840–1926, vol. II

Wombwell, Sir Philip; see Wombwell, Sir F. P. A. W.

Womersley, Rt Hon. Sir Walter James, 1st Bt, 1878–1961, vol. VI

Wonham, Rear-Adm. (S) Charles Scrivener, 1870–1946, vol. IV

Wonnacott, Ven. Thomas Oswald, 1869–1957, vol. V

Wontner, Arthur, 1875–1960, vol. V

Wood, Sir Alexander, died 1924, vol. II

Wood, Rt Rev. Alexander, died 1937, vol. III

Wood, Alexander, 1879–1950, vol. IV

Wood, Major Alexander Vaughan Leipsic, 1867–1933, vol. III

Wood, Alfred, 1836–1906, vol. I

Wood, Sir Alfred, 1878–1960, vol. V

Wood, Alfred Cecil, 1896–1968, vol. VI

Wood, Ven. Alfred Maitland, 1840–1918, vol. II

Wood, Allan Fergusson, 1876–1966, vol. VI

Wood, Rev. Andrew, 1833–1917, vol. II

Wood, Rear-Adm. Arthur Edmund, 1875–1961, vol. VI

Wood, Arthur Henry, 1870–1964, vol. VI

Wood, Sir Arthur Nicholas Lindsay, 2nd Bt (cr 1897), 1875–1939, vol. III

Wood, Captain Sir Basil Samuel Hill H.; see Hill-Wood.

Wood, Brooks Crompton, died 1946, vol. IV

Wood, Butler, 1854–1934, vol. III

Wood, Catherine Jane, died 1930, vol. III

Wood, Col Cecil Ernest, died 1932, vol. III

Wood, Cecil Godfrey, 1851–1906, vol. I

Wood, Rt Rev. Cecil John, 1874–1957, vol. V

Wood, Rev. Canon Cecil Thomas, 1903–1980, vol. VII

Wood, Sir (Charles) Edgar, 1877–1941, vol. IV

Wood, Charles Frederick, 1867–1937, vol. III

Wood, Charles Malcolm, 1846–1915, vol. I

Wood, Col Charles Michell Aloysius, 1873–1936, vol. III

Wood, Lt-Col Charles Peevor Boileau, died 1932, vol. III

Wood, Rt Rev. Claud Thomas Thellusson, 1885–1961, vol. VI

Wood, Lt-Col Cyril, 1852–1904, vol. I

Wood, Lt-Col David Edward, 1853–1927, vol. II

Wood, Sir David John Hatherley P., 7th Bt (cr 1837); see Page Wood.

Wood, Sir Edgar; see Wood, Sir C. E.

Wood, Rev. Edmund Gough De Salis, 1842–1932, vol. III

Wood, Edmund Walter Hanbury, 1898–1947, vol. IV

Wood, Sir Edward, 1839–1917, vol. II

Wood, Maj.-Gen. Edward Alexander, 1841–1898, vol. I

Wood, Brig.-Gen. Edward Allan, 1872–1930, vol. III

Wood, Sir (Edward) Graham, 1854–1930, vol. III

Wood, Edward Stephen, 1890–1948, vol. IV

Wood, Maj.-Gen. Sir Elliott, 1844–1931, vol. III

Wood, Eric Rawlinson, 1893–1977, vol. VII

Wood, Lt-Gen. Sir Ernest, 1894–1971, vol. VII
Wood, Ernest Clement, 1890–1970, vol. VI
Wood, Brig.-Gen. Ernest Joseph MacFarlane, 1867–1939, vol. III
Wood, Mrs Ethel Mary, *died* 1970, vol. VI
Wood, Field-Marshal Sir Evelyn, 1838–1919, vol. II
Wood, Hon. Col Evelyn Fitzgerald Michell, 1869–1943, vol. IV
Wood, Francis Derwent, 1871–1926, vol. II
Wood, Sir Frank, 1913–1974, vol. VII
Wood, Franklin Garrett, *died* 1978, vol. VII
Wood, Frederick Benjamin, 1849–1928, vol. II
Wood, George Arnold, 1865–1928, vol. II
Wood, Gervase E., 1877–1954, vol. V
Wood, Sir Graham; *see* Wood, Sir E. G.
Wood, Harrie Dalrymple, 1869–1937, vol. III
Wood, Col Hastings St Leger, 1856–1933, vol. III
Wood, Haydn, 1882–1959, vol. V
Wood, Col Henry, 1835–1919, vol. II
Wood, Col Henry, 1872–1940, vol. III
Wood, Henry Ernest, 1868–1946, vol. IV
Wood, Sir Henry Hastings Affleck, 1826–1904, vol. I
Wood, Sir Henry Joseph, 1869–1944, vol. IV
Wood, Rev. Henry Thellusson, *died* 1928, vol. II
Wood, Sir Henry Trueman, 1845–1929, vol. III
Wood, Herbert, 1893–1950, vol. IV
Wood, Herbert Duncan S.; *see* Searles-Wood.
Wood, Herbert George, 1879–1963, vol. VI
Wood, Hugh McKinnon, 1884–1955, vol. V
Wood, Rev. Hugh Singleton, 1859–1941, vol. IV
Wood, I. Hickory, *died* 1913, vol. I
Wood, Captain Sir Ian Lindsay, 3rd Bt (*cr* 1897), 1909–1946, vol. IV
Wood, J. S., 1853–1920, vol. II
Wood, James, *died* 1936, vol. III
Wood, Lt-Col Sir James L.; *see* Leigh-Wood.
Wood, Sir James Lockwood, *died* 1941, vol. IV
Wood, Rev. John, 1833–1929, vol. III
Wood, Sir John, 1st Bt (*cr* 1918), 1857–1951, vol. V
Wood, John, 1880–1952, vol. V
Wood, Sir John Arthur Haigh, 2nd Bt (*cr* 1918), 1888–1974, vol. VII
Wood, Sir John Barry, 1870–1933, vol. III
Wood, Lt-Col John Bruce, *died* 1927, vol. II
Wood, Hon. John Dennistoun, 1829–1914, vol. I (A)
Wood, John Gathorne, 1839–1929, vol. III
Wood, Captain John Lockhart, 1871–1915, vol. I
Wood, Lt-Col John Nicholas Price, 1877–1962, vol. VI
Wood, Major Sir John Page, 5th Bt (*cr* 1837), 1860–1912, vol. I
Wood, John Philip, *died* 1906, vol. I
Wood, Sir John Stuart Page, 6th Bt (*cr* 1837), 1898–1955, vol. V
Wood, John Vincent, 1905–1952, vol. V
Wood, Lt-Col John William Massey, 1855–1916, vol. II
Wood, Rev. Joseph, 1842–1921, vol. II
Wood, Josiah, 1843–1927, vol. II
Wood, Kenneth Spencer, 1897–1963, vol. VI
Wood, Rt Hon. Sir Kingsley, 1881–1943, vol. IV

Wood, Lawson, 1878–1957, vol. V
Wood, Leslie Stuart, 1873–1948, vol. IV
Wood, Sir Lindsay, 1st Bt (*cr* 1897), 1834–1920, vol. II
Wood, Rev. Llewellyn, *died* 1929, vol. III
Wood, Mary Hay, *died* 1934, vol. III
Wood, Sir Matthew, 4th Bt (*cr* 1837), 1857–1908, vol. I
Wood, Metcalfe, *died* 1944, vol. IV
Wood, Major Sir Murdoch McKenzie, 1881–1949, vol. IV
Wood, Oswald Edward, 1899–1974, vol. VII
Wood, Lt-Col Oswald Gillespie, 1851–1902, vol. I
Wood, Paul Hamilton, 1907–1962, vol. VI
Wood, Percival Arthur Gilbert, 1866–1945, vol. IV
Wood, Philip Francis, 1858–1939, vol. III
Wood, Brig.-Gen. Philip Richard, 1868–1945, vol. IV
Wood, Sir Richard, 1806–1900, vol. I
Wood, Gen. Robert E., 1879–1969, vol. VI
Wood, Robert Henry, 1860–1930, vol. III
Wood, Sir Robert Stanford, 1886–1963, vol. VI
Wood, Robert Williams, 1868–1955, vol. V
Wood, R(onald) McKinnon, 1892–1967, vol. VI
Wood, Major Sir Samuel Hill H.; *see* Hill-Wood.
Wood, Starr, 1870–1944, vol. IV
Wood, Stuart Zachary Taylor, 1889–1966, vol. VI
Wood, Sydney Herbert, 1884–1958, vol. V
Wood, Rev. Theodore, 1862–1923, vol. II
Wood, Col Thomas, 1853–1933, vol. III
Wood, Thomas, 1892–1950, vol. IV
Wood, Thomas Alfred, 1867–1944, vol. IV
Wood, Thomas Andrew Urquhart, 1914–1975, vol. VII
Wood, Thomas Barlow, 1869–1929, vol. III
Wood, Brig.-Gen. Thomas Birchall, 1865–1944, vol. IV
Wood, Rt Hon. Thomas M'Kinnon, 1855–1927, vol. II
Wood, Thomas Outterson, *died* 1930, vol. III
Wood, W. H., 1888–1954, vol. V
Wood, Walter, 1866–1961, vol. VI
Wood, Walter Gunnell, 1861–1942, vol. IV
Wood, Sir Wilfred William Hill H.; *see* Hill-Wood.
Wood, Wilfrid Burton, 1883–1943, vol. IV
Wood, Rev. William, 1829–1919, vol. II
Wood, William Alfred Rae, 1878–1970, vol. VI
Wood, William Charles Henry, *died* 1947, vol. IV (A), vol. V
Wood, William Francis John, 1876–1934, vol. III
Wood, William Henry Heton A.; *see* Arden Wood.
Wood, William K.; *see* King-Wood.
Wood, William L., 1879–1958, vol. V
Wood, William Thomas, 1877–1958, vol. V
Wood, Sir William Valentine, 1883–1959, vol. V
Wood, William Wightman, 1846–1914, vol. I
Wood, Sir William Wilkinson, 1879–1963, vol. VI
Wood, Lt-Col Wyndham Madden Pierpoint, *died* 1950, vol. IV
Wood, Zachary Taylor, 1860–1915, vol. I
Wood-Martin, William Gregory, 1847–1917, vol. II
Wood-Samuel, Rev. Richard, *died* 1939, vol. III
Wood-Seys, Roland Alex., 1854–1919, vol. II

Woodall, Sir Corbet, 1841–1916, vol. II
Woodall, Col Frederic, 1866–1956, vol. V
Woodall, Lt-Col Harold Whiteman, 1872–1951, vol. V
Woodall, William, 1832–1901, vol. I
Woodard, Rev. Canon Alfred Lambert, 1880–1971, vol. VII
Woodard, Rev. Lambert, 1848–1924, vol. II
Woodberry, George Edward, 1855–1930, vol. III
Woodbridge, 1st Baron, 1867–1949, vol. IV
Woodburn, Rt Hon. Arthur, 1890–1978, vol. VII
Woodburn, Rev. George, 1867–1947, vol. IV
Woodburn, Hon. Sir John, died 1902, vol. I
Woodburn, Lt-Col Thomas Stanley, 1881–1965, vol. VI
Woodcock, Eric Charles, 1904–1978, vol. VII
Woodcock, Rt Hon. George, 1904–1979, vol. VII
Woodcock, Col Herbert Charles, 1871–1950, vol. IV
Woodcock, Hubert Bayley Drysdale, 1867–1957, vol. V
Woodcock, T. A., 1897–1965, vol. VI
Woodcock, Brig.-Gen. Wilfrid James, 1878–1960, vol. V
Woodd, Ven. Henry Alexander, 1865–1954, vol. V
Woodeson, Sir James Brewis, 1917–1980, vol. VII
Woodfall, Robert, 1855–1920, vol. II
Woodford, Charles Morris, 1852–1927, vol. II
Woodford, James, 1893–1976, vol. VII
Woodford, Stewart Lyndon, 1835–1913, vol. I
Woodford, Thomas Gordon Charles, 1911–1962, vol. VI
Woodforde, Very Rev. Christopher, 1907–1962, vol. VI
Woodgate, Sir Alfred, 1860–1943, vol. IV
Woodgate, Maj.-Gen. Edward Robert Prevost, 1845–1900, vol. I
Woodgate, (Hubert) Leslie, 1902–1961, vol. VI
Woodgate, Leslie; see Woodgate, H. L.
Woodgate, Walter Bradford, 1840–1920, vol. II
Woodhall, Lt-Comdr Eric Langton, 1899–1940, vol. III
Woodham-Smith, Cecil (Blanche), 1896–1977, vol. VII
Woodhams, Herbert Martin, 1890–1965, vol. VI
Woodhead, Arthur Longden, 1862–1957, vol. V
Woodhead, Ernest, 1857–1944, vol. IV
Woodhead, Sir German Sims, 1855–1921, vol. II
Woodhead, Henry George Wandesford, 1883–1959, vol. V
Woodhead, Sir John Ackroyd, 1881–1973, vol. VII
Woodhouse, Albert Cyril, 1887–1940, vol. IV
Woodhouse, Arthur William Webster, 1867–1961, vol. VI
Woodhouse, Adm. Sir Charles Henry Lawrence, 1893–1978, vol. VII
Woodhouse, Rev. Frederick Charles, 1827–1905, vol. I
Woodhouse, Brig. Harold Lister, 1887–1960, vol. V
Woodhouse, Rear-Adm. Hector Roy Mackenzie, 1889–1971, vol. VII
Woodhouse, Rev. Henry George, 1852–1930, vol. III
Woodhouse, Herbert, 1859–1957, vol. V

Woodhouse, Rt Rev. John Walker, 1884–1955, vol. V
Woodhouse, Sir Percy, 1856–1931, vol. III
Woodhouse, Maj.-Gen. Sir Percy; see Woodhouse, Maj.-Gen. Sir T. P.
Woodhouse, Sir Stewart, 1846–1921, vol. II
Woodhouse, Thomas, 1862–1933, vol. III
Woodhouse, Maj.-Gen. Sir (Tom) Percy, 1857–1931, vol. III
Woodhouse, Vernon Kerslake, died 1936, vol. III
Woodhouse, William Bradley, 1873–1940, vol. III
Woodhouse, William John, 1866–1937, vol. III
Woodhull, Zula Maud, died 1940, vol. III
Woodifield, Col Anthony Hudson, 1867–1946, vol. IV
Wooding, Rt Hon. Sir Hugh Olliviere Beresford, 1904–1974, vol. VII
Wooding, John Conrad, 1901–1954, vol. V
Woodland, Col Arthur Law, 1849–1921, vol. II
Woodland, William Norton Ferrier, 1879–1952, vol. V
Woodley, Sir (Frederick George) Richard, died 1971, vol. VII
Woodley, Sir Richard; see Woodley, Sir F. G. R.
Woodlock, Rev. Francis, 1871–1940, vol. III
Woodman, Sir George Joseph, 1847–1915, vol. I
Woodman, John, 1888–1971, vol. VII
Woodnutt, Harold Frederick Martin; see Woodnutt, Mark.
Woodnutt, Mark, (Harold Frederick Martin Woodnutt), 1918–1974, vol. VII
Woodroffe, Brig.-Gen. Charles Richard, 1878–1965, vol. VI
Woodroffe, Hon. James T., 1838–1908, vol. I
Woodroffe, Sir John George, 1865–1936, vol. III
Woodroffe, Paul Vincent, 1875–1954, vol. V
Woodrooffe, Very Rev. Henry Reade, 1834–1913, vol. I
Woodruff, Douglas; see Woodruff, J. D.
Woodruff, Harold Addison, died 1966, vol. VI
Woodruff, (John) Douglas, 1897–1978, vol. VII
Woodruff, Keith Montague Cumberland, 1891–1978, vol. VII
Woodruff, Timothy Lester, 1858–1913, vol. I (A)
Woods, Albert, died 1944, vol. IV
Woods, Lt-Col Albert Edward, 1862–1938, vol. III
Woods, Sir Albert William, 1816–1904, vol. I
Woods, Rev. Vice-Adm. Alexander Riall Wadham, 1880–1954, vol. V
Woods, Alice, 1849–1941, vol. IV
Woods, Donald Devereux, 1912–1964, vol. VI
Woods, Maj.-Gen. Edward Ambrose, 1891–1957, vol. V
Woods, Rt Rev. Edward Sydney, 1877–1953, vol. V
Woods, Rt Rev. Frank Theodore, 1874–1932, vol. III
Woods, Rev. George Frederick, 1907–1966, vol. VI
Woods, Rev. George Saville, 1886–1951, vol. V
Woods, Col Harold, 1879–1952, vol. V
Woods, Henry, 1846–1921, vol. II
Woods, Henry, 1868–1952, vol. IV
Woods, Henry Charles, 1841–1931, vol. III
Woods, Henry Charles, 1881–1939, vol. III

Woods, Adm. Sir Henry Felix, 1843–1929, vol. III
Woods, Rev. Henry George, 1842–1915, vol. I
Woods, Hon. Henry John Bacon, 1842–1916, vol. II
Woods, Brig.-Gen. Hugh Kennedy, 1877–1964, vol. VI
Woods, Irene Charlotte, 1891–1976, vol. VII
Woods, Sir James Edward, 1850–1944, vol. IV
Woods, Hon. Lt-Col James Hossack, 1867–1941, vol. IV
Woods, Sir James William, died 1941, vol. IV
Woods, Sir John Harold Edmund, 1895–1962, vol. VI
Woods, Joseph Ainsworth, 1870–1947, vol. IV
Woods, Joseph Andrews, died 1925, vol. II
Woods, Margaret Louisa, 1856–1945, vol. IV
Woods, Matthew Snooke Grosvenor, 1838–1925, vol. II
Woods, Maurice Henry, 1882–1929, vol. III
Woods, Oliver Frederick John Bradley, 1911–1972, vol. VII
Woods, Percy, 1842–1922, vol. II
Woods, Col Philip James, 1880–1961, vol. VI
Woods, Sir Raymond Wybrow, 1882–1943, vol. IV
Woods, Richard Lennox, died 1918, vol. II
Woods, Sir Robert Henry, 1865–1938, vol. III
Woods, Sir Robert Stanton, 1877–1954, vol. V
Woods, Samuel, 1846–1915, vol. I (A)
Woods, Samuel Moses James, 1867–1931, vol. III
Woods, Walter Sainsbury, 1884–1960, vol. V (A)
Woods, Adm. Sir Wilfrid John Wentworth, 1906–1975, vol. VII
Woods, Sir Wilfrid Wentworth, 1876–1947, vol. IV
Woods, William, 1855–1932, vol. III
Woods, William Forster, 1865–1942, vol. IV
Woods, Col William Talbot, 1891–1975, vol. VII
Woods, William Wilson, 1884–1972, vol. VII
Woods Ballard, Lt-Col Basil, 1900–1980, vol. VII
Woodthorpe, John Frederick, 1897–1966, vol. VI
Woodthorpe, Ven. Robert Augustus, 1861–1931, vol. III
Woodthorpe, Col Robert Gosset, 1844–1898, vol. I
Woodville, Richard Caton, 1856–1927, vol. II
Woodward, Sir (Alfred) Chad (Turner), 1880–1957, vol. V
Woodward, Arthur Maurice, 1883–1973, vol. VII
Woodward, Sir Arthur Smith, 1864–1944, vol. IV
Woodward, Sir Chad; see Woodward, Sir A. C. T.
Woodward, Rt Rev. Clifford Salisbury, 1878–1959, vol. V
Woodward, Denys Cuthbert, 1902–1972, vol. VII
Woodward, Edward Gilbert, 1900–1950, vol. IV
Woodward, Lt-Col Edward Hamilton Everard, 1888–1976, vol. VII
Woodward, Maj.-Gen. Sir Edward Mabbott, 1861–1943, vol. IV
Woodward, Lt-Gen. Sir Eric Winslow, 1899–1967, vol. VI
Woodward, Sir (Ernest) Llewellyn, 1890–1971, vol. VII
Woodward, Col Francis Willoughby, 1872–1926, vol. II
Woodward, George Ernest, 1865–1939, vol. III
Woodward, Henry, 1832–1921, vol. II

Woodward, Rear-Adm. Sir Henry William, 1879–1959, vol. V
Woodward, Rev. Herbert Willoughby, 1854–1932, vol. III
Woodward, Horace Bolingbroke, 1848–1914, vol. I
Woodward, Joan, (Mrs L. T. Blakeman), 1916–1971, vol. VII
Woodward, Col John Henry, 1849–1918, vol. II
Woodward, Sir Lionel Mabbott, 1864–1925, vol. II
Woodward, Sir Llewellyn; see Woodward, Sir E. L.
Woodward, Marcus, died 1940, vol. III
Woodward, Oliver Holmes, 1885–1966, vol. VI
Woodward, Adm. Robert, 1838–1907, vol. I
Woodward, Robert Burns, 1917–1979, vol. VII
Woodward, Robert Simpson, 1849–1924, vol. II
Woodward, William Harrison, 1855–1941, vol. IV
Woodward-Nutt, Arthur Edgar, 1902–1980, vol. VII
Woodwark, Sir (Arthur) Stanley, died 1945, vol. IV
Woodwark, Col (George) Graham, 1874–1938, vol. III
Woodwark, Col Graham; see Woodwark, Col George G.
Woodwark, Sir Stanley; see Woodwark, Sir A. S.
Woodwright, Surg. Rear-Adm. Charles Sharman, 1870–1949, vol. IV
Woodyatt, Maj.-Gen. Nigel Gresley, 1861–1936, vol. III
Woof, Rowsby, 1883–1943, vol. IV
Woolacott, John Evans, 1862–1936, vol. III
Woolavington, 1st Baron, 1849–1935, vol. III
Woolcock, William James Uglow, 1878–1947, vol. IV
Wooldridge, George Henry, died 1957, vol. V
Wooldridge, Harry Ellis, 1845–1917, vol. II
Wooldridge, Henry, 1908–1975, vol. VII
Wooldridge, Sidney William, 1900–1963, vol. VI
Wooldridge, Walter Reginald, 1900–1966, vol. VI
Woolf, Albert Edward Mortimer, 1884–1957, vol. V
Woolf, Rev. Bertram Lee, died 1956, vol. V
Woolf, Charles H.; see Hyatt-Woolf.
Woolf, Leonard Sidney, 1880–1969, vol. VI
Woolf, Virginia, 1882–1941, vol. IV
Woolfe, Brig. Richard Dean Townsend, 1888–1966, vol. VI
Woolford, Sir Eustace Gordon, 1876–1966, vol. VI
Woolfryes, Surg.-Gen. Sir John Andrews, 1823–1912, vol. I
Woolgar, Alfred John, 1879–1968, vol. VI
Wooll, Edward, 1878–1970, vol. VI
Woollam, Rev. Canon J., 1827–1909, vol. I
Woollard, Herbert Henry, 1889–1939, vol. III
Woollcombe, Captain Charles George Ley, 1884–1962, vol. VI
Woollcombe, Lt-Gen. Sir Charles Louis, 1857–1934, vol. III
Woollcombe, Rt Rev. Henry St John Stirling, 1869–1941, vol. IV
Woollcombe, Adm. Louis Charles Stirling, 1872–1951, vol. V
Woollcombe, Major Malcolm Louis, 1891–1968, vol. VI
Woollcombe, Adm. Maurice, 1868–1930, vol. III

Woollcott, Alexander, 1887–1943, vol. IV
Woollen, James, 1854–1921, vol. II
Woolley, Charles, 1846–1922, vol. II
Woolley, Lt-Col Sir Charles Augustus, 1859–1936, vol. III
Woolley, Paymaster Rear-Adm. Charles Edward Allen, 1863–1940, vol. III
Woolley, Sir (Charles) Leonard, 1880–1960, vol. V
Woolley, Frank Edward, 1887–1978, vol. VII
Woolley, Rev. Geoffrey Harold, 1892–1968, vol. VI
Woolley, Howard Mark, 1879–1971, vol. VII
Woolley, Sir Leonard; see Woolley, Sir C. L.
Woolley, Rev. Reginald Maxwell, 1877–1931, vol. III
Woolley, Samuel Walter, 1865–1927, vol. II
Woolley-Hart, Arthur, 1859–1941, vol. IV
Woolmer, Rt Rev. Laurence Henry, 1906–1977, vol. VII
Woolmer, Ronald Francis, 1908–1962, vol. VI
Woolner, Alfred Cooper, died 1936, vol. III
Woolnough, Rev. Canon Howard Frank, 1886–1973, vol. VII
Woolnough, Walter George, 1876–1958, vol. V
Woolrych, H. R., 1858–1917, vol. II
Wools-Sampson, Col Sir Aubrey, died 1924, vol. II
Woolston, Thomas Henry, 1855–1927, vol. II
Woolton, 1st Earl of, 1883–1964, vol. VI
Woolton, 2nd Earl of, 1922–1969, vol. VI
Woolveridge, Air Cdre Harry Leonard, 1887–1960, vol. V
Woon, Gen. Sir John Blaxall, 1856–1938, vol. III
Woosnam, Ven. Charles Maxwell, 1856–1930, vol. III
Woosnam, R. B., died 1915, vol. I
Wootten, Aubrey Francis Wootten, 1866–1923, vol. II
Wootten, Maj.-Gen. Sir George Frederick, 1893–1970, vol. VI
Wootten, Maj.-Gen. Richard Montague, 1889–1979, vol. VII
Wootton, Hubert Arthur, 1884–1947, vol. IV
Wootton-Davies, James Henry, 1884–1964, vol. VI
Worboys, Sir Arthur Thomas, died 1966, vol. VI
Worboys, Sir Walter John, 1900–1969, vol. VI
Wordie, Sir James Mann, 1889–1962, vol. VI
Wordingham, Charles Henry, 1866–1925, vol. II
Wordsworth, Rev. Christopher, 1848–1938, vol. III
Wordsworth, Dame Elizabeth, 1840–1932, vol. III
Wordsworth, Rt Rev. John, 1843–1911, vol. I
Wordsworth, William, 1835–1917, vol. II
Wordsworth, William Christopher, 1878–1950, vol. IV
Wordsworth, Captain Sir William Henry Laycock, 1880–1960, vol. V
Worgan, Lt-Gen. John, 1821–1909, vol. I
Worgan, Brig.-Gen. Rivers Berney, died 1936, vol. III
Worgan, Col Sydney Drummond, 1872–1950, vol. IV
Workman, Charles Rufus Marshall, died 1942, vol. IV
Workman, Fanny Bullock, died 1925, vol. II
Workman, Harold, 1897–1975, vol. VII
Workman, Rev. Herbert Brook, 1862–1951, vol. V

Workman, Mark, 1864–1936, vol. III
Workman, Walter Percy, 1863–1918, vol. II
Workman, William Arthur, 1877–1956, vol. V
Workman, William Hunter, 1847–1937, vol. III
Workman, William Thomas, died 1971, vol. VII
Workman-Macnaghten, Rt Hon. Sir Francis Edmund; see Macnaghten.
Worley, Sir Arthur, 1st Bt, 1871–1937, vol. III
Worley, Frederick Palliser, 1880–1960, vol. V (A)
Worley, Sir Newnham Arthur, 1892–1976, vol. VII
Worlledge, Rev. Arthur John, 1848–1919, vol. II
Worlledge, Sir John Leonard, 1895–1968, vol. VI
Wormald, Francis, 1904–1972, vol. VII
Wormald, Sir John, 1859–1933, vol. III
Wormall, Arthur, 1900–1964, vol. VI
Wormell, Richard, 1838–1914, vol. I
Worms, 2nd Baron de, 1829–1912, vol. I
Worms, 3rd Baron de, 1869–1938, vol. III
Worms, Percy George de, 1873–1941, vol. IV
Wornum, George Grey, 1888–1957, vol. V
Wornum, Ralph Selden, 1847–1910, vol. I
Worrall, Arthur Hardey, 1868–1960, vol. V
Worrell, Most Rev. Clarendon Lamb, 1853–1934, vol. III
Worrell, Sir Frank Mortimer Maglinne, 1924–1967, vol. VI
Worrell, John Austin, 1852–1927, vol. II
Worsfold, Sir Thomas Cato, 1st Bt, died 1936, vol. III
Worsfold, William Basil, 1858–1939, vol. III
Worsley, Lord; Charles Sackville Pelham, 1887–1914, vol. I
Worsley, Lady; (Alexandra Mary Freesia), 1890–1963, vol. VI
Worsley, Rev. Edward, 1844–1923, vol. II
Worsley, Comdr Frank Arthur, 1872–1943, vol. IV
Worsley, Col Henry Robert Brown, 1833–1902, vol. I
Worsley, Philip Ernest T. C.; see Tindal-Carill-Worsley.
Worsley, Ralph Marcus Meaburn, 1887–1939, vol. III
Worsley, Rev. Richard, 1889–1972, vol. VII
Worsley, Lt-Col Richard Stanley, 1879–1917, vol. II
Worsley, Major Ronald Henry Warton, 1886–1932, vol. III
Worsley, Col Sidney John, 1895–1974, vol. VII
Worsley, Col Sir William Arthington, 4th Bt, 1890–1973, vol. VII
Worsley, Sir William Cayley, 2nd Bt, 1828–1897, vol. I
Worsley, Sir William Henry Arthington, 3rd Bt, 1861–1936, vol. III
Worsley-Gough, Lt-Col Henry Worsley; see Gough.
Worsley-Taylor, Sir Francis Edward, 4th Bt, 1874–1958, vol. V
Worsley-Taylor, Sir Henry Wilson, 1st Bt, 1847–1924, vol. II
Worsley-Taylor, Lt-Col Sir James, 2nd Bt, 1872–1933, vol. III
Worsley-Taylor, Captain Sir John Godfrey, 3rd Bt, 1915–1952, vol. V

738

Worsnop, Bernard Lister, 1892–1980, vol. VII
Worster-Drought, Charles, *died* 1971, vol. VII
Worswick, Thomas, *died* 1932, vol. III
Wort, Sir Alfred William Ewart, 1883–1976, vol. VII
Worth, Arthur Hovenden, 1877–1955, vol. V
Worth, Claud, *died* 1936, vol. III
Wortham, Maj.-Gen. Geoffrey Christopher Hale, 1913–1967, vol. VI
Wortham, Col Harold Charles Webster Hale, 1878–1939, vol. III
Wortham, Hugh Evelyn, 1884–1959, vol. V
Wortham, Brig. Philip William Temple Hale, 1874–1955, vol. V
Worthington, Albert Octavius, 1844–1918, vol. II
Worthington, Arthur Furley, 1874–1964, vol. VI
Worthington, Arthur Mason, 1852–1916, vol. II
Worthington, Charles Edward, 1897–1970, vol. VI
Worthington, Col Edward Bruen, 1860–1945, vol. IV
Worthington, Col Sir Edward Scott, 1876–1953, vol. V
Worthington, Frank, 1874–1964, vol. VI
Worthington, Maj.-Gen. Frederic Frank, 1889–1967, vol. VI
Worthington, Henry Hugo, 1857–1924, vol. II
Worthington, Sir Hubert, 1886–1963, vol. VI
Worthington, John Morton, 1883–1956, vol. V
Worthington, Sir John Vigers, 1872–1951, vol. V
Worthington, Sir Percy Scott, 1864–1939, vol. III
Worthington, Rear-Adm. Roger Ernest, 1889–1967, vol. VI
Worthington, Thomas, 1850–1933, vol. III
Worthington, William Barton, 1854–1939, vol. III
Worthington-Evans, Rt Hon. Sir Laming, 1st Bt, 1868–1931, vol. III
Worthington-Evans, Sir Shirley; *see* Worthington-Evans, Sir W. S. W.
Worthington-Evans, Sir (William) Shirley (Worthington), 2nd Bt, 1904–1971, vol. VII
Wortley, Hon. Clare Euphemia S.; *see* Stuart-Wortley.
Wortley, Maj.-Gen. Hon. Edward James Montagu S.; *see* Stuart-Wortley.
Wortley, Rev. Edward Jocelyn, *died* 1928, vol. II
Wortley, Edward Jocelyn, 1884–1942, vol. IV
Wortley, Hon. Mrs Edward S.; *see* Stuart Wortley, Violet.
Wortley, Harry Almond Saville, 1885–1947, vol. IV
Wortley, Lt-Gen. Hon. Sir Richard Montagu S.; *see* Stuart-Wortley.
Worton, Albert Samuel, 1874–1940, vol. III
Wotherspoon, (George) Ralph (Howard), 1897–1979, vol. VII
Wotherspoon, Ralph; *see* Wotherspoon, G. R. H.
Wotherspoon, Robert Andrew, 1912–1975, vol. VII
Wragg, Sir Herbert, *died* 1956, vol. V
Wragg, Hon. Sir Walter Thomas, 1842–1913, vol. I
Wragge, Clement Lindley, 1852–1922, vol. II
Wragge, Robert Horton Vernon, 1854–1933, vol. III
Wraight, Ernest Alfred, 1879–1946, vol. IV

Wraith, Col Ernest Arnold, 1876–1937, vol. III
Wrangel, Count Herman, 1857–1934, vol. III
Wrangham, Rev. Francis, *died* 1941, vol. IV
Wratislaw, Albert Charles, 1862–1938, vol. III
Wratislaw, Adm. Henry Rushworth, 1832–1913, vol. I
Wraxall, 1st Baron, 1873–1931, vol. III
Wraxall, Sir Charles Frederick Lascelles, 7th Bt, 1896–1951, vol. V
Wraxall, Sir Morville William, 6th Bt, 1862–1902, did not have an entry in Who's Who.
Wraxall, Sir Morville William Lascelles, 8th Bt, 1922–1978, vol. VII
Wraxall, Sir Morville William Nathaniel, 5th Bt, 1834–1898 (this entry was not transferred to Who was Who).
Wray, Brig.-Gen. Cecil; *see* Wray, Brig.-Gen. J. C.
Wray, Vice-Adm. Fawcet, 1873–1932, vol. III
Wray, Rev. Frederick William, 1864–1943, vol. IV
Wray, Brig.-Gen. (John) Cecil, 1864–1947, vol. IV
Wray, Captain Kenneth Mackenzie, 1855–1927, vol. II
Wray, Leonard, *died* 1942, vol. IV
Wray, Captain Thomas Henry Roberts-, *died* 1943, vol. IV
Wray, W. Fitzwater, *died* 1938, vol. III
Wreford, Sir Ernest Henry, 1866–1938, vol. III
Wreford, George, 1843–1919, vol. II
Wreford-Brown, Captain Claude Wreford, 1876–1915, vol. I
Wren, Maj.-Gen. John, 1896–1958, vol. V
Wren, Percival Christopher, 1885–1941, vol. IV
Wren, Walter, *died* 1898, vol. I
Wrenbury, 1st Baron, 1845–1935, vol. III
Wrenbury, 2nd Baron, 1890–1940, vol. III
Wrench, Sir Charles Arthur, 1875–1948, vol. IV
Wrench, Edward Mason, 1833–1912, vol. I
Wrench, Sir Evelyn; *see* Wrench, Sir J. E. L.
Wrench, Rt Hon. Frederick Stringer, 1849–1926, vol. II
Wrench, Hylda Henrietta, (Lady Wrench), *died* 1955, vol. V
Wrench, Sir (John) Evelyn (Leslie), 1882–1966, vol. VI
Wrench, John Mervyn Dallas, 1883–1961, vol. VI
Wrench, Mollie Louise S.; *see* Stanley-Wrench.
Wrenfordsley, Sir Henry Thomas, *died* 1908, vol. I
Wrenn, Charles Leslie, 1895–1969, vol. VI
Wrey, Rev. Sir Albany Bourchier Sherard, 13th Bt, 1861–1948, vol. IV
Wrey, Sir Bourchier Robert Sherard, 11th Bt, 1855–1917, vol. II
Wrey, Sir Henry Bourchier Toke, 10th Bt, 1829–1900, vol. I
Wrey, Sir Philip Bourchier Sherard, 12th Bt, 1858–1936, vol. III
Wrey, Captain William Bourchier Sherard, 1865–1926, vol. II
Wright, Baron (Life Peer); Robert Alderson Wright, 1869–1964, vol. VI
Wright of Ashton under Lyne, Baron (Life Peer); Lewis Tatham Wright, 1903–1974, vol. VII
Wright, Adam Henry, 1846–1930, vol. III

Wright, Albert Allen, 1846–1905, vol. I
Wright, Albert Ernest, 1902–1960, vol. V
Wright, Comdr Alexander Galloway, 1874–1943, vol. IV
Wright, Sir Alexander Kemp, 1859–1933, vol. III
Wright, Sir Almroth Edward, 1861–1947, vol. IV
Wright, Sir Andrew Barkworth, 1895–1971, vol. VII
Wright, Brig.-Gen. Archibald John Arnott, 1851–1943, vol. IV
Wright, Arnold, died 1941, vol. IV
Wright, Rev. Arthur, 1831–1920, vol. II
Wright, Rev. Arthur, 1843–1924, vol. II
Wright, Arthur Alban, 1887–1967, vol. VI
Wright, Sir Arthur Cory C.; see Cory-Wright.
Wright, A(rthur) Dickson, died 1976, vol. VII
Wright, Arthur Robinson, 1862–1932, vol. III
Wright, Lt-Col Bache Allen, 1874–1932, vol. III
Wright, Bernard Arker, 1893–1973, vol. VII
Wright, Sir Bernard Swanwick, 1876–1961, vol. VI
Wright, Cecily Gertrude, died 1942, vol. IV
Wright, Col Sir Charles; see Wright, Col Sir W. C.
Wright, Charles Edward, died 1945, vol. IV
Wright, Charles Henry, 1864–1941, vol. IV
Wright, Charles Henry Conrad, 1869–1957, vol. V
Wright, Rev. Charles Henry Hamilton, 1836–1909, vol. I
Wright, Charles Ichabod, 1828–1905, vol. I
Wright, Sir Charles Seymour, 1887–1975, vol. VII
Wright, Sir Charles Theodore Hagberg, 1862–1940, vol. III
Wright, Sir Cory Francis C.; see Cory-Wright.
Wright, Dickson; see Wright, A. D.
Wright, Dudley, 1868–1949, vol. IV
Wright, Dudley d'Auvergne, 1867–1948, vol. IV
Wright, Edward Fitzwalter, 1902–1957, vol. V
Wright, Edward Fortescue, 1858–1904, vol. I
Wright, Edward Perceval, 1834–1910, vol. I
Wright, Rev. Edwin Henry, 1843–1937, vol. III
Wright, Eric Blackwood, 1860–1940, vol. III
Wright, Ernest, 1882–1974, vol. VII
Wright, Fowler; see Wright, S. F.
Wright, Frank, 1853–1922, vol. II
Wright, Frank Arnold, 1874–1961, vol. VI
Wright, Frank Joseph Henry, 1901–1970, vol. VI
Wright, Frank Lloyd, 1869–1959, vol. V
Wright, Frank Trueman W.; see Wynyard-Wright.
Wright, Frederick Adam, 1869–1946, vol. IV
Wright, Lt-Col Frederick William, 1850–1927, vol. II
Wright, Sir Geoffrey C.; see Cory-Wright.
Wright, George, died 1913, vol. I
Wright, Sir George, died 1927, vol. II
Wright, Col George, 1860–1942, vol. IV
Wright, George Arthur, died 1920, vol. II
Wright, George Maurice, died 1956, vol. V
Wright, George Payling, 1898–1964, vol. VI
Wright, Rt Rev. George William, 1873–1956, vol. V
Wright, Lt-Col Guy Jefferys H.; see Hornsby-Wright.
Wright, H. C. Seppings, died 1937, vol. III
Wright, Harold, 1858–1908, vol. I
Wright, Harold Bell, 1872–1944, vol. IV

Wright, Harold Edward, 1868–1946, vol. IV
Wright, Rev. Harold Hall, 1859–1926, vol. II
Wright, Lt-Col Harry, 1856–1942, vol. IV
Wright, Major Hedley, died 1903, vol. I
Wright, Hedley Duncan, 1891–1942, vol. IV
Wright, Maj.-Gen. Henry Brooke Hagstromer, 1864–1948, vol. IV
Wright, Rev. Henry Dixon D.; see Dixon-Wright.
Wright, Sir Henry Edward, 1893–1966, vol. VI
Wright, Henry FitzHerbert, 1870–1947, vol. IV
Wright, Henry Robert, 1877–1951, vol. V
Wright, Henry Smith, 1839–1910, vol. I
Wright, Sir Herbert, 1874–1940, vol. III
Wright, Lt-Col Herbert James, 1888–1974, vol. VII
Wright, Huntley, 1869–1941, vol. IV
Wright, Sir James, 1823–1899, vol. I
Wright, James, died 1947, vol. IV
Wright, James Brown, 1861–1926, vol. II
Wright, John, 1857–1933, vol. III
Wright, Most Rev. John Charles, 1861–1933, vol. III
Wright, John George, 1897–1971, vol. VII
Wright, John Graham, 1873–1949, vol. IV
Wright, John Moncrieff, 1884–1971, vol. VII
Wright, Col Sir John Roper, 1st Bt, 1843–1926, vol. II
Wright, Sir Johnstone, 1883–1953, vol. V
Wright, Joseph, 1855–1930, vol. III
Wright, Joshua Butler, 1877–1939, vol. III
Wright, Kenneth Anthony, 1899–1975, vol. VII
Wright, Sir Leonard Morton, 1906–1967, vol. VI
Wright, Rev. Leslie, 1899–1972, vol. VII
Wright, Louise, died 1944, vol. IV
Wright, Mabel Osgood, 1859–1934, vol. III
Wright, Mark Robinson, 1854–1944, vol. IV
Wright, Sir Michael Robert, 1901–1976, vol. VII
Wright, Rear-Adm. Noel, 1890–1975, vol. VII
Wright, Sir Norman Charles, 1900–1970, vol. VI
Wright, Orville, 1871–1948, vol. IV
Wright, Percy Malcolm, 1906–1959, vol. V
Wright, Phillip Arundell, 1889–1970, vol. VI
Wright, R. Ramsay, 1852–1933, vol. III
Wright, Lt-Col Robert Ernest, 1884–1977, vol. VII
Wright, Sir Robert Patrick, 1857–1938, vol. III
Wright, Sir Robert Samuel, 1839–1904, vol. I
Wright, Col Robert Wallace, 1863–1928, vol. II
Wright, Adm. Sir Royston Hollis, 1908–1977, vol. VII
Wright, Samson, died 1956, vol. V
Wright, Samuel, 1895–1975, vol. VII
Wright, Samuel John, 1899–1975, vol. VII
Wright, Lt-Col Stephen, 1863–1936, vol. III
Wright, (Sydney) Fowler, 1874–1965, vol. VI
Wright, Sir Thomas, 1838–1905, vol. I
Wright, Gen. Sir Thomas, 1825–1910, vol. I
Wright, Thomas, 1859–1936, vol. III
Wright, Thomas G., 1878–1929, vol. III
Wright, Thomas Rowland Drake, 1853–1926, vol. II
Wright, Uriah John, 1840–1914, vol. I
Wright, Brig.-Gen. Wallace Duffield, died 1953, vol. V
Wright, Walter Page, 1864–1940, vol. III

Wright, Wilfrid Thomas Mermoud, 1882–1946, vol. IV

Wright, Willard Huntington, 1888–1939, vol. III

Wright, William, 1862–1931, vol. III

Wright, William, 1874–1937, vol. III

Wright, William Aldis, 1831–1914, vol. I

Wright, Col William Burgess, *died* 1930, vol. III

Wright, Col Sir (William) Charles, 2nd Bt, 1876–1950, vol. IV

Wright, Major William Gordon, 1883–1930, vol. III

Wright, William Hammond, 1871–1959, vol. V (A)

Wright, Rev. William Herbert Thomas, *died* 1929, vol. III

Wright, Rev. Canon William Joseph, 1881–1954, vol. V

Wright, Sir William Owen, 1882–1951, vol. V

Wright, Gen. Sir William Purvis, 1846–1910, vol. I

Wright, Sir William Shaw, 1843–1914, vol. I

Wright, Lt-Col Rev. William Thomas, *died* 1938, vol. III

Wright-Henderson, Rev. Patrick Arkley, 1841–1922, vol. II

Wrighton, Edward, 1880–1937, vol. III

Wrightson, Captain Charles Archibald Wise, 1874–1953, vol. V

Wrightson, Edmund Harry Paul Garmondsway, 1919–1972, vol. VII

Wrightson, Sir Guy; *see* Wrightson, Sir T. G.

Wrightson, John, 1840–1916, vol. II

Wrightson, Sir Thomas, 1st Bt, 1839–1921, vol. II

Wrightson, Sir Thomas Garmondsway, (Sir Guy), 2nd Bt, 1871–1950, vol. IV

Wrightson, Walsh, 1852–1935, vol. III

Wrigley, Hon. Brig.-Gen. Clement Carr, 1870–1934, vol. III

Wrigley, Sir John Crompton, 1888–1977, vol. VII

Wrigley, Rev. Joseph Henry, *died* 1938, vol. III

Wrigley, Leslie James, *died* 1933, vol. III

Wrinch, Dorothy, *died* 1976, vol. VII

Wrixon, Hon. Sir Henry John, 1839–1913, vol. I

Wrixon-Becher, Sir Eustace William Windham; *see* Becher.

Wrixon-Becher, Lt-Col Henry; *see* Becher.

Wrixon-Becher, Sir John; *see* Becher.

Wroblewski, Wladyslaw, 1875–1952, vol. V

Wrong, Edward Murray, 1889–1928, vol. II

Wrong, George Mackinnon, 1860–1948, vol. IV

Wrong, Humphrey Hume, 1894–1954, vol. V

Wrottesley, 3rd Baron, 1824–1910, vol. I

Wrottesley, 4th Baron, 1873–1962, vol. VI

Wrottesley, 5th Baron, 1918–1977, vol. VII

Wrottesley, Captain Francis Robert, 1877–1954, vol. V

Wrottesley, Rt Hon. Sir Frederic John, 1880–1948, vol. IV

Wroughton, Brig.-Gen. John Bartholomew, 1874–1940, vol. III

Wroughton, Philip, 1846–1910, vol. I

Wroughton, Major Philip Musgrave Neeld, 1887–1917, vol. II

Wroughton, William Musgrave, 1850–1928, vol. II

Wunderly, Sir Harry Wyatt, 1892–1971, vol. VII

Wurth, Wallace Charles, 1896–1960, vol. V (A)

Wurtzburg, Charles Edward, 1891–1952, vol. V

Wyard, Stanley, 1887–1946, vol. IV

Wyatt, Brig. Arthur Geoffrey, 1900–1960, vol. V

Wyatt, Col Ernest Robert Caldwell, 1880–1957, vol. V

Wyatt, Major Francis Ogilvy, 1871–1919, vol. II

Wyatt, Harold Frazer, *died* 1925, vol. II

Wyatt, Horace Matthew, 1876–1954, vol. V

Wyatt, James Montagu, 1883–1953, vol. V

Wyatt, Rev. Joseph Light, 1841–1936, vol. III

Wyatt, Brig.-Gen. Louis John, 1874–1955, vol. V

Wyatt, Sir Myles Dermot Norris, 1903–1968, vol. VI

Wyatt, Rev. Paul Williams, 1856–1935, vol. III

Wyatt, Sir Stanley, 1877–1968, vol. VI

Wyatt, Thomas Henry, 1841–1920, vol. II

Wyatt, Travers Carey, 1887–1954, vol. V

Wyatt, Sir William Henry, 1823–1898, vol. I

Wyatt-Paine, Wyatt, *died* 1935, vol. III

Wyatt-Smith, Stanley; *see* Smith.

Wyche, Rev. Cyrill John, 1867–1945, vol. IV

Wycherley, Sir Bruce; *see* Wycherley, Sir R. B.

Wycherley, Sir (Robert) Bruce, 1894–1965, vol. VI

Wyeth, Rex, 1914–1978, vol. VII

Wyfold, 1st Baron, 1851–1937, vol. III

Wyfold, 2nd Baron, 1880–1942, vol. IV

Wyke, Rt Hon. Sir Charles Lennox, 1815–1897, vol. I

Wykeham-Martin, Cornwallis Philip; *see* Martin.

Wykeham-Musgrave, Herbert Wenman, 1871–1931, vol. III

Wykes, John Arthur, 1891–1970, vol. VI

Wykes-Finch, Rev. William Robert, 1855–1922, vol. II

Wykes-Sneyd, Vice-Adm. Ralph Stuart, 1882–1951, vol. V

Wyld, Rev. Edwin G., *died* 1919, vol. II

Wyld, Henry Cecil Kennedy, 1870–1945, vol. IV

Wyldbore-Smith, Sir Edmund; *see* Smith.

Wylde, Rt Rev. Arnold Lomas, 1880–1958, vol. V

Wylde, Col Charles Fenwick, 1867–1946, vol. IV

Wylde, Gen. Edward Andrée, 1858–1925, vol. II

Wylde, Everard William, *died* 1911, vol. I

Wylde, Rev. John, 1841–1941, vol. IV

Wylde, John Truro, *died* 1927, vol. II

Wylde, Rev. Robert, *died* 1927, vol. II

Wylde, William Henry, 1819–1909, vol. I

Wyles, Lilian Mary Elizabeth, 1895–1975, vol. VII

Wyley, Col Sir William Fitzthomas, 1852–1940, vol. III

Wylie, Alexander, *died* 1921, vol. II

Wylie, Andrew, *died* 1935, vol. III

Wylie, Major Charles Hotham Montagu Doughty-, 1868–1915, vol. I

Wylie, David Storer, 1876–1965, vol. VI

Wylie, Sir Francis James, 1865–1952, vol. V

Wylie, Sir Francis Verner, 1891–1970, vol. VI

Wylie, Maj.-Gen. Henry, 1844–1918, vol. II

Wylie, Miss I. A. R., *died* 1959, vol. V

Wylie, James, 1875–1941, vol. IV

Wylie, James Hamilton, 1844–1914, vol. I

Wylie, Rt Hon. James Owens, 1845–1935, vol. III

Wylie, Brig.-Gen. James Scott, 1862–1937, vol. III

Wylie, John, *died* 1936, vol. III

Wylie, Major John Price, 1888–1939, vol. III
Wylie, Lt-Col Macleod, 1881–1952, vol. V
Wylie, Hon. William Evelyn, 1881–1964, vol. VI
Wyllarde, Dolf, died 1950, vol. IV
Wyllie, Lt-Col Alexander Keith, 1853–1928, vol. II
Wyllie, Charles W., died 1923, vol. II
Wyllie, Lt-Col Harold, 1880–1973, vol. VII
Wyllie, John, died 1916, vol. II
Wyllie, William Gifford, died 1969, vol. VI
Wyllie, Lt-Col Sir William Hutt Curzon, 1848–1909, vol. I
Wyllie, William Lionel, 1851–1931, vol. III
Wylly, Col Guy George Egerton, 1880–1962, vol. VI
Wylly, Col Harold Carmichael, 1858–1932, vol. III
Wylson, Oswald Cane, 1858–1925, vol. II
Wymark, Patrick Carl, (A. K. A. Cheeseman), 1926–1970, vol. VI
Wymer, Francis John, 1898–1976, vol. VII
Wyn-Harris, Sir Percy, 1903–1979, vol. VII
Wynch, Lionel Maling, 1864–1955, vol. V
Wyncoll, Col Charles Edward, 1857–1943, vol. IV
Wyndham, Sir Charles, 1837–1919, vol. II
Wyndham, Lt-Col Charles John, 1844–1930, vol. III
Wyndham, Rt Hon. George, 1863–1913, vol. I
Wyndham, Col Guy Percy, 1865–1941, vol. IV
Wyndham, Major Guy Richard Charles, 1896–1948, vol. IV
Wyndham, Henry Saxe, 1867–1940, vol. III
Wyndham, Horace Cowley, 1873–1970, vol. VI
Wyndham, Sir Hugh, 1836–1916, vol. II
Wyndham, Mary, (Lady Wyndham); see Moore, Mary.
Wyndham, Sir Percy, 1864–1943, vol. IV
Wyndham, Percy, 1867–1947, vol. IV
Wyndham, Hon. Percy Scawen, 1835–1911, vol. I
Wyndham, Lady Sibell Mary; see Grosvenor, Countess.
Wyndham, Col Walter George Crole, 1857–1948, vol. IV
Wyndham, Captain William, 1842–1930, vol. III
Wyndham, Hon. William Reginald, 1876–1914, vol. I
Wyndham White, Sir Eric, 1913–1980, vol. VII
Wynford, 3rd Baron, 1826–1899, vol. I
Wynford, 4th Baron, 1829–1903, vol. I
Wynford, 5th Baron, 1834–1904, vol. I
Wynford, 6th Baron, 1871–1940, vol. III
Wynford, 7th Baron, 1874–1943, vol. IV
Wynn, Hon. Charles Henry, 1847–1911, vol. I
Wynn, Hon. Frederick George, 1853–1932, vol. III
Wynn, Frederick R. W.; see Williams Wynn.
Wynn, Rt Rev. Harold Edward, 1889–1956, vol. V
Wynn, Col Sir Herbert Lloyd Watkin W.; see Williams-Wynn.
Wynn, Col Sir Robert William Herbert Watkin W.; see Williams-Wynn.
Wynn, Hon. Rowland Tempest Beresford, 1898–1977, vol. VII
Wynn, Rev. Walter, 1865–1951, vol. V
Wynn, Sir Watkin W.; see Williams-Wynn.
Wynn, William Henry, 1878–1956, vol. V

Wynn Parry, Hon. Sir Henry, 1899–1964, vol. VI
Wynn-Wynne, Major Reginald, 1857–1913, vol. I
Wynne, Hon. Agar, 1850–1934, vol. III
Wynne, Anthony; see Wilson, Robert McNair.
Wynne, Rev. Arthur Edwin, 1864–1964, vol. VI
Wynne, Gen. Sir Arthur Singleton, 1846–1936, vol. III
Wynne, Esmé; see Wynne-Tyson, D. E. E.
Wynne, Major Francis George, 1885–1918, vol. II
Wynne, Frederick Horton, 1877–1943, vol. IV
Wynne, Ven. G. R., 1838–1912, vol. I
Wynne, George, 1839–1912, vol. I
Wynne, Rt Hon. Sir Henry Arthur, 1867–1943, vol. IV
Wynne, Lt-Col Henry Ernest Singleton, 1877–1962, vol. VI
Wynne, May; see Knowles, Mabel Winifred.
Wynne, Pamela; see Scott, Winifred Mary.
Wynne, Major Reginald W.; see Wynn-Wynne.
Wynne, Sir Trevredyn Rashleigh, 1853–1942, vol. IV
Wynne, William Palmer, 1861–1950, vol. IV
Wynne, William Robert Maurice, 1840–1909, vol. I
Wynne-Edwards, Rev. John Rosindale, 1864–1943, vol. IV
Wynne-Edwards, Sir Robert Meredydd, 1897–1974, vol. VII
Wynne-Eyton, Alan John F.; see Fairbairn-Wynne-Eyton.
Wynne Finch, Col Sir William Heneage, 1893–1961, vol. VI
Wynne-Jones, Major Charles Llewelyn, 1890–1974, vol. VII
Wynne-Jones, Very Rev. Llewelyn, died 1936, vol. III
Wynne-Jones, Tom Neville, 1893–1979, vol. VII
Wynne-Tyson, Dorothy Estelle Esmé, 1898–1972, vol. VII
Wynter, Bryan Herbert, 1915–1975, vol. VII
Wynter, Brig.-Gen. Francis Arthur, 1870–1942, vol. IV
Wynter, Maj.-Gen. Henry Douglas, 1886–1945, vol. IV
Wynter, Brig. Henry Walter, 1882–1959, vol. V
Wynter, Walter Essex, 1860–1945, vol. IV
Wynter-Morgan, Air Cdre Wilfred, 1894–1968, vol. VI
Wynyard, Diana, 1906–1964, vol. VI
Wynyard, Major Edward George, 1861–1936, vol. III
Wynyard, Col Rowley, 1855–1931, vol. III
Wynyard-Wright, Frank Trueman, 1884–1979, vol. VII
Wyon, Sir Albert William, 1869–1937, vol. III
Wyon, Allan, 1843–1907, vol. I
Wyon, Rev. Allan Gairdner, 1882–1962, vol. VI
Wyrall, Everard; see Wyrall, R. E.
Wyrall, Reginald Everard, 1878–1933, vol. III
Wyse, Andrew Nicholas B.; see Bonaparte-Wyse.
Wyse, Henry Taylor, 1870–1951, vol. V
Wyse, Marjorie Anne E.; see Erskine-Wyse.
Wythes, Ernest James, 1868–1949, vol. IV
Wyvill, Marmaduke D'Arcy, 1849–1918, vol. II

Y

Yahuda, Abraham Shalom Ezekiel, 1877–1951, vol. V

Yahya Khan, Gen. Agha Muhammad, 1917–1980, vol. VII

Yain, Sir Lee Ah, 1874–1932, vol. III

Yakub, Moulvi Sir Mohammad, 1879–1942, vol. IV

Yaldwin, Lt-Col Alfred George, 1847–1905, vol. I

Yale, Col James Corbet, 1859–1936, vol. III

Yamagata, Aritomo, Field-Marshal Prince, 1838–1922, vol. II

Yamin Khan, Sir Mohammed, died 1966, vol. VI

Yapp, Sir Arthur Keysall, 1869–1936, vol. III

Yapp, Sir Frederick Charles, 1880–1958, vol. V

Yapp, Richard Henry, died 1929, vol. III

Yarborough, 4th Earl of, 1859–1936, vol. III

Yarborough, 5th Earl of, 1888–1948, vol. IV

Yarborough, 6th Earl of, 1893–1966, vol. VI

Yarborough, Countess of; (Marcia Amelia Mary); see Fauconberg and Conyers, Baroness.

Yarborough, George Eustace C.; see Cooke-Yarborough.

Yarborough, Rev. John James Cooke-, 1855–1941, vol. IV

Yarde-Buller, Brig.-Gen. Hon. Sir Henry, 1862–1928, vol. II

Yarde-Buller, Hon. Walter, 1859–1935, vol. III

Yardley, Captain John Henry Reginald, 1881–1938, vol. III

Yardley, Col John Watkins, 1858–1920, vol. II

Yardley, Samuel, 1839–1902, vol. I

Yarr, Maj.-Gen. Sir Thomas, 1862–1937, vol. III

Yarrow, Sir Alfred Fernandez, 1st Bt, 1842–1932, vol. III

Yarrow, Eleanor Cecilia, (Lady Yarrow), died 1953, vol. V

Yarrow, Sir Harold Edgar, 2nd Bt, 1884–1962, vol. VI

Yarworth-Jones, Sir William, 1870–1953, vol. V

Yashiro, Yukio, 1890–1975, vol. VII

Yate, Lt-Col Arthur Campbell, 1853–1929, vol. III

Yate, Col Sir Charles Edward, 1st Bt, 1849–1940, vol. III

Yate, Rev. George Edward, died 1908, vol. I

Yate-Lee, Lawford, 1838–1901, vol. I

Yates, Col Clarence Montague, 1881–1952, vol. V

Yates, Lt-Gen. Sir David P.; see Peel Yates.

Yates, Lt-Col Donald, 1893–1960, vol. VI (AI)

Yates, Dornford; see Mercer, Major Cecil William.

Yates, Lt-Col Hubert Peel, 1874–1938, vol. III

Yates, Bt-Col James Ainsworth, 1883–1929, vol. III

Yates, John Ernest, 1887–1969, vol. VI

Yates, Joseph Maghull, 1844–1916, vol. II

Yates, Rev. Thomas, 1873–1936, vol. III

Yates, Sir Thomas, 1896–1978, vol. VII

Yates, Victor Francis, 1900–1969, vol. VI

Yates, Walter Baldwyn, died 1947, vol. IV

Yates, Rev. Canon William R., 1870–1951, vol. V

Yatman, Col Arthur Hamilton, 1874–1947, vol. IV

Yatman, Brig.-Gen. Clement, 1871–1940, vol. III

Yeaman, Sir Ian David, 1889–1977, vol. VII

Yeames, William Frederick, 1835–1918, vol. II

Yearsley, Macleod; see Yearsley, P. M.

Yearsley, (Percival) Macleod, died 1951, vol. V

Yeatman-Biggs, Rt Rev. Huyshe Wolcott, 1845–1922, vol. II

Yeats, Gerald Aylmer L.; see Levett-Yeats.

Yeats, Jack Butler, died 1957, vol. V

Yeats, John Butler, 1839–1922, vol. II

Yeats, William Butler, 1865–1939, vol. III

Yeats-Brown, Francis, 1886–1944, vol. IV

Yeats-Brown, Montagu, 1834–1921, vol. II

Yeatts, Maurice William Walter Murray, 1894–1950, vol. IV

Yeaxlee, Basil Alfred, 1883–1967, vol. VI

Yeilding, Col William Richard, 1856–1934, vol. III

Yeld, Edward, 1839–1921, vol. II

Yellowlees, Henry, 1888–1971, vol. VII

Yelverton, Adm. Bentinck John Davies, died 1959, vol. V

Yelverton, Hon. Roger Dawson, died 1912, vol. I

Yelverton, William Henry Morgan, 1840–1909, vol. I

Yen, W. W., 1877–1950, vol. IV (A), vol. V

Yencken, Arthur F., 1894–1944, vol. IV

Yeo, Sir Alfred William, 1863–1928, vol. II

Yeo, Gerald Francis, 1845–1909, vol. I

Yeo, Rt Rev. Mgr Henry D., 1872–1952, vol. V

Yeo, J. Burney, died 1914, vol. I

Yeo, Sir William, 1896–1972, vol. VII

Yeo-Thomas, Wing Comdr Forest Frederick Edward, 1901–1964, vol. VI

Yeoman, Rev. Alexander Ross, 1874–1956, vol. V

Yeoman, Ven. Henry Walker, died 1897, vol. I

Yerburgh, Rev. Oswald Pryor W.; see Wardell-Yerburgh.

Yerburgh, Richard Eustre, 1847–1939, vol. III

Yerburgh, Robert Armstrong, 1853–1916, vol. II

Yerbury, Francis Rowland, 1885–1970, vol. VI

Yerbury, Air Vice-Marshal Richard Olyffe, 1914–1971, vol. VII

Yerkes, Charles Tyson, 1837–1905, vol. I

Yerkes, Robert Mearns, 1876–1956, vol. V

Yetts, W. Perceval, 1878–1957, vol. V

Yew, Loke, died 1917, vol. II

Yexley, Lionel, 1861–1933, vol. III

Yglesias, V. P., died 1911, vol. I

Yolland, John Horatio, 1863–1944, vol. IV

Yonge, Charlotte Mary, 1823–1901, vol. I

Yonge, Lt-Col Philip Caynton, 1877–1928, vol. II

Yool, Air Vice-Marshal William Munro, 1894–1978, vol. VII

York, Ven. George William, died 1944, vol. IV

York, Thomas John Pinches, 1898–1970, vol. VI

Yorke, Hon. Alexander Grantham, 1847–1911, vol. I

Yorke, Hon. Alfred Ernest Frederick, 1871–1928, vol. II

Yorke, Lt-Col Sir Arthur; see Yorke, Lt-Col Sir H. A.

Yorke, Curtis, died 1930, vol. III

Yorke, Dorothy, 1879–1946, vol. IV

Yorke, Francis Reginald Stevens, 1906–1962, vol. VI
Yorke, Lt-Col Sir (H.) Arthur, 1848–1930, vol. III
Yorke, Sir Henry Francis Redhead, 1842–1914, vol. I
Yorke, Henry Vincent; see Green, H.
Yorke, John Reginald, 1836–1912, vol. I
Yorke, Brig. Philip Gerard, 1882–1968, vol. VI
Yorke, Brig.-Gen. Ralph Maximilian, 1874–1951, vol. V
Yorke, Robert Langdon, 1887–1954, vol. V
Yorke, Simon, 1903–1966, vol. VI
Yorke, Vincent Wodehouse, 1869–1957, vol. V
Yorke, Warrington, 1883–1943, vol. IV
Yorstoun, Brig.-Gen. Archibald Morden C.; see Carthew-Yorstoun.
Yoshida, Shigeru, 1878–1967, vol. VI
Youard, Very Rev. Wilfrid Wadham, 1869–1964, vol. VI
Youens, Rev. Canon Fearnley Algernon Cyril, 1886–1967, vol. VI
Youens, Rt Rev. Laurence W., died 1939, vol. III
Youl, Sir James Arndell, 1809–1904, vol. I
Young, Rt Hon. Lord; George Young, 1819–1907, vol. I
Young, Sir Alastair Spencer Templeton, 2nd Bt (cr 1945), 1918–1963, vol. VI
Young, Sir Alban; see Young, Sir C. A.
Young, Hon. Sir Alexander; see Young, Hon. Sir J. A.
Young, (Alexander Bell) Filson, 1876–1938, vol. III
Young, Alfred, died 1900, vol. I
Young, Rev. Alfred, 1873–1940, vol. III
Young, Alfred Harry, died 1912, vol. I
Young, Sir Alfred Karney, 1865–1942, vol. IV
Young, Rev. Allan, 1925–1979, vol. VII
Young, Sir Allen William, 1827–1915, vol. I (A)
Young, Allyn Abbott, 1876–1929, vol. III
Young, Andrew, 1873–1937, vol. III
Young, Andrew, 1858–1943, vol. IV
Young, Rev. Canon Andrew John, 1885–1971, vol. VII
Young, Col Archibald, 1865–1931, vol. III
Young, Archibald, 1873–1939, vol. III
Young, Archibald Hope, 1863–1935, vol. III
Young, Lt-Col Arthur Davidson, 1862–1937, vol. III
Young, Col Sir Arthur Edwin, 1907–1979, vol. VII
Young, Captain Sir Arthur Henderson, 1854–1938, vol. III
Young, Arthur Primrose, 1885–1977, vol. VII
Young, Sir Arthur Stewart Leslie, 1st Bt (cr 1945), 1889–1950, vol. IV
Young, Rev. Augustus Blayney Russell, 1845–1941, vol. IV
Young, Maj.-Gen. Bernard Keith, 1892–1969, vol. VI
Young, Sir (Charles) Alban, 9th Bt (cr 1769), 1865–1944, vol. IV
Young, Col Charles Augustus, 1863–1944, vol. IV
Young, Rev. Canon Charles Edgar, 1897–1977, vol. VII
Young, Charles Edward Baring, 1850–1928, vol. II

Young, Maj.-Gen. Charles Frederic Gordon, 1859–1956, vol. V
Young, Christopher Alwyne Jack, 1912–1978, vol. VII
Young, Clyde, 1871–1948, vol. IV
Young, Sir Cyril Roe Muston, 4th Bt (cr 1821), 1881–1955, vol. V
Young, Rev. Daniel Eliott, 1851–1935, vol. III
Young, Daniel Henderson Lusk, 1861–1921, vol. II
Young, Lt-Col David Douglas, 1857–1940, vol. III
Young, Rev. Dinsdale Thomas, 1861–1938, vol. III
Young, Douglas, 1882–1967, vol. VI
Young, Sir Douglas; see Young, Sir J. D.
Young, Sir Douglas; see Young, Sir W. D.
Young, Rev. Egerton Ryerson, 1840–1909, vol. I
Young, Emily Hilda, 1880–1949, vol. IV
Young, Sir Eric; see Young, Sir T. E. B.
Young, Ernest, 1869–1952, vol. V
Young, Brig.-Gen. Ernest Douglas, 1872–1957, vol. V
Young, Ernest Herbert, 1878–1921, vol. II (A), vol. III
Young, Miss Evelyn Lucy, 1879–1960, vol. V
Young, F. E. Mills, died 1945, vol. IV
Young, Filson; see Young, A. B. F.
Young, Francis Brett, 1884–1954, vol. V
Young, Rev. Francis Samuel, 1871–1934, vol. III
Young, Francis Watson, 1851–1941, vol. IV
Young, Lt-Col Sir Frank Popham, 1863–1940, vol. III
Young, Captain Sir Frederic William, died 1927, vol. II
Young, Sir Frederick, 1817–1913, vol. I
Young, Frederick, 1890–1948, vol. IV
Young, Col Frederick de Bude, 1865–1920, vol. II
Young, Frederick George Charles, 1877–1955, vol. V
Young, Frederick Hugh, 1892–1969, vol. VI
Young, Sir Frederick William, 1876–1948, vol. IV
Young, Geoffrey Winthrop, 1876–1958, vol. V
Young, Sir George, 3rd Bt (cr 1813), 1837–1930, vol. III
Young, Sir George, 4th Bt (cr 1813), 1872–1952, vol. V
Young, George; see Young, Rt Hon. Lord.
Young, Rt Hon. George Charles Gillespie, 1876–1939, vol. III
Young, Very Rev. George Edward, died 1937, vol. III
Young, Brig.-Gen. George Frederick, 1846–1919, vol. II
Young, George Malcolm, 1882–1959, vol. V
Young, Sir George Peregrine, 5th Bt (cr 1813), 1908–1960, vol. V
Young, Mrs George Washington; see Nordica, Mme.
Young, Gerard Mackworth-, 1884–1965, vol. VI
Young, Gladys, died 1975, vol. VII
Young, Maj.-Gen. Gordon Drummond, 1896–1964, vol. VI
Young, Grace Chisholm, 1868–1944, vol. IV
Young, Lt-Col Harry Norman, 1874–1944, vol. IV

Young, Brig.-Gen. Henry Alfred, 1867–1941, vol. IV
Young, Henry Alfred, *died* 1942, vol. IV
Young, Brig. Henry Ayerst, 1895–1952, vol. V
Young, Hon. Henry Esson, 1867–1939, vol. III
Young, Brig.-Gen. Henry George, 1870–1956, vol. V
Young, Hilda Beatrice, (Sister Pauline), *died* 1967, vol. VI
Young, Major Sir Hubert Winthrop, 1885–1950, vol. IV
Young, Hugh Hampton, 1870–1945, vol. IV
Young, Hugo Joseph, 1847–1929, vol. III
Young, James, 1883–1963, vol. VI
Young, James, 1887–1975, vol. VII
Young, Hon. Sir (James) Alexander, 1875–1956, vol. V
Young, James Barclay Murdoch, 1897–1957, vol. V
Young, James Carleton, 1856–1918, vol. II
Young, Maj.-Gen. James Charles, 1858–1926, vol. II
Young, Gen. James Nowell, 1824–1917, vol. II
Young, Sir James Reid, 1888–1971, vol. VII
Young, Maj.-Gen. James Vernon, 1891–1961, vol. VI
Young, John, 1835–1902, vol. I
Young, Rt Hon. John, 1826–1915, vol. I (A)
Young, John, 1845–1925, vol. II
Young, Rev. John, 1844–1930, vol. III
Young, Sir (John) Douglas, 1883–1973, vol. VII
Young, Col Sir John Smith, 1843–1932, vol. III
Young, John Stirling, 1894–1971, vol. VII
Young, Brig.-Gen. Sir Julian Mayne, 1872–1961, vol. VI
Young, Brig.-Gen. Julius Ralph, 1864–1961, vol. VI
Young, Karl, 1879–1943, vol. IV
Young, Brig. Keith de Lorentz, 1889–1962, vol. VI
Young, Keith Downes, 1848–1929, vol. III
Young, M'Gregor, 1864–1942, vol. IV
Young, Sir Mark Aitchison, 1886–1974, vol. VII
Young, Morris Yudlevitz, *died* 1950, vol. IV
Young, Major Norman E., 1862–1902, vol. I
Young, Norman Egerton, 1892–1964, vol. VI
Young, Norwood, 1860–1943, vol. IV
Young, Comdr Oliver, 1855–1908, vol. I
Young, Owen D., 1874–1962, vol. VI
Young, Patrick Charles, 1880–1951, vol. V
Young, Maj.-Gen. Peter George Francis, 1912–1976, vol. VII
Young, Rt Rev. Richard, 1843–1905, vol. I
Young, Rt Hon. Robert, 1822–1917, vol. II
Young, Robert, 1860–1932, vol. III
Young, Maj.-Gen. Robert, 1877–1953, vol. V
Young, Sir Robert, 1872–1957, vol. V
Young, Sir Robert Arthur, 1871–1959, vol. V
Young, Robert Fitzgibbon, *died* 1960, vol. V
Young, Robert Magill, 1851–1925, vol. II
Young, Samuel, 1822–1918, vol. II
Young, Stephen, 1894–1972, vol. VII
Young, Sydney, 1857–1937, vol. III
Young, Thomas, 1896–1977, vol. VII
Young, Maj.-Gen. Thomas, 1893–1979, vol. VII
Young, Sir (Thomas) Eric (Boswell), 1891–1973, vol. VII

Young, Thomas Moffat, 1873–1946, vol. IV
Young, Lt-Col Walter Herbert, *died* 1940, vol. III
Young, Sir Walter James, 1872–1940, vol. III
Young, Rev. William, 1840–1915, vol. I (A)
Young, William, 1863–1942, vol. IV
Young, Sir William, 1875–1957, vol. V
Young, William, 1885–1965, vol. VI (AII)
Young, Sir William, 1905–1980, vol. VII
Young, William Arthur, 1867–1955, vol. V
Young, William Arthur, 1890–1955, vol. V
Young, Sir (William) Douglas, 1859–1943, vol. IV
Young, William Henry, 1863–1942, vol. IV
Young, William John, 1878–1942, vol. IV
Young, Sir William Lawrence, 8th Bt (*cr* 1769), 1864–1921, vol. II
Young, Sir William Mackworth, 1840–1924, vol. II
Young, Sir William Muston Need, 3rd Bt (*cr* 1821), 1847–1934, vol. III (A), vol. IV
Young, Rt Hon. William Robert, 1856–1933, vol. III
Young-Jamieson, Vice-Adm. Douglas, 1893–1955, vol. V
Younger of Leckie, 1st Viscount, 1851–1929, vol. III
Younger of Leckie, 2nd Viscount, 1880–1946, vol. IV
Younger, Brig. Arthur Allan Shakespear, 1881–1960, vol. V
Younger, Harry George, 1866–1951, vol. V
Younger, Sir James Paton, 1891–1974, vol. VII
Younger, Maj.-Gen. John Edward Talbot, 1888–1974, vol. VII
Younger, Rt Hon. Sir Kenneth Gilmour, 1908–1976, vol. VII
Younger, Robert; *see* Baron Blanesborough.
Younger, Robert Tannahill, 1860–1906, vol. I
Younger, Sir William, 1st Bt, 1862–1937, vol. III
Younger, Rev. William, 1869–1956, vol. V
Younger, Sir William Robert, 2nd Bt, 1888–1973, vol. VII
Younghusband, Arthur Delaval, 1854–1931, vol. III
Younghusband, Charles Wright, 1821–1899, vol. I
Younghusband, Sir Francis Edward, 1863–1942, vol. IV
Younghusband, Maj.-Gen. Sir George John, 1859–1944, vol. IV
Younghusband, Maj.-Gen. John William, 1823–1907, vol. I
Younghusband, Maj.-Gen. Leslie Napier, *died* 1939, vol. III
Younghusband, Gen. Robert Romer, 1819–1905, vol. I
Younghusband, Romer Edward, 1858–1933, vol. III
Youngman, Annie Mary, *died* 1919, vol. II
Youngman, William, 1880–1963, vol. VI
Yoxall, Sir James Henry, 1857–1925, vol. II
Ypres, 1st Earl of, 1852–1925, vol. II
Ypres, 2nd Earl of, 1881–1958, vol. V
Ysaye, Eugene, 1858–1931, vol. III
Ystwyth, 1st Baron, 1840–1935, vol. III
Yuill, Lt-Col Harry Hogg, 1886–1935, vol. III
Yule, Annie Henrietta, (Lady Yule), *died* 1950, vol. IV

Yule, Sir David, 1st Bt, 1858–1928, vol. II
Yule, George Udny, 1871–1951, vol. V
Yule, Col James Herbert, 1847–1920, vol. II
Yusuf, Sir Mohamad, *died* 1965, vol. VI (AII)
Yusuf, Nawab Sir Muhammad, *born* 1895, vol. VI
Yutang, Lin; *see* Lin Yutang.
Yves-Guyot, 1843–1928, vol. II

Z

Zacharewitsch, Michael, 1878–1953, vol. V
Zaehner, Robert Charles, 1913–1974, vol. VII
Zafar Ali, Sir, Khan Bahadur, Mirza, 1870–1942, vol. IV
Zaharoff, Sir Basil, 1850–1936, vol. III
Zambra, William Warren S.; *see* Shaw-Zambra.
Zammit, Salvatore Cachia, *died* 1918, vol. II
Zammit, Sir Temistocle, 1864–1935, vol. III
Zamora y Torres, Don Niceto Alcalá, 1877–1949, vol. IV
Zanardelli, Guiseppe, 1829–1903, vol. I
Zangwill, Edith Ayrton, *died* 1945, vol. IV
Zangwill, Israel, 1864–1926, vol. II
Zangwill, Louis, 1869–1938, vol. III
Zanuck, Darryl Francis, 1902–1979, vol. VII
Zanzibar, Sultan of, *died* 1902, vol. I
Zanzibar, Sultan of, 1879–1960, vol. V
Zaphiro, Photius Philip Constantine, 1877–1933, vol. III
Zaroubin, Georgi Nikolaevitch, 1900–1968, vol. VI
Zavertal, Hon. Captain Ladislao Joseph Philip Paul, 1849–1942, vol. IV
Zeal, Hon. Sir William Austin, 1830–1912, vol. I
Zealley, Sir Alec Thomas Sharland, 1893–1970, vol. VI
Zeiller, Charles Rene, 1847–1915, vol. I (A)
Zelie, Rev. John Sheridan, 1866–1942, vol. IV

Zepler, Eric Ernest, 1898–1980, vol. VII
Zeppelin, Count Ferdinand, 1838–1917, vol. II
Zernike, Frits, 1888–1966, vol. VI
Zetland, 1st Marquess of, 1844–1929, vol. III
Zetland, 2nd Marquess of, 1876–1961, vol. VI
Zeuner, Frederick Everard, 1905–1963, vol. VI
Zhukov, Marshal Georgi Konstantinovich, 1896–1974, vol. VII
Zichy-Woinarski, Casimir Julius, 1863–1935, vol. III
Ziegler, Karl, 1898–1973, vol. VII
Zielinski, Thaddeus, 1859–1944, vol. IV
Zigomala, Hilda, 1869–1946, vol. IV
Zilliacus, Konni, 1894–1967, vol. VI
Zimmer, George Frederick, 1854–1935, vol. III
Zimmermann, Agnes Marie, 1847–1925, vol. II
Zimmern, Sir Alfred, 1879–1957, vol. V
Zimmern, Alice, 1855–1939, vol. III
Zimmern, Helen, 1846–1934, vol. III
Zinkeisen, Anna Katrina, *died* 1976, vol. VII
Ziwer, Ahmad Pasha, 1864–1945, vol. IV
Zohrab, Gen. Sir Edward Henry, 1850–1909, vol. I
Zola, Emile, 1840–1902, vol. I
Zoppi, Count Vittorio, 1898–1967, vol. VI
Zorn, Anders Leonard, 1860–1920, vol. II
Zouche, 15th Baron, 1851–1914, vol. I
Zouche, Baroness (16th in line), 1860–1917 (this entry was not transferred to Who was Who).
Zouche, Baroness (17th in line), 1875–1965, vol. VI
Zukor, Adolph, 1873–1976, vol. VII
Zulfikar Ali Khan, Sir, 1875–1933, vol. III
Zuloaga, Ignacio, 1870–1945, vol. IV
Zulueta, Francis de, 1878–1958, vol. V
Zwar, Bernard T., 1876–1947, vol. IV
Zweig, Arnold, 1887–1968, vol. VI
Zweig, Stefan, *died* 1942, vol. IV
Zwemer, Rev. Samuel Marinus, 1867–1952, vol. V